# Holt McDougal

# Online Learning

## All the help you need, any time you need it.

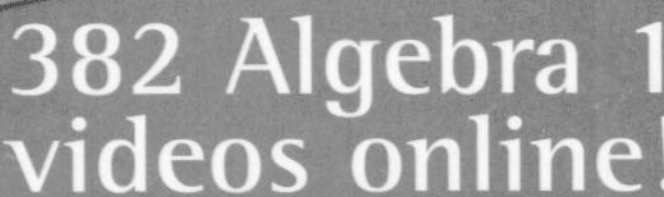


Lesson Tutorial Videos feature entertaining and enlightening videos that illustrate every example in your textbook!

**Premier Online Edition**
- Complete Student Edition
- Lesson Tutorial Videos for every example
- Interactive practice with feedback

**Extra Practice**
- Homework Help Online
- Intervention and enrichment exercises
- State test practice

**Online Tools**
- Graphing calculator
- TechKeys "How-to" tutorials on graphing calculators
- Algebra tiles
- Multilingual glossary

**For Parents**
- Algebra Refresher
- Parent Resources Online

Log on to **www.go.hrw.com** to see Holt McDougal online resources.

HOLT McDOUGAL

NORTH CAROLINA

# Algebra 1


Edward B. Burger

David J. Chard

Earlene J. Hall

Paul A. Kennedy

Steven J. Leinwand

Freddie L. Renfro

Dale G. Seymour

Bert K. Waits

HOLT McDOUGAL

a division of Houghton Mifflin Harcourt

Cover photo: Pamlico Sound Nags Head, North Carolina; © Ron Chapple/ Taxi/Getty Images

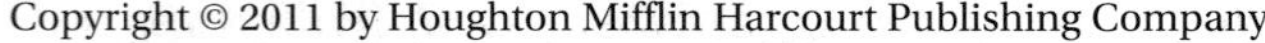

Cover photo: Orton Plantation near Wilmington, North Carolina; © George and Monserrate Schwartz/Alamy

Cover photo: basket of apples; © Lloyd Sutton Masterfile

Cover photo: The Wright Brothers Nation Memorial, North Carolina; © David Lyon Alamy



Printed in the U.S.A.

ISBN-13 978-0-030-99602-3
ISBN-10 0-030-99602-3

2 3 4 5 6 7 8 9 0914 15 14 13 12 11 10
4500239695

# Authors

**Edward B. Burger, Ph.D.** is Professor of Mathematics and Chair at Williams College and is the author of numerous articles, books, and videos. He has won several of the most prestigious writing and teaching awards offered by the Mathematical Association of America. Dr. Burger has appeared on NBC TV, National Public Radio, and has given innumerable mathematical performances around the world.

**Freddie L. Renfro, BA, MA,** has 35 years of experience in Texas education as a classroom teacher and director/coordinator of Mathematics PreK-12 for school districts in the Houston area. She has served as TEA TAAS/TAKS reviewer, team trainer for Texas Math Institutes, TEKS Algebra Institute writer, and presenter at math workshops.

**David J. Chard, Ph.D.,** is an Associate Dean of Curriculum and Academic Programs at the University of Oregon. He is the President of the Division for Research at the Council for Exceptional Children, is a member of the International Academy for Research on Learning Disabilities, and is the Principal Investigator on two major research projects for the U.S. Department of Education.

**Tom W. Roby, Ph.D.,** is Associate Professor of Mathematics and Director of the Quantitative Learning Center at the University of Connecticut. He founded and co-directed the Bay Area-based ACCLAIM professional development program. He also chaired the advisory board of the California Mathematics Project and reviewed content for the California Standards Tests.

**Paul A. Kennedy, Ph.D.,** is a professor in the Department of Mathematics at Colorado State University. Dr. Kennedy is a leader in mathematics education. His research focuses on developing algebraic thinking by using multiple representations and technology. He is the author of numerous publications.

**Dale G. Seymour** is a retired mathematics teacher, author, speaker and publisher. Dale founded Creative Publications in 1968, and went on to found two other mathematics publishing companies. Creating mathematical sculptures is one of his many hobbies.

**Steven J. Leinwand** spent 22 years as the Mathematics Supervisor with the Connecticut Department of Education. He is currently a Principal Research Analyst at the American Institutes for Research.

**Bert K. Waits, Ph.D.,** is a Professor Emeritus of Mathematics at The Ohio State University and co-founder of $T^3$ (Teachers Teaching with Technology), a national professional development program.

# North Carolina Teacher Advisory Panel

**Kiara A. Cox**
Math Teacher
Albemarle Road Middle School
Charlotte, NC

**Kristen Drum**
Math Teacher
Carrington Middle School
Durham, NC

**Charles Larrick**
Academic Facilitator
J.M. Alexander Middle School
Charlotte, NC

**Sarah M. Meyer**
Math Teacher
Northeast Middle School
Charlotte, NC

**Marcy Myers**
Math Facilitator
Southwest Middle School
Charlotte, NC

**Ivey Powell, Jr.**
Math Teacher
Parker Middle School
Rocky Mount, NC

**Malik Richardson**
Math Facilitator
Bishop Spaugh Community Academy
Charlotte, NC

**Jeffrey Vincent**
Curriculum Resource
Charlotte-Mecklenburg Schools
Charlotte, NC

# Contributing Writers

**Linda Antinone**
Paschal High School
Fort Worth, TX

**Carmen Whitman**
National Consultant
Pflugerville, TX

# Field Test Participants

**John Bakelaar**
Peeples Middle School
Jackson, MS

**Carey Carter**
Alvarado High School
Alvarado, TX

**Vicki Petty**
Central Middle School
Murfreesboro, TN

**Len Zigment**
Mesa Ridge High School
Colorado Springs, CO

# Reviewers

**John Bakelaar**
Assistant Principal
Whitten Middle School
Jackson, MS

**Jennifer Bauer**
Mathematics Instructional Leader
East Haven High School
East Haven, CT

**Doug Becker**
Mathematics Teacher
Gaylord High School
Gaylord, MI

**Joe Brady**
Mathematics Department Chair
Ensworth High School
Nashville, TN

**Sharon Butler**
Adjunct Faculty
Montgomery College of The Woodlands
Spring, TX

**Kathy Dean Davis**
Mathematics Department Chair, retired
Bowling Green Junior High
Bowling Green, KY

**Maureen "Willie" DiLaura**
Middle School Math Specialist, retired
Lockerman Middle School
Denton, MD

**Arlane Frederick**
Curriculum & Learning Specialist in Mathematics, retired
Kenmore-Town of Tonawanda UFSD
Buffalo, New York

**Marieta W. Harris**
Mathematics Specialist
Memphis, TN

**Connie Johnsen**
Mathematics Teacher
Harker Heights High School
Harker Heights, TX

**Mary Jones**
Mathematics Supervisor/Teacher
Grand Rapids Public Schools
Grand Rapids, MI

**Lendy Jones**
Algebra Teacher
Liberty Hill Middle School
Killeen, TX

**Mary Joy**
Algebra Teacher
Mayfield High School
Las Cruces, NM

**Vilma Martinez**
Algebra Teacher
Nikki Rowe High School
McAllen, TX

**Mende Mays**
Algebra Teacher
Crockett Junior High
Odessa, TX

**Rebecca Newburn**
Lead Math Teacher
Davidson Middle School
San Rafael, CA

**Vicki Petty**
Mathematics Teacher
Central Middle School
Murfreesboro, TN

**Susan Pippen**
Mathematics Department Chair
Hinsdale South High School
Darien, IL

**Elaine Rafferty**
Mathematics Learning Specialist
Charleston County SD
Charleston , SC

**Susan Rash**
Manager of Secondary Curriculum
Red Clay CSD
Wilmington, DE

**John Remensky**
Mathematics Department Chair
South Park High School
South Park, PA

**Raymond Seymour**
Mathematics Department Head, retired
Kirby Middle School
San Antonio, TX

**Jennifer J. Southers**
Mathematics Teacher
Hillcrest High School
Simpsonville, SC

**Jill Springer**
Mathematics Teacher
Henderson County High School
Henderson, KY

**Dr. Katherine Staltare**
Mathematics Consultant & Graduate Level
Course Developer
NYSUT, Effective Teaching Program
New York State

**Pam Walker**
Curriculum Teacher Specialist
Nacogdoches ISD
Nacogdoches, TX

**Larry Ward**
Mathematics Supervisor, retired
Carrollton-Farmers Branch ISD
Carrollton, TX

**Carmen Whitman**
Director, Mathematics for All Consulting
Pflugerville, TX

# Preparing for the EOC Test

***Holt McDougal Algebra 1*** provides many opportunities for you to prepare for the End-of-Course Algebra 1 Test.

## Countdown to EOC

**Use the Countdown to EOC to practice for your state test every day.**

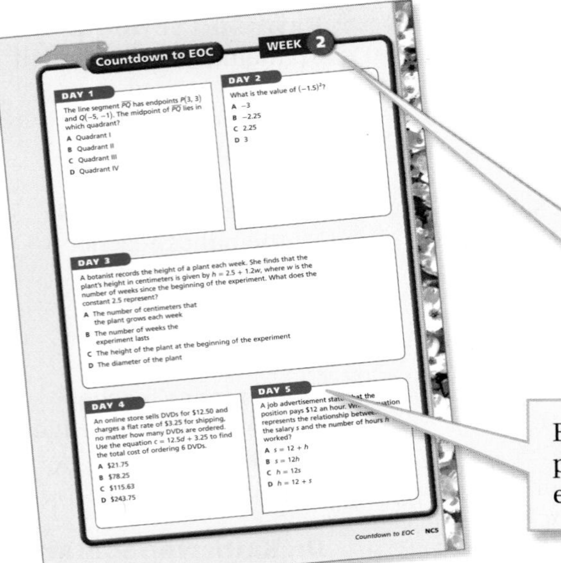

Countdown to EOC

WEEK 2

DAY 1

The line segment $\overline{PQ}$ has endpoints $P(3, 3)$ and $Q(-5, -1)$. The midpoint of $\overline{PQ}$ lies in which quadrant?

A Quadrant I
B Quadrant II
C Quadrant III
D Quadrant IV

DAY 2

What is the value of $(-1.5)^2$?

A $-3$
B $-2.25$
C $2.25$
D $3$

DAY 3

A botanist records the height of a plant each week. She finds that the plant's height in centimeters is given by $h = 2.5 + 1.2w$, where $w$ is the number of weeks since the beginning of the experiment. What does the constant 2.5 represent?

A The number of centimeters that the plant grows each week
B The number of weeks the experiment lasts
C The height of the plant at the beginning of the experiment
D The diameter of the plant

DAY 4

An online store sells DVDs for $12.50 and charges a flat rate of $3.25 for shipping, no matter how many DVDs are ordered. Use the equation $c = 12.5d + 3.25$ to find the total cost of ordering 6 DVDs.

A $21.75
B $78.25
C $115.63
D $243.75

DAY 5

A job advertisement stat... at the position pays $12 an hour. W... uation represents the relationship betwe... the salary $s$ and the number of hours $h$ worked?

A $s = 12 + h$
B $s = 12h$
C $h = 12s$
D $h = 12 + s$

Countdown to EOC NC5

### Step 1

✔ **Complete one item each day before you start the lesson.**

There are 24 pages of practice for the test. Each page is designed to be used in a week so that all practice will be completed before the test is given.

Each week's page has five practice test items, one for each day of the week.

## Standard Course of Study

**The North Carolina Objectives taught in each lesson are listed at the start of the lesson.**

### Step 2

✔ **Preview the objectives before you start the lesson.**

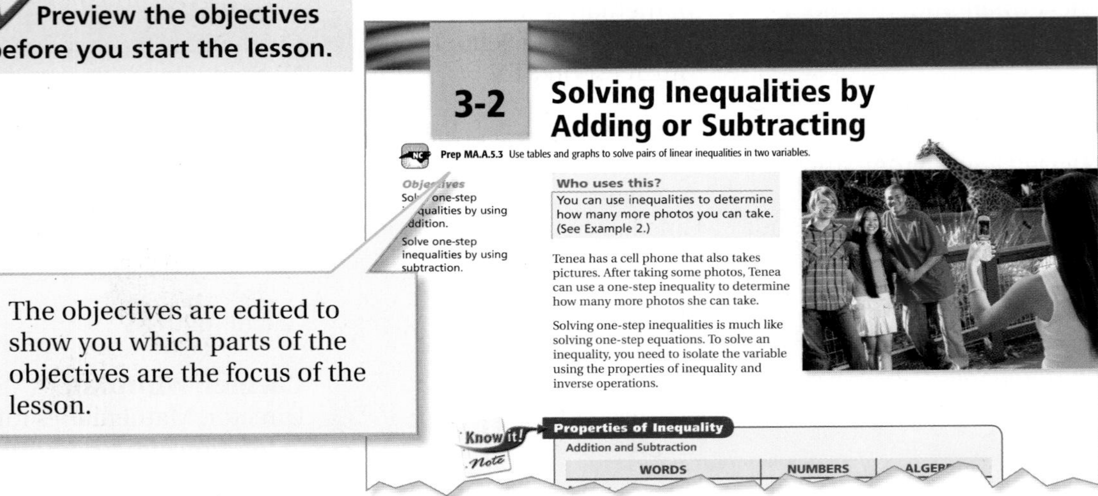

3-2 Solving Inequalities by Adding or Subtracting

Prep MA.A.5.3 Use tables and graphs to solve pairs of linear inequalities in two variables.

Objectives

Sol... one-step ...qualities by using ...ddition.

Solve one-step inequalities by using subtraction.

Who uses this?

You can use inequalities to determine how many more photos you can take. (See Example 2.)

Tenea has a cell phone that also takes pictures. After taking some photos, Tenea can use a one-step inequality to determine how many more photos she can take.

Solving one-step inequalities is much like solving one-step equations. To solve an inequality, you need to isolate the variable using the properties of inequality and inverse operations.

Know it! Note

Properties of Inequality

Addition and Subtraction

| WORDS | NUMBERS | ALGEB... |
|---|---|---|

The objectives are edited to show you which parts of the objectives are the focus of the lesson.

## SPIRAL REVIEW

**Use the Spiral Review for constant review of objectives taught in the current and previous lessons.**

# Step 3

**✔ Keep your skills fresh by practicing the objectives daily.**

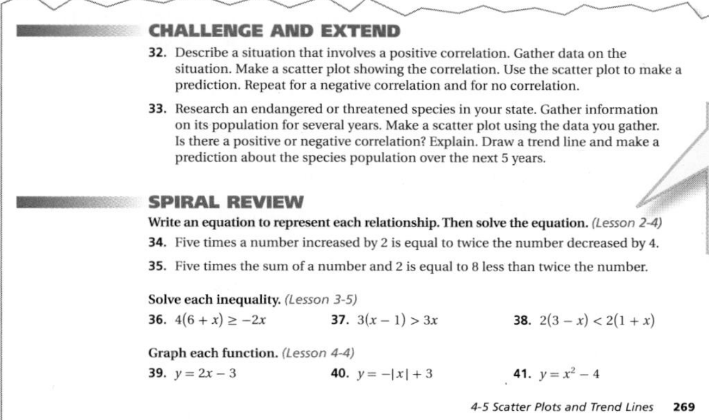

### CHALLENGE AND EXTEND

**32.** Describe a situation that involves a positive correlation. Gather data on the situation. Make a scatter plot showing the correlation. Use the scatter plot to make a prediction. Repeat for a negative correlation and for no correlation.

**33.** Research an endangered or threatened species in your state. Gather information on its population for several years. Make a scatter plot using the data you gather. Is there a positive or negative correlation? Explain. Draw a trend line and make a prediction about the species population over the next 5 years.

### SPIRAL REVIEW

**Write an equation to represent each relationship. Then solve the equation.** *(Lesson 2-4)*

**34.** Five times a number increased by 2 is equal to twice the number decreased by 4.

**35.** Five times the sum of a number and 2 is equal to 8 less than twice the number.

**Solve each inequality.** *(Lesson 3-5)*

**36.** $4(6 + x) \geq -2x$ **37.** $3(x - 1) > 3x$ **38.** $2(3 - x) < 2(1 + x)$

**Graph each function.** *(Lesson 4-4)*

**39.** $y = 2x - 3$ **40.** $y = -|x| + 3$ **41.** $y = x^2 - 4$

*4-5 Scatter Plots and Trend Lines* **269**

If you need help with a problem, go to the lesson referenced at the end of the problem.

# Step 4

**✔ After finishing each chapter, review your knowledge of the objectives.**

**Use the EOC Test Prep for review of objectives taught in the current and previous chapters.**

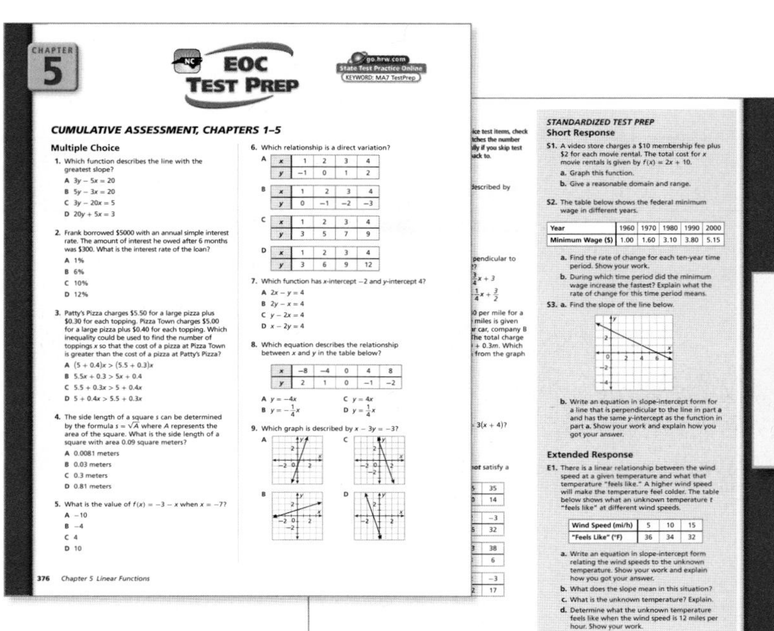

CHAPTER 5

EOC TEST PREP

go.hrw.com State Test Practice Online KEYWORD: MA7 TestPrep

*CUMULATIVE ASSESSMENT, CHAPTERS 1–5*

**Multiple Choice**

**1.** Which function describes the line with the greatest slope?

A $3y - 5x = 20$
B $5y - 3x = 20$
C $3y - 20x = 5$
D $20y + 5x = 3$

**2.** Frank borrowed $5000 with an annual simple interest rate. The amount of interest he owed after 6 months was $300. What is the interest rate of the loan?

A 1%
B 6%
C 10%
D 12%

**3.** Patty's Pizza charges $5.50 for a large pizza plus $0.30 for each topping. Pizza Town charges $5.00 for a large pizza plus $0.40 for each topping. Which inequality could be used to find the number of toppings $x$ so that the cost of a pizza at Pizza Town is greater than the cost of a pizza at Patty's Pizza?

A $(5 + 0.4)x > (5.5 + 0.3)x$
B $5.5x + 0.3 > 5x + 0.4$
C $5.5 + 0.3x > 5 + 0.4x$
D $5 + 0.4x > 5.5 + 0.3x$

**4.** The side length of a square $s$ can be determined by the formula $s = \sqrt{A}$ where $A$ represents the area of the square. What is the side length of a square with area 0.09 square meters?

A 0.0081 meters
B 0.03 meters
C 0.3 meters
D 0.81 meters

**5.** What is the value of $f(x) = -3 - x$ when $x = -7$?

A −10
B −4
C 4
D 10

**6.** Which relationship is a direct variation?

A

| x | 1 | 2 | 3 | 4 |
|---|---|---|---|---|
| y | −1 | 0 | 1 | 2 |

B

| x | 1 | 2 | 3 | 4 |
|---|---|---|---|---|
| y | 0 | −1 | −2 | −3 |

C

| x | 1 | 2 | 3 | 4 |
|---|---|---|---|---|
| y | 3 | 5 | 7 | 9 |

D

| x | 1 | 2 | 3 | 4 |
|---|---|---|---|---|
| y | 3 | 6 | 9 | 12 |

**7.** Which function has $x$-intercept −2 and $y$-intercept 4?

A $2x - y = 4$
B $2y - x = 4$
C $y - 2x = 4$
D $x - 2y = 4$

**8.** Which equation describes the relationship between $x$ and $y$ in the table below?

| x | −8 | −4 | 0 | 4 | 8 |
|---|---|---|---|---|---|
| y | 2 | 1 | 0 | −1 | −2 |

A $y = -4x$ C $y = 4x$
B $y = -\frac{1}{4}x$ D $y = \frac{1}{4}x$

**9.** Which graph is described by $x - 3y = -3$?

A B C D

376 *Chapter 5 Linear Functions*

*STANDARDIZED TEST PREP*

**Short Response**

**S1.** A video store charges a $10 membership fee plus $2 for each movie rental. The total cost for $x$ movie rentals is given by $f(x) = 2x + 10$.

a. Graph this function.
b. Give a reasonable domain and range.

**S2.** The table below shows the federal minimum wage in different years.

| Year | 1960 | 1970 | 1980 | 1990 | 2000 |
|---|---|---|---|---|---|
| Minimum Wage ($) | 1.00 | 1.60 | 3.10 | 3.80 | 5.15 |

a. Find the rate of change for each ten-year time period. Show your work.
b. During which time period did the minimum wage increase the fastest? Explain what the rate of change for this time period means.

**S3.** a. Find the slope of the line below.

b. Write an equation in slope-intercept form for a line that is perpendicular to the line in part a and has the same $y$-intercept as the function in part a. Show your work and explain how you got your answer.

**Extended Response**

**E1.** There is a linear relationship between the wind speed at a given temperature and what that temperature "feels like." A higher wind speed will make the temperature feel colder. The table below shows what an unknown temperature $t$ "feels like" at different wind speeds.

| Wind Speed (mi/h) | 5 | 10 | 15 |
|---|---|---|---|
| "Feels Like" (°F) | 36 | 34 | 32 |

a. Write an equation in slope-intercept form relating the wind speeds to the unknown temperature. Show your work and explain how you got your answer.
b. What does the slope mean in this situation?
c. What is the unknown temperature? Explain.
d. Determine what the unknown temperature feels like when the wind speed is 12 miles per hour. Show your work.

*Cumulative Assessment, Chapters 1–5* 377

These pages include practice with multiple choice items as seen on the EOC Test. They also include short response and extended response items.

# Countdown to EOC

## Week 1

### Day 1

Which expression represents the verbal phrase "the sum of three times a number and five"?

**A** $3(n + 5)$

**B** $3 + n \cdot 5$

**C** $3n + 5$

**D** $3 + (n + 5)$

### Day 2

Cell phone bills are based on a flat monthly fee and the number of minutes used. In the equation $c = 0.07m + 29.99$, what does the variable $m$ represent?

**A** The number of months billed

**B** The total amount of the bill

**C** The number of minutes used

**D** The phone number

### Day 3

Look at the table. Which equation ***best*** describes the relationship between the number of students and the number of tables in the cafeteria?

| Students ($n$) | Tables ($t$) |
|---|---|
| 720 | 18 |
| 600 | 15 |
| 960 | 24 |

**A** $n = 40t$

**B** $n = 35t + 90$

**C** $t = 40n$

**D** $n = 45t - 90$

### Day 4

What is the value of $\left(-\frac{1}{3}\right)^3$?

**A** $-\frac{1}{9}$

**B** $-\frac{1}{27}$

**C** $\frac{1}{27}$

**D** $\frac{1}{9}$

### Day 5

What is the solution to the equation $6.3 = m - 2.1$?

**A** 2.1

**B** 3

**C** 4.2

**D** 8.4

# Countdown to EOC — WEEK 2

## DAY 1

The line segment $\overline{PQ}$ has endpoints $P(3, 3)$ and $Q(-5, -1)$. The midpoint of $\overline{PQ}$ lies in which quadrant?

**A** Quadrant I

**B** Quadrant II

**C** Quadrant III

**D** Quadrant IV

## DAY 2

What is the value of $(-1.5)^2$?

**A** $-3$

**B** $-2.25$

**C** 2.25

**D** 3

## DAY 3

A botanist records the height of a plant each week. She finds that the plant's height in centimeters is given by $h = 2.5 + 1.2w$, where $w$ is the number of weeks since the beginning of the experiment. What does the constant 2.5 represent?

**A** The number of centimeters that the plant grows each week

**B** The number of weeks the experiment lasts

**C** The height of the plant at the beginning of the experiment

**D** The diameter of the plant

## DAY 4

An online store sells DVDs for $12.50 and charges a flat rate of $3.25 for shipping, no matter how many DVDs are ordered. Use the equation $c = 12.5d + 3.25$ to find the total cost of ordering 6 DVDs.

**A** $21.75

**B** $78.25

**C** $115.63

**D** $243.75

## DAY 5

A job advertisement states that the position pays $12 an hour. Which equation represents the relationship between the salary $s$ and the number of hours $h$ worked?

**A** $s = 12 + h$

**B** $s = 12h$

**C** $h = 12s$

**D** $h = 12 + s$

# Countdown to EOC WEEK 3

## DAY 1

What is the simplified form of the expression $3(2x - 4) - 5(x + 6)$?

**A** $x - 42$

**B** $x + 2$

**C** $x + 18$

**D** $11x - 42$

## DAY 2

Which property can be used to justify the equation shown below?

$$3x + 18 + 4x + 6 = 3x + 4x + 18 + 6$$

**A** Associative Property

**B** Commutative Property

**C** Distributive Property

**D** Addition Property of Equality

## DAY 3

Lydia received a gift card for $25.00 worth of smoothies from the Smoothie Spot. If the cost of each smoothie is $3.25, which table ***best*** describes *b*, the balance remaining on the gift card after she buys *n* smoothies?

**A**

| *n* | *b* |
|---|---|
| 1 | $21.75 |
| 3 | $15.25 |
| 4 | $12.00 |
| 7 | $2.25 |

**B**

| *n* | *b* |
|---|---|
| 2 | $18.50 |
| 4 | $12.00 |
| 6 | $6.50 |
| 8 | $0 |

**C**

| *n* | *b* |
|---|---|
| 1 | $21.75 |
| 2 | $18.50 |
| 5 | $15.25 |
| 7 | $12.00 |

**D**

| *n* | *b* |
|---|---|
| 2 | $18.50 |
| 3 | $15.25 |
| 5 | $7.75 |
| 6 | $4.50 |

## DAY 4

The band is trying to raise money to take a field trip to the Rock and Roll Hall of Fame. They decide to sell sweatshirts. The equation for the amount of money *a* that they will make for selling *t* sweatshirts is $a = 22t - 350$. In order to make at least $2100, how many sweatshirts do the band members need to sell?

**A** 112

**B** 111

**C** 80

**D** 79

## DAY 5

What is the solution to the equation $8x - 10 = 54$?

**A** 5.5

**B** 6.75

**C** 8

**D** 12

# Countdown to EOC WEEK 4

## DAY 1

What is the solution to the equation $6(m - 4) + 2m = -8$?

A $-2$

B $-\frac{1}{2}$

C $\frac{1}{2}$

D 2

## DAY 2

Stuart ran 40 yards in 5 seconds. What was his average speed in miles per hour? Round your answer to the nearest tenth.

A 8.0 mi/h

B 16.4 mi/h

C 24.0 mi/h

D 35.2 mi/h

## DAY 3

At a certain time of the day, a 24-foot tree casts an 18-foot shadow. How long is the shadow cast by a 4-foot mailbox at the same time of day?

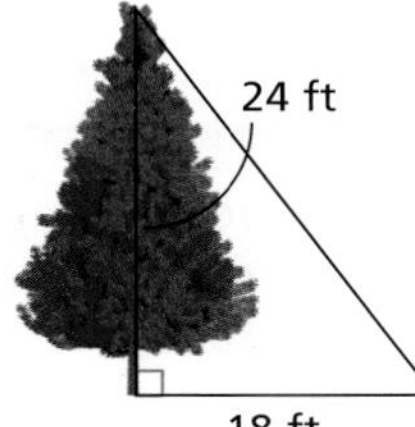


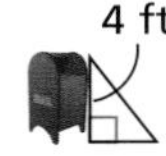


A 1.3 feet

B 3 feet

C 4.5 feet

D 5 feet

## DAY 4

In a test, a new hybrid car drove 619 yards on 1 ounce of gasoline. What is this rate in miles per gallon? Round your answer to the nearest tenth.

A 7.5 mi/gal

B 15.0 mi/gal

C 22.5 mi/gal

D 45.0 mi/gal

## DAY 5

What is the solution to the equation $6(x - 9) = -12x + 36$?

A $x = 5$

B $x = 2.5$

C $x = -1$

D $x = -5$

# Countdown to EOC — WEEK 5

## DAY 1

A scale model of a building is built exactly $\frac{1}{24}$ the size of the actual building. If the model is 18 inches tall, how tall is the actual building?

**A** 24 feet

**B** 36 feet

**C** 48 feet

**D** 432 feet

## DAY 2

Claire's father is 6 years more than 3 times her age. If her dad is 39 years old, how old is Claire?

**A** 15 years old

**B** 11 years old

**C** 7 years old

**D** 6 years old

## DAY 3

Josey set up the following equation to convert a speed. What units should she use for the resulting rate?

$$\frac{\textbf{60 mi}}{\textbf{1 h}} \bullet \frac{\textbf{5280 ft}}{\textbf{1 mi}} \bullet \frac{\textbf{1 h}}{\textbf{60 min}} = \textbf{5280}\ \boxed{?}$$

**A** ft/s

**B** ft/min

**C** mi/min

**D** mi/h

## DAY 4

What is the solution to $-8x - 3 = -4x + 5$?

**A** $-4$

**B** $-2$

**C** 2

**D** 4

## DAY 5

The cheerleaders are selling tickets to a pasta dinner to raise money for new competition outfits. They plan to charge $6 per person, and their total expenses for dinner are $135. Which value for the number of tickets sold would result in the cheerleaders ***not*** making a profit?

**A** 46

**B** 45

**C** 23

**D** 22

# Countdown to EOC WEEK 6

## DAY 1

Which equation matches the data in the table?

| $x$ | 3 | 1 | −2 | 6 |
|---|---|---|---|---|
| $y$ | 2 | 4 | 7 | −1 |

**A** $y = -x + 5$

**B** $y = 2x - 1$

**C** $y = x + 3$

**D** $y = -3x + 11$

## DAY 2

The drama club charges $3 admission to the one-act play festival. Their expenses are $115. In order for the club to make exactly $110 after expenses, how many people must attend the festival?

**A** 39

**B** 75

**C** 114

**D** 152

## DAY 3

Melissa's brother's age is 6 years less than twice her age. The sum of her age and her brother's age is 27. What is Melissa's age?

**A** 6

**B** 9

**C** 11

**D** 16

## DAY 4

Lara has a coupon for $4 off each pair of jeans that she buys. If she buys 5 pairs of jeans and each pair of jeans costs $$x$, which equation gives the total cost $c$ of the jeans?

**A** $c = 5(x - 4)$

**B** $c = 5x - 4$

**C** $c = 4(x - 5)$

**D** $c = 4x - 5$

## DAY 5

A bus company sells an annual bus pass for $8.50, and then charges a rider $0.25 per ride. Using the equation $c = 0.25b + 8.5$, how much will it cost for someone to ride the bus 38 times?

**A** $118.00

**B** $20.00

**C** $18.00

**D** $9.50

# Countdown to EOC — WEEK 7

## DAY 1

Which equation has the solution $x = -3$?

**A** $-3x + 4 = 10 - 5x$

**B** $2 = -3x + 11$

**C** $0 = 2(x - 4) + 14$

**D** $-13x = 6 + 5x$

## DAY 2

Which term best describes $\overline{AB}$ as it relates to circle A?

**A** chord

**B** circumference

**C** diameter

**D** radius

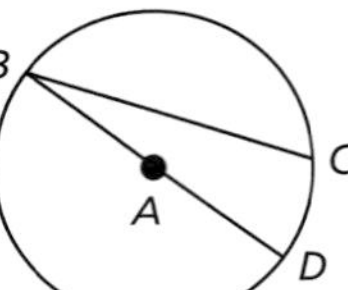


## DAY 3

Which graph shows a line where each value of $y$ is three more than half of $x$?

**A**

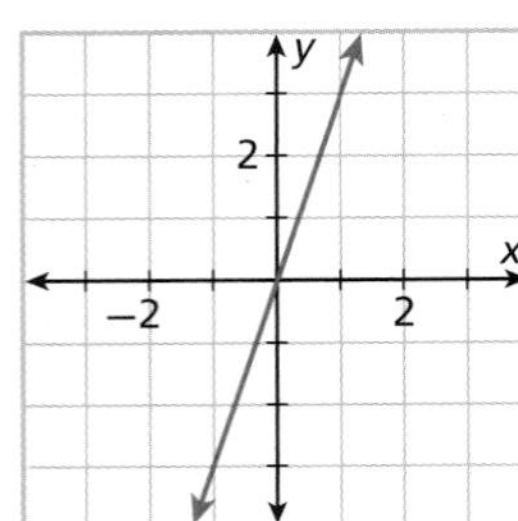

**C**

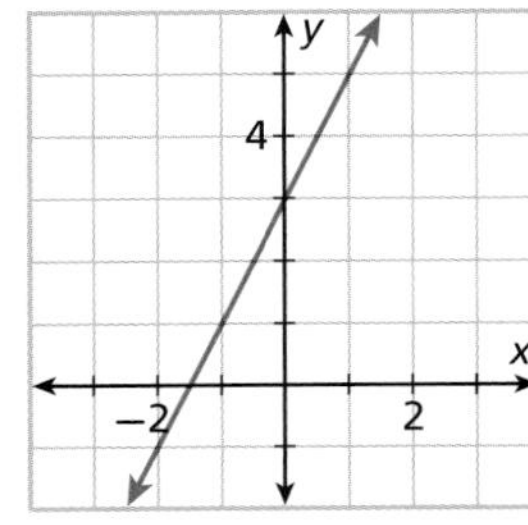

**B**

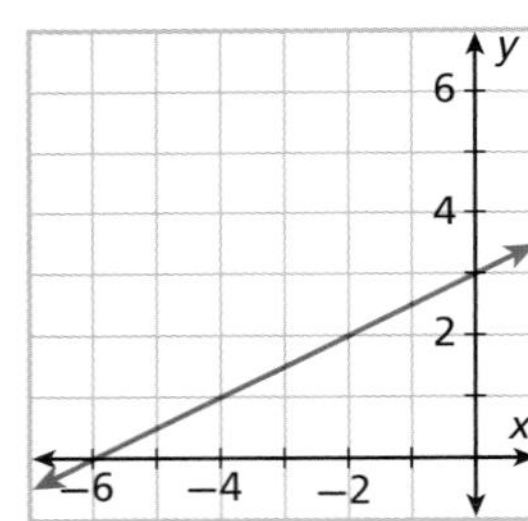

**D**

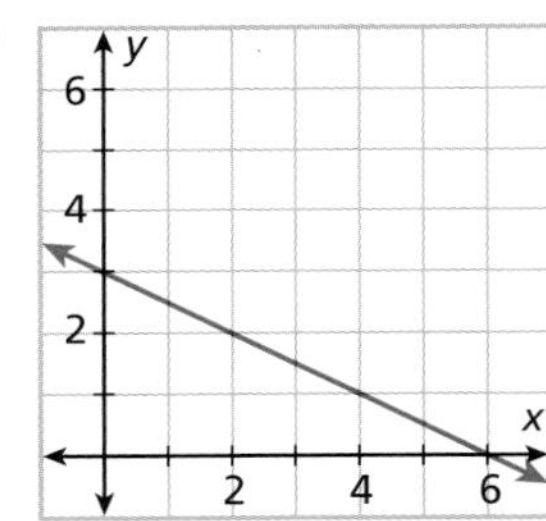

## DAY 4

What is the area of the composite figure?

**A** 8 square meters

**B** 21 square meters

**C** 25 square meters

**D** 45 square meters

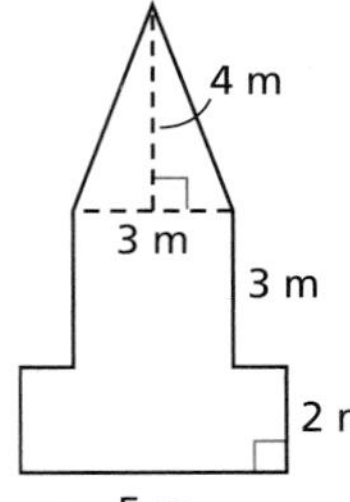


## DAY 5

The population $p$ of a small town is given by $p = 3550 + 85x$, where $x$ is the number of years after 1990. In what year was the population of the town 4825?

**A** 1995

**B** 2005

**C** 2011

**D** 2015

# Countdown to EOC — WEEK 8

## DAY 1

A swimming pool charges an annual $75 membership fee, and it costs $1.50 each time a member brings a guest. Which equation shows the yearly cost $y$ in terms of the number of guests $g$?

**A** $y = 75g + 1.5$

**B** $y = -1.5g + 75$

**C** $y = 1.5g + 75$

**D** $y = 1.5g + 75g$

## DAY 2

On a certain standardized test, the equation $s = 9q + 218$ is used to determine a student's score. In this equation, $s$ is the score and $q$ is the number of questions answered correctly. If the maximum score on the test is 650, how many questions are on the test?

**A** 96 questions

**B** 72 questions

**C** 48 questions

**D** 24 questions

## DAY 3

Which term best describes $\overline{BC}$ as it relates to circle A?

**A** chord

**B** circumference

**C** diameter

**D** radius

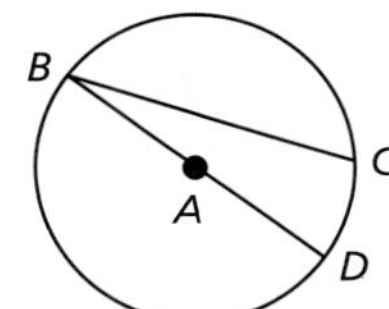


## DAY 4

A publishing company must ship boxes of a particular book to bookstores around the country. The boxes used for shipping can hold a maximum of 35 pounds. If the company wants to ship at least 10 books per box, what is the maximum weight of a book that can be put in the box?

**A** 3 pounds

**B** $3\frac{1}{2}$ pounds

**C** 4 pounds

**D** 25 pounds

## DAY 5

Which verbal description does ***not*** match the function $f(x) = -\frac{1}{3}x - 5$?

**A** The function value is the difference between $x$ times $-\frac{1}{3}$ and 5.

**B** The function value is 5 less than the product of $x$ and $-\frac{1}{3}$.

**C** The function value is $-\frac{1}{3}$ of $x$ subtracted from 5.

**D** The function value is $-\frac{1}{3}$ of $x$ decreased by 5.

## Countdown to EOC — WEEK 9

### DAY 1

Brian calculates the charge for each lawn he mows by using the function $f(t) = 4t + 5.5$, where $t$ is the number of hours spent mowing the lawn. He always works for at least one full hour. Which statement ***cannot*** be inferred from this information?

**A** Brian's hourly rate is \$4.

**B** Brian charges \$5.50 for all lawns.

**C** Brian uses \$5.50 worth of gas for each job.

**D** The minimum that Brian will make for each lawn is \$9.50.

### DAY 2

Which of the following relationships has a negative correlation?

**A** A person's height and weight

**B** The number of minutes spent studying and a test grade

**C** The outside temperature and the number of layers of clothes a person wears

**D** The number of years a person spent in school and the person's salary

### DAY 3

What is the best estimate for the number of participants in the snowboarding competition in 2007?

**A** 25

**B** 35

**C** 40

**D** 60

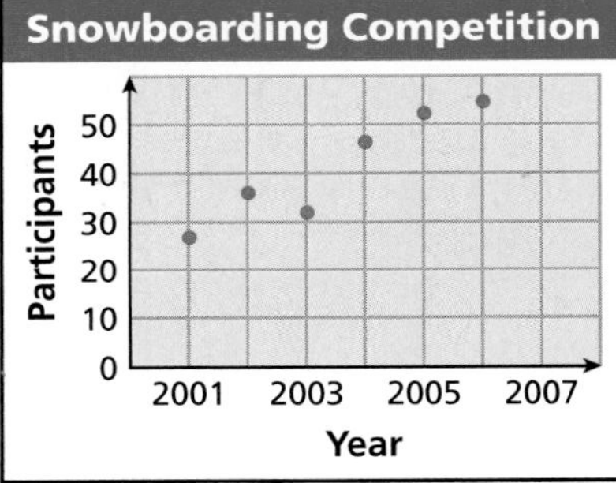


### DAY 4

Which function ***best*** matches the table?

| $x$ | −3 | 0 | 3 | 6 |
|---|---|---|---|---|
| $y$ | 2 | 4 | 6 | 8 |

**A** $y = -\frac{2}{3}x$

**B** $y = 2x + 4$

**C** $y = \frac{2}{3}x + 4$

**D** $y = \frac{1}{3}x + 3$

### DAY 5

Which of the following statements is true for all functions?

**A** Every element of the domain maps to only one element in the range.

**B** Every element of the range maps to only one element in the domain.

**C** A vertical line intersects the graph at more than one point.

**D** No range value is repeated more than once.

# Countdown to EOC WEEK 10

## DAY 1

A function relating two quantities is $f(x) = \frac{1}{5}x + 6$. What will always be true based on this function?

**A** $f(x)$ will be less than $x$.

**B** If $x$ is positive, then $f(x)$ will be positive.

**C** If $x$ is negative, then $f(x)$ will be negative.

**D** $f(x)$ will be greater than $x$.

## DAY 2

In the equation $p = -40q + 163$, which relationship between $p$ and $q$ is true?

**A** You cannot determine the relationship based on this information.

**B** $q$ is dependent on $p$.

**C** $p$ and $q$ are independent of each other.

**D** $p$ is dependent on $q$.

## DAY 3

What is the equation of the line shown?

**A** $y = 2x$

**B** $y = -2x$

**C** $y = \frac{1}{2}x$

**D** $y = -\frac{1}{2}x$

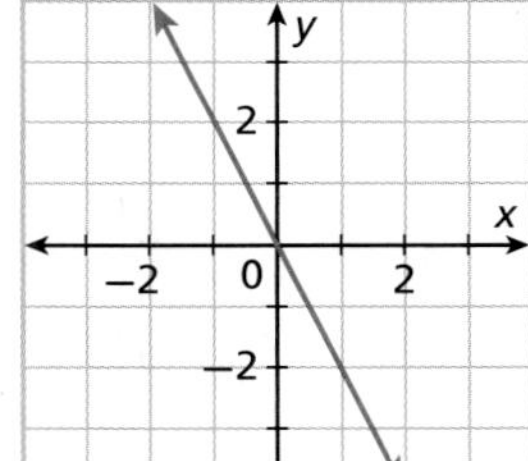


## DAY 4

What is the solution to $-8x - 3 = -4x + 5$?

**A** $x = -2$

**B** $x = 2$

**C** $x = 4$

**D** $x = -4$

## DAY 5

The sum of three consecutive integers is 54. What is the greatest of the three integers?

**A** 17

**B** 18

**C** 19

**D** 20

# Countdown to EOC

# WEEK 11

## DAY 1

In a picture, a monument is 4.5 inches tall and 2.5 inches wide. The actual monument is 60 feet wide. How tall is the actual monument?

**A** $33\frac{1}{3}$ feet

**B** 90 feet

**C** 108 feet

**D** 112.5 feet

## DAY 2

At a computer repair shop, the function $f(t) = 40t + 35$ is used to calculate fees, where $t$ is the number of hours technicians spend working on the computer. If you pay $315 to get your computer repaired, how long did the technician work on repairing your computer?

**A** 8.75 hours

**B** 7.875 hours

**C** 7.5 hours

**D** 7 hours

## DAY 3

The scatter plot shows the relationship between the size of a diamond in Carats and its retail price. What is the ***approximate*** retail price of a 0.30 Carat diamond?

**A** $400

**B** $600

**C** $800

**D** $1000

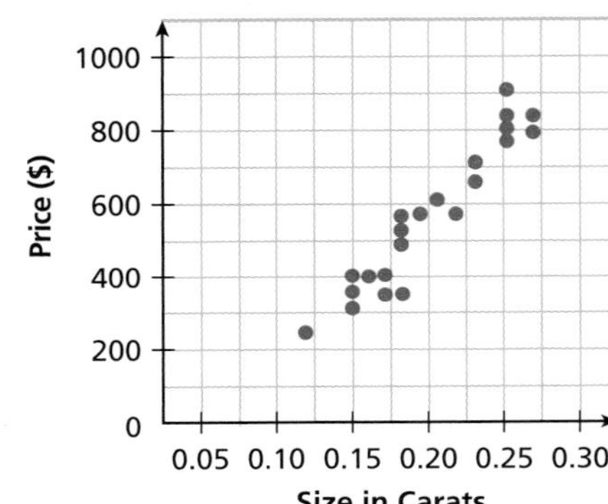


## DAY 4

The relationship between which two quantities can be represented by a linear function?

**A** The volume of a cube and its side length

**B** The perimeter of a rectangle and its area

**C** The perimeter of an equilateral triangle and its side length

**D** The area of a square and its side length

## DAY 5

David invests $1000 in an account that pays simple interest. The function $V(t)$ gives the value of the account after $t$ years. What type of function is $V(t)$?

**A** Exponential

**B** Linear

**C** Quadratic

**D** Rational

# Countdown to EOC WEEK 12

## DAY 1

Which function is equivalent to $2x - 3y = 9$?

**A** $y = -\frac{2}{3}x - 3$

**B** $y = \frac{2}{3}x - 3$

**C** $y = \frac{3}{2}x - 3$

**D** $y = -\frac{3}{2}x - 3$

## DAY 2

What is the range of the function shown in the table?

| $x$ | 1 | 3 | 5 | 8 |
|---|---|---|---|---|
| $f(x)$ | 2 | −2 | 0 | 2 |

**A** {1, 3, 5, 8}

**B** {4}

**C** {−2, 0, 2}

**D** {7}

## DAY 3

Which graph shows a linear function?

**A**

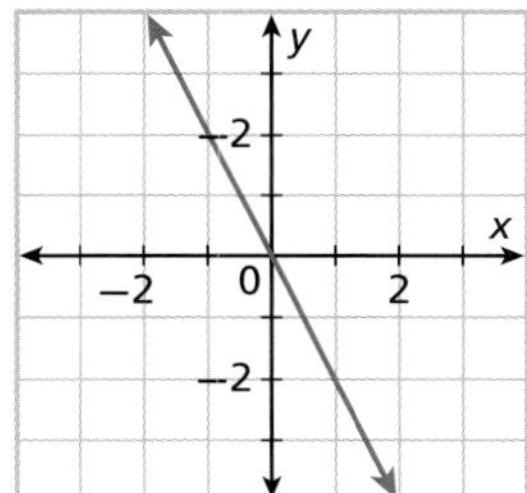


**C**

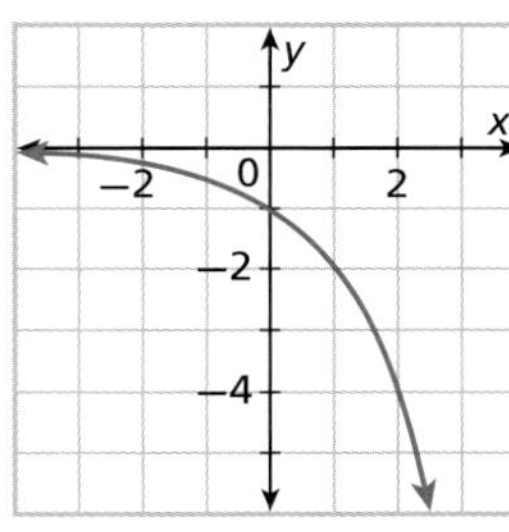


**B**

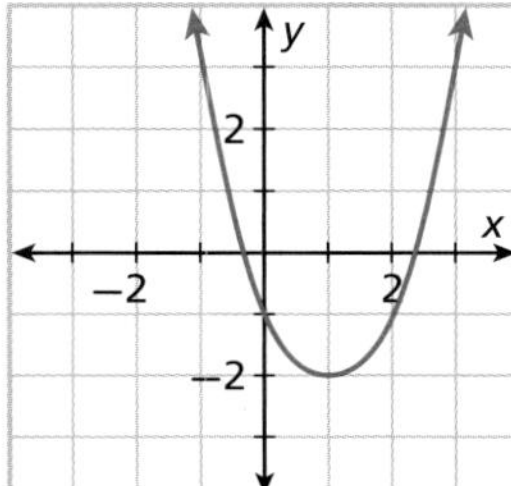


**D**

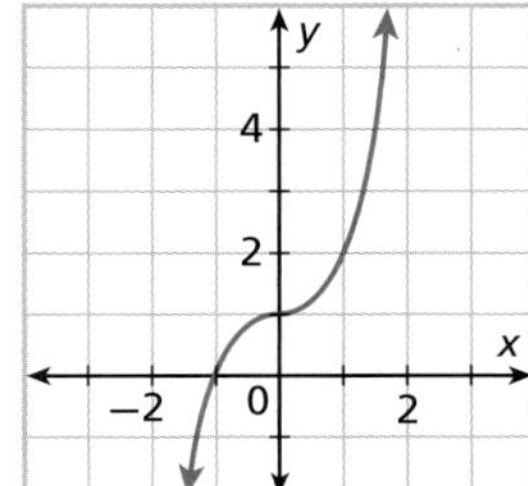


## DAY 4

What is the distance between the points $(1, 4)$ and $(-1, 3)$?

**A** 2

**B** $\sqrt{5}$

**C** $\sqrt{7}$

**D** 12

## DAY 5

An arithmetic sequence is given by the rule $a_n = 23 - 6n$. What is the common difference?

**A** −6

**B** 6

**C** 17

**D** 23

# Countdown to EOC

## WEEK 13

### DAY 1

A taxicab ride costs \$2.50 for the first mile and \$0.40 for each additional $\frac{1}{4}$-mile. If $x$ represents the number of quarter miles traveled, which function gives $y$, the cost of a taxicab ride at least 1 mile long?

**A** $y = 0.4x - 2.50$

**B** $y = 0.4(x - 4) - 2.50$

**C** $y = 0.4x + 2.50$

**D** $y = 0.4(x - 4) + 2.50$

### DAY 2

A taxi company charges a \$2.50 fee per ride plus an additional \$2.10 per mile traveled. On the graph, what would the \$2.50 fee represent?

**A** The slope

**B** The $x$-intercept

**C** The $y$-intercept

**D** The rate of increase

### DAY 3

Which description of the relationship between $x$ and $y$ ***best*** matches the graph below?

**A** The value of $y$ is 3 times the value of $x$.

**B** The value of $x$ is 2 more than the value of $y$.

**C** The value of $x$ is 2 less than the value of $y$.

**D** The value of $x$ is 3 times the value of $y$.

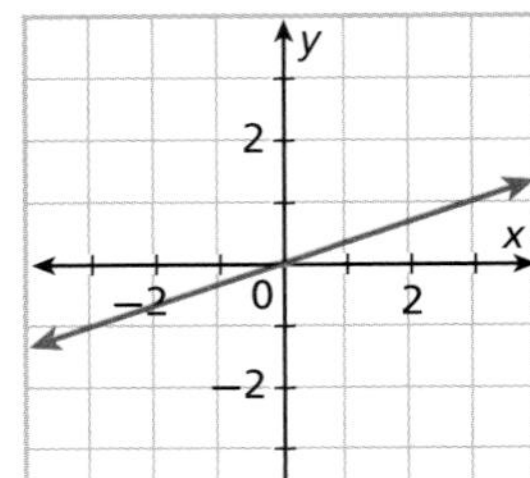


### DAY 4

In which relationship are the two quantities independent of one another?

**A** The amount of tax paid for an item and the price of the item

**B** The number of snacks bought from a snack machine and the amount of money in the machine

**C** The number of hours worked at \$6.50 per hour and the amount of money earned

**D** The age of a person and the number of televisions in their house

### DAY 5

The linear function $f(x) = 3x + 15$ models the cost of renting $x$ movies over the course of a year from a certain store. What range restrictions will there be if you graph this function?

**A** $f(x) \geq 0$

**B** $f(x) \geq 15$

**C** $f(x) > 0$

**D** $0 \leq f(x) \leq 15$

# Countdown to EOC

# WEEK 14

## DAY 1

Which function matches the data in the table?

| $x$ | −3 | 2 | 5 |
|---|---|---|---|
| $f(x)$ | 15 | 0 | 15 |

**A** $f(x) = -3x + 6$

**B** $f(x) = -5x$

**C** $f(x) = x^2 - 2x$

**D** $f(x) = 3x^2 - 12$

## DAY 2

A consultant charges her clients for her services based on an equation relating the total bill $f(h)$ to the number of hours worked $h$. The ***best*** interpretation of this function $f(h) = 125h + 150$ is:

**A** She charges \$150 per hour plus a \$125 flat fee.

**B** She charges \$125 per hour plus a \$150 flat fee.

**C** She charges \$275 per hour.

**D** Her hourly charges vary from \$125 to \$150 depending on the job.

## DAY 3

The solutions of what system of inequalities are shown in the graph?

**A** $\begin{cases} y > x - 3 \\ y \leq x + 1 \end{cases}$

**B** $\begin{cases} y \geq x - 3 \\ y < x + 1 \end{cases}$

**C** $\begin{cases} y < x - 3 \\ y \geq x + 1 \end{cases}$

**D** $\begin{cases} y \leq x - 3 \\ y > x + 1 \end{cases}$

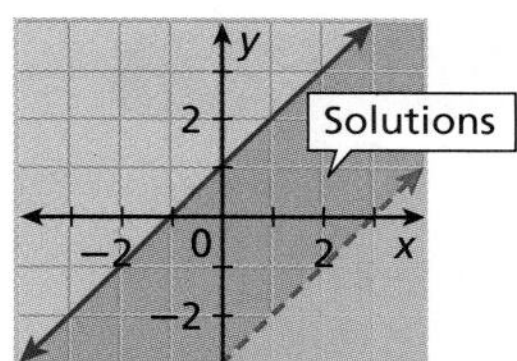


## DAY 4

What is the range of the function $f(x) = 2x + 3$?

**A** All real numbers

**B** $f(x) \geq 3$

**C** $f(x) \geq 0$

**D** $f(x) \geq -3$

## DAY 5

What is the median of the following data set?

15, 12, 14, 28, 18, 12, 20

**A** 12

**B** 15

**C** 16

**D** 17

## DAY 1

Which graph shows a linear function?

A

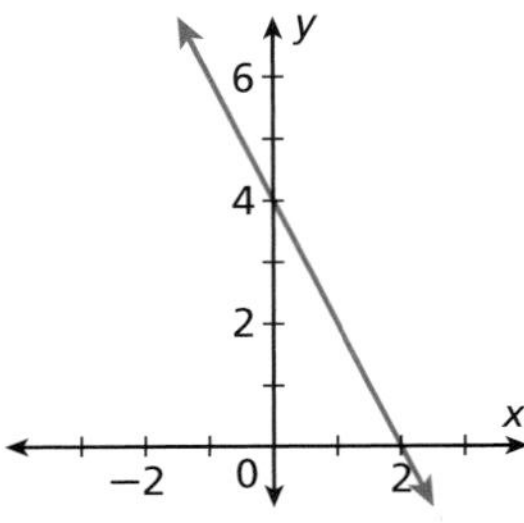

C

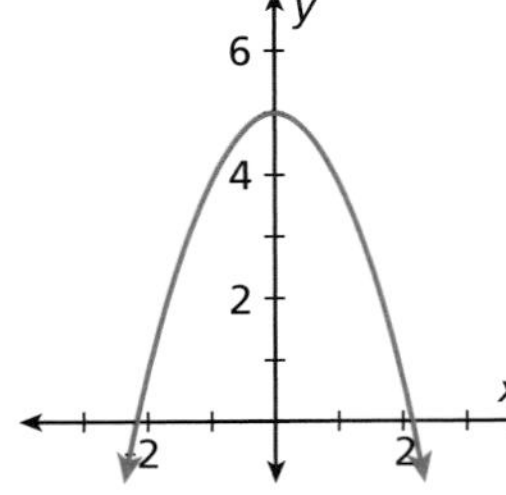

B

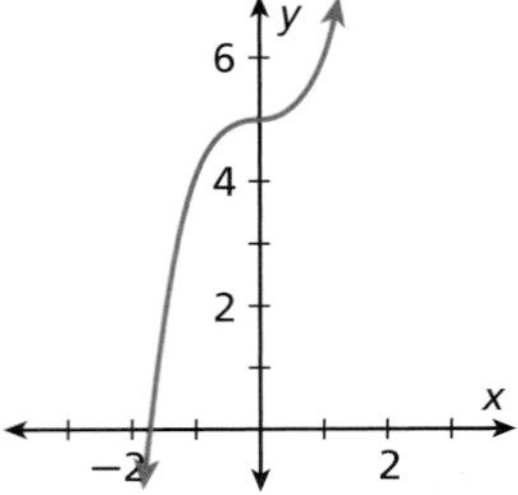

D

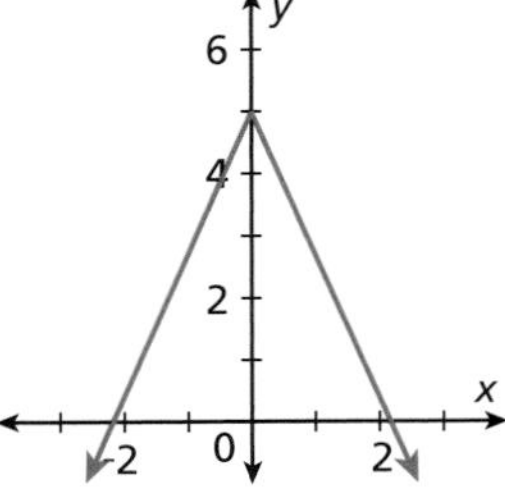

## DAY 2

A rectangle has width $x - 2$ and length $x + 4$. Which polynomial gives the area of the rectangle?

**A** $4x + 8$

**B** $x^2 - 8$

**C** $x^2 + 2x - 8$

**D** $x^2 + 8x - 8$

## DAY 3

What is the value of $\left(\frac{1}{4}\right)^{-3}$?

**A** $-64$

**B** $-\frac{1}{64}$

**C** $\frac{1}{64}$

**D** 64

## DAY 4

What is the solution to the system of equations?

$$\begin{cases} 3x - 4y = 19 \\ y = 2x - 11 \end{cases}$$

**A** $(5, -1)$

**B** $(-5, -21)$

**C** $(5, 1)$

**D** $(-5, -8.5)$

## DAY 5

When $x$ is 4, $y$ is 20. If $y$ varies directly as $x$, what is the constant of variation?

**A** $\frac{1}{5}$

**B** 5

**C** 16

**D** 80

# Countdown to EOC — WEEK 16

## DAY 1

Suppose $y$ varies directly as $x$, and $y = 12$ when $x = 5$. What is the value of $y$ when $x = 8$?

**A** 3.3

**B** 7.5

**C** 15

**D** 19.2

## DAY 2

What is the equation of the line shown?

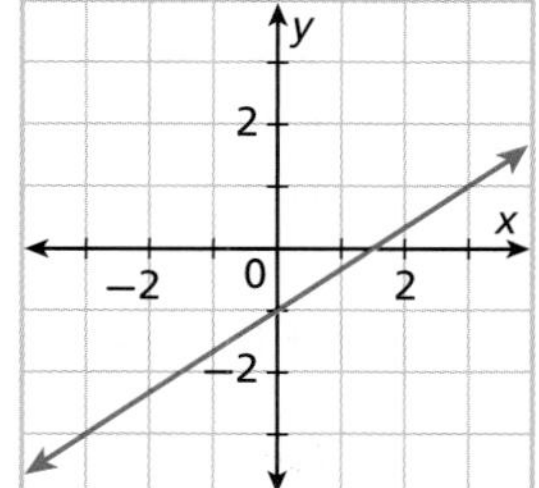


**A** $y = \frac{3}{2}x + 1$

**B** $y = -\frac{3}{2}x - 1$

**C** $y = \frac{2}{3}x - 1$

**D** $y = -\frac{2}{3}x$

## DAY 3

Which of the following statements accurately describes the function shown in the graph?

**A** The function decreases over both intervals shown.

**B** The function decreases over the first shown interval and increases over the second.

**C** The function increases over the first shown interval and decreases over the second.

**D** The function increases over both intervals shown.

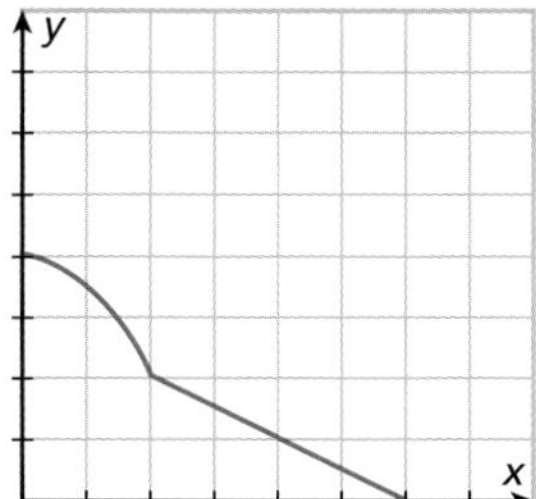


## DAY 4

Your school is selling candles to raise money. If profit $y$ is related to the number of items sold $x$, what are reasonable restrictions on the domain?

**A** $y \geq 0$

**B** No restrictions

**C** $x \geq 0$

**D** $0 \leq y \leq 2000$

## DAY 5

What is the solution to the system of equations graphed below?

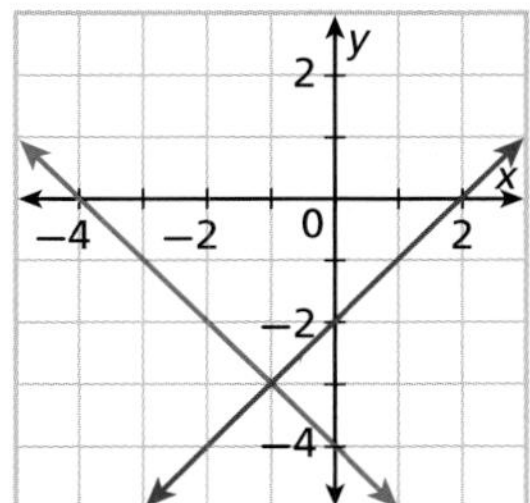


**A** $(-1, 3)$

**B** $(-1, -3)$

**C** $(-3, -1)$

**D** $(3, -1)$

## DAY 1

A store manager increases the wholesale cost of an item by 35%. Which statement ***best*** represents the functional relationship between the wholesale cost of the item and the markup on the item?

**A** The markup is dependent on the wholesale cost.

**B** The wholesale cost is dependent on the markup.

**C** The markup and the wholesale cost are independent of each other.

**D** The relationship cannot be determined.

## DAY 2

What is the factored form of the expression $4x^2 - 12x + 9$?

**A** $(2x - 3)^2$

**B** $(2x + 3)(2x - 3)$

**C** $(4x - 3)(x - 3)$

**D** $(2x + 3)^2$

## DAY 3

The scatter plot shows the percent of households at various income levels that own a car. What is a reasonable estimate for the percent of households with incomes of $50,000 that own a car?

**A** 50%

**B** 65%

**C** 77%

**D** 85%

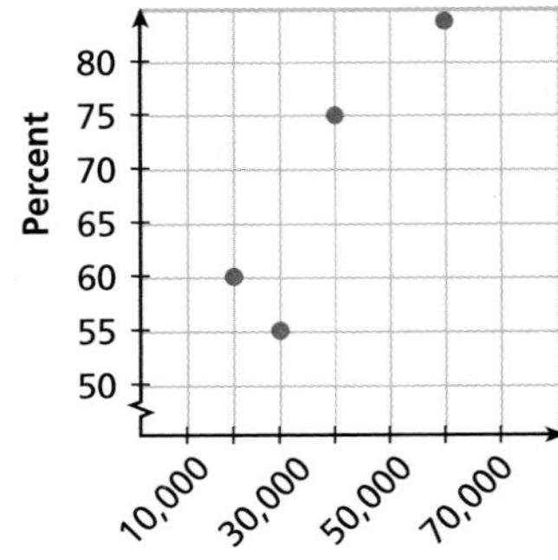


## DAY 4

What is the slope of the line with equation $3x - 5y = 12$?

**A** $-3$

**B** $-\frac{3}{5}$

**C** $\frac{3}{5}$

**D** 3

## DAY 5

Joy and a friend start a business. What linear function relates the total income and each partner's share of the profit based on the data in the table?

| Total Income ($t$) | Profit Share ($p$) |
|---|---|
| $350.00 | $50.00 |
| $425.00 | $87.50 |
| $500.00 | $125.00 |

**A** $p = \frac{1}{2}t - 125$

**B** $p = \frac{1}{4}t - 37.5$

**C** $p = t - 300$

**D** $p = \frac{1}{7}t$

# Countdown to EOC — WEEK 18

## DAY 1

What is the range of the function $f(x) = 2x^2 + 1$ if the domain is $\{-2, 0, 3\}$?

**A** $\{1, 9, 19\}$

**B** $\{0, 8, 18\}$

**C** $\{-9, 1, 19\}$

**D** $\{-2, 0, 3\}$

## DAY 2

Which function has a *y*-intercept of $-2$ and a graph whose slope is $\frac{5}{4}$?

**A** $5x + 4y = 2$

**B** $y = \frac{5}{4}x + 2$

**C** $y = -\frac{5}{4}x + 2$

**D** $y = \frac{5}{4}x - 2$

## DAY 3

The graph shows the relationship between a person's height and weight. Which of the following statements would be an invalid conclusion for this data?

**A** The graph shows data for 20 people.

**B** A person who is tall is likely to have a higher weight.

**C** There is a positive correlation between height and weight.

**D** A person who has a lower weight has a fast metabolism.

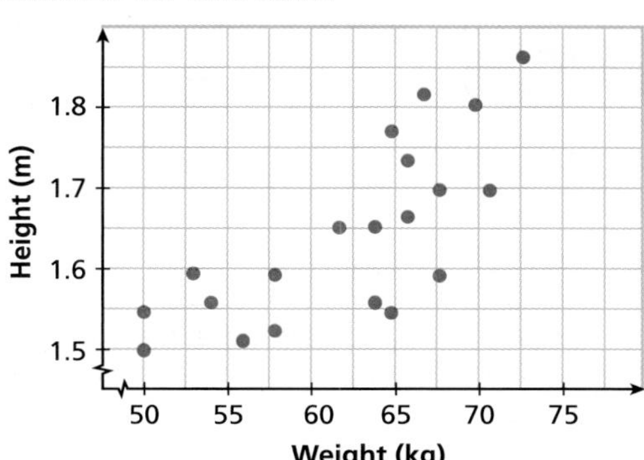


## DAY 4

Which table shows a relation that is a function?

**A**

| x | −1 | 0 | 0 | 1 | 3 |
|---|---|---|---|---|---|
| y | 4 | 4 | 5 | 6 | 9 |

**B**

| x | 6 | 6 | 6 | 6 | 6 |
|---|---|---|---|---|---|
| y | −4 | −6 | −8 | −10 | −12 |

**C**

| x | −4 | −2 | 0 | 2 | 4 |
|---|---|---|---|---|---|
| y | −1 | −1 | −1 | −1 | −1 |

**D**

| x | −3 | −3 | −2 | −1 | 0 |
|---|---|---|---|---|---|
| y | 0 | 1 | 2 | 3 | 4 |

## DAY 5

The graph shows the distance that a person is from home while driving at a constant speed. What quantity is represented by the *y*-intercept?

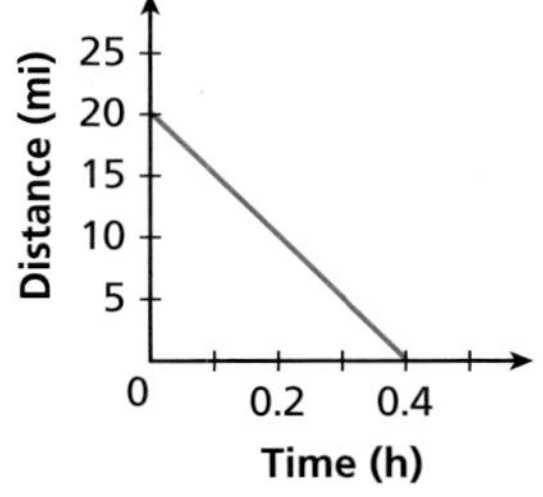


**A** The speed at which the person is driving

**B** The distance from home at the start

**C** The amount of time it takes to get home

**D** The distance from home at the end

# Countdown to EOC

## WEEK 19

### DAY 1

Assuming that the graph below has the same *x*- and *y*-scale, which is the ***best*** estimate for the solution to the system?

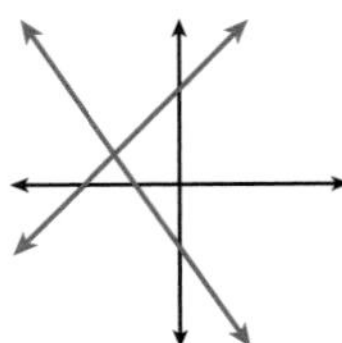

**A** $(-5, 10)$

**B** $(-4, 2)$

**C** $(3, -6)$

**D** $(8, -4)$

### DAY 2

The value of a car *t* years after it is purchased is given by the function $V(t) = 18{,}000(0.88)^t$. ***Approximately*** what is the value of the car 4 years after it is purchased?

**A** \$4,500

**B** \$9,500

**C** \$10,800

**D** \$15,800

### DAY 3

Which graph shows a function from the family $f(x) = x^2$?

**A**

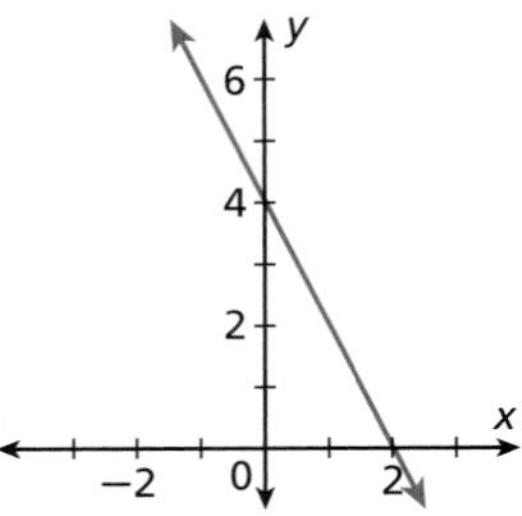


**C**

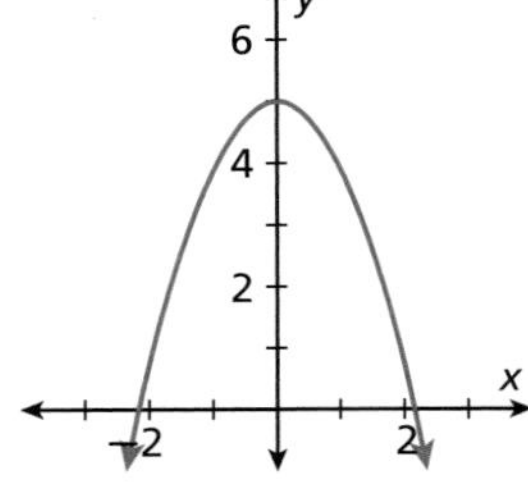


**B**

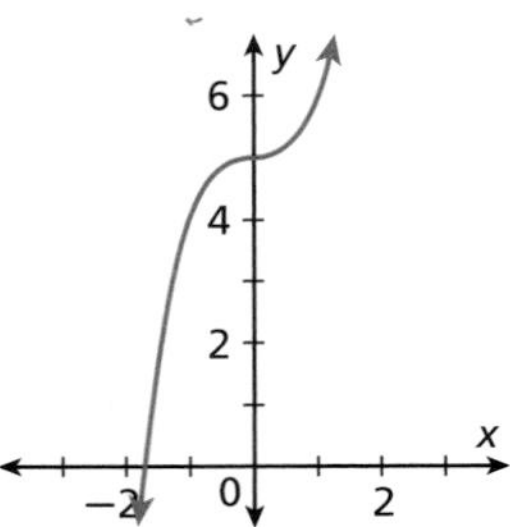


**D**

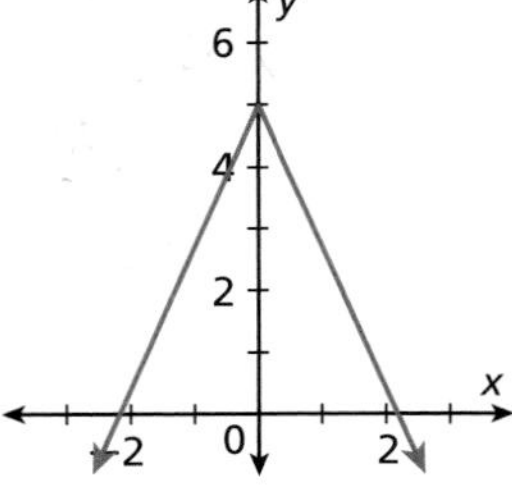


### DAY 4

Miguel earns a 15% commission on his sales in addition to a salary of \$500 a week. His earnings can be modeled by the equation $p = 0.15s + 500$. What restrictions on the values of *p* and *s* ***best*** fit this situation?

**A** $p \geq 0$, *s* can be any value.

**B** $s \geq 0$, *p* can be any value.

**C** $s \geq 500$, $p \geq 0$

**D** $s \geq 0$, $p \geq 500$

### DAY 5

If $f(x) = \frac{1}{2}x$, what ***best*** describes the relationship between *x* and $f(x)$?

**A** As the value of *x* increases by 1, the value of $f(x)$ will increase by 2.

**B** As the value of *x* increases by 1, the value of $f(x)$ will remain the same.

**C** As the value of *x* increases by 1, the value of $f(x)$ will increase by $\frac{1}{2}$.

**D** The value of *x* will not affect the value of $f(x)$.

# Countdown to EOC

# WEEK 20

## DAY 1

On Saturday, Suzie's Pretzel Stand sells a total of 12 items. Suzie charges \$3 for a pretzel and \$2 for a milkshake. If she took in \$32 on Saturday, which system of equations can be used to determine how many pretzels and how many milkshakes were sold?

**A** $\begin{cases} 3x + 2y = 12 \\ x + y = 32 \end{cases}$

**B** $\begin{cases} 3x - 2y = 32 \\ x + y = 12 \end{cases}$

**C** $\begin{cases} 3x - 2y = 12 \\ x + y = 32 \end{cases}$

**D** $\begin{cases} x + y = 12 \\ 3x + 2y = 32 \end{cases}$

## DAY 2

Which expression represents the volume of the pyramid?

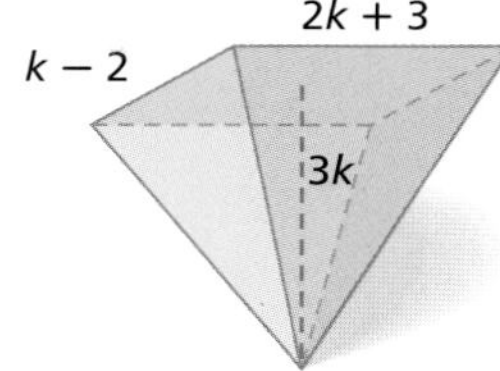


**A** $6k + 1$

**B** $2k^2 + 2k - 6$

**C** $2k^3 - k^2 - 6k$

**D** $6k^3 + 3k^2 - 18k$

## DAY 3

What is the surface area of the cylinder? Round your answer to the nearest tenth.

**A** 150.8 $ft^2$

**B** 179.1 $ft^2$

**C** 207.3 $ft^2$

**D** 226.2 $ft^2$

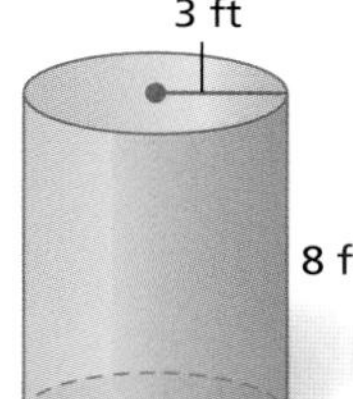


## DAY 4

A quadrilateral has one pair of parallel sides and two congruent diagonals. What is the best classification for this quadrilateral?

**A** parallelogram

**B** rectangle

**C** rhombus

**D** trapezoid

## DAY 5

What is the ratio of the volume of a pyramid to the volume of a prism with the same base area and height?

**A** 1:3

**B** 1:2

**C** 2:1

**D** 3:1

# Countdown to EOC

# WEEK 21

## DAY 1

What is the measure of $\angle 3$ in the regular hexagon below?

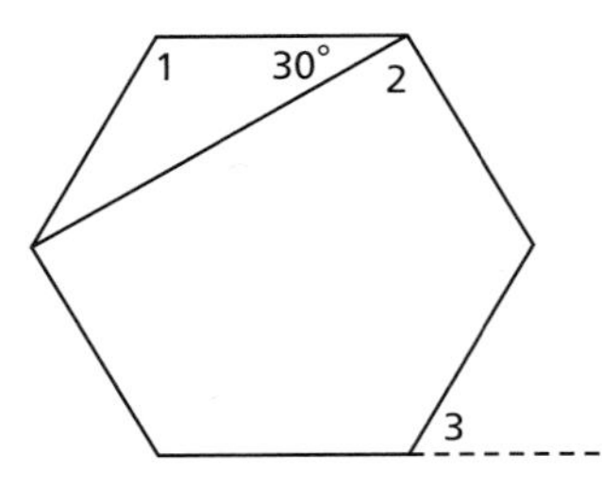


**A** 30°

**B** 60°

**C** 90°

**D** 120°

## DAY 2

How do the graphs of the functions $f(x) = x^2 - 5$ and $g(x) = x^2 + 4$ relate to each other?

**A** The graph of $f(x)$ is 9 units to the left of the graph of $g(x)$.

**B** The graph of $f(x)$ is 1 unit below the graph of $g(x)$.

**C** The graph of $f(x)$ is 9 units below the graph of $g(x)$.

**D** The graph of $f(x)$ is 1 unit to the left of the graph of $g(x)$.

## DAY 3

The graph shows the proposed balance in Jake's bank account if Jake saves an average of $15 a week. Which statement would ***not*** be true if the slope of the line were to increase?

**A** Jake is saving more money per week.

**B** Jake started with more money in his bank account.

**C** It will take less time for Jake's bank balance to reach $120.

**D** After 6 weeks Jake will have more than $90 in his bank account.

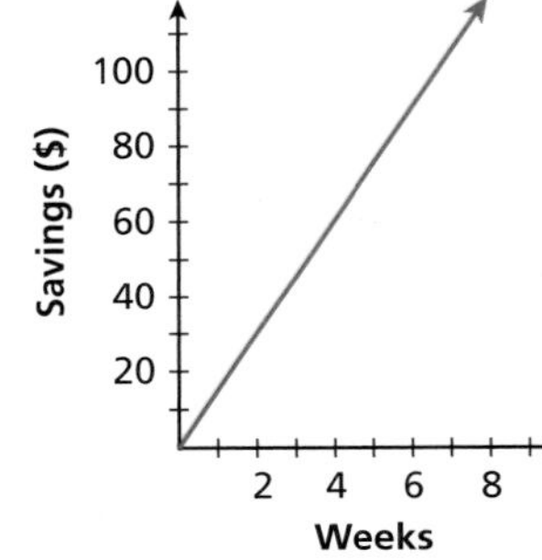


## DAY 4

Ron has a rectangular box that is 12 inches wide, 18 inches long, and 2 inches deep. What is the surface area of the box?

**A** 144 square inches

**B** 432 square inches

**C** 504 square inches

**D** 552 square inches

## DAY 5

What is the value of the expression $\left(\frac{10^2}{10^{-4} \cdot 10^5}\right)^{-2}$?

**A** $-100$

**B** $-\frac{1}{100}$

**C** $\frac{1}{100}$

**D** 100

# Countdown to EOC — WEEK 22

## DAY 1

Over what interval does the function increase?

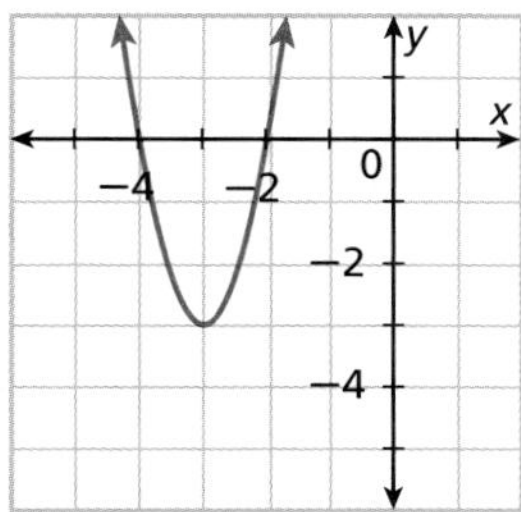


A $x < -3$

B $x < 0$

C $x > 0$

D $x > -3$

## DAY 2

Over what interval does the function decrease?

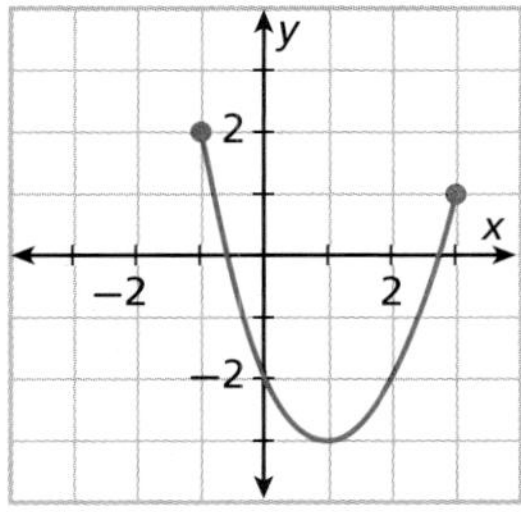


A $x < -1$

B $-1 < x < 1$

C $1 < x < 3$

D $x > 3$

## DAY 3

Which of the following statements is true?

A The function increases over the interval $0 < x < 2$.

B The function decreases over the interval $0 < x < 2$.

C The rate of increase is greatest just before the function peaks.

D The rate of increase is greatest just after $x = 0$.

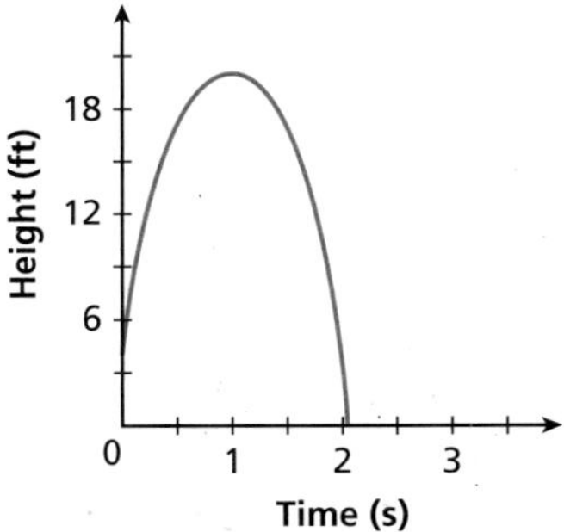


## DAY 4

What is the factored form of $x^2 - 49$?

A $(x + 7)(x - 7)$

B $(x - 7)^2$

C $(x + 7)^2$

D $(x + 49)(x - 1)$

## DAY 5

Which of the following data sets has the greatest interquartile range?

A 3, 4, 6, 5, 7, 5, 7

B 8, 8, 8, 8, 8, 8, 8

C 10, 3, 11, 11, 12, 11, 11

D 2, 1, 2, 6, 4, 5, 6

# Countdown to EOC

## WEEK 23

### DAY 1

What effect does the outlier have on the mean of the given data set?

2 3 4 4 4 5 5 5 22

**A** The outlier decreases the mean by 2.

**B** The outlier increases the mean by 0.5.

**C** The outlier increases the mean by 2.

**D** The outlier increases the mean by 22.

### DAY 2

What is the quotient when $6x^5 - 8x^3 + 4x$ is divided by $2x$?

**A** $3x^4 - 4x + 2$

**B** $4x^3 - 6x^2 + 2$

**C** $3x^5 - 4x^3 + 2x$

**D** $3x^4 - 4x^2 + 2$

### DAY 3

The graph shows the height of water coming out of a fountain over time. Based on the shape of the graph, which type of function below most likely models this situation?

**A** Exponential

**B** Linear

**C** Quadratic

**D** Radical

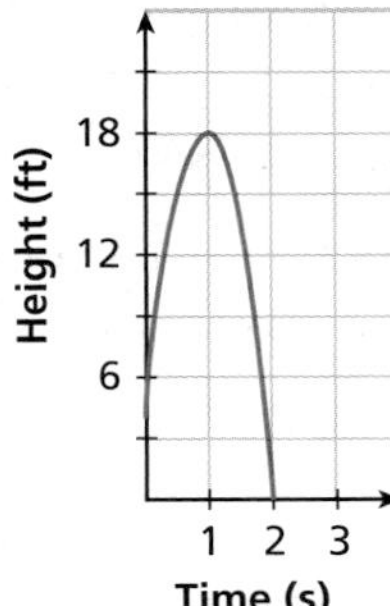


### DAY 4

What is the factored form of $2x^2 + 7x + 3$?

**A** $(2x + 3)(x + 1)$

**B** $(2x + 1)(x + 3)$

**C** $(2x - 1)(x - 3)$

**D** $(2x - 3)(x - 1)$

### DAY 5

Find the product: $(4 + \sqrt{5})(5 - \sqrt{5})$

**A** 20

**B** $20 - \sqrt{5}$

**C** $15 + \sqrt{5}$

**D** $15 + 5\sqrt{5}$

# Countdown to EOC

## WEEK 24

### DAY 1

A circular lawn with a radius of 50 feet is divided into 5 equal sectors. What is the area of each sector? Round your answer to the nearest square foot.

**A** 314 square feet

**B** 785 square feet

**C** 1570 square feet

**D** 7850 square feet

### DAY 2

Latoya invests $2500 in an account that pays compound interest. The function $A(t)$ gives the value of the account after $t$ years. What type of function is $A(t)$?

**A** Exponential

**B** Linear

**C** Quadratic

**D** Rational

### DAY 3

Which situation ***cannot*** be described by a linear function?

**A** The amount of commission earned on a sale if the commission rate is 12%

**B** The area of a square given its side length

**C** The cost of renting a car if the charge is $25 plus $0.15 per mile

**D** The amount paid for babysitting *h* hours if you charge $8.25 per hour

### DAY 4

Suppose $y$ varies inversely as $x$, and $y = 8$ when $x = 4$. What is the value of $y$ when $x = 2$?

**A** 16

**B** 10

**C** 4

**D** 1

### DAY 5

Which of the following relationships between $x$ and $y$ is neither a direct variation nor an inverse variation?

**A** $y = 25x$

**B** $y = \frac{12}{x}$

**C** $xy = 80$

**D** $x + y = 1$

# North Carolina

## The Tar Heel State

Lake Waccamaw

State capitol, Raleigh

Cape Hatteras

## North Carolina Standard Course of Study for High School Math Level A

*North Carolina's Essential Standards and Clarifying Objectives have the following coding scheme:*

| MA. | N. | 1. | 1 |
|---|---|---|---|
| Level | Strand | Number | Clarifying Objective |

**Key to Strands:**

N – Number and Operations
A – Algebra
G – Geometry
S – Statistics and Probability
D – Discrete Mathematics

State bird, cardinal

State flower, flowering dogwood

# North Carolina Standard Course of Study

Charlotte

## Number and Operations

| | |
|---|---|
| **MA.N.1** | Use ratios and rates to solve problems. |
| **MA.N.1.1** | Use proportions to solve problems. |
| **MA.N.1.2** | Select appropriate units and explain the result based on the problem being solved. |
| **MA.N.2** | Use properties of exponents to simplify expressions. |
| **MA.N.2.1** | Represent numerical expressions with exponents in their simplest forms. |
| **MA.N.2.2** | Represent algebraic expressions with exponents in their simplest forms. |
| **MA.N.2.3** | Use strategies to compute square roots and cube roots of numbers that are not perfect squares or perfect cubes. |

Grandfather Mountain, Linville

### Algebra

**MA.A.1** Use appropriate properties and strategies to combine and factor algebraic expressions.

**MA.A.1.1** Execute all operations with algebraic expressions (division by monomials only).

**MA.A.1.2** Use associative, commutative and distributive properties to combine algebraic expressions.

**MA.A.1.3** Analyze quadratic expressions to determine their factors.

**MA.A.2** Use direct and indirect variation to solve problems.

**MA.A.2.1** Use substitution strategies to solve equations involving direct and inverse variation.

**MA.A.2.2** Use literal equations to represent direct and indirect variation.

**MA.A.2.3** Explain the effect that an increase or decrease in one variable will have on the other variables.

**MA.A.3** Analyze patterns of change in functional relationships.

**MA.A.3.1** Differentiate between linear, quadratic and exponential patterns of change.

**MA.A.3.2** Identify intervals of increase or decrease.

**MA.A.3.3** Explain the rate of increase or decrease on an interval.

**MA.A.4** Understand functions based on mathematical and real-world phenomena.

**MA.A.4.1** Categorize relations as functions or "not functions".

**MA.A.4.2** Use appropriate terminology and notation (function, domain, range and intercepts) associated with functions.

**MA.A.4.3** Interpret the relationship of constants and coefficients for data presented in graphs, tables and equations.

**MA.A.4.4** Represent linear functions in a variety of equivalent forms (including point-slope).

**MA.A.4.5** Use graphs, tables and symbols to solve linear equations.

**MA.A.4.6** Use tables and graphs to solve exponential equations.

**MA.A.4.7** Use graphs, tables, and properties to solve quadratic equations.

**MA.A.5** Use strategies to find solutions for linear and exponential relationships.

**MA.A.5.1** Represent linear and exponential relationships in the form of models.

**MA.A.5.2** Use strategies to solve systems of linear equations in two variables, graphically and symbolically.

**MA.A.5.3** Use tables and graphs to solve pairs of linear inequalities in two variables.

**MA.A.5.4** Use tables and graphs to solve systems with linear and exponential inequalities.

*Charlotte skyline*

# North Carolina

Bodie Island Light House, Outer Banks

## Geometry

**MA.G.1** Analyze properties of geometric shapes in the Cartesian coordinate system.

**MA.G.1.1** Use strategies to calculate the slope, distance between points, coordinates of the midpoints and the distance from a point to a line.

**MA.G.1.2** Use geometric properties to identify geometric shapes.

**MA.G.2** Use formulas to solve problems involving area and volume.

**MA.G.2.1** Recognize examples of chord, tangent and secant in visual displays.

**MA.G.2.2** Use formulas to solve problems involving the areas of polygons.

**MA.G.2.3** Understand the 3:1 relationship between volumes of right circular cylinders and cones with the same height and circular base and between the volume of a prism and pyramid with the same base area and height.

**MA.G.2.4** Use formulas to solve problems involving volume of right prisms, pyramids, circular cylinders and right circular cones.

**MA.G.2.5** Represent the relationship between the surface area of prisms, cylinders and pyramids to the sum of the area(s) of their base(s) and lateral surfaces using planar nets to illustrate and sum the relevant measures.

*Great Smoky Mountains National Park*

*Great Smoky Mountains National Park*

## Statistics and Probability

**MA.S.1** Analyze statistical distributions in terms of the relationships among shape, center, spread and outliers.

**MA.S.1.1** Explain the effect of an outlier on the mean, median and range of various graphical displays.

**MA.S.1.2** Compare shape, center, and spread of univariate data using graphical displays, quartiles, percentiles, outliers, means and standard deviations.

**MA.S.2** Infer trends in bivariate data.

**MA.S.2.1** Use formal strategies for placement of lines of best fit to model bivariate data.

**MA.S.2.2** Infer trends in bivariate data displayed in scatter plots to determine informally if the data is best fit with a linear, exponential or quadratic model.

## Discrete

**MA.D.1** Use vertex-edge graphs to route and optimize critical paths.

**MA.D.1.1** Apply the properties of vertex-edge graphs.

**MA.D.1.2** Use vertex-edge graphs and algorithmic thinking (a step-by-step plan) to model and solve problems involving efficient route, Euler Circuits, and Hamiltonian Circuits.

Blue Ridge Parkway
Wright Brothers National Memorial
Pullen Park, Raleigh
North Carolina Black Bear
North Carolina beach

# Foundations for Algebra

## Tools for Success

# Equations

## Tools for Success

CHAPTER 3

# Inequalities

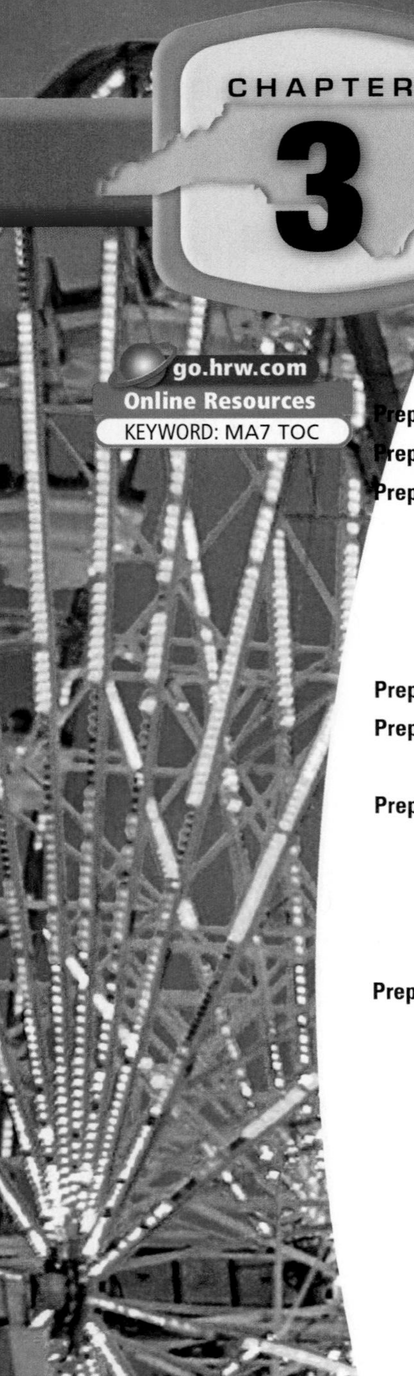




## Tools for Success

CHAPTER 4

# Functions



go.hrw.com
Online Resources
KEYWORD: MA7 TOC

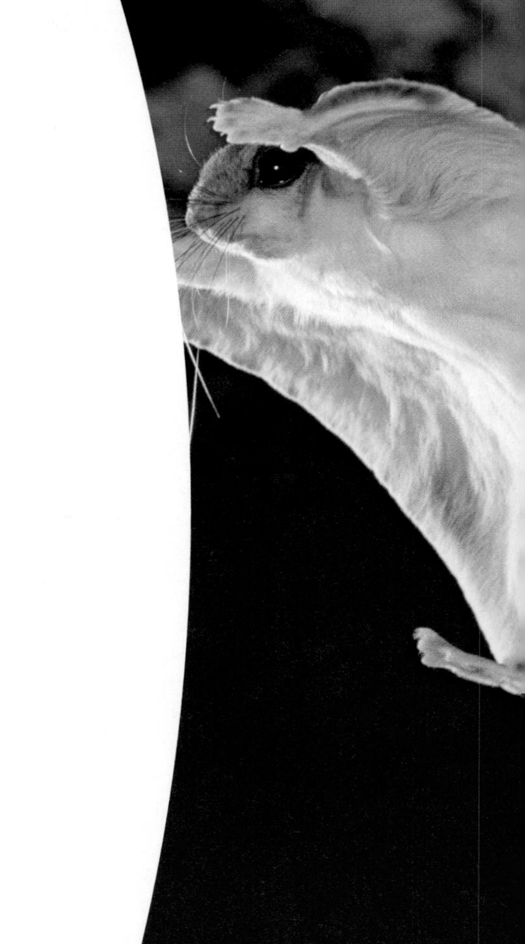

## Tools for Success

# Linear Functions



go.hrw.com
Online Resources
KEYWORD: MA7 TOC

## Tools for Success

# Systems of Equations and Inequalities

CHAPTER 6

go.hrw.com
Online Resources
KEYWORD: MA7 TOC

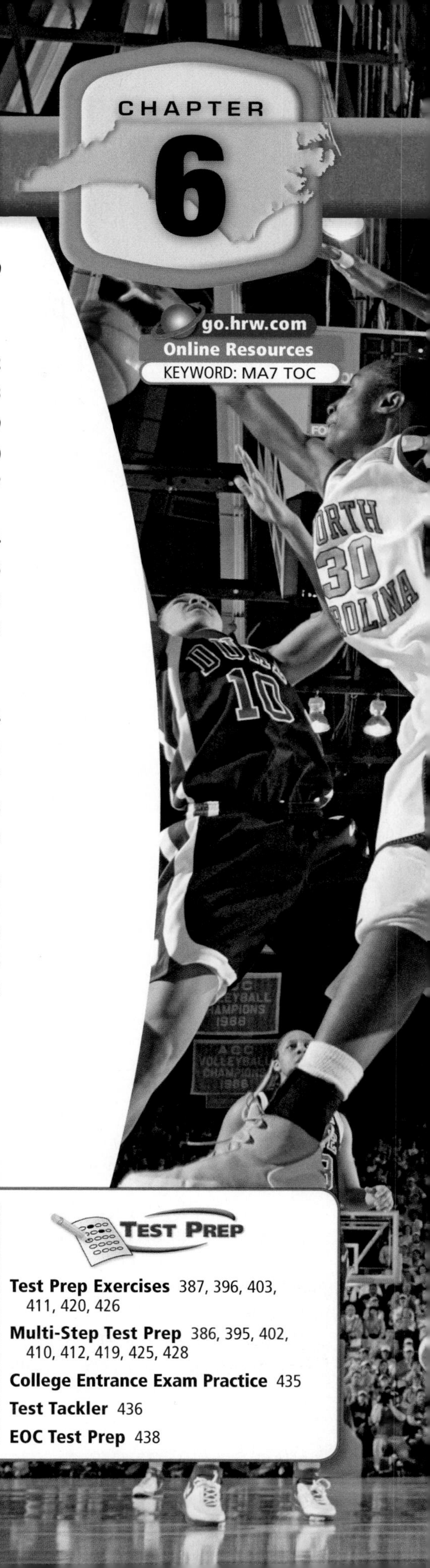

## Tools for Success

# Exponents and Polynomials



## Tools for Success

CHAPTER 8

# Factoring Polynomials

## Tools for Success

# Quadratic Functions and Equations

go.hrw.com
Online Resources
KEYWORD: MA7 TOC



## Tools for Success

CHAPTER 10

# Data Analysis and Probability

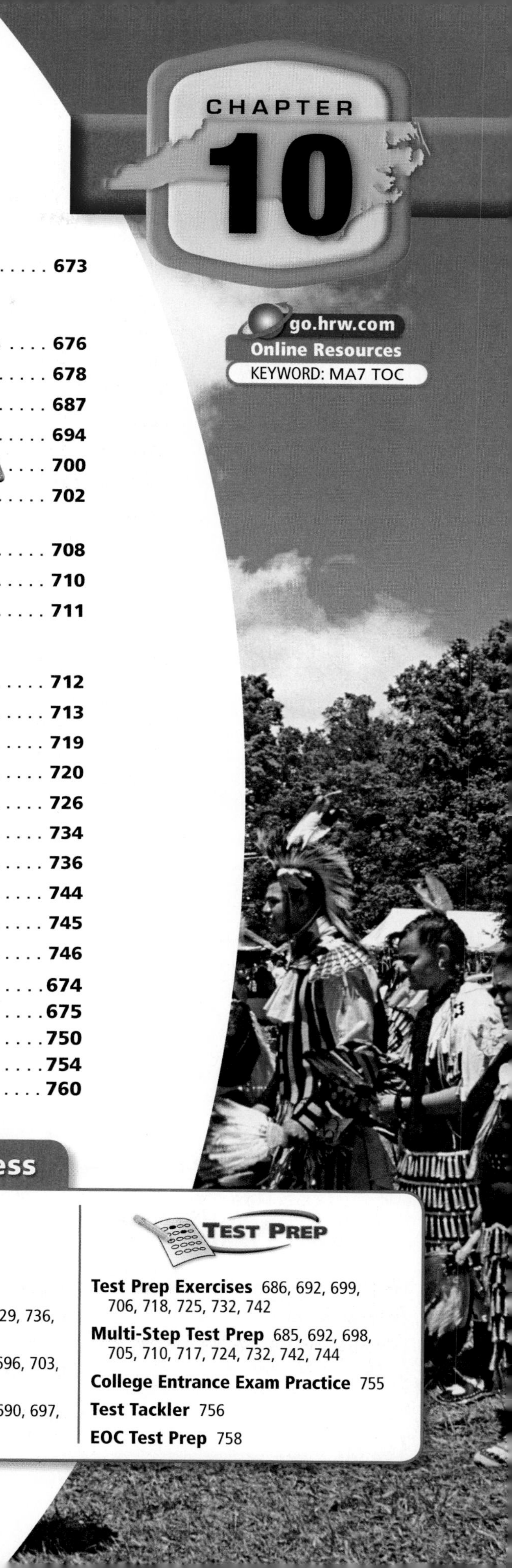

go.hrw.com
Online Resources
KEYWORD: MA7 TOC

# Exponential and Radical Functions

go.hrw.com
Online Resources
KEYWORD: MA7 TOC



## Tools for Success

CHAPTER 12

# Rational Functions and Equations



go.hrw.com
Online Resources
KEYWORD: MA7 TOC

## Tools for Success

# WHO USES MATHEMATICS?

The Career Path features are a set of interviews with young adults who are either preparing for or just beginning in different career fields. These people share what math courses they studied in high school, how math is used in their field, and what options the future holds. Also, many exercises throughout the book highlight the different skills used in various career fields.

## Career Path

go.hrw.com
Career Resources Online
KEYWORD: MA7 Career

### Career Applications

**CULINARY ARTS** *p. 200*

If you enjoy preparing food, you might be interested in a culinary arts program. Besides cooking, you can also learn business skills, like how to start and run your own catering business. See page 200 to find out what math courses will help prepare you for this career.

**DATA MINING** *p. 347*

Read the Career Path on page 347 to learn what courses a data mining major may take and what careers are available in this field. For example, do you like to keep track of sports statistics? If so, a background in data mining can help you find work with a professional sports team.

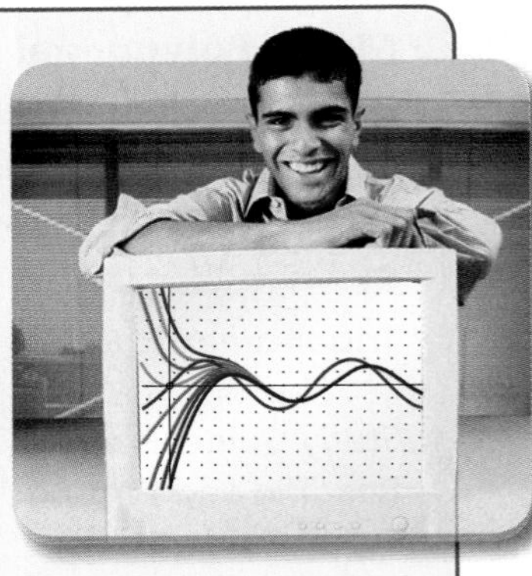

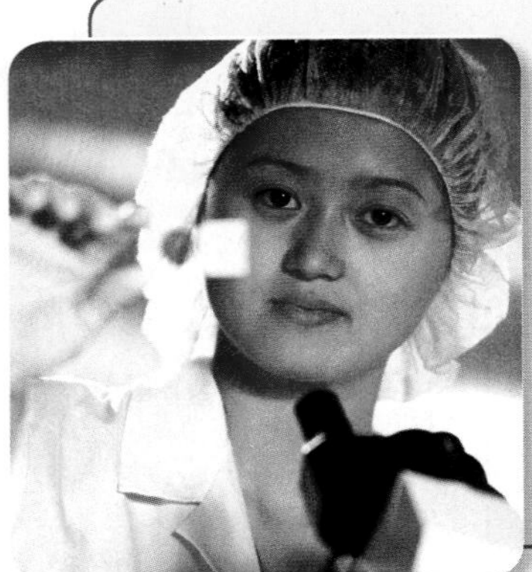

**BIOSTATISTICS** *p. 743*

The Career Path on page 743 describes the education and experience needed to be a successful biostatistician. One important job biostatisticians do is research and test medications to ensure that they are both effective and safe for human use.

# WHY LEARN MATHEMATICS?

Links to interesting topics may accompany real-world applications in the examples or exercises. For a complete list of all applications in *Holt McDougal Algebra 1*, see page S149 in the Index.

**LINK — Number Theory**

Fibonacci numbers occur frequently throughout nature. The number of petals on many flowers are numbers of the Fibonacci sequence. Two petals on a flower are rare but 3, 5, and even 34 petals are common.

**Find the given term of each arithmetic sequence.**

**34.** 2.5, 8.5, 14.5, 20.5, ...; 30th term

**35.** 189.6, 172.3, 155, 137.7, ...; 18th term

**36.** $\frac{1}{4}, \frac{3}{4}, \frac{5}{4}, \frac{7}{4}, \ldots$; 15th term

**37.** $\frac{2}{3}, \frac{11}{12}, \frac{7}{6}, \frac{17}{12}, \ldots$; 25th term

**38. Number Theory** The sequence 1, 1, 2, 3, 5, 8, 13, ... is a famous sequence called the Fibonacci sequence. After the first two terms, each term is the sum of the previous two terms.

a. Write the first 10 terms of the Fibonacci sequence. Is the Fibonacci sequence arithmetic? Explain.

b. Notice that the third term is divisible by 2. Are the 6th and 9th terms also divisible by 2? What conclusion can you draw about every third term? Why is this true?

c. Can you find any other patterns? (*Hint:* Look at every 4th and 5th term.)

**39. Entertainment** Seats in a concert hall are arranged in the pattern shown.

a. The numbers of seats in the rows form an arithmetic sequence. Write a rule for the arithmetic sequence.

b. How many seats are in the 15th row?

## LINKS Real-World



**LINK — Biology**

When bleeding occurs, platelets (which appear green in the image above) help to form a clot to reduce blood loss. Calcium and vitamin K are also necessary for clot formation.



**LINK — Engineering**

This arched bridge spans a river near the city of Yokote in northwestern Japan.



**LINK — Travel**

Building began on the Tower of Pisa, located in Pisa, Italy, in 1173. The tower started leaning after the third story was added. At the fifth story, attempts were made to correct the leaning. The tower was finally complete in 1350.

# Focus on Problem Solving

## The Problem-Solving Plan

To be a good problem solver you need a good problem-solving plan. Using a problem-solving plan along with a problem-solving strategy helps you organize your work and correctly solve the problem. The plan used in this book is outlined below.

### UNDERSTAND the Problem

- **What are you asked to find?** Make sure you understand exactly what the problem is asking. Restate the problem in your own words.
- **What information is given in the problem?** List every piece of information the problem gives you.
- **Is all the information relevant?** Sometimes problems have extra information that is not needed to solve the problem. Try to determine what is and is not needed. This helps you stay organized when you are making a plan.
- **Were you given enough information to solve the problem?** Sometimes there simply is not enough information to solve the problem. List what else you need to know to solve the problem.

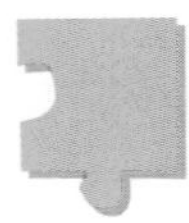

### Make a PLAN

- **What problem-solving strategy or strategies can you use to help you solve the problem?** Think about strategies you have used in the past to solve problems. Would any of them be helpful in solving this problem?
- **Create a step-by-step plan of how you will solve the problem.** Write out your plan in words to help you get a clearer idea of how to solve the problem mathematically.

### SOLVE

- **Use your plan to solve the problem.** Translate your plan from words to math. Show each step in your solution and write your answer in a complete sentence.

### LOOK BACK

- **Did you completely answer the question that was asked?** Be sure you answered the question that was asked and that your answer is complete.
- **Is your answer reasonable?** Your answer should make sense.
- **Could you have used a different strategy to solve the problem?** Solving the problem again with a different strategy is a good way to check your answer.
- **Did you learn anything that could help you solve similar problems in the future?** You may want to take notes about this kind of problem and the strategy you used to solve it.

# Using the Problem-Solving Plan

The feeder at an animal shelter needs 125 pounds of food to feed the rescued dogs for a month. A local grocery store is having a special—buy two 10-pound bags of dog food and get a 3.5-pound bag free. What is the fewest number of 10-pound bags the feeder can buy to have enough dog food for the month?

## UNDERSTAND the Problem

**List the important information in the problem.**

At least 125 pounds of dog food are needed for one month.
If the feeder buys two 10-pound bags of dog food, she gets a 3.5-pound bag free.

**What is the problem asking you to find?**

The fewest number of 10-pound bags the feeder needs to buy to have 125 pounds of dog food.

## Make a PLAN

**Choose a strategy.**

You can **make a table** to organize the number of bags purchased, the number of pounds in those bags, the number of free pounds, and the total number of pounds. Make a table and work out one column at a time until there are at least 125 pounds of food.

## SOLVE

**Use the strategy.**

*For every even number of bags, increase the number of free pounds by 3.5.*

| Number of Bags | 1 | 2 | 3 | 4 | 5 | 6 | 7 | 8 | 9 | 10 | 11 |
|---|---|---|---|---|---|---|---|---|---|---|---|
| Pounds | 10 | 20 | 30 | 40 | 50 | 60 | 70 | 80 | 90 | 100 | 110 |
| Free Pounds | 0 | 3.5 | 3.5 | 7 | 7 | 10.5 | 10.5 | 14 | 14 | 17.5 | 17.5 |
| Total Pounds | 10 | 23.5 | 33.5 | 47 | 57 | 70.5 | 80.5 | 94 | 104 | 117.5 | **127.5** |

The fewest number of bags the feeder must buy is 11.

## LOOK BACK

**Check your answer.**

Multiply the number of bags purchased by the weight of each bag. This is the number of pounds paid for: $11 \times 10 = 110$.

Then divide the number of bags purchased by 2, and multiply the whole number result by 3.5. This is the number of free pounds received because of the special: $11 \div 2 = 5.5$, $5 \times 3.5 = 17.5$.
Add the pounds: $110 + 17.5 = 127.5$.
The feeder only needs 125 pounds, so this is enough.

# How to Study Algebra 1

This book has many features designed to help you learn and study effectively. Becoming familiar with these features will prepare you for greater success on your exams.

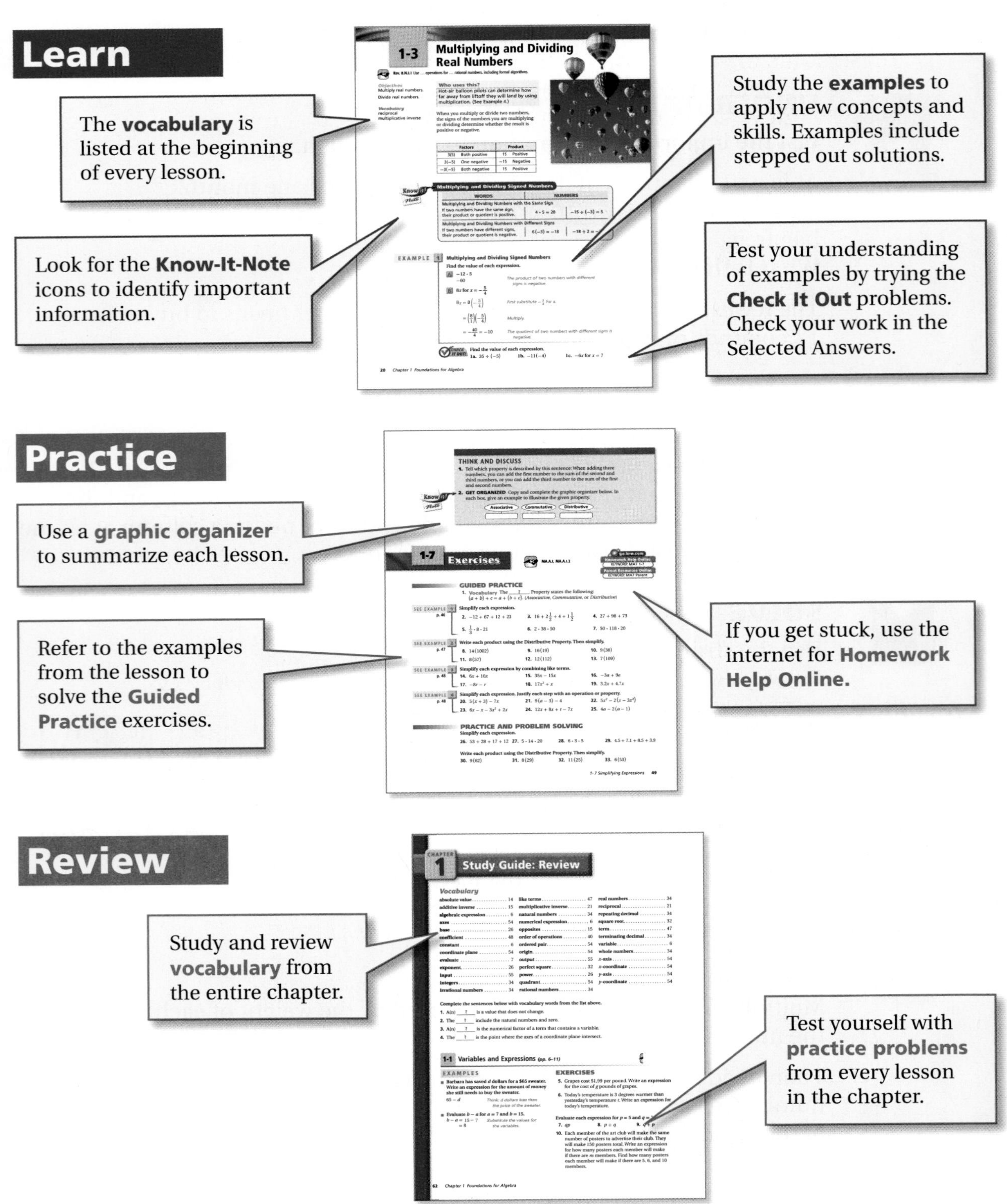

# Scavenger Hunt

Use this scavenger hunt to discover a few of the many tools in ***Holt McDougal Algebra 1*** that you can use to become an independent learner. On a separate sheet of paper, write the answers to each question below. Within each answer, one letter will be in a yellow box. After you have answered every question, identify the letters that would be in yellow boxes and rearrange them to reveal the answer to the question at the bottom of the page.

1. What is the first **Vocabulary** term in the Study Guide: Preview for Chapter 2?

2. What keyword should you enter for **Homework Help** for Lesson 6-3?

3. In Lesson 7-3, what is **Example 1** teaching you to find?

4. What are you asked to give an example of in the **Know-It Note** on page 543?

5. What college major is listed for the **Career Path** on page 547?

6. To what school subject is **Exercise 44** on page 456 linked?

7. In the **Study Guide: Review** for Chapter 10, what sport do Questions 4 and 5 refer to?

8. In Chapter 5's **Test Tackler**, what multiple choice strategy is described?

## FACT!

Algebra was used to build what ancient structures?

CHAPTER 1

# Foundations for Algebra

## 1A The Language of Algebra

## 1B The Tools of Algebra



### Why Learn This?

You can use square roots to determine the size of a square flower garden. The Latham Garden at Tryon Palace in New Bern, NC, is shown.

go.hrw.com

**Chapter Project Online**

KEYWORD: MA7 ChProj

## Vocabulary

**Match each term on the left with a definition on the right.**

1. difference
2. factor
3. perimeter
4. area

A. the distance around a figure
B. a number that is multiplied by another number to form a product
C. a result of division
D. the number of square units a figure covers
E. a result of subtraction

## Whole Number Operations

**Add, subtract, multiply, or divide.**

5. $23 + 6$
6. $156 \div 12$
7. $18 \times 96$
8. $85 - 62$

## Add and Subtract Decimals

**Add or subtract.**

9. $2.18 + 6.9$
10. $0.32 - 0.18$
11. $29.34 + 0.27$
12. $4 - 1.82$

## Multiply Decimals

**Multiply.**

13. $0.7 \times 0.6$
14. $2.5 \times 0.1$
15. $1.5 \times 1.5$
16. $3.04 \times 0.12$

## Divide Decimals

**Divide.**

17. $6.15 \div 3$
18. $8.64 \div 2$
19. $7.2 \div 0.4$
20. $92.7 \div 0.3$

## Multiply and Divide Fractions

**Multiply or divide. Give your answer in simplest form.**

21. $\frac{3}{5} \times \frac{1}{2}$
22. $\frac{2}{3} \div \frac{1}{6}$
23. $\frac{7}{8} \times \frac{4}{7}$
24. $4 \div \frac{2}{3}$

## Add and Subtract Fractions

**Add or subtract. Give your answer in simplest form.**

25. $\frac{2}{5} + \frac{2}{5}$
26. $\frac{3}{8} - \frac{1}{8}$
27. $\frac{1}{2} + \frac{1}{4}$
28. $\frac{2}{3} - \frac{4}{9}$

CHAPTER 1

# Study Guide: Preview

## Where You've Been

**Previously, you**

- learned words related to mathematical operations.
- identified numbers on a real number line.
- performed operations on whole numbers, decimals, and fractions.
- plotted points in the coordinate plane.

## In This Chapter

**You will study**

- how to evaluate and simplify expressions.
- properties of the real number system.
- the order of operations.
- patterns formed by points plotted in the coordinate plane.

## Where You're Going

**You can use the skills learned in this chapter**

- to form a solid foundation for the rest of this algebra course.
- in other classes, such as Biology, History, and Physics.
- to determine final costs, stock values, and profit.

## *Key Vocabulary/Vocabulario*

| | |
|---|---|
| additive inverse | inverso aditivo |
| coefficient | coeficiente |
| constant | constante |
| coordinate plane | plano cartesiano |
| irrational numbers | números irracionales |
| like terms | términos semejantes |
| origin | origen |
| rational numbers | números racionales |
| variable | variable |

## *Vocabulary Connections*

To become familiar with some of the vocabulary terms in the chapter, consider the following. You may refer to the chapter, the glossary, or a dictionary if you like.

1. The word **variable** comes from the word *vary*. What does *vary* mean? Which of the key vocabulary terms above has the opposite meaning?
2. Another word for *inverse* is *reverse*. The word *additive* relates to the operation of addition. What do you think an **additive inverse** is?
3. The prefix *ir-* means "not." What relationship do you think **rational numbers** and **irrational numbers** may have?
4. To *originate* means "to begin at." What do you think the **origin** of a coordinate plane is?

## Reading Strategy: Use Your Book for Success

Understanding how your textbook is organized will help you locate and use helpful information.

Pay attention to the **margin notes.** Know-It Note icons point out key information. Writing Math notes, Helpful Hints, and Caution notes help you understand concepts and avoid common mistakes.

**Writing Math**
These expressions mean "2 times $y$":
$2y$ $2(y)$

**Helpful Hint**
A replacement set
a set of numbers t
can be substituted

**Caution!**
In the expression
$-5^2$, 5 is the base
because the nega

The **Glossary** is found in the back of your textbook. Use it as a resource when you need the definition of an unfamiliar word or property.

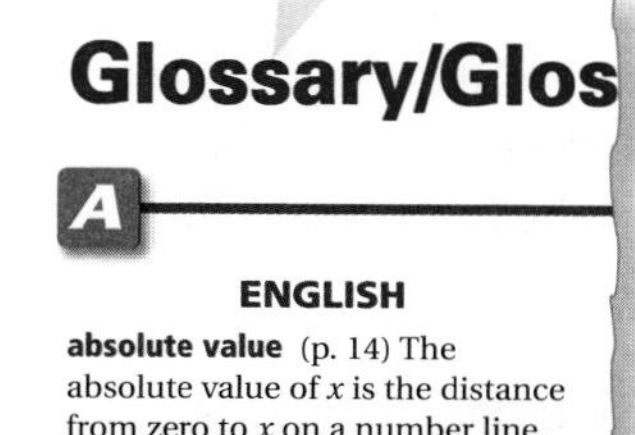


The **Index** is located at the end of your textbook. Use it to locate the page where a particular concept is taught.

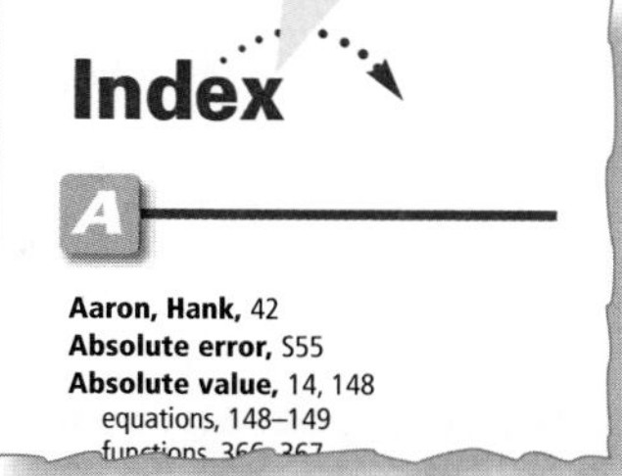


The **Skills Bank** is found in the back of your textbook. These pages review concepts from previous math courses, including geometry skills.

## Try This

**Use your textbook for the following problems.**

1. Use the index to find the page where each word is defined: *algebraic expression, like terms, ordered pair, real numbers.*
2. What mnemonic device is taught in a Helpful Hint in Lesson 1-6, Order of Operations?
3. Use the glossary to find the definition of each word: *additive inverse, constant, perfect square, reciprocal.*
4. Where can you review the concepts of area and perimeter?

# 1-1 Variables and Expressions

**Rev. 6.A.1.1** Use verbal descriptions ... to represent problem situations.

***Objectives***
Translate between words and algebra.

Evaluate algebraic expressions.

***Vocabulary***
variable
constant
numerical expression
algebraic expression
evaluate

**Why learn this?**
Variables and expressions can be used to determine how many plastic drink bottles must be recycled to make enough carpet for a house.

A home that is "green built" uses many recycled products, including carpet made from recycled plastic drink bottles. You can determine how many square feet of carpet can be made from a certain number of plastic drink bottles by using *variables, constants,* and *expressions.*

A **variable** is a letter or symbol used to represent a value that can change.

A **constant** is a value that does not change.

A **numerical expression** may contain only constants and operations.

An **algebraic expression** may contain variables, constants, and operations.

You will need to translate between algebraic expressions and words to be successful in math. The table below shows some of the ways to write mathematical operations with words.

Plus, sum, increased by

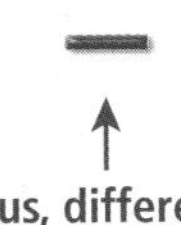

Minus, difference, less than

Times, product, equal groups of

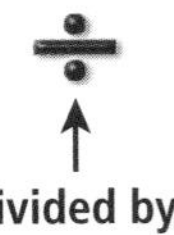

Divided by, quotient

## EXAMPLE 1 Translating from Algebraic Symbols to Words

**Writing Math**

These expressions all mean "2 times $y$":

| | |
|---|---|
| $2y$ | $2(y)$ |
| $2 \cdot y$ | $(2)(y)$ |
| $2 \times y$ | $(2)y$ |

**Give two ways to write each algebraic expression in words.**

**A** $x + 3$
the sum of $x$ and 3
$x$ increased by 3

**B** $m - 7$
the difference of $m$ and 7
7 less than $m$

**C** $2 \cdot y$
2 times $y$
the product of 2 and $y$

**D** $k \div 5$
$k$ divided by 5
the quotient of $k$ and 5

**Give two ways to write each algebraic expression in words.**

**1a.** $4 - n$ **1b.** $\frac{t}{5}$ **1c.** $9 + q$ **1d.** $3(h)$

To translate words into algebraic expressions, look for words that indicate the action that is taking place.

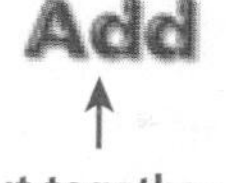

| Add | Subtract | Multiply | Divide |
|---|---|---|---|
| ↑ | ↑ | ↑ | ↑ |
| Put together, combine | Find how much more or less | Put together equal groups | Separate into equal groups |

## EXAMPLE 2 Translating from Words to Algebraic Symbols

**A** **Eve reads 25 pages per hour. Write an expression for the number of pages she reads in $h$ hours.**

$h$ represents the number of hours that Eve reads.

$25 \cdot h$ or $25h$ *Think: h groups of 25 pages.*

**B** **Sam is 2 years younger than Sue, who is $y$ years old. Write an expression for Sam's age.**

$y$ represents Sue's age.

$y - 2$ *Think: "younger than" means "less than."*

**C** **William runs a mile in 12 minutes. Write an expression for the number of miles that William runs in $m$ minutes.**

$m$ represents the total time William runs.

$\frac{m}{12}$ *Think: How many groups of 12 are in m?*

**2a.** Lou drives at 65 mi/h. Write an expression for the number of miles that Lou drives in $t$ hours.

**2b.** Miriam is 5 cm taller than her sister, who is $m$ cm tall. Write an expression for Miriam's height in centimeters.

**2c.** Elaine earns \$32 per day. Write an expression for the amount that she earns in $d$ days.

To **evaluate** an expression is to find its value. To evaluate an algebraic expression, substitute numbers for the variables in the expression and then simplify the expression.

## EXAMPLE 3 Evaluating Algebraic Expressions

**Evaluate each expression for $x = 8$, $y = 5$, and $z = 4$.**

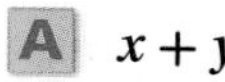

**A** $x + y$

$x + y = 8 + 5$ *Substitute 8 for x and 5 for y.*

$= 13$ *Simplify.*

**B** $\frac{x}{z}$

$\frac{x}{z} = \frac{8}{4}$ *Substitute 8 for x and 4 for z.*

$= 2$ *Simplify.*

**Evaluate each expression for $m = 3$, $n = 2$, and $p = 9$.**

**3a.** $mn$ **3b.** $p - n$ **3c.** $p \div m$

## EXAMPLE 4 *Recycling Application*

**Approximately fourteen 20-ounce plastic drink bottles must be recycled to produce 1 square foot of carpet.**

**a. Write an expression for the number of bottles needed to make *c* square feet of carpet.**

The expression $14c$ models the number of bottles needed to make $c$ square feet of carpet.

**b. Find the number of bottles needed to make 40, 120, and 224 square feet of carpet.**

Evaluate $14c$ for $c = 40$, 120, and 224.

| $c$ | $14c$ |
|---|---|
| 40 | $14(40) = 560$ |
| 120 | $14(120) = 1680$ |
| 224 | $14(224) = 3136$ |

To make 40 $ft^2$ of carpet, 560 bottles are needed.
To make 120 $ft^2$ of carpet, 1680 bottles are needed.
To make 224 $ft^2$ of carpet, 3136 bottles are needed.

**Helpful Hint**

A replacement set is a set of numbers that can be substituted for a variable. The replacement set in Example 4 is {40, 120, 224}.

**4.** To make one sweater, sixty-three 20-ounce plastic drink bottles must be recycled.

**a.** Write an expression for the number of bottles needed to make *s* sweaters.

**b.** Find the number of bottles needed to make 12, 25, and 50 sweaters.

### THINK AND DISCUSS

**1.** Write two ways to suggest each of the following, using words or phrases: addition, subtraction, multiplication, division.

**2.** Explain the difference between a numerical expression and an algebraic expression.

**3. GET ORGANIZED** Copy and complete the graphic organizer. Next to each operation, write a word phrase in the left box and its corresponding algebraic expression in the right box.

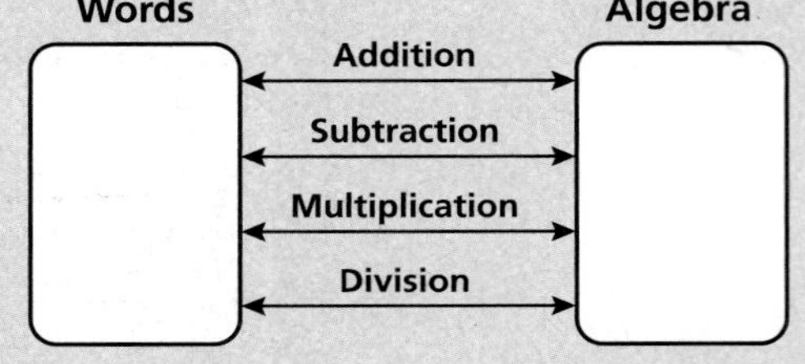


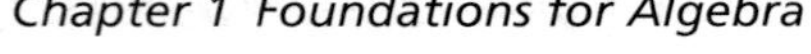

# 1-1 Exercises

Rev. 6.A.1.1

go.hrw.com
Homework Help Online
KEYWORD: MA7 1-1
Parent Resources Online
KEYWORD: MA7 Parent

## GUIDED PRACTICE

1. **Vocabulary** A(n) ___?___ is a value that can change. (*algebraic expression*, *constant*, or *variable*)

SEE EXAMPLE 1 p. 6

**Give two ways to write each algebraic expression in words.**

2. $n - 5$
3. $\frac{f}{3}$
4. $c + 15$
5. $9 - y$
6. $\frac{x}{12}$
7. $t + 12$
8. $8x$
9. $x - 3$

SEE EXAMPLE 2 p. 7

10. George drives at 45 mi/h. Write an expression for the number of miles George travels in $h$ hours.
11. The length of a rectangle is 4 units greater than its width $w$. Write an expression for the length of the rectangle.

SEE EXAMPLE 3 p. 7

**Evaluate each expression for $a = 3$, $b = 4$, and $c = 2$.**

12. $a - c$
13. $ab$
14. $b \div c$
15. $ac$

SEE EXAMPLE 4 p. 8

16. Brianna practices the piano 30 minutes each day.
    a. Write an expression for the number of hours she practices in $d$ days.
    b. Find the number of hours Brianna practices in 2, 4, and 10 days.

## PRACTICE AND PROBLEM SOLVING

**Independent Practice**

| For Exercises | See Example |
|---|---|
| 17–24 | 1 |
| 25–26 | 2 |
| 27–30 | 3 |
| 31 | 4 |

**Extra Practice**
Skills Practice p. S4
Application Practice p. S28

**Give two ways to write each algebraic expression in words.**

17. $5p$
18. $4 - y$
19. $3 + x$
20. $3y$
21. $-3s$
22. $r \div 5$
23. $14 - t$
24. $x + 0.5$
25. Friday's temperature was 20° warmer than Monday's temperature $t$. Write an expression for Friday's temperature.
26. Ann sleeps 8 hours per night. Write an expression for the number of hours Ann sleeps in $n$ nights.

**Evaluate each expression for $r = 6$, $s = 5$, and $t = 3$.**

27. $r - s$
28. $s + t$
29. $r \div t$
30. $sr$
31. Jim is paid for overtime when he works more than 40 hours per week.
    a. Write an expression for the number of hours he works overtime when he works $h$ hours.
    b. Find the number of hours Jim works overtime when he works 40, 44, 48, and 52 hours.

32. **Write About It** Write a paragraph that explains to another student how to evaluate an expression.

**Write an algebraic expression for each verbal expression. Then write a real-world situation that could be modeled by the expression.**

33. the product of 2 and $x$
34. $b$ less than 17
35. 10 more than $y$

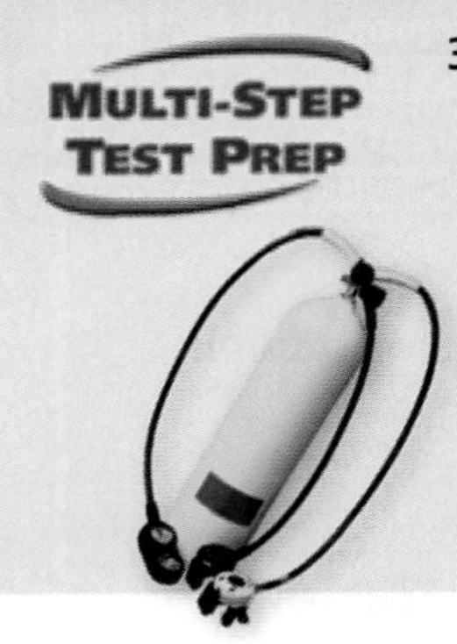


**36.** This problem will prepare you for the Multi-Step Test Prep on page 38.

The air around you puts pressure on your body equal to 14.7 pounds per square inch (psi). When you are underwater, the water exerts additional pressure on your body. For each foot you are below the surface of the water, the pressure increases by 0.445 psi.

a. What does 14.7 represent in the expression $14.7 + 0.445d$?

b. What does $d$ represent in the expression?

c. What is the total pressure exerted on a person's body when $d = 8$ ft?

**37. Geometry** The length of a rectangle is 9 inches. Write an expression for the area of the rectangle if the width is $w$ inches. Find the area of the rectangle when the width is 1, 8, 9, and 11 inches.

**38. Geometry** The perimeter of any rectangle is the sum of its lengths and widths. The area of any rectangle is the length $\ell$ times the width $w$.

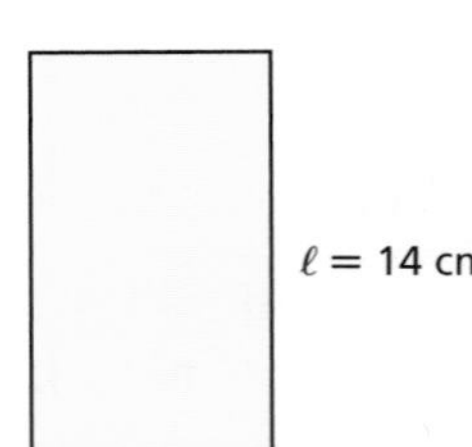


a. Write an expression for the perimeter of a rectangle.

b. Find the perimeter of the rectangle shown.

c. Write an expression for the area of a rectangle.

d. Find the area of the rectangle shown.

**Complete each table. Evaluate the expression for each value of $x$.**

**39.**

| $x$ | $x + 12$ |
|---|---|
| 1 | |
| 2 | |
| 3 | |
| 4 | |

**40.**

| $x$ | $10x$ |
|---|---|
| 1 | |
| 5 | |
| 10 | |
| 15 | |

**41.**

| $x$ | $x \div 2$ |
|---|---|
| 12 | |
| 20 | |
| 26 | |
| 30 | |

A crater on Canada's Devon Island is geologically similar to the surface of Mars. However, the temperature on Devon Island is about 37°F in summer, and the average summer temperature on Mars is −85°F.

**42. Astronomy** An object's weight on Mars can be found by multiplying 0.38 by the object's weight on Earth.

a. An object weighs $p$ pounds on Earth. Write an expression for its weight on Mars.

b. Dana weighs 120 pounds, and her bicycle weighs 44 pounds. How much would Dana and her bicycle together weigh on Mars?

**43. Meteorology** Use the bar graph to write an expression for the average annual precipitation in New York, New York.

a. The average annual precipitation in New York is $m$ inches more than the average annual precipitation in Houston, Texas.

b. The average annual precipitation in New York is $s$ inches less than the average annual precipitation in Miami, Florida.

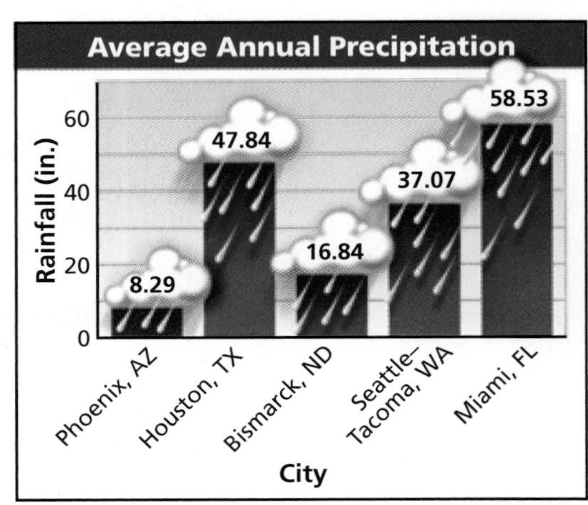

44. **Critical Thinking** Compare algebraic expressions and numerical expressions. Give examples of each.

**Write an algebraic expression for each verbal expression. Then evaluate the algebraic expression for the given values of $x$.**

| | Verbal | Algebraic | $x = 12$ | $x = 14$ |
|---|---|---|---|---|
| | $x$ reduced by 5 | $x - 5$ | $12 - 5 = 7$ | $14 - 5 = 9$ |
| **45.** | 7 more than $x$ | ■ | ■ | ■ |
| **46.** | The quotient of $x$ and 2 | ■ | ■ | ■ |
| **47.** | The sum of $x$ and 3 | ■ | ■ | ■ |

Rev. 6.A.1.1

48. Claire has had her driver's license for 3 years. Bill has had his license for $b$ fewer years than Claire. Which expression can be used to show the number of years Bill has had his driver's license?

Ⓐ $3 + b$ Ⓑ $b + 3$ Ⓒ $3 - b$ Ⓓ $b < 3$

49. Which expression represents $x$?

Ⓕ $12 - 5$ Ⓗ $7 - x$

Ⓖ $x + 5$ Ⓙ $12 - x$

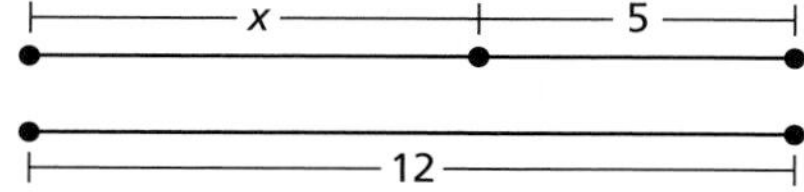


50. Which situation is best modeled by the expression $25 - x$?

Ⓐ George places $x$ more video games on a shelf with 25 games.

Ⓑ Sarah has driven $x$ miles of a 25-mile trip.

Ⓒ Amelia paid 25 dollars of an $x$ dollar lunch that she shared with Ariel.

Ⓓ Jorge has 25 boxes full of $x$ baseball cards each.

## CHALLENGE AND EXTEND

**Evaluate each expression for the given values of the variables.**

**51.** $2ab$; $a = 6$, $b = 3$ **52.** $2x + y$; $x = 4$, $y = 5$ **53.** $3x \div 6y$; $x = 6$, $y = 3$

**54.** **Multi-Step** An Internet service provider charges \$9.95/month for the first 20 hours and \$0.50 for each additional hour. Write an expression representing the charges for $h$ hours of use in one month when $h$ is more than 20 hours. What is the charge for 35 hours?

## SPIRAL REVIEW

**The sum of the angle measures in a triangle is 180°. Find the measure of the third angle given the other two angle measures.** *(Previous course)*

**55.** 45° and 90° **56.** 120° and 20° **57.** 30° and 60°

**Write an equivalent fraction for each percent.** *(Previous course)*

**58.** 25% **59.** 50% **60.** 75% **61.** 100%

**Find a pattern and use it to give the next three numbers.** *(Previous course)*

**62.** 4, 12, 20, 28, … **63.** 3, 9, 27, 81, 243, … **64.** 2, 3, 5, 8, 12, …

# Create a Table to Evaluate Expressions

You can use a graphing calculator to quickly evaluate expressions for many values of the variable.

*Use with Lesson 1-1*

## Activity 1

**Evaluate $2x + 7$ for $x = 25, 125, 225, 325,$ and 425.**

1. Press Y= and enter **2X+7** for **Y1**.

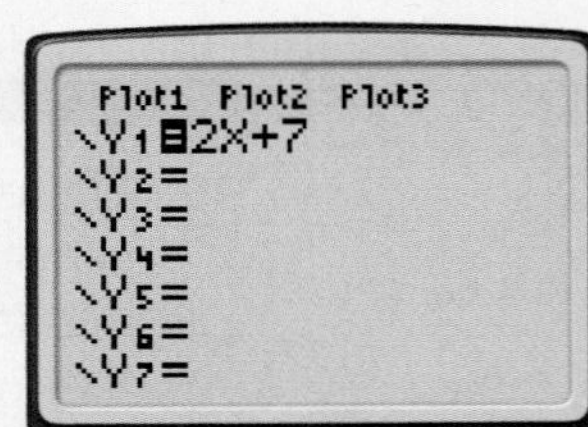


2. Determine a pattern for values of $x$.
   The $x$-values start with 25 and increase by 100.

3. Press 2nd WINDOW (TBLSET) to view the *Table Setup* window.
   Enter **25** as the starting value in **TblStart=**.
   Enter **100** as the amount by which $x$ changes in **△Tbl=**.

4. Press 2nd GRAPH (TABLE) to create a table of values.
   The first column shows values of $x$ starting with 25 and increasing by 100.
   The second column shows values of the expression $2x + 7$ when $x$ is equal to the value in the first column.
   You can use the arrow keys to view the table when $x$ is greater than 625.

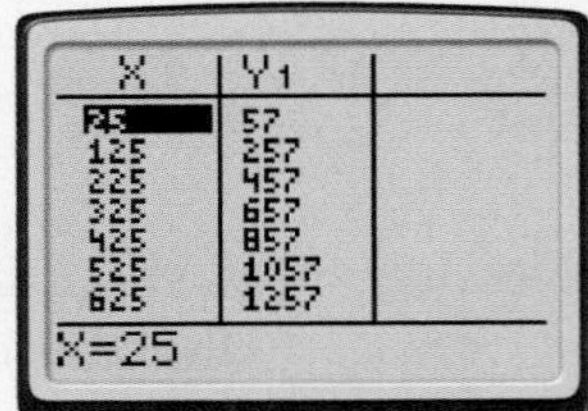


## Try This

1. Use the table feature of a graphing calculator to evaluate $5x - 7$ for $x = 4, 6, 8, 10,$ and 12.
   a. What value did you enter in **TblStart=?**
   b. What value did you enter in **△Tbl=?**
2. Use the table feature of a graphing calculator to evaluate $3x + 4$ for $x = -5, -1, 3,$ 7, and 11.
   a. What value did you enter in **TblStart=?**
   b. What value did you enter in **△Tbl=?**

You can also use a spreadsheet program to evaluate expressions.

## Activity 2

**Evaluate $2x + 7$ for $x = 3, 5, 7, 9$, and 11.**

1. In the first column, enter the values 3, 5, 7, 9, and 11.

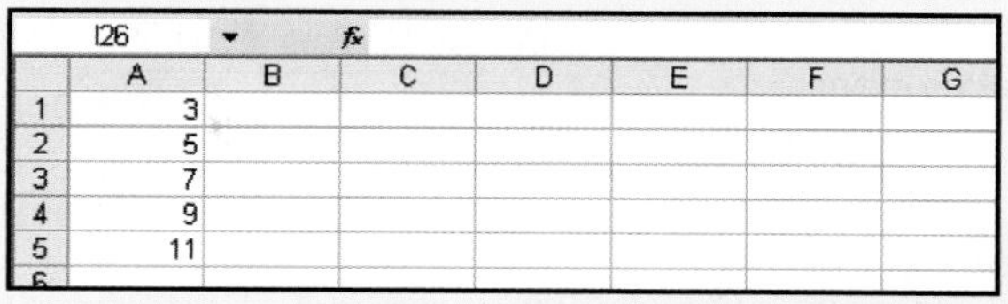

|  | A | B | C | D | E | F | G |
|---|---|---|---|---|---|---|---|
| 1 | 3 |  |  |  |  |  |  |
| 2 | 5 |  |  |  |  |  |  |
| 3 | 7 |  |  |  |  |  |  |
| 4 | 9 |  |  |  |  |  |  |
| 5 | 11 |  |  |  |  |  |  |

2. Enter the expression in cell B1.

   To do this, type the following:
   = 2 * A1 + 7

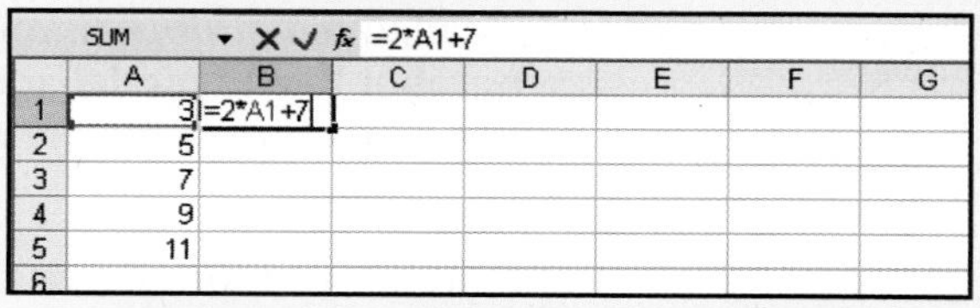

SUM ▾ ✕ ✓ fx =2*A1+7

|  | A | B | C | D | E | F | G |
|---|---|---|---|---|---|---|---|
| 1 | 3 | =2*A1+7 |  |  |  |  |  |
| 2 | 5 |  |  |  |  |  |  |
| 3 | 7 |  |  |  |  |  |  |
| 4 | 9 |  |  |  |  |  |  |
| 5 | 11 |  |  |  |  |  |  |

3. Press Enter.

   The value of $2x + 7$ when $x = 3$ appears in cell B1.

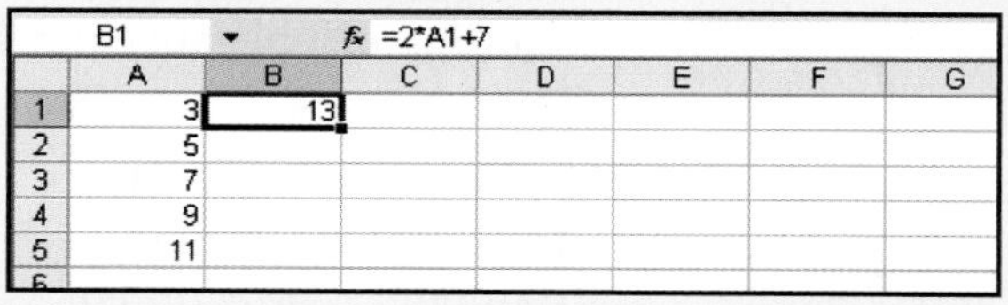

B1 ▾ fx =2*A1+7

|  | A | B | C | D | E | F | G |
|---|---|---|---|---|---|---|---|
| 1 | 3 | 13 |  |  |  |  |  |
| 2 | 5 |  |  |  |  |  |  |
| 3 | 7 |  |  |  |  |  |  |
| 4 | 9 |  |  |  |  |  |  |
| 5 | 11 |  |  |  |  |  |  |

4. Copy the formula into cells B2, B3, B4, and B5.

   Use the mouse to click on the lower right corner of cell B1. Hold down the mouse button and drag the cursor through cell B5.

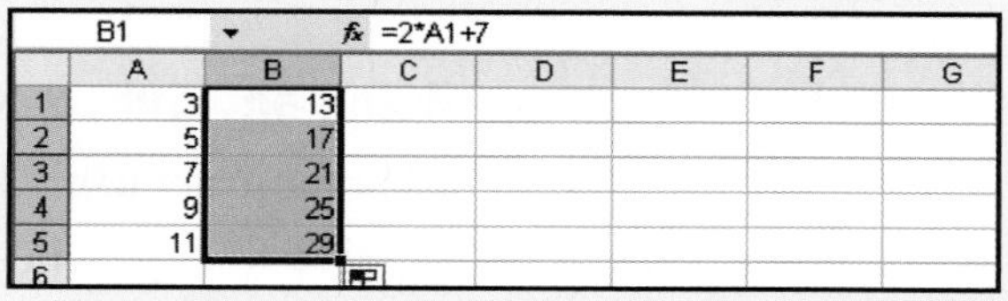

   For each row in column B, the number that is substituted for $x$ is the value in the same row of column A.

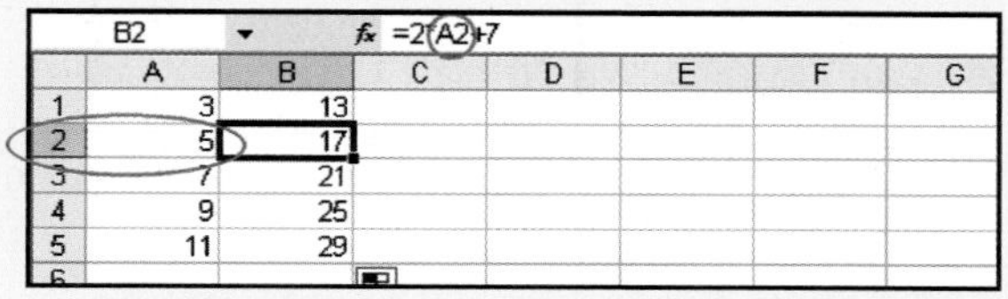

   You can continue the table by entering more values in column A and copying the formula from B1 into more cells in column B.

B1 ▾ fx =2*A1+7

|  | A | B | C | D | E | F | G |
|---|---|---|---|---|---|---|---|
| 1 | 3 | 13 |  |  |  |  |  |
| 2 | 5 | 17 |  |  |  |  |  |
| 3 | 7 | 21 |  |  |  |  |  |
| 4 | 9 | 25 |  |  |  |  |  |
| 5 | 11 | 29 |  |  |  |  |  |

B2 ▾ fx =2*A2+7

|  | A | B | C | D | E | F | G |
|---|---|---|---|---|---|---|---|
| 1 | 3 | 13 |  |  |  |  |  |
| 2 | 5 | 17 |  |  |  |  |  |
| 3 | 7 | 21 |  |  |  |  |  |
| 4 | 9 | 25 |  |  |  |  |  |
| 5 | 11 | 29 |  |  |  |  |  |

## Try This

**3.** Use a spreadsheet program to evaluate $-2x + 9$ for $x = -5, -2, 1, 4$, and 7.

**a.** What values did you enter in column A?

**b.** What did you type in cell B1?

**4.** Use a spreadsheet program to evaluate $7x - 10$ for $x = 2, 7, 12, 17$, and 22.

**a.** What values did you enter in column A?

**b.** What did you type in cell B1?

# 1-2 Adding and Subtracting Real Numbers

**Rev. 8.N.1.1** Use … operations for … rational numbers, including formal algorithms.

***Objectives***
Add real numbers.

Subtract real numbers.

***Vocabulary***
absolute value
opposites
additive inverse

**Why learn this?**
The total length of a penguin's dive can be determined by adding real numbers. (See Example 4.)

All the numbers on a number line are called *real numbers*. You can use a number line to model addition and subtraction of real numbers.

**Addition**
To model addition of a positive number, move right. To model addition of a negative number, move left.

**Subtraction**
To model subtraction of a positive number, move left. To model subtraction of a negative number, move right.

**EXAMPLE 1** **Adding and Subtracting Numbers on a Number Line**

**Add or subtract using a number line.**

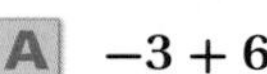

**A** $-3 + 6$

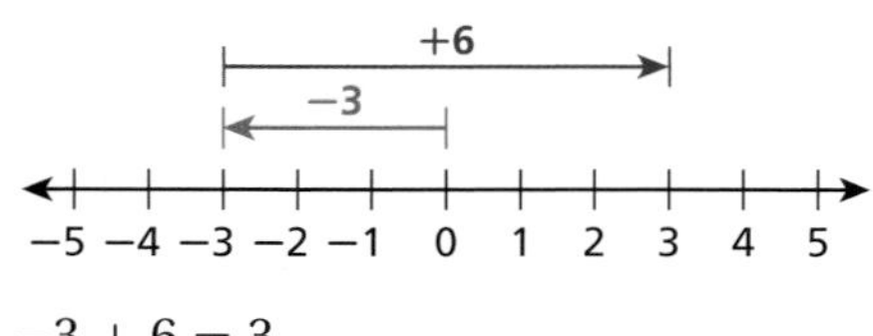


*Start at 0. Move left to −3.*

*To add 6, move right 6 units.*

$-3 + 6 = 3$

**B** $-2 - (-9)$

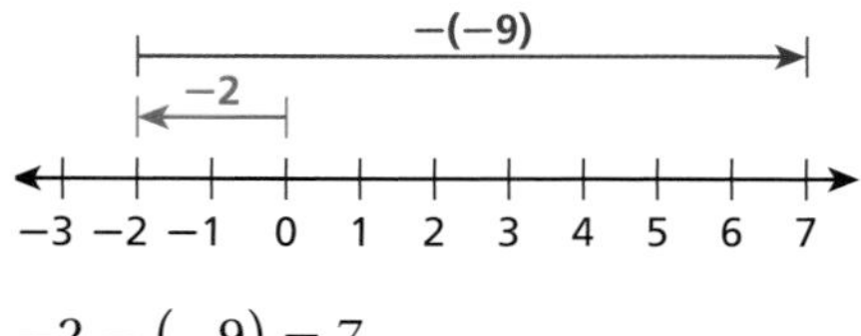


*Start at 0. Move left to −2.*

*To subtract −9, move right 9 units.*

$-2 - (-9) = 7$

**Add or subtract using a number line.**

**1a.** $-3 + 7$ **1b.** $-3 - 7$ **1c.** $-5 - (-6.5)$

The **absolute value** of a number is its distance from zero on a number line. The absolute value of 5 is written as $|5|$.

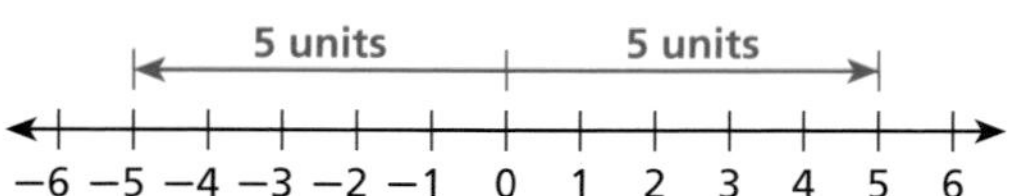


$|5| = 5$

$|-5| = 5$

## Adding Real Numbers

| WORDS | NUMBERS | |
|---|---|---|
| **Adding Numbers with the Same Sign**<br>If two numbers have the same sign, add their absolute values and use the sign of the numbers. | $3 + 6$<br>$9$ | $-2 + (-9)$<br>$-11$ |
| **Adding Numbers with Different Signs**<br>If two numbers have different signs, find the difference of their absolute values and use the sign of the number with the greater absolute value. | $-8 + 12$<br>$4$ | $3 + (-15)$<br>$-12$ |

### EXAMPLE 2 Adding Real Numbers

**Add.**

**A** $\mathbf{-3 + (-16)}$

$-3 + (-16)$ — *When the signs of the numbers are the same, find the sum of their absolute values: 3 + 16 = 19.*

$-19$ — *Both numbers are negative, so the sum is negative.*

**B** $\mathbf{x + 7}$ **for** $\mathbf{x = -13}$

$x + 7 = (-13) + 7$ — *First substitute −13 for x.*

$(-13) + 7$ — *When the signs are different, find the difference of the absolute values: 13 − 7 = 6.*

$-6$ — *Use the sign of the number with the greater absolute value. The sum is negative.*

**Add.**

**2a.** $-5 + (-7)$ **2b.** $-13.5 + (-22.3)$ **2c.** $x + (-68)$ for $x = 52$

Two numbers are **opposites** if their sum is 0. A number and its opposite are the same distance from zero. They have the same absolute value.

A number and its opposite are **additive inverses**. To subtract signed numbers, you can use additive inverses. Subtracting a number is the same as adding the opposite of the number.

Additive inverses

$$11 - 6 = 5 \qquad 11 + (-6) = 5$$

Subtracting 6 is the same as adding the inverse of 6.

## Subtracting Real Numbers

| WORDS | NUMBERS | ALGEBRA |
|---|---|---|
| To subtract a number, add its opposite. Then follow the rules for adding signed numbers. | $3 - 8 = 3 + (-8)$<br>$8 - 3 = 5$<br>$\lvert -8 \rvert > \lvert 3 \rvert$<br>$-5$ | $a - b = a + (-b)$ |

## EXAMPLE 3 Subtracting Real Numbers

**Subtract.**

**A** $7 - 10$

| | |
|---|---|
| $7 - 10 = 7 + (-10)$ | *To subtract 10, add −10.* |
| | *When the signs of the numbers are different, subtract the absolute values: 10 − 7 = 3.* |
| $-3$ | *Use the sign of the number with the greater absolute value. The sum is negative.* |

**B** $-3 - (-12)$

| | |
|---|---|
| $-3 - (-12) = -3 + 12$ | *To subtract −12, add 12.* |
| | *When the signs of the numbers are different, subtract the absolute values: 12 − 3 = 9.* |
| $9$ | *Use the sign of the number with the greater absolute value. The sum is positive.* |

**C** $x - 22$ **for** $x = -11$

| | |
|---|---|
| $x - 22 = -11 - 22$ | *First substitute −11 for x.* |
| $-11 + (-22)$ | *To subtract 22, add −22.* |
| | *When the signs of the numbers are the same, add the absolute values: 11 + 22 = 33.* |
| $-33$ | *Both numbers are negative, so the sum is negative.* |

**Helpful Hint**

On many scientific and graphing calculators, there is one button to express the opposite of a number and a different button to express subtraction.

**Subtract.**

**3a.** $13 - 21$ **3b.** $\frac{1}{2} - \left(-3\frac{1}{2}\right)$ **3c.** $x - (-12)$ for $x = -14$

## EXAMPLE 4 *Biology Application*

**An emperor penguin stands on an iceberg that extends 10 feet above the water. Then the penguin dives to an elevation of −67 feet to catch a fish. What is the total length of the penguin's dive?**

Find the difference in the elevations of the iceberg and the fish.

| elevation of iceberg | minus | elevation of fish |
|---|---|---|
| 10 | − | −67 |

$10 - (-67)$

| | |
|---|---|
| $10 - (-67) = 10 + 67$ | *To subtract −67, add 67.* |
| $= 77$ | *Find the sum of the absolute values.* |

The total length of the penguin's dive is 77 feet.

**4. What if...?** The tallest known iceberg in the North Atlantic rose 550 feet above the ocean's surface. How many feet would it be from the top of the tallest iceberg to the wreckage of the *Titanic*, which is at an elevation of −12,468 feet?

## THINK AND DISCUSS

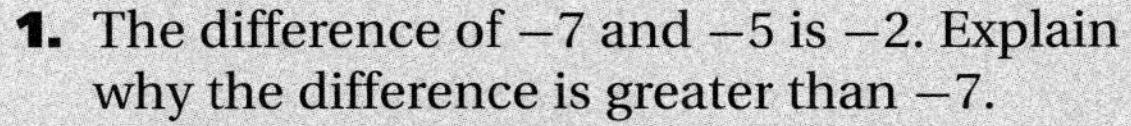

1. The difference of $-7$ and $-5$ is $-2$. Explain why the difference is greater than $-7$.

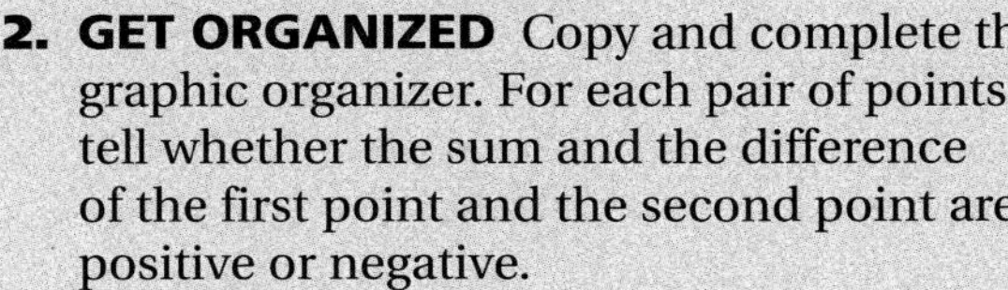

2. **GET ORGANIZED** Copy and complete the graphic organizer. For each pair of points, tell whether the sum and the difference of the first point and the second point are positive or negative.

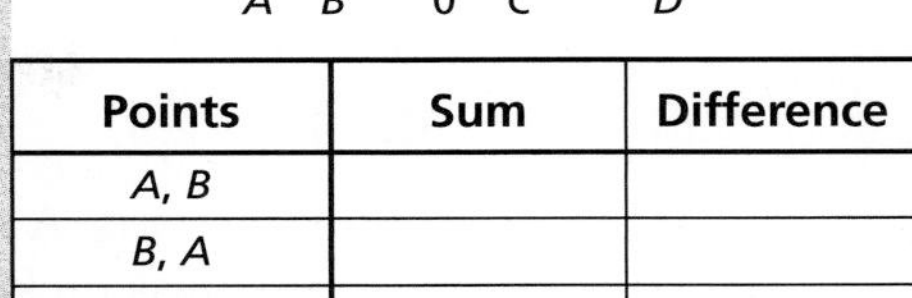


| Points | Sum | Difference |
|---|---|---|
| *A, B* | | |
| *B, A* | | |
| *C, B* | | |
| *D, A* | | |

# 1-2 Exercises

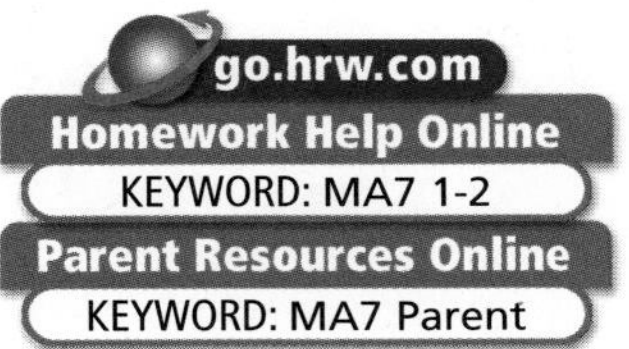


## GUIDED PRACTICE

1. **Vocabulary** The sum of a number and its ___?___ is always zero. (*opposite* or *absolute value*)

SEE EXAMPLE 1 p. 14

**Add or subtract using a number line.**

2. $-4 + 7$
3. $-3.5 - 5$
4. $5.6 - 9.2$
5. $3 - \left(-6\frac{1}{4}\right)$

SEE EXAMPLE 2 p. 15

**Add.**

6. $91 + (-11)$
7. $4\frac{3}{4} + \left(-3\frac{3}{4}\right)$
8. $15.6 + x$ for $x = -17.9$

SEE EXAMPLE 3 p. 16

**Subtract.**

9. $23 - 36$
10. $4.3 - 8.4$
11. $x - 2\frac{4}{5}$ for $x = 1\frac{1}{5}$

SEE EXAMPLE 4 p. 16

12. **Economics** The Dow Jones Industrial Average (DJIA) reports the average prices of stocks for 30 companies. Use the table to determine the total decrease in the DJIA for the two days.

| DJIA 1987 | |
|---|---|
| Friday, Oct. 16 | −108.35 |
| Monday, Oct. 19 | −507.99 |

## PRACTICE AND PROBLEM SOLVING

**Independent Practice**

| For Exercises | See Example |
|---|---|
| 13–16 | 1 |
| 17–19 | 2 |
| 20–22 | 3 |
| 23 | 4 |

**Extra Practice**
Skills Practice p. S4
Application Practice p. S28

**Add or subtract using a number line.**

13. $-2 + 6$
14. $6 + (-2)$
15. $\frac{1}{4} - 12$
16. $-\frac{2}{5} + 6$

**Add.**

17. $-18 + (-12)$
18. $-2.3 + 3.5$
19. $x + 29$ for $x = -15$

**Subtract.**

20. $12 - 22$
21. $-\frac{3}{4} - \left(-\frac{1}{4}\right)$
22. $38 - x$ for $x = 24.6$
23. **Meteorology** A meteorologist reported that the day's high temperature was 17°F and the low temperature was −6°F. What was the difference between the day's high and low temperatures?

**Evaluate the expression $n + (-5)$ for each value of $n$.**

**24.** $n = 312$ **25.** $n = 5.75$ **26.** $n = -\frac{7}{12}$ **27.** $n = -7\frac{2}{5}$

**Add or subtract.**

**28.** $-8 - 3$ **29.** $-9 + (-3)$ **30.** $16 - (-16)$ **31.** $100 - 63$

**32.** $5.2 - 2.5$ **33.** $-4.7 - (-4.7)$ **34.** $\frac{2}{5} - \frac{7}{8}$ **35.** $\frac{2}{5} - \frac{3}{10}$

**36. Business** A restaurant manager lost $415 in business during the month of January. Business picked up in February, and he ended that month with a profit of $1580.

**a.** What was the manager's profit after January and February?

**b. What if...?** The restaurant lost $245 in business during the month of March. What was the manager's profit after January, February, and March?

**Compare. Write $<$, $>$, or $=$.**

**37.** $-4 - (-6)$ ■ $-7 - 3$ **38.** $|-51|$ ■ $|0|$ **39.** $3 - (-3)$ ■ $0 - (-3)$

**40.** $-3 - 8$ ■ $-22 + 11$ **41.** $|-10 + 5|$ ■ $|-15|$ **42.** $9 + (-8)$ ■ $-12 + 13$

**43. Travel** Death Valley National Park is located in California. Use the table to determine the difference in elevation between the highest and lowest locations.

| Death Valley National Park | |
|---|---|
| **Location** | **Elevation (ft)** |
| Badwater | −282 |
| Emigrant Pass | 5,318 |
| Furnace Creek Airport | −210 |
| Telescope Creek | 11,049 |

**Critical Thinking Use examples to explain whether each statement is sometimes, always, or never true.**

**44.** The difference between two negative numbers is positive.

**45.** The sum of two negative numbers is negative.

**46.** The difference of a negative number and a positive number is negative.

**47. ///ERROR ANALYSIS///** Which is incorrect? Explain the error.

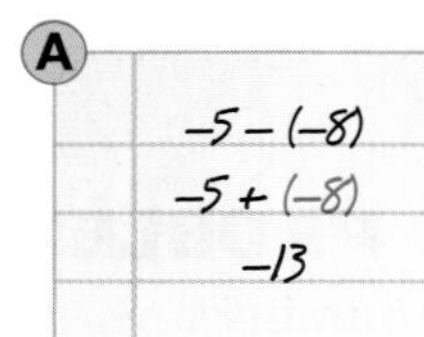


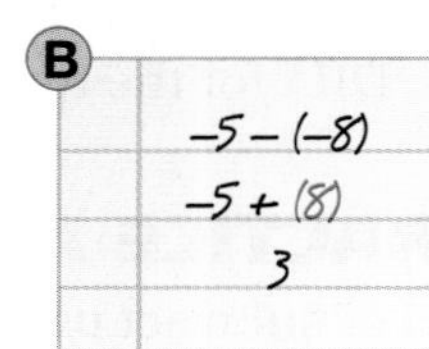


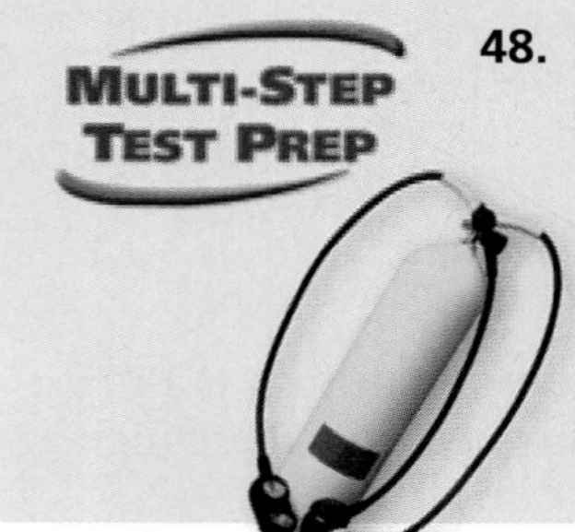


**48.** This problem will prepare you for the Multi-Step Test Prep on page 38.

**a.** A plane flies at a height of 1800 feet over a 150-foot-tall building. How far above the building is the plane? Draw a diagram to explain your answer.

**b.** The same plane flies over a diver who is 80 feet below the surface of the water. How far is the plane above the diver? Draw a diagram to explain your answer.

**c.** Subtract the diver's altitude of −80 feet from the plane's altitude of 1800 feet. Explain why this distance is greater than 1800 feet.

**49. Write About It** Use the following examples to explain why addition and subtraction are called inverse operations:

$8 + (-2) = 8 - 2 \qquad 8 - (-2) = 8 + 2$

## TEST PREP

Rev. 8.N.1.1

**50.** A rectangle has a length of 23.8 cm and a width of 14.5 cm. What is its perimeter?

Ⓐ 9.3 cm  Ⓑ 38.3 cm  Ⓒ 62.1 cm  Ⓓ 76.6 cm

**51.** At midnight, the temperature was −12°F. By noon, the temperature had risen 25°F. During the afternoon, it fell 10°F and fell another 3°F by midnight. What was the final temperature?

Ⓕ 0°F  Ⓖ 3°F  Ⓗ 12°F  Ⓙ 24°F

**52.** The table shows the amounts Mr. Espinosa spent on lunch each day one week. What is the total amount Mr. Espinosa spent for lunch this week?

| Day | Monday | Tuesday | Wednesday | Thursday | Friday |
|---|---|---|---|---|---|
| Amount ($) | 5.40 | 4.16 | 7.07 | 5.40 | 9.52 |

Ⓐ $21.83  Ⓑ $22.03  Ⓒ $31.55  Ⓓ $36.95

## CHALLENGE AND EXTEND

**Find the value of each expression.**

**53.** $-1\frac{1}{5} + (-7.8)$  **54.** $-\frac{1}{5} + 2.1$  **55.** $9.75 + \left(-7\frac{3}{4}\right)$  **56.** $-2\frac{3}{10} + 8.5$

**For each pattern shown below, describe a rule for finding the next term. Then use your rule to write the next 3 terms.**

**57.** 14, 10, 6, 2, ...  **58.** $-2, -\frac{8}{5}, -\frac{6}{5}, -\frac{4}{5}, \ldots$

**59. Geography** Sam visited two volcanoes and two caves. Cotapaxi, a volcano in Ecuador, has an elevation of 19,347 ft. Sangay, also in Ecuador, has an elevation of 17,159 ft. The main entrance of Sistema Huautla, a cave in Mexico, has an elevation of 5051 ft. The main entrance of Sistema Cheve, also in Mexico, has an elevation of 9085 ft. What is the average elevation of these places?

## SPIRAL REVIEW

**Give the area of the figure described.** *(Previous course)*

**60.** rectangle; $\ell = 12$ cm, $w = 5$ cm  **61.** triangle; $b = 8$ in., $h = 11$ in.

**Find the length of the third side of the triangle.** *(Previous course)*

**62.** perimeter = 12 cm

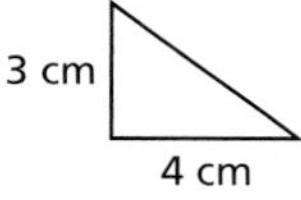


**63.** perimeter = 30 cm

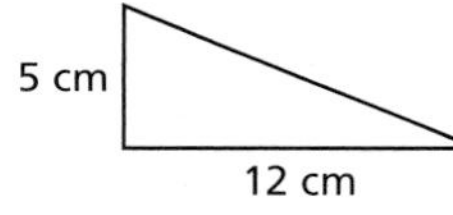


**64.** perimeter = 56 cm

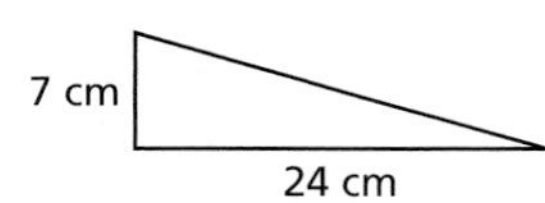


**Evaluate each expression for $x = 8$, $y = 4$, and $z = 2$.** *(Lesson 1-1)*

**65.** $x + y$  **66.** $\frac{x}{z}$  **67.** $x - y$  **68.** $\frac{y}{z}$

# 1-3 Multiplying and Dividing Real Numbers

**Rev. 8.N.1.1** Use … operations for … rational numbers, including formal algorithms.

*Objectives*
Multiply real numbers.
Divide real numbers.

*Vocabulary*
reciprocal
multiplicative inverse

**Who uses this?**
Hot-air balloon pilots can determine how far away from liftoff they will land by using multiplication. (See Example 4.)

When you multiply or divide two numbers, the signs of the numbers you are multiplying or dividing determine whether the result is positive or negative.

| Factors | | Product | |
|---|---|---|---|
| 3(5) | Both positive | 15 | Positive |
| 3(−5) | One negative | −15 | Negative |
| −3(−5) | Both negative | 15 | Positive |

**Multiplying and Dividing Signed Numbers**

| WORDS | NUMBERS | |
|---|---|---|
| **Multiplying and Dividing Numbers with the Same Sign** | | |
| If two numbers have the same sign, their product or quotient is positive. | $4 \cdot 5 = 20$ | $-15 \div (-3) = 5$ |
| **Multiplying and Dividing Numbers with Different Signs** | | |
| If two numbers have different signs, their product or quotient is negative. | $6(-3) = -18$ | $-18 \div 2 = -9$ |

## EXAMPLE 1 Multiplying and Dividing Signed Numbers

**Find the value of each expression.**

**A** $-12 \cdot 5$

$-60$ — *The product of two numbers with different signs is negative.*

**B** $8x$ for $x = -\frac{5}{4}$

$8x = 8\left(-\frac{5}{4}\right)$ — *First substitute $-\frac{5}{4}$ for x.*

$= \left(\frac{8}{1}\right)\left(-\frac{5}{4}\right)$ — *Multiply.*

$= -\frac{40}{4} = -10$ — *The quotient of two numbers with different signs is negative.*

**Find the value of each expression.**

**1a.** $35 \div (-5)$ **1b.** $-11(-4)$ **1c.** $-6x$ for $x = 7$

Two numbers are **reciprocals** if their product is 1. A number and its reciprocal are called **multiplicative inverses**. To divide by a number, you can multiply by its multiplicative inverse.

Multiplicative inverses

$$10 \div 5 = 2 \qquad 10 \cdot \frac{1}{5} = \frac{10}{5} = 2$$

Dividing by 5 is the same as multiplying by the reciprocal of 5, $\frac{1}{5}$.

Dividing by a nonzero number is the same as multiplying by the reciprocal of the number.

## EXAMPLE 2 Dividing by Fractions

**Helpful Hint**

You can write the reciprocal of a number by switching the numerator and denominator. A number written without a denominator has a denominator of 1.

**Divide.**

**A** $-\frac{4}{5} \div \left(-\frac{8}{15}\right)$

$-\frac{4}{5} \div \left(-\frac{8}{15}\right) = -\frac{4}{5}\left(-\frac{15}{8}\right)$ *To divide by $-\frac{8}{15}$, multiply by $-\frac{15}{8}$.*

$= \frac{(-4)(-15)}{5(8)}$ *Multiply the numerators and multiply the denominators.*

$= \frac{60}{40} = \frac{3}{2}$ *$-\frac{4}{5}$ and $-\frac{8}{15}$ have the same sign, so the quotient is positive.*

**B** $-4 \div 9\frac{1}{4}$

$-4 \div 9\frac{1}{4} = -\frac{4}{1} \div \frac{37}{4}$ *Write 4 as a fraction with a denominator of 1. Write $9\frac{1}{4}$ as an improper fraction.*

$= -\frac{4}{1} \cdot \frac{4}{37}$ *To divide by $\frac{37}{4}$, multiply by $\frac{4}{37}$.*

$= -\frac{4(4)}{1(37)} = -\frac{16}{37}$ *$-4$ and $9\frac{1}{4}$ have different signs, so the quotient is negative.*

**Divide.**

**2a.** $-\frac{3}{4} \div -9$ **2b.** $\frac{3}{10} \div \left(-\frac{6}{5}\right)$ **2c.** $-\frac{5}{6} \div 1\frac{2}{3}$

No number can be multiplied by 0 to give a product of 1, so 0 has no reciprocal. Because of this, division by 0 is not possible. We say that division by 0 is undefined.

**Properties of Zero**

| WORDS | NUMBERS | ALGEBRA |
|---|---|---|
| **Multiplication by Zero** The product of any number and 0 is 0. | $\frac{1}{3} \cdot 0 = 0 \quad 0(-17) = 0$ | $a \cdot 0 = 0 \quad 0 \cdot a = 0$ |
| **Zero Divided by a Number** The quotient of 0 and any nonzero number is 0. | $\frac{0}{6} = 0 \quad 0 \div \frac{2}{3} = 0$ | $\frac{0}{a} = 0 \quad a \neq 0$ |
| **Division by Zero** Division by 0 is undefined. | $12 \div 0 \quad \frac{-5}{0}$ Undefined | $a \div 0 \quad \frac{a}{0}$ Undefined |

## EXAMPLE 3 Multiplying and Dividing with Zero

**Multiply or divide if possible.**

**A** $0 \div 16.568$ — *Zero is divided by a nonzero number.*
0 — *The quotient of zero and any nonzero number is 0.*

**B** $63\frac{7}{8} \div 0$ — *A number is divided by zero.*
undefined — *Division by zero is undefined.*

**C** $1 \cdot 0$ — *A number is multiplied by zero.*
0 — *The product of any number and 0 is 0.*

**Multiply or divide.**

**3a.** $0 \div \left(-8\frac{1}{6}\right)$ **3b.** $2.040 \div 0$ **3c.** $(-12{,}350)(0)$

## EXAMPLE 4 *Recreation Application*

**A hot-air balloon is taken for a 2.5-hour trip. The wind speed (and the speed of the balloon) is 4.75 mi/h. The balloon travels in a straight line. How many miles away from the liftoff site will the balloon land?**

Find the distance traveled at a rate of 4.75 mi/h for 2.5 hours. To find distance, multiply rate by time.

| rate | times | time |
|---|---|---|
| 4.75 | • | 2.5 |

$4.75 \cdot 2.5$
$11.875$

The hot-air balloon will land 11.875 miles from the liftoff site.

**4.** **What if...?** On another hot-air balloon trip, the wind speed is 5.25 mi/h. The trip is planned for 1.5 hours. The balloon travels in a straight line. How many miles away from the liftoff site will the balloon land?

## THINK AND DISCUSS

**1.** Explain how to use mental math to find the missing value: $\frac{4}{5} \cdot ? = 1$.

**2.** **GET ORGANIZED** Copy and complete the graphic organizer. In each blank, write "pos" or "neg" to indicate positive or negative.

| Multiplying and Dividing Numbers | |
|---|---|
| **Multiplication** | **Division** |
| pos × ___ = pos | pos ÷ ___ = pos |
| pos × ___ = neg | pos ÷ ___ = neg |
| neg × ___ = neg | neg ÷ ___ = neg |
| neg × ___ = pos | neg ÷ ___ = pos |

# 1-3 Exercises

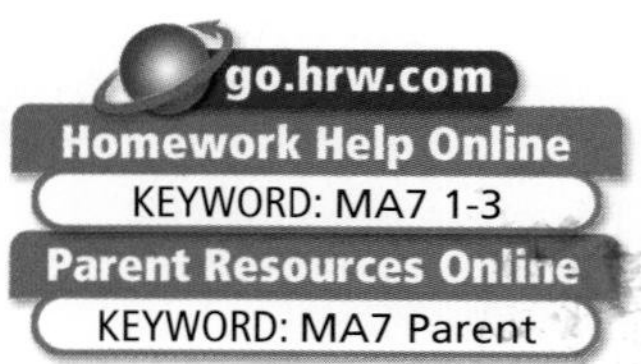


## GUIDED PRACTICE

1. **Vocabulary** How do you find the *reciprocal* of $\frac{1}{2}$?

SEE EXAMPLE 1 p. 20

**Find the value of each expression.**

2. $-72 \div (-9)$
3. $11(-11)$
4. $-7.2 \div x$ for $x = 3.6$

SEE EXAMPLE 2 p. 21

**Divide.**

5. $5 \div \frac{5}{7}$
6. $\frac{4}{5} \div \left(-\frac{8}{5}\right)$
7. $\frac{2}{3} \div \left(-\frac{1}{3}\right)$
8. $\frac{16}{25} \div \frac{4}{5}$

SEE EXAMPLE 3 p. 22

**Multiply or divide if possible.**

9. $3.8 \div 0$
10. $0(-27)$
11. $0 \div \frac{2}{3}$
12. $\frac{7}{8} \div 0$

SEE EXAMPLE 4 p. 22

13. **Entertainment** It is estimated that 7 million people saw off-Broadway shows in 2002. Assume that the average price of a ticket was \$30. How much money was spent on tickets for off-Broadway shows in 2002?

## PRACTICE AND PROBLEM SOLVING

**Independent Practice**

| For Exercises | See Example |
|---|---|
| 14–16 | 1 |
| 17–20 | 2 |
| 21–24 | 3 |
| 25 | 4 |

**Extra Practice**

Skills Practice p. S4
Application Practice p. S28

**Find the value of each expression.**

14. $-30 \div (-6)$
15. $8(-4)$
16. $x(-12)$ for $x = -25$

**Divide.**

17. $\frac{3}{20} \div \left(-\frac{1}{4}\right)$
18. $\frac{9}{14} \div \frac{15}{28}$
19. $4\frac{1}{2} \div 1\frac{1}{2}$
20. $2\frac{3}{4} \div \left(-1\frac{1}{2}\right)$

**Multiply or divide if possible.**

21. $0 \cdot 15$
22. $-0.25 \div 0$
23. $0 \div 1$
24. $\frac{0}{1} \div 3$

25. **Weather** A cold front changes the temperature by −3°F each day. If the temperature started at 0°F, what will the temperature be after 5 days?

**Multiply or divide.**

26. $21 \div (-3)$
27. $-100 \div 25$
28. $-6 \div (-14)$
29. $-6.2(10)$
30. $\frac{1}{2} \div \frac{1}{2}$
31. $-3.75(-5)$
32. $-12\frac{1}{2}(-3)$
33. $17\left(\frac{1}{17}\right)$

34. **Critical Thinking** What positive number is the same as its reciprocal?

**Evaluate each expression for $a = 4$, $b = -3$, and $c = -2$.**

35. $ab$
36. $a \div c$
37. $bc$
38. $c \div a$

**Let $p$ represent a positive number, $n$ represent a negative number, and $z$ represent zero. Tell whether each expression is positive, negative, zero, or undefined.**

39. $pn$
40. $pnz$
41. $\frac{n}{p}$
42. $-pz$
43. $-\frac{p}{n}$
44. $-(pn)$
45. $\frac{pn}{z}$
46. $\frac{z}{n}$

**Evaluate the expression $y \div \frac{3}{4}$ for each value of $y$.**

**47.** $y = \frac{3}{4}$ **48.** $y = -\frac{9}{16}$ **49.** $y = \frac{3}{8}$ **50.** $y = -2\frac{1}{4}$

**Evaluate the expression $\frac{1}{2} \div m$ for each value of $m$.**

**51.** $m = -\frac{5}{2}$ **52.** $m = \frac{7}{8}$ **53.** $m = \frac{4}{9}$ **54.** $m = -5$

LINK

**Diving**

Florida is home to more than 300 freshwater springs, some of which are explored by cave divers. This chamber of the Diepolder Cave system is about 250 feet deep.

**55. Education** Benjamin must have 120 credit hours of instruction to receive his college degree. Benjamin wants to graduate in 8 semesters without attending summer sessions. How many credit hours must Benjamin take each semester to graduate in 8 semesters?

**56. Diving** An underwater exploration team is swimming at a depth of $-15$ feet. Then they dive to an underwater cave that is at 8 times this depth. What is the depth of the underwater cave?

**Compare. Write <, >, or =.**

**57.** $10\left(-\frac{1}{2}\right)$ ▒ $20 \div 4$ **58.** $16 \div (-2)$ ▒ $-2(-4)$ **59.** $5(-2.4)$ ▒ $-2\frac{2}{3} \div 3$

**60.** $\frac{3}{4} \div \left(-\frac{1}{2}\right)$ ▒ $20 \div 4$ **61.** $2.1(-3.4)$ ▒ $2.1(-3.4)$ **62.** $0\left(-\frac{3}{5}\right)$ ▒ $\frac{1}{2} \div \frac{1}{2}$

**63. Critical Thinking** There is a relationship between the number of negative factors and the sign of the product.

**a.** What is the sign of the product of an even number of negative factors?

**b.** What is the sign of the product of an odd number of negative factors?

**c.** Explain why the number of negative factors affects the sign of the product.

**d.** Does the number of positive factors affect the sign of the product? Explain.

**Write each division expression as a multiplication expression.**

**64.** $12 \div (-3)$ **65.** $75 \div 15$ **66.** $\frac{80}{-8}$ **67.** $\frac{-121}{11}$

**Determine whether each statement is sometimes, always, or never true.**

**68.** The quotient of two negative numbers is negative.

**69.** The quotient of two numbers with the same sign has that sign.

**70.** The product of two numbers with different signs is positive.

**71. Write About It** The product of two factors is positive. One of the factors is negative. Explain how you can determine the sign of the second factor.

**MULTI-STEP TEST PREP**

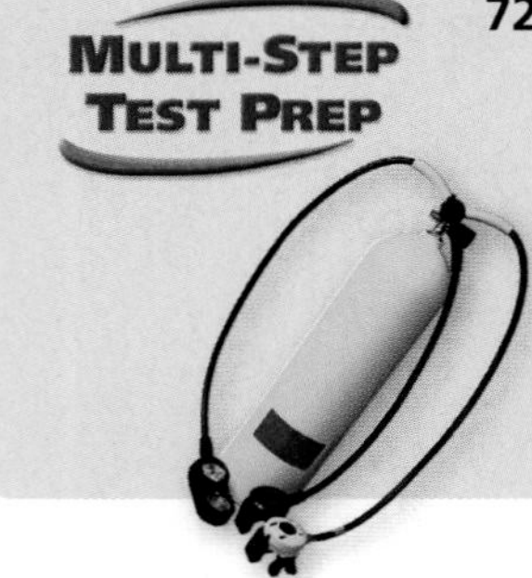

**72.** This problem will prepare you for the Multi-Step Test Prep on page 38.

**a.** You swam 20 feet in 5 seconds. Use the formula $r = \frac{d}{t}$ to determine how fast you were swimming. Explain how you found your answer.

**b.** A diver descended at a rate of 15 feet per minute. Make a table to show the diver's depth after 1, 2, and 5 minutes.

**c.** Show two ways to find how far the diver descended in 5 minutes. Remember that multiplication is repeated addition.

73. In which situation below would you multiply 5 • 35 to find the final balance?

Rev. 8.N.1.1

(A) Marc had $35 in his bank account, and for 5 weeks, he withdrew $5 a week.
(B) Marc opened a new bank account, and for the first 5 months, he deposited $35 a month.
(C) Marc opened a bank account with $35. For 5 weeks, he deposited $5 a week.
(D) Marc withdrew $35 a month from his bank account for 5 months.

74. Robyn is buying carpet for her bedroom floor, which is a 15-foot-by-12-foot rectangle. If carpeting costs $1.25 per square foot, how much will it cost Robyn to carpet her bedroom?

(F) $68 (G) $144 (H) $180 (J) $225

75. **Short Response** In music notation, a half note is played $\frac{1}{2}$ the length of a whole note. A quarter note is played $\frac{1}{4}$ the length of a whole note. In a piece of music, the clarinets play 8 half notes. In the same length of time, the flutes play $x$ quarter notes. Determine how many quarter notes the flutes play. Explain your method.

## CHALLENGE AND EXTEND

**Find the value of each expression.**

76. $(-2)(-2)(-2)$
77. $\frac{5}{7} \cdot \frac{5}{7}$
78. $5\left(-\frac{4}{5}\right)\left(-\frac{3}{4}\right)$
79. $\left|-\frac{1}{4}\right| \cdot |20|$
80. $5 \cdot 4 \cdot 3 \cdot 2 \cdot 1$
81. $\left|-\frac{2}{5}\right| \cdot \left|\frac{5}{2}\right|$
82. $\frac{1}{2} \cdot \frac{2}{3} \cdot \frac{3}{4} \cdot \frac{4}{5}$
83. $\left(-\frac{3}{4}\right)\left(-\frac{3}{4}\right)\left(-\frac{3}{4}\right)$
84. $(2^3)^2$

**For each pattern shown below, verbally describe a rule for finding the next term. Then use your rule to write the next 3 terms.**

85. $-1, 2, -4, 8, \ldots$
86. $\frac{1}{63}, -\frac{1}{21}, \frac{1}{7}, -\frac{3}{7}, \ldots$
87. $-5, 10, -15, 20, -25, \ldots$
88. $0.5, 0.25, 0.125, 0.0625, \ldots$

89. A cleaning service charges $49.00 to clean a one-bedroom apartment. If the work takes longer than 2 hours, the service charges $18.00 for each additional hour. What would be the total cost for a job that took 4 hours to complete?

## SPIRAL REVIEW

**Identify each polygon.** *(Previous course)*

90. 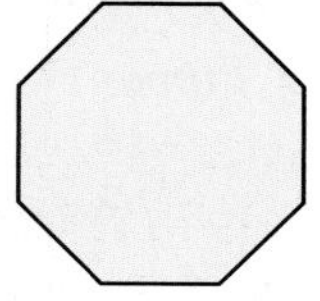
91. 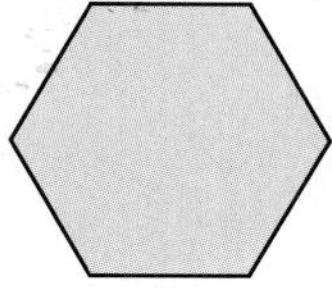
92. 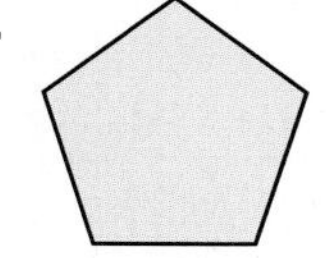
93. 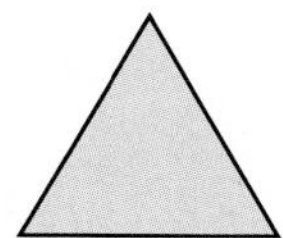

94. A prepaid phone card has a credit of 200 minutes. Write an expression for the number of minutes left on the card after $t$ minutes have been used. *(Lesson 1-1)*

**Add or subtract.** *(Lesson 1-2)*

95. $12 - 18$
96. $-6 + 14$
97. $3 - (-5)$
98. $11 + (-8)$

# 1-4 Powers and Exponents

**Rev. 6.N.5** Understand large ... numbers using exponents and exponential notation.

***Objective***
Evaluate expressions containing exponents.

***Vocabulary***
power
base
exponent

**Who uses this?**
Biologists use exponents to model the growth patterns of living organisms.

When bacteria divide, their number increases exponentially. This means that the number of bacteria is multiplied by the same factor each time the bacteria divide. Instead of writing repeated multiplication to express a product, you can use a power.

A **power** is an expression written with an *exponent* and a *base* or the value of such an expression. $3^2$ is an example of a power.

When a number is raised to the second power, we usually say it is "squared." The area of a *square* is $s \cdot s = s^2$, where $s$ is the side length.

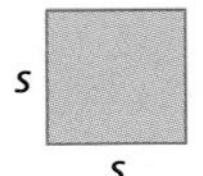


When a number is raised to the third power, we usually say it is "cubed." The volume of a *cube* is $s \cdot s \cdot s = s^3$, where $s$ is the side length.

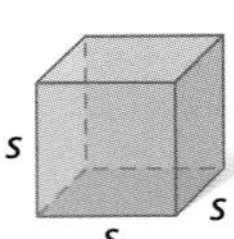


**EXAMPLE 1** **Writing Powers for Geometric Models**

**Write the power represented by each geometric model.**

**A** 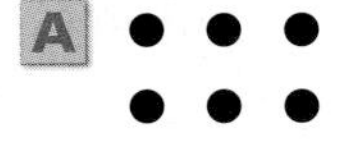
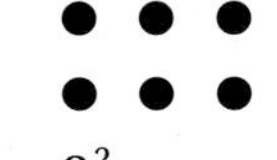

$3^2$

*There are 3 rows of 3 dots. 3 × 3*
*The factor 3 is used 2 times.*

**B** 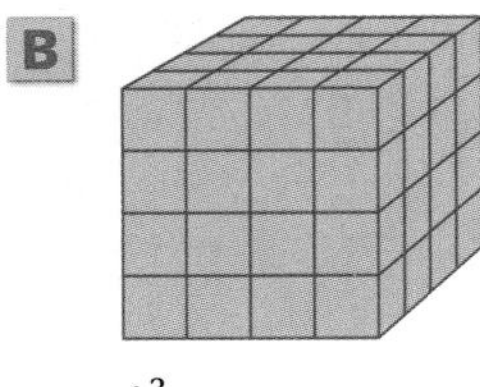

$4^3$

*The figure is 4 cubes long, 4 cubes wide, and 4 cubes tall. 4 × 4 × 4*
*The factor 4 is used 3 times.*

**Write the power represented by each geometric model.**

**1a.** 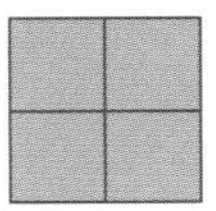

**1b.** 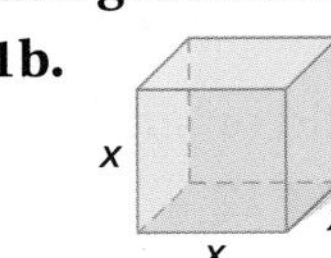

There are no easy geometric models for numbers raised to exponents greater than 3, but you can still write them using repeated multiplication or a base and exponent.

| Reading Exponents | | | |
|---|---|---|---|
| **Words** | **Multiplication** | **Power** | **Value** |
| 3 to the first power | 3 | $3^1$ | 3 |
| 3 to the second power, or 3 squared | $3 \cdot 3$ | $3^2$ | 9 |
| 3 to the third power, or 3 cubed | $3 \cdot 3 \cdot 3$ | $3^3$ | 27 |
| 3 to the fourth power | $3 \cdot 3 \cdot 3 \cdot 3$ | $3^4$ | 81 |
| 3 to the fifth power | $3 \cdot 3 \cdot 3 \cdot 3 \cdot 3$ | $3^5$ | 243 |

## EXAMPLE 2 Evaluating Powers

**Simplify each expression.**

**A** $(-2)^3$

$(-2)(-2)(-2)$ *Use −2 as a factor 3 times.*

$-8$

**Caution!**

In the expression $-5^2$, 5 is the base because the negative sign is not in parentheses.
In the expression $(-2)^3$, −2 is the base because of the parentheses.

**B** $-5^2$

$-1 \cdot 5 \cdot 5$ *Think of a negative sign in front of a power as multiplying by −1. Find the product of −1 and two 5's.*

$-1 \cdot 25$

$-25$

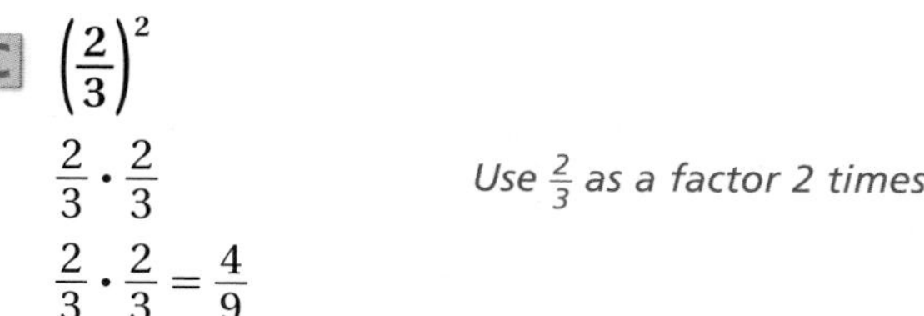

**C** $\left(\frac{2}{3}\right)^2$

$\frac{2}{3} \cdot \frac{2}{3}$ *Use $\frac{2}{3}$ as a factor 2 times.*

$\frac{2}{3} \cdot \frac{2}{3} = \frac{4}{9}$

**Simplify each expression.**

**2a.** $(-5)^3$ **2b.** $-6^2$ **2c.** $\left(\frac{3}{4}\right)^3$

## EXAMPLE 3 Writing Powers

**Write each number as a power of the given base.**

**A** **8; base 2**

$2 \cdot 2 \cdot 2$ *The product of three 2's is 8.*

$2^3$

**B** **−125; base −5**

$(-5)(-5)(-5)$ *The product of three −5's is −125.*

$(-5)^3$

**Write each number as a power of the given base.**

**3a.** 64; base 8 **3b.** −27; base −3

## EXAMPLE 4 Problem-Solving Application

**A certain bacterium splits into 2 bacteria every hour. There is 1 bacterium on a slide. If each bacterium on the slide splits once per hour, how many bacteria will be on the slide after 6 hours?**

### 1 Understand the Problem

The **answer** will be the number of bacteria on the slide after 6 hours.
List the **important information:**

- There is 1 bacterium on a slide that divides into 2 bacteria.
- Each bacterium then divides into 2 more bacteria.

### 2 Make a Plan

Draw a diagram to show the number of bacteria after each hour.

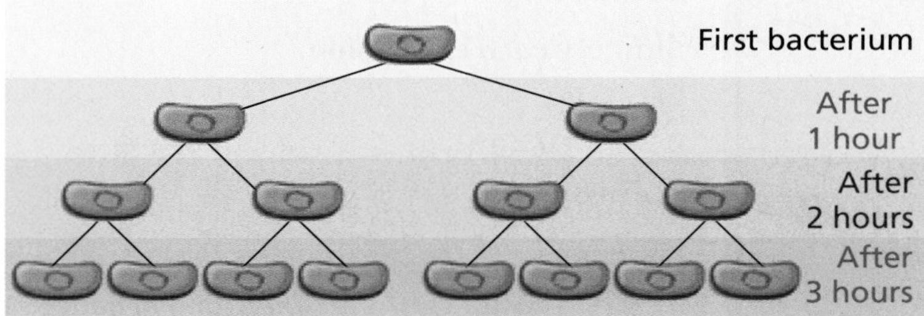


### 3 Solve

Notice that after each hour, the number of bacteria is a power of 2.

After 1 hour: $1 \cdot \mathbf{2} = 2$ or $2^1$ bacteria on the slide
After 2 hours: $2 \cdot \mathbf{2} = 4$ or $2^2$ bacteria on the slide
After 3 hours: $4 \cdot \mathbf{2} = 8$ or $2^3$ bacteria on the slide
So, after the 6th hour, there will be $\mathbf{2^6}$ bacteria.
$2^6 = 2 \cdot 2 \cdot 2 \cdot 2 \cdot 2 \cdot 2 = 64$ *Multiply six 2's.*
After 6 hours, there will be 64 bacteria on the slide.

### 4 Look Back

The numbers become too large for a diagram quickly, but a diagram helps you recognize a pattern. Then you can write the numbers as powers of 2.

**4. What if...?** How many bacteria will be on the slide after 8 hours?

## THINK AND DISCUSS

**1.** Express $8^3$ in words two ways.

**2. GET ORGANIZED** Copy and complete the graphic organizer. In each box, give an example and tell whether the expression is positive or negative.

| | Even Exponent | Odd Exponent |
|---|---|---|
| Positive Base | | |
| Negative Base | | |

# 1-4 Exercises

go.hrw.com
Homework Help Online
KEYWORD: MA7 1-4
Parent Resources Online
KEYWORD: MA7 Parent

## GUIDED PRACTICE

1. **Vocabulary** What does the *exponent* in the expression $5^6$ tell you?

SEE EXAMPLE 1 p. 26

**Write the power represented by each geometric model.**

2. 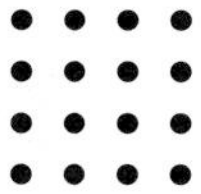 (dot array) 3. 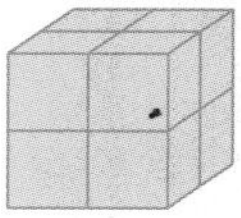 (cube) 4. 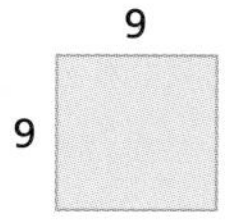 (square, 9 by 9)

SEE EXAMPLE 2 p. 27

**Simplify each expression.**

5. $7^2$ 6. $(-2)^4$ 7. $(-2)^5$ 8. $-\left(\frac{1}{2}\right)^4$

SEE EXAMPLE 3 p. 27

**Write each number as a power of the given base.**

9. 81; base 9 10. 100,000; base 10 11. −64; base −4
12. 10; base 10 13. 81; base 3 14. 36; base −6

SEE EXAMPLE 4 p. 28

15. **Technology** Jan wants to predict the number of hits she will get on her Web page. Her Web page received 3 hits during the first week it was posted. If the number of hits triples every week, how many hits will the Web page receive during the 5th week?

## PRACTICE AND PROBLEM SOLVING

| Independent Practice | |
|---|---|
| For Exercises | See Example |
| 16–18 | 1 |
| 19–22 | 2 |
| 23–28 | 3 |
| 29 | 4 |

**Extra Practice**
Skills Practice p. S4
Application Practice p. S28

**Write the power represented by each geometric model.**

16.
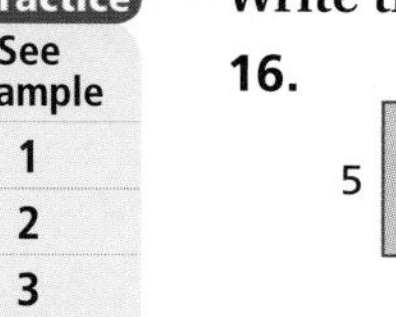

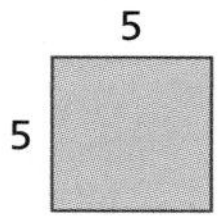

17.

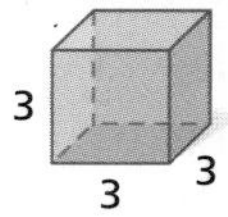

18.
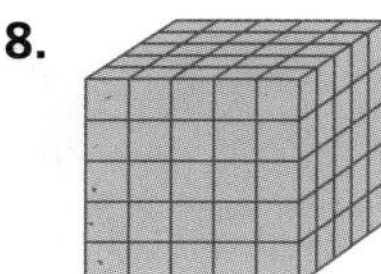

**Simplify each expression.**

19. $3^3$ 20. $(-4)^2$ 21. $-4^2$ 22. $\left(-\frac{3}{5}\right)^2$

**Write each number as a power of the given base.**

23. 49; base 7 24. 1000; base 10 25. −8; base −2
26. 1,000,000; base 10 27. 64; base 4 28. 343; base 7

29. **Biology** Protozoa are single-celled organisms. *Paramecium aurelia* is one type of protozoan. The number of *Paramecium aurelia* protozoa doubles every 1.25 days. There was one protozoan on a slide 5 days ago. How many protozoa are on the slide now?

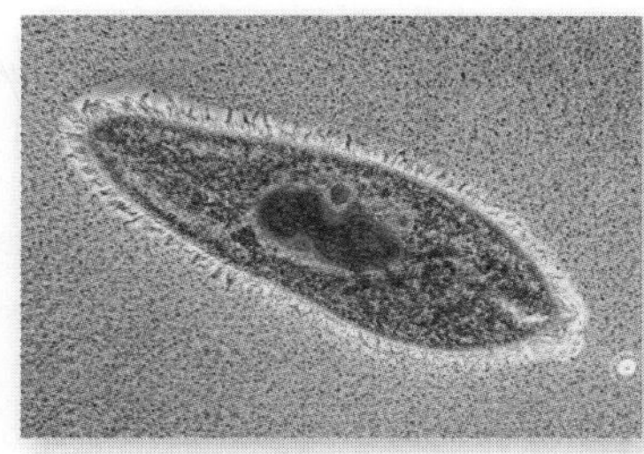

30. **Write About It** A classmate says that any number raised to an even power is positive. Give examples to explain whether your classmate is correct.

**Compare. Write <, >, or =.**

31. $3^2$ ▒ $3^3$ 32. $5^2$ ▒ $2^5$ 33. $4^2$ ▒ $2^4$ 34. $1^9$ ▒ $1^4$
35. $-2^3$ ▒ $(-2)^3$ 36. $-3^2$ ▒ $(-3)^2$ 37. $10^2$ ▒ $2^6$ 38. $2^2$ ▒ $4^1$

Write each expression as repeated multiplication. Then simplify the expression.

39. $2^3$  40. $1^7$  41. $(-4)^3$  42. $-4^3$

43. $(-1)^3$  44. $(-1)^4$  45. $\left(\frac{1}{3}\right)^3$  46. $-2.2^2$

47. **Geometry** The diagram shows an ornamental tile design.

a. What is the area of the whole tile?

b. What is the area of the white square?

c. What is the area of the two shaded regions?

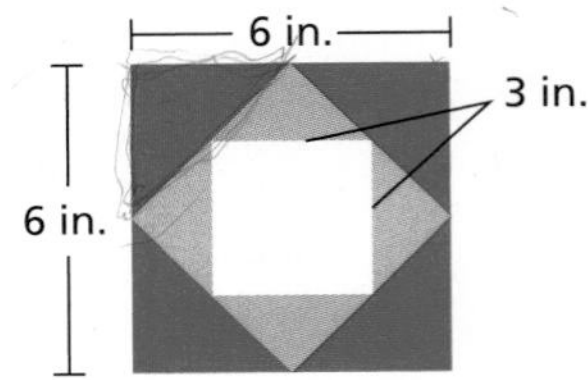


Write each expression using a base and an exponent.

48. $3 \cdot 3 \cdot 3 \cdot 3$  49. $6 \cdot 6$  50. $8 \cdot 8 \cdot 8 \cdot 8 \cdot 8$

51. $(-1)(-1)(-1)(-1)$  52. $(-7)(-7)(-7)$  53. $\left(\frac{1}{9}\right)\left(\frac{1}{9}\right)\left(\frac{1}{9}\right)$

54. **Art** A painting is made of 3 concentric squares. The side length of the largest square is 24 cm. What is the area of the painting?

55. **Estimation** A box is shaped like a cube with edges 22.7 centimeters long. What is the approximate volume of the box?

Write the exponent that makes each equation true.

56. $2^{\blacksquare} = 4$  57. $4^{\blacksquare} = 16$  58. $(-2)^{\blacksquare} = 16$  59. $5^{\blacksquare} = 625$

60. $-2^{\blacksquare} = -8$  61. $10^{\blacksquare} = 100$  62. $5^{\blacksquare} = 125$  63. $3^{\blacksquare} = 81$

64. **Entertainment** Mark and Becky play a coin toss game. Both start with one point. Every time the coin comes up heads, Mark doubles his score. Every time the coin comes up tails, Becky triples her score. The results of their game so far are shown in the table.

a. What is Mark's score?

b. What is Becky's score?

c. **What if...?** If they toss the coin 50 more times, who do you think will win? Why?

| Coin Toss Results | |
|---|---|
| Heads | Tails |
| ✓ | ✓ |
| ✓ | ✓ |
| ✓ | ✓ |
| ✓ | |
| ✓ | |

65. **Critical Thinking** The number of zeros in powers of 10 follow a pattern.

a. Evaluate each of the following: $10^2$, $10^3$, $10^4$.

b. Explain what relationship you see between the exponent of a power of 10 and the number of zeros in the answer.

**MULTI-STEP TEST PREP**

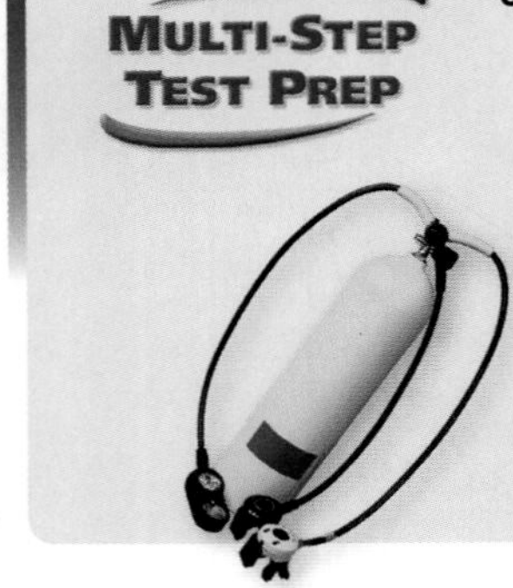

66. This problem will prepare you for the Multi-Step Test Prep on page 38.

The formula $p = \frac{F}{A}$ shows that pressure $p$ is the amount of force $F$ exerted over an area $A$ in square units.

a. A 50-pound bag of flour sits on a block and exerts a force over an area of 100 in$^2$. What is the pressure exerted on the block by the bag of flour?

b. A weight exerts 64 pounds on each square foot of a diver's body. What force is exerted on each square *inch* of the diver's body? (*Hint:* Determine how many square inches are in one square foot.)

Rev. 6.N.5

**67.** Which of the following is equal to $9^2$?

Ⓐ $9 \cdot 2$ Ⓑ 27 Ⓒ $3^4$ Ⓓ $-9^2$

**68.** Which power represents the same value as the product $(-16)(-16)(-16)(-16)$?

Ⓕ $(-16)4$ Ⓖ $(-16)^4$ Ⓗ $-16^4$ Ⓙ $-(16 \cdot 4)$

**69.** A number raised to the third power is negative. What is true about the number?

Ⓐ The number is positive.
Ⓑ The number is negative.
Ⓒ The number is even.
Ⓓ The number is odd.

**70.** A pattern exists as a result of raising $-1$ to consecutive whole numbers. Which is the best representation of the value of $-1$ raised to the 100th power?

| $(-1)^n$ | $(-1)^1$ | $(-1)^2$ | $(-1)^3$ | $(-1)^4$ | $(-1)^5$ | $(-1)^6$ |
|---|---|---|---|---|---|---|
| Value | $-1$ | 1 | $-1$ | 1 | $-1$ | 1 |

Ⓕ $-1^{100}$ Ⓖ $-1$ Ⓗ 1 Ⓙ 0

## CHALLENGE AND EXTEND

**Simplify each expression.**

**71.** $(2^2)(2^2)(2^2)$ **72.** $(2^3)(2^3)(2^3)$ **73.** $(-4^2)(-4^2)(-4^2)(-4^2)$

**74. Design** The diagram shows the layout of a pool and the surrounding path. The path is 2.5 feet wide.

**a.** What is the total area of the pool and path?

**b.** What is the area of the pool?

**c.** What is the area of the path?

**d.** One bag of pebbles covers 10 square feet. How many bags of pebbles are needed to cover the path?

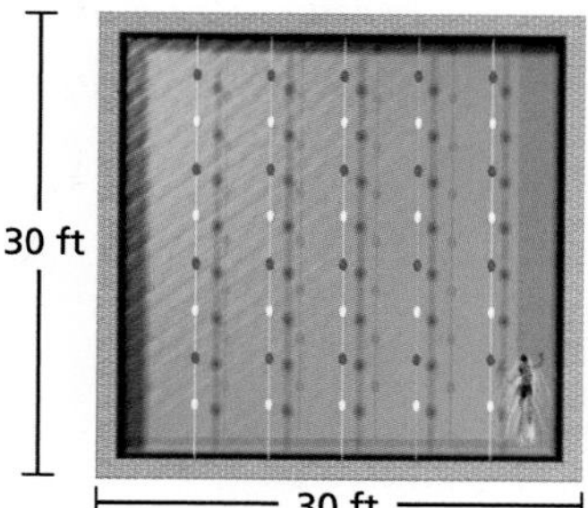


**75.** Exponents and powers have special properties.

**a.** Write both $4^2$ and $4^3$ as a product of 4's.

**b.** Write the product of the two expressions from part **a.** Write this product as a power of 4.

**c. Write About It** Add the exponents in the expressions $4^2$ and $4^3$. Describe any relationship you see between your answer to part **b** and the sum of the exponents.

## SPIRAL REVIEW

**Find the mean of each data set by dividing the sum of the data by the number of items in the data set.** *(Previous course)*

**76.** 7, 7, 8, 8 **77.** 1, 3, 5, 7, 9 **78.** 10, 9, 9, 12, 12

**Give two ways to write each algebraic expression in words.** *(Lesson 1-1)*

**79.** $5 - x$ **80.** $6n$ **81.** $c \div d$ **82.** $a + b$

**Multiply or divide if possible.** *(Lesson 1-3)*

**83.** $\frac{4}{5} \div \frac{8}{25}$ **84.** $0 \div \frac{6}{7}$ **85.** $-20(-14)$ **86.** $\frac{1}{2}\left(-\frac{4}{5}\right)$

# 1-5 Square Roots and Real Numbers

**MA.N.2.3** Use strategies to compute square roots … of numbers that are not perfect squares ...

***Objectives***

Evaluate expressions containing square roots.

Classify numbers within the real number system.

***Vocabulary***

square root
perfect square
real numbers
natural numbers
whole numbers
integers
rational numbers
terminating decimal
repeating decimal
irrational numbers

**Why learn this?**

Square roots are used to find the side length of a square when you know the area of the square, like when covering a square plot with flower seeds. (See Example 2.)

Deep down inside, Coach Knott had always wanted to be a math teacher.



A number that is multiplied by itself to form a product is called a **square root** of that product. The operations of squaring and finding a square root are inverse operations.

The radical symbol, $\sqrt{\phantom{x}}$, is used to represent square roots. Positive real numbers have two square roots.

$$4 \cdot 4 = 4^2 = 16 \rightarrow \sqrt{16} = 4 \leftarrow \text{Positive square root of 16}$$

$$(-4)(-4) = (-4)^2 = 16 \rightarrow -\sqrt{16} = -4 \leftarrow \text{Negative square root of 16}$$

The nonnegative square root is represented by $\sqrt{\phantom{x}}$. The negative square root is represented by $-\sqrt{\phantom{x}}$.

A **perfect square** is a number whose positive square root is a *whole number.* Some examples of perfect squares are shown in the table.

| 0 | 1 | 4 | 9 | 16 | 25 | 36 | 49 | 64 | 81 | 100 |
|---|---|---|---|---|---|---|---|---|---|---|
| $0^2$ | $1^2$ | $2^2$ | $3^2$ | $4^2$ | $5^2$ | $6^2$ | $7^2$ | $8^2$ | $9^2$ | $10^2$ |

## EXAMPLE 1 Finding Square Roots of Perfect Squares

**Find each square root.**

**A** $\sqrt{49}$

$7^2 = 49$ *Think: What number squared equals 49?*

$\sqrt{49} = 7$ *Positive square root → positive 7*

**B** $-\sqrt{36}$

$6^2 = 36$ *Think: What is the opposite of the square root of 36?*

$-\sqrt{36} = -6$ *Negative square root → negative 6*

**Reading Math**

The expression $\sqrt{-36}$ does not represent a real number because there is no real number that can be multiplied by itself to form a product of $-36$.

**Find each square root.**

**1a.** $\sqrt{4}$ **1b.** $-\sqrt{25}$

The square roots of many numbers, like $\sqrt{15}$, are not whole numbers. A calculator can approximate the value of $\sqrt{15}$ as 3.872983346... Without a calculator, you can use square roots of perfect squares to help estimate the square roots of other numbers.

## EXAMPLE 2 *Problem-Solving Application*

PROBLEM SOLVING

**Nancy wants to plant wildflowers in a square-shaped plot. She has enough wildflower seeds to cover 19 ft$^2$. Estimate to the nearest tenth the side length of a square plot with an area of 19 ft$^2$.**

### 1 Understand the Problem

The **answer** will be the side length of the square garden.

List the **important information:**

- The garden has an area of 19 feet.

### 2 Make a Plan

The side length of the square is $\sqrt{19}$ because $\sqrt{19} \cdot \sqrt{19} = 19$. 19 is not a perfect square, so $\sqrt{19}$ is not a whole number. Estimate $\sqrt{19}$ to the nearest tenth.

Find the two whole numbers that $\sqrt{19}$ is between. 19 is between the perfect squares 16 and 25, so $\sqrt{19}$ is between $\sqrt{16}$ and $\sqrt{25}$, or between 4 and 5. 19 is closer to 16 than to 25, so $\sqrt{19}$ is closer to 4 than to 5.

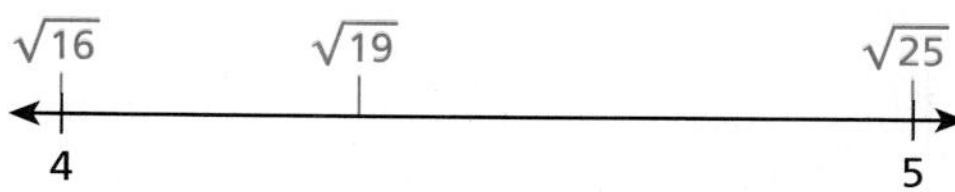


You can use a guess-and-check method to estimate $\sqrt{19}$.

### 3 Solve

| | | | |
|---|---|---|---|
| Guess 4.3: | $4.3^2 = 18.49$ | too low | *$\sqrt{19}$ is greater than 4.3.* |
| Guess 4.4: | $4.4^2 = 19.36$ | too high | *$\sqrt{19}$ is less than 4.4.* |

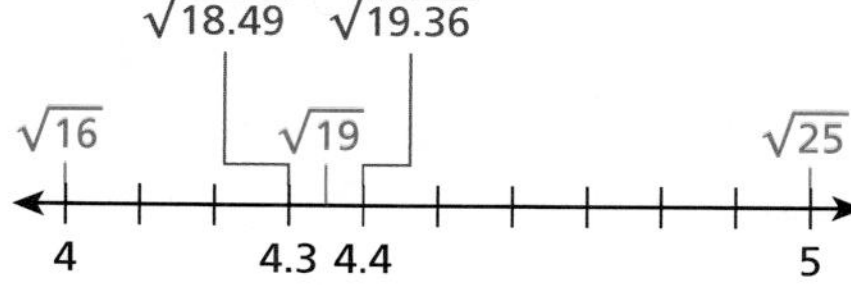


Because 19 is closer to 19.36 than to 18.49, $\sqrt{19}$ is closer to 4.4 than to 4.3.

$\sqrt{19} \approx 4.4$

**Writing Math**

The symbol ≈ means approximately equal to.

### 4 Look Back

A square garden with a side length of 4.4 ft would have an area of 19.36 ft$^2$. 19.36 is close to 19, so 4.4 ft is a reasonable estimate.

2. **What if...?** Nancy decides to buy more wildflower seeds and now has enough to cover 38 ft$^2$. What is the side length of a square garden with an area of 38 ft$^2$?

All numbers that can be represented on the number line are called **real numbers** and can be classified according to their characteristics.

**Real Numbers**

Rational Numbers ($\mathbb{Q}$): $\frac{27}{4}$, $0.\overline{3}$, $-\frac{10}{11}$, $4.5$, $\frac{5}{9}$

Integers ($\mathbb{Z}$): $-3$, $-2$, $-1$

Whole Numbers ($\mathbb{W}$): $0$

Natural Numbers ($\mathbb{N}$): $1$, $2$, $3$

Irrational Numbers: $\sqrt{17}$, $-\sqrt{11}$, $\sqrt{2}$, $e$, $\pi$

- **Natural numbers** are the counting numbers: 1, 2, 3, …
- **Whole numbers** are the natural numbers and zero: 0, 1, 2, 3, …
- **Integers** are whole numbers and their opposites: −3, −2, −1, 0, 1, 2, 3, …
- **Rational numbers** can be expressed in the form $\frac{a}{b}$, where $a$ and $b$ are both integers and $b \neq 0$: $\frac{1}{2}, \frac{7}{1}, \frac{9}{10}$
- **Terminating decimals** are rational numbers in decimal form that have a finite number of digits: 1.5, 2.75, 4.0
- **Repeating decimals** are rational numbers in decimal form that have a block of one or more digits that repeats continuously: $1.\overline{3}$, $0.\overline{6}$, $2.\overline{14}$, $6.2\overline{7}$
- **Irrational numbers** cannot be expressed in the form $\frac{a}{b}$. They include square roots of whole numbers that are not perfect squares and nonterminating decimals that do not repeat: $\sqrt{2}$, $\sqrt{11}$, $\pi$

## EXAMPLE 3 Classifying Real Numbers

**Write all classifications that apply to each real number.**

**A** $\frac{8}{9}$

$8 \div 9 = 0.888\ldots = 0.\overline{8}$ — *$\frac{8}{9}$ can be written as a repeating decimal.*

rational number, repeating decimal

**B** 18

$18 = \frac{18}{1} = 18.0$ — *18 can be written as a fraction and a decimal.*

rational number, terminating decimal, integer, whole number, natural number

**C** $\sqrt{20}$

$\sqrt{20} = 4.472135\ldots$ — *The digits of $\sqrt{20}$ continue with no pattern.*

irrational number

**Reading Math**

Note the symbols for the sets of numbers.

$\mathbb{R}$: real numbers
$\mathbb{Q}$: rational numbers
$\mathbb{Z}$: integers
$\mathbb{W}$: whole numbers
$\mathbb{N}$: natural numbers

**Write all classifications that apply to each real number.**

**3a.** $7\frac{4}{9}$ **3b.** $-12$ **3c.** $\sqrt{10}$

## THINK AND DISCUSS

**1.** Write $\frac{2}{3}$ and $\frac{3}{5}$ as decimals. Identify what number classifications the two numbers share and how their classifications are different.

Know it! Note

**2. GET ORGANIZED** Copy the graphic organizer and use the flowchart to classify each of the given numbers. Write each number in the box with the most specific classification that applies. $4, \sqrt{25}, 0, \frac{1}{3}, -15, -2.25, \frac{1}{4}, \sqrt{21}, 2^4, (-1)^2$

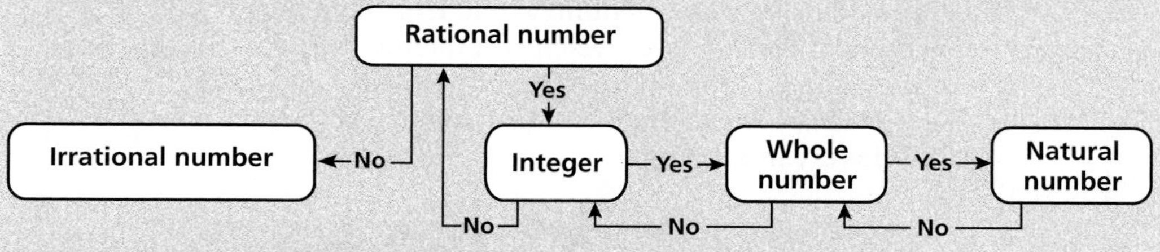


# 1-5 Exercises

MA.N.2.3

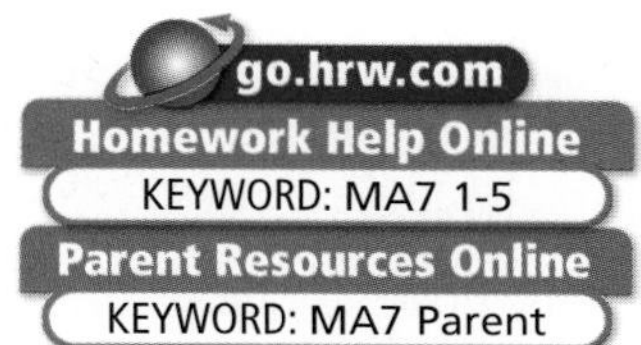


## GUIDED PRACTICE

1. **Vocabulary** Give an example of an *integer* that is not a *whole number*.

SEE EXAMPLE 1 p. 32

**Find each square root.**

2. $\sqrt{64}$
3. $\sqrt{225}$
4. $-\sqrt{1}$
5. $\sqrt{169}$

SEE EXAMPLE 2 p. 33

6. A contractor is told that a potential client's kitchen floor is in the shape of a square. The area of the floor is 45 $\text{ft}^2$. Find the side length of the floor to the nearest tenth.

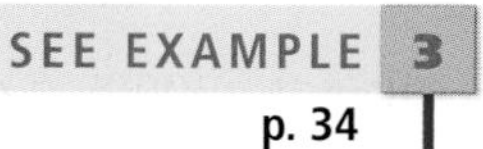
SEE EXAMPLE 3 p. 34

**Write all classifications that apply to each real number.**

7. $-27$
8. $\frac{1}{6}$
9. $\sqrt{12}$
10. $-6.8$

## PRACTICE AND PROBLEM SOLVING

**Independent Practice**

| For Exercises | See Example |
|---|---|
| 11–14 | 1 |
| 15 | 2 |
| 16–19 | 3 |

**Extra Practice**

Skills Practice p. S4
Application Practice p. S28

**Find each square root.**

11. $\sqrt{121}$
12. $\sqrt{9}$
13. $-\sqrt{100}$
14. $\sqrt{400}$

15. Mr. and Mrs. Phillips are going to build a new home with a foundation that is in the shape of a square. The house will cover 222 square yards. Find the length of the side of the house to the nearest tenth of a yard.

**Write all classifications that apply to each real number.**

16. $\frac{5}{12}$
17. $\sqrt{49}$
18. $-3$
19. $\sqrt{18}$

**Compare. Write <, >, or =.**

20. $\sqrt{88}$ ▒ 9
21. 8 ▒ $\sqrt{63}$
22. 6 ▒ $\sqrt{40}$
23. $\sqrt{169}$ ▒ 13

**Geometry** Give the side length of each square. Round your answer to the nearest whole number, if necessary.

**24.** Area = $81 \text{ cm}^2$

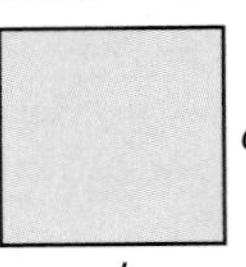


**25.** Area = $34 \text{ in}^2$

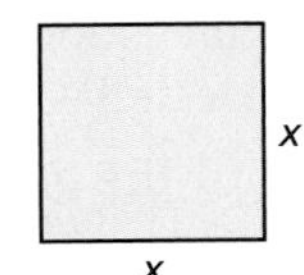


**26.** Area = $169 \text{ m}^2$

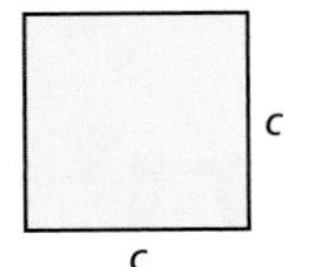


**Travel** During a cross-country road trip, Madeline recorded the distance between several major cities and the time it took to travel between those cities. Find Madeline's average speed for each leg of the trip and classify that number.

**Madeline's Cross-Country Road Trip**

| | | Distance (mi) | Time (h) | Speed (mi/h) | Classification |
|---|---|---|---|---|---|
| **27.** | Portland, ME, to Memphis, TN | 1485 | 33 | ▒ | ▒ |
| **28.** | Memphis, TN, to Denver, CO | 1046 | 27 | ▒ | ▒ |
| **29.** | Denver, CO, to Boise, ID | 831 | 24 | ▒ | ▒ |
| **30.** | Boise, ID, to Portland, OR | 424 | 9 | ▒ | ▒ |

**Determine whether each statement is sometimes, always, or never true.**

**31.** Natural numbers are whole numbers.

**32.** Negative numbers are integers.

**33.** Mixed numbers are rational numbers.

**34.** A positive number has two square roots.

**Tell whether whole numbers, integers, or rational numbers are the most reasonable to describe each. Explain your answer.**

**35.** number of pets

**36.** body temperature

**37.** recipe measurements

**38.** money owed

**39.** distances

**40.** home runs

**41. Critical Thinking** Tell how you would classify the square roots of all positive integers that are not perfect squares.

**42. Write About It** Tell whether the square root of an integer is sometimes, always, or never an integer. Explain.

**MULTI-STEP TEST PREP**

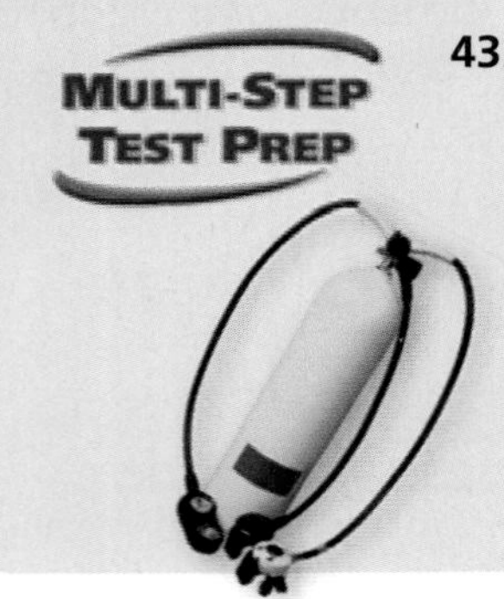

**43.** This problem will prepare you for the Multi-Step Test Prep on page 38.

The equation $a^2 + b^2 = c^2$ relates the lengths of the sides of a right triangle. Sides $a$ and $b$ make the right angle of the triangle.

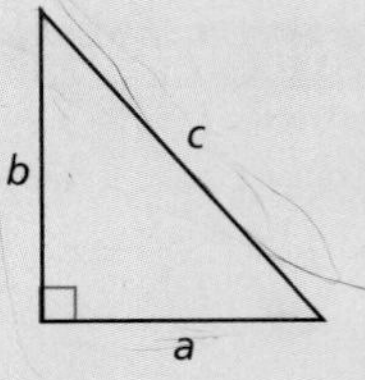


**a.** What is the value of $c^2$ when $a = 5$ and $b = 12$? Determine the square root of $c^2$ to find the value of $c$.

**b.** A diver is a horizontal distance of 50 feet from a boat and 120 feet beneath the surface of the water. What distance will the diver swim if he swims diagonally to the boat?

**44. Entertainment** In a game called Pente, players place different-colored stones on a grid. Each player tries to make rows of 5 or more stones in their color while preventing their opponent(s) from doing the same. The square game board has 324 squares on it. How many squares are on each side of the board?

MA.N.2.3

45. Which point on the number line is closest to $-\sqrt{11}$?

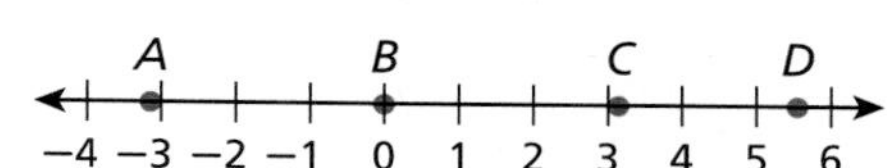


(A) A (B) B (C) C (D) D

46. What is the area of the figure at right?

(F) 24 cm$^2$ (H) 104 cm$^2$

(G) 52 cm$^2$ (J) 576 cm$^2$

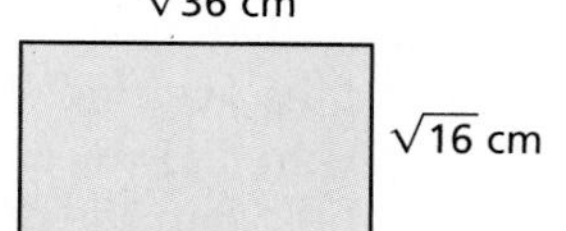


47. Which number is closest to $\sqrt{111}$?

(A) −50 (B) 10

(C) −10 (D) 50

## CHALLENGE AND EXTEND

**Find each square root.**

**48.** $\sqrt{0.81}$ **49.** $\sqrt{0.25}$ **50.** $\sqrt{1.69}$ **51.** $\sqrt{2.25}$

**Number Theory Use the following information for Exercises 52 and 53.**

A set of numbers is said to be *closed* under a certain operation if, when you perform the operation on any two numbers in the set, the result is also a number in the set.

The set of real numbers is closed under addition. This means that when you add any two real numbers, the sum is also a real number.

**52.** Is the set of real numbers closed under subtraction? Explain.

**53.** Is the set of whole numbers closed under subtraction? Explain.

## SPIRAL REVIEW

**Use the formula $V = \ell wh$ to find the volume of a rectangular prism with the given dimensions.** *(Previous course)*

**54.** $\ell = 3$ cm, $w = 2$ cm, $h = 5$ cm **55.** $\ell = 7$ in., $w = 4$ in., $h = 6$ in.

**Add or subtract.** *(Lesson 1-2)*

**56.** $-14 + (-16)$ **57.** $-\frac{1}{4} - \left(-\frac{3}{4}\right)$ **58.** $25 - x$ when $x = 17.6$

**Evaluate each expression.** *(Lesson 1-4)*

**59.** $-3^4$ **60.** $\left(-\frac{2}{5}\right)^3$ **61.** $14^2$ **62.** $4^3$

CHAPTER 1

# MULTI-STEP TEST PREP

SECTION 1A

## The Language of Algebra

**Under Pressure** Atmospheric pressure is 14.7 pounds per square inch (psi). Underwater, the water exerts additional pressure. The total pressure on a diver underwater is the atmospheric pressure plus the water pressure.

1. As a diver moves downward in the water, the water pressure increases by 14.7 psi for approximately every 33 ft of water. Make a table to show the total pressure on a diver at 0, 33, 66, and 99 ft below the surface of the water. At what depth would the total pressure equal 73.5 psi? Explain your method.

2. A diver is 40 ft below the surface of the water when a hot-air balloon flies over her. The hot-air balloon is 849 ft above the surface of the water. Draw a diagram and write an expression to find the distance between the diver and the balloon when the balloon is directly above her.

3. The diver swam 62.5 ft in 5 minutes. How fast was she swimming? What total distance will she have traveled after an additional 4 minutes if she maintains this same speed?

4. The total pressure on each square foot of the diver's body is given by the expression $2116.8 + 64.145d$, where $d$ is the depth in feet. At a depth of 66 ft, what is the total pressure on each square foot of her body? What is the total pressure on each square *inch* of her body at this depth? How does your answer compare to your results for part **a?**

5. The diver realizes that she has drifted horizontally about 30 ft from the boat she left. She is at a depth of 40 ft from the surface. What is the diver's diagonal distance from the boat?

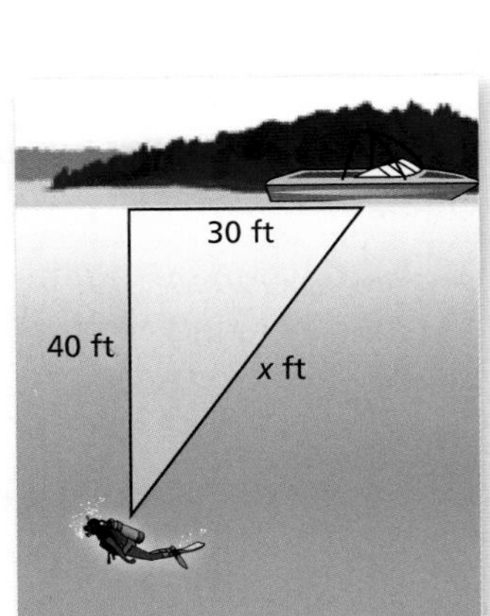

# READY TO GO ON?

CHAPTER 1

SECTION 1A

## Quiz for Lessons 1-1 Through 1-5

### 1-1 Variables and Expressions

**Give two ways to write each algebraic expression in words.**

1. $4 + n$
2. $m - 9$
3. $\frac{g}{2}$
4. $4z$
5. Bob earns $15 per hour. Write an expression for the amount of money he earns in $h$ hours.
6. A soccer practice is 90 minutes long. Write an expression for the number of minutes left after $m$ minutes have elapsed.

**Evaluate each expression for $x = 3$, $y = 6$, and $z = 2$.**

7. $y \div z$
8. $xy$
9. $x + y$
10. $x - z$

### 1-2 Adding and Subtracting Real Numbers

**Add or subtract.**

11. $81 + (-15)$
12. $27 - 32$
13. $2 - \left(-1\frac{1}{4}\right)$
14. $x + (-14)$ for $x = -7$
15. Brandon's bank statement shows a balance of −$45.00. What will the balance be after Brandon deposits $70.00?

### 1-3 Multiplying and Dividing Real Numbers

**Find the value of each expression if possible.**

16. $9(-9)$
17. $6 \div \frac{3}{5}$
18. $9.6 \div 0$
19. $-\frac{1}{2}x$ for $x = -\frac{1}{2}$
20. Simon drove for $2\frac{1}{2}$ hours to get from his house to the beach. Simon averaged 55 miles per hour on the trip. What is the distance from Simon's house to the beach?

### 1-4 Powers and Exponents

**Simplify each expression.**

21. $(-3)^2$
22. $-3^2$
23. $\left(-\frac{2}{3}\right)^3$
24. $\left(-\frac{1}{2}\right)^5$
25. The number of bytes in a kilobyte is 2 to the 10th power. Express this number in two ways.

### 1-5 Square Roots and Real Numbers

**Find each square root.**

26. $\sqrt{225}$
27. $-\sqrt{49}$
28. $\sqrt{144}$
29. $\sqrt{\frac{16}{25}}$
30. Mindy is building a patio that is in the shape of a square. The patio will cover 56 square yards. Find the length of a side of the patio to the nearest tenth of a yard.

**Classify each real number. Write all classifications that apply.**

31. $\frac{1}{11}$
32. $\sqrt{12}$
33. $\sqrt{400}$
34. $-6$

# 1-6 Order of Operations

**Rev. 8.N.1.1** Use … operations for all rational numbers, including formal algorithms.

***Objective***
Use the order of operations to simplify expressions.

***Vocabulary***
order of operations

**Who uses this?**
Sports statisticians use the order of operations to calculate data. (See Example 5.)

A baseball player must run to first, second, and third bases before running back to home plate. In math, some tasks must be done in a certain order.

When a numerical or algebraic expression contains more than one operation symbol, the **order of operations** tells you which operation to perform first.

| Order of Operations | |
|---|---|
| First: | Perform operations inside grouping symbols. |
| Second: | Simplify powers. |
| Third: | Perform multiplication and division from left to right. |
| Fourth: | Perform addition and subtraction from left to right. |

Grouping symbols include parentheses ( ), brackets [ ], and braces { }. If an expression contains more than one set of grouping symbols, simplify the expression inside the innermost set first. Follow the order of operations within that set of grouping symbols and then work outward.

## EXAMPLE 1 Simplifying Numerical Expressions

**Simplify each expression.**

**A** $-4^2 + 24 \div 3 \cdot 2$

$-4^2 + 24 \div 3 \cdot 2$ — *There are no grouping symbols.*

$-16 + 24 \div 3 \cdot 2$ — *Simplify powers. The exponent applies only to the 4.*

$-16 + 8 \cdot 2$ — *Divide.*

$-16 + 16$ — *Multiply.*

$0$ — *Add.*

**B** $4\left[25 - (5-2)^2\right]$

$4\left[25 - (5-2)^2\right]$ — *There are two sets of grouping symbols.*

$4\left[25 - 3^2\right]$ — *Perform the operations in the innermost set.*

$4\left[25 - 9\right]$ — *Simplify powers.*

$4 \cdot 16$ — *Perform the operations inside the brackets.*

$64$ — *Multiply.*

**Helpful Hint**

The first letters of these words can help you remember the order of operations.

| | |
|---|---|
| **P**lease | **P**arentheses |
| **E**xcuse | **E**xponents |
| **M**y | **M**ultiply/ |
| **D**ear | **D**ivide |
| **A**unt | **A**dd/ |
| **S**ally | **S**ubtract |

**Simplify each expression.**

**1a.** $8 \div \frac{1}{2} \cdot 3$ **1b.** $5.4 - 3^2 + 6.2$ **1c.** $-20 \div \left[-2(4+1)\right]$

## EXAMPLE 2 Evaluating Algebraic Expressions

**Evaluate each expression for the given value of *x*.**

**A** $21 - x + 2 \cdot 5$ **for** $x = 7$

| | |
|---|---|
| $21 - x + 2 \cdot 5$ | |
| $21 - 7 + 2 \cdot 5$ | *First substitute 7 for x.* |
| $21 - 7 + 10$ | *Multiply.* |
| $14 + 10$ | *Subtract.* |
| $24$ | *Add.* |

**B** $5^2(30 - x)$ **for** $x = 24$

| | |
|---|---|
| $5^2(30 - x)$ | |
| $5^2(30 - 24)$ | *First substitute 24 for x.* |
| $5^2(6)$ | *Perform the operation inside the parentheses.* |
| $25(6)$ | *Simplify powers.* |
| $150$ | *Multiply.* |

**Evaluate each expression for the given value of *x*.**

**2a.** $14 + x^2 \div 4$ for $x = 2$ **2b.** $(x \cdot 2^2) \div (2 + 6)$ for $x = 6$

Fraction bars, radical symbols, and absolute-value symbols can also be used as grouping symbols. Remember that a fraction bar indicates division.

## EXAMPLE 3 Simplifying Expressions with Other Grouping Symbols

**Simplify each expression.**

**A** $\dfrac{-22 - 2^2}{5 - 3}$

| | |
|---|---|
| $\dfrac{(-22 - 2^2)}{(5 - 3)}$ | *The fraction bar acts as a grouping symbol. Simplify the numerator and the denominator before dividing.* |
| $\dfrac{-22 - 4}{5 - 3}$ | *Simplify the power in the numerator.* |
| $\dfrac{-26}{5 - 3}$ | *Subtract to simplify the numerator.* |
| $\dfrac{-26}{2}$ | *Subtract to simplify the denominator.* |
| $-13$ | *Divide.* |

> **Helpful Hint**
>
> You may need to add grouping symbols to simplify expressions when using a scientific or graphing calculator.
> To simplify $\frac{2 + 3}{5 - 4}$ with a calculator, enter $(2 + 3) \div (5 - 4)$.

**B** $|10 - 5^2| \div 5$

| | |
|---|---|
| $\lvert 10 - 5^2 \rvert \div 5$ | *The absolute-value symbols act as grouping symbols.* |
| $\lvert 10 - 25 \rvert \div 5$ | *Simplify the power.* |
| $\lvert -15 \rvert \div 5$ | *Subtract within the absolute-value symbols.* |
| $15 \div 5$ | *Write the absolute value of −15.* |
| $3$ | *Divide.* |

**Simplify each expression.**

**3a.** $\dfrac{5 + 2(-8)}{(-2)^3 - 3}$ **3b.** $|4 - 7|^2 \div (-3)$ **3c.** $3\sqrt{50 - 1}$

You may need to use grouping symbols when translating from words to numerical or algebraic expressions. Remember that operations inside grouping symbols are performed first.

## EXAMPLE 4 Translating from Words to Math

**Remember!**

Look for words that imply mathematical operations.

*difference* → subtract
*sum* → add
*product* → multiply
*quotient* → divide

**Translate each word phrase into a numerical or algebraic expression.**

**A** **one half times the difference of −5 and 3**

$\frac{1}{2}(-5 - 3)$ *Use parentheses so that the difference is evaluated first.*

**B** **the square root of the quotient of −12 and *n***

$\sqrt{\frac{-12}{n}}$ *Show the square root of a quotient.*

4. Translate the word phrase into a numerical or algebraic expression: the product of 6.2 and the sum of 9.4 and 8.

## EXAMPLE 5 *Sports Application*

**Hank Aaron's last season in the Major Leagues was in 1976. A player's total number of bases can be found using the expression $S + 2D + 3T + 4H$. Use the table to find Hank Aaron's total bases for 1976.**

**HANK AARON**
1976 Statistics

| Base Hits | Number |
|---|---|
| Single (S) | 44 |
| Double (D) | 8 |
| Triple (T) | 0 |
| Home run (H) | 10 |

$S + 2D + 3T + 4H$

$44 + 2(8) + 3(0) + 4(10)$ *First substitute values for each variable.*

$44 + 16 + 0 + 40$ *Multiply.*

$60 + 0 + 40$ *Add from left to right.*

$100$ *Add.*

Hank Aaron's total number of bases for 1976 was 100.

5. Another formula for a player's total number of bases is $\text{Hits} + D + 2T + 3H$. Use this expression to find Hank Aaron's total bases for 1959, when he had 223 hits, 46 doubles, 7 triples, and 39 home runs.

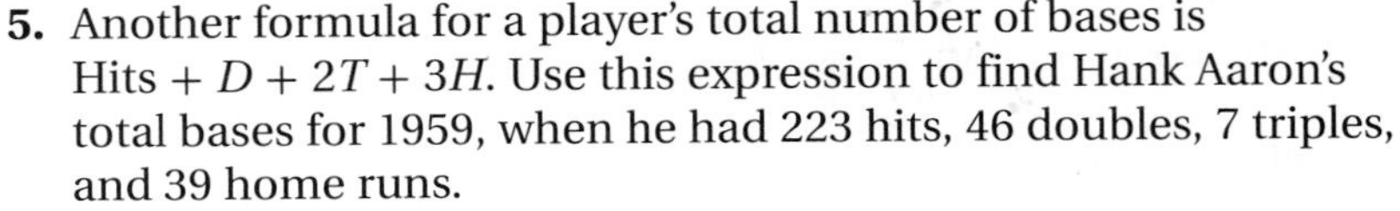

### THINK AND DISCUSS

1. Explain whether you always perform addition before subtraction when simplifying a numerical or algebraic expression.

2. **GET ORGANIZED** Copy and complete the graphic organizer. In each box, show how grouping symbols can be placed so that the expression is equal to the number shown.

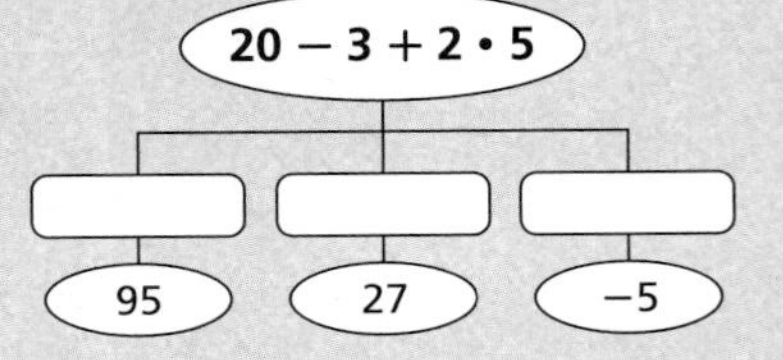

# 1-6 Exercises

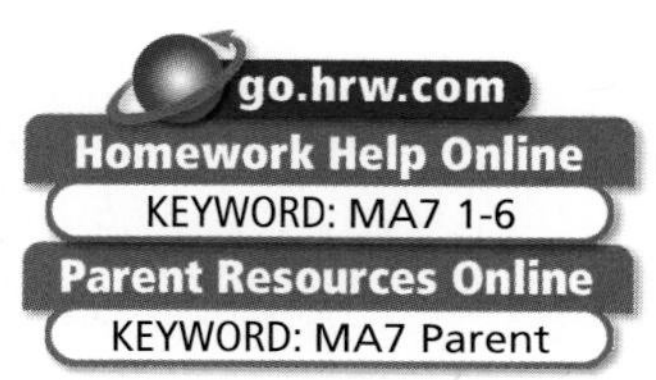


## GUIDED PRACTICE

1. **Vocabulary** Explain why the *order of operations* is necessary for simplifying numerical expressions.

SEE EXAMPLE 1 p. 40

**Simplify each expression.**

2. $5 - 12 \div (-2)$
3. $30 - 5 \cdot 3$
4. $50 - 6 + 8$
5. $12 \div (-4)(3)$
6. $(5 - 8)(3 - 9)$
7. $16 + \left[5 - \left(3 + 2^2\right)\right]$

SEE EXAMPLE 2 p. 41

**Evaluate each expression for the given value of the variable.**

8. $5 + 2x - 9$ for $x = 4$
9. $30 \div 2 - d$ for $d = 14$
10. $51 - 91 + g$ for $g = 20$
11. $2(3 + n)$ for $n = 4$
12. $4(b - 4)^2$ for $b = 5$
13. $12 + \left[20(5 - k)\right]$ for $k = 1$

SEE EXAMPLE 3 p. 41

**Simplify each expression.**

14. $24 \div |4 - 10|$
15. $4.5 - \sqrt{2(4.5)}$
16. $5(2) + 16 \div |-4|$
17. $\frac{0 - 24}{6 + 2}$
18. $\frac{2 + 3(6)}{2^2}$
19. $-44 \div \sqrt{12 \div 3}$

SEE EXAMPLE 4 p. 42

**Translate each word phrase into a numerical or algebraic expression.**

20. 5 times the absolute value of the sum of $s$ and $-2$
21. the product of 12 and the sum of $-2$ and 6
22. 14 divided by the sum of 52 and $-3$

SEE EXAMPLE 5 p. 42

23. **Geometry** The surface area of a cylinder can be found using the expression $2\pi r(h + r)$. Find the surface area of the cylinder shown. (Use 3.14 for $\pi$ and give your final answer rounded to the nearest tenth.)

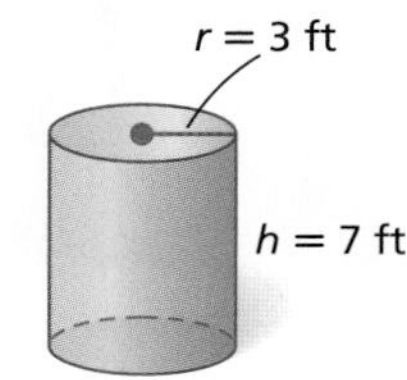


## PRACTICE AND PROBLEM SOLVING

**Independent Practice**

| For Exercises | See Example |
|---|---|
| 24–32 | 1 |
| 33–41 | 2 |
| 42–49 | 3 |
| 50–53 | 4 |
| 54 | 5 |

**Extra Practice**

Skills Practice p. S5

Application Practice p. S28

**Simplify each expression.**

24. $3 + 4(-5)$
25. $20 - 4 + 5 - 2$
26. $41 + 12 \div 2$
27. $3(-9) + (-2)(-6)$
28. $10^2 \div (10 - 20)$
29. $(6 + 2 \cdot 3) \div (9 - 7)^2$
30. $-9 - (-18) + 6$
31. $15 \div (2 - 5)$
32. $5(1 - 2) - (3 - 2)$

**Evaluate each expression for the given value of the variable.**

33. $-6(3 - p)$ for $p = 7$
34. $5 + (r + 2)^2$ for $r = 4$
35. $13 - \left[3 + (j - 12)\right]$ for $j = 5$
36. $(-4 - a)^2$ for $a = -3$
37. $7 - (21 - h)^2$ for $h = 25$
38. $10 + \left[8 \div (q - 3)\right]$ for $q = 2$
39. $(4r - 2) + 7$ for $r = 3$
40. $-2(11b - 3)$ for $b = 5$
41. $7x(3 + 2x)$ for $x = -1$

**Simplify each expression.**

42. $-4|2.5 - 6|$
43. $\frac{8 - 8}{2 - 1}$
44. $\frac{3 + |8 - 10|}{2}$
45. $\sqrt{3^2 - 5} \div 8$
46. $\frac{-18 - 36}{-9}$
47. $\frac{6|5 - 7|}{14 - 2}$
48. $\sqrt{5^2 - 4^2}$
49. $(-6 + 24) \div |-3|$

**Translate each word phrase into a numerical or an algebraic expression.**

50. the product of 7 and the sum of 2 and $d$

51. the difference of 3 and the quotient of 2 and 5

52. the square root of the sum of 5 and $-4$

53. the difference of 8 and the absolute value of the product of 3 and 5

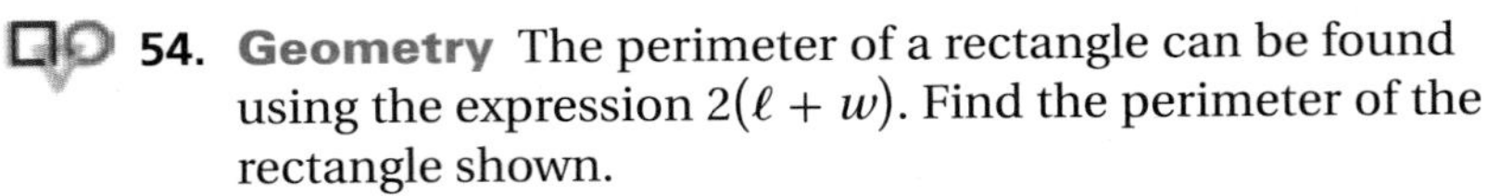

54. **Geometry** The perimeter of a rectangle can be found using the expression $2(\ell + w)$. Find the perimeter of the rectangle shown.

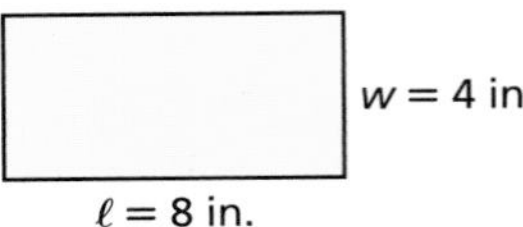


55. Simplify each expression.
   a. $50 + 10 \div 2$  b. $50 \cdot 10 - 2$  c. $50 \cdot 10 \div 2$
   d. $50 \div 10 \cdot 2$  e. $50 - 10 \cdot 2$  f. $50 + 10 \cdot 2$

**Translate each word phrase into a numerical or algebraic expression.**

56. the difference of 8 and the product of 4 and $n$

57. 2 times the sum of 9 and the opposite of $x$

58. two-thirds of the difference of $-2$ and 8

59. the square root of 7 divided by the product of 3 and 10

LINK **Sports**

In 2004, Paul Hamm became the first American to win a gold medal in the men's all-around competition at the Olympics. He won by a margin of 0.012 point.

60. **Sports** At the 2004 Summer Olympics, U.S. gymnast Paul Hamm received the scores shown in the table during the individual all-around competition.

**2004 Summer Olympics Individual Scores for Paul Hamm**

| Event | Floor | Pommel horse | Rings | Vault | Parallel bars | Horizontal bar |
|---|---|---|---|---|---|---|
| Score | 9.725 | 9.700 | 9.587 | 9.137 | 9.837 | 9.837 |

   a. Write a numerical expression to show the average of Hamm's scores. (*Hint:* The average of a set of values is the sum of the values divided by the number of values.)
   b. Simplify the expression to find Hamm's average score.

61. **Critical Thinking** Are parentheses required when translating the word phrase "the sum of 8 and the product of 3 and 2" into a numerical phrase? Explain.

**Translate each word phrase into a numerical expression. Then simplify.**

62. the sum of 8 and the product of $-3$ and 5

63. the difference of the product of 3 and 5 and the product of 6 and 2

64. the product of $\frac{2}{3}$ and the absolute value of the difference of 3 and $-12$

**MULTI-STEP TEST PREP**

65. This problem will prepare you for the Multi-Step Test Prep on page 60.
   a. Find the area of each face of the prism. Find the sum of these areas to find the total surface area of the prism.
   b. The total surface area of a prism is described by the expression $2(\ell w) + 2(\ell h) + 2(wh)$. Explain how this expression relates to the sum you found in part **a.**
   c. Use the expression above to find the total surface area of the prism. Explain why your answers to parts **a** and **c** should be equal.

3 in. 4 in. 5 in.

**66. Geometry** The area of a trapezoid is equal to the average of its bases times its height. Use the expression $\left(\frac{b_1 + b_2}{2}\right)h$ to determine the area of the trapezoid.

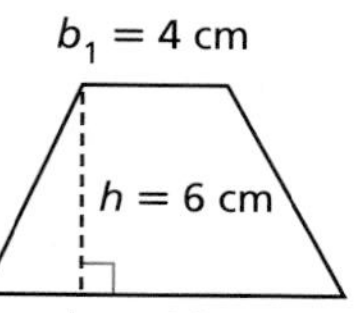


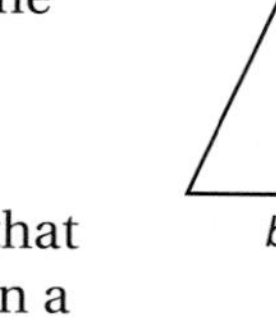

**67. Write About It** Many everyday processes must be done in a certain order to be completed successfully. Describe a process that requires several steps, and tell why the steps must be followed in a certain order.

Rev. 8.N.1.1

**68.** Cara's family rented a car for their 3-day vacation to the Grand Canyon. They paid \$29.00 per day and \$0.12 for each mile driven. Which expression represents Cara's family's cost to rent the car for 3 days and drive 318 miles?

Ⓐ $29 + 0.12(318)$

Ⓑ $29 + 3 + 0.12 + 318$

Ⓒ $29(3) + 0.12(318)$

Ⓓ $3[9 + 0.12(318)]$

**69.** The perimeter of the Norman window shown is approximated by the expression $2(3 + 8) + 3.14(3)$. Which is the closest approximation of the perimeter of the window?

Ⓕ 23.4 ft

Ⓖ 28.4 ft

Ⓗ 31.4 ft

Ⓙ 51.4 ft

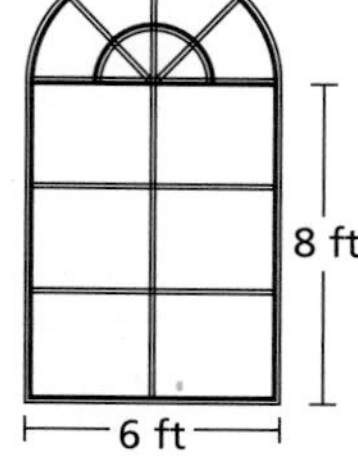


**70. Gridded Response** Evaluate $\sqrt{\frac{54 - (-2)(5)}{20 - 4^2}}$.

## CHALLENGE AND EXTEND

**Simplify each expression.**

**71.** $\frac{3 + 9 \cdot 2}{2 - 3^2}$

**72.** $\left[(-6 \cdot 4) \div -6 \cdot 4\right]^2$

**73.** $\sqrt{\frac{8 + 10^2}{13 + (-10)}}$

**74.** Use the numbers 2, 4, 5, and 8 to write an expression that has a value of 5. You may use any operations, and you must use each of the numbers at least once.

**75.** Use the numbers 2, 5, 6, and 9 to write an expression that has a value of 1. You may use any operations, and you must use each of the numbers at least once.

**76.** If the value of $(\otimes + 5)^2$ is 81, what is the value of $(\otimes + 5)^2 + 1$?

**77.** If the value of $(\otimes + 1)^2 - 3$ is 22, what is the value of $(\otimes + 1)^2 - 5$?

## SPIRAL REVIEW

**Identify each angle as acute, right, obtuse, or straight.** *(Previous course)*

**78.** 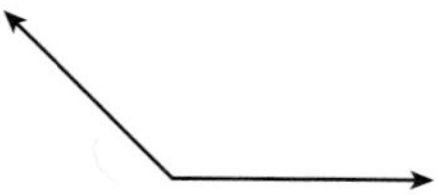

**79.** 

**80.** 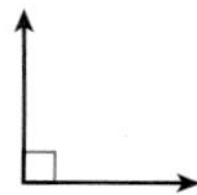

**Add or subtract.** *(Lesson 1-2)*

**81.** $51 - (-49)$

**82.** $-5 + \left(-1\frac{1}{3}\right)$

**83.** $-3 + (-8)$

**84.** 2.9

**Find each square root.** *(Lesson 1-5)*

**85.** $\sqrt{64}$

**86.** $\sqrt{324}$

**87.** $\sqrt{\frac{36}{49}}$

**88.** $-$

# 1-7 Simplifying Expressions

**MA.A.1** Use appropriate properties and strategies to combine ... algebraic expressions. *Also* **MA.A.1.2**

***Objectives***
Use the Commutative, Associative, and Distributive Properties to simplify expressions.

Combine like terms.

***Vocabulary***
term
like terms
coefficient

**Who uses this?**
Triathletes can use the Commutative, Associative, and Distributive Properties to calculate overall times mentally.

A triathlon is an endurance race that includes swimming, biking, and running. The winner is determined by adding the times for each of the three events.

The Commutative and Associative Properties of Addition and Multiplication allow you to rearrange an expression to simplify it.

**Properties of Addition and Multiplication**

| WORDS | NUMBERS | | ALGEBRA | |
|---|---|---|---|---|
| **Commutative Property**<br>You can add numbers in any order and multiply numbers in any order. | $2 + 7 = 7 + 2$<br>$3 \cdot 9 = 9 \cdot 3$ | | $a + b = b + a$<br>$ab = ba$ | |
| **Associative Property**<br>When you are only adding or multiplying, you can group any of the numbers together. | $6 + 8 + 2$<br>$= (6 + 8) + 2$<br>$= 6 + (8 + 2)$ | $7 \cdot 4 \cdot 5$<br>$= (7 \cdot 4) \cdot 5$<br>$= 7 \cdot (4 \cdot 5)$ | $a + b + c$<br>$= (a + b) + c$<br>$= a + (b + c)$ | $abc$<br>$= (ab)c$<br>$= a(bc)$ |

**EXAMPLE 1** **Using the Commutative and Associative Properties**

**Simplify each expression.**

**A** $4 \cdot 9 \cdot 25$

$9 \cdot 4 \cdot 25$ — *Use the Commutative Property.*

$9 \cdot (4 \cdot 25)$ — *Use the Associative Property to make groups of compatible numbers.*

$9 \cdot 100$

$900$

**B** $25 + 48 + 75$

$25 + 75 + 48$ — *Use the Commutative Property.*

$(25 + 75) + 48$ — *Use the Associative Property to make groups of compatible numbers.*

$100 + 48$

$148$

**Helpful Hint**
Compatible numbers help you do math mentally. Try to make multiples of 5 or 10. They are simpler to use when multiplying.

**Simplify each expression.**

**1a.** $15\frac{1}{3} + 4 + 1\frac{2}{3}$ **1b.** $410 + 58 + 90 + 2$ **1c.** $\frac{1}{2} \cdot 7 \cdot 8$

## Student to Student

### Commutative and Associative Properties

**Lorna Anderson**
Pearson High School

*I used to get the Commutative and Associative Properties mixed up.*

*To remember the Commutative Property, I think of people commuting back and forth from work. When people commute, they move. I can move the numbers around without changing the value of the expression.*

*For the Associative Property, I think of associating with my friends. They're the group I hang out with. In math, it's about how numbers are grouped.*

The Distributive Property is used with addition to simplify expressions.

### Distributive Property

| WORDS | NUMBERS | ALGEBRA |
|---|---|---|
| You can multiply a number by a sum or multiply by each number in the sum and then add. The result is the same. | $3(4 + 8) = 3(4) + 3(8)$ | $a(b + c) = ab + ac$ |

The Distributive Property also works with subtraction because subtraction is the same as adding the opposite.

### EXAMPLE 2 Using the Distributive Property with Mental Math

**Write each product using the Distributive Property. Then simplify.**

**A** $15(103)$

| | |
|---|---|
| $15(100 + 3)$ | *Rewrite 103 as 100 + 3.* |
| $15(100) + 15(3)$ | *Use the Distributive Property.* |
| $1500 + 45$ | *Multiply.* |
| $1545$ | *Add.* |

**B** $6(19)$

| | |
|---|---|
| $6[20 + (-1)]$ | *Rewrite 19 as 20 + (–1).* |
| $6(20) + 6(-1)$ | *Use the Distributive Property.* |
| $120 + (-6)$ | *Multiply.* |
| $114$ | *Add.* |

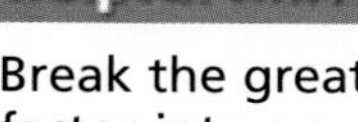

**Helpful Hint**

Break the greater factor into a sum that contains a multiple of 10.

**Write each product using the Distributive Property. Then simplify.**

**2a.** $9(52)$ **2b.** $12(98)$ **2c.** $7(34)$

The **terms** of an expression are the parts to be added or subtracted. **Like terms** are terms that contain the same variables raised to the same powers. Constants are also like terms.

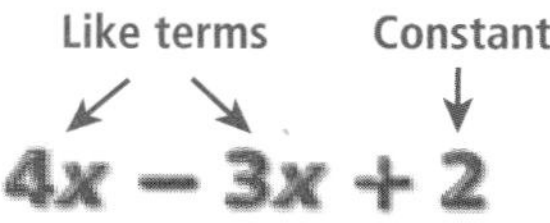

A **coefficient** is a number multiplied by a variable. Like terms can have different coefficients. A variable written without a coefficient has a coefficient of 1.

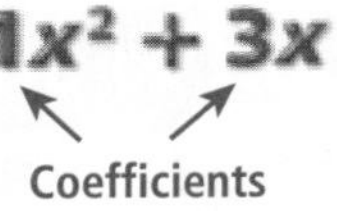


Using the Distributive Property can help you combine like terms. You can factor out the common factor to simplify the expression.

$$7x^2 - 4x^2 = (7 - 4)x^2$$ *Factor out $x^2$ from both terms.*

$$= (3)x^2$$ *Perform operations in parentheses.*

$$= 3x^2$$

Notice that you can combine like terms by adding or subtracting the coefficients and keeping the variables and exponents the same.

## EXAMPLE 3 Combining Like Terms

**Simplify each expression by combining like terms.**

**A** $12x + 30x$

$12x + 30x$ *12x and 30x are like terms.*

$42x$ *Add the coefficients.*

> **Caution!**
> Add or subtract only the coefficients.
> $6.8y^2 - y^2 \neq 6.8$

**B** $6.8y^2 - y^2$

$6.8y^2 - y^2$ *A variable without a coefficient has a coefficient of 1.*

$6.8y^2 - 1y^2$ *$6.8y^2$ and $1y^2$ are like terms.*

$5.8y^2$ *Subtract the coefficients.*

**C** $4n + 11n^2$

$4n + 11n^2$ *4n and $11n^2$ are not like terms.*

$4n + 11n^2$ *Do not combine the terms.*

**CHECK IT OUT!** **Simplify each expression by combining like terms.**

**3a.** $16p + 84p$ **3b.** $-20t - 8.5t$ **3c.** $3m^2 + m^3$

## EXAMPLE 4 Simplifying Algebraic Expressions

**Simplify $2(x + 6) + 3x$. Justify each step with an operation or property.**

| | Procedure | Justification |
|---|---|---|
| 1. | $2(x + 6) + 3x$ | |
| 2. | $2(x) + 2(6) + 3x$ | Distributive Property |
| 3. | $2x + 12 + 3x$ | Multiply. |
| 4. | $2x + 3x + 12$ | Commutative Property |
| 5. | $(2x + 3x) + 12$ | Associative Property |
| 6. | $5x + 12$ | Combine like terms. |

**CHECK IT OUT!** **Simplify each expression. Justify each step with an operation or property.**

**4a.** $6(x - 4) + 9$ **4b.** $-12x - 5x + 3a + x$

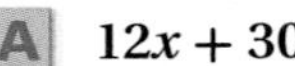

## THINK AND DISCUSS

1. Tell which property is described by this sentence: When adding three numbers, you can add the first number to the sum of the second and third numbers, or you can add the third number to the sum of the first and second numbers.

2. **GET ORGANIZED** Copy and complete the graphic organizer below. In each box, give an example to illustrate the given property.

| Associative | Commutative | Distributive |
|---|---|---|
| | | |

# 1-7 Exercises

MA.A.1, MA.A.1.2

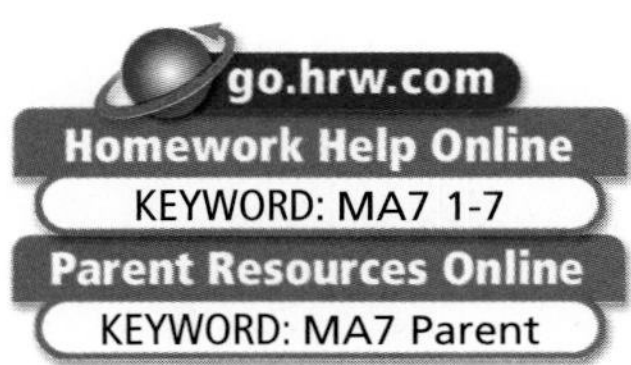


## GUIDED PRACTICE

1. **Vocabulary** The ____?____ Property states the following: $(a + b) + c = a + (b + c)$. (*Associative*, *Commutative*, or *Distributive*)

SEE EXAMPLE 1 p. 46

**Simplify each expression.**

2. $-12 + 67 + 12 + 23$
3. $16 + 2\frac{1}{2} + 4 + 1\frac{1}{2}$
4. $27 + 98 + 73$
5. $\frac{1}{3} \cdot 8 \cdot 21$
6. $2 \cdot 38 \cdot 50$
7. $50 \cdot 118 \cdot 20$

SEE EXAMPLE 2 p. 47

**Write each product using the Distributive Property. Then simplify.**

8. $14(1002)$
9. $16(19)$
10. $9(38)$
11. $8(57)$
12. $12(112)$
13. $7(109)$

SEE EXAMPLE 3 p. 48

**Simplify each expression by combining like terms.**

14. $6x + 10x$
15. $35x - 15x$
16. $-3a + 9a$
17. $-8r - r$
18. $17x^2 + x$
19. $3.2x + 4.7x$

SEE EXAMPLE 4 p. 48

**Simplify each expression. Justify each step with an operation or property.**

20. $5(x + 3) - 7x$
21. $9(a - 3) - 4$
22. $5x^2 - 2(x - 3x^2)$
23. $6x - x - 3x^2 + 2x$
24. $12x + 8x + t - 7x$
25. $4a - 2(a - 1)$

## PRACTICE AND PROBLEM SOLVING

**Simplify each expression.**

26. $53 + 28 + 17 + 12$
27. $5 \cdot 14 \cdot 20$
28. $6 \cdot 3 \cdot 5$
29. $4.5 + 7.1 + 8.5 + 3.9$

**Write each product using the Distributive Property. Then simplify.**

30. $9(62)$
31. $8(29)$
32. $11(25)$
33. $6(53)$

| Independent Practice | |
|---|---|
| For Exercises | See Example |
| 26–29 | 1 |
| 30–33 | 2 |
| 34–37 | 3 |
| 38–43 | 4 |

**Extra Practice**
Skills Practice p. S5
Application Practice p. S28

**Simplify each expression by combining like terms.**

**34.** $3x + 9x$ **35.** $14x^2 - 5x^2$ **36.** $-7x + 8x$ **37.** $3x^2 - 4$

**Simplify each expression. Justify each step with an operation or property.**

**38.** $4(y + 6) + 9$ **39.** $-7(x + 2) + 4x$ **40.** $3x + 2 - 2x - 1$

**41.** $5x - 3x + 3x^2 + 9x$ **42.** $8x + 2x - 3y - 9x$ **43.** $7y - 3 + 6y - 7$

**44. Estimation** Tavon bought a binder, 3 spiral notebooks, and a pen. The binder cost \$4.89, the notebooks cost \$1.99 each, and the pen cost \$2.11. About how much did Tavon spend on school supplies?

**45. Sports** In a triathlon, athletes race in swimming, biking, and running events. The athlete with the shortest total time to complete the events is the winner.

**Times from Triathlon**

| Athlete | Swim (min:s) | Bike (min:s) | Run (min:s) |
|---|---|---|---|
| Amy | 18:51 | 45:17 | 34:13 |
| Julie | 17:13 | 40:27 | 23:32 |
| Mardi | 19:09 | 38:58 | 25:32 |
| Sabine | 13:09 | 31:37 | 19:01 |

**a.** Find the total time for each athlete. (*Hint:* 1 minute = 60 seconds)

**b.** Use the total times for the athletes to determine the order in which they finished the triathlon.

**Name the property that is illustrated in each equation.**

**46.** $5 + x = x + 5$ **47.** $x - 2 = -2 + x$ **48.** $2 + (3 + y) = (2 + 3) + y$

**49.** $3(2r - 7) = 3(2r) - 3(7)$ **50.** $(2 + g) + 3 = 2 + (g + 3)$ **51.** $45x - 35 = 5(9x) - 5(7)$

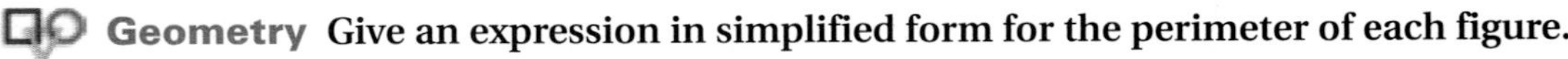

**Geometry** **Give an expression in simplified form for the perimeter of each figure.**

**52.** Rectangle with sides $2w$ and $w$

**53.** Triangle with sides $4p$, $8 - p$, and $3p + 1$

**54.** Parallelogram with sides $2s + 3$ and $2s + 3$

**55. Critical Thinking** Evaluate $a - (b - c)$ and $(a - b) - c$ for $a = 10$, $b = 7$, and $c = 3$. Based on your answers, explain whether there is an Associative Property of Subtraction.

**56. Write About It** Describe a real-world situation that can be represented by the Distributive Property. Translate your situation into an algebraic expression. Define each variable you use.

**57.** This problem will prepare you for the Multi-Step Test Prep on page 60.

**a.** The diagram shows a pattern of shapes that can be folded to make a cylinder. How is the length $\ell$ of the rectangle related to the circumference of (distance around) each circle?

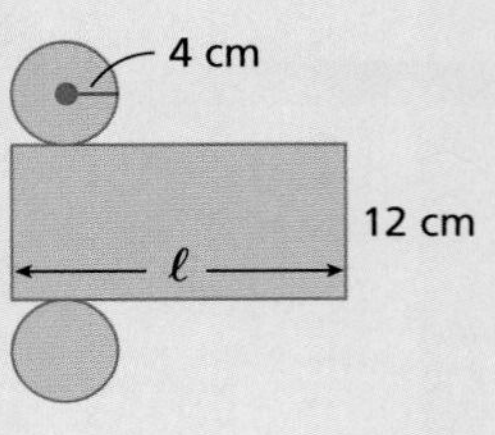


**b.** An expression for the circumference of each circle is $2\pi r$. Write an expression for the area of the rectangle.

**c.** Use these expressions to write an expression for the total area of the figures. Leave the symbol $\pi$ in your expression.

TEST PREP

MA.A.1, MA.A.1.2

**58.** Ariel has 19 more CDs than her sister Tiffany has. Victor has 3 times as many CDs as Ariel has. Which expression can be used to show how many CDs the three have in total?

(A) $19 + 3x$ (B) $51 + 3x$ (C) $76 + 3x$ (D) $76 + 5x$

**59.** Which expression can be used to represent the perimeter of the rectangle?

(F) $16k$ (H) $3k + 13$

(G) $32k$ (J) $6k + 26$

$3 + k$

$2(k + 5)$

**60.** Which equation is an example of the Distributive Property?

(A) $(25 + 18) + 33 = 25 + (18 + 33)$

(B) $33 + (25 \cdot 18) = (25 \cdot 18) + 33$

(C) $33 \cdot 25 + 33 \cdot 18 = 33 \cdot (25 + 18)$

(D) $3 + 25 \cdot 33 + 18 = 18 + 33 \cdot 25 + 33$

## CHALLENGE AND EXTEND

**Simplify.**

**61.** $4[3(x + 9) + 2]$

**62.** $-3[(x - 2) + 5(x - 2)]$

**63.** $(2b + 5) - (8b + 6) + 3(b - 2)$

**64.** $\frac{1}{2}[(10 - g) + (-6 + 3g)]$

**65.** Fill in the missing justifications.

| Procedure | Justification |
|---|---|
| $11e - 7 - 3e = 11e + (-7) + (-3)e$ | Definition of subtraction |
| $= 11e + (-3)e + (-7)$ | a. ? |
| $= [11e + (-3)e] + (-7)$ | b. ? |
| $= [11 + (-3)]e + (-7)$ | c. ? |
| $= 8e + (-7)$ | d. ? |
| $= 8e - 7$ | Definition of subtraction |

**66.** Fill in the missing justifications.

| Procedure | Justification |
|---|---|
| $\frac{a + b}{c} = \frac{1}{c}(a + b)$ | Definition of division |
| $= \frac{1}{c}(a) + \frac{1}{c}(b)$ | a. ? |
| $= \frac{a}{c} + \frac{b}{c}$ | b. ? |

## SPIRAL REVIEW

**Give the area of the figure described.** *(Previous course)*

**67.** square; $s = 6$ ft

**68.** parallelogram; $b = 7$ mm, $h = 13$ mm

**Evaluate each expression.** *(Lesson 1-4)*

**69.** $2^6$

**70.** $18^2$

**71.** $-\left(\frac{1}{2}\right)^3$

**72.** $\left(-\frac{1}{2}\right)^2$

**Simplify each expression.** *(Lesson 1-6)*

**73.** $3 + 4 - 10 \div 2 + 1$

**74.** $\frac{8^2 - 6^2}{8^2 + 6^2}$

**75.** $2 - [6 - 8 \div (3 + 1)]$

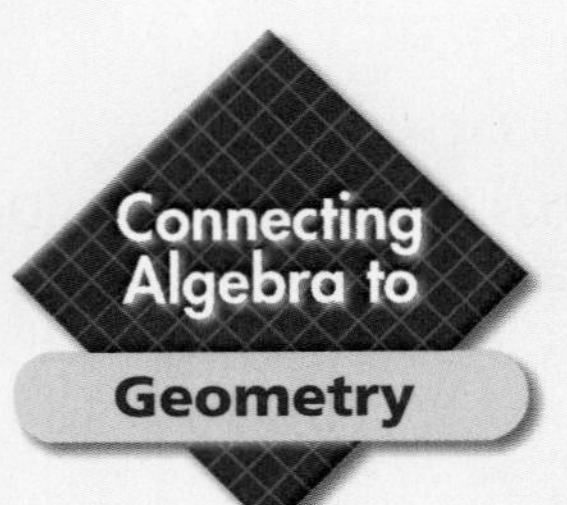


**See Skills Bank page S60**

# Perimeter

The distance around a geometric figure is called the *perimeter*. You can use what you have learned about combining like terms to simplify expressions for perimeter.

**MA.A.1** Use appropriate properties and strategies to combine … algebraic expressions. *Also* **MA.A.1.2**

A closed figure with straight sides is called a *polygon*. To find the perimeter of a polygon, add the lengths of the sides.

## Example 1

**A Write an expression for the perimeter of the quadrilateral.**

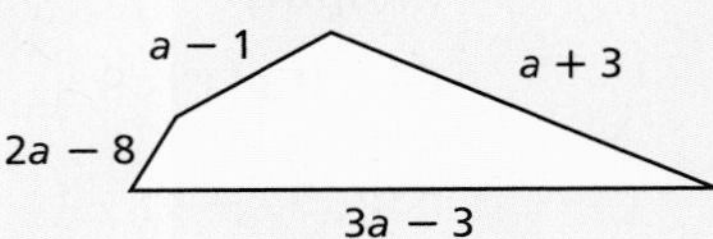


Add the lengths of the four sides.

$P = (a + 3) + (2a - 8) + (3a - 3) + (a - 1)$

Combine like terms to simplify.

$P = (a + 2a + 3a + a) + (3 - 8 - 3 - 1)$

$= 7a - 9$ *This is a general expression for the perimeter.*

**B Find the perimeter of this quadrilateral for $a = 5$.**

Substitute 5 for $a$.

$P = 7(5) - 9$ *Multiply; then subtract.*

$= 35 - 9$

$= 26$ *This is the perimeter when $a = 5$.*

## Try This

**Write and simplify an expression for the perimeter of each figure.**

1\.

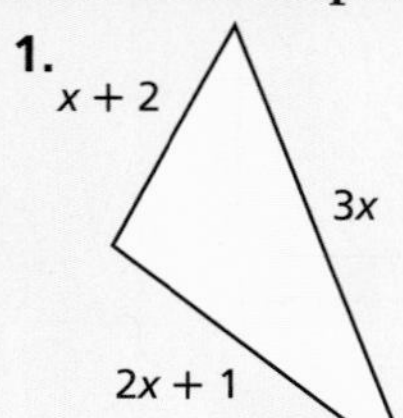


2\.

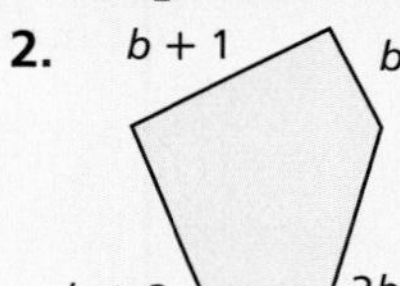
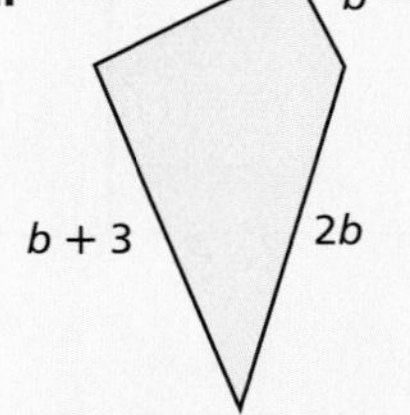


3\.

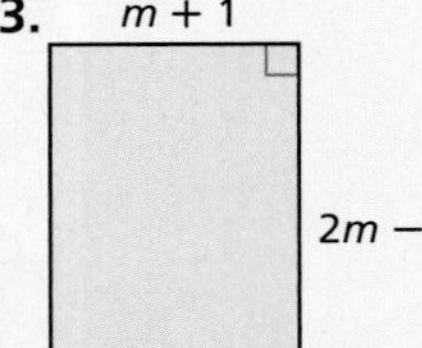


**Find the perimeter of each figure for the given value of the variable.**

4\. $k = 3$

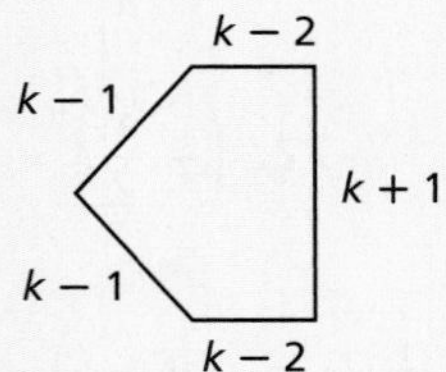


5\. $n = 10$

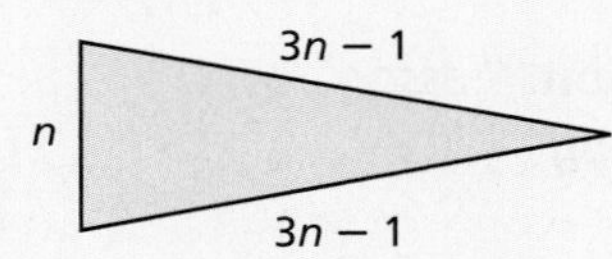


6\. $y = 4$

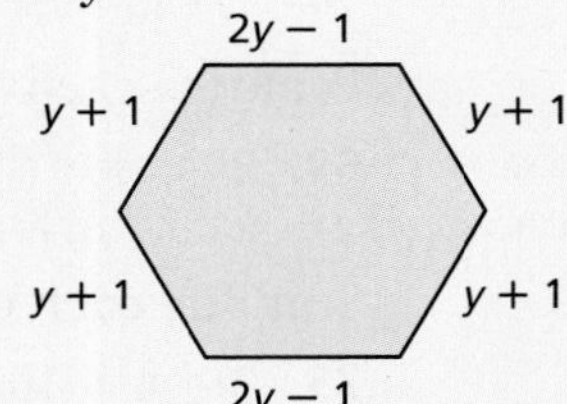

Combining like terms is one way to explore what happens to the perimeter when you double the sides of a triangle or other polygon.

## Example 2

**What happens to the perimeter of this triangle when you double the length of each side?**

Write an expression for the perimeter of the smaller triangle. Combine like terms to simplify the expression.

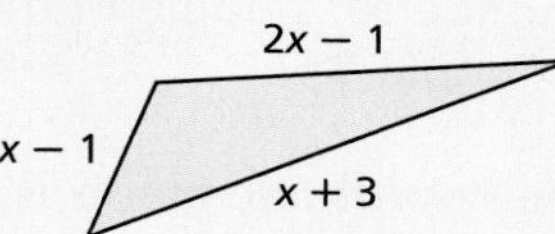


$(x - 1) + (2x - 1) + (x + 3)$

$(x + 2x + x) + (-1 - 1 + 3)$

$4x + 1$ *Perimeter of small triangle*

Double the length of each side of the triangle.

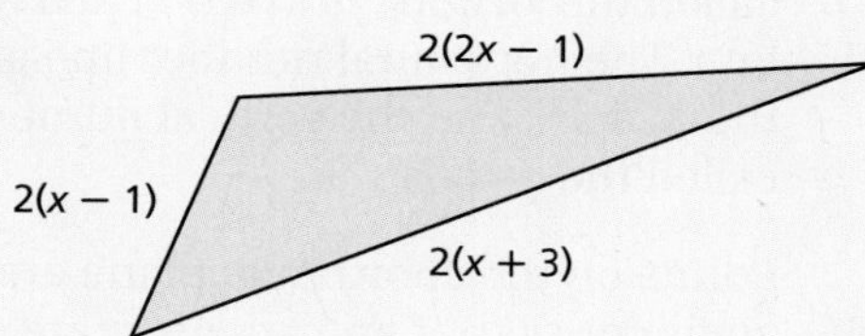


$2(x - 1) = 2x - 2$

$2(2x - 1) = 4x - 2$

$2(x + 3) = 2x + 6$

Find the perimeter of the larger triangle. Combine like terms to simplify.

$(2x - 2) + (4x - 2) + (2x + 6)$ *Add the lengths of the sides.*

$(2x + 4x + 2x) + (-2 - 2 + 6)$ *Use the Associative Property and combine like terms.*

$8x + 2$ *Perimeter of large triangle*

Use the Distributive Property to show that the new perimeter is twice the original perimeter.

$8x + 2 = 2(4x + 1)$

## Try This

**Each set of expressions represents the side lengths of a triangle. Use the Distributive Property to show that doubling the side lengths doubles the perimeter.**

**7.** $2p + 1$, $3p + 2$, $5p$

**8.** $c - 1$, $2c + 1$, $3c - 1$

**9.** $w + 5$, $w + 5$, $3w - 1$

**10.** $h - 2$, $3h$, $2h + 3$

**Solve each problem.**

**11.** Use the triangles in Example 2. Find the side lengths and perimeters for $x = 5$.

**12.** The sides of a quadrilateral are $2x - 1$, $x + 3$, $3x + 1$, and $x - 1$. Double the length of each side. Then find an expression for the perimeter of the new figure.

**13.** What happens to the perimeter of this trapezoid when you triple the length of each side? Use the variables *a*, *b*, *b*, and *c* for the lengths of the sides. Explain your answer using the Distributive Property.

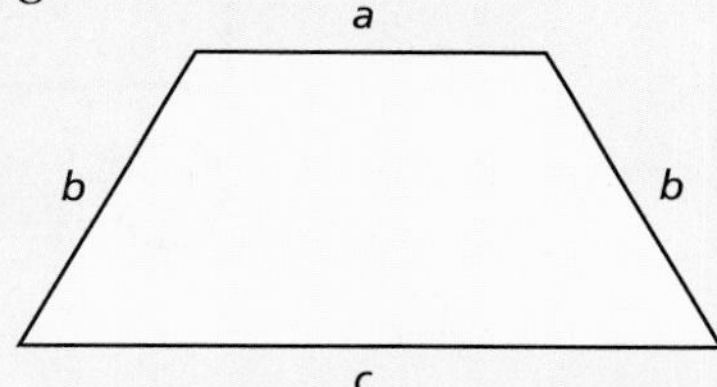

# 1-8 Introduction to Functions

**Prep MA.G.1.1** Use strategies to calculate the slope, distance between points, coordinates of the midpoints and the distance from a point to a line.

***Objectives***

Graph ordered pairs in the coordinate plane.

Graph functions from ordered pairs.

***Vocabulary***

coordinate plane
axes
origin
*x*-axis
*y*-axis
ordered pair
*x*-coordinate
*y*-coordinate
quadrant
input
output

**Why learn this?**

You can use functions to determine how the cost of a caricature is affected by the number of people in the picture. (See Example 3.)

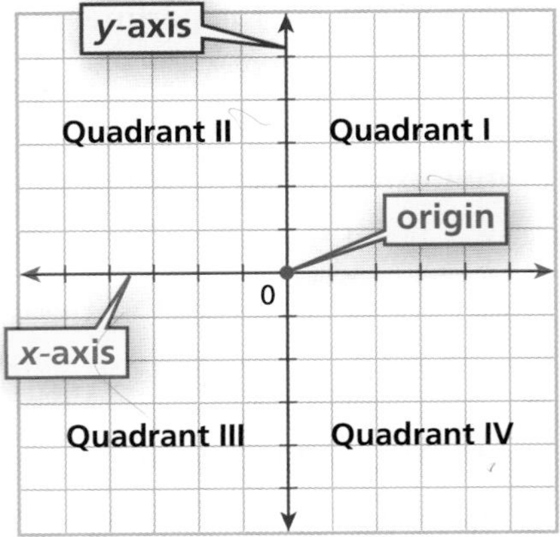


The **coordinate plane** is formed by the intersection of two perpendicular number lines called **axes**. The point of intersection, called the **origin**, is at 0 on each number line. The horizontal number line is called the ***x*-axis**, and the vertical number line is called the ***y*-axis**.

Points on the coordinate plane are described using ordered pairs. An **ordered pair** consists of an ***x*-coordinate** and a ***y*-coordinate** and is written $(x, y)$. Points are often named by a capital letter.

## EXAMPLE 1 Graphing Points in the Coordinate Plane

**Graph each point.**

**A** $M(3, 4)$

Start at the origin.

Move 3 units right and 4 units up.

**B** $N(-2, 0)$

Start at the origin. Move 2 units left.

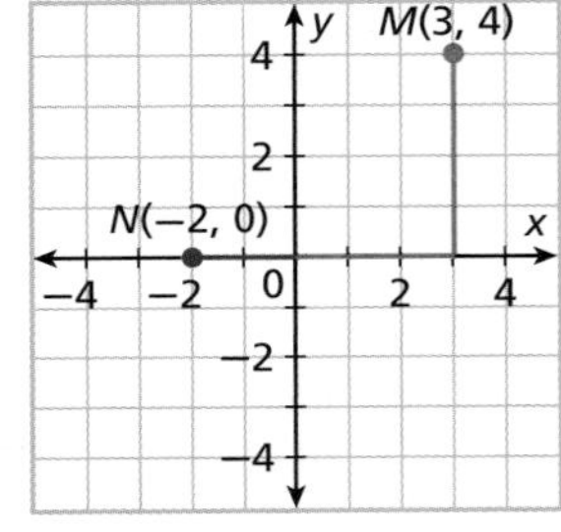


**Reading Math**

The *x*-coordinate tells how many units to move left or right from the origin. The *y*-coordinate tells how many units to move up or down.

**Graph each point.**

**1a.** $R(2, -3)$ **1b.** $S(0, 2)$ **1c.** $T(-2, 6)$

Look at the graph at the top of this lesson. The axes divide the coordinate plane into four **quadrants**. Points that lie on an axis are not in any quadrant.

## EXAMPLE 2 Locating Points in the Coordinate Plane

**Name the quadrant in which each point lies.**

**A** $P$

Quadrant III

**B** $Q$

Quadrant II

**C** $R$

no quadrant ($x$-axis)

**D** $S$

Quadrant IV

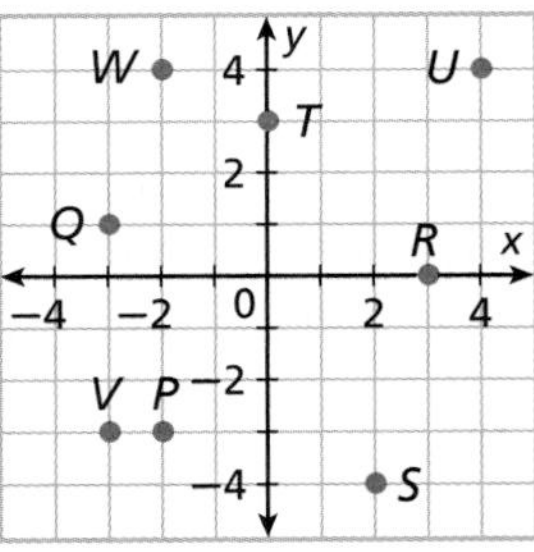

**Name the quadrant in which each point lies.**

**2a.** $T$ **2b.** $U$ **2c.** $V$ **2d.** $W$

An equation that contains two variables can be used as a rule to generate ordered pairs. When you substitute a value for $x$, you generate a value for $y$. The value substituted for $x$ is called the **input**, and the value generated for $y$ is called the **output**.

Output ↓ Input ↓

$$y = 10x + 5$$

In a *function*, the value of $y$ (the output) is determined by the value of $x$ (the input). All of the equations in this lesson represent functions.

## EXAMPLE 3 Art Application

**A caricature artist charges his clients a $5 setup fee plus $10 for every person in a picture. Write a rule for the artist's fee. Write ordered pairs for the artist's fee when there are 1, 2, 3, and 4 people in the picture.**

Let $y$ represent the artist's fee and $x$ represent the number of people in a picture.

> **Writing Math**
>
> The artist's fee is determined by the number of people in the picture, so the number of people is the input and the artist's fee is the output.

| Artist's fee | is | $5 | plus | $10 | for each | person. |
|---|---|---|---|---|---|---|
| $y$ | $=$ | 5 | $+$ | 10 | $\cdot$ | $x$ |

$y = 5 + 10x$

| Number of People in Picture | Rule | Charges | Ordered Pair |
|---|---|---|---|
| $x$ (input) | $y = 5 + 10x$ | $y$ (output) | $(x, y)$ |
| 1 | $y = 5 + 10(1)$ | 15 | (1, 15) |
| 2 | $y = 5 + 10(2)$ | 25 | (2, 25) |
| 3 | $y = 5 + 10(3)$ | 35 | (3, 35) |
| 4 | $y = 5 + 10(4)$ | 45 | (4, 45) |

3. **What if...?** The artist increased his fees to a $10 setup fee plus $20 for every person. Write a rule for the new fee. Find the fee when there are 1, 2, 3, and 4 people.

When you graph ordered pairs generated by a function, they may create a pattern.

## EXAMPLE 4 Generating and Graphing Ordered Pairs

**Generate ordered pairs for each function using the given values for $x$. Graph the ordered pairs and describe the pattern.**

**A** $y = 4x - 3; x = -1, 0, 1, 2$

| Input | Output | Ordered Pair |
|---|---|---|
| $x$ | $y$ | $(x, y)$ |
| −1 | $4(-1) - 3 = -7$ | (−1, −7) |
| 0 | $4(0) - 3 = -3$ | (0, −3) |
| 1 | $4(1) - 3 = 1$ | (1, 1) |
| 2 | $4(2) - 3 = 5$ | (2, 5) |

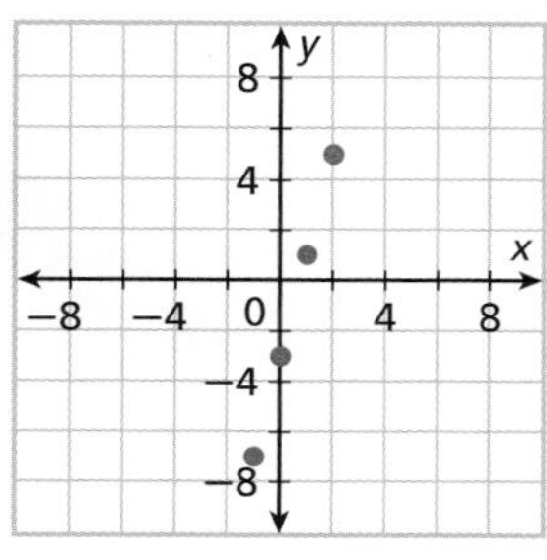


The points form a straight line.

**Generate ordered pairs for each function using the given values for $x$. Graph the ordered pairs and describe the pattern.**

**B** $y = 2x^2 + 1; x = -2, -1, 0, 1, 2$

| Input | Output | Ordered Pair |
|---|---|---|
| $x$ | $y$ | $(x, y)$ |
| $-2$ | $2(-2)^2 + 1 = 9$ | $(-2, 9)$ |
| $-1$ | $2(-1)^2 + 1 = 3$ | $(-1, 3)$ |
| $0$ | $2(0)^2 + 1 = 1$ | $(0, 1)$ |
| $1$ | $2(1)^2 + 1 = 3$ | $(1, 3)$ |
| $2$ | $2(2)^2 + 1 = 9$ | $(2, 9)$ |

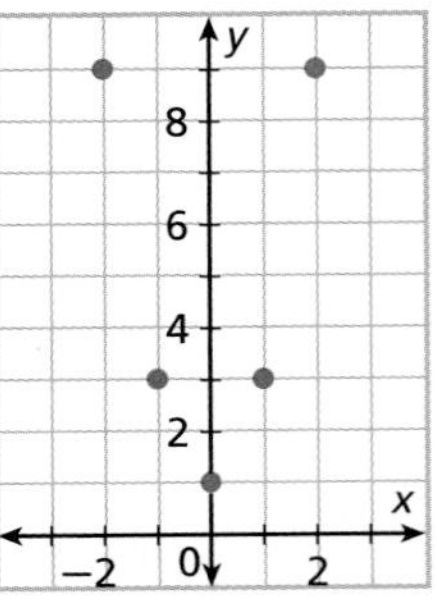

The points form a U shape.

**C** $y = |x + 3|; x = -5, -4, -3, -2, -1$

| Input | Output | Ordered Pair |
|---|---|---|
| $x$ | $y$ | $(x, y)$ |
| $-5$ | $\lvert -5 + 3 \rvert = \lvert -2 \rvert = 2$ | $(-5, 2)$ |
| $-4$ | $\lvert -4 + 3 \rvert = \lvert -1 \rvert = 1$ | $(-4, 1)$ |
| $-3$ | $\lvert -3 + 3 \rvert = \lvert 0 \rvert = 0$ | $(-3, 0)$ |
| $-2$ | $\lvert -2 + 3 \rvert = \lvert 1 \rvert = 1$ | $(-2, 1)$ |
| $-1$ | $\lvert -1 + 3 \rvert = \lvert 2 \rvert = 2$ | $(-1, 2)$ |

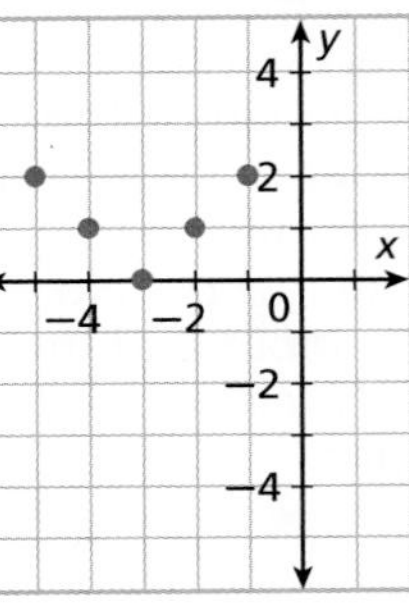

The points form a V shape.

**Generate ordered pairs for each function using the given values for $x$. Graph the ordered pairs and describe the pattern.**

**4a.** $y = \frac{1}{2}x - 4; x = -4, -2, 0, 2, 4$

**4b.** $y = 3x^2 + 3; x = -3, -1, 0, 1, 3$

**4c.** $y = |x - 2|; x = 0, 1, 2, 3, 4$

In Chapter 4, you will learn more about functions. You will study the relationship between the shape of a graph and the rule that generates the ordered pairs.

## THINK AND DISCUSS

1. Describe how to graph the ordered pair $(-3, 6)$.
2. Give an example of a point that lies on the $y$-axis.
3. **GET ORGANIZED** Copy and complete the graphic organizer. In each blank, write "positive" or "negative."

| Quadrant II<br>$x$ is ?.<br>$y$ is ?. | Quadrant I<br>$x$ is ?.<br>$y$ is ?. |
|---|---|
| $x$ is ?.<br>$y$ is ?.<br>Quadrant III | $x$ is ?.<br>$y$ is ?.<br>Quadrant IV |

The Coordinate Plane

# 1-8 Exercises

Prep MA.G.1.1

go.hrw.com
Homework Help Online
KEYWORD: MA7 1-8
Parent Resources Online
KEYWORD: MA7 Parent

## GUIDED PRACTICE

1. **Vocabulary** Explain why the order in an *ordered pair* is important.

SEE EXAMPLE 1 p. 54

**Graph each point.**

2. $J(4, 5)$ 3. $K(-3, 2)$ 4. $L(6, 0)$ 5. $M(1, -7)$

SEE EXAMPLE 2 p. 54

**Name the quadrant in which each point lies.**

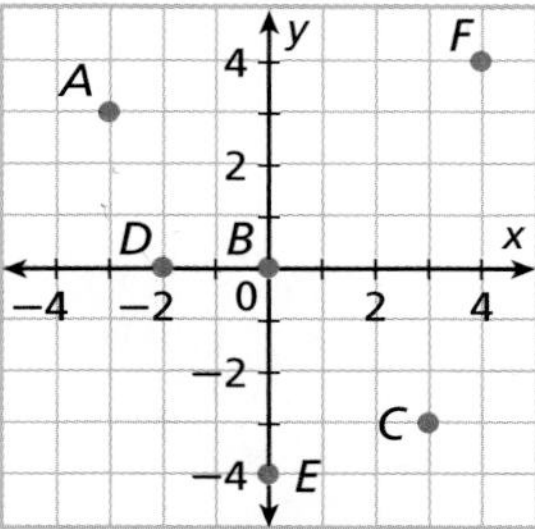


6. $A$ 7. $B$ 8. $C$
9. $D$ 10. $E$ 11. $F$

SEE EXAMPLE 3 p. 55

12. **Multi-Step** The number of counselors at a summer camp must be equal to $\frac{1}{4}$ the number of campers. Write a rule for the number of counselors that must be at the camp. Write ordered pairs for the number of counselors when there are 76, 100, 120, and 168 campers.

SEE EXAMPLE 4 p. 55

**Generate ordered pairs for each function for $x = -2, -1, 0, 1$, and 2. Graph the ordered pairs and describe the pattern.**

13. $y = x + 2$ 14. $y = -x$ 15. $y = -2|x|$ 16. $y = \frac{1}{2}x^2$

## PRACTICE AND PROBLEM SOLVING

**Independent Practice**

| For Exercises | See Example |
|---|---|
| 17–20 | 1 |
| 21–26 | 2 |
| 27 | 3 |
| 28–31 | 4 |

**Extra Practice**

Skills Practice p. S5
Application Practice p. S28

**Graph each point.**

17. $D(2, 8)$ 18. $E(-2, -7)$ 19. $F(0, -5)$ 20. $G(4, -4)$

**Name the quadrant in which each point lies.**

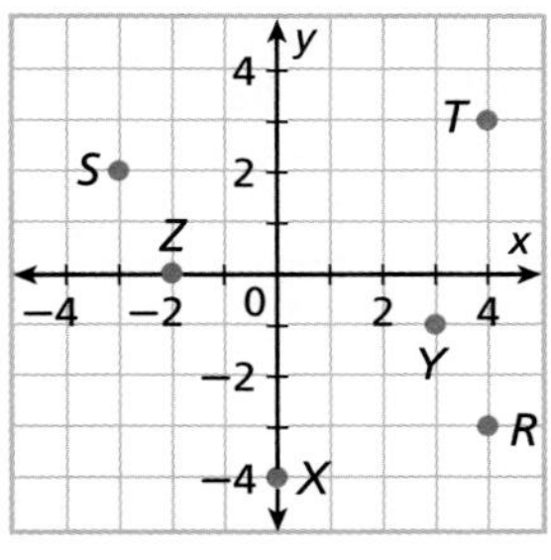


21. $X$ 22. $Y$ 23. $Z$
24. $R$ 25. $S$ 26. $T$

27. **Multi-Step** Jeremy's wages include a \$500 base salary plus $\frac{1}{10}$ of his sales. Write a rule for the total amount of Jeremy's paycheck. Write ordered pairs for the amount of Jeremy's paycheck when his sales are \$500, \$3000, \$5000, and \$7500.

**Generate ordered pairs for each function for $x = -2, -1, 0, 1$, and 2. Graph the ordered pairs and describe the pattern.**

28. $y = 6 - 2x$ 29. $y = -(x^2)$ 30. $y = 3|x|$ 31. $y = x^2 + 3$

**Geometry** **Graph each point and connect them in the order they are listed. Connect the last point to the first. Describe the figure drawn.**

32. $(-1, 1), (4, 1), (4, -4), (-1, -4)$
33. $(-6, 3), (2, -2), (-7, -3)$
34. $(4, 4), (6, 2), (5, -1), (3, -1), (2, 2)$
35. $(-6, 5), (4, 5), (4, 7), (-6, 7)$

36. **Multi-Step** The salary at Beth's company is \$32,000 for someone with no experience and increases by \$2700 per year of experience. Write a rule for the salary at Beth's company. Write ordered pairs for the salaries for employees with 0, 2, 5, and 7 years of experience.

**37.** This problem will prepare you for the Multi-Step Test Prep on page 60.

**a.** A room decorator wants to purchase fabric. Each yard of fabric costs \$2.90. Write a rule for the cost of the fabric. Let $c$ equal the total cost and $f$ equal the number of yards of fabric.

**b.** Which variable is the input and which variable is the output?

**c.** Make a table showing the cost of 1, 2, 3, 4, and 5 yards of fabric.

**d.** How many whole yards can the decorator purchase if she has \$21.00?

**Write an equation for each rule. Use the given values for $x$ to generate ordered pairs. Graph the ordered pairs and describe the pattern.**

**38.** $y$ is equal to 3 more than the absolute value of $x$; $x = -2, -1, 0, 1$, and 2.

**39.** $y$ is equal to the sum of one half of $x$ and $-3$; $x = -4, -2, 0, 2$, and 4.

**40.** $y$ is equal to the sum of $x$ squared and 1; $x = -5, -3, -1, 1, 3$, and 5.

**41. Business** An events planner is preparing for a 5K race. She will buy enough water bottles for 50 volunteers, plus $1\frac{1}{2}$ times the number of runners who preregister for the race.

**a.** Write an equation for the number of water bottles the planner should buy.

**b.** Generate ordered pairs for the number of water bottles the event planner will buy for the following numbers of preregistered runners: 100, 150, 200, 250, and 300.

**Math History**

The coordinate plane is also called the Cartesian plane. This name comes from the mathematician Rene Descartes (1596–1650), who is credited with discovering the coordinate plane.

**Give the coordinates of three points that fit the given description. Graph the points and describe the pattern.**

**42.** The $x$-coordinate is 1 less than the $y$-coordinate.

**43.** The sum of the $x$-coordinate and $y$-coordinate is 5.

**44.** The $x$-coordinate is 2 times the $y$-coordinate.

**45.** The quotient of the $x$-coordinate and $y$-coordinate is 3.

**46. Critical Thinking** Lance wrote five ordered pairs for which the $y$-coordinate was the opposite of the $x$-coordinate. Then he graphed the ordered pairs. What pattern did the points make?

**47. Write About It** Graph the point $(4, 2)$.

**a.** How is graphing the point $(4, 2)$ different from graphing the point $(2, 4)$?

**b.** How is graphing the point $(4, 2)$ different from graphing the point $(-4, -2)$?

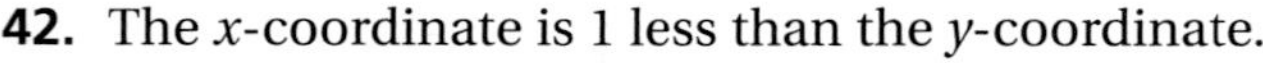

**48.** ///ERROR ANALYSIS/// Two students graphed the point $(4, 6)$. Which is incorrect? Explain the error.

A

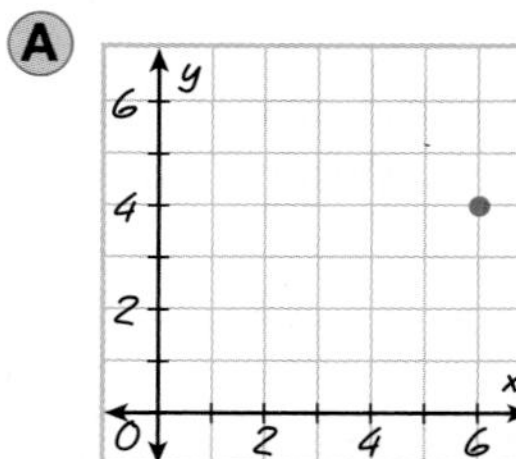


B

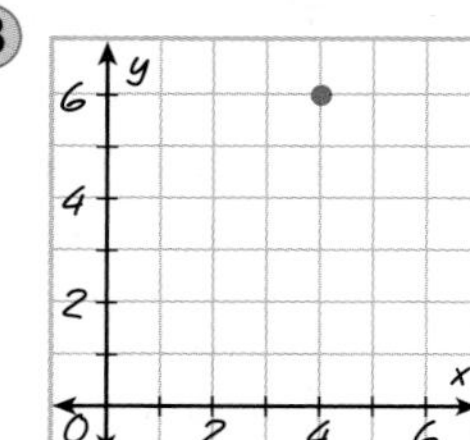


**49.** Generate ordered pairs for $y = x$, graph the points, and connect them to make a line. Do the same for $y = x + 2$ using the same values for $x$. How is the line for $y = x + 2$ different from the line for $y = x$?

50. Which equation could be used to generate the ordered pairs $(2, 7)$ and $(6, 9)$?

**Prep MA.G.1.1**

Ⓐ $y = 9 - x$ Ⓑ $y = \frac{3}{2}x^2 + 1$ Ⓒ $y = \frac{1}{2}x + 6$ Ⓓ $y = x + 5$

51. Which table of ordered pairs is generated when the values 1, 2, 3, and 4 are substituted for $x$ in the equation $y = 2x - 4$?

Ⓕ

| $x$ | $y$ |
|---|---|
| 1 | −3 |
| 2 | −2 |
| 3 | −1 |
| 4 | 0 |

Ⓖ

| $x$ | $y$ |
|---|---|
| 1 | −2 |
| 2 | 0 |
| 3 | 2 |
| 4 | 4 |

Ⓗ

| $x$ | $y$ |
|---|---|
| 1 | −2 |
| 2 | 0 |
| 3 | 1 |
| 4 | 2 |

Ⓙ

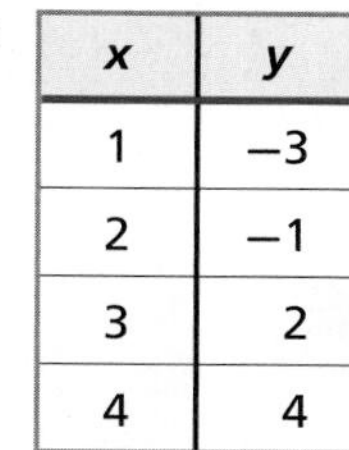

| $x$ | $y$ |
|---|---|
| 1 | −3 |
| 2 | −1 |
| 3 | 2 |
| 4 | 4 |

52. For which point on the graph is $x > \frac{7}{2}$ and $y < \frac{8}{3}$?

Ⓐ $A$ Ⓒ $C$

Ⓑ $B$ Ⓓ $D$

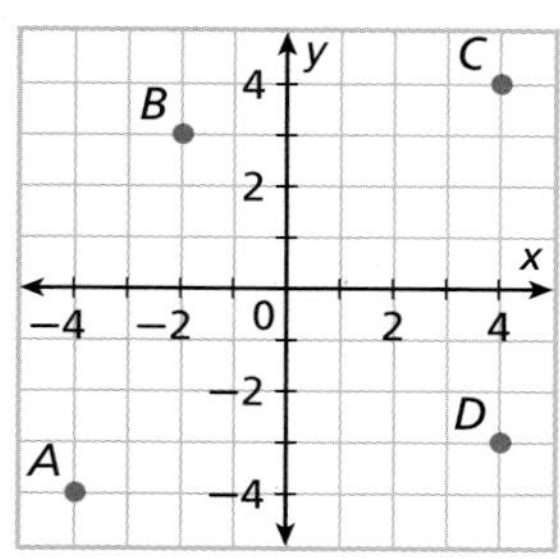


53. Which ordered pair describes the point $(2, 5)$ shifted 3 units right and 2 units down?

Ⓕ (0, 8) Ⓗ (5, 3)

Ⓖ (2, 3) Ⓙ (5, 5)

## CHALLENGE AND EXTEND

**Graph each point.**

54. $W(x + 4, y - 8)$ for $x = 5$ and $y = 2$

55. $X(5 - x, y^2)$ for $x = -1$ and $y = 3$

56. $Y(x + y, y - x)$ for $x = 6$ and $y = 3$

57. $Z(xy, x^2y)$ for $x = -1$ and $y = 4$

58. Graph several ordered pairs that have an $x$-coordinate of 3. Describe the pattern.

59. Graph several ordered pairs that have a $y$-coordinate of 6. Describe the pattern.

60. Find the perimeter of a rectangle whose vertices have the coordinates $A(3, 6)$, $B(3, -2)$, $C(-1, -2)$, and $D(-1, 6)$.

61. **Multi-Step** The coordinates of three vertices of a rectangle are $J(-4, -2)$, $K(2, -2)$, and $L(2, 5)$. Find the coordinates of the fourth vertex. What is the area of the rectangle?

## SPIRAL REVIEW

**Give the name of each figure.** *(Previous course)*

62. 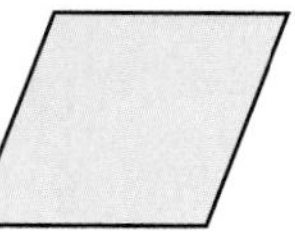

63. 

64. 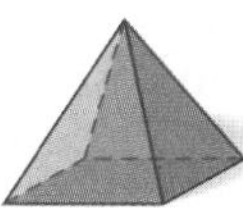

65. 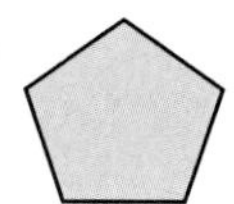

**Classify each real number. Write all classifications that apply.** *(Lesson 1-5)*

66. $\sqrt{36}$

67. $\sqrt{6}$

68. $\frac{1}{9}$

69. $-32$

**Simplify each expression.** *(Lesson 1-7)*

70. $\frac{1}{5} \cdot 18 \cdot 25$

71. $x^2 + 3x$

72. $2a - b + a + 4b$

CHAPTER 1

SECTION 1B

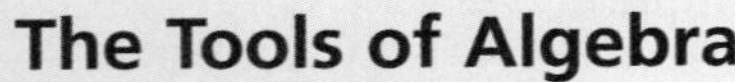

## The Tools of Algebra

**Design Time** Lori's family and Marie's family are redecorating a room in each other's home. They have three days for the decorating project, which will be filmed for a local TV show.

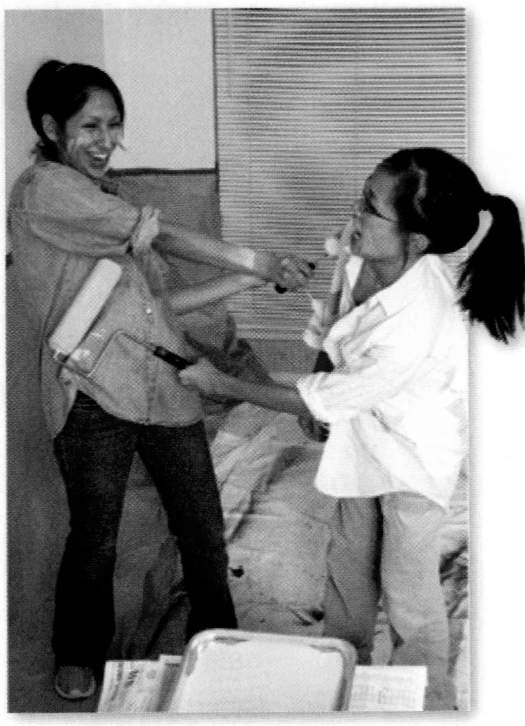

1. Lori decides to paint Marie's room a shade of blue. She measures the height and width of each wall in the rectangular room. She finds that two walls have a width of 12 feet and the other two have a width of 14 feet. The ceiling is 9 feet high. Find the area of each wall. Find the total area of all four walls plus the ceiling.

2. One gallon of paint covers 400 square feet. How many gallons are needed if Lori wants to apply 2 coats of paint to all the walls and the ceiling?

3. Lori decided to build a bedside table in the shape of a cylinder and cover it with yellow fabric on the top and the side. The fabric costs \$2.50 per square yard. The table has a radius of 1 foot and a height of 2 feet. What is the cost to cover the table? Use 3.14 for $\pi$.

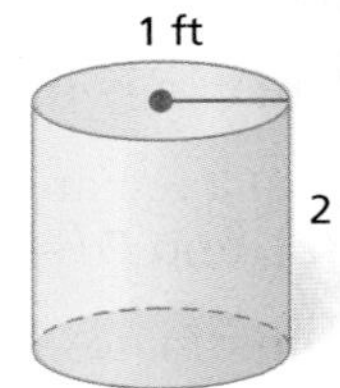


4. Lori will fill a vase with multicolored beads and place it on the bedside table. The vase is in the approximate shape of a cone. The height of the vase is 10 inches, and the radius of the vase at the top is 3 inches. Find the volume of the vase. Use 3.14 for $\pi$. (*Hint:* The formula for the volume of a cone is $V = \frac{1}{3}\pi r^2 h$, where $r$ is the radius of the cone and $h$ is the height of the cone.)

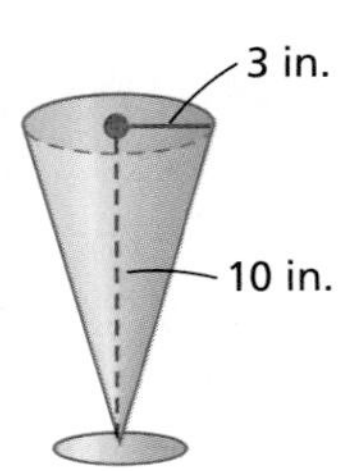


5. Lori wants to create a border around the room using stickers. She can purchase a package of 5 stickers for \$6.00. Make a table to show the cost of 1, 2, 3, 4, and 5 packages of stickers. Make another table to show the cost based on the number of stickers (not the number of packages). How many stickers can Lori purchase if she has \$32 left in her budget?

## Quiz for Lessons 1-6 Through 1-8

### 1-6 Order of Operations

**Simplify each expression.**

1. $-6 + 12 \div (-3)$
2. $30 - 9 + 4$
3. $(6 - 8) \cdot (7 - 5)$
4. $8 \cdot [8 - (4 - 2)]$
5. $\frac{23 - 3 \cdot 5}{4}$
6. $|3 - 9| \div 2 + 5$

**Translate each word phrase into a numerical expression.**

7. the quotient of 16 and the difference of 9 and $-7$
8. the product of 5 and the sum of 6 and 4
9. The area of a trapezoid can be found using the expression $\frac{1}{2}(b_1 + b_2)h$. Find the area of the trapezoid shown.

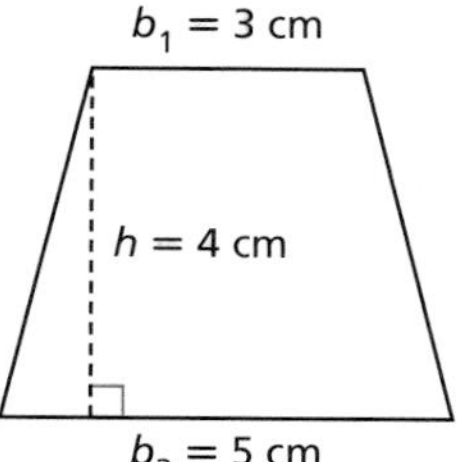


### 1-7 Simplifying Expressions

**Simplify each expression.**

10. $75 + 32 + 25$
11. $5 \cdot 18 \cdot 20$
12. $\frac{1}{4} \cdot 19 \cdot 8$

**Write each product using the Distributive Property. Then simplify.**

13. $7(67)$
14. $9(29)$
15. $17(18)$
16. $8(106)$

**Simplify each expression.**

17. $4k + 15k$
18. $x^2 + 22x^2$
19. $-2g + 5g$

**Simplify each expression. Justify each step.**

20. $3(x + 2) - 3x$
21. $x - 6x^2 + 3x + 4x^2$
22. $-2(3x + 2y + 4x - 5y)$

### 1-8 Introduction to Functions

**Graph each point.**

23. $A(0, -3)$
24. $B(-2, -3)$
25. $C(1, 4)$

**Name the quadrant in which each point lies.**

26. $A$
27. $B$
28. $C$
29. $D$
30. $E$
31. $F$

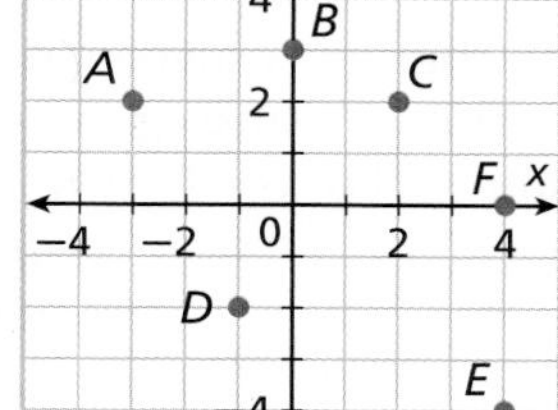


**Generate ordered pairs for each function for $x = -2, -1, 0, 1,$ and 2. Graph the ordered pairs and describe the pattern.**

32. $y = x^2 + 1$
33. $y = x - 1$
34. $y = -|x|$
35. $y = 3x + 3$
36. A swimming pool contains 30,000 gallons of water. The pool is drained at a rate of 100 gallons per minute. Write a rule for the amount of water in the pool when $x$ minutes have gone by. Find the amount of water in the pool when 30 minutes have gone by.

CHAPTER 1

# Study Guide: Review

## Vocabulary



**Complete the sentences below with vocabulary words from the list above.**

1. A(n) ___?___ is a value that does not change.
2. The ___?___ include the natural numbers and zero.
3. A(n) ___?___ is the numerical factor of a term that contains a variable.
4. The ___?___ is the point where the axes of a coordinate plane intersect.

## 1-1 Variables and Expressions *(pp. 6–11)*

Rev. 6.A.1.1

### EXAMPLES

- **Barbara has saved *d* dollars for a $65 sweater. Write an expression for the amount of money she still needs to buy the sweater.**

  $65 - d$ — *Think: d dollars less than the price of the sweater.*

- **Evaluate $b - a$ for $a = 7$ and $b = 15$.**

  $b - a = 15 - 7$ — *Substitute the values for the variables.*
  $= 8$

### EXERCISES

5. Grapes cost $1.99 per pound. Write an expression for the cost of *g* pounds of grapes.
6. Today's temperature is 3 degrees warmer than yesterday's temperature *t*. Write an expression for today's temperature.

**Evaluate each expression for $p = 5$ and $q = 1$.**

7. $qp$
8. $p \div q$
9. $q + p$
10. Each member of the art club will make the same number of posters to advertise their club. They will make 150 posters total. Write an expression for how many posters each member will make if there are *m* members. Find how many posters each member will make if there are 5, 6, and 10 members.

## 1-2 Adding and Subtracting Real Numbers *(pp. 14–19)*

Rev. 8.N.1.1

### EXAMPLES

**Add or subtract.**

- $-4 + (-9)$

  $-4 + (-9)$ — *The signs are the same.*
  $4 + 9 = 13$ — *Add the absolute values and use the sign of the numbers.*
  $-13$

- $-8 - (-3)$

  $-8 - (-3)$
  $-8 + 3$ — *To subtract −3, add 3.*
  $-5$

### EXERCISES

**Add or subtract.**

**11.** $-2 + (-12)$ **12.** $-6 + 1.4$ **13.** $9\frac{1}{4} + \left(-4\frac{3}{4}\right)$

**14.** $\frac{1}{2} - \frac{3}{2}$ **15.** $-8 - 16$ **16.** $6.7 - (-7.6)$

**17.** $3\frac{1}{3} - x$ when $x = -1\frac{2}{3}$

**18.** A trail starts at an elevation of 2278 feet. It descends 47 feet to a campsite. What is the elevation of the campsite?

## 1-3 Multiplying and Dividing Real Numbers *(pp. 20–25)*

Rev. 8.N.1.1

### EXAMPLES

**Multiply or divide.**

- $-12(9)$

  $-12(9) = -108$

- $-\frac{5}{6} \div \left(-\frac{3}{4}\right)$

  $-\frac{5}{6} \div \left(-\frac{3}{4}\right) = -\frac{5}{6}\left(-\frac{4}{3}\right)$
  $= \frac{(-5)(-4)}{6(3)}$
  $= \frac{20}{18} = \frac{10}{9}$

### EXERCISES

**Multiply or divide if possible.**

**19.** $-5(-18)$ **20.** $0 \cdot 10$ **21.** $-4(3.8)$

**22.** $-56 \div 7$ **23.** $0 \div 0.75$ **24.** $9 \div 0$

**Divide.**

**25.** $4 \div \frac{4}{9}$ **26.** $-\frac{1}{2} \div \frac{3}{4}$ **27.** $\frac{6}{7} \div \frac{2}{5}$

**28.** An exercise program recommends that a person walk at least 10,000 steps every day. At this rate, how many steps would the person walk in 1 year?

## 1-4 Powers and Exponents *(pp. 26–31)*

Rev. 6.N.5

### EXAMPLES

- **Simplify $-3^4$.**

  $-3^4 = -1 \cdot 3 \cdot 3 \cdot 3 \cdot 3$ — *Find the product of −1 and four 3's.*
  $= -81$

- **Write −216 as a power of −6.**

  $-216 = (-6)(-6)(-6)$ — *The product of three −6's is −216.*
  $= (-6)^3$

### EXERCISES

**Write each expression as repeated multiplication. Then simplify the expression.**

**29.** $4^3$ **30.** $(-3)^3$ **31.** $(-3)^4$

**32.** $-5^2$ **33.** $\left(\frac{2}{3}\right)^3$ **34.** $\left(-\frac{4}{5}\right)^2$

**Write each number as a power of the given base.**

**35.** 16; base 2 **36.** −1000; base −10

**37.** 64; base −8 **38.** 12; base 12

**39.** The interior of a safe is shaped like a cube with edges 9 inches long. What is the volume of the interior of the safe?

## 1-5 Square Roots and Real Numbers *(pp. 32–37)*

MA.N.2.3

### EXAMPLES

**Find each square root.**

■ $-\sqrt{64}$

$8^2 = 64$

$-\sqrt{64} = -8$

■ $\sqrt{\frac{16}{81}}$

$\left(\frac{4}{9}\right)^2 = \frac{4}{9} \cdot \frac{4}{9} = \frac{16}{81}$

$\sqrt{\frac{16}{81}} = \frac{4}{9}$

■ **Classify −7. Write all classifications that apply.**

$-7 = \frac{-7}{1} = -7.0$

rational number, terminating decimal, integer

### EXERCISES

**Find each square root.**

**40.** $\sqrt{36}$ **41.** $\sqrt{196}$ **42.** $-\sqrt{49}$

**43.** $-\sqrt{144}$ **44.** $\sqrt{\frac{25}{36}}$ **45.** $\sqrt{\frac{1}{169}}$

**Classify each real number. Write all the classifications that apply.**

**46.** 21 **47.** 0 **48.** −13

**49.** 0.8 **50.** $\sqrt{3}$ **51.** $\frac{5}{6}$

**52.** A tabletop is shaped like a square with an area of 13 square feet. Find the length of one side of the table to the nearest tenth of a foot.

## 1-6 Order of Operations *(pp. 40–45)*

Rev. 8.N.1.1

### EXAMPLES

■ **Simplify $18 - 3\left(\frac{15-7}{4}\right)^2$.**

| | |
|---|---|
| $18 - 3\left(\frac{15-7}{4}\right)^2$ | |
| $18 - 3\left(\frac{8}{4}\right)^2$ | *Simplify the numerator.* |
| $18 - 3(2)^2$ | *Simplify inside parentheses.* |
| $18 - 3 \cdot 4$ | *Evaluate powers.* |
| $18 - 12$ | *Multiply.* |
| $6$ | *Subtract.* |

■ **Evaluate $-5\sqrt{40 - x} + 12$ for $x = 4$.**

| | |
|---|---|
| $-5\sqrt{40 - 4} + 12$ | *Substitute the value for x.* |
| $-5\sqrt{36} + 12$ | *Simplify inside the square root symbol.* |
| $-5(6) + 12$ | *Evaluate the square root.* |
| $-30 + 12$ | *Multiply.* |
| $-18$ | *Add.* |

### EXERCISES

**Simplify each expression.**

**53.** $5 \cdot 4 + 3$ **54.** $17 + 3(-3)$

**55.** $[8 + (2 - 6)^2] \div 4$ **56.** $\frac{4^2 - 11}{10}$

**57.** $|12 - 3 \cdot 7| \cdot (-2)$ **58.** $\sqrt{4 \cdot 5 + 5} - 5$

**Evaluate each expression for the given value of $x$.**

**59.** $48 - x + 29$ for $x = 15$

**60.** $x + 4 \cdot 6 - 10$ for $x = -4$

**61.** $8(x - 8)^3$ for $x = 9$

**62.** $[(3 - x)^2 + 4] \div 2$ for $x = 7$

**Translate each word phrase into a numerical or algebraic expression.**

**63.** the sum of 8 and the product of 7 and −2

**64.** the quotient of 12 and the sum of 8 and 3

**65.** 4 times the square root of $x$ less than 20

**66.** The expression $16t^2 + vt$ can be used to find the distance in feet traveled by a falling object. The initial speed is $v$ (ft/s), and time is $t$ (s). Find the distance traveled in 3 s by a falling object with an initial speed of 8 ft/s. *(Note: This expression neglects air resistance.)*

## 1-7 Simplifying Expressions *(pp. 46–51)*

MA.A.1, MA.A.1.2

### EXAMPLES

**Simplify each expression.**

- $-6f^2 - 8f + 3f^2$

  $-6f^2 + 3f^2 - 8f$ — *Commutative Property*

  $-3f^2 - 8f$ — *Combine like terms.*

- $3x - 4y$

  $3x - 4y$ — *There are no like terms. It cannot be simplified.*

- $5x^2 - 3(x - 2) - x$

  $5x^2 - 3x - 3(-2) - x$ — *Distributive Property*

  $5x^2 - 3x + 6 - x$ — *Multiply.*

  $5x^2 - 3x - x + 6$ — *Commutative Property*

  $5x^2 - 4x + 6$ — *Combine like terms.*

### EXERCISES

**Simplify each expression.**

**67.** $18 + 26 - 8 + 4$

**68.** $60 \cdot 27 \cdot \frac{1}{6}$

**Write each product using the Distributive Property. Then simplify.**

**69.** $13(103)$

**70.** $18(99)$

**Simplify each expression.**

**71.** $20x - 16x$

**72.** $2y^2 + 5y^2$

**73.** $6(x + 4) - 2x$

**74.** $-2(x^2 - 1) + 4x^2$

**75.** $-2y + 3y^2 - 3y + y$

**76.** $7y + 3y - a - 2y$

**77.** Rita bought a sandwich, 2 bottles of water, and an apple for lunch. The sandwich cost $4.99, the bottles of water cost $1.48 each, and the apple cost $0.89. About how much did Rita spend on lunch?

## 1-8 Introduction to Functions *(pp. 54–59)*

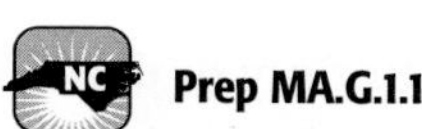


### EXAMPLES

- **Generate ordered pairs for the function using the given values for $x$. Graph the ordered pairs and describe the pattern.**

  $y = x + 2$; $x = -4, -3, -2, -1, 0$

| Input | Output | Ordered Pair |
|---|---|---|
| $x$ | $y$ | $(x, y)$ |
| $-4$ | $-4 + 2 = -2$ | $(-4, -2)$ |
| $-3$ | $-3 + 2 = -1$ | $(-3, -1)$ |
| $-2$ | $-2 + 2 = 0$ | $(-2, 0)$ |
| $-1$ | $-1 + 2 = 1$ | $(-1, 1)$ |
| $0$ | $0 + 2 = 2$ | $(0, 2)$ |

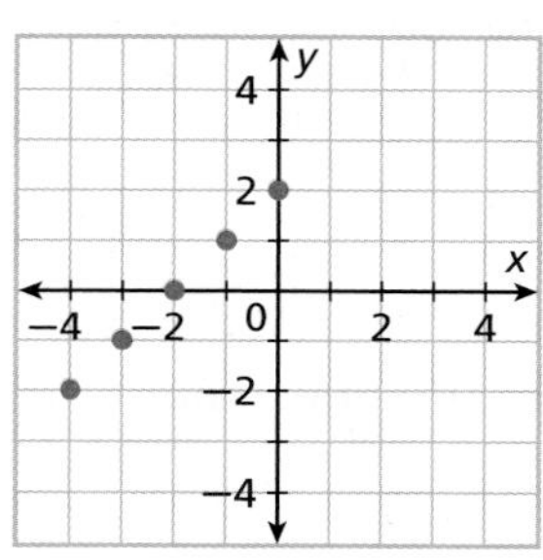


The points form a straight line.

### EXERCISES

**Graph each point.**

**78.** $A(2, 3)$

**79.** $B(-1, 4)$

**80.** $C(0, 8)$

**81.** $D(5, -3)$

**Name the quadrant in which each point lies.**

**82.** $R$

**83.** $S$

**84.** $T$

**85.** $U$

**86.** $V$

**87.** $W$

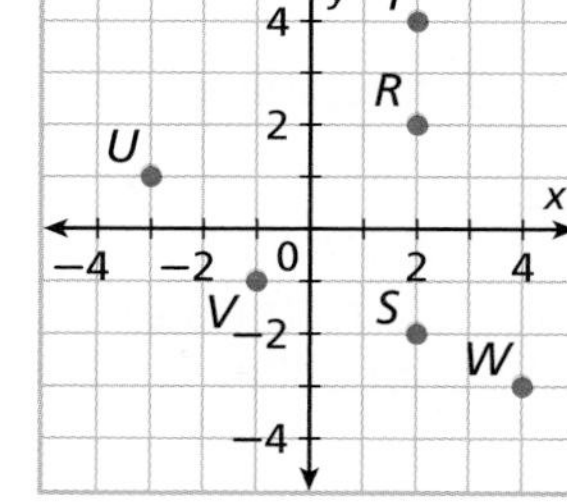


**88.** The price of an item with tax is equal to the price of the item plus $\frac{1}{20}$ of the price. Write a rule for the price with tax. Find the price with tax of items that cost $2, $15, $30, and $40.

**89.** Generate ordered pairs for the function $y = \frac{1}{4}x^2$ for $x = -4, -1, 0, 1$, and $4$. Graph the ordered pairs and describe the pattern.

CHAPTER 1

# CHAPTER TEST

**Evaluate each expression for $a = 2$, $b = 3$, and $c = 6$.**

**1.** $c - a$  **2.** $ab$  **3.** $c \div a$  **4.** $\frac{c}{b}$  **5.** $b - a$

**6.** Write two verbal expressions for $n - 5$.

**7.** Nate runs 8 miles each week. Write an expression for the number of miles he runs in $n$ weeks. Find the number of miles Nate runs in 5 weeks.

**Add or subtract.**

**8.** $-5 + 8$  **9.** $-3 - 4$  **10.** $4 + (-7)$  **11.** $7 - x$ for $x = -2$

**The table shows the lowest temperatures recorded in four states.**

**12.** What is the difference between the lowest temperatures in Alaska and Hawaii?

**13.** What is the difference between the lowest temperatures in Nebraska and Texas?

| Lowest Temperatures in Four States | |
|---|---|
| **Location** | **Temperature (°F)** |
| Prospect Creek, Alaska | −80 |
| Camp Clarke, Nebraska | −47 |
| Mauna Kea, Hawaii | 12 |
| Seminole, Texas | −23 |

**Multiply or divide if possible.**

**14.** $(-3)(-6)$  **15.** $-\frac{1}{2} \div \frac{1}{4}$  **16.** $12 \div (-3)$  **17.** $x \div -4$ for $x = 0$

**Simplify each expression.**

**18.** $5^4$  **19.** $\left(-\frac{4}{5}\right)^3$  **20.** $2^5$  **21.** $-6^2$

**Classify each real number. Write all classifications that apply.**

**22.** 30  **23.** $\sqrt{6}$  **24.** $-12$  **25.** $\frac{1}{2}$

**Evaluate each expression for the given value of $x$.**

**26.** $\frac{-2 - 6}{x^2}$ for $x = 2$  **27.** $8(x - 1)^2$ for $x = 11$  **28.** $22 + [-2(19 - x)]$ for $x = 7$

**29.** Does the phrase "2 times the sum of a number and 5" represent the same expression as the phrase "the sum of 2 times a number and 5"? Explain why or why not.

**Simplify each expression.**

**30.** $5\frac{1}{4} + 7 + 2\frac{3}{4}$  **31.** $-2(x + 5) + 4x$  **32.** $3x + 2x^2 - x$

**Graph each point.**

**33.** $W(1, -3)$  **34.** $X(-3, 0)$  **35.** $Y(5, 3)$  **36.** $Z(0, -2)$

**37.** Generate ordered pairs for $y = 2x - 1$ for $x = -2, -1, 0, 1, 2$. Graph the ordered pairs and describe the pattern.

CHAPTER 1

## FOCUS ON SAT

The SAT* is a 3-hour test that is often used to predict academic success at the college level. SAT scores are used to compare the math and verbal reasoning skills of students from all over the world.

**You may want to time yourself as you take this practice test. It should take you about 8 minutes to complete.**

HOT TIP! In each section of SAT questions, the easier questions are at the beginning of the section and harder questions come later. Answer as many of the easy questions as you can first, and then move on to the more challenging questions.

**1.** The number 0 is NOT an example of which of the following?

**(A)** Real numbers

**(B)** Rational numbers

**(C)** Whole numbers

**(D)** Integers

**(E)** Natural numbers

**2.** A clothing store opens with 75 pairs of jeans on a sale table. By noon, 10 pairs have been sold. As of 2:00, another 8 pairs have been sold. A clerk then restocks with 12 pairs. Receipts show that 18 pairs of jeans were sold after 2:00. How many pairs of jeans are left at the end of the day?

**(A)** 51

**(B)** 27

**(C)** 123

**(D)** 36

**(E)** 23

**3.** If Jack is three times as old as his sister Judy, which of the following expressions represents Jack's age if Judy is $j$ years old?

**(A)** $3j > j$

**(B)** $3j$

**(C)** $j + 3$

**(D)** $3 - j$

**(E)** $\frac{1}{3}j$

**4.** Which of the following is equal to $-3^4$?

**(A)** $-64$

**(B)** 12

**(C)** $-12$

**(D)** 81

**(E)** $-81$

**5.** What is the result after applying the following sequence of operations to a number $n$ in the given order?

1. Subtract 2.
2. Divide by 3.
3. Add 7.
4. Multiply by $-1$.

**(A)** $\frac{n-2}{3} + 7(-1)$

**(B)** $\frac{(-n-2)+7}{3}$

**(C)** $-\left(-\frac{2}{3} + 7\right)n$

**(D)** $-\left(\frac{n-2}{3} + 7\right)$

**(E)** $n - \frac{2}{3} + 7(-1)$

**6.** Which property is illustrated by the equation $8(7) + 8(6) = 8(7 + 6)$?

**(A)** Distributive Property

**(B)** Associative Property of Multiplication

**(C)** Commutative Property of Addition

**(D)** Commutative Property of Multiplication

**(E)** Associative Property of Addition

CHAPTER 1

# TEST TACKLER

Standardized Test Strategies

## Gridded Response: Fill in Answer Grids Correctly

When responding to a test item that requires you to place your answer in a grid, you must fill out the grid on your answer sheet correctly, or the item will be marked as incorrect.

### EXAMPLE 1

**Gridded Response: Simplify the expression $12^2 - 3(10 + 4)$.**

| 1 | 0 | 2 | | |
|---|---|---|---|---|

$$12^2 - 3(10 + 4)$$
$$12^2 - 3(14)$$
$$144 - 3(14)$$
$$144 - 42$$
$$102$$

The expression simplifies to 102.

- Write your answer in the answer boxes at the top of the grid.
- Put only one digit in each box. Do not leave a blank box in the middle of an answer.
- Shade the bubble for each digit in the same column as the digit in the answer box.

### EXAMPLE 2

**Gridded Response: Evaluate the expression $ba \div c$ for $a = -7$, $b = 2$, and $c = -6$.**

| 7 | / | 3 | | |
|---|---|---|---|---|

$$ba \div c$$
$$(-7)(2) \div (-6)$$
$$-14 \div (-6)$$
$$\frac{7}{3} = 2\frac{1}{3} = 2.\overline{3}$$

The expression simplifies to $\frac{7}{3}$, $2\frac{1}{3}$, or $2.\overline{3}$.

- Mixed numbers and repeating decimals cannot be gridded, so you must grid the answer as $\frac{7}{3}$.
- Write your answer in the answer boxes at the top of the grid.
- Put only one digit or symbol in each box. On some grids, the fraction bar and the decimal point have a designated box. Do not leave a blank box in the middle of an answer.
- Shade the bubble for each digit or symbol in the same column as the digit in the answer box.

**On many grids you cannot grid a negative number because the grid does not include the negative sign. If you get a negative answer to a test item, you may need to recalculate the problem.**

**Read each sample and then answer the questions that follow.**

**Sample A**
A student correctly evaluated an expression and got $\frac{8}{15}$ as a result. Then the student filled in the grid as shown.

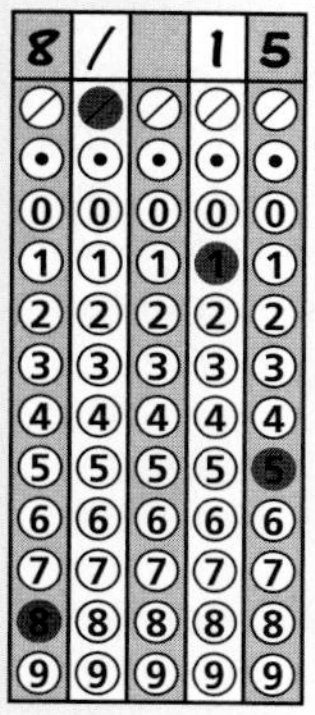

1. What error did the student make when filling out the grid?
2. Explain how to fill in the answer correctly.

**Sample B**
The square root of 6.25 is 2.5. This answer is displayed in the grid.

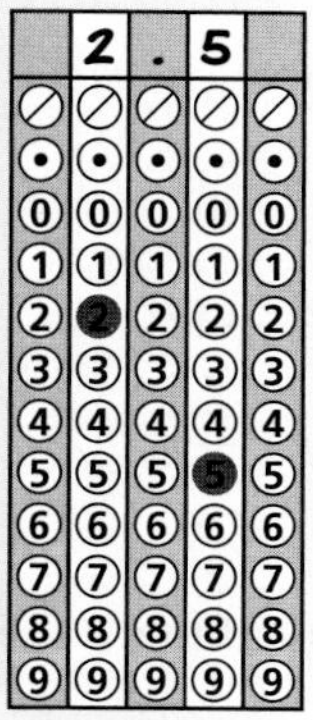

3. What error did the student make when filling in the grid?
4. Explain how to fill in the answer correctly.

**Sample C**
A student correctly simplified the expression $2\frac{1}{8} + 3\frac{5}{8} + \frac{7}{8}$. Then the student filled in the grid as shown.

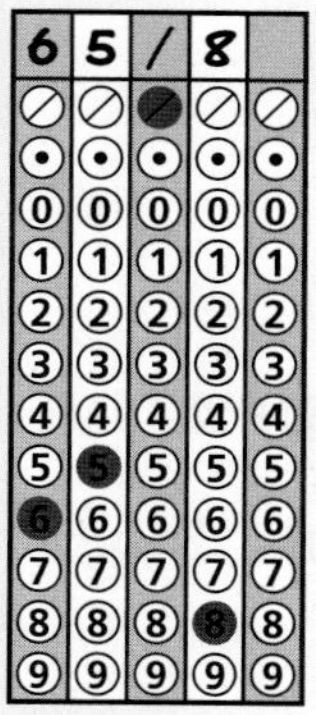

5. What answer does the grid show?
6. Explain why you cannot fill in a mixed number.
7. Write the answer $6\frac{5}{8}$ in two forms that could be entered in the grid correctly.

**Sample D**
A student added $-10$ and 25 and got an answer of 15. Then the student filled in the grid as shown.

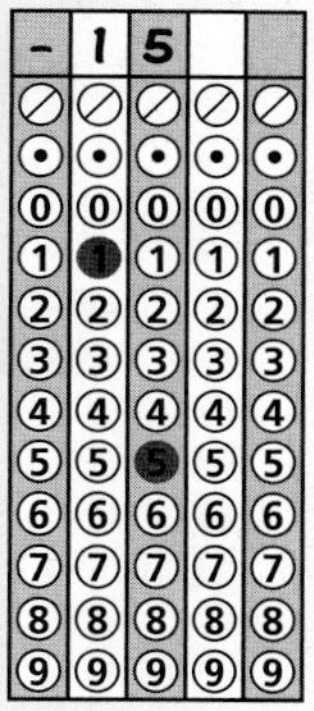

8. What error does the grid show?
9. Another student got an answer of $-15$. Explain why the student knew this answer was wrong.

CHAPTER 1

go.hrw.com
State Test Practice Online
KEYWORD: MA7 TestPrep

## CUMULATIVE ASSESSMENT, CHAPTER 1

### Multiple Choice

1. Eric is collecting gifts for a charity event. He needs 150 gifts. So far he has collected $x$ gifts. Which expression represents how many gifts Eric still needs to collect?

   A $150 + x$ C $x - 150$

   B $150 - x$ D $150 \div x$

2. An online store sells birdhouses for $34.95 each. For each order, there is a one-time shipping and handling fee of $7.50. Which expression can be used to represent the cost of ordering $x$ birdhouses?

   A $x + 34.95 + 7.50$

   B $(34.95 + 7.50)x$

   C $7.50x + 34.95$

   D $34.95x + 7.50$

3. Which equation could have generated the table?

| $x$ | $y$ |
|---|---|
| −2 | 5 |
| −1 | 2 |
| 0 | 1 |
| 1 | 2 |
| 2 | 5 |

   A $y = -2x + 1$

   B $y = x + 1$

   C $y = |2x| + 1$

   D $y = x^2 + 1$

4. The equation $C = \frac{5}{9}(F - 32)$ relates the Celsius temperature $C$ to the Fahrenheit temperature $F$. What is the Celsius temperature if the Fahrenheit temperature is $-13$ degrees?

   A −45 °C

   B −39.2 °C

   C −25 °C

   D −10.6 °C

5. Janis's band has been offered 12 percent of total food and drink sales if they play for the Kozmic Coffee House Friday and Saturday. The band would like to buy a new $400 amp. If the average customer spends $9, how many customers need to spend money on the two nights so that the band can get their amp?

   A 44

   B 45

   C 370

   D 371

6. The volume of a sphere with radius $r$ is $\frac{4\pi r^3}{3}$. The radius of a ball is 4 inches. What is the volume of the ball in cubic inches?

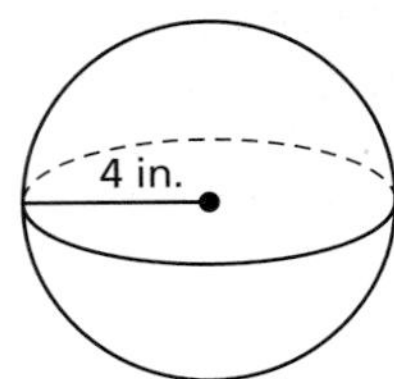


   A $16\pi \text{ in}^3$

   B $\frac{64\pi}{3} \text{ in}^3$

   C $\frac{256\pi}{3} \text{ in}^3$

   D $\frac{4096\pi}{3} \text{ in}^3$

7. At one time, a U.S. dollar had the same value as 11.32 Mexican pesos. How many Mexican pesos were equal to 16 U.S. dollars at that time?

   A 1.41 pesos

   B 4.68 pesos

   C 27.32 pesos

   D 181.12 pesos

**Read each question carefully. Be sure you understand what the question is asking before looking at the answer choices or beginning your calculations.**

**8.** What is the value of the function $y = 4x^2 + 8$ when $x = 3$?

A 20

B 32

C 44

D 76

**9.** Tickets to a festival cost \$5.00 each, and lunch costs \$8.50 per person. Renting a bus to and from the festival costs \$47.00. Which expression can be used to represent the cost of *x* people going to the festival? (Assume that the *x* people will fit on one bus.)

A $5.00 + 8.50 + 47.00$

B $5.00x + 8.50 + 47.00$

C $5.00 + 8.50x + 47.00$

D $5.00x + 8.50x + 47.00$

**10.** Tara has found that her business runs most efficiently when the number of supervisors is equal to $\frac{1}{5}$ of the number of office workers. Tara currently has 200 office workers in her employ. Given that number, which ordered pair below shows the most efficient relationship of office workers to supervisors?

A (200, 1000)

B (200, 40)

C (40, 200)

D (40, 8)

**11.** The area of a circle with radius *r* is $\pi r^2$. What is the area of the robot sumo-wrestling ring shown below? Use 3.14 for $\pi$. Round your answer to the nearest tenth.

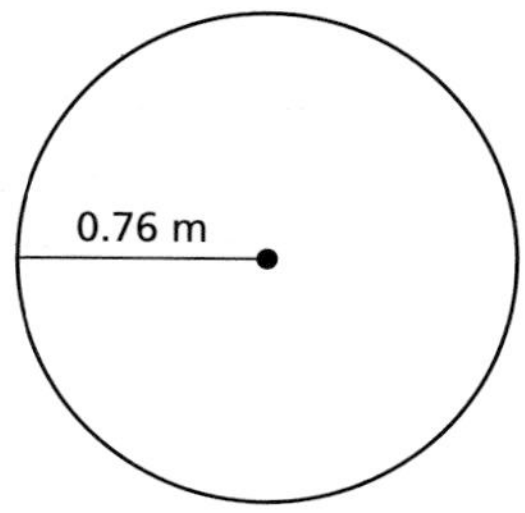


A 9.9 $m^2$

B 7.5 $m^2$

C 2.4 $m^2$

D 1.8 $m^2$

## *STANDARDIZED TEST PREP*

## Short Response

**S1.** Dee is using a coordinate plane to make a map of her town. Each square on the grid represents 1 square mile. She plots her house at the origin. Her school is 3 miles east and 2 miles north of her house.

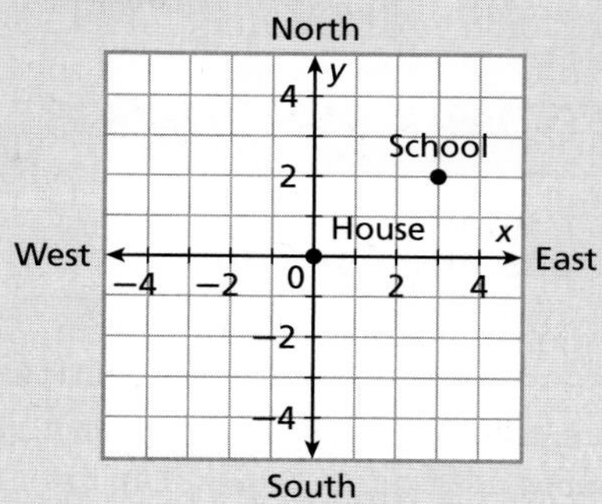


**a.** Write an ordered pair to show where Dee plotted the point for her school.

**b.** The post office is 4 miles east of Dee's house. Write an ordered pair to show where Dee should plot a point for the post office.

**c.** The bank is 3 miles north and 3 miles west of the school. Which is closer to Dee's house, the post office or the bank? Explain your answer.

**S2.** As part of a challenge problem, a math teacher writes the following expression on the board:

$$-(-x)$$

**a.** If *x* is 12, what is the value of the expression?

**b.** If *x* is a negative number, is the value of the expression positive or negative? Explain how you found your answer.

**c.** Simplify the expression.

## Extended Response

**E1.** Fatima enrolled in a traveler rewards program. She begins with 10,000 bonus points. For every trip she takes, she collects 3000 bonus points.

**a.** Write an expression for the number of bonus points Fatima has after *x* trips.

**b.** Make a table showing the number of bonus points Fatima has after 0, 1, 2, 3, 4, and 5 trips.

**c.** Graph the ordered pairs from the table. Describe the pattern formed by the points.

**d.** When Fatima has collected 20,000 bonus points, she gets a free vacation. How many trips does Fatima need to take to get a free vacation?

CHAPTER 2

# Equations

## Why Learn This?

A common use of equations and proportional relationships is the construction of scale models, such as this model of a Duncan Phyfe chair in Thomasville, NC.

go.hrw.com
Chapter Project Online
KEYWORD: MA7 ChProj

# ARE YOU READY?

## Vocabulary

**Match each term on the left with a definition on the right.**

1. constant
2. expression
3. order of operations
4. variable

A. a mathematical phrase that contains operations, numbers, and/or variables

B. a mathematical statement that two expressions are equivalent

C. a process for evaluating expressions

D. a symbol used to represent a quantity that can change

E. a value that does not change

## Order of Operations

**Simplify each expression.**

5. $(7 - 3) \div 2$
6. $4 \cdot 6 \div 3$
7. $12 - 3 + 1$
8. $2 \cdot 10 \div 5$
9. $125 \div 5^2$
10. $7 \cdot 6 + 5 \cdot 4$

## Add and Subtract Integers

**Add or subtract.**

11. $-15 + 19$
12. $-6 - (-18)$
13. $6 + (-8)$
14. $-12 + (-3)$

## Add and Subtract Fractions

**Perform each indicated operation. Give your answer in the simplest form.**

15. $\frac{1}{4} + \frac{2}{3}$
16. $1\frac{1}{2} - \frac{3}{4}$
17. $\frac{3}{8} + \frac{2}{3}$
18. $\frac{3}{2} - \frac{2}{3}$

## Evaluate Expressions

**Evaluate each expression for the given value of the variable.**

19. $2x + 3$ for $x = 7$
20. $3n - 5$ for $n = 7$
21. $13 - 4a$ for $a = 2$
22. $3y + 5$ for $y = 5$

## Connect Words and Algebra

23. Janie bought 4 apples and 6 bananas. Each apple cost $0.75, and each banana cost $0.60. Write an expression representing the total cost.
24. A rectangle has a width of 13 inches and a length of $\ell$ inches. Write an expression representing the area of the rectangle.
25. Write a phrase that could be modeled by the expression $n + 2n$.

CHAPTER 2

# Study Guide: Preview

## Where You've Been

**Previously, you**

- practiced using operations in algebra.
- used variables to represent quantities.
- wrote expressions to represent situations.
- simplified and evaluated expressions.

## In This Chapter

**You will study**

- how to use inverse operations to solve equations containing variables.
- writing equations to represent situations.
- simplifying equations before solving.

## Where You're Going

**You can use the skills in this chapter**

- to compare unit prices for consumer products.
- to calculate percentages in taxes, tips, interest, and commissions.
- to create or interpret scale models and drawings.
- to solve problems in science courses and all future math courses.

## *Key Vocabulary/Vocabulario*

| | |
|---|---|
| equation | ecuación |
| formula | fórmula |
| identity | identidad |
| indirect measurement | medición indirecta |
| literal equation | ecuación literal |
| percent | porcentaje |
| percent change | porcentaje de cambio |
| proportion | proporción |
| ratio | razón |
| unit rate | tasa unitaria |

## *Vocabulary Connections*

To become familiar with some of the vocabulary terms in the chapter, consider the following. You may refer to the chapter, the glossary, or a dictionary if you like.

1. The word **equation** begins with the root *equa-*. List some other words that begin with *equa-*. What do all these words have in common?
2. The word *literal* means "of letters." How might a **literal equation** be different from an equation like $3 + 5 = 8$?
3. One definition of **identity** is "exact sameness." An equation consists of two expressions. If an equation is an *identity,* what do you think is true about the expressions?
4. The word *per* means "for each," and the word *cent* means "hundred." How can you use these meanings to understand the term **percent**?

# Reading and Writing Math

CHAPTER 2

## Study Strategy: Use Your Own Words

Explaining a concept using your own words will help you better understand it. For example, learning to solve equations might seem difficult if the textbook doesn't use the same words that you would use.

As you work through each lesson:

- Identify the important ideas from the explanation in the book.
- Use your own words to explain the important ideas you identified.

| What Arturo Reads | What Arturo Writes |
| --- | --- |
| To evaluate an expression is to find its value. | *Evaluate an expression*—find the value. |
| To evaluate an algebraic expression, substitute numbers for the variables in the expression and then simplify the expression. | Substitute a number for each variable (letter), and find the answer. |
| A replacement set is a set of numbers that can be substituted for a variable. | *Replacement set*—numbers that can be substituted for a letter. |

### Try This

**Rewrite each paragraph in your own words.**

1. Two numbers are opposites if their sum is 0. A number and its opposite are on opposite sides of zero on a number line, but are the same distance from zero.
2. The Commutative and Associative Properties of Addition and Multiplication allow you to rearrange an expression to simplify it.
3. The terms of an expression are the parts to be added or subtracted. Like terms are terms that contain the same variables raised to the same powers. Constants are also like terms.

# Model One-Step Equations

You can use algebra tiles and an equation mat to model and solve equations. To find the value of the variable, place or remove tiles to get the $x$-tile by itself on one side of the mat. You must place or remove the same number of yellow tiles or the same number of red tiles on both sides.

*Use with Lesson 2-1*

**Prep MA.A.4.5** Use graphs, tables and symbols to solve linear equations.

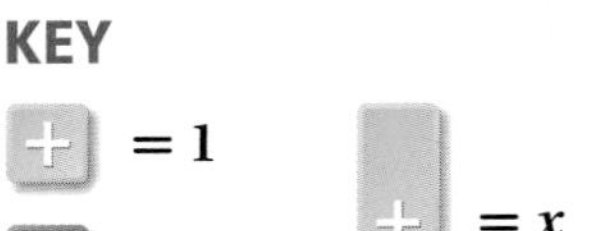


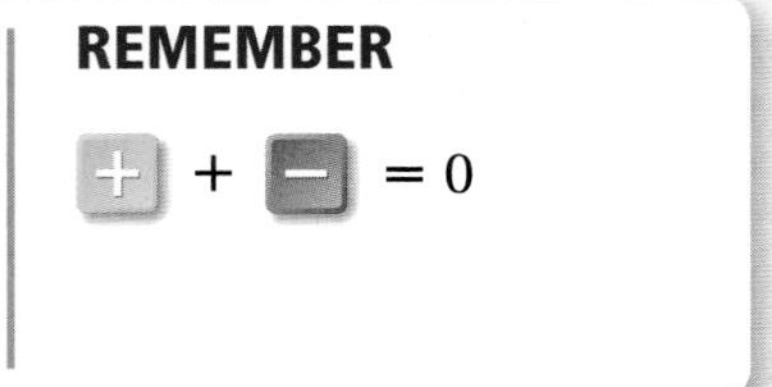


## Activity

**Use algebra tiles to model and solve $x + 6 = 2$.**

| MODEL | | ALGEBRA |
|---|---|---|
| | *Model x + 6 on the left side of the mat and 2 on the right side of the mat.* | $x + 6 = 2$ |
| | *Place 6 red tiles on both sides of the mat. This represents adding −6 to both sides of the equation.* | $x + 6 + (-6) = 2 + (-6)$ |
| | *Remove zero pairs from both sides of the mat.* | $x + \mathbf{0} = \mathbf{0} + (-4)$ |
| | *One x-tile is equivalent to 4 red tiles.* | $x = -4$ |

## Try This

**Use algebra tiles to model and solve each equation.**

**1.** $x + 2 = 5$ **2.** $x - 7 = 8$ **3.** $x - 5 = 9$ **4.** $x + 4 = 7$

# 2-1 Solving Equations by Adding or Subtracting

 **MA.A.4.5** Use ... symbols to solve linear equations.

***Objective***
Solve one-step equations in one variable by using addition or subtraction.

***Vocabulary***
equation
solution of an equation

**Who uses this?**
Athletes can use an equation to estimate their maximum heart rates. (See Example 4.)

An **equation** is a mathematical statement that two expressions are equal. A **solution of an equation** is a value of the variable that makes the equation true.

To find solutions, *isolate the variable*. A variable is isolated when it appears by itself on one side of an equation, and not at all on the other side. Isolate a variable by using inverse operations, which "undo" operations on the variable.

| Inverse Operations | |
|---|---|
| **Operation** | **Inverse Operation** |
| Addition | Subtraction |
| Subtraction | Addition |

An equation is like a balanced scale. To keep the balance, perform the same operation on both sides.

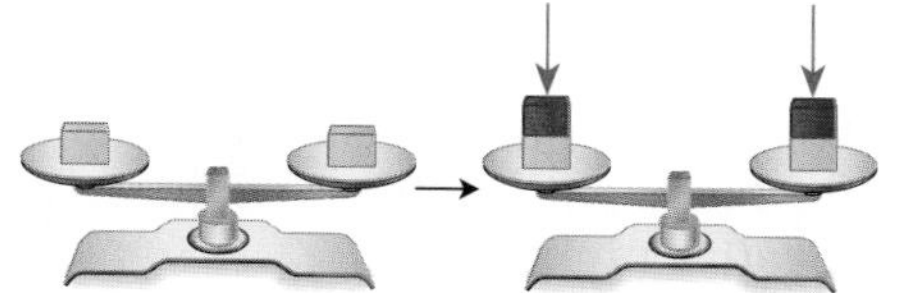

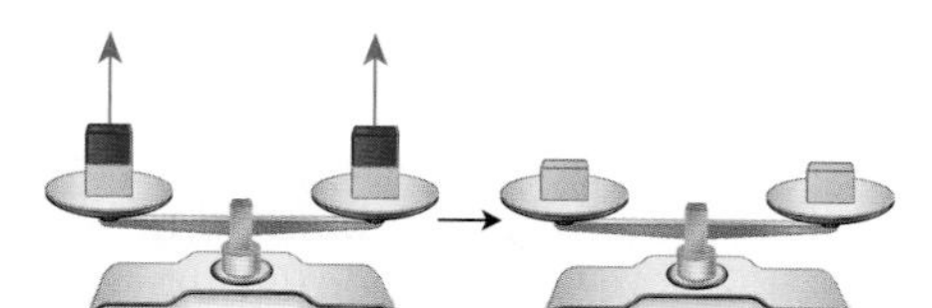

## EXAMPLE 1 Solving Equations by Using Addition

**Solve each equation.**

**A** $x - 10 = 4$

$$\begin{aligned} x - 10 &= 4 \\ \underline{+10} &\quad \underline{+10} \\ x &= 14 \end{aligned}$$

*Since 10 is subtracted from x, add 10 to both sides to undo the subtraction.*

*Check* 

$$\begin{array}{c|c} x - 10 & 4 \\ \hline 14 - 10 & 4 \\ 4 & 4 \checkmark \end{array}$$

*To check your solution, substitute 14 for x in the original equation.*

**B** $\frac{2}{5} = m - \frac{1}{5}$

$$\begin{aligned} \frac{2}{5} &= m - \frac{1}{5} \\ \underline{+\frac{1}{5}} &\quad \underline{+\frac{1}{5}} \\ \frac{3}{5} &= m \end{aligned}$$

*Since $\frac{1}{5}$ is subtracted from m, add $\frac{1}{5}$ to both sides to undo the subtraction.*

**Writing Math**

Solutions are sometimes written in a *solution set*. For Example 1A, the solution set is {14}. For Example 1B, the solution set is $\left\{\frac{3}{5}\right\}$.

**Solve each equation. Check your answer.**

**1a.** $n - 3.2 = 5.6$ **1b.** $-6 = k - 6$ **1c.** $16 = m - 9$

## EXAMPLE 2 Solving Equations by Using Subtraction

**Solve each equation. Check your answer.**

**A** $x + 7 = 9$

$$\begin{aligned} x + 7 &= \phantom{-}9 \\ \underline{\phantom{x+}-7} &\quad \underline{-7} \\ x \quad &= \phantom{-}2 \end{aligned}$$

*Since 7 is added to x, subtract 7 from both sides to undo the addition.*

*Check* $\begin{array}{c|c} x + 7 = 9 & \\ \hline 2 + 7 & 9 \\ 9 & 9 \checkmark \end{array}$

*To check your solution, substitute 2 for x in the original equation.*

**B** $0.7 = r + 0.4$

$$\begin{aligned} 0.7 &= r + 0.4 \\ \underline{-0.4} &\quad \underline{-0.4} \\ 0.3 &= r \end{aligned}$$

*Since 0.4 is added to r, subtract 0.4 from both sides to undo the addition.*

*Check* $\begin{array}{c|c} 0.7 = r + 0.4 & \\ \hline 0.7 & 0.3 + 0.4 \\ 0.7 & 0.7 \checkmark \end{array}$

*To check your solution, substitute 0.3 for r in the original equation.*

**Solve each equation. Check your answer.**

**2a.** $d + \frac{1}{2} = 1$ **2b.** $-5 = k + 5$ **2c.** $6 + t = 14$

Remember that subtracting is the same as adding the opposite. When solving equations, you will sometimes find it easier to add an opposite to both sides instead of subtracting. For example, this method may be useful when the equation contains negative numbers.

## EXAMPLE 3 Solving Equations by Adding the Opposite

**Solve $-8 + b = 2$.**

$$\begin{aligned} -8 + b &= \phantom{+}2 \\ \underline{+8 \phantom{+b}} &\quad \underline{+8} \\ b &= 10 \end{aligned}$$

*Since −8 is added to b, add 8 to both sides.*

CHECK IT OUT!

**Solve each equation. Check your answer.**

**3a.** $-2.3 + m = 7$ **3b.** $-\frac{3}{4} + z = \frac{5}{4}$ **3c.** $-11 + x = 33$

### Student to Student

### *Zero As a Solution*

**Ama Walker**
Carson High School

*I used to get confused when I got a solution of 0. But my teacher reminded me that 0 is a number just like any other number, so it can be a solution of an equation. Just check your answer and see if it works.*

$$\begin{aligned} x + 6 &= \phantom{-}6 \\ \underline{\phantom{x}-6} &\quad \underline{-6} \\ x \quad &= \phantom{-}0 \end{aligned}$$

*Check* $\begin{array}{c|c} x + 6 = 6 & \\ \hline 0 + 6 & 6 \\ 6 & 6 \checkmark \end{array}$

## EXAMPLE 4 *Fitness Application*

**A person's maximum heart rate is the highest rate, in beats per minute, that the person's heart should reach. One method to estimate maximum heart rate states that your age added to your maximum heart rate is 220. Using this method, write and solve an equation to find the maximum heart rate of a 15-year-old.**

| Age | added to | maximum heart rate | is | 220. |
|---|---|---|---|---|
| $a$ | $+$ | $r$ | $=$ | 220 |

$$a + r = 220$$ *Write an equation to represent the relationship.*

$$15 + r = 220$$ *Substitute 15 for a. Since 15 is added to r, subtract 15 from both sides to undo the addition.*

$$\underline{-15 \quad\quad -15}$$

$$r = 205$$

The maximum heart rate for a 15-year-old is 205 beats per minute. Since age added to maximum heart rate is 220, the answer should be less than 220. So 205 is a reasonable answer.

4. **What if...?** Use the method above to find a person's age if the person's maximum heart rate is 185 beats per minute.

The properties of equality allow you to perform inverse operations, as in the previous examples. These properties say that you can perform the same operation on both sides of an equation.

**Properties of Equality**

| WORDS | NUMBERS | ALGEBRA |
|---|---|---|
| **Addition Property of Equality**<br>You can add the same number to both sides of an equation, and the statement will still be true. | $3 = 3$<br>$3 + 2 = 3 + 2$<br>$5 = 5$ | $a = b$<br>$a + c = b + c$ |
| **Subtraction Property of Equality**<br>You can subtract the same number from both sides of an equation, and the statement will still be true. | $7 = 7$<br>$7 - 5 = 7 - 5$<br>$2 = 2$ | $a = b$<br>$a - c = b - c$ |

### THINK AND DISCUSS

1. Identify each of the following as an *expression* or *equation*. Explain your reasoning.

   **a.** $2t = 3$ **b.** $xy^2 + x + 3$ **c.** $-5 - n = 0$

2. **GET ORGANIZED** Copy and complete the graphic organizer. In each box, write an example of an equation that can be solved by using the given property, and solve it.

# 2-1 Exercises

MA.A.4.5

go.hrw.com
**Homework Help Online**
KEYWORD: MA7 2-1
**Parent Resources Online**
KEYWORD: MA7 Parent

## GUIDED PRACTICE

1. **Vocabulary** Will the *solution of an equation* such as $x - 3 = 9$ be a variable or a number? Explain.

**Solve each equation. Check your answer.**

SEE EXAMPLE 1 p. 77

2. $s - 5 = 3$
3. $17 = w - 4$
4. $k - 8 = -7$
5. $x - 3.9 = 12.4$
6. $8.4 = y - 4.6$
7. $\frac{3}{8} = t - \frac{1}{8}$

SEE EXAMPLE 2 p. 78

8. $t + 5 = -25$
9. $9 = s + 9$
10. $42 = m + 36$
11. $2.8 = z + 0.5$
12. $b + \frac{2}{3} = 2$
13. $n + 1.8 = 3$

SEE EXAMPLE 3 p. 78

14. $-10 + d = 7$
15. $20 = -12 + v$
16. $-46 + q = 5$
17. $2.8 = -0.9 + y$
18. $-\frac{2}{3} + c = \frac{2}{3}$
19. $-\frac{5}{6} + p = 2$

SEE EXAMPLE 4 p. 79

20. **Geology** In 1673, the Hope diamond was reduced from its original weight by about 45 carats, resulting in a diamond weighing about 67 carats. Write and solve an equation to find how many carats the original diamond weighed. Show that your answer is reasonable.

## PRACTICE AND PROBLEM SOLVING

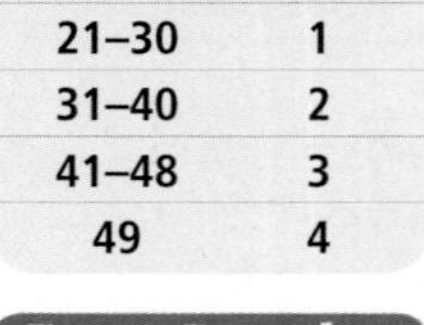

**Independent Practice**

| For Exercises | See Example |
|---|---|
| 21–30 | 1 |
| 31–40 | 2 |
| 41–48 | 3 |
| 49 | 4 |

**Extra Practice**
Skills Practice p. S6
Application Practice p. S29

**Solve each equation. Check your answer.**

21. $1 = k - 8$
22. $u - 15 = -8$
23. $x - 7 = 10$
24. $-9 = p - 2$
25. $\frac{3}{7} = p - \frac{1}{7}$
26. $q - 0.5 = 1.5$
27. $6 = t - 4.5$
28. $4\frac{2}{3} = r - \frac{1}{3}$
29. $6 = x - 3$
30. $1.75 = k - 0.75$
31. $19 + a = 19$
32. $4 = 3.1 + y$
33. $m + 20 = 3$
34. $-12 = c + 3$
35. $v + 2300 = -800$
36. $b + 42 = 300$
37. $3.5 = n + 4$
38. $b + \frac{1}{2} = \frac{1}{2}$
39. $x + 5.34 = 5.39$
40. $2 = d + \frac{1}{4}$
41. $-12 + f = 3$
42. $-9 = -4 + g$
43. $-1200 + j = 345$
44. $90 = -22 + a$
45. $26 = -4 + y$
46. $1\frac{3}{4} = -\frac{1}{4} + w$
47. $-\frac{1}{6} + h = \frac{1}{6}$
48. $-5.2 + a = -8$
49. **Finance** Luis deposited \$500 into his bank account. He now has \$4732. Write and solve an equation to find how much was in his account before the deposit. Show that your answer is reasonable.
50. **ERROR ANALYSIS** Below are two possible solutions to $x + 12.5 = 21.6$. Which is incorrect? Explain the error.

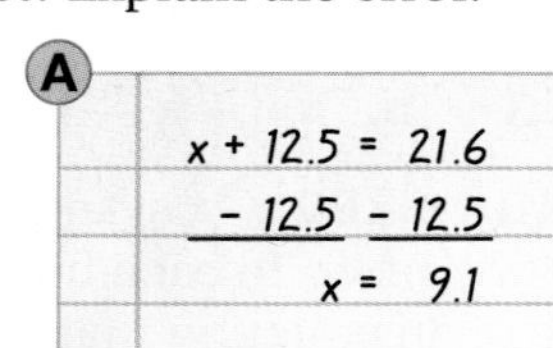


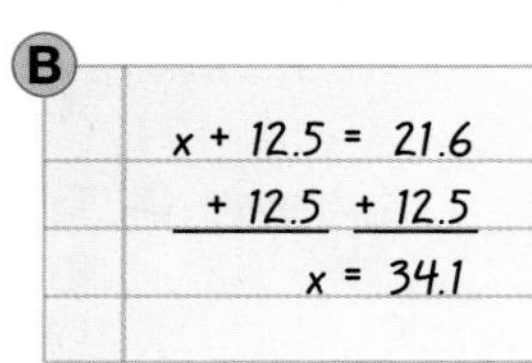

**Write an equation to represent each relationship. Then solve the equation.**

**51.** Ten less than a number is equal to 12.

**52.** A number decreased by 13 is equal to 7.

**53.** Eight more than a number is 16.

**54.** A number minus 3 is –8.

**55.** The sum of 5 and a number is 6.

**56.** Two less than a number is –5.

**57.** The difference of a number and 4 is 9.

**LINK**

**Geology**

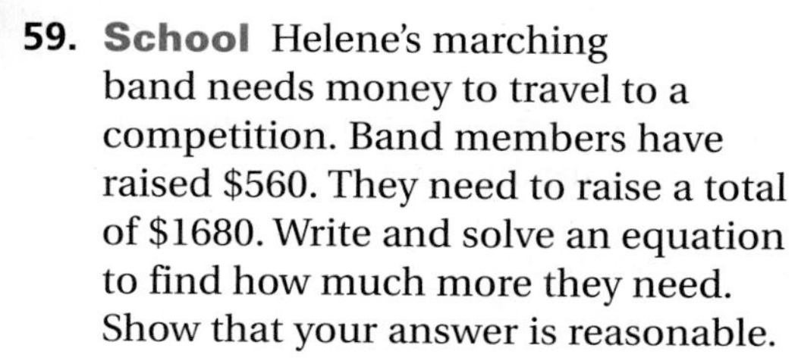

The ocean depths are home to many odd-looking creatures. The anglerfish pictured above, known as the common black devil, may appear menacing but reaches a maximum length of only about 5 inches.

**58.** **Geology** The sum of the Atlantic Ocean's average depth (in feet) and its greatest depth is 43,126. Use the information in the graph to write and solve an equation to find the average depth of the Atlantic Ocean. Show that your answer is reasonable.

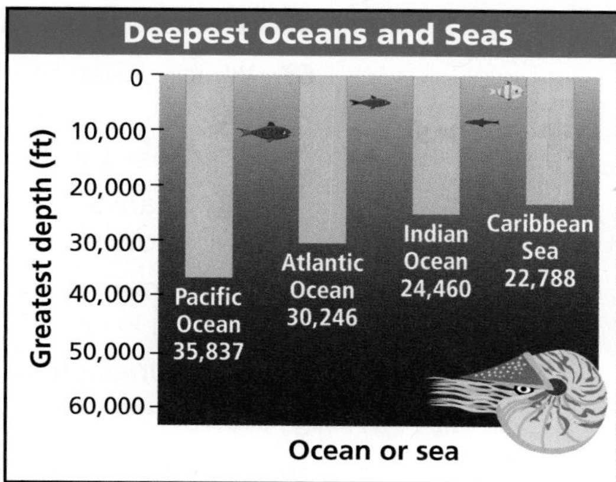


**59.** **School** Helene's marching band needs money to travel to a competition. Band members have raised \$560. They need to raise a total of \$1680. Write and solve an equation to find how much more they need. Show that your answer is reasonable.

**60.** **Economics** When you receive a loan to make a purchase, you often must make a down payment in cash. The amount of the loan is the purchase cost minus the down payment. Riva made a down payment of \$1500 on a used car. She received a loan of \$2600. Write and solve an equation to find the cost of the car. Show that your answer is reasonable.

**Geometry** **The angles in each pair are complementary. Write and solve an equation to find each value of $x$. (*Hint:* The measures of complementary angles add to 90°.)**

**61.**

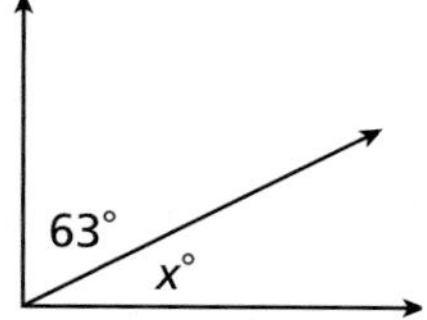


**62.**

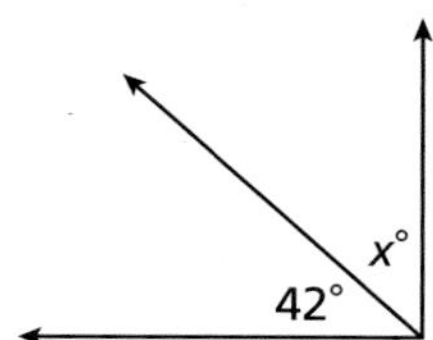


**63.**

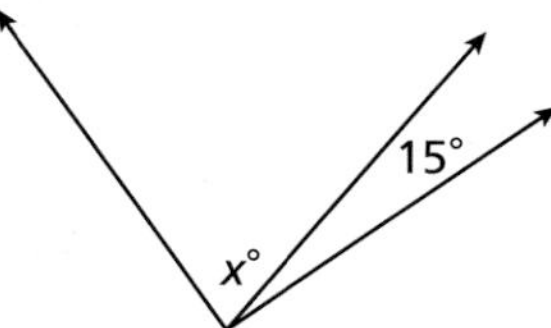


**MULTI-STEP TEST PREP**

**64.** This problem will prepare you for the Multi-Step Test Prep on page 112.

*Rates* are often used to describe how quickly something is moving or changing.

**a.** A wildfire spreads at a rate of 1000 acres per day. How many acres will the fire cover in 2 days? Show that your answer is reasonable.

**b.** How many acres will the fire cover in 5 days? Explain how you found your answer.

**c.** Another wildfire spread for 7 days and covered a total of 780 square miles. How can you estimate the number of square miles the fire covered per day?

65. **Statistics** The range of a set of scores is 28, and the lowest score is 47. Write and solve an equation to find the highest score. (*Hint:* In a data set, the range is the difference between the highest and the lowest values.) Show that your answer is reasonable.

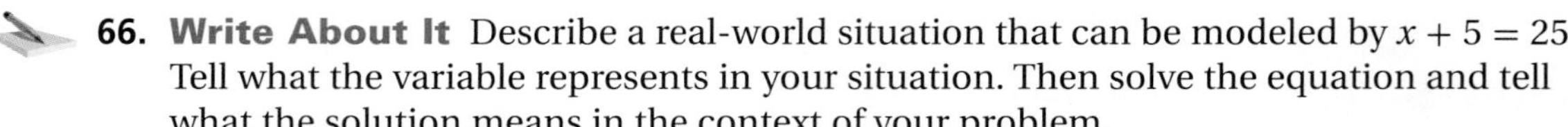

66. **Write About It** Describe a real-world situation that can be modeled by $x + 5 = 25$. Tell what the variable represents in your situation. Then solve the equation and tell what the solution means in the context of your problem.

67. **Critical Thinking** Without solving, tell whether the solution of $-3 + z = 10$ will be greater than 10 or less than 10. Explain.

MA.A.4.5

68. Which situation is best represented by $x - 32 = 8$?

(A) Logan withdrew $32 from her bank account. After her withdrawal, her balance was $8. How much was originally in her account?

(B) Daniel has 32 baseball cards. Joseph has 8 fewer baseball cards than Daniel. How many baseball cards does Joseph have?

(C) Room A contains 32 desks. Room B has 8 fewer desks. How many desks are in Room B?

(D) Janelle bought a bag of 32 craft sticks for a project. She used 8 craft sticks. How many craft sticks does she have left?

69. For which equation is $a = 8$ a solution?

(F) $15 - a = 10$ (G) $10 + a = 23$ (H) $a - 18 = 26$ (J) $a + 8 = 16$

70. **Short Response** Julianna used a gift card to pay for an $18 haircut. The remaining balance on the card was $22.

**a.** Write an equation that can be used to determine the original value of the card.

**b.** Solve your equation to find the original value of the card.

## CHALLENGE AND EXTEND

**Solve each equation. Check your answer.**

71. $\left(3\frac{1}{5}\right) + b = \frac{4}{5}$ 72. $x - \frac{7}{4} = \frac{2}{3}$ 73. $x + \frac{7}{4} = \frac{2}{3}$ 74. $x - \frac{4}{9} = \frac{4}{9}$

75. If $p - 4 = 2$, find the value of $5p - 20$. 76. If $t + 6 = 21$, find the value of $-2t$.

77. If $x + 3 = 15$, find the value of $18 + 6x$. 78. If $2 + n = -11$, find the value of $6n$.

## SPIRAL REVIEW

**Multiply or divide.** *(Lesson 1-3)*

79. $-63 \div (-7)$ 80. $\frac{3}{7} \div \left(-\frac{4}{7}\right)$ 81. $(-12)(-6)$

**Give the side length of a square with the given area.** *(Lesson 1-5)*

82. $225\ \text{m}^2$ 83. $36\ \text{ft}^2$ 84. $100\ \text{cm}^2$

**Simplify each expression.** *(Lesson 1-6)*

85. $8[-5 - (3 + 2)]$ 86. $1 - [4^2 - (12 - 15)^2]$ 87. $\frac{-12 + (-6)}{6}$

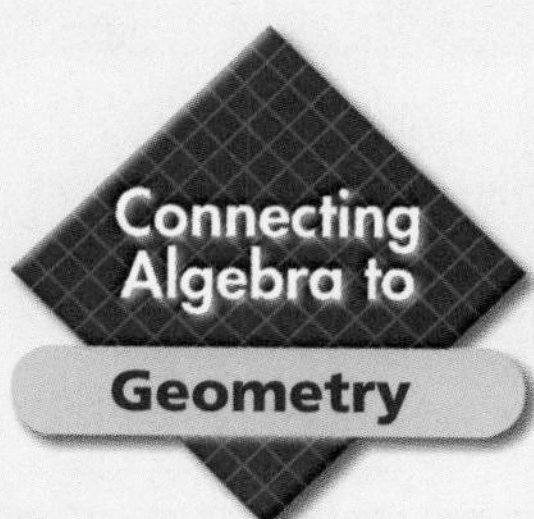


# Area of Composite Figures

See Skills Bank page S61

Review the area formulas for squares, rectangles, and triangles in the table below.

**MA.A.4.5** Use … symbols to solve linear equations. *Also* **MA.G.2.2**

| Squares | Rectangles | Triangles |
|---|---|---|
| $s$ | $\ell$, $w$ | $h$, $b$ |
| $A = s^2$ | $A = \ell w$ | $A = \frac{1}{2}bh$ |

A *composite figure* is a figure that is composed of basic shapes. You can divide composite figures into combinations of squares, rectangles, and triangles to find their areas.

## Example

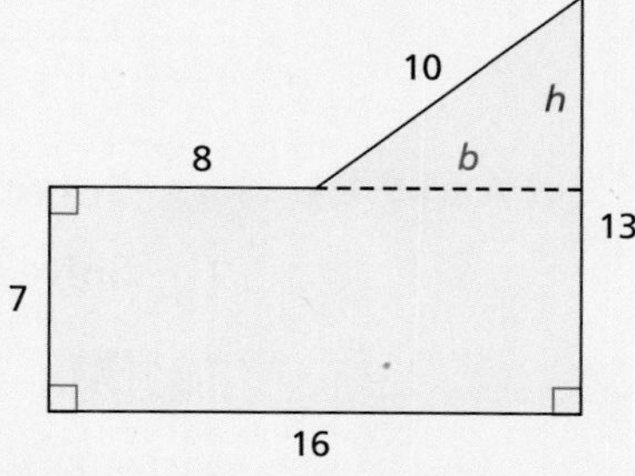


**Find the area of the figure shown.**

Divide the figure into a rectangle and a right triangle. Notice that you do not know the base or the height of the triangle. Use $b$ and $h$ to represent these lengths.

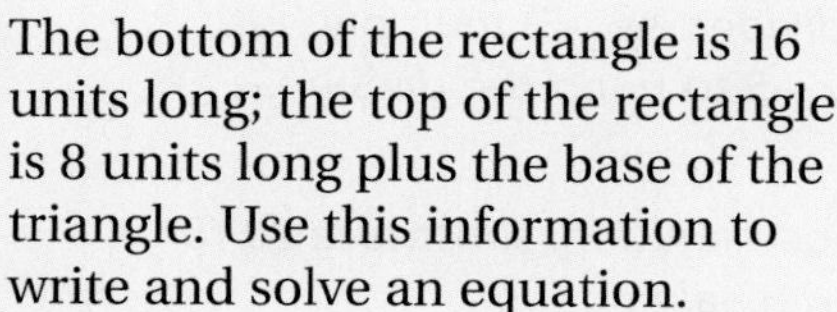

The bottom of the rectangle is 16 units long; the top of the rectangle is 8 units long plus the base of the triangle. Use this information to write and solve an equation.

$$\begin{aligned} b + 8 &= 16 \\ -8 &\quad -8 \\ b &= 8 \end{aligned}$$

The right side of the figure is 13 units long: 7 units from the rectangle plus the height of the triangle. Use this information to write and solve an equation.

$$\begin{aligned} h + 7 &= 13 \\ -7 &\quad -7 \\ h &= 6 \end{aligned}$$

The area of the figure is the sum of the areas of the rectangle and the triangle.

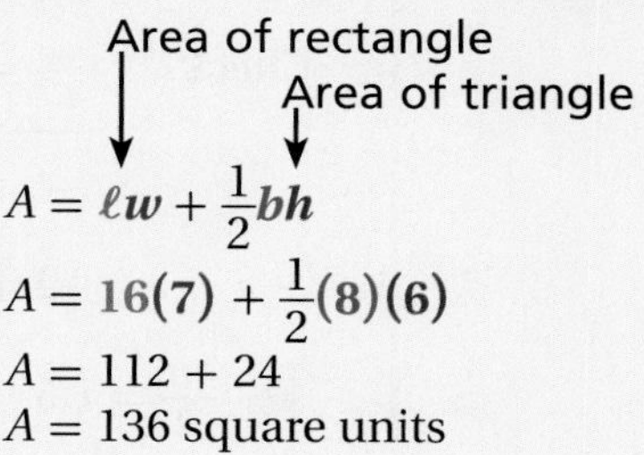


$A = \ell w + \frac{1}{2}bh$

$A = 16(7) + \frac{1}{2}(8)(6)$

$A = 112 + 24$

$A = 136$ square units

## Try This

**Find the area of each composite figure.**

**1.**

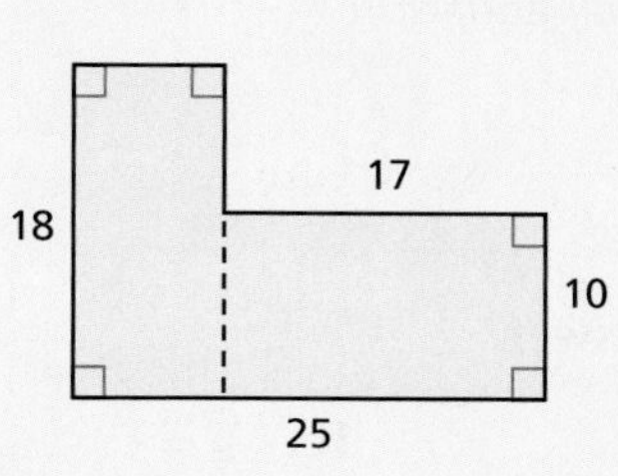


**2.**

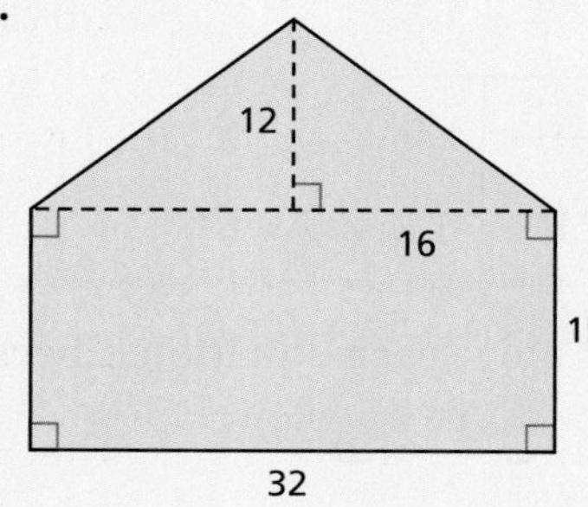


**3.**

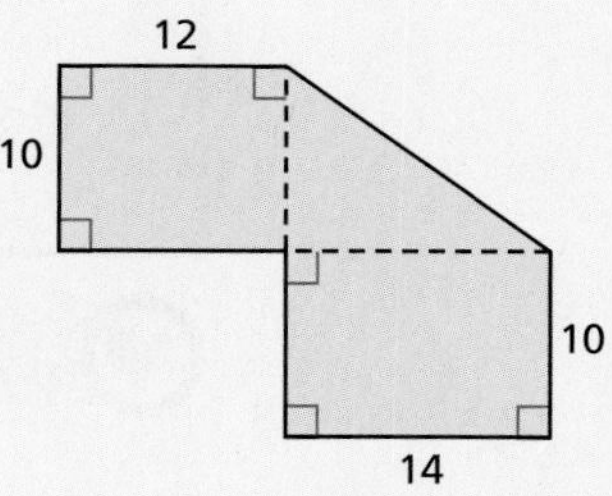

# 2-2 Solving Equations by Multiplying or Dividing

**MA.A.4.5** Use ... symbols to solve linear equations.

***Objective***
Solve one-step equations in one variable by using multiplication or division.

**Who uses this?**
Pilots can make quick calculations by solving one-step equations. (See Example 4.)

Solving an equation that contains multiplication or division is similar to solving an equation that contains addition or subtraction. Use inverse operations to undo the operations on the variable.

Remember that an equation is like a balanced scale. To keep the balance, whatever you do on one side of the equation, you must also do on the other side.

| Inverse Operations | |
|---|---|
| **Operation** | **Inverse Operation** |
| Multiplication | Division |
| Division | Multiplication |

## EXAMPLE 1 Solving Equations by Using Multiplication

**Solve each equation. Check your answer.**

**A** $-4 = \frac{k}{-5}$

$$(-5)(-4) = (-5)\left(\frac{k}{-5}\right)$$ *Since k is divided by −5, multiply both sides by −5 to undo the division.*

$$20 = k$$

*Check* $-4 = \frac{k}{-5}$ *To check your solution, substitute 20 for k in the original equation.*

$$-4 \;\Big|\; \frac{20}{-5}$$

$$-4 \;\Big|\; -4 \checkmark$$

**B** $\frac{m}{3} = 1.5$

$$(3)\left(\frac{m}{3}\right) = (3)(1.5)$$ *Since m is divided by 3, multiply both sides by 3 to undo the division.*

$$m = 4.5$$

*Check* $\frac{m}{3} = 1.5$ *To check your solution, substitute 1.5 for m in the original equation.*

$$\frac{4.5}{3} \;\Big|\; 1.5$$

$$1.5 \;\Big|\; 1.5 \checkmark$$

**Solve each equation. Check your answer.**

**1a.** $\frac{p}{5} = 10$ **1b.** $-13 = \frac{y}{3}$ **1c.** $\frac{c}{8} = 7$

**EXAMPLE 2** **Solving Equations by Using Division**

**Solve each equation. Check your answers.**

**A** $7x = 56$

$$\frac{7x}{7} = \frac{56}{7}$$
$$x = 8$$

*Since x is multiplied by 7, divide both sides by 7 to undo the multiplication.*

*Check* $7x = 56$

| 7(8) | 56 |
|---|---|
| 56 | 56 ✓ |

*To check your solution, substitute 8 for x in the original equation.*

**B** $13 = -2w$

$$\frac{13}{-2} = \frac{-2w}{-2}$$
$$-6.5 = w$$

*Since w is multiplied by −2, divide both sides by −2 to undo the multiplication.*

*Check* $13 = -2w$

| 13 | −2(−6.5) |
|---|---|
| 13 | 13 ✓ |

*To check your solution, substitute −6.5 for w in the original equation.*

**Solve each equation. Check your answer.**

**2a.** $16 = 4c$ **2b.** $0.5y = -10$ **2c.** $15k = 75$

Remember that dividing is the same as multiplying by the reciprocal. When solving equations, you will sometimes find it easier to multiply by a reciprocal instead of dividing. This is often true when an equation contains fractions.

**EXAMPLE 3** **Solving Equations That Contain Fractions**

**Solve each equation.**

**A** $\frac{5}{9}v = 35$

$$\left(\frac{9}{5}\right)\frac{5}{9}v = \left(\frac{9}{5}\right)35$$
$$v = 63$$

*The reciprocal of $\frac{5}{9}$ is $\frac{9}{5}$. Since v is multiplied by $\frac{5}{9}$, multiply both sides by $\frac{9}{5}$.*

**B** $\frac{5}{2} = \frac{4y}{3}$

$$\frac{5}{2} = \frac{4y}{3}$$
$$\frac{5}{2} = \frac{4}{3}y$$

*$\frac{4y}{3}$ is the same as $\frac{4}{3}y$.*

$$\left(\frac{3}{4}\right)\frac{5}{2} = \left(\frac{3}{4}\right)\frac{4}{3}y$$
$$\frac{15}{8} = y$$

*The reciprocal of $\frac{4}{3}$ is $\frac{3}{4}$. Since y is multiplied by $\frac{4}{3}$, multiply both sides by $\frac{3}{4}$.*

**Solve each equation. Check your answer.**

**3a.** $-\frac{1}{4} = \frac{1}{5}b$ **3b.** $\frac{4j}{6} = \frac{2}{3}$ **3c.** $\frac{1}{6}w = 102$

**EXAMPLE 4** ***Aviation Application***

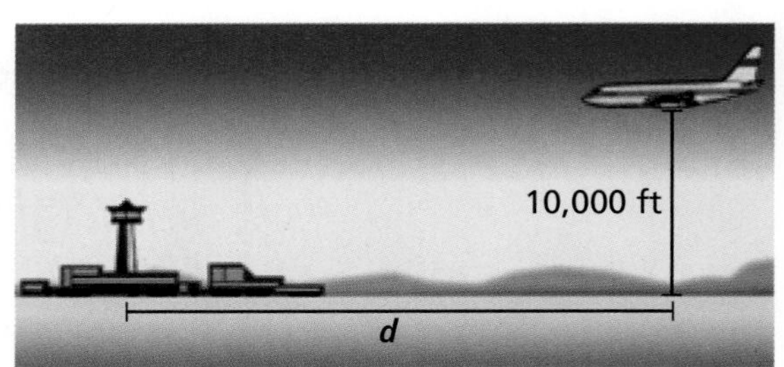


**The distance in miles from the airport that a plane should begin descending, divided by 3, equals the plane's height above the ground in thousands of feet. If a plane is 10,000 feet above the ground, write and solve an equation to find the distance at which the pilot should begin descending.**

**Caution!**

The equation uses the plane's height above the ground in *thousands* of feet. So substitute 10 for *h*, not 10,000.

**Distance** **divided by 3** **equals** **height in thousands of feet.**

$$\frac{d}{3} = h$$ *Write an equation to represent the relationship.*

$$\frac{d}{3} = 10$$ *Substitute 10 for h. Since d is divided by 3, multiply both sides by 3 to undo the division.*

$$(3)\frac{d}{3} = (3)10$$

$$d = 30$$

The pilot should begin descending 30 miles from the airport.

**4.** **What if...?** A plane began descending 45 miles from the airport. Use the equation above to find how high the plane was flying when the descent began.

You have now used four properties of equality to solve equations. These properties are summarized in the box below.

Know it! Note

**Properties of Equality**

| WORDS | NUMBERS | ALGEBRA |
|---|---|---|
| **Addition Property of Equality**<br>You can add the same number to both sides of an equation, and the statement will still be true. | $3 = 3$<br>$3 + 2 = 3 + 2$<br>$5 = 5$ | $a = b$<br>$a + c = b + c$ |
| **Subtraction Property of Equality**<br>You can subtract the same number from both sides of an equation, and the statement will still be true. | $7 = 7$<br>$7 - 5 = 7 - 5$<br>$2 = 2$ | $a = b$<br>$a - c = b - c$ |
| **Multiplication Property of Equality**<br>You can multiply both sides of an equation by the same number, and the statement will still be true. | $6 = 6$<br>$6(3) = 6(3)$<br>$18 = 18$ | $a = b$<br>$ac = bc$ |
| **Division Property of Equality**<br>You can divide both sides of an equation by the same nonzero number, and the statement will still be true. | $8 = 8$<br>$\frac{8}{4} = \frac{8}{4}$<br>$2 = 2$ | $a = b$<br>$(c \neq 0)$<br>$\frac{a}{c} = \frac{b}{c}$ |

## THINK AND DISCUSS

**1.** Tell how the Multiplication and Division Properties of Equality are similar to the Addition and Subtraction Properties of Equality.

**2. GET ORGANIZED** Copy and complete the graphic organizer. In each box, write an example of an equation that can be solved by using the given property, and solve it.

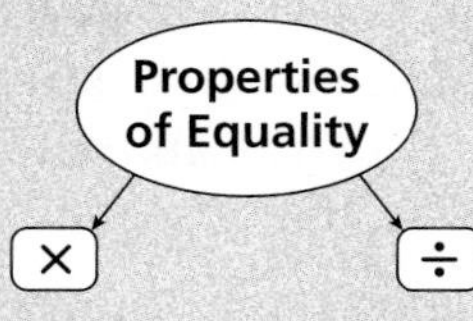


# 2-2 Exercises

MA.A.4.5

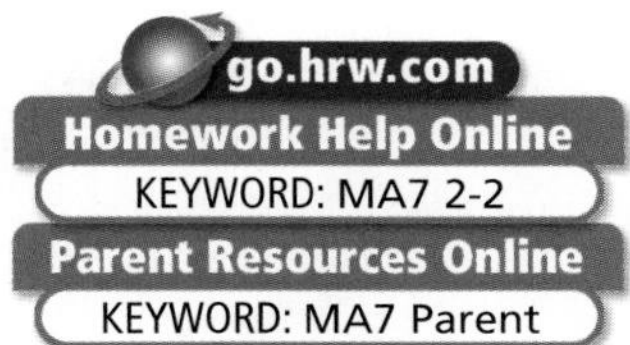


## GUIDED PRACTICE

SEE EXAMPLE 1 p. 84

**Solve each equation. Check your answer.**

**1.** $\frac{k}{4} = 8$ **2.** $\frac{z}{3} = -9$ **3.** $-2 = \frac{w}{-7}$

**4.** $6 = \frac{t}{-5}$ **5.** $\frac{g}{1.9} = 10$ **6.** $2.4 = \frac{b}{5}$

SEE EXAMPLE 2 p. 85

**7.** $4x = 28$ **8.** $-64 = 8c$ **9.** $-9j = -45$

**10.** $84 = -12a$ **11.** $4m = 10$ **12.** $2.8 = -2h$

SEE EXAMPLE 3 p. 85

**13.** $\frac{1}{2}d = 7$ **14.** $15 = \frac{5}{6}f$ **15.** $\frac{2}{3}s = -6$

**16.** $9 = -\frac{3}{8}r$ **17.** $\frac{1}{10} = \frac{4}{5}y$ **18.** $\frac{1}{4}v = -\frac{3}{4}$

SEE EXAMPLE 4 p. 86

**19. Recreation** The Baseball Birthday Batter Package at a minor league ballpark costs \$192. The package includes tickets, drinks, and cake for a group of 16 children. Write and solve an equation to find the cost per child.

**20. Nutrition** An orange contains about 80 milligrams of vitamin C, which is 10 times as much as an apple contains. Write and solve an equation to find the amount of vitamin C in an apple.

## PRACTICE AND PROBLEM SOLVING

**Solve each equation. Check your answer.**

**21.** $\frac{x}{2} = 12$ **22.** $-40 = \frac{b}{5}$ **23.** $-\frac{j}{6} = 6$ **24.** $-\frac{n}{3} = -4$

**25.** $-\frac{q}{5} = 30$ **26.** $1.6 = \frac{d}{3}$ **27.** $\frac{v}{10} = 5.5$ **28.** $\frac{h}{8.1} = -4$

**29.** $5t = -15$ **30.** $49 = 7c$ **31.** $-12 = -12u$ **32.** $-7m = 63$

**33.** $-52 = -4c$ **34.** $11 = -2z$ **35.** $5f = 1.5$ **36.** $-8.4 = -4n$

| Independent Practice | |
|---|---|
| For Exercises | See Example |
| 21–28 | 1 |
| 29–36 | 2 |
| 37–44 | 3 |
| 45 | 4 |

**Extra Practice**
Skills Practice p. S6
Application Practice p. S29

**Solve each equation. Check your answer.**

37. $\frac{5}{2}k = 5$
38. $-9 = \frac{3}{4}d$
39. $-\frac{5}{8}b = 10$
40. $-\frac{4}{5}g = -12$
41. $\frac{4}{7}t = -2$
42. $-\frac{4}{5}p = \frac{2}{3}$
43. $\frac{2}{3} = -\frac{1}{3}q$
44. $-\frac{5}{8} = -\frac{3}{4}a$

45. **Finance** After taxes, Alexandra's take-home pay is $\frac{7}{10}$ of her salary before taxes. Write and solve an equation to find Alexandra's salary before taxes for the pay period that resulted in \$392 of take-home pay.

46. **Earth Science** Your weight on the Moon is about $\frac{1}{6}$ of your weight on Earth. Write and solve an equation to show how much a person weighs on Earth if he weighs 16 pounds on the Moon. How could you check that your answer is reasonable?

47. **ERROR ANALYSIS** For the equation $\frac{x}{3} = 15$, a student found the value of $x$ to be 5. Explain the error. What is the correct answer?

**Geometry The perimeter of a square is given. Write and solve an equation to find the length of each side of the square.**

48. $P = 36$ in.
49. $P = 84$ in.
50. $P = 100$ yd
51. $P = 16.4$ cm

**LINK**

**Statistics**

American Robert P. Wadlow (1918–1940) holds the record for world's tallest man—8 ft 11.1 in. He also holds world records for the largest feet and hands.

*Source: Guinness World Records 2005*

**Write an equation to represent each relationship. Then solve the equation.**

52. Five times a number is 45.
53. A number multiplied by negative 3 is 12.
54. A number divided by 4 is equal to 10.
55. The quotient of a number and 3 is negative 8.

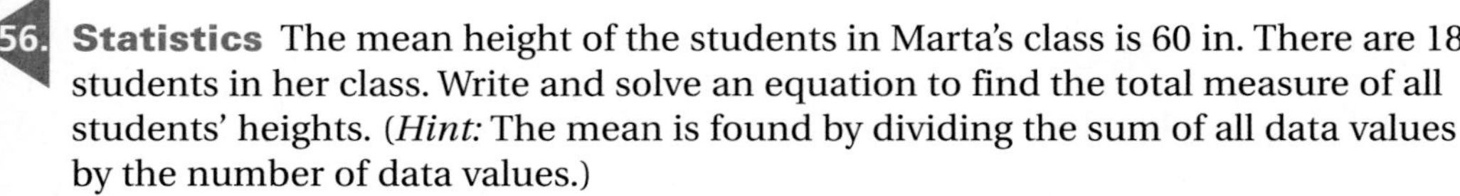

56. **Statistics** The mean height of the students in Marta's class is 60 in. There are 18 students in her class. Write and solve an equation to find the total measure of all students' heights. (*Hint:* The mean is found by dividing the sum of all data values by the number of data values.)

57. **Finance** Lisa earned \$6.25 per hour at her after-school job. Each week she earned \$50. Write and solve an equation to show how many hours she worked each week.

58. **Critical Thinking** Will the solution of $\frac{x}{2.1} = 4$ be greater than 4 or less than 4? Explain.

59. **Consumer Economics** Dion's long-distance phone bill was \$13.80. His long-distance calls cost \$0.05 per minute. Write and solve an equation to find the number of minutes he was charged for. Show that your answer is reasonable.

60. **Nutrition** An 8 oz cup of coffee has about 184 mg of caffeine. This is 5 times as much caffeine as in a 12 oz soft drink. Write and solve an equation to find about how much caffeine is in a 12 oz caffeinated soft drink. Round your answer to the nearest whole number. Show that your answer is reasonable.

**Use the equation $8y = 4x$ to find $y$ for each value of $x$.**

| | $x$ | $4x$ | $8y = 4x$ | $y$ |
|---|---|---|---|---|
| 61. | −4 | $4(-4) = -16$ | $8y = -16$ | |
| 62. | −2 | | | |
| 63. | 0 | | | |
| 64. | 2 | | | |

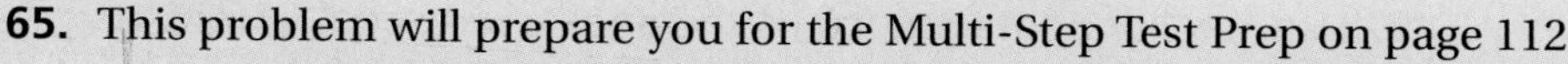

**MULTI-STEP TEST PREP**

65. This problem will prepare you for the Multi-Step Test Prep on page 112.

a. The formula for the mean of a data set is mean $= \frac{\text{sum of data values}}{\text{number of data values}}$. One summer, there were 1926 wildfires in Arizona. Which value does this number represent in the formula?

b. The mean number of acres burned by each wildfire was 96.21. Which value does this number represent in the formula?

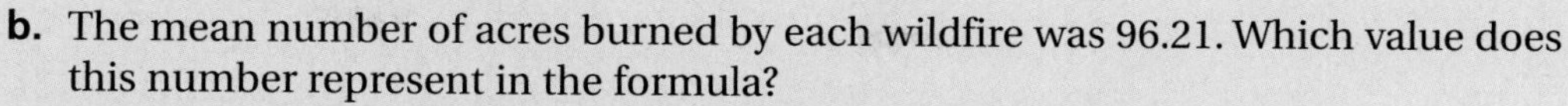

c. Use the formula and information given to find how many acres were burned by wildfires in Arizona that summer. Round your answer to the nearest acre. Show that your answer is reasonable.

**Solve each equation. Check your answer.**

66. $\frac{m}{6} = 1$ 67. $4x = 28$ 68. $1.2h = 14.4$ 69. $\frac{1}{5}x = 121$

70. $2w = 26$ 71. $4b = \frac{3}{4}$ 72. $5y = 11$ 73. $\frac{n}{1.9} = 3$

**Biology** **Use the table for Exercises 74 and 75.**

| Average Weight | | | |
|---|---|---|---|
| Animal | At Birth (g) | Adult Female (g) | Adult Male (g) |
| Hamster | 2 | 130 | 110 |
| Guinea pig | 85 | 800 | 1050 |
| Rat | 5 | 275 | 480 |

74. The mean weight of an adult male rat is 16 times the mean weight of an adult male mouse. Write and solve an equation to find the mean weight of an adult male mouse. Show that your answer is reasonable.

75. On average, a hamster at birth weighs $\frac{2}{3}$ the weight of a gerbil at birth. Write and solve an equation to find the average weight of a gerbil at birth. Show that your answer is reasonable.

76. **Write About It** Describe a real-world situation that can be modeled by $3x = 42$. Solve the equation and tell what the solution means in the context of your problem.

**TEST PREP**

NC MA.A.4.5

77. Which situation does NOT represent the equation $\frac{d}{2} = 10$?

(A) Leo bought a box of pencils. He gave half of them to his brother. They each got 10 pencils. How many pencils were in the box Leo bought?

(B) Kasey evenly divided her money from baby-sitting into two bank accounts. She put $10 in each account. How much did Kasey earn?

(C) Gilbert cut a piece of ribbon into 2-inch strips. When he was done, he had ten 2-inch strips. How long was the ribbon to start?

(D) Mattie had 2 more CDs than her sister Leona. If Leona had 10 CDs, how many CDs did Mattie have?

78. Which equation below shows a correct first step for solving $3x = -12$?

(F) $3x + 3 = -12 + 3$ (H) $3(3x) = 3(-12)$

(G) $3x - 3 = -12 - 3$ (J) $\frac{3x}{3} = \frac{-12}{3}$

79. In a regular pentagon, all of the angles are equal in measure. The sum of the angle measures is 540°. Which of the following equations could be used to find the measure of each angle?

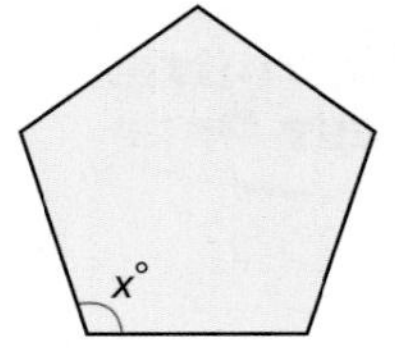


(A) $\frac{x}{540} = 5$ (C) $540x = 5$

(B) $5x = 540$ (D) $\frac{x}{5} = 540$

80. For which equation is $m = 10$ a solution?

(F) $5 = 2m$ (G) $5m = 2$ (H) $\frac{m}{2} = 5$ (J) $\frac{m}{10} = 2$

81. **Short Response** Luisa bought 6 cans of cat food that each cost the same amount. She spent a total of $4.80.

a. Write an equation to determine the cost of one can of cat food. Tell what each part of your equation represents.

b. Solve your equation to find the cost of one can of cat food. Show each step.

## CHALLENGE AND EXTEND

**Solve each equation.**

82. $\left(3\frac{1}{5}\right)b = \frac{4}{5}$ 83. $\left(1\frac{1}{3}\right)x = 2\frac{2}{3}$ 84. $\left(5\frac{4}{5}\right)x = -52\frac{1}{5}$

85. $\left(-2\frac{9}{10}\right)k = -26\frac{1}{10}$ 86. $\left(1\frac{2}{3}\right)w = 15\frac{1}{3}$ 87. $\left(2\frac{1}{4}\right)d = 4\frac{1}{2}$

**Find each indicated value.**

88. If $2p = 4$, find the value of $6p + 10$. 89. If $6t = 24$, find the value of $-5t$.

90. If $3x = 15$, find the value of $12 - 4x$. 91. If $\frac{n}{2} = -11$, find the value of $6n$.

92. To isolate $x$ in $ax = b$, what should you divide both sides by?

93. To isolate $x$ in $\frac{x}{a} = b$, what operation should you perform on both sides of the equation?

94. **Travel** The formula $d = rt$ gives the distance $d$ that is traveled at a rate $r$ in time $t$.

a. If $d = 400$ and $r = 25$, what is the value of $t$?

b. If $d = 400$ and $r = 50$, what is the value of $t$?

c. **What if...?** How did $t$ change when $r$ increased from 25 to 50?

d. **What if...?** If $r$ is doubled while $d$ remains the same, what is the effect on $t$?

## SPIRAL REVIEW

**Find each square root.** *(Lesson 1-5)*

95. $\sqrt{144}$ 96. $\sqrt{196}$ 97. $\sqrt{625}$ 98. $-\sqrt{9}$

**Write and solve an equation that could be used to answer each question.** *(Lesson 2-1)*

99. Lisa's age plus Sean's age is 17. Sean is 11 years old. How old is Lisa?

100. The length of a rectangle is 6 feet more than the width of the rectangle. The length is 32 feet. What is the width of the rectangle?

**Solve each equation.** *(Lesson 2-1)*

101. $2 = a - 4$ 102. $x - 12 = -3$ 103. $z - 5 = 11$ 104. $-4 = x + 5$

# Solve Equations by Graphing

You can use graphs to solve equations. As you complete this activity, you will learn some of the connections between a graph and an equation.

**MA.A.4.5** Use graphs…to solve linear equations.

*Use with Lesson 2-3*

## Activity

**Solve $3x - 4 = 5$.**

1. Press [Y=]. In $Y_1$, enter the left side of the equation, $3x - 4$.

   [Y=] 3 [X,T,θ,n] [–] 4 [ENTER]

2. Press [GRAPH]. Press [TRACE]. The display will show the $x$- and $y$-values of a point on the line. Press the right arrow key several times. Notice that the $x$- and $y$-values change.

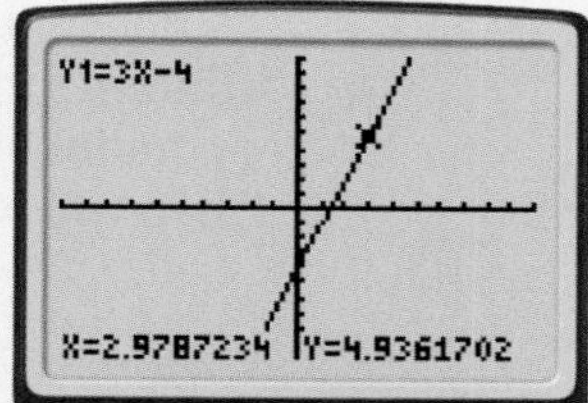


3. Continue to trace until the $y$-value is close to 5, the right side of the equation. The corresponding $x$-value, 2.9787…, is an approximation of the solution. The solution is about 3.

4. While still in trace mode, to check, press **3** [ENTER]. The display will show the value of the function when $x = 3$. When $x = 3$, $y = 5$. So 3 is the solution. You can also check this solution by substituting 3 for $x$ in the equation:

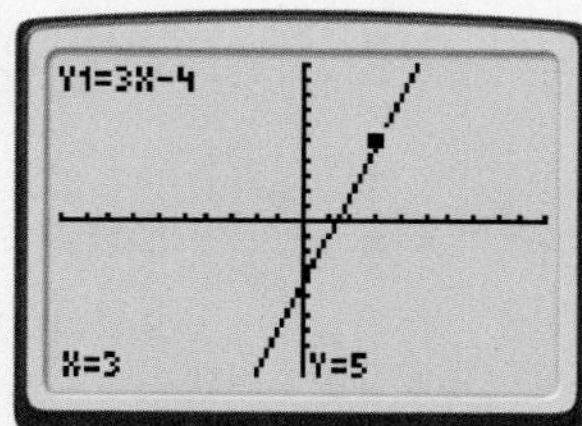


*Check*

| $3x - 4$ | $= 5$ |
|---|---|
| $3(3) - 4$ | $5$ |
| $9 - 4$ | $5$ |
| $5$ | $5$ ✓ |

## Try This

1. Solve $3x - 4 = 2$, $3x - 4 = 17$, and $3x - 4 = -7$ by graphing.
2. Trace to any point on the line. What do the $x$- and $y$-values mean in terms of the equation?
3. What do you think the line in the graph represents?
4. Describe a procedure for finding the solution of $3x - 4 = y$ for any value of $y$.
5. Solve $\frac{1}{2}x - 7 = -4$, $\frac{1}{2}x - 7 = 0$, and $\frac{1}{2}x - 7 = 2$ by graphing.

# 2-3 Solving Two-Step and Multi-Step Equations

**MA.A.4.5** Use … symbols to solve linear equations.

***Objective***
Solve equations in one variable that contain more than one operation.

**Why learn this?**
Equations containing more than one operation can model real-world situations, such as the cost of a music club membership.

Alex belongs to a music club. In this club, students can buy a student discount card for \$19.95. This card allows them to buy CDs for \$3.95 each. After one year, Alex has spent \$63.40.

To find the number of CDs $c$ that Alex bought, you can solve an equation.

Cost of discount card

Cost per CD → $3.95c + 19.95 = 63.40$ ← Total cost

Notice that this equation contains multiplication and addition. Equations that contain more than one operation require more than one step to solve. Identify the operations in the equation and the order in which they are applied to the variable. Then use inverse operations and work backward to undo them one at a time.

$$3.95c + 19.95 = 63.40$$

**Operations in the Equation**

1. First $c$ is **multiplied** by 3.95.
2. Then 19.95 is **added**.

**To Solve**

1. **Subtract** 19.95 from both sides of the equation.
2. Then **divide** both sides by 3.95.

## EXAMPLE 1 Solving Two-Step Equations

**Solve $10 = 6 - 2x$. Check your answer.**

$10 = 6 - 2x$ — *First x is multiplied by −2. Then 6 is added.*

$\underline{-6}\quad\underline{-6}$ — *Work backward: Subtract 6 from both sides.*

$4 = -2x$ — *Since x is multiplied by −2, divide both sides by −2 to undo the multiplication.*

$\frac{4}{-2} = \frac{-2x}{-2}$

$-2 = 1x$

$-2 = x$

*Check* $10 = 6 - 2x$

| | |
|---|---|
| 10 | $6 - 2(-2)$ |
| 10 | $6 - (-4)$ |
| 10 | 10 ✓ |

**Solve each equation. Check your answer.**

**1a.** $-4 + 7x = 3$ **1b.** $1.5 = 1.2y - 5.7$ **1c.** $\frac{n}{7} + 2 = 2$

## EXAMPLE 2 Solving Two-Step Equations That Contain Fractions

**Solve $\frac{q}{15} - \frac{1}{5} = \frac{3}{5}$.**

**Method 1** Use fraction operations.

$$\frac{q}{15} - \frac{1}{5} = \frac{3}{5}$$

*Since $\frac{1}{5}$ is subtracted from $\frac{q}{15}$, add $\frac{1}{5}$ to both sides to undo the subtraction.*

$$\underline{\quad +\frac{1}{5} \quad} \quad \underline{+\frac{1}{5}}$$

$$\frac{q}{15} = \frac{4}{5}$$

*Since q is divided by 15, multiply both sides by 15 to undo the division.*

$$15\left(\frac{q}{15}\right) = 15\left(\frac{4}{5}\right)$$

$$q = \frac{15 \cdot 4}{5}$$

*Simplify.*

$$q = \frac{60}{5}$$

$$q = 12$$

**Method 2** Multiply by the least common denominator (LCD) to clear the fractions.

$$\frac{q}{15} - \frac{1}{5} = \frac{3}{5}$$

$$15\left(\frac{q}{15} - \frac{1}{5}\right) = 15\left(\frac{3}{5}\right)$$

*Multiply both sides by 15, the LCD of the fractions.*

$$15\left(\frac{q}{15}\right) - 15\left(\frac{1}{5}\right) = 15\left(\frac{3}{5}\right)$$

*Distribute 15 on the left side.*

$$q - 3 = 9$$

*Simplify.*

$$\underline{+3} \quad \underline{+3}$$

*Since 3 is subtracted from q, add 3 to both sides to undo the subtraction.*

$$q = 12$$

**Solve each equation. Check your answer.**

**2a.** $\frac{2x}{5} - \frac{1}{2} = 5$ **2b.** $\frac{3}{4}u + \frac{1}{2} = \frac{7}{8}$ **2c.** $\frac{1}{5}n - \frac{1}{3} = \frac{8}{3}$

Equations that are more complicated may have to be simplified before they can be solved. You may have to use the Distributive Property or combine like terms before you begin using inverse operations.

## EXAMPLE 3 Simplifying Before Solving Equations

**Solve each equation.**

**A** $6x + 3 - 8x = 13$

$$6x + 3 - 8x = 13$$

$$6x - 8x + 3 = 13$$

*Use the Commutative Property of Addition.*

$$-2x + 3 = 13$$

*Combine like terms.*

$$\underline{\quad -3} \quad \underline{-3}$$

*Since 3 is added to −2x, subtract 3 from both sides to undo the addition.*

$$-2x = 10$$

$$\frac{-2x}{-2} = \frac{10}{-2}$$

*Since x is multiplied by −2, divide both sides by −2 to undo the multiplication.*

$$x = -5$$

**Helpful Hint**

You can think of an opposite sign as a coefficient of $-1$.
$-(x + 2) = -1(x + 2)$ and $-x = -1x$.

**Solve each equation.**

**B** $9 = 6 - (x + 2)$

$9 = 6 + (-1)(x + 2)$ *Write subtraction as addition of the opposite.*

$9 = 6 + (-1)(x) + (-1)(2)$ *Distribute $-1$ on the right side.*

$9 = 6 - x - 2$ *Simplify.*

$9 = 6 - 2 - x$ *Use the Commutative Property of Addition.*

$9 = 4 - x$ *Combine like terms.*

$\underline{-4} \quad \underline{-4}$ *Since 4 is added to $-x$, subtract 4 from both sides to undo the addition.*

$5 = -x$

$\frac{5}{-1} = \frac{-x}{-1}$ *Since $x$ is multiplied by $-1$, divide both sides by $-1$ to undo the multiplication.*

$-5 = x$

**Solve each equation. Check your answer.**

**3a.** $2a + 3 - 8a = 8$

**3b.** $-2(3 - d) = 4$

**3c.** $4(x - 2) + 2x = 40$

## EXAMPLE 4

### *Problem-Solving Application*

**Alex belongs to a music club. In this club, students can buy a student discount card for \$19.95. This card allows them to buy CDs for \$3.95 each. After one year, Alex has spent \$63.40. Write and solve an equation to find how many CDs Alex bought during the year.**

**1 Understand the Problem**

The **answer** will be the number of CDs that Alex bought during the year.

**List the important information:**

- Alex paid \$19.95 for a student discount card.
- Alex pays \$3.95 for each CD purchased.
- After one year, Alex has spent \$63.40.

**2 Make a Plan**

Let $c$ represent the number of CDs that Alex purchased. That means Alex has spent \$3.95$c$. However, Alex must also add the amount spent on the card. Write an equation to represent this situation.

| total cost | = | cost of compact discs | + | cost of discount card |
|---|---|---|---|---|
| 63.40 | = | $3.95c$ | + | 19.95 |

### Solve

$$63.40 = 3.95c + 19.95$$
$$\underline{-19.95 \qquad\qquad -19.95}$$
$$43.45 = 3.95c$$
$$\frac{43.45}{3.95} = \frac{3.95c}{3.95}$$
$$11 = c$$

*Since 19.95 is added to 3.95c, subtract 19.95 from both sides to undo the addition.*

*Since c is multiplied by 3.95, divide both sides by 3.95 to undo the multiplication.*

Alex bought 11 CDs during the year.

### Look Back

Check that the answer is reasonable. The cost per CD is about \$4, so if Alex bought 11 CDs, this amount is about $11(4) = \$44$.

Add the cost of the discount card, which is about \$20: $44 + 20 = 64$. So the total cost was about \$64, which is close to the amount given in the problem, \$63.40.

**4.** Sara paid \$15.95 to become a member at a gym. She then paid a monthly membership fee. Her total cost for 12 months was \$735.95. How much was the monthly fee?

## EXAMPLE 5 Solving Equations to Find an Indicated Value

**If $3a + 12 = 30$, find the value of $a + 4$.**

**Step 1** Find the value of $a$.

$$3a + 12 = 30$$
$$\underline{-12 \quad -12}$$
$$3a = 18$$
$$\frac{3a}{3} = \frac{18}{3}$$
$$a = 6$$

*Since 12 is added to 3a, subtract 12 from both sides to undo the addition.*

*Since a is multiplied by 3, divide both sides by 3 to undo the multiplication.*

**Step 2** Find the value of $a + 4$.

$a + 4$

$6 + 4$ — *To find the value of a + 4, substitute 6 for a.*

$10$ — *Simplify.*

**5.** If $2x + 4 = -24$, find the value of $3x$.

## THINK AND DISCUSS

**1.** Explain the steps you would follow to solve $2x + 1 = 7$. How is this procedure different from the one you would follow to solve $2x - 1 = 7$?

Know it! Note

**2. GET ORGANIZED** Copy and complete the graphic organizer. In each box, write and solve a multi-step equation. Use addition, subtraction, multiplication, and division at least one time each.

| Solving Multi-Step Equations | |
|---|---|
| | |

# 2-3 Exercises

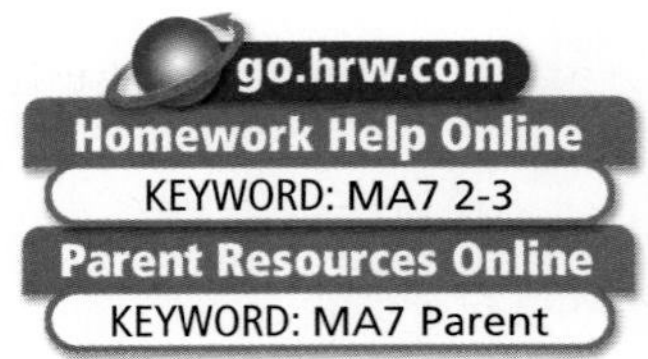


## GUIDED PRACTICE

SEE EXAMPLE 1 p. 92

**Solve each equation. Check your answer.**

1. $4a + 3 = 11$
2. $8 = 3r - 1$
3. $42 = -2d + 6$
4. $x + 0.3 = 3.3$
5. $15y + 31 = 61$
6. $9 - c = -13$

SEE EXAMPLE 2 p. 93

7. $\frac{x}{6} + 4 = 15$
8. $\frac{1}{3}y + \frac{1}{4} = \frac{5}{12}$
9. $\frac{2}{7}j - \frac{1}{7} = \frac{3}{14}$
10. $15 = \frac{a}{3} - 2$
11. $4 - \frac{m}{2} = 10$
12. $\frac{x}{8} - \frac{1}{2} = 6$

SEE EXAMPLE 3 p. 93

13. $28 = 8x + 12 - 7x$
14. $2y - 7 + 5y = 0$
15. $2.4 = 3(m + 4)$
16. $3(x - 4) = 48$
17. $4t + 7 - t = 19$
18. $5(1 - 2w) + 8w = 15$

SEE EXAMPLE 4 p. 94

19. **Transportation** Paul bought a student discount card for the bus. The card cost $7 and allows him to buy daily bus passes for $1.50. After one month, Paul spent $29.50. How many daily bus passes did Paul buy?

SEE EXAMPLE 5 p. 95

20. If $3x - 13 = 8$, find the value of $x - 4$.
21. If $3(x + 1) = 7$, find the value of $3x$.
22. If $-3(y - 1) = 9$, find the value of $\frac{1}{2}y$.
23. If $4 - 7x = 39$, find the value of $x + 1$.

## PRACTICE AND PROBLEM SOLVING

**Independent Practice**

| For Exercises | See Example |
|---|---|
| 24–29 | 1 |
| 30–35 | 2 |
| 36–41 | 3 |
| 42 | 4 |
| 43–46 | 5 |

**Extra Practice**

Skills Practice p. S6
Application Practice p. S29

**Solve each equation. Check your answer.**

24. $5 = 2g + 1$
25. $6h - 7 = 17$
26. $0.6v + 2.1 = 4.5$
27. $3x + 3 = 18$
28. $0.6g + 11 = 5$
29. $32 = 5 - 3t$
30. $2d + \frac{1}{5} = \frac{3}{5}$
31. $1 = 2x + \frac{1}{2}$
32. $\frac{z}{2} + 1 = \frac{3}{2}$
33. $\frac{2}{3} = \frac{4j}{6}$
34. $\frac{3}{4} = \frac{3}{8}x - \frac{3}{2}$
35. $\frac{1}{5} - \frac{x}{5} = -\frac{2}{5}$
36. $6 = -2(7 - c)$
37. $5(h - 4) = 8$
38. $-3x - 8 + 4x = 17$
39. $4x + 6x = 30$
40. $2(x + 3) = 10$
41. $17 = 3(p - 5) + 8$
42. **Consumer Economics** Jennifer is saving money to buy a bike. The bike costs $245. She has $125 saved, and each week she adds $15 to her savings. How long will it take her to save enough money to buy the bike?
43. If $2x + 13 = 17$, find the value of $3x + 1$.
44. If $-(x - 1) = 5$, find the value of $-4x$.
45. If $5(y + 10) = 40$, find the value of $\frac{1}{4}y$.
46. If $9 - 6x = 45$, find the value of $x - 4$.

**Geometry** **Write and solve an equation to find the value of $x$ for each triangle. (*Hint:* The sum of the angle measures in any triangle is 180°.)**

47. 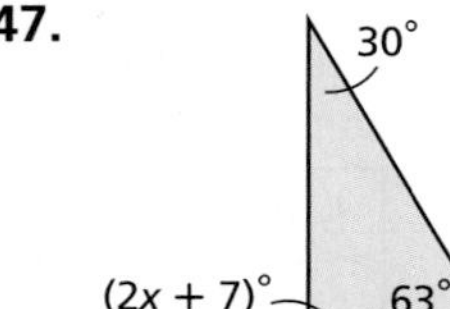


48. 115°, x°, x°

49. 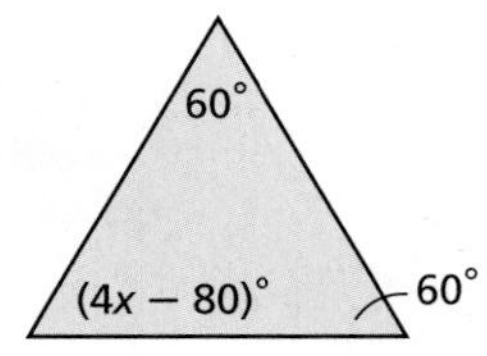

**LINK History**

Martin Luther King Jr. entered college at age 15. During his life he earned 3 degrees and was awarded 20 honorary degrees.

*Source:* lib.lsu.edu

**Write an equation to represent each relationship. Solve each equation.**

**50.** Seven less than twice a number equals 19.

**51.** Eight decreased by 3 times a number equals 2.

**52.** The sum of two times a number and 5 is 11.

**53.** **History** In 1963, Dr. Martin Luther King Jr. began his famous "I have a dream" speech with the words "Five score years ago, a great American, in whose symbolic shadow we stand, signed the Emancipation Proclamation." The proclamation was signed by President Abraham Lincoln in 1863.

**a.** Using the dates given, write and solve an equation that can be used to find the number of years in a score.

**b.** How many score would represent 60?

**Solve each equation. Check your answer.**

**54.** $3t + 44 = 50$

**55.** $3(x - 2) = 18$

**56.** $15 = \frac{c}{3} - 2$

**57.** $2x + 6.5 = 15.5$

**58.** $3.9w - 17.9 = -2.3$

**59.** $17 = x - 3(x + 1)$

**60.** $5x + 9 = 39$

**61.** $15 + 5.5m = 70$

**Biology** **Use the graph for Exercises 62 and 63.**

**62.** The height of an ostrich is 20 inches more than 4 times the height of a kiwi. Write and solve an equation to find the height of a kiwi. Show that your answer is reasonable.

**63.** Five times the height of a kakapo minus 70 equals the height of an emu. Write and solve an equation to find the height of a kakapo. Show that your answer is reasonable.

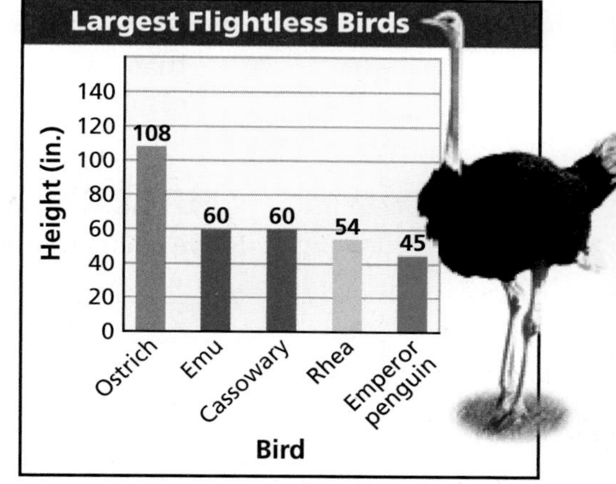


*Source: The Top Ten of Everything*

**64.** The sum of two consecutive whole numbers is 57. What are the two numbers? (*Hint:* Let $n$ represent the first number. Then $n + 1$ is the next consecutive whole number.)

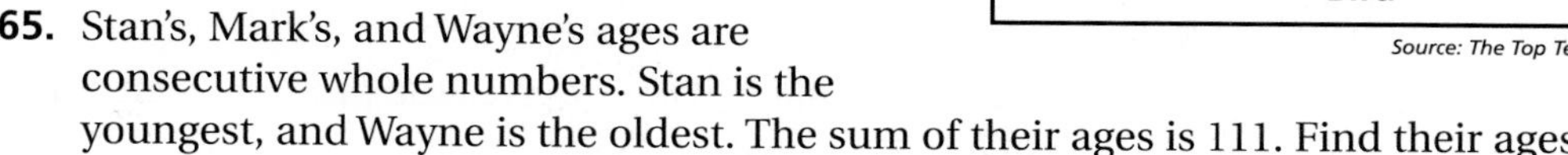

**65.** Stan's, Mark's, and Wayne's ages are consecutive whole numbers. Stan is the youngest, and Wayne is the oldest. The sum of their ages is 111. Find their ages.

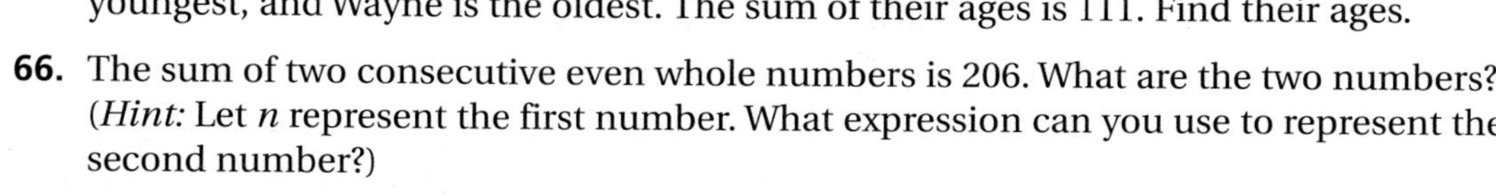

**66.** The sum of two consecutive even whole numbers is 206. What are the two numbers? (*Hint:* Let $n$ represent the first number. What expression can you use to represent the second number?)

**MULTI-STEP TEST PREP**

**67.** This problem will prepare you for the Multi-Step Test Prep on page 112.

**a.** The cost of fighting a certain forest fire is \$225 per acre. Complete the table.

**b.** Write an equation for the relationship between the cost $c$ of fighting the fire and the number of acres $n$.

**Cost of Fighting Fire**

| Acres | Cost ($) |
|---|---|
| 100 | 22,500 |
| 200 | ■ |
| 500 | ■ |
| 1000 | ■ |
| 1500 | ■ |
| $n$ | ■ |

68. **Critical Thinking** The equation $2(m - 8) + 3 = 17$ has more than one solution method. Give at least two different "first steps" to solve this equation.

69. **Write About It** Write a series of steps that you can use to solve any multi-step equation.

MA.A.4.5

70. Lin sold 4 more shirts than Greg. Fran sold 3 times as many shirts as Lin. In total, the three sold 51 shirts. Which represents the number of shirts Greg sold?

Ⓐ $3g = 51$ Ⓑ $3 + g = 51$ Ⓒ $8 + 5g = 51$ Ⓓ $16 + 5g = 51$

71. If $\frac{4m - 3}{7} = 3$, what is the value of $7m - 5$?

Ⓕ 6 Ⓖ 10.5 Ⓗ 37 Ⓙ 68.5

72. The equation $c = 48 + 0.06m$ represents the cost $c$ of renting a car and driving $m$ miles. Which statement best describes this cost?

Ⓐ The cost is a flat rate of \$0.06 per mile.

Ⓑ The cost is \$0.48 for the first mile and \$0.06 for each additional mile.

Ⓒ The cost is a \$48 fee plus \$0.06 per mile.

Ⓓ The cost is a \$6 fee plus \$0.48 per mile.

73. **Gridded Response** A telemarketer earns \$150 a week plus \$2 for each call that results in a sale. Last week she earned a total of \$204. How many of her calls resulted in sales?

## CHALLENGE AND EXTEND

**Solve each equation. Check your answer.**

74. $\frac{9}{2}x + 18 + 3x = \frac{11}{2}$

75. $\frac{15}{4}x - 15 = \frac{33}{4}$

76. $(x + 6) - (2x + 7) - 3x = -9$

77. $(4x + 2) - (12x + 8) + 2(5x - 3) = 6 + 11$

78. Find a value for $b$ so that the solution of $4x + 3b = -1$ is $x = 2$.

79. Find a value for $b$ so that the solution of $2x - 3b = 0$ is $x = -9$.

80. **Business** The formula $p = nc - e$ gives the profit $p$ when a number of items $n$ are each sold at a cost $c$ and expenses $e$ are subtracted.

a. If $p = 2500$, $n = 2000$, and $e = 800$, what is the value of $c$?

b. If $p = 2500$, $n = 1000$, and $e = 800$, what is the value of $c$?

c. **What if...?** If $n$ is divided in half while $p$ and $e$ remain the same, what is the effect on $c$?

## SPIRAL REVIEW

**Write all classifications that apply to each real number.** *(Lesson 1-5)*

81. $\sqrt{3}$

82. $-58$

83. $2\frac{1}{3}$

84. $0.17$

**Write each product using the Distributive Property. Then simplify.** *(Lesson 1-7)*

85. $8(61)$

86. $9(28)$

87. $11(28)$

88. $13(21)$

**Solve each equation.** *(Lesson 2-1)*

89. $17 = k + 4$

90. $x - 18 = 3$

91. $a + 6 = -12$

92. $-7 = q - 7$

# Model Equations with Variables on Both Sides

Algebra tile models can help you understand how to solve equations with variables on both sides.

*Use with Lesson 2-4*

 **Prep MA.A.4.5** Use graphs, tables and symbols to solve linear equations.

**KEY**

$= 1$

$= -1$

 $= x$ 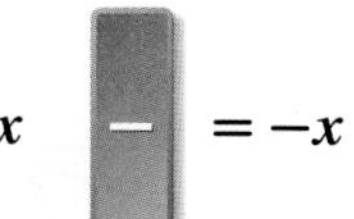 $= -x$

**REMEMBER**

$+ \; = 0$

## Activity

**Use algebra tiles to model and solve $5x - 2 = 2x + 10$.**

| MODEL | | ALGEBRA |
|---|---|---|
| | *Model 5x − 2 on the left side of the mat and 2x + 10 on the right side.* *Remember that 5x − 2 is the same as 5x + (−2).* | $5x - 2 = 2x + 10$ |
| | *Remove 2 x-tiles from both sides. This represents subtracting 2x from both sides of the equation.* | $5x - 2 - \mathbf{2x} = 2x - \mathbf{2x} + 10$<br>$3x - 2 = 10$ |
| | *Place 2 yellow tiles on both sides. This represents adding 2 to both sides of the equation.* *Remove zero pairs.* | $3x - 2 + \mathbf{2} = 10 + \mathbf{2}$<br>$3x = 12$ |
| | *Separate each side into 3 equal groups.* *Each group is $\frac{1}{3}$ of the side.* *One x-tile is equivalent to 4 yellow tiles.* | $\frac{1}{3}(3x) = \frac{1}{3}(12)$<br>$x = 4$ |

## Try This

**Use algebra tiles to model and solve each equation.**

**1.** $3x + 2 = 2x + 5$ **2.** $5x + 12 = 2x + 3$ **3.** $9x - 5 = 6x + 13$ **4.** $x = -2x + 9$

# 2-4 Solving Equations with Variables on Both Sides

**MA.A.4.5** Use … symbols to solve linear equations. *Also* **MA.A.1.1**

***Objective***
Solve equations in one variable that contain variable terms on both sides.

***Vocabulary***
identity
contradiction

**Why learn this?**
You can compare prices and find the best value.

Many phone companies offer low rates for long-distance calls without requiring customers to sign up for their services. To compare rates, solve an equation with variables on both sides.

To solve an equation like this, use inverse operations to "collect" variable terms on one side of the equation.

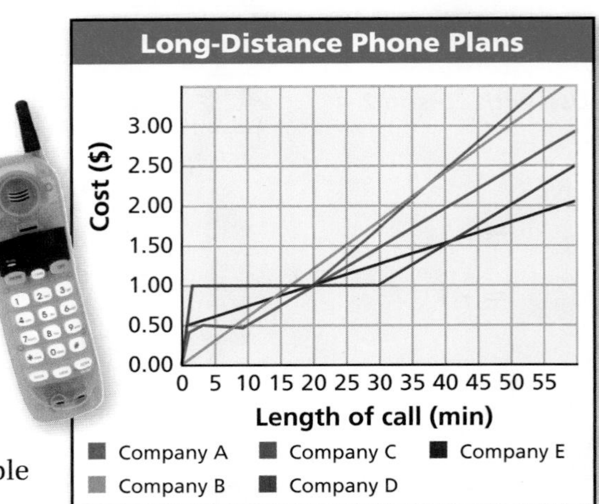


## EXAMPLE 1 Solving Equations with Variables on Both Sides

**Solve each equation.**

**A** $7k = 4k + 15$

$$\begin{aligned} 7k &= 4k + 15 \\ -4k &\quad -4k \\ \hline 3k &= 15 \end{aligned}$$

*To collect the variable terms on one side, subtract 4k from both sides.*

$$\frac{3k}{3} = \frac{15}{3}$$
$$k = 5$$

*Since k is multiplied by 3, divide both sides by 3 to undo the multiplication.*

**B** $5x - 2 = 3x + 4$

$$\begin{aligned} 5x - 2 &= 3x + 4 \\ -3x &\quad -3x \\ \hline 2x - 2 &= 4 \end{aligned}$$

*To collect the variable terms on one side, subtract 3x from both sides.*

$$\begin{aligned} +2 &\quad +2 \\ \hline 2x &= 6 \end{aligned}$$

*Since 2 is subtracted from 2x, add 2 to both sides to undo the subtraction.*

$$\frac{2x}{2} = \frac{6}{2}$$
$$x = 3$$

*Since x is multiplied by 2, divide both sides by 2 to undo the multiplication.*

***Check*** $5x - 2 = 3x + 4$

| $5(3) - 2$ | $3(3) + 4$ |
|---|---|
| $15 - 2$ | $9 + 4$ |
| $13$ | $13$ ✓ |

*To check your solution, substitute 3 for x in the original equation.*

**Helpful Hint**
Equations are often easier to solve when the variable has a positive coefficient. Keep this in mind when deciding on which side to "collect" variable terms.

**Solve each equation. Check your answer.**

**1a.** $4b + 2 = 3b$ **1b.** $0.5 + 0.3y = 0.7y - 0.3$

To solve more complicated equations, you may need to first simplify by using the Distributive Property or combining like terms.

## EXAMPLE 2 Simplifying Each Side Before Solving Equations

**Solve each equation.**

**A** $2(y+6) = 3y$

$$\begin{aligned} 2(y+6) &= 3y \\ 2(y) + 2(6) &= 3y \\ 2y + 12 &= 3y \\ -2y \quad &\quad -2y \\ 12 &= y \end{aligned}$$

*Distribute 2 to the expression in parentheses.*

*To collect the variable terms on one side, subtract 2y from both sides.*

*Check*

| $2(y+6)$ | $= 3y$ |
|---|---|
| $2(12+6)$ | $3(12)$ |
| $2(18)$ | $36$ |
| $36$ | $36$ ✓ |

*To check your solution, substitute 12 for y in the original equation.*

**B** $3 - 5b + 2b = -2 - 2(1-b)$

$$\begin{aligned} 3 - 5b + 2b &= -2 - 2(1-b) \\ 3 - 5b + 2b &= -2 - 2(1) - 2(-b) \\ 3 - 5b + 2b &= -2 - 2 + 2b \\ 3 - 3b &= -4 + 2b \\ +3b \quad &\quad +3b \\ 3 \quad &= -4 + 5b \\ +4 \quad &\quad +4 \\ 7 \quad &= \quad 5b \\ \frac{7}{5} &= \frac{5b}{5} \\ 1.4 &= b \end{aligned}$$

*Distribute −2 to the expression in parentheses.*

*Combine like terms.*

*Add 3b to both sides.*

*Since −4 is added to 5b, add 4 to both sides.*

*Since b is multiplied by 5, divide both sides by 5.*

**Solve each equation. Check your answer.**

**2a.** $\frac{1}{2}(b+6) = \frac{3}{2}b - 1$ **2b.** $3x + 15 - 9 = 2(x+2)$

An **identity** is an equation that is true for all values of the variable. An equation that is an identity has infinitely many solutions. A **contradiction** is an equation that is not true for any value of the variable. It has no solutions.

### Identities and Contradictions

| WORDS | NUMBERS | ALGEBRA |
|---|---|---|
| **Identity**<br>When solving an equation, if you get an equation that is always true, the original equation is an identity, and it has infinitely many solutions. | $2 + 1 = 2 + 1$<br>$3 = 3$ ✓ | $2 + x = 2 + x$<br>$-x \quad -x$<br>$2 \quad = 2$ ✓ |
| **Contradiction**<br>When solving an equation, if you get a false equation, the original equation is a contradiction, and it has no solutions. | $1 = 1 + 2$<br>$1 = 3$ ✗ | $x = x + 3$<br>$-x \quad -x$<br>$0 = \quad 3$ ✗ |

## EXAMPLE 3 Infinitely Many Solutions or No Solutions

**Writing Math**

The solution set for Example 3B is an empty set—it contains no elements. The empty set can be written as ∅ or {}.

**Solve each equation.**

**A** $x + 4 - 6x = 6 - 5x - 2$

$x + 4 - 6x = 6 - 5x - 2$ *Identify like terms.*

$4 - 5x = 4 - 5x$ *Combine like terms on the left and the right.*

$\underline{+5x} \quad \underline{+5x}$ *Add 5x to both sides.*

$4 = 4$ ✓ *True statement*

The equation $x + 4 - 6x = 6 - 5x - 2$ is an identity. All values of $x$ will make the equation true. All real numbers are solutions.

**B** $-8x + 6 + 9x = -17 + x$

$-8x + 6 + 9x = -17 + x$ *Identify like terms.*

$x + 6 = -17 + x$ *Combine like terms.*

$\underline{-x} \quad \underline{-x}$ *Subtract x from both sides.*

$6 = -17$ ✗ *False statement*

The equation $-8x + 6 + 9x = -17 + x$ is a contradiction. There is no value of $x$ that will make the equation true. There are no solutions.

**Solve each equation.**

**3a.** $4y + 7 - y = 10 + 3y$ **3b.** $2c + 7 + c = -14 + 3c + 21$

## EXAMPLE 4 *Consumer Application*

**The long-distance rates of two phone companies are shown in the table. How long is a call that costs the same amount no matter which company is used? What is the cost of that call?**

| Phone Company | Charges |
|---|---|
| Company A | 36¢ plus 3¢ per minute |
| Company B | 6¢ per minute |

Let $m$ represent minutes, and write expressions for each company's cost.

| When is | 36¢ | plus | 3¢ per minute | times number of minutes | the same as | 6¢ per minute | times number of minutes | ? |
|---|---|---|---|---|---|---|---|---|
| | 36 | + | 3 | (m) | = | 6 | (m) | |

$36 + 3m = 6m$

$\underline{-3m} \quad \underline{-3m}$ *To collect the variable terms on one side, subtract 3m from both sides.*

$36 = 3m$

$\frac{36}{3} = \frac{3m}{3}$ *Since m is multiplied by 3, divide both sides by 3 to undo the multiplication.*

$12 = m$

The charges will be the same for a 12-minute call using either phone service. To find the cost of this call, evaluate either expression for $m = 12$:

$$36 + 3m = 36 + 3(12) = 36 + 36 = 72 \qquad 6m = 6(12) = 72$$

The cost of a 12-minute call through either company is 72¢.

**4.** Four times Greg's age, decreased by 3 is equal to 3 times Greg's age, increased by 7. How old is Greg?

## THINK AND DISCUSS

1. Tell which of the following is an identity. Explain your answer.

   a. $4(a + 3) - 6 = 3(a + 3) - 6$  b. $8.3x - 9 + 0.7x = 2 + 9x - 11$

2. **GET ORGANIZED** Copy and complete the graphic organizer. In each box, write an example of an equation that has the indicated number of solutions.

An equation with variables on both sides can have...

| one solution: | many solutions: | no solution: |
|---|---|---|

# 2-4 Exercises

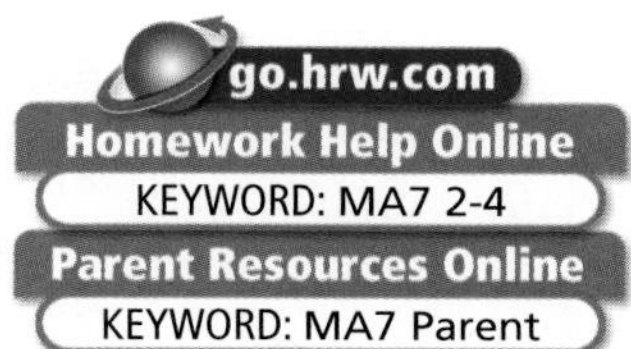


## GUIDED PRACTICE

1. **Vocabulary** An equation that has no solution is called a(n) ___?___. (*identity* or *contradiction*)

SEE EXAMPLE 1 p. 100

**Solve each equation. Check your answer.**

2. $2c - 5 = c + 4$
3. $8r + 4 = 10 + 2r$
4. $2x - 1 = x + 11$
5. $28 - 0.3y = 0.7y - 12$

SEE EXAMPLE 2 p. 101

6. $-2(x + 3) = 4x - 3$
7. $3c - 4c + 1 = 5c + 2 + 3$
8. $5 + 3(q - 4) = 2(q + 1)$
9. $5 - (t + 3) = -1 + 2(t - 3)$

SEE EXAMPLE 3 p. 102

10. $7x - 4 = -2x + 1 + 9x - 5$
11. $8x + 6 - 9x = 2 - x - 15$
12. $6y = 8 - 9 + 6y$
13. $6 - 2x - 1 = 4x + 8 - 6x - 3$

SEE EXAMPLE 4 p. 102

14. **Consumer Economics** A house-painting company charges \$376 plus \$12 per hour. Another painting company charges \$280 plus \$15 per hour.
    a. How long is a job for which both companies will charge the same amount?
    b. What will that cost be?

## PRACTICE AND PROBLEM SOLVING

**Solve each equation. Check your answer.**

15. $7a - 17 = 4a + 1$
16. $2b - 5 = 8b + 1$
17. $4x - 2 = 3x + 4$
18. $2x - 5 = 4x - 1$
19. $8x - 2 = 3x + 12.25$
20. $5x + 2 = 3x$
21. $3c - 5 = 2c + 5$
22. $-17 - 2x = 6 - x$
23. $3(t - 1) = 9 + t$
24. $5 - x - 2 = 3 + 4x + 5$
25. $2(x + 4) = 3(x - 2)$
26. $3m - 10 = 2(4m - 5)$
27. $5 - (n - 4) = 3(n + 2)$
28. $6(x + 7) - 20 = 6x$
29. $8(x + 1) = 4x - 8$
30. $x - 4 - 3x = -2x - 3 - 1$
31. $-2(x + 2) = -2x + 1$
32. $2(x + 4) - 5 = 2x + 3$

| Independent Practice | |
|---|---|
| For Exercises | See Example |
| 15–22 | 1 |
| 23–29 | 2 |
| 30–32 | 3 |
| 33 | 4 |

**Extra Practice**

Skills Practice p. S6
Application Practice p. S29

33. **Sports** Justin and Tyson are beginning an exercise program to train for football season. Justin weighs 150 lb and hopes to gain 2 lb per week. Tyson weighs 195 lb and hopes to lose 1 lb per week.
    a. If the plan works, in how many weeks will the boys weigh the same amount?
    b. What will that weight be?

**Write an equation to represent each relationship. Then solve the equation.**

34. Three times the sum of a number and 4 is the same as 18 more than the number.
35. A number decreased by 30 is the same as 14 minus 3 times the number.
36. Two less than 2 times a number is the same as the number plus 64.

**Solve each equation. Check your answer.**

37. $2x - 2 = 4x + 6$
38. $3x + 5 = 2x + 2$
39. $4x + 3 = 5x - 4$
40. $-\frac{2}{5}p + 2 = \frac{1}{5}p + 11$
41. $5x + 24 = 2x + 15$
42. $5x - 10 = 14 - 3x$
43. $12 - 6x = 10 - 5x$
44. $5x - 7 = -6x - 29$
45. $1.8x + 2.8 = 2.5x + 2.1$
46. $2.6x + 18 = 2.4x + 22$
47. $1 - 3x = 2x + 8$
48. $\frac{1}{2}(8 - 6h) = h$
49. $3(x + 1) = 2x + 7$
50. $9x - 8 + 4x = 7x + 16$
51. $3(2x - 1) + 5 = 6(x + 1)$
52. **Travel** Rapid Rental Car company charges a $40 rental fee, $15 for gas, and $0.25 per mile driven. For the same car, Capital Cars charges $45 for rental and gas and $0.35 per mile.
    a. Find the number of miles for which the companies' charges will be the same. Then find that charge. Show that your answers are reasonable.
    b. The Barre family estimates that they will drive about 95 miles during their vacation to Hershey, Pennsylvania. Which company should they rent their car from? Explain.
    c. **What if...?** The Barres have extended their vacation and now estimate that they will drive about 120 miles. Should they still rent from the same company as in part **b**? Why or why not?
    d. Give a general rule for deciding which company to rent from.
53. **Geometry** The triangles shown have the same perimeter. What is the value of $x$?

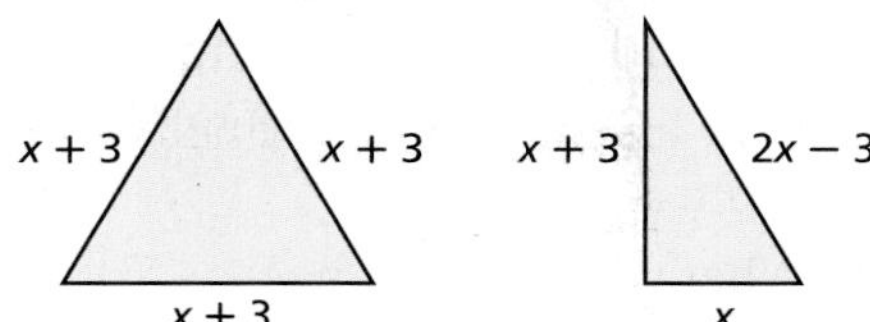


**MULTI-STEP TEST PREP**

54. This problem will prepare you for the Multi-Step Test Prep on page 112.
    a. A fire currently covers 420 acres and continues to spread at a rate of 60 acres per day. How many total acres will be covered in the next 2 days? Show that your answer is reasonable.
    b. Write an expression for the total area covered by the fire in $d$ days.
    c. The firefighters estimate that they can put out the fire at a rate of 80 acres per day. Write an expression for the total area that the firefighters can put out in $d$ days.
    d. Set the expressions in parts **b** and **c** equal. Solve for $d$. What does $d$ represent?

A cheetah's body is well designed for fast running. Its tail acts like a boat's rudder to help it make sharp turns. Its spine acts like a spring to propel it forward.

*Source:* www.cheetahspot.com

55. **Critical Thinking** Write an equation with variables on both sides that has no solution.

56. **Biology** The graph shows the maximum recorded speeds of the four fastest mammals.

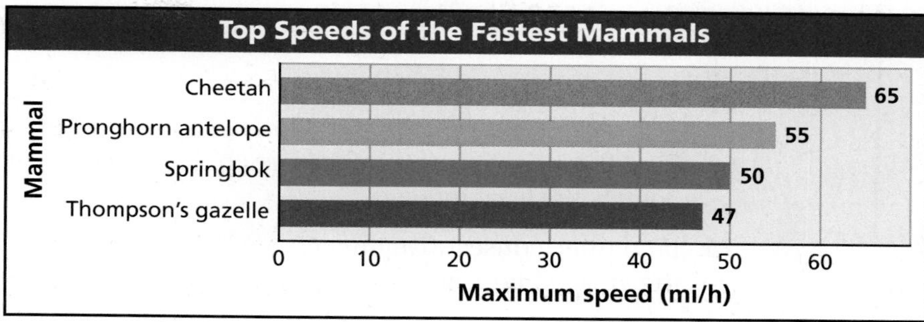


*Source: The Top 10 of Everything*

a. Write an expression for the distance in miles that a Thompson's gazelle can run at top speed in $x$ hours.

b. Write an expression for the distance in miles that a cheetah can run at top speed in $x$ hours.

c. A cheetah and a Thompson's gazelle are running at their top speeds. The cheetah is one mile behind the gazelle. Write an expression for the distance the cheetah must run to catch up with the gazelle.

d. Write and solve an equation that represents how long the cheetah will have to run at top speed to catch up with the gazelle.

e. A cheetah can maintain its top speed for only 300 yards. Will the cheetah be able to catch the gazelle? Explain.

57. **Write About It** Write a series of steps that you can use to solve any equation with variables on both sides.

## TEST PREP

MA.A.4.5, MA.A.1.1

58. Lindsey's monthly magazine subscription costs \$1.25 per issue. Kenzie's monthly subscription costs \$1.50 per issue, but she received her first 2 issues free. Which equation can be used to find the number of months after which the girls will have paid the same amount?

   (A) $1.25m = 1.50m - 2$  
   (B) $1.25m = 1.50m - 2m$  
   (C) $1.25m = 1.50(m - 2)$  
   (D) $1.25m = 3m - 1.50$

59. What is the numerical solution of the equation *7 times a number equals 3 less than 5 times that number*?

   (F) $-1.5$  (G) $0.25$  (H) $\frac{2}{3}$  (J) $4$

60. Three packs of markers cost \$9.00 less than 5 packs of markers. Which equation best represents this situation?

   (A) $5x + 9 = 3x$  (B) $3x + 9 = 5x$  (C) $3x - 9 = 5x$  (D) $9 - 3x = 5x$

61. Nicole has \$120. If she saves \$20 per week, in how many days will she have \$500?

   (F) 19  (G) 25  (H) 133  (J) 175

62. **Gridded Response** Solve $-2(x - 1) + 5x = 2(2x - 1)$.

## CHALLENGE AND EXTEND

**Solve each equation.**

**63.** $4x + 2[4 - 2(x + 2)] = 2x - 4$

**64.** $\frac{x+5}{2} + \frac{x-1}{2} = \frac{x-1}{3}$

**65.** $\frac{2}{3}w - \frac{1}{4} = \frac{2}{3}\left(w - \frac{1}{4}\right)$

**66.** $-5 - 7 - 3f = -f - 2(f + 6)$

**67.** $\frac{2}{3}x + \frac{1}{2} = \frac{3}{5}x - \frac{5}{6}$

**68.** $x - \frac{1}{4} = \frac{x}{3} + 7\frac{3}{4}$

**69.** Find three consecutive integers such that twice the greatest integer is 2 less than 3 times the least integer.

**70.** Find three consecutive integers such that twice the least integer is 12 more than the greatest integer.

**71.** Rob had twice as much money as Sam. Then Sam gave Rob 1 quarter, 2 nickels, and 3 pennies. Rob then gave Sam 8 dimes. If they now have the same amount of money, how much money did Rob originally have? Check your answer.

## SPIRAL REVIEW

**Write an expression for the perimeter of each figure.** *(Lesson 1-1)*

**72.** square with side $x$ cm

**73.** equilateral triangle with side $y$ cm

**Multiply or divide.** *(Lesson 1-3)*

**74.** $6.1 \div 0$

**75.** $3(-21)$

**76.** $0 \div \frac{7}{8}$

**77.** $\frac{2}{5} \div \frac{1}{10}$

**78.** $5 \div (-5)$

**79.** $\frac{-16}{-8}$

**80.** $-1000 \div (-0.001)$

**81.** $500(-0.25)$

**Solve each equation.** *(Lesson 2-3)*

**82.** $4x - 44 = 8$

**83.** $2(x - 3) = 24$

**84.** $-1 = \frac{x}{4} - 3$

**85.** $2x + 6 = 12$

## Career Path

go.hrw.com
Career Resources Online
KEYWORD: MA7 Career

**Beth Simmons**
Biology major

**Q: What math classes did you take in high school?**

**A:** Algebra 1 and 2, Geometry, and Precalculus

**Q: What math classes have you taken in college?**

**A:** Two calculus classes and a calculus-based physics class

**Q: How do you use math?**

**A:** I use math a lot in physics. Sometimes I would think a calculus topic was totally useless, and then we would use it in physics class! In biology, I use math to understand populations.

**Q: What career options are you considering?**

**A:** When I graduate, I could teach, or I could go to graduate school and do more research. I have a lot of options.

# 2-5 Solving for a Variable

**Ext. MA.A.4.5** Use ... symbols to solve linear equations.

***Objectives***
Solve a formula for a given variable.

Solve an equation in two or more variables for one of the variables.

***Vocabulary***
formula
literal equation

**Who uses this?**
Athletes can "rearrange" the distance formula to calculate their average speed.

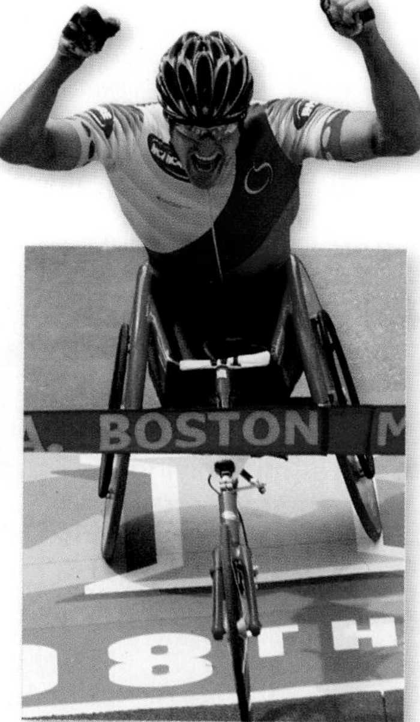


Many wheelchair athletes compete in marathons, which cover about 26.2 miles. Using the time $t$ it took to complete the race, the distance $d$, and the *formula* $d = rt$, racers can find their average speed $r$.

A **formula** is an equation that states a rule for a relationship among quantities.

In the formula $d = rt$, $d$ is isolated. You can "rearrange" a formula to isolate any variable by using inverse operations. This is called *solving for a variable.*

| Solving for a Variable | |
|---|---|
| **Step 1** | Locate the variable you are asked to solve for in the equation. |
| **Step 2** | Identify the operations on this variable and the order in which they are applied. |
| **Step 3** | Use inverse operations to undo operations and isolate the variable. |

## EXAMPLE 1 *Sports Application*

**In 2004, Ernst Van Dyk won the wheelchair race of the Boston Marathon with a time of about 1.3 hours. The race was about 26.2 miles. What was his average speed? Use the formula $d = rt$ and round your answer to the nearest tenth.**

**Helpful Hint**

A number divided by itself equals 1. For $t \neq 0$, $\frac{t}{t} = 1$.

The question asks for speed, so first solve the formula $d = rt$ for $r$.

$d = rt$ — *Locate r in the equation.*

$\frac{d}{t} = \frac{rt}{t}$ — *Since r is multiplied by t, divide both sides by t to undo the multiplication.*

$\frac{d}{t} = r$, or $r = \frac{d}{t}$

Now use this formula and the information given in the problem.

$r = \frac{d}{t} \approx \frac{26.2}{1.3}$

$\approx 20.2$

Van Dyk's average speed was about 20.2 miles per hour.

**1.** Solve the formula $d = rt$ for $t$. Find the time in hours that it would take Van Dyk to travel 26.2 miles if his average speed was 18 miles per hour. Round to the nearest hundredth.

## EXAMPLE 2 Solving Formulas for a Variable

**A** **The formula for a Fahrenheit temperature in terms of degrees Celsius is $F = \frac{9}{5}C + 32$. Solve for $C$.**

$$F = \frac{9}{5}C + 32$$ *Locate C in the equation.*

$$\underline{-32} \quad \underline{\quad -32}$$ *Since 32 is added to $\frac{9}{5}C$, subtract 32 from both sides to undo the addition.*

$$F - 32 = \frac{9}{5}C$$

$$\left(\frac{5}{9}\right)(F - 32) = \left(\frac{5}{9}\right)\frac{9}{5}C$$ *Since C is multiplied by $\frac{9}{5}$, divide both sides by $\frac{9}{5}$ (multiply by $\frac{5}{9}$) to undo the multiplication.*

$$\frac{5}{9}(F - 32) = C$$

**Remember!**

Dividing by a fraction is the same as multiplying by the reciprocal.

**B** **The formula for a person's typing speed is $s = \frac{w - 10e}{m}$, where $s$ is speed in words per minute, $w$ is number of words typed, $e$ is number of errors, and $m$ is number of minutes typing. Solve for $w$.**

$$s = \frac{w - 10e}{m}$$ *Locate w in the equation.*

$$m(s) = m\left(\frac{w - 10e}{m}\right)$$ *Since w − 10e is divided by m, multiply both sides by m to undo the division.*

$$ms = w - 10e$$

$$\underline{+10e} \quad \underline{+10e}$$ *Since 10e is subtracted from w, add 10e to both sides to undo the subtraction.*

$$ms + 10e = w$$

**2.** The formula for an object's final velocity $f$ is $f = i - gt$, where $i$ is the object's initial velocity, $g$ is acceleration due to gravity, and $t$ is time. Solve for $i$.

A formula is a type of *literal equation*. A **literal equation** is an equation with two or more variables. To solve for one of the variables, use inverse operations.

## EXAMPLE 3 Solving Literal Equations for a Variable

**A** **Solve $m - n = 5$ for $m$.**

$$m - n = 5$$ *Locate m in the equation.*

$$\underline{+n \quad +n}$$ *Since n is subtracted from m, add n to both sides to undo the subtraction.*

$$m = 5 + n$$

**B** **Solve $\frac{m}{k} = x$ for $k$.**

$$\frac{m}{k} = x$$ *Locate k in the equation.*

$$k\left(\frac{m}{k}\right) = kx$$ *Since k appears in the denominator, multiply both sides by k.*

$$m = kx$$

$$\frac{m}{x} = \frac{kx}{x}$$ *Since k is multiplied by x, divide both sides by x to undo the multiplication.*

$$\frac{m}{x} = k$$

**3a.** Solve $5 - b = 2t$ for $t$.

**3b.** Solve $D = \frac{m}{V}$ for $V$.

## THINK AND DISCUSS

1. Describe a situation in which a formula could be used more easily if it were "rearranged." Include the formula in your description.
2. Explain how to solve $P = 2\ell + 2w$ for $w$.

3. **GET ORGANIZED** Copy and complete the graphic organizer. Write a formula that is used in each subject. Then solve the formula for each of its variables.

| Common Formulas | |
|---|---|
| **Subject** | **Formula** |
| Geometry | |
| Physical science | |
| Earth science | |

Ext. MA.A.4.5

# 2-5 Exercises

go.hrw.com
Homework Help Online
KEYWORD: MA7 2-5
Parent Resources Online
KEYWORD: MA7 Parent

## GUIDED PRACTICE

SEE EXAMPLE 1 p. 107

1. **Vocabulary** Explain why a *formula* is a type of *literal equation*.
2. **Construction** The formula $a = 46c$ gives the floor area $a$ in square meters that can be wired using $c$ circuits.
   a. Solve $a = 46c$ for $c$.
   b. If a room is 322 square meters, how many circuits are required to wire this room?

SEE EXAMPLE 2 p. 108

3. The formula for the volume of a rectangular prism with length $\ell$, width $w$, and height $h$ is $V = \ell wh$. Solve this formula for $w$.

SEE EXAMPLE 3 p. 108

4. Solve $st + 3t = 6$ for $s$.
5. Solve $m - 4n = 8$ for $m$.
6. Solve $\frac{f+4}{g} = 6$ for $f$.
7. Solve $b + c = \frac{10}{a}$ for $a$.

## PRACTICE AND PROBLEM SOLVING

**Independent Practice**

| For Exercises | See Example |
|---|---|
| 8 | 1 |
| 9 | 2 |
| 10–13 | 3 |

**Extra Practice**

Skills Practice p. S7
Application Practice p. S29

8. **Geometry** The formula $C = 2pr$ relates the circumference $C$ of a circle to its radius $r$. (Recall that $p$ is the constant ratio of circumference to diameter.)
   a. Solve $C = 2pr$ for $r$.
   b. If a circle's circumference is 15 inches, what is its radius? Leave the symbol $p$ in your answer.

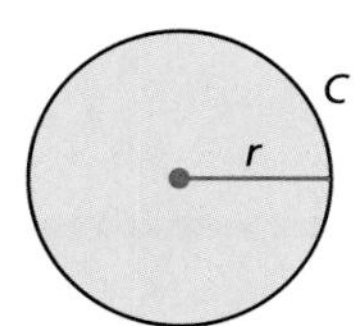


*C is the distance around the circle.*

*r is the distance from the center of the circle to any point on the circle.*

9. **Finance** The formula $A = P + I$ shows that the total amount of money $A$ received from an investment equals the principal $P$ (the original amount of money invested) plus the interest $I$. Solve this formula for $I$.
10. Solve $-2 = 4r + s$ for $s$.
11. Solve $xy - 5 = k$ for $x$.
12. Solve $\frac{m}{n} = p - 6$ for $n$.
13. Solve $\frac{x-2}{y} = z$ for $y$.

**Solve for the indicated variable.**

14. $S = 180n - 360$ for $n$
15. $\frac{x}{5} - g = a$ for $x$
16. $A = \frac{1}{2}bh$ for $b$
17. $y = mx + b$ for $x$
18. $a = 3n + 1$ for $n$
19. $PV = nRT$ for $T$
20. $T + M = R$ for $T$
21. $M = T - R$ for $T$
22. $PV = nRT$ for $R$
23. $2a + 2b = c$ for $b$
24. $5p + 9c = p$ for $c$
25. $ax + r = 7$ for $r$
26. $3x + 7y = 2$ for $y$
27. $4y + 3x = 5$ for $x$
28. $y = 3x + 3b$ for $b$

29. **Estimation** The table shows the flying time and distance traveled for five flights on a certain airplane.
    a. Use the data in the table to write a rule that *estimates* the relationship between flying time $t$ and distance traveled $d$.
    b. Use your rule from part **a** to estimate the time that it takes the airplane to fly 1300 miles.
    c. Solve your rule for $d$.
    d. Use your rule from part **c** to estimate the distance the airplane can fly in 8 hours.

**Flying Times**

| Flight | Time (h) | Distance (mi) |
|---|---|---|
| A | 2 | 1018 |
| B | 3 | 1485 |
| C | 4 | 2103 |
| D | 5 | 2516 |
| E | 6 | 2886 |

30. **Sports** To find a baseball pitcher's earned run average (ERA), you can use the formula $Ei = 9r$, where $E$ represents ERA, $i$ represents number of innings pitched, and $r$ represents number of earned runs allowed. Solve the equation for $E$. What is a pitcher's ERA if he allows 5 earned runs in 18 innings pitched?

31. **Meteorology** For altitudes up to 36,000 feet, the relationship between temperature and altitude can be described by the formula $t = -0.0035a + g$, where $t$ is the temperature in degrees Fahrenheit, $a$ is the altitude in feet, and $g$ is the ground temperature in degrees Fahrenheit. Solve this formula for $a$.

32. **Write About It** In your own words, explain how to solve a literal equation for one of the variables.

33. **Critical Thinking** How is solving $a - ab = c$ for $a$ different from the problems in this lesson? How might you solve this equation for $a$?

**MULTI-STEP TEST PREP**

34. This problem will prepare you for the Multi-Step Test Prep on page 112.
    a. Suppose firefighters can extinguish a wildfire at a rate of 60 acres per day. Use this information to complete the table.
    b. Use the last row in the table to write an equation for acres $A$ extinguished in terms of the number of days $d$.
    c. Graph the points in the table with *Days* on the horizontal axis and *Acres* on the vertical axis. Describe the graph.

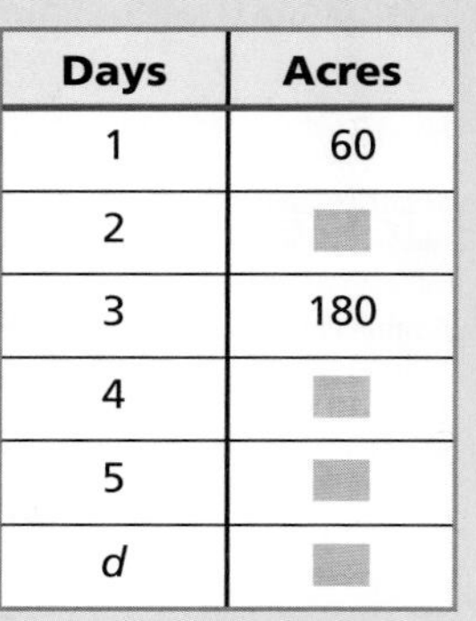

| Days | Acres |
|---|---|
| 1 | 60 |
| 2 | |
| 3 | 180 |
| 4 | |
| 5 | |
| $d$ | |

35. Which equation is the result of solving $9 + 3x = 2y$ for $x$?

Ext. MA.A.4.5

Ⓐ $\frac{9 + 3y}{2} = x$ Ⓑ $\frac{2}{3}y - 9 = x$ Ⓒ $x = \frac{2}{3}y - 3$ Ⓓ $x = 2y - 3$

36. Which of the following is a correct method for solving $2a - 5b = 10$ for $b$?

Ⓕ Add $5b$ to both sides, then divide both sides by 2.

Ⓖ Subtract $5b$ from both sides, then divide both sides by 2.

Ⓗ Divide both sides by 5, then add $2a$ to both sides.

Ⓙ Subtract $2a$ from both sides, then divide both sides by $-5$.

37. The formula for the volume of a rectangular prism is $V = \ell wh$. Anna wants to make a cardboard box with a length of 7 inches, a width of 5 inches, and a volume of 210 cubic inches. Which variable does Anna need to solve for in order to build her box?

Ⓐ $V$ Ⓑ $\ell$ Ⓒ $w$ Ⓓ $h$

## CHALLENGE AND EXTEND

**Solve for the indicated variable.**

38. $3.3x + r = 23.1$ for $x$ 39. $\frac{2}{5}a - \frac{3}{4}b = c$ for $a$ 40. $\frac{3}{5}x + 1.4y = \frac{2}{5}$ for $y$

41. $t = \frac{d}{500} + \frac{1}{2}$ for $d$ 42. $s = \frac{1}{2}gt^2$ for $g$ 43. $v^2 = u^2 + 2as$ for $s$

44. Solve $y = mx + 6$ for $m$. What can you say about $y$ if $m = 0$?

45. **Entertainment** The formula $S = \frac{h \cdot w \cdot f \cdot t}{35{,}000}$ gives the approximate size in kilobytes (Kb) of a compressed video. The variables $h$ and $w$ represent the height and width of the frame measured in pixels, $f$ is the number of frames per second (fps) the video plays, and $t$ is the time the video plays in seconds. Estimate the time a movie trailer will play if it has a frame height of 320 pixels, has a frame width of 144 pixels, plays at 15 fps, and has a size of 2370 Kb.

## SPIRAL REVIEW

46. Jill spent $\frac{1}{4}$ of the money she made baby-sitting. She made \$40 baby-sitting. How much did she spend? *(Previous course)*

47. In one class, $\frac{3}{5}$ of the students are boys. There are 30 students in the class. How many are girls? *(Previous course)*

**Evaluate each expression for the given value of $x$.** *(Lesson 1-6)*

48. $3 + 2 \cdot x + 4$ for $x = 3$ 49. $24 \div 4 - x$ for $x = 12$ 50. $43 - 62 + x$ for $x = 15$

**Solve each equation.** *(Lesson 2-1)*

51. $18 = -2 + w$ 52. $2 = -3 + c$ 53. $-8 + k = 4$ 54. $-15 + a = -27$

# MULTI-STEP TEST PREP

## Equations and Formulas

**All Fired Up** A large forest fire in the western United States burns for 14 days, spreading to cover approximately 3850 acres. Firefighters do their best to contain the fire, but hot temperatures and high winds may prompt them to request additional support.

1. The fire spreads at an average rate of how many acres per day?
2. Officials estimate that the fire will spread to cover 9075 acres before it is contained. At this rate, how many more days will it take for the fire to cover an area of 9075 acres? Answer this question using at least two different methods.
3. Additional help arrives, and the firefighters contain the fire in 7 more days. In total, how many acres does the fire cover before it is contained?
4. If the fire had spread to cover an area of 7000 acres, it would have reached Bowman Valley. Explain how the graph shows that firefighters stopped the spread of the fire before it reached Bowman Valley.

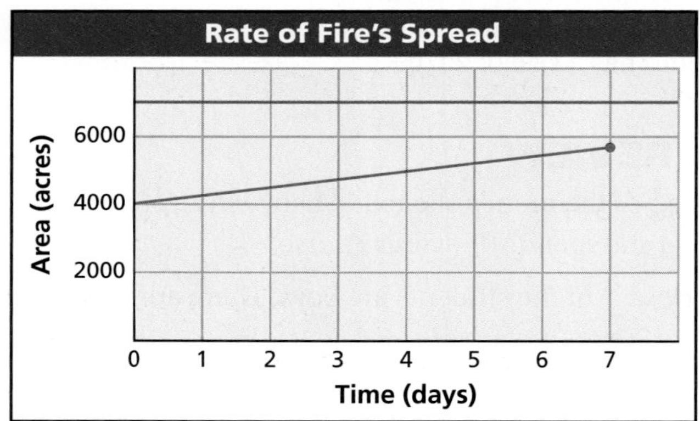


5. The total cost of fighting the fire for 21 days was approximately \$1,440,000. What was the approximate cost per acre of fighting the fire?

# READY TO GO ON?

## Quiz for Lessons 2-1 Through 2-5

### 2-1 Solving Equations by Adding or Subtracting

**Solve each equation.**

**1.** $x - 32 = -18$ **2.** $1.1 = m - 0.9$ **3.** $j + 4 = -17$ **4.** $\frac{9}{8} = g + \frac{1}{2}$

**5.** When she first purchased it, Soledad's computer had 400 GB of hard drive space. After six months, there were only 313 GB available. Write and solve an equation to find the amount of hard drive space that Soledad used in the first six months.

### 2-2 Solving Equations by Multiplying or Dividing

**Solve each equation.**

**6.** $\frac{h}{3} = -12$ **7.** $-2.8 = \frac{w}{-3}$ **8.** $42 = 3c$ **9.** $-0.1b = 3.7$

**10.** A fund-raiser raised \$2400, which was $\frac{3}{5}$ of the goal. Write and solve an equation to find the amount of the goal.

### 2-3 Solving Two-Step and Multi-Step Equations

**Solve each equation.**

**11.** $2r + 20 = 200$ **12.** $\frac{3}{5}k + 5 = 7$ **13.** $5n + 6 - 3n = -12$ **14.** $4(x - 7) = 2$

**15.** A taxicab company charges \$2.10 plus \$0.80 per mile. Carmen paid a fare of \$11.70. Write and solve an equation to find the number of miles she traveled.

### 2-4 Solving Equations with Variables on Both Sides

**Solve each equation.**

**16.** $4x - 3 = 2x + 5$ **17.** $3(2x - 5) = 2(3x - 2)$

**18.** $2(2t - 3) = 6(t + 2)$ **19.** $7(x + 5) = -7(x + 5)$

**20.** On the first day of the year, Diego had \$700 in his savings account and started spending \$35 a week. His brother Juan had \$450 and started saving \$15 a week. After how many weeks will the brothers have the same amount? What will that amount be?

### 2-5 Solving for a Variable

**21.** Solve $2x + 3y = 12$ for $x$. **22.** Solve $\frac{x}{r} = v$ for $x$.

**23.** Solve $5j + s = t - 2$ for $t$. **24.** Solve $h + p = 3(k - 8)$ for $k$.

**25.** The formula for the area of a triangle is $A = \frac{1}{2}bh$. Solve the formula for $h$. If the area of a triangle is 48 $cm^2$, and its base measures 12 cm, what is the height of the triangle?

# 2-6 Rates, Ratios, and Proportions

 **MA.N.1** Use ratios and rates to solve problems. *Also* **MA.N.1.2**

***Objectives***

Write and use ratios, rates, and unit rates.

Write and solve proportions.

***Vocabulary***

ratio
rate
scale
unit rate
conversion factor
proportion
cross products
scale drawing
scale model

**Why learn this?**

Ratios and proportions are used to draw accurate maps. (See Example 5.)

A **ratio** is a comparison of two quantities by division. The ratio of $a$ to $b$ can be written $a{:}b$ or $\frac{a}{b}$, where $b \neq 0$. Ratios that name the same comparison are said to be *equivalent.*

A statement that two ratios are equivalent, such as $\frac{1}{12} = \frac{2}{24}$, is called a **proportion**.

## EXAMPLE 1 Using Ratios

**The ratio of faculty members to students at a college is 1:15. There are 675 students. How many faculty members are there?**

**Reading Math**

Read the proportion $\frac{1}{15} = \frac{x}{675}$ as "1 is to 15 as $x$ is to 675."

$\frac{\text{faculty}}{\text{students}} \begin{matrix}\rightarrow\\ \rightarrow\end{matrix} \frac{1}{15}$ *Write a ratio comparing faculty to students.*

$\frac{1}{15} = \frac{x}{675}$ *Write a proportion. Let x be the number of faculty members.*

$675\left(\frac{x}{675}\right) = 675\left(\frac{1}{15}\right)$ *Since x is divided by 675, multiply both sides of the equation by 675.*

$x = 45$

There are 45 faculty members.

1. The ratio of games won to games lost for a baseball team is 3:2. The team won 18 games. How many games did the team lose?

A **rate** is a ratio of two quantities with different units, such as $\frac{34 \text{ mi}}{2 \text{ gal}}$. Rates are usually written as *unit rates.* A **unit rate** is a rate with a second quantity of 1 unit, such as $\frac{17 \text{ mi}}{1 \text{ gal}}$, or 17 mi/gal. You can convert any rate to a unit rate.

## EXAMPLE 2 Finding Unit Rates

**Takeru Kobayashi of Japan ate 53.5 hot dogs in 12 minutes to win a contest. Find the unit rate. Round your answer to the nearest hundredth.**

$\frac{53.5}{12} = \frac{x}{1}$ *Write a proportion to find an equivalent ratio with a second quantity of 1.*

$4.46 \approx x$ *Divide on the left side to find x.*

The unit rate is approximately 4.46 hot dogs per minute.

2. Cory earns \$52.50 in 7 hours. Find the unit rate.

A rate such as $\frac{12 \text{ in.}}{1 \text{ ft}}$, in which the two quantities are equal but use different units, is called a **conversion factor**. To convert a rate from one set of units to another, multiply by a conversion factor.

## EXAMPLE 3 Converting Rates

**Helpful Hint**

In Example 3A, "1 km" appears to divide out, leaving "degrees per meter," which are the units asked for. Use this strategy of "dividing out" units when converting rates.

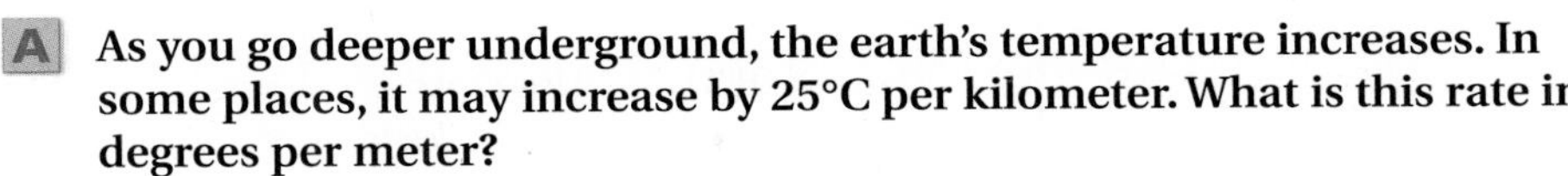

**A** **As you go deeper underground, the earth's temperature increases. In some places, it may increase by 25°C per kilometer. What is this rate in degrees per meter?**

$$\frac{25°\text{C}}{1 \text{ km}} \cdot \frac{1 \text{ km}}{1000 \text{ m}}$$ *To convert the second quantity in a rate, multiply by a conversion factor with that unit in the first quantity.*

$$\frac{0.025°\text{C}}{1 \text{ m}}$$

The rate is 0.025°C per meter.

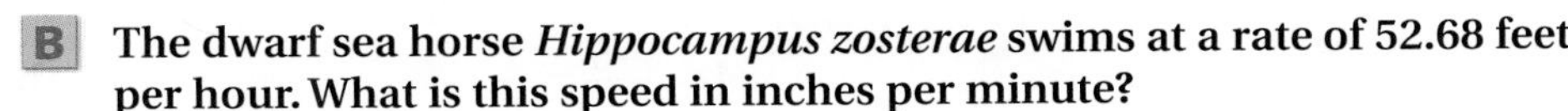

**B** **The dwarf sea horse *Hippocampus zosterae* swims at a rate of 52.68 feet per hour. What is this speed in inches per minute?**

**Step 1** Convert the speed to inches per hour.

$$\frac{52.68 \text{ ft}}{1 \text{ h}} \cdot \frac{12 \text{ in.}}{1 \text{ ft}}$$ *To convert the first quantity in a rate, multiply by a conversion factor with that unit in the second quantity.*

$$\frac{632.16 \text{ in.}}{1 \text{ h}}$$

The speed is 632.16 inches per hour.

**Step 2** Convert this speed to inches per minute.

$$\frac{632.16 \text{ in.}}{1 \text{ h}} \cdot \frac{1 \text{ h}}{60 \text{ min}}$$ *To convert the second quantity in a rate, multiply by a conversion factor with that unit in the first quantity.*

$$\frac{10.536 \text{ in.}}{1 \text{ min}}$$

The speed is 10.536 inches per minute.

*Hippocampus zosterae*

Check that the answer is reasonable. The answer is about 10 in./min.

- There are 60 min in 1 h, so 10 in./min is $60(10) = 600$ in./h.
- There are 12 in. in 1 ft, so 600 in./h is $\frac{600}{12} = 50$ ft/h. This is close to the rate given in the problem, 52.68 ft/h.

**CHECK IT OUT!** 3. A cyclist travels 56 miles in 4 hours. What is the cyclist's speed in feet per second? Round your answer to the nearest tenth, and show that your answer is reasonable.

In the proportion $\frac{a}{b} = \frac{c}{d}$, the products $a \cdot d$ and $b \cdot c$ are called **cross products**. You can solve a proportion for a missing value by using the Cross Products Property.

Know it! Note

**Cross Products Property**

| WORDS | NUMBERS | ALGEBRA |
|---|---|---|
| In a proportion, cross products are equal. | $\frac{2}{3} \times \frac{4}{6}$<br>$2 \cdot 6 = 3 \cdot 4$ | If $\frac{a}{b} = \frac{c}{d}$ and $b \neq 0$ and $d \neq 0$, then $ad = bc$. |

## EXAMPLE 4 Solving Proportions

**Solve each proportion.**

**A** $\frac{5}{9} = \frac{3}{w}$

$\frac{5}{9} \times \frac{3}{w}$

$5(w) = 9(3)$ *Use cross products.*

$5w = 27$

$\frac{5w}{5} = \frac{27}{5}$ *Divide both sides by 5.*

$w = \frac{27}{5}$

**B** $\frac{8}{x+10} = \frac{1}{12}$

$\frac{8}{x+10} \times \frac{1}{12}$

$8(12) = 1(x+10)$ *Use cross products.*

$96 = x + 10$

$\underline{-10} \quad \underline{-10}$ *Subtract 10 from both sides.*

$86 = x$

**Solve each proportion.**

**4a.** $\frac{-5}{2} = \frac{y}{8}$ **4b.** $\frac{g+3}{5} = \frac{7}{4}$

A **scale** is a ratio between two sets of measurements, such as 1 in:5 mi. A **scale drawing** or **scale model** uses a scale to represent an object as smaller or larger than the actual object. A map is an example of a scale drawing.

## EXAMPLE 5 Scale Drawings and Scale Models

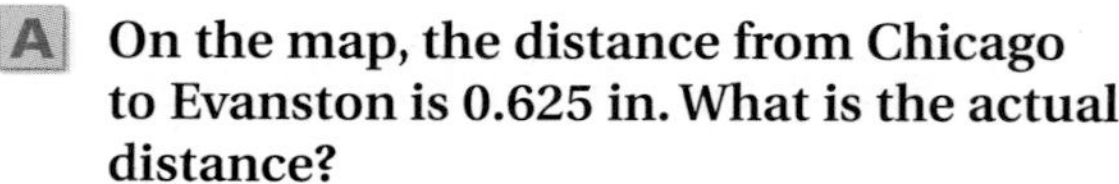

**A** **On the map, the distance from Chicago to Evanston is 0.625 in. What is the actual distance?**

$\frac{\text{map}}{\text{actual}} \begin{matrix}\rightarrow \\ \rightarrow\end{matrix} \frac{1 \text{ in.}}{18 \text{ mi}}$ *Write the scale as a fraction.*

$\frac{1}{18} \times \frac{0.625}{x}$ *Let x be the actual distance.*

$x \cdot 1 = 18(0.625)$ *Use cross products to solve.*

$x = 11.25$

The actual distance is 11.25 mi.

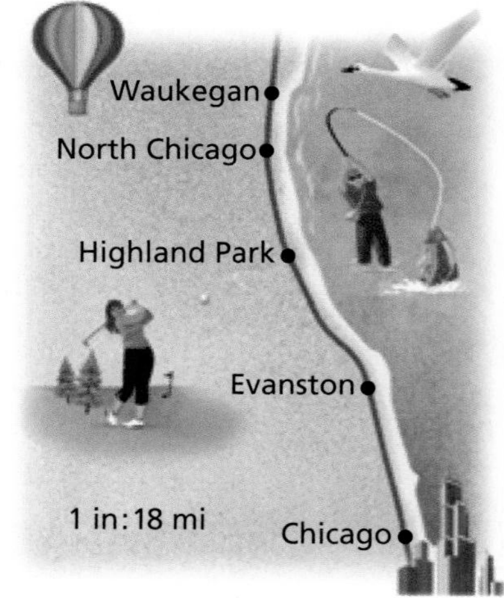


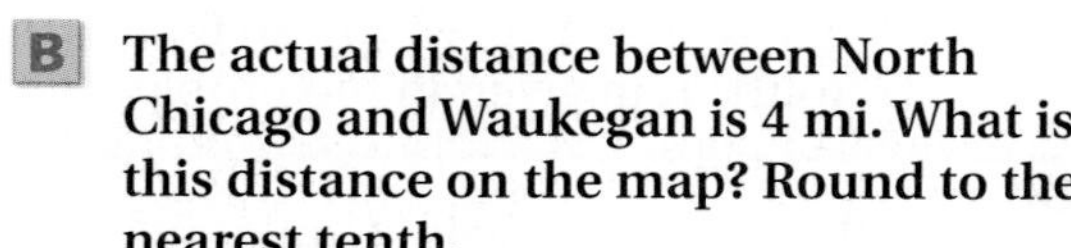

**B** **The actual distance between North Chicago and Waukegan is 4 mi. What is this distance on the map? Round to the nearest tenth.**

$\frac{\text{map}}{\text{actual}} \begin{matrix}\rightarrow \\ \rightarrow\end{matrix} \frac{1 \text{ in.}}{18 \text{ mi}}$ *Write the scale as a fraction.*

$\frac{1}{18} \times \frac{x}{4}$ *Let x be the distance on the map.*

$4 = 18x$ *Use cross products to solve the proportion.*

$\frac{4}{18} = \frac{18x}{18}$ *Since x is multiplied by 18, divide both sides by 18 to undo the multiplication.*

$0.2 \approx x$ *Round to the nearest tenth.*

The distance on the map is about 0.2 in.

**Reading Math**

A scale written without units, such as 32:1, means that 32 units of any measure correspond to 1 unit of that same measure.

**5.** A scale model of a human heart is 16 ft long. The scale is 32:1. How many inches long is the actual heart it represents?

## THINK AND DISCUSS

1. Explain two ways to solve the proportion $\frac{t}{4} = \frac{3}{5}$.
2. How could you show that the answer to Example 5A is reasonable?

3. **GET ORGANIZED** Copy and complete the graphic organizer. In each box, write an example of each use of ratios.

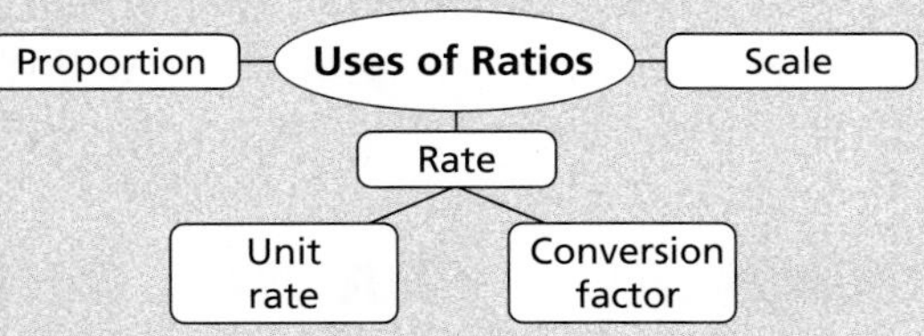


# 2-6 Exercises

MA.N.1, MA.N.1.2

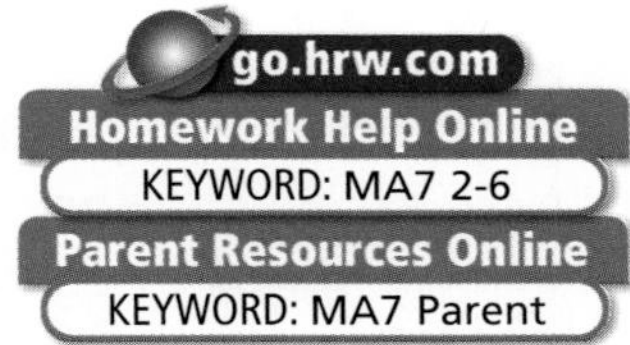


## GUIDED PRACTICE

1. **Vocabulary** What does it mean when two ratios form a *proportion*?

SEE EXAMPLE 1 p. 114

2. The ratio of the sale price of a jacket to the original price is 3 : 4. The original price is \$64. What is the sale price?
3. **Chemistry** The ratio of hydrogen atoms to oxygen atoms in water is 2 : 1. If an amount of water contains 341 trillion atoms of oxygen, how many hydrogen atoms are there?

SEE EXAMPLE 2 p. 114

**Find each unit rate.**

4. A computer's fan rotates 2000 times in 40 seconds.
5. Twelve cows produce 224,988 pounds of milk.
6. A yellow jacket can fly 4.5 meters in 9 seconds.

SEE EXAMPLE 3 p. 115

7. Lydia wrote $4\frac{1}{2}$ pages of her science report in one hour. What was her writing rate in pages per minute?
8. A model airplane flies 18 feet in 2 seconds. What is the airplane's speed in miles per hour? Round your answer to the nearest hundredth.
9. A vehicle uses 1 tablespoon of gasoline to drive 125 yards. How many miles can the vehicle travel per gallon? Round your answer to the nearest mile. (*Hint:* There are 256 tablespoons in a gallon.)

SEE EXAMPLE 4 p. 116

**Solve each proportion.**

10. $\frac{3}{z} = \frac{1}{8}$
11. $\frac{x}{3} = \frac{1}{5}$
12. $\frac{b}{4} = \frac{3}{2}$
13. $\frac{f+3}{12} = \frac{7}{2}$
14. $\frac{-1}{5} = \frac{3}{2d}$
15. $\frac{3}{14} = \frac{s-2}{21}$
16. $\frac{-4}{9} = \frac{7}{x}$
17. $\frac{3}{s-2} = \frac{1}{7}$
18. $\frac{10}{h} = \frac{52}{13}$

19. **Archaeology** Stonehenge II in Hunt, Texas, is a scale model of the ancient construction in Wiltshire, England. The scale of the model to the original is 3:5. The Altar Stone of the original construction is 4.9 meters tall. Write and solve a proportion to find the height of the model of the Altar Stone.

Alfred Sheppard, one of the builders of Stonehenge II.

## PRACTICE AND PROBLEM SOLVING

**Independent Practice**

| For Exercises | See Example |
|---|---|
| 20–21 | 1 |
| 22–23 | 2 |
| 24–25 | 3 |
| 26–37 | 4 |
| 38 | 5 |

**Extra Practice**

Skills Practice p. S7

Application Practice p. S29

20. **Gardening** The ratio of the height of a bonsai ficus tree to the height of a full-size ficus tree is 1:9. The bonsai ficus is 6 inches tall. What is the height of a full-size ficus?

21. **Manufacturing** At one factory, the ratio of defective light bulbs produced to total light bulbs produced is about 3:500. How many light bulbs are expected to be defective when 12,000 are produced?

**Find each unit rate.**

22. Four gallons of gasoline weigh 25 pounds.

23. Fifteen ounces of gold cost $6058.50.

24. **Biology** The tropical giant bamboo can grow 11.9 feet in 3 days. What is this rate of growth in inches per hour? Round your answer to the nearest hundredth, and show that your answer is reasonable.

25. **Transportation** The maximum speed of the Tupolev Tu-144 airliner is 694 m/s. What is this speed in kilometers per hour?

**Solve each proportion.**

26. $\frac{v}{6} = \frac{1}{2}$ 27. $\frac{2}{5} = \frac{4}{y}$ 28. $\frac{2}{h} = \frac{-5}{6}$ 29. $\frac{3}{10} = \frac{b+7}{20}$

30. $\frac{5t}{9} = \frac{1}{2}$ 31. $\frac{2}{3} = \frac{6}{q-4}$ 32. $\frac{x}{8} = \frac{7.5}{20}$ 33. $\frac{3}{k} = \frac{45}{18}$

34. $\frac{6}{a} = \frac{15}{17}$ 35. $\frac{9}{2} = \frac{5}{x+1}$ 36. $\frac{3}{5} = \frac{x}{100}$ 37. $\frac{38}{19} = \frac{n-5}{20}$

38. **Science** The image shows a dust mite as seen under a microscope. The scale of the drawing to the dust mite is 100:1. Use a ruler to measure the length of the dust mite in the image in millimeters. What is the actual length of the dust mite?

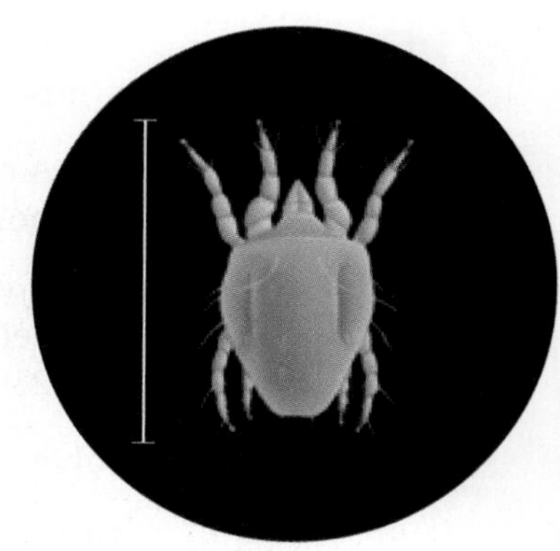

39. **Finance** On a certain day, the exchange rate was 60 U.S. dollars for 50 euro. How many U.S. dollars were 70 euro worth that day? Show that your answer is reasonable.

40. **Environmental Science** An environmental scientist wants to estimate the number of carp in a pond. He captures 100 carp, tags all of them, and releases them. A week later, he captures 85 carp and records how many have tags. His results are shown in the table. Write and solve a proportion to estimate the number of carp in the pond.

| Status | Number Captured |
|---|---|
| Tagged | 20 |
| Not tagged | 65 |

41. **ERROR ANALYSIS** Below is a bonus question that appeared on an algebra test and a student's response.

> The ratio of junior varsity members to varsity members on the track team is 3:5. There are 24 members on the team. Write a proportion to find the number of junior varsity members.
>
> $\frac{3}{5} = \frac{x}{24}$

The student did not receive the bonus points. Why is this proportion incorrect?

**LINK Sports**

The records for the women's 100-meter dash and the women's 200-meter dash were set by Florence Griffith-Joyner, known as "Flo Jo." She is still referred to as the world's fastest woman.

42. **Sports** The table shows world record times for women's races of different distances.
  a. Find the speed in meters per second for each race. Round your answers to the nearest hundredth.
  b. Which race has the fastest speed? the slowest?
  c. **Critical Thinking** Give a possible reason why the speeds are different.

| World Records (Women) | |
|---|---|
| Distance (m) | Times (s) |
| 100 | 10.5 |
| 200 | 21.3 |
| 800 | 113.3 |
| 5000 | 864.7 |

43. **Entertainment** Lynn, Faith, and Jeremy are film animators. In one 8-hour day, Lynn rendered 203 frames, Faith rendered 216 frames, and Jeremy rendered 227 frames. How many more frames per hour did Faith render than Lynn did?

**Solve each proportion.**

44. $\frac{x-1}{3} = \frac{x+1}{5}$
45. $\frac{m}{3} = \frac{m+4}{7}$
46. $\frac{1}{x-3} = \frac{3}{x-5}$
47. $\frac{a}{2} = \frac{a-4}{30}$
48. $\frac{3}{2y} = \frac{16}{y+2}$
49. $\frac{n+3}{5} = \frac{n-1}{2}$
50. $\frac{1}{y} = \frac{1}{6y-1}$
51. $\frac{2}{n} = \frac{4}{n+3}$
52. $\frac{5t-3}{-2} = \frac{t+3}{2}$
53. $\frac{3}{d+3} = \frac{4}{d+12}$
54. $\frac{3x+5}{14} = \frac{x}{3}$
55. $\frac{5}{2n} = \frac{8}{3n-24}$

56. **Decorating** A particular shade of paint is made by mixing 5 parts red paint with 7 parts blue paint. To make this shade, Shannon mixed 12 quarts of blue paint with 8 quarts of red paint. Did Shannon mix the correct shade? Explain.

57. **Write About It** Give three examples of proportions. How do you know they are proportions? Then give three nonexamples of proportions. How do you know they are not proportions?

58. This problem will prepare you for the Multi-Step Test Prep on page 146.
  a. Marcus is shopping for a new jacket. He finds one with a price tag of \$120. Above the rack is a sign that says that he can take off $\frac{1}{5}$. Find out how much Marcus can deduct from the price of the jacket.
  b. What price will Marcus pay for the jacket?
  c. Copy the model below. Complete it by placing numerical values on top and the corresponding fractional parts below.

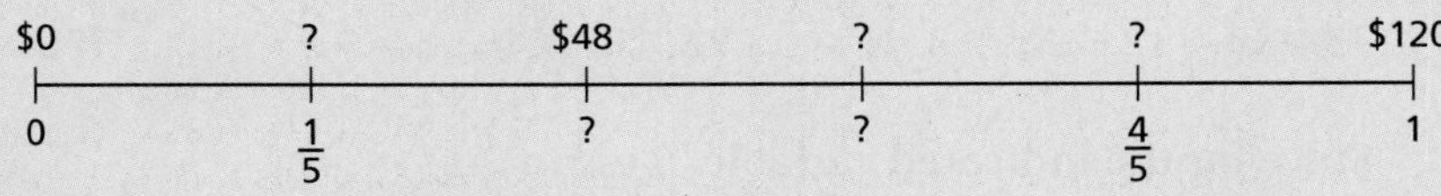


  d. Explain how this model shows proportional relationships.

## TEST PREP

MA.N.1, MA.N.1.2

**59.** One day the U.S. dollar was worth approximately 100 yen. An exchange of 2500 yen was made that day. What was the value of the exchange in dollars?

Ⓐ \$25 Ⓑ \$400 Ⓒ \$2500 Ⓓ \$40,000

**60.** Brett walks at a speed of 4 miles per hour. He walks for 20 minutes in a straight line at this rate. Approximately what distance does Brett walk?

Ⓕ 0.06 miles Ⓖ 1.3 miles Ⓗ 5 miles Ⓙ 80 miles

**61.** A shampoo company conducted a survey and found that 3 out of 8 people use their brand of shampoo. Which proportion could be used to find the expected number of users $n$ in a city of 75,000 people?

Ⓐ $\frac{3}{8} = \frac{75{,}000}{n}$ Ⓑ $\frac{3}{75{,}000} = \frac{n}{8}$ Ⓒ $\frac{8}{3} = \frac{n}{75{,}000}$ Ⓓ $\frac{3}{8} = \frac{n}{75{,}000}$

**62.** A statue is 3 feet tall. The display case for a model of the statue can fit a model that is no more than 9 inches tall. Which of the scales below allows for the tallest model of the statue that will fit in the display case?

Ⓕ 2:1 Ⓖ 1:1 Ⓗ 1:3 Ⓙ 1:4

## CHALLENGE AND EXTEND

**63. Geometry** Complementary angles are two angles whose measures add up to 90°. The ratio of the measures of two complementary angles is 4:5. What are the measures of the angles?

**64.** A customer wanted 24 feet of rope. The clerk at the hardware store used what she thought was a yardstick to measure the rope, but the yardstick was actually 2 inches too short. How many inches were missing from the customer's piece of rope?

**65. Population** The population density of Jackson, Mississippi, is 672.2 people per square kilometer. What is the population density in people per square meter? Show that your answer is reasonable. (*Hint:* There are 1000 meters in 1 kilometer. How many square meters are in 1 square kilometer?)

## SPIRAL REVIEW

**Evaluate each expression.** *(Lesson 1-4)*

**66.** $8^2$ **67.** $(-3)^3$ **68.** $(-3)^2$ **69.** $-\left(\frac{1}{2}\right)^5$

**Write the power represented by each geometric model.** *(Lesson 1-4)*

**70.**

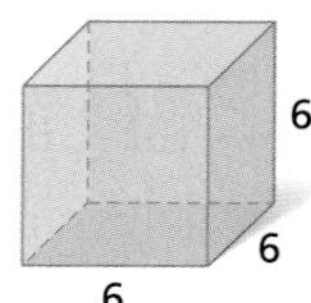


**71.**

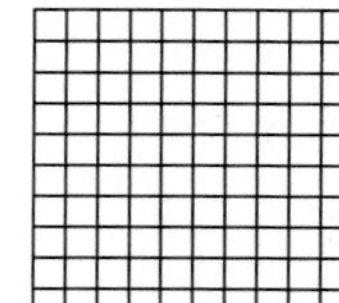

**72.**

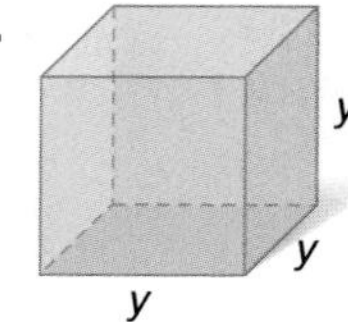


**Solve each equation. Check your answer.** *(Lesson 2-4)*

**73.** $2x - 12 = 5x + 3$ **74.** $3a - 4 = 6 - 7a$ **75.** $3x - 4 = 2x + 4$

**Solve for the indicated variable.** *(Lesson 2-5)*

**76.** $y = mx + b$ for $b$ **77.** $PV = nRT$ for $V$ **78.** $A = \frac{1}{2}bh$ for $h$

# 2-7 Applications of Proportions

**MA.N.1** Use ratios ... to solve problems. **MA.N.1.1** Use proportions to solve problems. *Also* **MA.N.1.2**

***Objectives***

Use proportions to solve problems involving geometric figures.

Use proportions and similar figures to measure objects indirectly.

***Vocabulary***

similar
corresponding sides
corresponding angles
indirect measurement
scale factor

**Why learn this?**

Proportions can be used to find the heights of tall objects, such as totem poles, that would otherwise be difficult to measure. (See Example 2.)

**Similar** figures have exactly the same shape but not necessarily the same size.

**Corresponding sides** of two figures are in the same relative position, and **corresponding angles** are in the same relative position. Two figures are similar if and only if the lengths of corresponding sides are proportional and all pairs of corresponding angles have equal measures.

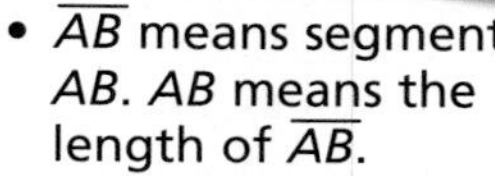

**Reading Math**

- $\overline{AB}$ means segment $AB$. $AB$ means the length of $\overline{AB}$.
- $\angle A$ means angle $A$. $m\angle A$ means the measure of angle $A$.

$$\frac{AB}{DE} = \frac{BC}{EF} = \frac{AC}{DF}$$

$m\angle A = m\angle D$
$m\angle B = m\angle E$
$m\angle C = m\angle F$

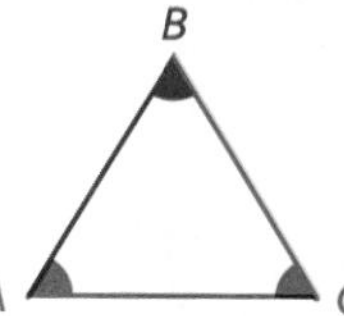


When stating that two figures are similar, use the symbol ~. For the triangles above, you can write $\triangle ABC \sim \triangle DEF$. Make sure corresponding vertices are in the same order. It would be incorrect to write $\triangle ABC \sim \triangle EFD$.

You can use proportions to find missing lengths in similar figures.

## EXAMPLE 1 Finding Missing Measures in Similar Figures

**Find the value of *x* in each diagram.**

**A** $\triangle RST \sim \triangle BCD$

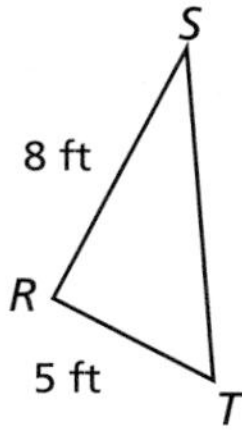


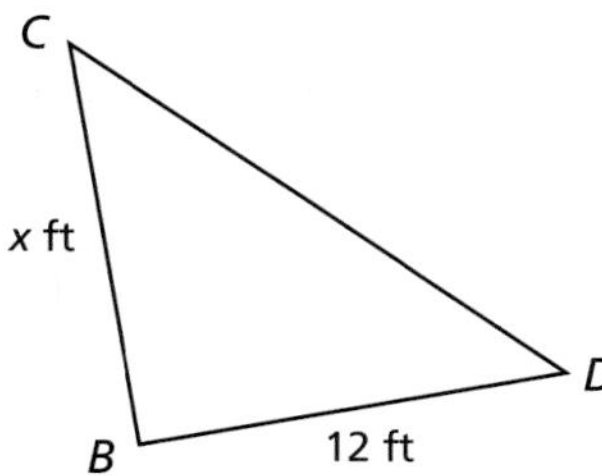


*R* corresponds to *B*, *S* corresponds to *C*, and *T* corresponds to *D*.

$\frac{5}{12} = \frac{8}{x}$ — $\frac{RT}{BD} = \frac{RS}{BC}$

$5x = 96$ — *Use cross products.*

$\frac{5x}{5} = \frac{96}{5}$ — *Since x is multiplied by 5, divide both sides by 5 to undo the multiplication.*

$x = 19.2$

The length of $\overline{BC}$ is 19.2 ft.

**Find the value of $x$ in each diagram.**

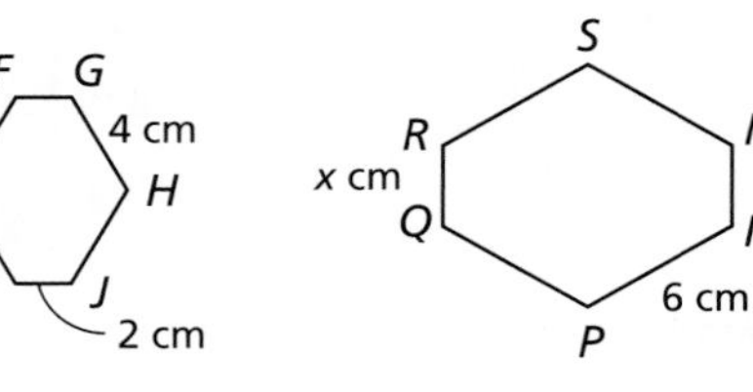


**B** ***FGHJKL ~ MNPQRS***

$$\frac{6}{4} = \frac{x}{2} \qquad \frac{NP}{GH} = \frac{RQ}{KJ}$$

$$4x = 12 \qquad \textit{Use cross products.}$$

$$\frac{4x}{4} = \frac{12}{4}$$ *Since x is multiplied by 4, divide both sides by 4 to undo the multiplication.*

$$x = 3$$

The length of $\overline{QR}$ is 3 cm.

**1.** Find the value of $x$ in the diagram if *ABCD ~ WXYZ*.

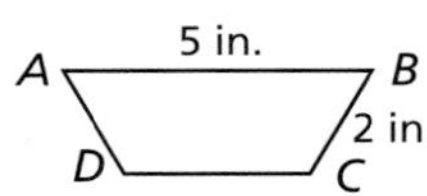


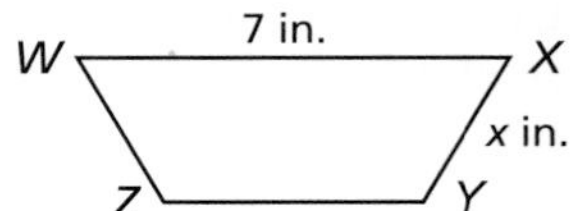


You can solve a proportion involving similar triangles to find a length that is not easily measured. This method of measurement is called **indirect measurement**. If two objects form right angles with the ground, you can apply indirect measurement using their shadows.

## EXAMPLE 2 *Measurement Application*

**A totem pole casts a shadow 45 feet long at the same time that a 6-foot-tall man casts a shadow that is 3 feet long. Write and solve a proportion to find the height of the totem pole.**

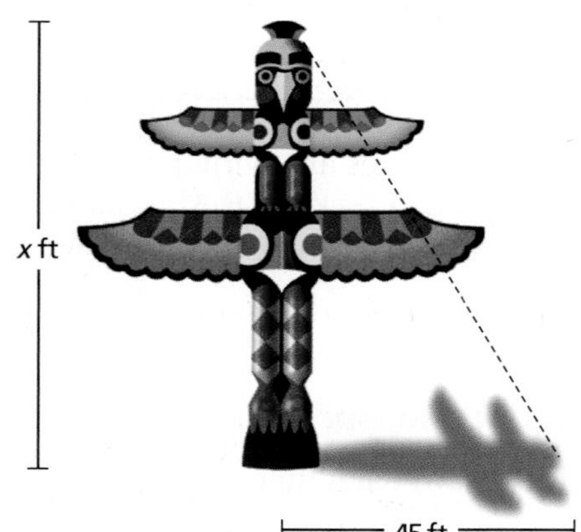


*Both the man and the totem pole form right angles with the ground, and their shadows are cast at the same angle. You can form two similar right triangles.*

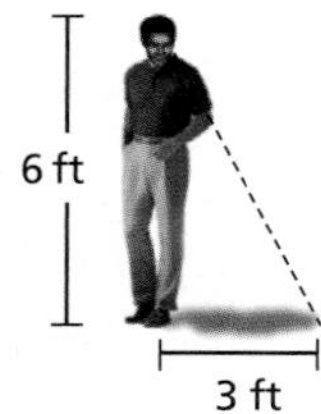


$$\frac{6}{x} = \frac{3}{45} \qquad \frac{\textit{man's height}}{\textit{pole's height}} = \frac{\textit{man's shadow}}{\textit{pole's shadow}}$$

$$3x = 270 \qquad \textit{Use cross products.}$$

$$\frac{3x}{3} = \frac{270}{3}$$ *Since x is multiplied by 3, divide both sides by 3 to undo the multiplication.*

$$x = 90$$

The totem pole is 90 feet tall.

**Helpful Hint**

A height of 90 ft seems reasonable for a totem pole. If you got 900 or 9000 ft, that would not be reasonable, and you should check your work.

**2a.** A forest ranger who is 150 cm tall casts a shadow 45 cm long. At the same time, a nearby tree casts a shadow 195 cm long. Write and solve a proportion to find the height of the tree.

**2b.** A woman who is 5.5 feet tall casts a shadow 3.5 feet long. At the same time, a building casts a shadow 28 feet long. Write and solve a proportion to find the height of the building.

If every dimension of a figure is multiplied by the same number, the result is a similar figure. The multiplier is called a **scale factor**.

**EXAMPLE 3** **Changing Dimensions**

**A** **Every dimension of a 2-by-4-inch rectangle is multiplied by 1.5 to form a similar rectangle. How is the ratio of the perimeters related to the ratio of corresponding sides? How is the ratio of the areas related to the ratio of corresponding sides?**

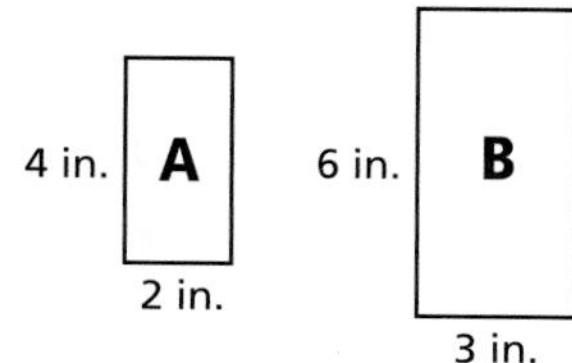


| | Rectangle A | Rectangle B |
|---|---|---|
| $P = 2\ell + 2w$ | $2(2) + 2(4) = 12$ | $2(6) + 2(3) = 18$ |
| $A = \ell w$ | $4(2) = 8$ | $6(3) = 18$ |

Sides: $\frac{4}{6} = \frac{2}{3}$ Perimeters: $\frac{12}{18} = \frac{2}{3}$ Areas: $\frac{8}{18} = \frac{4}{9} = \left(\frac{2}{3}\right)^2$

The ratio of the perimeters is equal to the ratio of corresponding sides. The ratio of the areas is the square of the ratio of corresponding sides.

**Helpful Hint**

A scale factor between 0 and 1 reduces a figure. A scale factor greater than 1 enlarges it.

**B** **Every dimension of a cylinder with radius 4 cm and height 6 cm is multiplied by $\frac{1}{2}$ to form a similar cylinder. How is the ratio of the volumes related to the ratio of corresponding dimensions?**

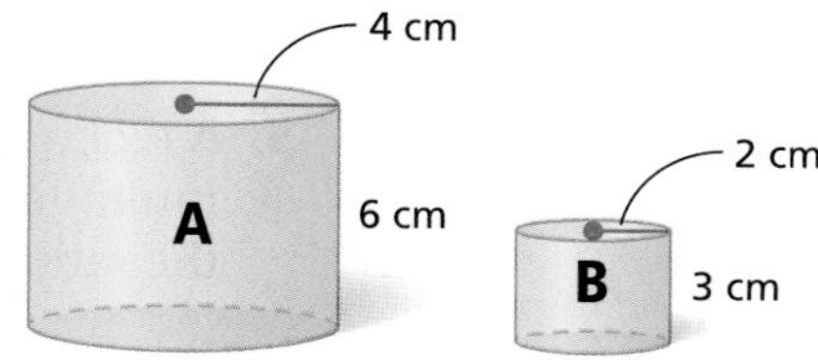


| | Cylinder A | Cylinder B |
|---|---|---|
| $V = \pi r^2 h$ | $\pi(4)^2(6) = 96\pi$ | $\pi(2)^2(3) = 12\pi$ |

Radii: $\frac{4}{2} = \frac{2}{1} = 2$ Heights: $\frac{6}{3} = \frac{2}{1} = 2$ Volumes: $\frac{96\pi}{12\pi} = \frac{8}{1} = 8 = 2^3$

The ratio of the volumes is the cube of the ratio of corresponding dimensions.

3. A rectangle has width 12 inches and length 3 inches. Every dimension of the rectangle is multiplied by $\frac{1}{3}$ to form a similar rectangle. How is the ratio of the perimeters related to the ratio of the corresponding sides?

## THINK AND DISCUSS

1. Name some pairs of real-world items that appear to be similar figures.

2. **GET ORGANIZED** Copy and complete the graphic organizer. In the top box, sketch and label two similar triangles. Then list the corresponding sides and angles in the bottom boxes.

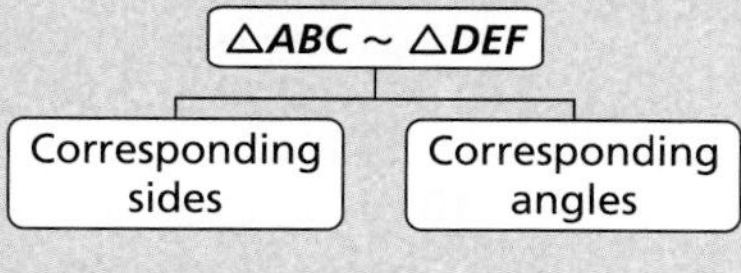

# 2-7 Exercises

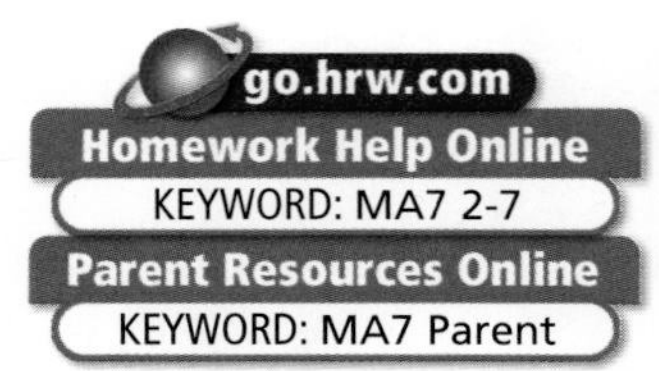


## GUIDED PRACTICE

1. **Vocabulary** What does it mean for two figures to be *similar*?

SEE EXAMPLE 1 p. 121

**Find the value of $x$ in each diagram.**

2. $\triangle ABC \sim \triangle DEF$

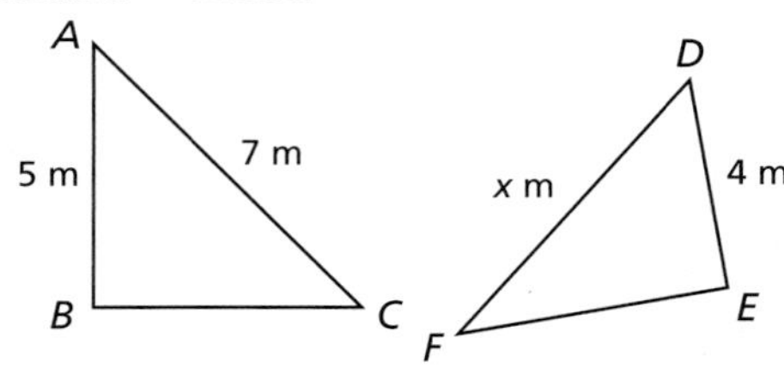


3. $RSTV \sim WXYZ$

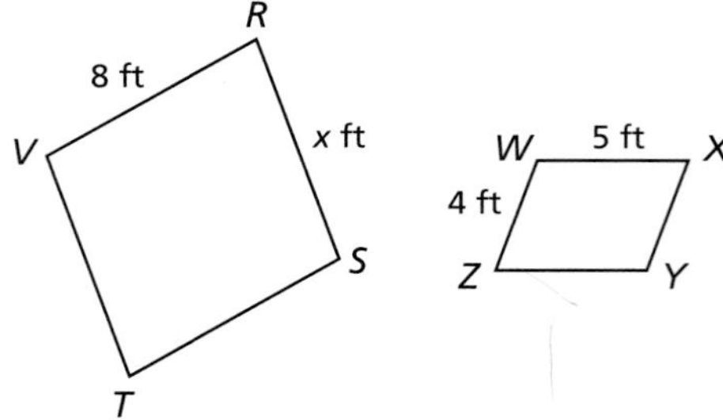


SEE EXAMPLE 2 p. 122

4. Roger is 5 feet tall and casts a shadow 3.5 feet long. At the same time, the flagpole outside his school casts a shadow 14 feet long. Write and solve a proportion to find the height of the flagpole.

SEE EXAMPLE 3 p. 123

5. A rectangle has length 12 feet and width 8 feet. Every dimension of the rectangle is multiplied by $\frac{3}{4}$ to form a similar rectangle. How is the ratio of the areas related to the ratio of corresponding sides?

## PRACTICE AND PROBLEM SOLVING

**Independent Practice**

| For Exercises | See Example |
|---|---|
| 6–7 | 1 |
| 8 | 2 |
| 9 | 3 |

**Extra Practice**

Skills Practice p. S7
Application Practice p. S29

**Find the value of $x$ in each diagram.**

6. $\triangle LMN \sim \triangle RST$

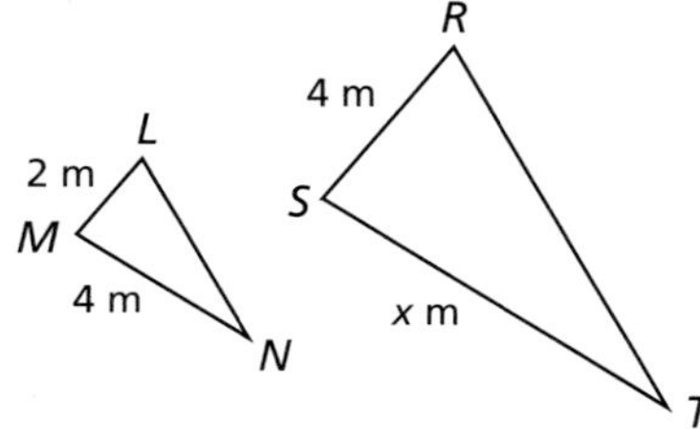


7. prism $A \sim$ prism $B$

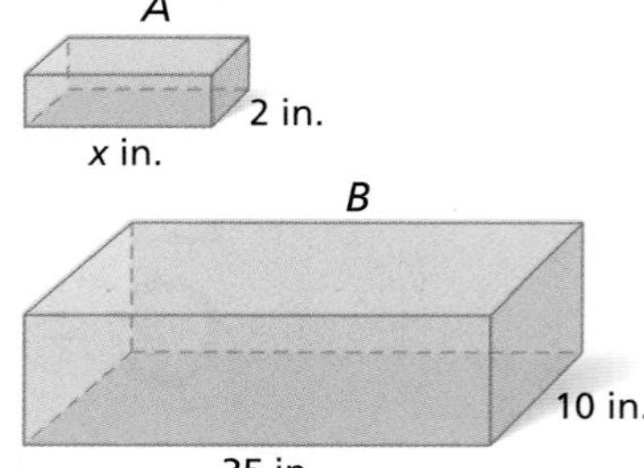


8. Write and solve a proportion to find the height of the taller tree in the diagram at right.

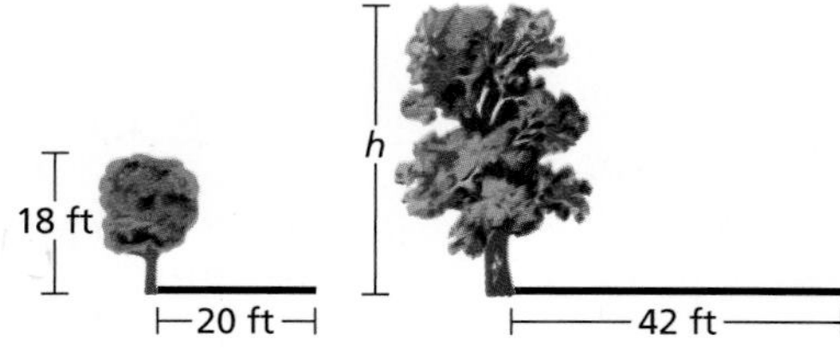


9. A triangle has side lengths of 5 inches, 12 inches, and 15 inches. Every dimension is multiplied by $\frac{1}{5}$ to form a new triangle. How is the ratio of the perimeters related to the ratio of corresponding sides?

10. **Hobbies** For a baby shower gift, Heather crocheted a baby blanket whose length was $2\frac{1}{2}$ feet and whose width was 2 feet. She plans to crochet a proportionally larger similar blanket for the baby's mother. If she wants the length of the mother's blanket to be $6\frac{1}{4}$ feet, what should the width be? Show that your answer is reasonable.

11. **Real Estate** Refer to the home builder's advertisement. The family rooms in both models are rectangular. How much carpeting is needed to carpet the family room in the Weston model?

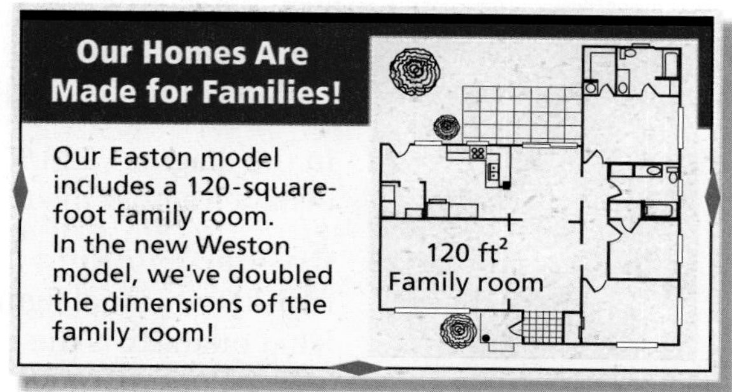


12. A rectangle has an area of 16 $ft^2$. Every dimension is multiplied by a scale factor, and the new rectangle has an area of 64 $ft^2$. What was the scale factor?

13. A cone has a volume of $98\pi$ $cm^3$. Every dimension is multiplied by a scale factor, and the new cone has a volume of $6272\pi$ $cm^3$. What was the scale factor?

**Find the value of $x$ in each diagram.**

14. $FGHJK \sim MNPQR$

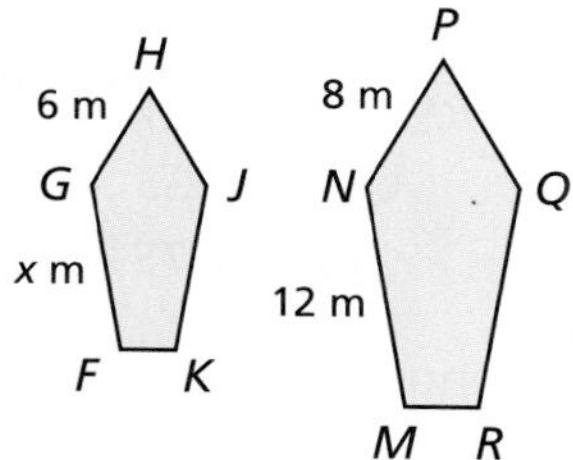


15. cylinder $A \sim$ cylinder $B$

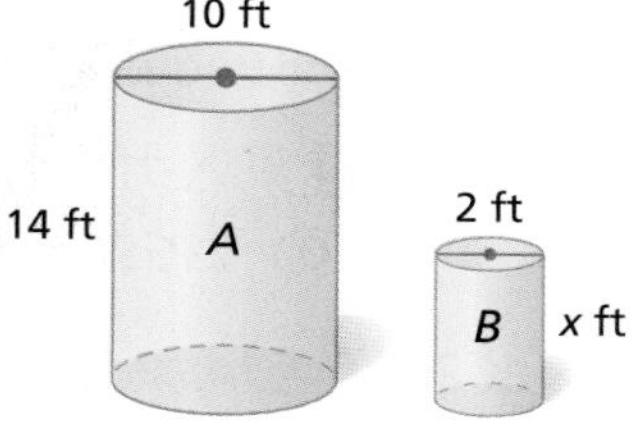


16. $\triangle BCD \sim \triangle FGD$

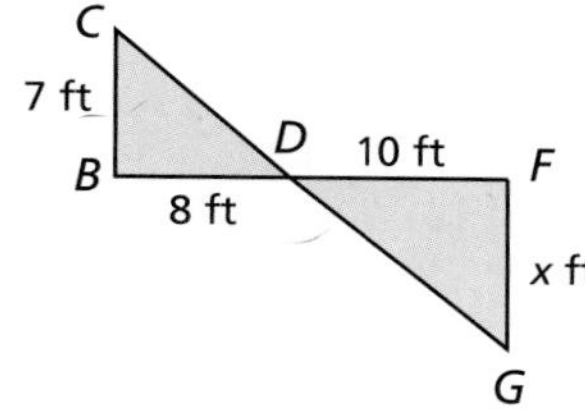


17. $\triangle RST \sim \triangle QSV$

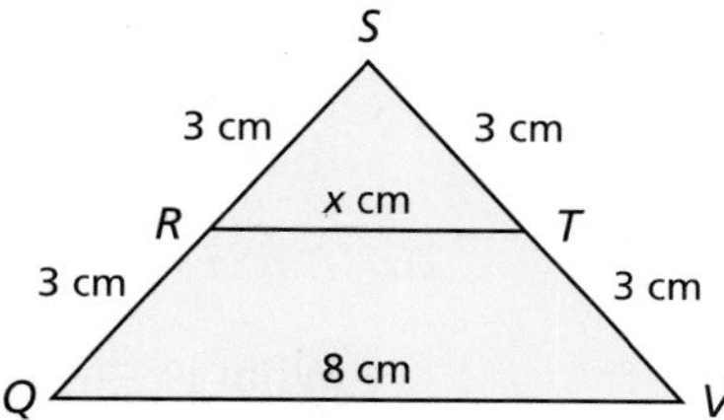


18. A tower casts a 450 ft shadow at the same time that a 4 ft child casts a 6 ft shadow. Write and solve a proportion to find the height of the tower.

19. **Write About It** At Pizza Palace, a pizza with a diameter of 8 inches costs \$6.00. The restaurant manager says that a 16-inch pizza should be priced at \$12.00 because it is twice as large. Do you agree? Explain why or why not.

**MULTI-STEP TEST PREP**

20. This problem will prepare you for the Multi-Step Test Prep on page 146.

Another common application of proportion is *percents*. A percent is a ratio of a number to 100. For example, $80\% = \frac{80}{100}$.

a. Write 12%, 18%, 25%, 67%, and 98% as ratios.

b. Percents can also be written as decimals. Write each of your ratios from part **a** as a decimal.

c. What do you notice about a percent and its decimal equivalent?

You will learn more about percents and their connections to proportions in upcoming lessons.

21. A lighthouse casts a shadow that is 36 meters long. At the same time, a person who is 1.5 meters tall casts a shadow that is 4.5 meters long. Write and solve a proportion to find the height of the lighthouse.

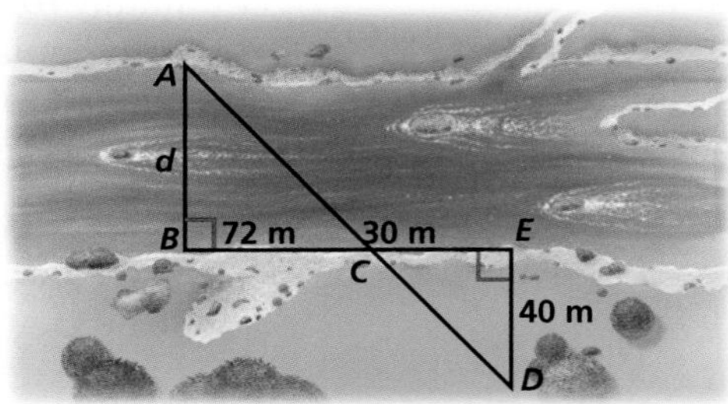


22. In the diagram, $\triangle ABC \sim \triangle DEC$. What is the distance across the river from $A$ to $B$?

23. **Critical Thinking** If every dimension of a two-dimensional figure is multiplied by $k$, by what quantity is the area multiplied?

## TEST PREP

MA.N.1, MA.N.1.1, MA.N.1.2

24. A beach ball holds 800 cubic inches of air. Another beach ball has a radius that is half that of the larger ball. How much air does the smaller ball hold?

 (A) 400 cubic inches
 (B) 200 cubic inches
 (C) 100 cubic inches
 (D) 80 cubic inches

25. For two similar triangles, $\frac{SG}{MW} = \frac{GT}{WR} = \frac{TS}{RM}$. Which statement below is NOT correct?

 (F) $\triangle SGT \sim \triangle MWR$
 (G) $\triangle GST \sim \triangle MRW$
 (H) $\triangle TGS \sim \triangle RWM$
 (J) $\triangle GTS \sim \triangle WRM$

26. **Gridded Response** A rectangle has length 5 centimeters and width 3 centimeters. A similar rectangle has length 7.25 centimeters. What is the width in centimeters of this rectangle?

## CHALLENGE AND EXTEND

27. Find the values of $w$, $x$, and $y$ given that $\triangle ABC \sim \triangle DEF \sim \triangle GHJ$.

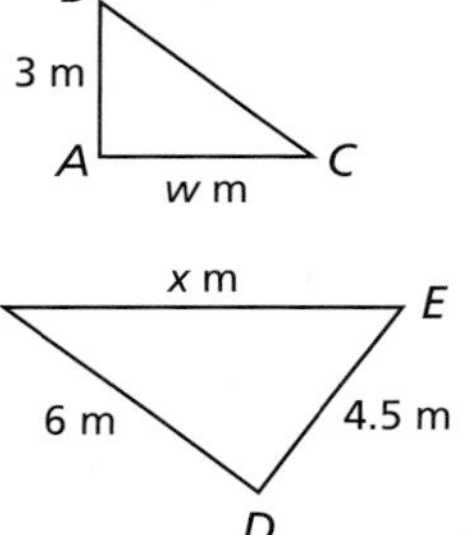


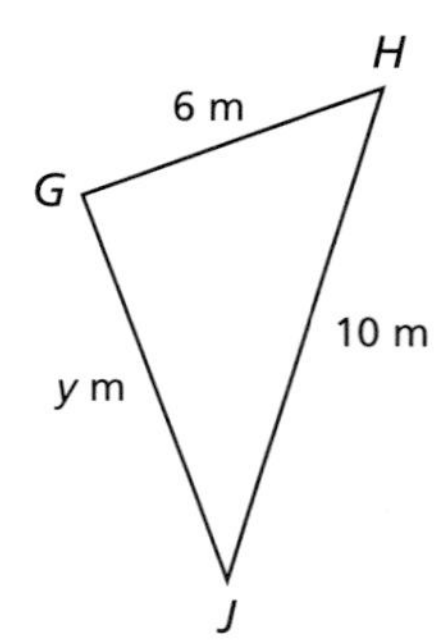


28. $\triangle RST \sim \triangle VWX$ and $\frac{RT}{VX} = b$.

 What is $\frac{\text{area of } \triangle RST}{\text{area of } \triangle VWX}$?

29. **Multi-Step** Rectangles $A$ and $B$ are similar. The area of $A$ is 30.195 cm$^2$. The length of $B$ is 6.1 cm. Each dimension of $B$ is $\frac{2}{3}$ the corresponding dimension of $A$. What is the perimeter of $B$?

## SPIRAL REVIEW

**Add or subtract.** *(Lesson 1-2)*

30. $-9 - 2$ 31. $-7 + (-5)$ 32. $12 - (-18)$ 33. $19 - 65$

**Generate ordered pairs for each function for $x = -2, -1, 0, 1, 2$.** *(Lesson 1-8)*

34. $y = 2x$ 35. $y = x^2$ 36. $y = 6 - x$ 37. $y = 3x - 1$

**Solve each proportion.** *(Lesson 2-6)*

38. $\frac{x}{8} = \frac{1}{4}$ 39. $\frac{6}{x} = \frac{3}{16}$ 40. $\frac{5}{12} = \frac{-4}{f}$ 41. $\frac{3}{10} = \frac{x+1}{15}$

# 2-8 Percents

**MA.N.1** Use ratios … to solve problems. **MA.N.1.1** Use proportions to solve problems.

***Objective***
Solve problems involving percents.

***Vocabulary***
percent

**Who uses this?**
Jewelers use percents to determine the purity of precious metals. (See Example 4.)

A **percent** is a ratio that compares a number to 100. For example, $25\% = \frac{25}{100}$.

To find the fraction equivalent of a percent, write the percent as a ratio with a denominator of 100. Then simplify.

$$25\% = \frac{25}{100} = \frac{1}{4}$$

To find the decimal equivalent of a percent, divide by 100.

$$25\% = \frac{25}{100} = 0.25$$

Know it! Note

**Some Common Equivalents**

| **Percent** | 10% | 20% | 25% | $33\frac{1}{3}\%$ | 40% | 50% | 60% | $66\frac{2}{3}\%$ | 75% | 80% | 100% |
|---|---|---|---|---|---|---|---|---|---|---|---|
| **Fraction** | $\frac{1}{10}$ | $\frac{1}{5}$ | $\frac{1}{4}$ | $\frac{1}{3}$ | $\frac{2}{5}$ | $\frac{1}{2}$ | $\frac{3}{5}$ | $\frac{2}{3}$ | $\frac{3}{4}$ | $\frac{4}{5}$ | 1 |
| **Decimal** | 0.1 | 0.2 | 0.25 | $0.\overline{3}$ | 0.4 | 0.5 | 0.6 | $0.\overline{6}$ | 0.75 | 0.8 | 1.0 |

The greatest percent shown in the table is 100%, or 1. But percents can be greater than 100%. For example, $120\% = \frac{120}{100} = 1.2$. You can also find percents that are less than 1%. For example, $0.5\% = \frac{0.5}{100} = 0.005$.

You can use the proportion $\frac{\text{part}}{\text{whole}} = \frac{\text{percent}}{100}$ to find unknown values.

## EXAMPLE 1 Finding the Part

**A** **Find 50% of 20.**

**Method 1** Use a proportion.

$\frac{\text{part}}{\text{whole}} = \frac{\text{percent}}{100}$ *Use the percent proportion.*

$\frac{x}{20} = \frac{50}{100}$ *Let x represent the part.*

$100x = 1000$ *Find the cross products.*

$x = 10$ *Since x is multiplied by 100, divide both sides by 100 to undo the multiplication.*

50% of 20 is 10.

***Check*** 50% is the same as $\frac{1}{2}$, and $\frac{1}{2}$ of 20 is 10. 

**B** **Find 105% of 72.**

**Method 2** Use an equation.

$x = 105\% \text{ of } 72$ *Write an equation. Let x represent the part.*

$x = 1.05(72)$ *Write the percent as a decimal and multiply.*

$x = 75.6$

105% of 72 is 75.6.

**1a.** Find 20% of 60. **1b.** Find 210% of 8. **1c.** Find 4% of 36.

## EXAMPLE 2 Finding the Percent

**Helpful Hint**

Before solving, decide what is a reasonable answer. For Example 2A, 50% of 60 is 30, so the answer will be less than 50% of 60.

**A** **What percent of 60 is 15?**

**Method 1** Use a proportion.

$\frac{\text{part}}{\text{whole}} = \frac{\text{percent}}{100}$ *Use the percent proportion.*

$\frac{15}{60} = \frac{x}{100}$ *Let x represent the percent.*

$60x = 1500$ *Find the cross products.*

$\frac{60x}{60} = \frac{1500}{60}$ *Since x is multiplied by 60, divide both sides by 60 to undo the multiplication.*

$x = 25$

15 is 25% of 60.

**B** **440 is what percent of 400?**

**Method 2** Use an equation.

$440 = x \cdot 400$ *Write an equation. Let x represent the percent.*

$440 = 400x$ *Since x is multiplied by 400, divide both sides by 400 to undo the multiplication.*

$\frac{440}{400} = \frac{400x}{400}$

$1.1 = x$ *The answer is a decimal.*

$110\% = x$ *Write the decimal as a percent. This answer is reasonable; 440 is more than 100% of 400.*

440 is 110% of 400.

**2a.** What percent of 35 is 7? **2b.** 27 is what percent of 9?

## EXAMPLE 3 Finding the Whole

**A** **40% of what number is 14?**

**Method 1** Use a proportion.

$\frac{\text{part}}{\text{whole}} = \frac{\text{percent}}{100}$ *Use the percent proportion.*

$\frac{14}{x} = \frac{40}{100}$ *Let x represent the whole.*

$40x = 1400$ *Find the cross products.*

$\frac{40x}{40} = \frac{1400}{40}$ *Since x is multiplied by 40, divide both sides by 40 to undo the multiplication.*

$x = 35$

40% of 35 is 14.

**B** **40 is 0.8% of what number?**

**Method 2** Use an equation.

$$40 = 0.8\% \text{ of } x$$ *Write an equation. Let x represent the whole.*

$$40 = 0.008 \cdot x$$ *Write the percent as a decimal.*

$$\frac{40}{0.008} = \frac{0.008x}{0.008}$$ *Since x is multiplied by 0.008, divide both sides by 0.008 to undo the multiplication.*

$$5000 = x$$

40 is 0.8% of 5000.

**3a.** 120% of what number is 90? **3b.** 48 is 15% of what number?

**EXAMPLE 4** ***Career Application***

**Jewelers use the karat system to determine the amount of pure gold in jewelry. Pure gold is 24 karat, meaning the item is 100% gold. A 14-karat gold ring contains 14 parts gold and 10 parts other metal. What percent of the ring is gold? Round your answer to the nearest percent.**

$$\frac{\text{part}}{\text{whole}} = \frac{\text{percent}}{100}$$ *Use the percent proportion.*

$$\frac{14}{24} = \frac{x}{100}$$ *Let x represent the percent.*

$$24x = 1400$$ *Find the cross products.*

$$\frac{24x}{24} = \frac{1400}{24}$$ *Since x is multiplied by 24, divide both sides by 24 to undo the multiplication.*

$$x = 58.\overline{3}$$

A 14-karat gold ring is approximately 58% gold.

**4.** Use the information above to find the number of karats in a bracelet that is 42% gold. Round your answer to the nearest whole number.

## THINK AND DISCUSS

**1.** Describe the numerical value of the percent when the part is greater than the whole. Give an example.

**2.** 64% of a number is 32. Is the number greater than or less than 32? Explain.

**3. GET ORGANIZED** Copy and complete the graphic organizer. In each box, write and solve an example using the given method.

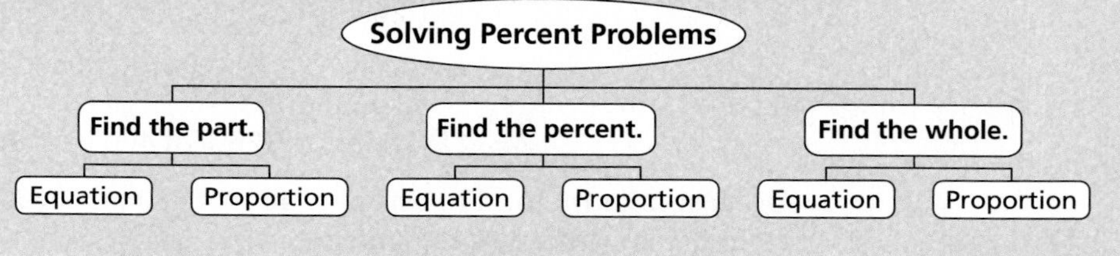

# 2-8 Exercises

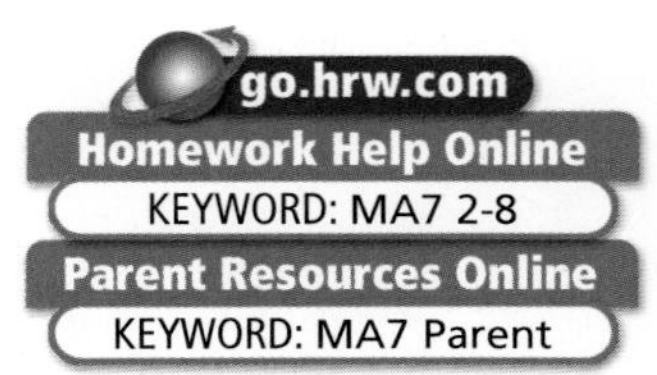


## GUIDED PRACTICE

1. **Vocabulary** In your own words, write a definition of *percent*.

SEE EXAMPLE 1 p. 127

2. Find 75% of 40.
3. Find $12\frac{1}{2}$% of 168.
4. Find 115% of 57.
5. Find 70% of 8.

SEE EXAMPLE 2 p. 128

6. What percent of 40 is 25?
7. What percent of 225 is 180?
8. 57 is what percent of 30?
9. 1 is what percent of 8?

SEE EXAMPLE 3 p. 128

10. 28 is 32% of what number?
11. 4% of what number is 7?
12. 16 is 10% of what number?
13. 105% of what number is 37.8?

SEE EXAMPLE 4 p. 129

14. **Nutrition** A certain granola bar has 2 grams of fiber. This is 8% of the recommended daily value. How many grams of fiber are recommended daily?

## PRACTICE AND PROBLEM SOLVING

**Independent Practice**

| For Exercises | See Example |
|---|---|
| 15–18 | 1 |
| 19–22 | 2 |
| 23–26 | 3 |
| 27 | 4 |

**Extra Practice**

Skills Practice p. S7
Application Practice p. S29

**Find each value. Round to the nearest tenth if necessary.**

15. 60% of 80
16. 35% of 90
17. $\frac{1}{2}$% of 500
18. 210% of 30
19. What percent of 52 is 13?
20. What percent of 9 is 27?
21. 11 is what percent of 22?
22. 5 is what percent of 67?
23. 36 is 90% of what number?
24. 8.2 is 2% of what number?
25. $4\frac{1}{2}$% of what number is 23?
26. 16% of what number is 94?
27. **Nutrition** A certain can of iced tea contains 4% of the recommended daily allowance of sodium. The recommended daily allowance is 2500 milligrams. How many milligrams of sodium are in the can of iced tea?

**Write each decimal or fraction as a percent.**

28. $\frac{5}{4}$
29. 0.02
30. 0.27
31. $\frac{2}{25}$
32. $\frac{7}{7}$
33. 0.64
34. $\frac{31}{100}$
35. 0.85
36. 0.003
37. $\frac{17}{20}$

**Write each percent as a decimal and as a fraction.**

38. 23%
39. 52%
40. 12.5%
41. 90%
42. 87.2%
43. 112%
44. 29%
45. 6%
46. 1.5%
47. $\frac{3}{5}$%
48. **Estimation** To estimate 26% of 400, think:

$$26\% \text{ is close to } 25\% \text{ and } 25\% = \frac{1}{4}$$

$$\frac{1}{4} \text{ of } 400 = 100.$$

Therefore, 26% of 400 is about 100.

Use a similar method to estimate 48% of 610 and 73% of 820. Then check your estimates by finding each percent.

**49. Critical Thinking** Which is greater, 0.5 or $\frac{1}{2}$%? Explain.

**Write each list in order from least to greatest.**

**50.** $\frac{1}{20}$, 5.3%, 5.1, 0.005, $\frac{1}{2}$

**51.** 1.1, 11%, $\frac{1}{10}$, 0.001, 1%

**52.** $\frac{3}{8}$, 29%, $\frac{2}{5}$, 0.25, 38%

**53.** 0.49, 82%, 0.94, $\frac{4}{5}$, $\frac{5}{9}$

**54. Biology** On average, sloths spend 16.5 hours per day sleeping. What percent of the day do sloths spend sleeping? Round your answer to the nearest percent.

**55. Entertainment** The numbers of various types of movies rented over a period of time are indicated in the graph.

a. What percent of the movies rented were comedies?

b. What type of movie made up 25% of the rentals?

c. What percent of the movies rented were in the "other" category?

d. **What if...?** If 25 of the comedy rentals had instead been action rentals, what percent of the movies rented would have been comedies? Round your answer to the nearest tenth.

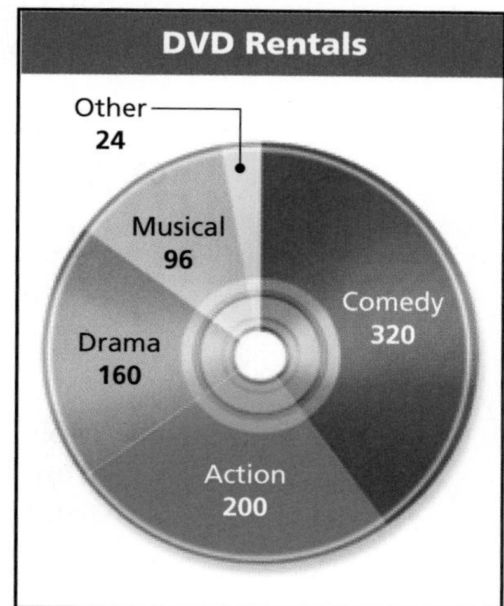


**56. Multi-Step** According to the 2000 U.S. Census, 138,053,563 Americans are male, and 143,368,343 Americans are female. About what percent of the population is male? female? Round your answers to the nearest percent.

**57.** Complete each statement in the table below. Describe any patterns you see in the completed table.

| | | |
|---|---|---|
| 1% of 400 is 4. | 100% of ▒ is 12. | ▒% of 80 is 20. |
| 2% of ▒ is 4. | 50% of ▒ is 12. | ▒% of 40 is 20. |
| 4% of ▒ is 4. | 25% of ▒ is 12. | ▒% of 20 is 20. |
| 8% of ▒ is 4. | 12.5% of ▒ is 12. | ▒% of 10 is 20. |

**58. Write About It** Explain the advantages of using the proportion method to solve percent problems. Then, explain the advantages of using the equation method to solve percent problems.

**MULTI-STEP TEST PREP**

**59.** This problem will prepare you for the Multi-Step Test Prep on page 146.

Kathryn found a new dress at the mall. The price tag reads \$90. The sign above the rack of dresses says that all items on the rack are 40% off.

a. Set up a proportion to find 40% of \$90. This is the amount of the discount.

b. How much will Kathryn pay for the dress? Show that your answer is reasonable.

c. Copy and complete the model below. Explain how this model can help you answer the above questions in another way.

| \$0 | \$9 | \$18 | ? | ? | ? | ? | ? | ? | ? | \$90 |
|---|---|---|---|---|---|---|---|---|---|---|
| 0% | 10% | 20% | ? | ? | 50% | ? | ? | ? | ? | 100% |

## TEST PREP

MA.N.1, MA.N.1.1

60. Which proportion can be used to find 14% of 60?

Ⓐ $\frac{x}{100} = \frac{60}{14}$ Ⓑ $\frac{14}{100} = \frac{60}{x}$ Ⓒ $\frac{x}{100} = \frac{14}{60}$ Ⓓ $\frac{14}{100} = \frac{x}{60}$

61. Raul surveyed 35 students about their preferred lunch. Fourteen preferred chicken. Half of those students preferred chicken with barbecue sauce. What percent should Raul report as preferring chicken with barbecue sauce?

Ⓕ 20% Ⓖ 40% Ⓗ 50% Ⓙ 80%

62. After an election in a small town, the newspaper reported that 42% of the registered voters actually voted. If 12,000 people voted, which equation can be used to find the number of registered voters?

Ⓐ $v = 42 \cdot 12{,}000$ Ⓑ $v = 0.42 \cdot 12{,}000$ Ⓒ $42v = 12{,}000$ Ⓓ $0.42v = 12{,}000$

63. Which list is in order from least to greatest?

Ⓕ $\frac{1}{2}$, 20%, 33%, 0.625, $\frac{1}{8}$, 1 Ⓗ $\frac{1}{8}$, $\frac{1}{2}$, 0.625, 1, 20%, 30%

Ⓖ $\frac{1}{8}$, 20%, 33%, $\frac{1}{2}$, 0.625, 1 Ⓙ 0.625, $\frac{1}{8}$, $\frac{1}{2}$, 1, 20%, 30%

64. Moises saves 8% of his weekly paycheck in his savings account. He deposited $18.80 from his last paycheck into his savings account. Which is the best estimate of the total amount of Moises's last paycheck?

Ⓐ $26 Ⓑ $100 Ⓒ $160 Ⓓ $200

## CHALLENGE AND EXTEND

**Find each value. Round to the nearest tenth if necessary.**

65. What percent of 16 is 2.75?

66. 22 is 73.5% of what number?

67. 121.3% of 73 is what number?

68. What percent of 8000 is 6525?

69. Find 10% of 8 and 8% of 10. What do you notice? Try this with several other pairs of numbers. Do you think this relationship will be true for all pairs of numbers? Why or why not?

70. **Chemistry** A chemist has 20 milliliters of a solution that is 40% acid. She wants to increase the acid content of the solution to make it a 50%-acid solution. How many milliliters of pure acid should she add to the solution? (*Hint:* Begin by finding the number of milliliters of acid in the original solution.)

## SPIRAL REVIEW

**Simplify each expression.** *(Lesson 1-7)*

71. $32 + 47 + 28 + 13$

72. $4 \cdot 23 \cdot 25$

73. $8 \cdot 4 \cdot 5$

74. $44 + 27 + 56$

75. A picture has a width of 4 in. and a length of 6 in. It is enlarged on a copier, and the new length is 9 in. What is the new width? *(Lesson 2-7)*

76. A picture has a width of 4 in. and a length of 6 in. It is reduced on a copier, and the new length is 4.8 in. What is the new width? *(Lesson 2-7)*

77. A rectangle has an area of 9 ft$^2$. Every dimension is multiplied by a scale factor, and the new rectangle has an area of 81 ft$^2$. What was the scale factor? *(Lesson 2-7)*

# 2-9 Applications of Percents

**MA.N.1** Use ratios and rates to solve problems. **MA.N.1.1** Use proportions to solve problems.

***Objectives***
Use common applications of percents.

Estimate with percents.

***Vocabulary***
commission
interest
sales tax
principal
tip

**Who uses this?**
Sales representatives use percents to calculate their total pay.

A **commission** is money paid to a person or a company for making a sale. Usually the commission is a percent of the sale amount.

## EXAMPLE 1 *Business Application*

**Ms. Barns earns a base salary of $42,000 plus a 1.5% commission on sales. Her total sales one year were $700,000. Find her total pay for the year.**

| | |
|---|---|
| total pay = base salary + commission | *Write the formula for total pay.* |
| = base salary + % of total sales | *Write the formula for commission.* |
| = 42,000 + 1.5% of 700,000 | *Substitute values given in the problem.* |
| = 42,000 + (0.015)(700,000) | *Write the percent as a decimal.* |
| = 42,000 + 10,500 | *Multiply.* |
| = 52,500 | *Add.* |

Ms. Barns's total pay was $52,500.

**Caution!**
You must convert a percent to a decimal or a fraction before doing any calculations with it.

**CHECK IT OUT!** **1.** A telemarketer earns $350 per week plus a 12% commission on sales. Find her total pay for a week in which her sales are $940.

**Interest** is the amount of money charged for borrowing money, or the amount of money earned when saving or investing money. **Principal** is the amount borrowed or invested. Simple interest is interest paid only on the principal.

**Simple Interest Paid Annually**

$$I = Prt$$

Simple interest → $I$; Principal → $P$; Interest rate per year as a decimal → $r$; Time in years → $t$

## EXAMPLE 2 *Finance Application*

**A** **Find the simple interest paid annually for 2 years on a $900 loan at 16% per year.**

| | |
|---|---|
| $I = Prt$ | *Write the formula for simple interest.* |
| $I = (900)(0.16)(2)$ | *Substitute known values. Write the interest rate as a decimal.* |
| $I = 288$ | |

The amount of interest is $288.

**Helpful Hint**

When you are using the formula $I = Prt$ to find simple interest paid annually, $t$ represents time in years. One month is $\frac{1}{12}$ year. In Example 2B, $t = \frac{3}{12}$.

**B** **After 3 months the simple interest earned annually on an investment of $7000 was $63. Find the interest rate.**

$I = Prt$ *Write the formula for simple interest.*

$63 = (7000)(r)\left(\frac{3}{12}\right)$ *Substitute the given values.*

$63 = 1750r$ *Multiply $7000\left(\frac{3}{12}\right)$. Since r is multiplied by 1750, divide both sides by 1750 to undo the multiplication.*

$\frac{63}{1750} = \frac{1750r}{1750}$

$0.036 = r$

The interest rate is 3.6%.

**2a.** Find the simple interest earned after 2 years on an investment of $3000 at 4.5% interest earned annually.

**2b.** The simple interest paid on a loan after 6 months was $306. The annual interest rate was 8%. Find the principal.

A **tip** is an amount of money added to a bill for service. It is usually a percent of the bill before *sales tax* is added. **Sales tax** is a percent of an item's cost.

Sales tax and tips are sometimes estimated instead of calculated exactly. When estimating percents, use percents that you can calculate mentally.

- Find 10% of a number by moving the decimal point one place to the left.
- Find 1% of a number by moving the decimal point two places to the left.
- Find 5% of a number by finding $\frac{1}{2}$ of 10% of the number.

## EXAMPLE 3 Estimating with Percents

**A** **The dinner check for Maria's family is $67.95. Estimate a 15% tip.**

**Step 1** First round $67.95 to $70.

**Step 2** Think: 15% = 10% + 5%

10% of $70 = $7.00 *Move the decimal point one place left.*

**Step 3** Think: 5% = 10% ÷ 2

= $7.00 ÷ 2 = $3.50

**Step 4** 15% = 10% + 5%

= $7.00 + $3.50 = $10.50

The tip should be about $10.50.

**Helpful Hint**

A 6.25% sales tax rate means that for every $100 you spend, you would pay $6.25 in sales tax.

**B** **The sales tax rate is 6.25%. Estimate the sales tax on a shirt that costs $29.50.**

**Step 1** First round 6.25% to 6% and $29.50 to $30.

**Step 2** Think: 6% = 6(1%)

1% of $30 = $0.30 *Move the decimal point 2 places left.*

**Step 3** 6% = 6(1%)

= 6($0.30) = $1.80

The sales tax is about $1.80.

**3a.** Estimate a 15% tip on a check for $21.98.

**3b.** Estimate the tax on shoes that cost $68.50 when the sales tax rate is 8.25%

## THINK AND DISCUSS

1. Explain how commission, interest, sales tax, and tips are alike.
2. When the sales tax rate is 8.25%, the tax on a \$10 purchase is \$0.83. Is the tax on \$20 twice as much? Explain.

3. **GET ORGANIZED** Copy and complete the graphic organizer. In each box, write an example of each type of application and find the answer.

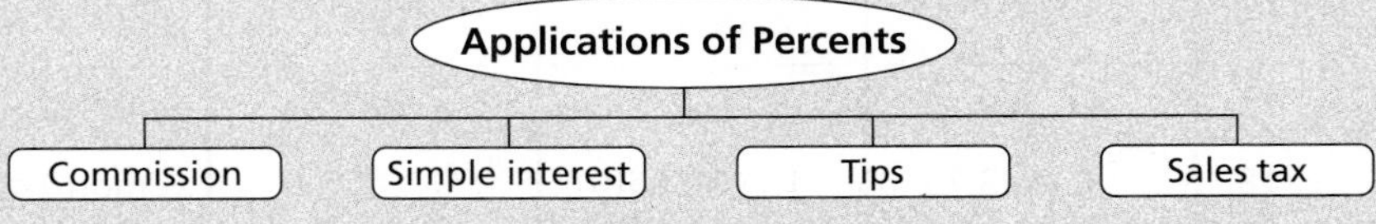


MA.N.1, MA.N.1.1

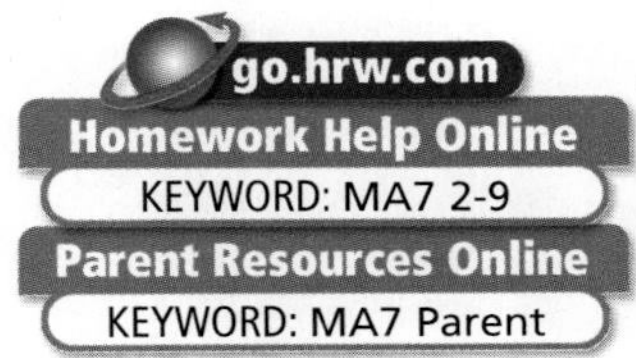


## GUIDED PRACTICE

1. **Vocabulary** How are *commission* and *tips* alike? How are they different?

SEE EXAMPLE 1 p. 133

2. A sales representative earns a 2.5% commission on sales. Find the commission earned when the total sales are \$80,700.
3. Karen earns a salary of \$28,600 per year plus a 4.25% commission on sales. Find her total earnings for a year when the sales are \$310,000.

SEE EXAMPLE 2 p. 133

4. Find the amount of simple interest earned after 2 years on \$480 invested at a 7% annual interest rate.
5. Find the number of years it would take for \$1200 to earn simple interest of \$324 at an annual interest rate of 6% per year.
6. Find the total amount owed after 6 months on a loan of \$900 at an annual simple interest rate of 8.5%.

SEE EXAMPLE 3 p. 134

7. Estimate a 15% tip on a \$42.65 check.
8. Estimate the tax on a \$198 stereo when the sales tax is 5.25%.

## PRACTICE AND PROBLEM SOLVING

**Independent Practice**

| For Exercises | See Example |
|---|---|
| 9–10 | 1 |
| 11–13 | 2 |
| 14–15 | 3 |

**Extra Practice**

Skills Practice p. S7
Application Practice p. S29

9. A boat salesperson earns a 2.5% commission on the sale of each boat. Find the commission earned on a boat that sells for \$18,500.
10. A cell phone distributor earns a yearly salary of \$28,000 plus a 17.5% commission on sales. Find the total earnings for a year when the sales are \$38,000.
11. Find the simple interest paid after 3 months on a loan of \$9700 borrowed at an annual interest rate of 11%.
12. After 8 months, \$750 simple interest was owed on a loan of \$9000. Find the annual interest rate.

13. How long will it take \$680 to earn \$102 in simple interest at an annual interest rate of 3%?

14. Estimate the tip on a \$19.65 check using a tip rate of 15%.

15. Estimate the tax on tires that cost \$498 with a 6.25% sales tax.

**Use $I = Prt$ to complete the table. All interest rates are annual.**

| | $I$ = | $P$ × | $r$ × | $t$ |
|---|---|---|---|---|
| 16. | ■ | \$8275 | 13% | 3 years |
| 17. | \$3969 | ■ | 10.5% | 9 months |
| 18. | \$23.75 | \$950 | ■ | 6 months |
| 19. | \$380 | \$4750 | 4% | ■ |

**LINK Technology**

Koopa is a Gulf Coast box turtle from Hartford, Connecticut. His paintings have sold for hundreds of dollars at online auctions.

20. Chris has \$21.50. He wants a book for \$5.85 and a CD for \$14.99. The sales tax is 6.25%.
   a. How could Chris estimate whether he has enough to buy the book and the CD?
   b. Does he have enough money to buy the book and the CD?

21. **Technology** An online auction company charges sellers a commission fee of 5.25% of an item's final selling price. If you sell an item for \$55, what fee will you pay to the auction company? Show that your answer is reasonable.

22. **Business** Sometimes business partners do not share the ownership of a business equally. Instead, they each own a percent of the business, and each receives that percent of the profits. Alvarez, Brown, and Chow are partners in a business that earned \$500,000. Alvarez owns 40% of the business. Chow received \$175,000.
   a. How much money did Alvarez and Brown each receive?
   b. What percent of the business is owned by Brown? by Chow?

23. **Write About It** Lewis invested \$1000 at 3% annual simple interest for 4 years. Lisa invested \$1000 at 4% annual simple interest for 3 years. Explain why Lewis and Lisa earned the same amount of interest.

24. **Critical Thinking** To estimate a tip of 15%, Amy tips \$1.00 for every \$6.00 in the total bill. Is this method reasonable? Why or why not?

25. **/// ERROR ANALYSIS ///** Which solution is incorrect? Explain the error.

A
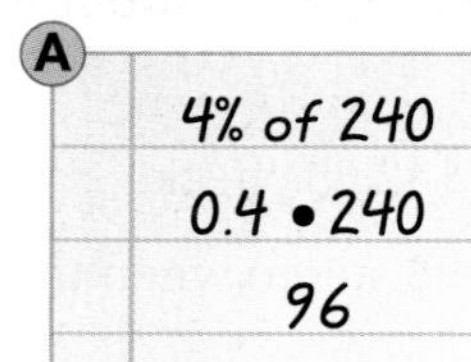


B
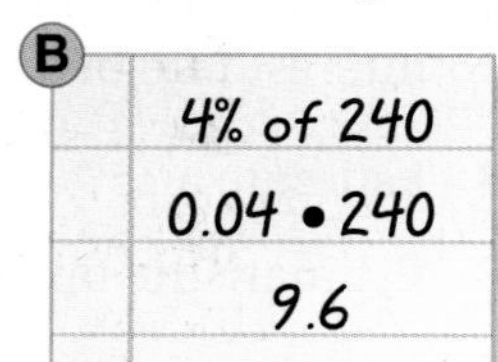

26. This problem will prepare you for the Multi-Step Test Prep on page 146.
   a. Juan is shopping for a new CD player. He finds one he likes for \$225. The sales tax is 7.5%. What will be the total cost of the CD player?
   b. The salesperson tells Juan that a sale starts tomorrow, and the CD player will be reduced to \$157.50. What is the total cost, including tax, that Juan will pay if he buys the CD player tomorrow?
   c. How much will Juan save if he buys the CD player tomorrow?

MA.N.1, MA.N.1.1

27. Which account earns the most simple interest after 1 year? Assume that interest is paid annually.
    - (A) \$5000 at 8% per year
    - (B) \$10,000 at 4% per year
    - (C) \$8000 at 4.8% per year
    - (D) \$4000 at 10.2% per year

28. Craig earns \$200 per week plus 8% commission on sales. Joan earns \$150 per week plus 12% commission on sales. Last week, both had sales of \$1500. Who earned more money?
    - (F) Craig earned more than Joan.
    - (G) Joan earned more than Craig.
    - (H) Both earned the same amount.
    - (J) Cannot be determined

29. **Short Response** If 2% of a number is 300, what is 6% of the number? Explain how you got your answer.

## CHALLENGE AND EXTEND

30. **Multi-Step** A lunch check for Mark and a friend was \$19.50 before the 6% sales tax was added. Mark wants to leave a tip of at least 20%. He has no coins, and he does not want to wait for change. What is the least amount he should leave to pay the check, tax, and tip?

31. The final cost of an item was \$50. This included 6% sales tax. What was the price of the item before tax?

**Finance A stockbroker earns a commission based on the amount of a transaction according to the table below.**

| Stockbroker's Commissions | | | | |
|---|---|---|---|---|
| **Transaction** | \$0–\$10,000 | For each additional dollar up to \$20,000 | For each additional dollar up to \$40,000 | For each additional dollar over \$40,000 |
| **Commission** | 0.5% | 0.4% | 0.3% | 0.2% |

**For example, the commission on a transaction of \$11,000 is 0.5% of \$10,000 plus 0.4% of \$1000. Use the table for Exercises 32–34.**

32. Find the amount of commission earned on a transaction of \$15,000.
33. Find the amount of commission earned on a transaction of \$21,000.
34. Find the amount of commission earned on a transaction of \$100,000.

## SPIRAL REVIEW

**Write an expression for each statement.** *(Lesson 1-1)*

35. 2 less than $x$
36. the sum of one half of $x$ and $-1$

**Compare. Write $<$, $>$, or $=$.** *(Lesson 1-5)*

37. $\sqrt{65}$ ▒ 8
38. 7 ▒ $\sqrt{51}$
39. 9 ▒ $\sqrt{80}$
40. $\sqrt{196}$ ▒ 14

**Find each value. Round to the nearest tenth if necessary.** *(Lesson 2-8)*

41. 40% of 60 is what number?
42. What percent of 26 is 13?
43. 22 is what percent of 99?
44. 80% of what number is 64?

# 2-10 Percent Increase and Decrease

**MA.N.1** Use ratios and rates to solve problems. **MA.N.1.1** Use proportions to solve problems.

*Objective*
Find percent increase and decrease.

*Vocabulary*
percent change
percent increase
percent decrease
discount
markup

**Who uses this?**
Consumers can use percent change to determine how much money they can save. (See Example 3.)

"May I suggest you read the sign again, Sir."

A **percent change** is an increase or decrease given as a percent of the original amount. **Percent increase** describes an amount that has grown and **percent decrease** describes an amount that has been reduced.

**Percent Change**

$$\text{percent change} = \frac{\text{amount of increase or decrease}}{\text{original amount}}, \text{ expressed as a percent}$$

**EXAMPLE 1** **Finding Percent Increase or Decrease**

**Find each percent change. Tell whether it is a percent increase or decrease.**

**A** **from 25 to 49**

$$\text{percent change} = \frac{\text{amount of increase}}{\text{original amount}}$$

$$= \frac{49 - 25}{25}$$

$$= \frac{24}{25} \qquad \textit{Simplify the numerator.}$$

$$= 0.96$$

$$= 96\% \qquad \textit{Write the answer as a percent.}$$

25 to 49 is an increase, so a change from 25 to 49 is a 96% increase.

**Helpful Hint**

Before solving, decide what is a reasonable answer. For Example 1A, 25 to 50 would be a 100% increase. So 25 to 49 should be slightly less than 100%.

**B** **from 50 to 45**

$$\text{percent change} = \frac{\text{amount of decrease}}{\text{original amount}}$$

$$= \frac{50 - 45}{50}$$

$$= \frac{5}{50} \qquad \textit{Simplify the numerator.}$$

$$= \frac{1}{10} \qquad \textit{Simplify the fraction.}$$

$$= 10\% \qquad \textit{Write the answer as a percent.}$$

50 to 45 is a decrease, so a change from 50 to 45 is a 10% decrease.

**Find each percent change. Tell whether it is a percent increase or decrease.**

**1a.** from 200 to 110 **1b.** from 25 to 30 **1c.** from 80 to 115

## EXAMPLE  Finding the Result of a Percent Increase or Decrease

**A** **Find the result when 30 is increased by 20%.**

$0.20(30) = 6$ *Find 20% of 30. This is the amount of the increase.*

$30 + 6 = 36$ *It is a percent increase, so add 6 to the original amount.*

30 increased by 20% is 36.

**B** **Find the result when 65 is decreased by 80%.**

$0.80(65) = 52$ *Find 80% of 65. This is the amount of the decrease.*

$65 - 52 = 13$ *It is a percent decrease, so subtract 52 from 65.*

65 decreased by 80% is 13.

**2a.** Find the result when 72 is increased by 25%.

**2b.** Find the result when 10 is decreased by 40%.

Common applications of percent change are *discounts* and *markups*.

A **discount** is an amount by which an original price is reduced.

**discount** = % of **original price**

final price = **original price** − **discount**

A **markup** is an amount by which a wholesale cost is increased.

**markup** = % of **wholesale cost**

final price = **wholesale cost** + **markup**

## EXAMPLE 3 Discounts

**A** **Admission to the museum is $8. Students receive a 15% discount. How much is the discount? How much do students pay?**

**Method 1** A discount is a percent decrease. So find $8 decreased by 15%.

$0.15(8) = 1.20$ *Find 15% of 8. This is the amount of the discount.*

$8 - 1.20 = 6.80$ *Subtract 1.20 from 8. This is the student price.*

**Method 2** Subtract percent discount from 100%.

$100\% - 15\% = 85\%$ *Students pay 85% of the regular price, $8.*

$0.85(8) = 6.80$ *Find 85% of 8. This is the student price.*

$8 - 6.80 = 1.20$ *Subtract 6.80 from 8. This is the amount of the discount.*

By either method, the discount is $1.20. Students pay $6.80.

**Helpful Hint**

Before solving, decide what is a reasonable answer. For Example 3A, a 25% discount is $2 off. So a 15% discount will be less than $2 off.

**B** **Christo used a coupon and paid $7.35 for a pizza that normally costs $10.50. Find the percent discount.**

$\$10.50 - \$7.35 = \$3.15$ *Think: 3.15 is what percent of 10.50? Let x represent the percent.*

$3.15 = x(10.50)$

$\frac{3.15}{10.50} = \frac{x \cdot 10.50}{10.50}$ *Since x is multiplied by 10.50, divide both sides by 10.50 to undo the multiplication.*

$0.3 = x$

$30\% = x$ *Write the answer as a percent.*

The discount is 30%.

**3a.** A $220 bicycle was on sale for 60% off. Find the sale price.

**3b.** Ray paid $12 for a $15 T-shirt. What was the percent discount?

## EXAMPLE  4 Markups

**A Kaleb buys necklaces at a wholesale cost of $48 each. He then marks up the price by 75% and sells the necklaces. What is the amount of the markup? What is the selling price?**

**Method 1**

A markup is a percent increase. So find $48 increased by 75%.

$0.75(48) = 36$ *Find 75% of 48. This is the amount of the markup.*

$48 + 36 = 84$ *Add to 48. This is the selling price.*

**Method 2**

Add percent markup to 100%.

$100\% + 75\% = 175\%$ *The selling price is 175% of the wholesale price, $48.*

$1.75(48) = \mathbf{84}$ *Find 175% of 48. This is the selling price.*

$\mathbf{84} - 48 = 36$ *Subtract from 84. This is the amount of the markup.*

By either method, the amount of the markup is $36. The selling price is $84.

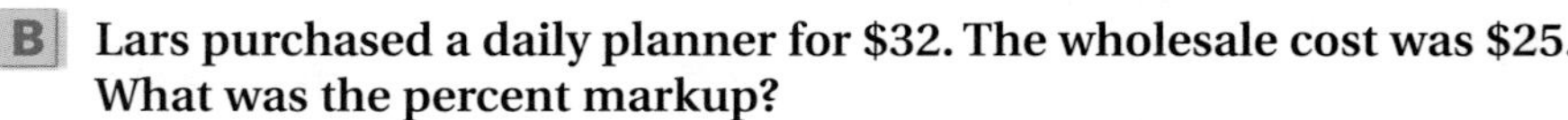

**B Lars purchased a daily planner for $32. The wholesale cost was $25. What was the percent markup?**

$32 - 25 = 7$ *Find the amount of the markup.*

$7 = x(25)$ *Think: 7 is what percent of 25? Let x represent the percent.*

$\frac{7}{25} = \frac{25x}{25}$ *Since x is multiplied by 25, divide both sides by 25 to undo the multiplication.*

$0.28 = x$

$28\% = x$ *Write the answer as a percent.*

The markup was 28%.

**4a.** A video game has a 70% markup. The wholesale cost is $9. What is the selling price?

**4b.** What is the percent markup on a car selling for $21,850 that had a wholesale cost of $9500?

## THINK AND DISCUSS

1. 80% of a number is the same as a ?% decrease from that number. A 30% increase from a number is the same as ?% of that number.
2. A markup of 200% will result in a final cost that is how many times the wholesale cost?
3. What information would you need to find the percent change in your school's population over the last ten years?

4. **GET ORGANIZED** Copy and complete the graphic organizer. In each box, write and solve an example of the given type of problem.

| Percent Increase | Percent Decrease | Discount | Markup |
|---|---|---|---|
| | | | |

# 2-10 Exercises

MA.N.1, MA.N.1.1

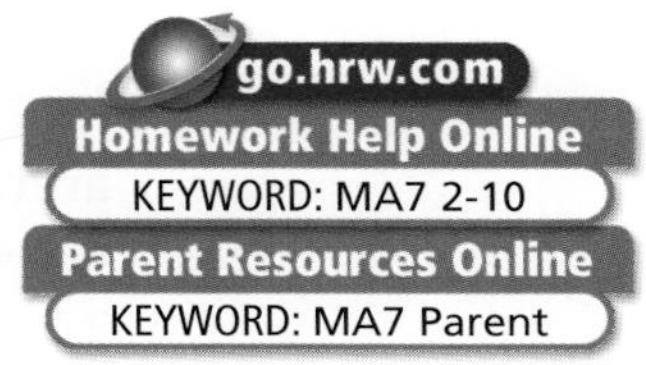


## GUIDED PRACTICE

1. **Vocabulary** Compare *percent increase* and *percent decrease.*

SEE EXAMPLE 1 p. 138

**Find each percent change. Tell whether it is a percent increase or decrease**

2. 25 to 45
3. 10 to 8
4. 400 to 300
5. 16 to 18
6. 40 to 50
7. 50 to 40

SEE EXAMPLE 2 p. 138

8. Find the result when 40 is increased by 85%.
9. Find the result when 60 is increased by 3%.
10. Find the result when 350 is decreased by 10%.
11. Find the result when 16 is decreased by 50%.

SEE EXAMPLE 3 p. 139

12. What is the final price on a $185 leather jacket that is on sale for 40% off?
13. Neal bought a book on sale for $3.60. It was originally priced at $12. What was Neal's discount as a percent?

SEE EXAMPLE 4 p. 140

14. Yolanda bought a video that was priced at a 65% markup over the manufacturer's cost of $12. What was Yolanda's cost?
15. Randy sells hats for $12.35. The wholesale cost of each hat is $6.50. What is Randy's markup as a percent?

## PRACTICE AND PROBLEM SOLVING

**Independent Practice**

| For Exercises | See Example |
|---|---|
| 16–27 | 1 |
| 28–31 | 2 |
| 32–33 | 3 |
| 34–35 | 4 |

**Extra Practice**

Skills Practice p. S7
Application Practice p. S29

**Find each percent change. Tell whether it is a percent increase or decrease.**

16. 50 to 60
17. 4 to 3
18. 96 to 84
19. 9 to 45
20. 32 to 30
21. 15 to 19.5
22. 150 to 180
23. 17 to 14.45
24. 20 to 15
25. 265 to 318
26. 35 to 105
27. 300 to 275
28. Find the result when 24 is increased by 75%.
29. Find the result when 240 is increased by 5%.
30. Find the result when 30 is decreased by 85%.
31. Find the result when 8 is decreased by 5%.
32. The cost of Hisako's school supplies was $49.80. She had a coupon for 30% off the entire purchase. What was the final price?
33. With the purchase of 10 greeting cards, Addie received a discount. She paid $26.35 for the cards that would normally have cost $31. What percent discount did Addie receive?
34. Irma sells boxing gloves in her sporting goods store for a 9% markup over the manufacturer's cost of $40. What is the selling price of the gloves?
35. Bottled water in a certain vending machine costs $1.50. This price is a markup from the wholesale cost of $0.20. What is the markup as a percent?
36. **Critical Thinking** Is the percent increase from 50 to 80 the same as the percent decrease from 80 to 50? Why or why not?

**Multi-Step** **The graph shows the average height of a child from birth to age 4. Use the graph for Exercises 37–39.**

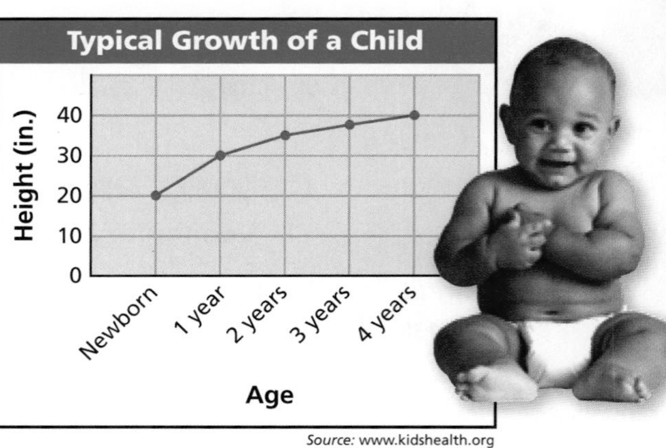

Source: www.kidshealth.org

**37.** By what percent does a child's height increase from birth to age 1 year?

**38.** By what percent does a child's height increase from birth to age 4 years?

**39.** **Estimation** Estimate the amount and percent of increase in a child's height from age 2 to age 3. Show that your estimate is reasonable.

**40.** **Employment** Last summer, Duncan charged $20 to mow a lawn in his neighborhood. This summer, he'll charge $23. What is the percent increase in Duncan's price? Show that your answer is reasonable.

**Copy and complete the table.**

| | Original Amount | New Amount | Percent Change |
|---|---|---|---|
| **41.** | 12 | ■ | 50% increase |
| **42.** | $48 | $42.24 | ■ |
| **43.** | $4\frac{1}{2}$ | $13\frac{1}{2}$ | ■ |
| **44.** | 8525 | ■ | 20% decrease |

**Find each missing number.**

**45.** 20 increased by ■% is 24.

**46.** 80 decreased by ■% is 76.

**47.** 120 decreased by 50% is ■.

**48.** 200 increased by ■% is 210.

**49.** **Nutrition** A can of soup had 480 mg of sodium per serving. The sodium was reduced to 360 mg per serving so that the soup could be advertised as "low sodium." What was the percent change in sodium content?

**50.** **Write About It** Dana is shopping for shoes at a store advertising "everything 45% off." Describe a method she could use to estimate the discount and final price on a pair of shoes.

**MULTI-STEP TEST PREP**

**51.** This problem will prepare you for the Multi-Step Test Prep on page 146.

**a.** Robert finds a shirt on a sale rack. All items on the rack are 40% off. The price on his shirt is missing. When the clerk scans the bar code, he tells Robert that the sale price of the shirt is $18. What percent of the original price is $18?

**b.** Set up a proportion to find the original price of the shirt.

**c.** Copy and complete the model below and explain how it helps you to solve this problem in another way.

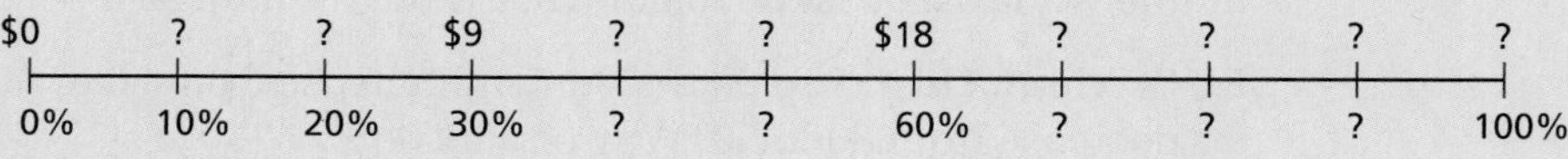

## TEST PREP

MA.N.1, MA.N.1.1

52. Lucia gets film developed at Photo King, where 24 prints cost \$7.80. This week, Photo King is having a sale, and 24 prints cost \$6.63. What percent of the regular cost will Lucia save?

  (A) 15% (B) 17% (C) 25% (D) 85%

53. Which of these does NOT represent "200 decreased by 45%"?

  (F) 200(0.55) (G) 110 (H) 200 − 0.45 (J) 200(1 − 0.45)

54. Which of these represents a 15% increase?

  (A) A price is marked up from \$12.50 to \$15.
  (B) Joanna's bank account balance grew from \$127.50 to \$150.
  (C) A baseball card's value rose from \$6 to \$6.15.
  (D) Luis's hourly wage was raised from \$8 to \$9.20.

55. The original price of an item was \$199. During a sale, the price was reduced by 45%. Then, during a clearance sale, the price was reduced an additional 20%. What was the final price?

  (F) \$71.91 (G) \$87.56 (H) \$98.97 (J) \$101.89

56. **Gridded Response** A skateboard that sells for \$65 is on sale for 15% off. What is the sale price in dollars?

## CHALLENGE AND EXTEND

**Find each missing number.**

57. ▢ increased by 15% is 230.
58. ▢ increased by 50% is 48.
59. ▢ decreased by 20% is 500.
60. ▢ decreased by 70% is 4.35.
61. The label on a bottle of orange juice says "now 25% more." The bottle has 80 fluid ounces of juice. What was the original volume? Show that your answer is reasonable.
62. Angelina paid \$21 for a backpack that was 30% off. What was the original price? Show that your answer is reasonable.
63. **Multi-Step** Mr. Hansen owns a bookstore. He buys used books at 25% of the cover price and sells them at a 45% markup of what he paid. Jerry sold Mr. Hansen three books with cover prices of \$7.95, \$5.95, and \$12.10. If Jerry bought back his books, how much would he pay?

## SPIRAL REVIEW

**Find the complement and the supplement of each angle.** *(Previous course)*

64. 65°
65. 10°
66. 45°
67. 30°

**Solve each equation.** *(Lessons 2-1 and 2-2)*

68. $-15 + x = -3$
69. $x + 16 = -4$
70. $r - 3 = 6$
71. $n - (-10) = 67$
72. $98 = 7z$
73. $\frac{x}{3} = 12$
74. $-x = 4$
75. $\frac{x}{5} = -20$

**Estimate each amount.** *(Lesson 2-9)*

76. the tip on a \$60.65 check using a tip rate of 15%
77. the tax on a \$70 DVD player when the sales tax is 6%

# Explore Changes in Population

You can use percents to describe changes in populations. A population may grow by a certain percent or decrease by a certain percent. Explore changing populations in these activities.

*Use with Lesson 2-10*

**MA.N.1** Use ... rates to solve problems. *Also* **MA.A.3, MA.A.3.2, Prep MA.A.3.1**

## Activity 1

A team of biologists is studying a population of deer. There are 32 deer in the first year of the study. Due to a lack of predators, the biologists find that the herd grows by 50% every year.

1. Copy and complete the table. The first two rows have been completed for you.

| Year | Percent Increase | Amount of Increase | Population |
|---|---|---|---|
| 1 | | | 32 |
| 2 | 50% | $0.50 \cdot 32 = 16$ | $32 + 16 = 48$ |
| 3 | 50% | ■ | ■ |
| 4 | 50% | ■ | ■ |
| 5 | 50% | ■ | ■ |
| 6 | 50% | ■ | ■ |

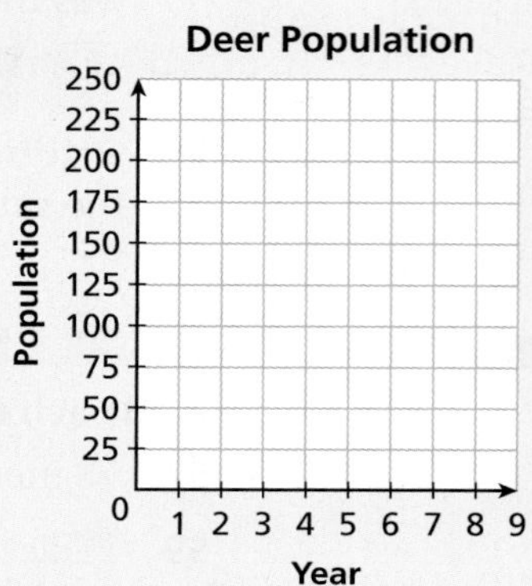


2. Describe the percent increase from year to year.
3. Describe the amount of increase from year to year.
4. Copy the grid above onto graph paper. Plot the year and the population of deer on the graph as six ordered pairs (year, population). Connect the points with a smooth curve.
5. Describe the shape of your graph.

## Try This

A researcher places 10 bacteria on a dish. This species increases by 100% every hour.

1. Copy and complete the table below.

| Hour | 0 | 1 | 2 | 3 | 4 | 5 |
|---|---|---|---|---|---|---|
| Amount of Increase | | ■ | ■ | ■ | ■ | ■ |
| Bacteria | 10 | ■ | ■ | ■ | ■ | ■ |

2. Graph points from the table as (hour, bacteria). Connect the points with a smooth curve.
3. Compare this graph with the graph of the deer population.
4. Why does the amount of increase change when the percent of increase stays the same?

## Activity 2

A second team of biologists is studying a population of wolves. There are 3125 wolves in the first year. The biologists find that this population decreases by 40% every year.

1. **Make a Prediction** Based on your results in Activity 1, what do you think will happen to the amount of decrease each year?

2. Copy and complete the table below. The first two rows have been completed for you.

| Year | Percent Decrease | Amount of Decrease | Population |
|---|---|---|---|
| 1 | | | 3125 |
| 2 | 40% | $0.40 \cdot 3125 = 1250$ | $3125 - 1250 = 1875$ |
| 3 | 40% | ■ | ■ |
| 4 | 40% | ■ | ■ |
| 5 | 40% | ■ | ■ |
| 6 | 40% | ■ | ■ |

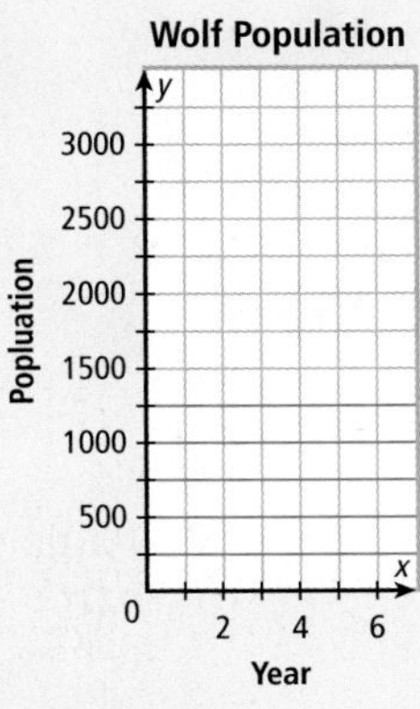


3. What happens to the amount of decrease in the wolf population from year to year? Was your prediction from Problem 1 correct?

4. **Make a Prediction** Copy the grid above onto graph paper. Based on your results in Activity 1, what do you think the graph of ordered pairs (year, population) will look like?

5. Plot the year and the population of wolves on the graph as six ordered pairs (year, population). Connect the points with a smooth curve.

6. Describe the shape of your graph. Was your prediction from Problem 4 correct?

## Try This

A half-life is the amount of time it takes half of an amount of radioactive substance to decay into another substance. Tritium is a radioactive form of hydrogen with a half-life of 12.3 years. In other words, after one half-life of 12.3 years, an amount of tritium will have decreased by 50%.

5. Suppose you start with 128 grams of tritium. Copy and complete the table below.
6. Make a graph that shows how much tritium is left after 0, 1, 2, 3, 4, and 5 half-lives.
7. Compare this graph with the graph of the wolf population.

| Half-lives | 0 | 1 | 2 | 3 | 4 | 5 |
|---|---|---|---|---|---|---|
| Percent Decrease | 0 | 50% | 50% | 50% | 50% | 50% |
| Amount of Decrease (g) | | ■ | ■ | ■ | ■ | ■ |
| Tritium Remaining (g) | 128 | ■ | ■ | ■ | ■ | ■ |

8. Describe the graph of a population that increases by a fixed percent. Why does the graph have this shape?
9. Describe the graph of a population that decreases by a fixed percent. Why does the graph have this shape?

# MULTI-STEP TEST PREP

## Percentages

**Bargain Hunters** Maria is on her high school's lacrosse team, and her friend Paula is on the softball team. The girls notice an advertisement in the newspaper for a clearance sale at their favorite sporting goods store. The ad shows an additional $\frac{1}{4}$ off the already reduced prices of 60% off. Maria and Paula head to the store to shop for bargains.

1. Maria finds a lacrosse stick with a regular price of $65. Find the sale price of the lacrosse stick prior to the additional $\frac{1}{4}$ off.
2. Find the sale price of Maria's lacrosse stick with the additional $\frac{1}{4}$ off.
3. Paula says that with the extra $\frac{1}{4}$ off, the total discount is 85% off. Maria thinks the discount is less than that. Who is correct? Explain your reasoning.
4. Paula finds a softball glove with a price tag that is not readable. The sales clerk scans the bar code and says the sale price, including the extra $\frac{1}{4}$ off, is $16.50. What was the original price of the softball glove? Show your reasoning.
5. Sales tax is 7.8%. Find the total amount that the girls will pay for the lacrosse stick and the softball glove together, including tax.

# READY TO GO ON?

CHAPTER 2
SECTION 2B

## Quiz for Lessons 2-6 Through 2-10

### 2-6 Rates, Ratios, and Proportions

1. Last week, the ratio of laptops to desktops sold at a computer store was 2:3. Eighteen desktop models were sold. How many laptop models were sold?
2. Anita read 150 pages in 5 hours. What is her reading rate in pages per minute?

**Find the unit rate.**

3. Twenty-six crackers contain 156 Calories.
4. A store developed 1024 photographs in 8 hours.

**Solve each proportion.**

5. $\frac{-18}{n} = \frac{9}{2}$
6. $\frac{d}{5} = \frac{2}{4}$
7. $\frac{4}{12} = \frac{r+2}{16}$
8. $\frac{-3}{7} = \frac{6}{x+6}$

### 2-7 Applications of Proportions

**Find the value of *n* in each diagram.**

9. $\triangle RST \sim \triangle XYZ$

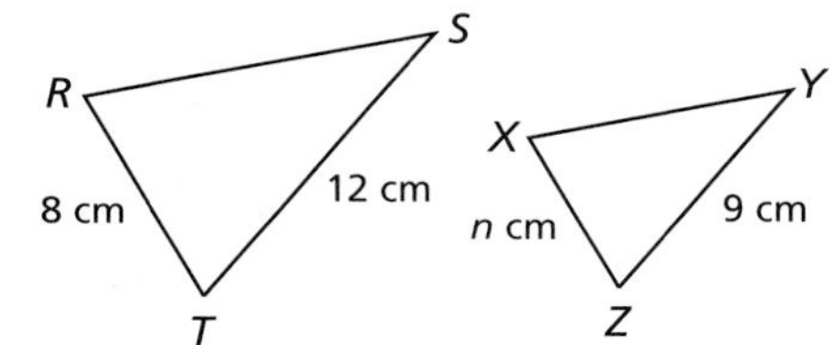


10. $ABCD \sim FGHJ$

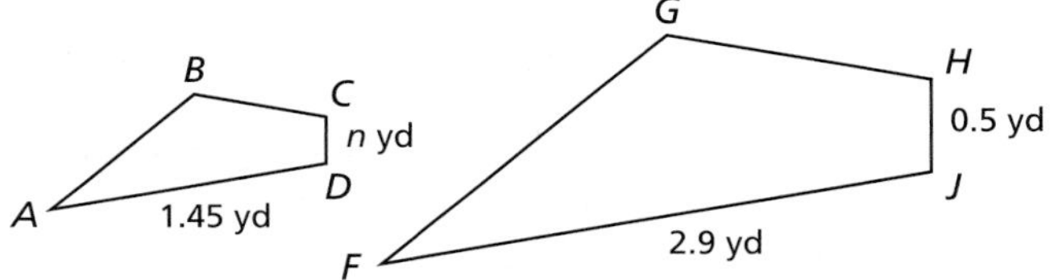


### 2-8 Percents

11. Find 40% of 25.
12. Find 130% of 9.
13. 35 is what percent of 70?
14. What percent of 400 is 640?
15. 16 is 80% of what number?
16. 200% of what number is 28?
17. A volunteer at the zoo is responsible for feeding the animals in 15 exhibits in the reptile house. This represents 20% of the total exhibits in the reptile house. How many exhibits are in the reptile house?

### 2-9 Applications of Percents

18. Peter earns \$32,000 per year plus a 2.5% commission on his jewelry sales. Find Peter's total salary for the year when his sales are valued at \$420,000.
19. Estimate the tax on a \$21,899 car when the tax rate is 5%.

### 2-10 Percent Increase and Decrease

**Find each percent change. Tell whether it is a percent increase or decrease.**

20. from 60 to 66
21. from 48 to 12
22. from 200 to 80
23. from 9.8 to 14.7
24. Andrea purchased a picture frame for \$14.56. This price was a 30% markup from the wholesale cost. What was the wholesale cost?

EXTENSION

# Solving Absolute-Value Equations

**Ext. MA.A.4.5** Use … symbols to solve linear equations.

***Objective***
Solve equations in one variable that contain absolute-value expressions.

The absolute value of a number is that number's distance from zero on a number line. For example, $|-5| = 5$.

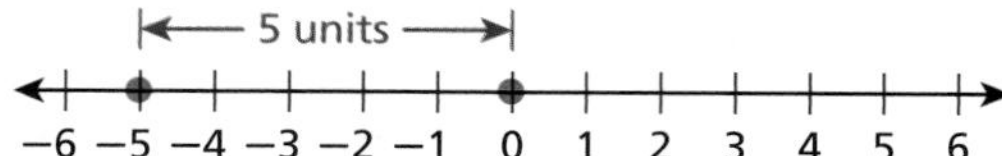


Both 5 and −5 are a distance of 5 units from 0, so both 5 and −5 have an absolute value of 5.

To write this using algebra, you would write $|x| = 5$. This equation asks, "What values of $x$ have an absolute value of 5?" The solutions are 5 and −5. Notice this equation has two solutions.

## Absolute-Value Equations

| WORDS | NUMBERS |
|---|---|
| The equation $|x| = a$ asks, what values of $x$ have an absolute value of $a$? The solutions are $a$ and the opposite of $a$. | $|x| = 5$<br>$x = 5$ or $x = -5$ |
| **GRAPH** | **ALGEBRA** |
| ⟵ $a$ units ⟶⟵ $a$ units ⟶<br>$-a$ 0 $a$ | $|x| = a$<br>$x = a$ or $x = -a$<br>$(a \geq 0)$ |

To solve absolute-value equations, perform inverse operations to isolate the absolute-value expression on one side of the equation. Then you must consider two cases.

**EXAMPLE 1** **Solving Absolute-Value Equations**

**Writing Math**
Solution sets are efficient when an equation has more than one solution. The solution set for Example 1A is $\{-4, 4\}$.

**Solve each equation. Check your answer.**

**A** $|x| = 4$

$|x| = 4$ *Think: What numbers are 4 units from 0?*

*Rewrite the equation as two cases.*

| **Case 1** | **Case 2** |
|---|---|
| $x = 4$ | $x = -4$ |

The solutions are 4 and −4.

***Check***

| $|x| = 4$ | |
|---|---|
| $|4|$ | 4 |
| 4 | 4 ✓ |

| $|x| = 4$ | |
|---|---|
| $|-4|$ | 4 |
| 4 | 4 ✓ |

**Solve each equation. Check your answer.**

**B** $4|x+2| = 20$

$$\frac{4|x+2|}{4} = \frac{20}{4}$$

$$|x+2| = 5$$

*Since $|x + 2|$ is multiplied by 4, divide both sides by 4 to undo the multiplication.*

*Think: What numbers are 5 units from 0?*

| Case 1 | Case 2 |
|---|---|
| $x + 2 = 5$ | $x + 2 = -5$ |
| $-2 \quad -2$ | $-2 \quad -2$ |
| $x = 3$ | $x = -7$ |

*Rewrite the equation as two cases. Since 2 is added to x, subtract 2 from both sides of each equation.*

The solutions are 3 and −7.

*Check*

| $4\lvert x+2\rvert$ | $= 20$ |
|---|---|
| $4\lvert 3+2\rvert$ | 20 |
| $4\lvert 5\rvert$ | 20 |
| $4(5)$ | 20 |
| 20 | 20 ✓ |

| $4\lvert x+2\rvert$ | $= 20$ |
|---|---|
| $4\lvert -7+2\rvert$ | 20 |
| $4\lvert -5\rvert$ | 20 |
| $4(5)$ | 20 |
| 20 | 20 ✓ |

**Solve each equation. Check your answer.**

**1a.** $|x| - 3 = 4$ **1b.** $|x - 2| = 8$

Not all absolute-value equations have two solutions. If the absolute-value expression equals 0, there is one solution. If an equation states that an absolute-value is negative, there are no solutions.

## EXAMPLE 2 Special Cases of Absolute-Value Equations

**Solve each equation.**

**A** $|x+3| + 4 = 4$

$$|x+3| + 4 = 4$$
$$\underline{-4 \quad -4}$$
$$|x+3| = 0$$

*Since 4 is added to $|x + 3|$, subtract 4 from both sides to undo the addition.*

$$x + 3 = 0$$
$$\underline{-3 \quad -3}$$
$$x = -3$$

*There is only one case. Since 3 is added to x, subtract 3 from both sides to undo the addition.*

*Check*

| $\lvert x+3\rvert + 4$ | $= 4$ |
|---|---|
| $\lvert -3+3\rvert + 4$ | 4 |
| $\lvert 0\rvert + 4$ | 4 |
| $0 + 4$ | 4 |
| 4 | 4 ✓ |

*To check your solution, substitute −3 for x in the original equation.*

**B** $5 = |x+2| + 8$

$$5 = |x+2| + 8$$
$$\underline{-8 \quad -8}$$
$$-3 = |x+2| \text{ ✗}$$

*Since 8 is added to $|x + 2|$, subtract 8 from both sides to undo the addition.*

*Absolute value cannot be negative.*

This equation has no solution.

**Remember!**

Absolute value must be nonnegative because it represents distance.

**Solve each equation.**

**2a.** $2 - |2x - 5| = 7$ **2b.** $-6 + |x - 4| = -6$

EXTENSION

# Exercises

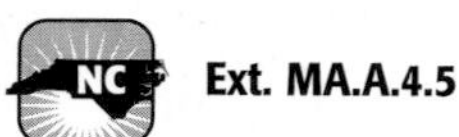
Ext. MA.A.4.5

**Solve each equation. Check your answer.**

**1.** $|x| = 6$
**2.** $-8 = |x|$
**3.** $|x| = 0$
**4.** $9 = |x + 5|$
**5.** $|3x| + 2 = 8$
**6.** $2|x| = 18$
**7.** $|x + 3| - 6 = 2$
**8.** $18 = 3|x - 1|$
**9.** $|2x - 4| = 22$
**10.** $|x| = \frac{1}{2}$
**11.** $|x| - 7 = 50$
**12.** $-2|x| = -4$
**13.** $5|x| = 15$
**14.** $3|x| - 12 = 18$
**15.** $2|x| - 10 = 22$
**16.** $2|x + 3| = 18$
**17.** $|5x - 10| + 5 = 15$
**18.** $|x - 3| + 14 = 7$
**19.** $|x| + 7 = 21 - 9$
**20.** $|3x| + 8 = 9$
**21.** $2|x + 1| + 4 = 12$
**22.** $|x + 4| = -7$
**23.** $7 = |3x + 9| + 7$
**24.** $5|x + 7| + 14 = 8$

**25.** The two numbers that are 5 units from 3 on the number line are represented by the absolute-value equation $|n - 3| = 5$. What are these two numbers? Graph the solutions.

**26.** Write and solve an absolute-value equation that represents the two numbers $x$ that are 2 units from 7 on a number line. Graph the solutions.

**27.** **Manufacturing** A quality control inspector at a bolt factory examines random bolts that come off the assembly line. Any bolt whose diameter differs by more than 0.04 mm from 6.5 mm is sent back. Let $d$ equal the actual diameter of a bolt. Solve the equation $|d - 6.5| = 0.04$ to find the maximum and minimum diameters of an acceptable bolt.

**28.** **Communication** Barry's walkie-talkie has a range of 2 mi. Barry is traveling on a straight highway and is at mile marker 207. Write and solve an absolute-value equation to find the minimum and maximum mile marker that Barry's walkie-talkie will reach.

**29.** **Space Shuttle** The diameter of a valve for the space shuttle must be within 0.001 mm of 5 mm. Write and solve an absolute-value equation to find the boundary values for acceptable diameters of the valve.

5 mm

**Solve each equation. Check your answer.**

**30.** $|x| + 2 = 4$
**31.** $|x - 42.04| = 23.24$
**32.** $|3x + 1| = 13$
**33.** $|-2x - 5.75| = 13.25$
**34.** $\left|\frac{2}{3}x - \frac{2}{3}\right| = \frac{2}{3}$
**35.** $|4x| + 7 = 7$
**36.** $6 - |x| = 0$
**37.** $8 = 7 - |x|$
**38.** $|x| + 6 = 12 - 6$
**39.** $9 = 7 - |x + 2|$
**40.** $|2x| = -12 + 6$
**41.** $|x - 3.8| = 6.5$

**42.** Write an absolute-value equation whose solutions are graphed on the number line below.

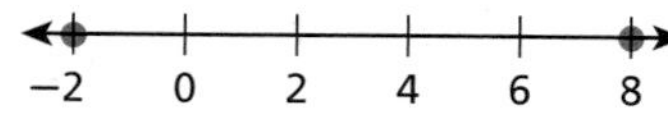

43. **Temperature** A thermostat is set so that the temperature in a laboratory freezer stays within 2.5°F of 2°F. Write and solve an absolute-value equation to find the maximum and minimum temperatures in the freezer.

44. **Construction** A brick company guarantees to fill a contractor's order to within 5% accuracy. A contractor orders 1500 bricks. Write and solve an absolute-value equation to find the maximum and minimum number of bricks guaranteed by the brick company.

45. **Sports** According to a height and weight chart, Bruce's ideal wrestling weight is 168 pounds. Bruce wants to keep his weight within 3 pounds of his ideal weight. Write and solve an absolute-value equation to find Bruce's maximum and minimum weights.

46. **Recreation** To ensure safety, boaters must be aware of wind conditions while they are on the water. A particular instrument gives wind speed within a certain amount of the true wind speed, as shown in the table.

| Measured Wind Speed (mi/h) | True Wind Speed (mi/h) |
|---|---|
| 20 | 15–25 |
| 22 | 17–27 |
| 24 | 19–29 |
| 26 | 21–31 |
| 28 | 23–33 |
| 30 | 25–35 |

a. Use the table to write an absolute-value equation for the minimum and maximum possible true wind speeds $t$ when the measured wind speed is 24 mi/h.

b. Solve your equation from part **a** and check that it is correct by comparing it to the values given in the table when measured wind speed is 24 mi/h.

c. Will your equation work for all of the values in the table? Explain.

d. Explain what your equation says about the measurements given by the instrument.

47. **Write About It** Although $|5w - 6| = -21$ has no solutions, write two cases and carry out the steps to solve each case. What do you find when you check your answers by substituting them into the original equation?

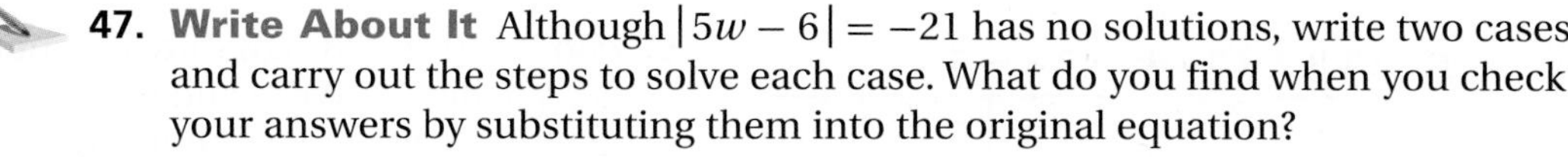

48. **ERROR ANALYSIS** Find and explain the error below. What is the correct answer?

$-3|x + 6| = -9$
$-3x - 18 = -9$
$-3x = 9$
$x = -3$

49. **Write About It** Do you agree with the following statement? *To solve an absolute-value equation, you always need to solve two equations.* Why or why not?

50. **Challenge** The perimeter of a rectangle is 100. The length of the rectangle is $|2x - 4|$ inches and the width is $x$ inches. What are the possible values of $x$? Explain.

CHAPTER 2

# Study Guide: Review

## Vocabulary



**Complete the sentences below with vocabulary words from the list above.**

1. A formula is a type of a(n) ___?___.
2. A(n) ___?___ is used to compare two quantities by division.

## 2-1 Solving Equations by Adding or Subtracting *(pp. 77–82)*

 MA.A.4.5

### EXAMPLES

**Solve each equation. Check your answer.**

- $x - 12 = -8.3$
  $\quad +12 \quad +12$
  $x = 3.7$

  *Check* $x - 12 = -8.3$

  | $3.7 - 12$ | $-8.3$ |
  |---|---|
  | $-8.3$ | $-8.3$ ✓ |

- $-7.8 = 5 + t$
  $\quad -5 \quad -5$
  $-12.8 = t$

  *Check* $-7.8 = 5 + t$

  | $-7.8$ | $5 + (-12.8)$ |
  |---|---|
  | $-7.8$ | $-7.8$ ✓ |

### EXERCISES

**Solve each equation. Check your answer.**

3. $b - 16 = 20$
4. $4 + x = 2$
5. $9 + a = -12$
6. $-7 + y = 11$
7. $z - \frac{1}{4} = \frac{7}{8}$
8. $w + \frac{2}{3} = 3$
9. Robin needs 108 signatures for her petition. So far, she has 27. Write and solve an equation to determine how many more signatures she needs.

## 2-2 Solving Equations by Multiplying or Dividing *(pp. 84–90)*

 MA.A.4.5

### EXAMPLES

**Solve each equation.**

- $\frac{z}{2.4} = 12$
  $(2.4)\frac{z}{2.4} = (2.4)12$
  $z = 28.8$

- $-8x = 148$
  $\frac{-8x}{-8} = \frac{148}{-8}$
  $x = -18.5$

### EXERCISES

**Solve each equation. Check your answer.**

10. $35 = 5x$
11. $-3n = 10$
12. $-30 = \frac{n}{3}$
13. $\frac{x}{-5} = -2.6$
14. $5y = 0$
15. $-4.6r = 9.2$

## 2-3 Solving Two-Step and Multi-Step Equations *(pp. 92–98)*

### EXAMPLE

■ Solve $\frac{3x}{5} - \frac{x}{4} + \frac{1}{2} = \frac{6}{5}$.

$$\frac{3x}{5} - \frac{x}{4} + \frac{1}{2} = \frac{6}{5}$$

$$20\left(\frac{3x}{5} - \frac{x}{4} + \frac{1}{2}\right) = 20\left(\frac{6}{5}\right)$$ *Multiply by the LCD.*

$$12x - 5x + 10 = 24$$

$$7x + 10 = 24$$ *Combine like terms.*

$$\underline{-10 \quad -10}$$

$$7x = 14$$

$$\frac{7x}{7} = \frac{14}{7}$$

$$x = 2$$

### EXERCISES

**Solve each equation. Check your answer.**

**16.** $4t - 13 = 57$

**17.** $5 - 2y = 15$

**18.** $\frac{k}{5} - 6 = 2$

**19.** $\frac{5}{6}f - \frac{3}{4}f + \frac{3}{4} = \frac{1}{2}$

**20.** $7x - 19x = 6$

**21.** $4 + 3a - 6 = 43$

**22.** If $8n + 22 = 70$, find the value of $3n$.

**23.** If $0 = 6n - 36$, find the value of $n - 5$.

**24.** The sum of the measures of two angles is 180°. One angle measures $3a$ and the other angle measures $2a - 25$ Find $a$. Then find the measure of each angle.

## 2-4 Solving Equations with Variables on Both Sides *(pp. 100–106)*

MA.A.4.5, MA.A.1.1

### EXAMPLE

■ Solve $x + 7 = 12 + 3x - 7x$.

$$x + 7 = 12 + 3x - 7x$$

$$x + 7 = 12 - 4x$$ *Combine like terms.*

$$\underline{+4x \qquad +4x}$$

$$5x + 7 = 12$$

$$\underline{-7 \quad -7}$$

$$5x = 5$$

$$\frac{5x}{5} = \frac{5}{5}$$

$$x = 1$$

### EXERCISES

**Solve each equation. Check your answer.**

**25.** $4x + 2 = 3x$

**26.** $-3r - 8 = -5r - 12$

**27.** $-a - 3 + 7 = 3a$

**28.** $-(x - 4) = 2x + 6$

**29.** $\frac{2}{3}n = 4n - \frac{10}{3}n - \frac{1}{2}$

**30.** $0.2(7 + 2t) = 0.4t + 1.4$

**31.** One photo shop charges $0.36 per print. Another photo shop charges $2.52 plus $0.08 per print. Juan finds that the cost of developing his photos is the same at either shop. How many photos does Juan have to develop?

## 2-5 Solving for a Variable *(pp. 107–111)*

### EXAMPLE

■ Solve $A = P + Prt$ for $r$.

$$A = P + Prt$$

$$\underline{-P \quad -P}$$

$$A - P = Prt$$

$$\frac{A - P}{Pt} = \frac{Prt}{Pt}$$

$$\frac{A - P}{Pt} = r$$

### EXERCISES

**Solve for the indicated variable.**

**32.** $C = \frac{360}{n}$ for $n$

**33.** $S = \frac{n}{2}(a + \ell)$ for $a$

**34.** $0.25x + y = 225$ for $x$

**35.** The formula $a = \frac{d}{g}$ gives the average gas mileage $a$ of a vehicle that uses $g$ gallons of gas to travel $d$ miles. Use the formula to find how many gallons of gas a vehicle with an average gas mileage of 20.2 miles per gallon will use to travel 75 miles. Round your answer to the nearest tenth.

## 2-6 Rates, Ratios, and Proportions *(pp. 114–120)*

### EXAMPLES

- **The ratio of skateboarders to bikers in an extreme sports contest is 7:2. There are 91 skateboarders. How many bikers are there?**

$\frac{\text{skateboarders}}{\text{bikers}} \rightarrow \frac{7}{2}$ *Write a proportion.*

$\frac{7}{2} = \frac{91}{x}$ *Let x be the number of bikers.*

$7 \cdot x = 2 \cdot 91$ *Use cross products.*

$7x = 182$

$\frac{7x}{7} = \frac{182}{7}$ *Solve for x.*

$x = 26$

There are 26 bikers.

- **Solve $\frac{3w-7}{21} = \frac{3}{7}$.**

$\frac{3w-7}{21} = \frac{3}{7}$

$7(3w-7) = 21(3)$ *Use cross products*

$21w - 49 = 63$

$+49 \quad +49$

$21w = 112$

$\frac{21w}{21} = \frac{112}{21}$

$w = \frac{16}{3}$

### EXERCISES

**36.** In the ninth grade there are 320 students and 20 teachers. What is the student-to-teacher ratio?

**37.** A recipe for a casserole calls for 2 cups of rice. The recipe makes 6 servings of casserole. How many cups of rice will you need to make 10 servings of casserole?

**Find each unit rate. Round your answer to the nearest hundredth.**

**38.** Teresa can buy 18 golf balls for $32.99.

**39.** A 15 oz bottle of juice costs $2.75.

**Convert each rate. Round your answer to the nearest hundredth if necessary.**

**40.** 30 cm/s to m/h

**41.** 75 ft/s to mi/min

**Solve each proportion. Check your answer.**

**42.** $\frac{n}{8} = \frac{2}{10}$

**43.** $\frac{2}{9} = \frac{12}{x}$

**44.** $\frac{3}{k} = \frac{9}{15}$

**45.** $\frac{1}{3} = \frac{x}{x-6}$

**46.** The distance from Durango, Colorado, to Denver, Colorado, is approximately 385 miles. The scale on a map is 0.25 in : 25 mi. How far apart should the two cities be located on the map?

## 2-7 Applications of Proportions *(pp. 121–126)*

### EXAMPLE

- **When Janelle stood next to the Washington Monument, she cast a 1.2-foot-long shadow, and the monument cast a 111-foot-long shadow. Janelle is 6 feet tall. How tall is the monument?**

$\frac{x}{111} = \frac{6}{1.2}$ *Write a proportion.*

$1.2x = 666$ *Use cross products.*

$\frac{1.2x}{1.2} = \frac{666}{1.2}$ *Solve for x.*

$x = 555$

The monument is 555 feet tall.

### EXERCISES

**47.** Find the value of $x$ in the diagram.

$\triangle ABC \sim \triangle DEF$

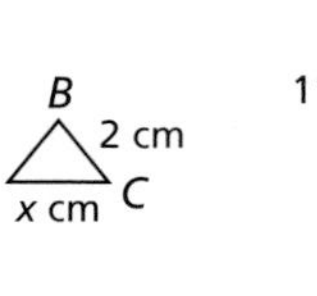


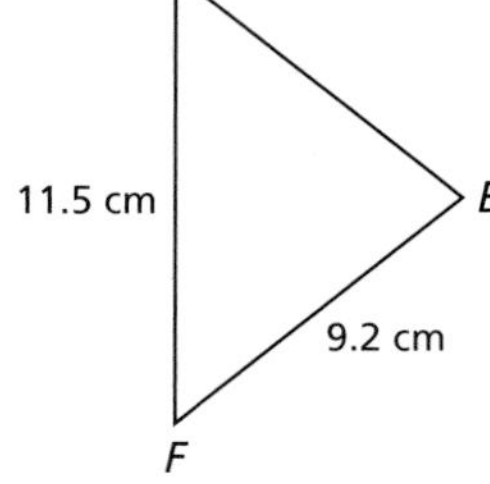


**48.** A tree casts a shadow that is 14 ft long at the same time that a nearby 2-foot-tall pole casts a shadow that is 1.75 ft long. How tall is the tree?

**49.** A circle has a radius of 9 inches. The radius is multiplied by $\frac{2}{3}$ to form a second circle. How is the ratio of the areas related to the ratio of the radii?

## 2-8 Percents *(pp. 127–132)*

### EXAMPLE

- **Earth's surface area is about 197 million square miles. About 58 million square miles is land. What percent is water?**

197 million − 58 million = 139 million

$$\frac{\text{part}}{\text{whole}} = \frac{\text{percent}}{100} \longrightarrow \frac{139}{197} = \frac{n}{100}$$

$197n = 13{,}900$ *Use cross products.*

$n = 70.56$

About 71% of Earth's surface area is water.

### EXERCISES

**50.** Find 2.3% of 230.

**51.** Find 115% of 2700.

**52.** What percent of 18 is 12? Round your answer to the nearest tenth of a percent.

**53.** What percent of 14 is 56?

**54.** 90% of what number is 120? Round the number to the nearest tenth.

**55.** 90 is 37.5% of what number?

**56.** A student answered 32 questions correctly and 8 incorrectly. What percent of the questions were answered correctly?

## 2-9 Applications of Percents *(pp. 133–137)*

### EXAMPLE

- **After 10 months, the simple interest earned on $3000 was $52.50. Find the interest rate.**

$I = Prt$

$52.5 = 3000(r)\left(\frac{10}{12}\right)$ *Substitute.*

$52.5 = 2500r$ *Multiply.*

$\frac{52.5}{2500} = \frac{2500r}{2500}$ *Solve for r.*

$0.021 = r$

The interest rate is 2.1%. *Write as a percent.*

### EXERCISES

**57.** A salesperson earns a base salary of $36,000 plus $2\frac{1}{2}$% commission on sales. His total sales for one year was $500,000. Find the salesperson's total pay for that year.

**58.** Find the simple interest paid for 10 years on a $10,000 loan at 9% per year.

**59.** The sales tax rate is 8%. Estimate the tax on a jacket that costs $69.95.

## 2-10 Percent Increase and Decrease *(pp. 138–143)*

### EXAMPLES

**Find each percent change. Tell whether it is a percent increase or decrease.**

- from 50 to 56

$$\text{percent change} = \frac{\text{amount of increase}}{\text{original amount}} = \frac{56-50}{50} = \frac{6}{50} = 0.12 = 12\%$$

The change is a 12% increase.

- from 120 to 72

$$\text{percent change} = \frac{\text{amount of decrease}}{\text{original amount}} = \frac{120-72}{120} = \frac{48}{120} = 0.40 = 40\%$$

The change is a 40% decrease.

### EXERCISES

**Find each percent change. Tell whether it is a percent increase or decrease. Round your answer to the nearest percent.**

**60.** from 19 to 26

**61.** from 42 to 28

**62.** Find the result when 65 is increased by 40%.

**63.** Find the result when 150 is decreased by 15%.

**64.** Tom sells sunglasses that he buys wholesale for $2.50 each. He then marks up the price 150%. What is the amount of the markup? What is the selling price?

**65.** The original price of a shirt was $79.99. It is on sale for $49.99. What is the percent discount? Round to the nearest tenth.

CHAPTER 2

**Solve each equation.**

**1.** $y - 7 = 2$

**2.** $x + 12 = 19$

**3.** $-5 + z = 8$

**4.** $9x = 72$

**5.** $\frac{m}{-8} = -2.5$

**6.** $\frac{7}{8}a = 42$

**7.** $15 = 3 - 4x$

**8.** $\frac{2a}{3} + \frac{1}{5} = \frac{7}{6}$

**9.** $8 - (b - 2) = 11$

**10.** $-2x + 4 = 5 - 3x$

**11.** $3(q - 2) + 2 = 5q - 7 - 2q$

**12.** $5z = -3(z + 7)$

**Solve for the indicated variable.**

**13.** $r - 2s = 14$ for $s$

**14.** $V = \frac{1}{3}bh$ for $b$

**15.** $P = 2(\ell + w)$ for $\ell$

**16.** The ratio of red marbles to blue marbles in a bag is 4:7. There are 16 red marbles. How many blue marbles are there?

**Find each unit rate. Round to the nearest hundredth if necessary.**

**17.** A store sells 3 videotapes for $4.99.

**18.** Twenty-five students use 120 sheets of paper.

**Solve each proportion.**

**19.** $\frac{5}{4} = \frac{x}{12}$

**20.** $\frac{8}{2z} = \frac{15}{60}$

**21.** $\frac{x + 10}{10} = \frac{18}{12}$

**22.** The scale on a map is 1 inch:500 miles. If two cities are 875 miles apart, how far apart are they on the map?

**Find the value of $x$ in each diagram. Round your answer to the nearest tenth.**

**23.** $\triangle EFG \sim \triangle RTS$

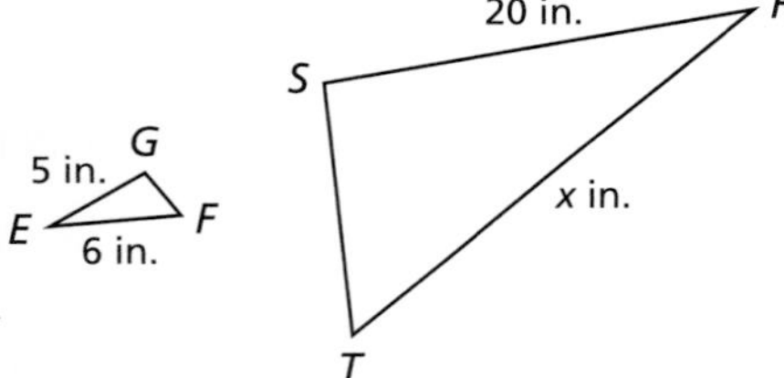


**24.** $HJKL \sim WXYZ$

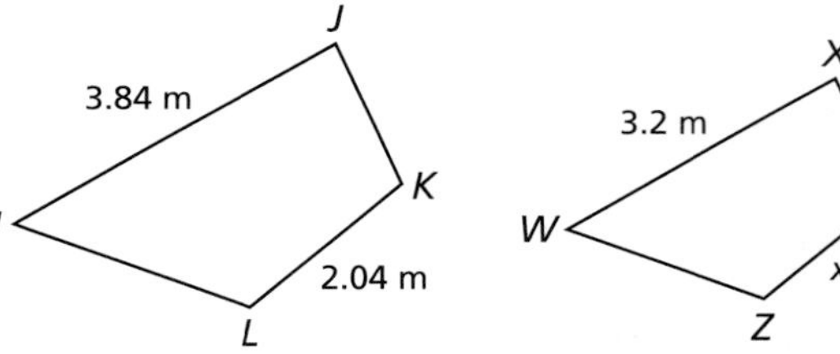


**25.** What is 23% of 46?

**26.** 37.5 is 60% of what number?

**27.** What percent of 175 is 35?

**28.** Find the simple interest earned after 5 years on an investment of $2000 at 3.2% per year.

**29.** A lunch check is $27.95. Estimate a 15% tip.

**Find each percent change. Tell whether it is a percent increase or decrease.**

**30.** from 180 to 234

**31.** from 12 to 48

**32.** from 56 to 21

CHAPTER 2

## *FOCUS ON ACT*

The ACT Mathematics Test is one of four tests in the ACT. You have 60 minutes to answer 60 multiple-choice questions. The questions cover material typically taught through the end of eleventh grade. You will need to know some basic formulas.

**There is no penalty for guessing on the ACT. If you are unsure of the correct answer, eliminate as many answer choices as possible. Then make your best guess. Be sure you have marked an answer for every question before time runs out.**

**You may want to time yourself as you take this practice test. It should take you about 6 minutes to complete.**

**1.** At a certain high school, the ratio of left-handed to right-handed basketball players is 1:4. If there are a total of 20 players on the team, how many players are right-handed?

**(A)** 1

**(B)** 4

**(C)** 5

**(D)** 12

**(E)** 16

**2.** If $y - 3 = \frac{2}{5}(x + 1)$, then $x = ?$

**(F)** $\frac{5(y-3)-2}{2}$

**(G)** $y - \frac{22}{5}$

**(H)** $\frac{2(y-3)}{5} - 1$

**(J)** $\frac{2(y+1)+15}{5}$

**(K)** $\frac{5}{2}y - 4$

**3.** What is $\frac{1}{5}\%$ of 20?

**(A)** 0.004

**(B)** 0.04

**(C)** 0.4

**(D)** 4

**(E)** 100

**4.** If $x - 3 = 4 - 2(x + 5)$, then $x = ?$

**(F)** $-3$

**(G)** $-1$

**(H)** 1

**(J)** $\frac{3}{2}$

**(K)** $\frac{11}{3}$

**5.** If $\triangle ABC \sim \triangle DEF$, what is the length of $\overline{AC}$?

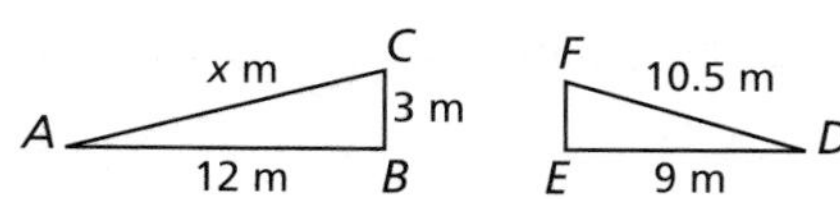


**(A)** 2.6 meters

**(B)** 3.5 meters

**(C)** 7 meters

**(D)** 14 meters

**(E)** 15 meters

**6.** A movie theater makes 30% of its revenue from concession sales. If concession sales were $174,000, what was the total revenue?

**(F)** $52,200

**(G)** $121,800

**(H)** $248,570

**(J)** $580,000

**(K)** $746,000

CHAPTER 2

# TEST TACKLER

Standardized Test Strategies

## Multiple Choice: Eliminate Answer Choices

You can answer some problems without doing many calculations. Use logic to eliminate answer choices and save time.

### EXAMPLE 1

**Which number is the square of 123,765?**

Ⓐ 15,317,775,225 Ⓒ 15,317,775,230

Ⓑ 15,317,775,233 Ⓓ 15,317,775,227

*Your calculator will not help you on this question. Due to rounding, any of the answer choices are possible.*

*But you can use this fact to eliminate three of the answer choices:*

*The square of any number ending in 5 is also a number ending in 5.*

The only answer choice that ends in 5 is A, 15,317,775,225.

### EXAMPLE 2

**What is a possible area of the wooden triangle shown?**

Ⓕ 11 square feet Ⓗ 14 square feet

Ⓖ 20 square feet Ⓙ 24 square feet

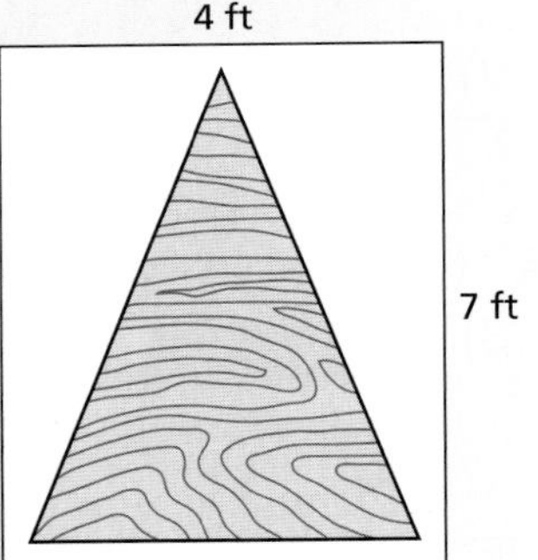


*The triangle is inside a rectangle with an area of $7 \times 4 = 28$ square feet.*

*If the triangle had the same base and height as the rectangle, its area would be half the area of the rectangle, 14 square feet.*

*However, the triangle fits inside the rectangle, so its area must be less than 14 square feet.*

The only answer choice that is less than 14 square feet is F, 11 square feet.

**Try to eliminate unreasonable answer choices. Some choices may be too great or too small, have incorrect units, or not be divisible by a necessary number.**

**Read each test item and answer the questions that follow.**

**Item A**

**The top speed of a three-toed sloth is 0.12 miles per hour. About how many feet can a sloth travel in an hour?**

Ⓐ 0.12 feet
Ⓑ 600 feet
Ⓒ 2.27 feet
Ⓓ 7500 inches

1. Are there any answer choices you can eliminate immediately? If so, which choices and why?
2. Describe how you can use estimation to find the correct answer.

**Item B**

**A city park is shaped like a triangle. The Liberty Street side of the park is 120 feet long, and the First Avenue side is 50 feet long.**

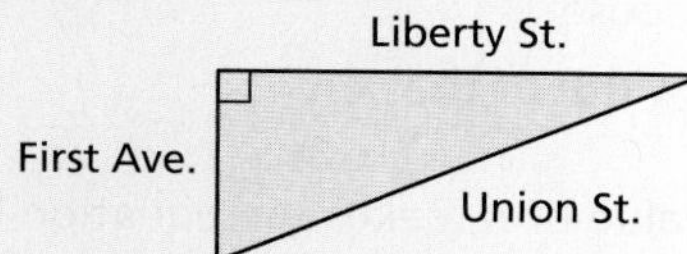


**What is the approximate length of the side of the park that faces Union Street?**

Ⓕ 25 feet
Ⓖ 110 inches
Ⓗ 65 feet
Ⓙ 130 feet

3. Can any of the answer choices be eliminated immediately? If so, which choices and why?
4. Are there any properties you can use to solve this problem? If so, what are they?
5. Describe how to find the correct answer without doing any calculations.

**Item C**

**Approximately how long will the average 18-year-old have slept in his lifetime?**

Ⓐ 6 weeks
Ⓑ 6 months
Ⓒ 6 years
Ⓓ 6 decades

6. Which answer choice can be eliminated immediately? Why?
7. Explain how to use mental math to solve this problem.

**Item D**

**Sheila's paychecks for February and March were equal. If she worked every day during both months, for which month was her daily pay lower?**

Ⓕ February
Ⓖ March
Ⓗ Her daily pay did not change.
Ⓙ Cannot be determined

8. What do you need to know to solve this problem?
9. Describe how you can find the correct answer.

**Item E**

**Greg tripled the number of baseball cards he had last week. Which of these could be the number of cards Greg has now?**

Ⓐ 100
Ⓑ 200
Ⓒ 150
Ⓓ 250

10. The number of cards that Greg has now must be divisible by what number? How can you tell if a number is divisible by this number?
11. Describe how to find the answer to this problem.

CHAPTER 2

## CUMULATIVE ASSESSMENT, CHAPTERS 1–2

### Multiple Choice

**1.** What operation does ◊ represent if $x \lozenge 2.2 = 4.5$ when $x = 9.9$?

A Addition

B Subtraction

C Multiplication

D Division

**2.** A couple earns \$4819.25 a month. They pay 9.5% of their monthly income as the monthly payment on their car. To the nearest dollar, how much does the couple pay for their monthly car payment?

A \$458 C \$4578

B \$507 D \$4810

**3.** Every dimension of cylinder *A* is multiplied by 4 to make cylinder *B*. What is the ratio of the volume of cylinder *A* to the volume of cylinder *B*?

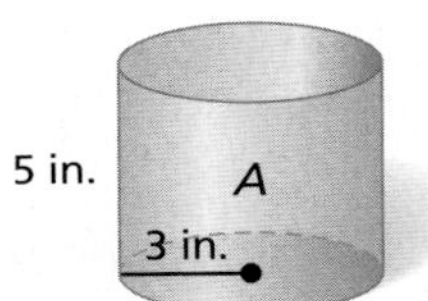


A $\frac{1}{64}$ C $\frac{1}{4}$

B $\frac{1}{16}$ D $\frac{1}{3}$

**4.** A clock loses 5 minutes every day. How much time will it lose in 2 hours?

A 0.417 second C 240 seconds

B 25 seconds D 600 seconds

**5.** A statue is 8 feet tall. The display case for a model of the statue is 18 inches tall. Which scale allows for the tallest model of the statue that will fit in the display case?

A 1 inch:2 inches C 1 inch:5 inches

B 1 inch:7 inches D 1 inch:10 inches

**6.** What is the value of $-|6^2|$?

A $-36$ C $-8$

B $-12$ D $-3$

**7.** Mr. Phillips wants to install hardwood flooring in his den. The flooring costs \$25.86 per square yard. The blueprint below shows his house. What other information do you need in order to find the total cost of the flooring?

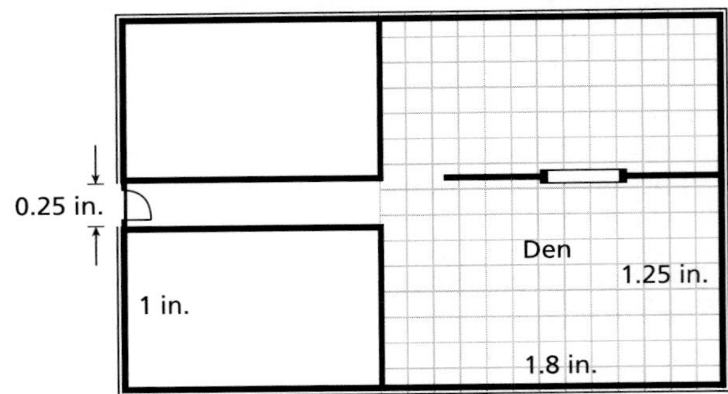


A The lengths and widths of the adjoining rooms in the blueprint

B The total area of the blueprint

C The scale of inches in the blueprint to yards in the house

D The width of the den

**8.** What value of *n* makes the equation below have no solution?

$$2x + 2 = nx - 3$$

A $-2$

B 0

C 2

D 3

**9.** Which of the equations below represents the second step of the solution process?

Step 1: $3(5x - 2) + 27 = -24$
Step 2: ☐
Step 3: $15x + 21 = -24$
Step 4: $15x = -45$
Step 5: $x = -3$

A $3(5x + 27) - 2 = -24$

B $3(5x + 25) = -24$

C $15x - 2 + 27 = -24$

D $15x - 6 + 27 = -24$

**If you are stuck on a problem, skip it and come back later. Another problem might remind you of something that will help. If you feel yourself become tense, take a few deep breaths to relax.**

**10.** Cass drove 3 miles to school, and then she drove $m$ miles to a friend's house. The total mileage for these two trips was 8 miles. Which equation ***cannot*** be used to determine the number of miles Cass drove?

**A** $3 + m = 8$

**B** $3 - m = 8$

**C** $8 - 3 = m$

**D** $8 - m = 3$

**11.** If $\frac{20}{x} = \frac{4}{x-5}$, which of the following is a true statement?

**A** $x(x - 5) = 80$

**B** $20x = 4(x - 5)$

**C** $20(x - 5) = 4x$

**D** $24 = 2x - 5$

**12.** Melissa invested her savings in a retirement account that pays simple interest. A portion of her account record is shown below. What is the interest rate on Melissa's account?

| Date | Transaction | Amount | Balance |
|---|---|---|---|
| 8/1 | Beginning deposit | \$6000.00 | \$6000.00 |
| 8/31 | Interest payment | \$192.00 | \$6192.00 |
| 9/1 | Withdrawal | \$1000.00 | \$5192.00 |
| 9/30 | Interest payment | \$166.14 | \$5358.14 |

**A** 3.2%

**B** 0.032%

**C** \$833.86

**D** \$25.86

**13.** A bike rental shop charges a one-time charge of \$8 plus an hourly fee to rent a bike. Dan paid \$24.50 to rent a bike for $5\frac{1}{2}$ hours. What is the bike shop's hourly fee?

**A** \$6.00

**B** \$4.45

**C** \$3.00

**D** \$1.81

### *STANDARDIZED TEST PREP*

## Short Response

**S1.** Alex buys 5 calendars to give as gifts. Each calendar has the same price. When the cashier rings up Alex's calendars, the total cost before tax is \$58.75.

**a.** Write and solve an equation to find the cost of each calendar.

**b.** The total cost of Alex's calendars after tax is \$63.45. Find the percent sales tax. Show your work and explain in words how you found your answer.

**c.** Alex's friend Keisha buys some calendars for the same price. She uses her 15% discount card. The total cost before tax is \$39.95. How many calendars did Keisha buy? Show your work and explain in words how you found your answer.

**S2.** Is the percent increase from 50 to 100 the same as the percent decrease from 100 to 50? Explain your reasoning in words.

## Extended Response

**E1.** Korena is putting a decorative border around her rectangular flower garden. The total perimeter of the garden is 200 feet.

**a.** Draw three different rectangles that could represent Korena's flower garden. Label the dimensions of your rectangles.

**b.** Use the table to show the lengths and widths of five different rectangles that could represent Korena's flower garden. Do not use any of your rectangles from part **a.**

**Possible Dimensions of Korena's Garden**

| Length ($\ell$) | Width ($w$) | Perimeter ($P$) |
|---|---|---|
| | | |
| | | |
| | | |
| | | |
| | | |

**c.** The length of Korena's garden is 4 times its width. Explain how to use the perimeter formula $P = 2\ell + 2w$ to find the dimensions of Korena's garden.

**d.** Find the dimensions of Korena's garden.

## Snakes of North Carolina

North Carolina is home to 37 species of snakes. The greatest number of different species can be found in the Coastal Plain region, where 36 of the species live. Although several of the state's snake species are venomous, nonvenomous snakes are far more common in all parts of the state.

**1.** Among snake species found in North Carolina, 6 species are venomous. What percent of the species are nonvenomous? Round to the nearest percent.

**2.** The skin that a snake sheds is usually 25% longer than the snake itself. A park ranger finds the skin of a rat snake that is 4.5 feet long. What was the length of the snake?

Eastern Coral Snake

**For 3 and 4, use the graph.**

**3.** The maximum length of a pine snake divided by 3 equals the typical length of a scarlet snake. Write and solve an equation to find the maximum length of a pine snake.

**4.** The typical length of a copperhead is 4 cm less than 4 times the typical length of a worm snake.

  **a.** Write an equation you can use to find the typical length of a worm snake.

  **b.** Solve the equation.

  **c.** The typical length of a ringneck snake is 160% of the length of a worm snake. What is the typical length of a ringneck snake?

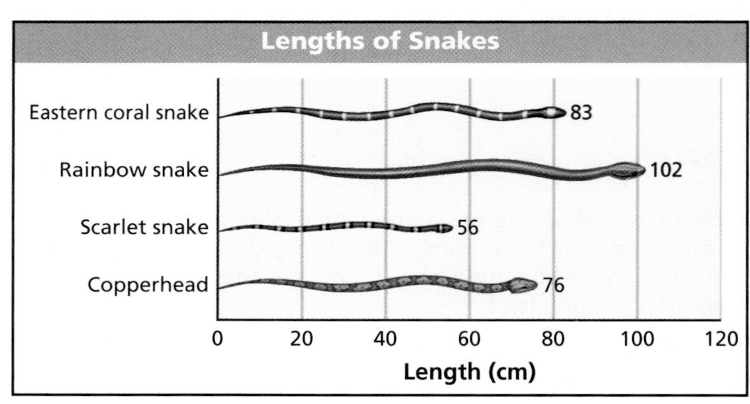

# Wright Brothers National Memorial

An airplane flight lasting 20 seconds and covering 120 feet may not seem like much of a journey. However, this was the time and distance of the world's first successful flight on December 17, 1903, at Kitty Hawk. Today, the Wright Brothers National Memorial honors this historic achievement of Orville and Wilbur Wright.

**1.** The memorial features a monument to the Wright Brothers. At the same time that the monument casts a shadow that is 36 feet long, a visitor who is 5 feet tall casts a shadow that is 3 feet long. How tall is the monument?

**2.** The Wright Brothers' airplane, the *Flyer*, was 21 feet long and $9\frac{1}{4}$ feet tall. A scale model of the plane is built using the scale 1 in:3 ft.

**a.** How long is the model?

**b.** Will the model fit in a box that is 3 inches tall? Why or why not?

**The Wright Brothers made four flights on December 17, 1903, as shown in the diagram. Use the diagram for 3 and 4.**

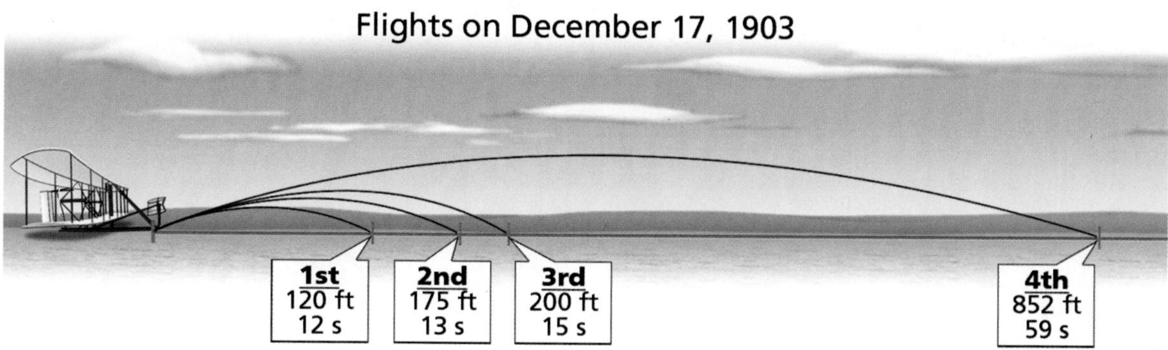


**3. a.** What was the average speed of the airplane during the first flight?

**b.** Express this speed in miles per hour.

**4.** Suppose that during the third flight the airplane had been able to continue at the same speed and travel a total of 500 feet. Write and solve a proportion to find out how long the flight would have taken.

CHAPTER 3

# Inequalities

## Why Learn This?

You can use inequalities to determine how many points are needed to win a competition at the North Carolina State Fair in Raleigh.

go.hrw.com
Chapter Project Online
KEYWORD: MA7 ChProj

# ARE YOU READY?

## Vocabulary

**Match each term on the left with a definition on the right.**

1. equation
2. evaluate
3. inverse operations
4. like terms
5. solution of an equation

A. mathematical phrase that contains operations, numbers, and/or variables
B. mathematical statement that two expressions are equivalent
C. value of a variable that makes a statement true
D. terms that contain the same variable raised to the same power
E. to find the value of an expression
F. operations that undo each other

## Evaluate Expressions

**Evaluate each expression for $a = 2$ and $b = 6$.**

6. $b - a$
7. $ab$
8. $b \div a$
9. $a + b$

## Compare and Order Real Numbers

**Compare. Write <, >, or =.**

10. 10 ▒ 21
11. 5.27 ▒ 5.23
12. 20% ▒ 0.2
13. $\frac{1}{3}$ ▒ $\frac{2}{5}$

## Combine Like Terms

**Simplify each expression by combining like terms.**

14. $6x + x$
15. $-8a + 3a$
16. $9x^2 - 15x^2$
17. $2.1x + 4.3x$

## Distributive Property

**Simplify each expression.**

18. $2(x + 3)$
19. $(3 - d)5$
20. $4(r - 1)$
21. $3(4 + m)$

## Solve One-Step Equations

**Solve.**

22. $s - 3 = 8$
23. $-7x = 21$
24. $y + 11 = 2$
25. $\frac{h}{2} = 6$
26. $t + 2 = -2$
27. $6x = 42$
28. $r - 8 = -13$
29. $\frac{y}{3} = -12$

# CHAPTER 3 Study Guide: Preview

## Where You've Been

**Previously, you**

- learned the properties of equality.
- solved equations by using inverse operations.
- solved equations with variables on both sides.

## In This Chapter

**You will study**

- the properties of inequality.
- how to solve inequalities by using inverse operations.
- how to solve inequalities with variables on both sides.
- how to solve compound inequalities.

## Where You're Going

**You can use the skills in this chapter**

- in all your future math classes, including Geometry.
- in other classes, such as Health, Chemistry, Physics, and Economics.
- in the real world to plan a budget, to find cost-efficient services, and to set financial goals.

## *Key Vocabulary/Vocabulario*

| | |
|---|---|
| compound inequality | desigualdad compuesta |
| inequality | desigualdad |
| intersection | intersección |
| solution of an inequality | solución de una desigualdad |
| union | unión |

## *Vocabulary Connections*

To become familiar with some of the vocabulary terms in the chapter, consider the following. You may refer to the chapter, the glossary, or a dictionary if you like.

1. The prefix *in*- means "not." An *equality* states that two things are equal. Use these meanings to write your own definition for the word **inequality**.
2. The word *compound* means "consisting of two or more parts." What do you think a **compound inequality** might be?
3. The **intersection** of two roads is the place where the two roads overlap. What do you think the *intersection* of two graphs would be?
4. The word **union** begins with the root *uni*-. List some other words that begin with *uni*-. What do all of these words have in common?

## Study Strategy: Use Your Notes Effectively

Taking notes helps you arrange, organize, and process information from your textbook and class lectures. In addition to taking notes, you need to use your notes before and after class effectively.

**Step 1: Before Class**

- Review your notes from the last class.
- Then preview the next lesson and write down any questions you have.

**Step 2: During Class**

- Write down main ideas.
- If you miss something, leave a blank and keep taking notes. Fill in any holes later.
- Use diagrams and abbreviations. Make sure you will understand any abbreviations later.

**Step 3: After Class**

- Fill in the holes you left during class.
- Highlight or circle the most important ideas, such as vocabulary, formulas, or procedures.
- Use your notes to quiz yourself.

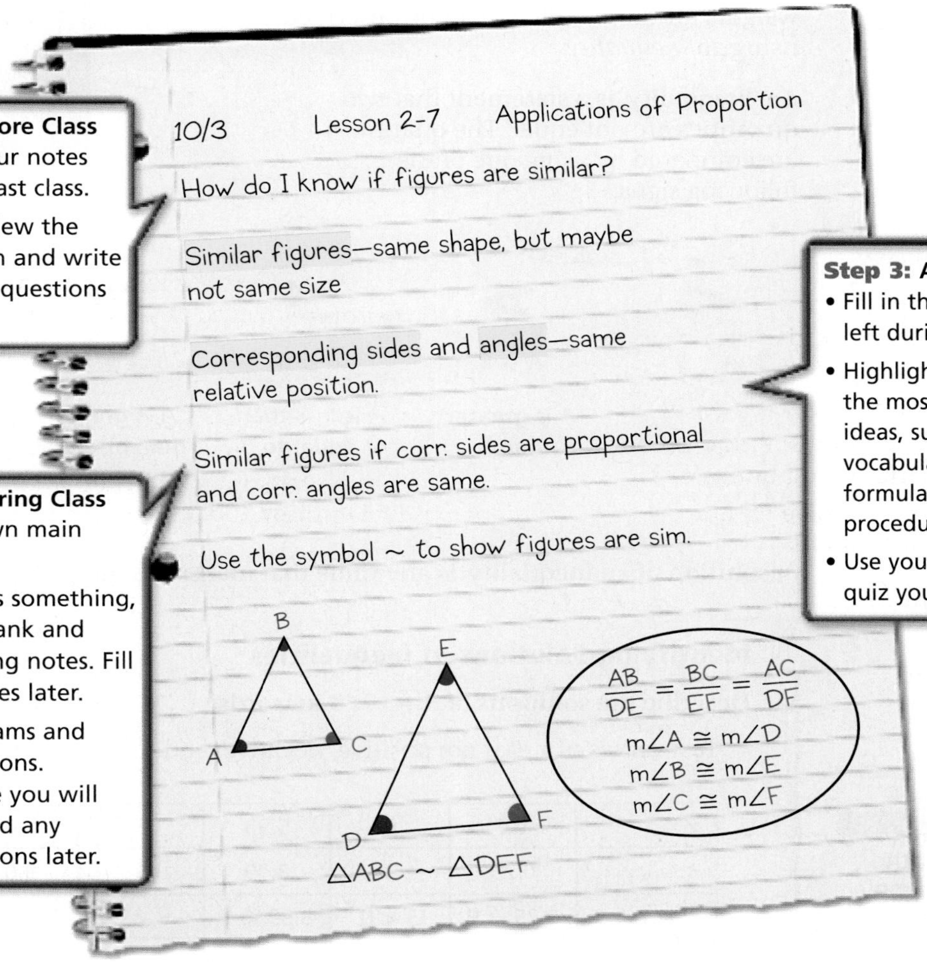

10/3 Lesson 2-7 Applications of Proportion

How do I know if figures are similar?

Similar figures—same shape, but maybe not same size

Corresponding sides and angles—same relative position.

Similar figures if corr. sides are proportional and corr. angles are same.

Use the symbol ~ to show figures are sim.

$$\frac{AB}{DE} = \frac{BC}{EF} = \frac{AC}{DF}$$

$m\angle A \cong m\angle D$

$m\angle B \cong m\angle E$

$m\angle C \cong m\angle F$

$\triangle ABC \sim \triangle DEF$

### Try This

1. Look at the next lesson in your textbook. Write down some questions you have about the material in that lesson. Leave space between each question so that you can write the answers during the next class.
2. Look at the notes you took during the last class. List three ways you can improve your note-taking skills.

# 3-1 Graphing and Writing Inequalities

**Prep MA.A.5.3** Use tables and graphs to solve pairs of linear inequalities in two variables.

***Objectives***
Identify solutions of inequalities in one variable.

Write and graph inequalities in one variable.

***Vocabulary***
inequality
solution of an inequality

**Who uses this?**
Members of a crew team can use inequalities to be sure they fall within a range of weights. (See Example 4.)

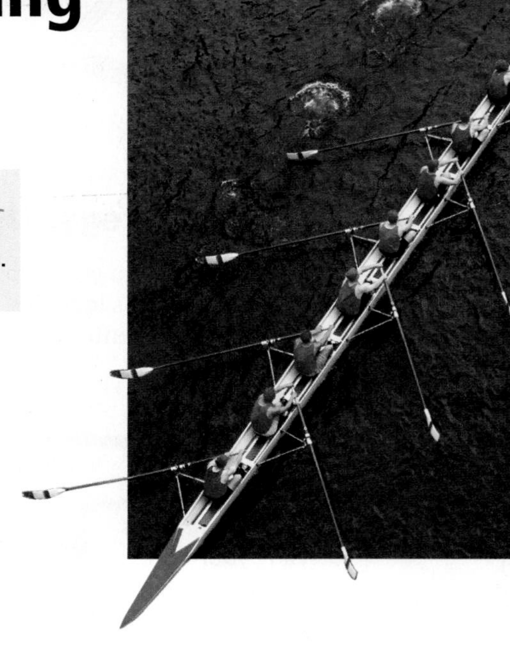

The athletes on a lightweight crew team must weigh 165 pounds or less. The acceptable weights for these athletes can be described using an *inequality*.

An **inequality** is a statement that two quantities are not equal. The quantities are compared by using one of the following signs:

| $<$ | $>$ | $\leq$ | $\geq$ | $\neq$ |
|---|---|---|---|---|
| $A < B$ | $A > B$ | $A \leq B$ | $A \geq B$ | $A \neq B$ |
| *A* is less than *B*. | *A* is greater than *B*. | *A* is less than or equal to *B*. | *A* is greater than or equal to *B*. | *A* is not equal to *B*. |

A **solution of an inequality** is any value that makes the inequality true.

**EXAMPLE 1** **Identifying Solutions of Inequalities**

**Describe the solutions of $3 + x < 9$ in words.**

Test values of $x$ that are positive, negative, and 0.

| $x$ | $-2.75$ | 0 | 5.99 | 6 | 6.01 | 6.1 |
|---|---|---|---|---|---|---|
| $3 + x$ | 0.25 | 3 | 8.99 | 9 | 9.01 | 9.1 |
| $3 + x \overset{?}{<} 9$ | $0.25 \overset{?}{<} 9$ | $3 \overset{?}{<} 9$ | $8.99 \overset{?}{<} 9$ | $9 \overset{?}{<} 9$ | $9.01 \overset{?}{<} 9$ | $9.1 \overset{?}{<} 9$ |
| **Solution?** | Yes | Yes | Yes | No | No | No |

*When the value of x is a number less than 6, the value of 3 + x is less than 9.*
*When the value of x is 6, the value of 3 + x is equal to 9.*
*When the value of x is a number greater than 6, the value of 3 + x is greater than 9.*

It appears that the solutions of $3 + x < 9$ are numbers less than 6.

**Writing Math**

The solutions of the inequality in Example 1 can be written in *set-builder notation* as $\{x | x < 6\}$, which is read as "the set of all real numbers $x$ such that $x$ is less than 6."

**CHECK IT OUT!** **1.** Describe the solutions of $2p > 8$ in words.

An inequality like $3 + x < 9$ has too many solutions to list. You can use a graph on a number line to show all the solutions.

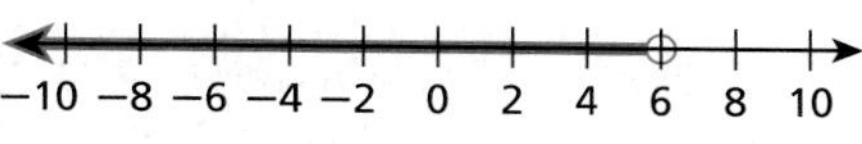


The solutions are shaded and an arrow shows that the solutions continue past those shown on the graph. To show that an endpoint is a solution, draw a solid circle at the number. To show that an endpoint is not a solution, draw an empty circle.

## Graphing Inequalities

| WORDS | ALGEBRA | GRAPH |
|---|---|---|
| All real numbers less than 5 | $x < 5$ | −4 −3 −2 −1 0 1 2 3 4 5 6 |
| All real numbers greater than −1 | $x > -1$ | −4 −3 −2 −1 0 1 2 3 4 5 6 |
| All real numbers less than or equal to $\frac{1}{2}$ | $x \le \frac{1}{2}$ | $-2$ $-1\frac{1}{2}$ $-1$ $-\frac{1}{2}$ $0$ $\frac{1}{2}$ $1$ |
| All real numbers greater than or equal to 0 | $x \ge 0$ | −4 −3 −2 −1 0 1 2 3 4 5 6 |

## EXAMPLE 2 Graphing Inequalities

**Graph each inequality.**

**A** $b < -1.5$

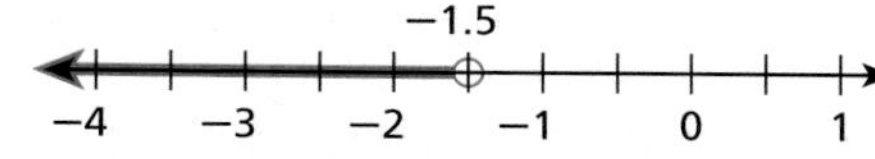


*Draw an empty circle at −1.5.*

*Shade all the numbers less than −1.5 and draw an arrow pointing to the left.*

**B** $r \ge 2$

−4 −3 −2 −1 0 1 2 3 4 5 6

*Draw a solid circle at 2.*

*Shade all the numbers greater than 2 and draw an arrow pointing to the right.*

**Graph each inequality.**

**2a.** $c > 2.5$ **2b.** $2^2 - 4 \ge w$ **2c.** $m \le -3$

## Student to Student

### *Graphing Inequalities*

**Victor Solomos**
Palmer High School

*To know which direction to shade a graph, I write inequalities with the variable on the left side of the inequality symbol. I know that the symbol has to point to the same number after I rewrite the inequality.*

*For example, I write $4 < y$ as $y > 4$.*

*Now the inequality symbol points in the direction that I should draw the shaded arrow on my graph.*

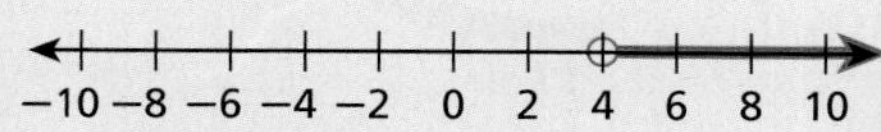

## EXAMPLE 3 Writing an Inequality from a Graph

**Write the inequality shown by each graph.**

**A**

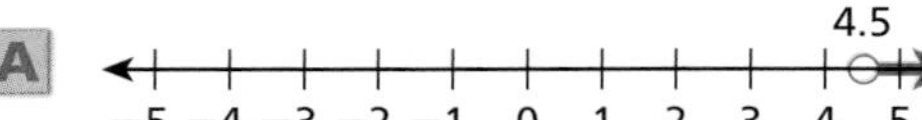


*Use any variable. The arrow points to the right, so use either > or ≥.*
*The empty circle at 4.5 means that 4.5 is not a solution, so use >.*

$h > 4.5$

**B**

−5 −4 −3 −2 −1 0 1 2 3 4 5

*Use any variable. The arrow points to the left, so use either < or ≤.*
*The solid circle at −3 means that −3 is a solution, so use ≤.*

$m \leq -3$

**3.** Write the inequality shown by the graph.

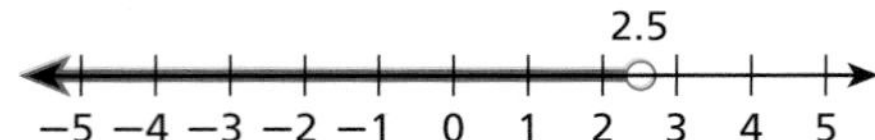


## EXAMPLE 4 *Sports Application*

**The members of a lightweight crew team can weigh no more than 165 pounds each. Define a variable and write an inequality for the acceptable weights of the team members. Graph the solutions.**

> **Reading Math**
> "No more than" means "less than or equal to."
> "At least" means "greater than or equal to."

Let $w$ represent the weights that are allowed.

| Athletes may weigh | no more than | 165 pounds. |
|---|---|---|
| $w$ | $\leq$ | 165 |

$w \leq 165$

165
0 30 60 90 120 150 180

Stop the graph at 0 because a person's weight must be a positive number.

**4.** A store's employees earn at least \$8.25 per hour. Define a variable and write an inequality for the amount the employees may earn per hour. Graph the solutions.

### THINK AND DISCUSS

**1.** Compare the solutions of $x > 2$ and $x \geq 2$.

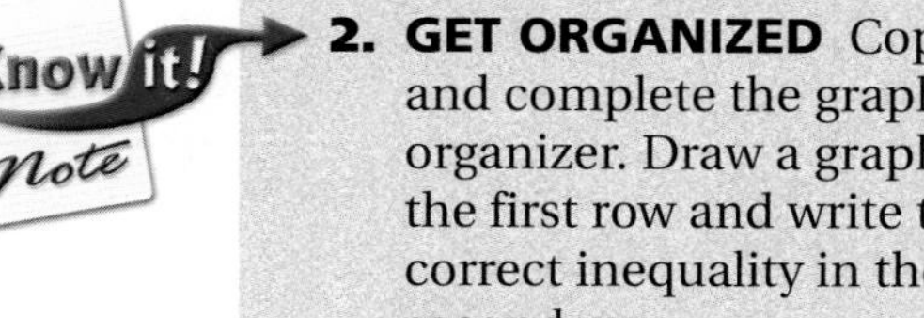


**2. GET ORGANIZED** Copy and complete the graphic organizer. Draw a graph in the first row and write the correct inequality in the second row.

| Inequality | Graph |
|---|---|
| $x > 1$ | |
| | −5 −4 −3 −2 −1 0 1 |

# 3-1 Exercises

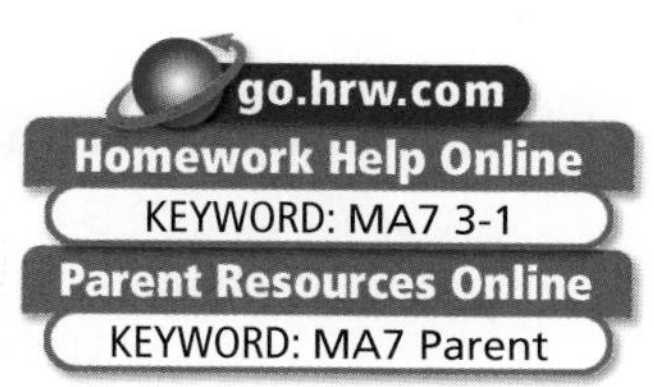


## GUIDED PRACTICE

1. **Vocabulary** How is a *solution of an inequality* like a solution of an equation?

SEE EXAMPLE 1 p. 168

**Describe the solutions of each inequality in words.**

2. $g - 5 \geq 6$
3. $-2 < h + 1$
4. $20 > 5t$
5. $5 - x \leq 2$

SEE EXAMPLE 2 p. 169

**Graph each inequality.**

6. $x < -5$
7. $c \geq 3\frac{1}{2}$
8. $(4 - 2)^3 > m$
9. $p \geq \sqrt{17 + 8}$

SEE EXAMPLE 3 p. 170

**Write the inequality shown by each graph.**

10. −6 −5 −4 −3 −2 −1 0 1 2 3 4
11. $-8\frac{1}{2}$ −9 −8 −7 −6 −5 −4 −3 −2 −1 0 1
12. 5.5 −4 −3 −2 −1 0 1 2 3 4 5 6
13. −7 −12 −10 −8 −6 −4 −2 0
14. −4 −3 −2 −1 0 1 2 3 4 5 6
15. −2 0 2 4 6 8 10 12 14 16 18

SEE EXAMPLE 4 p. 170

**Define a variable and write an inequality for each situation. Graph the solutions.**

16. There must be at least 20 club members present in order to hold a meeting.
17. A trainer advises an athlete to keep his heart rate under 140 beats per minute.

## PRACTICE AND PROBLEM SOLVING

**Independent Practice**

| For Exercises | See Example |
|---|---|
| 18–21 | 1 |
| 22–25 | 2 |
| 26–31 | 3 |
| 32–33 | 4 |

**Extra Practice**
Skills Practice p. S8
Application Practice p. S30

**Describe the solutions of each inequality in words.**

18. $-2t > -8$
19. $0 > w - 2$
20. $3k > 9$
21. $\frac{1}{2}b \leq 6$

**Graph each inequality.**

22. $7 < x$
23. $t \leq -\frac{1}{2}$
24. $d > 4(5 - 8)$
25. $t \leq 3^2 - 2^2$

**Write the inequality shown by each graph.**

26.
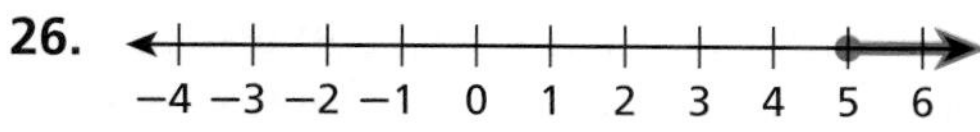


27. −11 −16 −14 −12 −10 −8 −6 −4
28. −3.5 −6 −5 −4 −3 −2 −1 0 1 2 3 4
29. −3.3 −5 −4 −3 −2 −1 0 1 2 3 4 5
30. −5 −4 −3 −2 −1 0 1 2 3 4 5
31.
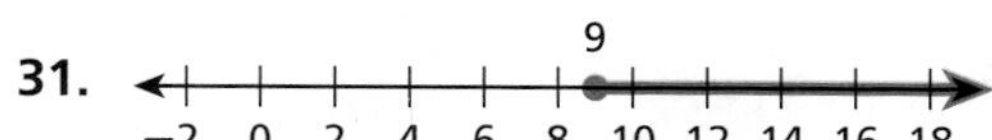


**Define a variable and write an inequality for each situation. Graph the solutions.**

32. The maximum speed allowed on Main Street is 25 miles per hour.
33. Applicants must have at least 5 years of experience.

**Write each inequality in words.**

**34.** $x > 7$ **35.** $h < -5$ **36.** $d \leq 23$ **37.** $r \geq -2$

**Write each inequality with the variable on the left. Graph the solutions.**

**38.** $19 < g$ **39.** $17 \geq p$ **40.** $10 < e$ **41.** $0 < f$

**Define a variable and write an inequality for each situation. Graph the solutions.**

**42.** The highest temperature ever recorded on Earth was 135.9°F at Al Aziziyah, Libya, on September 13, 1922.

**43.** Businesses with profits less than $10,000 per year will be shut down.

**44.** You must be at least 46 inches tall to ride the Indiana Jones Adventure ride at Disney's California Adventure Park.

**45.** Due to a medical condition, a hiker can hike only in areas with an elevation no more than 5000 feet above sea level.

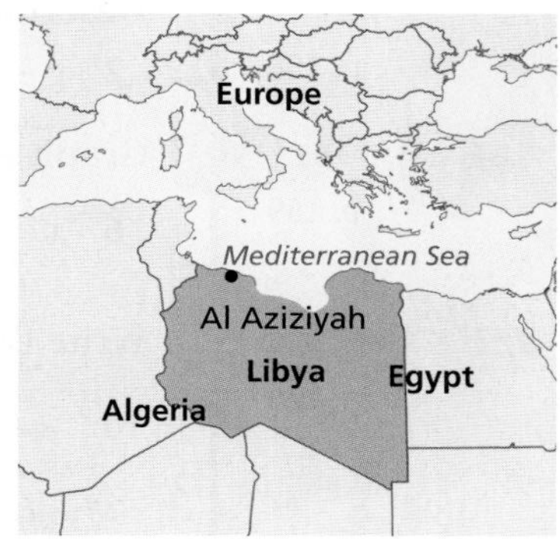


**Write a real-world situation that could be described by each inequality.**

**46.** $x \geq 0$ **47.** $x < 10$ **48.** $x \leq 12$ **49.** $x > 8.5$

**Match each inequality with its graph.**

**50.** $x \geq 5$ **A.** −2 −1 0 1 2 3 4 5 6 7 8

**51.** $x < 5$ **B.**

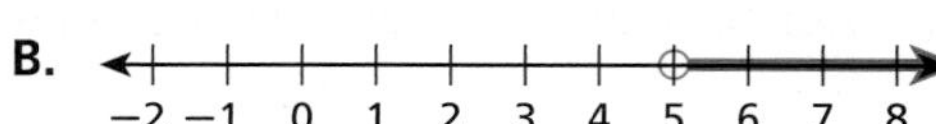


**52.** $x > 5$ **C.** −2 −1 0 1 2 3 4 5 6 7 8

**53.** $x \leq 5$ **D.** −2 −1 0 1 2 3 4 5 6 7 8

**54.** **///ERROR ANALYSIS///** Two students graphed the inequality $4 > b$. Which graph is incorrect? Explain the error.

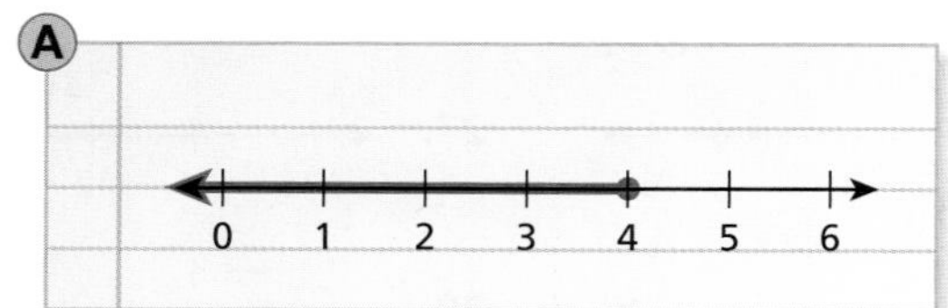


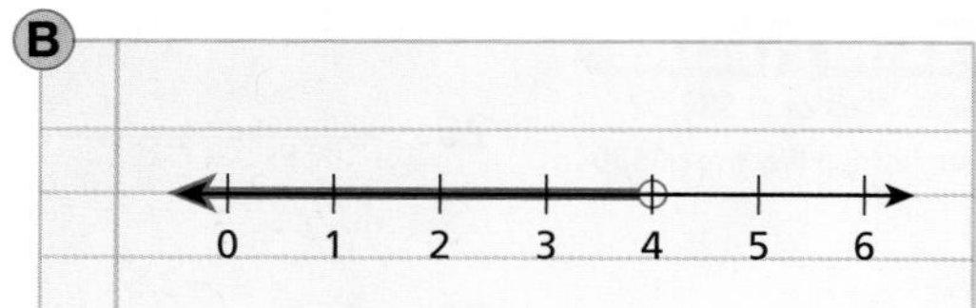


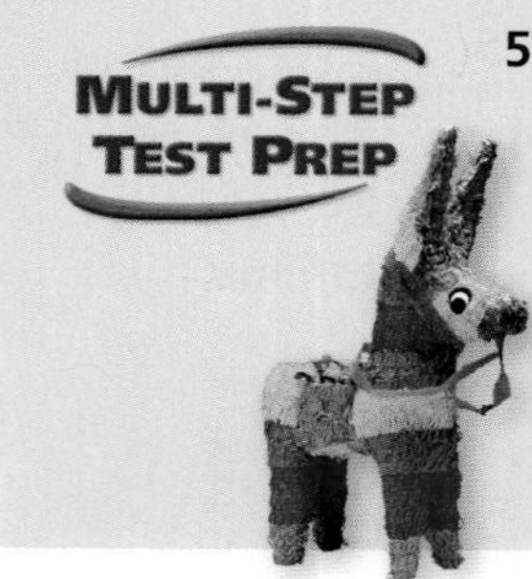


**55.** This problem will prepare you for the Multi-Step Test Prep on page 186.

**a.** Mirna earned $125 baby-sitting during the spring break. She needs to save $90 for the German Club trip. She wants to spend the remainder of the money shopping. Write an inequality to show how much she can spend.

**b.** Graph the inequality you wrote in part **a.**

**c.** Mirna spends $15 on a bracelet. Write an inequality to show how much money she has left to spend.

**56. Critical Thinking** Graph all positive integer solutions of the inequality $x < 5$.

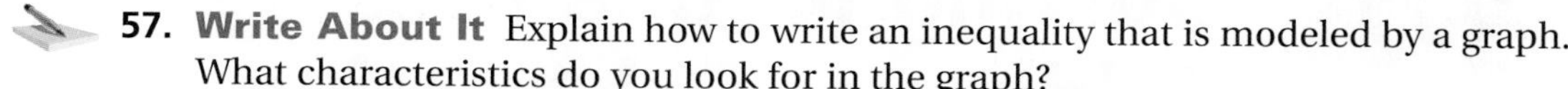

**57. Write About It** Explain how to write an inequality that is modeled by a graph. What characteristics do you look for in the graph?

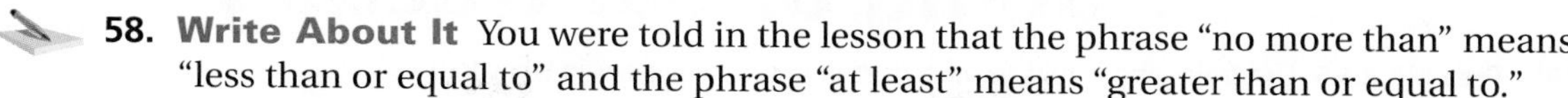

**58. Write About It** You were told in the lesson that the phrase "no more than" means "less than or equal to" and the phrase "at least" means "greater than or equal to."

**a.** What does the phrase "at most" mean?

**b.** What does the phrase "no less than" mean?

NC Prep MA.A.5.3

**59.** Which is NOT a solution of the inequality $5 - 2x \geq -3$?

Ⓐ 0 Ⓑ 2 Ⓒ 4 Ⓓ 5

**60.** Which is NOT a solution of the inequality $3 - x < 2$?

Ⓕ 1 Ⓖ 2 Ⓗ 3 Ⓙ 4

**61.** Which graph represents the solutions of $-2 \leq 1 - t$?

Ⓐ
−5 −4 −3 −2 −1 0 1 2 3 4 5

Ⓒ 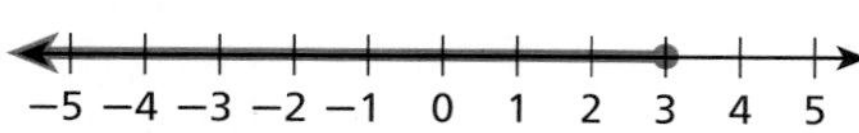


Ⓑ 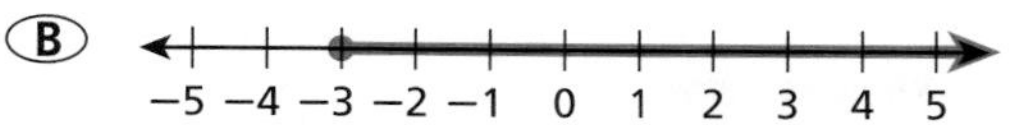


Ⓓ 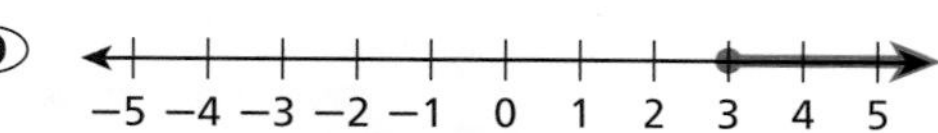


## CHALLENGE AND EXTEND

**Give a value for $x$ and a value for $y$ that make each inequality true.**

**62.** $x + y \leq |x + y|$ **63.** $x^2 < xy$ **64.** $x - y \geq y - x$

**Complete each statement. Write < or >.**

**65.** If $a > b$, then $b$ ▒ $a$. **66.** If $x > y$ and $y > z$, then $x$ ▒ $z$.

**67.** Name a value of $x$ that makes the statement $0.35 < x < 1.27$ true.

**68.** Is $\frac{5}{6}$ a solution of $x < 1$? How many solutions of $x < 1$ are between 0 and 1?

**69. Write About It** Explain how to graph all the solutions of $x \neq 5$.

## SPIRAL REVIEW

**Add or subtract.** *(Lesson 1-2)*

**70.** $-7 + 5$ **71.** $6 - (-4)$ **72.** $8 - 13$ **73.** $12 + (-5)$

**Simplify each expression.** *(Lesson 1-7)*

**74.** $x + 3x$ **75.** $x + (x + 1) + (x + 2)$ **76.** $5 + (x + 3) + 5 + 2(x + 3)$

**77.** There are twice as many girls in Sally's class as boys. Write a rule for the number of girls in Sally's class. Find the number of girls if there are 8 boys. *(Lesson 1-8)*

**78.** A video club charges a $12 membership fee plus $2.00 for each movie rental. Write a rule for the cost of renting $x$ videos. Find the cost of renting 3, 7, and 15 videos. *(Lesson 1-8)*

**Solve each equation. Check your answer.** *(Lesson 2-4)*

**79.** $2b - 6 = b + 3$ **80.** $-3(2 - x) = 5x + 2$ **81.** $2(y + 1) = 2y + 1$

# 3-2 Solving Inequalities by Adding or Subtracting

**Prep MA.A.5.3** Use tables and graphs to solve pairs of linear inequalities in two variables.

***Objectives***

Solve one-step inequalities by using addition.

Solve one-step inequalities by using subtraction.

**Who uses this?**

You can use inequalities to determine how many more photos you can take. (See Example 2.)

Tenea has a cell phone that also takes pictures. After taking some photos, Tenea can use a one-step inequality to determine how many more photos she can take.

Solving one-step inequalities is much like solving one-step equations. To solve an inequality, you need to isolate the variable using the properties of inequality and inverse operations.

**Properties of Inequality**

**Addition and Subtraction**

| WORDS | NUMBERS | ALGEBRA |
|---|---|---|
| **Addition**<br>You can add the same number to both sides of an inequality, and the statement will still be true. | $3 < 8$<br>$3 + 2 < 8 + 2$<br>$5 < 10$ | $a < b$<br>$a + c < b + c$ |
| **Subtraction**<br>You can subtract the same number from both sides of an inequality, and the statement will still be true. | $9 < 12$<br>$9 - 5 < 12 - 5$<br>$4 < 7$ | $a < b$<br>$a - c < b - c$ |

**These properties are also true for inequalities that use the symbols >, ≥, and ≤.**

EXAMPLE 1

## Using Addition and Subtraction to Solve Inequalities

**Solve each inequality and graph the solutions.**

**Helpful Hint**

Use an inverse operation to "undo" the operation in an inequality. If the inequality contains addition, use subtraction to undo the addition.

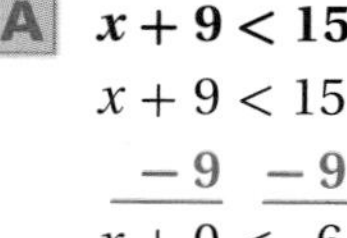

**A** $x + 9 < 15$

$$\begin{aligned} x + 9 &< 15 \\ -9 \quad & \;\; -9 \\ x + 0 &< 6 \\ x &< 6 \end{aligned}$$

*Since 9 is added to x, subtract 9 from both sides to undo the addition.*

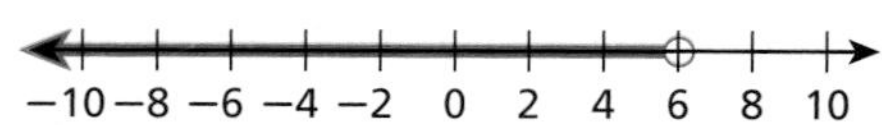


**B** $d - 3 > -6$

$$\begin{aligned} d - 3 &> -6 \\ +3 \quad & \;\; +3 \\ d + 0 &> -3 \\ d &> -3 \end{aligned}$$

*Since 3 is subtracted from d, add 3 to both sides to undo the subtraction.*

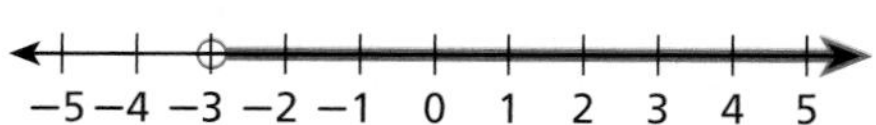

**Solve each inequality and graph the solutions.**

**C** $\mathbf{0.7 \geq n - 0.4}$

$$
\begin{aligned}
0.7 &\geq n - 0.4 \\
\underline{+0.4} \quad & \quad \underline{+0.4} \\
1.1 &\geq n - 0 \\
n &\leq 1.1
\end{aligned}
$$

*Since 0.4 is subtracted from n, add 0.4 to both sides to undo the subtraction.*

1.1

−5 −4 −3 −2 −1 0 1 2 3 4 5

**Solve each inequality and graph the solutions.**

**1a.** $s + 1 \leq 10$ **1b.** $2\frac{1}{2} > -3 + t$ **1c.** $q - 3.5 < 7.5$

Since there can be an infinite number of solutions to an inequality, it is not possible to check all the solutions. You can check the endpoint and the direction of the inequality symbol.

The solutions of $x + 9 < 15$ are given by $x < 6$.

**Step 1** Check the endpoint.

Substitute 6 for $x$ in the related equation $x + 9 = 15$. The endpoint should be a solution of the equation.

| $x + 9 = 15$ | |
|---|---|
| $6 + 9$ | 15 |
| 15 | 15 ✓ |

**Step 2** Check the inequality symbol.

Substitute a number less than 6 for $x$ in the original inequality. The number you choose should be a solution of the inequality.

| $x + 9 < 15$ | | |
|---|---|---|
| $4 + 9$ | $<$ | 15 |
| 13 | $<$ | 15 ✓ |

## EXAMPLE 2 *Problem Solving Application*

**The memory in Tenea's camera phone allows her to take up to 20 pictures. Tenea has already taken 16 pictures. Write, solve, and graph an inequality to show how many more pictures Tenea could take.**

### 1 Understand the Problem

The **answer** will be an inequality and a graph that show all the possible numbers of pictures that Tenea can take.

**List the important information:**

- Tenea can take up to, or *at most,* 20 pictures.
- Tenea has taken 16 pictures already.

### 2 Make a Plan

Write an inequality.

Let $p$ represent the remaining number of pictures Tenea can take.

| Number taken | plus | number remaining | is at most | 20 pictures. |
|---|---|---|---|---|
| 16 | + | $p$ | $\leq$ | 20 |

 **Solve**

$$\begin{array}{rl} 16 + p \leq & 20 \\ \underline{-16} & \underline{-16} \\ p \leq & 4 \end{array}$$

*Since 16 is added to p, subtract 16 from both sides to undo the addition.*

It is not reasonable for Tenea to take a negative or fractional number of pictures, so graph the nonnegative integers less than or equal to 4.

Tenea could take 0, 1, 2, 3, or 4 more pictures.

 **Look Back**

***Check*** Check the endpoint, 4.

$$\begin{array}{r|l} \multicolumn{2}{c}{16 + p = 20} \\ \hline 16 + 4 & 20 \\ 20 & 20 \checkmark \end{array}$$

Check a number less than 4.

$$\begin{array}{r|c|l} \multicolumn{3}{c}{16 + p \leq 20} \\ \hline 16 + 2 & \leq & 20 \\ 18 & \leq & 20 \checkmark \end{array}$$

Adding 0, 1, 2, 3, or 4 more pictures will not exceed 20.

**2.** The Recommended Daily Allowance (RDA) of iron for a female in Sarah's age group (14–18 years) is 15 mg per day. Sarah has consumed 11 mg of iron today. Write and solve an inequality to show how many more milligrams of iron Sarah can consume without exceeding the RDA.

## EXAMPLE 3 *Sports Application*

**Josh can bench press 220 pounds. He wants to bench press at least 250 pounds. Write and solve an inequality to determine how many more pounds Josh must lift to reach his goal. Check your answer.**

Let $p$ represent the number of additional pounds Josh must lift.

| 220 pounds | plus | additional pounds | is at least | 250 pounds. |
|---|---|---|---|---|
| 220 | + | $p$ | $\geq$ | 250 |

$$\begin{array}{rl} 220 + p \geq & 250 \\ \underline{-220} & \underline{-220} \\ p \geq & 30 \end{array}$$

*Since 220 is added to p, subtract 220 from both sides to undo the addition.*

***Check*** Check the endpoint, 30.

$$\begin{array}{r|l} \multicolumn{2}{c}{220 + p = 250} \\ \hline 220 + 30 & 250 \\ 250 & 250 \checkmark \end{array}$$

Check a number greater than 30.

$$\begin{array}{r|c|l} \multicolumn{3}{c}{220 + p \geq 250} \\ \hline 220 + 40 & \geq & 250 \\ 260 & \geq & 250 \checkmark \end{array}$$

Josh must lift at least 30 additional pounds to reach his goal.

**3. What If...?** Josh wants to try to break the school record of 282 pounds. Write and solve an inequality to determine how many more pounds Josh needs to break the school record. Check your answer.

## THINK AND DISCUSS

1. Show how to check your solution to Example 1B.
2. Explain how the Addition and Subtraction Properties of Inequality are like the Addition and Subtraction Properties of Equality.

3. **GET ORGANIZED** Copy and complete the graphic organizer. In each box, write an inequality that you must use the specified property to solve. Then solve and graph the inequality.

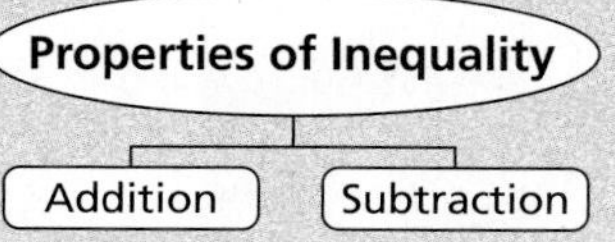


## 3-2 Exercises

### GUIDED PRACTICE

SEE EXAMPLE 1 p. 174

**Solve each inequality and graph the solutions.**

1. $12 < p + 6$
2. $w + 3 \geq 4$
3. $-5 + x \leq -20$
4. $z - 2 > -11$

SEE EXAMPLE 2 p. 175

5. **Health** For adults, the maximum safe water temperature in a spa is 104°F. The water temperature in Bill's spa is 102°F. The temperature is increased by $t$°F. Write, solve, and graph an inequality to show the values of $t$ for which the water temperature is still safe.

SEE EXAMPLE 3 p. 176

6. **Consumer Economics** A local restaurant will deliver food to your house if the purchase amount of your order is at least $25.00. The total for part of your order is $17.95. Write and solve an inequality to determine how much more you must spend for the restaurant to deliver your order.

### PRACTICE AND PROBLEM SOLVING

**Independent Practice**

| For Exercises | See Example |
|---|---|
| 7–10 | 1 |
| 11 | 2 |
| 12 | 3 |

**Extra Practice**

Skills Practice p. S8

Application Practice p. S30

**Solve each inequality and graph the solutions.**

7. $a - 3 \geq 2$
8. $2.5 > q - 0.8$
9. $-45 + x < -30$
10. $r + \frac{1}{4} \leq \frac{3}{4}$

11. **Engineering** The maximum load for a certain elevator is 2000 pounds. The total weight of the passengers on the elevator is 1400 pounds. A delivery man who weighs 243 pounds enters the elevator with a crate of weight $w$. Write, solve, and graph an inequality to show the values of $w$ that will not exceed the weight limit of the elevator.

12. **Transportation** The gas tank in Mindy's car holds at most 15 gallons. She has already filled the tank with 7 gallons of gas. She will continue to fill the tank with $g$ gallons more. Write and solve an inequality that shows all values of $g$ that Mindy can add to the car's tank.

**Write an inequality to represent each statement. Solve the inequality and graph the solutions.**

13. Ten less than a number $x$ is greater than 32.
14. A number $n$ increased by 6 is less than or equal to 4.
15. A number $r$ decreased by 13 is at most 15.

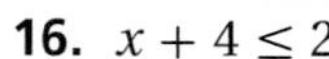

**Solve each inequality and graph the solutions.**

**16.** $x + 4 \leq 2$ **17.** $-12 + q > 39$ **18.** $x + \frac{3}{5} < 7$ **19.** $4.8 \geq p + 4$

**20.** $-12 \leq x - 12$ **21.** $4 < 206 + c$ **22.** $y - \frac{1}{3} > \frac{2}{3}$ **23.** $x + 1.4 \geq 1.4$

**LINK**

**Health**

Special-effects contact lenses are sometimes part of costumes for movies. All contact lenses should be worn under an eye doctor's supervision.

**24.** Use the inequality $s + 12 \geq 20$ to fill in the missing numbers.

**a.** $s \geq$ ▢ **b.** $s +$ ▢ $\geq 30$ **c.** $s - 8 \geq$ ▢

**25. Health** A particular type of contact lens can be worn up to 30 days in a row. Alex has been wearing these contact lenses for 21 days. Write, solve, and graph an inequality to show how many more days Alex could wear his contact lenses.

**Solve each inequality and match the solution to the correct graph.**

**26.** $1 \leq x - 2$

**A.** 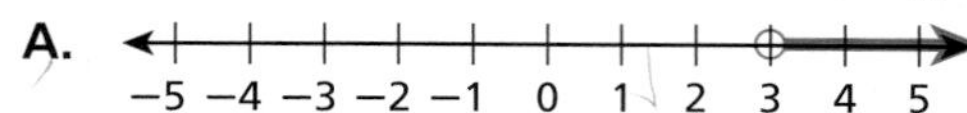

**27.** $8 > x - (-5)$

**B.** 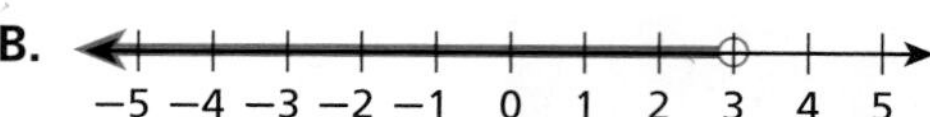

**28.** $x + 6 > 9$

**C.** 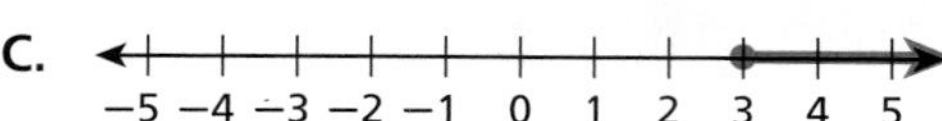

**29.** $-4 \geq x - 7$

**D.** 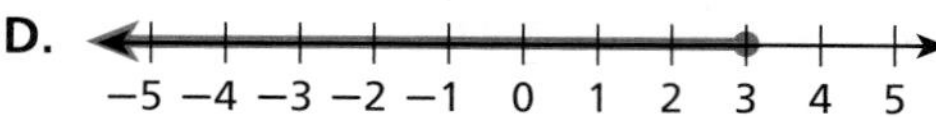

**30. Estimation** Is $x < 10$ a reasonable estimate for the solutions to the inequality $11.879 + x < 21.709$? Explain your answer.

**31. Sports** At the Seattle Mariners baseball team's home games, there are 45,611 seats in the four areas listed in the table. Suppose all the suite level and club level seats during a game are filled. Write and solve an inequality to determine how many people $p$ could be sitting in the other types of seats.

**Mariners Home Game Seating**

| Type of Seat | Number of Seats |
|---|---|
| Main bowl | 24,399 |
| Upper bowl | 16,022 |
| Club level | 4,254 |
| Suite level | 936 |

**32. Critical Thinking** Recall that in Chapter 2 a balance scale was used to model solving equations. Describe how a balance scale could model solving inequalities.

**33. Critical Thinking** Explain why $x + 4 \geq 6$ and $x - 4 \geq -2$ have the same solutions.

**34. Write About It** How do the solutions of $x + 2 \geq 3$ differ from the solutions of $x + 2 > 3$? How do the graphs of the solutions differ?

**MULTI-STEP TEST PREP**

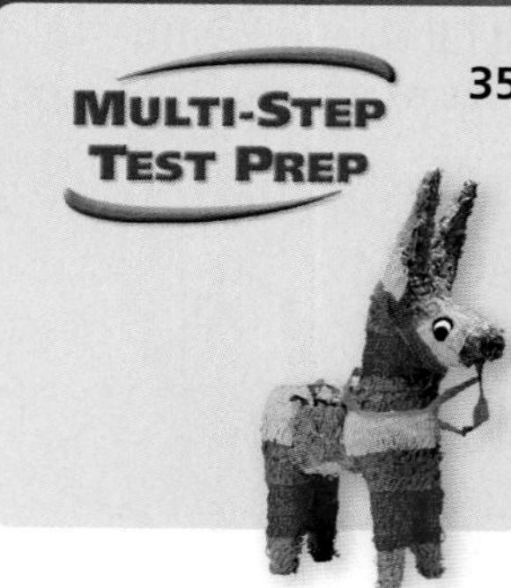

**35.** This problem will prepare you for the Multi-Step Test Prep on page 186.

**a.** Daryl finds that the distance from Columbus, Ohio, to Washington, D.C, is 411 miles. What is the round-trip distance?

**b.** Daryl can afford to drive a total of 1000 miles. Write an inequality to show the number of miles $m$ he can drive while in Washington, D.C.

**c.** Solve the inequality and graph the solutions on a number line. Show that your answer is reasonable.

36. Which is a reasonable solution of $4.7367 + p < 20.1784$?

Ⓐ 15 Ⓑ 16 Ⓒ 24 Ⓓ 25

37. Which statement can be modeled by $x + 3 \leq 12$?

Ⓕ Sam has 3 bottles of water. Together, Sam and Dave have at most 12 bottles of water.

Ⓖ Jennie sold 3 cookbooks. To earn a prize, Jennie must sell at least 12 cookbooks.

Ⓗ Peter has 3 baseball hats. Peter and his brothers have fewer than 12 baseball hats.

Ⓙ Kathy swam 3 laps in the pool this week. She must swim more than 12 laps.

38. Which graph represents the solutions of $p + 3 < 1$?

Ⓐ 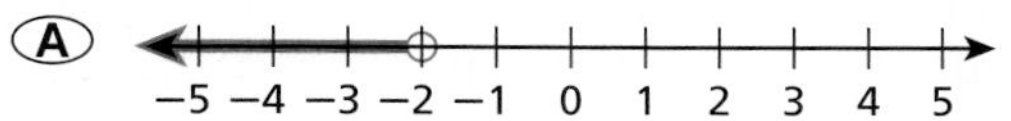


Ⓒ 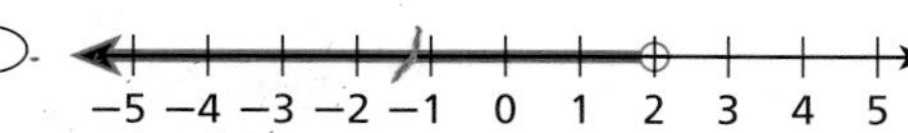


Ⓑ 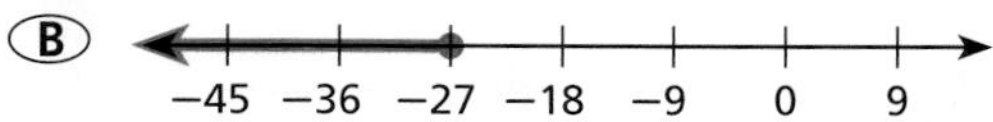


Ⓓ −5 −4 −3 −2 −1 0 1 2 3 4 5

39. Which inequality does NOT have the same solutions as $n + 12 \leq 26$?

Ⓕ $n \leq 14$ Ⓖ $n + 6 \leq 20$ Ⓗ $10 \geq n - 4$ Ⓙ $n - 12 \leq 14$

## CHALLENGE AND EXTEND

**Solve each inequality and graph the solutions.**

40. $6\frac{9}{10} \geq 4\frac{4}{5} + x$

41. $r - 1\frac{2}{5} \leq 3\frac{7}{10}$

42. $6\frac{2}{3} + m > 7\frac{1}{6}$

**Determine whether each statement is *sometimes, always,* or *never* true. Explain.**

43. $a + b > a - b$

44. If $a > c$, then $a + b > c + b$.

45. If $a > b$ and $c > d$, then $a + c > b + d$.

46. If $x + b > c$ and $x > 0$ have the same solutions, what is the relationship between $b$ and $c$?

## SPIRAL REVIEW

**Solve each equation for the indicated variable.** *(Lesson 2-5)*

47. $2x + 3y = 9$ for $y$

48. $P = 4s$ for $s$

49. $2a + ab = c$ for $a$

50. $p + e = f$ for $e$

51. $2s - k = 11$ for $k$

52. $5m + n = 0$ for $m$

**Find the value of $x$ in each diagram of similar figures.** *(Lesson 2-7)*

53. 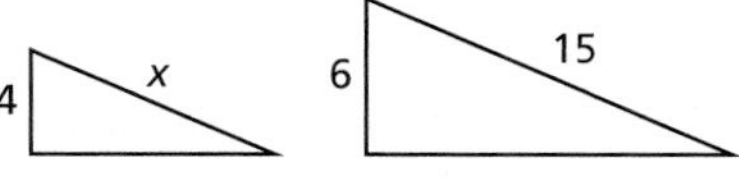


54. 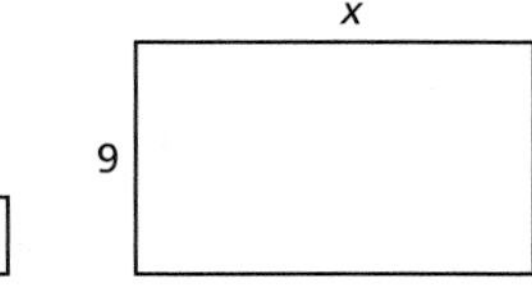


**Write the inequality shown by each graph.** *(Lesson 3-1)*

55. −4 −3 −2 −1 0 1 2 3 4 5 6

56. 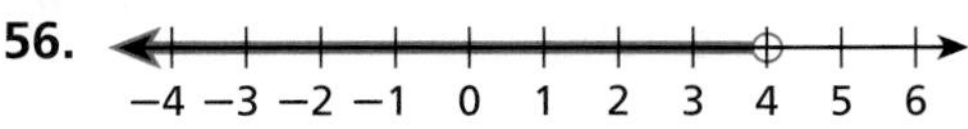

# 3-3 Solving Inequalities by Multiplying or Dividing

**Prep MA.A.5.3** Use tables and graphs to solve pairs of linear inequalities in two variables.

*Objectives*
Solve one-step inequalities by using multiplication.

Solve one-step inequalities by using division.

**Who uses this?**

You can solve an inequality to determine how much you can buy with a certain amount of money. (See Example 3.)

**"This is all I have, so I'll take 3 pencils, 3 notebooks, a binder, and 0.9 calculators."**

Jonny Hawkins/CartoonResource.com

Remember, solving inequalities is similar to solving equations. To solve an inequality that contains multiplication or division, undo the operation by dividing or multiplying both sides of the inequality by the same number.

The rules below show the properties of inequality for multiplying or dividing by a positive number. The rules for multiplying or dividing by a negative number appear later in this lesson.

## Properties of Inequality

**Multiplication and Division by Positive Numbers**

| WORDS | NUMBERS | ALGEBRA |
|---|---|---|
| **Multiplication**<br>You can multiply both sides of an inequality by the same *positive* number, and the statement will still be true. | $7 < 12$<br>$7(3) < 12(3)$<br>$21 < 36$ | If $a < b$ and $c > 0$, then $ac < bc$. |
| **Division**<br>You can divide both sides of an inequality by the same *positive* number, and the statement will still be true. | $15 < 35$<br>$\frac{15}{5} < \frac{35}{5}$<br>$3 < 7$ | If $a < b$ and $c > 0$, then $\frac{a}{c} < \frac{b}{c}$. |

**These properties are also true for inequalities that use the symbols >, ≥, and ≤.**

## EXAMPLE 1 Multiplying or Dividing by a Positive Number

**Solve each inequality and graph the solutions.**

**A** $3x > -27$

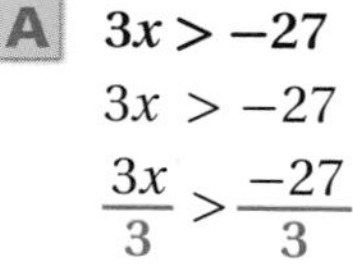

$$3x > -27$$

$$\frac{3x}{3} > \frac{-27}{3}$$

*Since x is multiplied by 3, divide both sides by 3 to undo the multiplication.*

$$1x > -9$$

$$x > -9$$

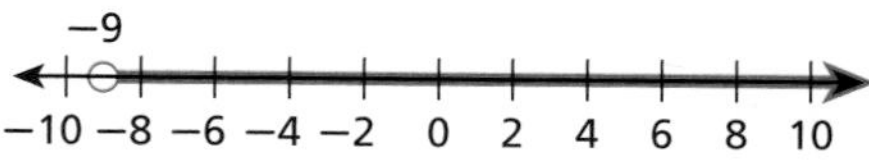

**Solve each inequality and graph the solutions.**

**B** $\frac{2}{3}r < 6$

$$\frac{2}{3}r < 6$$

*Since r is multiplied by $\frac{2}{3}$, multiply both sides by the reciprocal of $\frac{2}{3}$.*

$$\frac{3}{2}\left(\frac{2}{3}r\right) < \frac{3}{2}(6)$$

$$r < 9$$

9

−8 −6 −4 −2 0 2 4 6 8 10 12

**Solve each inequality and graph the solutions.**

**1a.** $4k > 24$ **1b.** $-50 \geq 5q$ **1c.** $\frac{3}{4}g > 27$

If you multiply or divide both sides of an inequality by a negative number, the resulting inequality is not a true statement. You need to reverse the inequality symbol to make the statement true.

| | |
|---|---|
| $5 > -3$ | *5 is **greater than** −3.* |
| $5(-2)\ \square\ -3(-2)$ | *Multiply both sides by −2.* |
| $-10\ \square\ 6$ | *You know that −10 is less than 6, so use the symbol for **less than**.* |
| $-10 < 6$ | |

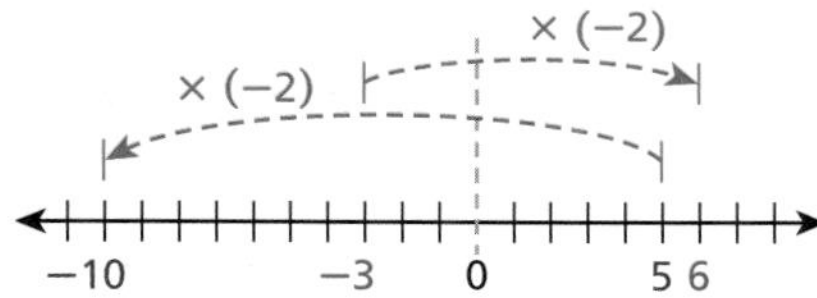


*Multiplying both sides by a negative number changes the sign of both sides of the inequality.*

This means there is another set of properties of inequality for multiplying or dividing by a negative number.

Know it! Note

## Properties of Inequality

**Multiplication and Division by Negative Numbers**

| WORDS | NUMBERS | ALGEBRA |
|---|---|---|
| **Multiplication**<br>If you multiply both sides of an inequality by the same *negative* number, you must reverse the inequality symbol for the statement to still be true. | $8 > 4$<br>$8(-2) < 4(-2)$<br>$-16 < -8$<br>$-16 < -8$ | If $a > b$ and $c < 0$, then $ac < bc$. |
| **Division**<br>If you divide both sides of an inequality by the same *negative* number, you must reverse the inequality symbol for the statement to still be true. | $12 > 4$<br>$\frac{12}{-4} < \frac{4}{-4}$<br>$-3 < -1$<br>$-3 < -1$ | If $a > b$ and $c < 0$, then $\frac{a}{c} < \frac{b}{c}$. |

**These properties are also true for inequalities that use the symbols <, ≥, and ≤.**

## EXAMPLE 2 Multiplying or Dividing by a Negative Number

**Caution!**

Do not change the direction of the inequality symbol just because you see a negative sign. For example, you do not change the symbol when solving $4x < -24$.

**Solve each inequality and graph the solutions.**

**A** $-8x > 72$

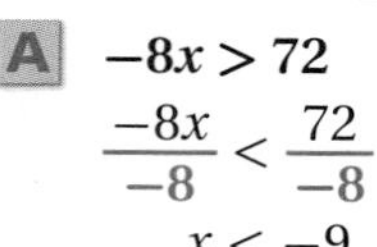

$$\frac{-8x}{-8} < \frac{72}{-8}$$ *Since x is multiplied by −8, divide both sides by −8. Change > to <.*

$$x < -9$$

−15 −12 −9 −6 −3 0 3

**B** $-3 \le \frac{x}{-5}$

$$-5(-3) \ge -5\left(\frac{x}{-5}\right)$$ *Since x is divided by −5, multiply both sides by −5. Change ≤ to ≥.*

$$15 \ge x \text{ (or } x \le 15)$$

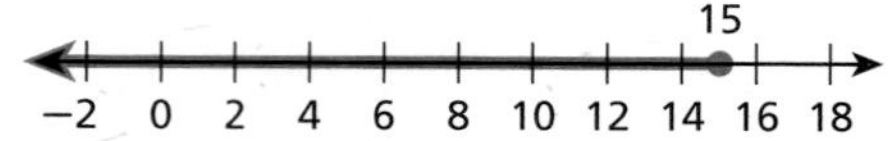

**Solve each inequality and graph the solutions.**

**2a.** $10 \ge -x$ **2b.** $4.25 > -0.25h$

## EXAMPLE 3 *Consumer Application*

**Ryan has a $16 gift card for a health store where a smoothie costs $2.50 with tax. What are the possible numbers of smoothies that Ryan can buy?**

Let $s$ represent the number of smoothies Ryan can buy.

| $2.50 | times | number of smoothies | is at most | $16.00. |
|---|---|---|---|---|
| 2.50 | • | $s$ | ≤ | 16.00 |

$$2.50s \le 16.00$$

$$\frac{2.50s}{2.50} \le \frac{16.00}{2.50}$$ *Since s is multiplied by 2.50, divide both sides by 2.50. The symbol does not change.*

$$s \le 6.4$$ *Ryan can buy only a whole number of smoothies.*

Ryan can buy 0, 1, 2, 3, 4, 5, or 6 smoothies.

**3.** A pitcher holds 128 ounces of juice. What are the possible numbers of 10-ounce servings that one pitcher can fill?

## THINK AND DISCUSS

**1.** Compare the Multiplication and Division Properties of Inequality and the Multiplication and Division Properties of Equality.

**2. GET ORGANIZED** Copy and complete the graphic organizer. In each cell, write and solve an inequality.

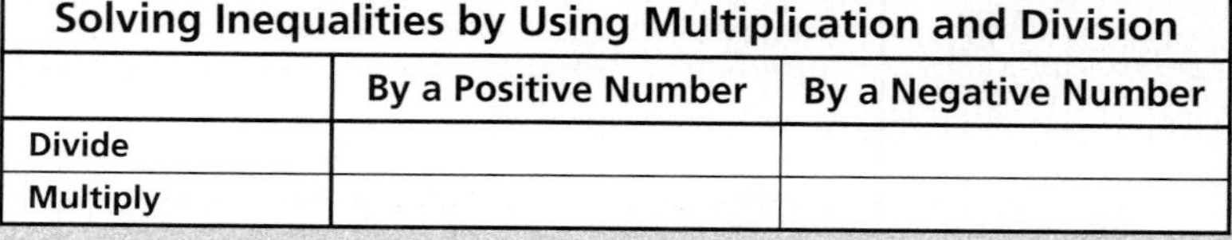

| Solving Inequalities by Using Multiplication and Division | | |
|---|---|---|
| | By a Positive Number | By a Negative Number |
| Divide | | |
| Multiply | | |

# 3-3 Exercises

Prep MA.A.5.3

go.hrw.com
Homework Help Online
KEYWORD: MA7 3-3
Parent Resources Online
KEYWORD: MA7 Parent

## GUIDED PRACTICE

SEE EXAMPLE 1 p. 180

**Solve each inequality and graph the solutions.**

1. $3b > 27$
2. $-40 \geq 8b$
3. $\frac{d}{3} > 6$
4. $24d \leq 6$
5. $1.1m \leq 1.21$
6. $\frac{2}{3}k > 6$
7. $9s > -18$
8. $\frac{4}{5} \geq \frac{r}{2}$

SEE EXAMPLE 2 p. 182

9. $-2x < -10$
10. $\frac{b}{-2} \geq 8$
11. $-3.5n < 1.4$
12. $4 > -8g$
13. $\frac{d}{-6} < \frac{1}{2}$
14. $-10h \geq -6$
15. $12 > \frac{t}{-6}$
16. $-\frac{1}{2}m \geq -7$

SEE EXAMPLE 3 p. 182

17. **Travel** Tom saved \$550 to go on a school trip. The cost for a hotel room, including tax, is \$80 per night. Write an inequality to show the number of nights Tom can stay at the hotel.

## PRACTICE AND PROBLEM SOLVING

**Independent Practice**

| For Exercises | See Example |
|---|---|
| 18–29 | 1 |
| 30–41 | 2 |
| 42 | 3 |

**Extra Practice**

Skills Practice p. S8
Application Practice p. S30

**Solve each inequality and graph the solutions.**

18. $10 < 2t$
19. $\frac{1}{3}j \leq 4$
20. $-80 < 8c$
21. $21 > 3d$
22. $\frac{w}{4} \geq -2$
23. $\frac{h}{4} \leq \frac{2}{7}$
24. $6y < 4.2$
25. $12c \leq -144$
26. $\frac{4}{5}x \geq \frac{2}{5}$
27. $6b \geq \frac{3}{5}$
28. $-25 > 10p$
29. $\frac{b}{8} \leq -2$
30. $-9a > 81$
31. $\frac{1}{2} < \frac{r}{-3}$
32. $-6p > 0.6$
33. $\frac{y}{-4} > -\frac{1}{2}$
34. $-\frac{1}{6}f < 5$
35. $-2.25t < -9$
36. $24 \leq -10w$
37. $-11z > 121$
38. $\frac{3}{5} < \frac{f}{-5}$
39. $-k \geq 7$
40. $-2.2b < -7.7$
41. $16 \geq -\frac{4}{3}p$
42. **Camping** The rope Roz brought with her camping gear is 54 inches long. Roz needs to cut shorter pieces of rope that are each 18 inches long. What are the possible number of pieces Roz can cut?

**Solve each inequality and graph the solutions.**

43. $-8x < 24$
44. $3t \leq 24$
45. $\frac{1}{4}x < 5$
46. $\frac{4}{5}p \geq -24$
47. $54 \leq -9p$
48. $3t > -\frac{1}{2}$
49. $-\frac{3}{4}b > -\frac{3}{2}$
50. $216 > 3.6r$

**Write an inequality for each statement. Solve the inequality and graph the solutions.**

51. The product of a number and 7 is not less than 21.
52. The quotient of $h$ and $-6$ is at least 5.
53. The product of $-\frac{4}{5}$ and $b$ is at most $-16$.
54. Ten is no more than the quotient of $t$ and 4.
55. **Write About It** Explain how you know whether to reverse the inequality symbol when solving an inequality.

56. **Geometry** The area of a rectangle is at most 21 square inches. The width of the rectangle is 3.5 inches. What are the possible measurements for the length of the rectangle?

**Solve each inequality and match the solution to the correct graph.**

57. $-0.5t \geq 1.5$

58. $\frac{1}{9}t \leq -3$

59. $-13.5 \leq -4.5t$

60. $\frac{t}{-6} \leq -\frac{1}{2}$

A. 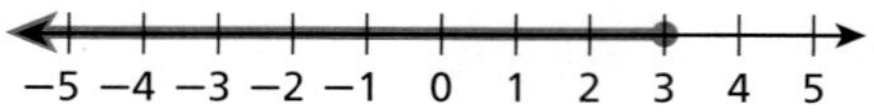
−5 −4 −3 −2 −1 0 1 2 3 4 5

B. 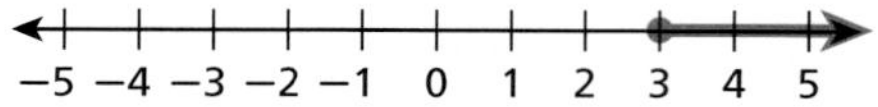
−5 −4 −3 −2 −1 0 1 2 3 4 5

C. 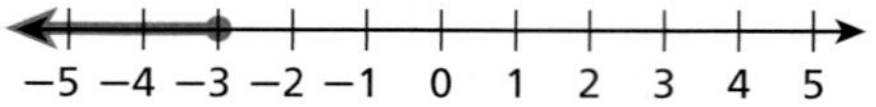
−5 −4 −3 −2 −1 0 1 2 3 4 5

D. 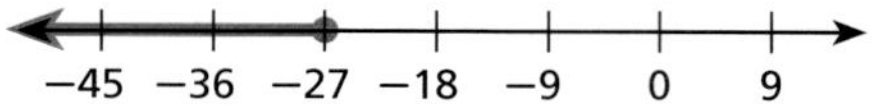
−45 −36 −27 −18 −9 0 9

**LINK**

**Animals**

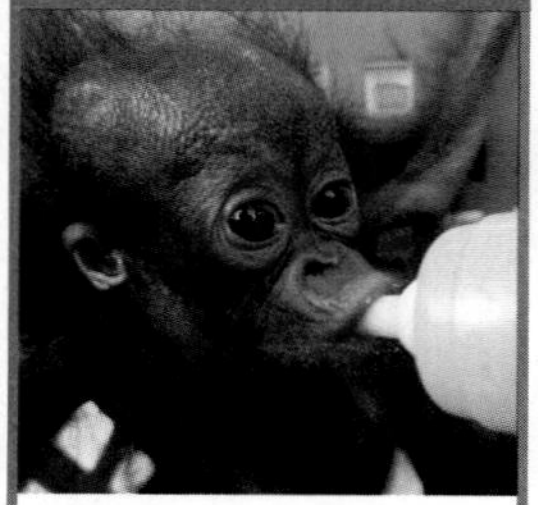

Orangutans weigh about 3.5 pounds at birth. As adults, female orangutans can weigh as much as 110 pounds, and male orangutans can weigh up to 300 pounds.

61. **Animals** A wildlife shelter in North Carolina is home to native species of birds, mammals, and reptiles. If cat chow is sold in 20 lb bags, what is the least number of bags of cat chow needed for one year at this shelter?

**Food Consumed at a Wildlife Shelter per Week**

| Type of Food | Amount of Food (lb) |
|---|---|
| Grapes | 4 |
| Mixed seed | 10 |
| Peanuts | 5 |
| Cat chow | 10 |
| Kitten chow | 5 |

62. **Education** In order to earn an A in a college math class, a student must score no less than 90% of all possible points. One semester, students with at least 567 points earned an A in the class. Write an inequality to show the numbers of points possible.

63. **Critical Thinking** Explain why you cannot solve an inequality by multiplying both sides by zero.

64. **/// ERROR ANALYSIS ///** Two students have different answers for a homework problem. Which answer is incorrect? Explain the error.

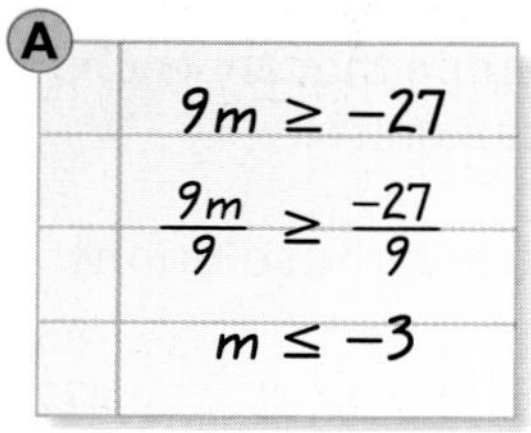
A
9m ≥ −27
9m/9 ≥ −27/9
m ≤ −3

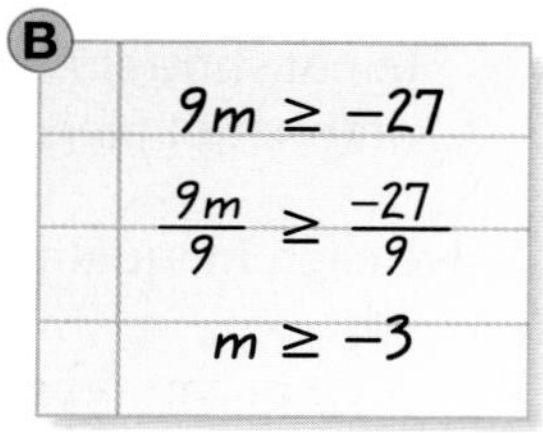
B
9m ≥ −27
9m/9 ≥ −27/9
m ≥ −3

65. Jan has a budget of $800 for catering. The catering company charges $12.50 per guest. Write and solve an inequality to show the numbers of guests Jan can invite.

**MULTI-STEP TEST PREP**

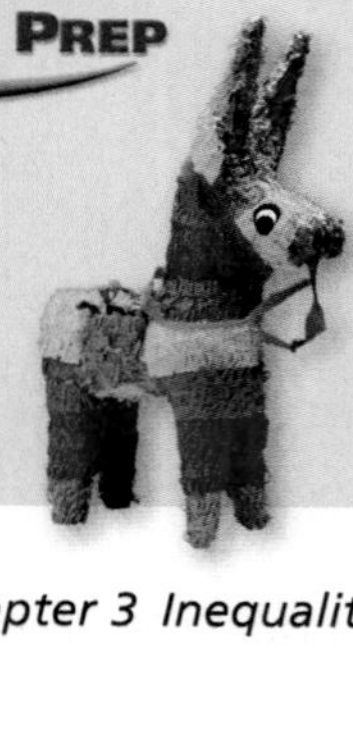

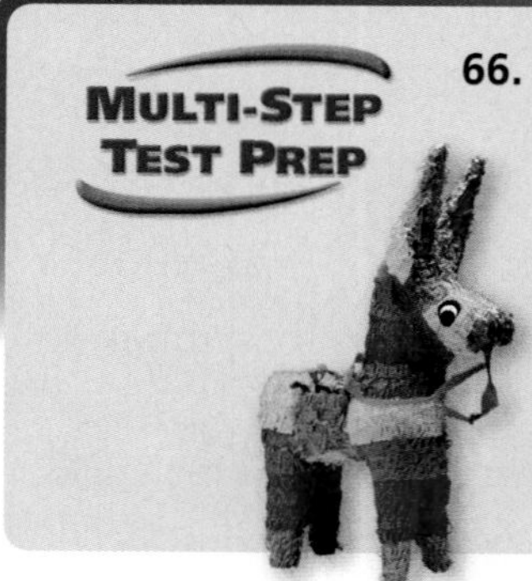

66. This problem will prepare you for the Multi-Step Test Prep on page 186.

**a.** The Swimming Club can spend a total of $250 for hotel rooms for its spring trip. One hotel costs $75 per night. Write an inequality to find the number of rooms the club can reserve at this hotel. Let $n$ be the number of rooms.

**b.** Solve the inequality you wrote in part **a.** Graph the solutions on a number line. Make sure your answer is reasonable.

**c.** Another hotel offers a rate of $65 per night. Does this allow the club to reserve more rooms? Explain your reasoning.

Prep MA.A.5.3

67. Which inequality does NOT have the same solutions as $-\frac{2}{3}y > 4$?

Ⓐ $12 < -2y$

Ⓑ $\frac{y}{2} < -12$

Ⓒ $-\frac{3}{4}y > \frac{9}{2}$

Ⓓ $-3y > 18$

68. The solutions of which inequality are NOT represented by the following graph?

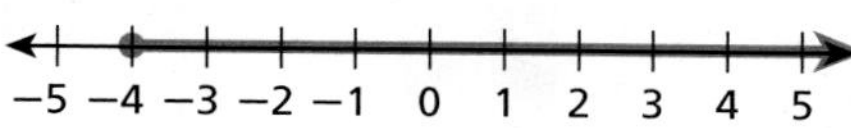


Ⓕ $\frac{x}{2} \geq -2$

Ⓖ $-5x \geq 20$

Ⓗ $3x \geq -12$

Ⓙ $-7x \leq 28$

69. Which inequality can be used to find the number of 39-cent stamps you can purchase for $4.00?

Ⓐ $0.39s \geq 4.00$

Ⓑ $0.39s \leq 4.00$

Ⓒ $\frac{s}{0.39} \leq 4.00$

Ⓓ $\frac{4.00}{0.39} \leq s$

70. **Short Response** Write three different inequalities that have the same solutions as $x > 4$. Show your work and explain each step.

## CHALLENGE AND EXTEND

**Solve each inequality.**

71. $2\frac{1}{3} \leq -\frac{5}{6}g$

72. $\frac{2x}{3} < 8.25$

73. $2\frac{5}{8}m > \frac{7}{10}$

74. $3\frac{3}{5}f \geq 14\frac{2}{5}$

75. **Estimation** What is the greatest possible integer solution of the inequality $3.806x < 19.902$?

76. **Critical Thinking** The Transitive Property of Equality states that if $a = b$ and $b = c$, then $a = c$. Is there a Transitive Property of Inequality using the symbol $<$? Give an example to support your answer.

77. **Critical Thinking** The Symmetric Property of Equality states that if $a = b$, then $b = a$. Is there a Symmetric Property of Inequality? Give an example to support your answer.

## SPIRAL REVIEW

**Write the power represented by each geometric model.** *(Lesson 1-4)*

78. ● ● ●
● ● ●
● ● ●

79. 

80. 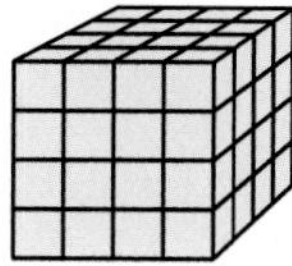

**Find the unit rate.** *(Lesson 2-6)*

81. Twelve gallons of gas cost $22.68.

82. A tree grows four feet in six years.

83. A student types 105 words in 3 minutes.

**Solve each inequality and graph the solutions.** *(Lesson 3-2)*

84. $x + 5 \geq 3$

85. $t - \frac{1}{4} < \frac{3}{4}$

86. $4 > x - 1$

87. $6 > b - 8$

CHAPTER 3

SECTION 3A

## Simple Inequalities

**Remember the Alamo!** The Spanish Club is planning a trip for next summer. They plan to travel from Fort Worth, Texas, to San Antonio, Texas. They can spend only $550 for the entire trip.

1. The treasurer of the club budgets $60 for gasoline. The current gas price is $1.95/gallon. The school van gets an average of 20 miles per gallon of gasoline. Determine how many miles they can drive on this budget. Round your answer to the nearest mile.
2. The distance from Fort Worth to San Antonio is 266 miles. Write an inequality that can be used to solve for the number of miles $m$ that they can drive while in San Antonio. Solve your inequality and graph the solutions.
3. The treasurer budgeted $200 for hotel rooms for one night. The club chose a hotel that charges $58 per night. Write an inequality that can be used to solve for the number of rooms they can reserve $n$. What is the maximum number of rooms that they can reserve in the hotel?
4. Use the maximum number of rooms you found in part **3.** How much will the club spend on hotel rooms?
5. The club members plan to spend $80 on food. They also want to see attractions in San Antonio, such as SeaWorld and the Alamo.

   Write an inequality that can be solved to find the amount of money available for seeing attractions. What is the maximum amount the club can spend seeing attractions?
6. Write a summary of the budget for the Spanish Club trip. Include the amount they plan to spend on gasoline, hotel rooms, food, and attractions.

# READY TO GO ON?

## Quiz for Lessons 3-1 Through 3-3

### 3-1 Graphing and Writing Inequalities

**Describe the solutions of each inequality in words.**

**1.** $-2 < r$ **2.** $t - 1 \leq 7$ **3.** $2s \geq 6$ **4.** $4 > 5 - x$

**Graph each inequality.**

**5.** $x > -2$ **6.** $m \leq 1\frac{1}{2}$ **7.** $g < \sqrt{8 + 1}$ **8.** $h \geq 2^3$

**Write the inequality shown by each graph.**

**9.** 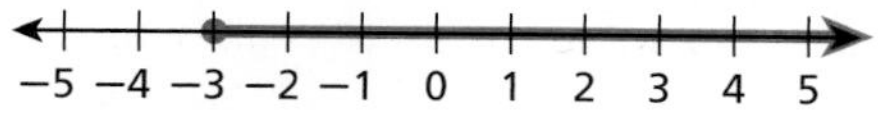


**10.** 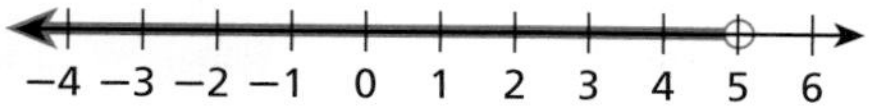


**11.** 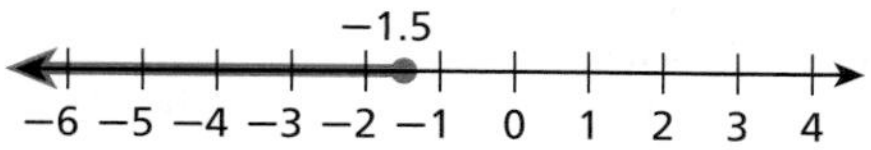


**Write an inequality for each situation and graph the solutions.**

**12.** You must purchase at least 5 tickets to receive a discount.

**13.** Children under 13 are not admitted to certain movies without an adult.

**14.** A cell phone plan allows up to 250 free minutes per month.

### 3-2 Solving One-Step Inequalities by Adding and Subtracting

**Solve each inequality and graph the solutions.**

**15.** $k + 5 \leq 7$ **16.** $4 > p - 3$ **17.** $r - 8 \geq -12$ **18.** $-3 + p < -6$

**19.** Allie must sell at least 50 gift baskets for the band fund-raiser. She already sold 36 baskets. Write and solve an inequality to determine how many more baskets Allie must sell for the fund-raiser.

**20.** Dante has at most \$12 to spend on entertainment each week. So far this week, he spent \$7.50. Write and solve an inequality to determine how much money Dante can spend on entertainment the rest of the week.

### 3-3 Solving One-Step Inequalities by Multiplying and Dividing

**Solve each inequality and graph the solutions.**

**21.** $-4x < 8$ **22.** $\frac{d}{3} \geq -3$ **23.** $\frac{3}{4}t \leq 12$ **24.** $8 > -16c$

**25.** A spool of ribbon is 80 inches long. Riley needs to cut strips of ribbon that are 14 inches long. What are the possible numbers of strips that Riley can cut?

# 3-4 Solving Two-Step and Multi-Step Inequalities

**Prep MA.A.5.3** Use tables and graphs to solve pairs of linear inequalities in two variables.

***Objective***
Solve inequalities that contain more than one operation.

**Who uses this?**
Contestants at a county fair can solve an inequality to find how many pounds a prize-winning pumpkin must weigh. (See Example 3.)

At the county fair, contestants can enter contests that judge animals, recipes, crops, art projects, and more. Sometimes an average score or average weight is used to determine the winner of the blue ribbon. A contestant can use a multi-step inequality to determine what score or weight is needed in order to win.

Inequalities that contain more than one operation require more than one step to solve. Use inverse operations to undo the operations in the inequality one at a time.

## EXAMPLE 1 Solving Multi-Step Inequalities

**Solve each inequality and graph the solutions.**

**A** $160 + 4f \leq 500$

$160 + 4f \leq 500$
$\underline{-160 \qquad -160}$ *Since 160 is added to 4f, subtract 160 from both sides to undo the addition.*

$4f \leq 340$ *Since f is multiplied by 4, divide both sides by 4 to undo the multiplication.*

$\frac{4f}{4} \leq \frac{340}{4}$

$f \leq 85$

85
0 10 20 30 40 50 60 70 80 90 100

**Remember!**
Subtracting a number is the same as adding its opposite.
$7 - 2t = 7 + (-2t)$

**B** $7 - 2t \leq 21$

$7 - 2t \leq 21$
$\underline{-7 \qquad -7}$ *Since 7 is added to −2t, subtract 7 from both sides to undo the addition.*

$-2t \leq 14$ *Since t is multiplied by −2, divide both sides by −2 to undo the multiplication.*

$\frac{-2t}{-2} \geq \frac{14}{-2}$ *Change ≤ to ≥.*

$t \geq -7$

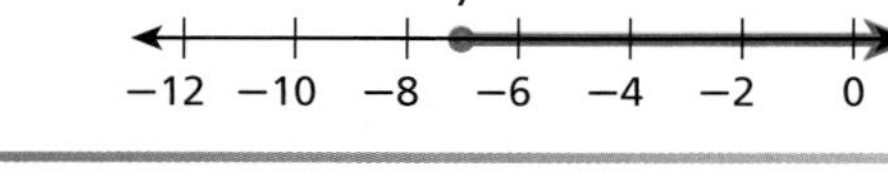

**Solve each inequality and graph the solutions.**

**1a.** $-12 \geq 3x + 6$ **1b.** $\frac{x + 5}{-2} > 3$ **1c.** $\frac{1 - 2n}{3} \geq 7$

To solve more complicated inequalities, you may first need to simplify the expressions on one or both sides by using the order of operations, combining like terms, or using the Distributive Property.

## EXAMPLE 2 Simplifying Before Solving Inequalities

**Solve each inequality and graph the solutions.**

**A** $-4 + (-8) < -5c - 2$

$-12 < -5c - 2$ — *Combine like terms. Since 2 is subtracted from −5c, add 2 to both sides to undo the subtraction.*

$\underline{+2 \qquad\quad +2}$

$-10 < -5c$ — *Since c is multiplied by −5, divide both sides by −5 to undo the multiplication. Change < to >.*

$\frac{-10}{-5} > \frac{-5c}{-5}$

$2 > c$ (or $c < 2$)

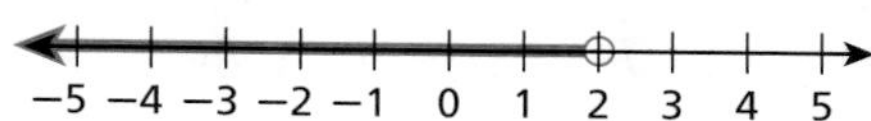


**B** $-3(3 - x) < 4^2$

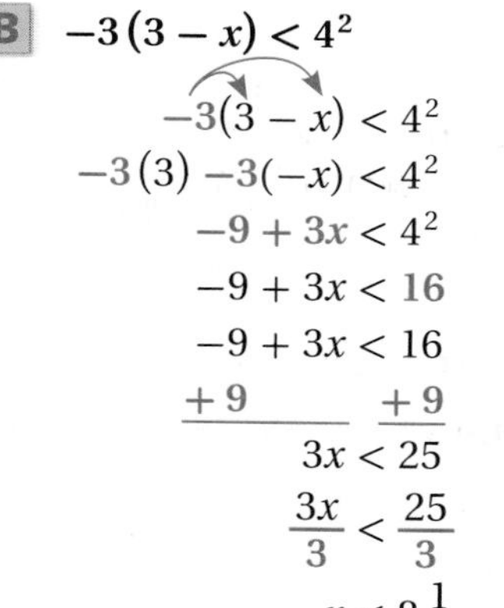

$-3(3 - x) < 4^2$

$-3(3) - 3(-x) < 4^2$

$-9 + 3x < 4^2$ — *Distribute −3 on the left side.*

$-9 + 3x < 16$ — *Simplify the right side.*

$-9 + 3x < 16$ — *Since −9 is added to 3x, add 9 to both sides to undo the addition.*

$\underline{+9 \qquad\quad +9}$

$3x < 25$ — *Since x is multiplied by 3, divide both sides by 3 to undo the multiplication.*

$\frac{3x}{3} < \frac{25}{3}$

$x < 8\frac{1}{3}$

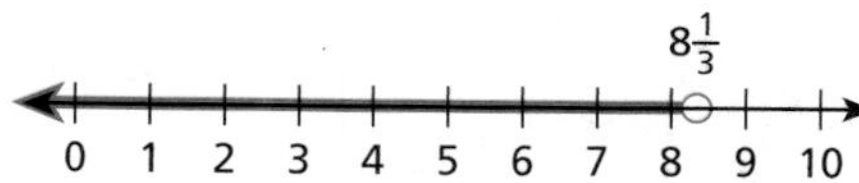


**C** $\frac{4}{5}x + \frac{1}{2} > \frac{3}{5}$

$10\left(\frac{4}{5}x + \frac{1}{2}\right) > 10\left(\frac{3}{5}\right)$ — *Multiply both sides by 10, the LCD of the fractions.*

$10\left(\frac{4}{5}x\right) + 10\left(\frac{1}{2}\right) > 10\left(\frac{3}{5}\right)$ — *Distribute 10 on the left side.*

$8x + 5 > 6$ — *Since 5 is added to 8x, subtract 5 from both sides to undo the addition.*

$\underline{\quad -5 \quad -5}$

$8x \quad > 1$

$\frac{8x}{8} > \frac{1}{8}$ — *Since x is multiplied by 8, divide both sides by 8 to undo the multiplication.*

$x > \frac{1}{8}$

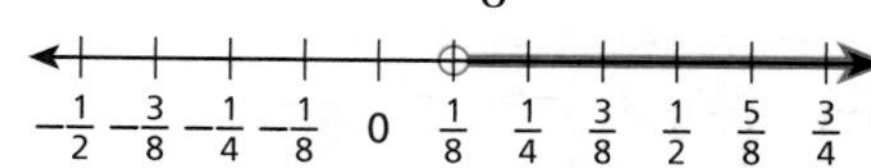

**Solve each inequality and graph the solutions.**

**2a.** $2m + 5 > 5^2$ **2b.** $3 + 2(x + 4) > 3$ **2c.** $\frac{5}{8} < \frac{3}{8}x - \frac{1}{4}$

## EXAMPLE 3 Gardening Application

**To win the blue ribbon for the Heaviest Pumpkin Crop at the county fair, the average weight of John's two pumpkins must be greater than 819 lb. One of his pumpkins weighs 887 lb. What is the least number of pounds the second pumpkin could weigh in order for John to win the blue ribbon?**

Let $p$ represent the weight of the second pumpkin. The average weight of the pumpkins is the sum of each weight divided by 2.

| (887 | plus | p) | divided by | 2 | must be greater than | 819. |
|---|---|---|---|---|---|---|
| (887 | + | p) | ÷ | 2 | > | 819 |

$$\frac{887 + p}{2} > 819$$

*Since 887 + p is divided by 2, multiply both sides by 2 to undo the division.*

$$2\left(\frac{887 + p}{2}\right) > 2(819)$$

$$887 + p > 1638$$

*Since 887 is added to p, subtract 887 from both sides to undo the addition.*

$$\underline{-887} \qquad \underline{-887}$$

$$p > 751$$

The second pumpkin must weigh more than 751 pounds.

***Check*** Check the endpoint, 751.

$$\frac{887 + p}{2} = 819$$

| | |
|---|---|
| $\frac{887 + 751}{2}$ | 819 |
| $\frac{1638}{2}$ | 819 |
| 819 | 819 ✓ |

Check a number greater than 751.

$$\frac{887 + p}{2} > 819$$

| | | |
|---|---|---|
| $\frac{887 + 755}{2}$ | > | 819 |
| $\frac{1642}{2}$ | > | 819 |
| 821 | > | 819 ✓ |

**3.** The average of Jim's two test scores must be at least 90 to make an A in the class. Jim got a 95 on his first test. What grades can Jim get on his second test to make an A in the class?

## THINK AND DISCUSS

**1.** The inequality $v \geq 25$ states that 25 is the ___?___. (*value of v, minimum value of v,* or *maximum value of v*)

**2.** Describe two sets of steps for solving the inequality $\frac{x+5}{3} > 7$.

**3. GET ORGANIZED** Copy and complete the graphic organizer.

Solving Multi-Step Equations and Inequalities

How are they alike? | How are they different?

# 3-4 Exercises

Prep MA.A.5.3

go.hrw.com
Homework Help Online
KEYWORD: MA7 3-4
Parent Resources Online
KEYWORD: MA7 Parent

## GUIDED PRACTICE

SEE EXAMPLE 1 p. 188

**Solve each inequality and graph the solutions.**

**1.** $2m + 1 > 13$ **2.** $2d + 21 \leq 11$ **3.** $6 \leq -2x + 2$ **4.** $4c - 7 > 5$

**5.** $\frac{4 + x}{3} > -4$ **6.** $1 < 0.2x - 0.7$ **7.** $\frac{3 - 2x}{3} \leq 7$ **8.** $2x + 5 \geq 2$

SEE EXAMPLE 2 p. 189

**9.** $4(x + 2) > 6$ **10.** $\frac{1}{4}x + \frac{2}{3} < \frac{3}{4}$ **11.** $4 - x + 6^2 \geq 21$

**12.** $4 - x > 3(4 - 2)$ **13.** $0.2(x - 10) > -1.8$ **14.** $3(j + 41) \leq 35$

SEE EXAMPLE 3 p. 190

**15. Business** A sales representative is given a choice of two paycheck plans. One choice includes a monthly base pay of \$300 plus 10% commission on his sales. The second choice is a monthly salary of \$1200. For what amount of sales would the representative make more money with the first plan?

## PRACTICE AND PROBLEM SOLVING

**Independent Practice**

| For Exercises | See Example |
|---|---|
| 16–27 | 1 |
| 28–36 | 2 |
| 37 | 3 |

**Extra Practice**

Skills Practice p. S9
Application Practice p. S30

**Solve each inequality and graph the solutions.**

**16.** $4r - 9 > 7$ **17.** $3 \leq 5 - 2x$ **18.** $\frac{w + 3}{2} > 6$ **19.** $11w + 99 < 77$

**20.** $9 \geq \frac{1}{2}v + 3$ **21.** $-4x - 8 > 16$ **22.** $8 - \frac{2}{3}z \leq 2$ **23.** $f + 2\frac{1}{2} < -2$

**24.** $\frac{3n - 8}{5} \geq 2$ **25.** $-5 > -5 - 3w$ **26.** $10 > \frac{5 - 3p}{2}$ **27.** $2v + 1 > 2\frac{1}{3}$

**28.** $4(x + 3) > -24$ **29.** $4 > x - 3(x + 2)$ **30.** $-18 \geq 33 - 3h$

**31.** $-2 > 7x - 2(x - 4)$ **32.** $9 - (9)^2 > 10x - x$ **33.** $2a - (-3)^2 \geq 13$

**34.** $6 - \frac{x}{3} + 1 > \frac{2}{3}$ **35.** $12(x - 3) + 2x > 6$ **36.** $15 \geq 19 + 2(q - 18)$

**37. Communications** One cell phone company offers a plan that costs \$29.99 and includes unlimited night and weekend minutes. Another company offers a plan that costs \$19.99 and charges \$0.35 per minute during nights and weekends. For what numbers of night and weekend minutes does the second company's plan cost more than the first company's plan?

**Solve each inequality and graph the solutions.**

**38.** $-12 > -4x - 8$ **39.** $5x + 4 \leq 14$ **40.** $\frac{2}{3}x - 5 > 7$

**41.** $x - 3x > 2 - 10$ **42.** $5 - x - 2 > 3$ **43.** $3 < 2x - 5(x + 3)$

**44.** $\frac{1}{6} - \frac{2}{3}m \geq \frac{1}{4}$ **45.** $4 - (r - 2) > 3 - 5$ **46.** $0.3 - 0.5n + 1 \geq 0.4$

**47.** $6^2 > 4(x + 2)$ **48.** $-4 - 2n + 4n > 7 - 2^2$ **49.** $\frac{1}{4}(p - 10) \geq 6 - 4$

**50.** Use the inequality $-4t - 8 \leq 12$ to fill in the missing numbers.

**a.** $t \geq$ ■ **b.** $t + 4 \geq$ ■ **c.** $t -$ ■ $\geq 0$

**d.** $t + 10 \geq$ ■ **e.** $3t \geq$ ■ **f.** $\frac{t}{■} \geq -5$

**Write an inequality for each statement. Solve the inequality and graph the solutions.**

**51.** One-half of a number, increased by 9, is less than 33.

**52.** Six is less than or equal to the sum of 4 and $-2x$.

**53.** The product of 4 and the sum of a number and 12 is at most 16.

**54.** The sum of half a number and two-thirds of the number is less than 14.

**Solve each inequality and match the solution to the correct graph.**

**55.** $4x - 9 \geq 7$

**56.** $-6 \geq 3(x - 2)$

**57.** $-2x - 6 \geq -4 + 2$

**58.** $\frac{1}{2} - \frac{1}{3}x \leq \left(\frac{2}{3} + \frac{1}{3}\right)^2$

**A.** −5 −4 −3 −2 −1 0 1 2 3 4 5

**B.** −5 −4 −3 −2 −1 0 1 2 3 4 5

**C.** $-\frac{3}{2}$ −5 −4 −3 −2 −1 0 1 2 3 4 5

**D.** −5 −4 −3 −2 −1 0 1 2 3 4 5

**59. Entertainment** A digital video recorder (DVR) records television shows on an internal hard drive. To use a DVR, you need a subscription with a DVR service company. Two companies advertise their charges for a DVR machine and subscription service.

For what numbers of months will a consumer pay less for the machine and subscription at Easy Electronics than at Cable Solutions?

**60. Geometry** The area of the triangle shown is less than 55 square inches.

**a.** Write an inequality that can be used to find $x$.

**b.** Solve the inequality you wrote in part **a.**

**c.** What is the maximum height of the triangle?

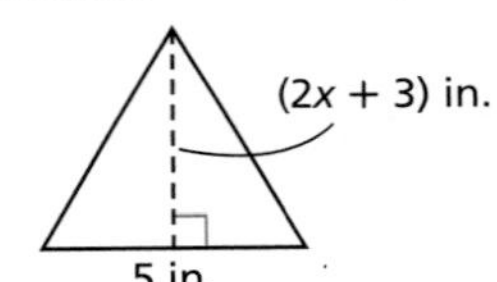


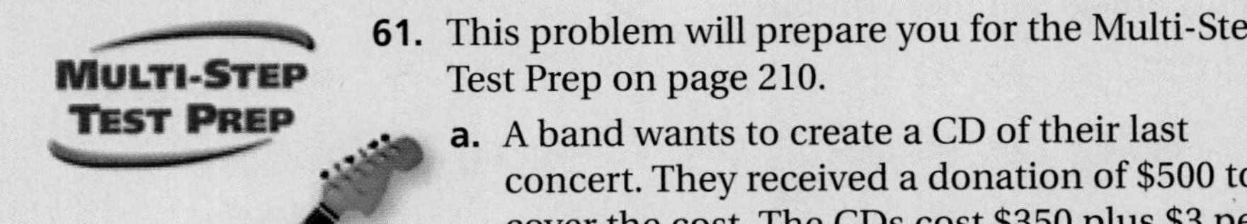

**MULTI-STEP TEST PREP**

**61.** This problem will prepare you for the Multi-Step Test Prep on page 210.

**a.** A band wants to create a CD of their last concert. They received a donation of $500 to cover the cost. The CDs cost $350 plus $3 per CD. Complete the table to find a relationship between the number of CDs and the total cost.

| Number | Process | Cost |
|---|---|---|
| 1 | 350 + 3 | 353 |
| 2 | | |
| 3 | | |
| 10 | | |
| $n$ | | |

**b.** Write an equation for the cost $C$ of the CDs based on the number of CDs $n$.

**c.** Write an inequality that can be used to determine how many CDs can be made with the $500 donation. Solve the inequality and determine how many CDs the band can have made from the $500 donation.

62. **Critical Thinking** What is the least whole number that is a solution of $4r - 4.9 > 14.95$?

63. **Write About It** Describe two sets of steps to solve $2(x + 3) > 10$.

## TEST PREP

Prep MA.A.5.3

64. What are the solutions of $3y > 2x + 4$ when $y = 6$?

Ⓐ $7 > x$ Ⓑ $x > 7$ Ⓒ $x > 11$ Ⓓ $11 > x$

65. Cecilia has $30 to spend at a carnival. Admission costs $5.00, lunch will cost $6.00, and each ride ticket costs $1.25. Which inequality represents the number of ride tickets $x$ that Cecilia can buy?

Ⓕ $30 - (5 - 6) + 1.25x \leq 30$ Ⓗ $30 - (5 + 6) \leq 1.25x$

Ⓖ $5 + 6 + 1.25x \leq 30$ Ⓙ $30 + 1.25x \leq 5 + 6$

66. Which statement is modeled by $2p + 5 < 11$?

Ⓐ The sum of 5 and 2 times $p$ is at least 11.

Ⓑ Five added to the product of 2 and $p$ is less than 11.

Ⓒ Two times $p$ plus 5 is at most 11.

Ⓓ The product of 2 and $p$ added to 5 is 11.

67. **Gridded Response** A basketball team scored 8 points more in its second game than in its first. In its third game, the team scored 42 points. The total number of points scored in the three games was more than 150. What is the least number of points the team might have scored in its *second* game?

## CHALLENGE AND EXTEND

**Solve each inequality and graph the solutions.**

68. $3(x + 2) - 6x + 6 \leq 0$ 69. $-18 > -(2x + 9) - 4 + x$ 70. $\frac{2 + x}{2} - (x - 1) > 1$

**Write an inequality for each statement. Graph the solutions.**

71. $x$ is a positive number. 72. $x$ is a negative number.

73. $x$ is a nonnegative number. 74. $x$ is not a positive number.

75. $x$ times negative 3 is positive. 76. The opposite of $x$ is greater than 2.

## SPIRAL REVIEW

**Find each square root.** *(Lesson 1-5)*

77. $\sqrt{49}$ 78. $-\sqrt{144}$ 79. $\sqrt{\frac{4}{9}}$

80. $\sqrt{196}$ 81. $-\sqrt{1}$ 82. $\sqrt{10{,}000}$

83. Video rental store A charges a membership fee of $25 and $2 for each movie rental. Video rental store B charges a membership fee of $10 and $2.50 for each movie. Find the number of movie rentals for which both stores' charges are the same. *(Lesson 2-4)*

**Solve each inequality and graph the solutions.** *(Lesson 3-3)*

84. $2x < -8$ 85. $\frac{a}{-2} \leq -3$ 86. $\frac{1}{4} < \frac{t}{12}$

# 3-5 Solving Inequalities with Variables on Both Sides

**Prep MA.A.5.3** Use tables and graphs to solve pairs of linear inequalities in two variables.

***Objective***
Solve inequalities that contain variable terms on both sides.

**Who uses this?**
Business owners can use inequalities to find the most cost-efficient services. (See Example 2.)

Some inequalities have variable terms on both sides of the inequality symbol. You can solve these inequalities like you solved equations with variables on both sides.

Use the properties of inequality to "collect" all the variable terms on one side and all the constant terms on the other side.

**EXAMPLE 1 Solving Inequalities with Variables on Both Sides**

**Solve each inequality and graph the solutions.**

**A** $x < 3x + 8$

$x < 3x + 8$ — *To collect the variable terms on one side, subtract x from both sides.*

$-x \quad -x$

$0 < 2x + 8$ — *Since 8 is added to 2x, subtract 8 from both sides to undo the addition.*

$-8 \quad -8$

$-8 < 2x$

$\frac{-8}{2} < \frac{2x}{2}$ — *Since x is multiplied by 2, divide both sides by 2 to undo the multiplication.*

$-4 < x$ (or $x > -4$)

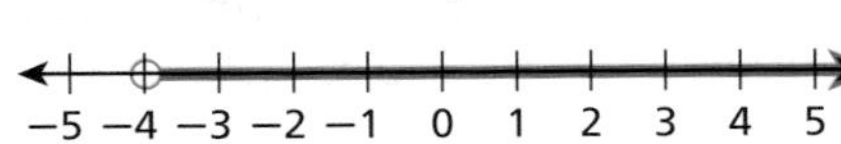

**Helpful Hint**

Your first step can also be to subtract 3x from both sides to get $-2x < 8$. When you divide by a negative number, remember to reverse the inequality symbol.

**B** $6x - 1 \leq 3.5x + 4$

$6x - 1 \leq 3.5x + 4$ — *Subtract 6x from both sides.*

$-6x \quad -6x$

$-1 \leq -2.5x + 4$ — *Since 4 is added to −2.5x, subtract 4 from both sides to undo the addition.*

$-4 \quad -4$

$-5 \leq -2.5x$

$\frac{-5}{-2.5} \geq \frac{-2.5x}{-2.5}$ — *Since x is multiplied by −2.5, divide both sides by−2.5 to undo the multiplication. Reverse the inequality symbol.*

$2 \geq x$

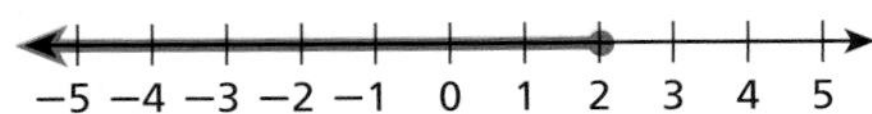

**Solve each inequality and graph the solutions.**

**1a.** $4x \geq 7x + 6$ **1b.** $5t + 1 < -2t - 6$

## EXAMPLE 2 Business Application

**The *Daily Info* charges a fee of \$650 plus \$80 per week to run an ad. The *People's Paper* charges \$145 per week. For how many weeks will the total cost at *Daily Info* be less expensive than the cost at *People's Paper*?**

Let $w$ be the number of weeks the ad runs in the paper.

| *Daily Info* fee | plus | \$80 per week | times | number of weeks | is less expensive than | *People's Paper* charge per week | times | number of weeks. |
|---|---|---|---|---|---|---|---|---|
| \$650 | + | \$80 | • | $w$ | < | \$145 | • | $w$ |

$$650 + 80w < 145w$$

$$\underline{-80w \quad\quad -80w}$$ *Subtract 80w from both sides.*

$$650 < 65w$$ *Since w is multiplied by 65, divide both sides by 65 to undo the multiplication.*

$$\frac{650}{65} < \frac{65w}{65}$$

$$10 < w$$

The total cost at *Daily Info* is less than the cost at *People's Paper* if the ad runs for more than 10 weeks.

**CHECK IT OUT!** 2. A-Plus Advertising charges a fee of \$24 plus \$0.10 per flyer to print and deliver flyers. Print and More charges \$0.25 per flyer. For how many flyers is the cost at A-Plus Advertising less than the cost at Print and More?

You may need to simplify one or both sides of an inequality before solving it. Look for like terms to combine and places to use Distributive Property.

## EXAMPLE 3 Simplifying Each Side Before Solving

**Solve each inequality and graph the solutions.**

**A** $6(1 - x) < 3x$

$$6(1 - x) < 3x$$ *Distribute 6 on the left side of the inequality.*

$$6(1) - 6(x) < 3x$$ *Add 6x to both sides so that the coefficient of x is positive.*

$$6 - 6x < 3x$$

$$\underline{+6x \quad\quad +6x}$$

$$6 < 9x$$

$$\frac{6}{9} < \frac{9x}{9}$$ *Since x is multiplied by 9, divide both sides by 9 to undo the multiplication.*

$$\frac{2}{3} < x$$

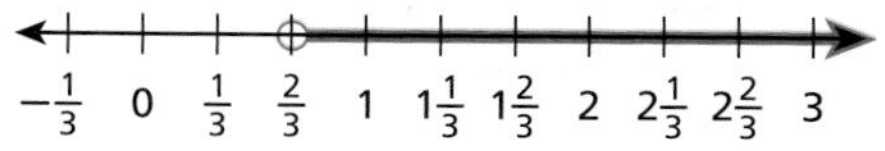

**Helpful Hint**

In Example 3B, you can also multiply each term in the inequality by a power of 10 to clear the decimals.

$10(-0.2x) + 10(0.9) \geq 10(1.6x)$

$-2x + 9 \geq 16x$

**Solve each inequality and graph the solutions.**

**B** $-0.2x + 0.9 \geq 1.6x$

$$\begin{aligned} -0.2x + 0.9 &\geq 1.6x \\ \underline{+0.2x \qquad} & \quad \underline{+0.2x} \\ 0.9 &\geq 1.8x \end{aligned}$$

*Since $-0.2x$ is added to 0.9, subtract $-0.2x$ from both sides. Subtracting $-0.2x$ is the same as adding 0.2x.*

$$\frac{0.9}{1.8} \geq \frac{1.8x}{1.8}$$

*Since x is multiplied by 1.8, divide both sides by 1.8 to undo the multiplication.*

$$\frac{1}{2} \geq x$$

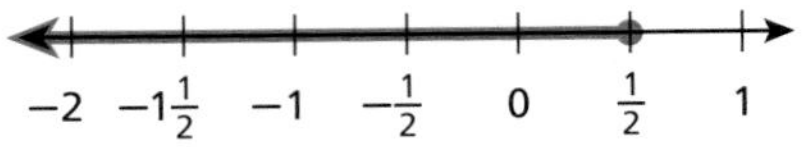

Number line: $-2$, $-1\frac{1}{2}$, $-1$, $-\frac{1}{2}$, $0$, $\frac{1}{2}$, $1$

**Solve each inequality and graph the solutions.**

**3a.** $5(2 - r) \geq 3(r - 2)$

**3b.** $0.5x - 0.3 + 1.9x < 0.3x + 6$

There are special cases of inequalities called *identities* and *contradictions*.

**Know it! Note**

## Identities and Contradictions

| WORDS | ALGEBRA |
|---|---|
| **Identity**<br>When solving an inequality, if you get a statement that is always true, the original inequality is an identity, and all real numbers are solutions. | $1 + x < 7 + x$<br>$\underline{-x \qquad -x}$<br>$1 < 7$ ✓ |
| **Contradiction**<br>When solving an inequality, if you get a false statement, the original inequality is a contradiction, and it has no solutions. | $x + 7 < x$<br>$\underline{-x \qquad -x}$<br>$7 < 0$ ✗ |

**These properties are also true for inequalities that use the symbols >, ≥, and ≤.**

## EXAMPLE 4 Identities and Contradictions

**Solve each inequality.**

**A** $x + 5 \geq x + 3$

$$\begin{aligned} x + 5 &\geq x + 3 \\ \underline{-x \qquad} & \quad \underline{-x \qquad} \\ 5 &\geq \quad 3 \checkmark \end{aligned}$$

*Subtract x from both sides.*

*True statement*

All values of $x$ make the inequality true.
All real numbers are solutions.

**B** $2x + 6 < 5 + 2x$

$$\begin{aligned} 2x + 6 &< 5 + 2x \\ \underline{-2x \qquad} & \quad \underline{\qquad -2x} \\ 6 &< 5 \ ✗ \end{aligned}$$

*Subtract 2x from both sides.*

*False statement*

No values of $x$ make the inequality true.
There are no solutions.

**Solve each inequality.**

**4a.** $4(y - 1) \geq 4y + 2$

**4b.** $x - 2 < x + 1$

## THINK AND DISCUSS

1. Explain how you would collect the variable terms to solve the inequality $5c - 4 > 8c + 2$.

2. **GET ORGANIZED** Copy and complete the graphic organizer. In each box, give an example of an inequality of the indicated type.

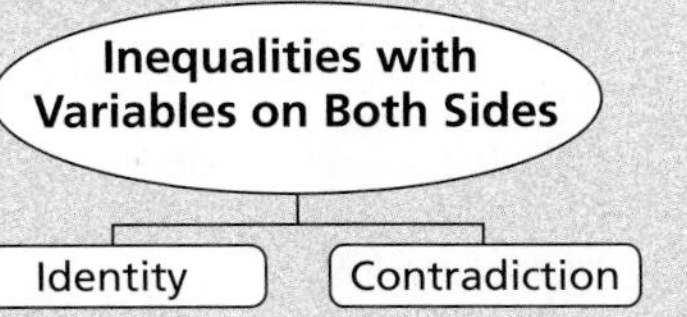


# 3-5 Exercises

Prep MA.A.5.3

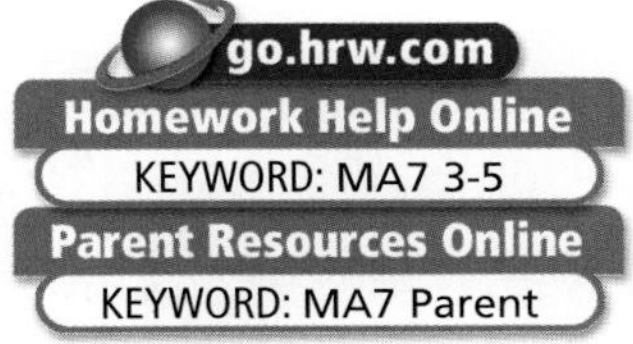


## GUIDED PRACTICE

SEE EXAMPLE 1 p. 194

**Solve each inequality and graph the solutions.**

1. $2x > 4x - 6$
2. $7y + 1 \leq y - 5$
3. $27x + 33 > 58x - 29$
4. $-3r < 10 - r$
5. $5c - 4 > 8c + 2$
6. $4.5x - 3.8 \geq 1.5x - 2.3$

SEE EXAMPLE 2 p. 195

7. **School** The school band will sell pizzas to raise money for new uniforms. The supplier charges \$100 plus \$4 per pizza. If the band members sell the pizzas for \$7 each, how many pizzas will they have to sell to make a profit?

SEE EXAMPLE 3 p. 195

**Solve each inequality and graph the solutions.**

8. $5(4 + x) \leq 3(2 + x)$
9. $-4(3 - p) > 5(p + 1)$
10. $2(6 - x) < 4x$
11. $4x > 3(7 - x)$
12. $\frac{1}{2}f + \frac{3}{4} \geq \frac{1}{4}f$
13. $-36.72 + 5.65t < 0.25t$

SEE EXAMPLE 4 p. 196

**Solve each inequality.**

14. $2(x - 2) \leq -2(1 - x)$
15. $4(y + 1) < 4y + 2$
16. $4v + 1 < 4v - 7$
17. $b - 4 \geq b - 6$
18. $3(x - 5) > 3x$
19. $2k + 7 \geq 2(k + 14)$

## PRACTICE AND PROBLEM SOLVING

**Solve each inequality and graph the solutions.**

20. $3x \leq 5x + 8$
21. $9y + 3 > 4y - 7$
22. $1.5x - 1.2 < 3.1x - 2.8$
23. $7 + 4b \geq 3b$
24. $7 - 5t < 4t - 2$
25. $2.8m - 5.2 > 0.8m + 4.8$

26. **Geometry** Write and solve an inequality to find the values of $x$ for which the area of the rectangle is greater than the area of the triangle.

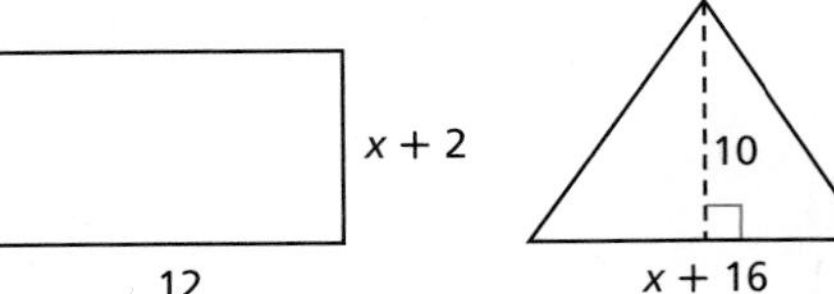

| Independent Practice | |
|---|---|
| For Exercises | See Example |
| 25 | 1 |
| 26 | 2 |
| 27–32 | 3 |
| 33–38 | 4 |

**Extra Practice**
Skills Practice p. S9
Application Practice p. S30

**Solve each inequality and graph the solutions.**

**27.** $4(2 - x) \le 5(x - 2)$ **28.** $-3(n + 4) < 6(1 - n)$ **29.** $9(w + 2) \le 12w$

**30.** $4.5 + 1.3t > 3.8t - 3$ **31.** $\frac{1}{2}r + \frac{2}{3} \ge \frac{1}{3}r$ **32.** $2(4 - n) < 3n - 7$

**Solve each inequality.**

**33.** $3(2 - x) < -3(x - 1)$ **34.** $7 - y > 5 - y$ **35.** $3(10 + z) \le 3z + 36$

**36.** $-5(k - 1) \ge 5(2 - k)$ **37.** $4(x - 1) \le 4x$ **38.** $3(v - 9) \ge 15 + 3v$

**Solve each inequality and graph the solutions.**

**39.** $3t - 12 > 5t + 2$ **40.** $-5(y + 3) - 6 < y + 3$

**41.** $3x + 9 - 5x < x$ **42.** $18 + 9p > 12p - 31$

**43.** $2(x - 5) < -3x$ **44.** $-\frac{2}{5}x \le \frac{4}{5} - \frac{3}{5}x$

**45.** $-2(x - 7) - 4 - x < 8x + 32$ **46.** $-3(2r - 4) \ge 2(5 - 3r)$

**47.** $-7x - 10 + 5x \ge 3(x + 4) + 8$ **48.** $-\frac{1}{3}(n + 8) + \frac{1}{3}n \le 1 - n$

**Recreation**

The American Kitefliers Association has over 4000 members in 35 countries. Kitefliers participate in festivals, competitions, and kite-making workshops.

**49. Recreation** A red kite is 100 feet off the ground and is rising at 8 feet per second. A blue kite is 180 feet off the ground and is rising at 5 feet per second. How long will it take for the red kite to be higher than the blue kite? Round your answer to the nearest second.

**50. Education** The table shows the enrollment in Howard High School and Phillips High School for three school years.

| School Enrollment | | | |
|---|---|---|---|
| | Year 1 | Year 2 | Year 3 |
| Howard High School | 1192 | 1188 | 1184 |
| Philipps High School | 921 | 941 | 961 |

**a.** How much did the enrollment change each year at Howard?

**b.** Use the enrollment in year 1 and your answer from part **a** to write an expression for the enrollment at Howard in any year $x$.

**c.** How much did the enrollment change each year at Phillips?

**d.** Use the enrollment in year 1 and your answer from part **c** to write an expression for the enrollment at Phillips in any year $x$.

**e.** Assume that the pattern in the table continues. Use your expressions from parts **b** and **d** to write an inequality that can be solved to find the year in which the enrollment at Phillips High School will be greater than the enrollment at Howard High School. Solve your inequality and graph the solutions.

**MULTI-STEP TEST PREP**

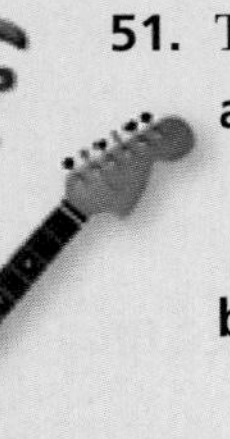

**51.** This problem will prepare you for the Multi-Step Test Prep on page 210.

**a.** The school orchestra is creating a CD of their last concert. The cost of creating the CDs is $400 + 4.50 per CD. Write an expression for the cost of creating the CDs based on the number of CDs $n$.

**b.** The orchestra plans to sell the CDs for $12. Write an expression for the amount the orchestra earns from the sale of $n$ CDs.

**c.** In order for the orchestra to make a profit, the amount they make selling the CDs must be greater than the cost of creating the CDs. Write an inequality that can be solved to find the number of CDs the orchestra must sell in order to make a profit. Solve your inequality.

**Write an inequality to represent each relationship. Solve your inequality.**

52. Four more than twice a number is greater than two-thirds of the number.

53. Ten less than five times a number is less than six times the number decreased by eight.

54. The sum of a number and twenty is less than four times the number decreased by one.

55. Three-fourths of a number is greater than or equal to five less than the number.

56. **Entertainment** Use the table to determine how many movies you would have to rent for Video View to be less expensive than Movie Place.

| | Membership Fee ($) | Cost per Rental ($) |
|---|---|---|
| **Movie Place** | None | 2.99 |
| **Video View** | 19.99 | 1.99 |

57. **Geometry** In an acute triangle, all angles measure less than 90°. Also, the sum of the measures of any two angles is greater than the measure of the third angle. Can the measures of an acute triangle be $x$, $x - 1$, and $2x$? Explain.

58. **Write About It** Compare the steps you would follow to solve an inequality to the steps you would follow to solve an equation.

59. **Critical Thinking** How can you tell just by looking at the inequality $x > x + 1$ that it has no solutions?

60. **///ERROR ANALYSIS///** Two students solved the inequality $5x < 3 - 4x$. Which is incorrect? Explain the error.

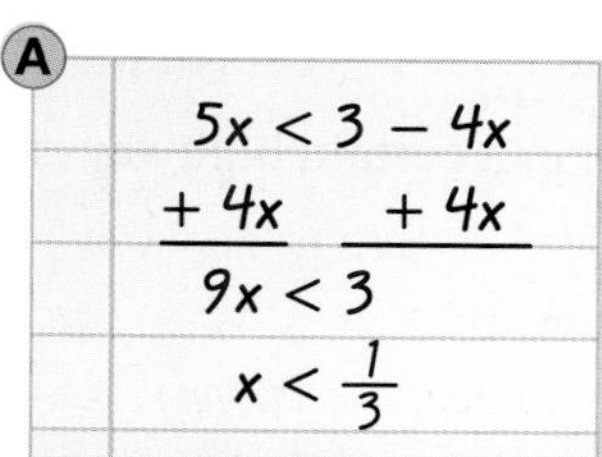


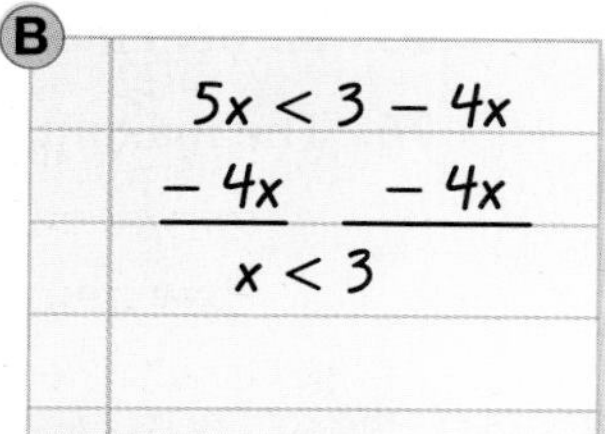

Prep MA.A.5.3

61. If $a - b > a + b$, which statement is true?

Ⓐ The value of $a$ is positive.
Ⓑ The value of $b$ is positive.
Ⓒ The value of $a$ is negative.
Ⓓ The value of $b$ is negative.

62. If $-a < b$, which statement is always true?

Ⓕ $a < b$  Ⓖ $a > b$  Ⓗ $a < -b$  Ⓙ $a > -b$

63. Which is a solution of the inequality $7(2 - x) > 4(x - 2)$?

Ⓐ −2  Ⓑ 2  Ⓒ 4  Ⓓ 7

64. Which is the graph of $-3x < -6$?

Ⓕ −5 −4 −3 −2 −1 0 1 2 3 4 5

Ⓗ
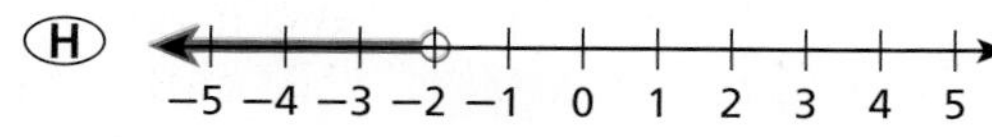


Ⓖ −5 −4 −3 −2 −1 0 1 2 3 4 5

Ⓙ −5 −4 −3 −2 −1 0 1 2 3 4 5

65. **Short Response** Write a real-world situation that could be modeled by the inequality $7x + 4 > 4x + 13$. Explain how the inequality relates to your situation.

## CHALLENGE AND EXTEND

**Solve each inequality.**

66. $2\frac{1}{2} + 2x \geq 5\frac{1}{2} + 2\frac{1}{2}x$

67. $1.6x - 20.7 > 6.3x - (-2.2x)$

68. $1.3x - 7.5x < 8.5x - 29.4$

69. $-4w + \frac{-8 - 37}{9} \leq \frac{75 - 3}{9} + 3w$

70. Replace the square and circle with numbers so that the inequality is an identity. $\square - 2x < \bigcirc - 2x$

71. Replace the square and circle with numbers so that the inequality is a contradiction. $\square - 2x < \bigcirc - 2x$

72. **Critical Thinking** Explain whether there are any numbers that can replace the square and circle so that the inequality is an identity. $\square + 2x < \bigcirc + x$

## SPIRAL REVIEW

73. The ratio of the width of a rectangle to the length is 2:5. The length is 65 inches. Find the width. *(Lesson 2-6)*

74. Find the simple interest paid after 6 months on a loan of $5000 borrowed at a rate of 9%. *(Lesson 2-9)*

**Define a variable and write an inequality for each situation. Graph the solutions.** *(Lesson 3-1)*

75. Participants must be at least 14 years old.

76. The maximum speed on a certain highway is 60 miles per hour.

## Career Path

go.hrw.com
Career Resources Online
KEYWORD: MA7 Career

**Katie Flannigan**
Culinary Arts program

**Q: What math classes did you take in high school?**

A: Algebra 1, Geometry, and Algebra 2

**Q: What math classes have you taken since high school?**

A: I have taken a basic accounting class and a business math class.

**Q: How do you use math?**

A: I use math to estimate how much food I need to buy. I also use math when adjusting recipe amounts to feed large groups of people.

**Q: What are your future plans?**

A: I plan to start my own catering business. The math classes I took will help me manage the financial aspects of my business.

Use with Lesson 3-6

# Truth Tables and Compound Statements

A compound statement is formed by combining two or more simple statements. A compound statement is either true or false depending on whether its simple statements are true or false.

## Activity 1

• Let *P* be "Cindy is at least 17 years old."  • Let *Q* be "Cindy has a driver's license."

| If... | then *P* is | and *Q* is | so *P* AND *Q* is |
|---|---|---|---|
| Cindy is 18 years old. Cindy has a driver's license. | True | True | True |
| Cindy is 17 years old. Cindy does not have a driver's license. | True | False | False |
| Cindy is 16 years old. Cindy has a driver's license. | False | True | False |
| Cindy is 15 years old. Cindy does not have a driver's license. | False | False | False |

*P* **AND** *Q* is true when ___?___.

## Try This

**For each pair of simple statements, tell whether *P* AND *Q* is true or false.**

**1.** *P:* Many birds can fly; *Q:* A zebra is an animal.

## Activity 2

• Let *P* be "Paul plays tennis."  • Let *Q* be "Paul has brown eyes."

| If... | then *P* is | and *Q* is | so *P* OR *Q* is |
|---|---|---|---|
| Paul plays tennis. Paul has brown eyes. | True | True | True |
| Paul plays tennis. Paul has green eyes. | True | False | True |
| Paul does not play tennis. Paul has brown eyes. | False | True | True |
| Paul does not play tennis. Paul has green eyes. | False | False | False |

*P* **OR** *Q* is true when ___?___.

## Try This

**For each pair of simple statements, tell whether *P* OR *Q* is true or false.**

**2.** *P:* The number 12 is even; *Q:* The number 12 is a composite number.

# 3-6 Solving Compound Inequalities

**Prep MA.A.5.3** Use tables and graphs to solve pairs of linear inequalities in two variables.

***Objectives***
Solve compound inequalities in one variable.

Graph solution sets of compound inequalities in one variable.

***Vocabulary***
compound inequality
intersection
union

**Who uses this?**

A lifeguard can use compound inequalities to describe the safe pH levels in a swimming pool. (See Example 1.)

The inequalities you have seen so far are simple inequalities. When two simple inequalities are combined into one statement by the words AND or OR, the result is called a **compound inequality**.

**Know it! Note** — **Compound Inequalities**

| WORDS | ALGEBRA | GRAPH |
|---|---|---|
| All real numbers greater than 2 AND less than 6 | $x > 2$ AND $x < 6$<br>$2 < x < 6$ | 0 2 4 6 8 |
| All real numbers greater than or equal to 2 AND less than or equal to 6 | $x \geq 2$ AND $x \leq 6$<br>$2 \leq x \leq 6$ | 0 2 4 6 8 |
| All real numbers less than 2 OR greater than 6 | $x < 2$ OR $x > 6$ | 0 2 4 6 8 |
| All real numbers less than or equal to 2 OR greater than or equal to 6 | $x \leq 2$ OR $x \geq 6$ | 0 2 4 6 8 |

**EXAMPLE 1** ***Chemistry Application***

**A water analyst recommends that the pH level of swimming pool water be between 7.2 and 7.6 inclusive. Write a compound inequality to show the pH levels that are within the recommended range. Graph the solutions.**

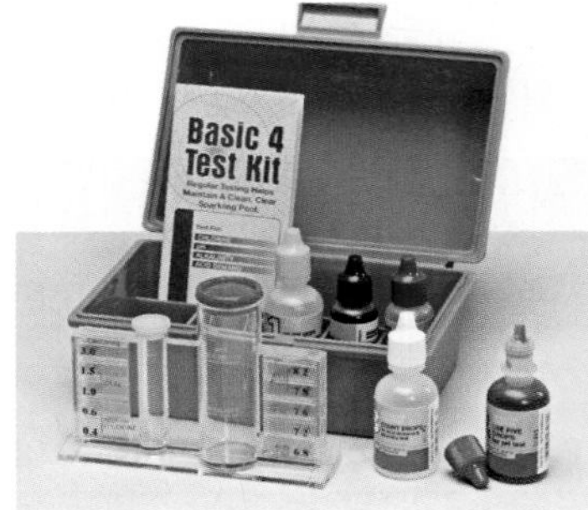


**Helpful Hint**

The phrase "between 7.2 and 7.6 *inclusive*" means that the numbers 7.2 and 7.6 are included in the solutions. Use a solid circle for endpoints that are solutions.

Let $p$ be the pH level of swimming pool water.

| 7.2 | is less than or equal to | pH level | is less than or equal to | 7.6 |
|---|---|---|---|---|
| 7.2 | $\leq$ | $p$ | $\leq$ | 7.6 |

$7.2 \leq p \leq 7.6$

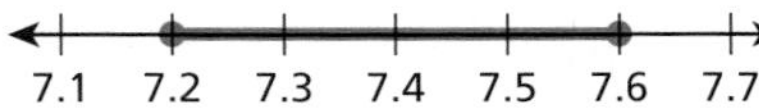

**1.** The free chlorine level in a pool should be between 1.0 and 3.0 parts per million inclusive. Write a compound inequality to show the levels that are within this range. Graph the solutions.

In this diagram, oval $A$ represents some integer solutions of $x < 10$, and oval $B$ represents some integer solutions of $x > 0$. The overlapping region represents numbers that belong in both ovals. Those numbers are solutions of *both* $x < 10$ *and* $x > 0$.

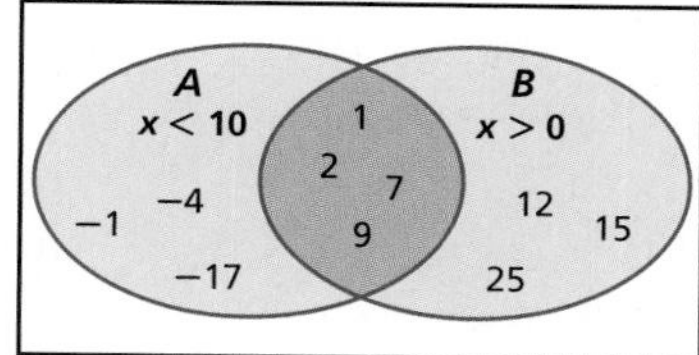


You can graph the solutions of a compound inequality involving AND by using the idea of an overlapping region. The overlapping region is called the **intersection** and shows the numbers that are solutions of both inequalities.

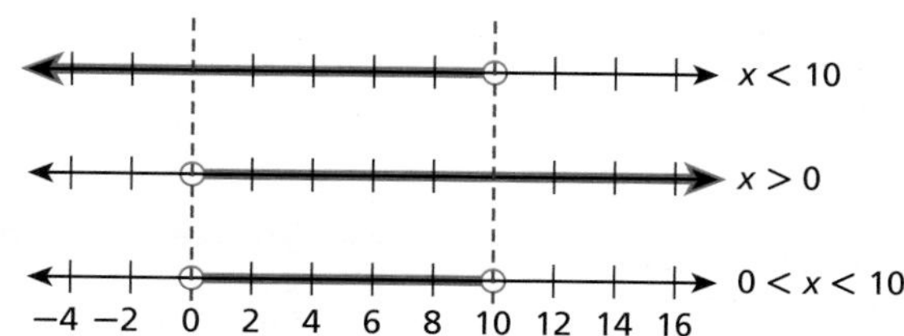


## EXAMPLE 2 Solving Compound Inequalities Involving AND

**Solve each compound inequality and graph the solutions.**

**A** $4 \le x + 2 \le 8$

$4 \le x + 2$ AND $x + 2 \le 8$ — *Write the compound inequality using AND.*

$\underline{-2 \quad\quad -2}$ $\quad$ $\underline{-2 \quad -2}$ — *Solve each simple inequality.*

$2 \le x$ AND $x \le 6$

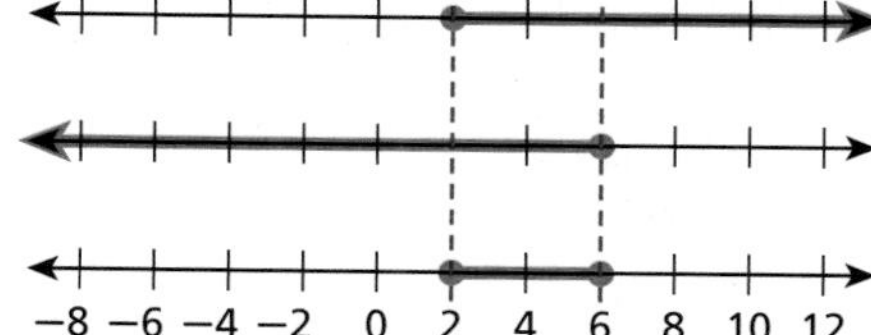


**Remember!**

The statement $-5 \le 2x + 3 \le 9$ consists of two inequalities connected by AND. Example 2B shows a "shorthand" method.

**B** $-5 \le 2x + 3 < 9$

$-5 \le 2x + 3 < 9$ — *Since 3 is added to 2x, subtract 3 from each part of the inequality.*

$\underline{-3 \quad\quad -3 \quad -3}$

$-8 \le 2x < 6$

$\frac{-8}{2} \le \frac{2x}{2} < \frac{6}{2}$ — *Since x is multiplied by 2, divide each part of the inequality by 2.*

$-4 \le x < 3$

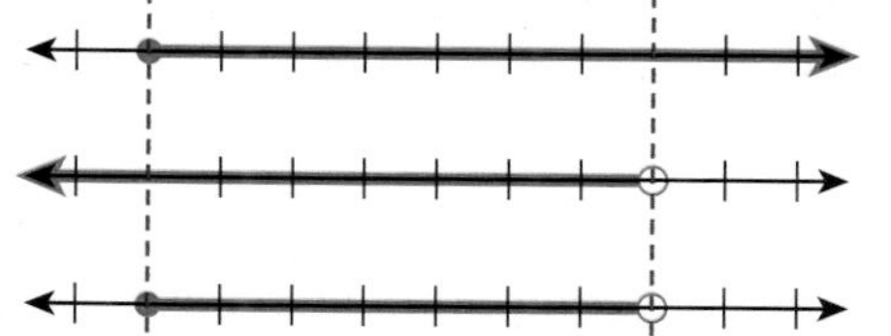

**Solve each compound inequality and graph the solutions.**

**2a.** $-9 < x - 10 < -5$ $\quad$ **2b.** $-4 \le 3n + 5 < 11$

In this diagram, circle $A$ represents some integer solutions of $x < 0$, and circle $B$ represents some integer solutions of $x > 10$. The combined shaded regions represent numbers that are solutions of *either* $x < 0$ *or* $x > 10$.

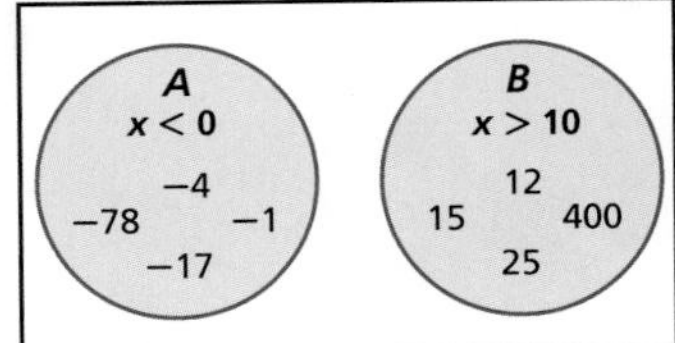


You can graph the solutions of a compound inequality involving OR by using the idea of combining regions. The combined regions are called the **union** and show the numbers that are solutions of either inequality.

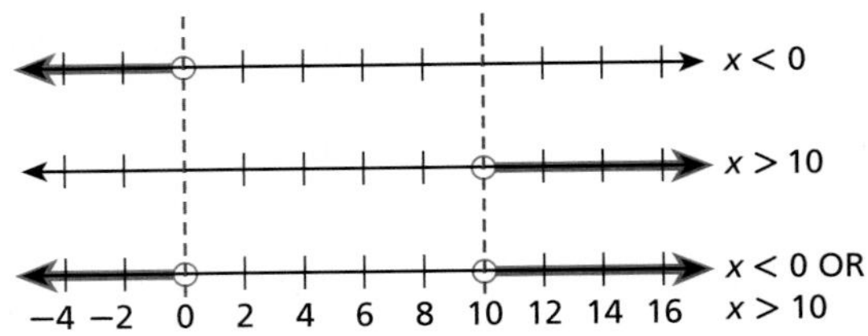


## EXAMPLE 3 Solving Compound Inequalities Involving OR

**Solve each compound inequality and graph the solutions.**

**A** $-4 + a > 1$ **OR** $-4 + a < -3$

$-4 + a > 1$ OR $-4 + a < -3$

$\underline{+4 \quad\quad +4} \quad \underline{+4 \quad\quad +4}$ *Solve each simple inequality.*

$a > 5$ OR $a < 1$

*Graph a > 5.*

*Graph a < 1.*

−4 −3 −2 −1 0 1 2 3 4 5 6

*Graph the union by combining the regions.*

**B** $2x \leq 6$ **OR** $3x > 12$

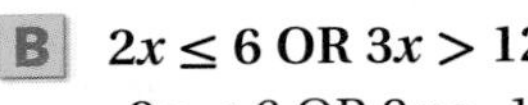

$2x \leq 6$ OR $3x > 12$

$\frac{2x}{2} \leq \frac{6}{2}$ $\frac{3x}{3} > \frac{12}{3}$ *Solve each simple inequality.*

$x \leq 3$ OR $x > 4$

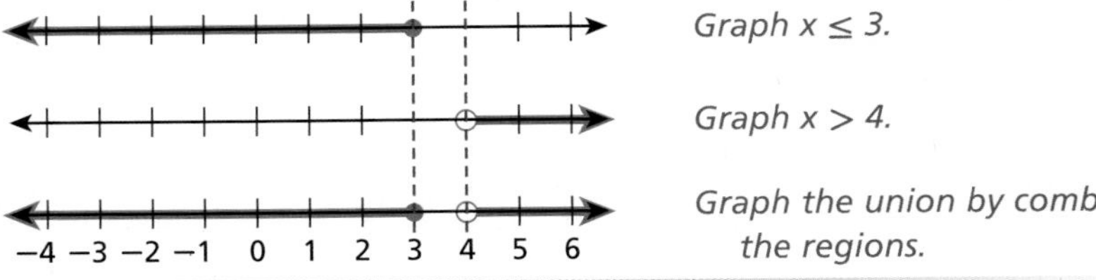

**Solve each compound inequality and graph the solutions.**

**3a.** $2 + r < 12$ OR $r + 5 > 19$

**3b.** $7x \geq 21$ OR $2x < -2$

Every solution of a compound inequality involving AND must be a solution of both parts of the compound inequality. If no numbers are solutions of *both* simple inequalities, then the compound inequality has no solutions.

The solutions of a compound inequality involving OR are not always two separate sets of numbers. There may be numbers that are solutions of both parts of the compound inequality.

## EXAMPLE 4 Writing a Compound Inequality from a Graph

**Write the compound inequality shown by each graph.**

**A**

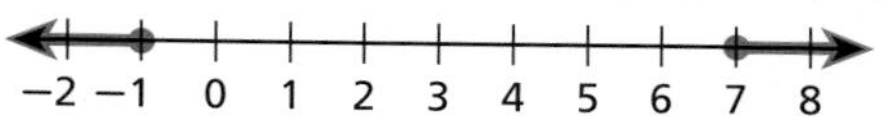


*The shaded portion of the graph is not between two values, so the compound inequality involves OR.*

*On the left, the graph shows an arrow pointing left, so use either $<$ or $\leq$. The solid circle at $-1$ means $-1$ is a solution, so use $\leq$.*

$x \leq -1$

*On the right, the graph shows an arrow pointing right, so use either $>$ or $\geq$. The solid circle at 7 means 7 is a solution, so use $\geq$.*

$x \geq 7$

The compound inequality is $x \leq -1$ OR $x \geq 7$.

**B**

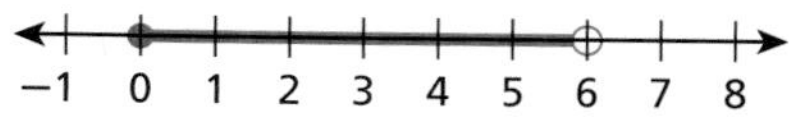


*The shaded portion of the graph is between the values 0 and 6, so the compound inequality involves AND.*

*The shaded values are to the right of 0, so use $>$ or $\geq$. The solid circle at 0 means 0 is a solution, so use $\geq$.*

$x \geq 0$

*The shaded values are to the left of 6, so use $<$ or $\leq$. The empty circle at 6 means 6 is not a solution, so use $<$.*

$x < 6$

The compound inequality is $x \geq 0$ AND $x < 6$.

**Helpful Hint**

The compound inequality in Example 4B can also be written with the variable between the two endpoints.
$0 \leq x < 6$

**Write the compound inequality shown by the graph.**

**4a.**

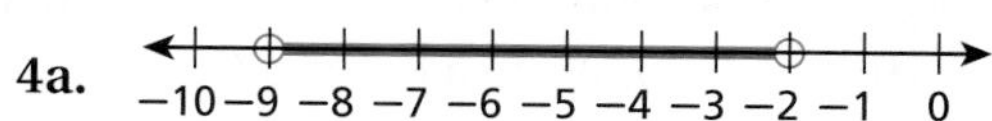


**4b.** −5 −4 −3 −2 −1 0 1 2 3 4 5

### THINK AND DISCUSS

**1.** Describe how to write the compound inequality $y > 4$ AND $y \leq 12$ without using the joining word AND.

**2. GET ORGANIZED** Copy and complete the graphic organizers. Write three solutions in each of the three sections of the diagram. Then write each of your nine solutions in the appropriate column or columns of the table.

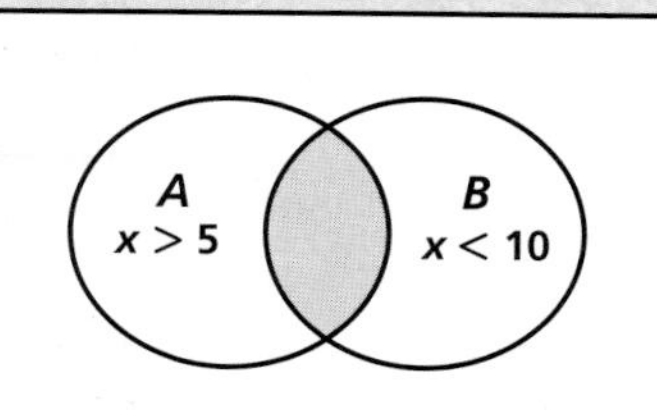


| $x > 5$ AND $x < 10$ | $x > 5$ OR $x < 10$ |
| --- | --- |
| | |

# 3-6 Exercises

Prep MA.A.5.3

go.hrw.com
**Homework Help Online**
KEYWORD: MA7 3-6
**Parent Resources Online**
KEYWORD: MA7 Parent

## GUIDED PRACTICE

1. **Vocabulary** The graph of a(n) ___?___ shows all values that are solutions to both simple inequalities that make a compound inequality. (*union* or *intersection*)

SEE EXAMPLE 1 p. 202

2. **Biology** An iguana needs to live in a warm environment. The temperature in a pet iguana's cage should be between 70° F and 95°F inclusive. Write a compound inequality to show the temperatures that are within the recommended range. Graph the solutions.

SEE EXAMPLE 2 p. 203

**Solve each compound inequality and graph the solutions.**

3. $-3 < x + 2 < 7$
4. $5 \le 4x + 1 \le 13$
5. $2 < x + 2 < 5$
6. $11 < 2x + 3 < 21$

SEE EXAMPLE 3 p. 204

7. $x + 2 < -6$ OR $x + 2 > 6$
8. $r - 1 < 0$ OR $r - 1 > 4$
9. $n + 2 < 3$ OR $n + 3 > 7$
10. $x - 1 < -1$ OR $x - 5 > -1$

SEE EXAMPLE 4 p. 205

**Write the compound inequality shown by each graph.**

11. 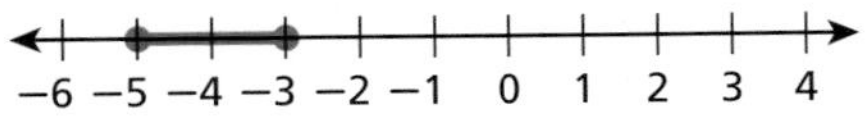

12. 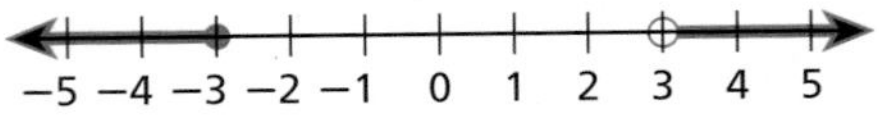

13. 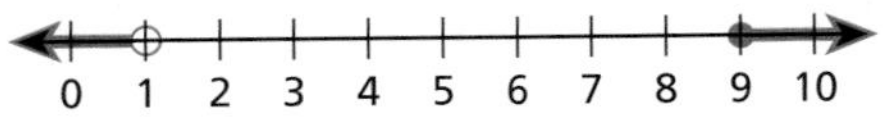

14. 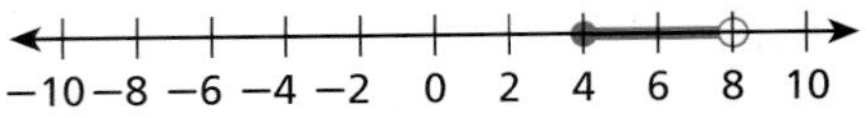

## PRACTICE AND PROBLEM SOLVING

**Independent Practice**

| For Exercises | See Example |
|---|---|
| 15 | 1 |
| 16–19 | 2 |
| 20–23 | 3 |
| 24–27 | 4 |

**Extra Practice**
Skills Practice p. S9
Application Practice p. S30

15. **Meteorology** Earth's atmosphere is made of several layers. A layer called the stratosphere extends from about 16 km above Earth's surface to about 50 km above Earth's surface. Write a compound inequality to show the altitudes that are within the range of the stratosphere. Graph the solutions.

**Solve each compound inequality and graph the solutions.**

16. $-1 < x + 1 < 1$
17. $1 \le 2n - 5 \le 7$
18. $-2 < x - 2 < 2$
19. $5 < 3x - 1 < 17$
20. $x - 4 < -7$ OR $x + 3 > 4$
21. $2x + 1 < 1$ OR $x + 5 > 8$
22. $x + 1 < 2$ OR $x + 5 > 8$
23. $x + 3 < 0$ OR $x - 2 > 0$

**Write the compound inequality shown by each graph.**

24. 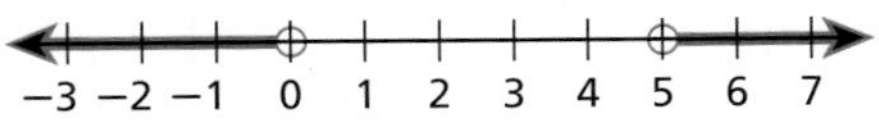

25. 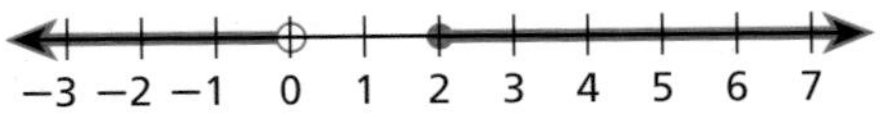

26. 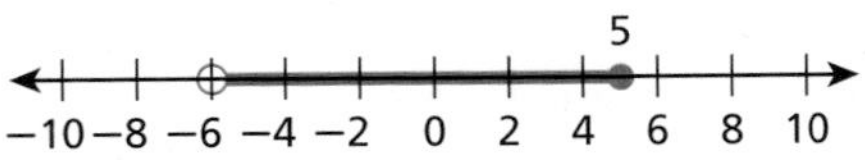

27. 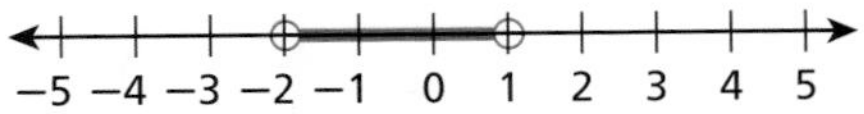

28. **Music** A typical acoustic guitar has a range of three octaves. When the guitar is tuned to "concert pitch," the range of frequencies for those three octaves is between 82.4 Hz and 659.2 Hz inclusive. Write a compound inequality to show the frequencies that are within the range of a typical acoustic guitar. Graph the solutions.

29. This problem will prepare you for the Multi-Step Test Prep on page 210. Jenna's band is going to record a CD at a recording studio. They will pay \$225 to use the studio for one day and \$80 per hour for sound technicians. Jenna has \$200 and hopes to raise an additional \$350 by taking pre-orders for the CDs.

   a. Explain how the inequality $200 \leq 225 + 80n \leq 550$ can be used to find the number of hours Jenna and her band can afford to use the studio and sound technicians.

   b. Solve the inequality. Are there any numbers in the solution set that are not reasonable in this situation?

   c. How much more money does Jenna need to raise if she wants to use the studio and sound technicians for 6 hours?

**Write and graph a compound inequality for the numbers described.**

30. all real numbers between $-6$ and 6

31. all real numbers less than or equal to 2 and greater than or equal to 1

32. all real numbers greater than 0 and less than 15

33. all real numbers between $-10$ and 10 inclusive

**Chemistry**

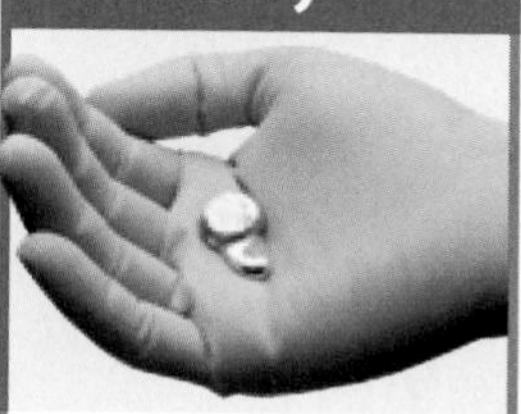

The element gallium is in a solid state at room temperature but becomes a liquid at about 30°C. Gallium stays in a liquid state until it reaches a temperature of about 2204°C.

34. **Transportation** The cruise-control function on Georgina's car should keep the speed of the car within 3 mi/h of the set speed. Write a compound inequality to show the acceptable speeds $s$ if the set speed is 55 mi/h. Graph the solutions.

35. **Chemistry** Water is not a liquid if its temperature is above 100°C or below 0°C. Write a compound inequality for the temperatures $t$ when water is not a liquid.

**Solve each compound inequality and graph the solutions.**

36. $5 \leq 4b - 3 \leq 9$

37. $-3 < x - 1 < 4$

38. $r + 2 < -2$ OR $r - 2 > 2$

39. $2a - 5 < -5$ OR $3a - 2 > 1$

40. $x - 4 \geq 5$ AND $x - 4 \leq 5$

41. $n - 4 < -2$ OR $n + 1 > 6$

42. **Sports** The ball used in a soccer game may not weigh more than 16 ounces or less than 14 ounces at the start of the match. After $1\frac{1}{2}$ ounces of air was added to a ball, the ball was approved for use in a game. Write and solve a compound inequality to show how much the ball might have weighed before the air was added.

43. **Meteorology** Tornado damage is rated using the Fujita scale shown in the table. A tornado has a wind speed of 200 miles per hour. Write and solve a compound inequality to show how many miles per hour the wind speed would need to increase for the tornado to be rated "devastating" but not "incredible."

**Fujita Tornado Scale**

| Category | Type | Wind Speed (mi/h) |
|---|---|---|
| F0 | Weak | 40 to 72 |
| F1 | Moderate | 73 to 112 |
| F2 | Significant | 113 to 157 |
| F3 | Severe | 158 to 206 |
| F4 | Devastating | 207 to 260 |
| F5 | Incredible | 261 to 318 |

44. Give a real world situation that can be described by a compound inequality. Write the inequality that describes your situation.

45. **Write About It** How are the graphs of the compound inequality $x < 3$ AND $x < 7$ and the compound inequality $x < 3$ OR $x < 7$ different? How are the graphs alike? Explain.

46. **Critical Thinking** If there is no solution to a compound inequality, does the compound inequality involve OR or AND? Explain.

## TEST PREP

Prep MA.A.5.3

47. Which of the following describes the solutions of $-x + 1 > 2$ OR $x - 1 > 2$?
   (A) all real numbers greater than 1 or less than 3
   (B) all real numbers greater than 3 or less than 1
   (C) all real numbers greater than $-1$ or less than 3
   (D) all real numbers greater than 3 or less than $-1$

48. Which of the following is a graph of the solutions of $x - 3 < 2$ AND $x + 3 > 2$?

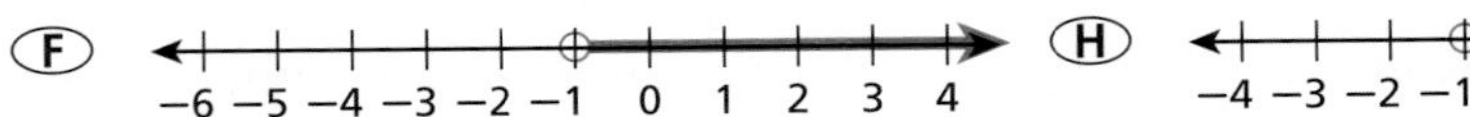

49. Which compound inequality is shown by the graph?

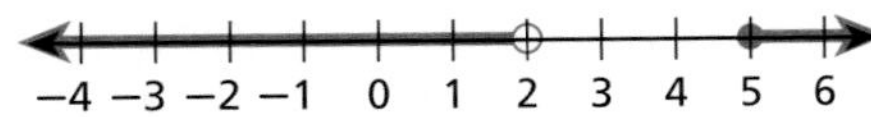

   (A) $x \leq 2$ OR $x > 5$
   (B) $x < 2$ OR $x \geq 5$
   (C) $x \leq 2$ OR $x \geq 5$
   (D) $x \geq 2$ OR $x > 5$

50. Which of the following is a solution of $x + 1 \geq 3$ AND $x + 1 \leq 3$?
   (F) 0 (G) 1 (H) 2 (J) 3

## CHALLENGE AND EXTEND

**Solve and graph each compound inequality.**

51. $2c - 10 < 5 - 3c < 7c$

52. $5p - 10 < p + 6 < 3p$

53. $2s \leq 18 - s$ OR $5s \geq s + 36$

54. $9 - x \geq 5x$ OR $20 - 3x \leq 17$

55. Write a compound inequality that represents all values of $x$ that are NOT solutions to $x < -1$ OR $x > 3$.

56. For the compound inequality $x + 2 \geq a$ AND $x - 7 \leq b$, find values of $a$ and $b$ for which the only solution is $x = 1$.

## SPIRAL REVIEW

**Simplify each expression. Justify each step.** *(Lesson 1-7)*

57. $4(x - 3) + 7$

58. $5x - 4y - x + 3y$

59. $6a - 3(a - 1)$

**Generate ordered pairs for each function for $x = -2, -1, 0, 1$, and 2. Graph the ordered pairs and describe the pattern.** *(Lesson 1-8)*

60. $y = -2x + 2$

61. $y = x^2 - 1$

62. $y = x^2 + (-2)$

**Solve each inequality and graph the solutions.** *(Lesson 3-4)*

63. $3m - 5 < 1$

64. $2(x + 4) > 6$

65. $11 \leq 7 - 2x$

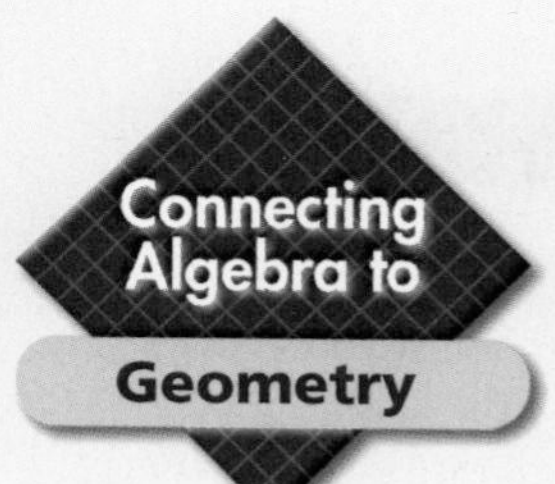


# Triangle Inequality

For any triangle, the sum of the lengths of any two sides is greater than the length of the third side.

*See Skills Bank page S60*

The sides of this triangle are labeled $a$, $b$, and $c$. You can use the Triangle Inequality to write three statements about the triangle.

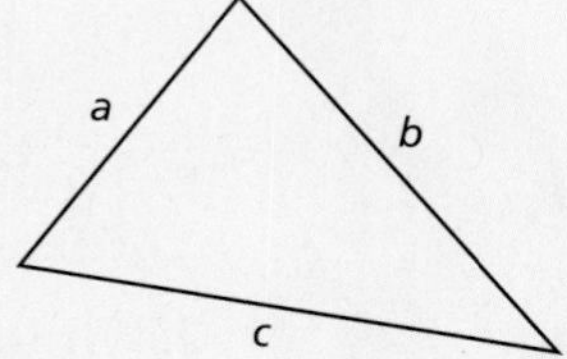


$a + b > c$ $\quad a + c > b$ $\quad b + c > a$

Unless all three of the inequalities are true, the lengths $a$, $b$, and $c$ cannot form a triangle.

## Example 1

**Can three side lengths of 25 cm, 15 cm, and 5 cm form a triangle?**

**a.** $25 + 15 > 5$
$40 > 5$ *True*

**b.** $25 + 5 > 15$
$30 > 15$ *True*

**c.** $15 + 5 > 25$
$20 > 25$ *False*

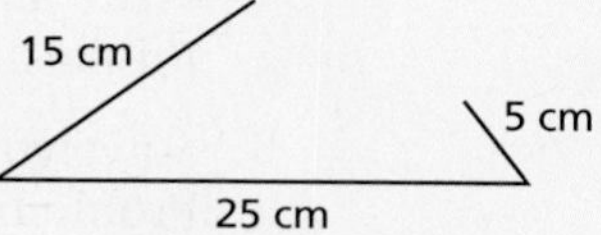


One of the inequalities is false, so the three lengths will not make a triangle. The situation is shown in the figure to the right.

## Example 2

**Two sides of a triangle measure 8 ft and 10 ft. What is the range of lengths of the third side?**

Start by writing three statements about the triangle. Use $x$ for the unknown side length.

**a.** $8 + 10 > x$
$18 > x$
*The third side must be shorter than 18 ft.*

**b.** $8 + x > 10$
$8 + x - 8 > 10 - 8$
$x > 2$
*The third side must be longer than 2 ft.*

**c.** $x + 10 > 8$
$x + 10 - 10 > 8 - 10$
$x > -2$
*This provides no new useful information.*

From part **a,** the third side must be shorter than 18 ft. And from part **b,** it must be longer than 2 ft. An inequality showing this is $2 < x < 18$.

## Try This

**Decide whether the three lengths given can form a triangle. If not, explain.**

**1.** 14 ft, 30 ft, 10 ft

**2.** 11 cm, 8 cm, 17 cm

**3.** $6\frac{1}{2}$ yd, 3 yd, $2\frac{3}{4}$ yd

**Write a compound inequality for the range of lengths of the third side of each triangle.**

**4.**

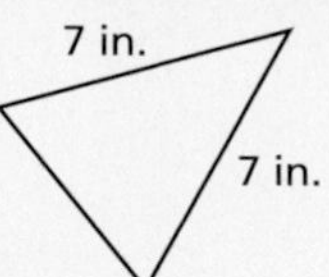


**5.**

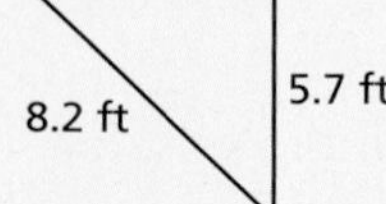


**6.**

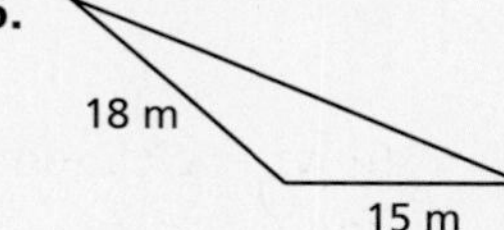

## Multi-Step and Compound Inequalities

**Guitar Picks** Cullen and his band are interested in recording a CD of their music. The recording studio charges $450 to record the music and then charges $5 for each CD. The band is required to spend at least $1000 for the total of the recording and CD charges.

1. Write an equation for the cost $C$ of the CDs based on the number of CDs $n$.
2. Write an inequality that can be used to determine the minimum number of CDs that must be burned at this studio to meet the $1000 total.
3. Solve your inequality from Problem 2.
4. The band orders the minimum number of CDs found in Problem 3. They want to sell the CDs and make at least as much money as they spent for the recording studio and making the CDs. Write an inequality that can be solved to determine the minimum amount the band should charge for their CDs.
5. Solve your inequality from Problem 4.
6. If the band has 30 more CDs made than the minimum number found in Problem 4 and charges the minimum price found in Problem 5, will they make a profit? If so, how much profit will the band make?

# READY TO GO ON?

CHAPTER 3

SECTION 3B

## Quiz for Lessons 3-4 Through 3-6

### 3-4 Solving Two-Step and Multi-Step Inequalities

**Solve each inequality and graph the solutions.**

**1.** $2x + 3 < 9$

**2.** $3t - 2 > 10$

**3.** $7 \geq 1 - 6r$

**Solve each inequality.**

**4.** $2(x - 3) > -1$

**5.** $\frac{1}{3}a + \frac{1}{2} > \frac{2}{3}$

**6.** $2^2 - x > 4(3 - 5)$

**7.** $24b + 5 - 6b \leq 41$

**8.** $-7(7 + x) \geq -50$

**9.** $11d - (-2) < -15d$

**10.** $15 < 5(m - 7)$

**11.** $2 + (-6) > 8p$

**12.** The average of Mindy's two test scores must be at least 92 to make an A in the class. Mindy got an 88 on her first test. What scores can she get on her second test to make an A in the class?

### 3-5 Solving Inequalities with Variables on Both Sides

**Solve each inequality and graph the solutions.**

**13.** $5x < 3x + 8$

**14.** $6p - 3 > 9p$

**15.** $r - 8 \geq 3r - 12$

**Solve each inequality.**

**16.** $3(y + 6) > 2(y + 4)$

**17.** $4(5 - g) \geq g$

**18.** $5(t + 3) < 5t - 3$

**19.** $-2(6 + h) < 3(1 + h)$

**20.** $4x < 4(x - 1)$

**21.** $3(1 - x) \geq -3(x + 2)$

**22.** $9d > 3(1 - d)$

**23.** $16(s - 2) \leq 4(4s - 5)$

**24.** $5q \leq 2(q + 3)$

**25.** $3n > 5(n - 2)$

**26.** Phillip has \$100 in the bank and deposits \$18 per month. Gil has \$145 in the bank and deposits \$15 per month. For how many months will Gil have a larger bank balance than Phillip?

### 3-6 Solving Compound Inequalities

**Solve each compound inequality and graph the solutions.**

**27.** $-2 \leq x + 3 < 9$

**28.** $m + 2 < -1$ OR $m - 2 > 6$

**29.** $-3 \geq x - 1$ AND $x - 5 > 2$

**30.** $-2 > r + 2$ OR $r + 4 < 5$

**31.** $-2x > -8$ AND $x + 7 \geq 6$

**32.** $5 > y + 9$ OR $y - 4 > 2$

**33.** It is recommended that a certain medicine be stored in temperatures above 32° F and below 70° F. Write a compound inequality to show the acceptable storage temperatures for this medicine.

EXTENSION

# Solving Absolute-Value Inequalities

**Prep MA.A.5.3** Use tables and graphs to solve pairs of linear inequalities in two variables.

***Objective***
Solve inequalities in one variable involving absolute-value expressions.

When an inequality contains an absolute-value expression, it can be written as a compound inequality. The inequality $|x| < 5$ describes all real numbers whose distance from 0 is less than 5 units. The solutions are all numbers between $-5$ and 5, so $|x| < 5$ can be written as $-5 < x < 5$, which is the compound inequality $x > -5$ AND $x < 5$.

**Absolute-Value Inequalities Involving <**

| WORDS | NUMBERS |
|---|---|
| The inequality $\lvert x\rvert < a$ (when $a > 0$) asks, "What values of $x$ have an absolute value less than $a$?" The solutions are numbers between $-a$ and $a$. | $\lvert x\rvert < 5$<br>$-5 < x < 5$<br>$x > -5$ AND $x < 5$ |
| **GRAPH** | **ALGEBRA** |
| ← $a$ units →← $a$ units →<br>$-a$ 0 $a$ | $\lvert x\rvert < a$ (when $a > 0$)<br>$-a < x < a$<br>$x > -a$ AND $x < a$ |

**The same properties are true for inequalities that use the symbol ≤.**

**EXAMPLE 1**

## Solving Absolute-Value Inequalities Involving <

**Solve each inequality and graph the solutions. Then write the solutions as a compound inequality.**

**A** $|x| + 3 < 12$

$$\begin{aligned} |x| + 3 &< 12 \\ -3 \quad &\;\; -3 \\ |x| &< 9 \end{aligned}$$

*Since 3 is added to $|x|$, subtract 3 from both sides to undo the addition.*

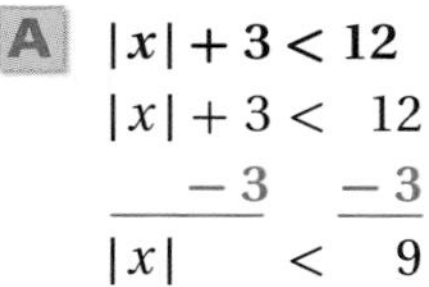


*Think, "The distance from x to 0 is less than 9 units."*

$x > -9$ AND $x < 9$

$-9 < x < 9$

*Write as a compound inequality.*

**Helpful Hint**

Just like solving absolute-value equations, when you solve absolute-value inequalities, isolate the absolute-value expression.

**B** $|x| - 7 < -3$

$$\begin{aligned} |x| - 7 &< -3 \\ +7 \quad &\;\; +7 \\ |x| &< 4 \end{aligned}$$

*Since 7 is subtracted from $|x|$, add 7 to both sides to undo the subtraction.*

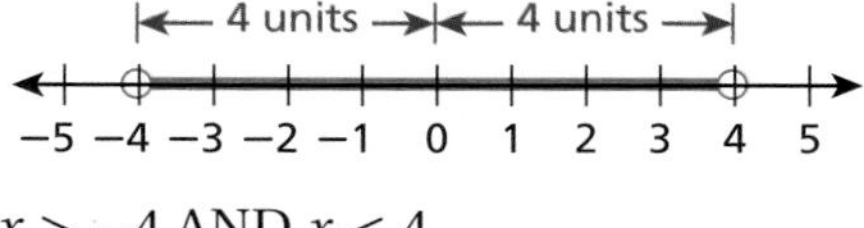


*Think, "The distance from x to 0 is less than 4 units."*

$x > -4$ AND $x < 4$

$-4 < x < 4$

*Write as a compound inequality.*

**Solve each inequality and graph the solutions. Then write the solutions as a compound inequality.**

**C** $\mathbf{2|x| \le 6}$

$\frac{2|x|}{2} \le \frac{6}{2}$ — *Since |x| is multiplied by 2, divide both sides by 2.*

$|x| \le 3$

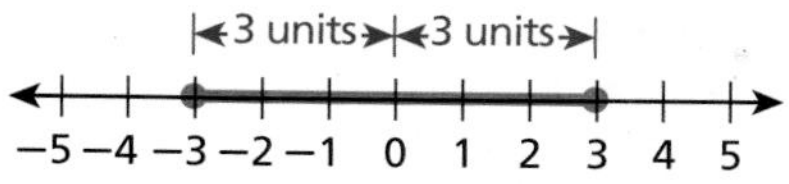


*Think, "The distance from x to 0 is less than or equal to 3 units."*

$x \ge -3$ AND $x \le 3$ — *Write as a compound inequality.*

$-3 \le x \le 3$

**D** $\mathbf{|x+3| - 4.5 \le 7.5}$

$|x+3| - 4.5 \le 7.5$ — *Since 4.5 is subtracted from |x + 3|, add 4.5 to both sides.*

$\quad\quad\quad\;\; +4.5 \quad +4.5$

$|x+3| \le 12$

*Think, "The distance from x to −3 is less than or equal to 12 units."*

$x + 3 \ge -12$ AND $x + 3 \le 12$ — *x + 3 is between −12 and 12, inclusive.*

$\quad -3 \quad -3 \quad\quad -3 \quad -3$

$x \ge -15$ AND $x \le 9$

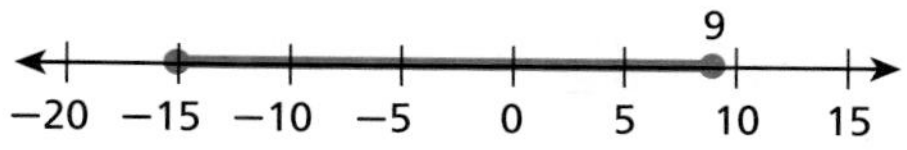


$x \ge -15$ AND $x \le 9$ — *Write as a compound inequality.*

$-15 \le x \le 9$

**CHECK IT OUT!** **Solve each inequality and graph the solutions. Then write the solutions as a compound inequality.**

**1a.** $|x| + 12 < 15$

**1b.** $|x| - 6 < -5$

The inequality $|x| > 5$ describes all real numbers whose distance from 0 is greater than 5 units. The solutions are all numbers less than −5 or greater than 5. The inequality $|x| > 5$ can be written as the compound inequality $x < -5$ OR $x > 5$.

**Know it! Note**

## Absolute-Value Inequalities Involving >

| WORDS | NUMBERS |
|---|---|
| The inequality $|x| > a$ (when $a > 0$) asks, "What values of $x$ have an absolute value greater than $a$?" The solutions are numbers less than $-a$ or greater than $a$. | $|x| > 5$<br>$x < -5$ OR $x > 5$ |
| **GRAPH** | **ALGEBRA** |
| 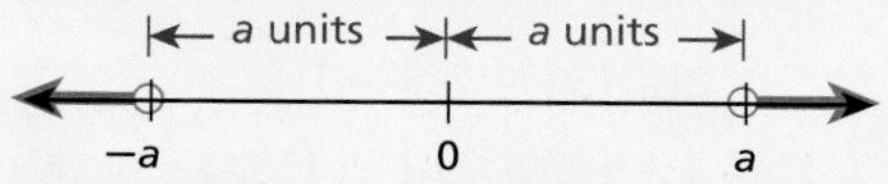 | $|x| > a$ (when $a > 0$)<br>$x < -a$ OR $x > a$ |



**The same properties are true for inequalities that use the symbol ≥.**

## EXAMPLE 2 Solving Absolute-Value Inequalities Involving >

**Solve each inequality and graph the solutions. Then write the solutions as a compound inequality.**

**A** $|x| + 5 > 14$

$|x| + 5 > 14$ — *Since 5 is added to $|x|$, subtract 5 from both sides to undo the addition.*

$\quad\; -5 \;\; -5$

$|x| \qquad > 9$

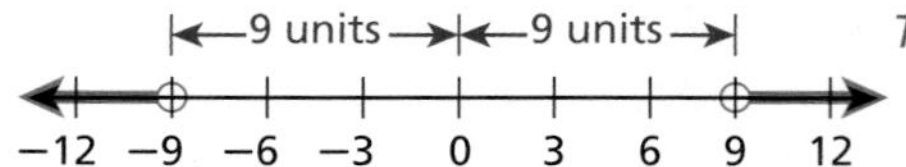


*Think, "The distance from x to 0 is greater than 9 units."*

$x < -9$ OR $x > 9$ — *Write as a compound inequality.*

**B** $|x| - 20 > -13$

$|x| - 20 > -13$ — *Since 20 is subtracted from $|x|$, add 20 to both sides to undo the subtraction.*

$\quad\; +20 \;\; +20$

$|x| \qquad > 7$

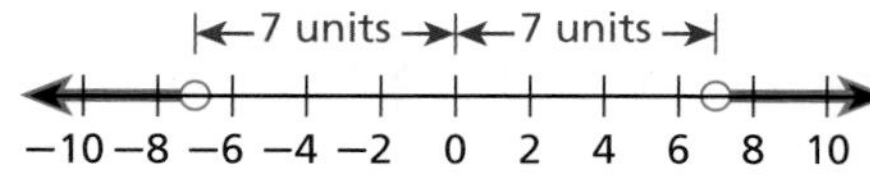


*Think, "The distance from x to 0 is greater than 7 units."*

$x < -7$ OR $x > 7$ — *Write as a compound inequality.*

**C** $|x - 8| + 5 \geq 11$

$|x - 8| + 5 \geq \; 11$ — *Since 5 is added to $|x - 8|$, subtract 5 from both sides to undo the addition.*

$\qquad\quad -5 \quad -5$

$|x - 8| \quad \geq \quad 6$

*Think, "The distance from x to 8 is greater than or equal to 6 units."*

$x - 8 \leq -6$ OR $x - 8 \geq 6$

$x - 8 \leq -6$ OR $x - 8 \geq \; 6$ — *Solve the two inequalities.*

$\;\; +8 \;\; +8 \qquad\quad +8 \;\; +8$

$x \quad \leq \; 2$ OR $x \quad \geq \; 14$

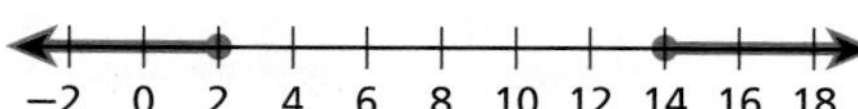


$x \leq 2$ OR $x \geq 14$ — *Write as a compound inequality.*

**Solve each inequality and graph the solutions. Then write the solutions as a compound inequality.**

**2a.** $|x| + 10 \geq 12$

**2b.** $|x| - 7 > -1$

**2c.** $\left|x + 2\frac{1}{2}\right| + \frac{1}{2} \geq 4$

EXTENSION

# Exercises

**Solve each absolute-value inequality and graph the solutions.**

1. $|x| - 5 \leq -2$
2. $|x| - 6 > 16$
3. $|x + 1| - 7.8 < 6.2$
4. $|x + 5| - 4\frac{1}{2} \geq 7\frac{1}{2}$
5. $|3x| + 2 < 8$
6. $|x| + 2.9 > 8.6$

**Write and solve an absolute-value inequality for each expression. Graph the solutions on a number line.**

7. all numbers whose absolute value is less than or equal to 15
8. all numbers that have an absolute value greater than 7
9. all numbers less than 3 units from 2 on the number line
10. all numbers at least 2 units from 8 on the number line
11. Find all values of $x$ that make $|x - 5|$

    a. less than 11.  b. at least 4.  c. less than or equal to 8.

**Tell whether the given value of $x$ is a solution of the inequality.**

12. $|x| > 3$; $x = -5$
13. $|2x| \leq 8$; $x = 6$
14. $|x - 1.2| < 5.4$; $x = 6.6$
15. $\left|x + 3\frac{1}{2}\right| - 2\frac{1}{4} \geq 5\frac{1}{4}$; $x = -11$

**Write an absolute-value inequality for each graph.**

16. −5 −4 −3 −2 −1 0 1 2 3 4 5

17. −5 −4 −3 −2 −1 0 1 2 3 4 5

18. $-6\frac{1}{2}$ $6\frac{1}{2}$ −10 −8 −6 −4 −2 0 2 4 6 8 10

19. −7 7 −10 −8 −6 −4 −2 0 2 4 6 8 10

20. **ERROR ANALYSIS** A student solved the absolute-value inequality below. Find and explain the error(s) in the student's work. What is the correct answer?

$$|x - 6| + 3 \geq 8$$
$$|x - 6| + 3 \geq 8$$
$$\underline{\quad -3 \quad -3}$$
$$|x - 6| \geq 5$$
$$-5 \geq x - 6 \geq 5$$
$$\underline{+6 \qquad +6 \qquad +6}$$
$$1 \geq x \geq 11$$

21. **Write About It** Describe how to use an absolute-value inequality to find all the values on a number line that are within 5 units of −6.

CHAPTER 3

# Study Guide: Review

## Vocabulary



**Complete the sentences below with vocabulary words from the list above.**

1. A(n) ___?___ is a mathematical statement that two quantities are not equal.
2. The numbers that are solutions to either inequality of a compound inequality is the ___?___.
3. A statement formed by combining two simple inequalities with the words AND or OR is a(n) ___?___.
4. The numbers that are solutions to both inequalities of a compound inequality is the ___?___.
5. Any value that makes the inequality true is a(n) ___?___.

## 3-1 Graphing and Writing Inequalities *(pp. 168–173)*

**Prep for MA.A.5.3**

### EXAMPLES

■ **Graph the inequality $y > -1$.**

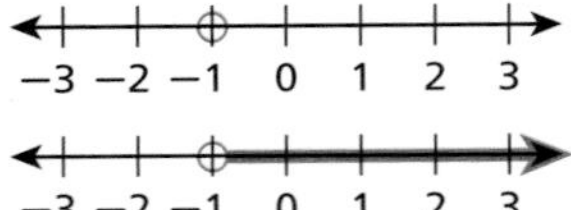


*Draw an empty circle at −1.*

*Shade all the numbers greater than −1.*

■ **Write the inequality shown by the graph.**

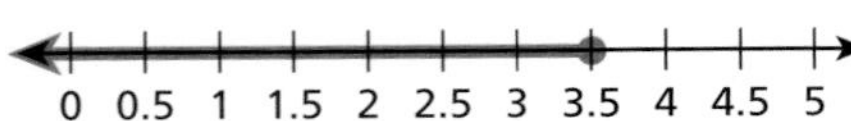


$n \le 3.5$ *Use the variable n.*
*The arrow points left, so use either $<$ or $\le$. The closed circle means 3.5 is a solution, so use $\le$.*

■ **Write an inequality for the situation and graph the solutions.**

Applicants for a driver's permit must be at least 16 years old.

| age | must be at least | 16 years |
|---|---|---|
| $a$ | $\ge$ | 16 |

0 2 4 6 8 10 12 14 16 18 20

### EXERCISES

**Graph each inequality.**

6. $x > -3$
7. $p \le 4$
8. $-1 > t$
9. $r \ge 9.5$
10. $2(3 - 5) < k$
11. $w < 3$

**Write the inequality shown by each graph.**

12. 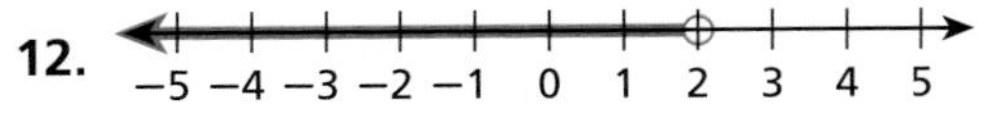


13. −3.5; −4 −3 −2 −1 0 1

14. −12 −10 −8 −6 −4 −2 0

**Define a variable and write an inequality for each situation. Graph the solutions.**

15. The temperature must be at least 72°F.
16. No more than 12 students were present.
17. It takes less than 30 minutes to complete the lab activity.

## 3-2 Solving Inequalities by Adding or Subtracting *(pp. 174–179)*  Prep for MA.A.5.3

### EXAMPLES

**Solve each inequality and graph the solutions.**

- **$x + 6 > 2$**

$$\begin{aligned} x + 6 &> 2 \\ -6 & \quad -6 \\ x &> -4 \end{aligned}$$

*Since 6 is added to x, subtract 6 from both sides.*

−5 −4 −3 −2 −1 0 1 2 3 4 5

- **$n - 1.3 < 3.2$**

$$\begin{aligned} n - 1.3 &< 3.2 \\ +1.3 & \quad +1.3 \\ n &< 4.5 \end{aligned}$$

*Since 1.3 is subtracted from x, add 1.3 to both sides.*

0 0.5 1 1.5 2 2.5 3 3.5 4 4.5 5

### EXERCISES

**Solve each inequality and graph the solutions.**

**18.** $t + 3 < 10$

**19.** $k - 7 \leq -5$

**20.** $-1 < m + 4$

**21.** $x + 2.3 \geq 6.8$

**22.** $w - 3 < 6.5$

**23.** $4 > a - 1$

**24.** $h - \frac{1}{4} < \frac{3}{4}$

**25.** $5 > 7 + v$

**26.** Tammy wants to run at least 10 miles per week. So far this week, she ran 4.5 miles. Write and solve an inequality to determine how many more miles Tammy must run this week to reach her goal.

**27.** Rob has a gift card for $50. So far, he has selected a shirt that costs $32. Write and solve an inequality to determine the amount Rob could spend without exceeding the gift card limit.

## 3-3 Solving Inequalities by Multiplying or Dividing *(pp. 180–185)*  Prep for MA.A.5.3

### EXAMPLES

- **Solve $\frac{p}{-3} \leq 6$ and graph the solutions.**

$$\frac{p}{-3} \leq 6$$

*Since p is divided by −3, multiply both sides by −3.*

$$-3 \cdot \frac{p}{-3} \geq -3 \cdot 6$$

$$p \geq -18$$

*Change ≤ to ≥.*

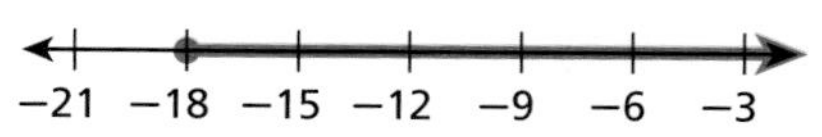


- **What possible numbers of pizzas that cost $5.50 each can be purchased with $30?**

Let $n$ represent the number of pizzas that can be purchased.

| $5.50 | times | number of pizzas | is at most | $30. |
|---|---|---|---|---|
| 5.50 | • | $n$ | ≤ | 30 |

$$5.50n \leq 30$$

*Since n is multiplied by 5.50, divide both sides by 5.50.*

$$\frac{5.50n}{5.50} \leq \frac{30}{5.50}$$

$$n \leq 5\frac{5}{11}$$

Only a whole number of pizzas can be purchased, so 0, 1, 2, 3, 4, or 5 pizzas can be purchased.

### EXERCISES

**Solve each inequality and graph the solutions.**

**28.** $3a \leq 15$

**29.** $-18 < 6t$

**30.** $\frac{p}{4} > 2$

**31.** $\frac{2}{5}x \leq -10$

**32.** $-3n < -18$

**33.** $\frac{g}{-2} > 6$

**34.** $-2k < 14$

**35.** $-3 > \frac{1}{3}r$

**36.** $27 < -9h$

**37.** $-0.4g > -1$

**38.** What are the possible numbers of notebooks costing $1.39 that can be purchased with $10?

**39.** The senior class is selling lanyards as a fundraiser. The profit for each lanyard is $0.75. Write and solve an inequality to determine the number of lanyards the class must sell to make a profit of at least $250.

Prep for MA.A.5.3

### EXAMPLES

**Solve each inequality and graph the solution.**

■ **$18 + 3t > -12$**

$$18 + 3t > -12$$
$$\underline{-18 \qquad -18}$$
$$3t > -30$$

*Since 18 is added to 3t, subtract 18 from both sides.*

$$\frac{3t}{3} > \frac{-30}{3}$$
$$t > -10$$

*Since t is multiplied by 3, divide both sides by 3.*

−12 −10 −8 −6 −4 −2 0

■ **$3^2 - 5 \le 2(1 + x)$**

$$3^2 - 5 \le 2(1 + x)$$
$$9 - 5 \le 2(1 + x)$$

*Simplify the left side using order of operations.*

$$4 \le 2(1 + x)$$
$$4 \le 2(1) + 2(x)$$

*Distribute 2 on the right side.*

$$4 \le 2 + 2x$$
$$\underline{-2 \quad -2}$$
$$2 \le 2x$$

*Since 2 is added to 2x, subtract 2 from both sides*

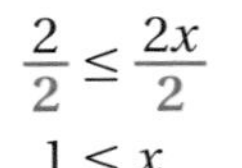

$$\frac{2}{2} \le \frac{2x}{2}$$
$$1 \le x$$

*Since x is multiplied by 2, divide both sides by 2.*

■ **Car rental company A charges \$45 per day to rent a certain car. Car rental company B charges \$30 per day plus \$0.20 per mile to rent a similar car. For how many miles is the cost at car rental company B more than the cost at car rental company A?**

Let $m$ represent the number of miles traveled per day.

| \$30 | plus | \$0.20 | times | $m$ | is more than | \$45. |
|---|---|---|---|---|---|---|
| 30 | + | 0.20 | • | $m$ | > | 45 |

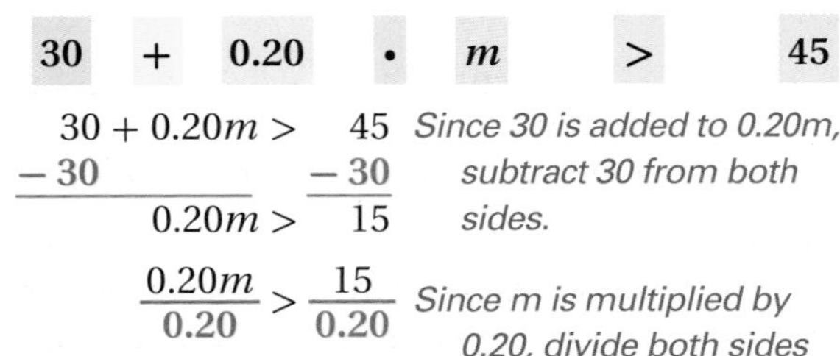

$$30 + 0.20m > 45$$
$$\underline{-30 \qquad\qquad -30}$$
$$0.20m > 15$$

*Since 30 is added to 0.20m, subtract 30 from both sides.*

$$\frac{0.20m}{0.20} > \frac{15}{0.20}$$
$$m > 75$$

*Since m is multiplied by 0.20, divide both sides by 0.20.*

The cost at company B is higher for more than 75 miles.

### EXERCISES

**Solve each inequality and graph the solutions.**

**40.** $3x + 4 < 19$

**41.** $7 \le 2t - 5$

**42.** $\frac{m + 3}{2} > -4$

**43.** $9 - 3r > -9$

**44.** $\frac{5 - 4p}{7} < 3$

**45.** $5 < 2g + 19$

**46.** $2(x + 5) < 8$

**47.** $-4(2 - 5) > (-3)^2 - h$

**48.** $\frac{1}{5}x + \frac{1}{2} > \frac{4}{5}$

**49.** $0.5(b - 2) \le 4$

**50.** $\frac{1}{3}y - \frac{1}{2} > \frac{2}{3}$

**51.** $6 - 0.2n < 9$

**52.** Carl's Cable Company charges \$55 for monthly service plus \$4 for each pay-per-view movie. Teleview Cable Company charges \$110 per month with no fee for movies. For what number of movies is the cost of Carl's Cable Company less than the cost of Teleview?

**Use the table for Exercise 53.**

| Month | Account Balance (\$) |
|---|---|
| 1 | 245 |
| 2 | 275 |
| 3 | 305 |
| 4 | 335 |

**53.** If the pattern continues, for how many months will the account balance be less than \$1000?

**54.** Company A has a sales position with a yearly salary of \$42,000. Company B has a similar sales position with a salary of \$39,000 plus 1% commission on yearly sales. For what amount of yearly sales is the salary at company A greater than the salary and commission at company B?

## 3-5 Solving Inequalities with Variables on Both Sides *(pp. 194–200)* Prep for MA.A.5.3

### EXAMPLES

■ **Solve $b + 16 < 3b$ and graph the solutions.**

$b + 16 > 3b$ *Subtract b from both sides so that the coefficient of b is positive.*

$\underline{-b \qquad -b}$

$16 > 2b$

$\frac{16}{2} > \frac{2b}{2}$ *Since b is multiplied by 2, divide both sides by 2.*

$8 > b$

−8 −6 −4 −2 0 2 4 6 8 10 12

**Solve each inequality.**

■ $3(1 - k) > 4 - 3k$

$3(1) - 3(k) > 4 - 3k$ *Distribute the 3.*

$3 - 3k > 4 - 3k$

$\underline{+3k \qquad +3k}$ *Add 3k to both sides.*

$3 > 4$ *False statement*

There are no solutions.

■ $12x - 1 > 12x - 19$ *Subtract 12x from both sides.*

$\underline{-12x \qquad -12x}$

$-1 > -19$ *True statement*

All real numbers are solutions.

### EXERCISES

**Solve the inequality and graph the solutions.**

**55.** $5 + 2m < -3m$

**56.** $y \leq 6 + 4y$

**57.** $4c - 7 > 9c + 8$

**58.** $-3(2 - q) \geq 6(q + 1)$

**59.** $2(5 - x) < 3x$

**60.** $3.5t - 1.8 < 1.6t + 3.9$

**Solve each inequality.**

**61.** $d - 2 < d - 4$

**62.** $2(1 - x) > -2(1 + x)$

**63.** $4(1 - p) < 4(2 + p)$

**64.** $3w + 1 > 3(w - 1)$

**65.** $5(4 - k) < 5k$

**66.** $3(c + 1) > 3c + 5$

**67.** Hanna has a savings account with a balance of \$210 and deposits \$16 per month. Faith has a savings account with a balance of \$175 and deposits \$20 per month. Write and solve an inequality to determine the number of months Hanna's account balance will be greater than Faith's account balance.

## 3-6 Solving Compound Inequalities *(pp. 202–208)*

Prep for MA.A.5.3

### EXAMPLES

**Solve each compound inequality and graph the solutions.**

■ $-3 < c + 5 \leq 11$ *Since 5 is added to c, subtract 5 from each part of the inequality.*

$\underline{-5 \qquad -5 \quad -5}$

$-8 < c \leq 6$

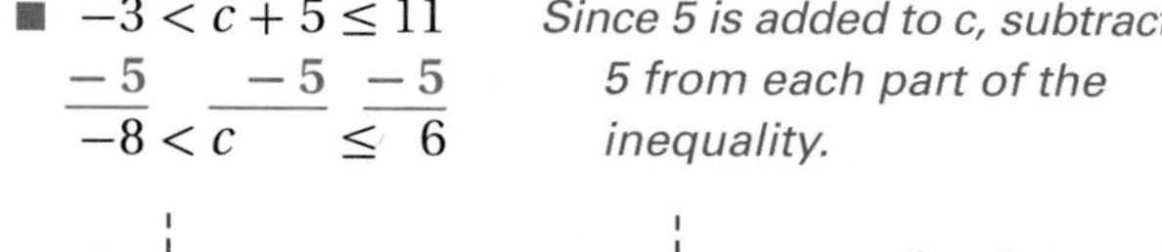

*Graph $c > -8$ and $c \leq 6$.*

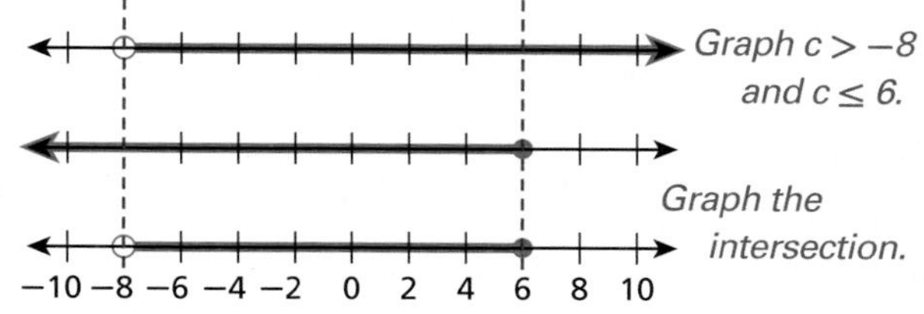

*Graph the intersection.*

−10 −8 −6 −4 −2 0 2 4 6 8 10

■ $-2 + t \geq 2$ OR $t + 3 < 1$ *Solve the simple inequalities.*

$\underline{+2 \qquad +2} \qquad \underline{-3 \quad -3}$

$t \geq 4$ OR $t < -2$

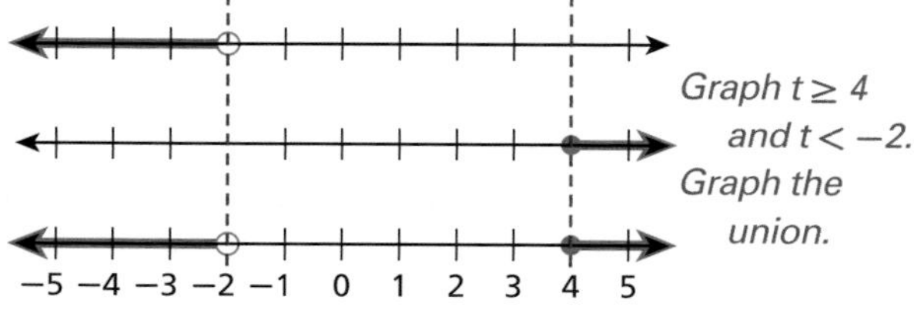

*Graph $t \geq 4$ and $t < -2$.*

*Graph the union.*

−5 −4 −3 −2 −1 0 1 2 3 4 5

### EXERCISES

**Solve each compound inequality and graph the solutions.**

**68.** $-4 < t + 6 < 10$

**69.** $-8 < k - 2 \leq 5$

**70.** $-3 + r > 4$ OR $r + 1 < -1$

**71.** $n - 4 > 5$ AND $2 > n + 3$

**72.** $p + 8 > 6$ AND $12 \geq p + 7$

**73.** $3 < s + 9$ OR $1 > s - 4$

**74.** One day, the high temperature was 84°F and the low temperature was 68°F. Write a compound inequality to represent the day's temperatures.

**75.** The table shows formulas for the recommended heart rates during exercise for a person who is *a* years old. Write and solve a compound inequality to determine the heart rate range for a 16-year-old person.

| Recommended Heart Rate Range | |
|---|---|
| Lower Limit | $0.5 \times (220 - a)$ |
| Upper Limit | $0.9 \times (220 - a)$ |

CHAPTER 3

# CHAPTER TEST

**Describe the solutions of each inequality in words.**

**1.** $-6 \le m$ **2.** $3t > 12$ **3.** $-x \ge 2$ **4.** $2 + b \le 10$

**Graph each inequality.**

**5.** $b > -3$ **6.** $2.5 < c$ **7.** $y \le -\sqrt{25}$ **8.** $3 - (4 + 7) \ge h$

**Write the inequality shown by each graph.**

**9.**
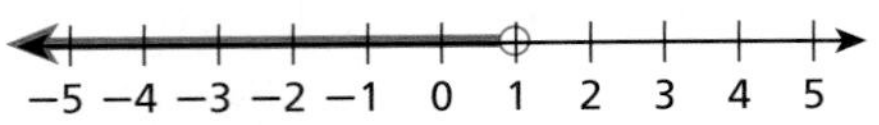


**10.**
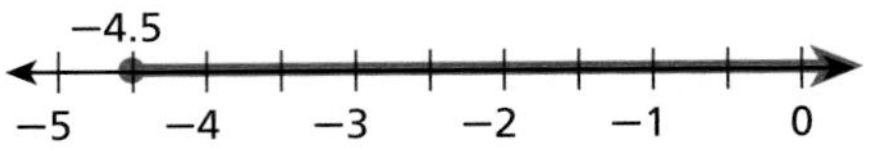


**Write an inequality for the situation and graph the solutions.**

**11.** Madison must run a mile in no more than 9 minutes to qualify for the race.

**Solve each inequality and graph the solutions.**

**12.** $d - 5 > -7$ **13.** $f + 4 < -3$ **14.** $4.5 \ge s + 3.2$ **15.** $g + (-2) \le 9$

**16.** Students need at least 75 hours of volunteer service to meet their graduation requirement. Samir has already completed 48 hours. Write and solve an inequality to determine how many more hours he needs to complete.

**Solve each inequality and graph the solutions.**

**17.** $-2c \le 2$ **18.** $3 > \frac{k}{2}$ **19.** $\frac{4}{5}x \le -8$ **20.** $\frac{b}{3} > -7$

**21.** Marco needs to buy premium gasoline for his car. He has \$20 in his wallet. Write and solve an inequality to determine how many gallons of gas Marco can buy.

| Gasoline Prices (\$) | | |
|---|---|---|
| Regular | Plus | Premium |
| 2.05 | 2.12 | 2.25 |

**Solve each inequality and graph the solutions.**

**22.** $3x - 8 < 4$ **23.** $-2(c - 3) > 4$ **24.** $5 \le \frac{3}{4}n - 2^4$ **25.** $3 - 2a \le -15 + (-9)$

**Solve each inequality.**

**26.** $2k - 6 > 3k + 2$ **27.** $2(5 - f) \le f + 12$ **28.** $\frac{3}{2}d \le -\frac{1}{2}d + 6$

**29.** Dion needs to rent a moving van for the day. Company A charges \$75 plus \$0.25 for every mile driven. Company B charges \$50 plus \$0.75 for each mile. For how many miles is company B less expensive than company A?

**Solve each compound inequality and graph the solutions.**

**30.** $-1 \le x - 3 < 3$ **31.** $t + 7 < 3$ OR $t - 1 > 4$ **32.** $d - 2 < 5$ AND $d + 1 \ge 7$

**33.** The driving school instructor has asked Lina to stay within 2 miles of the posted speed limits. The current road has a speed limit of 45 mi/h. Write a compound inequality to show Lina's acceptable speeds *s*.

## FOCUS ON SAT STUDENT-PRODUCED RESPONSES

Ten questions on the SAT require you to enter your answer in a special grid like the one shown. You do not have to write your answer in the boxes at the top of the grid, but doing this may help you avoid errors when filling in the grid. The circles must be filled in correctly for you to receive credit.

**You cannot enter a zero in the first column of the grid. This is to encourage you to give a more accurate answer when you need to round. For example, $\frac{1}{16}$ written as a decimal is 0.0625. This should be entered in the grid as .063 instead of 0.06.**

**You may want to time yourself as you take this practice test. It should take you about 9 minutes to complete.**

**1.** Mailing a standard-sized letter in 2005 by first-class mail cost \$0.37 for a letter weighing 1 ounce or less and \$0.23 for each additional ounce. How much did it cost, in dollars, to send a standard-sized letter that weighed 3 ounces?

**2.** If $p = q - 2$ and $\frac{q}{3} = 9$, what is the value of $p$?

**3.** Give the maximum value of $x$ if $12 - 3(x + 1) \geq \frac{1}{2}(3 - 5)$.

**4.** Give the minimum value of $x$ if $2x + y \leq 7x - 9$ and $y = -3$.

**5.** For what integer value of $x$ is $2x - 9 < 5$ and $x - 1 > 4$?

**6.** What is the minimum value of $z$ that satisfies the inequality $z - 7.3 \geq 4.1$?

**7.** To be eligible for financial aid, Alisa must work at least 15 hours per week in a work-study program. She wants to spend at least 5 more hours studying than working each week. What is the minimum number of hours per day (Monday through Friday) that she must study to meet this goal and be eligible for financial aid?

**8.** For all real numbers $a$ and $b$, define the operation # as follows:

$$a \# b = 2a - b$$

Given $a = 3$ and $a \# b = 1$, what is the value of $b$?

CHAPTER 3

# TEST TACKLER

## Standardized Test Strategies

## Short Response: Understand Short Response Scores

To answer a short-response question completely, you must show how you solved the problem and explain your answer. Short response questions are scored using a 2-point scoring rubric. A sample scoring rubric is provided below.

### EXAMPLE 1

**Short Response** An online company offers free shipping if the cost of the order is at least $35. Your order currently totals $26.50. Write an inequality to show how much more you need to spend to qualify for free shipping. Solve the inequality and explain what your answer means.

**2-point response:**

Let c be the amount I must add to my order.
c plus the amount I already ordered must be at least $35.
c + 26.50 ≥ 35

$c + 26.50 \geq 35$

$c + 26.50 - 26.50 \geq 35 - 26.50$

$c \geq 8.50$

Check:
$8.50 + 26.50 \geq 35$ ✓

To get free shipping on the order, I must spend at least $8.50 more since $8.50 + $26.50 is at least $35.

*The student wrote and solved an inequality correctly. The student defined the variable used in the inequality, answered the question in a complete sentence, and showed an explanation for the work done.*

**1-point response:**

$c + 26.50 > 35$

$c > 8.50$

$8.50

*The student did not define the variable. The student gave a correct answer, but the inequality symbol shown in the student's work is incorrect. No explanation was given.*

**0-point response:**

$9.25

*The student gave an answer that satisfies the problem, but the student did not show any work or give explanation.*

**Scoring Rubric:**

**2 points:** The student writes and correctly solves an inequality, showing all work. Student defines the variable, answers the question in a complete sentence, and provides an explanation.

**1 point:** The student writes and correctly solves an inequality but does not show all work, does not define the variable, or does not provide an explanation.

**1 point:** The student writes and solves an inequality but gives an incorrect answer. The student shows all work and provides an explanation for the answer.

**0 points:** The student gives no response or provides a solution without showing any work or explanation.

**Read short-response test items carefully. If you are allowed to write in the test booklet, underline or circle the parts of the question that tell you what your answer must include. Be sure to explain how you get your answer in complete sentences.**

**Read each sample and answer the questions that follow by using the scoring rubric below.**

### Scoring Rubric:

**2 points:** The student demonstrates a thorough understanding of the concept, correctly answers the question, and provides a complete explanation.

**1 point:** The student correctly answers the question but does not show all work or does not provide an explanation.

**1 point:** The student makes minor errors resulting in an incorrect solution but shows and explains understanding of the concept.

**0 points:** The student gives a response but shows no work or explanation, or the student gives no response.

**Sample A**

**Short Response** Write a real-world situation that can be modeled by the inequality $25s - 75 \geq 250$. Solve for s and explain how the value of s relates to your situation.

**Student's Answer**

*A painter rents a booth at the county fair for $75. The artist sells his paintings for $25 each. If he makes at least $250 in profit, he can buy a new easel.*

*The artist has to sell at least 13 paintings.*

1. What score should the student's answer receive? Explain your reasoning.
2. What additional information, if any, should the student's answer include in order to receive full credit?

**Sample B**

**Short Response** How do the solutions of $3s - 10 < 15 - 2s$ and $-34 + 9s \leq 4s - 9$ differ? How are the solutions alike? Include a graph in your explanation.

**Student's Answer**

Solve both inequalities.

$$3s - 10 < 15 - 2s$$
$$+2s \qquad +2s$$
$$5s - 10 < 15$$
$$+10 \quad +10$$
$$5s < 25$$
$$\frac{5s}{5} < \frac{25}{5}$$
$$s < 5$$

$$-34 + 9s \leq 4s - 9$$
$$-4s \quad -4s$$
$$-34 + 5s \leq -9$$
$$+34 \qquad +34$$
$$5s \leq 25$$
$$\frac{5s}{5} \leq \frac{25}{5}$$
$$s \leq 5$$

Blue graph: $s < 5$ Red graph: $s \leq 5$

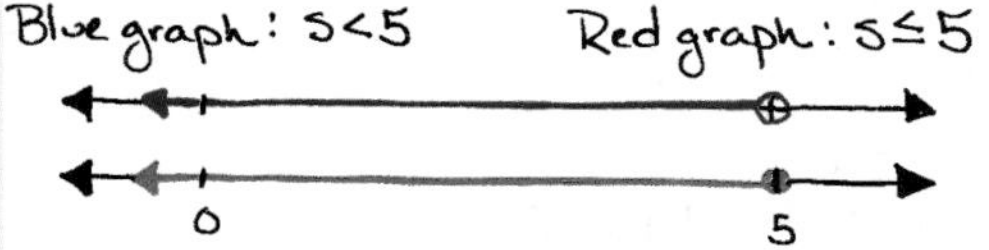


3. What score should the student's answer receive? Explain your reasoning.
4. What additional information, if any, should the student's answer include in order to receive full credit?

**Sample C**

**Short Response** Explain the difference between the solution of the equation $x - 6 = 2x + 9$ and the solutions of the inequality $x - 6 < 2x + 9$.

**Student's Answer**

*The equation has a solution of x = –15, and the inequality has a solution of x > –15. The equation is true only when x equals –15. The inequality is true for all values greater than –15.*

5. What score should the student's answer receive? Explain your reasoning.
6. What additional information, if any, should the student's answer include in order to receive full credit?

CHAPTER 3

# CUMULATIVE ASSESSMENT, CHAPTERS 1–3

## Multiple Choice

1. Billie borrowed \$5,000. The annual interest rate is 14.5%. After three years, how much simple interest has Billie paid on her loan?
   - A \$217,500.00
   - B \$2,175.00
   - C \$1,450.00
   - D \$217.50

2. If $t + 8 = 2$, find the value of $2t$.
   - A $-12$
   - B $-6$
   - C 12
   - D 20

3. The length of the rectangle is $2(x + 1)$ meters and the perimeter is 60 meters. Find the length of the rectangle in meters.

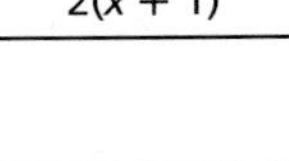


   - A 12 meters
   - B 26 meters
   - C 28 meters
   - D 56 meters

4. An art store is selling tubes of oil paint for 30% off. The regular price is \$8.50 per tube. Sales tax is 8% of the purchase price. Selma has \$25 to spend on oil paint. What is the greatest number of tubes she can buy?
   - A 3
   - B 4
   - C 5
   - D 6

5. What is the value of the function $y = 8x^2 - 7$ at $x = 6$?
   - A 281
   - B 288
   - C 505
   - D 512

6. On March 28, 2008, Eamon Sullivan set a world record by swimming 50 meters in 21.28 seconds. A shortfin mako shark can swim at a speed of 20 kilometers per hour. At these rates, would Sullivan or a mako shark win a 50-meter race, and by how many seconds?
   - A Sullivan, by about 1 second
   - B Sullivan, by about 9 seconds
   - C the shark, by about 6 seconds
   - D the shark, by about 12 seconds

7. Which graph shows the solutions of $-2(1 - x) < 3(x - 2)$?

A

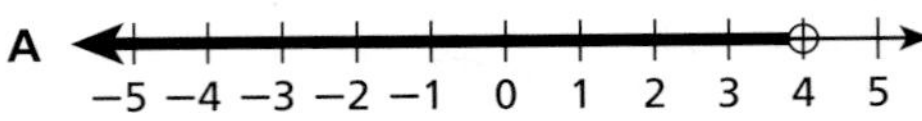


B

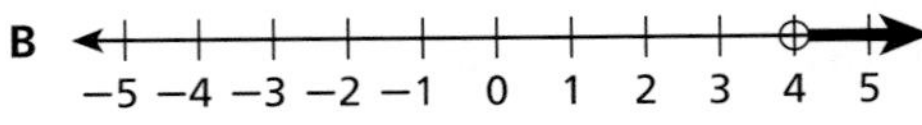


C −5 −4 −3 −2 −1 0 1 2 3 4 5

D −5 −4 −3 −2 −1 0 1 2 3 4 5

8. Which compound inequality has no solution?
   - A $x > 1$ OR $x < -2$
   - B $x < 1$ AND $x > -2$
   - C $x < 1$ OR $x < -2$
   - D $x > 1$ AND $x < -2$

9. Which proportion could be used to determine the ratio of the areas of these similar rectangles?

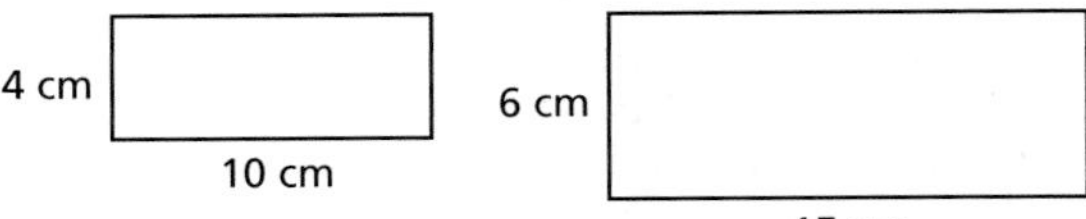


   - A $\frac{2}{3}$
   - B $\frac{2}{5}$
   - C $\frac{4}{9}$
   - D $\frac{4}{25}$

**To check your answer, use a different method to solve the problem from the one you originally used. If you made a mistake the first time, you are unlikely to make the same mistake when you solve the problem a different way.**

**10.** On the German autobahn, the recommended speed is 130 kilometers per hour. Approximately what is this speed in feet per second? (*Hint:* 1.6 kilometers $\approx$ 1 mile)

**A** 0.023 foot/second

**B** 119.167 feet/second

**C** 305.067 feet/second

**D** 7150 feet/second

**11.** The sum of the measures of any two sides of a triangle must be greater than the measure of the third side. What is the greatest possible integer value for x?

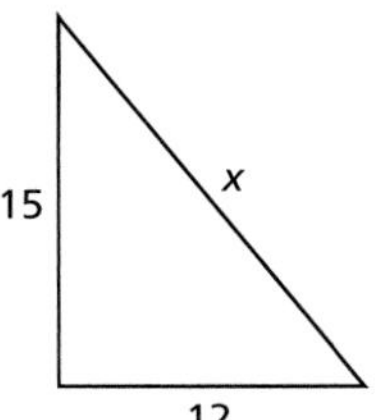


**A** 27

**B** 26

**C** 20

**D** 19

**12.** After 2 years, the simple interest paid on an investment of $2500 was $175. What percent was the interest rate?

**A** 0.035%

**B** 3.5%

**C** 7%

**D** 28.57%

**13.** The radius of a circle can be determined by the formula $r = \sqrt{\frac{A}{\pi}}$. What is the radius of a circle that has an area $A$ of 314 square meters? (Use 3.14 for $\pi$.)

**A** 5.6 m

**B** 10 m

**C** 100 m

**D** 177.2 m

***STANDARDIZED TEST PREP***

## Short Response

**S1.** Write 2 different inequalities that have the same solution as $n > 3$ such that

**a.** the first inequality uses the symbol $>$ and requires addition or subtraction to solve.

**b.** the second inequality uses the symbol $<$ and requires multiplication or division to solve.

**S2.** Alison has twice as many videogames as Kyle. Maurice has 5 more videogames than Alison. The total number of videogames is less than 40.

**a.** Write an inequality to represent this situation.

**b.** Solve the inequality to determine the greatest number of videogames Maurice could have.

**S3.** Donna's Deli delivers lunches for $7 per person plus a $35 delivery fee. Larry's Lunches delivers lunches for $11 per person.

**a.** Write an expression to represent the cost of $x$ lunches from Donna's Deli. Write an expression to represents the cost of ordering $x$ lunches from Larry's Lunches.

**b.** Write an inequality to determine the number of lunches for which the cost of Larry's Lunches is less than the cost of Donna's Deli.

**c.** Solve the inequality and explain what the answer means. Which restaurant charges less for an order of 10 lunches?

## Extended Response

**E1.** Aleya has two employment opportunities. Company A offered her a yearly salary of $31,000. Company B offered her a similar position with a yearly salary of $27,000 plus 2.5% commission on her total sales for the year.

**a.** Let $x$ represent Aleya's total sales for the year at company B. Write an expression to represent the total income after one year at company B.

**b.** Use your expression from part **a** to write an inequality that could be solved to determine the amount of sales for which the yearly income at company A would be greater than that at company B.

**c.** Solve the inequality from part **b** and explain the meaning of the solution in relation to Aleya's decision to work for company A or company B.

**d.** How much more than the salary at company A would Aleya make after one year at company B if her total sales for the year was $200,000?

CHAPTER 4

# Functions



## Why Learn This?

Scientists can use data along with functions to model and make predictions about populations of animals, such as the Southern Flying Squirrel found in Western North Carolina.

Chapter Project Online
KEYWORD: MA7 ChProject

# Are You Ready?

## Vocabulary

**Match each term on the left with a definition on the right.**

1. absolute value
2. algebraic expression
3. input
4. output
5. $x$-axis

A. a letter used to represent a value that can change
B. the value generated for $y$
C. a group of numbers, symbols, and variables with one or more operations
D. the distance of a number from zero on the number line
E. the horizontal number line in the coordinate plane
F. a value substituted for $x$

## Ordered Pairs

**Graph each point on the same coordinate plane.**

6. $(-2, 4)$
7. $(0, -5)$
8. $(1, -3)$
9. $(4, 2)$
10. $(3, -2)$
11. $(-1, -2)$
12. $(-1, 3)$
13. $(-4, 0)$

## Function Tables

**Generate ordered pairs for each function for $x = -2, -1, 0, 1, 2$.**

14. $y = -2x - 1$
15. $y = x + 1$
16. $y = -x^2$
17. $y = \frac{1}{2}x + 2$
18. $y = (x + 1)^2$
19. $y = (x - 1)^2$

## Solve Multi-Step Equations

**Solve each equation. Check your answer.**

20. $17x - 15 = 12$
21. $-7 + 2t = 7$
22. $-6 = \frac{p}{3} + 9$
23. $5n - 10 = 35$
24. $3r - 14 = 7$
25. $9 = \frac{x}{2} + 1$
26. $-2.4 + 1.6g = 5.6$
27. $34 - 2x = 12$
28. $2(x + 5) = -8$

## Solve for a Variable

**Solve each equation for the indicated variable.**

29. $A = \ell w$ for $w$
30. $V = \ell wh$ for $w$
31. $A = bh$ for $h$
32. $C = 2\pi r$ for $r$
33. $I = Prt$ for $P$
34. $V = \frac{1}{3}\ell wh$ for $h$

# CHAPTER 4 Study Guide: Preview

## Where You've Been

**Previously, you**

- were introduced to functions when you generated and graphed ordered pairs.
- stated rules for relationships among values.
- represented and interpreted data using bar graphs and circle graphs.

## In This Chapter

**You will study**

- relationships between variables and determine whether a relation is a function.
- relationships in function notation.
- how trend lines on scatter plots can help you make predictions.

## Where You're Going

**You can use the skills in this chapter**

- to find values of a function from a graph.
- to analyze data and make predictions in other courses, such as Chemistry.
- to calculate total earnings for a certain hourly rate.

## *Key Vocabulary/Vocabulario*

| | |
|---|---|
| arithmetic sequence | sucesión aritmética |
| common difference | diferencia común |
| correlation | correlación |
| dependent variable | variable dependiente |
| domain | dominio |
| function | función |
| function notation | notación de función |
| independent variable | variable independiente |
| no correlation | sin correlación |
| range | rango |
| relation | relación |
| scatter plot | diagrama de dispersión |
| sequence | sucesión |

## *Vocabulary Connections*

To become familiar with some of the vocabulary terms in the chapter, consider the following. You may refer to the chapter, the glossary, or a dictionary if you like.

1. What does the word *dependent* mean? What do you think is true about the value of a **dependent variable**?
2. A *function* is a special type of relation and *notation* is a method of writing. What do you suppose is meant by **function notation**?
3. The word *correlation* means "relationship." What might it mean if two sets of data have **no correlation**?
4. What does it mean when someone says that two people have something in *common*? If *difference* is the answer to a subtraction problem, what might it mean for a list of numbers to have a **common difference**?

CHAPTER 4

## Reading Strategy: Read and Interpret Math Symbols

It is essential that as you read through each lesson of the textbook, you can interpret mathematical symbols.

### Common Math Symbols

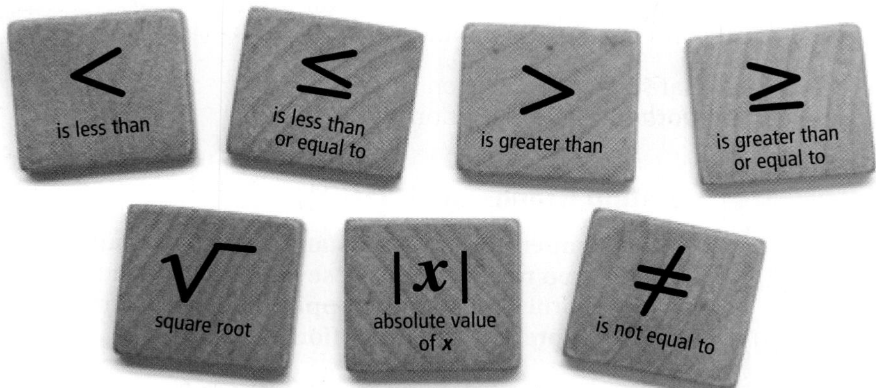


**You must be able to translate symbols into words . . .**

| Using Symbols | Using Words |
|---|---|
| $3\left(\frac{x}{12}\right) - 1 = 21$ | Three times the quotient of $x$ and 12, minus 1 equals 21. |
| $25x + 6 \geq 17$ | Twenty-five times $x$ plus 6 is greater than or equal to 17. |
| $\lvert x \rvert > 14$ | The absolute value of $x$ is greater than 14. |
| $\sqrt{60 + x} \leq 40$ | The square root of the sum of 60 and $x$ is less than or equal to 40. |

**. . . and words into symbols.**

| Using Words | Using Symbols |
|---|---|
| The height of the shed is at least 9 feet. | $h \geq 9$ ft |
| The distance is at most one tenth of a mile. | $d \leq 0.1$ mi |
| The silo contains more than 600 cubic feet of corn. | $c > 600$ ft$^3$ |

**Try This**

**Translate the symbols into words.**

1. $x \leq \sqrt{10}$
2. $\lvert x \rvert + 2 > 45$
3. $-5 \leq x < 8$
4. $-6 - \frac{1}{5}x = -32$

**Translate the words into symbols.**

5. There are less than 15 seconds remaining.
6. The tax rate is 8.25 percent of the cost.
7. Ann counted over 100 pennies.
8. Joe can spend at least $22 but no more than $30.

# 4-1 Graphing Relationships

**Prep MA.A.4** Understand functions based on ... real-world phenomena.

***Objectives***
Match simple graphs with situations.

Graph a relationship.

***Vocabulary***
continuous graph
discrete graph

**Who uses this?**
Cardiologists can use graphs to analyze their patients' heartbeats. (See Example 2.)

Graphs can be used to illustrate many different situations. For example, trends shown on a cardiograph can help a doctor see how the patient's heart is functioning.

To relate a graph to a given situation, use key words in the description.

## EXAMPLE 1 Relating Graphs to Situations

**The air temperature was constant for several hours at the beginning of the day and then rose steadily for several hours. It stayed the same temperature for most of the day before dropping sharply at sundown. Choose the graph that best represents this situation.**

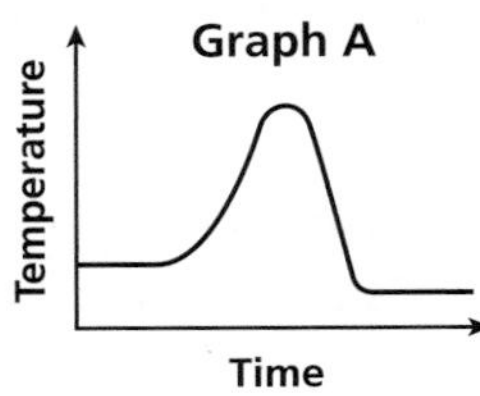


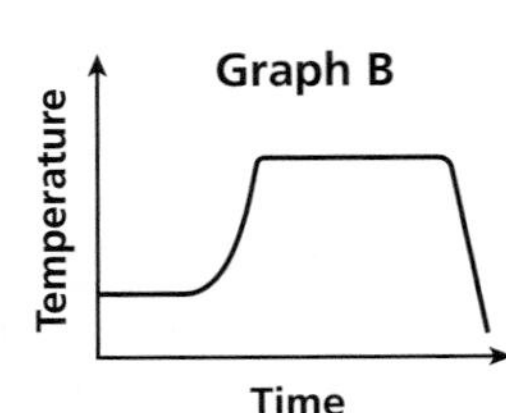


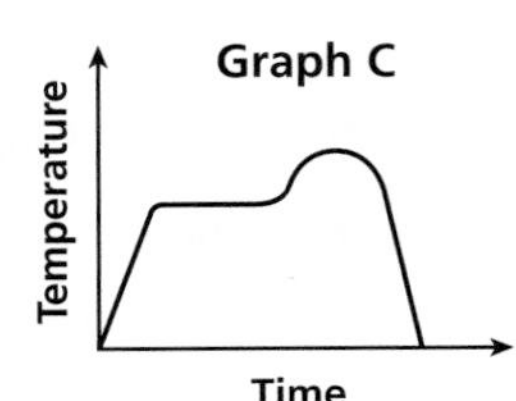


**Step 1** Read the graphs from left to right to show time passing.

**Step 2** List key words in order and decide which graph shows them.

| Key Words | Segment Description... | Graphs... |
|---|---|---|
| Was constant | Horizontal | Graphs A and B |
| Rose steadily | **Slanting upward** | Graphs A and B |
| Stayed the same | Horizontal | Graph B |
| Dropped sharply | **Slanting downward** | Graph B |

**Step 3** Pick the graph that shows all the key phrases in order.

horizontal, **slanting upward,**
horizontal, **slanting downward**

The correct graph is B.

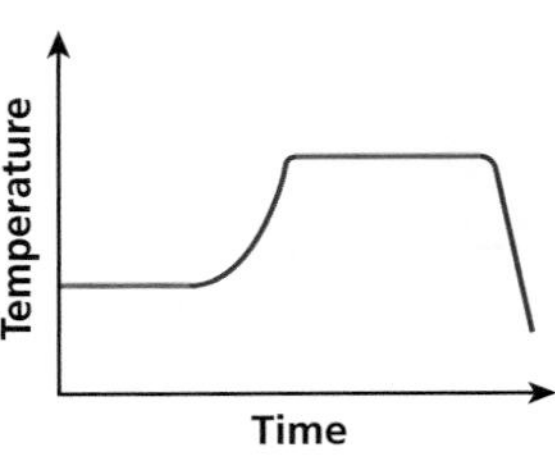

**1.** The air temperature increased steadily for several hours and then remained constant. At the end of the day, the temperature increased slightly again before dropping sharply. Choose the graph above that best represents this situation.

As seen in Example 1, some graphs are connected lines or curves called **continuous graphs**. Some graphs are only distinct points. These are called **discrete graphs**.

The graph on theme-park attendance is an example of a discrete graph. It consists of distinct points because each year is distinct and people are counted in whole numbers only. The values between the whole numbers are not included, since they have no meaning for the situation.

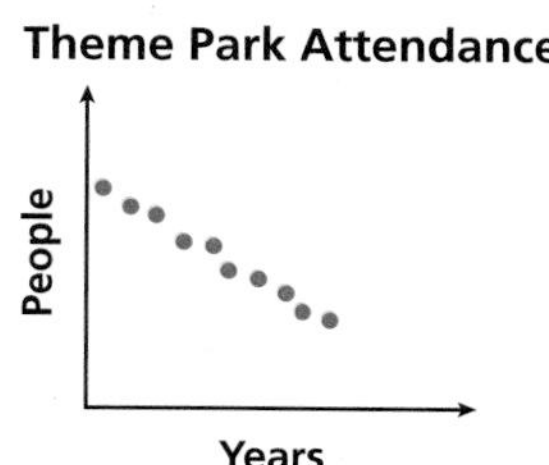


**EXAMPLE 2** **Sketching Graphs for Situations**

**Sketch a graph for each situation. Tell whether the graph is continuous or discrete.**

**Helpful Hint**

When sketching or interpreting a graph, pay close attention to the labels on each axis.

**A** **Simon is selling candles to raise money for the school dance. For each candle he sells, the school will get $2.50. He has 10 candles that he can sell.**

*The amount earned (y-axis) increases by $2.50 for each candle Simon sells (x-axis).*

*Since Simon can only sell whole candles or none at all, the graph is 11 distinct points.*

The graph is discrete.

**B** **Angelique's heart rate is being monitored while she exercises on a treadmill. While walking, her heart rate remains the same. As she increases her pace, her heart rate rises at a steady rate. When she begins to run, her heart rate increases more rapidly and then remains high while she runs. As she decreases her pace, her heart rate slows down and returns to her normal rate.**

As time passes during her workout (moving left to right along the $x$-axis), her heart rate ($y$-axis) does the following:

- **remains the same**,
- **rises at a steady rate**,
- **increases more rapidly** (**steeper** than previous segment),
- **remains high**,
- **slows down**,
- and then returns to her **normal rate**.

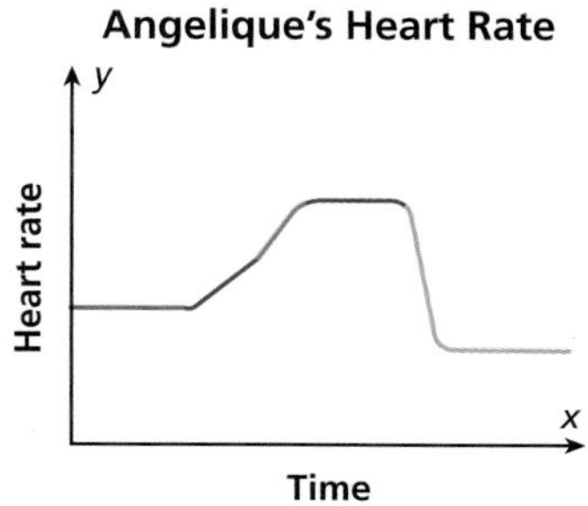


The graph is continuous.

**Sketch a graph for each situation. Tell whether the graph is continuous or discrete.**

**2a.** Jamie is taking an 8-week keyboarding class. At the end of each week, she takes a test to find the number of words she can type per minute. She improves each week.

**2b.** Henry begins to drain a water tank by opening a valve. Then he opens another valve. Then he closes the first valve. He leaves the second valve open until the tank is empty.

Both graphs show a relationship about a child going down a slide. **Graph A** represents the child's *distance from the ground* related to time. **Graph B** represents the child's *speed* related to time.

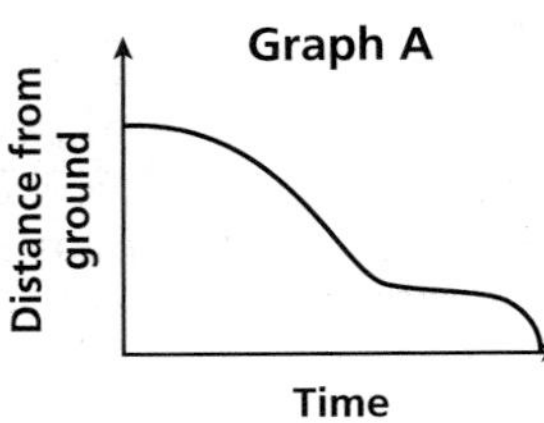


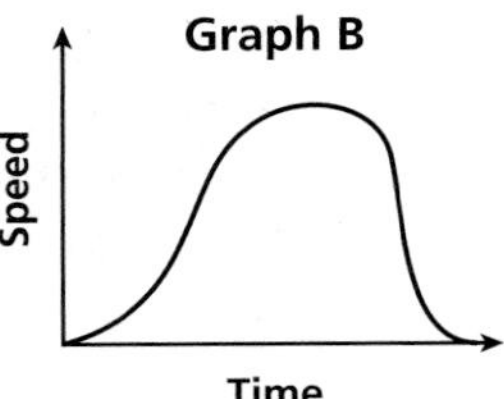


## EXAMPLE 3 Writing Situations for Graphs

**Write a possible situation for the given graph.**

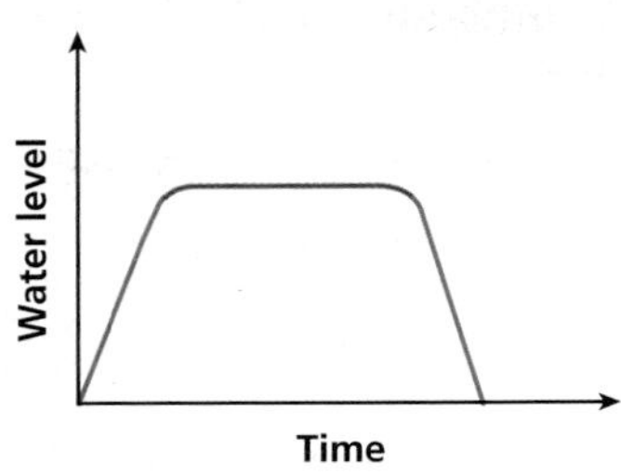


**Step 1** Identify labels.
$x$-axis: time    $y$-axis: water level

**Step 2** Analyze sections.
Over time, the water level does the following:

- increases steadily,
- **remains unchanged**,
- and then decreases steadily.

**Possible Situation:**

A watering can is filled with water. It **sits for a while** until the flowers are planted. The water in the can is then emptied on top of the planted flowers.

**3.** Write a possible situation for the given graph.

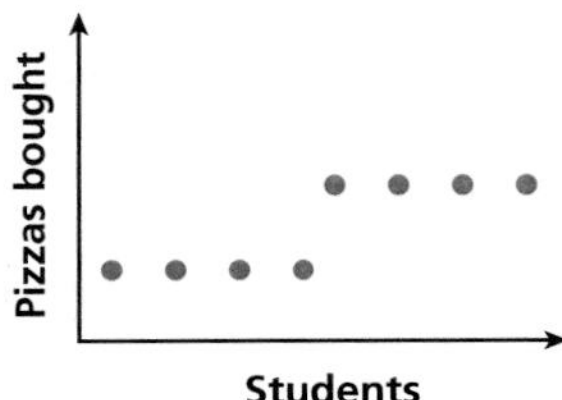


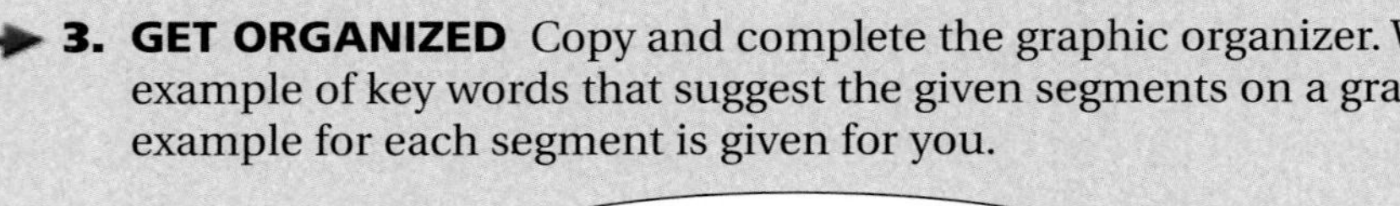

## THINK AND DISCUSS

**1.** Should a graph of age related to height be a continuous graph or a discrete graph? Explain.

**2.** Give an example of a situation that, when graphed, would include a horizontal segment.

**3. GET ORGANIZED** Copy and complete the graphic organizer. Write an example of key words that suggest the given segments on a graph. One example for each segment is given for you.

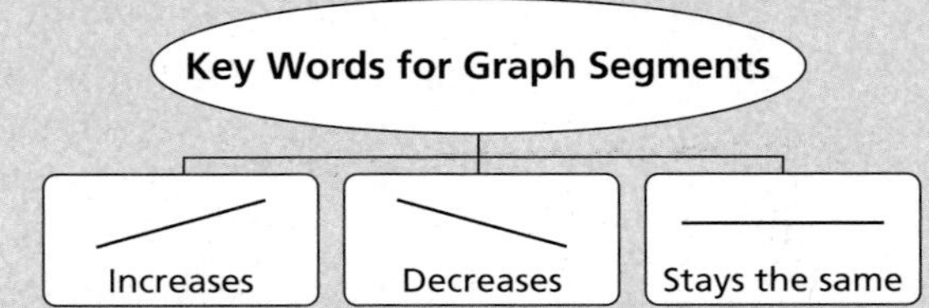

# 4-1 Exercises

## GUIDED PRACTICE

**Vocabulary** **Apply the vocabulary from this lesson to answer each question.**

1. A ___?___ graph is made of connected lines or curves. (*continuous* or *discrete*)
2. A ___?___ graph is made of only distinct points. (*continuous* or *discrete*)

SEE EXAMPLE 1
p. 230

**Choose the graph that best represents each situation.**

3. A person alternates between running and walking.
4. A person gradually speeds up to a constant running pace.
5. A person walks, gradually speeds up to a run, and then slows back down to a walk.

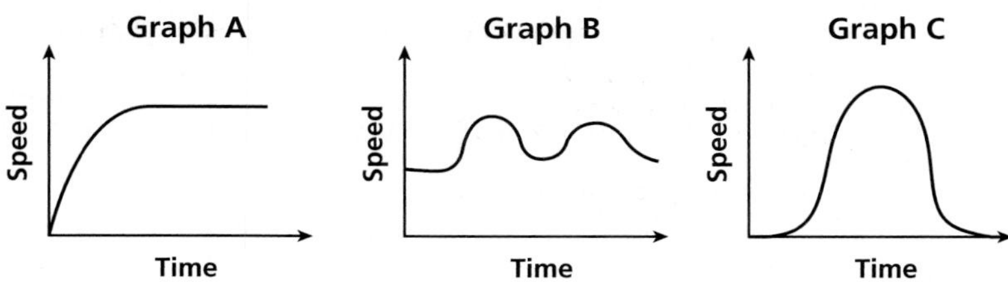


SEE EXAMPLE 2
p. 231

6. Maxine is buying extra pages for her photo album. Each page holds exactly 8 photos. Sketch a graph to show the maximum number of photos she can add to her album if she buys 1, 2, 3, or 4 extra pages. Tell whether the graph is continuous or discrete.

SEE EXAMPLE 3
p. 232

**Write a possible situation for each graph.**

7. 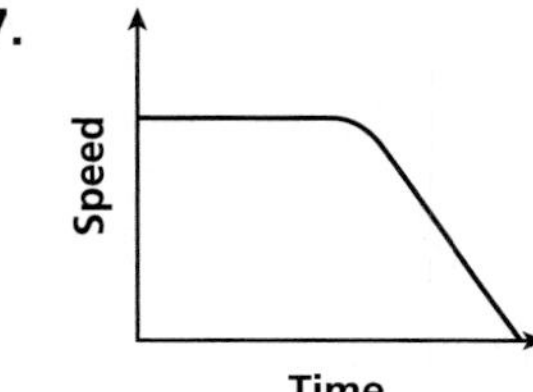


8. 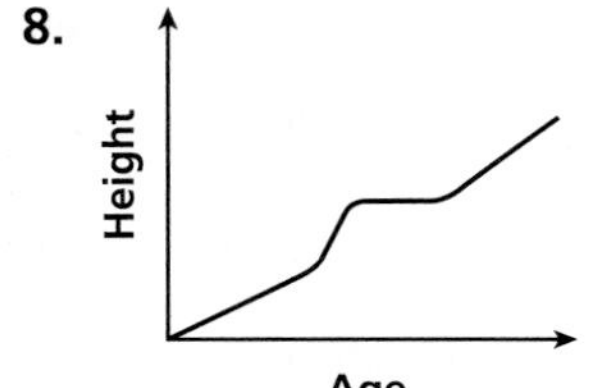


9. 

## PRACTICE AND PROBLEM SOLVING

**Independent Practice**

| For Exercises | See Example |
|---|---|
| 10–12 | 1 |
| 13 | 2 |
| 14–16 | 3 |

**Extra Practice**

Skills Practice p. S10
Application Practice p. S31

**Choose the graph that best represents each situation.**

10. A flag is raised up a flagpole quickly at the beginning and then more slowly near the top.
11. A flag is raised up a flagpole in a jerky motion, using a hand-over-hand method.
12. A flag is raised up a flagpole at a constant rate of speed.

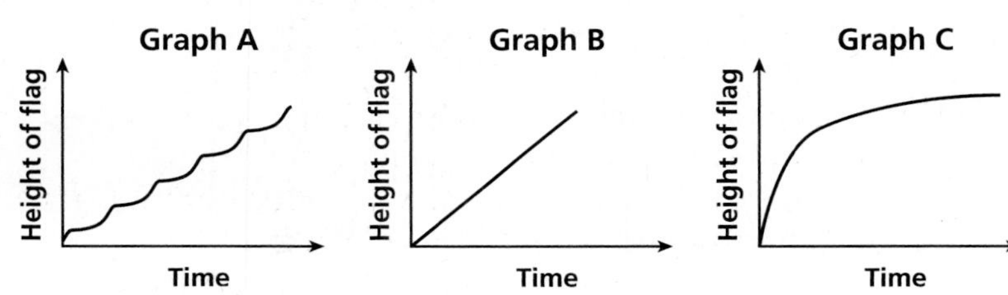

13. For six months, a puppy gained weight at a steady rate. Sketch a graph to illustrate the weight of the puppy during that time period. Tell whether the graph is continuous or discrete.

**Write a possible situation for each graph.**

14.

Distance from home

Time

15.

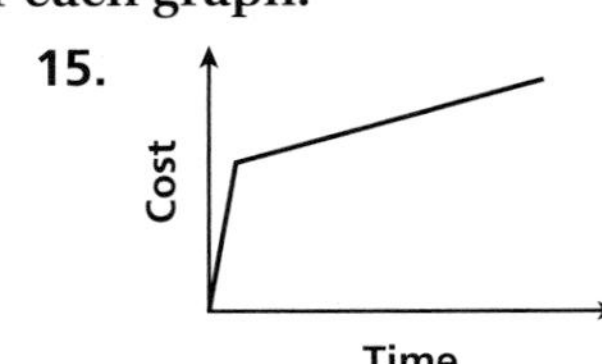


16.

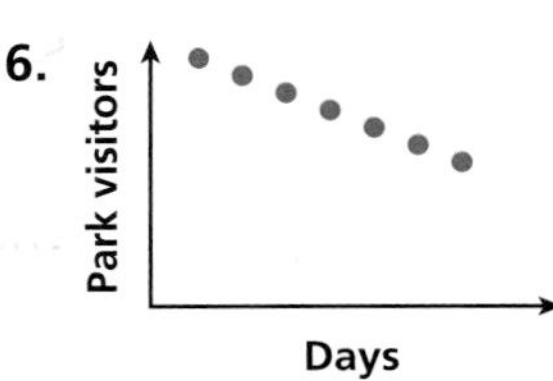


17. **Data Collection** Use a graphing calculator and motion detector for the following.
   a. On a coordinate plane, draw a graph relating distance away from a starting point walking at various speeds and time.
   b. Using the motion detector as the starting point, walk away from the motion detector to make a graph on the graphing calculator that matches the one you drew.
   c. Compare your walking speeds to each change in steepness on the graph.

18. **Sports** The graph shows the speed of a horse during and after a race. Use it to describe the changing pace of the horse during the race.

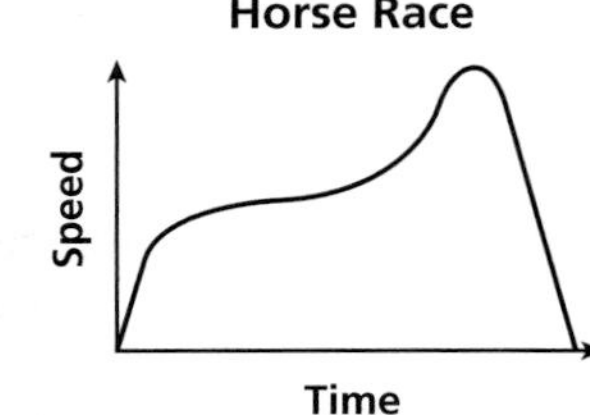


19. **Recreation** You hike up a mountain path starting at 10 A.M. You camp overnight and then walk back down the same path at the same pace at 10 A.M. the next morning. On the same set of axes, graph the relationship between distance from the top of the mountain and the time of day for both the hike up and the hike down. What does the point of intersection of the graphs represent?

**LINK**

**Sports**

On November 1, 1938, the underdog Seabiscuit beat the heavily favored Triple-Crown winner War Admiral in a historic horse race at Pimlico Race Course in Baltimore, Maryland.

20. **Critical Thinking** Suppose that you sketched a graph of speed related to time for a brick being dropped from the top of a building. Then you sketched a graph for speed related to time for a ball that was rolled down a hill and then came to rest. How would the graphs be the same? How would they be different?

21. **Write About It** Describe a real-life situation that could be represented by a graph that has distinct points. Then describe a real-life situation that could be represented by a connected graph.

**MULTI-STEP TEST PREP**

22. This problem will prepare you for the Multi-Step Test Prep on page 260.

A rectangular pool that is 4 feet deep at all places is being filled at a constant rate.

   a. Sketch a graph to show the depth of the water as it increases over time.
   b. The side view of another swimming pool is shown. If the pool is being filled at a constant rate, sketch a graph to show the depth of the water as it increases over time.

## Test Prep

Prep MA.A.4

23. Which situation would NOT be represented by a graph with distinct points?
   Ⓐ Amount of money earned based on the number of cereal bars sold
   Ⓑ Number of visitors per day for one week to a grocery store
   Ⓒ The amount of iced tea in a pitcher at a restaurant during the lunch hour
   Ⓓ The total cost of buying 1, 2, or 3 CDs at the music store

24. Which situation is best represented by the graph?
   Ⓕ A snowboarder starts at the bottom of the hill and takes a ski lift to the top.
   Ⓖ A cruise boat travels at a steady pace from the port to its destination.
   Ⓗ An object dropped from the top of a building gains speed at a rapid pace before hitting the ground.
   Ⓙ A marathon runner starts at a steady pace and then runs faster at the end of the race before stopping at the finish line.

Speed

Time

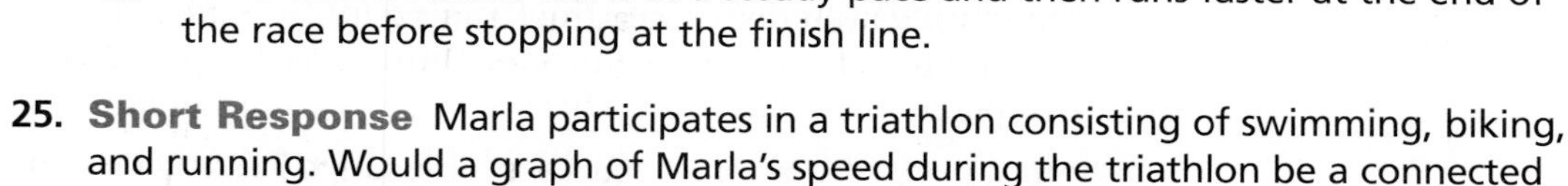

25. **Short Response** Marla participates in a triathlon consisting of swimming, biking, and running. Would a graph of Marla's speed during the triathlon be a connected graph or distinct points? Explain.

## CHALLENGE AND EXTEND

**Pictured are three vases and graphs representing the height of water as it is poured into each of the vases at a constant rate. Match each vase with the correct graph.**

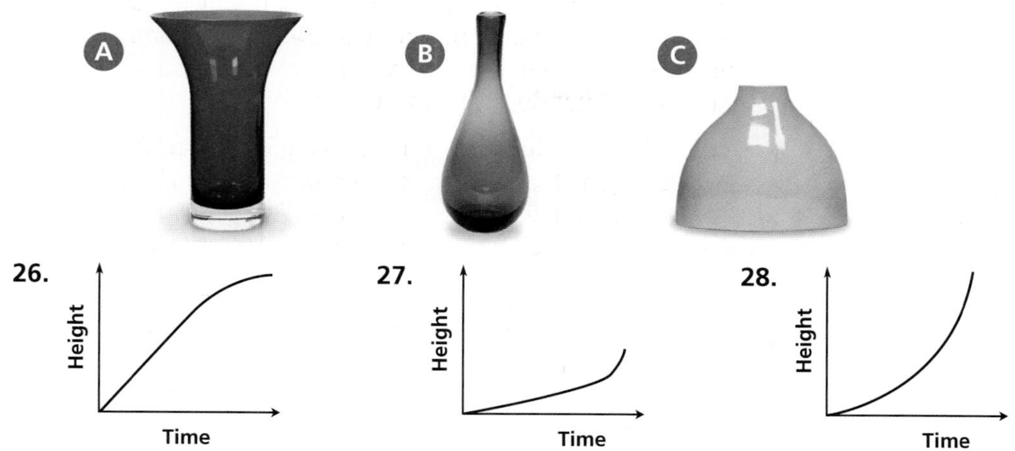


## SPIRAL REVIEW

**Evaluate each expression.** *(Lesson 1-4)*

29. $-2^3$ 30. $4^4$ 31. $\left(\frac{1}{3}\right)^2$

**Generate ordered pairs for each function for $x = -2, -1, 0, 1,$ and $2$. Graph the ordered pairs and describe the pattern.** *(Lesson 1-8)*

32. $y = x - 2$ 33. $2x + y = 1$ 34. $y = |x - 1|$ 35. $y = x^2 + 2$

**Write and solve an equation to represent each relationship.** *(Lesson 2-1)*

36. A number increased by 11 is equal to 3.
37. Five less than a number is equal to $-2$.

# 4-2 Relations and Functions

**MA.A.4.1** Categorize relations as functions or "not functions". **MA.A.4.2** Use appropriate terminology ... associated with functions.

***Objectives***

Identify functions.

Find the domain and range of relations and functions.

***Vocabulary***

relation
domain
range
function

**Why learn this?**

You can use a relation to show finishing positions and scores in a track meet.

In Lesson 4-1, you saw relationships represented by graphs. Relationships can also be represented by a set of ordered pairs called a **relation**.

In the scoring system of some track meets, for **first place** you get **5** points, for **second place** you get **3** points, for **third place** you get **2** points, and for **fourth place** you get **1** point. This scoring system is a relation, so it can be shown as ordered pairs, $\{(1, 5), (2, 3), (3, 2), (4, 1)\}$. You can also show relations in other ways, such as tables, graphs, or *mapping diagrams*.

**EXAMPLE 1** **Showing Multiple Representations of Relations**

**Express the relation for the track meet scoring system, $\{(1, 5), (2, 3), (3, 2), (4, 1)\}$, as a table, as a graph, and as a mapping diagram.**

**Table**

| Track Scoring | |
|---|---|
| Place | Points |
| 1 | 5 |
| 2 | 3 |
| 3 | 2 |
| 4 | 1 |

*Write all x-values under "Place" and all y-values under "Points."*

**Graph**

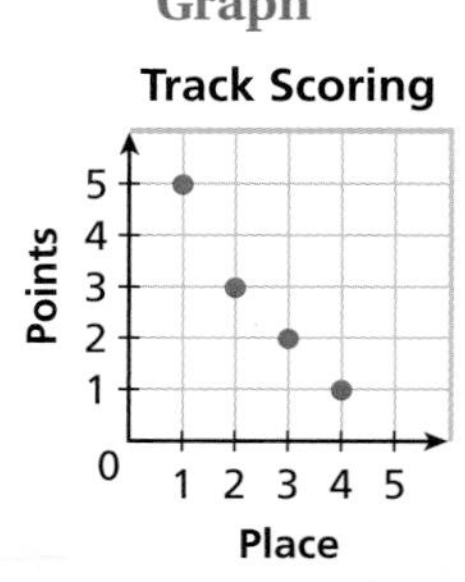


*Use the x- and y-values to plot the ordered pairs.*

**Mapping Diagram**

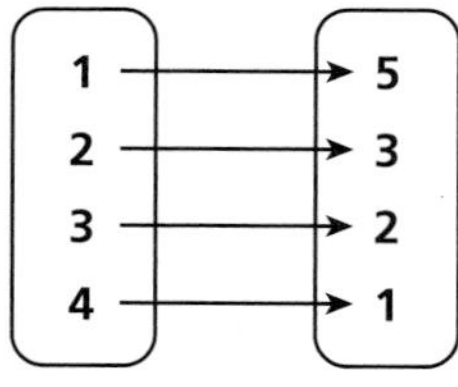


*Write all x-values under "Place" and all y-values under "Points." Draw an arrow from each x-value to its corresponding y-value.*

**1.** Express the relation $\{(1, 3)\ (2, 4), (3, 5)\}$ as a table, as a graph, and as a mapping diagram.

The **domain** of a relation is the set of first coordinates (or $x$-values) of the ordered pairs. The **range** of a relation is the set of second coordinates (or $y$-values) of the ordered pairs. The domain of the track meet scoring system is $\{1, 2, 3, 4\}$. The range is $\{5, 3, 2, 1\}$.

## EXAMPLE 2 Finding the Domain and Range of a Relation

**Give the domain and range of the relation.**

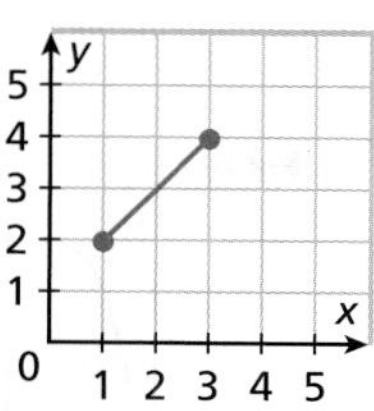


The domain is all $x$-values from 1 through 3, inclusive.

The range is all $y$-values from 2 through 4, inclusive.

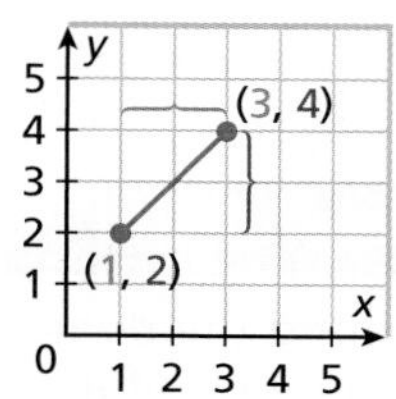


D: $1 \le x \le 3$ R: $2 \le y \le 4$

**Give the domain and range of each relation.**

**2a.**

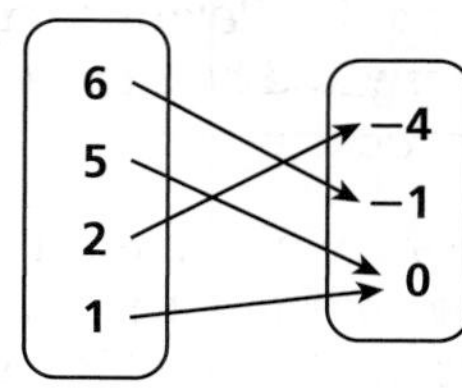


**2b.**

| x | y |
|---|---|
| 1 | 1 |
| 4 | 4 |
| 8 | 1 |

A **function** is a special type of relation that pairs each domain value with exactly one range value.

## EXAMPLE 3 Identifying Functions

**Give the domain and range of each relation. Tell whether the relation is a function. Explain.**

**A**

| Field Trip | |
|---|---|
| Students $x$ | Buses $y$ |
| 75 | 2 |
| 68 | 2 |
| 125 | 3 |

D: $\{75, 68, 125\}$

R: $\{2, 3\}$

*Even though 2 is in the range twice, it is written only once when you are giving the range.*

This relation is a function. Each domain value is paired with exactly one range value.

**Writing Math**

When there is a finite number of values in a domain or range, list the values inside braces.

**B**

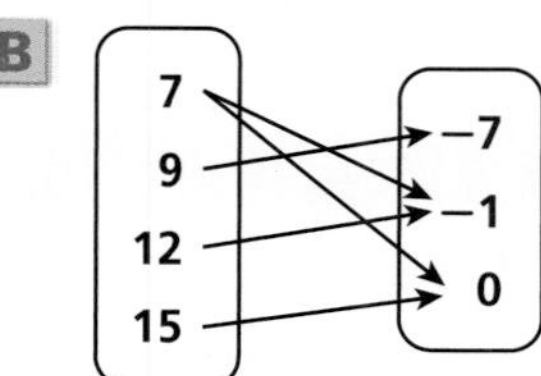


*Use the arrows to determine which domain values correspond to each range value.*

D: $\{7, 9, 12, 15\}$

R: $\{-7, -1, 0\}$

This relation is not a function. Each domain value does not have exactly one range value. The domain value 7 is paired with the range values $-1$ and 0.

**Give the domain and range of each relation. Tell whether the relation is a function. Explain.**

**C**

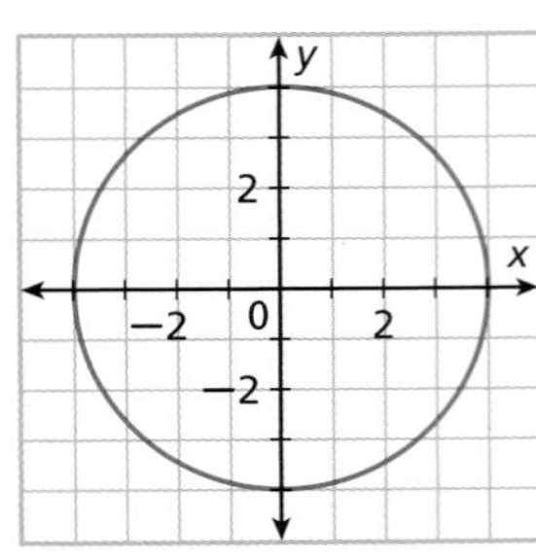

*Draw in lines to see the domain and range values.*

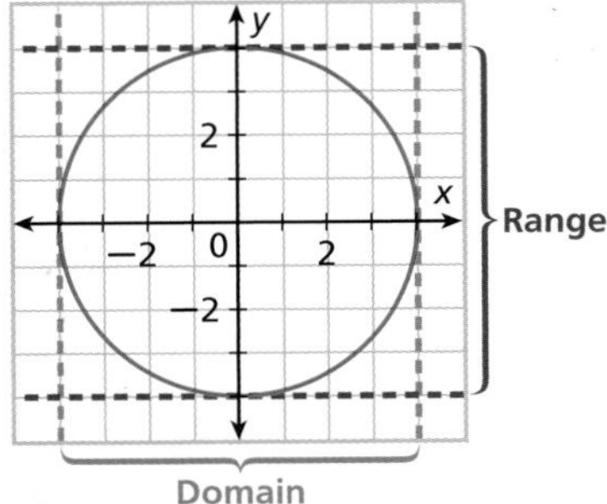


D: $-4 \le x \le 4$ R: $-4 \le y \le 4$

| x | 4 | 0 | 0 | −4 |
|---|---|---|---|---|
| y | 0 | 4 | −4 | 0 |

*To compare domain and range values, make a table using points from the graph.*

This relation is not a function because there are several domain values that have more than one range value. For example, the domain value 0 is paired with both 4 and −4.

### Helpful Hint

To find the domain and range of a graph, it may help to draw in lines to see the *x*- and *y*-values.

**Give the domain and range of each relation. Tell whether the relation is a function and explain.**

**3a.** $\{(8, 2), (-4, 1), (-6, 2), (1, 9)\}$ **3b.**

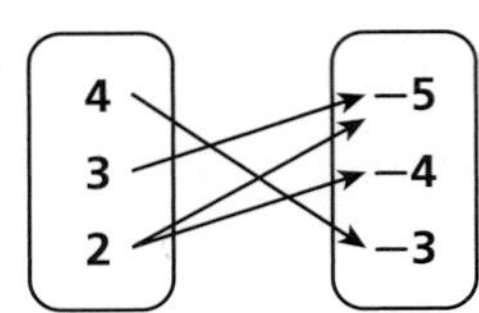


## Student to Student

*Functions*

**Eric Dawson**
Boone High School

*I decide whether a list of ordered pairs is a function by looking at the x-values. If they're all different, then it's a function.*

| *(1, 6), (2, 5), (6, 5), (0, 8)* | *(5, 6), (7, 2), (5, 8), (6, 3)* |
|---|---|
| ***All different x-values*** | ***Same x-value*** (with different *y*-values) |
| *Function* | *Not a function* |

## THINK AND DISCUSS

1. Describe how to tell whether a set of ordered pairs is a function.
2. Can the graph of a vertical line segment represent a function? Explain.

3. **GET ORGANIZED** Copy and complete the graphic organizer by explaining when a relation is a function and when it is not a function.

| A relation is... | |
|---|---|
| A function if... | Not a function if... |

# 4-2 Exercises

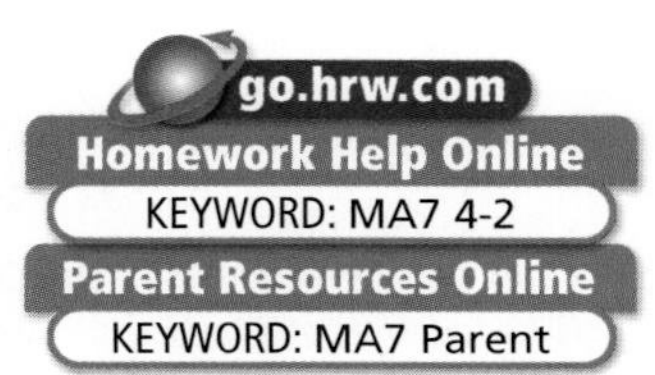


## GUIDED PRACTICE

**Vocabulary** **Apply the vocabulary from this lesson to answer each question.**

1. Use a mapping diagram to show a relation that is not a *function*.
2. The set of $x$-values for a relation is also called the __?__. (*domain* or *range*)

SEE EXAMPLE 1
p. 236

**Express each relation as a table, as a graph, and as a mapping diagram.**

3. $\{(1, 1), (1, 2)\}$
4. $\left\{(-1, 1), \left(-2, \frac{1}{2}\right), \left(-3, \frac{1}{3}\right), \left(-4, \frac{1}{4}\right)\right\}$
5. $\{(-1, 1), (-3, 3), (5, -5), (-7, 7)\}$
6. $\{(0, 0), (2, -4), (2, -2)\}$

SEE EXAMPLE 2
p. 237

**Give the domain and range of each relation.**

7. $\{(-5, 7), (0, 0), (2, -8), (5, -20)\}$
8. $\{(1, 2), (2, 4), (3, 6), (4, 8), (5, 10)\}$
9.

| $x$ | 3 | 5 | 2 | 8 | 6 |
|---|---|---|---|---|---|
| $y$ | 9 | 25 | 4 | 81 | 36 |

10. 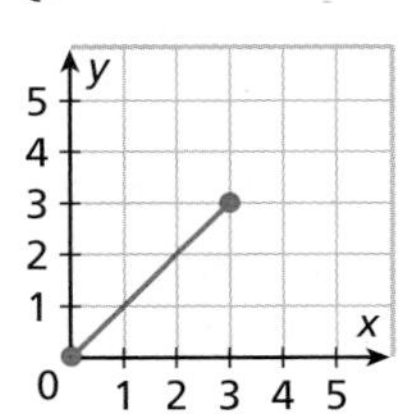


SEE EXAMPLE 3
p. 237

**Multi-Step** **Give the domain and range of each relation. Tell whether the relation is a function. Explain.**

11. $\{(1, 3), (1, 0), (1, -2), (1, 8)\}$
12. $\{(-2, 1), (-1, 2), (0, 3), (1, 4)\}$
13.

| $x$ | −2 | −1 | 0 | 1 | 2 |
|---|---|---|---|---|---|
| $y$ | 1 | 1 | 1 | 1 | 1 |

14.

## PRACTICE AND PROBLEM SOLVING

**Independent Practice**

| For Exercises | See Example |
|---|---|
| 15–16 | 1 |
| 17–18 | 2 |
| 19–20 | 3 |

**Extra Practice**

Skills Practice p. S10
Application Practice p. S31

**Express each relation as a table, as a graph, and as a mapping diagram.**

15. $\{(-2, -4), (-1, -1), (0, 0), (1, -1), (2, -4)\}$
16. $\left\{(2, 1), \left(2, \frac{1}{2}\right), (2, 2), \left(2, 2\frac{1}{2}\right)\right\}$

**Give the domain and range of each relation.**

17. 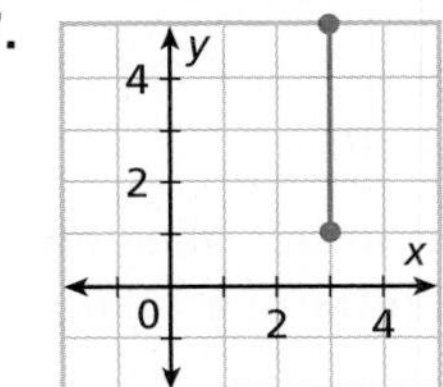


18.

| $x$ | $y$ |
|---|---|
| 4 | 4 |
| 5 | 5 |
| 6 | 6 |
| 7 | 7 |
| 8 | 8 |

**Multi-Step** **Give the domain and range of each relation. Tell whether the relation is a function. Explain.**

**19.**

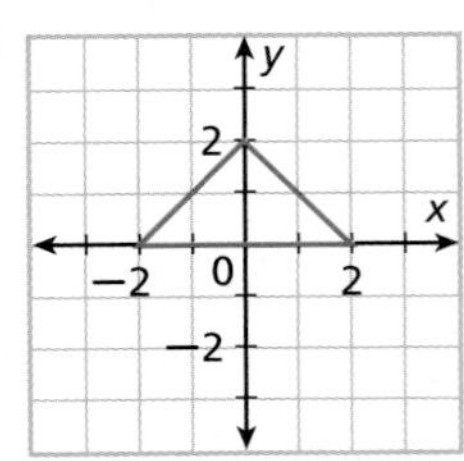


**20.**

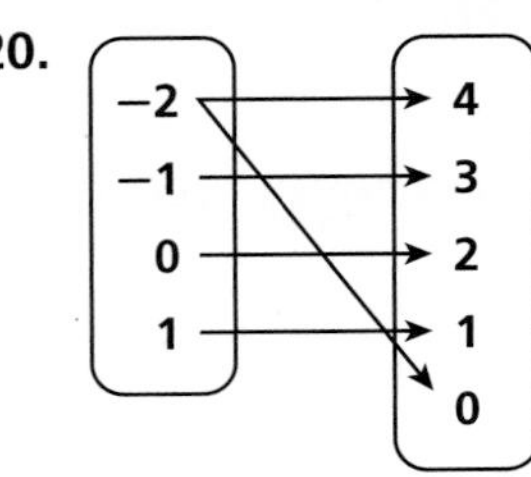


21. **Consumer Application** An electrician charges a base fee of \$75 plus \$50 for each hour of work. Create a table that shows the amount the electrician charges for 1, 2, 3, and 4 hours of work. Let $x$ represent the number of hours and $y$ represent the amount charged for $x$ hours. Is this relation a function? Explain.

22. **Geometry** Write a relation as a set of ordered pairs in which the $x$-value represents the length of a side of a square and the $y$-value represents the area of the square. Use a domain of 2, 4, 6, 9, and 11.

23. **Multi-Step** Create a mapping diagram to display the numbers of days in 1, 2, 3, and 4 weeks. Is this relation a function? Explain.

24. **Nutrition** The illustrations list the number of grams of fat and the number of Calories from fat for selected foods.
    a. Create a graph for the relation between grams of fat and Calories from fat.
    b. Is this relation a function? Explain.

**Hamburger**
Fat (g): 14
Fat (Cal): 126

**Cheeseburger**
Fat (g): 18
Fat (Cal): 162

**Grilled chicken filet**
Fat (g): 3.5
Fat (Cal): 31.5

**Breaded chicken filet**
Fat (g): 11
Fat (Cal): 99

**Taco salad**
Fat (g): 19
Fat (Cal): 171

25. **Recreation** A shop rents canoes for a \$7 equipment fee and \$2 per hour, with a maximum cost of \$15 per day. Express the number of hours $x$ and the cost $y$ as a relation in table form, and find the cost to rent a canoe for 1, 2, 3, 4, and 5 hours. Is this relation a function? Explain.

26. **Health** You can burn about 6 Calories a minute bicycling. Let $x$ represent the number of minutes bicycled, and let $y$ represent the number of Calories burned.
    a. Write ordered pairs to show the number of Calories burned if you bicycle for 60, 120, 180, 240, or 300 minutes. Graph the ordered pairs.
    b. Find the domain and range of the relation.
    c. Does this graph represent a function? Explain.

27. **Critical Thinking** For a function, can the number of elements in the range be greater than the number of elements in the domain? Explain.

28. **Critical Thinking** Tell whether each statement is true or false. If false, explain why.
    a. All relations are functions.
    b. All functions are relations.

**MULTI-STEP TEST PREP**

29. This problem will prepare you for the Multi-Step Test Prep on page 260.
    a. The graph shows the number of gallons being pumped into a pool over a 5-hour time period. Find the domain and range of the graph.
    b. Does the graph represent a function? Explain.
    c. Give the time and volume as ordered pairs at 2 hours and at 3 hours 30 minutes.

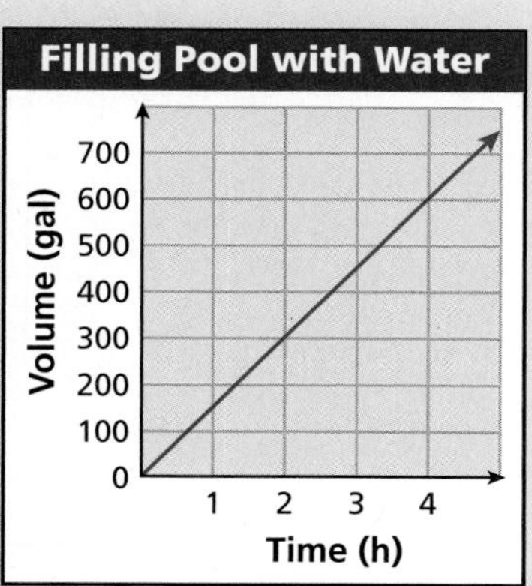


30. **ERROR ANALYSIS** When asked whether the relation $\{(-4, 16), (-2, 4), (0, 0), (2, 4)\}$ is a function, a student stated that the relation is not a function because 4 appears twice. What error did the student make? How would you explain to the student why this relation is a function?

31. **Write About It** Describe a real-world situation using a relation that is NOT a function. Create a mapping diagram to show why the relation is not a function.

**TEST PREP**

**MA.A.4.1, MA.A.4.2**

32. Which of the following relations is NOT a function?

Ⓐ $\{(6, 2), (-1, 2), (-3, 2), (-5, 2)\}$

Ⓑ
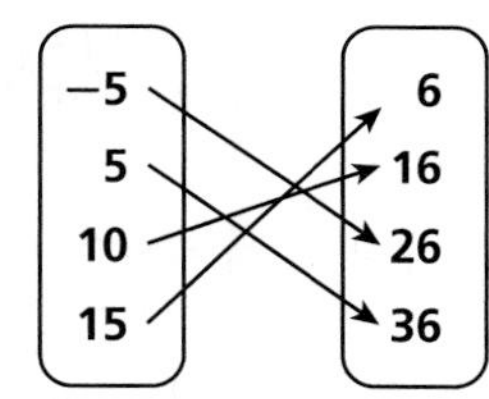


Ⓒ

| $x$ | 3 | 5 | 7 |
|---|---|---|---|
| $y$ | 1 | 15 | 30 |

Ⓓ
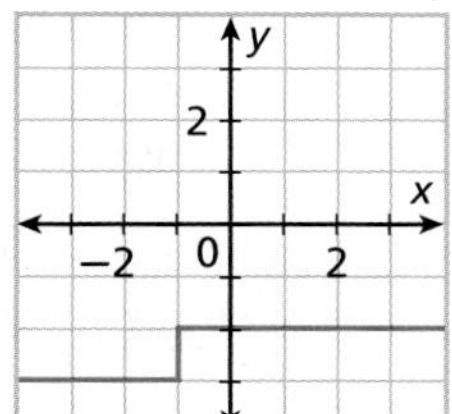


33. Which is NOT a correct way to describe the function $\{(-3, 2), (1, 8), (-1, 5), (3, 11)\}$?

Ⓕ
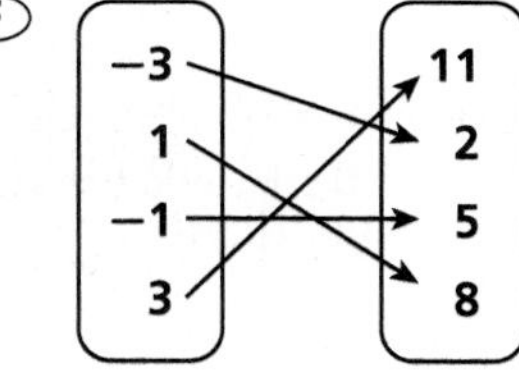


Ⓗ Domain: $\{-3, 1, -1, 3\}$

Range: $\{2, 8, 5, 11\}$

Ⓖ
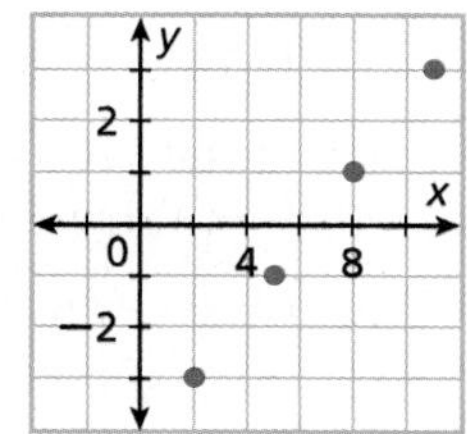


Ⓙ

| $x$ | $y$ |
|---|---|
| −3 | 2 |
| −1 | 5 |
| 1 | 8 |
| 3 | 11 |

**34.** Which graph represents a function?

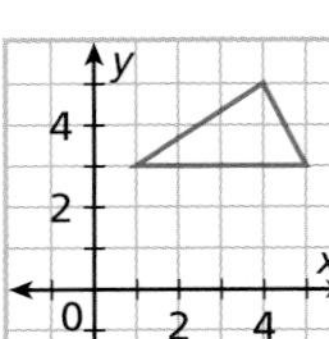

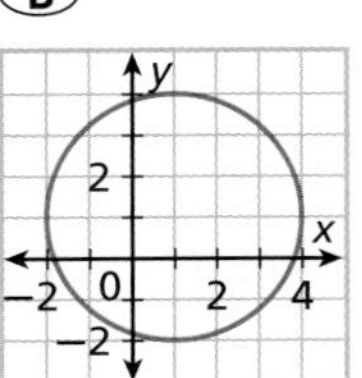
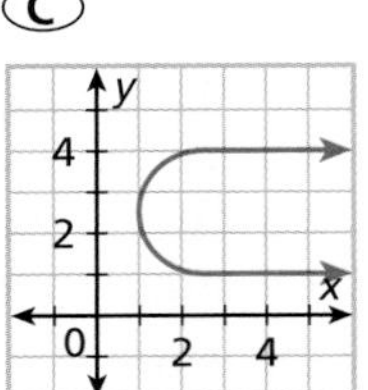

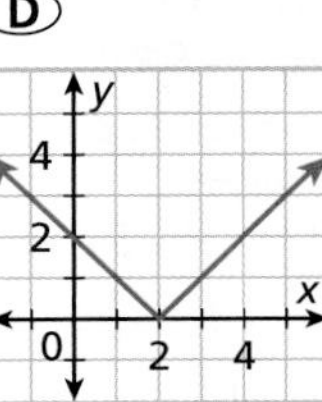

**35. Extended Response** Use the table for the following.

| *x* | −3 | −1 | 0 | 1 | 3 |
|---|---|---|---|---|---|
| *y* | 5 | 7 | 9 | 11 | 13 |

**a.** Express the relation as ordered pairs.

**b.** Give the domain and range of the relation.

**c.** Does the relation represent a function? Explain your answer.

## CHALLENGE AND EXTEND

**36.** What values of $a$ make the relation $\{(a, 1), (2, 3), (4, 5)\}$ a function? Explain.

**37.** What values of $b$ make the relation $\{(5, 6), (7, 8), (9, b)\}$ a function? Explain.

**38.** The *inverse* of a relation is created by interchanging the $x$- and $y$- coordinates of each ordered pair in the relation.

**a.** Find the inverse of the following relation: $\{(-2, 5), (0, 4), (3, -8), (7, 5)\}$.

**b.** Is the original relation a function? Why or why not? Is the inverse of the relation a function? Why or why not?

**c.** The statement "If a relation is a function, then the inverse of the relation is also a function" is sometimes true. Give an example of a relation and its inverse that are both functions. Also give an example of a relation and its inverse that are both not functions.

## SPIRAL REVIEW

**39.** The ratio of the width of a rectangle to its length is 3 : 4. The length of the rectangle is 36 cm. Write and solve a proportion to find the rectangle's width. *(Lesson 2-6)*

**40.** A scale drawing of a house is drawn with a scale of 1 in. : 16 ft. Find the actual length of a hallway that is $\frac{5}{8}$ in. on the scale drawing. *(Lesson 2-6)*

**41.** Penny wants to drink at least 64 ounces of water today. She has consumed 45 ounces of water so far. Write, solve, and graph an inequality to determine how many more ounces of water Penny must drink to reach her goal. *(Lesson 3-2)*

**42.** The local pizza parlor sold the following number of pizzas over 10 days. Sketch a graph for the situation. Tell whether the graph is continuous or discrete. *(Lesson 4-1)*

| Time (days) | 1 | 2 | 3 | 4 | 5 | 6 | 7 | 8 | 9 | 10 |
|---|---|---|---|---|---|---|---|---|---|---|
| Pizzas Sold | 5 | 11 | 2 | 4 | 8 | 10 | 3 | 6 | 12 | 1 |

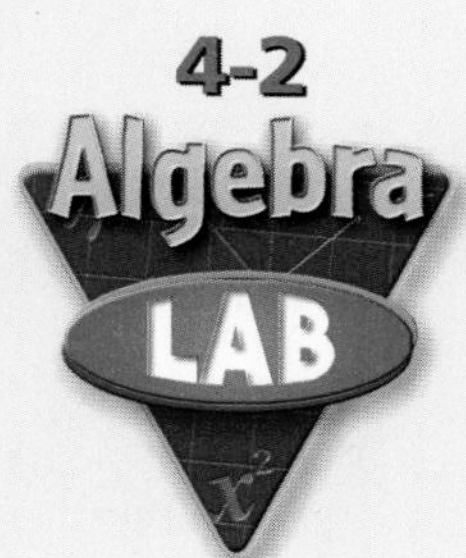

Use with Lesson 4-2

# The Vertical-Line Test

The *vertical-line test* can be used to visually determine whether a graphed relation is a function.

 **MA.A.4.1** Categorize relations as functions or "not functions".

## Activity

1. Look at the values in Table 1. Is every $x$-value paired with exactly one $y$-value? If not, what $x$-value(s) are paired with more than one $y$-value?

2. Is the relation a function? Explain.

3. Graph the points from the Table 1. Draw a vertical line through each point of the graph. Does any vertical line touch more than one point?

**Table 1**

| $x$ | $y$ |
|---|---|
| −2 | −5 |
| −1 | −3 |
| 0 | −1 |
| 1 | 1 |
| 2 | 3 |
| 3 | 5 |

4. Look at the values in Table 2. Is every $x$-value paired with exactly one $y$-value? If not, what $x$-value(s) are paired with more than one $y$-value?

5. Is the relation a function? Explain.

6. Graph the points from the Table 2. Draw a vertical line through each point of the graph. Does any vertical line touch more than one point?

7. What is the $x$-value of the two points that are on the same vertical line? Is that $x$-value paired with more than one $y$-value?

8. Write a statement describing how to use a vertical line to tell if a relation is a function. This is called the vertical-line test.

9. Why does the vertical-line test work?

**Table 2**

| $x$ | $y$ |
|---|---|
| −2 | −3 |
| 1 | 4 |
| 0 | 5 |
| 1 | 2 |
| 2 | 3 |
| 3 | 5 |

## Try This

**Use the vertical-line test to determine whether each relation is a function. If a relation is not a function, list two ordered pairs that show the same $x$-value with two different $y$-values.**

1. 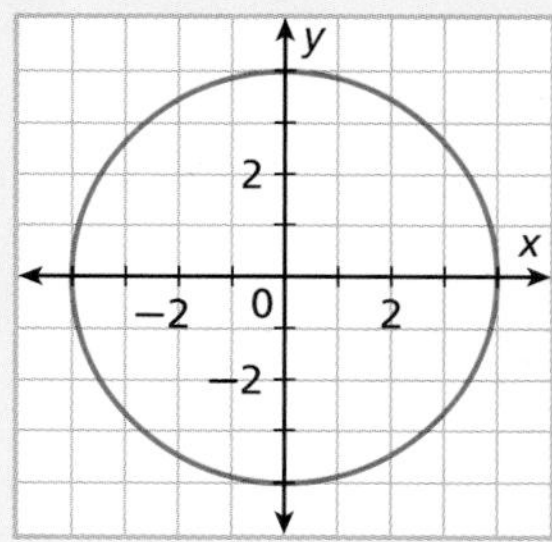


2. 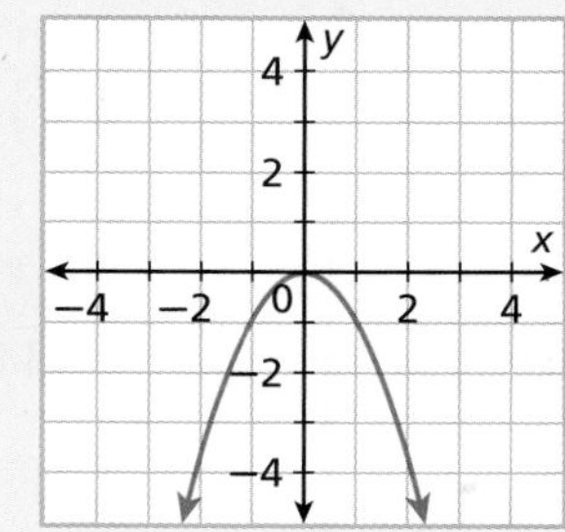


3. 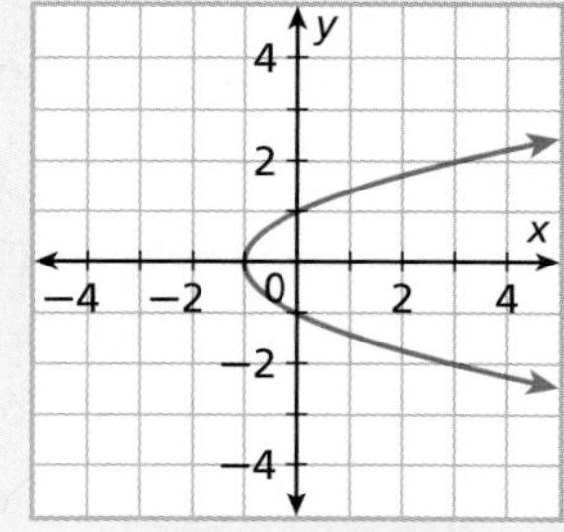

# Model Variable Relationships

*Use with Lesson 4-3*

You can use models to represent an algebraic relationship. Using these models, you can write an algebraic expression to help describe and extend patterns.

**MA.A.4** Understand functions based on mathematical and real-world phenomena.

**The diagrams below represent the side views of tables. Each has a tabletop and a base. Copy and complete the chart using the pattern shown in the diagrams.**

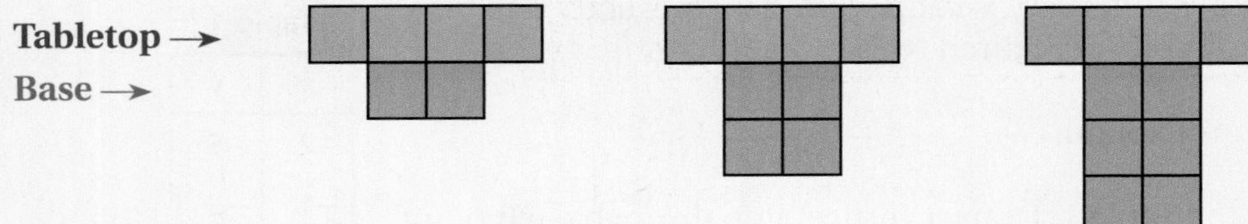


| TERM NUMBER | FIGURE | DESCRIPTION OF FIGURE | EXPRESSION FOR NUMBER OF BLOCKS | VALUE OF TERM (NUMBER OF BLOCKS) | ORDERED PAIR |
|---|---|---|---|---|---|
| 1 | | length of table top = 4<br>height of base = 1 | $4 + (2)1$ | 6 | (1, 6) |
| 2 | | length of table top = 4<br>height of base = 2 | | 8 | |
| 3 | | length of table top = 4<br>height of base = 3 | | 10 | |
| 4 | | | | | |
| 5 | | | | | |
| $n$ | | | | | |

## Try This

1. Explain why you must multiply the height of the base by 2.
2. What does the ordered pair (1, 6) mean?
3. Does the ordered pair (10, 24) belong in this pattern? Why or why not?
4. Which expression from the table describes how you would find the total number of blocks for any term number $n$?
5. Use your rule to find the 25th term in this pattern.

# 4-3 Writing Functions

**MA.A.4.2** Use appropriate terminology and notation … associated with functions.

***Objectives***

Identify independent and dependent variables.

Write an equation in function notation and evaluate a function for given input values.

***Vocabulary***

independent variable
dependent variable
function rule
function notation

**Why learn this?**

You can use a function rule to calculate how much money you will earn for working specific amounts of time.

Suppose Tasha baby-sits and charges \$5 per hour.

| Time Worked (h) $x$ | 1 | 2 | 3 | 4 |
|---|---|---|---|---|
| Amount Earned (\$) $y$ | 5 | 10 | 15 | 20 |

The amount of money Tasha earns is \$5 times the number of hours she works. Write an equation using two different variables to show this relationship.

Amount earned is \$5 times the number of hours worked.

$$y \quad = 5 \quad \cdot \quad x$$

Tasha can use this equation to find how much money she will earn for any number of hours she works.

**EXAMPLE 1** **Using a Table to Write an Equation**

**Determine a relationship between the $x$- and $y$-values. Write an equation.**

| $x$ | 1 | 2 | 3 | 4 |
|---|---|---|---|---|
| $y$ | −2 | −1 | 0 | 1 |

**Step 1** List possible relationships between the first $x$- and $y$-values.

$1 - 3 = -2$ or $1(-2) = -2$

**Step 2** Determine if one relationship works for the remaining values.

$2 - 3 = -1$ ✓ $\quad 2(-2) \neq -1$ ✗

$3 - 3 = 0$ ✓ $\quad 3(-2) \neq 0$ ✗

$4 - 3 = 1$ ✓ $\quad 4(-2) \neq 1$ ✗

The first relationship works. The value of $y$ is 3 less than $x$.

**Step 3** Write an equation.

$y = x - 3$ *The value of y is 3 less than x.*

**1.** Determine a relationship between the $x$- and $y$-values in the relation $\{(1, 3), (2, 6), (3, 9), (4, 12)\}$. Write an equation.

The equation in Example 1 describes a function because for each $x$-value (input), there is only one $y$-value (output).

The input of a function is the **independent variable**. The **output** of a function is the **dependent variable**. The value of the dependent variable *depends* on, or is a function of, the value of the independent variable. For Tasha, the amount she earns depends on, or is a function of, the amount of time she works.

## EXAMPLE 2 Identifying Independent and Dependent Variables

**Helpful Hint**

There are several different ways to describe the variables of a function.

| Independent Variable | Dependent Variable |
|---|---|
| *x*-values | *y*-values |
| Domain | Range |
| Input | Output |
| $x$ | $f(x)$ |

**Identify the independent and dependent variables in each situation.**

**A In the winter, more electricity is used when the temperature goes down, and less is used when the temperature rises.**

The **amount of electricity** used *depends on* the temperature.

Dependent: **amount of electricity** Independent: temperature

**B The cost of shipping a package is based on its weight.**

The **cost** of shipping a package *depends on* its weight.

Dependent: **cost** Independent: weight

**C The faster Ron walks, the quicker he gets home.**

The **time** it takes Ron to get home *depends on* the speed he walks.

Dependent: **time** Independent: speed

**Identify the independent and dependent variables in each situation.**

**2a.** A company charges \$10 per hour to rent a jackhammer.

**2b.** Camryn buys $p$ pounds of apples at \$0.99 per pound.

An algebraic expression that defines a function is a **function rule**. $5 \cdot x$ in the equation about Tasha's earnings is a function rule.

If $x$ is the independent variable and $y$ is the dependent variable, then **function notation** for $y$ is $f(x)$, read "$f$ of $x$," where $f$ names the function. When an equation in two variables describes a function, you can use function notation to write it.

**The dependent variable is a function of the independent variable.**

| | | | |
|---|---|---|---|
| $y$ | **is** | **a function of** | $x$. |
| $y$ | $=$ | $f$ | $(x)$ |

Since $y = f(x)$, Tasha's earnings, $y = 5x$, can be rewritten in function notation by substituting $f(x)$ for $y$: $f(x) = 5x$. Sometimes you will see functions written using $y$, and sometimes you will see functions written using $f(x)$.

## EXAMPLE 3 Writing Functions

**Identify the independent and dependent variables. Write a rule in function notation for each situation.**

**A A lawyer's fee is \$200 per hour for her services.**

The **fee** for the lawyer depends on how many hours she works.

Dependent: **fee** Independent: hours

Let $h$ represent the number of hours the lawyer works.

The function for the lawyer's fee is $f(h) = 200h$.

**Identify the independent and dependent variables. Write a rule in function notation for each situation.**

**B** **The admission fee to a local carnival is \$8. Each ride costs \$1.50.**

The **total cost** depends on the number of rides ridden, plus \$8.

Dependent: **total cost** Independent: number of rides

Let $r$ represent the number of rides ridden.

The function for the total cost of the carnival is $f(r) = 1.50r + 8$.

**Identify the independent and dependent variables. Write a rule in function notation for each situation.**

**3a.** Steven buys lettuce that costs \$1.69/lb.

**3b.** An amusement park charges a \$6.00 parking fee plus \$29.99 per person.

You can think of a function as an **input-output** machine. For Tasha's earnings, $f(x) = 5x$, if you input a value $x$, the output is $5x$.

If Tasha wanted to know how much money she would earn by working 6 hours, she could input 6 for $x$ and find the output. This is called *evaluating the function.*

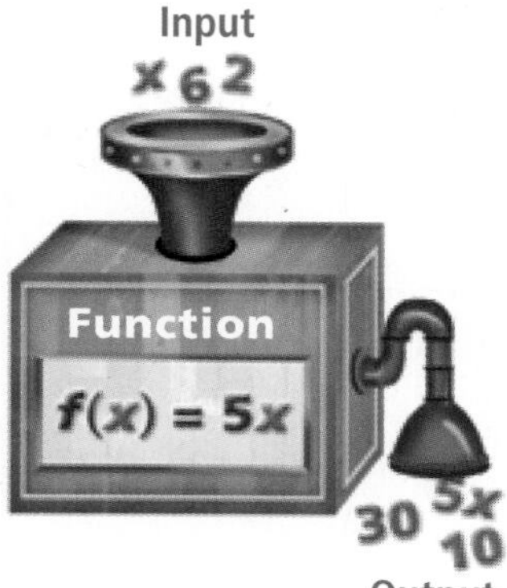


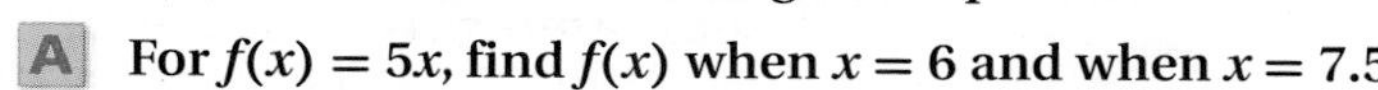

EXAMPLE 4

## Evaluating Functions

**Evaluate each function for the given input values.**

**A** **For $f(x) = 5x$, find $f(x)$ when $x = 6$ and when $x = 7.5$.**

| | |
|---|---|
| $f(x) = 5x$ | $f(x) = 5x$ |
| $f(6) = 5(6)$ *Substitute 6 for x.* | $f(7.5) = 5(7.5)$ *Substitute 7.5 for x.* |
| $= 30$ *Simplify.* | $= 37.5$ *Simplify.* |

**B** **For $g(t) = 2.30t + 10$, find $g(t)$ when $t = 2$ and when $t = -5$.**

| | |
|---|---|
| $g(t) = 2.30t + 10$ | $g(t) = 2.30t + 10$ |
| $g(2) = 2.30(2) + 10$ | $g(-5) = 2.30(-5) + 10$ |
| $= 4.6 + 10$ | $= -11.5 + 10$ |
| $= 14.6$ | $= -1.5$ |

**C** **For $h(x) = \frac{1}{2}x - 3$, find $h(x)$ when $x = 12$ and when $x = -8$.**

| | |
|---|---|
| $h(x) = \frac{1}{2}x - 3$ | $h(x) = \frac{1}{2}x - 3$ |
| $h(12) = \frac{1}{2}(12) - 3$ | $h(-8) = \frac{1}{2}(-8) - 3$ |
| $= 6 - 3$ | $= -4 - 3$ |
| $= 3$ | $= -7$ |

**Reading Math**

Functions can be named with any letter; *f*, *g*, and *h* are the most common. You read $f(6)$ as "*f* of 6," and $g(2)$ as "*g* of 2."

**Evaluate each function for the given input values.**

**4a.** For $h(c) = 2c - 1$, find $h(c)$ when $c = 1$ and $c = -3$.

**4b.** For $g(t) = \frac{1}{4}t + 1$, find $g(t)$ when $t = -24$ and $t = 400$.

When a function describes a real-world situation, every real number is not always reasonable for the domain and range. For example, a number representing the length of an object cannot be negative, and only whole numbers can represent a number of people.

### EXAMPLE 5 Finding the Reasonable Domain and Range of a Function

**Manuel has already sold \$20 worth of tickets to the school play. He has 4 tickets left to sell at \$2.50 per ticket. Write a function rule to describe how much money Manuel can collect from selling tickets. Find a reasonable domain and range for the function.**

| Money collected from ticket sales | is | \$2.50 | per | ticket | plus | the \$20 already sold. |
|---|---|---|---|---|---|---|
| $f(x)$ | $=$ | \$2.50 | $\cdot$ | $x$ | $+$ | 20 |

If he sells $x$ more tickets, he will have collected $f(x) = 2.50x + 20$ dollars.

Manuel has only 4 tickets left to sell, so he could sell 0, 1, 2, 3, or 4 tickets. A reasonable domain is $\{0, 1, 2, 3, 4\}$.

Substitute these values into the function rule to find the range values.

| $x$ | 0 | 1 | 2 | 3 | 4 |
|---|---|---|---|---|---|
| $f(x)$ | $2.50(0) + 20 = 20$ | $2.50(1) + 20 = 22.50$ | $2.50(2) + 20 = 25$ | $2.50(3) + 20 = 27.50$ | $2.50(4) + 20 = 30$ |

A reasonable range for this situation is $\{\$20, \$22.50, \$25, \$27.50, \$30\}$.

5. The settings on a space heater are the whole numbers from 0 to 3. The total number of watts used for each setting is 500 times the setting number. Write a function rule to describe the number of watts used for each setting. Find a reasonable domain and range for the function.

## THINK AND DISCUSS

1. When you input water into an ice machine, the output is ice cubes. Name another real-world object that has an input and an output.
2. How do you identify the independent and dependent variables in a situation?
3. Explain how to find reasonable domain values for a function.

4. **GET ORGANIZED** Copy and complete the graphic organizer. Use the rule $y = x + 3$ and the domain $\{-2, -1, 0, 1, 2\}$.

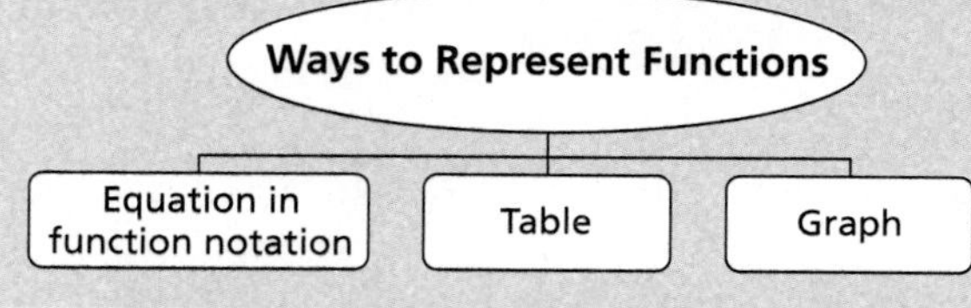

# 4-3 Exercises

MA.A.4.2

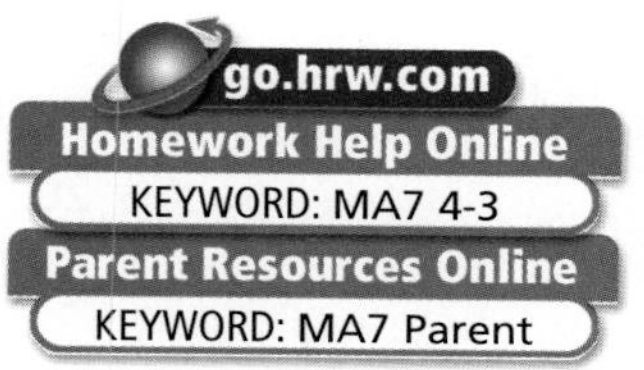


## GUIDED PRACTICE

**Vocabulary** **Apply the vocabulary from this lesson to answer each question.**

1. The output of a function is the __?__ variable. (*independent* or *dependent*)
2. An algebraic expression that defines a function is a __?__. (*function rule* or *function notation*)

SEE EXAMPLE 1 p. 245

**Determine a relationship between the $x$- and $y$-values. Write an equation.**

3.

| $x$ | 1 | 2 | 3 | 4 |
|---|---|---|---|---|
| $y$ | $-1$ | 0 | 1 | 2 |

4. $\{(1, 4), (2, 7), (3, 10), (4, 13)\}$

SEE EXAMPLE 2 p. 246

**Identify the independent and dependent variables in each situation.**

5. A small-size bottle of water costs \$1.99 and a large-size bottle of water costs \$3.49.
6. An employee receives 2 vacation days for every month worked.

SEE EXAMPLE 3 p. 246

**Identify the independent and dependent variables. Write a rule in function notation for each situation.**

7. An air-conditioning technician charges customers \$75 per hour.
8. An ice rink charges \$3.50 for skates and \$1.25 per hour.

SEE EXAMPLE 4 p. 247

**Evaluate each function for the given input values.**

9. For $f(x) = 7x + 2$, find $f(x)$ when $x = 0$ and when $x = 1$.
10. For $g(x) = 4x - 9$, find $g(x)$ when $x = 3$ and when $x = 5$.
11. For $h(t) = \frac{1}{3}t - 10$, find $h(t)$ when $t = 27$ and when $t = -15$.

SEE EXAMPLE 5 p. 248

12. A construction company uses beams that are 2, 3, or 4 meters long. The measure of each beam must be converted to centimeters. Write a function rule to describe the situation. Find a reasonable domain and range for the function. (*Hint*: 1 m = 100 cm)

## PRACTICE AND PROBLEM SOLVING

**Independent Practice**

| For Exercises | See Example |
|---|---|
| 13–14 | 1 |
| 15–16 | 2 |
| 17–19 | 3 |
| 20–22 | 4 |
| 23 | 5 |

**Extra Practice**

Skills Practice p. S10
Application Practice p. S31

**Determine a relationship between the $x$- and $y$-values. Write an equation.**

13.

| $x$ | 1 | 2 | 3 | 4 |
|---|---|---|---|---|
| $y$ | $-2$ | $-4$ | $-6$ | $-8$ |

14. $\{(1, -1), (2, -2), (3, -3), (4, -4)\}$

**Identify the independent and dependent variables in each situation.**

15. Gardeners buy fertilizer according to the size of a lawn.
16. The cost to gift wrap an order is \$3 plus \$1 per item wrapped.

**Identify the independent and dependent variables. Write a rule in function notation for each situation.**

17. To rent a DVD, a customer must pay \$3.99 plus \$0.99 for every day that it is late.
18. Stephen charges \$25 for each lawn he mows.
19. A car can travel 28 miles per gallon of gas.

**Evaluate each function for the given input values.**

**20.** For $f(x) = x^2 - 5$, find $f(x)$ when $x = 0$ and when $x = 3$.

**21.** For $g(x) = x^2 + 6$, find $g(x)$ when $x = 1$ and when $x = 2$.

**22.** For $f(x) = \frac{2}{3}x + 3$, find $f(x)$ when $x = 9$ and when $x = -3$.

**23.** A mail-order company charges \$5 per order plus \$2 per item in the order, up to a maximum of 4 items. Write a function rule to describe the situation. Find a reasonable domain and range for the function.

**LINK**

**Transportation**

Air Force One refers to two specially configured Boeing 747-200B airplanes. The radio call sign when the president is aboard either aircraft or any Air Force aircraft is "Air Force One."

**24.** **Transportation** Air Force One can travel 630 miles per hour. Let $h$ be the number of hours traveled. The function rule $d = 630h$ gives the distance $d$ in miles that Air Force One travels in $h$ hours.

a. Identify the independent and dependent variables. Write $d = 630h$ in function notation.

b. What are reasonable values for the domain and range in the situation described?

c. How far can Air Force One travel in 12 hours?

**25.** Complete the table for $g(z) = 2z - 5$.

| $z$ | 1 | 2 | 3 | 4 |
|---|---|---|---|---|
| $g(z)$ | | | | |

**26.** Complete the table for $h(x) = x^2 + x$.

| $x$ | 0 | 1 | 2 | 3 |
|---|---|---|---|---|
| $h(x)$ | | | | |

**27.** **Estimation** For $f(x) = 3x + 5$, estimate the output when $x = -6.89$, $x = 1.01$, and $x = 4.67$.

**28.** **Transportation** A car can travel 30 miles on a gallon of gas and has a 20-gallon gas tank. Let $g$ be the number of gallons of gas the car has in its tank. The function rule $d = 30g$ gives the distance $d$ in miles that the car travels on $g$ gallons.

a. What are reasonable values for the domain and range in the situation described?

b. How far can the car travel on 12 gallons of gas?

**29.** **Critical Thinking** Give an example of a real-life situation for which the reasonable domain consists of 1, 2, 3, and 4 and the reasonable range consists of 2, 4, 6, and 8.

**30.** **///ERROR ANALYSIS///** Rashid saves \$150 each month. He wants to know how much he will have saved in 2 years. He writes the rule $s = m + 150$ to help him figure out how much he will save, where $s$ is the amount saved and $m$ is the number of months he saves. Explain why his rule is incorrect.

**31.** **Write About It** Give a real-life situation that can be described by a function. Explain which is the independent variable and which is the dependent variable.

**MULTI-STEP TEST PREP**

**32.** This problem will prepare you for the Multi-Step Test Prep on page 260.

The table shows the volume $v$ of water pumped into a pool after $t$ hours.

a. Determine a relationship between the time and the volume of water and write an equation.

b. Identify the independent and dependent variables.

c. If the pool holds 10,000 gallons, how long will it take to fill?

**Amount of Water in Pool**

| Time (h) | Volume (gal) |
|---|---|
| 0 | 0 |
| 1 | 1250 |
| 2 | 2500 |
| 3 | 3750 |
| 4 | 5000 |

MA.A.4.2

**33.** Marsha buys $x$ pens at \$0.70 per pen and one pencil for \$0.10. Which function gives the total amount Marsha spends?

Ⓐ $c(x) = 0.70x + 0.10x$
Ⓑ $c(x) = 0.70x + 1$
Ⓒ $c(x) = (0.70 + 0.10)x$
Ⓓ $c(x) = 0.70x + 0.10$

**34.** Belle is buying pizzas for her daughter's birthday party, using the prices in the table. Which equation best describes the relationship between the total cost $c$ and the number of pizzas $p$?

| Pizzas | Total Cost ($) |
|---|---|
| 5 | 26.25 |
| 10 | 52.50 |
| 15 | 78.75 |

Ⓕ $c = 26.25p$
Ⓖ $c = 5.25p$
Ⓗ $c = p + 26.25$
Ⓙ $c = 6p - 3.75$

**35.** **Gridded Response** What is the value of $f(x) = 5 - \frac{1}{2}x$ when $x = 3$?

## CHALLENGE AND EXTEND

**36.** The formula to convert a temperature that is in degrees Celsius $x$ to degrees Fahrenheit $f(x)$ is $f(x) = \frac{9}{5}x + 32$. What are reasonable values for the domain and range when you convert to Fahrenheit the temperature of water as it rises from 0° to 100° Celsius?

**37.** **Math History** In his studies of the motion of free-falling objects, Galileo Galilei found that regardless of its mass, an object will fall a distance $d$ that is related to the square of its travel time $t$ in seconds. The modern formula that describes free-fall motion is $d = \frac{1}{2}gt^2$, where $g$ is the acceleration due to gravity and $t$ is the length of time in seconds the object falls. Find the distance an object falls in 3 seconds. (*Hint*: Research to find acceleration due to gravity in meters per second squared.)

## SPIRAL REVIEW

**Solve each equation. Check your answer.** *(Lesson 2-3)*

**38.** $5x + 2 - 7x = -10$ **39.** $3(2 - y) = 15$ **40.** $\frac{2}{3}p - \frac{1}{2} = \frac{1}{6}$

**Find the value of $x$ in each diagram.** *(Lesson 2-7)*

**41.** $\triangle ABC \sim \triangle DEF$

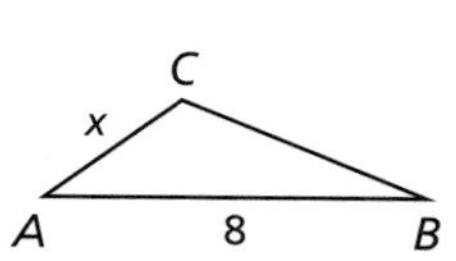


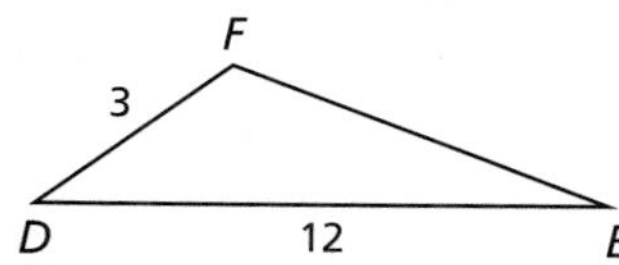


**42.** $QRST \sim LMNP$

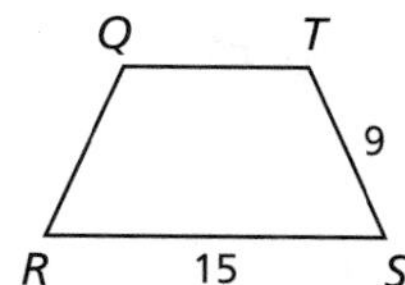


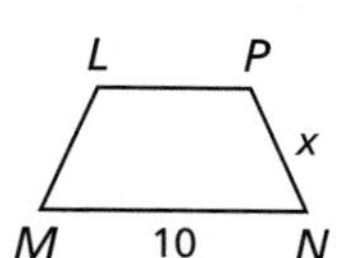


**Give the domain and range of each relation. Tell whether the relation is a function and explain.** *(Lesson 4-2)*

**43.**

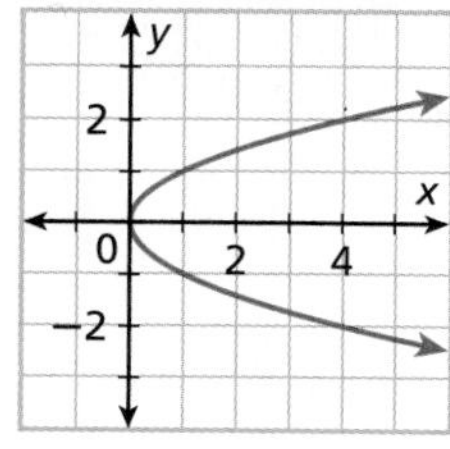


**44.**

| $x$ | $y$ |
|---|---|
| −3 | 4 |
| −1 | 2 |
| 0 | 0 |
| 1 | 2 |
| 3 | −4 |

# 4-4 Graphing Functions

**MA.A.4** Understand functions based on mathematical and real-world phenomena.

***Objectives***

Graph functions given a limited domain.

Graph functions given a domain of all real numbers.

**Who uses this?**

Scientists can use a function to make conclusions about rising sea level.

Sea level is rising at an approximate rate of 2.5 millimeters per year. If this rate continues, the function $y = 2.5x$ can describe how many millimeters $y$ sea level will rise in the next $x$ years.

One way to understand functions such as the one above is to graph them. You can graph a function by finding ordered pairs that satisfy the function.

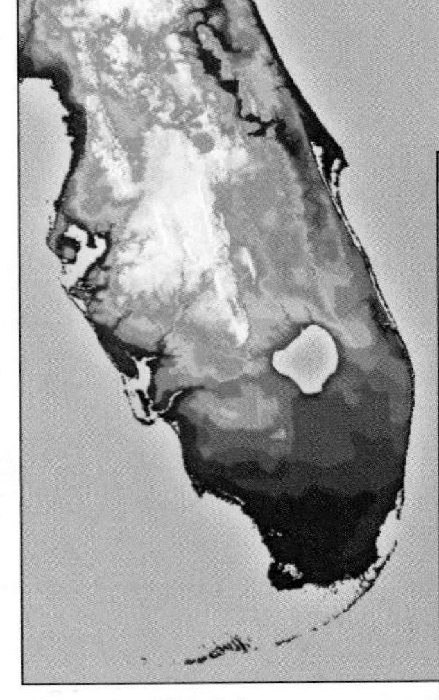

Current Florida coastline.

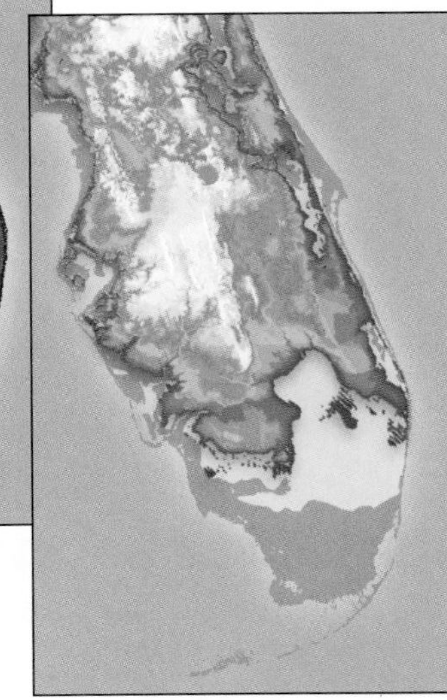

Possible Florida coastline in 2400 years.

## EXAMPLE 1 Graphing Solutions Given a Domain

**Graph each function for the given domain.**

**A** $-x + 2y = 6$; D: $\{-4, -2, 0, 2\}$

**Step 1** Solve for $y$ since you are given values of the domain, or $x$.

$$-x + 2y = 6$$

$$\underline{+x \qquad\quad +x}$$ *Add x to both sides.*

$$2y = x + 6$$

$$\frac{2y}{2} = \frac{x+6}{2}$$ *Since y is multiplied by 2, divide both sides by 2.*

$$y = \frac{x}{2} + \frac{6}{2}$$ *Rewrite $\frac{x+6}{2}$ as two separate fractions.*

$$y = \frac{1}{2}x + 3$$ *Simplify.*

**Helpful Hint**

Sometimes solving for $y$ first makes it easier to substitute values of $x$ and solve to find an ordered pair.

To review solving for a variable, see Lesson 2-5.

**Step 2** Substitute the given values of the domain for $x$ and find values of $y$.

| $x$ | $y = \frac{1}{2}x + 3$ | $(x, y)$ |
|---|---|---|
| $-4$ | $y = \frac{1}{2}(-4) + 3 = 1$ | $(-4, 1)$ |
| $-2$ | $y = \frac{1}{2}(-2) + 3 = 2$ | $(-2, 2)$ |
| $0$ | $y = \frac{1}{2}(0) + 3 = 3$ | $(0, 3)$ |
| $2$ | $y = \frac{1}{2}(2) + 3 = 4$ | $(2, 4)$ |

**Step 3** Graph the ordered pairs.

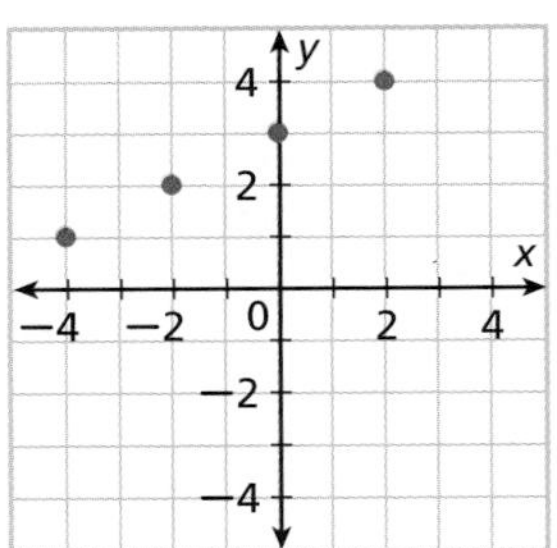

**Graph each function for the given domain.**

**B** $f(x) = |x|$; D: {−2, −1, 0, 1, 2}

**Step 1** Use the given values of the domain to find values of $f(x)$.

| $x$ | $f(x) = \|x\|$ | $(x, f(x))$ |
|---|---|---|
| −2 | $f(x) = \|-2\| = 2$ | (−2, 2) |
| −1 | $f(x) = \|-1\| = 1$ | (−1, 1) |
| 0 | $f(x) = \|0\| = 0$ | (0, 0) |
| 1 | $f(x) = \|1\| = 1$ | (1, 1) |
| 2 | $f(x) = \|2\| = 2$ | (2, 2) |

**Step 2** Graph the ordered pairs.

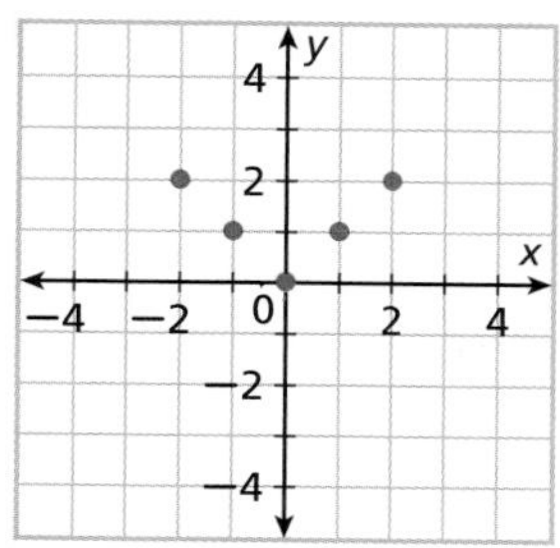

**Graph each function for the given domain.**

**1a.** $-2x + y = 3$; D: {−5, −3, 1, 4}

**1b.** $f(x) = x^2 + 2$; D: {−3, −1, 0, 1, 3}

If the domain of a function is all real numbers, any number can be used as an input value. This process will produce an infinite number of ordered pairs that satisfy the function. Therefore, arrowheads are drawn at both "ends" of a smooth line or curve to represent the infinite number of ordered pairs. If a domain is not given, assume that the domain is all real numbers.

| Graphing Functions Using a Domain of All Real Numbers | |
|---|---|
| **Step 1** | Use the function to generate ordered pairs by choosing several values for $x$. |
| **Step 2** | Plot enough points to see a pattern for the graph. |
| **Step 3** | Connect the points with a line or smooth curve. |

## EXAMPLE 2 Graphing Functions

**Graph each function.**

**A** $2x + 1 = y$

**Step 1** Choose several values of $x$ and generate ordered pairs.

| $x$ | $2x + 1 = y$ | $(x, y)$ |
|---|---|---|
| −3 | $2(-3) + 1 = -5$ | (−3, −5) |
| −2 | $2(-2) + 1 = -3$ | (−2, −3) |
| −1 | $2(-1) + 1 = -1$ | (−1, −1) |
| 0 | $2(0) + 1 = 1$ | (0, 1) |
| 1 | $2(1) + 1 = 3$ | (1, 3) |
| 2 | $2(2) + 1 = 5$ | (2, 5) |
| 3 | $2(3) + 1 = 7$ | (3, 7) |

**Step 2** Plot enough points to see a pattern.

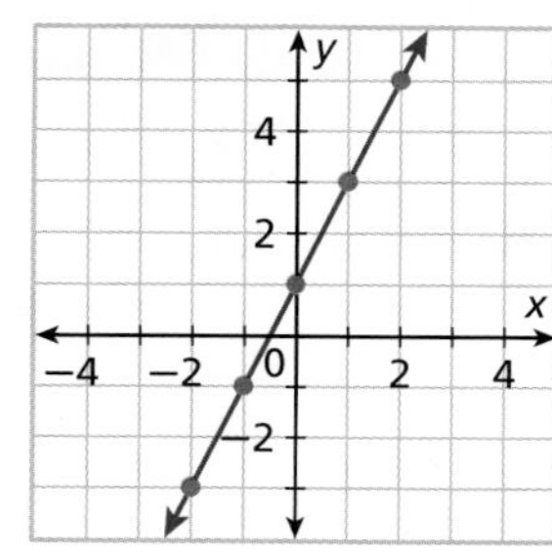

**Helpful Hint**

When choosing values of $x$, be sure to choose both positive and negative values. You may not need to graph all the points to see the pattern.

**Step 3** The ordered pairs appear to form a line. **Draw a line** through all the points to show all the ordered pairs that satisfy the function. Draw arrowheads on both "ends" of the line.

**Graph each function.**

**B** $y = x^2$

**Step 1** Choose several values of $x$ and generate ordered pairs.

| $x$ | $y = x^2$ | $(x, y)$ |
|---|---|---|
| −3 | $y = (-3)^2 = 9$ | $(-3, 9)$ |
| −2 | $y = (-2)^2 = 4$ | $(-2, 4)$ |
| −1 | $y = (-1)^2 = 1$ | $(-1, 1)$ |
| 0 | $y = (0)^2 = 0$ | $(0, 0)$ |
| 1 | $y = (1)^2 = 1$ | $(1, 1)$ |
| 2 | $y = (2)^2 = 4$ | $(2, 4)$ |

**Step 2** Plot enough points to see a pattern.

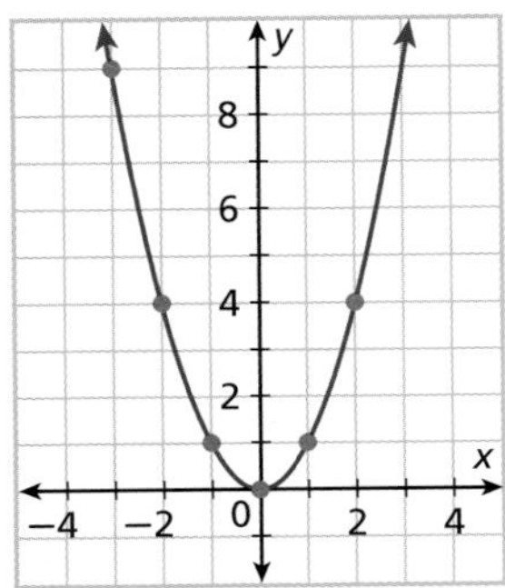


**Step 3** The ordered pairs appear to form an almost U-shaped graph. **Draw a smooth curve** through the points to show all the ordered pairs that satisfy the function. Draw arrowheads on the "ends" of the curve.

*Check* If the graph is correct, any point on it should satisfy the function. Choose an ordered pair on the graph that was not in your table. $(3, 9)$ is on the graph. Check whether it satisfies $y = x^2$.

| $y = x^2$ | | |
|---|---|---|
| 9 | $3^2$ | *Substitute the values for x and y into the function. Simplify.* |
| 9 | 9 ✓ | *The ordered pair (3, 9) satisfies the function.* |

**Graph each function.**

**2a.** $f(x) = 3x - 2$ **2b.** $y = |x - 1|$

**EXAMPLE 3**

## Finding Values Using Graphs

**Use a graph of the function $f(x) = \frac{1}{3}x + 2$ to find the value of $f(x)$ when $x = 6$. Check your answer.**

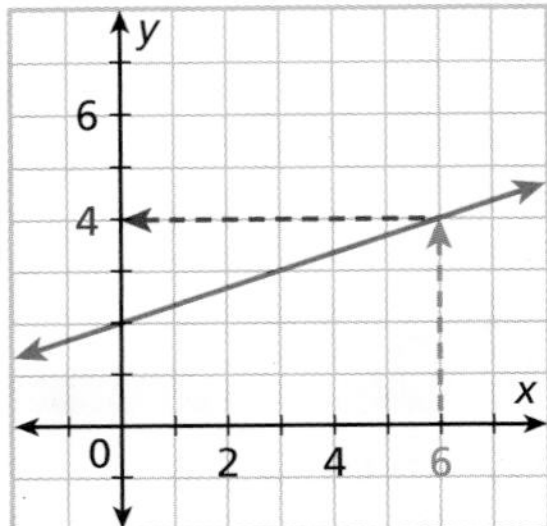


Locate 6 on the $x$-axis. Move up to the graph of the function. Then move **left** to the $y$-axis to find the corresponding value of $y$.

$f(x) = 4$

*Check* Use substitution.

| $f(x) = \frac{1}{3}x + 2$ | | |
|---|---|---|
| 4 | $\frac{1}{3}(6) + 2$ | *Substitute the values for x and y into the function.* |
| 4 | $2 + 2$ | *Simplify.* |
| 4 | 4 ✓ | *The ordered pair (4, 6) satisfies the function.* |

**Writing Math**

"The value of $y$ is 4 when $x = 6$" can also be written as $f(6) = 4$.

**3.** Use the graph above to find the value of $x$ when $f(x) = 3$. Check your answer.

Recall that in real-world situations you may have to limit the domain to make answers reasonable. For example, quantities such as time, distance, and number of people can be represented using only nonnegative values. When both the domain and the range are limited to nonnegative values, the function is graphed only in Quadrant I.

## EXAMPLE  Problem-Solving Application

**The function $y = 2.5x$ describes how many millimeters sea level $y$ rises in $x$ years. Graph the function. Use the graph to estimate how many millimeters sea level will rise in 3.5 years.**

### 1 Understand the Problem

The **answer** is a graph that can be used to find the value of $y$ when $x$ is 3.5.

**List the important information:**

- The function $y = 2.5x$ describes how many millimeters sea level rises.

### 2 Make a Plan

Think: What values should I use to graph this function? Both, the number of years sea level has risen and the distance sea level rises, cannot be negative. Use only nonnegative values for both the domain and the range. The function will be graphed in Quadrant I.

### 3 Solve

Choose several nonnegative values of $x$ to find values of $y$. Then graph the ordered pairs.

| $x$ | $y = 2.5x$ | $(x, y)$ |
|---|---|---|
| 0 | $y = 2.5(0) = 0$ | $(0, 0)$ |
| 1 | $y = 2.5(1) = 2.5$ | $(1, 2.5)$ |
| 2 | $y = 2.5(2) = 5$ | $(2, 5)$ |
| 3 | $y = 2.5(3) = 7.5$ | $(3, 7.5)$ |
| 4 | $y = 2.5(4) = 10$ | $(4, 10)$ |

*Draw a line through the points to show all the ordered pairs that satisfy this function.*

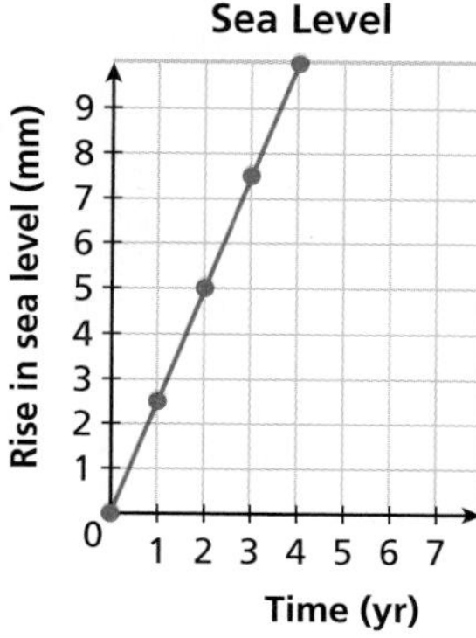


Use the graph to estimate the $y$-value when $x$ is 3.5. Sea level will rise about 8.75 millimeters in 3.5 years.

###  Look Back

As the number of years increases, sea level also increases, so the graph is reasonable. When $x$ is between 3 and 4, $y$ is between 7.5 and 10. Since 3.5 is between 3 and 4, it is reasonable to estimate $y$ to be 8.75 when $x$ is 3.5.

4. The fastest recorded Hawaiian lava flow moved at an average speed of 6 miles per hour. The function $y = 6x$ describes the distance $y$ the lava moved on average in $x$ hours. Graph the function. Use the graph to estimate how many miles the lava moved after 5.5 hours.

## THINK AND DISCUSS

1. How do you find the range of a function if the domain is all real numbers?
2. Explain how to use a graph to find the value of a function for a given value of $x$.

3. **GET ORGANIZED** Copy and complete the graphic organizer. Explain how to graph a function for each situation.

| Graphing a Function | |
|---|---|
| Not a real-world situation | Real-world situation |

# 4-4 Exercises

MA.A.4

go.hrw.com
Homework Help Online
KEYWORD: MA7 4-4
Parent Resources Online
KEYWORD: MA7 Parent

## GUIDED PRACTICE

SEE EXAMPLE 1 p. 252

Graph each function for the given domain.

1. $3x - y = 1$; D: $\{-3, -1, 0, 4\}$
2. $f(x) = -|x|$; D: $\{-5, -3, 0, 3, 5\}$
3. $f(x) = x + 4$; D: $\{-5, -3, 0, 4\}$
4. $y = x^2 - 1$; D: $\{-3, -1, 0, 1, 3\}$

SEE EXAMPLE 2 p. 253

Graph each function.

5. $f(x) = 6x + 4$
6. $y = \frac{1}{2}x + 4$
7. $x + y = 0$
8. $y = |x| - 4$
9. $f(x) = 2x^2 - 7$
10. $y = -x^2 + 5$

SEE EXAMPLE 3 p. 254

11. Use a graph of the function $f(x) = \frac{1}{2}x - 2$ to find the value of $y$ when $x = 2$. Check your answer.

SEE EXAMPLE 4 p. 255

12. **Oceanography** The floor of the Atlantic Ocean is spreading at an average rate of 1 inch per year. The function $y = x$ describes the number of inches $y$ the ocean floor spreads in $x$ years. Graph the function. Use the graph to estimate the number of inches the ocean floor will spread in $10\frac{1}{2}$ years.

## PRACTICE AND PROBLEM SOLVING

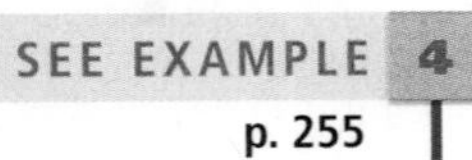

| Independent Practice | |
|---|---|
| For Exercises | See Example |
| 13–16 | 1 |
| 17–24 | 2 |
| 25–26 | 3 |
| 27 | 4 |

Extra Practice
Skills Practice p. S12
Application Practice p. S31

Graph each function for the given domain.

13. $2x + y = 4$; D: $\{-3, -1, 4, 7\}$
14. $y = |x| - 1$; D: $\{-4, -2, 0, 2, 4\}$
15. $f(x) = -7x$; D: $\{-2, -1, 0, 1\}$
16. $y = (x + 1)^2$; D: $\{-2, -1, 0, 1, 2\}$

Graph each function.

17. $y = -3x + 5$
18. $f(x) = 3x$
19. $x + y = 8$
20. $f(x) = 2x + 2$
21. $y = -|x| + 10$
22. $f(x) = -5 + x^2$
23. $y = |x + 1| + 1$
24. $y = (x - 2)^2 - 1$
25. Use a graph of the function $f(x) = -2x - 3$ to find the value of $y$ when $x = -4$. Check your answer.
26. Use a graph of the function $f(x) = \frac{1}{3}x + 1$ to find the value of $y$ when $x = 6$. Check your answer.

27. **Transportation** An electric motor scooter can travel at 0.25 miles per minute. The function $y = 0.25x$ describes the number of miles $y$ the scooter can travel in $x$ minutes. Graph the function. Use the graph to estimate the number of miles an electric motor scooter travels in 15 minutes.

**Graph each function.**

28. $f(x) = x - 1$
29. $12 - x - 2y = 0$
30. $3x - y = 13$
31. $y = x^2 - 2$
32. $x^2 - y = -4$
33. $2x^2 = f(x)$
34. $f(x) = |2x| - 2$
35. $y = |-x|$
36. $-|2x + 1| = y$

37. Find the value of $x$ so that $(x, 12)$ satisfies $y = 4x + 8$.
38. Find the value of $x$ so that $(x, 6)$ satisfies $y = -x - 4$.
39. Find the value of $y$ so that $(-2, y)$ satisfies $y = -2x^2$.

**For each function, determine whether the given points are on the graph.**

40. $y = 7x - 2$; $(1, 5)$ and $(2, 10)$
41. $y = |x| + 2$; $(3, 5)$ and $(-1, 3)$
42. $y = x^2$; $(1, 1)$ and $(-3, -9)$
43. $y = \frac{1}{4}x - 2$; $\left(1, -\frac{3}{4}\right)$ and $(4, -1)$
44. **ERROR ANALYSIS** Student A says that $(3, 2)$ is on the graph of $y = 4x - 5$, but student B says that it is not. Who is incorrect? Explain the error.

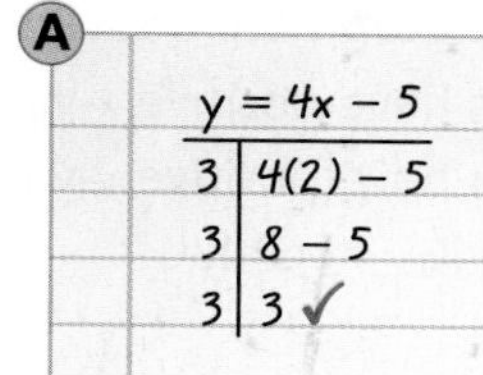


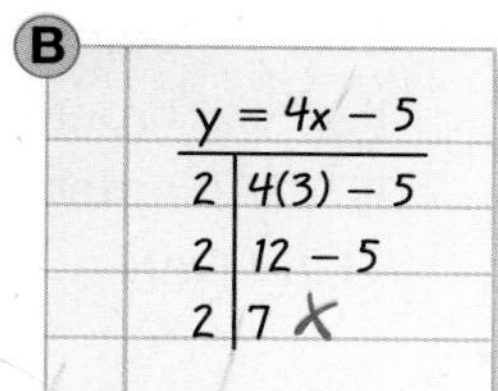


**Determine whether $(0, -7)$, $\left(-6, -\frac{5}{3}\right)$, and $(-2, -3)$ lie on the graph of each function.**

45. $x + 3y = -11$
46. $y + |x| = -1$
47. $x^2 - y = 7$

**For each function, find three ordered pairs that lie on the graph of the function.**

48. $-6 = 3x + 2y$
49. $y = 1.1x + 2$
50. $y = \frac{4}{5}x$
51. $y = 3x - 1$
52. $y = |x| + 6$
53. $y = x^2 - 5$
54. **Critical Thinking** Graph the functions $y = |x|$ and $y = -|x|$. Describe how they are alike. How are they different?

**MULTI-STEP TEST PREP**

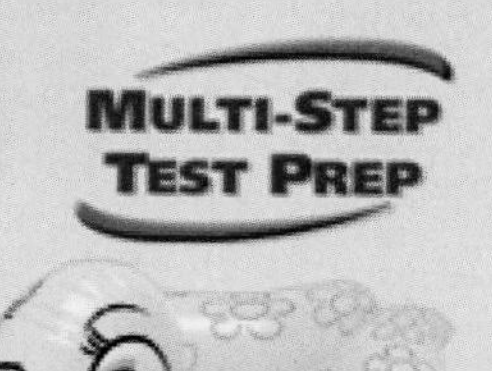

55. This problem will prepare you for the Multi-Step Test Prep on page 260.

A pool containing 10,000 gallons of water is being drained. Every hour, the volume of the water in the pool decreases by 1500 gallons.

a. Write an equation to describe the volume $v$ of water in the pool after $h$ hours.
b. How much water is in the pool after 1 hour?
c. Create a table of values showing the volume of the water in gallons in the pool as a function of the time in hours and graph the function.

56. **Estimation** Estimate the value of $y$ from the graph when $x = 2.117$.

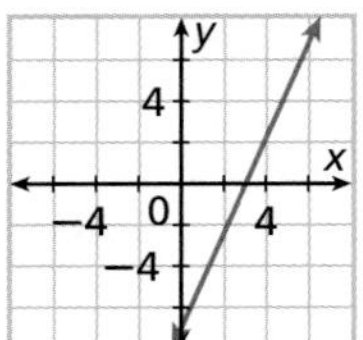


57. **Write About It** Why is a graph a convenient way to show the ordered pairs that satisfy a function?

**TEST PREP**

MA.A.4

58. Which function is graphed?

Ⓐ $2y - 3x = 2$ Ⓒ $y = 2x - 1$
Ⓑ $5x + y = 1$ Ⓓ $y = 5x + 8$

59. Which ordered pair is NOT on the graph of $y = 4 - |x|$?

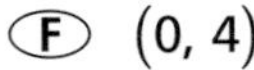

Ⓕ (0, 4) Ⓗ (−1, 3)
Ⓖ (4, 0) Ⓙ (3, −1)

60. Which function has (3, 2) on its graph?

Ⓐ $2x - 3y = 12$ Ⓒ $y = -\frac{2}{3}x + 4$
Ⓑ $-2x - 3y = 12$ Ⓓ $y = -\frac{3}{2}x + 4$

61. Which statement(s) is true about the function $y = x^2 + 1$?

I. All points on the graph are above the origin.
II. All ordered pairs have positive $x$-values.
III. All ordered pairs have positive $y$-values.

Ⓕ I Only Ⓖ II Only Ⓗ I and II Ⓙ I and III

## CHALLENGE AND EXTEND

62. Graph the function $y = x^3$. Make sure you have enough ordered pairs to see the shape of the graph.

63. The temperature of a liquid that started at 64°F is increasing by 4°F per hour. Write a function that describes the temperature of the liquid over time. Graph the function to show the temperatures over the first 10 hours.

## SPIRAL REVIEW

**Write the power represented by each geometric model.** *(Lesson 1-4)*

64. 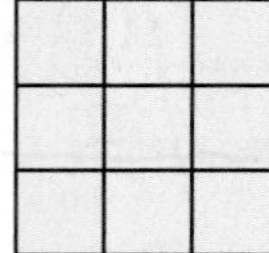

65. 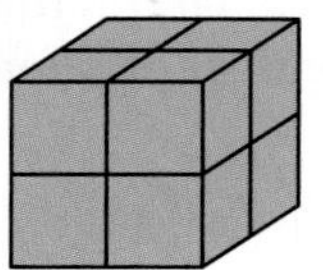

66. 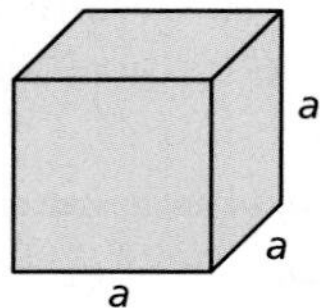


**Solve each inequality and graph the solutions.** *(Lesson 3-3)*

67. $5p < -20$

68. $18 > -9k$

69. $\frac{3}{4}b \geq 15$

**Evaluate each function for the given input values.** *(Lesson 4-3)*

70. For $f(x) = -2x - 3$, find $f(x)$ when $x = -4$ and when $x = 2$.

71. For $h(t) = \frac{2}{3}t + 1$, find $h(t)$ when $t = -6$ and when $t = 9$.

# Connect Function Rules, Tables, and Graphs

You can use a graphing calculator to understand the connections among function rules, tables, and graphs.

*Use with Lesson 4-4*

**MA.A.4.4** Represent linear functions in a variety of equivalent forms…

go.hrw.com
**Lab Resources Online**
KEYWORD: MA7 Lab4

## Activity

**Make a table of values for the function $f(x) = 4x + 3$ when the domain is all real numbers. Then graph the function.**

1. Press Y= and enter the function rule **4x + 3**.

2. Press 2nd WINDOW (TBLSET). Make sure **Indpnt: Auto** and **Depend: Auto** are selected.

3. To view the table, press 2nd GRAPH (TABLE). The $x$-values and the corresponding $y$-values appear in table form. Use the up and down arrow keys to scroll through the table.

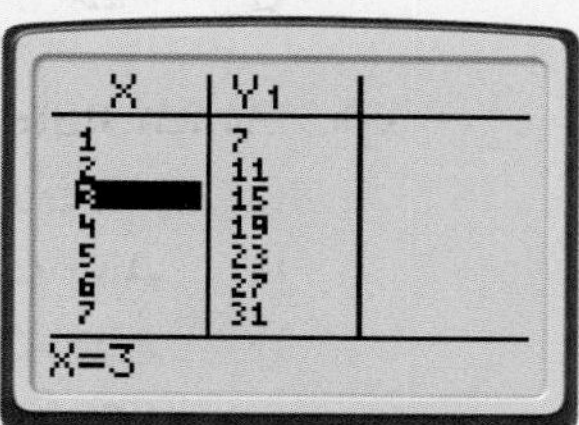


4. To view the table with the graph, press MODE and select **G-T** view. Press ENTER. Be sure to use the standard window.

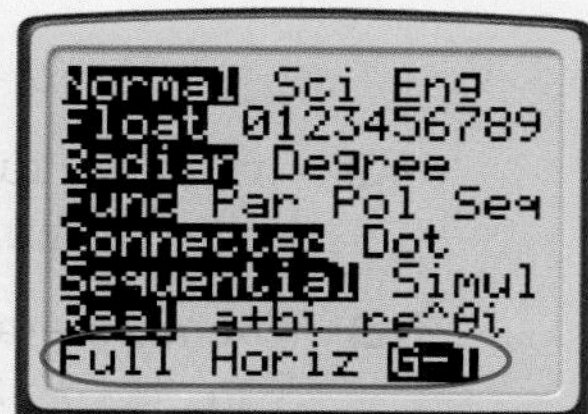


5. Press TRACE to see both the graph and a table of values.

6. Press the left arrow key several times to move the cursor. Notice that the point on the graph and the values in the table correspond.

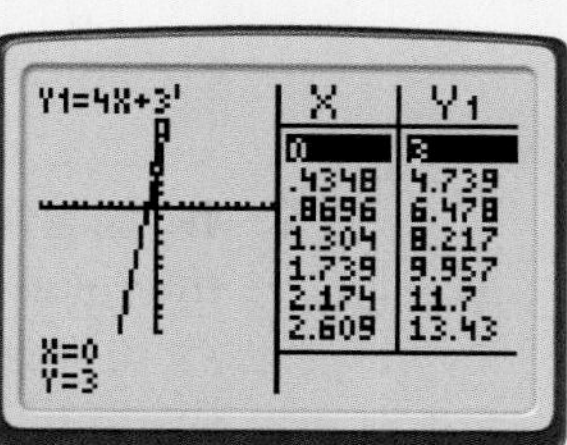


## Try This

**Make a table of values for each function. Then graph the function.**

1. $f(x) = 2x - 1$
2. $f(x) = 1.5x$
3. $f(x) = \frac{1}{2}x + 2$
4. Explain the relationship between a function rule and its table of values and the graph of the function.

## Function Concepts

**Down the Drain** The graph shows the relationship between the number of hours that have passed since a pool began to drain and the amount of water in the pool.

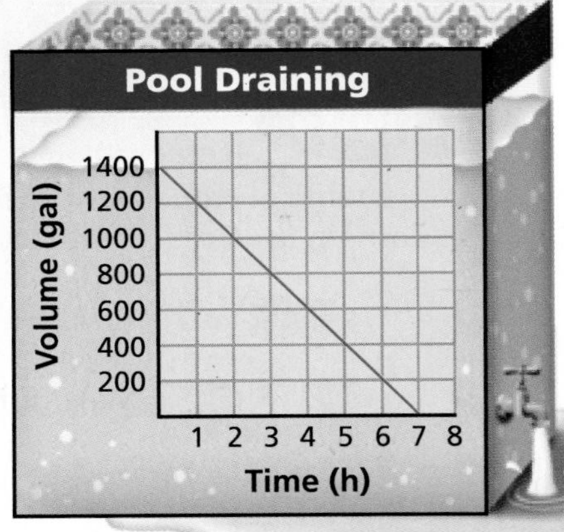


1. Describe in words the relationship between the amount of water in the pool and the number of hours that have passed since the pool began to drain.
2. What are the domain and range for the graph?
3. Use the graph to determine how much water is in the pool after 3 hours. How much water is in the pool after $4\frac{1}{2}$ hours?
4. Copy and complete the table.

| Draining Pool | |
|---|---|
| **Time (h)** | **Volume (gal)** |
| 0 | 1400 |
| 1 | |
| 2 | |
| 3 | |
| 4 | |
| 5 | |
| 6 | |
| 7 | |

5. Write an equation to describe the relationship between the volume $V$ and the time $t$. Use the equation to find how much water is in the pool after 5.2 hours.

# READY TO GO ON?

CHAPTER 4

SECTION 4A

## Quiz for Lessons 4-1 Through 4-4

### 4-1 Graphing Relationships

**Choose the graph that best represents each situation.**

1. A person bungee jumps from a high platform.
2. A person jumps on a trampoline in a steady motion.
3. Xander takes a quiz worth 100 points. Each question is worth 20 points. Sketch a graph to show his possible score if he misses 1, 2, 3, 4, or 5 questions.

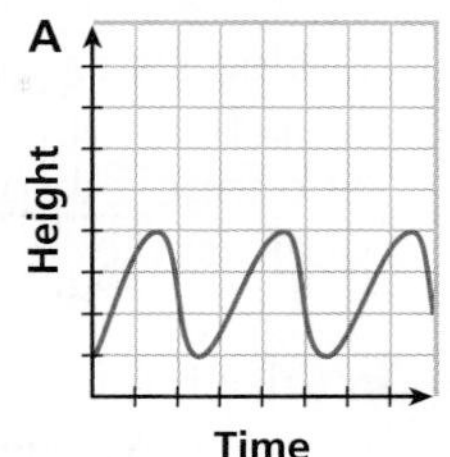


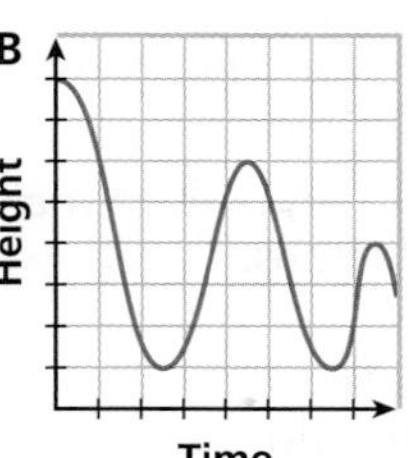


### 4-2 Relations and Functions

**Give the domain and range of each relation. Tell whether the relation is a function. Explain.**

4.

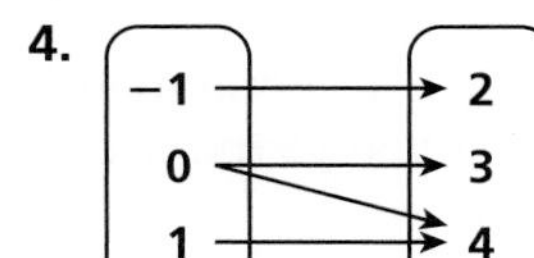


5.

| $x$ | −2 | −2 | 0 | 2 | 2 |
|---|---|---|---|---|---|
| $y$ | 3 | 3 | 3 | 3 | 3 |

6.

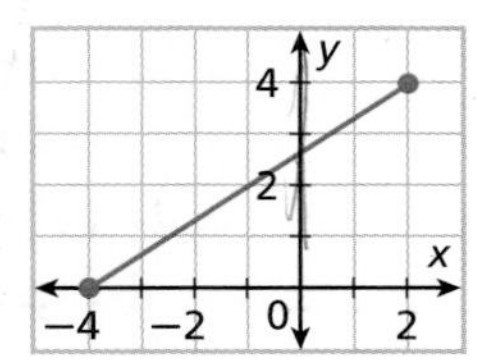


### 4-3 Writing Functions

**Determine a relationship between the $x$- and $y$-values. Write an equation.**

7.

| $x$ | 1 | 2 | 3 | 4 |
|---|---|---|---|---|
| $y$ | −6 | −5 | −4 | −3 |

8.

| $x$ | 1 | 2 | 3 | 4 |
|---|---|---|---|---|
| $y$ | −3 | −6 | −9 | −12 |

9. A printer can print 8 pages per minute. Identify the dependent and independent variables for the situation. Write a rule in function notation.

**Evaluate each function for the given input values.**

10. For $f(x) = 3x - 1$, find $f(x)$ when $x = 2$.
11. For $g(x) = x^2 - x$, find $g(x)$ when $x = -2$.
12. A photographer charges a sitting fee of \$15 plus \$3 for each pose. Write a function to describe the situation. Find a reasonable domain and range for up to 5 poses.

### 4-4 Graphing Functions

**Graph each function for the given domain.**

13. $2x - y = 3$; D: $\{-2, 0, 1, 3\}$
14. $y = 4 - x^2$; D: $\{-1, 0, 1, 2\}$
15. $y = 3 - 2x$; D: $\{-1, 0, 1, 3\}$

**Graph each function.**

16. $x + y = 6$
17. $y = |x| - 3$
18. $y = x^2 + 1$
19. The function $y = 8x$ represents how many miles $y$ a certain storm travels in $x$ hours. Graph the function and estimate the number of miles the storm travels in 10.5 h.

# 4-5 Scatter Plots and Trend Lines

**MA.S.2** Infer trends in bivariate data. *Also* **Prep MA.S.2.1, Prep MA.S.2.2**

***Objectives***
Create and interpret scatter plots.

Use trend lines to make predictions.

***Vocabulary***
scatter plot
correlation
positive correlation
negative correlation
no correlation
trend line

**Who uses this?**
Ecologists can use scatter plots to help them analyze data about endangered species, such as ocelots. (See Example 1.)

In this chapter, you have examined relationships between sets of ordered pairs, or data. Displaying data visually can help you see relationships.

A **scatter plot** is a graph with points plotted to show a possible relationship between two sets of data. A scatter plot is an effective way to display some types of data.

**EXAMPLE 1** **Graphing a Scatter Plot from Given Data**

**The table shows the number of species added to the list of endangered and threatened species in the United States during the given years. Graph a scatter plot using the given data.**

| Increase in List | | | | | | | |
|---|---|---|---|---|---|---|---|
| Calendar Year | 1996 | 1997 | 1998 | 1999 | 2000 | 2001 | 2002 |
| Species | 91 | 79 | 62 | 11 | 39 | 10 | 9 |

*Source:* U.S. Fish and Wildlife Service

**Species Added to List**

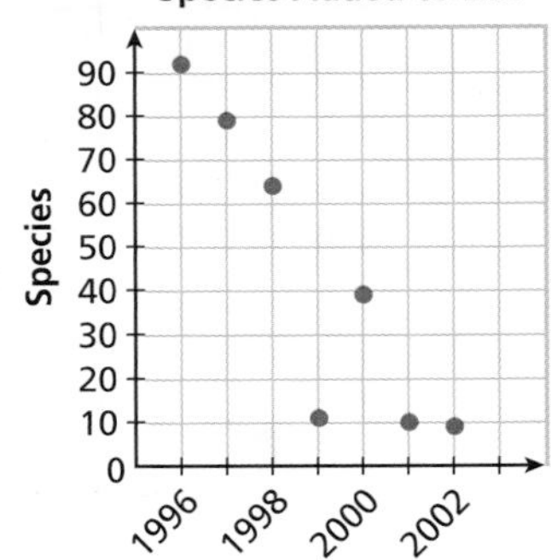


*Use the table to make ordered pairs for the scatter plot.*

*The x-value represents the calendar year and the y-value represents the number of species added.*

*Plot the ordered pairs.*

**Helpful Hint**
The point (2000, 39) tells you that in the year 2000, the list increased by 39 species.

**1.** The table shows the number of points scored by a high school football team in the first four games of a season. Graph a scatter plot using the given data.

| Game | 1 | 2 | 3 | 4 |
|---|---|---|---|---|
| Score | 6 | 21 | 46 | 34 |

A **correlation** describes a relationship between two data sets. A graph may show the correlation between data. The correlation can help you analyze trends and make predictions. There are three types of correlations between data.

Know it! Note

## Correlations

| Positive Correlation | Negative Correlation | No Correlation |
|---|---|---|
| Both sets of data values increase. | One set of data values increases as the other set decreases. | There is no relationship between the data sets. |

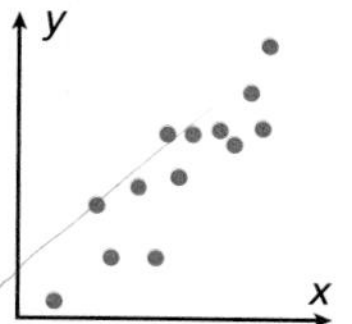


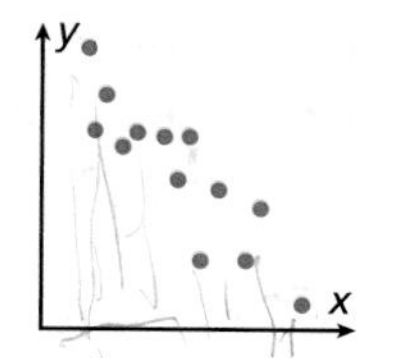


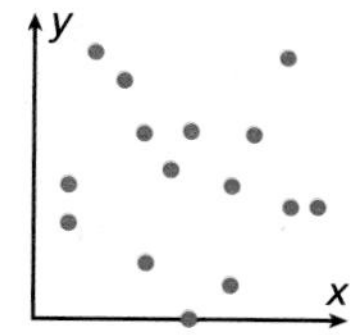


In the endangered species graph, as time increases, the number of new species added decreases. So the correlation between the data is negative.

## EXAMPLE 2 Describing Correlations from Scatter Plots

**Describe the correlation illustrated by the scatter plot.**

**TV Watching and Test Scores**

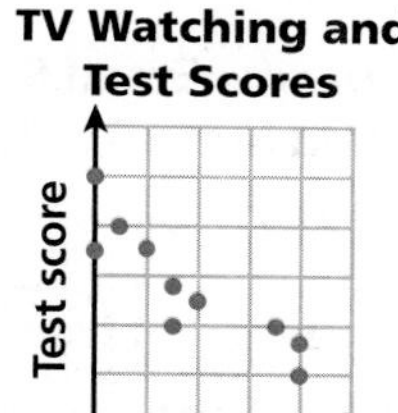


**Watching TV (h)**

*As the number of hours spent watching TV increased, test scores decreased.*

There is a negative correlation between the two data sets.

2. Describe the correlation illustrated by the scatter plot.

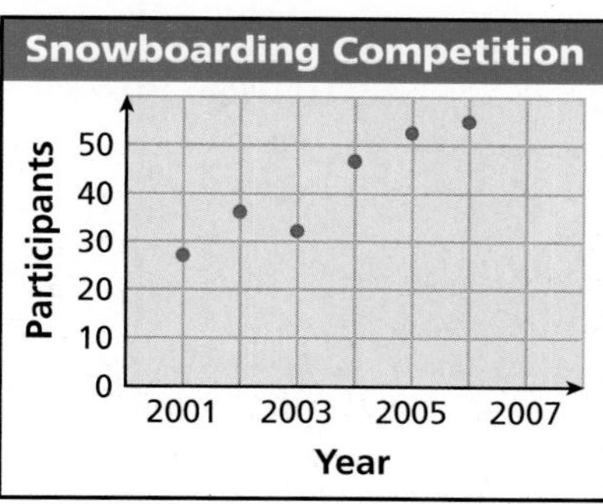


## EXAMPLE 3 Identifying Correlations

**Identify the correlation you would expect to see between each pair of data sets. Explain.**

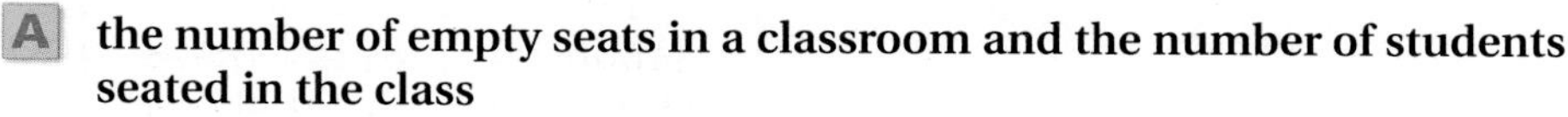

**A the number of empty seats in a classroom and the number of students seated in the class**

You would expect to see a negative correlation. As the number of students increases, the number of empty seats decreases.

**B the number of pets a person owns and the number of books that person read last year**

You would expect to see no correlation. The number of pets a person owns has nothing to do with how many books the person has read.

**Identify the correlation you would expect to see between each pair of data sets. Explain.**

**C** **the monthly rainfall and the depth of water in a reservoir**

You would expect to see a positive correlation. As more rain falls, there is more water in the reservoir.

**CHECK IT OUT!** **Identify the correlation you would expect to see between each pair of data sets. Explain.**

**3a.** the temperature in Houston and the number of cars sold in Boston

**3b.** the number of members in a family and the size of the family's grocery bill

**3c.** the number of times you sharpen your pencil and the length of your pencil

## EXAMPLE 4 Matching Scatter Plots to Situations

**Choose the scatter plot that best represents the relationship between the number of days since a sunflower seed was planted and the height of the plant. Explain.**

Graph A

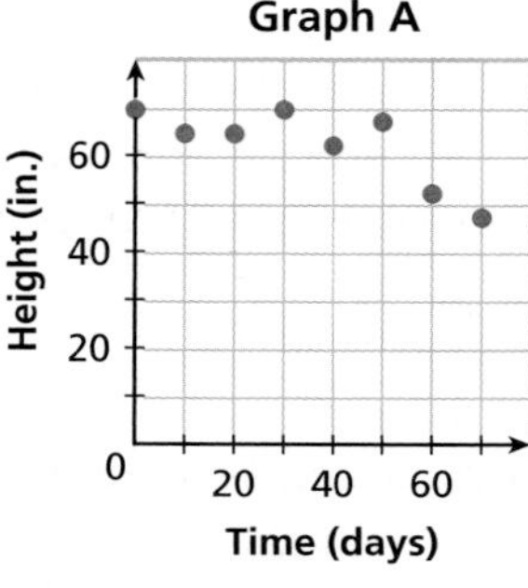


Graph B

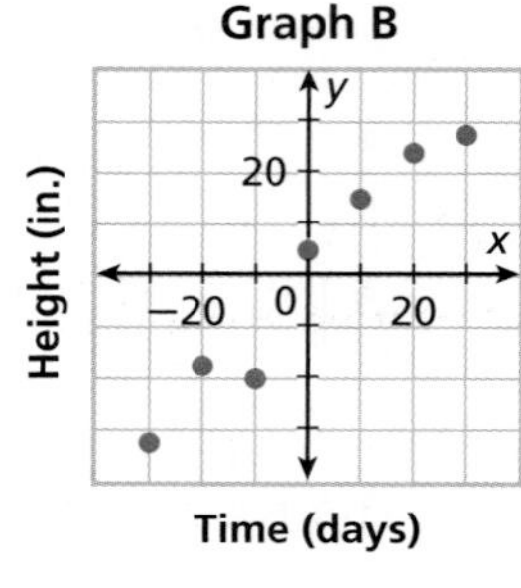


Graph C

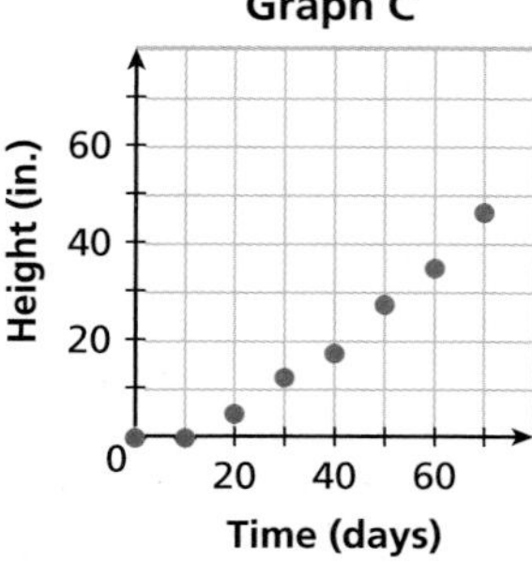


*There will be a positive correlation between the number of days and the height because the plant will grow each day.*

*Neither the number of days nor the plant heights can be negative.*

*This graph shows all positive coordinates and a positive correlation, so it could represent the data sets.*

Graph A has a negative correlation, so it is incorrect.

Graph B shows negative values, so it is incorrect.

Graph C is the correct scatter plot.

**CHECK IT OUT!** **4.** Choose the scatter plot that best represents the relationship between the number of minutes since a pie has been taken out of the oven and the temperature of the oven. Explain.

Graph A

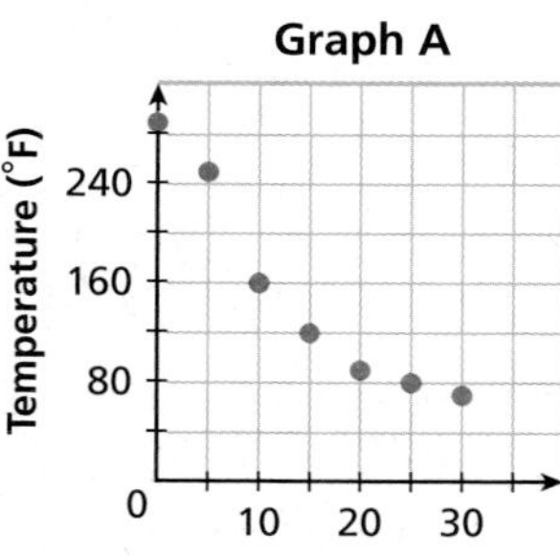


Graph B

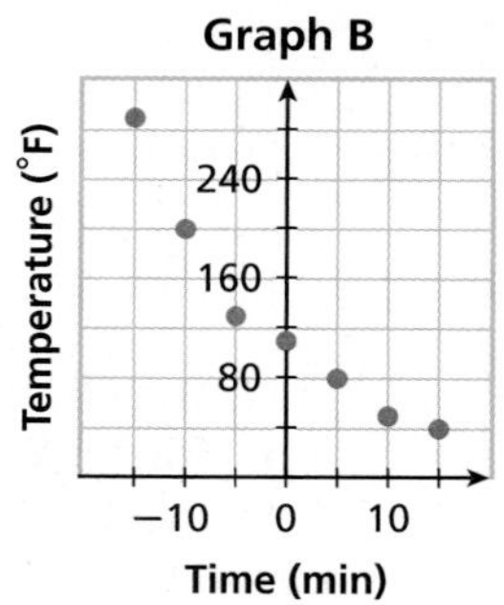


Graph C

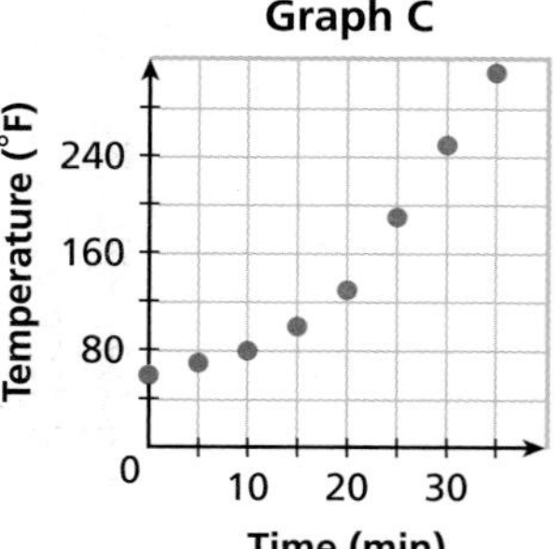

You can graph a function on a scatter plot to help show a relationship in the data. Sometimes the function is a straight line. This line, called a **trend line** helps show the correlation between data sets more clearly. It can also be helpful when making predictions based on the data.

## EXAMPLE 5 *Fund-raising Application*

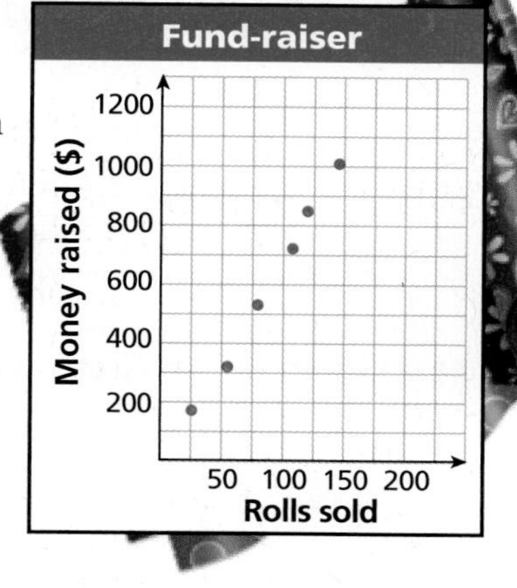


**The scatter plot shows a relationship between the total amount of money collected and the total number of rolls of wrapping paper sold as a school fund-raiser. Based on this relationship, predict how much money will be collected when 175 rolls have been sold.**

Draw a trend line and use it to make a prediction.

Fund-raiser

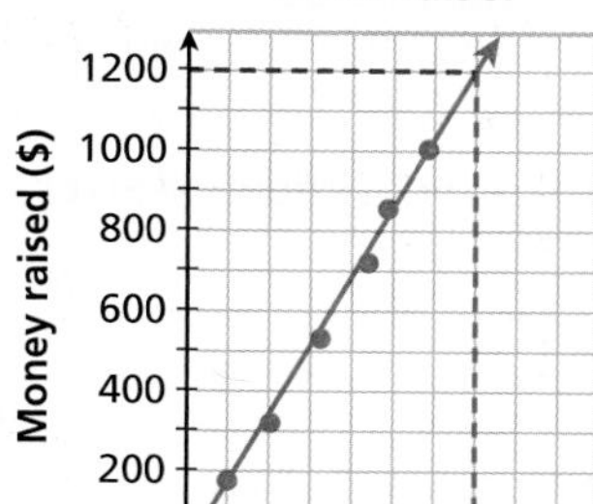


*Draw a line that has about the same number of points above and below it. Your line may or may not go through data points.*

*Find the point on the line whose x-value is 175. The corresponding y-value is 1200.*

Based on the data, $1200 is a reasonable prediction of how much money will be collected when 175 rolls have been sold.

**5.** Based on the trend line above, predict how many wrapping paper rolls need to be sold to raise $500.

## THINK AND DISCUSS

**1.** Is it possible to make a prediction based on a scatter plot with no correlation? Explain your answer.

**2. GET ORGANIZED** Copy and complete the graphic organizer with either a scatter plot, or a real-world example, or both.

| | Graph | Example |
|---|---|---|
| Positive Correlation | | |
| Negative Correlation | | The amount of water in a watering can and the number of flowers watered |
| No Correlation | | |

# 4-5 Exercises

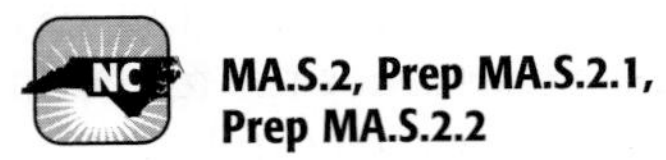


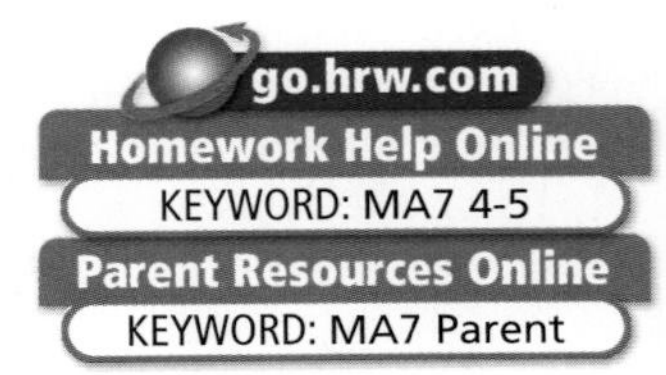


## GUIDED PRACTICE

**Vocabulary** **Apply the vocabulary from this lesson to answer each question.**

1. Give an example of a graph that is not a *scatter plot.*
2. How is a scatter plot that shows *no correlation* different from a scatter plot that shows a *negative correlation*?
3. Does a *trend line* always pass through every point on a scatter plot? Explain.

SEE EXAMPLE 1 p. 263

**Graph a scatter plot using the given data.**

4.

| Garden Statue | Cupid | Gnome | Lion | Flamingo | Wishing well |
|---|---|---|---|---|---|
| Height (in.) | 32 | 18 | 35 | 28 | 40 |
| Price ($) | 50 | 25 | 80 | 15 | 75 |

SEE EXAMPLE 2 p. 264

**Describe the correlation illustrated by each scatter plot.**

5.

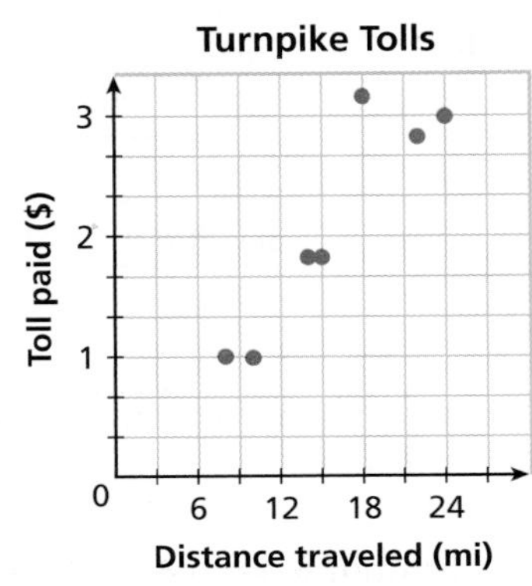


6.

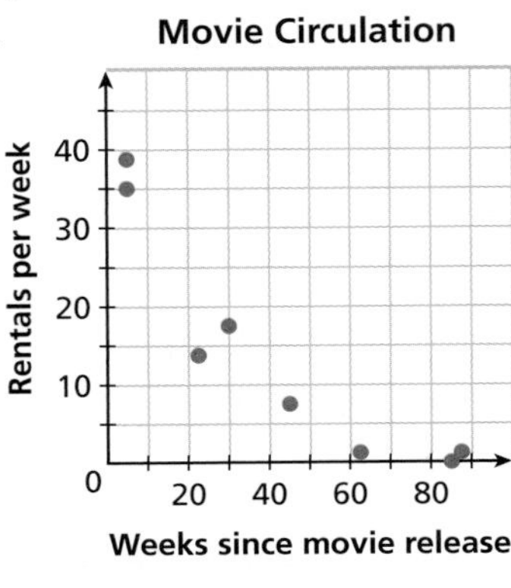


SEE EXAMPLE 3 p. 264

**Identify the correlation you would expect to see between each pair of data sets. Explain.**

7. the volume of water poured into a container and the amount of empty space left in the container
8. a person's shoe size and the length of the person's hair
9. the outside temperature and the number of people at the beach

SEE EXAMPLE 4 p. 265

**Choose the scatter plot that best represents the described relationship. Explain.**

10. age of car and number of miles traveled
11. age of car and sales price of car
12. age of car and number of states traveled to

Graph A

Graph B

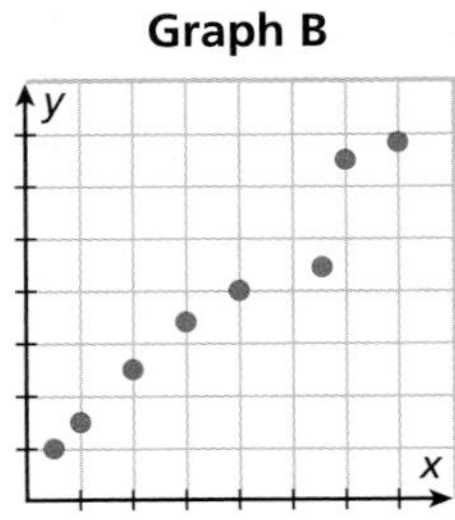


Graph C

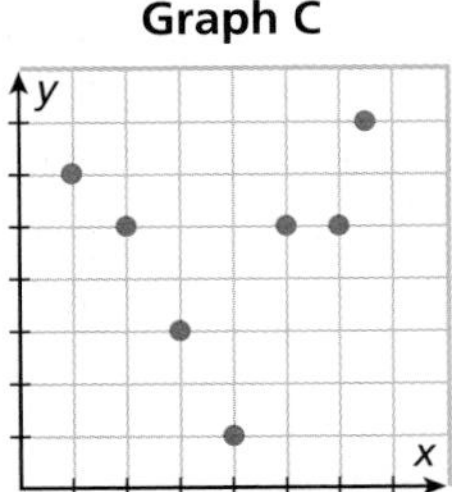

SEE EXAMPLE 5
p. 266

13. **Transportation** The scatter plot shows the total number of miles passengers flew on U.S. domestic flights in the month of April for the years 1997–2004. Based on this relationship, predict how many miles passengers will fly in April 2008.

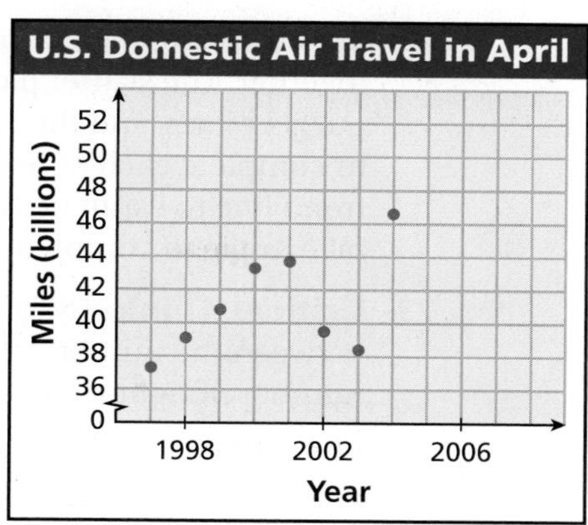


## PRACTICE AND PROBLEM SOLVING

**Independent Practice**

| For Exercises | See Example |
|---|---|
| 14 | 1 |
| 15–16 | 2 |
| 17–18 | 3 |
| 19–20 | 4 |
| 21 | 5 |

**Extra Practice**

Skills Practice p. S12
Application Practice p. S31

**Graph a scatter plot using the given data.**

14.

| Train Arrival Time | 6:45 A.M. | 7:30 A.M. | 8:15 A.M. | 9:45 A.M. | 10:30 A.M. |
|---|---|---|---|---|---|
| Passengers | 160 | 148 | 194 | 152 | 64 |

**Describe the correlation illustrated by each scatter plot.**

15.

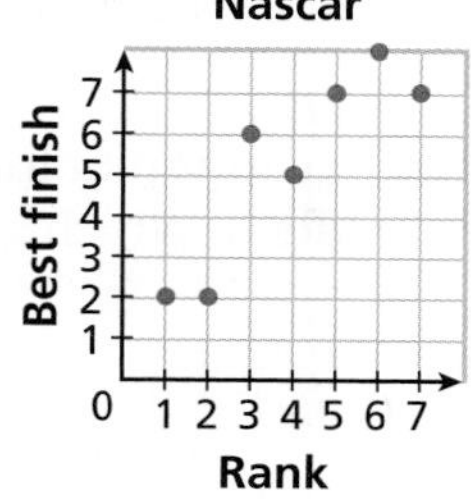


16.

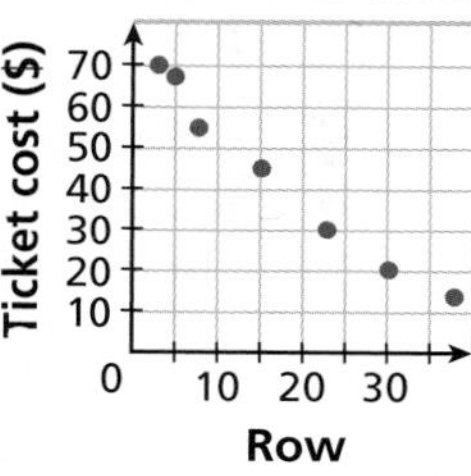


**Identify the correlation you would expect to see between each pair of data sets. Explain.**

17. the speed of a runner and the distance she can cover in 10 minutes

18. the year a car was made and the total mileage

**Choose the scatter plot that best represents the described relationship. Explain.**

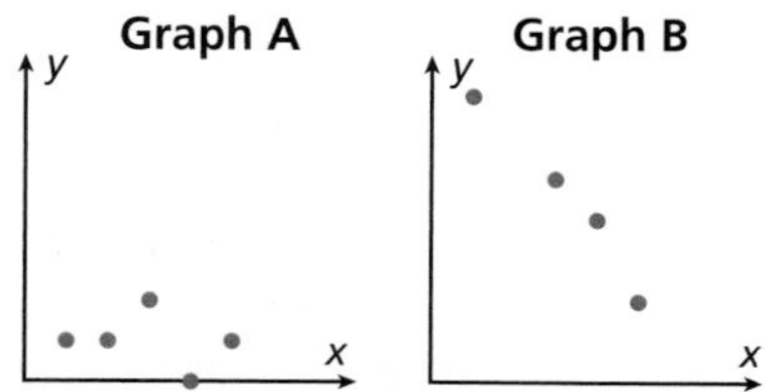


19. the number of college classes taken and the number of roommates

20. the number of college classes taken and the hours of free time.

21. **Ecology** The scatter plot shows a projection of the average ocelot population living in Laguna Atascosa National Wildlife Refuge near Brownsville, Texas. Based on this relationship, predict the number of ocelots living at the wildlife refuge in 2014 if nothing is done to help manage the ocelot population.

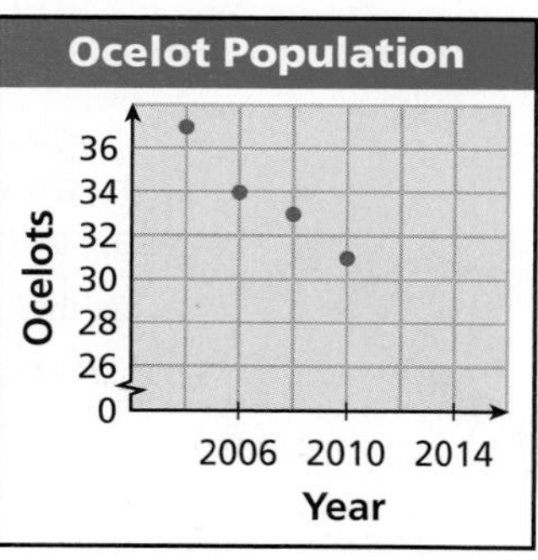


**LINK Ecology**

The ocelot population in Texas is dwindling due in part to their habitat being destroyed. The ocelot population at Laguna Atascosa National Wildlife Refuge is monitored by following 5–10 ocelots yearly by radio telemetry.

22. **Estimation** Angie enjoys putting jigsaw puzzles together. The scatter plot shows the number of puzzle pieces and the time in minutes it took her to complete each of her last six puzzles. Use the trend line to estimate the time in minutes it will take Angie to complete a 1200-piece puzzle.

23. **Critical Thinking** Describe the correlation between the number of left shoes sold and the number of right shoes sold.

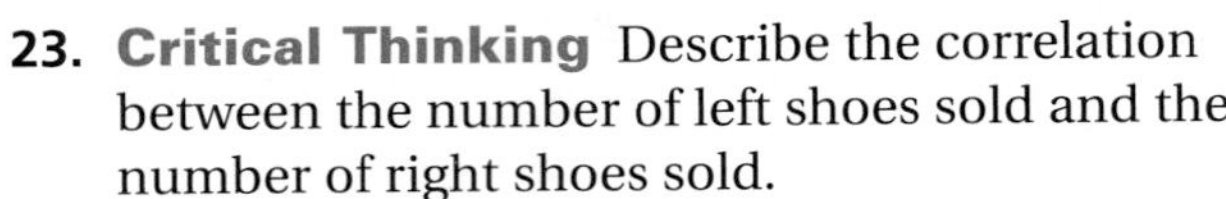

24. Roma had guests for dinner at her house eight times and has recorded the number of guests and the total cost for each meal in the table.

| Guests | 3 | 4 | 4 | 6 | 6 | 7 | 8 | 8 |
|---|---|---|---|---|---|---|---|---|
| Cost ($) | 30 | 65 | 88 | 90 | 115 | 160 | 150 | 162 |

a. Graph a scatter plot of the data.
b. Describe the correlation.
c. Draw a trend line.
d. Based on the trend line you drew, predict the cost of dinner for 11 guests.
e. **What if...?** Suppose that each cost in the table increased by $5. How will this affect the cost of dinner for 11 guests?

25. **ERROR ANALYSIS** Students graphed a scatter plot for the temperature of hot bath water and time if no new water is added. Which graph is incorrect? Explain the error.

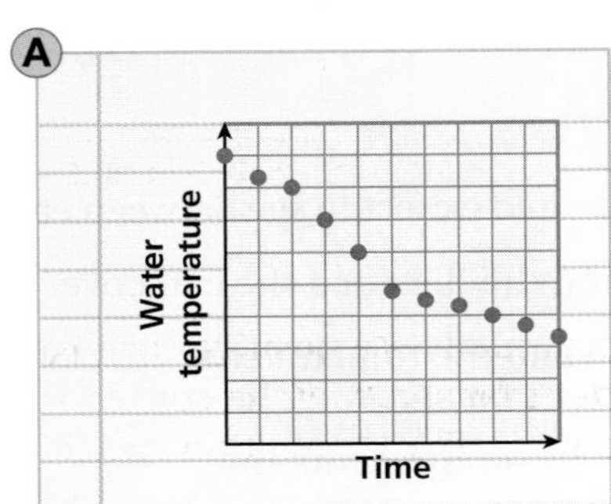


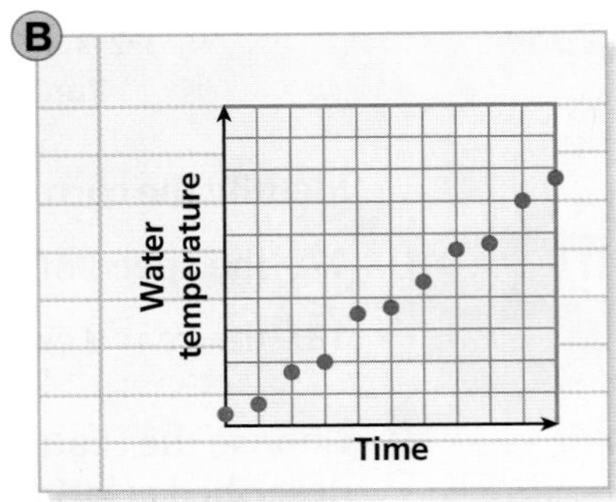


26. **Critical Thinking** Will more people or fewer people buy an item if the price goes up? Explain the relationship and describe the correlation.

**MULTI-STEP TEST PREP**

STATE

27. This problem will prepare you for the Multi-Step Test Prep on page 278.

Juan and his parents are visiting a university 205 miles from their home. As they travel, Juan uses the car odometer and his watch to keep track of the distance.

a. Make a scatter plot for this data set.
b. Describe the correlation. Explain.
c. Draw a trend line for the data and predict the distance Juan would have traveled going to a university 4 hours away.

| Time (min) | Distance (mi) |
|---|---|
| 0 | 0 |
| 30 | 28 |
| 60 | 58 |
| 90 | 87 |
| 120 | 117 |
| 150 | 148 |
| 180 | 178 |
| 210 | 205 |

28. **Write About It** Conduct a survey of your classmates to find the number of siblings they have and the number of pets they have. Predict whether there will be a positive, negative, or no correlation. Then graph the data in a scatter plot. What is the relationship between the two data sets? Was your prediction correct?

## TEST PREP

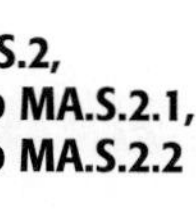

MA.S.2,
Prep MA.S.2.1,
Prep MA.S.2.2

29. Which graph is the best example of a negative correlation?

Ⓐ 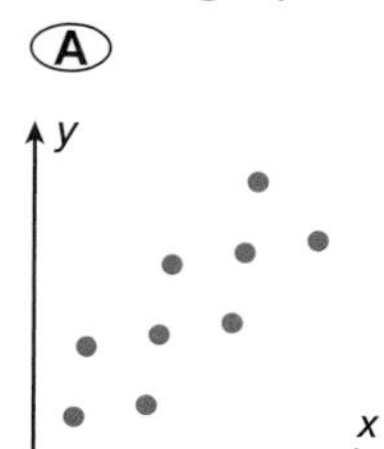


Ⓑ 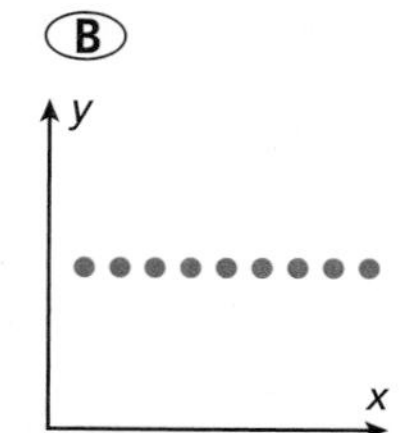


Ⓒ 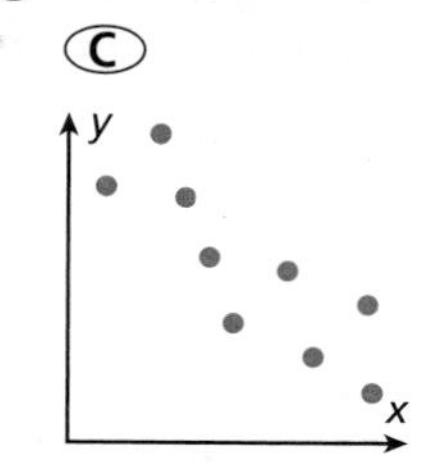


Ⓓ 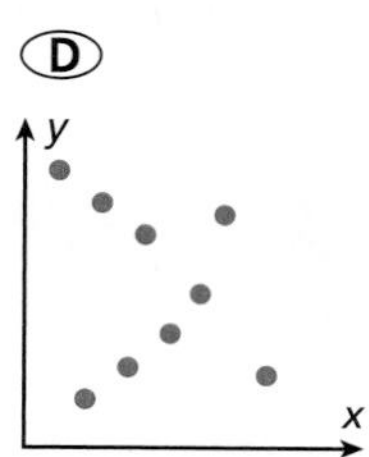


30. Which situation best describes a positive correlation?
    - Ⓕ The amount of rainfall on Fridays
    - Ⓖ The height of a candle and the amount of time it stays lit
    - Ⓗ The price of a pizza and the number of toppings added
    - Ⓙ The temperature of a cup of hot chocolate and the length of time it sits

31. **Short Response** Write a real-world situation for the graph. Explain your answer.

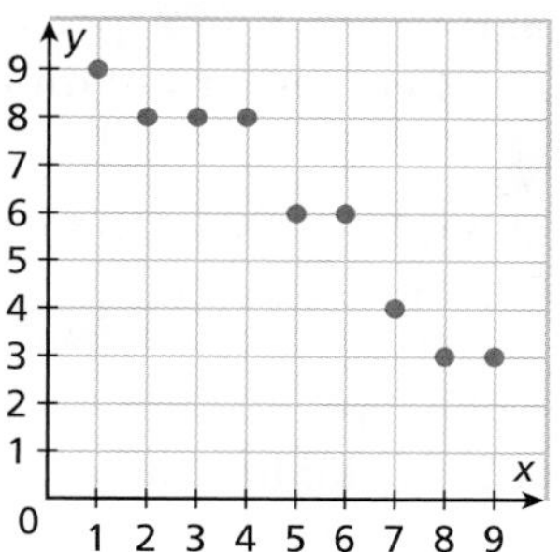


## CHALLENGE AND EXTEND

32. Describe a situation that involves a positive correlation. Gather data on the situation. Make a scatter plot showing the correlation. Use the scatter plot to make a prediction. Repeat for a negative correlation and for no correlation.

33. Research an endangered or threatened species in your state. Gather information on its population for several years. Make a scatter plot using the data you gather. Is there a positive or negative correlation? Explain. Draw a trend line and make a prediction about the species population over the next 5 years.

## SPIRAL REVIEW

**Write an equation to represent each relationship. Then solve the equation.** *(Lesson 2-4)*

34. Five times a number increased by 2 is equal to twice the number decreased by 4.

35. Five times the sum of a number and 2 is equal to 8 less than twice the number.

**Solve each inequality.** *(Lesson 3-5)*

36. $4(6 + x) \geq -2x$ 37. $3(x - 1) > 3x$ 38. $2(3 - x) < 2(1 + x)$

**Graph each function.** *(Lesson 4-4)*

39. $y = 2x - 3$ 40. $y = -|x| + 3$ 41. $y = x^2 - 4$

# Interpret Scatter Plots and Trend Lines

You can use a graphing calculator to graph a trend line on a scatter plot.

*Use with Lesson 4-5*

**MA.S.2** Infer trends in bivariate data. **MA.S.2.1** Use formal strategies for placement of lines of best fit to model bivariate data.

go.hrw.com
**Lab Resources Online**
KEYWORD: MA7 Lab 4

## Activity

**The table shows the dosage of a particular medicine as related to a person's weight. Graph a scatter plot of the given data. Draw the trend line. Then predict the dosage for a person weighing 240 pounds.**

| Weight (lb) | 90 | 100 | 110 | 125 | 140 | 155 | 170 | 180 | 200 |
|---|---|---|---|---|---|---|---|---|---|
| Dosage (mg) | 20 | 25 | 30 | 35 | 40 | 53 | 60 | 66 | 75 |

1. First enter the data. Press STAT and select **1: Edit**. In **L1**, enter the first weight. Press ENTER. Continue entering all weights. Use ▶ to move to **L2**. Enter the first dosage. Press ENTER. Continue entering all dosages.

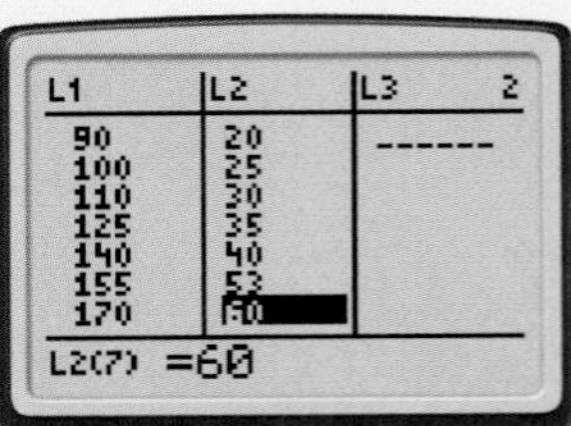


2. To view the scatter plot, press 2nd Y=. Select **Plot 1**. Select **On**, the first plot type, and the plot mark +. Press ZOOM. Select **9: ZoomStat**. You should see a scatter plot of the data.

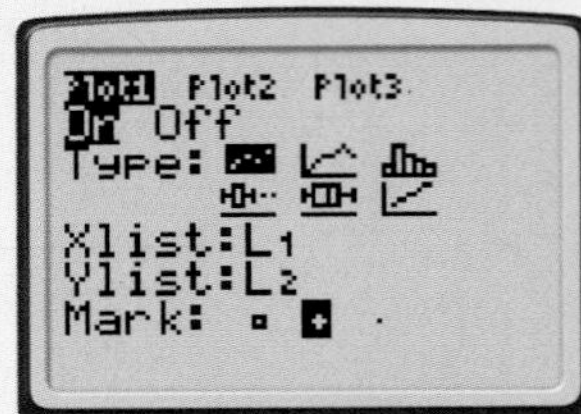


3. To find the trend line, press STAT and select the **CALC** menu. Select **LinReg (ax+b)**. Press ENTER. This gives you the values of $a$ and $b$ in the trend line.

4. To enter the equation for the trend line, press Y=, then input **.5079441502x − 26.78767453**. Press GRAPH.

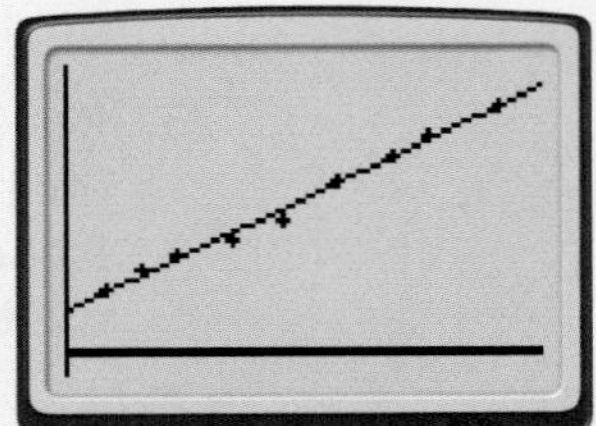

5. Now predict the dosage when the weight is 240 pounds. Press VARS. Select **Y-VARS** menu and select **1:Function**. Select **1:Y1**. Enter **(240)**. Press ENTER. The dosage is about 95 milligrams.

## Try This

1. The table shows the price of a stock over an 8-month period. Graph a scatter plot of the given data. Draw the trend line. Then predict what the price of one share of stock will be in the twelfth month.

| Month | 1 | 2 | 3 | 4 | 5 | 6 | 7 | 8 |
|---|---|---|---|---|---|---|---|---|
| Price ($) | 32 | 35 | 37 | 41 | 46 | 50 | 54 | 59 |

# Median-Fit Line

*See Skills Bank page S72*

You have learned about trend lines. Now you will learn about another line of fit called the median-fit line.

**MA.S.2** Infer trends in bivariate data. **MA.S.2.1** Use formal strategies for placement of lines of best fit to model bivariate data.

## Example

**At a water raft rental shop, a group of up to four people can rent a single raft. The table shows the number of rafts rented to different groups of people one morning. Find the median-fit line for the data.**

| People $x$ | 1 | 2 | 4 | 5 | 5 | 5 | 7 | 9 | 10 | 11 | 12 | 15 |
|---|---|---|---|---|---|---|---|---|---|---|---|---|
| Rafts Rented $y$ | 1 | 1 | 1 | 3 | 4 | 5 | 4 | 7 | 5 | 3 | 4 | 6 |

1. Plot the points on a coordinate plane.

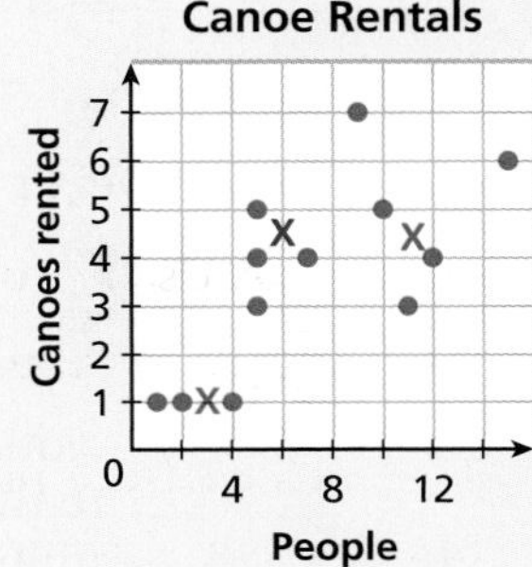


2. Divide the data into three sections of equal size. Find the medians of the $x$-values and the $y$-values for each section. Plot the three median points with an X.

| 1 | 2 | 4 | 5 | 5 | 5 | 7 | 9 | 10 | 11 | 12 | 15 |
|---|---|---|---|---|---|---|---|---|---|---|---|
| 1 | 1 | 1 | 3 | 4 | 5 | 4 | 7 | 5 | 3 | 4 | 6 |

Median point: (3, 1) | **Median point: (6, 4.5)** | Median point: (11.5, 4.5)

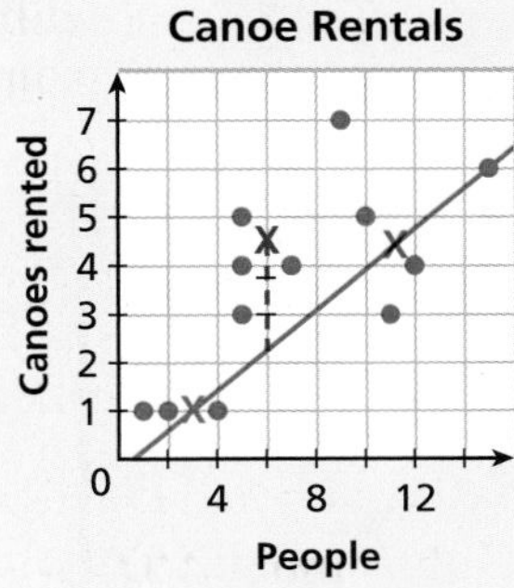


3. Connect the outside, or first and third, median points with a line.

4. Lightly draw a dashed line straight down from the middle median point to the line just drawn. Mark the dashed line to create three equal segments.

5. Keeping your ruler parallel to the first line you drew, move your ruler to the mark closest to the line. Draw the line. This is the median-fit line.

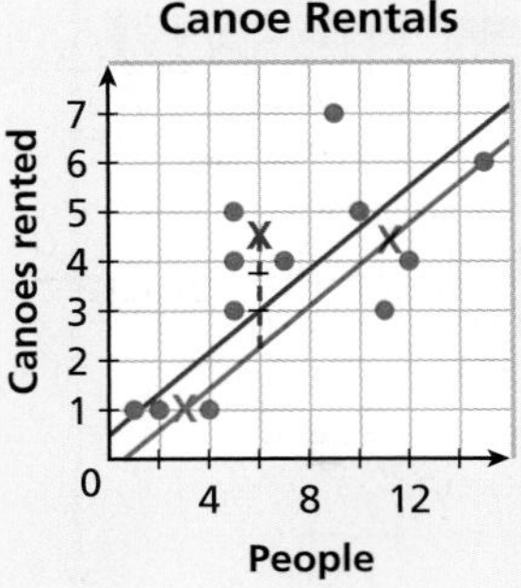


## Try This

1. A manager at a restaurant kept track one afternoon of the number of people in a party and the time it took to seat them. Find the median-fit line for the data.
2. Use your median-fit line to predict the time it took to seat a party of 6.

| People $x$ | 3 | 7 | 8 | 8 | 10 | 12 |
|---|---|---|---|---|---|---|
| Wait Time $y$ (min) | 1 | 5 | 3 | 9 | 6 | 6 |

# 4-6 Arithmetic Sequences

**MA.A.3** Analyze patterns of change in functional relationships.

***Objectives***

Recognize and extend an arithmetic sequence.

Find a given term of an arithmetic sequence.

***Vocabulary***

sequence
term
arithmetic sequence
common difference

**Why learn this?**

The distance between you and a lightning strike can be approximated by using an arithmetic sequence.

During a thunderstorm, you can estimate your distance from a lightning strike by counting the number of seconds from the time you see the lightning until the time you hear the thunder.

When you list the times and distances in order, each list forms a sequence. A **sequence** is a list of numbers that often forms a pattern. Each number in a sequence is a **term**.

| Time (s) | 1 | 2 | 3 | 4 | 5 | 6 | 7 | 8 |
|---|---|---|---|---|---|---|---|---|
| Distance (mi) | 0.2 | 0.4 | 0.6 | 0.8 | 1.0 | 1.2 | 1.4 | 1.6 |

$+0.2 \quad +0.2 \quad +0.2 \quad +0.2 \quad +0.2 \quad +0.2 \quad +0.2$

Notice that in the distance sequence, you can find the next term by adding 0.2 to the previous term. When the terms of a sequence differ by the same nonzero number $d$, the sequence is an **arithmetic sequence** and $d$ is the **common difference**. So the distances in the table form an arithmetic sequence with common difference 0.2.

**EXAMPLE 1** **Identifying Arithmetic Sequences**

**Determine whether each sequence appears to be an arithmetic sequence. If so, find the common difference and the next three terms in the sequence.**

**A** **12, 8, 4, 0, ...**

**Step 1** Find the difference between successive terms.

12, 8, 4, 0, ...

$-4 \quad -4 \quad -4$

*You add −4 to each term to find the next term. The common difference is −4.*

**Step 2** Use the common difference to find the next 3 terms.

12, 8, 4, 0, −4, −8, −12

$-4 \quad -4 \quad -4$

The sequence appears to be an arithmetic sequence with a common difference of −4. The next 3 terms are −4, −8, −12.

**Reading Math**

The three dots at the end of a sequence are called an ellipsis. They mean that the sequence continues and can be read as "and so on."

**B** **1, 4, 9, 16, ...**

Find the difference between successive terms.

1, 4, 9, 16, ...

$+3 \quad +5 \quad +7$

*The difference between successive terms is not the same.*

This sequence is not an arithmetic sequence.

**Determine whether each sequence appears to be an arithmetic sequence. If so, find the common difference and the next three terms.**

**1a.** $-\frac{3}{4}, -\frac{1}{4}, \frac{1}{4}, \frac{3}{4}, \ldots$

**1b.** $\frac{2}{3}, \frac{1}{3}, -\frac{1}{3}, -\frac{2}{3}, \ldots$

**1c.** $-4, -2, 1, 5, \ldots$

**1d.** $4, 1, -2, -5, \ldots$

The variable $a$ is often used to represent terms in a sequence. The variable $a_9$, read "$a$ sub 9," is the ninth term in a sequence. To designate any term, or the $n$th term, in a sequence, you write $a_n$, where $n$ can be any number.

| 1 | 2 | 3 | 4... | $n$ | ← Position |
|---|---|---|---|---|---|
| ↓ | ↓ | ↓ | ↓ | | |
| 3, | 5, | 7, | 9... | | ← Term |
| $a_1$ | $a_2$ | $a_3$ | $a_4$ | $a_n$ | |

The sequence above starts with 3. The common difference $d$ is 2. You can use the first term and the common difference to write a rule for finding $a_n$.

| Words | Numbers | Algebra |
|---|---|---|
| 1st term | 3 | $a_1$ |
| 2nd term | $3 + (1)2 = 5$ | $a_1 + 1d$ |
| 3nd term | $3 + (2)2 = 7$ | $a_1 + 2d$ |
| 4th term | $3 + (3)2 = 9$ | $a_1 + 3d$ |
| ⋮ | ⋮ | ⋮ |
| $n$th term | $3 + (n - 1)2$ | $a_1 + (n - 1)d$ |

The pattern in the table shows that to find the $n$th term, add the **first term** to the product of $(n - 1)$ and the **common difference**.

**Finding the $n$th Term of an Arithmetic Sequence**

The $n$th term of an arithmetic sequence with **common difference $d$** and **first term $a_1$** is

$$a_n = a_1 + (n - 1)d.$$

## EXAMPLE 2 Finding the $n$th Term of an Arithmetic Sequence

**Find the indicated term of each arithmetic sequence.**

**A** **22nd term: 5, 2, −1, −4, ...**

**Step 1** Find the common difference.

5, 2, −1, −4, ... *The common difference is −3.*

−3 −3 −3

**Step 2** Write a rule to find the 22nd term.

| | |
|---|---|
| $a_n = a_1 + (n - 1)d$ | *Write the rule to find the nth term.* |
| $a_{22} = 5 + (22 - 1)(-3)$ | *Substitute 5 for $a_1$, 22 for n, and −3 for d.* |
| $= 5 + (21)(-3)$ | *Simplify the expression in parentheses.* |
| $= 5 - 63$ | *Multiply.* |
| $= -58$ | *Add.* |

The 22nd term is −58.

**Find the indicated term of each arithmetic sequence.**

**B** **15th term: $a_1 = 7$; $d = 3$**

$a_n = a_1 + (n - 1)d$ — *Write the rule to find the nth term.*

$a_{15} = 7 + (15 - 1)3$ — *Substitute 7 for $a_1$, 15 for n, and 3 for d.*

$= 7 + (14)3$ — *Simplify the expression in parentheses.*

$= 7 + 42$ — *Multiply.*

$= 49$ — *Add.*

The 15th term is 49.

**Find the indicated term of each arithmetic sequence.**

**2a.** 60th term: 11, 5, −1, −7, … **2b.** 12th term: $a_1 = 4.2$; $d = 1.4$

## EXAMPLE 3 *Travel Application*

**The odometer on a car reads 60,473. Every day, the car is driven 54 miles. What is the odometer reading 20 days later?**

**Step 1** Determine whether the situation appears to be arithmetic.

The sequence for the situation is arithmetic because the odometer reading will increase by 54 miles per day.

**Step 2** Find $d$, $a_1$, and $n$.

Since the odometer reading will increase by 54 miles per day, $d = 54$.

Since the odometer reading is 60,473 miles, $a_1 = 60{,}473$.

Since you want to find the odometer reading 20 days later, you will need to find the 21st term of the sequence, so $n = 21$.

**Step 3** Find the odometer reading for $a_n$.

$a_n = a_1 + (n - 1)d$ — *Write the rule to find the nth term.*

$a_{21} = 60{,}473 + (21 - 1)54$ — *Substitute 60,473 for $a_1$, 54 for d, and 21 for n.*

$= 60{,}473 + (20)54$ — *Simplify the expression in parentheses.*

$= 60{,}473 + 1080$ — *Multiply.*

$= 61{,}553$ — *Add.*

The odometer will read 61,553 miles 20 days later.

**3.** Each time a truck stops, it drops off 250 pounds of cargo. It started with a load of 2000 pounds. How much does the load weigh after the fifth stop?

## THINK AND DISCUSS

**1.** Explain how to determine if a sequence appears to be arithmetic.

**2. GET ORGANIZED** Copy and complete the graphic organizer with steps for finding the *n*th term of an arithmetic sequence.

Finding the *n*th Term of an Arithmetic Sequence

# 4-6 Exercises

MA.A.3

go.hrw.com
Homework Help Online
KEYWORD: MA7 4-6
Parent Resources Online
KEYWORD: MA7 Parent

## GUIDED PRACTICE

1. **Vocabulary** When trying to find the $n$th term of an arithmetic sequence you must first know the ___?___. (*common difference* or *sequence*)

SEE EXAMPLE 1 p. 272

**Multi-Step Determine whether each sequence appears to be an arithmetic sequence. If so, find the common difference and the next three terms.**

2. 2, 8, 14, 20, …
3. 2.1, 1.4, 0.7, 0, …
4. 1, 1, 2, 3, …
5. 0.1, 0.3, 0.9, 2.7, …

SEE EXAMPLE 2 p. 273

**Find the indicated term of each arithmetic sequence.**

6. 21st term: 3, 8, 13, 18, …
7. 18th term: $a_1 = -2$; $d = -3$

SEE EXAMPLE 3 p. 274

8. **Shipping** To package and ship an item, it costs \$5 for shipping supplies and \$0.75 for each pound the package weighs. What is the cost of shipping a 12-pound package?

## PRACTICE AND PROBLEM SOLVING

**Independent Practice**

| For Exercises | See Example |
|---|---|
| 9–12 | 1 |
| 13–14 | 2 |
| 15 | 3 |

**Extra Practice**

Skills Practice p. S11
Application Practice p. S31

**Multi-Step Determine whether each sequence appears to be an arithmetic sequence. If so, find the common difference and the next three terms.**

9. −1, 10, −100, 1,100, …
10. 0, −2, −4, −6, …
11. −22, −31, −40, −49, …
12. 0.2, 0.5, 0.9, 1.1, …

**Find the indicated term of each arithmetic sequence.**

13. 31st term: 1.40, 1.55, 1.70, …
14. 50th term: $a_1 = 2.2$ ; $d = 1.1$

15. **Travel** Rachel signed up for a frequent-flier program and received 3000 bonus miles. She earns 1300 frequent-flier miles each time she purchases a round-trip ticket. How many frequent-flier miles will she have after 5 round-trips?

**Find the common difference for each arithmetic sequence.**

16. 0, 6, 12, 18, …
17. $\frac{1}{2}, \frac{3}{4}, 1, \frac{5}{4}, \ldots$
18. 107, 105, 103, 101, …
19. 7.9, 5.7, 3.5, 1.3, …
20. $\frac{1}{5}, \frac{2}{5}, \frac{3}{5}, \frac{4}{5}, \ldots$
21. 4.25, 4.32, 4.39, 4.46, …

**Find the next four terms in each arithmetic sequence.**

22. −4, −7, −10, −13, …
23. $\frac{1}{8}, 0, -\frac{1}{8}, -\frac{1}{4}, \ldots$
24. 505, 512, 519, 526, …
25. 1.8, 1.3, 0.8, 0.3, …
26. $\frac{2}{3}, \frac{4}{3}, 2, \frac{8}{3}, \ldots$
27. −1.1, −0.9, −0.7, −0.5

**Find the given term of each arithmetic sequence.**

28. 5, 10, 15, 20, …; 17th term
29. 121, 110, 99, 88, …; 10th term
30. −2, −5, −8, −11, …; 41st term
31. −30, −22, −14, −6, …; 20th term

32. **Critical Thinking** Is the sequence $5a - 1, 3a - 1, a - 1, -a - 1, \ldots$ arithmetic? If not, explain why not. If so, find the common difference and the next three terms.

33. **Recreation** The rates for a go-cart course are shown.

a. Explain why the relationship described on the flyer could be an arithmetic sequence.

b. Find the cost for 1, 2, 3, and 4 laps. Write a rule to find the $n$th term of the sequence.

c. How much would 15 laps cost?

d. **What if...?** After 9 laps, you get the 10th one free. Will the sequence still be arithmetic? Explain.

**LINK**

**Number Theory**

Fibonacci numbers occur frequently throughout nature. The number of petals on many flowers are numbers of the Fibonacci sequence. Two petals on a flower are rare but 3, 5, and even 34 petals are common.

**Find the given term of each arithmetic sequence.**

34. 2.5, 8.5, 14.5, 20.5, ...; 30th term

35. 189.6, 172.3, 155, 137.7, ...; 18th term

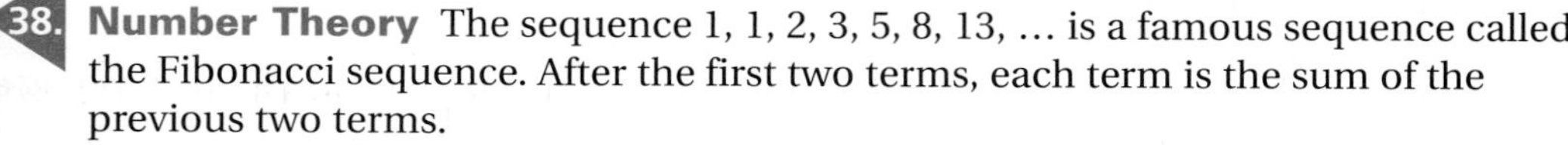

36. $\frac{1}{4}, \frac{3}{4}, \frac{5}{4}, \frac{7}{4}, \ldots$; 15th term

37. $\frac{2}{3}, \frac{11}{12}, \frac{7}{6}, \frac{17}{12}, \ldots$; 25th term

38. **Number Theory** The sequence 1, 1, 2, 3, 5, 8, 13, ... is a famous sequence called the Fibonacci sequence. After the first two terms, each term is the sum of the previous two terms.

a. Write the first 10 terms of the Fibonacci sequence. Is the Fibonacci sequence arithmetic? Explain.

b. Notice that the third term is divisible by 2. Are the 6th and 9th terms also divisible by 2? What conclusion can you draw about every third term? Why is this true?

c. Can you find any other patterns? (*Hint:* Look at every 4th and 5th term.)

39. **Entertainment** Seats in a concert hall are arranged in the pattern shown.

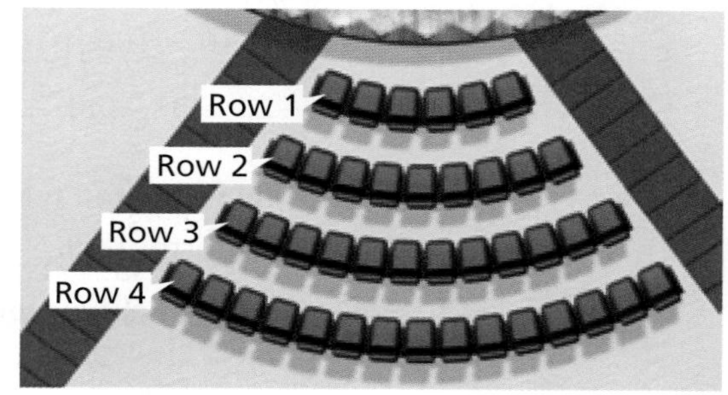


a. The numbers of seats in the rows form an arithmetic sequence. Write a rule for the arithmetic sequence.

b. How many seats are in the 15th row?

c. A ticket costs $40. Suppose every seat in the first 10 rows is filled. What is the total revenue from those seats?

d. **What if...?** An extra chair is added to each row. Write the new rule for the arithmetic sequence and find the new total revenue from the first 10 rows.

40. **Write About It** Explain how to find the common difference of an arithmetic sequence. How can you determine whether the arithmetic sequence has a positive common difference or a negative common difference?

41. This problem will prepare you for the Multi-Step Test Prep on page 278.

Juan is traveling to visit universities. He notices mile markers along the road. He records the mile marker every 10 minutes. His father is driving at a constant speed.

a. Copy and complete the table.

b. Write the rule for the sequence.

c. What does the common difference represent?

d. If this sequence continues, find the mile marker for time interval 10.

| Time Interval | Mile Marker |
|---|---|
| 1 | 520 |
| 2 | 509 |
| 3 | 498 |
| 4 | |
| 5 | |
| 6 | |

MA.A.3

42. What are the next three terms in the arithmetic sequence −21, −12, −3, 6, ... ?

Ⓐ 9, 12, 15 Ⓑ 15, 24, 33 Ⓒ 12, 21, 27 Ⓓ 13, 20, 27

43. What is the common difference for the data listed in the second column?

Ⓕ −1.8 Ⓗ 2.8

Ⓖ 1.8 Ⓙ −3.6

| Altitude (ft) | Boiling Point of Water (°F) |
|---|---|
| 1000 | 210.2 |
| 2000 | 208.4 |
| 3000 | 206.6 |

44. Which of the following sequences is NOT arithmetic?

Ⓐ −4, 2, 8, 14, ... Ⓑ 9, 4, −1, −6, ... Ⓒ 2, 4, 8, 16, ... Ⓓ $\frac{1}{3}, 1\frac{1}{3}, 2\frac{1}{3}, 3\frac{1}{3}, \ldots$

## CHALLENGE AND EXTEND

45. The first term of an arithmetic sequence is 2, and the common difference is 9. Find two consecutive terms of the sequence that have a sum of 355. What positions in the sequence are the terms?

46. The 60th term of an arithmetic sequence is 106.5, and the common difference is 1.5. What is the first term of the sequence?

47. **Athletics** Verona is training for a marathon. The first part of her training schedule is shown below.

| Session | 1 | 2 | 3 | 4 | 5 | 6 |
|---|---|---|---|---|---|---|
| Distance Run (mi) | 3.5 | 5 | 6.5 | 8 | 9.5 | 11 |

a. If Verona continues this pattern, during which training session will she run 26 miles? Is her training schedule an arithmetic sequence? Explain.

b. If Verona's training schedule starts on a Monday and she runs every third day, on which day will she run 26 miles?

## SPIRAL REVIEW

48. Three sides of a triangle are represented by $x$, $x + 3$ and $x + 5$. The perimeter of the triangle is 35 units. Solve for $x$. *(Lesson 2-3)*

49. The length of a rectangle is 2 and the width is represented by $x + 4$. The area of the rectangle is 40 square units. Solve for $x$. *(Lesson 2-3)*

**Solve each compound inequality and graph the solutions.** *(Lesson 3-6)*

50. $4 < 2n + 6 \leq 20$

51. $t + 5 > 7$ OR $2t - 8 < -12$

**Describe the correlation illustrated by each scatter plot.** *(Lesson 4-5)*

52. Household Televisions

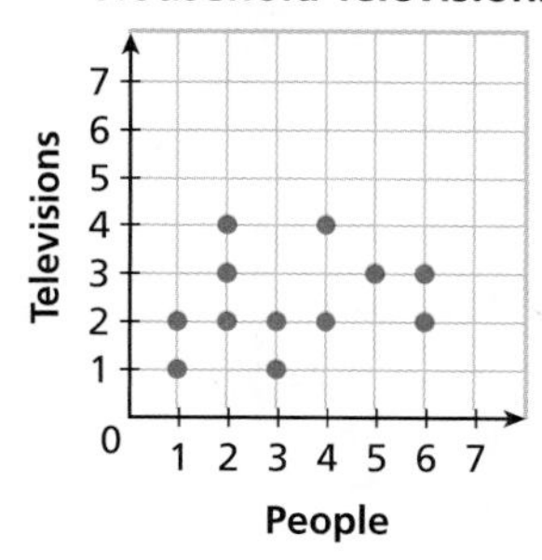


53. Safe Heart Rate

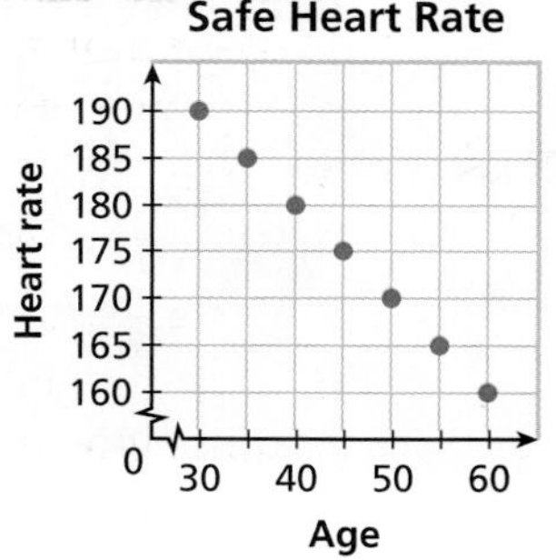

CHAPTER 4

# MULTI-STEP TEST PREP

SECTION 4B

STATE

## Applying Functions

**College Knowledge** Myra is helping her brother plan a college visit 10 hours away from their home. She creates a table listing approximate travel times and distances from their home.

1. Create a scatter plot for the data.
2. Draw a trend line through the data.
3. Based on the trend line, how many miles will they have traveled after 5 hours?
4. If Myra's brother decided to visit a college 13 hours away from their home, approximately how many miles will they travel?
5. To find the average speed for the entire trip, find $\frac{\text{change in distance}}{\text{change in time}}$ between the initial ordered pair and the final ordered pair. Include the units.

| Time (h) | Distance (mi) |
|---|---|
| 0 | 0 |
| 2 | 123 |
| 3 | 190 |
| 4 | 207 |
| 6 | 355 |
| 8 | 472 |
| 10 | 657 |

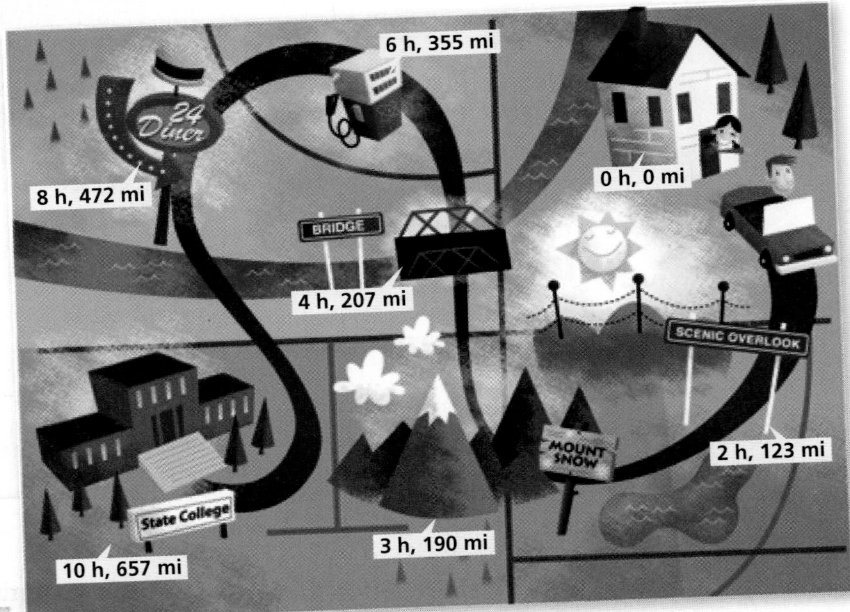

# READY TO GO ON?

CHAPTER 4

SECTION 4B

## Quiz for Lessons 4-5 Through 4-6

### 4-5 Scatter Plots and Trend Lines

**The table shows the time it takes different people to read a given number of pages.**

| Pages Read | 2 | 6 | 6 | 8 | 8 | 10 | 10 |
|---|---|---|---|---|---|---|---|
| Time (min) | 10 | 15 | 20 | 15 | 30 | 25 | 30 |

1. Graph a scatter plot using the given data.
2. Describe the correlation illustrated by the scatter plot.

**Choose the scatter plot that best represents the described relationship. Explain.**

3. number of movie tickets sold and number of available seats
4. number of movie tickets sold and amount of concession sales
5. number of movie tickets sold and length of movie

Graph A

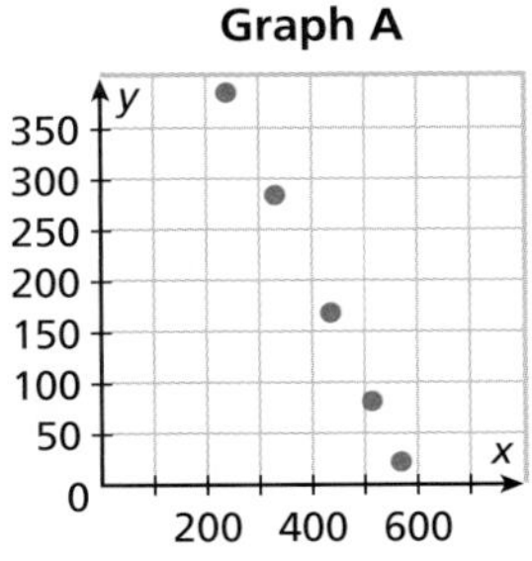


Graph B

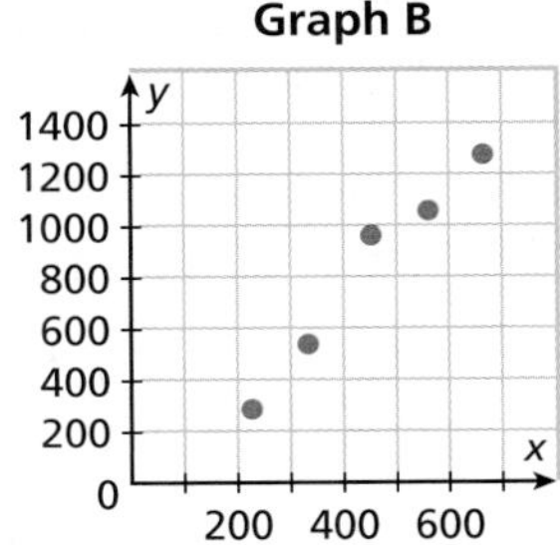


Graph C

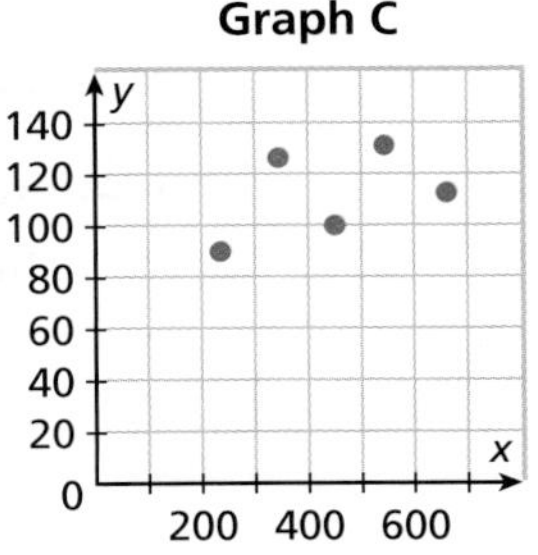


6. The scatter plot shows the estimated annual sales for an electronics and appliance chain of stores for the years 2004–2009. Based on this relationship, predict the annual sales in 2012.

Estimated Annual Sales

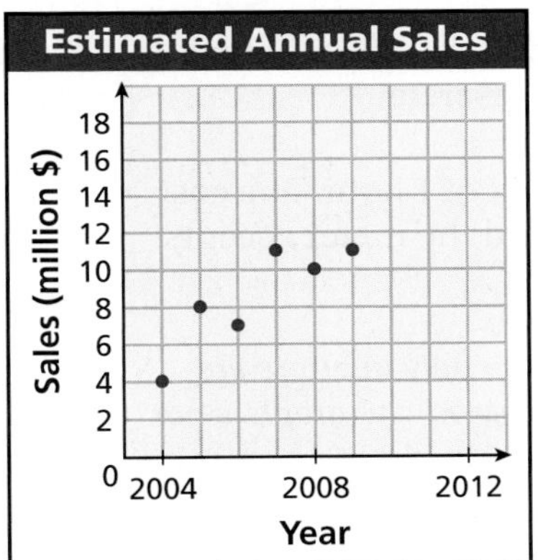


### 4-6 Arithmetic Sequences

**Determine whether each sequence appears to be an arithmetic sequence. If so, find the common difference and the next three terms.**

7. 7, 3, −1, −5, ...
8. 3, 6, 12, 24, ...
9. −3.5, −2, −0.5, 1, ...

**Find the indicated term of the arithmetic sequence.**

10. 31st term: 12, 7, 2, −3, ...
11. 22nd term: $a_1 = 6$; $d = 4$
12. With no air resistance, an object would fall 16 feet during the first second, 48 feet during the second second, 80 feet during the third second, 112 feet during the fourth second, and so on. How many feet will the object fall during the ninth second?

CHAPTER 4

# Study Guide: Review

## Vocabulary



**Complete the sentences below with vocabulary words from the list above.**

1. The set of $x$-coordinates of the ordered pairs of a relation is called the ___?___.
2. If one set of data values increases as another set of data values decreases, the relationship can be described as having a(n) ___?___.
3. A sequence is an ordered list of numbers where each number is a(n) ___?___.

## 4-1 Graphing Relationships *(pp. 230–235)*

### EXAMPLES

**Sketch a graph for each situation. Tell whether the graph is continuous or discrete.**

- A parking meter has a limit of 1 hour. The cost is $0.25 per 15 minutes and the meter accepts quarters only.

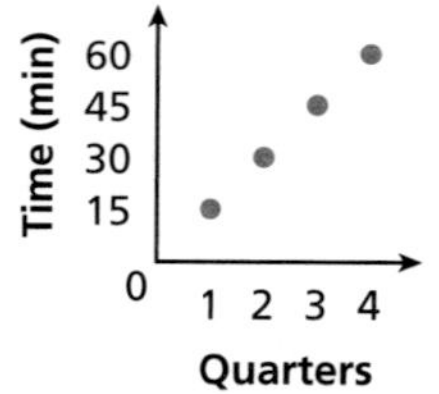


*Since only quarters are accepted, the graph is not connected.*

The graph is discrete.

- Ian bought a cup of coffee. At first, he sipped slowly. As it cooled, he drank more quickly. The last bit was cold, and he dumped it out.

As time passes the coffee was sipped slowly, **drank more quickly,** and then dumped out.

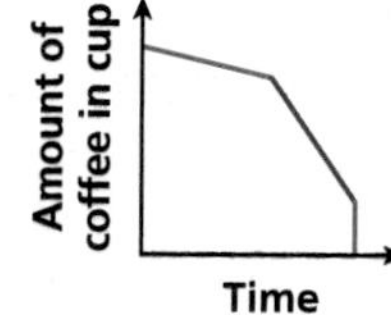


The graph is continuous.

### EXERCISES

**Sketch a graph for each situation. Tell whether the graph is continuous or discrete.**

4. A girl was walking home at a steady pace. Then she stopped to talk to a friend. After her friend left, she jogged the rest of the way home.
5. A ball is dropped from a second story window and bounces to a stop on the patio below.
6. Jason was on the second floor when he got a call to attend a meeting on the sixth floor. He took the stairs. After the meeting, he took the elevator to the first floor.

**Write a possible situation for each graph.**

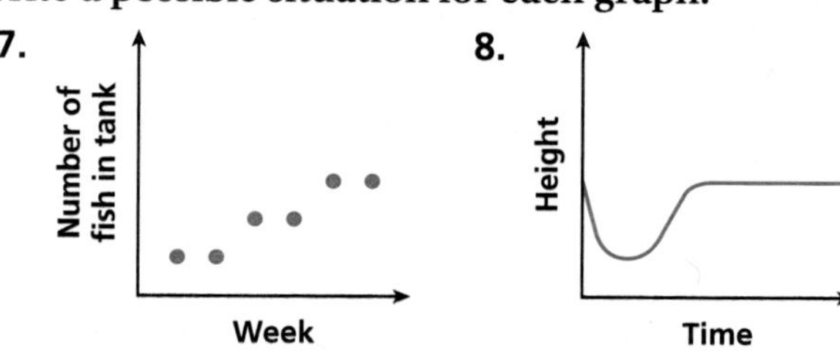

## 4-2 Relations and Functions (pp. 236–242)

MA.A.4.1, MA.A.4.2

### EXAMPLES

- Express the relation $\{(2, 15), (4, 12), (5, 7), (7, 2)\}$ as a table, as a graph, and as a mapping diagram.

Table

| x | y |
|---|---|
| 2 | 15 |
| 4 | 12 |
| 5 | 7 |
| 7 | 2 |

Graph

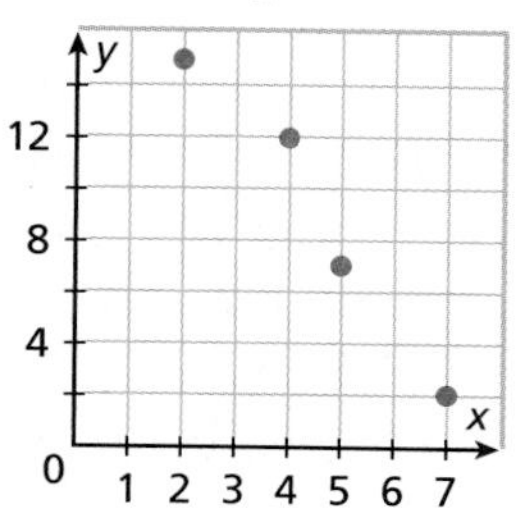

Mapping Diagram

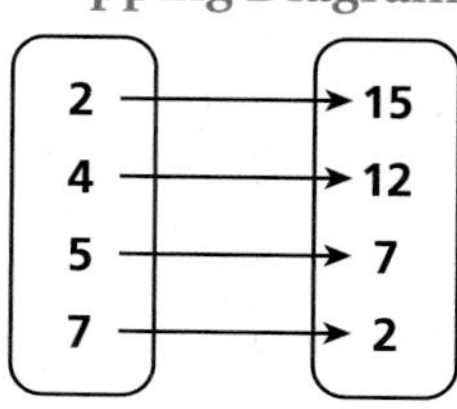

Give the domain and range of each relation. Tell whether the relation is a function. Explain.

- 

| x | y |
|---|---|
| −3 | 0 |
| −2 | 0 |
| −1 | 1 |

D: $\{-3, -2, -1\}$

R: $\{0, 1\}$

The relation is a function because each domain value is paired with exactly one range value.

- 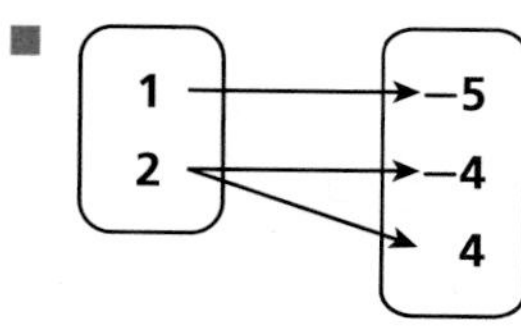

D: $\{1, 2\}$

R: $\{-5, -4, 4\}$

The relation is not a function because one domain value is paired with two range values.

- 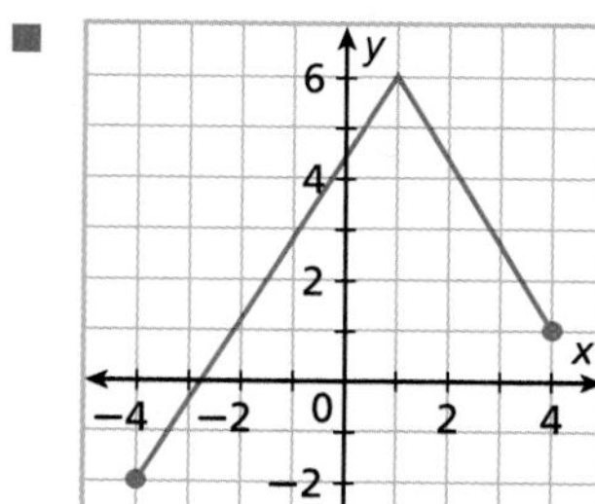

D: $-4 \le x \le 4$

R: $-2 \le y \le 6$

The relation is a function because every $x$-value is paired with exactly one $y$-value.

### EXERCISES

Express each relation as a table, as a graph, and as a mapping diagram.

9. $\{(-1, 0), (0, 1), (2, 1)\}$
10. $\{(-2, -1), (-1, 1), (2, 3), (3, 4)\}$

Give the domain and range of each relation.

11. $\{(-4, 5), (-2, 3), (0, 1), (2, -1)\}$
12. $\{(-2, -1) (-1, 0), (0, -1), (1, 0), (2, -1)\}$
13.

| x | 0 | 1 | 4 | 1 | 4 |
|---|---|---|---|---|---|
| y | 0 | −1 | −2 | 1 | 2 |

14. 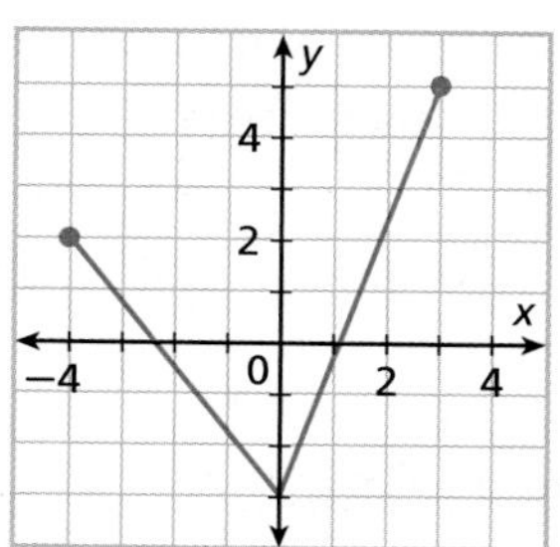

Give the domain and range of each relation. Tell whether the relation is a function. Explain.

15. $\{(-5, -3), (-3, -2), (-1, -1), (1, 0)\}$
16. 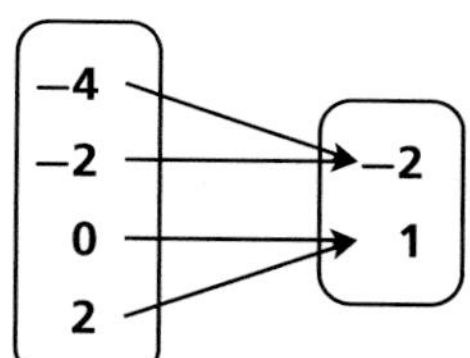
17.

| x | 1 | 2 | 3 | 4 | 1 |
|---|---|---|---|---|---|
| y | 3 | 2 | 1 | 0 | −1 |

18. A local parking garage charges $5.00 for the first hour plus $1.50 for each additional hour or part of an hour. Write a relation as a set of ordered pairs in which the $x$-value represents the number of hours and the $y$-value represents the cost for $x$ hours. Use a domain of 1, 2, 3, 4, 5. Is this relation a function? Explain.
19. A baseball coach is taking the team for ice cream. Four students can ride in each car. Create a mapping diagram to show the number of cars needed to transport 8, 10, 14, and 16 students. Is this relation a function? Explain.

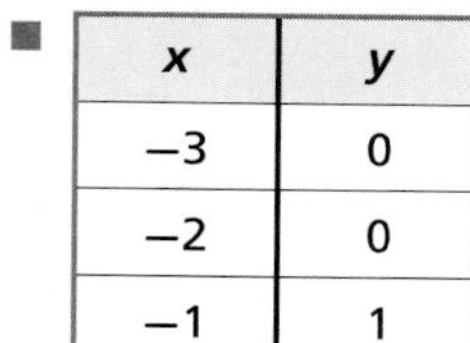

## 4-3 Writing Functions *(pp. 245–251)*

MA.A.4.2

### EXAMPLES

■ **Determine a relationship between the $x$- and $y$-values in the table. Write an equation.**

| $x$ | 1 | 2 | 3 | 4 |
|---|---|---|---|---|
| $y$ | −3 | −6 | −9 | −12 |

*What are possible relationships between the x-values and the y-values?*

$1 - 4 = -3$ $\quad$ $1(-3) = -3$

$2 - 4 \neq -6$ ✗ $\quad$ $2(-3) = -6$ ✓

$3(-3) = -9$ ✓

$4(-3) = -12$ ✓

$y = -3x$ $\quad$ *Write an equation.*

**Identify the independent and dependent variables. Write a rule in function notation for the situation.**

■ Nia earns \$5.25 per hour.

Nia's **pay** depends on the **number of hours** she works.

Dependent: **pay**

Independent: **hours**

Let $h$ represent the number of hours Nia works.

The function for Nia's pay is $f(h) = 5.25h$.

### EXERCISES

**Determine the relationship between the $x$- and $y$-values. Write an equation.**

20.

| $x$ | 1 | 2 | 3 | 4 |
|---|---|---|---|---|
| $y$ | −6 | −5 | −4 | −3 |

21. $\{(1, 9), (2, 18), (3, 27), (4, 36)\}$

**Identify the independent and dependent variables. Write a rule in function notation for the situation.**

22. A baker spends \$6 on ingredients for each cake he bakes.
23. Tim will buy twice as many CDs as Raul.

**Evaluate each function for the given input values.**

24. For $f(x) = -2x + 4$, find $f(x)$ when $x = -5$.
25. For $g(n) = -n^2 - 2$, find $g(n)$ when $n = -3$.
26. For $h(t) = 7 - |t + 3|$, find $h(t)$ when $t = -4$ and when $t = 5$.

## 4-4 Graphing Functions *(pp. 252–258)*

MA.A.4

### EXAMPLE

■ **Graph the function $y = 3x - 1$.**

**Step 1** Choose several values of $x$ to generate ordered pairs.

| $x$ | $y = 3x - 1$ | $y$ |
|---|---|---|
| −1 | $y = 3(-1) - 1 = -4$ | −4 |
| 0 | $y = 3(0) - 1 = -1$ | −1 |
| 1 | $y = 3(1) - 1 = 2$ | 2 |
| 2 | $y = 3(2) - 1 = 5$ | 5 |

**Step 2** Plot enough points to see a pattern.

**Step 3** Draw a line through the points to show all the ordered pairs that satisfy this function.

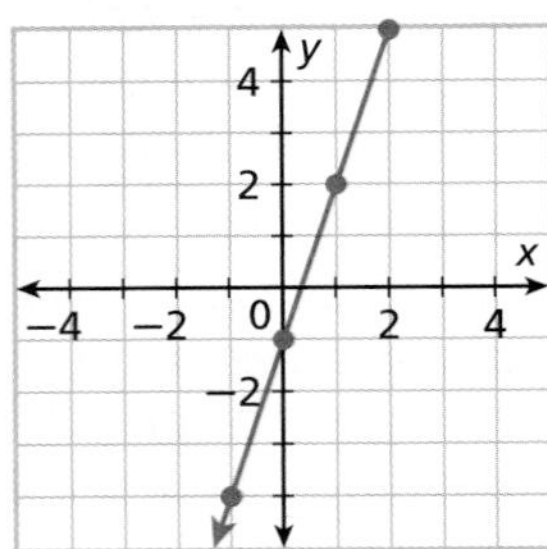


### EXERCISES

**Graph each function for the domain $\{-2, -1, 1, 2\}$.**

27. $4x + y = 2$
28. $y = (1 - x)^2$

**Graph each function.**

29. $3x - y = 1$
30. $y = 2 - |x|$
31. $y = x^2 - 6$
32. $y = |x + 5| + 1$
33. The function $y = 6.25x$ describes the amount of money $y$ Peter gets paid after $x$ hours. Graph the function. Use the graph to estimate how much money Peter gets paid after 7 hours.

## 4-5 Scatter Plots and Trend Lines *(pp. 262–269)*

MA.S.2, Prep MA.S.2.1, Prep MA.S.2.2

### EXAMPLE

- **The graph shows the amount of money in a savings account. Based on this relationship, predict how much money will be in the account in month 7.**

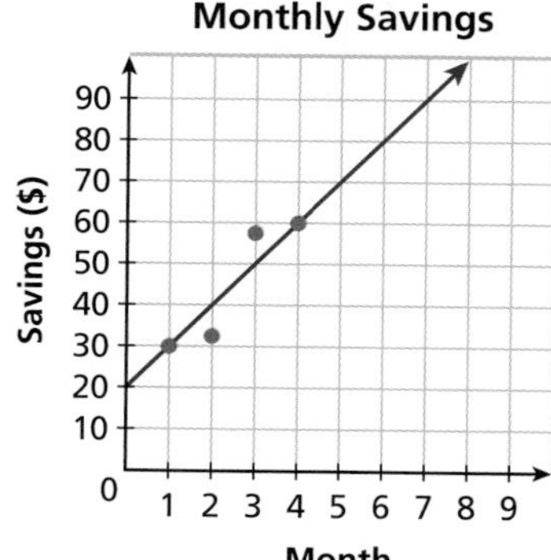


*Draw a line that has about the same number of points above and below it. Your line may or may not go through data points.*

*Find the point on the line whose x-value is 7.*

Based on the data, $90 is a reasonable prediction.

### EXERCISES

**34.** The table shows the value of a car for the given years. Graph a scatter plot using the given data. Describe the correlation illustrated by the scatter plot.

| Year | 2000 | 2001 | 2002 | 2003 |
|---|---|---|---|---|
| Value (thousand $) | 28 | 25 | 23 | 20 |

**35.** The graph shows the results of a 2003–2004 survey on class size at the given grade levels. Based on this relationship, predict the class size for the 9th grade.

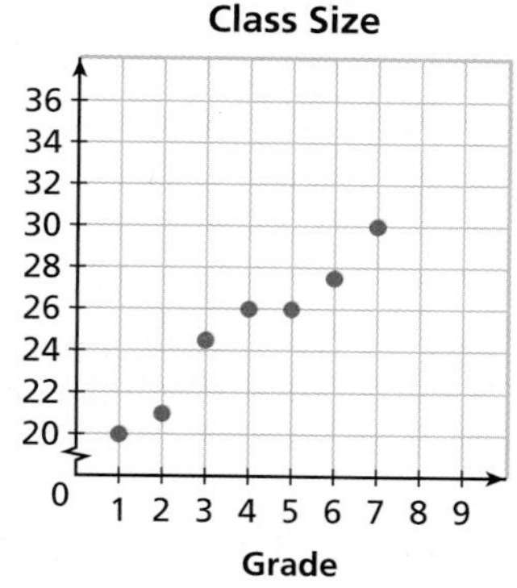


## 4-6 Arithmetic Sequences *(pp. 272–277)*

### EXAMPLES

- **Determine whether the sequence appears to be arithmetic. If so, find the common difference and the next three terms.**

  **−8, −5 ,−2 , 1,...**

  **Step 1** Find the difference between successive terms.

  −8, −5, −2, 1,...
  +3 +3 +3

  *The common difference is 3.*

  **Step 2** Use the common difference to find the next 3 terms.

  −8, −5, −2, 1, 4, 7, 10
  +3 +3 +3

- **Find the indicated term of the arithmetic sequence. 18th term: $a_1 = -4$; $d = 6$**

  $a_n = a_1 + (n - 1)d$ *Write the rule.*

  $a_{18} = -4 + (18 - 1)6$ *Substitute.*

  $= -4 + (17)6$ *Simplify.*

  $= -4 + 102$ *Simplify.*

  $= 98$

  The 18th term is 98.

### EXERCISES

**Determine whether each sequence appears to be arithmetic. If so, find the common difference and the next three terms.**

**36.** 20, 14, 8, 2,...

**37.** −15, −12, −9, −4,...

**38.** 5, 4, 2, −1,...

**39.** −8, −5.5, −3, −0.5,...

**Find the indicated term of each arithmetic sequence.**

**40.** 31st term: −15, −11, −7, −3,...

**41.** 24th term: $a_1 = 7$; $d = -3$

**42.** 17th term: $a_1 = -20$; $d = 2.5$

**43.** Marie has $180 in a savings account. She plans to deposit $12 per week. Assuming that she does not withdraw any money from her account, what will her balance be in 20 weeks?

**44.** The table shows the temperature at the given heights above sea level. Find the temperature at 8000 feet above sea level.

| Height Above Sea Level (thousand feet) | 1 | 2 | 3 | 4 |
|---|---|---|---|---|
| Temperature (°C) | 30 | 23.5 | 17 | 10.5 |

CHAPTER 4

# CHAPTER TEST

**Choose the graph that best represents each situation.**

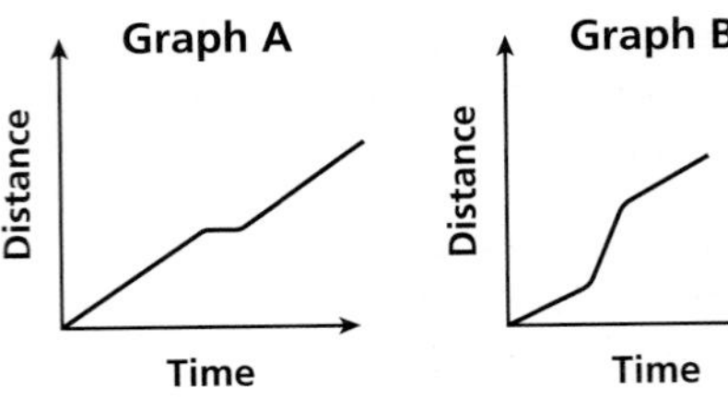


1. A person walks leisurely, stops, and then continues walking.
2. A person jogs, then runs, and then jogs again.

**Give the domain and range for each relation. Tell whether the relation is a function. Explain.**

3. 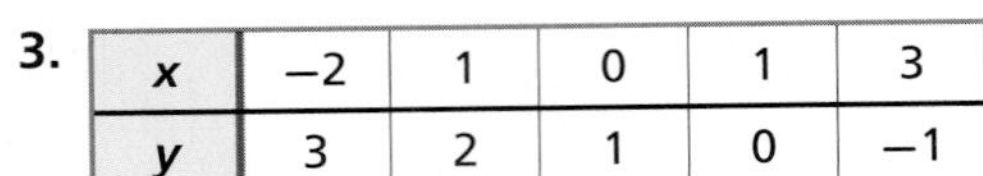

| $x$ | $-2$ | 1 | 0 | 1 | 3 |
|---|---|---|---|---|---|
| $y$ | 3 | 2 | 1 | 0 | $-1$ |

4. (graph)

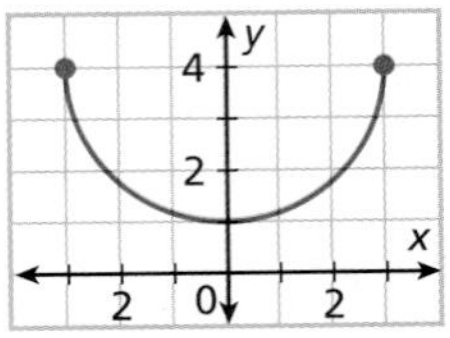

5. Bowling costs \$3 per game plus \$2.50 for shoe rental. Identify the independent and dependent variables. Write a rule in function notation for the situation.

**Evaluate each function for the given input values.**

6. For $f(x) = -3x + 4$, find $f(x)$ when $x = -2$.
7. For $f(x) = 2x^2$, find $f(x)$ when $x = -3$.
8. An engraver charges a \$10 fee plus \$6 for each line of engraving. Write a function to describe the situation. Find a reasonable domain and range for the function for up to 8 lines.

**Graph each function for the given domain.**

9. $3x + y = 4$; D: $\{-2, -1, 0, 1, 2\}$
10. $y = |x - 1|$; D: $\{-3, 0, 1, 3, 5\}$
11. $y = x^2 - 1$; D: $\{-2, -1, 0, 1, 2\}$

**Graph each function.**

12. $y = x - 5$
13. $y = x^2 - 5$
14. $y = |x| + 3$
15. The function $y = 30x$ describes the amount of interest $y$ earned in a savings account in $x$ years. Graph the function. Use the graph to estimate the total amount of interest earned in 7 years.

**The table shows possible recommendations for the number of hours of sleep that children should get every day.**

| Age (yr) | 1 | 2 | 3 | 4 | 5 | 14 |
|---|---|---|---|---|---|---|
| Sleep Needed (h) | 14 | 13 | 12 | 12 | 11 | 9 |

16. Graph a scatter plot of the given data.
17. Describe the correlation illustrated by the scatter plot.
18. Predict how many hours of sleep a 16-year-old needs.

**Determine whether each sequence appears to be an arithmetic sequence. If so, find the common difference and the next three terms.**

19. 11, 6, 1, –4,...
20. –4, –3, –1, 2,...
21. 7, 21, 30, 45,...

**Find the indicated term of the arithmetic sequence.**

22. 32nd term: 18, 11, 4, –3,...
23. 24th term: $a_1 = 4$; $d = 6$
24. Mandy's new job has a starting salary of \$16,000 and annual increases of \$800. How much will she earn during her fifth year?

CHAPTER 4

## *FOCUS ON ACT*

Questions on the ACT Mathematics Test do not require the use of a calculator, but you may bring one to use with the test. Make sure that it is a calculator that is on the approved list for the ACT.

**You may want to time yourself as you take this practice test. It should take you about 6 minutes to complete.**

**When taking the test, you will be more comfortable using a calculator that you are used to. If you already have a calculator, make sure it is one of the permitted calculators. If you plan to use a new one, make sure to practice using it before the test.**

**1.** The soccer team is ordering new uniforms. There is a one-time setup charge of \$50.00, and each uniform costs \$23.50. Which of the following best describes the total cost $C$ for ordering uniforms for $p$ players?

**(A)** $C = 23.50p$

**(B)** $C = 50p$

**(C)** $C = 73.50p$

**(D)** $C = 23.50p + 50$

**(E)** $C = 50p + 23.50$

**2.** In the given relation, what domain value corresponds to the range value $-2$?
$\{(-1, 2), (-2, 4), (2, 5), (0, -2), (2, 0)\}$

**(F)** $-2$

**(G)** 0

**(H)** 2

**(J)** 4

**(K)** 5

**3.** Evaluate $h(x) = \frac{1}{2}(5 - 6x) + 9x$ when $x = \frac{2}{3}$.

**(A)** $\frac{9}{2}$

**(B)** $\frac{13}{2}$

**(C)** 7

**(D)** $\frac{19}{2}$

**(E)** $\frac{23}{2}$

**4.** What is the seventh term of the arithmetic sequence $-4, -1, 2 \ldots$?

**(F)** 5

**(G)** 10

**(H)** 11

**(J)** 14

**(K)** 17

**5.** The graph of which function is shown below?

**(A)** $y = -3x - 5$

**(B)** $y = -\frac{1}{3}x - \frac{5}{3}$

**(C)** $y = -5x - 3$

**(D)** $y = 3x - 5$

**(E)** $y = 5x + 3$

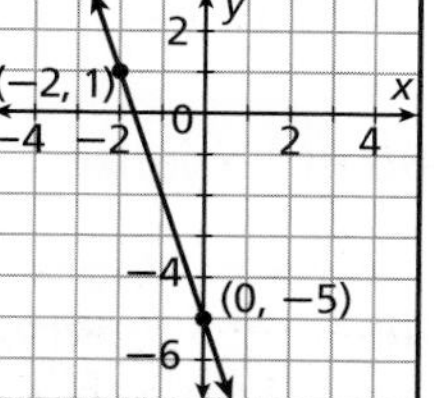


**6.** Which of the following relations is NOT a function?

**(F)** $\{(0, 1), (1, 2), (2, 3), (3, 4)\}$

**(G)** $\{(1, 2), (2, 2), (3, 3), (4, 3)\}$

**(H)** $\{(0, 2), (2, 4), (4, 1), (1, 3)\}$

**(J)** $\{(1, 3), (4, 2), (2, 0), (3, 4)\}$

**(K)** $\{(0, 2), (1, 3), (4 ,3), (1, 2)\}$

CHAPTER 4

# TEST TACKLER

Standardized Test Strategies

## Extended Response: Understand the Scores

Extended response test items are typically multipart questions that require a high level of thinking. The responses are scored using a 4-point rubric. To receive full credit, you must correctly answer all parts of the question and provide a clear explanation. A partial answer is worth 2 to 3 points, an incorrect solution is worth 1 point, and no response is worth 0 points.

### EXAMPLE 1

**Extended Response** A train traveling from Boston, Massachusetts, to Richmond, Virginia, averages about 55 miles per hour. Define the variables, write an equation, make a table, and draw a graph to show the distance the train travels in 0 to 5 hours.

Here are examples of four different responses and their scores using the rubric shown.

**4-point response:**

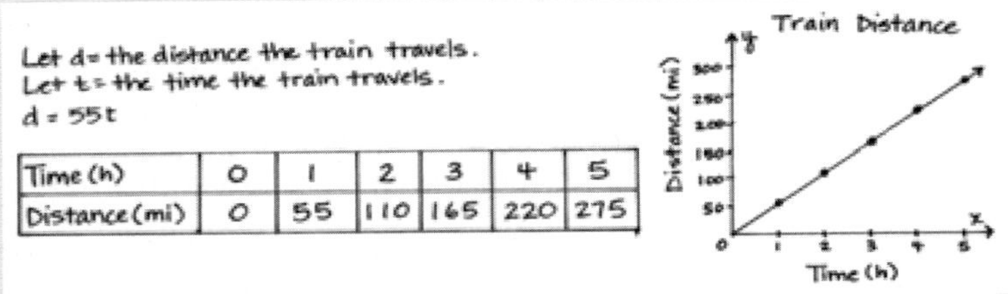
Let d = the distance the train travels.
Let t = the time the train travels.
d = 55t

| Time (h) | 0 | 1 | 2 | 3 | 4 | 5 |
|---|---|---|---|---|---|---|
| Distance (mi) | 0 | 55 | 110 | 165 | 220 | 275 |



**3-point response:**

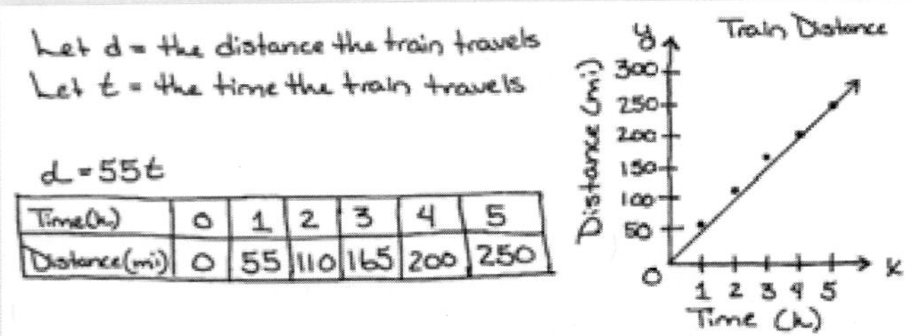
Let d = the distance the train travels
Let t = the time the train travels

d = 55t

| Time (h) | 0 | 1 | 2 | 3 | 4 | 5 |
|---|---|---|---|---|---|---|
| Distance (mi) | 0 | 55 | 110 | 165 | 200 | 250 |



*The student shows all of the work, but there are two minor computation errors when $t = 4$ and $t = 5$.*

**2-point response:**

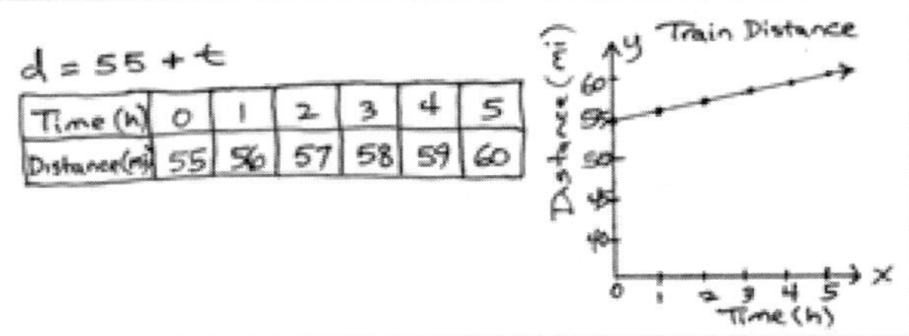
d = 55 + t

| Time (h) | 0 | 1 | 2 | 3 | 4 | 5 |
|---|---|---|---|---|---|---|
| Distance (mi) | 55 | 56 | 57 | 58 | 59 | 60 |



*The student writes an incorrect equation and uses it to create an incorrect table and graph.*

**1-point response:**

d = 55t

*The student does not answer two parts of the question.*

Never leave an extended-response test item blank. At least try to define variables or write equations where appropriate. You will get some points just for trying.

**Read each test item and answer the questions that follow using the rubric below.**

**Scoring Rubric:**

**4 points:** The student shows all of the work, correctly answers all parts of the question, and provides a clear explanation.

**3 points:** The student shows most of the work and provides a clear explanation but has a minor computation error, or the student shows all of the work and arrives at a correct solution but does not provide a clear explanation.

**2 points:** The student makes major errors resulting in an incorrect solution, or the student gives a correct solution but does not show any work nor provide an explanation.

**1 point:** The student shows no work and gives an incorrect solution.

**0 points:** The student gives no response.

**Item A**

**Extended Response** Draw a graph that is a function. Explain why it is a function. Then draw a graph that is NOT a function. Explain why it is not a function.

1. What should be included in a 4-point response?
2. Explain how would you score the response below.

Function — Not a function

The first graph is a function because each x-value has exactly one y-value. When $x=1$, $y=1$. The second graph is not a function because there is more than one y-value for each x-value. When $x=1$, $y=1$, and $y=-1$. Therefore, the second graph is not a function.

**Item B**

**Extended Response** A car travels at a steady rate of 60 miles per hour. Identify the independent and dependent variables. Describe the domain and range. Write an equation to describe the situation.

3. Ana wrote the response below.

The equation is $y = 60x$. The independent variable is time and the dependent variable is distance. The domain and range are all real numbers.

Explain how would you score Ana's response.

4. If you did not give Ana full credit, what should be added to Ana's response, if anything, so that it receives full credit?

**Item C**

**Extended Response** Lara bought 8 notebooks and 4 binders. She spent $14 total without tax. How much did each notebook cost if each binder cost $2.50? Write an equation and find the solution.

5. Explain how would you score the response below.

*Let s = the cost of each notebook.*
*Let b = the cost of each binder.*
$8s + 4b = 14$
$8s + 4(2.50) = 14$
$8s + 10 = 14$
$8s = 4$
$s = 2$ *The notebooks cost $2 each*

6. If you did not give the response full credit, what should be added to the response, if anything, so that it receives full credit?

CHAPTER 4

## CUMULATIVE ASSESSMENT, CHAPTERS 1–4

### Multiple Choice

**1.** Evaluate: $y = |x| - 25$ when $x = -3$.

A $-28$  
B $-22$  
C $-7$  
D $4$

**2.** Benito has $x$ apples. He cuts each apple in half and gives each half to a different horse. Which expression represents the number of horses Benito feeds?

A $x \cdot \frac{1}{2}$  
B $x \div \frac{1}{2}$  
C $x \cdot 1\frac{1}{2}$  
D $x \div 1\frac{1}{2}$

**3.** A scale model of a car has a scale of 1:20. The length of the actual car is 196 inches. What is the length of the model car?

A 4.9 inches  
B 9.8 inches  
C 24 inches  
D 98 inches

**4.** If $4 - a = -6$, what is the value of $\frac{2a}{a^3}$?

A $\frac{1}{50}$  
B $\frac{1}{2}$  
C 8  
D 10

**5.** There are $f$ flowers in a bouquet. One-half of the flowers are roses. One-third of the roses are red. There are 5 red roses in the bouquet. How many total flowers are in the bouquet?

A 10  
B 15  
C 25  
D 30

**6.** What is the value of $x$ when $3(x + 7) - 6x = 4 - (x + 1)$?

A 1  
B 4.5  
C 8  
D 9

**7.** Which statement is represented by the inequality $3f + 2 > -16$?

A Two added to 3 times $f$ is at least $-16$.  
B Three times the sum of $f$ and 2 is at most $-16$.  
C The sum of 2 and 3 times $f$ is more than $-16$.  
D The product of $3f$ and 2 is no more than $-16$.

**8.** WalkieTalkie phone company charges $18.00 for basic phone service per month and $0.15 per minute for long distance calls. Arena Calls charges $80.00 per month with no fee for long distance calls. What is the minimum number of minutes of long distance calls for which the cost of WalkieTalkie is more than the cost of Arena Calls per month?

A 341  
B 362  
C 414  
D 434

**9.** A bird flies from the ground to the top of a tree, sits there and sings for a while, flies down to the top of a picnic table to eat crumbs, and then flies back to the top of the tree to sing some more. Which graph best represents this situation?

A

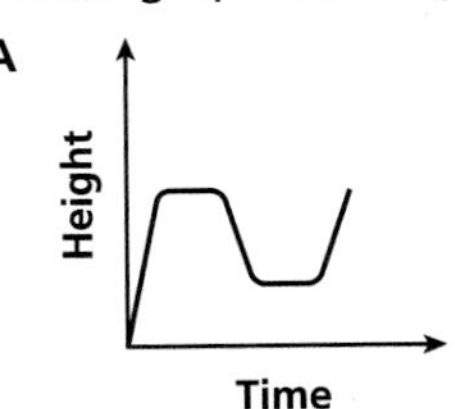


C

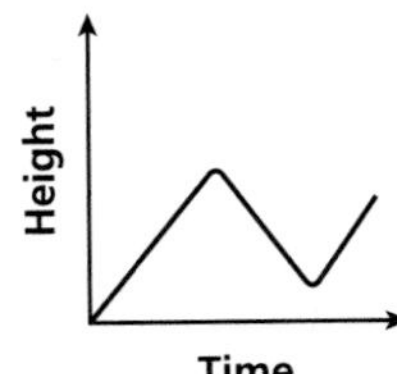


B

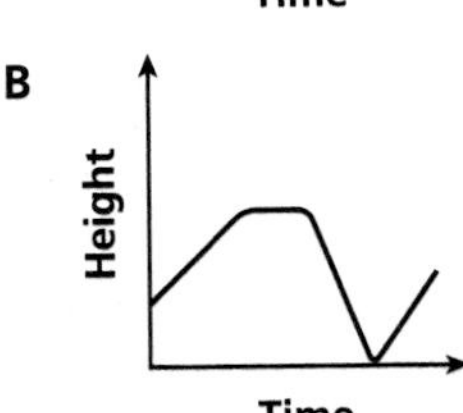


D

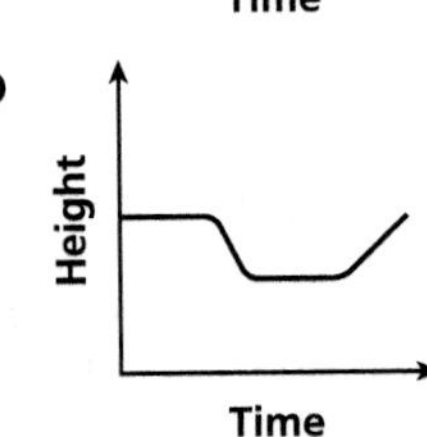


**10.** Which relation is ***not*** a function?

A $\{(1, -5), (3, 1), (-5, 4), (4, -2)\}$  
B $\{(2, 7), (3, 7), (4, 7), (5, 8)\}$  
C $\{(1, -5), (-1, 6), (1, 5), (6, -3)\}$  
D $\{(3, -2), (5, -6), (7, 7), (8, 8)\}$

**If possible, use the same calculator you usually use in math class. A timed test is not the right place to figure out where buttons are and how they work. Also, replace your batteries the night before the test. If your batteries run out, you may be given a replacement calculator you are not familiar with.**

**11.** The graph below shows a function.

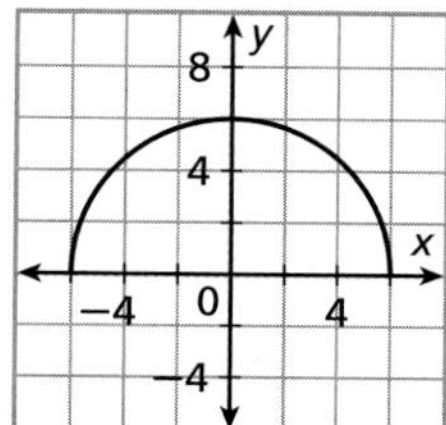


What is the domain of the function?

**A** $x \geq 0$

**B** $x \geq -6$

**C** $0 \leq x \leq 6$

**D** $-6 \leq x \leq 6$

**12.** Which situation best describes a negative correlation?

**A** The speed of a runner and the time it takes to run a race

**B** The number of apples in a bag and the weight of the bag of apples

**C** The time it takes to repair a car and the amount of the bill

**D** The number of people in a household and the amount of mail in their mailbox

**13.** Which of the following is a solution of $x + 1 \leq \frac{3}{2}$ AND $x - 1 \geq -\frac{5}{4}$?

**A** $\frac{3}{2}$ **C** $-\frac{1}{3}$

**B** $\frac{1}{3}$ **D** $-\frac{3}{2}$

**14.** Evaluate: $h(4)$ for $h(x) = x^3 + 2x$.

**A** 72 **C** 64

**B** 68 **D** 33

**15.** Lupe wants to know the height of the tree in her front yard. She knows that she is 5.2 feet tall, and her shadow measures 3.5 feet long. The tree's shadow is 15.2 feet long. To the nearest tenth of a foot, how tall is the tree?

**A** 13.8 feet

**B** 16.6 feet

**C** 22.6 feet

**D** 26.6 feet

## *STANDARDIZED TEST PREP*
## Short Response

**S1.** A function is graphed below.

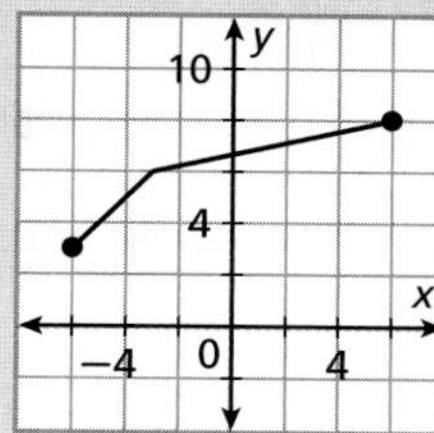


What is the domain and range of the function?

**S2.** Rory made a pentagon by cutting two triangles from a square piece of cardboard as shown.

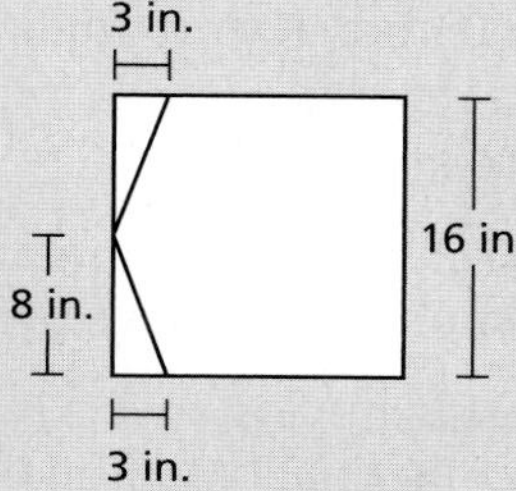


What is the area of the pentagon? Show your work or explain how you got your answer.

**S3.** The manager of a new restaurant needs at most 12 servers. He has already hired 7 servers.

**a.** Write and solve an inequality to determine how many more servers the manager could hire.

**b.** Graph the solutions to the inequality you solved in part **a.**

**S4.** Study the sequence below.

18, 24.5, 31, 37.5, 44,...

**a.** Could this sequence be arithmetic? Explain.

**b.** Find the 100th term of the sequence. Show your work.

## Extended Response

**E1.** A relation is shown in the table.

| *x* | *y* |
|---|---|
| 2 | 12 |
| 3 | 15 |
| 3 | 18 |
| 5 | 40 |
| 6 | 64 |

**a.** Express the relation as a mapping diagram.

**b.** Is the relation a function? Explain why or why not.

**c.** Write a possible real-life situation for the relation.

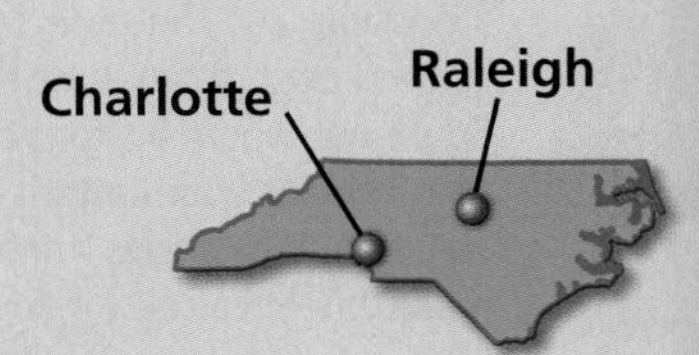


## Charlotte Area Transit System

With a fleet of 200 buses, a historic trolley, and a new rail line, the Charlotte Area Transit System (CATS) is probably the best way to get around North Carolina's largest city. The system includes more than 40 routes and transports more than 18 million passengers per year.

**For 1–4, use the table shown.**

| CATS Fares and Passes | |
|---|---|
| Single ride | \$1.30 |
| Weekly pass (unlimited rides) | \$13 |
| Monthly pass (unlimited rides) | \$52 |

**1.** Write a function using function notation that gives the total cost of $x$ single rides on CATS.

**2.** Joshua is considering buying a weekly pass. Write and solve an inequality to find out how many times he can ride during one week for less than the cost of a pass.

**3.** Elena has already spent \$22 on fares this month. She plans on riding $x$ additional times during the month.

**a.** Write a function for the total cost of Elena's rides for the month.

**b.** Graph the function.

**c.** Explain how to use your graph to estimate Elena's total cost if she rides 4 more times.

**d.** Elena would like to spend no more than \$30 on rides this month. Use your graph to estimate how many additional times she can ride and stay within her budget.

**4.** Each week, Lamar spends between \$6.50 and \$10.40 inclusive on fares.

**a.** Write a compound inequality to show the amount Lamar spends each week.

**b.** How many times does Lamar ride each week?

## The Carolina Hurricanes

Since their debut in 1997, the Carolina Hurricanes have brought the fast-paced excitement of the National Hockey League to fans in their hometown of Raleigh and throughout North Carolina. In 2006, the Hurricanes won the Stanley Cup and gave the state its first major-league sports championship.

1. The table shows the total number of goals the Hurricanes scored and the number of games the team won in its first ten seasons. Make a scatter plot of the data.
2. Describe the correlation in the scatter plot.
3. Suppose that the Hurricanes score 275 goals next season. Predict how many games they will win. Explain how you made your prediction.
4. Andrea made a scatter plot showing the number of goals the team scored in each season and the number of games the team lost during each season. Describe the correlation you would expect to see in her scatter plot.
5. During the 2006–2007 season, the Hurricanes' average attendance at home games was 17,387. Suppose that the team's average attendance increases by 108 in each of the following seasons. Use an arithmetic sequence to find the team's average attendance 12 seasons later.

**Carolina Hurricanes Data**

| Season | Goals Scored | Number of Wins |
|---|---|---|
| 1997–98 | 200 | 33 |
| 1998–99 | 210 | 34 |
| 1999–00 | 217 | 37 |
| 2000–01 | 212 | 38 |
| 2001–02 | 217 | 35 |
| 2002–03 | 171 | 22 |
| 2003–04 | 172 | 28 |
| 2005–06 | 294 | 52 |
| 2006–07 | 241 | 40 |

**(There were no NHL games played in the 2004-2005 season.)**

# Linear Functions



## Why Learn This?

The South Face of Stone Mountain has a steep incline that can be modeled by a linear function.

go.hrw.com

Chapter Project Online

KEYWORD: MA7 ChProj

# ARE YOU READY?

## Vocabulary

**Match each term on the left with a definition on the right.**

1. coefficient
2. coordinate plane
3. transformation
4. perpendicular

A. a change in the size or position of a figure
B. forming right angles
C. a two-dimensional system formed by the intersection of a horizontal number line and a vertical number line
D. an ordered pair of numbers that gives the location of a point
E. a number multiplied by a variable

## Ordered Pairs

**Graph each point on the same coordinate plane.**

5. $A(2, 5)$
6. $B(-1, -3)$
7. $C(-5, 2)$
8. $D(4, -4)$
9. $E(-2, 0)$
10. $F(0, 3)$
11. $G(8, 7)$
12. $H(-8, -7)$

## Solve for a Variable

**Solve each equation for the indicated variable.**

13. $2x + y = 8$; $y$
14. $5y = 5x - 10$; $y$
15. $2y = 6x - 8$; $y$
16. $10x + 25 = 5y$; $y$

## Evaluate Expressions

**Evaluate each expression for the given value of the variable.**

17. $4g - 3$; $g = -2$
18. $8p - 12$; $p = 4$
19. $4x + 8$; $x = -2$
20. $-5t - 15$; $t = 1$

## Connect Words and Algebra

21. The value of a stock begins at \$0.05 and increases by \$0.01 each month. Write an equation representing the value of the stock $v$ in any month $m$.
22. Write a situation that could be modeled by the equation $b = 100 - s$.

## Rates and Unit Rates

**Find each unit rate.**

23. 322 miles on 14 gallons of gas
24. \$14.25 for 3 pounds of deli meat
25. 32 grams of fat in 4 servings
26. 120 pictures on 5 rolls of film

CHAPTER 5

# Study Guide: Preview

## Where You've Been

**Previously, you**

- wrote equations in function notation.
- graphed functions.
- identified the domain and range of functions.
- identified independent and dependent variables.

## In This Chapter

**You will study**

- writing and graphing linear functions.
- identifying and interpreting the components of linear graphs, including the $x$-intercept, $y$-intercept, and slope.
- graphing and analyzing families of functions.

## Where You're Going

**You can use the skills in this chapter**

- to solve systems of linear equations in Chapter 6.
- to identify rates of change in linear data in biology and economics.
- to make calculations and comparisons in your personal finances.

## Key Vocabulary/Vocabulario

| | |
|---|---|
| constant of variation | constante de variación |
| direct variation | variación directa |
| family of functions | familia de funciones |
| linear function | función lineal |
| parallel lines | líneas paralelas |
| perpendicular lines | líneas perpendiculares |
| slope | pendiente |
| transformation | transformación |
| $x$-intercept | intersección con el eje $x$ |
| $y$-intercept | intersección con el eje $y$ |

## Vocabulary Connections

To become familiar with some of the vocabulary terms in the chapter, consider the following. You may refer to the chapter, the glossary, or a dictionary if you like.

1. What shape do you think is formed when a **linear function** is graphed on a coordinate plane?
2. The meaning of *intercept* is similar to the meaning of *intersection*. What do you think an **$x$-intercept** might be?
3. **Slope** is a word used in everyday life, as well as in mathematics. What is your understanding of the word *slope*?
4. A family is a group of related people. Use this concept to define **family of functions**.

## Study Strategy: Use Multiple Representations

Representing a math concept in more than one way can help you understand it more clearly. As you read the explanations and example problems in your text, note the use of tables, lists, graphs, diagrams, and symbols, as well as words to explain a concept.

**From Lesson 4-4:**

In this example from Chapter 4, the given function is described using an equation, a table, ordered pairs, and a graph.

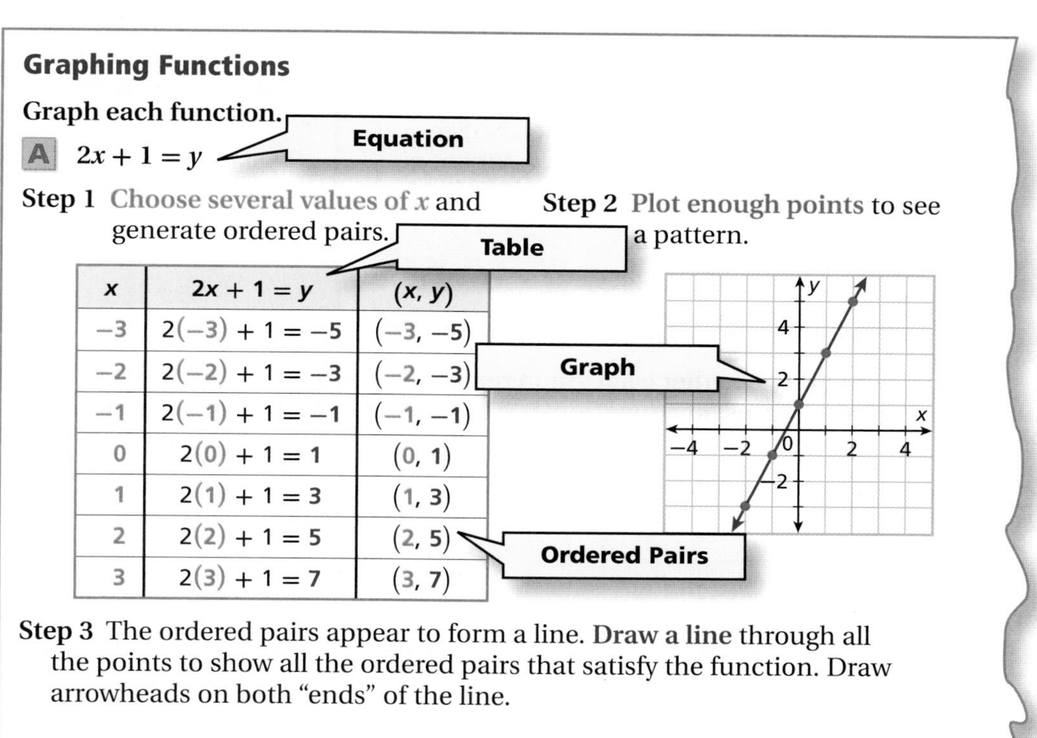

### Graphing Functions

**Graph each function.**

**A** $2x + 1 = y$ — Equation

**Step 1** Choose several values of $x$ and generate ordered pairs. — Table

| $x$ | $2x + 1 = y$ | $(x, y)$ |
|---|---|---|
| −3 | $2(-3) + 1 = -5$ | $(-3, -5)$ |
| −2 | $2(-2) + 1 = -3$ | $(-2, -3)$ |
| −1 | $2(-1) + 1 = -1$ | $(-1, -1)$ |
| 0 | $2(0) + 1 = 1$ | $(0, 1)$ |
| 1 | $2(1) + 1 = 3$ | $(1, 3)$ |
| 2 | $2(2) + 1 = 5$ | $(2, 5)$ |
| 3 | $2(3) + 1 = 7$ | $(3, 7)$ |

**Step 2** Plot enough points to see a pattern.



**Step 3** The ordered pairs appear to form a line. **Draw a line** through all the points to show all the ordered pairs that satisfy the function. Draw arrowheads on both "ends" of the line.

## Try This

1. If an employee earns \$8.00 an hour, $y = 8x$ gives the total pay $y$ the employee will earn for working $x$ hours. For this equation, make a table of ordered pairs and a graph. Explain the relationships between the equation, the table, and the graph. How does each one describe the situation?
2. What situations might make one representation more useful than another?

# 5-1 Identifying Linear Functions

**MA.A.4.4** Represent linear functions in a variety of equivalent forms ... *Also* **MA.A.4.2, MA.A.5.1**

***Objectives***
Identify linear functions and linear equations.

Graph linear functions that represent real-world situations and give their domain and range.

***Vocabulary***
linear function
linear equation

**Why learn this?**
Linear functions can describe many real-world situations, such as distances traveled at a constant speed.

Most people believe that there is no speed limit on the German autobahn. However, many stretches have a speed limit of 120 km/h. If a car travels continuously at this speed, $y = 120x$ gives the number of kilometers $y$ that the car would travel in $x$ hours. Solutions are shown in the graph.

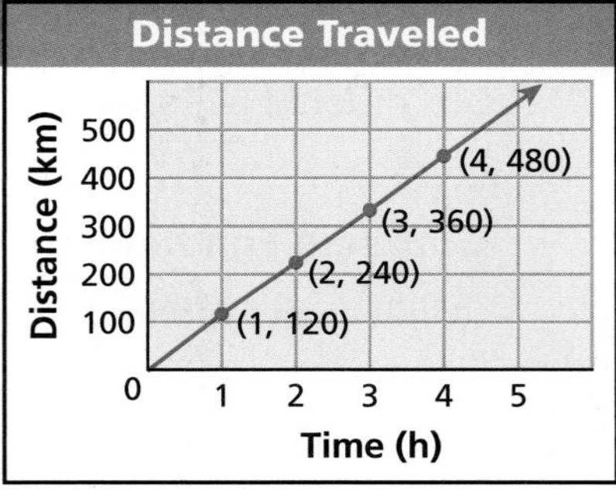


The graph represents a function because each domain value ($x$-value) is paired with exactly one range value ($y$-value). Notice that the graph is a straight line. A function whose graph forms a straight line is called a **linear function**.

## EXAMPLE 1 Identifying a Linear Function by Its Graph

**Identify whether each graph represents a function. Explain. If the graph does represent a function, is the function linear?**

**A**

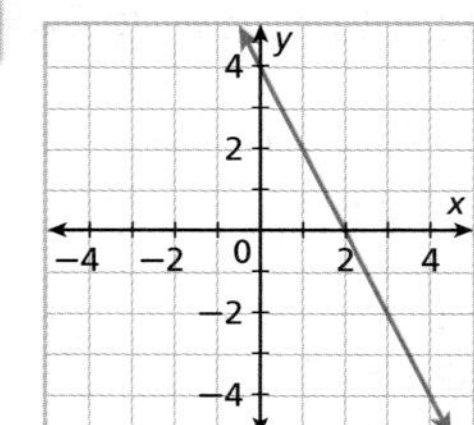

*Each domain value is paired with exactly one range value. The graph forms a line.*

linear function

**B**

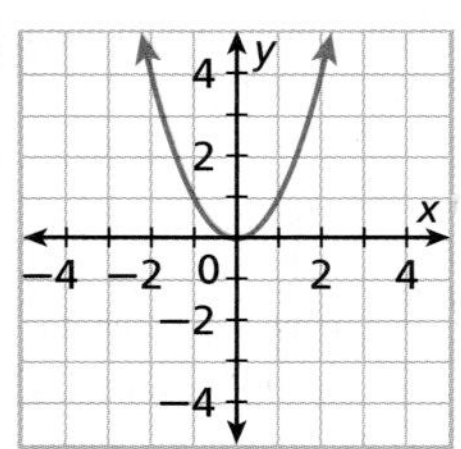

*Each domain value is paired with exactly one range value. The graph is not a line.*

not a linear function

**C**

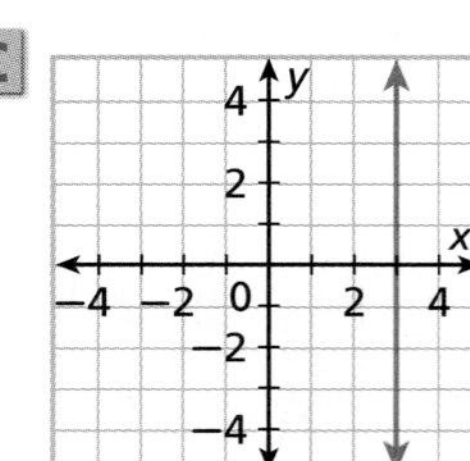

*The only domain value, 3, is paired with many different range values.*

not a function

**Identify whether each graph represents a function. Explain. If the graph does represent a function, is the function linear?**

**1a.**

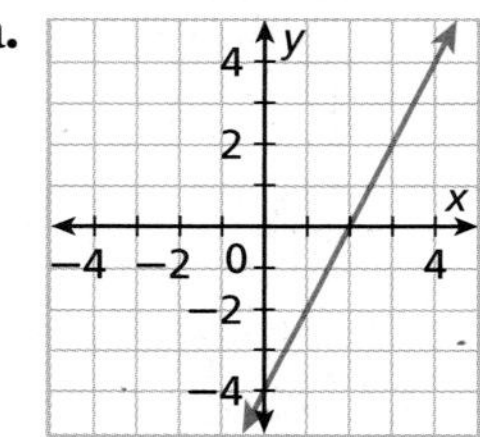

**1b.**

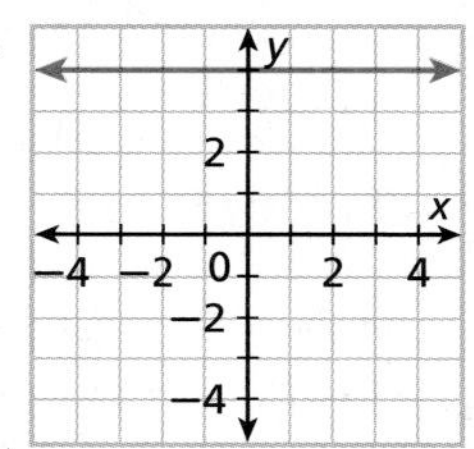

**1c.**

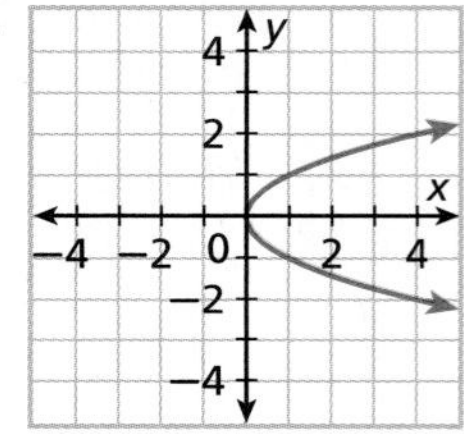

You can sometimes identify a linear function by looking at a table or a list of ordered pairs. In a linear function, a constant change in $x$ corresponds to a constant change in $y$.

**Caution!**

If you find a constant change in the $y$-values, check for a constant change in the $x$-values. Both need to be constant for the function to be linear.

| | $x$ | $y$ | |
|---|---|---|---|
| | −2 | 7 | |
| +1 | −1 | 4 | −3 |
| +1 | 0 | 1 | −3 |
| +1 | 1 | −2 | −3 |
| +1 | 2 | −5 | −3 |

In this table, a constant change of +1 in $x$ corresponds to a constant change of −3 in $y$. These points satisfy a linear function.

*The points from this table lie on a line.*

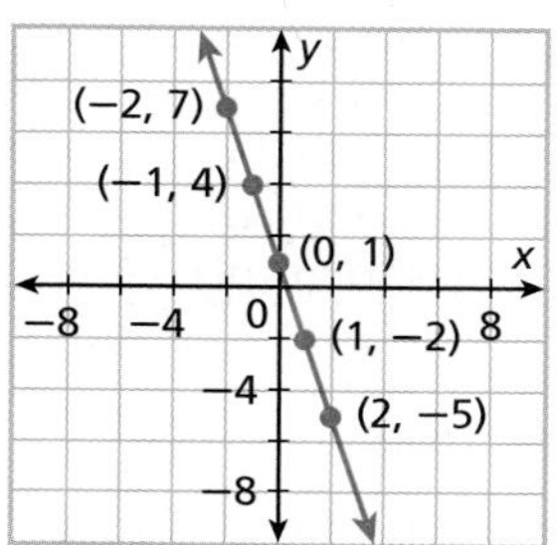


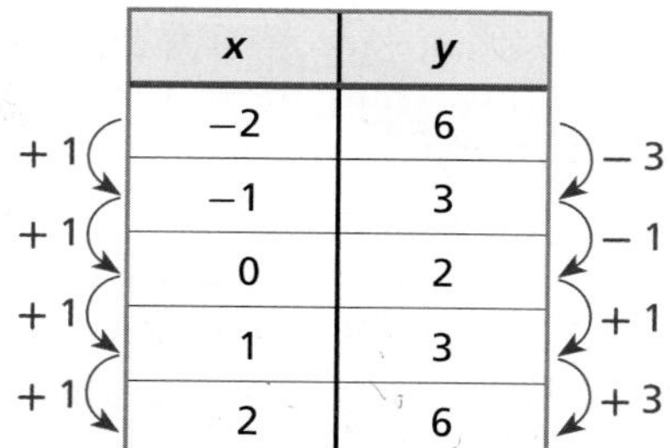

| | $x$ | $y$ | |
|---|---|---|---|
| | −2 | 6 | |
| +1 | −1 | 3 | −3 |
| +1 | 0 | 2 | −1 |
| +1 | 1 | 3 | +1 |
| +1 | 2 | 6 | +3 |

In this table, a constant change of +1 in $x$ does *not* correspond to a constant change in $y$. These points do *not* satisfy a linear function.

*The points from this table do not lie on a line.*

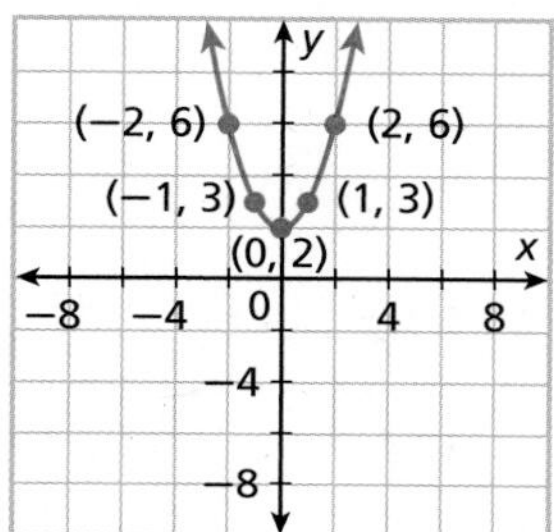


EXAMPLE 2

## Identifying a Linear Function by Using Ordered Pairs

**Tell whether each set of ordered pairs satisfies a linear function. Explain.**

**A** 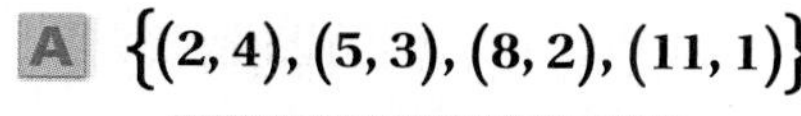 $\{(2, 4), (5, 3), (8, 2), (11, 1)\}$

| | $x$ | $y$ | |
|---|---|---|---|
| | 2 | 4 | |
| +3 | 5 | 3 | −1 |
| +3 | 8 | 2 | −1 |
| +3 | 11 | 1 | −1 |

*Write the ordered pairs in a table. Look for a pattern.*

*A constant change of +3 in x corresponds to a constant change of −1 in y.*

These points satisfy a linear function.

**B** $\{(-10, 10), (-5, 4), (0, 2), (5, 0)\}$

| | $x$ | $y$ | |
|---|---|---|---|
| | −10 | 10 | |
| +5 | −5 | 4 | −6 |
| +5 | 0 | 2 | −2 |
| +5 | 5 | 0 | −2 |

*Write the ordered pairs in a table. Look for a pattern.*

*A constant change of +5 in x corresponds to different changes in y.*

These points do not satisfy a linear function.

**2.** Tell whether the set of ordered pairs $\{(3, 5), (5, 4), (7, 3), (9, 2), (11, 1)\}$ satisfies a linear function. Explain.

Another way to determine whether a function is linear is to look at its equation. A function is linear if it is described by a *linear equation*. A **linear equation** is any equation that can be written in the *standard form* shown below.

### Standard Form of a Linear Equation

$Ax + By = C$ where $A$, $B$, and $C$ are real numbers and $A$ and $B$ are not both 0

Notice that when a linear equation is written in standard form
- $x$ and $y$ both have exponents of 1.
- $x$ and $y$ are not multiplied together.
- $x$ and $y$ do not appear in denominators, exponents, or radical signs.

| Linear | | Not Linear | |
|---|---|---|---|
| $3x + 2y = 10$ | *Standard form* | $3xy + x = 1$ | *$x$ and $y$ are multiplied.* |
| $y - 2 = 3x$ | *Can be written as $3x - y = -2$* | $x^3 + y = -1$ | *$x$ has an exponent other than 1.* |
| $-y = 5x$ | *Can be written as $5x + y = 0$* | $x + \frac{6}{y} = 12$ | *$y$ is in a denominator.* |

For any two points, there is exactly one line that contains them both. This means you need only two ordered pairs to graph a line.

## EXAMPLE 3 Graphing Linear Functions

- $y - x = y + (-x)$
- $y + (-x) = -x + y$
- $-x = -1x$
- $y = 1y$

**Tell whether each function is linear. If so, graph the function.**

**A** $y = x + 3$

$$y = x + 3$$ *Write the equation in standard form.*

$$\underline{-x \quad -x}$$ *Subtraction Property of Equality*

$$y - x = 3$$

$$-x + y = 3$$ *The equation is in standard form ($A = -1$, $B = 1$, $C = 3$).*

The equation can be written in standard form, so the function is linear.

To graph, choose three values of $x$, and use them to generate ordered pairs. (You only need two, but graphing three points is a good check.)

Plot the points and connect them with a straight line.

| $x$ | $y = x + 3$ | $(x, y)$ |
|---|---|---|
| 0 | $y = 0 + 3 = 3$ | $(0, 3)$ |
| 1 | $y = 1 + 3 = 4$ | $(1, 4)$ |
| 2 | $y = 2 + 3 = 5$ | $(2, 5)$ |

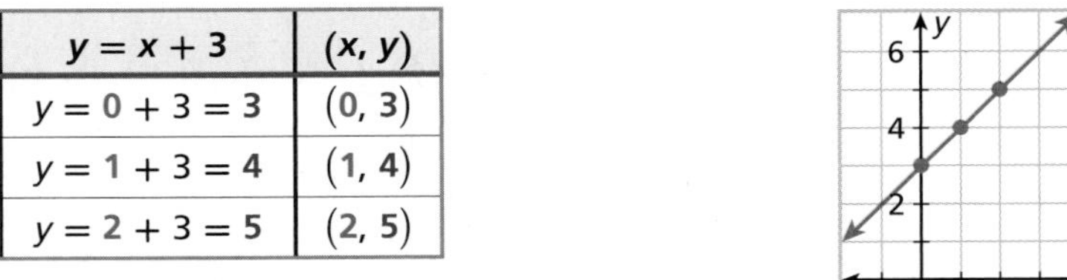


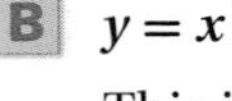

**B** $y = x^2$

This is not linear, because $x$ has an exponent other than 1.

**Tell whether each function is linear. If so, graph the function.**

**3a.** $y = 5x - 9$ **3b.** $y = 12$ **3c.** $y = 2^x$

For linear functions whose graphs are not horizontal, the domain and range are all real numbers. However, in many real-world situations, the domain and range must be restricted. For example, some quantities cannot be negative, such as time.

Sometimes domain and range are restricted even further to a set of points. For example, a quantity such as number of people can only be whole numbers. When this happens, the graph is not actually connected because every point on the line is not a solution. However, you may see these graphs shown connected to indicate that the linear pattern, or trend, continues.

## EXAMPLE 4 *Career Application*

**Sue rents a manicure station in a salon and pays the salon owner \$5.50 for each manicure she gives. The amount Sue pays each day is given by $f(x) = 5.50x$, where $x$ is the number of manicures. Graph this function and give its domain and range.**

*Choose several values of x and make a table of ordered pairs.*

| $x$ | $f(x) = 5.50x$ |
|---|---|
| 0 | $f(0) = 5.50(0) = 0$ |
| 1 | $f(1) = 5.50(1) = 5.50$ |
| 2 | $f(2) = 5.50(2) = 11.00$ |
| 3 | $f(3) = 5.50(3) = 16.50$ |
| 4 | $f(4) = 5.50(4) = 22.00$ |
| 5 | $f(5) = 5.50(5) = 27.50$ |

*Graph the ordered pairs.*

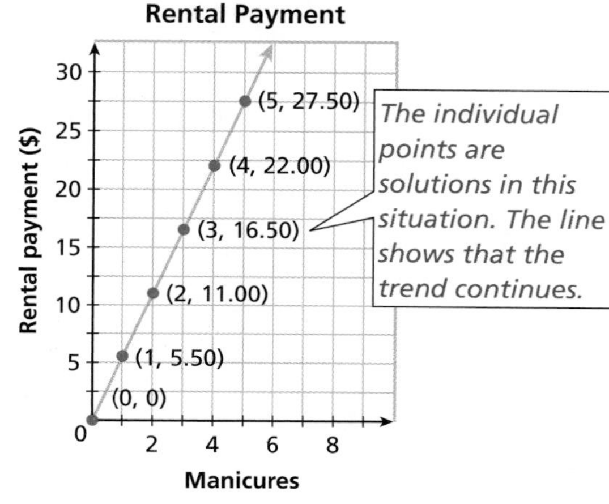


The number of manicures must be a whole number, so the domain is $\{0, 1, 2, 3, \ldots\}$. The range is $\{0, 5.50, 11.00, 16.50, \ldots\}$.

**Remember!**

$f(x) = y$, so in Example 4, graph the function values (dependent variable) on the $y$-axis.

**CHECK IT OUT!**

4. **What if...?** At another salon, Sue can rent a station for \$10.00 per day plus \$3.00 per manicure. The amount she would pay each day is given by $f(x) = 3x + 10$, where $x$ is the number of manicures. Graph this function and give its domain and range.

## THINK AND DISCUSS

1. Suppose you are given five ordered pairs that satisfy a function. When you graph them, four lie on a straight line, but the fifth does not. Is the function linear? Why or why not?
2. In Example 4, why is every point on the line not a solution?

3. **GET ORGANIZED** Copy and complete the graphic organizer. In each box, describe how to use the information to identify a linear function. Include an example.

Determining Whether a Function Is Linear
- From its graph
- From its equation
- From a list of ordered pairs

## 5-1 Exercises

MA.A.4.4, MA.A.4.2, MA.A.5.1

go.hrw.com
Homework Help Online
KEYWORD: MA7 5-1
Parent Resources Online
KEYWORD: MA7 Parent

### GUIDED PRACTICE

1. **Vocabulary** Is the *linear equation* $3x - 2 = y$ in standard form? Explain.

SEE EXAMPLE 1 p. 296

**Identify whether each graph represents a function. Explain. If the graph does represent a function, is the function linear?**

2. 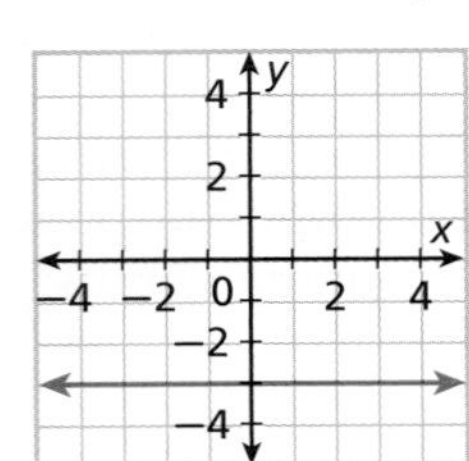

3. 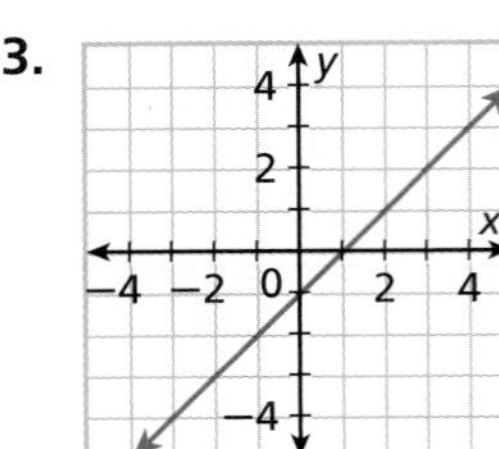

4. 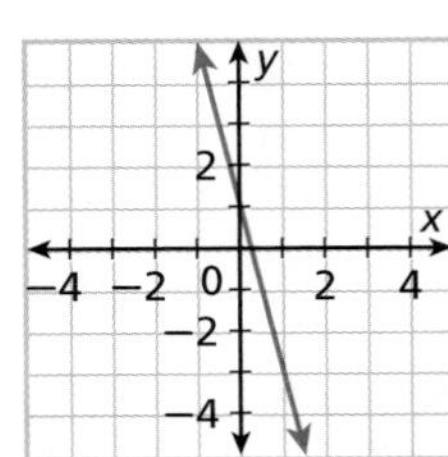

SEE EXAMPLE 2 p. 297

**Tell whether the given ordered pairs satisfy a linear function. Explain.**

5.

| x | 5 | 4 | 3 | 2 | 1 |
|---|---|---|---|---|---|
| y | 0 | 2 | 4 | 6 | 8 |

6.

| x | 1 | 4 | 9 | 16 | 25 |
|---|---|---|---|---|---|
| y | 1 | 2 | 3 | 4 | 5 |

7. $\{(0, 5), (-2, 3), (-4, 1), (-6, -1), (-8, -3)\}$

8. $\{(2, -2), (-1, 0), (-4, 1), (-7, 3), (-10, 6)\}$

SEE EXAMPLE 3 p. 298

**Tell whether each function is linear. If so, graph the function.**

9. $2x + 3y = 5$

10. $2y = 8$

11. $\frac{x^2 + 3}{5} = y$

12. $\frac{x}{5} = \frac{y}{3}$

SEE EXAMPLE 4 p. 299

13. **Transportation** A train travels at a constant speed of 75 mi/h. The function $f(x) = 75x$ gives the distance that the train travels in $x$ hours. Graph this function and give its domain and range.

14. **Entertainment** A movie rental store charges a $6.00 membership fee plus $2.50 for each movie rented. The function $f(x) = 2.50x + 6$ gives the cost of renting $x$ movies. Graph this function and give its domain and range.

### PRACTICE AND PROBLEM SOLVING

**Independent Practice**

| For Exercises | See Example |
|---|---|
| 15–17 | 1 |
| 18–20 | 2 |
| 21–24 | 3 |
| 25 | 4 |

**Extra Practice**

Skills Practice p. S12
Application Practice p. S32

**Identify whether each graph represents a function. Explain. If the graph does represent a function, is the function linear?**

15. 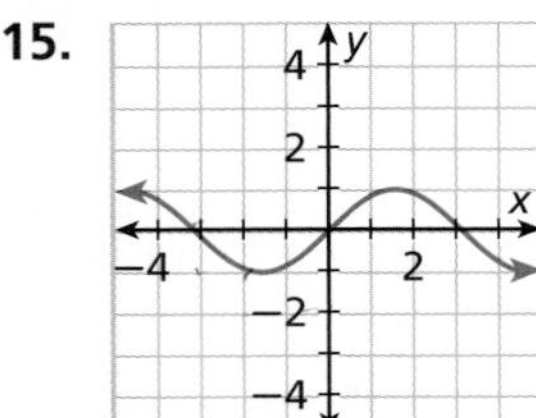

16. 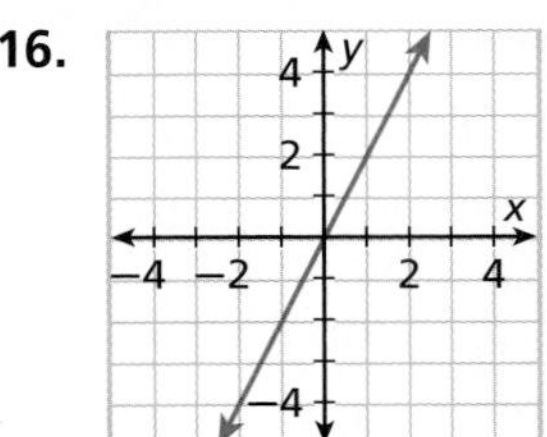

17. 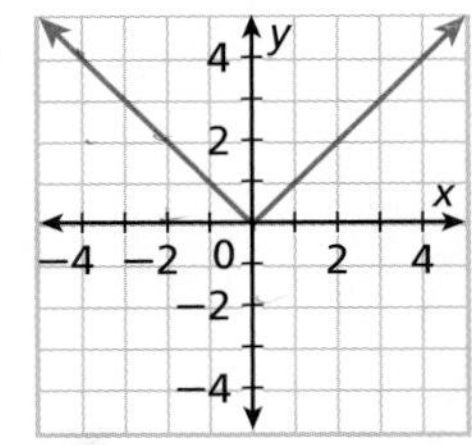

**Tell whether the given ordered pairs satisfy a linear function. Explain.**

18.

| x | −3 | 0 | 3 | 6 | 9 |
|---|---|---|---|---|---|
| y | −2 | −1 | 0 | 2 | 4 |

19.

| x | −1 | 0 | 1 | 2 | 3 |
|---|---|---|---|---|---|
| y | −3 | −2 | −1 | 0 | 1 |

20. $\{(3, 4), (0, 2), (-3, 0), (-6, -2), (-9, -4)\}$

**Tell whether each function is linear. If so, graph the function.**

**21.** $y = 5$ **22.** $4y - 2x = 0$ **23.** $\frac{3}{x} + 4y = 10$ **24.** $5 + 3y = 8$

**25. Transportation** The gas tank in Tony's car holds 15 gallons, and the car can travel 25 miles for each gallon of gas. When Tony begins with a full tank of gas, the function $f(x) = -\frac{1}{25}x + 15$ gives the amount of gas $f(x)$ that will be left in the tank after traveling $x$ miles (if he does not buy more gas). Graph this function and give its domain and range.

**Tell whether the given ordered pairs satisfy a function. If so, is it a linear function?**

**26.** $\{(2, 5), (2, 4), (2, 3), (2, 2), (2, 1)\}$ **27.** $\{(-8, 2), (-6, 0), (-4, -2), (-2, -4), (0, -6)\}$

**28.**

| x | −10 | −6 | −2 | 2 | 4 |
|---|---|---|---|---|---|
| y | 0 | 0.25 | 0.50 | 0.75 | 1 |

**29.**

| x | −5 | −1 | 3 | 7 | 11 |
|---|---|---|---|---|---|
| y | 1 | 1 | 1 | 1 | 1 |

**Tell whether each equation is linear. If so, write the equation in standard form and give the values of *A*, *B*, and *C*.**

**30.** $2x - 8y = 16$ **31.** $y = 4x + 2$ **32.** $2x = \frac{y}{3} - 4$ **33.** $\frac{4}{x} = y$

**34.** $\frac{x + 4}{2} = \frac{y - 4}{3}$ **35.** $x = 7$ **36.** $xy = 6$ **37.** $3x - 5 + y = 2y - 4$

**38.** $y = -x + 2$ **39.** $5x = 2y - 3$ **40.** $2y = -6$ **41.** $y = \sqrt{x}$

**Graph each linear function.**

**42.** $y = 3x + 7$ **43.** $y = x + 25$ **44.** $y = 8 - x$ **45.** $y = 2x$

**46.** $-2y = -3x + 6$ **47.** $y - x = 4$ **48.** $y - 2x = -3$ **49.** $x = 5 + y$

**50. Measurement** One inch is equal to approximately 2.5 centimeters. Let $x$ represent inches and $y$ represent centimeters. Write an equation in standard form relating $x$ and $y$. Give the values of *A*, *B*, and *C*.

**51. Wages** Molly earns $8.00 an hour at her job.

**a.** Let $x$ represent the number of hours that Molly works. Write a function using $x$ and $f(x)$ that describes Molly's pay for working $x$ hours.

**b.** Graph this function and give its domain and range.

**52. Write About It** For $y = 2x - 1$, make a table of ordered pairs and a graph. Describe the relationships between the equation, the table, and the graph.

**53. Critical Thinking** Describe a real-world situation that can be represented by a linear function whose domain and range must be limited. Give your function and its domain and range.

**MULTI-STEP TEST PREP**

**54.** This problem will prepare you for the Multi-Step Test Prep on page 332.

**a.** Juan is running on a treadmill. The table shows the number of Calories Juan burns as a function of time. Explain how you can tell that this relationship is linear by using the table.

**b.** Create a graph of the data.

**c.** How can you tell from the graph that the relationship is linear?

| Time (min) | Calories |
|---|---|
| 3 | 27 |
| 6 | 54 |
| 9 | 81 |
| 12 | 108 |
| 15 | 135 |
| 18 | 162 |
| 21 | 189 |

55. **Physical Science** A ball was dropped from a height of 100 meters. Its height above the ground in meters at different times after its release is given in the table. Do these ordered pairs satisfy a linear function? Explain.

| Time (s) | 0 | 1 | 2 | 3 |
|---|---|---|---|---|
| Height (m) | 100 | 90.2 | 60.8 | 11.8 |

56. **Critical Thinking** Is the equation $x = 9$ a linear equation? Does it describe a linear function? Explain.

## TEST PREP

MA.A.4.4, MA.A.4.2, MA.A.5.1

57. Which is NOT a linear function?

Ⓐ $y = 8x$ Ⓑ $y = x + 8$ Ⓒ $y = \frac{8}{x}$ Ⓓ $y = 8 - x$

58. The speed of sound in 0°C air is about 331 feet per second. Which function could be used to describe the distance in feet $d$ that sound will travel in air in $s$ seconds?

Ⓕ $d = s + 331$ Ⓖ $d = 331s$ Ⓗ $s = 331d$ Ⓙ $s = 331 - d$

59. **Extended Response** Write your own linear function. Show that it is a linear function in at least three different ways. Explain any connections you see between your three methods.

## CHALLENGE AND EXTEND

60. What equation describes the $x$-axis? the $y$-axis? Do these equations represent linear functions?

**Geometry** Copy and complete each table below. Then tell whether the table shows a linear relationship.

61.

| Perimeter of a Square | |
|---|---|
| Side Length | Perimeter |
| 1 | |
| 2 | |
| 3 | |
| 4 | |

62.

| Area of a Square | |
|---|---|
| Side Length | Area |
| 1 | |
| 2 | |
| 3 | |
| 4 | |

63.

| Volume of a Cube | |
|---|---|
| Side Length | Volume |
| 1 | |
| 2 | |
| 3 | |
| 4 | |

## SPIRAL REVIEW

**Simplify each expression.** *(Lesson 1-4)*

64. $8^2$ 65. $(-1)^3$ 66. $(-4)^4$ 67. $\left(\frac{1}{3}\right)^2$

**Solve each equation. Check your answer.** *(Lesson 2-4)*

68. $6m + 5 = 3m - 4$ 69. $2(t - 4) = 3 - (3t + 1)$ 70. $9y + 5 - 2y = 2y + 5 - y + 3$

**Find the value of $x$ in each diagram.** *(Lesson 2-7)*

71. $\triangle ABC \sim \triangle DEF$

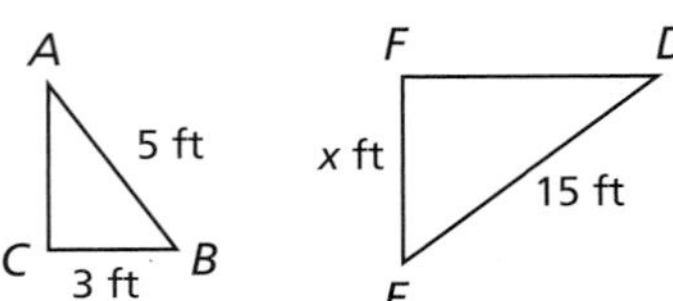


72. $ABCD \sim QRST$

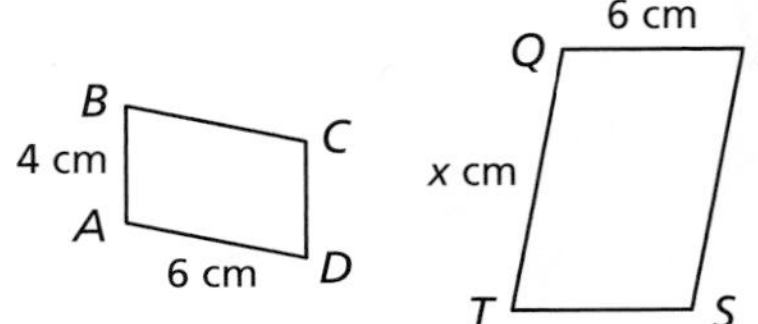

# 5-2 Using Intercepts

**MA.A.4.2** Use appropriate terminology and notation...associated with functions. *Also* **MA.A.4.4, MA.A.5.1, MA.A.4.5**

***Objectives***

Find $x$- and $y$-intercepts and interpret their meanings in real-world situations.

Use $x$- and $y$-intercepts to graph lines.

***Vocabulary***

$y$-intercept

$x$-intercept

**Who uses this?**

Divers can use intercepts to determine the time a safe ascent will take.

A diver explored the ocean floor 120 feet below the surface and then ascended at a rate of 30 feet per minute. The graph shows the diver's elevation below sea level during the ascent.

The **$y$-intercept** is the $y$-coordinate of the point where the graph intersects the $y$-axis. The $x$-coordinate of this point is always 0.

The **$x$-intercept** is the $x$-coordinate of the point where the graph intersects the $x$-axis. The $y$-coordinate of this point is always 0.

*The x-intercept is 4. It represents the time that the diver reaches the surface, or when depth = 0.*

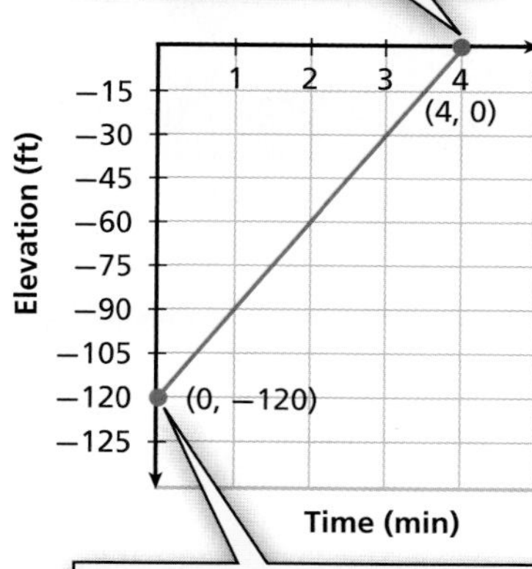


*The y-intercept is −120. It represents the diver's elevation at the start of the ascent, when time = 0.*

**EXAMPLE**  **Finding Intercepts**

**Find the $x$- and $y$-intercepts.**

**A**

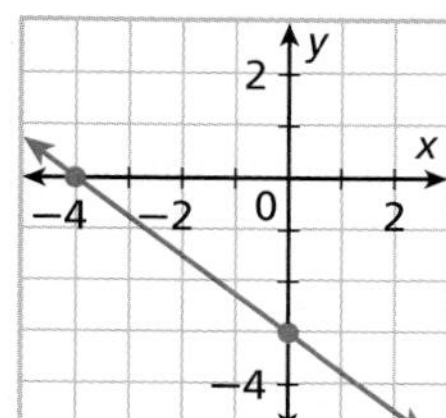


*The graph intersects the y-axis at (0, −3).*
The $y$-intercept is −3.

*The graph intersects the x-axis at (−4, 0).*
The $x$-intercept is −4.

**B** $3x - 2y = 12$

To find the $x$-intercept, replace $y$ with 0 and solve for $x$.

$$3x - 2y = 12$$
$$3x - 2(0) = 12$$
$$3x - 0 = 12$$
$$3x = 12$$
$$\frac{3x}{3} = \frac{12}{3}$$
$$x = 4$$

The $x$-intercept is 4.

To find the $y$-intercept, replace $x$ with 0 and solve for $y$.

$$3x - 2y = 12$$
$$3(0) - 2y = 12$$
$$0 - 2y = 12$$
$$-2y = 12$$
$$\frac{-2y}{-2} = \frac{12}{-2}$$
$$y = -6$$

The $y$-intercept is −6.

**Find the $x$- and $y$-intercepts.**

**1a.**

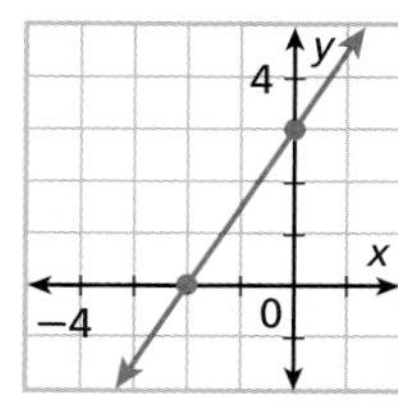


**1b.** $-3x + 5y = 30$

**1c.** $4x + 2y = 16$

## Student to Student

### *Finding Intercepts*

**Madison Stewart**
Jefferson High School

*I use the "cover-up" method to find intercepts. To use this method, make sure the equation is in standard form first.*

*If I have $4x - 3y = 12$:*

*First, I cover $4x$ with my finger and solve the equation I can still see.*

$$\text{☝} - 3y = 12$$
$$y = -4$$

*The y-intercept is $-4$.*

*Then I cover $-3y$ with my finger and do the same thing.*

$$4x \text{ ☝} = 12$$
$$x = 3$$

*The x-intercept is 3.*

## EXAMPLE 2 *Travel Application*

**The Sandia Peak Tramway in Albuquerque, New Mexico, travels a distance of about 4500 meters to the top of Sandia Peak. Its speed is 300 meters per minute. The function $f(x) = 4500 - 300x$ gives the tram's distance in meters from the top of the peak after $x$ minutes. Graph this function and find the intercepts. What does each intercept represent?**

*Neither time nor distance can be negative, so choose several nonnegative values for x. Use the function to generate ordered pairs.*

| $x$ | 0 | 2 | 5 | 10 | 15 |
|---|---|---|---|---|---|
| $f(x) = 4500 - 300x$ | 4500 | 3900 | 3000 | 1500 | 0 |

*Graph the ordered pairs. Connect the points with a line.*

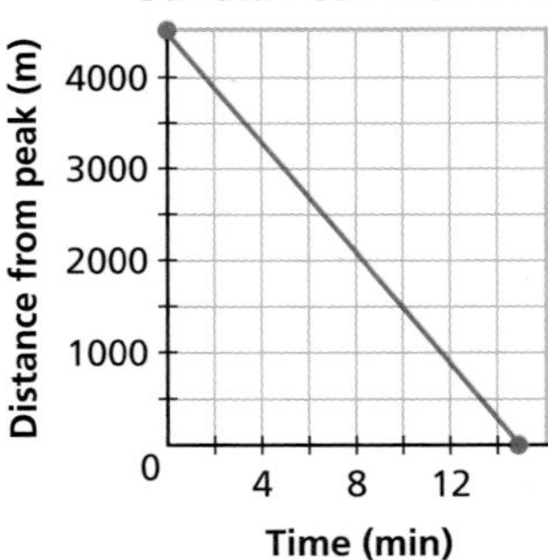


- $y$-intercept: 4500. This is the starting distance from the top (time = 0).
- $x$-intercept: 15. This the time when the tram reaches the peak (distance = 0).

**Caution!**

The graph is not the path of the tram. Even though the line is descending, the graph describes the distance from the peak as the tram goes *up* the mountain.

**2.** The school store sells pens for \$2.00 and notebooks for \$3.00. The equation $2x + 3y = 60$ describes the number of pens $x$ and notebooks $y$ that you can buy for \$60.

**a.** Graph the function and find its intercepts.

**b.** What does each intercept represent?

Remember, to graph a linear function, you need to plot only two ordered pairs. It is often simplest to find the ordered pairs that contain the intercepts.

## EXAMPLE 3 Graphing Linear Equations by Using Intercepts

**Use intercepts to graph the line described by each equation.**

**A** $2x - 4y = 8$

**Step 1** Find the intercepts.

***x*-intercept:**

$$2x - 4y = 8$$
$$2x - 4(0) = 8$$
$$2x = 8$$
$$\frac{2x}{2} = \frac{8}{2}$$
$$x = 4$$

***y*-intercept:**

$$2x - 4y = 8$$
$$2(0) - 4y = 8$$
$$-4y = 8$$
$$\frac{-4y}{-4} = \frac{8}{-4}$$
$$y = -2$$

**Step 2** Graph the line.

*Plot (4, 0) and (0, −2).*

*Connect with a straight line.*

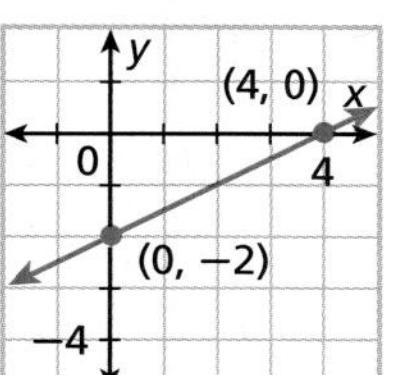


### Helpful Hint

You can use a third point to check your line. Either choose a point from your graph and check it in the equation, or use the equation to generate a point and check that it is on your graph.

**B** $\frac{2}{3}y = 4 - \frac{1}{2}x$

**Step 1** Write the equation in standard form.

$$6\left(\frac{2}{3}y\right) = 6\left(4 - \frac{1}{2}x\right)$$ *Multiply both sides by 6, the LCD of the fractions, to clear the fractions.*

$$4y = 24 - 3x$$

$$3x + 4y = 24$$ *Write the equation in standard form.*

**Step 2** Find the intercepts.

***x*-intercept:**

$$3x + 4y = 24$$
$$3x + 4(0) = 24$$
$$3x = 24$$
$$\frac{3x}{3} = \frac{24}{3}$$
$$x = 8$$

***y*-intercept:**

$$3x + 4y = 24$$
$$3(0) + 4y = 24$$
$$4y = 24$$
$$\frac{4y}{4} = \frac{24}{4}$$
$$y = 6$$

**Step 3** Graph the line.

*Plot (8, 0) and (0, 6).*

*Connect with a straight line.*

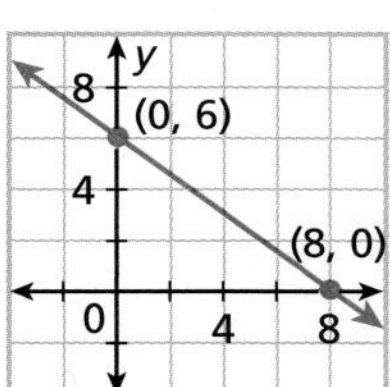

**Use intercepts to graph the line described by each equation.**

**3a.** $-3x + 4y = -12$

**3b.** $y = \frac{1}{3}x - 2$

## THINK AND DISCUSS

1. A function has *x*-intercept 4 and *y*-intercept 2. Name two points on the graph of this function.
2. What is the *y*-intercept of $2.304x + y = 4.318$? What is the *x*-intercept of $x - 92.4920y = -21.5489$?

3. **GET ORGANIZED** Copy and complete the graphic organizer.

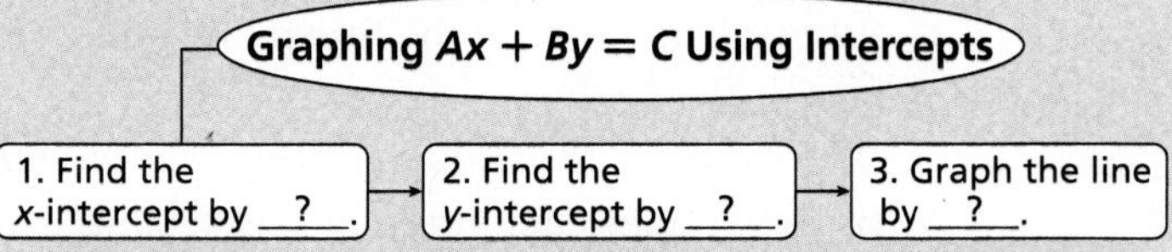

# 5-2 Exercises

go.hrw.com
**Homework Help Online**
KEYWORD: MA7 5-2
**Parent Resources Online**
KEYWORD: MA7 Parent

## GUIDED PRACTICE

1. **Vocabulary** The ___?___ is the $y$-coordinate of the point where a graph crosses the $y$-axis. ($x$-*intercept* or $y$-*intercept*)

SEE EXAMPLE 1
p. 303

**Find the $x$- and $y$-intercepts.**

2. 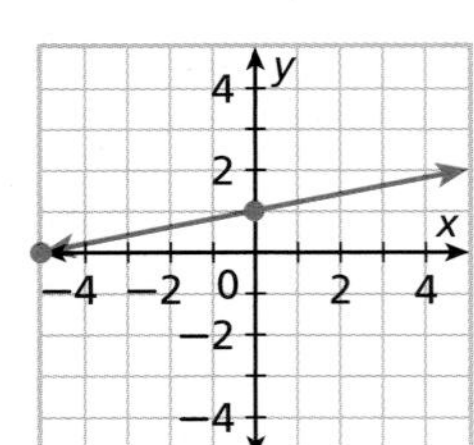

3. 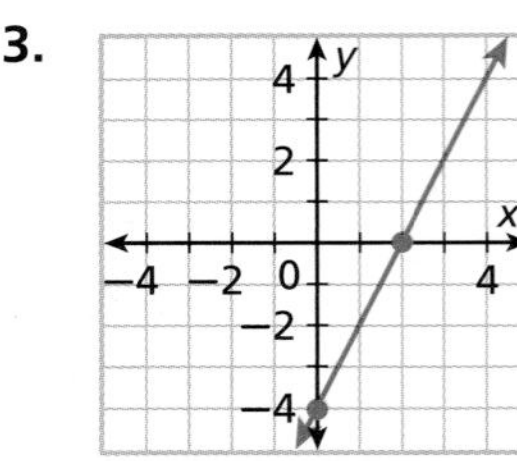

4. 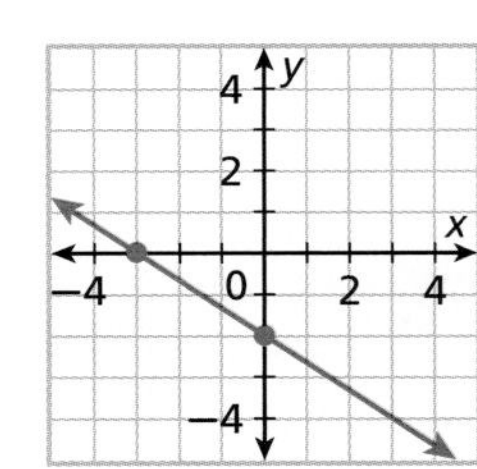

5. $2x - 4y = 4$
6. $-2y = 3x - 6$
7. $4y + 5x = 2y - 3x + 16$

SEE EXAMPLE 2
p. 304

8. **Biology** To thaw a specimen stored at $-25°C$, the temperature of a refrigeration tank is raised 5°C every hour. The temperature in the tank after $x$ hours can be described by the function $f(x) = -25 + 5x$.
   a. Graph the function and find its intercepts.
   b. What does each intercept represent?

SEE EXAMPLE 3
p. 305

**Use intercepts to graph the line described by each equation.**

9. $4x - 5y = 20$
10. $y = 2x + 4$
11. $\frac{1}{3}x - \frac{1}{4}y = 2$
12. $-5y + 2x = -10$

## PRACTICE AND PROBLEM SOLVING

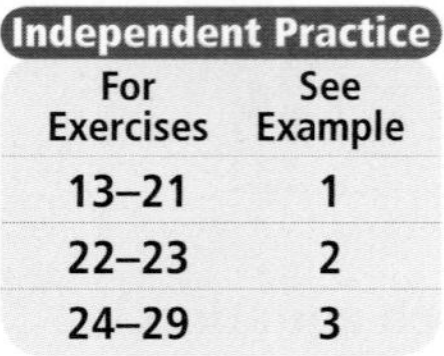

**Independent Practice**

| For Exercises | See Example |
|---|---|
| 13–21 | 1 |
| 22–23 | 2 |
| 24–29 | 3 |

**Extra Practice**
Skills Practice p. S12
Application Practice p. S32

**Find the $x$- and $y$-intercepts.**

13. 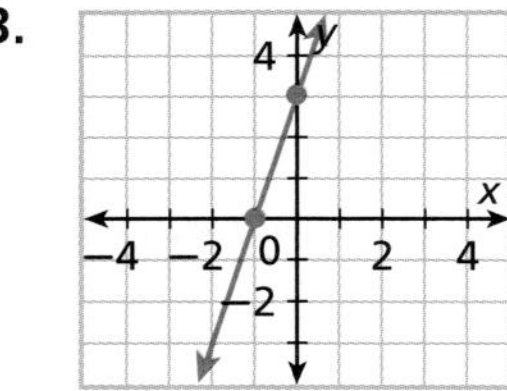

14. 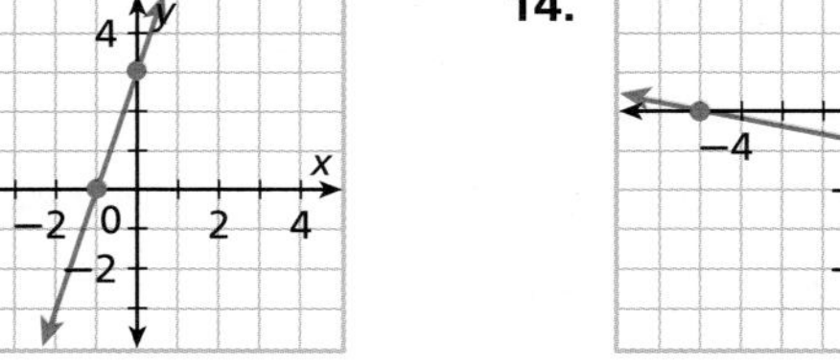

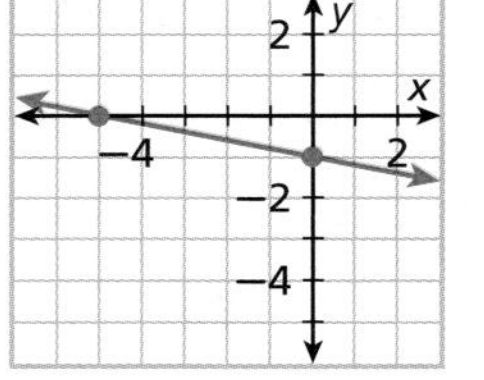

15.

16. $6x + 3y = 12$
17. $4y - 8 = 2x$
18. $-2y + x = 2y - 8$
19. $4x + y = 8$
20. $y - 3x = -15$
21. $2x + y = 10x - 1$
22. **Environmental Science** A fishing lake was stocked with 300 bass. Each year, the population decreases by 25. The population of bass in the lake after $x$ years is represented by the function $f(x) = 300 - 25x$.
    a. Graph the function and find its intercepts.
    b. What does each intercept represent?
23. **Sports** Julie is running a 5-kilometer race. She ran 1 kilometer every 5 minutes. Julie's distance from the finish line after $x$ minutes is represented by the function $f(x) = 5 - \frac{1}{5}x$.
    a. Graph the function and find its intercepts.
    b. What does each intercept represent?

**Use intercepts to graph the line described by each equation.**

**24.** $4x - 6y = 12$ **25.** $2x + 3y = 18$ **26.** $\frac{1}{2}x - 4y = 4$

**27.** $y - x = -1$ **28.** $5x + 3y = 15$ **29.** $x - 3y = -1$

**Biology**

Bamboo is the world's fastest-growing woody plant. Some varieties can grow more than 30 centimeters a day and up to 40 meters tall.

**30. Biology** A bamboo plant is growing 1 foot per day. When you first measure it, it is 4 feet tall.

a. Write an equation to describe the height $y$, in feet, of the bamboo plant $x$ days after you measure it.

b. What is the $y$-intercept?

c. What is the meaning of the $y$-intercept in this problem?

**31. Estimation** Look at the scatter plot and trend line.

a. Estimate the $x$- and $y$-intercepts.

b. What is the real-world meaning of each intercept?

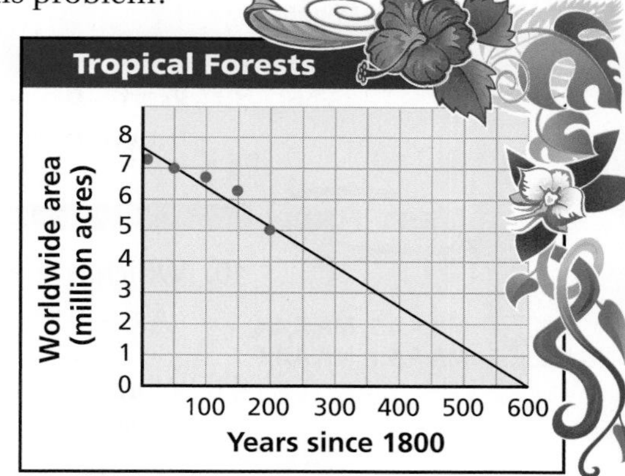


**32. Personal Finance** A bank employee notices an abandoned checking account with a balance of $412. If the bank charges a $4 monthly fee for the account, the function $b = 412 - 4m$ shows the balance $b$ in the account after $m$ months.

a. Graph the function and give its domain and range. (*Hint:* The bank will keep charging the monthly fee even after the account is empty.)

b. Find the intercepts. What does each intercept represent?

c. When will the bank account balance be 0?

**33. Critical Thinking** Complete the following to learn about intercepts and horizontal and vertical lines.

a. Graph $x = -6$, $x = 1$, and $x = 5$. Find the intercepts.

b. Graph $y = -3$, $y = 2$, and $y = 7$. Find the intercepts.

c. Write a rule describing the intercepts of functions whose graphs are horizontal and vertical lines.

**Match each equation with a graph.**

**34.** $-2x - y = 4$ **35.** $y = 4 - 2x$ **36.** $2y + 4x = 8$ **37.** $4x - 2y = 8$

**A.**

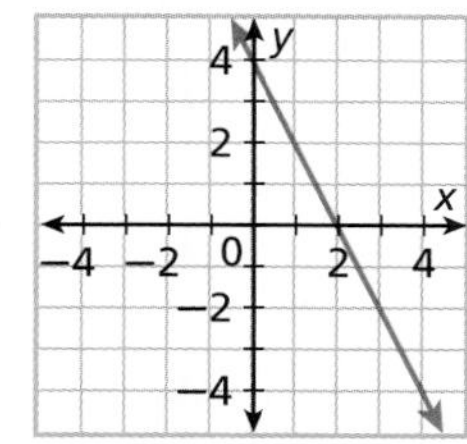


**B.**

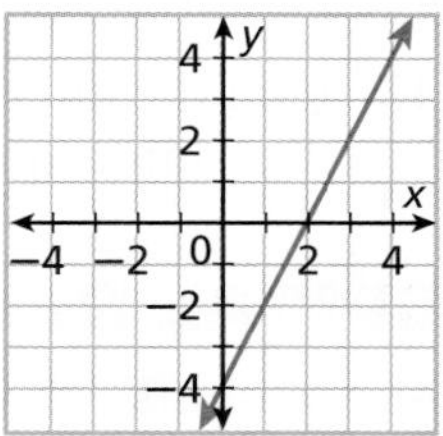


**C.**

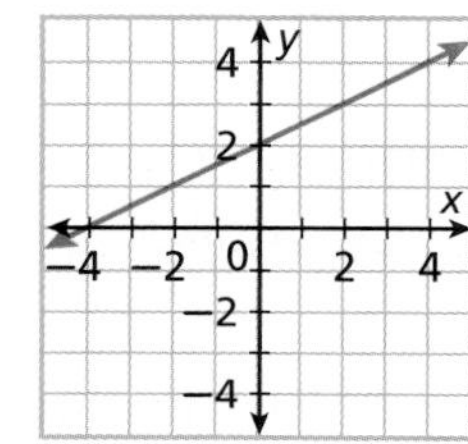


**D.**

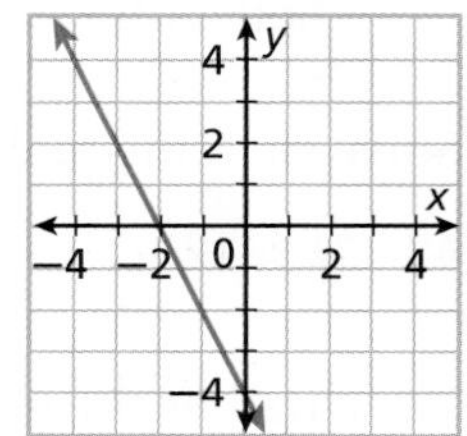

**38.** This problem will prepare you for the Multi-Step Test Prep on page 332.

Kristyn rode a stationary bike at the gym. She programmed the timer for 20 minutes. The display counted backward to show how much time remained in her workout. It also showed her mileage.

**a.** What are the intercepts?

**b.** What do the intercepts represent?

| Time Remaining (min) | Distance Covered (mi) |
|---|---|
| 20 | 0 |
| 16 | 0.35 |
| 12 | 0.70 |
| 8 | 1.05 |
| 4 | 1.40 |
| 0 | 1.75 |

**39. Write About It** Write a real-world problem that could be modeled by a linear function whose $x$-intercept is 5 and whose $y$-intercept is 60.

NC MA.A.4.2, MA.A.4.4, MA.A.5.1, MA.A.4.5

**40.** Which is the $x$-intercept of $-2x = 9y - 18$?

Ⓐ $-9$ Ⓑ $-2$ Ⓒ 2 Ⓓ 9

**41.** Which of the following situations could be represented by the graph?

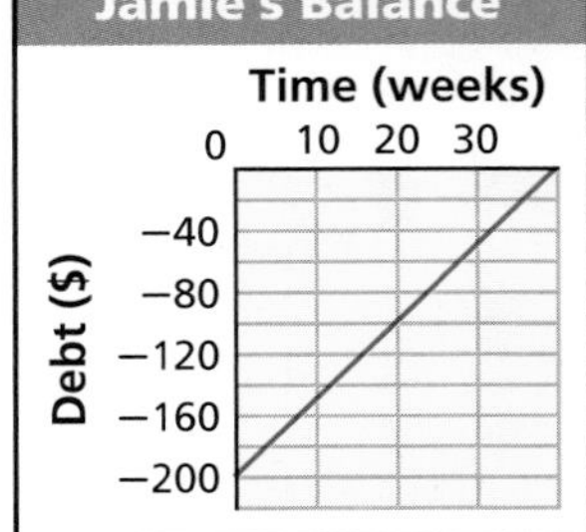


Ⓕ Jamie owed her uncle \$200. Each week for 40 weeks she paid him \$5.

Ⓖ Jamie owed her uncle \$200. Each week for 5 weeks she paid him \$40.

Ⓗ Jamie owed her uncle \$40. Each week for 5 weeks she paid him \$200.

Ⓙ Jamie owed her uncle \$40. Each week for 200 weeks she paid him \$5.

**42. Gridded Response** What is the $y$-intercept of $60x + 55y = 660$?

## CHALLENGE AND EXTEND

**Use intercepts to graph the line described by each equation.**

**43.** $\frac{1}{2}x + \frac{1}{5}y = 1$ **44.** $0.5x - 0.2y = 0.75$ **45.** $y = \frac{3}{8}x + 6$

**46.** For any linear equation $Ax + By = C$, what are the intercepts?

**47.** Find the intercepts of $22x - 380y = 20{,}900$. Explain how to use the intercepts to determine appropriate scales for the graph.

## SPIRAL REVIEW

**48.** Marlon's fish tank is 80% filled with water. Based on the measurements shown, what volume of the tank is NOT filled with water? *(Lesson 2-8)*

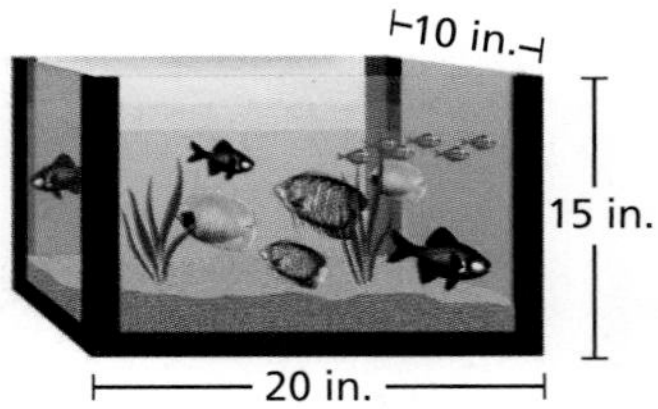


**Solve each inequality and graph the solutions.** *(Lesson 3-3)*

**49.** $3c > 12$ **50.** $-4 \geq \frac{t}{2}$ **51.** $\frac{1}{2}m \geq -3$ **52.** $-2w > 14$

**Tell whether the given ordered pairs satisfy a linear function. Explain.** *(Lesson 5-1)*

**53.** $\{(-2, 0), (0, 3), (2, 6), (4, 9), (6, 12)\}$ **54.** $\{(0, 0), (1, 1), (4, 2), (9, 3), (16, 4)\}$

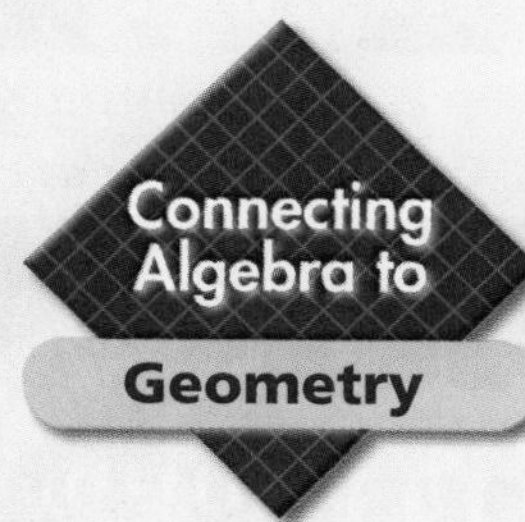


# Area in the Coordinate Plane

See Skills Bank page S61

Lines in the coordinate plane can form the sides of polygons. You can use points on these lines to help you find the areas of these polygons.

**MA.A.4.2** Use appropriate terminology and notation…associated with functions. *Also* **MA.A.4.5, MA.G.2.2**

## Example

**Find the area of the triangle formed by the $x$-axis, the $y$-axis, and the line described by $3x + 2y = 18$.**

**Step 1** Find the intercepts of $3x + 2y = 18$.

| $x$-intercept: | $y$-intercept: |
|---|---|
| $3x + 2y = 18$ | $3x + 2y = 18$ |
| $3x + 2(0) = 18$ | $3(0) + 2y = 18$ |
| $3x = 18$ | $2y = 18$ |
| $x = 6$ | $y = 9$ |

**Step 2** Use the intercepts to graph the line. The $x$-intercept is 6, so plot $(6, 0)$. The $y$-intercept is 9, so plot $(0, 9)$. Connect with a straight line. Then shade the triangle formed by the line and the axes, as described.

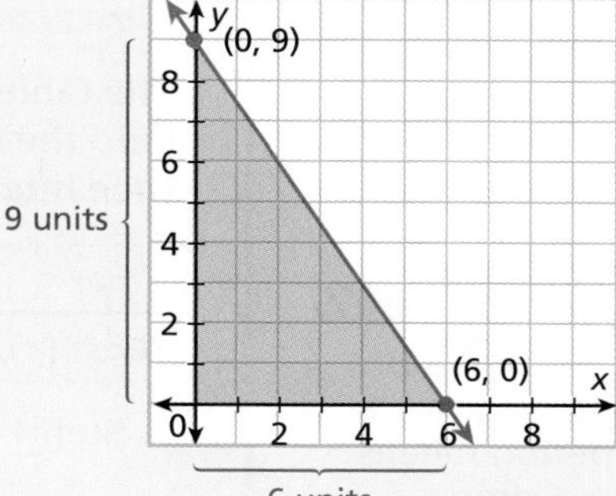


**Step 3** Recall that the area of a triangle is given by $A = \frac{1}{2}bh$.

- The length of the base is 6.
- The height is 9.

**Step 4** Substitute these values into the formula.

$A = \frac{1}{2}bh$

$A = \frac{1}{2}(6)(9)$    *Substitute into the area formula.*

$= \frac{1}{2}(54)$    *Simplify.*

$= 27$

The area of the triangle is 27 square units.

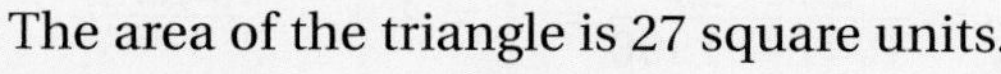

## Try This

1. Find the area of the triangle formed by the $x$-axis, the $y$-axis, and the line described by $3x + 2y = 12$.
2. Find the area of the triangle formed by the $x$-axis, the $y$-axis, and the line described by $y = 6 - x$.
3. Find the area of the polygon formed by the $x$-axis, the $y$-axis, the line described by $y = 6$, and the line described by $x = 4$.

# 5-3 Rate of Change and Slope

**MA.A.3** Analyze patterns of change in functional relationships. *Also* **MA.A.3.2, MA.A.3.3**

***Objectives***

Find rates of change and slopes.

Relate a constant rate of change to the slope of a line.

***Vocabulary***

rate of change
rise
run
slope

**Why learn this?**

Rates of change can be used to find how quickly costs have increased.

In 1985, the cost of sending a 1-ounce letter was 22 cents. In 1988, the cost was 25 cents. How fast did the cost change from 1985 to 1988? In other words, at what *rate* did the cost change?

A **rate of change** is a ratio that compares the amount of change in a dependent variable to the amount of change in an independent variable.

$$\text{rate of change} = \frac{\textbf{change in dependent variable}}{\textbf{change in independent variable}}$$

**EXAMPLE 1** ***Consumer Application***

**The table shows the cost of mailing a 1-ounce letter in different years. Find the rate of change in cost for each time interval. During which time interval did the cost increase at the greatest rate?**

| Year | 1985 | 1988 | 1990 | 1991 | 2004 |
|---|---|---|---|---|---|
| Cost (¢) | 22 | 25 | 25 | 29 | 37 |

**Step 1** Identify the dependent and independent variables.

**dependent: cost** **independent: year**

**Step 2** Find the rates of change.

1985 to 1988 $\frac{\text{change in cost}}{\text{change in years}} = \frac{25-22}{1988-1985} = \frac{3}{3} = 1$ $\frac{\textit{1 cent}}{\textit{year}}$

1988 to 1990 $\frac{\text{change in cost}}{\text{change in years}} = \frac{25-25}{1990-1988} = \frac{0}{2} = 0$ $\frac{\textit{0 cents}}{\textit{year}}$

1990 to 1991 $\frac{\text{change in cost}}{\text{change in years}} = \frac{29-25}{1991-1990} = \frac{4}{1} = 4$ $\frac{\textit{4 cents}}{\textit{year}}$

1991 to 2004 $\frac{\text{change in cost}}{\text{change in years}} = \frac{37-29}{2004-1991} = \frac{8}{13}$ $\frac{\frac{8}{13}\textit{ cent}}{\textit{year}}$

The cost increased at the greatest rate from 1990 to 1991.

A rate of change of 1 cent per year for a 3-year period means that the *average* change was 1 cent per year. The *actual* change in each year may have been different.

**1.** The table shows the balance of a bank account on different days of the month. Find the rate of change during each time interval. During which time interval did the balance decrease at the greatest rate?

| Day | 1 | 6 | 16 | 22 | 30 |
|---|---|---|---|---|---|
| Balance ($) | 550 | 285 | 210 | 210 | 175 |

## EXAMPLE 2 Finding Rates of Change from a Graph

**Graph the data from Example 1 and show the rates of change.**

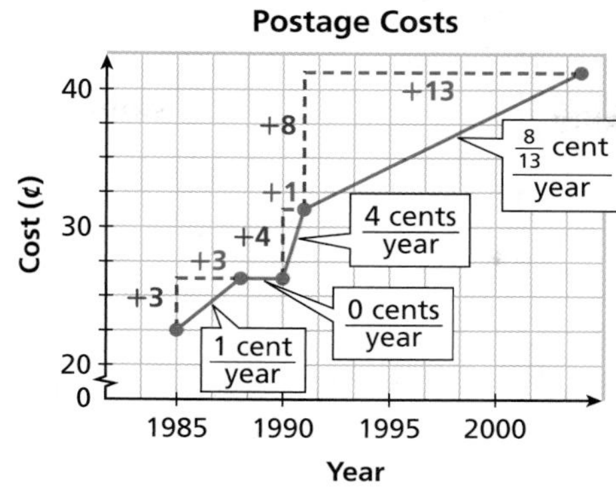


*Graph the ordered pairs. The vertical blue segments show the changes in the dependent variable, and the horizontal green segments show the changes in the independent variable.*

*Notice that the greatest rate of change is represented by the steepest of the red line segments.*

*Also notice that between 1988 and 1990, when the cost did not change, the red line segment is horizontal.*

**2.** Graph the data from Check It Out Problem 1 and show the rates of change.

If all of the connected segments have the same rate of change, then they all have the same steepness and together form a straight line. The constant rate of change of a line is called the *slope* of the line.

**Know it! Note**

### Slope of a Line

The **rise** is the difference in the ***y*-values** of two points on a line.

The **run** is the difference in the ***x*-values** of two points on a line.

The **slope** of a line is the ratio of rise to run for any two points on the line.

$$\text{slope} = \frac{\text{rise}}{\text{run}} = \frac{\text{change in } y}{\text{change in } x}$$

(Remember that $y$ is the **dependent variable** and $x$ is the **independent variable.**)

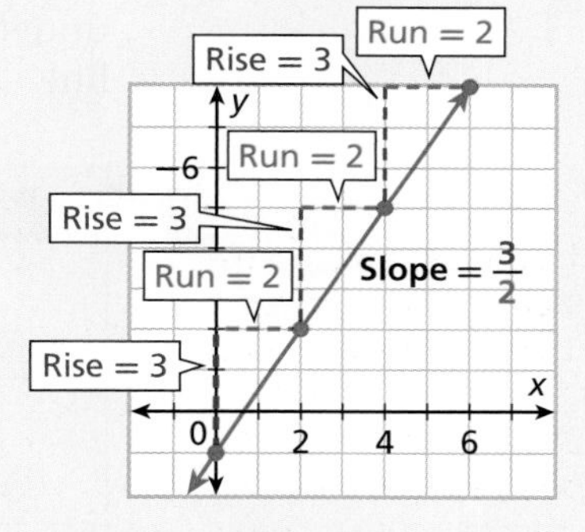


## EXAMPLE 3 Finding Slope

**Find the slope of the line.**

**Caution!**

Pay attention to the scales on the axes. One square on the grid may not represent 1 unit. In Example 3, each square represents $\frac{1}{2}$ unit.

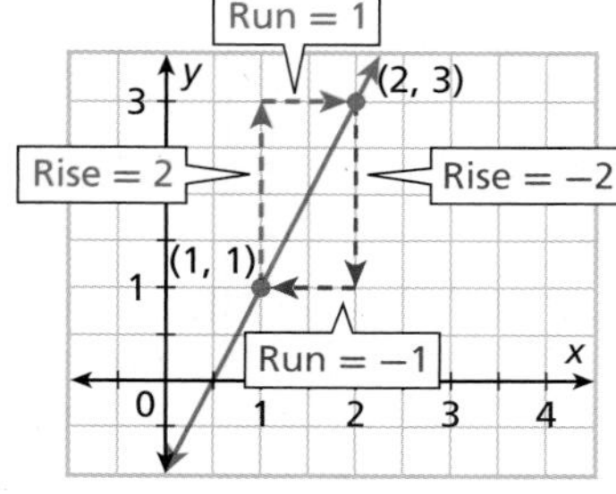


*Begin at one point and count vertically to find the rise.*

*Then count horizontally to the second point to find the run.*

$$\text{slope} = \frac{2}{1} = 2$$

*It does not matter which point you start with. The slope is the same.*

$$\text{slope} = \frac{-2}{-1} = 2$$

**3.** Find the slope of the line that contains $(0, -3)$ and $(5, -5)$.

## EXAMPLE 4 Finding Slopes of Horizontal and Vertical Lines

**Find the slope of each line.**

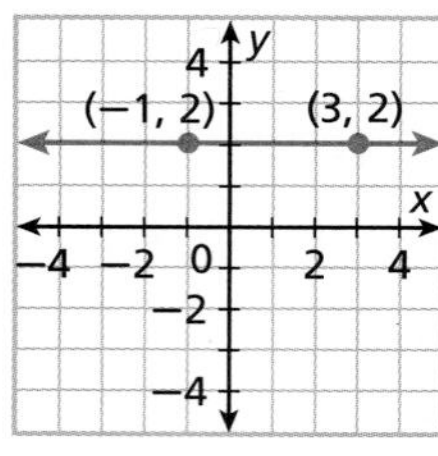


$\frac{\text{rise}}{\text{run}} = \frac{0}{4} = 0$

The slope is 0.

B

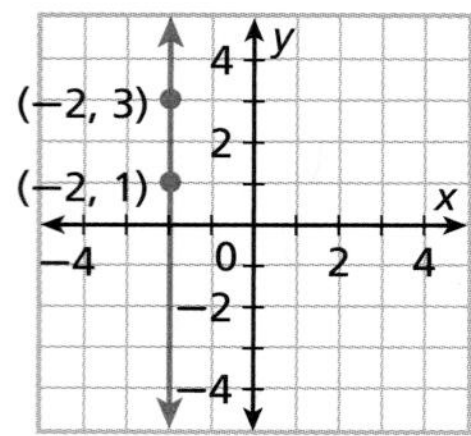


$\frac{\text{rise}}{\text{run}} = \frac{2}{0}$ *You cannot divide by 0.*

The slope is undefined.

**Find the slope of each line.**

**4a.**

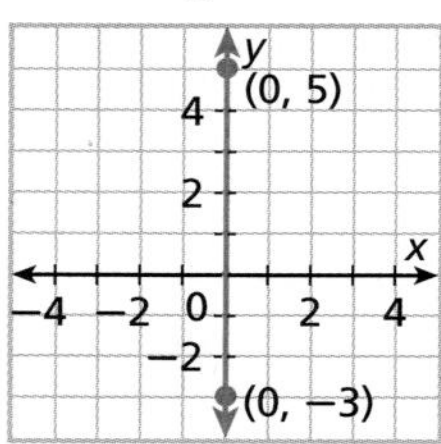


**4b.**

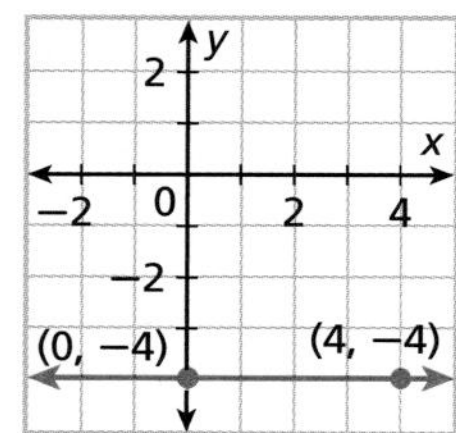


As shown in the previous examples, slope can be positive, negative, zero, or undefined. You can tell which of these is the case by looking at the graph of a line—you do not need to calculate the slope.

| Positive Slope | Negative Slope | Zero Slope | Undefined Slope |
|---|---|---|---|
| | | | |
| Line rises from left to right. | Line falls from left to right. | Horizontal line | Vertical line |

## EXAMPLE 5 Describing Slope

**Tell whether the slope of each line is positive, negative, zero, or undefined.**

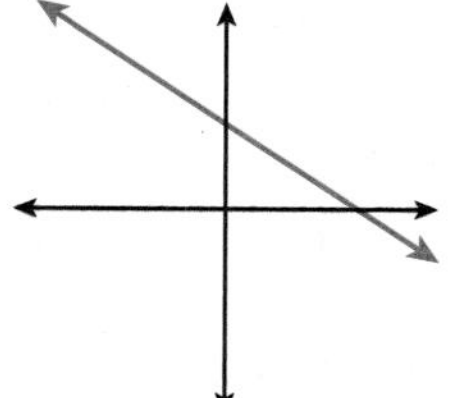

*The line falls from left to right.*

The slope is negative.

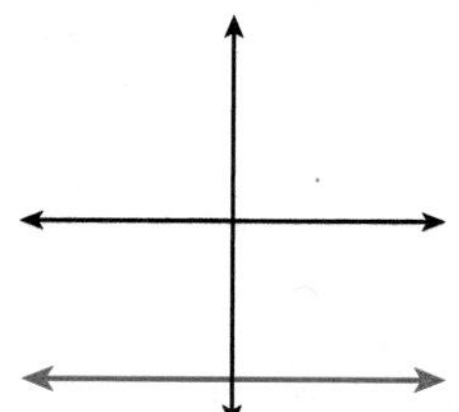

*The line is horizontal.*

The slope is 0.

**Tell whether the slope of each line is positive, negative, zero, or undefined.**

**5a.**

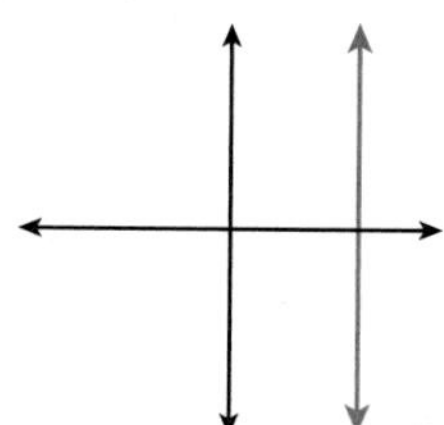

**5b.**

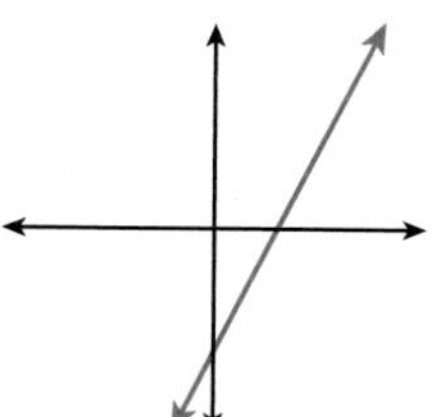

Remember that the slope of a line is its steepness. Some lines are steeper than others. As the absolute value of the slope increases, the line becomes steeper. As the absolute value of the slope decreases, the line becomes less steep.

| Comparing Slopes | | |
|---|---|---|
| 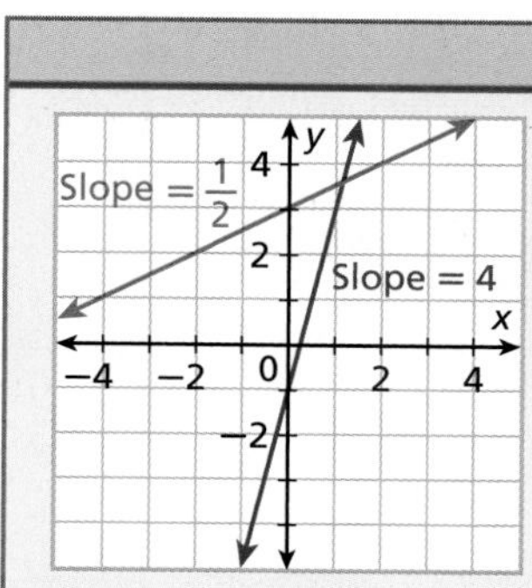  | 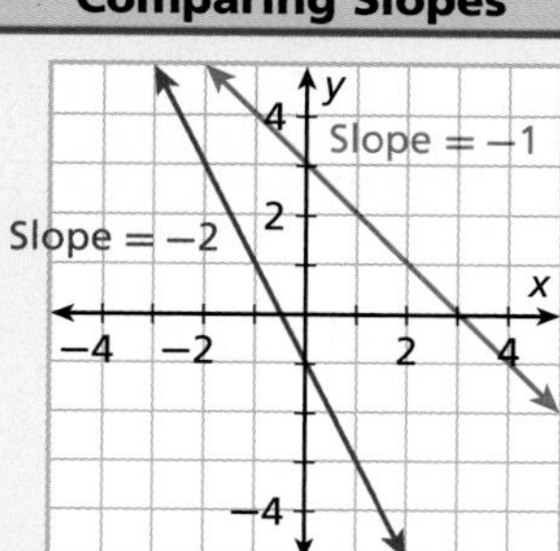  | Slope = −3<br>Slope = $\frac{3}{4}$ |
| The line with slope **4** is steeper than the line with slope $\frac{1}{2}$. | The line with slope **−2** is steeper than the line with slope **−1**. | The line with slope **−3** is steeper than the line with slope $\frac{3}{4}$. |
| $\lvert 4 \rvert > \left\lvert \frac{1}{2} \right\rvert$ | $\lvert -2 \rvert > \lvert -1 \rvert$ | $\lvert -3 \rvert > \left\lvert \frac{3}{4} \right\rvert$ |

## THINK AND DISCUSS

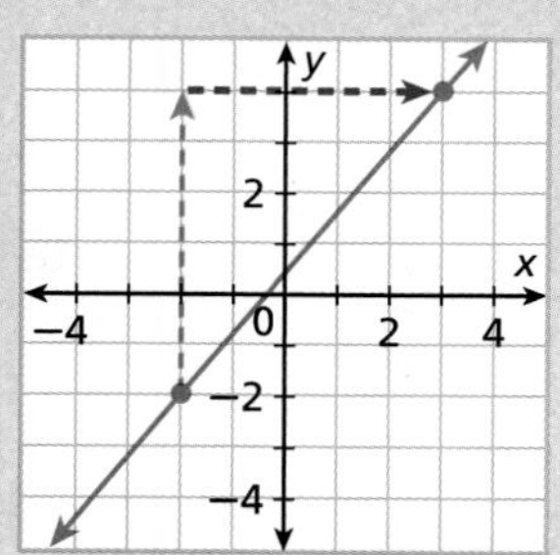

1. What is the rise shown in the graph? What is the run? What is the slope?
2. The rate of change of the profits of a company over one year is negative. How have the profits of the company changed over that year?
3. Would you rather climb a hill with a slope of 4 or a hill with a slope of $\frac{5}{2}$? Explain your answer.

Know it! Note

4. **GET ORGANIZED** Copy and complete the graphic organizer. In each box, sketch a line whose slope matches the given description.

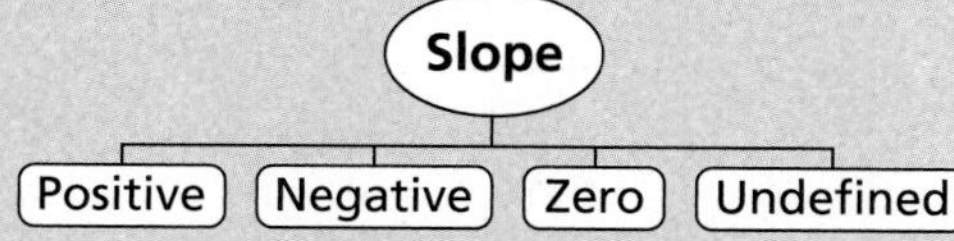

# 5-3 Exercises

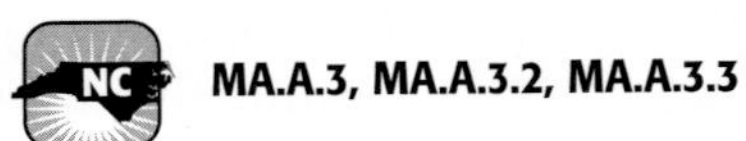


go.hrw.com
Homework Help Online
KEYWORD: MA7 5-3
Parent Resources Online
KEYWORD: MA7 Parent

## GUIDED PRACTICE

1. **Vocabulary** The *slope* of any nonvertical line is __?__. (*positive* or *constant*)

SEE EXAMPLE 1
p. 310

2. The table shows the volume of gasoline in a gas tank at different times. Find the rate of change for each time interval. During which time interval did the volume decrease at the greatest rate?

| Time (h) | 0 | 1 | 3 | 6 | 7 |
|---|---|---|---|---|---|
| Volume (gal) | 12 | 9 | 5 | 1 | 1 |

SEE EXAMPLE 2
p. 311

3. The table shows a person's heart rate over time. Graph the data and show the rates of change.

| Time (min) | 0 | 2 | 5 | 7 | 10 |
|---|---|---|---|---|---|
| Heart Rate (beats/min) | 64 | 92 | 146 | 84 | 64 |

SEE EXAMPLE 3
p. 311

**Find the slope of each line.**

4. 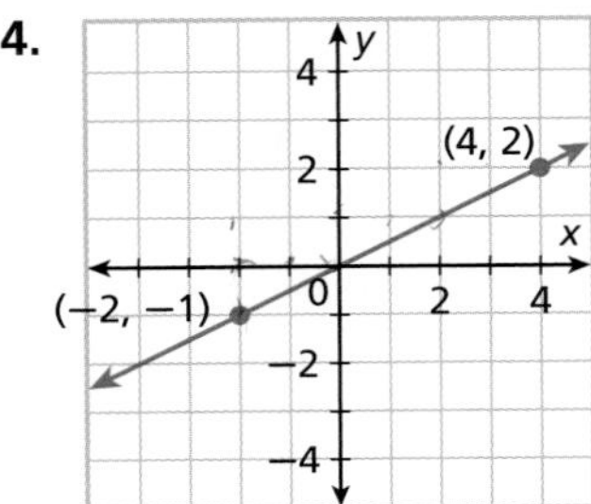


5. 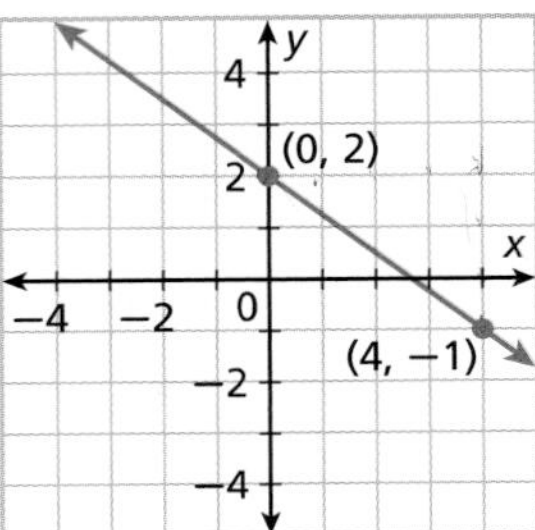


SEE EXAMPLE 4
p. 312

6. 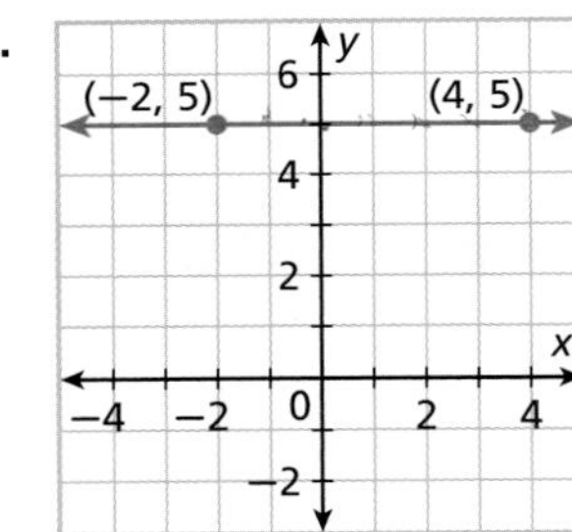


7. 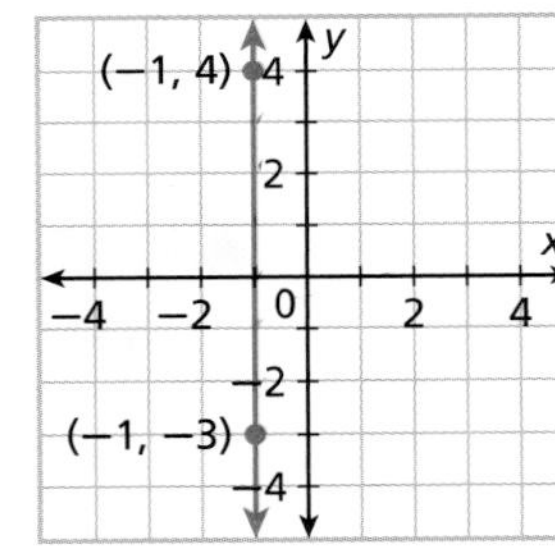


SEE EXAMPLE 5
p. 312

**Tell whether the slope of each line is positive, negative, zero, or undefined.**

8. 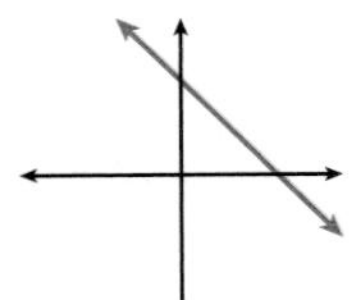

9. 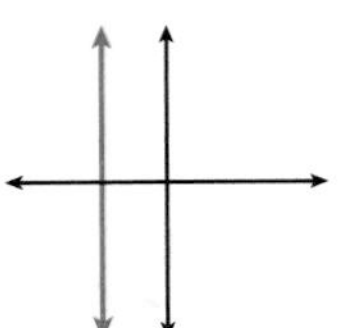

10. 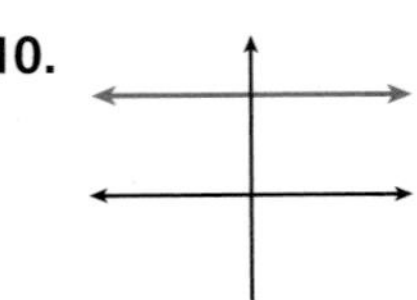

11. 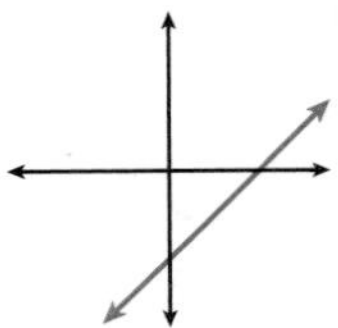

## PRACTICE AND PROBLEM SOLVING

**Independent Practice**

| For Exercises | See Example |
|---|---|
| 12 | 1 |
| 13 | 2 |
| 14–15 | 3 |
| 16–17 | 4 |
| 18–19 | 5 |

**Extra Practice**

Skills Practice p. S12
Application Practice p. S32

12. The table shows the length of a baby at different ages. Find the rate of change for each time interval. Round your answers to the nearest tenth. During which time interval did the baby have the greatest growth rate?

| Age (mo) | 3 | 9 | 18 | 26 | 33 |
|---|---|---|---|---|---|
| Length (in.) | 23.5 | 27.5 | 31.6 | 34.5 | 36.7 |

13. The table shows the distance of an elevator from the ground floor at different times. Graph the data and show the rates of change.

| Time (s) | 0 | 15 | 23 | 30 | 35 |
|---|---|---|---|---|---|
| Distance (m) | 30 | 70 | 0 | 45 | 60 |

**Find the slope of each line.**

14.

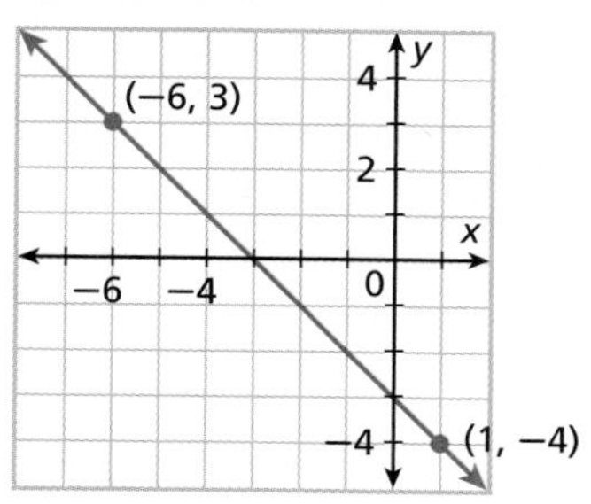


15.

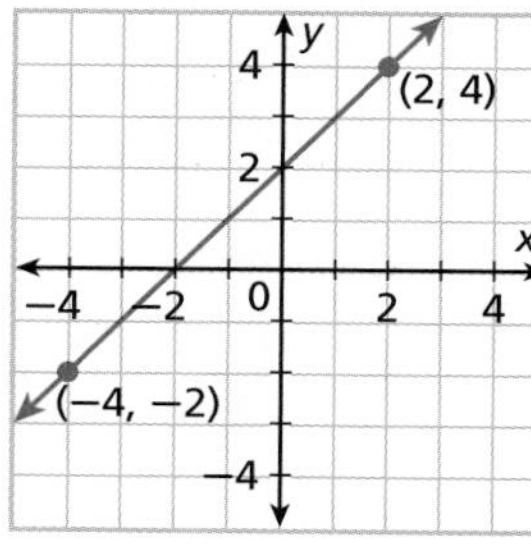


16.

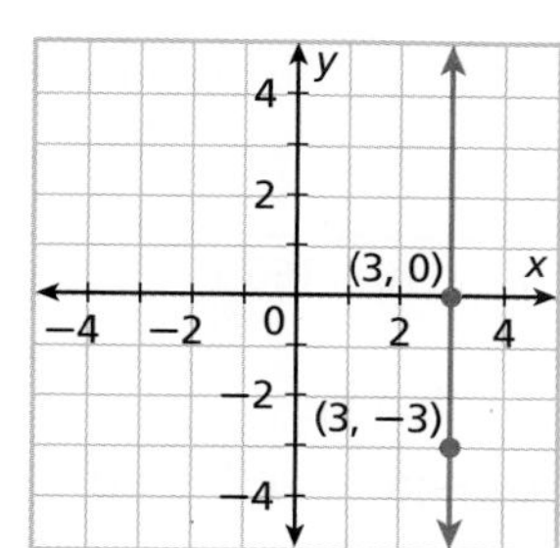


17.

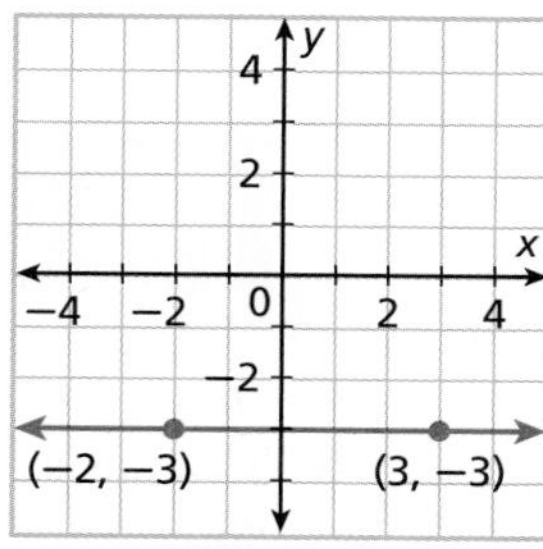


**Tell whether the slope of each line is positive, negative, zero, or undefined.**

18.

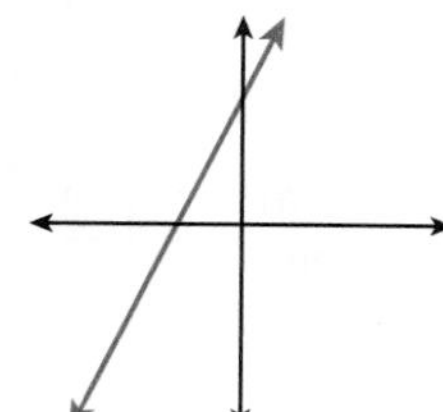

19.

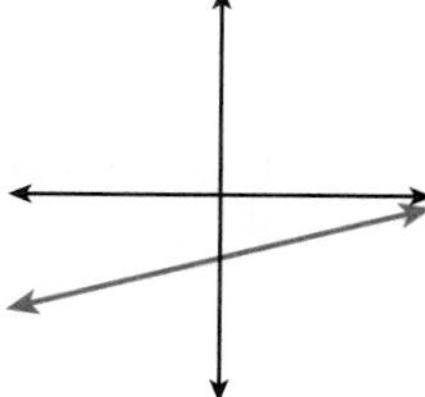

**LINK Travel**

The Incline Railway's climb up Lookout Mountain has been called "America's Most Amazing Mile." A round-trip on the railway lasts about 1.5 hours.

20. **Travel** The Lookout Mountain Incline Railway in Chattanooga, Tennessee, is the steepest passenger railway in the world. A section of the railway has a slope of about 0.73. In this section, a vertical change of 1 unit corresponds to a horizontal change of what length? Round your answer to the nearest hundredth.

21. **Critical Thinking** In Lesson 5-1, you learned that in a linear function, a constant change in $x$ corresponds to a constant change in $y$. How is this related to slope?

22. This problem will prepare you for the Multi-Step Test Prep on page 332.
  a. The graph shows a relationship between a person's age and his or her estimated maximum heart rate in beats per minute. Find the slope.
  b. Describe the rate of change in this situation.

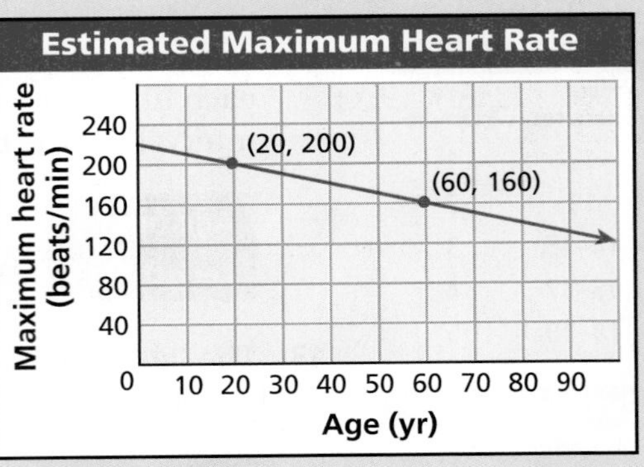


23. **Construction** Most staircases in use today have 9-inch treads and $8\frac{1}{2}$-inch risers. What is the slope of a staircase with these measurements?

24. A ladder is leaned against a building. The bottom of the ladder is 9 feet from the building. The top of the ladder is 16 feet above the ground.
  a. Draw a diagram to represent this situation.
  b. What is the slope of the ladder?

Tread

Riser

25. **Write About It** Why will the slope of any horizontal line be 0? Why will the slope of any vertical line be undefined?

26. The table shows the distance traveled by a car during a five-hour road trip.

| Time (h) | 0 | 1 | 2 | 3 | 4 | 5 |
|---|---|---|---|---|---|---|
| Distance (mi) | 0 | 40 | 80 | 80 | 110 | 160 |

  a. Graph the data and show the rates of change.
  b. The rate of change represents the average speed. During which hour was the car's average speed the greatest?

27. **Estimation** The graph shows the number of files scanned by a computer virus detection program over time.
  a. Estimate the coordinates of point $A$.
  b. Estimate the coordinates of point $B$.
  c. Use your answers from parts **a** and **b** to estimate the rate of change (in files per second) between points $A$ and $B$.

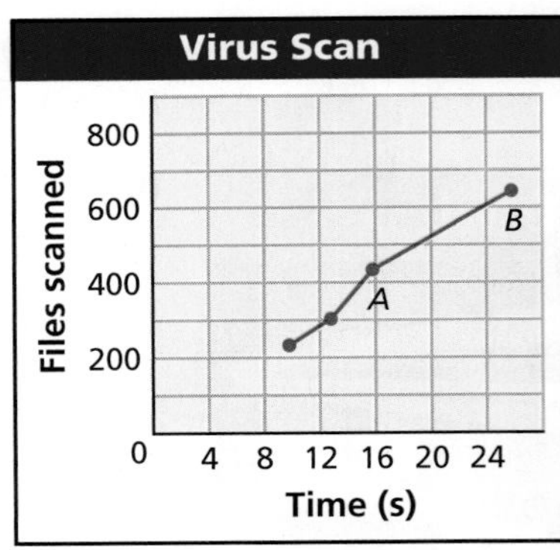

28. **Data Collection** Use a graphing calculator and a motion detector for the following. Set the equipment so that the graph shows distance on the $y$-axis and time on the $x$-axis.
  a. Experiment with walking in front of the motion detector. How must you walk to graph a straight line? Explain.
  b. Describe what you must do differently to graph a line with a positive slope vs. a line with a negative slope.
  c. How can you graph a line with slope 0? Explain.

MA.A.3, MA.A.3.2, MA.A.3.3

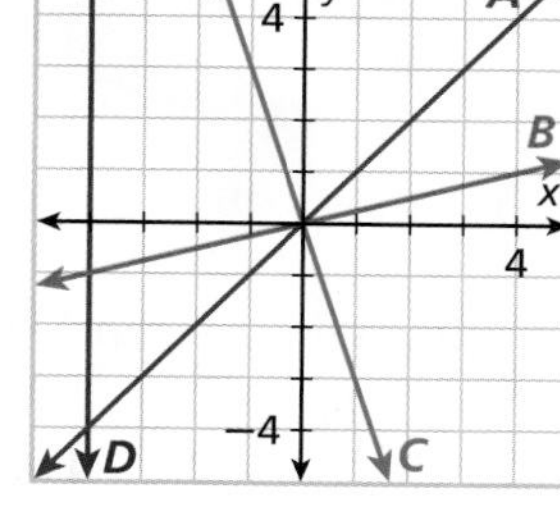


29. The slope of which line has the greatest absolute value?
    - (A) line $A$
    - (B) line $B$
    - (C) line $C$
    - (D) line $D$

30. For which line is the run equal to 0?
    - (A) line $A$
    - (B) line $B$
    - (C) line $C$
    - (D) line $D$

31. Which line has a slope of 4?

(F)

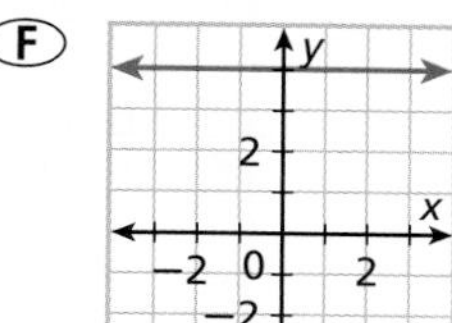

(H)

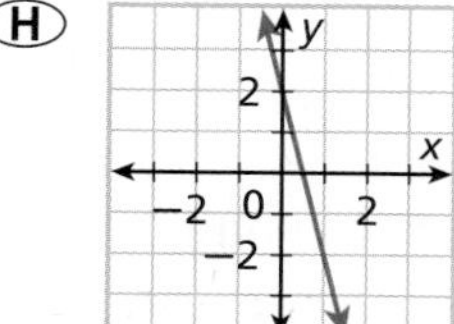

(G)

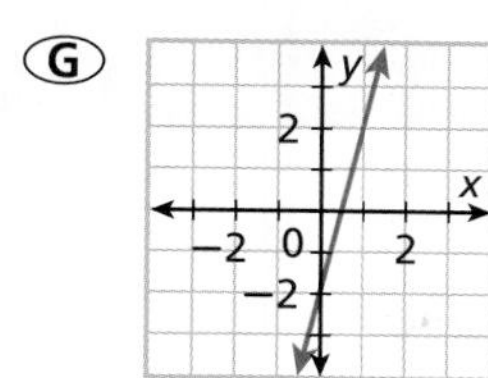

(J)

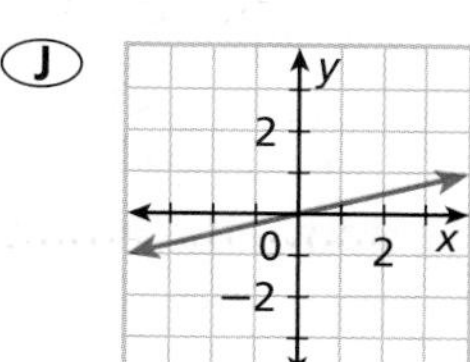

## CHALLENGE AND EXTEND

32. **Recreation** Tara and Jade are hiking up a hill. Each has a different stride. The run for Tara's stride is 32 inches, and the rise is 8 inches. The run for Jade's stride is 36 inches. What is the rise of Jade's stride?

33. **Economics** The table shows cost in dollars charged by an electric company for various amounts of energy in kilowatt-hours.

| Energy (kWh) | 0 | 200 | 400 | 600 | 1000 | 2000 |
|---|---|---|---|---|---|---|
| Cost ($) | 3 | 3 | 31 | 59 | 115 | 150 |

   a. Graph the data and show the rates of change.
   b. Compare the rates of change for each interval. Are they all the same? Explain.
   c. What do the rates of change represent?
   d. Describe in words the electric company's billing plan.

## SPIRAL REVIEW

**Add or subtract.** *(Lesson 1-2)*

34. $-5 + 15$

35. $9 - 11$

36. $-5 - (-25)$

**Find the domain and range of each relation, and tell whether the relation is a function.** *(Lesson 4-2)*

37. $\{(3, 4), (3, 2), (3, 0), (3, -2)\}$

38.

| $x$ | 0 | 2 | 4 | −2 | −4 |
|---|---|---|---|---|---|
| $y$ | 0 | 2 | 4 | 2 | 4 |

**Find the $x$- and $y$-intercepts.** *(Lesson 5-2)*

39. $2x + y = 6$

40. $y = -3x - 9$

41. $2y = -4x + 1$

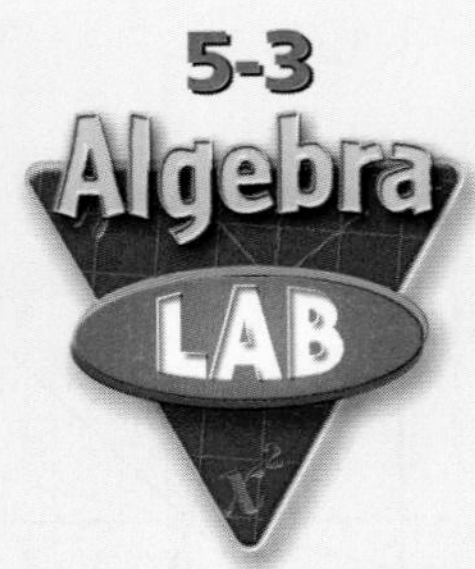

Use with Lesson 5-3

# Explore Constant Changes

There are many real-life situations in which the amount of change is constant. In these activities, you will explore what happens when

- a quantity increases by a constant amount.
- a quantity decreases by a constant amount.

**MA.A.3** Analyze patterns of change in functional relationships.
*Also* **Prep MA.A.4.3, MA.A.5.1**

## Activity 1

Janice has read 7 books for her summer reading club. She plans to read 2 books each week for the rest of the summer. The table shows the total number of books that Janice will have read after different numbers of weeks have passed.

| Janice's Summer Reading | |
|---|---|
| **Week** | **Total Books Read** |
| 0 | 7 |
| 1 | 9 |
| 2 | 11 |
| 3 | 13 |
| 4 | 15 |
| 5 | 17 |

1. What number is added to the number of books in each row to get the number of books in the next row?
2. What does your answer to Problem 1 represent in Janice's situation? Describe the meaning of the constant change.
3. Graph the ordered pairs from the table. Describe how the points are related.
4. Look again at your answer to Problem 1. Explain how this number affects your graph.

## Try This

At a particular college, a full-time student must take at least 12 credit hours per semester and may take up to 18 credit hours per semester. Tuition costs $200 per credit hour.

| Tuition Costs | |
|---|---|
| **Credit Hours** | **Cost ($)** |
| 12 | ■ |
| 13 | ■ |
| 14 | ■ |
| 15 | ■ |
| 16 | ■ |
| 17 | ■ |
| 18 | ■ |

1. Copy and complete the table by using the information above.
2. What number is added to the cost in each row to get the cost in the next row?
3. What does your answer to Problem 2 above represent in the situation? Describe the meaning of the constant change.
4. Graph the ordered pairs from the table. Describe how the points are related.
5. Look again at your answer to Problem 2. Explain how this number affects the shape of your graph.
6. Compare your graphs from Activity 1 and Problem 4. How are they alike? How are they different?
7. **Make a Conjecture** Describe the graph of any situation that involves repeated addition of a positive number. Why do you think your description is correct?

## Activity 2

An airplane is 3000 miles from its destination. The plane is traveling at a rate of 540 miles per hour. The table shows how far the plane is from its destination after various amounts of time have passed.

| Airplane's Distance | |
|---|---|
| **Time (h)** | **Distance to Destination (mi)** |
| 0 | 3000 |
| 1 | 2460 |
| 2 | 1920 |
| 3 | 1380 |
| 4 | 840 |

1. What number is subtracted from the distance in each row to get the distance in the next row?
2. What does your answer to Problem 1 represent in the situation? Describe the meaning of the constant change.
3. Graph the ordered pairs from the table. Describe how the points are related.
4. Look again at your answer to Problem 1. Explain how this number affects your graph.

## Try This

A television game show begins with 20 contestants. Each week, the players vote 2 contestants off the show.

| Game Show | |
|---|---|
| **Week** | **Contestants Remaining** |
| 0 | 20 |
| 1 | ■ |
| 2 | ■ |
| 3 | ■ |
| 4 | ■ |
| 5 | ■ |
| 6 | ■ |

8. Copy and complete the table by using the information above.
9. What number is subtracted from the number of contestants in each row to get the number of contestants in the next row?
10. What does your answer to Problem 9 represent in the situation? Describe the meaning of the constant change.
11. Graph the ordered pairs from the table. Describe how the points are related.
12. Look again at your answer to Problem 9. Explain how this number affects the shape of your graph.
13. Compare your graphs from Activity 2 and Problem 11. How are they alike? How are they different?
14. **Make a Conjecture** Describe the graph of any situation that involves repeated subtraction of a positive number. Why do you think your description is correct?
15. Compare your two graphs from Activity 1 with your two graphs from Activity 2. How are they alike? How are they different?
16. **Make a Conjecture** How are graphs of situations involving repeated subtraction different from graphs of situations involving repeated addition? Explain your answer.

# 5-4 The Slope Formula

**MA.G.1.1** Use strategies to calculate the slope... **MA.A.3** Analyze patterns of change in functional relationships. *Also* **MA.A.3.3, MA.A.5.1, MA.A.4.5**

***Objective***
Find slope by using the slope formula.

**Why learn this?**
You can use the slope formula to find how quickly a quantity, such as the amount of water in a reservoir, is changing. (See Example 3.)

In Lesson 5-3, slope was described as the constant rate of change of a line. You saw how to find the slope of a line by using its graph.

There is also a formula you can use to find the slope of a line, which is usually represented by the letter $m$. To use this formula, you need the coordinates of two different points on the line.

**Slope Formula**

| WORDS | FORMULA | EXAMPLE |
|---|---|---|
| The slope of a line is the ratio of the difference in $y$-values to the difference in $x$-values between any two different points on the line. | If $(x_1, y_1)$ and $(x_2, y_2)$ are any two different points on a line, the slope of the line is $m = \frac{y_2 - y_1}{x_2 - x_1}$. | If $(2, -3)$ and $(1, 4)$ are two points on a line, the slope of the line is $m = \frac{4-(-3)}{1-2} = \frac{7}{-1} = -7$. |

**EXAMPLE 1** **Finding Slope by Using the Slope Formula**

**Reading Math**
The small numbers to the bottom right of the variables are called subscripts. Read $x_1$ as "$x$ sub one" and $y_2$ as "$y$ sub two."

**Find the slope of the line that contains $(4, -2)$ and $(-1, 2)$.**

$m = \frac{y_2 - y_1}{x_2 - x_1}$ *Use the slope formula.*

$= \frac{2-(-2)}{-1-4}$ *Substitute $(4, -2)$ for $(x_1, y_1)$ and $(-1, 2)$ for $(x_2, y_2)$.*

$= \frac{4}{-5}$ *Simplify.*

$= -\frac{4}{5}$

The slope of the line that contains $(4, -2)$ and $(-1, 2)$ is $-\frac{4}{5}$.

**1a.** Find the slope of the line that contains $(-2, -2)$ and $(7, -2)$.

**1b.** Find the slope of the line that contains $(5, -7)$ and $(6, -4)$.

**1c.** Find the slope of the line that contains $\left(\frac{3}{4}, \frac{7}{5}\right)$ and $\left(\frac{1}{4}, \frac{2}{5}\right)$.

Sometimes you are not given two points to use in the formula. You might have to choose two points from a graph or a table.

## EXAMPLE 2 Finding Slope from Graphs and Tables

**Each graph or table shows a linear relationship. Find the slope.**

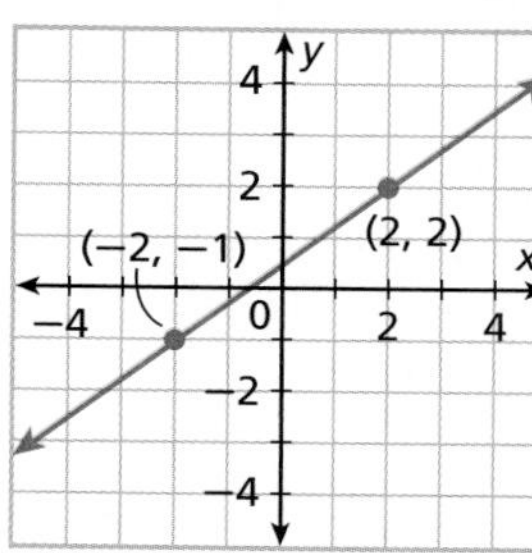


*Let (2, 2) be $(x_1, y_1)$ and (−2, −1) be $(x_2, y_2)$.*

$$m = \frac{y_2 - y_1}{x_2 - x_1}$$ *Use the slope formula.*

$$= \frac{-1 - 2}{-2 - 2}$$ *Substitute (2, 2) for $(x_1, y_1)$ and (−2, −1) for $(x_2, y_2)$.*

$$= \frac{-3}{-4}$$ *Simplify.*

$$= \frac{3}{4}$$

**B**

| x | 2 | 2 | 2 | 2 |
|---|---|---|---|---|
| y | 0 | 1 | 3 | 5 |

**Step 1** Choose any two points from the table. Let (2, 0) be $(x_1, y_1)$ and (2, 3) be $(x_2, y_2)$.

**Step 2** Use the slope formula.

$$m = \frac{y_2 - y_1}{x_2 - x_1}$$ *Use the slope formula.*

$$= \frac{3 - 0}{2 - 2}$$ *Substitute (2, 0) for $(x_1, y_1)$ and (2, 3) for $(x_2, y_2)$.*

$$= \frac{3}{0}$$ *Simplify.*

The slope is undefined.

**Each graph or table shows a linear relationship. Find the slope.**

**2a.**

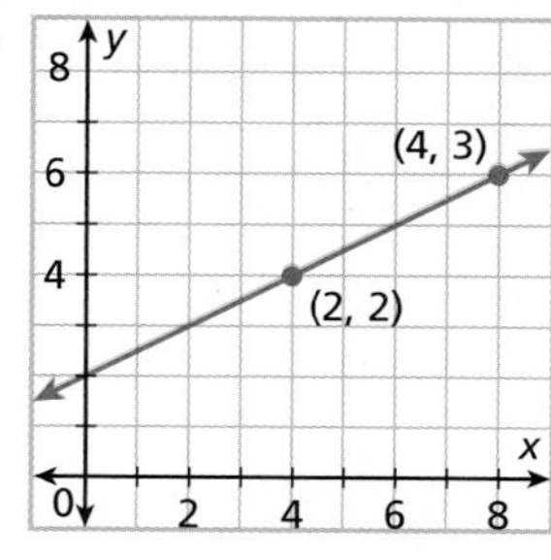

**2b.**

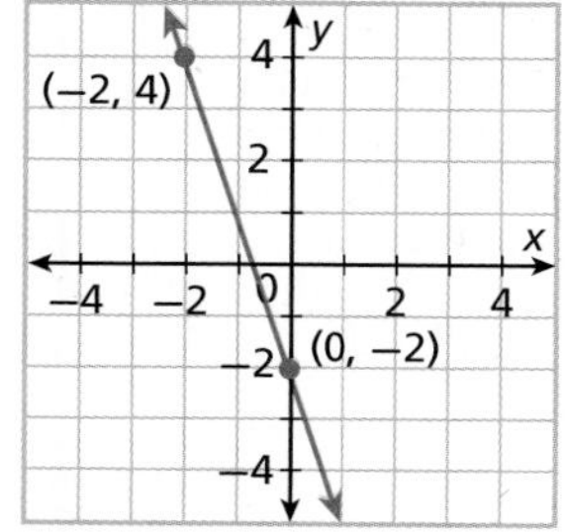


**2c.**

| x | 0 | 2 | 5 | 6 |
|---|---|---|---|---|
| y | 1 | 5 | 11 | 13 |

**2d.**

| x | −2 | 0 | 2 | 4 |
|---|---|---|---|---|
| y | 3 | 0 | −3 | −6 |

Remember that slope is a rate of change. In real-world problems, finding the slope can give you information about how quantity is changing.

## EXAMPLE 3 Application

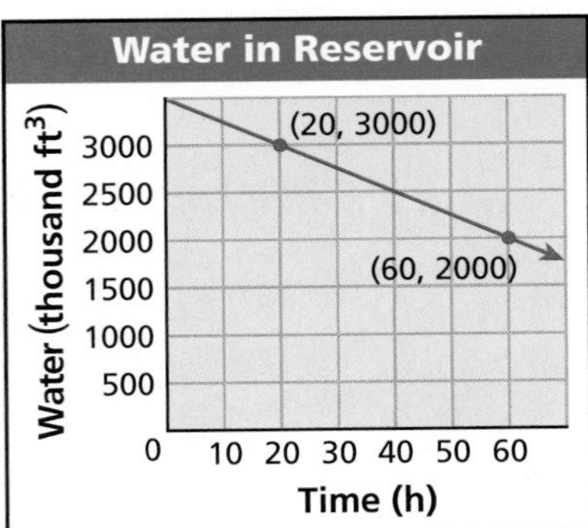


**The graph shows how much water is in a reservoir at different times. Find the slope of the line. Then tell what the slope represents.**

**Step 1** Use the slope formula.

$$m = \frac{y_2 - y_1}{x_2 - x_1}$$

$$= \frac{2000 - 3000}{60 - 20}$$

$$= \frac{-1000}{40} = -25$$

**Step 2** Tell what the slope represents.

In this situation, $y$ represents **volume of water** and $x$ represents **time**.

So slope represents $\frac{\text{change in volume}}{\text{change in time}}$ in units of $\frac{\text{thousands of cubic feet}}{\text{hours}}$.

A slope of $-25$ means the amount of water in the reservoir is decreasing (negative change) at a rate of 25 thousand cubic feet each hour.

**3.** The graph shows the height of a plant over a period of days. Find the slope of the line. Then tell what the slope represents.

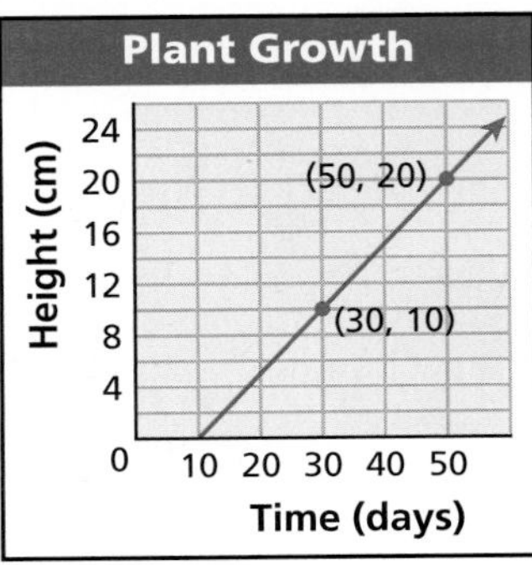


If you know the equation that describes a line, you can find its slope by using any two ordered-pair solutions. It is often easiest to use the ordered pairs that contain the intercepts.

## EXAMPLE 4 Finding Slope from an Equation

**Find the slope of the line described by $6x - 5y = 30$.**

**Step 1** Find the $x$-intercept.

$$6x - 5y = 30$$

$$6x - 5(0) = 30 \quad \textit{Let } y = 0.$$

$$6x = 30$$

$$\frac{6x}{6} = \frac{30}{6}$$

$$x = 5$$

**Step 2** Find the $y$-intercept.

$$6x - 5y = 30$$

$$6(0) - 5y = 30 \quad \textit{Let } x = 0.$$

$$-5y = 30$$

$$\frac{-5y}{-5} = \frac{30}{-5}$$

$$y = -6$$

**Step 3** The line contains $(5, 0)$ and $(0, -6)$. Use the slope formula.

$$m = \frac{y_2 - y_1}{x_2 - x_1} = \frac{-6 - 0}{0 - 5} = \frac{-6}{-5} = \frac{6}{5}$$

**4.** Find the slope of the line described by $2x + 3y = 12$.

## THINK AND DISCUSS

1. The slope of a line is the difference of the ___?___ divided by the difference of the ___?___ for any two points on the line.
2. Two points lie on a line. When you substitute their coordinates into the slope formula, the value of the denominator is 0. Describe this line.

3. **GET ORGANIZED** Copy and complete the graphic organizer. In each box, describe how to find slope using the given method.

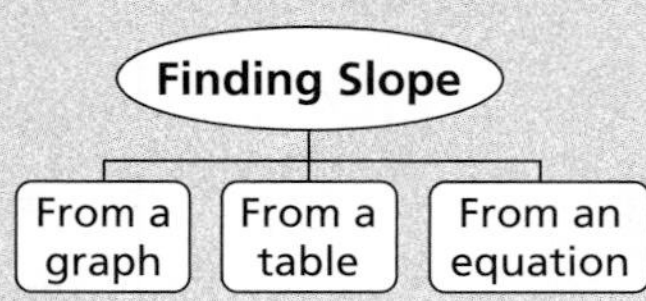


# 5-4 Exercises

**MA.G.1.1, MA.A.3, MA.A.3.3, MA.A.5.1, MA.A.4.5**

## GUIDED PRACTICE

SEE EXAMPLE 1 p. 320

**Find the slope of the line that contains each pair of points.**

1. $(3, 6)$ and $(6, 9)$
2. $(2, 7)$ and $(4, 4)$
3. $(-1, -5)$ and $(-9, -1)$

SEE EXAMPLE 2 p. 321

**Each graph or table shows a linear relationship. Find the slope.**

4.

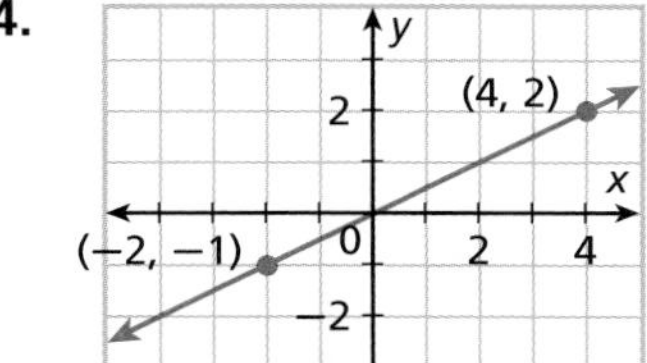


5.

| x | y |
|---|---|
| 0 | 25 |
| 2 | 45 |
| 4 | 65 |
| 6 | 85 |

SEE EXAMPLE 3 p. 322

**Find the slope of each line. Then tell what the slope represents.**

6.

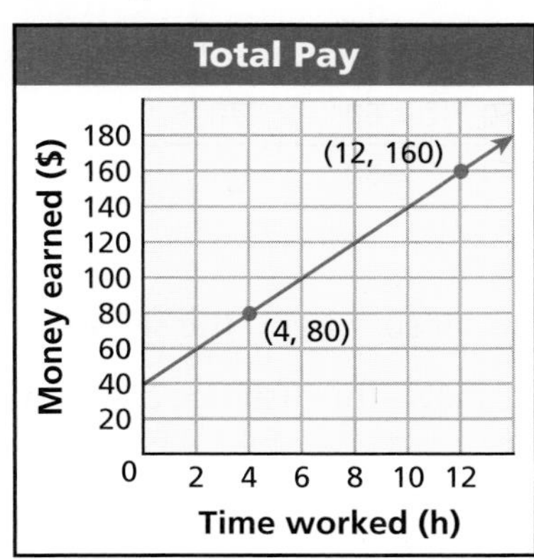


7.

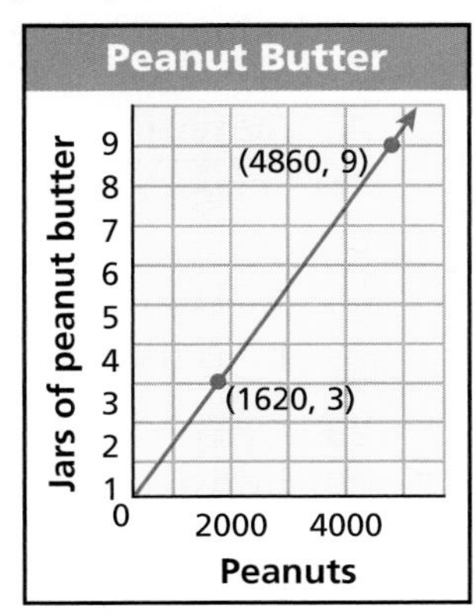


SEE EXAMPLE 4 p. 322

**Find the slope of the line described by each equation.**

8. $8x + 2y = 96$
9. $5x = 90 - 9y$
10. $5y = 160 + 9x$

## PRACTICE AND PROBLEM SOLVING

**Independent Practice**

| For Exercises | See Example |
|---|---|
| 11–13 | 1 |
| 14–15 | 2 |
| 16–17 | 3 |
| 18–20 | 4 |

**Extra Practice**

Skills Practice p. S12
Application Practice p. S32

**Find the slope of the line that contains each pair of points.**

**11.** (2, 5) and (3, 1) **12.** (−9, −5) and (6, −5) **13.** (3, 4) and (3, −1)

**Each graph or table shows a linear relationship. Find the slope.**

**14.**

| x | y |
|---|---|
| 1 | 18.5 |
| 2 | 22 |
| 3 | 25.5 |
| 4 | 29 |

**15.**

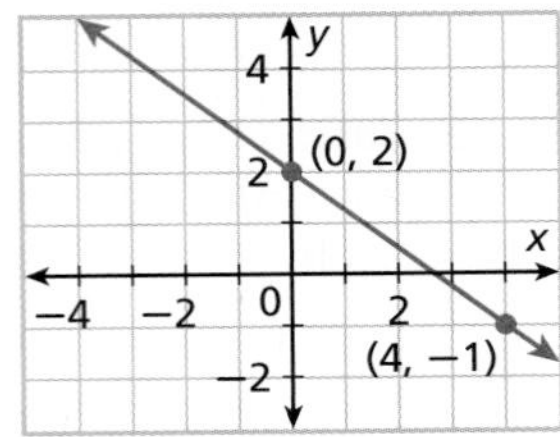


**Find the slope of each line. Then tell what the slope represents.**

**16.**

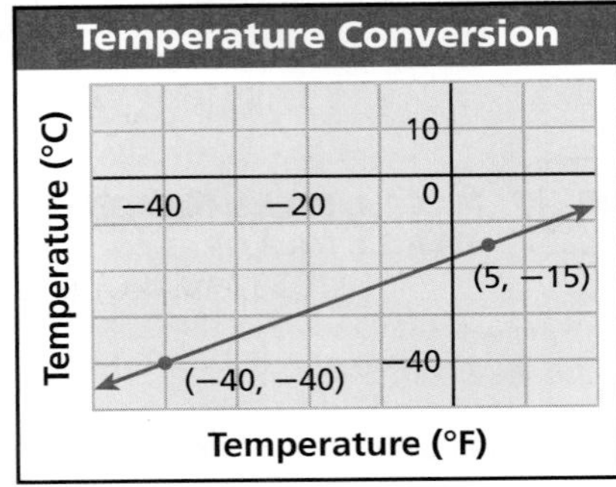


**17.**

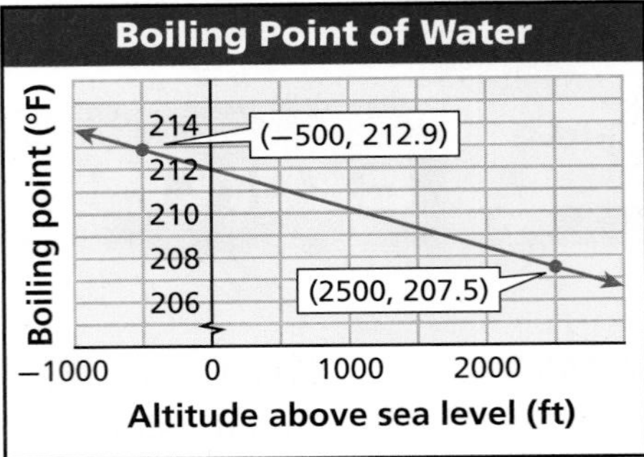


**Find the slope of the line described by each equation.**

**18.** $7x + 13y = 91$ **19.** $5y = 130 - 13x$ **20.** $7 - 3y = 9x$

**21.** **ERROR ANALYSIS** Two students found the slope of the line that contains $(-6, 3)$ and $(2, -1)$. Who is incorrect? Explain the error.

**A**

$$m = \frac{-1-3}{2-(-6)} = \frac{-4}{8} = -\frac{1}{2}$$

**B**

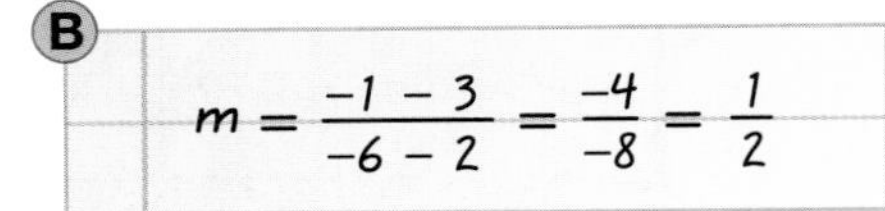

$$m = \frac{-1-3}{-6-2} = \frac{-4}{-8} = \frac{1}{2}$$

**22. Environmental Science** The table shows how the number of cricket chirps per minute changes with the air temperature.

| Temperature (°F) | 40 | 50 | 60 | 70 | 80 | 90 |
|---|---|---|---|---|---|---|
| Chirps per minute | 0 | 40 | 80 | 120 | 160 | 200 |

a. Find the rates of change.

b. Is the graph of the data a line? If so, what is the slope? If not, explain why not.

**23. Critical Thinking** The graph shows the distance traveled by two cars.

a. Which car is going faster? How much faster?

b. How are the speeds related to slope?

c. At what rate is the distance between the cars changing?

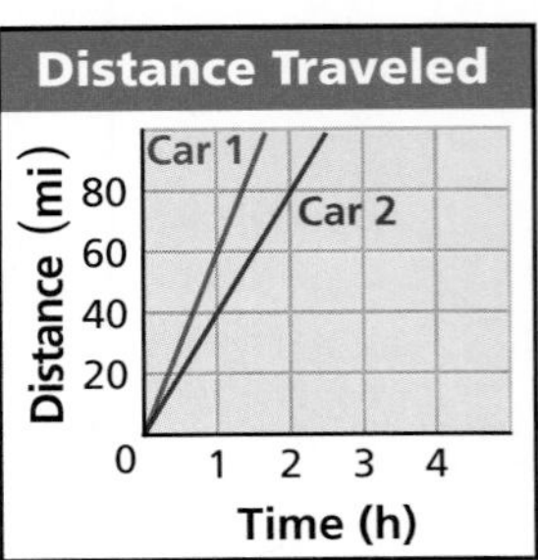

**24. Write About It** You are given the coordinates of two points on a line. Describe two different ways to find the slope of that line.

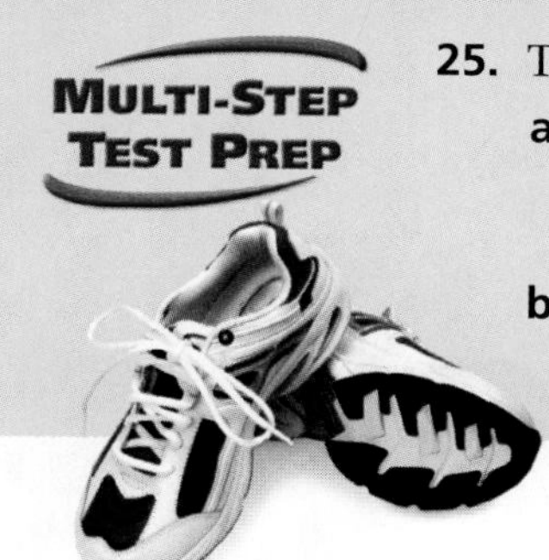


25. This problem will prepare you for the Multi-Step Test Prep on page 332.
   a. One way to estimate your maximum heart rate is to subtract your age from 220. Write a function to describe the relationship between maximum heart rate $y$ and age $x$.
   b. The graph of this function is a line. Find its slope. Then tell what the slope represents.

MA.G.1.1, MA.A.3, MA.A.3.3, MA.A.5.1, MA.A.4.5

26. The equation $2y + 3x = -6$ describes a line with what slope?

   Ⓐ $\frac{3}{2}$  Ⓑ 0  Ⓒ $\frac{1}{2}$  Ⓓ $-\frac{3}{2}$

27. A line with slope $-\frac{1}{3}$ could pass through which of the following pairs of points?

   Ⓕ $\left(0, -\frac{1}{3}\right)$ and $(1, 1)$  Ⓗ $(0, 0)$ and $\left(-\frac{1}{3}, -\frac{1}{3}\right)$

   Ⓖ $(-6, 5)$ and $(-3, 4)$  Ⓙ $(5, -6)$ and $(4, 3)$

28. **Gridded Response** Find the slope of the line that contains $(-1, 2)$ and $(5, 5)$.

## CHALLENGE AND EXTEND

**Find the slope of the line that contains each pair of points.**

29. $(a, 0)$ and $(0, b)$  30. $(2x, y)$ and $(x, 3y)$  31. $(x, y)$ and $(x + 2, 3 - y)$

**Find the value of $x$ so that the points lie on a line with the given slope.**

32. $(x, 2)$ and $(-5, 8)$, $m = -1$  33. $(4, x)$ and $(6, 3x)$, $m = \frac{1}{2}$

34. $(1, -3)$ and $(3, x)$, $m = -1$  35. $(-10, -4)$ and $(x, x)$, $m = \frac{1}{7}$

36. A line contains the point $(1, 2)$ and has a slope of $\frac{1}{2}$. Use the slope formula to find another point on this line.

37. The points $(-2, 4)$, $(0, 2)$, and $(3, x - 1)$ all lie on the same line. What is the value of $x$? (*Hint:* Remember that the slope of a line is constant for any two points on the line.)

## SPIRAL REVIEW

**Solve each equation. Check your answer.** *(Lesson 2-1)*

38. $k - 3.14 = 1.71$  39. $-7 = p - 12$  40. $25 = f - 16$

41. $-2 = 9 + n$  42. $\frac{1}{5} + x = \frac{3}{5}$  43. $a - \frac{1}{2} = \frac{3}{2}$

**Tell whether the given ordered pairs satisfy a linear function.** *(Lesson 5-1)*

44. $\{(1, 1), (2, 4), (3, 9), (4, 16)\}$  45. $\{(9, 0), (8, -5), (5, -20), (3, -30)\}$

**Use the intercepts to graph the line described by each equation.** *(Lesson 5-2)*

46. $x - y = 5$  47. $3x + y = 9$  48. $y = 5x + 10$

# 5-5 Direct Variation

**MA.A.2** Use direct ... variation to solve problems. *Also* **MA.A.2.1, MA.A.2.2, MA.A.2.3, MA.A.5.1, MA.A.4.5**

***Objective***
Identify, write, and graph direct variation.

***Vocabulary***
direct variation
constant of variation

**Who uses this?**
Chefs can use direct variation to determine ingredients needed for a certain number of servings.

Paella is a rice dish that originated in Valencia, Spain.

A recipe for paella calls for 1 cup of rice to make 5 servings. In other words, a chef needs 1 cup of rice for every 5 servings.

| **Rice (c) $x$** | 1 | 2 | 3 | 4 |
|---|---|---|---|---|
| **Servings $y$** | 5 | 10 | 15 | 20 |

The equation $y = 5x$ describes this relationship. In this relationship, the number of servings *varies directly* with the number of cups of rice.

A **direct variation** is a special type of linear relationship that can be written in the form $y = kx$, where $k$ is a nonzero constant called the **constant of variation**.

## EXAMPLE 1 Identifying Direct Variations from Equations

**Tell whether each equation represents a direct variation. If so, identify the constant of variation.**

**A** $y = 4x$

This equation represents a direct variation because it is in the form $y = kx$. The constant of variation is 4.

**B** $-3x + 5y = 0$

$-3x + 5y = 0$ *Solve the equation for y.*

$\underline{+3x \qquad\quad +3x}$ *Since −3x is added to y, add 3x to both sides.*

$5y = 3x$

$\frac{5y}{5} = \frac{3x}{5}$ *Since y is multiplied by 5, divide both sides by 5.*

$y = \frac{3}{5}x$

This equation represents a direct variation because it can be written in the form $y = kx$. The constant of variation is $\frac{3}{5}$.

**C** $2x + y = 10$

$2x + y = 10$ *Solve the equation for y.*

$\underline{-2x \qquad\quad -2x}$ *Since 2x is added to y, subtract 2x from both sides.*

$y = -2x + 10$

This equation does not represent a direct variation because it cannot be written in the form $y = kx$.

**Tell whether each equation represents a direct variation. If so, identify the constant of variation.**

**1a.** $3y = 4x + 1$ **1b.** $3x = -4y$ **1c.** $y + 3x = 0$

What happens if you solve $y = kx$ for $k$?

$y = kx$

$\frac{y}{x} = \frac{kx}{x}$ *Divide both sides by x (x ≠ 0).*

$\frac{y}{x} = k$

So, in a direct variation, the ratio $\frac{y}{x}$ is equal to the constant of variation. Another way to identify a direct variation is to check whether $\frac{y}{x}$ is the same for each ordered pair (except where $x = 0$).

## EXAMPLE 2 Identifying Direct Variations from Ordered Pairs

**Tell whether each relationship is a direct variation. Explain.**

| x | 1 | 3 | 5 |
|---|---|---|---|
| y | 6 | 18 | 30 |

**Method 1** Write an equation.

$y = 6x$ *Each y-value is 6 times the corresponding x-value.*

This is a direct variation because it can be written as $y = kx$, where $k = 6$.

**Method 2** Find $\frac{y}{x}$ for each ordered pair.

$\frac{6}{1} = 6$ $\frac{18}{3} = 6$ $\frac{30}{5} = 6$

This is a direct variation because $\frac{y}{x}$ is the same for each ordered pair.

| x | 2 | 4 | 8 |
|---|---|---|---|
| y | −2 | 0 | 4 |

**Method 1** Write an equation.

$y = x - 4$ *Each y-value is 4 less than the corresponding x-value.*

This is not a direct variation because it cannot be written as $y = kx$.

**Method 2** Find $\frac{y}{x}$ for each ordered pair.

$\frac{-2}{2} = -1$ $\frac{0}{4} = 0$ $\frac{4}{8} = \frac{1}{2}$

This is not a direct variation because $\frac{y}{x}$ is not the same for all ordered pairs.

**Tell whether each relationship is a direct variation. Explain.**

**2a.**

| x | y |
|---|---|
| −3 | 0 |
| 1 | 3 |
| 3 | 6 |

**2b.**

| x | y |
|---|---|
| 2.5 | −10 |
| 5 | −20 |
| 7.5 | −30 |

**2c.**

| x | y |
|---|---|
| −2 | 5 |
| 1 | 3 |
| 4 | 1 |

If you know one ordered pair that satisfies a direct variation, you can write the equation. You can also find other ordered pairs that satisfy the direct variation.

## EXAMPLE 3 Writing and Solving Direct Variation Equations

**The value of $y$ varies directly with $x$, and $y = 6$ when $x = 12$. Find $y$ when $x = 27$.**

**Method 1** Find the value of $k$ and then write the equation.

| | |
|---|---|
| $y = kx$ | *Write the equation for a direct variation.* |
| $6 = k(12)$ | *Substitute 6 for y and 12 for x. Solve for k.* |
| $\frac{1}{2} = k$ | *Since k is multiplied by 12, divide both sides by 12.* |

The equation is $y = \frac{1}{2}x$. When $x = 27$, $y = \frac{1}{2}(27) = 13.5$.

**Method 2** Use a proportion.

| | |
|---|---|
| $\frac{6}{12} = \frac{y}{27}$ | *In a direct variation, $\frac{y}{x}$ is the same for all values of x and y.* |
| $12y = 162$ | *Use cross products.* |
| $y = 13.5$ | *Since y is multiplied by 12, divide both sides by 12.* |

**3.** The value of $y$ varies directly with $x$, and $y = 4.5$ when $x = 0.5$. Find $y$ when $x = 10$.

## EXAMPLE 4 Graphing Direct Variations

**The three-toed sloth is an extremely slow animal. On the ground, it travels at a speed of about 6 feet per minute. Write a direct variation equation for the distance $y$ a sloth will travel in $x$ minutes. Then graph.**

**Step 1** Write a direct variation equation.

| distance | = | 6 feet per minute | times | number of minutes |
|---|---|---|---|---|
| $y$ | = | 6 | $\cdot$ | $x$ |

**Step 2** Choose values of $x$ and generate ordered pairs.

| $x$ | $y = 6x$ | $(x, y)$ |
|---|---|---|
| 0 | $y = 6(0) = 0$ | (0, 0) |
| 1 | $y = 6(1) = 6$ | (1, 6) |
| 2 | $y = 6(2) = 12$ | (2, 12) |

**Step 3** Graph the points and connect.

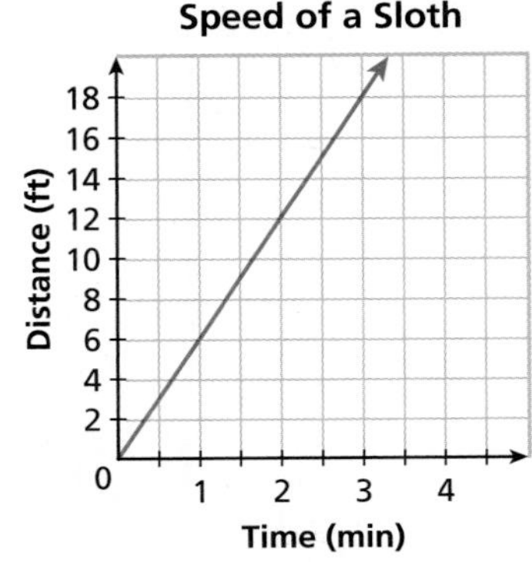

**4.** The perimeter $y$ of a square varies directly with its side length $x$. Write a direct variation equation for this relationship. Then graph.

Look at the graph in Example 4. It passes through (0, 0) and has a slope of 6. The graph of any direct variation $y = kx$

- is a line through (0, 0).
- has a slope of $k$.

## THINK AND DISCUSS

1. How do you know that a direct variation is linear?
2. Why does the graph of any direct variation pass through (0, 0)?

3. **GET ORGANIZED** Copy and complete the graphic organizer. In each box, describe how you can use the given information to identify a direct variation.

| Recognizing a Direct Variation | | |
|---|---|---|
| From an Equation | From Ordered Pairs | From a Graph |

# 5-5 Exercises

MA.A.2, MA.A.2.1, MA.A.2.2, MA.A.2.3, MA.A.5.1, MA.A.4.5

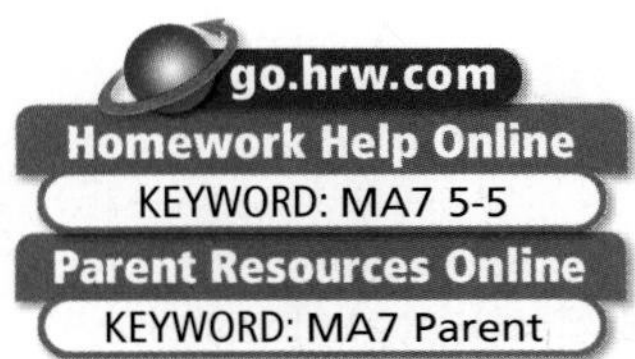


## GUIDED PRACTICE

1. **Vocabulary** If $x$ varies directly with $y$, then the relationship between the two variables is said to be a ___?___. (*direct variation* or *constant of variation*)

SEE EXAMPLE 1 p. 326

**Tell whether each equation represents a direct variation. If so, identify the constant of variation.**

2. $y = 4x + 9$
3. $2y = -8x$
4. $x + y = 0$

SEE EXAMPLE 2 p. 327

**Tell whether each relationship is a direct variation. Explain.**

5.

| $x$ | 10 | 5 | 2 |
|---|---|---|---|
| $y$ | 12 | 7 | 4 |

6.

| $x$ | 3 | −1 | −4 |
|---|---|---|---|
| $y$ | −6 | 2 | 8 |

SEE EXAMPLE 3 p. 328

7. The value of $y$ varies directly with $x$, and $y = -3$ when $x = 1$. Find $y$ when $x = -6$.
8. The value of $y$ varies directly with $x$, and $y = 6$ when $x = 18$. Find $y$ when $x = 12$.

SEE EXAMPLE 4 p. 328

9. **Wages** Cameron earns $5 per hour at her after-school job. The total amount of her paycheck varies directly with the amount of time she works. Write a direct variation equation for the amount of money $y$ that she earns for working $x$ hours. Then graph.

## PRACTICE AND PROBLEM SOLVING

**Tell whether each equation represents a direct variation. If so, identify the constant of variation.**

10. $y = \frac{1}{6}x$
11. $4y = x$
12. $x = 2y - 12$

**Tell whether each relationship is a direct variation. Explain.**

13.

| $x$ | 6 | 9 | 17 |
|---|---|---|---|
| $y$ | 13.2 | 19.8 | 37.4 |

14.

| $x$ | −6 | 3 | 12 |
|---|---|---|---|
| $y$ | 4 | −2 | −8 |

| Independent Practice | |
|---|---|
| For Exercises | See Example |
| 10–12 | 1 |
| 13–14 | 2 |
| 15–16 | 3 |
| 17 | 4 |

**Extra Practice**

Skills Practice p. S13
Application Practice p. S32

15. The value of $y$ varies directly with $x$, and $y = 8$ when $x = -32$. Find $y$ when $x = 64$.

16. The value of $y$ varies directly with $x$, and $y = \frac{1}{2}$ when $x = 3$. Find $y$ when $x = 1$.

17. While on his way to school, Norman saw that the cost of gasoline was $2.50 per gallon. Write a direct variation equation to describe the cost $y$ of $x$ gallons of gas. Then graph.

**Tell whether each relationship is a direct variation. Explain your answer.**

18. The equation $-15x + 4y = 0$ relates the length of a videotape in inches $x$ to its approximate playing time in seconds $y$.

19. The equation $y - 2.00x = 2.50$ relates the cost $y$ of a taxicab ride to distance $x$ of the cab ride in miles.

**Each ordered pair is a solution of a direct variation. Write the equation of direct variation. Then graph your equation and show that the slope of the line is equal to the constant of variation.**

| | | | |
|---|---|---|---|
| 20. $(2, 10)$ | 21. $(-3, 9)$ | 22. $(8, 2)$ | 23. $(1.5, 6)$ |
| 24. $(7, 21)$ | 25. $(1, 2)$ | 26. $(2, -16)$ | 27. $\left(\frac{1}{7}, 1\right)$ |
| 28. $(-2, 9)$ | 29. $(9, -2)$ | 30. $(4, 6)$ | 31. $(3, 4)$ |
| 32. $(5, 1)$ | 33. $(1, -6)$ | 34. $\left(-1, \frac{1}{2}\right)$ | 35. $(7, 2)$ |

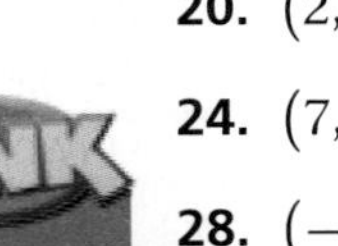


**Astronomy**

The Mars rover *Spirit* landed on Mars in January 2004 and immediately began sending photos of the planet's surface back to Earth.

36. **Astronomy** Weight varies directly with gravity. A Mars lander weighed 767 pounds on Earth but only 291 pounds on Mars. Its accompanying Mars rover weighed 155 pounds on Mars. How much did it weigh on Earth? Round your answer to the nearest pound.

37. **Environment** Mischa bought an energy-efficient washing machine. She will save about 15 gallons of water per wash load.
    a. Write an equation of direct variation to describe how many gallons of water $y$ Mischa saves for $x$ loads of laundry she washes.
    b. Graph your direct variation from part **a.** Is every point on the graph a solution in this situation? Why or why not?
    c. If Mischa does 2 loads of laundry per week, how many gallons of water will she have saved at the end of a year?

38. **Critical Thinking** If you double an $x$-value in a direct variation, will the corresponding $y$-value double? Explain.

39. **Write About It** In a direct variation $y = kx$, $k$ is sometimes called the "constant of proportionality." How are proportions related to direct variations?

**MULTI-STEP TEST PREP**

40. This problem will prepare you for the Multi-Step Test Prep on page 332.

    Rhea exercised on a treadmill at the gym. When she was finished, the display showed that she had walked at an average speed of 3 miles per hour.
    a. Write an equation that gives the number of miles $y$ that Rhea would cover in $x$ hours if she walked at this speed.
    b. Explain why this is a direct variation and find the value of $k$. What does this value represent in Rhea's situation?

## TEST PREP

MA.A.2, MA.A.2.1, MA.A.2.2, MA.A.2.3, MA.A.5.1, MA.A.4.5

41. Which equation does NOT represent a direct variation?

Ⓐ $y = \frac{1}{3}x$ Ⓑ $y = -2x$ Ⓒ $y = 4x + 1$ Ⓓ $6x - y = 0$

42. Identify which set of data represents a direct variation.

Ⓕ

| x | 1 | 2 | 3 |
|---|---|---|---|
| y | 1 | 2 | 3 |

Ⓗ

| x | 1 | 2 | 3 |
|---|---|---|---|
| y | 3 | 5 | 7 |

Ⓖ

| x | 1 | 2 | 3 |
|---|---|---|---|
| y | 0 | 1 | 2 |

Ⓙ

| x | 1 | 2 | 3 |
|---|---|---|---|
| y | 3 | 4 | 5 |

43. Two yards of fabric cost $13, and 5 yards of fabric cost $32.50. Which equation relates the cost of the fabric $c$ to its length $\ell$?

Ⓐ $c = 2.6\ell$ Ⓑ $c = 6.5\ell$ Ⓒ $c = 13\ell$ Ⓓ $c = 32.5\ell$

44. **Gridded Response** A car is traveling at a constant speed. After 3 hours, the car has traveled 180 miles. If the car continues to travel at the same constant speed, how many hours will it take to travel a total of 270 miles?

## CHALLENGE AND EXTEND

45. **Transportation** The function $y = 20x$ gives the number of miles $y$ that a gasoline-powered sport-utility vehicle (SUV) can travel on $x$ gallons of gas. The function $y = 60x$ gives the number of miles $y$ that a gas-electric hybrid car can travel on $x$ gallons of gas.
    a. If you drive 120 miles, how much gas will you save by driving the hybrid instead of the SUV?
    b. Graph both functions on the same coordinate plane. Will the lines ever meet? Explain.
    c. **What if...?** Shannon drives 15,000 miles in one year. How many gallons of gas will she use if she drives the SUV? the hybrid?

46. Suppose the equation $ax + by = c$, where $a$, $b$, and $c$ are real numbers, describes a direct variation. What do you know about the value of $c$?

## SPIRAL REVIEW

**Solve for the indicated variable.** *(Lesson 2-5)*

47. $p + 4q = 7; p$ 48. $\frac{s-5}{t} = 2; s$ 49. $xy + 2y = 4; x$

**Determine a relationship between the x- and y-values and write an equation.** *(Lesson 4-3)*

50.

| x | y |
|---|---|
| 1 | −5 |
| 2 | −4 |
| 3 | −3 |
| 4 | −2 |

51.

| x | y |
|---|---|
| 1 | −2 |
| 2 | −4 |
| 3 | −6 |
| 4 | −8 |

52.

| x | y |
|---|---|
| −3 | 9 |
| −2 | 6 |
| −1 | 3 |
| 0 | 0 |

**Find the slope of the line described by each equation.** *(Lesson 5-4)*

53. $4x + y = -9$ 54. $6x - 3y = -9$ 55. $5x = 10y - 5$

CHAPTER 5

# MULTI-STEP TEST PREP

SECTION 5A

## Characteristics of Linear Functions

**Heart Health** People who exercise need to be aware of their maximum heart rate.

1. One way to estimate your maximum heart rate $m$ is to subtract 85% of your age in years from 217. Create a table of values that shows the maximum heart rates for people ages 13 to 18. Then write an equation to describe the data in the table.
2. Use your table from Problem 1 to graph the relationship between age and maximum heart rate. What are the intercepts? What is the slope?
3. What do the intercepts represent in this situation?
4. What does the slope represent? Explain why the slope is negative.
5. Another formula for estimating maximum heart rate is $m = 206.3 - 0.711a$, where $a$ represents age in years. Describe how this equation is different from your equation in Problem 1. Include slope and intercepts in your description.
6. Which equation gives a higher maximum heart rate?
7. To be exercising in your *aerobic training zone* means that your heart rate is 70% to 80% of your maximum heart rate. Write two equations that someone could use to estimate the range of heart rates that are within his or her aerobic training zone. Use your equation for maximum heart rate from Problem 1.

# READY TO GO ON?

CHAPTER 5

SECTION 5A

## Quiz for Lessons 5-1 Through 5-5

### 5-1 Identifying Linear Functions

**Tell whether the given ordered pairs satisfy a linear function. Explain.**

1.

| $x$ | −2 | −1 | 0 | 1 | 2 |
|---|---|---|---|---|---|
| $y$ | 1 | 0 | 1 | 4 | 9 |

2. $\{(-3, 8), (-2, 6), (-1, 4), (0, 2), (1, 0)\}$

### 5-2 Using Intercepts

3. A baby pool that held 120 gallons of water is draining at a rate of 6 gal/min. The function $f(x) = 120 - 6x$ gives the amount of water in the pool after $x$ minutes. Graph the function and find its intercepts. What does each intercept represent?

**Use intercepts to graph the line described by each equation.**

4. $2x - 4y = 16$

5. $-3y + 6x = -18$

6. $y = -3x + 3$

### 5-3 Rate of Change and Slope

7. The chart gives the amount of water in a rain gauge in inches at various times. Graph this data and show the rates of change.

| Time (h) | 1 | 2 | 3 | 4 | 5 |
|---|---|---|---|---|---|
| Rain (in.) | 0.2 | 0.4 | 0.7 | 0.8 | 1.0 |

### 5-4 The Slope Formula

**Find the slope of each line. Then tell what the slope represents.**

8.

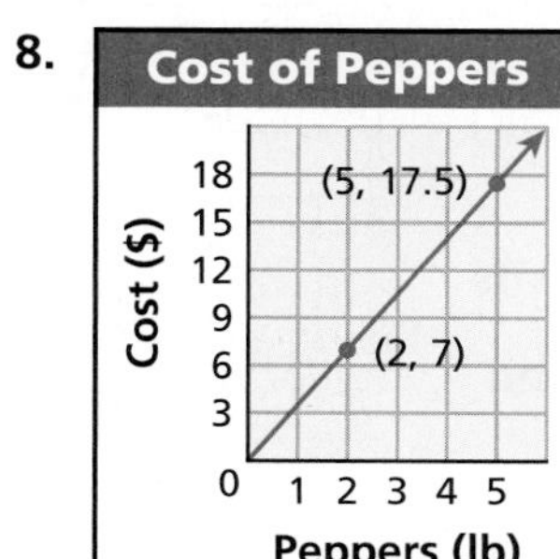


9.

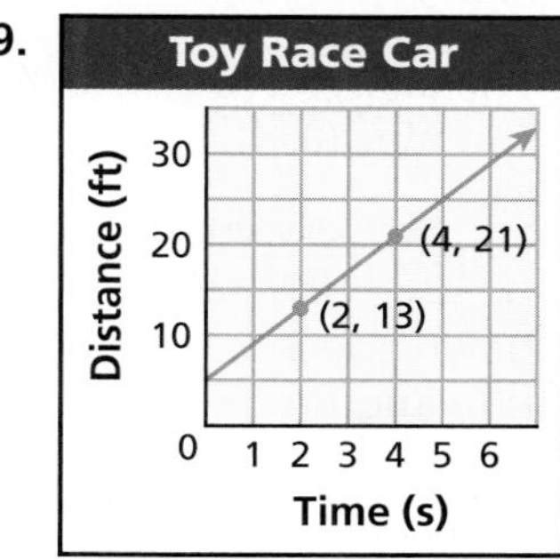


10.

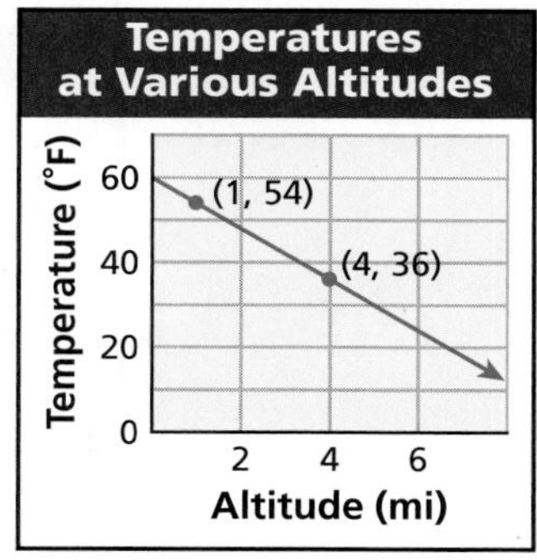


### 5-5 Direct Variation

**Tell whether each relationship is a direct variation. If so, identify the constant of variation.**

11.

| $x$ | 1 | 4 | 8 | 12 |
|---|---|---|---|---|
| $y$ | 3 | 6 | 10 | 14 |

12.

| $x$ | −6 | −2 | 0 | 3 |
|---|---|---|---|---|
| $y$ | −3 | −1 | 0 | 1.5 |

13. The value of $y$ varies directly with $x$, and $y = 10$ when $x = 4$. Find $x$ when $y = 14$.

# 5-6 Slope-Intercept Form

**MA.A.4.4** Represent linear functions in a variety of equivalent forms... *Also* **MA.A.4.3, MA.A.5.1, MA.A.4.5, MA.A.4.2**

***Objectives***

Write a linear equation in slope-intercept form.

Graph a line using slope-intercept form.

**Who uses this?**

Consumers can use slope-intercept form to model and calculate costs, such as the cost of renting a moving van. (See Example 4.)

You have seen that you can graph a line if you know two points on the line. Another way is to use the point that contains the $y$-intercept and the slope of the line.

## EXAMPLE 1 Graphing by Using Slope and $y$-intercept

**Graph each line given the slope and $y$-intercept.**

**A** slope $= \frac{3}{4}$; $y$-intercept $= -2$

**Step 1** The $y$-intercept is $-2$, so the line contains $(0, -2)$. Plot $(0, -2)$.

**Step 2** Slope $= \frac{\text{change in } y}{\text{change in } x} = \frac{3}{4}$. Count **3 units up** and **4 units right** from $(0, -2)$ and plot another point.

**Step 3** Draw the line through the two points.

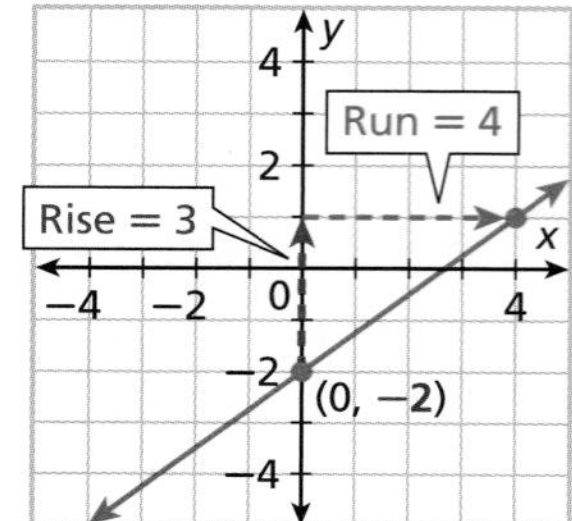


**B** slope $= -2$, $y$-intercept $= 4$

**Step 1** The $y$-intercept is 4, so the line contains $(0, 4)$. Plot $(0, 4)$.

**Step 2** Slope $= \frac{\text{change in } y}{\text{change in } x} = \frac{-2}{1}$. Count **2 units down** and **1 unit right** from $(0, 4)$ and plot another point.

**Step 3** Draw the line through the two points.

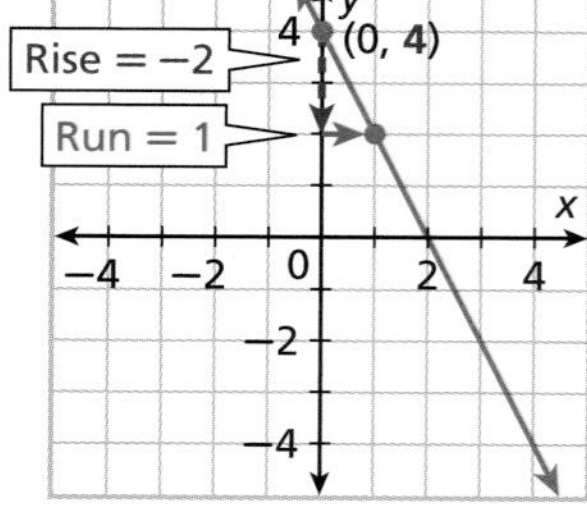


**Writing Math**

Any integer can be written as a fraction with 1 in the denominator.

$-2 = \frac{-2}{1}$

**Graph each line given the slope and $y$-intercept.**

**1a.** slope $= 2$, $y$-intercept $= -3$ **1b.** slope $= -\frac{2}{3}$, $y$-intercept $= 1$

If you know the slope of a line and the $y$-intercept, you can write an equation that describes the line.

**Step 1** If a line has slope 2 and the $y$-intercept is 3, then $m = 2$ and $(0, 3)$ is on the line. Substitute these values into the slope formula.

*Slope formula* $\rightarrow m = \frac{y_2 - y_1}{x_2 - x_1}$ $\quad 2 = \frac{y - 3}{x - 0}$ $\leftarrow$ *Since you don't know* $(x_2, y_2)$, *use* $(x, y)$.

**Step 2** Solve for $y$: $2 = \dfrac{y-3}{x-0}$

$2 = \dfrac{y-3}{x}$ *Simplify the denominator.*

$2 \cdot x = \left(\dfrac{y-3}{x}\right) \cdot x$ *Multiplication Property of Equality*

$2x = y - 3$

$\underline{+3} \quad \underline{+3}$ *Addition Property of Equality*

$2x + 3 = y$, or $y = 2x + 3$

**Slope-Intercept Form of a Linear Equation**

If a line has **slope** $m$ and the **y-intercept** is $b$, then the line is described by the equation $y = mx + b$.

Any linear equation can be written in slope-intercept form by solving for $y$ and simplifying. In this form, you can immediately see the slope and $y$-intercept. Also, you can quickly graph a line when the equation is written in slope-intercept form.

**Remember!**

Subtraction is the same as addition of the opposite.

$-12x - \frac{1}{2} =$

$-12x + \left(-\frac{1}{2}\right)$

## EXAMPLE 2 Writing Linear Equations in Slope-Intercept Form

**Write the equation that describes each line in slope-intercept form.**

**A** slope $= \frac{1}{3}$, $y$-intercept $= 6$

$y = mx + b$ *Substitute the given values for m and b.*

$y = \frac{1}{3}x + 6$ *Simplify if necessary.*

**B** slope $= -12$, $y$-intercept $= -\frac{1}{2}$

$y = mx + b$

$y = -12x + \left(-\frac{1}{2}\right)$

$y = -12x - \frac{1}{2}$

**C** slope $= 1$, $y$-intercept $= 0$

$y = mx + b$ *Substitute the given*

$y = 1x + 0$ *values for m and b.*

$y = x$ *Simplify.*

**D** slope $= 0$, $y$-intercept $= -5$

$y = mx + b$

$y = 0x + (-5)$

$y = -5$

**E** slope $= 4$, $(2, 5)$ is on the line

**Step 1** Find the $y$-intercept.

$y = mx + b$ *Write the slope-intercept form.*

$5 = 4(2) + b$ *Substitute 4 for m, 2 for x, and 5 for y.*

$5 = 8 + b$ *Solve for b. Use the Subtraction Property of Equality.*

$\underline{-8} \quad \underline{-8}$

$-3 = b$

**Step 2** Write the equation.

$y = mx + b$ *Write the slope-intercept form.*

$y = 4x + (-3)$ *Substitute 4 for m and −3 for b.*

$y = 4x - 3$

**2.** A line has slope 8 and $(3, -1)$ is on the line. Write the equation that describes this line in slope-intercept form.

## EXAMPLE 3 Using Slope-Intercept Form to Graph

**Write each equation in slope-intercept form. Then graph the line described by the equation.**

**A** $y = 4x - 3$

$y = 4x - 3$ is in the form $y = mx + b$.

slope: $m = 4 = \frac{4}{1}$

$y$-intercept: $b = -3$

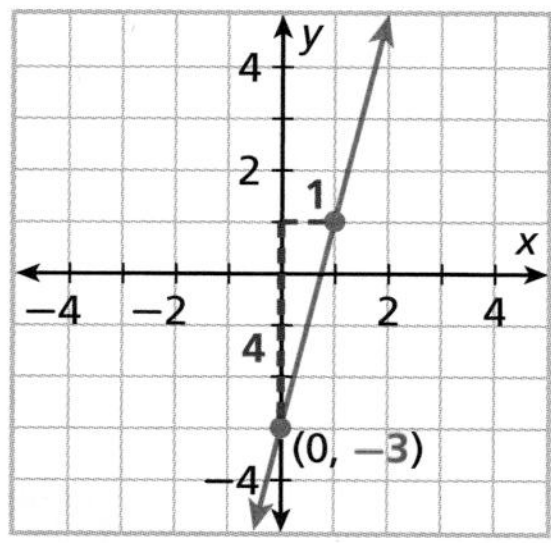


**Step 1** Plot $(0, -3)$.

**Step 2** Count **4 units up** and **1 unit right** and plot another point.

**Step 3** Draw the line connecting the two points.

**B** $y = -\frac{2}{3}x + 2$

$y = -\frac{2}{3}x + 2$ is in the form $y = mx + b$.

slope: $m = -\frac{2}{3} = \frac{-2}{3}$

$y$-intercept: $b = 2$

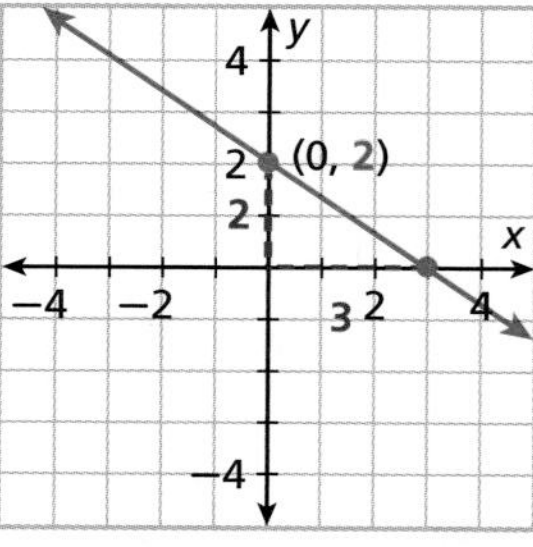


**Step 1** Plot $(0, 2)$

**Step 2** Count **2 units down** and **3 units right** and plot another point.

**Step 3** Draw the line connecting the two points.

**Helpful Hint**

To divide $(8 - 3x)$ by 2, you can multiply by $\frac{1}{2}$ and use the Distributive Property.

$$\frac{8 - 3x}{2} = \frac{1}{2}(8 - 3x)$$
$$= \frac{1}{2}(8) + \frac{1}{2}(-3x)$$
$$= 4 - \frac{3}{2}x$$

**C** $3x + 2y = 8$

**Step 1** Write the equation in slope-intercept form by solving for $y$.

$$3x + 2y = 8$$
$$\underline{-3x \qquad -3x}$$ *Subtraction Property of Equality*
$$2y = 8 - 3x$$

$$\frac{2y}{2} = \frac{8 - 3x}{2}$$ *Division Property of Equality*

$$y = 4 - \frac{3}{2}x$$ $\frac{3x}{2} = \frac{3}{2}x$

$$y = -\frac{3}{2}x + 4$$ *Write the equation in the form $y = mx + b$.*

**Step 2** Graph the line.

$y = -\frac{3}{2}x + 4$ is in the form $y = mx + b$.

slope: $m = -\frac{3}{2} = \frac{-3}{2}$

$y$-intercept: $b = 4$

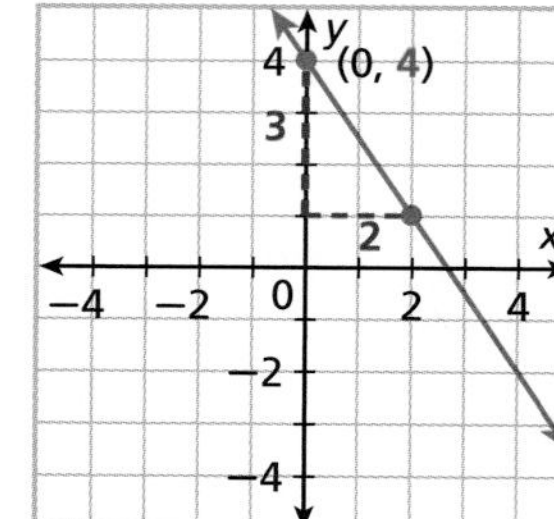


- Plot $(0, 4)$.
- Then count **3 units down** and **2 units right** and plot another point.
- Draw the line connecting the two points.

**Write each equation in slope-intercept form. Then graph the line described by the equation.**

**3a.** $y = \frac{2}{3}x$ **3b.** $6x + 2y = 10$ **3c.** $y = -4$

## EXAMPLE 4 *Consumer Application*

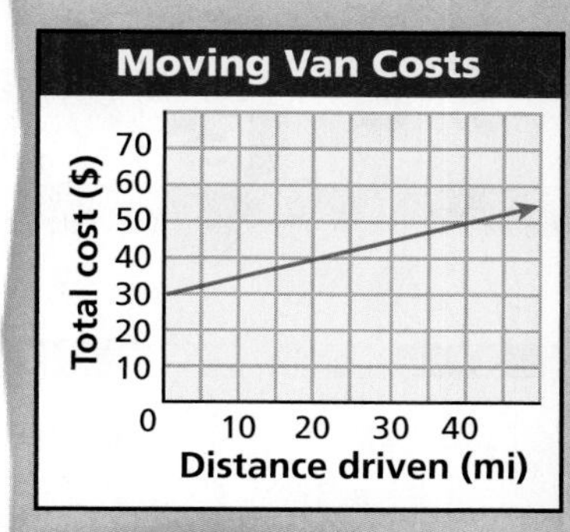


**To rent a van, a moving company charges \$30.00 plus \$0.50 per mile. The cost as a function of the number of miles driven is shown in the graph.**

**a. Write an equation that represents the cost as a function of the number of miles.**

| Cost | is | \$0.50 per mile | times | miles | plus | \$30.00 |
|---|---|---|---|---|---|---|
| $y$ | $=$ | 0.5 | $\cdot$ | $x$ | $+$ | 30 |

An equation is $y = 0.5x + 30$.

**b. Identify the slope and $y$-intercept and describe their meanings.**

The $y$-intercept is 30. This is the cost for 0 miles, or the initial fee of \$30.00.

The slope is 0.5. This is the rate of change of the cost: \$0.50 per mile.

**c. You are moving a distance of 150 miles and have budgeted \$100 for renting the van. Is this enough money? Explain.**

$y = 0.5x + 30 = 0.5(150) + 30 = 105$ *Substitute 150 for x.*

The cost for 150 miles is \$105. You have not budgeted enough money to rent the van.

4. A caterer charges a \$200 fee plus \$18 per person served. The cost as a function of the number of guests is shown in the graph.

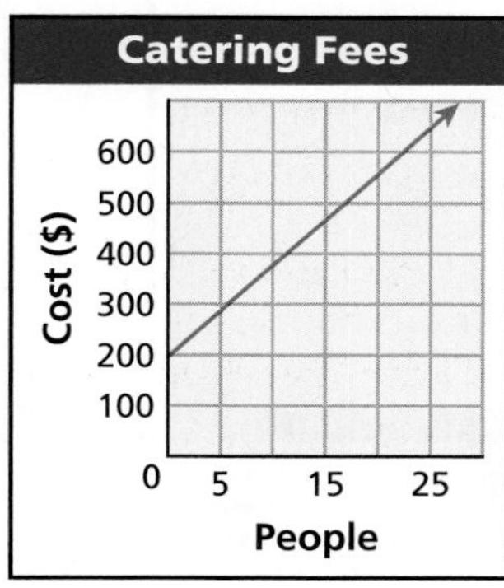


   a. Write an equation that represents the cost as a function of the number of guests.
   b. Identify the slope and $y$-intercept and describe their meanings.
   c. If you have \$4000, can you hold an event for 200 guests? Explain.

## THINK AND DISCUSS

1. If a linear function has a $y$-intercept of $b$, at what point does its graph cross the $y$-axis?
2. Where does the line described by $y = 4.395x - 23.75$ cross the $y$-axis?

3. **GET ORGANIZED** Copy and complete the graphic organizer.

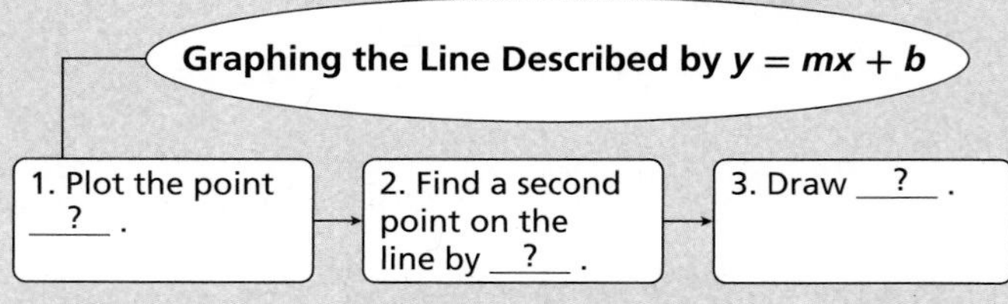

# 5-6 Exercises

MA.A.4.4, MA.A.4.3, MA.A.5.1, MA.A.4.5, MA.A.4.2

go.hrw.com
Homework Help Online
KEYWORD: MA7 5-6
Parent Resources Online
KEYWORD: MA7 Parent

## GUIDED PRACTICE

SEE EXAMPLE 1 p. 334

**Graph each line given the slope and $y$-intercept.**

1. slope $= \frac{1}{3}$, $y$-intercept $= -3$
2. slope $= 0.5$, $y$-intercept $= 3.5$
3. slope $= 5$, $y$-intercept $= -1$
4. slope $= -2$, $y$-intercept $= 2$

SEE EXAMPLE 2 p. 335

**Write the equation that describes each line in slope-intercept form.**

5. slope $= 8$, $y$-intercept $= 2$
6. slope $= \frac{1}{2}$, $y$-intercept $= -6$
7. slope $= 0$, $y$-intercept $= -3$
8. slope $= 5$, the point $(2, 7)$ is on the line

SEE EXAMPLE 3 p. 336

**Write each equation in slope-intercept form. Then graph the line described by the equation.**

9. $y = \frac{2}{5}x - 6$
10. $3x - y = 1$
11. $2x + y = 4$

SEE EXAMPLE 4 p. 337

12. Helen is in a bicycle race. She has already biked 10 miles and is now biking at a rate of 18 miles per hour. Her distance as a function of time is shown in the graph.
    a. Write an equation that represents the distance Helen has biked as a function of time.
    b. Identify the slope and $y$-intercept and describe their meanings.
    c. How far will Helen have biked after 2 hours?

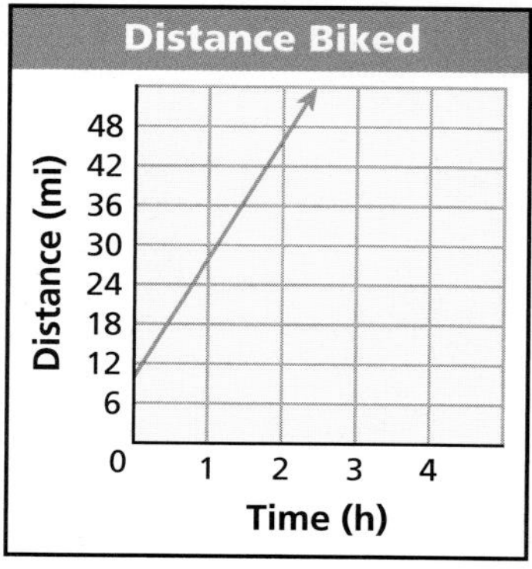


## PRACTICE AND PROBLEM SOLVING

| Independent Practice | |
|---|---|
| For Exercises | See Example |
| 13–16 | 1 |
| 17–20 | 2 |
| 21–29 | 3 |
| 30 | 4 |

**Extra Practice**
Skills Practice p. S13
Application Practice p. S32

**Graph each line given the slope and $y$-intercept.**

13. slope $= \frac{1}{4}$, $y$-intercept $= 7$
14. slope $= -6$, $y$-intercept $= -3$
15. slope $= 1$, $y$-intercept $= -4$
16. slope $= -\frac{4}{5}$, $y$-intercept $= 6$

**Write the equation that describes each line in slope-intercept form.**

17. slope $= 5$, $y$-intercept $= -9$
18. slope $= -\frac{2}{3}$, $y$-intercept $= 2$
19. slope $= -\frac{1}{2}$, $(6, 4)$ is on the line
20. slope $= 0$, $(6, -8)$ is on the line

**Write each equation in slope-intercept form. Then graph the line described by the equation.**

21. $y = -\frac{1}{2}x + 3$
22. $y = \frac{1}{3}x - 5$
23. $y = x + 6$
24. $6x + 3y = 12$
25. $y = \frac{7}{2}$
26. $4x + y = 9$
27. $-\frac{1}{2}x + y = 4$
28. $\frac{2}{3}x + y = 2$
29. $2x + y = 8$

**30. Fitness** Pauline's health club has an enrollment fee of \$175 and costs \$35 per month. Total cost as a function of number of membership months is shown in the graph.

a. Write an equation that represents the total cost as a function of months.

b. Identify the slope and $y$-intercept and describe their meanings.

c. Find the cost of one year of membership.

**Health Club Membership Costs**

Cost (\$): 0, 50, 100, 150, 200, 250

Months: 1, 2, 3, 4

**31. ERROR ANALYSIS** Two students wrote $3x + 2y = 5$ in slope-intercept form. Who is incorrect? Describe the error.

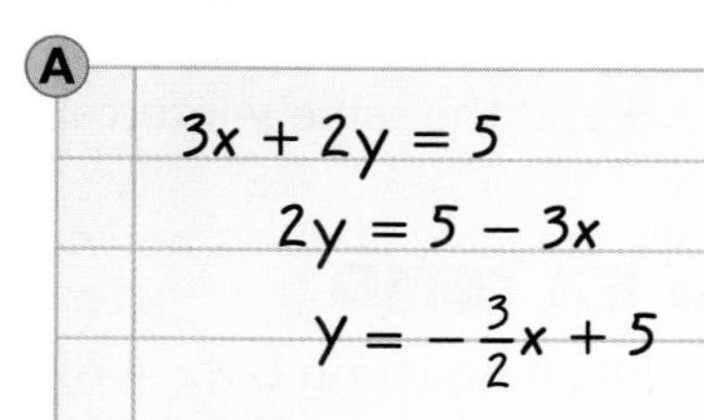


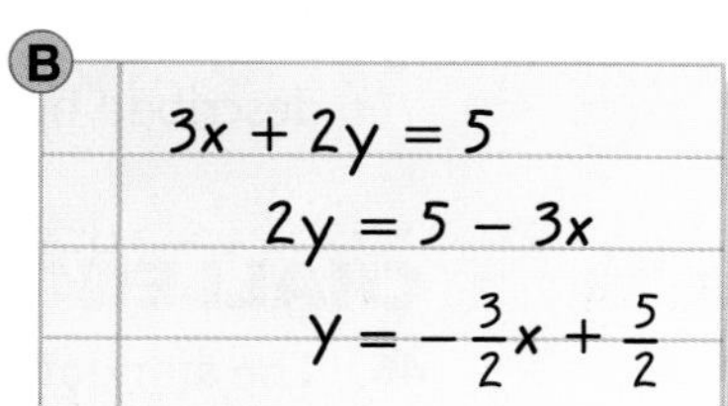


**Critical Thinking Tell whether each situation is possible or impossible. If possible, draw a sketch of the graphs. If impossible, explain.**

**32.** Two different lines have the same slope.

**33.** Two different linear functions have the same $y$-intercept.

**34.** Two intersecting lines have the same slope.

**35.** A linear function does not have a $y$-intercept.

**Match each equation with its corresponding graph.**

**36.** $y = 2x - 1$

**37.** $y = \frac{1}{2}x - 1$

**38.** $y = -\frac{1}{2}x + 1$

**A.**

**B.**

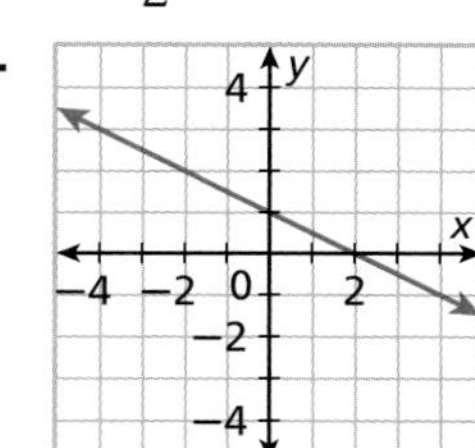


**C.**

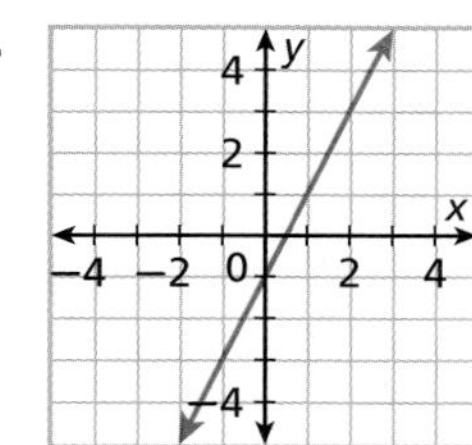


**39. Write About It** Write an equation that describes a vertical line. Can you write this equation in slope-intercept form? Why or why not?

**40.** This problem will prepare you for the Multi-Step Test Prep on page 364.

a. Ricardo and Sam walk from Sam's house to school. Sam lives 3 blocks from Ricardo's house. The graph shows their distance from Ricardo's house as they walk to school. Create a table of these values.

b. Find an equation for the distance as a function of time.

c. What are the slope and $y$-intercept? What do they represent in this situation?

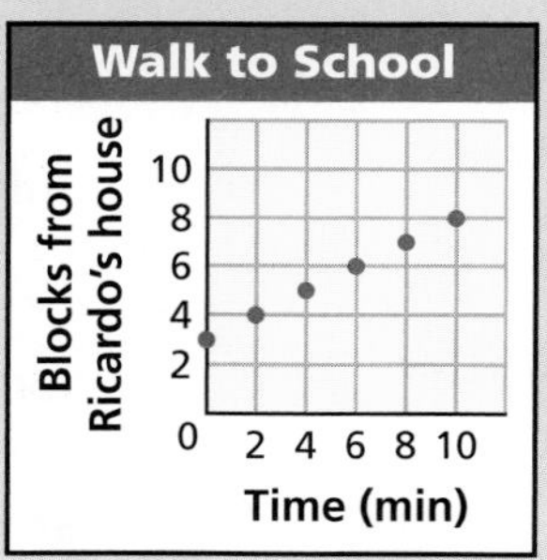

## TEST PREP

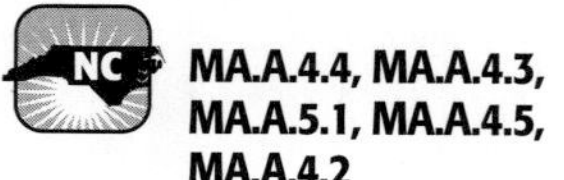

MA.A.4.4, MA.A.4.3, MA.A.5.1, MA.A.4.5, MA.A.4.2

**41.** Which function has the same $y$-intercept as $y = \frac{1}{2}x - 2$?

(A) $2x + 3y = 6$ (B) $x + 4y = -8$ (C) $-\frac{1}{2}x + y = 4$ (D) $\frac{1}{2}x - 2y = -2$

**42.** What is the slope-intercept form of $x - y = -8$?

(F) $y = -x - 8$ (G) $y = x - 8$ (H) $y = -x + 8$ (J) $y = x + 8$

**43.** Which function has a $y$-intercept of 3?

(A) $2x - y = 3$ (B) $2x + y = 3$ (C) $2x + y = 6$ (D) $y = 3x$

**44.** **Gridded Response** What is the slope of the line described by $-6x = -2y + 5$?

**45.** **Short Response** Write a function whose graph has the same slope as the line described by $3x - 9y = 9$ and the same $y$-intercept as $8x - 2y = 6$. Show your work.

## CHALLENGE AND EXTEND

**46.** The standard form of a linear equation is $Ax + By = C$. Rewrite this equation in slope-intercept form. What is the slope? What is the $y$-intercept?

**47.** What value of $n$ in the equation $nx + 5 = 3y$ would give a line with slope $-2$?

**48.** If $b$ is the $y$-intercept of a linear function whose graph has slope $m$, then $y = mx + b$ describes the line. Below is an incomplete justification of this statement. Fill in the missing information.

| Statements | Reasons |
|---|---|
| 1. $m = \dfrac{y_1 - x_1}{y_2 - x_2}$ | 1. Slope formula |
| 2. $m = \dfrac{y - b}{x - 0}$ | 2. By definition, if $b$ is the $y$-intercept, then $(\blacksquare, b)$ is a point on the line. $(x, y)$ is any other point on the line. |
| 3. $m = \dfrac{y - b}{x}$ | 3. ___?___ |
| 4. $m\blacksquare = y - b$ | 4. Multiplication Property of Equality (Multiply both sides of the equation by $x$.) |
| 5. $mx + b = y$, or $y = mx + b$ | 5. ___?___ |

## SPIRAL REVIEW

**Define a variable and write an inequality for each situation. Graph the solutions.** *(Lesson 3-1)*

**49.** Molly has, at most, 2 hours to work out at the gym today.

**50.** Mishenko is hoping to save at least $300 this month.

**Solve each inequality.** *(Lesson 3-5)*

**51.** $3n \leq 2n + 8$ **52.** $4x - 4 > 2(x + 5)$ **53.** $2(2t + 1) > 6t + 8$

**Tell whether each equation is a direct variation. If so, identify the constant of variation.** *(Lesson 5-5)*

**54.** $12x = 3y$ **55.** $y = -2x + 6$ **56.** $y = -x$

# 5-7 Point-Slope Form

**MA.A.4.4** Represent linear functions in a variety of equivalent forms (including point-slope). *Also* **MA.G.1.1, MA.A.4.3, MA.A.5.1, MA.A.4.5**

***Objectives***

Graph a line and write a linear equation using point-slope form.

Write a linear equation given two points.

**Why learn this?**

You can use point-slope form to represent a cost function, such as the cost of placing a newspaper ad. (See Example 5.)

In Lesson 5-6, you saw that if you know the slope of a line and the $y$-intercept, you can graph the line. You can also graph a line if you know its slope and any point on the line.

## EXAMPLE 1 Using Slope and a Point to Graph

**Graph the line with the given slope that contains the given point.**

**A** **slope = 3; (1, 1)**

**Step 1** Plot (1, 1).

**Step 2** Use the slope to move from (1, 1) to another point.

$$\text{slope} = \frac{\text{change in } y}{\text{change in } x} = 3 = \frac{3}{1}$$

Move **3 units up** and **1 unit right** and plot another point.

**Step 3** Draw the line connecting the two points.

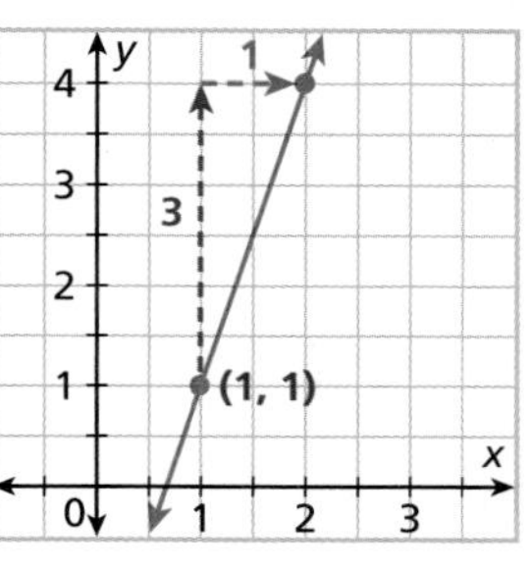


**Helpful Hint**

For a negative fraction, you can write the negative sign in one of three places.

$$-\frac{1}{2} = \frac{-1}{2} = \frac{1}{-2}$$

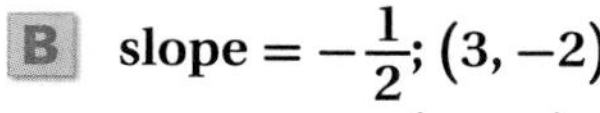

**B** **slope = $-\frac{1}{2}$; (3, −2)**

**Step 1** Plot (3, −2).

**Step 2** Use the slope to move from (3, −2) to another point.

$$\text{slope} = \frac{\text{change in } y}{\text{change in } x} = \frac{1}{-2} = -\frac{1}{2}$$

Move **1 unit up** and **2 units left** and plot another point.

**Step 3** Draw the line connecting the two points.

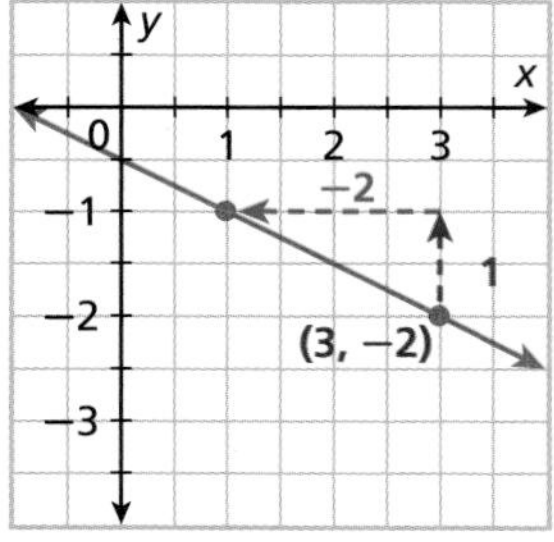


**C** **slope = 0; (3, 2)**

A line with slope of 0 is horizontal.

Draw the horizontal line through (3, 2).

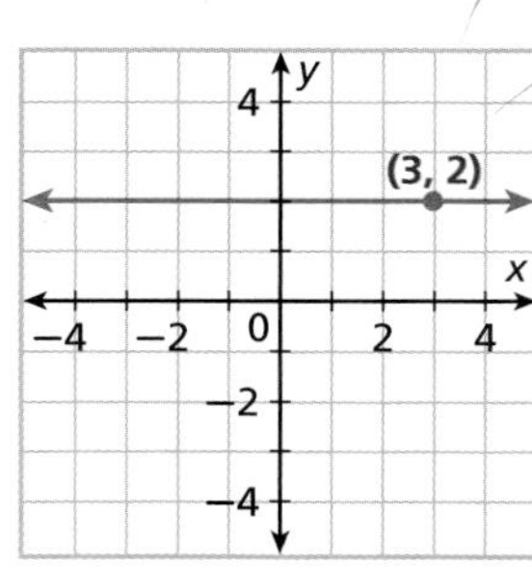

**1.** Graph the line with slope −1 that contains (2, −2).

If you know the slope and any point on the line, you can write an equation of the line by using the slope formula. For example, suppose a line has a slope of 3 and contains $(2, 1)$. Let $(x, y)$ be any other point on the line.

Slope formula

$$m = \frac{y_2 - y_1}{x_2 - x_1} \longrightarrow 3 = \frac{y-1}{x-2}$$ *Substitute into the slope formula.*

$$3(x-2) = \left(\frac{y-1}{x-2}\right)(x-2)$$ *Multiplication Property of Equality*

$$3(x-2) = y - 1$$ *Simplify.*

$$y - 1 = 3(x-2)$$

**Point-Slope Form of a Linear Equation**

The line with slope $m$ that contains the point $(x_1, y_1)$ can be described by the equation $y - y_1 = m(x - x_1)$.

## EXAMPLE 2 Writing Linear Equations in Point-Slope Form

**Write an equation in point-slope form for the line with the given slope that contains the given point.**

**A** slope $= \frac{5}{2}$; $(-3, 0)$

$$y - y_1 = m(x - x_1)$$
$$y - 0 = \frac{5}{2}[x - (-3)]$$
$$y - 0 = \frac{5}{2}(x + 3)$$

**B** slope $= -7$; $(4, 2)$

$$y - y_1 = m(x - x_1)$$
$$y - 2 = -7(x - 4)$$

**C** slope $= 0$; $(-2, -3)$

$$y - y_1 = m(x - x_1)$$
$$y - (-3) = 0[x - (-2)]$$
$$y + 3 = 0(x + 2)$$

**Write an equation in point-slope form for the line with the given slope that contains the given point.**

**2a.** slope $= 2$; $\left(\frac{1}{2}, 1\right)$ **2b.** slope $= 0$; $(3, -4)$

## EXAMPLE 3 Writing Linear Equations in Slope-Intercept Form

**Write an equation in slope-intercept form for the line with slope $-4$ that contains $(-1, -2)$.**

**Step 1** Write the equation in point-slope form: $y - y_1 = m(x - x_1)$

$$y - (-2) = -4[x - (-1)]$$

**Step 2** Write the equation in slope-intercept form by solving for $y$.

$$y - (-2) = -4[x - (-1)]$$

$$y + 2 = -4(x + 1)$$ *Rewrite subtraction of negative numbers as addition.*

$$y + 2 = -4x - 4$$ *Distributive Property*

$$\underline{-2} \qquad \underline{-2}$$ *Subtraction Property of Equality*

$$y = -4x - 6$$

**3.** Write an equation in slope-intercept form for the line with slope $\frac{1}{3}$ that contains $(-3, 1)$.

## EXAMPLE 4 Using Two Points to Write an Equation

**Write an equation in slope-intercept form for the line through the two points.**

**A** $(1, -4)$ **and** $(3, 2)$

**Step 1** Find the slope.

$$m = \frac{y_2 - y_1}{x_2 - x_1} = \frac{2 - (-4)}{3 - 1} = \frac{6}{2} = 3$$

**Step 2** Substitute the slope and one of the points into the point-slope form.

$$y - y_1 = m(x - x_1)$$

$$y - 2 = 3(x - 3) \quad \textit{Choose (3, 2).}$$

**Step 3** Write the equation in slope-intercept form.

$$y - 2 = 3(x - 3)$$

$$y - 2 = 3x - 9$$

$$\underline{+2} \quad \underline{+2}$$

$$y = 3x - 7$$

**B** $(4, -7)$ **and** $(0, 5)$

**Step 1** Find the slope.

$$m = \frac{y_2 - y_1}{x_2 - x_1} = \frac{5 - (-7)}{0 - 4} = \frac{12}{-4} = -3$$

**Step 2** Substitute the slope and one of the points into the point-slope form.

$$y - y_1 = m(x - x_1)$$

$$y - (-7) = -3(x - 4) \quad \textit{Choose (4, −7).}$$

$$y + 7 = -3(x - 4)$$

**Step 3** Write the equation in slope-intercept form.

$$y + 7 = -3(x - 4)$$

$$y + 7 = -3x + 12$$

$$\underline{-7} \quad \underline{-7}$$

$$y = -3x + 5$$

**Helpful Hint**

After Step 1 of Example 4B, you could have written the equation in slope-intercept form immediately, because one of the given points contained the *y*-intercept.

**Write an equation in slope-intercept form for the line through the two points.**

**4a.** $(1, -2)$ and $(3, 10)$

**4b.** $(6, 3)$ and $(0, -1)$

## EXAMPLE 5 *Problem-Solving Application*

PROBLEM SOLVING

**The cost to place an ad in a newspaper for one week is a linear function of the number of lines in the ad. The costs for 3, 5, and 10 lines are shown. Write an equation in slope-intercept form that represents the function. If you have $50, can you place an ad that is 18 lines long? Explain.**

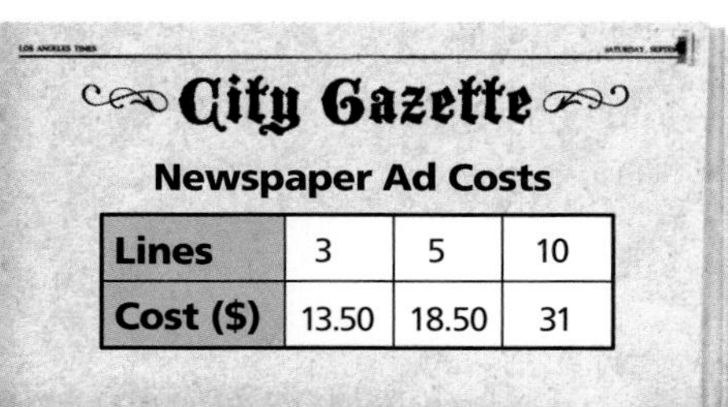

City Gazette

**Newspaper Ad Costs**

| Lines | 3 | 5 | 10 |
|---|---|---|---|
| Cost ($) | 13.50 | 18.50 | 31 |

### 1 Understand the Problem

- The **answer** will have two parts—an equation in slope-intercept form and whether you can place an ad that is 18 lines long.
- The ordered pairs given in the table—(3, 13.50), (5, 18.50), and (10, 31)—satisfy the equation.

### Make a Plan

You can use two of the ordered pairs to find the slope. Then use point-slope form to write the equation. Finally, write the equation in slope-intercept form.

**3 Solve**

**Step 1** Choose any two ordered pairs from the table to find the slope.

$$m = \frac{y_2 - y_1}{x_2 - x_1} = \frac{\mathbf{18.50} - \mathbf{13.50}}{\mathbf{5} - \mathbf{3}} = \frac{5}{2} = 2.5 \quad \textit{Use (3, 13.50) and (5, 18.50).}$$

**Step 2** Substitute the slope and any ordered pair from the table into the point-slope form.

$y - y_1 = m(x - x_1)$

$y - \mathbf{31} = \mathbf{2.5}(x - \mathbf{10})$ *Use (10, 31).*

**Step 3** Write the equation in slope-intercept form by solving for $y$.

$y - 31 = 2.5(x - 10)$

$y - 31 = 2.5x - 25$ *Distributive Property*

$y = 2.5x + 6$ *Addition Property of Equality*

**Step 4** Find the cost of an ad containing 18 lines by substituting 18 for $x$.

$y = 2.5x + 6 = 2.5(\mathbf{18}) + 6 = 51$

The cost of an ad containing 18 lines is \$51. Since you have only \$50, you cannot place an ad containing 18 lines.

**Look Back**

If the equation is correct, the ordered pairs that you did not use in Step 2 will be solutions. Substitute (3, 13.50) and (5, 18.50) into the equation.

| $y = 2.5x + 6$ | |
|---|---|
| **13.50** | $2.5(\mathbf{3}) + 6$ |
| 13.5 | $7.5 + 6$ |
| 13.5 | 13.5 ✓ |

| $y = 2.5x + 6$ | |
|---|---|
| **18.50** | $2.5(\mathbf{5}) + 6$ |
| 18.5 | $12.5 + 6$ |
| 18.5 | 18.5 ✓ |

**5. What if...?** At a different newspaper, the costs to place an ad for one week are shown. Write an equation in slope-intercept form that represents this linear function. If you have \$65, can you place an ad that is 21 lines long? Explain.

| Lines | Cost (\$) |
|---|---|
| 3 | 12.75 |
| 5 | 17.25 |
| 10 | 28.50 |

## THINK AND DISCUSS

**1.** How are point-slope form and slope-intercept form alike? different?

**2.** When is point-slope form useful? When is slope-intercept form useful?

**3. GET ORGANIZED** Copy and complete the graphic organizer. In each box, describe how to find the equation of a line by using the given method.

**Writing the Equation of a Line**

- If you know two points on the line
- If you know the slope and *y*-intercept
- If you know the slope and a point on the line

# 5-7 Exercises

MA.A.4.4, MA.G.1.1, MA.A.4.3, MA.A.5.1, MA.A.4.5

go.hrw.com
Homework Help Online
KEYWORD: MA7 5-7
Parent Resources Online
KEYWORD: MA7 Parent

## GUIDED PRACTICE

SEE EXAMPLE 1 p. 341

**Graph the line with the given slope that contains the given point.**

1. slope $= 1$; $(1, 0)$
2. slope $= -1$; $(3, 1)$
3. slope $= -2$; $(-4, -2)$

SEE EXAMPLE 2 p. 342

**Write an equation in point-slope form for the line with the given slope that contains the given point.**

4. slope $= \frac{1}{5}$; $(2, -6)$
5. slope $= -4$; $(1, 5)$
6. slope $= 0$; $(3, -7)$

SEE EXAMPLE 3 p. 342

**Write an equation in slope-intercept form for the line with the given slope that contains the given point.**

7. slope $= -\frac{1}{3}$; $(-3, 8)$
8. slope $= 2$; $(1, 1)$
9. slope $= \frac{1}{3}$; $(-6, -2)$
10. slope $= 2$; $(-1, 1)$
11. slope $= 3$; $(2, -7)$
12. slope $= -4$; $(4, 2)$

SEE EXAMPLE 4 p. 343

**Write an equation in slope-intercept form for the line through the two points.**

13. $(-2, 2)$ and $(2, -2)$
14. $(0, -4)$ and $(1, -6)$
15. $(1, 1)$ and $(-5, 3)$
16. $(-3, 1)$ and $(0, 10)$
17. $(7, 8)$ and $(6, 9)$
18. $(0, -2)$ and $(2, 8)$

SEE EXAMPLE 5 p. 343

19. **Measurement** An oil tank is being filled at a constant rate. The depth of the oil is a function of the number of minutes the tank has been filling, as shown in the table. Write an equation in slope-intercept form that represents this linear function. Then find the depth of the oil after one-half hour.

| Time (min) | Depth (ft) |
|---|---|
| 0 | 3 |
| 10 | 5 |
| 15 | 6 |

## PRACTICE AND PROBLEM SOLVING

**Independent Practice**

| For Exercises | See Example |
|---|---|
| 20–22 | 1 |
| 23–28 | 2 |
| 29–34 | 3 |
| 35–40 | 4 |
| 41 | 5 |

**Extra Practice**

Skills Practice p. S13
Application Practice p. S32

**Graph the line with the given slope that contains the given point.**

20. slope $= -\frac{1}{2}$; $(-3, 4)$
21. slope $= \frac{3}{5}$; $(1, -2)$
22. slope $= 4$; $(-1, 0)$

**Write an equation in point-slope form for the line with the given slope that contains the given point.**

23. slope $= \frac{2}{9}$; $(-1, 5)$
24. slope $= 0$; $(4, -2)$
25. slope $= 8$; $(1, 8)$
26. slope $= \frac{1}{2}$; $(-8, 3)$
27. slope $= 3$; $(4, 7)$
28. slope $= -2$; $(-1, 3)$

**Write an equation in slope-intercept form for the line with the given slope that contains the given point.**

29. slope $= -\frac{2}{7}$; $(14, -3)$
30. slope $= \frac{4}{5}$; $(-15, 1)$
31. slope $= -\frac{1}{4}$; $(4, -1)$
32. slope $= -6$; $(9, 3)$
33. slope $= -5$; $(2, 3)$
34. slope $= \frac{1}{5}$; $(-5, -2)$

**Write an equation in slope-intercept form for the line through the two points.**

35. $(7, 8)$ and $(-7, 6)$
36. $(2, 7)$ and $(-4, 4)$
37. $(-1, 2)$ and $(4, -23)$
38. $(4, -1)$ and $(-8, -10)$
39. $(0, 11)$ and $(-7, -3)$
40. $(1, 27)$ and $(-2, 12)$

As altitude increases, the amount of breathable oxygen decreases. At elevations above 8000 feet, this can cause altitude sickness. To prevent this, mountain climbers often use tanks containing a mixture of air and pure oxygen.

41. **Science** At higher altitudes, water boils at lower temperatures. This relationship between altitude and boiling point is linear. The table shows some altitudes and the corresponding boiling points. Write an equation in slope-intercept form that represents this linear function. Then find the boiling point at 6000 feet.

| Boiling Point of Water | |
|---|---|
| Altitude (ft) | Temperature (°F) |
| 1000 | 210 |
| 1500 | 209 |
| 3000 | 206 |

**The tables show linear relationships between $x$ and $y$. Copy and complete the tables.**

42.

| $x$ | −2 | 0 | | 7 |
|---|---|---|---|---|
| $y$ | −18 | | 12 | 27 |

43.

| $x$ | −4 | 1 | 0 | |
|---|---|---|---|---|
| $y$ | 14 | 4 | | −6 |

44. **///ERROR ANALYSIS///** Two students used point-slope form to find an equation that describes the line with slope −3 through $(-5, 2)$. Who is incorrect? Explain the error.

A

$y - y_1 = m(x - x_1)$

$y - 2 = -3(x - 5)$

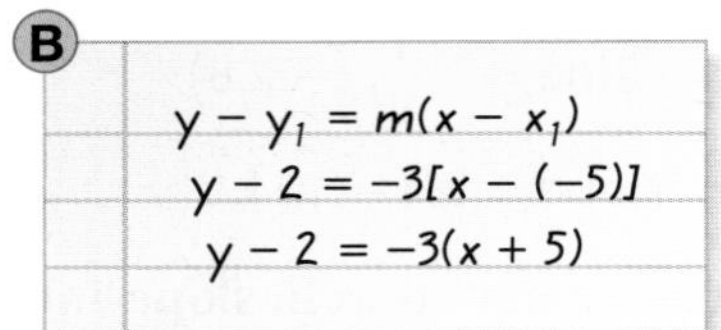


45. **Critical Thinking** Compare the methods for finding the equation that describes a line when you know
- a point on the line and the slope of the line.
- two points on the line.

How are the methods alike? How are they different?

46. **Write About It** Explain why the first statement is false but the second is true.
- All linear equations can be written in point-slope form.
- All linear equations that describe functions can be written in point-slope form.

47. **Multi-Step** The table shows the mean combined (verbal and math) SAT scores for several different years.

| Years Since 1980 | 0 | 5 | 10 | 17 | 21 |
|---|---|---|---|---|---|
| Mean Combined Score | 994 | 1009 | 1001 | 1016 | 1020 |

a. Make a scatter plot of the data and add a trend line to your graph.
b. Use your trend line to estimate the slope and $y$-intercept, and write an equation in slope-intercept form.
c. What do the slope and $y$-intercept represent in this situation?

48. This problem will prepare you for the Multi-Step Test Prep on page 364.
a. Stephen is walking from his house to his friend Sharon's house. When he is 12 blocks away, he looks at his watch. He looks again when he is 8 blocks away and finds that 6 minutes have passed. Write two ordered pairs for these data in the form (time, blocks).
b. Write a linear equation for these two points.
c. What is the total amount of time it takes Stephen to reach Sharon's house? Explain how you found your answer.

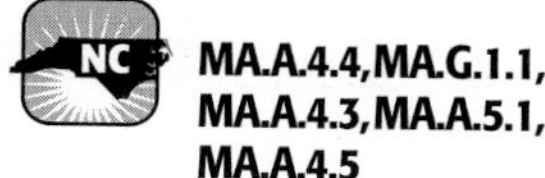

MA.A.4.4, MA.G.1.1, MA.A.4.3, MA.A.5.1, MA.A.4.5

**49.** Which equation describes the line through $(-5, 1)$ with slope of 1?

Ⓐ $y + 1 = x - 5$
Ⓑ $y + 5 = x - 1$
Ⓒ $y - 1 = -5(x - 1)$
Ⓓ $y - 1 = x + 5$

**50.** A line contains (4, 4) and (5, 2). What are the slope and $y$-intercept?

Ⓕ slope = −2 ; $y$-intercept = 2
Ⓖ slope = 1.2 ; $y$-intercept = −2
Ⓗ slope = −2; $y$-intercept = 12
Ⓙ slope = 12; $y$-intercept = 1.2

## CHALLENGE AND EXTEND

**51.** A linear function has the same $y$-intercept as $x + 4y = 8$ and its graph contains the point $(2, 7)$. Find the slope and $y$-intercept.

**52.** Write the equation of a line in slope-intercept form that contains $\left(\frac{3}{4}, \frac{1}{2}\right)$ and has the same slope as the line described by $y + 3x = 6$.

**53.** Write the equation of a line in slope-intercept form that contains $\left(-\frac{1}{2}, -\frac{1}{3}\right)$ and $\left(1\frac{1}{2}, 1\right)$.

## SPIRAL REVIEW

**Solve each compound inequality and graph the solutions.** *(Lesson 3-6)*

**54.** $-4 \le x + 2 \le 1$

**55.** $m - 5 > -7$ AND $m + 1 < 2$

**Graph each function.** *(Lesson 4-4)*

**56.** $y = x - 3$

**57.** $y = x^2 + 5$

**58.** $y = |2x|$

**Write the equation that describes each line in slope-intercept form.** *(Lesson 5-6)*

**59.** slope = 3, $y$-intercept = −5

**60.** slope = −2, the point $(2, 4)$ is on the line

## Career Path

go.hrw.com
Career Resources Online
KEYWORD: MA7 Career

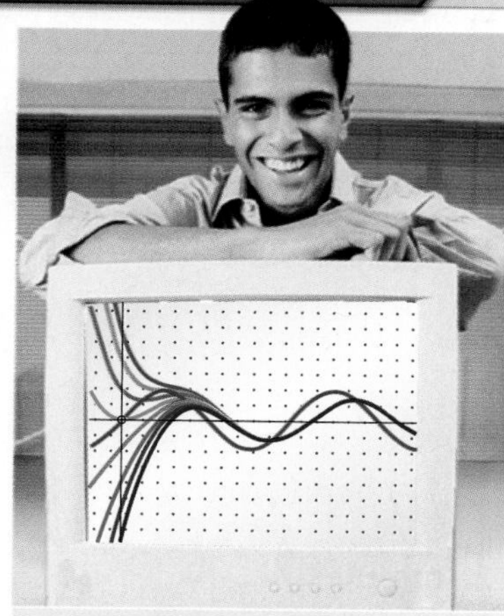

**Michael Raynor**
Data mining major

**Q: What math classes did you take in high school?**

**A:** Algebra 1 and 2, Geometry, and Statistics

**Q: What math classes have you taken in college?**

**A:** Applied Statistics, Data Mining Methods, Web Mining, and Artificial Intelligence

**Q: How do you use math?**

**A:** Once for a class, I used software to analyze basketball statistics. What I learned helped me develop strategies for our school team.

**Q: What are your future plans?**

**A:** There are many options for people with data mining skills. I could work in banking, pharmaceuticals, or even the military. But my dream job is to develop game strategies for an NBA team.

# Interpreting Trend Lines

Review the definitions for slope and $y$-intercept. Also review the equation for slope-intercept form in the table below.

**MA.A.4.4** Represent linear functions in a variety of equivalent forms (including point-slope). *Also* **MA.G.1.1, MA.A.4.3, MA.A.5.1, MA.S.2, Prep MA.S.2.1**

| Slope | $y$-intercept | Slope-Intercept Form |
|---|---|---|
| If $(x_1, y_1)$ and $(x_2, y_2)$ are any two points on a line, then the slope is $m = \frac{y_2 - y_1}{x_2 - x_1}$. | The $y$-coordinate of the point where a graph intersects the $y$-axis | $y = mx + b$, where $m$ is the slope and $b$ is the $y$-intercept |

In Chapter 4 you learned how to draw trend lines on scatter plots. Now you will learn how to find the equations of trend lines.

## Example

**Write an equation for the trend line on the scatter plot.**

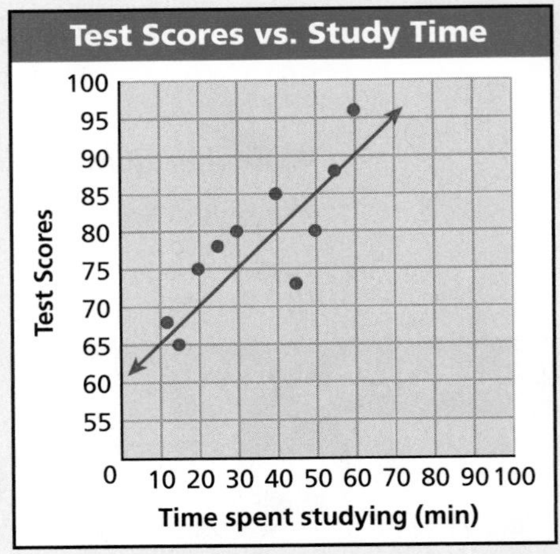


Two points on the trend line are $(30, 75)$ and $(60, 90)$.

To find the slope of the line that contains $(30, 75)$ and $(60, 90)$, use the slope formula.

$m = \frac{y_2 - y_1}{x_2 - x_1}$ *Use the slope formula.*

$m = \frac{90 - 75}{60 - 30}$ *Substitute (30, 75) for $(x_1, y_1)$ and (60, 90) for $(x_2, y_2)$.*

$m = \frac{15}{30}$ *Simplify.*

$m = \frac{1}{2}$

It appears that the trend line has a $y$-intercept of about 60.

$y = mx + b$ *Slope-intercept form*

$y = \frac{1}{2}x + 60$ *Substitute the values of m and b.*

## Try This

1. In the example above, what is the meaning of the slope?
2. What does the $y$-intercept represent?
3. Use the equation to predict the test score of a student who spent 25 minutes studying.
4. Use the table to create a scatter plot. Draw a trend line and find the equation of your trend line. Tell the meaning of the slope and $y$-intercept. Then use your equation to predict the race time of a runner who ran 40 miles in training.

| Distance Run in Training (mi) | 12 | 15 | 16 | 18 | 21 | 23 | 24 | 25 | 33 |
|---|---|---|---|---|---|---|---|---|---|
| Race Time (min) | 65 | 64 | 55 | 58 | 55 | 50 | 50 | 47 | 36 |

# 5-8 Slopes of Parallel and Perpendicular Lines

**MA.G.1.1** Use strategies to calculate the slope… *Also* **MA.A.4.3, MA.A.4.4, MA.A.5.1, MA.G.1, MA.G.1.2**

***Objectives***
Identify and graph parallel and perpendicular lines.

Write equations to describe lines parallel or perpendicular to a given line.

***Vocabulary***
parallel lines
perpendicular lines

**Why learn this?**
Parallel lines and their equations can be used to model costs, such as the cost of a booth at a farmers' market.

To sell at a particular farmers' market for a year, there is a \$100 membership fee. Then you pay \$3 for each hour that you sell at the market. However, if you were a member the previous year, the membership fee is reduced to \$50.

- The **red** line shows the total cost if you are a new member.
- The **blue** line shows the total cost if you are a returning member.

These two lines are *parallel.* **Parallel lines** are lines in the same plane that have no points in common. In other words, they do not intersect.

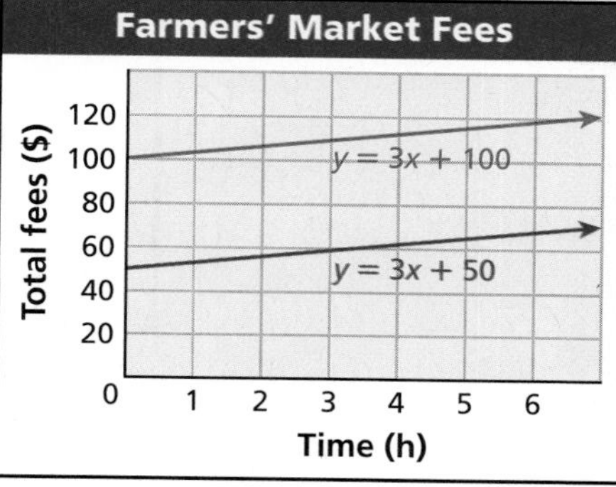


**Know it! Note**

**Parallel Lines**

| | | |
|---|---|---|
| **WORDS** | Two different nonvertical lines are parallel if and only if they have the same slope. | All different vertical lines are parallel. |
| **GRAPH** | $y = \frac{1}{2}x + 5$; $y = \frac{1}{2}x + 1$ | $x = -2$; $x = 4$ |

## EXAMPLE 1 Identifying Parallel Lines

**Identify which lines are parallel.**

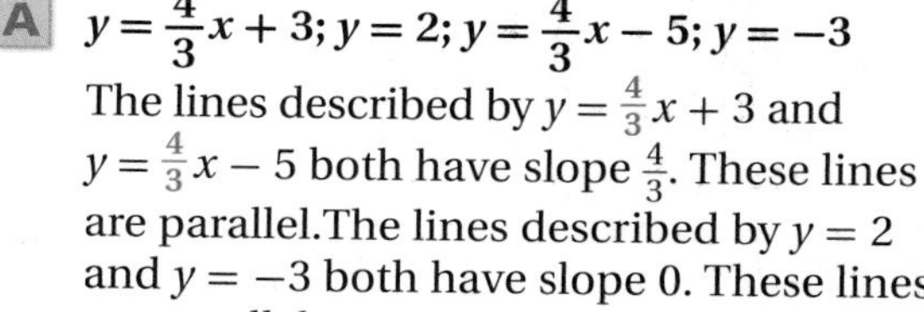

**A** $y = \frac{4}{3}x + 3$; $y = 2$; $y = \frac{4}{3}x - 5$; $y = -3$

The lines described by $y = \frac{4}{3}x + 3$ and $y = \frac{4}{3}x - 5$ both have slope $\frac{4}{3}$. These lines are parallel. The lines described by $y = 2$ and $y = -3$ both have slope 0. These lines are parallel.

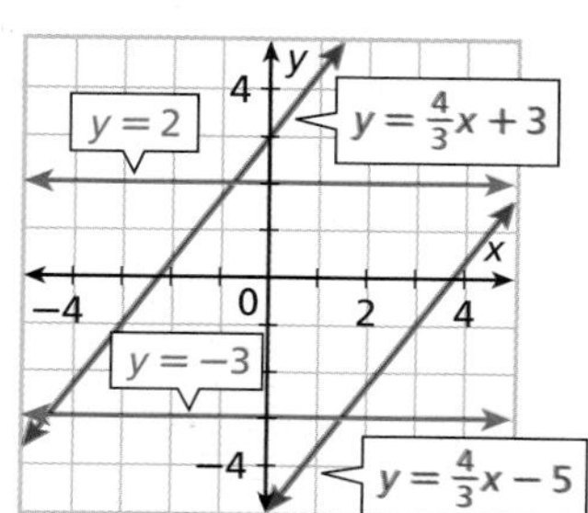

**Identify which lines are parallel.**

**B** $y = 3x + 2$; $y = -\frac{1}{2}x + 4$; $x + 2y = -4$; $y - 5 = 3(x - 1)$

Write all equations in slope-intercept form to determine the slopes.

| $y = 3x + 2$ <br> slope-intercept form ✓ | $y = -\frac{1}{2}x + 4$ <br> slope-intercept form ✓ |
|---|---|
| $x + 2y = -4$ <br> $\underline{-x \qquad -x}$ <br> $2y = -x - 4$ <br> $\frac{2y}{2} = \frac{-x - 4}{2}$ <br> $y = -\frac{1}{2}x - 2$ | $y - 5 = 3(x - 1)$ <br> $y - 5 = 3x - 3$ <br> $\underline{+5 \qquad +5}$ <br> $y \quad = 3x + 2$ |

The lines described by $y = 3x + 2$ and $y - 5 = 3(x - 1)$ have the same slope, but they are not parallel lines. They are the same line.

The lines described by $y = -\frac{1}{2}x + 4$ and $x + 2y = -4$ represent parallel lines. They each have slope $-\frac{1}{2}$.

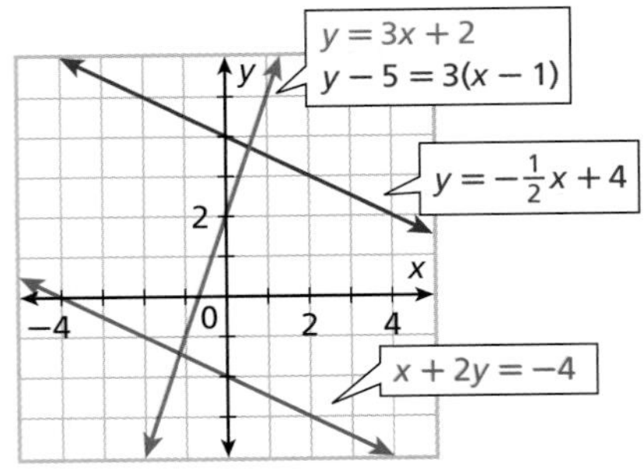

**Identify which lines are parallel.**

**1a.** $y = 2x + 2$; $y = 2x + 1$; $y = -4$; $x = 1$

**1b.** $y = \frac{3}{4}x + 8$; $-3x + 4y = 32$; $y = 3x$; $y - 1 = 3(x + 2)$

**EXAMPLE 2** Geometry

Remember!

In a parallelogram, opposite sides are parallel.

### *Geometry Application*

**Show that *ABCD* is a parallelogram.**

*Use the ordered pairs and the slope formula to find the slopes of $\overline{AB}$ and $\overline{CD}$.*

$$\text{slope of } \overline{AB} = \frac{7 - 5}{4 - (-1)} = \frac{2}{5}$$

$$\text{slope of } \overline{CD} = \frac{3 - 1}{4 - (-1)} = \frac{2}{5}$$

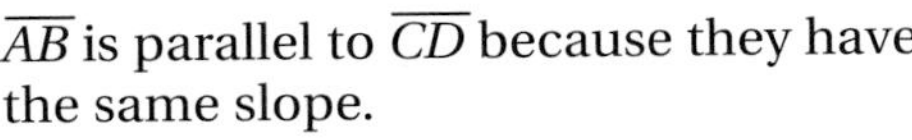

$\overline{AB}$ is parallel to $\overline{CD}$ because they have the same slope.

$\overline{AD}$ is parallel to $\overline{BC}$ because they are both vertical.

Therefore, *ABCD* is a parallelogram because both pairs of opposite sides are parallel.

**2.** Show that the points $A(0, 2)$, $B(4, 2)$, $C(1, -3)$, and $D(-3, -3)$ are the vertices of a parallelogram.

**Perpendicular lines** are lines that intersect to form right angles (90°).

Know it! Note

## Perpendicular Lines

| | | |
|---|---|---|
| **WORDS** | Two nonvertical lines are perpendicular if and only if the product of their slopes is −1. | Vertical lines are perpendicular to horizontal lines. |
| **GRAPH** | $y = -\frac{2}{3}x + 3$; $y = \frac{3}{2}x - 2$ | $y = 3$; $x = 2$ |

## EXAMPLE 3 Identifying Perpendicular Lines

**Identify which lines are perpendicular: $x = -2$; $y = 1$; $y = -4x$; $y + 2 = \frac{1}{4}(x + 1)$.**

The graph described by $x = -2$ is a vertical line, and the graph described by $y = 1$ is a horizontal line. These lines are perpendicular.

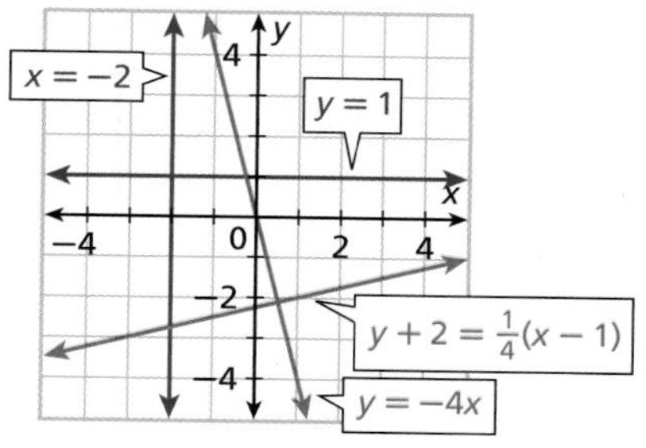


The slope of the line described by $y = -4x$ is $-4$. The slope of the line described by $y + 2 = \frac{1}{4}(x - 1)$ is $\frac{1}{4}$.

$$(-4)\left(\frac{1}{4}\right) = -1$$

These lines are perpendicular because the product of their slopes is −1.

**3.** Identify which lines are perpendicular: $y = -4$; $y - 6 = 5(x + 4)$; $x = 3$; $y = -\frac{1}{5}x + 2$.

## EXAMPLE 4 Geometry Application

Geometry

**Show that $PQR$ is a right triangle.**

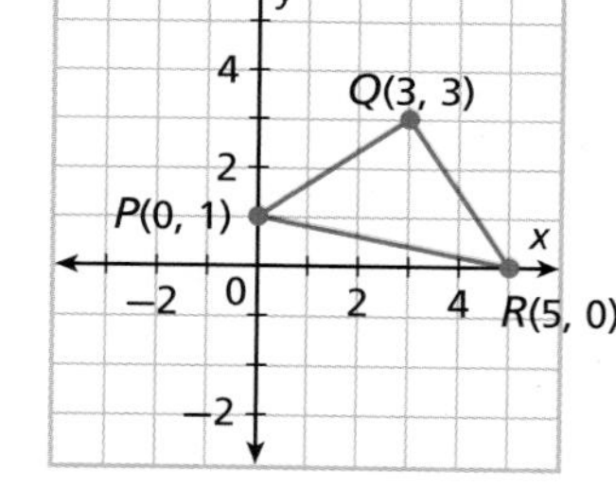


If $PQR$ is a right triangle, $\overline{PQ}$ will be perpendicular to $\overline{QR}$.

slope of $\overline{PQ} = \frac{3 - 1}{3 - 0} = \frac{2}{3}$

slope of $\overline{QR} = \frac{3 - 0}{3 - 5} = \frac{3}{-2} = -\frac{3}{2}$

$\overline{PQ}$ is perpendicular to $\overline{QR}$ because $\frac{2}{3}\left(-\frac{3}{2}\right) = -1$.

Therefore, $PQR$ is a right triangle because it contains a right angle.

**Helpful Hint**

A right triangle contains one right angle. In Example 4, ∠P and ∠R are clearly not right angles, so the only possibility is ∠Q.

**4.** Show that $P(1, 4)$, $Q(2, 6)$, and $R(7, 1)$ are the vertices of a right triangle.

EXAMPLE 5 **Writing Equations of Parallel and Perpendicular Lines**

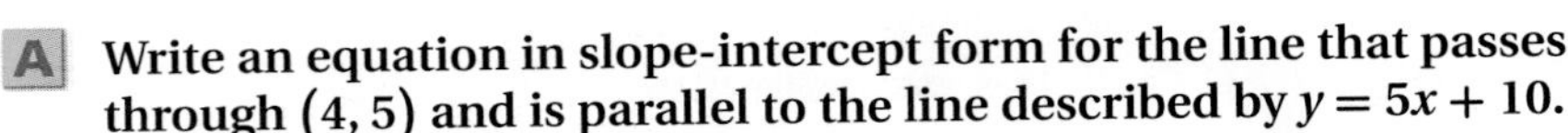

**A** **Write an equation in slope-intercept form for the line that passes through $(4, 5)$ and is parallel to the line described by $y = 5x + 10$.**

**Step 1** Find the slope of the line.

$y = 5x + 10$ *The slope is 5.*

The parallel line also has a slope of 5.

**Step 2** Write the equation in point-slope form.

$y - y_1 = m(x - x_1)$ *Use point-slope form.*

$y - 5 = 5(x - 4)$ *Substitute 5 for m, 4 for $x_1$, and 5 for $y_1$.*

**Step 3** Write the equation in slope-intercept form.

$y - 5 = 5(x - 4)$

$y - 5 = 5x - 20$ *Distributive Property*

$y = 5x - 15$ *Addition Property of Equality*

> **Helpful Hint**
>
> If you know the slope of a line, the slope of a perpendicular line will be the "opposite reciprocal."
>
> $\frac{2}{3} \rightarrow -\frac{3}{2}$
>
> $\frac{1}{5} \rightarrow -5$
>
> $-7 \rightarrow \frac{1}{7}$

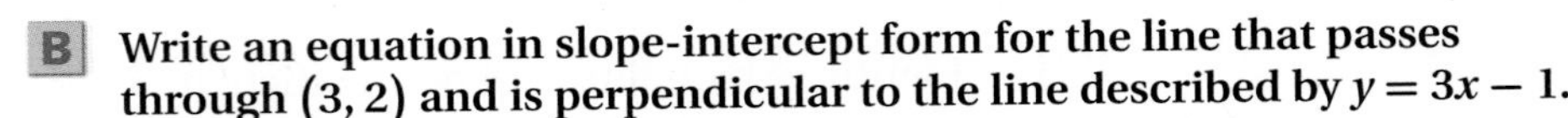

**B** **Write an equation in slope-intercept form for the line that passes through $(3, 2)$ and is perpendicular to the line described by $y = 3x - 1$.**

**Step 1** Find the slope of the line.

$y = 3x - 1$ *The slope is 3.*

The perpendicular line has a slope of $-\frac{1}{3}$, because $3\left(-\frac{1}{3}\right) = -1$.

**Step 2** Write the equation in point-slope form.

$y - y_1 = m(x - x_1)$ *Use point-slope form.*

$y - 2 = -\frac{1}{3}(x - 3)$ *Substitute $-\frac{1}{3}$ for m, 3 for $x_1$, and 2 for $y_1$.*

**Step 3** Write the equation in slope-intercept form.

$y - 2 = -\frac{1}{3}(x - 3)$

$y - 2 = -\frac{1}{3}x + 1$ *Distributive Property*

$y = -\frac{1}{3}x + 3$ *Addition Property of Equality*

**5a.** Write an equation in slope-intercept form for the line that passes through $(5, 7)$ and is parallel to the line described by $y = \frac{4}{5}x - 6$.

**5b.** Write an equation in slope-intercept form for the line that passes through $(-5, 3)$ and is perpendicular to the line described by $y = 5x$.

## THINK AND DISCUSS

1. Are the lines described by $y = \frac{1}{2}x$ and $y = 2x$ perpendicular? Explain.
2. Describe the slopes and y-intercepts when two nonvertical lines are parallel.

3. **GET ORGANIZED** Copy and complete the graphic organizer. In each box, sketch an example and describe the slopes.

| Parallel lines | Perpendicular lines |
|---|---|

# 5-8 Exercises

MA.G.1.1, MA.A.4.3, MA.A.4.4, MA.A.5.1, MA.G.1.2

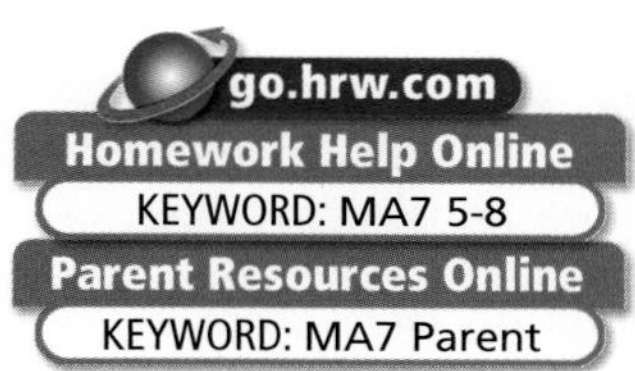


## GUIDED PRACTICE

1. **Vocabulary** ___?___ lines have the same slope. (*Parallel* or *Perpendicular*)

SEE EXAMPLE 1 p. 349

**Identify which lines are parallel.**

2. $y = 6$; $y = 6x + 5$; $y = 6x - 7$; $y = -8$
3. $y = \frac{3}{4}x - 1$; $y = -2x$; $y - 3 = \frac{3}{4}(x - 5)$; $y - 4 = -2(x + 2)$

SEE EXAMPLE 2 p. 350

4. **Geometry** Show that *ABCD* is a trapezoid. (*Hint:* In a trapezoid, exactly one pair of opposite sides is parallel.)

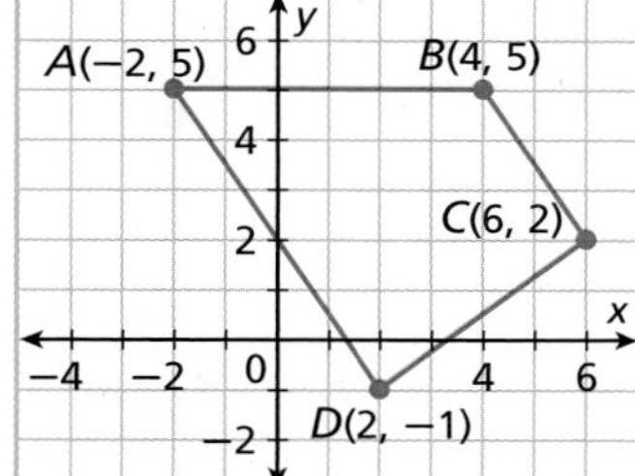


SEE EXAMPLE 3 p. 351

**Identify which lines are perpendicular.**

5. $y = \frac{2}{3}x - 4$; $y = -\frac{3}{2}x + 2$; $y = -1$; $x = 3$
6. $y = -\frac{3}{7}x - 4$; $y - 4 = -7(x + 2)$;
   $y - 1 = \frac{1}{7}(x - 4)$; $y - 7 = \frac{7}{3}(x - 3)$

SEE EXAMPLE 4 p. 351

7. **Geometry** Show that *PQRS* is a rectangle. (*Hint:* In a rectangle, all four angles are right angles.)

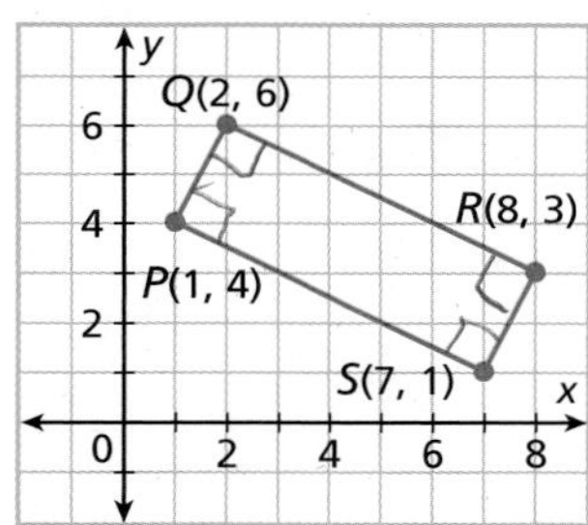


SEE EXAMPLE 5 p. 352

8. Write an equation in slope-intercept form for the line that passes through (5, 0) and is perpendicular to the line described by $y = -\frac{5}{2}x + 6$.

## PRACTICE AND PROBLEM SOLVING

**Independent Practice**

| For Exercises | See Example |
|---|---|
| 9–11 | 1 |
| 12 | 2 |
| 13–15 | 3 |
| 16 | 4 |
| 17 | 5 |

**Extra Practice**

Skills Practice p. S13
Application Practice p. S32

**Identify which lines are parallel.**

9. $x = 7$; $y = -\frac{5}{6}x + 8$; $y = -\frac{5}{6}x - 4$; $x = -9$
10. $y = -x$; $y - 3 = -1(x + 9)$; $y - 6 = \frac{1}{2}(x - 14)$; $y + 1 = \frac{1}{2}x$
11. $y = -3x + 2$; $y = \frac{1}{2}x - 1$; $-x + 2y = 17$; $3x + y = 27$
12. **Geometry** Show that *LMNP* is a parallelogram.

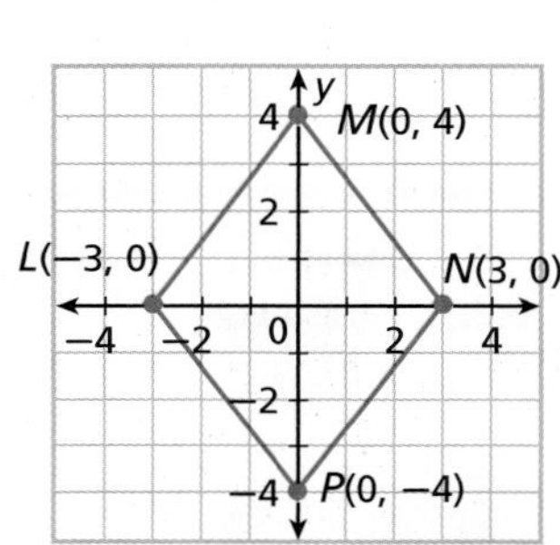


**Identify which lines are perpendicular.**

13. $y = 6x$; $y = \frac{1}{6}x$; $y = -\frac{1}{6}x$; $y = -6x$
14. $y - 9 = 3(x + 1)$; $y = -\frac{1}{3}x + 5$; $y = 0$; $x = 6$
15. $x - 6y = 15$; $y = 3x - 2$; $y = -3x - 3$; $y = -6x - 8$; $3y = -x - 11$

 16. **Geometry** Show that $ABC$ is a right triangle.

17. Write an equation in slope-intercept form for the line that passes through $(0, 0)$ and is parallel to the line described by $y = -\frac{6}{7}x + 1$.

$A(-7, -2)$, $B(-3, -3)$, $C(-4, -7)$

**Without graphing, tell whether each pair of lines is parallel, perpendicular, or neither.**

18. $x = 2$ and $y = -5$

19. $y = 7x$ and $y - 28 = 7(x - 4)$

20. $y = 2x - 1$ and $y = \frac{1}{2}x + 2$

21. $y - 3 = \frac{1}{4}(x - 3)$ and $y + 13 = \frac{1}{4}(x + 1)$

**Write an equation in slope-intercept form for the line that is parallel to the given line and that passes through the given point.**

22. $y = 3x - 7$; $(0, 4)$

23. $y = \frac{1}{2}x + 5$; $(4, -3)$

24. $4y = x$; $(4, 0)$

25. $y = 2x + 3$; $(1, 7)$

26. $5x - 2y = 10$; $(3, -5)$

27. $y = 3x - 4$; $(-2, 7)$

28. $y = 7$; $(2, 4)$

29. $x + y = 1$; $(2, 3)$

30. $2x + 3y = 7$; $(4, 5)$

31. $y = 4x + 2$; $(5, -3)$

32. $y = \frac{1}{2}x - 1$; $(0, -4)$

33. $3x + 4y = 8$; $(4, -3)$

**Write an equation in slope-intercept form for the line that is perpendicular to the given line and that passes through the given point.**

34. $y = -3x + 4$; $(6, -2)$

35. $y = x - 6$; $(-1, 2)$

36. $3x - 4y = 8$; $(-6, 5)$

37. $5x + 2y = 10$; $(3, -5)$

38. $y = 5 - 3x$; $(2, -4)$

39. $-10x + 2y = 8$; $(4, -3)$

40. $2x + 3y = 7$; $(4, 5)$

41. $4x - 2y = -6$; $(3, -2)$

42. $-2x - 8y = 16$; $(4, 5)$

43. $y = -2x + 4$; $(-2, 5)$

44. $y = x - 5$; $(0, 5)$

45. $x + y = 2$; $(8, 5)$

46. Write an equation describing the line that is parallel to the $y$-axis and that is 6 units to the right of the $y$-axis.

47. Write an equation describing the line that is perpendicular to the $y$-axis and that is 4 units below the $x$-axis.

48. **Critical Thinking** Is it possible for two linear functions whose graphs are parallel lines to have the same $y$-intercept? Explain.

49. **Estimation** Estimate the slope of a line that is perpendicular to the line through $(2.07, 8.95)$ and $(-1.9, 25.07)$.

 50. **Write About It** Explain in words how to write an equation in slope-intercept form that describes a line parallel to $y - 3 = -6(x - 3)$.

**MULTI-STEP TEST PREP**

51. This problem will prepare you for the Multi-Step Test Prep on page 364.
    a. Flora walks from her home to the bus stop at a rate of 50 steps per minute. Write a rule that gives her distance from home (in steps) as a function of time.
    b. Flora's neighbor Dan lives 30 steps closer to the bus stop. He begins walking at the same time and at the same pace as Flora. Write a rule that gives Dan's distance from *Flora's* house as a function of time.
    c. Will Flora meet Dan along the walk? Use a graph to help explain your answer.

52. Which describes a line parallel to the line described by $y = -3x + 2$?

MA.G.1.1, MA.A.4.3, MA.A.4.4, MA.A.5.1, MA.G.1.2

Ⓐ $y = -3x$  Ⓑ $y = \frac{1}{3}x$  Ⓒ $y = 2 - 3x$  Ⓓ $y = \frac{1}{3}x + 2$

53. Which describes a line passing through (3, 3) that is perpendicular to the line described by $y = \frac{3}{5}x + 2$?

Ⓕ
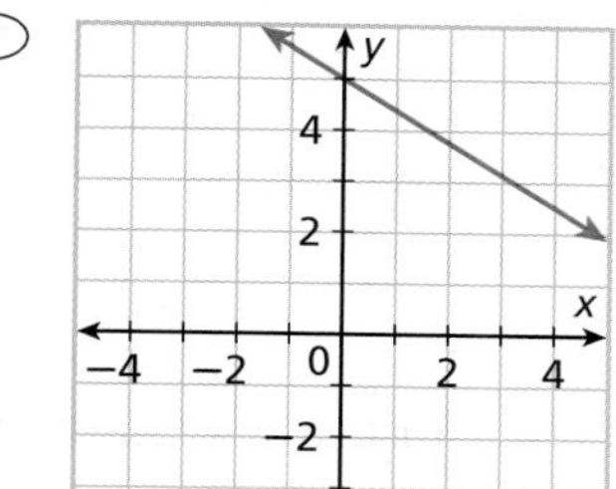


Ⓗ

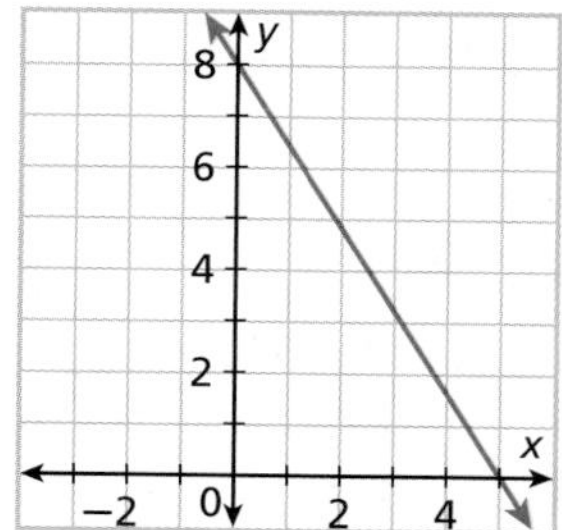


Ⓖ $y = \frac{5}{3}x - 2$  Ⓙ $y = \frac{3}{5}x + \frac{6}{5}$

54. **Gridded Response** The graph of a linear function $f(x)$ is parallel to the line described by $2x + y = 5$ and contains the point $(6, -2)$. What is the $y$-intercept of $f(x)$?

## CHALLENGE AND EXTEND

55. Three or more points that lie on the same line are called *collinear points.* Explain why the points $A$, $B$, and $C$ must be collinear if the line containing $A$ and $B$ has the same slope as the line containing $B$ and $C$.

56. The lines described by $y = (a + 12)x + 3$ and $y = 4ax$ are parallel. What is the value of $a$?

57. The lines described by $y = (5a + 3)x$ and $y = -\frac{1}{2}x$ are perpendicular. What is the value of $a$?

58. **Geometry** The diagram shows a square in the coordinate plane. Use the diagram to show that the diagonals of a square are perpendicular.

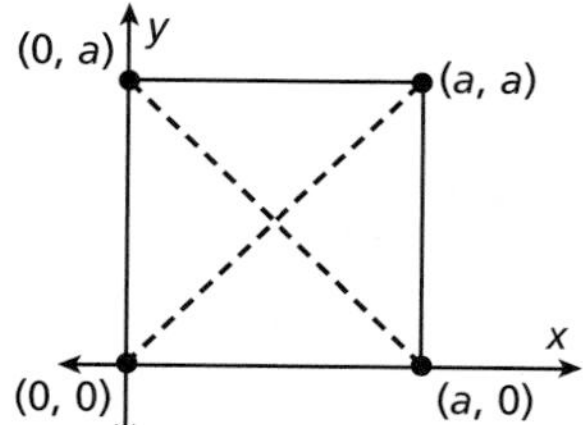


## SPIRAL REVIEW

59. The record high temperature for a given city is 112°F. The morning temperature today was 94°F and the temperature will increase $t$ degrees. Write and solve an inequality to find all values of $t$ that would break the record for the high temperature. *(Lesson 3-2)*

**Graph each function.** *(Lesson 4-4)*

60. $y = -3x + 5$  61. $y = x - 1$  62. $y = x^2 - 3$

**Write an equation in slope-intercept form for the line with the given slope that contains the given point.** *(Lesson 5-7)*

63. slope $= \frac{2}{3}$; $(6, -1)$  64. slope $= -5$; $(2, 4)$  65. slope $= -\frac{1}{2}$; $(-1, 0)$

66. slope $= -\frac{1}{3}$; $(2, 7)$  67. slope $= 0$; $(-3, 3)$  68. slope $= \frac{1}{5}$; $(-4, -2)$

Use with Lesson 5-9

# The Family of Linear Functions

A *family of functions* is a set of functions whose graphs have basic characteristics in common. For example, all linear functions form a family. You can use a graphing calculator to explore families of functions.

**MA.A.4.3** Interpret the relationship of constants and coefficients for data presented in graphs...and equations.

go.hrw.com
Lab Resources Online
KEYWORD: MA7 LAB5

## Activity

**Graph the lines described by $y = x - 2$, $y = x - 1$, $y = x$, $y = x + 1$, $y = x + 2$, $y = x + 3$, and $y = x + 4$. How does the value of $b$ affect the graph described by $y = x + b$?**

1. All of the functions are in the form $y = x + b$. Enter them into the Y= editor.

   Y= X,T,θ,n − 2 ENTER

   X,T,θ,n − 1 ENTER

   and so on.

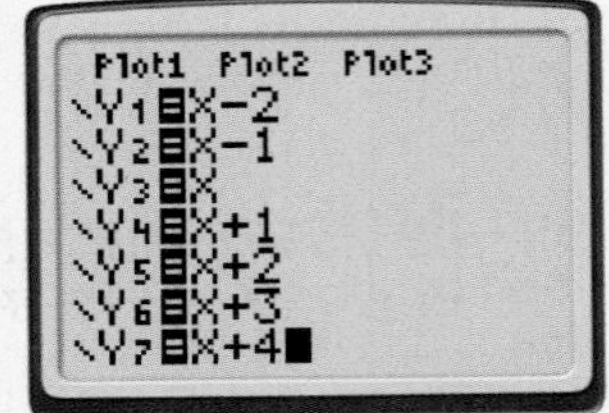


2. Press ZOOM and select **6:Zstandard.** Think about the different values of $b$ as you watch the graphs being drawn. Notice that the lines are all parallel.

3. It appears that the value of $b$ in $y = x + b$ shifts the graph up or down—up if $b$ is positive and down if $b$ is negative.

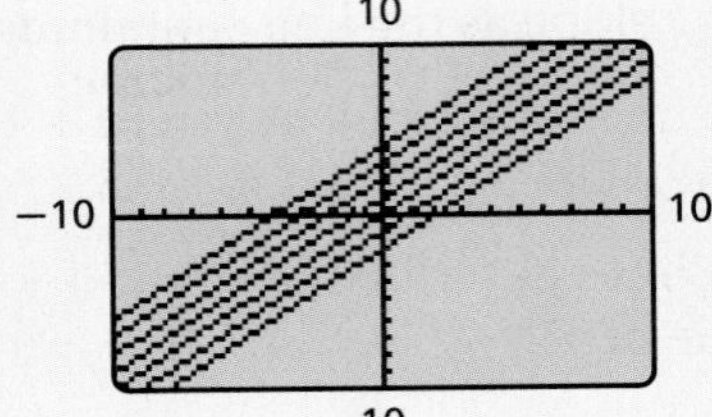


## Try This

1. Make a prediction about the lines described by $y = 2x - 3$, $y = 2x - 2$, $y = 2x - 1$, $y = 2x$, $y = 2x + 1$, $y = 2x + 2$, and $y = 2x + 3$. Then graph. Was your prediction correct?
2. Now use your calculator to explore what happens to the graph of $y = mx$ when you change the value of $m$.
   a. **Make a Prediction** How do you think the lines described by $y = -2x$, $y = -x$, $y = x$, and $y = 2x$ will be related? How will they be alike? How will they be different?
   b. Graph the functions given in part **a**. Was your prediction correct?
   c. How is the effect of $m$ different when $m$ is positive from when $m$ is negative?

# 5-9 Transforming Linear Functions

**MA.A.4.3** Interpret the relationship of constants and coefficients for data presented in graphs...and equations. *Also* **MA.A.5.1**

***Objective***
Describe how changing slope and $y$-intercept affect the graph of a linear function.

***Vocabulary***
family of functions
parent function
transformation
translation
rotation
reflection

**Who uses this?**
Business owners can use transformations to show the effects of price changes, such as the price of trophy engraving. (See Example 5.)

A **family of functions** is a set of functions whose graphs have basic characteristics in common. For example, all linear functions form a family because all of their graphs are the same basic shape.

A **parent function** is the most basic function in a family. For linear functions, the parent function is $f(x) = x$.

The graphs of all other linear functions are *transformations* of the graph of the parent function, $f(x) = x$. A **transformation** is a change in position or size of a figure.

There are three types of transformations—*translations, rotations,* and *reflections.*

Look at the four functions and their graphs below.

**Remember!**
Function notation—$f(x)$, $g(x)$, and so on—can be used in place of $y$.
$y = f(x)$

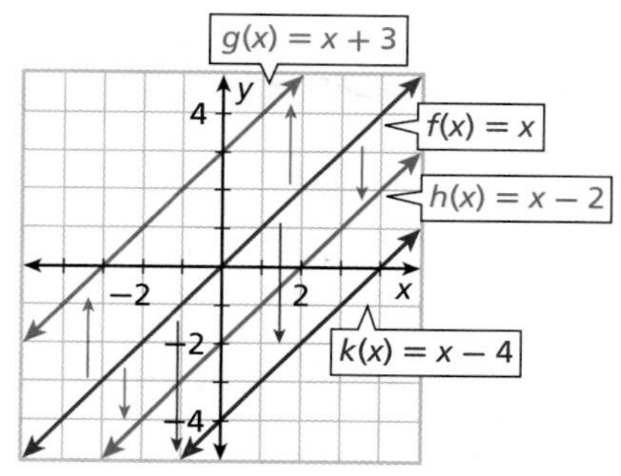


Notice that all of the lines above are parallel. The slopes are the same but the $y$-intercepts are different.

The graphs of $g(x) = x + 3$, $h(x) = x - 2$, and $k(x) = x - 4$ are vertical *translations* of the graph of the parent function, $f(x) = x$. A **translation** is a type of transformation that moves every point the same distance in the same direction. You can think of a translation as a "slide."

**Vertical Translation of a Linear Function**

When the $y$-intercept $b$ is changed in the function $f(x) = mx + b$, the graph is translated vertically.

- If $b$ increases, the graph is translated up.
- If $b$ decreases, the graph is translated down.

## EXAMPLE 1 Translating Linear Functions

**Graph $f(x) = x$ and $g(x) = x - 5$. Then describe the transformation from the graph of $f(x)$ to the graph of $g(x)$.**

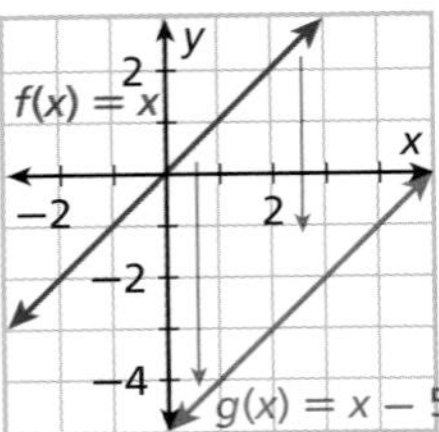


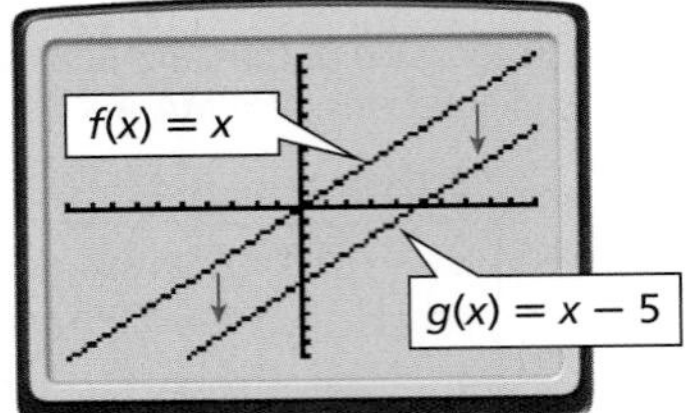


The graph of $g(x) = x - 5$ is the result of translating the graph of $f(x) = x$ 5 units down.

1. Graph $f(x) = x + 4$ and $g(x) = x - 2$. Then describe the transformation from the graph of $f(x)$ to the graph of $g(x)$.

The graphs of $g(x) = 3x$, $h(x) = 5x$, and $k(x) = \frac{1}{2}x$ are *rotations* of the graph of $f(x) = x$. A **rotation** is a transformation about a point. You can think of a rotation as a "turn." The $y$-intercepts are the same, but the slopes are different.

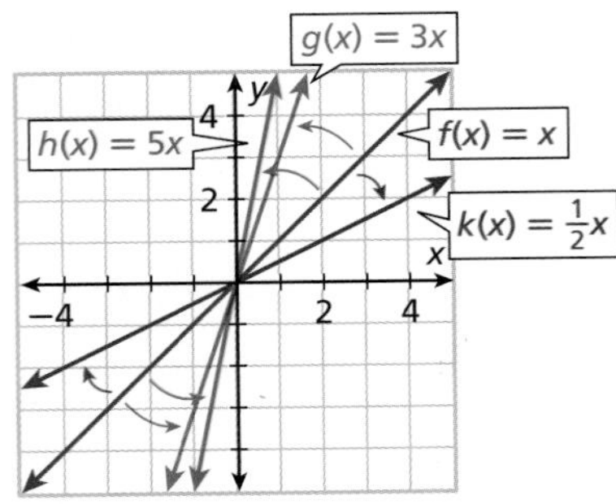


### Know it! Note — Rotation of a Linear Function

When the slope $m$ is changed in the function $f(x) = mx + b$ it causes a rotation of the graph about the point $(0, b)$, which changes the line's steepness.

## EXAMPLE 2 Rotating Linear Functions

**Graph $f(x) = x + 2$ and $g(x) = 2x + 2$. Then describe the transformation from the graph of $f(x)$ to the graph of $g(x)$.**

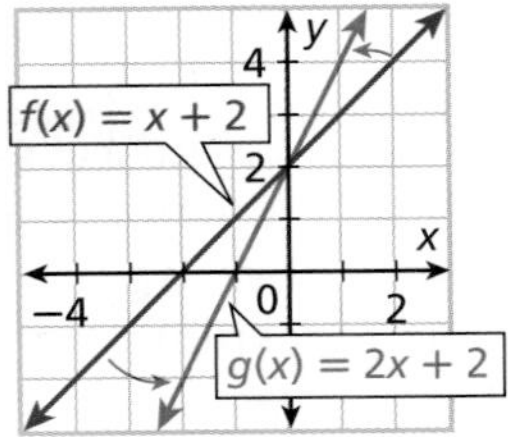


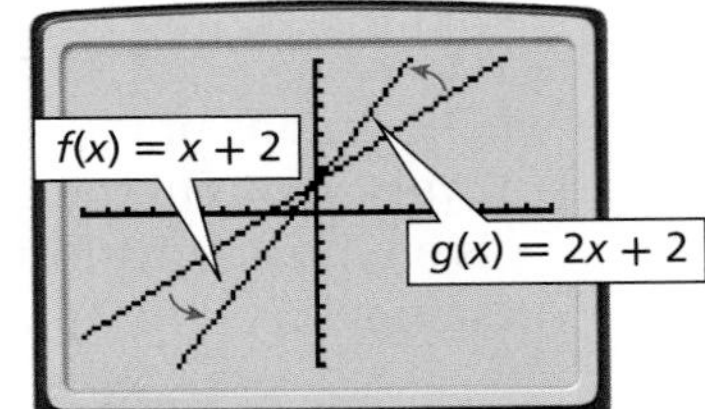


The graph of $g(x) = 2x + 2$ is the result of rotating the graph of $f(x) = x + 2$ about $(0, 2)$. The graph of $g(x)$ is steeper than the graph of $f(x)$.

2. Graph $f(x) = 3x - 1$ and $g(x) = \frac{1}{2}x - 1$. Then describe the transformation from the graph of $f(x)$ to the graph of $g(x)$.

The diagram shows the *reflection* of the graph of $f(x) = 2x$ across the $y$-axis, producing the graph of $g(x) = -2x$. A **reflection** is a transformation across a line that produces a mirror image. You can think of a reflection as a "flip" over a line.

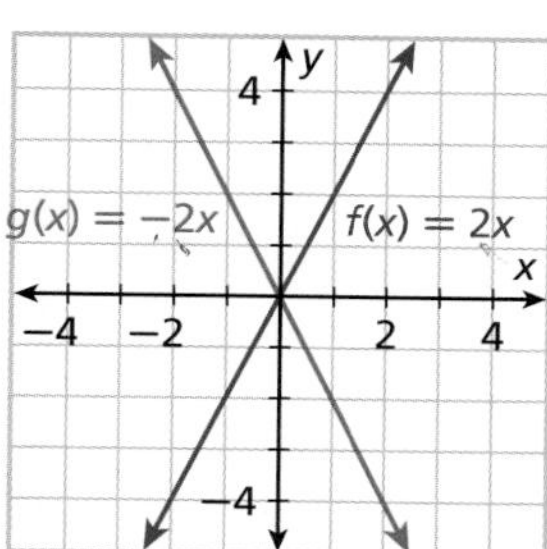


## Know it! Note: Reflection of a Linear Function

When the slope $m$ is multiplied by $-1$ in $f(x) = mx + b$, the graph is reflected across the $y$-axis.

## EXAMPLE 3 Reflecting Linear Functions

**Graph $f(x)$. Then reflect the graph of $f(x)$ across the $y$-axis. Write a function $g(x)$ to describe the new graph.**

**A** $f(x) = x$

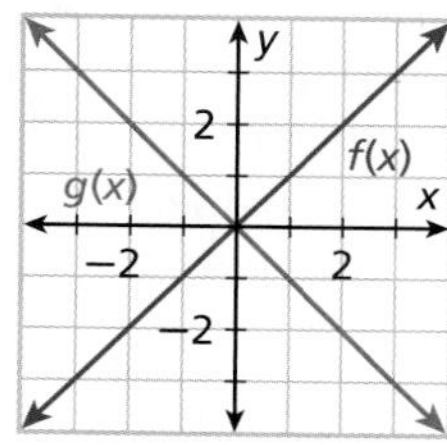


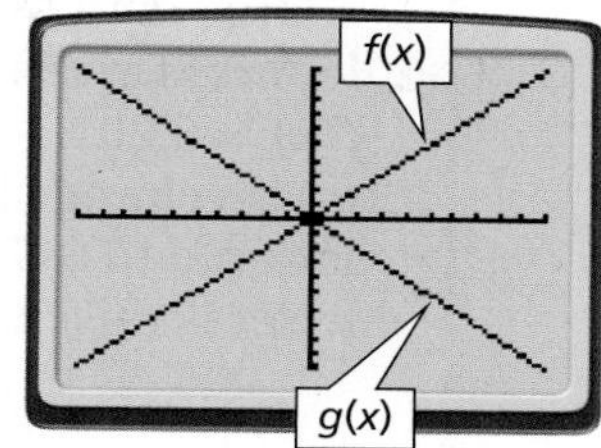


To find $g(x)$, multiply the value of $m$ by $-1$.

In $f(x) = x$, $m = 1$.

$1(-1) = -1$ *This is the value of m for g(x).*

$g(x) = -x$

**B** $f(x) = -4x - 1$

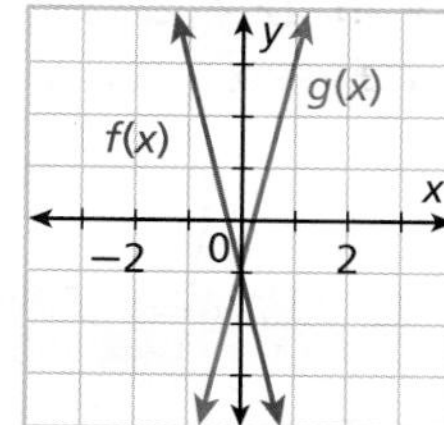


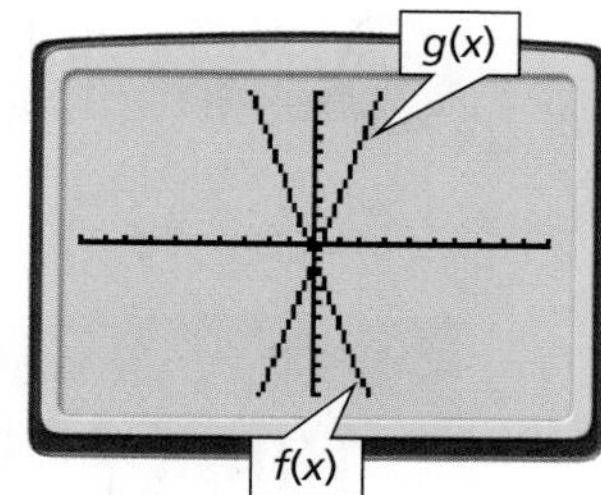


To find $g(x)$, multiply the value of $m$ by $-1$.

In $f(x) = -4x - 1$, $m = -4$.

$-4(-1) = 4$ *This is the value of m for g(x).*

$g(x) = 4x - 1$

**3.** Graph $f(x) = \frac{2}{3}x + 2$. Then reflect the graph of $f(x)$ across the $y$-axis. Write a function $g(x)$ to describe the new graph.

## EXAMPLE 4 Multiple Transformations of Linear Functions

**Graph $f(x) = x$ and $g(x) = 3x + 1$. Then describe the transformations from the graph of $f(x)$ to the graph of $g(x)$.**

Find transformations of $f(x) = x$ that will result in $g(x) = 3x + 1$:

- Multiply $f(x)$ by 3 to get $h(x) = 3x$. This rotates the graph about $(0, 0)$ and makes it steeper.
- Then add 1 to $h(x)$ to get $g(x) = 3x + 1$. This translates the graph 1 unit up.

The transformations are a rotation and a translation.

4. Graph $f(x) = x$ and $g(x) = -x + 2$. Then describe the transformations from the graph of $f(x)$ to the graph of $g(x)$.

## EXAMPLE 5 *Business Application*

**A trophy company charges $175 for a trophy plus $0.20 per letter for the engraving. The total charge for a trophy with $x$ letters is given by the function $f(x) = 0.20x + 175$. How will the graph change if the trophy's cost is lowered to $172? if the charge per letter is raised to $0.50?**

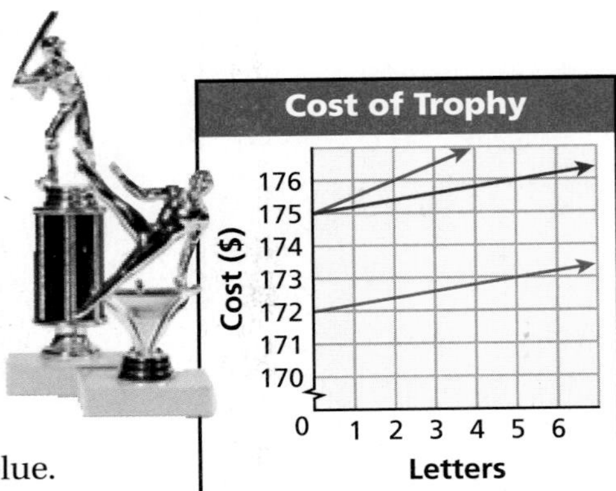


$f(x) = 0.20x + 175$ is graphed in blue.

If the trophy's cost is lowered to $172, the new function is $g(x) = 0.20x + 172$. The original graph will be translated 3 units down.

If the charge per letter is raised to $0.50, the new function is $h(x) = 0.50x + 175$. The original graph will be rotated about $(0, 175)$ and become steeper.

5. **What if...?** How will the graph change if the charge per letter is lowered to $0.15? if the trophy's cost is raised to $180?

### THINK AND DISCUSS

1. Describe the graph of $f(x) = x + 3.45$
2. Look at the graphs in Example 5. For each line, is every point on the line a solution in this situation? Explain.

3. **GET ORGANIZED** Copy and complete the graphic organizer. In each box, sketch a graph of the given transformation of $f(x) = x$, and label it with a possible equation.

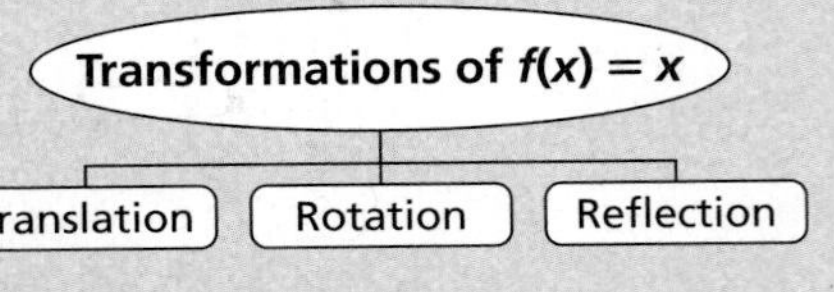

# 5-9 Exercises

MA.A.4.3, MA.A.5.1

go.hrw.com
Homework Help Online
KEYWORD: MA7 5-9
Parent Resources Online
KEYWORD: MA7 Parent

## GUIDED PRACTICE

**Vocabulary** **Apply the vocabulary from this lesson to answer each question.**

1. Changing the value of $b$ in $f(x) = mx + b$ results in a __?__ of the graph. (*translation* or *reflection*)

2. Changing the value of $m$ in $f(x) = mx + b$ results in a __?__ of the graph. (*translation* or *rotation*)

**Graph $f(x)$ and $g(x)$. Then describe the transformation from the graph of $f(x)$ to the graph of $g(x)$.**

SEE EXAMPLE 1 p. 358

3. $f(x) = x$, $g(x) = x - 4$
4. $f(x) = x$, $g(x) = x + 1$
5. $f(x) = x$, $g(x) = x + 2$
6. $f(x) = x$, $g(x) = x - 6.5$

SEE EXAMPLE 2 p. 358

7. $f(x) = x$, $g(x) = \frac{1}{4}x$
8. $f(x) = \frac{1}{5}x + 3$, $g(x) = x + 3$
9. $f(x) = 2x - 2$, $g(x) = 4x - 2$
10. $f(x) = x + 1$, $g(x) = \frac{1}{2}x + 1$

**Graph $f(x)$. Then reflect the graph of $f(x)$ across the $y$-axis. Write a function $g(x)$ to describe the new graph.**

SEE EXAMPLE 3 p. 359

11. $f(x) = -\frac{1}{5}x$
12. $f(x) = 2x + 4$
13. $f(x) = \frac{1}{3}x - 6$
14. $f(x) = 5x - 1$

**Graph $f(x)$ and $g(x)$. Then describe the transformations from the graph of $f(x)$ to the graph of $g(x)$.**

SEE EXAMPLE 4 p. 360

15. $f(x) = x$, $g(x) = 2x - 2$
16. $f(x) = x$, $g(x) = \frac{1}{3}x + 1$
17. $f(x) = -x - 1$, $g(x) = -4x$
18. $f(x) = -x$, $g(x) = -\frac{1}{2}x - 3$

SEE EXAMPLE 5 p. 360

19. **Entertainment** For large parties, a restaurant charges a reservation fee of \$25, plus \$15 per person. The total charge for a party of $x$ people is $f(x) = 15x + 25$. How will the graph of this function change if the reservation fee is raised to \$50? if the per-person charge is lowered to \$12?

## PRACTICE AND PROBLEM SOLVING

| Independent Practice | |
|---|---|
| For Exercises | See Example |
| 20–21 | 1 |
| 22–23 | 2 |
| 24–25 | 3 |
| 26–27 | 4 |
| 28 | 5 |

**Extra Practice**
Skills Practice p. S13
Application Practice p. S32

**Graph $f(x)$ and $g(x)$. Then describe the transformation(s) from the graph of $f(x)$ to the graph of $g(x)$.**

20. $f(x) = x$, $g(x) = x + \frac{1}{2}$
21. $f(x) = x$, $g(x) = x - 4$
22. $f(x) = \frac{1}{5}x - 1$, $g(x) = \frac{1}{10}x - 1$
23. $f(x) = x + 2$, $g(x) = \frac{2}{3}x + 2$

**Graph $f(x)$. Then reflect the graph of $f(x)$ across the $y$-axis. Write a function $g(x)$ to describe the new graph.**

24. $f(x) = 6x$
25. $f(x) = -3x - 2$

**Graph $f(x)$ and $g(x)$. Then describe the transformations from the graph of $f(x)$ to the graph of $g(x)$.**

26. $f(x) = 2x$, $g(x) = 4x - 1$
27. $f(x) = -7x + 5$, $g(x) = -14x$

28. **School** The number of chaperones on a field trip must include 1 teacher for every 4 students, plus 2 parents total. The function describing the number of chaperones for a trip of $x$ students is $f(x) = \frac{1}{4}x + 2$. How will the graph change if the number of parents is reduced to 0? if the number of teachers is raised to 1 for every 3 students?

**Describe the transformation(s) on the graph of $f(x) = x$ that result in the graph of $g(x)$. Graph $f(x)$ and $g(x)$, and compare the slopes and intercepts.**

29. $g(x) = -x$
30. $g(x) = x + 8$
31. $g(x) = 3x$
32. $g(x) = -\frac{2}{7}x$
33. $g(x) = 6x - 3$
34. $g(x) = -2x + 1$

**Sketch the transformed graph. Then write a function to describe your graph.**

35. Rotate the graph of $f(x) = -x + 2$ until it has the same steepness in the opposite direction.

36. Reflect the graph of $f(x) = x - 1$ across the $y$-axis, and then translate it 4 units down.

37. Translate the graph of $f(x) = \frac{1}{6}x - 10$ six units up.

LINK

**Hobbies**

Seattle librarian Nancy Pearl started the first citywide reading program, "If All Seattle Reads the Same Book," in 1998. Many cities have since emulated this program, attempting to unite communities by having everyone read the same book at the same time.

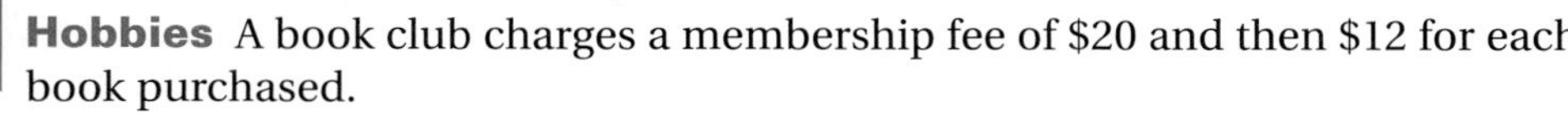

38. **Hobbies** A book club charges a membership fee of \$20 and then \$12 for each book purchased.
   a. Write and graph a function to represent the cost $y$ of membership in the club based on the number of books purchased $x$.
   b. **What if...?** Write and graph a second function to represent the cost of membership if the club raises its membership fee to \$30.
   c. Describe the relationship between your graphs from parts **a** and **b.**

**Describe the transformation(s) on the graph of $f(x) = x$ that result in the graph of $g(x)$.**

39. $g(x) = x - 9$
40. $g(x) = -x$
41. $g(x) = 5x$
42. $g(x) = -\frac{2}{3}x + 1$
43. $g(x) = -2x$
44. $g(x) = \frac{1}{5}x$

45. **Careers** Kelly works as a salesperson. She earns a weekly base salary plus a commission that is a percent of her total sales. Her total weekly pay is described by $f(x) = 0.20x + 300$, where $x$ is total sales in dollars.
   a. What is Kelly's weekly base salary?
   b. What percent of total sales does Kelly receive as commission?
   c. **What if...?** What is the change in Kelly's salary plan if the weekly pay function changes to $g(x) = 0.25x + 300$? to $h(x) = 0.2x + 400$?

46. **Critical Thinking** To transform the graph of $f(x) = x$ into the graph of $g(x) = -x$, you can reflect the graph of $f(x)$ across the $y$-axis. Find another transformation that will have the same result.

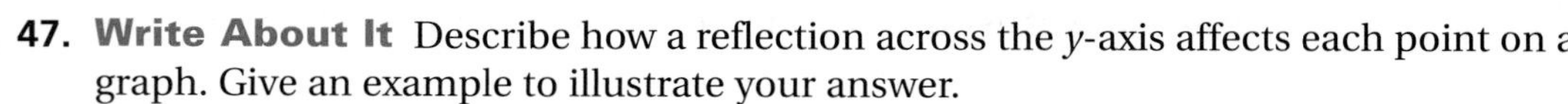

47. **Write About It** Describe how a reflection across the $y$-axis affects each point on a graph. Give an example to illustrate your answer.

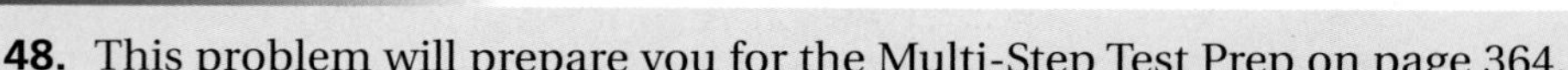

**MULTI-STEP TEST PREP**

48. This problem will prepare you for the Multi-Step Test Prep on page 364.
   a. Maria is walking from school to the softball field at a rate of 3 feet per second. Write a rule that gives her distance from school (in feet) as a function of time (in seconds). Then graph.
   b. Give a real-world situation that could be described by a line parallel to the one in part **a.**
   c. What does the $y$-intercept represent in each of these situations?

MA.A.4.3, MA.A.5.1

49. Which best describes the effect on $f(x) = 2x - 5$ if the slope changes to 10?

(A) Its graph becomes less steep.
(B) Its graph moves 15 units up.
(C) Its graph makes 10 complete rotations.
(D) The $x$-intercept becomes $\frac{1}{2}$.

50. Given $f(x) = 22x - 182$, which does NOT describe the effect of increasing the $y$-intercept by 182?

(F) The new line passes through the origin.
(G) The new $x$-intercept is 0.
(H) The new line is parallel to the original.
(J) The new line is steeper than the original.

## CHALLENGE AND EXTEND

51. You have seen that the graph of $g(x) = x + 3$ is the result of translating the graph of $f(x) = x$ three units up. However, you can also think of this as a *horizontal* translation—that is, a translation left or right. Graph $g(x) = x + 3$. Describe the horizontal translation of the graph of $f(x) = x$ to get the graph of $g(x) = x + 3$.

52. If $c > 0$, how can you describe the translation that transforms the graph of $f(x) = x$ into the graph of $g(x) = x + c$ as a horizontal translation? $g(x) = x - c$ as a horizontal translation?

## SPIRAL REVIEW

**Give an expression in simplest form for the perimeter of each figure.** *(Lesson 1-7)*

53.
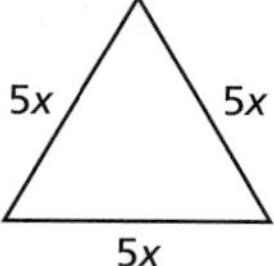


54.
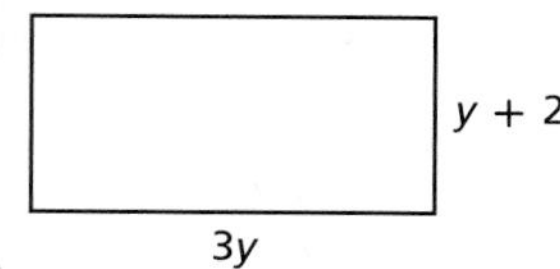


**Identify the correlation you would expect to see between each pair of data sets. Explain.** *(Lesson 4-5)*

55. the temperature and the number of people at the local ice cream parlor

56. the amount of electricity used and the total electric bill

57. the number of miles driven after a fill-up and the amount of gasoline in the tank

**Identify which lines are parallel.** *(Lesson 5-8)*

58. $y = -2x + 3$; $y = 2x$; $y = -2$; $y = -2x - 4$; $y = \frac{1}{2}x$; $y - 1 = -\frac{1}{2}(x + 6)$

59. $y = \frac{3}{5}x + 8$; $y = -\frac{3}{5}x$; $y + 1 = -\frac{3}{5}(x - 2)$; $y = \frac{5}{3}x + 9$; $y = 3x + 5$

**Identify which lines are perpendicular.** *(Lesson 5-8)*

60. $3x - 5y = 5$; $5y = -2x - 15$; $y = 3x + 5$; $5x + 3y = -21$; $y = \frac{5}{2}x - 2$

61. $x = 4$; $2y + x = 6$; $3x - y = 12$; $y = 2x + 3$; $y = -3$

CHAPTER 5

# MULTI-STEP TEST PREP

SECTION 5B

## Using Linear Functions

**Take a Walk!** All intersections in Durango, Colorado, have crossing signals with timers. Once the signal changes to walk, the timer begins at 28 seconds and counts down to show how much time pedestrians have to cross the street.

1. Pauline counted her steps as she crossed the street. She counted 15 steps with 19 seconds remaining. When she reached the opposite side of the street, she had counted a total of 30 steps and had 10 seconds remaining. Copy and complete the table below using these values.

| Time Remaining (s) | 28 | ■ | ■ |
|---|---|---|---|
| Steps | 0 | ■ | ■ |

2. Find the average rate of change for Pauline's walk.
3. Sketch a graph of the points in the table, or plot them on your graphing calculator.
4. Find an equation that describes the line through the points.
5. How would the graph change if Pauline increased her speed? What if she decreased her speed?

# READY TO GO ON?



## Quiz for Lessons 5-6 Through 5-9

### 5-6 Slope-Intercept Form

**Graph each line given the slope and $y$-intercept.**

1. slope $= \frac{1}{4}$; $y$-intercept $= 2$
2. slope $= -3$; $y$-intercept $= 5$
3. slope $= -1$; $y$-intercept $= -6$

**Write each equation in slope-intercept form, and then graph.**

4. $2x + y = 5$
5. $2x - 6y = 6$
6. $3x + y = 3x - 4$
7. **Entertainment** At a chili cook-off, people pay a \$3.00 entrance fee and \$0.50 for each bowl of chili they taste. The graph shows the total cost per person as a function of the number of bowls of chili tasted.

   a. Write a rule that gives the total cost per person as a function of the number of bowls of chili tasted.

   b. Identify the slope and $y$-intercept and describe their meanings in this situation.

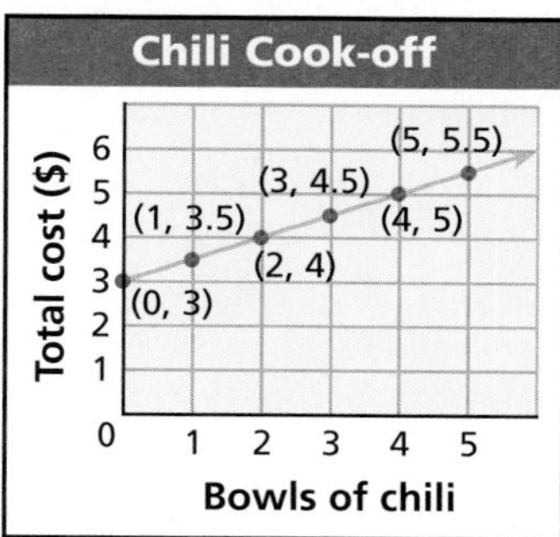


### 5-7 Point-Slope Form

**Graph the line with the given slope that contains the given point.**

8. slope $= -3$; $(0, 3)$
9. slope $= -\frac{2}{3}$; $(-3, 5)$
10. slope $= 2$; $(-3, -1)$

**Write an equation in slope-intercept form for the line through the two points.**

11. $(3, 1)$ and $(4, 3)$
12. $(-1, -1)$ and $(1, 7)$
13. $(1, -4)$ and $(-2, 5)$

### 5-8 Slopes of Parallel and Perpendicular Lines

**Identify which lines are parallel.**

14. $y = -2x$; $y = 2x + 1$; $y = 2x$; $y = 2(x + 5)$
15. $-3y = x$; $y = -\frac{1}{3}x + 1$; $y = -3x$; $y + 2 = x + 4$

**Identify which lines are perpendicular.**

16. $y = -4x - 1$; $y = \frac{1}{4}x$; $y = 4x - 6$; $x = -4$
17. $y = -\frac{3}{4}x$; $y = \frac{3}{4}x - 3$; $y = \frac{4}{3}x$; $y = 4$; $x = 3$
18. Write an equation in slope-intercept form for the line that passes through $(5, 2)$ and is parallel to the line described by $3x - 5y = 15$.
19. Write an equation in slope-intercept form for the line that passes through $(3, 5)$ and is perpendicular to the line described by $y = -\frac{3}{2}x - 2$.

### 5-9 Transforming Linear Functions

**Graph $f(x)$ and $g(x)$. Then describe the transformation(s) from the graph of $f(x)$ to the graph of $g(x)$.**

20. $f(x) = 5x$, $g(x) = -5x$
21. $f(x) = \frac{1}{2}x - 1$, $g(x) = \frac{1}{2}x + 4$
22. An attorney charges an initial fee of \$250 and then \$150 per hour. The total bill after $x$ hours is $f(x) = 150x + 250$. How will the graph of this function change if the initial fee is reduced to \$200? if the hourly rate is increased to \$175?

EXTENSION

# Absolute-Value Functions

**MA.A.4.2** Use appropriate terminology...associated with functions. *Also* **MA.A.4.3**

***Objectives***
Graph absolute-value functions.

Identify characteristics of absolute-value functions and their graphs.

***Vocabulary***
absolute-value function
axis of symmetry
vertex

An **absolute-value function** is a function whose rule contains an absolute-value expression. A table and graph for $y = |x|$ are shown below.

| $x$ | $y = \|x\|$ |
|---|---|
| −2 | 2 |
| −1 | 1 |
| 0 | 0 |
| 1 | 1 |
| 2 | 2 |

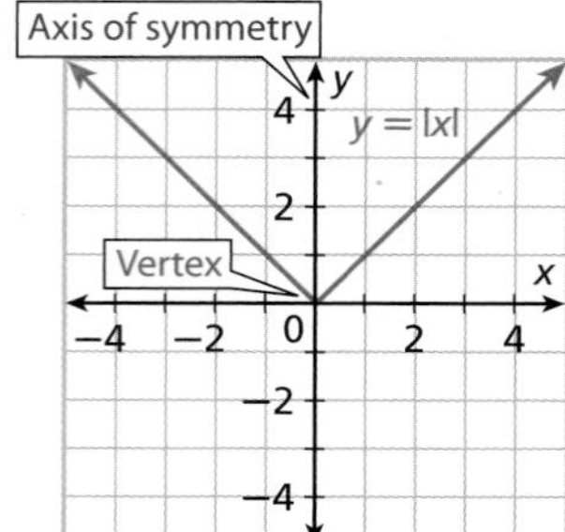


Absolute-value graphs are V-shaped. The **axis of symmetry** is the line that divides the graph into two congruent halves. The **vertex** is the "corner" point.

From the graph of $y = |x|$, you can tell that
- the **axis of symmetry** is the $y$-axis $(x = 0)$.
- the **vertex** is $(0, 0)$.
- the domain ($x$-values) is the set of all real numbers.
- the range ($y$-values) is described by $y \geq 0$.
- $y = |x|$ is a function because each domain value has exactly one range value.
- the $x$-intercept and the $y$-intercept are both 0.

EXAMPLE 1

### Absolute-Value Functions

**Graph $y = |x| - 1$ and label the axis of symmetry and the vertex. Identify the intercepts, and give the domain and range.**

*Choose positive, negative, and zero values for x, and find ordered pairs.*

| $x$ | −2 | −1 | 0 | 1 | 2 |
|---|---|---|---|---|---|
| $y = \|x\| - 1$ | 1 | 0 | −1 | 0 | 1 |

*Plot the ordered pairs and connect them.*

From the graph, you can tell that
- the **axis of symmetry** is the $y$-axis $(x = 0)$.
- the **vertex** is $(0, -1)$.
- the $x$-intercepts are 1 and −1.
- the $y$-intercept is −1.
- the domain is all real numbers.
- the range is described by $y \geq -1$.

1. Graph $f(x) = 3|x|$ and label the axis of symmetry and the vertex. Identify the intercepts, and give the domain and range.

## EXAMPLE 2 *Sports Application*

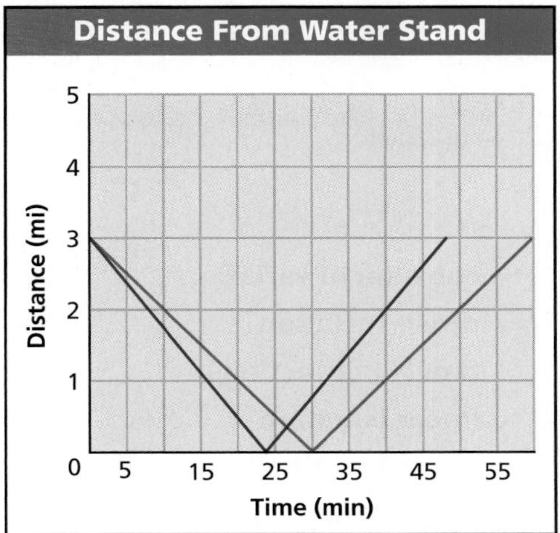


**In a charity race, there is a water stand for the runners halfway between the start and finish lines. The function $y = \left|\frac{x}{8} - 3\right|$ models Riley's distance $y$ in miles from the water stand $x$ minutes into the race.**

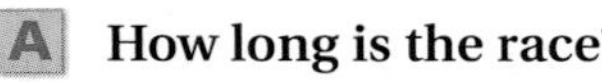

**A How long is the race?**

$y = \left|\frac{x}{8} - 3\right|$ is graphed in blue.

At the start of the race ($x = 0$), Riley is 3 mi from the water stand. The water stand is halfway between the start and finish lines, so the race is 6 mi.

**B How much time does it take Riley to reach the water stand?**

When Riley reaches the water stand, $y = 0$. This happens when $x = 24$. It takes Riley 24 min to reach the water stand.

**C The function $y = \left|\frac{x}{10} - 3\right|$ models Dean's distance from the water stand during the same race. Compare Dean's graph to Riley's graph. What can you conclude about Dean's speed?**

$y = \left|\frac{x}{10} - 3\right|$ is graphed in red. Both graphs start at the same point, but Dean's graph is shifted to the right. It takes him more time to reach the water stand and to finish the race. Therefore, he must be running more slowly than Riley.

2. How would the graph be different for someone who runs faster than Riley?

## EXTENSION Exercises

**MA.A.4.2, MA.A.4.3**

**Graph each absolute-value function and label the axis of symmetry and the vertex. Identify the intercepts, and give the domain and range.**

1. $y = |x| + 3$
2. $y = |x + 3|$
3. $y = \frac{1}{2}|x|$
4. $y = |x - 3|$

**Tell whether each statement is sometimes, always, or never true.**

5. The absolute value of a number is negative.
6. An absolute-value function has an $x$-intercept.
7. An absolute-value function has two $y$-intercepts.
8. **Multi-Step** Graph $y = |x|$, $y = |x| + 5$, and $y = |x| - 6$ on the same coordinate plane. Then make a conjecture, in terms of a transformation, about the graph of $y = |x| + k$, for any value of $k$.
9. **Multi-Step** Graph $y = |x|$, $y = |x - 4|$, and $y = |x + 3|$ on the same coordinate plane. Then make a conjecture, in terms of a transformation, about the graph of $y = |x - h|$, for any value of $h$.

CHAPTER 5

# Study Guide: Review

## Vocabulary

**constant of variation** . . . . . . . . 326
**direct variation** . . . . . . . . . . . . . 326
**family of functions** . . . . . . . . . 357
**linear equation** . . . . . . . . . . . . . 298
**linear function** . . . . . . . . . . . . . 296
**parallel lines** . . . . . . . . . . . . . . . 349
**parent function** . . . . . . . . . . . . . 357
**perpendicular lines** . . . . . . . . . 351
**rate of change** . . . . . . . . . . . . . . 310
**reflection** . . . . . . . . . . . . . . . . . . 359
**rise** . . . . . . . . . . . . . . . . . . . . . . . . 311
**rotation** . . . . . . . . . . . . . . . . . . . . 358
**run** . . . . . . . . . . . . . . . . . . . . . . . . 311
**slope** . . . . . . . . . . . . . . . . . . . . . . . 311
**transformation** . . . . . . . . . . . . . . 357
**translation** . . . . . . . . . . . . . . . . . 357
***x*-intercept** . . . . . . . . . . . . . . . . 303
***y*-intercept** . . . . . . . . . . . . . . . . 303

**Complete the sentences below with vocabulary words from the list above. Words may be used more than once.**

**1.** A(n) __?__ is a "slide," a(n) __?__ is a "turn," and a(n) __?__ is a "flip."

**2.** The $x$-coordinate of the point that contains the __?__ is always 0.

**3.** In the equation $y = mx + b$, the value of $m$ is the __?__ , and the value of $b$ is the __?__ .

## 5-1 Identifying Linear Functions *(pp. 296–302)*

MA.A.4.4, MA.A.4.2, MA.A.5.1

### EXAMPLES

**Tell whether each function is linear. If so, graph the function.**

■ $y = -3x + 2$

$$\begin{aligned} y &= -3x + 2 \\ +3x \quad & \; +3x \\ 3x + y &= 2 \end{aligned}$$

*Write the equation in standard form.*

This is a linear function.

*Generate ordered pairs.*

| $x$ | $y = -3x + 2$ | $(x, y)$ |
|---|---|---|
| −2 | $y = -3(-2) + 2 = 8$ | (−2, 8) |
| 0 | $y = -3(0) + 2 = 2$ | (0, 2) |
| 2 | $y = -3(2) + 2 = -4$ | (2, −4) |

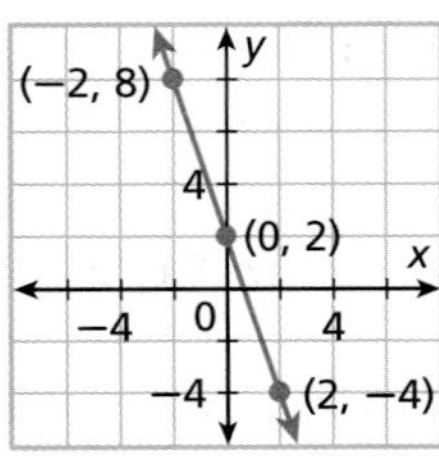


*Plot the points and connect them with a straight line.*

■ $y = 2x^3$

This is not a linear function because $x$ has an exponent other than 1.

### EXERCISES

**Tell whether the given ordered pairs satisfy a linear function. Explain.**

**4.**

| $x$ | $y$ |
|---|---|
| −3 | 3 |
| −1 | 1 |
| 1 | 1 |
| 3 | 3 |

**5.**

| $x$ | $y$ |
|---|---|
| 0 | −3 |
| 1 | −1 |
| 2 | 1 |
| 3 | 3 |

**6.** $\{(-2, 5), (-1, 3), (0, 1), (1, -1), (2, -3)\}$

**7.** $\{(1, 7), (3, 6), (6, 5), (9, 4), (13, 3)\}$

**Each equation below is linear. Write each equation in standard form and give the values of $A$, $B$, and $C$.**

**8.** $y = -5x + 1$

**9.** $\frac{x + 2}{2} = -3y$

**10.** $4y = 7x$

**11.** $9 = y$

**12.** Helene is selling cupcakes for \$0.50 each. The function $f(x) = 0.5x$ gives the total amount of money Helene makes after selling $x$ number of cupcakes. Graph this function and give its domain and range.

## 5-2 Using Intercepts *(pp. 303–308)*

MA.A.4.2, MA.A.4.4, MA.A.5.1, MA.A.4.5

### EXAMPLE

■ **Find the $x$- and $y$-intercepts of $2x + 5y = 10$.**

| Let $y = 0$. | Let $x = 0$. |
|---|---|
| $2x + 5(0) = 10$ | $2(0) + 5y = 10$ |
| $2x + 0 = 10$ | $0 + 5y = 10$ |
| $2x = 10$ | $5y = 10$ |
| $\frac{2x}{2} = \frac{10}{2}$ | $\frac{5y}{5} = \frac{10}{5}$ |
| $x = 5$ | $y = 2$ |
| The $x$-intercept is 5. | The $y$-intercept is 2. |

### EXERCISES

**Find the $x$- and $y$-intercepts.**

**13.**

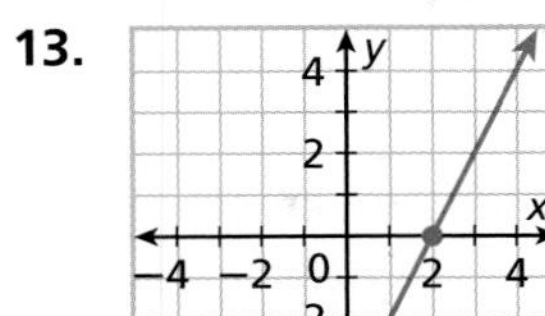

**14.**

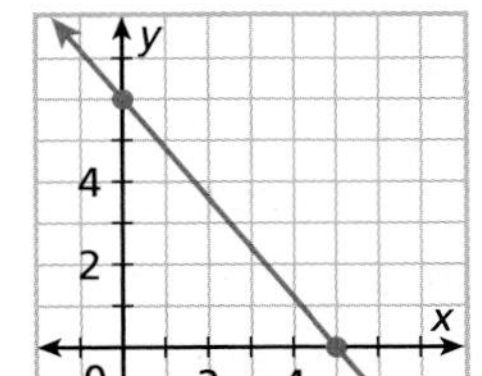

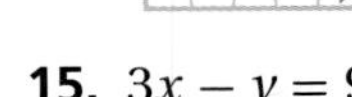

**15.** $3x - y = 9$

**16.** $-2x + y = 1$

**17.** $-x + 6y = 18$

**18.** $3x - 4y = 1$

## 5-3 Rate of Change and Slope *(pp. 310–317)*

MA.A.3, MA.A.3.2, MA.A.3.3

### EXAMPLE

■ **Find the slope.**

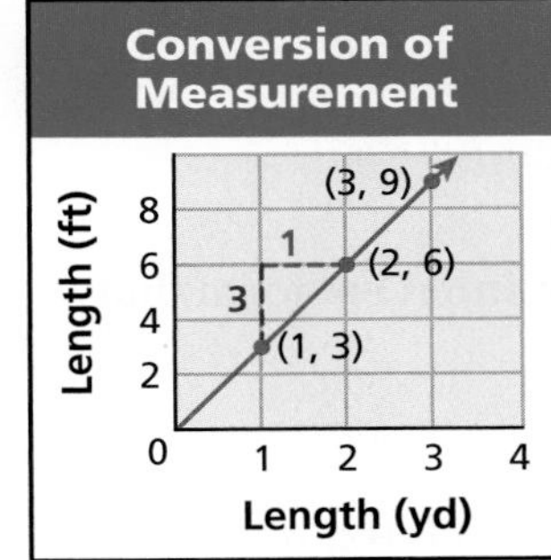


$$\text{slope} = \frac{\text{change in } y}{\text{change in } x} = \frac{3}{1} = 3$$

### EXERCISES

**19.** Graph the data and show the rates of change.

| Time (s) | Distance (ft) |
|---|---|
| 0 | 0 |
| 1 | 16 |
| 2 | 64 |
| 3 | 144 |
| 4 | 256 |

**20.** Find the slope of the line graphed below.

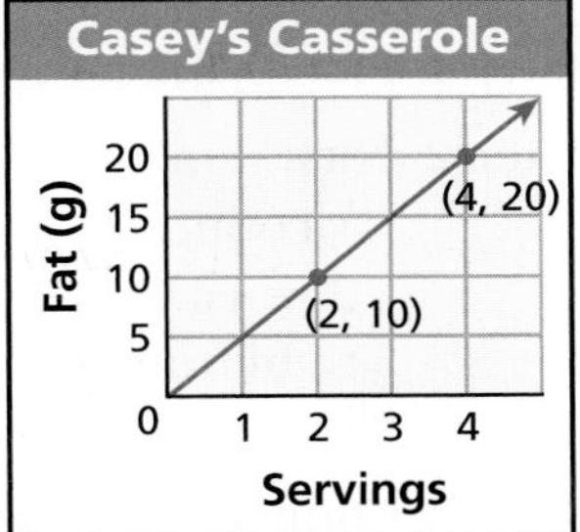


## 5-4 The Slope Formula *(pp. 320–325)*

MA.G.1.1, MA.A.3, MA.A.3.3, MA.A.5.1, MA.A.4.5

### EXAMPLE

■ **Find the slope of the line described by $2x - 3y = 6$.**

**Step 1** Identify the $x$- and $y$-intercepts.

| Let $y = 0$. | Let $x = 0$. |
|---|---|
| $2x - 3(0) = 6$ | $2(0) - 3y = 6$ |
| $2x = 6$ | $-3y = 6$ |
| $x = 3$ | $y = -2$ |

The line contains $(3, 0)$ and $(0, -2)$.

**Step 2** Use the slope formula.

$$m = \frac{y_2 - y_1}{x_2 - x_1} = \frac{-2 - 0}{0 - 3} = \frac{-2}{-3} = \frac{2}{3}$$

### EXERCISES

**Find the slope of the line described by each equation.**

**21.** $4x + 3y = 24$

**22.** $y = -3x + 6$

**23.** $x + 2y = 10$

**24.** $3x = y + 3$

**25.** $y + 2 = 7x$

**26.** $16x = 4y + 1$

**Find the slope of the line that contains each pair of points.**

**27.** $(1, 2)$ and $(2, -3)$

**28.** $(4, -2)$ and $(-5, 7)$

**29.** $(-3, -6)$ and $(4, 1)$

**30.** $\left(\frac{1}{2}, 2\right)$ and $\left(\frac{3}{4}, \frac{5}{2}\right)$

**31.** $(2, 2)$ and $(2, 7)$

**32.** $(1, -3)$ and $(5, -3)$

## 5-5 Direct Variation *(pp. 326–331)*

MA.A.2, MA.A.2.1, MA.A.2.2, MA.A.2.3, MA.A.5.1, MA.A.4.5

### EXAMPLE

- **Tell whether $6x = -4y$ is a direct variation. If so, identify the constant of variation.**

$6x = -4y$

$\frac{6x}{-4} = \frac{-4y}{-4}$ *Solve the equation for y.*

$-\frac{6}{4}x = y$

$y = -\frac{3}{2}x$ *Simplify.*

This equation is a direct variation because it can be written in the form $y = kx$, where $k = -\frac{3}{2}$.

### EXERCISES

**Tell whether each equation is a direct variation. If so, identify the constant of variation.**

**33.** $y = -6x$ **34.** $x - y = 0$

**35.** $y + 4x = 3$ **36.** $2x = -4y$

**37.** The value of $y$ varies directly with $x$, and $y = -8$ when $x = 2$. Find $y$ when $x = 3$.

**38.** Maleka charges \$8 per hour for baby-sitting. The amount of money she makes varies directly with the number of hours she baby-sits. The equation $y = 8x$ tells how much she earns $y$ for baby-sitting $x$ hours. Graph this direct variation.

## 5-6 Slope-Intercept Form *(pp. 334–340)*

MA.A.4.4, MA.A.4.3, MA.A.5.1, MA.A.4.5, MA.A.4.2

### EXAMPLE

- **Graph the line with slope $= -\frac{4}{5}$ and $y$-intercept $= 8$.**

**Step 1** Plot $(0, 8)$.

**Step 2** For a slope of $\frac{-4}{5}$, count 4 down and 5 right from $(0, 8)$. Plot another point.

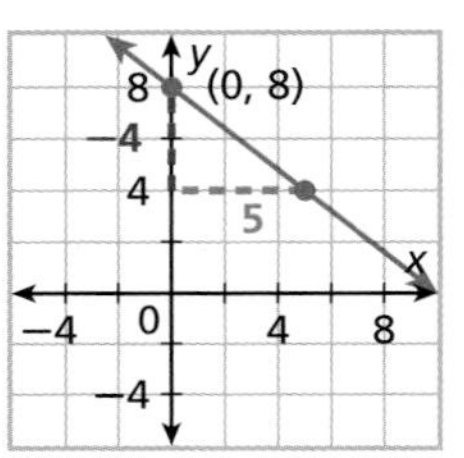


**Step 3** Connect the two points with a line.

### EXERCISES

**Graph each line given the slope and $y$-intercept.**

**39.** slope $= -\frac{1}{2}$; $y$-intercept $= 4$

**40.** slope $= 3$; $y$-intercept $= -7$

**Write the equation in slope-intercept form that describes each line.**

**41.** slope $= \frac{1}{3}$, $y$-intercept $= 5$

**42.** slope $= 4$, the point $(1, -5)$ is on the line

## 5-7 Point-Slope Form *(pp. 341–347)*

MA.A.4.4, MA.G.1.1, MA.A.4.3, MA.A.5.1, MA.A.4.5

### EXAMPLE

- **Write an equation in slope-intercept form for the line through $(4, -1)$ and $(-2, 8)$.**

$m = \frac{y_2 - y_1}{x_2 - x_1} = \frac{8-(-1)}{-2-4} = \frac{9}{-6} = -\frac{3}{2}$ *Find the slope.*

$y - y_1 = m(x - x_1)$ *Substitute into the point-slope form.*

$y - 8 = -\frac{3}{2}[x - (-2)]$

$y - 8 = -\frac{3}{2}(x + 2)$ *Solve for y.*

$y - 8 = -\frac{3}{2}x - 3$

$y = -\frac{3}{2}x + 5$

### EXERCISES

**Graph the line with the given slope that contains the given point.**

**43.** slope $= \frac{1}{2}$; $(4, -3)$ **44.** slope $= -1$; $(-3, 1)$

**Write an equation in point-slope form for the line with the given slope through the given point.**

**45.** slope $= 2$; $(1, 3)$ **46.** slope $= -5$; $(-6, 4)$

**Write an equation in slope-intercept form for the line through the two points.**

**47.** $(1, 4)$ and $(3, 8)$ **48.** $(0, 3)$ and $(-2, 5)$

**49.** $(-2, 4)$ and $(-1, 6)$ **50.** $(-3, 2)$ and $(5, 2)$

## 5-8 Slopes of Parallel and Perpendicular Lines (pp. 349–355)

MA.G.1.1, MA.A.4.3, MA.A.4.4, MA.A.5.1, MA.G.1, MA.G.1.2

### EXAMPLE

■ **Write an equation in slope-intercept form for the line that passes through $(4, -2)$ and is perpendicular to the line described by $y = -4x + 3$.**

**Step 1** Find the slope of $y = -4x + 3$.
The slope is $-4$. The perpendicular line has a slope of $\frac{1}{4}$.

**Step 2** Write the equation.
The perpendicular line has a slope of $\frac{1}{4}$ and contains $(4, -2)$.

$$y - y_1 = m(x - x_1)$$
$$y + 2 = \frac{1}{4}(x - 4)$$

**Step 3** Write the equation in slope-intercept form.

$$y + 2 = \frac{1}{4}(x - 4)$$

$$y + 2 = \frac{1}{4}x - 1 \quad \textit{Distribute } \frac{1}{4}.$$

$$y = \frac{1}{4}x - 3 \quad \textit{Subtract 2 from both sides.}$$

### EXERCISES

**Identify which lines are parallel.**

51. $y = -\frac{1}{3}x;\ y = 3x + 2;\ y = -\frac{1}{3}x - 6;\ y = 3$

52. $y - 2 = -4(x - 1);\ y = 4x - 4;\ y = \frac{1}{4}x;\ y = -4x - 2$

**Identify which lines are perpendicular.**

53. $y - 1 = -5(x - 6);\ y = \frac{1}{5}x + 2;\ y = 5;\ y = 5x + 8$

54. $y = 2x;\ y - 2 = 3(x + 1);\ y = \frac{2}{3}x - 4;\ y = -\frac{1}{3}x$

55. Show that $ABC$ is a right triangle.

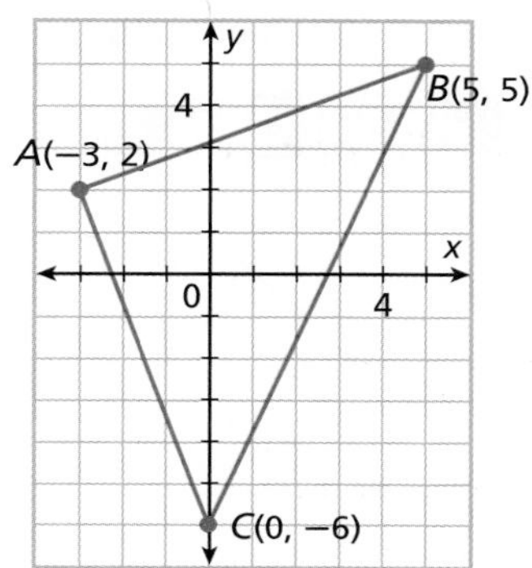


56. Write an equation in slope-intercept form for the line that passes through $(1, -1)$ and is parallel to the line described by $y = 2x - 4$.

## 5-9 Transforming Linear Functions (pp. 357–363)

MA.A.4.3, MA.A.5.1

### EXAMPLE

■ **Graph $f(x) = \frac{1}{2}x$ and $g(x) = 4x + 2$. Then describe the transformation(s) from the graph of $f(x)$ to the graph of $g(x)$.**

Find transformations on $f(x) = \frac{1}{2}x$ that will result in $g(x) = 4x + 2$.

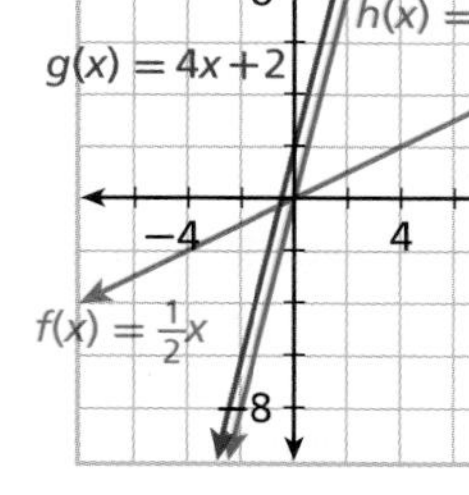


- Multiply $f(x) = \frac{1}{2}x$ by 8 to get $h(x) = 4x$. This rotates the graph about $(0, 0)$, making it steeper.
- Then add 2 to $h(x) = 4x$ to get $g(x) = 4x + 2$. This translates the graph 2 units up.

The transformations are rotation and translation.

### EXERCISES

**Graph $f(x)$ and $g(x)$. Then describe the transformation(s) from the graph of $f(x)$ to the graph of $g(x)$.**

57. $f(x) = x,\ g(x) = x + 4$

58. $f(x) = x,\ g(x) = x - 1$

59. $f(x) = 3x,\ g(x) = 2x$

60. $f(x) = \frac{1}{2}x + 1,\ g(x) = 5x + 1$

61. $f(x) = 4x,\ g(x) = -4x$

62. $f(x) = \frac{1}{3}x - 2,\ g(x) = -\frac{1}{3}x - 2$

63. The entrance fee at a carnival is \$3 and each ride costs \$1. The total cost for $x$ rides is $f(x) = x + 3$. How will the graph of this function change if the entrance fee is increased to \$5? if the cost per ride is increased to \$2?

# CHAPTER 5 CHAPTER TEST

**Tell whether the given ordered pairs satisfy a linear function. Explain.**

1. $\{(0, 0), (1, 1), (2, 4), (3, 9), (4, 16)\}$

2. 

| $x$ | −3 | −1 | 1 | 3 | 5 |
|---|---|---|---|---|---|
| $y$ | 6 | 3 | 0 | −3 | −6 |

3. Lily plans to volunteer at the tutoring center for 45 hours. She can tutor 3 hours per week. The function $f(x) = 45 - 3x$ gives the number of hours she will have left to tutor after $x$ weeks. Graph the function and find its intercepts. What does each intercept represent?

4. Use intercepts to graph the line described by $2x - 3y = 6$.

**Find the slope of each line. Then tell what the slope represents.**

5. 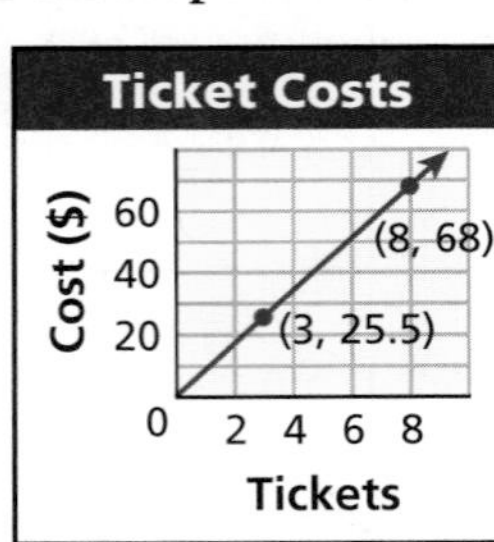


6. 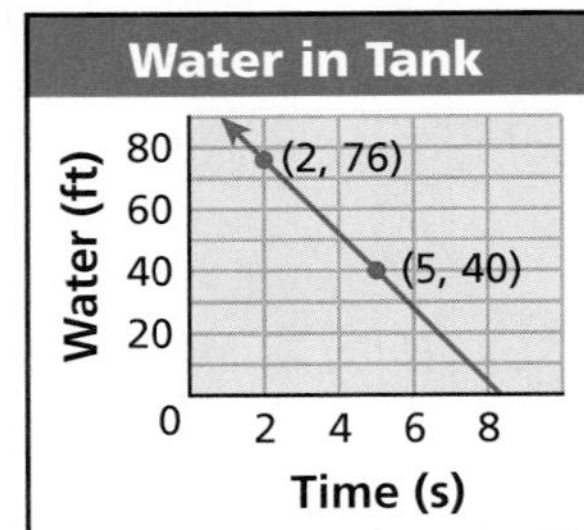


7. 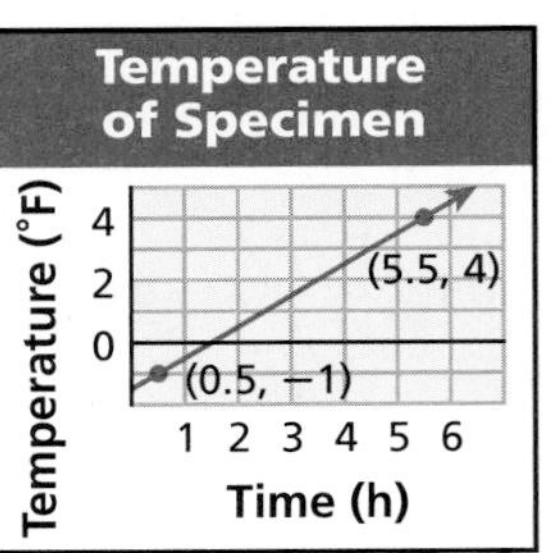


**Tell whether each relationship is a direct variation. If so, identify the constant of variation.**

8. 

| $x$ | −1 | 2 | 5 | 9 |
|---|---|---|---|---|
| $y$ | 4 | 7 | 10 | 14 |

9. 

| $x$ | −2 | 2 | 6 | 10 |
|---|---|---|---|---|
| $y$ | 1 | −1 | −3 | −5 |

10. Write the equation $2x - 2y = 4$ in slope-intercept form, and then graph.

11. Graph the line with slope $\frac{1}{3}$ that contains the point $(-4, -3)$.

12. Write an equation in slope-intercept form for the line through $(-1, 1)$ and $(0, 3)$.

13. Identify which lines are parallel: $y = -\frac{1}{2}x + 3$; $y = \frac{1}{2}x + 1$; $y = 2x$; $x + 2y = 4$.

14. Identify which lines are perpendicular: $y - 2 = 3x$; $y + 4x = -1$; $y = -\frac{1}{3}x + 5$; $y = \frac{1}{3}x - 4$.

15. Write an equation in slope-intercept form for the line that passes through $(0, 6)$ and is parallel to the line described by $y = 2x + 3$.

16. Write an equation in slope-intercept form for the line that passes through $(4, 6)$ and is perpendicular to the line described by $y = x - 3$.

**Graph $f(x)$ and $g(x)$. Then describe the transformation(s) from the graph of $f(x)$ to the graph of $g(x)$.**

17. $f(x) = 8x$, $g(x) = 4x$

18. $f(x) = -x + 2$, $g(x) = -x - 1$

19. $f(x) = 3x$, $g(x) = 6x - 1$

20. An airport parking lot charges an entry fee of \$2.00 plus \$2.50 for every hour that your car is parked. The total charge for parking $x$ hours is $f(x) = 2.5x + 2$. How will the graph of this function change if the entry fee is increased to \$3.50? If the hourly rate is reduced to \$2.25?

CHAPTER 5

## FOCUS ON SAT

SAT scores are based on the total number of items answered correctly minus a fraction of the number of multiple-choice questions answered incorrectly. No points are subtracted for questions unanswered.

**On the SAT, there is a penalty for guessing on multiple-choice items. Guess only when you can eliminate at least one of the answer choices.**

**You may want to time yourself as you take this practice test. It should take you about 7 minutes to complete.**

**1.** The line through $A(1, -3)$ and $B(-2, d)$ has slope $-2$. What is the value of $d$?

**(A)** $-\frac{3}{2}$

**(B)** $-1$

**(C)** $\frac{1}{2}$

**(D)** 3

**(E)** 5

**2.** The ordered pairs $\{(0, -3), (4, -1), (6, 0), (10, 2)\}$ satisfy a pattern. Which is NOT true?

**(A)** The pattern is linear.

**(B)** The pattern can be described by $2x - 4y = 12$.

**(C)** The ordered pairs lie on a line.

**(D)** $(-4, 1)$ satisfies the same pattern.

**(E)** The set of ordered pairs is a function.

**3.** If $y$ varies directly as $x$, what is the value of $x$ when $y = 72$?

| *x* | 7 | 12 | |
|---|---|---|---|
| *y* | 28 | 48 | 72 |

**(A)** 17

**(B)** 18

**(C)** 24

**(D)** 28

**(E)** 36

**4.** The line segment between the points $(4, 0)$ and $(2, -2)$ forms one side of a rectangle. Which of the following coordinates could determine another vertex of that rectangle?

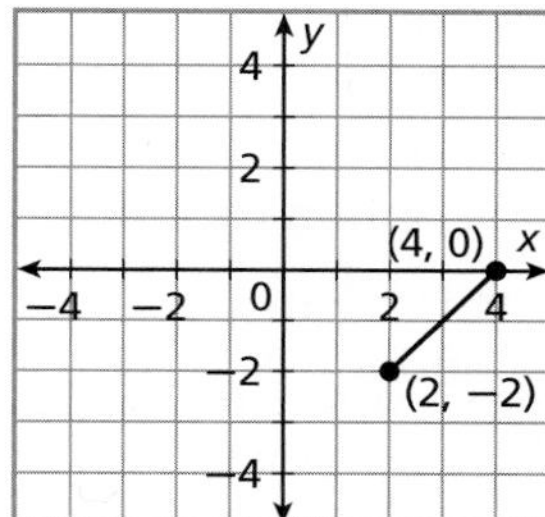


**(A)** $(-2, 6)$

**(B)** $(-2, -2)$

**(C)** $(0, 6)$

**(D)** $(1, 2)$

**(E)** $(4, 6)$

**5.** Which of the following has the same slope as the line described by $2x - 3y = 3$?

**(A)** $3x - 2y = 2$

**(B)** $\frac{2}{3}x - y = -2$

**(C)** $2x - 2y = 3$

**(D)** $\frac{1}{3}x - 2y = -2$

**(E)** $-2x - 3y = 2$

CHAPTER 5

# TEST TACKLER

Standardized Test Strategies

## Multiple Choice: Recognize Distracters

In multiple-choice items, the options that are incorrect are called *distracters*. This is an appropriate name, because these incorrect options can distract you from the correct answer.

Test writers create distracters by using common student errors. Beware! Even if the answer you get when you work the problem is one of the options, it may not be the correct answer.

### EXAMPLE 1

**What is the $y$-intercept of $4x + 10 = -2y$?**

Ⓐ 10 Ⓒ $-2.5$

Ⓑ 5 Ⓓ $-5$

**Look at each option carefully.**

Ⓐ This is a distracter. The $y$-intercept would be 10 if the function was $4x + 10 = y$. A common error is to ignore the coefficient of $y$.

Ⓑ This is a distracter. Another common error is to divide by 2 instead of $-2$ when solving for $y$.

Ⓒ This is a distracter. One of the most common errors students make is confusing the $x$-intercept and the $y$-intercept. This distracter is actually the *$x$-intercept* of the given line.

Ⓓ This is the correct answer.

### EXAMPLE 2

**What is the equation of a line with a slope of $-4$ that contains $(2, -3)$?**

Ⓕ $y - 3 = -4(x - 2)$ Ⓗ $y + 3 = -4(x - 2)$

Ⓖ $y - 2 = -4(x + 3)$ Ⓙ $y + 4 = -3(x - 2)$

**Look at each option carefully.**

Ⓕ This is a distracter. Students often make errors with positive and negative signs. You would get this answer if you simplified $y - (-3)$ as $y - 3$.

Ⓖ This is a distracter. You would get this answer if you switched the $x$-coordinate and the $y$-coordinate.

Ⓗ This is the correct answer.

Ⓙ This is a distracter. You would get this answer if you substituted the given values incorrectly in the point-slope equation.

When you calculate an answer to a multiple-choice test item, try to solve the problem again with a different method to make sure your answer is correct.

**Read each test item and answer the questions that follow.**

**Item A**

**A line contains $(1, 2)$ and $(-2, 14)$. What are the slope and $y$-intercept?**

(A) Slope $= -4$; $y$-intercept $= -2$

(B) Slope $= 4$; $y$-intercept $= 6$

(C) Slope $= -\frac{1}{4}$; $y$-intercept $= 1$

(D) Slope $= -4$; $y$-intercept $= 6$

1. What common error does the slope in choice B represent?
2. The slope given in choice A is correct, but the $y$-intercept is not. What error was made when finding the $y$-intercept?
3. What formula can you use to find the slope of a line? How was this formula used incorrectly to get the slope in choice C?

**Item B**

**Which of these functions has a graph that is NOT parallel to the line described by $y = \frac{1}{2}x + 4$?**

(F) $y = 6 - \frac{1}{2}x$

(G) $y = \frac{1}{2}x + 6$

(H) $-2y = -x + 1$

(J) $2y = x$

4. When given two linear functions, describe how to determine whether their graphs are parallel.
5. Which is the correct answer? Describe the errors a student might make to get each of the distracters.

**Item C**

**Which of these lines has a slope of $-3$?**

(A)
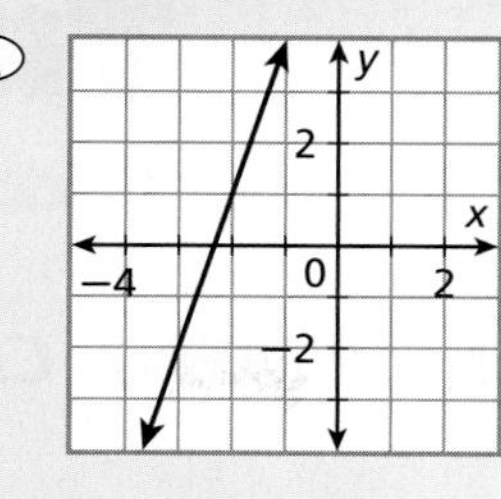


(C)
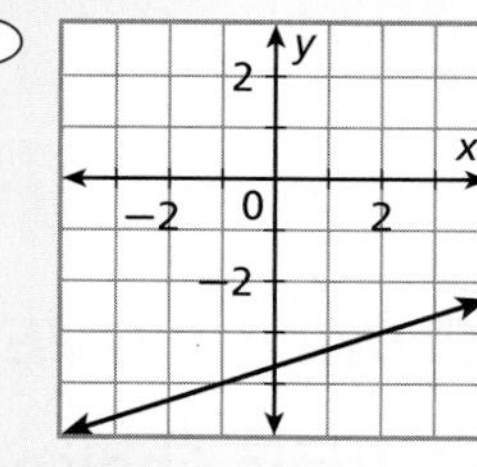


(B)
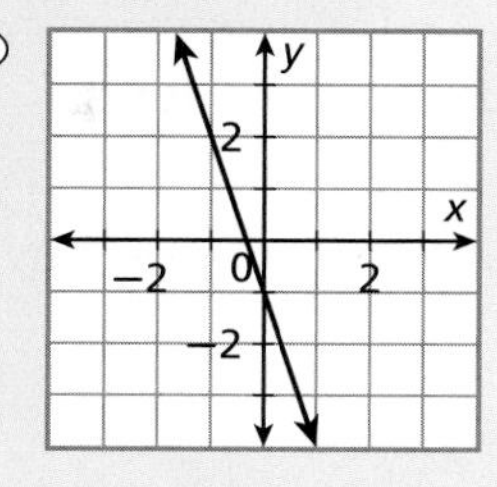


(D)
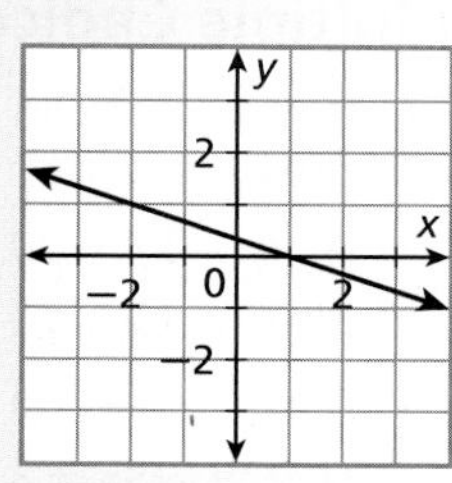


6. Which two answer choices can be eliminated immediately? Why?
7. Decribe how to find the slope of a line from its graph.
8. What common error does choice A represent?
9. What common error does choice D represent?
10. Which is the correct answer?

**Item D**

**Which is NOT a linear function?**

(F) $f(x) = 4 + x$

(G) $f(x) = -x - 4$

(H) $f(x) = 4x^2$

(J) $f(x) = \frac{1}{4}x$

11. When given a function rule, how can you tell if the function is linear?
12. What part of the function given in choice G might make someone think it is not linear?
13. What part of the function given in choice J might make someone think it is not linear?
14. What part of the function given in choice H makes it NOT linear?

CHAPTER 5

go.hrw.com
State Test Practice Online
KEYWORD: MA7 TestPrep

# CUMULATIVE ASSESSMENT, CHAPTERS 1–5

## Multiple Choice

**1.** Which function describes the line with the greatest slope?

A $3y - 5x = 20$

B $5y - 3x = 20$

C $3y - 20x = 5$

D $20y + 5x = 3$

**2.** Frank borrowed \$5000 with an annual simple interest rate. The amount of interest he owed after 6 months was \$300. What is the interest rate of the loan?

A 1%

B 6%

C 10%

D 12%

**3.** Patty's Pizza charges \$5.50 for a large pizza plus \$0.30 for each topping. Pizza Town charges \$5.00 for a large pizza plus \$0.40 for each topping. Which inequality could be used to find the number of toppings $x$ so that the cost of a pizza at Pizza Town is greater than the cost of a pizza at Patty's Pizza?

A $(5 + 0.4)x > (5.5 + 0.3)x$

B $5.5x + 0.3 > 5x + 0.4$

C $5.5 + 0.3x > 5 + 0.4x$

D $5 + 0.4x > 5.5 + 0.3x$

**4.** The side length of a square $s$ can be determined by the formula $s = \sqrt{A}$ where $A$ represents the area of the square. What is the side length of a square with area 0.09 square meters?

A 0.0081 meters

B 0.03 meters

C 0.3 meters

D 0.81 meters

**5.** What is the value of $f(x) = -3 - x$ when $x = -7$?

A $-10$

B $-4$

C 4

D 10

**6.** Which relationship is a direct variation?

A

| x | 1 | 2 | 3 | 4 |
|---|---|---|---|---|
| y | −1 | 0 | 1 | 2 |

B

| x | 1 | 2 | 3 | 4 |
|---|---|---|---|---|
| y | 0 | −1 | −2 | −3 |

C

| x | 1 | 2 | 3 | 4 |
|---|---|---|---|---|
| y | 3 | 5 | 7 | 9 |

D

| x | 1 | 2 | 3 | 4 |
|---|---|---|---|---|
| y | 3 | 6 | 9 | 12 |

**7.** Which function has $x$-intercept $-2$ and $y$-intercept 4?

A $2x - y = 4$

B $2y - x = 4$

C $y - 2x = 4$

D $x - 2y = 4$

**8.** Which equation describes the relationship between $x$ and $y$ in the table below?

| x | −8 | −4 | 0 | 4 | 8 |
|---|---|---|---|---|---|
| y | 2 | 1 | 0 | −1 | −2 |

A $y = -4x$

B $y = -\frac{1}{4}x$

C $y = 4x$

D $y = \frac{1}{4}x$

**9.** Which graph is described by $x - 3y = -3$?

A

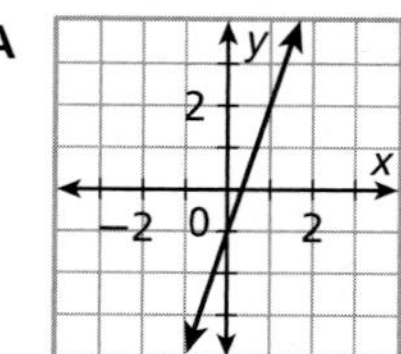


C

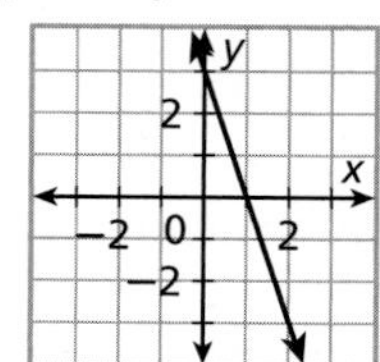


B

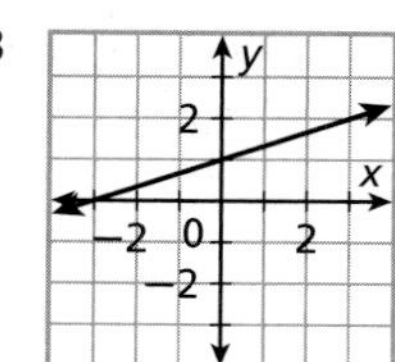


D

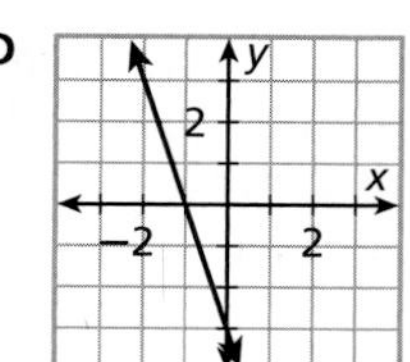

**When answering multiple-choice test items, check that the test item number matches the number on your answer sheet, especially if you skip test items that you plan to come back to.**

**10.** Which line is parallel to the line described by $2x + 3y = 6$?

A $3x + 2y = 6$

B $3x - 2y = -6$

C $2x + 3y = -6$

D $2x - 3y = 6$

**11.** Which function's graph is ***not*** perpendicular to the line described by $4x - y = -2$?

A $y + \frac{1}{4}x = 0$

B $\frac{1}{2}x = 10 - 2y$

C $3y = \frac{3}{4}x + 3$

D $y = -\frac{1}{4}x + \frac{3}{2}$

**12.** Company A charges \$30 plus \$0.40 per mile for a car rental. The total charge for $m$ miles is given by $f(m) = 30 + 0.4m$. For a similar car, company B charges \$30 plus \$0.30 per mile. The total charge for $m$ miles is given by $g(m) = 30 + 0.3m$. Which best describes the transformation from the graph of $f(m)$ to the graph of $g(m)$?

A Translation up

B Translation down

C Rotation

D Reflection

**13.** What is the $y$-intercept of $y - 2 = 3(x + 4)$?

A $-\frac{14}{3}$

B $-2$

C 6

D 14

**14.** Which set of ordered pairs does ***not*** satisfy a linear function?

A

| $x$ | 5 | 10 | 15 | 25 | 35 |
|---|---|---|---|---|---|
| $y$ | 2 | 4 | 6 | 10 | 14 |

B

| $x$ | 13 | 10 | 7 | 2 | −3 |
|---|---|---|---|---|---|
| $y$ | 8 | 14 | 20 | 26 | 32 |

C

| $x$ | 3 | 13 | 23 | 33 | 38 |
|---|---|---|---|---|---|
| $y$ | 20 | 16 | 12 | 8 | 6 |

D

| $x$ | 17 | 12 | 7 | 2 | −3 |
|---|---|---|---|---|---|
| $y$ | −3 | 2 | 7 | 12 | 17 |

## *STANDARDIZED TEST PREP*

## Short Response

**S1.** A video store charges a \$10 membership fee plus \$2 for each movie rental. The total cost for $x$ movie rentals is given by $f(x) = 2x + 10$.

**a.** Graph this function.

**b.** Give a reasonable domain and range.

**S2.** The table below shows the federal minimum wage in different years.

| Year | 1960 | 1970 | 1980 | 1990 | 2000 |
|---|---|---|---|---|---|
| Minimum Wage (\$) | 1.00 | 1.60 | 3.10 | 3.80 | 5.15 |

**a.** Find the rate of change for each ten-year time period. Show your work.

**b.** During which time period did the minimum wage increase the fastest? Explain what the rate of change for this time period means.

**S3. a.** Find the slope of the line below.

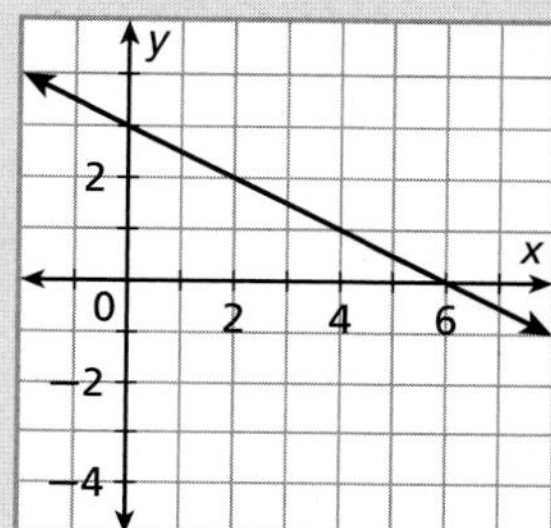


**b.** Write an equation in slope-intercept form for a line that is perpendicular to the line in part **a** and has the same $y$-intercept as the function in part **a**. Show your work and explain how you got your answer.

## Extended Response

**E1.** There is a linear relationship between the wind speed at a given temperature and what that temperature "feels like." A higher wind speed will make the temperature feel colder. The table below shows what an unknown temperature $t$ "feels like" at different wind speeds.

| Wind Speed (mi/h) | 5 | 10 | 15 |
|---|---|---|---|
| "Feels Like" (°F) | 36 | 34 | 32 |

**a.** Write an equation in slope-intercept form relating the wind speeds to the unknown temperature. Show your work and explain how you got your answer.

**b.** What does the slope mean in this situation?

**c.** What is the unknown temperature? Explain.

**d.** Determine what the unknown temperature feels like when the wind speed is 12 miles per hour. Show your work.

CHAPTER 6

# Systems of Equations and Inequalities

## Why Learn This?

You can solve a system of equations to decide how many tickets you can buy at different prices for a Duke vs. UNC women's basketball game.

go.hrw.com
Chapter Project Online
KEYWORD: MA7 ChProj

## Vocabulary

**Match each term on the left with a definition on the right.**

1. inequality
2. linear equation
3. ordered pair
4. slope
5. solution of an equation

A. a pair of numbers $(x, y)$ that represent the coordinates of a point
B. a statement that two quantities are not equal
C. the $y$-value of the point at which the graph of an equation crosses the $y$-axis
D. a value of the variable that makes the equation true
E. the ratio of the vertical change to the horizontal change for a nonvertical line
F. an equation whose graph is a straight line

## Graph Linear Functions

**Graph each function.**

6. $y = \frac{3}{4}x + 1$
7. $y = -3x + 5$
8. $y = x - 6$
9. $x + y = 4$
10. $y = -\frac{2}{3}x + 4$
11. $y = -5$

## Solve Multi-Step Equations

**Solve each equation.**

12. $-7x - 18 = 3$
13. $12 = -3n + 6$
14. $\frac{1}{2}d + 30 = 32$
15. $-2p + 9 = -3$
16. $33 = 5y + 8$
17. $-3 + 3x = 27$

## Solve for a Variable

**Solve each equation for $y$.**

18. $7x + y = 4$
19. $y + 2 = -4x$
20. $8 = x - y$
21. $x + 2 = y - 5$
22. $2y - 3 = 12x$
23. $y + \frac{3}{4}x = 4$

## Evaluate Expressions

**Evaluate each expression for the given value of the variable.**

24. $t - 5$ for $t = 7$
25. $9 - 2a$ for $a = 4$
26. $\frac{1}{2}x - 2$ for $x = 14$
27. $n + 15$ for $n = 37$
28. $9c + 4$ for $c = \frac{1}{3}$
29. $16 + 3d$ for $d = 5$

## Solve and Graph Inequalities

**Solve and graph each inequality.**

30. $b - 9 \geq 1$
31. $-2x < 10$
32. $3y \leq -3$
33. $\frac{1}{3}y \leq 5$

CHAPTER 6

# Study Guide: Preview

## Where You've Been

### Previously, you

- solved one-step and multi-step equations.
- solved one-step and multi-step inequalities.
- graphed linear equations on a coordinate plane.

## In This Chapter

### You will study

- how to find a solution that satisfies two linear equations.
- how to find solutions that satisfy two linear inequalities.
- how to graph one or more linear inequalities on a coordinate plane.

## Where You're Going

### You can use the skills in this chapter

- to determine which purchases are better deals.
- in other classes, such as Economics and Chemistry.
- to solve linear equations that involve three or more variables in future math classes.

## *Key Vocabulary/Vocabulario*

| | |
|---|---|
| consistent system | sistema consistente |
| dependent system | sistema dependiente |
| inconsistent system | sistema inconsistente |
| independent system | sistema independiente |
| linear inequality | desigualdad lineal |
| solution of a linear inequality | solución de una desigualdad lineal |
| system of linear equations | sistema de ecuaciones lineales |

## *Vocabulary Connections*

To become familiar with some of the vocabulary terms in the chapter, consider the following. You may refer to the chapter, the glossary, or a dictionary if you like.

1. The word *system* means "a group." How do you think a **system of linear equations** is different from a linear equation?
2. A **consistent system** has *at least one* solution. How many solutions do you think an **inconsistent system** has?
3. A **dependent system** has infinitely many solutions. Which vocabulary term above means a system with *exactly one* solution?
4. In Chapters 4 and 5, you saw that a solution of a linear equation was the ordered pair that made the equation true. Modify this to define **solution of a linear inequality**.

CHAPTER 6

## Writing Strategy: Write a Convincing Argument/Explanation

The Write About It icon  appears throughout the book. These icons identify questions that require you to write a complete argument or explanation. Writing a convincing argument or explanation shows that you have a solid understanding of a concept.

To be effective, an argument or explanation should include

- evidence, work, or facts.
- a complete response that will answer or explain.

**From Lesson 2-9**

**23. Write About It** Lewis invested \$1000 at 3% simple interest for 4 years. Lisa invested \$1000 at 4% simple interest for 3 years. Explain why Lewis and Lisa earned the same amount of interest.

**Step 1** **Identify what you need to answer or explain.**
Explain why Lewis and Lisa earned the same amount of interest.

**Step 2** **Give evidence, work, or facts that are needed to answer the question.**
Use the formula for simple interest to find the amount of interest earned: $I = Prt$.

**Lewis:** $P = 1000$, $r = 0.03$, $t = 4$

$$I = Prt = 1000(0.03)(4) = 120$$
$$I = 1000(0.12) = \$120$$

**Lisa:** $P = 1000$, $r = 0.04$, $t = 3$

$$I = Prt = 1000(0.04)(3) = 120$$
$$I = 1000(0.12) = \$120$$

**Step 3** **Write a complete response that answers or explains.**
Lewis and Lisa both invested the same amount of money, \$1000. They earned the same amount of interest because $0.04 \times 3$ and $0.03 \times 4$ both equal 0.12. They both earned $0.12 \times \$1000$, or \$120.

### Try This

**Write a convincing argument or explanation.**

1. What is the least whole number that is a solution of $12x + 15.4 > 118.92$? Explain.
2. Which equation has an error? Explain the error.

**A.** $4(6 \cdot 5) = (4)6 \cdot (4)5$ **B.** $4(6 \cdot 5) = (4 \cdot 6)5$

# Solve Linear Equations by Using a Spreadsheet

You can use a spreadsheet to answer "What if...?" questions. By changing one or more values, you can quickly model different scenarios.

*Use with Lesson 6-1*

**MA.A.4.5** Use...tables...to solve linear equations.

go.hrw.com
**Lab Resources Online**
KEYWORD: MA7 Lab6

## Activity

**Company Z makes DVD players. The company's costs are \$400 per week plus \$20 per DVD player. Each DVD player sells for \$45. How many DVD players must company Z sell in one week to make a profit?**

Let $n$ represent the number of DVD players company Z sells in one week.

$c = 400 + 20n$ *The total cost is \$400 plus \$20 times the number of DVD players made.*

$s = 45n$ *The total sales income is \$45 times the number of DVD players sold.*

$p = s - c$ *The total profit is the sales income minus the total cost.*

1. Set up your spreadsheet with columns for number of DVD players, total cost, total income, and profit.

2. Under Number of DVD Players, enter 1 in cell A2.

3. Use the equations above to enter the formulas for total cost, total sales, and total profit in row 2.
   - In cell B2, enter the formula for total cost.
   - In cell C2, enter the formula for total sales income.
   - In cell D2, enter the formula for total profit.

Company Z Profit

| | A | B | C | D |
|---|---|---|---|---|
| 1 | Number of DVD Players | Total Cost (\$) | Total Income (\$) | Profit (\$) |
| 2 | 1 | 420 | 45 | -375 |

= 400 + 20*A2 = 45*A2 = C2 – B2

4. Fill columns A, B, C, and D by selecting cells A1 through D1, clicking the small box at the bottom right corner of cell D2, and dragging the box down through several rows.

5. Find the point where the profit is \$0. This is known as the breakeven point, where total cost and total income are the same.

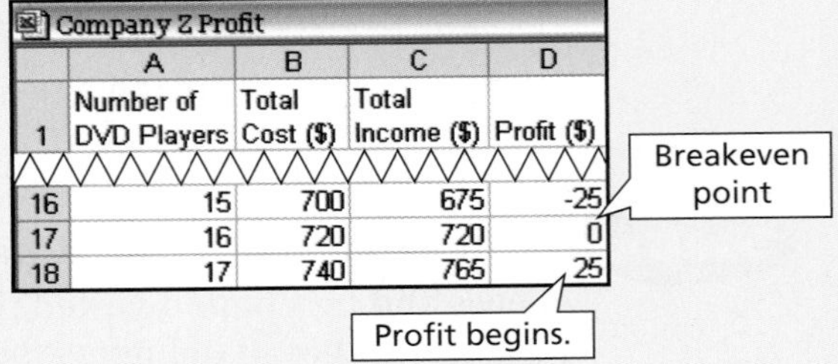
Company Z Profit

| | A | B | C | D |
|---|---|---|---|---|
| 1 | Number of DVD Players | Total Cost (\$) | Total Income (\$) | Profit (\$) |
| 16 | 15 | 700 | 675 | -25 |
| 17 | 16 | 720 | 720 | 0 |
| 18 | 17 | 740 | 765 | 25 |



Company Z must sell 17 DVD players to make a profit. The profit is \$25.

## Try This

**For Exercises 1 and 2, use the spreadsheet from the activity.**

1. If company Z sells 10 DVD players, will they make a profit? Explain. What if they sell 16?
2. Company Z makes a profit of \$225 dollars. How many DVD players did they sell?

**For Exercise 3, make a spreadsheet.**

3. Company Y's costs are \$400 per week plus \$20 per DVD player. They want the breakeven point to occur with sales of 8 DVD players. What should the sales price be?

# 6-1 Solving Systems by Graphing

**MA.A.5.2** Use strategies to solve systems of linear equations in two variables graphically... *Also* **MA.A.5.1**

***Objectives***

Identify solutions of systems of linear equations in two variables.

Solve systems of linear equations in two variables by graphing.

***Vocabulary***

system of linear equations

solution of a system of linear equations

**Why learn this?**

You can compare costs by graphing a system of linear equations. (See Example 3.)

Sometimes there are different charges for the same service or product at different places. For example, Bowl-o-Rama charges $2.50 per game plus $2 for shoe rental while Bowling Pinz charges $2 per game plus $4 for shoe rental. A *system of linear equations* can be used to compare these charges.

A **system of linear equations** is a set of two or more linear equations containing two or more variables. A **solution of a system of linear equations** with two variables is an ordered pair that satisfies each equation in the system. So, if an ordered pair is a solution, it will make both equations true.

## EXAMPLE 1 Identifying Solutions of Systems

**Tell whether the ordered pair is a solution of the given system.**

**A** $(4, 1); \begin{cases} x + 2y = 6 \\ x - y = 3 \end{cases}$

| $x + 2y = 6$ | |
|---|---|
| $(4) + 2(1)$ | 6 |
| $4 + 2$ | 6 |
| 6 | 6 ✓ |

| $x - y = 3$ | |
|---|---|
| $(4) - (1)$ | 3 |
| 3 | 3 ✓ |

*Substitute 4 for x and 1 for y in each equation in the system.*

The ordered pair $(4, 1)$ makes both equations true.

$(4, 1)$ is a solution of the system.

**B** $(-1, 2); \begin{cases} 2x + 5y = 8 \\ 3x - 2y = 5 \end{cases}$

| $2x + 5y = 8$ | |
|---|---|
| $2(-1) + 5(2)$ | 8 |
| $-2 + 10$ | 8 |
| 8 | 8 ✓ |

| $3x - 2y = 5$ | |
|---|---|
| $3(-1) - 2(2)$ | 5 |
| $-3 - 4$ | 5 |
| $-7$ | 5 ✗ |

*Substitute −1 for x and 2 for y in each equation in the system.*

The ordered pair $(-1, 2)$ makes one equation true, but not the other.

$(-1, 2)$ is not a solution of the system.

**Helpful Hint**

If an ordered pair does not satisfy the first equation in the system, there is no need to check the other equations.

CHECK IT OUT! **Tell whether the ordered pair is a solution of the given system.**

**1a.** $(1, 3); \begin{cases} 2x + y = 5 \\ -2x + y = 1 \end{cases}$

**1b.** $(2, -1); \begin{cases} x - 2y = 4 \\ 3x + y = 6 \end{cases}$

All solutions of a linear equation are on its graph. To find a solution of a system of linear equations, you need a point that each line has in common. In other words, you need their point of intersection.

$$\begin{cases} y = 2x - 1 \\ y = -x + 5 \end{cases}$$

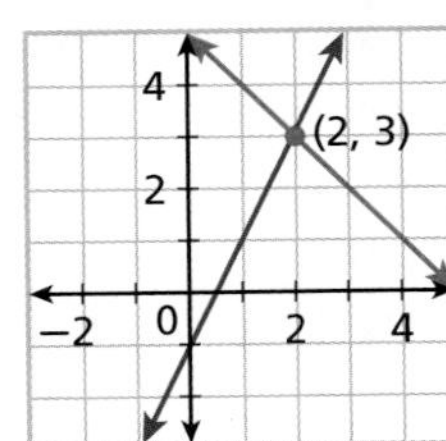


The point $(2, 3)$ is where the two lines intersect and is a solution of both equations, so $(2, 3)$ is the solution of the system.

## EXAMPLE 2 Solving a System of Linear Equations by Graphing

**Helpful Hint**

Sometimes it is difficult to tell exactly where the lines cross when you solve by graphing. It is good to confirm your answer by substituting it into both equations.

**Solve each system by graphing. Check your answer.**

$$\begin{cases} y = x - 3 \\ y = -x - 1 \end{cases}$$

*Graph the system.*

The solution appears to be at $(1, -2)$.

***Check***

Substitute $(1, -2)$ into the system.

| $y = x - 3$ | |
|---|---|
| $(-2)$ | $(1) - 3$ |
| $-2$ | $-2$ ✓ |

| $y = -x - 1$ | |
|---|---|
| $(-2)$ | $-(1) - 1$ |
| $-2$ | $-2$ ✓ |

$(1, -2)$ is a solution of the system.

$$\begin{cases} x + y = 0 \\ y = -\frac{1}{2}x + 1 \end{cases}$$

$$\begin{aligned} x + y &= 0 \\ \underline{-x} \quad &\underline{-x} \\ y &= -x \end{aligned}$$

*Rewrite the first equation in slope-intercept form.*

*Graph using a calculator and then use the intersection command.*

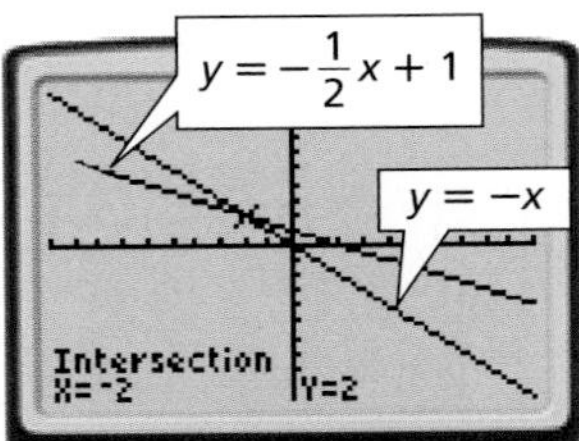


***Check*** Substitute $(-2, 2)$ into the system.

| $x + y = 0$ | |
|---|---|
| $(-2) + (2)$ | $0$ |
| $0$ | $0$ ✓ |

| $y = -\frac{1}{2}x + 1$ | |
|---|---|
| $(2)$ | $-\frac{1}{2}(-2) + 1$ |
| $2$ | $1 + 1$ |
| $2$ | $2$ ✓ |

The solution is $(-2, 2)$.

**Solve each system by graphing. Check your answer.**

**2a.** $\begin{cases} y = -2x - 1 \\ y = x + 5 \end{cases}$

**2b.** $\begin{cases} y = \frac{1}{3}x - 3 \\ 2x + y = 4 \end{cases}$

## EXAMPLE 3 Problem-Solving Application

PROBLEM SOLVING

**Bowl-o-Rama charges $2.50 per game plus $2 for shoe rental, and Bowling Pinz charges $2 per game plus $4 for shoe rental. For how many games will the cost to bowl be the same at both places? What is that cost?**

### 1 Understand the Problem

The **answer** will be the number of games played for which the total cost is the same at both bowling alleys. **List the important information:**

- Game price: Bowl-o-Rama $2.50 Bowling Pinz: $2
- Shoe-rental fee: Bowl-o-Rama $2 Bowling Pinz: $4

### 2 Make a Plan

Write a system of equations, one equation to represent the price at each company. Let $x$ be the number of games played and $y$ be the total cost.

| | Total cost | is | price per game | times | games | plus | shoe rental. |
|---|---|---|---|---|---|---|---|
| Bowl-o-Rama | $y$ | $=$ | 2.5 | $\cdot$ | $x$ | $+$ | 2 |
| Bowling Pinz | $y$ | $=$ | 2 | $\cdot$ | $x$ | $+$ | 4 |

### 3 Solve

Graph $y = 2.5x + 2$ and $y = 2x + 4$. The lines appear to intersect at $(4, 12)$. So, the cost at both places will be the same for 4 games bowled and that cost will be $12.

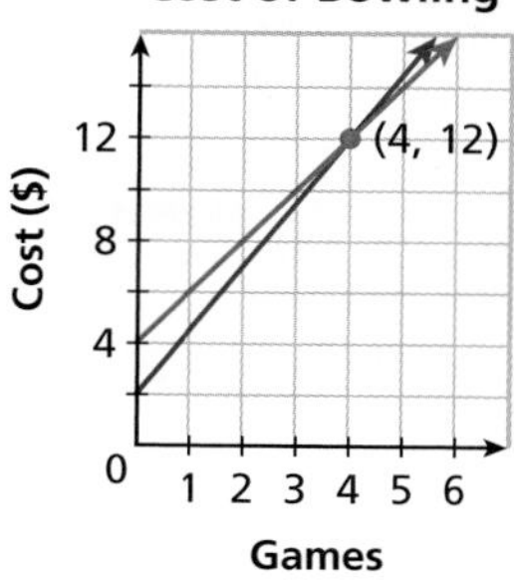


### 4 Look Back

Check $(4, 12)$ using both equations.

Cost of bowling 4 games at Bowl-o-Rama:
$\$2.5(4) + \$2 = 10 + 2 = 12$ ✓

Cost of bowling 4 games at Bowling Pinz:
$\$2(4) + \$4 = 8 + 4 = 12$ ✓

3. Video club A charges $10 for membership and $3 per movie rental. Video club B charges $15 for membership and $2 per movie rental. For how many movie rentals will the cost be the same at both video clubs? What is that cost?

## THINK AND DISCUSS

1. Explain how to use a graph to solve a system of linear equations.
2. Explain how to check a solution of a system of linear equations.
3. **GET ORGANIZED** Copy and complete the graphic organizer. In each box, write a step for solving a linear system by graphing. More boxes may be added.

Solving a Linear System by Graphing

1. → 2. → 3.

# 6-1 Exercises

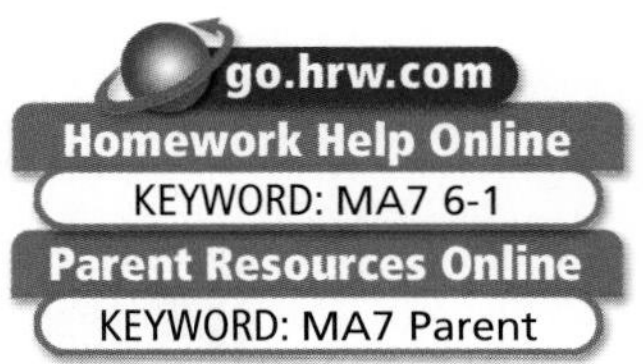


## GUIDED PRACTICE

1. **Vocabulary** Describe a *solution of a system of linear equations.*

SEE EXAMPLE 1 p. 383

**Tell whether the ordered pair is a solution of the given system.**

2. $(2, -2); \begin{cases} 3x + y = 4 \\ x - 3y = -4 \end{cases}$
3. $(3, -1); \begin{cases} x - 2y = 5 \\ 2x - y = 7 \end{cases}$
4. $(-1, 5); \begin{cases} -x + y = 6 \\ 2x + 3y = 13 \end{cases}$

SEE EXAMPLE 2 p. 384

**Solve each system by graphing. Check your answer.**

5. $\begin{cases} y = \frac{1}{2}x \\ y = -x + 3 \end{cases}$
6. $\begin{cases} y = x - 2 \\ 2x + y = 1 \end{cases}$
7. $\begin{cases} -2x - 1 = y \\ x + y = 3 \end{cases}$

SEE EXAMPLE 3 p. 385

8. To deliver mulch, Lawn and Garden charges \$30 per cubic yard of mulch plus a \$30 delivery fee. Yard Depot charges \$25 per cubic yard of mulch plus a \$55 delivery fee. For how many cubic yards will the cost be the same? What will that cost be?

## PRACTICE AND PROBLEM SOLVING

**Independent Practice**

| For Exercises | See Example |
|---|---|
| 9–11 | 1 |
| 12–15 | 2 |
| 16 | 3 |

**Extra Practice**

Skills Practice p. S14
Application Practice p. S33

**Tell whether the ordered pair is a solution of the given system.**

9. $(1, -4); \begin{cases} x - 2y = 8 \\ 4x - y = 8 \end{cases}$
10. $(-2, 1); \begin{cases} 2x + 3y = -7 \\ 3x + y = -5 \end{cases}$
11. $(5, 2); \begin{cases} 2x + y = 12 \\ -3y - x = -11 \end{cases}$

**Solve each system by graphing. Check your answer.**

12. $\begin{cases} y = \frac{1}{2}x + 2 \\ y = -x - 1 \end{cases}$
13. $\begin{cases} y = x \\ y = -x + 6 \end{cases}$
14. $\begin{cases} -2x - 1 = y \\ x = -y + 3 \end{cases}$
15. $\begin{cases} x + y = 2 \\ y = x - 4 \end{cases}$

16. **Multi-Step** Angelo runs 7 miles per week and increases his distance by 1 mile each week. Marc runs 4 miles per week and increases his distance by 2 miles each week. In how many weeks will Angelo and Marc be running the same distance? What will that distance be?

17. **School** The school band sells carnations on Valentine's Day for \$2 each. They buy the carnations from a florist for \$0.50 each, plus a \$16 delivery charge.
    a. Write a system of equations to describe the situation.
    b. Graph the system. What does the solution represent?
    c. Explain whether the solution shown on the graph makes sense in this situation. If not, give a reasonable solution.

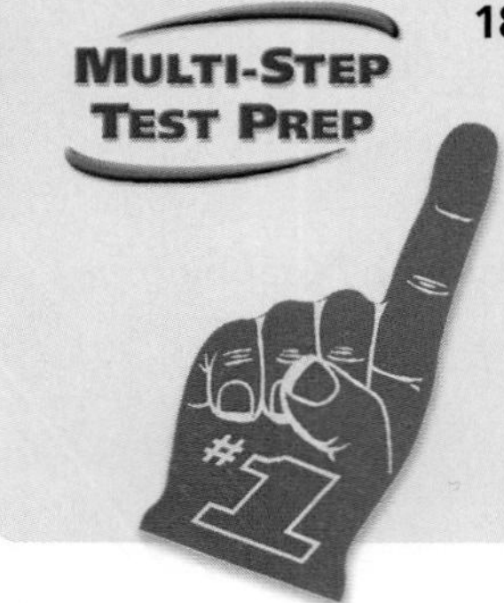


18. This problem will prepare you for the Multi-Step Test Prep on page 412.
    a. The Warrior baseball team is selling hats as a fund-raiser. They contacted two companies. Hats Off charges a \$50 design fee and \$5 per hat. Top Stuff charges a \$25 design fee and \$6 per hat. Write an equation for each company's pricing.
    b. Graph the system of equations from part **a.** For how many hats will the cost be the same? What is that cost?
    c. Explain when it is cheaper for the baseball team to use Top Stuff and when it is cheaper to use Hats Off.

**Graphing Calculator** Use a graphing calculator to graph and solve the systems of equations in Exercises 19–22. Round your answer to the nearest tenth.

19. $\begin{cases} y = 4.7x + 2.1 \\ y = 1.6x - 5.4 \end{cases}$

20. $\begin{cases} 4.8x + 0.6y = 4 \\ y = -3.2x + 2.7 \end{cases}$

21. $\begin{cases} y = \frac{5}{4}x - \frac{2}{3} \\ \frac{8}{3}x + y = \frac{5}{9} \end{cases}$

22. $\begin{cases} y = 6.9x + 12.4 \\ y = -4.1x - 5.3 \end{cases}$

**LINK**

**Landscaping**

Middleton Place Gardens, South Carolina, are the United States' oldest landscaped gardens. The gardens were established in 1741 and opened to the public in the 1920s.

23. **Landscaping** The gardeners at Middleton Place Gardens want to plant a total of 45 white and pink hydrangeas in one flower bed. In another flower bed, they want to plant 120 hydrangeas. In this bed, they want 2 times the number of white hydrangeas and 3 times the number of pink hydrangeas as in the first bed. Use a system of equations to find how many white and how many pink hydrangeas the gardeners should buy altogether.

24. **Fitness** Rusty burns 5 Calories per minute swimming and 11 Calories per minute jogging. In the morning, Rusty burns 200 Calories walking and swims for $x$ minutes. In the afternoon, Rusty will jog for $x$ minutes. How many minutes must he jog to burn at least as many Calories $y$ in the afternoon as he did in the morning? Round your answer up to the next whole number of minutes.

25. A tree that is 2 feet tall is growing at a rate of 1 foot per year. A 6-foot tall tree is growing at a rate of 0.5 foot per year. In how many years will the trees be the same height?

26. **Critical Thinking** Write a real-world situation that could be represented by the system $\begin{cases} y = 3x + 10 \\ y = 5x + 20 \end{cases}$.

27. **Write About It** When you graph a system of linear equations, why does the intersection of the two lines represent the solution of the system?

**TEST PREP**

MA.A.5.2, MA.A.5.1

28. Taxi company A charges \$4 plus \$0.50 per mile. Taxi company B charges \$5 plus \$0.25 per mile. Which system best represents this problem?

(A) $\begin{cases} y = 4x + 0.5 \\ y = 5x + 0.25 \end{cases}$

(B) $\begin{cases} y = 0.5x + 4 \\ y = 0.25x + 5 \end{cases}$

(C) $\begin{cases} y = -4x + 0.5 \\ y = -5x + 0.25 \end{cases}$

(D) $\begin{cases} y = -0.5x + 4 \\ y = -0.25x + 5 \end{cases}$

29. Which system of equations represents the given graph?

(F) $\begin{cases} y = 2x - 1 \\ y = \frac{1}{3}x + 3 \end{cases}$

(G) $\begin{cases} y = -2x + 1 \\ y = 2x - 3 \end{cases}$

(H) $\begin{cases} y = 2x + 1 \\ y = \frac{1}{3}x - 3 \end{cases}$

(J) $\begin{cases} y = -2x - 1 \\ y = 3x - 3 \end{cases}$

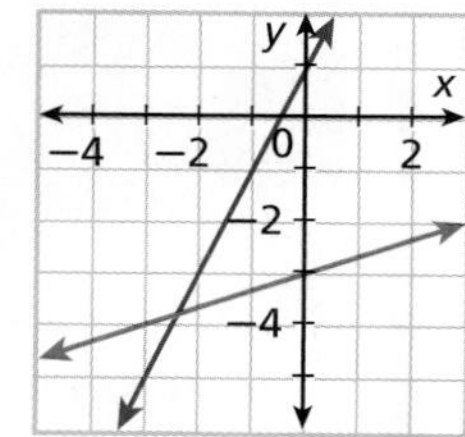


30. **Gridded Response** Which value of $b$ will make the system $y = 2x + 2$ and $y = 2.5x + b$ intersect at the point $(2, 6)$?

## CHALLENGE AND EXTEND

**31. Entertainment** If the pattern in the table continues, in what month will the number of sales of VCRs and DVD players be the same? What will that number be?

| Total Number Sold | | | | |
|---|---|---|---|---|
| Month | 1 | 2 | 3 | 4 |
| VCRs | 500 | 490 | 480 | 470 |
| DVD Players | 250 | 265 | 280 | 295 |

**32.** Long Distance Inc. charges a \$1.45 connection charge and \$0.03 per minute. Far Away Calls charges a \$1.52 connection charge and \$0.02 per minute.

**a.** For how many minutes will a call cost the same from both companies? What is that cost?

**b.** When is it better to call using Long Distance Inc.? Far Away Calls? Explain.

**c. What if...?** Long Distance Inc. raised its connection charge to \$1.50 and Far Away Calls decreased its connection charge by 2 cents. How will this affect the graphs? Now which company is better to use for calling long distance? Why?

## SPIRAL REVIEW

**Solve each equation.** *(Lesson 2-2)*

**33.** $18 = \frac{3}{7}x$ **34.** $-\frac{x}{5} = 12$ **35.** $-6y = -13.2$ **36.** $\frac{2}{5} = \frac{y}{12}$

**Describe the solutions of each inequality in words.** *(Lesson 3-1)*

**37.** $3c < 15$ **38.** $\frac{1}{3}x \geq 9$ **39.** $5 + a > 11$

**Solve each inequality and graph the solutions.** *(Lesson 3-4)*

**40.** $4(2x + 1) > 28$ **41.** $3^3 + 9 \leq -4c$ **42.** $\frac{1}{8}x + \frac{3}{5} \leq \frac{3}{8}$

## Career Path

Career Resources Online
KEYWORD: MA7 Career

**Ethan Reynolds**
Applied Sciences major

**Q: What math classes did you take in high school?**

**A:** Career Math, Algebra, and Geometry

**Q: What are you studying and what math classes have you taken?**

**A:** I am really interested in aviation. I am taking Statistics and Trigonometry. Next year I will take Calculus.

**Q: How is math used in aviation?**

**A:** I use math to interpret aeronautical charts. I also perform calculations involving wind movements, aircraft weight and balance, and fuel consumption. These skills are necessary for planning and executing safe air flights.

**Q: What are your future plans?**

**A:** I could work as a commercial or corporate pilot or even as a flight instructor. I could also work toward a bachelor's degree in aviation management, air traffic control, aviation electronics, aviation maintenance, or aviation computer science.

# Model Systems of Linear Equations

You can use algebra tiles to model and solve some systems of linear equations.

*Use with Lesson 6-2*

**Prep MA.A.5.2** Use strategies to solve systems of linear equations in two variables...symbolically.

**KEY**

[+] = 1

[−] = −1

[+ long tile] = $x$  [− long tile] = $-x$

**REMEMBER**
When two expressions are equal, you can substitute one for the other in any expression or equation.

## Activity

**Use algebra tiles to model and solve** $\begin{cases} y = 2x - 3 \\ x + y = 9 \end{cases}$.

| MODEL | | ALGEBRA |
|---|---|---|
| $x$ $y$ 9 | *The first equation is solved for y. Model the second equation, x + y = 9, by substituting 2x − 3 for y.* | $x + y = 9$<br>$x + (2x - 3) = 9$<br>$3x - 3 = 9$ |
| | *Add 3 yellow tiles on both sides of the mat. This represents adding 3 to both sides of the equation.*<br>*Remove zero pairs.* | $3x - 3 = 9$<br>$+3 \quad +3$<br>$3x = 12$ |
| | *Divide each group into 3 equal groups. Align one x-tile with each group on the right side. One x-tile is equivalent to 4 yellow tiles. x = 4* | $\frac{3x}{3} = \frac{12}{3}$<br>$x = 4$ |

To solve for $y$, substitute 4 for $x$ in one of the equations:

$$\begin{aligned} y &= 2x - 3 \\ &= 2(4) - 3 \\ &= 5 \end{aligned}$$

The solution is (4, 5).

## Try This

**Model and solve each system of equations.**

**1.** $\begin{cases} y = x + 3 \\ 2x + y = 6 \end{cases}$

**2.** $\begin{cases} 2x + 3 = y \\ x + y = 6 \end{cases}$

**3.** $\begin{cases} 2x + 3y = 1 \\ x = -1 - y \end{cases}$

**4.** $\begin{cases} y = x + 1 \\ 2x - y = -5 \end{cases}$

# 6-2 Solving Systems by Substitution

**MA.A.5.2** Use strategies to solve systems of linear equations in two variables...symbolically. *Also* **MA.A.5.1**

***Objective***
Solve systems of linear equations in two variables by substitution.

**Why learn this?**

You can solve systems of equations to help select the best value among high-speed Internet providers. (See Example 3.)

Sometimes it is difficult to identify the exact solution to a system by graphing. In this case, you can use a method called *substitution*.

The goal when using substitution is to reduce the system to one equation that has only one variable. Then you can solve this equation by the methods taught in Chapter 2.

| Solving Systems of Equations by Substitution | |
|---|---|
| **Step 1** | Solve for one variable in at least one equation, if necessary. |
| **Step 2** | Substitute the resulting expression into the other equation. |
| **Step 3** | Solve that equation to get the value of the first variable. |
| **Step 4** | Substitute that value into one of the original equations and solve. |
| **Step 5** | Write the values from Steps 3 and 4 as an ordered pair, $(x, y)$, and check. |

## EXAMPLE 1 Solving a System of Linear Equations by Substitution

**Solve each system by substitution.**

**A** $\begin{cases} y = 2x \\ y = x + 5 \end{cases}$

**Step 1** $y = 2x$ — *Both equations are solved for y.*
$y = x + 5$

**Step 2** $y = x + 5$ — *Substitute 2x for y in the second equation.*
$2x = x + 5$

**Step 3** $-x \quad -x$ — *Solve for x. Subtract x from both sides to combine like terms.*
$x = 5$

**Step 4** $y = 2x$ — *Write one of the original equations.*
$y = 2(5)$ — *Substitute 5 for x.*
$y = 10$

**Step 5** $(5, 10)$ — *Write the solution as an ordered pair.*

***Check*** Substitute $(5, 10)$ into both equations in the system.

| $y = 2x$ | |
|---|---|
| **10** | $2(5)$ |
| 10 | 10 ✓ |

| $y = x + 5$ | |
|---|---|
| **10** | $5 + 5$ |
| 10 | 10 ✓ |

**Helpful Hint**

You can substitute the value of one variable into *either* of the original equations to find the value of the other variable.

**Solve each system by substitution.**

**B** $\begin{cases} 2x + y = 5 \\ y = x - 4 \end{cases}$

**Step 1** $y = x - 4$ — *The second equation is solved for y.*

**Step 2** $2x + y = 5$

$2x + (x - 4) = 5$ — *Substitute x − 4 for y in the first equation.*

**Step 3** $3x - 4 = 5$ — *Simplify. Then solve for x.*

$\underline{\quad +4 \quad +4}$ — *Add 4 to both sides.*

$3x = 9$

$\frac{3x}{3} = \frac{9}{3}$ — *Divide both sides by 3.*

$x = 3$

**Step 4** $y = x - 4$ — *Write one of the original equations.*

$y = 3 - 4$ — *Substitute 3 for x.*

$y = -1$

**Step 5** $(3, -1)$ — *Write the solution as an ordered pair.*

**C** 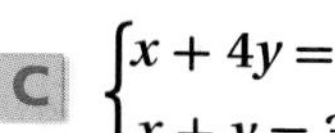

$\begin{cases} x + 4y = 6 \\ x + y = 3 \end{cases}$

**Step 1** $x + 4y = 6$ — *Solve the first equation for x by subtracting 4y from both sides.*

$\underline{\quad -4y \quad -4y}$

$x = 6 - 4y$

**Step 2** $x + y = 3$

$(6 - 4y) + y = 3$ — *Substitute 6 − 4y for x in the second equation.*

**Step 3** $6 - 3y = 3$ — *Simplify. Then solve for y.*

$\underline{-6 \qquad -6}$ — *Subtract 6 from both sides.*

$-3y = -3$

$\frac{-3y}{-3} = \frac{-3}{-3}$ — *Divide both sides by −3.*

$y = 1$

**Step 4** $x + y = 3$ — *Write one of the original equations.*

$x + 1 = 3$ — *Substitute 1 for y.*

$\underline{\quad -1 \quad -1}$ — *Subtract 1 from both sides.*

$x = 2$

**Step 5** $(2, 1)$ — *Write the solution as an ordered pair.*

**Helpful Hint**

Sometimes neither equation is solved for a variable. You can begin by solving either equation for either *x* or *y*.

**Solve each system by substitution.**

**1a.** $\begin{cases} y = x + 3 \\ y = 2x + 5 \end{cases}$ **1b.** $\begin{cases} x = 2y - 4 \\ x + 8y = 16 \end{cases}$ **1c.** $\begin{cases} 2x + y = -4 \\ x + y = -7 \end{cases}$

Sometimes you substitute an expression for a variable that has a coefficient. When solving for the second variable in this situation, you can use the Distributive Property.

## EXAMPLE 2 Using the Distributive Property

**Solve $\begin{cases} 4y - 5x = 9 \\ x - 4y = 11 \end{cases}$ by substitution.**

**Step 1** 
$$\begin{aligned} x - 4y &= 11 \\ +4y \quad & \quad +4y \\ x &= 4y + 11 \end{aligned}$$
*Solve the second equation for x by adding 4y to each side.*

**Step 2** 
$$4y - 5x = 9$$
$$4y - 5(4y + 11) = 9$$
*Substitute 4y + 11 for x in the first equation.*

**Step 3** 
$$4y - 5(4y) - 5(11) = 9$$
*Distribute −5 to the expression in the parentheses. Simplify. Solve for y.*
$$4y - 20y - 55 = 9$$
$$-16y - 55 = 9$$
$$+55 \quad +55$$
*Add 55 to both sides.*
$$-16y = 64$$
$$\frac{-16y}{-16} = \frac{64}{-16}$$
*Divide both sides by −16.*
$$y = -4$$

**Step 4** 
$$x - 4y = 11$$
*Write one of the original equations.*
$$x - 4(-4) = 11$$
*Substitute −4 for y.*
$$x + 16 = 11$$
*Simplify.*
$$-16 \quad -16$$
*Subtract 16 from both sides.*
$$x = -5$$

**Step 5** $(-5, -4)$ *Write the solution as an ordered pair.*

**Caution!**

When you solve one equation for a variable, you must substitute the value or expression into the *other* original equation, not the one that has just been solved.

**2.** Solve $\begin{cases} -2x + y = 8 \\ 3x + 2y = 9 \end{cases}$ by substitution.

### Student to Student — *Solving Systems by Substitution*

**Erika Chu**
Terrell High School

*I always look for a variable with a coefficient of 1 or −1 when deciding which equation to solve for x or y.*

*For the system*

$$\begin{cases} 2x + y = 14 \\ -3x + 4y = -10 \end{cases}$$

*I would solve the first equation for y because it has a coefficient of 1.*

$$2x + y = 14$$
$$y = -2x + 14$$

*Then I use substitution to find the values of x and y.*

$$-3x + 4y = -10$$
$$-3x + 4(-2x + 14) = -10$$
$$-3x + (-8x) + 56 = -10$$
$$-11x + 56 = -10$$
$$-11x = -66$$
$$x = 6$$

$$y = -2x + 14$$
$$y = -2(6) + 14 = 2$$

*The solution is* $(6, 2)$.

## EXAMPLE 3 Consumer Economics Application

**One high-speed Internet provider has a $50 setup fee and costs $30 per month. Another provider has no setup fee and costs $40 per month.**

**a. In how many months will both providers cost the same? What will that cost be?**

Write an equation for each option. Let $t$ represent the total amount paid and $m$ represent the number of months.

| | Total paid | is | setup fee | plus | cost per month | times | months. |
|---|---|---|---|---|---|---|---|
| Option 1 | $t$ | $=$ | 50 | $+$ | 30 | $\cdot$ | $m$ |
| Option 2 | $t$ | $=$ | 0 | $+$ | 40 | $\cdot$ | $m$ |

**Step 1** $t = 50 + 30m$ — *Both equations are solved for t.*

$t = 40m$

**Step 2** $50 + 30m = 40m$ — *Substitute 50 + 30m for t in the second equation.*

**Step 3** $\underline{\quad -30m \quad -30m}$ — *Solve for m. Subtract 30m from both sides to combine like terms.*

$50 = 10m$

$\frac{50}{10} = \frac{10m}{10}$ — *Divide both sides by 10.*

$5 = m$

**Step 4** $t = 40m$ — *Write one of the original equations.*

$= 40(5)$ — *Substitute 5 for m.*

$= 200$

**Step 5** $(5, 200)$ — *Write the solution as an ordered pair.*

In 5 months, the total cost for each option will be the same—$200.

**b. If you plan to cancel in 1 year, which is the cheaper provider? Explain.**

Option 1: $t = 50 + 30(12) = 410$ Option 2: $t = 40(12) = 480$

Option 1 is cheaper.

3. One cable television provider has a $60 setup fee and $80 per month, and the second has a $160 equipment fee and $70 per month.
   - **a.** In how many months will the cost be the same? What will that cost be?
   - **b.** If you plan to move in 6 months, which is the cheaper option? Explain.

## THINK AND DISCUSS

**1.** If you graphed the equations in Example 1A, where would the lines intersect?

**2. GET ORGANIZED** Copy and complete the graphic organizer. In each box, solve the system by substitution using the first step given. Show that each method gives the same solution.

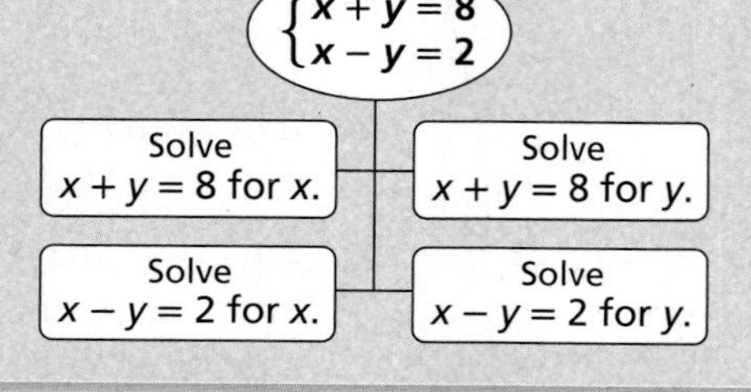

# 6-2 Exercises

MA.A.5.2, MA.A.5.1

go.hrw.com
Homework Help Online
KEYWORD: MA7 6-2
Parent Resources Online
KEYWORD: MA7 Parent

## GUIDED PRACTICE

**Solve each system by substitution.**

SEE EXAMPLE 1 p. 390

**1.** $\begin{cases} y = 5x - 10 \\ y = 3x + 8 \end{cases}$ **2.** $\begin{cases} 3x + y = 2 \\ 4x + y = 20 \end{cases}$ **3.** $\begin{cases} y = x + 5 \\ 4x + y = 20 \end{cases}$

SEE EXAMPLE 2 p. 392

**4.** $\begin{cases} x - 2y = 10 \\ \frac{1}{2}x - 2y = 4 \end{cases}$ **5.** $\begin{cases} y - 4x = 3 \\ 2x - 3y = 21 \end{cases}$ **6.** $\begin{cases} x = y - 8 \\ -x - y = 0 \end{cases}$

SEE EXAMPLE 3 p. 393

**7. Consumer Economics** The Strauss family is deciding between two lawn-care services. Green Lawn charges a \$49 startup fee, plus \$29 per month. Grass Team charges a \$25 startup fee, plus \$37 per month.

**a.** In how many months will both lawn-care services cost the same? What will that cost be?

**b.** If the family will use the service for only 6 months, which is the better option? Explain.

## PRACTICE AND PROBLEM SOLVING

| Independent Practice | |
|---|---|
| For Exercises | See Example |
| 8–10 | 1 |
| 11–16 | 2 |
| 17 | 3 |

**Extra Practice**
Skills Practice p. S14
Application Practice p. S33

**Solve each system by substitution.**

**8.** $\begin{cases} y = x + 3 \\ y = 2x + 4 \end{cases}$ **9.** $\begin{cases} y = 2x + 10 \\ y = -2x - 6 \end{cases}$ **10.** $\begin{cases} x + 2y = 8 \\ x + 3y = 12 \end{cases}$

**11.** $\begin{cases} 2x + 2y = 2 \\ -4x + 4y = 12 \end{cases}$ **12.** $\begin{cases} y = 0.5x + 2 \\ -y = -2x + 4 \end{cases}$ **13.** $\begin{cases} -x + y = 4 \\ 3x - 2y = -7 \end{cases}$

**14.** $\begin{cases} 3x + y = -8 \\ -2x - y = 6 \end{cases}$ **15.** $\begin{cases} x + 2y = -1 \\ 4x - 4y = 20 \end{cases}$ **16.** $\begin{cases} 4x = y - 1 \\ 6x - 2y = -3 \end{cases}$

**17. Recreation** Casey wants to buy a gym membership. One gym has a \$150 joining fee and costs \$35 per month. Another gym has no joining fee and costs \$60 per month.

**a.** In how many months will both gym memberships cost the same? What will that cost be?

**b.** If Casey plans to cancel in 5 months, which is the better option for him? Explain.

**Solve each system by substitution. Check your answer.**

**18.** $\begin{cases} x = 5 \\ x + y = 8 \end{cases}$ **19.** $\begin{cases} y = -3x + 4 \\ x = 2y + 6 \end{cases}$ **20.** $\begin{cases} 3x - y = 11 \\ 5y - 7x = 1 \end{cases}$

**21.** $\begin{cases} \frac{1}{2}x + \frac{1}{3}y = 6 \\ x - y = 2 \end{cases}$ **22.** $\begin{cases} x = 7 - 2y \\ 2x + y = 5 \end{cases}$ **23.** $\begin{cases} y = 1.2x - 4 \\ 2.2x + 5 = y \end{cases}$

**24.** The sum of two numbers is 50. The first number is 43 less than twice the second number. Write and solve a system of equations to find the two numbers.

**25. Money** A jar contains $n$ nickels and $d$ dimes. There are 20 coins in the jar, and the total value of the coins is \$1.40. How many nickels and how many dimes are in the jar? (*Hint:* Nickels are worth \$0.05 and dimes are worth \$0.10.)

26. **Multi-Step** Use the receipts below to write and solve a system of equations to find the cost of a large popcorn and the cost of a small drink.

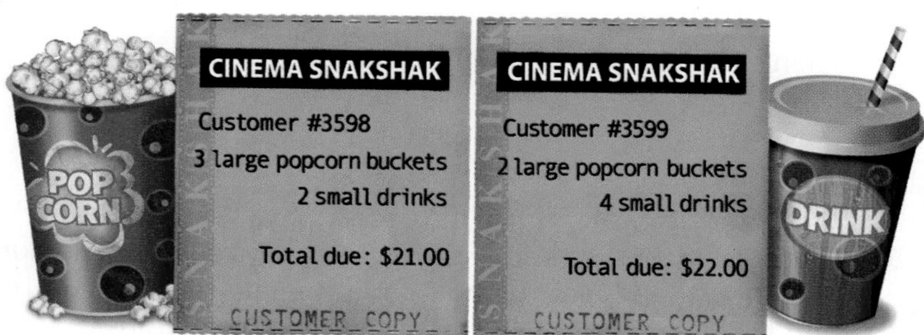


27. **Finance** Helene invested a total of $1000 in two simple-interest bank accounts. One account paid 5% annual interest; the other paid 6% annual interest. The total amount of interest she earned after one year was $58. Write and solve a system of equations to find the amount invested in each account. (*Hint:* Change the interest rates into decimals first.)

**Geometry** **Two angles whose measures have a sum of 90° are called complementary angles. For Exercises 28–30, $x$ and $y$ represent complementary angles. Find the measure of each angle.**

28. $\begin{cases} x + y = 90 \\ y = 4x - 10 \end{cases}$

29. $\begin{cases} x = 2y \\ x + y = 90 \end{cases}$

30. $\begin{cases} y = 2(x - 15) \\ x + y = 90 \end{cases}$

31. **Aviation** With a headwind, a small plane can fly 240 miles in 3 hours. With a tailwind, the plane can fly the same distance in 2 hours. Follow the steps below to find the rates of the plane and wind.

    a. Copy and complete the table. Let $p$ be the rate of the plane and $w$ be the rate of the wind.

| | Rate | • | Time | = | Distance |
|---|---|---|---|---|---|
| With Headwind | $p - w$ | • | ■ | = | 240 |
| With Tailwind | ■ | • | 2 | = | ■ |

    b. Use the information in each row to write a system of equations.

    c. Solve the system of equations to find the rates of the plane and wind.

32. **Write About It** Explain how to solve a system of equations by substitution.

33. **Critical Thinking** Explain the connection between the solution of a system solved by graphing and the solution to the same system solved by substitution.

**MULTI-STEP TEST PREP**

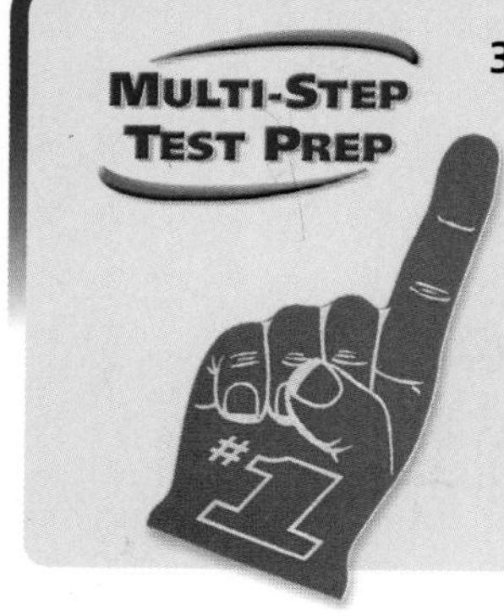

34. This problem will prepare you for the Multi-Step Test Prep on page 412.

    At the school store, Juanita bought 2 books and a backpack for a total of $26 before tax. Each book cost $8 less than the backpack.

    a. Write a system of equations that can be used to find the price of each book and the price of the backpack.

    b. Solve this system by substitution.

    c. Solve this system by graphing. Discuss advantages and disadvantages of solving by substitution and solving by graphing.

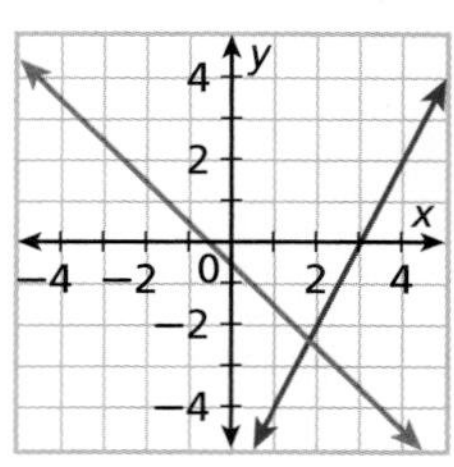


**35. Estimation** Use the graph to estimate the solution to $\begin{cases} 2x - y = 6 \\ x + y = -0.6 \end{cases}$. Round your answer to the nearest tenth. Then solve the system by substitution.

MA.A.5.2, MA.A.5.1

**36.** Elizabeth met 24 of her cousins at a family reunion. The number of male cousins $m$ was 6 less than twice the number of female cousins $f$. Which system can be used to find the number of male cousins and female cousins?

Ⓐ $\begin{cases} m + f = 24 \\ f = 2m - 6 \end{cases}$ Ⓑ $\begin{cases} m + f = 24 \\ f = 2m \end{cases}$ Ⓒ $\begin{cases} m = 24 + f \\ m = f - 6 \end{cases}$ Ⓓ $\begin{cases} f = 24 - m \\ m = 2f - 6 \end{cases}$

**37.** Which problem is best represented by the following system $\begin{cases} d = n + 5 \\ d + n = 12 \end{cases}$?

Ⓕ Roger has 12 coins in dimes and nickels. There are 5 more dimes than nickels.
Ⓖ Roger has 5 coins in dimes and nickels. There are 12 more dimes than nickels.
Ⓗ Roger has 12 coins in dimes and nickels. There are 5 more nickels than dimes.
Ⓙ Roger has 5 coins in dimes and nickels. There are 12 more nickels than dimes.

## CHALLENGE AND EXTEND

**38.** A car dealership has 378 cars on its lot. The ratio of new cars to used cars is 5:4. Write and solve a system of equations to find the number of new and used cars on the lot.

**Solve each system by substitution.**

**39.** $\begin{cases} 2r - 3s - t = 12 \\ s + 3t = 10 \\ t = 4 \end{cases}$ **40.** $\begin{cases} x + y + z = 7 \\ y + z = 5 \\ 2y - 4z = -14 \end{cases}$ **41.** $\begin{cases} a + 2b + c = 19 \\ -b + c = -5 \\ 3b + 2c = 15 \end{cases}$

## SPIRAL REVIEW

**Write a possible situation for the given graph.** *(Lesson 4-1)*

**42.**

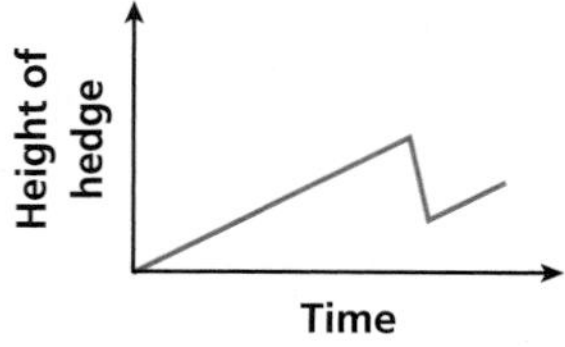


**43.**

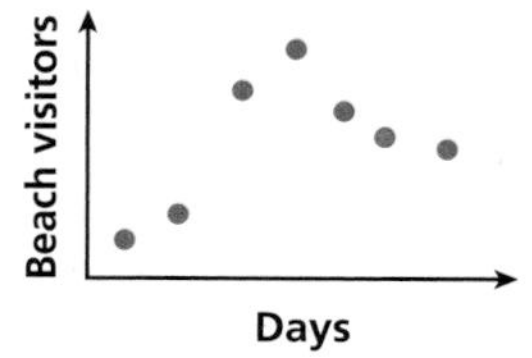


**44.**

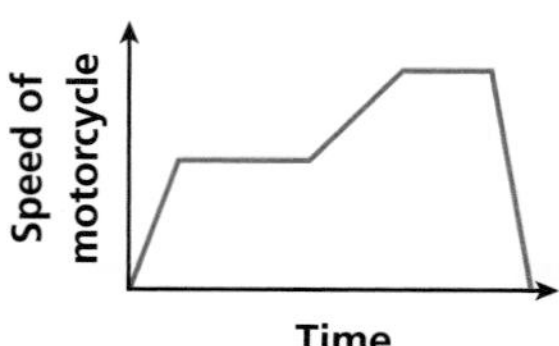


**Find the $x$- and $y$-intercepts.** *(Lesson 5-2)*

**45.** $6x - 2y = 12$ **46.** $-3y + x = 15$ **47.** $4y - 40 = -5x$

**Tell whether each ordered pair is a solution of the given system.** *(Lesson 6-1)*

**48.** $(3, 0); \begin{cases} 2x - y = -6 \\ x + y = 3 \end{cases}$ **49.** $(-1, 4); \begin{cases} y - 2x = 6 \\ x + 4y = 15 \end{cases}$ **50.** $(5, 6); \begin{cases} \frac{1}{3}y + x = 7 \\ 2x = 12 \end{cases}$

# 6-3 Solving Systems by Elimination

**MA.A.5.2** Use strategies to solve systems of linear equations in two variables...symbolically. *Also* **MA.A.5.1**

***Objectives***

Solve systems of linear equations in two variables by elimination.

Compare and choose an appropriate method for solving systems of linear equations.

**Why learn this?**

You can solve a system of linear equations to determine how many flowers of each type you can buy to make a bouquet. (See Example 4.)

Another method for solving systems of equations is *elimination*. Like substitution, the goal of elimination is to get one equation that has only one variable. To do this by elimination, you add the two equations in the system together.

Remember that an equation stays balanced if you add equal amounts to both sides. So if $5x + 2y = 1$, you can add $5x + 2y$ to one side of an equation and $1$ to the other side and the balance is maintained.

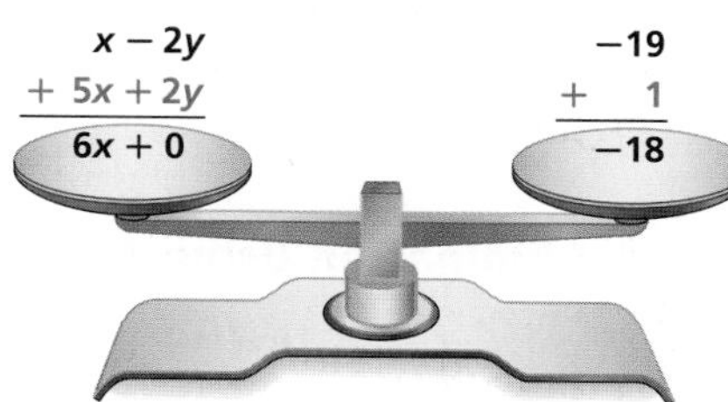


Since $-2y$ and $2y$ have **opposite coefficients**, the $y$-term is eliminated. The result is one equation that has only one variable: $6x = -18$.

When you use the elimination method to solve a system of linear equations, align all like terms in the equations. Then determine whether any like terms can be eliminated because they have opposite coefficients.

| Solving Systems of Equations by Elimination | |
|---|---|
| **Step 1** | Write the system so that like terms are aligned. |
| **Step 2** | Eliminate one of the variables and solve for the other variable. |
| **Step 3** | Substitute the value of the variable into one of the original equations and solve for the other variable. |
| **Step 4** | Write the answers from Steps 2 and 3 as an ordered pair, $(x, y)$, and check. |

Later in this lesson you will learn how to multiply one or more equations by a number in order to produce opposites that can be eliminated.

## EXAMPLE 1 Elimination Using Addition

Solve $\begin{cases} x - 2y = -19 \\ 5x + 2y = 1 \end{cases}$ by elimination.

**Step 1** $\begin{aligned} x - 2y &= -19 \\ +\ 5x + 2y &= \ \ 1 \end{aligned}$ — *Write the system so that like terms are aligned.*

**Step 2** $6x + 0 = -18$ — *Add the equations to eliminate the y-terms.*

$6x = -18$ — *Simplify and solve for x.*

$\frac{6x}{6} = \frac{-18}{6}$ — *Divide both sides by 6.*

$x = -3$

**Step 3** $x - 2y = -19$ — *Write one of the original equations.*

$-3 - 2y = -19$ — *Substitute −3 for x.*

$\underline{+3} \qquad \underline{+3}$ — *Add 3 to both sides.*

$-2y = -16$

$\frac{-2y}{-2} = \frac{-16}{-2}$ — *Divide both sides by −2.*

$y = 8$

**Step 4** $(-3, 8)$ — *Write the solution as an ordered pair.*

**Helpful Hint**

Check your answer.

| $x - 2y = -19$ | |
|---|---|
| $-3 - 2(8)$ | $-19$ |
| $-3 - 16$ | $-19$ |
| $-19$ | $-19$ ✓ |

| $5x + 2y = 1$ | |
|---|---|
| $5(-3) + 2(8)$ | $1$ |
| $-15 + 16$ | $1$ |
| $1$ | $1$ ✓ |

**1.** Solve $\begin{cases} y + 3x = -2 \\ 2y - 3x = 14 \end{cases}$ by elimination.

When two equations each contain the same term, you can subtract one equation from the other to solve the system. To subtract an equation, add the opposite of *each* term.

## EXAMPLE 2 Elimination Using Subtraction

Solve $\begin{cases} 3x + 4y = 18 \\ -2x + 4y = 8 \end{cases}$ by elimination.

**Step 1** $\begin{aligned} 3x + 4y &= 18 \\ -(-2x + 4y &= 8) \end{aligned}$

$\begin{aligned} 3x + 4y &= 18 \\ +\ 2x - 4y &= -8 \end{aligned}$ — *Add the opposite of each term in the second equation.*

**Step 2** $5x + 0 = 10$ — *Eliminate the y-term.*

$5x = 10$ — *Simplify and solve for x.*

$x = 2$

**Step 3** $-2x + 4y = 8$ — *Write one of the original equations.*

$-2(2) + 4y = 8$ — *Substitute 2 for x.*

$-4 + 4y = 8$

$\underline{+4} \qquad \underline{+4}$ — *Add 4 to both sides.*

$4y = 12$ — *Simplify and solve for y.*

$y = 3$

**Step 4** $(2, 3)$ — *Write the solution as an ordered pair.*

**Remember!**

Remember to check by substituting your answer into both original equations.

**2.** Solve $\begin{cases} 3x + 3y = 15 \\ -2x + 3y = -5 \end{cases}$ by elimination.

In some cases, you will first need to multiply one or both of the equations by a number so that one variable has opposite coefficients. This will be the new Step 1.

## EXAMPLE 3 Elimination Using Multiplication First

**Helpful Hint**

In Example 3A, you could have also multiplied the first equation by −3 to eliminate the $y$-term.

**Solve each system by elimination.**

**A** $\begin{cases} 2x + y = 3 \\ -x + 3y = -12 \end{cases}$

**Step 1**

$$\begin{aligned} 2x + y &= 3 \\ +2(-x + 3y &= -12) \end{aligned}$$

*Multiply each term in the second equation by 2 to get opposite x-coefficients.*

$$\begin{aligned} 2x + y &= 3 \\ +(-2x + 6y &= -24) \end{aligned}$$

*Add the new equation to the first equation.*

**Step 2**

$$7y = -21$$

$$y = -3$$

*Simplify and solve for y.*

**Step 3**

$2x + y = 3$ — *Write one of the original equations.*

$2x - 3 = 3$ — *Substitute −3 for y.*

$\quad +3 \quad +3$ — *Add 3 to both sides.*

$2x = 6$ — *Simplify and solve for x.*

$x = 3$

**Step 4** $(3, -3)$ — *Write the solution as an ordered pair.*

**Helpful Hint**

Use the techniques for finding a common denominator when trying to find values to multiply each equation by.

**B** $\begin{cases} 7x - 12y = -22 \\ 5x - 8y = -14 \end{cases}$

**Step 1**

$$\begin{aligned} 2(7x - 12y &= -22) \\ +(-3)(5x - 8y &= -14) \end{aligned}$$

*Multiply the first equation by 2 and the second equation by −3 to get opposite y-coefficients.*

$$\begin{aligned} 14x - 24y &= -44 \\ +(-15x + 24y &= 42) \end{aligned}$$

*Add the new equations to the first equation.*

**Step 2**

$$-x + 0 = -2$$

$$x = 2$$

*Simplify and solve for x.*

**Step 3**

$7x - 12y = -22$ — *Write one of the original equations.*

$7(2) - 12y = -22$ — *Substitute 2 for x.*

$14 - 12y = -22$

$-14 \quad -14$ — *Subtract 14 from both sides.*

$-12y = -36$ — *Simplify and solve for y.*

$y = 3$

**Step 4** $(2, 3)$ — *Write the solution as an ordered pair.*

**Solve each system by elimination.**

**3a.** $\begin{cases} 3x + 2y = 6 \\ -x + y = -2 \end{cases}$

**3b.** $\begin{cases} 2x + 5y = 26 \\ -3x - 4y = -25 \end{cases}$

## EXAMPLE 4 *Consumer Economics Application*

**Sam spent \$24.75 to buy 12 flowers for his mother. The bouquet contained roses and daisies. How many of each type of flower did Sam buy?**

Write a system. Use $r$ for the number of roses and $d$ for the number of daisies.

$2.50r + 1.75d = 24.75$ — *The cost of roses and daisies totals \$24.75.*

$r + d = 12$ — *The total number of roses and daisies is 12.*

**Step 1**

$$\begin{aligned} 2.50r + 1.75d &= 24.75 \\ +\,(-2.50)(r + d &= 12) \end{aligned}$$

*Multiply the second equation by −2.50 to get opposite r-coefficients.*

$$\begin{aligned} 2.50r + 1.75d &= \phantom{-}24.75 \\ +\,(-2.50r - 2.50d &= -30.00) \end{aligned}$$

*Add this equation to the first equation to eliminate the r-term.*

**Step 2**

$$\begin{aligned} -0.75d &= -5.25 \\ d &= 7 \end{aligned}$$

*Simplify and solve for d.*

**Step 3**

$r + d = 12$ — *Write one of the original equations.*

$r + 7 = 12$ — *Substitute 7 for d.*

$\underline{-7 \quad -7}$ — *Subtract 7 from both sides.*

$r = 5$

**Step 4**

$(5, 7)$ — *Write the solution as an ordered pair.*

Sam can buy 5 roses and 7 daisies.

4. **What if...?** Sally spent \$14.85 to buy 13 flowers. She bought lilies, which cost \$1.25 each, and tulips, which cost \$0.90 each. How many of each flower did Sally buy?

All systems can be solved in more than one way. For some systems, some methods may be better than others.

### Systems of Linear Equations

| METHOD | USE WHEN... | EXAMPLE |
|---|---|---|
| Graphing | • Both equations are solved for $y$.<br>• You want to estimate a solution. | $\begin{cases} y = 3x + 2 \\ y = -2x + 6 \end{cases}$ |
| Substitution | • A variable in either equation has a coefficient of 1 or −1.<br>• Both equations are solved for the same variable.<br>• Either equation is solved for a variable. | $\begin{cases} x + 2y = 7 \\ x = 10 - 5y \end{cases}$<br>or<br>$\begin{cases} x = 2y + 10 \\ x = 3y + 5 \end{cases}$ |
| Elimination | • Both equations have the same variable with the same or opposite coefficients.<br>• A variable term in one equation is a multiple of the corresponding variable term in the other equation. | $\begin{cases} 3x + 2y = 8 \\ 5x + 2y = 12 \end{cases}$<br>or<br>$\begin{cases} 6x + 5y = 10 \\ 3x + 2y = 15 \end{cases}$ |

## THINK AND DISCUSS

1. Explain how multiplying the second equation in a system by $-1$ and eliminating by adding is the same as elimination by subtraction. Give an example of a system for which this applies.
2. Explain why it does not matter which variable you solve for first when solving a system by elimination.

3. **GET ORGANIZED** Copy and complete the graphic organizer. In each box, write an example of a system of equations that you could solve using the given method.

Solving Systems of Linear Equations
- Substitution
- Elimination using addition or subtraction
- Elimination using multiplication

# 6-3 Exercises

MA.A.5.2, MA.A.5.1

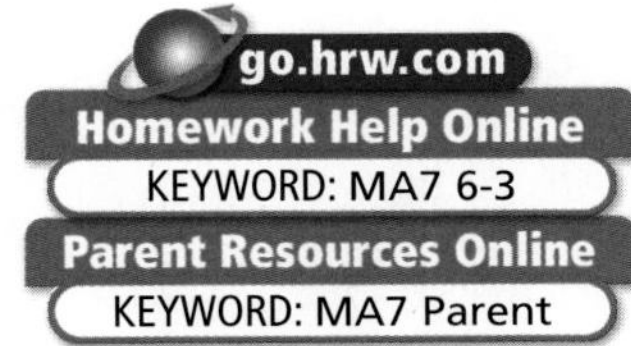



## GUIDED PRACTICE

**Solve each system by elimination.**

SEE EXAMPLE 1 p. 398

1. $\begin{cases} -x + y = 5 \\ x - 5y = -9 \end{cases}$
2. $\begin{cases} x + y = 12 \\ x - y = 2 \end{cases}$
3. $\begin{cases} 2x + 5y = -24 \\ 3x - 5y = 14 \end{cases}$

SEE EXAMPLE 2 p. 398

4. $\begin{cases} x - 10y = 60 \\ x + 14y = 12 \end{cases}$
5. $\begin{cases} 5x + y = 0 \\ 5x + 2y = 30 \end{cases}$
6. $\begin{cases} -5x + 7y = 11 \\ -5x + 3y = 19 \end{cases}$

SEE EXAMPLE 3 p. 399

7. $\begin{cases} 2x + 3y = 12 \\ 5x - y = 13 \end{cases}$
8. $\begin{cases} -3x + 4y = 12 \\ 2x + y = -8 \end{cases}$
9. $\begin{cases} 2x + 4y = -4 \\ 3x + 5y = -3 \end{cases}$

SEE EXAMPLE 4 p. 400

10. **Consumer Economics** Each family in a neighborhood is contributing \$20 worth of food to the neighborhood picnic. The Harlin family is bringing 12 packages of buns. The hamburger buns cost \$2.00 per package. The hot-dog buns cost \$1.50 per package. How many packages of each type of bun did they buy?

## PRACTICE AND PROBLEM SOLVING

**Independent Practice**

| For Exercises | See Example |
|---|---|
| 11–13 | 1 |
| 14–16 | 2 |
| 17–19 | 3 |
| 20 | 4 |

Skills Practice p. S14
Application Practice p. S33

**Solve each system by elimination.**

11. $\begin{cases} -x + y = -1 \\ 2x - y = 0 \end{cases}$
12. $\begin{cases} -2x + y = -20 \\ 2x + y = 48 \end{cases}$
13. $\begin{cases} 3x - y = -2 \\ -2x + y = 3 \end{cases}$
14. $\begin{cases} x - y = 4 \\ x - 2y = 10 \end{cases}$
15. $\begin{cases} x + 2y = 5 \\ 3x + 2y = 17 \end{cases}$
16. $\begin{cases} 3x - 2y = -1 \\ 3x - 4y = 9 \end{cases}$
17. $\begin{cases} x - y = -3 \\ 5x + 3y = 1 \end{cases}$
18. $\begin{cases} 9x - 3y = 3 \\ 3x + 8y = -17 \end{cases}$
19. $\begin{cases} 5x + 2y = -1 \\ 3x + 7y = 11 \end{cases}$
20. **Multi-Step** Mrs. Gonzalez bought centerpieces to put on each table at a graduation party. She spent \$31.50. There are 8 tables each requiring either a candle or vase. Candles cost \$3 and vases cost \$4.25. How many of each type did she buy?

 **21. Geometry** The difference between the length and width of a rectangle is 2 units. The perimeter is 40 units. Write and solve a system of equations to determine the length and width of the rectangle. (*Hint:* The perimeter of a rectangle is $2\ell + 2w$.)

**22. ERROR ANALYSIS** Which is incorrect? Explain the error.

**A**

$$\begin{cases} x + y = -3 \\ 3x + y = 3 \end{cases} \qquad \begin{array}{r} x + y = -3 \\ \underline{-(3x + y = 3)} \\ -2x = 0 \\ x = 0 \end{array}$$

**B**

$$\begin{cases} x + y = -3 \\ 3x + y = 3 \end{cases} \qquad \begin{array}{r} x + y = -3 \\ \underline{-(3x + y = 3)} \\ -2x = -6 \\ x = 3 \end{array}$$

**23. Chemistry** A chemist has a bottle of a 1% acid solution and a bottle of a 5% acid solution. She wants to mix the two solutions to get 100 mL of a 4% acid solution. Follow the steps below to find how much of each solution she should use.

| | 1% Solution | + | 5% Solution | = | 4% Solution |
|---|---|---|---|---|---|
| **Amount of Solution (mL)** | $x$ | + | $y$ | = | ■ |
| **Amount of Acid (mL)** | $0.01x$ | + | ■ | = | $0.04(100)$ |

**a.** Copy and complete the table.

**b.** Use the information in the table to write a system of equations.

**c.** Solve the system of equations to find how much she will use from each bottle to get 100 mL of a 4% acid solution.

**LINK Math History**

In 1247, Ch'in Chiu-Shao wrote *Mathematical Treatise in Nine Sections.* Its contents included solving systems of equations and the Chinese Remainder Theorem.

**Critical Thinking** **Which method would you use to solve each system? Explain.**

**24.** $\begin{cases} \frac{1}{2}x - 5y = 30 \\ \frac{1}{2}x + 7y = 6 \end{cases}$

**25.** $\begin{cases} -x + 2y = 3 \\ 4x - 5y = -3 \end{cases}$

**26.** $\begin{cases} 3x - y = 10 \\ 2x - y = 7 \end{cases}$

**27.** $\begin{cases} 3y + x = 10 \\ x = 4y + 2 \end{cases}$

**28.** $\begin{cases} y = -4x \\ y = 2x + 3 \end{cases}$

**29.** $\begin{cases} 2x + 6y = 12 \\ 4x + 5y = 15 \end{cases}$

**30. Business** A local boys club sold 176 bags of mulch and made a total of $520. They did not sell any of the expensive cocoa mulch. Use the table to determine how many bags of each type of mulch they sold.

| Mulch Prices ($) | |
|---|---|
| Cocoa | 4.75 |
| Hardwood | 3.50 |
| Pine Bark | 2.75 |

**MULTI-STEP TEST PREP**

**31.** This problem will prepare you for the Multi-Step Test Prep on page 412.

**a.** The school store is running a promotion on school supplies. Different supplies are placed on two shelves. You can purchase 3 items from shelf A and 2 from shelf B for $16. Or you can purchase 2 items from shelf A and 3 from shelf B for $14. Write a system of equations that can be used to find the individual prices for the supplies on shelf A and on shelf B.

**b.** Solve the system of equations by elimination.

**c.** If the supplies on shelf A are normally $6 each and the supplies on shelf B are normally $3 each, how much will you save on each package plan from part **a**?

32. **Write About It** Solve the system $\begin{cases} 3x + y = 1 \\ 2x + 4y = -6 \end{cases}$. Explain how you can check your solution algebraically and graphically.

## TEST PREP

MA.A.5.2, MA.A.5.1

33. A math test has 25 problems. Some are worth 2 points, and some are worth 3 points. The test is worth 60 points total. Which system can be used to determine the number of 2-point problems and the number of 3-point problems on the test?

Ⓐ $\begin{cases} x + y = 25 \\ 2x + 3y = 60 \end{cases}$ Ⓑ $\begin{cases} x + y = 60 \\ 2x + 3y = 25 \end{cases}$ Ⓒ $\begin{cases} x - y = 25 \\ 2x + 3y = 60 \end{cases}$ Ⓓ $\begin{cases} x - y = 60 \\ 2x - 3y = 25 \end{cases}$

34. An electrician charges \$15 plus \$11 per hour. Another electrician charges \$10 plus \$15 per hour. For what amount of time will the cost be the same? What is that cost?

Ⓕ 1 hour; \$25

Ⓖ $1\frac{1}{4}$ hours; \$28.75

Ⓗ $1\frac{1}{2}$ hours; \$30

Ⓙ $1\frac{3}{4}$ hours; \$32.50

35. **Short Response** Three hundred and fifty-eight tickets to the school basketball game on Friday were sold. Student tickets were \$1.50, and nonstudent tickets were \$3.25. The school made \$752.25.

**a.** Write a system of linear equations that could be used to determine how many student and how many nonstudent tickets were sold. Define the variables you use.

**b.** Solve the system you wrote in part **a.** How many student and how many nonstudent tickets were sold?

## CHALLENGE AND EXTEND

**Solve each system by any method.**

36. $\begin{cases} x + 16\frac{1}{2} = -\frac{3}{4}y \\ y = \frac{1}{2}x \end{cases}$ 37. $\begin{cases} 2x + y + z = 17 \\ \frac{1}{2}z = 5 \\ x - y = 5 \end{cases}$ 38. $\begin{cases} x - 2y - z = -1 \\ -x + 2y + 4z = -11 \\ 2x + y + z = 1 \end{cases}$

39. The sum of the digits of a two-digit number is 5. If the number is multiplied by 3, the result is 42. Write and solve a system of equations to find the number. (*Hint:* One equation involves the digits in the number. The other equation involves the values of the digits.)

## SPIRAL REVIEW

**Determine a relationship between the *x*- and *y*-values. Write an equation.** (*Lesson 4-3*)

40.

| *x* | 1 | 2 | 3 | 4 |
|---|---|---|---|---|
| *y* | 6 | 7 | 8 | 9 |

41.

| *x* | 1 | 2 | 3 | 4 |
|---|---|---|---|---|
| *y* | 3 | 6 | 9 | 12 |

42.

| *x* | 1 | 2 | 3 | 4 |
|---|---|---|---|---|
| *y* | −9 | −8 | −7 | −6 |

**Tell whether each equation is a direct variation. If so, identify the constant of variation.** (*Lesson 5-5*)

43. $x = 2y$ 44. $y = -6x$ 45. $y - 1 = x$

**Solve each system by substitution.** (*Lesson 6-2*)

46. $\begin{cases} y = x - 1 \\ x + y = 10 \end{cases}$ 47. $\begin{cases} x = y - 5 \\ 2x + 1 = y \end{cases}$ 48. $\begin{cases} y = 2x - 1 \\ x - y = 3 \end{cases}$

# Solving Classic Problems

You can use systems of linear equations to solve some "classic" math problems that are common in textbooks and puzzle books.

*See Skills Bank page S52*

**MA.A.5.2** Use strategies to solve systems of linear equations in two variables, graphically and symbolically.

## Example 1

**Yuri is twice as old as Zack. Four years from now, the sum of their ages will be 23. How old is Yuri?**

**Step 1** Write a system. Let $y$ represent Yuri's age. Let $z$ represent Zack's age.

Yuri is twice as old as Zack.

$$y = 2z$$

In 4 years, the sum of their ages will be 23.

$$(y + 4) + (z + 4) = 23$$
$$y + z + 8 = 23$$
$$y + z = 15$$

**Step 2** Solve the equations for $y$.

$$\begin{cases} y = 2z \\ y + z = 15 \end{cases} \rightarrow \begin{cases} y = 2z \\ y = -z + 15 \end{cases}$$

**Step 3** Graph $y = 2z$ and $y = -z + 15$.

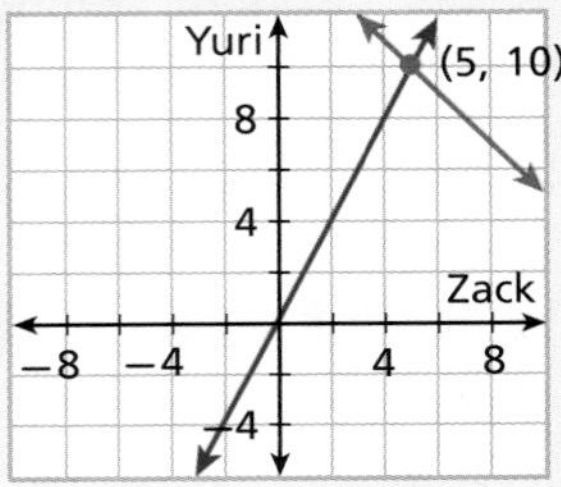


The lines appear to intersect at $(5, 10)$.

The solution $(5, 10)$ means that Yuri is 10 years old.

## Example 2

**Mandy has 11 coins in dimes and quarters. The value of her coins is \$2.15. How many dimes does she have?**

**Step 1** Write a system. Let $d$ be the number of dimes. Let $q$ be the number of quarters.

The total number of coins is 11.

$$q + d = 11$$

The value of the coins is \$2.15.

$$0.25q + 0.10d = 2.15$$
$$100(0.25q + 0.10d = 2.15)$$
$$25q + 10d = 215$$
$$5q + 2d = 43$$

**Step 2** Solve the first equation for $d$.

$$d = 11 - q$$

**Step 3** Substitute $11 - q$ for $d$ in the second equation.

$$5q + 2(11 - q) = 43$$
$$3q + 22 = 43 \quad \textit{Distribute 2 and then combine like terms.}$$
$$3q = 21$$
$$q = 7 \quad \textit{Solve for q.}$$

**Step 4** Substitute 7 for $q$ in one of the original equations.

$$q + d = 11$$
$$7 + d = 11$$
$$d = 4$$

The solution $(4, 7)$ means that there are 4 dimes and 7 quarters. Mandy has 4 dimes.

## Example 3

**When the digits of a two-digit number are reversed, the new number is 45 less than the original number. The sum of the digits is 7. What is the original number?**

**Step 1** Write expressions for the original number and the new number. Let $a$ represent the tens digit. Let $b$ represent the ones digit.

The original number: $10a + b$

The new number: $10b + a$

**Step 2** Write a system.

The new number is 45 less than the original number.

$$10b + a = (10a + b) - 45$$
$$9b - 9a = -45$$
$$b - a = -5 \rightarrow a - b = 5$$

The sum of the digits is 7.

$$a + b = 7$$

**Step 3** Add the equations to eliminate the $b$-term. Solve for $a$.

$$\begin{array}{r} a - b = 5 \\ + (a + b = 7) \\ \hline 2a \quad = 12 \end{array}$$
$$a = 6$$

**Step 4** Substitute 6 for $a$ in one of the original equations.

$$a + b = 7$$
$$6 + b = 7$$
$$b = 1$$

The solution is $(6, 1)$. This means that 6 is the tens digit and 1 is the ones digit. The original number is 61.

*Check* Check your solution using the original problem.
The sum of the digits is 7: $6 + 1 = 7$ ✓
When the digits are reversed, the new number is 45 less than the original number: $16 = 61 - 45$ ✓

## Try This

**Solve.**

1. The sum of the digits of a two-digit number is 17. When the digits are reversed, the new number is 9 more than the original number. What is the original number?
2. Vic has 14 coins in nickels and quarters. The value of his coins is $1.70. How many quarters does he have?
3. Grace is 8 years older than her brother Sam. The sum of their ages is 24. How old is Grace?

# 6-4 Solving Special Systems

**MA.A.5.2** Use strategies to solve systems of linear equations in two variables, graphically and symbolically. *Also* **MA.A.5.1**

***Objectives***

Solve special systems of linear equations in two variables.

Classify systems of linear equations and determine the number of solutions.

***Vocabulary***

inconsistent system
consistent system
independent system
dependent system

**Why learn this?**

Linear systems can be used to analyze business growth, such as comic book sales. (See Example 4.)

In Lesson 6-1, you saw that when two lines intersect at a point, there is exactly one solution to the system. Systems with at least one solution are called **consistent**.

When the two lines in a system do not intersect, they are parallel lines. There are no ordered pairs that satisfy both equations, so there is no solution. A system that has no solution is an **inconsistent system**.

## EXAMPLE 1 Systems with No Solution

Solve $\begin{cases} y = x - 1 \\ -x + y = 2 \end{cases}$.

**Method 1** Compare slopes and $y$-intercepts.

$y = x - 1 \rightarrow y = 1x - 1$ *Write both equations in slope-intercept form.*

$-x + y = 2 \rightarrow y = 1x + 2$ *The lines are parallel because they have the same slope and different y-intercepts.*

This system has no solution so it is an inconsistent system.

**Remember!**

For help recalling identities and contradictions, see Lesson 2-4.

**Method 2** Solve the system algebraically. Use the substitution method because the first equation is solved for $y$.

$-x + (x - 1) = 2$ *Substitute x − 1 for y in the second equation, and solve.*

$-1 = 2$ ✗ *False. The equation is a contradiction.*

This system has no solution so it is an inconsistent system.

***Check*** Graph the system to confirm that the lines are parallel.

*The lines appear to be parallel.*

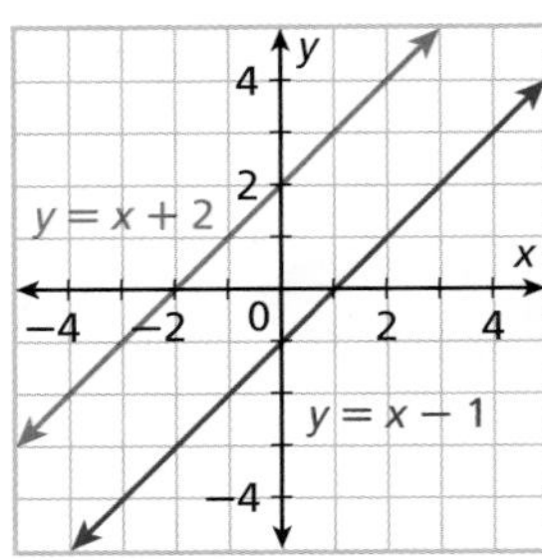

**1.** Solve $\begin{cases} y = -2x + 5 \\ 2x + y = 1 \end{cases}$.

If two linear equations in a system have the same graph, the graphs are coincident lines, or the same line. There are infinitely many solutions of the system because every point on the line represents a solution of both equations.

**Caution!**

0 = 0 is a true statement. It does not mean the system has zero solutions or no solution.

## EXAMPLE 2 Systems with Infinitely Many Solutions

**Solve** $\begin{cases} y = 2x + 1 \\ 2x - y + 1 = 0 \end{cases}$.

**Method 1** Compare slopes and $y$-intercepts.

$$y = 2x + 1 \rightarrow y = 2x + 1$$
$$2x - y + 1 = 0 \rightarrow y = 2x + 1$$

*Write both equations in slope-intercept form. The lines have the same slope and the same y-intercept.*

If this system were graphed, the graphs would be the same line. There are infinitely many solutions.

**Method 2** Solve the system algebraically. Use the elimination method.

$$y = 2x + 1 \rightarrow -2x + y = 1$$ *Write equations to line up like terms.*

$$2x - y + 1 = 0 \rightarrow \underline{2x - y = -1}$$ *Add the equations.*

$$0 = 0 \checkmark$$ *True. The equation is an identity.*

There are infinitely many solutions.

**2.** Solve $\begin{cases} y = x - 3 \\ x - y - 3 = 0 \end{cases}$.

Consistent systems can either be independent or dependent.

- An **independent system** has exactly one solution. The graph of an independent system consists of two intersecting lines.
- A **dependent system** has infinitely many solutions. The graph of a dependent system consists of two coincident lines.

### Classification of Systems of Linear Equations

| CLASSIFICATION | CONSISTENT AND INDEPENDENT | CONSISTENT AND DEPENDENT | INCONSISTENT |
|---|---|---|---|
| Number of Solutions | Exactly one | Infinitely many | None |
| Description | Different slopes | Same slope, same $y$-intercept | Same slope, different $y$-intercepts |
| Graph | Intersecting lines | Coincident lines | Parallel lines |

## EXAMPLE 3 Classifying Systems of Linear Equations

**Classify each system. Give the number of solutions.**

**A** $\begin{cases} 2y = x + 2 \\ -\frac{1}{2}x + y = 1 \end{cases}$

$2y = x + 2 \rightarrow y = \frac{1}{2}x + 1$ *Write both equations in slope-intercept form.*

$-\frac{1}{2}x + y = 1 \rightarrow y = \frac{1}{2}x + 1$ *The lines have the same slope and the same y-intercepts. They are the same.*

The system is consistent and dependent. It has infinitely many solutions.

**B** $\begin{cases} y = 2(x - 1) \\ y = x + 1 \end{cases}$

$y = 2(x - 1) \rightarrow y = 2x - 2$ *Write both equations in slope-intercept form.*

$y = x + 1 \rightarrow y = 1x + 1$ *The lines have different slopes. They intersect.*

The system is consistent and independent. It has one solution.

**Classify each system. Give the number of solutions.**

**3a.** $\begin{cases} x + 2y = -4 \\ -2(y + 2) = x \end{cases}$ **3b.** $\begin{cases} y = -2(x - 1) \\ y = -x + 3 \end{cases}$ **3c.** $\begin{cases} 2x - 3y = 6 \\ y = \frac{2}{3}x \end{cases}$

## EXAMPLE 4 *Business Application*

**The sales manager at Comics Now is comparing its sales with the sales of its competitor, Dynamo Comics. If the sales patterns continue, will the sales for Comics Now ever equal the sales for Dynamo Comics? Explain.**

| Comic Books Sold per Year (thousands) POW! | 2005 | 2006 | 2007 | 2008 |
|---|---|---|---|---|
| Comics Now | 130 | 170 | 210 | 250 |
| Dynamo Comics | 180 | 220 | 260 | 300 |

Use the table to write a system of linear equations. Let $y$ represent the sales total and $x$ represent the increase in sales.

| | Sales total | equals | increase in sales per year | times | years | plus | beginning sales. |
|---|---|---|---|---|---|---|---|
| Comics Now | $y$ | = | 40 | • | $x$ | + | 130 |
| Dynamo Comics | $y$ | = | 40 | • | $x$ | + | 180 |

**Helpful Hint**

The increase in sales is the difference between sales each year.

$\begin{cases} y = 40x + 130 \\ y = 40x + 180 \end{cases}$

$y = 40x + 130$ *Both equations are in slope-intercept form.*

$y = 40x + 180$ *The lines have the same slope, but different y-intercepts.*

The graphs of the two equations are parallel lines, so there is no solution. If the patterns continue, sales for the two companies will never be equal.

**4.** Matt has \$100 in a checking account and deposits \$20 per month. Ben has \$80 in a checking account and deposits \$30 per month. Will the accounts ever have the same balance? Explain.

## THINK AND DISCUSS

1. Describe the graph of a system of equations that has infinitely many solutions. Compare the slopes and $y$-intercepts.
2. What methods can be used to determine the number of solutions of a system of linear equations?

3. **GET ORGANIZED** Copy and complete the graphic organizer. In each box, write the word that describes a system with that number of solutions and sketch a graph.

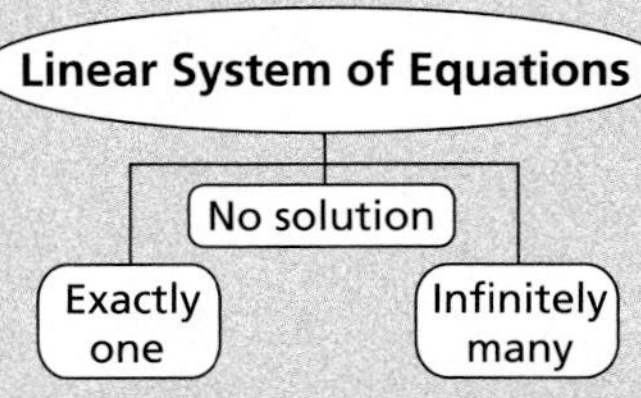


# 6-4 Exercises

MA.A.5.2, MA.A.5.1

go.hrw.com
Homework Help Online
KEYWORD: MA7 6-4
Parent Resources Online
KEYWORD: MA7 Parent

## GUIDED PRACTICE

1. **Vocabulary** A ___?___ system can be independent or dependent. (*consistent* or *inconsistent*)

**Solve each system of linear equations.**

SEE EXAMPLE 1 p. 406

2. $\begin{cases} y = x + 1 \\ -x + y = 3 \end{cases}$
3. $\begin{cases} 3x + y = 6 \\ y = -3x + 2 \end{cases}$
4. $\begin{cases} -y = 4x + 1 \\ 4x + y = 2 \end{cases}$

SEE EXAMPLE 2 p. 407

5. $\begin{cases} y = -x + 3 \\ x + y - 3 = 0 \end{cases}$
6. $\begin{cases} y = 2x - 4 \\ 2x - y - 4 = 0 \end{cases}$
7. $\begin{cases} -7x + y = -2 \\ 7x - y = 2 \end{cases}$

SEE EXAMPLE 3 p. 408

**Classify each system. Give the number of solutions.**

8. $\begin{cases} y = 2(x + 3) \\ -2y = 2x + 6 \end{cases}$
9. $\begin{cases} y = -3x - 1 \\ 3x + y = 1 \end{cases}$
10. $\begin{cases} 9y = 3x + 18 \\ \frac{1}{3}x - y = -2 \end{cases}$

SEE EXAMPLE 4 p. 408

11. **Athletics** Micah walks on a treadmill at 4 miles per hour. He has walked 2 miles when Luke starts running at 6 miles per hour on the treadmill next to him. If their rates continue, will Luke's distance ever equal Micah's distance? Explain.

## PRACTICE AND PROBLEM SOLVING

**Solve each system of linear equations.**

12. $\begin{cases} y = 2x - 2 \\ -2x + y = 1 \end{cases}$
13. $\begin{cases} x + y = 3 \\ y = -x - 1 \end{cases}$
14. $\begin{cases} x + 2y = -4 \\ y = -\frac{1}{2}x - 4 \end{cases}$
15. $\begin{cases} -6 + y = 2x \\ y = 2x - 36 \end{cases}$

16. $\begin{cases} y = -2x + 3 \\ 2x + y - 3 = 0 \end{cases}$
17. $\begin{cases} y = x - 2 \\ x - y - 2 = 0 \end{cases}$
18. $\begin{cases} x + y = -4 \\ y = -x - 4 \end{cases}$
19. $\begin{cases} -9x - 3y = -18 \\ 3x + y = 6 \end{cases}$

**Independent Practice**

| For Exercises | See Example |
|---|---|
| 12–15 | 1 |
| 16–19 | 2 |
| 20–22 | 3 |
| 23 | 4 |

**Extra Practice**

Skills Practice p. S15

Application Practice p. S33

**Classify each system. Give the number of solutions.**

20. $\begin{cases} y = -x + 5 \\ x + y = 5 \end{cases}$

21. $\begin{cases} y = -3x + 2 \\ y = 3x \end{cases}$

22. $\begin{cases} y - 1 = 2x \\ y = 2x - 1 \end{cases}$

23. **Sports** Mandy is skating at 5 miles per hour. Nikki is skating at 6 miles per hour and started 1 mile behind Mandy. If their rates stay the same, will Mandy catch up with Nikki? Explain.

24. **Multi-Step** Photocopier A can print 35 copies per minute. Photocopier B can print 35 copies per minute. Copier B is started and makes 10 copies. Copier A is then started. If the copiers continue, will the number of copies from machine A ever equal the number of copies from machine B? Explain.

**LINK**

**Geology**

Geodes are rounded, hollow rock formations. Most are partially or completely filled with layers of colored quartz crystals. The world's largest geode was discovered in Spain in 2000. It is 26 feet long and 5.6 feet high.

25. **Entertainment** One week Trey rented 4 DVDs and 2 video games for $18. The next week he rented 2 DVDs and 1 video game for $9. Find the rental costs for each video game and DVD. Explain your answer.

26. Rosa bought 1 pound of cashews and 2 pounds of peanuts for $10. At the same store, Sabrina bought 2 pounds of cashews and 1 pound of peanuts for $11. Find the cost per pound for cashews and peanuts.

27. **Geology** Pam and Tommy collect geodes. Pam's parents gave her 2 geodes to start her collection, and she buys 4 every year. Tommy has 2 geodes that were given to him for his birthday. He buys 4 every year. If Pam and Tommy continue to buy the same amount of geodes per year, when will Tommy have as many geodes as Pam? Explain your answer.

28. Use the data given in the tables.

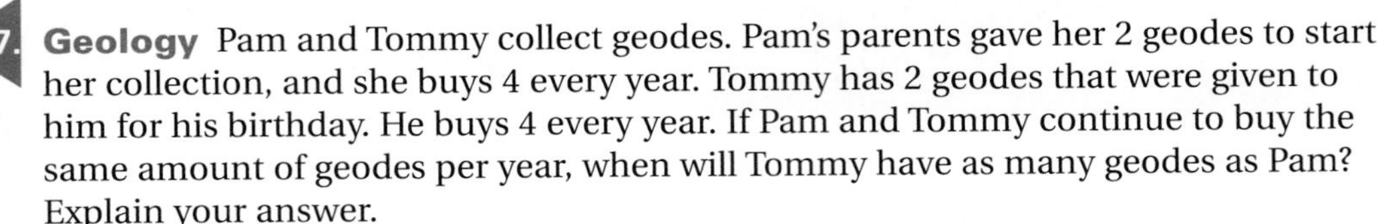

| $x$ | 3 | 4 | 5 | 6 |
|---|---|---|---|---|
| $y$ | 6 | 8 | 10 | 12 |

| $x$ | 12 | 13 | 14 | 15 |
|---|---|---|---|---|
| $y$ | 24 | 26 | 28 | 30 |

a. Write an equation to describe the data in each table.

b. Graph the system of equations from part **a**. Describe the graph.

c. How could you have predicted the graph by looking at the equations?

d. **What if...?** Each $y$-value in the second table increases by 1. How does this affect the graphs of the two equations? How can you tell how the graphs would be affected without actually graphing?

29. **Critical Thinking** Describe the graphs of two equations if the result of solving the system by substitution or elimination is the statement $1 = 3$.

30. This problem will prepare you for the Multi-Step Test Prep on page 412.

The Crusader pep club is selling team buttons that support the sports teams. They contacted Buttons, Etc. which charges $50 plus $1.10 per button, and Logos, which charges $40 plus $1.10 per button.

a. Write an equation for each company's cost.

b. Use the system from part **a** to find when the price for both companies is the same. Explain.

c. What part of the equation should the pep club negotiate to change so that the cost of Buttons, Etc. is the same as Logos? What part of the equation should change in order to get a better price?

31. **ERROR ANALYSIS** Student A says there is no solution to the graphed system of equations. Student B says there is one solution. Which student is incorrect? Explain the error.

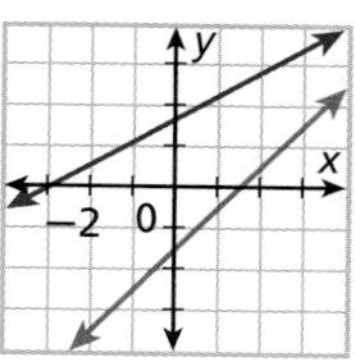


32. **Write About It** Compare the graph of a system that is consistent and independent with the graph of a system that is consistent and dependent.

33. Which of the following classifications fit the following system?

**MA.A.5.2, MA.A.5.1**

$$\begin{cases} 2x - y = 3 \\ 6x - 3y = 9 \end{cases}$$

(A) Inconsistent and independent

(B) Consistent and independent

(C) Inconsistent and dependent

(D) Consistent and dependent

34. Which of the following would be enough information to classify a system of two linear equations?

(F) The graphs have the same slope.

(G) The $y$-intercepts are the same.

(H) The graphs have different slopes.

(J) The $y$-intercepts are different.

## CHALLENGE AND EXTEND

35. What conditions are necessary for the system $\begin{cases} y = 2x + p \\ y = 2x + q \end{cases}$ to have infinitely many solutions? no solution?

36. Solve the systems in parts **a** and **b.** Use this information to make a conjecture about all solutions that exist for the system in part **c.**

**a.** $\begin{cases} 3x + 4y = 0 \\ 4x + 3y = 0 \end{cases}$

**b.** $\begin{cases} 2x + 5y = 0 \\ 5x + 2y = 0 \end{cases}$

**c.** $\begin{cases} ax + by = 0 \\ bx + ay = 0 \end{cases}$, for $a > 0$, $b > 0$, $a \neq b$

## SPIRAL REVIEW

**Use the map to find the actual distances between each pair of cities.** *(Lesson 2-6)*

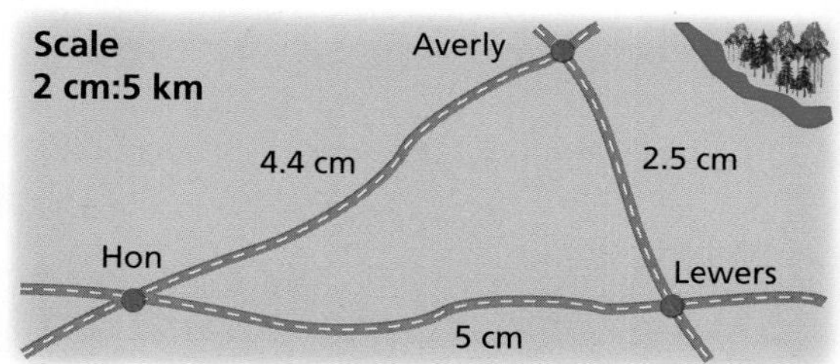


37. from Hon to Averly

38. from Averly to Lewers

**Determine if each sequence appears to be an arithmetic sequence. If so, find the common difference and the next three terms.** *(Lesson 4-6)*

39. 1, 3, 5, 9, ...

40. 1, 5, 9, 13, ...

41. $0, -1\frac{1}{2}, -3, -4\frac{1}{2}, \ldots$

**Solve each system by graphing.** *(Lesson 6-1)*

42. $\begin{cases} y = x - 2 \\ y = -x + 4 \end{cases}$

43. $\begin{cases} y = 2x \\ x + y = -6 \end{cases}$

44. $\begin{cases} y = -\frac{1}{2}x \\ y - x = 9 \end{cases}$

CHAPTER 6

SECTION 6A

# MULTI-STEP TEST PREP

## Systems of Equations

**We've Got Spirit** Some cheerleaders are going to sell spirit bracelets and foam fingers to raise money for traveling to away games.

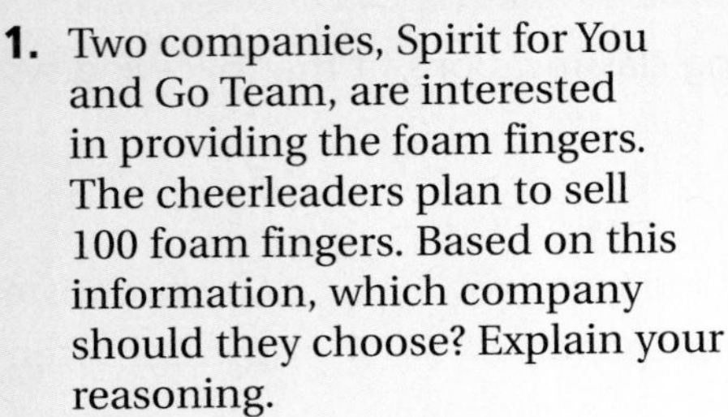


1. Two companies, Spirit for You and Go Team, are interested in providing the foam fingers. The cheerleaders plan to sell 100 foam fingers. Based on this information, which company should they choose? Explain your reasoning.

| Company | Design fee | Cost per item |
|---|---|---|
| Spirit for You | \$35 | \$2.50 |
| Go Team | \$20 | \$3.00 |

2. The cheerleaders sold foam fingers for \$5 and spirit bracelets for \$4. They sold 40 more foam fingers than bracelets, and they earned \$965. Write a system of equations to describe this situation.
3. Solve this system using at least two different methods. Explain each method.
4. Using the company you chose in Problem 1, how much profit did the cheerleaders make from the foam fingers alone? (*Hint:* profit = amount earned − expenses)
5. What is the maximum price the cheerleaders could pay for each spirit bracelet in order to make a total profit of \$500?

# READY TO GO ON?

CHAPTER 6

SECTION 6A

## Quiz for Lessons 6-1 Through 6-4

### 6-1 Solving Systems by Graphing

**Tell whether the ordered pair is a solution of the given system.**

1. $(-2, 1); \begin{cases} y = -2x - 3 \\ y = x + 3 \end{cases}$

2. $(9, 2); \begin{cases} x - 4y = 1 \\ 2x - 3y = 3 \end{cases}$

3. $(3, -1); \begin{cases} y = -\frac{1}{3}x \\ y + 2x = 5 \end{cases}$

**Solve each system by graphing.**

4. $\begin{cases} y = x + 5 \\ y = \frac{1}{2}x + 4 \end{cases}$

5. $\begin{cases} y = -x - 2 \\ 2x - y = 2 \end{cases}$

6. $\begin{cases} \frac{2}{3}x + y = -3 \\ 4x + y = 7 \end{cases}$

7. **Banking** Christiana and Marlena opened their first savings accounts on the same day. Christiana opened her account with $50 and plans to deposit $10 every month. Marlena opened her account with $30 and plans to deposit $15 every month. After how many months will their two accounts have the same amount of money? What will that amount be?

### 6-2 Solving Systems by Substitution

**Solve each system by substitution.**

8. $\begin{cases} y = -x + 5 \\ 2x + y = 11 \end{cases}$

9. $\begin{cases} 4x - 3y = -1 \\ 3x - y = -2 \end{cases}$

10. $\begin{cases} y = -x \\ y = -2x - 5 \end{cases}$

### 6-3 Solving Systems by Elimination

**Solve each system by elimination.**

11. $\begin{cases} x + 3y = 15 \\ 2x - 3y = -6 \end{cases}$

12. $\begin{cases} x + y = 2 \\ 2x + y = -1 \end{cases}$

13. $\begin{cases} -2x + 5y = -1 \\ 3x + 2y = 11 \end{cases}$

14. It takes Akira 10 minutes to make a black and white drawing and 25 minutes for a color drawing. On Saturday he made a total of 9 drawings in 2 hours. Write and solve a system of equations to determine how many drawings of each type Akira made.

### 6-4 Solving Special Systems

**Solve each system of linear equations.**

15. $\begin{cases} y = -2x - 6 \\ 2x + y = 5 \end{cases}$

16. $\begin{cases} x + y = 2 \\ 2x + 2y = -6 \end{cases}$

17. $\begin{cases} y = -2x + 4 \\ 2x + y = 4 \end{cases}$

**Classify each system. Give the number of solutions.**

18. $\begin{cases} 3x = -6y + 3 \\ 2y = -x + 1 \end{cases}$

19. $\begin{cases} y = -4x + 2 \\ 4x + y = -2 \end{cases}$

20. $\begin{cases} 4x - 3y = 8 \\ y = 4(x + 2) \end{cases}$

# 6-5 Solving Linear Inequalities

**Prep MA.A.5.3** Use … graphs to solve pairs of linear inequalities in two variables. *Also* **MA.A.5.1**

***Objective***
Graph and solve linear inequalities in two variables.

***Vocabulary***
linear inequality
solution of a linear inequality

**Who uses this?**
Consumers can use linear inequalities to determine how much food they can buy for an event. (See Example 3.)

A **linear inequality** is similar to a linear equation, but the equal sign is replaced with an inequality symbol. A **solution of a linear inequality** is any ordered pair that makes the inequality true.

## EXAMPLE 1 Identifying Solutions of Inequalities

**Tell whether the ordered pair is a solution of the inequality.**

**A** $(7, 3); y < x - 1$

$$\begin{array}{c|c|c} y & < & x - 1 \\ \hline 3 & & 7 - 1 \\ 3 & < & 6 \checkmark \end{array}$$

*Substitute (7, 3) for (x, y).*

$(7, 3)$ is a solution.

**B** $(4, 5); y > 3x + 2$

$$\begin{array}{c|c|c} y & > & 3x + 2 \\ \hline 5 & & 3(4) + 2 \\ 5 & & 12 + 2 \\ 5 & > & 14 \text{ ✗} \end{array}$$

*Substitute (4, 5) for (x, y).*

$(4, 5)$ is not a solution.

**Tell whether the ordered pair is a solution of the inequality.**

**1a.** $(4, 5); y < x + 1$

**1b.** $(1, 1); y > x - 7$

A linear inequality describes a region of a coordinate plane called a *half-plane*. All points in the region are solutions of the linear inequality. The boundary line of the region is the graph of the related equation.

When the inequality is written as $y \leq$ or $y \geq$, the points on the boundary line are solutions of the inequality, and the line is **solid**.

When the inequality is written as $y <$ or $y >$, the points on the boundary line are not solutions of the inequality, and the line is **dashed**.

When the inequality is written as $y >$ or $y \geq$, the points **above** the boundary line are solutions of the inequality.

When the inequality is written as $y <$ or $y \leq$, the points **below** the boundary line are solutions of the inequality.

| Graphing Linear Inequalities | |
|---|---|
| **Step 1** | Solve the inequality for *y* (slope-intercept form). |
| **Step 2** | Graph the boundary line. Use a solid line for ≤ or ≥. Use a dashed line for < or >. |
| **Step 3** | Shade the half-plane above the line for *y* > or *y* ≥. Shade the half-plane below the line for *y* < or *y* ≤. Check your answer. |

## EXAMPLE 2 Graphing Linear Inequalities in Two Variables

**Graph the solutions of each linear inequality.**

**A** $y < 3x + 4$

**Step 1** The inequality is already solved for $y$.

**Step 2** Graph the boundary line $y = 3x + 4$. Use a dashed line for $<$.

**Step 3** The inequality is $<$, so shade below the line.

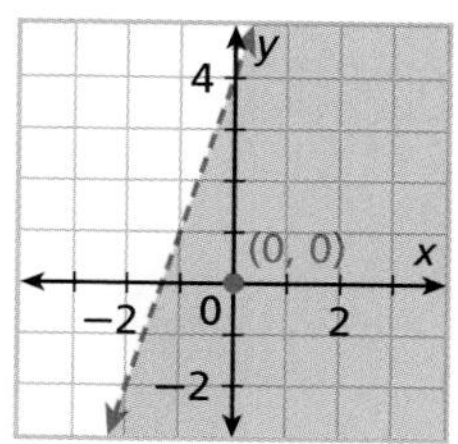


### Helpful Hint

The point (0, 0) is a good test point to use if it does not lie on the boundary line.

*Check*

| $y$ | | $<$ | $3x + 4$ |
|---|---|---|---|
| $0$ | | | $3(0) + 4$ |
| $0$ | | | $0 + 4$ |
| $0$ | $<$ | | $4$ ✓ |

*Substitute (0, 0) for (x, y) because it is not on the boundary line.*

*The point (0, 0) satisfies the inequality, so the graph is shaded correctly.*

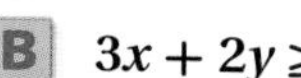
**B** $3x + 2y \geq 6$

**Step 1** Solve the inequality for $y$.

$$3x + 2y \geq 6$$
$$\underline{-3x} \qquad \underline{-3x}$$
$$2y \geq -3x + 6$$
$$y \geq -\frac{3}{2}x + 3$$

*Addition Property of Inequality*

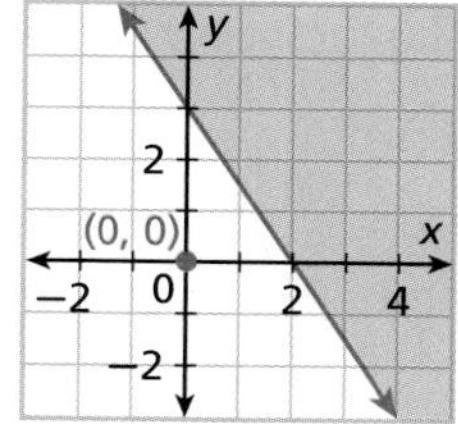


**Step 2** Graph the boundary line $y = -\frac{3}{2}x + 3$. Use a solid line for $\geq$.

**Step 3** The inequality is $\geq$, so shade above the line.

*Check*

| $y$ | | $\geq$ | $\frac{3}{2}x + 3$ |
|---|---|---|---|
| $0$ | | | $\frac{3}{2}(0) + 3$ |
| $0$ | | | $0 + 3$ |
| $0$ | $\geq$ | | $3$ ✗ |

*A false statement means that the half-plane containing (0, 0) should NOT be shaded. (0, 0) is not one of the solutions, so the graph is shaded correctly.*

**Graph the solutions of each linear inequality.**

**2a.** $4x - 3y > 12$ **2b.** $2x - y - 4 > 0$ **2c.** $y \geq -\frac{2}{3}x + 1$

## EXAMPLE 3 — *Consumer Economics Application*

**Sarah can spend at most \$7.50 on vegetables. Broccoli costs \$1.25 per bunch and carrots cost \$0.75 per package.**

**a. Write a linear inequality to describe the situation.**

Let $x$ represent the number of bunches of broccoli and let $y$ represent the number of packages of carrots.

Write an inequality. Use $\le$ for "at most."

| Cost of broccoli | plus | cost of carrots | is at most | \$7.50. |
|---|---|---|---|---|
| $1.25x$ | $+$ | $0.75y$ | $\le$ | $7.50$ |

Solve the inequality for $y$.

$$1.25x + 0.75y \le 7.50$$

$$100(1.25x + 0.75y) \le 100(7.50)$$ *You can multiply both sides of the inequality by 100 to eliminate the decimals.*

$$125x + 75y \le 750$$

$$\underline{-125x \qquad\quad -125x}$$ *Subtraction Property of Inequality*

$$75y \le 750 - 125x$$

$$\frac{75y}{75} \le \frac{750 - 125x}{75}$$ *Division Property of Inequality*

$$y \le 10 - \frac{5}{3}x$$

**b. Graph the solutions.**

**Step 1** Since Sarah cannot buy a negative amount of vegetables, the system is graphed only in Quadrant I. Graph the boundary line $y = -\frac{5}{3}x + 10$. Use a solid line for $\le$.

**Step 2** Shade below the line. Sarah must buy whole numbers of bunches or packages. All the points on or below the line with whole number coordinates are the different combinations of broccoli and carrots that Sarah can buy.

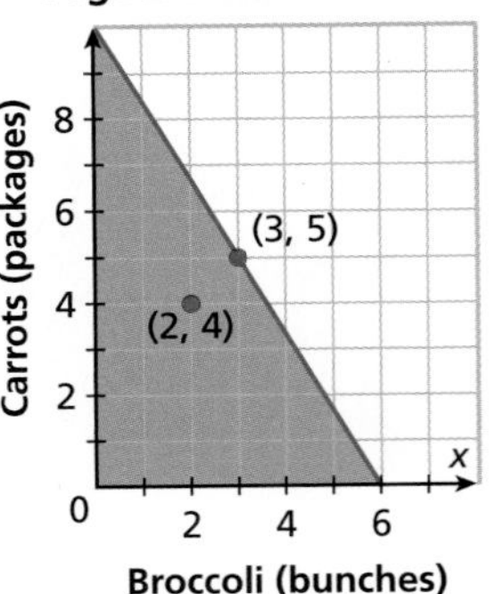


**c. Give two combinations of vegetables that Sarah can buy.**

Two different combinations that Sarah could buy for \$7.50 or less are 2 bunches of broccoli and 4 packages of carrots, or 3 bunches of broccoli and 5 packages of carrots.

3. **What if...?** Dirk is going to bring two types of olives to the Honor Society induction and can spend no more than \$6. Green olives cost \$2 per pound and black olives cost \$2.50 per pound.
   - **a.** Write a linear inequality to describe the situation.
   - **b.** Graph the solutions.
   - **c.** Give two combinations of olives that Dirk could buy.

## EXAMPLE 4 Writing an Inequality from a Graph

**Write an inequality to represent each graph.**

**A**

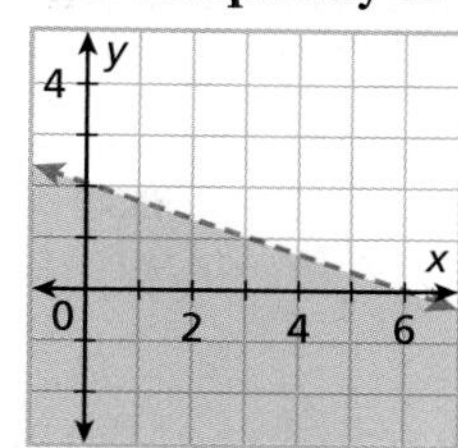


$y$-intercept: 2; slope: $-\frac{1}{3}$

Write an equation in slope-intercept form.

$$y = mx + b \longrightarrow y = -\frac{1}{3}x + 2$$

The graph is shaded *below* a *dashed* boundary line.

Replace = with < to write the inequality $y < -\frac{1}{3}x + 2$.

**B**

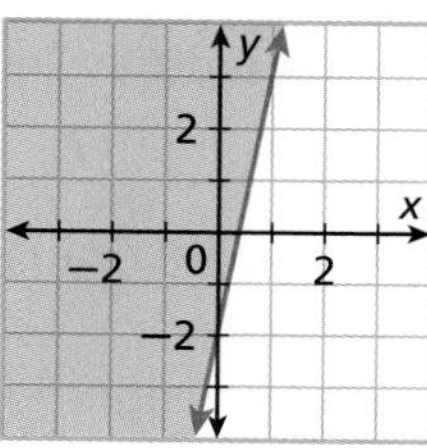


$y$-intercept: $-2$; slope: 5

Write an equation in slope-intercept form.

$$y = mx + b \longrightarrow y = 5x + (-2)$$

The graph is shaded *above* a *solid* boundary line.

Replace = with ≥ to write the inequality $y \geq 5x - 2$.

**C**

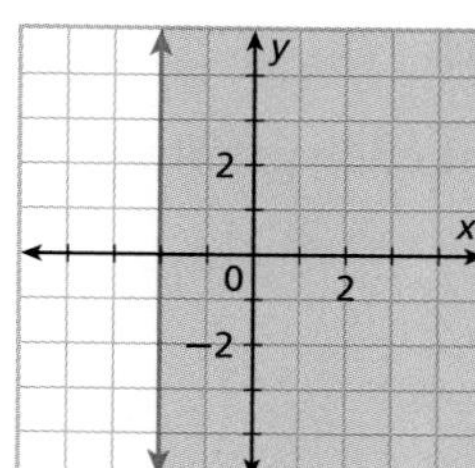


$y$-intercept: none; slope: undefined

The graph is a vertical line at $x = -2$.

The graph is shaded on the *right* side of a *solid* boundary line.

Replace = with ≥ to write the inequality $x \geq -2$.

**Write an inequality to represent each graph.**

**4a.**

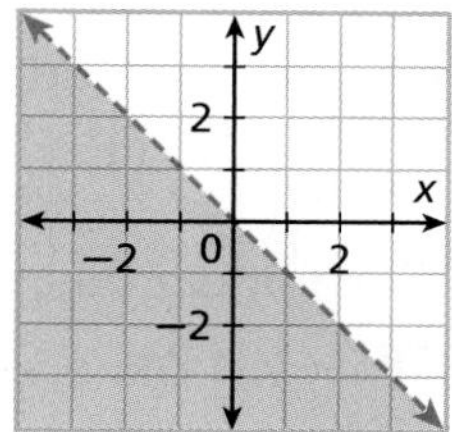


**4b.**

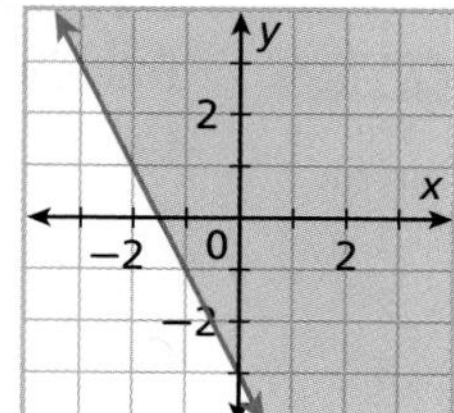


### THINK AND DISCUSS

1. Tell how graphing a linear inequality is the same as graphing a linear equation. Tell how it is different.
2. Explain how you would write a linear inequality from a graph.
3. **GET ORGANIZED** Copy and complete the graphic organizer.

| Inequality | $y < 5x + 2$ | $y > 7x - 3$ | $y \leq 9x + 1$ | $y \geq -3x - 2$ |
|---|---|---|---|---|
| Symbol | < | | | |
| Boundary Line | Dashed | | | |
| Shading | Below | | | |

# 6-5 Exercises

Prep MA.A.5.3, MA.A.5.1

go.hrw.com
Homework Help Online
KEYWORD: MA7 6-5
Parent Resources Online
KEYWORD: MA7 Parent

## GUIDED PRACTICE

1. **Vocabulary** Can a *solution of a linear inequality* lie on a dashed boundary line? Explain.

SEE EXAMPLE 1 p. 414

**Tell whether the ordered pair is a solution of the given inequality.**

2. $(0, 3)$; $y \le -x + 3$
3. $(2, 0)$; $y > -2x - 2$
4. $(-2, 1)$; $y < 2x + 4$

SEE EXAMPLE 2 p. 415

**Graph the solutions of each linear inequality.**

5. $y \le -x$
6. $y > 3x + 1$
7. $-y < -x + 4$
8. $-y \ge x + 1$

SEE EXAMPLE 3 p. 416

9. **Multi-Step** Jack is making punch with orange juice and pineapple juice. He can make at most 16 cups of punch.
   a. Write an inequality to describe the situation.
   b. Graph the solutions.
   c. Give two possible combinations of cups of orange juice and pineapple juice that Jack can use in his punch.

SEE EXAMPLE 4 p. 417

**Write an inequality to represent each graph.**

10.

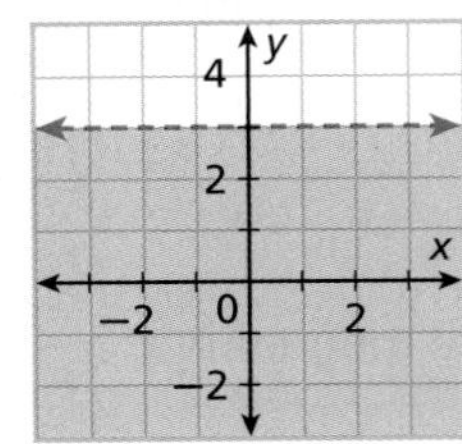


11.

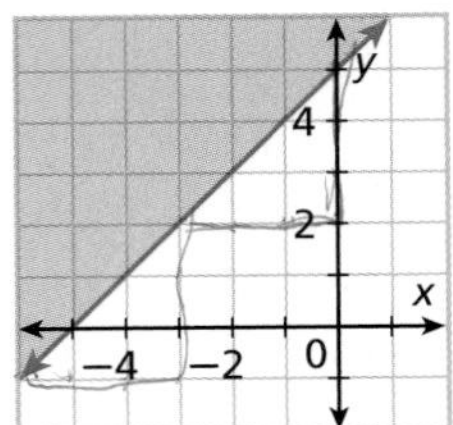


## PRACTICE AND PROBLEM SOLVING

| Independent Practice | |
|---|---|
| For Exercises | See Example |
| 12–14 | 1 |
| 15–18 | 2 |
| 19 | 3 |
| 20–21 | 4 |

**Extra Practice**
Skills Practice p. S15
Application Practice p. S33

**Tell whether the ordered pair is a solution of the given inequality.**

12. $(2, 3)$; $y \ge 2x + 3$
13. $(1, -1)$; $y < 3x - 3$
14. $(0, 7)$; $y > 4x + 7$

**Graph the solutions of each linear inequality.**

15. $y > -2x + 6$
16. $-y \ge 2x$
17. $x + y \le 2$
18. $x - y \ge 0$

19. **Multi-Step** Beverly is serving hamburgers and hot dogs at her cookout. Hamburger meat costs \$3 per pound, and hot dogs cost \$2 per pound. She wants to spend no more than \$30.
   a. Write an inequality to describe the situation.
   b. Graph the solutions.
   c. Give two possible combinations of pounds of hamburger and hot dogs that Beverly can buy.

**Write an inequality to represent each graph.**

20.

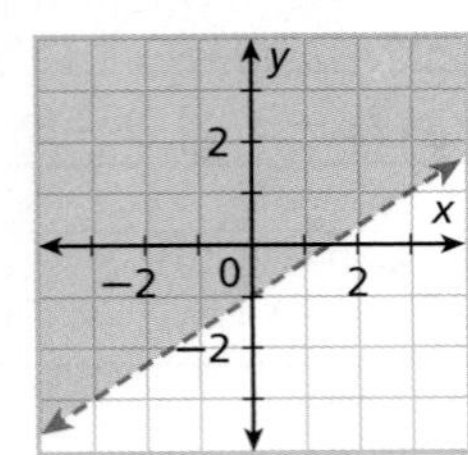


21.

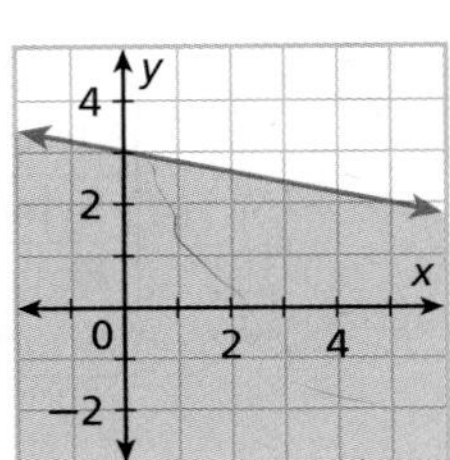

22. **Business** An electronics store makes \$125 profit on every DVD player it sells and \$100 on every CD player it sells. The store owner wants to make a profit of at least \$500 a day selling DVD players and CD players.

  a. Write a linear inequality to determine the number of DVD players $x$ and the number of CD players $y$ that the owner needs to sell to meet his goal.

  b. Graph the linear inequality.

  c. Describe the possible values of $x$. Describe the possible values of $y$.

  d. List three possible combinations of DVD players and CD players that the owner could sell to meet his goal.

**Graph the solutions of each linear inequality.**

23. $y \leq 2 - 3x$ 24. $-y < 7 + x$ 25. $2x - y \leq 4$ 26. $3x - 2y > 6$

27. **Geometry** Marvin has 18 yards of fencing that he can use to put around a rectangular garden.

  a. Write a linear inequality that describes the possible lengths and widths of the garden.

  b. Graph the inequality and list three possible solutions to the problem.

  c. What are the dimensions of the largest *square* garden that can be fenced in with whole-number dimensions?

28. **Hobbies** Stephen wants to buy yellow tangs and clown fish for his saltwater aquarium. He wants to spend no more than \$77 on fish. At the store, yellow tangs cost \$15 each and clown fish cost \$11 each. Write and graph a linear inequality to find the number of yellow tangs $x$ and the number of clown fish $y$ that Stephen could purchase. Name a solution of your inequality that is not reasonable for the situation. Explain.

**Graph each inequality on a coordinate plane.**

29. $y > 1$ 30. $-2 < x$ 31. $x \geq -3$ 32. $y \leq 0$

33. $0 \geq x$ 34. $-12 + y > 0$ 35. $x + 7 < 7$ 36. $-4 \geq x - y$

37. **School** At a high school football game, tickets at the gate cost \$7 per adult and \$4 per student. Write a linear inequality to determine the number of adult and student tickets that need to be sold so that the amount of money taken in at the gate is at least \$280. Graph the inequality and list three possible solutions.

38. **Critical Thinking** Why must a region of a coordinate plane be shaded to show all solutions of a linear inequality?

39. **Write About It** Give a real-world situation that can be described by a linear inequality. Then graph the inequality and give two solutions.

**MULTI-STEP TEST PREP**

40. This problem will prepare you for the Multi-Step Test Prep on page 428. Gloria is making teddy bears. She is making boy and girl bears. She has enough stuffing to create 50 bears. Let $x$ represent the number of girl bears and $y$ represent the number of boy bears.

  a. Write an inequality that shows the possible number of boy and girl bears Gloria can make.

  b. Graph the inequality.

  c. Give three possible solutions for the numbers of boy and girl bears that can be made.

41. **ERROR ANALYSIS** Student A wrote $y < 2x - 1$ as the inequality represented by the graph. Student B wrote $y \leq 2x - 1$ as the inequality represented by the graph. Which student is incorrect? Explain the error.

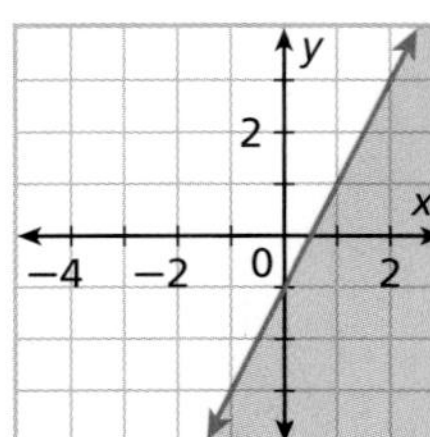


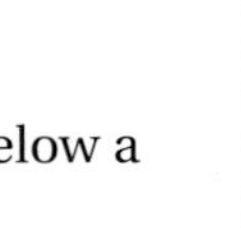

42. **Write About It** How do you decide to shade above or below a boundary line? What does this shading represent?

## TEST PREP

Prep MA.A.5.3, MA.A.5.1

43. Which point is a solution of the inequality $y > -x + 3$?

Ⓐ (0, 3) Ⓑ (1, 4) Ⓒ (−1, 4) Ⓓ (0, −3)

44. Which inequality is represented by the graph at right?

Ⓕ $2x + y \geq 3$ Ⓗ $2x + y \leq 3$

Ⓖ $2x + y > 3$ Ⓙ $2x + y < 3$

45. Which of the following describes the graph of $3 \leq x$?

Ⓐ The boundary line is dashed, and the shading is to the right.

Ⓑ The boundary line is dashed, and the shading is to the left.

Ⓒ The boundary line is solid, and the shading is to the right.

Ⓓ The boundary line is solid, and the shading is to the left.

## CHALLENGE AND EXTEND

**Graph each inequality.**

46. $0 \geq -6 - 2x - 5y$ 47. $y > |x|$ 48. $y \geq |x - 3|$

49. A linear inequality has the points (0, 3) and (−3, 1.5) as solutions on the boundary line. Also, the point (1, 1) is not a solution. Write the linear inequality.

50. Two linear inequalities are graphed on the same coordinate plane. The point (0, 0) is a solution of both inequalities. The entire coordinate plane is shaded except for Quadrant I. What are the two inequalities?

## SPIRAL REVIEW

**Tell whether each function is linear. If so, graph the function.** *(Lesson 5-1)*

51. $y = 2x - 4$ 52. $y = x^2 + 2$ 53. $y = 3$

**Write an equation in slope-intercept form for the line through the two points.** *(Lesson 5-7)*

54. (0, 9) and (5, 2) 55. (−5, −2) and (7, 7) 56. (0, 0) and (−8, −10)

57. (−1, −2) and (1, 4) 58. (2, 2) and (6, 5) 59. (−3, 2) and (3, −1)

**Solve each system by elimination.** *(Lesson 6-3)*

60. $\begin{cases} x + 6y = 14 \\ x - 6y = -10 \end{cases}$ 61. $\begin{cases} x + y = 13 \\ 3x + y = 9 \end{cases}$ 62. $\begin{cases} 2x - 4y = 18 \\ 5x - y = 36 \end{cases}$

63. $\begin{cases} 2y + x = 12 \\ y - 2x = 1 \end{cases}$ 64. $\begin{cases} 2y - 6x = -8 \\ y = -5x + 12 \end{cases}$ 65. $\begin{cases} 2x + 3y = 33 \\ y = \frac{1}{4}x \end{cases}$

# 6-6 Solving Systems of Linear Inequalities

**MA.A.5.3** Use ... graphs to solve pairs of linear inequalities in two variables. *Also* **MA.A.5.1**

***Objective***
Graph and solve systems of linear inequalities in two variables.

***Vocabulary***
system of linear inequalities
solution of a system of linear inequalities

**Who uses this?**
The owner of a surf shop can use systems of linear inequalities to determine how many surfboards and wakeboards need to be sold to make a certain profit. (See Example 4.)

A **system of linear inequalities** is a set of two or more linear inequalities containing two or more variables. The **solutions of a system of linear inequalities** consists of all the ordered pairs that satisfy all the linear inequalities in the system.

**EXAMPLE 1** **Identifying Solutions of Systems of Linear Inequalities**

**Tell whether the ordered pair is a solution of the given system.**

**Remember!**
An ordered pair must be a solution of all inequalities to be a solution of the system.

**A** $(2, 1);\ \begin{cases} y < -x + 4 \\ y \le x + 1 \end{cases}$

$(2, 1)$

$$\begin{array}{c|c|c} \multicolumn{3}{c}{y < -x + 4} \\ \hline 1 & & -2 + 4 \\ 1 & < & 2\ \checkmark \end{array}$$

$(2, 1)$

$$\begin{array}{c|c|c} \multicolumn{3}{c}{y \le x + 1} \\ \hline 1 & & 2 + 1 \\ 1 & \le & 3\ \checkmark \end{array}$$

$(2, 1)$ is a solution to the system because it satisfies both inequalities.

**B** $(2, 0);\ \begin{cases} y \ge 2x \\ y < x + 1 \end{cases}$

$(2, 0)$

$$\begin{array}{c|c|c} \multicolumn{3}{c}{y \ge 2x} \\ \hline 0 & & 2(2) \\ 0 & \ge & 4\ \times \end{array}$$

$(2, 0)$

$$\begin{array}{c|c|c} \multicolumn{3}{c}{y < x + 1} \\ \hline 0 & & 2 + 1 \\ 0 & < & 3\ \checkmark \end{array}$$

$(2, 0)$ is not a solution to the system because it does not satisfy both inequalities.

**Tell whether the ordered pair is a solution of the given system.**

**1a.** $(0, 1);\ \begin{cases} y < -3x + 2 \\ y \ge x - 1 \end{cases}$  **1b.** $(0, 0);\ \begin{cases} y > -x + 1 \\ y > x - 1 \end{cases}$

To show all the solutions of a system of linear inequalities, graph the solutions of each inequality. The solutions of the system are represented by the overlapping shaded regions. Below are graphs of Examples 1A and 1B.

**Example 1A**

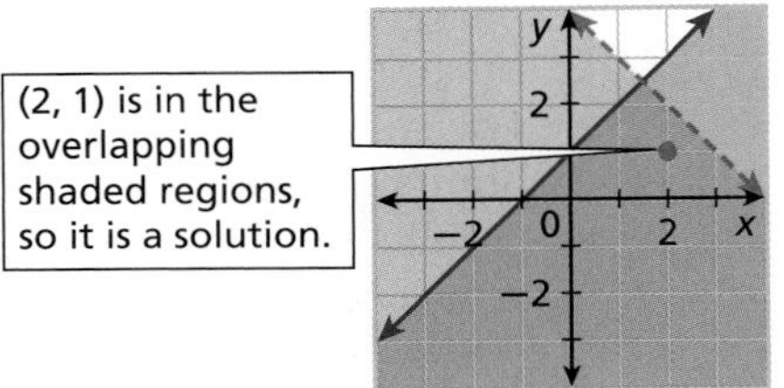


**Example 1B**

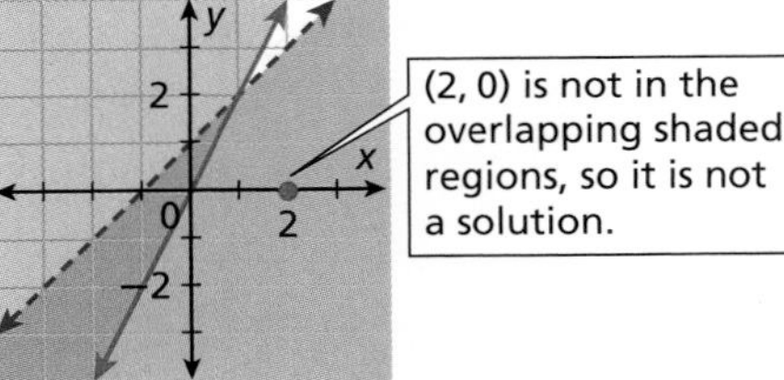

## EXAMPLE 2 Solving a System of Linear Inequalities by Graphing

**Graph the system of linear inequalities. Give two ordered pairs that are solutions and two that are not solutions.**

$$\begin{cases} 8x + 4y \le 12 \\ y > \frac{1}{2}x - 2 \end{cases}$$

$8x + 4y \le 12$ *Write the first inequality in slope-intercept form.*

$4y \le -8x + 12$

$y \le -2x + 3$

*Graph the system.*

$$\begin{cases} y \le -2x + 3 \\ y > \frac{1}{2}x - 2 \end{cases}$$

(−3, 4) satisfies both inequalities.

(−1, 1) satisfies both inequalities.

(2, −1) satisfies only $y \le -2x + 3$.

(2, −4) satisfies only $y \le -2x + 3$.

$(-1, 1)$ and $(-3, 4)$ are solutions.
$(2, -1)$ and $(2, -4)$ are not solutions.

**Graph each system of linear inequalities. Give two ordered pairs that are solutions and two that are not solutions.**

**2a.** $\begin{cases} y \le x + 1 \\ y > 2 \end{cases}$ **2b.** $\begin{cases} y > x - 7 \\ 3x + 6y \le 12 \end{cases}$

In Lesson 6-4, you saw that in systems of linear equations, if the lines are parallel, there are no solutions. With systems of linear inequalities, that is not always true.

## EXAMPLE 3 Graphing Systems with Parallel Boundary Lines

**Graph each system of linear inequalities.**

**A** $\begin{cases} y < 2x - 3 \\ y > 2x + 2 \end{cases}$

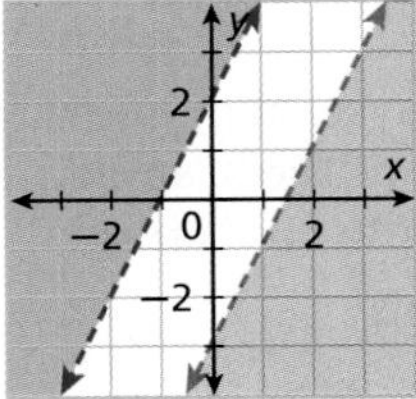

This system has no solution.

**B** $\begin{cases} y > x - 3 \\ y \le x + 1 \end{cases}$

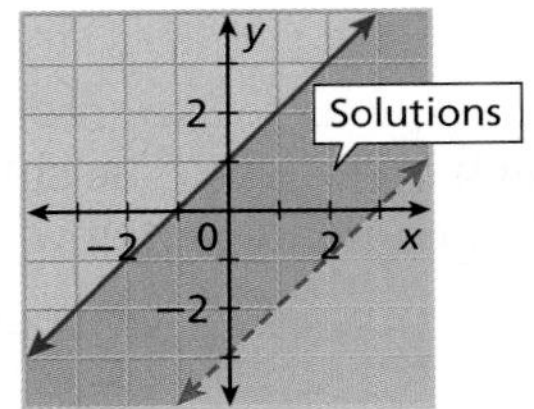


The solutions are all points between the parallel lines and on the solid line.

**C** $\begin{cases} y \le -3x - 2 \\ y \le -3x + 4 \end{cases}$

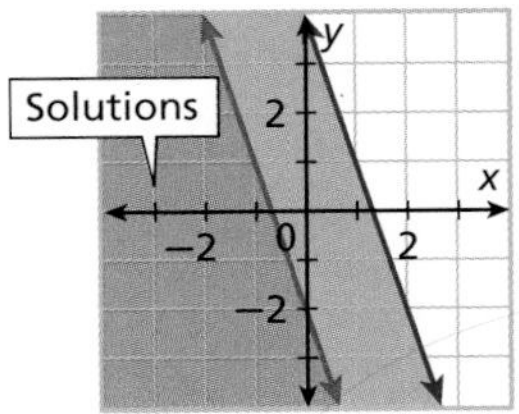


The solutions are the same as the solutions of $y \le -3x - 2$.

**Graph each system of linear inequalities.**

**3a.** $\begin{cases} y > x + 1 \\ y \leq x - 3 \end{cases}$ **3b.** $\begin{cases} y \geq 4x - 2 \\ y \leq 4x + 2 \end{cases}$ **3c.** $\begin{cases} y > -2x + 3 \\ y > -2x \end{cases}$

## EXAMPLE 4 *Business Application*

**A surf shop makes the profits given in the table. The shop owner sells at least 10 surfboards and at least 20 wakeboards per month. He wants to earn at least $2000 a month. Show and describe all possible combinations of surfboards and wakeboards that the store owner needs to sell to meet his goals. List two possible combinations.**

| Profit per Board Sold ($) | |
|---|---|
| Surfboard | 150 |
| Wakeboard | 100 |

**Step 1** Write a system of inequalities.

Let $x$ represent the number of surfboards and $y$ represent the number of wakeboards.

$x \geq 10$ — *He sells at least 10 surfboards.*

$y \geq 20$ — *He sells at least 20 wakeboards.*

$150x + 100y \geq 2000$ — *He wants to earn a total of at least $2000.*

**Step 2** Graph the system.

The graph should be in only the first quadrant because sales are not negative.

**Step 3** Describe all possible combinations.

To meet the sales goals, the shop could sell any combination represented by an ordered pair of whole numbers in the solution region. Answers must be whole numbers because the shop cannot sell part of a surfboard or wakeboard.

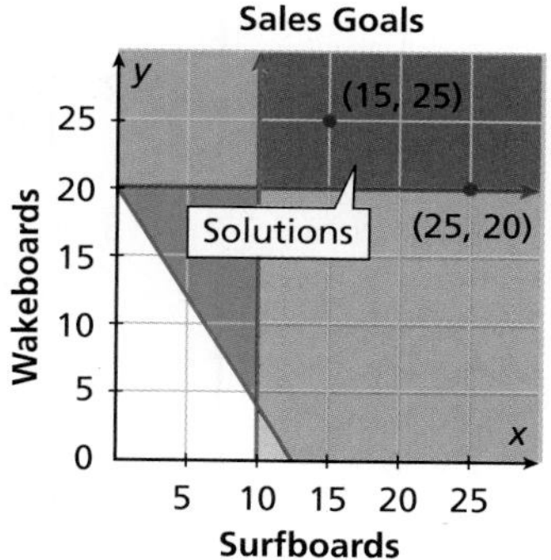


**Step 4** List two possible combinations.

Two possible combinations are:

15 surfboards and 25 wakeboards

25 surfboards and 20 wakeboards

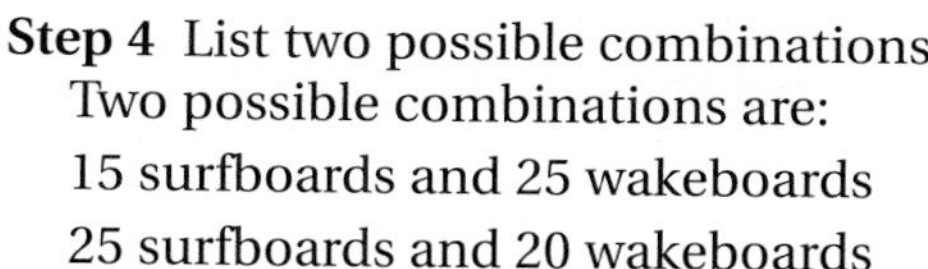

**Caution!**

An ordered pair solution of the system need not have whole numbers, but answers to many application problems may be restricted to whole numbers.

**4.** At her party, Alice is serving pepper jack cheese and cheddar cheese. She wants to have at least 2 pounds of each. Alice wants to spend at most $20 on cheese. Show and describe all possible combinations of the two cheeses Alice could buy. List two possible combinations.

| Price per Pound ($) | |
|---|---|
| Pepper Jack | 4 |
| Cheddar | 2 |

## THINK AND DISCUSS

**1.** How would you write a system of linear inequalities from a graph?

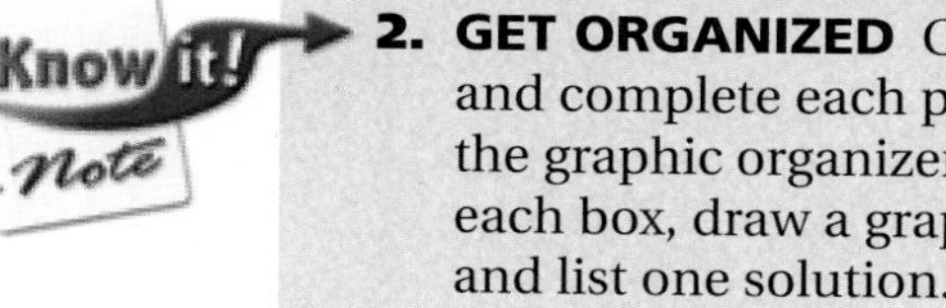


**2. GET ORGANIZED** Copy and complete each part of the graphic organizer. In each box, draw a graph and list one solution.

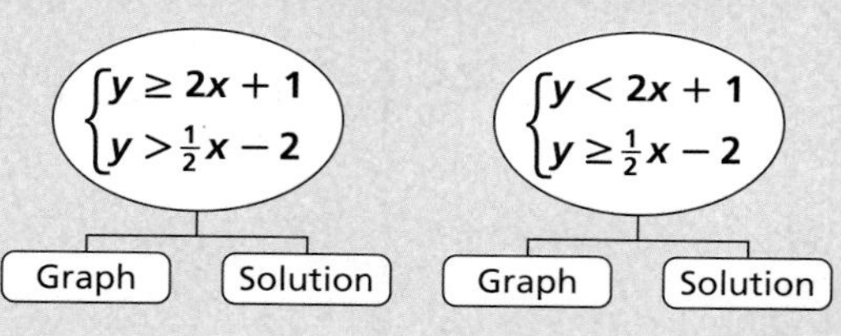

# 6-6 Exercises

MA.A.5.3, MA.A.5.1

go.hrw.com
Homework Help Online
KEYWORD: MA7 6-6
Parent Resources Online
KEYWORD: MA7 Parent

## GUIDED PRACTICE

1. **Vocabulary** A solution of a system of inequalities is a solution of ___?___ of the inequalities in the system. (*at least one* or *all*)

SEE EXAMPLE 1 p. 421

**Tell whether the ordered pair is a solution of the given system.**

2. $(0, 0); \begin{cases} y < -x + 3 \\ y < x + 2 \end{cases}$

3. $(0, 0); \begin{cases} y < 3 \\ y > x - 2 \end{cases}$

4. $(1, 0); \begin{cases} y > 3x \\ y \leq x + 1 \end{cases}$

SEE EXAMPLE 2 p. 422

**Graph each system of linear inequalities. Give two ordered pairs that are solutions and two that are not solutions.**

5. $\begin{cases} y < 2x - 1 \\ y > 2 \end{cases}$

6. $\begin{cases} x < 3 \\ y > x - 2 \end{cases}$

7. $\begin{cases} y \geq 3x \\ 3x + y \geq 3 \end{cases}$

8. $\begin{cases} 2x - 4y \leq 8 \\ y > x - 2 \end{cases}$

SEE EXAMPLE 3 p. 422

**Graph each system of linear inequalities.**

9. $\begin{cases} y > 2x + 3 \\ y < 2x \end{cases}$

10. $\begin{cases} y \leq -3x - 1 \\ y \geq -3x + 1 \end{cases}$

11. $\begin{cases} y > 4x - 1 \\ y \leq 4x + 1 \end{cases}$

12. $\begin{cases} y < -x + 3 \\ y > -x + 2 \end{cases}$

13. $\begin{cases} y > 2x - 1 \\ y > 2x - 4 \end{cases}$

14. $\begin{cases} y \leq -3x + 4 \\ y \leq -3x - 3 \end{cases}$

SEE EXAMPLE 4 p. 423

15. **Business** Sandy makes \$2 profit on every cup of lemonade that she sells and \$1 on every cupcake that she sells. Sandy wants to sell at least 5 cups of lemonade and at least 5 cupcakes per day. She wants to earn at least \$25 per day. Show and describe all the possible combinations of lemonade and cupcakes that Sandy needs to sell to meet her goals. List two possible combinations.

## PRACTICE AND PROBLEM SOLVING

**Independent Practice**

| For Exercises | See Example |
|---|---|
| 16–18 | 1 |
| 19–22 | 2 |
| 23–28 | 3 |
| 29 | 4 |

**Extra Practice**
Skills Practice p. S15
Application Practice p. S33

**Tell whether the ordered pair is a solution of the given system.**

16. $(0, 0); \begin{cases} y > -x - 1 \\ y < 2x + 4 \end{cases}$

17. $(0, 0); \begin{cases} x + y < 3 \\ y > 3x - 4 \end{cases}$

18. $(1, 0); \begin{cases} y > 3x \\ y > 3x + 1 \end{cases}$

**Graph each system of linear inequalities. Give two ordered pairs that are solutions and two that are not solutions.**

19. $\begin{cases} y < -3x - 3 \\ y \geq 0 \end{cases}$

20. $\begin{cases} y < -1 \\ y > 2x - 1 \end{cases}$

21. $\begin{cases} y > 2x + 4 \\ 6x + 2y \geq -2 \end{cases}$

22. $\begin{cases} 9x + 3y \leq 6 \\ y > x \end{cases}$

**Graph each system of linear inequalities.**

23. $\begin{cases} y < 3 \\ y > 5 \end{cases}$

24. $\begin{cases} y < x - 1 \\ y > x - 2 \end{cases}$

25. $\begin{cases} x \geq 2 \\ x \leq 2 \end{cases}$

26. $\begin{cases} y > -4x - 3 \\ y < -4x + 2 \end{cases}$

27. $\begin{cases} y > -1 \\ y > 2 \end{cases}$

28. $\begin{cases} y \leq 2x + 1 \\ y \leq 2x - 4 \end{cases}$

29. **Multi-Step** Linda works at a pharmacy for \$15 an hour. She also baby-sits for \$10 an hour. Linda needs to earn at least \$90 per week, but she does not want to work more than 20 hours per week. Show and describe the number of hours Linda could work at each job to meet her goals. List two possible solutions.

30. **Farming** Tony wants to plant at least 40 acres of corn and at least 50 acres of soybeans. He wants no more than 200 acres of corn and soybeans. Show and describe all the possible combinations of the number of acres of corn and of soybeans Tony could plant. List two possible combinations.

**Graph each system of linear inequalities.**

31. $\begin{cases} y \geq -3 \\ y \geq 2 \end{cases}$

32. $\begin{cases} y > -2x - 1 \\ y > -2x - 3 \end{cases}$

33. $\begin{cases} x \leq -3 \\ x \geq 1 \end{cases}$

34. $\begin{cases} y < 4 \\ y > 0 \end{cases}$

**Write a system of linear inequalities to represent each graph.**

35. 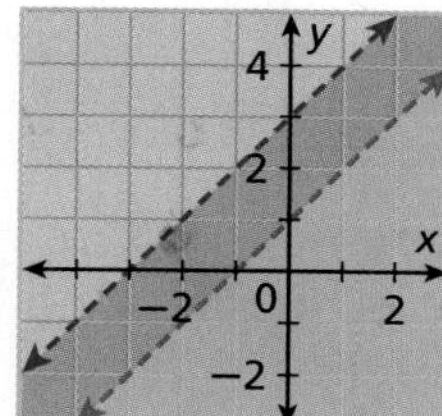


36. 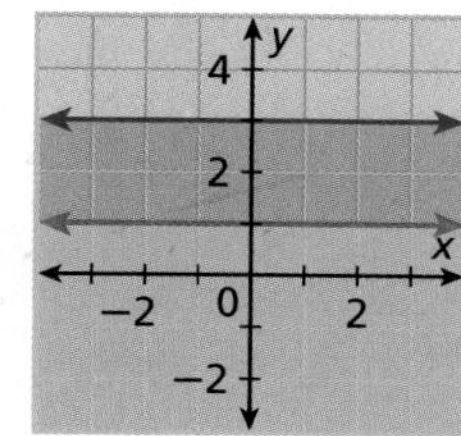


37. 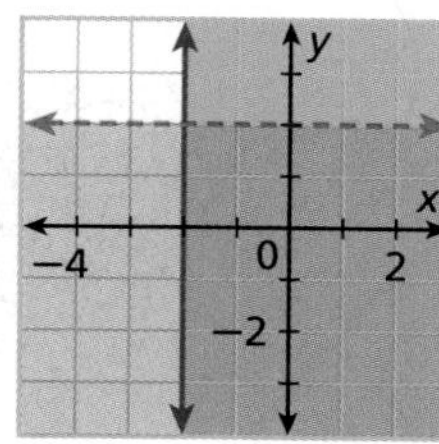


**LINK**

**Military**

In 1959, the first class graduated from the Air Force Academy. The first class that included women graduated in 1980.

38. **Military** For males to enter the United States Air Force Academy, located in Colorado Springs, CO, they must be at least 17 but less than 23 years of age. Their standing height must be not less than 60 inches and not greater than 80 inches. Graph all possible heights and ages for eligible male candidates. Give three possible combinations.

39. **ERROR ANALYSIS** Two students wrote a system of linear inequalities to describe the graph. Which student is incorrect? Explain the error.

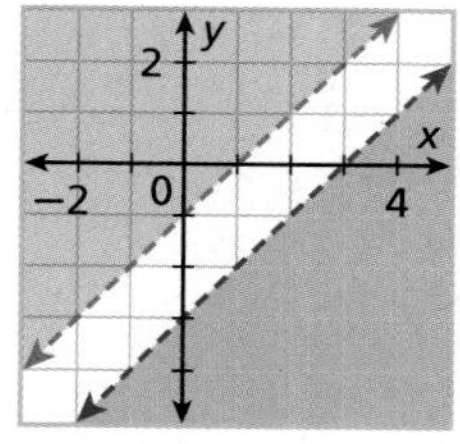


A
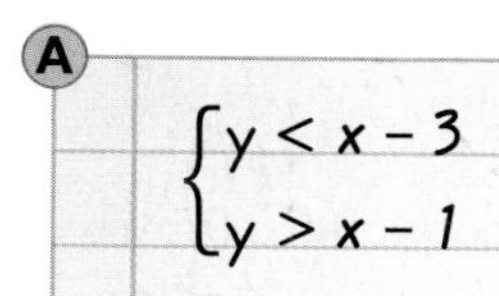


B
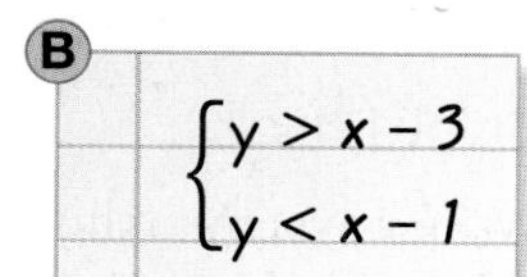


40. **Recreation** Vance wants to fence in a rectangular area for his dog. He wants the length of the rectangle to be at least 30 feet and the perimeter to be no more than 150 feet. Graph all possible dimensions of the rectangle.

41. **Critical Thinking** Can the solutions of a system of linear inequalities be the points on a line? Explain.

**MULTI-STEP TEST PREP**

42. This problem will prepare you for the Multi-Step Test Prep on page 428.

Gloria is starting her own company making teddy bears. She has enough bear bodies to create 40 bears. She will make girl bears and boy bears.

a. Write an inequality to show this situation.

b. Gloria will charge \$15 for girl bears and \$12 for boy bears. She wants to earn at least \$540 a week. Write an inequality to describe this situation.

c. Graph this situation and locate the solution region.

43. **Write About It** What must be true of the boundary lines in a system of two linear inequalities if there is no solution of the system? Explain.

## TEST PREP

MA.A.5.3, MA.A.5.1

44. Which point is a solution of $\begin{cases} 2x + y \geq 3 \\ y \geq -2x + 1 \end{cases}$?

   (A) (0, 0) (B) (0, 1) (C) (1, 0) (D) (1, 1)

45. Which system of inequalities best describes the graph?

   (F) $\begin{cases} y < 2x - 3 \\ y > 2x + 1 \end{cases}$ (H) $\begin{cases} y < 2x - 3 \\ y < 2x + 1 \end{cases}$

   (G) $\begin{cases} y > 2x - 3 \\ y < 2x + 1 \end{cases}$ (J) $\begin{cases} y > 2x - 3 \\ y > 2x + 1 \end{cases}$

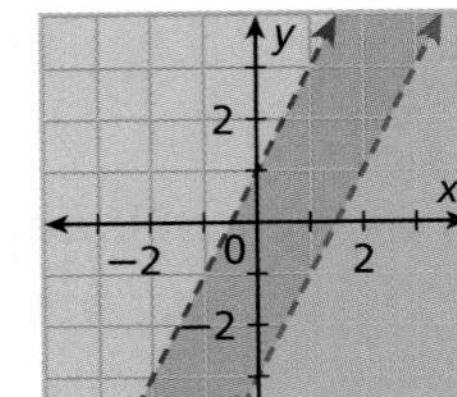


46. **Short Response** Graph and describe $\begin{cases} y + x > 2 \\ y \leq -3x + 4 \end{cases}$. Give two possible solutions of the system.

## CHALLENGE AND EXTEND

47. **Estimation** Graph the given system of inequalities. Estimate the area of the overlapping solution regions.
$$\begin{cases} y \geq 0 \\ y \leq x + 3.5 \\ y \leq -x + 3.5 \end{cases}$$

48. Write a system of linear inequalities for which $(-1, 1)$ and $(1, 4)$ are solutions and $(0, 0)$ and $(2, -1)$ are not solutions.

49. Graph $|y| < 1$.

50. Write a system of linear inequalities for which the solutions are all the points in the third quadrant.

## SPIRAL REVIEW

**Use the diagram to find each of the following.** *(Lesson 1-6)*

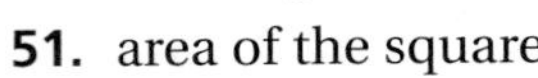

51. area of the square

52. area of the yellow triangle

53. combined area of the blue triangles

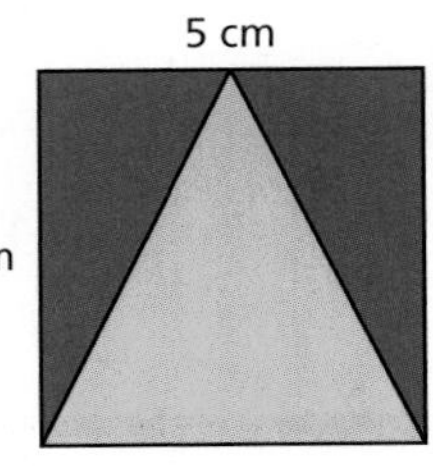


**Tell whether the given ordered pairs satisfy a linear function.** *(Lesson 5-1)*

54. $\{(3, 8), (4, 6), (5, 4), (6, 2), (7, 0)\}$

55. $\{(6, 1), (7, 2), (8, 4), (9, 7), (10, 11)\}$

56. $\{(2, 10), (7, 9), (12, 8), (17, 7), (22, 6)\}$

57. $\{(1, -9), (3, -7), (5, -5), (7, -3), (9, -1)\}$

**Graph the solutions of each linear inequality.** *(Lesson 6-5)*

58. $y \leq 2x - 1$

59. $-\frac{1}{4}x + y > 6$

60. $5 - x \geq 0$

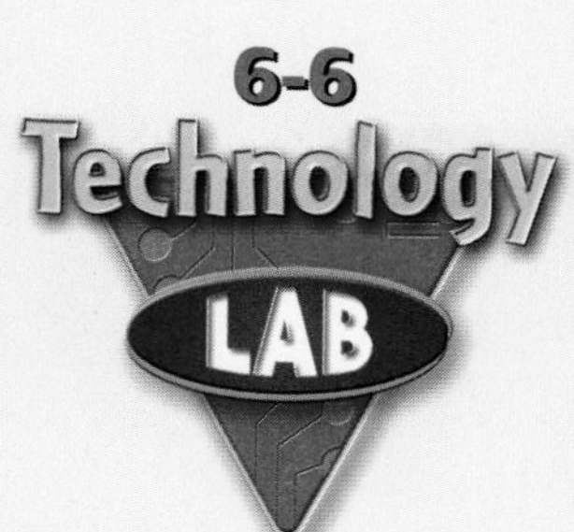


# Solve Systems of Linear Inequalities

A graphing calculator gives a visual solution to a system of linear inequalities.

*Use with Lesson 6-6*

**MA.A.5.3** Use tables and graphs to solve pairs of linear inequalities in two variables.

## Activity

**Graph the system** $\begin{cases} y > 2x - 4 \\ 2.75y - x < 6 \end{cases}$**. Give two ordered pairs that are solutions.**

1. Write the first boundary line in slope-intercept form.

   $y > 2x - 4 \quad \longrightarrow \quad y = 2x - 4$

2. Press **Y=** and enter $2x - 4$ for **Y1**.

   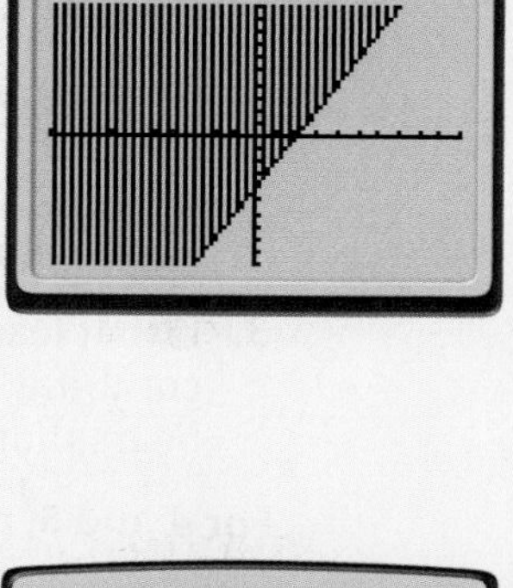
   

   The inequality contains the symbol >. The solution region is above the boundary line. Press ◀ to move the cursor to the left of **Y1**. Press **ENTER** until the icon that looks like a region above a line appears. Press **GRAPH**.

3. Solve the second inequality for $y$.

   $2.75y - x < 6$

   $2.75y < x + 6$

   $y < \dfrac{x + 6}{2.75} \quad \longrightarrow \quad y = \dfrac{x + 6}{2.75}$

4. Press **Y=** and enter $(x + 6)/2.75$ for **Y2**.

   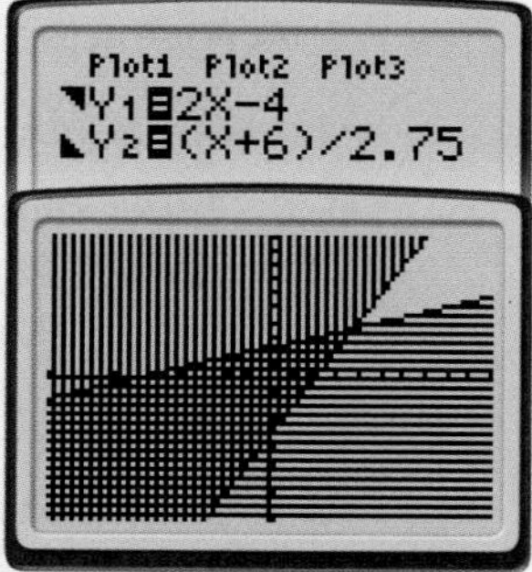
   

   The inequality contains the symbol <. The solution region is below the boundary line. Press ◀ to move the cursor to the left of **Y2**. Press **ENTER** until the icon that looks like a region below a line appears. Press **GRAPH**.

5. The solutions of the system are represented by the overlapping shaded regions. The points (0, 0) and (−1, 0) are in the shaded region.

*Check* Test (0, 0) and (−1, 0) in both inequalities.

| | (0, 0) | (−1, 0) |
|---|---|---|
| $y > 2x - 4$ | $0 \overset{?}{>} 2(0) - 4$<br>$0 > -4$ ✓ | $0 \overset{?}{>} 2(-1) - 4$<br>$0 > -6$ ✓ |
| $2.75y - x < 6$ | $2.75(0) - 0 \overset{?}{<} 6$<br>$0 < 6$ ✓ | $2.75(0) - (-1) \overset{?}{<} 6$<br>$1 < 6$ ✓ |

## Try This

**Graph each system. Give two ordered pairs that are solutions.**

**1.** $\begin{cases} x + 5y > -10 \\ x - y < 4 \end{cases}$ **2.** $\begin{cases} y > x - 2 \\ y \le x + 2 \end{cases}$ **3.** $\begin{cases} y > x - 2 \\ y \le 3 \end{cases}$ **4.** $\begin{cases} y < x - 3 \\ y - 3 > x \end{cases}$

CHAPTER 6

# MULTI-STEP TEST PREP

SECTION 6B

## Equations and Formulas

**Bearable Sales** Gloria makes teddy bears. She dresses some as girl bears with dresses and bows and some as boy bears with bow ties. She is running low on supplies. She has only 100 eyes, 30 dresses, and 60 ties that can be used as bows on the girls and bow ties on the boys.

1. Write the inequalities that describe this situation. Let $x$ represent the number of boy bears and $y$ represent the number of girl bears.
2. Graph the inequalities and locate the region showing the number of boy and girl bears Gloria can make.
3. List at least three combinations of girl and boy bears that Gloria can make.

**For 4 and 5, use the table.**

4. Using the boundary line in your graph from Problem 2, copy and complete the table with the corresponding number of girl bears.
5. Gloria sells the bears for profit. She makes a profit of \$8 for the girl bears and \$5 for the boy bears. Use the table from Problem 4 to find the profit she makes for each given combination.
6. Which combination is the most profitable? Explain. Where does it lie on the graph?

| Bear Combinations | |
|---|---|
| **Boy** | **Girl** |
| 0 | ■ |
| 10 | ■ |
| 20 | ■ |
| 30 | ■ |
| 40 | ■ |
| 50 | ■ |

# READY TO GO ON?



## Quiz for Lessons 6-5 Through 6-6

### 6-5 Solving Linear Inequalities

**Tell whether the ordered pair is a solution of the inequality.**

1. $(3, -2); y < -2x + 1$
2. $(2, 1); y \geq 3x - 5$
3. $(1, -6); y \leq 4x - 10$

**Graph the solutions of each linear inequality.**

4. $y \geq 4x - 3$
5. $3x - y < 5$
6. $2x + 3y < 9$
7. $y \leq -\frac{1}{2}x$
8. Theo's mother has given him at most $150 to buy clothes for school. The pants cost $30 each and the shirts cost $15 each. How many of each can he buy? Write a linear inequality to describe the situation. Graph the linear inequality and give three possible combinations of pants and shirts Theo could buy.

**Write an inequality to represent each graph.**

9. 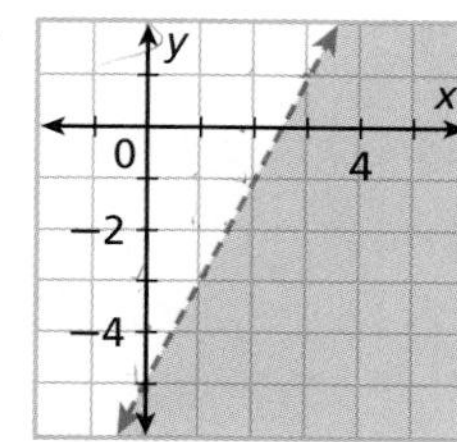


10. 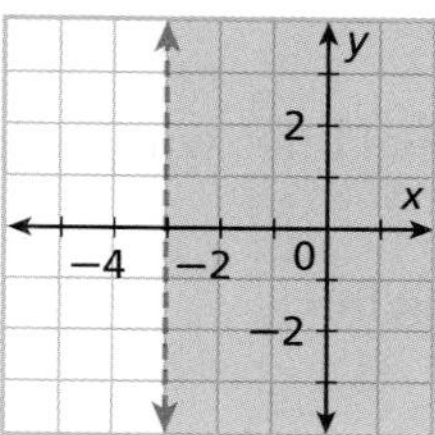


11. 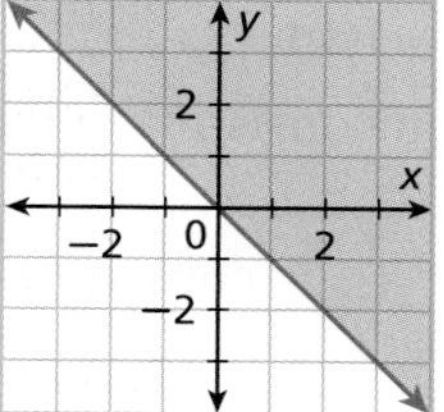


### 6-6 Solving Systems of Linear Inequalities

**Tell whether the ordered pair is a solution of the given system.**

12. $(-3, -1); \begin{cases} y > -2 \\ y < x + 4 \end{cases}$
13. $(-3, 0); \begin{cases} y \leq x + 4 \\ y \geq -2x - 6 \end{cases}$
14. $(0, 0); \begin{cases} y \geq 3x \\ 2x + y < -1 \end{cases}$

**Graph each system of linear inequalities. Give two ordered pairs that are solutions and two that are not solutions.**

15. $\begin{cases} y > -2 \\ y < x + 3 \end{cases}$
16. $\begin{cases} x + y \leq 2 \\ 2x + y \geq -1 \end{cases}$
17. $\begin{cases} 2x - 5y \leq -5 \\ 3x + 2y < 10 \end{cases}$

**Graph each system of linear inequalities and describe the solutions.**

18. $\begin{cases} y \geq x + 1 \\ y \geq x - 4 \end{cases}$
19. $\begin{cases} y \geq 2x - 1 \\ y < 2x - 3 \end{cases}$
20. $\begin{cases} y < -3x + 5 \\ y > -3x - 2 \end{cases}$
21. A grocer sells mangos for $4/lb and apples for $3/lb. The grocer starts with 45 lb of mangos and 50 lb of apples each day. The grocer's goal is to make at least $300 by selling mangos and apples each day. Show and describe all possible combinations of mangos and apples that could be sold to meet the goal. List two possible combinations.

CHAPTER 6

# Study Guide: Review

## Vocabulary



**Complete the sentences below with vocabulary words from the list above.**

1. A(n) ___?___ is a system that has exactly one solution.
2. A set of two or more linear equations that contain the same variable(s) is a(n) ___?___.
3. The ___?___ consists of all the ordered pairs that satisfy all the inequalities in the system.
4. A system consisting of equations of parallel lines with different $y$-intercepts is a(n) ___?___.
5. A(n) ___?___ consists of two intersecting lines.

## 6-1 Solving Systems by Graphing *(pp. 383–388)*

MA.A.5.2, MA.A.5.1

### EXAMPLE

■ Solve $\begin{cases} y = 2x - 2 \\ x + 2y = 16 \end{cases}$ by graphing.

**Check your answer.**

$\begin{cases} y = 2x - 2 \\ y = -\frac{1}{2}x + 8 \end{cases}$ *Write the second equation in slope-intercept form.*

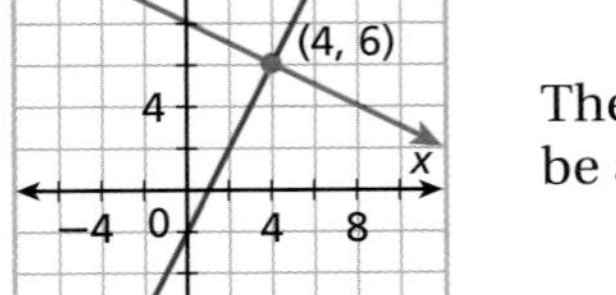


The solution appears to be at $(4, 6)$.

| $y = 2x - 2$ | |
|---|---|
| 6 | $2(4) - 2$ |
| 6 | 6 ✓ |

| $x + 2y = 16$ | |
|---|---|
| $4 + 2(6)$ | 16 |
| 16 | 16 ✓ |

The ordered pair $(4, 6)$ makes both equations true, so it is a solution of the system.

### EXERCISES

**Tell whether the ordered pair is a solution of the given system.**

6. $(0, -5)$; $\begin{cases} y = -6x + 5 \\ x - y = 5 \end{cases}$

7. $(4, 3)$; $\begin{cases} x - 2y = -2 \\ y = \frac{1}{2}x + 1 \end{cases}$

8. $\left(1\frac{3}{4}, 7\frac{1}{4}\right)$; $\begin{cases} x + y = 9 \\ 2y = 6x + 4 \end{cases}$

9. $(-1, -1)$; $\begin{cases} y = -2x + 5 \\ 3y = 6x + 3 \end{cases}$

**Solve each system by graphing. Check your answer.**

10. $\begin{cases} y = 3x + 2 \\ y = -2x - 3 \end{cases}$

11. $\begin{cases} y = -\frac{1}{3}x + 5 \\ 2x - 2y = -2 \end{cases}$

12. Raheel is comparing the cost of two parking garages. Garage A charges a flat fee of \$6 per car plus \$0.50 per hour. Garage B charges a flat fee of \$2 per car plus \$1 per hour. After how many hours will the cost at garage A be the same as the cost at garage B? What will that cost be?

## 6-2 Solving Systems by Substitution *(pp. 390–396)*

### EXAMPLE

■ Solve $\begin{cases} 2x - 3y = -2 \\ y - 3x = 10 \end{cases}$ by substitution.

**Step 1** $y - 3x = 10$ — *Solve the second equation for y.*

$y = 3x + 10$

**Step 2** $2x - 3y = -2$ — *Substitute 3x + 10 for y in the first equation.*

$2x - 3(3x + 10) = -2$

**Step 3** — *Solve for x.*

$2x - 9x - 30 = -2$

$-7x - 30 = -2$

$-7x = 28$

$x = -4$

**Step 4** $y - 3x = 10$ — *Substitute −4 for x.*

$y - 3(-4) = 10$

$y + 12 = 10$ — *Find the value of y.*

$y = -2$

**Step 5** $(-4, -2)$ — *Write the solution as an ordered pair.*

To check the solution, substitute $(-4, -2)$ into both equations in the system.

### EXERCISES

**Solve each system by substitution.**

**13.** $\begin{cases} y = x + 3 \\ y = 2x + 12 \end{cases}$

**14.** $\begin{cases} y = -4x \\ y = 2x - 3 \end{cases}$

**15.** $\begin{cases} 2x + y = 4 \\ 3x + y = 3 \end{cases}$

**16.** $\begin{cases} x + y = -1 \\ y = -2x + 3 \end{cases}$

**17.** $\begin{cases} x = y - 7 \\ -y - 2x = 8 \end{cases}$

**18.** $\begin{cases} \frac{1}{2}x + y = 9 \\ 3x - 4y = -6 \end{cases}$

**19.** The Nash family's car needs repairs. Estimates for parts and labor from two garages are shown below.

| Garage | Parts ($) | Labor ($ per hour) |
|---|---|---|
| Motor Works | 650 | 70 |
| Jim's Car Care | 800 | 55 |

For how many hours of labor will the total cost of fixing the car be the same at both garages? What will that cost be? Which garage will be cheaper if the repairs require 8 hours of labor? Explain.

## 6-3 Solving Systems by Elimination *(pp. 397–403)*

### EXAMPLE

■ Solve $\begin{cases} 2x - 3y = -8 \\ x + 4y = 7 \end{cases}$ by elimination.

**Step 1** — *Multiply the second equation by −2.*

$2x - 3y = -8$

$+(-2)(x + 4y = 7)$

— *Eliminate the x-term.*

$2x - 3y = -8$

$+(-2x - 8y = -14)$

**Step 2** $0x - 11y = -22$ — *Solve for y.*

$y = 2$

**Step 3** — *Substitute 2 for y. Simplify and solve for x.*

$2x - 3y = -8$

$2x - 3(2) = -8$

$2x - 6 = -8$

$2x = -2$

$x = -1$

**Step 4** $(-1, 2)$ — *Write the solution as an ordered pair.*

To check the solution, substitute $(-1, 2)$ into both equations in the system.

### EXERCISES

**Solve each system by elimination.**

**20.** $\begin{cases} 4x + y = -1 \\ 2x - y = -5 \end{cases}$

**21.** $\begin{cases} x + 2y = -1 \\ x + y = 2 \end{cases}$

**22.** $\begin{cases} x + y = 12 \\ 2x + 5y = 27 \end{cases}$

**23.** $\begin{cases} 3x - 2y = -6 \\ \frac{1}{3}x + 3y = 9 \end{cases}$

**Solve each system by any method. Explain why you chose each method. Check your answer.**

**24.** $\begin{cases} 3x + y = 2 \\ y = -4x \end{cases}$

**25.** $\begin{cases} y = \frac{1}{3}x - 6 \\ y = -2x + 1 \end{cases}$

**26.** $\begin{cases} 2y = -3x \\ y = -2x + 2 \end{cases}$

**27.** $\begin{cases} x - y = 0 \\ 3x + y = 8 \end{cases}$

## 6-4 Solving Special Systems *(pp. 406–411)*

MA.A.5.2, MA.A.5.1

### EXAMPLES

**Classify each system. Give the number of solutions.**

■ $\begin{cases} y = 3x + 4 \\ 6x - 2y = -8 \end{cases}$

Use the substitution method because the first equation is solved for $y$.

$6x - 2(3x + 4) = -8$ *Substitute 3x + 4 for y in the second equation.*

$6x - 6x - 8 = -8$

$-8 = -8$ ✓ *True.*

*The equation is an identity. There are infinitely many solutions.*

This system is **consistent** and **dependent.** The two lines are coincident (the same line) because they have identical slopes and $y$-intercepts.

■ $\begin{cases} y = 2x - 1 \\ 2x - y = -2 \end{cases}$

Compare slopes and $y$-intercepts. Write both equations in slope-intercept form.

$\begin{cases} y = 2x - 1 & \Rightarrow y = 2x - 1 \\ 2x - y = -2 & \Rightarrow y = 2x + 2 \end{cases}$

*The lines have the same slope and different y-intercepts. The lines are parallel.*

The lines never intersect, so this system is **inconsistent**. It has **no solution.**

■ $\begin{cases} 2x - y = 6 \\ y = x - 1 \end{cases}$

Write both equations in slope-intercept form.

$\begin{cases} 2x - y = 6 & \Rightarrow y = 2x - 6 \\ y = x - 1 & \Rightarrow y = 1x - 1 \end{cases}$

*The lines intersect because they have different slopes.*

The system is **consistent** and **independent.** There is **one solution:** $(5, 4)$.

### EXERCISES

**Solve each system of linear equations.**

**28.** $\begin{cases} y = \frac{1}{4}x - 3 \\ y = \frac{1}{4}x + 5 \end{cases}$

**29.** $\begin{cases} y = -x + 4 \\ x + y = 4 \end{cases}$

**30.** $\begin{cases} y = 3x + 2 \\ y = 2x \end{cases}$

**31.** $\begin{cases} -4x - y = 6 \\ \frac{1}{2}y = -2x - 3 \end{cases}$

**32.** $\begin{cases} x + 2y = 8 \\ y = -\frac{1}{2}x + 4 \end{cases}$

**33.** $\begin{cases} y - 2x = -1 \\ y + 2x = -5 \end{cases}$

**34.** Tristan and his friend Marco just started DVD collections. They continue to get DVDs at the rate shown in the table below. Will Tristan ever have the same number of DVDs as Marco? Explain.

| DVD Collections | | | |
|---|---|---|---|
| | Month 1 | Month 2 | Month 3 |
| Tristan | 2 | 7 | 12 |
| Marco | 8 | 12 | 16 |

**Classify each system. Give the number of solutions.**

**35.** $\begin{cases} y = \frac{1}{2}x + 2 \\ y = \frac{1}{4}x - 8 \end{cases}$

**36.** $\begin{cases} y = 3x - 7 \\ y = 3x + 2 \end{cases}$

**37.** $\begin{cases} 2x + y = 2 \\ y - 2 = -2x \end{cases}$

**38.** $\begin{cases} -3x - y = -5 \\ y = -3x - 5 \end{cases}$

**39.** $\begin{cases} 2x + 3y = 1 \\ 3x + 2y = 1 \end{cases}$

**40.** $\begin{cases} x + \frac{1}{2}y = 3 \\ 2x = 6 - y \end{cases}$

**41.** The two parallel lines graphed below represent a system of equations. Classify the system and give the number of solutions.

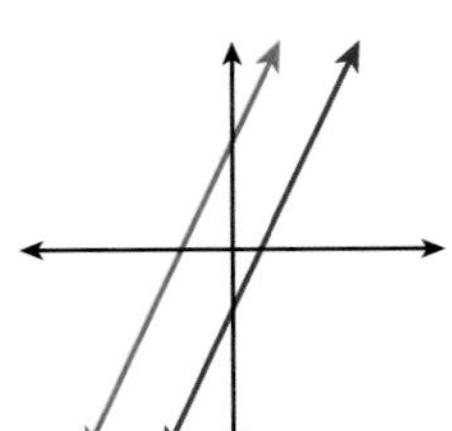

## 6-5 Solving Linear Inequalities *(pp. 414–420)*

Prep MA.A.5.3, MA.A.5.1

### EXAMPLE

- **Graph the solutions of $x - 2y < 6$.**

**Step 1** Solve the inequality for $y$.

$$x - 2y < 6$$
$$-2y < -x + 6$$
$$y > \frac{1}{2}x - 3$$

**Step 2** Graph $y = \frac{1}{2}x - 3$. Use a dashed line for $>$.

**Step 3** The inequality is $>$, so shade above the boundary line.

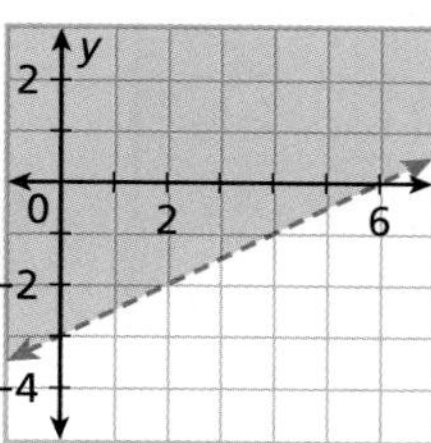


***Check*** Substitute $(0, 0)$ for $(x, y)$ because it is not on the boundary line.

| $x - 2y$ | $< 6$ |
|---|---|
| $0 - 2(0)$ | $6$ |
| $0$ | $< 6$ ✓ |

*$(0, 0)$ satisfies the inequality, so the graph is shaded correctly.*

### EXERCISES

**Tell whether the ordered pair is a solution of the inequality.**

**42.** $(0, -3)$; $y < 2x - 3$

**43.** $(2, -1)$; $y \geq x - 3$

**44.** $(6, 0)$; $y > -3x + 4$

**45.** $(10, 10)$; $y \leq x - 3$

**Graph the solutions of each linear inequality.**

**46.** $y < -2x + 5$

**47.** $x - y \geq 2$

**48.** $-x + 2y \geq 6$

**49.** $y > -4x$

**50.** $x + y + 4 > 0$

**51.** $5 - y \geq 2x$

**52.** The Mathematics Club is selling pizza and lemonade to raise money for a trip. They estimate that the trip will cost at least \$450. If they make \$2 on each slice of pizza and \$1 on each bottle of lemonade, how many of each do they need to sell to have enough money for their trip? Write an inequality to describe the situation. Graph and then give two combinations of the number of pizza slices and number of lemonade bottles they need to sell.

## 6-6 Solving Systems of Linear Inequalities *(pp. 421–426)*

MA.A.5.3, MA.A.5.1

### EXAMPLES

- **Graph $\begin{cases} y < -x + 5 \\ y \geq 2x - 3 \end{cases}$. Give two ordered pairs that are solutions and two that are not solutions.**

Graph both inequalities.

The solutions of the system are represented by the overlapping shaded regions.

The points $(0, 0)$ and $(-2, 2)$ are solutions of the system.

The points $(3, -2)$ and $(4, 4)$ are not solutions.

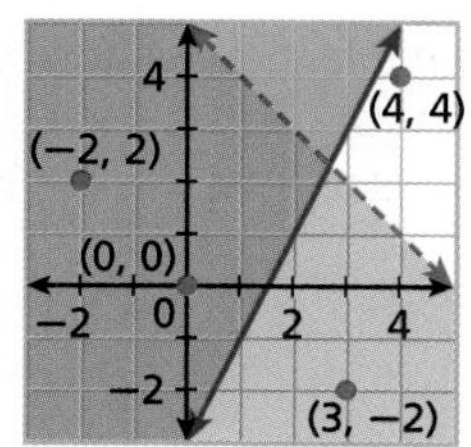


### EXERCISES

**Tell whether the ordered pair is a solution of the given system.**

**53.** $(3, 3)$; $\begin{cases} y > -2x + 9 \\ y \geq x \end{cases}$

**54.** $(-1, 0)$; $\begin{cases} 2x - y > -5 \\ y \leq -3x - 3 \end{cases}$

**Graph each system of linear inequalities. Give two ordered pairs that are solutions and two that are not solutions.**

**55.** $\begin{cases} y \geq x + 4 \\ y > 6x - 3 \end{cases}$

**56.** $\begin{cases} y \leq -2x + 8 \\ y > 3x - 5 \end{cases}$

**57.** $\begin{cases} -x + 2y > 6 \\ x + y < 4 \end{cases}$

**58.** $\begin{cases} x - y > 7 \\ x + 3y \leq 15 \end{cases}$

**Graph each system of linear inequalities.**

**59.** $\begin{cases} y > -x - 6 \\ y < -x + 5 \end{cases}$

**60.** $\begin{cases} 4x + 2y \geq 10 \\ 6x + 3y < -9 \end{cases}$

CHAPTER 6

# CHAPTER TEST

**Tell whether the ordered pair is a solution of the given system.**

1. $(1, -4); \begin{cases} y = -4x \\ y = 2x - 2 \end{cases}$

2. $(0, -1); \begin{cases} 3x - y = 1 \\ x + 5y = -5 \end{cases}$

3. $(3, 2); \begin{cases} x - 2y = -1 \\ -3x + 2y = 5 \end{cases}$

**Solve each system by graphing.**

4. $\begin{cases} y = x - 3 \\ y = -2x - 3 \end{cases}$

5. $\begin{cases} 2x + y = -8 \\ y = \frac{1}{3}x - 1 \end{cases}$

6. $\begin{cases} y = -x + 4 \\ x = y + 2 \end{cases}$

**Solve each system by substitution.**

7. $\begin{cases} y = -6 \\ y = -2x - 2 \end{cases}$

8. $\begin{cases} -x + y = -4 \\ y = 2x - 11 \end{cases}$

9. $\begin{cases} x - 3y = 3 \\ 2x = 3y \end{cases}$

10. The costs for services at two kennels are shown in the table. Joslyn plans to board her dog and have him bathed once during his stay. For what number of days will the cost for boarding and bathing her dog at each kennel be the same? What will that cost be? If Joslyn plans a week-long vacation, which is the cheaper service? Explain.

| Kennel Costs | | |
|---|---|---|
| | Boarding ($ per day) | Bathing ($) |
| Pet Care | 30 | 15 |
| Fido's | 28 | 27 |

**Solve each system by elimination.**

11. $\begin{cases} 3x - y = 7 \\ 2x + y = 3 \end{cases}$

12. $\begin{cases} 4x + y = 0 \\ x + y = -3 \end{cases}$

13. $\begin{cases} 2x + y = 3 \\ x - 2y = -1 \end{cases}$

**Classify each system. Give the number of solutions.**

14. $\begin{cases} y = 6x - 1 \\ 6x - y = 1 \end{cases}$

15. $\begin{cases} y = -3x - 3 \\ 3x + y = 3 \end{cases}$

16. $\begin{cases} 2x - y = 1 \\ -4x + y = 1 \end{cases}$

**Graph the solutions of each linear inequality.**

17. $y < 2x - 5$

18. $-y \geq 8$

19. $y > \frac{1}{3}x$

**Graph each system of linear inequalities. Give two ordered pairs that are solutions and two that are not solutions.**

20. $\begin{cases} y > \frac{1}{2}x - 5 \\ y \leq 4x - 1 \end{cases}$

21. $\begin{cases} y > -x + 4 \\ 3x - y > 3 \end{cases}$

22. $\begin{cases} y \geq 2x \\ y - 2x < 6 \end{cases}$

23. Ezra and Tava sold at least 150 coupon books. Ezra sold at most 30 books more than twice the number Tava sold. Show and describe all possible combinations of the numbers of coupon books Ezra and Tava sold. List two possible combinations.

CHAPTER 6

## *FOCUS ON ACT*

Four scores are reported for the ACT Mathematics Test: one score based on all 60 problems and one for each content area. The three content areas are: Pre-Algebra/ Elementary Algebra, Intermediate Algebra/Coordinate Geometry, and Plane Geometry/Trigonometry.

**Taking classes that cover the content areas on the ACT is a good idea. This way you will have skills from each area of the test. Preparation over a long term is better than cramming at the last minute.**

**You may want to time yourself as you take this practice test. It should take you about 5 minutes to complete.**

**1.** Which system of inequalities is represented by the graph?

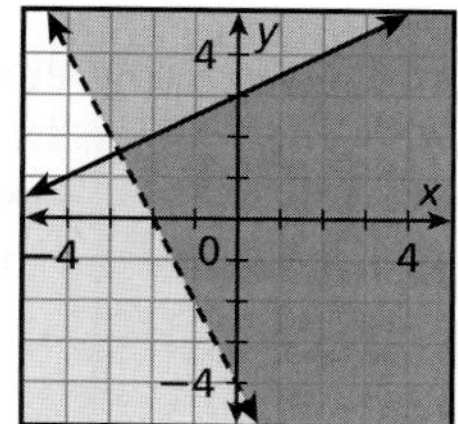


**(A)** $\begin{cases} -x + 2y < 6 \\ 2x + y > -4 \end{cases}$

**(B)** $\begin{cases} x - 2y \leq 6 \\ 2x - y \geq 4 \end{cases}$

**(C)** $\begin{cases} -x + 2y \leq 6 \\ 2x + y \geq 4 \end{cases}$

**(D)** $\begin{cases} -x + 2y \leq 6 \\ 2x + y > -4 \end{cases}$

**(E)** $\begin{cases} x - 2y \leq 6 \\ 2x - y > 4 \end{cases}$

**2.** What is the solution for $y$ in the given system?

$\begin{cases} 4x + 3y = 1 \\ -4x + 3y = -7 \end{cases}$

**(F)** $-1$

**(G)** 0

**(H)** 1

**(J)** 2

**(K)** 6

**3.** Wireless phone company A charges \$20 per month plus \$0.12 per minute. Wireless phone company B charges \$50 per month plus \$0.06 per minute. For how many minutes of calls will the monthly bills be the same?

**(A)** 80 minutes

**(B)** 100 minutes

**(C)** 160 minutes

**(D)** 250 minutes

**(E)** 500 minutes

**4.** Which of the following systems of equations does NOT have a solution?

**(F)** $\begin{cases} x + 5y = 30 \\ -4x + 5y = 10 \end{cases}$

**(G)** $\begin{cases} x + 5y = -30 \\ -4x + 5y = 10 \end{cases}$

**(H)** $\begin{cases} x + 5y = -30 \\ -4x + 5y = -10 \end{cases}$

**(J)** $\begin{cases} -4x + 5y = -10 \\ -8x + 10y = -20 \end{cases}$

**(K)** $\begin{cases} -4x + 5y = -10 \\ -4x + 5y = -30 \end{cases}$

CHAPTER 6

# TEST TACKLER

Standardized Test Strategies

## Any Question Type: Read the Problem for Understanding

Standardized test questions may vary in format including multiple choice, gridded response, and short or extended response. No matter what format the test uses, read each question carefully and critically. Do not rush. Be sure you completely understand what you are asked to do and what your response should include.

### EXAMPLE 1

#### Extended Response

**An interior decorator charges a consultation fee of $50 plus $12 per hour. Another interior decorator charges a consultation fee of $5 plus $22 per hour. Write a system of equations to find the amount of time for which the cost of both decorators will be the same. Graph the system. After how many hours will the cost be the same for both decorators? What will the cost be?**

**Read the problem again.**

**What information are you given?**

the consultation fees and hourly rates of two decorators

**What are you asked to do?**

1. Write a system of equations.
2. Graph the system.
3. Interpret the solution to the system.

**What should your response include?**

1. a system of equations with variables defined
2. a graph of the system
3. the time when the cost is the same for both decorators
4. the cost at that time

Read each test item and answer the questions that follow.

**Item A**
**Short Response** Which value of $b$ will make the lines intersect at the point $(-2, 14)$?

$$\begin{cases} y = -6x + 2 \\ y = 4x + b \end{cases}$$

1. What information are you given?
2. What are you asked to do?
3. Ming's answer to this test problem was $y = 4x + 22$. Did Ming answer correctly? Explain.

**Item B**
**Extended Response** Solve the system by using elimination. Explain how you can check your solution algebraically and graphically.

$$\begin{cases} 4x + 10y = -48 \\ 6x - 10y = 28 \end{cases}$$

4. What method does the problem ask you to use to solve the system of equations?
5. What methods does the problem ask you to use to check your solution?
6. How many parts are there to this problem? List what needs to be included in your response.

**Item C**
**Gridded Response** What is the $x$-coordinate of the solution to this system? $\begin{cases} y = 6x + 9 \\ y = 12x - 15 \end{cases}$

7. What question is being asked?
8. A student correctly found the solution of the system to be $(4, 33)$. What should the student mark on the grid so that the answer is correct?

After you answer each item, read the item again to be sure your response includes everything that is asked for.

**Item D**
**Short Response** Write an inequality to represent the graph below. Give a real-world situation that this inequality could describe.

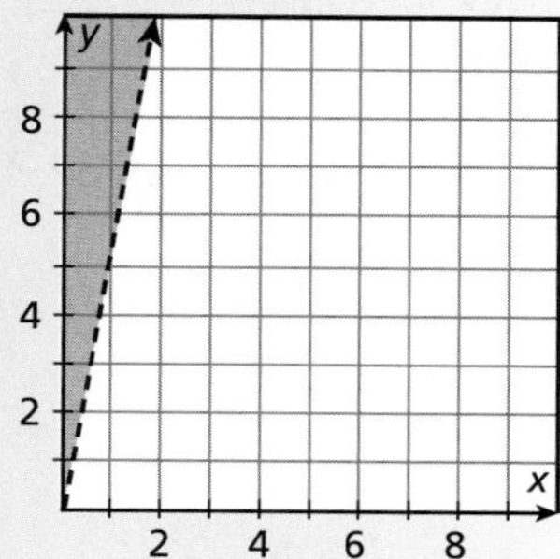


9. As part of his answer, a student wrote the following response:

The point (1, 5) is not a solution to the inequality because it lies on the line, but (2, 12) is a solution because it lies above the line.

Is his response appropriate? Explain.

10. What should the response include so that it answers all parts of the problem?

**Item E**
**Multiple Choice** Taylor bikes 50 miles per week and increases her distance by 2 miles each week. Josie bikes 30 miles per week and increases her distance by 10 miles each week. In how many weeks will Taylor and Josie be biking the same distance?

Ⓐ 2.5 weeks
Ⓑ 7.5 weeks
Ⓒ 55 weeks
Ⓓ 110 weeks

11. What question is being asked?
12. Carson incorrectly selected option C as his answer. What question did he most likely answer?

CHAPTER 6

go.hrw.com
State Test Practice Online
KEYWORD: MA7 TestPrep

# CUMULATIVE ASSESSMENT, CHAPTERS 1–6

## Multiple Choice

**1.** What is the value of $f(x) = 3x^2 + 2x$ when $x = -5$?

**A** $-85$

**B** $-40$

**C** 65

**D** 85

**2.** Which of the problems below could be solved by finding the solution of this system?

$$\begin{cases} 2x + 2y = 56 \\ y = \frac{1}{3}x \end{cases}$$

**A** The area of a rectangle is 56. The width is one-third the length. Find the length of the rectangle.

**B** The area of a rectangle is 56. The length is one-third the perimeter. Find the length of the rectangle.

**C** The perimeter of a rectangle is 56. The length is one-third more than the width. Find the length of the rectangle.

**D** The perimeter of a rectangle is 56. The width is one-third the length. Find the length of the rectangle.

**3.** What is the slope of a line perpendicular to a line that passes through (3, 8) and (1, −4)?

**A** $-\frac{1}{6}$ **C** 2

**B** $-\frac{1}{2}$ **D** 6

**4.** Which inequality is graphed below?

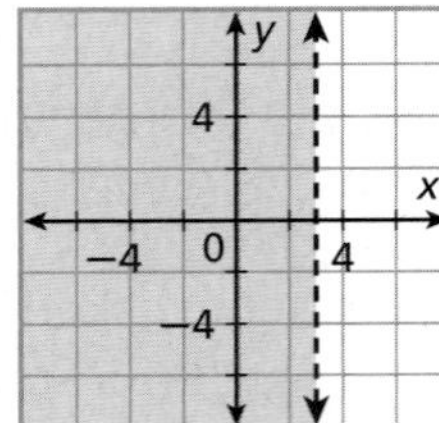


**A** $-x > -3$ **C** $2x < -6$

**B** $-y > -3$ **D** $3y < 9$

**5.** A chemist has a bottle of a 10% acid solution and a bottle of a 30% acid solution. He mixes the solutions together to get 500 mL of a 25% acid solution. How much of the 30% solution did he use?

**A** 125 mL **C** 375 mL

**B** 150 mL **D** 450 mL

**6.** Which ordered pair is NOT a solution of the system graphed below?

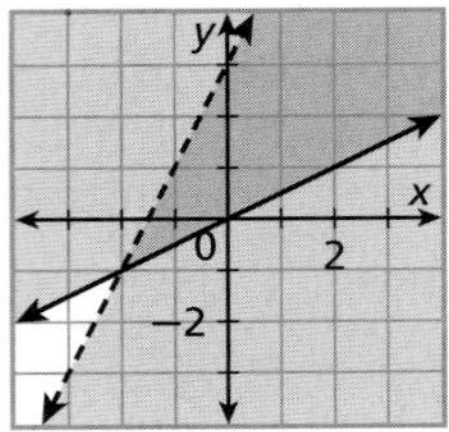


**A** (0, 0) **C** (1, 1)

**B** (0, 3) **D** (2, 1)

**7.** Henrick wants to take his friends to the drive-in movies. One drive-in charges $10 per vehicle, plus $1.25 per person. Another drive-in charges $5 per vehicle and $2.50 per person. What is the number of people for which both drive-in theatres charge the same price?

**A** 4 people **C** 10 people

**B** 7 people **D** 15 people

**8.** Which ordered pair is a solution of this system?

$$\begin{cases} 2x - y = -2 \\ \frac{1}{3}y = x \end{cases}$$

**A** (0, 2) **C** (2, 6)

**B** (1, 3) **D** (3, 8)

**9.** Where does the graph of $5x - 10y = 30$ cross the $y$-axis?

**A** (0, −3) **C** (6, 0)

**B** $\left(0, \frac{1}{2}\right)$ **D** (0, −6)

**Most standardized tests allow you to write in your test booklet. Cross out each answer choice you eliminate. This may keep you from accidentally marking an answer other than the one you think is right. However, don't draw in your math book!**

**10.** Hillary needs markers and poster board for a project. The markers are $0.79 each and the poster board is $1.89 per sheet. She needs at least 4 sheets of poster board. Hillary has $15 to spend on project materials. Which system models this information?

A $\begin{cases} p \geq 4 \\ 0.79m + 1.89p \leq 15 \end{cases}$

B $\begin{cases} 0.79m \geq 1.89p \\ 4p \leq 15 \end{cases}$

C $\begin{cases} 4p \geq 1.89 \\ m + 4p \leq 15 \end{cases}$

D $\begin{cases} p + m \leq 15 \\ 0.79m + 1.89p \geq 4 \end{cases}$

**11.** A family went to see a play. Adult tickets cost $12 each and children's tickets cost $7 each. Eight people went to the play, and they paid a total of $81. How many adults and how many children went to the play?

**A** 3 adults, 5 children

**B** 4 adults, 4 children

**C** 5 adults, 3 children

**D** 7 adults, 1 child

**12.** What is an equation for the line that passes through (5, 3) and is perpendicular to the line described by $y = -3x - 3$?

**A** $y = -3x + 18$ **C** $y = \frac{1}{3}x + \frac{4}{3}$

**B** $y = -\frac{1}{3}x + \frac{14}{3}$ **D** $y = 3x + 12$

**13.** Anastasia collects statues and pedestals. Three pedestals weigh the same as five statues. The total weight of 2 pedestals and 7 statues is 310 pounds. What is the weight of a statue?

**A** 30 pounds **C** 70 pounds

**B** 50 pounds **D** 90 pounds

**14.** What value of $k$ will make the system $y - 5x = -1$ and $y = kx + 3$ inconsistent?

**A** $-5$ **C** 3

**B** $-1$ **D** 5

*STANDARDIZED TEST PREP*

## Short Response

**S1.** The data in the table represents a linear relationship between $x$ and $y$. Find the missing $y$-value. Explain your answer.

| $x$ | $y$ |
|---|---|
| $-3$ | $-15$ |
| $-1$ | $-7$ |
| 0 | $-3$ |
| 2 | ■ |
| 5 | 17 |

**S2.** Graph $y > \frac{-x}{3} - 1$ on a coordinate plane. Name one point that is a solution of the inequality.

**S3.** Marc and his brother Ty start saving money at the same time. Marc has $145 and will add $10 to his savings every week. Ty has $20 and will add $15 to his savings every week. After how many weeks will Marc and Ty have the same amount saved? What is that amount? Show your work.

**S4.** A movie producer is looking for extras to act as office employees in his next movie. The producer needs extras that are at least 40 years old but less than 70 years old. They should be at least 60 inches tall but less than 75 inches tall. Graph all the possible combinations of ages and heights for extras that match the producer's needs. Let $x$ represent age and $y$ represent height. Show your work.

**S5.** Graph the system $\begin{cases} y < -2x + 3 \\ y \geq 6x + 6 \end{cases}$.

**a.** Is (0, 0) a solution of the system you graphed? Explain why or why not.

**b.** Is (−4, 5) a solution of the system you graphed? Explain why or why not.

## Extended Response

**E1.** Every year, Erin knits scarves and sells them at the craft fair. This year she used $6 worth of yarn for each scarf. She also paid $50 to rent a table at the fair. She sold every scarf for $10.

**a.** Write a system of linear equations to represent the amount Erin spent and the amount she collected. Tell what your variables represent. Tell what each equation in the system represents.

**b.** Use any method to solve the system you wrote in part **a.** Show your work. How many scarves did Erin need to sell to make a profit? Explain.

**c.** Describe two ways you could check your solution to part **b.** Check your solution by using one of those ways. Show your work.

## Cherokee Bear Zoo

The Smoky Mountains of North Carolina are the natural habitat of the American black bear. While it may be unusual to see a black bear in the wild, visitors to western North Carolina are guaranteed to spot some at the Cherokee Bear Zoo, where black bears share the spotlight with grizzlies and other wild animals.

1. A black bear can gain weight rapidly as it prepares to hibernate for the winter. The graph shows the weight of a black bear during the weeks of preparation. What is the slope of the line? What does it represent?

**Black Bear Weight Before Hibernation**

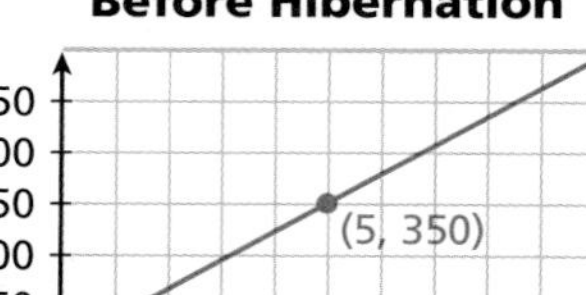

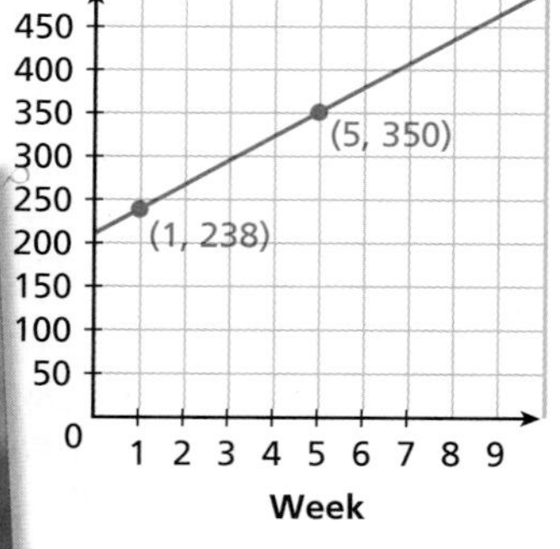

2. Write an equation that gives the bear's weight $y$ as a function of the week $x$.
3. Is the relationship a direct variation? Why or why not?
4. What is the $y$-intercept of the graph? What does it represent?
5. The bear goes into hibernation in the 11th week. What is the bear's weight at this time?
6. During hibernation, the number of heartbeats $h$ varies directly with the number of minutes $m$, and $h = 50$ when $m = 5$. Find the number of heartbeats in 3 minutes.

## Lafayette's Tour

North Carolina has dozens of scenic byways. Lafayette's Tour, in the northeast corner of the state, is one of the longest and most popular. The route, which traces the 1825 voyage of General Lafayette, takes motorists past historic sites and examples of classic southern architecture.

1. Allison and Kendall are driving Lafayette's Tour in separate cars. The diagram at the bottom of the page shows the distances they have already driven and their average rates.
   a. Write an equation that gives Allison's total distance $y$ as a function of the number of additional hours $x$ that she drives.
   b. Write an equation that gives Kendall's total distance $y$ as a function of the number of additional hours $x$ that he drives.
2. Graph the two equations on the same coordinate plane.
3. What is the slope of each line that you graphed? Explain why this slope makes sense.
4. How many additional hours does it take for Kendall to pass Allison?
5. It takes Allison 4 hours to complete the rest of the drive along Lafayette's Tour. How long is Lafayette's Tour?

**Medoc Mountain State Park is on Lafayette's Tour.**

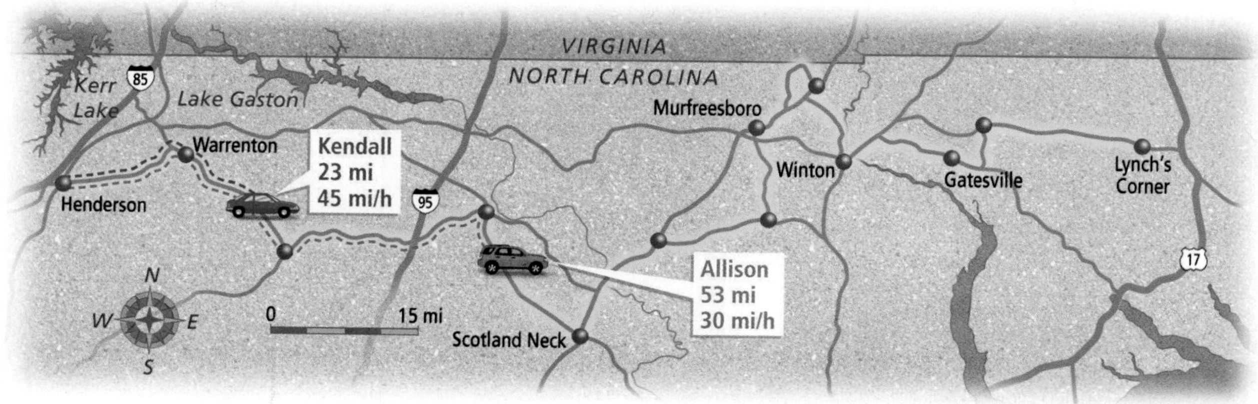

# Exponents and Polynomials



## Why Learn This?

Polynomials can be used to plan fireworks displays, such as this one in Chapel Hill, NC.

go.hrw.com
Chapter Project Online
KEYWORD: MA7 ChProj

# ARE YOU READY?

## Vocabulary

**Match each term on the left with a definition on the right.**

1. Associative Property
2. coefficient
3. Commutative Property
4. exponent
5. like terms

A. a number that is raised to a power
B. a number multiplied by a variable
C. a property of addition and multiplication that states you can add or multiply numbers in any order
D. the number of times a base is used as a factor
E. terms that contain the same variables raised to the same powers
F. a property of addition and multiplication that states you can group the numbers in any order

## Exponents

**Write each expression using a base and an exponent.**

6. $4 \cdot 4 \cdot 4 \cdot 4 \cdot 4 \cdot 4 \cdot 4$
7. $5 \cdot 5$
8. $(-10)(-10)(-10)(-10)$
9. $x \cdot x \cdot x$
10. $k \cdot k \cdot k \cdot k \cdot k$
11. 9

## Evaluate Powers

**Evaluate each expression.**

12. $3^4$
13. $-12^2$
14. $5^3$
15. $2^5$
16. $4^3$
17. $(-1)^6$

## Multiply Decimals

**Multiply.**

18. $0.006 \times 10$
19. $25{,}250 \times 100$
20. $2.4 \times 6.5$

## Combine Like Terms

**Simplify each expression.**

21. $6 + 3p + 14 + 9p$
22. $8y - 4x + 2y + 7x - x$
23. $(12 + 3w - 5) + 6w - 3 - 5w$
24. $6n - 14 + 5n$

## Squares and Square Roots

**Tell whether each number is a perfect square. If so, identify its positive square root.**

25. 42
26. 81
27. 36
28. 50
29. 100
30. 4
31. 1
32. 12

CHAPTER 7

# Study Guide: Preview

## Where You've Been

**Previously, you**

- wrote and evaluated exponential expressions.
- simplified algebraic expressions by combining like terms.

## In This Chapter

**You will study**

- properties of exponents.
- powers of 10 and scientific notation.
- how to add, subtract, and multiply polynomials by using properties of exponents and combining like terms.

## Where You're Going

**You can use the skills in this chapter**

- to model area, perimeter, and volume in geometry.
- to express very small or very large quantities in science classes such as Chemistry, Physics, and Biology.
- in the real world to model business profits and population growth or decline.

## *Key Vocabulary/Vocabulario*

| | |
|---|---|
| binomial | binomio |
| degree of a monomial | grado de un monomio |
| degree of a polynomial | grado de un polinomio |
| leading coefficient | coeficiente principal |
| monomial | monomio |
| perfect-square trinomial | trinomio cuadrado perfecto |
| polynomial | polinomio |
| scientific notation | notación científica |
| standard form of a polynomial | forma estándar de un polinomio |
| trinomial | trinomio |

## *Vocabulary Connections*

To become familiar with some of the vocabulary terms in the chapter, consider the following. You may refer to the chapter, the glossary, or a dictionary if you like.

1. Very large and very small numbers are often encountered in the sciences. If *notation* means a method of writing something, what might **scientific notation** mean?
2. A **polynomial** written in standard form may have more than one algebraic term. What do you think the **leading coefficient** of a polynomial is?
3. A simple definition of **monomial** is "an expression with exactly one term." If the prefix *mono-* means "one" and the prefix *bi-* means "two," define the word **binomial**.
4. What words do you know that begin with the prefix *tri-*? What do they all have in common? Define the word **trinomial** based on the prefix *tri-* and the information given in Problem 3.

Reading and Writing Math

CHAPTER 7

## Reading Strategy: Read and Understand the Problem

Follow this strategy when solving word problems.

- Read the problem through once.
- Identify exactly what the problem asks you to do.
- Read the problem again, slowly and carefully, to break it into parts.
- Highlight or underline the key information.
- Make a plan to solve the problem.

**From Lesson 6-6**

**29. Multi-Step** Linda works at a pharmacy for $15 an hour. She also baby-sits for $10 an hour. Linda needs to earn at least $90 per week, but she does not want to work more than 20 hours per week. Show and describe the number of hours Linda could work at each job to meet her goals. List two possible solutions.

| | | |
|---|---|---|
| **Step 1** | **Identify exactly what the problem asks you to do.** | • Show and describe the number of hours Linda can work at each job and earn at least $90 per week, without working more than 20 hours per week.<br>• List two possible solutions of the system. |
| **Step 2** | **Break the problem into parts. Highlight or underline the key information.** | • Linda has two jobs. She makes **$15 per hour** at one job and **$10 per hour** at the other job.<br>• She wants to earn **at least $90 per week.**<br>• She does **not** want to work **more than 20 hours per week.** |
| **Step 3** | **Make a plan to solve the problem.** | • Write a system of inequalities.<br>• Solve the system.<br>• Identify two possible solutions of the system. |

### Try This

**For the problem below,**

**a. identify exactly what the problem asks you to do.**

**b. break the problem into parts. Highlight or underline the key information.**

**c. make a plan to solve the problem.**

1. The difference between the length and the width of a rectangle is 14 units. The area is 120 square units. Write and solve a system of equations to determine the length and the width of the rectangle. (*Hint:* The formula for the area of a rectangle is $A = \ell w$.)

# 7-1 Integer Exponents

**MA.N.2.1** Represent numerical expressions with exponents in their simplest forms. *Also* **MA.N.2.2**

***Objectives***

Evaluate expressions containing zero and integer exponents.

Simplify expressions containing zero and integer exponents.

**Who uses this?**

Manufacturers can use negative exponents to express very small measurements.

In 1930, the Model A Ford was one of the first cars to boast precise craftsmanship in mass production. The car's pistons had a diameter of $3\frac{7}{8}$ inches; this measurement could vary by at most $10^{-3}$ inch.

You have seen positive exponents. Recall that to simplify $3^2$, use 3 as a factor 2 times: $3^2 = 3 \cdot 3 = 9$.

But what does it mean for an exponent to be negative or 0? You can use a table and look for a pattern to figure it out.

**Remember!**

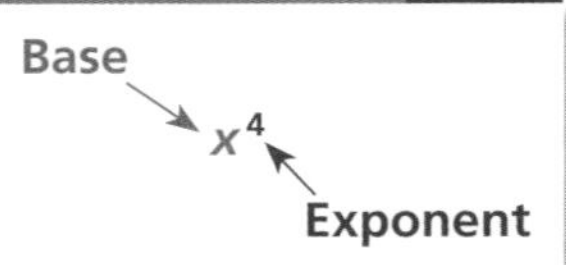


| Power | $5^5$ | $5^4$ | $5^3$ | $5^2$ | $5^1$ | $5^0$ | $5^{-1}$ | $5^{-2}$ |
|---|---|---|---|---|---|---|---|---|
| Value | 3125 | 625 | 125 | 25 | 5 | | | |

÷ 5   ÷ 5   ÷ 5   ÷ 5

When the exponent decreases by one, the value of the power is divided by 5. Continue the pattern of dividing by 5:

$$5^0 = \frac{5}{5} = 1 \qquad 5^{-1} = \frac{1}{5} = \frac{1}{5^1} \qquad 5^{-2} = \frac{1}{5} \div 5 = \frac{1}{25} = \frac{1}{5^2}$$

**Know it! Note**

**Integer Exponents**

| WORDS | NUMBERS | ALGEBRA |
|---|---|---|
| **Zero exponent**—Any nonzero number raised to the zero power is 1. | $3^0 = 1 \quad 123^0 = 1$ <br> $(-16)^0 = 1 \quad \left(\frac{3}{7}\right)^0 = 1$ | If $x \neq 0$, then $x^0 = 1$. |
| **Negative exponent**—A nonzero number raised to a negative exponent is equal to 1 divided by that number raised to the opposite (positive) exponent. | $3^{-2} = \frac{1}{3^2} = \frac{1}{9}$ <br> $2^{-4} = \frac{1}{2^4} = \frac{1}{16}$ | If $x \neq 0$ and $n$ is an integer, then $x^{-n} = \frac{1}{x^n}$. |

**Reading Math**

$2^{-4}$ is read "2 to the negative fourth power."

Notice the phrase "nonzero number" in the table above. This is because $0^0$ and 0 raised to a negative power are both undefined. For example, if you use the pattern given above the table with a base of 0 instead of 5, you would get $0^0 = \frac{0}{0}$. Also, $0^{-6}$ would be $\frac{1}{0^6} = \frac{1}{0}$. Since division by 0 is undefined, neither value exists.

## EXAMPLE 1 Manufacturing Application

**The diameter for the Model A Ford piston could vary by at most $10^{-3}$ inch. Simplify this expression.**

$$10^{-3} = \frac{1}{10^3} = \frac{1}{10 \cdot 10 \cdot 10} = \frac{1}{1000}$$

$10^{-3}$ inch is equal to $\frac{1}{1000}$ inch, or 0.001 inch.

**1.** A sand fly may have a wingspan up to $5^{-3}$ m. Simplify this expression.

## EXAMPLE 2 Zero and Negative Exponents

**Caution!**

In $(-3)^{-4}$, the base is negative because the negative sign is inside the parentheses.

In $-3^{-4}$ the base (3) is positive.

**Simplify.**

**A** $2^{-3}$

$$2^{-3} = \frac{1}{2^3} = \frac{1}{2 \cdot 2 \cdot 2} = \frac{1}{8}$$

**B** $5^0$

$5^0 = 1$ *Any nonzero number raised to the zero power is 1.*

**C** $(-3)^{-4}$

$$(-3)^{-4} = \frac{1}{(-3)^4} = \frac{1}{(-3)(-3)(-3)(-3)} = \frac{1}{81}$$

**D** $-3^{-4}$

$$-3^{-4} = -\frac{1}{3^4} = -\frac{1}{3 \cdot 3 \cdot 3 \cdot 3} = -\frac{1}{81}$$

**Simplify.**

**2a.** $10^{-4}$ **2b.** $(-2)^{-4}$ **2c.** $(-2)^{-5}$ **2d.** $-2^{-5}$

## EXAMPLE 3 Evaluating Expressions with Zero and Negative Exponents

**Evaluate each expression for the given value(s) of the variable(s).**

**A** $x^{-1}$ **for** $x = 2$

$2^{-1}$ *Substitute 2 for x.*

$2^{-1} = \frac{1}{2^1} = \frac{1}{2}$ *Use the definition $x^{-n} = \frac{1}{x^n}$.*

**B** $a^0b^{-3}$ **for** $a = 8$ **and** $b = -2$

$8^0 \cdot (-2)^{-3}$ *Substitute 8 for a and −2 for b.*

$1 \cdot \frac{1}{(-2)^3}$ *Evaluate expressions with exponents.*

$1 \cdot \frac{1}{(-2)(-2)(-2)}$ *Write the power in the denominator as a product.*

$1 \cdot \frac{1}{-8}$ *Evaluate the power in the denominator.*

$-\frac{1}{8}$ *Simplify.*

**Evaluate each expression for the given value(s) of the variable(s).**

**3a.** $p^{-3}$ for $p = 4$ **3b.** $8a^{-2}b^0$ for $a = -2$ and $b = 6$

What if you have an expression with a negative exponent in a denominator, such as $\frac{1}{x^{-8}}$?

| | |
|---|---|
| $x^{-n} = \frac{1}{x^n}$, or $\frac{1}{x^n} = x^{-n}$ | *Definition of negative exponent* |
| $\frac{1}{x^{-8}} = x^{-(-8)}$ | *Substitute −8 for n.* |
| $= x^8$ | *Simplify the exponent on the right side.* |

So if a base with a negative exponent is in a denominator, it is equivalent to the same base with the opposite (positive) exponent in the numerator.

An expression that contains negative or zero exponents is not considered to be simplified. Expressions should be rewritten with only positive exponents.

## EXAMPLE 4 Simplifying Expressions with Zero and Negative Exponents

**Simplify.**

**A** $3y^{-2}$

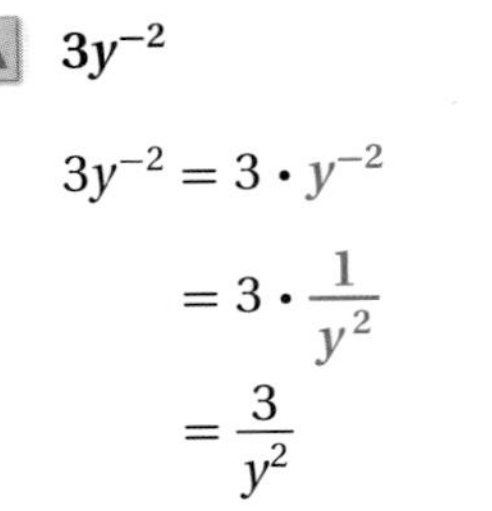

$$3y^{-2} = 3 \cdot y^{-2} = 3 \cdot \frac{1}{y^2} = \frac{3}{y^2}$$

**B** $\frac{-4}{k^{-4}}$

$$\frac{-4}{k^{-4}} = -4 \cdot \frac{1}{k^{-4}} = -4 \cdot k^4 = -4k^4$$

**C** $\frac{x^{-3}}{a^0y^5}$

$$\frac{x^{-3}}{a^0y^5} = \frac{1}{x^3 \cdot 1 \cdot y^5} = \frac{1}{x^3y^5}$$

*$a^0 = 1$ and $x^{-3} = \frac{1}{x^3}$.*

**Simplify.**

**4a.** $2r^0m^{-3}$ **4b.** $\frac{r^{-3}}{7}$ **4c.** $\frac{g^4}{h^{-6}}$

### THINK AND DISCUSS

**1.** Complete each equation: $2b^? = \frac{2}{b^2}$, $\frac{s^{-3}}{k^?} = \frac{1}{s^3}$, $?^{-2} = \frac{1}{t^2}$

**2. GET ORGANIZED** Copy and complete the graphic organizer. In each box, describe how to simplify, and give an example.

Simplifying Expressions with Negative Exponents

- For a negative exponent in the numerator . . .
- For a negative exponent in the denominator . . .

# 7-1 Exercises

MA.N.2.1, MA.N.2.2

go.hrw.com
Homework Help Online
KEYWORD: MA7 7-1
Parent Resources Online
KEYWORD: MA7 Parent

## GUIDED PRACTICE

SEE EXAMPLE 1 p. 447

1. **Medicine** A typical virus is about $10^{-7}$ m in size. Simplify this expression.

SEE EXAMPLE 2 p. 447

**Simplify.**

2. $6^{-2}$ 3. $3^0$ 4. $-5^{-2}$ 5. $3^{-3}$ 6. $1^{-8}$
7. $-8^{-3}$ 8. $10^{-2}$ 9. $(4.2)^0$ 10. $(-3)^{-3}$ 11. $4^{-2}$

SEE EXAMPLE 3 p. 447

**Evaluate each expression for the given value(s) of the variable(s).**

12. $b^{-2}$ for $b = -3$
13. $(2t)^{-4}$ for $t = 2$
14. $(m - 4)^{-5}$ for $m = 6$
15. $2x^0y^{-3}$ for $x = 7$ and $y = -4$

SEE EXAMPLE 4 p. 448

**Simplify.**

16. $4m^0$ 17. $3k^{-4}$ 18. $\frac{7}{r^{-7}}$ 19. $\frac{x^{10}}{d^{-3}}$
20. $2x^0y^{-4}$ 21. $\frac{f^{-4}}{g^{-6}}$ 22. $\frac{c^4}{d^{-3}}$ 23. $p^7q^{-1}$

## PRACTICE AND PROBLEM SOLVING

| Independent Practice | |
|---|---|
| For Exercises | See Example |
| 24 | 1 |
| 25–36 | 2 |
| 37–42 | 3 |
| 43–57 | 4 |

**Extra Practice**
Skills Practice p. S16
Application Practice p. S34

24. **Biology** One of the smallest bats is the northern blossom bat, which is found from Southeast Asia to Australia. This bat weighs about $2^{-1}$ ounce. Simplify this expression.

**Simplify.**

25. $8^0$ 26. $5^{-4}$ 27. $3^{-4}$ 28. $-9^{-2}$
29. $-6^{-2}$ 30. $7^{-2}$ 31. $\left(\frac{2}{5}\right)^0$ 32. $13^{-2}$
33. $(-3)^{-1}$ 34. $(-4)^2$ 35. $\left(\frac{1}{2}\right)^{-2}$ 36. $-7^{-1}$

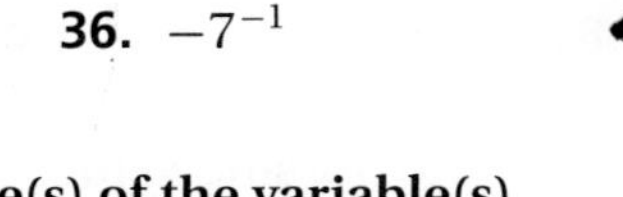

**Evaluate each expression for the given value(s) of the variable(s).**

37. $x^{-4}$ for $x = 4$
38. $\left(\frac{2}{3}v\right)^{-3}$ for $v = 9$
39. $(10 - d)^0$ for $d = 11$
40. $10m^{-1}n^{-5}$ for $m = 10$ and $n = -2$
41. $(3ab)^{-2}$ for $a = \frac{1}{2}$ and $b = 8$
42. $4w^vx^v$ for $w = 3$, $v = 0$, and $x = -5$

**Simplify.**

43. $k^{-4}$ 44. $2z^{-8}$ 45. $\frac{1}{2b^{-3}}$ 46. $c^{-2}d$ 47. $-5x^{-3}$
48. $4x^{-6}y^{-2}$ 49. $\frac{2f^0}{7g^{-10}}$ 50. $\frac{r^{-5}}{s^{-1}}$ 51. $\frac{s^5}{t^{-12}}$ 52. $\frac{3w^{-5}}{x^{-6}}$
53. $b^0c^0$ 54. $\frac{2}{3}m^{-1}n^5$ 55. $\frac{q^{-2}r^0}{s^0}$ 56. $\frac{a^{-7}b^2}{c^3d^{-4}}$ 57. $\frac{h^3k^{-1}}{6m^2}$

**Evaluate each expression for $x = 3, y = -1$, and $z = 2$.**

**58.** $z^{-5}$ **59.** $(x + y)^{-4}$ **60.** $(yz)^0$ **61.** $(xyz)^{-1}$

**62.** $(xy - 3)^{-2}$ **63.** $x^{-y}$ **64.** $(yz)^{-x}$ **65.** $xy^{-4}$

**66.** **/// ERROR ANALYSIS ///** Look at the two equations below. Which is incorrect? Explain the error.

A

$5x^{-3} = \frac{1}{5x^3}$

B

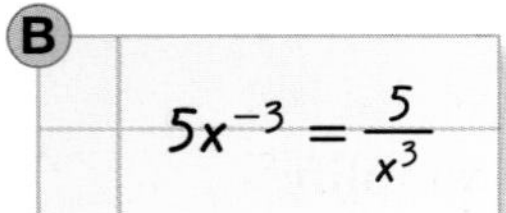


**Simplify.**

**67.** $a^3b^{-2}$ **68.** $c^{-4}d^3$ **69.** $v^0w^2y^{-1}$ **70.** $(a^2b^{-7})^0$ **71.** $-5y^{-6}$

**72.** $\frac{2a^{-5}}{b^{-6}}$ **73.** $\frac{2a^3}{b^{-1}}$ **74.** $\frac{m^2}{n^{-3}}$ **75.** $\frac{x^{-8}}{3y^{12}}$ **76.** $-\frac{20p^{-1}}{5q^{-3}}$

LINK

**Biology**

When bleeding occurs, platelets (which appear green in the image above) help to form a clot to reduce blood loss. Calcium and vitamin K are also necessary for clot formation.

**77.** **Biology** Human blood contains red blood cells, white blood cells, and platelets. The table shows the sizes of these components. Simplify each expression.

**Blood Components**

| Part | Size (m) |
|---|---|
| Red blood cell | $125{,}000^{-1}$ |
| White blood cell | $3(500)^{-2}$ |
| Platelet | $3(1000)^{-2}$ |

**Tell whether each statement is sometimes, always, or never true.**

**78.** If $n$ is a positive integer, then $x^{-n} = \frac{1}{x^n}$.

**79.** If $x$ is positive, then $x^{-n}$ is negative.

**80.** If $n$ is zero, then $x^{-n}$ is 1.

**81.** If $n$ is a negative integer, then $x^{-n} = 1$.

**82.** If $x$ is zero, then $x^{-n}$ is 1.

**83.** If $n$ is an integer, then $x^{-n} > 1$.

**84.** **Critical Thinking** Find the value of $2^3 \cdot 2^{-3}$. Then find the value of $3^2 \cdot 3^{-2}$. Make a conjecture about the value of $a^n \cdot a^{-n}$.

**85.** **Write About It** Explain in your own words why $2^{-3}$ is the same as $\frac{1}{2^3}$.

**Find the missing value.**

**86.** $\frac{1}{4} = 2^{\blacksquare}$ **87.** $9^{-2} = \frac{1}{\blacksquare}$ **88.** $\frac{1}{64} = \blacksquare^{-2}$ **89.** $\frac{\blacksquare}{3} = 3^{-1}$

**90.** $7^{-2} = \frac{1}{\blacksquare}$ **91.** $10^{\blacksquare} = \frac{1}{1000}$ **92.** $3 \cdot 4^{-2} = \frac{3}{\blacksquare}$ **93.** $2 \cdot \frac{1}{5} = 2 \cdot 5^{\blacksquare}$

**94.** This problem will prepare you for the Multi-Step Test Prep on page 474.

**a.** The product of the frequency $f$ and the wavelength $w$ of light in air is a constant $v$. Write an equation for this relationship.

**b.** Solve this equation for wavelength. Then write this equation as an equation with $f$ raised to a negative exponent.

**c.** The units for frequency are hertz (Hz). One hertz is one cycle per second, which is often written as $\frac{1}{s}$. Rewrite this expression using a negative exponent.

## TEST PREP

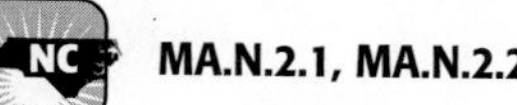

MA.N.2.1, MA.N.2.2

95. Which is NOT equivalent to the other three?

Ⓐ $\frac{1}{25}$ Ⓑ $5^{-2}$ Ⓒ 0.04 Ⓓ $-25$

96. Which is equal to $6^{-2}$?

Ⓕ $6(-2)$ Ⓖ $(-6)(-6)$ Ⓗ $-\frac{1}{6 \cdot 6}$ Ⓙ $\frac{1}{6 \cdot 6}$

97. Simplify $\frac{a^3b^{-2}}{c^{-1}}$.

Ⓐ $\frac{a^3c}{b^2}$ Ⓑ $\frac{a^3b^2}{-c}$ Ⓒ $\frac{a^3}{-b^2c}$ Ⓓ $\frac{c}{a^3b^2}$

98. **Gridded Response** Simplify $\left[2^{-2} + (6 + 2)^0\right]$.

99. **Short Response** If $a$ and $b$ are real numbers and $n$ is a positive integer, write a simplified expression for the product $a^{-n} \cdot b^0$ that contains only positive exponents. Explain your answer.

## CHALLENGE AND EXTEND

100. **Multi-Step** Copy and complete the table of values below. Then graph the ordered pairs and describe the shape of the graph.

| $x$ | −4 | −3 | −2 | −1 | 0 | 1 | 2 | 3 | 4 |
|---|---|---|---|---|---|---|---|---|---|
| $y = 2^x$ | ▒ | ▒ | ▒ | ▒ | ▒ | ▒ | ▒ | ▒ | ▒ |

101. **Multi-Step** Copy and complete the table. Then write a rule for the values of $1^n$ and $(-1)^n$ when $n$ is any negative integer.

| $n$ | −1 | −2 | −3 | −4 | −5 |
|---|---|---|---|---|---|
| $1^n$ | ▒ | ▒ | ▒ | ▒ | ▒ |
| $(-1)^n$ | ▒ | ▒ | ▒ | ▒ | ▒ |

## SPIRAL REVIEW

**Solve each equation.** *(Lesson 2-3)*

102. $6x - 4 = 8$

103. $-9 = 3(p - 1)$

104. $\frac{y}{5} - 8 = -12$

105. $1.5h - 5 = 1$

106. $2w + 6 - 3w = -10$

107. $-12 = \frac{1}{2}n + 2 - n$

**Identify the independent and dependent variables. Write a rule in function notation for each situation.** *(Lesson 4-3)*

108. Pink roses cost $1.50 per stem.

109. For dog-sitting, Beth charges a $30 flat fee plus $10 a day.

**Write the equation that describes each line in slope-intercept form.** *(Lesson 5-6)*

110. slope = 3, $y$-intercept = −4

111. slope = $\frac{1}{3}$, $y$-intercept = 5

112. slope = 0, $y$-intercept = $\frac{2}{3}$

113. slope = −4, the point $(1, 5)$ is on the line

# 7-2 Powers of 10 and Scientific Notation

**MA.N.2.1** Represent numerical expressions with exponents in their simplest forms.

Nucleus of a silicon atom

***Objectives***

Evaluate and multiply by powers of 10.

Convert between standard notation and scientific notation.

***Vocabulary***

scientific notation

**Why learn this?**

Powers of 10 can be used to read and write very large and very small numbers, such as the masses of atomic particles. (See Exercise 30.)

The table shows relationships between several powers of 10.

| Power | $10^3$ | $10^2$ | $10^1$ | $10^0$ | $10^{-1}$ | $10^{-2}$ | $10^{-3}$ |
|---|---|---|---|---|---|---|---|
| Value | 1000 | 100 | 10 | 1 | $\frac{1}{10} = 0.1$ | $\frac{1}{100} = 0.01$ | $\frac{1}{1000} = 0.001$ |

(Moving right: ÷ 10 at each step. Moving left: × 10 at each step.)

- Each time you **divide by 10**, the exponent decreases by 1 and the decimal point moves one place to the left.
- Each time you **multiply by 10**, the exponent increases by 1 and the decimal point moves one place to the right.

**Know it! Note**

## Powers of 10

| WORDS | NUMBERS |
|---|---|
| **Positive Integer Exponent**<br>If $n$ is a positive integer, find the value of $10^n$ by starting with 1 and moving the decimal point $n$ places to the right. | $10^4 = 1\,0,0\,0\,0$<br>4 places |
| **Negative Integer Exponent**<br>If $n$ is a positive integer, find the value of $10^{-n}$ by starting with 1 and moving the decimal point $n$ places to the left. | $10^{-6} = \frac{1}{10^6} = 0.0\,0\,0\,0\,0\,1$<br>6 places |

**EXAMPLE 1**

### Evaluating Powers of 10

**Find the value of each power of 10.**

**A** $10^{-3}$

*Start with 1 and move the decimal point three places to the left.*

0.001 (written 0. 0 0 1 with arrow showing the move)

0.001

**B** $10^2$

*Start with 1 and move the decimal point two places to the right.*

1 0 0

100

**C** $10^0$

*Start with 1 and move the decimal point zero places.*

1

**Writing Math**

You may need to add zeros to the right or left of a number in order to move the decimal point in that direction.

CHECK IT OUT! Find the value of each power of 10.

**1a.** $10^{-2}$ **1b.** $10^{5}$ **1c.** $10^{10}$

**EXAMPLE 2** **Writing Powers of 10**

**Reading Math**

If you do not see a decimal point in a number, it is understood to be at the end of the number.

**Write each number as a power of 10.**

**A** **10,000,000**

*The decimal point is seven places to the right of 1, so the exponent is 7.*

$10^{7}$

**B** **0.001**

*The decimal point is three places to the left of 1, so the exponent is −3.*

$10^{-3}$

**C** **10**

*The decimal point is one place to the right of 1, so the exponent is 1.*

$10^{1}$

**Write each number as a power of 10.**

**2a.** 100,000,000 **2b.** 0.0001 **2c.** 0.1

You can also move the decimal point to find the product of any number and a power of 10. You start with the number instead of starting with 1.

| Multiplying by Powers of 10 | |
|---|---|
| If the exponent is a positive integer, move the decimal point to the right. | $125 \times 10^{5} = 12{,}500{,}000$ (5 places) |
| If the exponent is a negative integer, move the decimal point to the left. | $36.2 \times 10^{-3} = 0.0362$ (3 places) |

**EXAMPLE 3** **Multiplying by Powers of 10**

**Find the value of each expression.**

**A** $97.86 \times 10^{6}$

97.8 6 0 0 0 0 *Move the decimal point 6 places to the right.*

97,860,000

**B** $19.5 \times 10^{-4}$

0 0 1 9.5 *Move the decimal point 4 places to the left.*

0.00195

**Find the value of each expression.**

**3a.** $853.4 \times 10^{5}$ **3b.** $0.163 \times 10^{-2}$

**Scientific notation** is a method of writing numbers that are very large or very small. A number written in scientific notation has two parts that are multiplied.

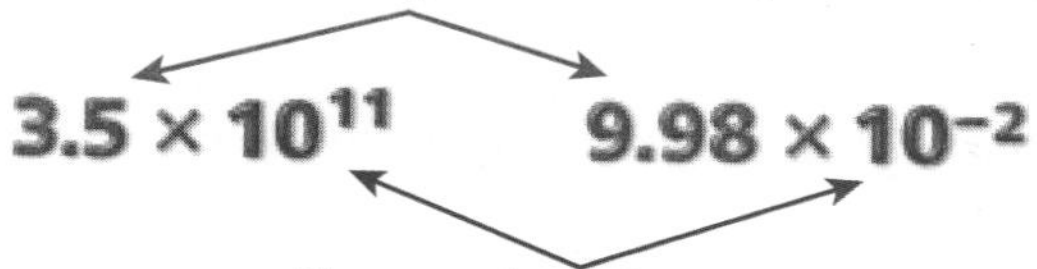

## EXAMPLE 4 Astronomy Application

**Jupiter has a diameter of about 143,000 km. Its shortest distance from Earth is about $5.91 \times 10^8$ km, and its average distance from the Sun is about 778,400,000 km. Jupiter's orbital speed is approximately $1.3 \times 10^4$ m/s.**

143,000 km

**Reading Math**

*Standard form* refers to the usual way that numbers are written—not in scientific notation.

**A Write Jupiter's shortest distance from Earth in standard form.**

$5.91 \times 10^8$

5.9 1 0 0 0 0 0 0 — *Move the decimal point 8 places to the right.*

591,000,000 km

**B Write Jupiter's average distance from the Sun in scientific notation.**

778,400,000

7 7 8, 4 0 0, 0 0 0 — *Count the number of places you need to move the decimal point to get a number between 1 and 10.*

8 places

$7.784 \times 10^8$ km — *Use that number as the exponent of 10.*

**4a.** Use the information above to write Jupiter's diameter in scientific notation.

**4b.** Use the information above to write Jupiter's orbital speed in standard form.

## EXAMPLE 5 Comparing and Ordering Numbers in Scientific Notation

**Order the list of numbers from least to greatest.**

$1.2 \times 10^{-1}, 8.2 \times 10^4, 6.2 \times 10^5, 2.4 \times 10^5, 1 \times 10^{-1}, 9.9 \times 10^{-4}$

**Step 1** List the numbers in order by powers of 10.

$9.9 \times 10^{-4}, 1.2 \times 10^{-1}, 1 \times 10^{-1}, 8.2 \times 10^4, 6.2 \times 10^5, 2.4 \times 10^5$

**Step 2** Order the numbers that have the same power of 10.

$9.9 \times 10^{-4}, 1 \times 10^{-1}, 1.2 \times 10^{-1}, 8.2 \times 10^4, 2.4 \times 10^5, 6.2 \times 10^5$

**5.** Order the list of numbers from least to greatest.
$5.2 \times 10^{-3}, 3 \times 10^{14}, 4 \times 10^{-3}, 2 \times 10^{-12}, 4.5 \times 10^{30}, 4.5 \times 10^{14}$

## THINK AND DISCUSS

**1.** Tell why $34.56 \times 10^4$ is not correctly written in scientific notation.

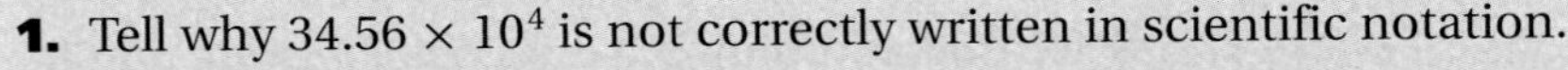

**2. GET ORGANIZED** Copy and complete the graphic organizer.

Powers of 10 and Scientific Notation

| A negative exponent corresponds to moving the decimal point ___?___. | A positive exponent corresponds to moving the decimal point ___?___. |
|---|---|

# 7-2 Exercises

## GUIDED PRACTICE

1. **Vocabulary** Explain how you can tell whether a number is written in *scientific notation.*

SEE EXAMPLE 1 p. 452

**Find the value of each power of 10.**

2. $10^6$ 3. $10^{-5}$ 4. $10^{-4}$ 5. $10^8$

SEE EXAMPLE 2 p. 453

**Write each number as a power of 10.**

6. 10,000 7. 0.000001 8. 100,000,000,000,000,000

SEE EXAMPLE 3 p. 453

**Find the value of each expression.**

9. $650.3 \times 10^6$ 10. $48.3 \times 10^{-4}$ 11. $92 \times 10^{-3}$

SEE EXAMPLE 4 p. 454

12. **Astronomy** A light-year is the distance that light travels in a year and is equivalent to $9.461 \times 10^{12}$ km. Write this distance in standard form.

SEE EXAMPLE 5 p. 454

13. Order the list of numbers from least to greatest.
$8.5 \times 10^{-1}$, $3.6 \times 10^8$, $5.85 \times 10^{-3}$, $2.5 \times 10^{-1}$, $8.5 \times 10^8$

## PRACTICE AND PROBLEM SOLVING

**Independent Practice**

| For Exercises | See Example |
|---|---|
| 14–17 | 1 |
| 18–20 | 2 |
| 21–24 | 3 |
| 25–26 | 4 |
| 27 | 5 |

**Extra Practice**

Skills Practice p. S16
Application Practice p. S34

**Find the value of each power of 10.**

14. $10^3$ 15. $10^{-9}$ 16. $10^{-12}$ 17. $10^{14}$

**Write each number as a power of 10.**

18. 0.01 19. 1,000,000 20. 0.000000000000001

**Find the value of each expression.**

21. $9.2 \times 10^4$ 22. $1.25 \times 10^{-7}$ 23. $42 \times 10^{-5}$ 24. $0.05 \times 10^7$

25. **Biology** The human body is made of about $1 \times 10^{13}$ cells. Write this number in standard form.

26. **Statistics** At the beginning of the twenty-first century, the population of China was about 1,287,000,000. Write this number in scientific notation.

27. Order the list of numbers from least to greatest.
$2.13 \times 10^{-1}$, $3.12 \times 10^2$, $1.23 \times 10^{-3}$, $2.13 \times 10^1$, $1.32 \times 10^{-3}$, $3.12 \times 10^{-3}$

28. **Health** Donnell is allergic to pollen. The diameter of a grain of pollen is between $1.2 \times 10^{-5}$ m and $9 \times 10^{-5}$ m. Donnell's air conditioner has a filter that removes particles larger than $3 \times 10^{-7}$ m. Will the filter remove pollen? Explain.

29. **Entertainment** In the United States, a CD is certified platinum if it sells 1,000,000 copies. A CD that has gone 2 times platinum has sold 2,000,000 copies. How many copies has a CD sold if it has gone 27 times platinum? Write your answer in scientific notation.

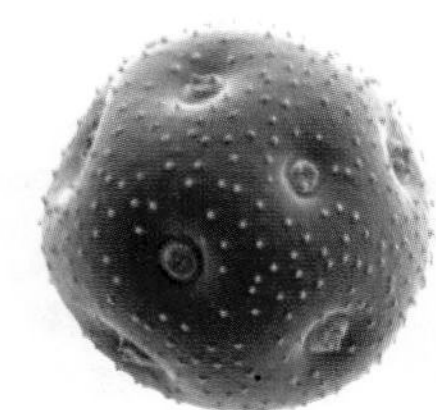

Grain of pollen, enlarged 1050 times

**Write each number in scientific notation.**

30. 40,080,000 31. 235,000 32. 170,000,000,000
33. 0.0000006 34. 0.000077 35. 0.0412

**State whether each number is written in scientific notation. If not, write it in scientific notation.**

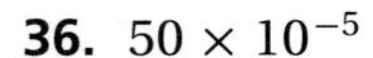

**36.** $50 \times 10^{-5}$ **37.** $8.1 \times 10^{-2}$ **38.** 1,200,000 **39.** $0.25 \times 10^{3}$

**40.** 0.1 **41.** $7 \times 10^{8}$ **42.** 48,000 **43.** $3.5 \times 10^{-6}$

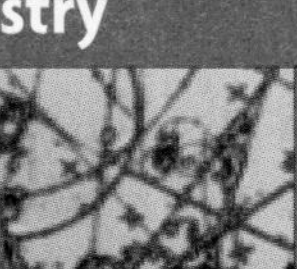

**LINK**

**Chemistry**

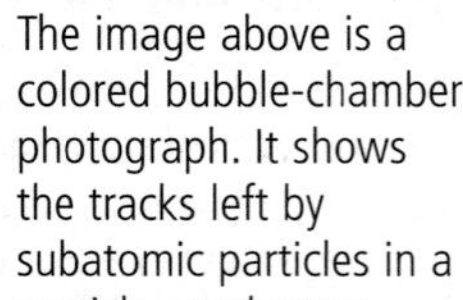

The image above is a colored bubble-chamber photograph. It shows the tracks left by subatomic particles in a particle accelerator.

**44. Chemistry** Atoms are made of three elementary particles: protons, electrons, and neutrons. The mass of a proton is about $1.67 \times 10^{-27}$ kg. The mass of an electron is about 0.000000000000000000000000000000911 kg. The mass of a neutron is about $1.68 \times 10^{-27}$ kg. Which particle has the least mass? (*Hint:* Compare the numbers after they are written in scientific notation.)

**45. Communication** This bar graph shows the increase of cellular telephone subscribers worldwide.

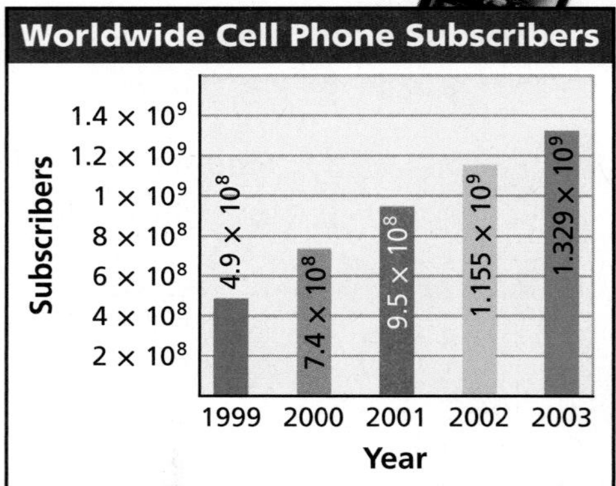


a. Write the number of subscribers for the following years in standard form: 1999, 2000, and 2003.

b. Zorah looks at the bar graph and says, "It looks like the number of cell phone subscribers nearly doubled from 2000 to 2003." Do you agree with Zorah? Use scientific notation to explain your answer.

**46. Measurement** In the metric system, the basic unit for measuring length is the meter (m). Other units for measuring length are based on the meter and powers of 10, as shown in the table.

| Selected Metric Lengths | |
|---|---|
| 1 millimeter (mm) = $10^{-3}$ m | 1 dekameter (dam) = $10^{1}$ m |
| 1 centimeter (cm) = $10^{-2}$ m | 1 hectometer (hm) = $10^{2}$ m |
| 1 decimeter (dm) = $10^{-1}$ m | 1 kilometer (km) = $10^{3}$ m |

a. Which lengths in the table are longer than a meter? Which are shorter than a meter? How do you know?

b. Evaluate each power of 10 in the table to check your answers to part **a.**

**47. Critical Thinking** Recall that $\frac{1}{10^3} = 10^{-3}$. Based on this information, complete the following statement: Dividing a number by $10^3$ is equivalent to multiplying by ▒.

**48. Write About It** When you change a number from scientific notation to standard form, explain how you know which way to move the decimal point and how many places to move it.

**MULTI-STEP TEST PREP**

**49.** This problem will prepare you for the Multi-Step Test Prep on page 474.

a. The speed of light is approximately $3 \times 10^{8}$ m/s. Write this number in standard form.

b. Why do you think it would be better to express this number in scientific notation rather than standard form?

c. The wavelength of a shade of red light is 0.00000068 meters. Write this number in scientific notation.

## TEST PREP

MA.N.2.1

50. There are about $3.2 \times 10^7$ seconds in one year. What is this number in standard form?

    (A) 0.000000032
    (B) 0.00000032
    (C) 32,000,000
    (D) 320,000,000

51. Which expression is the scientific notation for 82.35?

    (F) $8.235 \times 10^1$ (G) $823.5 \times 10^{-1}$ (H) $8.235 \times 10^{-1}$ (J) $0.8235 \times 10^2$

52. Which statement is correct for the list of numbers below?
    $2.35 \times 10^{-8}$, 0.000000029, $1.82 \times 10^8$, 1,290,000,000, $1.05 \times 10^9$

    (A) The list is in increasing order.
    (B) If 0.000000029 is removed, the list will be in increasing order.
    (C) If 1,290,000,000 is removed, the list will be in increasing order.
    (D) The list is in decreasing order.

## CHALLENGE AND EXTEND

53. **Technology** The table shows estimates of computer storage. A CD-ROM holds 700 MB. A DVD-ROM holds 4.7 GB. Estimate how many times more storage a DVD has than a CD. Explain how you found your answer.

| Computer Storage |
|---|
| 1 kilobyte (KB) ≈ 1000 bytes |
| 1 megabyte (MB) ≈ 1 million bytes |
| 1 gigabyte (GB) ≈ 1 billion bytes |

54. For parts **a–d**, use what you know about multiplying by powers of 10 and the Commutative and Associative Properties of Multiplication to find each product. Write each answer in scientific notation.

    **a.** $(3 \times 10^2)(2 \times 10^3)$ **b.** $(5 \times 10^8)(1.5 \times 10^{-6})$
    **c.** $(2.2 \times 10^{-8})(4 \times 10^{-3})$ **d.** $(2.5 \times 10^{-12})(2 \times 10^6)$
    **e.** Based on your answers to parts **a–d**, write a rule for multiplying numbers in scientific notation.
    **f.** Does your rule work when you multiply $(6 \times 10^3)(8 \times 10^5)$? Explain.

## SPIRAL REVIEW

**Define a variable and write an inequality for each situation. Graph the solutions.** *(Lesson 3-1)*

55. Melanie must wait at least 45 minutes for the results of her test.

56. Ulee's dog can lose no more than 8 pounds to stay within a healthy weight range.

57. Charlene must spend more than $50 to get the advertised discount.

**Solve each system by elimination.** *(Lesson 6-3)*

58. $\begin{cases} x + y = 8 \\ x - y = 2 \end{cases}$ 59. $\begin{cases} 2x + y = -3 \\ 2x + 3y = -1 \end{cases}$ 60. $\begin{cases} x - 6y = -3 \\ 3x + 4y = 13 \end{cases}$

**Evaluate each expression for the given value(s) of the variable(s).** *(Lesson 7-1)*

61. $t^{-4}$ for $t = 2$ 62. $(-8m)^0$ for $m = -5$ 63. $3a^{-3}b^0$ for $a = 5$ and $b = 6$

Use with Lesson 7-3

# Explore Properties of Exponents

You can use patterns to find some properties of exponents.

**MA.N.2.1** Represent numerical expressions with exponents in their simplest forms.
**MA.N.2.2** Represent algebraic expressions with exponents in their simplest forms.

## Activity 1

1. Copy and complete the table below.

| $3^2 \cdot 3^3 = (3 \cdot 3)(3 \cdot 3 \cdot 3) = 3^{\blacksquare}$ |
|---|
| $5^4 \cdot 5^2 = (\blacksquare \cdot \blacksquare \cdot \blacksquare \cdot \blacksquare)(\blacksquare \cdot \blacksquare) = 5^{\blacksquare}$ |
| $4^3 \cdot 4^3 = (\blacksquare \cdot \blacksquare \cdot \blacksquare)(\blacksquare \cdot \blacksquare \cdot \blacksquare) = \blacksquare^{\blacksquare}$ |
| $2^3 \cdot 2^2 = (\blacksquare \cdot \blacksquare \cdot \blacksquare)(\blacksquare \cdot \blacksquare) = \blacksquare^{\blacksquare}$ |
| $6^3 \cdot 6^4 = (\quad)(\quad) =$ |

2. Examine your completed table. Look at the two exponents in each factor and the exponent in the final answer. What pattern do you notice?

3. Use your pattern to make a conjecture: $a^m \cdot a^n = a^{\blacksquare}$.

## Try This

**Use your conjecture to write each product below as a single power.**

**1.** $5^3 \cdot 5^5$ **2.** $7^2 \cdot 7^2$ **3.** $10^8 \cdot 10^4$ **4.** $8^7 \cdot 8^3$

**5.** Make a table similar to the one above to explore what happens when you multiply more than two powers that have the same base. Then write a conjecture in words to summarize what you find.

## Activity 2

1. Copy and complete the table below.

| $(2^3)^2 = 2^3 \cdot 2^3 = (\blacksquare \cdot \blacksquare \cdot \blacksquare)(\blacksquare \cdot \blacksquare \cdot \blacksquare) = 2^{\blacksquare}$ |
|---|
| $(2^2)^3 = \blacksquare \cdot \blacksquare \cdot \blacksquare = (\blacksquare \cdot \blacksquare)(\blacksquare \cdot \blacksquare)(\blacksquare \cdot \blacksquare) = \blacksquare^{\blacksquare}$ |
| $(4^2)^4 = \blacksquare \cdot \blacksquare \cdot \blacksquare \cdot \blacksquare = (\blacksquare \cdot \blacksquare)(\blacksquare \cdot \blacksquare)(\blacksquare \cdot \blacksquare)(\blacksquare \cdot \blacksquare) = \blacksquare^{\blacksquare}$ |
| $(3^4)^2 = \blacksquare \cdot \blacksquare = (\blacksquare \cdot \blacksquare \cdot \blacksquare \cdot \blacksquare)(\blacksquare \cdot \blacksquare \cdot \blacksquare \cdot \blacksquare) = \blacksquare^{\blacksquare}$ |
| $(6^3)^4 =$ |

2. Examine your completed table. Look at the two exponents in the original expression and the exponent in the final answer. What pattern do you notice?

3. Use your pattern to make a conjecture: $(a^m)^n = a^{\blacksquare}$.

## Try This

**Use your conjecture to write each product below as a single power.**

**6.** $(5^3)^2$ **7.** $(7^2)^2$ **8.** $(3^3)^4$ **9.** $(9^7)^3$

**10.** Make a table similar to the one in Activity 2 to explore what happens when you raise a power to two powers, for example, $\left[(4^2)^3\right]^3$. Then write a conjecture in words to summarize what you find.

## Activity 3

**1** Copy and complete the table below.

| |
|---|
| $(ab)^3 = (ab)(ab)(ab) = (a \cdot a \cdot a)(b \cdot b \cdot b) = a^{\blacksquare} b^{\blacksquare}$ |
| $(mn)^4 = (\blacksquare)(\blacksquare)(\blacksquare)(\blacksquare) = (\blacksquare \cdot \blacksquare \cdot \blacksquare \cdot \blacksquare)(\blacksquare \cdot \blacksquare \cdot \blacksquare \cdot \blacksquare) = \blacksquare^{\blacksquare} \blacksquare^{\blacksquare}$ |
| $(xy)^2 = (\blacksquare)(\blacksquare) = (\blacksquare \cdot \blacksquare)(\blacksquare \cdot \blacksquare) = \blacksquare^{\blacksquare} \blacksquare^{\blacksquare}$ |
| $(cd)^5 = (\blacksquare)(\blacksquare)(\blacksquare)(\blacksquare)(\blacksquare) = (\blacksquare \cdot \blacksquare \cdot \blacksquare \cdot \blacksquare \cdot \blacksquare)(\blacksquare \cdot \blacksquare \cdot \blacksquare \cdot \blacksquare \cdot \blacksquare) = \blacksquare^{\blacksquare} \blacksquare^{\blacksquare}$ |
| $(pq)^6 =$ |

**2** Examine your completed table. Look at the original expression and the final answer. What pattern do you notice?

**3** Use your pattern to make a conjecture: $(ab)^n = a^{\blacksquare} b^{\blacksquare}$.

## Try This

**Use your conjecture to write each power below as a product.**

**11.** $(rs)^8$ **12.** $(yz)^9$ **13.** $(ab)^7$ **14.** $(xz)^{12}$

**15.** Look at the first row of your table. What property or properties allow you to write $(ab)(ab)(ab)$ as $(a \cdot a \cdot a)(b \cdot b \cdot b)$?

**16.** Make a table similar to the one above to explore what happens when you raise a product containing more than two factors to a power, for example, $(xyz)^7$. Then write a conjecture in words to summarize what you find.

# 7-3 Multiplication Properties of Exponents

**MA.N.2.1** Represent numerical expressions with exponents in their simplest forms.
*Also* **MA.N.2.2**

***Objective***
Use multiplication properties of exponents to evaluate and simplify expressions.

**Who uses this?**
Astronomers can multiply expressions with exponents to find the distance between objects in space. (See Example 2.)

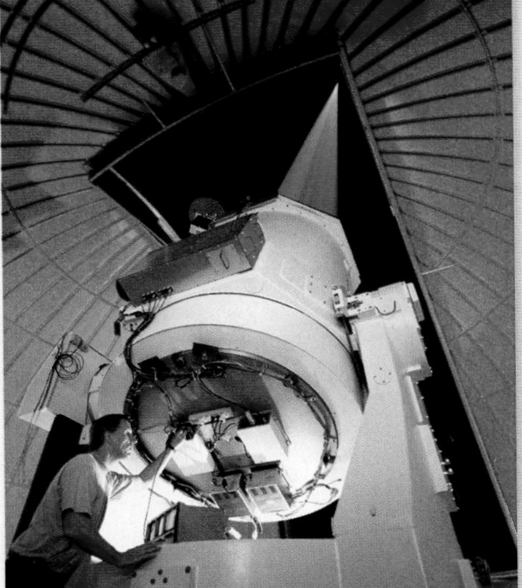

You have seen that exponential expressions are useful when writing very small or very large numbers. To perform operations on these numbers, you can use properties of exponents. You can also use these properties to simplify your answer.

In this lesson, you will learn some properties that will help you simplify exponential expressions containing multiplication.

**Simplifying Exponential Expressions**

**An exponential expression is completely simplified if...**

- There are no negative exponents.
- The same base does not appear more than once in a product or quotient.
- No powers are raised to powers.
- No products are raised to powers.
- No quotients are raised to powers.
- Numerical coefficients in a quotient do not have any common factor other than 1.

| Examples | Nonexamples |
|---|---|
| $\frac{b}{a}$ $\quad x^3$ $\quad z^{12}$ $\quad a^4b^4$ $\quad \frac{s^5}{t^5}$ $\quad \frac{5a^2}{2b}$ | $a^{-2}ba$ $\quad x \cdot x^2$ $\quad (z^3)^4$ $\quad (ab)^4$ $\quad \left(\frac{s}{t}\right)^5$ $\quad \frac{10a^2}{4b}$ |

Products of powers with the same base can be found by writing each power as repeated multiplication.

$$3^5 \cdot 3^2 = (3 \cdot 3 \cdot 3 \cdot 3 \cdot 3) \cdot (3 \cdot 3) = 3^7$$

Notice the relationship between the exponents in the factors and the exponent in the product: $5 + 2 = 7$.

**Product of Powers Property**

| WORDS | NUMBERS | ALGEBRA |
|---|---|---|
| The product of two powers with the same base equals that base raised to the sum of the exponents. | $6^7 \cdot 6^4 = 6^{7+4} = 6^{11}$ | If $a$ is any nonzero real number and $m$ and $n$ are integers, then $a^m \cdot a^n = a^{m+n}$. |

## EXAMPLE 1 Finding Products of Powers

**Simplify.**

**A** $2^5 \cdot 2^6$

$2^5 \cdot 2^6$

$2^{5+6}$ — *Since the powers have the same base, keep the base and add the exponents.*

$2^{11}$

**B** $4^2 \cdot 3^{-2} \cdot 4^5 \cdot 3^6$

$4^2 \cdot 3^{-2} \cdot 4^5 \cdot 3^6$

$(4^2 \cdot 4^5) \cdot (3^{-2} \cdot 3^6)$ — *Group powers with the same base together.*

$4^{2+5} \cdot 3^{-2+6}$ — *Add the exponents of powers with the same base.*

$4^7 \cdot 3^4$

**C** $a^4 \cdot b^5 \cdot a^2$

$a^4 \cdot b^5 \cdot a^2$

$(a^4 \cdot a^2) \cdot b^5$ — *Group powers with the same base together.*

$a^6 \cdot b^5$ — *Add the exponents of powers with the same base.*

$a^6b^5$

**D** $y^2 \cdot y \cdot y^{-4}$

$(y^2 \cdot y^1) \cdot y^{-4}$ — *Group the first two powers.*

$y^3 \cdot y^{-4}$ — *The first two powers have the same base, so add the exponents.*

$y^{-1}$ — *The two remaining powers have the same base, so add the exponents.*

$\frac{1}{y}$ — *Write with a positive exponent.*

**Remember!**

A number or variable written without an exponent actually has an exponent of 1.

$10 = 10^1$

$y = y^1$

**Simplify.**

**1a.** $7^8 \cdot 7^4$

**1b.** $3^{-3} \cdot 5^8 \cdot 3^4 \cdot 5^2$

**1c.** $m \cdot n^{-4} \cdot m^4$

**1d.** $x \cdot x^{-1} \cdot x^{-3} \cdot x^{-4}$

## EXAMPLE 2 *Astronomy Application*

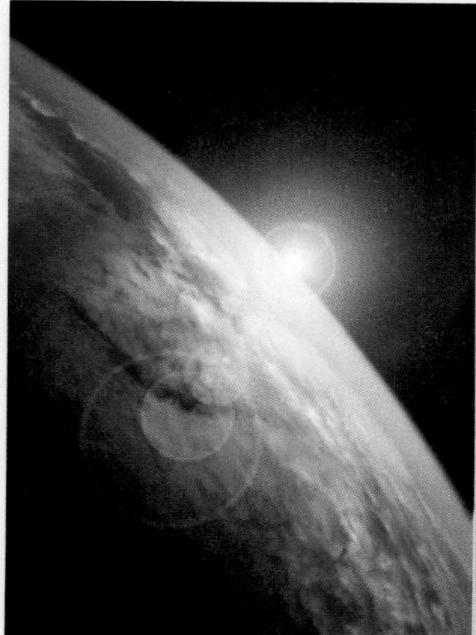

**Light from the Sun travels at about $1.86 \times 10^5$ miles per second. It takes about 500 seconds for the light to reach Earth. Find the approximate distance from the Sun to Earth. Write your answer in scientific notation.**

distance = rate × time

$= (1.86 \times 10^5) \times 500$

$= (1.86 \times 10^5) \times (5 \times 10^2)$ — *Write 500 in scientific notation.*

$= (1.86 \times 5) \times (10^5 \times 10^2)$ — *Use the Commutative and Associative Properties to group.*

$= 9.3 \times 10^7$ — *Multiply within each group.*

The Sun is about $9.3 \times 10^7$ miles from Earth.

**2.** Light travels at about $1.86 \times 10^5$ miles per second. Find the approximate distance that light travels in one hour. Write your answer in scientific notation.

To find a power of a power, you can use the meaning of exponents.

$$(4^3)^2 = 4^3 \cdot 4^3 = (4 \cdot 4 \cdot 4) \cdot (4 \cdot 4 \cdot 4) = 4^6$$

Notice the relationship between the exponents in the original power and the exponent in the final power: $3 \cdot 2 = 6$.

**Power of a Power Property**

| WORDS | NUMBERS | ALGEBRA |
|---|---|---|
| A power raised to another power equals that base raised to the product of the exponents. | $(6^7)^4 = 6^{7 \cdot 4} = 6^{28}$ | If $a$ is any nonzero real number and $m$ and $n$ are integers, then $(a^m)^n = a^{mn}$. |

## EXAMPLE 3 Finding Powers of Powers

**Simplify.**

**A** $(7^4)^3$

$7^{4 \cdot 3}$ *Use the Power of a Power Property.*

$7^{12}$ *Simplify.*

**B** $(3^6)^0$

$3^{6 \cdot 0}$ *Use the Power of a Power Property.*

$3^0$ *Zero multiplied by any number is zero.*

$1$ *Any number raised to the zero power is 1.*

**C** $(x^2)^{-4} \cdot x^5$

$x^{2 \cdot (-4)} \cdot x^5$ *Use the Power of a Power Property.*

$x^{-8} \cdot x^5$ *Simplify the exponent of the first term.*

$x^{-8+5}$ *Since the powers have the same base, add the exponents.*

$x^{-3}$

$\frac{1}{x^3}$ *Write with a positive exponent.*

**Simplify.**

**3a.** $(3^4)^5$ **3b.** $(6^0)^3$ **3c.** $(a^3)^4 \cdot (a^{-2})^{-3}$

## Student to Student

### *Multiplication Properties of Exponents*

**Briana Tyler**
Memorial High School

*Sometimes I can't remember when to add exponents and when to multiply them. When this happens, I write everything in expanded form.*

*For example, I would write $x^2 \cdot x^3$ as $(x \cdot x)(x \cdot x \cdot x) = x^5$. Then $x^2 \cdot x^3 = x^{2+3} = x^5$.*

*I would write $(x^2)^3$ as $x^2 \cdot x^2 \cdot x^2$, which is $(x \cdot x)(x \cdot x)(x \cdot x) = x^6$.*

*Then $(x^2)^3 = x^{2 \cdot 3} = x^6$.*

*This way I get the right answer even if I forget the properties.*

Powers of products can be found by using the meaning of an exponent.

$$(8x)^3 = 8x \cdot 8x \cdot 8x = 8 \cdot 8 \cdot 8 \cdot x \cdot x \cdot x = 8^3x^3 = 512x^3$$

Know it! Note

### Power of a Product Property

| WORDS | NUMBERS | ALGEBRA |
|---|---|---|
| A product raised to a power equals the product of each factor raised to that power. | $(2 \cdot 4)^3 = 2^3 \cdot 4^3$<br>$= 8 \cdot 64$<br>$= 512$ | If $a$ and $b$ are any nonzero real numbers and $n$ is any integer, then $(ab)^n = a^nb^n$. |

## EXAMPLE 4 Finding Powers of Products

**Simplify.**

**A** $(-3x)^2$

| | |
|---|---|
| $(-3)^2 \cdot x^2$ | *Use the Power of a Product Property.* |
| $9x^2$ | *Simplify.* |

**Caution!**

In Example 4B, the negative sign is not part of the base.
$-(3x)^2 = -1 \cdot (3x)^2$

**B** $-(3x)^2$

| | |
|---|---|
| $-(3^2 \cdot x^2)$ | *Use the Power of a Product Property.* |
| $-(9 \cdot x^2)$ | *Simplify.* |
| $-9x^2$ | |

**C** $(x^{-2} \cdot y^0)^3$

| | |
|---|---|
| $(x^{-2})^3 \cdot (y^0)^3$ | *Use the Power of a Product Property.* |
| $x^{-2 \cdot 3} \cdot y^{0 \cdot 3}$ | *Use the Power of a Power Property.* |
| $x^{-6} \cdot y^0$ | *Simplify.* |
| $x^{-6} \cdot 1$ | *Write $y^0$ as 1.* |
| $\frac{1}{x^6}$ | *Write with a positive exponent.* |

**Simplify.**

**4a.** $(4p)^3$ **4b.** $(-5t^2)^2$ **4c.** $(x^2y^3)^4 \cdot (x^2y^4)^{-4}$

## THINK AND DISCUSS

**1.** Explain why $(a^2)^3$ and $a^2 \cdot a^3$ are not equivalent expressions.

**2. GET ORGANIZED** Copy and complete the graphic organizer. In each box, supply the missing exponents. Then give an example for each property.

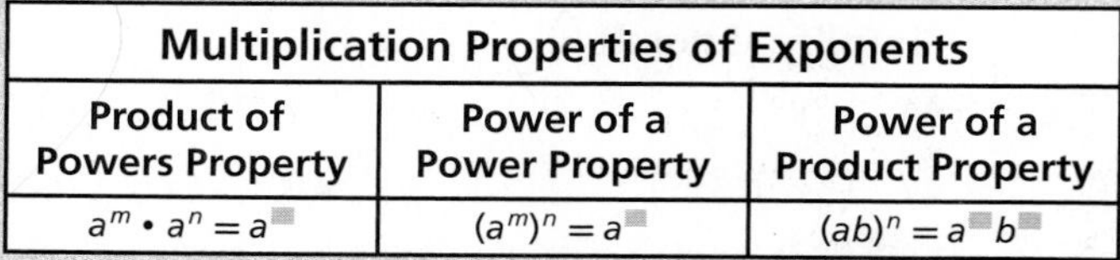

| Multiplication Properties of Exponents | | |
|---|---|---|
| Product of Powers Property | Power of a Power Property | Power of a Product Property |
| $a^m \cdot a^n = a^{■}$ | $(a^m)^n = a^{■}$ | $(ab)^n = a^{■}b^{■}$ |

# 7-3 Exercises

MA.N.2.1, MA.N.2.2

go.hrw.com
Homework Help Online
KEYWORD: MA7 7-3
Parent Resources Online
KEYWORD: MA7 Parent

## GUIDED PRACTICE

SEE EXAMPLE 1 p. 460

Simplify.

1. $2^2 \cdot 2^3$
2. $5^3 \cdot 5^3$
3. $n^6 \cdot n^2$
4. $x^2 \cdot x^{-3} \cdot x^4$

SEE EXAMPLE 2 p. 461

5. **Science** If you traveled in space at a speed of 1000 miles per hour, how far would you travel in $7.5 \times 10^5$ hours? Write your answer in scientific notation.

SEE EXAMPLE 3 p. 462

Simplify.

6. $(x^2)^5$
7. $(y^4)^8$
8. $(p^3)^3$
9. $(3^{-2})^2$
10. $(a^{-3})^4 \cdot (a^7)^2$
11. $xy \cdot (x^2)^3 \cdot (y^3)^4$

SEE EXAMPLE 4 p. 463

12. $(2t)^5$
13. $(6k)^2$
14. $(r^2s)^7$
15. $(-2x^5)^3$
16. $-(2x^5)^3$
17. $(a^2b^2)^5 \cdot (a^{-5})^2$

## PRACTICE AND PROBLEM SOLVING

**Independent Practice**

| For Exercises | See Example |
|---|---|
| 18–21 | 1 |
| 22 | 2 |
| 23–28 | 3 |
| 29–34 | 4 |

**Extra Practice**
Skills Practice p. S16
Application Practice p. S34

Simplify.

18. $3^3 \cdot 2^3 \cdot 3$
19. $6 \cdot 6^2 \cdot 6^3 \cdot 6^2$
20. $a^5 \cdot a^0 \cdot a^{-5}$
21. $x^7 \cdot x^{-6} \cdot y^{-3}$

22. **Geography** Rhode Island is the smallest state in the United States. Its land area is about $2.9 \times 10^{10}$ square feet. Alaska, the largest state, is about $5.5 \times 10^2$ times as large as Rhode Island. What is the land area of Alaska in square feet? Write your answer in scientific notation.

Simplify.

23. $(2^3)^3$
24. $(3^6)^0$
25. $(x^2)^{-1}$
26. $(b^4)^6 \cdot b$
27. $b \cdot (a^3)^4 \cdot (b^{-2})^3$
28. $(x^4)^2 \cdot (x^{-1})^{-4}$
29. $(3x)^3$
30. $(5w^8)^2$
31. $(p^4q^2)^7$
32. $(-4x^3)^4$
33. $-(4x^3)^4$
34. $(x^3y^4)^3 \cdot (xy^3)^{-2}$

Find the missing exponent in each expression.

35. $a^{■}a^4 = a^{10}$
36. $(a^{■})^4 = a^{12}$
37. $(a^2b^{■})^4 = a^8b^{12}$
38. $(a^3b^6)^{■} = \frac{1}{a^9b^{18}}$
39. $(b^2)^{-4} = \frac{1}{b^{■}}$
40. $a^{■} \cdot a^6 = a^6$

 **Geometry** Write an expression for the area of each figure.

41. 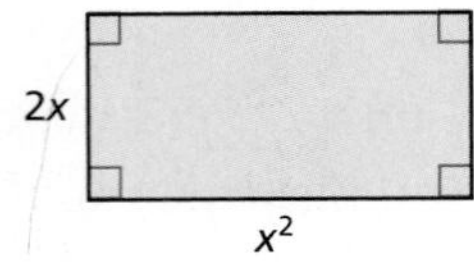


42. 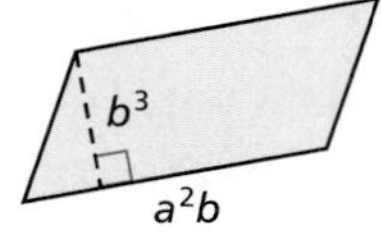


43. 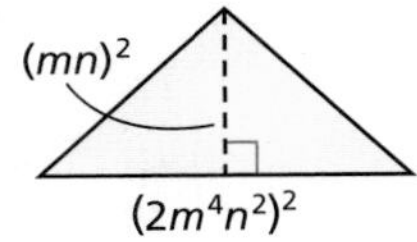


Simplify, if possible.

44. $x^6y^5$
45. $(2x^2)^2 \cdot (3x^3)^3$
46. $x^2 \cdot y^{-3} \cdot x^{-2} \cdot y^{-3}$
47. $(5x^2)(5x^2)^2$
48. $-(x^2)^4(-x^2)^4$
49. $a^3 \cdot a^0 \cdot 3a^3$
50. $(ab)^3(ab)^{-2}$
51. $10^2 \cdot 10^{-4} \cdot 10^5$
52. $(x^2y^2)^2(x^2y)^{-2}$

**53. Astronomy** The graph shows the approximate time it takes light from the Sun, which travels at a speed of $1.86 \times 10^5$ miles per second, to reach several planets. Find the approximate distance from the Sun to each planet in the graph. Write your answers in scientific notation. (*Hint:* Remember $d = rt$.)

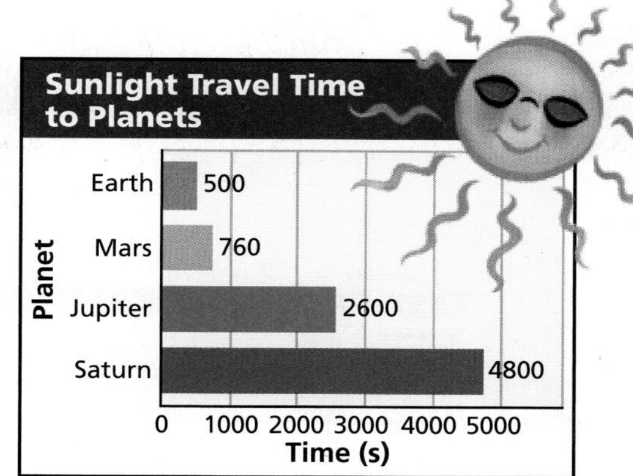


**54. Geometry** The volume of a rectangular prism can be found by using the formula $V = \ell wh$ where $\ell$, $w$, and $h$ represent the length, width, and height of the prism. Find the volume of a rectangular prism whose dimensions are $3a^2$, $4a^5$, and $4a^2b^2$.

**55. ///ERROR ANALYSIS///** Explain the error in each simplification below. What is the correct answer in each case?

**a.** $x^2 \cdot x^4 = x^8$ **b.** $(x^4)^5 = x^9$ **c.** $(x^2)^3 = x^{2^3} = x^8$

**Simplify.**

**56.** $(-3x^2)(5x^{-3})$ **57.** $(a^4b)(a^3b^{-6})$ **58.** $(6w^5)(2v^2)(w^6)$

**59.** $(3m^7)(m^2n)(5m^3n^8)$ **60.** $(b^2)^{-2}(b^4)^5$ **61.** $(3st)^2t^5$

**62.** $(2^2)^2(x^5y)^3$ **63.** $(-t)(-t)^2(-t^4)$ **64.** $(2m^2)(4m^4)(8n)^2$

**65. Estimation** Estimate the value of each expression. Explain how you estimated.

**a.** $[(-3.031)^2]^3$ **b.** $(6.2085 \times 10^2) \times (3.819 \times 10^{-5})$

**66. Physical Science** The speed of sound at sea level is about 344 meters per second. The speed of light is about $8.7 \times 10^5$ times faster than the speed of sound. What is the speed of light in meters per second? Write your answer in scientific notation and in standard form.

**67. Write About It** Is $(x^2)^3$ equal to $(x^3)^2$? Explain.

**68. Biology** A newborn baby has about 26,000,000,000 cells. An adult has about $1.9 \times 10^3$ times as many cells as a baby. About how many cells does an adult have? Write your answer in scientific notation.

**Simplify.**

**69.** $(-4k)^2 + k^2$ **70.** $-3z^3 + (-3z)^3$ **71.** $(2x^2)^2 + 2(x^2)^2$

**72.** $(2r)^2s^2 + 6(rs)^2 + 1$ **73.** $(3a)^2b^3 + 3(ab)^2(2b)$ **74.** $(x^2)(x^2)(x^2) + 3x^2$

**75.** This problem will prepare you for the Multi-Step Test Prep on page 474.

**a.** The speed of light $v$ is the product of the frequency $f$ and the wavelength $w$: ($v = fw$). Wavelengths are often measured in *nanometers*. *Nano* means $10^{-9}$, so 1 nanometer $= 10^{-9}$ meters. What is 600 nanometers in meters? Write your answer in scientific notation.

**b.** Use your answer from part ***a*** to find the speed of light in meters per second if $f = 5 \times 10^{14}$ Hz.

**c.** Explain why you can rewrite $(6 \times 10^{-7})(5 \times 10^{14})$ as $(6 \times 5)(10^{-7})(10^{14})$.

**Critical Thinking** Rewrite each expression so that it has only one exponent. (*Hint:* You may use parentheses.)

76. $c^3d^3$ 77. $36a^2b^2$ 78. $\frac{8a^3}{b^3}$ 79. $\frac{k^{-2}}{4m^2n^2}$

## TEST PREP

MA.N.2.1, MA.N.2.2

80. Which of the following is equivalent to $x^2 \cdot x^0$?
 (A) 0 (B) 1 (C) $x^2$ (D) $x^{20}$

81. Which of the following is equivalent to $(3 \times 10^5)(4 \times 10^2)$?
 (F) $7 \times 10^7$ (G) $7 \times 10^{10}$ (H) $1.2 \times 10^8$ (J) $1.2 \times 10^{11}$

82. What is the value of $n^3$ when $n = 4 \times 10^5$?
 (A) $1.2 \times 10^9$ (B) $1.2 \times 10^{16}$ (C) $6.4 \times 10^9$ (D) $6.4 \times 10^{16}$

83. Which represents the area of the triangle?
 (F) $6x^2$ (H) $7x^2$
 (G) $12x^2$ (J) $24x^2$

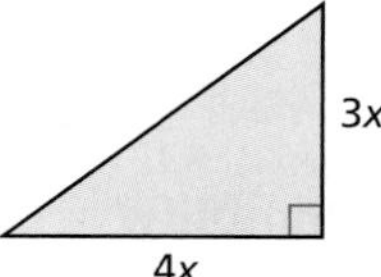


## CHALLENGE AND EXTEND

**Simplify.**

84. $3^2 \cdot 3^x$ 85. $(3^2)^x$ 86. $(x^yz)^2$

87. $(x+1)^{-2}(x+1)^3$ 88. $(x+1)^2(x+1)^{-3}$ 89. $(x^y \cdot x^z)^3$

90. $(4^x)^x$ 91. $(x^x)^x$ 92. $(3x)^{2y}$

**Find the value of *x*.**

93. $5^x \cdot 5^4 = 5^8$ 94. $7^3 \cdot 7^x = 7^{12}$ 95. $(4^x)^3 = 4^{12}$ 96. $(6^2)^x = 6^{16}$

97. **Multi-Step** The edge of a cube measures $1.2 \times 10^{-2}$ m. What is the volume of the cube in cubic centimeters?

## SPIRAL REVIEW

**Find the value of *x* in each diagram.** *(Lesson 2-7)*

98. $\square ABCD \sim \square WXYZ$ 99. $\triangle ABC \sim \triangle RST$

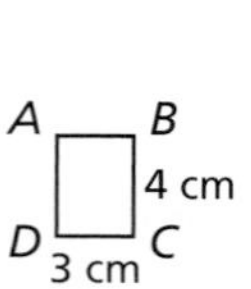


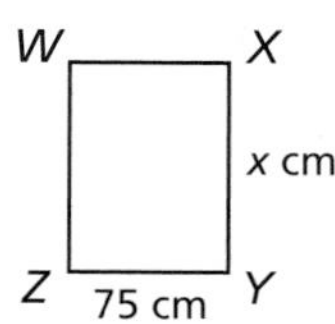


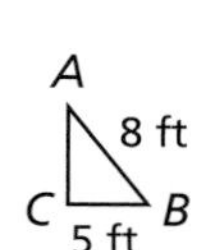


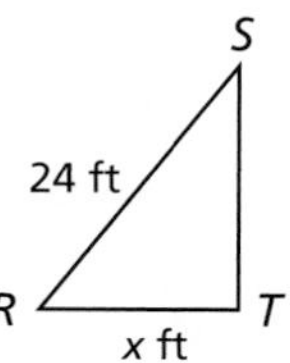


**Determine whether each sequence appears to be an arithmetic sequence. If so, find the common difference and the next three terms.** *(Lesson 4-6)*

100. 5, 1, −3, −7, … 101. −3, −2, 0, 3, … 102. 0.4, 1.0, 1.6, 2.2, …

**Write each number in standard form.** *(Lesson 7-2)*

103. $7.8 \times 10^6$ 104. $4.95 \times 10^{-4}$ 105. $983 \times 10^{-1}$ 106. $0.06 \times 10^8$

# 7-4 Division Properties of Exponents

**MA.N.2.1** Represent numerical expressions with exponents in their simplest forms.
*Also* **MA.N.2.2**

***Objective***
Use division properties of exponents to evaluate and simplify expressions.

**Who uses this?**
Economists can use expressions with exponents to calculate national debt statistics. (See Example 3.)

A quotient of powers with the same base can be found by writing the powers in factored form and dividing out common factors.

$$\frac{3^5}{3^3} = \frac{\cancel{3} \cdot \cancel{3} \cdot \cancel{3} \cdot 3 \cdot 3}{\cancel{3} \cdot \cancel{3} \cdot \cancel{3}} = 3 \cdot 3 = 3^2$$

Notice the relationship between the exponents in the original quotient and the exponent in the final answer: $5 - 3 = 2$.

**Quotient of Powers Property**

| WORDS | NUMBERS | ALGEBRA |
|---|---|---|
| The quotient of two nonzero powers with the same base equals the base raised to the difference of the exponents. | $\frac{6^7}{6^4} = 6^{7-4} = 6^3$ | If $a$ is a nonzero real number and $m$ and $n$ are integers, then $\frac{a^m}{a^n} = a^{m-n}$. |

## EXAMPLE 1 Finding Quotients of Powers

**Simplify.**

**A** $\frac{3^8}{3^2}$

$$\frac{3^8}{3^2} = 3^{8-2}$$
$$= 3^6 = 729$$

**B** $\frac{x^5}{x^5}$

$$\frac{x^5}{x^5} = x^{5-5}$$
$$= x^0 = 1$$

**Helpful Hint**

$3^6 = 729$
Both $3^6$ and 729 are considered to be simplified.

**C** $\frac{a^5b^9}{(ab)^4}$

$$\frac{a^5b^9}{(ab)^4} = \frac{a^5b^9}{a^4b^4}$$
$$= a^{5-4} \cdot b^{9-4}$$
$$= a^1 \cdot b^5$$
$$= ab^5$$

**D** $\frac{2^3 \cdot 3^2 \cdot 5^7}{2 \cdot 3^4 \cdot 5^5}$

$$\frac{2^3 \cdot 3^2 \cdot 5^7}{2 \cdot 3^4 \cdot 5^5} = 2^{3-1} \cdot 3^{2-4} \cdot 5^{7-5}$$
$$= 2^2 \cdot 3^{-2} \cdot 5^2$$
$$= \frac{2^2 \cdot 5^2}{3^2}$$
$$= \frac{4 \cdot 25}{9} = \frac{100}{9}$$

**Simplify.**

**1a.** $\frac{2^9}{2^7}$ **1b.** $\frac{y}{y^4}$ **1c.** $\frac{m^5n^4}{(m^5)^2n}$ **1d.** $\frac{3^5 \cdot 2^4 \cdot 4^3}{3^4 \cdot 2^2 \cdot 4^6}$

## EXAMPLE 2 Dividing Numbers in Scientific Notation

**Simplify $(2 \times 10^8) \div (8 \times 10^5)$ and write the answer in scientific notation.**

$$(2 \times 10^8) \div (8 \times 10^5) = \frac{2 \times 10^8}{8 \times 10^5}$$

$$= \frac{2}{8} \times \frac{10^8}{10^5}$$ *Write as a product of quotients.*

$$= 0.25 \times 10^{8-5}$$ *Simplify each quotient.*

$$= 0.25 \times 10^3$$ *Simplify the exponent.*

$$= 2.5 \times 10^{-1} \times 10^3$$ *Write 0.25 in scientific notation as $2.5 \times 10^{-1}$.*

$$= 2.5 \times 10^{-1+3}$$ *The second two terms have the same base, so add the exponents.*

$$= 2.5 \times 10^2$$ *Simplify the exponent.*

**Writing Math**

You can "split up" a quotient of products into a product of quotients:

$$\frac{a \times c}{b \times d} = \frac{a}{b} \times \frac{c}{d}$$

Example:

$$\frac{3 \times 4}{5 \times 7} = \frac{3}{5} \times \frac{4}{7} = \frac{12}{35}$$

**2.** Simplify $(3.3 \times 10^6) \div (3 \times 10^8)$ and write the answer in scientific notation.

## EXAMPLE 3 *Economics Application*

**In the year 2000, the United States public debt was about $5.6 \times 10^{12}$ dollars. The population of the United States in that year was about $2.8 \times 10^8$ people. What was the average debt per person? Give your answer in standard form.**

To find the average debt per person, divide the total debt by the number of people.

$$\frac{\text{total debt}}{\text{number of people}} = \frac{5.6 \times 10^{12}}{2.8 \times 10^8}$$

$$= \frac{5.6}{2.8} \times \frac{10^{12}}{10^8}$$ *Write as a product of quotients.*

$$= 2 \times 10^{12-8}$$ *Simplify each quotient.*

$$= 2 \times 10^4$$ *Simplify the exponent.*

$$= 20{,}000$$ *Write in standard form.*

The average debt per person was about $20,000.

**3.** In 1990, the United States public debt was about $3.2 \times 10^{12}$ dollars. The population of the United States in 1990 was about $2.5 \times 10^8$ people. What was the average debt per person? Write your answer in standard form.

A power of a quotient can be found by first writing factors and then writing the numerator and denominator as powers.

$$\left(\frac{2}{3}\right)^3 = \frac{2}{3} \cdot \frac{2}{3} \cdot \frac{2}{3} = \frac{2 \cdot 2 \cdot 2}{3 \cdot 3 \cdot 3} = \frac{2^3}{3^3}$$

Notice that the exponents in the final answer are the same as the exponent in the original expression.

## Positive Power of a Quotient Property

| WORDS | NUMBERS | ALGEBRA |
|---|---|---|
| A quotient raised to a positive power equals the quotient of each base raised to that power. | $\left(\frac{3}{5}\right)^4 = \frac{3}{5} \cdot \frac{3}{5} \cdot \frac{3}{5} \cdot \frac{3}{5} = \frac{3 \cdot 3 \cdot 3 \cdot 3}{5 \cdot 5 \cdot 5 \cdot 5} = \frac{3^4}{5^4}$ | If $a$ and $b$ are nonzero real numbers and $n$ is a positive integer, then $\left(\frac{a}{b}\right)^n = \frac{a^n}{b^n}$. |

**EXAMPLE 4** **Finding Positive Powers of Quotients**

**Simplify.**

**A** $\left(\frac{3}{4}\right)^3$

$\left(\frac{3}{4}\right)^3 = \frac{3^3}{4^3}$ *Use the Power of a Quotient Property.*

$= \frac{27}{64}$ *Simplify.*

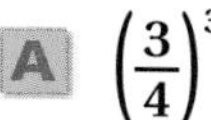

**B** $\left(\frac{2x^3}{yz}\right)^3$

$\left(\frac{2x^3}{yz}\right)^3 = \frac{(2x^3)^3}{(yz)^3}$ *Use the Power of a Quotient Property.*

$= \frac{2^3(x^3)^3}{y^3z^3}$ *Use the Power of a Product Property: $(2x^3)^3 = 2^3(x^3)^3$ and $(yz)^3 = y^3z^3$.*

$= \frac{8x^9}{y^3z^3}$ *Simplify $2^3$ and use the Power of a Power Property: $(x^3)^3 = x^{3 \cdot 3} = x^9$.*

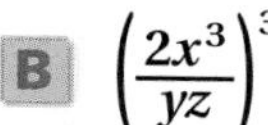

**Simplify.**

**4a.** $\left(\frac{2^3}{3^2}\right)^2$ **4b.** $\left(\frac{ab^4}{c^2d^3}\right)^5$ **4c.** $\left(\frac{a^3b}{a^2b^2}\right)^3$

Remember that $x^{-n} = \frac{1}{x^n}$. What if $x$ is a fraction?

$\left(\frac{a}{b}\right)^{-n} = \frac{1}{\left(\frac{a}{b}\right)^n} = 1 \div \left(\frac{a}{b}\right)^n$ *Write the fraction as division.*

$= 1 \div \frac{a^n}{b^n}$ *Use the Power of a Quotient Property.*

$= 1 \cdot \frac{b^n}{a^n}$ *Multiply by the reciprocal.*

$= \frac{b^n}{a^n}$ *Simplify.*

$= \left(\frac{b}{a}\right)^n$ *Use the Power of a Quotient Property.*

Therefore, $\left(\frac{a}{b}\right)^{-n} = \left(\frac{b}{a}\right)^n$.

## Negative Power of a Quotient Property

| WORDS | NUMBERS | ALGEBRA |
|---|---|---|
| A quotient raised to a negative power equals the reciprocal of the quotient raised to the opposite (positive) power. | $\left(\frac{2}{3}\right)^{-4} = \left(\frac{3}{2}\right)^{4} = \frac{3^4}{2^4}$ | If $a$ and $b$ are nonzero real numbers and $n$ is a positive integer, then $\left(\frac{a}{b}\right)^{-n} = \left(\frac{b}{a}\right)^{n} = \frac{b^n}{a^n}$. |

**EXAMPLE 5** **Finding Negative Powers of Quotients**

**Simplify.**

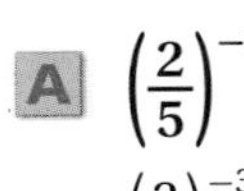

**A** $\left(\frac{2}{5}\right)^{-3}$

$$\left(\frac{2}{5}\right)^{-3} = \left(\frac{5}{2}\right)^{3}$$ *Rewrite with a positive exponent.*

$$= \frac{5^3}{2^3}$$ *Use the Power of a Quotient Property.*

$$= \frac{125}{8}$$ *$5^3 = 125$ and $2^3 = 8$.*

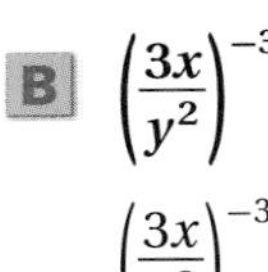

**B** $\left(\frac{3x}{y^2}\right)^{-3}$

$$\left(\frac{3x}{y^2}\right)^{-3} = \left(\frac{y^2}{3x}\right)^{3}$$ *Rewrite with a positive exponent.*

$$= \frac{(y^2)^3}{(3x)^3}$$ *Use the Power of a Quotient Property.*

*Use the Power of a Power Property: $(y^2)^3 = y^{2 \cdot 3} = y^6$.*

$$= \frac{y^6}{3^3x^3}$$ *Use the Power of a Product Property: $(3x)^3 = 3^3x^3$.*

$$= \frac{y^6}{27x^3}$$ *Simplify the denominator.*

**C** $\left(\frac{3}{4}\right)^{-1}\left(\frac{2x}{3y}\right)^{-2}$

$$\left(\frac{3}{4}\right)^{-1}\left(\frac{2x}{3y}\right)^{-2} = \left(\frac{4}{3}\right)^{1}\left(\frac{3y}{2x}\right)^{2}$$ *Rewrite each fraction with a positive exponent.*

$$= \frac{4}{3} \cdot \frac{(3y)^2}{(2x)^2}$$ *Use the Power of a Quotient Property.*

$$= \frac{4}{3} \cdot \frac{3^2y^2}{2^2x^2}$$ *Use the Power of a Product Property: $(3y)^2 = 3^2y^2$ and $(2x)^2 = 2^2x^2$.*

$$= \frac{{}^1\cancel{4}}{{}_1\cancel{3}} \cdot \frac{\cancel{9}^3y^2}{{}_1\cancel{4}x^2}$$ *Divide out common factors.*

$$= \frac{3y^2}{x^2}$$

**Helpful Hint**

Whenever all of the factors in the numerator or the denominator divide out, replace them with 1.

**Simplify.**

**5a.** $\left(\frac{4}{3^2}\right)^{-3}$ **5b.** $\left(\frac{2a}{b^2c^3}\right)^{-4}$ **5c.** $\left(\frac{s}{3}\right)^{-2}\left(\frac{9s^2}{t}\right)^{-1}$

## THINK AND DISCUSS

1. Compare the Quotient of Powers Property and the Product of Powers Property. Then compare the Power of a Quotient Property and the Power of a Product Property.

2. **GET ORGANIZED** Copy and complete the graphic organizer. In each cell, supply the missing information. Then give an example for each property.

| If *a* and *b* are nonzero real numbers and *m* and *n* are integers, then... | | |
|---|---|---|
| $\frac{a^m}{a^n} = \blacksquare$ | $\left(\frac{a}{b}\right)^n = \frac{\blacksquare}{\blacksquare}$ | $\left(\frac{a}{b}\right)^{-n} = \left(\frac{\blacksquare}{\blacksquare}\right)^{\blacksquare}$ |

# 7-4 Exercises

MA.N.2.1, MA.N.2.2

go.hrw.com
Homework Help Online
KEYWORD: MA7 7-4
Parent Resources Online
KEYWORD: MA7 Parent

### GUIDED PRACTICE

SEE EXAMPLE 1 p. 467

Simplify.

1. $\frac{5^8}{5^6}$
2. $\frac{2^2 \cdot 3^4 \cdot 4^4}{2^9 \cdot 3^5}$
3. $\frac{15x^6}{5x^6}$
4. $\frac{a^5b^6}{a^3b^7}$

SEE EXAMPLE 2 p. 468

Simplify each quotient and write the answer in scientific notation.

5. $(2.8 \times 10^{11}) \div (4 \times 10^8)$
6. $(5.5 \times 10^3) \div (5 \times 10^8)$
7. $(1.9 \times 10^4) \div (1.9 \times 10^4)$

SEE EXAMPLE 3 p. 468

8. **Sports** A star baseball player earns an annual salary of \$8.1 × $10^6$. There are 162 games in a baseball season. How much does this player earn per game? Write your answer in standard form.

SEE EXAMPLE 4 p. 469

Simplify.

9. $\left(\frac{2}{5}\right)^2$
10. $\left(\frac{x^2}{xy^3}\right)^3$
11. $\left(\frac{a^3}{(a^3b)^2}\right)^2$
12. $\frac{y^{10}}{y}$

SEE EXAMPLE 5 p. 470

13. $\left(\frac{3}{4}\right)^{-2}$
14. $\left(\frac{2x}{y^3}\right)^{-4}$
15. $\left(\frac{2}{3}\right)^{-1}\left(\frac{3a}{2b}\right)^{-2}$
16. $\left(\frac{x^3}{y^2}\right)^{-4}$

### PRACTICE AND PROBLEM SOLVING

Simplify.

17. $\frac{3^9}{3^6}$
18. $\frac{5^4 \cdot 3^3}{5^2 \cdot 3^2}$
19. $\frac{x^8y^3}{x^3y^3}$
20. $\frac{x^8y^4}{x^9yz}$

Simplify each quotient and write the answer in scientific notation.

21. $(4.7 \times 10^{-3}) \div (9.4 \times 10^3)$
22. $(8.4 \times 10^9) \div (4 \times 10^{-5})$
23. $(4.2 \times 10^{-5}) \div (6 \times 10^{-3})$
24. $(2.1 \times 10^2) \div (8.4 \times 10^5)$

| Independent Practice | |
|---|---|
| For Exercises | See Example |
| 17–20 | 1 |
| 21–24 | 2 |
| 25 | 3 |
| 26–29 | 4 |
| 30–33 | 5 |

**Extra Practice**
Skills Practice p. S16
Application Practice p. S34

25. **Astronomy** The mass of Earth is about $3 \times 10^{-3}$ times the mass of Jupiter. The mass of Earth is about $6 \times 10^{24}$ kg. What is the mass of Jupiter? Give your answer in scientific notation.

**Simplify.**

26. $\left(\frac{2}{3}\right)^4$
27. $\left(\frac{a^4}{b^2}\right)^3$
28. $\left(\frac{a^3b^2}{ab^3}\right)^6$
29. $\left(\frac{xy^2}{x^3y}\right)^3$
30. $\left(\frac{1}{7}\right)^{-3}$
31. $\left(\frac{x^2}{y^5}\right)^{-5}$
32. $\left(\frac{8w^7}{16}\right)^{-1}$
33. $\left(\frac{1}{4}\right)^{-2}\left(\frac{6x}{7}\right)^{-2}$

**Simplify, if possible.**

34. $\frac{x^6}{x^5}$
35. $\frac{8d^5}{4d^3}$
36. $\frac{x^2y^3}{a^2b^3}$
37. $\frac{(3x^3)^3}{(6x^2)^2}$
38. $\frac{(5x^2)^3}{5x^2}$
39. $\left(\frac{c^2a^3}{a^5}\right)^2$
40. $\left(\frac{3a}{a^3 \cdot a^0}\right)^3$
41. $\left(\frac{-p^4}{-5p^3}\right)^{-2}$
42. $\left(\frac{b^{-2}}{b^3}\right)^2$
43. $\left(\frac{10^2}{10^{-5} \cdot 10^5}\right)^{-1}$
44. $\left(\frac{x^2y^2}{x^2y}\right)^{-3}$
45. $\frac{(-x^2)^4}{-(x^2)^4}$

46. **Critical Thinking** How can you use the Quotient of a Power Property to explain the definition of $x^{-n}$? (*Hint:* Think of $\frac{1}{x^n}$ as $\frac{x^0}{x^n}$.)

47. **Geography** *Population density* is the number of people per unit of area. The area of the United States is approximately $9.37 \times 10^6$ square kilometers. The table shows population data from the U. S. Census Bureau.

| United States Population | |
|---|---|
| Year | Population (to nearest million) |
| 2000 | $2.81 \times 10^8$ |
| 1995 | $2.66 \times 10^8$ |
| 1990 | $2.48 \times 10^8$ |

Write the approximate population density (people per square kilometer) for each of the given years in scientific notation. Round decimals to the nearest hundredth.

48. **Chemistry** The pH of a solution is a number that describes the concentration of hydrogen ions in that solution. For example, if the concentration of hydrogen ions in a solution is $10^{-4}$, that solution has a pH of 4.

Lemon juice
pH 2

Apples
pH 3

Water
pH 7

Ammonia
pH 11

a. What is the concentration of hydrogen ions in lemon juice?
b. What is the concentration of hydrogen ions in water?
c. How many times more concentrated are the hydrogen ions in lemon juice than in water?

49. **Write About It** Explain how to simplify $\frac{4^5}{4^2}$. How is it different from simplifying $\frac{4^2}{4^5}$?

**Find the missing exponent(s).**

50. $\frac{x^{\blacksquare}}{x^4} = x^2$
51. $\frac{x^7}{x^{\blacksquare}} = x^4$
52. $\left(\frac{a^2}{b^{\blacksquare}}\right)^4 = \frac{a^8}{b^{12}}$
53. $\left(\frac{x^4}{y^{\blacksquare}}\right)^{-1} = \frac{y^3}{x^{\blacksquare}}$

**Multi-Step Test Prep**

**54.** This problem will prepare you for the Multi-Step Test Prep on page 474.

**a.** Yellow light has a wavelength of 589 nm. A nanometer (nm) is $10^{-9}$ m. What is 589 nm in meters? Write your answer in scientific notation.

**b.** The speed of light in air, $v$, is $3 \times 10^8$ m/s, and $v = fw$, where $f$ represents the frequency in hertz (Hz) and $w$ represents the wavelength in meters. What is the frequency of yellow light?

## Test Prep

MA.N.2.1, MA.N.2.2

**55.** Which of the following is equivalent to $(8 \times 10^6) \div (4 \times 10^2)$?

Ⓐ $2 \times 10^3$ Ⓑ $2 \times 10^4$ Ⓒ $4 \times 10^3$ Ⓓ $4 \times 10^4$

**56.** Which of the following is equivalent to $\left(\frac{x^{12}}{3xy^4}\right)^{-2}$?

Ⓕ $\frac{9y^8}{x^{22}}$ Ⓖ $\frac{3y^8}{x^{22}}$ Ⓗ $\frac{3y^6}{x^{12}}$ Ⓙ $\frac{6y^8}{x^{26}}$

**57.** Which of the following is equivalent to $\frac{(-3x)^4}{-(3x)^4}$?

Ⓐ $-1$ Ⓑ $1$ Ⓒ $-81x^4$ Ⓓ $\frac{1}{81x^4}$

## CHALLENGE AND EXTEND

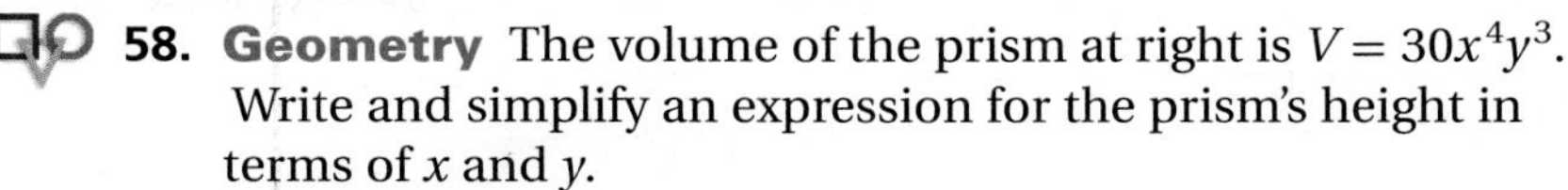

**58. Geometry** The volume of the prism at right is $V = 30x^4y^3$. Write and simplify an expression for the prism's height in terms of $x$ and $y$.

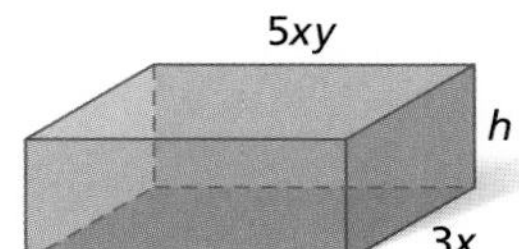


**59.** Simplify $\frac{3^{2x}}{3^{2x-1}}$.

**60.** Simplify $\frac{(x+1)^2}{(x+1)^3}$.

**61.** Copy and complete the table below to show how the Quotient of Powers Property can be found by using the Product of Powers Property.

| Statements | Reasons |
|---|---|
| 1. $a^{m-n} = a^{\blacksquare + \blacksquare}$ | 1. Subtraction is addition of the opposite. |
| 2. $= a^{\blacksquare} \cdot a^{\blacksquare}$ | 2. Product of Powers Property |
| 3. $= a^m \cdot \frac{1}{a^n}$ | 3. ____?____ |
| 4. $= \frac{a^m}{\blacksquare}$ | 4. Multiplication can be written as division. |

## SPIRAL REVIEW

**Find each square root.** *(Lesson 1-5)*

**62.** $\sqrt{36}$ **63.** $\sqrt{1}$ **64.** $-\sqrt{49}$ **65.** $\sqrt{144}$

**Solve each equation.** *(Lesson 2-4)*

**66.** $-2(x-1) + 4x = 5x + 3$ **67.** $x - 1 - (4x + 3) = 5x$

**Simplify.** *(Lesson 7-3)*

**68.** $3^2 \cdot 3^3$ **69.** $k^5 \cdot k^{-2} \cdot k^{-3}$ **70.** $(4t^5)^2$ **71.** $-(5x^4)^3$

# MULTI-STEP TEST PREP

## Exponents

**I See the Light!** The speed of light is the product of its frequency $f$ and its wavelength $w$. In air, the speed of light is $3 \times 10^8$ m/s.

1. Write an equation for the relationship described above, and then solve this equation for frequency. Write this equation as an equation with $w$ raised to a negative exponent.

2. Wavelengths of visible light range from 400 to 700 nanometers ($10^{-9}$ meters). Use a graphing calculator and the relationship you found in Problem 1 to graph frequency as a function of wavelength. Sketch the graph with the axes clearly labeled. Describe your graph.

3. The speed of light in water is $\frac{3}{4}$ of its speed in air. Find the speed of light in water.

4. When light enters water, some colors bend more than others. How much the light bends depends on its wavelength. This is what creates a rainbow. The frequency of green light is about $5.9 \times 10^{14}$ cycles per second. Find the wavelength of green light in water.

5. When light enters water, colors with shorter wavelengths bend more than colors with longer wavelengths. Violet light has a frequency of $7.5 \times 10^{14}$ cycles per second, and red light has a frequency of $4.6 \times 10^{14}$ cycles per second. Which of these colors of light will bend more when it enters water? Justify your answer.

# READY TO GO ON?

CHAPTER 7

SECTION 7A

## Quiz for Lessons 7-1 Through 7-4

### 7-1 Integer Exponents

**Evaluate each expression for the given value(s) of the variable(s).**

1. $t^{-6}$ for $t = 2$
2. $n^{-3}$ for $n = -5$
3. $x^{-3}y$ for $x = 4$ and $y = -2$
4. $p^0$ for $p = 9$
5. $(5 - d)^{-7}$ for $d = 6$
6. $r^0 s^{-2}$ for $r = 8$ and $s = 10$

**Simplify.**

7. $5k^{-3}$
8. $\dfrac{x^4}{y^{-6}}$
9. $8f^{-4} g^0$
10. $\dfrac{a^{-3}}{b^{-2}}$

11. **Measurement** Metric units can be written in terms of a base unit. The table shows some of these equivalencies. Simplify each expression.

| Selected Metric Prefixes | | | | | |
|---|---|---|---|---|---|
| Milli- | Centi- | Deci- | Deka- | Hecto- | Kilo- |
| $10^{-3}$ | $10^{-2}$ | $10^{-1}$ | $10^1$ | $10^2$ | $10^3$ |

### 7-2 Powers of 10 and Scientific Notation

12. Find the value of $10^4$.
13. Write 0.0000001 as a power of 10.
14. Write 100,000,000,000 as a power of 10.
15. Find the value of $82.1 \times 10^4$.
16. **Measurement** The lead in a mechanical pencil has a diameter of 0.5 mm. Write this number in scientific notation.

### 7-3 Multiplication Properties of Exponents

**Simplify.**

17. $2^2 \cdot 2^5$
18. $3^5 \cdot 3^{-3}$
19. $p^4 \cdot p^5$
20. $a^3 \cdot a^{-6} \cdot a^{-2}$

21. **Biology** A swarm of locusts was estimated to contain $2.8 \times 10^{10}$ individual insects. If each locust weighs about 2.5 grams, how much did this entire swarm weigh? Write your answer in scientific notation and in standard form.

**Simplify.**

22. $(3x^4)^3$
23. $(m^3n^2)^5$
24. $(-4d^7)^2$
25. $(cd^6)^3 \cdot (c^5d^2)^2$

### 7-4 Division Properties of Exponents

**Simplify.**

26. $\dfrac{6^9}{6^7}$
27. $\dfrac{12a^5}{3a^2}$
28. $\dfrac{x^4y^8}{x^6y^6}$
29. $\dfrac{5m^2n^4}{m^2n}$
30. $\left(\dfrac{3}{5}\right)^3$
31. $\left(\dfrac{4p^3}{2pq^4}\right)^2$
32. $\left(\dfrac{5}{6}\right)^{-2}$
33. $\left(\dfrac{x^3y^4}{xy^5}\right)^{-3}$

**Simplify each quotient and write the answer in scientific notation.**

34. $(8 \times 10^9) \div (2 \times 10^6)$
35. $(3.5 \times 10^5) \div (7 \times 10^8)$
36. $(1 \times 10^4) \div (4 \times 10^4)$

# 7-5 Polynomials

**Prep MA.A.1.1** Execute all operations with algebraic expressions (division by monomials only). *Also* **Prep MA.A.1, Prep MA.A.1.2**

***Objectives***

Classify polynomials and write polynomials in standard form.

Evaluate polynomial expressions.

***Vocabulary***

monomial
degree of a monomial
polynomial
degree of a polynomial
standard form of a polynomial
leading coefficient
quadratic
cubic
binomial
trinomial

**Who uses this?**

Pyrotechnicians can use polynomials to plan complex fireworks displays. (See Example 5.)

A **monomial** is a number, a variable, or a product of numbers and variables with whole-number exponents.

| Monomials | Not Monomials |
|---|---|
| $5 \quad x \quad -7xy \quad 0.5x^4$ | $-0.3x^{-2} \quad 4x - y \quad \frac{2}{x^3}$ |

The **degree of a monomial** is the sum of the exponents of the variables. A constant has degree 0.

## EXAMPLE 1 Finding the Degree of a Monomial

**Find the degree of each monomial.**

**A** $-2a^2b^4$

The degree is 6. *Add the exponents of the variables: 2 + 4 = 6*

**B** 4

$4x^0$ *There is no variable, but you can write 4 as $4x^0$.*

The degree is 0.

**C** $8y$

$8y^1$ *A variable written without an exponent has exponent 1.*

The degree is 1.

**Remember!**

The *terms* of an expression are the parts being added or subtracted. See Lesson 1-7.

**Find the degree of each monomial.**

**1a.** $1.5k^2m$ **1b.** $4x$ **1c.** $2c^3$

A **polynomial** is a monomial or a sum or difference of monomials. The **degree of a polynomial** is the degree of the term with the greatest degree.

## EXAMPLE 2 Finding the Degree of a Polynomial

**Find the degree of each polynomial.**

**A** $4x - 18x^5$

$4x$: degree 1 $\quad -18x^5$: degree 5 *Find the degree of each term.*

The degree of the polynomial is the greatest degree, 5.

**Find the degree of each polynomial.**

**B** $0.5x^2y + 0.25xy + 0.75$

$0.5x^2y$: degree 3 $\quad$ $0.25xy$: degree 2 $\quad$ $0.75$: degree 0

The degree of the polynomial is the greatest degree, 3.

**C** $6x^4 + 9x^2 - x + 3$

$6x^4$: degree 4 $\quad$ $9x^2$: degree 2 $\quad$ $-x$: degree 1 $\quad$ 3: degree 0

The degree of the polynomial is the greatest degree, 4.

**Find the degree of each polynomial.**

**2a.** $5x - 6$ **2b.** $x^3y^2 + x^2y^3 - x^4 + 2$

The terms of a polynomial may be written in any order. However, polynomials that contain only one variable are usually written in *standard form.*

The **standard form of a polynomial** that contains one variable is written with the terms in order from greatest degree to least degree. When written in standard form, the coefficient of the first term is called the **leading coefficient**.

## EXAMPLE 3 Writing Polynomials in Standard Form

**Write each polynomial in standard form. Then give the leading coefficient.**

**A** $20x - 4x^3 + 2 - x^2$

*Find the degree of each term. Then arrange them in descending order.*

$$\underbrace{20x}_{1}\ \underbrace{-4x^3}_{3}\ \underbrace{+2}_{0}\ \underbrace{-x^2}_{2} \rightarrow \underbrace{-4x^3}_{3}\ \underbrace{-x^2}_{2}\ \underbrace{+20x}_{1}\ \underbrace{+2}_{0}$$

Degree: 1 3 0 2 → 3 2 1 0

The standard form is $-4x^3 - x^2 + 20x + 2$. The leading coefficient is $-4$.

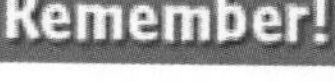

A variable written without a coefficient has a coefficient of 1.

$y^5 = 1y^5$

**B** $y^3 + y^5 + 4y$

*Find the degree of each term. Then arrange them in descending order.*

$$\underbrace{y^3}_{3}\ \underbrace{+y^5}_{5}\ \underbrace{+4y}_{1} \rightarrow \underbrace{y^5}_{5}\ \underbrace{+y^3}_{3}\ \underbrace{+4y}_{1}$$

Degree: 3 5 1 → 5 3 1

The standard form is $y^5 + y^3 + 4y$. The leading coefficient is 1.

**Write each polynomial in standard form. Then give the leading coefficient.**

**3a.** $16 - 4x^2 + x^5 + 9x^3$ **3b.** $18y^5 - 3y^8 + 14y$

Some polynomials have special names based on their degree and the number of terms they have.

| Degree | Name |
|---|---|
| 0 | Constant |
| 1 | Linear |
| 2 | **Quadratic** |
| 3 | **Cubic** |
| 4 | Quartic |
| 5 | Quintic |
| 6 or more | 6th degree, 7th degree, and so on |

| Terms | Name |
|---|---|
| 1 | Monomial |
| 2 | **Binomial** |
| 3 | **Trinomial** |
| 4 or more | Polynomial |

## EXAMPLE 4 Classifying Polynomials

**Classify each polynomial according to its degree and number of terms.**

**A** $5x - 6$

Degree: 1 Terms: 2 $5x - 6$ is a linear **binomial.**

**B** $y^2 + y + 4$

Degree: 2 Terms: 3 $y^2 + y + 4$ is a quadratic **trinomial.**

**C** $6x^7 + 9x^2 - x + 3$

Degree: 7 Terms: 4 $6x^7 + 9x^2 - x + 3$ is a 7th-degree **polynomial.**

**Classify each polynomial according to its degree and number of terms.**

**4a.** $x^3 + x^2 - x + 2$ **4b.** 6 **4c.** $-3y^8 + 18y^5 + 14y$

## EXAMPLE 5 *Physics Application*

**A firework is launched from a platform 6 feet above the ground at a speed of 200 feet per second. The firework has a 5-second fuse. The height of the firework in feet is given by the polynomial $-16t^2 + 200t + 6$, where $t$ is the time in seconds. How high will the firework be when it explodes?**

Substitute the time for $t$ to find the firework's height.

$-16t^2 + 200t + 6$

$-16(5)^2 + 200(5) + 6$ *The time is 5 seconds.*

$-16(25) + 200(5) + 6$

$-400 + 1000 + 6$ *Evaluate the polynomial by using the order of operations.*

606

When the firework explodes, it will be 606 feet above the ground.

**5. What if...?** Another firework with a 5-second fuse is launched from the same platform at a speed of 400 feet per second. Its height is given by $-16t^2 + 400t + 6$. How high will this firework be when it explodes?

### THINK AND DISCUSS

**1.** Explain why each expression is not a polynomial: $2x^2 + 3x^{-3}$; $1 - \frac{a}{b}$.

**2. GET ORGANIZED** Copy and complete the graphic organizer. In each circle, write an example of the given type of polynomial.

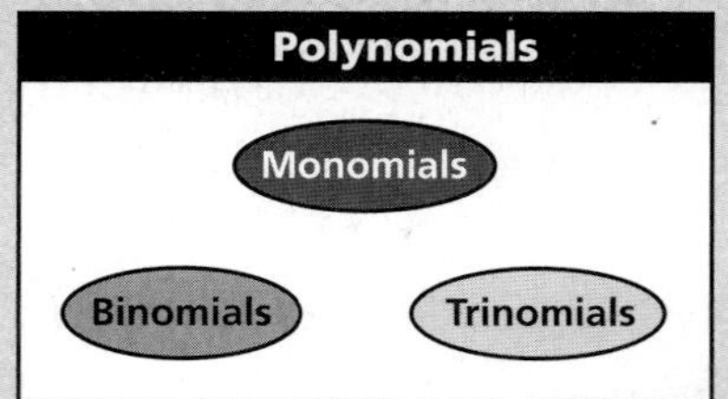

# 7-5 Exercises

go.hrw.com
Homework Help Online
KEYWORD: MA7 7-5
Parent Resources Online
KEYWORD: MA7 Parent

## GUIDED PRACTICE

**Vocabulary** Match each polynomial on the left with its classification on the right.

1. $2x^3 + 6$
2. $3x^3 + 4x^2 - 7$
3. $5x^2 - 2x + 3x^4 - 6$

a. quartic polynomial
b. quadratic polynomial
c. cubic trinomial
d. cubic binomial

SEE EXAMPLE 1 p. 476

Find the degree of each monomial.

4. $10^6$
5. $-7xy^2$
6. $0.4n^8$
7. $2$

SEE EXAMPLE 2 p. 476

Find the degree of each polynomial.

8. $x^2 - 2x + 1$
9. $0.75a^2b - 2a^3b^5$
10. $15y - 84y^3 + 100 - 3y^2$
11. $r^3 + r^2 - 5$
12. $a^3 + a^2 - 2a$
13. $3k^4 + k^3 - 2k^2 + k$

SEE EXAMPLE 3 p. 477

Write each polynomial in standard form. Then give the leading coefficient.

14. $-2b + 5 + b^2$
15. $9a^8 - 8a^9$
16. $5s^2 - 3s + 3 - s^7$
17. $2x + 3x^2 - 1$
18. $5g - 7 + g^2$
19. $3c^2 + 5c^4 + 5c^3 - 4$

SEE EXAMPLE 4 p. 478

Classify each polynomial according to its degree and number of terms.

20. $x^2 + 2x + 3$
21. $x - 7$
22. $8 + k + 5k^4$
23. $q^2 + 6 - q^3 + 3q^4$
24. $5k^2 + 7k^3$
25. $2a^3 + 4a^2 - a^4$

SEE EXAMPLE 5 p. 478

26. **Geometry** The surface area of a cone is approximated by the polynomial $3.14r^2 + 3.14r\ell$, where $r$ is the radius and $\ell$ is the slant height. Find the approximate surface area of this cone.

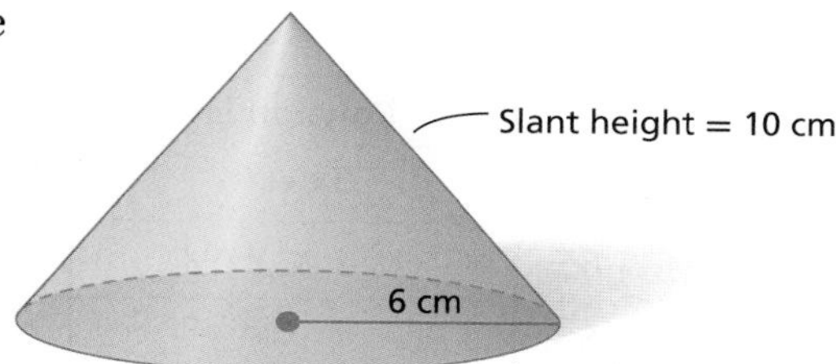


## PRACTICE AND PROBLEM SOLVING

**Independent Practice**

| For Exercises | See Example |
|---|---|
| 27–34 | 1 |
| 35–40 | 2 |
| 41–49 | 3 |
| 50–57 | 4 |
| 58 | 5 |

**Extra Practice**

Skills Practice p. S17
Application Practice p. S34

Find the degree of each monomial.

27. $3y^4$
28. $6k$
29. $2a^3b^2c$
30. $325$
31. $2y^4z^3$
32. $9m^5$
33. $p$
34. $5$

Find the degree of each polynomial.

35. $a^2 + a^4 - 6a$
36. $3^2b - 5$
37. $3.5y^2 - 4.1y - 6$
38. $-5f^4 + 2f^6 + 10f^8$
39. $4n^3 - 2n$
40. $4r^3 + 4r^6$

Write each polynomial in standard form. Then give the leading coefficient.

41. $2.5 + 4.9t^3 - 4t^2 + t$
42. $8a - 10a^2 + 2$
43. $x^7 - x + x^3 - x^5 + x^{10}$
44. $-m + 7 - 3m^2$
45. $3x^2 + 5x - 4 + 5x^3$
46. $-2n + 1 - n^2$
47. $4d + 3d^2 - d^3 + 5$
48. $3s^2 + 12s^3 + 6$
49. $4x^2 - x^5 - x^3 + 1$

Hybrid III is the crash test dummy used by the Insurance Institute for Highway Safety. During a crash test, sensors in the dummy's head, neck, chest, legs, and feet measure and record forces. Engineers study this data to help design safer cars.

**Classify each polynomial according to its degree and number of terms.**

**50.** $12$ **51.** $6k$ **52.** $3.5x^3 - 4.1x - 6$ **53.** $4g + 2g^2 - 3$

**54.** $2x^2 - 6x$ **55.** $6 - s^3 - 3s^4$ **56.** $c^2 + 7 - 2c^3$ **57.** $-y^2$

**58. Transportation** The polynomial $3.675v + 0.096v^2$ is used by transportation officials to estimate the stopping distance in feet for a car whose speed is $v$ miles per hour on flat, dry pavement. What is the stopping distance for a car traveling at 30 miles per hour?

**Tell whether each statement is sometimes, always, or never true.**

**59.** A monomial is a polynomial.

**60.** A trinomial is a 3rd-degree polynomial.

**61.** A binomial is a trinomial.

**62.** A polynomial has two or more terms.

**63. Geometry** A piece of 8.5-by-11-inch cardboard has identical squares cut from its corners. It is then folded into a box with no lid. The volume of the box in cubic inches is $4c^3 - 39c^2 + 93.5c$, where $c$ is the side length of the missing squares in inches.

**a.** What is the volume of the box if $c = 1$ in.?

**b.** What is the volume of the box if $c = 1.5$ in.?

**c.** What is the volume of the box if $c = 4.25$ in.?

**d. Critical Thinking** Does your answer to part **c** make sense? Explain why or why not.

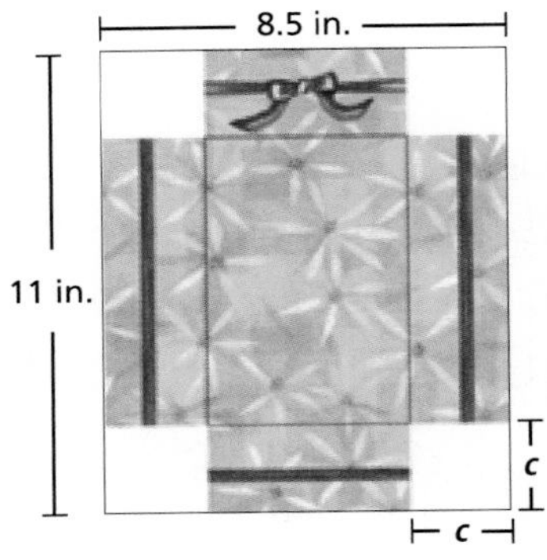


**Copy and complete the table by evaluating each polynomial for the given values of $x$.**

| | Polynomial | $x = -2$ | $x = 0$ | $x = 5$ |
|---|---|---|---|---|
| **64.** | $5x - 6$ | $5(-2) - 6 = -16$ | $5(0) - 6 = -6$ | |
| **65.** | $x^5 + x^3 + 4x$ | | | |
| **66.** | $-10x^2$ | | | |

**Give one example of each type of polynomial.**

**67.** quadratic trinomial **68.** linear binomial **69.** constant monomial

**70.** cubic monomial **71.** quintic binomial **72.** 12th-degree trinomial

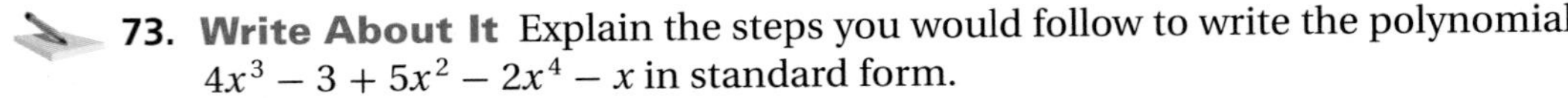

**73. Write About It** Explain the steps you would follow to write the polynomial $4x^3 - 3 + 5x^2 - 2x^4 - x$ in standard form.

**74.** This problem will prepare you for the Multi-Step Test Prep on page 508.

**a.** The perimeter of the rectangle shown is $12x + 6$. What is the degree of this polynomial?

**b.** The area of the rectangle is $8x^2 + 12x$. What is the degree of this polynomial?

$2x + 3$

$4x$

75. **ERROR ANALYSIS** Two students evaluated $4x - 3x^5$ for $x = -2$. Which is incorrect? Explain the error.

**A**

$4(-2) - 3(-2)^5$
$-8 + 6^5$
$-8 + 7776$
$7768$

**B**

$4(-2) - 3(-2)^5$
$-8 - 3(-32)$
$-8 + 96$
$88$

**TEST PREP**

NC Prep MA.A.1.1, Prep MA.A.1, Prep MA.A.1.2

76. Which polynomial has the highest degree?

Ⓐ $3x^8 - 2x^7 + x^6$ Ⓑ $5x - 100$ Ⓒ $25x^{10} + 3x^5 - 15$ Ⓓ $134x^2$

77. What is the value of $-3x^3 + 4x^2 - 5x + 7$ when $x = -1$?

Ⓕ 3 Ⓖ 13 Ⓗ 9 Ⓙ 19

78. **Short Response** A toy rocket is launched from the ground at 75 feet per second. The polynomial $-16t^2 + 75t$ gives the rocket's height in feet after $t$ seconds. Make a table showing the rocket's height after 1 second, 2 seconds, 3 seconds, and 4 seconds. At which of these times will the rocket be the highest?

## CHALLENGE AND EXTEND

79. **Medicine** Doctors and nurses use growth charts and formulas to tell whether a baby is developing normally. The polynomial $0.016m^3 - 0.390m^2 + 4.562m + 50.310$ gives the average length in centimeters of a baby boy between 0 and 10 months of age, where $m$ is the baby's age in months.

   **a.** What is the average length of a 2-month-old baby boy? a 5-month-old baby boy? Round your answers to the nearest centimeter.

   **b.** What is the average length of a newborn (0-month-old) baby boy?

   **c.** How could you find the answer to part **b** without doing any calculations?

80. Consider the binomials $4x^5 + x$, $4x^4 + x$, and $4x^3 + x$.

   **a.** Without calculating, which binomial has the greatest value for $x = 5$?

   **b.** Are there any values of $x$ for $4x^3 + x$ which will have the greatest value? Explain.

## SPIRAL REVIEW

81. Jordan is allowed 90 minutes of screen time per day. Today, he has already used $m$ minutes. Write an expression for the remaining number of minutes Jordan has today. *(Lesson 1-1)*

82. Pens cost $0.50 each. Giselle bought $p$ pens. Write an expression for the total cost of Giselle's pens. *(Lesson 1-1)*

**Classify each system. Give the number of solutions.** *(Lesson 6-4)*

83. $\begin{cases} y = -4x + 5 \\ 4x + y = 2 \end{cases}$ 84. $\begin{cases} 2x + 8y = 10 \\ 4y = -x + 5 \end{cases}$ 85. $\begin{cases} y = 3x + 2 \\ y = -5x - 6 \end{cases}$

**Simplify.** *(Lesson 7-4)*

86. $\dfrac{4^7}{4^4}$ 87. $\dfrac{x^6y^4}{x^4y^9}$ 88. $\left(\dfrac{2v^4}{vw^5}\right)^2$ 89. $\left(\dfrac{2p}{p^3}\right)^{-4}$

7-6 Algebra LAB

Use with Lesson 7-6

# Model Polynomial Addition and Subtraction

You can use algebra tiles to model polynomial addition and subtraction.

**MA.A.1** Use appropriate … strategies to combine … algebraic expressions. *Also* **MA.A.1.1**

go.hrw.com
Lab Resources Online
KEYWORD: MA7 LAB7

**KEY**

 = 1 = −1 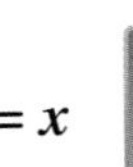 $= x$ 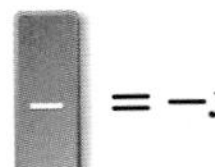 $= -x$  $= x^2$ 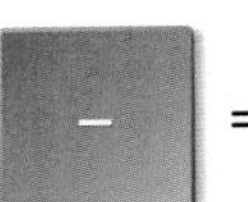 $= -x^2$

## Activity 1

**Use algebra tiles to find $(2x^2 - x) + (x^2 + 3x - 1)$.**

| MODEL | | ALGEBRA |
|---|---|---|
| | *Use tiles to represent all terms from both expressions.* | $(2x^2 - x) + (x^2 + 3x - 1)$ |
| | *Rearrange tiles so that like tiles are together. Like tiles are the same size and shape.* | $(2x^2 + x^2) + (-x + 3x) - 1$ |
| | *Remove any zero pairs.* | $3x^2 - x + x + 2x - 1$ |
| | *The remaining tiles represent the sum.* | $3x^2 + 2x - 1$ |

## Try This

**Use algebra tiles to find each sum.**

1. $(-2x^2 + 1) + (-x^2)$
2. $(3x^2 + 2x + 5) + (x^2 - x - 4)$
3. $(x - 3) + (2x - 2)$
4. $(5x^2 - 3x - 6) + (x^2 + 3x + 6)$
5. $-5x^2 + (2x^2 + 5x)$
6. $(x^2 - x - 1) + (6x - 3)$

**Use algebra tiles to find $(2x^2 + 6) - 4x^2$.**

| MODEL | ALGEBRA |
|---|---|
| *Use tiles to represent the terms in the first expression.* | $2x^2 + 6$ |
| To subtract $4x^2$, you would remove 4 yellow $x^2$-tiles, but there are not enough to do this. Remember that subtraction is the same as adding the opposite, so rewrite $(2x^2 + 6) - 4x^2$ as $(2x^2 + 6) + (-4x^2)$. | |
| *Add 4 red $x^2$-tiles.* | $2x^2 + 6 + (-4x^2)$ |
| *Rearrange tiles so that like tiles are together.* | $2x^2 + (-4x^2) + 6$ |
| *Remove zero pairs.* | $2x^2 + (-2x^2) + (-2x^2) + 6$ |
| *The remaining tiles represent the difference.* | $-2x^2 + 6$ |

## Try This

**Use algebra tiles to find each sum.**

**7.** $(6x^2 + 4x) - 3x^2$ **8.** $(2x^2 + x - 7) - 5x$ **9.** $(3x + 6) - 6$

**10.** $(8x + 5) - (-2x)$ **11.** $(x^2 + 2x) - (-4x^2 + x)$ **12.** $(3x^2 - 4) - (x^2 + 6x)$

**13.**  represents a zero pair. Use algebra tiles to model two other zero pairs.

**14.** When is it not necessary to "add the opposite" for polynomial subtraction using algebra tiles?

# 7-6 Adding and Subtracting Polynomials

**MA.A.1.1** Execute … operations with algebraic expressions…
*Also* **MA.A.1, MA.A.1.2**

***Objective***
Add and subtract polynomials.

**Who uses this?**
Business owners can add and subtract polynomials that model profit. (See Example 4.)

"This one pretty much sums it up."

© Mike Baldwin / Cornered
www.cartoonstock.com

Just as you can perform operations on numbers, you can perform operations on polynomials. To add or subtract polynomials, combine like terms.

## EXAMPLE 1 Adding and Subtracting Monomials

**Add or subtract.**

**A** $15m^3 + 6m^2 + 2m^3$

| | |
|---|---|
| $15m^3 + 6m^2 + 2m^3$ | *Identify like terms.* |
| $15m^3 + 2m^3 + 6m^2$ | *Rearrange terms so that like terms are together.* |
| $17m^3 + 6m^2$ | *Combine like terms.* |

**B** $3x^2 + 5 - 7x^2 + 12$

| | |
|---|---|
| $3x^2 + 5 - 7x^2 + 12$ | *Identify like terms.* |
| $3x^2 - 7x^2 + 5 + 12$ | *Rearrange terms so that like terms are together.* |
| $-4x^2 + 17$ | *Combine like terms.* |

**C** $0.9y^5 - 0.4y^5 + 0.5x^5 + y^5$

| | |
|---|---|
| $0.9y^5 - 0.4y^5 + 0.5x^5 + y^5$ | *Identify like terms.* |
| $0.9y^5 - 0.4y^5 + y^5 + 0.5x^5$ | *Rearrange terms so that like terms are together.* |
| $1.5y^5 + 0.5x^5$ | *Combine like terms.* |

**D** $2x^2y - x^2y - x^2y$

| | |
|---|---|
| $2x^2y - x^2y - x^2y$ | *All terms are like terms.* |
| $0$ | *Combine.* |

**Remember!**
Like terms are constants or terms with the same variable(s) raised to the same power(s). To review combining like terms, see Lesson 1-7.

**CHECK IT OUT!** **Add or subtract.**

**1a.** $2s^2 + 3s^2 + s$

**1b.** $4z^4 - 8 + 16z^4 + 2$

**1c.** $2x^8 + 7y^8 - x^8 - y^8$

**1d.** $9b^3c^2 + 5b^3c^2 - 13b^3c^2$

Polynomials can be added in either vertical or horizontal form.

In vertical form, align the like terms and add:

$$\begin{array}{r} 5x^2 + 4x + 1 \\ +\ 2x^2 + 5x + 2 \\ \hline 7x^2 + 9x + 3 \end{array}$$

In horizontal form, use the Associative and Commutative Properties to regroup and combine like terms:

$$(5x^2 + 4x + 1) + (2x^2 + 5x + 2)$$
$$= (5x^2 + 2x^2) + (4x + 5x) + (1 + 2)$$
$$= 7x^2 + 9x + 3$$

## EXAMPLE 2 Adding Polynomials

**Add.**

**A** $(2x^2 - x) + (x^2 + 3x - 1)$

| | |
|---|---|
| $(2x^2 - x) + (x^2 + 3x - 1)$ | *Identify like terms.* |
| $(2x^2 + x^2) + (-x + 3x) + (-1)$ | *Group like terms together.* |
| $3x^2 + 2x - 1$ | *Combine like terms.* |

**B** $(-2ab + b) + (2ab + a)$

| | |
|---|---|
| $(-2ab + b) + (2ab + a)$ | *Identify like terms.* |
| $(-2ab + 2ab) + b + a$ | *Group like terms together.* |
| $0 + b + a$ | *Combine like terms.* |
| $b + a$ | *Simplify.* |

**C** $(4b^5 + 8b) + (3b^5 + 6b - 7b^5 + b)$

| | |
|---|---|
| $(4b^5 + 8b) + (3b^5 + 6b - 7b^5 + b)$ | *Identify like terms.* |
| $(4b^5 + 8b) + (-4b^5 + 7b)$ | *Combine like terms in the second polynomial.* |
| $\begin{array}{r} 4b^5 + 8b \\ + -4b^5 + 7b \\ \hline 0 \quad + 15b \end{array}$ | *Use the vertical method.* <br> *Combine like terms.* |
| $15b$ | *Simplify.* |

**D** $(20.2y^2 + 6y + 5) + (1.7y^2 - 8)$

| | |
|---|---|
| $(20.2y^2 + 6y + 5) + (1.7y^2 - 8)$ | *Identify like terms.* |
| $\begin{array}{r} 20.2y^2 + 6y + 5 \\ + 1.7y^2 + 0y - 8 \\ \hline 21.9y^2 + 6y - 3 \end{array}$ | *Use the vertical method.* <br> *Write 0y as a placeholder in the second polynomial.* <br> *Combine like terms.* |

### Writing Math

When you use the Associative and Commutative Properties to rearrange the terms, the sign in front of each term must stay with that term.

**2.** Add $(5a^3 + 3a^2 - 6a + 12a^2) + (7a^3 - 10a)$.

To subtract polynomials, remember that subtracting is the same as adding the opposite. To find the opposite of a polynomial, you must write the opposite of *each* term in the polynomial:

$$-(2x^3 - 3x + 7) = -2x^3 + 3x - 7$$

## EXAMPLE 3 Subtracting Polynomials

**Subtract.**

**A** $(2x^2 + 6) - (4x^2)$

| | |
|---|---|
| $(2x^2 + 6) + (-4x^2)$ | *Rewrite subtraction as addition of the opposite.* |
| $(2x^2 + 6) + (-4x^2)$ | *Identify like terms.* |
| $(2x^2 - 4x^2) + 6$ | *Group like terms together.* |
| $-2x^2 + 6$ | *Combine like terms.* |

**B** $(a^4 - 2a) - (3a^4 - 3a + 1)$

| | |
|---|---|
| $(a^4 - 2a) + (-3a^4 + 3a - 1)$ | *Rewrite subtraction as addition of the opposite.* |
| $(a^4 - 2a) + (-3a^4 + 3a - 1)$ | *Identify like terms.* |
| $(a^4 - 3a^4) + (-2a + 3a) - 1$ | *Group like terms together.* |
| $-2a^4 + a - 1$ | *Combine like terms.* |

Subtract.

**C** $(3x^2 - 2x + 8) - (x^2 - 4)$

$(3x^2 - 2x + 8) + (-x^2 + 4)$ *Rewrite subtraction as addition of the opposite.*

$(3x^2 - 2x + 8) + (-x^2 + 4)$ *Identify like terms.*

$$\begin{array}{r} 3x^2 - 2x + 8 \\ + -x^2 + 0x + 4 \\ \hline 2x^2 - 2x + 12 \end{array}$$

*Use the vertical method.*
*Write 0x as a placeholder.*
*Combine like terms.*

**D** $(11z^3 - 2z) - (z^3 - 5)$

$(11z^3 - 2z) + (-z^3 + 5)$ *Rewrite subtraction as addition of the opposite.*

$(11z^3 - 2z) + (-z^3 + 5)$ *Identify like terms.*

$$\begin{array}{r} 11z^3 - 2z + 0 \\ + -z^3 + 0z + 5 \\ \hline 10z^3 - 2z + 5 \end{array}$$

*Use the vertical method.*
*Write 0 and 0z as placeholders.*
*Combine like terms.*

3. Subtract $(2x^2 - 3x^2 + 1) - (x^2 + x + 1)$.

## EXAMPLE 4 Business Application

The profits of two different manufacturing plants can be modeled as shown, where $x$ is the number of units produced at each plant.

**Eastern:**
$-0.03x^2 + 25x - 1500$

**Southern:**
$-0.02x^2 + 21x - 1700$

**Write a polynomial that represents the difference of the profits at the eastern plant and the profits at the southern plant.**

$(-0.03x^2 + 25x - 1500)$ *Eastern plant profits*

$-(-0.02x^2 + 21x - 1700)$ *Southern plant profits*

$$\begin{array}{r} (-0.03x^2 + 25x - 1500) \\ +(+0.02x^2 - 21x + 1700) \\ \hline -0.01x^2 + 4x + 200 \end{array}$$

*Write subtraction as addition of the opposite.*
*Combine like terms.*

4. Use the information above to write a polynomial that represents the total profits from both plants.

## THINK AND DISCUSS

1. Identify the like terms in the following list: $-12x^2, -4.7y, \frac{1}{5}x^2y, y, 3xy^2, -9x^2, 5x^2y, -12x$
2. Describe how to find the opposite of $9t^2 - 5t + 8$.
3. **GET ORGANIZED** Copy and complete the graphic organizer. In each box, write an example that shows how to perform the given operation.

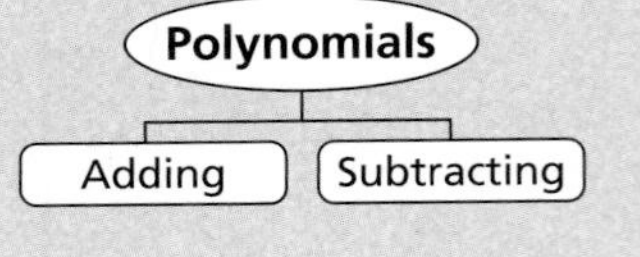

# 7-6 Exercises

MA.A.1.1, MA.A.1, MA.A.1.2

go.hrw.com
Homework Help Online
KEYWORD: MA7 7-6
Parent Resources Online
KEYWORD: MA7 Parent

## GUIDED PRACTICE

SEE EXAMPLE 1 p. 484

Add or subtract.

1. $7a^2 - 10a^2 + 9a$
2. $13x^2 + 9y^2 - 6x^2$
3. $0.07r^4 + 0.32r^3 + 0.19r^4$
4. $\frac{1}{4}p^3 + \frac{2}{3}p^3$
5. $5b^3c + b^3c - 3b^3c$
6. $-8m + 5 - 16 + 11m$

SEE EXAMPLE 2 p. 485

Add.

7. $(5n^3 + 3n + 6) + (18n^3 + 9)$
8. $(3.7q^2 - 8q + 3.7) + (4.3q^2 - 2.9q + 1.6)$
9. $(-3x + 12) + (9x^2 + 2x - 18)$
10. $(9x^4 + x^3) + (2x^4 + 6x^3 - 8x^4 + x^3)$

SEE EXAMPLE 3 p. 485

Subtract.

11. $(6c^4 + 8c + 6) - (2c^4)$
12. $(16y^2 - 8y + 9) - (6y^2 - 2y + 7y)$
13. $(2r + 5) - (5r - 6)$
14. $(-7k^2 + 3) - (2k^2 + 5k - 1)$

SEE EXAMPLE 4 p. 486

15. **Geometry** Write a polynomial that represents the measure of angle $ABD$.

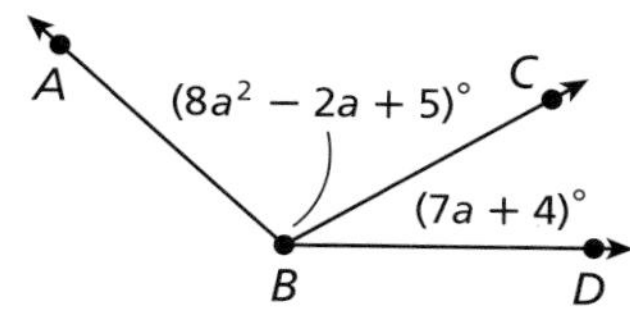


## PRACTICE AND PROBLEM SOLVING

| Independent Practice | |
|---|---|
| For Exercises | See Example |
| 16–24 | 1 |
| 25–28 | 2 |
| 29–32 | 3 |
| 33–34 | 4 |

**Extra Practice**
Skills Practice p. S17
Application Practice p. S34

Add or subtract.

16. $4k^3 + 6k^2 + 9k^3$
17. $5m + 12n^2 + 6n - 8m$
18. $2.5a^4 - 8.1b^4 - 3.6b^4$
19. $2d^5 + 1 - d^5$
20. $7xy - 4x^2y - 2xy$
21. $-6x^3 + 5x + 2x^3 + 4x^3$
22. $x^2 + x + 3x + 2x^2$
23. $3x^3 - 4 - x^3 - 1$
24. $3b^3 - 2b - 1 - b^3 - b$

Add.

25. $(2t^2 - 8t) + (8t^2 + 9t)$
26. $(-7x^2 - 2x + 3) + (4x^2 - 9x)$
27. $(x^5 - x) + (x^4 + x)$
28. $(-2z^3 + z + 2z^3 + z) + (3z^3 - 5z^2)$

Subtract.

29. $(t^3 + 8t^2) - (3t^3)$
30. $(3x^2 - x) - (x^2 + 3x - x)$
31. $(5m + 3) - (6m^3 - 2m^2)$
32. $(3s^2 + 4s) - (-10s^2 + 6s)$
33. **Photography** The measurements of a photo and its frame are shown in the diagram. Write a polynomial that represents the width of the photo.
34. **Geometry** The length of a rectangle is represented by $4a + 3b$, and its width is represented by $7a - 2b$. Write a polynomial for the perimeter of the rectangle.

**Add or subtract.**

**35.** $(2t - 7) + (-t + 2)$

**36.** $(4m^2 + 3m) + (-2m^2)$

**37.** $(4n - 2) - 2n$

**38.** $(-v - 7) - (-2v)$

**39.** $(4x^2 + 3x - 6) + (2x^2 - 4x + 5)$

**40.** $(2z^2 - 3z - 3) + (2z^2 - 7z - 1)$

**41.** $(5u^2 + 3u + 7) - (u^3 + 2u^2 + 1)$

**42.** $(-7h^2 - 4h + 7) - (7h^2 - 4h + 11)$

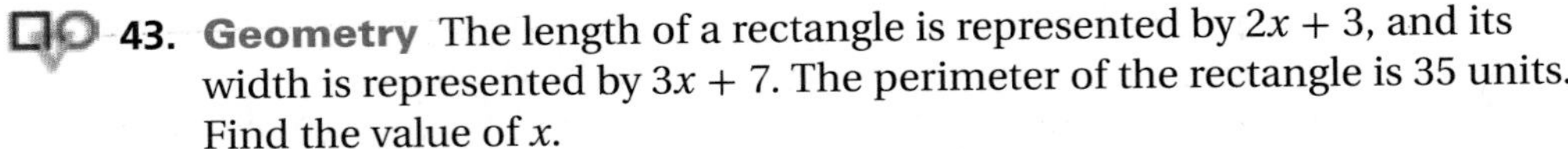

**43. Geometry** The length of a rectangle is represented by $2x + 3$, and its width is represented by $3x + 7$. The perimeter of the rectangle is 35 units. Find the value of $x$.

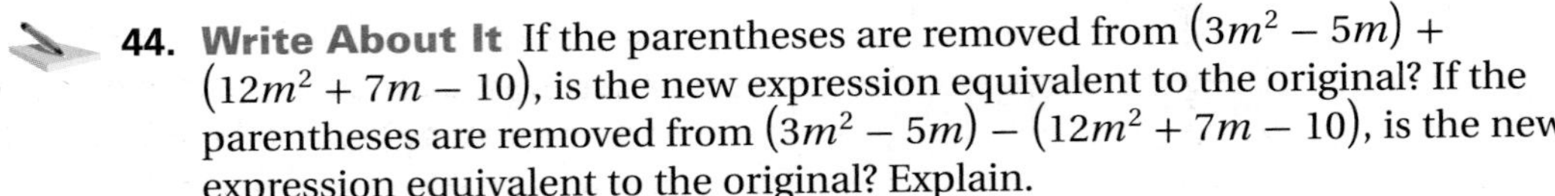

**44. Write About It** If the parentheses are removed from $(3m^2 - 5m) + (12m^2 + 7m - 10)$, is the new expression equivalent to the original? If the parentheses are removed from $(3m^2 - 5m) - (12m^2 + 7m - 10)$, is the new expression equivalent to the original? Explain.

**45. ///ERROR ANALYSIS///** Two students found the sum of the polynomials $(-3n^4 + 6n^3 + 4n^2)$ and $(8n^4 - 3n^2 + 9n)$. Which is incorrect? Explain the error.

**A**

$$\begin{array}{r} -3n^4 + 6n^3 + 4n^2 + 0n \\ +8n^4 + 0n^3 - 3n^2 + 9n \\ \hline 5n^4 + 6n^3 + n^2 + 9n \end{array}$$

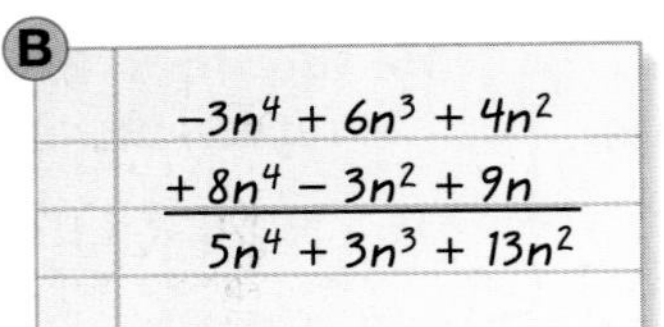

**B**

$$\begin{array}{r} -3n^4 + 6n^3 + 4n^2 \\ +8n^4 - 3n^2 + 9n \\ \hline 5n^4 + 3n^3 + 13n^2 \end{array}$$

**Copy and complete the table by finding the missing polynomials.**

| | Polynomial 1 | Polynomial 2 | Sum |
|---|---|---|---|
| **46.** | $x^2 - 6$ | $3x^2 - 10x + 2$ | ■ |
| **47.** | $12x + 5$ | ■ | $15x + 11$ |
| **48.** | ■ | $5x^4 + 8$ | $6x^4 - 3x^2 - 1$ |
| **49.** | $7x^3 - 6x - 3$ | ■ | $7x^3 + 11$ |
| **50.** | $2x^3 + 5x^2$ | $7x^3 - 5x^2 + 1$ | ■ |
| **51.** | ■ | $x + x^2 + 6$ | $3x^2 + 2x + 1$ |

**52. Critical Thinking** Does the order in which you add polynomials affect the sum? Does the order in which you subtract polynomials affect the difference? Explain.

**MULTI-STEP TEST PREP**

**53.** This problem will prepare you for the Multi-Step Test Prep on page 508.

**a.** Ian plans to build a fenced dog pen. At first, he planned for the pen to be a square of length $x$ on each side, but then he decided that a square may not be best. He added 4 to the length and subtracted 3 from the width. Draw a diagram to show the dimensions of the new pen.

**b.** Write a polynomial that represents the amount of fencing that Ian will need for the new dog pen.

**c.** How much fencing will Ian need if $x = 15$?

54. What is the missing term?

MA.A.1.1, MA.A.1, MA.A.1.2

$(-14y^2 + 9y^2 - 12y + 3) + (2y^2 + \blacksquare - 6y - 2) = (-3y^2 - 15y + 1)$

Ⓐ $-6y$ Ⓑ $-3y$ Ⓒ $3y$ Ⓓ $6y$

55. Which is NOT equivalent to $-5t^3 - t$?

Ⓕ $-(5t^3 + t)$ Ⓗ $(t^3 + 6t) - (6t^3 + 7t)$

Ⓖ $(2t^3 - 4t) - (-7t - 3t)$ Ⓙ $(2t^3 - 3t^2 + t) - (7t^3 - 3t^2 + 2t)$

56. **Extended Response** Tammy plans to put a wallpaper border around the perimeter of her room. She will not put the border across the doorway, which is 3 feet wide.

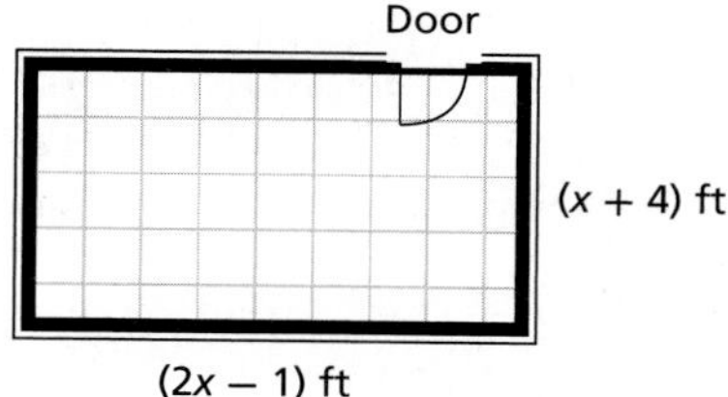


a. Write a polynomial that represents the number of feet of wallpaper border that Tammy will need.

b. A local store has 50 feet of the border that Tammy has chosen. What is the greatest whole-number value of $x$ for which this amount would be enough for Tammy's room? Justify your answer.

c. Determine the dimensions of Tammy's room for the value of $x$ that you found in part **b.**

## CHALLENGE AND EXTEND

57. **Geometry** The legs of the isosceles triangle at right measure $(x^3 + 5)$ units. The perimeter of the triangle is $(2x^3 + 3x^2 + 8)$ units. Write a polynomial that represents the measure of the base of the triangle.

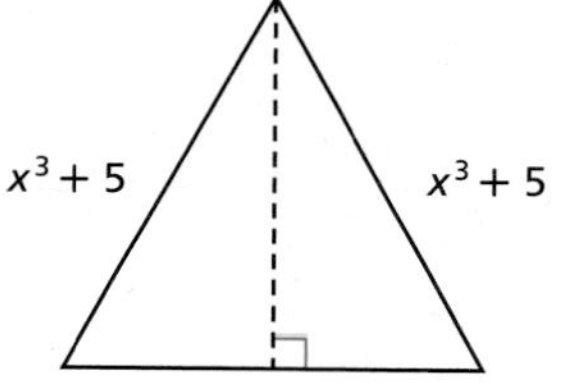


58. Write two polynomials whose sum is $4m^3 + 3m$.

59. Write two polynomials whose difference is $4m^3 + 3m$.

60. Write three polynomials whose sum is $4m^3 + 3m$.

61. Write two monomials whose sum is $4m^3 + 3m$.

62. Write three trinomials whose sum is $4m^3 + 3m$.

## SPIRAL REVIEW

**Solve each inequality and graph the solutions.** *(Lesson 3-2)*

63. $d + 5 \geq -2$ 64. $15 < m - 11$ 65. $-6 + t < -6$

**Write each equation in slope-intercept form. Then graph the line described by each equation.** *(Lesson 5-6)*

66. $3x + y = 8$ 67. $2y = \frac{1}{2}x + 6$ 68. $y = 4(-x + 1)$

**Simplify.** *(Lesson 7-3)*

69. $b^4 \cdot b^7$ 70. $cd^4 \cdot (c^{-5})^3$ 71. $(-3z^6)^2$ 72. $(j^3k^{-5})^3 \cdot (k^2)^4$

Use with Lesson 7-7

# Model Polynomial Multiplication

You can use algebra tiles to multiply polynomials. Use the length and width of a rectangle to represent the factors. The area of the rectangle represents the product.

**MA.A.1** Use appropriate … strategies to combine … algebraic expressions. *Also* **MA.A.1.1**

**KEY**

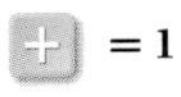 $= 1$

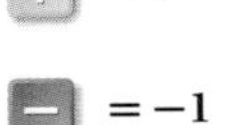 $= -1$

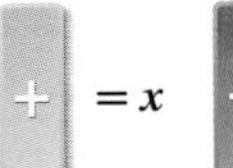 $= x$ 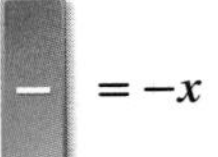 $= -x$  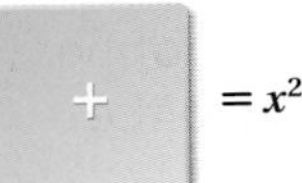 $= x^2$

**REMEMBER**
- The product of two values with the same sign is positive.
- The product of two values with different signs is negative.

## Activity 1

**Use algebra tiles to find $2(x + 1)$.**

| MODEL | | ALGEBRA |
|---|---|---|
| 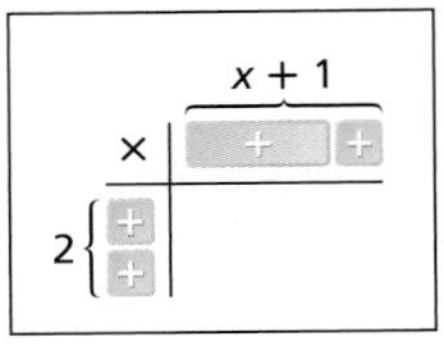 | *Place the first factor in a column along the left side of the grid. This will be the width of the rectangle.* *Place the second factor across the top of the grid. This will be the length of the rectangle.* | $2(x + 1)$ |
| 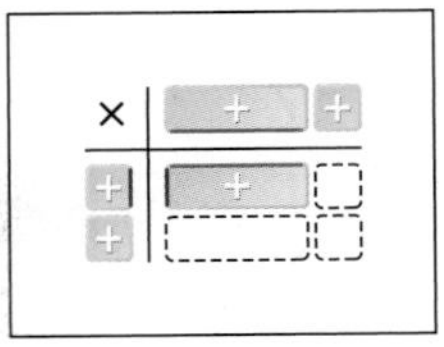 | *Fill in the grid with tiles that have the same width as the tiles in the left column and the same length as the tiles in the top row.* | |
| 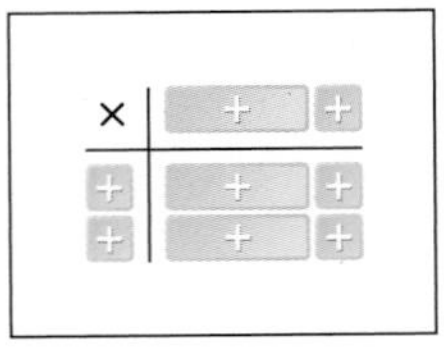 | *The area of the rectangle inside the grid represents the product.* | $x + x + 1 + 1$<br>$2x + 2$ |

The rectangle has an area of $2x + 2$, so $2(x + 1) = 2x + 2$. Notice that this is the same product you would get by using the Distributive Property to multiply $2(x + 1)$.

**Use algebra tiles to find each product.**

**1.** $3(x + 2)$ **2.** $2(2x + 1)$ **3.** $3(x + 1)$ **4.** $3(2x + 2)$

## Activity 2

**Use algebra tiles to find $2x(x - 3)$.**

| MODEL | | ALGEBRA |
|---|---|---|
| | *Place tiles to form the length and width of a rectangle and fill in the rectangle.* *The product of two values with the same sign (same color) is positive (yellow).* *The product of two values with different signs (different colors) is negative (red).* | $2x(x - 3)$ |
| | *The area of the rectangle inside the grid represents the product.* *The rectangle has an area of $2x^2 - 6x$, so $2x(x - 3) = 2x^2 - 6x$.* | $x^2 + x^2 - x - x - x - x - x - x$ <br> $2x^2 - 6x$ |

## Try This

**Use algebra tiles to find each product.**

**5.** $3x(x - 2)$ **6.** $x(2x - 1)$ **7.** $x(x + 1)$ **8.** $(8x + 5)(-2x)$

## Activity 3

**Use algebra tiles to find $(x + 1)(x - 2)$.**

| MODEL | | ALGEBRA |
|---|---|---|
| | *Place tiles for each factor to form the length and width of a rectangle.* *Fill in the grid and remove any zero pairs.* | $(x + 1)(x - 2)$ <br> $x^2 - x - x + x - 1 - 1$ |
| | *The area inside the grid represents the product.* *The remaining area is $x^2 - x - 2$, so $(x + 1)(x - 2) = x^2 - x - 2$.* | $x^2 - x - 1 - 1$ <br> $x^2 - x - 2$ |

## Try This

**Use algebra tiles to find each product.**

**9.** $(x + 2)(x - 3)$ **10.** $(x - 1)(x + 3)$ **11.** $(x - 2)(x - 3)$ **12.** $(x + 1)(x + 2)$

# 7-7 Multiplying Polynomials

**MA.A.1.1** Execute … operations with algebraic expressions…
*Also* **MA.A.1, MA.A.1.2, MA.N.2.2, MA.G.2.2**

***Objective***
Multiply polynomials.

**Why learn this?**
You can multiply polynomials to write expressions for areas, such as the area of a dulcimer. (See Example 5.)

To multiply monomials and polynomials, you will use some of the properties of exponents that you learned earlier in this chapter.

## EXAMPLE 1 Multiplying Monomials

**Multiply.**

**A** $(5x^2)(4x^3)$

$(5x^2)(4x^3)$

$(5 \cdot 4)(x^2 \cdot x^3)$ *Group factors with like bases together.*

$20x^5$ *Multiply.*

**B** $(-3x^3y^2)(4xy^5)$

$(-3x^3y^2)(4xy^5)$

$(-3 \cdot 4)(x^3 \cdot x)(y^2 \cdot y^5)$ *Group factors with like bases together.*

$-12x^4y^7$ *Multiply.*

**C** $\left(\frac{1}{2}a^3b\right)(a^2c^2)(6b^2)$

$\left(\frac{1}{2}a^3b\right)(a^2c^2)(6b^2)$

$\left(\frac{1}{2} \cdot 6\right)(a^3 \cdot a^2)(b \cdot b^2)(c^2)$ *Group factors with like bases together.*

$3a^5b^3c^2$ *Multiply.*

**Remember!**
When multiplying powers with the same base, keep the base and add the exponents.
$x^2 \cdot x^3 = x^{2+3} = x^5$

**Multiply.**

**1a.** $(3x^3)(6x^2)$ **1b.** $(2r^2t)(5t^3)$ **1c.** $\left(\frac{1}{3}x^2y\right)(12x^3z^2)(y^4z^5)$

To multiply a polynomial by a monomial, use the Distributive Property.

## EXAMPLE 2 Multiplying a Polynomial by a Monomial

**Multiply.**

**A** $5(2x^2 + x + 4)$

$5(2x^2 + x + 4)$

$(5)2x^2 + (5)x + (5)4$ *Distribute 5.*

$10x^2 + 5x + 20$ *Multiply.*

**Multiply.**

**B** $2x^2y(3x - y)$

$(2x^2y)(3x - y)$

$(2x^2y)3x + (2x^2y)(-y)$ — *Distribute $2x^2y$.*

$(2 \cdot 3)(x^2 \cdot x)y + 2(-1)(x^2)(y \cdot y)$ — *Group like bases together.*

$6x^3y - 2x^2y^2$ — *Multiply.*

**C** $4a(a^2b + 2b^2)$

$4a(a^2b + 2b^2)$

$(4a)a^2b + (4a)2b^2$ — *Distribute 4a.*

$(4)(a \cdot a^2)(b) + (4 \cdot 2)(a)(b^2)$ — *Group like bases together.*

$4a^3b + 8ab^2$ — *Multiply.*

**Multiply.**

**2a.** $2(4x^2 + x + 3)$ **2b.** $3ab(5a^2 + b)$ **2c.** $5r^2s^2(r - 3s)$

To multiply a binomial by a binomial, you can apply the Distributive Property more than once:

$$(x + 3)(x + 2) = x(x + 2) + 3(x + 2)$$ *Distribute x and 3.*

$$= x(x + 2) + 3(x + 2)$$

$$= x(x) + x(2) + 3(x) + 3(2)$$ *Distribute x and 3 again.*

$$= x^2 + 2x + 3x + 6$$ *Multiply.*

$$= x^2 + 5x + 6$$ *Combine like terms.*

Another method for multiplying binomials is called the FOIL method.

1. Multiply the **F**irst terms. $(x+3)(x+2) \rightarrow x \cdot x = x^2$ (F)
2. Multiply the **O**uter terms. $(x+3)(x+2) \rightarrow x \cdot 2 = 2x$ (O)
3. Multiply the **I**nner terms. $(x+3)(x+2) \rightarrow 3 \cdot x = 3x$ (I)
4. Multiply the **L**ast terms. $(x+3)(x+2) \rightarrow 3 \cdot 2 = 6$ (L)

$$(x+3)(x+2) = \underset{F}{x^2} + \underset{O}{2x} + \underset{I}{3x} + \underset{L}{6} = x^2 + 5x + 6$$

## EXAMPLE 3 Multiplying Binomials

**Multiply.**

**A** $(x+2)(x-5)$

$(x+2)(x-5)$

$x(x-5)+2(x-5)$ *Distribute x and 2.*

$x(x)+x(-5)+2(x)+2(-5)$ *Distribute x and 2 again.*

$x^2-5x+2x-10$ *Multiply.*

$x^2-3x-10$ *Combine like terms.*

**Helpful Hint**

In the expression $(x+5)^2$, the base is $(x+5)$.

$(x+5)^2 =$
$(x+5)(x+5)$

**B** $(x+5)^2$

$(x+5)(x+5)$ *Write as a product of two binomials.*

$(x\cdot x)+(x\cdot 5)+(5\cdot x)+(5\cdot 5)$ *Use the FOIL method.*

$x^2+5x+5x+25$ *Multiply.*

$x^2+10x+25$ *Combine like terms.*

**C** $(3a^2-b)(a^2-2b)$

$3a^2(a^2)+3a^2(-2b)-b(a^2)-b(-2b)$ *Use the FOIL method.*

$3a^4-6a^2b-a^2b+2b^2$ *Multiply.*

$3a^4-7a^2b+2b^2$ *Combine like terms.*

**3a.** $(a+3)(a-4)$ **3b.** $(x-3)^2$ **3c.** $(2a-b^2)(a+4b^2)$

To multiply polynomials with more than two terms, you can use the Distributive Property several times. Multiply $(5x+3)$ by $(2x^2+10x-6)$:

$$\begin{aligned}(5x+3)(2x^2+10x-6) &= 5x(2x^2+10x-6)+3(2x^2+10x-6)\\ &= 5x(2x^2+10x-6)+3(2x^2+10x-6)\\ &= 5x(2x^2)+5x(10x)+5x(-6)+3(2x^2)+3(10x)+3(-6)\\ &= 10x^3+50x^2-30x+6x^2+30x-18\\ &= 10x^3+56x^2-18\end{aligned}$$

You can also use a rectangle model to multiply polynomials with more than two terms. This is similar to finding the area of a rectangle with length $(2x^2+10x-6)$ and width $(5x+3)$:

| | $2x^2$ | $+10x$ | $-6$ |
|---|---|---|---|
| $5x$ | $10x^3$ | $50x^2$ | $-30x$ |
| $+3$ | $6x^2$ | $30x$ | $-18$ |

*Write the product of the monomials in each row and column.*

To find the product, add all of the terms inside the rectangle by combining like terms and simplifying if necessary.

$$10x^3+6x^2+50x^2+30x-30x-18$$
$$10x^3+56x^2-18$$

Another method that can be used to multiply polynomials with more than two terms is the vertical method. This is similar to methods used to multiply whole numbers.

$$\begin{array}{r}2x^2 + 10x - 6\\ \times \quad 5x + 3\\ \hline 6x^2 + 30x - 18\\ + 10x^3 + 50x^2 - 30x \quad\\ \hline 10x^3 + 56x^2 + 0x - 18\\ 10x^3 + 56x^2 \quad\quad - 18\end{array}$$

*Multiply each term in the top polynomial by 3.*

*Multiply each term in the top polynomial by 5x, and align like terms.*

*Combine like terms by adding vertically.*

*Simplify.*

## EXAMPLE 4 Multiplying Polynomials

**Helpful Hint**

A polynomial with *m* terms multiplied by a polynomial with *n* terms has a product that, before simplifying, has *mn* terms. In Example 4A, there are 2 • 3, or 6, terms before simplifying.

**Multiply.**

**A** $(x + 2)(x^2 - 5x + 4)$

$(x + 2)(x^2 - 5x + 4)$

$x(x^2 - 5x + 4) + 2(x^2 - 5x + 4)$ — *Distribute x and 2.*

$x(x^2) + x(-5x) + x(4) + 2(x^2) + 2(-5x) + 2(4)$ — *Distribute x and 2 again.*

$x^3 + 2x^2 - 5x^2 - 10x + 4x + 8$ — *Simplify.*

$x^3 - 3x^2 - 6x + 8$ — *Combine like terms.*

**B** $(3x - 4)(-2x^3 + 5x - 6)$

$(3x - 4)(-2x^3 + 5x - 6)$

$$\begin{array}{r}-2x^3 + 0x^2 + 5x - 6\\ \times \quad\quad 3x - 4\\ \hline 8x^3 + 0x^2 - 20x + 24\\ + -6x^4 + 0x^3 + 15x^2 - 18x \quad\quad\\ \hline -6x^4 + 8x^3 + 15x^2 - 38x + 24\end{array}$$

*Add $0x^2$ as a placeholder.*

*Multiply each term in the top polynomial by −4.*

*Multiply each term in the top polynomial by 3x, and align like terms.*

*Combine like terms by adding vertically.*

**C** $(x - 2)^3$

$[(x - 2)(x - 2)](x - 2)$ — *Write as the product of three binomials.*

$[x \cdot x + x(-2) - 2 \cdot x - 2(-2)](x - 2)$ — *Use the FOIL method on the first two factors.*

$(x^2 - 2x - 2x + 4)(x - 2)$ — *Multiply.*

$(x^2 - 4x + 4)(x - 2)$ — *Combine like terms.*

$(x - 2)(x^2 - 4x + 4)$ — *Use the Commutative Property of Multiplication.*

$x(x^2 - 4x + 4) + (-2)(x^2 - 4x + 4)$ — *Distribute x and −2.*

$x(x^2) + x(-4x) + x(4) + (-2)(x^2)$
$\quad + (-2)(-4x) + (-2)(4)$ — *Distribute x and −2 again.*

$x^3 - 4x^2 + 4x - 2x^2 + 8x - 8$ — *Simplify.*

$x^3 - 6x^2 + 12x - 8$ — *Combine like terms.*

**Multiply.**

**D** $(2x + 3)(x^2 - 6x + 5)$

| | $x^2$ | $-6x$ | $+5$ |
|---|---|---|---|
| $2x$ | $2x^3$ | $-12x^2$ | $10x$ |
| $+3$ | $3x^2$ | $-18x$ | $15$ |

*Write the product of the monomials in each row and column.*

$2x^3 + 3x^2 - 12x^2 - 18x + 10x + 15$ *Add all terms inside the rectangle.*

$2x^3 - 9x^2 - 8x + 15$ *Combine like terms.*

**Multiply.**

**4a.** $(x + 3)(x^2 - 4x + 6)$

**4b.** $(3x + 2)(x^2 - 2x + 5)$

## EXAMPLE 5 *Music Application*

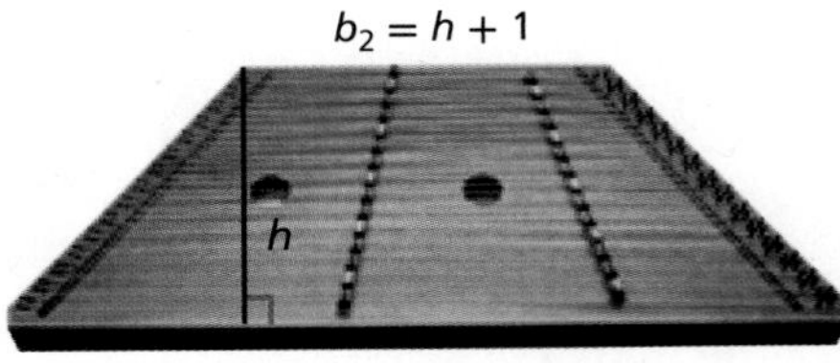


**A dulcimer is a musical instrument that is sometimes shaped like a trapezoid.**

**A** **Write a polynomial that represents the area of the dulcimer shown.**

$A = \frac{1}{2}h(b_1 + b_2)$ *Write the formula for area of a trapezoid.*

$= \frac{1}{2}h[(2h - 1) + (h + 1)]$ *Substitute $2h - 1$ for $b_1$ and $h + 1$ for $b_2$.*

$= \frac{1}{2}h(3h)$ *Combine like terms.*

$= \frac{3}{2}h^2$ *Simplify.*

The area is represented by $\frac{3}{2}h^2$.

**B** **Find the area of the dulcimer when the height is 22 inches.**

$A = \frac{3}{2}h^2$ *Use the polynomial from part **a**.*

$= \frac{3}{2}(22)^2$ *Substitute 22 for h.*

$= \frac{3}{2}(484) = 726$

The area is 726 square inches.

**5.** The length of a rectangle is 4 meters shorter than its width.

**a.** Write a polynomial that represents the area of the rectangle.

**b.** Find the area of the rectangle when the width is 6 meters.

## THINK AND DISCUSS

**1.** Compare the vertical method for multiplying polynomials with the vertical method for multiplying whole numbers.

**2. GET ORGANIZED** Copy and complete the graphic organizer. In each box, multiply two polynomials using the given method.

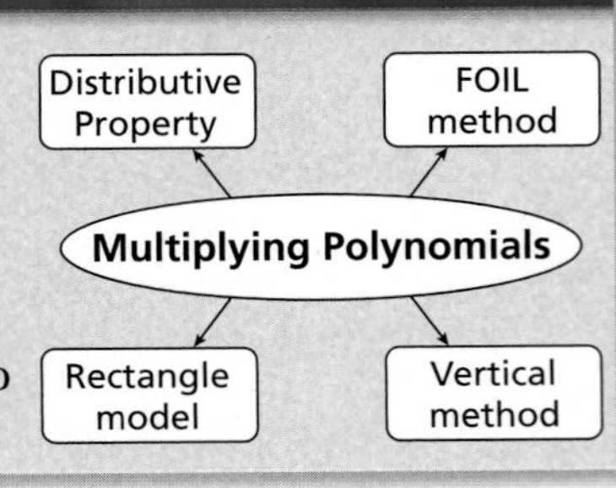

# 7-7 Exercises

MA.A.1.1, MA.A.1, MA.A.1.2, MA.N.2.2, MA.G.2.2

go.hrw.com
Homework Help Online
KEYWORD: MA7 7-7
Parent Resources Online
KEYWORD: MA7 Parent

## GUIDED PRACTICE

SEE EXAMPLE 1 p. 492

**Multiply.**

1. $(2x^2)(7x^4)$
2. $(-5mn^3)(4m^2n^2)$
3. $(6rs^2)(s^3t^2)\left(\frac{1}{2}r^4t^3\right)$
4. $\left(\frac{1}{3}a^5\right)(12a)$
5. $(-3x^4y^2)(-7x^3y)$
6. $(-2pq^3)(5p^2q^2)(-3q^4)$

SEE EXAMPLE 2 p. 492

7. $4(x^2 + 2x + 1)$
8. $3ab(2a^2 + 3b^3)$
9. $2a^3b(3a^2b + ab^2)$
10. $-3x(x^2 - 4x + 6)$
11. $5x^2y(2xy^3 - y)$
12. $5m^2n^3 \cdot mn^2(4m - n)$

SEE EXAMPLE 3 p. 494

13. $(x + 1)(x - 2)$
14. $(x + 1)^2$
15. $(x - 2)^2$
16. $(y - 3)(y - 5)$
17. $(4a^3 - 2b)(a - 3b^2)$
18. $(m^2 - 2mn)(3mn + n^2)$

SEE EXAMPLE 4 p. 495

19. $(x + 5)(x^2 - 2x + 3)$
20. $(3x + 4)(x^2 - 5x + 2)$
21. $(2x - 4)(-3x^3 + 2x - 5)$
22. $(-4x + 6)(2x^3 - x^2 + 1)$
23. $(x - 5)(x^2 + x + 1)$
24. $(a + b)(a - b)(b - a)$

SEE EXAMPLE 5 p. 496

25. **Photography** The length of a rectangular photograph is 3 inches less than twice the width.
    a. Write a polynomial that represents the area of the photograph.
    b. Find the area of the photograph when the width is 4 inches.

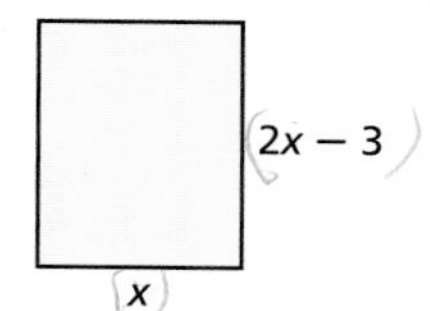


## PRACTICE AND PROBLEM SOLVING

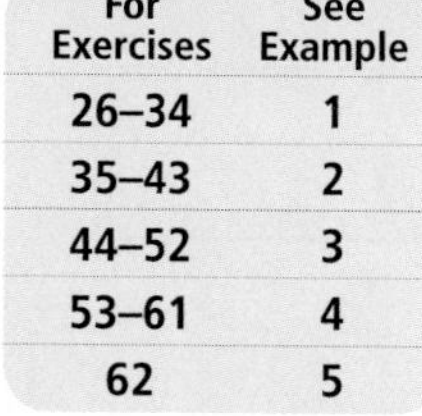

**Independent Practice**

| For Exercises | See Example |
|---|---|
| 26–34 | 1 |
| 35–43 | 2 |
| 44–52 | 3 |
| 53–61 | 4 |
| 62 | 5 |

**Extra Practice**

Skills Practice p. S17
Application Practice p. S34

**Multiply.**

26. $(3x^2)(8x^5)$
27. $(-2r^3s^4)(6r^2s)$
28. $(15xy^2)\left(\frac{1}{3}x^2z^3\right)(y^3z^4)$
29. $(-2a^3)(-5a)$
30. $(6x^3y^2)(-2x^2y)$
31. $(-3a^2b)(-2b^3)(-a^3b^2)$
32. $(7x^2)(xy^5)(2x^3y^2)$
33. $(-4a^3bc^2)(a^3b^2c)(3ab^4c^5)$
34. $(12mn^2)(2m^2n)(mn)$
35. $9s(s + 6)$
36. $9(2x^2 - 5x)$
37. $3x(9x^2 - 4x)$
38. $3(2x^2 + 5x + 4)$
39. $5s^2t^3(2s - 3t^2)$
40. $x^2y^3 \cdot 5x^2y(6x + y^2)$
41. $-5x(2x^2 - 3x - 1)$
42. $-2a^2b^3(3ab^2 - a^2b)$
43. $-7x^3y \cdot x^2y^2(2x - y)$
44. $(x + 5)(x - 3)$
45. $(x + 4)^2$
46. $(m - 5)^2$
47. $(5x - 2)(x + 3)$
48. $(3x - 4)^2$
49. $(5x + 2)(2x - 1)$
50. $(x - 1)(x - 2)$
51. $(x - 8)(7x + 4)$
52. $(2x + 7)(3x + 7)$
53. $(x + 2)(x^2 - 3x + 5)$
54. $(2x + 5)(x^2 - 4x + 3)$
55. $(5x - 1)(-2x^3 + 4x - 3)$
56. $(x - 3)(x^2 - 5x + 6)$
57. $(2x^2 - 3)(4x^3 - x^2 + 7)$
58. $(x - 4)^3$
59. $(x - 2)(x^2 + 2x + 1)$
60. $(2x + 10)(4 - x + 6x^3)$
61. $(1 - x)^3$

62. **Geometry** The length of the rectangle at right is 3 feet longer than its width.
    a. Write a polynomial that represents the area of the rectangle.
    b. Find the area of the rectangle when the width is 5 feet.

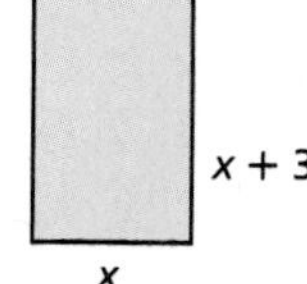


63. A square tabletop has side lengths of $(4x - 6)$ units. Write a polynomial that represents the area of the tabletop.

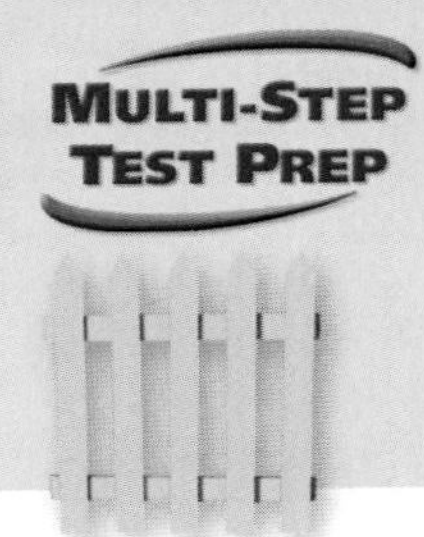


64. This problem will prepare you for the Multi-Step Test Prep on page 508.
   a. Marie is creating a garden. She designs a rectangular garden with a length of $(x + 4)$ feet and a width of $(x + 1)$ feet. Draw a diagram of Marie's garden with the length and width labeled.
   b. Write a polynomial that represents the area of Marie's garden.
   c. What is the area when $x = 4$?

65. Copy and complete the table below.

| | A | Degree of A | B | Degree of B | A • B | Degree of A • B |
|---|---|---|---|---|---|---|
| | $2x^2$ | 2 | $3x^5$ | 5 | $6x^7$ | 7 |
| a. | $5x^3$ | ■ | $2x^2 + 1$ | ■ | ■ | ■ |
| b. | $x^2 + 2$ | ■ | $x^2 - x$ | ■ | ■ | ■ |
| c. | $x - 3$ | ■ | $x^3 - 2x^2 + 1$ | ■ | ■ | ■ |

   d. Use the results from the table to complete the following: The product of a polynomial of degree $m$ and a polynomial of degree $n$ has a degree of ■.

**Geometry** **Write a polynomial that represents the area of each rectangle.**

66.

67.

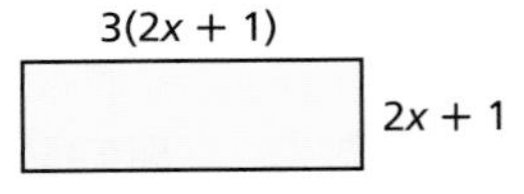


68.

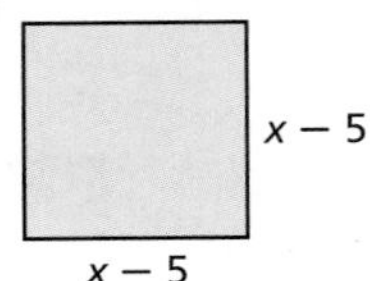

**Sports**

Team handball is a game with elements of soccer and basketball. It originated in Europe in the 1900s and was first played at the Olympics in 1936 with teams of 11 players. Today, a handball team consists of seven players—six court players and one goalie.

69. **Sports** The length of a regulation team handball court is twice its width.

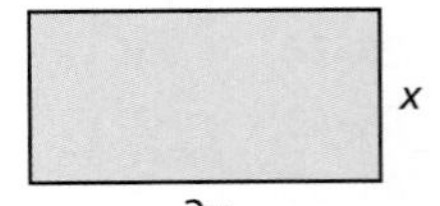


   a. Write a polynomial that represents the area of the court.
   b. The width of a team handball court is 20 meters. Find the area of the court.

**Multiply.**

70. $(1.5a^3)(4a^6)$
71. $(2x + 5)(x - 6)$
72. $(3g - 1)(g + 5)$
73. $(4x - 2y)(2x - 3y)$
74. $(x + 3)(x - 3)$
75. $(1.5x - 3)(4x + 2)$
76. $(x - 10)(x + 4)$
77. $x^2(x + 3)$
78. $(x + 1)(x^2 + 2x)$
79. $(x - 4)(2x^2 + x - 6)$
80. $(a + b)(a - b)^2$
81. $(2p - 3q)^3$

82. **Multi-Step** A rectangular swimming pool is 25 feet long and 10 feet wide. It is surrounded by a fence that is $x$ feet from each side of the pool.
   a. Draw a diagram of this situation.
   b. Write expressions for the length and width of the fenced region. (*Hint:* How much longer is one side of the fenced region than the corresponding side of the pool?)
   c. Write an expression for the area of the fenced region.

83. **Write About It** Explain why the FOIL method can be used to multiply only two binomials at a time.

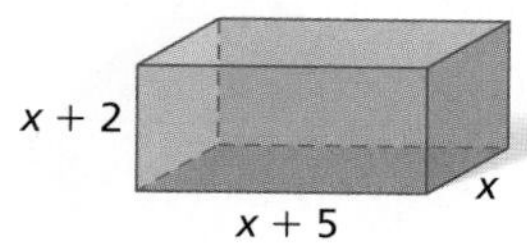


**84. Geometry** Write a polynomial that represents the volume of the rectangular prism.

**85. Critical Thinking** Is there any value for $x$ that would make the statement $(x + 3)^3 = x^3 + 3^3$ true? Give an example to justify your answer.

**86. Estimation** The length of a rectangle is 1 foot more than its width. Write a polynomial that represents the area of the rectangle. Estimate the width of the rectangle if its area is 25 square feet.

## TEST PREP

**MA.A.1.1, MA.A.1, MA.A.1.2, MA.N.2.2, MA.G.2.2**

**87.** Which of the following products is equal to $a^2 - 5a - 6$?

Ⓐ $(a - 1)(a - 5)$ Ⓑ $(a - 2)(a - 3)$ Ⓒ $(a + 1)(a - 6)$ Ⓓ $(a + 2)(a - 3)$

**88.** Which of the following is equal to $2a(a^2 - 1)$?

Ⓕ $2a^2 - 2a$ Ⓖ $2a^3 - 1$ Ⓗ $2a^3 - 2a$ Ⓙ $2a^2 - 1$

**89.** What is the degree of the product of $3x^3y^2z$ and $x^2yz$?

Ⓐ 5 Ⓑ 6 Ⓒ 7 Ⓓ 10

## CHALLENGE AND EXTEND

**Simplify.**

**90.** $6x^2 - 2(3x^2 - 2x + 4)$ **91.** $x^2 - 2x(x + 3)$ **92.** $x(4x - 2) + 3x(x + 1)$

**93.** The diagram shows a sandbox and the frame that surrounds it.

$x + 5$
$x + 1$
$x + 3$
$x - 1$

**a.** Write a polynomial that represents the area of the sandbox.

**b.** Write a polynomial that represents the area of the frame that surrounds the sandbox.

**94. Geometry** The side length of a square is $(8 + 2x)$ units. The area of this square is the same as the perimeter of another square with a side length of $(x^2 + 48)$ units. Find the value of $x$.

**95.** Write a polynomial that represents the product of three consecutive integers. Let $x$ represent the first integer.

**96.** Find $m$ and $n$ so that $x^m(x^n + x^{n-2}) = x^5 + x^3$.

**97.** Find $a$ so that $2x^a(5x^{2a-3} + 2x^{2a+2}) = 10x^3 + 4x^8$

## SPIRAL REVIEW

**98.** A stop sign is 2.5 meters tall and casts a shadow that is 3.5 meters long. At the same time, a flagpole casts a shadow that is 28 meters long. How tall is the flagpole? *(Lesson 2-7)*

**Graph the solutions of each linear inequality.** *(Lesson 6-5)*

**99.** $y \leq x - 2$ **100.** $4x - 2y < 10$ **101.** $-y \geq -3x + 1$

**Classify each polynomial according to its degree and number of terms.** *(Lesson 7-5)*

**102.** $6x - 1$ **103.** $5x^2$ **104.** $4m^2 - 12m + 3 + 5m^3$

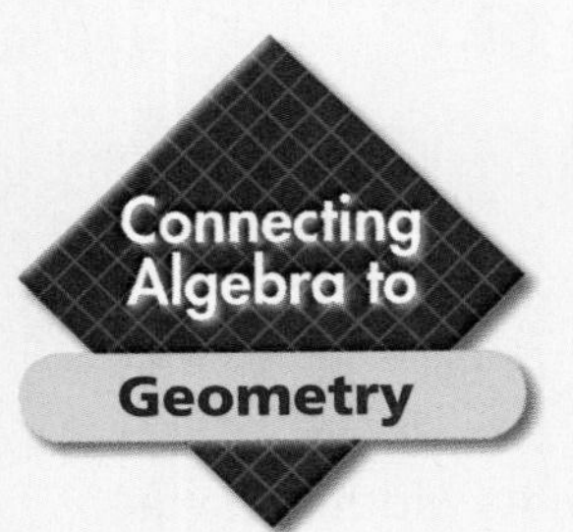


# Volume and Surface Area

*See Skills Bank pages S66–S67*

The volume $V$ of a three-dimensional figure is the amount of space it occupies. The surface area $S$ is the total area of the two-dimensional surfaces that make up the figure.

**MA.G.2.4** Use formulas to solve problems involving volume of right prisms, pyramids, circular cylinders and right circular cones. *Also* **MA.A.1.1, MA.A.1, MA.A.1.2, MA.N.2.2**

**Rectangular Prism**

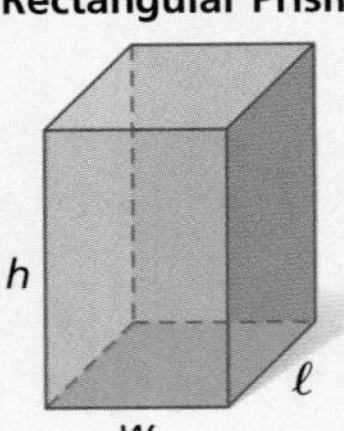


$V = \ell wh$
$S = 2(\ell w + \ell h + wh)$

**Cylinder**

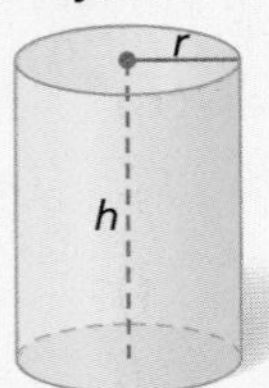


$V = \pi r^2 h$
$S = 2\pi r^2 + 2\pi rh$

**Cone**

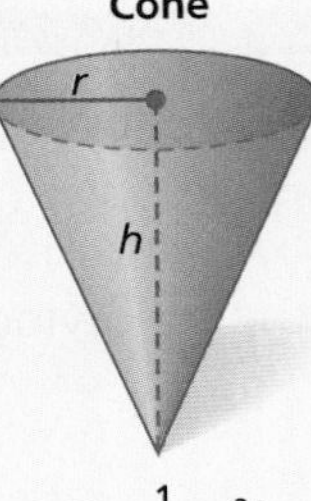


$V = \frac{1}{3}\pi r^2 h$

**Pyramid**

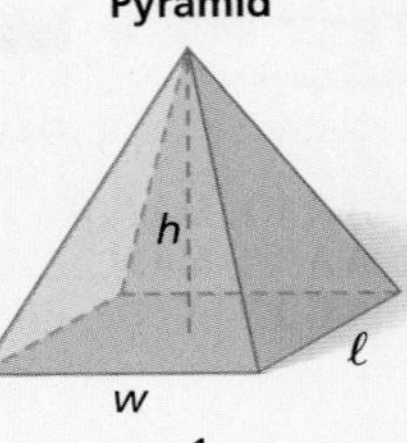


$V = \frac{1}{3}\ell wh$

## Example

**Write and simplify a polynomial expression for the volume of the cone. Leave the symbol $\pi$ in your answer.**

$V = \frac{1}{3}\pi r^2 h$ — *Choose the correct formula.*

$= \frac{1}{3}\pi(6p)^2(p+1)$ — *Substitute 6p for r and p + 1 for h.*

$= \frac{1}{3}\pi(36p^2)(p+1)$ — *Use the Power of a Product Property.*

$= \frac{1}{3}(36)\pi[p^2(p+1)]$ — *Use the Associative Property of Multiplication.*

$= 12\pi p^2(p+1)$ — *Distribute $12\pi p^2$.*

$= 12\pi p^3 + 12\pi p^2$

p + 1
6p

## Try This

**Write and simplify a polynomial expression for the volume of each figure.**

**1.**

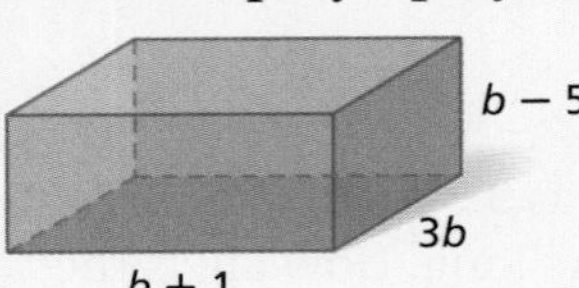


**2.**

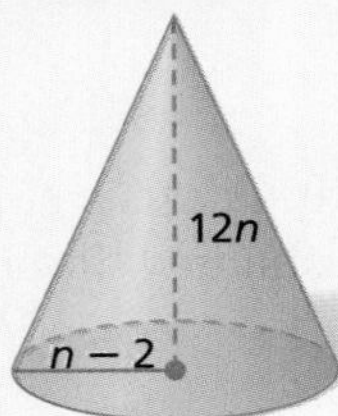


**3.**

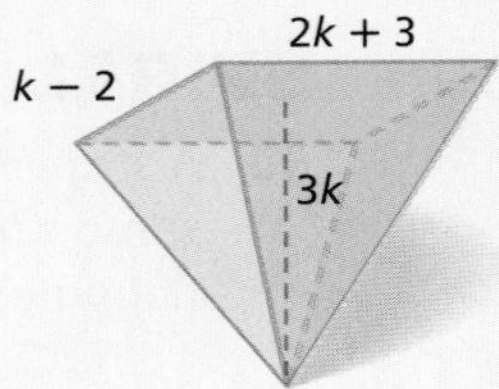


**Write and simplify a polynomial expression for the surface area of each figure.**

**4.**

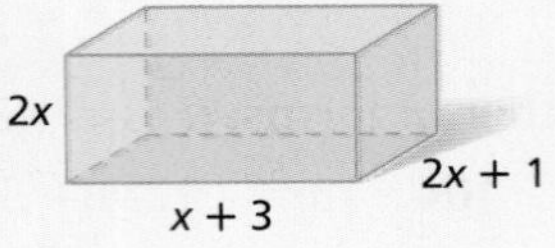


**5.**

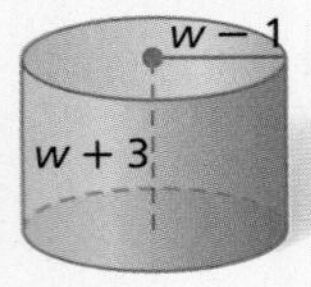


**6.**

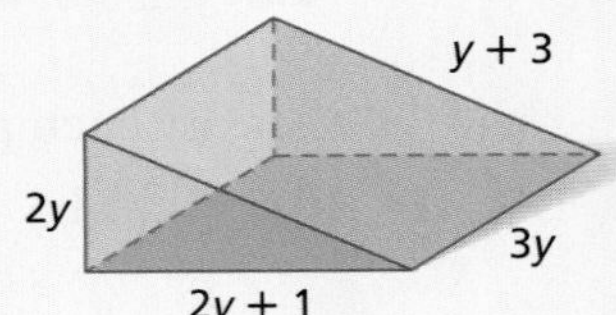

# 7-8 Special Products of Binomials

**MA.A.1.1** Execute ... operations with algebraic expressions... *Also* **MA.A.1, MA.A.1.2, MA.N.2.2, MA.G.2.2**

***Objective***
Find special products of binomials.

***Vocabulary***
perfect-square trinomial
difference of two squares

**Why learn this?**
You can use special products to find areas, such as the area of a deck around a pond. (See Example 4.)

Imagine a square with sides of length $(a + b)$:

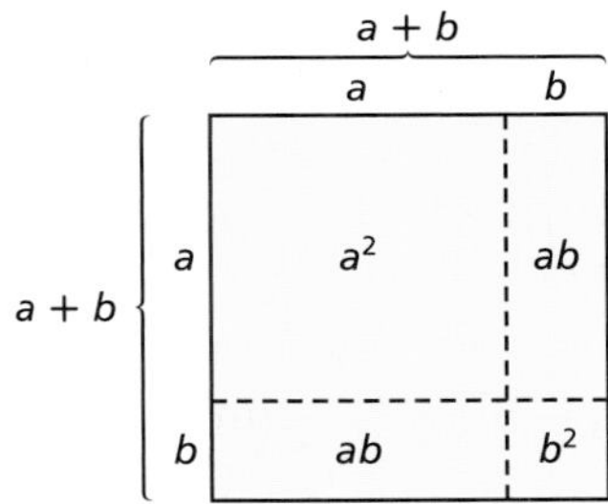


The area of this square is $(a + b)(a + b)$, or $(a + b)^2$. The area of this square can also be found by adding the areas of the smaller squares and rectangles inside. The sum of the areas inside is $\mathbf{a^2 + ab + ab + b^2}$.

This means that $(a + b)^2 = \mathbf{a^2 + 2ab + b^2}$.

You can use the FOIL method to verify this:

$$(a + b)^2 = (a + b)(a + b) = a^2 + \mathbf{ab} + \mathbf{ab} + b^2$$

F L I O

$$= a^2 + 2ab + b^2$$

A trinomial of the form $a^2 + 2ab + b^2$ is called a *perfect-square trinomial*. A **perfect-square trinomial** is a trinomial that is the result of squaring a binomial.

## EXAMPLE 1 Finding Products in the Form $(a + b)^2$

**Multiply.**

**A** $(x + 4)^2$

$(a + b)^2 = a^2 + 2ab + b^2$ — *Use the rule for $(a + b)^2$.*

$(x + 4)^2 = x^2 + 2(x)(4) + 4^2$ — *Identify a and b: $a = x$ and $b = 4$.*

$= x^2 + 8x + 16$ — *Simplify.*

**B** $(3x + 2y)^2$

$(a + b)^2 = a^2 + 2ab + b^2$ — *Use the rule for $(a + b)^2$.*

$(3x + 2y)^2 = (3x)^2 + 2(3x)(2y) + (2y)^2$ — *Identify a and b: $a = 3x$ and $b = 2y$.*

$= 9x^2 + 12xy + 4y^2$ — *Simplify.*

**Multiply.**

**C** $(4 + s^2)^2$

$(a + b)^2 = a^2 + 2ab + b^2$ — *Use the rule for $(a + b)^2$.*

$(4 + s^2)^2 = (4)^2 + 2(4)(s^2) + (s^2)^2$ — *Identify a and b: $a = 4$ and $b = s^2$.*

$= 16 + 8s^2 + s^4$ — *Simplify.*

**D** $(-m + 3)^2$

$(a + b)^2 = a^2 + 2ab + b^2$ — *Use the rule for $(a + b)^2$.*

$(-m + 3)^2 = (-m)^2 + 2(-m)(3) + 3^2$ — *Identify a and b: $a = -m$ and $b = 3$.*

$= m^2 - 6m + 9$ — *Simplify.*

**Multiply.**

**1a.** $(x + 6)^2$ **1b.** $(5a + b)^2$ **1c.** $(1 + c^3)^2$

You can use the FOIL method to find products in the form $(a - b)^2$:

F L I O

$$(a - b)^2 = (a - b)(a - b) = a^2 - ab - ab + b^2$$
$$= a^2 - 2ab + b^2$$

A trinomial of the form $a^2 - 2ab + b^2$ is also a perfect-square trinomial because it is the result of squaring the binomial $(a - b)$.

## EXAMPLE 2 Finding Products in the Form $(a - b)^2$

**Multiply.**

**A** $(x - 5)^2$

$(a - b)^2 = a^2 - 2ab + b^2$ — *Use the rule for $(a - b)^2$.*

$(x - 5)^2 = x^2 - 2(x)(5) + 5^2$ — *Identify a and b: $a = x$ and $b = 5$.*

$= x^2 - 10x + 25$ — *Simplify.*

**B** $(6a - 1)^2$

$(a - b)^2 = a^2 - 2ab + b^2$ — *Use the rule for $(a - b)^2$.*

$(6a - 1)^2 = (6a)^2 - 2(6a)(1) + (1)^2$ — *Identify a and b: $a = 6a$ and $b = 1$.*

$= 36a^2 - 12a + 1$ — *Simplify.*

**C** $(4c - 3d)^2$

$(a - b)^2 = a^2 - 2ab + b^2$ — *Use the rule for $(a - b)^2$.*

$(4c - 3d)^2 = (4c)^2 - 2(4c)(3d) + (3d)^2$ — *Identify a and b: $a = 4c$ and $b = 3d$.*

$= 16c^2 - 24cd + 9d^2$ — *Simplify.*

**D** $(3 - x^2)^2$

$(a - b)^2 = (a)^2 - 2ab + b^2$ — *Use the rule for $(a - b)^2$.*

$(3 - x^2)^2 = (3)^2 - 2(3)(x^2) + (x^2)^2$ — *Identify a and b: $a = 3$ and $b = x^2$.*

$= 9 - 6x^2 + x^4$ — *Simplify.*

**Multiply.**

**2a.** $(x - 7)^2$ **2b.** $(3b - 2c)^2$ **2c.** $(a^2 - 4)^2$

You can use an area model to see that $(a + b)(a - b) = a^2 - b^2$.

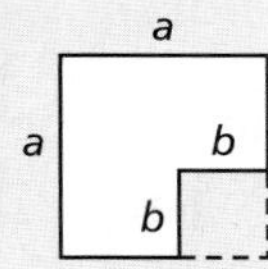


Begin with a square with area $a^2$. Remove a square with area $b^2$. The area of the new figure is $a^2 - b^2$.

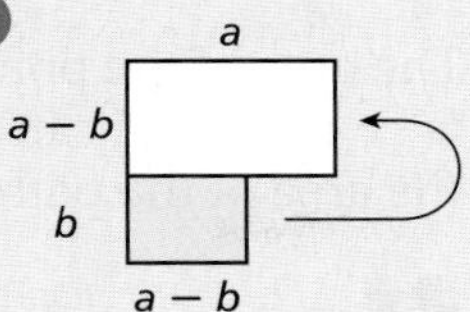


Then remove the smaller rectangle on the bottom. Turn it and slide it up next to the top rectangle.

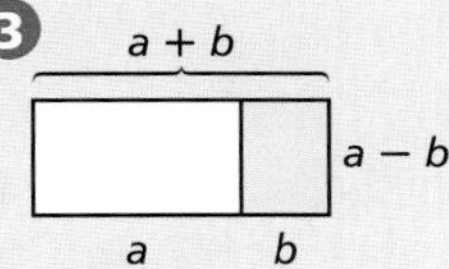


The new arrangement is a rectangle with length $a + b$ and width $a - b$. Its area is $(a + b)(a - b)$.

So $(a + b)(a - b) = a^2 - b^2$. A binomial of the form $a^2 - b^2$ is called a **difference of two squares**.

## EXAMPLE 3 Finding Products in the Form $(a + b)(a - b)$

**Multiply.**

**A** $(x + 6)(x - 6)$

$(a + b)(a - b) = a^2 - b^2$ — *Use the rule for $(a + b)(a - b)$.*

$(x + 6)(x - 6) = x^2 - 6^2$ — *Identify a and b: $a = x$ and $b = 6$.*

$= x^2 - 36$ — *Simplify.*

**B** $(x^2 + 2y)(x^2 - 2y)$

$(a + b)(a - b) = a^2 - b^2$ — *Use the rule for $(a + b)(a - b)$.*

$(x^2 + 2y)(x^2 - 2y) = (x^2)^2 - (2y)^2$ — *Identify a and b: $a = x^2$ and $b = 2y$.*

$= x^4 - 4y^2$ — *Simplify.*

**C** $(7 + n)(7 - n)$

$(a + b)(a - b) = a^2 - b^2$ — *Use the rule for $(a + b)(a - b)$.*

$(7 + n)(7 - n) = 7^2 - n^2$ — *Identify a and b: $a = 7$ and $b = n$.*

$= 49 - n^2$ — *Simplify.*

**Multiply.**

**3a.** $(x + 8)(x - 8)$ **3b.** $(3 + 2y^2)(3 - 2y^2)$ **3c.** $(9 + r)(9 - r)$

## EXAMPLE 4 *Problem-Solving Application*

**A square koi pond is surrounded by a gravel path. Write an expression that represents the area of the path.**

### 1 Understand the Problem

The **answer** will be an expression that represents the area of the path.

**List the important information:**

- The pond is a square with a side length of $x - 2$.
- The path has a side length of $x + 2$.

## Make a Plan

The area of the pond is $(x-2)^2$. The total area of the path plus the pond is $(x+2)^2$. You can subtract the area of the pond from the total area to find the area of the path.

## Solve

**Step 1** Find the total area.

$$(x+2)^2 = x^2 + 2(x)(2) + 2^2$$ *Use the rule for $(a+b)^2$: $a = x$ and $b = 2$.*

$$= x^2 + 4x + 4$$

**Step 2** Find the area of the pond.

$$(x-2)^2 = x^2 - 2(x)(2) + 2^2$$ *Use the rule for $(a-b)^2$: $a = x$ and $b = 2$.*

$$= x^2 - 4x + 4$$

**Remember!**

To subtract a polynomial, add the opposite of *each* term.

**Step 3** Find the area of the path.

| area of path | = | total area | − | area of pond |
|---|---|---|---|---|
| $a$ | = | $x^2 + 4x + 4$ | − | $(x^2 - 4x + 4)$ |

$= x^2 + 4x + 4 - x^2 + 4x - 4$ *Identify like terms.*

$= (x^2 - x^2) + (4x + 4x) + (4 - 4)$ *Group like terms together.*

$= 8x$

The area of the path is $8x$. *Combine like terms.*

## Look Back

Suppose that $x = 10$. Then one side of the path is 12, and the total area is $12^2$, or 144. Also, if $x = 10$, one side of the pond is 8, and the area of the pond is $8^2$, or 64. This means the area of the path is $144 - 64 = 80$.

According to the solution above, the area of the path is $8x$. If $x = 10$, then $8x = 8(10) = 80$. ✓

**4.** Write an expression that represents the area of the swimming pool at right.

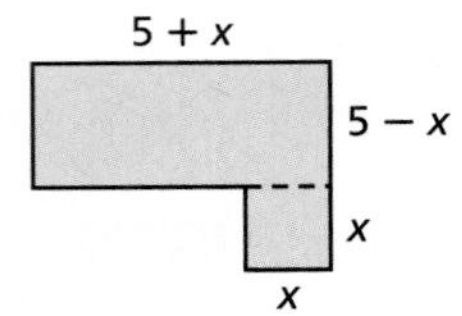

**Special Products of Binomials**

**Perfect-Square Trinomials**

$$(a+b)^2 = (a+b)(a+b) = a^2 + 2ab + b^2$$
$$(a-b)^2 = (a-b)(a-b) = a^2 - 2ab + b^2$$

**Difference of Two Squares**

$$(a+b)(a-b) = a^2 - b^2$$

## THINK AND DISCUSS

1. Use the FOIL method to verify that $(a + b)(a - b) = a^2 - b^2$.
2. When a binomial is squared, the middle term of the resulting trinomial is twice the ___?___ of the first and last terms.
3. **GET ORGANIZED** Copy and complete the graphic organizer. Complete the special product rules and give an example of each.

| Special Products of Binomials | | |
|---|---|---|
| Perfect-Square Trinomials | | Difference of Two Squares |
| $(a + b)^2 = ?$ | $(a - b)^2 = ?$ | $(a + b)(a - b) = ?$ |

# 7-8 Exercises

MA.A.1.1, MA.A.1, MA.A.1.2, MA.N.2.2, MA.G.2.2

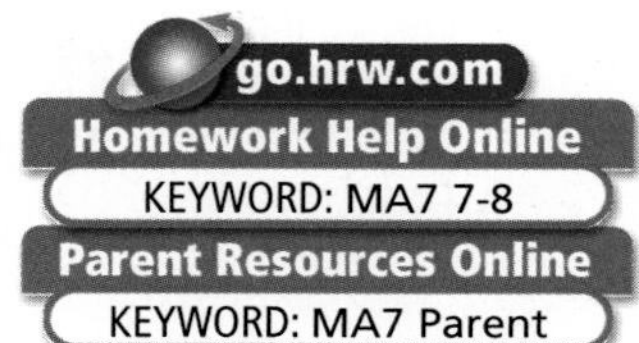


## GUIDED PRACTICE

1. **Vocabulary** In your own words, describe a *perfect-square trinomial*.

SEE EXAMPLE 1 p. 501

**Multiply.**

2. $(x + 7)^2$
3. $(2 + x)^2$
4. $(x + 1)^2$
5. $(2x + 6)^2$
6. $(5x + 9)^2$
7. $(2a + 7b)^2$

SEE EXAMPLE 2 p. 502

8. $(x - 6)^2$
9. $(x - 2)^2$
10. $(2x - 1)^2$
11. $(8 - x)^2$
12. $(6p - q)^2$
13. $(7a - 2b)^2$

SEE EXAMPLE 3 p. 503

14. $(x + 5)(x - 5)$
15. $(x + 6)(x - 6)$
16. $(5x + 1)(5x - 1)$
17. $(2x^2 + 3)(2x^2 - 3)$
18. $(9 - x^3)(9 + x^3)$
19. $(2x - 5y)(2x + 5y)$

SEE EXAMPLE 4 p. 503

20. **Geometry** Write a polynomial that represents the area of the figure.

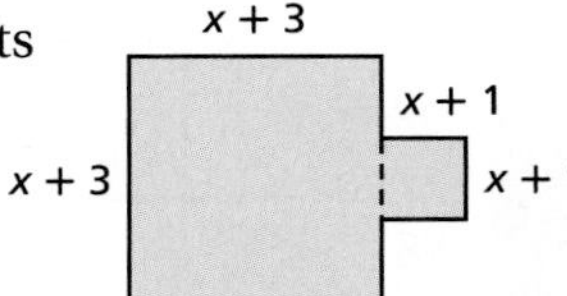


## PRACTICE AND PROBLEM SOLVING

| Independent Practice | |
|---|---|
| For Exercises | See Example |
| 21–26 | 1 |
| 27–32 | 2 |
| 33–38 | 3 |
| 39 | 4 |

**Extra Practice**
Skills Practice p. S17
Application Practice p. S34

**Multiply.**

21. $(x + 3)^2$
22. $(4 + z)^2$
23. $(x^2 + y^2)^2$
24. $(p + 2q^3)^2$
25. $(2 + 3x)^2$
26. $(r^2 + 5t)^2$
27. $(s^2 - 7)^2$
28. $(2c - d^3)^2$
29. $(a - 8)^2$
30. $(5 - w)^2$
31. $(3x - 4)^2$
32. $(1 - x^2)^2$
33. $(a - 10)(a + 10)$
34. $(y + 4)(y - 4)$
35. $(7x + 3)(7x - 3)$
36. $(x^2 - 2)(x^2 + 2)$
37. $(5a^2 + 9)(5a^2 - 9)$
38. $(x^3 + y^2)(x^3 - y^2)$

39. **Entertainment** Write a polynomial that represents the area of the circular puzzle. Remember that the formula for area of a circle is $A = \pi r^2$, where $r$ is the radius of the circle. Leave the symbol $\pi$ in your answer.

40. **Multi-Step** A square has sides that are $(x - 1)$ units long and a rectangle has a length of $x$ units and a width of $(x - 2)$ units.
    a. What are the possible values of $x$? Explain.
    b. Which has the greater area, the square or the rectangle?
    c. What is the difference in the areas?

**Multiply.**

41. $(x + y)^2$
42. $(x - y)^2$
43. $(x^2 + 4)(x^2 - 4)$
44. $(x^2 + 4)^2$
45. $(x^2 - 4)^2$
46. $(1 - x)^2$
47. $(1 + x)^2$
48. $(1 - x)(1 + x)$
49. $(x^3 - a^3)(x^3 - a^3)$
50. $(5 + n)(5 + n)$
51. $(6a - 5b)(6a + 5b)$
52. $(r - 4t^4)(r - 4t^4)$

**Copy and complete the tables to verify the special products of binomials.**

| | a | b | $(a - b)^2$ | $a^2 - 2ab + b^2$ |
|---|---|---|---|---|
| | 1 | 4 | $(1 - 4)^2 = 9$ | $1^2 - 2(1)(4) + 4^2 = 9$ |
| 53. | 2 | 4 | ■ | ■ |
| 54. | 3 | 2 | ■ | ■ |

| | a | b | $(a + b)^2$ | $a^2 + 2ab + b^2$ |
|---|---|---|---|---|
| 55. | 1 | 4 | ■ | ■ |
| 56. | 2 | 5 | ■ | ■ |
| 57. | 3 | 0 | ■ | ■ |

| | a | b | $(a + b)(a - b)$ | $a^2 - b^2$ |
|---|---|---|---|---|
| 58. | 1 | 4 | ■ | ■ |
| 59. | 2 | 3 | ■ | ■ |
| 60. | 3 | 2 | ■ | ■ |

LINK

**Math History**

Beginning about 3000 B.C.E., the Babylonians lived in what is now Iraq and Turkey. Around 575 B.C.E., they built the Ishtar Gate to serve as one of eight main entrances into the city of Babylon. The image above is a relief sculpture from a restoration of the Ishtar Gate.

61. **Math History** The Babylonians used tables of squares and the formula $ab = \frac{(a + b)^2 - (a - b)^2}{4}$ to multiply two numbers. Use this formula to find the product $35 \cdot 24$.

62. **Critical Thinking** Find a value of $c$ that makes $16x^2 - 24x + c$ a perfect-square trinomial.

63. **ERROR ANALYSIS** Explain the error below. What is the correct product?
$(a - b)^2 = a^2 - b^2$

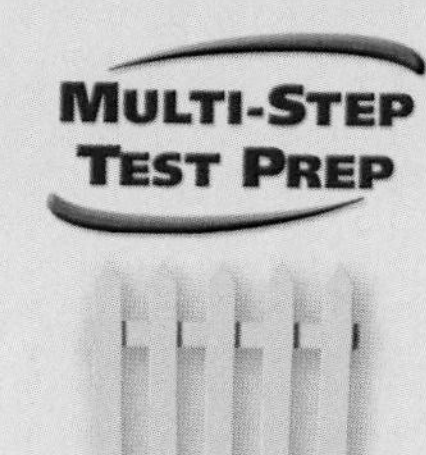


**64.** This problem will prepare you for the Multi-Step Test Prep on page 508.

**a.** Michael is fencing part of his yard. He started with a square of length $x$ on each side. He then added 3 feet to the length and subtracted 3 feet from the width. Make a sketch to show the fenced area with the length and width labeled.

**b.** Write a polynomial that represents the area of the fenced region.

**c.** Michael bought a total of 48 feet of fencing. What is the area of his fenced region?

**65. Critical Thinking** The polynomial $ax^2 - 49$ is a difference of two squares. Find all possible values of $a$ between 1 and 100 inclusive.

**66. Write About It** When is the product of two binomials also a binomial? Explain and give an example.

## TEST PREP

NC MA.A.1.1, MA.A.1, MA.A.1.2, MA.N.2.2, MA.G.2.2

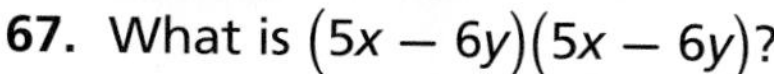

**67.** What is $(5x - 6y)(5x - 6y)$?

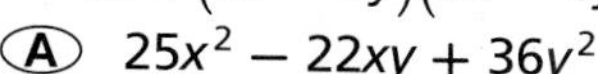

Ⓐ $25x^2 - 22xy + 36y^2$
Ⓑ $25x^2 - 60xy + 36y^2$
Ⓒ $25x^2 + 22xy + 36y^2$
Ⓓ $25x^2 + 60xy + 36y^2$

**68.** Which product is represented by the model?

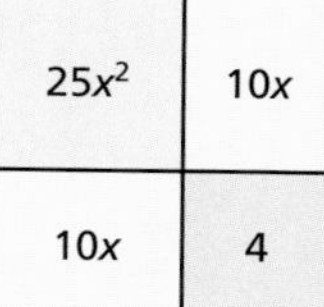


Ⓕ $(2x + 5)(2x + 5)$
Ⓖ $(5x - 2)(5x - 2)$
Ⓗ $(5x + 2)(5x - 2)$
Ⓙ $(5x + 2)(5x + 2)$

**69.** If $a + b = 12$ and $a^2 - b^2 = 96$ what is the value of $a$?

Ⓐ 2 Ⓑ 4 Ⓒ 8 Ⓓ 10

**70.** If $rs = 15$ and $(r + s)^2 = 64$, what is the value of $r^2 + s^2$?

Ⓕ 25 Ⓖ 30 Ⓗ 34 Ⓙ 49

## CHALLENGE AND EXTEND

**71.** Multiply $(x + 4)(x + 4)(x - 4)$.

**72.** Multiply $(x + 4)(x - 4)(x - 4)$.

**73.** If $x^2 + bx + c$ is a perfect-square trinomial, what is the relationship between $b$ and $c$?

**74.** You can multiply two numbers by rewriting the numbers as the difference of two squares. For example:

$$36 \cdot 24 = (30 + 6)(30 - 6) = 30^2 - 6^2 = 900 - 36 = 864$$

Use this method to multiply $27 \cdot 19$. Explain how you rewrote the numbers.

## SPIRAL REVIEW

**75.** The square paper that Yuki is using to make an origami frog has an area of 165 cm². Find the side length of the paper to the nearest centimeter. *(Lesson 1-5)*

**Use intercepts to graph the line described by each equation.** *(Lesson 5-2)*

**76.** $2x + 3y = 6$

**77.** $y = -3x + 9$

**78.** $\frac{1}{2}x + y = 4$

**Add or subtract.** *(Lesson 7-6)*

**79.** $3x^2 + 8x - 2x + 9x^2$

**80.** $(8m^4 + 2n - 3m^3 + 6) + (9m^3 + 5 - 4m^4)$

**81.** $(2p^3 + p) - (5p^3 + 9p)$

**82.** $(12t - 3t^2 + 10) - (-5t^2 - 7 - 4t)$

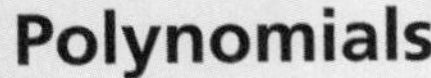

## Polynomials

**Don't Fence Me In** James has 500 feet of fencing to enclose a rectangular region on his farm for some sheep.

1. Make a sketch of three possible regions that James could enclose and give the corresponding areas.
2. If the length of the region is $x$, find an expression for the width.
3. Use your answer to Problem 2 to write an equation for the area of the region.
4. Graph your equation from Problem 3 on your calculator. Sketch the graph.
5. James wants his fenced region to have the largest area possible using 500 feet of fencing. Find this area using the graph or a table of values.
6. What are the length and width of the region with the area from Problem 5? Describe this region.

# READY TO GO ON?

CHAPTER 7

SECTION 7B

## Quiz for Lessons 7-5 Through 7-8

### 7-5 Polynomials

**Write each polynomial in standard form and give the leading coefficient.**

1. $4r^2 + 2r^6 - 3r$
2. $y^2 + 7 - 8y^3 + 2y$
3. $-12t^3 - 4t + t^4$
4. $n + 3 + 3n^2$
5. $2 + 3x^3$
6. $-3a^2 + 16 + a^7 + a$

**Classify each polynomial according to its degree and number of terms.**

7. $2x^3 + 5x - 4$
8. $5b^2$
9. $6p^2 + 3p - p^4 + 2p^3$
10. $x^2 + 12 - x$
11. $-2x^3 - 5 + x - 2x^7$
12. $5 - 6b^2 + b - 4b^4$

13. **Business** The function $C(x) = x^3 - 15x + 14$ gives the cost to manufacture $x$ units of a product. What is the cost to manufacture 900 units?

### 7-6 Adding and Subtracting Polynomials

**Add or subtract.**

14. $(10m^3 + 4m^2) + (7m^2 + 3m)$
15. $(3t^2 - 2t) + (9t^2 + 4t - 6)$
16. $(12d^6 - 3d^2) + (2d^4 + 1)$
17. $(6y^3 + 4y^2) - (2y^2 + 3y)$
18. $(7n^2 - 3n) - (5n^2 + 5n)$
19. $(b^2 - 10) - (-5b^3 + 4b)$

20. **Geometry** The measures of the sides of a triangle are shown as polynomials. Write a simplified polynomial to represent the perimeter of the triangle.

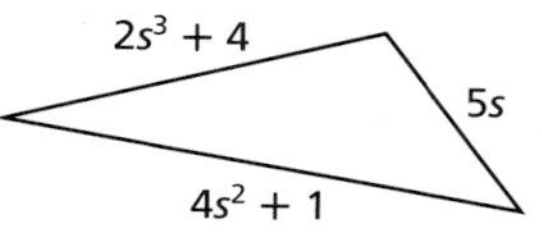


### 7-7 Multiplying Polynomials

**Multiply.**

21. $2h^3 \cdot 5h^5$
22. $(s^8t^4)(-6st^3)$
23. $2ab(5a^3 + 3a^2b)$
24. $(3k + 5)^2$
25. $(2x^3 + 3y)(4x^2 + y)$
26. $(p^2 + 3p)(9p^2 - 6p - 5)$

27. **Geometry** Write a simplified polynomial expression for the area of a parallelogram whose base is $(x + 7)$ units and whose height is $(x - 3)$ units.

### 7-8 Special Products of Binomials

**Multiply.**

28. $(d + 9)^2$
29. $(3 + 2t)^2$
30. $(2x + 5y)^2$
31. $(m - 4)^2$
32. $(a - b)^2$
33. $(3w - 1)^2$
34. $(c + 2)(c - 2)$
35. $(5r + 6)(5r - 6)$

36. **Sports** A child's basketball has a radius of $(x - 5)$ inches. Write a polynomial that represents the surface area of the basketball. (The formula for the surface area of a sphere is $S = 4\pi r^2$, where $r$ represents the radius of the sphere.) Leave the symbol $\pi$ in your answer.

CHAPTER 7

# Study Guide: Review

## Vocabulary



**Complete the sentences below with vocabulary words from the list above.**

1. A(n) __?__ polynomial is a polynomial of degree 3.
2. When a polynomial is written with the terms in order from highest to lowest degree, it is in __?__.
3. A(n) __?__ is a number, a variable, or a product of numbers and variables with whole-number exponents.
4. A(n) __?__ is a polynomial with three terms.
5. __?__ is a method of writing numbers that are very large or very small.

## 7-1 Integer Exponents *(pp. 446–451)*

MA.N.2.1, MA.N.2.2

### EXAMPLES

Simplify.

■ $-2^{-4}$

$-2^{-4} = -\frac{1}{2^4} = -\frac{1}{2 \cdot 2 \cdot 2 \cdot 2} = -\frac{1}{16}$

■ $3^0$

$3^0 = 1$ *Any nonzero number raised to the zero power is 1.*

■ **Evaluate $r^3s^{-4}$ for $r = -3$ and $s = 2$.**

$r^3s^{-4}$

$(-3)^3(2)^{-4} = \frac{(-3)(-3)(-3)}{2 \cdot 2 \cdot 2 \cdot 2} = -\frac{27}{16}$

■ **Simplify $\frac{a^{-3}b^4}{c^{-2}}$.**

$\frac{a^{-3}b^4}{c^{-2}} = \frac{b^4c^2}{a^3}$

### EXERCISES

6. The diameter of a certain bearing is $2^{-5}$ in. Evaluate this expression.

**Simplify.**

7. $(3.6)^0$
8. $(-1)^{-4}$
9. $5^{-3}$
10. $10^{-4}$

**Evaluate each expression for the given value(s) of the variable(s).**

11. $b^{-4}$ for $b = 2$
12. $\left(\frac{2}{5}b\right)^{-4}$ for $b = 10$
13. $-2p^3q^{-3}$ for $p = 3$ and $q = -2$

**Simplify.**

14. $m^{-2}$
15. $bc^0$
16. $-\frac{1}{2}x^{-2}y^{-4}$
17. $\frac{2b^6}{c^{-4}}$
18. $\frac{3a^2c^{-2}}{4b^0}$
19. $\frac{q^{-1}r^{-2}}{s^{-3}}$

## 7-2 Powers of 10 and Scientific Notation *(pp. 452–457)*

### EXAMPLES

- **Write 1,000,000 as a power of 10.**

  1,000,000 — *The decimal point is 6 places to the right of 1.*

  $1{,}000{,}000 = 10^6$

- **Find the value of $386.21 \times 10^5$.**

  386.2 1 0 0 0 — *Move the decimal point 5 places to the right.*

  38,621,000

- **Write 0.000000041 in scientific notation.**

  0.0 0 0 0 0 0 0 4 1 — *Move the decimal point 8 places to the right to get a number between 1 and 10.*

  $4.1 \times 10^{-8}$

### EXERCISES

**Find the value of each power of 10.**

**20.** $10^7$ **21.** $10^{-5}$

**Write each number as a power of 10.**

**22.** 100 **23.** 0.00000000001

**Find the value of each expression.**

**24.** $3.25 \times 10^5$ **25.** $0.18 \times 10^4$

**26.** $17 \times 10^{-2}$ **27.** $299 \times 10^{-6}$

**28.** Order the list of numbers from least to greatest. $6.3 \times 10^{-3}$, $1.2 \times 10^4$, $5.8 \times 10^{-7}$, $2.2 \times 10^2$

**29.** In 2003, the average daily value of shares traded on the New York Stock Exchange was about $\$3.85 \times 10^{10}$. Write this amount in standard form.

## 7-3 Multiplication Properties of Exponents *(pp. 460–466)*

### EXAMPLES

**Simplify.**

- $5^3 \cdot 5^{-2}$

  $5^3 \cdot 5^{-2}$ — *The powers have the same base.*

  $5^{3+(-2)}$ — *Add the exponents.*

  $5^1$

  $5$

- $a^4 \cdot b^{-3} \cdot b \cdot a^{-2}$

  $a^4 \cdot b^{-3} \cdot b \cdot a^{-2}$ — *Use properties to group factors.*

  $(a^4 \cdot a^{-2}) \cdot (b^{-3} \cdot b)$

  $a^2 \cdot b^{-2}$ — *Add the exponents of powers with the same base.*

  $\dfrac{a^2}{b^2}$ — *Write with a positive exponent.*

- $(a^{-3}b^2)^{-2}$

  $(a^{-3})^{-2} \cdot (b^2)^{-2}$ — *Power of a Product Property*

  $a^6 \cdot b^{-4}$ — *Power of a Power Property*

  $\dfrac{a^6}{b^4}$ — *Write with a positive exponent.*

### EXERCISES

**Simplify.**

**30.** $5^3 \cdot 5^6$ **31.** $2^6 \cdot 3 \cdot 2^{-3} \cdot 3^3$

**32.** $b^2 \cdot b^8$ **33.** $r^4 \cdot r$

**34.** $(x^3)^4$ **35.** $(s^3)^0$

**36.** $(2^3)^{-1}$ **37.** $(5^2)^{-2}$

**38.** $(4b^3)^{-2}$ **39.** $(g^3h^2)^4$

**40.** $(-x^2y)^2$ **41.** $-(x^2y)^2$

**42.** $(x^2y^3)(xy^3)^4$ **43.** $(j^2k^3)(j^4k^6)$

**44.** $(5^3 \cdot 5^{-2})^{-1}$ **45.** $(mn^3)^5(mn^5)^3$

**46.** $(4 \times 10^8)(2 \times 10^3)$ **47.** $(3 \times 10^2)(3 \times 10^5)$

**48.** $(5 \times 10^3)(2 \times 10^6)$ **49.** $(7 \times 10^5)(4 \times 10^9)$

**50.** $(3 \times 10^{-4})(2 \times 10^5)$ **51.** $(3 \times 10^{-8})(6 \times 10^{-1})$

**52.** In 2003, Wyoming's population was about $5.0 \times 10^5$. California's population was about $7.1 \times 10$ times as large as Wyoming's. What was the approximate population of California? Write your answer in scientific notation.

## 7-4 Division Properties of Exponents *(pp. 467–473)*

### EXAMPLES

■ **Simplify $\frac{x^9}{x^2}$.**

$\frac{x^9}{x^2} = x^{9-2}$ *The powers have the same base.*

$x^7$ *Subtract the exponents.*

■ **Write $(3 \times 10^{12}) \div (6 \times 10^7)$ in scientific notation.**

$$(3 \times 10^{12}) \div (6 \times 10^7) = \frac{(3 \times 10^{12})}{(6 \times 10^7)}$$
$$= \frac{3}{6} \times \frac{10^{12}}{10^7}$$
$$= 0.5 \times 10^{12-7}$$
$$= 0.5 \times 10^5$$
$$= 5 \times 10^{-1} \times 10^5$$
$$= 5 \times 10^4$$

### EXERCISES

**Simplify.**

53. $\frac{2^8}{2^2}$

54. $\frac{(-2)^5}{(-2)^3}$

55. $\frac{m^6}{m}$

56. $\frac{p^5}{p^5}$

57. $\frac{2^6 \cdot 4 \cdot 7^3}{2^5 \cdot 4^4 \cdot 7^2}$

58. $\frac{24b^6}{4b^5}$

59. $\frac{t^4v^5}{tv}$

60. $\left(\frac{1}{2}\right)^{-4}$

**Simplify each quotient and write the answer in scientific notation.**

61. $(2.5 \times 10^8) \div (0.5 \times 10^7)$

62. $(2 \times 10^{10}) \div (8 \times 10^2)$

63. $(8.2 \times 10^{15}) \div (4.1 \times 10^{11})$

64. $(4.5 \times 10^{15}) \div (2 \times 10^8)$

## 7-5 Polynomials *(pp. 476–481)*

Prep MA.A.1.1, Prep MA.A.1, Prep MA.A.1.2

### EXAMPLES

■ **Find the degree of the polynomial $3x^2 + 8x^5$.**

$3x^2 + 8x^5$ *$8x^5$ has the highest degree.*

The degree is 5.

■ **Write the polynomial $6y - 4y^3 + 2y^2 - 1$ in standard form. Then give the leading coefficient,**

The standard form is $-4y^3 + 2y^2 + 6y - 1$.

The leading coefficient is $-4$.

■ **Classify the polynomial $y^3 - 2y$ according to its degree and number of terms.**

Degree: 3
Terms: 2

The polynomial $y^3 - 2y$ is a **cubic binomial.**

### EXERCISES

**Find the degree of each polynomial.**

65. $5$

66. $8st^3 + 10st$

67. $3z^6 - 4z + 12$

68. $6h - 4 + 2h^7$

69. $5k - 5k^2 - 2$

70. $b - 6$

**Write each polynomial in standard form. Then give the leading coefficient.**

71. $2n - 4 + 3n^2$

72. $2a - a^4 - a^6 + 3a^3$

73. $1 - t - 5t^2$

74. $12v + 6v^4 + 3$

75. $5 + x - 2x^2$

76. $-w^3 - 2w^6 + w^2 - w$

**Classify each polynomial according to its degree and number of terms.**

77. $2s - 6$

78. $-8p^5$

79. $3n^2 - 5n + 7$

80. $6g^3 + 4g^2 - 8g - 2$

81. $-m^4 - m^2 - 1$

82. $2$

83. $8 - 2r^3 + r^5$

84. $-2x^3 - 5 + x - 2x^7$

## 7-6 Adding and Subtracting Polynomials *(pp. 484–489)*

MA.A.1.1, MA.A.1, MA.A.1.2

### EXAMPLES

**Add.**

- $(h^3 - 2h) + (3h^2 + 4h) - 2h^3$

  $(h^3 - 2h) + (3h^2 + 4h) - 2h^3$

  $(h^3 - 2h^3) + (3h^2) + (4h - 2h)$

  $-h^3 + 3h^2 + 2h$

**Subtract.**

- $(n^3 + 5 - 6n^2) - (3n^2 - 7)$

  $(n^3 + 5 - 6n^2) + (-3n^2 + 7)$

  $(n^3 + 5 - 6n^2) + (-3n^2 + 7)$

  $n^3 + (-6n^2 - 3n^2) + (5 + 7)$

  $n^3 - 9n^2 + 12$

### EXERCISES

**Add or subtract.**

85. $3t + 5 - 7t - 2$
86. $4x^5 - 6x^6 + 2x^5 - 7x^5$
87. $-h^3 - 2h^2 + 4h^3 - h^2 + 5$
88. $(3m - 7) + (2m^2 - 8m + 6)$
89. $(12 + 6p) - (p - p^2 + 4)$
90. $(3z - 9z^2 + 2) + (2z^2 - 4z + 8)$
91. $(10g - g^2 + 3) - (-4g^2 + 8g - 1)$
92. $(-5x^3 + 2x^2 - x + 5) - (-5x^3 + 3x^2 - 5x - 3)$

## 7-7 Multiplying Polynomials *(pp. 492–499)*

MA.A.1.1, MA.A.1, MA.A.1.2, MA.N.2.2, MA.G.2.2

### EXAMPLES

**Multiply.**

- $(2x - 4)(3x + 5)$

  $2x(3x) + 2x(5) - 4(3x) - 4(5)$

  $6x^2 + 10x - 12x - 20$

  $6x^2 - 2x - 20$

- $(b - 2)(b^2 + 4b - 5)$

  $b(b^2) + b(4b) - b(5) - 2(b^2) - 2(4b) - 2(-5)$

  $b^3 + 4b^2 - 5b - 2b^2 + (-8b) + 10$

  $b^3 + 2b^2 - 13b + 10$

### EXERCISES

**Multiply.**

93. $(2r)(4r)$
94. $(3a^5)(2ab)$
95. $(-3xy)(-6x^2y)$
96. $(3s^3t^2)(2st^4)\left(\frac{1}{2}s^2t^8\right)$
97. $2(x^2 - 4x + 6)$
98. $-3ab(ab - 2a^2b + 5a)$
99. $(a + 3)(a - 6)$
100. $(b - 9)(b + 3)$
101. $(x - 10)(x - 2)$
102. $(t - 1)(t + 1)$
103. $(2q + 6)(4q + 5)$
104. $(5g - 8)(4g - 1)$

## 7-8 Special Products of Binomials *(pp. 501–507)*

MA.A.1.1, MA.A.1, MA.A.1.2, MA.N.2.2, MA.G.2.2

### EXAMPLES

**Multiply.**

- $(2h - 6)^2$

  $(2h - 6)^2 = (2h)^2 + 2(2h)(-6) + (-6)^2$

  $4h^2 - 24h + 36$

- $(4x - 3)(4x + 3)$

  $(4x - 3)(4x + 3) = (4x)^2 - 3^2$

  $16x^2 - 9$

### EXERCISES

**Multiply.**

105. $(p - 4)^2$
106. $(x + 12)^2$
107. $(m + 6)^2$
108. $(3c + 7)^2$
109. $(2r - 1)^2$
110. $(3a - b)^2$
111. $(2n - 5)^2$
112. $(h - 13)^2$
113. $(x - 1)(x + 1)$
114. $(z + 15)(z - 15)$
115. $(c^2 - d)(c^2 + d)$
116. $(3k^2 + 7)(3k^2 - 7)$

CHAPTER 7

Evaluate each expression for the given value(s) of the variable(s).

1. $\left(\frac{1}{3}b\right)^{-2}$ for $b = 12$

2. $\left(14 - a^0b^2\right)^{-3}$ for $a = -2$ and $b = 4$

Simplify.

3. $2r^{-3}$

4. $-3f^0g^{-1}$

5. $m^2n^{-3}$

6. $\frac{1}{2}s^{-5}t^3$

Write each number as a power of 10.

7. 0.0000001

8. 10,000,000,000,000

9. 1

Find the value of each expression.

10. $1.25 \times 10^{-5}$

11. $10^8 \times 10^{-11}$

12. $325 \times 10^{-2}$

13. **Technology** In 2002, there were approximately 544,000,000 Internet users worldwide. Write this number in scientific notation.

Simplify.

14. $\left(f^4\right)^3$

15. $\left(4b^2\right)^0$

16. $\left(a^3b^6\right)^6$

17. $-\left(x^3\right)^5 \cdot \left(x^2\right)^6$

Simplify each quotient and write the answer in scientific notation.

18. $\left(3.6 \times 10^9\right) \div \left(6 \times 10^4\right)$

19. $\left(3 \times 10^{12}\right) \div \left(9.6 \times 10^{16}\right)$

Simplify.

20. $\frac{y^4}{y}$

21. $\frac{d^2f^5}{\left(d^3\right)^2f^{-4}}$

22. $\frac{2^5 \cdot 3^3 \cdot 5^4}{2^8 \cdot 3^2 \cdot 5^4}$

23. $\left(\frac{4s}{3t}\right)^{-2} \cdot \left(\frac{2s}{6t}\right)^2$

24. **Geometry** The surface area of a cone is approximated by the polynomial $3.14r^2 + 3.14r\ell$, where $r$ is the radius and $\ell$ is the slant height. Find the approximate surface area of a cone when $\ell = 5$ cm and $r = 3$ cm.

Add or subtract.

25. $3a - 4b + 2a$

26. $\left(2b^2 - 4b^3\right) - \left(6b^3 + 8b^2\right)$

27. $-9g^2 + 3g - 4g^3 - 2g + 3g^2 - 4$

Multiply.

28. $-5\left(r^2s - 6\right)$

29. $(2t - 7)(t + 4)$

30. $\left(4g - 1\right)\left(4g^2 - 5g - 3\right)$

31. $(m + 6)^2$

32. $(3t - 7)(3t + 7)$

33. $\left(3x^2 - 7\right)^2$

34. **Carpentry** Carpenters use a tool called a *speed square* to help them mark right angles. A speed square is a right triangle.

   a. Write a polynomial that represents the area of the speed square shown.

   b. Find the area when $x = 4.5$ in.

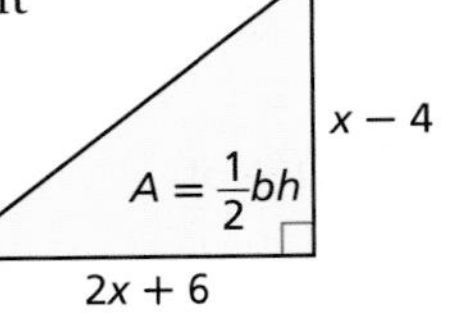

# COLLEGE ENTRANCE EXAM PRACTICE

CHAPTER 7

## *FOCUS ON SAT*

When you receive your SAT scores, you will find a percentile for each score. The percentile tells you what percent of students scored lower than you on the same test. Your percentile at the national and state levels may differ because of the different groups being compared.

**You may want to time yourself as you take this practice test. It should take you about 7 minutes to complete.**

**You may use some types of calculators on the math section of the SAT. For about 40% of the test items, a graphing or scientific calculator is recommended. Bring a calculator that you are comfortable using. You won't have time to figure out how a new calculator works.**

---

**1.** If $(x + 1)(x + 4) - (x - 1)(x - 2) = 0$, what is the value of $x$?

**(A)** $-1$

**(B)** $-\frac{1}{4}$

**(C)** $0$

**(D)** $\frac{1}{4}$

**(E)** $1$

---

**2.** Which of the following is equal to $4^5$?

**I.** $3^5 \times 1^5$

**II.** $2^{10}$

**III.** $4^0 \times 4^5$

**(A)** I only

**(B)** II only

**(C)** I and II only

**(D)** II and III only

**(E)** I, II, and III

---

**3.** If $x^{-4} = 81$, then $x =$

**(A)** $-3$

**(B)** $\frac{1}{4}$

**(C)** $\frac{1}{3}$

**(D)** $3$

**(E)** $9$

---

**4.** What is the value of $2x^3 - 4x^2 + 3x + 1$ when $x = -2$?

**(A)** $-37$

**(B)** $-25$

**(C)** $-5$

**(D)** $7$

**(E)** $27$

---

**5.** What is the area of a rectangle with a length of $x - a$ and a width of $x + b$?

$x - a$

$x + b$

**(A)** $x^2 - a^2$

**(B)** $x^2 + b^2$

**(C)** $x^2 - abx + ab$

**(D)** $x^2 - ax - bx - ab$

**(E)** $x^2 + bx - ax - ab$

---

**6.** For integers greater than 0, define the following operations.

$$a \square b = 2a^2 + 3b$$

$$a \triangle b = 5a^2 - 2b$$

What is $(a \square b) + (a \triangle b)$?

**(A)** $7a^2 + b$

**(B)** $-3a^2 + 5b$

**(C)** $7a^2 - b$

**(D)** $3a^2 - 5b$

**(E)** $-3a^2 - b$

CHAPTER 7

# TEST TACKLER

Standardized Test Strategies

## Any Question Type: Use a Diagram

When a test item includes a diagram, use it to help solve the problem. Gather as much information from the drawing as possible. However, keep in mind that diagrams are not always drawn to scale and can be misleading.

### EXAMPLE 1

**Multiple Choice** **What is the height of the triangle when $x = 4$ and $y = 1$?**

Ⓐ 2 Ⓒ 8

Ⓑ 4 Ⓓ 16

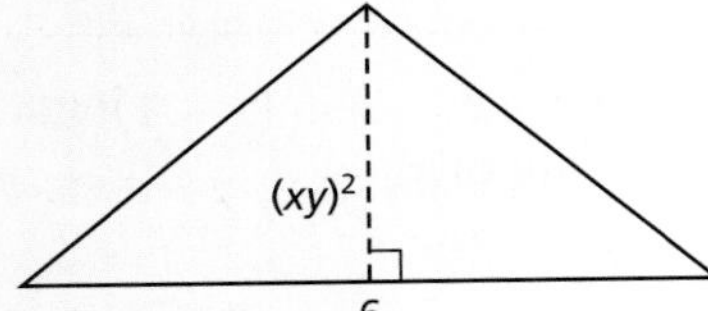


*In the diagram, the height appears to be less than 6, so you might eliminate choices C and D. However, doing the math shows that the height is actually greater than 6. Do not rely solely on visual information. Always use the numbers given in the problem.*

The height of the triangle is $(xy)^2$.
When $x = 4$ and $y = 1$, $(xy)^2 = (4 \cdot 1)^2 = (4)^2 = 16$.
Choice D is the correct answer.

If a test item does not have a diagram, draw a quick sketch of the problem situation. Label your diagram with the data given in the problem.

### EXAMPLE 2

**Short Response** **A square placemat is lying in the middle of a rectangular table. The side length of the placemat is $\left(\frac{x}{2}\right)$. The length of the table is $12x$, and the width is $8x$. Write a polynomial to represent the area of the placemat. Then write a polynomial to represent the area of the table that surrounds the placemat.**

*Use the information in the problem to draw and label a diagram. Then write the polynomials.*

12x
8x
$\frac{x}{2}$
$\frac{x}{2}$

$$\text{area of placemat} = s^2 = \left(\frac{x}{2}\right)^2 = \left(\frac{x}{2}\right)\left(\frac{x}{2}\right) = \frac{x^2}{4}$$

$$\text{area of table} = \ell w = (12x)(8x) = 96x^2$$

$$\text{area of table} - \text{area of placemat} = 96x^2 - \frac{x^2}{4} = \frac{384x^2 - x^2}{4} = \frac{383x^2}{4}$$

The area of the placemat is $\frac{x^2}{4}$.

The area of the table that surrounds the placemat is $\frac{383x^2}{4}$.

If a given diagram does not reflect the problem, draw a sketch that is more accurate. If a test item does not have a diagram, use the given information to sketch your own. Try to make your sketch as accurate as possible.

**Read each test item and answer the questions that follow.**

**Item A**

**Short Response** The width of a rectangle is 1.5 feet more than 4 times its length. Write a polynomial expression for the area of the rectangle. What is the area when the length is 16.75 feet?

1. What is the unknown measure in this problem?
2. How will drawing a diagram help you solve the problem?
3. Draw and label a sketch of the situation.

**Item B**

**Multiple Choice** Rectangle *ABDC* is similar to rectangle *MNPO*. If the width of rectangle *ABDC* is 8, what is its length?

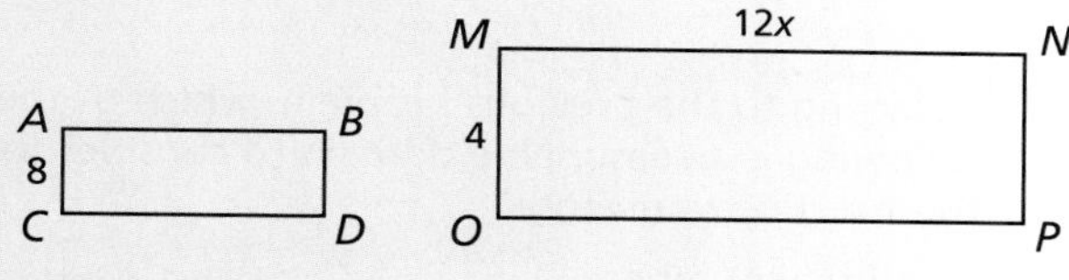


Ⓐ 2

Ⓑ $2x$

Ⓒ $24x$

Ⓓ 24

4. Look at the dimensions in the diagram. Do you think that the length of rectangle *ABDC* is greater or less than the length of rectangle *MNPO*?
5. Do you think the drawings reflect the information in the problem accurately? Why or why not?
6. Draw your own sketch to match the information in the problem.

**Item C**

**Short Response** Write a polynomial expression for the area of triangle *QRP*. Write a polynomial expression for the area of triangle *MNP*. Then use these expressions to write a polynomial expression for the area of *QRNM*.

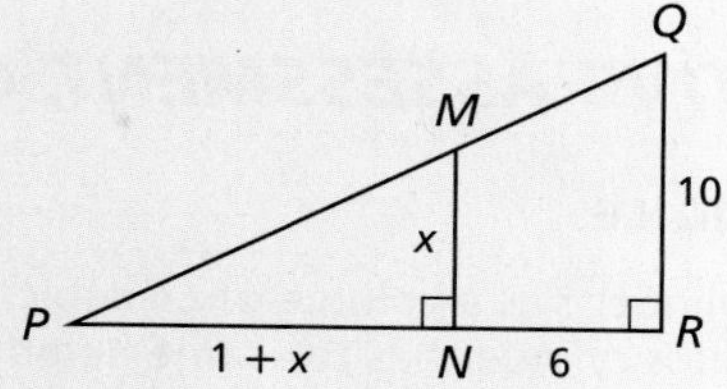


7. Describe how redrawing the figure can help you better understand the information in the problem.
8. After reading this test item, a student redrew the figure as shown below. Is this a correct interpretation of the original figure? Explain.

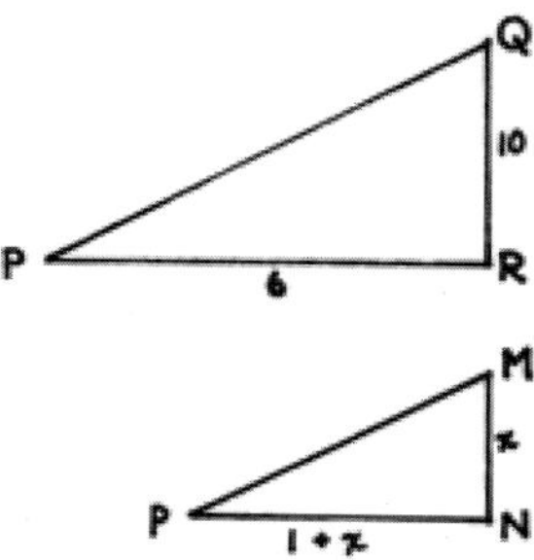


**Item D**

**Multiple Choice** The measure of angle *XYZ* is $(x^2 + 10x + 15)°$. What is the measure of angle *XYW*?

Ⓕ $(6x + 15)°$

Ⓖ $(2x^2 + 14x + 15)°$

Ⓗ $(14x + 15)°$

Ⓙ $(6x^2 + 15)°$

9. What information does the diagram provide that the problem does not?
10. Will the measure of angle *XYW* be less than or greater than the measure of angle *XYZ*? Explain.

CHAPTER 7

go.hrw.com
State Test Practice Online
KEYWORD: MA7 TestPrep

## CUMULATIVE ASSESSMENT, CHAPTERS 1–7

### Multiple Choice

**1.** A plastic cylinder has a volume of 64 cubic inches. A glass cylinder has the same height as the plastic cylinder, but its radius is half the radius of the plastic cylinder. What is the volume of the glass cylinder?

A 4 in$^3$

B 16 in$^3$

C 32 in$^3$

D 64 in$^3$

**2.** Which expression represents the phrase *eight less than the product of a number and two*?

A $2 - 8x$

B $8 - 2x$

C $2x - 8$

D $\frac{x}{2} - 8$

**3.** Which is a solution of the inequality $7 - 3(x - 3) > 2(x + 3)$?

A 0

B 2

C 5

D 12

**4.** Janet is ordering game cartridges from an online retailer. The retailer's prices, including shipping and handling, are given in the table below.

| Game Cartridges | Total Cost ($) |
|---|---|
| 1 | 54.95 |
| 2 | 104.95 |
| 3 | 154.95 |
| 4 | 204.95 |

Which of the following best describes why the relation given in the table is or is not a function?

A The relation is not a function because each number of game cartridges is assigned one price.

B The relation is a function because the Total Cost is increasing.

C The relation is a function because each number of game cartridges is assigned one price.

D The relation is not a function because there are only four ordered pairs in the table.

**5.** When given two variables $x$ and $y$, what does it mean when $x$ is called the independent variable?

A The value of $x$ does not affect the value of $y$.

B The value of $x$ is not restricted in any way by the value of $y$.

C The value of $y$ is not restricted in any way by the value of $x$.

D The standard notation requires only a $y$ variable.

**6.** The average full-time editor for a national newspaper writes 2 articles per week. Each article is read by an average of 3845 people. Let $T$ stand for the total number of times that ***all*** of an editor's articles have been read $w$ weeks into the year. Which equation below best represents $T$?

A $T = 7690$

B $T = 7690 + w$

C $T = 7690w$

D $T = 7690w^2$

**7.** Referring to the previous problem, which of the following is a reasonable domain to consider for the function you chose?

A All real numbers

B $0 \leq w \leq 7690$

C $0 \leq w \leq 52$

D $0 \leq w \leq 25$

**8.** Which equation describes a line parallel to $y = 5 - 2x$?

A $y = -2x + 8$

B $y = 2x - 5$

C $y = 5 + \frac{1}{2}x$

D $y = 5 - \frac{1}{2}x$

**Test writers develop multiple-choice test options with distracters. Distracters are incorrect options that are based on common student errors. Be cautious! Even if the answer you calculated is one of the options, it may not be the correct answer. Always check your work carefully.**

**9.** Jennifer has a pocketful of change, all in nickels and quarters. She has 11 coins with a total value of $1.15. Which system of equations below can be used to find the number of each type of coin?

**A** $\begin{cases} n + q = 11 \\ n + q = 1.15 \end{cases}$

**B** $\begin{cases} n + q = 11 \\ 5n + 25q = 1.15 \end{cases}$

**C** $\begin{cases} 5n + 25q = 11 \\ n + q = 1.15 \end{cases}$

**D** $\begin{cases} n + q = 11 \\ 0.05n + 0.25q = 1.15 \end{cases}$

**10.** A square has sides of length $x - 4$. A rectangle has a length of $x + 2$ and width of $2x - 1$. What is the total combined area of the square and the rectangle?

**A** $10x - 14$

**B** $4x - 3$

**C** $3x^2 - 5x + 14$

**D** $3x^2 + 3x - 18$

**11.** In 1867, the United States purchased the Alaska Territory from Russia for about $\$7.2 \times 10^6$. The total area of the territory was approximately $6.5 \times 10^5$ square miles. Assuming the cost is dependent on the number of square miles, what is the constant of variation?

**A** 1

**B** 12

**C** $6 \times 10^5$

**D** $7.2 \times 10^6$

**12.** Referring to the previous problem, what does the constant of variation represent?

**A** The cost of the Alaska Territory

**B** The total area of the Alaska Territory

**C** The cost per square mile for the Alaska Territory

**D** The constant of variation has no real-life significance in this case.

### *STANDARDIZED TEST PREP*

## Short Response

**S1.** A sweater that normally sells for $35 was marked down 20% and placed on the sale rack. Later, the sweater was marked down an additional 30% and placed on the clearance rack.

**a.** Find the price of the sweater while on the sale rack. Show your work.

**b.** Find the price of the sweater while on the clearance rack. Show your work.

**S2.** A set of positive integers $(a, b, c)$ is called a *Pythagorean triple* if $a^2 + b^2 = c^2$.

**a.** Find $a^2$, $b^2$, and $c^2$ when $a = 2x$, $b = x^2 - 1$, and $c = x^2 + 1$. Show your work.

**b.** Is $(2x, x^2 - 1, x^2 + 1)$ a Pythagorean triple? Explain your reasoning.

**S3.** Ron is making an ice sculpture. The block of ice is in the shape of a rectangular prism with a length of $(x + 2)$ inches, a width of $(x - 2)$ inches, and a height of $2x$ inches.

**a.** Write and simplify a polynomial expression for the volume of the block of ice. Show your work.

**b.** The final volume of the ice sculpture is $(x^3 + 4x^2 - 10x + 1)$ cubic inches. Write an expression for the volume of ice that Ron carved away. Show your work.

**S4.** Simplify the expression $(3 \cdot a^2 \cdot b^{-4} \cdot a \cdot b^{-3})^{-3}$ using two different methods. Show that the results are the same.

## Extended Response

**E1.** Look at the pentagon below.

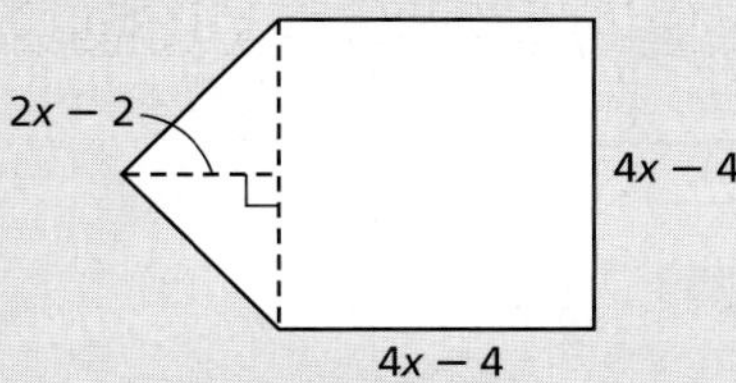


**a.** Write and simplify an expression that represents the area of the pentagon. Show your work or explain your answer.

**b.** Show one method of checking that your expression in part **a** is correct.

**c.** The triangular part of the pentagon can be rearranged to form a square. Write the area of this square as the square of a binomial.

**d.** Expand the product that you wrote in part **c**. What type of polynomial is this?

**e.** Is the square of a binomial ever a binomial? Explain your reasoning.

CHAPTER 8

# Factoring Polynomials

## 8A Factoring Methods

## 8B Applying Factoring Methods



### Why Learn This?

When given the area of a rectangle, such as the Spring Canal Garden and Fountain at the Daniel Stowe Botanical Garden in Belmont, NC, as a polynomial, you can sometimes factor to find the dimensions of the rectangle.

go.hrw.com
Chapter Project Online
KEYWORD: MA7 ChProj

# ARE YOU READY?

## Vocabulary

**Match each term on the left with a definition on the right.**

1. binomial
2. composite number
3. factor
4. multiple
5. prime number

A. a whole number greater than 1 that has more than two whole-number factors
B. a polynomial with two terms
C. the product of any number and a whole number
D. a number that is written as the product of its prime factors
E. a whole number greater than 1 that has exactly two factors, itself and 1
F. a number that is multiplied by another number to get a product

## Multiples

**Write the first four multiples of each number.**

6. 3
7. 4
8. 8
9. 15

## Factors

**Tell whether the second number is a factor of the first number.**

10. 20, 5
11. 50, 6
12. 120, 8
13. 245, 7

## Prime and Composite Numbers

**Tell whether each number is prime or composite. If the number is composite, write it as the product of two numbers.**

14. 2
15. 7
16. 10
17. 38
18. 115
19. 147
20. 151
21. 93

## Multiply Monomials and Polynomials

**Simplify.**

22. $2(x+5)$
23. $3h(h+1)$
24. $xy(x^2-xy^3)$
25. $6m(m^2-4m-1)$

## Multiply Binomials

**Find each product.**

26. $(x+3)(x+8)$
27. $(b-7)(b+1)$
28. $(2p-5)(p-1)$
29. $(3n+4)(2n+3)$

CHAPTER 8

# Study Guide: Preview

## Where You've Been

**Previously, you**

- used properties of exponents to evaluate and simplify expressions.
- added and subtracted polynomials by combining like terms.
- multiplied polynomials.

## In This Chapter

**You will study**

- greatest common factors.
- how to factor polynomials.
- how to factor special products.
- how to choose a factoring method.

## Where You're Going

**You can use the skills in this chapter**

- in geometry to solve area problems.
- in physics to solve quadratic equations.
- in the real world to calculate dimensions in landscaping, construction, or design work.

## *Key Vocabulary/Vocabulario*

| | |
|---|---|
| greatest common factor | máximo común divisor |
| prime factorization | factorización prima |

## *Vocabulary Connections*

To become familiar with the vocabulary terms in the chapter, consider the following. You may refer to the chapter, the glossary, or a dictionary if you like.

1. The word *factor* refers to a number or polynomial that is multiplied by another number or polynomial to form a product. What do you think the word *factor* means when it is used as a verb (action word)?
2. List some words that end with the suffixes *-ize* or *-ization*. What does the ending *-ization* seem to mean? What do you think *factorization* means?
3. The words *prime, primer, primary*, and *primitive* all come from the same root word. What are the meanings of these words? How can their meanings help you understand what a *prime factor* is?
4. What is a prime number? How might the **prime factorization** of a number differ from another factorization?
5. What does the word *common* mean? How can you use this meaning to understand the term **greatest common factor**?

CHAPTER 8

## Reading Strategy: Read a Lesson for Understanding

To help you learn new concepts, you should read each lesson with a purpose. As you read a lesson, make notes. Include the main ideas of the lesson and any questions you have. In class, listen for explanations of the vocabulary, clarification of the examples, and answers to your questions.

### Reading Tips

*Objectives*
Evaluate and multiply by powers of 10.
Convert between standard notation and scientific notation.

The objectives tell you the main idea of the lesson.

*If a power of 10 has a negative integer exponent, does that make the number negative?*
*How do I enter numbers written in scientific notation into my calculator?*

Write down questions you have as you read the lesson.

**EXAMPLE 1 Evaluating Powers of 10**

**Find the value of each power of 10.**

**A** $10^{-3}$

*Start with 1 and move the decimal point three places to the left.*

0. 0 0 1

0.001

Work through the examples and write down any questions you have.

CHECK IT OUT!

Practice what you've learned in the Check It Out sections.

### Try This

**Read Lesson 8-1 prior to your next class. Then answer the questions below.**

1. What are the lesson objectives?
2. What vocabulary, formulas, and symbols are new?
3. Which examples, if any, are unclear?
4. What questions do you have about the lesson?

# 8-1 Factors and Greatest Common Factors

**Prep MA.A.1** Use appropriate properties and strategies to … factor algebraic expressions. *Also* **Prep MA.A.1.3**

***Objectives***

Write the prime factorization of numbers.

Find the GCF of monomials.

***Vocabulary***

prime factorization

greatest common factor

**Who uses this?**

Web site designers who sell electronic greeting cards can use the greatest common factor of numbers to design their Web sites. (See Example 4.)

The whole numbers that are multiplied to find a product are called factors of that product. A number is divisible by its factors.

**Remember!**

A prime number has exactly two factors, itself and 1. The number 1 is not prime because it only has one factor.

You can use the factors of a number to write the number as a product. The number 12 can be factored several ways.

**Factorizations of 12**

$1 \cdot 12 \quad 2 \cdot 6 \quad 3 \cdot 4 \quad 1 \cdot 4 \cdot 3 \quad 2 \cdot 2 \cdot 3$

The order of the factors does not change the product, but there is only one example above that cannot be factored further. The circled factorization is the **prime factorization** because all the factors are prime numbers. The prime factors can be written in any order, and, except for changes in the order, there is only one way to write the prime factorization of a number.

## EXAMPLE 1 Writing Prime Factorizations

**Write the prime factorization of 60.**

**Method 1** Factor tree

*Choose any two factors of 60 to begin. Keep finding factors until each branch ends in a prime factor.*

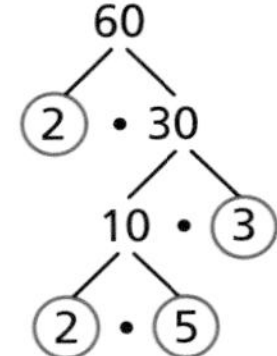


$60 = 2 \cdot 2 \cdot 5 \cdot 3$

**Method 2** Ladder diagram

*Choose a prime factor of 60 to begin. Keep dividing by prime factors until the quotient is 1.*

| | |
|---|---|
| 2 | 60 |
| 3 | 30 |
| 2 | 10 |
| 5 | 5 |
| | 1 |

$60 = 2 \cdot 3 \cdot 2 \cdot 5$

The prime factorization of 60 is $2 \cdot 2 \cdot 3 \cdot 5$ or $2^2 \cdot 3 \cdot 5$.

**Write the prime factorization of each number.**

**1a.** 40 **1b.** 33 **1c.** 49 **1d.** 19

Factors that are shared by two or more whole numbers are called common factors. The greatest of these common factors is called the **greatest common factor**, or GCF.

Factors of 12: 1, 2, 3, 4, 6, 12
Factors of 32: 1, 2, 4, 8, 16, 32
Common factors: 1, 2, (4)
The greatest of the common factors is 4.

## EXAMPLE 2 Finding the GCF of Numbers

**Find the GCF of each pair of numbers.**

**A** **24 and 60**

**Method 1** List the factors.

factors of 24: 1, 2, 3, 4, 6, 8, (12), 24 — *List all the factors.*
factors of 60: 1, 2, 3, 4, 5, 6, 10, (12), 15, 20, 30, 60 — *Circle the GCF.*

The GCF of 24 and 60 is 12.

**B** **18 and 27**

**Method 2** Use prime factorization.

$18 = 2 \cdot 3 \cdot 3$ — *Write the prime factorization of each number.*
$27 = 3 \cdot 3 \cdot 3$ — *Align the common factors.*
$3 \cdot 3 = 9$

The GCF of 18 and 27 is 9.

**Find the GCF of each pair of numbers.**

**2a.** 12 and 16 **2b.** 15 and 25

You can also find the GCF of monomials that include variables. To find the GCF of monomials, write the prime factorization of each coefficient and write all powers of variables as products. Then find the product of the common factors.

## EXAMPLE 3 Finding the GCF of Monomials

**Find the GCF of each pair of monomials.**

**A** **$3x^3$ and $6x^2$**

$3x^3 = 3 \cdot x \cdot x \cdot x$ — *Write the prime factorization of each coefficient and write powers as products.*
$6x^2 = 2 \cdot 3 \cdot x \cdot x$ — *Align the common factors.*
$3 \cdot x \cdot x = 3x^2$ — *Find the product of the common factors.*

The GCF of $3x^3$ and $6x^2$ is $3x^2$.

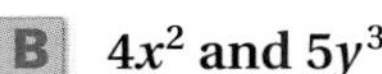

**B** **$4x^2$ and $5y^3$**

$4x^2 = 2 \cdot 2 \cdot x \cdot x$ — *Write the prime factorization of each coefficient and write powers as products.*
$5y^3 = 5 \cdot y \cdot y \cdot y$ — *Align the common factors.*
*There are no common factors other than 1.*

The GCF of $4x^2$ and $5y^3$ is 1.

**Helpful Hint**

If two terms contain the same variable raised to different powers, the GCF will contain that variable raised to the lower power.

**Find the GCF of each pair of monomials.**

**3a.** $18g^2$ and $27g^3$ **3b.** $16a^6$ and $9b$ **3c.** $8x$ and $7v^2$

## EXAMPLE 4 *Technology Application*

**Garrison is creating a Web page that offers electronic greeting cards. He has 24 special occasion designs and 42 birthday designs. The cards will be displayed with the same number of designs in each row. Special occasion and birthday designs will not appear in the same row. How many rows will there be if Garrison puts the greatest possible number of designs in each row?**

The 24 special occasion designs and 42 birthday designs must be divided into groups of equal size. The number of designs in each row must be a common factor of 24 and 42.

factors of 24: 1, 2, 3, 4, (6), 8, 12, 24
factors of 42: 1, 2, 3, (6), 7, 14, 21, 42

*Find the common factors of 24 and 42.*

The GCF of 24 and 42 is 6.

The greatest possible number of designs in each row is 6. Find the number of rows of each group of designs when there are 6 designs in each row.

$$\frac{\text{24 special occasion designs}}{\text{6 designs per row}} = 4 \text{ rows}$$

$$\frac{\text{42 birthday designs}}{\text{6 designs per row}} = 7 \text{ rows}$$

When the greatest possible number of designs is in each row, there are 11 rows in total.

**4.** Adrianne is shopping for a CD storage unit. She has 36 CDs by pop music artists and 48 CDs by country music artists. She wants to put the same number of CDs on each shelf without putting pop music and country music CDs on the same shelf. If Adrianne puts the greatest possible number of CDs on each shelf, how many shelves does her storage unit need?

## THINK AND DISCUSS

**1.** Describe two ways you can find the prime factorization of a number.

**2. GET ORGANIZED** Copy and complete the graphic organizer. Show how to write the prime factorization of $100x^2$ by filling in each box.

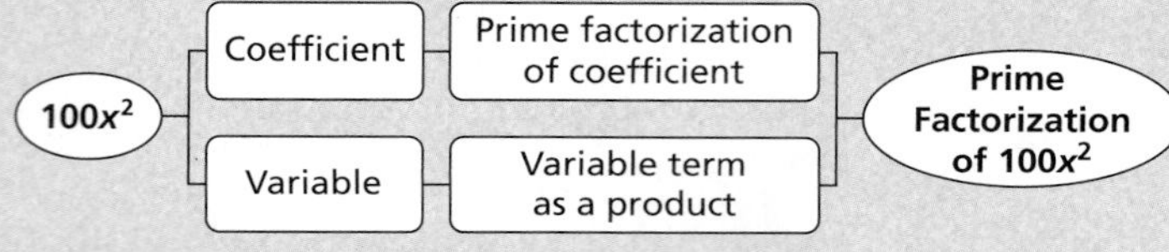

# 8-1 Exercises

Prep MA.A.1, Prep MA.A.1.3

go.hrw.com
Homework Help Online
KEYWORD: MA7 8-1
Parent Resources Online
KEYWORD: MA7 Parent

## GUIDED PRACTICE

1. **Vocabulary** Define the term *greatest common factor* in your own words.

SEE EXAMPLE 1 p. 524

**Write the prime factorization of each number.**

2. 20 3. 36 4. 27 5. 54
6. 96 7. 7 8. 100 9. 75

SEE EXAMPLE 2 p. 525

**Find the GCF of each pair of numbers.**

10. 12 and 60 11. 14 and 49 12. 55 and 121

SEE EXAMPLE 3 p. 525

**Find the GCF of each pair of monomials.**

13. $6x^2$ and $5x^2$ 14. $15y^3$ and $-20y$ 15. $13q^4$ and $2p^2$

SEE EXAMPLE 4 p. 526

16. Samantha is making beaded necklaces using 54 glass beads and 18 clay beads. She wants each necklace to have the same number of beads, but each necklace will have only one type of bead. If she puts the greatest possible number of beads on each necklace, how many necklaces can she make?

## PRACTICE AND PROBLEM SOLVING

**Independent Practice**

| For Exercises | See Example |
|---|---|
| 17–24 | 1 |
| 25–27 | 2 |
| 28–30 | 3 |
| 31 | 4 |

**Extra Practice**
Skills Practice p. S18
Application Practice p. S35

**Write the prime factorization of each number.**

17. 18 18. 64 19. 12 20. 150
21. 17 22. 226 23. 49 24. 63

**Find the GCF of each pair of numbers.**

25. 36 and 63 26. 14 and 15 27. 30 and 40

**Find the GCF of each pair of monomials.**

28. $8a^2$ and 11 29. $9s$ and $63s^3$ 30. $-64n^4$ and $24n^2$

31. José is making fruit-filled tart shells for a party. He has 72 raspberries and 108 blueberries. The tarts will each have the same number of berries. Raspberries and blueberries will not be in the same tart. If he puts the greatest possible number of fruits in each tart, how many tarts can he make?

**Find the GCF of each pair of products.**

32. $3 \cdot 5 \cdot t$ and $2 \cdot 2 \cdot 5 \cdot t \cdot t$ 33. $-1 \cdot 2 \cdot 2 \cdot x \cdot x$ and $2 \cdot 2 \cdot 7 \cdot x \cdot x \cdot x$
34. $2 \cdot 2 \cdot 2 \cdot 11 \cdot x \cdot x \cdot x$ and $3 \cdot 11$ 35. $2 \cdot 5 \cdot n \cdot n \cdot n$ and $-1 \cdot 2 \cdot 3 \cdot n$

36. **Write About It** The number 2 is even and is prime. Explain why all other prime numbers are odd numbers.

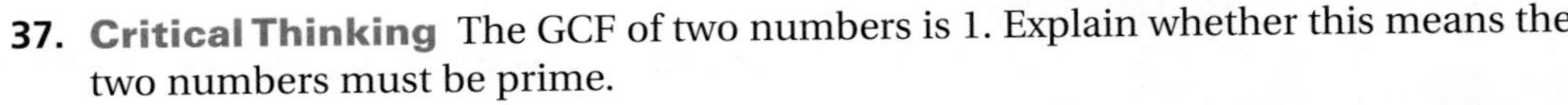

37. **Critical Thinking** The GCF of two numbers is 1. Explain whether this means the two numbers must be prime.

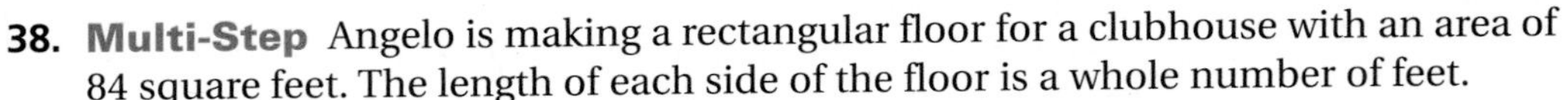

38. **Multi-Step** Angelo is making a rectangular floor for a clubhouse with an area of 84 square feet. The length of each side of the floor is a whole number of feet.

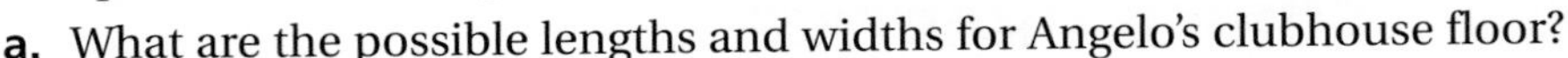

a. What are the possible lengths and widths for Angelo's clubhouse floor?
b. What is the minimum perimeter for the clubhouse floor?
c. What is the maximum perimeter for the clubhouse floor?

**LINK**

**Music**

DCI is a nonprofit organization that oversees drum and bugle corps performances and competitions for youths between the ages of 14 and 21.

39. **Music** The Cavaliers and the Blue Devils are two of the marching bands that are members of Drum Corps International (DCI). DCI bands are made up of percussionists, brass players, and color guard members who use flags and other props.

In 2004, there were 35 color guard members in the Cavaliers and 40 in the Blue Devils. The two color guards will march in rows with the same number of people in each row without mixing the guards together. If the greatest possible number of people are in each row, how many rows will there be?

**For each set of numbers, determine which two numbers have a GCF greater than 1, and find that GCF.**

40. 11, 12, 14
41. 8, 20, 63
42. 16, 21, 27
43. 32, 63, 105
44. 25, 35, 54
45. 35, 54, 72

46. **Number Sense** The prime factorization of 24 is $2^3 \cdot 3$. Without performing any calculations or using a diagram, write the prime factorization of 48. Explain your reasoning.

**Fill in each diagram. Then write the prime factorization of the number.**

47.

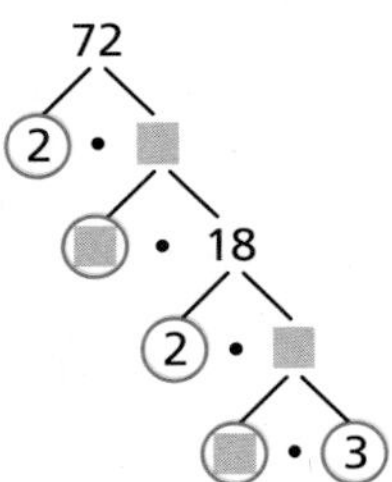


48.

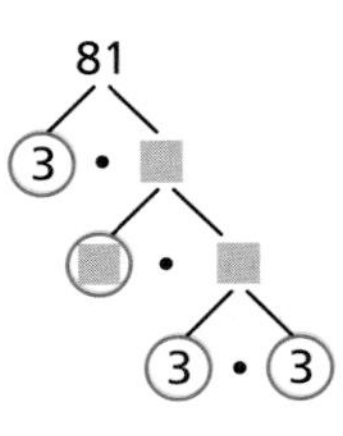


49.

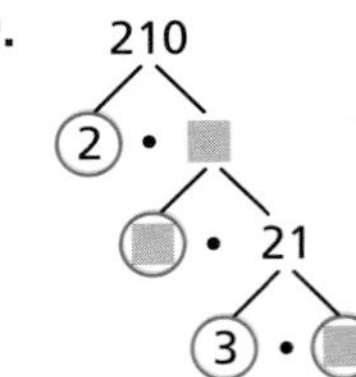


50.
■ | 56
2 | 28
2 | ■
■ | 7
1

51.
■ | 108
■ | 54
3 | ■
■ | 9
3 | 3
1

52.
2 | 136
■ | 68
2 | ■
■ | 17
1

53.
2 | 48
2 | ■
■ | 12
2 | ■
■ | 3
1

54.
■ | 140
2 | ■
■ | 35
7 | 7
1

55.
2 | 40
■ | 20
■ | ■
5 | ■
1

56. This problem will prepare you for the Multi-Step Test Prep on page 556. The equation for the motion of an object with constant acceleration is $d = vt + \frac{1}{2}at^2$ where $d$ is distance traveled in feet, $v$ is starting velocity in ft/s, $a$ is acceleration in ft/s$^2$, and $t$ is time in seconds.

    a. A toy car begins with a velocity of 2 ft/s and accelerates at 2 ft/s$^2$. Write an expression for the distance the toy car travels after $t$ seconds.

    b. What is the GCF of the terms of your expression from part **a**?

Prep MA.A.1, Prep MA.A.1.3

57. Which set of numbers has a GCF greater than 6?

    (A) 18, 24, 36 (B) 30, 35, 40 (C) 11, 29, 37 (D) 16, 24, 48

58. The slope of a line is the GCF of 48 and 12. The $y$-intercept is the GCF of the slope and 8. Which equation describes the line?

    (F) $y = 12x + 4$ (G) $y = 6x + 2$ (H) $y = 4x + 4$ (J) $y = 3x + 1$

59. **Extended Response** Patricia is making a dog pen in her back yard. The pen will be rectangular and have an area of 24 square feet. Draw and label a diagram that shows all possible whole-number dimensions for the pen. Find the perimeter of each rectangle you drew. Which dimensions should Patricia use in order to spend the least amount of money on fencing materials? Explain your reasoning.

## CHALLENGE AND EXTEND

**Find the GCF of each set.**

60. $4n^3, 16n^2, 8n$
61. $27y^3, 18y^2, 81y$
62. $100, 25s^5, 50s$
63. $2p^4r, 8p^3r^2, 16p^2r^3$
64. $2x^3y, 8x^2y^2, 17xy^3$
65. $8a^4b^3, 4a^3b^3, 12a^2b^3$
66. **Geometry** The area of a triangle is 10 in$^2$. What are the possible whole-number dimensions for the base and height of the triangle?
67. **Number Sense** The GCF of three different numbers is 7. The sum of the three numbers is 105. What are the three numbers?
68. **Critical Thinking** Find three different *composite* numbers whose GCF is 1. (*Hint:* A composite number has factors other than 1 and itself.)

## SPIRAL REVIEW

**Find each value. Round to the nearest tenth if necessary.** *(Lesson 2-8)*

69. 40% of 60
70. 250% of 16
71. What percent of 80 is 20?

**Determine if each sequence could be an arithmetic sequence. If so, find the common difference and use it to find the next three terms.** *(Lesson 4-6)*

72. 3, 7, 11, 15, ...
73. −4, −8, −16, −32, ...
74. 1.5, 1, 0.5, 0, ...
75. Write a simplified polynomial expression for the perimeter of the triangle. *(Lesson 7-6)*

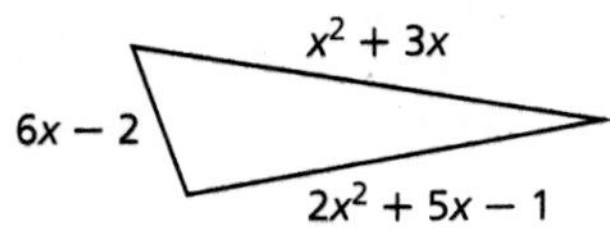

Use with Lesson 8-2

# Model Factoring

You can use algebra tiles to write a polynomial as the product of its factors. This process is called factoring. Factoring is the reverse of multiplying.

**MA.A.1** Use appropriate...strategies to ... factor algebraic expressions. *Also* **Prep MA.A.1.3**

**KEY**

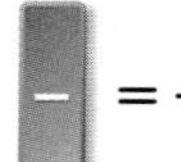

= 1, = −1

$= x$, $= -x$, $= x^2$

## Activity

**Use algebra tiles to factor $4x + 8$.**

| MODEL | | ALGEBRA |
|---|---|---|
| | *Model $4x + 8$.* | $4x + 8$ |
| $x + 2$; $x$; $4$ | *Arrange the tiles into a rectangle. The total area represents $4x + 8$. The length and width represent the factors. The rectangle has a width of $x + 2$ and a length of 4.* | $4x + 8 = 4(x + 2)$ |

**Use algebra tiles to factor $x^2 - 2x$.**

| MODEL | | ALGEBRA |
|---|---|---|
| | *Model $x^2 - 2x$.* | $x^2 - 2x$ |
| $x - 2$; $x$; $x$ | *Arrange the tiles into a rectangle. The total area represents $x^2 - 2x$. The length and width represent the factors. The rectangle has a width of $x - 2$ and a length of $x$.* | $x^2 - 2x = x(x - 2)$ |

## Try This

**Use algebra tiles to factor each polynomial.**

**1.** $3x + 9$ **2.** $2x + 8$ **3.** $4x - 12$ **4.** $3x - 12$

**5.** $2x^2 + 2x$ **6.** $x^2 + 4x$ **7.** $x^2 - 3x$ **8.** $2x^2 - 4x$

# 8-2 Factoring by GCF

**MA.A.1** Use appropriate properties and strategies to … factor algebraic expressions. *Also* **MA.A.1.3**

***Objective***
Factor polynomials by using the greatest common factor.

**Why learn this?**
You can determine the dimensions of a solar panel by factoring an expression representing the panel's area. (See Example 2.)

Recall that the Distributive Property states that $ab + ac = a(b + c)$. The Distributive Property allows you to "factor" out the GCF of the terms in a polynomial to write a factored form of the polynomial.

A polynomial is in its factored form when it is written as a product of monomials and polynomials that cannot be factored further. The polynomial $2(3x - 4x)$ is not fully factored because the terms in the parentheses have a common factor of $x$.

**Writing Math**
Aligning common factors can help you find the greatest common factor of two or more terms.

## EXAMPLE 1 Factoring by Using the GCF

**Factor each polynomial. Check your answer.**

**A** $4x^2 - 3x$

$4x^2 = 2 \cdot 2 \cdot \boxed{x} \cdot x$
$3x = 3 \cdot \boxed{x}$ — *Find the GCF.*

$x$ — *The GCF of $4x^2$ and $3x$ is x.*

$4x(x) - 3(x)$ — *Write terms as products using the GCF as a factor.*

$x(4x - 3)$ — *Use the Distributive Property to factor out the GCF.*

***Check*** $x(4x - 3)$ — *Multiply to check your answer.*
$4x^2 - 3x$ ✓ — *The product is the original polynomial.*

**B** $10y^3 + 20y^2 - 5y$

$10y^3 = 2 \cdot \boxed{5} \cdot \boxed{y} \cdot y \cdot y$ — *Find the GCF.*
$20y^2 = 2 \cdot 2 \cdot \boxed{5} \cdot \boxed{y} \cdot y$
$5y = \boxed{5} \cdot \boxed{y}$

$5 \cdot y = 5y$ — *The GCF of $10y^3$, $20y^2$, and $5y$ is $5y$.*

$2y^2(5y) + 4y(5y) - 1(5y)$ — *Write terms as products using the GCF as a factor.*

$5y(2y^2 + 4y - 1)$ — *Use the Distributive Property to factor out the GCF.*

***Check*** $5y(2y^2 + 4y - 1)$ — *Multiply to check your answer.*
$10y^3 + 20y^2 - 5y$ ✓ — *The product is the original polynomial.*

**Factor each polynomial. Check your answer.**

**C** $-12x - 8x^2$

$-1(12x + 8x^2)$ — *Both coefficients are negative. Factor out −1.*

$12x = \boxed{2} \cdot \boxed{2} \cdot 3 \cdot \boxed{x}$ — *Find the GCF.*

$8x^2 = \boxed{2} \cdot \boxed{2} \cdot 2 \cdot \boxed{x} \cdot x$

$2 \cdot 2 \cdot x = 4x$ — *The GCF of 12x and $8x^2$ is 4x.*

$-1[3(4x) + 2x(4x)]$ — *Write each term as a product using the GCF.*

$-1[4x(3 + 2x)]$ — *Use the Distributive Property to factor out the GCF.*

$-1(4x)(3 + 2x)$

$-4x(3 + 2x)$

***Check***

$-4x(3 + 2x) = -12x - 8x^2$ ✓ — *Multiply to check your answer.*

**D** $5x^2 + 7$

$5x^2 = 5 \cdot x \cdot x$ — *Find the GCF.*

$7 = 7$

$5x^2 + 7$ — *There are no common factors other than 1.*

The polynomial cannot be factored further.

> **Caution!**
>
> When you factor out −1 as the first step, be sure to include it in all the other steps as well.

CHECK IT OUT!

**Factor each polynomial. Check your answer.**

**1a.** $5b + 9b^3$ **1b.** $9d^2 - 8^2$

**1c.** $-18y^3 - 7y^2$ **1d.** $8x^4 + 4x^3 - 2x^2$

To write expressions for the length and width of a rectangle with area expressed by a polynomial, you need to write the polynomial as a product. You can write a polynomial as a product by factoring it.

## EXAMPLE 2 *Science Application*

**Mandy's calculator is powered by solar energy. The area of the solar panel is $(7x^2 + x)$ cm². Factor this polynomial to find possible expressions for the dimensions of the solar panel.**

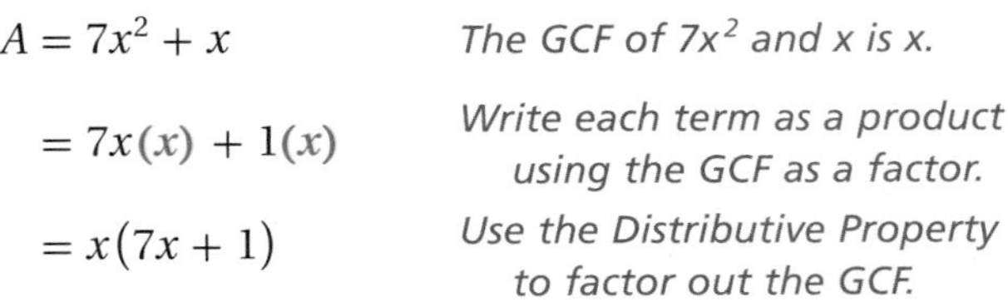

$A = 7x^2 + x$ — *The GCF of $7x^2$ and x is x.*

$= 7x(x) + 1(x)$ — *Write each term as a product using the GCF as a factor.*

$= x(7x + 1)$ — *Use the Distributive Property to factor out the GCF.*

Possible expressions for the dimensions of the solar panel are $x$ cm and $(7x + 1)$ cm.

CHECK IT OUT!

**2. What if...?** The area of the solar panel on another calculator is $(2x^2 + 4x)$ cm². Factor this polynomial to find possible expressions for the dimensions of the solar panel.

Sometimes the GCF of terms is a binomial. This GCF is called a common binomial factor. You factor out a common binomial factor the same way you factor out a monomial factor.

## EXAMPLE 3 Factoring Out a Common Binomial Factor

**Factor each expression.**

**A** $7(x-3)-2x(x-3)$

$7(x-3)-2x(x-3)$ — *The terms have a common binomial factor of $(x-3)$.*

$(x-3)(7-2x)$ — *Factor out $(x-3)$.*

**B** $-t(t^2+4)+(t^2+4)$

$-t(t^2+4)+(t^2+4)$ — *The terms have a common binomial factor of $(t^2+4)$.*

$-t(t^2+4)+1(t^2+4)$ — *$(t^2+4)=1(t^2+4)$*

$(t^2+4)(-t+1)$ — *Factor out $(t^2+4)$.*

**C** $9x(x+4)-5(4+x)$

$9x(x+4)-5(4+x)$ — *$(x+4)=(4+x)$, so the terms have a common binomial factor of $(x+4)$.*

$9x(x+4)-5(x+4)$

$(x+4)(9x-5)$ — *Factor out $(x+4)$.*

**D** $-3x^2(x+2)+4(x-7)$

$-3x^2(x+2)+4(x-7)$ — *There are no common factors.*

The expression cannot be factored.

**Factor each expression.**

**3a.** $4s(s+6)-5(s+6)$

**3b.** $7x(2x+3)+(2x+3)$

**3c.** $3x(y+4)-2y(x+4)$

**3d.** $5x(5x-2)-2(5x-2)$

You may be able to factor a polynomial by grouping. When a polynomial has four terms, you can make two groups and factor out the GCF from each group.

## EXAMPLE 4 Factoring by Grouping

**Factor each polynomial by grouping. Check your answer.**

**A** $12a^3-9a^2+20a-15$

$(12a^3-9a^2)+(20a-15)$ — *Group terms that have a common number or variable as a factor.*

$3a^2(4a-3)+5(4a-3)$ — *Factor out the GCF of each group.*

$3a^2(4a-3)+5(4a-3)$ — *$(4a-3)$ is another common factor.*

$(4a-3)(3a^2+5)$ — *Factor out $(4a-3)$.*

*Check* $(4a-3)(3a^2+5)$ — *Multiply to check your solution.*

$4a(3a^2)+4a(5)-3(3a^2)-3(5)$

$12a^3+20a-9a^2-15$

$12a^3-9a^2+20a-15$ ✓ — *The product is the original polynomial.*

**Factor each polynomial by grouping. Check your answer.**

**B** $9x^3 + 18x^2 + x + 2$

| | |
|---|---|
| $(9x^3 + 18x^2) + (x + 2)$ | *Group terms.* |
| $9x^2(x + 2) + 1(x + 2)$ | *Factor out the GCF of each group.* |
| $9x^2(x + 2) + 1(x + 2)$ | *$(x + 2)$ is a common factor.* |
| $(x + 2)(9x^2 + 1)$ | *Factor out $(x + 2)$.* |
| ***Check*** $(x + 2)(9x^2 + 1)$ | *Multiply to check your solution.* |
| $x(9x^2) + x(1) + 2(9x^2) + 2(1)$ | |
| $9x^3 + x + 18x^2 + 2$ | |
| $9x^3 + 18x^2 + x + 2$ ✓ | *The product is the original polynomial.* |

**Factor each polynomial by grouping. Check your answer.**

**4a.** $6b^3 + 8b^2 + 9b + 12$ **4b.** $4r^3 + 24r + r^2 + 6$

**Helpful Hint**

If two quantities are opposites, their sum is 0.

$(5 - x) + (x - 5)$
$5 - x + x - 5$
$-x + x + 5 - 5$
$0 + 0$
$0$

Recognizing opposite binomials can help you factor polynomials. The binomials $(5 - x)$ and $(x - 5)$ are opposites. Notice $(5 - x)$ can be written as $-1(x - 5)$.

| | |
|---|---|
| $-1(x - 5) = (-1)(x) + (-1)(-5)$ | *Distributive Property* |
| $= -x + 5$ | *Simplify.* |
| $= 5 - x$ | *Commutative Property of Addition* |
| So, $(5 - x) = -1(x - 5)$. | |

## EXAMPLE 5 Factoring with Opposites

**Factor $3x^3 - 15x^2 + 10 - 2x$.**

| | |
|---|---|
| $3x^3 - 15x^2 + 10 - 2x$ | |
| $(3x^3 - 15x^2) + (10 - 2x)$ | *Group terms.* |
| $3x^2(x - 5) + 2(5 - x)$ | *Factor out the GCF of each group.* |
| $3x^2(x - 5) + 2(-1)(x - 5)$ | *Write $(5 - x)$ as $-1(x - 5)$.* |
| $3x^2(x - 5) - 2(x - 5)$ | *Simplify. $(x - 5)$ is a common factor.* |
| $(x - 5)(3x^2 - 2)$ | *Factor out $(x - 5)$.* |

**Factor each polynomial. Check your answer.**

**5a.** $15x^2 - 10x^3 + 8x - 12$ **5b.** $8y - 8 - x + xy$

## THINK AND DISCUSS

**1.** Explain how finding the GCF of monomials helps you factor a polynomial.

**2. GET ORGANIZED** Copy and complete the graphic organizer.

**Factoring by GCF**

1. Find the __?__ common factor. → 2. Write each term as a __?__ using the GCF. → 3. Use the __?__ to factor out the GCF. → 4. Check by __?__.

# 8-2 Exercises

MA.A.1, MA.A.1.3

go.hrw.com
Homework Help Online
KEYWORD: MA7 8-2
Parent Resources Online
KEYWORD: MA7 Parent

## GUIDED PRACTICE

SEE EXAMPLE 1 p. 531

**Factor each polynomial. Check your answer.**

1. $15a - 5a^2$
2. $10g^3 - 3g$
3. $-35x + 42$
4. $-4x^2 - 6x$
5. $12h^4 + 8h^2 - 6h$
6. $3x^2 - 9x + 3$
7. $9m^2 + m$
8. $14n^3 + 7n + 7n^2$
9. $36f + 18f^2 + 3$
10. $-15b^2 + 7b$

SEE EXAMPLE 2 p. 532

11. **Physics** A model rocket is fired vertically into the air at 320 ft/s. The expression $-16t^2 + 320t$ gives the rocket's height after $t$ seconds. Factor this expression.

SEE EXAMPLE 3 p. 533

**Factor each expression.**

12. $5(m - 2) - m(m - 2)$
13. $2b(b + 3) + 5(b + 3)$
14. $4(x - 3) - x(y + 2)$

SEE EXAMPLE 4 p. 533

**Factor each polynomial by grouping. Check your answer.**

15. $x^3 + 4x^2 + 2x + 8$
16. $6x^3 + 4x^2 + 3x + 2$
17. $4b^3 - 6b^2 + 10b - 15$
18. $2m^3 + 4m^2 + 6m + 12$
19. $7r^3 - 35r^2 + 6r - 30$
20. $10a^3 + 4a^2 + 5a + 2$

SEE EXAMPLE 5 p. 534

21. $2r^2 - 6r + 12 - 4r$
22. $6b^2 - 3b + 4 - 8b$
23. $14q^2 - 21q + 6 - 4q$
24. $3r - r^2 + 2r - 6$
25. $2m^3 - 6m^2 + 9 - 3m$
26. $6a^3 - 9a^2 - 12 + 8a$

## PRACTICE AND PROBLEM SOLVING

**Independent Practice**

| For Exercises | See Example |
|---|---|
| 27–35 | 1 |
| 36 | 2 |
| 37–42 | 3 |
| 43–48 | 4 |
| 49–54 | 5 |

**Extra Practice**

Skills Practice p. S18
Application Practice p. S35

**Factor each polynomial. Check your answer.**

27. $9y^2 + 45y$
28. $36d^3 + 24$
29. $-14x^4 + 5x^2$
30. $-15f - 10f^2$
31. $-4d^4 + d^3 - 3d^2$
32. $14x^3 + 63x^2 - 7x$
33. $21c^2 + 14c$
34. $33d^3 + 22d + 11$
35. $-5g^3 - 15g^2$
36. **Finance** After $t$ years, the amount of money in a savings account that earns simple interest is $P + Prt$, where $P$ is the starting amount and $r$ is the yearly interest rate. Factor this expression.

**Factor each expression.**

37. $6a(a - 2) - 5b(b + 4)$
38. $-4x(x + 2) + 9(x + 2)$
39. $6y(y - 7) + (y - 7)$
40. $a(x - 3) + 2b(x - 3)$
41. $-3(2 + b) + 4b(b + 2)$
42. $5(3x - 2) + x(3x - 2)$

**Factor each polynomial by grouping. Check your answer.**

43. $2a^3 - 8a^2 + 3a - 12$
44. $x^3 + 3x^2 + 5x + 15$
45. $6x^3 + 18x^2 + x + 3$
46. $7x^3 + 2x^2 + 28x + 8$
47. $n^3 - 2n^2 + 5n - 10$
48. $10b^3 - 16b^2 + 25b - 40$
49. $2m^3 - 2m^2 + 3 - 3m$
50. $2d^3 - d^2 - 3 + 6d$
51. $6f^3 - 8f^2 + 20 - 15f$
52. $5k^2 - k^3 + 3k - 15$
53. $b^3 - 2b - 8 + 4b^2$
54. $20 - 15x - 6x^2 + 8x$

**Fill in the missing part of each factorization.**

55. $16v + 12v^2 = 4v(4 + ■)$

56. $15x - 25x^2 = 5x(3 - ■)$

57. $-16k^3 - 24k^2 = -8k^2(■ + 3)$

58. $-x - 10 = -1(■ + 10)$

**Copy and complete the table.**

| | Polynomial | Number of Terms | Name | Completely Factored Form |
|---|---|---|---|---|
| | $3y + 3x + 9$ | 3 | trinomial | $3(y + x + 3)$ |
| **59.** | $x^2 + 5x$ | ■ | ■ | ■ |
| **60.** | $28c^2 - 49c$ | ■ | ■ | ■ |
| **61.** | $a^4 + a^3 + a^2$ | ■ | ■ | ■ |
| **62.** | $36 + 99r - 40r^2 - 110r^3$ | ■ | ■ | ■ |

63. **Personal Finance** The final amount of money earned by a certificate of deposit (CD) after $n$ years can be represented by the expression $Px^n$, where $P$ is the original amount contributed and $x$ is the interest rate.

| Year | Amount of CD |
|---|---|
| 2004 | \$100.00 |
| 2005 | \$200.00 |
| 2006 | \$400.00 |

Justin's aunt purchased CDs to help him pay for college. The table shows the amount of the CD she purchased each year. In 2007, she will pay \$800.00 directly to the college.

a. Each CD has the same interest rate. Write expressions for the value of the CDs purchased in 2004, 2005, and 2006 when Justin starts college in 2007.

b. Write a polynomial to represent the total value of the CDs purchased in 2004, 2005, and 2006 plus the amount paid to the college in 2007.

c. Factor the polynomial in part **c** by grouping. Evaluate the factored form of the polynomial when the interest rate is 1.09.

64. **Write About It** Describe how to find the area of the figure shown. Show each step and write your answer in factored form.

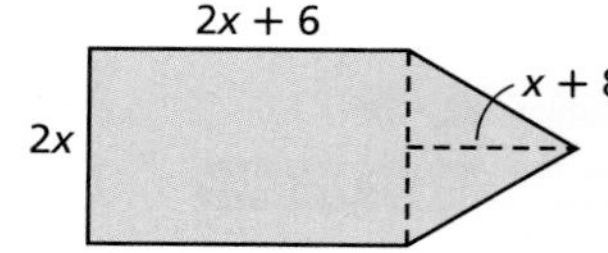


65. **Critical Thinking** Show two methods of factoring the expression $3a - 3b - 4a + 4b$.

66. **Geometry** The area of the triangle is represented by the expression $\frac{1}{2}(x^3 - 2x + 2x^2 - 4)$. The height of the triangle is $x + 2$. Write an expression for the base of the triangle. (*Hint:* The formula for the area of a triangle is $A = \frac{1}{2}bh$.)

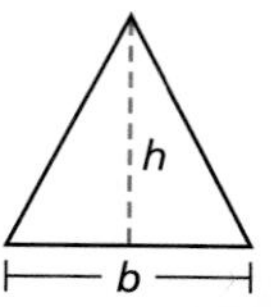


67. **Write About It** Explain how you know when two binomials are opposites.

68. This problem will prepare you for the Multi-Step Test Prep on page 556.

a. The Multiplication Property of Zero states that the product of any number and 0 is 0. What must be true about either $a$ or $b$ to make $ab = 0$?

b. A toy car's distance in feet from the starting point is given by the equation $d = t(3 - t)$. Explain why $t(3 - t) = 0$ means that either $t = 0$ or $(3 - t) = 0$.

c. When $d = 0$, the car is at the starting point. Use the fact that $t = 0$ or $(3 - t) = 0$ when $d = 0$ to find the two times when the car is at the starting point.

**Fill in each blank with a property or definition that justifies the step.**

**69.** $7x^3 + 2x + 21x^2 + 6 = 7x^3 + 21x^2 + 2x + 6$ **a.** ___?___

$= (7x^3 + 21x^2) + (2x + 6)$ **b.** ___?___

$= 7x^2(x + 3) + 2(x + 3)$ **c.** ___?___

$= (x + 3)(7x^2 + 2)$ **d.** ___?___

**70.** **/// ERROR ANALYSIS ///** Which factorization of $3n^3 - n^2$ is incorrect? Explain.

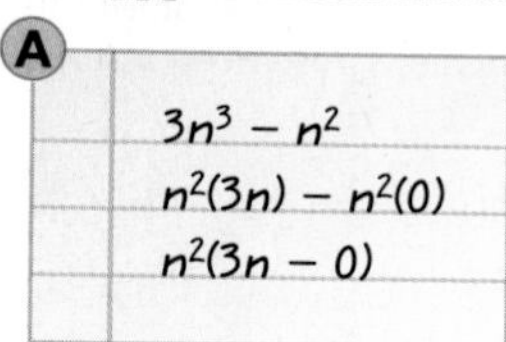


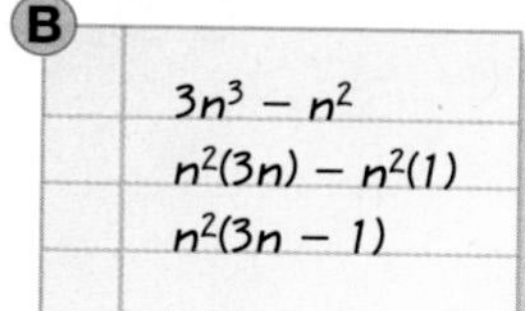

MA.A.1, MA.A.1.3

**71.** Which is the complete factorization of $24x^3 - 12x^2$?

(A) $6(4x^3 - 2x^2)$ (B) $12(2x^3 - x^2)$ (C) $12x(2x^2 - x)$ (D) $12x^2(2x - 1)$

**72.** Which is NOT a factor of $18x^2 + 36x$?

(F) 1 (G) $4x$ (H) $x + 2$ (J) $18x$

**73.** The area of a rectangle is represented by the polynomial $x^2 + 3x - 6x - 18$. Which of the following could represent the length and width of the rectangle?

(A) Length: $x + 3$; width: $x + 6$

(B) Length: $x - 3$; width: $x - 6$

(C) Length: $x + 3$; width: $x - 6$

(D) Length: $x - 3$; width: $x + 6$

## CHALLENGE AND EXTEND

**Factor each polynomial.**

**74.** $6ab^2 - 24a^2$ **75.** $-72a^2b^2 - 45ab$ **76.** $-18a^2b^2 + 21ab$

**77.** $ab + bc + ad + cd$ **78.** $4y^2 + 8ay - y - 2a$ **79.** $x^3 - 4x^2 + 3x - 12$

**80. Geometry** The area between two concentric circles is called an *annulus*. The formula for area of an annulus is $A = \pi R^2 - \pi r^2$, where $R$ is the radius of the larger circle and $r$ is the radius of the smaller circle.

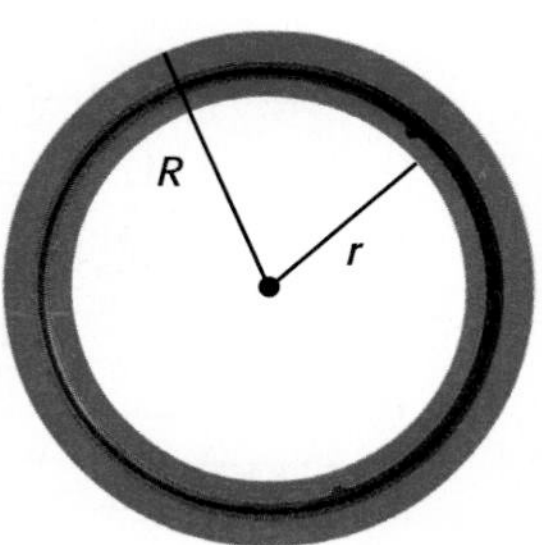


a. Factor the formula for area of an annulus by using the GCF.

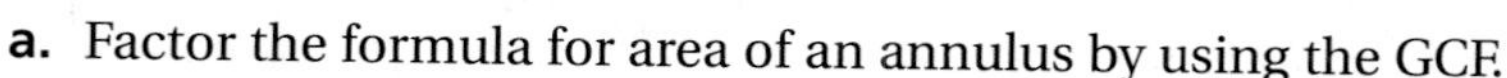

b. Use the factored form to find the area of an annulus with $R = 12$ cm and $r = 5$ cm.

## SPIRAL REVIEW

**81.** The coordinates of the vertices of a quadrilateral are $A(-2, 5)$, $B(6, 5)$, $C(4, -3)$, and $D(-4, -3)$. Use slope to show that $ABCD$ is a parallelogram. *(Lesson 5-8)*

**82.** Graph the data in the table and show the rates of change. *(Lesson 5-3)*

| Time (yr) | 1998 | 1999 | 2002 | 2004 | 2005 |
|---|---|---|---|---|---|
| Profit (million \$) | 0.6 | 0.8 | 1.3 | 1.9 | 2.4 |

**Write the prime factorization of each number.** *(Lesson 8-1)*

**83.** 52 **84.** 75 **85.** 24 **86.** 28

Use with Lesson 8-3

# Model Factorization of Trinomials

You can use algebra tiles to write a trinomial as a product of two binomials. This is called factoring a trinomial.

**MA.A.1** Use appropriate ... strategies to ... factor algebraic expressions. *Also* **Prep MA.A.1.3**

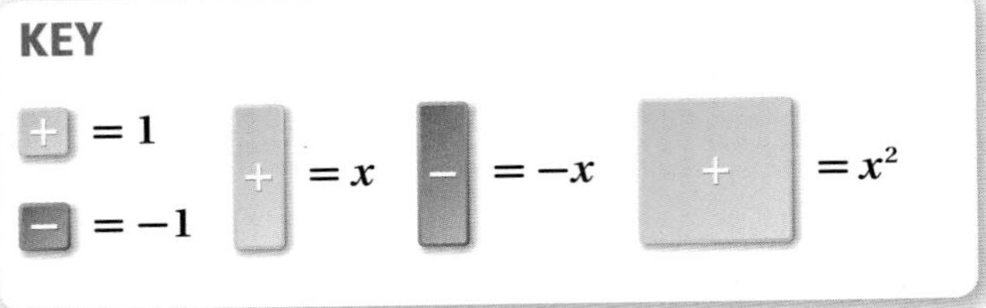


## Activity 1

**Use algebra tiles to factor $x^2 + 7x + 6$.**

| MODEL | | ALGEBRA |
|---|---|---|
| | *Model $x^2 + 7x + 6$.* | $x^2 + 7x + 6$ |
| | *Try to arrange all of the tiles in a rectangle. Start by placing the $x^2$-tile in the upper left corner.* *Arrange the unit tiles in a rectangle so that the top left corner of this rectangle touches the bottom right corner of the $x^2$-tile.* *Arrange the x-tiles so that all the tiles together make one large rectangle.* *This arrangement does not work because two x-tiles are left over.* | $x^2 + 7x + 6 \neq (x + 2)(x + 3)$ |
| | *Rearrange the unit tiles to form another rectangle.* *Fill in the empty spaces with x-tiles. All 7 x-tiles fit. This is the correct arrangement.* *The total area represents the trinomial. The length and width represent the factors.* | $x^2 + 7x + 6 = (x + 1)(x + 6)$ |

The rectangle has width $x + 1$ and length $x + 6$. So $x^2 + 7x + 6 = (x + 1)(x + 6)$.

## Try This

**Use algebra tiles to factor each trinomial.**

**1.** $x^2 + 2x + 1$ **2.** $x^2 + 3x + 2$ **3.** $x^2 + 6x + 5$ **4.** $x^2 + 6x + 9$

**5.** $x^2 + 5x + 4$ **6.** $x^2 + 6x + 8$ **7.** $x^2 + 5x + 6$ **8.** $x^2 + 8x + 12$

## Activity 2

**Use algebra tiles to factor $x^2 + x - 2$.**

| MODEL | | ALGEBRA |
|---|---|---|
| | *Model $x^2 + x - 2$.* | $x^2 + x - 2$ |
| | *Start by placing the $x^2$-tile in the upper left corner.* *Arrange the unit tiles in a rectangle so that the top left corner of this rectangle touches the bottom right corner of the $x^2$-tile.* *To make a rectangle, you need to fill in the empty spaces, but there aren't enough x-tiles to fill in the empty spaces.* | |
| | *Add a zero pair. Arrange the x-tiles to complete the rectangle.* *Remember that the product of two positive values is positive and the product of a positive and a negative value is negative.* | |
| | *The total area represents the trinomial. The length and width represent the factors.* | $x^2 + x - 2 = (x - 1)(x + 2)$ |

The rectangle has width $x - 1$ and length $x + 2$. So, $x^2 + x - 2 = (x - 1)(x + 2)$.

## Try This

**9.** Why can you add one red $-x$-tile and one yellow $x$-tile?

**Use algebra tiles to factor each polynomial.**

**10.** $x^2 - x - 2$ **11.** $x^2 - 2x - 3$ **12.** $x^2 - 5x + 4$ **13.** $x^2 - 7x + 10$

**14.** $x^2 - 2x + 1$ **15.** $x^2 - 6x + 5$ **16.** $x^2 + 5x - 6$ **17.** $x^2 + 3x - 4$

**18.** $x^2 - x - 6$ **19.** $x^2 + 3x - 10$ **20.** $x^2 - 2x - 8$ **21.** $x^2 + x - 12$

# 8-3 Factoring $x^2 + bx + c$

**MA.A.1** Use appropriate properties and strategies to ... factor algebraic expressions. *Also* **MA.A.1.3**

***Objective***
Factor quadratic trinomials of the form $x^2 + bx + c$.

**Why learn this?**
Factoring polynomials will help you find the dimensions of rectangular shapes, such as a fountain. (See Exercise 71.)

In Chapter 7, you learned how to multiply two binomials using the Distributive Property or the FOIL method. In this lesson, you will learn how to factor a trinomial into two binomials.

Notice that when you multiply $(x + 2)(x + 5)$, the constant term in the trinomial is the product of the constants in the binomials.

$$(x + 2)(x + 5) = x^2 + 7x + 10$$

You can use this fact to factor a trinomial into its binomial factors. Look for two numbers that are factors of the constant term in the trinomial. Write two binomials with those numbers, and then multiply to see if you are correct.

**EXAMPLE 1** **Factoring Trinomials by Guess and Check**

**Factor $x^2 + 19x + 60$ by guess and check.**

$(\blacksquare + \blacksquare)(\blacksquare + \blacksquare)$ *Write two sets of parentheses.*

$(x + \blacksquare)(x + \blacksquare)$ *The first term is $x^2$, so the variable terms have a coefficient of 1.*

The constant term in the trinomial is 60.

$(x + 1)(x + 60) = x^2 + 61x + 60$ ✗ *Try factors of 60 for the constant terms in the binomials.*

$(x + 2)(x + 30) = x^2 + 32x + 60$ ✗

$(x + 3)(x + 20) = x^2 + 23x + 60$ ✗

$(x + 4)(x + 15) = x^2 + 19x + 60$ ✓

The factors of $x^2 + 19x + 60$ are $(x + 4)$ and $(x + 15)$.

$x^2 + 19x + 60 = (x + 4)(x + 15)$

**Remember!**
When you multiply two binomials, multiply:
**F**irst terms
**O**uter terms
**I**nner terms
**L**ast terms

**Factor each trinomial by guess and check.**

**1a.** $x^2 + 10x + 24$ **1b.** $x^2 + 7x + 12$

The guess and check method is usually not the most efficient method of factoring a trinomial. Look at the product of $(x + 3)$ and $(x + 4)$.

$$\overset{x^2 \quad 12}{(x+3)(x+4)} = x^2 + 7x + 12$$

$3x$

$4x$

The coefficient of the middle term is the sum of 3 and 4. The third term is the product of 3 and 4.

**Factoring $x^2 + bx + c$**

| WORDS | EXAMPLE |
|---|---|
| To factor a quadratic trinomial of the form $x^2 + bx + c$, find two factors of $c$ whose sum is $b$. | To factor $x^2 + 9x + 18$, look for factors of 18 whose sum is 9. |

| Factors of 18 | Sum | |
|---|---|---|
| 1 and 18 | 19 ✗ | |
| 2 and 9 | 11 ✗ | |
| 3 and 6 | 9 ✓ | $x^2 + 9x + 18 = (x + 3)(x + 6)$ |

When $c$ is positive, its factors have the same sign. The sign of $b$ tells you whether the factors are positive or negative. When $b$ is positive, the factors are positive, and when $b$ is negative, the factors are negative.

EXAMPLE **2**

## Factoring $x^2 + bx + c$ When $c$ Is Positive

**Factor each trinomial. Check your answer.**

**A** $x^2 + 6x + 8$

$(x + \square)(x + \square)$ *$b = 6$ and $c = 8$; look for factors of 8 whose sum is 6.*

| Factors of 8 | Sum | |
|---|---|---|
| 1 and 8 | 9 | ✗ |
| 2 and 4 | 6 | ✓ |

*The factors needed are 2 and 4.*

$(x + 2)(x + 4)$

***Check*** $(x + 2)(x + 4) = x^2 + 4x + 2x + 8$ *Use the FOIL method.*

$= x^2 + 6x + 8$ ✓ *The product is the original polynomial.*

**B** $x^2 + 5x + 6$

$(x + \square)(x + \square)$ *$b = 5$ and $c = 6$; look for factors of 6 whose sum is 5.*

| Factors of 6 | Sum | |
|---|---|---|
| 1 and 6 | 7 | ✗ |
| 2 and 3 | 5 | ✓ |

*The factors needed are 2 and 3.*

$(x + 2)(x + 3)$

***Check*** $(x + 2)(x + 3) = x^2 + 3x + 2x + 6$ *Use the FOIL method.*

$= x^2 + 5x + 6$ ✓ *The product is the original polynomial.*

**Factor each trinomial. Check your answer.**

**C** $x^2 - 10x + 16$

$(x + \blacksquare)(x + \blacksquare)$

*$b = -10$ and $c = 16$; look for factors of 16 whose sum is $-10$.*

| Factors of 16 | Sum | |
|---|---|---|
| $-1$ and $-16$ | $-17$ | ✗ |
| $-2$ and $-8$ | $-10$ | ✓ |
| $-4$ and $-4$ | $-8$ | ✗ |

*The factors needed are $-2$ and $-8$.*

$(x - 2)(x - 8)$

*Check* $(x - 2)(x - 8) = x^2 - 8x - 2x + 16$ *Use the FOIL method.*

$= x^2 - 10x + 16$ ✓ *The product is the original polynomial.*

**Factor each trinomial. Check your answer.**

**2a.** $x^2 + 8x + 12$

**2b.** $x^2 - 5x + 6$

**2c.** $x^2 + 13x + 42$

**2d.** $x^2 - 13x + 40$

When $c$ is negative, its factors have opposite signs. The sign of $b$ tells you which factor is positive and which is negative. The factor with the greater absolute value has the same sign as $b$.

## EXAMPLE 3 Factoring $x^2 + bx + c$ When $c$ Is Negative

**Factor each trinomial.**

**A** $x^2 + 7x - 18$

$(x + \blacksquare)(x + \blacksquare)$

*$b = 7$ and $c = -18$; look for factors of $-18$ whose sum is 7. The factor with the greater absolute value is positive.*

| Factors of $-18$ | Sum | |
|---|---|---|
| $-1$ and 18 | 17 | ✗ |
| $-2$ and 9 | 7 | ✓ |
| $-3$ and 6 | 3 | ✗ |

*The factors needed are $-2$ and 9.*

$(x - 2)(x + 9)$

**Helpful Hint**

If you have trouble remembering the rules for which factor is positive and which is negative, you can try all the factor pairs and check their sums.

**B** $x^2 - 5x - 24$

$(x + \blacksquare)(x + \blacksquare)$

*$b = -5$ and $c = -24$; look for factors of $-24$ whose sum is $-5$. The factor with the greater absolute value is negative.*

| Factors of $-24$ | Sum | |
|---|---|---|
| 1 and $-24$ | $-23$ | ✗ |
| 2 and $-12$ | $-10$ | ✗ |
| 3 and $-8$ | $-5$ | ✓ |
| 4 and $-6$ | $-2$ | ✗ |

*The factors needed are 3 and $-8$.*

$(x + 3)(x - 8)$

**Factor each trinomial. Check your answer.**

**3a.** $x^2 + 2x - 15$ **3b.** $x^2 - 6x + 8$ **3c.** $x^2 - 8x - 20$

A polynomial and the factored form of the polynomial are equivalent expressions. When you evaluate these two expressions for the same value of the variable, the results are the same.

## EXAMPLE 4 Evaluating Polynomials

**Factor $n^2 + 11n + 24$. Show that the original polynomial and the factored form have the same value for $n = 0, 1, 2, 3,$ and $4$.**

$n^2 + 11n + 24$

$(n + \square)(n + \square)$ *$b = 11$ and $c = 24$; look for factors of 24 whose sum is 11.*

| Factors of 24 | Sum | |
|---|---|---|
| 1 and 24 | 25 | ✗ |
| 2 and 12 | 14 | ✗ |
| 3 and 8 | 11 | ✓ |
| 4 and 6 | 10 | ✗ |

*The factors needed are 3 and 8.*

$(n + 3)(n + 8)$

Evaluate the original polynomial and the factored form for $n = 0, 1, 2, 3,$ and $4$.

| $n$ | $n^2 + 11n + 24$ |
|---|---|
| 0 | $0^2 + 11(0) + 24 = 24$ |
| 1 | $1^2 + 11(1) + 24 = 36$ |
| 2 | $2^2 + 11(2) + 24 = 50$ |
| 3 | $3^2 + 11(3) + 24 = 66$ |
| 4 | $4^2 + 11(4) + 24 = 84$ |

| $n$ | $(n + 3)(n + 8)$ |
|---|---|
| 0 | $(0 + 3)(0 + 8) = 24$ |
| 1 | $(1 + 3)(1 + 8) = 36$ |
| 2 | $(2 + 3)(2 + 8) = 50$ |
| 3 | $(3 + 3)(3 + 8) = 66$ |
| 4 | $(4 + 3)(4 + 8) = 84$ |

The original polynomial and the factored form have the same value for the given values of $n$.

4. Factor $n^2 - 7n + 10$. Show that the original polynomial and the factored form have the same value for $n = 0, 1, 2, 3,$ and $4$.

## THINK AND DISCUSS

1. Explain in your own words how to factor $x^2 + 9x + 14$. Show how to check your answer.
2. Explain how you can determine the signs of the factors of $c$ when factoring a trinomial of the form $x^2 + bx + c$.

3. **GET ORGANIZED** Copy and complete the graphic organizer. In each box, write an example of a trinomial with the given properties and factor it.

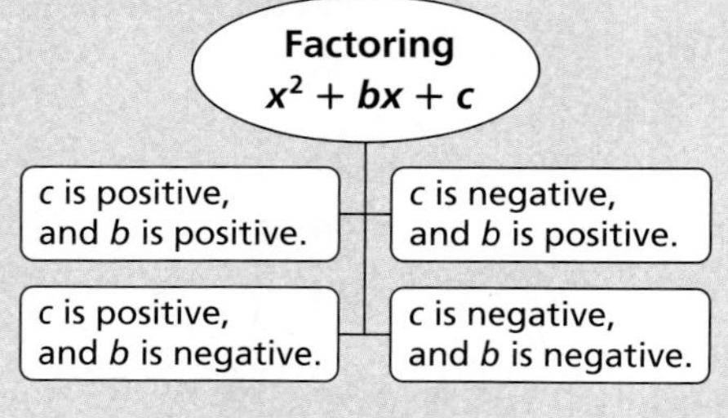

# 8-3 Exercises

MA.A.1, MA.A.1.3

go.hrw.com
Homework Help Online
KEYWORD: MA7 8-3
Parent Resources Online
KEYWORD: MA7 Parent

## GUIDED PRACTICE

SEE EXAMPLE 1 p. 540

**Factor each trinomial by guess and check.**

**1.** $x^2 + 13x + 36$ **2.** $x^2 + 11x + 24$ **3.** $x^2 + 14x + 40$

SEE EXAMPLE 2 p. 541

**Factor each trinomial. Check your answer.**

**4.** $x^2 + 4x + 3$ **5.** $x^2 + 10x + 16$ **6.** $x^2 + 15x + 44$

**7.** $x^2 - 7x + 6$ **8.** $x^2 - 9x + 14$ **9.** $x^2 - 11x + 24$

SEE EXAMPLE 3 p. 542

**10.** $x^2 - 6x - 7$ **11.** $x^2 + 6x - 27$ **12.** $x^2 + x - 30$

**13.** $x^2 - x - 2$ **14.** $x^2 - 3x - 18$ **15.** $x^2 - 4x - 45$

SEE EXAMPLE 4 p. 543

**16.** Factor $n^2 + 6n - 7$. Show that the original polynomial and the factored form have the same value for $n = 0, 1, 2, 3,$ and 4.

## PRACTICE AND PROBLEM SOLVING

**Independent Practice**

| For Exercises | See Example |
|---|---|
| 17–19 | 1 |
| 20–25 | 2 |
| 26–31 | 3 |
| 32 | 4 |

**Extra Practice**

Skills Practice p. S18
Application Practice p. S35

**Factor each trinomial by guess and check.**

**17.** $x^2 + 13x + 30$ **18.** $x^2 + 11x + 28$ **19.** $x^2 + 16x + 48$

**Factor each trinomial. Check your answer.**

**20.** $x^2 + 12x + 11$ **21.** $x^2 + 16x + 28$ **22.** $x^2 + 15x + 36$

**23.** $x^2 - 6x + 5$ **24.** $x^2 - 9x + 18$ **25.** $x^2 - 12x + 32$

**26.** $x^2 + x - 12$ **27.** $x^2 + 4x - 21$ **28.** $x^2 + 9x - 36$

**29.** $x^2 - 12x - 13$ **30.** $x^2 - 10x - 24$ **31.** $x^2 - 2x - 35$

**32.** Factor $n^2 - 12n - 45$. Show that the original polynomial and the factored form have the same value for $n = 0, 1, 2, 3,$ and 4.

**Match each trinomial with its correct factorization.**

**33.** $x^2 + 3x - 10$ **A.** $(x - 2)(x - 5)$

**34.** $x^2 - 7x + 10$ **B.** $(x + 1)(x + 10)$

**35.** $x^2 - 9x - 10$ **C.** $(x - 2)(x + 5)$

**36.** $x^2 + 11x + 10$ **D.** $(x + 1)(x - 10)$

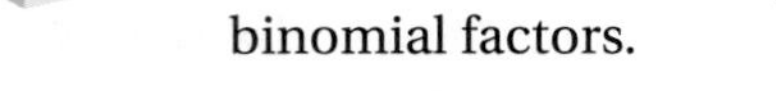

**37. Write About It** Compare multiplying binomials with factoring polynomials into binomial factors.

**Factor each trinomial. Check your answer.**

**38.** $x^2 + x - 20$ **39.** $x^2 - 11x + 18$ **40.** $x^2 - 4x - 21$

**41.** $x^2 + 10x + 9$ **42.** $x^2 - 12x + 32$ **43.** $x^2 + 13x + 42$

**44.** $x^2 - 7x + 12$ **45.** $x^2 + 11x + 18$ **46.** $x^2 - 6x - 27$

**47.** $x^2 + 5x - 24$ **48.** $x^2 - 10x + 21$ **49.** $x^2 + 4x - 45$

**50.** Factor $n^2 + 11n + 28$. Show that the original polynomial and the factored form have the same value for $n = 0, 1, 2, 3,$ and 4.

51. **Estimation** The graph shows the areas of rectangles with dimensions $(x + 1)$ yards and $(x + 2)$ yards. Estimate the value of $x$ for a rectangle with area 9 square yards.

Area (yd²)
40
30
20
10
0
1 2 3 4
x-values

52. **Geometry** The area of a rectangle in square feet can be represented by $x^2 + 8x + 12$. The length is $(x + 6)$ ft. What is the width of the rectangle?

53. **Remodeling** A homeowner wants to enlarge a closet that has an area of $(x^2 + 3x + 2)$ ft². The length is $(x + 2)$ ft. After construction, the area will be $(x^2 + 8x + 15)$ ft² with a length of $(x + 3)$ ft.

   a. Find the dimensions of the closet before construction.
   b. Find the dimensions of the closet after construction.
   c. By how many feet will the length and width increase after construction?

LINK

**Art**

The Dutch painter Theo van Doesburg (1883–1931) is most famous for his paintings composed of lines and rectangles, such as the one shown above.

**Art** **Write the polynomial modeled and then factor.**

54.
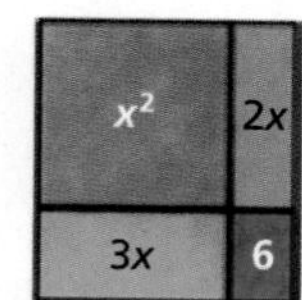


55.
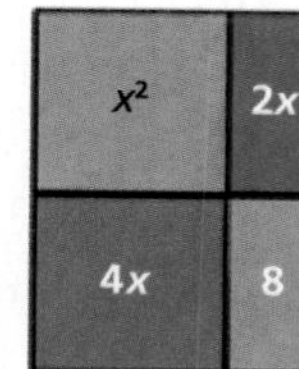


56.
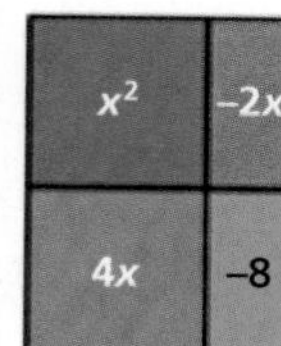


**Copy and complete the table.**

| | $x^2 + bx + c$ | Sign of $c$ | Binomial Factors | Signs of Numbers in Binomials |
|---|---|---|---|---|
| | $x^2 + 4x + 3$ | Positive | $(x + 1)(x + 3)$ | Both positive |
| 57. | $x^2 - 4x + 3$ | ▇ | $(x ▇ 1)(x ▇ 3)$ | ▇ |
| 58. | $x^2 + 2x - 3$ | ▇ | $(x ▇ 1)(x ▇ 3)$ | ▇ |
| 59. | $x^2 - 2x - 3$ | ▇ | $(x ▇ 1)(x ▇ 3)$ | ▇ |

60. **Geometry** A rectangle has area $x^2 + 6x + 8$. The length is $x + 4$. Find the width of the rectangle. Could the rectangle be a square? Explain why or why not.

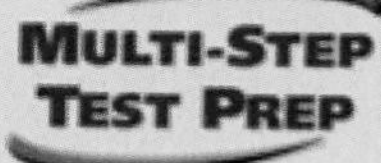


61. This problem will prepare you for the Multi-Step Test Prep on page 556. The equation for the motion of an object with constant acceleration is $d = vt + \frac{1}{2}at^2$ where $d$ is distance traveled in feet, $v$ is starting velocity in feet per second, $a$ is acceleration in feet per second squared, and $t$ is time in seconds.

   a. Janna has two toy race cars on a track. One starts with a velocity of 0 ft/s and accelerates at 2 ft/s². Write an equation for the distance the car travels in time $t$.
   b. The second car travels at a constant speed of 4 ft/s. Write an equation for the distance the second car travels in time $t$. (*Hint:* When speed is constant, the acceleration is 0 ft/s².)
   c. By setting the equations equal to each other you can determine when the cars have traveled the same distance: $t^2 = 4t$. This can be written as $t^2 - 4t = 0$. Factor the left side of the equation.

62. **Construction** The length of a platform is $(x + 7)$ ft. The area of the platform is $(x^2 + 9x + 14)$ ft$^2$. Find the width of the platform.

**Tell whether each statement is true or false. If false, explain.**

63. The third term in a factorable trinomial is equal to the product of the constants in its binomial factors.

64. The constants in the binomial factors of $x^2 + x - 2$ are both negative.

65. The correct factorization of $x^2 - 3x - 4$ is $(x + 4)(x - 1)$.

66. All trinomials of the form $x^2 + bx + c$ can be factored.

**Fill in the missing part of each factorization.**

67. $x^2 - 6x + 8 = (x - 2)(x - \blacksquare)$

68. $x^2 - 2x - 8 = (x + 2)(x - \blacksquare)$

69. $x^2 + 2x - 8 = (x - 2)(x + \blacksquare)$

70. $x^2 + 6x + 8 = (x + 2)(x + \blacksquare)$

71. **Construction** The area of a rectangular fountain is $(x^2 + 12x + 20)$ ft$^2$. The width is $(x + 2)$ ft.
    a. Find the length of the fountain.
    b. A 2-foot walkway is built around the fountain. Find the dimensions of the outside border of the walkway.
    c. Find the total area covered by the fountain and walkway.

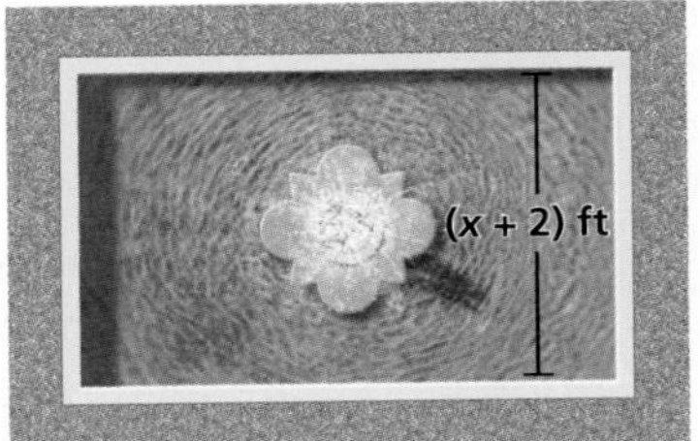


72. **Critical Thinking** Find all possible values of $b$ so that $x^2 + bx + 6$ can be factored into binomial factors.

## TEST PREP

MA.A.1, MA.A.1.3

73. Which is the correct factorization of $x^2 - 10x - 24$?
    (A) $(x - 4)(x - 6)$
    (B) $(x + 4)(x - 6)$
    (C) $(x - 2)(x + 12)$
    (D) $(x + 2)(x - 12)$

74. Which value of $b$ would make $x^2 + bx - 20$ factorable?
    (F) 9
    (G) 12
    (H) 19
    (J) 21

75. Which value of $b$ would NOT make $x^2 + bx - 36$ factorable?
    (A) 5
    (B) 9
    (C) 15
    (D) 16

76. **Short Response** What are the factors of $x^2 + 2x - 24$? Show and explain each step of factoring the polynomial.

## CHALLENGE AND EXTEND

**Factor each trinomial.**

77. $x^4 + 18x^2 + 81$

78. $y^4 - 5y^2 - 24$

79. $d^4 + 22d^2 + 21$

80. $(u + v)^2 + 2(u + v) - 3$

81. $(de)^2 - (de) - 20$

82. $(m - n)^2 - 4(m - n) - 45$

83. Find all possible values of $b$ such that, when $x^2 + bx + 28$ is factored, both constants in the binomials are positive.

84. Find all possible values of $b$ such that, when $x^2 + bx + 32$ is factored, both constants in the binomials are negative.

85. The area of Beth's rectangular garden is $(x^2 + 13x + 42)$ ft². The width is $(x + 6)$ ft.

| Item | Cost |
|---|---|
| Fertilizer | 0.28 ($/ft²) |
| Fencing | 2.00 ($/ft) |

a. What is the length of the garden?
b. Find the perimeter in terms of $x$.
c. Find the cost to fence the garden when $x$ is 5.
d. Find the cost of fertilizer when $x$ is 5.
e. Find the total cost to fence and fertilize Beth's garden when $x$ is 5.

## SPIRAL REVIEW

86. Choose the situation that best describes the graph. *(Lesson 4-1)*

A. An object increases speed, stops, and then moves in reverse.
B. An object starts at rest, increases speed steadily, maintains constant speed, and then comes to an immediate stop.
C. An object increases speed quickly, then increases speed slowly, and then comes to an immediate stop.

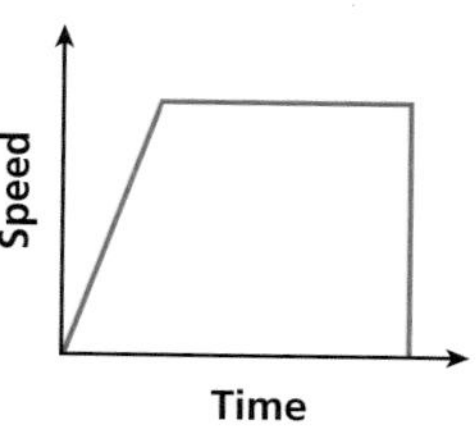


**Simplify.** *(Lesson 7-3)*

87. $x^3x^2$

88. $m^8n^3m^{-12}$

89. $(t^4)^3$

90. $(-2xy^3)^5$

**Factor each polynomial by grouping.** *(Lesson 8-2)*

91. $x^3 + 2x^2 + 5x + 10$

92. $2n^3 - 8n^2 - 3n + 12$

93. $2p^4 - 4p^3 + 7p - 14$

94. $x^3 - 4x^2 + x - 4$

## Career Path

go.hrw.com
Career Resources Online
KEYWORD: MA7 Career

**Jessica Rubino**
***Environmental Sciences major***

**Q: What math classes did you take in high school?**
A: Algebra 1, Algebra 2, and Geometry

**Q: What college math classes have you taken?**
A: I took several computer modeling and programming classes as well as Statistics and Probability.

**Q: How is math used in some of your projects?**
A: Computer applications help me analyze data collected from a local waste disposal site. I used my mathematical knowledge to make recommendations on how to preserve surrounding water supplies.

**Q: What plans do you have for the future?**
A: I enjoy my studies in the area of water pollution. I would also like to research more efficient uses of natural energy resources.

# 8-4 Factoring $ax^2 + bx + c$

**MA.A.1** Use appropriate properties and strategies to ... factor algebraic expressions. *Also* **MA.A.1.3**

***Objective***
Factor quadratic trinomials of the form $ax^2 + bx + c$.

**Why learn this?**
The height of a football that has been kicked can be modeled by a factored polynomial. (See Exercise 69.)

In the previous lesson you factored trinomials of the form $x^2 + bx + c$. Now you will factor trinomials of the form $ax^2 + bx + c$, where $a \neq 0$.

When you multiply $(3x + 2)(2x + 5)$, the coefficient of the $x^2$-term is the product of the coefficients of the $x$-terms. Also, the constant term in the trinomial is the product of the constants in the binomials.

$$(3x+2)(2x+5) = 6x^2 + 19x + 10$$

To factor a trinomial like $ax^2 + bx + c$ into its binomial factors, write two sets of parentheses: $(\square x + \square)(\square x + \square)$.

Write two numbers that are factors of $a$ next to the $x$'s and two numbers that are factors of $c$ in the other blanks. Multiply the binomials to see if you are correct.

## EXAMPLE 1 Factoring $ax^2 + bx + c$ by Guess and Check

**Factor $4x^2 + 16x + 15$ by guess and check.**

$(\square + \square)(\square + \square)$ *Write two sets of parentheses.*

$(\square x + \square)(\square x + \square)$ *The first term is $4x^2$, so at least one variable term has a coefficient other than 1.*

The coefficient of the $x^2$-term is 4. The constant term in the trinomial is 15.

*Try factors of 4 for the coefficients and factors of 15 for the constant terms.*

$(1x + 15)(4x + 1) = 4x^2 + 61x + 15$ ✗

$(1x + 5)(4x + 3) = 4x^2 + 23x + 15$ ✗

$(1x + 3)(4x + 5) = 4x^2 + 17x + 15$ ✗

$(1x + 1)(4x + 15) = 4x^2 + 19x + 15$ ✗

$(2x + 15)(2x + 1) = 4x^2 + 32x + 15$ ✗

$(2x + 5)(2x + 3) = 4x^2 + 16x + 15$ ✓

The factors of $4x^2 + 16x + 15$ are $(2x + 5)$ and $(2x + 3)$.

$4x^2 + 16x + 15 = (2x + 5)(2x + 3)$

**Factor each trinomial by guess and check.**

**1a.** $6x^2 + 11x + 3$ **1b.** $3x^2 - 2x - 8$

So, to factor $ax^2 + bx + c$, check the factors of $a$ and the factors of $c$ in the binomials. The sum of the products of the outer and inner terms should be $b$.

Product = $a$ — Product = $c$

$$(\blacksquare x + \blacksquare)(\blacksquare x + \blacksquare) = ax^2 + bx + c$$

Sum of outer and inner products = $b$

Since you need to check all the factors of $a$ and all the factors of $c$, it may be helpful to make a table. Then check the products of the outer and inner terms to see if the sum is $b$. You can multiply the binomials to check your answer.

## EXAMPLE 2 Factoring $ax^2 + bx + c$ When $c$ Is Positive

**Factor each trinomial. Check your answer.**

**A** $2x^2 + 11x + 12$

$(\blacksquare x + \blacksquare)(\blacksquare x + \blacksquare)$ *$a = 2$ and $c = 12$; Outer + Inner = 11*

| Factors of 2 | Factors of 12 | Outer + Inner |
|---|---|---|
| 1 and 2 | 1 and 12 | $1(12) + 2(1) = 14$ ✗ |
| 1 and 2 | 12 and 1 | $1(1) + 2(12) = 25$ ✗ |
| 1 and 2 | 2 and 6 | $1(6) + 2(2) = 10$ ✗ |
| 1 and 2 | 6 and 2 | $1(2) + 2(6) = 14$ ✗ |
| 1 and 2 | 3 and 4 | $1(4) + 2(3) = 10$ ✗ |
| 1 and 2 | 4 and 3 | $1(3) + 2(4) = 11$ ✓ |

$(x + 4)(2x + 3)$

*Check* $(x + 4)(2x + 3) = 2x^2 + 3x + 8x + 12$ *Use the FOIL method.*

$= 2x^2 + 11x + 12$ ✓

**Remember!**

When $b$ is negative and $c$ is positive, the factors of $c$ are both negative.

**B** $5x^2 - 14x + 8$

$(\blacksquare x + \blacksquare)(\blacksquare x + \blacksquare)$ *$a = 5$ and $c = 8$; Outer + Inner = −14*

| Factors of 5 | Factors of 8 | Outer + Inner |
|---|---|---|
| 1 and 5 | −1 and −8 | $1(-8) + 5(-1) = -13$ ✗ |
| 1 and 5 | −8 and −1 | $1(-1) + 5(-8) = -41$ ✗ |
| 1 and 5 | −2 and −4 | $1(-4) + 5(-2) = -14$ ✓ |

$(x - 2)(5x - 4)$

*Check* $(x - 2)(5x - 4) = 5x^2 - 4x - 10x + 8$ *Use the FOIL method.*

$= 5x^2 - 14x + 8$ ✓

**Factor each trinomial. Check your answer.**

**2a.** $6x^2 + 17x + 5$ **2b.** $9x^2 - 15x + 4$ **2c.** $3x^2 + 13x + 12$

When $c$ is negative, one factor of $c$ will be positive and the other factor will be negative. Only some of the factors are shown in the examples, but you may need to check all of the possibilities.

## EXAMPLE 3 Factoring $ax^2 + bx + c$ When $c$ Is Negative

**Factor each trinomial. Check your answer.**

**A** $4y^2 + 7y - 2$

$(\square y + \square)(\square y + \square)$ *$a = 4$ and $c = -2$; Outer + Inner = 7*

| Factors of 4 | Factors of −2 | Outer + Inner |
|---|---|---|
| 1 and 4 | 1 and −2 | $1(-2) + (4)1 = 2$ ✗ |
| 1 and 4 | −1 and 2 | $(1)2 + 4(-1) = -2$ ✗ |
| 1 and 4 | 2 and −1 | $1(-1) + (4)2 = 7$ ✓ |

$(y + 2)(4y - 1)$

**Check** $(y + 2)(4y - 1) = 4y^2 - y + 8y - 2$ *Use the FOIL method.*

$= 4y^2 + 7y - 2$ ✓

**B** $4x^2 + 19x - 5$

$(\square x + \square)(\square x + \square)$ *$a = 4$ and $c = -5$; Outer + Inner = 19*

| Factors of 4 | Factors of −5 | Outer + Inner |
|---|---|---|
| 1 and 4 | 1 and −5 | $1(-5) + (4)1 = -1$ ✗ |
| 1 and 4 | −1 and 5 | $(1)5 + 4(-1) = 1$ ✗ |
| 1 and 4 | 5 and −1 | $1(-1) + (4)5 = 19$ ✓ |

$(x + 5)(4x - 1)$

**Check** $(x + 5)(4x - 1) = 4x^2 - x + 20x - 5$ *Use the FOIL method.*

$= 4x^2 + 19x - 5$ ✓

**C** $2x^2 - 7x - 15$

$(\square x + \square)(\square x + \square)$ *$a = 2$ and $c = -15$; Outer + Inner = −7*

| Factors of 2 | Factors of −15 | Outer + Inner |
|---|---|---|
| 1 and 2 | 1 and −15 | $1(-15) + (2)1 = -13$ ✗ |
| 1 and 2 | −1 and 15 | $(1)15 + 2(-1) = 13$ ✗ |
| 1 and 2 | 3 and −5 | $1(-5) + (2)3 = 1$ ✗ |
| 1 and 2 | −3 and 5 | $(1)5 + 2(-3) = -1$ ✗ |
| 1 and 2 | 5 and −3 | $1(-3) + (2)5 = 7$ ✗ |
| 1 and 2 | −5 and 3 | $(1)3 + 2(-5) = -7$ ✓ |

$(x - 5)(2x + 3)$

**Check** $(x - 5)(2x + 3) = 2x^2 + 3x - 10x - 15$ *Use the FOIL method.*

$= 2x^2 - 7x - 15$ ✓

**Factor each trinomial. Check your answer.**

**3a.** $6x^2 + 7x - 3$ **3b.** $4n^2 - n - 3$

## Student to Student

### Factoring $ax^2 + bx + c$

**Reggie Wilson**
Franklin High School

*I like to use a box to help me factor trinomials. I look for factors of ac that add to b. Then I arrange the terms in a box and factor.*

*To factor $6x^2 + 7x + 2$, first I find the factors I need.*

$ac = 2(6) = 12 \quad b = 7$

| Factors of 12 | Sum |
|---|---|
| 1 and 12 | 13 |
| 2 and 6 | 8 |
| 3 and 4 | 7 |

*Then I rewrite the trinomial as $6x^2 + 3x + 4x + 2$.*

*Now I arrange $6x^2 + 3x + 4x + 2$ in a box and factor out the common factors from each row and column.*

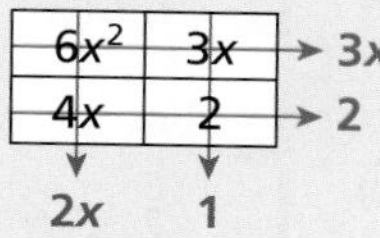


*The factors are $(2x + 1)$ and $(3x + 2)$.*

When the leading coefficient is negative, factor out $-1$ from each term before using other factoring methods.

### EXAMPLE 4 Factoring $ax^2 + bx + c$ When $a$ Is Negative

**Factor $-2x^2 - 15x - 7$.**

$-1(2x^2 + 15x + 7)$ *Factor out −1.*

$-1(\square x + \square)(\square x + \square)$ *$a = 2$ and $c = 7$; Outer + Inner = 15*

| Factors of 2 | Factors of 7 | Outer + Inner | |
|---|---|---|---|
| 1 and 2 | 1 and 7 | $(1)7 + (2)1 = 9$ | ✗ |
| 1 and 2 | 7 and 1 | $(1)1 + (2)7 = 15$ | ✓ |

$(x + 7)(2x + 1)$

$-1(x + 7)(2x + 1)$

**Caution!**
When you factor out $-1$ in an early step, you must carry it through the rest of the steps.

**Factor each trinomial. Check your answer.**

**4a.** $-6x^2 - 17x - 12$ **4b.** $-3x^2 - 17x - 10$

## THINK AND DISCUSS

**1.** Let $a$, $b$, and $c$ be positive. If $ax^2 + bx + c$ is the product of two binomials, what do you know about the signs of the numbers in the binomials?

**2. GET ORGANIZED** Copy and complete the graphic organizer. Write each of the following trinomials in the appropriate box and factor each one.
$3x^2 + 10x - 8 \quad 3x^2 + 10x + 8$
$3x^2 - 10x + 8 \quad 3x^2 - 10x - 8$

| Factoring $ax^2 + bx + c$ | |
|---|---|
| $c > 0$ | |
| $b > 0$ | $b < 0$ |
| | |
| $c < 0$ | |
| $b < 0$ | $b > 0$ |
| | |

# 8-4 Exercises

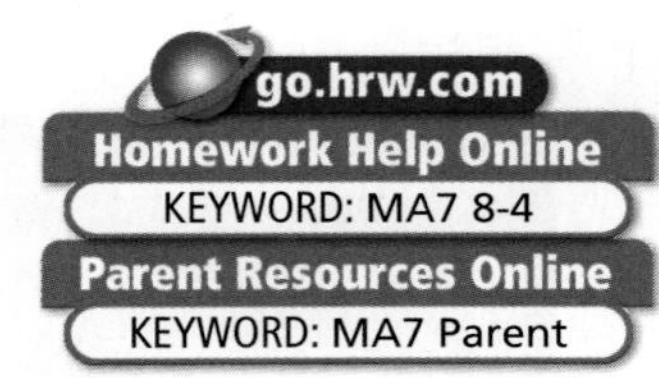


## GUIDED PRACTICE

Factor each trinomial by guess and check.

SEE EXAMPLE 1 p. 548

1. $2x^2 + 9x + 10$
2. $5x^2 + 31x + 6$
3. $5x^2 + 7x - 6$
4. $6x^2 + 37x + 6$
5. $3x^2 - 14x - 24$
6. $6x^2 + x - 2$

SEE EXAMPLE 2 p. 549

Factor each trinomial. Check your answer.

7. $5x^2 + 11x + 2$
8. $2x^2 + 11x + 5$
9. $4x^2 - 9x + 5$
10. $2y^2 - 11y + 14$
11. $5x^2 + 9x + 4$
12. $3x^2 + 7x + 2$

SEE EXAMPLE 3 p. 550

13. $4a^2 + 8a - 5$
14. $15x^2 + 4x - 3$
15. $2x^2 + x - 6$
16. $6n^2 - 11n - 10$
17. $10x^2 - 9x - 1$
18. $7x^2 - 3x - 10$

SEE EXAMPLE 4 p. 551

19. $-2x^2 + 5x + 12$
20. $-4n^2 - 16n + 9$
21. $-5x^2 + 7x + 6$
22. $-6x^2 + 13x - 2$
23. $-4x^2 - 8x + 5$
24. $-5x^2 + x + 18$

## PRACTICE AND PROBLEM SOLVING

**Independent Practice**

| For Exercises | See Example |
|---|---|
| 25–33 | 1 |
| 34–42 | 2 |
| 43–48 | 3 |
| 49–51 | 4 |

**Extra Practice**

Skills Practice p. S19
Application Practice p. S35

Factor each trinomial by guess and check.

25. $9x^2 + 9x + 2$
26. $2x^2 + 7x + 5$
27. $3n^2 + 8n + 4$
28. $10d^2 + 17d + 7$
29. $4c^2 - 17c + 15$
30. $6x^2 + 14x + 4$
31. $8x^2 + 22x + 5$
32. $6x^2 - 13x + 6$
33. $5x^2 + 9x - 18$

Factor each trinomial. Check your answer.

34. $6x^2 + 23x + 7$
35. $10n^2 - 17n + 7$
36. $3x^2 + 11x + 6$
37. $7x^2 + 15x + 2$
38. $3n^2 + 4n + 1$
39. $3x^2 - 19x + 20$
40. $6x^2 + 11x + 4$
41. $4x^2 - 31x + 21$
42. $10x^2 + 31x + 15$
43. $12y^2 + 17y - 5$
44. $3x^2 + 10x - 8$
45. $4x^2 + 4x - 3$
46. $2n^2 - 7n - 4$
47. $3x^2 - 4x - 15$
48. $3n^2 - n - 4$
49. $-4x^2 - 4x + 15$
50. $-3x^2 + 16x - 16$
51. $-3x^2 - x + 2$

**Geometry** For Exercises 52–54, write the polynomial modeled and then factor.

52.

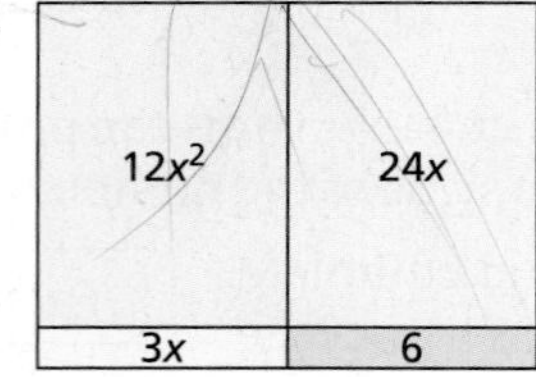


53.

| $2x^2$ | $-x$ |
|---|---|
| $-4x$ | 2 |

54.

| $5x^2$ | $-4x$ |
|---|---|
| $35x$ | $-28$ |

Factor each trinomial, if possible.

55. $9n^2 + 17n + 8$
56. $2x^2 - 7x - 4$
57. $4x^2 - 12x + 5$
58. $5x^2 - 4x + 12$
59. $3x^2 + 14x + 16$
60. $-3x^2 - 11x + 4$
61. $6x^2 - x - 12$
62. $10a^2 + 11a + 3$
63. $4x^2 - 12x + 9$

64. **Geometry** The area of a rectangle is $6x^2 + 11x + 5$ cm². The width is $(x + 1)$ cm. What is the length of the rectangle?

$(x + 1)$ cm

65. **Write About It** Write a paragraph describing how to factor $6x^2 + 13x + 6$. Show each step you would take and explain your steps.

**Complete each factorization.**

66.
$$8x^2 + 18x - 5$$
$$8x^2 + 20x - 2x - 5$$
$$(8x^2 + 20x) - (2x + 5)$$
$$\blacksquare(\blacksquare + \blacksquare) - \blacksquare(2x + 5)$$
$$(\blacksquare - \blacksquare)(2x + 5)$$

67.
$$4x^2 + 9x + 2$$
$$4x^2 + 8x + x + 2$$
$$(4x^2 + 8x) + (x + 2)$$
$$\blacksquare(\blacksquare + \blacksquare) + \blacksquare(x + 2)$$
$$(\blacksquare + \blacksquare)(x + 2)$$

68. **Gardening** The length of Rebecca's rectangular garden was two times the width $w$. Rebecca increased the length and width of the garden so that the area of the new garden is $(2w^2 + 7w + 6)$ square yards. By how much did Rebecca increase the length and the width of the garden?

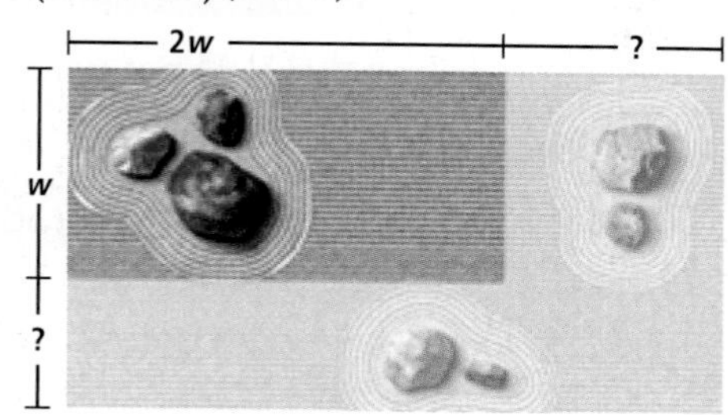


69. **Physics** The height of a football that has been thrown or kicked can be described by the expression $-16t^2 + vt + h$ where $t$ is the time in seconds, $v$ is the initial upward velocity, and $h$ is the initial height in feet.

a. Write an expression for the height of a football at time $t$ when the initial upward velocity is 20 feet per second and the initial height is 6 feet.

b. Factor your expression from part **a.**

c. Find the height of the football after 1 second.

70. **ERROR ANALYSIS** A student attempted to factor $2x^2 + 11x + 12$ as shown. Find and explain the error.

$2x^2 + 11x + 12$

| Factors of 12 | Sum | |
|---|---|---|
| 1 and 12 | 13 | ✓ |
| 2 and 6 | 8 | ✗ |
| 3 and 4 | 7 | ✗ |

$(2x + 1)(x + 12)$

**MULTI-STEP TEST PREP**

71. This problem will prepare you for the Multi-Step Test Prep on page 552. The equation $d = 2t^2$ gives the distance from the start point of a toy boat that starts at rest and accelerates at 4 cm/s². The equation $d = 10t - 8$ gives the distance from the start point of a second boat that starts at rest 8 cm behind the first boat and travels at a constant rate of 10 cm/s.

a. By setting the equations equal to each other, you can determine when the cars are the same distance from the start point: $2t^2 = 10t - 8$. Use properties of algebra to collect all terms on the left side of the equation, leaving 0 on the right side.

b. Factor the expression on the left side of the equation.

c. The boats are the same distance from the start point at $t = 1$ and $t = 4$. Explain how the factors you found in part **b** were used to find these two times.

**Match each trinomial with its correct factorization.**

**72.** $6x^2 - 29x - 5$ **A.** $(x + 5)(6x + 1)$

**73.** $6x^2 - 31x + 5$ **B.** $(x - 5)(6x - 1)$

**74.** $6x^2 + 31x + 5$ **C.** $(x + 5)(6x - 1)$

**75.** $6x^2 + 29x - 5$ **D.** $(x - 5)(6x + 1)$

**76.** **Critical Thinking** The quadratic trinomial $ax^2 + bx + c$ has $a > 0$ and can be factored into the product of two binomials.

**a.** Explain what you know about the signs of the constants in the factors if $c > 0$.

**b.** Explain what you know about the signs of the constants in the factors if $c < 0$.

MA.A.1, MA.A.1.3

**77.** What value of $b$ would make $3x^2 + bx - 8$ factorable?

Ⓐ 3 Ⓑ 10 Ⓒ 11 Ⓓ 25

**78.** Which product of binomials is represented by the model?

Ⓕ $(x + 4)(3x + 5)$ Ⓗ $(x + 3)(5x + 4)$

Ⓖ $(x + 4)(5x + 3)$ Ⓙ $(x + 5)(3x + 4)$

| $5x^2$ | $4x$ |
|---|---|
| $15x$ | 12 |

**79.** Which binomial is a factor of $24x^2 - 49x + 2$?

Ⓐ $x - 2$ Ⓑ $x - 1$ Ⓒ $x + 1$ Ⓓ $x + 2$

**80.** Which value of $c$ would make $2x^2 + x + c$ NOT factorable?

Ⓕ $-15$ Ⓖ $-9$ Ⓗ $-6$ Ⓙ $-1$

## CHALLENGE AND EXTEND

**Factor each trinomial. Check your answer.**

**81.** $1 + 4x + 4x^2$ **82.** $1 - 14x + 49x^2$ **83.** $1 + 18x + 81x^2$

**84.** $25 + 30x + 9x^2$ **85.** $4 + 20x + 25x^2$ **86.** $4 - 12x + 9x^2$

**87.** Find all possible values of $b$ such that $3x^2 + bx + 2$ can be factored.

**88.** Find all possible values of $b$ such that $3x^2 + bx - 2$ can be factored.

**89.** Find all possible values of $b$ such that $5x^2 + bx + 1$ can be factored.

## SPIRAL REVIEW

**90.** Archie makes \$12 per hour and is paid for whole numbers of hours. The function $f(x) = 12x$ gives the amount of money that Archie makes in $x$ hours. Graph this function and give its domain and range. *(Lesson 5-1)*

**Graph each system of linear inequalities. Give two ordered pairs that are solutions and two that are not solutions.** *(Lesson 6-6)*

**91.** $\begin{cases} y < -2x + 1 \\ y > 3x - 5 \end{cases}$ **92.** $\begin{cases} y \geq -x + 2 \\ y \leq x - 3 \end{cases}$ **93.** $\begin{cases} y \leq -4x \\ y > 2x - 6 \end{cases}$

**Factor each trinomial. Check your answer.** *(Lesson 8-3)*

**94.** $x^2 + 6x + 8$ **95.** $x^2 - 8x - 9$ **96.** $x^2 - 8x + 12$

# Use a Graph to Factor Polynomials

You can use a graphing calculator to help factor polynomials.

*Use with Lesson 8-4*

**MA.A.1** Use appropriate properties and strategies to ... factor algebraic expressions. *Also* **MA.A.1.3**

go.hrw.com
**Lab Resources Online**
KEYWORD: MA7 Lab8

## Activity

**Factor $x^2 - 3x - 4$ using algebra and check your factorization using a graphing calculator.**

**1** $x^2 - 3x - 4$

$(x + \blacksquare)(x + \blacksquare)$ *$b = -3$ and $c = -4$; look for factors of $-4$ whose sum is $-3$.*

$(x - 4)(x + 1)$ *$-4(1) = -4; -4 + 1 = -3$*

**2** Press Y= and enter $x^2 - 3x - 4$ for **Y1.**

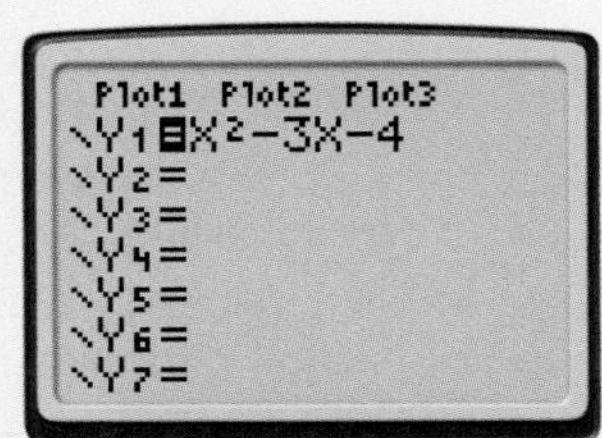


**3** Press GRAPH to view the graph of the equation.

**4** Press TRACE and use the left and right buttons to move the cursor along the graph. The graph appears to cross the $x$-axis at $x = -1$ and $x = 4$.

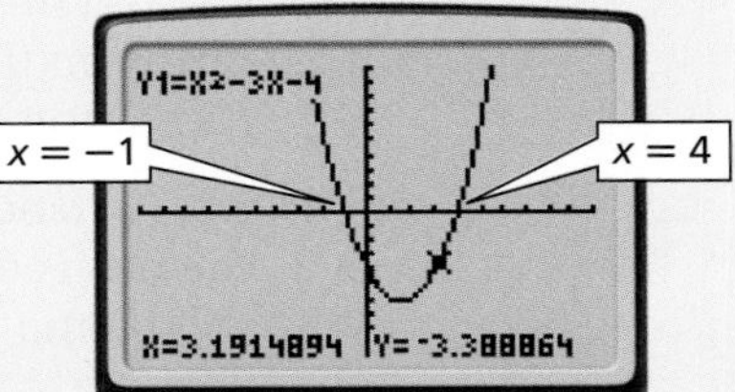


**5** To find the value of $y$ at $x = -1$, enter $-1$ and press ENTER while in *Trace* mode. The calculator gives you a value for $y$. Then enter 4 to find the value of $y$ at $x = 4$.

The calculator tells you that $y = 0$ at $x = -1$ and at $x = 4$.

Notice that for a function with a binomial factor of the form $(x - a)$, it appears that $a$ is an $x$-intercept.

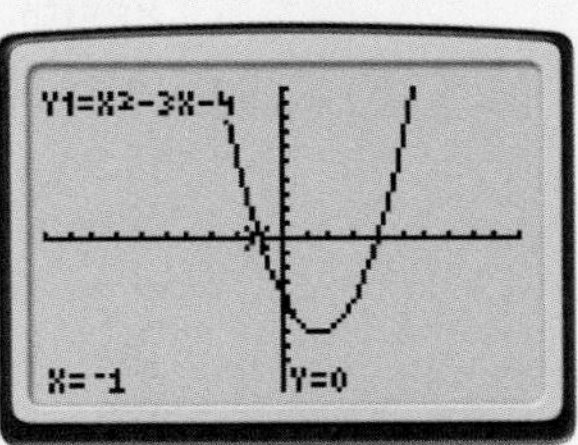


## Try This

**Graph each trinomial and use the graph to predict the factors. Then factor each trinomial using algebra.**

**1.** $x^2 - x - 2$ **2.** $x^2 + 5x + 6$ **3.** $x^2 + x - 12$

**4.** $x^2 + 12x - 64$ **5.** $x^2 - 4x - 5$ **6.** $3x^2 + 16x - 12$

CHAPTER 8

# MULTI-STEP TEST PREP

SECTION 8A

## Factoring

**Red Light, Green Light** The equation for the motion of an object with constant acceleration is $d = vt + \frac{1}{2}at^2$ where $d$ is distance traveled in meters, $v$ is starting velocity in m/s, $a$ is acceleration in $\text{m/s}^2$, and $t$ is time in seconds.

1. A car is stopped at a traffic light. The light changes to green and the driver starts to drive, accelerating at a rate of $4\ \text{m/s}^2$. Write an equation for the distance the car travels in time $t$.
2. A bus is traveling at a speed of 15 m/s. The driver approaches the same traffic light in another traffic lane. He does not brake, and continues at the same speed. Write an equation for the distance the bus travels in time $t$. (*Hint:* At a constant speed, the acceleration is $0\ \text{m/s}^2$.)
3. Set the equations equal to each other so you can determine when the car and bus are the same distance from the intersection. Collect all the terms on the left side of this new equation, leaving 0 on the right side. Factor the expression on the left side of the equation.
4. Let $t = 0$ be the point at which the car is just starting to drive and the bus is even with the car. Find the other time when the vehicles will be the same distance from the intersection.
5. What distance will the two vehicles have traveled when they are again at the same distance from the intersection?
6. A truck traveling at 16 m/s is 24 meters behind the bus at $t = 0$. The equation $d = -24 + 16t$ gives the position of the truck. At what time will the truck be the same distance from the intersection as the bus? What will that distance be?

# READY TO GO ON?

CHAPTER 8

SECTION 8A

## Quiz for Lessons 8-1 Through 8-4

### 8-1 Factors and Greatest Common Factors

**Write the prime factorization of each number.**

**1.** 54 **2.** 42 **3.** 50 **4.** 120 **5.** 44 **6.** 78

**Find the GCF of each pair of monomials.**

**7.** $6p^3$ and $2p$

**8.** $12x^3$ and $18x^4$

**9.** $-15$ and $20s^4$

**10.** $3a$ and $4b^2$

**11.** Brent is making a wooden display case for his baseball collection. He has 24 balls from American League games and 30 balls from National League games. He wants to display the same number of baseballs in each row and does not want to put American League baseballs in the same row as National League baseballs. How many rows will Brent need in the display case to put the greatest number of baseballs possible in each row?

### 8-2 Factoring by GCF

**Factor each polynomial. Check your answer.**

**12.** $2d^3 + 4d$

**13.** $m^2 - 8m^5$

**14.** $12x^4 - 8x^3 - 4x^2$

**15.** $3k^2 + 6k - 3$

**16.** The surface area of a cone can be found using the expression $s\pi r + \pi r^2$, where $s$ represents the slant height and $r$ represents the radius of the base. Factor this expression.

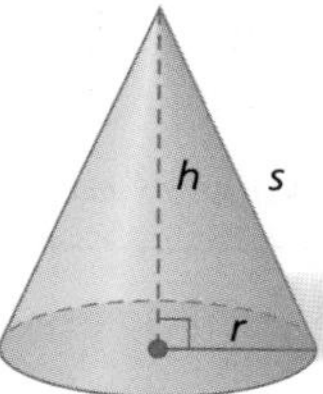


**Factor each polynomial by grouping. Check your answer.**

**17.** $w^3 - 4w^2 + w - 4$

**18.** $3x^3 + 6x^2 - 4x - 8$

**19.** $2p^3 - 6p^2 + 15 - 5p$

**20.** $n^3 - 6n^2 + 5n - 30$

### 8-3 Factoring $x^2 + bx + c$

**Factor each trinomial. Check your answer.**

**21.** $n^2 + 9n + 20$ **22.** $d^2 - 6d - 7$ **23.** $x^2 - 6x + 8$

**24.** $y^2 + 7y - 30$ **25.** $k^2 - 6k + 5$ **26.** $c^2 - 10c + 24$

**27.** Simplify and factor the polynomial $n(n + 3) - 4$. Show that the original polynomial and the factored form describe the same sequence of numbers for $n = 0, 1, 2, 3,$ and $4$.

### 8-4 Factoring $ax^2 + bx + c$

**Factor each trinomial. Check your answer.**

**28.** $2x^2 + 11x + 5$ **29.** $3n^2 + 16n + 21$ **30.** $5y^2 - 7y - 6$

**31.** $4g^2 - 10g + 6$ **32.** $6p^2 - 18p - 24$ **33.** $12d^2 + 7d - 12$

**34.** The area of a rectangle is $(8x^2 + 8x + 2)$ cm$^2$. The width is $(2x + 1)$ cm. What is the length of the rectangle?

# 8-5 Factoring Special Products

**MA.A.1** Use appropriate properties and strategies to … factor algebraic expressions. *Also* **MA.A.1.3**

***Objectives***

Factor perfect-square trinomials.

Factor the difference of two squares.

**Who uses this?**

Urban planners can use the area of a square park to find its length and width. (See Example 2.)

You studied the patterns of some special products of binomials in Chapter 7. You can use those patterns to factor certain polynomials.

A trinomial is a perfect square if:

- The **first** and **last** terms are perfect squares.
- The **middle** term is two times one factor from the first term and one factor from the last term.

$$9x^2 + 12x + 4$$

$$3x \cdot 3x \quad 2(3x \cdot 2) \quad 2 \cdot 2$$

**Perfect-Square Trinomials**

| PERFECT-SQUARE TRINOMIAL | EXAMPLES |
|---|---|
| $a^2 + 2ab + b^2 = (a + b)(a + b) = (a + b)^2$ | $x^2 + 6x + 9 = (x + 3)(x + 3) = (x + 3)^2$ |
| $a^2 - 2ab + b^2 = (a - b)(a - b) = (a - b)^2$ | $x^2 - 2x + 1 = (x - 1)(x - 1) = (x - 1)^2$ |

## EXAMPLE 1 Recognizing and Factoring Perfect-Square Trinomials

**Determine whether each trinomial is a perfect square. If so, factor. If not, explain.**

**A** $x^2 + 12x + 36$

$$x^2 + 12x + 36$$

$$x \cdot x \quad 2(x \cdot 6) \quad 6 \cdot 6$$

*The trinomial is a perfect square. Factor.*

**Method 1** Factor.

$x^2 + 12x + 36$

| Factors of 36 | Sum | |
|---|---|---|
| 1 and 36 | 37 | ✗ |
| 2 and 18 | 20 | ✗ |
| 3 and 12 | 15 | ✗ |
| 4 and 9 | 13 | ✗ |
| 6 and 6 | 12 | ✓ |

$(x + 6)(x + 6)$

**Method 2** Use the rule.

$x^2 + 12x + 36$   *$a = x$, $b = 6$*

$x^2 + 2(x)(6) + 6^2$   *Write the trinomial as $a^2 + 2ab + b^2$.*

$(x + 6)^2$   *Write the trinomial as $(a + b)^2$.*

**Determine whether each trinomial is a perfect square. If so, factor. If not, explain.**

**B** $4x^2 - 12x + 9$

$$4x^2 - 12x + 9$$

$2x \cdot 2x \quad 2(2x \cdot 3) \quad 3 \cdot 3$ — *The trinomial is a perfect square. Factor.*

| | |
|---|---|
| $4x^2 - 12x + 9$ | *$a = 2x, b = 3$* |
| $(2x)^2 - 2(2x)(3) + 3^2$ | *$a^2 - 2ab + b^2$* |
| $(2x - 3)^2$ | *$(a - b)^2$* |

**C** $x^2 + 9x + 16$

$$x^2 + 9x + 16$$

$x \cdot x \quad 2(x \cdot 4) \quad 4 \cdot 4$ — *$2(x \cdot 4) \neq 9x$*

$x^2 + 9x + 16$ is not a perfect-square trinomial because $9x \neq 2(x \cdot 4)$.

**Helpful Hint**

You can check your answer by using the FOIL method.

For Example 1B, $(2x - 3)^2 =$ $(2x - 3)(2x - 3) =$ $4x^2 - 6x - 6x + 9 =$ $4x^2 - 12x + 9$

**Determine whether each trinomial is a perfect square. If so, factor. If not, explain.**

**1a.** $x^2 + 4x + 4$ **1b.** $x^2 - 14x + 49$ **1c.** $9x^2 - 6x + 4$

## EXAMPLE 2 *Problem-Solving Application*

**The park in the center of the Place des Vosges in Paris, France, is in the shape of a square. The area of the park is $(25x^2 + 70x + 49)$ ft². The side length of the park is in the form $cx + d$, where $c$ and $d$ are whole numbers. Find an expression in terms of $x$ for the perimeter of the park. Find the perimeter when $x = 8$ ft.**

### 1 Understand the Problem

The **answer** will be an expression for the perimeter of the park and the value of the expression when $x = 8$.

List the **important information:**

- The park is a square with area $(25x^2 + 70x + 49)$ ft².
- The side length of the park is in the form $cx + d$, where $c$ and $d$ are whole numbers.

### 2 Make a Plan

The formula for the area of a square is area $= (\text{side})^2$.

Factor $25x^2 + 70x + 49$ to find the side length of the park. Write a formula for the perimeter of the park, and evaluate the expression for $x = 8$.

### 3 Solve

$$\begin{aligned} &25x^2 + 70x + 49 && a = 5x,\ b = 7 \\ &(5x)^2 + 2(5x)(7) + 7^2 && \text{Write the trinomial as } a^2 + 2ab + b^2. \\ &(5x + 7)^2 && \text{Write the trinomial as } (a + b)^2. \end{aligned}$$

$$25x^2 + 70x + 49 = (5x + 7)(5x + 7)$$

The side length of the park is $(5x + 7)$ ft and $(5x + 7)$ ft.

Write a formula for the perimeter of the park.

$$\begin{aligned} P &= 4s && \text{Write the formula for the perimeter of a square.} \\ &= 4(5x + 7) && \text{Substitute the side length for } s. \\ &= 20x + 28 && \text{Distribute 4.} \end{aligned}$$

An expression for the perimeter of the park in feet is $20x + 28$.

Evaluate the expression when $x = 8$.

$$\begin{aligned} P &= 20x + 28 \\ &= 20(8) + 28 && \text{Substitute 8 for } x. \\ &= 188 \end{aligned}$$

When $x = 8$ ft, the perimeter of the park is 188 ft.

### 4 Look Back

For a square with a perimeter of 188 ft, the side length is $\frac{188}{4} = 47$ ft and the area is $47^2 = 2209$ ft$^2$.

Evaluate $25x^2 + 70x + 49$ for $x = 8$:

$$\begin{aligned} &25(8)^2 + 70(8) + 49 \\ &1600 + 560 + 49 \\ &2209\ \checkmark \end{aligned}$$

**2. What if...?** A company produces square sheets of aluminum, each of which has an area of $(9x^2 + 6x + 1)$ m$^2$. The side length of each sheet is in the form $cx + d$, where $c$ and $d$ are whole numbers. Find an expression in terms of $x$ for the perimeter of a sheet. Find the perimeter when $x = 3$ m.

In Chapter 7 you learned that the difference of two squares has the form $a^2 - b^2$. The difference of two squares can be written as the product $(a + b)(a - b)$. You can use this pattern to factor some polynomials.

A polynomial is a difference of two squares if:

- There are two terms, one subtracted from the other.
- Both terms are perfect squares.

$$\underset{2x \cdot 2x}{4x^2} - \underset{3 \cdot 3}{9}$$

**Difference of Two Squares**

| DIFFERENCE OF TWO SQUARES | EXAMPLE |
| --- | --- |
| $a^2 - b^2 = (a + b)(a - b)$ | $x^2 - 9 = (x + 3)(x - 3)$ |

**EXAMPLE 3** **Recognizing and Factoring the Difference of Two Squares**

**Determine whether each binomial is a difference of two squares. If so, factor. If not, explain.**

> **Reading Math**
> Recognize a difference of two squares: the coefficients of variable terms are perfect squares, powers on variable terms are even, and constants are perfect squares.

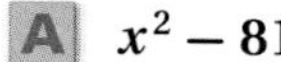

**A** $x^2 - 81$

$$x^2 - 81$$

$x \cdot x \quad 9 \cdot 9$ *The polynomial is a difference of two squares.*

$x^2 - 9^2$ *$a = x$, $b = 9$*

$(x + 9)(x - 9)$ *Write the polynomial as $(a + b)(a - b)$.*

$x^2 - 81 = (x + 9)(x - 9)$

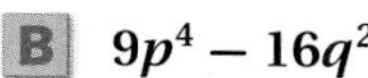

**B** $9p^4 - 16q^2$

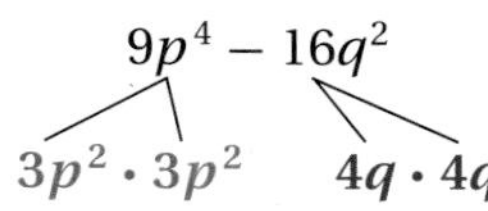

$$9p^4 - 16q^2$$

$3p^2 \cdot 3p^2 \quad 4q \cdot 4q$ *The polynomial is a difference of two squares.*

$(3p^2)^2 - (4q)^2$ *$a = 3p^2$, $b = 4q$*

$(3p^2 + 4q)(3p^2 - 4q)$ *Write the polynomial as $(a + b)(a - b)$.*

$9p^4 - 16q^2 = (3p^2 + 4q)(3p^2 - 4q)$

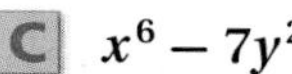

**C** $x^6 - 7y^2$

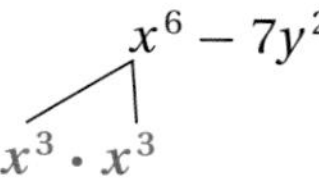

$$x^6 - 7y^2$$

$x^3 \cdot x^3$ *$7y^2$ is not a perfect square.*

$x^6 - 7y^2$ is not the difference of two squares because $7y^2$ is not a perfect square.

**Determine whether the binomial is a difference of two squares. If so, factor. If not, explain.**

**3a.** $1 - 4x^2$ **3b.** $p^8 - 49q^6$ **3c.** $16x^2 - 4y^5$

## THINK AND DISCUSS

1. The binomial $1 - x^4$ is a difference of two squares. Use the rule to identify $a$ and $b$ in $1 - x^4$.
2. The polynomial $x^2 + 8x + 16$ is a perfect-square trinomial. Use the rule to identify $a$ and $b$ in $x^2 + 8x + 16$.

3. **GET ORGANIZED** Copy and complete the graphic organizer. Write an example of each type of special product and factor it.

| Special Product | Factored Form |
|---|---|
| Perfect-square trinomial with positive coefficient of middle term | |
| Perfect-square trinomial with negative coefficient of middle term | |
| Difference of two squares | |

# 8-5 Exercises

MA.A.1, MA.A.1.3

go.hrw.com
Homework Help Online
KEYWORD: MA7 8-5
Parent Resources Online
KEYWORD: MA7 Parent

## GUIDED PRACTICE

SEE EXAMPLE 1 p. 558

**Determine whether each trinomial is a perfect square. If so, factor. If not, explain.**

1. $x^2 - 4x + 4$
2. $x^2 - 4x - 4$
3. $9x^2 - 12x + 4$
4. $x^2 + 2x + 1$
5. $x^2 - 6x + 9$
6. $x^2 - 6x - 9$

SEE EXAMPLE 2 p. 559

7. **City Planning** A city purchases a rectangular plot of land with an area of $(x^2 + 24x + 144)$ yd$^2$ for a park. The dimensions of the plot are of the form $ax + b$, where $a$ and $b$ are whole numbers. Find an expression for the perimeter of the park. Find the perimeter when $x = 10$ yd.

SEE EXAMPLE 3 p. 561

**Determine whether each binomial is a difference of two squares. If so, factor. If not, explain.**

8. $1 - 4x^2$
9. $s^2 - 4^2$
10. $81x^2 - 1$
11. $4x^4 - 9y^2$
12. $x^8 - 50$
13. $x^6 - 9$

## PRACTICE AND PROBLEM SOLVING

**Independent Practice**

| For Exercises | See Example |
|---|---|
| 14–19 | 1 |
| 20 | 2 |
| 21–26 | 3 |

**Determine whether the trinomial is a perfect square. If so, factor. If not, explain.**

14. $4x^2 - 4x + 1$
15. $4x^2 - 4x - 1$
16. $36x^2 - 12x + 1$
17. $25x^2 + 10x + 4$
18. $9x^2 + 18x + 9$
19. $16x^2 - 40x + 25$

20. **Measurement** You are given a sheet of paper and told to cut out a rectangular piece with an area of $(4x^2 - 44x + 121)$ mm$^2$. The dimensions of the rectangle have the form $ax - b$, where $a$ and $b$ are whole numbers. Find an expression for the perimeter of the rectangle you cut out. Find the perimeter when $x = 41$ mm.

**Determine whether each binomial is a difference of two squares. If so, factor. If not, explain.**

21. $1^2 - 4x^2$
22. $25m^2 - 16n^2$
23. $4x - 9y$
24. $49p^{12} - 9q^6$
25. $9^2 - 100x^4$
26. $x^3 - y^3$

**Find the missing term in each perfect-square trinomial.**

27. $x^2 + 14x + \blacksquare$
28. $9x^2 + \blacksquare + 25$
29. $\blacksquare - 36y + 81$

**Factor each polynomial using the rule for perfect-square trinomials or the rule for a difference of two squares. Tell which rule you used.**

30. $x^2 - 8x + 16$
31. $100x^2 - 81y^2$
32. $36x^2 + 24x + 4$
33. $4r^6 - 25s^6$
34. $49x^2 - 70x + 25$
35. $x^{14} - 144$

36. **Write About It** What is similar about a perfect-square trinomial and a difference of two squares? What is different?
37. **Critical Thinking** Describe two ways to create a perfect-square trinomial.
38. For what value of $b$ would $(x + b)(x + b)$ be the factored form of $x^2 - 22x + 121$?
39. For what value of $c$ are the factors of $x^2 + cx + 256$ the same?

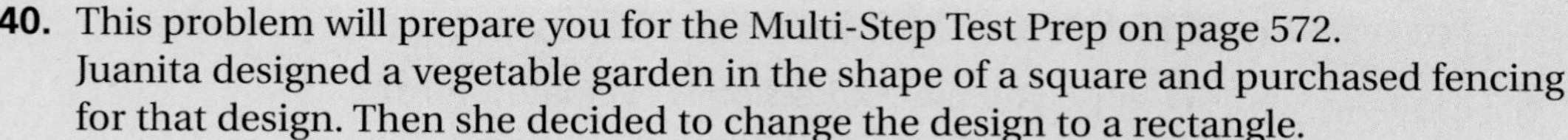

**40.** This problem will prepare you for the Multi-Step Test Prep on page 572. Juanita designed a vegetable garden in the shape of a square and purchased fencing for that design. Then she decided to change the design to a rectangle.

**a.** The square garden had an area of $x^2$ ft$^2$. The area of the rectangular garden is $(x^2 - 25)$ ft$^2$. Factor the expression for the area of the rectangular garden.

**b.** The rectangular garden must have the same perimeter as the square garden, so Juanita added a number of feet to the length and subtracted the same number of feet from the width. Use your factors from part **a** to determine how many feet were added to the length and subtracted from the width.

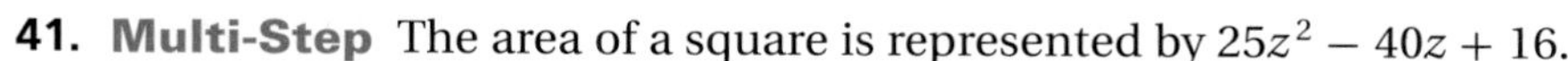

**c.** If the original length of the square garden was 8 feet, what are the length and width of the new garden?

**41. Multi-Step** The area of a square is represented by $25z^2 - 40z + 16$.

**a.** What expression represents the length of a side of the square?

**b.** What expression represents the perimeter of the square?

**c.** What are the length of a side, the perimeter, and the area of the square when $z = 3$?

**42. Multi-Step** A small rectangle is drawn inside a larger rectangle as shown.

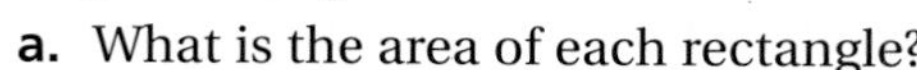

**a.** What is the area of each rectangle?

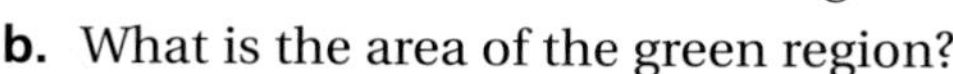

**b.** What is the area of the green region?

**c.** Factor the expression for the area of the green region. (*Hint:* First factor out the common factor of 3 and then factor the binomial.)

**43.** Evaluate each expression for the values of $x$.

| | $x$ | $x^2 + 10x + 25$ | $(x + 5)^2$ | $(x - 5)^2$ | $x^2 - 10x + 25$ | $x^2 - 25$ |
|---|---|---|---|---|---|---|
| **a.** | $-5$ | | | | | |
| **b.** | $-1$ | | | | | |
| **c.** | 0 | | | | | |
| **d.** | 1 | | | | | |
| **e.** | 5 | | | | | |

**44.** In the table above, which columns have equivalent values? Explain why.

**45. Geometry** A model for the difference of two squares is shown below. Copy and complete the second figure by writing the missing labels.

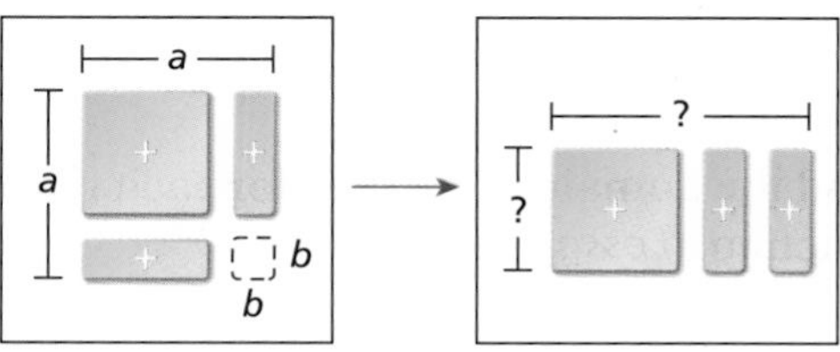


**46. ERROR ANALYSIS** Two students factored $25x^4 - 9y^2$. Which is incorrect? Explain the error.

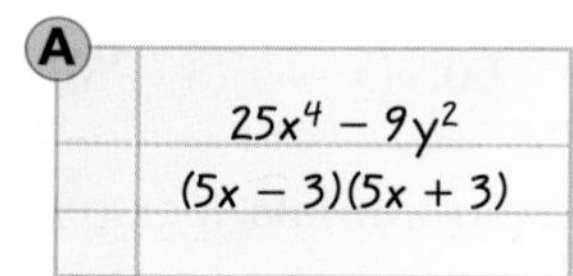

**A**

$25x^4 - 9y^2$

$(5x - 3)(5x + 3)$

**B**

$25x^4 - 9y^2$

$(5x^2 - 3y)(5x^2 + 3y)$

MA.A.1, MA.A.1.3

**47.** A polynomial expression is evaluated for the $x$- and $y$-values shown in the table. Which expression was evaluated to give the values shown in the third column?

| $x$ | $y$ | Value of Expression |
|---|---|---|
| 0 | 0 | 0 |
| −1 | −1 | 0 |
| 1 | 1 | 0 |
| 1 | −1 | 4 |

Ⓐ $x^2 - y^2$
Ⓑ $x^2 + 2xy + y^2$
Ⓒ $x^2 - 2xy + y^2$
Ⓓ None of the above

**48.** The area of a square is $4x^2 + 20x + 25$. Which expression can also be used to model the area of the square?

Ⓕ $(2x - 5)(5 - 2x)$
Ⓖ $(2x + 5)(2x - 5)$
Ⓗ $(2x - 5)^2$
Ⓙ $(2x + 5)^2$

**49.** **Gridded Response** Evaluate the polynomial expression $x^2 - 18x + 81$ for $x = 10$.

## CHALLENGE AND EXTEND

**50.** The binomial $81x^4 - 16$ can be factored using the rule for a difference of two squares.

a. Fill in the factorization: $81x^4 - 16$
$(9x^2 + ■)(■ - ■)$

b. One binomial from part **a** can be further factored. Identify the binomial and factor it.

c. Write your own binomial that can be factored twice as the difference of two squares.

**51.** The expression $4 - (v + 2)^2$ is the difference of two squares, because it fits the rule $a^2 - b^2$.

a. Identify $a$ and $b$ in the expression.

b. Factor and simplify $4 - (v + 2)^2$.

**The *difference of cubes* is an expression of the form $a^3 - b^3$. It can be factored according to the rule $a^3 - b^3 = (a + b)(a^2 - ab + b^2)$. For each binomial, identify $a$ and $b$, and factor using the rule.**

**52.** $x^3 - 1$ **53.** $27y^3 - 64$ **54.** $n^6 - 8$

## SPIRAL REVIEW

**Find the domain and range for each relation and tell whether the relation is a function.** *(Lesson 4-2)*

**55.** $\{(5, 2), (4, 1), (3, 0), (2, -1)\}$ **56.** $\{(-3, 6), (-1, 6), (1, 6), (3, 6)\}$

**57.** $\{(2, -8), (2, -2), (2, 4), (2, 10)\}$ **58.** $\{(-2, 4), (-1, 1), (0, 0), (1, 1)\}$

**Multiply.** *(Lesson 7-7)*

**59.** $2a(3a^2 + 7a - 5)$ **60.** $(x + 3)(x - 8)$ **61.** $(t - 4)^2$

**Find the GCF of each pair of monomials.** *(Lesson 8-1)*

**62.** $9m^2$ and $3m^2$ **63.** $8c^2$ and $8d^2$ **64.** $-12x^3y$ and $16y^2$

# Mental Math

Recognizing patterns of special products can help you perform multiplication mentally.

*See Skills Bank page S52*

Remember these special products that you studied in Chapters 7 and 8.

| Patterns of Special Products | |
|---|---|
| **Difference of Two Squares** | $(a + b)(a - b) = a^2 - b^2$ |
| **Perfect-Square Trinomial** | $(a + b)^2 = a^2 + 2ab + b^2$<br>$(a - b)^2 = a^2 - 2ab + b^2$ |

## Example 1

**Simplify $17^2 - 7^2$.**

This expression is a difference of two squares with $a = 17$ and $b = 7$.

$a^2 - b^2 = (a + b)(a - b)$ *Write the rule for a difference of two squares.*

$17^2 - 7^2 = (17 + 7)(17 - 7)$ *Substitute 17 for a and 7 for b.*

$= (24)(10)$ *Simplify each group.*

$= 240$

## Example 2

**Simplify $14^2 + 2(14)(6) + 6^2$.**

This expression is a perfect-square trinomial with $a = 14$ and $b = 6$.

$a^2 + 2ab + b^2 = (a + b)^2$ *Write the rule for a perfect-square trinomial.*

$14^2 + 2(14)(6) + 6^2 = (14 + 6)^2$ *Substitute 14 for a and 6 for b.*

$= (20)^2$ *Simplify.*

$= 400$

## Try This

**Simplify each expression using the rules for special products.**

1. $18^2 - 12^2$
2. $11^2 + 2(11)(14) + 14^2$
3. $22^2 - 18^2$
4. $38^2 - 2(38)(27) + 27^2$
5. $29^2 - 2(29)(17) + 17^2$
6. $55^2 + 2(55)(45) + 45^2$
7. $14^2 - 9^2$
8. $13^2 - 12^2$
9. $14^2 + 2(14)(16) + 16^2$

# 8-6 Choosing a Factoring Method

**MA.A.1** Use appropriate properties and strategies to … factor algebraic expressions. *Also* **MA.A.1.3**

***Objectives***

Choose an appropriate method for factoring a polynomial.

Combine methods for factoring a polynomial.

**Why learn this?**

You will need to factor polynomials to solve quadratic equations, which have many applications in physics. (See Exercise 42.)

The height of a leaping ballet dancer can be modeled by a quadratic polynomial. Solving an equation that involves that polynomial may require factoring the polynomial.

Recall that a polynomial is in its fully factored form when it is written as a product that cannot be factored further.

## EXAMPLE 1 Determining Whether a Polynomial Is Completely Factored

**Tell whether each polynomial is completely factored. If not, factor it.**

**A** $2x(x^2 + 4)$

$2x(x^2 + 4)$ *Neither $2x$ nor $x^2 + 4$ can be factored further.*

$2x(x^2 + 4)$ is completely factored.

**Caution!**

$x^2 + 4$ is a *sum* of squares, and cannot be factored.

**B** $(2x + 6)(x + 5)$

$(2x + 6)(x + 5)$ *$2x + 6$ can be further factored.*

$2(x + 3)(x + 5)$ *Factor out 2, the GCF of $2x$ and 6.*

$2(x + 3)(x + 5)$ is completely factored.

**CHECK IT OUT!** **Tell whether the polynomial is completely factored. If not, factor it.**

**1a.** $5x^2(x - 1)$ **1b.** $(4x + 4)(x + 1)$

To factor a polynomial completely, you may need to use more than one factoring method. Use the steps below to factor a polynomial completely.

| Factoring Polynomials | |
|---|---|
| **Step 1** | Check for a greatest common factor. |
| **Step 2** | Check for a pattern that fits the difference of two squares or a perfect-square trinomial. |
| **Step 3** | To factor $x^2 + bx + c$, look for two numbers whose sum is $b$ and whose product is $c$.<br>To factor $ax^2 + bx + c$, check factors of $a$ and factors of $c$ in the binomial factors. The sum of the products of the outer and inner terms should be $b$. |
| **Step 4** | Check for common factors. |

## EXAMPLE 2 Factoring by GCF and Recognizing Patterns

**Factor $-2xy^2 + 16xy - 32x$ completely. Check your answer.**

$-2xy^2 + 16xy - 32x$

$-2x(y^2 - 8y + 16)$ *Factor out the GCF. $y^2 - 8y + 16$ is a perfect-square trinomial of the form $a^2 - 2ab + b^2$.*

$-2x(y - 4)^2$ *$a = y, b = 4$*

*Check* $-2x(y - 4)^2 = -2x(y^2 - 8y + 16)$

$= -2xy^2 + 16xy - 32x$ ✓

**CHECK IT OUT!** **Factor each polynomial completely. Check your answer.**

**2a.** $4x^3 + 16x^2 + 16x$ **2b.** $2x^2y - 2y^3$

If none of the factoring methods work, the polynomial is said to be unfactorable.

## EXAMPLE 3 Factoring by Multiple Methods

**Factor each polynomial completely.**

**A** $2x^2 + 5x + 4$

$2x^2 + 5x + 4$ *The GCF is 1 and there is no pattern.*

$(\square x + \square)(\square x + \square)$ *$a = 2$ and $c = 4$; Outer + Inner = 5*

| Factors of 2 | Factors of 4 | Outer + Inner | |
|---|---|---|---|
| 1 and 2 | 1 and 4 | $(1)4 + (2)1 = 6$ | ✗ |
| 1 and 2 | 4 and 1 | $(1)1 + (2)4 = 9$ | ✗ |
| 1 and 2 | 2 and 2 | $(1)2 + (2)2 = 6$ | ✗ |

$2x^2 + 5x + 4$ is unfactorable.

**Helpful Hint**

For a polynomial of the form $ax^2 + bx + c$, if there are no numbers whose sum is $b$ and whose product is $ac$, then the polynomial is unfactorable.

**B** $3n^4 - 15n^3 + 12n^2$

$3n^2(n^2 - 5n + 4)$ *Factor out the GCF. There is no pattern.*

$(n + \square)(n + \square)$ *$b = -5$ and $c = 4$; look for factors of 4 whose sum is $-5$.*

| Factors of 4 | Sum | |
|---|---|---|
| $-1$ and $-4$ | $-5$ | ✓ |
| $-2$ and $-2$ | $-4$ | ✗ |

*The factors needed are $-1$ and $-4$.*

$3n^2(n - 1)(n - 4)$

**C** $4x^3 + 18x^2 + 20x$

$2x(2x^2 + 9x + 10)$ *Factor out the GCF. There is no pattern.*

$(\square x + \square)(\square x + \square)$ *$a = 2$ and $c = 10$; Outer + Inner = 9*

| Factors of 2 | Factors of 10 | Outer + Inner | |
|---|---|---|---|
| 1 and 2 | 1 and 10 | $(1)10 + (2)1 = 12$ | ✗ |
| 1 and 2 | 10 and 1 | $(1)1 + (2)10 = 21$ | ✗ |
| 1 and 2 | 2 and 5 | $(1)5 + (2)2 = 9$ | ✓ |

$(x + 2)(2x + 5)$

$2x(x + 2)(2x + 5)$

**D** $p^5 - p$

| | |
|---|---|
| $p(p^4 - 1)$ | *Factor out the GCF.* |
| $p(p^2 + 1)(p^2 - 1)$ | *$p^4 - 1$ is a difference of two squares.* |
| $p(p^2 + 1)(p + 1)(p - 1)$ | *$p^2 - 1$ is a difference of two squares.* |

**Factor each polynomial completely. Check your answer.**

**3a.** $3x^2 + 7x + 4$ **3b.** $2p^5 + 10p^4 - 12p^3$

**3c.** $9q^6 + 30q^5 + 24q^4$ **3d.** $2x^4 + 18$

## Methods to Factor Polynomials

| | |
|---|---|
| **Any Polynomial—Look for the greatest common factor.** | |
| $ab - ac = a(b - c)$ | $6x^2y + 10xy^2 = 2xy(3x + 5y)$ |
| **Binomials—Look for a difference of two squares.** | |
| $a^2 - b^2 = (a + b)(a - b)$ | $x^2 - 9y^2 = (x + 3y)(x - 3y)$ |
| **Trinomials—Look for perfect-square trinomials and other factorable trinomials.** | |
| $a^2 + 2ab + b^2 = (a + b)^2$<br>$a^2 - 2ab + b^2 = (a - b)^2$ | $x^2 + 4x + 4 = (x + 2)^2$<br>$x^2 - 2x + 1 = (x - 1)^2$ |
| $x^2 + bx + c = (x + \square)(x + \square)$<br>$ax^2 + bx + c = (\square x + \square)(\square x + \square)$ | $x^2 + 3x + 2 = (x + 1)(x + 2)$<br>$6x^2 + 7x + 2 = (2x + 1)(3x + 2)$ |
| **Polynomials of Four or More Terms—Factor by grouping.** | |
| $ax + bx + ay + by = x(a + b) + y(a + b)$<br>$= (x + y)(a + b)$ | $2x^3 + 4x^2 + x + 2 = (2x^3 + 4x^2) + (x + 2)$<br>$= 2x^2(x + 2) + 1(x + 2)$<br>$= (x + 2)(2x^2 + 1)$ |

## THINK AND DISCUSS

**1.** Give an expression that includes a polynomial that is not completely factored.

**2.** Give an example of an unfactorable binomial and an unfactorable trinomial.

**3. GET ORGANIZED** Copy the graphic organizer. Draw an arrow from each expression to the method you would use to factor it.

**Factoring Methods**

| Polynomial | Method |
|---|---|
| **1.** $16x^4 - 25y^8$ | **A.** Factoring out the GCF |
| **2.** $x^2 + 10x + 25$ | **B.** Factoring by grouping |
| **3.** $9t^2 + 27t + 18t^4$ | **C.** Unfactorable |
| **4.** $a^2 + 3a - 7a - 21$ | **D.** Difference of two squares |
| **5.** $100b^2 + 81$ | **E.** Perfect-square trinomial |

# 8-6 Exercises

MA.A.1, MA.A.1.3

go.hrw.com
Homework Help Online
KEYWORD: MA7 8-6
Parent Resources Online
KEYWORD: MA7 Parent

## GUIDED PRACTICE

SEE EXAMPLE 1 p. 566

Tell whether each polynomial is completely factored. If not, factor it.

1. $3x(9x^2 + 1)$
2. $2(4x^3 - 3x^2 - 8x)$
3. $2k^2(4 - k^3)$
4. $(2x + 3)(3x - 5)$
5. $4(4p^4 - 1)$
6. $a(a^3 + 2ab + b^2)$

SEE EXAMPLE 2 p. 567

Factor each polynomial completely. Check your answer.

7. $3x^5 - 12x^3$
8. $4x^3 + 8x^2 + 4x$
9. $8pq^2 + 8pq + 2p$
10. $18rs^2 - 2r$
11. $mn^5 - m^3n$
12. $2x^2y - 20xy + 50y$

SEE EXAMPLE 3 p. 567

13. $6x^4 - 3x^3 - 9x^2$
14. $3y^2 + 14y + 4$
15. $p^5 + 3p^3 + p^2 + 3$
16. $7x^5 + 21x^4 - 28x^3$
17. $2z^2 + 11z + 6$
18. $9p^2 - q^2 + 3p$

## PRACTICE AND PROBLEM SOLVING

**Independent Practice**

| For Exercises | See Example |
|---|---|
| 19–24 | 1 |
| 25–30 | 2 |
| 31–36 | 3 |

**Extra Practice**

Skills Practice p. S19
Application Practice p. S35

Tell whether each polynomial is completely factored. If not, factor it.

19. $2x(y^3 - 4y^2 + 5y)$
20. $2r(25r^6 - 36)$
21. $3n^2(n^2 - 25)$
22. $2m(m + 1)(m + 4)$
23. $2y^2(4x^2 + 9)$
24. $4(7g + 9h^2)$

Factor each polynomial completely. Check your answer.

25. $-4x^3 + 24x^2 - 36x$
26. $24r^2 - 6r^4$
27. $5d^2 - 60d + 135$
28. $4y^8 + 36y^7 + 81y^6$
29. $98x^3 - 50xy^2$
30. $4x^3y - 4x^2y - 8xy$
31. $5x^2 - 10x + 14$
32. $121x^2 + 36y^2$
33. $p^4 - 16$
34. $4m^6 - 30m^5 + 36m^4$
35. $2k^3 + 3k^2 + 6k + 9$
36. $ab^4 - 16a$

Write an expression for each situation. Factor your expression.

37. the square of Ella's age plus 12 times Ella's age plus 36
38. the square of the distance from point A to point B minus 81
39. the square of the number of seconds Bob can hold his breath minus 16 times the number of seconds plus 28
40. three times the square of apples on a tree minus 22 times the number of apples plus 35
41. the square of Beth's score minus 49
42. **Physics** The height in meters of a ballet dancer's center of mass when she leaps can be modeled by the polynomial $-5t^2 + 30t + 1$, where $t$ is time in seconds after the jump. Tell whether the polynomial is fully factored when written as $-1(5t^2 - 30t - 1)$. Explain.

43. **Write About It** When asked to factor a polynomial completely, you first determine that the terms in the polynomial do not share any common factors. What would be your next step?

Factor and simplify each expression.

44. $12(x + 1)^2 + 60(x + 1) + 75$
45. $(2x + 3)^2 - (x - 4)^2$
46. $45x(x - 2)^2 + 60x(x - 2) + 20x$
47. $(3x - 5)^2 - (y + 2)^2$

**MULTI-STEP TEST PREP**

48. This problem will prepare you for the Multi-Step Test Prep on page 568.
    a. The area of a Marci's rectangular flower garden is $(x^2 + 2x - 15)$ ft². Factor this expression for area.
    b. Draw a diagram of the garden and label the length and width with your factors from part **a.**
    c. Find the length and width of the flower garden if $x = 7$ ft.

49. **Critical Thinking** Show two methods of factoring $4x^2 - 100$.

50. **Estimation** Estimate the value of $2x^2 + 5xy + 3y^2$ when $x = -10.1$ and $y = 10.05$. (*Hint:* Factor the expression first.)

51. **/// ERROR ANALYSIS ///** Examine the factorization shown. Explain why the factorization is incorrect.

$12x^2 - 12x - 3$
$3(4x^2 - 4x - 1)$
$3(2x - 1)(2x - 1)$

**LINK**

**Math History**

Blaise Pascal was a French mathematician who lived in the 1600s.

**Math History** **Use the following information for Exercises 52–54.**

The triangle at right is called *Pascal's Triangle*. The triangle starts with 1 and each of the other numbers in the triangle is the sum of the two numbers in the row above it.

| Row | | | | | | | | | | | |
|---|---|---|---|---|---|---|---|---|---|---|---|
| 0 | | | | | | 1 | | | | | |
| 1 | | | | | 1 | | 1 | | | | |
| 2 | | | | 1 | | 2 | | 1 | | | |
| 3 | | | 1 | | 3 | | 3 | | 1 | | |
| 4 | | 1 | | 4 | | 6 | | 4 | | 1 | |
| 5 | 1 | | 5 | | 10 | | 10 | | 5 | | 1 |

Pascal's Triangle can be used to write the product of a binomial raised to an integer power. The numbers in each row give you the coefficients of each term in the product.

$$(a + b)^3 = a^3 + 3a^2b + 3ab^2 + b^3$$

The numbers in row 3 are 1, 3, 3, 1. These are the coefficients of the terms in the product $(a + b)^3$. The power of $a$ decreases in each term and the power of $b$ increases in each term.

Use the patterns you see in Pascal's Triangle to write the power of the binomial $a + b$ given by each product.

52. $a^6 + 6a^5b + 15a^4b^2 + 20a^3b^3 + 15a^2b^4 + 6ab^5 + b^6 = (a + b)^{■}$

53. $a^8 + 8a^7b + 28a^6b^2 + 56a^5b^3 + 70a^4b^4 + 56a^3b^5 + 28a^2b^6 + 8ab^7 + b^8 = (a + b)^{■}$

54. $a^7 + 7a^6b + 21a^5b^2 + 35a^4b^3 + 35a^3b^4 + 21a^2b^5 + 7ab^6 + b^7 = (a + b)^{■}$

**TEST PREP**

MA.A.1, MA.A.1.3

55. Which expression equals $6x^2 + 7x - 10$?
    Ⓐ $(6x + 2)(x - 5)$
    Ⓑ $(2x + 5)(3x - 2)$
    Ⓒ $(x + 2)(6x - 5)$
    Ⓓ $(3x + 2)(2x - 5)$

56. What is the complete factorization of $16x^{12} - 256$?
    Ⓕ $16(x^6 + 4)(x^6 - 4)$
    Ⓖ $(4x^6 + 16)(4x^6 - 16)$
    Ⓗ $16(x^6 + 4)(x^3 + 2)(x^3 - 2)$
    Ⓙ $(4x^6 + 16)(2x^3 + 4)(2x^3 - 4)$

57. Which of the expressions below represents the fifth step of the factorization?

**Step 1:** $40a^3 - 60a^2 - 10a + 15$

**Step 2:** $5(8a^3 - 12a^2 - 2a + 3)$

**Step 3:** $5[(8a^3 - 12a^2) - (2a - 3)]$

**Step 4:** $5[4a^2(2a - 3) - 1(2a - 3)]$

**Step 5:** 

**Step 6:** $5(2a - 3)(2a + 1)(2a - 1)$

Ⓐ $5(2a - 3)(2a + 3)(4a^2 - 1)$

Ⓑ $5(2a - 3)(4a^2 + 1)$

Ⓒ $5(2a - 3)(4a^2 - 1)$

Ⓓ $5(2a - 3)(2a - 3)(4a^2 - 1)$

58. **Short Response** Use the polynomial $8x^3 + 24x^2 + 18x$ for the following.
   a. Factor the polynomial. Explain each step and tell whether you used any rules for special products.
   b. Explain another set of steps that could be used to factor the polynomial.

## CHALLENGE AND EXTEND

59. **Geometry** The volume of the cylinder shown is represented by the expression $72\pi p^3 + 48\pi p^2 + 8\pi p$. The height of the cylinder is $8p$.
   a. Factor the expression for volume.
   b. What expression represents the radius of the cylinder?
   c. If the radius is 4 cm, what are the height and volume of the cylinder?

$V = \pi r^2 h$

**Factor.**

60. $g^7 + g^3 + g^5 + g^4$

61. $h^2 + h^8 + h^6 + h^4$

62. $x^{n+2} + x^{n+1} + x^n$

63. $x^{n+5} + x^{n+4} + x^{n+3}$

64. **Geometry** The rectangular prism has the dimensions shown.
   a. Write expressions for the height and length of the prism using $w$.
   b. Write a polynomial that represents the volume of the prism using $w$.

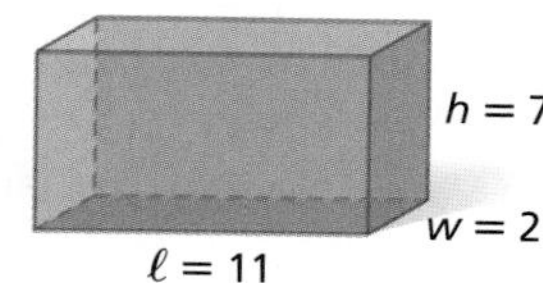


## SPIRAL REVIEW

**Simplify each expression by combining like terms.** *(Lesson 1-7)*

65. $-6n + 4n$

66. $5x^2 - 8x + 4x^2$

67. $2.6r + 9.7r$

**Write and solve a proportion to answer each question.** *(Lesson 2-6)*

68. The ratio of fiction to nonfiction books on Jessika's shelf is 3 to 4. If Jessika has 12 nonfiction books, how many fiction books does she have?

69. The scale of a model car is 23:2. If the steering wheel on the model car has a diameter of 3 cm, what is the diameter of the steering wheel on the actual car?

**Factor each trinomial.** *(Lesson 8-4)*

70. $2x^2 + 13x + 15$

71. $4x^2 + 4x - 3$

72. $6x^2 - 11x - 10$

CHAPTER 8

SECTION 8B

## Factoring

**Shaping the Environment** The Environmental Awareness Club is going to plant a garden on the front lawn of the school. Henry suggests a garden in the shape of a square. Theona suggests a rectangular shape.

Width = ?

Length = 12 m

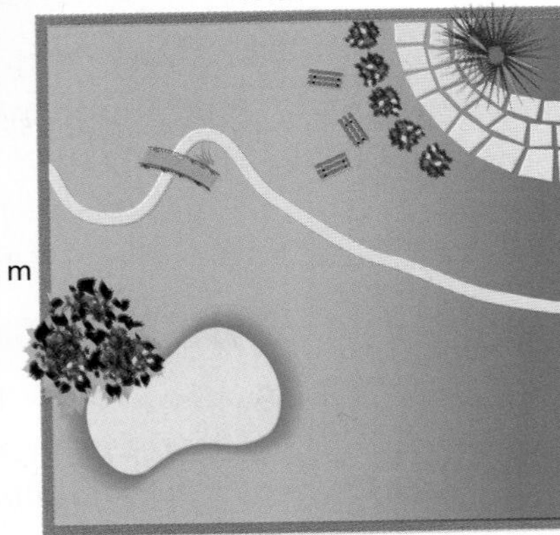

1. Henry's plans include a square garden with an area of $(x^2 + 12x + 36)$ m$^2$. Write expressions for the length and width of the square garden.
2. A drawing of the square garden shows a length of 12 m. What is the width of the square garden? What is the value of $x$? What is the total area of the square garden?
3. Theona's plans include a rectangular garden with an area of $(x^2 + 14x + 24)$ m$^2$. Write expressions for the length and width of the rectangular garden.
4. A drawing of the rectangular garden shows that the length is 6 m longer than the length of the square garden. What is the width of the rectangular garden? How much shorter is the width of the rectangular garden than the square garden?
5. Find the perimeter of each garden in terms of $x$.
6. Which plan should the club choose if they want the garden that covers the most area? Which plan should the club choose if they want the garden that requires the least fencing around it? Explain your reasoning.

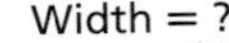


Length = (12 + 6) m

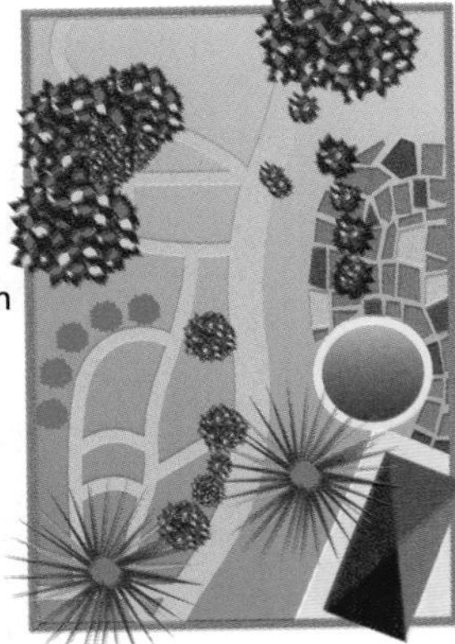

# READY TO GO ON?

CHAPTER 8

SECTION 8B

## Quiz for Lessons 8-5 Through 8-6

### 8-5 Factoring Special Products

**Determine whether each trinomial is a perfect square. If so, factor. If not, explain.**

1. $x^2 + 8x + 16$
2. $4x^2 - 20x + 25$
3. $x^2 + 3x + 9$
4. $2x^2 - 4x + 4$
5. $9x^2 - 12x + 4$
6. $x^2 - 12x - 36$
7. An architect is designing rectangular windows with an area of $(x^2 + 20x + 100)$ ft$^2$. The dimensions of the windows are of the form $ax + b$, where $a$ and $b$ are whole numbers. Find an expression for the perimeter of the windows. Find the perimeter of a window when $x = 4$ ft.

**Determine whether each trinomial is a difference of two squares. If so, factor. If not, explain.**

8. $x^2 - 121$
9. $4t^2 - 20$
10. $1 - 9y^4$
11. $25m^2 - 4m^6$
12. $16x^2 + 49$
13. $r^4 - t^2$
14. The area of a square is $(36d^2 - 36d + 9)$ in$^2$.
    a. What expression represents the length of a side of the square?
    b. What expression represents the perimeter of the square?
    c. What are the length of a side, the perimeter, and the area of the square when $d = 2$ in.?

### 8-6 Choosing a Factoring Method

**Tell whether each polynomial is completely factored. If not, factor it.**

15. $5(x^2 + 3x + 1)$
16. $6x(5x^2 - x)$
17. $3t(t^4 - 9)$
18. $2(m^2 - 10m + 25)$
19. $3(2y^2 - 5)(y + 1)$
20. $(2n + 6)(n - 4)$

**Factor each polynomial completely. Check your answer.**

21. $3x^3 - 12x^2 + 12x$
22. $16m^3 - 4m$
23. $5x^3y - 45xy$
24. $3t^2 + 5t - 1$
25. $3c^2 + 12c - 63$
26. $x^5 - 81x$

**Write an expression for each situation. Then factor your expression.**

27. the difference of the square of a board's length and 36
28. the square of Michael's age minus 8 times Michael's age plus 16
29. two times the square of a car's speed plus 2 times the car's speed minus 12
30. three times the cube of Jessie's height plus 3 times the square of Jessie's height minus 6 times Jessie's height
31. Write an expression for the area of the shaded region. Then factor the expression.

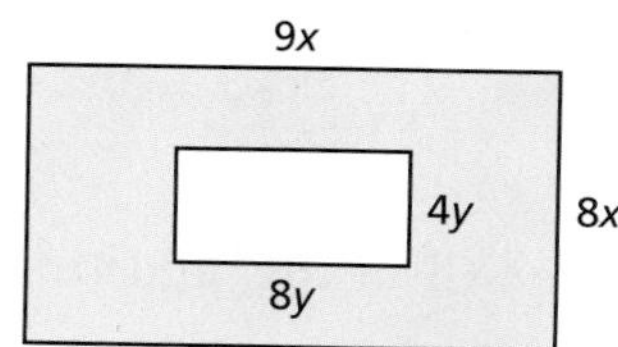

CHAPTER 8

# Study Guide: Review

## Vocabulary

greatest common factor ..... 525

prime factorization ......... 524

**Complete the sentences below with vocabulary words from the list above.**

1. A number written as a product so that each of its factors has no factors other than 1 and itself is the ___?___.
2. The ___?___ of two monomials is the greatest of the factors that the monomials share.

## 8-1 Factors and Greatest Common Factors *(pp. 524–529)*

**Prep MA.A.1, Prep MA.A.1.3**

### EXAMPLES

■ **Write the prime factorization of 84.**

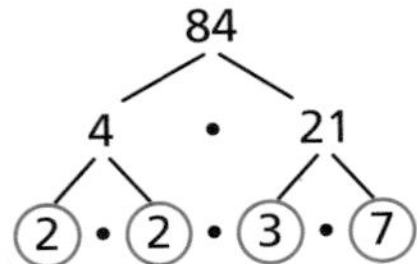


*Write as a product. Continue until all factors are prime.*

■ **Write the prime factorization of 75.**

$$\begin{array}{r|l} 3 & 75 \\ 5 & 25 \\ 5 & 5 \\ & 1 \end{array}$$

*Keep dividing by prime factors until the quotient is 1.*

$75 = 3 \cdot 5 \cdot 5 = 3 \cdot 5^2$

■ **Find the GCF of 36 and 90.**

$36 = 2 \cdot \boxed{2} \cdot \boxed{3} \cdot \boxed{3}$

$90 = \boxed{2} \cdot \boxed{3} \cdot \boxed{3} \cdot 5$

$2 \cdot 3 \cdot 3 = 18$

*Write the prime factorization of each number.*
*Find the product of the common factors.*

The GCF of 36 and 90 is 18.

■ **Find the GCF of $10x^5$ and $4x^2$.**

$10x^5 = \boxed{2} \cdot 5 \cdot \boxed{x} \cdot \boxed{x} \cdot x \cdot x \cdot x$

$4x^2 = \boxed{2} \cdot 2 \cdot \boxed{x} \cdot \boxed{x}$

$2 \cdot \quad x \cdot x = 2x^2$

*Write the prime factorization of each coefficient.*
*Write powers as products.*
*Find the product of the common factors.*

The GCF of $10x^5$ and $4x^2$ is $2x^2$.

### EXERCISES

**Write the prime factorization of each number.**

3. 12
4. 20
5. 32
6. 23
7. 40
8. 64
9. 66
10. 114

**Find the GCF of each pair of numbers.**

11. 15 and 50
12. 36 and 132
13. 29 and 30
14. 54 and 81
15. 20 and 48

**Find the GCF of each pair of monomials.**

16. $9m$ and 3
17. $4x$ and $2x^2$
18. $-18b^4$ and $27b^2$
19. $100r$ and $25r^5$
20. A hardware store carries 42 types of boxed nails and 36 types of boxed screws. The store manager wants to build a rack so that he can display the hardware in rows. He wants to put the same number of boxes in each row, but he wants no row to contain both nails and screws. What is the greatest number of boxes that he can display in one row? How many rows will there be if the manager puts the greatest number of boxes in each row?

## 8-2 Factoring by GCF (pp. 531–537)

### EXAMPLES

■ **Factor $3t^3 - 9t^2$. Check your answer.**

$3t^3 = 3 \cdot t \cdot t \cdot t$
$9t^2 = 3 \cdot 3 \cdot t \cdot t$ *Find the GCF.*

GCF: $3 \cdot t \cdot t = 3t^2$

$3t^3 - 9t^2 = 3t^2(t) - 3t^2(3)$
$= 3t^2(t - 3)$ *Factor out the GCF.*

***Check*** $3t^2(t - 3) = 3t^3 - 9t^2$ ✓

■ **Factor $-12s - 6s^3$. Check your answer.**

$-1(12s + 6s^3)$ *Factor out $-1$.*

$12s = 2 \cdot 2 \cdot 3 \cdot s$
$6s^3 = 2 \cdot \quad 3 \cdot s \cdot s \cdot s$ *Find the GCF.*

GCF: $2 \cdot 3 \cdot s = 6s$

$-1(12s + 6s^3)$

$1[(6s)(2) + (6s)(s^2)]$

$-1[(6s)(2 + s^2)]$

$-6s(2 + s^2)$ *Factor out the GCF.*

***Check*** $-6s(2 + s^2) = -12s - 6s^3$ ✓

■ **Factor $5(x - 7) + 3x(x - 7)$.**

$5(x - 7) + 3x(x - 7)$ *The terms have a common factor of $(x - 7)$.*

$(x - 7)(5 + 3x)$ *Factor out $(x - 7)$.*

■ **Factor $6b^3 + 8b + 15b^2 + 20$ by grouping.**

$(6b^3 + 8b) + (15b^2 + 20)$ *Group terms that have a common factor.*

$2b(3b^2 + 4) + 5(3b^2 + 4)$ *Factor each group.*

$(3b^2 + 4)(2b + 5)$ *Factor out $(3b^2 + 4)$.*

■ **Factor $2m^3 - 6m^2 + 15 - 5m$. Check your answer.**

$(2m^3 - 6m^2) + (15 - 5m)$ *Group terms.*
$2m^2(m - 3) + 5(3 - m)$ *Factor each group.*

$2m^2(m - 3) + 5(-1)(m - 3)$ *Rewrite $(3 - m)$ as $(-1)(m - 3)$.*

$2m^2(m - 3) - 5(m - 3)$ *Simplify.*
$(m - 3)(2m^2 - 5)$ *Factor out $(m - 3)$.*

***Check*** $(m - 3)(2m^2 - 5)$

$2m^3 - 5m - 6m^2 + 15$
$2m^3 - 6m^2 + 15 - 5m$ ✓

### EXERCISES

**Factor each polynomial. Check your answer.**

**21.** $5x - 15x^3$ **22.** $-16b + 32$

**23.** $-14v - 21$ **24.** $4a^2 - 12a - 8$

**25.** $5g^5 - 10g^3 - 15g$ **26.** $40p^2 - 10p + 30$

**27.** A civil engineer needs the area of a rectangular lot to be $(6x^2 + 5x)$ ft$^2$. Factor this polynomial to find expressions for the dimensions of the lot.

**Factor each expression.**

**28.** $2x(x - 4) + 9(x - 4)$

**29.** $t(3t + 5) - 6(3t + 5)$

**30.** $5(6 - n) - 3n(6 - n)$

**31.** $b(b + 4) + 2(b + 4)$

**32.** $x^2(x - 3) + 7(x - 3)$

**Factor each polynomial.**

**33.** $n^3 + n - 4n^2 - 4$

**34.** $6b^2 - 8b + 15b - 20$

**35.** $2h^3 - 7h + 14h^2 - 49$

**36.** $3t^2 + 18t + t + 6$

**37.** $10m^3 + 15m^2 - 2m - 3$

**38.** $8p^3 + 4p - 6p^2 - 3$

**39.** $5r - 10 + 2r - r^2$

**40.** $b^3 - 5b + 15 - 3b^2$

**41.** $6t - t^3 - 4t^2 + 24$

**42.** $12h - 3h^2 + h - 4$

**43.** $d - d^2 + d - 1$

**44.** $6b - 5b^2 + 10b - 12$

**45.** $5t - t^2 - t + 5$

**46.** $8b^2 - 2b^3 - 5b + 20$

**47.** $3r - 3r^2 - 1 + r$

**48.** Write an expression for the area of each of the two rectangles shown. Then write and factor an expression for the combined area.

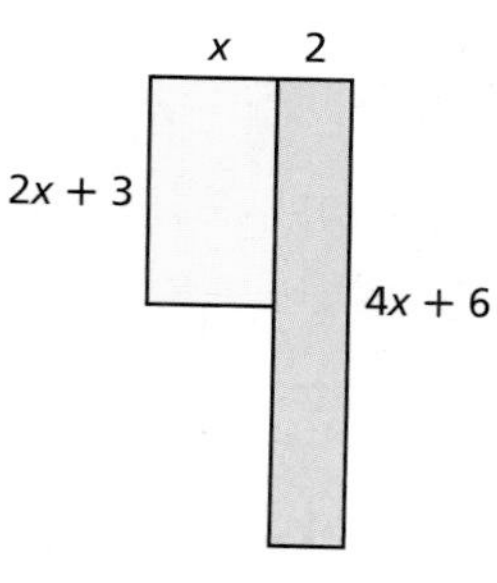

## 8-3 Factoring $x^2 + bx + c$ (pp. 540–547)

### EXAMPLES

**Factor each trinomial. Check your answer.**

■ $x^2 + 14x + 45$

$(x + \square)(x + \square)$ *Look for factors of 45 whose sum is 14.*

$(x + 9)(x + 5)$

*Check* $(x + 9)(x + 5) = x^2 + 5x + 9x + 45$

$= x^2 + 14x + 45$ ✓

■ $x^2 + 6x - 27$

$(x + \square)(x - \square)$ *Look for factors of −27 whose sum is 6.*

$(x + 9)(x - 3)$

*Check* $(x + 9)(x - 3) = x^2 - 3x + 9x - 27$

$= x^2 + 6x - 27$ ✓

### EXERCISES

**Factor each trinomial. Check your answer.**

**49.** $x^2 + 6x + 5$
**50.** $x^2 + 6x + 8$
**51.** $x^2 + 8x + 15$
**52.** $x^2 - 8x + 12$
**53.** $x^2 + 10x + 25$
**54.** $x^2 - 13x + 22$
**55.** $x^2 + 24x + 80$
**56.** $x^2 - 26x + 120$
**57.** $x^2 + 5x - 84$
**58.** $x^2 - 5x - 24$
**59.** $x^2 - 3x - 28$
**60.** $x^2 + 4x - 5$
**61.** $x^2 + x - 6$
**62.** $x^2 + x - 20$
**63.** $x^2 - 2x - 48$
**64.** $x^2 - 5x - 36$
**65.** $x^2 - 6x - 72$
**66.** $x^2 - 3x - 70$
**67.** $x^2 + 14x - 120$
**68.** $x^2 + 6x - 7$

**69.** The rectangle shown has an area of $(y^2 + 8y + 15)$ m². What is the width of the rectangle?

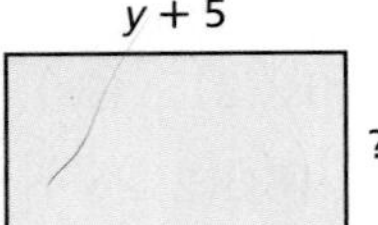


## 8-4 Factoring $ax^2 + bx + c$ (pp. 548–553)

### EXAMPLES

**Factor each trinomial.**

■ $6x^2 + 17x + 5$

$(\square x + \square)(\square x + \square)$ *a = 6 and c = 5; Outer + Inner = 17*

| Factors of 6 | Factors of 5 | Outer + Inner |
|---|---|---|
| 1 and 6 | 5 and 1 | $(1)1 + (6)5 = 31$ |
| 2 and 3 | 1 and 5 | $(2)5 + (3)1 = 13$ |
| 2 and 3 | 5 and 1 | $(2)1 + (3)5 = 17$ |

$(2x + 5)(3x + 1)$

■ $2n^2 - n - 10$

$(\square n + \square)(\square n + \square)$ *a = 2 and c = −10; Outer + Inner = −1*

| Factors of 2 | Factors of −10 | Outer + Inner |
|---|---|---|
| 1 and 2 | 1 and −10 | $1(-10) + 2(1) = -8$ |
| 1 and 2 | −1 and 10 | $1(10) + 2(-1) = 8$ |
| 1 and 2 | 2 and −5 | $1(-5) + 2(2) = -1$ |

$(1n + 2)(2n - 5) = (n + 2)(2n - 5)$

### EXERCISES

**Factor each trinomial. Check your answer.**

**70.** $2x^2 + 11x + 5$
**71.** $3x^2 + 10x + 7$
**72.** $2x^2 - 3x + 1$
**73.** $3x^2 + 8x + 4$
**74.** $5x^2 + 28x + 15$
**75.** $6x^2 - 19x + 15$
**76.** $4x^2 + 13x + 10$
**77.** $3x^2 + 10x + 8$
**78.** $7x^2 - 37x + 10$
**79.** $9x^2 + 18x + 8$
**80.** $2x^2 - x - 1$
**81.** $3x^2 - 11x - 4$
**82.** $2x^2 - 11x + 5$
**83.** $7x^2 - 19x - 6$
**84.** $5x^2 - 9x - 2$
**85.** $-6x^2 - x + 2$
**86.** $6x^2 - x - 5$
**87.** $6x^2 + 17x - 14$
**88.** $-4x^2 + 8x + 5$
**89.** $-10x^2 + 11x + 6$

**90.** Write the polynomial modeled and then factor.

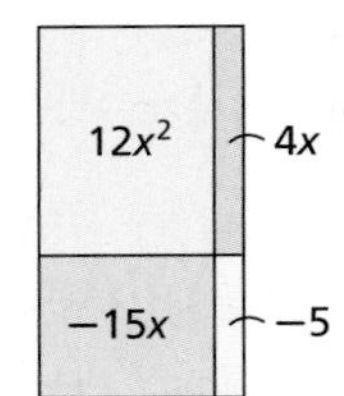

## 8-5 Factoring Special Products *(pp. 558–564)*

### EXAMPLES

- **Determine whether $x^2 + 18x + 81$ is a perfect square. If so, factor. If not, explain.**

$x^2 + 18x + 81$

$x \cdot x \quad 2(x \cdot 9) \quad 9 \cdot 9$

*The trinomial is of the form $a^2 + 2ab + b^2$, so it is a perfect-square trinomial.*

$x^2 + 18x + 81 = (x + 9)^2$

- **Determine whether $49x^4 - 25y^6$ is a difference of two squares. If so, factor. If not, explain.**

$49x^4 - 25y^6$

$7x^2 \cdot 7x^2 \quad 5y^3 \cdot 5y^3$ *The binomial is a difference of two squares.*

$(7x^2)^2 - (5y^3)^2$ *$a = 7x^2$, $b = 5x^3$*

$(7x^2 + 5y^3)(7x^2 - 5y^3)$ *Write the binomial as $(a + b)(a - b)$.*

$49x^4 - 25y^6 = (7x^2 + 5y^3)(7x^2 - 5y^3)$

### EXERCISES

**Determine whether each trinomial is a perfect square. If so, factor. If not, explain.**

91. $x^2 + 12x + 36$
92. $x^2 + 5x + 25$
93. $4x^2 - 2x + 1$
94. $9x^2 + 12x + 4$
95. $16x^2 + 8x + 4$
96. $x^2 + 14x + 49$

**Determine whether each binomial is a difference of two squares. If so, factor. If not, explain.**

97. $100x^2 - 81$
98. $x^2 - 2$
99. $5x^4 - 10y^6$
100. $(-12)^2 - (x^3)^2$
101. $121b^2 + 9c^8$
102. $100p^2 - 25q^2$

**Factor each polynomial using the pattern of perfect-square trinomials or the difference of two squares. Tell which pattern you used.**

103. $x^2 - 25$
104. $x^2 + 20x + 100$
105. $j^2 - k^4$
106. $9x^2 - 42x + 49$
107. $81x^2 + 144x + 64$
108. $16b^4 - 121c^6$

## 8-6 Choosing a Factoring Method *(pp. 566–571)*

### EXAMPLES

- **Tell whether $(3x - 9)(x + 4)$ is completely factored. If not, factor it.**

$(3x - 9)(x + 4)$ *$3x - 9$ can be factored.*

$3(x - 3)(x + 4)$ *Factor out 3, the GCF of $3x$ and 9.*

- $3ab^2 - 48a$

$3a(b^2 - 16)$ *Factor out the GCF.*

$3a(b + 4)(b - 4)$ *Factor the difference of two squares.*

*Check* $3a(b + 4)(b - 4) = 3a(b^2 - 16)$

$= 3ab^2 - 48a$ ✓

- $2m^3 + 4m^2 - 48m$

$2m(m^2 + 2m - 24)$ *Factor out the GCF.*

$2m(m - 4)(m + 6)$ *Factor the trinomial.*

*Check* $2m(m - 4)(m + 6)$

$2m(m^2 + 2m - 24)$

$2m^3 + 4m^2 - 48m$ ✓

### EXERCISES

**Tell whether each polynomial is completely factored. If not, factor it.**

109. $4x^2 + 10x + 6 = (4x + 6)(x + 1)$
110. $3y^2 + 75 = 3(y^2 + 25)$
111. $b^4 - 81 = (b^2 + 9)(b^2 - 9)$
112. $x^2 - 6x + 9 = (x - 3)^2$

**Factor each polynomial completely. Check your answer.**

113. $4x^2 - 64$
114. $3b^5 - 6b^4 - 24b^3$
115. $a^4b^3 - a^2b^5$
116. $t^{20} - t^4$
117. $5x^2 + 20x + 15$
118. $2x^4 - 50x^2$
119. $8t + 32 + 2st + 8s$
120. $25m^3 - 90m^2 - 40m$
121. $32x^4 - 48x^3 + 8x^2 - 12x$
122. $6s^4t + 12s^3t^2 + 6s^2t^3$
123. $10m^3 + 4m^2 - 90m - 36$

CHAPTER 8

# Chapter Test

**Find the GCF of each pair of monomials.**

1. $3t^4$ and $8t^2$
2. $2y^3$ and $-12y$
3. $15n^5$ and $9n^4$
4. Write the prime factorization of 360.
5. A coin collector is arranging a display of three types of nickels. The types of nickels and number of each type are shown in the table. The collector wants to arrange them in rows with the same number in each row without having different types in the same row. How many rows will she need if she puts the greatest possible number of nickels in each row?

| Type of Nickel | Number of Nickels |
|---|---|
| Liberty | 16 |
| Buffalo | 24 |
| Jefferson | 40 |

**Factor each expression.**

6. $24m^2 + 4m^3$
7. $9x^5 - 12x$
8. $-2r^4 - 6$
9. $3(c - 5) + 4c(c - 5)$
10. $10x^3 + 4x - 25x^2 - 10$
11. $4y^3 - 4y^2 - 3 + 3y$
12. A model rocket is shot vertically from a deck into the air at a speed of 50 m/s. The expression $-5t^2 + 50t + 5$ gives the approximate height of the rocket after $t$ seconds. Factor this expression.

**Factor each trinomial.**

13. $x^2 + 6x + 5$
14. $x^2 - 4x - 21$
15. $x^2 - 8x + 15$
16. $2x^2 + 9x + 7$
17. $2x^2 + 9x - 18$
18. $-3x^2 - 2x + 8$

**Determine whether each trinomial is a perfect square. If so, factor. If not, explain.**

19. $a^2 + 14a + 49$
20. $2x^2 + 10x + 25$
21. $9t^2 - 6t + 1$

**Determine whether each binomial is a difference of two squares. If so, factor. If not, explain.**

22. $b^2 - 16$
23. $25y^2 - 10$
24. $9a^2 - b^{10}$
25. A company is producing rectangular sheets of plastic. Each has an area of $(9x^2 + 30x + 25)$ ft². The dimensions of each sheet are of the form $ax + b$, where $a$ and $b$ are whole numbers. Find an expression for the perimeter of a sheet. Find the perimeter when $x = 4$ ft.

**Tell whether each polynomial is completely factored. If not, factor it.**

26. $(6x - 3)(x + 5)$
27. $(v^5 + 10)(v^5 - 10)$
28. $(2b + 3)(3b - 2)$

**Factor each polynomial completely.**

29. $8x^3 + 72x^2 + 160x$
30. $3x^5 - 27x^3$
31. $8x^3 + 64x^2 - 20x - 160$
32. $cd^4 - c^7d^6$
33. $100x^2 - 80x + 16$
34. $7m^8 - 7$

# COLLEGE ENTRANCE EXAM PRACTICE

CHAPTER 8

## FOCUS ON ACT

The ACT Mathematics test booklet usually has writing space for scratch work. You may not bring your own scratch paper to the testing center. Remember that any scratch work done in the test booklet is for your use only and will not be scored. Be sure to transfer your final answer to the answer sheet.

If you are unsure how to solve a problem, look through the answer choices. They may provide you with a clue to the solution method. It may take longer to work backward from the answer choices, so make sure you monitor your time.

**You may want to time yourself as you take this practice test. It should take you about 6 minutes to complete.**

**1.** What is the value of $c^2 - d^2$ if $c + d = 7$ and $c - d = -2$?

**(A)** $-14$

**(B)** $-5$

**(C)** $5$

**(D)** $14$

**(E)** $45$

**2.** Which of the following is the complete factorization of $6a^3b + 3a^2b^3$?

**(F)** $6a^3b^3$

**(G)** $9a^5b^4$

**(H)** $3ab(2a^2 + ab^2)$

**(J)** $3a^2b(2a + b^2)$

**(K)** $(6a^3b)(3a^2b^3)$

**3.** Which of the following is a factor of $x^2 + 3x - 18$?

**(A)** $x + 2$

**(B)** $x + 3$

**(C)** $x + 6$

**(D)** $x + 9$

**(E)** $x + 18$

**4.** The binomial $x - 3$ is NOT a factor of which of the following trinomials?

**(F)** $2x^2 - x - 3$

**(G)** $2x^2 - 5x - 3$

**(H)** $2x^2 - 8x + 6$

**(J)** $3x^2 - 6x - 9$

**(K)** $3x^2 - 10x + 3$

**5.** For what value of $n$ is $4x^2 + 20x + n^2 = (2x + n)^2$ true for any real number $x$?

**(A)** 4

**(B)** 5

**(C)** 8

**(D)** 10

**(E)** 25

**6.** What is the factored form of $x^2 + \frac{2x}{3} + \frac{x}{2} + \frac{2}{6}$?

**(F)** $\left(x + \frac{1}{3}\right)\left(x + \frac{1}{2}\right)$

**(G)** $\left(x + \frac{1}{2}\right)\left(x + \frac{2}{3}\right)$

**(H)** $\left(x + \frac{2}{3}\right)\left(x + \frac{1}{6}\right)$

**(J)** $(x + 2)\left(x + \frac{1}{3}\right)$

**(K)** $\left(x + \frac{1}{3}\right)\left(x + \frac{2}{3}\right)$

CHAPTER 8

# TEST TACKLER

Standardized Test Strategies

## Any Question Type: Translate Words to Math

When reading a word problem, look for key words and context clues to help you translate the words into a mathematical equation or expression.

Some key words, such as those shown in this table, represent certain mathematical operations.

| Action | Math Operation |
|---|---|
| Combining, increasing | Addition |
| Decreasing, reducing | Subtraction |
| Increasing or decreasing by a factor | Multiplication |
| Separating | Division |

### EXAMPLE 1

**Short Response** **The polynomial $x^2 + 7x + 12$ represents the area of a rectangle in square meters. The width is $(x + 3)$ meters. Find the combined measure of the length and the width.**

Use action words and context clues to translate the words into equations.

$x^2 + 7x + 12$ represents the **area of a rectangle** in square meters.

$x^2 + 7x + 12 \quad = \quad A$

The width is $(x + 3)$ meters.

$w = (x + 3)$

Find the **combined measure** of the **length** and the width.

$m = \ell + w$

Now use the equations to solve the problem.

$A = \ell w$ — *Write the formula for area of a rectangle.*

$x^2 + 7x + 12 = \ell(x + 3)$ — *Substitute $x^2 + 7x + 12$ for A and $(x + 3)$ for w.*

$(x + \boxed{?})(x + 3)$ — *Factor $x^2 + 7x + 12$ to find an expression for the length.*

$(x + 4)(x + 3)$ — *$3(4) = 12$; $3 + 4 = 7$*

The length is $(x + 4)$.

$m = \ell + w$ — *Write the equation for the combined measure of the length and width.*

$m = (x + 4) + (x + 3)$ — *Substitute $(x + 4)$ for $\ell$ and $(x + 3)$ for w.*

$m = 2x + 7$ — *Combine like terms.*

The combined measure of the length and width is $(2x + 7)$ meters.

Sometimes you cannot write an expression or equation in the order that the key words appear. For example, the expression "4 years younger than Maria" is written mathematically as $m - 4$.

Read each test item and answer the questions that follow.

**Item A**

**Short Response** The width of Alvin's rectangular mural is 6 times the length $x$. Alvin plans to make a new mural with an area of $(6x^2 - 24x + 24)$ square meters. By how much did Alvin decrease the area of the mural? Show your work.

1. What key words or context clues are in the first sentence of the test item? Use these clues to write an expression that represents the width of the rectangle.
2. Write an equation to represent the area of Alvin's first mural.
3. What math operation does the key word *decrease* represent?

**Item B**

**Multiple Choice** Which factored expression represents the phrase shown below?

*the square of the number of hours it takes to empty a cistern minus 20 times the number of hours plus 64*

Ⓐ $(h - 16)(h - 4)$ Ⓒ $(h - 8)(h - 8)$

Ⓑ $(h^2 - 20)(h - 64)$ Ⓓ $(h - 16)(h + 4)$

4. Which word in the phrase tells you to use an exponent in your expression?
5. What is the unknown value in the expression? Define a variable to represent this value.
6. Identify other key words and the mathematical operation phrase each one represents.

**Item C**

**Multiple Choice** A company owns two packaging plants. The polynomial $0.05x^2 + 16x - 9400$ models one plant's profit, where $x$ is the number of units packaged. The polynomial $-0.01x^2 + 17x - 5400$ models the other plant's profit. If $x$ is 25,000, what is the total profit of both plants?

Ⓐ $-\$5,830,300$

Ⓑ $\$25,810,200$

Ⓒ $\$31,640,500$

Ⓓ $\$37,471,000$

7. What mathematical symbol does the word *models* represent?
8. Write an equation for each plant that can be used to determine its profit $P$.
9. What mathematical operation does the term "total profit" represent?

**Item D**

**Gridded Response** One of the bases of a trapezoid is 12 meters greater than its height. The other base is 4 meters less than its height. Find the area of the trapezoid when the height is 6 meters.

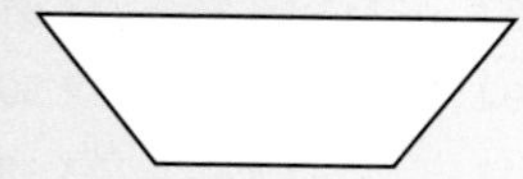

10. Identify the unknown dimension, and assign it a variable.
11. A student is unsure how many bases a trapezoid has. Identify the context clues that can help this student.
12. Make a list of the key words in the problem, and link each word to its mathematical meaning.
13. Write an expression for each base of the trapezoid.

## CUMULATIVE ASSESSMENT, CHAPTERS 1–8

### Multiple Choice

1. A rectangle has an area of $(x^2 + 5x - 24)$ square units. Which of the following are possible expressions for the length and the width of the rectangle?

   A Length: $(x - 24)$ units; width: $(x + 1)$ units

   B Length: $(x - 4)$ units; width: $(x + 6)$ units

   C Length: $(x - 3)$ units; width: $(x + 8)$ units

   D Length: $(x + 12)$ units; width: $(x - 2)$ units

2. If $\frac{2}{3}x - 9 = 3$, what is the value of the expression $8x - 3$?

   A $-75$ C 61

   B $-35$ D 141

3. The table below shows the cost of filling a 15-gallon tank with gas in different years.

| Year | Cost per Tank ($) |
|---|---|
| 1982 | 45.00 |
| 1987 | 21.81 |
| 1992 | 22.50 |
| 1997 | 23.18 |
| 2002 | 24.54 |
| 2007 | 45.68 |

   What would the slope of a trend line for this data represent?

   A The yearly change in the cost per tank

   B The price per tank of gas

   C The change in years

   D The cost of filling a 15-gallon tank with gas

4. What is the numerical solution to the equation *five less than three times a number equals four more than eight times the number?*

   A $-\frac{9}{5}$ C $-\frac{1}{5}$

   B $\frac{1}{11}$ D $\frac{1}{5}$

5. Which of the following expressions is equivalent to $x^2 - 8x + 16$?

   A $(x + 4)^2$ C $(x + 8)(x + 2)$

   B $(x + 4)(x - 4)$ D $(x - 4)^2$

6. An amusement park has two jumping attractions called moonbounces in the shape of similar cubes. The larger moonbounce has a volume of 4800 cubic feet. The smaller moonbounce is half the length of the larger one. What is the volume of the smaller moonbounce?

   A 300 cubic feet

   B 600 cubic feet

   C 1200 cubic feet

   D 2400 cubic feet

7. What is the value of $y$ if the line through $(1, -1)$ and $(2, 2)$ is parallel to the line through $(-2, 1)$ and $(-1, y)$?

   A $-8$ C 3

   B $-2$ D 4

8. Which of the following shows the complete factorization of $2x^3 + 4x^2 - 6x$?

   A $(2x^2 - 2x)(x + 3)$

   B $2x(x^2 + 2x - 3)$

   C $2x(x - 1)(x + 3)$

   D $2(x^3 + 2x^2 - 3x)$

9. Which graph shows the solution set of the compound inequality $-9 \le 5 - 2x \le 13$?

   A 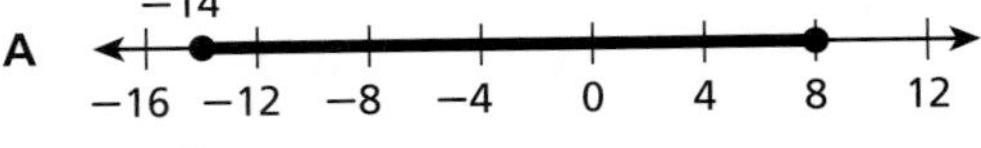


   B 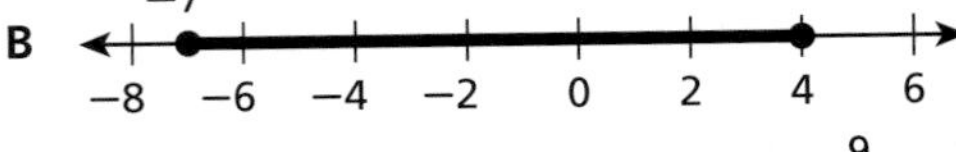


   C 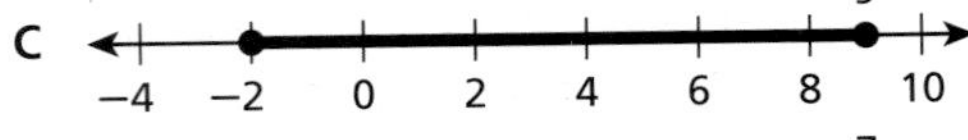


   D 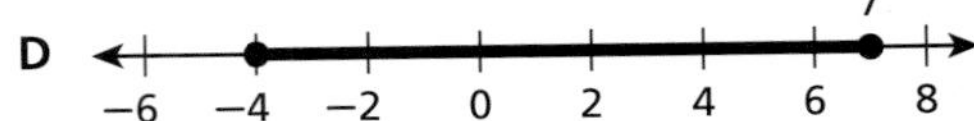

**Many standardized test booklets have a page listing commonly used formulas and basic measurement facts. Before the test begins, ask if you can remove the page from the booklet. If allowed, place the page nearby for easy reference.**

**10.** Which point lies on the graph of both functions?

$f(x) = 2x - 10$
$g(x) = 10 - 2x$

A (5, 0)
B (1, −8)
C (0, 0)
D (2, 6)

**11.** Hayley plans to solve the system of equations below.

$$\begin{cases} x + 3y = 8 \\ 5x - y = 8 \end{cases}$$

Which of the following does ***not*** show an equation Hayley can use to solve the system of equations?

A $x + 3(5x - 8) = 8$
B $5(8 - 3y) - y = 8$
C $x = 8 - 3y$
D $5x - (-x + 8) = 8$

**12.** Which value of $b$ would make $x^2 + bx - 2$ factorable?

A −2
B −1
C 0
D 3

**13.** The complete factorization of $-12x^3 + 14x^2 + 6x$ is $-2x(ax + 1)(2x - 3)$. What is the value of $a$?

A 6
B 3
C 2
D −3

**14.** The expression $x^2 + x + b$ is a perfect-square trinomial. What is the value of $b$?

A $\frac{1}{4}$
B 1
C 2
D 4

**15.** Margaret is buying a $35 sweater that is on sale for 20% off. What is the total price of the sweater when 5% sales tax is added?

A $45.60
B $36.75
C $29.40
D $28.00

## *STANDARDIZED TEST PREP*

### Short Response

**S1.** The area of a certain circle is $\pi(9x^2 + 6x + 1)$ square centimeters. Find an expression for the length of the circle's radius. Explain how you found your answer.

**S2.** A rectangle has an area of $(x^2 - 25)$ square feet.

**a.** Use factoring to write possible equations for the length and width of the rectangle.

**b.** Use your equations from part **a** to write an expression for the perimeter of the rectangle. Simplify the expression.

**c.** Use your equations from parts **a** and **b** to find the perimeter and the area of the rectangle when $x = 10$ feet. Show your work.

**S3.** Write the numbers 57,000,000,000 and 19,000 in scientific notation. Then show how to divide 57,000,000,000 by 19,000 using properties of exponents.

**S4.** Show that you can factor the expression $x^2y - 12 + 3y - 4x^2$ by grouping in two different ways.

### Extended Response

**E1.** The diagram below can be used to show that the expression $(a + b)^2$ is equivalent to the expression $a^2 + 2ab + b^2$.

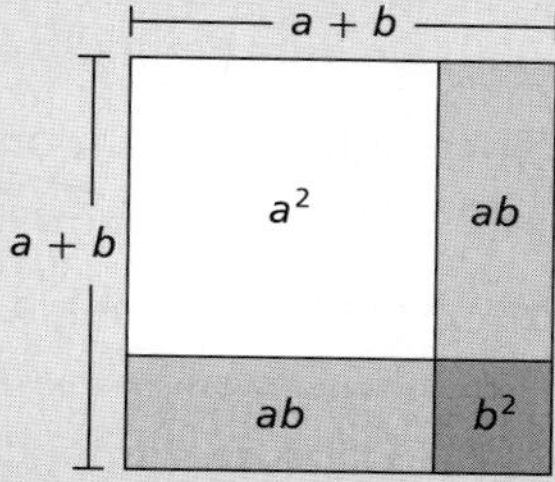


**a.** Make a diagram similar to the one above to model the expression $(a + b + c)^2$. Label each distinct area.

**b.** Use the labels from your diagram to write an expression equivalent to $(a + b + c)^2$.

**c.** Show that your expression in part **b** is equivalent to $(a + b + c)^2$ by evaluating each expression for $a = 4$, $b = 2$, and $c = 1$.

**d.** Factor $x^2 + y^2 + 9 + 2xy + 6x + 6y$. Show or explain how you found your answer.

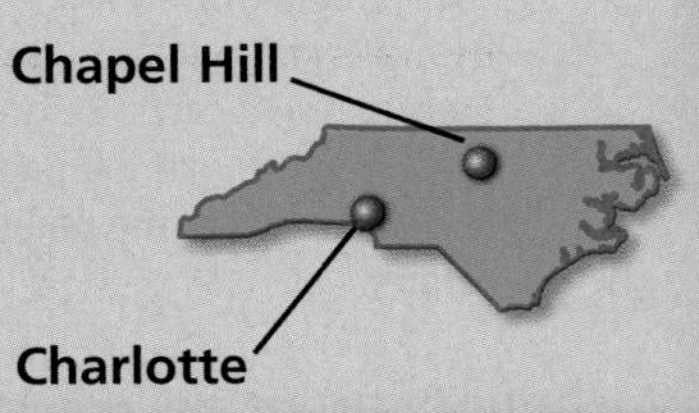


## Morehead Planetarium

Morehead Planetarium opened in 1949 as the first planetarium in the South. Located on the campus of the University of North Carolina in Chapel Hill, the facility remains one of the nation's best places to take a virtual trip into outer space.

**The table lists some of the stars that can be seen at the planetarium's monthly skywatching sessions. Use the table for 1–5.**

**1.** Write the distance of Arcturus from Earth in standard form.

**2.** Write the names of the stars in order from closest to Earth to farthest from Earth.

**3.** The star Deneb is 60 times as far from Earth as Vega. How far is Deneb from Earth?

**4.** What is the average of Vega's distance from Earth and Procyon's distance from Earth?

**5.** A light-year is the distance light can travel in one year—9,500,000,000,000 kilometers.

   **a.** Write the distance light travels in one year in scientific notation.

   **b.** How many light years from Earth is Pollux?

**Seven of the Brightest Stars as Seen From Earth**

| Name | Distance from Earth (km) |
|---|---|
| Sirius | $8.2 \times 10^{13}$ |
| Arcturus | $3.2 \times 10^{14}$ |
| Vega | $2.4 \times 10^{14}$ |
| Procyon | $1.1 \times 10^{14}$ |
| Altair | $1.5 \times 10^{14}$ |
| Spica | $2.1 \times 10^{15}$ |
| Pollux | $3.8 \times 10^{14}$ |

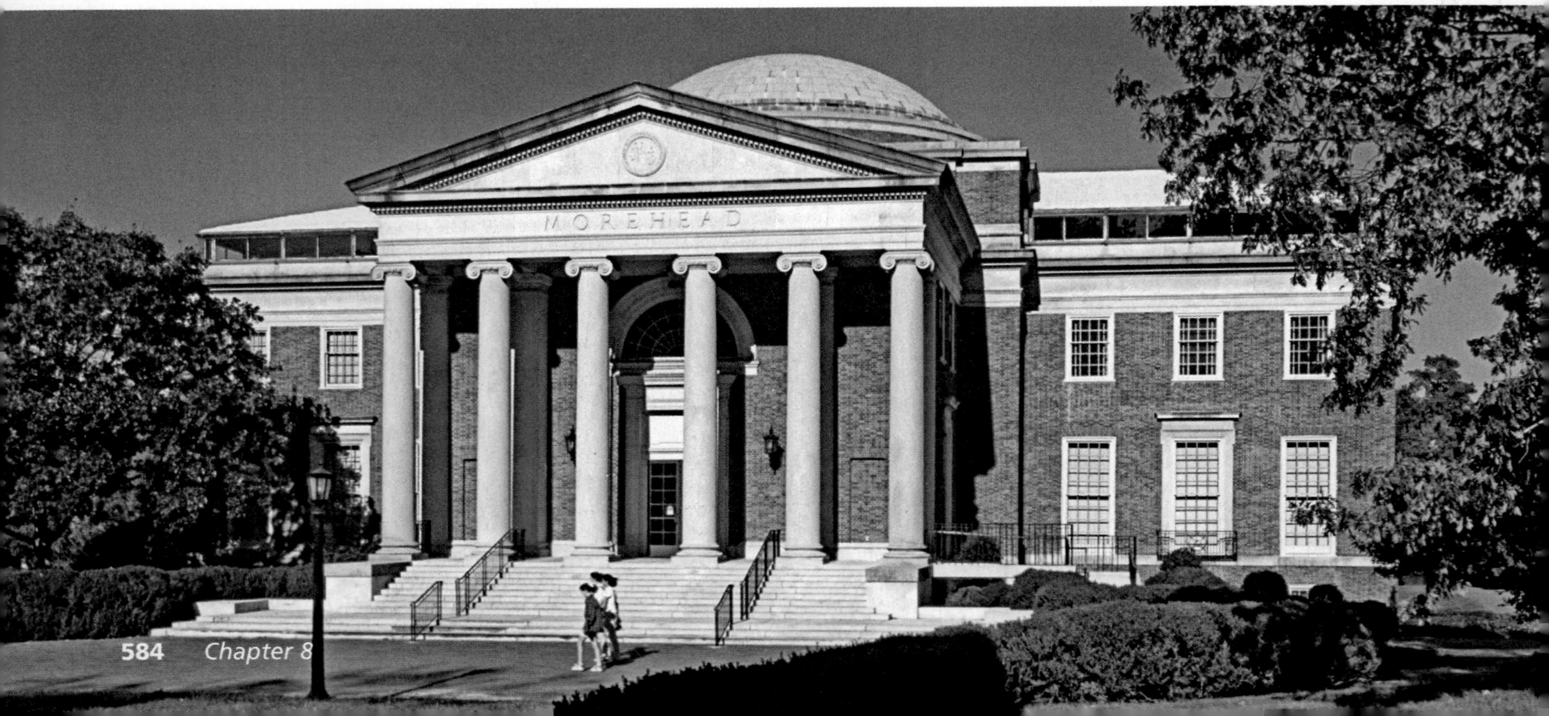

# Carolina Panthers

The Carolina Panthers football team has its home stadium in Charlotte. The stadium covers 1.6 million square feet, stands 13 stories tall, and seats 73,504 fans. High-tech video panels located around the stadium make it easy to follow the action on the field.

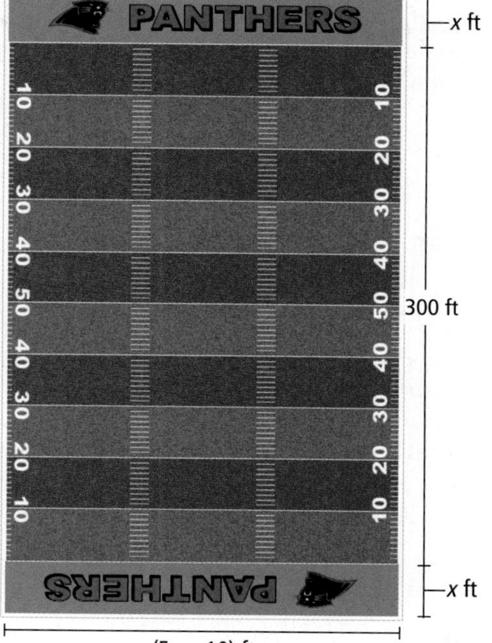


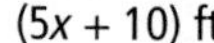


1. The figure shows the dimensions of the rectangular playing field. Write a polynomial that represents the perimeter of the field.
2. Write a polynomial that represents the area of the field.
3. The perimeter of the field is 1040 ft. Write and solve an equation to find the value of $x$. Then give the dimensions of the field.
4. A manufacturer makes square tarpaulins to cover the field in case of rain. The area of each tarpaulin is $(y^2 + 40y + 400)$ ft$^2$.
   a. Factor $y^2 + 40y + 400$ to write possible expressions for the length and width of a tarpaulin.
   b. Use your expressions from part **a** and suppose $y = 20$. How many tarpaulins are needed to cover the field? (Assume the tarpaulins can be arranged to cover the field without overlap.)
5. The stadium includes a rectangular delay-of-game clock that has an area of $(t^2 - 2t - 3)$ ft$^2$. The length is $(t + 1)$ ft.
   a. Write an expression for the width of the clock.
   b. What is the width of the clock if its perimeter is 28 ft?

CHAPTER 9

# Quadratic Functions and Equations

## Why Learn This?

Physicists can use quadratic equations to model how the height of water changes as it falls over Whitewater Falls in the Nantahala National Forest.

go.hrw.com
Chapter Project Online
KEYWORD: MA7 ChProj

# ARE YOU READY?

## Vocabulary

**Match each term on the left with a definition on the right.**

1. factoring
2. quadratic
3. trinomial
4. $x$-intercept

A. the process of writing a number or an algebraic expression as a product

B. the $x$-coordinate of the point where the graph intersects the $x$-axis

C. a polynomial with three terms

D. a polynomial with degree 2

E. the first number of an ordered pair of numbers that describes the location of a point on the coordinate plane

## Graph Functions

**Graph each function for the given domain.**

5. $y = -2x + 8$; D: $\{-4, -2, 0, 2, 4\}$
6. $y = (x + 1)^2$; D: $\{-3, -2, -1, 0, 1\}$
7. $y = x^2 + 3$; D: $\{-2, -1, 0, 1, 2\}$
8. $y = 2x^2$; D: all real numbers

## Multiply Binomials

**Find each product.**

9. $(m + 2)(m + 5)$
10. $(y - 7)(y + 2)$
11. $(2a + 4)(5a + 6)$
12. $(x + 1)(x + 1)$
13. $(t + 5)(t + 5)$
14. $(3n - 8)(3n - 8)$

## Factor Trinomials

**Factor each polynomial completely.**

15. $x^2 - 2x + 1$
16. $x^2 - x - 2$
17. $x^2 - 6x + 5$
18. $x^2 - x - 12$
19. $x^2 - 9x + 18$
20. $x^2 - 7x - 18$

## Squares and Square Roots

**Find the square root of each expression.**

21. $\sqrt{36}$
22. $\sqrt{121}$
23. $-\sqrt{64}$
24. $\sqrt{16}\sqrt{81}$
25. $\sqrt{\frac{9}{25}}$
26. $-\sqrt{6(24)}$

## Solve Multi-Step Equations

**Solve each equation.**

27. $3m + 5 = 11$
28. $3t + 4 = 10$
29. $5n + 13 = 28$
30. $2(k - 4) + k = 7$
31. $10 = \frac{r}{3} + 8$
32. $2(y - 6) = 8.6$

CHAPTER 9

# Study Guide: Preview

## Where You've Been

**Previously, you**

- identified and graphed linear functions.
- transformed linear functions.
- solved linear equations.
- factored quadratic polynomials, including perfect-square trinomials.

## In This Chapter

**You will study**

- identifying and graphing quadratic functions.
- transforming quadratic equations.
- solving quadratic equations.
- using factoring to graph quadratic functions and solve quadratic equations.

## Where You're Going

**You can use the skills in this chapter**

- to determine the maximum height of a ball thrown into the air.
- to graph higher-degree polynomials in future math classes, including Algebra 2.
- to solve problems about the height of launched or thrown objects in Physics.

## *Key Vocabulary/Vocabulario*

| | |
|---|---|
| axis of symmetry | eje de simetría |
| completing the square | completar el cuadrado |
| maximum | máximo |
| minimum | mínimo |
| parabola | parábola |
| quadratic equation | ecuación cuadrática |
| quadratic function | función cuadrática |
| vertex | vértice |
| zero of a function | cero de una función |

## *Vocabulary Connections*

To become familiar with some of the vocabulary terms in the chapter, consider the following. You may refer to the chapter, the glossary, or a dictionary if you like.

1. The value of a function is determined by its rule. The rule is an algebraic expression. What is true about the algebraic expression that determines a **quadratic function**?
2. The shape of a **parabola** is similar to the shape of an open parachute. Predict the shape of a *parabola*.
3. A **minimum** is a point on the graph of a curve with the least $y$-coordinate. How might a **maximum** be described?
4. An axis is an imaginary line. Use this information and your understanding of symmetry to define the term **axis of symmetry**.

## Study Strategy: Learn Vocabulary

Mathematics has a vocabulary all its own. Many new terms appear on the pages of your textbook. Learn these new terms as they are introduced. They will give you the necessary tools to understand new concepts.

Some tips to learning new vocabulary include:

- Look at the **context** in which a new word appears.
- Use **prefixes** or **suffixes** to figure out the word's meaning.
- Relate the new term to familiar **everyday words.** Keep in mind that a word's mathematical meaning may not exactly match its everyday meaning.

polynomial = many
intersection = overlap
conversion = change

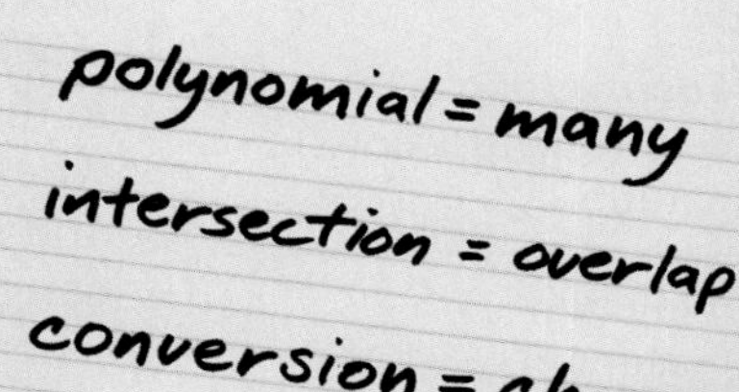

| Vocabulary Word | Study Tip | Definition |
|---|---|---|
| **Polynomial** | The prefix "poly-" means many. | One monomial or the sum or the difference of monomials |
| **Intersection** | Relate it to the meaning of the "intersection of two roads". | The overlapping region that shows the solution to a system of equations |
| **Conversion Factor** | Relate it to the word "convert", which means change or alter. | Used to convert a measurement to different units |

**Complete the chart.**

| | Vocabulary Word | Study Tips | Definition |
|---|---|---|---|
| **1.** | Trinomial | ▒ | ▒ |
| **2.** | Independent system | ▒ | ▒ |
| **3.** | Variable | ▒ | ▒ |

**Use the context of each sentence to define the underlined word. Then relate the word to everyday words.**

**4.** If two linear equations in a system have the same graph, the graphs are called coincident lines, or simply the same line.

**5.** In the formula $d = rt$, $d$ is isolated.

# 9-1 Identifying Quadratic Functions

**MA.A.3.1** Differentiate between linear [and] quadratic … patterns of change.
*Also* **MA.A.4.2, MA.A.4.3**

***Objectives***
Identify quadratic functions and determine whether they have a minimum or maximum.

Graph a quadratic function and give its domain and range.

***Vocabulary***
quadratic function
parabola
vertex
minimum
maximum

**Why learn this?**
The height of a soccer ball after it is kicked into the air can be described by a quadratic function. (See Exercise 51.)

The function $y = x^2$ is shown in the graph. Notice that the graph is not linear. This function is a *quadratic function*. A **quadratic function** is any function that can be written in the standard form $y = ax^2 + bx + c$, where $a$, $b$, and $c$ are real numbers and $a \neq 0$. The function $y = x^2$ can be written as $y = 1x^2 + 0x + 0$, where $a = 1$, $b = 0$, and $c = 0$.

In Lesson 5-1, you identified linear functions by finding that a constant change in $x$ corresponded to a constant change in $y$. The differences between $y$-values for a **constant change in $x$-values** are called ***first differences***.

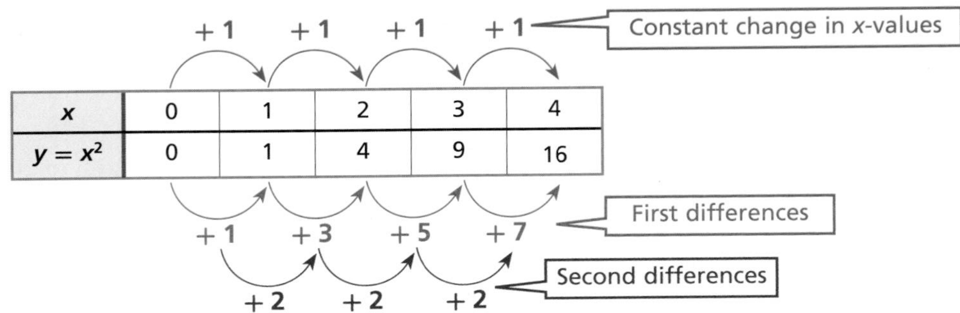

| $x$ | 0 | 1 | 2 | 3 | 4 |
|---|---|---|---|---|---|
| $y = x^2$ | 0 | 1 | 4 | 9 | 16 |



Notice that the quadratic function $y = x^2$ does not have constant first differences. It has constant ***second differences***. This is true for all quadratic functions.

## EXAMPLE 1 Identifying Quadratic Functions

**Tell whether each function is quadratic. Explain.**

**A**

| $x$ | $y$ |
|---|---|
| −4 | 8 |
| −2 | 2 |
| 0 | 0 |
| 2 | 2 |
| 4 | 8 |

$x$: +2, +2, +2, +2
First differences in $y$: −6, −2, +2, +6
Second differences: +4, +4, +4

*Since you are given a table of ordered pairs with a constant change in x-values, see if the second differences are constant.*

*Find the first differences, then find the second differences.*

The function is quadratic. The second differences are constant.

**B** $y = -3x + 20$ *Since you are given an equation, use $y = ax^2 + bx + c$.*

This is not a quadratic function because the value of $a$ is 0.

**Caution!**
Be sure there is a constant change in $x$-values before you try to find first or second differences.

**Helpful Hint**

Only $a$ cannot equal 0. It is okay for the values of $b$ and $c$ to be 0.

**Tell whether each function is quadratic. Explain.**

**C** $y + 3x^2 = -4$

$$\begin{aligned} y + 3x^2 &= -4 \\ -3x^2 \quad & \quad -3x^2 \\ y &= -3x^2 - 4 \end{aligned}$$

*Try to write the function in the form $y = ax^2 + bx + c$ by solving for y. Subtract $3x^2$ from both sides.*

This is a quadratic function because it can be written in the form $y = ax^2 + bx + c$ where $a = -3$, $b = 0$, and $c = -4$.

**Tell whether each function is quadratic. Explain.**

**1a.** $\{(-2, 4), (-1, 1), (0, 0), (1, 1), (2, 4)\}$ **1b.** $y + x = 2x^2$

The graph of a quadratic function is a curve called a **parabola**. To graph a quadratic function, generate enough ordered pairs to see the shape of the parabola. Then connect the points with a smooth curve.

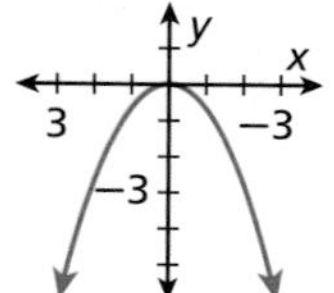


## EXAMPLE 2 Graphing Quadratic Functions by Using a Table of Values

**Use a table of values to graph each quadratic function.**

 $y = 2x^2$

| $x$ | $y = 2x^2$ |
|---|---|
| −2 | 8 |
| −1 | 2 |
| 0 | 0 |
| 1 | 2 |
| 2 | 8 |

*Make a table of values. Choose values of x and use them to find values of y.*

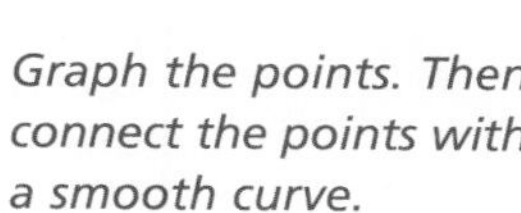

*Graph the points. Then connect the points with a smooth curve.*

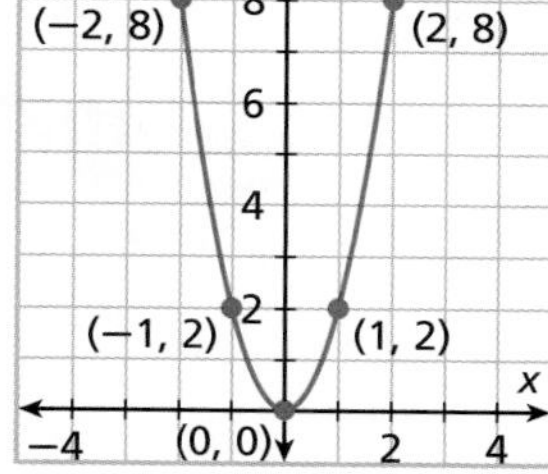


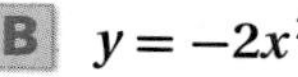

**B** $y = -2x^2$

| $x$ | $y = -2x^2$ |
|---|---|
| −2 | −8 |
| −1 | −2 |
| 0 | 0 |
| 1 | −2 |
| 2 | −8 |

*Make a table of values. Choose values of x and use them to find values of y.*

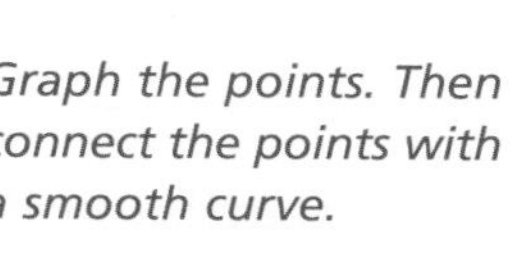

*Graph the points. Then connect the points with a smooth curve.*

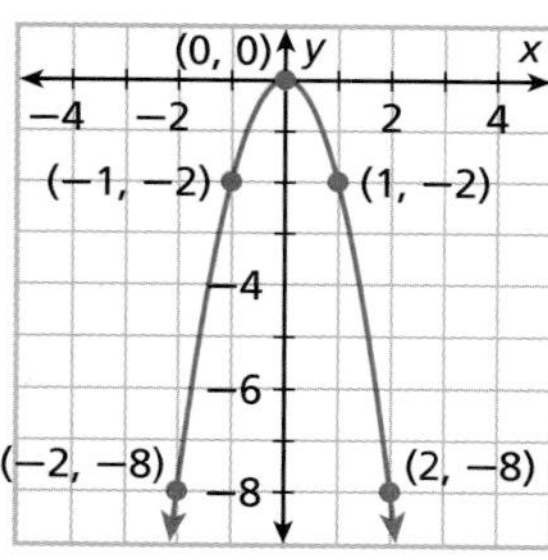

**Use a table of values to graph each quadratic function.**

**2a.** $y = x^2 + 2$ **2b.** $y = -3x^2 + 1$

As shown in the graphs in Examples 2A and 2B, some parabolas open upward and some open downward. Notice that the only difference between the two equations is the value of $a$. When a quadratic function is written in the form $y = ax^2 + bx + c$, the value of $a$ determines the direction a parabola opens.

- A parabola opens **upward** when $a > 0$.
- A parabola opens **downward** when $a < 0$.

## EXAMPLE 3 Identifying the Direction of a Parabola

**Tell whether the graph of each quadratic function opens upward or downward. Explain.**

**A** $y = 4x^2$

$y = 4x^2$

$a = 4$ *Identify the value of a.*

Since $a > 0$, the parabola opens upward.

**B** $2x^2 + y = 5$

$$\begin{aligned} 2x^2 + y &= 5 \\ \underline{-2x^2 \qquad} &\quad \underline{-2x^2} \\ y &= -2x^2 + 5 \\ a &= -2 \end{aligned}$$

*Write the function in the form $y = ax^2 + bx + c$ by solving for y. Subtract $2x^2$ from both sides.*

*Identify the value of a.*

Since $a < 0$, the parabola opens **downward**.

**Tell whether the graph of each quadratic function opens upward or downward. Explain.**

**3a.** $f(x) = -4x^2 - x + 1$ **3b.** $y - 5x^2 = 2x - 6$

The highest or lowest point on a parabola is the **vertex**. If a parabola opens upward, the vertex is the lowest point. If a parabola opens downward, the vertex is the highest point.

### Minimum and Maximum Values

| | | |
|---|---|---|
| **WORDS** | If $a > 0$, the parabola opens upward, and the $y$-value of the vertex is the **minimum** value of the function. | If $a < 0$, the parabola opens downward, and the $y$-value of the vertex is the **maximum** value of the function. |
| **GRAPHS** | $y = x^2 + 6x + 9$ 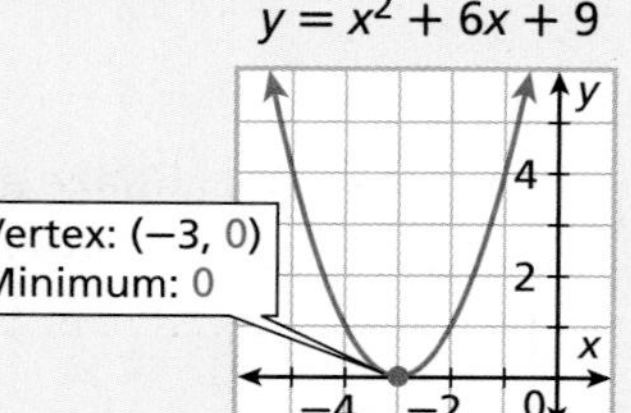 | $y = -x^2 + 6x - 4$ 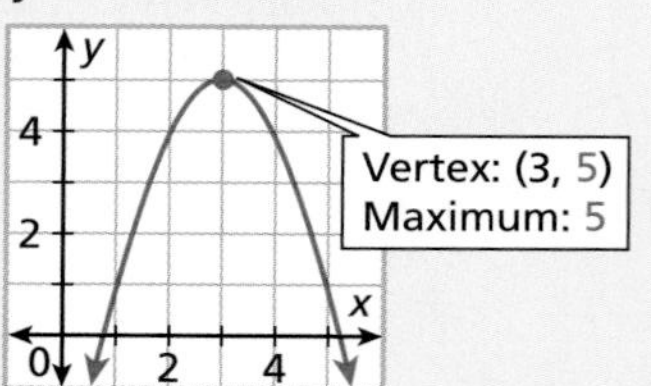 |



## EXAMPLE 4 Identifying the Vertex and the Minimum or Maximum

**Identify the vertex of each parabola. Then give the minimum or maximum value of the function.**

**A**

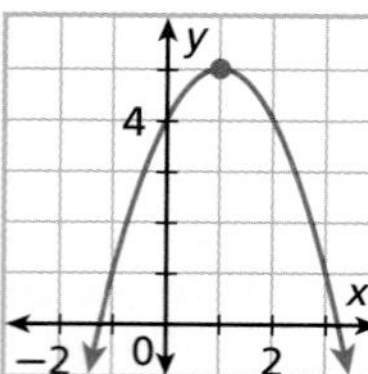

The vertex is $(1, 5)$, and the maximum is 5.

**B**

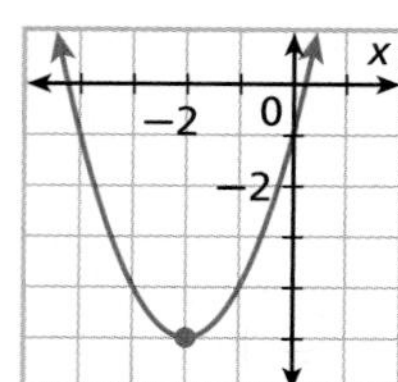

The vertex is $(-2, -5)$, and the minimum is $-5$.

**Identify the vertex of each parabola. Then give the minimum or maximum value of the function.**

**4a.**

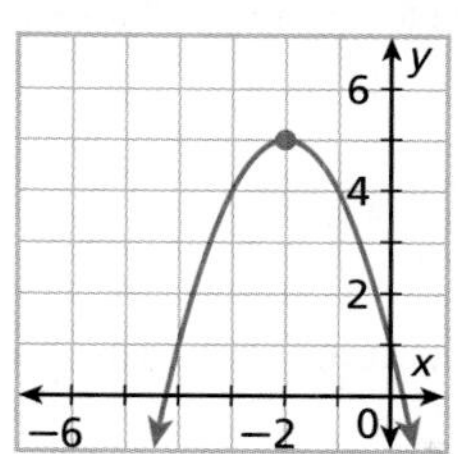

**4b.**

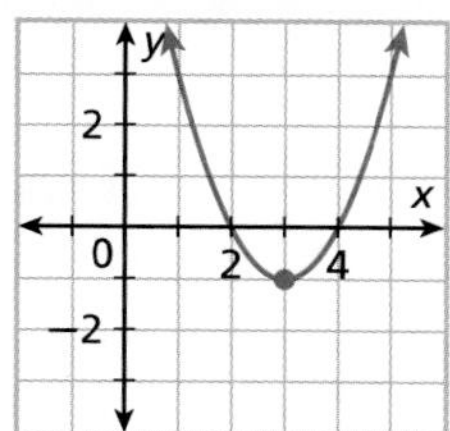

**Caution!**

You may not be able to see the entire graph, but that does not mean the graph stops. Remember that the arrows indicate that the graph continues.

Unless a specific domain is given, you may assume that the domain of a quadratic function is all real numbers. You can find the range of a quadratic function by looking at its graph.

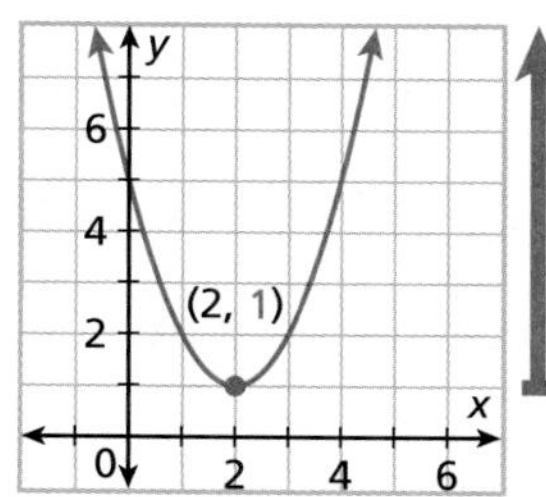

For the graph of $y = x^2 - 4x + 5$, the **range** begins at the minimum value of the function, where $y = 1$. All the $y$-values of the function are greater than or equal to 1. So the range is $y \geq 1$.

## EXAMPLE 5 Finding Domain and Range

**Find the domain and range.**

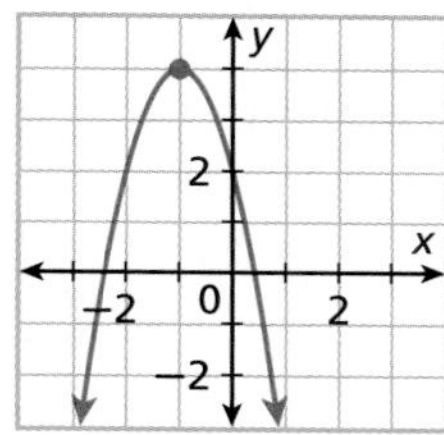

**Step 1** The graph opens downward, so identify the maximum.

The vertex is $(-1, 4)$, so the maximum is 4.

**Step 2** Find the domain and range.

D: all real numbers

R: $y \leq 4$

**Find the domain and range.**

**5a.**

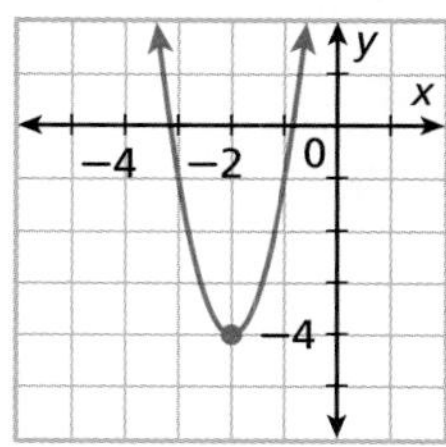

**5b.**

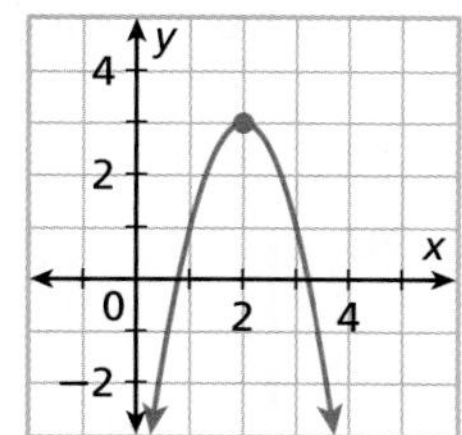

## THINK AND DISCUSS

**1.** How can you identify a quadratic function from ordered pairs? from looking at the function rule?

**2. GET ORGANIZED** Copy and complete the graphic organizer below. In each box, describe a way of identifying quadratic functions.

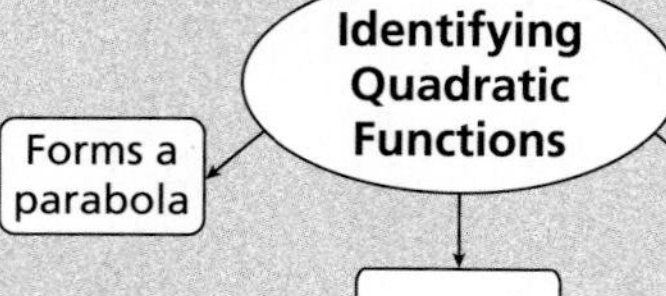

# 9-1 Exercises

MA.A.3.1, MA.A.4.2, MA.A.4.3

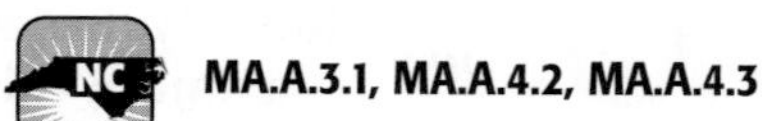


Homework Help Online
KEYWORD: MA7 9-1
Parent Resources Online
KEYWORD: MA7 Parent

## GUIDED PRACTICE

1. **Vocabulary** The $y$-value of the vertex of a parabola that opens upward is the ___?___ value of the function. (*maximum* or *minimum*)

SEE EXAMPLE 1 p. 590

**Tell whether each function is quadratic. Explain.**

2. $y + 6x = -14$
3. $2x^2 + y = 3x - 1$
4.

| $x$ | −4 | −3 | −2 | −1 | 0 |
|---|---|---|---|---|---|
| $y$ | 39 | 18 | 3 | −6 | −9 |

5. $\{(-10, 15), (-9, 17), (-8, 19), (-7, 21), (-6, 23)\}$

SEE EXAMPLE 2 p. 591

**Use a table of values to graph each quadratic function.**

6. $y = 4x^2$
7. $y = \frac{1}{2}x^2$
8. $y = -x^2 + 1$
9. $y = -5x^2$

SEE EXAMPLE 3 p. 592

**Tell whether the graph of each quadratic function opens upward or downward. Explain.**

10. $y = -3x^2 + 4x$
11. $y = 1 - 2x + 6x^2$
12. $y + x^2 = -x - 2$
13. $y + 2 = x^2$
14. $y - 2x^2 = -3$
15. $y + 2 + 3x^2 = 1$

SEE EXAMPLE 4 p. 592

**Identify the vertex of each parabola. Then give the minimum or maximum value of the function.**

16.
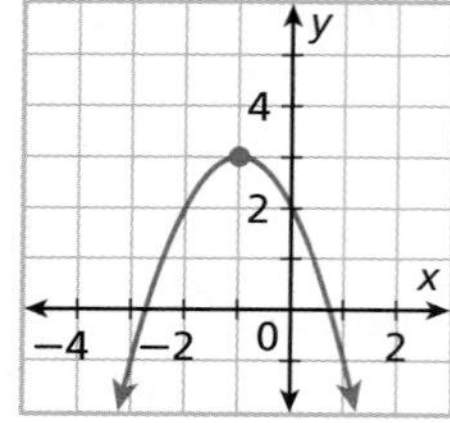

17.
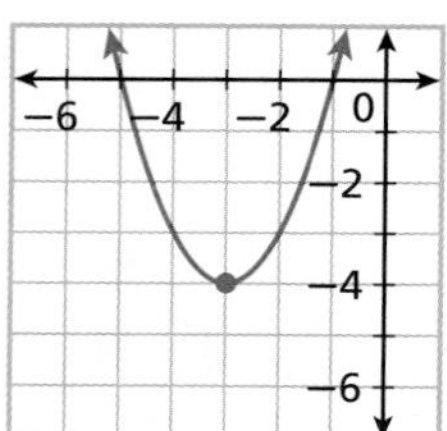

SEE EXAMPLE 5 p. 593

**Find the domain and range.**

18.
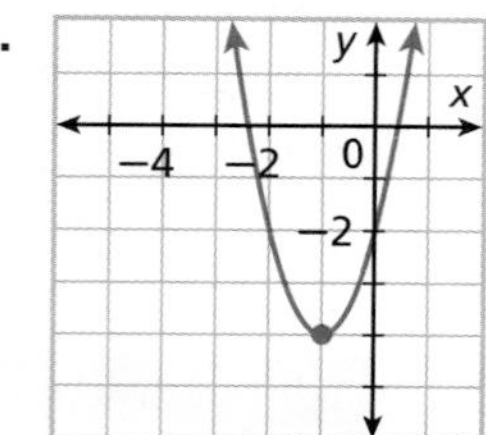

19.
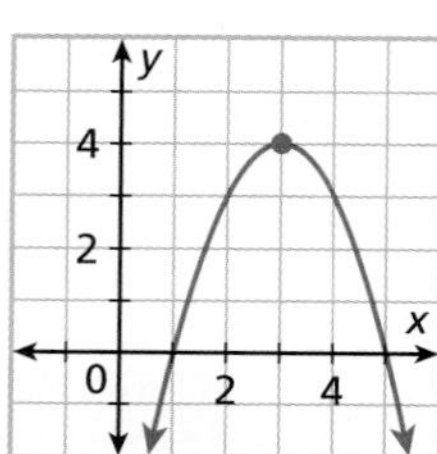

20.
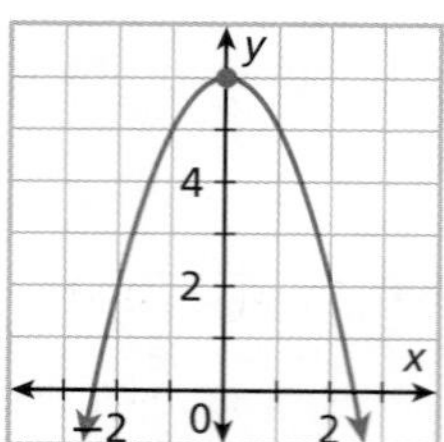

21.
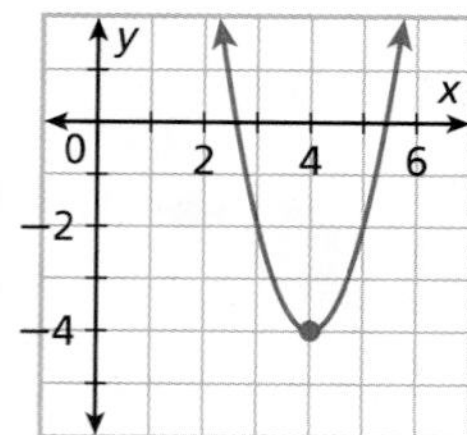

## PRACTICE AND PROBLEM SOLVING

| Independent Practice | |
|---|---|
| For Exercises | See Example |
| 22–25 | 1 |
| 26–29 | 2 |
| 30–32 | 3 |
| 33–34 | 4 |
| 35–38 | 5 |

**Extra Practice**

Skills Practice p. S20
Application Practice p. S36

**Tell whether each function is quadratic. Explain.**

**22.**

| $x$ | −2 | −1 | 0 | 1 | 2 |
|---|---|---|---|---|---|
| $y$ | −1 | 0 | 4 | 9 | 15 |

**23.** $-3x^2 + x = y - 11$

**24.** $\{(0, -3), (1, -2), (2, 1), (3, 6), (4, 13)\}$

**25.** $y = \frac{2}{3}x - \frac{4}{9} + \frac{1}{6}x^2$

**Use a table of values to graph each quadratic function.**

**26.** $y = x^2 - 5$ **27.** $y = -\frac{1}{2}x^2$ **28.** $y = -2x^2 + 2$ **29.** $y = 3x^2 - 2$

**Tell whether the graph of each quadratic function opens upward or downward. Explain.**

**30.** $y = 7x^2 - 4x$ **31.** $x - 3x^2 + y = 5$ **32.** $y = -\frac{2}{3}x^2$

**Identify the vertex of each parabola. Then give the minimum or maximum value of the function.**

**33.**

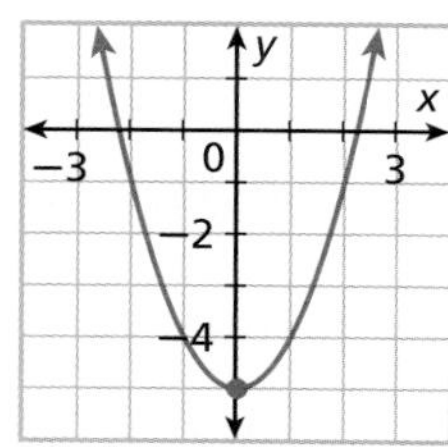


**34.**

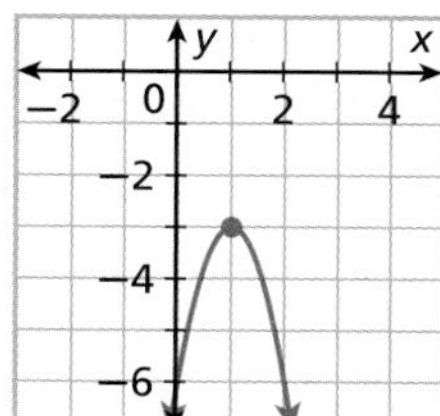


**Find the domain and range.**

**35.**

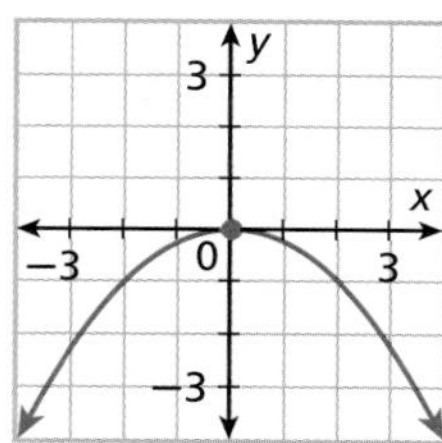


**36.**

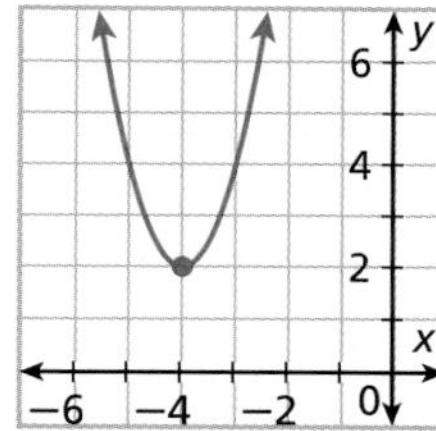


**37.**

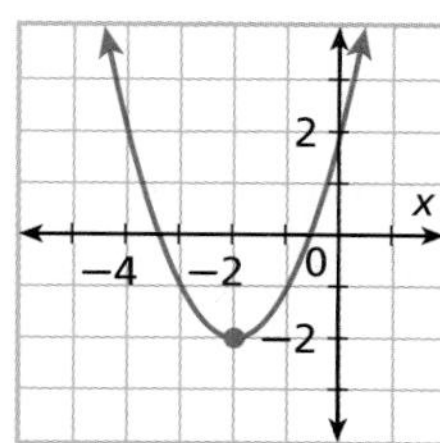


**38.**

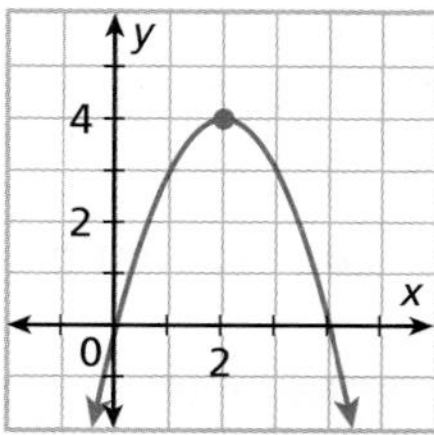


**Tell whether each statement is sometimes, always, or never true.**

**39.** The graph of a quadratic function is a straight line.

**40.** The range of a quadratic function is the set of all real numbers.

**41.** The highest power in a quadratic function is 2.

**42.** The graph of a quadratic function contains the point $(0, 0)$.

**43.** The vertex of a parabola occurs at the minimum value of the function.

**44.** The graph of a quadratic function that has a minimum opens upward.

Tell whether each function is quadratic. If it is, write the function in standard form. If not, explain why not.

**45.** $y = 3x - 1$

**46.** $y = 2x^2 - 5 + 3x$

**47.** $y = (x + 1)^2$

**48.** $y = 5 - (x - 1)^2$

**49.** $y = 3x^2 - 9$

**50.** $y = (x + 1)^3 - x^2$

**51.** **Estimation** **The graph shows the approximate height $y$ in meters of a volleyball $x$ seconds after it is served.**

**a.** Estimate the time it takes for the volleyball to reach its greatest height.

**b.** Estimate the greatest height that the volleyball reaches.

**c.** **Critical Thinking** If the domain of a quadratic function is all real numbers, why is the domain of this function limited to nonnegative numbers?

Volleyball's Height

VOLLEY

Height (m): 0.5, 1, 1.5, 2, 2.5, 3

Time (s): 0, 0.5, 1

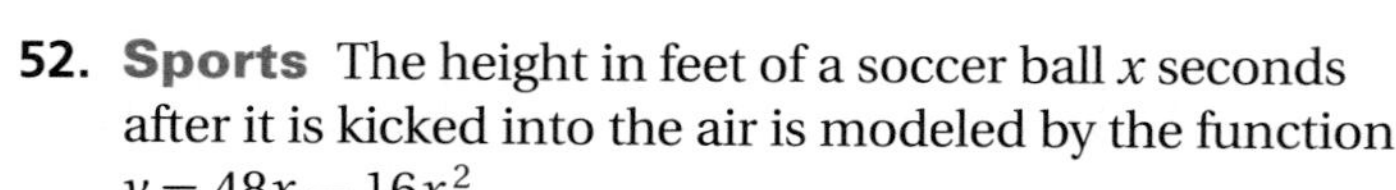

**52.** **Sports** The height in feet of a soccer ball $x$ seconds after it is kicked into the air is modeled by the function $y = 48x - 16x^2$.

**a.** Graph the function.

**b.** In this situation, what values make sense for the domain?

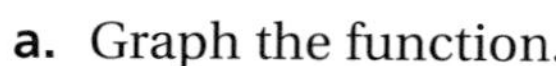

**c.** Does the soccer ball ever reach a height of 50 ft? How do you know?

Tell whether each function is linear, quadratic, or neither.

**53.** $y = \frac{1}{2}x - x^2$

**54.** $y = \frac{1}{2}x - 3$

**55.** $y + 3 = -x^2$

**56.** $y - 2x^2 = 0$

**57.** $y = \frac{1}{2}x(x^2)$

**58.** $y = \frac{3}{x^2}$

**59.** $y = \frac{3}{2}x$

**60.** $x^2 + 2x + 1 = y$

**61.** **Marine Biology** A scientist records the motion of a dolphin as it jumps from the water. The function $h(t) = -16t^2 + 32t$ models the dolphin's height in feet above the water after $t$ seconds.

**a.** Graph the function.

**b.** What domain makes sense for this situation?

**c.** What is the dolphin's maximum height above the water?

**d.** How long is the dolphin out of the water?

**62.** **Write About It** Explain how to tell the difference between a linear function and a quadratic function when given each of the following:

**a.** ordered pairs **b.** the function rule **c.** the graph

**MULTI-STEP TEST PREP**

**63.** This problem will prepare you for the Multi-Step Test Prep on page 620.

A rocket team is using simulation software to create and study water bottle rockets. The team begins by simulating the launch of a rocket without a parachute. The table gives data for one rocket design.

**a.** Show that the data represent a quadratic function.

**b.** Graph the function.

**c.** The acceleration due to gravity is $9.8\ \text{m/s}^2$. How is this number related to the data for this water bottle rocket?

| Time (s) | Height (m) |
|---|---|
| 0 | 0 |
| 1 | 34.3 |
| 2 | 58.8 |
| 3 | 73.5 |
| 4 | 78.4 |
| 5 | 73.5 |
| 6 | 58.8 |
| 7 | 34.3 |
| 8 | 0 |

64. **Critical Thinking** Given the function $-3 - y = x^2 + x$, why is it incorrect to state that the parabola opens upward and has a minimum?

MA.A.3.1, MA.A.4.2, MA.A.4.3

65. Which of the following is the graph of a quadratic function?

Ⓐ
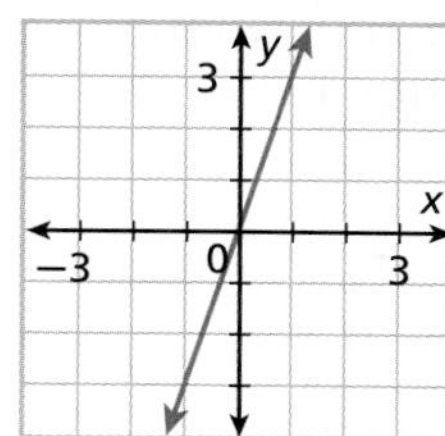


Ⓒ
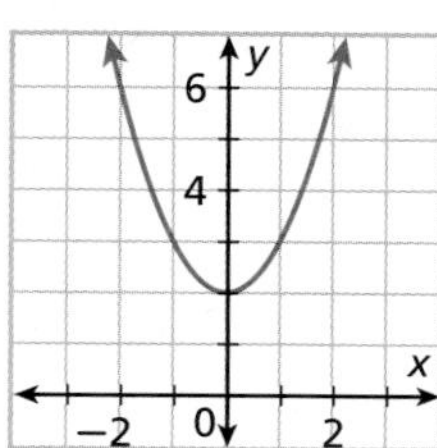


Ⓑ
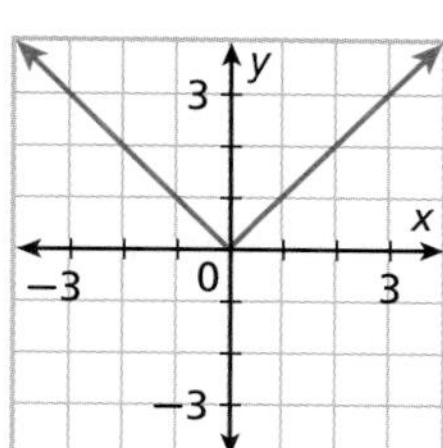


Ⓓ
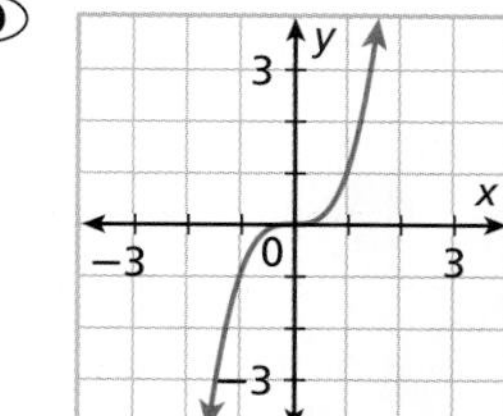


66. Which of the following quadratic functions has a maximum?

Ⓕ $2x^2 - y = 3x - 2$

Ⓖ $y = x^2 + 4x + 16$

Ⓗ $y - x^2 + 6 = 9x$

Ⓙ $y + 3x^2 = 9$

67. **Short Response** Is the function $f(x) = 5 - 2x^2 + 3x$ quadratic? Explain your answer by using two different methods of identification.

## CHALLENGE AND EXTEND

68. **Multi-Step** A rectangular picture measuring 6 in. by 10 in. is surrounded by a frame with uniform width $x$. Write a quadratic function to show the combined area of the picture and frame.

69. **Graphing Calculator** Use a graphing calculator to find the domain and range of the quadratic functions $y = x^2 - 4$ and $y = -(x + 2)^2$.

## SPIRAL REVIEW

**Write each number as a power of the given base.** *(Lesson 1-4)*

70. 10,000; base 10

71. 16; base −2

72. $\frac{8}{27}$; base $\frac{2}{3}$

73. A map shows a scale of 1 inch:3 miles. On the map, the distance from Lin's home to the park is $14\frac{1}{4}$ inches. What is the actual distance? *(Lesson 2-6)*

**Write a function to describe the situation. Find a reasonable domain and range for the function.** *(Lesson 4-3)*

74. Camp Wildwood has collected \$400 in registration fees. It can enroll another 3 campers for \$25 each.

75. Sal works between 30 and 35 hours per week. He earns \$9 per hour.

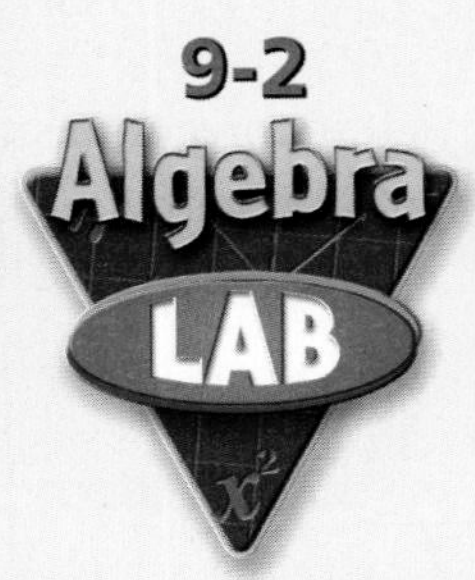


*Use with Lesson 9-2*

# Explore the Axis of Symmetry

Every graph of a quadratic function is a parabola that is symmetric about a vertical line through its vertex called the *axis of symmetry*.

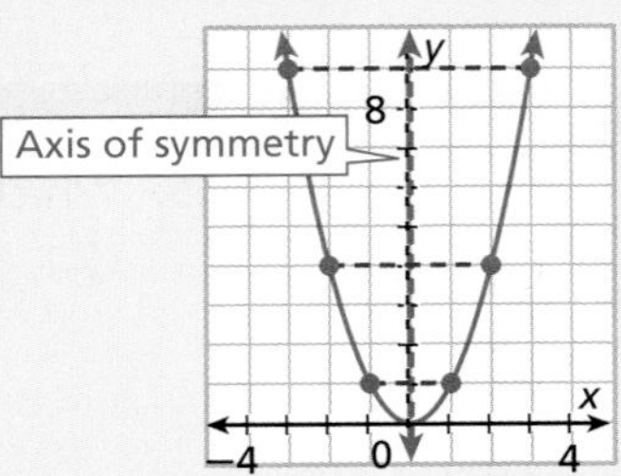


There is a relationship between $a$ and $b$ in the quadratic function and the equation of the axis of symmetry.

**MA.A.4.3** Interpret the relationship of ... coefficients for data presented in graphs...and equations.

## Activity

**1** Complete the table.

| Function | $y = 1x^2 - 2x - 3$ | $y = -2x^2 - 8x - 6$ | $y = -1x^2 + 4x$ |
|---|---|---|---|
| Graph | | | |
| $a$ | 1 | | |
| $b$ | −2 | | |
| $\frac{b}{a}$ | | | |
| Axis of Symmetry (from graph) | $x = 1$ | | |

**2** Compare the axis of symmetry with $\frac{b}{a}$ in your chart. What can you multiply $\frac{b}{a}$ by to get the number in the equation of the axis of symmetry? (*Hint:* Write and solve an equation to find the value.) Check your answer for each function.

**3** Use your answer from Problem 2 to complete the equation of the axis of symmetry of a quadratic function. $x =$ ___?___

## Try This

**For the graph of each quadratic function, find the equation of the axis of symmetry.**

**1.** $y = 2x^2 + 12x - 7$

**2.** $y = 4x^2 + 8x - 12$

**3.** $y = 5x^2 - 20x + 10$

**4.** $y = -3x^2 + 9x + 1$

**5.** $y = x^2 - 7$

**6.** $y = 3x^2 + x + 4$

# 9-2 Characteristics of Quadratic Functions

**MA.A.4.2** Use appropriate terminology … associated with functions.

***Objectives***

Find the zeros of a quadratic function from its graph.

Find the axis of symmetry and the vertex of a parabola.

***Vocabulary***

zero of a function

axis of symmetry

**Who uses this?**

Engineers can use characteristics of quadratic functions to find the height of the arch supports of bridges. (See Example 5.)

Recall that an $x$-intercept of a function is a value of $x$ when $y = 0$. A **zero of a function** is an $x$-value that makes the function equal to 0. So a zero of a function is the same as an $x$-intercept of a function. Since a graph intersects the $x$-axis at the point or points containing an $x$-intercept these intersections are also at the zeros of the function. A quadratic function may have one, two, or no zeros.

## EXAMPLE 1 Finding Zeros of Quadratic Functions From Graphs

**Find the zeros of each quadratic function from its graph. Check your answer.**

**A** $y = x^2 - x - 2$

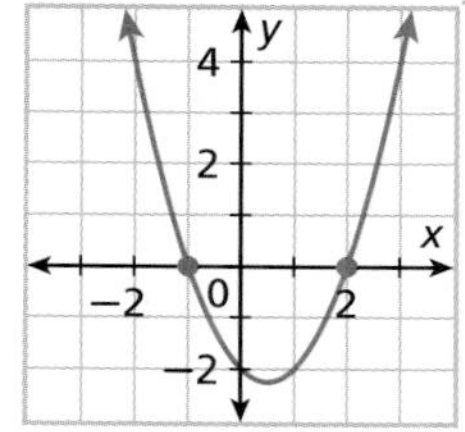

The zeros appear to be $-1$ and 2.

***Check***

$y = x^2 - x - 2$

$y = (-1)^2 - (-1) - 2$

$= 1 + 1 - 2 = 0$ ✓

$y = 2^2 - 2 - 2$

$= 4 - 2 - 2 = 0$ ✓

**B** $y = -2x^2 + 4x - 2$

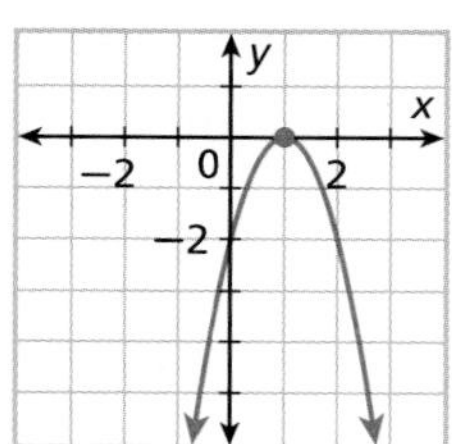

The only zero appears to be 1.

***Check***

$y = -2x^2 + 4x - 2$

$y = -2(1)^2 + 4(1) - 2$

$= -2(1) + 4 - 2$

$= -2 + 4 - 2$

$= 0$ ✓

**C** $y = \frac{1}{4}x^2 + 1$

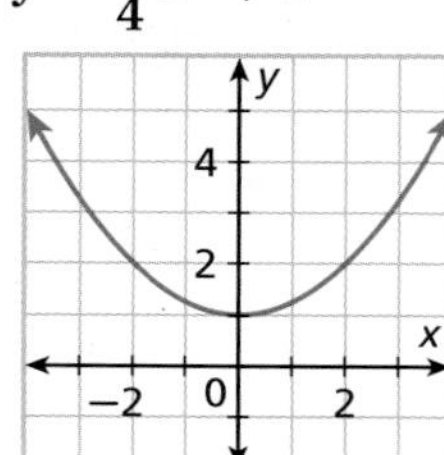

The graph does not cross the $x$-axis, so there are no zeros of this function.

**Helpful Hint**

Notice that if a parabola has only one zero, the zero is the $x$-coordinate of the vertex.

**Find the zeros of each quadratic function from its graph. Check your answer.**

**1a.** $y = -4x^2 - 2$

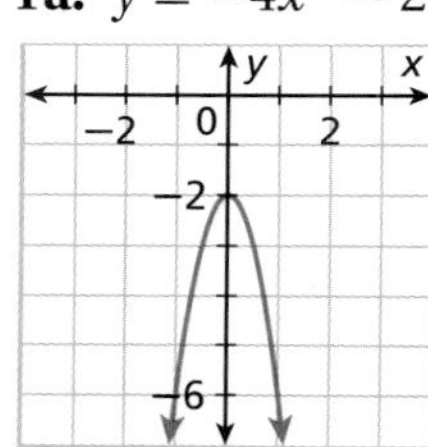

**1b.** $y = x^2 - 6x + 9$

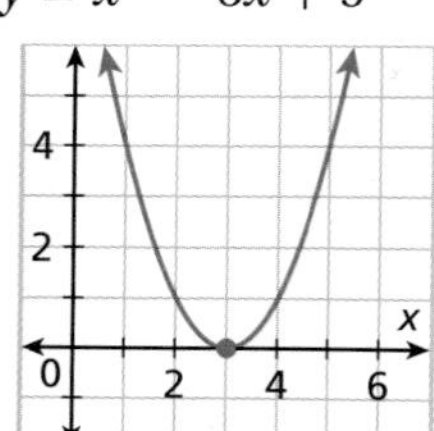

A vertical line that divides a parabola into two symmetrical halves is the **axis of symmetry**. The axis of symmetry always passes through the vertex of the parabola. You can use the zeros to find the axis of symmetry.

**Know it! Note**

## Finding the Axis of Symmetry by Using Zeros

| WORDS | NUMBERS | GRAPH |
|---|---|---|
| **One Zero**<br>If a function has one zero, use the $x$-coordinate of the vertex to find the axis of symmetry. | Vertex: $(3, 0)$<br>Axis of symmetry: $x = 3$ | $x = 3$; $(3, 0)$ |
| **Two Zeros**<br>If a function has two zeros, use the average of the two zeros to find the axis of symmetry. | $\frac{-4 + 0}{2} = \frac{-4}{2} = -2$<br>Axis of symmetry: $x = -2$ | $x = -2$; $(-4, 0)$; $(0, 0)$ |

**EXAMPLE 2** **Finding the Axis of Symmetry by Using Zeros**

**Find the axis of symmetry of each parabola.**

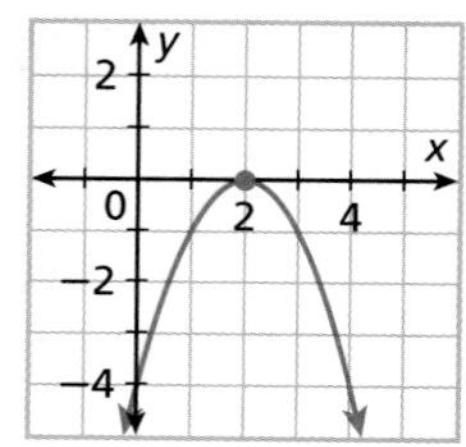


$(2, 0)$ *Identify the x-coordinate of the vertex.*

The axis of symmetry is $x = 2$.

**B**

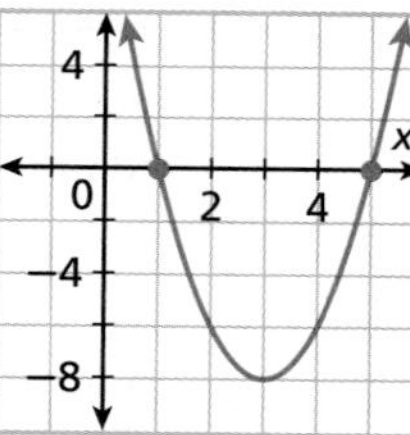


$\frac{1 + 5}{2} = \frac{6}{2} = 3$ *Find the average of the zeros.*

The axis of symmetry is $x = 3$.

**CHECK IT OUT!** **Find the axis of symmetry of each parabola.**

**2a.**

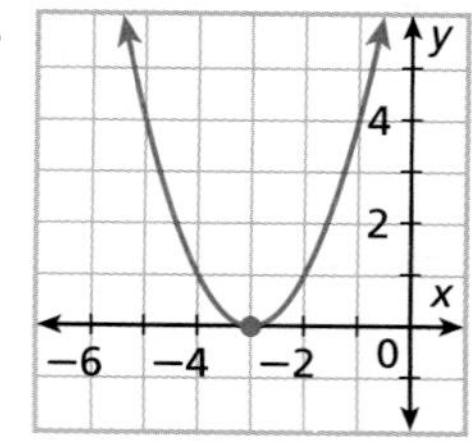


**2b.**

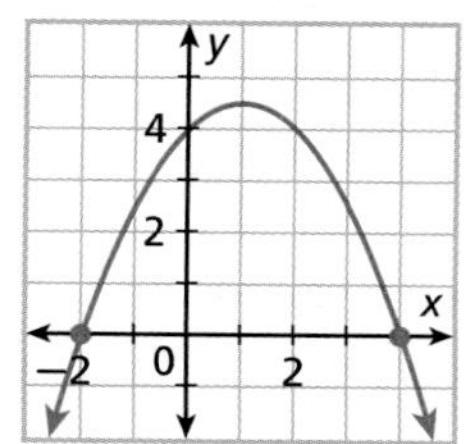

If a function has no zeros or they are difficult to identify from a graph, you can use a formula to find the axis of symmetry. The formula works for all quadratic functions.

Know it! Note

**Finding the Axis of Symmetry by Using the Formula**

| FORMULA | EXAMPLE |
|---|---|
| For a quadratic function $y = ax^2 + bx + c$, the axis of symmetry is the vertical line $x = -\frac{b}{2a}$. | $y = 2x^2 + 4x + 5$<br>$x = -\frac{b}{2a}$<br>$= -\frac{4}{2(2)} = -1$<br>The axis of symmetry is $x = -1$. |

## EXAMPLE 3 Finding the Axis of Symmetry by Using the Formula

**Find the axis of symmetry of the graph of $y = x^2 + 3x + 4$.**

**Step 1** Find the values of $a$ and $b$.

$y = 1x^2 + 3x + 4$

$a = 1, b = 3$

**Step 2** Use the formula $x = -\frac{b}{2a}$.

$x = -\frac{3}{2(1)} = -\frac{3}{2} = -1.5$

The axis of symmetry is $x = -1.5$.

**3.** Find the axis of symmetry of the graph of $y = 2x^2 + x + 3$.

Once you have found the axis of symmetry, you can use it to identify the vertex.

| Finding the Vertex of a Parabola |
|---|
| **Step 1** To find the $x$-coordinate of the vertex, find the axis of symmetry by using zeros or the formula. |
| **Step 2** To find the corresponding $y$-coordinate, substitute the $x$-coordinate of the vertex into the function. |
| **Step 3** Write the vertex as an ordered pair. |

## EXAMPLE 4 Finding the Vertex of a Parabola

**Find the vertex.**

**A** $y = -x^2 - 2x$

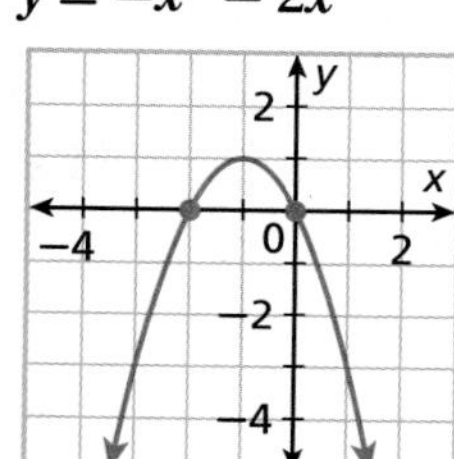


**Step 1** Find the $x$-coordinate.

The zeros are $-2$ and $0$.

$x = \frac{-2 + 0}{2} = \frac{-2}{2} = -1$

**Step 2** Find the corresponding $y$-coordinate.

$y = -x^2 - 2x$ *Use the function rule.*

$= -(-1)^2 - 2(-1) = 1$ *Substitute −1 for x.*

**Step 3** Write the ordered pair.

$(-1, 1)$

The vertex is $(-1, 1)$.

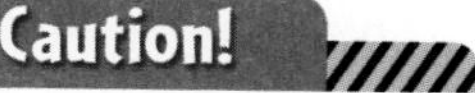


In Example 4A Step 2, use the order of operations to simplify the function.
$-(-1)^2 = -(1) = -1$

**Find the vertex.**

**B** $y = 5x^2 - 10x + 3$

**Step 1** Find the $x$-coordinate.

$a = 5, b = -10$ — *Identify a and b.*

$x = -\frac{b}{2a}$

$= -\frac{-10}{2(5)} = -\frac{-10}{10} = 1$ — *Substitute 5 for a and −10 for b.*

The $x$-coordinate of the vertex is 1.

**Step 2** Find the corresponding $y$-coordinate.

$y = 5x^2 - 10x + 3$ — *Use the function rule.*

$= 5(1)^2 - 10(1) + 3$ — *Substitute 1 for x.*

$= 5 - 10 + 3$

$= -2$

**Step 3** Write the ordered pair.

The vertex is $(1, -2)$.

**4.** Find the vertex of the graph of $y = x^2 - 4x - 10$.

## EXAMPLE 5 *Architecture Application*

**The height above water level of a curved arch support for a bridge can be modeled by $f(x) = -0.007x^2 + 0.84x + 0.8$, where $x$ is the distance in feet from where the arch support enters the water. Can a sailboat that is 24 feet tall pass under the bridge? Explain.**

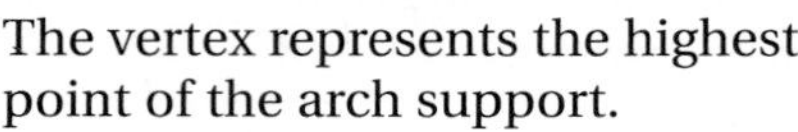

The vertex represents the highest point of the arch support.

**Step 1** Find the $x$-coordinate.

$a = -0.007, b = 0.84$ — *Identify a and b.*

$x = -\frac{b}{2a}$

$= -\frac{0.84}{2(-0.007)} = 60$ — *Substitute −0.007 for a and 0.84 for b.*

**Step 2** Find the corresponding $y$-coordinate.

$f(x) = -0.007x^2 + 0.84x + 0.8$ — *Use the function rule.*

$= -0.007(60)^2 + 0.84(60) + 0.8$ — *Substitute 60 for x.*

$= 26$

Since the height of the arch support is 26 feet, the sailboat can pass under the bridge.

**5.** The height of a small rise in a roller coaster track is modeled by $f(x) = -0.07x^2 + 0.42x + 6.37$, where $x$ is the distance in feet from a support pole at ground level. Find the height of the rise.

## THINK AND DISCUSS

1. How do you find the zeros of a function from its graph?
2. Describe how to find the axis of symmetry of a quadratic function if its graph does not cross the $x$-axis

3. **GET ORGANIZED** Copy and complete the graphic organizer. In each box, sketch a graph that fits the given description.

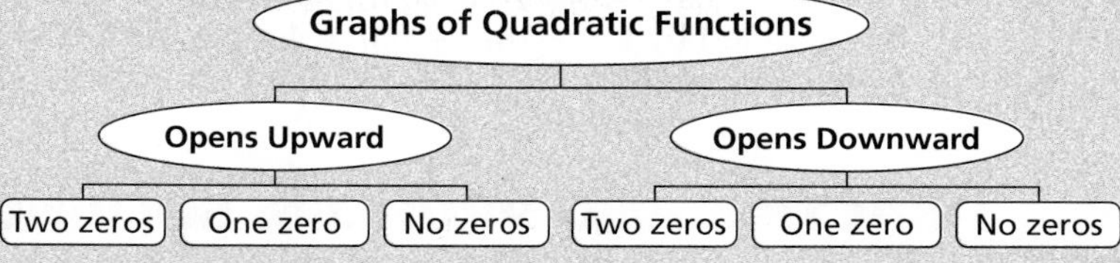


# 9-2 Exercises

MA.A.4.2

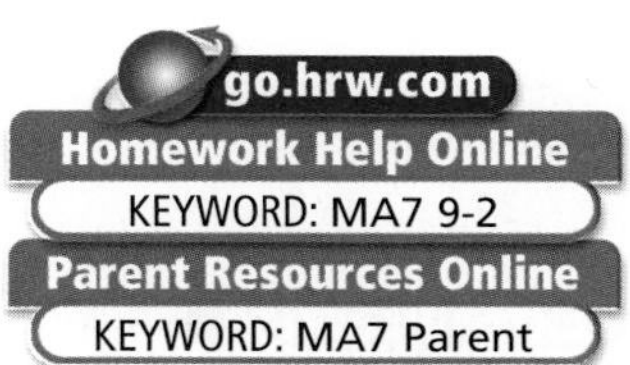


## GUIDED PRACTICE

**Vocabulary Apply the vocabulary from this lesson to answer each question.**

1. Why is the *zero of a function* the same as an $x$-intercept of a function?
2. Where is the *axis of symmetry* of a parabola located?

SEE EXAMPLE 1
p. 599

**Find the zeros of each quadratic function from its graph. Check your answer.**

3. $y = x^2 + 2x + 1$

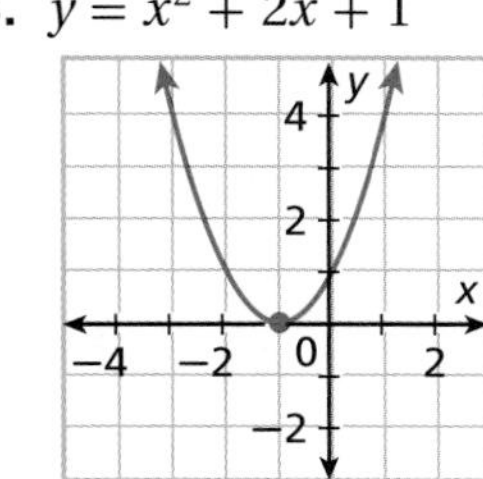

4. $y = 9 - x^2$

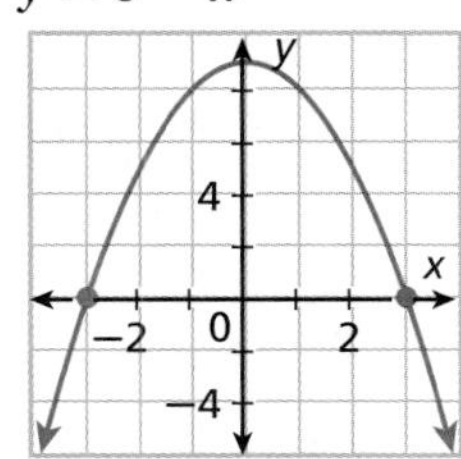

5. $y = -x^2 - x - 4$

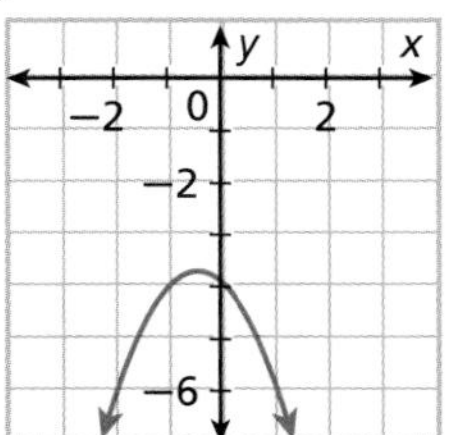

SEE EXAMPLE 2
p. 600

**Find the axis of symmetry of each parabola.**

6.

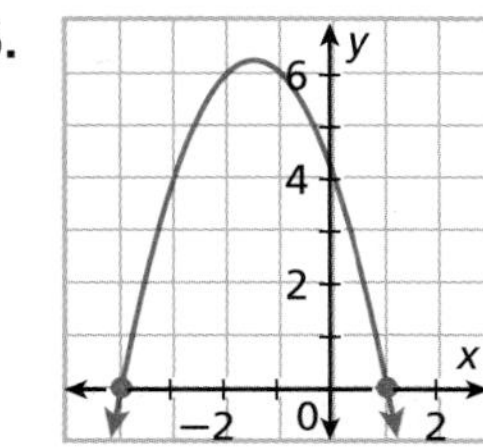

7.

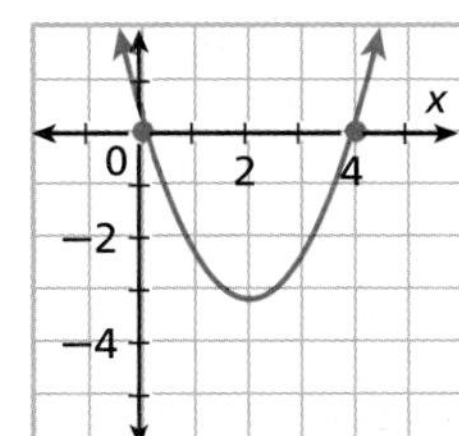

8.

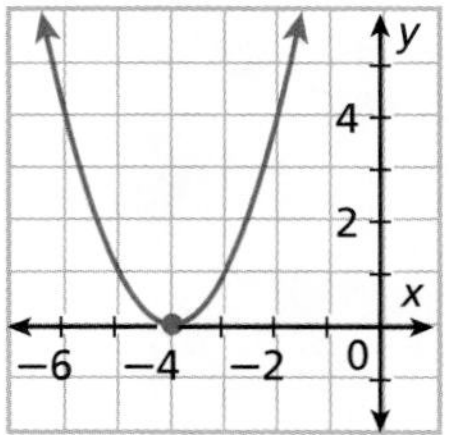

SEE EXAMPLE 3
p. 601

**For each quadratic function, find the axis of symmetry of its graph.**

9. $y = x^2 + 4x - 7$
10. $y = 3x^2 - 18x + 1$
11. $y = 2x^2 + 3x - 4$
12. $y = -3x^2 + x + 5$

SEE EXAMPLE 4
p. 601

**Find the vertex of each parabola.**

13. $y = -5x^2 + 10x + 3$

14. $y = x^2 + 4x - 7$

15. $y = \frac{1}{2}x^2 + 2x$

16. $y = -x^2 + 6x + 1$

17.
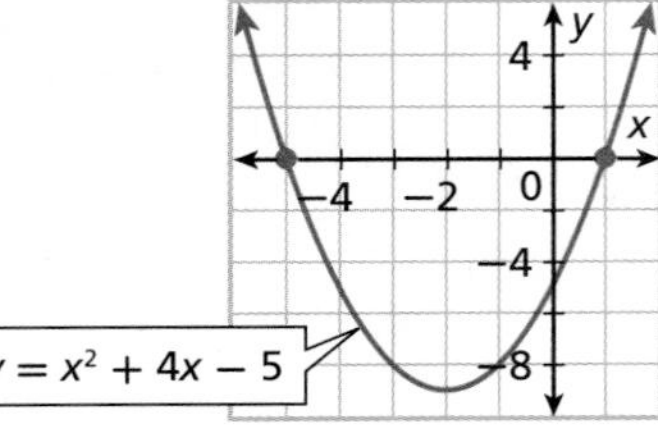


SEE EXAMPLE 5
p. 602

18. **Archery** The height in feet above the ground of an arrow after it is shot can be modeled by $y = -16t^2 + 63t + 4$. Can the arrow pass over a tree that is 68 feet tall? Explain.

## PRACTICE AND PROBLEM SOLVING

**Independent Practice**

| For Exercises | See Example |
|---|---|
| 19–21 | 1 |
| 22–24 | 2 |
| 25–28 | 3 |
| 29–33 | 4 |
| 34 | 5 |

**Extra Practice**

Skills Practice p. S20
Application Practice p. S36

**Find the zeros of each quadratic function from its graph. Check your answer.**

19. $y = \frac{1}{4}x^2 - x + 3$

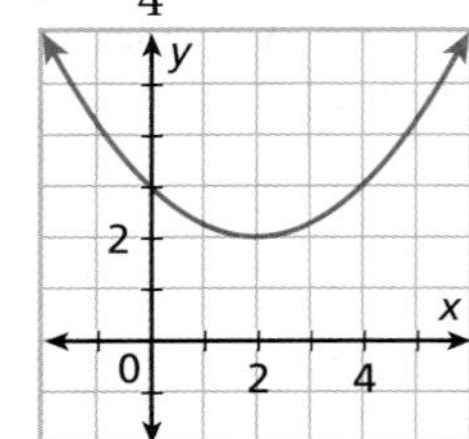

20. $y = -\frac{1}{3}x^2$

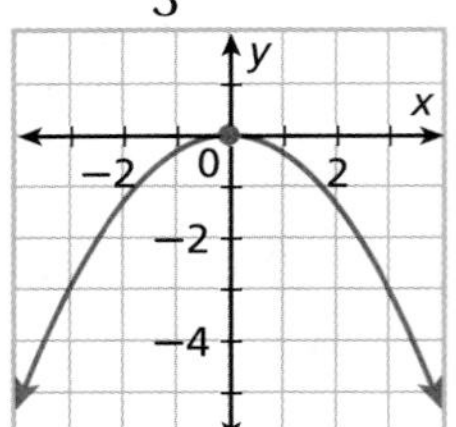

21. $y = x^2 + 10x + 16$

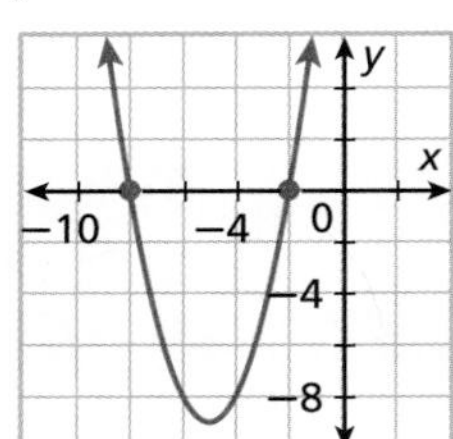

**Find the axis of symmetry of each parabola.**

22.
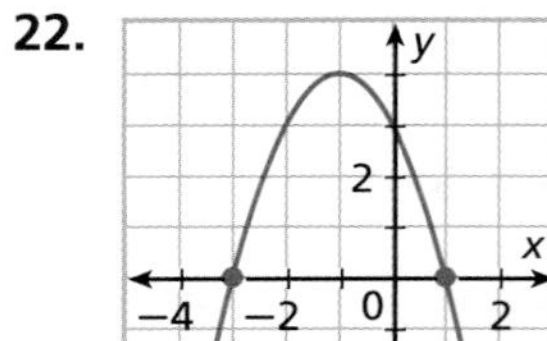

23.
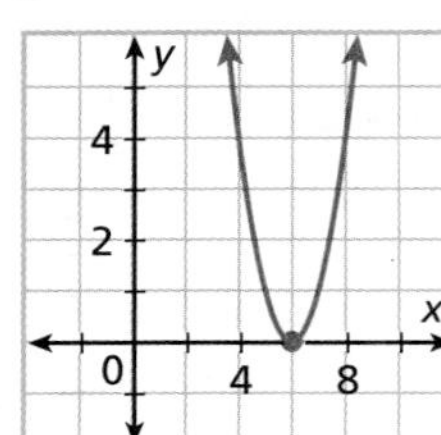

24.
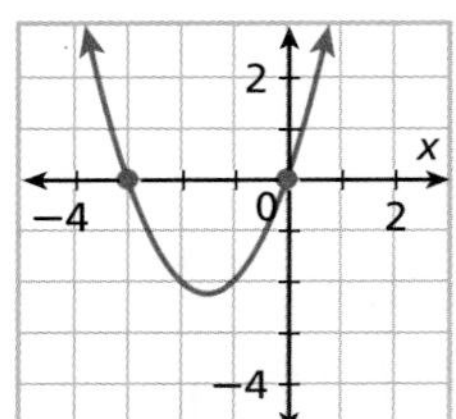

**For each quadratic function, find the axis of symmetry of its graph.**

25. $y = x^2 + x + 2$

26. $y = 3x^2 - 2x - 6$

27. $y = \frac{1}{2}x^2 - 5x + 4$

28. $y = -2x^2 + \frac{1}{3}x - \frac{3}{4}$

**Find the vertex of each parabola.**

29. $y = x^2 + 7x$

30. $y = -x^2 + 8x + 16$

31. $y = -2x^2 - 8x - 3$

32. $y = -x^2 + \frac{1}{2}x + 2$

33.
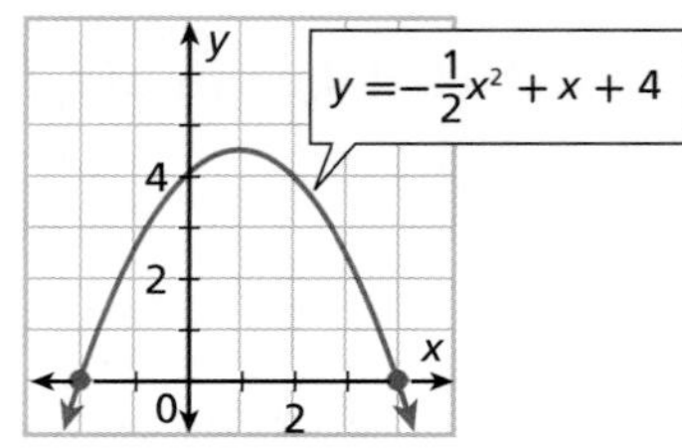


**LINK Engineering**

This arched bridge spans a river near the city of Yokote in northwestern Japan.

34. **Engineering** The height in feet of the curved arch support for a pedestrian bridge over a creek can be modeled by $f(x) = -0.628x^2 + 4.5x$, where $x$ is the distance in feet from where the arch support enters the water. If there is a flood that raises the level of the creek by 5.5 feet, will the top of the arch support be above the water? Explain.

35. **Critical Thinking** What conclusion can be drawn about the axis of symmetry of any quadratic function for which $b = 0$?

36. This problem will prepare you for the Multi-Step Test Prep on page 620.
 a. Use the graph of the height of a water bottle rocket to estimate the coordinates of the parabola's vertex.
 b. What does the vertex represent?
 c. Find the zeros of the function. What do they represent?
 d. Find the axis of symmetry. How is it related to the vertex and the zeros?

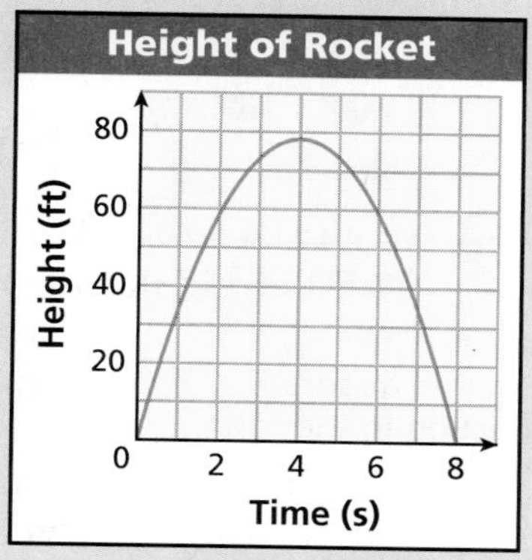

**Graphing Calculator** **Tell how many zeros each quadratic function has.**

37. $y = 8x^2 - 4x + 2$

38. $0 = y + 16x^2$

39. $\frac{1}{4}x^2 - 7x - 12 = y - 4$

40. **Write About It** If you are given the axis of symmetry of a quadratic function and know that the function has two zeros, how would you describe the location of the two zeros?

NC MA.A.4.2

41. Which function has the zeros shown in the graph?
 Ⓐ $y = x^2 + 2x + 8$
 Ⓑ $y = x^2 - 2x - 8$
 Ⓒ $y = x^2 + 2x - 8$
 Ⓓ $y = 2x^2 - 2x + 8$

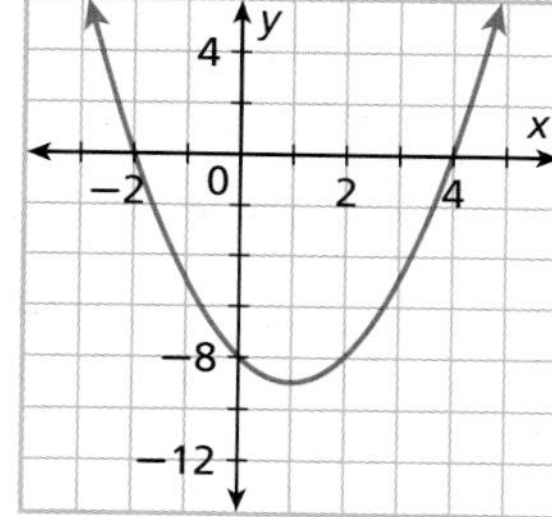


42. Which of the following functions has a graph with an axis of symmetry of $x = -\frac{1}{2}$?
 Ⓕ $y = 2x^2 - 2x + 5$
 Ⓖ $2x + 5 = 2x^2 - y$
 Ⓗ $2x^2 + y = 2x + 5$
 Ⓙ $2x - y = 5 - 2x^2$

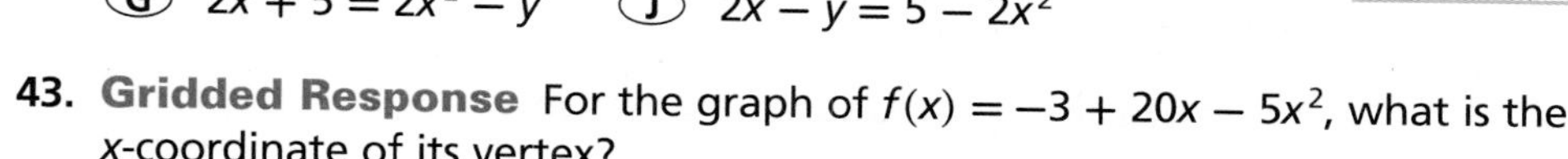

43. **Gridded Response** For the graph of $f(x) = -3 + 20x - 5x^2$, what is the $x$-coordinate of its vertex?

## CHALLENGE AND EXTEND

44. Describe the domain and range of a quadratic function that has exactly one zero and whose graph opens downward.

45. **Graphing Calculator** The height in feet of a parabolic bridge support is modeled by $f(x) = -0.01x^2 + 20$, where $y = -5$ represents ground level and the $x$-axis represents the middle of the bridge. Find the height and the width of the bridge support.

## SPIRAL REVIEW

46. The value of $y$ varies directly with $x$, and $y = -4$ when $x = 2$. Find $y$ when $x = 6$. *(Lesson 5-5)*

**Write each equation in slope-intercept form.** *(Lesson 5-6)*

47. $2x + y = 3$

48. $4y = 12x - 8$

49. $10 - 5y = 20x$

**Tell whether each function is quadratic. Explain.** *(Lesson 9-1)*

50. $y = 5x - 7$

51. $x^2 - 5x = 2 + y$

52. $y = -x^2 - 6x$

# 9-3 Graphing Quadratic Functions

**MA.A.4.2** Use appropriate terminology and notation...associated with functions.
*Also* **MA.A.4.3**

***Objective***
Graph a quadratic function in the form $y = ax^2 + bx + c$.

**Why use this?**
Graphs of quadratic functions can help you determine how high an object is tossed or kicked. (See Exercise 14.)

Recall that a $y$-intercept is the $y$-coordinate of the point where a graph intersects the $y$-axis. The $x$-coordinate of this point is always 0. For a quadratic function written in the form $y = ax^2 + bx + c$, when $x = 0$, $y = c$. So the $y$-intercept of a quadratic function is $c$.

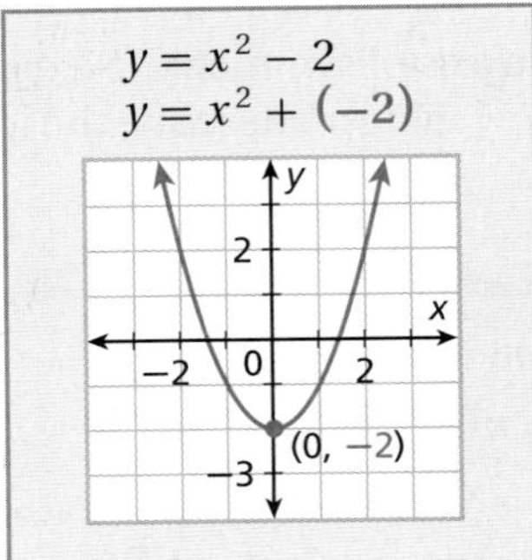


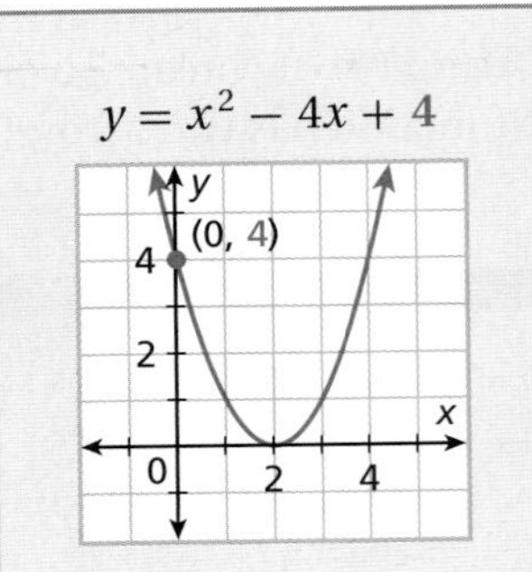


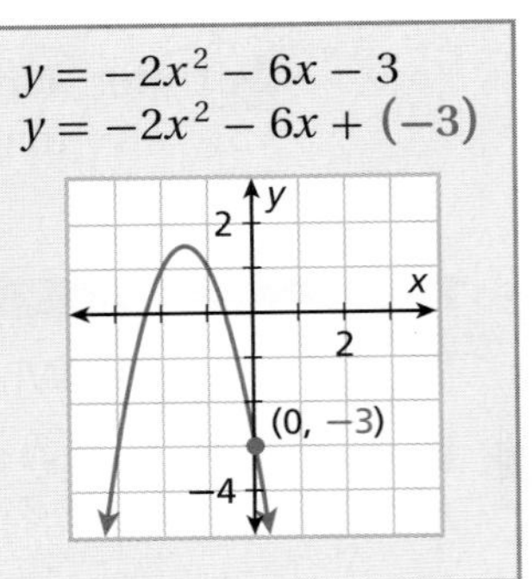


In the previous lesson, you found the axis of symmetry and vertex of a parabola. You can use these characteristics, the $y$-intercept, and symmetry to graph a quadratic function.

## EXAMPLE 1 Graphing a Quadratic Function

**Graph $y = x^2 - 4x - 5$.**

**Step 1** Find the axis of symmetry.

$x = -\frac{-4}{2(1)}$ *Use $x = -\frac{b}{2a}$. Substitute 1 for a and −4 for b.*

$= 2$ *Simplify.*

The axis of symmetry is $x = 2$.

**Step 2** Find the vertex.

$y = x^2 - 4x - 5$

$= 2^2 - 4(2) - 5$ *The x-coordinate of the vertex is 2. Substitute 2 for x.*

$= 4 - 8 - 5$ *Simplify.*

$= -9$ *The y-coordinate is −9.*

The vertex is $(2, -9)$.

**Step 3** Find the $y$-intercept.

$y = x^2 - 4x - 5$

$y = x^2 - 4x + (-5)$ *Identify c.*

The $y$-intercept is $-5$; the graph passes through $(0, -5)$.

**Step 4** Find two more points on the same side of the axis of symmetry as the point containing the $y$-intercept.

Since the axis of symmetry is $x = 2$, choose $x$-values less than 2.

| | | |
|---|---|---|
| Let $x = 1$. | | Let $x = -1$. |
| $y = 1^2 - 4(1) - 5$ | *Substitute x-coordinates.* | $y = (-1)^2 - 4(-1) - 5$ |
| $= 1 - 4 - 5$ | *Simplify.* | $= 1 + 4 - 5$ |
| $= -8$ | | $= 0$ |

Two other points are $(1, -8)$ and $(-1, 0)$.

## Helpful Hint

Because a parabola is symmetrical, each point is the same number of units away from the axis of symmetry as its reflected point.

**Step 5** Graph the **axis of symmetry**, the **vertex**, the point containing the **$y$-intercept**, and **two other points**.

**Step 6** **Reflect** the points across the axis of symmetry. Connect the points with a smooth curve.

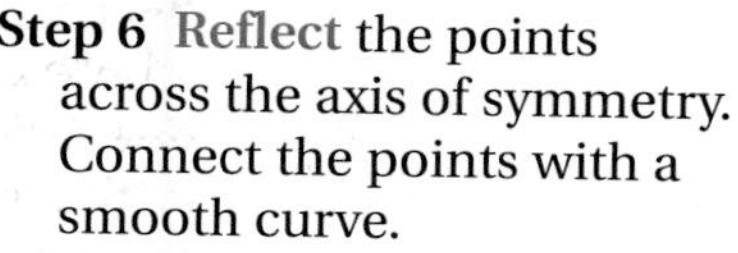

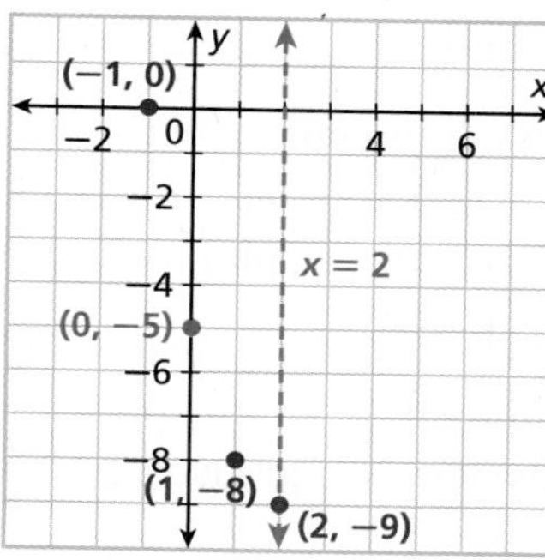


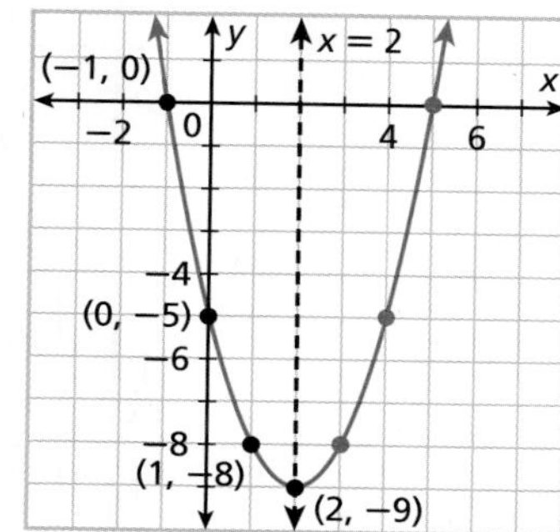

**Graph each quadratic function.**

**1a.** $y = 2x^2 + 6x + 2$

**1b.** $y + 6x = x^2 + 9$

## EXAMPLE 2 Problem-Solving Application

**The height in feet of a football that is kicked can be modeled by the function $f(x) = -16x^2 + 64x$, where $x$ is the time in seconds after it is kicked. Find the football's maximum height and the time it takes the football to reach this height. Then find how long the football is in the air.**

### 1 Understand the Problem

The **answer** includes three parts: the maximum height, the time to reach the maximum height, and the time to reach the ground.

**List the important information:**

- The function $f(x) = -16x^2 + 64x$ models the approximate height of the football after $x$ seconds.

## Remember!

The vertex is the highest or lowest point on a parabola. Therefore, in the example, it gives the maximum height of the football.

###  Make a Plan

Find the vertex of the graph because the maximum height of the football and the time it takes to reach it are the coordinates of the vertex. The football will hit the ground when its height is 0, so find the zeros of the function. You can do this by graphing.

## 3 Solve

**Step 1** Find the axis of symmetry.

$x = -\frac{64}{2(-16)}$ *Use $x = -\frac{b}{2a}$. Substitute −16 for a and 64 for b.*

$= -\frac{64}{-32} = 2$ *Simplify.*

The axis of symmetry is $x = 2$.

**Step 2** Find the vertex.

$y = -16x^2 + 64x$

$= -16(2)^2 + 64(2)$ *The x-coordinate of the vertex is 2. Substitute 2 for x.*

$= -16(4) + 128$ *Simplify.*

$= -64 + 128$

$= 64$ *The y-coordinate is 64.*

The vertex is $(2, 64)$.

**Step 3** Find the $y$-intercept.

$y = -16x^2 + 64x + 0$ *Identify c.*

The $y$-intercept is 0; the graph passes through $(0, 0)$.

**Step 4** Find another point on the same side of the axis of symmetry as the point containing the $y$-intercept.

Since the axis of symmetry is $x = 2$, choose an $x$-value that is less than 2. Let $x = 1$.

$y = -16(1)^2 + 64(1)$ *Substitute 1 for x.*

$= -16 + 64$ *Simplify.*

$= 48$

Another point is $(1, 48)$.

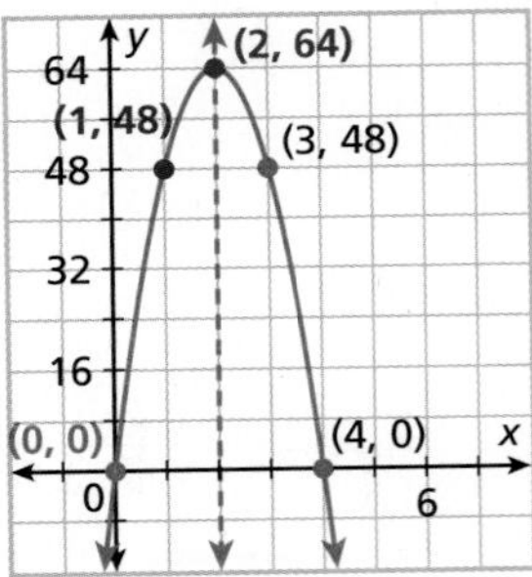


**Step 5** Graph the axis of symmetry, the vertex, the point containing the $y$-intercept, and the other point. Then reflect the points across the axis of symmetry. Connect the points with a smooth curve.

The vertex is $(2, 64)$. So at 2 seconds, the football has reached its maximum height of 64 feet. The graph shows the zeros of the function are 0 and 4. At 0 seconds the football has not yet been kicked, and at 4 seconds it reaches the ground. The football is in the air for 4 seconds.

## 4 Look Back

Check by substituting $(2, 64)$ and $(4, 0)$ into the function.

| | |
|---|---|
| $64 = -16(2)^2 + 64(2)$ | $0 = -16(4)^2 + 64(4)$ |
| $64 = -64 + 128$ | $0 = -256 + 256$ |
| $64 = 64$ ✓ | $0 = 0$ ✓ |

2. As Molly dives into her pool, her height in feet above the water can be modeled by the function $f(x) = -16x^2 + 24x$, where $x$ is the time in seconds after she begins diving. Find the maximum height of her dive and the time it takes Molly to reach this height. Then find how long it takes her to reach the pool.

## THINK AND DISCUSS

1. Explain how to find the $y$-intercept of a quadratic function that is written in the form $ax^2 - y = bx + c$.
2. Explain how to graph a quadratic function.
3. What do you think the vertex and zeros of the function will tell you for the situation in the Check It Out for Example 2?

4. **GET ORGANIZED** Copy and complete the graphic organizer using your own quadratic function.

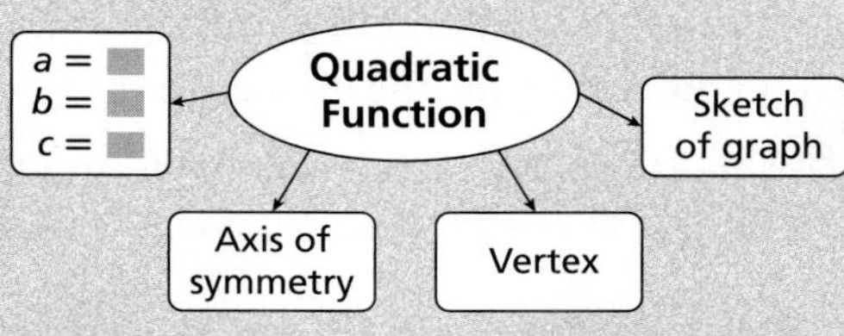


# 9-3 Exercises

MA.A.4.2, MA.A.4.3

## GUIDED PRACTICE

SEE EXAMPLE 1 p. 606

**Graph each quadratic function.**

1. $y = x^2 - 2x - 3$
2. $-y - 3x^2 = -3$
3. $y = 2x^2 + 2x - 4$
4. $y = x^2 + 4x - 8$
5. $y + x^2 + 5x + 2 = 0$
6. $y = 4x^2 + 2$

SEE EXAMPLE 2 p. 607

7. **Multi-Step** The height in feet of a golf ball that is hit from the ground can be modeled by the function $f(x) = -16x^2 + 96x$, where $x$ is the time in seconds after the ball is hit. Find the ball's maximum height and the time it takes the ball to reach this height. Then find how long the ball is in the air.

## PRACTICE AND PROBLEM SOLVING

| Independent Practice | |
|---|---|
| For Exercises | See Example |
| 8–13 | 1 |
| 14 | 2 |

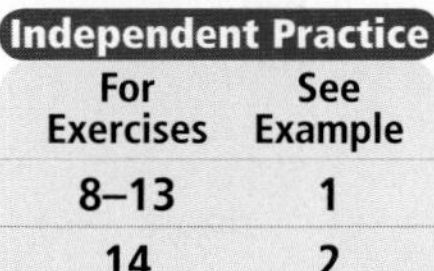


**Graph each quadratic function.**

8. $y = -4x^2 + 12x - 5$
9. $y = 3x^2 + 12x + 9$
10. $y - 7x^2 - 14x = 3$
11. $y = -x^2 + 2x$
12. $y - 1 = 4x^2 + 8x$
13. $y = -2x^2 - 3x + 4$
14. **Multi-Step** A juggler tosses a ring into the air. The height of the ring in feet above the juggler's hands can be modeled by the function $f(x) = -16x^2 + 16x$, where $x$ is the time in seconds after the ring is tossed. Find the ring's maximum height above the juggler's hands and the time it takes the ring to reach this height. Then find how long the ring is in the air.

**For each quadratic function, find the axis of symmetry and the vertex of its graph.**

15. $y = x^2 - 8x$
16. $y = -x^2 + 6x - 4$
17. $y = 4 - 3x^2$
18. $y = -2x^2 - 4$
19. $y = -x^2 - x - 4$
20. $y = x^2 + 8x + 16$

Building began on the Tower of Pisa, located in Pisa, Italy, in 1173. The tower started leaning after the third story was added. At the fifth story, attempts were made to correct the leaning. The tower was finally complete in 1350.

**Graph each quadratic function. On your graph, label the coordinates of the vertex. Draw and label the axis of symmetry.**

**21.** $y = -x^2$ **22.** $y = -x^2 + 4x$ **23.** $y = x^2 - 6x + 4$

**24.** $y = x^2 - x$ **25.** $y = 3x^2 - 4$ **26.** $y = -2x^2 - 16x - 25$

**27.** **Travel** While on a vacation in Italy, Rudy visited the Leaning Tower of Pisa. When he leaned over the railing to look down from the tower, his sunglasses fell off. The height in meters of the sunglasses as they fell can be approximated by the function $y = -5x^2 + 50$, where $x$ is the time in seconds.

a. Graph the function. (*Hint:* Use a graphing calculator.)

b. What is a reasonable domain and range?

c. How long did it take for the glasses to reach the ground?

**28.** **/// ERROR ANALYSIS ///** Two students found the equation of the axis of symmetry for the graph of $f(x) = -x^2 - 2x + 1$. Who is incorrect? Explain the error.

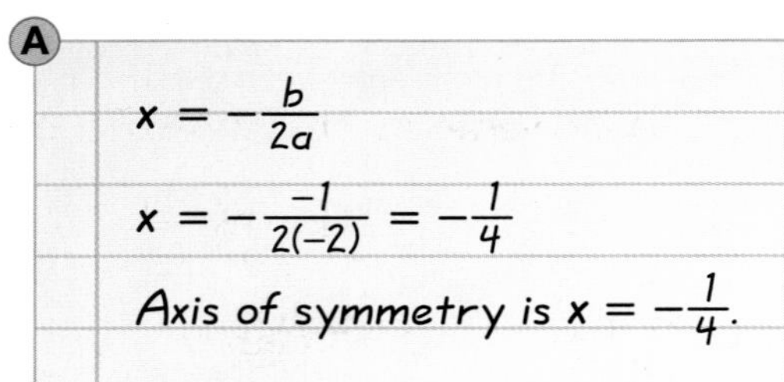


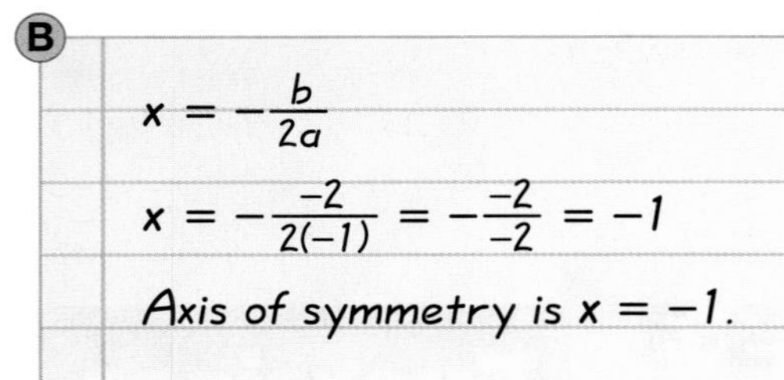


**29.** **Critical Thinking** The point $(5, 4)$ lies on the graph of a quadratic function whose axis of symmetry is $x = 2$. Find another point on the graph. Explain how you found the point.

**Engineering** **Use the graph for Exercises 30–32. The velocity $v$ in centimeters per second of a fluid flowing in a pipe varies according to the radius $r$ of the pipe.**

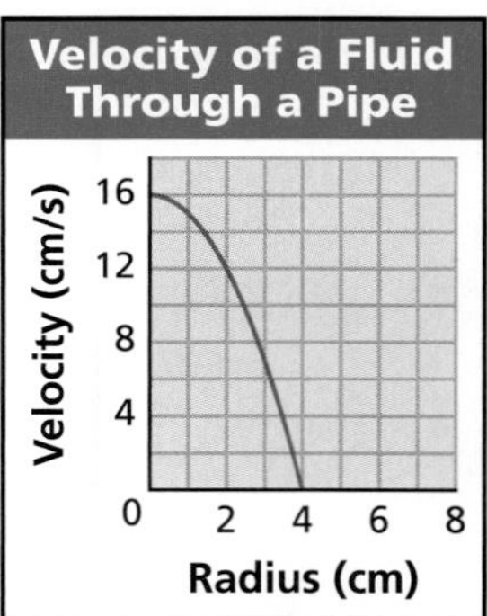


**30.** Find the radius of the pipe when the velocity is 7 cm/s.

**31.** Find the velocity of the fluid when the radius is 2 cm.

**32.** What is a reasonable domain for this function? Explain.

**33.** **Critical Thinking** The graph of a quadratic function has the vertex $(0, 5)$. One point on the graph is $(1, 6)$. Find another point on the graph. Explain how you found the point.

**34.** **Write About It** Explain how the vertex and the range can help you graph a quadratic function.

**MULTI-STEP TEST PREP**

**35.** This problem will prepare you for the Multi-Step Test Prep on page 620. A water bottle rocket is shot upward with an initial velocity of $v_i = 45$ ft/s from the roof of a school, which is at $h_i$, 50 ft above the ground. The equation $h = -\frac{1}{2}at^2 + v_i t + h_i$ models the rocket's height as a function of time. The acceleration due to gravity $a$ is 32 ft/s².

a. Write the equation for height as a function of time for this situation.

b. Find the vertex of this parabola.

c. Sketch the graph of this parabola and label the vertex.

d. What do the coordinates of the vertex represent in terms of time and height?

36. Copy and complete the table for each function.

| Function | Graph Opens | Axis of Symmetry | Vertex | Zeros | Domain and Range |
|---|---|---|---|---|---|
| $y = x^2 + 4$ | | $x =$ | ( , ) | | D: <br> R: |
| $y = -x^2 + 4$ | | $x =$ | ( , ) | | D: <br> R: |
| $y + 8 - x^2 = -2x$ | | $x =$ | ( , ) | | D: <br> R: |

NC MA.A.4.2, MA.A.4.3

37. Which is the axis of symmetry for the graph of $f(x) = 6 - 5x + \frac{1}{2}x^2$?

Ⓐ $x = 5$ Ⓑ $x = \frac{1}{20}$ Ⓒ $x = -5$ Ⓓ $x = -\frac{1}{20}$

38. What are the coordinates of the vertex for the graph of $f(x) = x^2 - 5x + 6$?

Ⓕ $\left(-\frac{5}{2}, -\frac{1}{4}\right)$ Ⓖ $\left(-\frac{5}{2}, \frac{1}{4}\right)$ Ⓗ $\left(\frac{5}{2}, \frac{1}{4}\right)$ Ⓙ $\left(\frac{5}{2}, -\frac{1}{4}\right)$

39. Which function's graph has an axis of symmetry of $x = 1$ and a vertex of $(1, 8)$?

Ⓐ $y = -x^2 + x + 8$ Ⓒ $y = 2x^2 - 4x - 8$

Ⓑ $y = x^2 + 8x + 1$ Ⓓ $y = -3x^2 + 6x + 5$

40. **Short Response** Graph $y = x^2 + 3x + 2$. What are the zeros, the axis of symmetry, and the coordinates of the vertex? Show your work.

## CHALLENGE AND EXTEND

41. The graph of a quadratic function has its vertex at $(1, -4)$ and one zero of the function is 3. Find the other zero. Explain how you found the other zero.

42. The $x$-intercepts of a quadratic function are 3 and $-3$. The $y$-intercept is 6. What are the coordinates of the vertex? Does the function have a maximum or a minimum? Explain.

## SPIRAL REVIEW

**Find the $x$- and $y$-intercepts.** *(Lesson 5-2)*

43.
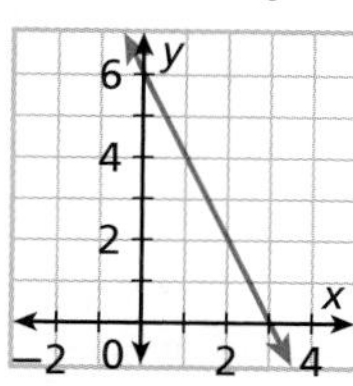


44.
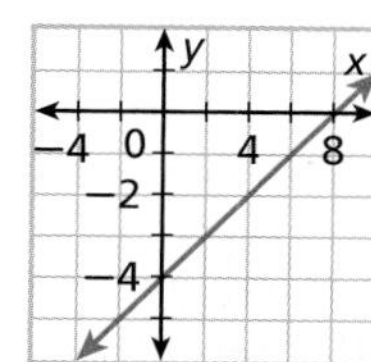


45.
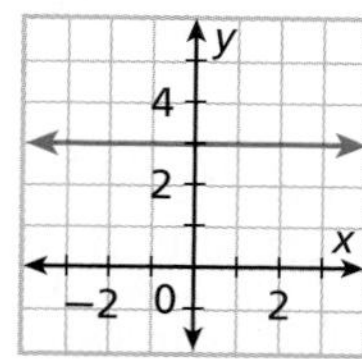


**Solve each system by using any method.** *(Lessons 6-1, 6-2, and 6-3)*

46. $\begin{cases} 3x - y = 2 \\ x + 4y = 18 \end{cases}$

47. $\begin{cases} 2x + 3y = 3 \\ 4x - y = 13 \end{cases}$

48. $\begin{cases} -2x + 3y = 12 \\ 6x + y = 4 \end{cases}$

**For each function, find the vertex of its graph.** *(Lesson 9-2)*

49. $y = x^2 + 2x - 15$

50. $y = -3x^2 + 12x - 4$

51. $y = -2x - x^2 + 3$

# The Family of Quadratic Functions

*Use with Lesson 9-4*

In Chapter 5, you learned that functions whose graphs share the same basic characteristics form a *family of functions*. All quadratic functions form a family because their graphs are all parabolas. You can use a graphing calculator to explore the family of quadratic functions.

**MA.A.4.3** Interpret the relationship of constants and coefficients for data presented in graphs...and equations.

## Activity

**Describe how the value of $a$ affects the graph of $y = ax^2$.**

1. Press Y=. Enter $\mathbf{Y_1}$ through $\mathbf{Y_4}$ as shown.

   Notice that $\mathbf{Y_2}$ represents the parent function $y = x^2$. To make it stand out from the other functions, change its line style. When you enter $\mathbf{Y_2}$, move the cursor to the line style indicator by pressing ◄. Then press ENTER to cycle through the choices until a thicker line appears.

2. Press GRAPH.

   Keep in mind the values of $a$ as the functions are graphed. The graphing calculator will graph the functions in order.

   Notice that the graph of $y = \frac{1}{2}x^2$ is wider than the graph of the parent function. The graphs of $y = 2x^2$ and $y = 3x^2$ are narrower than the graph of the parent function.

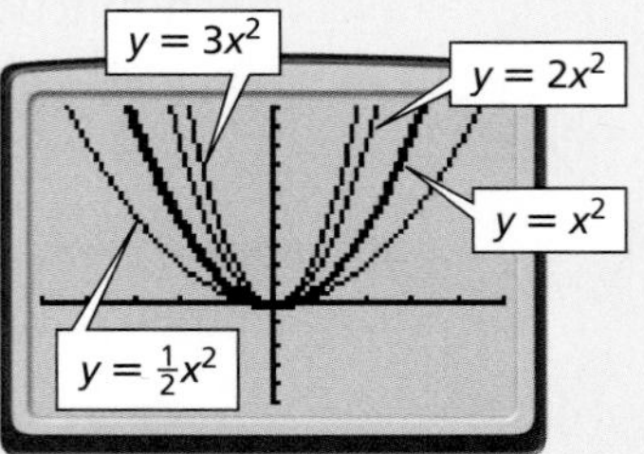


## Try This

1. How would the graph of $y = 6x^2$ compare with the graph of the parent function?
2. How would the graph of $y = \frac{1}{5}x^2$ compare with the graph of the parent function?
3. **Make a Conjecture** Make a conjecture about the effect of $a$ on the graph of $y = ax^2$.

**Consider the graphs of $y = -\frac{1}{2}x^2$, $y = -x^2$, $y = -2x^2$, and $y = -3x^2$.**

4. Describe the differences in the graphs.
5. How would the graph of $y = -8x^2$ compare with the graph of $y = -x^2$?
6. How do these results affect your conjecture from Problem 3?

**Consider the graphs of $y = x^2 - 1$, $y = x^2$, $y = x^2 + 2$, and $y = x^2 + 4$.**

7. Describe the differences in the graphs.
8. How would the graph of $y = x^2 - 7$ compare with the graph of the parent function?
9. **Make a Conjecture** Make a conjecture about the effect of $c$ on the graph of $y = x^2 + c$.

# 9-4 Transforming Quadratic Functions

**MA.A.4.3** Interpret the relationship of constants and coefficients for data presented in graphs…and equations.

***Objective***
Graph and transform quadratic functions.

**Why learn this?**
You can compare how long it takes raindrops to reach the ground from different heights. (See Exercise 18.)

**Remember!**
You saw in Lesson 5-9 that the graphs of all linear functions are transformations of the linear parent function, $y = x$.

The quadratic parent function is $f(x) = x^2$. The graph of all other quadratic functions are transformations of the graph of $f(x) = x^2$.

For the parent function $f(x) = x^2$:

- The axis of symmetry is $x = 0$, or the $y$-axis.
- The vertex is $(0, 0)$.
- The function has only one zero, 0.

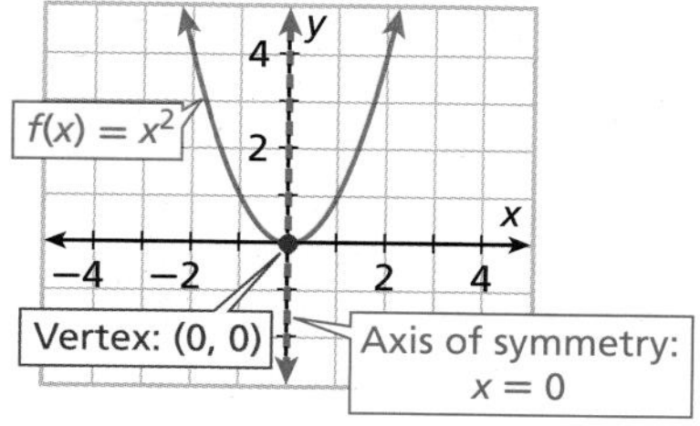


**Compare the coefficients in the following functions.**

$f(x) = x^2 \qquad g(x) = \frac{1}{2}x^2$

$h(x) = -3x^2$

$f(x) = 1x^2 + 0x + 0$

$g(x) = \frac{1}{2}x^2 + 0x + 0$

$h(x) = -3x^2 + 0x + 0$

| Same | Different |
|---|---|
| • $b = 0$<br>• $c = 0$ | • Value of $a$ |

**Compare the graphs of the same functions.**

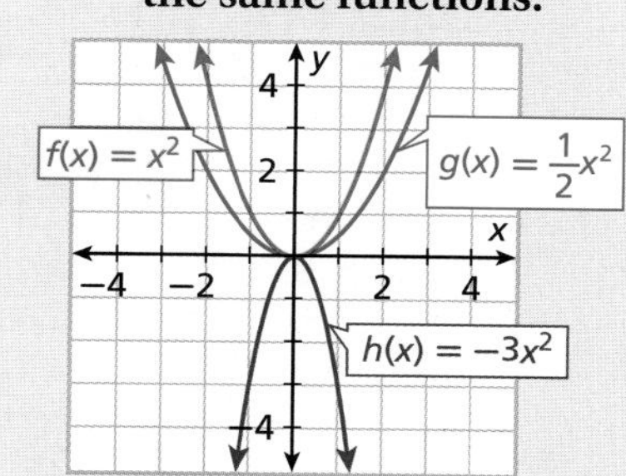


| Same | Different |
|---|---|
| • Axis of symmetry is $x = 0$.<br>• Vertex is $(0, 0)$. | • Widths of parabolas |

The value of $a$ in a quadratic function determines not only the direction a parabola opens, but also the width of the parabola.

**Know it! Note**

## Width of a Parabola

| WORDS | EXAMPLES |
|---|---|
| The graph of $f(x) = ax^2$ is narrower than the graph of $f(x) = x^2$ if $\lvert a \rvert > 1$ and wider if $\lvert a \rvert < 1$. | Compare the graphs of $g(x)$ and $h(x)$ with the graph of $f(x)$.<br>$\lvert -2 \rvert$ ? 1    $\left\lvert \frac{1}{4} \right\rvert$ ? 1<br>$2 > 1$    $\frac{1}{4} < 1$<br>narrower    wider<br>$f(x) = x^2$, $h(x) = \frac{1}{4}x^2$, $g(x) = -2x^2$ |

## EXAMPLE 1 Comparing Widths of Parabolas

**Order the functions from narrowest graph to widest.**

**A** $f(x) = -2x^2, g(x) = \frac{1}{3}x^2, h(x) = 4x^2$

**Step 1** Find $|a|$ for each function.

$|-2| = 2$ $\quad \left|\frac{1}{3}\right| = \frac{1}{3}$ $\quad |4| = 4$

**Step 2** Order the functions.

$h(x) = 4x^2$

$f(x) = -2x^2$

$g(x) = \frac{1}{3}x^2$

*The function with the narrowest graph has the greatest $|a|$.*

***Check*** Use a graphing calculator to compare the graphs.

$h(x) = 4x^2$ has the narrowest graph, and $g(x) = \frac{1}{3}x^2$ has the widest graph. ✓

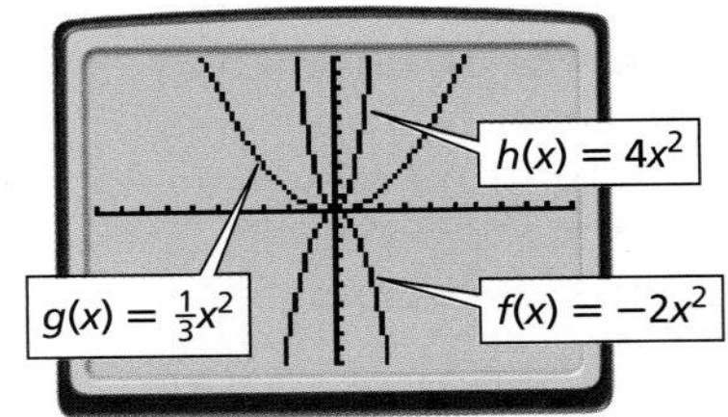


**B** $f(x) = 2x^2, g(x) = -2x^2$

**Step 1** Find $|a|$ for each function.

$|2| = 2$ $\quad |-2| = 2$

**Step 2** Order the functions from narrowest graph to widest.

Since the absolute values are equal, the graphs are the same width.

**Order the functions from narrowest graph to widest.**

**1a.** $f(x) = -x^2, g(x) = \frac{2}{3}x^2$

**1b.** $f(x) = -4x^2, g(x) = 6x^2, h(x) = 0.2x^2$

**Compare the coefficients in the following functions.**

$f(x) = x^2$ $\quad g(x) = x^2 - 4$

$h(x) = x^2 + 3$

$f(x) = 1x^2 + 0x + 0$

$g(x) = 1x^2 + 0x + -4$

$h(x) = 1x^2 + 0x + 3$

| Same | Different |
|---|---|
| • $a = 1$<br>• $b = 0$ | • Value of $c$ |

**Compare the graphs of the same functions.**

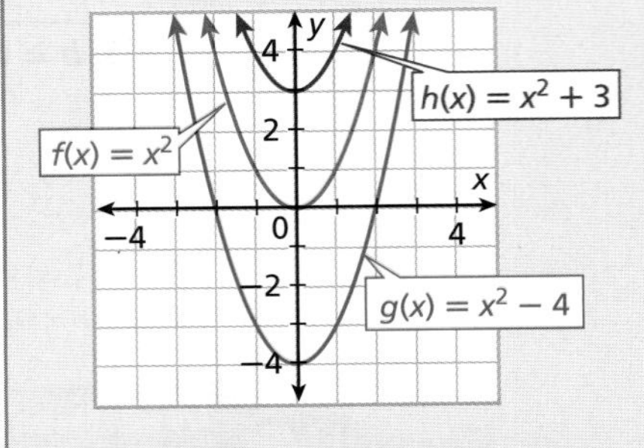


| Same | Different |
|---|---|
| • Axis of symmetry is $x = 0$.<br>• Width of parabola | • Vertex of parabola |

The value of $c$ makes these graphs look different. The value of $c$ in a quadratic function determines not only the value of the $y$-intercept but also a vertical translation of the graph of $f(x) = ax^2$ up or down the $y$-axis.

## Vertical Translations of a Parabola

The graph of the function $f(x) = x^2 + c$ is the graph of $f(x) = x^2$ translated vertically.

- If $c > 0$, the graph of $f(x) = x^2$ is translated $c$ units **up**.
- If $c < 0$, the graph of $f(x) = x^2$ is translated $c$ units **down**.

**EXAMPLE 2** Comparing Graphs of Quadratic Functions

**Compare the graph of each function with the graph of $f(x) = x^2$.**

**Helpful Hint**

When comparing graphs, it is helpful to draw them on the same coordinate plane.

 $g(x) = -\frac{1}{3}x^2 + 2$

**Method 1** Compare the graphs.

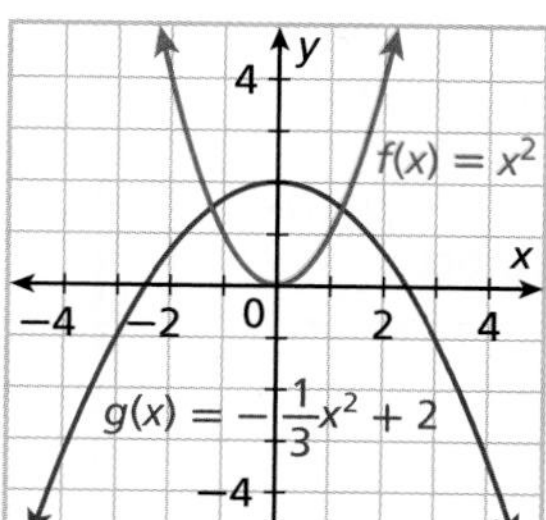


- The graph of $g(x) = -\frac{1}{3}x^2 + 2$ is **wider** than the graph of $f(x) = x^2$.
- The graph of $g(x) = -\frac{1}{3}x^2 + 2$ opens **downward**, and the graph of $f(x) = x^2$ opens **upward**.
- The axis of symmetry is the same.
- The vertex of $f(x) = x^2$ is $(0, 0)$. The vertex of $g(x) = -\frac{1}{3}x^2 + 2$ is translated **2 units up** to $(0, 2)$.

**B** $g(x) = 2x^2 - 3$

**Method 2** Use the functions.

- Since $|2| > |1|$, the graph of $g(x) = 2x^2 - 3$ is **narrower** than the graph of $f(x) = x^2$.
- Since $-\frac{b}{2a} = 0$ for both functions, the axis of symmetry is the same.
- The vertex of $f(x) = x^2$ is $(0, 0)$. The vertex of $g(x) = 2x^2 - 3$ is translated **3 units down** to $(0, -3)$.

***Check*** Use a graph to verify all comparisons.

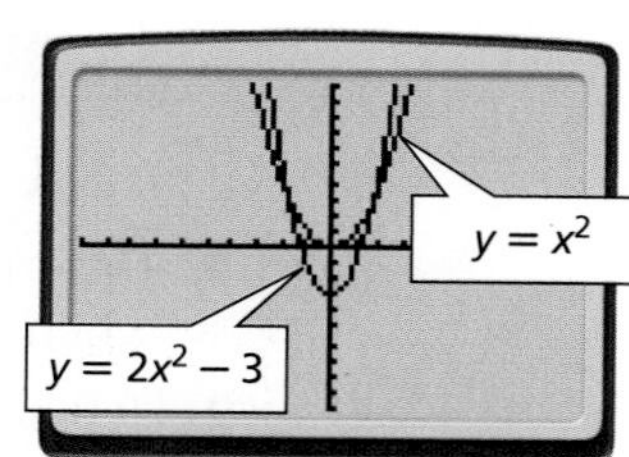

**Compare the graph of each function with the graph of $f(x) = x^2$.**

**2a.** $g(x) = -x^2 - 4$ **2b.** $g(x) = 3x^2 + 9$ **2c.** $g(x) = \frac{1}{2}x^2 + 2$

The quadratic function $h(t) = -16t^2 + c$ can be used to approximate the height $h$ in feet above the ground of a falling object $t$ seconds after it is dropped from a height of $c$ feet. This model is used only to approximate the height of falling objects because it does not account for air resistance, wind, and other real-world factors.

## EXAMPLE 3 Physics Application

**Two identical water balloons are dropped from different heights as shown in the diagram.**

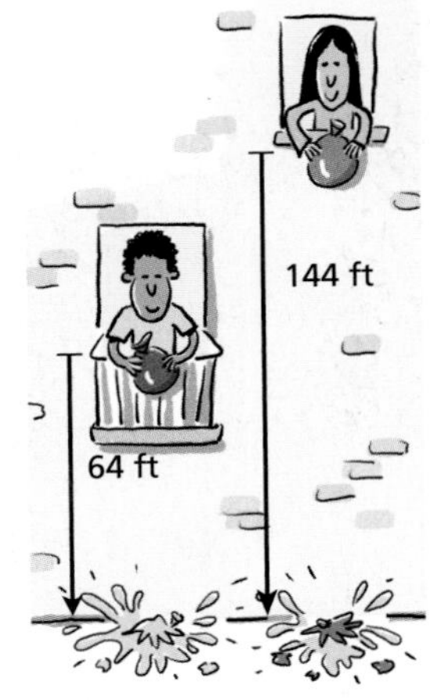


**a. Write the two height functions and compare their graphs.**

**Step 1** Write the height functions.
The $y$-intercept $c$ represents the original height.

$h_1(t) = -16t^2 + 64$ *Dropped from 64 feet*
$h_2(t) = -16t^2 + 144$ *Dropped from 144 feet*

**Caution!**

Remember that the graphs shown here represent the *height* of the objects over time, not the *paths* of the objects.

**Step 2** Use a graphing calculator.
Since time and height cannot be negative, set the window for nonnegative values.

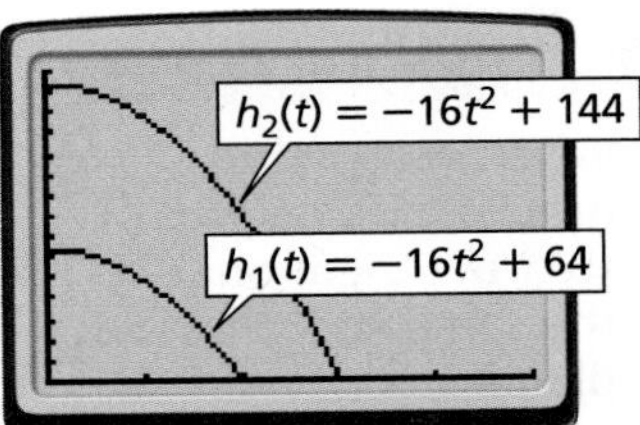


The graph of $h_2$ is a vertical translation of the graph of $h_1$. Since the balloon in $h_2$ is dropped from 80 feet higher than the one in $h_1$, the $y$-intercept of $h_2$ is 80 units higher.

**b. Use the graphs to tell when each water balloon reaches the ground.**

The zeros of each function are when the water balloons reach the ground.

The water balloon dropped from 64 feet reaches the ground in 2 seconds. The water balloon dropped from 144 feet reaches the ground in 3 seconds.

***Check*** These answers seem reasonable because the water balloon dropped from a greater height should take longer to reach the ground.

**3.** Two tennis balls are dropped, one from a height of 16 feet and the other from a height of 100 feet.

**a.** Write the two height functions and compare their graphs.

**b.** Use the graphs to tell when each tennis ball reaches the ground.

## THINK AND DISCUSS

**1.** Describe how the graph of $y = x^2 + c$ differs from the graph of $y = x^2$ when the value of $c$ is positive and when the value of $c$ is negative.

**2.** Tell how to determine whether a graph of a function is wider or narrower than the graph of $f(x) = x^2$.

**3. GET ORGANIZED** Copy and complete the graphic organizer by explaining how each change affects the graph $y = ax^2 + c$.

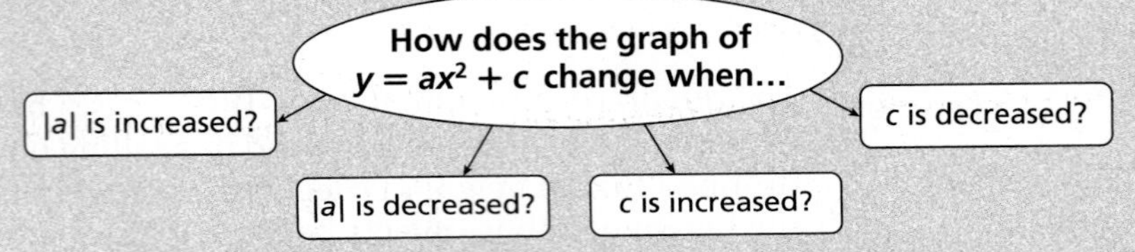

# 9-4 Exercises

go.hrw.com
Homework Help Online
KEYWORD: MA7 9-4
Parent Resources Online
KEYWORD: MA7 Parent

## GUIDED PRACTICE

SEE EXAMPLE 1 p. 614

**Order the functions from narrowest graph to widest.**

1. $f(x) = 3x^2$, $g(x) = 2x^2$
2. $f(x) = 5x^2$, $g(x) = -5x^2$
3. $f(x) = \frac{3}{4}x^2$, $g(x) = -2x^2$, $h(x) = -8x^2$
4. $f(x) = x^2$, $g(x) = -\frac{4}{5}x^2$, $h(x) = 3x^2$

SEE EXAMPLE 2 p. 615

**Compare the graph of each function with the graph of $f(x) = x^2$.**

5. $g(x) = x^2 + 6$
6. $g(x) = -2x^2 + 5$
7. $g(x) = \frac{1}{3}x^2$
8. $g(x) = -\frac{1}{4}x^2 - 2$

SEE EXAMPLE 3 p. 616

9. **Multi-Step** Two baseballs are dropped, one from a height of 16 feet and the other from a height of 256 feet.
   a. Write the two height functions and compare their graphs.
   b. Use the graphs to tell when each baseball reaches the ground.

## PRACTICE AND PROBLEM SOLVING

**Independent Practice**

| For Exercises | See Example |
|---|---|
| 10–13 | 1 |
| 14–17 | 2 |
| 18 | 3 |

**Extra Practice**

Skills Practice p. S20
Application Practice p. S36

**Order the functions from narrowest graph to widest.**

10. $f(x) = x^2$, $g(x) = 4x^2$
11. $f(x) = -2x^2$, $g(x) = \frac{1}{2}x^2$
12. $f(x) = -x^2$, $g(x) = -\frac{5}{8}x^2$, $h(x) = \frac{1}{2}x^2$
13. $f(x) = -5x^2$, $g(x) = -\frac{3}{8}x^2$, $h(x) = 3x^2$

**Compare the graph of each function with the graph of $f(x) = x^2$.**

14. $g(x) = \frac{1}{2}x^2 - 10$
15. $g(x) = -4x^2 - 2$
16. $g(x) = \frac{2}{3}x^2 - 9$
17. $g(x) = -\frac{1}{5}x^2 + 1$
18. **Multi-Step** A raindrop falls from a cloud at an altitude of 10,000 ft. Another raindrop falls from a cloud at an altitude of 14,400 ft.
    a. Write the two height functions and compare their graphs.
    b. Use the graphs to tell when each raindrop reaches the ground.

**Tell whether each statement is sometimes, always, or never true.**

19. The graphs of $f(x) = ax^2$ and $g(x) = -ax^2$ have the same width.
20. The function $f(x) = ax^2 + c$ has three zeros.
21. The graph of $y = ax^2 + 1$ has its vertex at the origin.
22. The graph of $y = -x^2 + c$ intersects the $x$-axis.

23. **Data Collection** Use a graphing calculator and a motion detector to graph the height of a falling object over time.
    a. Find a function to model the height of the object while it is in motion.
    b. **Critical Thinking** Explain why the value of $a$ in your function is not $-16$.

**Write a function to describe each of the following.**

**24.** The graph of $f(x) = x^2 + 10$ is translated 10 units down.

**25.** The graph of $f(x) = 3x^2 - 2$ is translated 4 units down.

**26.** The graph of $f(x) = 0.5x^2$ is narrowed.

**27.** The graph of $f(x) = -5x^2$ is narrowed and translated 2 units up.

**28.** The graph of $f(x) = x^2 - 7$ is widened and has no $x$-intercept.

**Match each function to its graph.**

**29.** $f(x) = 4x^2 - 3$ **30.** $f(x) = \frac{1}{4}x^2 - 3$ **31.** $f(x) = 4x^2 + 3$ **32.** $f(x) = -\frac{1}{4}x^2 - 3$

**A.** 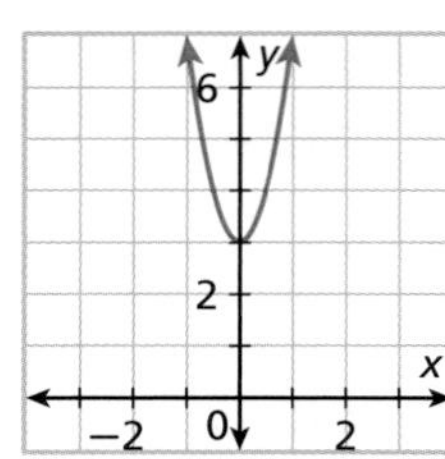

**B.** 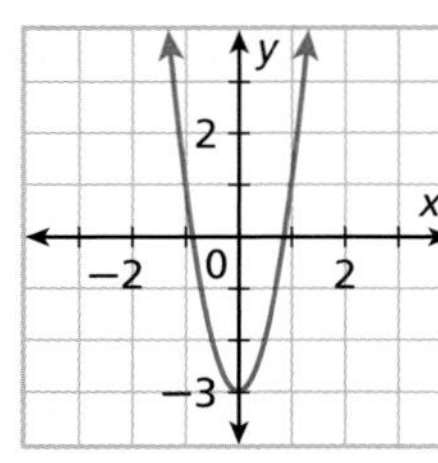

**C.** 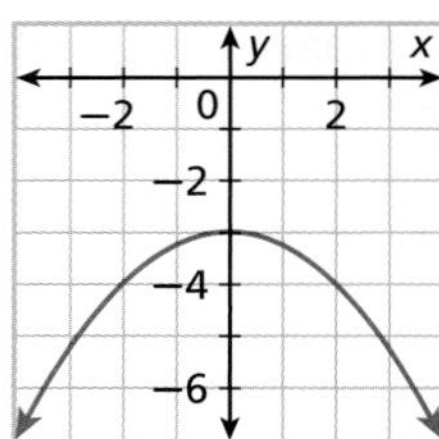

**D.** 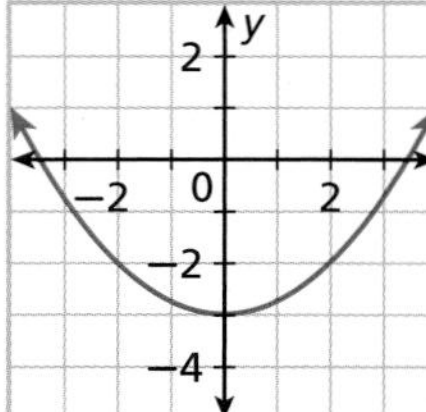

**33. Critical Thinking** For what values of $a$ and $c$ will $f(x) = ax^2 + c$ have one zero?

**34. Physics** The graph compares the heights of two identical coconuts that fell from different trees.

**a.** What are the starting heights of each coconut?

**b.** What is a possible function for the blue graph?

**c.** Estimate the time for each coconut to reach the ground.

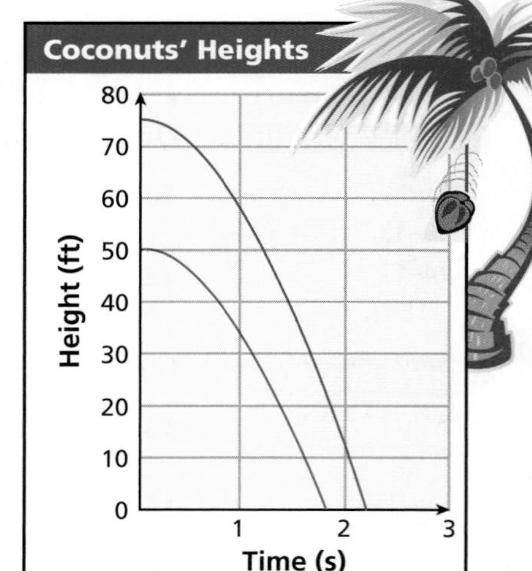


**35.** Give an example of a quadratic function for each description.

**a.** Its graph opens upward.

**b.** Its graph has the same width as in part **a,** but the graph opens downward.

**c.** Its graph is narrower than the graph in part **a.**

**36. Critical Thinking** Describe how the effect that the value of $c$ has on the graph of $y = x^2 + c$ is similar to the effect that the value of $b$ has on the graph of $y = x + b$.

**37. Write About It** Explain how you know, without graphing, what the graph of $f(x) = \frac{1}{10}x^2 - 5$ looks like.

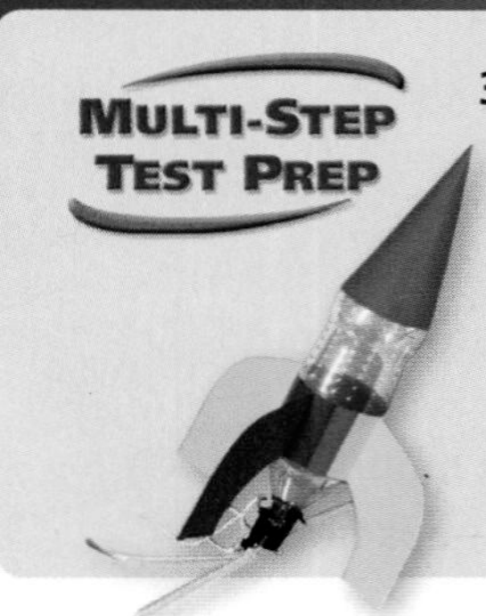


**38.** This problem will prepare you for the Multi-Step Test Prep on page 620.

**a.** Use a graphing calculator to graph $y = (x - 3)^2$. Compare this graph to the graph of $y = x^2$. How does this differ from $y = x^2 - 3$?

**b.** The equation $h = -16(x - 2)^2 + 64$ describes the height in feet of a water bottle rocket as a function of time. What is the highest point that the rocket will reach? When will it return to the ground?

**c.** How can the vertex be located from the equation? from the graph?

39. Which function's graph is the result of shifting the graph of $f(x) = -x^2 - 4$ 3 units down?

MA.A.4.3

Ⓐ $g(x) = -x^2 - 1$

Ⓑ $g(x) = -\frac{1}{3}x^2 - 4$

Ⓒ $g(x) = -4x^2 - 4$

Ⓓ $g(x) = -x^2 - 7$

40. Which of the following is true when the graph of $f(x) = x^2 + 4$ is transformed into the graph of $g(x) = 2x^2 + 4$?

Ⓕ The new function has more zeroes than the old function.

Ⓖ Both functions have the same vertex.

Ⓗ The function is translated up.

Ⓙ The axis of symmetry changes.

41. **Gridded Response** For what value of $c$ will $f(x) = x^2 + c$ have one zero?

## CHALLENGE AND EXTEND

42. **Graphing Calculator** Graph the functions $f(x) = (x + 1)^2$, $g(x) = (x + 4)^2$, $h(x) = (x - 2)^2$, and $k(x) = (x - 5)^2$. Make a conjecture about the result of transforming the graph of $f(x) = x^2$ into the graph of $f(x) = (x - h)^2$.

43. Using the function $f(x) = x^2$, write each new function:
    a. The graph is translated 7 units down.
    b. The graph is reflected across the $x$-axis and translated 2 units up.
    c. Each $y$-value is halved, and then the graph is translated 1 unit up.

## SPIRAL REVIEW

44. Justify each step. *(Lesson 1-7)*

| Procedure | Justification |
|---|---|
| $5x - 2(4 - x)$ | |
| $5x - 2(4 - x) = 5x - 8 + 2x$ | a. ? |
| $= 5x + 2x - 8$ | b. ? |
| $= (5x + 2x) - 8$ | c. ? |
| $= 7x - 8$ | d. ? |

**Describe the correlation illustrated by each scatter plot.** *(Lesson 4-5)*

45.

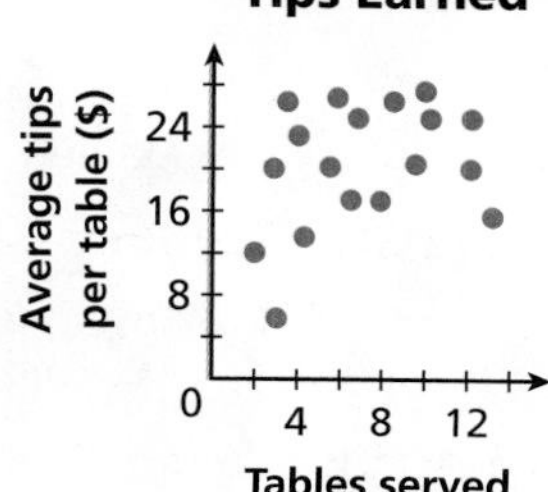


46.

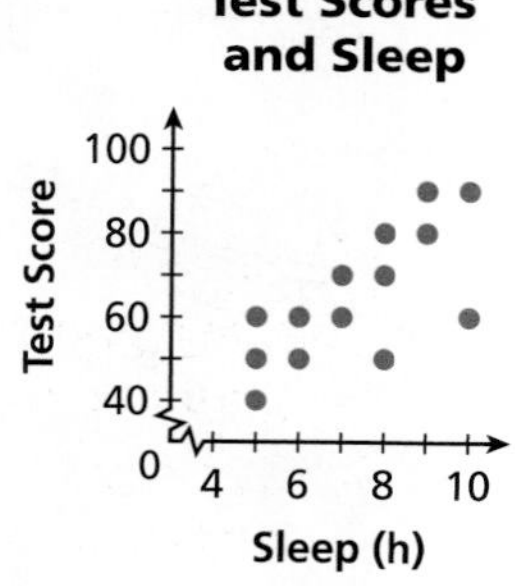


**Graph each quadratic function.** *(Lesson 9-3)*

47. $y = 2x^2 - 1$

48. $y = x^2 - 2x - 2$

49. $y = -3x^2 - x + 6$

CHAPTER 9

SECTION 9A

## Quadratic Functions

**The Sky's the Limit** The Physics Club is using computer simulation software to design a water bottle rocket that doesn't have a parachute. The data for their current design are shown in the table.

| Time (s) | Height (ft) |
|---|---|
| 0 | 0 |
| 1 | 80 |
| 2 | 128 |
| 3 | 144 |
| 4 | 128 |
| 5 | 80 |

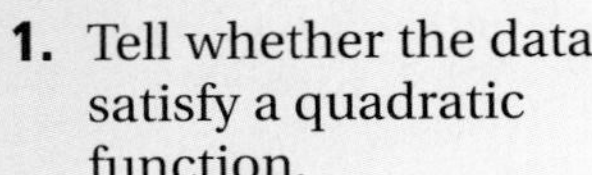

1. Tell whether the data satisfy a quadratic function.
2. Graph the function from Problem 1.

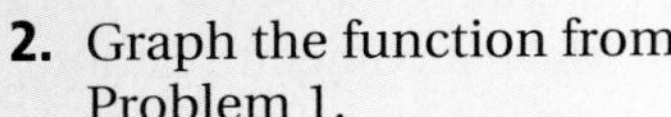

3. Find and label the zeros, axis of symmetry, and vertex.
4. Explain what the $x$- and $y$-coordinates of the vertex represent in the context of the problem.
5. Estimate how many seconds it will take the rocket to reach 110 feet. Explain.

# READY TO GO ON?

## Quiz for Lessons 9-1 Through 9-4

### 9-1 Identifying Quadratic Functions

**Tell whether each function is quadratic. Explain.**

1. $y + 2x^2 = 3x$
2. $x^2 + y = 4 + x^2$
3. $(-2, 12)(-1, 3)(0, 0)(1, 3)$

**Tell whether the graph of each quadratic function opens upward or downward and whether the parabola has a maximum or a minimum.**

4. $y = -x^2 - 7x + 18$
5. $y - 2x^2 = 4x + 3$
6. $f(x) = 5x - 0.5x^2$
7. Graph the function $y = \frac{1}{2}x^2 - 2$ and give the domain and range.

### 9-2 Characteristics of Quadratic Functions

**Find the zeros of each function from its graph. Then find its the axis of symmetry.**

8.
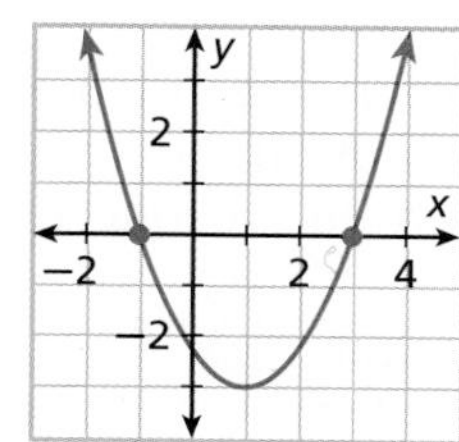


9.
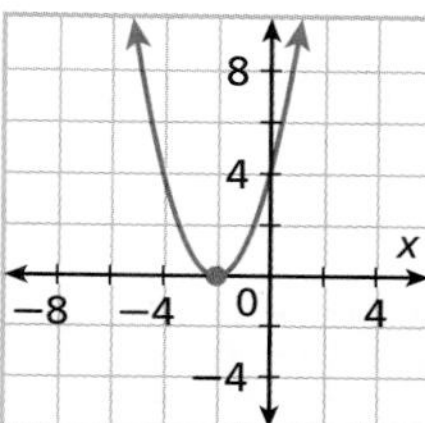


10.
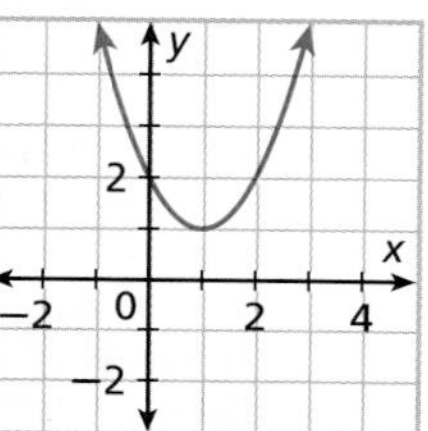


**Find the vertex of each parabola.**

11. $y = x^2 + 6x + 2$
12. $y = 3 + 4x - 2x^2$
13. $y = 3x^2 + 12x - 12$
14. The height in feet of the curved roof of an aircraft hangar can be modeled by $y = -0.02x^2 + 1.6x$, where $x$ is the distance in feet from one wall at ground level. How tall is the hangar?

### 9-3 Graphing Quadratic Functions

**Graph each quadratic function.**

15. $y = x^2 + 3x + 9$
16. $y = x^2 - 2x - 15$
17. $y = x^2 - 2x - 8$
18. $y = 2x^2 - 6$
19. $y = 4x^2 + 8x - 2$
20. $y = 2x^2 + 10x + 1$

### 9-4 Transforming Quadratic Functions

**Compare the graph of each function with the graph of $f(x) = x^2$.**

21. $g(x) = x^2 - 2$
22. $g(x) = \frac{2}{3}x^2$
23. $g(x) = 5x^2 + 3$
24. $g(x) = -x^2 + 4$
25. The pilot of a hot-air balloon drops a sandbag onto a target from a height of 196 feet. Later, he drops an identical sandbag from a height of 676 feet.
    a. Write the two height functions and compare their graphs. Use $h(t) = -16t^2 + c$, where $c$ is the height of the balloon.
    b. Use the graphs to tell when each sandbag will reach the ground.

# 9-5 Solving Quadratic Equations by Graphing

**MA.A.4.7** Use graphs…to solve quadratic equations.

***Objective***
Solve quadratic equations by graphing.

***Vocabulary***
quadratic equation

**Who uses this?**

Dolphin trainers can use solutions of quadratic equations to plan the choreography for their shows. (See Example 2.)

Every quadratic function has a related *quadratic equation*. A **quadratic equation** is an equation that can be written in the standard form $ax^2 + bx + c = 0$, where $a$, $b$, and $c$ are real numbers and $a \neq 0$.

When writing a quadratic function as its related quadratic equation, you replace $y$ with 0. So $y = 0$.

$$y = ax^2 + bx + c$$
$$0 = ax^2 + bx + c$$
$$ax^2 + bx + c = 0$$

One way to solve a quadratic equation in standard form is to graph the related function and find the $x$-values where $y = 0$. In other words, find the zeros of the related function. Recall that a quadratic function may have two, one, or no zeros.

| Solving Quadratic Equations by Graphing |
|---|
| **Step 1** Write the related function. |
| **Step 2** Graph the related function. |
| **Step 3** Find the zeros of the related function. |

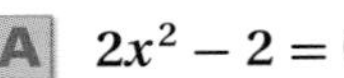


## Solving Quadratic Equations by Graphing

**Solve each equation by graphing the related function.**

**A** $2x^2 - 2 = 0$

**Step 1** Write the related function.

$2x^2 - 2 = y$, or $y = 2x^2 + 0x - 2$

**Step 2** Graph the function.

- The axis of symmetry is $x = 0$.
- The vertex is $(0, -2)$.
- Two other points are $(1, 0)$ and $(2, 6)$.
- Graph the points and reflect them across the axis of symmetry.

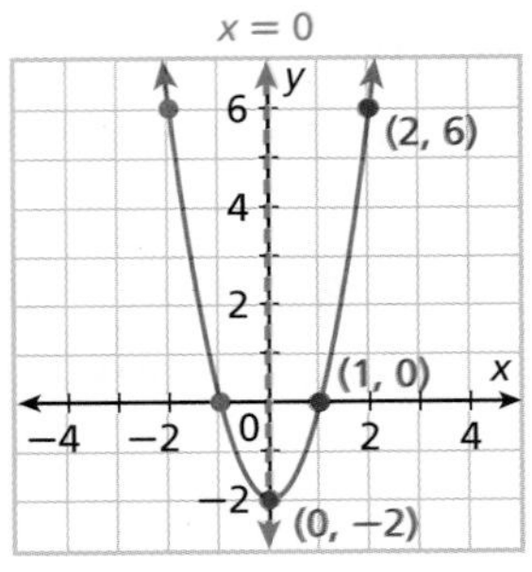


**Step 3** Find the zeros.

The zeros appear to be −1 and 1.

*Check*

| $2x^2 - 2 = 0$ | |
|---|---|
| $2(-1)^2 - 2$ | 0 |
| $2(1) - 2$ | 0 |
| $2 - 2$ | 0 |
| 0 | 0 ✓ |

*Substitute −1 and 1 for x in the quadratic equation.*

| $2x^2 - 2 = 0$ | |
|---|---|
| $2(1)^2 - 2$ | 0 |
| $2(1) - 2$ | 0 |
| $2 - 2$ | 0 |
| 0 | 0 ✓ |

**Solve each equation by graphing the related function.**

**B** $-x^2 - 4x - 4 = 0$

**Step 1** Write the related function.

$y = -x^2 - 4x - 4$

**Step 2** Graph the function.

- The axis of symmetry is $x = -2$.
- The vertex is $(-2, 0)$.
- The $y$-intercept is $-4$.
- Another point is $(-1, -1)$.
- Graph the points and **reflect** them across the axis of symmetry.

**Step 3** Find the zeros.

The only zero appears to be $-2$.

***Check***

$$\begin{array}{c|l} y = & -x^2 - 4x - 4 \\ \hline 0 & -(-2)^2 - 4(-2) - 4 \\ 0 & -(4) + 8 - 4 \\ 0 & -4 + 4 \\ 0 & 0 \checkmark \end{array}$$

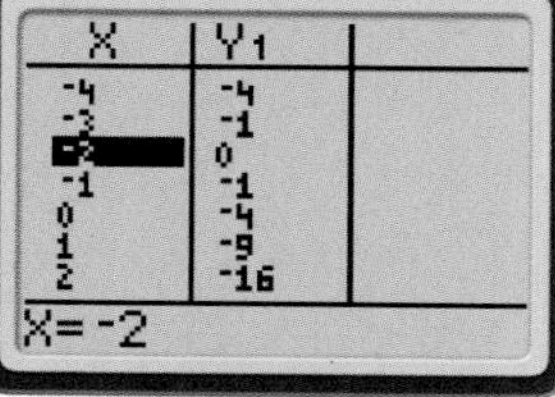


You can also confirm the solution by using the **Table** function. Enter the equation and press 2nd GRAPH (TABLE). When $y = 0$, $x = -2$. The $x$-intercept is $-2$.

**C** $x^2 + 5 = 4x$

**Step 1** Write the related function.

$x^2 - 4x + 5 = 0$

$y = x^2 - 4x + 5$

**Step 2** Graph the function.

Use a graphing calculator.

**Step 3** Find the zeros.

The function appears to have no zeros.

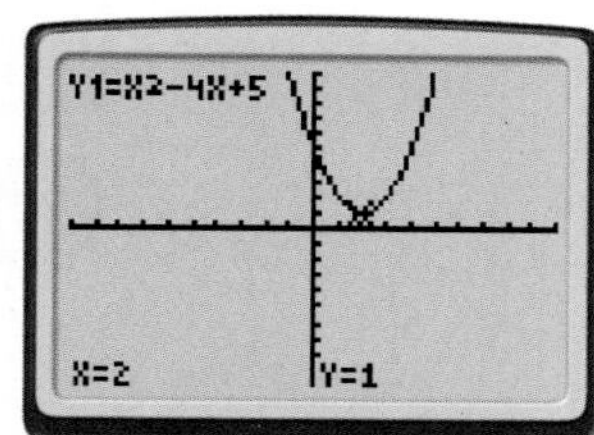


The equation has no real-number solutions.

***Check reasonableness*** Use the table function.

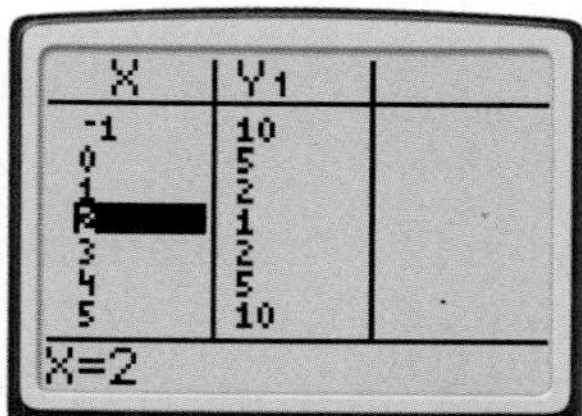


*There are no zeros in the Y1 column. Also, the signs of the values in this column do not change. The function appears to have no zeros.*

**Solve each equation by graphing the related function.**

**1a.** $x^2 - 8x - 16 = 2x^2$

**1b.** $6x + 10 = -x^2$

**1c.** $-x^2 + 4 = 0$

## EXAMPLE 2 Aquatics Application

**A dolphin jumps out of the water. The quadratic function $y = -16x^2 + 20x$ models the dolphin's height above the water after $x$ seconds. About how long is the dolphin out of the water?**

When the dolphin leaves the water, its height is 0, and when the dolphin reenters the water, its height is 0. So solve $0 = -16x^2 + 20x$ to find the times when the dolphin leaves and reenters the water.

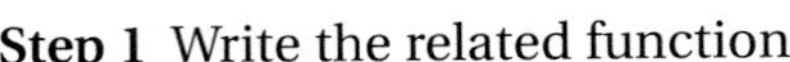

**Step 1** Write the related function.

$0 = -16x^2 + 20x$

$y = -16x^2 + 20x$

**Step 2** Graph the function.

Use a graphing calculator.

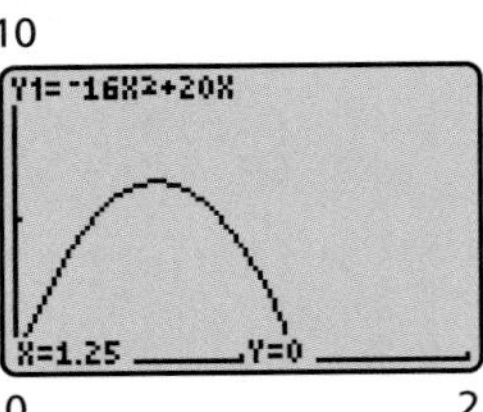


**Step 3** Use TRACE to estimate the zeros.

The zeros appear to be 0 and 1.25.

The dolphin leaves the water at 0 seconds and reenters the water at 1.25 seconds.

The dolphin is out of the water for about 1.25 seconds.

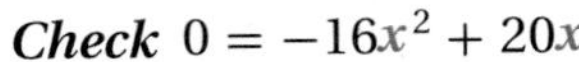

*Check* $0 = -16x^2 + 20x$

| | |
|---|---|
| 0 | $-16(1.25)^2 + 20(1.25)$ |
| 0 | $-16(1.5625) + 25$ |
| 0 | $-25 + 25$ |
| 0 | 0 ✓ |

*Substitute 1.25 for x in the quadratic equation.*

2. **What if...?** Another dolphin jumps out of the water. The quadratic function $y = -16x^2 + 32x$ models the dolphin's height above the water after $x$ seconds. About how long is the dolphin out of the water?

## THINK AND DISCUSS

1. Describe the graph of a quadratic function whose related quadratic equation has only one solution.
2. Describe the graph of a quadratic function whose related quadratic equation has no real solutions.
3. Describe the graph of a quadratic function whose related quadratic equation has two solutions.

4. **GET ORGANIZED** Copy and complete the graphic organizer. In each of the boxes, write the steps for solving quadratic equations by graphing.

Solving a Quadratic Equation by Graphing

| 1. | 2. | 3. |
|---|---|---|

# 9-5 Exercises

MA.A.4.7

go.hrw.com
Homework Help Online
KEYWORD: MA7 9-5
Parent Resources Online
KEYWORD: MA7 Parent

## GUIDED PRACTICE

1. **Vocabulary** Write two words related to the graph of the related function that can be used to find the solution of a *quadratic equation*.

SEE EXAMPLE 1 p. 622

**Solve each equation by graphing the related function.**

2. $x^2 - 4 = 0$
3. $x^2 = 16$
4. $-2x^2 - 6 = 0$
5. $-x^2 + 12x - 36 = 0$
6. $-x^2 = -9$
7. $2x^2 = 3x^2 - 2x - 8$
8. $x^2 - 6x + 9 = 0$
9. $8x = -4x^2 - 4$
10. $x^2 + 5x + 4 = 0$
11. $x^2 + 2 = 0$
12. $x^2 - 6x = 7$
13. $x^2 + 5x = -8$

SEE EXAMPLE 2 p. 624

14. **Sports** A baseball coach uses a pitching machine to simulate pop flies during practice. The baseball is shot out of the pitching machine with a velocity of 80 feet per second. The quadratic function $y = -16x^2 + 80x$ models the height of the baseball after $x$ seconds. How long is the baseball in the air?

## PRACTICE AND PROBLEM SOLVING

**Independent Practice**

| For Exercises | See Example |
|---|---|
| 15–23 | 1 |
| 24 | 2 |

**Extra Practice**

Skills Practice p. S21
Application Practice p. S36

**Solve each equation by graphing the related function.**

15. $-x^2 + 16 = 0$
16. $3x^2 = -7$
17. $5x^2 - 12x + 10 = x^2 + 10x$
18. $x^2 + 10x + 25 = 0$
19. $-4x^2 - 24x = 36$
20. $-9x^2 + 10x - 9 = -8x$
21. $-x^2 - 1 = 0$
22. $3x^2 - 27 = 0$
23. $4x^2 - 4x + 5 = 2x^2$
24. **Geography** Yosemite Falls in California is made of three smaller falls. The upper fall drops 1450 feet. The height $h$ in feet of a water droplet falling from the upper fall to the next fall is modeled by $h(t) = -16t^2 + 1450$, where $t$ is the time in seconds after the initial fall. Estimate the time it takes for the droplet to reach the next cascade.

**Tell whether each statement is always, sometimes, or never true.**

25. If the graph of a quadratic function has its vertex at the origin, then the related quadratic equation has exactly one solution.
26. If the graph of a quadratic function opens upward, then the related quadratic equation has two solutions.
27. If the graph of a quadratic function has its vertex on the $x$-axis, then the related quadratic equation has exactly one solution.
28. If the graph of a quadratic function has its vertex in the first quadrant, then the related quadratic equation has two solutions.
29. A quadratic equation in the form $ax^2 - c = 0$, where $a < 0$ and $c > 0$, has two solutions.

30. **Graphing Calculator** A fireworks shell is fired from a mortar. Its height is modeled by the function $h(t) = -16(t - 7)^2 + 784$, where $t$ is the time in seconds and $h$ is the height in feet.
    a. Graph the function.
    b. If the shell is supposed to explode at its maximum height, at what height should it explode?
    c. If the shell does not explode, how long will it take to return to the ground?

31. **Athletics** The graph shows the height $y$ in feet of a gymnast jumping off a vault after $x$ seconds.

   a. How long does the gymnast stay in the air?

   b. What is the maximum height that the gymnast reaches?

   c. Explain why the function $y = -5x^2 + 10x$ cannot accurately model the gymnast's motion.

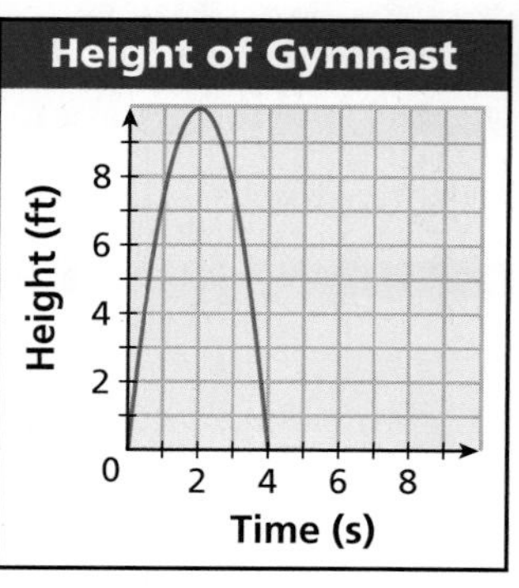


32. **Graphing Calculator** Use a graphing calculator to solve the equation $x^2 = x + 12$ by graphing $y_1 = x^2$ and $y_2 = x + 12$ and finding the $x$-coordinates of the points of intersection. (*Hint:* Find the points of intersection by using the 2nd CALC TRACE function after graphing.)

**LINK Biology**

Some species of kangaroos are able to jump 30 feet in distance and 6 feet in height.

33. **Biology** The quadratic function $y = -5x^2 + 7x$ approximates the height $y$ of a kangaroo $x$ seconds after it has jumped. About how long does it take the kangaroo to return to the ground?

**For Exercises 34–36, use the table to determine the solutions of the related quadratic equation.**

34.

| $x$ | $y$ |
|---|---|
| −2 | −1 |
| −1 | 0 |
| 0 | −1 |
| 1 | −4 |
| 2 | −9 |

35.

| $x$ | $y$ |
|---|---|
| −2 | −6 |
| −1 | 0 |
| 0 | 2 |
| 1 | 0 |
| 2 | −6 |

36.

| $x$ | $y$ |
|---|---|
| −2 | 6 |
| −1 | 3 |
| 0 | 2 |
| 1 | 3 |
| 2 | 6 |

37. **Geometry** The hypotenuse of a right triangle is 4 cm longer than one leg and 8 cm longer than the other leg. Let $x$ represent the length of the hypotenuse.

   a. Write an expression for the length of each leg in terms of $x$.

   b. Use the Pythagorean Theorem to write an equation that can be solved for $x$.

   c. Find the solutions of your equation from part **b.**

   d. **Critical Thinking** What do the solutions of your equation represent? Are both solutions reasonable? Explain.

38. **Write About It** Explain how to find solutions of a quadratic equation by analyzing a table of values.

39. **Critical Thinking** Explain why a quadratic equation in the form $ax^2 - c = 0$, where $a > 0$ and $c > 0$, will always have two solutions. Explain why a quadratic equation in the form $ax^2 + c = 0$, where $a > 0$ and $c > 0$, will never have any real-number solutions.

40. This problem will prepare you for the Multi-Step Test Prep on page 660. The quadratic equation $0 = -16t^2 + 80t$ gives the time $t$ in seconds when a golf ball is at height 0 feet.

   a. How long is the golf ball in the air?

   b. What is the maximum height of the golf ball?

   c. After how many seconds is the ball at its maximum height?

   d. What is the height of the ball after 3.5 seconds? Is there another time when the ball reaches that height? Explain.

MA.A.4.7

41. Use the graph to find the number of solutions of $-2x^2 + 2 = 0$.

Ⓐ 0 Ⓒ 2

Ⓑ 1 Ⓓ 3

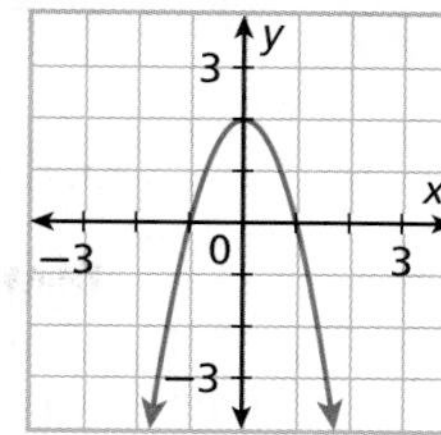

42. Which graph could be used to find the solutions of $x^2 = -4x + 12$?

Ⓕ

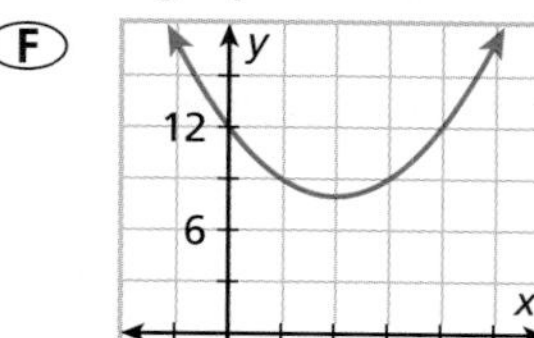

Ⓗ

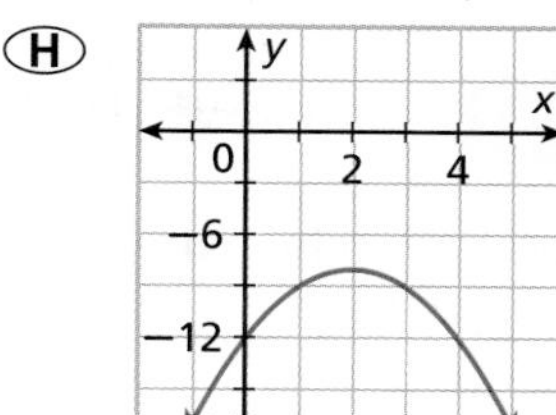

Ⓖ

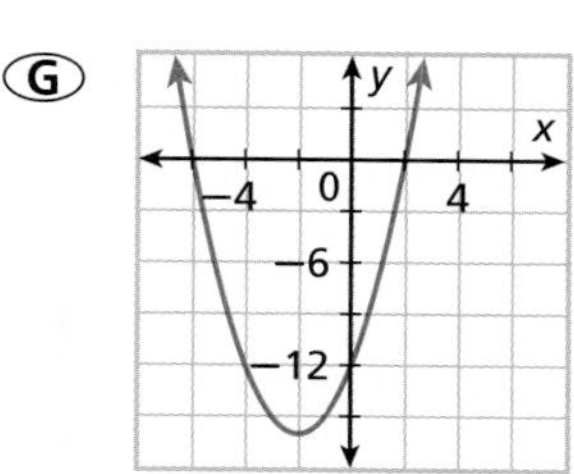

Ⓙ

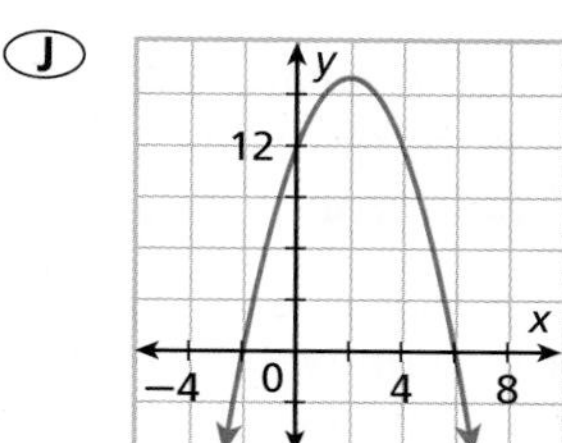

43. **Short Response** Find the solutions of $2x^2 + x - 1 = 0$ by graphing. Explain how the graph of the related function shows the solutions of the equation.

## CHALLENGE AND EXTEND

**Graphing Calculator** **Use a graphing calculator to find the solutions of each quadratic equation.**

44. $\frac{5}{16}x + \frac{1}{4}x^2 = \frac{3}{5}$

45. $1200x^2 - 650x - 100 = -200x - 175$

46. $\frac{1}{5}x + \frac{3}{4}x^2 = \frac{7}{12}$

47. $400x^2 - 100 = -300x + 456$

## SPIRAL REVIEW

**Write an equation in point-slope form for the line with the given slope that contains the given point.** *(Lesson 5-7)*

48. slope $= \frac{1}{2}$; $(2, 3)$

49. slope $= -3$; $(-2, 4)$

50. slope $= 0$; $(2, 1)$

**Simplify.** *(Lesson 7-4)*

51. $\frac{3^4}{3}$

52. $\frac{5^2 \cdot 2^4}{5 \cdot 2^2}$

53. $\frac{(x^4)^5}{(x^3)^3}$

54. $\left(\frac{x^3}{y^2}\right)^{-3}$

55. $\left(\frac{a^2b^3}{ab^2}\right)^3$

56. $\left(\frac{4s}{3t}\right)^{-2}$

57. $\left(\frac{2}{3}\right)^{-3} \cdot \left(\frac{a^3}{b}\right)^{-2}$

58. $\left(\frac{-k^2}{5k^3}\right)^{-3}$

**Compare the graph of each function with the graph of $f(x) = x^2$.** *(Lesson 9-4)*

59. $g(x) = 3x^2$

60. $g(x) = x^2 - 8$

61. $g(x) = \frac{3}{4}x^2 + 2$

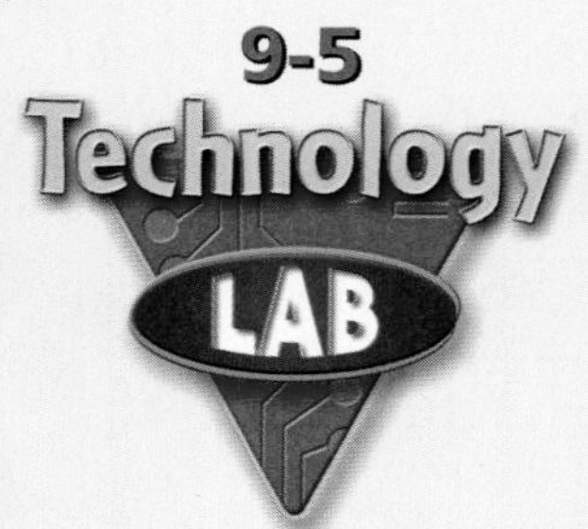


Use with Lesson 9-5

# Explore Roots, Zeros, and *x*-Intercepts

The solutions, or *roots*, of a quadratic equation are the $x$-intercepts, or zeros, of the related quadratic function. You can use tables or graphs on a graphing calculator to understand the connections between zeros, roots, and $x$-intercepts.

## Activity 1

**MA.A.4.7** Use graphs [and] tables…to solve quadratic equations. *Also* **MA.A.4.2**

**Solve $5x^2 + 8x - 4 = 0$ by using a table.**

1. Enter the related function in $\mathbf{Y_1}$.

2. Press 2nd GRAPH (TABLE) to use the **TABLE** function.

3. Scroll through the values by using ▲ and ▼. Look for values of 0 in the $\mathbf{Y_1}$ column. The corresponding $x$-value is a zero of the function. There is one zero at −2.

   Also look for places where the signs of nonzero $y$-values change. There is a zero between the corresponding $x$-values. So there is another zero somewhere between 0 and 1.

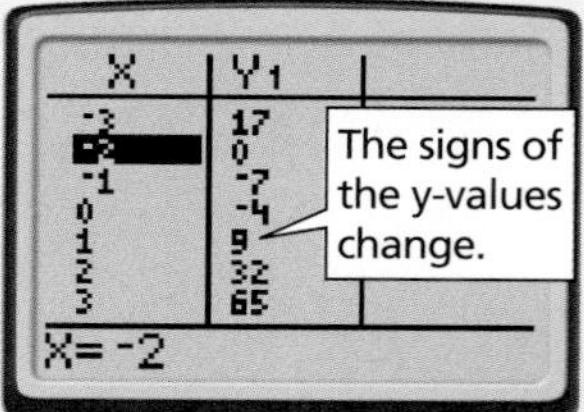


4. To get a better estimate of the zero, change the table settings. Press 2nd WINDOW (TBLSET) to view the **TABLE SETUP** screen. Set **TblStart = 0** and the step value **△Tbl = .1**. Press 2nd GRAPH (TABLE) to see the table again. The table will show you more $x$-values between 0 and 1.

5. Scroll through the values by using ▲ and ▼. The second zero is at 0.4.

   The zeros of the function, −2 and 0.4, are the solutions, or roots, of the equation $5x^2 + 8x - 4 = 0$. Check the solutions algebraically.

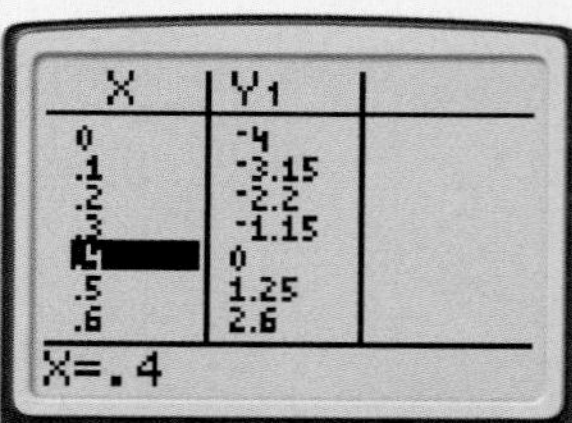


*Check*

| $5x^2 + 8x - 4 = 0$ | |
|---|---|
| $5(-2)^2 + 8(-2) - 4$ | $0$ |
| $5(4) - 16 - 4$ | $0$ |
| $20 - 16 - 4$ | $0$ |
| $0$ | $0$ ✓ |

| $5x^2 + 8x - 4 = 0$ | |
|---|---|
| $5(0.4)^2 + 8(0.4) - 4$ | $0$ |
| $5(0.16) + 3.2 - 4$ | $0$ |
| $0.8 + 3.2 - 4$ | $0$ |
| $0$ | $0$ ✓ |

## Try This

**Solve each equation by using a table.**

1. $x^2 - 4x - 5 = 0$
2. $x^2 - x - 6 = 0$
3. $2x^2 + x - 1 = 0$
4. $5x^2 - 6x - 8 = 0$
5. **Critical Thinking** How would you find the zero of a function that showed a sign change in the $y$-values between the $x$-values 1.2 and 1.3?
6. **Make a Conjecture** If you scrolled up and down the list and found only positive values, what might you conclude?

## Activity 2

**Solve $5x^2 + x - 8.4 = 0$ by using a table and a graph.**

1. Enter the related function in $\mathbf{Y_1}$.

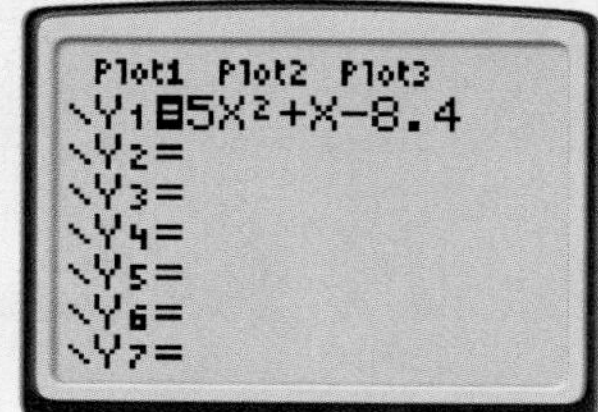


2. To view both the table and the graph at the same time, set your calculator to the Graph-Table mode. Press MODE and select **G-T**.

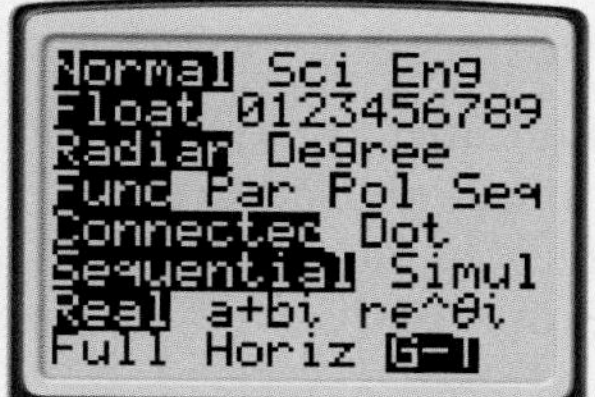


3. Press GRAPH. You should see the graph and the table. Notice that the function appears to have one negative zero and one positive zero near the $y$-axis.

4. To get a closer view of the graph, press ZOOM and select **4:ZDecimal**.

5. Press TRACE. Use ◀ to scroll to find the negative zero. The graph and the table show that the zero is $-1.4$.

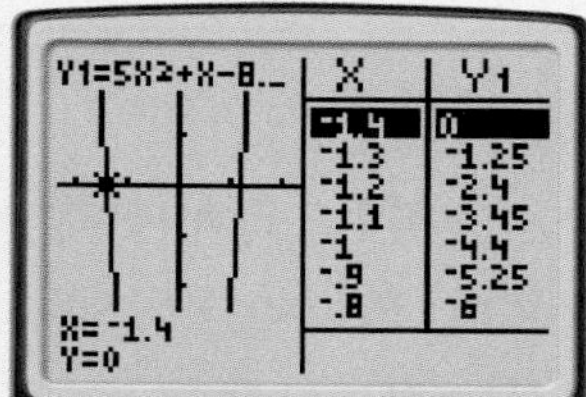


6. Use ▶ to scroll and find the positive zero. The graph and the table show that the zero is 1.2.

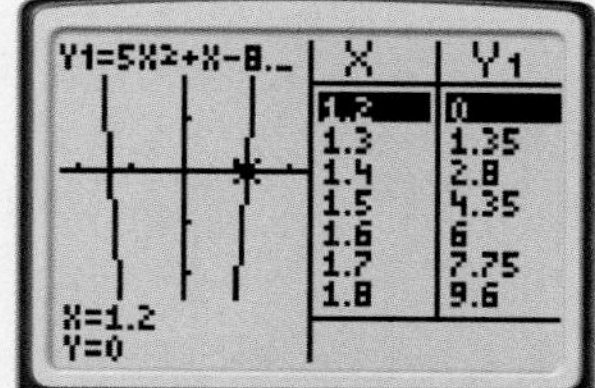


The solutions are $-1.4$ and 1.2. Check the solutions algebraically.

| $5x^2 + x - 8.4$ | $0$ |
|---|---|
| $5(-1.4)^2 + (-1.4) - 8.4$ | $0$ |
| $5(1.96) - 1.4 - 8.4$ | $0$ |
| $9.8 - 1.4 - 8.4$ | $0$ |
| $0$ | $0$ ✓ |

| $5x^2 + x - 8.4$ | $0$ |
|---|---|
| $5(1.2)^2 + (1.2) - 8.4$ | $0$ |
| $5(1.44) + 1.2 - 8.4$ | $0$ |
| $7.2 + 1.2 - 8.4$ | $0$ |
| $0$ | $0$ ✓ |

## Try This

**Solve each equation by using a table and a graph.**

**7.** $2x^2 - x - 3 = 0$ **8.** $5x^2 + 13x + 6 = 0$ **9.** $10x^2 - 3x - 4$ **10.** $x^2 - 2x - 0.96 = 0$

**11. Critical Thinking** Suppose that when you graphed a quadratic function, you could see only one side of the graph and one zero. What methods would you use to try to find the other zero?

# 9-6 Solving Quadratic Equations by Factoring

**MA.A.4.7** Use … properties to solve quadratic equations.

***Objective***
Solve quadratic equations by factoring.

**Who uses this?**
In order to determine how many seconds she will be in the air, a high diver can use a quadratic equation. (See Example 3.)

You have solved quadratic equations by graphing. Another method used to solve quadratic equations is to factor and use the Zero Product Property.

**Zero Product Property**

For all real numbers *a* and *b*,

| WORDS | NUMBERS | ALGEBRA |
|---|---|---|
| If the product of two quantities equals zero, at least one of the quantities equals zero. | $3(0) = 0$<br>$0(4) = 0$ | If $ab = 0$,<br>then $a = 0$ or $b = 0$. |

## EXAMPLE 1 Using the Zero Product Property

**Use the Zero Product Property to solve each equation. Check your answer.**

**A** $(x - 3)(x + 7) = 0$

$x - 3 = 0$ or $x + 7 = 0$ *Use the Zero Product Property.*

$x = 3$ or $x = -7$ *Solve each equation.*

The solutions are 3 and –7.

*Check*

| $(x-3)(x+7) = 0$ | |
|---|---|
| $(3-3)(3+7)$ | $0$ |
| $(0)(10)$ | $0$ |
| $0$ | $0$ ✓ |

*Substitute each solution for x into the original equation.*

| $(x-3)(x+7) = 0$ | |
|---|---|
| $(-7-3)(-7+7)$ | $0$ |
| $(-10)(0)$ | $0$ |
| $0$ | $0$ ✓ |

**B** $(x)(x - 5) = 0$

$x = 0$ or $x - 5 = 0$ *Use the Zero Product Property.*

$x = 5$ *Solve the second equation.*

The solutions are 0 and 5.

*Check*

| $(x)(x-5) = 0$ | |
|---|---|
| $(0)(0-5)$ | $0$ |
| $(0)(-5)$ | $0$ |
| $0$ | $0$ ✓ |

*Substitute each solution for x into the original equation.*

| $(x)(x-5) = 0$ | |
|---|---|
| $(5)(5-5)$ | $0$ |
| $(5)(0)$ | $0$ |
| $0$ | $0$ ✓ |

**Use the Zero Product Property to solve each equation. Check your answer.**

**1a.** $(x)(x + 4) = 0$ **1b.** $(x + 4)(x - 3) = 0$

If a quadratic equation is written in standard form, $ax^2 + bx + c = 0$, then to solve the equation, you may need to factor before using the Zero Product Property.

## EXAMPLE 2 Solving Quadratic Equations by Factoring

**Helpful Hint**

To review factoring techniques, see Lessons 8-3 through 8-5.

**Solve each quadratic equation by factoring.**

**A** $x^2 + 7x + 10 = 0$

| | |
|---|---|
| $(x + 5)(x + 2) = 0$ | *Factor the trinomial.* |
| $x + 5 = 0$ or $x + 2 = 0$ | *Use the Zero Product Property.* |
| $x = -5$ or $x = -2$ | *Solve each equation.* |

The solutions are $-5$ and $-2$.

***Check***

$$\begin{array}{r|l} x^2 + 7x + 10 & = 0 \\ \hline (-5)^2 + 7(-5) + 10 & 0 \\ 25 - 35 + 10 & 0 \\ 0 & 0 \checkmark \end{array} \qquad \begin{array}{r|l} x^2 + 7x + 10 & = 0 \\ \hline (-2)^2 + 7(-2) + 10 & 0 \\ 4 - 14 + 10 & 0 \\ 0 & 0 \checkmark \end{array}$$

**B** $x^2 + 2x = 8$

| | |
|---|---|
| $x^2 + 2x = 8$ <br> $-8 \quad -8$ <br> $x^2 + 2x - 8 = 0$ | *The equation must be written in standard form. So subtract 8 from both sides.* |
| $(x + 4)(x - 2) = 0$ | *Factor the trinomial.* |
| $x + 4 = 0$ or $x - 2 = 0$ | *Use the Zero Product Property.* |
| $x = -4$ or $x = 2$ | *Solve each equation.* |

The solutions are $-4$ and $2$.

***Check*** Graph the related quadratic function. The zeros of the related function should be the same as the solutions from factoring.

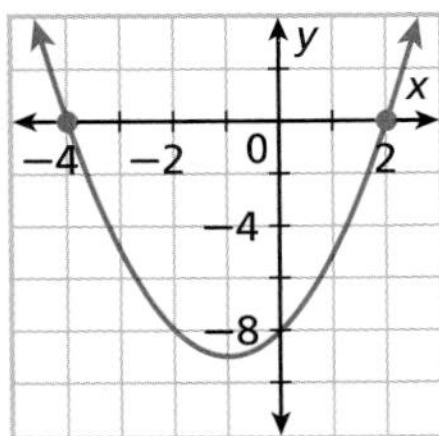


The graph of $y = x^2 + 2x - 8$ shows two zeros appear to be $-4$ and $2$, the same as the solutions from factoring. ✓

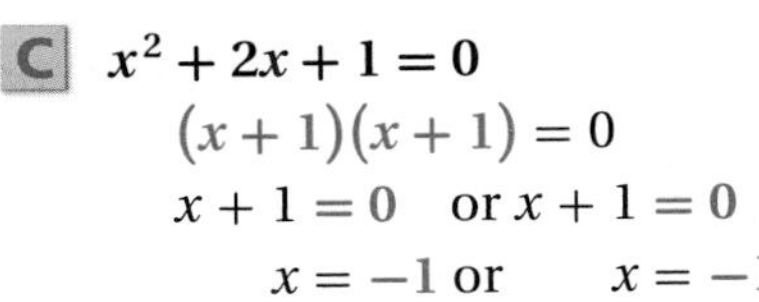

**C** $x^2 + 2x + 1 = 0$

| | |
|---|---|
| $(x + 1)(x + 1) = 0$ | *Factor the trinomial.* |
| $x + 1 = 0$ or $x + 1 = 0$ | *Use the Zero Product property.* |
| $x = -1$ or $x = -1$ | *Solve each equation.* |

Both factors result in the same solution, so there is one solution, $-1$.

***Check*** Graph the related quadratic function.

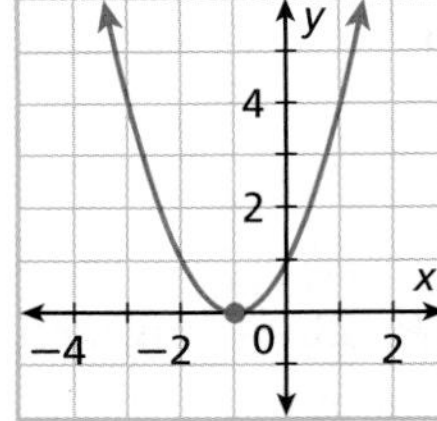


The graph of $y = x^2 + 2x + 1$ shows that one zero appears to be $-1$, the same as the solution from factoring. ✓

**Solve each quadratic equation by factoring.**

**D** $-2x^2 = 18 - 12x$

| | |
|---|---|
| $-2x^2 + 12x - 18 = 0$ | *Write the equation in standard form.* |
| $-2(x^2 - 6x + 9) = 0$ | *Factor out the GCF, −2.* |
| $-2(x-3)(x-3) = 0$ | *Factor the trinomial.* |
| $-2 \neq 0$ or $x - 3 = 0$ | *Use the Zero Product Property. −2 cannot equal 0.* |
| $x = 3$ | *Solve the remaining equation.* |

The only solution is 3.

*Check* $-2x^2 = 18 - 12x$

| | | |
|---|---|---|
| $-2(3)^2$ | $18 - 12(3)$ | *Substitute 3 into the original equation.* |
| $-18$ | $18 - 36$ | |
| $-18$ | $-18$ ✓ | |

**Helpful Hint**

$(x - 3)(x - 3)$ is a perfect square. Since both factors are the same, you solve only one of them.

**Solve each quadratic equation by factoring. Check your answer.**

**2a.** $x^2 - 6x + 9 = 0$  **2b.** $x^2 + 4x = 5$

**2c.** $30x = -9x^2 - 25$  **2d.** $3x^2 - 4x + 1 = 0$

## EXAMPLE 3 *Sports Application*

**The height of a diver above the water during a dive can be modeled by $h = -16t^2 + 8t + 48$, where $h$ is height in feet and $t$ is time in seconds. Find the time it takes for the diver to reach the water.**

| | |
|---|---|
| $h = -16t^2 + 8t + 48$ | |
| $0 = -16t^2 + 8t + 48$ | *The diver reaches the water when $h = 0$.* |
| $0 = -8(2t^2 - t - 6)$ | *Factor out the GCF, −8.* |
| $0 = -8(2t + 3)(t - 2)$ | *Factor the trinomial.* |
| $-8 \neq 0$, $2t + 3 = 0$ or $t - 2 = 0$ | *Use the Zero Product Property.* |
| $2t = -3$ or $t = 2$ | *Solve each equation.* |
| $t = -\frac{3}{2}$ ✗ | *Since time cannot be negative, $-\frac{3}{2}$ does not make sense in this situation.* |

It takes the diver 2 seconds to reach the water.

*Check* $0 = -16t^2 + 8t + 48$

| | | |
|---|---|---|
| 0 | $-16(2)^2 + 8(2) + 48$ | *Substitute 2 into the original equation.* |
| 0 | $-64 + 16 + 48$ | |
| 0 | 0 ✓ | |

**3. What if...?** The equation for the height above the water for another diver can be modeled by $h = -16t^2 + 8t + 24$. Find the time it takes this diver to reach the water.

## THINK AND DISCUSS

1. Explain two ways to solve $x^2 + x - 6 = 0$. How are these two methods similar?
2. For the quadratic equation $0 = (x + 2)(x - 6)$, what are the $x$-intercepts of the related function?

3. **GET ORGANIZED** Copy and complete the graphic organizer. In each box, write a step used to solve a quadratic equation by factoring.

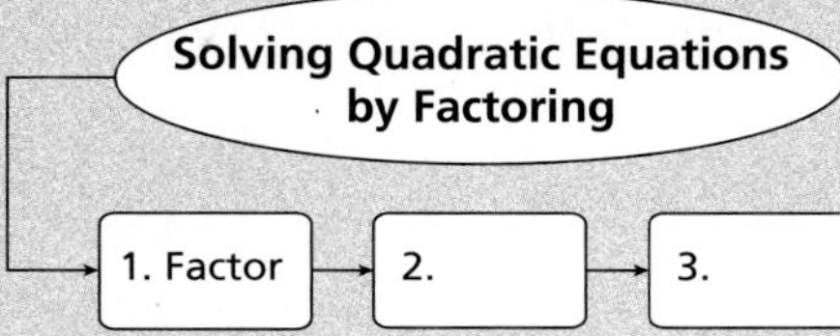


# 9-6 Exercises

## GUIDED PRACTICE

SEE EXAMPLE 1 p. 630

**Use the Zero Product Property to solve each equation. Check your answer.**

1. $(x + 2)(x - 8) = 0$
2. $(x - 6)(x - 5) = 0$
3. $(x + 7)(x + 9) = 0$
4. $(x)(x - 1) = 0$
5. $(x)(x + 11) = 0$
6. $(3x + 2)(4x - 1) = 0$

SEE EXAMPLE 2 p. 631

**Solve each quadratic equation by factoring. Check your answer.**

7. $x^2 + 4x - 12 = 0$
8. $x^2 - 8x - 9 = 0$
9. $x^2 - 5x + 6 = 0$
10. $x^2 - 3x = 10$
11. $x^2 + 10x = -16$
12. $x^2 + 2x = 15$
13. $x^2 - 8x + 16 = 0$
14. $-3x^2 = 18x + 27$
15. $x^2 + 36 = 12x$
16. $x^2 + 14x + 49 = 0$
17. $x^2 - 16x + 64 = 0$
18. $2x^2 + 6x = -18$

SEE EXAMPLE 3 p. 632

19. **Games** A group of friends tries to keep a beanbag from touching the ground without using their hands. Once the beanbag has been kicked, its height can be modeled by $h = -16t^2 + 14t + 2$, where $h$ is the height in feet above the ground and $t$ is the time in seconds. Find the time it takes the beanbag to reach the ground.

## PRACTICE AND PROBLEM SOLVING

**Independent Practice**

| For Exercises | See Example |
|---|---|
| 20–25 | 1 |
| 26–31 | 2 |
| 32 | 3 |

**Extra Practice**

Skills Practice p. S21
Application Practice p. S36

**Use the Zero Product Property to solve each equation. Check your answer.**

20. $(x - 8)(x + 6) = 0$
21. $(x + 4)(x + 7) = 0$
22. $(x - 2)(x - 5) = 0$
23. $(x - 9)(x) = 0$
24. $(x)(x + 25) = 0$
25. $(2x + 1)(3x - 1) = 0$

**Solve each quadratic equation by factoring. Check your answer.**

26. $x^2 + 8x + 15 = 0$
27. $x^2 - 2x - 8 = 0$
28. $x^2 - 4x + 3 = 0$
29. $x^2 + 10x + 25 = 0$
30. $x^2 - x = 12$
31. $-x^2 = 4x + 4$

32. **Multi-Step** The height of a flare can be approximated by the function $h = -16t^2 + 95t + 6$, where $h$ is the height in feet and $t$ is the time in seconds. Find the time it takes the flare to hit the ground.

**Determine the number of solutions of each equation.**

33. $(x + 8)(x + 8) = 0$
34. $(x - 3)(x + 3) = 0$
35. $(x + 7)^2 = 0$
36. $3x^2 + 12x + 9 = 0$
37. $x^2 + 12x + 40 = 4$
38. $(x - 2)^2 = 9$

39. **ERROR ANALYSIS** Which solution is incorrect? Explain the error.

A

$x^2 + x - 2 = 0$
$(x - 1)(x + 2) = 0$
$x = 1$ or $x = -2$

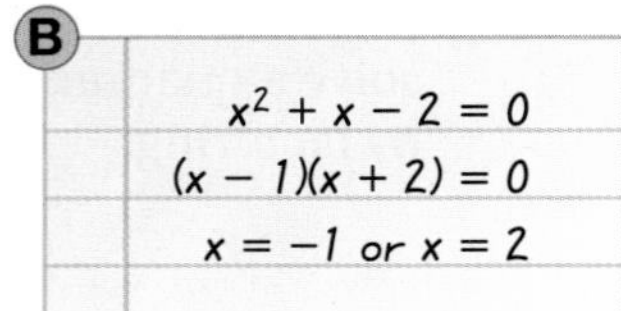
B

$x^2 + x - 2 = 0$
$(x - 1)(x + 2) = 0$
$x = -1$ or $x = 2$

40. **Number Theory** Write an equation that could be used to find two consecutive even integers whose product is 24. Let $x$ represent the first integer. Solve the equation and give the two integers.

41. **Geometry** The photo shows a traditional thatched house as found in Santana, Madeira in Portugal. The front of the house is in the shape of a triangle. Suppose the base of the triangle is 1 m less than its height and the area of the triangle is 15 $m^2$. Find the height of the triangle. (*Hint:* Use $A = \frac{1}{2}bh$.)

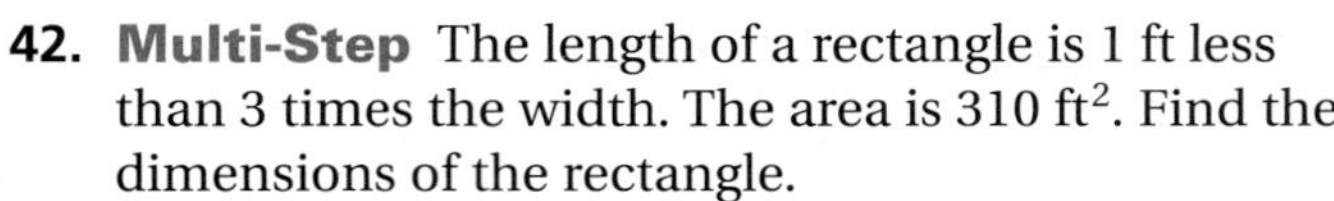

42. **Multi-Step** The length of a rectangle is 1 ft less than 3 times the width. The area is 310 $ft^2$. Find the dimensions of the rectangle.

43. **Physics** The height of a fireworks rocket in meters can be approximated by $h = -5t^2 + 30t$, where $h$ is the height in meters and $t$ is time in seconds. Find the time it takes the rocket to reach the ground after it has been launched.

44. **Geometry** One base of a trapezoid is the same length as the height of the trapezoid. The other base is 4 cm more than the height. The area of the trapezoid is 48 $cm^2$. Find the length of the shorter base. (*Hint:* Use $A = \frac{1}{2}h(b_1 + b_2)$.)

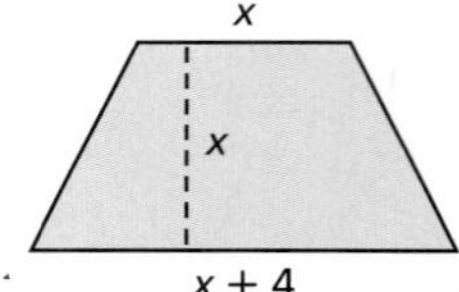


45. **Critical Thinking** Can you solve $(x - 2)(x + 3) = 5$ by solving $x - 2 = 5$ and $x + 3 = 5$? Why or why not?

46. **Write About It** Explain why you set each factor equal to zero when solving a quadratic equation by factoring.

**MULTI-STEP TEST PREP**

47. This problem will prepare you for the Multi-Step Test Prep on page 660.

A tee box is 48 feet above its fairway. Starting with an initial elevation of 48 ft at the tee box and an initial velocity of 32 ft/s, the quadratic equation $0 = -16t^2 + 32t + 48$ gives the time $t$ in seconds when a golf ball is at height 0 feet on the fairway.

a. Solve the quadratic equation by factoring to see how long the ball is in the air.
b. What is the height of the ball at 1 second?
c. Is the ball at its maximum height at 1 second? Explain.

MA.A.4.7

48. What are the solutions to $(x - 1)(2x + 5) = 0$?

Ⓐ $-1$ and $\frac{5}{2}$

Ⓑ $-1$ and $\frac{2}{5}$

Ⓒ $1$ and $-\frac{5}{2}$

Ⓓ $1$ and $-\frac{2}{5}$

49. Which graph could be used to solve the quadratic equation $x^2 - 5x + 6 = 0$?

Ⓕ

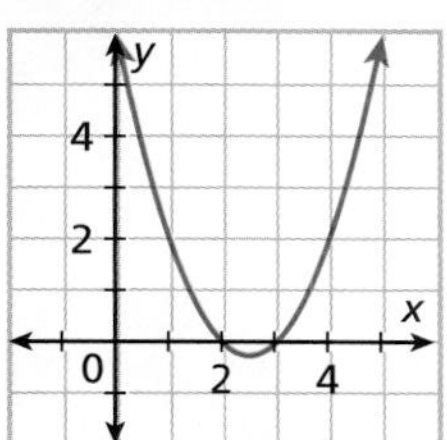

Ⓗ

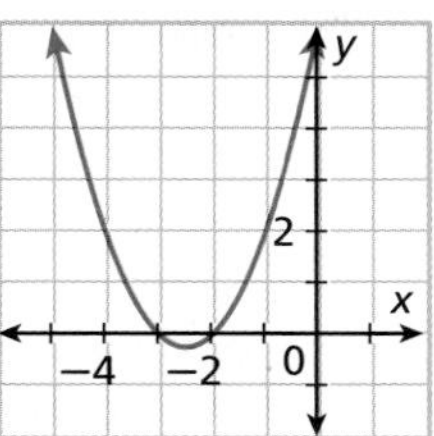


Ⓖ

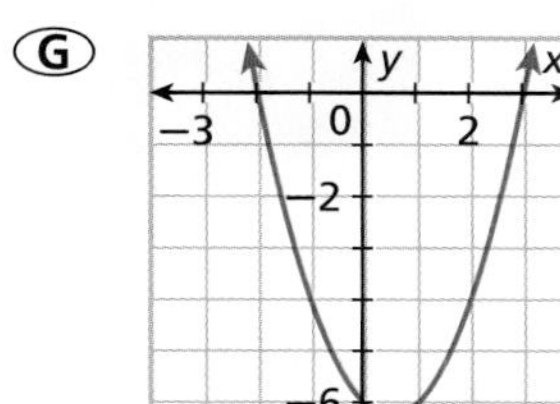


Ⓙ

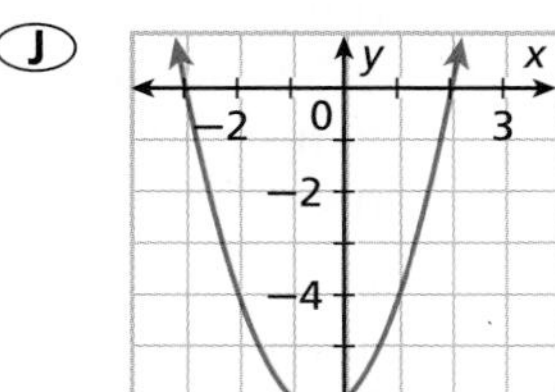


## CHALLENGE AND EXTEND

**Solve each quadratic equation by factoring.**

50. $6x^2 + 11x = 10$

51. $0.2x^2 + 1 = -1.2x$

52. $\frac{1}{3}x^2 = 2x - 3$

53. $75x - 45 = -30x^2$

54. $x^2 = -4(2x + 3)$

55. $\frac{x(x - 3)}{2} = 5$

**Geometry** **Use the diagram for Exercises 56–58.**

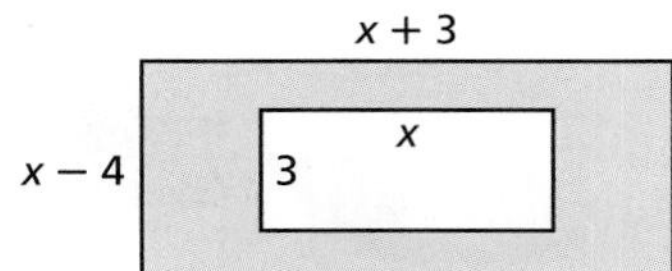


56. Write a polynomial to represent the area of the larger rectangle.

57. Write a polynomial to represent the area of the smaller rectangle.

58. Write a polynomial to represent the area of the shaded region, then solve for $x$ given that the area of the shaded region is 48 square units.

## SPIRAL REVIEW

**Write an algebraic expression for each situation.** *(Lesson 1-1)*

59. Veronica's height, if she is 4 inches shorter than her friend, and her friend is $f$ inches tall

60. The number of tires needed to build $m$ minivans, including 1 spare tire for each minivan.

**Find each square root.** *(Lesson 1-5)*

61. $\sqrt{121}$

62. $-\sqrt{64}$

63. $-\sqrt{100}$

64. $\sqrt{225}$

**Solve each equation by graphing the related function.** *(Lesson 9-5)*

65. $x^2 - 49 = 0$

66. $x^2 = x + 12$

67. $-x^2 + 8x = 15$

# 9-7 Solving Quadratic Equations by Using Square Roots

**MA.A.4.7** Use...properties to solve quadratic equations.
*Also* **MA.N.2.3, MA.G.2.2**

***Objective***
Solve quadratic equations by using square roots.

**Why learn this?**
Square roots can be used to find how much fencing is needed for a pen at a zoo. (See Example 4.)

Some quadratic equations cannot be easily solved by factoring. Square roots can be used to solve some of these quadratic equations. Recall from Lesson 1–5 that every positive real number has two square roots, one positive and one negative.

$$3(3) = 3^2 = 9 \longrightarrow \sqrt{9} = 3 \quad \leftarrow \text{Positive square root of 9}$$

$$(-3)(-3) = (-3)^2 = 9 \longrightarrow -\sqrt{9} = -3 \quad \leftarrow \text{Negative square root of 9}$$

The expression $\pm 3$ is read "plus or minus three."

When you take the square root of a positive real number and the sign of the square root is not indicated, you must find both the positive and negative square root. This is indicated by $\pm\sqrt{\ }$.

$$\pm\sqrt{9} = \pm 3 \quad \leftarrow \text{Positive and negative square roots of 9}$$

**Square-Root Property**

| WORDS | NUMBERS | ALGEBRA |
|---|---|---|
| To solve a quadratic equation in the form $x^2 = a$, take the square root of both sides. | $x^2 = 15$<br>$x = \pm\sqrt{15}$ | If $x^2 = a$ and $a$ is a positive real number, then $x = \pm\sqrt{a}$. |

## EXAMPLE 1 Using Square Roots to Solve $x^2 = a$

**Solve using square roots.**

**A** $x^2 = 16$

$x = \pm\sqrt{16}$ — *Solve for x by taking the square root of both sides. Use ± to show both square roots.*

$x = \pm 4$

The solutions are 4 and −4.

***Check***

| $x^2 = 16$ | |
|---|---|
| $(4)^2$ | 16 |
| 16 | 16 ✓ |

*Substitute 4 and −4 into the original equation.*

| $x^2 = 16$ | |
|---|---|
| $(-4)^2$ | 16 |
| 16 | 16 ✓ |

**Solve using square roots.**

**B** $x^2 = -4$

$x = \pm\sqrt{-4}$ *There is no real number whose square is negative.*

There is no real solution.

**Solve using square roots. Check your answer.**

**1a.** $x^2 = 121$ **1b.** $x^2 = 0$ **1c.** $x^2 = -16$

If a quadratic equation is not written in the form $x^2 = a$, use inverse operations to isolate $x^2$ before taking the square root of both sides.

## EXAMPLE 2 Using Square Roots to Solve Quadratic Equations

**Solve using square roots.**

**A** $x^2 + 5 = 5$

$$x^2 + 5 = 5$$

$$\underline{-5 \quad -5}$$ *Subtract 5 from both sides.*

$$x^2 = 0$$

$$x = \pm\sqrt{0} = 0$$ *Take the square root of both sides.*

The solution is 0.

**Helpful Hint**

The square root of 0 is neither positive nor negative. It is only 0.

**B** $4x^2 - 25 = 0$

$$4x^2 - 25 = 0$$

$$\underline{+25 \quad +25}$$ *Add 25 to both sides.*

$$\frac{4x^2}{4} = \frac{25}{4}$$ *Divide by 4 on both sides.*

$$x^2 = \frac{25}{4}$$

$$x = \pm\sqrt{\frac{25}{4}} = \pm\frac{5}{2}$$ *Take the square root of both sides. Use ± to show both square roots.*

The solutions are $\frac{5}{2}$ and $-\frac{5}{2}$.

*Check*

| $4x^2 - 25 = 0$ | |
|---|---|
| $4\left(\frac{5}{2}\right)^2 - 25$ | 0 |
| $\cancel{4}\left(\frac{25}{\cancel{4}}\right) - 25$ | 0 |
| $25 - 25$ | 0 ✓ |

| $4x^2 - 25 = 0$ | |
|---|---|
| $4\left(-\frac{5}{2}\right)^2 - 25$ | 0 |
| $\cancel{4}\left(\frac{25}{\cancel{4}}\right) - 25$ | 0 |
| $25 - 25$ | 0 ✓ |

**Solve by using square roots. Check your answer.**

**2a.** $100x^2 + 49 = 0$ **2b.** $36x^2 = 1$

When solving quadratic equations by using square roots, you may need to find the square root of a number that is not a perfect square. In this case, the answer is an irrational number. You can approximate the solutions.

## EXAMPLE 3 Approximating Solutions

**Solve. Round to the nearest hundredth.**

**A** $x^2 = 10$

$x = \pm\sqrt{10}$ *Take the square root of both sides.*

$x \approx \pm 3.16$ *Evaluate $\sqrt{10}$ on a calculator.*

The approximate solutions are 3.16 and −3.16.

**Solve. Round to the nearest hundredth.**

**B** $0 = -2x^2 + 80$

$$\begin{aligned} 0 &= -2x^2 + 80 \\ \underline{-80} \quad & \quad \underline{\quad\quad -80} \\ \frac{-80}{-2} &= \frac{-2x^2}{-2} \\ 40 &= x^2 \\ \pm\sqrt{40} &= x \\ x &\approx \pm 6.32 \end{aligned}$$

*Subtract 80 from both sides.*

*Divide by −2 on both sides.*

*Take the square root of both sides.*

*Evaluate $\sqrt{40}$ on a calculator.*

The approximate solutions are 6.32 and −6.32.

***Check*** Use a graphing calculator to support your answer.

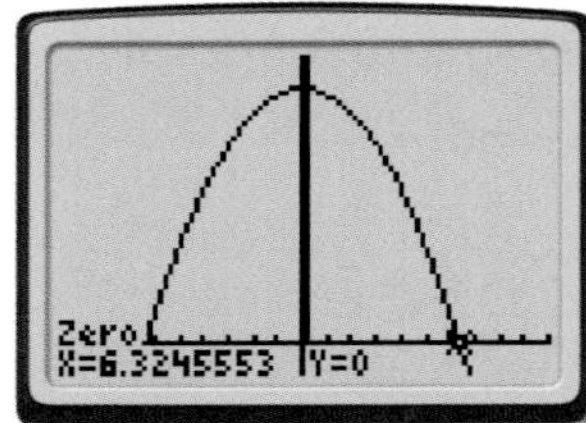


Use the zero function.
The approximate solutions are 6.32 and −6.32. ✓

**Solve. Round to the nearest hundredth.**

**3a.** $0 = 90 - x^2$ **3b.** $2x^2 - 64 = 0$ **3c.** $x^2 + 45 = 0$

## EXAMPLE 4 *Consumer Application*

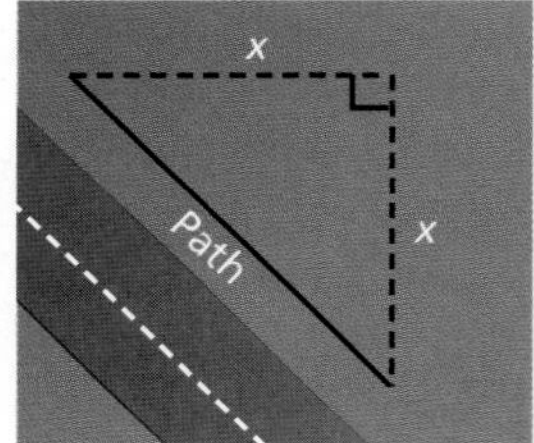


**A zookeeper is buying fencing to enclose a pen at the zoo. The pen is an isosceles right triangle. There is already a fence on the side that borders a path. The area of the pen will be 4500 square feet. The zookeeper can buy the fencing in whole feet only. How many feet of fencing should he buy?**

Let $x$ represent the length of one of the sides.

$\frac{1}{2}bh = A$ *Use the formula for area of a triangle.*

$\frac{1}{2}x(x) = 4500$ *Substitute x for both b and h and 4500 for A.*

$(2)\frac{1}{2}x^2 = 4500(2)$ *Simplify. Multiply both sides by 2.*

$x = \pm\sqrt{9000}$ *Take the square root of both sides.*

$x \approx \pm 94.9$ *Evaluate $\sqrt{9000}$ on a calculator.*

Negative numbers are not reasonable for length, so $x \approx 94.9$ is the only solution that makes sense. Therefore, the zookeeper needs 95 + 95, or 190, feet of fencing.

**Remember!**

An isosceles triangle has at least two sides of the same length.

**4.** A house is on a lot that is shaped like a trapezoid. The solid lines show the boundaries, where $x$ represents the width of the front yard. Find the width of the front yard, given that the area is 6000 square feet. Round to the nearest foot. (*Hint:* Use $A = \frac{1}{2}h(b_1 + b_2)$.)

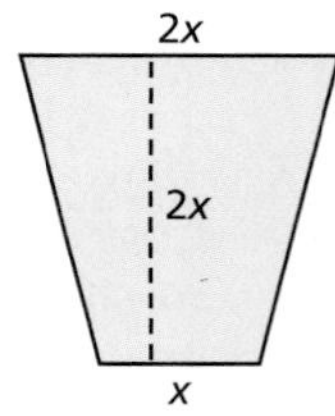

## THINK AND DISCUSS

1. Explain why there are no solutions to the quadratic equation $x^2 = -9$.
2. Describe how to estimate the solutions of $4 = x^2 - 16$. What are the approximate solutions?

3. **GET ORGANIZED** Copy and complete the graphic organizer. In each box, write an example of a quadratic equation with the given number of solutions. Solve each equation.

| Solving Quadratic Equations by Using Square Roots When the Equation Has... | | |
|---|---|---|
| No real solutions | One solution | Two solutions |

# 9-7 Exercises

MA.A.4.7, MA.N.2.3, MA.G.2.2

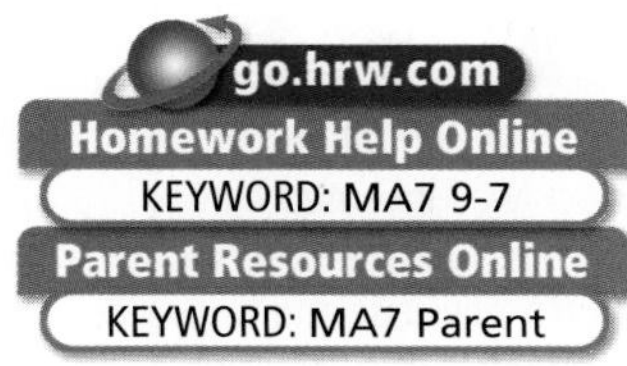


## GUIDED PRACTICE

SEE EXAMPLE 1 p. 636

**Solve using square roots. Check your answer.**

1. $x^2 = 225$
2. $x^2 = 49$
3. $x^2 = -100$
4. $x^2 = 400$
5. $-25 = x^2$
6. $36 = x^2$

SEE EXAMPLE 2 p. 637

7. $3x^2 - 75 = 0$
8. $0 = 81x^2 - 25$
9. $49x^2 + 64 = 0$
10. $16x^2 + 10 = 131$
11. $0 = 4x^2 - 16$
12. $100x^2 + 26 = 10$

SEE EXAMPLE 3 p. 637

**Solve. Round to the nearest hundredth.**

13. $3x^2 = 81$
14. $0 = x^2 - 60$
15. $100 - 5x^2 = 0$

SEE EXAMPLE 4 p. 638

16. **Geometry** The length of a rectangle is 3 times its width. The area of the rectangle is 170 square meters. Find the width. Round to the nearest tenth of a meter. (*Hint:* Use $A = bh$.)

## PRACTICE AND PROBLEM SOLVING

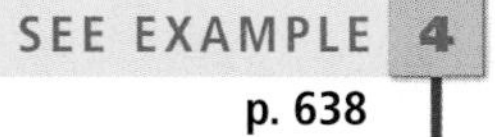


| For Exercises | See Example |
|---|---|
| 17–22 | 1 |
| 23–28 | 2 |
| 29–34 | 3 |
| 35 | 4 |

**Extra Practice**
Skills Practice p. S21
Application Practice p. S36

**Solve using square roots. Check your answer.**

17. $x^2 = 169$
18. $x^2 = 25$
19. $x^2 = -36$
20. $x^2 = 10{,}000$
21. $-121 = x^2$
22. $625 = x^2$
23. $4 - 81x^2 = 0$
24. $-4x^2 - 49 = 0$
25. $64x^2 - 5 = 20$
26. $9x^2 + 9 = 25$
27. $49x^2 + 1 = 170$
28. $81x^2 + 17 = 81$

**Solve. Round to the nearest hundredth.**

29. $4x^2 = 88$
30. $x^2 - 29 = 0$
31. $x^2 + 40 = 144$
32. $3x^2 - 84 = 0$
33. $50 - x^2 = 0$
34. $2x^2 - 10 = 64$

35. **Entertainment** For a scene in a movie, a sack of money is dropped from the roof of a 600 ft skyscraper. The height of the sack above the ground is given by $h = -16t^2 + 600$, where $t$ is the time in seconds. How long will it take the sack to reach the ground? Round to the nearest tenth of a second.

36. **Geometry** The area of a square is 196 $m^2$. Find the dimensions of the square.

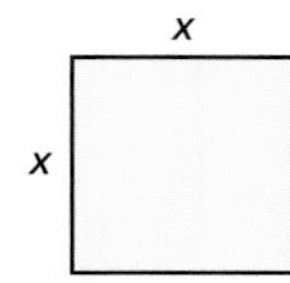


37. **Number Theory** If $a = 2b$ and $2ab = 36$, find all possible solutions for $a$ and $b$.

38. **Geometry** The geometric mean of two positive numbers $a$ and $b$ is the positive number $x$ such that $\frac{a}{x} = \frac{x}{b}$. Find the geometric mean of 2 and 18.

**LINK**

**Physics**

The first pendulum clock was invented by Christian Huygens, a Dutch physicist and mathematician, around 1656. Early pendulum clocks swung about 50° to the left and right. Modern pendulum clocks swing only 10° to 15°.

39. **Estimation** The area $y$ of any rectangle with side length $x$ and one side twice as long as the other is represented by $y = 2x^2$. Use the graph to estimate the dimensions of such a rectangle whose area is 35 square feet.

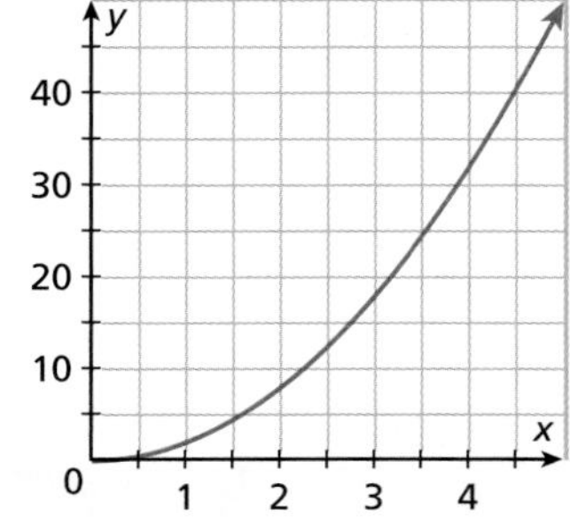


40. **Physics** The period of a pendulum is the amount of time it takes to swing back and forth one time. The relationship between the length of the pendulum $L$ in inches and the length of the period $t$ in seconds can be approximated by $L = 9.78t^2$. Find the period of a pendulum whose length is 60 inches. Round to the nearest tenth of a second.

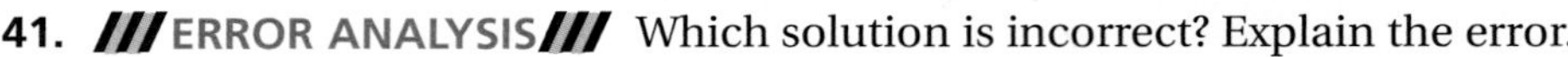

41. **/// ERROR ANALYSIS ///** Which solution is incorrect? Explain the error.

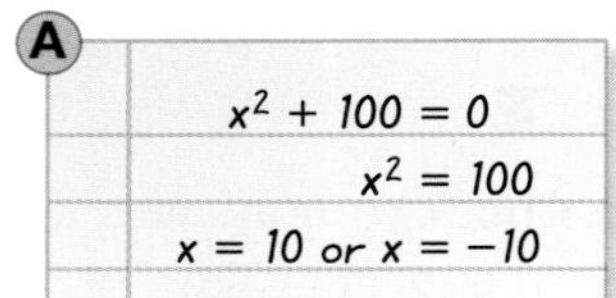


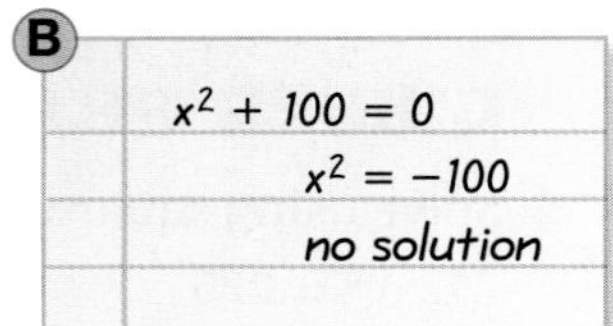


**Determine whether each statement is always, sometimes, or never true.**

42. There are two solutions to $x^2 = n$ when $n$ is positive.

43. If $n$ is a rational number, then the solutions to $x^2 = n$ are rational numbers.

44. **Multi-Step** The height in feet of a soccer ball kicked upward from the ground with initial velocity 60 feet per second is modeled by $h = -16t^2 + 60t$, where $t$ is the time in seconds. Find the time it takes for the ball to return to the ground. Round to the nearest tenth of a second.

45. **Critical Thinking** For the equation $x^2 = a$, describe the values of $a$ that will result in each of the following.

a. two solutions b. one solution c. no solution

**MULTI-STEP TEST PREP**

46. This problem will prepare you for the Multi-Step Test Prep on page 660.

The equation $d = 16t^2$ describes the distance $d$ in feet that a golf ball falls in relation to the number of seconds $t$ that it falls.

a. How many seconds will it take a golf ball to drop to the ground from a height of 4 feet?

b. Make a table and graph the related function.

c. How far will the golf ball drop in 1 second?

d. How many seconds will it take the golf ball to drop 64 feet?

For the quadratic equation $x^2 + a = 0$, determine whether each value of $a$ will result in two rational solutions. Explain.

**47.** $-\frac{1}{2}$ **48.** $\frac{1}{2}$ **49.** $-\frac{1}{4}$ **50.** $\frac{1}{4}$

**51. Write About It** Explain why the quadratic equation $x^2 + 4 = 0$ has no solutions but the quadratic equation $x^2 - 4 = 0$ has two solutions.

## TEST PREP

MA.A.4.7, MA.N.2.3, MA.G.2.2

**52.** The formula for finding the approximate volume of a cylinder is $V = 3.14r^2h$, where $r$ is the radius and $h$ is the height. The height of a cylinder is 100 cm, and the approximate volume is 1256 cm$^3$. Find the radius of the cylinder.

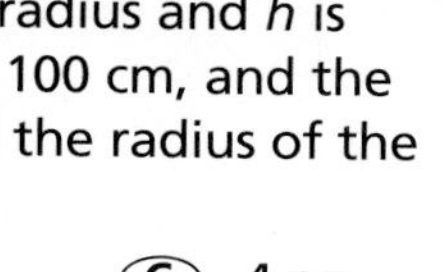

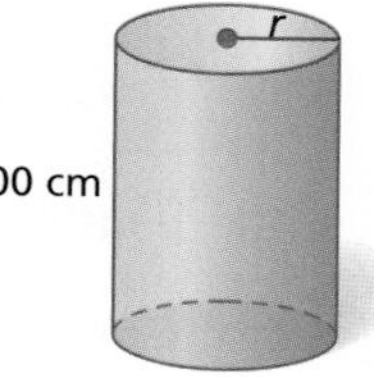


Ⓐ 400 cm
Ⓑ 20 cm
Ⓒ 4 cm
Ⓓ 2 cm

**53.** Which best describes the positive solution of $\frac{1}{2}x^2 = 20$?

Ⓕ Between 4 and 5
Ⓖ Between 5 and 6
Ⓗ Between 6 and 7
Ⓙ Between 7 and 8

**54.** Which best describes the solutions of $81x^2 - 169 = 0$?

Ⓐ Two rational solutions
Ⓑ Two irrational solutions
Ⓒ No solution
Ⓓ One solution

## CHALLENGE AND EXTEND

**Find the solutions of each equation without using a calculator.**

**55.** $288x^2 - 19 = -1$ **56.** $-75x^2 = -48$ **57.** $x^2 = \frac{128}{242}$

**58. Geometry** The Pythagorean Theorem states that $a^2 + b^2 = c^2$ if $a$ and $b$ represent the lengths of the legs of a right triangle and $c$ represents the length of the hypotenuse.

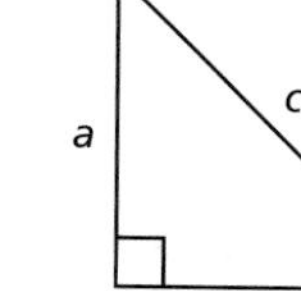


**a.** Find the length of the hypotenuse if the lengths of the legs are 9 cm and 12 cm.

**b.** Find the length of each leg of an isosceles right triangle whose hypotenuse is 10 cm. Round to the nearest tenth of a centimeter.

## SPIRAL REVIEW

**59.** The figures shown have the same perimeter. What is the value of $x$? *(Lesson 2-4)*

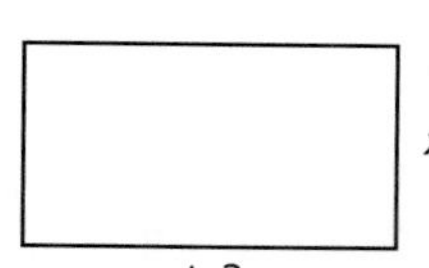


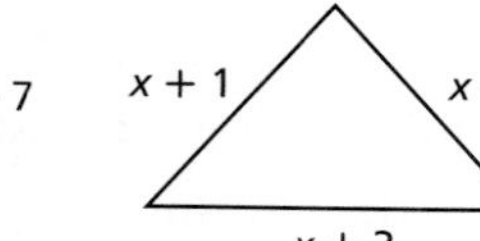


**60.** Identify which of the following lines are parallel:

$y = -2x + 3$, $2x - y = 8$, $6x - 2y = 10$, and $y + 4 = 2(3 - x)$. *(Lesson 5-8)*

**Solve each quadratic equation by factoring. Check your answer.** *(Lesson 9-6)*

**61.** $x^2 - 6x + 8 = 0$ **62.** $x^2 + 5x - 6 = 0$ **63.** $x^2 - 5x = 14$

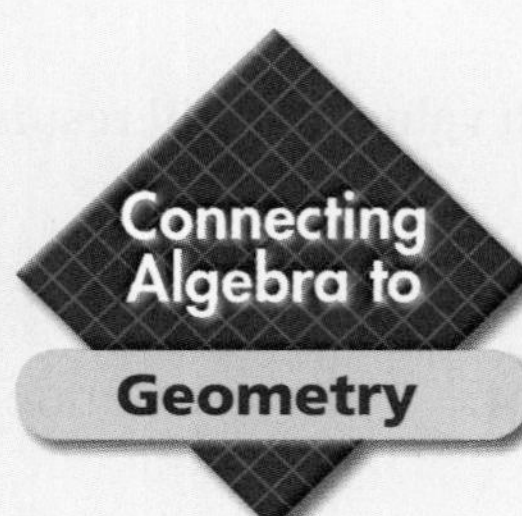


# The Distance Formula

*See Skills Bank page S68*

You can find the length of a vertical or horizontal line segment in the coordinate plane by subtracting coordinates.

**MA.G.1.1** Use strategies to calculate the … distance between points…

| WORDS | NUMBERS | ALGEBRA |
|---|---|---|
| The length of a vertical line segment is the absolute value of the difference between the $y$-coordinates of the endpoints. | $AB = \|2 - (-4)\| = \|6\| = 6$ | The distance between $P(x_1, y_1)$ and $Q(x_1, y_2)$ is $\|y_2 - y_1\|$. |
| The length of a horizontal line segment is the absolute value of the difference between the $x$-coordinates of the endpoints. | $CD = \|-2 - 3\| = \|-5\| = 5$ | The distance between $P(x_1, y_1)$ and $Q(x_2, y_1)$ is $\|x_2 - x_1\|$. |

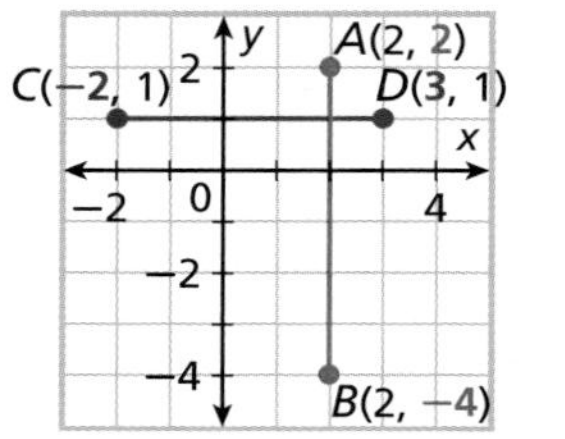

Graph labels: $A(2, 2)$, $C(-2, 1)$, $D(3, 1)$, $B(2, -4)$, $x$, $y$, $-2$, $0$, $4$, $2$, $-2$, $-4$

## Example 1

**Find the length of the line segment that connects $S(-4.5, 7.1)$ and $T(-4.5, 0.3)$.**

The $x$-coordinates are the same, so this is a vertical line segment. Subtract the $y$-coordinates and find the absolute value of the difference.

$|y_2 - y_1|$ *Formula for the length of a vertical line segment*

$|0.3 - 7.1|$ *Substitute.*

$|-6.8| = 6.8$ *Subtract and find the absolute value.*

## Try This

**Find the length of the line segment that connects each pair of points.**

1. $X(-1, 3)$ and $Y(4, 3)$
2. $M(5, -2)$ and $N(5, -8)$
3. $C(3, -1)$ and $D(3, 5)$
4. $P(14, -5)$ and $Q(25, -5)$
5. $A(-6, 0.5)$ and $B(-6, -4.3)$
6. $E(1.4, -0.7)$ and $F(3.8, -0.7)$

**Find the length of each segment.**

7. the altitude of $\triangle PQR$

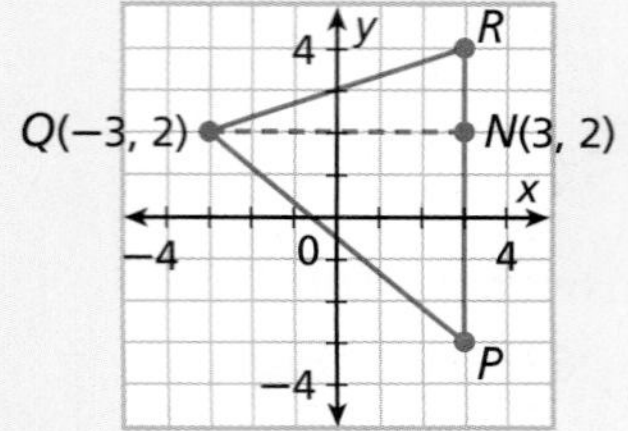


8. the height of parallelogram $EFGH$

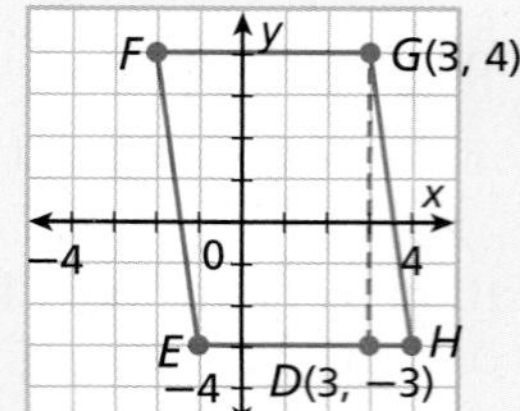


9. the height of trapezoid $ACDF$

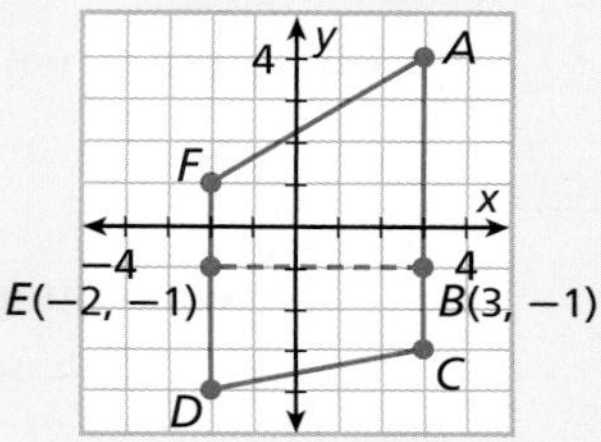

To find the length of a line segment that is not vertical or horizontal, such as $PQ$, think of it as the hypotenuse of a right triangle. Then you can use the Pythagorean Theorem.

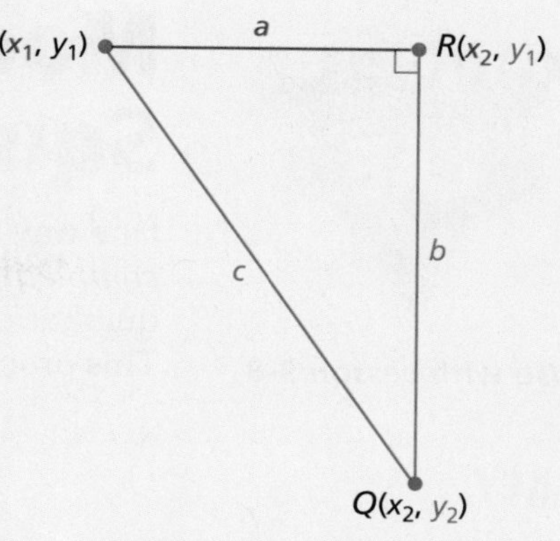


| | |
|---|---|
| $c^2 = a^2 + b^2$ | *Pythagorean Theorem* |
| $(PQ)^2 = (PR)^2 + (QR)^2$ | *Substitute.* |
| $PQ = \sqrt{(PR)^2 + (QR)^2}$ | *Solve for PQ. Use the positive square root to represent distance.* |
| $= \sqrt{\underbrace{(x_2 - x_1)^2}_{\text{Horizontal segment}} + \underbrace{(y_2 - y_1)^2}_{\text{Vertical segment}}}$ | *Use the Formula to find the length of each segment.* |

This is an example of the Distance Formula.

**The Distance Formula**

The distance between points $P$ and $Q$ with coordinates $P(x_1, y_1)$ and $Q(x_2, y_2)$ is given by

$$D = \sqrt{(x_2 - x_1)^2 + (y_2 - y_1)^2}.$$

## Example 2

**Find the length of the line segment that connects $H(20, -11)$ and $K(-4, 18)$.**

Use the Distance Formula. Let $(20, -11)$ be $(x_1, y_1)$ and $(-4, 18)$ be $(x_2, y_2)$.

| | |
|---|---|
| $D = \sqrt{(x_2 - x_1)^2 + (y_2 - y_1)^2}$ | *Write the formula.* |
| $= \sqrt{(\mathbf{-4} - \mathbf{20})^2 + [18 - (-11)]^2}$ | *Substitute.* |
| $= \sqrt{(-24)^2 + (29)^2}$ | *Find the differences.* |
| $= \sqrt{576 + 841}$ | *Square the differences.* |
| $= \sqrt{1417} \approx 37.64$ | *Use a calculator to find the square root.* |

## Try This

**Find the length of the line segment that connects each pair of points.**

**10.** $F(-8, 3)$ and $G(-11, -4)$ **11.** $S(30, -15)$ and $T(-55, 40)$ **12.** $W(0.5, 1.2)$ and $X(0.6, 2.5)$

**Find the length of each dashed line segment.**

**13.** the altitude of $\triangle WYZ$

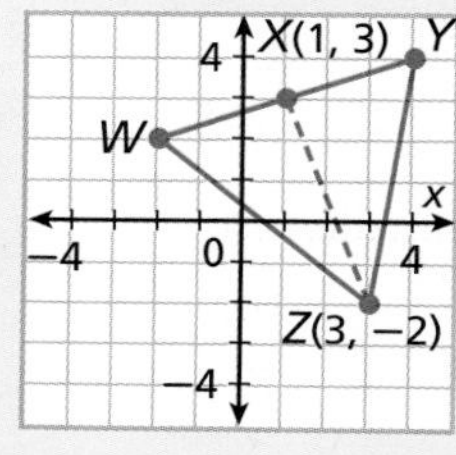


**14.** the height of parallelogram $ABCD$

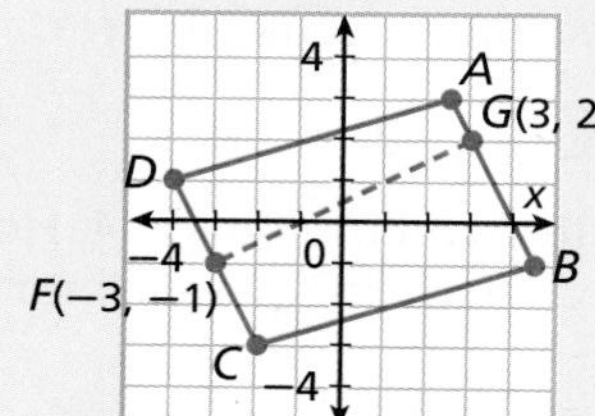


**15.** the height of trapezoid $LMNO$

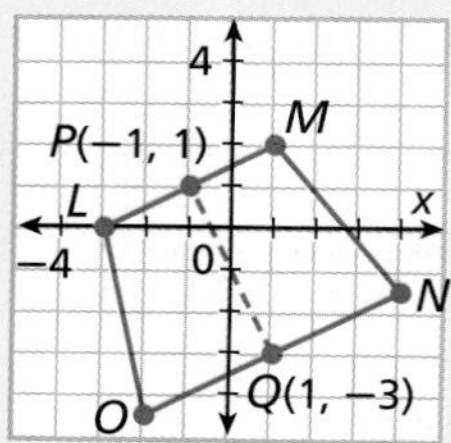

Use with Lesson 9-8

# Model Completing the Square

One way to solve a quadratic equation is by using a procedure called *completing the square.* In this procedure, you add something to a quadratic expression to make it a perfect-square trinomial. This procedure can be modeled with algebra tiles.

**Prep MA.A.4.7** Use graphs, tables, and properties to solve quadratic equations.

**KEY**

= 1   = $x$   = $x^2$

**Use algebra tiles to model $x^2 + 6x$. Add unit tiles to complete a perfect-square trinomial. Then write the new expression in factored form.**

| MODEL | ALGEBRA |
|---|---|
| *Arrange the tiles to form part of a large square.* *Part of the square is missing. How many one-tiles do you need to complete it?* | $x^2 + 6x$ |
| *Complete the square by placing 9 one-tiles on the mat.* *$x^2 + 6x + 9$ is a perfect-square trinomial.* | $x^2 + 6x + 9$ |
| $x + 3$, $x + 3$ *Use the length and the width of the square to rewrite the area expression in factored form.* | $(x + 3)^2$ |

## Try This

**Use algebra tiles to model each expression. Add unit tiles to complete a perfect-square trinomial. Then write the new expression in factored form.**

**1.** $x^2 + 4x$ **2.** $x^2 + 2x$ **3.** $x^2 + 10x$ **4.** $x^2 + 8x$

**5. Make a Conjecture** Examine the pattern in Problems 1–4. How many unit tiles would you have to add to make $x^2 + 12x$ a perfect-square trinomial?

# 9-8 Completing the Square

**MA.A.4.7** Use … properties to solve quadratic equations. *Also* **MA.G.2.2**

***Objective***
Solve quadratic equations by completing the square.

***Vocabulary***
completing the square

**Who uses this?**
Landscapers can solve quadratic equations to find dimensions of patios. (See Example 4.)

In the previous lesson, you solved quadratic equations by isolating $x^2$ and then using square roots. This method works if the quadratic equation, when written in standard form, is a perfect square.

When a trinomial is a perfect square, there is a relationship between the coefficient of the $x$-term and the constant term.

$$x^2 + 6x + 9 \qquad x^2 - 8x + 16$$

$$\left(\frac{6}{2}\right)^2 = 9 \qquad \left(\frac{-8}{2}\right)^2 = 16$$

*Divide the coefficient of the x-term by 2, then square the result to get the constant term.*

An expression in the form $x^2 + bx$ is not a perfect square. However, you can use the relationship shown above to add a term to $x^2 + bx$ to form a trinomial that is a perfect square. This is called **completing the square**.

**Completing the Square**

| WORDS | NUMBERS | ALGEBRA |
|---|---|---|
| To complete the square of $x^2 + bx$, add $\left(\frac{b}{2}\right)^2$ to the expression. This will form a perfect square trinomial. | $x^2 + 6x + \square$<br>$x^2 + 6x + \left(\frac{6}{2}\right)^2$<br>$x^2 + 6x + 9$<br>$(x + 3)^2$ | $x^2 + bx + \square$<br>$x^2 + bx + \left(\frac{b}{2}\right)^2$<br>$\left(x + \frac{b}{2}\right)^2$ |

## EXAMPLE 1 Completing the Square

**Complete the square to form a perfect square trinomial.**

**A** $x^2 + 10x + \square$

$x^2 + 10x$ — *Identify b.*

$\left(\frac{10}{2}\right)^2 = 5^2 = 25$ — *Find $\left(\frac{b}{2}\right)^2$.*

$x^2 + 10x + 25$ — *Add $\left(\frac{b}{2}\right)^2$ to the expression.*

**B** $x^2 - 9x + \square$

$x^2 + -9x$

$\left(\frac{-9}{2}\right)^2 = \frac{81}{4}$

$x^2 - 9x + \frac{81}{4}$

**Complete the square to form a perfect square trinomial.**

**1a.** $x^2 + 12x + \square$ **1b.** $x^2 - 5x + \square$ **1c.** $8x + x^2 + \square$

To solve a quadratic equation in the form $x^2 + bx = c$, first complete the square of $x^2 + bx$. Then you can solve using square roots.

| Solving a Quadratic Equation by Completing the Square |
|---|
| **Step 1** Write the equation in the form $x^2 + bx = c$. |
| **Step 2** Find $\left(\frac{b}{2}\right)^2$. |
| **Step 3** Complete the square by adding $\left(\frac{b}{2}\right)^2$ to both sides of the equation. |
| **Step 4** Factor the perfect-square trinomial. |
| **Step 5** Take the square root of both sides. |
| **Step 6** Write two equations, using both the positive and negative square root, and solve each equation. |

## EXAMPLE 2 Solving $x^2 + bx = c$ by Completing the Square

**Solve by completing the square.**

**A** $x^2 + 14x = 15$

**Step 1** $x^2 + 14x = 15$ — *The equation is in the form $x^2 + bx = c$.*

**Step 2** $\left(\frac{14}{2}\right)^2 = 7^2 = \mathbf{49}$ — *Find $\left(\frac{b}{2}\right)^2$.*

**Step 3** $x^2 + 14x + \mathbf{49} = 15 + \mathbf{49}$ — *Complete the square.*

**Step 4** $(x + 7)^2 = 64$ — *Factor and simplify.*

**Step 5** $x + 7 = \pm 8$ — *Take the square root of both sides.*

**Step 6** $x + 7 = 8$ or $x + 7 = -8$ — *Write and solve two equations.*
$x = 1$ or $x = -15$

The solutions are 1 and $-15$.

*Check*

| $x^2 + 14x$ | $= 15$ |
|---|---|
| $(1)^2 + 14(1)$ | 15 |
| $1 + 14$ | 15 |
| 15 | 15 ✓ |

| $x^2 + 14x$ | $= 15$ |
|---|---|
| $(-15)^2 + 14(-15)$ | 15 |
| $225 - 210$ | 15 |
| 15 | 15 ✓ |

**Helpful Hint**

$(x + 7)(x + 7) = (x + 7)^2$. So the square root of $(x + 7)^2$ is $x + 7$.

**B** $x^2 - 2x - 2 = 0$

**Step 1** $x^2 + (-2x) = 2$ — *Write in the form $x^2 + bx = c$.*

**Step 2** $\left(\frac{-2}{2}\right)^2 = (-1)^2 = \mathbf{1}$ — *Find $\left(\frac{b}{2}\right)^2$.*

**Step 3** $x^2 - 2x + \mathbf{1} = 2 + \mathbf{1}$ — *Complete the square.*

**Step 4** $(x - 1)^2 = 3$ — *Factor and simplify.*

**Step 5** $x - 1 = \pm\sqrt{3}$ — *Take the square root of both sides.*

**Step 6** $x - 1 = \sqrt{3}$ or $x - 1 = -\sqrt{3}$ — *Write and solve two equations.*
$x = 1 + \sqrt{3}$ or $x = 1 - \sqrt{3}$

The solutions are $1 + \sqrt{3}$ and $1 - \sqrt{3}$.

*Check* Use a graphing calculator to check your answer.

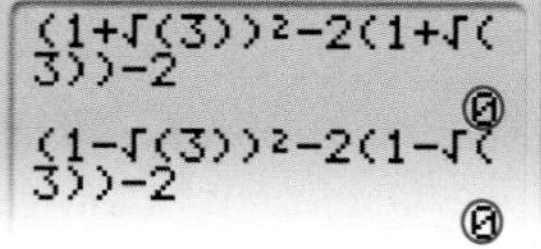


**Writing Math**

The expressions $1 + \sqrt{3}$ and $1 - \sqrt{3}$ can be written as one expression: $1 \pm \sqrt{3}$, which is read as "1 plus or minus the square root of 3."

**Solve by completing the square.**

**2a.** $x^2 + 10x = -9$ **2b.** $t^2 - 8t - 5 = 0$

## EXAMPLE 3 Solving $ax^2 + bx = c$ by Completing the Square

**Solve by completing the square.**

**A** $-2x^2 + 12x - 20 = 0$

**Step 1** $\frac{-2x^2}{-2} + \frac{12x}{-2} - \frac{20}{-2} = \frac{0}{-2}$ *Divide by −2 to make a = 1.*

$x^2 - 6x + 10 = 0$ *Write in the form $x^2 + bx = c$.*

$x^2 - 6x = -10$

$x^2 + (-6x) = -10$

**Step 2** $\left(\frac{-6}{2}\right)^2 = (-3)^2 = 9$ *Find $\left(\frac{b}{2}\right)^2$.*

**Step 3** $x^2 - 6x + 9 = -10 + 9$ *Complete the square.*

**Step 4** $(x - 3)^2 = -1$ *Factor and simplify.*

There is no real number whose square is negative, so there are no real solutions.

**B** $3x^2 - 10x = -3$

**Step 1** $\frac{3x^2}{3} - \frac{10}{3}x = \frac{-3}{3}$ *Divide by 3 to make a = 1.*

$x^2 - \frac{10}{3}x = -1$

$x^2 + \left(-\frac{10}{3}x\right) = -1$ *Write in the form $x^2 + bx = c$.*

**Step 2** $\left(-\frac{10}{3} \cdot \frac{1}{2}\right)^2 = \left(-\frac{10}{6}\right)^2 = \frac{100}{36} = \frac{25}{9}$ *Find $\left(\frac{b}{2}\right)^2$.*

**Step 3** $x^2 - \frac{10}{3}x + \frac{25}{9} = -1 + \frac{25}{9}$ *Complete the square.*

$x^2 - \frac{10}{3}x + \frac{25}{9} = -\frac{9}{9} + \frac{25}{9}$ *Rewrite using like denominators.*

**Step 4** $\left(x - \frac{5}{3}\right)^2 = \frac{16}{9}$ *Factor and simplify.*

**Step 5** $x - \frac{5}{3} = \pm\frac{4}{3}$ *Take the square root of both sides.*

**Step 6** $x - \frac{5}{3} = \frac{4}{3}$ or $x - \frac{5}{3} = -\frac{4}{3}$ *Write and solve two equations.*

$x = 3$ or $x = \frac{1}{3}$

The solutions are 3 and $\frac{1}{3}$.

**Remember!**

Dividing by 2 is the same as multiplying by $\frac{1}{2}$.

**Solve by completing the square.**

**3a.** $3x^2 - 5x - 2 = 0$ **3b.** $4t^2 - 4t + 9 = 0$

## EXAMPLE 4 *Problem-Solving Application*

PROBLEM SOLVING

**A landscaper is designing a rectangular brick patio. She has enough bricks to cover 144 square feet. She wants the length of the patio to be 10 feet greater than the width. What dimensions should she use for the patio? Round to the nearest hundredth of a foot.**

### 1 Understand the Problem

The **answer** will be the length and width of the patio.

**List the important information:**

- There are enough bricks to cover 144 square feet.
- One edge of the patio is to be 10 feet longer than the other edge.

### Make a Plan

Set the formula for the area of a rectangle equal to 144, the area of the patio. Solve the equation.

### Solve

Let $x$ be the width.
Then $x + 10$ is the length.

Use the formula for area of a rectangle.

| $\ell$ | $\cdot$ | $w$ | $=$ | $A$ |
|---|---|---|---|---|
| **length** | **times** | **width** | = | **area of patio** |
| $x + 10$ | $\cdot$ | $x$ | $=$ | $144$ |

**Step 1** $x^2 + 10x = 144$ — *Simplify.*

**Step 2** $\left(\frac{10}{2}\right)^2 = 5^2 = 25$ — *Find $\left(\frac{b}{2}\right)^2$.*

**Step 3** $x^2 + 10x + 25 = 144 + 25$ — *Complete the square by adding 25 to both sides.*

**Step 4** $(x + 5)^2 = 169$ — *Factor the perfect-square trinomial.*

**Step 5** $x + 5 = \pm 13$ — *Take the square root of both sides.*

**Step 6** $x + 5 = 13$ or $x + 5 = -13$ — *Write and solve two equations.*

$x = 8$ or $x = -18$

Negative numbers are not reasonable for length, so $x = 8$ is the only solution that makes sense.

The width is 8 feet, and the length is $8 + 10$, or 18, feet.

### Look Back

The length of the patio is 10 feet greater than the width. Also, $8(18) = 144$.

**4.** An architect designs a rectangular room with an area of 400 ft$^2$. The length is to be 8 ft longer than the width. Find the dimensions of the room. Round your answers to the nearest tenth of a foot.

## THINK AND DISCUSS

**1.** Tell how to solve a quadratic equation in the form $x^2 + bx + c = 0$ by completing the square.

**2. GET ORGANIZED** Copy and complete the graphic organizer. In each box, write and solve an example of the given type of quadratic equation.

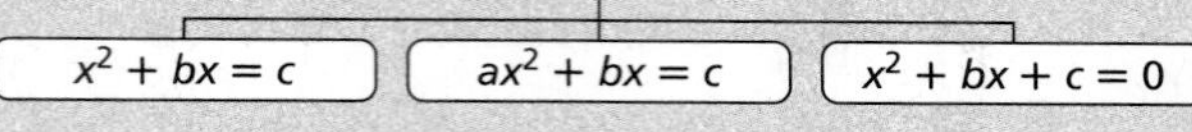

# 9-8 Exercises

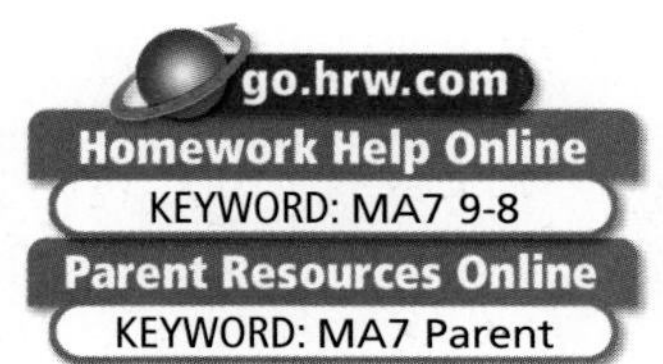


## GUIDED PRACTICE

1. **Vocabulary** Describe in your own words how to *complete the square* for the equation $1 = x^2 + 4x$.

SEE EXAMPLE 1 p. 645

**Complete the square to form a perfect square trinomial.**

2. $x^2 + 14x + \blacksquare$
3. $x^2 - 4x + \blacksquare$
4. $x^2 - 3x + \blacksquare$

SEE EXAMPLE 2 p. 647

**Solve by completing the square.**

5. $x^2 + 6x = -5$
6. $x^2 - 8x = 9$
7. $x^2 + x = 30$
8. $x^2 + 2x = 21$
9. $x^2 - 10x = -9$
10. $x^2 + 16x = 92$

SEE EXAMPLE 3 p. 647

11. $-x^2 - 5x = -5$
12. $-x^2 - 3x + 2 = 0$
13. $-6x = 3x^2 + 9$
14. $2x^2 - 6x = -10$
15. $-x^2 + 8x - 6 = 0$
16. $4x^2 + 16 = -24x$

SEE EXAMPLE 4 p. 647

17. **Multi-Step** The length of a rectangle is 4 meters longer than the width. The area of the rectangle is 80 square meters. Find the length and width. Round your answers to the nearest tenth of a meter.

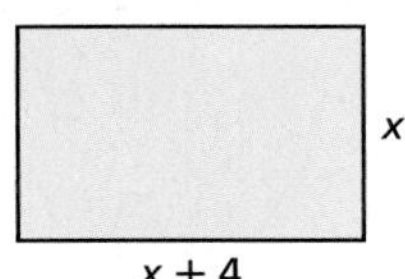


## PRACTICE AND PROBLEM SOLVING

| Independent Practice | |
|---|---|
| For Exercises | See Example |
| 18–20 | 1 |
| 21–26 | 2 |
| 27–32 | 3 |
| 33 | 4 |

**Extra Practice**
Skills Practice p. S21
Application Practice p. S36

**Complete the square to form a perfect square trinomial.**

18. $x^2 - 16x + \blacksquare$
19. $x^2 - 2x + \blacksquare$
20. $x^2 + 11x + \blacksquare$

**Solve by completing the square.**

21. $x^2 - 10x = 24$
22. $x^2 - 6x = -9$
23. $x^2 + 15x = -26$
24. $x^2 + 6x = 16$
25. $x^2 - 2x = 48$
26. $x^2 + 12x = -36$
27. $-x^2 + x + 6 = 0$
28. $2x^2 = -7x - 29$
29. $-x^2 - x + 1 = 0$
30. $3x^2 - 6x - 9 = 0$
31. $-x^2 = 15x + 30$
32. $2x^2 + 20x - 10 = 0$
33. **Geometry** The base of a parallelogram is 8 inches longer than twice the height. The area of the parallelogram is 64 square inches. What is the height?

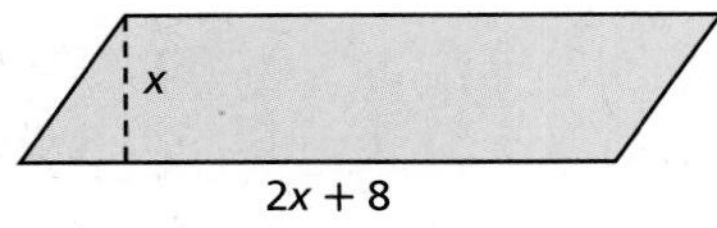


**Solve each equation by completing the square.**

34. $3x^2 + x = 10$
35. $x^2 = 2x + 6$
36. $2a^2 = 5a + 12$
37. $2x^2 + 5x = 3$
38. $4x = 7 - x^2$
39. $8x = -x^2 + 20$
40. **Hobbies** The height in feet $h$ of a water bottle rocket launched from a rooftop is given by the equation $h = -16t^2 + 320t + 32$, where $t$ is the time in seconds. After the rocket is fired, how long will it take to return to the ground? Solve by completing the square. Round your answer to the nearest tenth of a second.

**Complete each trinomial so that it is a perfect square.**

41. $x^2 + 18x + \blacksquare$
42. $x^2 - 100x + \blacksquare$
43. $x^2 - 7x + \blacksquare$
44. $x^2 + \blacksquare x + 4$
45. $x^2 - \blacksquare x + \frac{81}{4}$
46. $x^2 + \blacksquare x + \frac{1}{36}$

47. **Multi-Step** A roped-off area of width $x$ is created around a 34-by-10-foot rectangular museum display of Egyptian artifacts, as shown. The combined area of the display and the roped-off area is 640 square feet.

 a. Write an equation for the combined area.

 b. Find the width of the roped-off area.

48. **Graphing Calculator** Compare solving a quadratic equation by completing the square with finding the solutions on a graphing calculator.

 a. Complete the square to solve $2x^2 - 3x - 2 = 0$.

 b. Use your graphing calculator to graph $y = 2x^2 - 3x - 2$.

 c. Explain how to use this graph to find the solutions of $2x^2 - 3x - 2 = 0$.

 d. Compare the two methods of solving the equation. What are the advantages and disadvantages of each?

49. **ERROR ANALYSIS** Explain the error below. What is the correct answer?

$$x^2 + 4x = 77$$
$$x^2 + 4x + 4 = 77 + 4$$
$$(x + 2)^2 = 81$$
$$x + 2 = 9$$
$$x = 7$$

**Solve each equation by completing the square.**

| | | |
|---|---|---|
| 50. $5x^2 - 50x = 55$ | 51. $3x^2 + 36x = -27$ | 52. $28x - 2x^2 = 26$ |
| 53. $-36x = 3x^2 + 108$ | 54. $0 = 4x^2 + 32x + 44$ | 55. $16x + 40 = -2x^2$ |
| 56. $x^2 + 5x + 6 = 10x$ | 57. $x^2 + 3x + 18 = -3x$ | 58. $4x^2 + x + 1 = 3x^2$ |

59. **Write About It** Jamal prefers to solve $x^2 + 20x - 21 = 0$ by completing the square. Heather prefers to solve $x^2 + 11x + 18 = 0$ by factoring. Explain their reasoning.

60. **Critical Thinking** What should be done to the binomial $x^2 + y^2$ to make it a perfect-square trinomial? Explain.

61. This problem will prepare you for the Multi-Step Test Prep on page 660.

The function $h(t) = -16t^2 + vt + c$ models the height in feet of a golf ball after $t$ seconds when it is hit with initial velocity $v$ from initial height $c$ feet. A golfer stands on a tee box that is 32 feet above the fairway. He hits the golf ball from the tee at an initial velocity of 64 feet per second.

 a. Write an equation that gives the time $t$ when the golf ball lands on the fairway at height 0.

 b. What number would be added to both sides of the equation in part **a** to complete the square while solving for $t$?

 c. Solve the equation from part **a** by completing the square to find the time it takes the ball to reach the fairway. Round to the nearest tenth of a second.

62. **Write About It** Compare solving an equation of the form $x^2 + bx + c = 0$ by completing the square and solving an equation of the form $ax^2 + bx + c = 0$ by completing the square.

MA.A.4.7, MA.G.2.2

63. What value of $c$ will make $x^2 + 16x + c$ a perfect-square trinomial?

 Ⓐ 32  Ⓑ 64  Ⓒ 128  Ⓓ 256

64. What value of $b$ will make $x^2 + b + 25$ a perfect-square trinomial?

 Ⓕ 5  Ⓖ $5x$  Ⓗ 10  Ⓙ $10x$

65. Which of the following is closest to a solution of $3x^2 + 2x - 4 = 0$?

 Ⓐ 0  Ⓑ 1  Ⓒ 2  Ⓓ 3

66. **Short Response** Solve $x^2 - 8x - 20 = 0$ by completing the square. Explain each step in your solution.

## CHALLENGE AND EXTEND

**Solve each equation by completing the square.**

67. $6x^2 + 5x = 6$  68. $7x + 3 = 6x^2$  69. $4x = 1 - 3x^2$

70. What should be done to the binomial $ax^2 + bx$ to obtain a perfect-square trinomial?

71. Solve $ax^2 + bx = 0$ for $x$.

72. **Geometry** The hypotenuse of a right triangle is 20 cm. One of the legs is 4 cm longer than the other leg. Find the area of the triangle. (*Hint:* Use the Pythagorean Theorem.)

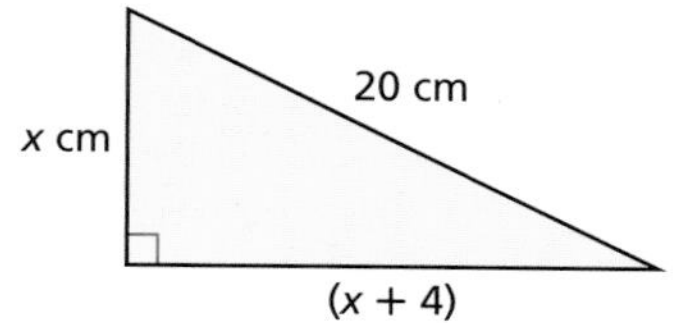


## SPIRAL REVIEW

**Graph the line with the given slope and y-intercepts.** *(Lesson 5-6)*

73. slope $= 4$, $y$-intercept $= -3$  74. slope $= -\frac{2}{3}$, $y$-intercept $= 4$

75. slope $= -2$, $y$-intercept $= -2$  76. slope $= -\frac{4}{3}$, $y$-intercept $= 0$

**Multiply.** *(Lesson 7-8)*

77. $(x - 4)^2$  78. $(x - 4)(x + 4)$  79. $(4 - t)^2$

80. $(2z + 3)^2$  81. $(8b^2 - 2)(8b^2 + 2)$  82. $(2x - 6)(2x + 6)$

**Solve using square roots.** *(Lesson 9-7)*

83. $5x^2 = 5$  84. $x^2 + 3 = 12$  85. $5x^2 = 80$

86. $9x^2 = 64$  87. $25 + x^2 = 250$  88. $64x^2 + 3 = 147$

**Solve. Round to the nearest hundredth.** *(Lesson 9-7)*

89. $12 = 5x^2$  90. $3x^2 - 4 = 15$  91. $x^2 - 7 = 19$

92. $6 + x^2 = 72$  93. $10x^2 - 10 = 12$  94. $2x^2 + 2 = 33$

# 9-9 The Quadratic Formula and the Discriminant

**MA.A.4.7** Use graphs…and properties to solve quadratic equations.
*Also* **MA.A.4.3**

***Objectives***

Solve quadratic equations by using the Quadratic Formula.

Determine the number of solutions of a quadratic equation by using the discriminant.

***Vocabulary***

discriminant

**Why learn this?**

You can use the discriminant to determine whether the weight in a carnival strength test will reach a certain height. (See Exercise 4.)

In the previous lesson, you completed the square to solve quadratic equations. If you complete the square of $ax^2 + bx + c = 0$, you can derive the *Quadratic Formula.* The Quadratic Formula is the only method that can be used to solve *any* quadratic equation.

| Numbers | | Algebra |
|---|---|---|
| $2x^2 + 6x + 1 = 0$ | | $ax^2 + bx + c = 0, a \neq 0$ |
| $\frac{2}{2}x^2 + \frac{6}{2}x + \frac{1}{2} = \frac{0}{2}$ | *Divide both sides by a.* | $\frac{a}{a}x^2 + \frac{b}{a}x + \frac{c}{a} = \frac{0}{a}$ |
| $x^2 + 3x + \frac{1}{2} = 0$ | | $x^2 + \frac{b}{a}x + \frac{c}{a} = 0$ |
| $x^2 + 3x = -\frac{1}{2}$ | *Subtract $\frac{c}{a}$ from both sides.* | $x^2 + \frac{b}{a}x = -\frac{c}{a}$ |
| $x^2 + 3x + \left(\frac{3}{2}\right)^2 = -\frac{1}{2} + \left(\frac{3}{2}\right)^2$ | *Complete the square.* | $x^2 + \frac{b}{a}x + \left(\frac{b}{2a}\right)^2 = -\frac{c}{a} + \left(\frac{b}{2a}\right)^2$ |
| $\left(x + \frac{3}{2}\right)^2 = \frac{9}{4} - \frac{1}{2}$ | *Factor and simplify.* | $\left(x + \frac{b}{2a}\right)^2 = \frac{b^2}{4a^2} - \frac{c}{a}$ |
| $\left(x + \frac{3}{2}\right)^2 = \frac{9}{4} - \frac{2}{4}$ | *Use common denominators.* | $\left(x + \frac{b}{2a}\right)^2 = \frac{b^2}{4a^2} - \frac{4ac}{4a^2}$ |
| $\left(x + \frac{3}{2}\right)^2 = \frac{7}{4}$ | *Simplify.* | $\left(x + \frac{b}{2a}\right)^2 = \frac{b^2 - 4ac}{4a^2}$ |
| $x + \frac{3}{2} = \pm\frac{\sqrt{7}}{2}$ | *Take square roots.* | $x + \frac{b}{2a} = \pm\frac{\sqrt{b^2 - 4ac}}{2a}$ |
| $x = -\frac{3}{2} \pm \frac{\sqrt{7}}{2}$ | *Subtract $\frac{b}{2a}$ from both sides.* | $x = -\frac{b}{2a} \pm \frac{\sqrt{b^2 - 4ac}}{2a}$ |
| $x = \frac{-3 \pm \sqrt{7}}{2}$ | *Simplify.* | $x = \frac{-b \pm \sqrt{b^2 - 4ac}}{2a}$ |

**Remember!**

To add fractions, you need a common denominator.

$$\frac{b^2}{4a^2} - \frac{c}{a} = \frac{b^2}{4a^2} - \frac{c}{a}\left(\frac{4a}{4a}\right)$$
$$= \frac{b^2}{4a^2} - \frac{4ac}{4a^2}$$
$$= \frac{b^2 - 4ac}{4a^2}$$

**The Quadratic Formula**

The solutions of $ax^2 + bx + c = 0$, where $a \neq 0$, are $x = \frac{-b \pm \sqrt{b^2 - 4ac}}{2a}$.

## EXAMPLE 1 Using the Quadratic Formula

**Solve using the Quadratic Formula.**

**A** $2x^2 + 3x - 5 = 0$

| | |
|---|---|
| $2x^2 + 3x + (-5) = 0$ | *Identify a, b, and c.* |
| $x = \frac{-b \pm \sqrt{b^2 - 4ac}}{2a}$ | *Use the Quadratic Formula.* |
| $x = \frac{-3 \pm \sqrt{3^2 - 4(2)(-5)}}{2(2)}$ | *Substitute 2 for a, 3 for b, and −5 for c.* |
| $x = \frac{-3 \pm \sqrt{9 - (-40)}}{4}$ | *Simplify.* |
| $x = \frac{-3 \pm \sqrt{49}}{4} = \frac{-3 \pm 7}{4}$ | *Simplify.* |
| $x = \frac{-3 + 7}{4}$ or $x = \frac{-3 - 7}{4}$ | *Write as two equations.* |
| $x = 1$ or $x = -\frac{5}{2}$ | *Solve each equation.* |

**Helpful Hint**

You can graph the related quadratic function to see if your solutions are reasonable.

**B** $2x = x^2 - 3$

| | |
|---|---|
| $1x^2 + (-2x) + (-3) = 0$ | *Write in standard form. Identify a, b, and c.* |
| $x = \frac{-(-2) \pm \sqrt{(-2)^2 - 4(1)(-3)}}{2(1)}$ | *Substitute 1 for a, −2 for b, and −3 for c.* |
| $x = \frac{2 \pm \sqrt{4 - (-12)}}{2}$ | *Simplify.* |
| $x = \frac{2 \pm \sqrt{16}}{2} = \frac{2 \pm 4}{2}$ | *Simplify.* |
| $x = \frac{2 + 4}{2}$ or $x = \frac{2 - 4}{2}$ | *Write as two equations.* |
| $x = 3$ or $x = -1$ | *Solve each equation.* |

Solve using the Quadratic Formula.

**1a.** $-3x^2 + 5x + 2 = 0$ **1b.** $2 - 5x^2 = -9x$

Many quadratic equations can be solved by graphing, factoring, taking the square root, or completing the square. Some cannot be solved by any of these methods, but you can always use the Quadratic Formula to solve any quadratic equation.

## EXAMPLE 2 Using the Quadratic Formula to Estimate Solutions

**Solve $x^2 - 2x - 4 = 0$ using the Quadratic Formula.**

$$x = \frac{-(-2) \pm \sqrt{(-2)^2 - 4(1)(-4)}}{2(1)}$$

$$x = \frac{2 \pm \sqrt{4 - (-16)}}{2} = \frac{2 \pm \sqrt{20}}{2}$$

$$x = \frac{2 + \sqrt{20}}{2} \quad \text{or} \quad x = \frac{2 - \sqrt{20}}{2}$$

Use a calculator: $x \approx 3.24$ or $x \approx -1.24$.

***Check reasonableness***

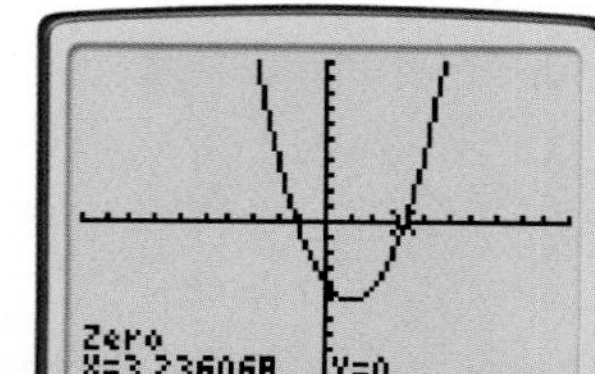

**2.** Solve $2x^2 - 8x + 1 = 0$ using the Quadratic Formula.

If the quadratic equation is in standard form, the **discriminant** of a quadratic equation is $b^2 - 4ac$, the part of the equation under the radical sign. Recall that quadratic equations can have two, one, or no real solutions. You can determine the number of solutions of a quadratic equation by evaluating its discriminant.

| Equation | $x^2 - 4x + 3 = 0$ | $x^2 + 2x + 1 = 0$ | $x^2 - 2x + 2 = 0$ |
|---|---|---|---|
| Discriminant | $a = 1, b = -4, c = 3$<br>$b^2 - 4ac$<br>$(-4)^2 - 4(1)(3)$<br>$16 - 12$<br>$4$<br>The discriminant is positive. | $a = 1, b = 2, c = 1$<br>$b^2 - 4ac$<br>$2^2 - 4(1)(1)$<br>$4 - 4$<br>$0$<br>The discriminant is zero. | $a = 1, b = -2, c = 2$<br>$b^2 - 4ac$<br>$(-2)^2 - 4(1)(2)$<br>$4 - 8$<br>$-4$<br>The discriminant is negative. |
| Graph of Related Function | Notice that the related function has two $x$-intercepts.<br>(1, 0) (3, 0) | Notice that the related function has one $x$-intercept.<br>(−1, 0) | Notice that the related function has no $x$-intercepts. |
| Number of Solutions | two real solutions | one real solution | no real solutions |

**The Discriminant of Quadratic Equation $ax^2 + bx + c = 0$**

If $b^2 - 4ac > 0$, the equation has two real solutions.

If $b^2 - 4ac = 0$, the equation has one real solution.

If $b^2 - 4ac < 0$, the equation has no real solutions.

## EXAMPLE 3 Using the Discriminant

**Find the number of solutions of each equation using the discriminant.**

**A** $3x^2 + 10x + 2 = 0$

$a = 3, b = 10, c = 2$

$b^2 - 4ac$

$10^2 - 4(3)(2)$

$100 - 24$

$76$

$b^2 - 4ac$ is positive.

There are two real solutions.

**B** $9x^2 - 6x + 1 = 0$

$a = 9, b = -6, c = 1$

$b^2 - 4ac$

$(-6)^2 - 4(9)(1)$

$36 - 36$

$0$

$b^2 - 4ac$ is zero.

There is one real solution.

**C** $x^2 + x + 1 = 0$

$a = 1, b = 1, c = 1$

$b^2 - 4ac$

$1^2 - 4(1)(1)$

$1 - 4$

$-3$

$b^2 - 4ac$ is negative.

There are no real solutions.

**Find the number of solutions of each equation using the discriminant.**

**3a.** $2x^2 - 2x + 3 = 0$ **3b.** $x^2 + 4x + 4 = 0$ **3c.** $x^2 - 9x + 4 = 0$

The height $h$ in feet of an object shot straight up with initial velocity $v$ in feet per second is given by $h = -16t^2 + vt + c$, where $c$ is the beginning height of the object above the ground.

## EXAMPLE 4 Physics Application

**Helpful Hint**

If the object is shot straight up from the ground, the initial height of the object above the ground equals 0.

**A weight 1 foot above the ground on a carnival strength test is shot straight up with an initial velocity of 35 feet per second. Will it ring the bell at the top of the pole? Use the discriminant to explain your answer.**

$h = -16t^2 + vt + c$

$20 = -16t^2 + 35t + 1$ *Substitute 20 for h, 35 for v, and 1 for c.*

$0 = -16t^2 + 35t + (-19)$ *Subtract 20 from both sides.*

$b^2 - 4ac$ *Evaluate the discriminant.*

$35^2 - 4(-16)(-19) = 9$ *Substitute −16 for a, 35 for b, and −19 for c.*

The discriminant is positive, so the equation has two solutions. The weight will reach a height of 20 feet so it will ring the bell.

**4. What if...?** Suppose the weight is shot straight up with an initial velocity of 20 feet per second. Will it ring the bell? Use the discriminant to explain your answer.

There is no one correct way to solve a quadratic equation. Many quadratic equations can be solved using several different methods.

## EXAMPLE 5 Solving Using Different Methods

**Solve $x^2 + 7x + 6 = 0$. Show your work.**

**Method 1** Solve by graphing.

$y = x^2 + 7x + 6$ *Write the related quadratic function and graph it.*

The solutions are the $x$-intercepts, $-6$ and $-1$.

**Method 2** Solve by factoring.

$x^2 + 7x + 6 = 0$

$(x + 6)(x + 1) = 0$ *Factor.*

$x + 6 = 0$ or $x - 1 = 0$ *Use the Zero Product Property.*

$x = -6$ or $x = -1$ *Solve each equation.*

**Method 3** Solve by completing the square.

$x^2 + 7x + 6 = 0$

$x^2 + 7x = -6$

$x^2 + 7x + \frac{49}{4} = -6 + \frac{49}{4}$ *Add $\left(\frac{b}{2}\right)^2$ to both sides.*

$\left(x + \frac{7}{2}\right)^2 = \frac{25}{4}$ *Factor and simplify.*

$x + \frac{7}{2} = \pm\frac{5}{2}$ *Take the square root of both sides.*

$x + \frac{7}{2} = \frac{5}{2}$ or $x + \frac{7}{2} = -\frac{5}{2}$ *Solve each equation.*

$x = -1$ or $x = -6$

**Method 4** Solve using the Quadratic Formula.

$1x^2 + 7x + 6 = 0$ *Identify a, b, and c.*

$x = \dfrac{-7 \pm \sqrt{7^2 - 4(1)(6)}}{2(1)}$ *Substitute 1 for a, 7 for b, and 6 for c.*

$x = \dfrac{-7 \pm \sqrt{49 - 24}}{2} = \dfrac{-7 \pm \sqrt{25}}{2} = \dfrac{-7 \pm 5}{2}$ *Simplify.*

$x = \dfrac{-7 + 5}{2}$ or $x = \dfrac{-7 - 5}{2}$ *Write as two equations.*

$x = -1$ or $x = -6$ *Solve each equation.*

**Solve. Show your work.**

**5a.** $x^2 + 7x + 10 = 0$ **5b.** $-14 + x^2 = 5x$ **5c.** $2x^2 + 4x - 21 = 0$

Notice that all of the methods in Example 5 produce the same solutions, $-1$ and $-6$. The only method you cannot use to solve $x^2 + 7x + 6 = 0$ is using square roots. Sometimes one method is better for solving certain types of equations. The table below gives some advantages and disadvantages of the different methods.

**Methods of Solving Quadratic Equations**

| METHOD | ADVANTAGES | DISADVANTAGES |
|---|---|---|
| Graphing | • Always works to give approximate solutions<br>• Can quickly see the number of solutions | • Cannot always get an exact solution |
| Factoring | • Good method to try first<br>• Straightforward if the equation is factorable | • Complicated if the equation is not easily factorable<br>• Not all quadratic equations are factorable. |
| Using square roots | • Quick when the equation has no *x*-term | • Cannot easily use when there is an *x*-term |
| Completing the square | • Always works | • Sometimes involves difficult calculations |
| Using the Quadratic Formula | • Always works<br>• Can always find exact solutions | • Other methods may be easier or less time consuming. |

**Student to Student**

***Solving Quadratic Equations***

**Binh Pham**
Johnson High School

*No matter what method I use, I like to check my answers for reasonableness by graphing.*

*I used the Quadratic Formula to solve $2x^2 - 7x - 10 = 0$. I found that $x \approx -1.09$ and $x \approx 4.59$. Then I graphed $y = 2x^2 - 7x - 10$. The x-intercepts appeared to be close to $-1$ and 4.5, so I knew my solutions were reasonable.*

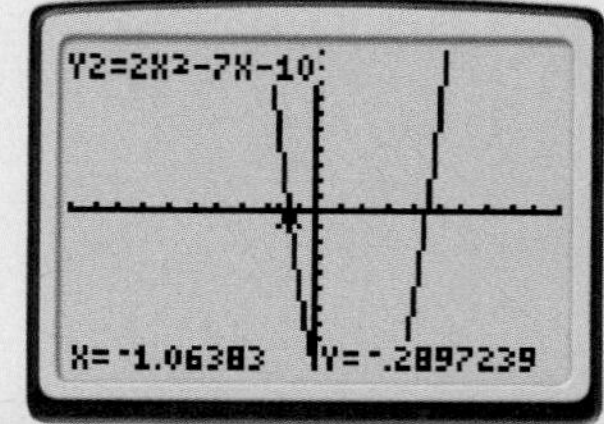

## THINK AND DISCUSS

1. Describe how to use the discriminant to find the number of solutions to a quadratic equation.
2. Choose a method to solve $x^2 + 5x + 4 = 0$ and explain why you chose that method.
3. Describe how the discriminant can be used to determine if an object will reach a given height.

4. **GET ORGANIZED** Copy and complete the graphic organizer. In each box, write the number of real solutions.

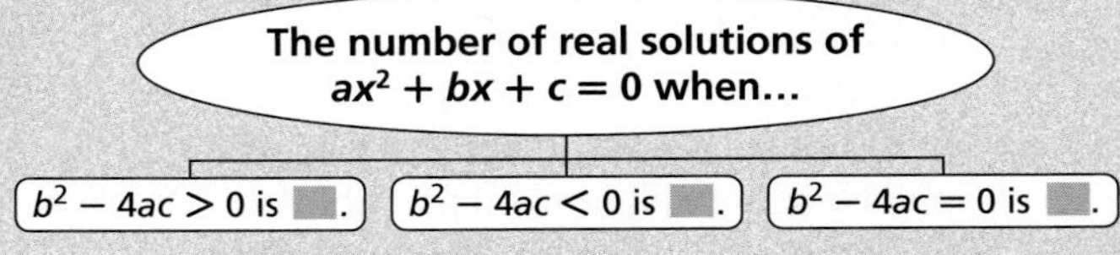


# 9-9 Exercises

MA.A.4.7, MA.A.4.3

## GUIDED PRACTICE

1. **Vocabulary** If the *discriminant* is negative, the quadratic equation has ___?___ solution(s). (*no*, *one*, or *two*)

SEE EXAMPLE 1 p. 653

**Solve using the Quadratic Formula.**

2. $x^2 - 5x + 4 = 0$
3. $2x^2 = 7x - 3$
4. $x^2 - 6x - 7 = 0$
5. $x^2 = -14x - 40$
6. $3x^2 - 2x = 8$
7. $4x^2 - 4x - 3 = 0$

SEE EXAMPLE 2 p. 653

8. $2x^2 - 6 = 0$
9. $x^2 + 6x + 3 = 0$
10. $x^2 - 7x + 2 = 0$
11. $3x^2 = -x + 5$
12. $x^2 - 4x - 7 = 0$
13. $2x^2 + x - 5 = 0$

SEE EXAMPLE 3 p. 654

**Find the number of solutions of each equation using the discriminant.**

14. $2x^2 + 4x + 3 = 0$
15. $x^2 + 4x + 4 = 0$
16. $2x^2 - 11x + 6 = 0$
17. $x^2 + x + 1 = 0$
18. $3x^2 = 5x - 1$
19. $-2x + 3 = 2x^2$
20. $2x^2 + 12x = -18$
21. $5x^2 + 3x = -4$
22. $8x = 1 - x^2$

SEE EXAMPLE 4 p. 655

23. **Hobbies** The height above the ground in meters of a model rocket on a particular launch can be modeled by the equation $h = -4.9t^2 + 102t + 100$, where $t$ is the time in seconds after its engine burns out 100 m above the ground. Will the rocket reach a height of 600 m? Use the discriminant to explain your answer.

SEE EXAMPLE 5 p. 655

**Solve. Show your work.**

24. $x^2 + x - 12 = 0$
25. $x^2 + 6x + 9 = 0$
26. $2x^2 - x - 1 = 0$
27. $4x^2 + 4x + 1 = 0$
28. $2x^2 + x - 7 = 0$
29. $9 = 2x^2 + 3x$

## PRACTICE AND PROBLEM SOLVING

**Independent Practice**

| For Exercises | See Example |
|---|---|
| 30–32 | 1 |
| 33–35 | 2 |
| 36–38 | 3 |
| 39 | 4 |
| 40–42 | 5 |

**Extra Practice**

Skills Practice p. S21

Application Practice p. S36

**Solve using the Quadratic Formula.**

**30.** $3x^2 = 13x - 4$ **31.** $x^2 - 10x + 9 = 0$ **32.** $1 = 3x^2 + 2x$

**33.** $x^2 - 4x + 1 = 0$ **34.** $3x^2 - 5 = 0$ **35.** $2x^2 + 7x = -4$

**Find the number of solutions of each equation using the discriminant.**

**36.** $3x^2 - 6x + 3 = 0$ **37.** $x^2 - 3x - 8 = 0$ **38.** $7x^2 + 6x + 2 = 0$

**39. Multi-Step** A gymnast who can stretch her arms up to reach 6 feet jumps straight up on a trampoline. The height of her feet above the trampoline can be modeled by the equation $h = -16x^2 + 12x$, where $x$ is the time in seconds after her jump. Do the gymnast's hands reach a height of 10 feet above the trampoline? Use the discriminant to explain. (*Hint:* Let $h = 10 - 6$, or 4.)

**Solve. Show your work.**

**40.** $x^2 + 4x + 3 = 0$ **41.** $x^2 + 2x = 15$ **42.** $x^2 - 12 = -x$

**Write each equation in standard form. Use the discriminant to determine the number of solutions. Then find any real solutions using the Quadratic Formula.**

**43.** $2x = 3 + 2x^2$ **44.** $x^2 = 2x + 9$ **45.** $2 = 7x + 4x^2$

**46.** $-7 = x^2$ **47.** $-12x = -9x^2 - 4$ **48.** $x^2 - 14 = 0$

**Multi-Step** **Use the discriminant to determine the number of $x$-intercepts. Then use the Quadratic Formula to find them.**

**49.** $y = 2x^2 - x - 21$ **50.** $y = 5x^2 + 12x + 8$ **51.** $y = x^2 - 10x + 25$

**52.** Copy and complete the table.

| Quadratic Equation | Discriminant | Number of Solutions |
|---|---|---|
| $x^2 + 12x - 20 = 0$ | ■ | ■ |
| $8x + x^2 = -16$ | ■ | ■ |
| $0.5x^2 + x - 3 = 0$ | ■ | ■ |
| $-3x^2 - 2x = 1$ | ■ | ■ |

**53. Sports** A diver begins on a platform 10 meters above the surface of the water. The diver's height is given by the equation $h(t) = -4.9t^2 + 3.5t + 10$, where $t$ is the time in seconds after the diver jumps.

**a.** How long does it take the diver to reach a point 1 meter above the water?

**b.** How many solutions does your equation from part **a** have?

**c.** Do all of the solutions to the equation make sense in the situation? Explain.

**54. Critical Thinking** How many solutions does the equation $x^2 = k$ have when $k > 0$, when $k < 0$, and when $k = 0$? Use the discriminant to explain.

**55. Write About It** How can you use the discriminant to save time?

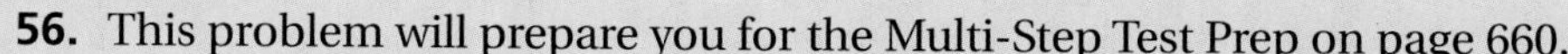

**MULTI-STEP TEST PREP**

56. This problem will prepare you for the Multi-Step Test Prep on page 660.

The equation $0 = -16t^2 + 80t + 20$ gives the time $t$ in seconds when a golf ball is at height 0 feet.

a. Will the height of the ball reach 130 feet? Explain.

b. Will the golf ball reach a height of 116 feet? If so, when?

c. Solve the given quadratic equation using the Quadratic Formula.

**TEST PREP**

MA.A.4.7, MA.A.4.3

57. How many solutions does $4x^2 - 3x + 1 = 0$ have?

Ⓐ 0 Ⓑ 1 Ⓒ 2 Ⓓ 4

58. For which of the following conditions does $ax^2 + bx + c = 0$ have two solutions?

I. $b^2 = 4ac$

II. $b^2 > 4ac$

III. $a = b, c = b$

Ⓕ I only Ⓖ II only Ⓗ III only Ⓙ II and III

59. **Extended Response** Use the equation $0 = x^2 + 2x + 1$ to answer the following.

a. How many solutions does the equation have?

b. Solve the equation by graphing.

c. Solve the equation by factoring.

d. Solve the equation by using the Quadratic Formula.

e. Explain which method was easiest for you. Why?

## CHALLENGE AND EXTEND

60. **Agriculture** A rancher has 80 yards of fencing to build a rectangular pen. Let $w$ be the width of the pen. Write an equation giving the area of the pen. Find the dimensions of the pen when the area is 400 square yards.

61. **Agriculture** A farmer wants to fence a four-sided field using an existing fence along the south side of the field. He has 1000 feet of fencing. He makes the northern boundary perpendicular to and twice as long as the western boundary. The eastern and western boundaries have to be parallel, but the northern and southern ones do not.

a. Can the farmer enclose an area of 125,000 square feet? Explain why or why not. (*Hint:* Use the formula for the area of a trapezoid, $A = \frac{1}{2}h(b_1 + b_2)$.)

b. What geometric shape will the field be?

## SPIRAL REVIEW

**Solve each equation by completing the square.** *(Lesson 9-8)*

62. $x^2 - 2x - 24 = 0$ 63. $x^2 + 6x = 40$ 64. $-3x^2 + 12x = 15$

**Factor each polynomial by grouping.** *(Lesson 8-2)*

65. $s^2r^3 + 5r^3 + 5t + s^2t$ 66. $b^3 - 4b^2 + 2b - 8$ 67. $n^5 - 6n^4 - 2n + 12$

**Order the functions from narrowest graph to widest.** *(Lesson 9-4)*

68. $f(x) = 0.2x^2, g(x) = 1.5x^2 + 4, h(x) = x^2 - 8$ 69. $f(x) = -\frac{1}{5}x^2 + 5, g(x) = \frac{1}{6}x^2$

CHAPTER 9

SECTION 9B

# MULTI-STEP TEST PREP

## Solving Quadratic Equations

**Seeing Green** A golf player hits a golf ball from a tee with an initial velocity of 80 feet per second. The height of the golf ball $t$ seconds after it is hit is given by $h = -16t^2 + 80t$.

1. How long is the golf ball in the air?
2. What is the maximum height of the golf ball?
3. How long after the golf ball is hit does it reach its maximum height?
4. What is the height of the golf ball after 3.5 seconds?
5. At what times is the golf ball 64 feet in the air? Explain.

# READY TO GO ON?

CHAPTER 9

SECTION 9B

## Quiz for Lessons 9-5 Through 9-9

### 9-5 Solving Quadratic Equations by Graphing

**Solve each equation by graphing the related function.**

1. $x^2 - 9 = 0$
2. $x^2 + 3x - 4 = 0$
3. $4x^2 + 8x = 32$
4. The height of a fireworks rocket launched from a platform 35 feet above the ground can be approximated by $h = -5t^2 + 30t + 35$, where $h$ is the height in meters and $t$ is the time in seconds. Find the time it takes the rocket to reach the ground after it is launched.

### 9-6 Solving Quadratic Equations by Factoring

**Use the Zero Product Property to solve each equation.**

5. $(x + 1)(x + 3) = 0$
6. $(x - 6)(x - 3) = 0$
7. $x(x + 3) = 18$
8. $(x + 2)(x - 5) = 60$

**Solve each quadratic equation by factoring.**

9. $x^2 - 4x - 32 = 0$
10. $x^2 - 8x + 15 = 0$
11. $x^2 + x = 6$
12. $-8x - 33 = -x^2$
13. The height of a soccer ball kicked from the ground can be approximated by the function $h = -16t^2 + 64t$, where $h$ is the height in feet and $t$ is the time in seconds. Find the time it takes for the ball to return to the ground.

### 9-7 Solving Quadratic Equations by Using Square Roots

**Solve using square roots.**

14. $3x^2 = 48$
15. $36x^2 - 49 = 0$
16. $-12 = x^2 - 21$
17. Solve $3x^2 + 5 = 21$. Round to the nearest hundredth.

### 9-8 Completing the Square

**Complete the square for each expression.**

18. $x^2 - 12x + \square$
19. $x^2 + 4x + \square$
20. $x^2 + 9x + \square$

**Solve by completing the square.**

21. $x^2 + 2x = 3$
22. $x^2 - 5 = 2x$
23. $x^2 + 7x = 8$
24. The length of a rectangle is 4 feet shorter than its width. The area of the rectangle is 42 square feet. Find the length and width. Round your answer to the nearest tenth of a foot.

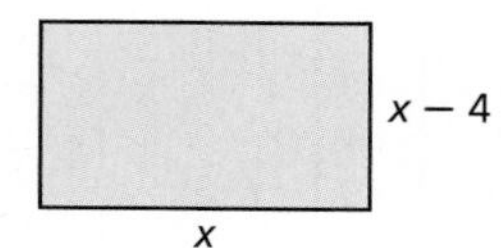


### 9-9 Using the Quadratic Formula and the Discriminant

**Solve using the Quadratic Formula. Round your answer to the nearest hundredth.**

25. $x^2 + 5x + 1 = 0$
26. $3x^2 + 1 = 2x$
27. $5x + 8 = 3x^2$

**Find the number of solutions of each equation using the discriminant.**

28. $2x^2 - 3x + 4 = 0$
29. $x^2 + 1 + 2x = 0$
30. $x^2 - 5 + 4x = 0$

CHAPTER 9

# Study Guide: Review

## Vocabulary

axis of symmetry . . . 600
completing the square . . . 645
discriminant . . . 654
maximum . . . 592
minimum . . . 592
parabola . . . 591
quadratic equation . . . 622
quadratic function . . . 590
vertex . . . 592
zero of a function . . . 599

**Complete the sentences below with vocabulary words from the list above.**

1. The ___?___ is the highest or lowest point on a parabola.
2. A quadratic function has a ___?___ if its graph opens upward and a ___?___ if its graph opens downward.
3. A ___?___ can also be called an $x$-intercept of the function.
4. Finding the ___?___ can tell you how many real-number solutions a quadratic equation has.
5. ___?___ is a process that results in a perfect-square trinomial.

## 9-1 Identifying Quadratic Functions *(pp. 590–597)*

MA.A.3.1, MA.A.4.2, MA.A.4.3

### EXAMPLE

■ **Use a table of values to graph $y = -5x^2 + 40x$.**

**Step 1** Make a table of values.
Choose values of $x$ and use them to find values of $y$.

| $x$ | 0 | 1 | 3 | 4 | 6 | 7 | 8 |
|---|---|---|---|---|---|---|---|
| $y$ | 0 | 35 | 75 | 80 | 60 | 35 | 0 |

**Step 2** Plot the points and connect them with a smooth curve.

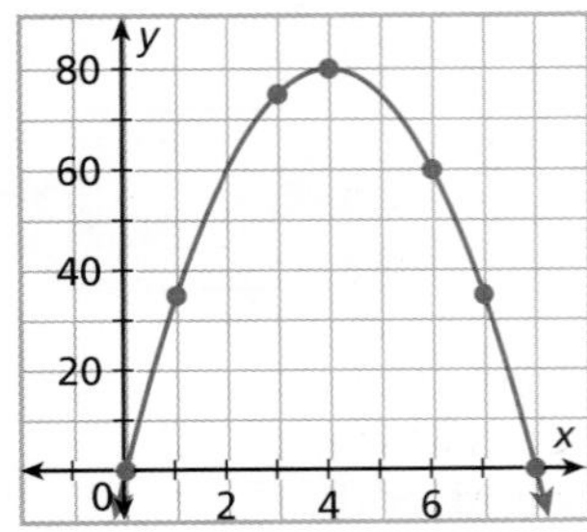


### EXERCISES

**Tell whether each function is quadratic. Explain.**

6. $y = 2x^2 + 9x - 5$
7. $y = -4x + 3$
8. $y = -\frac{1}{2}x^2$
9. $y = 5x^3 + 8$

**Use a table of values to graph each quadratic function.**

10. $y = 6x^2$
11. $y = -4x^2$
12. $y = \frac{1}{4}x^2$
13. $y = -3x^2$

**Tell whether the graph of each function opens upward or downward. Explain.**

14. $y = 5x^2 - 12$
15. $y = -x^2 + 3x - 7$
16. Identify the vertex of the parabola. Then give the minimum or maximum value of the function.

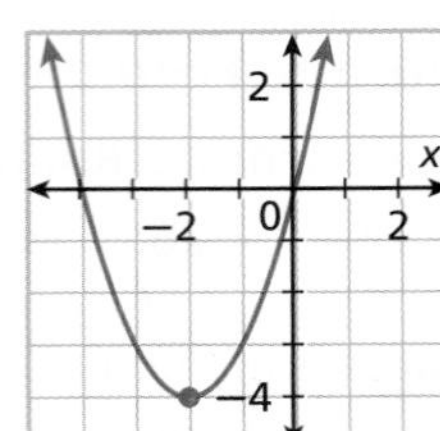

## 9-2 Characteristics of Quadratic Functions *(pp. 599–605)*

MA.A.4.2

### EXAMPLE

- **Find the zeros of $y = 2x^2 - 4x - 6$ from its graph. Then find the axis of symmetry and the vertex.**

$y = 2x^2 - 4x - 6$

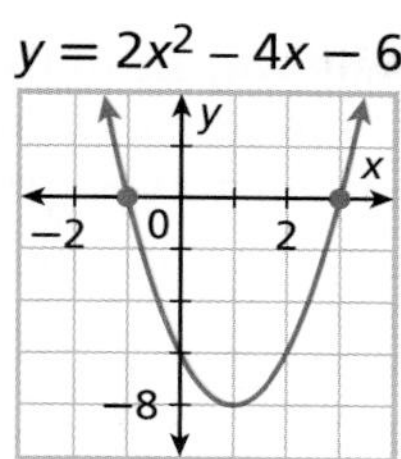

**Step 1** Use the graph to find the zeros.
The zeros are $-1$ and 3.

**Step 2** Find the axis of symmetry.

$x = \frac{-1+3}{2} = \frac{2}{2} = 1$ *Find the average of the zeros.*

The axis of symmetry is the vertical line $x = 1$.

**Step 3** Find the vertex.

$y = 2x^2 - 4x - 6$
$y = 2(1)^2 - 4(1) - 6$ *Substitute 1 into the function to find the y-value of the vertex.*
$y = -8$

The vertex is $(1, -8)$.

### EXERCISES

**Find the zeros of each quadratic function from its graph. Check your answer.**

**17.** $y = x^2 + 3x - 10$

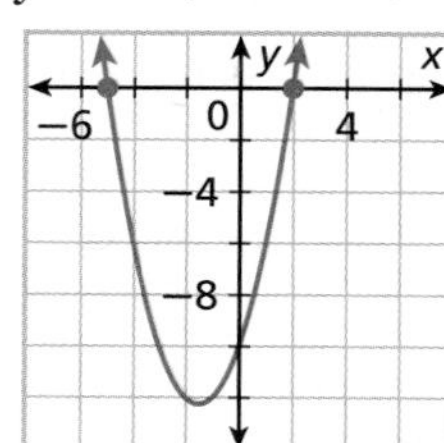

**18.** $y = x^2 - x - 2$

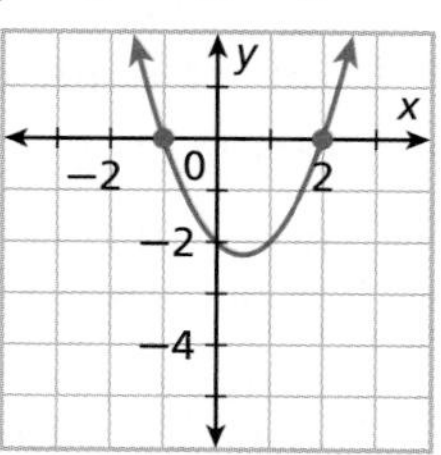

**Find the axis of symmetry and vertex of each parabola.**

**19.** $y = -x^2 + 12x - 32$

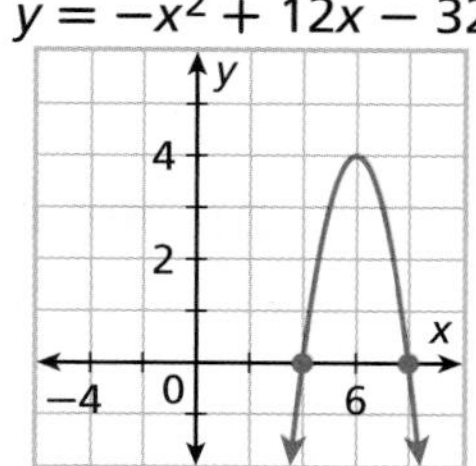

**20.** $y = 2x^2 + 4x - 16$

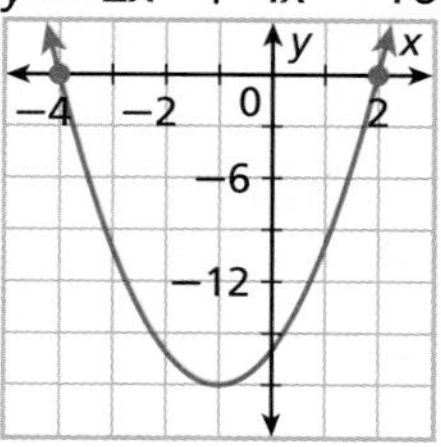

## 9-3 Graphing Quadratic Functions *(pp. 606–611)*

### EXAMPLE

- **Graph $y = 2x^2 - 8x - 10$.**

**Step 1** Find the axis of symmetry.

$x = \frac{-b}{2a} = \frac{-(-8)}{2(2)} = \frac{8}{4} = 2$

The axis of symmetry is $x = 2$.

**Step 2** Find the vertex.

$y = 2x^2 - 8x - 10$
$y = 2(2)^2 - 8(2) - 10$
$y = -18$

The vertex is $(2, -18)$.

**Step 3** Find the $y$-intercept.
$c = -10$

**Step 4** Find one more point on the graph.

$y = 2(-1)^2 - 8(-1) - 10 = 0$
Use $(-1, 0)$.

**Step 5** Graph the axis of symmetry and the points. **Reflect** the points and connect with a smooth curve.

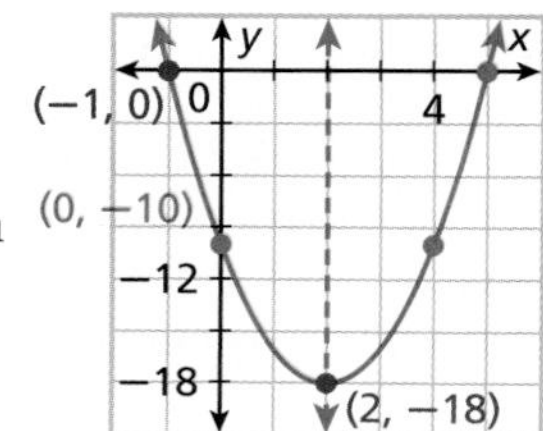


### EXERCISES

**Graph each quadratic function.**

**21.** $y = x^2 + 6x + 6$

**22.** $y = x^2 - 4x - 12$

**23.** $y = x^2 - 8x + 7$

**24.** $y = 2x^2 - 6x - 8$

**25.** $3x^2 + 6x = y - 3$

**26.** $2 - 4x^2 + y = 8x - 10$

**27.** Water that is sprayed upward from a sprinkler with an initial velocity of 20 m/s can be approximated by the function $y = -5x^2 + 20x$, where $y$ is the height of a drop of water $x$ seconds after it is released. Graph this function. Find the time it takes a drop of water to reach its maximum height, the water's maximum height, and the time it takes the water to reach the ground.

## 9-4 Transforming Quadratic Functions *(pp. 613–619)*

MA.A.4.3

### EXAMPLE

■ **Compare the graph of $g(x) = 3x^2 - 4$ with the graph of $f(x) = x^2$. Use the functions.**

- Both graphs open upward because $a > 0$.
- The axis of symmetry is the same, $x = 0$, because $b = 0$ in both functions.
- The graph of $g(x)$ is narrower than the graph of $f(x)$ because $|3| > |1|$.
- The vertex of $f(x)$ is $(0, 0)$. The vertex of $g(x)$ is translated 4 units down to $(0, -4)$.
- $f(x)$ has one zero at the origin. $g(x)$ has two zeros because the vertex is below the origin and the parabola opens upward.

### EXERCISES

**Compare the widths of the graphs of the given quadratic functions. Order functions with different widths from narrowest graph to widest.**

**28.** $f(x) = 2x^2$, $g(x) = 4x^2$

**29.** $f(x) = 6x^2$, $g(x) = -6x^2$

**30.** $f(x) = x^2$, $g(x) = \frac{1}{3}x^2$, $h(x) = 3x^2$

**Compare the graph of each function with the graph of $f(x) = x^2$.**

**31.** $g(x) = x^2 + 5$

**32.** $g(x) = 3x^2 - 1$

**33.** $g(x) = 2x^2 + 3$

## 9-5 Solving Quadratic Equations by Graphing *(pp. 622–627)*

MA.A.4.7

### EXAMPLE

■ **Solve $-4 = 4x^2 - 8x$ by graphing the related function.**

**Step 1** Write the equation in standard form:

$$0 = 4x^2 - 8x + 4.$$

**Step 2** Graph the related function:

$$y = 4x^2 - 8x + 4.$$

**Step 3** Find the zeros.
The only zero is 1. The solution is $x = 1$.

### EXERCISES

**Solve each equation by graphing the related function.**

**34.** $0 = x^2 + 4x + 3$

**35.** $0 = x^2 + 6x + 9$

**36.** $-4x^2 = 3$

**37.** $x^2 + 5 = 6x$

**38.** $-4x^2 = 64 - 32x$

**39.** $9 = 9x^2$

**40.** $-3x^2 + 2x = 5$

## 9-6 Solving Quadratic Equations by Factoring *(pp. 630–635)*

MA.A.4.7

### EXAMPLE

■ **Solve $3x^2 - 6x = 24$ by factoring.**

| | |
|---|---|
| $3x^2 - 6x = 24$ | *Write the equation in standard form.* |
| $3x^2 - 6x - 24 = 0$ | |
| $3(x^2 - 2x - 8) = 0$ | *Factor out 3.* |
| $3(x + 2)(x - 4) = 0$ | *Factor the trinomial.* |
| $3 \neq 0$, $x + 2 = 0$ or $x - 4 = 0$ | *Use the Zero Product Property.* |
| $x = -2$ or $x = 4$ | *Solve each equation.* |

### EXERCISES

**Solve each quadratic equation by factoring.**

**41.** $x^2 + 6x + 5 = 0$

**42.** $x^2 + 9x + 14 = 0$

**43.** $x^2 - 2x - 15 = 0$

**44.** $2x^2 - 2x - 4 = 0$

**45.** $x^2 + 10x + 25 = 0$

**46.** $4x^2 - 36x = -81$

**47.** A rectangle is 2 feet longer than it is wide. The area of the rectangle is 48 square feet. Write and solve an equation that can be used to find the width of the rectangle.

## 9-7 Solving Quadratic Equations by Using Square Roots *(pp. 636–641)*

MA.A.4.7

### EXAMPLE

- **Solve $2x^2 = 98$ using square roots.**

$\frac{2x^2}{2} = \frac{98}{2}$ *Divide both sides of the equation by 2 to isolate $x^2$.*

$x^2 = 49$

$x = \pm\sqrt{49}$ *Take the square root of both sides.*

$x = \pm 7$ *Use ± to show both roots.*

The solutions are −7 and 7.

### EXERCISES

**Solve using square roots.**

48. $5x^2 = 320$
49. $-x^2 + 144 = 0$
50. $x^2 = -16$
51. $x^2 + 7 = 7$
52. $2x^2 = 50$
53. $4x^2 = 25$
54. A rectangle is twice as long as it is wide. The area of the rectangle is 32 square feet. Find the rectangle's width.

## 9-8 Completing the Square *(pp. 645–651)*

MA.A.4.7, MA.G.2.2

### EXAMPLE

- **Solve $x^2 - 6x = -5$ by completing the square.**

$\left(\frac{-6}{2}\right)^2 = 9.$ *Find $\left(\frac{b}{2}\right)^2$.*

$x^2 - 6x + 9 = -5 + 9$ *Complete the square by adding $\left(\frac{b}{2}\right)^2$ to both sides.*

$x^2 - 6x + 9 = 4$

$(x - 3)^2 = 4$ *Factor the trinomial.*

$\sqrt{(x-3)^2} = \sqrt{4}$ *Take the square root of both sides.*

$x - 3 = \pm 2$ *Use the ± symbol.*

$x - 3 = 2$ or $x - 3 = -2$ *Solve each equation.*

$x = 5$ or $x = 1$

The solutions are 5 and 1.

### EXERCISES

**Solve by completing the square.**

55. $x^2 + 2x = 48$
56. $x^2 + 4x = 21$
57. $2x^2 - 12x + 10 = 0$
58. $x^2 - 10x = -20$
59. A homeowner is planning an addition to her house. She wants the new family room to have an area of 192 square feet. The contractor says that the length needs to be 4 more feet than the width. What will the dimensions of the new room be? Round your answer to the nearest hundredth of a foot.

## 9-9 Using the Quadratic Formula and the Discriminant *(pp. 652–659)*

MA.A.4.7, MA.A.4.3

### EXAMPLE

- **Solve $x^2 + 4x + 4 = 0$ using the Quadratic Formula.**

The equation $x^2 + 4x + 4 = 0$ is in standard form with $a = 1$, $b = 4$, and $c = 4$.

$x = \frac{-b \pm \sqrt{b^2 - 4ac}}{2a}$ *Write the Quadratic Formula.*

$= \frac{-4 \pm \sqrt{4^2 - 4(1)(4)}}{2(1)}$ *Substitute for a, b, and c.*

$= \frac{-4 \pm \sqrt{16 - 16}}{2}$ *Simplify.*

$= \frac{-4 \pm \sqrt{0}}{2} = \frac{-4}{2} = -2$

The solution is $x = -2$.

### EXERCISES

**Solve using the Quadratic Formula.**

60. $x^2 - 5x - 6 = 0$
61. $2x^2 - 9x - 5 = 0$
62. $4x^2 - 8x + 4 = 0$
63. $x^2 - 6x = -7$

**Find the number of solutions of each equation using the discriminant.**

64. $x^2 - 12x + 36 = 0$
65. $3x^2 + 5 = 0$
66. $2x^2 - 13x = -20$
67. $6x^2 - 20 = 15x + 1$

CHAPTER 9

**Tell whether each function is quadratic. Explain.**

**1.** (10, 50), (11, 71), (12, 94), (13, 119), (14, 146)

**2.** $3x^2 + y = 4 + 3x^2$

**3.** Tell whether the graph of $y = -2x^2 + 7x - 5$ opens upward or downward and whether the parabola has a maximum or a minimum.

**4.** Estimate the zeros of the quadratic function.

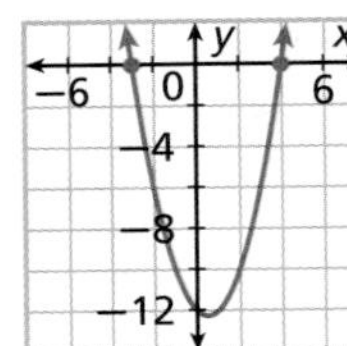


**5.** Find the axis of symmetry of the parabola.

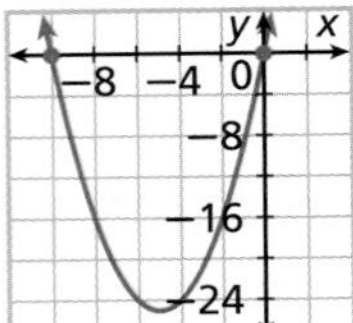


**6.** Find the vertex of the graph of $y = x^2 + 6x + 8$.

**7.** Graph the quadratic function $y = x^2 - 4x + 2$.

**Compare the graph of each function with the graph of $f(x) = x^2$.**

**8.** $g(x) = -x^2 - 2$

**9.** $h(x) = \frac{1}{3}x^2 + 1$

**10.** $g(x) = 3x^2 - 4$

**11.** A hammer is dropped from a 40-foot scaffold. Another one is dropped from a 60-foot scaffold.

**a.** Write the two height functions and compare their graphs. Use $h(t) = -16t^2 + c$, where $c$ is the height of the scaffold.

**b.** Use the graphs to estimate when each hammer will reach the ground.

**12.** A rocket is launched with an initial velocity of 110 m/s. The height of the rocket in meters is approximated by the quadratic equation $h = -5t^2 + 110t$ where $t$ is the time after launch in seconds. About how long does it take for the rocket to return to the ground?

**Solve by factoring.**

**13.** $x^2 + 6x + 5 = 0$

**14.** $x^2 - 12x = -36$

**15.** $x^2 - 81 = 0$

**Solve by using square roots.**

**16.** $-2x^2 = -72$

**17.** $9x^2 - 49 = 0$

**18.** $3x^2 + 12 = 0$

**Solve by completing the square.**

**19.** $x^2 + 10x = -21$

**20.** $x^2 - 6x + 4 = 0$

**21.** $2x^2 + 16x = 0$

**22.** A landscaper has enough cement to make a patio with an area of 150 square feet. The homeowner wants the length to be 6 feet longer than the width. What dimensions should be used for the patio? Round to the nearest tenth of a foot.

**Solve using the Quadratic Formula. Round to the nearest hundredth if necessary.**

**23.** $x^2 + 3x - 40 = 0$

**24.** $2x^2 + 7x = -5$

**25.** $8x^2 + 3x - 1 = 0$

**Find the number of solutions of each equation using the discriminant.**

**26.** $4x^2 - 4x + 1 = 0$

**27.** $2x^2 + 5x - 25 = 0$

**28.** $\frac{1}{2}x^2 + 8 = 0$

CHAPTER 9

## *FOCUS ON SAT SUBJECT TESTS*

In addition to the SAT, some colleges require the SAT Subject Tests for admission. Colleges that don't require the SAT Subject Tests may still use the scores to learn about your academic background and to place you in the appropriate college math class.

**Take the SAT Subject Test in mathematics while the material is still fresh in your mind. You are not expected to be familiar with all of the test content, but you should have completed at least three years of college-prep math.**

**You may want to time yourself as you take this practice test. It should take you about 6 minutes to complete.**

**1.** The graph below corresponds to which of the following quadratic functions?

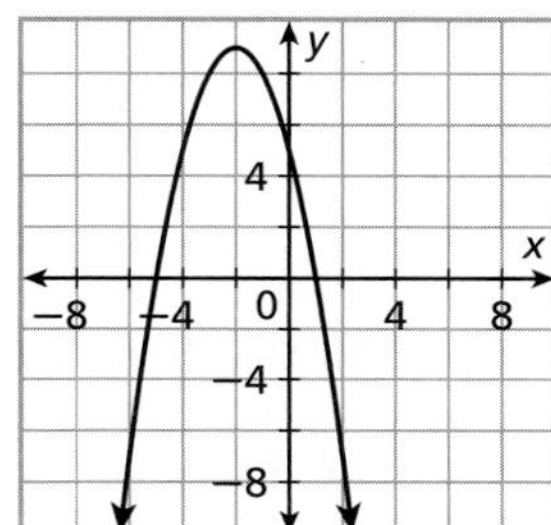


**(A)** $f(x) = x^2 + 4x - 5$

**(B)** $f(x) = -x^2 - 4x + 3$

**(C)** $f(x) = -x^2 + 5x - 4$

**(D)** $f(x) = -x^2 - 4x + 5$

**(E)** $f(x) = -x^2 - 3x + 5$

**2.** What is the sum of the solutions to the equation $9x^2 - 6x = 8$?

**(A)** $\frac{4}{3}$

**(B)** $\frac{2}{3}$

**(C)** $\frac{1}{3}$

**(D)** $-\frac{2}{3}$

**(E)** $-\frac{8}{3}$

**3.** If $h(x) = ax^2 + bx + c$, where $b^2 - 4ac < 0$ and $a < 0$, which of the following statements must be true?

**I.** The graph of $h(x)$ has no points in the first or second quadrants.

**II.** The graph of $h(x)$ has no points in the third or fourth quadrants.

**III.** The graph of $h(x)$ has points in all quadrants.

**(A)** I only

**(B)** II only

**(C)** III only

**(D)** I and II only

**(E)** None of the statements are true.

**4.** What is the axis of symmetry for the graph of a quadratic function whose zeros are −2 and 4?

**(A)** $x = -2$

**(B)** $x = 0$

**(C)** $x = 1$

**(D)** $x = 2$

**(E)** $x = 6$

**5.** How many real-number solutions does $0 = x^2 - 7x + 1$ have?

**(A)** None

**(B)** One

**(C)** Two

**(D)** All real numbers

**(E)** It is impossible to determine.

CHAPTER 9

# TEST TACKLER

## Standardized Test Strategies

## Extended Response: Explain Your Reasoning

Extended response test items often include multipart questions that evaluate your understanding of a math concept. To receive full credit, you must answer the problem correctly, show all of your work, and explain your reasoning. Use complete sentences and show your problem-solving method clearly.

### EXAMPLE 1

**Extended Response** **Given $\frac{1}{2}x^2 + y = 4x - 3$ and $y = 2x - 12x$, identify which is a quadratic function. Provide an explanation for your decision. For the quadratic function, tell whether the graph of the function opens upward or downward and whether the parabola has a maximum or a minimum. Explain your reasoning.**

*Read the solutions provided by two different students.*

**Student A**

The quadratic function is $\frac{1}{2}x^2 + y = 4x - 3$ because it can be written in standard form, $y = -\frac{1}{2}x^2 + 4x - 3$, where a, b, and c are real numbers and $a \neq 0$. The other function, $y = 2x - 12x$, is not quadratic because there is no $x^2$- term.

The graph of this function will open downward because a, which is equal to $-\frac{1}{2}$, is less than 0. Because the parabola opens downward, the graph will have a maximum.

*Excellent Explanation*

The response includes the correct answers along with a detailed explanation for each part of the problem. The explanation is written using complete sentences and is presented in an order that is easy to follow and to understand. It is obvious that this student knows how to determine and interpret a quadratic function.

**Student B**

$\frac{1}{2}x^2 + y = 4x - 3$ There is an $x^2$.

When I graphed the function on my calculator, I saw a parabola that opened downward.

It had a maximum.

*Poor Explanation*

The response includes the correct answers, but the explanation does not include details. The reason for defining the function as quadratic does not show knowledge of the concept. The student shows a lack of understanding of how to write and interpret a quadratic function in standard form.

**Include as many details as possible to support your reasoning. This increases the chance of getting full credit for your response.**

Read each test item and answer the questions that follow.

**Item A**

The height in feet of a tennis ball $x$ seconds after it is ejected from a serving machine is given by the ordered pairs $\{(0, 10), (0.5, 9), (1, 7), (1.5, 4), (2, 0)\}$. Determine whether the function is quadratic. Find its domain and range. Explain your answers.

1. What should a student include in the explanation to receive full credit?
2. Read the two explanations below. Which explanation is better? Why?

**Student A**

Range: $0 \le y \le 10$ Domain: $0 \le x \le 2$
Second differences are $-1$ : quadratic

**Student B**

The function is quadratic because the second differences are constant: $-1$. The domain and range are determined by the points $(0, 10)$ and $(2, 0)$. The range is $0 \le y \le 10$, and the domain is $0 \le x \le 2$.

**Item B**

The height of a golf ball can be approximated by the function $y = -5x^2 + 20x + 8$, where $y$ is the height in meters above the ground and $x$ is the time in seconds after the ball is hit. What is the maximum height of the ball? How long does it take for the ball to reach its maximum height? Explain.

3. A student correctly found the following answers. Use this information to write a clear and concise explanation.

Axis of symmetry is the vertical line at $x = 2$.
Vertex is at $(2, 28)$.
28 meters; 2 seconds
2 seconds versus 4 seconds

**Item C**

A science teacher set off a bottle rocket as part of a lab experiment. The function $h = -16t^2 + 96t$ represents the height in feet of a rocket that is shot out of a bottle with a vertical velocity of 96 feet per second. Find the time that the rocket is in the air. Explain how you found your answer.

4. Read the two responses below.
   a. Which student provided the better explanation? Why?
   b. What advice would you give the other student to improve his or her explanation?

**Student C**

Graph the function $h = -16t^2 + 96t$, and then find the zeros. The first zero is when $t = 0$, when the rocket is launched. The second zero is when the rocket hits the ground: $t = 6$. The difference between 6 and 0 is the time that the rocket is in the air: 6 seconds.

**Student D**

6 seconds.
Graph the function to find how long the rocket is in the air, and find the values where it crosses the x-axis.

**Item D**

The base of a parallelogram is 12 centimeters more than its height. The area of the parallelogram is 13 square centimeters. Explain how to determine the height and base of the figure. What is the height? What is the base?

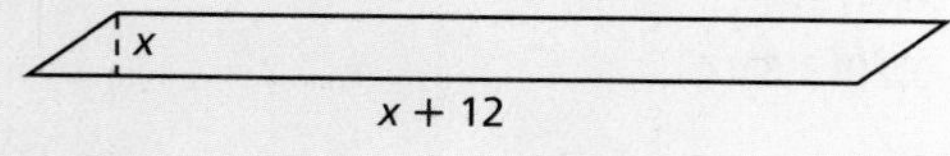


5. Read the following response. Identify any areas that need improvement. Rewrite the response so that it will receive full credit.

$x^2 + 12x + 36 = 49$ Complete the square.
$(x+6)^2 = 49$
$x + 6 = \sqrt{49}$
$x + 6 = \pm 7$; $x = 1$ or $-13$

base = 13, height = 1

CHAPTER 9

## CUMULATIVE ASSESSMENT, CHAPTERS 1–9

### Multiple Choice

1. The length of a rectangle is 2 units greater than the width. The area of the rectangle is 24 square units. What is the width?

   A 2 units

   B 4 units

   C 6 units

   D 12 units

2. Which function's graph is a translation of the graph of $f(x) = 3x^2 + 4$ seven units down?

   A $f(x) = -4x^2 + 4$

   B $f(x) = 10x^2 + 4$

   C $f(x) = 3x^2 - 3$

   D $f(x) = 3x^2 + 11$

3. The area of a circle is $\pi(9x^2 + 42x + 49)$. What is the circumference of the circle?

   A $\pi(3x + 7)$

   B $2\pi(3x + 7)$

   C $2\pi(3x + 7)^2$

   D $6x + 14$

4. CyberCafe charges a computer station rental fee of \$5, plus \$0.20 for each quarter-hour spent surfing. Which expression represents the total amount Carl will pay to use a computer station for three and a half hours?

   A $5 + 0.20(3.5)$

   B $5 + 0.20(3.5)(4)$

   C $5 + \frac{0.20}{3.5 \div 4}$

   D $5 + \frac{1}{4} \cdot \frac{0.20}{3.5}$

5. What is the midpoint of the line segment that connects the points $(-12, 4)$ and $(5, 7)$?

   A $(-3.5, 5.5)$

   B $(3.5, 5.5)$

   C $(-4, 6)$

   D $(4, 6)$

6. Which is a possible situation for the graph?

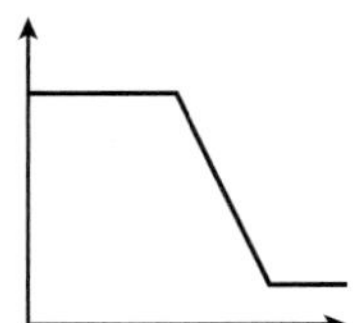

   A A car drives at a steady speed, slows down in a school zone, and then resumes its previous speed.

   B A child climbs the ladder of a slide and then slides down.

   C A person flies in an airplane for a while, parachutes out, and gets stuck in a tree.

   D The number of visitors increases in the summer, declines in the fall, and levels off in the winter.

7. Which of the following is the graph of $f(x) = -x^2 + 2$?

A
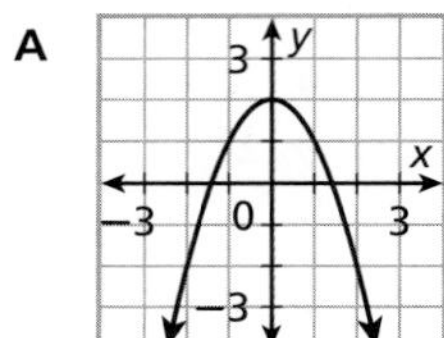


C
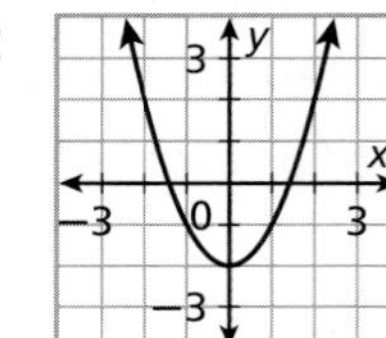


B
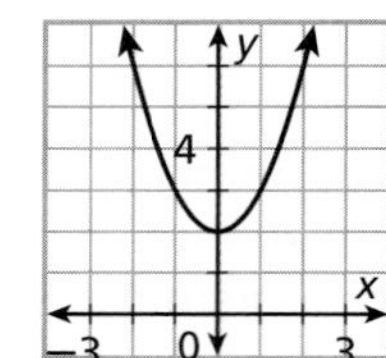


D
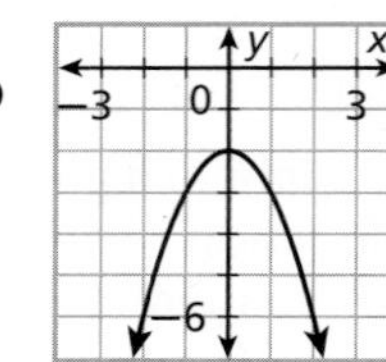


8. The value of $y$ varies directly with $x$, and $y = 40$ when $x = -5$. What is the value of $y$ when $x = 8$?

   A 25　　C $-8$

   B $-1$　　D $-64$

9. What is the slope of the line that passes through the points $(4, 7)$ and $(5, 3)$?

   A 4　　C $-4$

   B $\frac{1}{4}$　　D $-\frac{1}{4}$

**The problems on many standardized tests are ordered from least to most difficult, but all items are usually worth the same amount of points. If you are stuck on a question near the end of the test, your time may be better spent rechecking your answers to earlier questions.**

**10.** Putting Green Mini Golf charges a \$4 golf club rental fee plus \$1.25 per game. Good Times Golf charges a \$1.25 golf club rental fee plus \$3.75 per game. Which system of equations could be solved to determine for how many games the cost is the same at both places?

A $\begin{cases} y = 4x + 1.25 \\ y = 3.75 + 1.25x \end{cases}$

B $\begin{cases} y = 4 - 1.25x \\ y = -3.75 + 1.25x \end{cases}$

C $\begin{cases} y = 1.25x + 4 \\ y = 3.75x + 1.25 \end{cases}$

D $\begin{cases} y = 1.25x - 4 \\ y = 1.25x + 3.75 \end{cases}$

**11.** The graph of which function has an axis of symmetry of $x = -2$?

A $y = 2x^2 - x + 3$

B $y = 4x^2 + 2x + 3$

C $y = x^2 - 2x + 3$

D $y = x^2 + 4x + 3$

**12.** Which polynomial is the product of $x - 4$ and $x^2 - 4x + 1$?

A $-4x^2 + 17x - 4$

B $x^3 - 8x^2 + 17x - 4$

C $x^3 + 17x - 4$

D $x^3 - 15x + 4$

**13.** What is the discriminant of the equation $0 = -2x^2 + 3x + 4$?

A 41     C 35

B 40     D −44

**14.** Use the Quadratic Formula to find the positive solution of $4x^2 = 10x + 2$. Round your answer to the nearest hundredth.

A 4.07     C 2.12

B 3.85     D 2.69

## *STANDARDIZED TEST PREP*

## Short Response

**S1.** The data in the table shows ordered pair solutions to a linear function. Find the missing $y$-value. Show your work.

| $x$ | $y$ |
|---|---|
| −2 | −7 |
| −1 | −3 |
| 0 | |
| 1 | 5 |
| 2 | 9 |

**S2.** Answer the following questions using the function $f(x) = 2x^2 + 4x - 1$.

**a.** Make a table of values and give five points on the graph.

**b.** Find the axis of symmetry and vertex. Show all calculations.

**S3. a.** Show how to solve $x^2 - 2x - 8 = 0$ by graphing the related function. Show all your work.

**b.** Show another way to solve the equation in part **a**. Show all your work.

**S4.** What can you say about the value of $a$ if the graph of $y = ax^2 - 8$ has no $x$-intercepts? Explain.

## Extended Response

**E1.** The graph shows the quadratic function $f(x) = ax^2 + bx + c$.

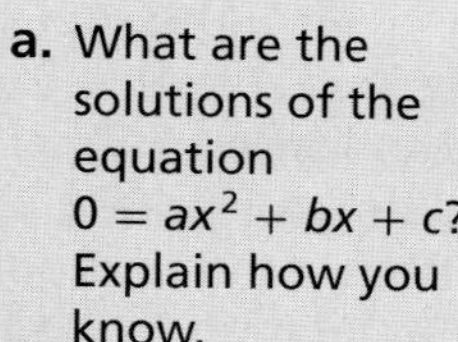

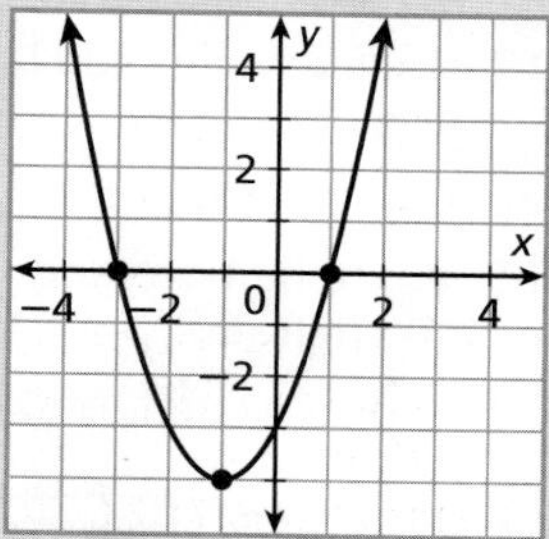


**a.** What are the solutions of the equation $0 = ax^2 + bx + c$? Explain how you know.

**b.** If the point $(-5, 12)$ lies on the graph of $f(x)$, the point $(a, 12)$ also lies on the graph. Find the value of $a$.

**c.** What do you know about the relationship between the values of $a$ and $b$? Use the coordinates of the vertex in your explanation.

**d.** Use what you know about solving quadratic equations by factoring to make a conjecture about the values of $a$, $b$, and $c$ in the function $f(x) = ax^2 + bx + c$.

CHAPTER 10

# Data Analysis and Probability

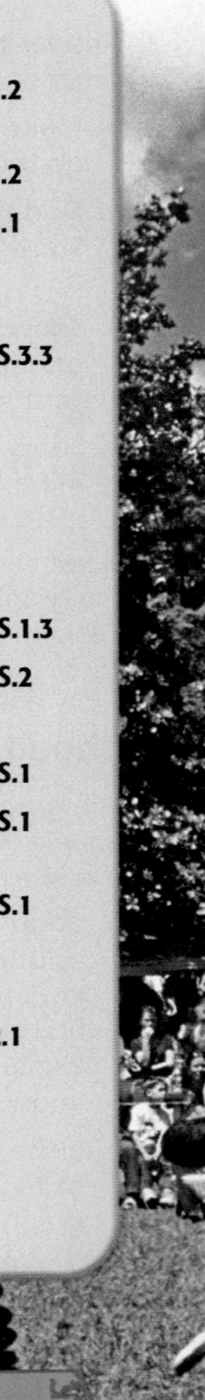



## Why Learn This?

You can use graphs to display data about populations, such as the Metrolina Native Americans shown here.

go.hrw.com
Chapter Project Online

KEYWORD: MA7 ChProj

# ARE YOU READY?

## Vocabulary

**Match each term on the left with a definition on the right.**

1. difference
2. factor
3. natural numbers
4. ratio
5. sum

A. the result of an addition
B. a number that is multiplied by another number to get a product
C. numbers that can be expressed in the form $\frac{a}{b}$, where $a$ and $b$ are both integers and $b \neq 0$
D. the result of a subtraction
E. a comparison of two quantities by division
F. the counting numbers: 1, 2, 3, …

## Solve Proportions

**Solve each proportion.**

6. $\frac{3}{4} = \frac{x}{12}$
7. $\frac{15}{9} = \frac{3}{x}$
8. $\frac{10}{20} = \frac{x}{100}$
9. $\frac{250}{1500} = \frac{x}{100}$

## Compare and Order Real Numbers

**Compare. Write <, >, or =.**

10. 20 ▒ 13
11. $\frac{2}{3}$ ▒ $\frac{1}{2}$
12. $\frac{3}{4}$ ▒ $\frac{7}{9}$
13. 0.75 ▒ $\frac{9}{12}$

**Order the numbers from least to greatest.**

14. $\frac{1}{2}, \frac{4}{5}, \frac{1}{8}, \frac{3}{4}, \frac{2}{3}$
15. $0.12, \frac{2}{5}, \frac{3}{4}, 0.3, \frac{1}{3}$

## Multiply Decimals

**Multiply.**

16. $0.25 \times 300$
17. $0.5 \times 4000$
18. $0.05 \times 200$
19. $0.125 \times 9600$

## Divide Decimals

**Divide.**

20. $435 \div 10$
21. $32 \div 100$
22. $777 \div 1000$
23. $295 \div 10{,}000$

## Fractions, Decimals, and Percents

**Write the equivalent decimal.**

24. $\frac{3}{5}$
25. 45%
26. $\frac{3}{4}$
27. 8%

**Write the equivalent percent.**

28. $\frac{1}{4}$
29. 0.2
30. 0.36
31. $\frac{1}{10}$

CHAPTER 10

# Study Guide: Preview

## Where You've Been

**Previously, you**

- read information from tables and graphs.
- added, subtracted, multiplied, and divided real numbers.
- worked with ratios and percents.

## In This Chapter

**You will study**

- how to organize data in tables, graphs, and plots.
- how to find the central tendency of a data set by calculating mean, median, and mode.
- writing experimental and theoretical probability as ratios, percents, and decimals.
- combinations, permutations, and factorials as extensions of multiplication.

## Where You're Going

**You can use the skills in this chapter**

- to present your findings from science laboratory experiments in an appropriate and accurate graphical form.
- to be more informed about statistical information in the news and not to be misled by how it is presented.

## *Key Vocabulary/Vocabulario*

| | |
|---|---|
| combination | combinación |
| compound event | suceso compuesto |
| dependent events | sucesos dependientes |
| experimental probability | probabilidad experimental |
| frequency | frecuencia |
| independent events | sucesos independientes |
| median | mediana |
| outlier | valor extremo |
| permutation | permutación |
| probability | probabilidad |
| quartile | cuartil |
| theoretical probability | probabilidad teórica |

## *Vocabulary Connections*

To become familiar with some of the vocabulary terms in the chapter, consider the following. You may refer to the chapter, the glossary, or a dictionary if you like.

1. The *median strip* is the middle region that divides a highway in half. Use this knowledge to define **median** as it relates to a set of data.
2. The word **quartile** starts with the prefix *quart-*. What are some other words that start with the prefix *quart-*? What do they all have in common?
3. **Probability** is the chance something will happen. Based on your understanding of the words *experiment* and *theory*, compare and contrast the terms **experimental probability** and **theoretical probability**.
4. A *compound word* is made up of two or more words. What do you think makes up a **compound event**?

# Reading and Writing Math

CHAPTER 10

## Reading Strategy: Read and Interpret Graphics

Knowing how to interpret figures, diagrams, charts, and graphs will help you gather the information you need to get the correct answer.

**What You See**

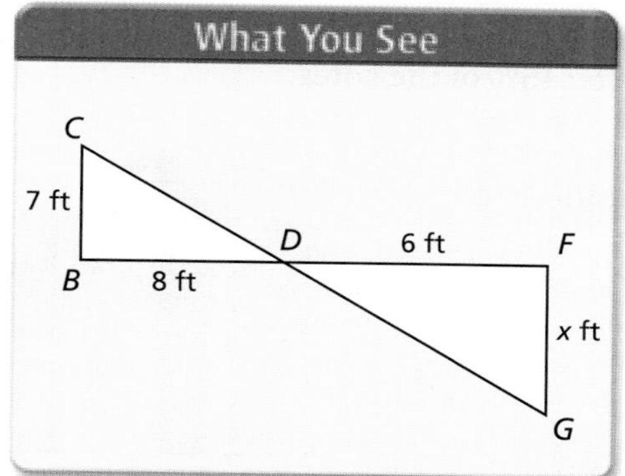


**How to Interpret**

✔ **Read all labels.**
$CB = 7$ ft; $BD = 8$ ft;
$DF = 6$ ft; $FG = x$ ft

✘ **Do not assume anything.**

It appears that $\overline{DF}$ is longer than $\overline{BD}$, but the labels indicate that it is shorter.

$\angle B$ and $\angle F$ appear to be 90°, but the diagram does not indicate this.

**What You See**

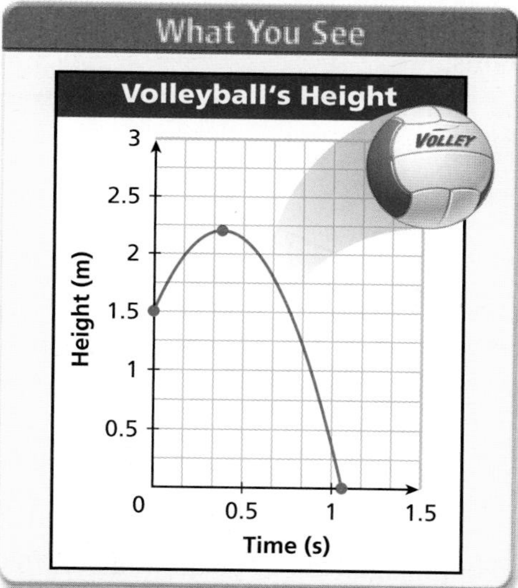


**How to Interpret**

✔ **Read the title.**
"Volleyball's Height"

✔ **Read each axis label.**

*x*-axis Indicates **time** measured in seconds

*y*-axis Indicates **height** measured in meters

✔ **Determine what information is represented.**

Each point on the graph gives the **height** of the ball at that **time**.

### Try This

**Look up each exercise in the text and answer the corresponding questions.**

1. Lesson 2-6 Exercise 42: What is the title of the table? What is the record for the 200-meter run?
2. Lesson 7-7 Exercise 69: What does $x$ represent in the diagram? Make a list of the information you know from the diagram.
3. Lesson 8-3 Exercise 51: What is represented by the $y$-axis? What is the $y$-value when $x$ equals 3.5? Is the graph linear? How do you know?
4. Lesson 9-8 Exercise 33: What does the dashed line represent? What facts about the parallelogram are given from the diagram?

# Bar and Circle Graphs

**MA.A.4.5** Use ... symbols to solve linear equations.

Data displayed in bar graphs and circle graphs can be used to solve equations. In these problems, parts of the graphs are missing.

*See Skills Bank page S52*

## Example 1

**The top part of this graph was torn off. If Warren received 15% of the votes, how many votes did Adams receive?**

Votes
80
60
40
20
0
52
65
42
28
Hansen
Adams
Warren
Sweeney
Marino
Candidate

**Step 1** Find the total number of votes. Let $t$ represent the total.

| 15% | of | the total votes | is | 42 votes. |
|---|---|---|---|---|
| 0.15 | • | $t$ | = | 42 |

$$0.15t = 42$$

$$t = 280 \text{ votes}$$

**Step 2** Find the number of votes Adams received.

Let $a$ represent the number of votes received by Adams. Let $h$, $w$, $s$, and $m$ represent the number of votes received by Hansen, Warren, Sweeney, and Marino.

$$t = a + h + w + s + m$$

$$280 = a + 52 + 42 + 65 + 28$$ *Substitute the numbers shown on the graph.*

$$280 = a + 187$$ *Simplify the right side of the equation.*

$$\underline{-187} \quad \underline{-187}$$

$$93 = a$$ *Subtract 187 from both sides.*

Adams received 93 votes.

## Try This

1. The missing bar is twice as tall as the bar for week 2. How many total miles did Kim bike in these five weeks?

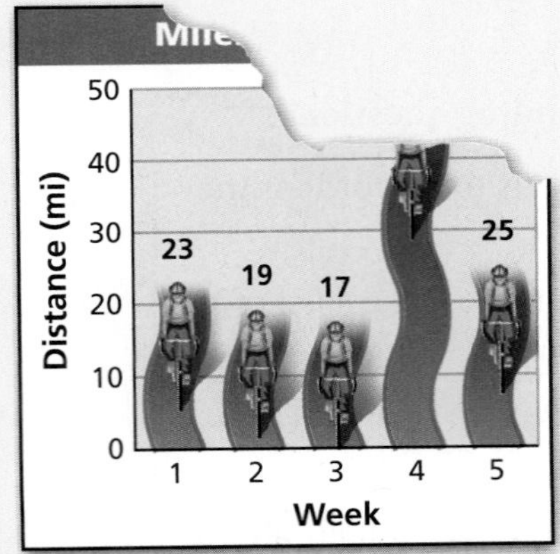


2. People aged 20–29 years walked 275 more miles than the oldest age group. Find the total miles walked by all age groups.

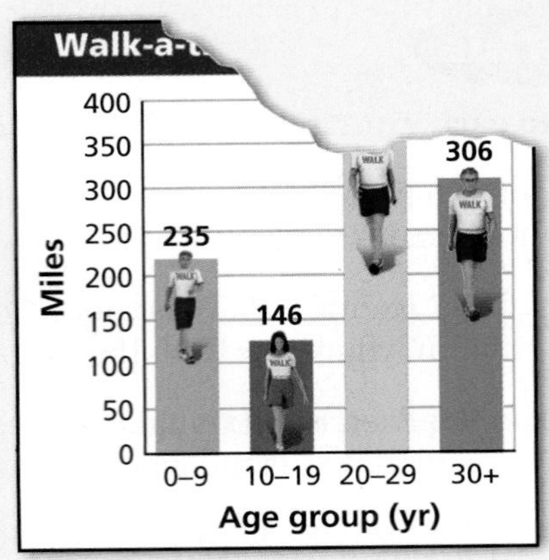

Remember that a circle graph represents all the data in a data set. The percent represented by each section is a part of the whole data set, so the sum of all the percents must be 100%.

## Example 2

**A survey asked people in a neighborhood to agree or disagree with the following statement:**

**"We need a traffic light at Jefferson Avenue and Third Street."**

**If 35% of the people disagreed with the statement, how many people had no opinion?**

**Opinion Survey**

Strongly agree 36
Agree 27
Disagree 63
Strongly disagree 45
No opinion ?

The number of people who answered "no opinion" is missing from the graph.

**Step 1** Find the total number of people who answered the survey. Let $t$ represent the total number of people.

| 35% | of | the total number of people | is | 63 people. |
|---|---|---|---|---|
| 0.35 | • | $t$ | = | 63 |

$0.35t = 63$

$t = 180$ people

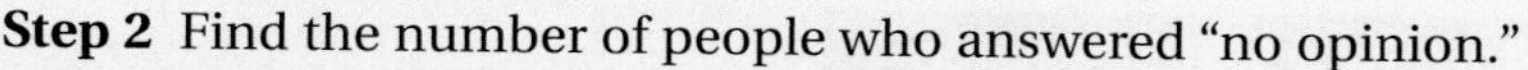

**Step 2** Find the number of people who answered "no opinion."

Let $n$ represent the number of "no opinion" answers. Let $d$, $s$, $g$, and $a$ represent the number of "disagree," "strongly disagree," "strongly agree," and "agree" answers.

$t = n + d + s + g + a$

$180 = n + 63 + 45 + 36 + 27$ *Substitute the numbers shown on the graph.*

$180 = n + 171$ *Simplify the right side of the equation.*

$\underline{-171} \quad \underline{-171}$

$9 = n$ *Subtract 171 from both sides.*

There were 9 people who had no opinion.

## Try This

**3.** The students in a junior high school voted on their choice for a field trip. Sixteen students voted for the natural history museum. How many students voted for the winning choice?

**Field Trip Vote**

Aquarium 25%
Zoo 20%
Museum 20%
Planetarium ?

**4.** At the fall dance recital, 40% of the tickets were sold to adults. What percent of the sales were to seniors?

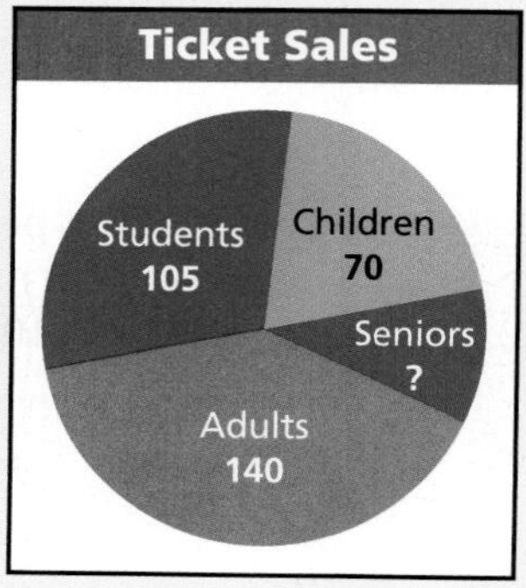

# 10-1 Organizing and Displaying Data

**MA.S.1.2** Compare shape, center, and spread of univariate data using graphical displays...

***Objectives***

Organize data in tables and graphs.

Choose a table or graph to display data.

***Vocabulary***

bar graph
line graph
circle graph

**Who uses this?**

Nutritionists can display health information about food in bar graphs.

*Bar graphs, line graphs,* and *circle graphs* can be used to present data in a visual way.

A **bar graph** displays data with vertical or horizontal bars. Bar graphs are a good way to display data that can be organized into categories. Using a bar graph, you can quickly compare the categories.

## EXAMPLE 1 Reading and Interpreting Bar Graphs

**Use the graph to answer each question.**

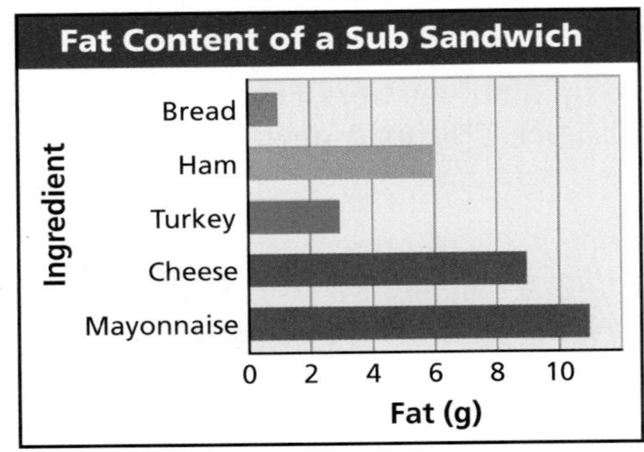


**A** **Which ingredient contains the most fat?**

mayonnaise — *The bar for mayonnaise is the longest.*

**B** **How many more grams of fat are in ham than in turkey?**

$6 - 3 = 3$ — *There are 6 grams of fat in ham and 3 grams of fat in turkey.*

**C** **How many total fat grams are in this sandwich?**

$1 + 6 + 3 + 9 + 11 = 30$ — *Add the number of fat grams for each ingredient.*

**D** **What percent of the total fat grams in this sandwich are from turkey?**

$\frac{3}{30} = \frac{1}{10} = 10\%$ — *Out of 30 total fat grams, 3 fat grams are from turkey.*

**Use the graph to answer each question.**

**1a.** Which ingredient contains the least amount of fat?

**1b.** Which ingredients contain at least 8 grams of fat?

A double-bar graph can be used to compare two data sets. A double-bar graph has a key to distinguish between the two sets of data.

## EXAMPLE 2 Reading and Interpreting Double Bar Graphs

**Use the graph to answer each question.**

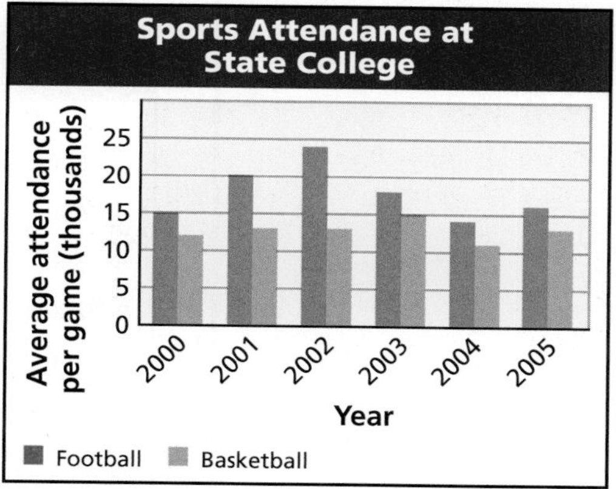


**A** **In which year did State College have the greatest average attendance for basketball?**

2003

*Find the tallest orange bar.*

**B** **On average, how many more people attended a football game than a basketball game in 2001?**

20,000 − 13,000 = 7000

*Find the height of each bar for 2001 and subtract.*

CHECK IT OUT! **2.** Use the graph to determine which years had the same average basketball attendance. What was the average attendance for those years?

A **line graph** displays data using line segments. Line graphs are a good way to display data that changes over a period of time.

## EXAMPLE 3 Reading and Interpreting Line Graphs

**Use the graph to answer each question.**

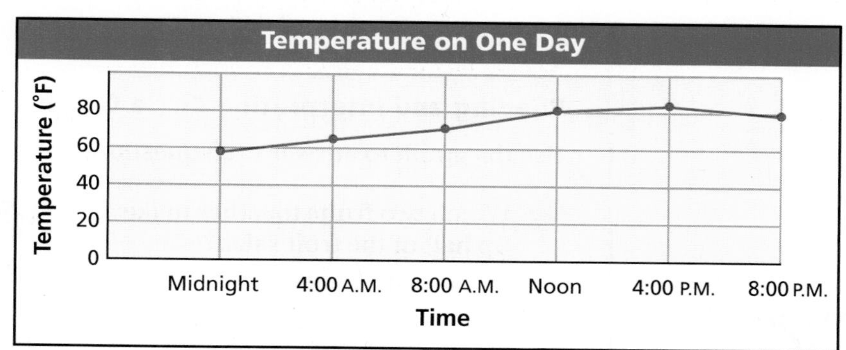


**A** **At what time was the temperature the warmest?**

4:00 P.M. *Identify the highest point.*

**B** **During which 4-hour time period did the temperature increase the most?**

From 8:00 A.M. to noon *Look for the segment with the greatest positive slope.*

**3.** Use the graph to estimate the difference in temperature between 4:00 A.M. and noon.

A double-line graph can be used to compare how two related data sets change over time. A double-line graph has a key to distinguish between the two sets of data.

**EXAMPLE 4** **Reading and Interpreting Double-Line Graphs**

**Use the graph to answer each question.**

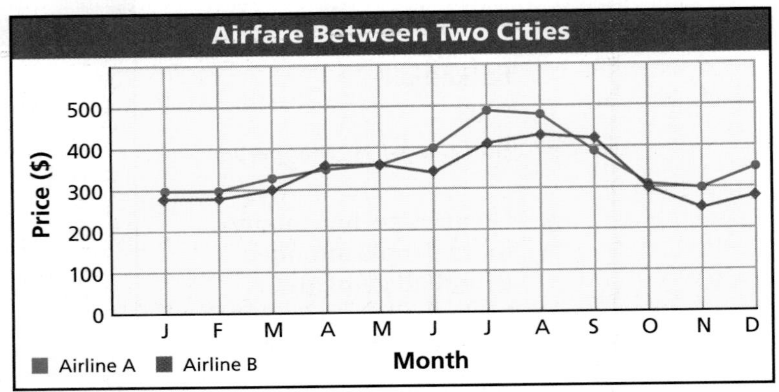


**A** **In which month(s) did airline B charge more than airline A?**

April and September *Identify the points when the purple line is higher than the blue line.*

**B** **During which month(s) did the airlines charge the same airfare?**

May *Look for the point where the data points overlap.*

**4.** Use the graph to describe the general trend of the data.

A **circle graph** shows parts of a whole. The entire circle represents 100% of the data and each sector represents a percent of the total. Circle graphs are good for comparing each category of data to the whole set.

**EXAMPLE 5** **Reading and Interpreting Circle Graphs**

**Use the graph to answer each question.**

**A** **Which two fruits together make up half of the fruit salad?**

bananas and strawberries

*Look for two fruits that together make up half of the circle.*

**B** **Which fruit is used more than any other?**

cantaloupe

*Look for the largest sector of the graph.*

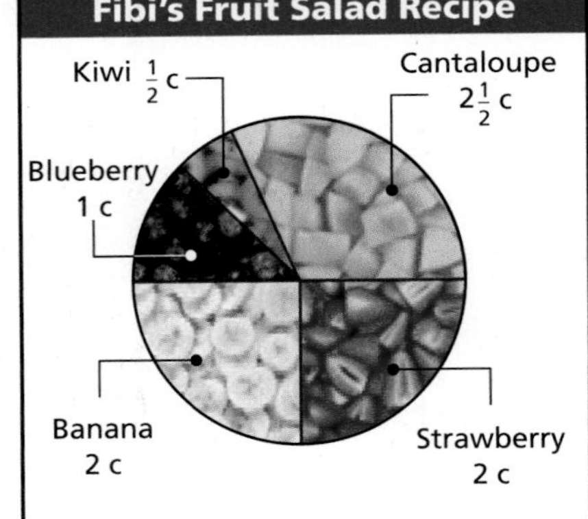


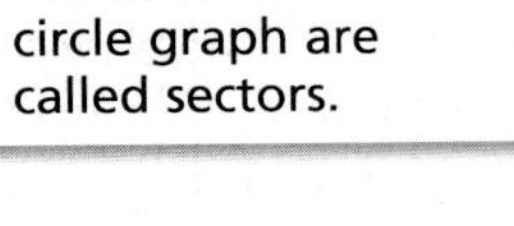


The sections of a circle graph are called sectors.

**5.** Use the graph to determine what percent of the fruit salad is cantaloupe.

## EXAMPLE 6 Choosing and Creating an Appropriate Display

**Use the given data to make a graph. Explain why you chose that type of graph.**

**A**

| Livestock Show Entries | |
|---|---|
| **Animal** | **Number** |
| Chicken | 38 |
| Goat | 10 |
| Horse | 32 |
| Pig | 12 |
| Sheep | 25 |

A bar graph is appropriate for this data because it will be a good way to compare categories.

**Step 1** Determine an appropriate scale and interval. The scale must include all of the data values. The scale is separated into equal parts, called intervals.

**Step 2** Use the data to determine the lengths of the bars. Draw bars of equal width. The bars should not touch.

**Step 3** Title the graph and label the horizontal and vertical scales.

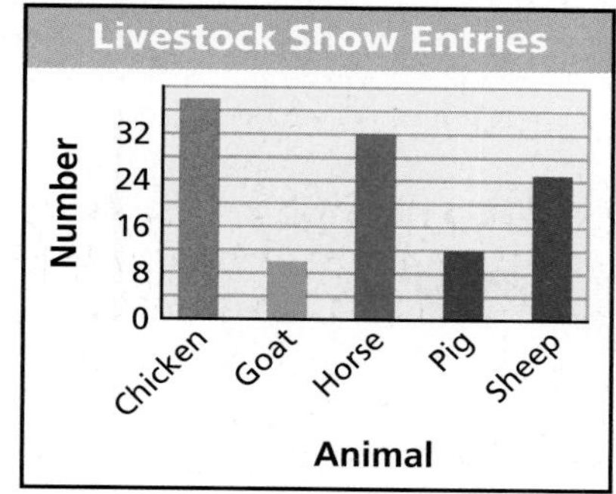


**B**

| Division of Crops | |
|---|---|
| **Crop** | **Area (acres)** |
| Corn | 70 |
| Fallow | 50 |
| Mixed vegetables | 10 |
| Soybeans | 40 |
| Wheat | 30 |

A circle graph is appropriate for this data because it shows categories as parts of a whole.

**Step 1** Calculate the percent of the total represented by each category.

Corn: $\frac{70}{200} = 0.35 = 35\%$

Soybeans: $\frac{40}{200} = 0.2 = 20\%$

Fallow: $\frac{50}{200} = 0.25 = 25\%$

Wheat: $\frac{30}{200} = 0.15 = 15\%$

Mixed vegetables: $\frac{10}{200} = 0.05 = 5\%$

**Step 2** Find the angle measure for each sector of the graph. Since there are 360° in a circle, multiply each percent by 360°.

Corn: $0.35 \times 360° = 126°$

Fallow: $0.25 \times 360° = 90°$

Mixed vegetables: $0.05 \times 360° = 18°$

Soybeans: $0.2 \times 360° = 72°$

Wheat: $0.15 \times 360° = 54°$

**Step 3** Use a compass to draw a circle. Mark the center and use a straightedge to draw one radius. Then use a protractor to draw each central angle.

**Step 4** Title the graph and label each sector.

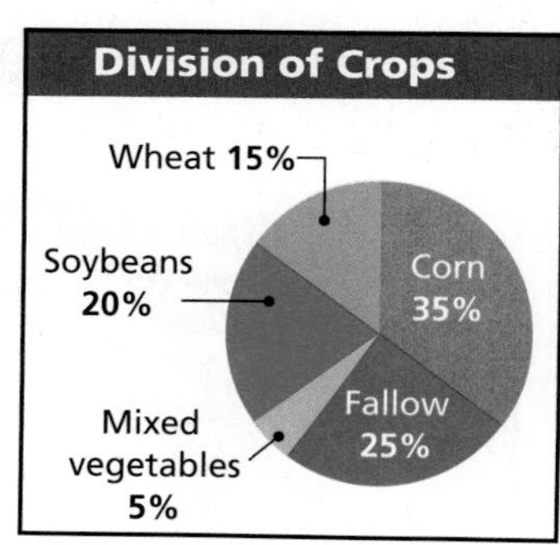

**Use the given data to make a graph. Explain why you chose that type of graph.**

| Chinnick College Enrollment | |
|---|---|
| **Year** | **Students** |
| 1930 | 586 |
| 1955 | 2,361 |
| 1980 | 15,897 |
| 2005 | 21,650 |

A line graph is appropriate for this data because it will show the change in enrollment over a period of time.

**Step 1** Determine the scale and interval for each set of data. Time should be plotted on the horizontal axis because it is independent.

**Step 2** Plot a point for each pair of values. Connect the points using line segments.

**Step 3** Title the graph and label the horizontal and vertical scales.

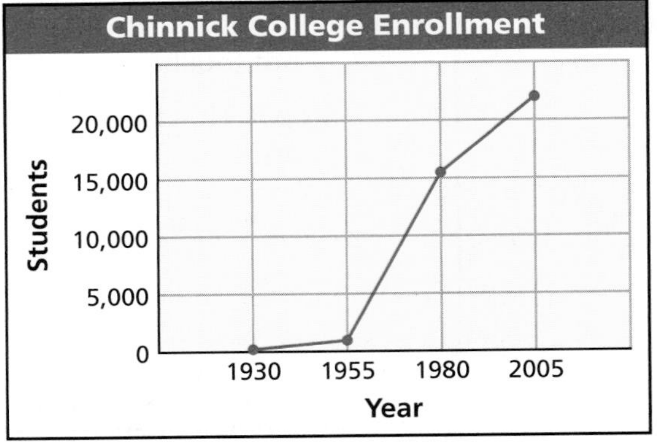

**6. Use the given data to make a graph. Explain why you chose that type of graph.**

The data below shows how Vera spends her time during a typical 5-day week during the school year.

| Vera's Schedule | | | | | | |
|---|---|---|---|---|---|---|
| **Activity** | Sleeping | Eating | School | Sports | Homework | Other |
| **Time (h)** | 45 | 8 | 30 | 10 | 10 | 17 |

## THINK AND DISCUSS

**1.** What are some comparisons you can make by looking at a bar graph?

**2.** Name some key components of a good line graph.

**3. GET ORGANIZED** Copy and complete the graphic organizer. In each box, tell which kind of graph is described.

Graph Type
- Compares categories
- Shows change over time
- Shows how a whole is divided in parts

# 10-1 Exercises

MA.S.1.2

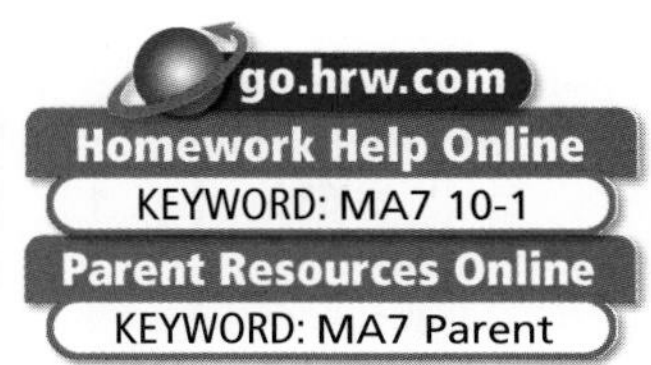


## GUIDED PRACTICE

**Vocabulary** **Use the vocabulary from this lesson to answer the following questions.**

1. In a *circle graph,* what does each sector represent?
2. In a *line graph,* how does the slope of a line segment relate to the rate of change?

SEE EXAMPLE 1 p. 678

**Use the bar graph for Exercises 3 and 4.**

3. Estimate the total number of animals at the shelter.
4. There are 3 times as many ___?___ as ___?___ at the animal shelter.

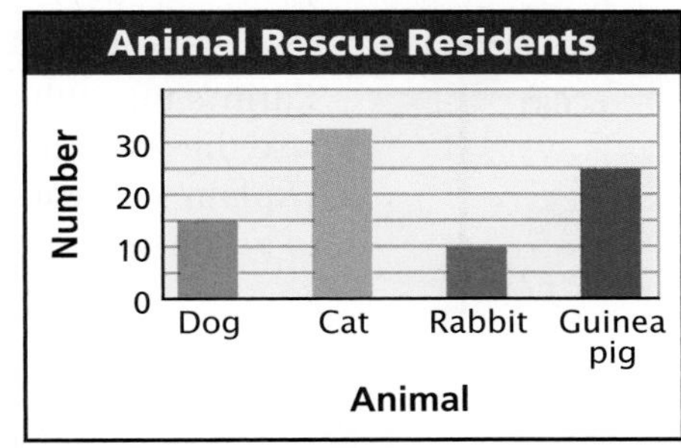


SEE EXAMPLE 2 p. 679

**Use the double-bar graph for Exercises 5–7.**

5. About how much more is a club level seat at stadium A than at stadium B?
6. Which type of seat is the closest in price at the two stadiums?
7. Describe one relationship between the ticket prices at stadium A and stadium B.

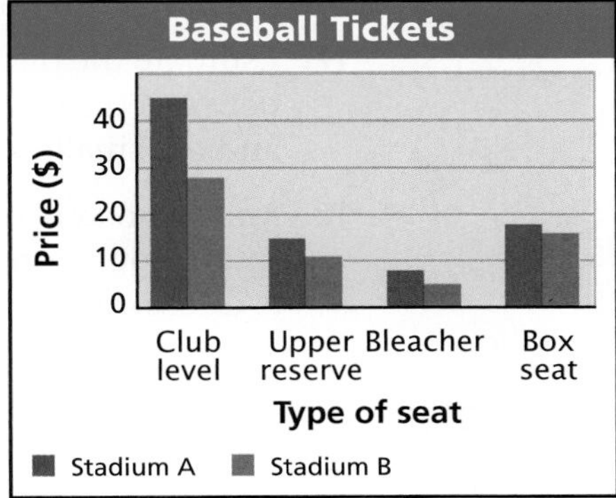


SEE EXAMPLE 3 p. 679

**Use the line graph for Exercises 8 and 9.**

8. Estimate the number of tickets sold during the week of the greatest sales.
9. Which one-week period of time saw the greatest change in sales?

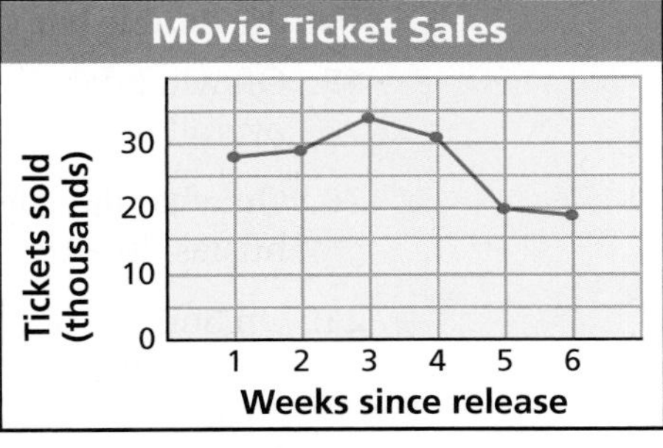


SEE EXAMPLE 4 p. 680

**Use the double-line graph for Exercises 10–12.**

10. When was the support for the two candidates closest?
11. Estimate the difference in voter support for the two candidates five weeks before the election.
12. Describe the general trend(s) of voter support for the two candidates.

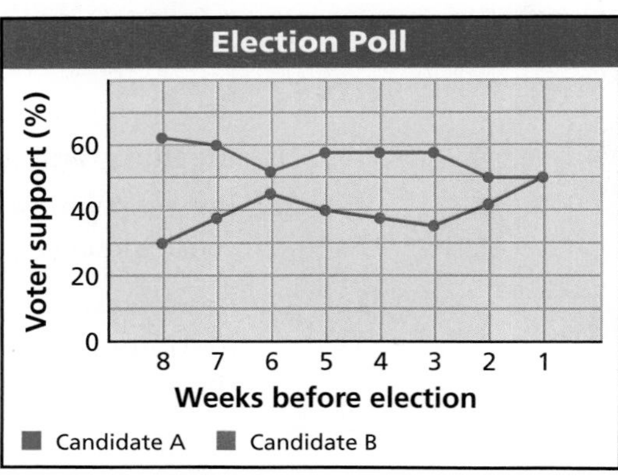

SEE EXAMPLE 5
p. 680

**Use the circle graph for Exercises 13–15.**

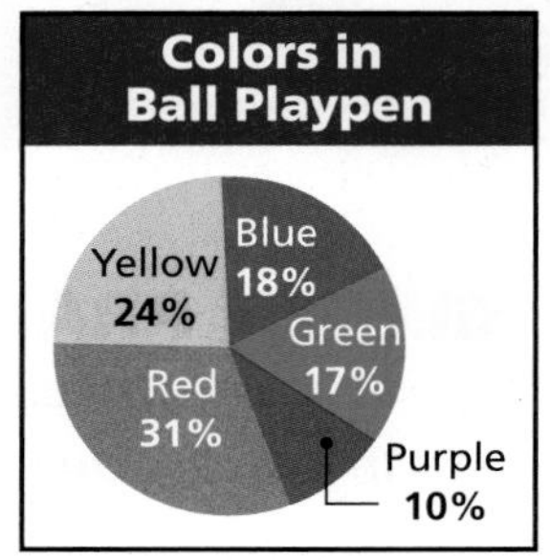


**13.** Which color is least represented in the ball playpen?

**14.** There are 500 balls in the playpen. How many are yellow?

**15.** Which two colors are approximately equally represented in the ball playpen?

SEE EXAMPLE 6
p. 681

**16.** The table shows the breakdown of Karim's monthly budget of $100. Use the given data to make a graph. Explain why you chose that type of graph.

| Item/Activity | Spending ($) |
|---|---|
| Clothing | 35 |
| Food | 25 |
| Entertainment | 25 |
| Other | 15 |

## PRACTICE AND PROBLEM SOLVING

**Independent Practice**

| For Exercises | See Example |
|---|---|
| 17–18 | 1 |
| 19–21 | 2 |
| 22–23 | 3 |
| 24–26 | 4 |
| 27–28 | 5 |
| 29 | 6 |

**Extra Practice**

Skills Practice p. S22
Application Practice p. S37

**Use the bar graph for Exercises 17 and 18.**

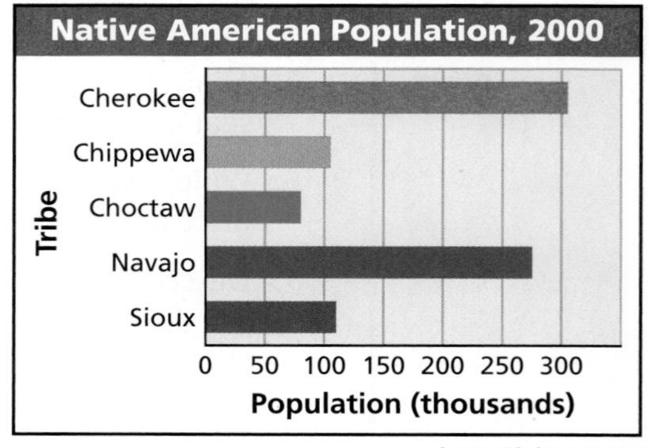


*Source*: U.S. Census Bureau

**17.** Estimate the difference in population between the tribes with the largest and the smallest population.

**18.** Approximately what percent of the total population shown in the table is Cherokee?

**Use the double bar graph for Exercises 19–21.**

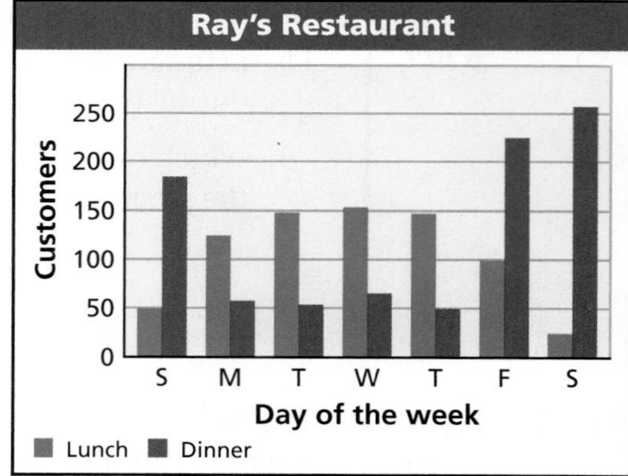


**19.** On what day did Ray do the most overall business?

**20.** On what day did Ray have the busiest lunch?

**21.** On Sunday, about how many times as great was the number of dinner customers as the number of lunch customers?

**Use the line graph for Exercises 22 and 23.**

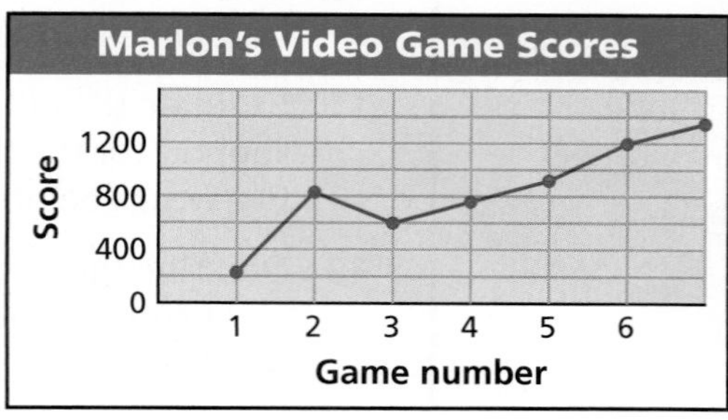


**22.** Between which two games did Marlon's score increase the most?

**23.** Between which three games did Marlon's score increase by about the same amount?

**Use the double-line graph for Exercises 24–26.**

**24.** What was the average value per share of Juan's two stocks in July 2004?

**25.** Which stock's value changed the most over any time period?

**26.** Describe the trend of the values of both stocks.

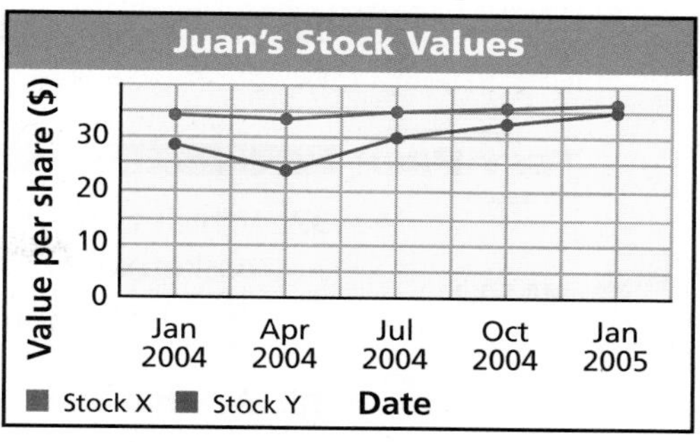


**Use the circle graph for Exercises 27 and 28.**

**27.** About what percent of the total number of cars are hopper cars?

**28.** About what percent of the total number of cars are gondola or tank cars?

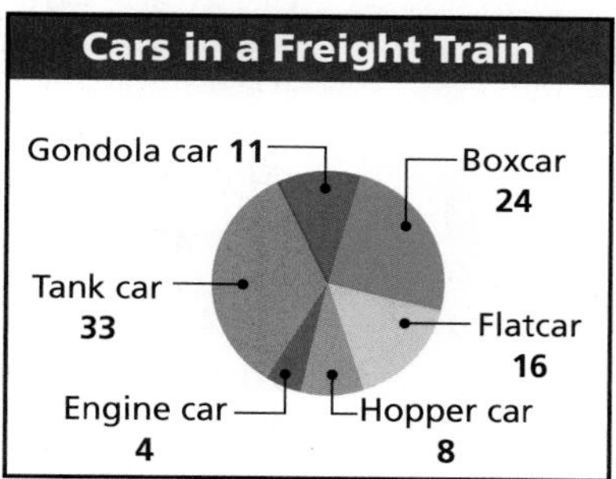


**29.** The table shows the weight of twin babies at various times from birth to four weeks old. Use the given data to make a graph. Explain why you chose that type of graph.

| Age (days) | Boy's Weight (lb) | Girl's Weight (lb) |
|---|---|---|
| 1 | 5.3 | 5.7 |
| 3 | 5.0 | 5.2 |
| 7 | 5.5 | 5.9 |
| 14 | 6.2 | 6.8 |
| 28 | 7.9 | 7.5 |

**Write *bar, double-bar, line, double-line,* or *circle* to indicate the type of graph that would best display the data described.**

**30.** attendance at a carnival each year over a ten-year period

**31.** attendance at two different carnivals each year over a ten-year period

**32.** attendance at five different carnivals during the same year

**33.** attendance at a carnival by age group as it relates to total attendance

**34. Critical Thinking** Give an example of real-world data that would best be displayed by each type of graph: line graph, circle graph, double-bar graph.

**35.** This problem will prepare you for the Multi-Step Test Prep on page 710.

The first modern Olympic Games took place in 1896 in Athens, Greece. The circle graph shows the total number of medals won by several countries at the Olympic Games of 1896.

**a.** Which country won the most medals? Estimate the percent of the medals won by this country.

**b.** Which country won the second most medals? Estimate the percent of the medals won by this country.

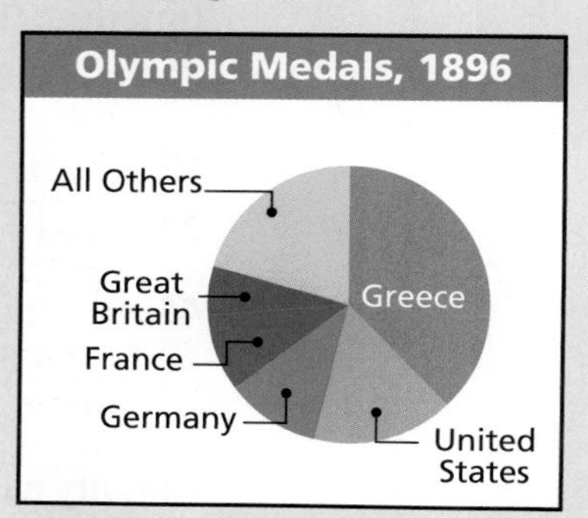

36. **Write About It** Explain how you could use a line graph to make predictions.

MA.S.1.2

37. Which type of graph would best display the contribution of each high school basketball player to the team, in terms of points scored?

(A) Bar graph (B) Line graph (C) Double-line graph (D) Circle graph

38. At what age did Marianna have 75% more magazine subscriptions than she did at age 40?

(F) 25

(G) 30

(H) 35

(J) 45

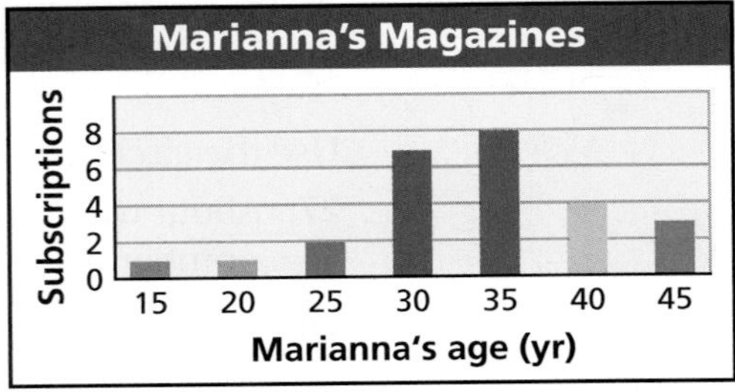


39. **Short Response** The table shows the number of students in each algebra class. Make a graph to display the data. Explain why you chose that type of graph.

| Teacher | Students |
|---|---|
| Mr. Abrams | 34 |
| Ms. Belle | 29 |
| Mr. Marvin | 25 |
| Ms. Swanson | 27 |

## CHALLENGE AND EXTEND

**Students and teachers at Lauren's school went on one of three field trips.**

40. On which trip were there more boys than girls?

41. A total of 60 people went to the museum. Estimate the number of girls who went to the museum.

42. Explain why it is not possible to determine whether fewer teachers went to the museum than to the zoo or the opera.

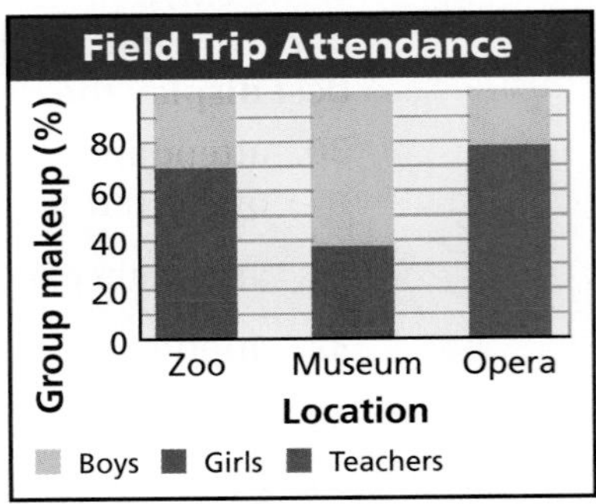


## SPIRAL REVIEW

**Find the domain and range for each relation and tell whether the relation is a function.** *(Lesson 4-2)*

43. $\{(-3, 3), (-1, 1), (0, 0), (1, 1), (3, 3)\}$

44.

| x | 1 | 2 | 3 | 4 | 5 |
|---|---|---|---|---|---|
| y | 2 | 4 | 6 | 8 | 10 |

45. Triangle $ABC$ has vertices on a coordinate plane as follows:

$A = (0, 5)$, $B = (3, 0)$, $C = (8, 3)$. Show that $\triangle ABC$ is a right triangle. *(Lesson 5-8)*

**Classify each polynomial according to its degree and number of terms.** *(Lesson 7-5)*

46. $24y$

47. $3x^2 + 6$

48. $4m - 18m^2 - 45m^3 + 120$

# 10-2 Frequency and Histograms

**MA.S.1.2** Compare shape, center, and spread of univariate data using graphical displays...

***Objectives***

Create stem-and-leaf plots.

Create frequency tables and histograms.

***Vocabulary***

stem-and-leaf plot
frequency
frequency table
histogram
cumulative frequency

**Why learn this?**

Stem-and-leaf plots can be used to organize data, like the number of students in elective classes. (See Example 1.)

A **stem-and-leaf** plot arranges data by dividing each data value into two parts. This allows you to see each data value.

The digits other than the last digit of each value are called a stem. → **2|3** ← The last digit of a value is called a leaf.

**Key: 2|3 means 23** ← The key tells you how to read each value.

## EXAMPLE 1 Making a Stem-and-Leaf Plot

**A** **The numbers of students in each of the elective classes at a school are given below. Use the data to make a stem-and-leaf plot.**

24, 14, 12, 25, 32, 18, 23, 24, 9, 18, 34, 28, 24, 27

**Number of Students in Elective Classes**

| Stem | Leaves |
|---|---|
| 0 | 9 |
| 1 | 2 4 8 8 |
| 2 | 3 4 4 4 5 7 8 |
| 3 | 2 4 |

*Key: 2|3 means 23*

*The tens digits are the stems.*

*The ones digits are the leaves. List the leaves from least to greatest within each row.*

*Title the graph and add a key.*

**B** **Marty's and Bill's scores for ten games of bowling are given below. Use the data to make a back-to-back stem-and-leaf plot.**

Marty: 137, 149, 167, 134, 121, 127, 143, 123, 168, 162

Bill: 129, 138, 141, 124, 139, 160, 149, 145, 128, 130

**Bowling Scores**

| Marty | | Bill |
|---|---|---|
| 7 3 1 | 12 | 4 8 9 |
| 7 4 | 13 | 0 8 9 |
| 9 3 | 14 | 1 5 9 |
| | 15 | |
| 8 7 2 | 16 | 0 |

*Key: |14|1 means 141*
*3|14| means 143*

*The first two digits are the stems.*

*The ones digits are the leaves.*

*Put Marty's scores on the left side and Bill's scores on the right.*

*Title the graph and add a key.*

*The graph shows that three of Marty's scores were higher than Bill's highest score.*

**Writing Math**

Stems are always consecutive numbers. In Example 1B, neither player has scores that start with 15, so there are no leaves in that row.

**1.** The temperatures in degrees Celsius for two weeks are given below. Use the data to make a stem-and-leaf plot.

7, 32, 34, 31, 26, 27, 23, 19, 22, 29, 30, 36, 35, 31

The **frequency** of a data value is the number of times it occurs. A **frequency table** shows the frequency of each data value. If the data is divided into intervals, the table shows the frequency of each interval.

EXAMPLE 2

## Making a Frequency Table

**The final scores for each golfer in a tournament are given below. Use the data to make a frequency table with intervals.**

77, 71, 70, 82, 75, 76, 72, 70, 77, 74, 71, 75, 68, 72, 75, 74

**Step 1** Identify the least and greatest values.

The least value is 68. The greatest value is 82.

**Step 2** Divide the data into equal intervals.

For this data set, use an interval of 3.

**Step 3** List the intervals in the first column of the table. Count the number of data values in each interval and list the count in the last column. Give the table a title.

**Golf Tournament Scores**

| Scores | Frequency |
|---|---|
| 68–70 | 3 |
| 71–73 | 4 |
| 74–76 | 6 |
| 77–79 | 2 |
| 80–82 | 1 |

**2.** The numbers of days of Maria's last 15 vacations are listed below. Use the data to make a frequency table with intervals.

4, 8, 6, 7, 5, 4, 10, 6, 7, 14, 12, 8, 10, 15, 12

A **histogram** is a bar graph used to display the frequency of data divided into equal intervals. The bars must be of equal width and should touch, but not overlap.

EXAMPLE 3

## Making a Histogram

**Use the frequency table in Example 2 to make a histogram.**

**Helpful Hint**

The intervals in a histogram must be of equal size.

**Step 1** Use the scale and interval from the frequency table.

**Step 2** Draw a bar for the number of scores in each interval.

All bars should be the same width. The bars should touch, but not overlap.

**Step 3** Title the graph and label the horizontal and vertical scales.

**3.** Make a histogram for the number of days of Maria's last 15 vacations.

4, 8, 6, 7, 5, 4, 10, 6, 7, 14, 12, 8, 10, 15, 12

**Cumulative frequency** shows the frequency of all data values less than or equal to a given value. You could just count the number of values, but if the data set has many values, you might lose track. Recording the data in a cumulative frequency table can help you keep track of the data values as you count.

### EXAMPLE 4 Making a Cumulative Frequency Table

**The heights in inches of the players on a school basketball team are given below.**

72, 68, 71, 70, 73, 69, 79, 76, 72, 75, 72, 74, 68, 70, 69, 75, 72, 71, 73, 76

**a. Use the data to make a cumulative frequency table.**

**Step 1** Choose intervals for the first column of the table.

**Step 2** Record the frequency of values in each interval for the second column.

**Step 3** Add the frequency of each interval to the frequencies of all the intervals before it. Put that number in the third column of the table.

**Step 4** Title the table.

**Basketball Players' Heights**

| Height (in.) | Frequency | Cumulative Frequency |
|---|---|---|
| 68–70 | 6 | 6 |
| 71–73 | 8 | 14 |
| 74–76 | 5 | 19 |
| 77–79 | 1 | 20 |

**b. How many players have heights under 74 in?**

All heights under 74 in. are displayed in the first two rows of the table, so look at the cumulative frequency shown in the second row.

There are 14 players with heights under 74 in.

**4.** The numbers of vowels in each sentence of a short essay are listed below.

33, 36, 39, 37, 34, 35, 43, 35, 28, 32, 36, 35, 29, 40, 33, 41, 37

**a.** Use the data to make a cumulative frequency table.

**b.** How many sentences contain 35 vowels or fewer?

## THINK AND DISCUSS

**1.** In a stem-and-leaf plot, the number of ___?___ is always the same as the number of data values. (*stems* or *leaves*)

**2.** Explain how to make a histogram from a stem-and-leaf plot.

**3. GET ORGANIZED** Copy and complete the graphic organizer.

Bar Graphs vs Histograms
- How are they alike?
- How are they different?

# 10-2 Exercises

MA.S.1.2

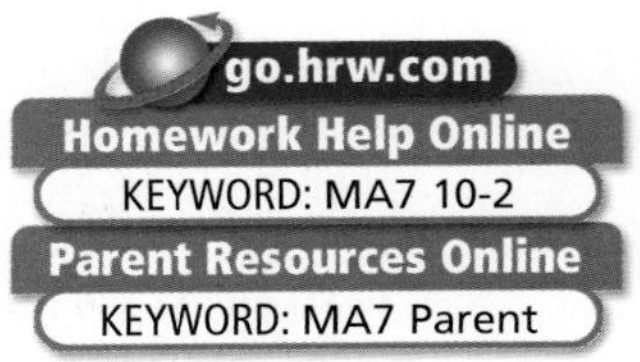


## GUIDED PRACTICE

1. **Vocabulary** A(n) ___?___ is a data display that shows individual data values. (*stem-and-leaf plot* or *histogram*)

SEE EXAMPLE 1
p. 687

2. **Sports** The ages of professional basketball players at the time the players were recruited are given. Use the data to make a stem-and-leaf plot.

| Ages When Recruited | | | | | | | | | | | |
|---|---|---|---|---|---|---|---|---|---|---|---|
| 21 | 23 | 21 | 18 | 22 | 19 | 24 | 22 | 21 | 22 | 20 | 21 |

3. **Weather** The average monthly rainfall for two cities (in inches) is given below. Use the data to make a back-to-back stem-and-leaf plot.

| Average Monthly Rainfall (in.) | | | | | | | | | | | | |
|---|---|---|---|---|---|---|---|---|---|---|---|---|
| Austin, TX | 1.9 | 2.4 | 1.9 | 3.0 | 3.6 | 3.3 | 1.9 | 2.1 | 3.2 | 3.5 | 2.2 | 2.3 |
| New York, NY | 3.3 | 3.1 | 3.9 | 3.7 | 4.2 | 3.3 | 4.1 | 4.1 | 3.6 | 3.3 | 4.2 | 3.6 |

SEE EXAMPLE 2
p. 688

4. **Sports** The finishing times of runners in a 5K race, to the nearest minute, are given. Use the data to make a frequency table with intervals.

| Finishing Times in 5K Race (to the nearest minute) | | | | | | | | |
|---|---|---|---|---|---|---|---|---|
| 19 | 25 | 23 | 29 | 32 | 30 | 21 | 22 | 24 |
| 19 | 28 | 26 | 31 | 34 | 30 | 28 | 25 | 24 |

SEE EXAMPLE 3
p. 688

5. **Biology** The breathing intervals of gray whales are given. Use the frequency table to make a histogram for the data.

| Breathing Intervals (min) | |
|---|---|
| **Interval** | **Frequency** |
| 5–7 | 4 |
| 8–10 | 7 |
| 11–13 | 7 |
| 14–16 | 8 |

SEE EXAMPLE 4
p. 689

6. The scores made by a group of eleventh-grade students on the mathematics portion of the SAT are given.

| Scores on Mathematics Portion of SAT | | | | | | | |
|---|---|---|---|---|---|---|---|
| 520 | 560 | 720 | 690 | 540 | 630 | 790 | 540 |
| 600 | 580 | 710 | 500 | 540 | 660 | 630 | |

   a. Use the data to make a cumulative frequency table.
   b. How many students scored 650 or higher on the mathematics portion of the SAT?

## PRACTICE AND PROBLEM SOLVING

7. The numbers of people who visited a park each day over two weeks during different seasons are given below. Use the data to make a back-to-back stem-and-leaf plot.

| Visitors to a Park | | | | | | | | | | | | | | |
|---|---|---|---|---|---|---|---|---|---|---|---|---|---|---|
| Summer | 25 | 25 | 26 | 27 | 27 | 57 | 59 | 22 | 23 | 29 | 22 | 23 | 54 | 53 |
| Winter | 11 | 12 | 13 | 9 | 30 | 27 | 4 | 19 | 14 | 19 | 21 | 33 | 35 | 9 |

| Independent Practice | |
|---|---|
| For Exercises | See Example |
| 7–8 | 1 |
| 9 | 2 |
| 10 | 3 |
| 11 | 4 |

**Extra Practice**

Skills Practice p. S22

Application Practice p. S37

8. **Weather** The daily high temperatures in degrees Fahrenheit in a town during one month are given. Use the data to make a stem-and-leaf plot.

| Daily High Temperatures (°F) | | | | | | | | | |
|---|---|---|---|---|---|---|---|---|---|
| 68 | 72 | 79 | 77 | 70 | 72 | 75 | 71 | 64 | 64 |
| 68 | 62 | 70 | 71 | 78 | 83 | 83 | 87 | 91 | 89 |
| 87 | 75 | 73 | 70 | 69 | 69 | 62 | 58 | 71 | 76 |

9. The overall GPAs of several high school seniors are given. Use the data to make a frequency table with intervals.

| Overall GPAs | | | | | | | | |
|---|---|---|---|---|---|---|---|---|
| 3.6 | 2.9 | 3.1 | 3.0 | 2.5 | 2.6 | 3.8 | 2.9 | |
| 2.2 | 2.9 | 3.1 | 3.3 | 3.6 | 3.0 | 2.3 | 2.8 | 2.9 |

10. **Chemistry** The atomic masses of the nonmetal elements are given in the table. Use the frequency table to make a histogram for the data.

| Atomic Masses of Nonmetal Elements | | | | | |
|---|---|---|---|---|---|
| Interval | 0–49.9 | 50–99.9 | 100–149.9 | 150–199.9 | 200–249.9 |
| Frequency | 11 | 3 | 2 | 0 | 2 |

**LINK**

**Automobiles**

Solar cars usually weigh between 330 and 880 pounds. A conventional car weighs over 4000 pounds.

11. The numbers of pretzels found in several samples of snack mix are given in the table.
    a. Use the data to make a cumulative frequency table.
    b. How many samples of snack mix had fewer than 42 pretzels?

| Numbers of Pretzels | | | | | |
|---|---|---|---|---|---|
| 42 | 39 | 39 | 38 | 40 | |
| 41 | 44 | 42 | 38 | 44 | |
| 47 | 36 | 40 | 40 | 43 | 38 |

12. **Automobiles** The table shows gas mileage for the most economical cars in July 2004, including three hybrids.

| Gas Mileage of Economical Cars | | | | | | | | | |
|---|---|---|---|---|---|---|---|---|---|
| Mileage in City (mi/gal) | 32 | 60 | 48 | 38 | 36 | 60 | 35 | 38 | 32 |
| Mileage on Highway (mi/gal) | 38 | 51 | 47 | 46 | 47 | 66 | 43 | 46 | 40 |

Make a back-to-back stem-and-leaf plot for the data.

13. Damien's math test scores are given in the table:
    a. Make a stem-and-leaf plot of Damien's test scores.
    b. Make a histogram of the test scores using intervals of 5.
    c. Make a histogram of the test scores using intervals of 10.
    d. Make a histogram of the test scores using intervals of 20.
    e. How does the size of the interval affect the appearance of the histogram?
    f. **Write About It** Which histogram makes Damien's grades look highest? Explain.

| Damien's Math Test Scores | | |
|---|---|---|
| 75 | 84 | 68 |
| 72 | 59 | 88 |
| 72 | 77 | 81 |
| 84 | 60 | 70 |

14. **///ERROR ANALYSIS///** Two students made stem-and-leaf plots for the following data: 530, 545, 550, 555, 570. Which is incorrect? Explain the error.

**A**

| Stem | Leaves |
|---|---|
| 53 | 0 |
| 54 | 5 |
| 55 | 0 5 |
| 57 | 0 |

Key: 52|5 means 525

**B**

| Stem | Leaves |
|---|---|
| 53 | 0 |
| 54 | 5 |
| 55 | 0 5 |
| 56 | |
| 57 | 0 |

Key: 52|5 means 525

15. This problem will prepare you for the Multi-Step Test Prep on page 710.
The 2004 Olympic results for women's weightlifting in the 48 kg weight class are 210, 205, 200, 190, 187.5, 182.5, 180, 177.5, 175, 172.5, 170, 167.5, and 165, measured in kilograms. Medals are awarded to the athletes who can lift the most weight.
   **a.** Create a frequency table beginning at 160 and using intervals of 10 kg.
   **b.** Create a histogram of the data.
   **c.** Tara Cunningham from the United States lifted 172.5 kg. Did she win a medal? How do you know?

16. **Entertainment** The top ten movies in United States theaters for the weekend of June 25–27, 2004, grossed the following amounts (in millions of dollars). Create a histogram for the data. Make the first interval 5–9.9.

| Ticket Sales (million $) | | | | |
|---|---|---|---|---|
| 23.9 | 19.7 | 18.8 | 13.5 | 13.1 |
| 11.2 | 10.2 | 7.5 | 6.1 | 5.1 |

17. **Critical Thinking** Margo's homework assignment is to make a data display of some data she finds in a newspaper. She found a frequency table with the given intervals.

Explain why Margo must be careful when drawing the bars of the histogram.

| Age |
|---|
| Under 18 |
| 18–30 |
| 31–54 |
| 55 and older |

MA.S.1.2

18. What data value occurs most often in the stem-and-leaf plot?

   Ⓐ 7　　Ⓒ 47
   Ⓑ 4.7　　Ⓓ 777

| Stem | Leaves |
|---|---|
| 3 | 2 3 4 4 7 9 |
| 4 | 0 1 5 7 7 7 8 |
| 5 | 1 2 2 3 |

*Key: 3|2 means 3.2*

19. The table shows the results of a survey about time spent on the Internet each month. Which statement is NOT supported by the data in the table?

| Time Spent on the Internet per Month | | |
|---|---|---|
| Time (h) | Frequency | Cumulative Frequency |
| 0–4 | 4 | 4 |
| 5–9 | 6 | 10 |
| 10–14 | 3 | 13 |
| 15–19 | 16 | 29 |
| 20–24 | 12 | 41 |
| 25–29 | 7 | 48 |
| 30–34 | 2 | 50 |

   Ⓕ The interval of 30 to 34 h/mo has the lowest frequency.
   Ⓖ More than half of those who responded spend more than 20 h/mo on the Internet.
   Ⓗ Only four people responded that they spend less than 5 h/mo on the Internet.
   Ⓙ Sixteen people responded that they spend less than 20 h/mo on the Internet.

20. The frequencies of starting salary ranges for college graduates are noted in the table. Which histogram best reflects the data?

| Starting Salaries | |
|---|---|
| **Salary Range ($)** | **Frequency** |
| 20,000–29,000 | 卌 卌 卌 卌 \|\| |
| 30,000–39,000 | 卌 卌 卌 卌 卌 卌 |
| 40,000–49,000 | 卌 卌 卌 \| |
| 50,000–59,000 | \| |

Ⓐ **Starting Salaries**

Frequency: 0, 10, 20, 30, 40; Salary range (thousand $): 20–29, 30–39, 40–49, 50–59

Ⓑ **Starting Salaries**

Frequency: 0, 10, 20, 30, 40; Salary range (thousand $): 20–29, 30–39, 40–49, 50–59

Ⓒ 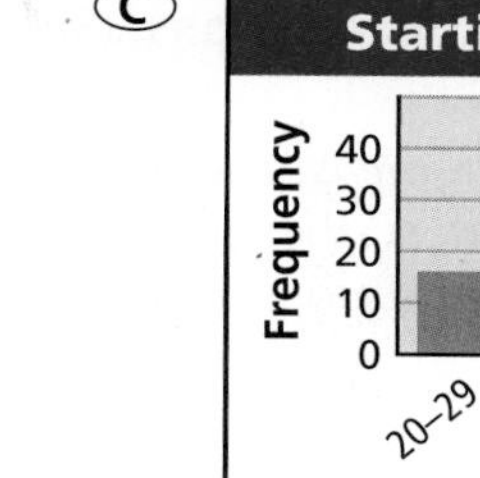


Ⓓ 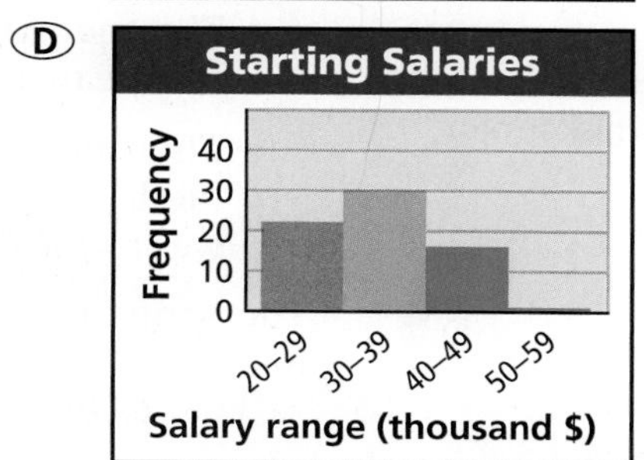


## CHALLENGE AND EXTEND

21. The cumulative frequencies of each interval have been given. Use this information to complete the frequency column.

| Interval | Frequency | Cumulative Frequency |
|---|---|---|
| 13–16 | ■ | 8 |
| 17–20 | ■ | 16 |
| 21–24 | ■ | 57 |
| 25–28 | ■ | 123 |

## SPIRAL REVIEW

**Solve each equation.** *(Lessons 2-3 and 2-4)*

22. $19 = -2c + 5$

23. $4(m + 2) = -1.2$

24. $2(x - 3) + 7 = 3x - 9$

25. The U.S. standard railroad gauge is 56.5 inches, which is the distance between the track's rails. Charles has a model train whose scale is 113:1. What is the distance between the rails on his model train track? *(Lesson 2-6)*

**Use the circle graph for Exercises 26–28.** *(Lesson 10-1)*

26. Which two types of gifts make up just over half of the donated gifts?

27. Which type of gift represents $\frac{1}{5}$ of the total donated gifts?

28. If there were 160 gifts donated, how many were books?

# 10-3 Data Distributions

**MA.S.1.1** Explain the effect of an outlier on the mean... *Also* **MA.S.1.2**

***Objectives***

Describe the central tendency of a data set.

Create box-and-whisker plots.

***Vocabulary***

mean
median
mode
range
outlier
quartile
interquartile range (IQR)
box-and-whisker plot

**Who uses this?**

Sports analysts examine data distributions. (See Example 3.)

A *measure of central tendency* describes how data clusters around a value.

- The **mean** is the sum of the values in the set divided by the number of values in the set.
- The **median** is the middle value when the values are in numerical order, or the mean of the two middle values if there are an even number of values.
- The **mode** is the value or values that occur most often. There may be one mode or more than one mode. If no value occurs more often than another, we say the data set has no mode.

The **range** of a set of data is the difference between the least and greatest values in the set. The range describes the spread of the data.

## EXAMPLE 1 Finding Mean, Median, Mode, and Range of a Data Set

**Find the mean, median, mode, and range of each data set.**

**A** **The number of hours Isaac did homework on six days: 3, 8, 4, 6, 5, 4.**

3, 4, 4, 5, 6, 8 — *Write the data in numerical order.*

**mean:** $\frac{3 + 4 + 4 + 5 + 6 + 8}{6} = \frac{30}{6}$ — *Add all the values and divide by the number of values.*

$= 5$

**median:** 3, 4, (4, 5), 6, 8 — *There are an even number of values. Find the mean of the two middle values.*

The median is 4.5.

**mode:** 4 — *4 occurs more often than any other value.*

**range:** $8 - 3 = 5$

**B** **The weight in pounds of Maria's five cats: 12, 14, 12, 16, 16.**

12, 12, 14, 16, 16 — *Write the data in numerical order.*

**mean:** $\frac{12 + 12 + 14 + 16 + 16}{5} = \frac{70}{5}$ — *Add all the values and divide by the number of values.*

$= 14$

**median:** 12, 12, (14), 16, 16 — *There are an odd number of values. Find the middle value.*

The median is 14.

**mode:** 12, 16 — *12 and 16 both occur more often than any other value.*

**range:** $16 - 12 = 4$

**Find the mean, median, mode, and range of each data set.**

**1a.** 8, 8, 14, 6 **1b.** 1, 5, 7, 2, 3 **1c.** 12, 18, 14, 17, 12, 18

A value that is very different from the other values in the set is called an **outlier**. In the data below, one value is much greater than the other values. This causes the mean to be greater than all of the other data values. In this case, either the median or mode would better describe the data.

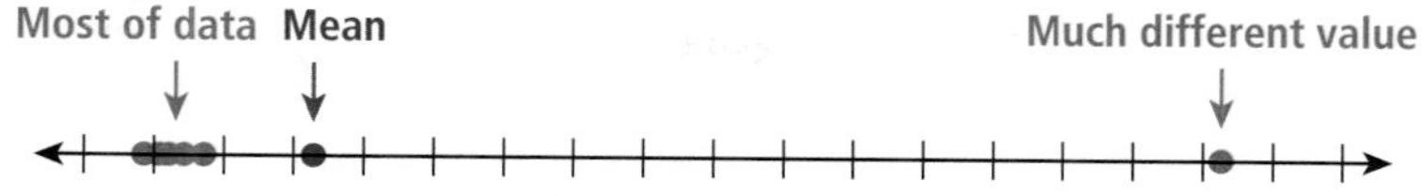


## EXAMPLE 2 Choosing a Measure of Central Tendency

**Niles scored 70, 74, 72, 71, 73 and 96 on six geography tests. Use the mean, median, and mode of his scores to answer each question.**

mean = 76 median = 72.5 mode: none

**A** **Which value gives Niles' test average?**

The average of Niles' scores is the mean, 76.

**B** **Which value best describes Niles' scores? Explain.**

The median score is the best description of Niles' six scores. Most of his scores were near 72.

The mean is higher than most of Niles' scores because he scored 96 on one test. Since there is no mode, it is not a good description of the data.

**2.** Josh scored 75, 75, 81, 84, and 85 on five tests. Use the mean, median, and mode of his scores to answer each question.

mean = 80 median = 81 mode = 75

**a.** Which value describes the score Josh received most often?

**b.** Which value best describes Josh's scores? Explain.

Measures of central tendency describe how data tends toward one value. You may also need to know how data is spread out across several values.

**Helpful Hint**

Mathematically, any value that is 1.5(IQR) less than the first quartile or 1.5(IQR) greater than the third quartile is an outlier.

**Quartiles** divide a data set into four equal parts. Each quartile contains one-fourth of the values in the set. The **interquartile range (IQR)** is the difference between the upper and lower quartiles. The IQR represents the middle half of the data.

Range: 9 − 1 = 8

IQR: 7 − 3 = 4

(1, 2, 2, 3, 3, 4, 4) 5, (6, 6, 7, 7, 8, 8, 9)

First quartile (Q1): 3

Median (Q2): 5

Third quartile (Q3): 7

A **box-and-whisker plot** can be used to show how the values in a data set are distributed. The minimum is the least value that is not an outlier. The maximum is the greatest value that is not an outlier. You need five values to make a box-and-whisker plot: the minimum, first quartile, median, third quartile, and maximum.

## EXAMPLE 3 *Sports Application*

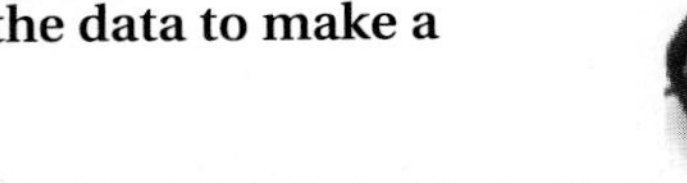

**The numbers of runs scored by a softball team in 19 games are given. Use the data to make a box-and-whisker plot.**

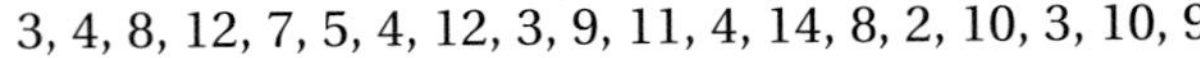

3, 4, 8, 12, 7, 5, 4, 12, 3, 9, 11, 4, 14, 8, 2, 10, 3, 10, 9

**Step 1** Order the data from least to greatest.

2, 3, 3, 3, 4, 4, 4, 5, 7, 8, 8, 9, 9, 10, 10, 11, 12, 12, 14

**Step 2** Identify the five needed values and determine whether there are any outliers.

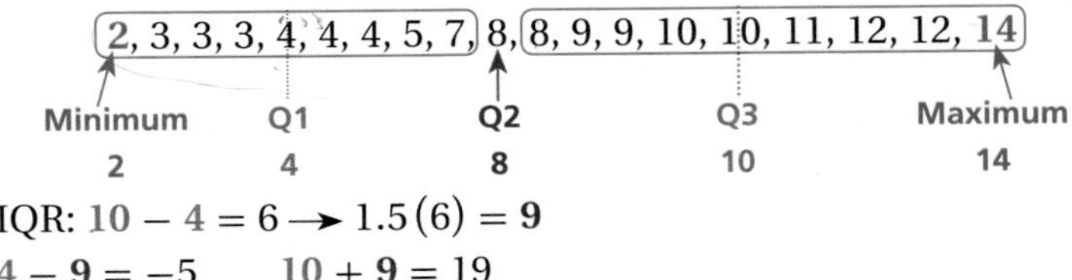


IQR: $10 - 4 = 6 \rightarrow 1.5(6) = 9$

$4 - 9 = -5 \qquad 10 + 9 = 19$

No values are less than −5 or greater than 19, so there are no outliers.

**Step 3** Draw a number line and plot a point above each of the five values you just identified. Draw a box through the lower and upper quartiles and a vertical line through the median. Draw lines from the box to the lower and upper extremes. (These are the whiskers.)

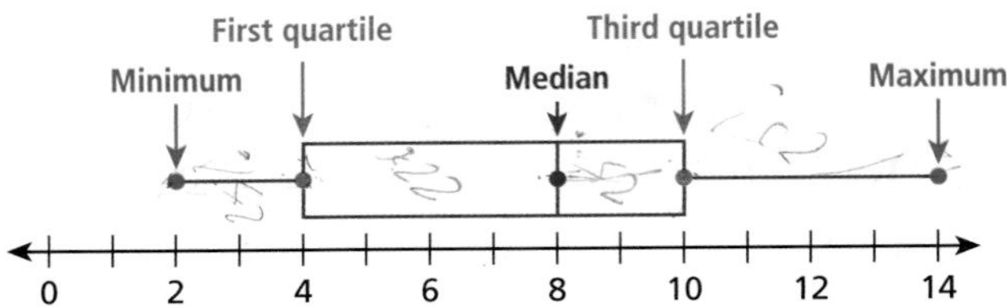


Half of the scores are between 4 and 10 runs per game. One-fourth of the scores are between 2 and 4. The greatest score earned by this team is 14.

**Writing Math**

An outlier is represented on a box-and-whisker plot by a point that is not connected to the box by whiskers.

**3.** Use the data to make a box-and-whisker plot.
13, 14, 18, 13, 12, 17, 15, 12, 13, 19, 11, 14, 14, 18, 22, 23

## THINK AND DISCUSS

**1.** Explain when the median is a value in the data set.

**2. GET ORGANIZED** Copy and complete the graphic organizer. Tell which measure of central tendency answers each question.

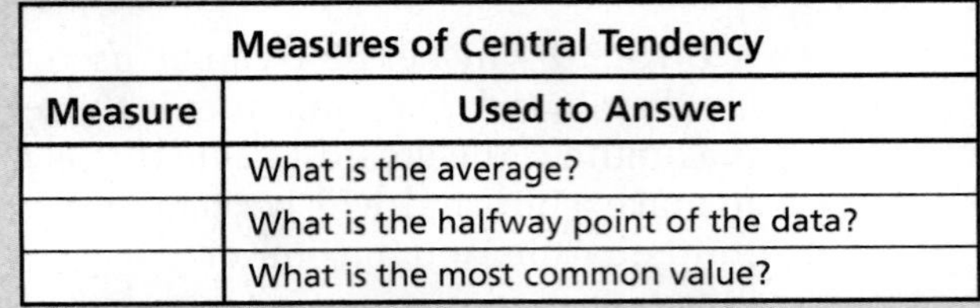

| Measures of Central Tendency | |
|---|---|
| **Measure** | **Used to Answer** |
| | What is the average? |
| | What is the halfway point of the data? |
| | What is the most common value? |

# 10-3 Exercises

## GUIDED PRACTICE

1. **Vocabulary** What is the difference between the *range* and the *interquartile range*?

SEE EXAMPLE 1 p. 694

**Find the mean, median, mode, and range of each data set.**

2. 85, 83, 85, 82
3. 12, 22, 33, 34, 44, 44
4. 10, 26, 25, 10, 20, 22, 25, 20
5. 71, 73, 75, 78, 78, 80, 85, 86

SEE EXAMPLE 2 p. 695

6. The distance between five students' homes and the school are 3, 2, 2, 2, and 15 miles. Use the mean, median, and mode of the distances to answer each question.

   mean = 4.8 median = 2 mode = 2

   **a.** Which value describes the distance between home and school that occurs most often?

   **b.** Which value best describes the distance between home and school? Explain.

SEE EXAMPLE 3 p. 696

**Use the data to make a box-and-whisker plot.**

7. 21, 31, 26, 24, 28, 26
8. 12, 13, 42, 62, 62, 82
9. 2, 1, 3, 1, 2, 6, 2, 4
10. 104, 68, 90, 96, 101, 106, 95, 88

## PRACTICE AND PROBLEM SOLVING

**Independent Practice**

| For Exercises | See Example |
|---|---|
| 11–14 | 1 |
| 15 | 2 |
| 16–19 | 3 |

**Extra Practice**

Skills Practice p. S22
Application Practice p. S37

**Find the mean, median, mode, and range of each data set.**

11. 75, 63, 89, 91
12. 1, 2, 2, 2, 3, 3, 3, 4
13. 19, 25, 31, 19, 34, 22, 31, 34
14. 58, 58, 60, 60, 60, 61, 63
15. **Sports** Lamont bowled 153, 145, 148, and 158 in four games. Use the mean, median, and mode of Lamont's bowling scores to answer each question.

    **a.** Which value describes Lamont's average score?

    **b.** Which value best describes Lamont's scores? Explain.

mean = 151
median = 150.5
mode: none

**Use the data to make a box-and-whisker plot.**

16. 62, 63, 62, 64, 68, 62, 62
17. 85, 90, 81, 100, 92, 85
18. 1, 2, 3, 4, 5, 6, 7, 8
19. 17, 13, 19, 17, 11, 17, 14, 11, 19, 12

**Find the mean, median, mode, and range of each data set.**

20. 1, 2, 3, 4, 5, 6, 7, 8, 9, 10
21. 5, 6, 6, 5, 5
22. 2.1, 4.3, 6.5, 1.2, 3.4
23. $0, \frac{1}{4}, \frac{1}{2}, \frac{3}{4}, 1$
24. 23, 25, 26, 25, 23
25. −3, −3, −3, −2, −2, −1
26. 1, 4, 9, 16, 25, 36
27. 51, 53, 51, 53, 51
28. 1, 0, 0, 0, 1, 1, 4
29. **Estimation** Estimate the mean of $16\frac{7}{8}$, $12\frac{1}{4}$, $22\frac{1}{10}$, $18\frac{5}{7}$, $19\frac{1}{3}$, and $13\frac{8}{11}$.
30. **Weather** The high temperatures in degrees Fahrenheit on 11 consecutive days were 68, 71, 75, 74, 77, 71, 73, 71, 72, 74, and 79. Find the mean, median, mode, and range of the temperatures. Then find the mean, median, mode, and range of the temperatures if the next day's temperature was 70°F. Describe the effect on the mean, median, mode, and range.

**31.** This problem will prepare you for the Multi-Step Test Prep on page 574.

In the 2004 Olympic games in Athens, the following results occurred for the men's pole vault finals: 5.95, 5.90, 5.85, 5.80, 5.75, 5.75, 5.75, 5.65, 5.65, 5.65, 5.55, 5.55, 5.55, 5.55, 5.55, 5.55. The results are heights in meters.

**a.** Find the mean, median, mode and range of this data set.

**b.** The gold medal was won by Timothy Mack of the United States. What was his height in the pole vault event?

**c.** Which measure of central tendency best describes the data set? Explain.

**32. Business** The salaries for eight people working for a small company are shown in the table. Determine the mean and median salaries. Which measure of central tendency best describes a typical salary of an employee at this company? Explain.

| Salaries ($) | |
|---|---|
| 20,000 | 25,000 |
| 20,000 | 30,000 |
| 23,000 | 35,000 |
| 25,000 | 100,000 |

**Use the data to make a box-and-whisker plot.**

**33.** 25, 28, 26, 16, 18, 15, 25, 28, 26, 16

**34.** 2, 3, 5, 7, 11, 13, 17, 19, 23, 29, 31

**35.** 1, 1, 1, 1, 2, 2, 2, 2, 3, 3, 4, 4, 4, 4, 4

**36. Sports** The table shows the attendance at 7 football games at Jefferson High School. Which measure of central tendency best shows the typical attendance at a football game?

| Attendance at Football Games | |
|---|---|
| Eagles vs. Bulldogs | 743 |
| Eagles vs. Panthers | 768 |
| Eagles vs. Coyotes | 835 |
| Eagles vs. Bears* | 1218 |
| Eagles vs. Colts | 797 |
| Eagles vs. Mustangs | 854 |

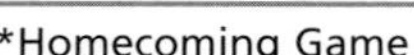
*Homecoming Game

**37. Write About It** Explain how an outlier with a large value will affect the mean. Explain how an outlier with a small value will affect the mean.

**38.** Allison has taken 5 tests worth 100 points each. Her scores are shown in the gradebook below. What score does she need on her next test to get an average of 90%?

| Student | Test 1 | Test 2 | Test 3 | Test 4 | Test 5 | Test 6 | Average |
|---|---|---|---|---|---|---|---|
| Allison | 88 | 85 | 89 | 92 | 90 | | |

**Tell whether each statement is *sometimes*, *always*, or *never* true.**

**39.** The mean is a value in the data set.

**40.** The median is a value in the data set.

**41.** The mode is a value in the data set.

**42.** The mean is affected by including an outlier.

**43.** The mode is affected by including an outlier.

44. **Critical Thinking** Consider the given data set: 1, 2, 3, 5, 8, 13, 21.

   a. Find the mean of the given data set.

   b. What happens to the mean of the data set if every number is increased by 2?

   c. What happens to the mean of the data set if every number is multiplied by 2?

MA.S.1.1, MA.S.1.2

45. Which value must be represented on a box-and-whisker plot?

   (A) Mean (B) Median (C) Mode (D) Range

46. Which value must be a value in a data set?

   (F) Mean (G) Median (H) Mode (J) Range

47. Which of the following could be used to find the mean, median, mode, and range of a data set?

   (A) Histogram
   (B) Frequency table
   (C) Stem-and-leaf plot
   (D) Box-and-whisker plot

## CHALLENGE AND EXTEND

48. List a set of data values with the following measures of central tendency: mean $= 8$ median $= 7$ mode $= 6$

49. For the box-and-whisker plot at right, how does the range of the lower half of the data differ from the range of the upper half of the data?

50. List a set of data values that can be represented by the box-and-whisker plot at right.

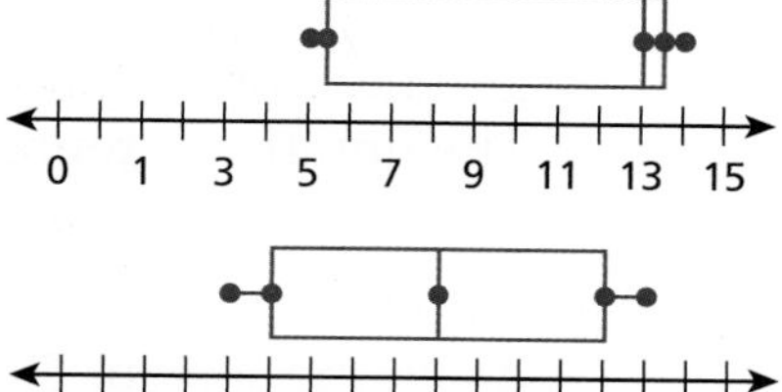


## SPIRAL REVIEW

**Find the slope of each line. Tell what rate the slope represents.** *(Lesson 5-3)*

51.

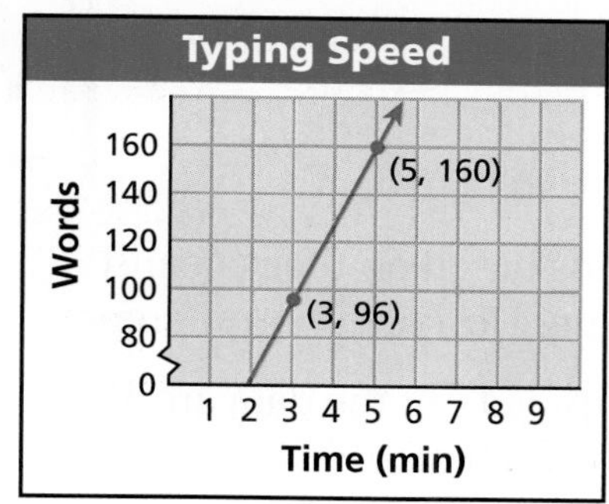


52.

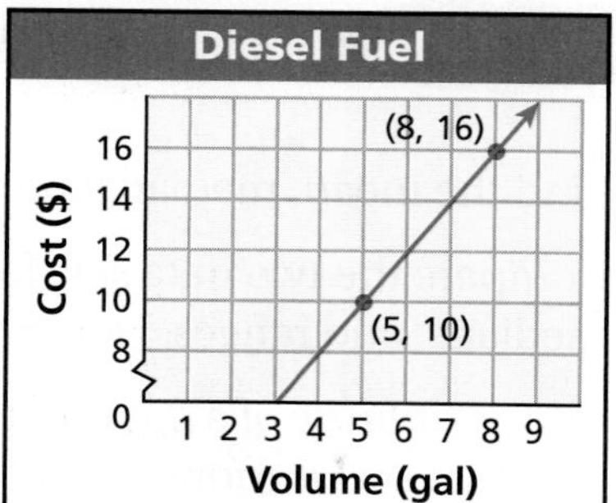


53. The length of a rectangle is one less than two times the width. The area is 15 yd$^2$. What are the dimensions of the rectangle? *(Lesson 9-6)*

54. The ages of the applicants for a driver's license one day are shown in the table. Create a stem-and-leaf plot of the data. *(Lesson 10-2)*

| Ages of Applicants | | | | | | | | | | | | | | |
|---|---|---|---|---|---|---|---|---|---|---|---|---|---|---|
| 17 | 16 | 21 | 16 | 16 | 17 | 35 | 16 | 18 | 17 | 16 | 16 | 23 | 18 | 30 |

# Explore Variability and the Effects of Outliers

You can use a graphing calculator to determine the mean, median, mode, and range of a set of data.

*Use with Lesson 10-3*

## Activity 1

The table shows the number of CDs sold online by two bands. Use a graphing calculator to analyze the data.

| Band | Jan | Feb | Mar | Apr | May | Jun |
|---|---|---|---|---|---|---|
| The Bulbs | 24 | 26 | 25 | 24 | 24 | 27 |
| Flash Pan | 25 | 33 | 39 | 24 | 24 | 5 |

1. Enter the data for the first band in the calculator. Press STAT and select **1:Edit**. Enter the data values for the first band under List 1 (**L1**). Press ENTER after each data value.

2. Find the mean of the data. Press STAT and move the cursor to the Calculate (**CALC**) menu. Select **1:1-Var Stats**, and then press 2nd L1 1 to calculate the statistics for List 1. The notation $\bar{x}$ represents the mean, so the mean is 25.

3. Find the median of the data. Use the down arrow to scroll down the screen. The median is 24.5.

4. Find the range of the data. The range is the difference between the greatest and least values: 27 – 24 = 3.

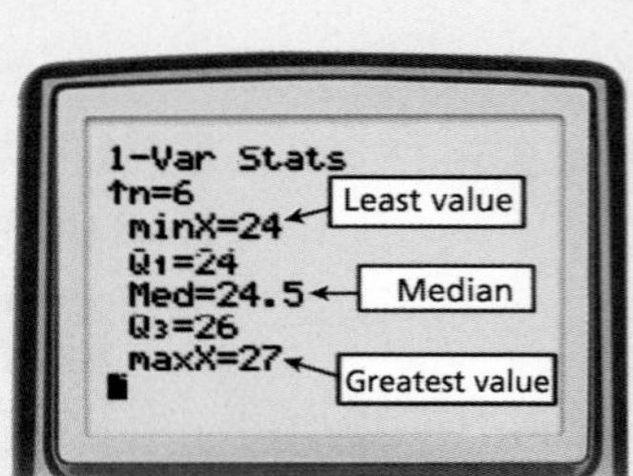

1. Find the mean, median, and range of the Flash Plan data.
2. Compare the two data sets for the two bands based on their means, medians, and ranges. How are they the same? How are they different?
3. The *variability* of a data set refers to how spread out the data are. Which of the two data sets is more variable? Explain how you know.
4. Why is it important to use more than one measure (such as mean) to describe data?
5. The table shows the number of times two bands performed during a six-year period. Use a graphing calculator to analyze the data. Compare the means, medians, and ranges of the data sets.

| Band | 2004 | 2005 | 2006 | 2007 | 2008 | 2009 |
|---|---|---|---|---|---|---|
| The Boxes | 31 | 28 | 47 | 56 | 77 | 67 |
| Wise Hope | 58 | 65 | 84 | 95 | 107 | 95 |

## Activity 2

The number of points scored by the Carolina Panthers football team in the last 12 games of the 2008 season are listed below. Use a graphing calculator to make a box-and-whisker plot of the data.

- 33, 28, 30, 38, 35, 28, 31, 17, 27, 30, 3, 34

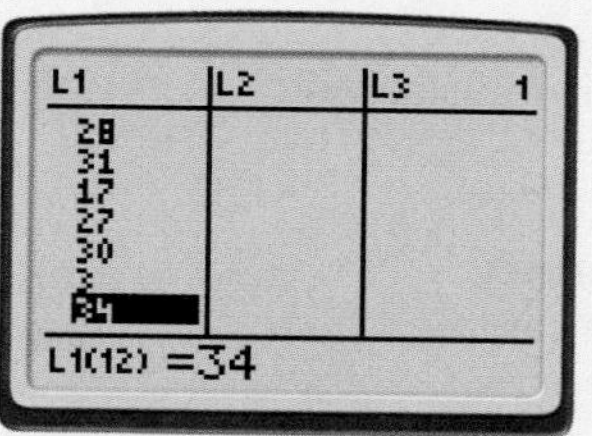


**1** To make a list of the data, press STAT, select **Edit**, and enter the values in List 1 **(L1)**. Press ENTER after each value.

**2** To use the **STAT PLOT** editor to set up the box-and-whisker plot, press 2nd [STAT PLOT] Y=, and then ENTER.
Press ENTER to select **Plot 1**.

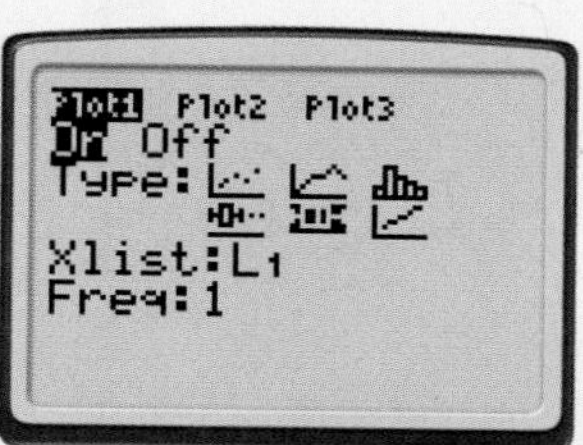


**3** Select **On**. Then use the arrow keys to choose the fifth type of graph, a box-and-whisker plot.
**Xlist** should be **L1** and **Freq:** should be 1.

**4** Press ZOOM and select **9: ZoomStat** to see the graph in the statistics window.

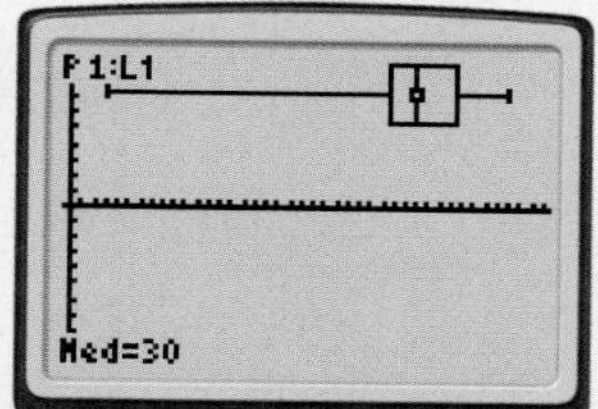


## Try This

**Find each value for the data set.**

**6.** minimum
**7.** first quartile
**8.** median
**9.** third quartile
**10.** maximum
**11.** mean

**12.** Identify the outlier in the data set and explain how you can tell that it is an outlier.

**Remove the outlier from the data set and create a new box-and-whisker plot. Find each value for the revised data set.**

**13.** minimum
**14.** first quartile
**15.** median
**16.** third quartile
**17.** maximum
**18.** mean

**19.** How does removing the outlier affect the measures of the data set?

**20.** How does removing the outlier affect the box-and-whisker plot?

# 10-4 Misleading Graphs and Statistics

**Rev. 8.S.3.3** Understand misuses of surveys, sampling, graphs, and statistics.

***Objectives***

Recognize misleading graphs.

Recognize misleading statistics.

***Vocabulary***

random sample

**Why learn this?**

A misleading graph can be used to distort the results of a student council election. (See Example 3.)

Graphs can be used to influence what people believe. The way data is displayed can influence how the data is interpreted.

## EXAMPLE 1 Misleading Bar Graphs

**The graph shows the size of tomatoes on plants that were treated with different fertilizers.**

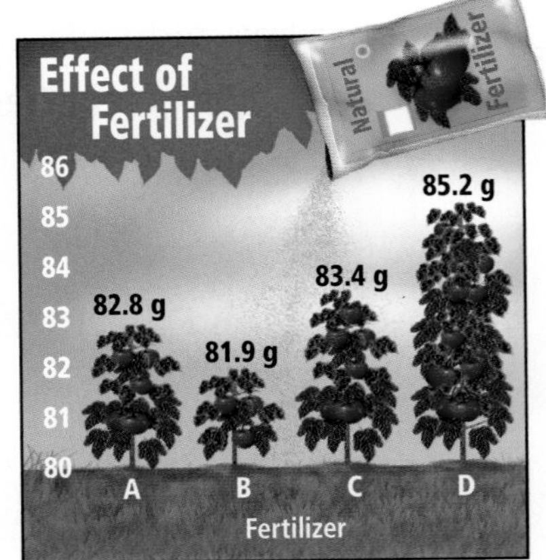


**A** **Explain why the graph is misleading.**

The scale on the vertical axis begins at 80. This exaggerates the differences between the sizes of the bars.

**B** **What might someone believe because of the graph?**

Someone might believe that the tomato treated with fertilizer D is much larger than the other tomatoes. It is only 3.3 grams larger than the tomato treated with fertilizer B.

1. Who might want to use the graph above? Explain.

## EXAMPLE 2 Misleading Line Graphs

**The graph shows the average price of gasoline in the U.S. in September.**

Average Gas Price in September

$1.60
$1.40
$1.20
$1.18
$1.16
$1.14
$1.12
$1.10
$1.00
1.08/gal
1.10/gal
1.24/gal
1.26/gal
1.43/gal
1993 1995 1997 1999 2001

**A** **Explain why the graph is misleading.**

The intervals on the vertical axis are not equal.

**B** **What might people be influenced to believe by the graph?**

Someone might believe that the price of gasoline increased the most between 1995 and 1997. However, the change between 1995 and 1997 was only $0.14/gal while the change between 1999 and 2001 was $0.17/gal.

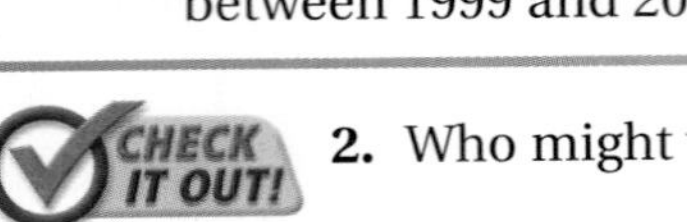

2. Who might want to use the graph above? Explain.

A circle graph compares each category of a data set to the whole. When any category is not represented in the graph, it may appear that another category represents a greater percentage of the total than it should.

## EXAMPLE 3 Misleading Circle Graphs

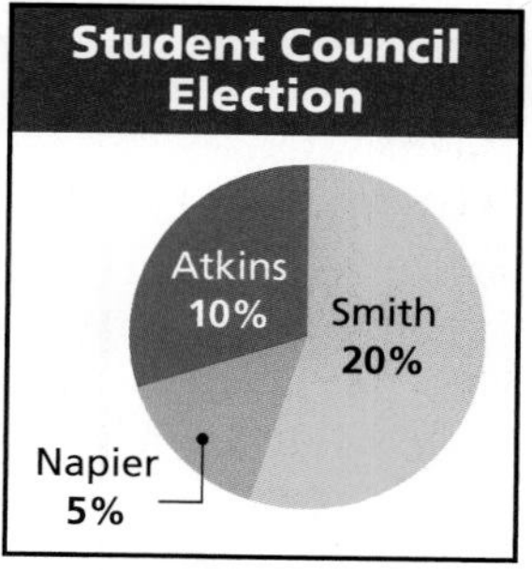


**The graph shows what percent of the total votes were received by three candidates for student council president.**

**A Explain why the graph is misleading.**

The sections of the graph do not add to 100%, so the votes for at least one of the candidates is not represented.

**B What might people be influenced to believe by the graph?**

Someone might believe that Smith won the election.

**3.** Who might want to use the graph above? Explain.

Statistics can be misleading because of the way the data is collected or the way the results are reported. A *random sample* is a good way to collect unbiased data. In a  **random sample**, all members of the group being surveyed have an equal chance of being selected.

## EXAMPLE 4 Misleading Statistics

**A researcher surveys people leaving a basketball game about what they like to watch on TV. Explain why the following statement is misleading: "80% of people like to watch sports on TV."**

The sample is biased because people who attend sporting events are more likely to watch sports on TV than people who watch TV but do not attend sporting events.

**4.** A researcher asks 4 people if they have seasonal allergies. Three people respond yes. Explain why the following statement is misleading: "75% of people have seasonal allergies."

### THINK AND DISCUSS

**1.** Give an example of a situation in which someone might intentionally try to make a graph misleading.

**2. GET ORGANIZED** Copy and complete the graphic organizer. Add more boxes if needed.

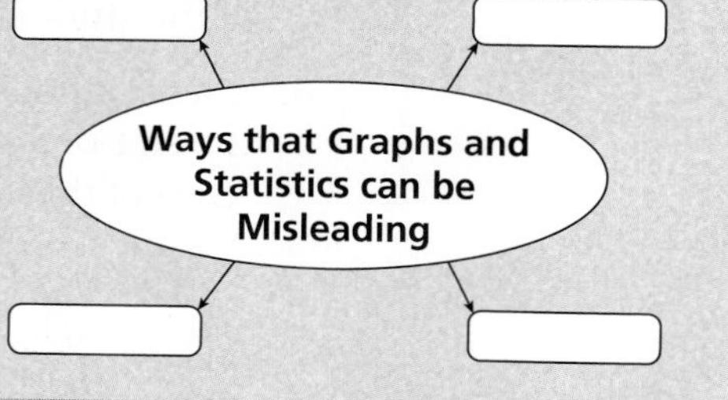

# 10-4 Exercises

## GUIDED PRACTICE

1. **Vocabulary** Explain in your own words what the term *random sample* means.

SEE EXAMPLE 1 p. 702

2. The graph shows the average salaries of employees at three companies.
   a. Explain why the graph is misleading.
   b. What might someone believe because of the graph?
   c. Who might want to use this graph?

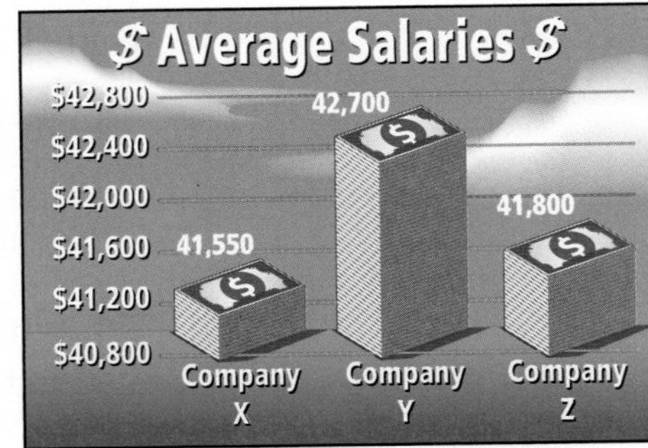


SEE EXAMPLE 2 p. 702

3. The graph shows hotel occupancy in San Francisco over four years.
   a. Explain why the graph is misleading.
   b. What might someone believe because of the graph?
   c. Who might want to use this graph?

SEE EXAMPLE 3 p. 703

4. The graph shows the nutritional information for a granola bar.
   a. Explain why the graph is misleading.
   b. What might someone believe because of the graph?
   c. Who might want to use this graph?

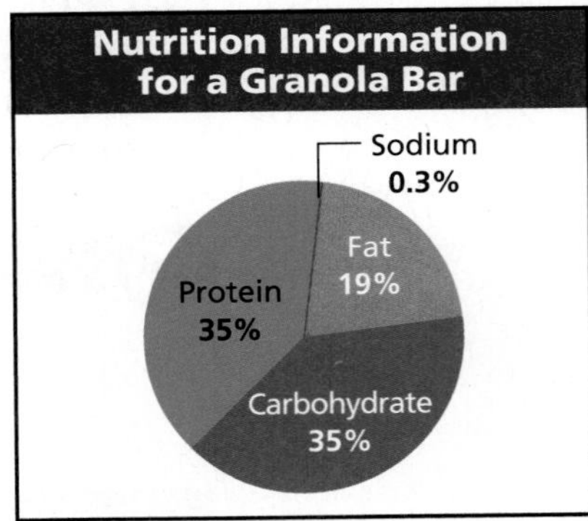


SEE EXAMPLE 4 p. 703

5. Three students were surveyed about their favorite teacher. Two students answer Mr. Gregory, and one answers Mr. Blaine. Explain why the following statement is misleading: "Mr. Gregory is the favorite teacher of a majority of the students."

6. A researcher surveys people at a shopping mall about whether they favor enlarging the size of the mall parking lot. Explain why the following statement is misleading: "85% of the community is in favor of enlarging the parking lot."

## PRACTICE AND PROBLEM SOLVING

| Independent Practice | |
|---|---|
| For Exercises | See Example |
| 7 | 1 |
| 8 | 2 |
| 9 | 3 |
| 10 | 4 |

**Extra Practice**

Skills Practice p. S22

Application Practice p. S37

7. The graph shows the median rent for men and women in a metropolitan area.
   a. Explain why the graph is misleading.
   b. What might someone believe because of the graph?
   c. Who might want to use this graph?

8. The graph shows the export prices of Colombian arabica coffee over nine years.
   a. Explain why the graph is misleading.
   b. What might someone believe because of the graph?
   c. Who might want to use this graph?

9. The graph shows how the state spent tax dollars during 1999 and 2000.
   a. Explain why the graph is misleading.
   b. What might someone believe because of the graph?
   c. Who might want to use this graph?

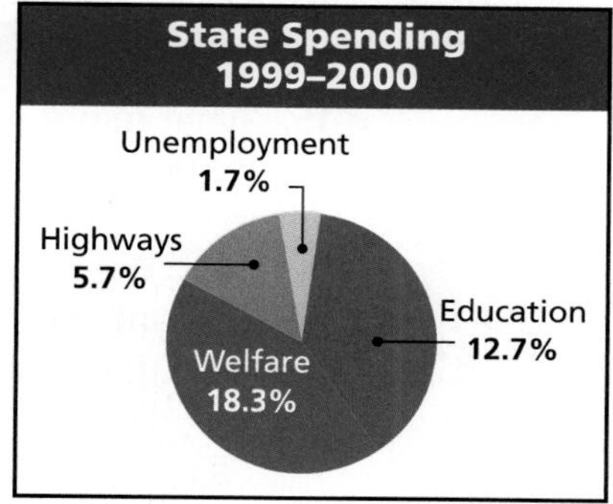


10. A college math course has one section with 240 students and 8 sections with 30 students. Explain why the following statement is misleading: "The average class size for the course is 53 students."

**MULTI-STEP TEST PREP**

11. This problem will prepare you for the Multi-Step Test Prep on page 710.

    The table shows scores from the women's gymnastics finals in the floor exercise at the 2004 Summer Olympic Games.
    a. Find the average score for the women in the finals.
    b. Why would it be misleading to say that this value is the average for women in the floor exercise?
    c. Make a graph for this data that could convince someone that the difference between the first place score and the eighth place score was very small.

| Rank | Name | Score |
|---|---|---|
| 1 | Catalina Ponor | 9.750 |
| 2 | Nicoleta Sofronie | 9.562 |
| 3 | Patricia Moreno | 9.487 |
| 4 | Fei Cheng | 9.412 |
| 5 | Daiane dos Santos | 9.375 |
| 6 | Mohini Bhardwaj | 9.312 |
| 7 | Kate Richardson | 9.312 |
| 8 | Alina Kozich | 8.500 |

12. **ERROR ANALYSIS** The graph shows the population of a city over time. Which conclusion is incorrect? Explain why the conclusion is incorrect and how the graph was misleading.

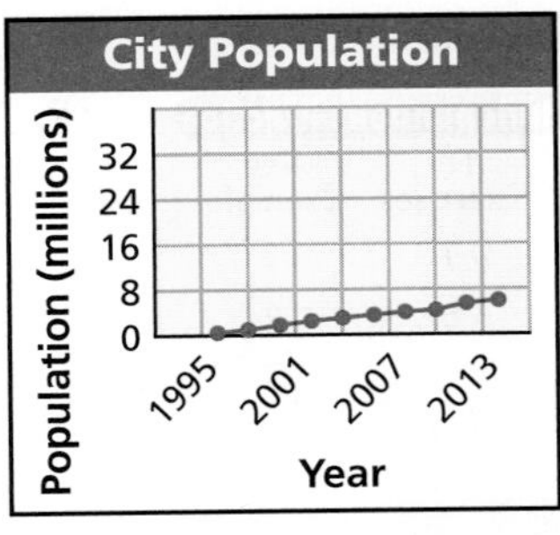


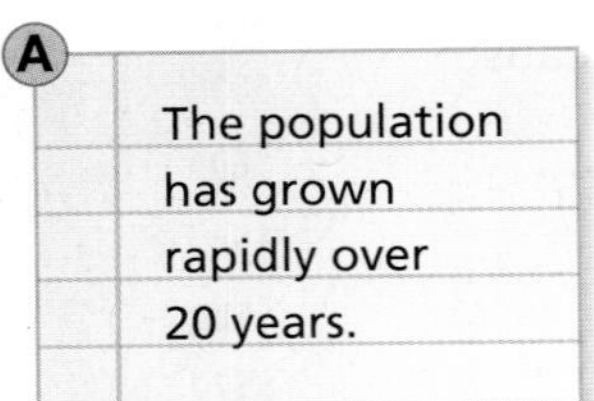


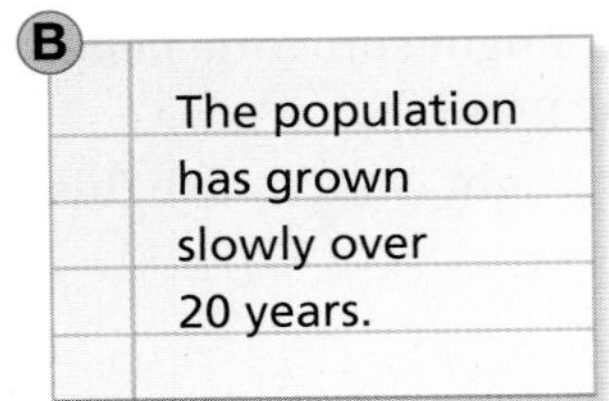


13. The table shows the average connection speeds of some broadband Internet service providers.

| Provider | Connection Speed (Kbps) |
|---|---|
| Speedy Online | 954 |
| TelQuick | 914 |
| Alacrity | 858 |

   a. Construct a display that suggests that Speedy Online is much faster than the other services.

   b. Construct a display that suggests that all of the services offer about the same connection speeds.

   c. **Write About It** Where might you expect to see your graph from part **b**? Explain.

14. **Critical Thinking** Explain how a graph can show truthful data but still be misleading.

**Rev. 8.S.3.3**

15. What might someone be influenced to believe because of the graph?

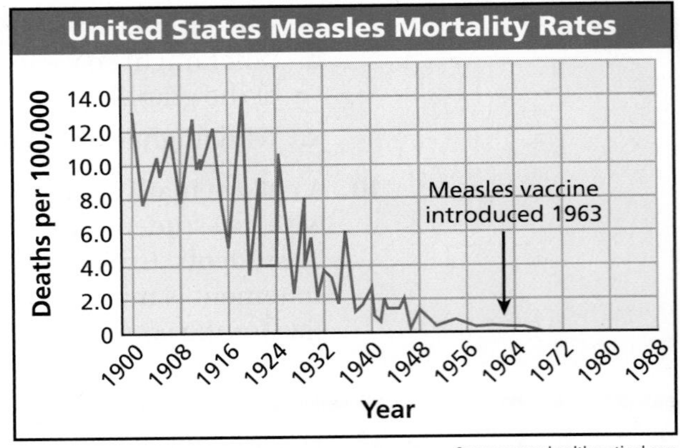


*Source:* www.healthsentinel.com

   Ⓐ The measles vaccine was introduced when the mortality rate was at its highest.

   Ⓑ The measles vaccine was unnecessary.

   Ⓒ The measles vaccine dramatically decreased the mortality rate.

   Ⓓ The measles vaccine increased the mortality rate.

16. The table shows the number of votes cast in the 2000 U.S. presidential election and in the 2002 French presidential election. What additional information is needed to determine whether the following statement is misleading?

| Country | Votes Cast |
|---|---|
| United States | 105,405,100 |
| France | 29,497,272 |

   "American voters are more likely to vote than French voters."

   Ⓕ The number of candidates in each election

   Ⓖ The legal voting age in France

   Ⓗ The number of registered voters in the United States in 2000 and France in 2002

   Ⓙ The number of polling locations in the United States in 2000 and France in 2002

## CHALLENGE AND EXTEND

17. **Logic** A fingerprint analyst is studying a fingerprint that was found in the chemistry lab. He reports that the fingerprint belongs to Dr. Arenson. Below are two questions the analyst was asked and the answers he gave.

**Question 1:** What are the chances that the fingerprint belongs to someone else who has the same fingerprint as Dr. Arenson?

**Answer:** One in several billion.

**Question 2:** What are the chances that the fingerprint was wrongly identified?

**Answer:** About 1 in 100.

a. What is the difference between the two questions?
b. What does the answer to question 1 lead you to believe?
c. Who do you think might have asked question 1?
d. What does the answer to question 2 lead you to believe?
e. Who do you think might have asked question 2?

**LINK History**

Florence Nightingale (1820–1910) served as a nurse in the Crimean War. In 1854, she brought the first female nurses to military hospitals.

18. **History** Graphs like the one at right were created by Florence Nightingale. Nightingale served as a nurse during the Crimean War and was concerned with the unsanitary conditions the soldiers lived in. Each "wedge" of the circle represents a month between April 1854 and March 1855.

a. What do you think Florence Nightingale wanted to show with this graph?
b. Who do you think Nightingale showed the graph to?

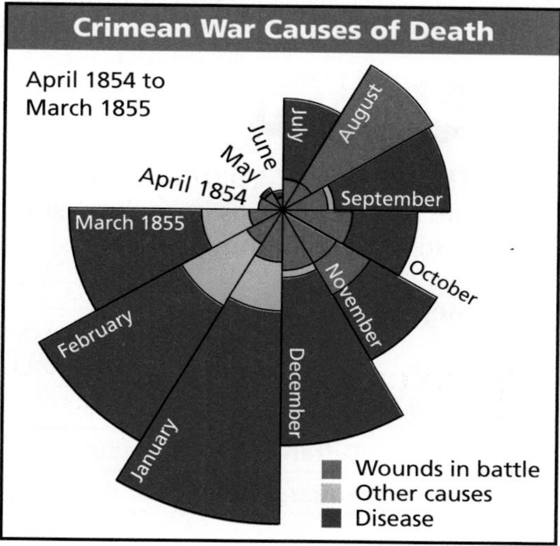


*Source:* The Florence Nightingale Museum

## SPIRAL REVIEW

**Write an inequality for each situation.** *(Lesson 3-1)*

19. The maximum weight for a certain truck load is 1500 pounds.

20. Isaac's research paper must be at least 12 pages.

21. A moving company will transport up to 20 boxes for no fee.

**Solve each inequality and graph the solutions.** *(Lesson 3-4)*

22. $2x - 3 < 7$
23. $3(t - 1) \geq -15$
24. $6 - n < 2n + 9$

25. The table shows the weight of a golden retriever at different ages. Choose a type of graph to display the given data. Make the graph, and explain why you chose that type of graph. *(Lesson 10-1)*

| Age (mo) | 1 | 3 | 6 | 12 |
|---|---|---|---|---|
| Weight (lb) | 8 | 23 | 45 | 66 |

# Standard Deviation and Percentiles

**MA.S.1.2** Compare shape, center, and spread of univariate data using ... percentiles...and standard deviations.

You have learned how to describe a data set using the mean, median, and mode. Sometimes you need other measures to describe a set of data. For example, the data sets {0, 20, 40} and {19, 20, 21} have the same mean and median, but the data sets are quite different.

**Variation** describes how data are spread out, or vary, from the mean or median. You have already seen one measure of variation, the range. Two other common measures of variation are the *variance* and the *standard deviation.*

**Variance:** average of the squared differences from the mean
**Standard deviation:** square root of the variance

A small standard deviation means the data are clustered near the mean. A large standard deviation means the data are spread out from the mean.

## Example 1

**The data set {72, 93, 84, 87, 92, 89, 82, 73} gives the number of games won by the Houston Astros in each season from 2000 to 2007. Find the variance and the standard deviation.**

**Step 1** Find the mean: $\frac{72 + 93 + 84 + 87 + 92 + 89 + 82 + 73}{8} = 84$

**Step 2** Find the difference of each data value and the mean. Square these differences.

| Data value | 72 | 93 | 84 | 87 | 92 | 89 | 82 | 73 |
|---|---|---|---|---|---|---|---|---|
| Difference from mean | −12 | 9 | 0 | 3 | 8 | 5 | −2 | −11 |
| Squared difference from mean | 144 | 81 | 0 | 9 | 64 | 25 | 4 | 121 |

**Step 3** Find the variance by adding the squared differences from Step 2 and dividing by the number of data values.

$$\frac{144 + 81 + 0 + 9 + 64 + 25 + 4 + 121}{8} = 56$$

**Step 4** Find the standard deviation by taking the square root of the variance: $\sqrt{56} \approx 7.5$

The variance is 56 and the standard deviation is approximately 7.5.

## Try This

1. The data set {91, 116, 93, 93, 63, 69, 78, 88} gives the number of games won by the Seattle Mariners in each season from 2000 to 2007.
   a. Find the variance and the standard deviation.
   b. Compare this data set to that of the Houston Astros. How are the data sets similar? How are they different, and what does this difference mean?
2. Susan and Katie each took 10 history quizzes. Both students have a mean score of 81. Susan's standard deviation is 2 and Katie's standard deviation is 15. What can you conclude?

A **percentile** is a measure that tells what percent of the total items in a data set are at or below that measure.

**Example 2**

**On a quiz taken by 30 students, a score of 85 is the 60th percentile. How many students scored 85 or lower? How many students scored higher than 85?**

If 85 is the 60th percentile, then 60% of the students scored 85 or lower.

$0.6 \times 30 = 18$ *Find 60% of 30, the total number of students.*

18 students scored 85 or lower.

$30 - 18 = 12$ *Subtract 18 from the total number of students to find how many students scored higher than 85.*

12 students scored higher than 85.

**Example 3**

**The heights of 12 students are given in the table. Find the percentile for each height.**

The maximum height in the table is **62** inches, so 62 is the **100th** percentile.

Find the percentile for each height by dividing the cumulative frequency for that height by the total number of students, **12**, and multiplying by 100. Round to the nearest whole number.

**Heights of Students**

| Height (in.) | Cumulative Frequency | Percentile |
|---|---|---|
| 57 | 1 | $\frac{1}{12} \times 100 \approx 8$ |
| 58 | 2 | $\frac{2}{12} \times 100 \approx 17$ |
| 59 | 5 | $\frac{5}{12} \times 100 \approx 42$ |
| 60 | 8 | $\frac{8}{12} \times 100 \approx 67$ |
| 61 | 10 | $\frac{10}{12} \times 100 \approx 83$ |
| 62 | 12 | 100 |

**Try This**

**3.** Mr. O'Donnell gave a 5-point quiz in his two algebra classes. The scores are listed in the tables. Copy the tables and complete the third column of each. Then compare the scores of the two classes.

**Quiz Scores – Class 1**

| Score | Cumulative Frequency | Percentile |
|---|---|---|
| 0 | 1 | ■ |
| 1 | 2 | ■ |
| 2 | 4 | ■ |
| 3 | 8 | ■ |
| 4 | 15 | ■ |
| 5 | 18 | ■ |

**Quiz Scores – Class 2**

| Score | Cumulative Frequency | Percentile |
|---|---|---|
| 0 | 1 | ■ |
| 1 | 2 | ■ |
| 2 | 8 | ■ |
| 3 | 9 | ■ |
| 4 | 12 | ■ |
| 5 | 18 | ■ |

CHAPTER 10

SECTION 10A

# MULTI-STEP TEST PREP

## Data Analysis

**USA! USA! USA!** In 708 B.C.E., the Olympic Games included the pentathlon. This event included the discus, javelin, long jump, running, and wrestling. The winner of the pentathlon was considered a "super athlete." The modern pentathlon of the Olympic Games includes five disciplines: target shooting, fencing, swimming, horseback riding, and cross-country running.

**1.** The pentathlon includes five events. What type of graph should be used to show what percent of this event is made up of each discipline?

**2.** Do you think the winner of the modern pentathlon must win each of the five events? Explain.

**3.** Thirty-two men competed in the modern pentathlon in the 2004 Olympic Games. The chart shows the total points for the competitors.

| Pentathlon Scores | | | | | | |
|---|---|---|---|---|---|---|
| 5480 | 5428 | 5392 | 5356 | 5340 | | |
| 5332 | 5320 | 5295 | 5276 | 5252 | 5200 | 5196 |
| 5192 | 5184 | 5180 | 5172 | 5144 | 5132 | 5084 |
| 5084 | 5068 | 5016 | 4976 | 4936 | 4932 | 4916 |
| 4904 | 4848 | 4732 | 4676 | 4420 | 4388 | |

Find the mean, median, and mode of this data set. Which value best describes the data? Explain.

**4.** Find the minimum, first quartile, third quartile, and maximum values of the data set above. Use these values and the median to make a box-and-whisker plot of the data.

# READY TO GO ON?

CHAPTER 10

SECTION 10A

## Quiz for Lessons 10-1 Through 10-4

### 10-1 Organizing and Displaying Data

**Use the circle graph for Problems 1–3.**

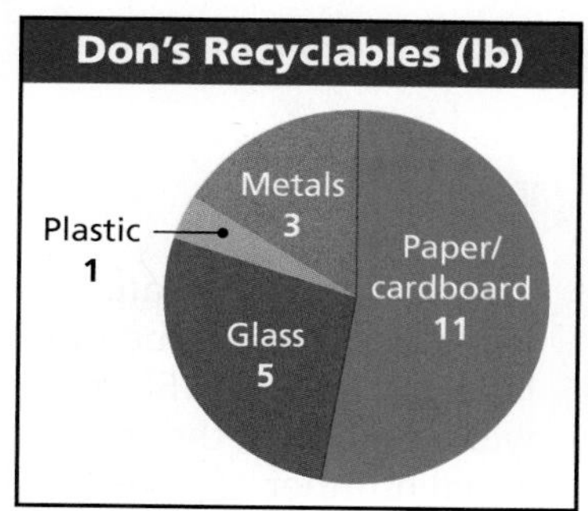


1. Which material represents over 50% of Don's recyclables?
2. How many pounds of materials does Don recycle?
3. What percent of Don's recyclables are glass?
4. The table shows the total proceeds for a fund-raiser at various times during the day. Choose a type of graph to display the given data. Make the graph, and explain why you chose that type of graph.

| Time | Total Proceeds (thousand $) | Time | Total Proceeds (thousand $) |
|---|---|---|---|
| 3:00 P.M. | 1.5 | 6:00 P.M. | 6.5 |
| 4:00 P.M. | 2 | 7:00 P.M. | 8 |
| 5:00 P.M. | 4 | 8:00 P.M. | 9.5 |

### 10-2 Frequency and Histograms

5. The Miller family is going to buy a new car. The approximate prices of the cars they are considering are given. Use the data to make a stem-and-leaf plot.

   $24,000, $28,000, $26,000, $32,000, $30,000, $41,000, $27,000, $22,000, $26,000, $33,000

6. The number of people at a caterer's last 12 parties are given below.

   16, 18, 17, 19, 15, 25, 18, 17, 18, 16, 17, 19

   a. Use the data to make a frequency table with intervals.

   b. Use your frequency table from part **a** to make a histogram.

### 10-3 Data Distributions

7. The daily high temperatures on 14 consecutive days in one city were 59°F, 49°F, 48°F, 46°F, 47°F, 51°F, 49°F, 43°F, 45°F, 52°F, 51°F, 51°F, 51°F, and 38°F.

   a. Find the mean, median, and mode of the temperatures.

   b. Which value describes the average high temperature for the 14 days?

   c. Which value best describes the high temperatures? Explain.

8. Use the temperature data above to make a box-and-whisker plot.

### 10-4 Misleading Graphs and Statistics

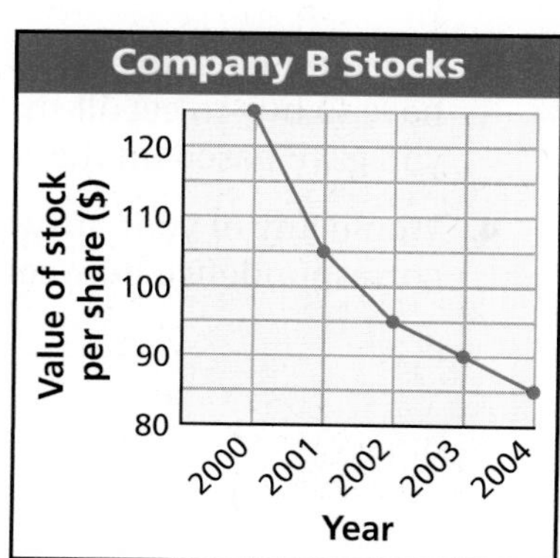


9. The graph shows the value of a company's stock over time. Explain why the graph is misleading. What might people believe because of the graph? Who might want to use this graph?
10. The results of an online survey of 230 people showed that 92% of the population felt very comfortable using technology. Explain why this statistic is misleading.

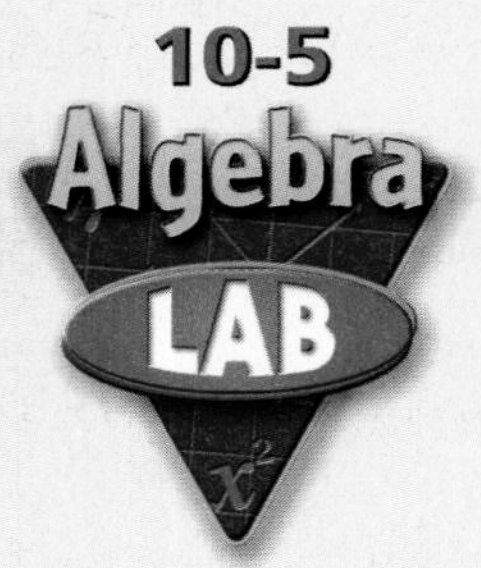


# Simulations

A simulation can be used to model an experiment that would be difficult or inconvenient to actually perform. In this lab, you will conduct simulations.

**Rev. 7.S.1.3** Interpret the actual outcomes from probability experiments for compound, independent situations.

*Use with Lesson 10-5*

## Activity

The local movie theater is offering an opportunity for customers to win a free night at the movies. To win, you must collect six different letters to spell CINEMA. Each movie ticket sold during this promotion will have one of the six letters stamped on the back of the ticket. An equal number of tickets will be stamped with each of the letters.

**1** Since there are six different letters that appear on the tickets an equal number of times, you can use a number cube to simulate collecting the six letters.

Each of the numbers on the number cube will represent a letter. Each roll of the number cube will represent purchasing one movie ticket, and the number rolled will represent the letter stamped on the ticket.

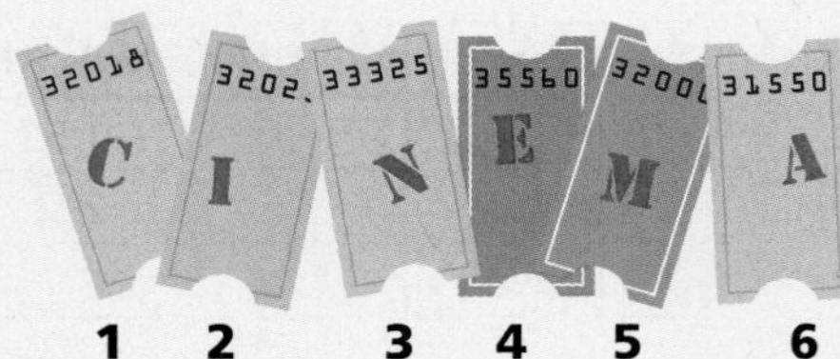


1 2 3 4 5 6

**2** The table shows the results of rolling the number cube until each number has been rolled once.

**a.** Based on the results shown in the table, how many rolls did it take to get all six numbers?

**b.** Based on the results in the table, how many movie tickets would you have to buy to get all six letters? If you purchased this number of tickets, would you be sure to win? Explain.

| Number on Cube | Letter on Ticket | Frequency |
|---|---|---|
| 1 | C | I |
| 2 | I | ~~IIII~~ I |
| 3 | N | IIII |
| 4 | E | II |
| 5 | M | II |
| 6 | A | III |

## Try This

1. Repeat the simulation four more times and record the results.
2. Find the average number of rolls from all five simulations $\left(\frac{\text{total number of rolls from 5 simulations}}{5}\right)$.
3. Based on your answer to Problem 2, how many movie tickets would you have to buy to get all six letters? Is this number different from the answer you gave based on the results in the table above?
4. Would any of your answers have been different if you had used a different correspondence between the numbers and letters? Explain.

# 10-5 Experimental Probability

**Rev. 6.S.2** Use strategies to identify sample spaces and probabilities.

***Objectives***
Determine the experimental probability of an event.

Use experimental probability to make predictions.

***Vocabulary***
experiment
trial
outcome
sample space
event
probability
experimental probability
prediction

**Why learn this?**

Experimental probability can be used by manufacturers for quality control. (See Example 4.)

An **experiment** is an activity involving chance. Each repetition or observation of an experiment is a **trial**, and each possible result is an **outcome**. The **sample space** of an experiment is the set of all possible outcomes.

| **Experiment** | Rolling a number cube | Tossing a coin | Spinning a game spinner |
|---|---|---|---|
| **Sample Space** | {1, 2, 3, 4, 5, 6} | {heads, tails} | {red, blue, green, yellow} |

**EXAMPLE 1** **Identifying Sample Spaces and Outcomes**

**Identify the sample space and the outcome shown for each experiment.**

**A** **tossing two coins**
Sample space: {HH, HT, TH, TT}
Outcome shown: heads, tails (H, T)

**B** **spinning a game spinner**
Sample space: {yellow, red, blue, green}
Outcome shown: green

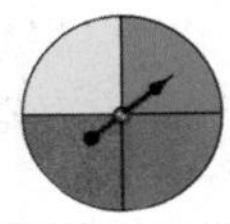

**1.** Identify the sample space and the outcome shown for the experiment: rolling a number cube.

An **event** is an outcome or set of outcomes in an experiment. **Probability** is the measure of how likely an event is to occur. Probabilities are written as fractions or decimals from 0 to 1, or as percents from 0% to 100%.

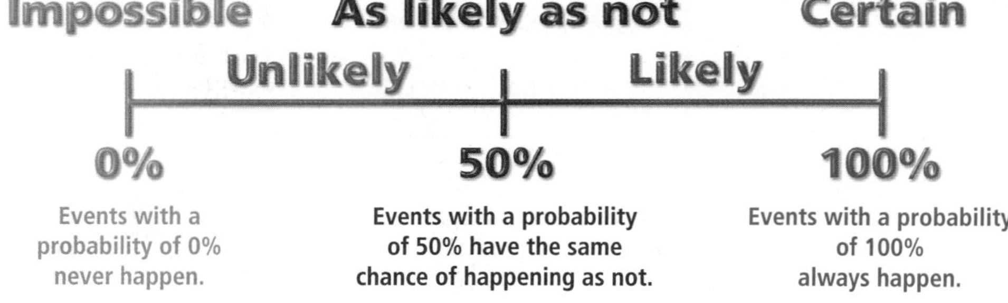

## EXAMPLE 2 Estimating the Likelihood of an Event

**Write *impossible, unlikely, as likely as not, likely,* or *certain* to describe each event.**

**A** **There are 31 days in August.**
August always has 31 days. This event is *certain.*

**B** **Carlos correctly guesses a number between 1 and 1000.**
Carlos must pick one outcome out of 1000 possible outcomes. This event is *unlikely.*

**C** **A coin lands heads up.**
Heads is one of two possible outcomes. This event is *as likely as not.*

**D** **Cecilia rolls a 10 on a standard number cube.**
A standard number cube is numbered 1 through 6. This event is *impossible.*

**2.** Write *impossible, unlikely, as likely as not, likely,* or *certain* to describe the event: Anthony rolls a number less than 7 on a standard number cube.

You can estimate the probability of an event by performing an experiment. The **experimental probability** of an event is the ratio of the number of times the event occurs to the number of trials. The more trials performed, the more accurate the estimate will be.

**Experimental Probability**

$$\text{experimental probability} = \frac{\text{number of times the event occurs}}{\text{number of trials}}$$

## EXAMPLE 3 Finding Experimental Probability

**An experiment consists of spinning a spinner. Use the results in the table to find the experimental probability of each event.**

| Outcome | Frequency |
|---|---|
| Red | 7 |
| Blue | 8 |
| Green | 5 |

**A** **spinner lands on blue**

$$\frac{\text{number of times the event occurs}}{\text{number of trials}} = \frac{8}{7+8+5} = \frac{8}{20} = \frac{2}{5}$$

**B** **spinner does not land on green**

When the spinner does not land on green, it must land on red or blue.

$$\frac{\text{number of times the event occurs}}{\text{number of trials}} = \frac{7+8}{7+8+5} = \frac{15}{20} = \frac{3}{4}$$

**Helpful Hint**

Probabilities can be expressed as fractions, decimals, or percents. For Example 3, the probabilities are:

3A: $\frac{2}{5} = 0.4 = 40\%$

3B: $\frac{3}{4} = 0.75 = 75\%$

**Use the information in Example 3 to find the experimental probability of each event.**

**3a.** spinner lands on red

**3b.** spinner does not land on red

You can use experimental probability to make *predictions*. A **prediction** is an estimate or guess about something that has not yet happened.

## EXAMPLE  4 *Quality Control Application*

**A manufacturer inspects 800 light bulbs and finds that 796 of them have no defects.**

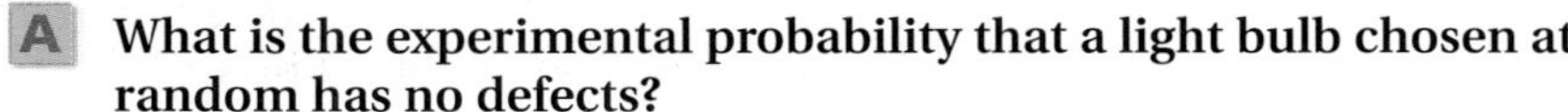

**A** **What is the experimental probability that a light bulb chosen at random has no defects?**

Find the experimental probability that a light bulb has no defects.

$$\frac{\text{number of times the event occurs}}{\text{number of trials}} = \frac{796}{800}$$

$$= 99.5\%$$

The experimental probability that a light bulb has no defects is 99.5%.

**B** **The manufacturer sent a shipment of 2400 light bulbs to a retail store. Predict the number of light bulbs in the shipment that are likely to have no defects.**

Find 99.5% of 2400.

$0.995(2400) = 2388$

The manufacturer predicts that 2388 light bulbs have no defects.

**4.** A manufacturer inspects 1500 electric toothbrush motors and finds 1497 to have no defects.

**a.** What is the experimental probability that a motor chosen at random will have no defects?

**b.** There are 35,000 motors in a warehouse. Predict the number of motors that are likely to have no defects.

## THINK AND DISCUSS

**1.** Explain the difference between an outcome and an event.

**2.** Is the experimental probability of an event always the same? Explain why or why not.

**3. GET ORGANIZED** Copy and complete the graphic organizer. In each box, write an example of an event that has the given likelihood.

Likelihood of an Event

Impossible | Unlikely | As likely as not | Likely | Certain

Rev. 6.S.2

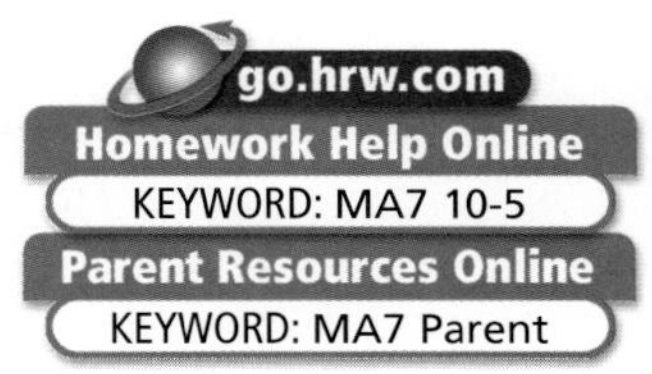


## GUIDED PRACTICE

1. **Vocabulary** Give an example of an *event* that has two possible *outcomes.*

SEE EXAMPLE 1 p. 713

**Identify the sample space and the outcome shown for each experiment.**

2. rolling a number cube
3. spinning a spinner
4. tossing 3 coins

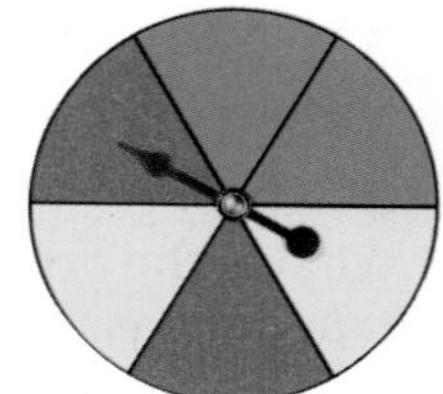

SEE EXAMPLE 2 p. 714

**Write *impossible, unlikely, as likely as not, likely,* or *certain* to describe each event.**

5. Peter was born in January. Thomas was born in June. Peter and Thomas have the same birthday.
6. The football team won 9 of its last 10 games. The team will win the next game.
7. A board game has a rule that if you roll the game cube and get a 6, you get an extra turn. You get an extra turn on your first roll.

SEE EXAMPLE 3 p. 714

**An experiment consists of rolling a number cube. Use the results in the table to find the experimental probability of each event.**

| Outcome | 1 | 2 | 3 | 4 | 5 | 6 |
|---|---|---|---|---|---|---|
| Frequency | 5 | 6 | 2 | 2 | 3 | 7 |

8. rolling a 6
9. rolling an even number
10. not rolling a 6

SEE EXAMPLE 4 p. 715

11. **Sports** One game of bowling consists of ten frames. Elyse usually rolls 3 strikes in each game.
    a. What is the experimental probability that Elyse will roll a strike on any frame?
    b. Predict the number of strikes Elyse will throw in 18 games.

## PRACTICE AND PROBLEM SOLVING

**Independent Practice**

| For Exercises | See Example |
|---|---|
| 12–14 | 1 |
| 15–17 | 2 |
| 18–20 | 3 |
| 21 | 4 |

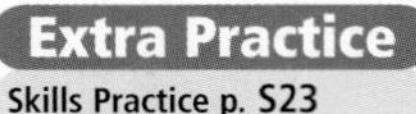
**Extra Practice**
Skills Practice p. S23
Application Practice p. S37

**Identify the sample space and the outcome shown for each experiment.**

12. tossing two coins
13. spinning a spinner
14. selecting a marble

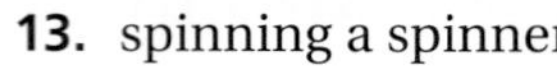
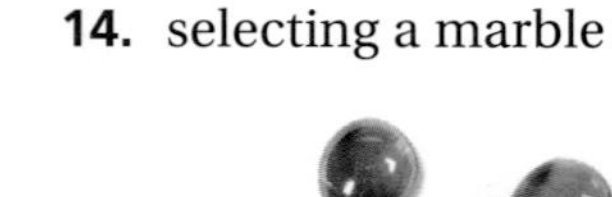

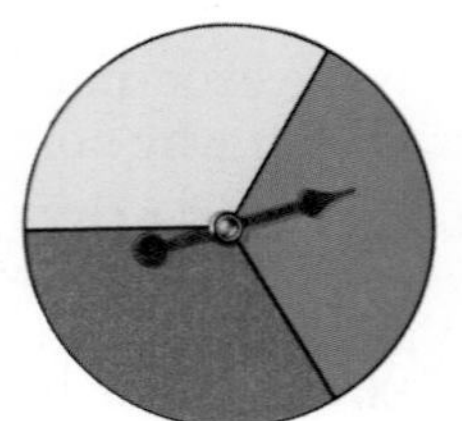

**Write *impossible, unlikely, as likely as not, likely,* or *certain* to describe each event.**

15. Marlo purchased a new pair of shoes. She takes one shoe out of the box. The shoe is for the left foot.

16. Sam takes the bus to school. The bus came late twice in the last two weeks. The bus will be late today.

17. Tammy dropped two quarters on the floor. At least one of them lands heads up.

**An experiment consists of randomly choosing a marble from a bag. Use the results in the table to find the experimental probability of each event.**

| Outcome | Frequency |
|---|---|
| Red | 4 |
| Blue | 6 |
| Green | 6 |
| Yellow | 9 |

18. choosing a yellow marble

19. choosing a blue marble

20. not choosing a green marble

21. **Sports** A ski lodge inspects 80 skis and finds 4 to be defective.
    a. What is the experimental probability that a ski chosen at random will be defective?
    b. The lodge has 420 skis. Predict the number of skis that are likely to be defective.

22. The table shows the results of a survey asking students the season of their birthday. What is the experimental probability that a student has a birthday during the summer?

| Season | Birthdays |
|---|---|
| Fall | 39 |
| Winter | 27 |
| Spring | 33 |
| Summer | 51 |

23. You and your friend can either go swimming or to a movie on Thursday. The weather forecast says there is a 70% chance of rain on Thursday. Should you plan on going swimming or to a movie? Explain.

24. **Critical Thinking** Tell why it is important to repeat an experiment many times.

25. **Write About It** Explain what it means for an event to have a 50-50 chance of happening.

26. How many outcomes are in the sample space for an experiment consisting of rolling two standard number cubes?

27. **Estimation** A manufacturing company produced 986 units in one day. Of those, 9 units were found to be defective. Estimate the experimental probability that a unit produced that day was defective. Then predict approximately how many units will be defective when 5680 units are produced in one week.

**MULTI-STEP TEST PREP**

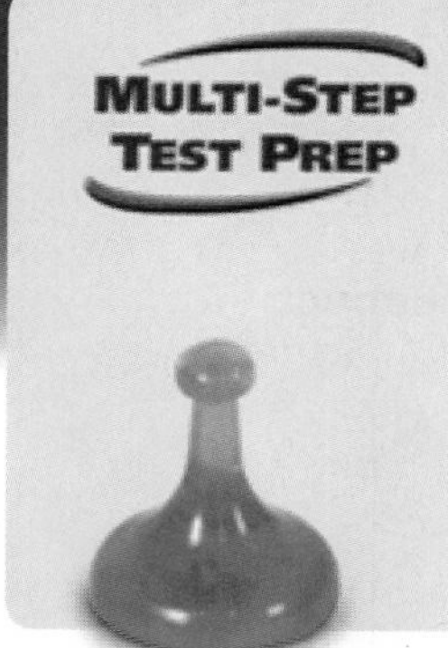

28. This problem will prepare you for the Multi-Step Test Prep on page 744.

    In a standard deck of cards, there are 13 cards in each of four suits: hearts, diamonds, clubs, and spades. The hearts and diamonds are red and the clubs and spades are black. Ricardo randomly drew cards from a standard deck of 52 cards. The table shows the results.

| Outcome | Frequency |
|---|---|
| Hearts | 7 |
| Diamonds | 7 |
| Clubs | 8 |
| Spades | 6 |

    a. Find the experimental probability of drawing a club.
    b. Find the experimental probability of drawing a black suit.

Rev. 6.S.2

29. Alex rolls two standard number cubes. What is the likelihood that the sum of the numbers is less than 4?

   Ⓐ Impossible  Ⓑ Unlikely  Ⓒ As likely as not  Ⓓ Likely

30. A community reported that $\frac{2}{3}$ of the residents had a pet and $\frac{1}{2}$ of the pet owners had a dog. If there are 84 residents in the community, how many residents are likely to have a dog?

   Ⓕ 14  Ⓖ 28  Ⓗ 42  Ⓙ 56

31. What is the probability that a number chosen at random from the list below will be a solution of the inequality $3x + 2 \leq 23$?

   −8, −7, −6, −5, −4, −3, −2, −1, 0, 1, 2, 3, 4, 5, 6, 7, 8, 9

   Ⓐ $\frac{17}{18}$  Ⓑ $\frac{8}{9}$  Ⓒ $\frac{1}{9}$  Ⓓ $\frac{1}{18}$

32. **Short Response** A coin was tossed 50 times. It landed showing heads 6 more times than it landed showing tails. What is the experimental probability of the coin landing on heads? Show your work.

## CHALLENGE AND EXTEND

**A coin is tossed 3 times. Use the sample space for this experiment to describe each event below as *impossible, unlikely, as likely as not, likely,* or *certain*. Justify each answer.**

33. At least 2 heads
34. 2 heads and 1 tail
35. 2 tails and 1 head
36. 3 tails
37. One coin is tossed 20 times.
   a. The experimental probability of the coin showing heads is 65%. How many times did the coin show tails?
   b. If the coin is tossed ten more times, how many more times must the coin land showing tails for the experimental probability of tails to be 50%?

## SPIRAL REVIEW

38. A sales representative earns 4.5% commission on sales. Find the commission earned when the total sales are $124,000. *(Lesson 2-9)*

39. Estimate the tax on a $255 printer when the tax rate is 5.5%. *(Lesson 2-9)*

**Compare the graph of each function to the graph of $f(x) = x^2$.** *(Lesson 9-4)*

40. $g(x) = \frac{1}{3}x^2$
41. $g(x) = -x^2$
42. $g(x) = x^2 - 12$

**The data shows the number of books read by seven students over the summer: 5, 5, 14, 2, 5, 5, 6.** *(Lesson 10-3)*

43. Give the mean, median, and mode of the data.
44. Which measure of central tendency best describes the data? Explain.
45. Create a box-and-whisker plot of the data.

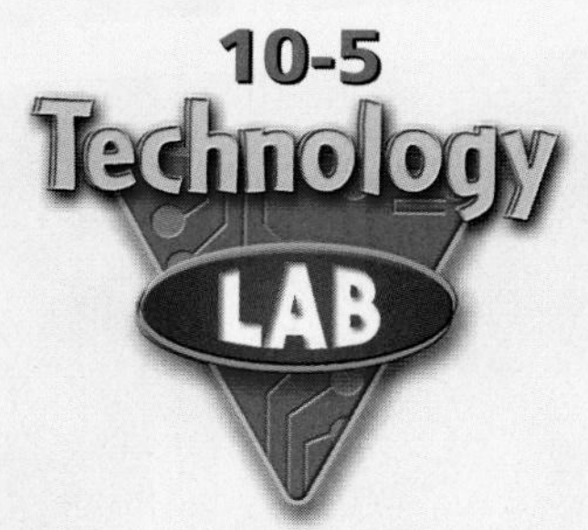


# Use Random Numbers

A calculator can be used to model an experiment that would be difficult or inconvenient to perform. To do this, you will use random numbers.

*Use with Lesson 10-5*

## Activity

You can use a calculator to explore the experimental probability that at least 2 people in a group of 6 people were born in the same month. Assume that all months are equally likely to be a person's birth month.

```
MATH NUM CPX PRB
1:rand
2:nPr
3:nCr
4:!
5:randInt(
6:randNorm(
7:randBin(
```

1. Represent each month with an integer. Since there are 12 months, use the numbers 1–12.

   To set your calculator up to generate random numbers, press MATH. Then use the arrow keys to highlight **PRB**. Select **5: randInt(**.

2. Now give the start number, 1, press ,, and give the end number, 12.

   Each time you press ENTER the calculator will return an integer from 1 to 12.

3. You are considering a group of 6 people. This means you need 6 random numbers.

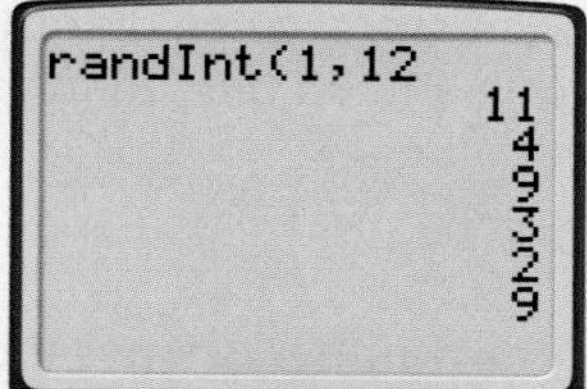


| | Person | | | | | |
|---|---|---|---|---|---|---|
| | 1 | 2 | 3 | 4 | 5 | 6 |
| **Trial 1** | 11 | 4 | 9 | 3 | 2 | 9 |
| **Trial 2** | 3 | 8 | 10 | 12 | 6 | 2 |

In the first trial, the number 9 appears twice. This means that two people have a birth day in the ninth month, September.

In the second trial, no number appears more than once. This means that none of the people were born in the same month.

## Try This

1. Repeat the experiment until you have 10 trials of the experiment. Count the number of trials in which a number appears more than once. Divide this number by the number of trials, 10, to find the experimental probability that at least 2 people in a group of 6 people will have the same birth month.
2. Gather the results from at least 100 trials of the experiment. (Either perform all of the trials yourself or combine data with your classmates.) Using your results, what is the experimental probability that at least 2 people in a group of 6 people will have the same birth month? Compare the results from 100 trials to the results of 10 trials.
3. How could you set up the experiment to find the experimental probability that at least 2 people in a group of 6 people will have the same birthday (same month and same date)?

# 10-6 Theoretical Probability

**Rev. 6.S.1** Understand the relationships between experimental and theoretical probabilities for simple events.

***Objectives***
Determine the theoretical probability of an event.

Convert between probabilities and odds.

***Vocabulary***
equally likely
theoretical probability
fair
complement
odds

**Why learn this?**
Theoretical probability can be used to determine the likelihood of different weather conditions. (See Example 2.)

A developing tornado near Amarillo, Texas.

When the outcomes in the sample space of an experiment have the same chance of occurring, the outcomes are said to be **equally likely**.

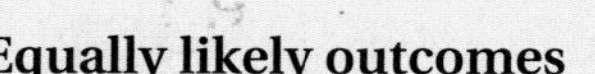

**Equally likely outcomes**

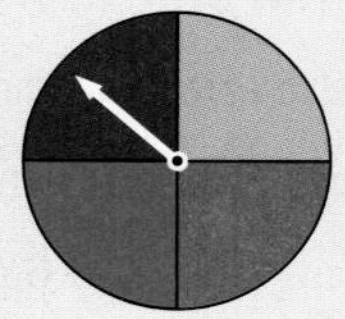

There is the same chance that the spinner will land on any of the colors.

**Not equally likely outcomes**

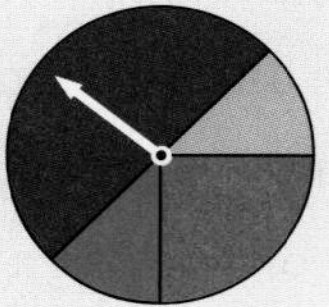

There is a greater chance that the spinner will land on blue than on any other color.

The **theoretical probability** of an event is the ratio of the number of ways the event can occur to the total number of equally likely outcomes.

**Theoretical Probability**

$$\text{theoretical probability} = \frac{\text{number of ways the event can occur}}{\text{total number of equally likely outcomes}}$$

An experiment in which all outcomes are equally likely is said to be **fair**. You can usually assume that experiments involving coins and number cubes are fair.

**EXAMPLE 1** **Finding Theoretical Probability**

**An experiment consists of rolling a number cube. Find the theoretical probability of each outcome.**

**A** **rolling a 3**

$$\frac{\text{number of ways the event can occur}}{\text{total number of equally likely outcomes}} = \frac{1}{6}$$ *There is one 3 on a number cube.*

$$= 0.1\overline{6}$$

$$= 16\frac{2}{3}\%$$

**Caution!**
The use of the word *experiment* does not necessarily mean you are looking for experimental probability.

**An experiment consists of rolling a number cube. Find the theoretical probability of each outcome.**

**B** **rolling a number greater than 3**

$$\frac{\text{number of ways the event can occur}}{\text{total number of equally likely outcomes}} = \frac{3}{6} = \frac{1}{2}$$ *There are 3 numbers greater than 3.*

$$= 0.5 = 50\%$$

**An experiment consists of rolling a number cube. Find the theoretical probability of each outcome.**

**1a.** rolling an even number **1b.** rolling a multiple of 3

When you toss a coin, there are two possible outcomes, heads or tails. The table below shows the theoretical probabilities and experimental results of tossing a coin 10 times.

**Reading Math**

The probability of an event can be written as *P*(event). *P*(heads) means "the probability that heads will be the outcome."

| | ***P*(heads)** | ***P*(tails)** | ***P*(heads) + *P*(tails)** |
|---|---|---|---|
| **Experimental Probability** | $\frac{3}{10}$ | $\frac{7}{10}$ | $\frac{3}{10} + \frac{7}{10} = \frac{10}{10} = 1$ |
| **Theoretical Probability** | $\frac{1}{2}$ | $\frac{1}{2}$ | $\frac{1}{2} + \frac{1}{2} = \frac{2}{2} = 1$ |

The sum of the probability of heads and the probability of tails is 1, or 100%. This is because it is certain that one of the two outcomes will always occur.

$$P(\text{event happening}) + P(\text{event not happening}) = 1$$

The **complement** of an event is all the outcomes in the sample space that are not included in the event. The sum of the probabilities of an event and its complement is 1, or 100%, because the event will either happen or not happen.

$$P(\text{event}) + P(\text{complement of event}) = 1$$

## EXAMPLE 2 Finding Probability by Using the Complement

**The weather forecaster predicts a 20% chance of snow. What is the probability that it will not snow?**

$P(\text{snow}) + P(\text{not snow}) = 100\%$ *Either it will snow or it will not snow.*

$20\% + P(\text{not snow}) = 100\%$

$-20\%$ $-20\%$ *Subtract 20% from both sides.*

$P(\text{not snow}) = 80\%$

CHECK IT OUT!

**2.** A jar has green, blue, purple, and white marbles. The probability of choosing a green marble is 0.2, the probability of choosing blue is 0.3, the probability of choosing purple is 0.1. What is the probability of choosing white?

**Odds** are another way to express the likelihood of an event. The *odds in favor of an event* describe the likelihood that the event will occur. The *odds against an event* describe the likelihood that the event will not occur.

Odds are usually written with a colon in the form $a:b$, but can also be written as $a$ to $b$ or $\frac{a}{b}$.

**Odds**

**ODDS IN FAVOR OF AN EVENT**

$$\text{odds in favor} = \frac{\text{number of ways an event can happen}}{\text{number of ways an event can fail to happen}} = a:b$$

**ODDS AGAINST AN EVENT**

$$\text{odds against} = \frac{\text{number of ways an event can fail to happen}}{\text{number of ways an event can happen}} = b:a$$

*a* represents the number of ways an event can occur.
*b* represents the number of ways an event can fail to occur.

The two numbers given as the odds will add up to the total number of possible outcomes. You can use this relationship to convert between odds and probabilities.

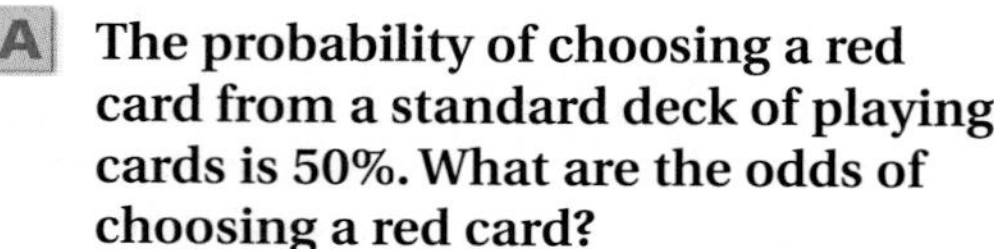


## Converting Between Odds and Probabilities

**A** **The probability of choosing a red card from a standard deck of playing cards is 50%. What are the odds of choosing a red card?**

*The probability of choosing a red card is 50%, so the probability of not drawing a red card is 100% − 50% = 50%.*

Odds in favor = 50 : 50, or 1 : 1

The odds in favor of choosing a red card are 1 : 1.

**Reading Math**

You may see an outcome called "favorable." This does not mean that the outcome is good or bad. A favorable outcome is the outcome you are looking for in a probability experiment.

**B** **The odds against choosing a green marble from a bag are 5 : 3. What is the probability of choosing a green marble?**

*The odds against green are 5:3, so the odds in favor of green are 3:5. This means there are 3 favorable outcomes and 5 unfavorable outcomes for a total of 8 possible outcomes.*

$$\frac{\text{number of ways event can happen}}{\text{total possible outcomes}} = \frac{3}{8}$$

The probability of choosing a green marble is $\frac{3}{8}$.

3. The odds in favor of winning a free drink are 1 : 24. What is the probability of winning a free drink?

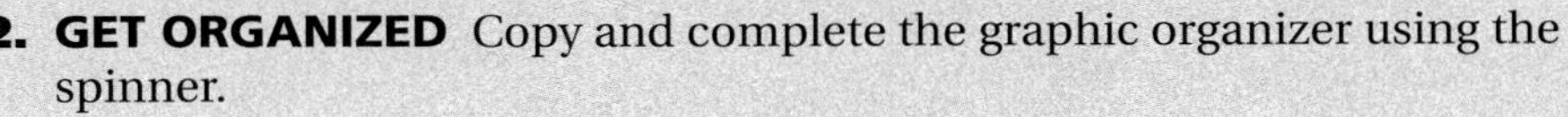

## THINK AND DISCUSS

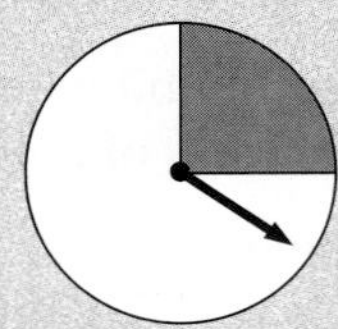



1. Tell how to find the probability of the complement of an event.
2. **GET ORGANIZED** Copy and complete the graphic organizer using the spinner.

| Probabilities on Spinner | |
|---|---|
| *P*(gray) | |
| *P*(not gray) | |
| Odds in favor of gray | |
| Odds against gray | |

# 10-6 Exercises

Rev. 6.S.1

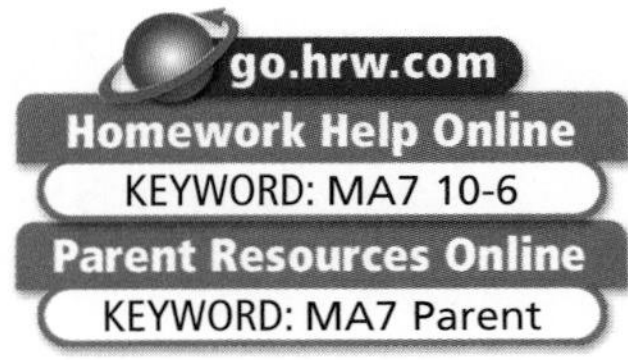



## GUIDED PRACTICE

1. **Vocabulary** All of the outcomes in the sample space that are not included in the event are called the ___?___. (*theoretical probability, complement,* or *odds*)

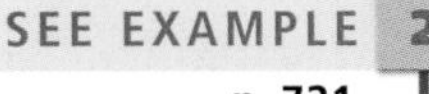

SEE EXAMPLE 1 p. 720

**Find the theoretical probability of each outcome.**

2. rolling a number divisible by 3 on a number cube
3. flipping 2 coins and both landing with tails showing
4. randomly choosing the letter S from the letters in STARS
5. rolling a prime number on a number cube

SEE EXAMPLE 2 p. 721

6. A spinner is green, red, and blue. The probability that a spinner will land on green is 15% and red is 35%. What is the probability the spinner will land on blue?

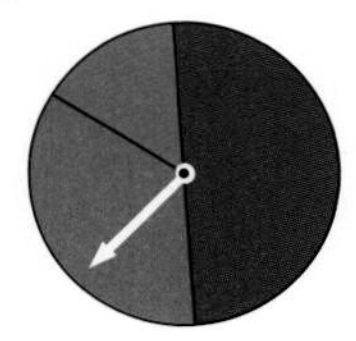

7. The probability of choosing a red marble from a bag is $\frac{1}{3}$. What is the probability of not choosing a red marble?
8. You have a $\frac{1}{50}$ chance of winning. What is the probability you will not win?
9. There is a $\frac{1}{10}$ chance that you will be chosen as class representative. What is the probability that you will not be chosen?

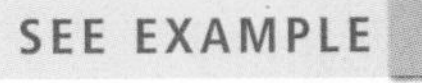

SEE EXAMPLE 3 p. 722

10. The odds against a spinner landing on blue are 3 : 1. What is the probability of the spinner landing on blue?
11. The probability of choosing an ace from a deck of cards is $\frac{1}{13}$. What are the odds of choosing an ace?
12. The probability of not winning a game is 80%. What are the odds of winning?
13. The odds in favor of a spinner landing on blue are 1 : 3. What is the probability of landing on blue?

## PRACTICE AND PROBLEM SOLVING

**Independent Practice**

| For Exercises | See Example |
|---|---|
| 14–16 | 1 |
| 17–19 | 2 |
| 20–22 | 3 |

**Extra Practice**

Skills Practice p. S23
Application Practice p. S37

**Find the theoretical probability of each outcome.**

**14.** rolling a 5 on a number cube

**15.** flipping 2 coins and 1 landing with heads showing, the other with tails showing

**16.** randomly choosing a blue marble from a bag of 5 blue marbles, 8 red marbles, and 7 yellow marbles

**17.** The probability of a spinner landing on yellow is $\frac{4}{9}$. What is the probability of it not landing on yellow?

**18.** There is a 3% probability of winning a game. Find the probability of not winning the game.

**19.** There is a 15% chance it will snow and a 15% chance it will rain. What is the probability that it will neither snow nor rain?

**20.** The odds against winning a contest are 99 : 1. What is the probability of not winning the contest?

**21.** The odds of choosing a white marble from a bag are 1 : 9. Find the probability of not choosing a white marble.

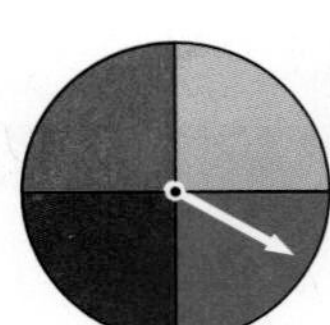

**22.** The probability of a spinner landing on green is 25%. What are the odds of the spinner not landing on green?

**Use the spinner for Exercises 23–28.**

**23.** $P(\text{red})$

**24.** $P(\text{green})$

**25.** $P(\text{not blue})$

**26.** odds in favor of yellow

**27.** odds against red

**28.** odds against green

**29. Write About It** A number cube is rolled. Which event has a greater theoretical probability: rolling a number less than 3 or rolling a number greater than three? Explain.

**30. ///ERROR ANALYSIS///** The odds in favor of an event are 1 : 4. Two students converted these odds into the probability of the event NOT happening. Which is incorrect? Explain the error.

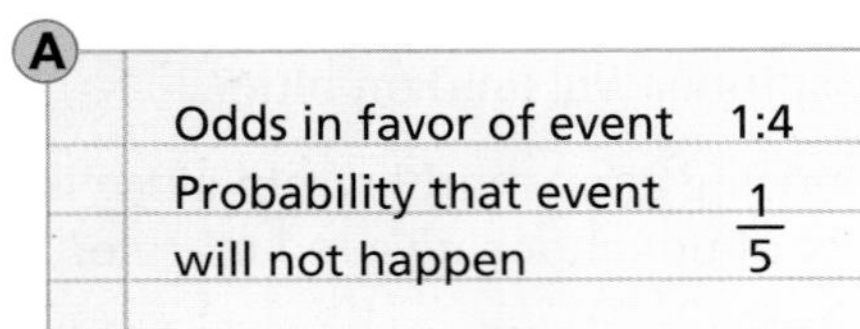

A

| | |
|---|---|
| Odds in favor of event | 1:4 |
| Probability that event will not happen | $\frac{1}{5}$ |

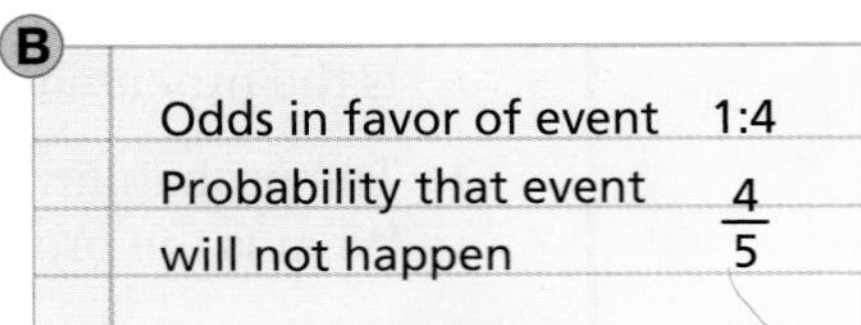

B

| | |
|---|---|
| Odds in favor of event | 1:4 |
| Probability that event will not happen | $\frac{4}{5}$ |

**31. Critical Thinking** The odds in favor of a certain event are the same as the odds against that event. What is the probability of the event occurring?

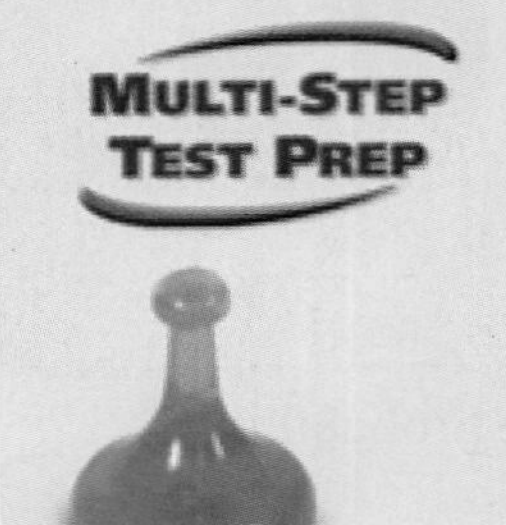

**MULTI-STEP TEST PREP**

**32.** This problem will prepare you for the Multi-Step Test Prep on page 744.

Chutes and Ladders is a children's game that uses a spinner with the numbers 1 through 6.

**a.** What is the probability of a spinning a 3?

**b.** What is the probability of spinning an odd number?

**c.** What is the probability of spinning a number that is less than or equal to 4?

33. **Write About It** Explain how to convert odds to probability.

34. **Geometry** The radius of each circle in the diagram is given. Find the probability that a point chosen at random will lie in the red area of the diagram.

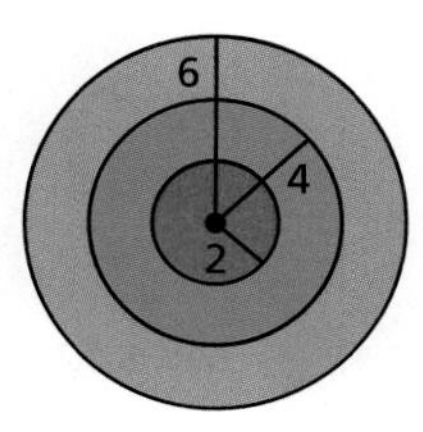

NC Rev. 6.S.1

35. Two coins are tossed. What is the probability that at least one of the coins lands with heads showing?

   (A) 25%  (B) $33\frac{1}{3}\%$  (C) 50%  (D) 75%

36. A standard number cube is rolled. Which has the greatest probability?

   (F) *P*(even)  (G) *P*(less than 5)  (H) *P*(not 2)  (J) *P*(greater than 3)

37. Find the probability that a point chosen at random would fall in the yellow area.

   (A) $\frac{1}{6}$  (C) $\frac{4}{9}$

   (B) $\frac{2}{9}$  (D) $\frac{2}{3}$

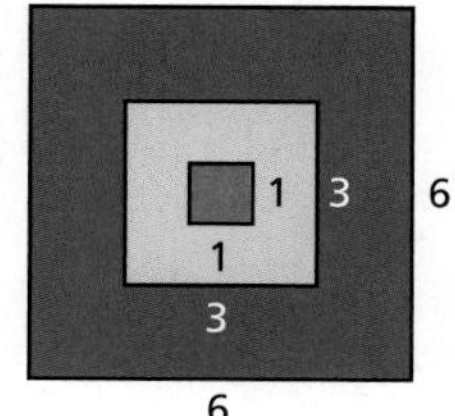


## CHALLENGE AND EXTEND

**Use the results of 3 coin-tossing experiments in the table for Exercise 38.**

38. Find the experimental probability for
   a. experiment 1.
   b. experiment 2.
   c. experiment 3.
   d. Find the theoretical probability of heads.

| | Experiment | | |
|---|---|---|---|
| | 1 | 2 | 3 |
| Number of Tosses | 10 | 100 | 1000 |
| Heads | 4 | 48 | 502 |

   e. **Write About It** How do the experimental probabilities of each experiment compare to the theoretical probability?

## SPIRAL REVIEW

39. The table shows the volume of water in an office water cooler over time. Find the rate of change for each time period. For which time period did the volume of water decrease at the slowest rate? *(Lesson 5-3)*

| Time of day | 7:00 A.M. | 9:00 A.M. | 1:00 P.M. | 4:00 P.M. | 5:00 P.M. |
|---|---|---|---|---|---|
| Volume (gal) | 4.2 | 3.8 | 2.7 | 1.2 | 0.8 |

**Factor each trinomial.** *(Lesson 8-4)*

40. $2x^2 + x - 21$  41. $4x^2 - 7x + 3$  42. $6x^2 + 23x + 20$

**An experiment consists of choosing a card out of a deck and recording the results. Use the table to find the experimental probability of each event.** *(Lesson 10-5)*

43. choosing a heart

44. choosing a heart or a diamond

45. not choosing a club

| Outcome | Frequency |
|---|---|
| Hearts | 2 |
| Diamonds | 6 |
| Spades | 5 |
| Clubs | 7 |

# 10-7 Independent and Dependent Events

**Rev. 8.S.1** Calculate the probabilities of dependent and independent events.

***Objectives***
Find the probability of independent events.

Find the probability of dependent events.

***Vocabulary***
independent events
dependent events

**Why learn this?**
You may need to understand independent and dependent events to determine the number of reading selections available.

Adam's teacher gives the class two lists of titles and asks each student to choose two of them to read. Adam can choose one title from each list or two titles from the same list.

**One title from each list**

| List 1 | List 2 |
|---|---|
| *Animal Farm* (circled) | *Never Cry Wolf* |
| *Ethan Frome* | *Night* |
| *Frankenstein* | *Things Fall Apart* |
| *Great Expectations* | *Wish You Well* |
| *Jane Eyre* | *Wuthering Heights* (circled) |

Choosing a title from one list does not affect the number of titles to choose from on the other list. The events are *independent.*

**Two titles from the same list**

| List (first choice) | List (second choice) |
|---|---|
| *Animal Farm* (circled) | ~~*Animal Farm*~~ |
| *Ethan Frome* | *Ethan Frome* |
| *Frankenstein* | *Frankenstein* (circled) |
| *Great Expectations* | *Great Expectations* |
| *Jane Eyre* | *Jane Eyre* |

Choosing a title from one of the lists changes the number of titles that can be chosen from the same list. The events are *dependent.*

Events are **independent events** if the occurrence of one event does not affect the probability of the other. Events are **dependent events** if the occurrence of one event does affect the probability of the other.

## EXAMPLE 1 Classifying Events as Independent or Dependent

**Tell whether each set of events is independent or dependent. Explain your answer.**

**A** **A dime lands heads up and a nickel lands heads up.**
The result of tossing a dime does not affect the result of tossing a nickel, so the events are independent.

**B** **You choose a colored game piece in a board game, and then your sister picks another color.**
Your sister cannot pick the same color you picked, and there are fewer game pieces for your sister to choose from after you choose, so the events are dependent.

**Tell whether each set of events is independent or dependent. Explain your answer.**

**1a.** A number cube lands showing an odd number. It is rolled a second time and lands showing 6.

**1b.** One student in your class is chosen for a project. Then another student in the class is chosen.

## Student to Student

### *Independent and Dependent Events*

**Lydia Delgado**
Northridge High School

*I use the everyday meanings of independent and dependent to remember their mathematical meanings.*

*The math class I take next year depends on which math classes I have already taken.*

*For dependent events, the occurrence of one affects the probability of the other.*

*The history class I take next year is independent from (does not depend on) which math classes I have taken.*

*For independent events, the occurrence of one does not affect the occurrence of the other.*

Suppose an experiment involves flipping two fair coins. The sample space of outcomes is shown by the tree diagram. Determine the theoretical probability of both coins landing heads up.

| 1st Coin | 2nd Coin |
|---|---|
| H | H |
| | T |
| T | H |
| | T |

There are four possible outcomes in the sample space: $\{(H, H), (H, T), (T, H), (T, T)\}$

Only one outcome includes both coins landing heads up.

The theoretical probability of both coins landing heads up is $\frac{1}{4}$.

Now look back at the separate theoretical probabilities of each coin landing heads up. The theoretical probability in each case is $\frac{1}{2}$. The product of these two probabilities is $\frac{1}{4}$, the same probability shown by the tree diagram.

To determine the probability of two independent events, multiply the probabilities of the two events.

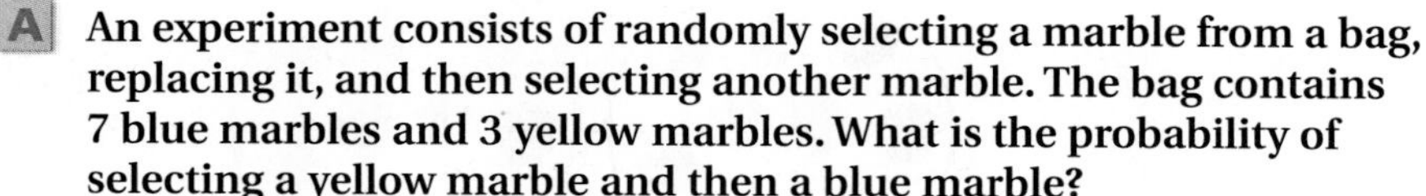

**Probability of Independent Events**

If $A$ and $B$ are independent events, then $P(A \text{ and } B) = P(A) \cdot P(B)$.

### EXAMPLE 2 Finding the Probability of Independent Events

**A** **An experiment consists of randomly selecting a marble from a bag, replacing it, and then selecting another marble. The bag contains 7 blue marbles and 3 yellow marbles. What is the probability of selecting a yellow marble and then a blue marble?**

Because the first marble is replaced after it is selected, the sample space for each selection is the same. The events are independent.

$$P(\text{yellow, blue}) = P(\text{yellow}) \cdot P(\text{blue})$$

$$= \frac{3}{10} \cdot \frac{7}{10}$$ *The probability of selecting yellow is $\frac{3}{10}$, and the probability of selecting blue is $\frac{7}{10}$.*

$$= \frac{21}{100}$$

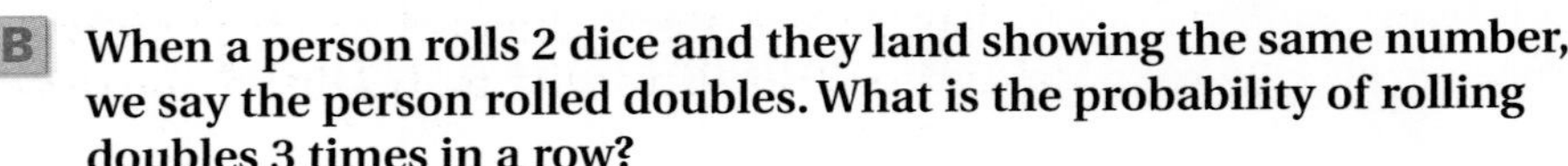

**B** **When a person rolls 2 dice and they land showing the same number, we say the person rolled doubles. What is the probability of rolling doubles 3 times in a row?**

The result of one roll does not affect any following rolls. The events are independent.

When you roll a pair of dice, there are 36 possible outcomes, six of which are doubles:

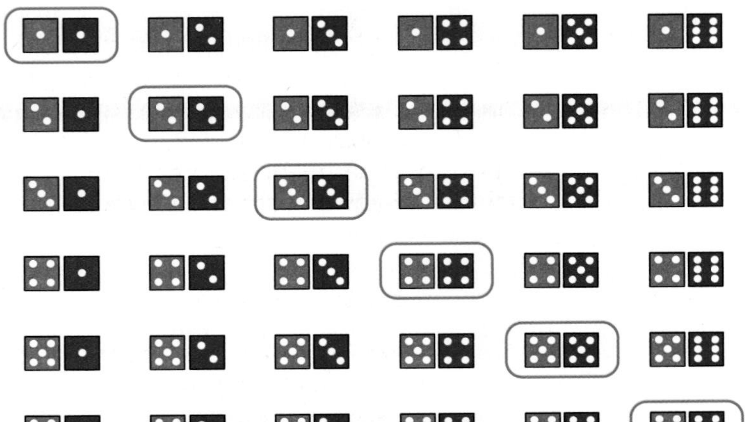

So, the probability of rolling doubles once is $P(\text{double}) = \frac{6}{36} = \frac{1}{6}$.

$$P(\text{double, double, double}) = P(\text{double}) \cdot P(\text{double}) \cdot P(\text{double})$$

$$= \frac{1}{6} \cdot \frac{1}{6} \cdot \frac{1}{6}$$

$$= \frac{1}{216}$$

**2.** An experiment consists of spinning the spinner twice. What is the probability of spinning two odd numbers?

Suppose an experiment involves drawing marbles from a bag. Determine the theoretical probability of drawing a red marble and then drawing a second red marble *without replacing the first one.*

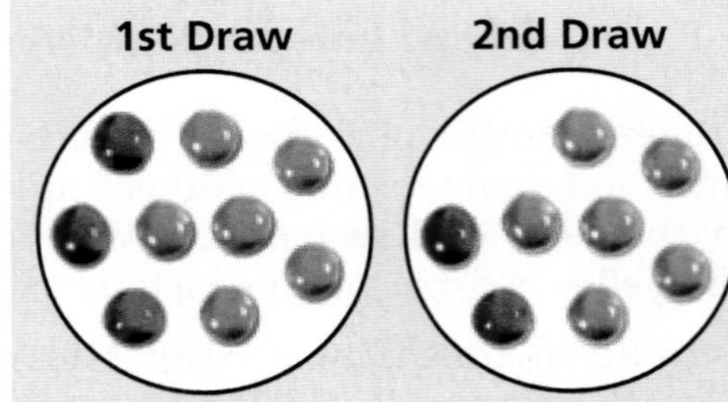


The sample space for the second draw is not the same as the sample space for the first draw. There are fewer marbles in the bag for the second draw.

This means the events are dependent.

Probability of drawing a red marble on the first draw $= \frac{3}{9} = \frac{1}{3}$

Probability of drawing a red marble on the second draw $= \frac{2}{8} = \frac{1}{4}$

To determine the probability of two dependent events, multiply the probability of the first event times the probability of the second event after the first event has occurred.

**Probability of Dependent Events**

If $A$ and $B$ are dependent events, then $P(A \text{ and } B) = P(A) \cdot P(B \text{ after } A)$.

## EXAMPLE 3 Problem-Solving Application

**There are 7 pink flowers and 5 yellow flowers in a bunch. Jane selects a flower at random, and then Leah selects a flower at random from the remaining flowers. What is the probability that Jane selects a pink flower and Leah selects a yellow flower?**

### 1 Understand the Problem

The **answer** will be the probability that a yellow flower is chosen after a pink flower is chosen.

List the **important information:**

- Jane chooses a pink flower from 7 pink flowers and 5 yellow flowers.
- Leah chooses a yellow flower from 6 pink flowers and 5 yellow flowers.

### 2 Make a Plan

Draw a diagram.

| Flowers Jane can choose from | | Flowers Leah can choose from | |
|---|---|---|---|
| ●●●●●●● | 7 pink | ●●●●●● | 6 pink |
| ○○○○○ | 5 yellow | ○○○○○ | 5 yellow |
| | 12 total | | 11 total |

After Jane selects a flower, the sample space changes. So the events are dependent.

### 3 Solve

$$P(\text{pink and yellow}) = P(\text{pink}) \cdot P(\text{yellow after pink})$$

$$= \frac{7}{12} \cdot \frac{5}{11}$$

*Jane selects one of 7 pink flowers from 12 total flowers. Then Leah selects one of 5 yellow flowers from the 11 flowers left.*

$$= \frac{35}{132}$$

The probability that Jane selects a pink flower and Leah selects a yellow flower is $\frac{35}{132}$.

### 4 Look Back

Drawing a diagram helps you see how the sample space changes. This means the events are dependent, so you can use the formula for probability of dependent events.

3. A bag has 10 red marbles, 12 white marbles, and 8 blue marbles. Two marbles are randomly drawn from the bag. What is the probability of drawing a blue marble and then a red marble?

### THINK AND DISCUSS

1. Give an example of two events that are dependent. Explain why the events are dependent.
2. **GET ORGANIZED** Copy and complete the graphic organizer.

| | Example | Probability |
|---|---|---|
| Dependent Events | $A =$<br>$B =$ | $P(A \text{ and } B) =$ |
| Independent Events | $A =$<br>$B =$ | $P(A \text{ and } B) =$ |

# 10-7 Exercises

Rev. 8.S.1

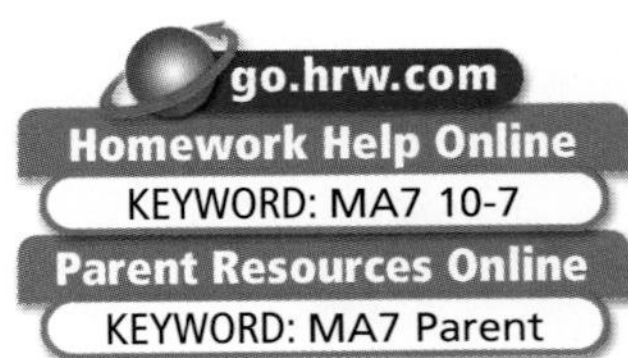


## GUIDED PRACTICE

1. **Vocabulary** Two events are ____?____ if the occurrence of one event affects the probability of the other event. (*independent* or *dependent*)

SEE EXAMPLE 1
p. 726

**Tell whether each set of events is independent or dependent. Explain your answers.**

2. You draw a heart from a deck of cards and set it aside. Then you draw a club from the deck of cards.
3. You guess "true" on two true-false questions.
4. Your brother calls you on the phone. You hang up the phone, and then your neighbor calls you.
5. You order from a menu, and then your friend orders a different meal.
6. A doctors' office schedules several patients. Then you make an appointment.

SEE EXAMPLE 2
p. 727

7. A coin is tossed three times. What is the probability of the coin landing heads up three times?
8. Seven cards are numbered from 1 to 7 and placed in a box. One card is selected at random and replaced. Another card is randomly selected. What is the probability of selecting two odd numbers?
9. Stacey rolls two number cubes. What is the probability that the sum of the numbers on the two number cubes is 7?
10. A number cube is rolled twice and a coin is tossed once. What is the probability of the coin landing heads up and the number cube landing with 2 showing both times?
11. A spinner with four equal sections of red, yellow, green, and blue is spun twice. What is the probability that it lands on yellow and then on green?

SEE EXAMPLE 3
p. 729

12. A bag contains 4 red marbles, 3 white marbles, and 6 blue marbles. What is the probability of randomly selecting a red marble, setting it aside, and then randomly selecting a white marble from the bag?

13. Seven cards are numbered from 1 to 7 and placed in a box. One card is selected at random and not replaced. Another card is randomly selected. What is the probability of selecting two odd numbers?

14. There are 15 boys and 14 girls in a room. Two of them are selected at random to take a survey. What is the probability that the two people selected will be girls?

## PRACTICE AND PROBLEM SOLVING

**Independent Practice**

| For Exercises | See Example |
|---|---|
| 15–16 | 1 |
| 17–19 | 2 |
| 20–22 | 3 |

**Extra Practice**
Skills Practice p. S23
Application Practice p. S37

**Tell whether each set of events is independent or dependent. Explain your answer.**

15. The teacher randomly selects two students from the class.

16. You roll a 3 on a number cube and choose a 3 from a deck of cards.

17. A number cube is rolled three times. What is the probability of rolling three even numbers?

18. Ten cards are numbered from 1 to 10 and placed in a box. One card is selected at random and replaced. Another card is randomly selected. What is the probability of selecting two even numbers?

19. Stacey rolls a number cube and flips a coin. What is the probability that she rolls a 5 and the coin lands heads up?

20. A bag contains 5 red marbles, 3 white marbles, and 4 blue marbles. What is the probability of randomly selecting a red marble, setting it aside, and then randomly selecting another red marble from the bag?

21. Ten cards are numbered from 1 to 10 and placed in a box. One card is selected at random and not replaced. Another card is randomly selected. What is the probability of selecting two even numbers?

22. A game has 6 colored playing pieces. They are red, yellow, green, blue, purple, and white. You and a friend pick your game piece without looking. What is the probability that your friend picks the blue piece and you pick the yellow piece?

**LINK**
**School**

On some standardized tests, there is no penalty for a wrong answer. On these tests, it is better to guess than to leave the answer blank, especially if some choices can be eliminated.

23. **School** On a multiple-choice test, each question has 4 possible answers. A student does not know the answers to three questions, so the student guesses.

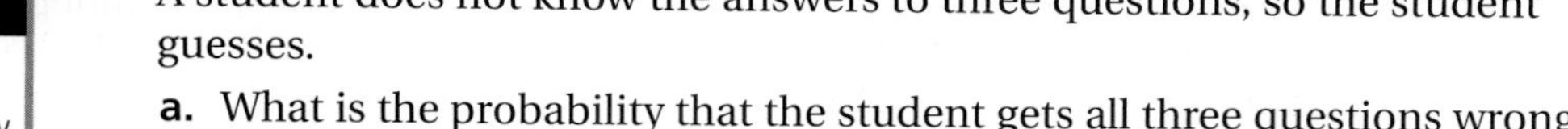

a. What is the probability that the student gets all three questions wrong?
b. What is the probability that the student gets all three questions right?

**Tell whether each set of events is independent or dependent. Explain your answer.**

24. Pick "Joe" from a box of names, replace it, and then pick "Craig."

25. Pick "Joe" from a box of names, set it aside, and then pick "Craig."

26. Roll a prime number on a number cube and get tails when flipping a coin.

27. Roll an even number, then an odd number, and then a 1 on a number cube.

MULTI-STEP TEST PREP

**28.** This problem will prepare you for the Multi-Step Test Prep on page 744. Yahtzee is a game that involves rolling five dice. On his or her turn, a player can roll up to three times to try to score points in various categories. Rolling a "Yahtzee" means rolling five of a kind, or five of the same number.

**a.** Juan has rolled twice and has three 5's showing. He rolls the remaining two dice. What is the probability that both dice will land showing 5?

**b.** Shauna has two 3's showing. She has one more roll with the remaining three dice. What is the probability that all three dice will land showing 3?

**c.** Mike rolls all five number cubes and all of them land showing 6. What is the probability of getting five 6's in one roll?

**29.** A bag contains 3 red, 5 blue, and 2 white marbles.

**a.** Find the probability of randomly picking a red marble, replacing it, and then picking a blue marble.

**b.** Find the probability of randomly picking a red marble, setting it aside, and then picking a blue marble.

**c.** Find the probability of randomly picking a red marble, replacing it, and then picking another red marble.

**d.** Find the probability of randomly picking a red marble, setting it aside, and then picking another red marble.

**30. Entertainment** Joe and Maria are playing a board game. On each turn, the player rolls two number cubes. Both players have two turns remaining.

**a.** Joe will win if he rolls double 6's on both turns. What is the probability that Joe will roll double 6's on both turns?

**b.** Maria will win if she rolls 2 on the first turn and 12 on the second turn. What is the probability that Maria will roll 2 on the first turn and 12 on the second turn?

**c. Write About It** Who has the better probability of winning? Explain.

**31.** Tamika has $2.50 in quarters in her pocket, including four state quarters. She reaches into her pocket and takes out two quarters, one at a time. What is the probability that they are both state quarters?

**32.** Ten cards are numbered 1 through 10 and placed in a bag. You draw a card, set it aside, and draw another card. What is the probability that you will draw two numbers that are divisible by 3?

**33. Critical Thinking** What is the probability of a coin landing heads up on two flips if it lands tails up on the first flip? Explain.

**34. Write About It** Explain what it means for two events to be independent.

## TEST PREP

**35.** A number cube is rolled twice. What is the probability of getting a 2 on both rolls?

Rev. 8.S.1

Ⓐ $\frac{1}{3}$ Ⓑ $\frac{1}{4}$ Ⓒ $\frac{1}{9}$ Ⓓ $\frac{1}{36}$

**36.** In baseball, Julio averages 3 hits in every 10 at bats. What is the probability that he will get hits in both of his next two at bats?

Ⓕ 0.03 Ⓖ 0.09 Ⓗ 0.3 Ⓙ 0.9

37. Two people from a group of 30 will be selected at random for a prize. Twenty people in the group are women. What is the probability that both people selected will be men?

(A) $\frac{3}{29}$ (B) $\frac{38}{87}$ (C) $\frac{56}{87}$ (D) $\frac{1}{10}$

38. Ravi has 10 pairs of socks in a drawer, but none of the pairs are matched up. Each pair is a different color, and one pair is blue. Ravi has to pick his socks in the dark so he does not wake his brother. Which expression can be used to find the probability that Ravi will choose a blue sock and then the matching sock?

(F) $\frac{1}{20} + \frac{1}{20}$ (G) $\frac{1}{10} \cdot \frac{1}{20}$ (H) $\frac{1}{20} + \frac{1}{19}$ (J) $\frac{1}{10} \cdot \frac{1}{19}$

## CHALLENGE AND EXTEND

39. **Basketball** Terrance has made 90% of the free throws he has attempted at basketball practice. What is the probability that he will make the next three free throws he attempts?

40. A number cube is rolled three times. What is the probability of rolling a 5 at least once?

**Geometry** **Use the grid for Exercises 41–44.**

On the grid at right, one small square represents 1% probability.

The pink area represents the probability that event *A* occurs.

The blue area represents the probability that event *B* occurs.

The area where the two colors overlap represents the probability that both events occur.

Use the grid to find each probability.

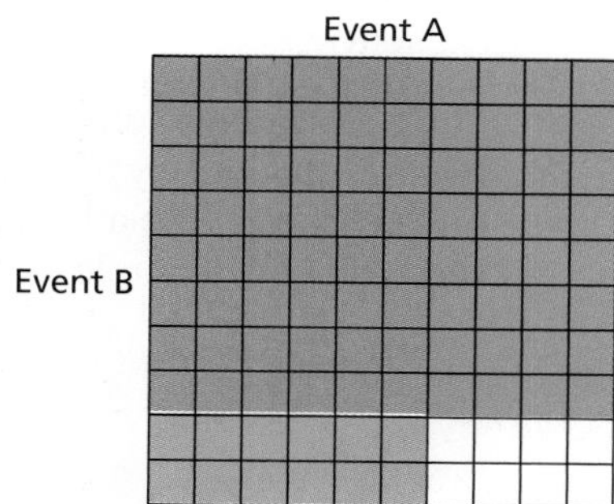


41. Event *A* occurs.

42. Event *B* occurs.

43. Event *A* occurs AND event *B* occurs.

44. Neither event *A* nor event *B* occurs.

## SPIRAL REVIEW

45. A tennis player serves 2 aces (unreturned serves) for every 17 serves. If the player serves 204 times in the next match, how many serves would you expect to be aces? *(Lesson 2-6)*

**Compare the graph of each function to the graph of $f(x) = x^2$.** *(Lesson 9-4)*

46. $g(x) = 4x^2 - 1$

47. $g(x) = \frac{1}{5}x^2$

48. $g(x) = -x^2 + 3$

**Find the theoretical probability of each outcome.** *(Lesson 10-6)*

49. Randomly selecting a blue marble out of a bag with 6 red and 9 blue marbles

50. Rolling a number less than 10 on a number cube

51. Randomly selecting A, E, I, O, or U from all letters of the alphabet

# Compound Events

*Use with Lesson 10-7*

When two events cannot happen at the same time, they are called *mutually exclusive* events. When two events can happen at the same time, they are called *inclusive* events. You can use sample spaces to determine the probabilities of mutually exclusive events and inclusive events.

When finding the probablity of a compound event, you should first determine whether the simple events involved are dependent or independent.

## Activity 1

**Rev. 8.S.1** Calculate the probabilities of dependent and independent events.

Suppose you are playing Monopoly and are "just visiting" the Jail. If you roll 7 on your next turn, you will land on Community Chest. If you roll 12, you will land on Chance. What is the probability that on your next roll you land on either Community Chest or Chance?

You cannot land on Community Chest and Chance at the same time, so the events are mutually exclusive. You cannot roll 7 and 12 at the same time, so those events are also mutually exclusive.

The table shows some of the totals when rolling two fair dice. Copy and complete the table. Use one color to circle all rolls with a total of 7. Use a second color to circle all rolls with a total of 12.

| + | 1 | 2 | 3 | 4 | 5 | 6 |
|---|---|---|---|---|---|---|
| **1** | 2 | 3 | 4 | 5 | | |
| **2** | 3 | 4 | | | | |
| **3** | 4 | 5 | | | | |
| **4** | 5 | | | | | |
| **5** | 6 | | | | | |
| **6** | 7 | | | | | |

## Try This

1. What is the total number of possible rolls?
2. What is the probability that the total will be 7?
3. What is the probability that the total will be 12?
4. What is the probability that the total will be 7 or 12?
5. What do you notice about the probabilities in Problems 2, 3, and 4?

**Suppose you are three spaces away from Community Chest and eight spaces away from Chance.**

6. What is the probability that on your next roll the total will be 3?
7. What is the probability that on your next roll the total will be 8?
8. What is the probability that on your next roll the total will be 3 or 8?
9. Complete the following statement:

   The probability that one of two mutually exclusive events will occur is the ___?___ of the probabilities of the individual events.

In this lab, you discovered this rule: If $A$ and $B$ are mutually exclusive events, then $P(A \text{ or } B) = P(A) + P(B)$.

## Activity 2

Suppose you are playing Yahtzee and on the last roll of your turn, you roll two of the five dice. You need to roll either a 1 or a 5 to make what is called a "small straight" (four consecutive numbers).

What is the probability that you will make a small straight?

You can roll a 1 and a 5 at the same time on different dice. These events are inclusive.

(If you roll a 1 and a 5, you will need to look at only four of the dice to make a small straight.)

There are three outcomes that involve rolling a 1 or rolling a 5.

| Case 1 | Case 2 | Case 3 |
|---|---|---|
| At least one 1 | At least one 5 | Both a 1 and a 5 |

## Try This

**10.** Find the probability of Case 1, rolling at least one 1.

**a.** What is the probability of rolling ⚀ on the first die and any number on the second die?

**b.** What is the probability of rolling any number on the first die and ⚀ on the second die?

**c.** What is the probability of rolling ⚀ on the first die and ⚀ on the second die?

**d.** Parts **a** and **b** both include rolling ⚀ on the first die and ⚀ on the second die. You need to count this outcome only once, so subtract the probability from part **c** from the sum of parts **a** and **b.**

**11.** Find the probability of Case 2, rolling at least one 5. (*Hint:* Repeat the steps in Problem 10.)

**12.** Find the probability of Case 3, rolling a 1 and a 5.

**13.** The probability of rolling a small straight, is the probability of rolling ⚀ *or* ⚄.

Subtract the probability of rolling both ⚀ *and* ⚄ from the sum of the probabilities of rolling ⚀ on one of the dice (Problem 10) and rolling ⚄ on one of the dice (Problem 11).

**14.** Complete the following statement:

The probability that one of two inclusive events will occur is the ___?___ of the probabilities of the individual events ___?___ the probability of the intersection of the two events.

In this lab, you discovered this rule:

If $A$ and $B$ are inclusive events, then $P(A \text{ or } B) = P(A) + P(B) - P(A \text{ and } B)$.

# 10-8 Combinations and Permutations

***Objectives***
Solve problems involving permutations.
Solve problems involving combinations.

***Vocabulary***
compound event
combination
permutation

**Who uses this?**
Security companies use permutations to create many security codes using a limited number of digits or letters. (See Exercise 8.)

Sometimes there are too many possible outcomes to make a tree diagram or a list. The *Fundamental Counting Principle* is one method of finding the number of possible outcomes.

**Fundamental Counting Principle**

If there are $m$ ways to choose a first item and $n$ ways to choose a second item after the first item has been chosen, then there are $m \cdot n$ ways to choose both items.

The Fundamental Counting Principle can also be used when there are more than two items to choose.

**EXAMPLE 1** **Using the Fundamental Counting Principle**

**A florist is arranging centerpieces that include 1 flower, 1 plant, and 1 vase. The florist has 2 kinds of vases, 2 kinds of plants, and 3 kinds of flowers to choose from. How many different centerpieces are possible?**

**Method 1** Use a tree diagram. *Follow each branch of the tree diagram to find all of the possible centerpieces.*

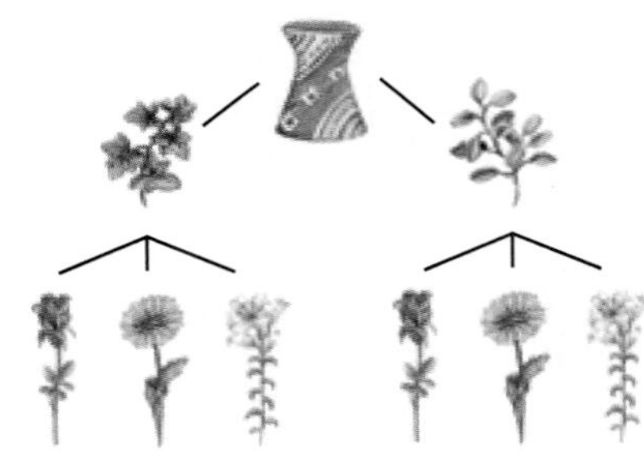

There are 12 possible centerpieces.

**Method 2** Use the Fundamental Counting Principle.

$2 \cdot 2 \cdot 3$ *There are 2 choices for the first item, 2 choices for the second item, and 3 choices for the third item.*

12

There are 12 possible centerpieces.

1. A voicemail system password is 1 letter followed by a 3-digit number less than 600. How many different voicemail passwords are possible?

**Remember!**

The sample space for an experiment is the set of all possible outcomes.

A **compound event** consists of two or more simple events, such as a rolled number cube landing with 3 showing and a tossed coin landing heads up. (A simple event has only one outcome, such as rolling a 3 on a number cube.) For some compound events, the order in which the simple events occur is important.

A **combination** is a grouping of outcomes in which the order does not matter. A **permutation** is an arrangement of outcomes in which the order does matter.

## EXAMPLE 2 Finding Combinations and Permutations

**Tell whether each situation involves combinations or permutations. Then give the number of possible outcomes.**

**A** **A street vendor sells cashews, peanuts, and almonds. How many different ways are there to mix two kinds of nuts?**

List all of the possible groupings:

| | | |
|---|---|---|
| cashews and peanuts | peanuts and almonds | almonds and cashews |
| peanuts and cashews | almonds and peanuts | cashews and almonds |

The order of the outcomes is not important, so this situation involves combinations. Eliminate the groupings that are duplicates.

| | | |
|---|---|---|
| cashews and peanuts | peanuts and almonds | almonds and cashews |
| ~~peanuts and cashews~~ | ~~almonds and peanuts~~ | ~~cashews and almonds~~ |

There are 3 different ways to mix two kinds of nuts.

**B** **Karen is painting her bedroom. She has orange, green, blue, and purple paint. She plans to use one color as a base coat and stencil a design with another color. How many different ways can she do this?**

List all of the possible groupings:

The order of the outcomes is important, because one color is painted on top of the other. This situation involves permutations.

There are 12 different ways for Karen to paint her room.

**Tell whether each situation involves combinations or permutations. Then give the number of possible outcomes.**

**2a.** Ingrid is stringing three different types of beads on a bracelet. How many ways can she use one bead of each type to string the next three beads?

**2b.** Nathan wants to order a sandwich with two of the following ingredients: mushroom, eggplant, tomato, and avocado. How many different sandwiches can Nathan choose?

**Helpful Hint**

The factorial of 0 is defined to be 1.
$0! = 1$

The factorial of a number is the product of the number and all the natural numbers less than the number. The factorial of 5 is written 5! and is read "five factorial." $5! = 5 \cdot 4 \cdot 3 \cdot 2 \cdot 1 = 120$. Factorials can be used to find the number of combinations and permutations that can be made from a set of choices.

Suppose you want to make a five-letter password from the letters *A, B, C, D,* and *E* without repeating a letter. You have 5 choices for the first letter, but only 4 choices for the second letter. You have one fewer choice for each letter of the password.

**5 choices × 4 choices × 3 choices × 2 choices × 1 choice = 120 permutations**

Suppose you want to make a three-letter password from the 5 letters *A, B, C, D,* and *E* without repeating a letter. Again, you have one fewer choice for each letter of the password.

**5 choices × 4 choices × 3 choices = 60 permutations**

The number of permutations is $\frac{5!}{2!}$, or $\frac{5 \cdot 4 \cdot 3 \cdot \cancel{2} \cdot \cancel{1}}{\cancel{2} \cdot \cancel{1}} = 5 \cdot 4 \cdot 3 = 60$.

**Permutations**

| | |
|---|---|
| **FORMULA** | The number of permutations of $n$ things chosen $r$ at a time: $_nP_r = \frac{n!}{(n-r)!}$. |
| **EXAMPLE** | A club will choose a president, a vice president, and a secretary from a list of 8 people. How many ways can the club choose the 3 officers?<br>The position that each person takes matters, so this situation involves permutations.<br>Think: There are 8 people, and the club will choose 3 of them. $_8P_3 = \frac{8!}{(8-3)!} = \frac{8!}{5!} = 336$ |

## EXAMPLE 3 Finding Permutations

**Lee brings 7 CDs numbered 1–7 to a party. How many different ways can he choose the first 4 CDs to play?**

*The order in which the CDs are played matters, so use the formula for permutations*

$$_7P_4 = \frac{7!}{(7-4)!} = \frac{7!}{3!}$$ *n = 7 and r = 4.*

$$= \frac{7 \cdot 6 \cdot 5 \cdot 4 \cdot \cancel{3} \cdot \cancel{2} \cdot \cancel{1}}{\cancel{3} \cdot \cancel{2} \cdot \cancel{1}}$$ *A number divided by itself is 1, so you can divide out common factors in the numerator and denominator.*

$$= 7 \cdot 6 \cdot 5 \cdot 4 = 840$$

There are 840 different ways Lee can choose to play the 4 CDs.

3. How many different ways can 9 people line up for a picture?

The formula for combinations also involves factorials.

Know it! Note

**Combinations**

| | |
|---|---|
| **FORMULA** | The number of combinations of $n$ things chosen $r$ at a time: $_nC_r = \frac{n!}{r!(n-r)!}$. |
| **EXAMPLE** | A club will form a 3-person committee from a list of 8 people. How many ways can the club choose the 3 people?<br>The position that each person takes does not matter, so this situation involves combinations.<br>Think: There are 8 people, and the club will choose 3 of them. $_8C_3 = \frac{8!}{3!(8-3)!} = \frac{8!}{3!5!} = 56$ |

## EXAMPLE 4 Finding Combinations

**There are 11 different cereals for sale at a grocery store. How many different ways can a shopper select 4 different cereals?**

*The order in which the cereals are selected does not matter, so use the formula for combinations.*

**Method 1** Use the formula for combinations.

$$_{11}C_4 = \frac{11!}{4!\,(11-4)!} = \frac{11!}{4!7!} \qquad \textit{n = 11 and r = 4.}$$

$$= \frac{11 \cdot 10 \cdot 9 \cdot 8 \cdot \cancel{7} \cdot \cancel{6} \cdot \cancel{5} \cdot \cancel{4} \cdot \cancel{3} \cdot \cancel{2} \cdot \cancel{1}}{(4 \cdot 3 \cdot 2 \cdot 1)(\cancel{7} \cdot \cancel{6} \cdot \cancel{5} \cdot \cancel{4} \cdot \cancel{3} \cdot \cancel{2} \cdot \cancel{1})}$$

$$= \frac{7920}{24} = 330$$

**Method 2** Use the **nCr** function of a calculator.

```
11 nCr 4
                330
```

There are 330 different ways the shopper can choose 4 different cereals.

**Helpful Hint**

You can also use a calculator to find permutations. Look for the **nPr** function on your calculator.

**4.** A basketball team has 12 members who can play any position. How many different ways can the coach choose 5 starting players?

## THINK AND DISCUSS

**1.** Explain how to find $\frac{10!}{9!}$ without a calculator.

Know it! Note

**2. GET ORGANIZED** Copy and complete the graphic organizer.

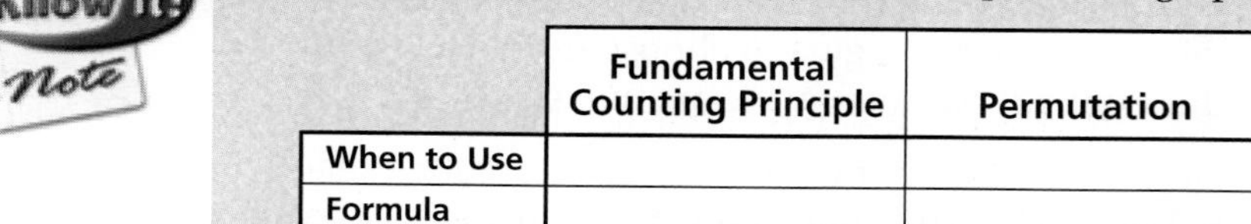

| | Fundamental Counting Principle | Permutation | Combination |
|---|---|---|---|
| **When to Use** | | | |
| **Formula** | | | |

# 10-8 Exercises

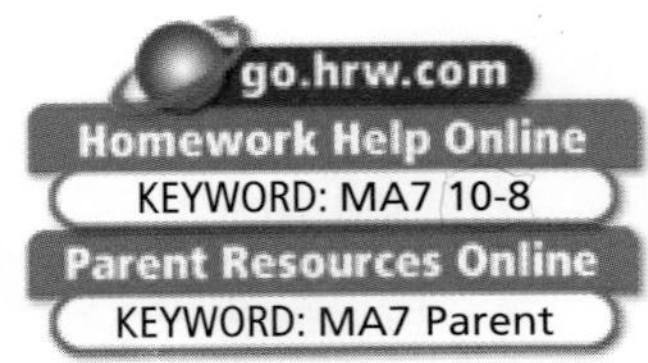


## GUIDED PRACTICE

1. **Vocabulary** A ____?____ is an arrangement of outcomes in which the order does not matter. (*compound event*, *permutation*, or *combination*)

SEE EXAMPLE 1 p. 736

2. The menu for a restaurant is shown. How many different meals with one salad, one soup, one entree, and one dessert are possible?

3. You have 4 colors of wrapping paper and 2 kinds of ribbon. How many different ways are there to use one color of paper and one type of ribbon to wrap a package?

SEE EXAMPLE 2 p. 737

**Tell whether each situation involves combinations or permutations. Then give the number of possible outcomes.**

4. How many different ways can 4 people be seated in a row of 4 seats?
5. How many different kinds of punch can be made from 2 of the following: cranberry juice, apple juice, orange juice, and grape juice?

SEE EXAMPLE 3 p. 738

6. An airport identification code is made up of three letters, like the examples shown. How many different airport identification codes are possible? (Assume any letter can be repeated and can appear in any position.)
7. A manager is scheduling interviews for job applicants. She has 8 time slots and 6 applicants to interview. How many different interview schedules are possible?
8. An e-mail server password must be 6 different lowercase letters. How many different e-mail server passwords are possible?

ABQ — Albuquerque International Airport, New Mexico

Dallas/Fort Worth International Airport, Texas

John F. Kennedy International Airport, New York

Los Angeles International Airport, California

ORD — O'Hare International Airport, Illinois

SEE EXAMPLE 4 p. 739

9. Francine is deciding which after-school clubs to join. She has time to participate in 3. How many different ways can Francine choose which 3 clubs to join?
10. Laura is making gift baskets. Each basket has 2 gifts, and she has 5 gifts to choose from. How many different gift baskets can Laura make?
11. How many different ways can a contest judge select 5 finalists from 20 contestants?

## PRACTICE AND PROBLEM SOLVING

**Independent Practice**

| For Exercises | See Example |
|---|---|
| 12–13 | 1 |
| 14–15 | 2 |
| 16–17 | 3 |
| 18–19 | 4 |

**Extra Practice**

Skills Practice p. S23
Application Practice p. S37

**12.** Maria looks in her closet and exclaims, "I have nothing to wear!" How many different outfits of one shirt, one pair of shorts, and one pair of sandals are possible using the items shown?

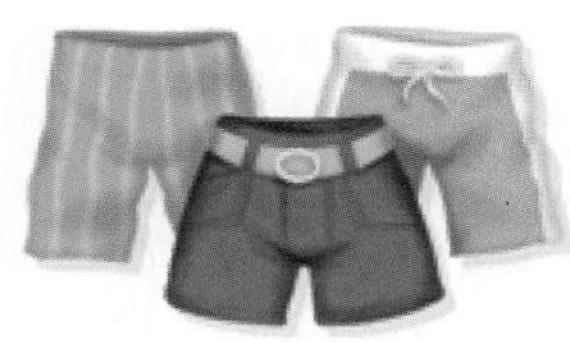

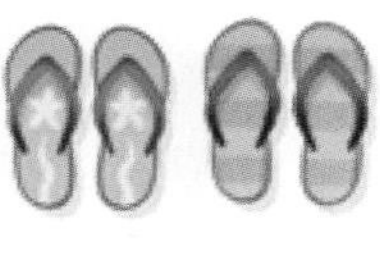

**13.** When a customer buys tickets for a concert, the ticket office assigns a confirmation code that is made up of 2 lowercase consonants, followed by 3 numbers. A letter or number may be repeated. How many different confirmation codes are possible?

**Tell whether each situation involves a combination or a permutation. Then give the number of possible outcomes.**

**14.** A team of archeologists divides a dig site into 3 areas. They dig one area at a time. How many different ways can they order the 3 areas?

**15.** To decide which team will lead the class discussion, a teacher writes the names of 5 students on slips of paper and puts them in a hat. Then she draws 2 names. How many teams of two are possible?

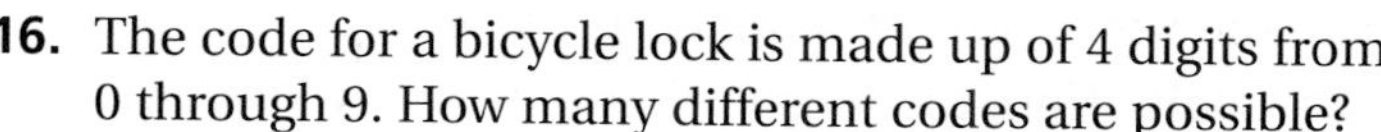

**16.** The code for a bicycle lock is made up of 4 digits from 0 through 9. How many different codes are possible?

**17.** A television station has 5 different commercials to play during the news. In how many different ways can they order the commercials?

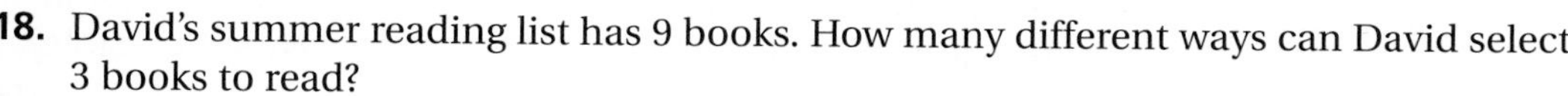

**18.** David's summer reading list has 9 books. How many different ways can David select 3 books to read?

**19.** Steve draws a hand of 7 cards from a deck of 52 different cards. How many different hands are possible?

**LINK — History**

Telephone "numbers" used to be made up of two letters and several digits. Calls were made by speaking the telephone number to a central operator, who then connected the call by hand.

**20.** **History** The North American Numbering Plan (NANP) was first used in 1947. It is a system for assigning telephone numbers and area codes.

**a.** Originally, the NANP allowed only 3-digit area codes whose first digit was not 0 or 1, and whose second digit was always 0 or 1. How many different area codes were possible under this system?

**b.** In 1995, because of increased demand, the NANP removed the restriction that the second digit of the area code must be 0 or 1. How many more area codes did this make possible?

**21.** **Critical Thinking** For $n = 6$ and $r = 2$, which is larger: ${}_nP_r$ or ${}_nC_r$? Explain why this is true.

**22.** **Write About It** Brian forgot the combination to open his locker. Explain why a "combination lock" should be called a "permutation lock."

**23.** **Write About It** You roll a number cube 6 times. Explain how to determine the number of possible outcomes. Would a tree diagram be useful in solving this problem? Explain why or why not.

24. This problem will prepare you for the Multi-Step Test Prep on page 744.

Many states have lotteries to raise money. In one lottery, the players choose 6 different numbers from the numbers 1–49. The order of the numbers does not matter.

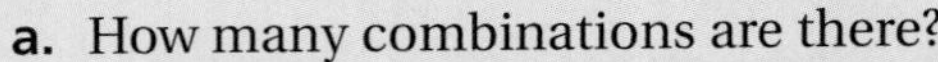

**a.** How many combinations are there?

**b.** The probability that your first number is on the winning ticket is $\frac{6}{49}$. The probability that your second number matches is $\frac{5}{48}$. The probabilities of the third, fourth, fifth, and sixth numbers matching are $\frac{4}{47}$, $\frac{3}{46}$, $\frac{2}{45}$, and $\frac{1}{44}$. The product of these probabilities is the probability of winning the lottery with one ticket. Find that probability. How does it relate to the number of combinations shown in part **a?**

25. **Technology** Nancy's password for her online banking program is made up of 6 letters. It does not matter whether the letters are uppercase or lowercase and any letter may be repeated.

**a.** What is the probability of someone correctly guessing Nancy's password?

**b.** How many hours would it take for someone to try all the possible passwords if the person could guess one password each second?

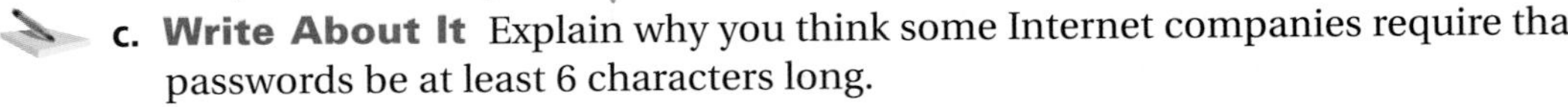

**c.** **Write About It** Explain why you think some Internet companies require that passwords be at least 6 characters long.

26. Which situation is best modeled by the expression ${}_{10}C_4$?

(A) Lisa's salon offers 10 kinds of shampoo and 4 kinds of conditioner. How many different ways can she shampoo and condition a client's hair?

(B) Sara has a box of 10 colored pencils. How many different ways can she choose 4 colored pencils from the box?

(C) A personal identification number (PIN) is a 4-digit number. Digits can be repeated in a PIN. How many different PINs are possible?

(D) There are 10 chairs placed around a table. How many different ways can 4 people seat themselves around the table?

27. Which of the following is equal to 4!?

(F) $10! - 6!$ (G) $\frac{8!}{2!}$ (H) $(2!)(2!)$ (J) $\frac{24!}{23!}$

28. Which table represents the values of ${}_xC_4$ for the given values of $x$?

(A)

| $x$ | ${}_xC_4$ |
|---|---|
| 5 | 5 |
| 6 | 30 |
| 7 | 210 |
| 8 | 1680 |

(B)

| $x$ | ${}_xC_4$ |
|---|---|
| 5 | 120 |
| 6 | 360 |
| 7 | 840 |
| 8 | 1680 |

(C)

| $x$ | ${}_xC_4$ |
|---|---|
| 5 | 5 |
| 6 | 15 |
| 7 | 35 |
| 8 | 70 |

(D)

| $x$ | ${}_xC_4$ |
|---|---|
| 5 | 30 |
| 6 | 90 |
| 7 | 210 |
| 8 | 240 |

29. **Short Response** The periodic table of the elements is a chart listing 112 different elements. Maria must give a presentation on 3 different elements from the periodic table. How many ways can she choose which elements to present? Show your work and explain each step.

## CHALLENGE AND EXTEND

**Simplify each expression.**

**30.** $\frac{8!}{3!}$ **31.** $\frac{7!4!}{6!}$ **32.** $\frac{{}_7P_5}{{}_7P_3}$

**33.** The chart shows the different toppings offered by a pizza shop.

**a.** How many different pizzas with 2 toppings are possible?

**b.** How many different pizzas with 6 toppings are possible?

**c.** What do you notice about your answers to parts **a** and **b**? Explain why you think this is.

**Pizza Ingredients**

- Extra Cheese
- Mushrooms
- Sausage
- Pineapple
- Green Peppers
- Pepperoni
- Onions
- Green Olives

**34.** Use the permutation and combination formulas you learned in this lesson.

**a.** What is the number of permutations when $n = r$?

**b.** What is the number of combinations when $n = r$?

**35.** You roll a number cube six times in a row. What is the probability that you roll the numbers 1 through 6 in order?

## SPIRAL REVIEW

**Simplify each expression.** *(Lesson 1-7)*

**36.** $4.9m + 3.8 - 2.1m - 3.9$ **37.** $4(2x - 1) + 9 - 3x$ **38.** $3a^2 - 5a - 7a^2$

**Identify the independent and dependent variables. Write a rule in function notation for each situation.** *(Lesson 4-3)*

**39.** A bathtub fills at a rate of 15 gallons per minute.

**40.** About 5 seeds should be planted per square inch.

**41.** A snow removal company charges a contract fee of $300 plus $80 per hour.

**42.** Five people responded that they spend the following amounts for haircuts during one year: $150, $120, $135, $0, and $145. A researcher concluded that "people spend an average of $110 per year on haircuts." Why is this statistic misleading? *(Lesson 10-4)*

## Career Path

go.hrw.com
Career Resources Online
KEYWORD: MA7 Career

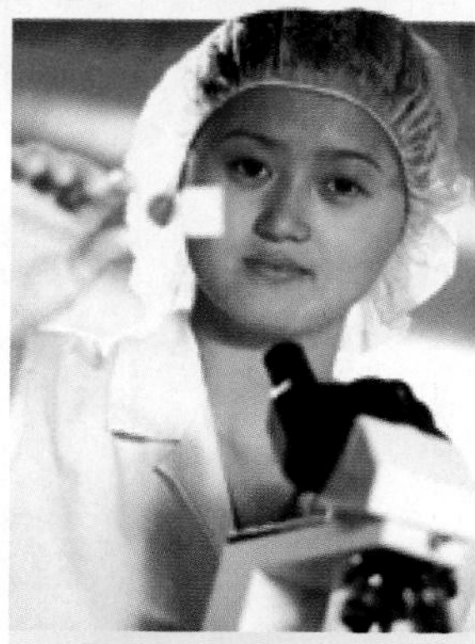

**Erika Sheehan**
Biostatistics major

**Q: What math classes did you take in high school?**

**A:** Algebra, Geometry, Precalculus, Calculus

**Q: What math classes have you taken in college?**

**A:** Statistics, Linear Algebra, Problem Solving

**Q: What do Biostatisticians do?**

**A:** Biostatisticians apply statistical methods to research scientific questions relating to health and medicine.

**Q: What are your plans for the future?**

**A:** After graduating, I would like to get a job at a pharmaceutical company testing the safety and effectiveness of new medicines.

CHAPTER 10

SECTION 10B

## Probability

**The Games People Play** Probability is involved in most board and card games.

1. There are 108 cards in a deck for the game Uno. The table shows the number of each type of card found in an Uno deck. What is the probability of randomly selecting a red card from a complete deck of Uno cards?

| Type of Card | Number in Deck |
|---|---|
| Blue cards, 0–9 | 19 |
| Green cards, 0–9 | 19 |
| Red cards, 0–9 | 19 |
| Yellow cards, 0–9 | 19 |
| Draw Two | 8 (2 in each color) |
| Reverse | 8 (2 in each color) |
| Skip | 8 (2 in each color) |
| Wild | 4 |
| Wild Draw Four | 4 |

2. Robert is playing Monopoly. He starts the game on the GO space. He wants to avoid the Income Tax space, which he will land on if he rolls a 4 with the two dice. What is the probability that he will land on the Income Tax space?

3. In the game Battleship, each player chooses locations for small ships on a 10-by-10 grid. Each player guesses grid spaces to try to locate the other player's ships. A correct guess equals a hit, and by hitting each space occupied by a ship, the ship is sunk. The battleship piece occupies four grid spaces. What is the probability that a player randomly guesses a correct grid space and hits the other player's battleship?

4. In the game Set, each card can be characterized in four ways. Cards are either red, green, or purple. The design on each card is either an oval, a squiggle, or a diamond. There are either one, two, or three of the design on the card. The designs are either solid, empty, or striped. How many different cards are possible?

## Quiz for Lessons 10-5 Through 10-8

### 10-5 Experimental Probability

**An experiment consists of pushing the random select button on a CD player for a disc with five tracks. Use the results in the table to find the experimental probability of each event.**

| Outcome | Frequency |
|---|---|
| Track 1 | 4 |
| Track 2 | 6 |
| Track 3 | 2 |
| Track 4 | 5 |
| Track 5 | 3 |

1. Selecting track 4
2. Selecting track 3
3. Not selecting track 2
4. Selecting an odd numbered track
5. Selecting one of the first 3 tracks
6. Ms. Bleakman checks 32 papers and finds 2 with no name. What is the experimental probability that a paper chosen at random will have no name? Ms. Bleakman has the papers of 176 students. Predict the number of papers she will find with no name.

### 10-6 Theoretical Probability

**Find the theoretical probability of each outcome.**

7. Landing on an odd number when spinning a spinner with 4 equal spaces marked 1, 4, 6, 8
8. Randomly selecting a vowel from all the letters in the word VOWELS
9. Picking a red marble out of a bag with 3 green, 5 blue, 2 red, and 6 yellow marbles
10. The probability of winning a certain prize is 5%. What are the odds of winning the prize?
11. The odds of choosing a winning ticket are 2 : 8. What is the probability of choosing a winning ticket?
12. The probability of snow is 70%. What are the odds of it not snowing?

### 10-7 Independent and Dependent Events

13. A physical education class has 12 boys and 18 girls. Each day, the teacher randomly selects a team captain. Assume that no student is absent. What is the probability that the team captain is a girl two days in a row?
14. After reading to a kindergarten class at the library, Tobey gives out stickers. He has 9 zoo animal stickers and 16 scratch-n-sniff stickers. If Tobey gives the stickers out at random, what is the probability that the first child gets a scratch-n-sniff sticker and the second child gets a zoo animal sticker?

### 10-8 Combinations and Permutations

15. Luisa is choosing a line-up of CDs to play from beginning to end at her party. She has 12 CDs from which to choose and time to play only 5. How many ways are there for Luisa to arrange the musical line-up?
16. Gavin is shopping for school clothes with his father. After trying on several shirts, Gavin has identified 8 shirts that he likes. His father says Gavin must narrow it down to 5 shirts. How many ways can Gavin choose 5 shirts from the 8 he likes?

EXTENSION

# Linear Models of Data

**MA.S.2.1** Use formal strategies for placement of lines of best fit to model bivariate data. *Also* **MA.A.5.1**

***Objectives***
Create linear models for data sets.

Describe the strength of a linear correlation between two variables.

***Vocabulary***
regression line
line of best fit
correlation coefficient

In Chapter 4, you made scatter plots of data. Then you modeled the data with trend lines that you drew by visually estimating. In this lesson, you will use a method called *linear regression* to compute the equation of a trend line. This type of trend line is called a **regression line** or a **line of best fit**.

## EXAMPLE 1 Finding the Equation of a Line of Best Fit

**The table shows the latitudes and average temperatures of several cities.**

| City | Latitude | Average Temperature (°C) |
|---|---|---|
| Barrow, Alaska, USA | 71.2° N | −12.7 |
| Yakutsk, Russia | 62.1° N | −10.1 |
| London, England | 51.3° N | 10.4 |
| Vancouver, British Columbia, Canada | 49.1° N | 9.8 |
| Chicago, Illinois, USA | 41.9° N | 10.3 |
| San Francisco, California, USA | 37.5° N | 13.8 |
| Memphis, Tennessee, USA | 35.0° N | 17.0 |
| Yuma, Arizona, USA | 32.7° N | 22.8 |
| Tindouf, Algeria | 27.7° N | 22.8 |
| Dakar, Senegal | 14.0° N | 24.5 |
| Mangalore, India | 12.5° N | 27.1 |

**A** **Find an equation for a line of best fit.**

Use your calculator.

To enter the data, press STAT and select **[1:Edit]**. Enter the latitudes in the L1 column and the average temperatures in the L2 column.

Then press STAT and choose **[CALC]**.

Choose **[4:LinReg(ax+b)]** and push ENTER.

An equation for a line of best fit is
$y \approx -0.68x + 39.32$.

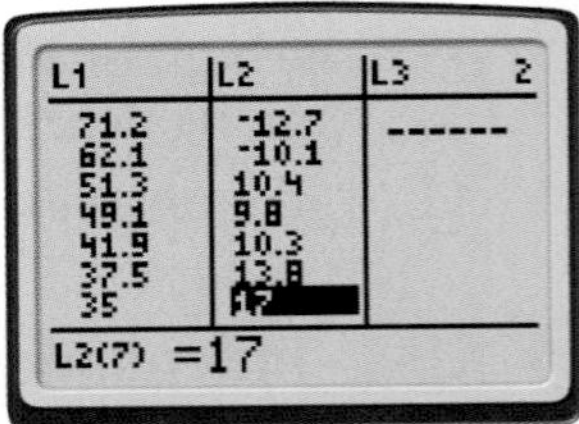


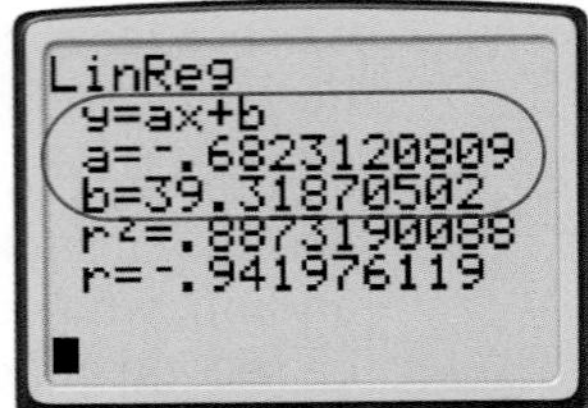


**B** **Quito, Ecuador, has an approximate latitude of 0°. Use your equation to predict Quito's average temperature.**

$y \approx -0.68x + 39.32$ *Write the equation.*

$y \approx -0.68(0) + 39.32$ *Substitute 0 for x.*

$y \approx 39.32$ *Simplify.*

The average temperature of Quito should be close to 39 °C.

**1.** The table shows the prices and the lengths in yards of several balls of yarn at Knit Mart.

| Length (yd) | 1680 | 100 | 153 | 99 | 109 | 109 | 176 | 100 | 1440 | 61 |
|---|---|---|---|---|---|---|---|---|---|---|
| Price ($) | 65.85 | 7.85 | 9.80 | 10.85 | 8.35 | 7.85 | 19.85 | 5.35 | 65.85 | 14.85 |

**a.** Find an equation for a line of best fit.

**b.** Knit Mart also sells yarn in a 1000-yard ball. Use your equation to predict the cost of this yarn.

In Example 1, you may have noticed the last value the calculator gives you, $r$. This is the *correlation coefficient.* The **correlation coefficient** $r$ is a measure of how well a model fits a data set (in other words, a measure of how closely the data points cluster around the graph).

## Properties of the Correlation Coefficient $r$

$r$ is a value in the range $-1 \le r \le 1$.

If $r = 1$, the data set forms a straight line with a positive slope.

If $r = 0$, the data set has no correlation.

If $r = -1$, the data set forms a straight line with a negative slope.

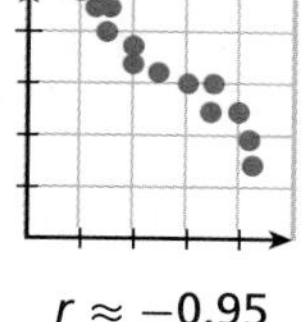

$r \approx -0.95$

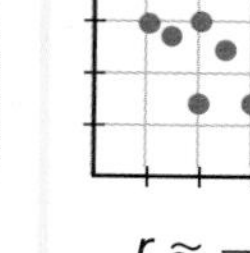

$r \approx -0.6$

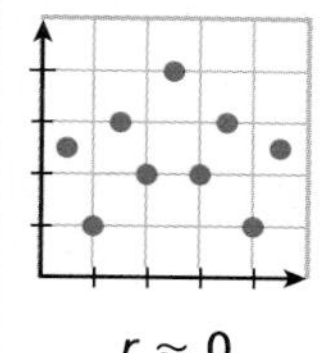

$r \approx 0$

$r \approx 0.6$

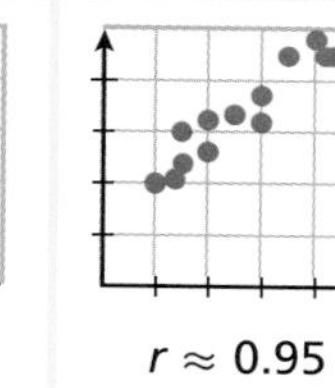

$r \approx 0.95$

**Helpful Hint**

$r$-values close to 1 or $-1$ indicate a very strong correlation. The closer $r$ is to 0, the weaker the correlation.

## EXAMPLE 2 Line of Best Fit and Correlation Coefficient

**There is a relationship between a city's population and the average time the city's citizens spend commuting to work each day, as shown in the table.**

| City | Population (thousands) | Average Commute Time (min) |
|---|---|---|
| Albuquerque, NM | 505 | 21.5 |
| Atlanta, GA | 486 | 31.1 |
| Austin, TX | 710 | 23.2 |
| Charlotte, NC | 630 | 25.1 |
| Chicago, IL | 2833 | 30.6 |
| Eugene, OR | 146 | 17.9 |
| Houston, TX | 2144 | 27.7 |
| Las Vegas, NV | 553 | 25.2 |
| New York/Newark, NY and NJ | 8496 | 34.0 |
| New Orleans, LA | 223 | 24.2 |
| San Francisco/Oakland, CA | 1141 | 24.6 |
| Washington, D.C. | 582 | 32.2 |

**A** **Find an equation for a line of best fit. How well does the line represent the data?**

Use your calculator.

Enter the data into the lists L1 and L2. Then press **STAT** and choose **[CALC]** at the top of the screen. Choose **[4:LinReg(ax+b)]** and push **ENTER**.

```
LinReg
 y=ax+b
 a=.001238619
 b=24.53739319
 r²=.366538653
 r=.6054243578
```

An equation for a line of best fit is $y \approx 0.001x + 24.5$. The value of $r$ is about 0.61, which indicates a moderate positive correlation.

**B** **The population of Jackson, Mississippi, is about 177,000. Use your equation to predict the average time a citizen of Jackson spends commuting to work. How accurate do you think your prediction is?**

$y \approx 0.001x + 24.5$ *Write the equation.*

$y \approx 0.001(177) + 24.5$ *Substitute 177 for x.*

$y \approx 24.7$ *Simplify.*

The average commute time in Jackson should be close to 24.7 min. You would expect this prediction to be somewhat close to the actual commute time in Jackson, since $r$ shows a moderate correlation. (In fact, the actual average commute time in Jackson is about 21.3 min.)

**2.** Kylie and Marcus designed a quiz to measure how much information adults retain after leaving school. The table below shows the quiz scores of several adults, matched with the number of years each person had been out of school.

| Time Out of School (yr) | 1 | 1 | 1 | 2 | 2 | 3 | 5 | 7 | 10 | 10 | 14 | 25 |
|---|---|---|---|---|---|---|---|---|---|---|---|---|
| Quiz Score | 85 | 94 | 98 | 75 | 80 | 77 | 63 | 56 | 45 | 50 | 34 | 33 |

**a.** Find an equation for a line of best fit. How well does the line represent the data?

**b.** Suppose Melanie has been out of school for 27 years. What score do you predict she would get on Kylie and Marcus's quiz? How accurate do you think your prediction is?

MA.S.2.1, MA.A.5.1

For Exercises 1 and 2:

**a. find an equation for a line of best fit and**

**b. tell how closely the data correlate.**

**1.** The table shows the number of books read by several students in an English class over a summer and the students' grades for the following semester.

| Books | 0 | 0 | 0 | 0 | 1 | 1 | 1 | 2 | 3 | 5 | 6 | 8 | 10 | 12 | 20 |
|---|---|---|---|---|---|---|---|---|---|---|---|---|---|---|---|
| Grade | 65 | 69 | 70 | 73 | 70 | 75 | 78 | 77 | 86 | 85 | 89 | 90 | 95 | 99 | 98 |

2. A negative correlation exists between the time Shawnda spends on homework during an evening and the amount of sleep she gets that night. The table shows data for several nights when Shawnda had homework.

| **Homework (h)** | 0.5 | 0.5 | 1 | 1 | 1 | 1.5 | 2 | 2 | 2.5 | 3 | 3 | 3 | 4 | 4.5 | 5 | 5 | 6 |
|---|---|---|---|---|---|---|---|---|---|---|---|---|---|---|---|---|---|
| **Sleep (h)** | 8 | 9 | 8 | 8.5 | 8.5 | 8 | 7.5 | 8 | 7.5 | 7 | 7 | 8 | 6.5 | 6.5 | 6 | 6.5 | 5 |

3. The table shows the number of customers at a coffee shop and the number of cookies sold for several days.

| **Customers** | 10 | 12 | 25 | 27 | 40 | 55 | 67 | 109 |
|---|---|---|---|---|---|---|---|---|
| **Cookies Sold** | 2 | 6 | 5 | 9 | 10 | 11 | 20 | 22 |

   a. Make a scatter plot of the data.
   b. Use your calculator to find a line of best fit and the correlation coefficient.
   c. What is the slope of the line of best fit? Describe the meaning of the slope in terms of the data.
   d. Describe what the correlation coefficient means in terms of the data.
   e. Use the equation for the line of best fit to predict the number of cookies sold on a day when 80 customers come to the coffee shop.
   f. Use the equation for the line of best fit to predict the number of customers on a day when 30 cookies are sold.
   g. For parts **e** and **f**, how accurate do you think your predictions are? Explain.

4. **Write About It** One data set has an $r$-value of $-0.78$. Another has an $r$-value of 0.65. Which $r$-value represents a stronger correlation? Why?

5. Match each scatter plot with its $r$-value.

I
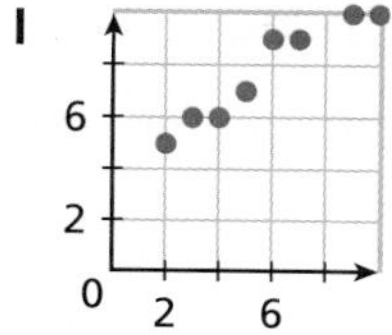

II
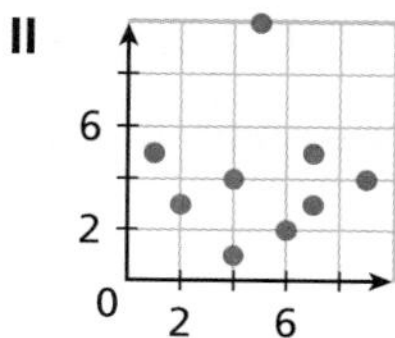

III
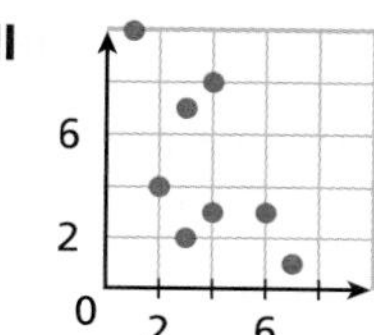

IV
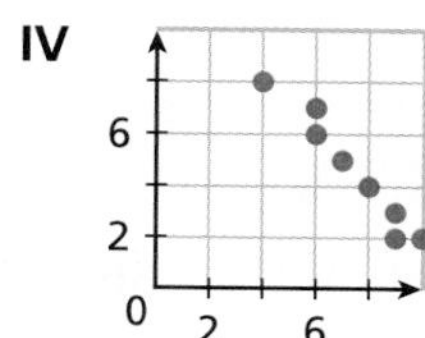

V
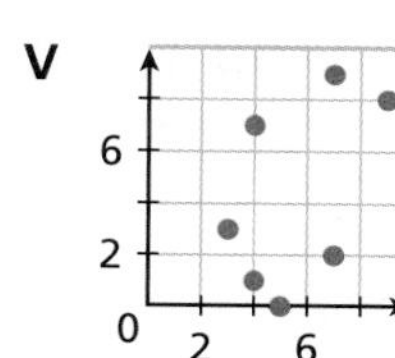

a. 0.49 b. $-0.64$ c. 0.96 d. $-0.98$ e. 0

6. Another method for finding a line of best fit for two sets of data is called the *quartile* points method. To use this method, first find the first quartile (Q1) and the third quartile (Q3) for each data set. If the data appear to have a negative correlation, then graph the quartile points fit line through (Q1 for the first set, Q3 for the second set) and (Q3 for the first set, Q1 for the second set). If the data appear to have a positive correlation, then graph the line through (Q1, Q1) and (Q3, Q3).

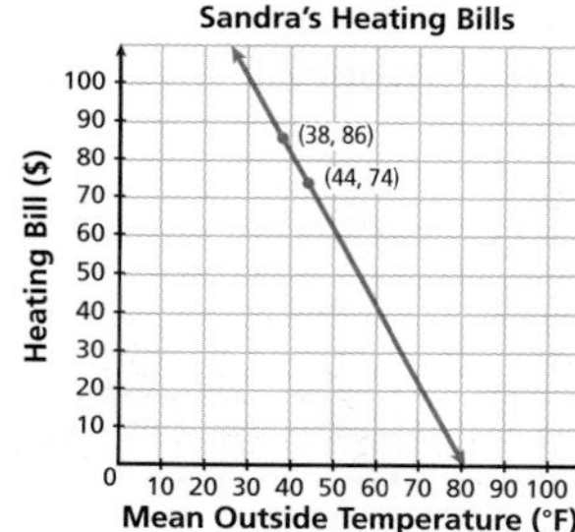


a. Graph the quartile points fit line for the given data.

b. Find the equation of your line from part a.

c. Use your equation to predict the heating bill for a month in which the average temperature is 40°F.

| **Sandra's Heating Bills** | | | | | | | |
|---|---|---|---|---|---|---|---|
| Mean Outside Temperature(°F) | 38 | 42 | 44 | 36 | 42 | 49 | 38 |
| Cookies Sold | 93 | 79 | 75 | 83 | 74 | 67 | 86 |

CHAPTER 10

# Study Guide: Review

## Vocabulary



**Complete the sentences below with vocabulary words from the list above.**

1. A(n) ___?___ is one possible result of an experiment.
2. The ___?___ is the difference between the upper and lower quartiles.
3. Two events are ___?___ if the occurrence of one event does not affect the probability of the other.

## 10-1 Organizing and Displaying Data *(pp. 678–686)*

MA.S.1.2

### EXAMPLE

**The circle graph shows the post-graduation plans for a high school's 500 graduating seniors.**

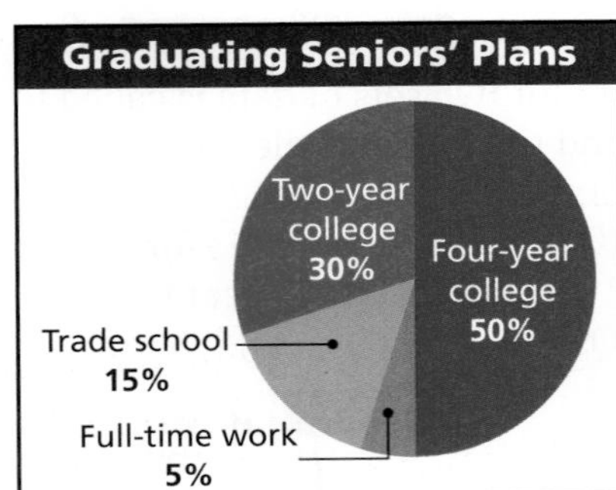


■ How many seniors plan to attend a four-year college?
50% of 500 *Find the percentage.*
$0.50 \times 500 = 250$
250 students plan to attend a four-year college.

### EXERCISES

**Use the double-bar graph for Exercises 4 and 5.**

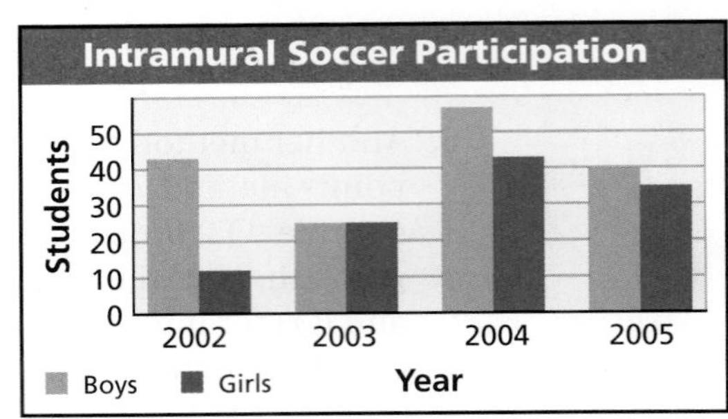


4. In which year did the same number of boys and girls participate?
5. How many more boys than girls participated during 2004?

## 10-2 Frequency and Histograms *(pp. 687–693)*

MA.S1.2

### EXAMPLE

- **The lives (in hours) of each light bulb in a test are given below. Use the data to make a frequency table and a histogram.**

  22, 28, 25, 21, 19, 21, 25,
  21, 22, 18, 20, 29, 25, 26

  *Identify the least and greatest values. Divide the data into equal intervals.*

| Light Bulb Life (h) | |
|---|---|
| **Life** | **Frequency** |
| 18–20 | 3 |
| 21–23 | 5 |
| 24–26 | 4 |
| 27–29 | 2 |

*Draw a bar for the number of hours in each interval. The bars touch, but do not overlap.*

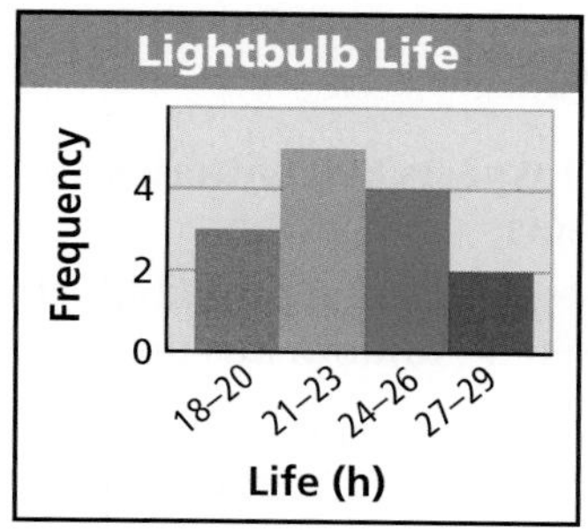


### EXERCISES

6. The weights of packages shipped by an online retailer are given below. Use the data to make a stem-and-leaf plot.

| Package Weight (lb) | | | | | | | | | | |
|---|---|---|---|---|---|---|---|---|---|---|
| 14 | 9 | 22 | 24 | 7 | 1 | 19 | 22 | 28 | 18 | 12 |

7. The numbers of people who attended two different plays are shown in the table below. Make a back-to-back stem-and-leaf plot.

| Play Attendance | |
|---|---|
| **Comedy Camp** | **Days and Days** |
| 104 62 83 102 104 120 81 126 122 | 103 105 80 135 109 128 82 132 139 |

8. The capacities of the gas tanks on several new vehicles are shown below. Use the data to make a frequency table with intervals.

| Gas Tank Capacity (gal) | | | | | | | | | | |
|---|---|---|---|---|---|---|---|---|---|---|
| 15 | 12 | 12 | 15 | 18 | 26 | 25 | 12 | 15 | 18 | 11 |
| 10 | 12 | 16 | 15 | 16 | 18 | 25 | 21 | 18 | 20 | 21 |

9. Use your frequency table from Exercise 9 to make a histogram.

## 10-3 Data Distributions *(pp. 694–699)*

MA.S.1.1, MA.S.1.2

### EXAMPLE

- **Consider the following ages of the winners of an art contest: 13, 15, 14, 18, 12, 10, 11, 13. Find the mean and mode of the data.**

  mean:

  $$\frac{10 + 11 + 12 + 13 + 13 + 14 + 15 + 18}{8}$$

  $$= \frac{106}{8}$$

  $$= 13.25$$

  mode: 13 *13 occurs most often.*

### EXERCISES

**Find the mean, median, mode, and range of each data set.**

10. Years of playing experience of the members of a musical ensemble:

    5, 14, 25, 7, 8, 10, 12, 33, 12

**Herman has five pairs of cowboy boots. The prices were \$120, \$137, \$120, \$145, and \$482.**
**mean: \$200.80 median: \$137 mode: \$120**

11. Which value best describes the price Herman paid? Explain.

**Use the data to make a box-and-whisker plot.**

12. 25, 28, 2, 24, 28, 21, 18, 29, 31, 12, 6, 19, 27, 3

## 10-4 Misleading Graphs and Statistics *(pp. 702–709)*

Rev. 8.S.3.3

### EXAMPLE

- **Explain why the graph is misleading.**

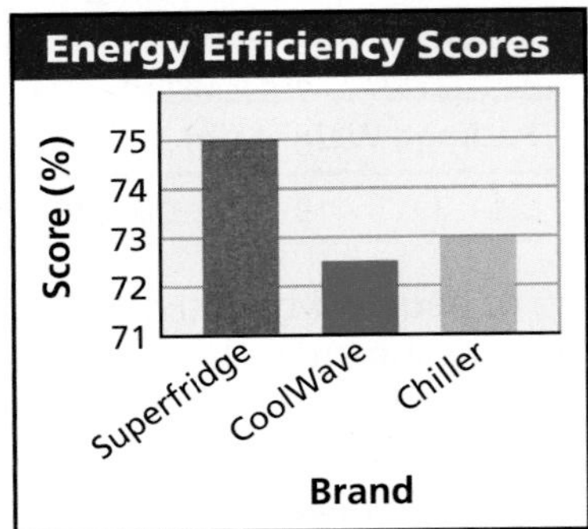


The vertical axis begins at 71. This exaggerates the difference in the heights of the bars.

### EXERCISES

**The graph shows the cost of admission to an amusement park over 20 years.**

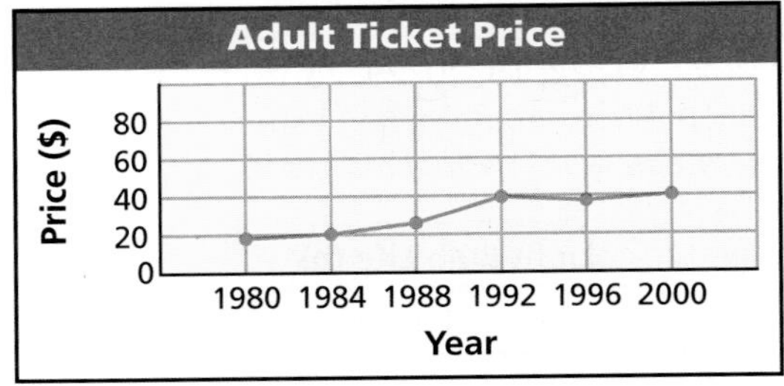


13. Explain why the graph is misleading.
14. What might someone believe because of the graph?

## 10-5 Experimental Probability *(pp. 713–718)*

Rev. 6.S.2

### EXAMPLES

**The manager of a photo processing lab inspects 500 photos and finds that 4 have flaws.**

- What is the experimental probability that a photo is flawed?

$$\frac{\text{number of times the event occurs}}{\text{number of trials}} = \frac{4}{500} = 0.8\%$$

- In one month, the lab processes 13,000 photos. Predict the number that are likely to be flawed.

$0.008 \cdot 13{,}000 = 104$ *Find 0.8% of 13,000*

104 photos are likely to be flawed.

### EXERCISES

**A manufacturer inspects 800 batteries and finds that 796 have no defects.**

15. What is the experimental probability that a battery chosen at random has no defects?
16. There are 25,000 batteries in storage. How many batteries are likely to have no defects?
17. Another storage area holds 50,000 batteries. How many batteries are likely to have a defect?

## 10-6 Theoretical Probability *(pp. 720–725)*

Rev. 6.S.1

### EXAMPLE

- **A jar contains red, green, brown, and blue marbles. The probability of choosing red is 0.30, of choosing green is 0.20, and of choosing brown is 0.25. Find the probability of choosing blue.**

$$P(\text{blue}) + P(\text{not blue}) = 1$$
$$P(\text{blue}) + P(\text{red, green, or brown}) = 1$$
$$P(\text{blue}) + (0.30 + 0.20 + 0.25) = 1$$
$$P(\text{blue}) + 0.75 = 1$$
$$P(\text{blue}) = 0.25$$

### EXERCISES

**Find the theoretical probability.**

18. Rolling a number less than 4 on a standard number cube
19. Randomly selecting a month that starts with "J" from all month names
20. Randomly selecting a vowel from the letters in EQUATION

## 10-7 Independent and Dependent Events *(pp. 726–733)*

Rev. 8.S.1

### EXAMPLES

**A hardware store shelf holds 12 cans of red paint, 4 cans of yellow paint, and 6 cans of black paint.**

- Syd selects one can at random and replaces it. Then she selects another can at random. What is the probability that Syd selects a red can and then a yellow can?

$$P(\text{red, yellow}) = P(\text{red}) \cdot P(\text{yellow})$$
$$= \frac{12}{22} \cdot \frac{4}{22} \quad \textit{Independent events}$$
$$= \frac{48}{484} = \frac{12}{121}$$

- Gene selects one can at random and then selects another can at random from the remaining cans. What is the probability that Gene selects two cans of black paint?

$$P(\text{black, black}) = P(\text{black}) \cdot P(\text{black after black})$$
$$= \frac{6}{22} \cdot \frac{5}{21} \quad \textit{Dependent events}$$
$$= \frac{30}{462} = \frac{5}{77}$$

### EXERCISES

**Tell whether each set of events is independent or dependent. Explain your answers.**

**21.** A computer generates a random number and then generates another random number.

**22.** You roll two number cubes. One is a 6 and the other is a 1.

**23.** Two audience members are called to the stage.

**A lottery machine contains different-colored balls. There are 64 green, 128 yellow, 1 golden, and 3 silver balls. Find the probability of each event.**

**24.** A yellow ball is drawn and set aside. Then a green ball is drawn.

**25.** A golden ball is drawn and set aside. Then another golden ball is drawn.

**26.** A green ball is drawn and replaced. Then another green ball is drawn.

## 10-8 Combinations and Permutations *(pp. 736–743)*

### EXAMPLES

**A sporting goods store carries sweatshirts for 8 local high school football teams.**

- How many different packages of 4 different high school sweatshirts are possible?

*Use a combination. The order does not matter.*

$${}_8C_4 = \frac{8!}{4!(8-4)!} = \frac{8!}{4!(4)!}$$
$$= \frac{8 \cdot 7 \cdot 6 \cdot 5 \cdot \cancel{4} \cdot \cancel{3} \cdot \cancel{2} \cdot \cancel{1}}{(4 \cdot 3 \cdot 2 \cdot 1)(\cancel{4} \cdot \cancel{3} \cdot \cancel{2} \cdot \cancel{1})} = \frac{1680}{24} = 70$$

Seventy different packages are possible.

- Three different high school sweatshirts will be hung in a row. How many displays are possible?

*Use a permutation. The order matters.*

$${}_8P_3 = \frac{8!}{(8-3)!} = \frac{8!}{5!} =$$
$$\frac{8 \cdot 7 \cdot 6 \cdot \cancel{5} \cdot \cancel{4} \cdot \cancel{3} \cdot \cancel{2} \cdot \cancel{1}}{\cancel{5} \cdot \cancel{4} \cdot \cancel{3} \cdot \cancel{2} \cdot \cancel{1}} = 336$$

There are 336 different possible displays.

### EXERCISES

**27.** A catering hall offers 4 different plates, 3 different silverware patterns, and 5 different types of glassware. How many place settings of one plate, one silverware pattern, and one type of glassware are possible?

**Tell whether each situation involves combinations or permutations. Then give the number of possible outcomes.**

**28.** Shelly is making up a 7-digit phone number to use in a play. She can choose any digit from 0–9 but does not want to repeat a number. How many different phone numbers are possible?

**29.** A restaurant offers 12 different appetizers. How many ways can a group of friends share 3 different appetizers?

**30.** A group of 15 friends is at an amusement park. In how many ways can a group be chosen to ride in a four-person gondola?

CHAPTER 10

# CHAPTER TEST

| Population of Oakville | |
|---|---|
| Year | Population |
| 1970 | 20,851 |
| 1980 | 14,229 |
| 1990 | 11,198 |
| 2000 | 9,579 |

1. The table shows the population of Oakville. Use the data to make a graph. Explain why you chose that type of graph.
2. Which ten-year period saw the greatest change in population?
3. Describe the trend in Oakville's population.

**The high temperatures in degrees Fahrenheit for two weeks are given: 64, 66, 63, 58, 59, 55, 51, 54, 61, 62, 68, 70, 63, 63.**

4. Use the data to make a stem-and-leaf plot.
5. Use the data to make a frequency table with intervals.
6. Use your frequency table from Problem 5 to make a histogram.

**The lengths of statements during a town council meeting are given.**

| Length of Statement (min) | | | | | | |
|---|---|---|---|---|---|---|
| 6 | 25 | 12 | 14 | 2 | 13 | 38 |
| 22 | 21 | 14 | 3 | 8 | 5 | 17 |

7. Find the mean, median, mode, and range of the data.
8. Use the data to make a box-and-whisker plot.

**A manufacturer inspects 500 watches and finds that 498 have no defects.**

9. What is the experimental probability that a watch chosen at random has no defects?
10. There are 30,000 watches in a warehouse. Predict the number of watches that are likely to have no defects.

**The graph shows how the money raised by a charity is spent.**

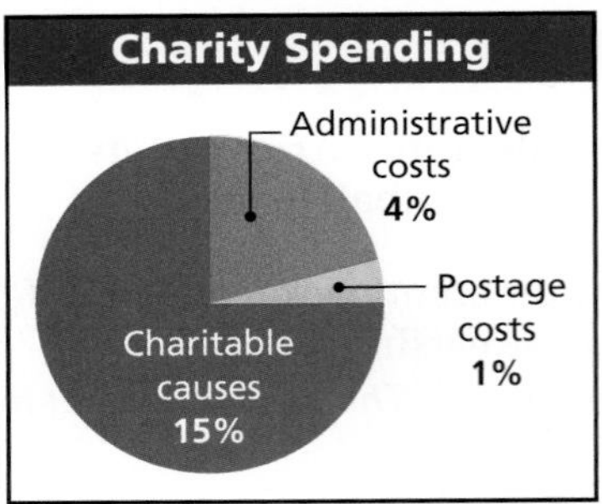


11. Explain why the graph is misleading.
12. What might someone believe because of the graph?
13. Who might want to use this graph?
14. An experiment consists of pulling one card out of a bag that has 12 cards, each with a different month of the year printed on it. What is the probability that the month begins with *A*?
15. The odds of spinning red on a spinner are 2:7. What is the probability of not spinning red?
16. A bag has 14 red marbles and 10 white marbles. Rosa randomly picks two marbles from the bag, one at a time. What is the probability that Rosa picks two white marbles?

**Tell whether each situation involves combinations or permutations. Then give the number of possible outcomes.**

17. Sara is ordering a deli platter for a party. The deli offers 9 kinds of meats. Sara must select 4 kinds for the platter. How many different platters can Sara choose?
18. Armando has 12 antique books. He will select 3 books and put one up for auction each day for three days. How many different ways can he do this?

# COLLEGE ENTRANCE EXAM PRACTICE

## FOCUS ON SAT MATHEMATICS SUBJECT TEST

There are two levels of SAT Subject Tests: Math Level I and Math Level II. Each test has 50 multiple-choice questions. The content of each test is very different. Getting a high score on one test does not mean you will get a high score on the other test.

**You can write all over the test book to sketch figures, do scratch work, or cross out incorrect answers to help you eliminate choices. Remember to mark your final answer on the answer sheet because the test book is not used for scoring.**

**You may want to time yourself as you take this practice test. It should take you about 6 minutes to complete.**

---

**1.** Which of the following represents the number of ways 6 committee members can be selected from a group of 25 teachers?

**(A)** ${}_{6}C_{25}$

**(B)** ${}_{19}C_{6}$

**(C)** ${}_{25}C_{6}$

**(D)** ${}_{6}P_{25}$

**(E)** ${}_{25}P_{6}$

**2.** Your friend randomly selects 2 movies from your collection to borrow. Your collection includes 9 comedies, 5 dramas, 3 mysteries, 1 musical, and 2 horror movies. What is the probability that both movies are comedies?

**(A)** $\frac{1}{36}$

**(B)** $\frac{18}{95}$

**(C)** $\frac{81}{400}$

**(D)** $\frac{2}{9}$

**(E)** $\frac{331}{380}$

**3.** A student's test scores are 88, 87, 82, 95, and 89. If the student needs an average test score of 90 to obtain a grade of A, what must the score be on the last test of the semester?

**(A)** 88

**(B)** 88.2

**(C)** 91

**(D)** 99

**(E)** 100

**4.** What is the probability of not getting a 2 on the spinner?

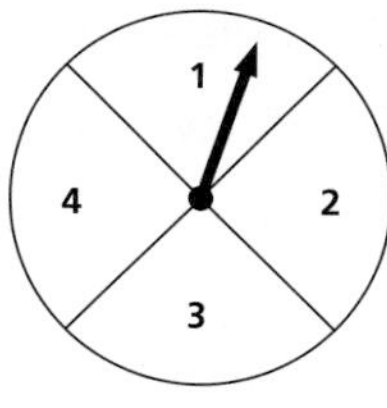


**(A)** 0.10

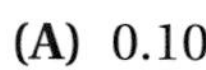

**(B)** 0.25

**(C)** 0.50

**(D)** 0.75

**(E)** 1

**5.** What is the value of $\frac{(n+1)!}{(n-1)!}$?

**(A)** $n^2 + n$

**(B)** $2n + 1$

**(C)** $n!$

**(D)** $n^2 - 1$

**(E)** $-1$

CHAPTER 10

# TEST TACKLER

Standardized Test Strategies

## Any Question Type: Spatial Reasoning

Some test questions include a three-dimensional figure. You must use spatial reasoning to correctly interpret the figure.

### EXAMPLE 1

**Which of the following shows the top view of the solid figure?**

(A) 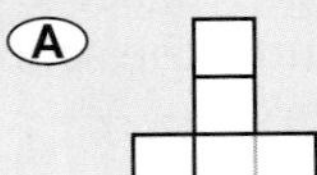

(B) 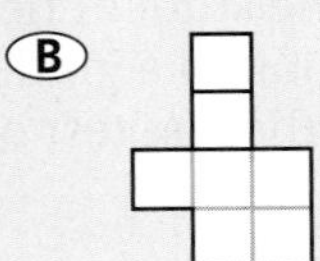

(C) 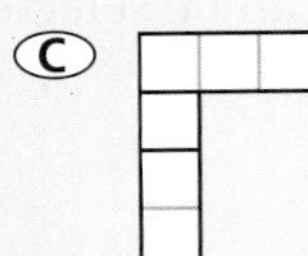

(D) 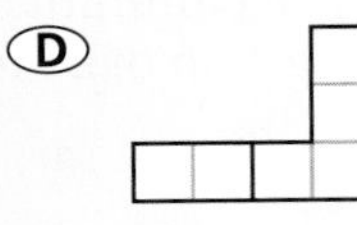

*Notice that the isometric drawing shows three sides of the figure: the top, front, and right side. Use the isometric drawing to make a foundation plan of the figure.*

*Count the number of cubes at the widest part of the figure and at the longest part of the figure.*

*The widest part is 3 cubes across.*
*The longest part is 4 cubes deep.*

*Draw a 3-by-4 grid.*

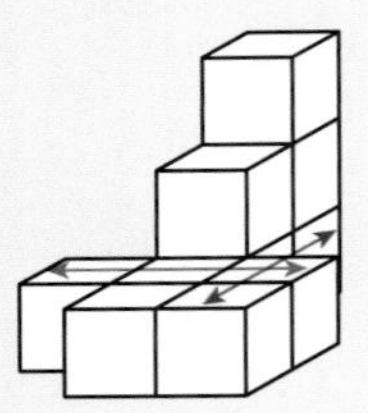

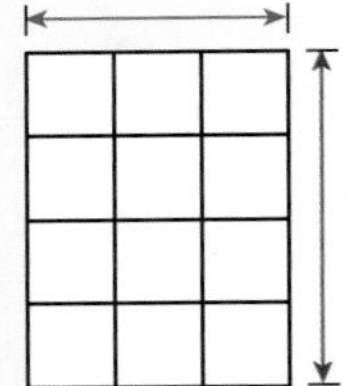

*Each cube on the bottom level of the figure corresponds to a square on the grid.*

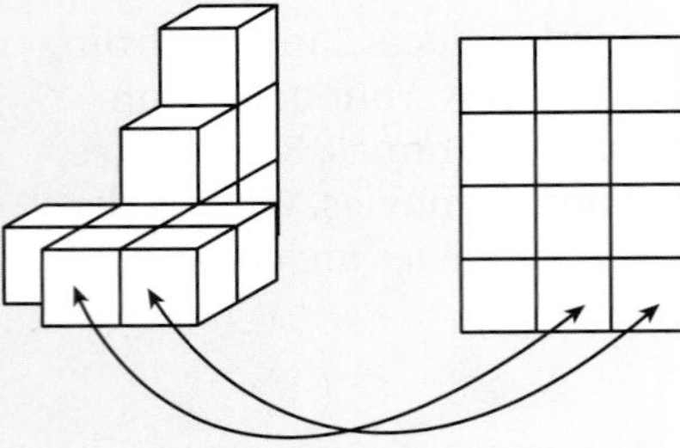

*Start at the front of the figure. Shade in each square of the grid that corresponds to a cube on the bottom level of the figure.*

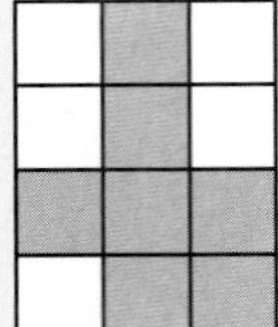

Using the foundation plan, you can see that choice B shows the top view of the solid.

Imagine that you are stacking blocks to help you to visualize the solid figure. Each square shown in the drawing represents a face of one block.

**Read each test item and answer the questions that follow.**

**Item A**

**Multiple Choice** **Which solid is represented by these top, side, and front views?**

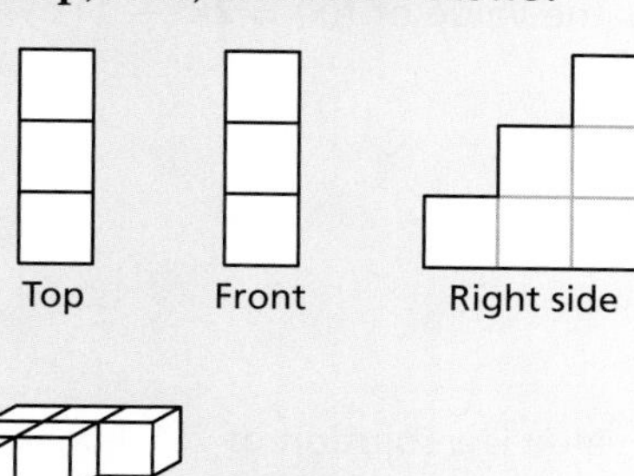


Ⓐ

Ⓑ

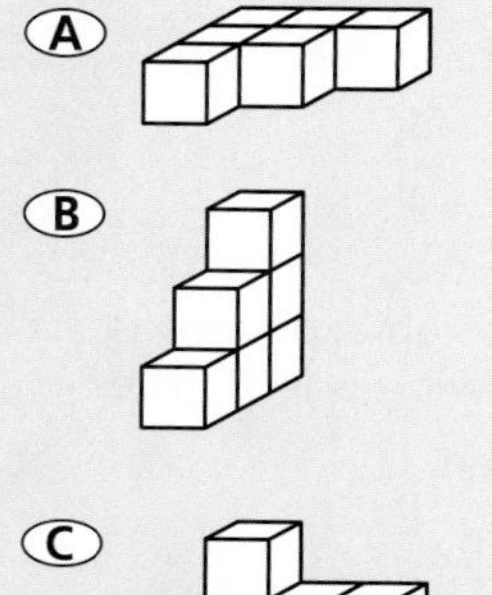

Ⓒ

Ⓓ

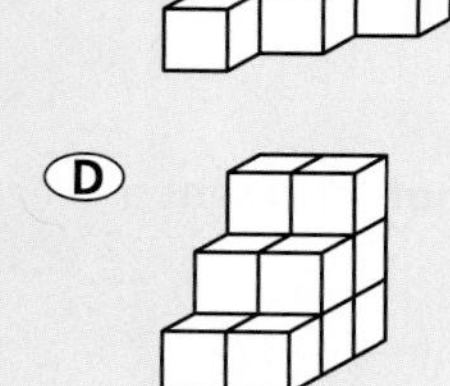

1. How many cubes can you see if you are looking down on the figure? How do you know?

2. How many cubes can you see if you are looking at the front of the figure? How do you know?

3. How many cubes high is the highest stack of the figure? Explain how you know.

4. Using your answers from Problems 1–3, what is the correct answer choice?

**Item B**

**Short Response** **The drawing shows a foundation plan of a solid figure made of stacked cubes. The numbers in the squares identify the number of cubes in each stack. Draw a three-dimensional view of this solid figure.**

| | | |
|---|---|---|
| 2 | 4 | 6 |
| 2 | 2 | 3 |
| 2 | 1 | 1 |

5. Draw the top view of the figure.

6. If you were to look at the figure from the right or from the front, how many cubes high is the highest stack? Explain how you know.

7. A student drew this figure as his response. Do you agree that this is the correct drawing? If so, explain how you know. If not, what did the student do wrong?

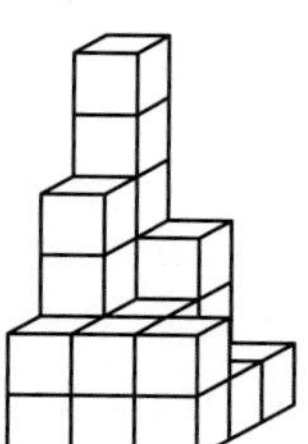

**Item C**

**Short Response** **Draw the top view and front view of the solid figure.**

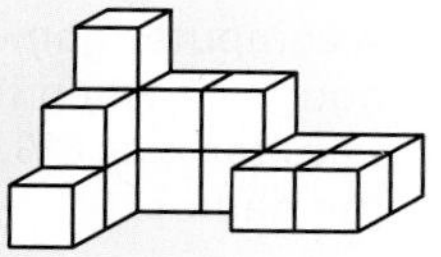

8. If you look down on the figure, how many cubes do you see?

9. Create a base plan or foundation plan for the figure.

10. Nolan drew his version of the top view of the figure. Is he correct? If not, show how you would change his drawing so that it is correct.

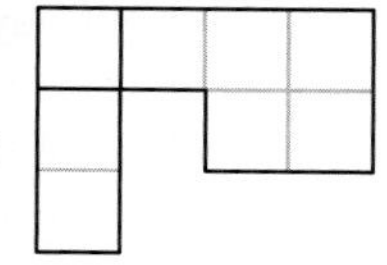

11. If you look at the figure from the front, how tall is the highest stack of cubes and how short is the shortest stack of cubes?

12. Draw the front view of the figure.

CHAPTER 10

# CUMULATIVE ASSESSMENT, CHAPTERS 1–10

## Multiple Choice

1. The ages of the first 20 people to finish a marathon are given below:

   21, 25, 31, 33, 35, 33, 32, 25, 24, 41, 23, 25, 26, 40, 31, 32, 30, 20, 19, 44.

   What is the interquartile range for the data?

   A 3
   B 6.5
   C 8.5
   D 25

2. Which function describes the line with the greatest slope?

   A $4x + 6y = 10$
   B $10x + 4y = 6$
   C $6x - 10y = 4$
   D $6x - 4y = 10$

3. A computer game normally sells for \$40. Niko bought it when it went on sale for 25% off. The sales tax was 6%. How much did Niko pay for the game?

   A \$10.60
   B \$12.40
   C \$31.80
   D \$32.40

4. Monique bought either a hat or scarf for each of her 12 friends. The hats cost \$22 each and the scarves cost \$19 each. She paid a total of \$252. How many hats and how many scarves did Monique buy?

   A 4 hats, 8 scarves
   B 7 hats, 5 scarves
   C 8 hats, 4 scarves
   D 5 hats, 7 scarves

5. What is an equation for the line that is parallel to the line described by $y = 7x + 5$ and that passes through (1, 3)?

   A $y = -7x + 10$
   B $y = -\frac{1}{7}x + \frac{22}{7}$
   C $y = \frac{1}{7}x + \frac{20}{7}$
   D $y = 7x - 4$

6. What is the value of $f(x) = 2x^2 - 11x$ when $x = -2$?

   A $-30$
   B $-14$
   C 14
   D 30

7. Which value is a solution of $2(1 - x) < 12$?

   A $-7$
   B $-6$
   C $-5$
   D $-4$

8. A negative number raised to an exponent is positive. Which of the following is NOT true?

   A The number could be even.
   B The number could be odd.
   C The exponent could be even.
   D The exponent could be odd.

9. Which of the following does ***not*** represent a function?

   A $\{(-4, 3), (-2, 1), (-2, -1), (-4, -3)\}$

   B
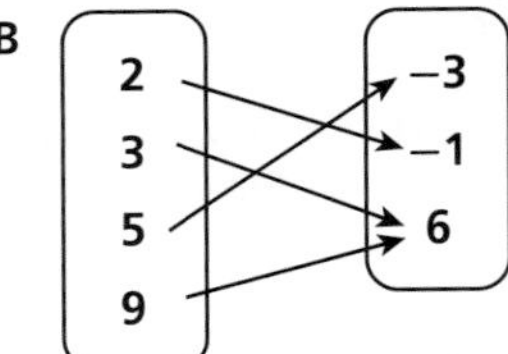


   C

| $x$ | −4 | −3 | −2 | −1 | 0 | 1 |
|---|---|---|---|---|---|---|
| $y$ | 4 | 3 | 2 | 1 | 0 | −1 |

   D
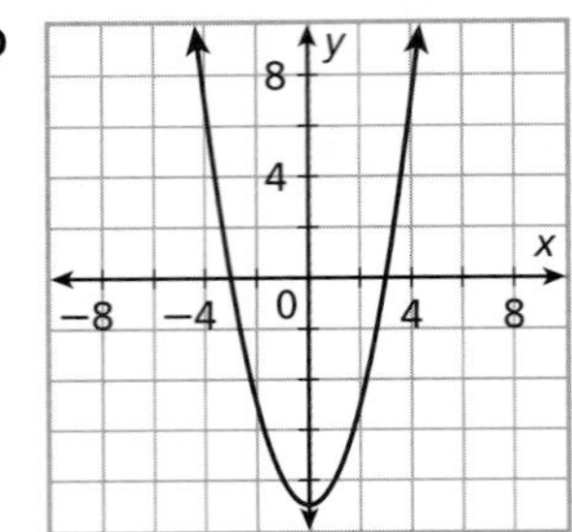

**If you are allowed to write in your test booklet, you may want to add additional information to a given diagram. Be sure to mark your answer on the answer sheet since your marks on the test booklet will not be graded.**

**10.** Which of these equations describes a line parallel to $x + 2y = 6$?

**A** $y = \frac{1}{2}x$

**B** $y = -\frac{1}{2}x + 4$

**C** $y = -2x + 6$

**D** $y = 2x + 3$

**11.** What is the probability that the spinner will ***not*** land on white?

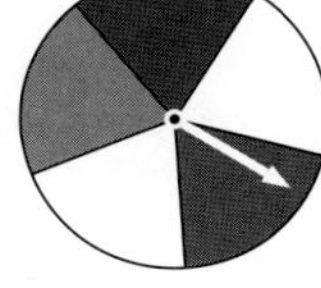

**A** 20%

**B** 40%

**C** 50%

**D** 60%

**12.** Which is a factor of $4x^2 + 24x + 36$?

**A** $x + 12$

**B** $2x + 6$

**C** $2x + 18$

**D** $4x + 18$

**13.** Yvette is choosing between two stores to get her family pictures taken. Say Cheese charges a $20 sitting fee and $14 per sheet of pictures. Picture Me charges a $12 sitting fee and $18 per sheet of pictures. For how many sheets will the total cost be the same at both stores?

**A** 2 **C** 4

**B** 3 **D** 5

**14.** Brian plays basketball. In the past, he has made 4 out of every 5 free throws. What is the probability that Brian will make the next two free throws?

**A** 0.04 **C** 0.4

**B** 0.16 **D** 0.64

**15.** A CD-ROM is storing $4.2 \times 10^8$ bytes of information. What is this number in standard form?

**A** 0.0000000042

**B** 0.00000042

**C** 420,000,000

**D** 4,200,000,000

***STANDARDIZED TEST PREP***

## Short Response

**S1.** An experiment consists of tossing 3 coins at the same time.

**a.** Identify the sample space.

**b.** What is the probability of tossing 2 tails and 1 head?

**c.** Which is more likely to occur: tossing exactly 1 tail or tossing at least 2 heads? Explain.

**S2.** If 8% of a number is 4, what is 12% of the number? Explain your reasoning.

**S3.** Nat surveyed 30 twelfth-grade students and found that 27 of them were in favor of allowing seniors to leave campus for lunch. As a result, Nat reported that "90% of the student body supports off-campus lunch privileges for seniors." Was Nat's statistic misleading? Explain.

**S4.** A service technician is scheduling house calls to make repairs. He has 9 time slots in his work day. He has 7 house calls to make. How many different schedules of his day are possible? Show and explain your work.

**S5.** Divide $(15x^2 + 8x - 12) \div (3x + 1)$ using long division. Show each step.

## Extended Response

**E1.** The ages of the first 15 people to enter a community center for bingo one evening are 77, 85, 76, 73, 69, 70, 84, 82, 76, 74, 89, 83, 68, 91, and 88.

**a.** Find the mean, median, mode, and range of the data.

**b.** Create a box-and-whisker plot of the data.

**c.** The sixteenth person to enter the center is 39 years old. Calculate the mean, median, mode, and range of the data with the 16 people.

**d.** Create a box-and-whisker plot with the 16 people.

**e.** When the sixteenth person was added, which measure of central tendency changed the most? Which measure changed the least? Explain.

**f.** How did the addition of the sixteenth person affect the box-and-whisker plot?

# North Carolina CONNECTION

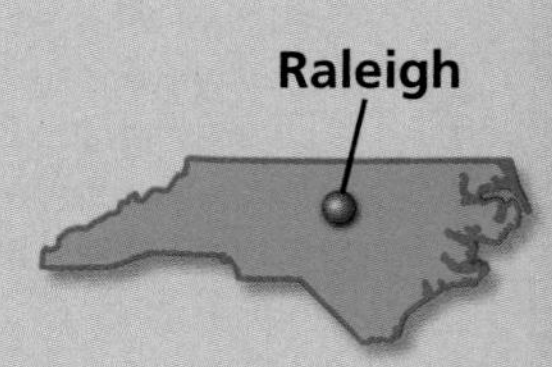


## Governors of North Carolina

The first governor of the state of North Carolina was Richard Caswell, who served from 1776 to 1780 and again from 1784 to 1787. Since then, more than five dozen different leaders have served as the state's top executive. The table provides data on North Carolina's governors from 1929 to 2001.

1. Use the data in the table to make a back-to-back stem-and-leaf plot.
2. Find the mean age at which the governors entered office. Find the mean age at which they left office.
3. A reporter uses the mode to describe the typical age at which the governors left office. Is this a good choice? Why or why not?
4. Make a box-and-whisker plot of the ages at which the governors took office. Then use the same number line to make a box-and-whisker plot of the ages at which the governors left office. The two box-and-whisker plots should appear one above the other.
5. Use any or all of the work you have done so far to help you describe the age of the "typical" governor of North Carolina during the period 1929 to 2001.

**Governors of North Carolina, 1929–2001**

| Name | Age Upon Entering Office | Age Upon Leaving Office |
|---|---|---|
| Oliver Gardner | 46 | 50 |
| John Ehringhaus | 50 | 54 |
| Clyde Hoey | 59 | 63 |
| J. Melville Broughton | 52 | 56 |
| R. Gregg Cherry | 53 | 57 |
| W. Kerr Scott | 52 | 56 |
| William Umstead | 57 | 59 |
| Luther Hodges | 56 | 63 |
| Terry Sanford | 43 | 47 |
| Dan Moore | 58 | 62 |
| Robert Scott | 39 | 43 |
| James Holshouser | 38 | 42 |
| James Hunt | 39 | 63 |
| James Martin | 49 | 57 |

North Carolina Executive Mansion, Raleigh

# North Carolina Symphony

For more than 75 years, the North Carolina Symphony has brought music to every corner of North Carolina as well as to the Kennedy Center in Washington, D.C., and Carnegie Hall in New York. The symphony, based in Raleigh, performs nearly 200 concerts per year, of which more than 50 are offered for free to schoolchildren around the state.

**For 1–4, use the diagram.**

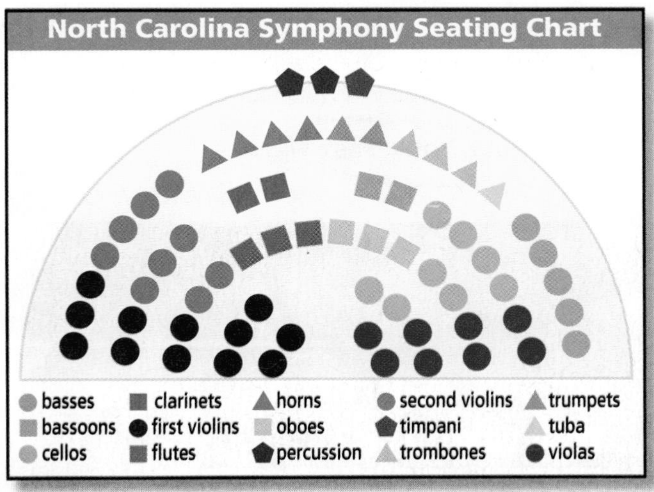


1. In how many different ways can the symphony's horn players sit in a row?
2. The symphony plans to perform Bach's *Brandenburg Concerto 3*. The concerto only requires three cello players. How many ways can the conductor choose the three cello players?
3. The cover of a program will feature the photos of one flute player, one oboe player, and one bass player. How many different combinations of photos are possible?
4. The director of the symphony wants to choose two musicians who play brass instruments to participate in a school program. The director places the names of the horn, trumpet, trombone, and tuba players in a hat and chooses two names without looking.
   a. What is the probability that the first name chosen is that of a trumpet player?
   b. What is the probability that both names are those of trumpet players?

# Exponential and Radical Functions



## Why Learn This?

Meteorologists can use radical equations to estimate the size of a storm and the length of time it will last.

go.hrw.com
Chapter Project Online
KEYWORD: MA7 ChProj

## Vocabulary

**Match each term on the left with a definition on the right.**

1. like terms
2. square root
3. domain
4. perfect square
5. exponent

A. the set of second elements of a relation
B. terms that contain the same variable raised to the same power
C. the set of first elements of a relation
D. a number that tells how many times a base is used as a factor
E. a number whose positive square root is a whole number
F. one of two equal factors of a number

## Evaluate Powers

**Find the value of each expression.**

**6.** $2^4$ **7.** $5^0$ **8.** $7 \cdot 3^2$ **9.** $3 \cdot 5^3$

**10.** $3^5$ **11.** $-6^2 + 8^1$ **12.** $40 \cdot 2^3$ **13.** $7^2 \cdot 3^1$

## Graph Functions

**Graph each function.**

**14.** $y = 8$ **15.** $y = x + 3$ **16.** $y = x^2 - 4$ **17.** $y = x^2 + 2$

## Fractions, Decimals, and Percents

**Write each percent as a decimal.**

**18.** 50% **19.** 25% **20.** 15.2% **21.** 200%

**22.** 1.9% **23.** 0.3% **24.** 0.1% **25.** 1.04%

## Squares and Square Roots

**Find each square root.**

**26.** $\sqrt{36}$ **27.** $\sqrt{81}$ **28.** $\sqrt{25}$ **29.** $\sqrt{64}$

## Pythagorean Theorem

**Find the length of the hypotenuse in each right triangle.**

**30.**

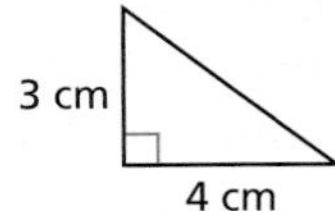


**31.**

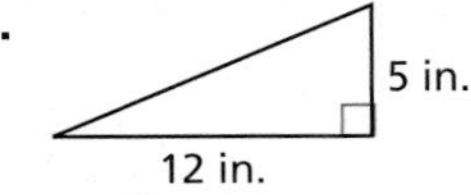


**32.**

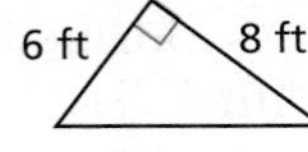


## Multiply Monomials and Polynomials

**Multiply.**

**33.** $5(2m - 3)$ **34.** $3x(8x + 9)$ **35.** $2t(3t - 1)$ **36.** $4r(4r - 5)$

CHAPTER 11

# Study Guide: Preview

## Where You've Been

**Previously, you**

- identified and extended arithmetic sequences.
- identified and graphed linear functions and quadratic functions.
- solved linear and quadratic equations.

## In This Chapter

**You will study**

- another type of sequence—geometric sequences.
- two more types of functions—exponential functions and square-root functions.
- radical equations.

## Where You're Going

**You can use the skills in this chapter**

- to analyze more complicated functions in later math courses, such as Calculus.
- to explore exponential growth and decay models that are used in science.
- to make informed decisions about finances.

## *Key Vocabulary/Vocabulario*

| | |
|---|---|
| common ratio | razón común |
| compound interest | interés compuesto |
| exponential decay | decrecimiento exponencial |
| exponential function | función exponencial |
| exponential growth | crecimiento exponencial |
| extraneous solution | solución extraña |
| geometric sequence | sucesión geométrica |
| like radicals | radicales semejantes |
| radical equation | ecuación radical |
| radical expression | expresión radical |
| radicand | radicando |
| square-root function | función de raíz cuadrada |

## *Vocabulary Connections*

To become familiar with some of the vocabulary terms in the chapter, consider the following. You may refer to the chapter, the glossary, or a dictionary if you like.

1. What does it mean when several items have something "in common"? What is a ratio? What do you think **common ratio** means?
2. In the division problem $2\overline{)50}$ (quotient 25), the *dividend* is 50. If a *radicand* is similar to a dividend, then what is the **radicand** in $\sqrt{16} = 4$?
3. A square-root sign is also known as a *radical.* Use this knowledge to define **radical expression** and **radical equation**.
4. The root word of *extraneous* is *extra. Extraneous* means *irrelevant* or *unrelated.* Use this information to define **extraneous solution**.

## Study Strategy: Remember Formulas

In math, there are many formulas, properties, and rules that you should commit to memory.

**To memorize a formula,** create flash cards. Write the name of the formula on one side of a card. Write the formula on the other side of the card. You might also include a diagram or an example if helpful. Study your flash cards on a regular basis.

### *Sample Flash Card*

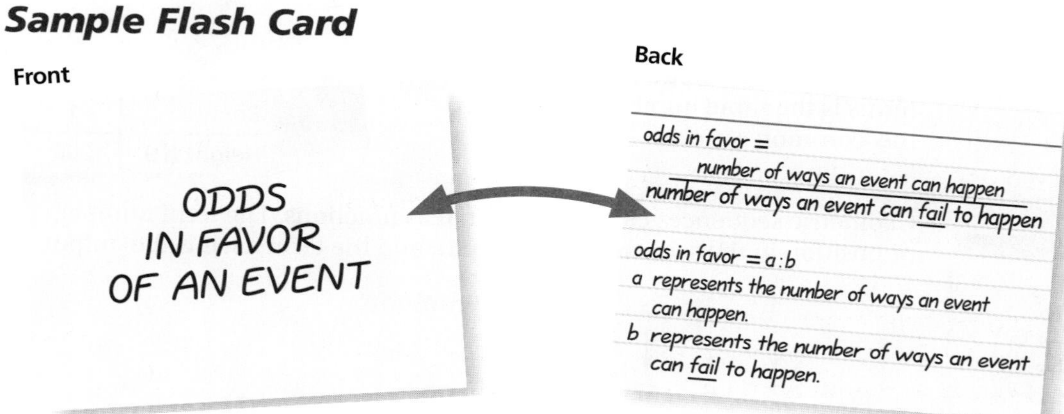


Knowing when and how to apply a mathematical formula is as important as memorizing the formula itself.

**To know what formula to apply,** read the problem carefully and look for key words.

### From Lesson 10-6

> The **probability** of choosing an ace from a deck of cards is $\frac{1}{13}$.
> What are the **odds of choosing an ace**?

The key words have been highlighted. The probability is given, and you are asked to find the odds. You should use the formula for *odds in favor of an event.*

### Try This

**Read each problem. Then write the formula(s) needed to solve it. What key words helped you identify the formula?**

1. A manufacturer inspects 450 computer chips and finds that 22 are defective. What is the experimental probability that a chip chosen at random is defective?
2. The area of a rectangular pool is 120 square feet. The length is 1 foot less than twice the width. What is the perimeter of the pool?

# 11-1 Geometric Sequences

**MA.A.3** Analyze patterns of change in functional relationships.

***Objectives***

Recognize and extend geometric sequences.

Find the *n*th term of a geometric sequence.

***Vocabulary***

geometric sequence

common ratio

**Who uses this?**

Bungee jumpers can use geometric sequences to calculate how high they will bounce.

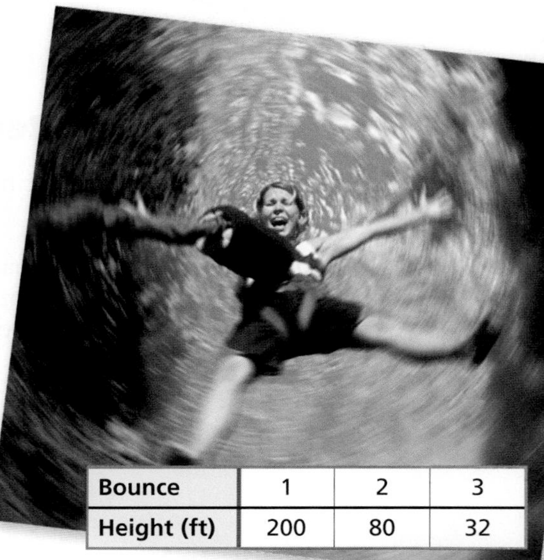

The table shows the heights of a bungee jumper's bounces.

| Bounce | 1 | 2 | 3 |
|---|---|---|---|
| Height (ft) | 200 | 80 | 32 |

The height of the bounces shown in the table form a *geometric sequence.* In a **geometric sequence**, the ratio of successive terms is the same number *r*, called the **common ratio**.

**Writing Math**

The variable *a* is often used to represent terms in a sequence. The variable $a_4$ (read "*a* sub 4") is the fourth term in a sequence.

Geometric sequences can be thought of as functions. The term number, or position in the sequence, is the input, and the term itself is the output.

| 1 | 2 | 3 | 4 | ← Position |
|---|---|---|---|---|
| ↓ | ↓ | ↓ | ↓ | |
| 3 | 6 | 12 | 24 | ← Term |
| $a_1$ | $a_2$ | $a_3$ | $a_4$ | |

To find a term in a geometric sequence, multiply the previous term by *r*.

**Finding a Term of a Geometric Sequence**

The *n*th term of a geometric sequence with common ratio *r* is

$$a_n = a_{n-1}r$$

**EXAMPLE 1 Extending Geometric Sequences**

**Find the next three terms in each geometric sequence.**

**A** **1, 3, 9, 27, ...**

**Step 1** Find the value of *r* by dividing each term by the one before it.

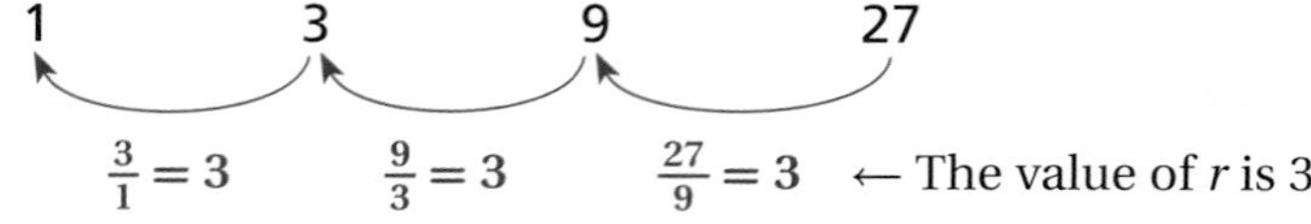



$\frac{3}{1} = 3$ $\quad \frac{9}{3} = 3$ $\quad \frac{27}{9} = 3$ ← The value of *r* is 3.

**Step 2** Multiply each term by 3 to find the next three terms.

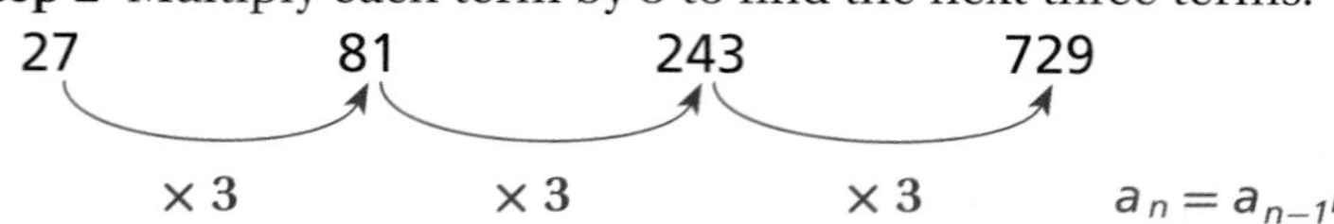



$\times 3$ $\quad \times 3$ $\quad \times 3$ $\quad a_n = a_{n-1}r$

The next three terms are 81, 243, and 729.

**Helpful Hint**

When the terms in a geometric sequence alternate between positive and negative, the value of $r$ is negative.

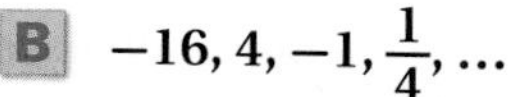


**Step 1** Find the value of $r$ by dividing each term by the one before it.

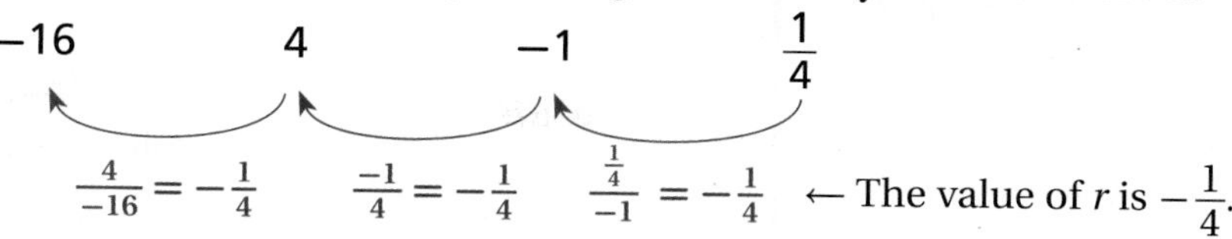


**Step 2** Multiply each term by $-\frac{1}{4}$ to find the next three terms.

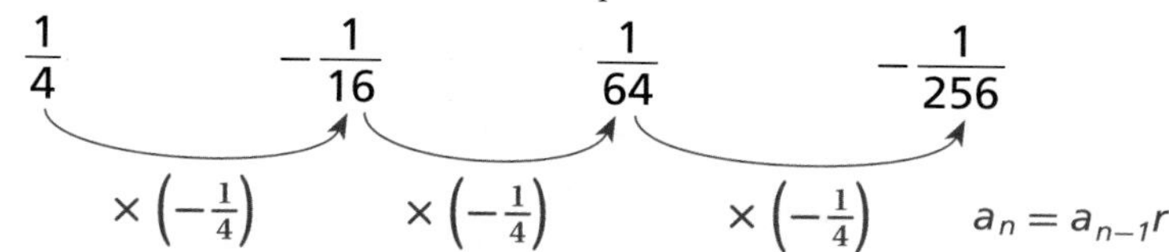


The next three terms are $-\frac{1}{16}$, $\frac{1}{64}$, and $-\frac{1}{256}$.

**Find the next three terms in each geometric sequence.**

**1a.** 5, −10, 20, −40, …

**1b.** 512, 384, 288, …

To find the output $a_n$ of a geometric sequence when $n$ is a large number, you need an equation, or function rule.

The pattern in the table shows that to get the $n$th term, multiply the first term by the common ratio raised to the power $n - 1$.

| Words | Numbers | Algebra |
|---|---|---|
| 1st term | 3 | $a_1$ |
| 2nd term | $3 \cdot 2^1 = 6$ | $a_1 \cdot r^1$ |
| 3rd term | $3 \cdot 2^2 = 12$ | $a_1 \cdot r^2$ |
| 4th term | $3 \cdot 2^3 = 24$ | $a_1 \cdot r^3$ |
| $n$th term | $3 \cdot 2^{n-1}$ | $a_1 \cdot r^{n-1}$ |

If the first term of a geometric sequence is $a_1$, the $n$th term is $a_n$, and the common ratio is $r$, then

$$a_n = a_1 r^{n-1}$$

$n$th term — $a_n$; 1st term — $a_1$; Common ratio — $r$

## EXAMPLE 2 Finding the $n$th Term of a Geometric Sequence

**A** **The first term of a geometric sequence is 128, and the common ratio is 0.5. What is the 10th term of the sequence?**

| | |
|---|---|
| $a_n = a_1 r^{n-1}$ | *Write the formula.* |
| $a_{10} = 128(0.5)^{10-1}$ | *Substitute 128 for $a_1$, 10 for n, and 0.5 for r.* |
| $= 128(0.5)^9$ | *Simplify the exponent.* |
| $= 0.25$ | *Use a calculator.* |

**B** **For a geometric sequence, $a_1 = 8$ and $r = 3$. Find the 5th term of this sequence.**

| | |
|---|---|
| $a_n = a_1 r^{n-1}$ | *Write the formula.* |
| $a_5 = 8(3)^{5-1}$ | *Substitute 8 for $a_1$, 5 for n, and 3 for r.* |
| $= 8(3)^4$ | *Simplify the exponent.* |
| $= 648$ | *Use a calculator.* |

**Caution!**

When writing a function rule for a sequence with a negative common ratio, remember to enclose $r$ in parentheses.
$-2^{12} \neq (-2)^{12}$

**C** **What is the 13th term of the geometric sequence 8, −16, 32, −64, … ?**

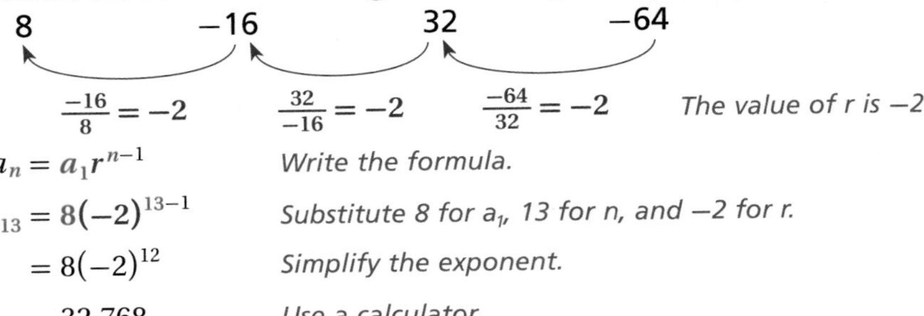


$\frac{-16}{8} = -2$ $\quad \frac{32}{-16} = -2$ $\quad \frac{-64}{32} = -2$ *The value of r is −2.*

$a_n = a_1 r^{n-1}$ *Write the formula.*

$a_{13} = 8(-2)^{13-1}$ *Substitute 8 for $a_1$, 13 for n, and −2 for r.*

$= 8(-2)^{12}$ *Simplify the exponent.*

$= 32{,}768$ *Use a calculator.*

The 13th term of the sequence is 32,768.

**2.** What is the 8th term of the sequence 1000, 500, 250, 125, … ?

## EXAMPLE 3 Sports Application

**A bungee jumper jumps from a bridge. The diagram shows the bungee jumper's height above the ground at the top of each bounce. The heights form a geometric sequence. What is the bungee jumper's height at the top of the 5th bounce?**

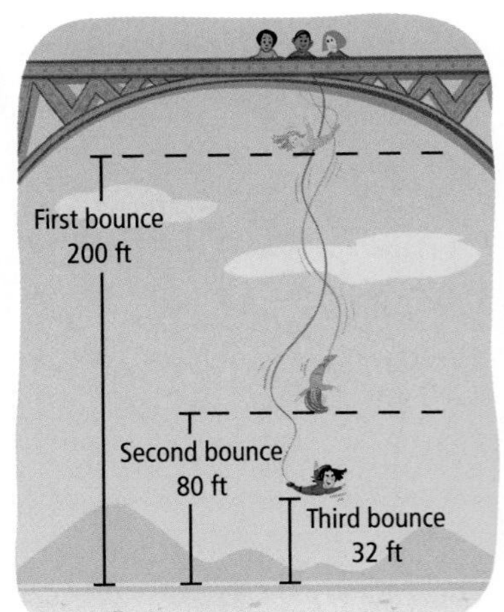


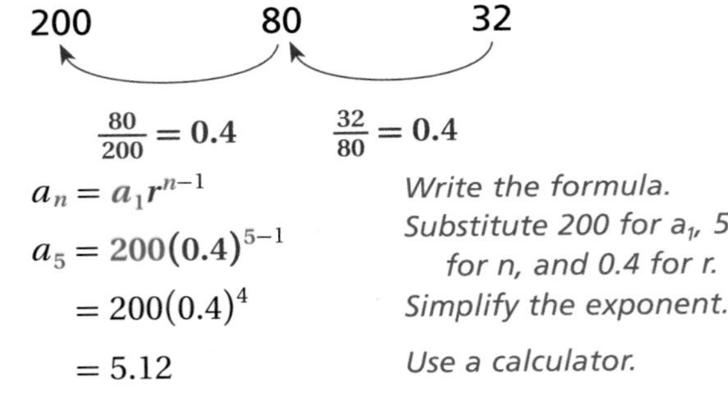


$\frac{80}{200} = 0.4$ $\quad \frac{32}{80} = 0.4$

$a_n = a_1 r^{n-1}$ *Write the formula.*

$a_5 = 200(0.4)^{5-1}$ *Substitute 200 for $a_1$, 5 for n, and 0.4 for r.*

$= 200(0.4)^4$ *Simplify the exponent.*

$= 5.12$ *Use a calculator.*

The height of the 5th bounce is 5.12 feet.

**3.** The table shows a car's value for 3 years after it is purchased. The values form a geometric sequence. How much will the car be worth in the 10th year?

| Year | Value ($) |
|---|---|
| 1 | 10,000 |
| 2 | 8,000 |
| 3 | 6,400 |

## THINK AND DISCUSS

**1.** How do you determine whether a sequence is geometric?

**2. GET ORGANIZED** Copy and complete the graphic organizer. In each box, write a way to represent the geometric sequence.

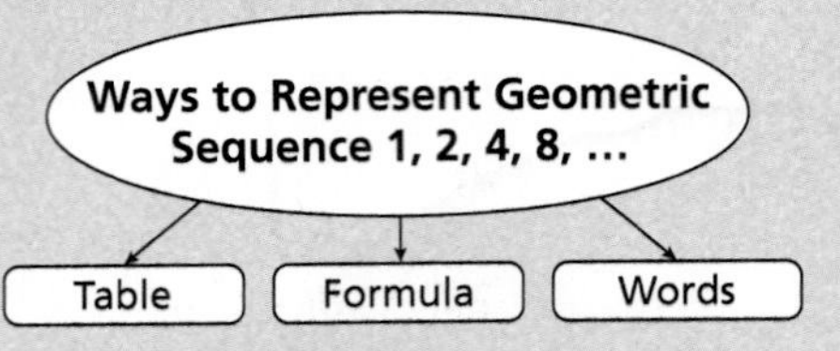

# 11-1 Exercises

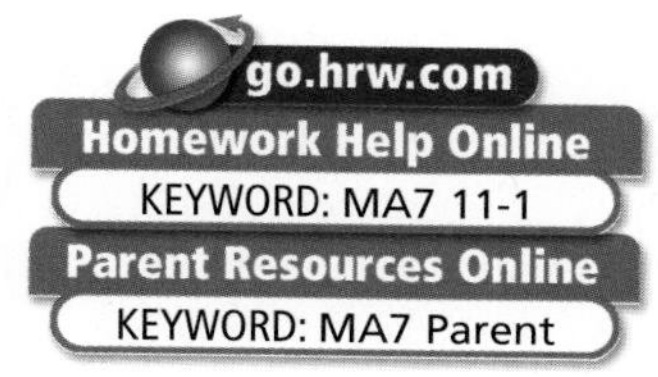


## GUIDED PRACTICE

1. **Vocabulary** What is the *common ratio* of a geometric sequence?

SEE EXAMPLE 1 p. 766

**Find the next three terms in each geometric sequence.**

2. 2, 4, 8, 16, …
3. 400, 200, 100, 50, …
4. 4, −12, 36, −108, …

SEE EXAMPLE 2 p. 767

5. The first term of a geometric sequence is 1, and the common ratio is 10. What is the 10th term of the sequence?
6. What is the 11th term of the geometric sequence 3, 6, 12, 24, … ?

SEE EXAMPLE 3 p. 768

7. **Sports** In the NCAA men's basketball tournament, 64 teams compete in round 1. Fewer teams remain in each following round, as shown in the graph, until all but one team have been eliminated. The numbers of teams in each round form a geometric sequence. How many teams compete in round 5?

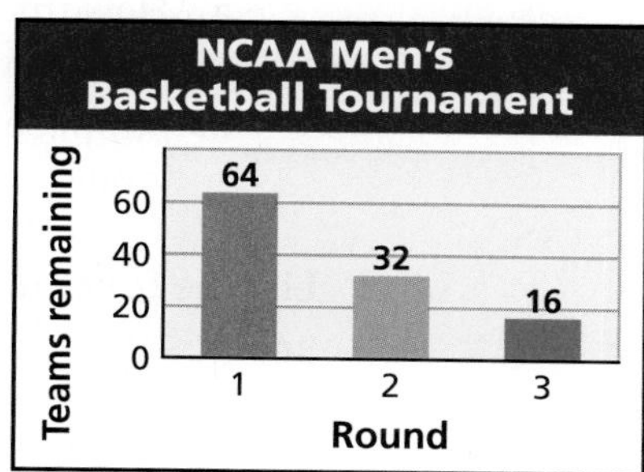


## PRACTICE AND PROBLEM SOLVING

**Independent Practice**

| For Exercises | See Example |
|---|---|
| 8–13 | 1 |
| 14–15 | 2 |
| 16 | 3 |

**Extra Practice**

Skills Practice p. S24
Application Practice p. S38

**Find the next three terms in each geometric sequence.**

8. −2, 10, −50, 250, …
9. 32, 48, 72, 108, …
10. 625, 500, 400, 320, …
11. 6, 42, 294, …
12. 6, −12, 24, −48, …
13. $40, 10, \frac{5}{2}, \frac{5}{8}, \ldots$
14. The first term of a geometric sequence is 18 and the common ratio is 3.5. What is the 5th term of the sequence?
15. What is the 14th term of the geometric sequence 1000, 100, 10, 1, … ?
16. **Physical Science** A ball is dropped from a height of 500 meters. The table shows the height of each bounce, and the heights form a geometric sequence. How high does the ball bounce on the 8th bounce? Round your answer to the nearest tenth of a meter.

| Bounce | Height (m) |
|---|---|
| 1 | 400 |
| 2 | 320 |
| 3 | 256 |

**Find the missing term(s) in each geometric sequence.**

17. 20, 40, ■, ■, …
18. ■, 6, 18, ■, …
19. 9, 3, 1, ■, …
20. 3, 12, ■, 192, ■, …
21. 7, 1, ■, ■, $\frac{1}{343}$, …
22. ■, 100, 25, ■, $\frac{25}{16}$, …
23. −3, ■, −12, 24, ■, …
24. ■, ■, 1, −3, 9, …
25. 1, 17, 289, ■, …

**Determine whether each sequence could be geometric. If so, give the common ratio.**

26. 2, 10, 50, 250, …
27. $15, 5, \frac{5}{3}, \frac{5}{9}, \ldots$
28. 6, 18, 24, 38, …
29. 9, 3, −1, −5, …
30. 7, 21, 63, 189, …
31. 4, 1, −2, −4, …

32. **Multi-Step** Billy earns money by mowing lawns for the summer. He offers two payment plans, as shown at right.

a. Do the payments for plan 2 form a geometric sequence? Explain.

b. If you were one of Billy's customers, which plan would you choose? (Assume that the summer is 10 weeks long.) Explain your choice.

Billy's Better Lawns
Weekly Lawn Care Service
TWO WAYS TO PAY!
Plan 1: Pay $150 for the entire summer.
Plan 2: Pay $1 the 1ST week, $2 the 2ND week, $4 the 3RD week, $8 the 4TH week, and so on.

33. **Measurement** When you fold a piece of paper in half, the thickness of the folded piece is twice the thickness of the original piece. A piece of copy paper is about 0.1 mm thick.

a. How thick is a piece of copy paper that has been folded in half 7 times?

b. Suppose that you could fold a piece of copy paper in half 12 times. How thick would it be? Write your answer in centimeters.

**List the first four terms of each geometric sequence.**

34. $a_1 = 3, a_n = 3(2)^{n-1}$

35. $a_1 = -2, a_n = -2(4)^{n-1}$

36. $a_1 = 5, a_n = 5(-2)^{n-1}$

37. $a_1 = 2, a_n = 2(2)^{n-1}$

38. $a_1 = 2, a_n = 2(5)^{n-1}$

39. $a_1 = 12, a_n = 12\left(\frac{1}{4}\right)^{n-1}$

40. **Critical Thinking** What happens to the terms of a geometric sequence when $r$ is doubled? Use an example to support your answer.

41. **Geometry** Fractals are geometric figures that are formed by repeating the same process over and over on a smaller and smaller scale. These are the steps to draw a square fractal.

**Step 1** (stage 0) Draw a large square.

**Step 2** (stage 1) Divide the square into four equal squares.

**Step 3** (stage 2) Divide each small square into four equal squares.

**Step 4** Repeat Step 3 indefinitely.

a. Draw stages 0, 1, 2, and 3 of the square fractal.

b. How many small squares are in each stage? Organize your data relating stage and number of small squares in a table.

c. Does the data in part **b** form a geometric sequence? Explain.

d. Write a rule to find the number of small squares in stage $n$.

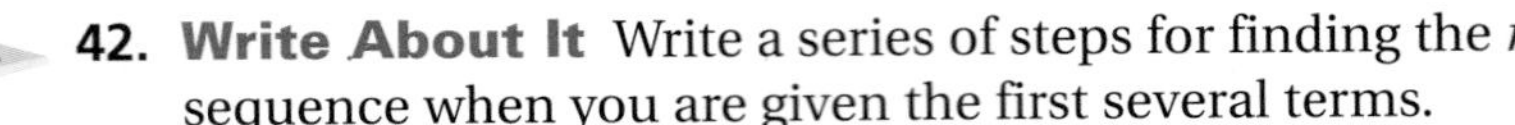

42. **Write About It** Write a series of steps for finding the $n$th term of a geometric sequence when you are given the first several terms.

43. This problem will prepare you for the Multi-Step Test Prep on page 796.

a. Three years ago, the annual tuition at a university was $3000. The following year, the tuition was $3300, and last year, the tuition was $3630. If the tuition has continued to grow in the same manner, what is the tuition this year? What do you expect it to be next year?

b. What is the common ratio?

c. What would you predict the tuition was 4 years ago? How did you find that value?

MA.A.3

44. Which of the following is a geometric sequence?

Ⓐ $\frac{1}{2}, 1, \frac{3}{2}, 2, \ldots$
Ⓑ $-2, -6, -10, -14, \ldots$
Ⓒ $3, 8, 13, 18, \ldots$
Ⓓ $5, 10, 20, 40, \ldots$

45. Which equation represents the $n$th term in the geometric sequence $2, -8, 32, -128, \ldots$?

Ⓕ $a_n = (-4)^n$ Ⓖ $a_n = (-4)^{n-1}$ Ⓗ $a_n = 2(-4)^n$ Ⓙ $a_n = 2(-4)^{n-1}$

46. The frequency of a musical note, measured in hertz (Hz), is called its pitch. The pitches of the A keys on a piano form a geometric sequence, as shown.

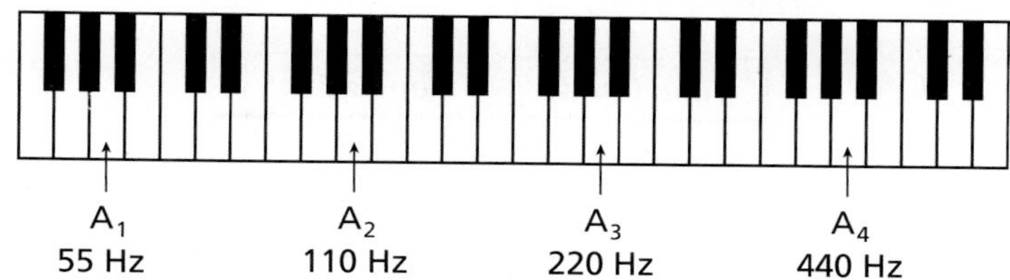


What is the frequency of $A_7$?

Ⓐ 880 Hz Ⓑ 1760 Hz Ⓒ 3520 Hz Ⓓ 7040 Hz

## CHALLENGE AND EXTEND

**Find the next three terms in each geometric sequence.**

47. $x, x^2, x^3, \ldots$

48. $2x^2, 6x^3, 18x^4, \ldots$

49. $\frac{1}{y^3}, \frac{1}{y^2}, \frac{1}{y}, \ldots$

50. $\frac{1}{(x+1)^2}, \frac{1}{x+1}, 1, \ldots$

51. The 10th term of a geometric sequence is 0.78125. The common ratio is −0.5. Find the first term of the sequence.

52. The first term of a geometric sequence is 12 and the common ratio is $\frac{1}{2}$. Is 0 a term in this sequence? Explain.

53. A geometric sequence starts with 14 and has a common ration of 0.4. Colin finds that another number in the sequence is 0.057344. Which term in the sequence did Colin find?

54. The first three terms of a sequence are 1, 2, and 4. Susanna said the 8th term of this sequence is 128. Paul said the 8th term is 29. Explain how the students found their answers. Why could these both be considered correct answers?

## SPIRAL REVIEW

**Solve each inequality and graph the solutions.** *(Lesson 3-2)*

55. $b - 4 > 6$

56. $-12 + x \leq -8$

57. $c + \frac{2}{3} < \frac{1}{3}$

**Graph the solutions of each linear inequality.** *(Lesson 6-5)*

58. $y < 2x - 4$

59. $3x + y > 6$

60. $-y \leq 2x + 1$

**Write a function to describe each of the following graphs.** *(Lesson 9-4)*

61. The graph of $f(x) = x^2 - 3$ translated 7 units up

62. The graph of $f(x) = 2x^2 + 6$ narrowed and translated 2 units down

# 11-2 Exponential Functions

**MA.A.3.1** Differentiate between linear ... and exponential patterns of change. *Also* MA.A.4.6, MA.A.5.1, MA.A.4.3

***Objectives***

Evaluate exponential functions.

Identify and graph exponential functions.

***Vocabulary***

exponential function

**Who uses this?**

Scientists model populations with exponential functions.

The table and the graph show an insect population that increases over time.

| Time (days) | Population |
|---|---|
| 0 | 2 |
| 1 | 6 |
| 2 | 18 |
| 3 | 54 |

$\times 3$ $\times 3$ $\times 3$

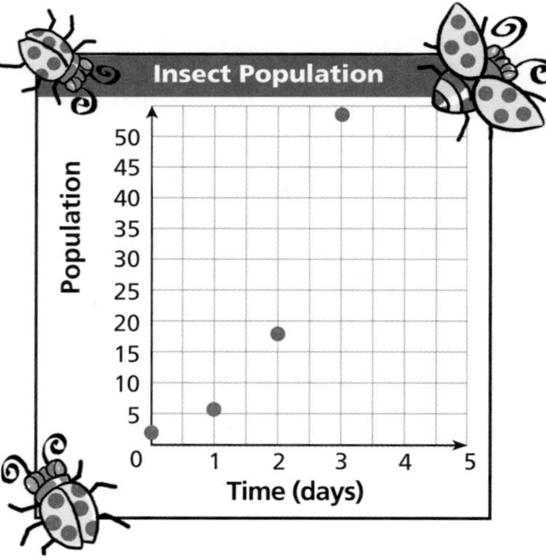


A function rule that describes the pattern above is $f(x) = 2(3)^x$. This type of function, in which the independent variable appears in an exponent, is an **exponential function**. Notice that 2 is the starting population and 3 is the amount by which the population is multiplied each day.

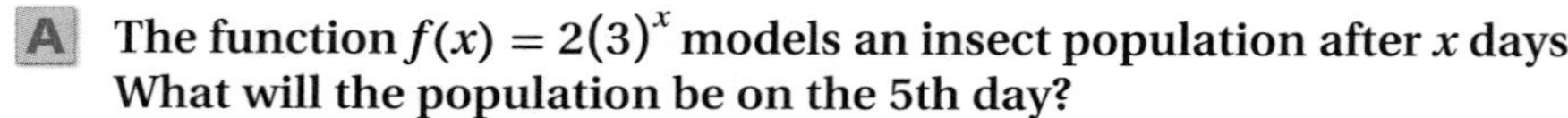


An exponential function has the form $f(x) = ab^x$, where $a \neq 0$, $b \neq 1$, and $b > 0$.

## EXAMPLE 1 Evaluating an Exponential Function

**A** **The function $f(x) = 2(3)^x$ models an insect population after $x$ days. What will the population be on the 5th day?**

$f(x) = 2(3)^x$ *Write the function.*

$f(5) = 2(3)^5$ *Substitute 5 for x.*

$= 2(243)$ *Evaluate $3^5$.*

$= 486$ *Multiply.*

There will be 486 insects on the 5th day.

**Helpful Hint**

In Example 1B, round your answer to the nearest whole number because there can only be a whole number of prairie dogs.

**B** **The function $f(x) = 1500(0.995)^x$, where $x$ is the time in years, models a prairie dog population. How many prairie dogs will there be in 8 years?**

$f(x) = 1500(0.995)^x$

$f(8) = 1500(0.995)^8$ *Substitute 8 for x.*

$\approx 1441$ *Use a calculator. Round to the nearest whole number.*

There will be about 1441 prairie dogs in 8 years.

1. The function $f(x) = 8(0.75)^x$ models the width of a photograph in inches after it has been reduced by 25% $x$ times. What is the width of the photograph after it has been reduced 3 times?

Remember that linear functions have constant first differences and quadratic functions have constant second differences. Exponential functions do not have constant differences, but they do have *constant ratios.*

As the $x$-values increase by a constant amount, the $y$-values are multiplied by a constant amount. This amount is the constant ratio and is the value of $b$ in $f(x) = ab^x$.

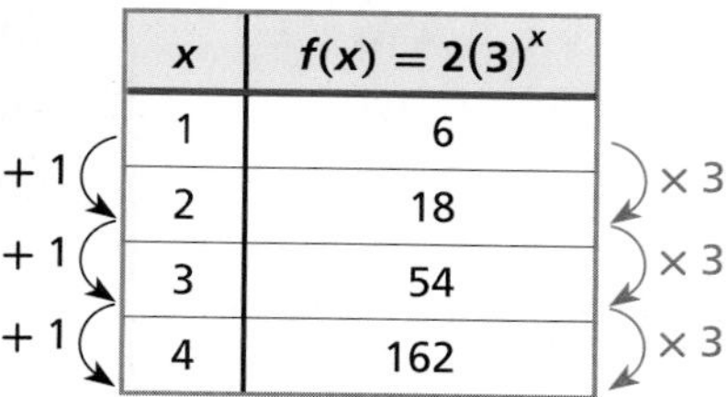

| $x$ | $f(x) = 2(3)^x$ |
|---|---|
| 1 | 6 |
| 2 | 18 |
| 3 | 54 |
| 4 | 162 |



## EXAMPLE 2 Identifying an Exponential Function

**Tell whether each set of ordered pairs satisfies an exponential function. Explain your answer.**

**A** $\{(-1, 1.5), (0, 3), (1, 6), (2, 12)\}$

| $x$ | $y$ |
|---|---|
| −1 | 1.5 |
| 0 | 3 |
| 1 | 6 |
| 2 | 12 |

+ 1, + 1, + 1; × 2, × 2, × 2

This is an exponential function. As the $x$-values increase by a constant amount, the $y$-values are multiplied by a constant amount.

**B** $\{(-1, -9), (1, 9), (3, 27), (5, 45)\}$

| $x$ | $y$ |
|---|---|
| −1 | −9 |
| 1 | 9 |
| 3 | 27 |
| 5 | 45 |

+ 2, + 2, + 2; × (−1), × 3, × $\frac{5}{3}$

This is *not* an exponential function. As the $x$-values increase by a constant amount, the $y$-values are *not* multiplied by a constant amount.

**Tell whether each set of ordered pairs satisfies an exponential function. Explain your answer.**

**2a.** $\{(-1, 1), (0, 0), (1, 1), (2, 4)\}$ **2b.** $\{(-2, 4), (-1, 2), (0, 1), (1, 0.5)\}$

To graph an exponential function, choose several values of $x$ (positive, negative, and 0) and generate ordered pairs. Plot the points and connect them with a smooth curve.

## EXAMPLE 3 Graphing $y = ab^x$ with $a > 0$ and $b > 1$

**Graph $y = 3(4)^x$.**

*Choose several values of $x$ and generate ordered pairs.*

| $x$ | $y = 3(4)^x$ |
|---|---|
| −1 | 0.75 |
| 0 | 3 |
| 1 | 12 |
| 2 | 48 |

*Graph the ordered pairs and connect with a smooth curve.*

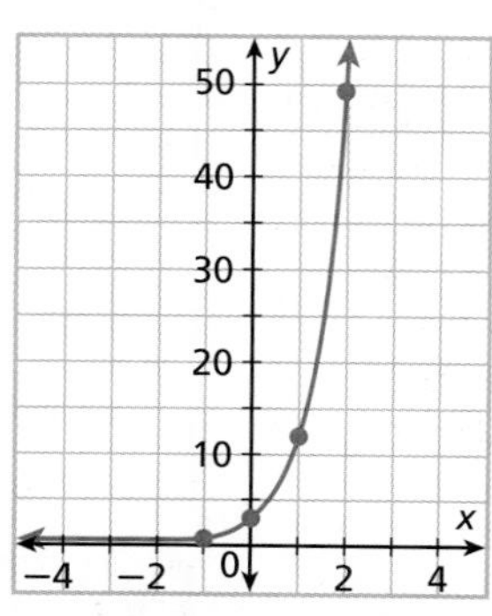

**3a.** Graph $y = 2^x$.

**3b.** Graph $y = 0.2(5)^x$.

## EXAMPLE 4 Graphing $y = ab^x$ with $a < 0$ and $b > 1$

**Graph $y = -5(2)^x$.**

*Choose several values of x and generate ordered pairs.*

| $x$ | $y = -5(2)^x$ |
|---|---|
| −1 | −2.5 |
| 0 | −5 |
| 1 | −10 |
| 2 | −20 |

*Graph the ordered pairs and connect with a smooth curve.*

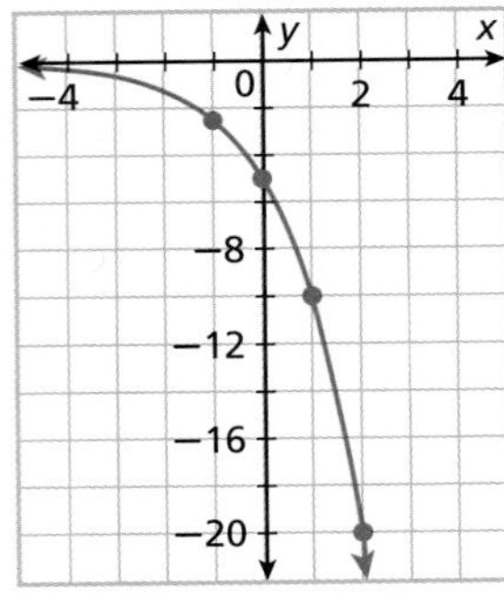

**4a.** Graph $y = -6^x$.

**4b.** Graph $y = -3(3)^x$.

## EXAMPLE 5 Graphing $y = ab^x$ with $0 < b < 1$

**Graph each exponential function.**

**A** $y = 3\left(\frac{1}{2}\right)^x$

*Choose several values of x and generate ordered pairs.*

| $x$ | $y = 3\left(\frac{1}{2}\right)^x$ |
|---|---|
| −1 | 6 |
| 0 | 3 |
| 1 | 1.5 |
| 2 | 0.75 |

*Graph the ordered pairs and connect with a smooth curve.*

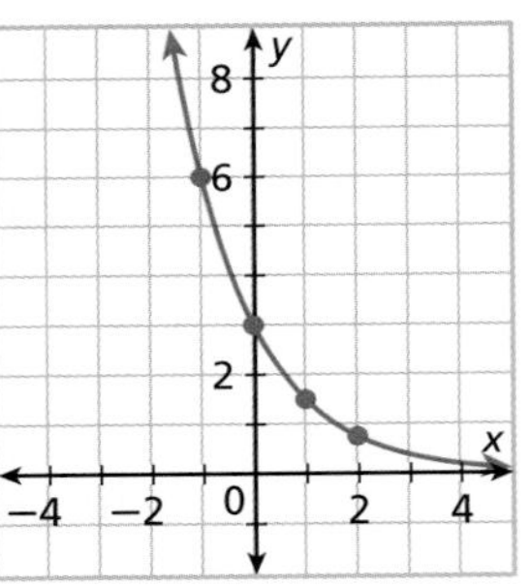

**B** $y = -2(0.4)^x$

*Choose several values of x and generate ordered pairs.*

| $x$ | $y = -2(0.4)^x$ |
|---|---|
| −2 | −12.5 |
| −1 | −5 |
| 0 | −2 |
| 1 | −0.8 |

*Graph the ordered pairs and connect with a smooth curve.*

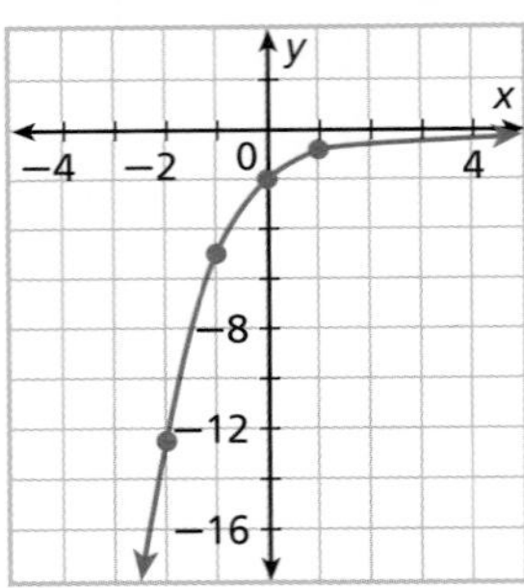

CHECK IT OUT!

**Graph each exponential function.**

**5a.** $y = 4\left(\frac{1}{4}\right)^x$

**5b.** $y = -2(0.1)^x$

The box summarizes the general shapes of exponential function graphs.

Know it! Note

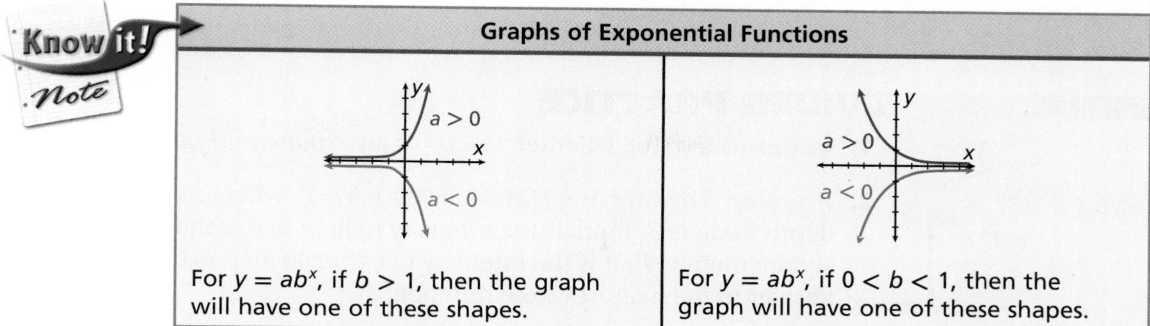


## EXAMPLE 6 *Statistics Application*

**In the year 2000, the world population was about 6 billion, and it was growing by 1.21% each year. At this growth rate, the function $f(x) = 6(1.0121)^x$ gives the population, in billions, $x$ years after 2000. Using this model, in about what year will the population reach 7 billion?**

*Enter the function into the* **Y=** *editor of a graphing calculator.*

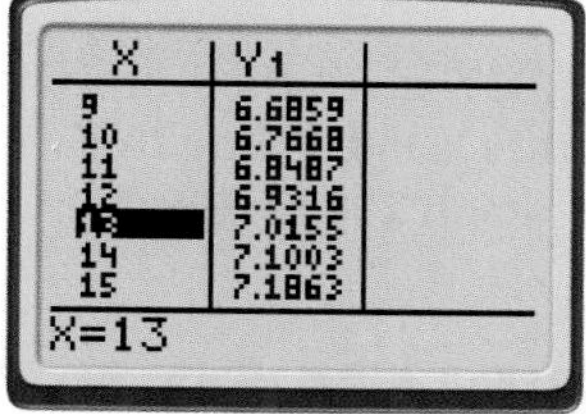


*Press* 2nd GRAPH (TABLE)*. Use the arrow keys to find a y-value as close to 7 as possible. The corresponding x-value is 13.*

The world population will reach 7 billion in about 2013.

**Caution!**

The function values give the population *in billions*, so a *y*-value of 7 means 7 billion.

CHECK IT OUT!

**6.** An accountant uses $f(x) = 12{,}330(0.869)^x$, where $x$ is the time in years since the purchase, to model the value of a car. When will the car be worth \$2000?

## THINK AND DISCUSS

**1.** How can you find the constant ratio of a set of exponential data?

Know it! Note

**2. GET ORGANIZED** Copy and complete the graphic organizer. In each box, give an example of an appropriate exponential function and sketch its graph.

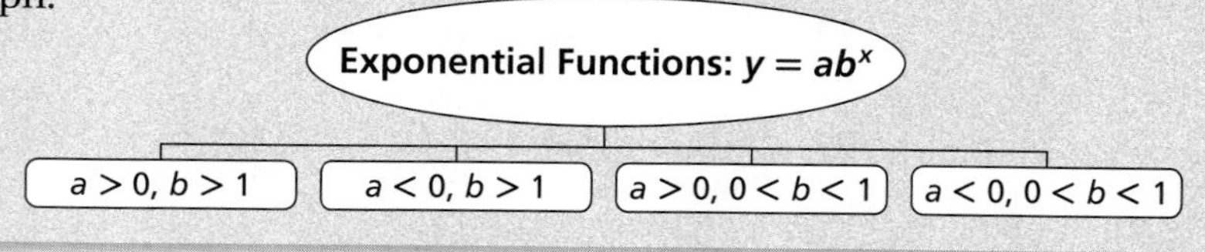

# 11-2 Exercises

MA.A.3.1, MA.A.4.6, MA.A.5.1, MA.A.4.3

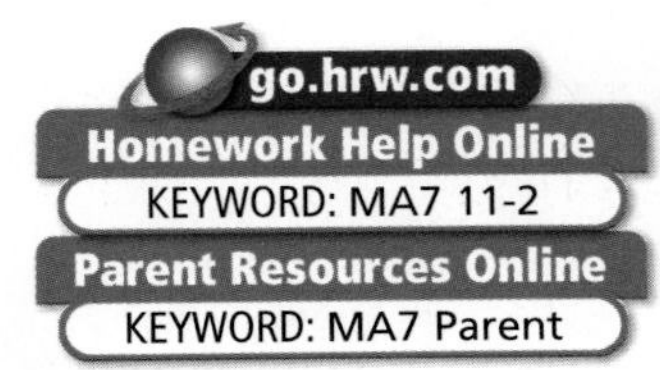


## GUIDED PRACTICE

1. **Vocabulary** Tell whether $y = 3x^4$ is an *exponential function*. Explain your answer.

SEE EXAMPLE 1 p. 772

2. **Physics** The function $f(x) = 50{,}000(0.975)^x$, where $x$ represents the underwater depth in meters, models the intensity of light below the water's surface in lumens per square meter. What is the intensity of light 200 meters below the surface? Round your answer to the nearest whole number.

SEE EXAMPLE 2 p. 773

**Tell whether each set of ordered pairs satisfies an exponential function. Explain your answer.**

3. $\{(-1, -1), (0, 0), (1, -1), (2, -4)\}$
4. $\{(0, 1), (1, 4), (2, 16), (3, 64)\}$

SEE EXAMPLE 3 p. 773

**Graph each exponential function.**

5. $y = 3^x$
6. $y = 5^x$
7. $y = 10(3)^x$
8. $y = 5(2)^x$

SEE EXAMPLE 4 p. 774

9. $y = -2(3)^x$
10. $y = -4(2)^x$
11. $y = -3(2)^x$
12. $y = 2(3)^x$

SEE EXAMPLE 5 p. 774

13. $y = -\left(\frac{1}{4}\right)^x$
14. $y = \left(\frac{1}{3}\right)^x$
15. $y = 2\left(\frac{1}{4}\right)^x$
16. $y = -2(0.25)^x$

SEE EXAMPLE 6 p. 775

17. The function $f(x) = 57.8(1.02)^x$ gives the number of passenger cars, in millions, in the United States $x$ years after 1960. Using this model, in about what year will the number of passenger cars reach 200 million?

## PRACTICE AND PROBLEM SOLVING

**Independent Practice**

| For Exercises | See Example |
|---|---|
| 18–20 | 1 |
| 21–24 | 2 |
| 25–27 | 3 |
| 28–30 | 4 |
| 31–33 | 5 |
| 34 | 6 |

**Extra Practice**
Skills Practice p. S24
Application Practice p. S38

18. **Sports** If a golf ball is dropped from a height of 27 feet, the function $f(x) = 27\left(\frac{2}{3}\right)^x$ gives the height in feet of each bounce, where $x$ is the bounce number. What will be the height of the 4th bounce?

19. Suppose the depth of a lake can be described by the function $y = 334(0.976)^x$, where $x$ represents the number of weeks from today. Today, the depth of the lake is 334 ft. What will the depth be in 6 weeks? Round your answer to the nearest whole number.

20. **Physics** A ball rolling down a slope travels continuously faster. Suppose the function $y = 1.3(1.41)^x$ describes the speed of the ball in inches per minute. How fast will the ball be rolling in 15 minutes? Round your answer to the nearest hundredth.

**Tell whether each set of ordered pairs satisfies an exponential function. Explain your answer.**

21. $\{(-2, 9), (-1, 3), (0, 1), \left(1, \frac{1}{3}\right)\}$
22. $\{(-1, 0), (0, 1), (1, 4), (2, 9)\}$
23. $\{(-1, -5), (0, -3), (1, -1), (2, 1)\}$
24. $\{(-3, 6.25), (-2, 12.5), (-1, 25), (0, 50)\}$

**Graph each exponential function.**

**25.** $y = 1.5^x$ **26.** $y = \frac{1}{3}(3)^x$ **27.** $y = 100(0.7)^x$

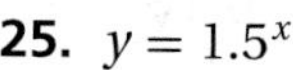

**28.** $y = -2(4)^x$ **29.** $y = -1(5)^x$ **30.** $y = -\frac{1}{2}(4)^x$

**31.** $y = 4\left(\frac{1}{2}\right)^x$ **32.** $y = -2\left(\frac{1}{3}\right)^x$ **33.** $y = 0.5(0.25)^x$

**LINK Technology**

Early silicon chips were about the size of your pinky finger and held one transistor. Today, chips the size of a baby's fingernail hold over 100 million transistors.

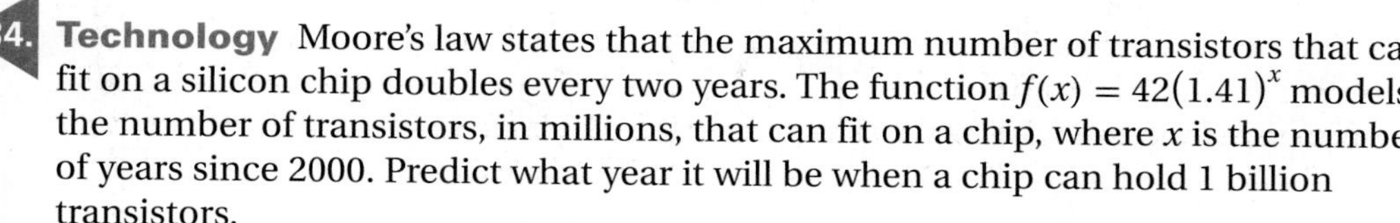

**34. Technology** Moore's law states that the maximum number of transistors that can fit on a silicon chip doubles every two years. The function $f(x) = 42(1.41)^x$ models the number of transistors, in millions, that can fit on a chip, where $x$ is the number of years since 2000. Predict what year it will be when a chip can hold 1 billion transistors.

**35. Multi-Step** A computer randomly creates three different functions. The functions are $y = (3.1x + 7)^2$, $y = 4.8(2)^x$, and $y = \frac{1}{5}(6)^x$. The computer then generates the $y$ value 38.4. Given the three different functions, determine which one is exponential *and* produces the generated number.

**36. Contests** As a promotion, a clothing store draws the name of one of its customers each week. The prize is a coupon for the store. If the winner is not present at the drawing, he or she cannot claim the prize, and the amount of the coupon increases for the following week's drawing. The function $f(x) = 20(1.2)^x$ gives the amount of the coupon in dollars after $x$ weeks of the prize going unclaimed.

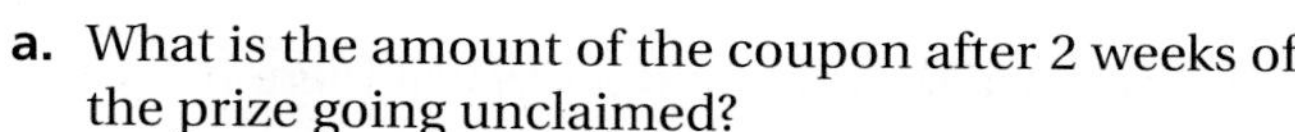

a. What is the amount of the coupon after 2 weeks of the prize going unclaimed?

b. After how many weeks of the prize going unclaimed will the amount of the coupon be greater than $100?

c. What is the original amount of the coupon?

d. Find the percent increase each week.

**37. Critical Thinking** In the definition of exponential function, the value of $b$ cannot be 1, and the value of $a$ cannot be 0. Why?

**Graphing Calculator Graph each group of functions on the same screen. How are their graphs alike? How are they different?**

**38.** $y = 2^x, y = 3^x, y = 4^x$ **39.** $y = \left(\frac{1}{2}\right)^x, y = \left(\frac{1}{3}\right)^x, y = \left(\frac{1}{4}\right)^x$

**Evaluate each of the following for the given value of $x$.**

**40.** $f(x) = 4^x; x = 3$ **41.** $f(x) = -(0.25)^x; x = 1.5$ **42.** $f(x) = 0.4(10)^x; x = -3$

**MULTI-STEP TEST PREP**

**43.** This problem will prepare you for the Multi-Step Test Prep on page 796.

a. The annual tuition at a community college since 2001 is modeled by the equation $C = 2000(1.08)^n$, where $C$ is the tuition cost and $n$ is the number of years since 2001. What was the tuition cost in 2001?

b. What is the annual percentage of tuition increase?

c. Find the tuition cost in 2006.

**44. Write About It** Your employer offers two salary plans. With plan A, your salary is $f(x) = 10{,}000(2x)$, where $x$ is the number of years you have worked for the company. With plan B, your salary is $g(x) = 10{,}000(2)^x$. Which plan would you choose? Why?

MA.A.3.1, MA.A.4.6, MA.A.5.1, MA.A.4.3

**45.** Which graph shows an exponential function?

Ⓐ 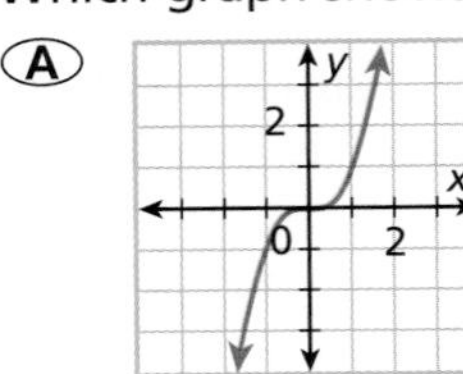

Ⓑ 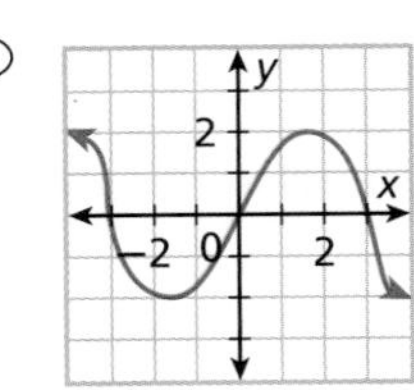

Ⓒ 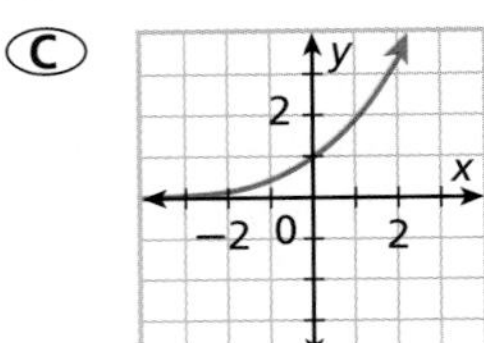

Ⓓ 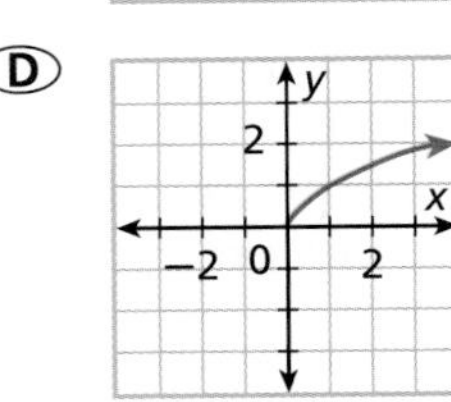

**46.** The function $f(x) = 15(1.4)^x$ represents the area in square inches of a photograph after it has been enlarged $x$ times by a factor of 140%. What is the area of the photograph after it has been enlarged 4 times?

Ⓕ 5.6 square inches

Ⓖ 57.624 square inches

Ⓗ 41.16 square inches

Ⓙ 560 square inches

**47.** Look at the pattern. How many squares will there be in the $n$th stage?

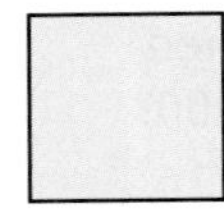
Stage 0

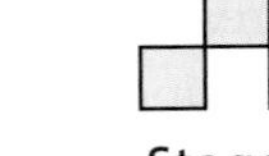
Stage 1

Stage 2

Ⓐ $5n$ Ⓑ $2.5 \cdot 2^n$ Ⓒ $25^{n-1}$ Ⓓ $5^n$

## CHALLENGE AND EXTEND

**Solve each equation.**

**48.** $4^x = 64$

**49.** $\left(\frac{1}{3}\right)^x = \frac{1}{27}$

**50.** $2^x = \frac{1}{16}$

**51.** Graph the following functions: $y = 2(2)^x$, $y = 3(2)^x$, $y = -2(2)^x$. Then make a conjecture about the relationship between the value of $a$ and the $y$-intercept of $y = ab^x$.

## SPIRAL REVIEW

**52.** The average of Roger's three test scores must be at least 90 to earn an A in his science class. Roger has scored 88 and 89 on his first two tests. Write and solve an inequality to find what he must score on the third test to earn an A. *(Lesson 3-4)*

**Find the missing term in each perfect-square trinomial.** *(Lesson 8-5)*

**53.** $x^2 + 10x + \blacksquare$

**54.** $4x^2 + \blacksquare + 64$

**55.** $\blacksquare + 42x + 49$

**56.** What is the 12th term of the sequence 4, 12, 36, 108, ...? *(Lesson 11-1)*

# Increasing and Decreasing Intervals

*Use with Lesson 11-2*

You can analyze the graph of a function to find the intervals where the function increases or decreases. A function is increasing when the $y$-values increase as the $x$-values increase. A function is decreasing when the $y$-values decrease as the $x$-values increase.

You can also analyze the rate at which a function increases or decreases. If the function appears very steep, then the rate of increase or decrease is great. If the function appears very level, then the rate is not great.

**MA.A.3** Analyze patterns of change in functional relationships. **MA.A.3.2** Identify intervals of increase or decrease.

## Activity

A graphing calculator can help determine the intervals for which a function is increasing or decreasing.

**1 Analyze the intervals and rates of increase or decrease for $f(x) = -x^2 - 4x + 3$.**

Graph the function. Use the TRACE function to move along the function from left to right. As you move, notice where the function values increase and where they begin to decrease.

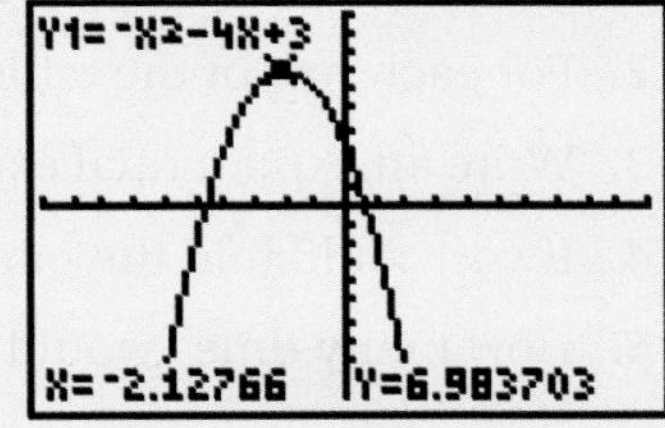


This function increases whenever $x$ is less than $-2$, then it begins to decrease. The function is increasing on the interval $x < -2$ and decreasing on the interval $x > -2$.

Both sides of the function are very steep, so the rates of increase and decrease are great.

**2 Analyze the intervals and rates of increase or decrease for $f(x) = -2(3)^x + 3$.**

The function always decreases, but the rate is very different. Notice that the left side of the function is relatively flat. The function is decreasing slowly. Around the point where $x = -1$, the function begins to decrease more rapidly. For $x$-values greater than $-1$, the rate of decrease is very great.

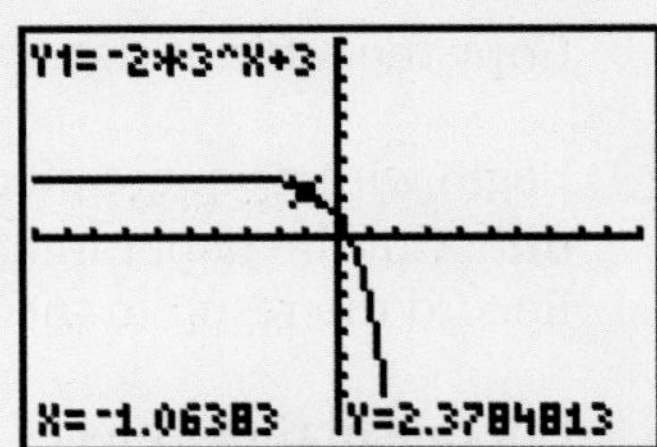


## Try This

**Analyze the intervals and rates of increase or decrease for each function.**

1. $f(x) = x^2 - 5x + 6$
2. $f(x) = -0.2x + 4$
3. $f(x) = \frac{1}{2}(4)^x - 4$
4. $f(x) = 9x - 5$
5. $f(x) = -5x^2 + 20x + 15$
6. $f(x) = -2(5)^x + 6$
7. **Draw a Conclusion** Consider a linear function, $f(x) = mx + b$, where $m$ is positive. What can you conclude about its intervals of increase or decrease?
8. **Draw a Conclusion** Consider a quadratic function $f(x) = ax^2 + bx + c$, where $a$ is negative. What can you conclude about its intervals of increase or decrease?

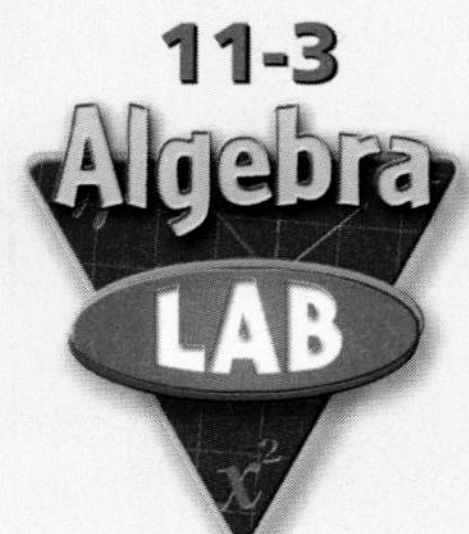


# Model Growth and Decay

You can fold and cut paper to model quantities that increase or decrease exponentially.

**MA.A.3** Analyze patterns of change in functional relationships.
**MA.A.5.1** Represent … exponential relationships in the form of models.

*Use with Lesson 11-3*

## Activity 1

| Folds | Regions |
|---|---|
| 0 | 1 |
| 1 | ■ |
| 2 | ■ |
| 3 | ■ |
| 4 | ■ |
| 5 | ■ |

1. Copy the table at right.
2. Fold a piece of notebook paper in half. Then open it back up. Count the number of regions created by the fold. Record your answer in the table.
3. Now fold the paper in half twice. Record the number of regions created by the folds in the table.
4. Repeat this process for 3, 4, and 5 folds.

## Try This

**1.** When the number of folds increases by 1, the number of regions ___?___ .

**2.** For each row of the table, write the number of regions as a power of 2.

**3.** Write an exponential expression for the number of regions formed by $n$ folds.

**4.** If you could fold the paper 8 times, how many regions would be formed?

**5.** How many times would you have to fold the paper to make 512 regions?

## Activity 2

| Cuts | Area |
|---|---|
| 0 | 1 |
| 1 | ■ |
| 2 | ■ |
| 3 | ■ |
| 4 | ■ |
| 5 | ■ |

1. Copy the table at right.
2. Begin with a square piece of paper. The area of the paper is 1 square unit. Cut the paper in half. Each piece has an area of $\frac{1}{2}$ square unit. Record the result in the table.
3. Cut one of those pieces in half again, and record the area of one of the new, smaller pieces in the table.
4. Repeat this process for 3, 4, and 5 cuts.

## Try This

**6.** When the number of cuts increases by 1, the area ___?___ .

**7.** For each row of the table, write the area as a power of 2.

**8.** Write an exponential expression for the area after $n$ cuts.

**9.** What would be the area after 7 cuts?

**10.** How many cuts would you have to make to get an area of $\frac{1}{256}$ square unit?

# 11-3 Exponential Growth and Decay

**MA.A.5.1** Represent … exponential relationships in the form of models. *Also* **MA.A.3**

***Objective***
Solve problems involving exponential growth and decay.

***Vocabulary***
exponential growth
compound interest
exponential decay
half-life

**Why learn this?**
Exponential growth and decay describe many real-world situations, such as the value of artwork. (See Example 1.)

**Exponential growth** occurs when a quantity increases by the same rate $r$ in each time period $t$. When this happens, the value of the quantity at any given time can be calculated as a function of the rate and the original amount.

**Exponential Growth**

An exponential growth function has the form $y = a(1 + r)^t$, where $a > 0$.

$y$ represents the final amount.
$a$ represents the original amount.
$r$ represents the rate of growth expressed as a decimal.
$t$ represents time.

## EXAMPLE 1 Exponential Growth

**Helpful Hint**
In Example 1, round to the nearest hundredth because the problem deals with money. This means you are rounding to the nearest cent.

**The original value of a painting is \$1400, and the value increases by 9% each year. Write an exponential growth function to model this situation. Then find the value of the painting in 25 years.**

**Step 1** Write the exponential growth function for this situation.

$y = a(1 + r)^t$ — *Write the formula.*

$= 1400(1 + \mathbf{0.09})^t$ — *Substitute 1400 for a and 0.09 for r.*

$= 1400(1.09)^t$ — *Simplify.*

**Step 2** Find the value in 25 years.

$y = 1400(1.09)^t$

$= 1400(1.09)^{25}$ — *Substitute 25 for t.*

$\approx 12{,}072.31$ — *Use a calculator and round to the nearest hundredth.*

The value of the painting in 25 years is \$12,072.31.

1. A sculpture is increasing in value at a rate of 8% per year, and its value in 2000 was \$1200. Write an exponential growth function to model this situation. Then find the sculpture's value in 2006.

A common application of exponential growth is *compound interest*. Recall that simple interest is earned or paid only on the principal. **Compound interest** is interest earned or paid on *both* the principal and previously earned interest.

### Compound Interest

$$A = P\left(1 + \frac{r}{n}\right)^{nt}$$

$A$ represents the balance after $t$ years.

$P$ represents the principal, or original amount.

$r$ represents the annual interest rate expressed as a decimal.

$n$ represents the number of times interest is compounded per year.

$t$ represents time in years.

## EXAMPLE 2 Finance Application

**Write a compound interest function to model each situation. Then find the balance after the given number of years.**

**A** **\$1000 invested at a rate of 3% compounded quarterly; 5 years**

**Step 1** Write the compound interest function for this situation.

$A = P\left(1 + \frac{r}{n}\right)^{nt}$ *Write the formula.*

$= 1000\left(1 + \frac{\mathbf{0.03}}{\mathbf{4}}\right)^{\mathbf{4}t}$ *Substitute 1000 for P, 0.03 for r, and 4 for n.*

$= 1000(1.0075)^{4t}$ *Simplify.*

**Step 2** Find the balance after 5 years.

$A = 1000(1.0075)^{4(5)}$ *Substitute 5 for t.*

$= 1000(1.0075)^{20}$

$\approx 1161.18$ *Use a calculator and round to the nearest hundredth.*

The balance after 5 years is \$1161.18.

**B** **\$18,000 invested at a rate of 4.5% compounded annually; 6 years**

**Step 1** Write the compound interest function for this situation.

$A = P\left(1 + \frac{r}{n}\right)^{nt}$ *Write the formula.*

$= 18{,}000\left(1 + \frac{\mathbf{0.045}}{\mathbf{1}}\right)^{t}$ *Substitute 18,000 for P, 0.045 for r, and 1 for n.*

$= 18{,}000(1.045)^{t}$ *Simplify.*

**Step 2** Find the balance after 6 years.

$A = 18{,}000(1.045)^{6}$ *Substitute 6 for t.*

$\approx 23{,}440.68$ *Use a calculator and round to the nearest hundredth.*

The balance after 6 years is \$23,440.68.

**Reading Math**

For compound interest,

- *annually* means "once per year" ($n = 1$).
- *quarterly* means "4 times per year" ($n = 4$).
- *monthly* means "12 times per year" ($n = 12$).

**Write a compound interest function to model each situation. Then find the balance after the given number of years.**

**2a.** \$1200 invested at a rate of 3.5% compounded quarterly; 4 years

**2b.** \$4000 invested at a rate of 3% compounded monthly; 8 years

**Exponential decay** occurs when a quantity decreases by the same rate $r$ in each time period $t$. Just like exponential growth, the value of the quantity at any given time can be calculated by using the rate and the original amount.

### Exponential Decay

An exponential decay function has the form $y = a(1 - r)^t$, where $a > 0$.

$y$ represents the final amount.

$a$ represents the original amount.

$r$ represents the rate of decay as a decimal.

$t$ represents time.

Notice an important difference between exponential growth functions and exponential decay functions. For exponential growth, the value inside the parentheses will be greater than 1 because $r$ is added to 1. For exponential decay, the value inside the parentheses will be less than 1 because $r$ is subtracted from 1.

## EXAMPLE 3 Exponential Decay

**The population of a town is decreasing at a rate of 1% per year. In 2000 there were 1300 people. Write an exponential decay function to model this situation. Then find the population in 2008.**

**Helpful Hint**

In Example 3, round your answer to the nearest whole number because there can only be a whole number of people.

**Step 1** Write the exponential decay function for this situation.

$y = a(1 - r)^t$ *Write the formula.*

$= 1300(1 - \mathbf{0.01})^t$ *Substitute 1300 for a and 0.01 for r.*

$= 1300(0.99)^t$ *Simplify.*

**Step 2** Find the population in 2008.

$y = 1300(0.99)^8$ *Substitute 8 for t.*

$\approx 1200$ *Use a calculator and round to the nearest whole number.*

The population in 2008 will be approximately 1200 people.

**3.** The fish population in a local stream is decreasing at a rate of 3% per year. The original population was 48,000. Write an exponential decay function to model this situation. Then find the population after 7 years.

A common application of exponential decay is *half-life*. The **half-life** of a substance is the time it takes for one-half of the substance to decay into another substance.

### Half-life

$A = P(0.5)^t$

$A$ represents the final amount.

$P$ represents the original amount.

$t$ represents the number of half-lives in a given time period.

## EXAMPLE 4 *Science Application*

**Fluorine-20 has a half-life of 11 seconds.**

**A** **Find the amount of fluorine-20 left from a 40-gram sample after 44 seconds.**

**Step 1** Find $t$, the number of half-lives in the given time period.

$\frac{44 \text{ s}}{11 \text{ s}} = 4$ *Divide the time period by the half-life. The value of t is 4.*

**Step 2** $A = P(0.5)^t$ *Write the formula.*

$= 40(0.5)^4$ *Substitute 40 for P and 4 for t.*

$= 2.5$ *Use a calculator.*

There are 2.5 grams of fluorine-20 remaining after 44 seconds.

**B** **Find the amount of fluorine-20 left from a 40-gram sample after 2.2 minutes. Round your answer to the nearest hundredth.**

**Step 1** Find $t$, the number of half-lives in the given time period.

$2.2(60) = 132$ *Find the number of seconds in 2.2 minutes.*

$\frac{132 \text{ s}}{11 \text{ s}} = 12$ *Divide the time period by the half-life. The value of t is* $\frac{132}{11} = 12$.

**Step 2** $A = P(0.5)^t$ *Write the formula.*

$= 40(0.5)^{12}$ *Substitute 40 for P and 12 for t.*

$\approx 0.01$ *Use a calculator. Round to the nearest hundredth.*

There is about 0.01 gram of fluorine-20 remaining after 2.2 minutes.

**4a.** Cesium-137 has a half-life of 30 years. Find the amount of cesium-137 left from a 100-milligram sample after 180 years.

**4b.** Bismuth-210 has a half-life of 5 days. Find the amount of bismuth-210 left from a 100-gram sample after 5 weeks. (*Hint:* Change 5 weeks to days.)

### THINK AND DISCUSS

1. Describe three real-world situations that can be described by exponential growth or exponential decay functions.
2. The population of a town after $t$ years can be modeled by $P = 1000(1.02)^t$. Is the population increasing or decreasing? By what percentage rate?
3. An exponential function is a function of the form $y = ab^x$. Explain why both exponential growth functions and exponential decay functions are exponential functions.

4. **GET ORGANIZED** Copy and complete the graphic organizer.

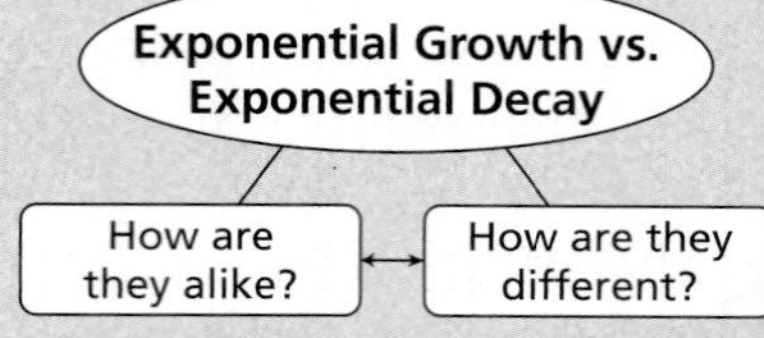

# 11-3 Exercises

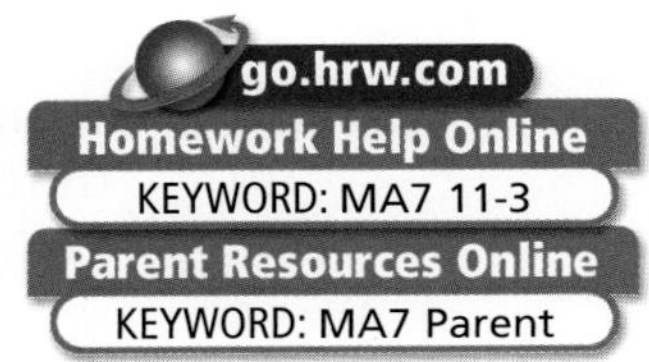


## GUIDED PRACTICE

1. **Vocabulary** The function $y = 0.68(2)^x$ is an example of ___?___. (*exponential growth* or *exponential decay*)

SEE EXAMPLE 1 p. 781

**Write an exponential growth function to model each situation. Then find the value of the function after the given amount of time.**

2. The cost of tuition at a college is $12,000 and is increasing at a rate of 6% per year; 4 years.
3. The number of student-athletes at a local high school is 300 and is increasing at a rate of 8% per year; 5 years.

SEE EXAMPLE 2 p. 782

**Write a compound interest function to model each situation. Then find the balance after the given number of years.**

4. $1500 invested at a rate of 3.5% compounded annually; 4 years
5. $4200 invested at a rate of 2.8% compounded quarterly; 6 years

SEE EXAMPLE 3 p. 783

**Write an exponential decay function to model each situation. Then find the value of the function after the given amount of time.**

6. The value of a car is $18,000 and is depreciating at a rate of 12% per year; 10 years.
7. The amount (to the nearest hundredth) of a 10-mg dose of a certain antibiotic decreases in your bloodstream at a rate of 16% per hour; 4 hours.

SEE EXAMPLE 4 p. 784

8. Bismuth-214 has a half-life of approximately 20 minutes. Find the amount of bismuth-214 left from a 30-gram sample after 1 hour.
9. Mendelevium-258 has a half-life of approximately 52 days. Find the amount of mendelevium-258 left from a 44-gram sample after 156 days.

## PRACTICE AND PROBLEM SOLVING

**Independent Practice**

| For Exercises | See Example |
|---|---|
| 10–13 | 1 |
| 14–17 | 2 |
| 18–19 | 3 |
| 20 | 4 |

**Extra Practice**

Skills Practice p. S24
Application Practice p. S38

**Write an exponential growth function to model each situation. Then find the value of the function after the given amount of time.**

10. Annual sales for a company are $149,000 and are increasing at a rate of 6% per year; 7 years.
11. The population of a small town is 1600 and is increasing at a rate of 3% per year; 10 years.
12. A new savings account starts at $700 and increases at 1.2% yearly; 8 years.
13. Membership of a local club grows at a rate of 7.8% yearly and currently has 30 members; 6 years.

**Write a compound interest function to model each situation. Then find the balance after the given number of years.**

14. $28,000 invested at a rate of 4% compounded annually; 5 years
15. $7000 invested at a rate of 3% compounded quarterly; 10 years
16. $3500 invested at a rate of 1.8% compounded monthly; 4 years
17. $12,000 invested at a rate of 2.6% compounded annually; 15 years

**Write an exponential decay function to model each situation. Then find the value of the function after the given amount of time.**

**18.** The population of a town is 18,000 and is decreasing at a rate of 2% per year; 6 years.

**19.** The value of a book is \$58 and decreases at a rate of 10% per year; 8 years.

**20.** The half-life of bromine-82 is approximately 36 hours. Find the amount of bromine-82 left from an 80-gram sample after 6 days.

**Identify each of the following functions as exponential growth or decay. Then give the rate of growth or decay as a percent.**

**21.** $y = 3(1.61)^t$ **22.** $y = 39(0.098)^t$ **23.** $y = a\left(\frac{2}{3}\right)^t$ **24.** $y = a\left(\frac{3}{2}\right)^t$

**25.** $y = a(1.1)^t$ **26.** $y = a(0.8)^t$ **27.** $y = a\left(\frac{5}{4}\right)^t$ **28.** $y = a\left(\frac{1}{2}\right)^t$

**Write an exponential growth or decay function to model each situation. Then find the value of the function after the given amount of time.**

**29.** The population of a country is 58,000,000 and grows by 0.1% per year; 3 years.

**30.** An antique car is worth \$32,000, and its value grows by 7% per year; 5 years.

**31.** An investment of \$8200 loses value at a rate of 2% per year; 7 years.

**32.** A new car is worth \$25,000, and its value decreases by 15% each year; 6 years.

**33.** The student enrollment in a local high school is 970 students and increases by 1.2% per year; 5 years.

Atlantic Ocean
North Sea
England
Testwood

**34. Archaeology** Carbon-14 dating is a way to determine the age of very old organic objects. Carbon-14 has a half-life of about 5700 years. An organic object with $\frac{1}{2}$ as much carbon-14 as its living counterpart died 5700 years ago. In 1999, archaeologists discovered the oldest bridge in England near Testwood, Hampshire. Carbon dating of the wood revealed that the bridge was 3500 years old. Suppose that when the bridge was built, the wood contained 15 grams of carbon-14. How much carbon-14 would it have contained when it was found by the archaeologists? Round to the nearest hundredth.

A computer-generated image of what the bridge at Testwood might have looked like

**35. ERROR ANALYSIS** Two students were asked to find the value of a \$1000-item after 3 years. The item was depreciating (losing value) at a rate of 40% per year. Which is incorrect? Explain the error.

**A**
$1000(0.6)^3$
\$216

**B**
$1000(0.4)^3$
\$64

**36. Critical Thinking** The value of a certain car can be modeled by the function $y = 20{,}000(0.84)^t$, where $t$ is time in years. Will the value ever be zero? Explain.

**37.** The value of a rare baseball card increases every year at a rate of 4%. Today, the card is worth \$300. The owner expects to sell the card as soon as the value is over \$600. How many years will the owner wait before selling the card? Round your answer to the nearest whole number.

**38.** This problem will prepare you for the Multi-Step Test Prep on page 796.

**a.** The annual tuition at a prestigious university was \$20,000 in 2002. It generally increases at a rate of 9% each year. Write a function to describe the cost as a function of the number of years since 2002. Use 2002 as year zero when writing the function rule.

**b.** What do you predict the cost of tuition will be in 2008?

**c.** Use a table of values to find the first year that the cost of the tuition will be more than twice the cost in 2002.

**39. Multi-Step** At bank A, \$600 is invested with an interest rate of 5% compounded annually. At bank B, \$500 is invested with an interest rate of 6% compounded quarterly. Which account will have a larger balance after 10 years? 20 years?

**40. Estimation** The graph shows the decay of 100 grams of sodium-24. Use the graph to estimate the number of hours it will take the sample to decay to 10 grams. Then estimate the half-life of sodium-24.

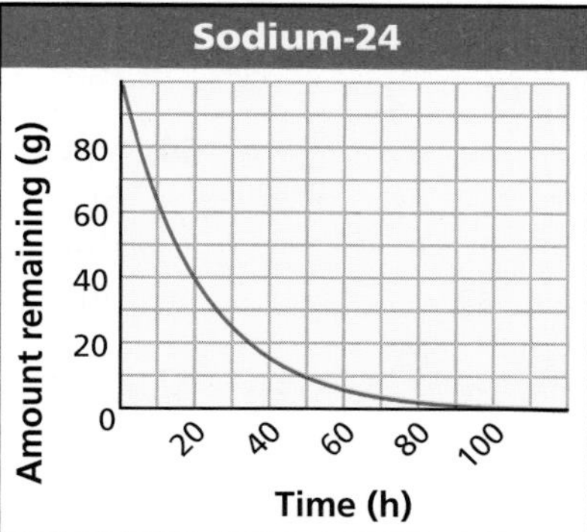

**41. Graphing Calculator** Use a graphing calculator to graph $y = 10(1 + r)^x$ for $r = 10\%$ and $r = 20\%$. Compare the two graphs. How does the value of $r$ affect the graphs?

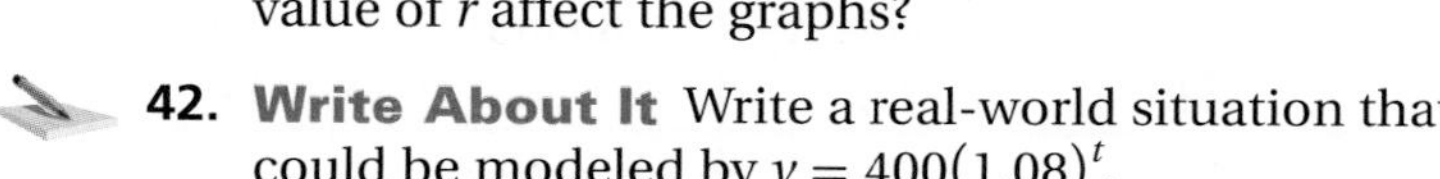

**42. Write About It** Write a real-world situation that could be modeled by $y = 400(1.08)^t$.

**43. Write About It** Write a real-world situation that could be modeled by $y = 800(0.96)^t$.

**44. Critical Thinking** The amount of water in a container doubles every minute. After 6 minutes, the container is full. Your friend says it was half full after 3 minutes. Do you agree? Why or why not?

MA.A.5.1, MA.A.3

**45.** A population of 500 is decreasing by 1% per year. Which function models this situation?

Ⓐ $y = 500(0.01)^t$ Ⓑ $y = 500(0.1)^t$ Ⓒ $y = 500(0.9)^t$ Ⓓ $y = 500(0.99)^t$

**46.** Which function is NOT an exponential decay model?

Ⓕ $y = 5\left(\frac{1}{3}\right)^x$ Ⓖ $y = -5\left(\frac{1}{3}\right)^x$ Ⓗ $y = 5(3)^{-x}$ Ⓙ $y = 5(3^{-1})^x$

**47.** Stephanie wants to save \$1000 for a down payment on a car that she wants to buy in 3 years. She opens a savings account that pays 5% interest compounded annually. About how much should Stephanie deposit now to have enough money for the down payment in 3 years?

Ⓐ \$295 Ⓑ \$333 Ⓒ \$500 Ⓓ \$865

**48. Short Response** In 2000, the population of a town was 1000 and was growing at a rate of 5% per year.

**a.** Write an exponential growth function to model this situation.

**b.** In what year will the population be 1300? Show how you found your answer.

## CHALLENGE AND EXTEND

**49.** You invest \$700 at a rate of 6% compounded quarterly. Use a graph to estimate the number of years it will take for your investment to increase to \$2300.

**50.** Omar invested \$500 at a rate of 4% compounded annually. How long will it take for Omar's money to double? How long would it take if the interest were 8% compounded annually?

**51.** An 80-gram sample of a radioactive substance decayed to 10 grams after 300 minutes. Find the half-life of the substance.

**52.** Praseodymium-143 has a half-life of 2 weeks. The original measurement for the mass of a sample was lost. After 6 weeks, 15 grams of praseodymium-143 remain. How many grams was the original sample?

**53.** Phillip invested some money in a business 8 years ago. Since then, his investment has grown at an average rate of 1.3% compounded quarterly. Phillip's investment is now worth \$250,000. How much was his original investment? Round your answer to the nearest dollar.

**54.** **Personal Finance** Anna has a balance of \$200 that she owes on her credit card. She plans to make a \$30 payment each month. There is also a 1.5% finance charge (interest) on the remaining balance each month. Copy and complete the table to answer the questions below. You may add more rows to the table as necessary.

| Month | Balance (\$) | Monthly Payment (\$) | Remaining Balance (\$) | 1.5% Finance Charge (\$) | New Balance (\$) |
|---|---|---|---|---|---|
| 1 | 200 | 30 | 170 | 2.55 | 172.55 |
| 2 | 172.55 | 30 | ■ | ■ | ■ |
| 3 | ■ | 30 | ■ | ■ | ■ |
| 4 | ■ | 30 | ■ | ■ | ■ |

**a.** How many months will it take Anna to pay the entire balance?

**b.** By the time Anna pays the entire balance, how much total interest will she have paid?

## SPIRAL REVIEW

**Write and solve a proportion for each situation.** *(Lesson 2-7)*

**55.** A daffodil that is 1.2 feet tall casts a shadow that is 1.5 feet long. At the same time, a nearby lamppost casts a shadow that is 20 feet long. What is the height of the the lamppost?

**56.** A green rectangular throw pillow measures 20 inches long by 10 inches wide. A proportionally similar yellow throw pillow is 12 inches long. What is the width of the yellow pillow?

**Graph each function.** *(Lesson 4-4)*

**57.** $f(x) = 2x + 1$ **58.** $f(x) = |x - 4|$ **59.** $f(x) = x^2 - 1$

**60.** The function $f(x) = 0.10(2)^x$ describes the total cost in dollars of a library book fine, where $x$ is the number of days that the book is overdue. What is the amount of the fine if a book is 4 days overdue? How many days overdue is a book if the fine is \$12.80? *(Lesson 11-2)*

# 11-4 Linear, Quadratic, and Exponential Models

**MA.S.2.2** Infer trends in bivariate data displayed in a scatter plot to determine informally if the data is best fit with a linear, exponential or quadratic model. *Also* **MA.A.3.1, MA.A.5.1, MA.A.4.3**

***Objectives***

Compare linear, quadratic, and exponential models.

Given a set of data, decide which type of function models the data and write an equation to describe the function.

**Why learn this?**

Different situations in sports can be described by linear, quadratic, or exponential models.

Look at the tables and graphs below. The data show three ways you have learned that variable quantities can be related. The relationships shown are linear, quadratic, and exponential.

**Linear**

| Training Heart Rate | |
|---|---|
| **Age (yr)** | **Beats/min** |
| 20 | 170 |
| 30 | 161.5 |
| 40 | 153 |
| 50 | 144.5 |

**Quadratic**

| Volleyball Height | |
|---|---|
| **Time (s)** | **Height (ft)** |
| 0.4 | 10.44 |
| 0.8 | 12.76 |
| 1 | 12 |
| 1.2 | 9.96 |

**Exponential**

| Volleyball Tournament | |
|---|---|
| **Round** | **Teams Left** |
| 1 | 16 |
| 2 | 8 |
| 3 | 4 |
| 4 | 2 |

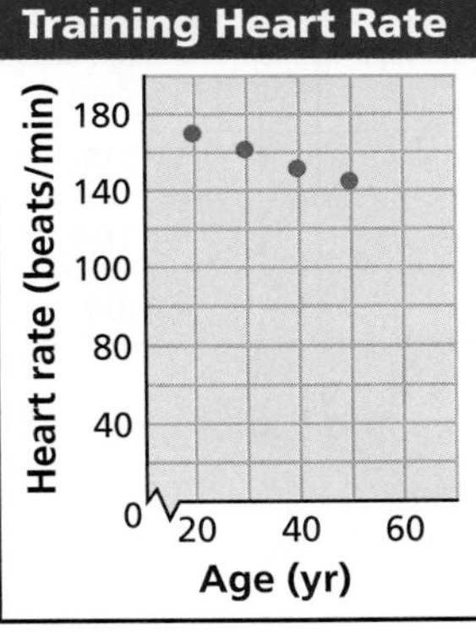


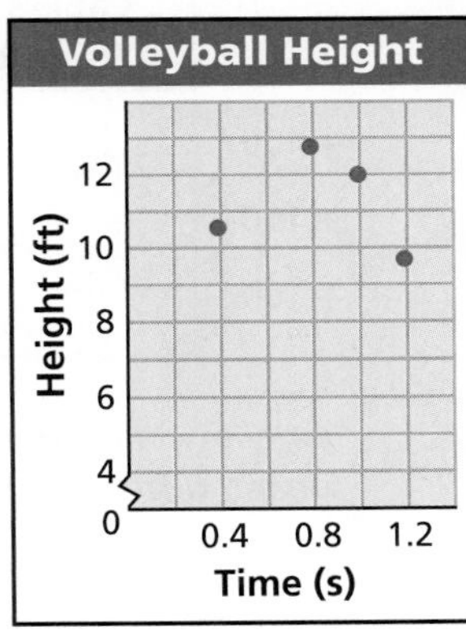


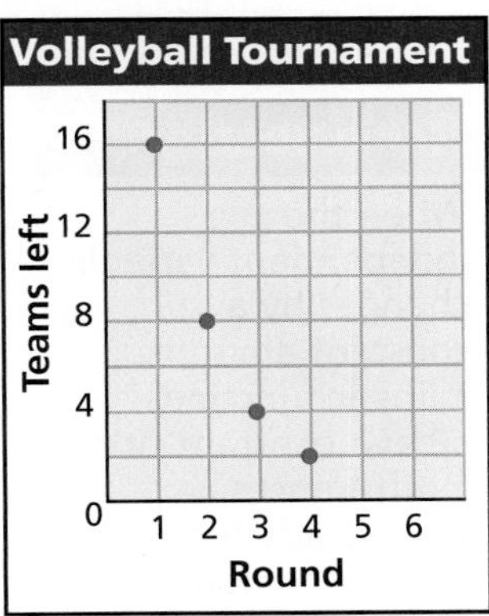


In the real world, people often gather data and then must decide what kind of relationship (if any) they think best describes their data.

## EXAMPLE 1 Graphing Data to Choose a Model

**Graph each data set. Which kind of model best describes the data?**

**A**

| Time (h) | 0 | 1 | 2 | 3 |
|---|---|---|---|---|
| **Bacteria** | 10 | 20 | 40 | 80 |

*Plot the data points and connect them.*

The data appear to be exponential.

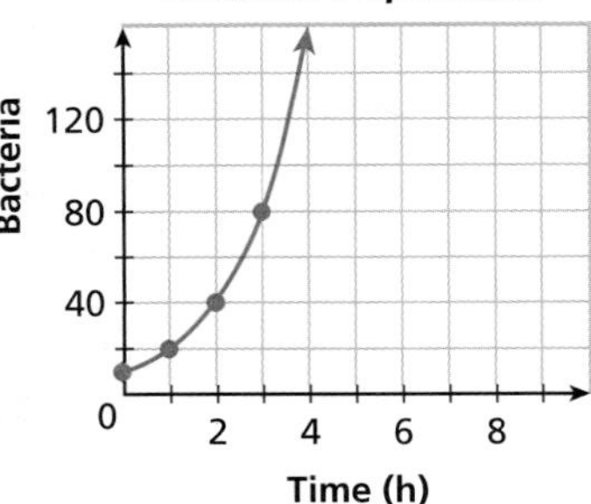

**Graph each data set. Which kind of model best describes the data?**

**B**

| °C | 0 | 5 | 10 | 15 | 20 |
|---|---|---|---|---|---|
| °F | 32 | 41 | 50 | 59 | 68 |

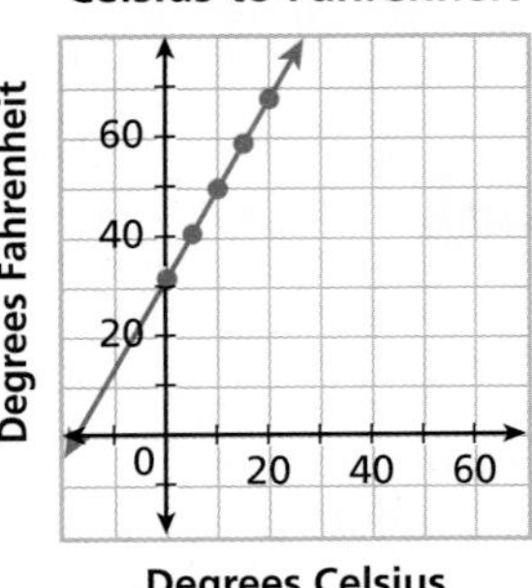


*Plot the data points and connect them.*

The data appear to be linear.

**CHECK IT OUT!** **Graph each data set. Which kind of model best describes the data?**

**1a.** $\{(-3, 0.30), (-2, 0.44), (0, 1), (1, 1.5), (2, 2.25), (3, 3.38)\}$

**1b.** $\{(-3, -14), (-2, -9), (-1, -6), (0, -5), (1, -6), (2, -9), (3, -14)\}$

Another way to decide which kind of relationship (if any) best describes a data set is to use patterns.

## EXAMPLE 2 Using Patterns to Choose a Model

**Look for a pattern in each data set to determine which kind of model best describes the data.**

**A**

| Height of Bridge Suspension Cables | |
|---|---|
| Cable's Distance from Tower (ft) | Cable's Height (ft) |
| 0 | 400 |
| 100 | 256 |
| 200 | 144 |
| 300 | 64 |

Distance: + 100, + 100, + 100. Height: − 144, − 112, − 80; second differences + 32, + 32.

*For every constant change in distance of +100 feet, there is a constant second difference of +32.*

The data appear to be quadratic.

**B**

| Value of a Car | |
|---|---|
| Car's Age (yr) | Value ($) |
| 0 | 20,000 |
| 1 | 17,000 |
| 2 | 14,450 |
| 3 | 12,282.50 |

Age: + 1, + 1, + 1. Value: × 0.85, × 0.85, × 0.85.

*For every constant change in age of +1 year, there is a constant ratio of 0.85.*

The data appear to be exponential.

**Remember!**

When the independent variable changes by a constant amount,
- linear functions have constant first differences.
- quadratic functions have constant second differences.
- exponential functions have a constant ratio.

**CHECK IT OUT!** **2.** Look for a pattern in the data set $\{(-2, 10), (-1, 1), (0, -2), (1, 1), (2, 10)\}$ to determine which kind of model best describes the data.

After deciding which model best fits the data, you can write a function. Recall the general forms of linear, quadratic, and exponential functions.

**General Forms of Functions**

| LINEAR | QUADRATIC | EXPONENTIAL |
|---|---|---|
| $y = mx + b$ | $y = ax^2 + bx + c$ | $y = ab^x$ |

EXAMPLE 3

## Problem-Solving Application

**Use the data in the table to describe how the ladybug population is changing. Then write a function that models the data. Use your function to predict the ladybug population after one year.**

| Ladybug Population | |
|---|---|
| Time (mo) | Ladybugs |
| 0 | 10 |
| 1 | 30 |
| 2 | 90 |
| 3 | 270 |

### 1 Understand the Problem

The **answer** will have three parts—a description, a function, and a prediction.

### 2 Make a Plan

Determine whether the data is linear, quadratic, or exponential. Use the general form to write a function. Then use the function to find the population after one year.

### 3 Solve

**Step 1** Describe the situation in words.

| Ladybug Population | | |
|---|---|---|
| Time (mo) | Ladybugs | |
| 0 | 10 | $\times 3$ |
| 1 | 30 | $\times 3$ |
| 2 | 90 | $\times 3$ |
| 3 | 270 | |

(Time increases by $+1$ each row.)

Each month, the ladybug population is multiplied by 3. In other words, the population triples each month.

**Step 2** Write the function.

There is a constant ratio of 3. The data appear to be exponential.

$y = ab^x$ *Write the general form of an exponential function.*

$y = a(3)^x$ *Substitute the constant ratio, 3, for b.*

$10 = a(3)^0$ *Choose an ordered pair from the table, such as (0, 10). Substitute for x and y.*

$10 = a(1)$ *Simplify.* $3^0 = 1$

$10 = a$ *The value of a is 10.*

$y = 10(3)^x$ *Substitute 10 for a in* $y = a(3)^x$.

**Helpful Hint**

You can choose any given ordered pair to substitute for $x$ and $y$. However, it is often easiest to choose an ordered pair that contains 0.

**Step 3** Predict the ladybug population after one year.

$y = 10(3)^x$ *Write the function.*

$= 10(3)^{12}$ *Substitute 12 for x (1 year = 12 mo).*

$= 5{,}314{,}410$ *Use a calculator.*

There will be 5,314,410 ladybugs after one year.

**Look Back**

You chose the ordered pair $(0, 10)$ to write the function. Check that every other ordered pair in the table satisfies your function.

| $y = 10(3)^x$ | |
|---|---|
| **30** | $10(3)^1$ |
| 30 | $10(3)$ |
| 30 | 30 ✓ |

| $y = 10(3)^x$ | |
|---|---|
| **90** | $10(3)^2$ |
| 90 | $10(9)$ |
| 90 | 90 ✓ |

| $y = 10(3)^x$ | |
|---|---|
| **270** | $10(3)^3$ |
| 270 | $10(27)$ |
| 270 | 270 ✓ |

**3.** Use the data in the table to describe how the oven temperature is changing. Then write a function that models the data. Use your function to predict the temperature after 1 hour.

| **Oven Temperature** | | | | |
|---|---|---|---|---|
| **Time (min)** | 0 | 10 | 20 | 30 |
| **Temperature (°F)** | 375 | 325 | 275 | 225 |

## Student to Student

### *Checking Units*

**Michael Gambhir**
Warren High School

*I used to get a lot of answers wrong because of the units. If a question asked for the value of something after 1 year, I would always just substitute 1 into the function.*

*I finally figured out that you have to check what x is. If x represents months and you're trying to find the value after 1 year, then you have to substitute 12, not 1, because there are 12 months in a year.*

## THINK AND DISCUSS

**1.** Do you think that every data set will be able to be modeled by a linear, quadratic, or exponential function? Why or why not?

**2.** In Example 3, is it certain that there will be 5,314,410 ladybugs after one year? Explain.

**3. GET ORGANIZED** Copy and complete the graphic organizer. In each box, list some characteristics and sketch a graph of each type of model.

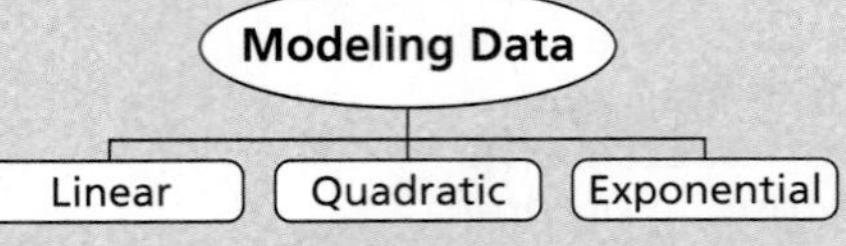

# 11-4 Exercises

MA.S.2.2, MA.A.3.1, MA.A.5.1, MA.A.4.3

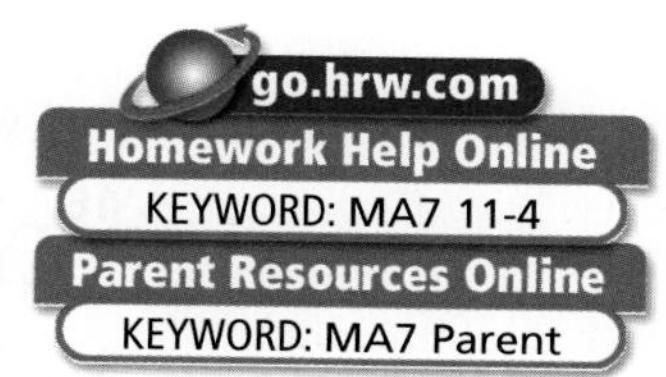


## GUIDED PRACTICE

SEE EXAMPLE 1 p. 789

**Graph each data set. Which kind of model best describes the data?**

1. $\{(-1, 4), (-2, 0.8), (0, 20), (1, 100), (-3, 0.16)\}$
2. $\{(0, 3), (1, 9), (2, 11), (3, 9), (4, 3)\}$
3. $\{(2, -7), (-2, -9), (0, -8), (4, -6), (6, -5)\}$

SEE EXAMPLE 2 p. 790

**Look for a pattern in each data set to determine which kind of model best describes the data.**

4. $\{(-2, 1), (-1, 2.5), (0, 3), (1, 2.5), (2, 1)\}$
5. $\{(-2, 0.75), (-1, 1.5), (0, 3), (1, 6), (2, 12)\}$
6. $\{(-2, 2), (-1, 4), (0, 6), (1, 8), (2, 10)\}$

SEE EXAMPLE 3 p. 791

7. **Consumer Economics** Use the data in the table to describe the cost of grapes. Then write a function that models the data. Use your function to predict the cost of 6 pounds of grapes.

| Total Cost of Grapes | | | | |
|---|---|---|---|---|
| Amount (lb) | 1 | 2 | 3 | 4 |
| Cost ($) | 1.79 | 3.58 | 5.37 | 7.16 |

## PRACTICE AND PROBLEM SOLVING

**Independent Practice**

| For Exercises | See Example |
|---|---|
| 8–10 | 1 |
| 11–13 | 2 |
| 14 | 3 |

**Extra Practice**
Skills Practice p. S24
Application Practice p. S38

**Graph each data set. Which kind of model best describes the data?**

8. $\{(-3, -5), (-2, -8), (-1, -9), (0, -8), (1, -5), (2, 0), (3, 7)\}$
9. $\{(-3, -1), (-2, 0), (-1, 1), (0, 2), (1, 3), (2, 4), (3, 5)\}$
10. $\{(0, 0.1), (2, 0.9), (3, 2.7), (4, 8.1)\}$

**Look for a pattern in each data set to determine which kind of model best describes the data.**

11. $\{(-2, 5), (-1, 4), (0, 3), (1, 2), (2, 1)\}$
12. $\{(-2, 12), (-1, 15), (0, 16), (1, 15), (2, 12)\}$
13. $\{(-2, 8), (-1, 4), (0, 2), (1, 1), (2, 0.5)\}$
14. **Business** Use the data in the table to describe how the company's sales are changing. Then write a function that models the data. Use your function to predict the amount of sales after 10 years.

| Company Sales | | | | |
|---|---|---|---|---|
| Year | 0 | 1 | 2 | 3 |
| Sales ($) | 25,000 | 30,000 | 36,000 | 43,200 |

15. **Multi-Step** Jay's hair grows about 6 inches each year. Write a function that describes the length $\ell$ in inches that Jay's hair will grow for each year $k$. Which kind of model best describes the function?

**Tell which kind of model best describes each situation.**

16. The height of a plant at weekly intervals over the last 6 weeks was 1 inches, 1.5 inches, 2 inches, 2.5 inches, 3 inches., and 3.5 inches.

17. The number of games a baseball player played in the last four years was 162, 162, 162, and 162.

18. The height of a ball in a certain time interval was recorded as 30.64 feet, 30.96 feet, 31 feet, 30.96 feet, and 30.64 feet.

**Write a function to model each set of data.**

19.

| $x$ | −1 | 0 | 1 | 2 | 4 |
|---|---|---|---|---|---|
| $y$ | 0.05 | 0.2 | 0.8 | 3.2 | 51.2 |

20.

| $x$ | −2 | 0 | 2 | 4 | 8 |
|---|---|---|---|---|---|
| $y$ | 5 | 4 | 3 | 2 | 0 |

**Tell which kind of model best describes each graph.**

21.

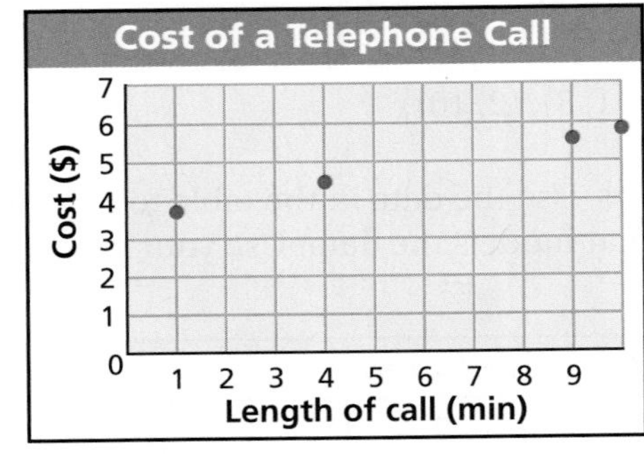


22.

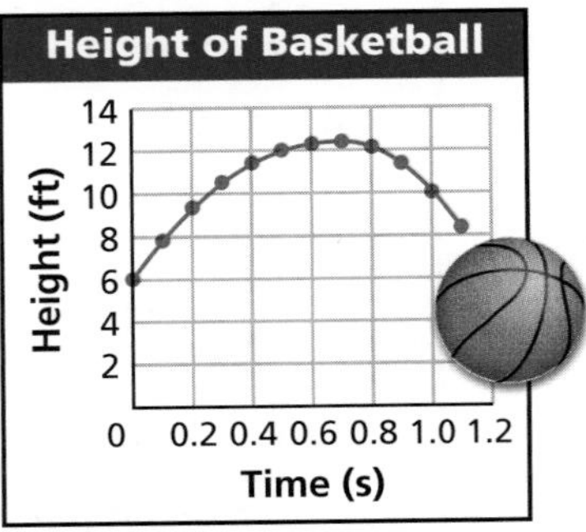


23. **Write About It** Write a set of data that you could model with an exponential function. Explain why the exponential model would work.

24. **ERROR ANALYSIS** A student concluded that the data set would best be modeled by a quadratic function. Explain the student's error.

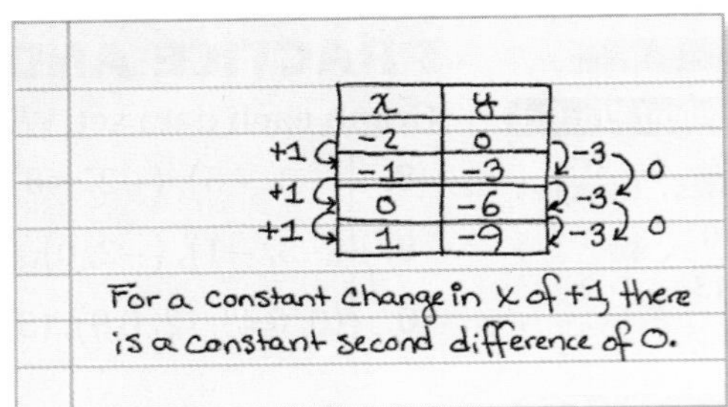


25. **Critical Thinking** Sometimes the graphs of quadratic data and exponential data can look very similar. Describe how you can tell them apart.

26. This problem will prepare you for the Multi-Step Test Prep on page 796.

a. Examine the two models that represent annual tuition for two colleges. Describe each model as linear, quadratic, or exponential.

b. Write a function rule for each model.

c. Both models have the same values for 2004. What does this mean?

d. Why do both models have the same value for year 1?

| Years After 2004 | Tuition at College 1 ($) | Tuition at College 2 ($) |
|---|---|---|
| 0 | 2000.00 | 2000.00 |
| 1 | 2200.00 | 2200.00 |
| 2 | 2400.00 | 2420.00 |
| 3 | 2600.00 | 2662.00 |
| 4 | 2800.00 | 2928.20 |

**MA.S.2.2, MA.A.3.1, MA.A.5.1, MA.A.4.3**

27. Which function best models the data: $\{(-4, -2), (-2, -1), (0, 0), (2, 1), (4, 2)\}$?

    (A) $y = \left(\frac{1}{2}\right)^x$ (B) $y = \frac{1}{2}x^2$ (C) $y = \frac{1}{2}x$ (D) $y = \left(\frac{1}{2}x\right)^2$

28. A city's population is increasing at a rate of 2% per year. Which type of model describes this situation?

    (F) Exponential (G) Quadratic (H) Linear (J) None of these

29. Which data set is best modeled by a linear function?

    (A) $\{(-2, 0), (-1, 2), (0, -4), (1, -1), (2, 2)\}$

    (B) $\{(-2, 2), (-1, 4), (0, 6), (1, 16), (2, 32)\}$

    (C) $\{(-2, 2), (-1, 4), (0, 6), (1, 8), (2, 10)\}$

    (D) $\{(-2, 0), (-1, 5), (0, 7), (1, 5), (2, 0)\}$

## CHALLENGE AND EXTEND

30. **Finance** An accountant estimates that a certain new automobile worth \$18,000 will lose value at a rate of 16% per year.
    a. Make a table that shows the worth of the car for years 0, 1, 2, 3, and 4. What is the real-world meaning of year 0?
    b. Which type of model best represents the data in your table? Explain.
    c. Write a function for your data.
    d. What is the value of the car after $5\frac{1}{2}$ years?
    e. What is the value of the car after 8 years?

31. **Pet Care** The table shows general guidelines for the weight of a Great Dane at various ages.
    a. None of the three models in this lesson—linear, quadratic, or exponential—fits this data exactly. Which of these is the *best* model for the data? Explain your choice.
    b. What would you predict for the weight of a Great Dane who is 1 year old?
    c. Do you think you could use your model to find the weight of a Great Dane at any age? Why or why not?

| Great Dane | |
|---|---|
| **Age (mo)** | **Weight (kg)** |
| 2 | 12 |
| 4 | 23 |
| 6 | 33 |
| 8 | 40 |
| 10 | 45 |

## SPIRAL REVIEW

**Write an algebraic expression for each situation.** *(Lesson 1-1)*

32. the total number of kilometers run by Helen in $n$ 5-kilometer races

33. the average gas mileage of a car that travels 145 miles on $g$ gallons of gasoline

34. Lorraine's height if she is $b$ inches shorter than Gene, who is 74 inches tall

**Solve by using square roots.** *(Lesson 9-7)*

35. $4x^2 = 100$ 36. $10 - x^2 = 10$ 37. $16x^2 + 5 = 86$

**Graph each exponential function.** *(Lesson 11-2)*

38. $y = 6^x$ 39. $y = -2(5)^x$ 40. $y = \left(\frac{1}{3}\right)^x$

CHAPTER 11

SECTION 11A

## Exponential Functions

**Dollars for Scholars** In 1980, the average annual tuition at two-year colleges was \$350. Since then, the cost of tuition has increased by an average of 9% each year.

1. Write a function rule that models the annual growth in tuition at two-year colleges since 1980. Let 1980 be year zero in your function. Identify the variables, and tell which is independent and which is dependent.
2. Use your function to determine the average annual tuition in 2006. Use a table and a graph to support your answer.
3. Use your function to predict the average annual tuition at two-year colleges for the year you plan to graduate from high school.
4. In what year is the average annual tuition twice as much as in 1980? Use a table and a graph to support your answer.
5. In what year does the average annual tuition reach \$1000? Use a table and a graph to support your answer.

# READY TO GO ON?

CHAPTER 11

SECTION 11A

## Quiz for Lessons 11-1 Through 11-4

### 11-1 Geometric Sequences

**Find the next three terms in each geometric sequence.**

1. 3, 6, 12, 24, ...
2. −1, 2, −4, 8, ...
3. −2400, −1200, −600, −300, ...
4. The first term of a geometric sequence is 2 and the common ratio is 3. What is the 8th term of the sequence?
5. The table shows the distance swung by a pendulum during its first three swings. The values form a geometric sequence. What will be the length of the 7th swing?

| Swing | Length (cm) |
|---|---|
| 1 | 1000 |
| 2 | 800 |
| 3 | 640 |

### 11-2 Exponential Functions

6. The function $f(x) = 3(1.1)^x$ gives the length (in inches) of an image after being enlarged by 10% $x$ times. What is the length of the image after it has been enlarged 4 times? Round your answer to the nearest hundredth.

**Graph each exponential function.**

7. $y = 3^x$
8. $y = 2(2)^x$
9. $y = -2(4)^x$
10. $y = -(0.5)^x$
11. The function $f(x) = 40(0.8)^x$ gives the amount of a medication in milligrams present in a patient's system $x$ hours after taking a 40-mg dose. In how many hours will there be less than 2 mg of the drug in a patient's system?

### 11-3 Exponential Growth and Decay

**Write a function to model each situation. Then find the value of the function after the given amount of time.**

12. Fiona's salary is $30,000, and she expects to receive a 3% raise each year; 10 years.
13. $2000 is invested at a rate of 4.5% compounded monthly; 3 years.
14. A $1200 computer is losing value at a rate of 20% per year; 4 years.
15. Strontium-90 has a half-life of 29 years. About how much strontium-90 will be left from a 100-mg sample after 290 years? Round your answer to the nearest thousandth.

### 11-4 Linear, Quadratic, and Exponential Models

**Graph each data set. Which kind of model best describes the data?**

16. $\{(-2, 5), (3, 10), (0, 1), (1, 2), (0.5, 1.25)\}$
17. $\{(0, 3), (2, 12), (-1, 1.5), (-3, 0.375), (4, 48)\}$

**Look for a pattern in each data set to determine which kind of model best describes the data.**

18. $\{(-2, -6), (-1, -5), (0, -4), (1, -3), (2, -2)\}$
19. $\{(-2, -24), (-1, -12), (0, -6), (1, -3)\}$
20. Use the data in the table to describe how the value of the stamp is changing. Then write a function that models the data. Use your function to predict the value of the stamp in 11 years.

| Value of Collectible Stamp | | | | |
|---|---|---|---|---|
| Year | 0 | 1 | 2 | 3 |
| Value ($) | 5.00 | 6.00 | 7.20 | 8.64 |

# 11-5 Square-Root Functions

**MA.A.4.2** Use appropriate terminology and notation...associated with functions. *Also.* **MA.A.4.3**

***Objectives***
Identify square-root functions and their domains and ranges.

Graph square-root functions.

***Vocabulary***
square-root function

**Who uses this?**
Astronauts can use square-root functions to calculate their speed in free fall.

Astronauts at NASA practice living in the weightlessness of space by training in the KC-135, also known as the "Vomit Comet." This aircraft flies to a certain altitude and then free falls for a period of time, simulating a zero-gravity environment.

The function $y = 8\sqrt{x}$ gives the speed in feet per second of an object in free fall after falling $x$ feet. This function is different from others you have seen so far. It contains a variable under the square-root sign, $\sqrt{\ }$.

**Square-Root Function**

| WORDS | EXAMPLES | NONEXAMPLES |
|---|---|---|
| A **square-root function** is a function whose rule contains a variable under a square-root sign. | $y = \sqrt{x}$<br>$y = \sqrt{2x + 1}$<br>$y = 3\sqrt{\frac{x}{2}} - 6$ | $y = x^2$<br>$y = \frac{2}{x + 1}$<br>$y = \sqrt{3}x$ |

## EXAMPLE 1 Evaluating Square-Root Functions

**A** **Find the speed of an object in free fall after it has fallen 4 feet.**

$y = 8\sqrt{x}$ *Write the speed function.*

$= 8\sqrt{4}$ *Substitute 4 for x.*

$= 8(2)$ *Simplify.*

$= 16$

After an object has fallen 4 feet, its speed is 16 ft/s.

**B** **Find the speed of an object in free fall after it has fallen 50 feet. Round your answer to the nearest tenth.**

$y = 8\sqrt{x}$ *Write the speed function.*

$= 8\sqrt{50}$ *Substitute 50 for x.*

$\approx 56.6$ *Use a calculator.*

After an object has fallen 50 feet, its speed is about 56.6 ft/s.

**Helpful Hint**

Check that your answer is reasonable. In Example 1B, $8\sqrt{49} = 8(7) = 56$, so $8\sqrt{50} \approx 56.6$ is reasonable.

CHECK IT OUT!

**1a.** Find the speed of an object in free fall after it has fallen 25 feet.

**1b.** Find the speed of an object in free fall after it has fallen 15 feet. Round your answer to the nearest hundredth.

Recall that the square root of a negative number is not a real number. The domain ($x$-values) of a square-root function is restricted to numbers that make the value under the radical sign greater than or equal to 0.

## EXAMPLE 2 Finding the Domain of Square-Root Functions

**Find the domain of each square-root function.**

**A** $y = \sqrt{x+4} - 3$

$x + 4 \geq 0$ — *The expression under the radical sign must be greater than or equal to 0.*

$\underline{-4 \quad -4}$ — *Solve the inequality. Subtract 4 from both sides.*

$x \geq -4$

The domain is the set of all real numbers greater than or equal to $-4$.

**B** $y = \sqrt{3(x-2)}$

$3(x-2) \geq 0$ — *The expression under the radical sign must be greater than or equal to 0.*

$3x - 6 \geq 0$ — *Solve the inequality. Distribute 3 on the left side.*

$\underline{+6 \quad +6}$ — *Add 6 to both sides.*

$3x \geq 6$

$x \geq 2$ — *Divide both sides by 3.*

The domain is the set of all real numbers greater than or equal to 2.

**Find the domain of each square-root function.**

**2a.** $y = \sqrt{2x-1}$ **2b.** $y = \sqrt{3x-5}$

The parent function for square-root functions, $f(x) = \sqrt{x}$, is graphed at right. Notice there are no $x$-values to the left of 0 because the domain is $x \geq 0$.

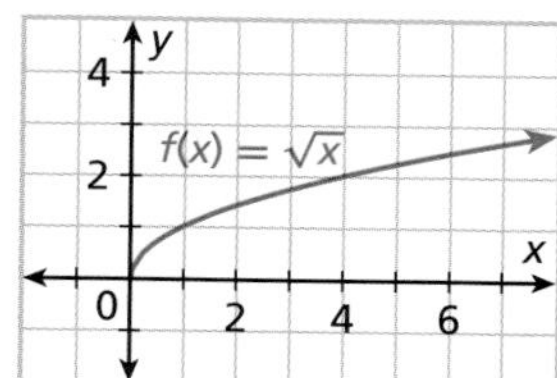

### Translations of the Graph of $f(x) = \sqrt{x}$

| The graph of $f(x) = \sqrt{x} + c$ is a vertical translation of the graph of $f(x) = \sqrt{x}$. | The graph of $f(x) = \sqrt{x-a}$ is a horizontal translation of the graph of $f(x) = \sqrt{x}$. |
|---|---|
| 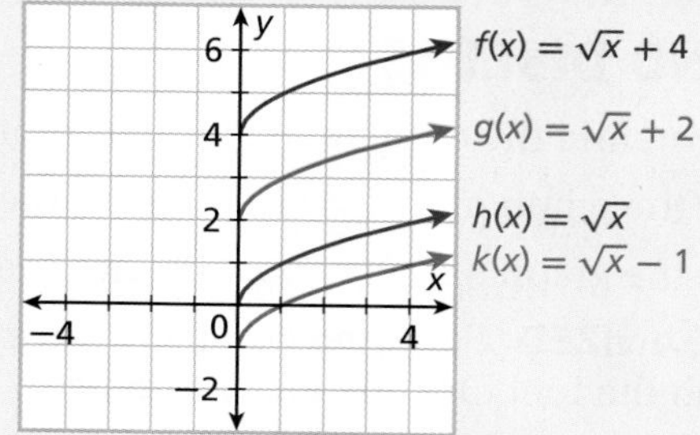 | 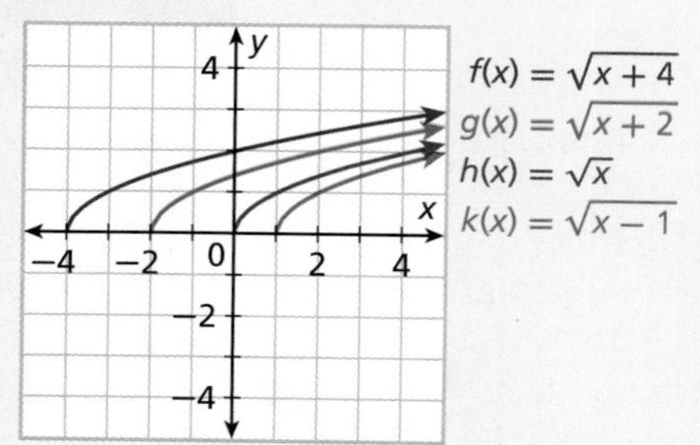 |
| The graph is translated $c$ units up for $c > 0$ and $c$ units down for $c < 0$. | The graph is translated $a$ units right for $a > 0$ and $a$ units left for $a < 0$. |





If a square-root function is given in one of these forms, you can graph the parent function $f(x) = \sqrt{x}$ and translate it vertically or horizontally.

## EXAMPLE 3 Graphing Square-Root Functions

**A** **Graph $f(x) = \sqrt{x - 4}$.**

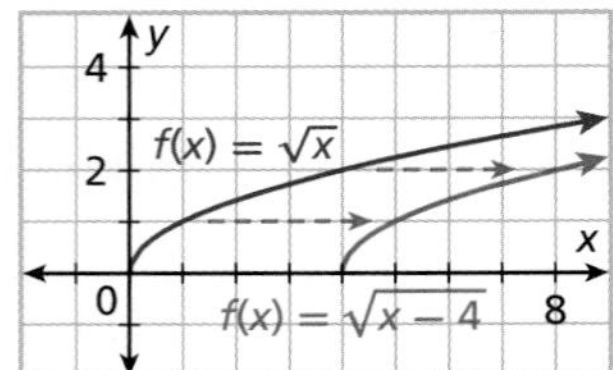


*Since this function is in the form $f(x) = \sqrt{x - a}$, you can graph it as a horizontal translation of the graph of $f(x) = \sqrt{x}$.*

*Graph $f(x) = \sqrt{x}$ and then shift the graph 4 units to the right.*

### Helpful Hint

In Example 3B, when generating ordered pairs, choose *x*-values that make the expression under the radical sign a perfect square.

**B** **Graph $f(x) = \sqrt{2x} + 3$.**

*This is not a horizontal or vertical translation of the graph of $f(x) = \sqrt{x}$.*

**Step 1** Find the domain of the function.

$2x \geq 0$ *The expression under the radical sign must be greater than or equal to 0.*

$x \geq 0$ *Solve the inequality by dividing both sides by 2.*

The domain is the set of all real numbers greater than or equal to 0.

**Step 2** Choose *x*-values greater than or equal to 0 and generate ordered pairs.

| x | $f(x) = \sqrt{2x} + 3$ |
|---|---|
| 0 | 3 |
| 2 | 5 |
| 8 | 7 |
| 18 | 9 |
| 32 | 11 |

**Step 3** Plot the points. Then connect them with a smooth curve.

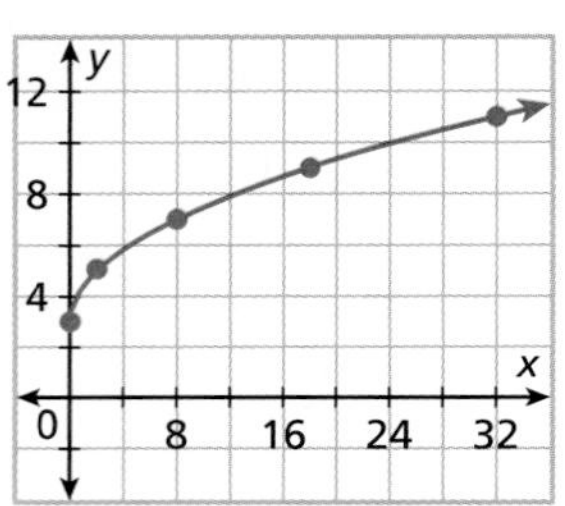

**Graph each square-root function.**

**3a.** $f(x) = \sqrt{x} + 2$ **3b.** $f(x) = 2\sqrt{x} + 3$

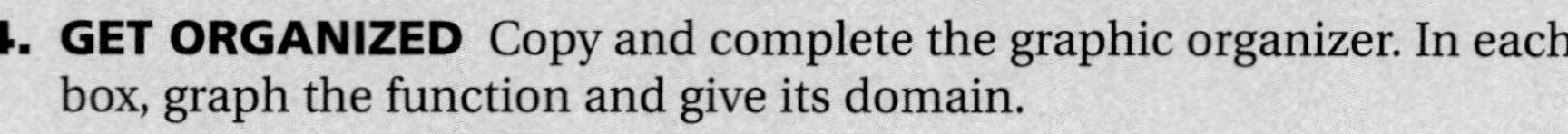

## THINK AND DISCUSS

1. How do you find the domain of a square-root function?
2. Compare the graph of $f(x) = \sqrt{x + 8}$ with the graph of $f(x) = \sqrt{x}$.
3. Compare the graph of $f(x) = \sqrt{x + 8}$ with the graph of $f(x) = \sqrt{x} + 8$.

4. **GET ORGANIZED** Copy and complete the graphic organizer. In each box, graph the function and give its domain.

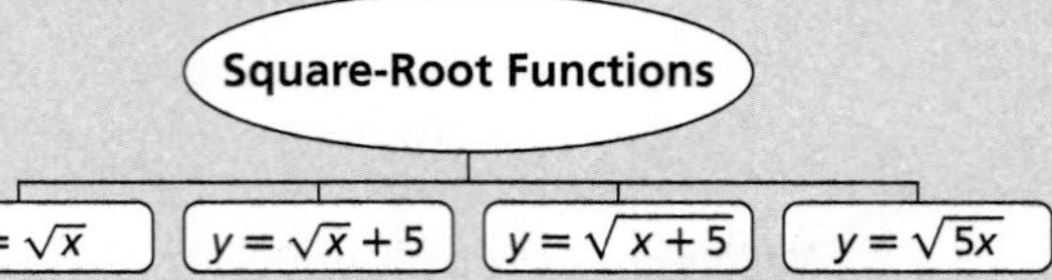

# 11-5 Exercises

MA.A.4.2, MA.A.4.3

go.hrw.com
Homework Help Online
KEYWORD: MA7 11-5
Parent Resources Online
KEYWORD: MA7 Parent

## GUIDED PRACTICE

1. **Vocabulary** Explain why $y = x + \sqrt{3}$ is not a *square-root function.*

SEE EXAMPLE 1 p. 798

2. **Geometry** In a right triangle, $c = \sqrt{a^2 + b^2}$, where $c$ is the length of the hypotenuse (the longest side) and $a$ and $b$ are the lengths of the other two sides, called the legs. What is the length of the hypotenuse of a right triangle if its legs measure 14 cm and 8 cm? Round your answer to the nearest hundredth.

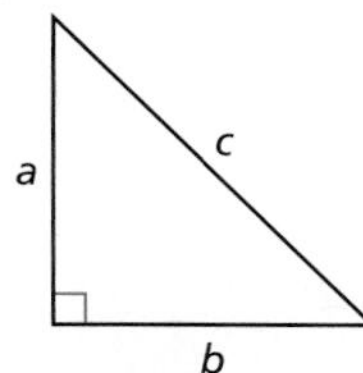


SEE EXAMPLE 2 p. 799

**Find the domain of each square-root function.**

3. $y = \sqrt{x + 6}$
4. $y = 4 - \sqrt{3 - x}$
5. $y = \sqrt{2x} - 5$
6. $y = \sqrt{x + 2}$
7. $y = \sqrt{3x + 9}$
8. $y = x + \sqrt{x - 5}$

SEE EXAMPLE 3 p. 800

**Graph each square-root function.**

9. $f(x) = \sqrt{x - 1}$
10. $f(x) = -\sqrt{2x}$
11. $f(x) = \sqrt{x} + 1$
12. $f(x) = \sqrt{x} - 12$
13. $f(x) = \sqrt{4 - x}$
14. $f(x) = \sqrt{x + 4}$

## PRACTICE AND PROBLEM SOLVING

**Independent Practice**

| For Exercises | See Example |
|---|---|
| 15 | 1 |
| 16–27 | 2 |
| 28–33 | 3 |

**Extra Practice**

Skills Practice p. S25
Application Practice p. S38

15. **Law Enforcement** At the scene of a car accident, police measure the length of the skid marks to estimate the speed that the car was traveling. On dry concrete, $f(x) = \sqrt{24x}$ gives the speed in mi/h when the length of the skid mark is $x$ feet. Find the speed that a car was traveling if it left a skid mark that was 104 ft long. Round your answer to the nearest hundredth.

**Find the domain of each square-root function.**

16. $y = \sqrt{8 - 2x}$
17. $y = 4 - \sqrt{\frac{x}{2}}$
18. $y = \sqrt{3x + 2}$
19. $y = \sqrt{-2x + 3}$
20. $y = 2\sqrt{x + 1} - 2$
21. $y = \sqrt{3(x + 2) - 1}$
22. $y = \sqrt{2(x + 4)} - 3$
23. $y = 7\sqrt{\frac{x}{5} - 8}$
24. $y = \sqrt{2(3x - 6)}$
25. $y = \sqrt{\frac{1}{3}(x - 9)}$
26. $y = \sqrt{2(x + 7) - 6}$
27. $y = 4 + \sqrt{3x + 2}$

**Graph each square-root function.**

28. $f(x) = \sqrt{x - 5}$
29. $f(x) = \sqrt{2x} - 4$
30. $f(x) = -1 - \sqrt{x}$
31. $f(x) = \sqrt{x} - 4$
32. $f(x) = 3\sqrt{x - 6}$
33. $f(x) = \frac{1}{2}\sqrt{x + 4}$

34. **Geometry** If you know a circle's area, you can use the formula $r = \sqrt{\frac{A}{\pi}}$ to find the radius. What is the radius of a circle whose area is 60 cm$^2$? Use 3.14 for $\pi$. Round your answer to the nearest hundredth of a centimeter.

35. **Graphing Calculator** Use a graphing calculator for the following.
    a. Graph $y = \sqrt{x}$, $y = \frac{1}{2}\sqrt{x}$, $y = 2\sqrt{x}$, $y = 3\sqrt{x}$, and $y = 4\sqrt{x}$ on the same screen.
    b. What is the domain of each function?
    c. What is the range of each function?
    d. Describe the characteristics of $y = a\sqrt{x}$ for $a > 0$.

**36. Graphing Calculator** Use a graphing calculator for the following.

a. Graph $y = -\sqrt{x}$, $y = -\frac{1}{2}\sqrt{x}$, $y = -2\sqrt{x}$, $y = -3\sqrt{x}$, and $y = -4\sqrt{x}$ on the same screen.

b. What is the domain of each function?

c. What is the range of each function?

d. Describe the characteristics of $y = a\sqrt{x}$ for $a < 0$.

**37.** The distance $d$ between two points $(x, y)$ and $(w, z)$ in the coordinate plane can be found by using the formula $d = \sqrt{(w - x)^2 + (z - y)^2}$. What is the distance between the points (2, 1) and (5, 3)? Round your answer to the nearest hundredth.

**LINK**

**Geology**

In December 2004, devastating tsunamis struck south and southeast Asia and eastern Africa. A worldwide relief effort ensued. Aid from the United States, both public and private, totaled over $2 billion in the year following the disaster.

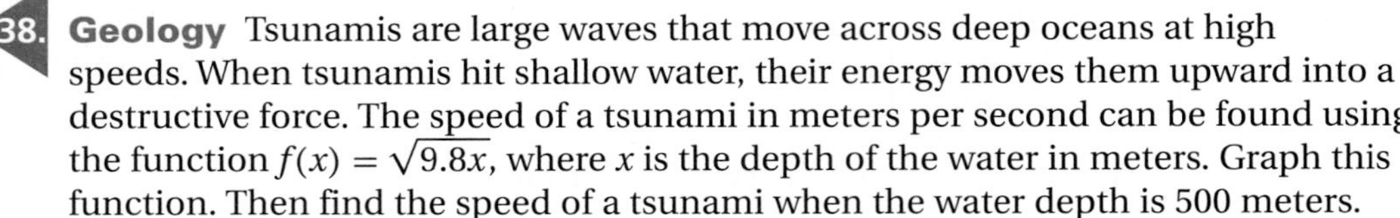

**38. Geology** Tsunamis are large waves that move across deep oceans at high speeds. When tsunamis hit shallow water, their energy moves them upward into a destructive force. The speed of a tsunami in meters per second can be found using the function $f(x) = \sqrt{9.8x}$, where $x$ is the depth of the water in meters. Graph this function. Then find the speed of a tsunami when the water depth is 500 meters.

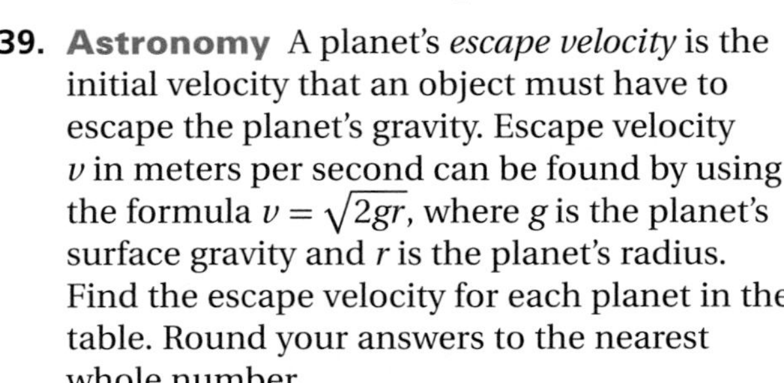

**39. Astronomy** A planet's *escape velocity* is the initial velocity that an object must have to escape the planet's gravity. Escape velocity $v$ in meters per second can be found by using the formula $v = \sqrt{2gr}$, where $g$ is the planet's surface gravity and $r$ is the planet's radius. Find the escape velocity for each planet in the table. Round your answers to the nearest whole number.

| Planet | $g$ (m/s$^2$) | $r$ (m) |
|---|---|---|
| Mercury | 3.7 | $2.4 \times 10^6$ |
| Venus | 8.8 | $6.1 \times 10^6$ |
| Earth | 9.8 | $6.4 \times 10^6$ |
| Mars | 3.7 | $3.4 \times 10^6$ |

**40. Geometry** The volume $V$ of a cylinder can be found by using the formula $V = \pi r^2 h$, where $r$ represents the radius of the cylinder and $h$ represents its height. Find the radius of a cylinder whose volume is 1212 in$^3$ and whose height is 10 inches. Use 3.14 for $\pi$.

**41. Write About It** Explain how to find the domain of a square-root function. Why is the domain not all real numbers?

**42. Multi-Step** For the function $y = \sqrt{3(x - 5)}$, find the value of $y$ that corresponds to the least possible value for $x$.

**43. Critical Thinking** Can the range of a square-root function be all real numbers? Explain.

**44.** This problem will prepare you for the Multi-Step Test Prep on page 830.

a. The Ocean Motion ride at Ohio's Cedar Point amusement park is a giant ship that swings like a pendulum. If a pendulum is under the influence of gravity only, then the time in seconds that it takes for one complete swing back and forth (called the pendulum's period) is $T = 2\pi\sqrt{\frac{\ell}{32}}$, where $\ell$ is the length of the pendulum in feet. What is the domain of this function?

b. What is the period of a pendulum whose length is 80 feet? Use 3.14 for $\pi$ and round your answer to the nearest hundredth.

c. The length of the Ocean Motion pendulum is about 80 feet. Do you think your answer to part **b** is its period? Explain why or why not.

MA.A.4.2,
MA.A.4.3

45. Which function is graphed at right?

Ⓐ $f(x) = \sqrt{x + 3}$ Ⓒ $f(x) = \sqrt{x - 3}$

Ⓑ $f(x) = \sqrt{x} + 3$ Ⓓ $f(x) = \sqrt{x} - 3$

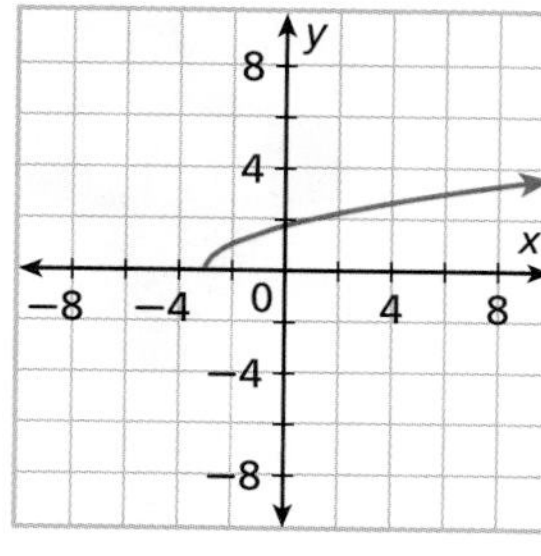


46. Which function has domain $x \geq 2$?

Ⓕ $y = \sqrt{2x}$ Ⓗ $y = \sqrt{\frac{x}{2}}$

Ⓖ $y = \sqrt{x + 2}$ Ⓙ $y = \sqrt{x - 2}$

47. The function $y = \sqrt{\frac{1}{5}x}$ gives the approximate time $y$ in seconds that it takes an object to fall to the ground from a height of $x$ meters. About how long will it take an object 25 meters above the ground to fall to the ground?

Ⓐ 11.2 seconds Ⓒ 2.2 seconds

Ⓑ 5 seconds Ⓓ 0.4 seconds

48. **Gridded Response** If $g(x) = \sqrt{4x} - 1$, what is $g(9)$?

## CHALLENGE AND EXTEND

**Find the domain of each function.**

49. $y = \sqrt{x^2 - 25}$ 50. $y = \sqrt{x^2 + 5x + 6}$ 51. $y = \sqrt{2x^2 + 5x - 12}$

**Find the domain and range of each function.**

52. $y = 2 - \sqrt{x + 3}$ 53. $y = 4 - \sqrt{3 - x}$ 54. $y = 6 - \sqrt{\frac{x}{2}}$

55. Give an example of a square-root function whose graph is above the $x$-axis.

56. Give an example of a square-root function whose graph is in Quadrant IV.

57. **Multi-Step** Justin is given the function $y = 3 - \sqrt{2(x - 5)}$ and $x = 2, 4, 5,$ and $7$. He notices that two of these values are not in the function's domain.

a. Which two values are not in the domain? How do you know?

b. What are the values of $y$ for the two given $x$-values that are in the domain?

## SPIRAL REVIEW

**Write each equation in slope-intercept form, and then graph.** *(Lesson 5-6)*

58. $2y = 4x - 8$ 59. $3x + 6y = 12$ 60. $2x = -y - 9$

**Find each product.** *(Lesson 7-8)*

61. $(3x - 1)^2$ 62. $(2x - 5)(2x + 5)$ 63. $(a - b^2c)^2$

64. $(x^2 + 2y)^2$ 65. $(3r - 2s)(3r + 2s)$ 66. $(a^3b^2 - c^4)(a^3b^2 + c^4)$

67. Blake invested \$42,000 at a rate of 5% compounded quarterly. Write a function to model this situation. Then find the value of Blake's investment after 3 years. *(Lesson 11-3)*

68. Lead-209 has a half-life of about 3.25 hours. Find the amount of lead-209 left from a 230-mg sample after 1 day. Round your answer to the nearest hundredth. *(Lesson 11-3)*

# Graph Radical Functions

You can use a graphing calculator to graph radical functions or to quickly check that a graph drawn by hand is reasonable.

**MA.A.4.3** Interpret the relationship of constants and coefficients for data presented in graphs…and equations.

*Use with Lesson 11-5*

## Activity

**Graph $f(x) = \sqrt{x-1}$ without using a graphing calculator. Then graph the same function on a graphing calculator and compare.**

**1** The graph will be a shift of the graph of the parent function $f(x) = \sqrt{x}$ one unit right. Graph $f(x) = \sqrt{x}$ and then shift the graph one unit right.

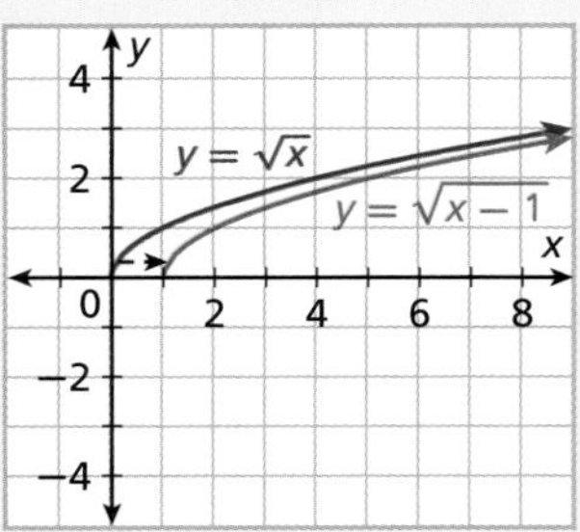


**2** Enter the function into the **Y=** editor.

Press WINDOW and enter −1 for **Xmin**, 9 for **Xmax**, −5 for **Ymin**, and 5 for **Ymax**.

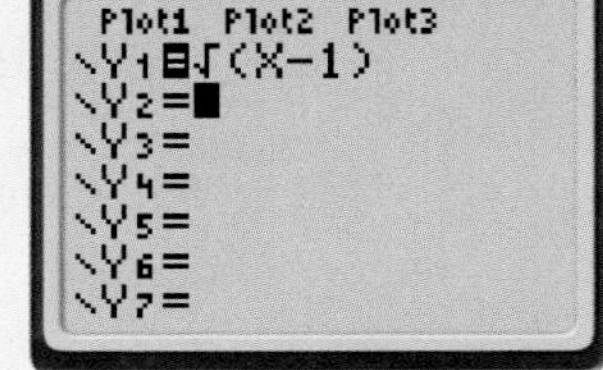


Press GRAPH and compare the graph on the screen to the graph done by hand.

The graph on the screen indicates that the graph done by hand is reasonable.

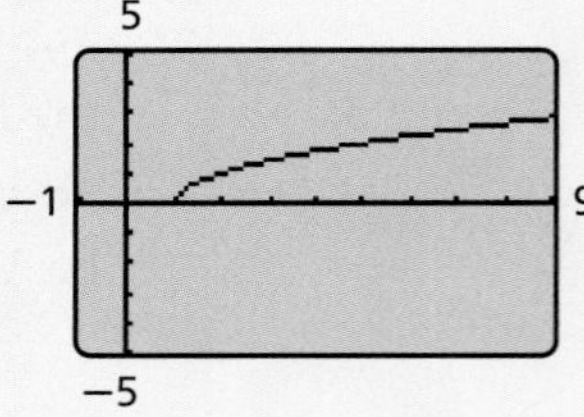


## Try This

1. Graph $f(x) = \sqrt{x+3}$ without using a graphing calculator. Then graph the same function on a graphing calculator and compare.
2. Graph $f(x) = \sqrt{x} - 2$ without using a graphing calculator. Then graph the same function on a graphing calculator and compare.
3. **Make a Conjecture** How do you think the graph of $f(x) = \sqrt{x+1} + 4$ compares to the graph of $f(x) = \sqrt{x}$? Use a graphing calculator to check your conjecture.
4. **Make a Conjecture** How do you think the graph of $f(x) = 2\sqrt{x}$ compares to the graph of $f(x) = \sqrt{x}$? Use a graphing calculator to check your conjecture.

# 11-6 Radical Expressions

**MA.N.2.3** Use strategies to compute square roots ... of numbers that are not perfect squares...

***Objective***
Simplify radical expressions.

***Vocabulary***
radical expression
radicand

**Why learn this?**
You can use a radical expression to find the length of a throw in baseball. (See Example 5.)

An expression that contains a radical sign ($\sqrt{\phantom{x}}$) is a **radical expression**. There are many different types of radical expressions, but in this course, you will only study radical expressions that contain square roots.

Examples of radical expressions:

$\sqrt{14}$ $\quad \sqrt{\ell^2 + w^2}$ $\quad \sqrt{2gd}$ $\quad \frac{\sqrt{d}}{4}$ $\quad 5\sqrt{2}$ $\quad \sqrt{18}$

The expression under a radical sign is the **radicand**. A radicand may contain numbers, variables, or both. It may contain one term or more than one term.

### Simplest Form of a Square-Root Expression

An expression containing square roots is in simplest form when
- the radicand has no perfect square factors other than 1.
- the radicand has no fractions.
- there are no square roots in any denominator.

Remember that positive numbers have two square roots, one positive and one negative. However, $\sqrt{\phantom{x}}$ indicates a nonnegative square root. When you simplify, be sure that your answer is not negative. To simplify $\sqrt{x^2}$, you should write $\sqrt{x^2} = |x|$, because you do not know whether $x$ is positive or negative.

Below are some simplified square-root expressions:

$\sqrt{x^2} = |x|$ $\quad \sqrt{x^3} = x\sqrt{x}$ $\quad \sqrt{x^4} = x^2$ $\quad \sqrt{x^5} = x^2\sqrt{x}$ $\quad \sqrt{x^6} = |x^3|$

## EXAMPLE 1 Simplifying Square-Root Expressions

**Simplify each expression.**

**A** $\sqrt{\frac{2}{72}}$

$\sqrt{\frac{2}{72}} = \sqrt{\frac{1}{36}}$

$= \frac{1}{6}$

**B** $\sqrt{3^2 + 4^2}$

$\sqrt{3^2 + 4^2} = \sqrt{9 + 16}$

$= \sqrt{25}$

$= 5$

**C** $\sqrt{x^2 + 8x + 16}$

$\sqrt{x^2 + 8x + 16} = \sqrt{(x+4)^2}$

$= |x + 4|$

**Simplify each expression.**

**1a.** $\sqrt{\frac{256}{4}}$ **1b.** $\sqrt{40 + 9}$ **1c.** $\sqrt{5^2 + 12^2}$ **1d.** $\sqrt{(3 - x)^2}$

## Product Property of Square Roots

| WORDS | NUMBERS | ALGEBRA |
|---|---|---|
| For any nonnegative real numbers *a* and *b*, the square root of *ab* is equal to the square root of *a* times the square root of *b*. | $\sqrt{4(25)} = \sqrt{100} = 10$<br>$\sqrt{4(25)} = \sqrt{4}\sqrt{25} = 2(5) = 10$ | $\sqrt{ab} = \sqrt{a}\sqrt{b}$, where $a \geq 0$ and $b \geq 0$ |

### EXAMPLE 2 Using the Product Property of Square Roots

**Simplify. All variables represent nonnegative numbers.**

**Helpful Hint**

When factoring the radicand, use factors that are perfect squares. In Example 2A, you could have factored 18 as 6 · 3, but this contains no perfect squares.

**A** $\sqrt{18}$

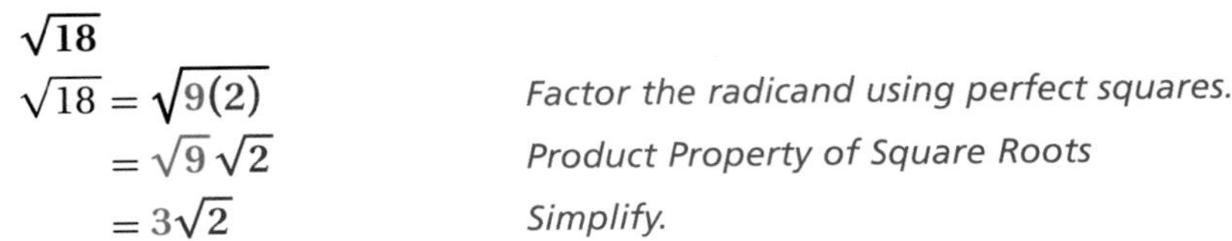

$\sqrt{18} = \sqrt{9(2)}$ *Factor the radicand using perfect squares.*

$= \sqrt{9}\sqrt{2}$ *Product Property of Square Roots*

$= 3\sqrt{2}$ *Simplify.*

**B** $\sqrt{x^4y^3}$

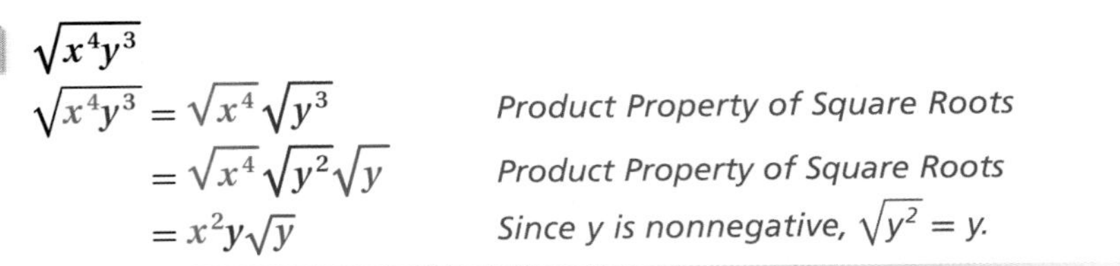

$\sqrt{x^4y^3} = \sqrt{x^4}\sqrt{y^3}$ *Product Property of Square Roots*

$= \sqrt{x^4}\sqrt{y^2}\sqrt{y}$ *Product Property of Square Roots*

$= x^2y\sqrt{y}$ *Since y is nonnegative, $\sqrt{y^2} = y$.*

**Simplify. All variables represent nonnegative numbers.**

**2a.** $\sqrt{128}$ **2b.** $\sqrt{x^3y^2}$ **2c.** $\sqrt{48a^2b}$

## Quotient Property of Square Roots

| WORDS | NUMBERS | ALGEBRA |
|---|---|---|
| For any real numbers *a* and *b* ($a \geq 0$ and $b > 0$), the square root of $\frac{a}{b}$ is equal to the square root of *a* divided by the square root of *b*. | $\sqrt{\frac{36}{4}} = \sqrt{9} = 3$<br>$\sqrt{\frac{36}{4}} = \frac{\sqrt{36}}{\sqrt{4}} = \frac{6}{2} = 3$ | $\sqrt{\frac{a}{b}} = \frac{\sqrt{a}}{\sqrt{b}}$, where $a \geq 0$ and $b > 0$ |

### EXAMPLE 3 Using the Quotient Property of Square Roots

**Simplify. All variables represent nonnegative numbers.**

**A** $\sqrt{\frac{5}{9}}$

$\sqrt{\frac{5}{9}} = \frac{\sqrt{5}}{\sqrt{9}}$ *Quotient Property of Square Roots*

$= \frac{\sqrt{5}}{3}$ *Simplify.*

**B** $\sqrt{\frac{a^5}{81a}}$

$\sqrt{\frac{a^5}{81a}} = \sqrt{\frac{a^4}{81}}$ *Simplify.*

$= \frac{\sqrt{a^4}}{\sqrt{81}}$ *Quotient Property of Square Roots*

$= \frac{a^2}{9}$ *Simplify.*

Simplify. All variables represent nonnegative numbers.

**3a.** $\sqrt{\frac{12}{27}}$ **3b.** $\sqrt{\frac{36}{x^4}}$ **3c.** $\sqrt{\frac{y^6}{4}}$

## EXAMPLE 4 Using the Product and Quotient Properties Together

**Simplify. All variables represent nonnegative numbers.**

**A** $\sqrt{\frac{80}{25}}$

$\frac{\sqrt{80}}{\sqrt{25}}$ *Quotient Property*

$\frac{\sqrt{16(5)}}{\sqrt{25}}$ *Write 80 as 16(5).*

$\frac{\sqrt{16}\sqrt{5}}{\sqrt{25}}$ *Product Property*

$\frac{4\sqrt{5}}{5}$ *Simplify.*

**B** $\sqrt{\frac{4x^5}{9}}$

$\frac{\sqrt{4x^5}}{\sqrt{9}}$ *Quotient Property*

$\frac{\sqrt{4}\sqrt{x^5}}{\sqrt{9}}$ *Product Property*

$\frac{\sqrt{4}\sqrt{x^4}\sqrt{x}}{\sqrt{9}}$

$\frac{2x^2\sqrt{x}}{3}$ *Simplify.*

**Caution!**

In the expression $\frac{4\sqrt{5}}{5}$, $\sqrt{5}$ and 5 are not common factors. $\frac{4\sqrt{5}}{5}$ is completely simplified.

Simplify. All variables represent nonnegative numbers.

**4a.** $\sqrt{\frac{20}{49}}$ **4b.** $\sqrt{\frac{z^5}{25y^2}}$ **4c.** $\sqrt{\frac{p^6}{q^{10}}}$

## EXAMPLE 5 *Sports Application*

**A baseball diamond is a square with sides of 90 feet. How far is a throw from third base to first base? Give the answer as a radical expression in simplest form. Then estimate the length to the nearest tenth of a foot.**

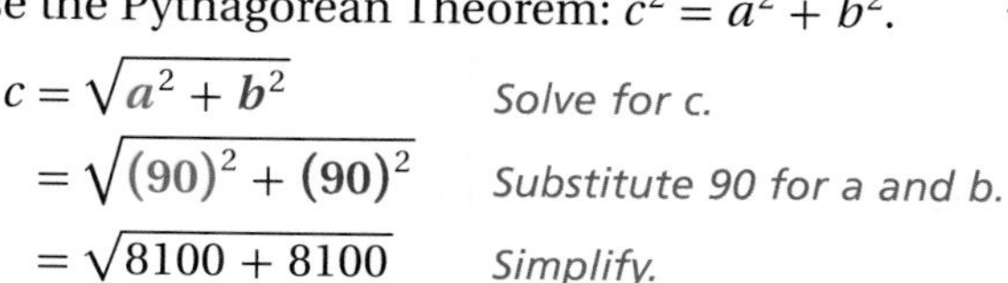


The distance from third base to first base is the hypotenuse of a right triangle. Use the Pythagorean Theorem: $c^2 = a^2 + b^2$.

$c = \sqrt{a^2 + b^2}$ *Solve for c.*

$= \sqrt{(90)^2 + (90)^2}$ *Substitute 90 for a and b.*

$= \sqrt{8100 + 8100}$ *Simplify.*

$= \sqrt{16{,}200}$

$= \sqrt{100(81)(2)}$ *Factor 16,200 using perfect squares.*

$= \sqrt{100}\sqrt{81}\sqrt{2}$ *Use the Product Property of Square Roots.*

$= 10(9)\sqrt{2}$

$= 90\sqrt{2}$ *Simplify.*

$\approx 127.3$ *Use a calculator and round to the nearest tenth.*

The distance is $90\sqrt{2}$, or about 127.3, feet.

**5.** A softball diamond is a square with sides of 60 feet. How long is a throw from third base to first base in softball? Give the answer as a radical expression in simplest form. Then estimate the length to the nearest tenth of a foot.

## THINK AND DISCUSS

1. Show two ways to evaluate $\sqrt{16(9)}$.

2. Show two ways to evaluate $\sqrt{\frac{100}{4}}$.

3. **GET ORGANIZED** Copy and complete the graphic organizer. In each box, write the property and give an example.

| | Product Property of Square Roots | Quotient Property of Square Roots |
|---|---|---|
| Words | | |
| Example | | |

# 11-6 Exercises

MA.N.2.3

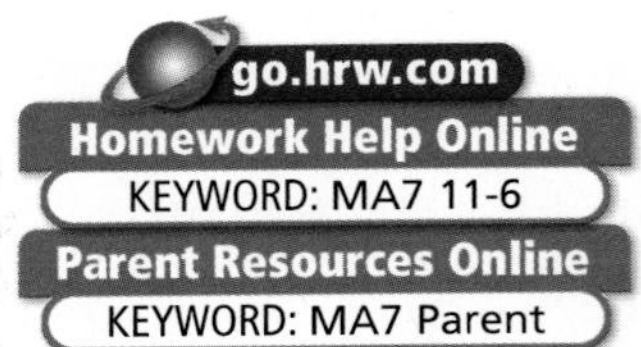



## GUIDED PRACTICE

1. **Vocabulary** In the expression $\sqrt{3x-6}+7$, what is the *radicand*?

SEE EXAMPLE 1 p. 805

**Simplify each expression.**

2. $\sqrt{81}$
3. $\sqrt{\frac{98}{2}}$
4. $\sqrt{(a+7)^2}$

SEE EXAMPLE 2 p. 806

**Simplify. All variables represent nonnegative numbers.**

5. $\sqrt{180}$
6. $\sqrt{40}$
7. $\sqrt{648}$
8. $\sqrt{m^5n^3}$
9. $\sqrt{32x^4y^3}$
10. $\sqrt{200a^2b}$

SEE EXAMPLE 3 p. 806

11. $\sqrt{\frac{17}{25}}$
12. $\sqrt{\frac{7}{16}}$
13. $\sqrt{\frac{6}{49}}$
14. $\sqrt{\frac{b}{c^2}}$
15. $\sqrt{\frac{4x^2}{36x}}$
16. $\sqrt{\frac{7a^4}{9a^3}}$

SEE EXAMPLE 4 p. 807

17. $\sqrt{\frac{108}{49}}$
18. $\sqrt{\frac{204}{25}}$
19. $\sqrt{\frac{512}{81}}$
20. $\sqrt{\frac{1}{36x^2}}$
21. $\sqrt{\frac{50x^2}{169}}$
22. $\sqrt{\frac{72x^7}{4x^4}}$

SEE EXAMPLE 5 p. 807

23. **Recreation** Your boat is traveling due north from a dock. Your friend's boat left at the same time from the same dock and is headed due east. After an hour, your friend calls and tells you that he has just stopped because of engine trouble. How far must you travel to meet your friend? Give your answer as a radical expression in simplest form. Then estimate the distance to the nearest mile.

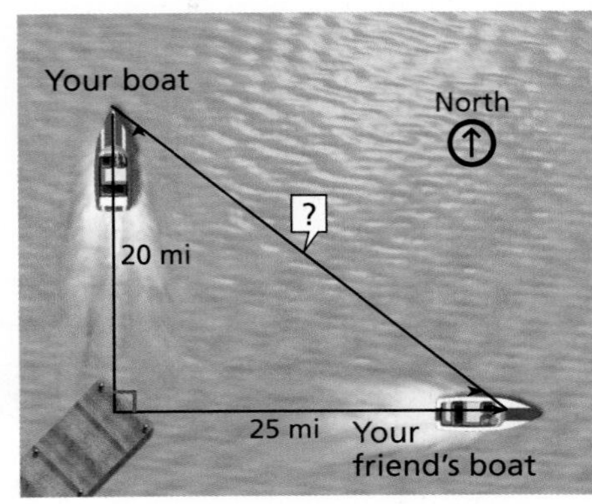

## PRACTICE AND PROBLEM SOLVING

**Independent Practice**

| For Exercises | See Example |
|---|---|
| 24–31 | 1 |
| 32–35 | 2 |
| 36–39 | 3 |
| 40–43 | 4 |
| 44 | 5 |

**Extra Practice**

Skills Practice p. S25

Application Practice p. S38

**Simplify.**

**24.** $\sqrt{100}$ **25.** $\sqrt{\frac{800}{2}}$ **26.** $\sqrt{3^2+4^2}$ **27.** $\sqrt{3 \cdot 27}$

**28.** $\sqrt{a^4}$ **29.** $\sqrt{(x+1)^2}$ **30.** $\sqrt{(5-x)^2}$ **31.** $\sqrt{(x-3)^2}$

**Simplify. All variables represent nonnegative numbers.**

**32.** $\sqrt{125}$ **33.** $\sqrt{4000}$ **34.** $\sqrt{216a^2b^2}$ **35.** $\sqrt{320r^2s^2}$

**36.** $\sqrt{\frac{15}{64}}$ **37.** $\sqrt{\frac{45}{4}}$ **38.** $\sqrt{\frac{64a^4}{4a^6}}$ **39.** $\sqrt{\frac{14z^3}{9z^3}}$

**40.** $\sqrt{\frac{128}{81}}$ **41.** $\sqrt{\frac{x^3}{y^6}}$ **42.** $\sqrt{\frac{150}{196x^2}}$ **43.** $\sqrt{\frac{192s^3}{49s}}$

**44. Amusement Parks** A thrill ride at an amusement park carries riders 160 feet straight up and then releases them for a free fall. The time $t$ in seconds that it takes an object in free fall to reach the ground is $t = \sqrt{\frac{d}{16}}$, where $d$ is the distance in feet that it falls. How long does it take the riders to reach the ground? Give your answer as a radical expression in simplest form. Then estimate the answer to the nearest tenth of a second.

**Simplify. All variables represent nonnegative numbers.**

**45.** $-4\sqrt{75}$ **46.** $-\sqrt{80}$ **47.** $5x\sqrt{63}$ **48.** $3\sqrt{48x}$

**49.** $2\sqrt{\frac{x^2}{4}}$ **50.** $\frac{1}{2}\sqrt{\frac{1}{25}}$ **51.** $3x\sqrt{\frac{x^5}{81}}$ **52.** $\frac{12}{x}\sqrt{\frac{x^2y}{36}}$

**Use the Product Property or the Quotient Property of Square Roots to write each expression as a single square root. Then simplify if possible.**

**53.** $\sqrt{12}\sqrt{3}$ **54.** $\sqrt{18}\sqrt{8}$ **55.** $\sqrt{10}\sqrt{5}$ **56.** $\sqrt{8}\sqrt{14}$

**57.** $\frac{\sqrt{33}}{\sqrt{11}}$ **58.** $\frac{\sqrt{24}}{\sqrt{2}}$ **59.** $\frac{\sqrt{60}}{\sqrt{3}}$ **60.** $\frac{\sqrt{72}}{\sqrt{9}}$

**61. Multi-Step** How many whole feet of fencing would be needed to enclose the triangular garden that is sketched at right? Explain your answer.

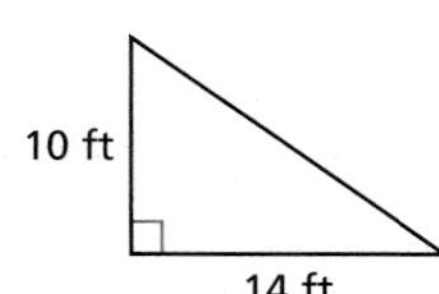

**62. Write About It** Write a series of steps that you could use to simplify $\sqrt{\frac{28}{49}}$.

**63.** This problem will prepare you for the Multi-Step Test Prep on page 830.

**a.** The vertical component of a roller coaster's speed in feet per second at the bottom of a hill is $v = \sqrt{64h}$, where $h$ is the hill's height in feet. Simplify this expression. Then estimate the velocity at the bottom of a 137-foot hill.

**b.** The distance along the track of a hill is $d = \sqrt{x^2 + h^2}$, where $x$ is the horizontal distance along the ground and $h$ is the hill's height. Where does this equation come from?

**c.** For the hill in part **a**, the horizontal distance along the ground is 103 feet. What is the distance along the track? Round your answer to the nearest tenth.

64. **Critical Thinking** The Product Property of Square Roots states that $\sqrt{ab} = \sqrt{a}\sqrt{b}$, where $a \geq 0$ and $b \geq 0$. Why must $a$ and $b$ be greater than or equal to zero?

Heron of Alexandria, Egypt, also called Hero, lived around 60 C.E. Heron's formula for the area of a triangle can be found in Book I of his *Metrica*.

65. **Architecture** The formula $d = \frac{\sqrt{6h}}{3}$ estimates the distance $d$ in miles that a person can see to the horizon from $h$ feet above the ground. Find the distance you could see to the horizon from the top of each building in the graph. Give your answers as radical expressions in simplest form and as estimates to the nearest tenth of a mile.

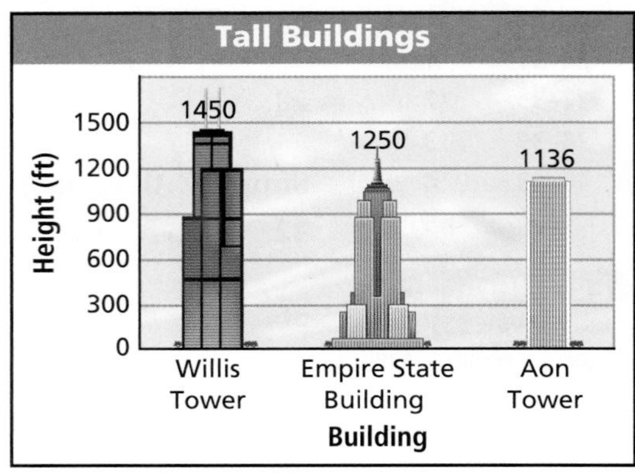


66. **Math History** Heron's formula for the area $A$ of a triangle is $A = \sqrt{s(s-a)(s-b)(s-c)}$, where $a$, $b$, and $c$ are the side lengths and $s = \frac{1}{2}(a + b + c)$. Find the area of a triangle with side lengths of 7 m, 9 m, and 12 m. Give your answer as a radical expression in simplest form and as an estimate to the nearest tenth.

MA.N.2.3

67. Which expression is in simplest form?
Ⓐ $\sqrt{49}$ Ⓑ $\sqrt{48}$ Ⓒ $\sqrt{35}$ Ⓓ $\sqrt{36}$

68. Which expression is equal to $\sqrt{60}$?
Ⓕ $2\sqrt{15}$ Ⓖ $6\sqrt{10}$ Ⓗ $15\sqrt{2}$ Ⓙ $10\sqrt{60}$

69. How long is the diagonal of a square whose area is 100 square feet?
Ⓐ $2\sqrt{10}$ feet Ⓑ 10 feet Ⓒ $10\sqrt{2}$ feet Ⓓ 20 feet

## CHALLENGE AND EXTEND

**Simplify. All variables represent nonnegative numbers.**

70. $\sqrt{4x + 16}$
71. $\sqrt{x^3 + x^2}$
72. $\sqrt{9x^3 - 18x^2}$

73. Let $x$ represent any real number (including negative numbers). Simplify each of the following expressions, using absolute-value symbols when necessary.
a. $\sqrt{x^2}$ b. $\sqrt{x^4}$ c. $\sqrt{x^6}$ d. $\sqrt{x^8}$ e. $\sqrt{x^{10}}$
f. For any nonnegative integer $n$, $\sqrt{x^{2n}} =$ ▒ if $n$ is even, and $\sqrt{x^{2n}} =$ ▒ if $n$ is odd.

## SPIRAL REVIEW

**Tell whether each relationship is a direct variation. Explain.** *(Lesson 5-5)*

74.

| x | 2 | 3 | 4 |
|---|---|---|---|
| y | 12 | 18 | 24 |

75.

| x | 2 | 3 | 4 |
|---|---|---|---|
| y | −6 | −5 | −4 |

76. Write an equation in slope-intercept form for the line through $(3, 1)$ and $(2, -5)$. *(Lesson 5-6)*

**Graph each data set. Which kind of model best describes the data?** *(Lesson 11-4)*

77. $\{(-3, 16), (-2, 8), (0, 2), (1, 1), (3, 0.25)\}$
78. $\{(-5, 15), (-2, -6), (0, -10), (3, -1), (4, 6)\}$

# 11-7 Adding and Subtracting Radical Expressions

**MA.N.2.3** Use strategies to compute square roots … of numbers that are not perfect squares...

***Objective***
Add and subtract radical expressions.

***Vocabulary***
like radicals

**Why learn this?**
You can add or subtract radical expressions to find perimeter. (See Example 3.)

Square-root expressions with the same radicand are examples of **like radicals**.

| **Like Radicals** | $2\sqrt{5}$ and $4\sqrt{5}$ | $6\sqrt{x}$ and $-2\sqrt{x}$ | $3\sqrt{4t}$ and $\sqrt{4t}$ |
|---|---|---|---|
| **Unlike Radicals** | 2 and $\sqrt{15}$ | $6\sqrt{x}$ and $\sqrt{6x}$ | $3\sqrt{2}$ and $2\sqrt{3}$ |

Like radicals can be combined by adding or subtracting. You can use the Distributive Property to show how this is done:

$$2\sqrt{5} + 4\sqrt{5} = (2 + 4)\sqrt{5} = 6\sqrt{5}$$

$$6\sqrt{x} - 2\sqrt{x} = (6 - 2)\sqrt{x} = 4\sqrt{x}$$

Notice that you can combine like radicals by adding or subtracting the numbers multiplied by the radical and keeping the radical the same.

**Helpful Hint**

Combining like radicals is similar to combining like terms.
$2\sqrt{5} + 4\sqrt{5} = 6\sqrt{5}$
$2x + 4x = 6x$

## EXAMPLE 1 Adding and Subtracting Square-Root Expressions

**Add or subtract.**

**A** $3\sqrt{7} + 8\sqrt{7}$

$3\sqrt{7} + 8\sqrt{7}$ — *The terms are like radicals.*

$11\sqrt{7}$

**B** $9\sqrt{y} - \sqrt{y}$

$9\sqrt{y} - 1\sqrt{y}$ — *$\sqrt{y} = 1\sqrt{y}$; the terms are like radicals.*

$8\sqrt{y}$

**C** $12\sqrt{2} - 4\sqrt{11}$

$12\sqrt{2} - 4\sqrt{11}$ — *The terms are unlike radicals. Do not combine.*

**D** $-8\sqrt{3d} + 6\sqrt{2d} + 10\sqrt{3d}$

$-8\sqrt{3d} + 6\sqrt{2d} + 10\sqrt{3d}$ — *Identify like radicals.*

$2\sqrt{3d} + 6\sqrt{2d}$ — *Combine like radicals.*

**Add or subtract.**

**1a.** $5\sqrt{7} - 6\sqrt{7}$ **1b.** $8\sqrt{3} - 5\sqrt{3}$

**1c.** $4\sqrt{n} + 4\sqrt{n}$ **1d.** $\sqrt{2s} - \sqrt{5s} + 9\sqrt{5s}$

Sometimes radicals do not appear to be like until they are simplified. Simplify all radicals in an expression before trying to identify like radicals.

## EXAMPLE 2 Simplifying Before Adding or Subtracting

**Simplify each expression.**

**A** $\sqrt{12} + \sqrt{27}$

| | |
|---|---|
| $\sqrt{4(3)} + \sqrt{9(3)}$ | *Factor the radicands using perfect squares.* |
| $\sqrt{4}\sqrt{3} + \sqrt{9}\sqrt{3}$ | *Product Property of Square Roots* |
| $2\sqrt{3} + 3\sqrt{3}$ | *Simplify.* |
| $5\sqrt{3}$ | *Combine like radicals.* |

**B** $3\sqrt{8} + \sqrt{45}$

| | |
|---|---|
| $3\sqrt{4(2)} + \sqrt{9(5)}$ | *Factor the radicands using perfect squares.* |
| $3\sqrt{4}\sqrt{2} + \sqrt{9}\sqrt{5}$ | *Product Property of Square Roots* |
| $3(2)\sqrt{2} + 3\sqrt{5}$ | *Simplify.* |
| $6\sqrt{2} + 3\sqrt{5}$ | *The terms are unlike radicals. Do not combine.* |

**Remember!**

When you write a radicand as a product, make at least one factor a perfect square.

**C** $5\sqrt{28x} - 8\sqrt{7x}$

| | |
|---|---|
| $5\sqrt{4(7x)} - 8\sqrt{7x}$ | *Factor 28x using a perfect square.* |
| $5\sqrt{4}\sqrt{7x} - 8\sqrt{7x}$ | *Product Property of Square Roots* |
| $5(2)\sqrt{7x} - 8\sqrt{7x}$ | *Simplify.* |
| $10\sqrt{7x} - 8\sqrt{7x}$ | |
| $2\sqrt{7x}$ | *Combine like radicals.* |

**D** $\sqrt{125b} + 3\sqrt{20b} - \sqrt{45b}$

| | |
|---|---|
| $\sqrt{25(5b)} + 3\sqrt{4(5b)} - \sqrt{9(5b)}$ | *Factor the radicands using perfect squares.* |
| $\sqrt{25}\sqrt{5b} + 3\sqrt{4}\sqrt{5b} - \sqrt{9}\sqrt{5b}$ | *Product Property of Square Roots* |
| $5\sqrt{5b} + 3(2)\sqrt{5b} - 3\sqrt{5b}$ | *Simplify.* |
| $5\sqrt{5b} + 6\sqrt{5b} - 3\sqrt{5b}$ | |
| $8\sqrt{5b}$ | *Combine like radicals.* |

**Simplify each expression.**

**2a.** $\sqrt{54} + \sqrt{24}$ **2b.** $4\sqrt{27} - \sqrt{18}$ **2c.** $\sqrt{12y} + \sqrt{27y}$

## EXAMPLE 3 *Geometry Application*

**Find the perimeter of the triangle. Give your answer as a radical expression in simplest form.**

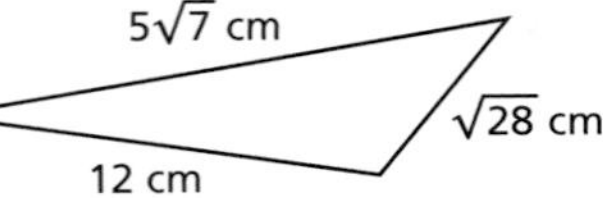


| | |
|---|---|
| $12 + 5\sqrt{7} + \sqrt{28}$ | *Write an expression for perimeter.* |
| $12 + 5\sqrt{7} + \sqrt{4(7)}$ | *Factor 28 using a perfect square.* |
| $12 + 5\sqrt{7} + \sqrt{4}\sqrt{7}$ | *Product Property of Square Roots* |
| $12 + 5\sqrt{7} + 2\sqrt{7}$ | *Simplify.* |
| $12 + 7\sqrt{7}$ | *Combine like radicals.* |

The perimeter is $\left(12 + 7\sqrt{7}\right)$ cm.

**3.** Find the perimeter of a rectangle whose length is $2\sqrt{b}$ inches and whose width is $3\sqrt{b}$ inches. Give your answer as a radical expression in simplest form.

## THINK AND DISCUSS

1. Rearrange the following into two groups of like radicals: $2\sqrt{6}$, $6\sqrt{5}$, $\sqrt{600}$, $\sqrt{150}$, $-\sqrt{20}$, $\sqrt{5}$.
2. Tell why you should simplify radicals when adding and subtracting expressions with radicals.

3. **GET ORGANIZED** Copy and complete the graphic organizer.

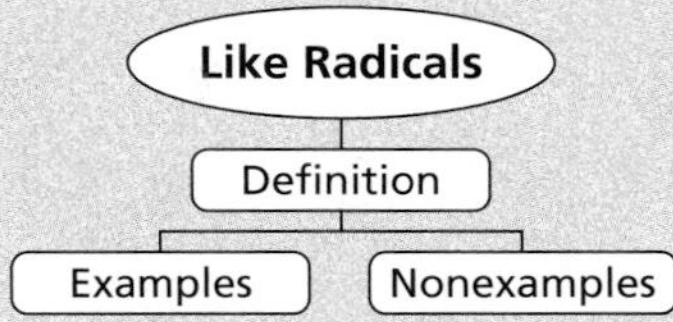


# 11-7 Exercises

MA.N.2.3

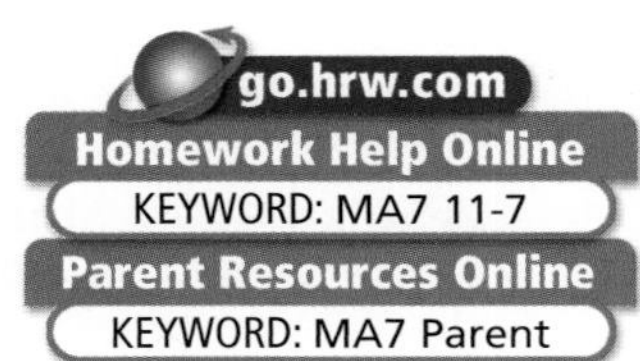


## GUIDED PRACTICE

1. **Vocabulary** Give an example of *like radicals*.

SEE EXAMPLE 1 p. 811

**Add or subtract.**

2. $14\sqrt{3} - 6\sqrt{3}$
3. $9\sqrt{5} + \sqrt{5}$
4. $6\sqrt{2} + 5\sqrt{2} - 15\sqrt{2}$
5. $3\sqrt{7} + 5\sqrt{2}$
6. $5\sqrt{a} - 9\sqrt{a}$
7. $9\sqrt{6a} + 6\sqrt{5a} - 4\sqrt{6a}$

SEE EXAMPLE 2 p. 812

**Simplify each expression.**

8. $\sqrt{32} - \sqrt{8}$
9. $4\sqrt{12} + \sqrt{75}$
10. $2\sqrt{3} + 5\sqrt{12} - \sqrt{27}$
11. $\sqrt{20x} - \sqrt{45x}$
12. $\sqrt{28c} + 9\sqrt{24c}$
13. $\sqrt{50t} - 2\sqrt{12t} + 3\sqrt{2t}$

SEE EXAMPLE 3 p. 812

14. **Geometry** Find the perimeter of the trapezoid shown. Give your answer as a radical expression in simplest form.

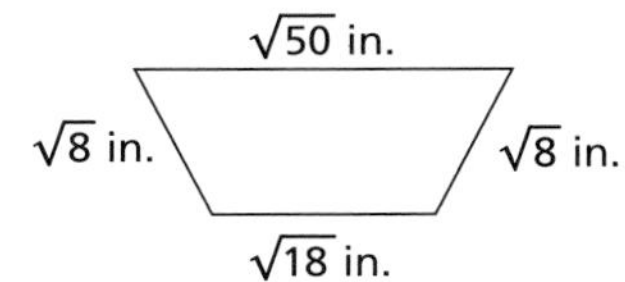


## PRACTICE AND PROBLEM SOLVING

| Independent Practice | |
|---|---|
| For Exercises | See Example |
| 15–20 | 1 |
| 21–29 | 2 |
| 30 | 3 |

**Extra Practice**
Skills Practice p. S25
Application Practice p. S38

**Add or subtract.**

15. $4\sqrt{3} + 2\sqrt{3}$
16. $\frac{1}{2}\sqrt{72} - 12$
17. $2\sqrt{11} + \sqrt{11} - 6\sqrt{11}$
18. $6\sqrt{7} + 7\sqrt{6}$
19. $-3\sqrt{n} - \sqrt{n}$
20. $2\sqrt{2y} + 3\sqrt{2y} - 2\sqrt{3y}$

**Simplify each expression.**

21. $\sqrt{175} + \sqrt{28}$
22. $2\sqrt{80} - \sqrt{20}$
23. $5\sqrt{8} - \sqrt{32} + 2\sqrt{18}$
24. $\sqrt{150r} + \sqrt{54r}$
25. $\sqrt{63x} - 4\sqrt{27x}$
26. $\sqrt{48p} + 3\sqrt{18p} - 2\sqrt{27p}$
27. $\sqrt{180j} - \sqrt{45j}$
28. $3\sqrt{90c} - \sqrt{40c}$
29. $2\sqrt{75m} - \sqrt{12m} - \sqrt{108m}$

30. **Fitness** What is the total length of the jogging path? Give your answer as a radical expression in simplest form.

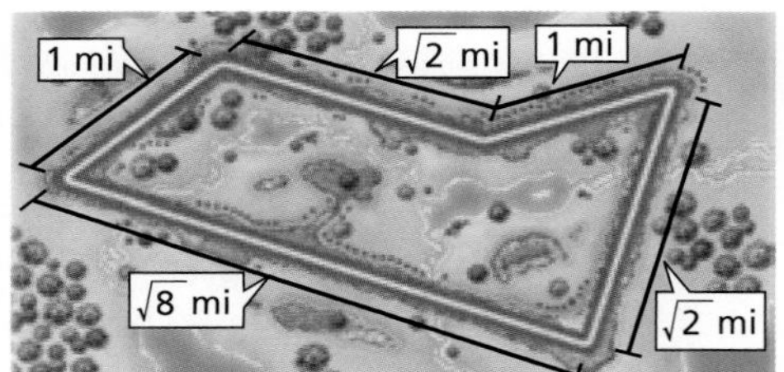


**Simplify each expression.**

31. $5\sqrt{7} + 7\sqrt{7}$
32. $18\sqrt{ab} - 10\sqrt{ab}$
33. $-3\sqrt{3} + 3\sqrt{3}$
34. $\sqrt{98} + \sqrt{128}$
35. $\sqrt{300} - \sqrt{27}$
36. $\sqrt{45x} + \sqrt{500x}$
37. $\frac{5}{2}\sqrt{8} + \frac{\sqrt{32}}{2}$
38. $\frac{1}{6}\sqrt{18} - \frac{\sqrt{2}}{2}$

39. **Geometry** Use the diagram to answer the following:

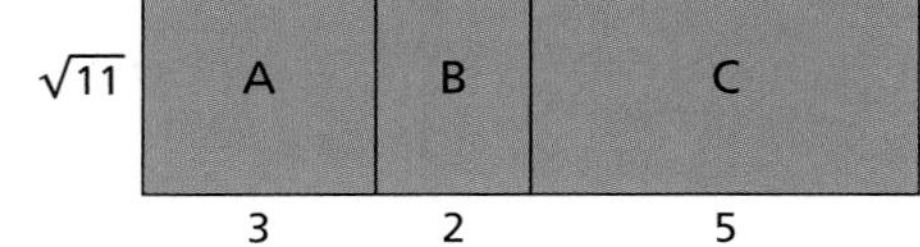


a. What is the area of section A? section B? section C?

b. What is the combined area of the three sections?

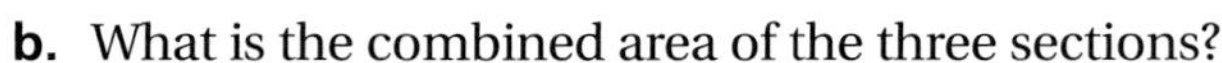

c. Explain how this model relates to adding like radicals.

**Simplify each expression.**

40. $\sqrt{450ab} - \sqrt{50ab}$
41. $\sqrt{12} + \sqrt{125} + \sqrt{25}$
42. $\sqrt{338} - \sqrt{18}$
43. $\sqrt{700x} - \sqrt{28x} - \sqrt{70x}$
44. $-3\sqrt{90} - 3\sqrt{160}$
45. $7\sqrt{80k} + 2\sqrt{20k} + \sqrt{45k}$
46. $\sqrt{24abc} + \sqrt{600abc}$
47. $\sqrt{12} + \sqrt{20} + \sqrt{27} + \sqrt{45}$

48. **///ERROR ANALYSIS///** Which expressions are simplified incorrectly? Explain the error in each incorrect simplification.

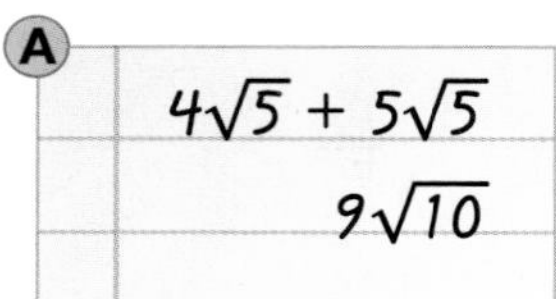


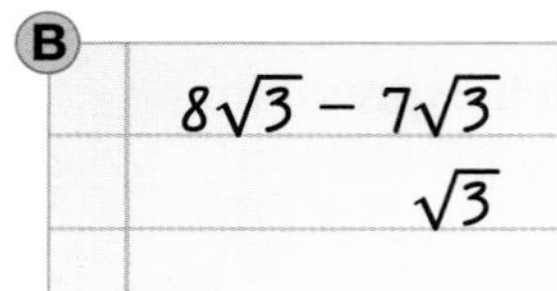


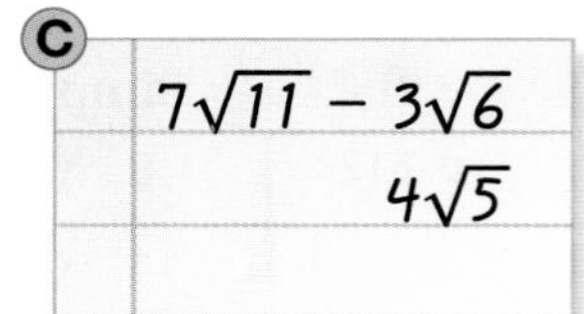

49. **Write About It** Tell how to identify like radicals. Give examples and nonexamples of like radicals in your answer.

**Complete each box to make a true statement.**

50. $5\sqrt{ab} + 2\sqrt{\square} - 3\sqrt{a} = 7\sqrt{ab} - 3\sqrt{a}$
51. $4\sqrt{x} - \sqrt{\square x} = \sqrt{x}$
52. $5\sqrt{2} - \sqrt{\square} + \sqrt{2} = 4\sqrt{2}$
53. $\sqrt{\square} + 8\sqrt{2} = 11\sqrt{2}$
54. $3\sqrt{3} + 2\sqrt{3} + \sqrt{\square} = 9\sqrt{3}$
55. $2x - \sqrt{\square} = -4x$

56. This problem will prepare you for the Multi-Step Test Prep on page 830.

a. The first Ferris wheel was designed by George W. Ferris and introduced at the 1893 Chicago World's Fair. Its diameter was 250 feet. What was its radius?

b. For a rider halfway up on the ride, the distance from the boarding point can be found by using the equation $d = \sqrt{2r^2}$, where $r$ is the radius of the wheel. Explain where this equation comes from. (*Hint:* Draw a picture.)

57. **Multi-Step** A square has an area of 48 $\text{in}^2$. Another square has an area of 12 $\text{in}^2$. Write a simplified radical expression for the perimeter of each square. Then write a simplified radical expression for the combined perimeters of the two squares.

58. **Critical Thinking** How are like radicals similar to like terms?

59. Which of the following expressions CANNOT be simplified?
   - (A) $3\sqrt{5} + 4\sqrt{5}$
   - (B) $5\sqrt{6} + 6\sqrt{5}$
   - (C) $2\sqrt{8} + 3\sqrt{2}$
   - (D) $3\sqrt{12} + \sqrt{27}$

60. What is $-5\sqrt{7x} + 6\sqrt{7x}$?
   - (F) $\sqrt{7x}$
   - (G) $\sqrt{14x^2}$
   - (H) $\sqrt{14x}$
   - (J) $7x$

61. What is $\sqrt{18} - \sqrt{2}$?
   - (A) $2\sqrt{2}$
   - (B) 4
   - (C) $4\sqrt{2}$
   - (D) $8\sqrt{2}$

## CHALLENGE AND EXTEND

**Simplify. All radicands represent nonnegative numbers.**

62. $5\sqrt{x-5} + 2\sqrt{x-5}$

63. $x\sqrt{x} + 2\sqrt{x}$

64. $4\sqrt{x-3} + \sqrt{25x-75}$

65. $2\sqrt{x+7} - \sqrt{4x+28}$

66. $\sqrt{4x^3 + 24x^2} + \sqrt{x^3 + 6x^2}$

67. $\sqrt{x^3 - x^2} + \sqrt{4x - 4}$

68. $\sqrt{x^3 + 2x^2} - \sqrt{x+2}$

69. $\sqrt{9x+9} - \sqrt{x^3 + 2x^2}$

70. **Geometry** Find the area of the trapezoid. Use the formula $A = \frac{1}{2}h(b_1 + b_2)$.

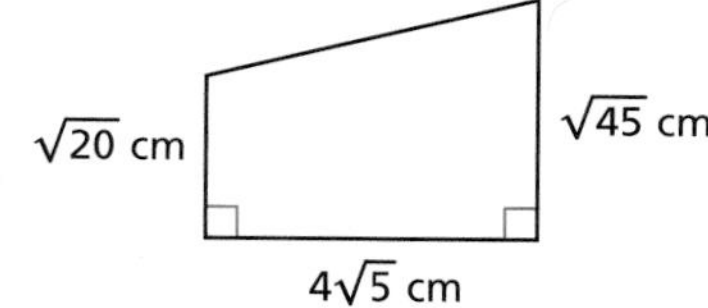


## SPIRAL REVIEW

71. Use slope to show that $ABCD$ is a parallelogram. *(Lesson 5-8)*

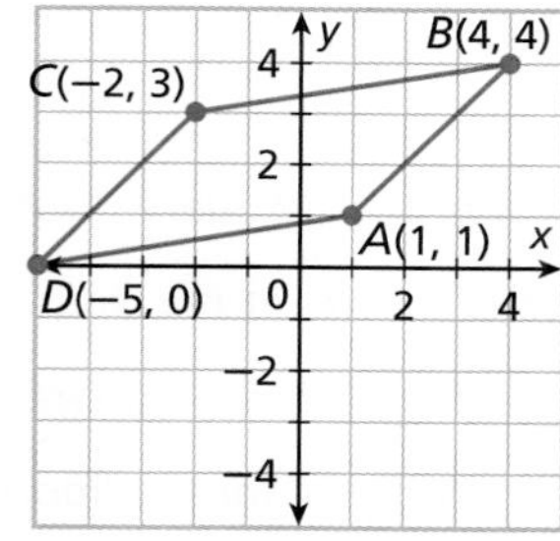


72. Use slope to show that $XYZ$ is a right triangle. *(Lesson 5-8)*

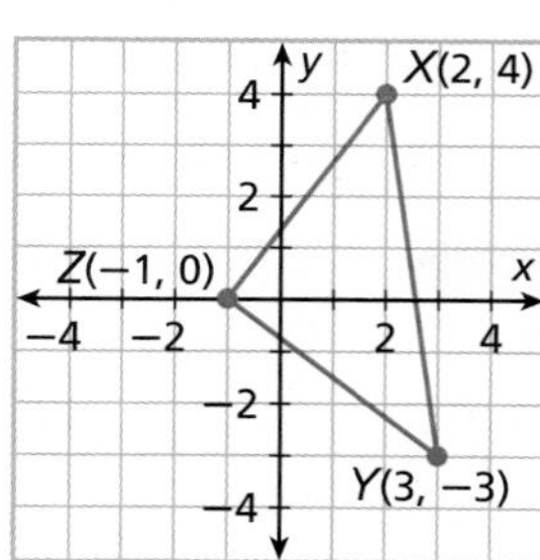


73. A number cube is rolled and a coin is tossed. What is the probability of rolling a 6 and tossing heads? *(Lesson 10-7)*

**Find the domain of each square-root function.** *(Lesson 11-5)*

74. $y = \sqrt{4x - 2}$

75. $y = -2\sqrt{x+3}$

76. $y = 1 + \sqrt{x+6}$

# 11-8 Multiplying and Dividing Radical Expressions

**MA.N.2.3** Use strategies to compute square roots … of numbers that are not perfect squares...

***Objectives***

Multiply and divide radical expressions.

Rationalize denominators.

**Who uses this?**

Electricians can divide radical expressions to find how much current runs through an appliance. (See Exercise 64.)

You can use the Product and Quotient Properties of square roots you have already learned to multiply and divide expressions containing square roots.



**EXAMPLE 1 Multiplying Square Roots**

**Multiply. Write each product in simplest form.**

**A** $\sqrt{3}\sqrt{6}$

| | |
|---|---|
| $\sqrt{3(6)}$ | *Product Property of Square Roots* |
| $\sqrt{18}$ | *Multiply the factors in the radicand.* |
| $\sqrt{9(2)}$ | *Factor 18 using a perfect-square factor.* |
| $\sqrt{9}\sqrt{2}$ | *Product Property of Square Roots* |
| $3\sqrt{2}$ | *Simplify.* |

**B** $(5\sqrt{3})^2$

| | |
|---|---|
| $5\sqrt{3} \cdot 5\sqrt{3}$ | *Expand the expression.* |
| $5(5)\sqrt{3}\sqrt{3}$ | *Commutative Property of Multiplication* |
| $25\sqrt{3(3)}$ | *Product Property of Square Roots* |
| $25\sqrt{9}$ | *Simplify the radicand.* |
| $25(3)$ | *Simplify the square root.* |
| $75$ | *Multiply.* |

**C** $2\sqrt{8x}\sqrt{4x}$

| | |
|---|---|
| $2\sqrt{8x(4x)}$ | *Product Property of Square Roots* |
| $2\sqrt{32x^2}$ | *Multiply the factors in the radicand.* |
| $2\sqrt{16(2)x^2}$ | *Factor 32 using a perfect-square factor.* |
| $2\sqrt{16}\sqrt{2}\sqrt{x^2}$ | *Product Property of Square Roots* |
| $2(4)\sqrt{2}(x)$ | |
| $8x\sqrt{2}$ | |

**Helpful Hint**

In Example 1C, $\sqrt{8x}$ and $\sqrt{4x}$ represent real numbers only if $x \geq 0$, so, in this case, $\sqrt{x^2} = x$.

**Multiply. Write each product in simplest form.**

**1a.** $\sqrt{5}\sqrt{10}$ **1b.** $(3\sqrt{7})^2$ **1c.** $\sqrt{2m}\sqrt{14m}$

EXAMPLE 2 **Using the Distributive Property**

**Multiply. Write each product in simplest form.**

**A** $\sqrt{2}\left(5+\sqrt{12}\right)$

| | |
|---|---|
| $\sqrt{2}\left(5+\sqrt{12}\right)$ | |
| $\sqrt{2}(5)+\sqrt{2}\sqrt{12}$ | *Distribute* $\sqrt{2}$. |
| $5\sqrt{2}+\sqrt{2(12)}$ | *Product Property of Square Roots* |
| $5\sqrt{2}+\sqrt{24}$ | *Multiply the factors in the second radicand.* |
| $5\sqrt{2}+\sqrt{4(6)}$ | *Factor 24 using a perfect-square factor.* |
| $5\sqrt{2}+\sqrt{4}\sqrt{6}$ | *Product Property of Square Roots* |
| $5\sqrt{2}+2\sqrt{6}$ | *Simplify.* |

**B** $\sqrt{3}\left(\sqrt{3}-\sqrt{5}\right)$

| | |
|---|---|
| $\sqrt{3}\left(\sqrt{3}-\sqrt{5}\right)$ | |
| $\sqrt{3}\sqrt{3}-\sqrt{3}\sqrt{5}$ | *Distribute* $\sqrt{3}$. |
| $\sqrt{3(3)}-\sqrt{3(5)}$ | *Product Property of Square Roots* |
| $\sqrt{9}-\sqrt{15}$ | *Simplify the radicands.* |
| $3-\sqrt{15}$ | *Simplify.* |

**Multiply. Write each product in simplest form.**

**2a.** $\sqrt{6}\left(\sqrt{8}-3\right)$ **2b.** $\sqrt{5}\left(\sqrt{10}+4\sqrt{3}\right)$

**2c.** $\sqrt{7k}\left(\sqrt{7}-5\right)$ **2d.** $5\sqrt{5}\left(-4+6\sqrt{5}\right)$

**Remember!**

**F**irst terms
**O**uter terms
**I**nner terms
**L**ast terms

See Lesson 7-7.

In Chapter 7, you learned to multiply binomials by using the FOIL method. The same method can be used to multiply square-root expressions that contain two terms.

F L I O

$$\left(4+\sqrt{3}\right)\left(5+\sqrt{3}\right)=4(5)+\underbrace{4\sqrt{3}+5\sqrt{3}}+\sqrt{3}\sqrt{3}$$
$$=20 \quad +9\sqrt{3} \quad +3 \quad = \quad 23+9\sqrt{3}$$

EXAMPLE 3 **Multiplying Sums and Differences of Radicals**

**Multiply. Write each product in simplest form.**

**A** $\left(4+\sqrt{5}\right)\left(3-\sqrt{5}\right)$

| | |
|---|---|
| $12-4\sqrt{5}+3\sqrt{5}-5$ | *Use the FOIL method.* |
| $7-\sqrt{5}$ | *Simplify by combining like terms.* |

**B** $\left(\sqrt{7}-5\right)^2$

| | |
|---|---|
| $\left(\sqrt{7}-5\right)\left(\sqrt{7}-5\right)$ | *Expand the expression.* |
| $7-5\sqrt{7}-5\sqrt{7}+25$ | *Use the FOIL method.* |
| $32-10\sqrt{7}$ | *Simplify by combining like terms.* |

**Multiply. Write each product in simplest form.**

**3a.** $\left(3+\sqrt{3}\right)\left(8-\sqrt{3}\right)$ **3b.** $\left(9+\sqrt{2}\right)^2$

**3c.** $\left(3-\sqrt{2}\right)^2$ **3d.** $\left(4-\sqrt{3}\right)\left(\sqrt{3}+5\right)$

A quotient with a square root in the denominator is **not** simplified. To simplify these expressions, multiply by a form of 1 to get a perfect-square radicand in the denominator. This is called *rationalizing the denominator.*

**EXAMPLE 4** **Rationalizing the Denominator**

**Simplify each quotient.**

**A** $\frac{\sqrt{7}}{\sqrt{2}}$

$\frac{\sqrt{7}}{\sqrt{2}}\left(\frac{\sqrt{2}}{\sqrt{2}}\right)$ *Multiply by a form of 1 to get a perfect-square radicand in the denominator.*

$\frac{\sqrt{14}}{\sqrt{4}}$ *Product Property of Square Roots*

$\frac{\sqrt{14}}{2}$ *Simplify the denominator.*

**Helpful Hint**

Use the square root in the denominator to find the appropriate form of 1 for multiplication.

**B** $\frac{\sqrt{7}}{\sqrt{8n}}$

$\frac{\sqrt{7}}{\sqrt{4(2n)}}$ *Write 8n using a perfect-square factor.*

$\frac{\sqrt{7}}{2\sqrt{2n}}$ *Simplify the denominator.*

$\frac{\sqrt{7}}{2\sqrt{2n}}\left(\frac{\sqrt{2n}}{\sqrt{2n}}\right)$ *Multiply by a form of 1 to get a perfect-square radicand in the denominator.*

$\frac{\sqrt{14n}}{2\sqrt{4n^2}}$ *Product Property of Square Roots*

$\frac{\sqrt{14n}}{2(2n)}$ *Simplify the square root in the denominator.*

$\frac{\sqrt{14n}}{4n}$ *Simplify the denominator.*

**Simplify each quotient.**

**4a.** $\frac{\sqrt{13}}{\sqrt{5}}$ **4b.** $\frac{\sqrt{7a}}{\sqrt{12}}$ **4c.** $\frac{2\sqrt{80}}{\sqrt{7}}$

## THINK AND DISCUSS

**1.** Explain why multiplying $\frac{\sqrt{6}}{\sqrt{5}}$ by $\frac{\sqrt{5}}{\sqrt{5}}$ does not change the value of $\frac{\sqrt{6}}{\sqrt{5}}$.

**2. GET ORGANIZED** Copy and complete the graphic organizer. In each box, give an example and show how to simplify it.

Multiplying Radical Expressions

| Multiplying two square roots | Using the Distributive Property | Using FOIL |
|---|---|---|

# 11-8 Exercises

MA.N.2.3

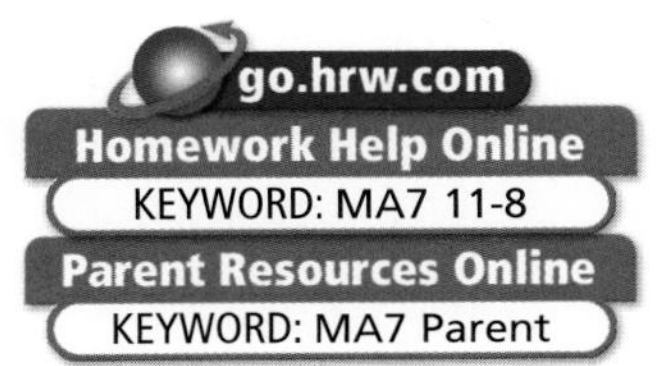


## GUIDED PRACTICE

SEE EXAMPLE 1 p. 816

**Multiply. Write each product in simplest form.**

1. $\sqrt{2}\sqrt{3}$
2. $\sqrt{3}\sqrt{8}$
3. $\left(5\sqrt{5}\right)^2$
4. $\left(4\sqrt{2}\right)^2$
5. $3\sqrt{3a}\sqrt{10}$
6. $2\sqrt{15p}\sqrt{3p}$

SEE EXAMPLE 2 p. 817

7. $\sqrt{6}\left(2+\sqrt{7}\right)$
8. $\sqrt{3}\left(5-\sqrt{3}\right)$
9. $\sqrt{7}\left(\sqrt{5}-\sqrt{3}\right)$
10. $\sqrt{2}\left(\sqrt{10}+8\sqrt{2}\right)$
11. $\sqrt{5y}\left(\sqrt{15}+4\right)$
12. $\sqrt{2t}\left(\sqrt{6t}-\sqrt{2t}\right)$

SEE EXAMPLE 3 p. 817

13. $\left(2+\sqrt{2}\right)\left(5+\sqrt{2}\right)$
14. $\left(4+\sqrt{6}\right)\left(3-\sqrt{6}\right)$
15. $\left(\sqrt{3}-4\right)\left(\sqrt{3}+2\right)$
16. $\left(5+\sqrt{3}\right)^2$
17. $\left(\sqrt{6}-5\sqrt{3}\right)^2$
18. $\left(6+3\sqrt{2}\right)^2$

SEE EXAMPLE 4 p. 818

**Simplify each quotient.**

19. $\frac{\sqrt{13}}{\sqrt{2}}$
20. $\frac{\sqrt{20}}{\sqrt{8}}$
21. $\frac{\sqrt{11}}{6\sqrt{3}}$
22. $\frac{\sqrt{28}}{\sqrt{3s}}$
23. $\frac{2}{\sqrt{7}}$
24. $\frac{3}{\sqrt{6}}$
25. $\frac{1}{\sqrt{5x}}$
26. $\frac{\sqrt{3}}{\sqrt{x}}$

## PRACTICE AND PROBLEM SOLVING

**Independent Practice**

| For Exercises | See Example |
|---|---|
| 27–32 | 1 |
| 33–38 | 2 |
| 39–44 | 3 |
| 45–52 | 4 |

**Extra Practice**

Skills Practice p. S25
Application Practice p. S38

**Multiply. Write each product in simplest form.**

27. $\sqrt{3}\sqrt{5}\sqrt{6}$
28. $3\sqrt{6}\left(5\sqrt{6}\right)$
29. $\left(2\sqrt{2}\right)^2$
30. $\left(3\sqrt{6}\right)^2$
31. $\sqrt{21d}\left(2\sqrt{3d}\right)$
32. $4\sqrt{5n}\left(2\sqrt{5n}\right)\left(3\sqrt{3n}\right)$
33. $\sqrt{5}\left(4-\sqrt{10}\right)$
34. $\sqrt{2}\left(\sqrt{6}+2\right)$
35. $\sqrt{2}\left(\sqrt{6}-\sqrt{10}\right)$
36. $3\sqrt{3}\left(\sqrt{8}-2\sqrt{6}\right)$
37. $\sqrt{3f}\left(\sqrt{3}+12\right)$
38. $\sqrt{8m}\left(\sqrt{10}+\sqrt{2m}\right)$
39. $\left(15+\sqrt{15}\right)\left(4+\sqrt{15}\right)$
40. $\left(\sqrt{6}+4\right)\left(\sqrt{2}-7\right)$
41. $\left(3-\sqrt{2}\right)\left(4+\sqrt{2}\right)$
42. $\left(\sqrt{5}-5\right)^2$
43. $\left(\sqrt{3}+8\right)^2$
44. $\left(2\sqrt{3}+4\sqrt{5}\right)^2$

**Simplify each quotient.**

45. $\frac{\sqrt{75}}{\sqrt{2}}$
46. $\frac{\sqrt{5}}{4\sqrt{8}}$
47. $\frac{\sqrt{27}}{3\sqrt{x}}$
48. $\frac{\sqrt{48k}}{\sqrt{5}}$
49. $\frac{\sqrt{49x}}{\sqrt{2}}$
50. $\frac{3\sqrt{27}}{\sqrt{b}}$
51. $\frac{\sqrt{12y}}{\sqrt{3}}$
52. $\frac{\sqrt{12t}}{\sqrt{6}}$

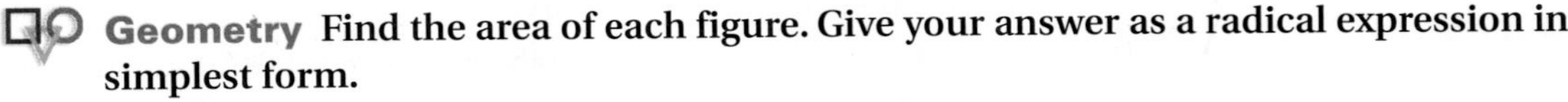

**Geometry** Find the area of each figure. Give your answer as a radical expression in simplest form.

53.

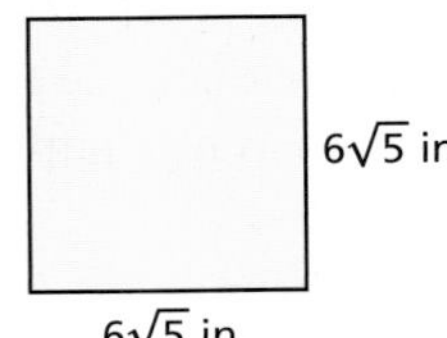


54.

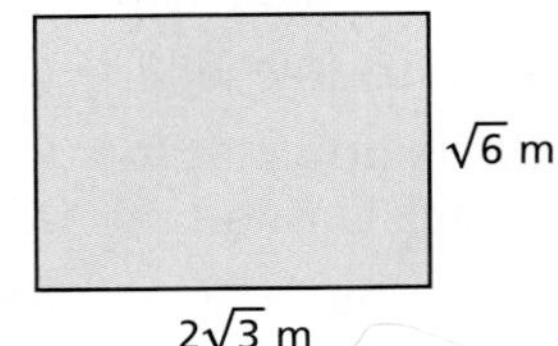


55.

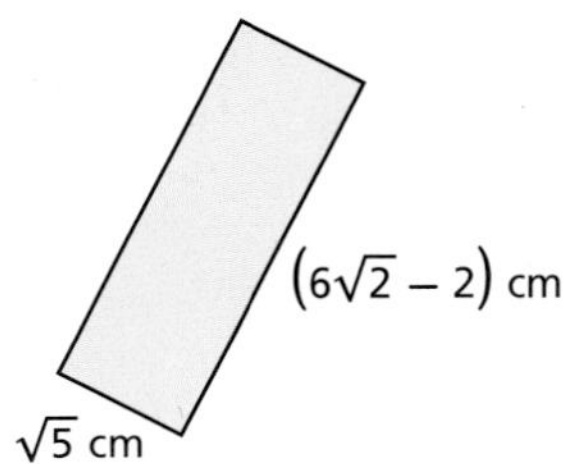

Simplify.

56. $\sqrt{3}\left(\frac{\sqrt{2}}{\sqrt{7}}\right)$

57. $\frac{15\sqrt{10}}{5\sqrt{3}}$

58. $\frac{6+\sqrt{18}}{3}$

59. $(\sqrt{3}-4)(\sqrt{3}+2)$

60. $\sqrt{2}(6+\sqrt{12})$

61. $\frac{\sqrt{1}+\sqrt{25}}{\sqrt{2}}$

62. $\frac{\sqrt{15}+\sqrt{10}}{\sqrt{5}}$

63. $\sqrt{12}(\sqrt{3}+8)^2$

64. $\sqrt{3}(4-2\sqrt{5})$

65. $(\sqrt{x}-\sqrt{y})^2$

66. $(\sqrt{x}-5)(3\sqrt{x}+7)$

67. $(\sqrt{3}+\sqrt{x})^2$

**LINK**

**Electricity**

People began using wind to generate electricity in the early twentieth century. A modern wind turbine is 120–180 feet tall and, depending on its construction, can generate up to 1 megawatt of power.

68. **Electricity** Electrical current in amps can be represented by $\frac{\sqrt{W}}{\sqrt{R}}$, where $W$ is power in watts and $R$ is resistance in ohms. How much electrical current is running through a microwave oven that has 850 watts of power and 5 ohms of resistance? Give the answer as a radical expression in simplest form. Then estimate the amount of current to the nearest tenth.

69. **Physics** The *period* of a pendulum is the amount of time it takes the pendulum to make one complete swing and return to its starting point. The period of a pendulum in seconds can be represented by $2\pi\sqrt{\frac{\ell}{32}}$, where $\ell$ is the length of the pendulum in feet. What is the period of a pendulum whose length is 3 feet? Give the answer as a radical expression in simplest form. Then estimate the period to the nearest tenth.

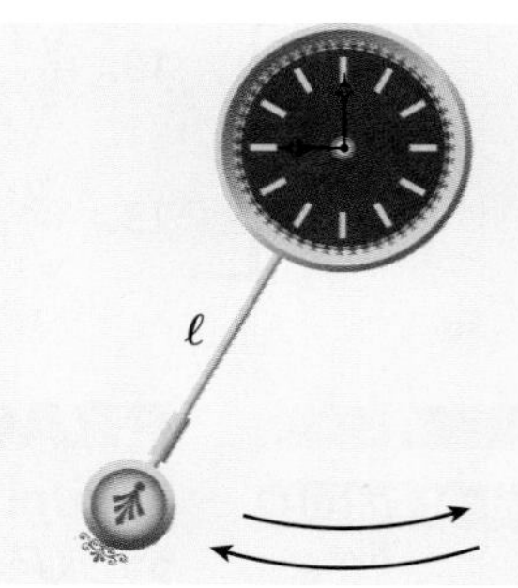


**Geometry** **Find the area of each triangle. Give the exact answer in simplest form. (*Hint:* The formula for the area of a triangle is $A=\frac{1}{2}bh$.)**

70.

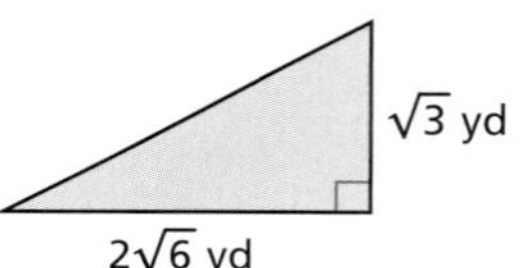


71.

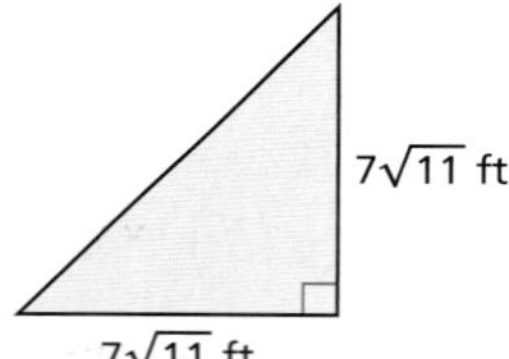


72.

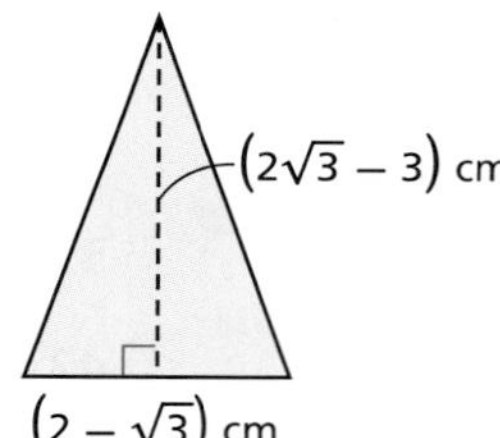

73. **Write About It** Describe an expression for which you would have to rationalize the denominator. How would you do it? Include an explanation of how you would choose what to multiply the original expression by.

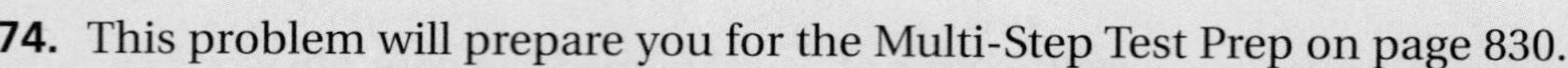

74. This problem will prepare you for the Multi-Step Test Prep on page 830.

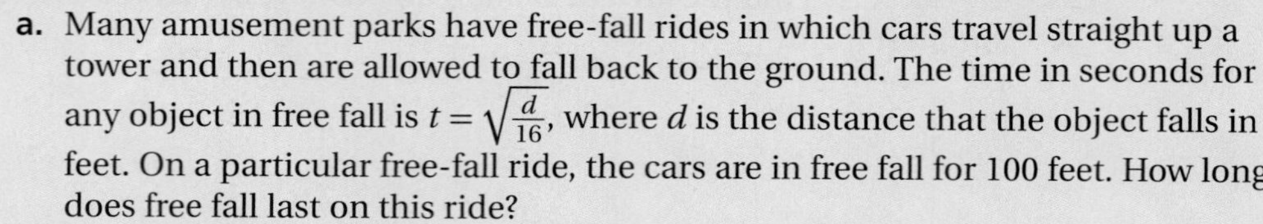

a. Many amusement parks have free-fall rides in which cars travel straight up a tower and then are allowed to fall back to the ground. The time in seconds for any object in free fall is $t=\sqrt{\frac{d}{16}}$, where $d$ is the distance that the object falls in feet. On a particular free-fall ride, the cars are in free fall for 100 feet. How long does free fall last on this ride?

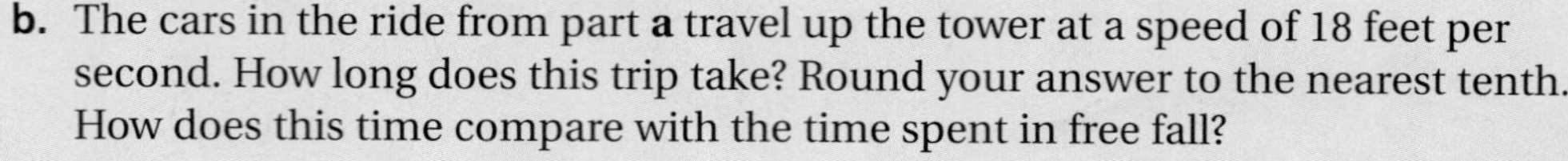

b. The cars in the ride from part **a** travel up the tower at a speed of 18 feet per second. How long does this trip take? Round your answer to the nearest tenth. How does this time compare with the time spent in free fall?

MA.N.2.3

**75.** What is the product of $3\sqrt{5}$ and $\sqrt{15}$?

Ⓐ $5\sqrt{3}$ Ⓑ $15\sqrt{3}$ Ⓒ $15\sqrt{15}$ Ⓓ $45\sqrt{5}$

**76.** Which of the following is the result of rationalizing the denominator in the expression $\frac{4}{3\sqrt{2}}$?

Ⓕ $\frac{\sqrt{2}}{3}$ Ⓖ $2\sqrt{2}$ Ⓗ $\frac{2\sqrt{2}}{3}$ Ⓙ $\frac{3\sqrt{2}}{2}$

**77.** Which of the following is equivalent to $(5\sqrt{10})^2$?

Ⓐ 50 Ⓑ 100 Ⓒ 125 Ⓓ 250

## CHALLENGE AND EXTEND

The expressions $\sqrt{a} + \sqrt{b}$ and $\sqrt{a} - \sqrt{b}$ are called *conjugates*. Using the FOIL method, conjugates can be multiplied as follows:

$$(\sqrt{a} - \sqrt{b})(\sqrt{a} + \sqrt{b}) = a + \sqrt{ab} - \sqrt{ab} - b = a - b$$

$$(\sqrt{3} - \sqrt{5})(\sqrt{3} + \sqrt{5}) = 3 + \sqrt{15} - \sqrt{15} - 5 = 3 - 5 = -2$$

Notice that the product does not contain any square roots. This means that you can use conjugates to rationalize denominators that contain sums or differences of square roots:

$$\frac{\sqrt{2}}{\sqrt{7} + \sqrt{2}}\left(\frac{\sqrt{7} - \sqrt{2}}{\sqrt{7} - \sqrt{2}}\right) = \frac{\sqrt{2}(\sqrt{7} - \sqrt{2})}{(\sqrt{7} + \sqrt{2})(\sqrt{7} - \sqrt{2})} = \frac{\sqrt{14} - \sqrt{4}}{7 - 2} = \frac{\sqrt{14} - 2}{5}$$

**Simplify.**

**78.** $\frac{4}{\sqrt{3} - \sqrt{2}}$ **79.** $\frac{8}{\sqrt{3} + \sqrt{5}}$ **80.** $\frac{\sqrt{5}}{\sqrt{10} + \sqrt{3}}$ **81.** $\frac{\sqrt{2} + \sqrt{3}}{\sqrt{2} - \sqrt{3}}$

**82.** $\frac{\sqrt{3}}{\sqrt{2} + \sqrt{3}}$ **83.** $\frac{\sqrt{2}}{\sqrt{8} + \sqrt{6}}$ **84.** $\frac{6}{\sqrt{2} + \sqrt{3}}$ **85.** $\frac{2}{\sqrt{6} - \sqrt{5}}$

**86. Geometry** One rectangle is $4\sqrt{6}$ feet long and $\sqrt{2}$ feet wide. Another rectangle is $8\sqrt{2}$ feet long and $2\sqrt{6}$ feet wide. How much more area does the larger rectangle cover than the smaller rectangle? (*Hint:* The formula for the area of a rectangle is $A = \ell w$.)

## SPIRAL REVIEW

**Describe the transformation(s) from the graph of $f(x)$ to the graph of $g(x)$.** *(Lesson 5-9)*

**87.** $f(x) = -2x + 3$; $g(x) = -2x - 1$ **88.** $f(x) = 4x$; $g(x) = 5x$

**Factor each polynomial completely. Check your answer.** *(Lesson 8-6)*

**89.** $x^2 + 7x - 30$ **90.** $6x^2 + 11x + 3$ **91.** $x^2 - 16$

**92.** $3x^2 + 30x + 75$ **93.** $2x^4 - 18$ **94.** $8x^3 - 20x^2 - 12x$

**Simplify. All variables represent nonnegative numbers.** *(Lesson 11-6)*

**95.** $\sqrt{360}$ **96.** $\sqrt{\frac{72}{16}}$ **97.** $\sqrt{\frac{49x^2}{64y^4}}$ **98.** $\sqrt{\frac{50a^7}{9a^3}}$

# 11-9 Solving Radical Equations

Ext. MA.N.2.3 Use strategies to compute square roots … of numbers that are not perfect squares...

***Objective***
Solve radical equations.

***Vocabulary***
radical equation
extraneous solution

**Who uses this?**
Meteorologists can use radical equations to estimate the size of a storm. (See Exercise 76.)

A **radical equation** is an equation that contains a variable within a radical. In this course, you will only study radical equations that contain square roots.

Recall that you use inverse operations to solve equations. For nonnegative numbers, squaring and taking the square root are inverse operations. When an equation contains a variable within a square root, square both sides of the equation to solve.

**Power Property of Equality**

| WORDS | NUMBERS | ALGEBRA |
|---|---|---|
| You can square both sides of an equation, and the resulting equation is still true. | $3 = 1 + 2$<br>$(3)^2 = (1 + 2)^2$<br>$9 = 9$ | If $a$ and $b$ are real numbers and $a = b$, then $a^2 = b^2$. |

## EXAMPLE 1 Solving Simple Radical Equations

**Solve each equation. Check your answer.**

**A** $\sqrt{x} = 8$

$(\sqrt{x})^2 = (8)^2$ *Square both sides.*

$x = 64$

*Check* $\sqrt{x} = 8$

$\sqrt{64}$ | $8$ *Substitute 64 for x in the original equation.*

$8$ | $8$ ✓ *Simplify.*

**B** $6 = \sqrt{4x}$

$(6)^2 = (\sqrt{4x})^2$ *Square both sides.*

$36 = 4x$

$9 = x$ *Divide both sides by 4.*

*Check* $6 = \sqrt{4x}$

$6$ | $\sqrt{4(9)}$ *Substitute 9 for x in the original equation.*

$6$ | $\sqrt{36}$ *Simplify.*

$6$ | $6$ ✓

**Solve each equation. Check your answer.**

**1a.** $\sqrt{x} = 6$ **1b.** $9 = \sqrt{27x}$ **1c.** $\sqrt{3x} = 1$

Some square-root equations do not have the square root isolated. To solve these equations, you may have to isolate the square root before squaring both sides. You can do this by using one or more inverse operations.

EXAMPLE 2

## Solving Radical Equations by Adding or Subtracting

**Solve each equation. Check your answer.**

**A** $\sqrt{x} + 3 = 10$

$\sqrt{x} = 7$ *Subtract 3 from both sides.*

$(\sqrt{x})^2 = (7)^2$ *Square both sides.*

$x = 49$

*Check* $\sqrt{x} + 3 = 10$

| | |
|---|---|
| $\sqrt{49} + 3$ | 10 |
| $7 + 3$ | 10 |
| 10 | 10 ✓ |

**B** $\sqrt{x - 5} = 4$

$(\sqrt{x - 5})^2 = (4)^2$ *Square both sides.*

$x - 5 = 16$

$x = 21$ *Add 5 to both sides.*

*Check* $\sqrt{x - 5} = 4$

| | |
|---|---|
| $\sqrt{21 - 5}$ | 4 |
| $\sqrt{16}$ | 4 |
| 4 | 4 ✓ |

**C** $\sqrt{2x - 1} + 4 = 7$

$\sqrt{2x - 1} = 3$ *Subtract 4 from both sides.*

$(\sqrt{2x - 1})^2 = (3)^2$ *Square both sides.*

$2x - 1 = 9$

$2x = 10$ *Add 1 to both sides.*

$x = 5$ *Divide both sides by 2.*

*Check* $\sqrt{2x - 1} + 4 = 7$

| | |
|---|---|
| $\sqrt{2(5) - 1} + 4$ | 7 |
| $\sqrt{10 - 1} + 4$ | 7 |
| $\sqrt{9} + 4$ | 7 |
| $3 + 4$ | 7 |
| 7 | 7 ✓ |

**Solve each equation. Check your answer.**

**2a.** $\sqrt{x} - 2 = 1$ **2b.** $\sqrt{x + 7} = 5$ **2c.** $\sqrt{3x + 7} - 1 = 3$

EXAMPLE 3

## Solving Radical Equations by Multiplying or Dividing

**Solve each equation. Check your answer.**

**A** $3\sqrt{x} = 21$

**Method 1**

$3\sqrt{x} = 21$

$\sqrt{x} = 7$ *Divide both sides by 3.*

$(\sqrt{x})^2 = (7)^2$ *Square both sides.*

$x = 49$

**Method 2**

$3\sqrt{x} = 21$

$(3\sqrt{x})^2 = 21^2$ *Square both sides.*

$9x = 441$

$x = 49$ *Divide both sides by 9.*

*Check* $3\sqrt{x} = 21$

| | | |
|---|---|---|
| $3\sqrt{49}$ | 21 | *Substitute 49 for x in the original equation.* |
| $3(7)$ | 21 | *Simplify.* |
| 21 | 21 ✓ | |

Solve each equation. Check your answer.

**B** $\dfrac{\sqrt{x}}{3} = 5$

**Method 1**

$\sqrt{x} = 15$ *Multiply both sides by 3.*

$(\sqrt{x})^2 = (15)^2$ *Square both sides.*

$x = 225$

**Method 2**

$\left(\dfrac{\sqrt{x}}{3}\right)^2 = (5)^2$ *Square both sides.*

$\dfrac{x}{9} = 25$

$x = 225$ *Multiply both sides by 9.*

***Check*** $\dfrac{\sqrt{x}}{3} = 5$

| $\dfrac{\sqrt{x}}{3}$ | $5$ | |
|---|---|---|
| $\dfrac{\sqrt{225}}{3}$ | $5$ | *Substitute 225 for x in the original equation.* |
| $\dfrac{15}{3}$ | $5$ | *Simplify.* |
| $5$ | $5$ ✓ | |

Solve each equation. Check your answer.

**3a.** $2\sqrt{x} = 22$ **3b.** $2 = \dfrac{\sqrt{x}}{4}$ **3c.** $\dfrac{2\sqrt{x}}{5} = 4$

## EXAMPLE 4 Solving Radical Equations with Square Roots on Both Sides

Solve each equation. Check your answer.

**A** $\sqrt{x+1} = \sqrt{3}$

$(\sqrt{x+1})^2 = (\sqrt{3})^2$ *Square both sides.*

$x + 1 = 3$

$x = 2$ *Subtract 1 from both sides.*

***Check*** $\sqrt{x+1} = \sqrt{3}$

| $\sqrt{x+1}$ | $\sqrt{3}$ |
|---|---|
| $\sqrt{2+1}$ | $\sqrt{3}$ |
| $\sqrt{3}$ | $\sqrt{3}$ ✓ |

**B** $\sqrt{x+8} - \sqrt{3x} = 0$

$\sqrt{x+8} = \sqrt{3x}$ *Add $\sqrt{3x}$ to both sides.*

$(\sqrt{x+8})^2 = (\sqrt{3x})^2$ *Square both sides.*

$x + 8 = 3x$

$8 = 2x$ *Subtract x from both sides.*

$4 = x$ *Divide both sides by 2.*

***Check*** $\sqrt{x+8} - \sqrt{3x} = 0$

| $\sqrt{x+8} - \sqrt{3x}$ | $0$ |
|---|---|
| $\sqrt{4+8} - \sqrt{3(4)}$ | $0$ |
| $\sqrt{12} - \sqrt{12}$ | $0$ |
| $0$ | $0$ ✓ |

Solve each equation. Check your answer.

**4a.** $\sqrt{3x+2} = \sqrt{x+6}$ **4b.** $\sqrt{2x-5} - \sqrt{6} = 0$

Squaring both sides of an equation may result in an **extraneous solution** — a number that is not a solution of the original equation.

Suppose your original equation is $x = 3$. $\qquad x = 3$

Square both sides. Now you have a new equation. $\qquad x^2 = 9$

Solve this new equation for $x$ by taking the square root of both sides. $\qquad \sqrt{x^2} = \sqrt{9}$; $x = 3$ or $x = -3$

Now there are two solutions of the new equation. One $(x = 3)$ is a solution of the original equation. The other $(x = -3)$ is extraneous—it is not a solution of the original equation. Because of extraneous solutions, it is important to check your answers.

## EXAMPLE 5 Extraneous Solutions

**Solve $\sqrt{6-x} = x$. Check your answer.**

$$\left(\sqrt{6-x}\right)^2 = (x)^2$$ *Square both sides.*

$$6 - x = x^2$$

$$x^2 + x - 6 = 0$$ *Write in standard form.*

$$(x-2)(x+3) = 0$$ *Factor.*

$$x - 2 = 0 \text{ or } x + 3 = 0$$ *Zero-Product Property*

$$x = 2 \text{ or } x = -3$$ *Solve for x.*

**Helpful Hint**

The equation in Example 5 has one solution. When all of the solutions of an equation are extraneous, the original equation has no solutions.

*Check*

| $\sqrt{6-x}$ | $= x$ |
|---|---|
| $\sqrt{6-2}$ | $2$ |
| $\sqrt{4}$ | $2$ |
| $2$ | $2$ ✓ |

*Substitute 2 for x in the equation.*

| $\sqrt{6-x}$ | $= x$ |
|---|---|
| $\sqrt{6-(-3)}$ | $-3$ |
| $\sqrt{9}$ | $-3$ |
| $3$ | $-3$ ✗ |

*Substitute −3 for x in the equation.*

$-3$ does not check; it is extraneous. The only solution is 2.

**Solve each equation. Check your answer.**

**5a.** $11 + \sqrt{5x} = 6$ **5b.** $x = \sqrt{-3x-2}$ **5c.** $x - 2 = \sqrt{x}$

## EXAMPLE 6 *Geometry Application*

Geometry

**A rectangle has an area of 52 square feet. Its length is 13 feet, and its width is $\sqrt{x}$ feet. What is the value of $x$? What is the width of the rectangle?**

$A = 52$ ft$^2$ $\sqrt{x}$ ft 13 ft

$$A = \ell w$$ *Use the formula for area of a rectangle.*

$$52 = 13\sqrt{x}$$ *Substitute 52 for A, 13 for ℓ, and $\sqrt{x}$ for w.*

$$\frac{52}{13} = \frac{13\sqrt{x}}{13}$$ *Divide both sides by 13.*

$$4 = \sqrt{x}$$

$$4^2 = \left(\sqrt{x}\right)^2$$ *Square both sides.*

$$16 = x$$

*Check* $A = \ell w$

| $52$ | $= 13\sqrt{x}$ |
|---|---|
| $52$ | $13\sqrt{16}$ |
| $52$ | $13(4)$ |
| $52$ | $52$ ✓ |

*Substitute 16 for x in the equation.*

The value of $x$ is 16. The width of the rectangle is $\sqrt{16} = 4$ feet.

**6.** A rectangle has an area of 15 cm$^2$. Its width is 5 cm, and its length is $\left(\sqrt{x+1}\right)$ cm. What is the value of $x$? What is the length of the rectangle?

## THINK AND DISCUSS

1. Compare the two methods used in Example 3A. Which method do you prefer? Why?
2. What is the first step to solve $\sqrt{x-2}+3=8$? Why?
3. **GET ORGANIZED** Copy and complete the graphic organizer. Write and solve a radical equation, using the boxes to show each step.

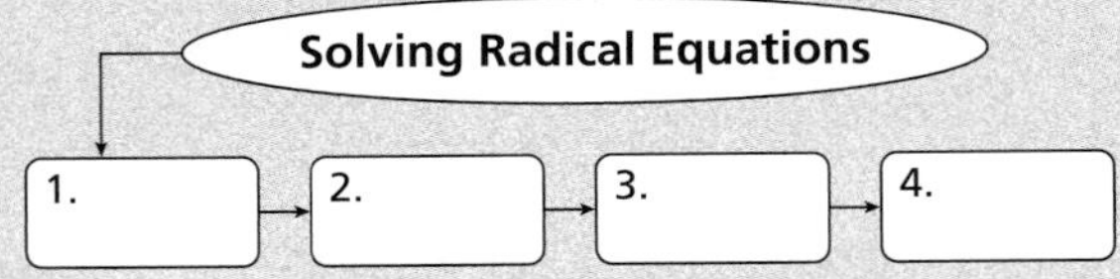


# 11-9 Exercises

Ext. MA.N.2.3

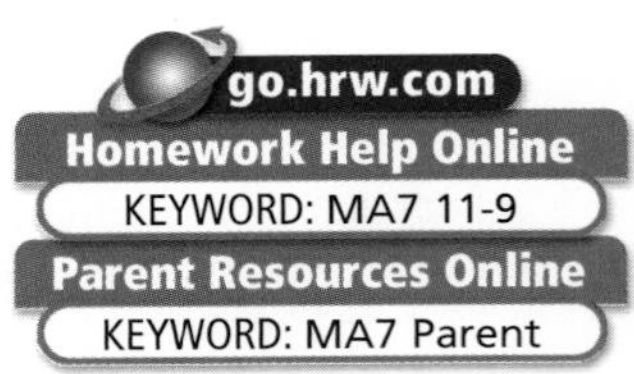


## GUIDED PRACTICE

1. **Vocabulary** Is $x=\sqrt{3}$ a *radical equation*? Why or why not?

SEE EXAMPLE 1 p. 822

**Solve each equation. Check your answer.**

2. $\sqrt{x}=7$
3. $4=\sqrt{-2y}$
4. $\sqrt{20a}=10$
5. $12=\sqrt{-x}$

SEE EXAMPLE 2 p. 823

6. $\sqrt{x}+6=11$
7. $\sqrt{2x-5}=7$
8. $\sqrt{2-a}=3$
9. $\sqrt{2x}-3=7$
10. $\sqrt{x-2}=3$
11. $\sqrt{x+3}=1$
12. $\sqrt{x-1}=2$
13. $\sqrt{4y+13}-1=6$

SEE EXAMPLE 3 p. 823

14. $-2\sqrt{x}=-10$
15. $\frac{\sqrt{a}}{2}=4$
16. $5\sqrt{-x}=20$
17. $\frac{3\sqrt{x}}{4}=3$
18. $\frac{5\sqrt{x}}{6}=10$
19. $2\sqrt{x}=8$
20. $\frac{\sqrt{x}}{3}=3$
21. $\frac{3\sqrt{x}}{2}=1$
22. $13\sqrt{2x}=26$
23. $\frac{\sqrt{x}}{5}=2$
24. $\frac{\sqrt{x-7}}{3}=1$
25. $4\sqrt{2x-1}=12$

SEE EXAMPLE 4 p. 824

**Solve each equation. Check your answer.**

26. $\sqrt{5-x}=\sqrt{6x-2}$
27. $\sqrt{x+7}=\sqrt{3x-19}$
28. $0=\sqrt{2x}-\sqrt{x+3}$
29. $\sqrt{x-5}=\sqrt{7-x}$
30. $\sqrt{-x}=\sqrt{2x+1}$
31. $\sqrt{3x+1}-\sqrt{2x+3}=0$

SEE EXAMPLE 5 p. 825

**Solve each equation. Check your answer.**

32. $\sqrt{x-5}+5=0$
33. $\sqrt{3x}+5=3$
34. $\sqrt{2-7x}=2x$
35. $x=\sqrt{12+x}$
36. $6+\sqrt{x-1}=4$
37. $\sqrt{6-3x}+2=x$
38. $\sqrt{x-2}=2-x$
39. $10+\sqrt{x}=5$

SEE EXAMPLE 6 p. 825

40. **Geometry** A trapezoid has an area of 14 cm$^2$. The length of one base is 4 cm and the length of the other base is 10 cm. The height is $\left(\sqrt{2x+3}\right)$ cm. What is the value of $x$? What is the height of the trapezoid? (*Hint:* The formula for the area of a trapezoid is $A=\frac{1}{2}(b_1+b_2)h$.)

## PRACTICE AND PROBLEM SOLVING

**Independent Practice**

| For Exercises | See Example |
|---|---|
| 41–44 | 1 |
| 45–48 | 2 |
| 49–52 | 3 |
| 53–58 | 4 |
| 59–66 | 5 |
| 67 | 6 |

**Extra Practice**

Skills Practice p. S25
Application Practice p. S38

**Solve each equation. Check your answer.**

**41.** $\sqrt{3x} = 12$ **42.** $2 = \sqrt{-2x}$ **43.** $\sqrt{-a} = 5$ **44.** $11 = \sqrt{c}$

**45.** $\sqrt{x-7} = 8$ **46.** $\sqrt{x} - 4 = 0$ **47.** $\sqrt{1-3x} = 5$ **48.** $\sqrt{5x+1} + 2 = 6$

**49.** $5\sqrt{x} = 30$ **50.** $\frac{\sqrt{2x}}{2} = 4$ **51.** $5\sqrt{-x} = 20$ **52.** $3\sqrt{3p} = 9$

**Solve each equation. Check your answer.**

**53.** $\sqrt{3x-13} = \sqrt{x+3}$ **54.** $\sqrt{x} - \sqrt{6-x} = 0$ **55.** $\sqrt{x+5} = \sqrt{2x-4}$

**56.** $\sqrt{4x-2} = \sqrt{3x+4}$ **57.** $\sqrt{5x-6} = \sqrt{16-6x}$ **58.** $\sqrt{12x-3} = \sqrt{4x+93}$

**Solve each equation. Check your answer.**

**59.** $\sqrt{x+6} = 1$ **60.** $-2\sqrt{x} = 6$ **61.** $x = \sqrt{2x+15}$ **62.** $\sqrt{6x} + 9 = 2$

**63.** $\sqrt{4-3x} = x$ **64.** $\sqrt{5x+4} = x - 4$ **65.** $\sqrt{2x+2} = 2x$ **66.** $\sqrt{x+3} + 10 = 7$

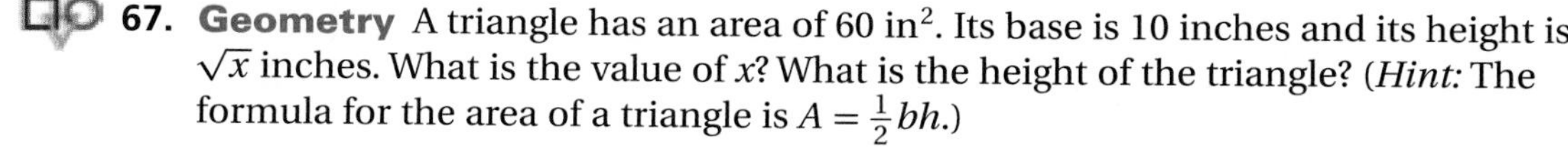

**67. Geometry** A triangle has an area of 60 $\text{in}^2$. Its base is 10 inches and its height is $\sqrt{x}$ inches. What is the value of $x$? What is the height of the triangle? (*Hint:* The formula for the area of a triangle is $A = \frac{1}{2}bh$.)

**Translate each sentence into an equation. Then solve the equation and check your answer.**

**68.** The square root of three times a number is nine.

**69.** The difference of the square root of a number and three is four.

**70.** The square root of the difference of a number and three is four.

**71.** A number is equal to the square root of the sum of that number and six.

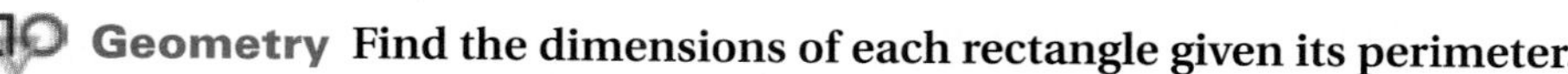

**Geometry** **Find the dimensions of each rectangle given its perimeter.**

**72.**

**73.**

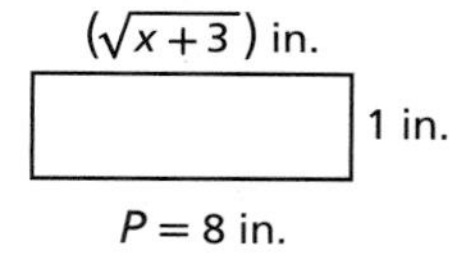


**74.**

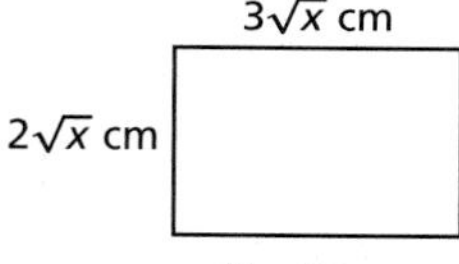


**75. Physics** The formula $v = \frac{\sqrt{2Em}}{m}$ describes the relationship between an object's mass $m$ in kilograms, its velocity $v$ in meters per second, and its kinetic energy $E$ in joules.

**a.** A baseball with a mass of 0.14 kg is thrown with a velocity of 28 m/s. How much kinetic energy does the baseball have?

**b.** What is the kinetic energy of an object at rest ($v = 0$)?

**76. Meteorology** The formula $t = \sqrt{\frac{d^2}{216}}$ gives the time $t$ in hours that a storm with diameter $d$ miles will last. What is the diameter of a storm that lasts 1 hour? Round your answer to the nearest hundredth.

**LINK**

**Meteorology**

This color-enhanced satellite image is from the National Hurricane Center. Images such as this one show the size of a storm and the area that it covers.

**77. Transportation** A sharp curve may require a driver to slow down to avoid going off the road. The equation $v = \sqrt{2.5r}$ describes the relationship between the radius $r$ in feet of an unbanked curve and the maximum velocity $v$ in miles per hour that a car can safely go around the curve. An engineer is designing a highway with a maximum speed limit of 65 mi/h. What is the radius of an unbanked curve for which this is the maximum safe speed?

78. **Write About It** Explain why it is important to check solutions when solving radical equations.

79. **Multi-Step** Solve for $x$ and $y$ in the equations $\sqrt{x} + \sqrt{y} = \sqrt{81}$ and $6\sqrt{y} = 24$. (*Hint:* Solve for $y$ first, and then use substitution to solve for $x$.)

**Tell whether the following statements are *always, sometimes,* or *never* true. If the answer is *sometimes,* give one example that is true and one that is false.**

80. If $a = b$, then $a^2 = b^2$.

81. If $a^2 = b^2$, then $a = b$.

82. When solving radical equations, the value of the variable is nonnegative.

83. **ERROR ANALYSIS** Two students solved $\sqrt{5 - x} = \sqrt{x + 9}$. Which is incorrect? Explain the error.

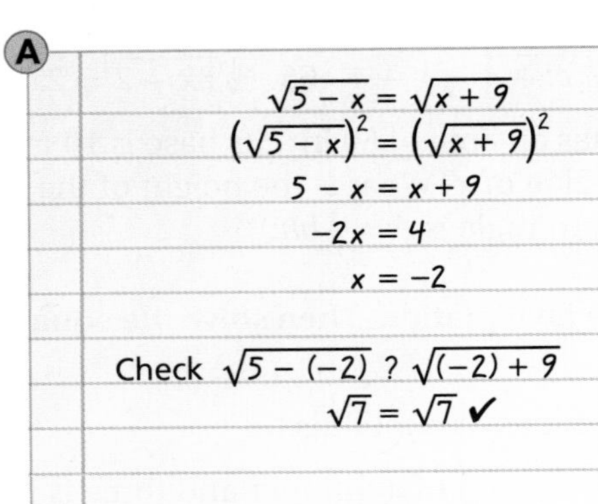


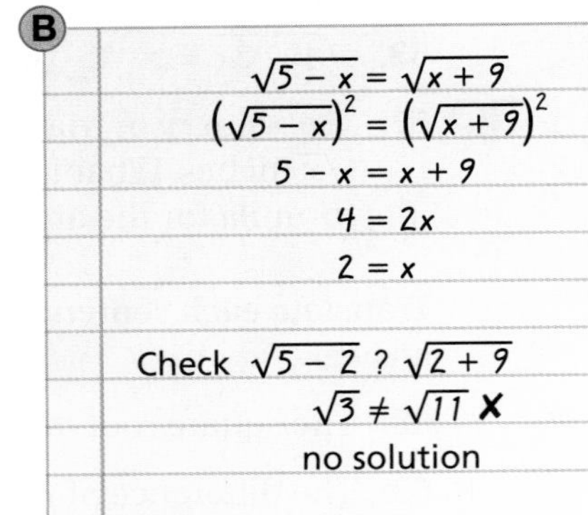


84. **Estimation** The relationship between a circle's radius and its area can be modeled by $r = \sqrt{\frac{A}{\pi}}$, where $r$ is the radius and $A$ is the area. Solutions to this equation are graphed at right. Use the graph to estimate the radius of a circle with an area of 29 m$^2$.

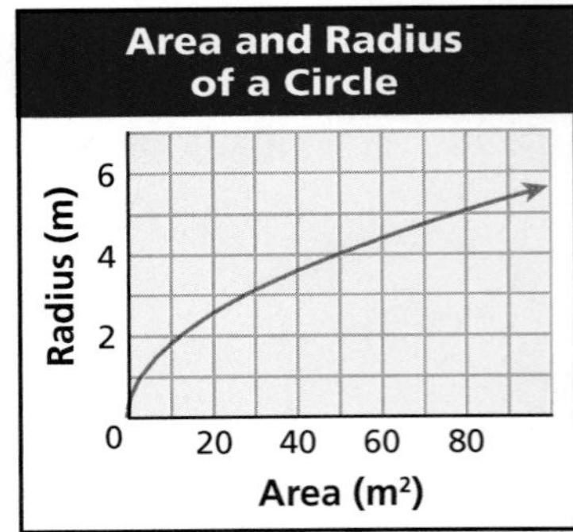


85. **Critical Thinking** Suppose that the equation $\sqrt{-x} = k$ has a solution. What does that tell you about the value of $x$? the value of $k$? Explain.

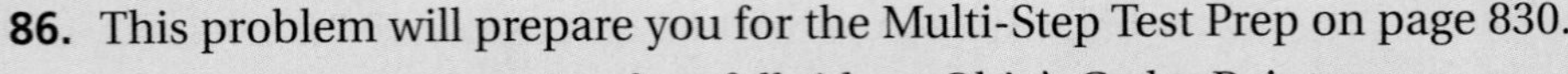

86. This problem will prepare you for the Multi-Step Test Prep on page 830.

   a. The Demon Drop is a free-fall ride at Ohio's Cedar Point amusement park. The maximum speed on the Demon Drop is 42 miles per hour. Convert this speed to feet per second. (*Hint:* There are 5280 feet in a mile.)

   b. The Demon Drop is 131 feet tall. Most of the drop is a vertical free fall, but near the bottom, the track curves so that the cars slow down gradually. The velocity of any object in free fall is $v = 8\sqrt{d}$, where $v$ is the velocity in feet per second and $d$ is the distance the object has fallen in feet. Use this equation and your answer to part **a** to estimate the free-fall distance.

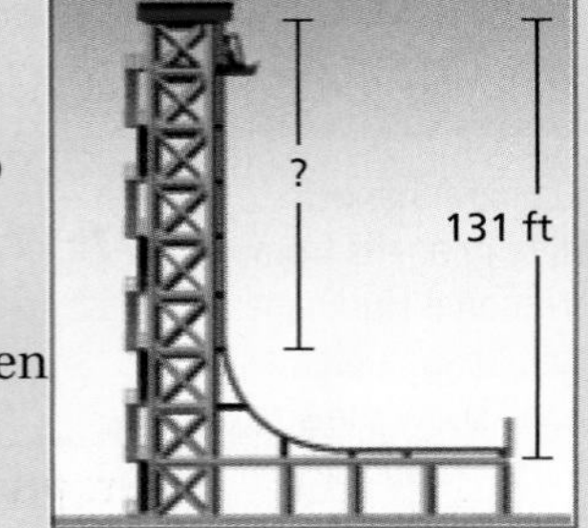

Ext. MA.N.2.3

**87.** Which of the following is the solution of $\sqrt{8-2x}-2=2$?

Ⓐ $-4$ Ⓑ $-2$ Ⓒ $2$ Ⓓ $4$

**88.** For which of the following values of $k$ does the equation $\sqrt{x+1}+k=0$ have no real solution?

Ⓕ $-2$ Ⓖ $-1$ Ⓗ $0$ Ⓙ $1$

**89.** Which of the following is the solution of $x=\sqrt{12-x}$?

Ⓐ $-4$ Ⓑ $-3$ Ⓒ $3$ Ⓓ $4$

**90.** Which of the following is the solution of $\sqrt{x+13}=5\sqrt{x-11}$?

Ⓕ $9$ Ⓖ $12$ Ⓗ $16$ Ⓙ $17$

**91.** Which of the following is an extraneous solution of $\sqrt{3x-2}=x-2$?

Ⓐ $1$ Ⓑ $2$ Ⓒ $3$ Ⓓ $6$

## CHALLENGE AND EXTEND

**Solve each equation. Check your answer.**

**92.** $\sqrt{x+3}=x+1$ **93.** $\sqrt{x-1}=x-1$ **94.** $x-1=\sqrt{2x+6}$

**95.** $\sqrt{x^2+5x+11}=x+3$ **96.** $\sqrt{x^2+9x+14}=x+4$ **97.** $x+2=\sqrt{x^2+5x+4}$

**98. Graphing Calculator** Solve $\sqrt{2x-2}=-\sqrt{x}$ and check your answer. Then use your graphing calculator for the following:

**a.** Graph $y=\sqrt{2x-2}$ and $y=-\sqrt{x}$ on the same screen. Make a sketch of the graphs.

**b.** Use the graphs in part **a** to explain your solution to $\sqrt{2x-2}=-\sqrt{x}$.

**99. Graphing Calculator** Solve $x=\sqrt{x+6}$ and check your answer. Then use your graphing calculator for the following:

**a.** Graph $y=x$ and $y=\sqrt{x+6}$ on the same screen. Make a sketch of the graphs.

**b.** Use the graphs in part **a** to explain your solution to $x=\sqrt{x+6}$.

**100.** Find the domain for the function $y=\frac{4}{\sqrt{x-2}}$. Is the domain for this function different from the domain for the function $y=\sqrt{x-2}$? Why or why not?

## SPIRAL REVIEW

**101.** On a map, the distance between two towns is 3.2 inches. If the map uses the scale 2.5 in : 40 mi, what is the actual distance between the towns? *(Lesson 2-6)*

**102.** In model railroading, O-scale trains use the scale 1 : 48. An O-scale boxcar measures 12.5 inches. How many feet long is the boxcar that it models? *(Lesson 2-6)*

**103.** The personal identification number (PIN) for a debit card is made up of four numbers. How many PINs are possible? *(Lesson 10-8)*

**104.** A dessert menu offers 6 different selections. The restaurant offers a dessert sampler that includes small portions of any 4 different choices from the dessert menu. How many different dessert samplers are possible? *(Lesson 10-8)*

**Graph each square-root function.** *(Lesson 11-5)*

**105.** $f(x)=\sqrt{x+3}$ **106.** $f(x)=\sqrt{3x-6}$ **107.** $f(x)=2\sqrt{x}+1$

## Radical Functions and Equations

ADMIT ONE 221948

**Eye in the Sky** The London Eye is a giant observation wheel in London, England. It carries people in enclosed capsules around its circumference. Opened on December 31, 1999, to welcome the new millennium, its diameter is 135 meters. On the London Eye, riders can see a distance of 40 kilometers.

1. What is the circumference of the London Eye? Use 3.14 for $\pi$.
2. The London Eye's velocity in meters per second can be found using the equation $v = \sqrt{0.001r}$, where $r$ is the radius of the wheel in meters. Find the velocity in meters per second. Round to the nearest hundredth.
3. Another way to find the velocity is to divide the distance around the wheel by the time for the ride. A ride on the London Eye lasts 30 minutes. Use this method to find the velocity of the wheel in meters per second to the nearest hundredth.
4. Are your answers to problems 2 and 3 the same? If not, explain any differences.
5. When a rider is at the highest point on the London Eye, how far is he from the bottom of the ride? Explain.
6. When a rider is at half the maximum height, her distance from the bottom of the ride can be found using the equation $d = \sqrt{2r^2}$. Explain where this equation comes from. Then find this distance. Round to the nearest hundredth.

# READY TO GO ON?

CHAPTER 11

SECTION 11B

## Quiz for Lessons 11-5 Through 11-9

### 11-5 Square-Root Functions

1. The distance in kilometers that a person can see to the horizon can be approximated by the formula $D = 113\sqrt{h}$, where $h$ is the person's height in kilometers above sea level. What is the distance to the horizon observed by a mountain climber who is 0.3 km above sea level?

**Find the domain of each square-root function.**

2. $y = \sqrt{3x} - 7$
3. $y = \sqrt{x - 5}$
4. $y = \sqrt{2x - 6}$

**Graph each square-root function.**

5. $f(x) = \sqrt{x - 6}$
6. $f(x) = \sqrt{x} + 5$
7. $f(x) = \sqrt{8 - 4x}$

### 11-6 Radical Expressions

**Simplify. All variables represent nonnegative numbers.**

8. $\sqrt{75}$
9. $\sqrt{\dfrac{300}{3}}$
10. $\sqrt{a^2b^3}$
11. $\sqrt{98xy^2}$
12. $\sqrt{\dfrac{32}{25}}$
13. $\sqrt{\dfrac{128}{121}}$
14. $\sqrt{\dfrac{4b^2}{81}}$
15. $\sqrt{\dfrac{75a^9}{49a^3}}$
16. How long is the diagonal of a rectangular television screen that is 19.2 inches long and 14.4 inches high?

### 11-7 Adding and Subtracting Radical Expressions

**Simplify each expression.**

17. $12\sqrt{7} - 5\sqrt{7}$
18. $3\sqrt{x} + 3\sqrt{x}$
19. $\sqrt{12} + \sqrt{75}$
20. $5\sqrt{50} + \sqrt{98}$
21. $4\sqrt{3} - 3\sqrt{4}$
22. $\sqrt{98x} + \sqrt{18x} - \sqrt{200x}$

### 11-8 Multiplying and Dividing Radical Expressions

**Multiply. Write each product in simplest form.**

23. $\sqrt{6}\sqrt{11}$
24. $\sqrt{3}\sqrt{8}$
25. $4\sqrt{12x}\sqrt{3x}$
26. $\left(3 - \sqrt{3}\right)\left(5 + \sqrt{3}\right)$

**Simplify each quotient.**

27. $\dfrac{\sqrt{19}}{\sqrt{3}}$
28. $\dfrac{\sqrt{14}}{\sqrt{8}}$
29. $\dfrac{\sqrt{6b}}{\sqrt{8}}$
30. $\dfrac{\sqrt{27}}{\sqrt{3t}}$

### 11-9 Solving Radical Equations

**Solve each equation. Check your answer.**

31. $\sqrt{x} - 4 = 21$
32. $-3\sqrt{x} = -12$
33. $\dfrac{5\sqrt{x}}{2} = 40$
34. $\sqrt{4x - 2} - \sqrt{43 - x} = 0$
35. $\sqrt{20 + x} = x$
36. $\sqrt{4x} + 12 = 10$

# Cube Roots

**MA.N.2.3** Use strategies to compute …cube roots of numbers that are not… perfect cubes.

***Objectives***
Simplify and evaluate expressions containing cube roots.
Estimate cube roots.

***Vocabulary***
cube root
perfect cube

Recall that the cube of a number is the number raised to the third power. It is called a cube because it represents the volume of a cube with edge lengths equal to that number. The drawing shows that 27 is the cube of 3, or $3^3 = 27$.

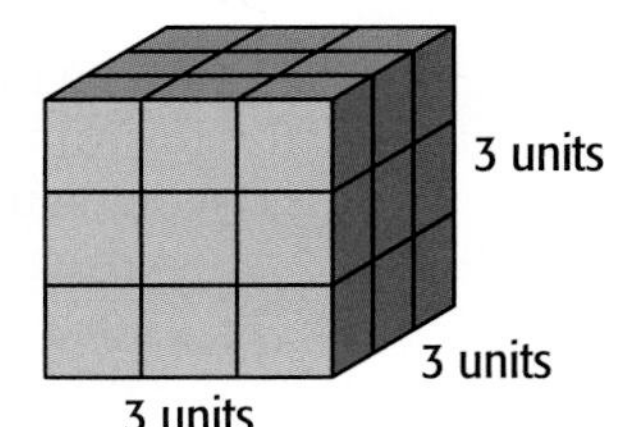


A number that is raised to the third power to form a product is a **cube root** of that product. 3 is a cube root of 27 because $3^3 = 27$. The symbol for a cube root is $\sqrt[3]{\phantom{x}}$ . Since $3^3 = 27$, $\sqrt[3]{27} = 3$.

Unlike square roots, every real number has exactly one cube root. It may be positive or negative. For example $\sqrt[3]{-27} = -3$ because $(-3)^3 = (-3)\cdot(-3)\cdot(-3) = -27$.

A **perfect cube** is a number whose cube root is an integer. Some perfect cubes are shown in the table.

| 1 | 8 | 27 | 64 | 125 | 216 | 343 | 512 | 729 | 1000 |
|---|---|---|---|---|---|---|---|---|---|
| $1^3$ | $2^3$ | $3^3$ | $4^3$ | $5^3$ | $6^3$ | $7^3$ | $8^3$ | $9^3$ | $10^3$ |

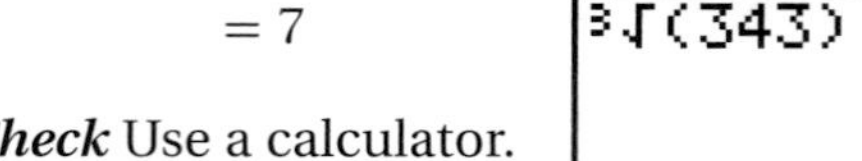


### Finding Cube Roots of Perfect Cubes

**Find each cube root.**

**A** $\sqrt[3]{343}$

$\sqrt[3]{343} = \sqrt[3]{7^3}$ *Think: What number cubed equals 343?*

$= 7$

*Check* Use a calculator.

```
3√(343)
                7
```

**Helpful Hint**

To enter a cube root on your graphing calculator, press  MATH and select 4: $\sqrt[3]{\phantom{x}}$ .

**B** $\sqrt[3]{-125}$

$\sqrt[3]{-125} = \sqrt[3]{(-5)^3}$ *Think: What number cubed equals –125?*

$= -5$

*Check* Use a calculator.

```
3√(-125)
               -5
```

**Find each cube root.**

**1a.** $\sqrt[3]{64}$ **1b.** $\sqrt[3]{-27}$

Cube roots of numbers that are not perfect cubes, such as 15, are not integers. A calculator can approximate $\sqrt[3]{15}$ as 2.466212074... Without a calculator, you can use the cube roots of perfect cubes to help estimate the cube roots of other numbers.

## EXAMPLE 2 Estimating Cube Roots

**Find the two integers that each cube root lies between.**

**A** $\sqrt[3]{567}$

Find two consecutive perfect cubes that 567 is between: $8^3 = 512$ and $9^3 = 729$.

567 is between 512 and 729, so $\sqrt[3]{567}$ is between 8 and 9.

***Check*** Use a calculator.

```
3√(567)
        8.276772529
```

**B** $\sqrt[3]{-195}$

Find two consecutive perfect cubes that –195 is between: $(-5)^3 = -125$ and $(-6)^3 = -216$.

–195 is between –125 and –216, so $\sqrt[3]{-195}$ is between –5 and –6.

***Check*** Use a calculator.

```
3√( -195)
        -5.798889998
```

**Find the two integers that each cube root lies between.**

**2a.** $\sqrt[3]{-100}$ **2b.** $\sqrt[3]{265}$

You can simplify cube-root expressions in much the same way that you simplify square-root expressions. The properties of square roots also apply to cube roots.

### Properties of Cube Roots

| WORDS | NUMBERS | ALGEBRA |
|---|---|---|
| **Product Property of Cube Roots**<br>For any real numbers *a* and *b*, the cube root of *ab* is equal to the cube root of *a* times the cube root of *b*. | $\sqrt[3]{8(27)} = \sqrt[3]{216} = 6$<br>$\sqrt[3]{8(27)} = \sqrt[3]{8}\sqrt[3]{27} = 2(3) = 6$ | $\sqrt[3]{ab} = \sqrt[3]{a}\sqrt[3]{b}$ |
| **Quotient Property of Cube Roots**<br>For any real numbers *a* and *b* ($b \neq 0$), the cube root of $\frac{a}{b}$ is equal to the cube root of *a* divided by the cube root of *b*. | $\sqrt[3]{\frac{64}{8}} = \sqrt[3]{8} = 2$<br>$\sqrt[3]{\frac{64}{8}} = \frac{\sqrt[3]{64}}{\sqrt[3]{8}} = \frac{4}{2} = 2$ | $\sqrt[3]{\frac{a}{b}} = \frac{\sqrt[3]{a}}{\sqrt[3]{b}}$, where $b \neq 0$ |

## EXAMPLE 3 Simplifying Cube-Root Expressions

**Simplify.**

**A** $\sqrt[3]{128}$

$\sqrt[3]{128} = \sqrt[3]{64(2)}$ *Factor perfect cubes in the radicand.*

$= \sqrt[3]{64}\sqrt[3]{2}$ *Product Property of Cube Roots*

$= 4\sqrt[3]{2}$ *Simplify.*

**B** $\dfrac{\sqrt[3]{-375}}{\sqrt[3]{-3}}$

$\dfrac{\sqrt[3]{-375}}{\sqrt[3]{-3}} = \sqrt[3]{\dfrac{-375}{-3}}$ *Quotient Property of Cube Roots*

$= \sqrt[3]{125}$ *Divide.*

$= 5$ *Simplify.*

**Simplify.**

**3a.** $\sqrt[3]{-54}$ **3b.** $\dfrac{\sqrt[3]{56}}{\sqrt[3]{7}}$

Cube-root expressions with the same radicand are like radicals. You can add and subtract cube-root expressions that contain like radicals.

## EXAMPLE 4 Adding and Subtracting Cube-Root Expressions

**Add or subtract.**

**A** $6\sqrt[3]{5} - 11\sqrt[3]{5}$

$6\sqrt[3]{5} - 11\sqrt[3]{5}$ *The terms are like radicals.*

$-5\sqrt[3]{5}$ *Subtract.*

**B** $2\sqrt[3]{24} + 4\sqrt[3]{3}$

$2\sqrt[3]{8(3)} + 4\sqrt[3]{3}$ *Factor perfect cubes in the radicand.*

$2\sqrt[3]{8}\sqrt[3]{3} + 4\sqrt[3]{3}$ *Product Property of Cube Roots*

$4\sqrt[3]{3} + 4\sqrt[3]{3}$ *Simplify. The terms are like radicals.*

$8\sqrt[3]{3}$

**Add or subtract.**

**4a.** $-8\sqrt[3]{9} + 7\sqrt[3]{9}$ **4b.** $7\sqrt[3]{2} - \sqrt[3]{250}$

EXTENSION

# Exercises

MA.N.2.3

Find each cube root.

1. $\sqrt[3]{27}$
2. $\sqrt[3]{-1000}$
3. $\sqrt[3]{216}$
4. $\sqrt[3]{-343}$
5. $\sqrt[3]{-1}$
6. $\sqrt[3]{729}$
7. $\sqrt[3]{512}$
8. $\sqrt[3]{-64}$

Find the two integers that each cube root lies between.

9. $\sqrt[3]{40}$
10. $\sqrt[3]{-85}$
11. $\sqrt[3]{750}$
12. $\sqrt[3]{300}$
13. $\sqrt[3]{-415}$
14. $\sqrt[3]{5}$
15. $\sqrt[3]{-222}$
16. $\sqrt[3]{80}$

Simplify.

17. $\sqrt[3]{250}$
18. $\sqrt[3]{-56}$
19. $\sqrt[3]{320}$
20. $\sqrt[3]{-686}$
21. $\sqrt[3]{\frac{-512}{64}}$
22. $\frac{\sqrt[3]{24}}{\sqrt[3]{81}}$
23. $\sqrt[3]{\frac{500}{125}}$
24. $\frac{\sqrt[3]{-40}}{\sqrt[3]{-216}}$

Add or subtract.

25. $2\sqrt[3]{10} + 7\sqrt[3]{10}$
26. $5\sqrt[3]{3} - \sqrt[3]{24}$
27. $-4\sqrt[3]{5} + 9\sqrt[3]{5}$
28. $-2\sqrt[3]{54} - 5\sqrt[3]{2}$
29. $8\sqrt[3]{9} + 4\sqrt[3]{72}$
30. $7\sqrt[3]{16} - 11\sqrt[3]{16}$

31. **Art** An artist created a sculpture in the shape of a cube that required 512 cubic feet of material. The artist now wants to paint the cube.
    a. Find an edge length of the cube.
    b. Find the surface area of the cube.
    c. The artist uses paint that costs $2.50 per square foot. How much will it cost to paint the cube?

32. **Geometry** The expression $\sqrt[3]{0.24V}$ can be used to approximate the radius of a sphere with a given volume $V$. Estimate the radius of a sphere that has a volume of 1458 cubic inches.

Compare the expressions. Write >, <, or =.

33. $\sqrt[3]{729}$ ■ $\sqrt{81}$
34. $2\sqrt{64}$ ■ $2\sqrt[3]{640}$
35. $\sqrt[3]{-1}$ ■ $\sqrt{1}$
36. $\sqrt[3]{500}$ ■ $7\sqrt[3]{4} - 2\sqrt[3]{4}$

37. **Critical Thinking** A positive number has two square roots, one that is positive and one that is negative. Is the same thing true for the cube root of a positive number? Explain.

38. **Write About It** Explain why you cannot take the square root of a negative number but you can take the cube root of a negative number.

CHAPTER 11

# Study Guide: Review

## Vocabulary



**Complete the sentences below with vocabulary words from the list above.**

1. $f(x) = \sqrt{2x}$ is an example of a(n) ___?___.
2. A(n) ___?___ function has the form $y = a(1 - r)^t$, where $a > 0$.
3. In the formula $a_n = a_1 r^{n-1}$, the variable $r$ represents the ___?___.
4. $f(x) = 2^x$ is an example of a(n) ___?___.

## 11-1 Geometric Sequences *(pp. 766–771)*

MA.A.3

### EXAMPLE

**What is the 10th term of the geometric sequence −6400, 3200, −1600, 800, ...?**

*Find the common ratio by dividing consecutive terms.*

$\frac{3200}{-6400} = -0.5 \quad \frac{-1600}{3200} = -0.5$

$a_n = a_1 r^{n-1}$ *Write the formula.*

$a_{10} = -6400(-0.5)^{10-1}$ *Substitute.*

$= -6400(-0.5)^9$ *Simplify.*

$= 12.5$

### EXERCISES

**Find the next three terms in each geometric sequence.**

5. 1, 3, 9, 27, ...
6. 3, −6, 12, −24, ...
7. 80, 40, 20, 10, ...
8. −1, −4, −16, −64, ...
9. The first term of a geometric sequence is 4 and the common ratio is 5. What is the 10th term?
10. What is the 15th term of the geometric sequence 4, 12, 36, 108, ...?

## 11-2 Exponential Functions *(pp. 772–778)*

MA.A.3.1, MA.A.4.6, MA.A.5.1, MA.A.4.3

### EXAMPLE

- **Tell whether the ordered pairs $\{(1, 4), (2, 16), (3, 36), (4, 64)\}$ satisfy an exponential function. Explain.**

| x | y |
|---|---|
| 1 | 4 |
| 2 | 16 |
| 3 | 36 |
| 4 | 64 |

*As the x-values increase by a constant amount, the y-values are not multiplied by a constant amount. This function is not exponential.*

### EXERCISES

**Tell whether each set of ordered pairs satisfies an exponential function. Explain.**

11. $\{(0, 1), (2, 9), (4, 81), (6, 729)\}$
12. $\{(-2, -8), (-1, -4), (0, 0), (1, 4)\}$

**Graph each exponential function.**

13. $y = 4^x$
14. $y = \left(\frac{1}{4}\right)^x$

# 11-3 Exponential Growth and Decay *(pp. 781–788)*

 MA.A.5.1

## EXAMPLE

**The value of a piece of antique furniture has been increasing at a rate of 2% per year. In 1990, its value was \$800. Write an exponential growth function to model the situation. Then find the value of the furniture in the year 2010.**

**Step 1** $y = a(1 + r)^t$ *Write the formula.*

$y = \mathbf{800}(1 + \mathbf{0.02})^t$ *Substitute.*

$y = 800(1.02)^t$ *Simplify.*

**Step 2** $y = 800(1.02)^{20}$ *Substitute 20 for t.*

$\approx 1188.76$ *Simplify and round.*

The furniture's value will be \$1188.76.

## EXERCISES

15. The number of students in the book club is increasing at a rate of 15% per year. In 2001, there were 9 students in the book club. Write an exponential growth function to model the situation. Then find the number of students in the book club in the year 2008.

16. The population of a small town is decreasing at a rate of 4% per year. In 1970, the population was 24,500. Write an exponential decay function to model the situation. Then find the population in the year 2020.

# 11-4 Linear, Quadratic, and Exponential Models *(pp. 789–795)*

 MA.S.2.2, MA.A.3.1, MA.A.5.1, MA.A.4.3

## EXAMPLE

- **Use the data in the table to describe how Jasmin's debt is changing. Then write a function that models the data. Use your function to predict Jasmin's debt after 8 years.**

| Jasmin's Debt | |
|---|---|
| **Years** | **Debt (\$)** |
| 1 | 130 |
| 2 | 260 |
| 3 | 520 |
| 4 | 1040 |

(Years: +1, +1, +1; Debt: × 2, × 2, × 2)

Jasmin's debt doubles every year.

For a constant change in time $(+1)$, there is a constant ratio of 2, so the data is exponential.

$y = ab^x$ *Write the general form.*

$y = a(2)^x$ *Substitute 2 for b.*

$130 = a(2)^1$ *Substitute (1, 130) for x and y.*

$a = 65$ *Solve for a.*

$y = 65(2)^x$ *Replace a and b in $y = ab^x$.*

$y = 65(2)^8$ *Substitute 8 for x.*

$y = 16{,}640$ *Simplify with a calculator.*

Jasmin's debt in 8 years will be \$16,640.

## EXERCISES

**Graph each data set. Which kind of model best describes the data?**

17. $\{(-2, -12), (-1, -3), (0, 0), (1, -3), (2, -12)\}$

18. $\{(-2, -2), (-1, 2), (0, 6), (1, 10), (2, 14)\}$

19. $\left\{\left(-2, -\frac{1}{4}\right), \left(-1, -\frac{1}{2}\right), (0, -1), (1, -2), (2, -4)\right\}$

**Look for a pattern in each data set to determine which kind of model best describes the data.**

20. $\{(0, 2), (1, 6), (2, 18), (3, 54), (4, 162)\}$

21. $\{(0, 0), (2, -20), (4, -80), (6, -180), (8, -320)\}$

22. $\{(-8, 5), (-4, 3), (0, 1), (4, -1), (8, -3)\}$

23. Write a function that models the data. Then use your function to predict how long the humidifier will produce steam with 10 quarts of water.

| Input and Output of a Humidifier | |
|---|---|
| **Water Volume (qt)** | **Steam Time (h)** |
| 3 | 4.5 |
| 4 | 6 |
| 5 | 7.5 |
| 6 | 9 |

## 11-5 Square-Root Functions *(pp. 798–803)*

MA.A.4.2, MA.A.4.3

### EXAMPLE

■ **Graph $f(x) = 3\sqrt{x-2}$.**

**Step 1** Find the domain of the function.

$x - 2 \geq 0$ *The radicand must be greater*

$x \geq 2$ *than or equal to 0.*

**Step 2** Generate ordered pairs.

| $x$ | $f(x) = 3\sqrt{x-2}$ |
|---|---|
| 2 | 0 |
| 3 | 3 |
| 6 | 6 |
| 11 | 9 |
| 18 | 12 |

*Choose x-values greater than or equal to 2 that form a perfect square under the radical sign.*

**Step 3** Plot and connect the points.

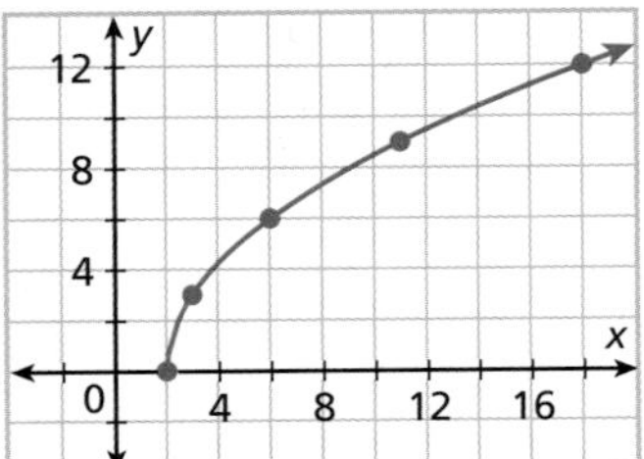


### EXERCISES

**24.** If you know the surface area $S$ of a cube, you can use the formula $\ell = \sqrt{\frac{S}{6}}$ to find the length $\ell$ of a side. What is the side length of a cube whose surface area is 135 $cm^2$? Round your answer to the nearest hundredth of a centimeter.

**Find the domain of each square-root function.**

**25.** $y = \sqrt{x} + 5$

**26.** $y = \sqrt{x+4}$

**27.** $y = 8 - \sqrt{3x}$

**28.** $y = 2\sqrt{x+2}$

**29.** $y = 1 + \sqrt{3x-4}$

**30.** $y = \sqrt{2x+6}$

**31.** $y = \sqrt{2x-7}$

**32.** $y = \sqrt{5x+18}$

**33.** $y = \sqrt{4x-3}$

**34.** $y = 3\sqrt{x-1}$

**Graph each square-root function.**

**35.** $f(x) = \sqrt{x} + 8$

**36.** $f(x) = \sqrt{x-3}$

**37.** $f(x) = -\sqrt{2x}$

**38.** $f(x) = \sqrt{x} - 1$

**39.** $f(x) = 2\sqrt{x+3}$

**40.** $f(x) = \sqrt{5-x}$

**41.** $f(x) = \sqrt{7-4x}$

**42.** $f(x) = 3\sqrt{x-1}$

**43.** $f(x) = 1 + \sqrt{x+1}$

**44.** $f(x) = \frac{1}{2}\sqrt{x-2}$

## 11-6 Radical Expressions *(pp. 805–810)*

MA.N.2.3

### EXAMPLES

**Simplify. All variables represent nonnegative numbers.**

■ $\sqrt{50x^4}$

$\sqrt{(25)(2)x^4}$ *Factor the radicand.*

$\sqrt{25}\sqrt{2}\sqrt{x^4}$ *Use the Product Property.*

$5x^2\sqrt{2}$ *Simplify.*

■ $\sqrt{\frac{16m^6}{64m^3}}$

$\sqrt{\frac{m^3}{4}}$ *Simplify the radicand.*

$\frac{\sqrt{m^3}}{\sqrt{4}}$ *Use the Quotient Property.*

$\frac{\sqrt{m^2}\sqrt{m}}{\sqrt{4}}$ *Use the Product Property.*

$\frac{m\sqrt{m}}{2}$ *Simplify.*

### EXERCISES

**Simplify. All variables represent nonnegative numbers.**

**45.** $\sqrt{121}$

**46.** $\sqrt{n^4}$

**47.** $\sqrt{(x+3)^2}$

**48.** $\sqrt{\frac{75}{3}}$

**49.** $\sqrt{36d^2}$

**50.** $\sqrt{y^6x}$

**51.** $\sqrt{12}$

**52.** $\sqrt{32ab^5}$

**53.** $\sqrt{\frac{5}{4}}$

**54.** $\sqrt{\frac{t^3}{100t}}$

**55.** $\sqrt{\frac{8}{18}}$

**56.** $\sqrt{\frac{32p^4}{49}}$

**57.** $\sqrt{\frac{s^2t^9}{s^4}}$

**58.** $\sqrt{\frac{72b^6}{225}}$

## 11-7 Adding and Subtracting Radical Expressions (pp. 811–815)

MA.N.2.3

### EXAMPLE

- **Simplify $\sqrt{50x} - \sqrt{2x} + \sqrt{12x}$.**

$$\sqrt{50x} - 1\sqrt{2x} + \sqrt{12x}$$
$$\sqrt{(25)(2)x} - 1\sqrt{2x} + \sqrt{(4)(3)x}$$
$$\sqrt{25}\sqrt{2x} - 1\sqrt{2x} + \sqrt{4}\sqrt{3x}$$
$$5\sqrt{2x} - 1\sqrt{2x} + 2\sqrt{3x}$$
$$4\sqrt{2x} + 2\sqrt{3x}$$

### EXERCISES

**Simplify each expression.**

**59.** $6\sqrt{7} + 3\sqrt{7}$
**60.** $4\sqrt{3} - \sqrt{3}$
**61.** $3\sqrt{2} + 2\sqrt{3}$
**62.** $9\sqrt{5t} - 8\sqrt{5t}$
**63.** $\sqrt{50} - \sqrt{18}$
**64.** $\sqrt{12} + \sqrt{20}$
**65.** $\sqrt{20x} - \sqrt{80x}$
**66.** $4\sqrt{54} - \sqrt{24}$

## 11-8 Multiplying and Dividing Radical Expressions (pp. 816–821)

MA.N.2.3

### EXAMPLES

- **Multiply $\left(\sqrt{3} + 6\right)^2$. Write the product in simplest form.**

$\left(\sqrt{3} + 6\right)^2$

$\left(\sqrt{3} + 6\right)\left(\sqrt{3} + 6\right)$ *Expand the expression.*

$3 + 6\sqrt{3} + 6\sqrt{3} + 36$ *Use the FOIL method.*

$39 + 12\sqrt{3}$ *Simplify.*

- **Simplify the quotient $\frac{\sqrt{5}}{\sqrt{3}}$.**

$\frac{\sqrt{5}}{\sqrt{3}}\left(\frac{\sqrt{3}}{\sqrt{3}}\right) = \frac{\sqrt{15}}{3}$ *Rationalize the denominator.*

### EXERCISES

**Multiply. Write each product in simplest form.**

**67.** $\sqrt{2}\sqrt{7}$
**68.** $\sqrt{3}\sqrt{6}$
**69.** $3\sqrt{2x}\sqrt{14}$
**70.** $\left(5\sqrt{6}\right)^2$
**71.** $\sqrt{2}\left(4 - \sqrt{8}\right)$
**72.** $\left(8 + \sqrt{7}\right)^2$

**Simplify each quotient.**

**73.** $\frac{4}{\sqrt{5}}$
**74.** $\frac{a\sqrt{9}}{\sqrt{2}}$
**75.** $\frac{\sqrt{8}}{2\sqrt{6}}$
**76.** $\frac{\sqrt{5}}{\sqrt{2n}}$
**77.** $\frac{\sqrt{18}}{\sqrt{12}}$
**78.** $\frac{-3}{\sqrt{3}}$

## 11-9 Solving Radical Equations (pp. 822–829)

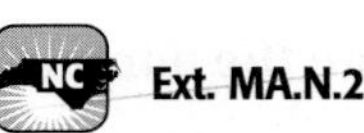
Ext. MA.N.2.3

### EXAMPLE

- **Solve $\sqrt{4x + 1} - 8 = -3$. Check your answer.**

$\sqrt{4x + 1} - 8 = -3$

$\sqrt{4x + 1} = 5$ *Add 8 to both sides.*

$\left(\sqrt{4x + 1}\right)^2 = (5)^2$ *Square both sides.*

$4x + 1 = 25$

$4x = 24$ *Subtract 1 from both sides.*

$x = 6$ *Divide both sides by 4.*

*Check* $\sqrt{4x + 1} - 8 = -3$

| | |
|---|---|
| $\sqrt{4(6) + 1} - 8$ | $-3$ |
| $\sqrt{25} - 8$ | $-3$ |
| $5 - 8$ | $-3$ |
| $-3$ | $-3$ ✓ |

### EXERCISES

**Solve each equation. Check your answer.**

**79.** $\sqrt{x} = 8$
**80.** $\sqrt{2x} = 4$
**81.** $\sqrt{x + 6} = 3$
**82.** $-3\sqrt{x} = -15$
**83.** $3\sqrt{-x} = 27$
**84.** $\frac{4\sqrt{x}}{5} = 8$
**85.** $\sqrt{x + 1} = \sqrt{3x - 5}$
**86.** $\sqrt{x - 2} + 4 = 3$
**87.** $12 = 4\sqrt{2x + 1}$
**88.** $\sqrt{x - 5} = \sqrt{7 - x}$
**89.** $\sqrt{x + 2} = 3$
**90.** $\sqrt{2x - 3} = 4$
**91.** $4\sqrt{x - 3} = 12$
**92.** $\sqrt{x + 6} = x$
**93.** $\sqrt{3x + 4} = x$
**94.** $\sqrt{2x + 6} = x - 1$

CHAPTER 11

# Chapter Test

**Find the next three terms in each geometric sequence.**

1. 2, 6, 18, 54, ...
2. 4800, 2400, 1200, 600, ...
3. −4, 20, −100, 500, ...

4. **Communication** If school is cancelled, the school secretary calls 2 families. Each of those families calls 2 other families. In the third round of calls, each of the 4 families calls 2 more families. If this pattern continues, how many families are called in the seventh round of calls?

**Graph each exponential function.**

5. $y = -2(4)^x$
6. $y = 3(2)^x$
7. $y = 4\left(\frac{1}{2}\right)^x$
8. $-\left(\frac{1}{3}\right)^x$

9. A teacher is repeatedly enlarging a diagram on a photocopier. The function $f(x) = 3(1.25)^x$ represents the length of the diagram, in centimeters, after $x$ enlargements. What is the length after 5 enlargements? Round to the nearest centimeter.

10. Chelsea invested $5600 at a rate of 3.6% compounded quarterly. Write a compound interest function to model the situation. Then find the balance after 6 years.

11. The number of trees in a forest is decreasing at a rate of 5% per year. The forest had 24,000 trees 15 years ago. Write an exponential decay function to model the situation. Then find the number of trees now.

**Look for a pattern in each data set to determine which kind of model best describes the data.**

12. $\{(-10, -17), (-5, -7), (0, 3), (5, 13), (10, 23)\}$
13. $\{(1, 3), (2, 9), (3, 27), (4, 81), (5, 243)\}$

14. Use the data in the table to describe how the bacteria population is changing. Then write a function that models the data. Use your function to predict the bacteria population after 10 hours.

| Bacteria Population | | | | |
|---|---|---|---|---|
| Time (h) | 0 | 1 | 2 | 3 |
| Bacteria | 6 | 18 | 54 | 162 |

**Find the domain of each square-root function.**

15. $y = 6 + \sqrt{x}$
16. $y = -2\sqrt{x + 9}$
17. $y = x + \sqrt{3x - 3}$

**Graph each square-root function.**

18. $f(x) = \sqrt{x} + 2$
19. $f(x) = \sqrt{x - 1}$
20. $f(x) = -3\sqrt{2x}$

**Simplify. All variables represent nonnegative numbers.**

21. $\sqrt{27}$
22. $\sqrt{75m^4}$
23. $\sqrt{\frac{x^6}{y^2}}$
24. $\sqrt{\frac{p^9}{144p}}$
25. $4\sqrt{10} - 2\sqrt{10}$
26. $5\sqrt{3y} + \sqrt{3y}$
27. $\sqrt{8} - \sqrt{50}$
28. $2\sqrt{75} - \sqrt{32} + \sqrt{48}$
29. $\sqrt{2}\sqrt{3m}$
30. $\frac{\sqrt{128d}}{\sqrt{5}}$
31. $\sqrt{3}\left(\sqrt{21} - 2\right)$
32. $\left(\sqrt{3} - 2\right)\left(\sqrt{3} + 4\right)$

**Solve each equation. Check your answer.**

33. $\sqrt{2x} = 6$
34. $\sqrt{3x + 4} - 2 = 5$
35. $\frac{2\sqrt{x}}{3} = 8$
36. $\sqrt{5x + 1} = \sqrt{2x - 2}$

# COLLEGE ENTRANCE EXAM PRACTICE

CHAPTER 11

## *FOCUS ON SAT MATHEMATICS SUBJECT TESTS*

Colleges use standardized test scores to confirm what your academic record indicates. Because courses and instruction differ from school to school, standardized tests are one way in which colleges try to compare students fairly when making admissions decisions.

**You may want to time yourself as you take this practice test. It should take you about 6 minutes to complete.**

**You will need to use a calculator on the SAT Mathematics Subject Tests. If you do not already have a graphing calculator, consider getting one because it may give you an advantage when solving some problems. Spend time getting used to your calculator before the test.**

---

**1.** What is the domain of $y = \sqrt{x - 4}$?

**(A)** $x \geq -2$

**(B)** $x \geq 2$

**(C)** $x \geq -4$

**(D)** $x \geq 4$

**(E)** $x > 4$

---

**2.** $\dfrac{\sqrt{8}\sqrt{3}}{\sqrt{5}} =$

**(A)** $2\sqrt{3}$

**(B)** $\dfrac{2\sqrt{3}}{5}$

**(C)** $\sqrt{12}$

**(D)** $\dfrac{4\sqrt{30}}{5}$

**(E)** $\dfrac{2\sqrt{30}}{5}$

---

**3.** If $\dfrac{\sqrt{6 - 3x}}{5} = 3$, what is the value of $x$?

**(A)** $-3$

**(B)** $-13$

**(C)** $-73$

**(D)** $-77$

**(E)** $-89$

---

**4.** The third term of a geometric sequence is 32 and the fifth term is 512. What is the eighth term of the sequence?

**(A)** 544

**(B)** 1232

**(C)** 8192

**(D)** 32,768

**(E)** 2,097,152

---

**5.** A band releases a new CD and tracks its sales. The table shows the number of copies sold each week (in thousands). Which type of function best models this data?

| CD Sales | |
|---|---|
| **Week** | **Copies Sold (thousands)** |
| 1 | 129.5 |
| 2 | 155 |
| 3 | 179.5 |
| 4 | 203 |
| 5 | 225.5 |
| 6 | 247 |

**(A)** Linear function

**(B)** Quadratic function

**(C)** Exponential function

**(D)** Square-root function

**(E)** Absolute-value function

CHAPTER 11

# TEST TACKLER

Standardized Test Strategies

## Multiple Choice: *None of the Above* or *All of the Above*

In some multiple-choice test items, one of the options is *None of the above* or *All of the above.* To answer these types of items, first determine whether each of the other options is true or false. If you find that more than one option is true, then the correct choice is likely to be *All of the above.* If none of the options are true, the correct choice is *None of the above.*

If you do not know how to solve the problem and have to guess, *All of the above* is most often correct, and *None of the above* is usually incorrect.

### EXAMPLE 1

**There are 8 players on the chess team. Which of the following expressions gives the number of ways in which the coach can choose 2 players to start the game?**

Ⓐ $_8C_2$

Ⓑ $\frac{8!}{2!(6!)}$

Ⓒ 28

Ⓓ All of the above

*Notice that choice D is* All of the above. *This means that you must look at each option. As you consider each option, mark it true or false in your test booklet.*

**A** Because order does not matter, this is a combination problem. The number of combinations of 8 players, taken 2 at a time, is given by $_nC_r$, where $n = 8$ and $r = 2$, so $_8C_2$ is a correct model of the combination. Choice A is true.

**B** The number of combinations of 8 players, taken 2 at a time, is given by $_nC_r = \frac{n!}{r!(n-r)!}$, where $n = 8$ and $r = 2$.

$$_nC_r = \frac{n!}{r!(n-r)!} = \frac{8!}{2!(8-2)!} = \frac{8!}{2!(6)!}$$

Choice B is a correct model of the combination. Choice B is also true. The answer is likely to be choice D, *All of the above*, but you should also check whether choice C is true.

**C** The number of combinations of 8 players, taken 2 at a time, is given by $_nC_r = \frac{n!}{r!(n-r)!}$, where $n = 8$ and $r = 2$.

$$_nC_r = \frac{n!}{r!(n-r)!} = \frac{8!}{2!(8-2)!} = \frac{8!}{2!(6)!} = 28$$

Choice C is a correct model of the combination. Choice C is true as well.

Because A, B, and C are all true, the correct response is D, *All of the above.*

Be careful of problems that contain more than one negative word, such as *no, not,* or *never.* Read the problem and each option twice before selecting an answer.

**Read each test item and answer the questions that follow.**

**Item A**

**The mean score on a test is 68. Which CANNOT be true?**

(A) Every score is 68.

(B) Half of the scores are 68, and half of the scores are 0.

(C) Half of the scores are 94, and half of the scores are 42.

(D) None of the above

1. What is the definition of *mean*?
2. If you find that an option is true, is that the correct response? Explain.
3. Willie determined that A and C could both be true, so he chose D as his response. Do you agree? Why or why not?

**Item B**

**What is the probability of rolling a 2 on a number cube?**

(F) $16.\overline{6}\%$

(G) $1 - P(\text{rolling } 1, 3, 4, 5, \text{ or } 6)$

(H) $\frac{1}{6}$

(J) All of the above

4. What is the complement of rolling a 2? Is choice G correct? Explain.
5. If you roll a number cube, how many possible outcomes are there? How does this information help you solve this problem?
6. Is the value given in choice H equivalent to any other choice? If so, which one(s)?
7. How many choices are true? What is the correct response to the test item?

**Item C**

**Suppose that a dart lands at a random point on the circular dartboard. Find the probability that the dart does NOT land inside the center circle.**

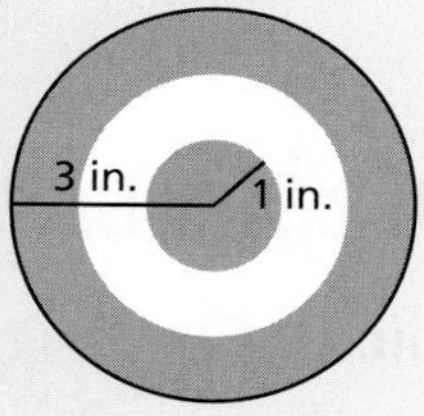


(A) $\frac{1}{9}$

(B) $8\pi$

(C) $\frac{8}{9}$

(D) None of the above

8. Kyle finds that choices A and B are both false. To save time, he selects choice D as his answer because he figures it is likely that choice C will also be false. Do you think Kyle made a wise decision? Why or why not?
9. What is the formula for the area of a circle? What is the total area of this dartboard? How can you determine the area of the dartboard outside the center circle?
10. Determine whether choices A, B, and C are true, and then give the correct response to this test item.

**Item D**

**Each gym member receives a 3-digit locker combination. Digits are from 0–9 and may repeat. What is the probability that you will receive a code consisting of three identical numbers?**

(F) $\frac{1}{100}$

(G) $\frac{10}{{}_{10}C_3}$

(H) ${}_{10}P_3 = \frac{10!}{7!}$

(J) All of the above

11. How can you determine whether choice J is the correct response to the test item?
12. Are the values given in choices F, G, and H equivalent? What does this tell you about choice J?

CHAPTER 11

go.hrw.com
State Test Practice Online
KEYWORD: MA7 TestPrep

## CUMULATIVE ASSESSMENT, CHAPTERS 1–11

### Multiple Choice

**1.** A sequence is defined by the rule $a_n = -3(2)^{n-1}$. What is the 5th term of the sequence?

A 5

B −30

C −48

D −216

**2.** Which could be the graph of $y = -2^x$?

A

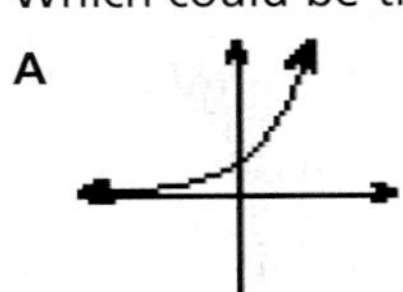

B

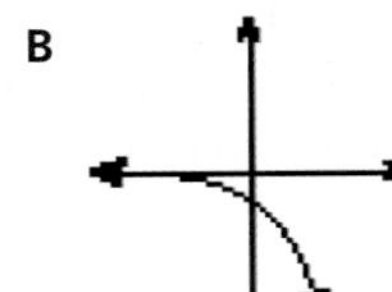

C

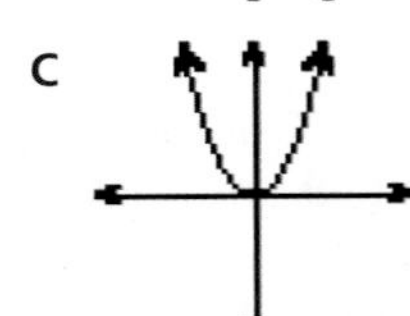

D

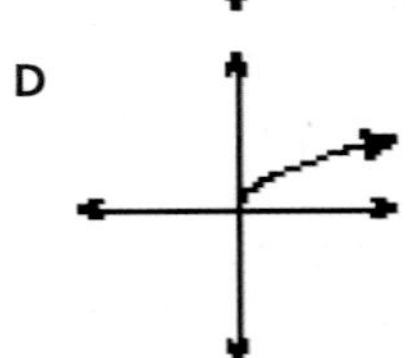

**3.** What is the slope of the line described by $4x - 3y = 12$?

A 4

B 3

C $\frac{4}{3}$

D $-\frac{3}{4}$

**4.** The odds in favor of a spinner landing on blue are 2:7. What is the probability of the spinner ***not*** landing on blue?

A $\frac{7}{9}$  C $\frac{2}{7}$

B $\frac{5}{7}$  D $\frac{2}{9}$

**5.** Which rule can be used to find the *n*th term $a_n$ in the sequence 8, 4, 2, 1, …?

A $a_n = 8\left(\frac{1}{2}\right)^n$  C $a_n = \left(\frac{1}{2}\right)^{n-1}$

B $a_n = 2(1)^n$  D $a_n = 8\left(\frac{1}{2}\right)^{n-1}$

**6.** Antwon invested $1250 at a rate of 5.2% compounded quarterly. After 5 years, what will be his balance to the nearest cent?

A $1333.40

B $1316.28

C $1467.35

D $1618.45

**7.** What is the solution to the system of equations below?

$$\begin{cases} 2x - y = 2 \\ y = 3x - 5 \end{cases}$$

A (4, 6)  C (2, 1)

B (3, 4)  D (0, 2)

**8.** What is the complete factorization of $2x^3 + 18x$?

A $2x(x^2 + 9)$

B $2x(x + 3)^2$

C $2x(x + 3)(x - 3)$

D $2(x^3 + 18)$

**9.** Which ordered pair lies on the graph of $y = 3(2)^{x+1}$?

A (−1, 0)  C (1, 12)

B (0, 9)  D (3, 24)

**When a test item gives an equation to be solved, it may be quicker to work backward from the answer choices by substituting them into the equation. If time remains, check your answer by solving the equation.**

**10.** A scientist was performing an experiment. Every minute, he recorded the number of bacteria. Which function models the data?

| Number of Bacteria | |
|---|---|
| **Time (min)** | **Bacteria** |
| 0 | 12 |
| 1 | 60 |
| 2 | 300 |
| 3 | 1500 |

A $y = 12x$

B $y = 12(5)^x$

C $y = 5(12)^x$

D $y = 12x^2 + 5x + 15$

**11.** Simplify: $(12 + \sqrt{20})(20 + \sqrt{12})$

A $272 + 4\sqrt{15}$

B $272 + 40\sqrt{5} + 24\sqrt{3} + 4\sqrt{15}$

C $240 + 80\sqrt{5} + 48\sqrt{3} + 16\sqrt{15}$

D $240 + 40\sqrt{5} + 24\sqrt{3} + 4\sqrt{15}$

**12.** The function $f(x) = 30{,}000(0.8)^x$ gives the value of a vehicle, where $x$ is the number of years after purchase. According to the function, what will be the value of the car 8 years after purchase? Round your answer to the nearest whole dollar.

A $5,033

B $19,200

C $50,300

D $192,000

**13.** Rosalind purchased a sewing machine at a 20%-off sale. The original selling price of the machine was $340. What was the sale price?

A $260

B $272

C $320

D $425

**14.** Jerome walked on a treadmill for 45 minutes at a speed of 4.2 miles per hour. How far did Jerome walk?

A 1.89 miles

B 2.1 miles

C 3.15 miles

D 5.6 miles

## *STANDARDIZED TEST PREP*

## Short Response

**S1.** The table shows the number of people newly infected by a certain virus with one person as the original source.

| Week | 1 | 2 | 3 | 4 | 5 | 6 | 7 |
|---|---|---|---|---|---|---|---|
| Newly Infected People | 1 | 3 | 9 | 27 | 81 | 243 | 729 |

**a.** Is the data set best described by a linear function, a quadratic function, or an exponential function? Write a function to model the data.

**b.** Use the function to predict the number of people that will become infected in the 10th week. Show your work.

**S2.** Ella and Mia went on a camping trip. The total cost for their trip was $124, which the girls divided evenly. Ella paid for 4 nights at the campsite and $30 for supplies. Mia paid for 2 nights at the campsite and $46 for supplies.

**a.** Write an equation that could be used to find the cost of one night's stay at the campsite. Explain what each variable in your equation represents.

**b.** Solve your equation from part **a** to find the cost of one night's stay at the campsite. Show your work.

## Extended Response

**E1.** Regina is beginning a training program to prepare for a race. In week 1, she will run 3 miles during each workout. Each week thereafter, she plans to increase the distance of her runs by 20%.

**a.** Write an equation to show the number of miles Regina plans to run during her workouts each week. Use the variable $n$ to represent the week number.

**b.** Make a table of values to show the distances of the runs in Regina's workouts for the first 6 weeks. Round each distance to the nearest hundredth of a mile. Then graph the points.

**c.** Explain how to use your equation from part **a** to determine how many miles Regina will run during each workout in week 8. Then find this number.

**d.** Explain how to the use your graph from part **b** to determine how many miles Regina will run during each workout in week 8. How does the graph verify the answer you found in part **c**?

CHAPTER 12

# Rational Functions and Equations



## Why Learn This?

Ratios and rational expressions can be used to explore perspective. An example of perspective is the apparent size difference in this photo between the near end and the far end of Boone Fork Bridge on the Tanawha Trail.

go.hrw.com
Chapter Project Online
KEYWORD: MA7 ChProj

# ARE YOU READY?

## Vocabulary

**Match each term on the left with a definition on the right.**

1. perfect-square trinomial
2. greatest common factor
3. monomial
4. polynomial
5. reciprocals

A. the greatest factor that is shared by two or more terms

B. a number, a variable, or a product of numbers and variables with whole-number exponents

C. two numbers whose product is 1

D. a polynomial with three terms

E. the sum or difference of monomials

F. a trinomial that is the result of squaring a binomial

## Simplify Fractions

**Simplify.**

**6.** $\frac{12}{4}$ **7.** $\frac{100}{36}$ **8.** $\frac{240}{18}$ **9.** $\frac{121}{66}$

## Add and Subtract Fractions

**Add or subtract.**

**10.** $\frac{1}{3}+\frac{1}{2}$ **11.** $\frac{7}{8}-\frac{1}{6}$ **12.** $\frac{3}{4}+\frac{2}{3}+\frac{1}{2}$ **13.** $\frac{5}{9}+\frac{1}{12}-\frac{1}{3}$

## Factor GCF from Polynomials

**Factor each polynomial.**

**14.** $x^2+2x$ **15.** $x^2+x$ **16.** $2x^2+x$ **17.** $x^2-x$

**18.** $3x^2+2x$ **19.** $4x^2-4$ **20.** $3x^2-6x$ **21.** $x^3-x^2$

## Properties of Exponents

**Simplify each expression.**

**22.** $4x \cdot 3x^2$ **23.** $-5 \cdot 2jk$ **24.** $-2a^3 \cdot 3a^4$ **25.** $3ab \cdot 4a^2b$

**26.** $2x \cdot 3y \cdot xy$ **27.** $a^2b \cdot 3ab^3$ **28.** $3rs \cdot 3rs^3$ **29.** $5m^2n^2 \cdot 4mn^2$

## Simplify Polynomial Expressions

**Simplify each expression.**

**30.** $4x-2y-8y$ **31.** $2r-4s+3s-8r$

**32.** $ab^2-ab+4ab^2+2a^2b+a^2b^2$ **33.** $3g(g-4)+g^2+g$

CHAPTER 12

# Study Guide: Preview

## Where You've Been

**Previously you**

- identified, wrote, and graphed equations of direct variation.
- identified and graphed quadratic, exponential, and square-root functions.
- used factoring to solve quadratic equations.
- simplified radical expressions and solved radical equations.

## In This Chapter

**You will study**

- how to identify, write, and graph equations of inverse variation.
- how to graph rational functions and simplify rational expressions.
- how to solve rational equations.

## Where You're Going

**You can use the skills in this chapter**

- to build upon your knowledge of graphing and transforming various types of functions.
- to solve problems involving inverse variation in classes such as Physics and Chemistry.
- to calculate costs when working with a fixed budget.

## Key Vocabulary/Vocabulario

| | |
|---|---|
| asymptote | asíntota |
| discontinuous function | función discontinua |
| excluded values | valores excluidos |
| inverse variation | variación inversa |
| rational equation | ecuación racional |
| rational expression | expresión racional |
| rational function | función racional |

## Vocabulary Connections

To become familiar with some of the vocabulary terms in the chapter, consider the following. You may refer to the chapter, the glossary, or a dictionary if you like.

1. What are some other words that mean the same as *continuous*? The prefix *dis-* generally means "not." Describe what the graph of a **discontinuous function** might look like.
2. What does it mean for someone or something to be *included* in a group? What about *excluded*? What might it mean for some values to be **excluded values** for a particular function?
3. A *direct variation* is a relationship between two variables, $x$ and $y$, that can be written in the form $y = kx$ where $k$ is a nonzero constant. The inverse of a number $x$ is $\frac{1}{x}$. Use this information to write the form of an **inverse variation**.
4. You learned in Chapter 1 that an *algebraic expression* is an expression that contains one or more variables, numbers, or operations. You also learned that a *rational number* is a number that can be written in the form of a fraction. Combine these terms to define **rational expression**. Give an example.

## Study Strategy: Prepare for Your Final Exam

Math is a cumulative subject, so your final exam will probably cover all of the material you have learned since the beginning of the course. Preparation is essential for you to be successful on your final exam. It may help you to make a study timeline like the one below.

**2 weeks before the final:**

- Look at previous exams and homework to determine areas I need to focus on; rework problems that were incorrect or incomplete.
- Make a list of all formulas, postulates, and theorems I need to know for the final.
- Create a practice exam using problems from the book that are similar to problems from each exam.

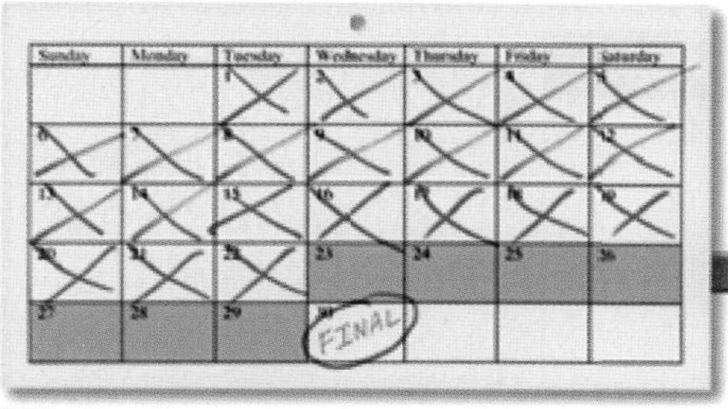

**1 week before the final:**

- Take the practice exam and check it. For each problem I miss, find 2 or 3 similar ones and work those.
- Work with a friend in the class to quiz each other on formulas, postulates, and theorems from my list.

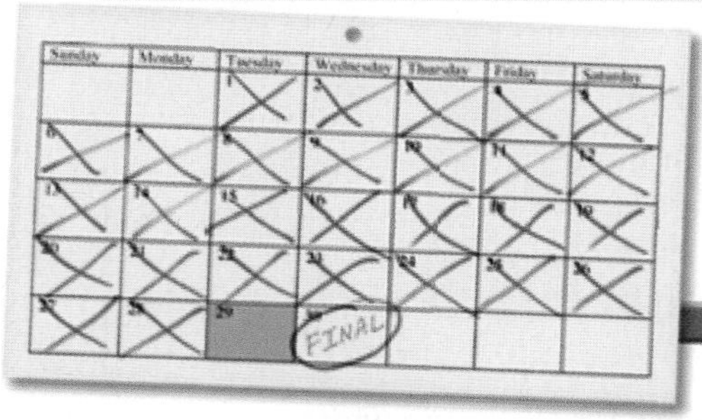

**1 day before the final:**

- Make sure I have pencils, calculator (check batteries!), ruler, compass, and protractor.

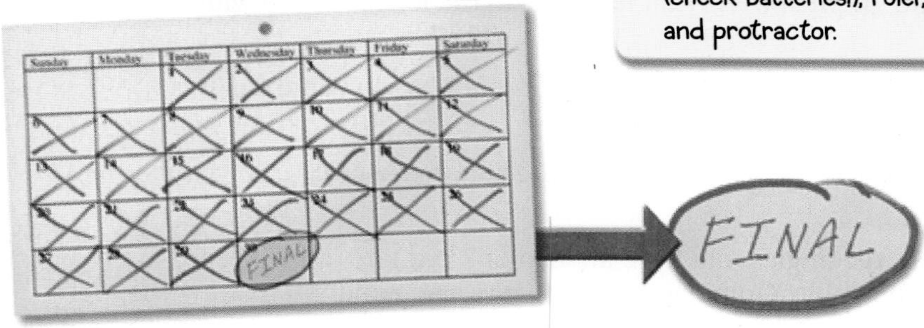

FINAL

**Try This**

1. Create a timeline that you will use to study for your final exam.

# Model Inverse Variation

The relationship between the width and the length of a rectangle with a constant area is an inverse variation. In this activity, you will study this relationship by modeling rectangles with square tiles or grid paper.

*Use with Lesson 12-1*

**Prep MA.A.2.1** Use substitution strategies to solve equations involving … inverse variation.

## Activity

Use 12 square tiles to form a rectangle with an area of 12 square units, or draw the rectangle on grid paper. Use a width of 1 unit and a length of 12 units.

Your rectangle should look like the one shown.

Using the same 12 square tiles, continue forming rectangles by changing the width and length until you have formed all the different rectangles you can that have an area of 12 square units. Copy and complete the table as you form each rectangle.

| Width ($x$) | Length ($y$) | Area ($xy$) |
|---|---|---|
| 1 | 12 | 12 |
| ▒ | ▒ | 12 |
| ▒ | ▒ | 12 |
| ▒ | ▒ | 12 |
| ▒ | ▒ | 12 |
| ▒ | ▒ | 12 |

Plot the ordered pairs from the table on a graph. Draw a smooth curve through the points.

## Try This

1. Look at the table and graph above. What happens to the length as the width increases? Why?
2. This type of relationship is called an *inverse variation*. Why do you think it is called that?
3. For each point, what does $xy$ equal? Complete the equation $xy =$ ▒. Solve this equation for $y$.
4. Form all the different rectangles that have an area of 24 square units. Record their widths and lengths in a table. Graph your results. Write an equation relating the width $x$ and length $y$.
5. **Make a Conjecture** Using the equations you wrote in 3 and 4, what do you think the equation of any inverse variation might look like when solved for $y$?

# 12-1 Inverse Variation

**MA.A.2** Use … indirect variation to solve problems. *Also* **MA.A.2.1, MA.A.2.2**

***Objective***
Identify, write, and graph inverse variations.

***Vocabulary***
inverse variation

**Why learn this?**
Inverse variation can be used to find the frequency at which a guitar string vibrates. (See Example 3.)

**Remember!**
A direct variation is an equation that can be written in the form $y = kx$, where $k$ is a nonzero constant.

A relationship that can be written in the form $y = \frac{k}{x}$, where $k$ is a nonzero constant and $x \neq 0$, is an **inverse variation**. The constant $k$ is the constant of variation.

Multiplying both sides of $y = \frac{k}{x}$ by $x$ gives $xy = k$. So, for any inverse variation, the product of $x$ and $y$ is a nonzero constant.

**Inverse Variations**

| WORDS | NUMBERS | ALGEBRA |
|---|---|---|
| $y$ varies inversely as $x$.<br>$y$ is inversely proportional to $x$. | $y = \frac{3}{x}$<br>$xy = 3$ | $y = \frac{k}{x}$<br>$xy = k (k \neq 0)$ |

There are two methods to determine whether a relationship between data is an inverse variation. You can write a function rule in $y = \frac{k}{x}$ form, or you can check whether $xy$ is constant for each ordered pair.

**EXAMPLE 1** **Identifying an Inverse Variation**

**Tell whether each relationship is an inverse variation. Explain.**

**A**

| x | y |
|---|---|
| 1 | 20 |
| 2 | 10 |
| 4 | 5 |

**Method 1** Write a function rule.

$y = \frac{20}{x}$ *Can write in $y = \frac{k}{x}$ form.*

The relationship is an inverse variation.

**Method 2** Find $xy$ for each ordered pair.

$1(20) = 20$, $2(10) = 20$, $4(5) = 20$

The product $xy$ is constant, so the relationship is an inverse variation.

**B**

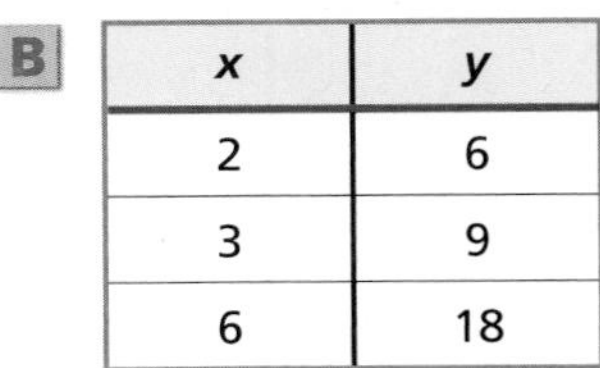

| x | y |
|---|---|
| 2 | 6 |
| 3 | 9 |
| 6 | 18 |

**Method 1** Write a function rule.

$y = 3x$ *Cannot write in $y = \frac{k}{x}$ form.*

The relationship is not an inverse variation.

**Method 2** Find $xy$ for each ordered pair.

$2(6) = 12$, $3(9) = 27$, $6(18) = 108$

The product $xy$ is not constant, so the relationship is not an inverse variation.

Tell whether each relationship is an inverse variation. Explain.

**C** $5xy = -21$

$\frac{5xy}{5} = \frac{-21}{5}$ *Find xy. Since xy is multiplied by 5, divide both sides by 5 to undo the multiplication.*

$xy = \frac{-21}{5}$ *Simplify.*

$xy$ equals the constant $\frac{-21}{5}$, so the relationship is an inverse variation.

**Tell whether each relationship is an inverse variation. Explain.**

**1a.**

| $x$ | $y$ |
|---|---|
| −12 | 24 |
| 1 | −2 |
| 8 | −16 |

**1b.**

| $x$ | $y$ |
|---|---|
| 3 | 3 |
| 9 | 1 |
| 18 | 0.5 |

**1c.** $2x + y = 10$

**Helpful Hint**

Since $k$ is a nonzero constant, $xy \neq 0$. Therefore, neither $x$ nor $y$ can equal 0, and no solution points will be on the $x$- or $y$-axes.

An inverse variation can also be identified by its graph. Some inverse variation graphs are shown. Notice that each graph has two parts that are not connected.

Also notice that none of the graphs contain $(0, 0)$. This is because $(0, 0)$ can never be a solution of an inverse variation equation.

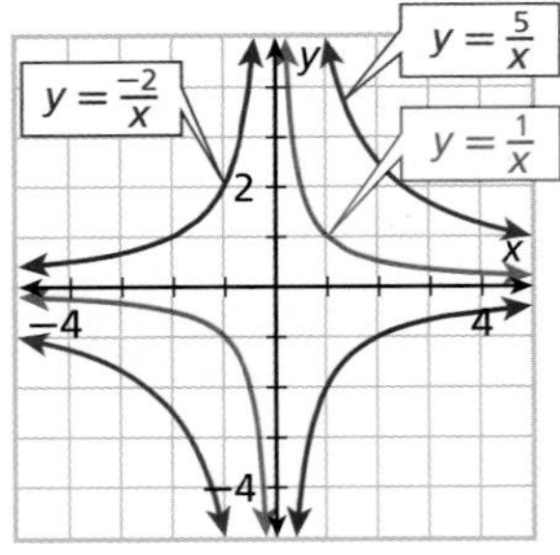


**EXAMPLE 2** **Graphing an Inverse Variation**

**Write and graph the inverse variation in which $y = 2$ when $x = 4$.**

**Step 1** Find $k$.

$k = xy$ *Write the rule for constant of variation.*

$= 4(2)$ *Substitute 4 for x and 2 for y.*

$= 8$

**Step 2** Use the value of $k$ to write an inverse variation equation.

$y = \frac{k}{x}$ *Write the rule for inverse variation.*

$y = \frac{8}{x}$ *Substitute 8 for k.*

**Step 3** Use the equation to make a table of values.

| $x$ | −4 | −2 | −1 | 0 | 1 | 2 | 4 |
|---|---|---|---|---|---|---|---|
| $y$ | −2 | −4 | −8 | undef. | 8 | 4 | 2 |

**Step 4** Plot the points and connect them with smooth curves.

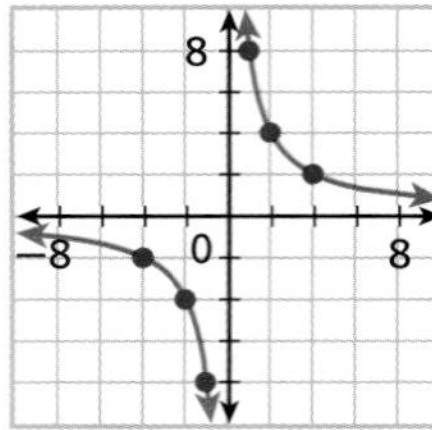

**2.** Write and graph the inverse variation in which $y = \frac{1}{2}$ when $x = 10$.

## EXAMPLE 3 Music Application

**The inverse variation $xy = 2400$ relates the vibration frequency $y$ in hertz (Hz) to the length $x$ in centimeters of a guitar string. Determine a reasonable domain and range and then graph this inverse variation. Use the graph to estimate the frequency of vibration when the string length is 100 centimeters.**

**Step 1** Solve the function for $y$ so you can graph it.

$xy = 2400$

$y = \frac{2400}{x}$ *Divide both sides by x.*

**Step 2** Decide on a reasonable domain and range.

$x > 0$ *Length is never negative and $x \neq 0$.*

$y > 0$ *Because x and xy are both positive, y is also positive.*

**Remember!**

Recall that sometimes domain and range are restricted in real-world situations.

**Step 3** Use values of the domain to generate reasonable ordered pairs.

| x | 20 | 40 | 60 | 120 |
|---|---|---|---|---|
| y | 120 | 60 | 40 | 20 |

**Step 4** Plot the points. Connect them with a smooth curve.

**Step 5** Find the $y$-value where $x = 100$. When the string length is 100 cm, the frequency of vibration is about 24 Hz.

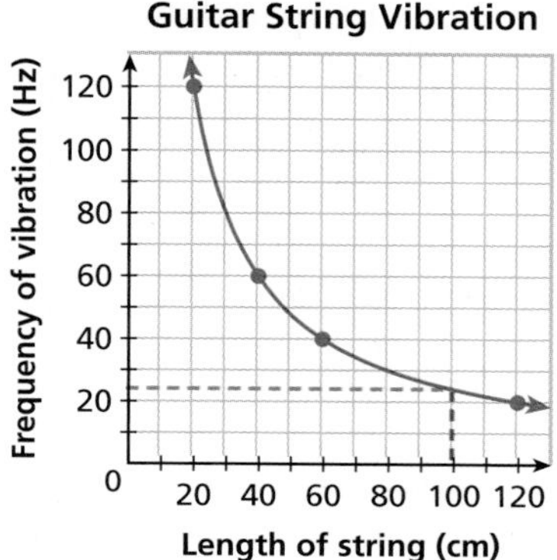

3. The inverse variation $xy = 100$ represents the relationship between the pressure $x$ in atmospheres (atm) and the volume $y$ in $mm^3$ of a certain gas. Determine a reasonable domain and range and then graph this inverse variation. Use the graph to estimate the volume of the gas when the pressure is 40 atmospheric units.

The fact that $xy = k$ is the same for every ordered pair in any inverse variation can help you find missing values in the relationship.

**Product Rule for Inverse Variation**

If $(x_1, y_1)$ and $(x_2, y_2)$ are solutions of an inverse variation, then $x_1y_1 = x_2y_2$.

## EXAMPLE  4 Using the Product Rule

**Let $x_1 = 3$, $y_1 = 2$, and $y_2 = 6$. Let $y$ vary inversely as $x$. Find $x_2$.**

$x_1y_1 = x_2y_2$ *Write the Product Rule for Inverse Variation.*

$(3)(2) = x_2(6)$ *Substitute 3 for $x_1$, 2 for $y_1$, and 6 for $y_2$.*

$6 = 6x_2$ *Simplify.*

$\frac{6}{6} = \frac{6x_2}{6}$ *Solve for $x_2$ by dividing both sides by 6.*

$1 = x_2$ *Simplify.*

CHECK IT OUT! **4.** Let $x_1 = 2$, $y_1 = -6$, and $x_2 = -4$. Let $y$ vary inversely as $x$. Find $y_2$.

**EXAMPLE 5** ***Physics Application***

**Boyle's law states that the pressure of a quantity of gas $x$ varies inversely as the volume of the gas $y$. The volume of air inside a bicycle pump is 5.2 in$^3$, and the pressure is 15.5 psi. Assuming no air escapes, what is the pressure of the air inside the pump after the handle is pushed in, and the air is compressed to a volume of 2.6 in$^3$?**

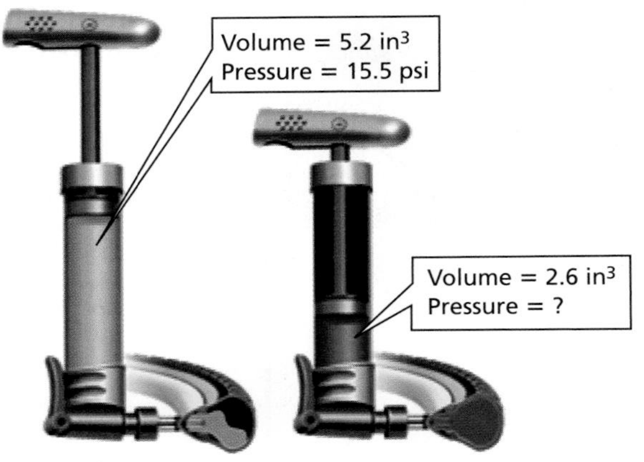


$x_1y_1 = x_2y_2$ *Use the Product Rule for Inverse Variation.*

$(5.2)(15.5) = (2.6)y_2$ *Substitute 5.2 for $x_1$, 15.5 for $y_1$, and 2.6 for $x_2$.*

$80.6 = 2.6y_2$ *Simplify.*

$\frac{80.6}{2.6} = \frac{2.6y_2}{2.6}$ *Solve for $y_2$ by dividing both sides by 2.6.*

$31 = y_2$ *Simplify.*

The pressure after the handle is pushed in is 31 psi.

**Reading Math**

In Example 5, $x_1$ and $y_1$ represent volume and pressure **before** the handle is pushed in, and $x_2$ and $y_2$ represent volume and pressure **after** the handle is pushed in.

CHECK IT OUT! **5.** On a balanced lever, weight varies inversely as the distance from the fulcrum to the weight. The diagram shows a balanced lever. How much does the child weigh?

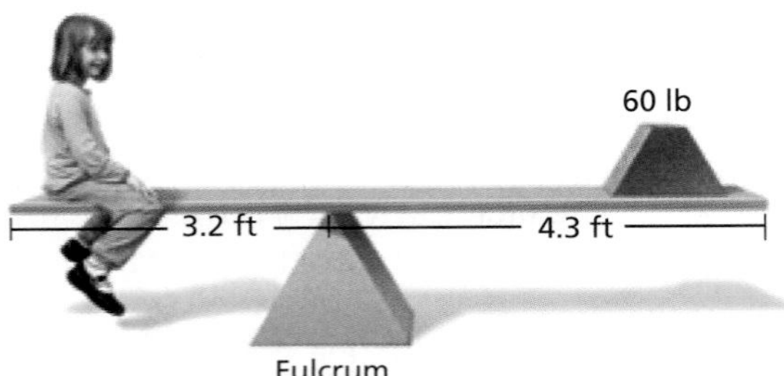


## THINK AND DISCUSS

**1.** Name two ways you can identify an inverse variation.

**2. GET ORGANIZED** Copy and complete the graphic organizer. In each box, write an example of the parts of the given inverse variation.

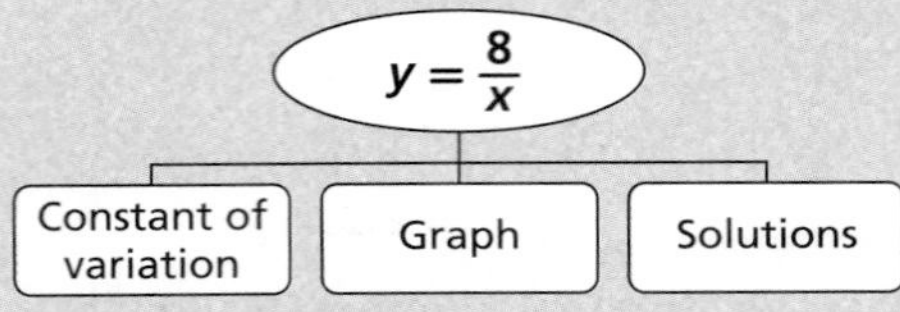

# 12-1 Exercises

MA.A.2, MA.A.2.1, MA.A.2.2

go.hrw.com
Homework Help Online
KEYWORD: MA7 12-1
Parent Resources Online
KEYWORD: MA7 Parent

## GUIDED PRACTICE

1. **Vocabulary** Describe the graph of an *inverse variation.*

SEE EXAMPLE 1 p. 851

**Tell whether each relationship is an inverse variation. Explain.**

2.

| x | y |
|---|---|
| 1 | 8 |
| 4 | 2 |
| 2 | 4 |

3.

| x | y |
|---|---|
| $\frac{1}{6}$ | 1 |
| $\frac{1}{3}$ | 2 |
| 2 | 12 |

4. $x + y = 8$

5. $4xy = 3$

SEE EXAMPLE 2 p. 852

6. Write and graph the inverse variation in which $y = 2$ when $x = 2$.
7. Write and graph the inverse variation in which $y = 6$ when $x = -1$.

SEE EXAMPLE 3 p. 853

8. **Travel** The inverse variation $xy = 30$ relates the constant speed $x$ in mi/h to the time $y$ in hours that it takes to travel 30 miles. Determine a reasonable domain and range and then graph this inverse variation. Use the graph to estimate how many hours it would take traveling 4 mi/h.

SEE EXAMPLE 4 p. 853

9. Let $x_1 = 3$, $y_1 = 12$, and $x_2 = 9$. Let $y$ vary inversely as $x$. Find $y_2$.
10. Let $x_1 = 1$, $y_1 = 4$, and $y_2 = 16$. Let $y$ vary inversely as $x$. Find $x_2$.

SEE EXAMPLE 5 p. 854

11. **Mechanics** The rotational speed of a gear varies inversely as the number of teeth on the gear. A gear with 12 teeth has a rotational speed of 60 rpm. How many teeth are on a gear that has a rotational speed of 45 rpm?

## PRACTICE AND PROBLEM SOLVING

**Independent Practice**

| For Exercises | See Example |
|---|---|
| 12–15 | 1 |
| 16–17 | 2 |
| 18 | 3 |
| 19–20 | 4 |
| 21 | 5 |

**Extra Practice**

Skills Practice p. S26
Application Practice p. S39

**Tell whether each relationship is an inverse variation. Explain.**

12.

| x | y |
|---|---|
| 3 | −3 |
| −5 | 5 |
| 7 | −7 |

13.

| x | y |
|---|---|
| 2 | 5 |
| 0.5 | 20 |
| 8 | 1.25 |

14. $x = \frac{13}{y}$

15. $y = 5x$

16. Write and graph the inverse variation in which $y = -2$ when $x = 5$.
17. Write and graph the inverse variation in which $y = -6$ when $x = -\frac{1}{3}$.
18. **Engineering** The inverse variation $xy = 12$ relates the current $x$ in amps to the resistance $y$ in ohms of a circuit attached to a 12-volt battery. Determine a reasonable domain and range and then graph this inverse variation. Use the graph to estimate the resistance of a circuit when the current is 5 amps.
19. Let $x_1 = -3$, $y_1 = -4$, and $y_2 = 6$. Let $y$ vary inversely as $x$. Find $x_2$.
20. Let $x_1 = 7$, $y_1 = 9$, and $x_2 = 6$. Let $y$ vary inversely as $x$. Find $y_2$.

LINK
**Winter Sports**

Snowshoes were originally made of wooden frames strung with animal intestines. Modern snowshoes are made with steel frames and may have cleats for gripping the snow.

21. **Home Economics** The length of fabric that June can afford varies inversely as the price per yard of the fabric. June can afford exactly 5 yards of fabric that costs \$10.50 per yard. How many yards of fabric that costs \$4.25 per yard can June buy? (Assume that she can only buy whole yards.)

22. **Winter Sports** When a person is snowshoeing, the pressure on the top of the snow in psi varies inversely as the area of the bottom of the snowshoe in square inches. The constant of variation is the weight of the person wearing the snowshoes in pounds.
    a. Helen weighs 120 pounds. About how much pressure does she put on top of the snow if she wears snowshoes that cover 360 in$^2$?
    b. Max weighs 207 pounds. If he exerts 0.4 psi of pressure on top of the snow, what is the area of the bottom of his snowshoes in square inches?

**Determine if each equation represents a direct variation, an inverse variation, or neither. Find the constant of variation when one exists.**

23. $y = 8x$ 24. $y = \frac{14}{x}$ 25. $y = \frac{1}{3}x - 2$ 26. $y = \frac{1}{5}x$

27. $y = 4\frac{3}{x}$ 28. $y = \frac{x}{2} + 7$ 29. $y = \frac{15}{x}$ 30. $y = 5x$

31. **Multi-Step** A track team is competing in a 10 km race. The distance will be evenly divided among the team members. Write an equation that represents the distance $d$ each runner will run if there are $n$ runners. Does this represent a direct variation, inverse variation, or neither?

**Determine whether each data set represents a direct variation, an inverse variation, or neither.**

32.

| x | 2 | 4 | 8 |
|---|---|---|---|
| y | 5 | 10 | 20 |

33.

| x | 6 | 12 | 15 |
|---|---|---|---|
| y | 6 | 8 | 9 |

34.

| x | 1 | 2 | 3 |
|---|---|---|---|
| y | 12 | 6 | 4 |

35. **Multi-Step** Your club awards one student a \$2000 scholarship each year, and each member contributes an equal amount. Your contribution $y$ depends on the number of members $x$. Write and graph an inverse variation equation that represents this situation. What are a reasonable domain and range?

36. **Estimation** Estimate the value of $y$ if $y$ is inversely proportional to $x$, $x = 4$, and the constant of variation is $6\pi$.

37. **Critical Thinking** Why will the point $(0, 0)$ never be a solution to an inverse variation?

38. **Write About It** Explain how to write an inverse variation equation of the form $y = \frac{k}{x}$ when values of $x$ and $y$ are known.

39. **Write About It** List all the mathematical terms you know that contain the word *inverse*. How are these terms all similar? How is *inverse variation* similar to these terms?

**MULTI-STEP TEST PREP**

40. This problem will prepare you for the Multi-Step Test Prep on page 876. The total number of workdays it takes to build the frame of a house varies inversely as the number of people working in a crew. Let $x$ be the number of people in the crew and let $y$ be the number of workdays.
    a. Find the constant of variation when $y = 75$ and $x = 2$.
    b. Write the rule for the inverse of variation equation.
    c. Graph the equation of this inverse variation.

## TEST PREP

MA.A.2, MA.A.2.1, MA.A.2.2

41. Which equation best represents the graph?

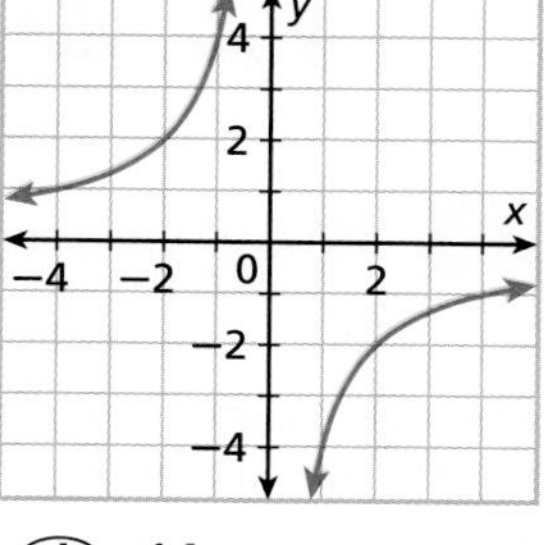


Ⓐ $y = -\frac{1}{4}x$  Ⓒ $y = -\frac{4}{x}$

Ⓑ $y = \frac{1}{4}x$  Ⓓ $y = \frac{4}{x}$

42. Determine the constant of variation if $y$ varies inversely as $x$ and $y = 2$ when $x = 7$.

Ⓕ $\frac{2}{7}$  Ⓖ $\frac{7}{2}$  Ⓗ 3.5  Ⓙ 14

43. Which of the following relationships does NOT represent an inverse variation?

Ⓐ

| $x$ | 2 | 4 | 5 |
|---|---|---|---|
| $y$ | 10 | 5 | 4 |

Ⓒ 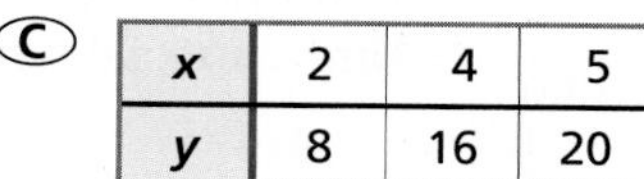

| $x$ | 2 | 4 | 5 |
|---|---|---|---|
| $y$ | 8 | 16 | 20 |

Ⓑ $y = \frac{17.5}{x}$  Ⓓ $\frac{11}{2} = xy$

44. **Gridded Response** At a carnival, the number of tickets Brad can buy is inversely proportional to the price of the tickets. He can afford 12 tickets that cost $2.50 each. How many tickets can Brad buy if each costs $3.00?

## CHALLENGE AND EXTEND

45. The definition of inverse variation says that $k$ is a nonzero constant. What function would $y = \frac{k}{x}$ represent if $k = 0$?

46. **Mechanics** A part of a car's braking system uses a lever to multiply the force applied to the brake pedal. The force at the end of a lever varies inversely with the distance from the fulcrum. Point $P$ is the end of the lever. A force of 2 lb is applied to the brake pedal. What is the force created at the point $P$?

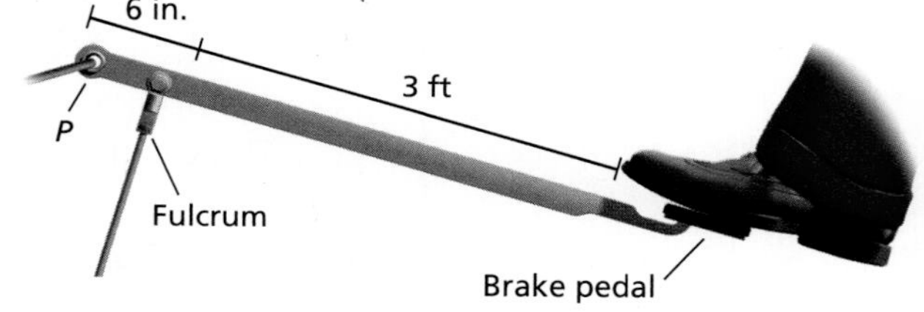


47. **Communication** The strength of a radio signal varies inversely with the square of the distance from the transmitter. A signal has a strength of 2000 watts when it is 4 kilometers from the transmitter. What is the strength of the signal 6 kilometers from the transmitter?

## SPIRAL REVIEW

**Find the domain and range for each relation. Tell whether the relation is a function.** *(Lesson 4-2)*

48. $\{(-2, -4), (-2, -2), (-2, 0), (-2, 2)\}$  49. $\{(-4, 5), (-2, 3), (0, 1), (2, 3), (4, 5)\}$

**Solve by completing the square.** *(Lesson 9-8)*

50. $x^2 + 12x = 45$  51. $d^2 - 6d - 7 = 0$  52. $2y^2 + 6y = -\frac{5}{2}$

53. A rectangle has a length of 6 cm and a width of 2 cm. Find the length of the diagonal and write it as a simplified radical expression. *(Lesson 11-6)*

# 12-2 Rational Functions

**MA.A.4.2** Use appropriate terminology...associated with functions. *Also* **MA.A.4.3**

***Objectives***
Identify excluded values of rational functions.

Graph rational functions.

***Vocabulary***
rational function
excluded value
discontinuous function
asymptote

**Who uses this?**
Gemologists can use rational functions to maximize reflected light. (See Example 4.)

A **rational function** is a function whose rule is a quotient of polynomials. The inverse variations you studied in the previous lesson are a special type of rational function.

Rational functions: $y = \frac{2}{x}$, $y = \frac{3}{4 - 2x}$, $y = \frac{1}{x^2}$

For any function involving $x$ and $y$, an **excluded value** is any $x$-value that makes the function value $y$ undefined. For a rational function, an excluded value is any value that makes the denominator equal 0.

## EXAMPLE 1 Identifying Excluded Values

**Identify the excluded value for each rational function.**

**A** $y = \frac{8}{x}$

$x = 0$ *Set the denominator equal to 0.*

The excluded value is 0.

**B** $y = \frac{3}{x + 3}$

$x + 3 = 0$ *Set the denominator equal to 0.*

$x = -3$ *Solve for x.*

The excluded value is $-3$.

**Identify the excluded value for each rational function.**

**1a.** $y = \frac{10}{x}$ **1b.** $y = \frac{4}{x - 1}$ **1c.** $y = -\frac{5}{x + 4}$

Most rational functions are **discontinuous functions**, meaning their graphs contain one or more jumps, breaks, or holes. This occurs at an excluded value.

One place that a graph of a rational function is discontinuous is at an *asymptote*. An **asymptote** is a line that a graph gets closer to as the absolute value of a variable increases. In the graph shown, both the $x$- and $y$-axes are asymptotes. The graphs of rational functions will get closer and closer to but never touch the asymptotes.

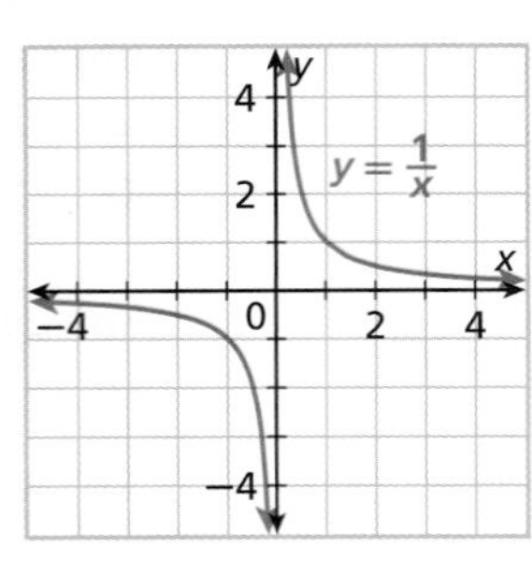

For rational functions, vertical asymptotes will occur at excluded values.

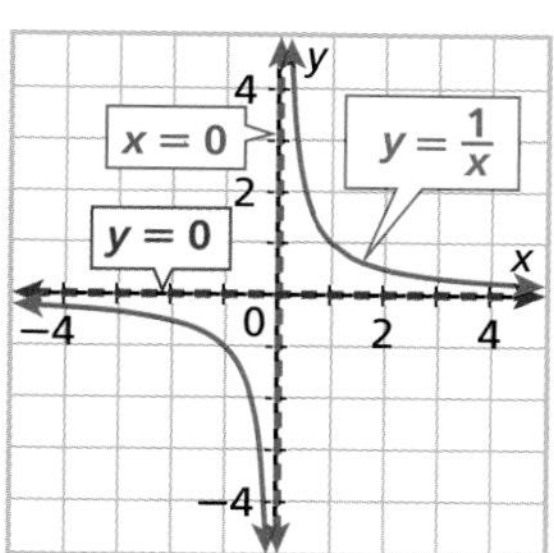


**Writing Math**

Vertical lines are written in the form $x = b$, and horizontal lines are written in the form $y = c$.

Look at the graph of $y = \frac{1}{x}$. The denominator is 0 when $x = 0$ so 0 is an excluded value. This means there is a vertical asymptote at $x = 0$. Notice the horizontal asymptote at $y = 0$.

Look at the graph of $y = \frac{1}{x-3} + 2$. Notice that the graph of the parent function $y = \frac{1}{x}$ has been translated **3 units right** and there is a vertical asymptote at $x = 3$. The graph has also been translated **2 units up** and there is a horizontal asymptote at $y = 2$.

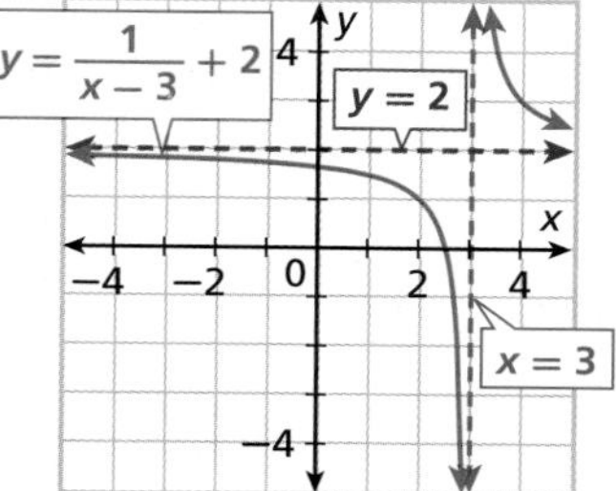


These translations lead to the following formulas for identifying asymptotes in rational functions.

## Identifying Asymptotes

| WORDS | EXAMPLES | |
|---|---|---|
| A rational function in the form $y = \frac{a}{x-b} + c$ has a vertical asymptote at the excluded value, or $x = b$, and a horizontal asymptote at $y = c$. | $y = \frac{2}{x}$ <br> $= \frac{2}{x-0} + 0$ <br> Vertical asymptote: $x = 0$ <br> Horizontal asymptote: $y = 0$ | $y = \frac{1}{x+2} + 4$ <br> $= \frac{1}{x-(-2)} + 4$ <br> Vertical asymptote: $x = -2$ <br> Horizontal asymptote: $y = 4$ |

## EXAMPLE 2 Identifying Asymptotes

**Identify the asymptotes.**

**A** $y = \frac{1}{x-6}$

**Step 1** Write in $y = \frac{1}{x-b} + c$ form.

$$y = \frac{1}{x-6} + 0$$

**Step 2** Identify the asymptotes.

vertical: $x = 6$

horizontal: $y = 0$

**B** $y = \frac{2}{3x-10} - 7$

**Step 1** Identify the vertical asymptote.

$3x - 10 = 0$ *Find the excluded value. Set the denominator equal to 0.*

$\underline{+10 \quad +10}$ *Add 10 to both sides.*

$3x = 10$

$x = \frac{10}{3}$ *Solve for x. $\frac{10}{3}$ is an excluded value.*

**Step 2** Identify the horizontal asymptote.

$c = -7$    *$-7$ can be written as $+(-7)$*

$y = -7$    *$y = c$*

vertical asymptote: $x = \frac{10}{3}$; horizontal asymptote: $y = -7$

**Identify the asymptotes.**

**2a.** $y = \dfrac{2}{x-5}$    **2b.** $y = \dfrac{1}{4x+16} + 5$    **2c.** $y = \dfrac{3}{x+77} - 15$

To graph a rational function in the form $y = \frac{a}{x-b} + c$ when $a = 1$, you can graph the asymptotes and then translate the parent function $y = \frac{1}{x}$. However, if $a \neq 1$, the graph is not a translation of the parent function. In this case, you can use the asymptotes and a table of values.

## EXAMPLE 3 Graphing Rational Functions Using Asymptotes

**Graph each function.**

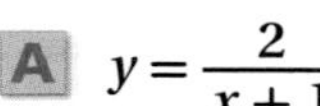

**A** $y = \dfrac{2}{x+1}$

Since the numerator is not 1, use the asymptotes and a table of values.

**Step 1** Identify the vertical and horizontal asymptotes.

vertical: $x = -1$    *Use $x = b$. $x + 1 = x - (-1)$, so $b = -1$.*

horizontal: $y = 0$    *Use $y = c$. $c = 0$*

**Step 2** Graph the asymptotes using dashed lines.

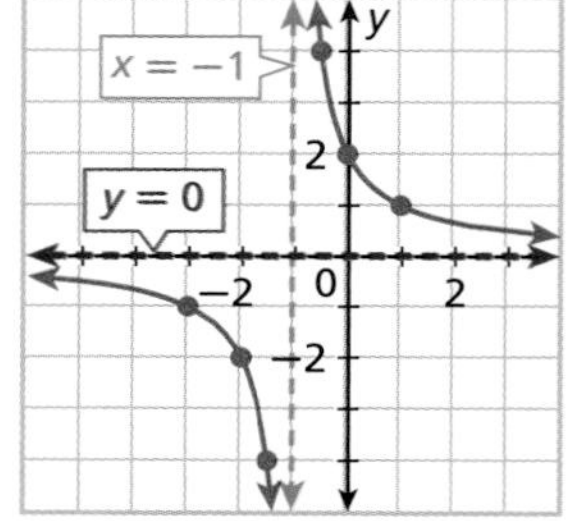


**Step 3** Make a table of values. Choose $x$-values on both sides of the vertical asymptote.

| $x$ | $-3$ | $-2$ | $-\frac{3}{2}$ | $-\frac{1}{2}$ | 0 | 1 |
|---|---|---|---|---|---|---|
| $y$ | $-1$ | $-2$ | $-4$ | 4 | 2 | 1 |

**Step 4** Plot the points and connect them with smooth curves. The curves will get very close to the asymptotes, but will not touch them.

**B** $y = \dfrac{1}{x-2} - 4$

Since the numerator is 1, use the asymptotes and translate $y = \frac{1}{x}$.

**Step 1** Identify the vertical and horizontal asymptotes.

vertical: $x = 2$    *Use $x = b$. $b = 2$*

horizontal: $y = -4$    *Use $y = c$. $c = -4$*

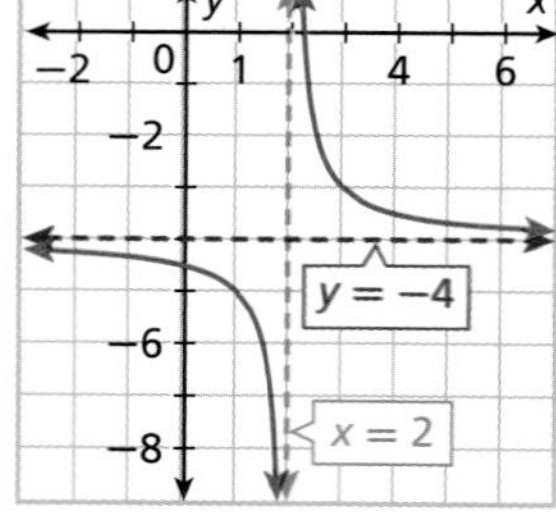


**Step 2** Graph the asymptotes using dashed lines.

**Step 3** Draw smooth curves to show the translation.

**Graph each function.**

**3a.** $y = \dfrac{1}{x+7} + 3$    **3b.** $y = \dfrac{2}{x-3} + 2$

## EXAMPLE 4 Gemology Application

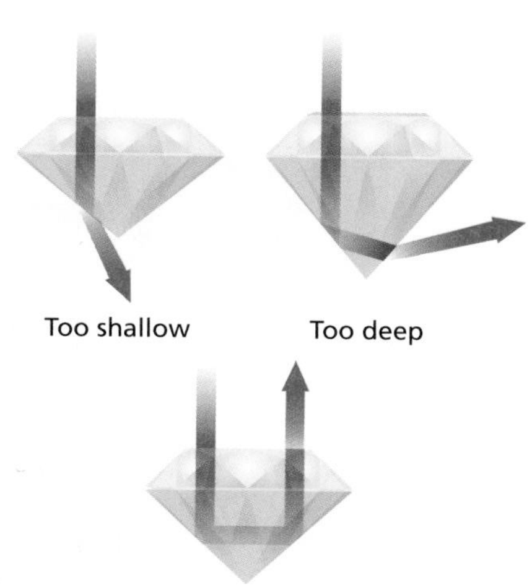


**Some diamonds are cut using ratios calculated by a mathematician, Marcel Tolkowsky, in 1919. The amount of light reflected up through the top of a diamond (brilliancy) can be maximized using the ratio between the width of the diamond and the depth of the diamond. A gemologist has a diamond with a width of 90 millimeters. If $x$ represents the depth of the diamond, then $y = \frac{90}{x}$ represents the brilliancy ratio $y$.**

**a. Describe the reasonable domain and range values.**

Both the depth of the diamond and the brilliancy ratio will be nonnegative, so nonnegative values are reasonable for the domain and range.

**b. Graph the function.**

**Step 1** Identify the vertical and horizontal asymptotes.

vertical: $x = 0$ *Use $x = b$. $b = 0$*

horizontal: $y = 0$ *Use $y = c$. $c = 0$*

**Step 2** Graph the asymptotes.
The asymptotes will be the $x$- and $y$-axes.

**Step 3** Since the domain is restricted to nonnegative values, only choose $x$-values on the right side of the vertical asymptote.

| Depth of Diamond (mm) | 2 | 10 | 20 | 45 |
|---|---|---|---|---|
| Brilliancy Ratio | 45 | 9 | 4.5 | 2 |

**Step 4** Plot the points and connect them with smooth curves.

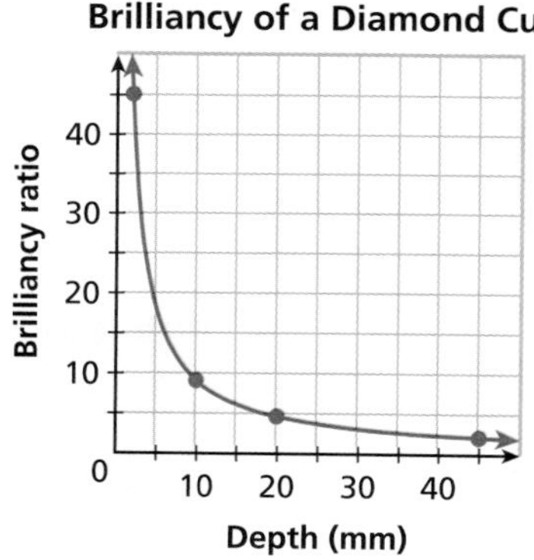

**4.** A librarian has a budget of $500 to buy copies of a software program. She will receive 10 free copies when she sets up an account with the supplier. The number of copies $y$ of the program that she can buy is given by $y = \frac{500}{x} + 10$, where $x$ is the price per copy.

**a.** Describe the reasonable domain and range values.

**b.** Graph the function.

The table shows some of the properties of the four families of functions you have studied and their graphs.

## Families of Functions

| LINEAR FUNCTION | QUADRATIC FUNCTION |
|---|---|
| $y = mx + b$ | $y = ax^2 + bx + c$ |
| • Parent function: $y = x$<br>• $m$ is the slope. It rotates the graph about $(0, b)$.<br>• $b$ is the $y$-intercept. It translates the graph of $y = x$ vertically. | • Parent function: $y = x^2$<br>• $a$ determines the width of the parabola and the direction it opens.<br>• $c$ translates the graph of $y = ax^2$ vertically.<br>• The axis of symmetry is the vertical line $x = -\frac{b}{2a}$. |
| | 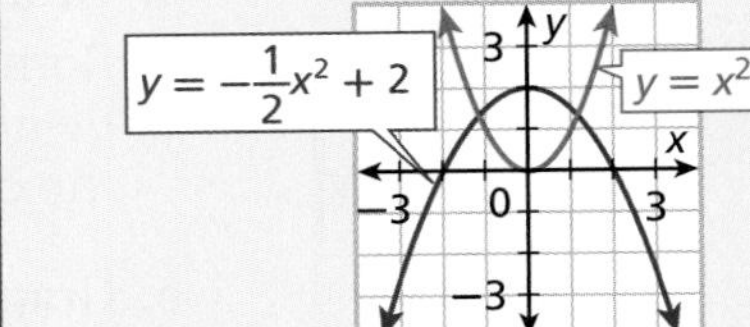  |
| **SQUARE-ROOT FUNCTION** | **RATIONAL FUNCTION** |
| $y = \sqrt{x - a} + b$ | $y = \frac{a}{x - b} + c$ |
| • Parent function: $y = \sqrt{x}$<br>• $a$ translates the graph of $y = \sqrt{x}$ horizontally.<br>• $b$ translates the graph of $y = \sqrt{x}$ vertically. | • Parent function: $y = \frac{1}{x}$<br>• $b$ translates the graph $y = \frac{1}{x}$ horizontally.<br>• $c$ translates the graph of $y = \frac{1}{x}$ vertically. |
| 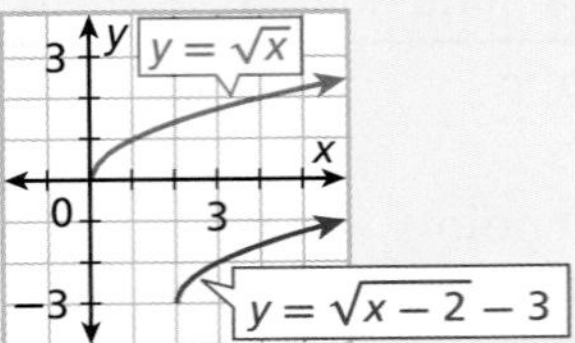  | 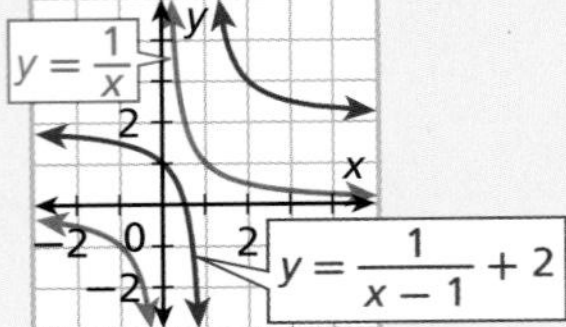  |

## THINK AND DISCUSS

1. Does $y = \frac{1}{x - 5}$ have any excluded values? Explain.
2. Tell how to find the vertical and horizontal asymptotes of $y = \frac{1}{x + 9} - 5$.
3. **GET ORGANIZED** Copy and complete the graphic organizer. In each box, find the asymptotes for the given rational function.

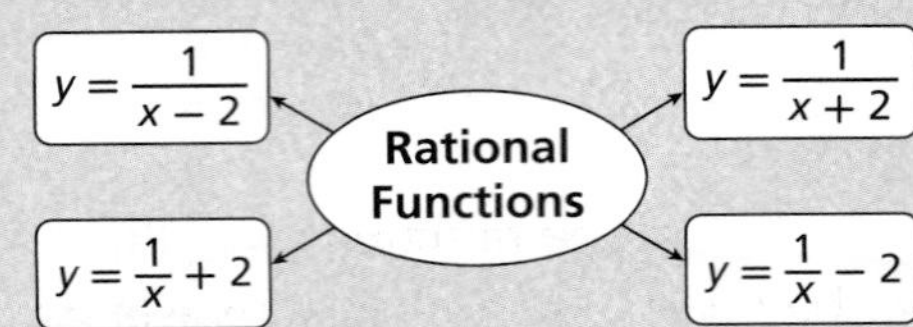

# 12-2 Exercises

MA.A.4.2, MA.A.4.3

go.hrw.com
Homework Help Online
KEYWORD: MA7 12-2
Parent Resources Online
KEYWORD: MA7 Parent

## GUIDED PRACTICE

1. **Vocabulary** An $x$-value that makes a function undefined is a(n) ___?___. (*asymptote* or *excluded value*)

SEE EXAMPLE 1 p. 858

**Identify the excluded value for each rational function.**

2. $y = \frac{4}{x}$
3. $y = \frac{2}{x+3}$
4. $y = -\frac{2}{x}$
5. $y = \frac{16}{x-4}$

SEE EXAMPLE 2 p. 859

**Identify the asymptotes.**

6. $y = \frac{1}{x-3}$
7. $y = \frac{4}{3x+15}$
8. $y = \frac{2}{3x-5} + 2$
9. $y = \frac{1}{x+9} - 10$

SEE EXAMPLE 3 p. 860

**Graph each function.**

10. $y = \frac{2}{x+6}$
11. $y = \frac{1}{x-2} - 6$
12. $y = \frac{1}{x} + 2$
13. $y = \frac{1}{x-3} - 2$

SEE EXAMPLE 4 p. 861

14. **Catering** A caterer has $100 in her budget for fruit. Slicing and delivery of each pound of fruit costs $5. If $x$ represents the cost per pound of the fruit itself, then $y = \frac{100}{x+5}$ represents the number of pounds $y$ she can buy.
    a. Describe the reasonable domain and range values.
    b. Graph the function.

## PRACTICE AND PROBLEM SOLVING

**Independent Practice**

| For Exercises | See Example |
|---|---|
| 15–18 | 1 |
| 19–22 | 2 |
| 23–26 | 3 |
| 27 | 4 |

**Extra Practice**

Skills Practice p. S26
Application Practice p. S39

**Identify the excluded value for each rational function.**

15. $y = \frac{7}{x}$
16. $y = \frac{1}{x-4}$
17. $y = -\frac{15}{x}$
18. $y = \frac{12}{x-5}$

**Identify the asymptotes.**

19. $y = \frac{9}{x-4}$
20. $y = \frac{2}{x+4}$
21. $y = \frac{7}{4x-12} + 4$
22. $y = \frac{7}{3x+5} - 9$

**Graph each function.**

23. $y = \frac{5}{x-5}$
24. $y = \frac{1}{x+5} - 6$
25. $y = \frac{1}{x+4}$
26. $y = \frac{1}{x-4} + 2$

27. **Business** A wholesaler is buying auto parts. He has $200 to spend. He receives 5 parts free with the order. The number of parts $y$ he can buy, if the average price of the parts is $x$ dollars, is $y = \frac{200}{x} + 5$.
    a. Describe the reasonable domain and range values.
    b. Graph the function.

**Find the excluded value for each rational function.**

28. $y = \frac{4}{x}$
29. $y = \frac{1}{x-7}$
30. $y = \frac{2}{x+4}$
31. $y = \frac{3}{2x+1}$

**Graph each rational function. Show the asymptotes.**

32. $y = \frac{1}{x-2}$
33. $y = \frac{2}{x} + 3$
34. $y = \frac{3}{x+1} + 2$
35. $y = \frac{1}{x-4} - 1$

36. **Multi-Step** The function $y = \frac{60}{x^2}$ relates the luminescence in lumens $y$ of a 60-watt lightbulb viewed from a distance of $x$ ft. Graph the function. Use the graph to find the luminescence of a 60-watt lightbulb viewed from a distance of 6 ft.

**Identify the asymptotes of each rational function.**

**37.** $y = \frac{7}{x+1}$ **38.** $y = \frac{1}{x} - 5$ **39.** $y = \frac{12}{x-2} + 5$ **40.** $y = \frac{18}{x+3} - 9$

**Match each graph with one of the following functions.**

**A.** $y = \frac{1}{x+1} + 2$ **B.** $y = \frac{1}{x+2} - 1$ **C.** $y = \frac{1}{x-2} + 1$

**41.**

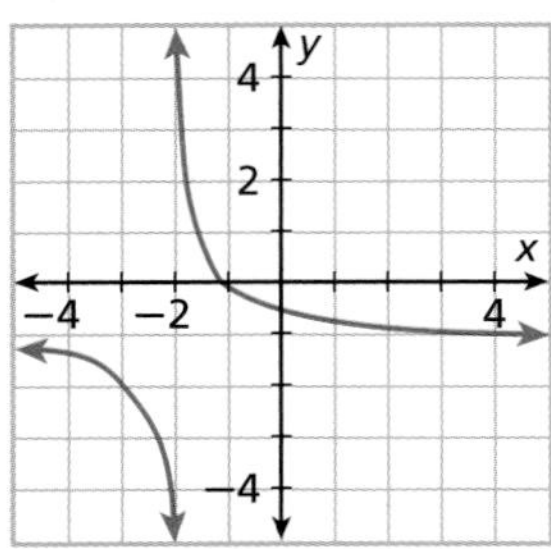

**42.**

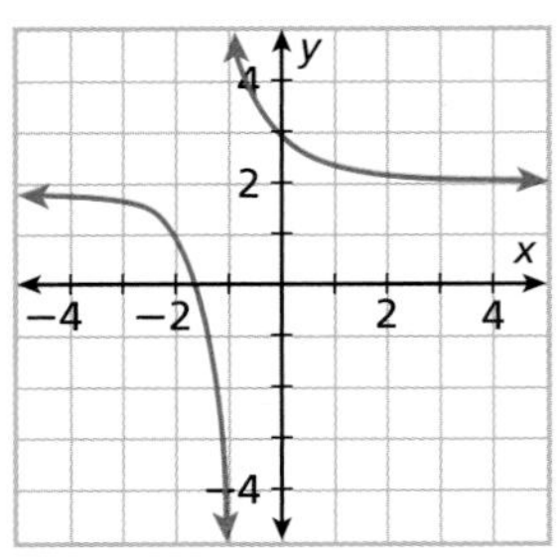

**43.**

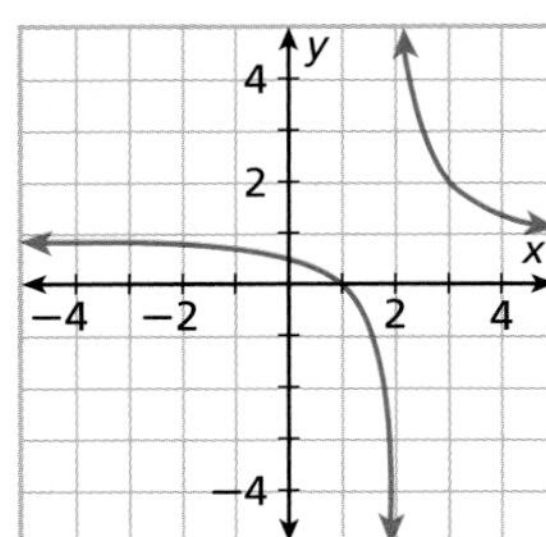

**44.** **ERROR ANALYSIS** In finding the horizontal asymptote of $y = \frac{1}{x+2} - 3$, student A said the asymptote is at $y = -3$, and student B said it is at $y = -2$. Who is incorrect? Explain the error.

**45. Finance** The time in months $y$ that it will take to pay off a bill of \$1200, when $x$ dollars are paid each month and the finance charge is \$15 per month, is $y = \frac{1200}{x-15}$. Describe the reasonable domain and range values and graph the function.

**46.** The table shows how long it takes different size landscaping teams to complete a project.

a. Graph the data.

b. Write a rational function to represent the data.

c. How many hours would it take 12 landscapers to complete the project?

| Landscapers | Time (h) |
|---|---|
| 2 | 30 |
| 4 | 15 |
| 5 | 12 |
| 10 | 6 |

**Graph each function. Compare its graph to the graph of $y = \frac{1}{x}$.**

**47.** $y = \frac{1}{x-6}$ **48.** $y = \frac{1}{x+7}$ **49.** $y = \frac{1}{x} + 4$ **50.** $y = \frac{1}{x-2} - 9$

**Find the domain that makes the range positive.**

**51.** $y = \frac{10}{x-2}$ **52.** $y = \frac{10}{x+2}$ **53.** $y = \frac{5}{5x+1}$ **54.** $y = \frac{4}{3x-7}$

**55. Critical Thinking** In which quadrants would you find the graph of $y = \frac{a}{x}$ when $a$ is positive? when $a$ is negative?

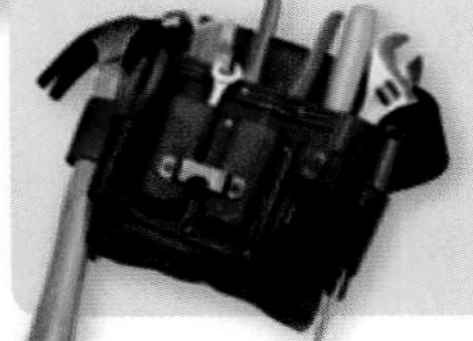

**56.** This problem will prepare you for the Multi-Step Test Prep on page 876.

It takes a total of 250 workdays to build a house for charity. For example, if 2 workers build the house, it takes them 125 actual construction days. If 10 workers are present, it takes 25 construction days to build the house.

a. Write a function that represents the number of construction days to build as a function of the number of workers.

b. What is the domain of this function?

c. Sketch a graph of the function.

57. **Write About It** Graph each pair of functions on a graphing calculator. Then make a conjecture about the relationship between the graphs of the rational functions $y = \frac{k}{x}$ and $y = \frac{-k}{x}$.

a. $y = \frac{1}{x}$; $y = \frac{-1}{x}$ b. $y = \frac{3}{x}$; $y = \frac{-3}{x}$ c. $y = \frac{5}{x}$; $y = \frac{-5}{x}$

## TEST PREP

NC MA.A.4.2, MA.A.4.3

58. Which function is graphed?

Ⓐ $y = \frac{2}{x + 3} - 4$ Ⓒ $y = \frac{2}{x - 3} + 4$

Ⓑ $y = \frac{2}{x + 4} - 3$ Ⓓ $y = \frac{2}{x - 4} + 3$

59. Which rational function has a graph with the horizontal asymptote $y = -1$?

Ⓕ $y = \frac{-1}{x}$ Ⓗ $y = \frac{1}{x + 1}$

Ⓖ $y = \frac{1}{x - 1}$ Ⓙ $y = \frac{1}{x} - 1$

60. **Short Response** Write a rational function whose graph is the same shape as the graph of $f(x) = \frac{1}{x}$, but is translated 2 units left and 3 units down. Graph the function.

## CHALLENGE AND EXTEND

61. Graph the equation $y = \frac{1}{x^2 + 1}$.

a. Does this equation represent a rational function? Explain.

b. What is the domain of the function?

c. What is the range of the function?

d. Is the graph discontinuous?

62. **Graphing Calculator** Are the graphs of $f(x) = \frac{(x - 3)(x - 1)}{(x - 3)}$ and $g(x) = x - 1$ identical? Explain. (*Hint:* Are there any excluded values?)

63. **Critical Thinking** Write the equation of the rational function that has a horizontal asymptote at $y = 3$ and a vertical asymptote at $x = -2$ and contains the point $(1, 4)$.

## SPIRAL REVIEW

**Solve each equation by graphing the related function.** *(Lesson 9-5)*

64. $4 - x^2 = 0$ 65. $3x^2 = x^2 + 2x + 12$ 66. $-x^2 = -6x + 9$

67. In the first five stages of a fractal design, a line segment has the following lengths, in centimeters: 240, 120, 60, 30, 15. Use this pattern and your knowledge of geometric sequences to determine the length of the segment in the tenth stage. *(Lesson 11-1)*

**Determine whether each function represents an inverse variation. Explain.** *(Lesson 12-1)*

68. $x + y = 12$

69.

| x | 30 | 60 | 90 | 120 |
|---|---|---|---|---|
| y | 10 | 20 | 30 | 40 |

70. $xy = -4$

# 12-3 Simplifying Rational Expressions

**MA.A.1.1** Execute … operations with algebraic expressions (division by a monomial only). *Also* **MA.A.1.3**

***Objectives***
Simplify rational expressions.

Identify excluded values of rational expressions.

***Vocabulary***
rational expression

**Why learn this?**
The shapes and sizes of plants and animals are partly determined by the ratio of surface area to volume.

If an animal's body is small and its surface area is large, the rate of heat loss will be high. Hummingbirds must maintain a high metabolism to compensate for the loss of body heat due to having a high surface-area-to-volume ratio. Formulas for surface-area-to-volume ratios are *rational expressions*.

A **rational expression** is an algebraic expression whose numerator and denominator are polynomials. The value of the polynomial expression in the denominator cannot be zero since division by zero is undefined. This means that rational expressions may have excluded values.

## EXAMPLE 1 Identifying Excluded Values

**Find any excluded values of each rational expression.**

**A** $\frac{5}{8r}$

$8r = 0$ *Set the denominator equal to 0.*

$r = \frac{0}{8} = 0$ *Solve for r by dividing both sides by 8.*

The excluded value is 0.

**B** $\frac{9d + 1}{d^2 - 2d}$

$d^2 - 2d = 0$ *Set the denominator equal to 0.*

$d(d - 2) = 0$ *Factor.*

$d = 0$ or $d - 2 = 0$ *Use the Zero Product Property.*

$d = 2$ *Solve for d.*

The excluded values are 0 and 2.

**C** $\frac{x + 4}{x^2 + 5x + 6}$

$x^2 + 5x + 6 = 0$ *Set the denominator equal to 0.*

$(x + 3)(x + 2) = 0$ *Factor.*

$x + 3 = 0$ or $x + 2 = 0$ *Use the Zero Product Property.*

$x = -3$ or $x = -2$ *Solve each equation for x.*

The excluded values are $-3$ and $-2$.

**Remember!**
To review the Zero Product Property, see Lesson 9-6.
To review factoring trinomials, see Chapter 8.

**Find any excluded values of each rational expression.**

**1a.** $\frac{12}{t + 5}$ **1b.** $\frac{3b}{b^2 + 5b}$ **1c.** $\frac{3k^2}{k^2 + 7k + 12}$

A rational expression is in its simplest form when the numerator and denominator have no common factors except 1. Remember that to simplify fractions you can divide out common factors that appear in both the numerator and the denominator. You can do the same to simplify rational expressions.

## EXAMPLE 2 Simplifying Rational Expressions

**Simplify each rational expression, if possible. Identify any excluded values.**

**Caution!**

Be sure to use the original denominator when finding excluded values. The excluded values may not be "seen" in the simplified denominator.

**A** $\dfrac{3t^3}{12t}$

$\dfrac{3t^3}{3 \cdot 4t}$ *Factor 12.*

$\dfrac{{}^1\cancel{3}t^{\cancel{3}2}}{{}_1\cancel{3} \cdot 4\cancel{t}^1}$ *Divide out common factors. Note that if t = 0, the expression is undefined.*

$\dfrac{t^2}{4};\ t \neq 0$ *Simplify. The excluded value is 0.*

**B** $\dfrac{3x^2 - 9x}{x - 3}$

$\dfrac{3x(x-3)}{x-3}$ *Factor the numerator.*

$\dfrac{3x\cancel{(x-3)}^1}{\cancel{x-3}^1}$ *Divide out common factors. Note that if x = 3, the expression is undefined.*

$3x;\ x \neq 3$ *Simplify. The excluded value is 3.*

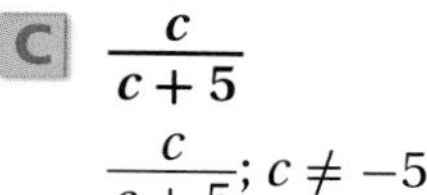

**C** $\dfrac{c}{c+5}$

$\dfrac{c}{c+5};\ c \neq -5$ *The numerator and denominator have no common factors. The excluded value is −5.*

**CHECK IT OUT!** **Simplify each rational expression, if possible. Identify any excluded values.**

**2a.** $\dfrac{5m^2}{15m}$ **2b.** $\dfrac{6p^3 + 12p}{p^2 + 2}$ **2c.** $\dfrac{3n}{n-2}$

From now on in this chapter, you may assume that the values of the variables that make the denominator equal to 0 are excluded values. You do not need to include excluded values in your answers unless they are asked for.

## EXAMPLE 3 Simplifying Rational Expressions with Trinomials

**Simplify each rational expression, if possible.**

**A** $\dfrac{k+1}{k^2 - 4k - 5}$

$\dfrac{k+1}{(k+1)(k-5)}$ *Factor the numerator and the denominator when possible.*

$\dfrac{\cancel{k+1}^1}{\cancel{(k+1)}^1(k-5)}$ *Divide out common factors.*

$\dfrac{1}{k-5}$ *Simplify.*

**B** $\dfrac{y^2 - 16}{y^2 - 8y + 16}$

$\dfrac{(y+4)(y-4)}{(y-4)(y-4)}$

$\dfrac{(y+4)\cancel{(y-4)}^1}{(y-4)\cancel{(y-4)}^1}$

$\dfrac{y+4}{y-4}$

**Simplify each rational expression, if possible.**

**3a.** $\dfrac{r+2}{r^2+7r+10}$ **3b.** $\dfrac{b^2-25}{b^2+10b+25}$

Recall from Chapter 8 that opposite binomials can help you factor polynomials. Recognizing opposite binomials can also help you simplify rational expressions.

Consider $\frac{x-3}{3-x}$. The numerator and denominator are opposite binomials. Therefore,

$$\frac{x-3}{3-x}=\frac{x-3}{-x+3}=\frac{\cancel{x-3}^{1}}{-1(\cancel{x-3})^{1}}=\frac{1}{-1}=-1.$$

## EXAMPLE 4 Simplifying Rational Expressions Using Opposite Binomials

**Simplify each rational expression, if possible.**

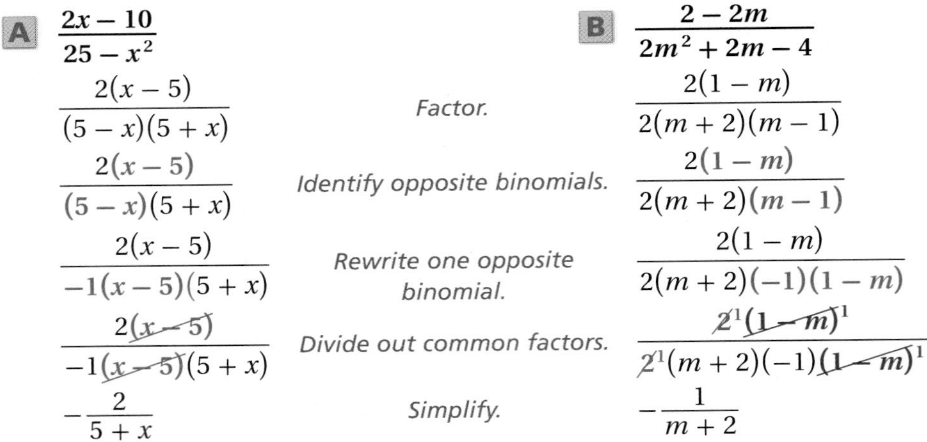

**A** $\dfrac{2x-10}{25-x^2}$

$\dfrac{2(x-5)}{(5-x)(5+x)}$ *Factor.*

$\dfrac{2(x-5)}{(5-x)(5+x)}$ *Identify opposite binomials.*

$\dfrac{2(x-5)}{-1(x-5)(5+x)}$ *Rewrite one opposite binomial.*

$\dfrac{2(\cancel{x-5})}{-1(\cancel{x-5})(5+x)}$ *Divide out common factors.*

$-\dfrac{2}{5+x}$ *Simplify.*

**B** $\dfrac{2-2m}{2m^2+2m-4}$

$\dfrac{2(1-m)}{2(m+2)(m-1)}$ *Factor.*

$\dfrac{2(1-m)}{2(m+2)(m-1)}$ *Identify opposite binomials.*

$\dfrac{2(1-m)}{2(m+2)(-1)(1-m)}$ *Rewrite one opposite binomial.*

$\dfrac{\cancel{2}^{1}(\cancel{1-m})^{1}}{\cancel{2}^{1}(m+2)(-1)(\cancel{1-m})^{1}}$ *Divide out common factors.*

$-\dfrac{1}{m+2}$ *Simplify.*

**Simplify each rational expression, if possible.**

**4a.** $\dfrac{3x-12}{16-x^2}$ **4b.** $\dfrac{6-2x}{2x^2-4x-6}$ **4c.** $\dfrac{3x-33}{x^2-121}$

## Student to Student

### *Simplifying Rational Expressions*

**Tanika Brown,** Washington High School

*When I can't tell if I'm allowed to divide out part of an expression, I substitute a number into the original expression and simplify it. Then I simplify the original expression by dividing out the term in question. I check by seeing if the results are the same.*

*For example, I'll use $x = 2$ to see if I can divide out $4x$ in $\frac{4x}{4x-7}$.*

*Substitute $x = 2$.*

$\dfrac{4x}{4x-7}$

$\dfrac{4(2)}{4(2)-7}$

$\dfrac{8}{8-7}=\dfrac{8}{1}=8$

*Divide out $4x$.*

$\dfrac{\cancel{4}^{1}\cancel{x}^{1}}{\cancel{4}^{1}\cancel{x}^{1}-7}$

$\dfrac{1}{1-7}$

$\dfrac{1}{-6}$

*$4x$ cannot be divided out because $8 \neq \frac{1}{-6}$.*

## EXAMPLE 5 Biology Application

**Desert plants must conserve water. Water evaporates from the surface of a plant. The volume determines how much water is in a plant. So the greater the surface-area-to-volume ratio, the less likely a plant is to survive in the desert. A barrel cactus is a desert plant that is close to spherical in shape.**

**a. What is the surface-area-to-volume ratio of a spherical barrel cactus? (*Hint:* For a sphere, $S = 4\pi r^2$ and $V = \frac{4}{3}\pi r^3$)**

$\dfrac{4\pi r^2}{\frac{4}{3}\pi r^3}$ *Write the ratio of surface area to volume.*

$\dfrac{4\cancel{\pi}^1 r^2}{\frac{4}{3}\cancel{\pi}^1 r^3}$ *Divide out common factors.*

$\dfrac{4\cancel{r^2}^1}{\frac{4}{3}\cancel{r^3}^1}$ *Use properties of exponents.*

$\dfrac{4}{r} \cdot \dfrac{3}{4}$ *Multiply by the reciprocal of $\frac{4}{3}$.*

$\dfrac{\cancel{4}^1}{r} \cdot \dfrac{3}{\cancel{4}^1}$ *Divide out common factors.*

$\dfrac{3}{r}$ *Simplify.*

**b. Which barrel cactus has a greater chance of survival in the desert, one with a radius of 4 inches or one with a radius of 7 inches? Explain.**

$\dfrac{3}{r} = \dfrac{3}{4}$ $\dfrac{3}{r} = \dfrac{3}{7}$ *Write the ratio of surface area to volume twice. Substitute 4 and 7 for r.*

$\dfrac{3}{4} > \dfrac{3}{7}$ *Compare the ratios.*

The barrel cactus with a radius of 7 inches has a greater chance of survival. Its surface-area-to-volume ratio is less than for a cactus with a radius of 4 inches.

**Remember!**

For two fractions with the same numerator, the value of the fraction with a greater denominator is less than the value of the other fraction.

$9 > 3$

$\dfrac{2}{9} < \dfrac{2}{3}$

**5.** Which barrel cactus has less of a chance to survive in the desert, one with a radius of 6 inches or one with a radius of 3 inches? Explain.

## THINK AND DISCUSS

**1.** Write a rational expression that has an excluded value that cannot be identified when the expression is in its simplified form.

**2. GET ORGANIZED** Copy and complete the graphic organizer. In each box, write and simplify one of the given rational expressions using the most appropriate method. $\frac{x-3}{x^2-6x+9}$, $\frac{5x^4}{x^2}$, $\frac{4-x}{x-4}$, $\frac{4x^2-4x}{8x}$

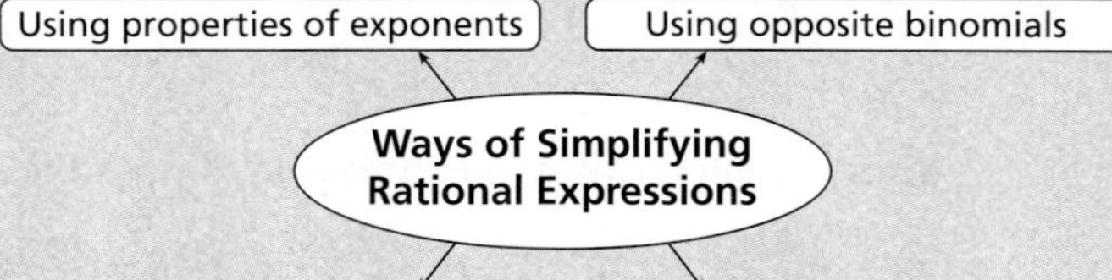

# 12-3 Exercises

MA.A.1.1, MA.A.1.3



## GUIDED PRACTICE

1. **Vocabulary** What is true about both the numerator and denominator of rational expressions?

SEE EXAMPLE 1 p. 866

**Find any excluded values of each rational expression.**

2. $\frac{5}{m}$
3. $\frac{x+2}{x^2-8x}$
4. $\frac{p^2}{p^2-2p-15}$

SEE EXAMPLE 2 p. 867

**Simplify each rational expression, if possible. Identify any excluded values.**

5. $\frac{4a^2}{8a}$
6. $\frac{2d^2+12d}{d+6}$
7. $\frac{2}{y+3}$
8. $\frac{10}{5-y}$
9. $\frac{2h}{2h+4}$
10. $\frac{3(x+4)}{6x}$

SEE EXAMPLE 3 p. 867

**Simplify each rational expression, if possible.**

11. $\frac{b+4}{b^2+5b+4}$
12. $\frac{s^2-4}{s^2+4s+4}$
13. $\frac{c^2+5c+6}{(c+3)(c-4)}$
14. $\frac{(x-2)(x+1)}{x^2+4x+3}$
15. $\frac{j^2-25}{j^2+2j-15}$
16. $\frac{p+1}{p^2-4p-5}$

SEE EXAMPLE 4 p. 868

17. $\frac{2n-16}{64-n^2}$
18. $\frac{8-4x}{2x^2-12x+16}$
19. $\frac{10-5r}{r^2-4r-12}$
20. $\frac{2x-14}{49-x^2}$
21. $\frac{5q-50}{100-q^2}$
22. $\frac{36-12a}{a^2+2a-15}$

SEE EXAMPLE 5 p. 869

23. **Construction** The side of a triangular roof will have the same height $h$ and base $b_2$ as the side of a trapezoidal roof.

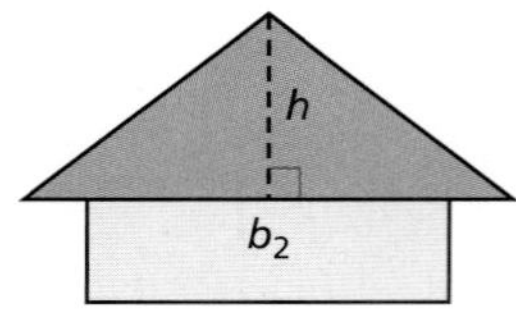


a. What is the ratio of the area of the triangular roof to the area of the trapezoidal roof?

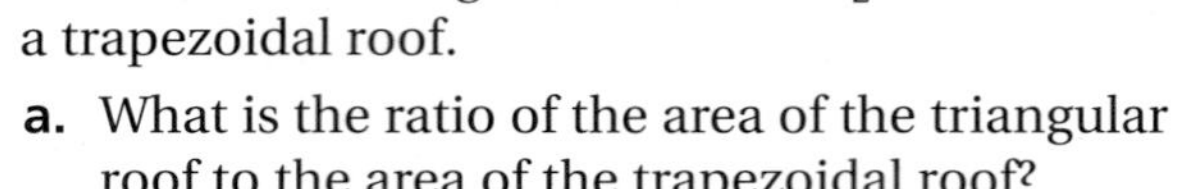

(*Hint:* For a triangle, $A = \frac{1}{2}b_2h$.
For a trapezoid, $A = \frac{b_1+b_2}{2}h$.)

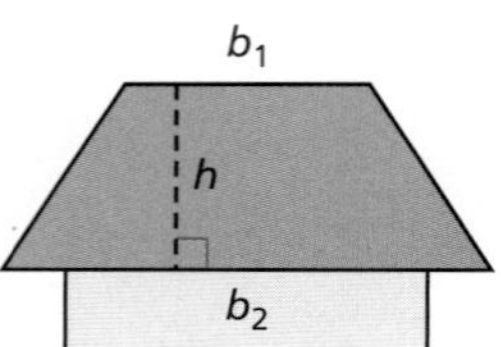


b. Compare the ratio from part **a** to what the ratio will be if $b_1$ is doubled for the trapezoidal roof and $b_2$ is doubled for both roofs.

## PRACTICE AND PROBLEM SOLVING

**Find any excluded values of each rational expression.**

24. $\frac{c}{c^2+c}$
25. $\frac{2}{-3x}$
26. $\frac{4}{x^2-3x-10}$
27. $\frac{n^2-1}{2n^2-7n-4}$

**Simplify each rational expression, if possible. Identify any excluded values.**

28. $\frac{4d^3+4d^2}{d+1}$
29. $\frac{3m^2}{m-4}$
30. $\frac{10y^4}{2y}$
31. $\frac{2t^2}{16t}$

**Independent Practice**

| For Exercises | See Example |
|---|---|
| 24–27 | 1 |
| 28–31 | 2 |
| 32–37 | 3 |
| 38–40 | 4 |
| 41 | 5 |

**Extra Practice**

Skills Practice p. S26
Application Practice p. S39

Simplify each rational expression, if possible.

32. $\frac{q-6}{q^2-9q+18}$

33. $\frac{z^2-2z+1}{z^2-1}$

34. $\frac{t-3}{t^2-5t+6}$

35. $\frac{p^2-6p-7}{p^2-4p-5}$

36. $\frac{x^2-1}{x^2+4x+3}$

37. $\frac{2x-4}{x^2-6x+8}$

38. $\frac{20-4x}{x^2-25}$

39. $\frac{3-3b}{3b^2+18b-21}$

40. $\frac{3v-36}{144-v^2}$

41. **Geometry** When choosing package sizes, a company wants a package that uses the least amount of material to hold the greatest volume of product.

a. What is the surface-area-to-volume ratio for a rectangular prism? (*Hint:* For a rectangular prism, $S = 2lw + 2lh + 2wh$ and $V = lwh$.)

b. Which box should the company choose? Explain.

**LINK**

**Biology**

As a result of a nation-wide policy of protection and reintroduction, the population of bald eagles in the lower 48 states grew from 417 nesting pairs in 1963 to more than 6400 nesting pairs in 2000.

*Source:* U.S. Fish and Wildlife Service

42. **Biology** The table gives information on two populations of animals that were released into the wild. Suppose 16 more predators and 20 more prey are released into the area. Write and simplify a rational expression to show the ratio of predator to prey.

| | Predator | Prey |
|---|---|---|
| Original Population | $x$ | $x$ |
| Population 5 Years Later | $4x$ | $5x$ |

Simplify each rational expression, if possible.

43. $\frac{p^2+12p+36}{12p+72}$

44. $\frac{3n^3+33n^2+15n}{3n^3+15n}$

45. $\frac{a}{2a+a}$

46. $\frac{j-5}{j^2-25}$

47. $\frac{6w^2+11w-7}{6w-3}$

48. $\frac{n^2-n-56}{n^2-16n+64}$

49. $\frac{(x+1)^2}{x^2+2x+1}$

50. $\frac{5}{(x+5)^2}$

51. $\frac{25-x^2}{x^2-3x-10}$

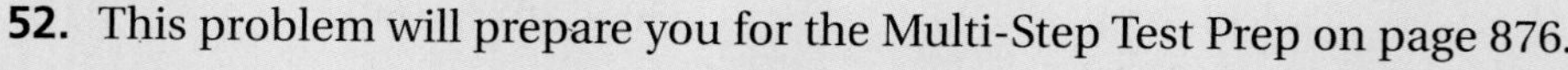

52. This problem will prepare you for the Multi-Step Test Prep on page 876.

It takes 250 workdays to build a house. The number of construction days is determined by the size of the crew. The crew includes one manager who supervises workers and checks for problems, but does not do any building.

a. The table shows the number of construction days as a function of the number of workers. Copy and complete the table.

b. Use the table to write a function that represents the number of construction days.

c. Identify the excluded values of the function.

| Crew Size ($x$) | $\frac{\text{Workdays}}{\text{Workers}}$ | Construction Days ($y$) |
|---|---|---|
| 2 | $\frac{250}{2-1}$ | 250 |
| 3 | $\frac{250}{3-1}$ | ■ |
| 6 | ■ | ■ |
| 11 | ■ | 25 |

53. **Geometry** Let $s$ represent the length of an edge of a cube.

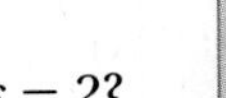
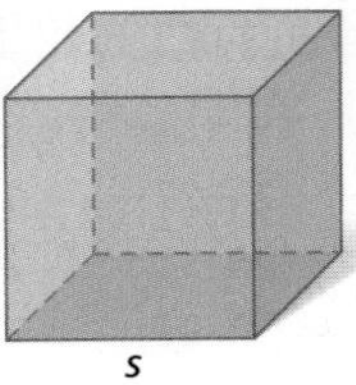


a. Write the ratio of a cube's surface area to volume in simplified form. (*Hint:* For a cube, $S = 6s^2$.)

b. What is the ratio of the cube's surface area to volume when $s = 2$?

c. What is the ratio of the cube's surface area to volume when $s = 6$?

54. **Write About It** Explain how to find excluded values for a rational expression.

55. **Critical Thinking** Give an example of a rational expression that has $x$ in both the numerator and denominator, but cannot be simplified.

## TEST PREP

MA.A.1.1, MA.A.1.3

56. Which expression is undefined for $x = 4$ and $x = -1$?

Ⓐ $\dfrac{x-1}{x+4}$ Ⓑ $\dfrac{x-4}{x+4}$ Ⓒ $\dfrac{x}{x^2+3x-4}$ Ⓓ $\dfrac{x}{x^2-3x-4}$

57. Which expression is the ratio of the area of a triangle to the area of a rectangle that has the same base and height?

Ⓕ $\dfrac{1}{2}$ Ⓖ $\dfrac{bh}{2}$ Ⓗ $\dfrac{(bh)^2}{2}$ Ⓙ 2

58. **Gridded Response** What is the excluded value for $\dfrac{x-4}{x^2-8x+16}$?

## CHALLENGE AND EXTEND

**Tell whether each statement is sometimes, always, or never true. Explain.**

59. A rational expression has an excluded value.

60. A rational expression has a square root in the numerator.

61. The graph of a rational function has at least one asymptote.

**Simplify each rational expression.**

62. $\dfrac{9v-6v^2}{4v^2-4v-3}$ 63. $\dfrac{2a^2-7a+3}{2a^2+9a-5}$ 64. $\dfrac{0.25y-0.10}{0.25y^2-0.04}$

**Identify any excluded values of each rational expression.**

65. $\dfrac{\frac{1}{4}x^2-7x+49}{\frac{1}{4}x^2-49}$ 66. $\dfrac{-80x+40x^2+40}{-30-30x^2+60x}$ 67. $\dfrac{6x+12}{12x+6x^2}$

## SPIRAL REVIEW

68. A rectangle has an area of 24 square feet. Every dimension is multiplied by a scale factor, and the new rectangle has an area of 864 square feet. What is the scale factor? *(Lesson 2-7)*

**Use intercepts to graph the line described by each equation.** *(Lesson 5-2)*

69. $5x - 3y = -15$ 70. $y = 8x - 8$ 71. $\frac{1}{2}x + y = 2$

**For each of the following, let $y$ vary inversely as $x$.** *(Lesson 12-1)*

72. $x_1 = 2$, $y_1 = 4$, and $x_2 = 1$. Find $y_2$. 73. $x_1 = 2$, $y_1 = -1$, and $y_2 = \frac{1}{3}$. Find $x_2$.

12-3 Technology LAB

# Graph Rational Functions

You can use a graphing calculator to graph rational functions and to compare graphs of rational functions before and after they are simplified.

*Use with Lesson 12-3*

**MA.A.4.2** Use appropriate terminology…associated with functions. *Also* **MA.A.4.3**

## Activity

**Simplify $y = \frac{x-1}{x^2-5x+4}$ and give any excluded values. Then graph both the original function and the simplified function and compare the graphs.**

1. Simplify the function and find the excluded values.

$$\frac{x-1}{x^2-5x+4} = \frac{x-1}{(x-1)(x-4)} = \frac{1}{x-4};\text{ excluded values: } 4, 1$$

2. Enter $y = \frac{x-1}{x^2-5x+4}$ and $y = \frac{1}{x-4}$ into your calculator as shown and press GRAPH.

3. To compare the graphs, press TRACE. At the top of the screen, you can see which graph the cursor is on. To change between graphs, press ▲ and ▼.

4. The graphs appear to be the same, but check the excluded values, 4 and 1. While on **Y1,** press 4 ENTER. Notice that there is no $y$-value at $x = 4$. The function is undefined.

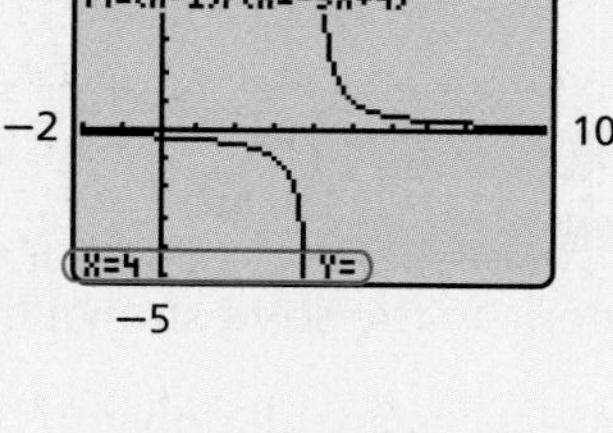


5. Press ▼ to switch to **Y2** and press 4 ENTER. This function is also undefined at $x = 4$. The graphs are the same at this excluded value.

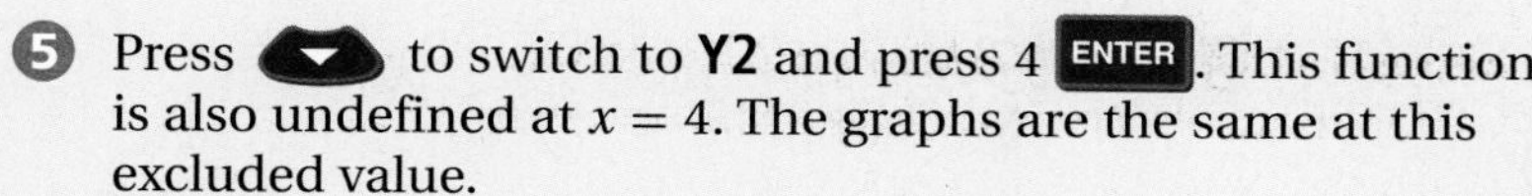
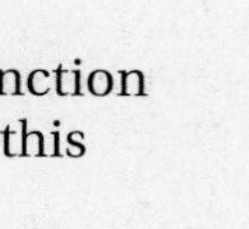

6. Return to **Y1** and press 1 ENTER. This function is undefined at $x = 1$. However, this is not a vertical asymptote. Instead, this graph has a "hole" at $x = 1$.

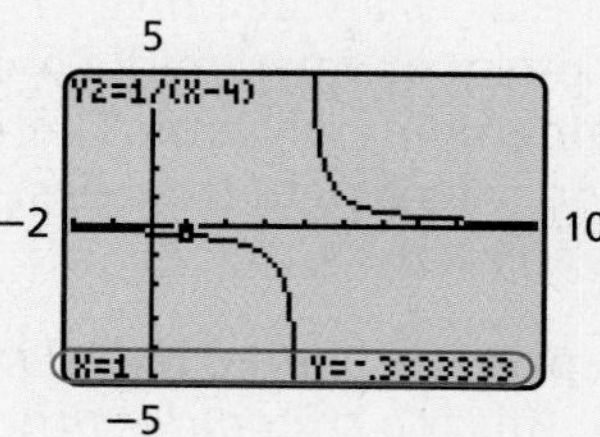


7. Switch to **Y2** and press 1 ENTER. This function is defined at $x = 1$. So the two graphs are the same except at $x = 1$.

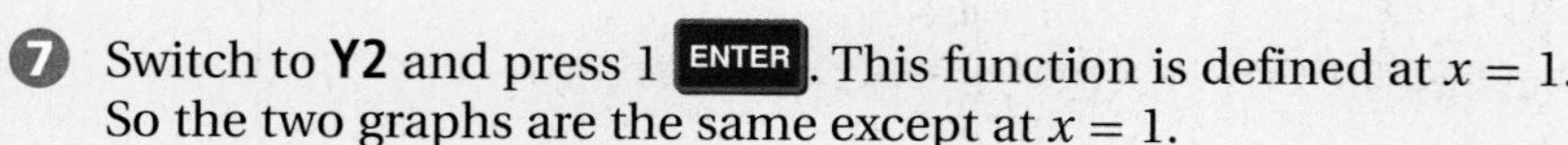

## Try This

1. Why is $x = 1$ an excluded value for one function but not for the other?
2. Are the functions $y = \frac{x-1}{x^2-5x+4}$ and $y = \frac{1}{x-4}$ truly equivalent for all values of $x$? Explain.
3. **Make a Conjecture** Complete each statement.
   **a.** If a value of $x$ is excluded from a function and its simplified form, it appears on the graph as a(n) ___?___.
   **b.** If a value of $x$ is excluded from a function but not its simplified form, it appears on the graph as a ___?___.

# Representing Solid Figures

A *net* is a flat pattern that can be folded to make a solid figure. The net shows all of the faces and surfaces of the solid.

See Skills Bank page S65

**Prep MA.G.2.5** Represent the relationship between the surface area of prisms, cylinders and pyramids to the sum of the area(s) of their base(s) and lateral surfaces using planar nets to illustrate and sum the relevant measures.

To identify the solid shown by a net, remember these properties of solids.

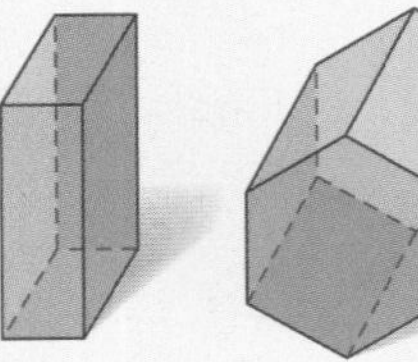

Prisms

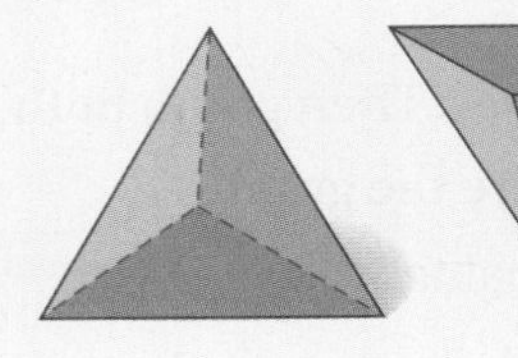

Pyramids

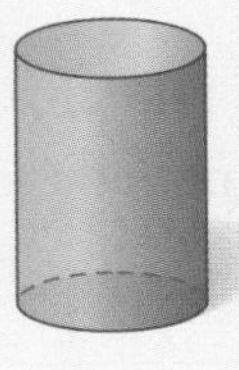

Cylinder

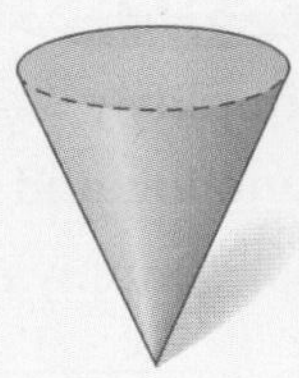

Cone

- A ***prism*** has two parallel, congruent bases that are polygons. The other faces are rectangles or parallelograms.
- A base of a ***pyramid*** is a polygon. The other faces are triangles.
- A ***cylinder*** has two congruent circles as its bases.
- A ***cone*** has one circle as its base.

## Example 1

**Identify the solid shown by this net.**

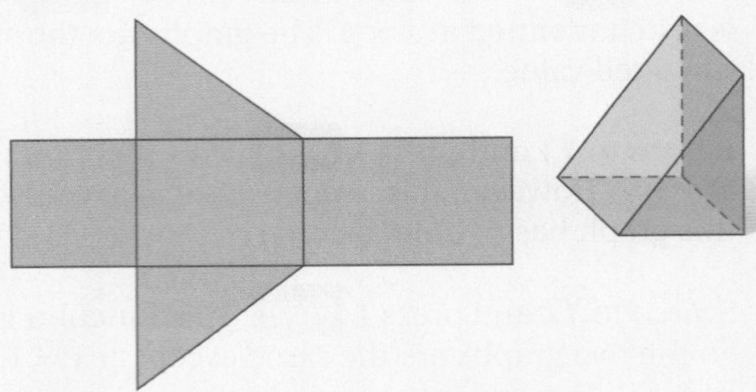

The faces are all polygons, so this is either a prism or a pyramid. Look for a pair of congruent polygons. There are two congruent right triangles. The solid is a *prism*.

A prism is named by the shape of its bases, so this is a *triangular prism*.

## Try This

**Identify the solid shown by each net.**

**1.**

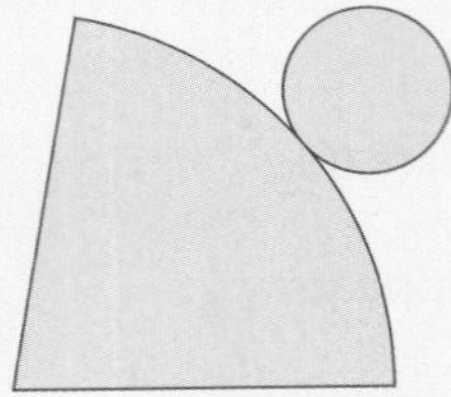

**2.**

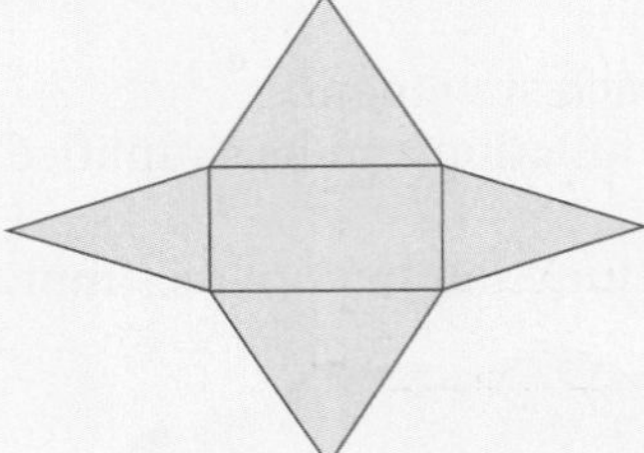

**3.**

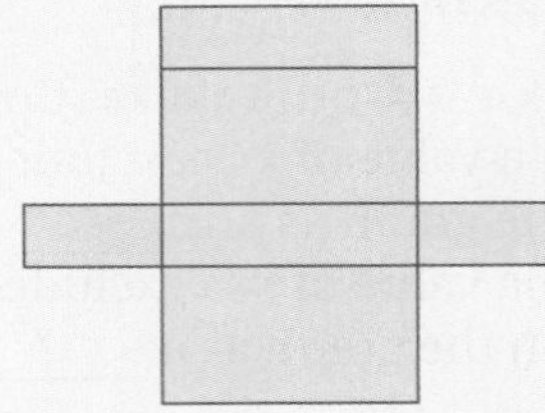

**Identify the solid shown by each net.**

**4.**

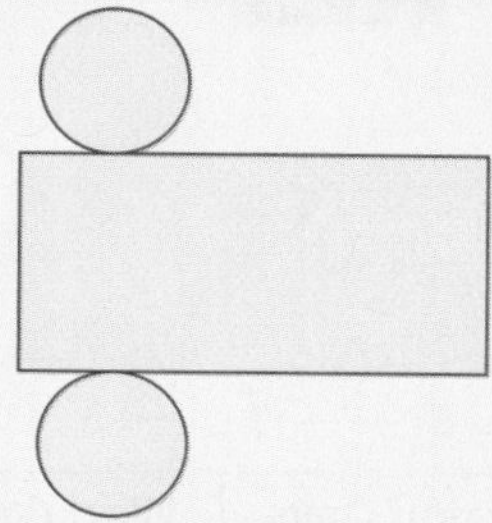

**5.**

**6.**

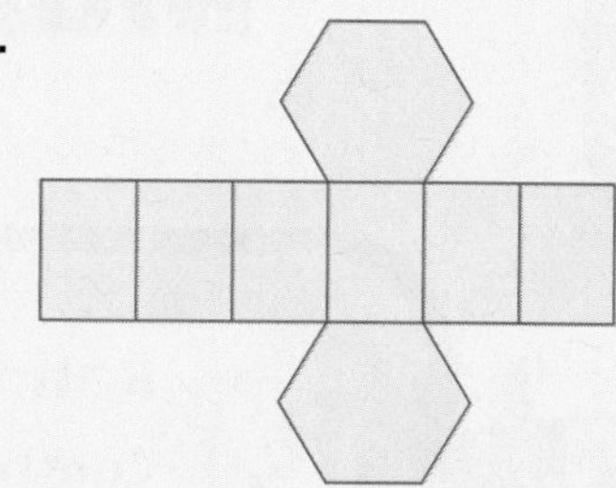

A foundation plan is a drawing that represents a solid made from cubes. The squares in the foundation plan are a top view of the solid. The number in each square shows the height of the solid at that point. The foundation plan shown is like a set of instructions for building the solid next to it.

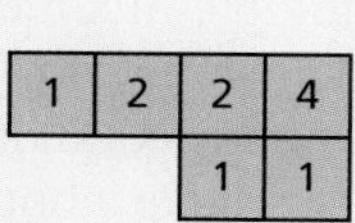


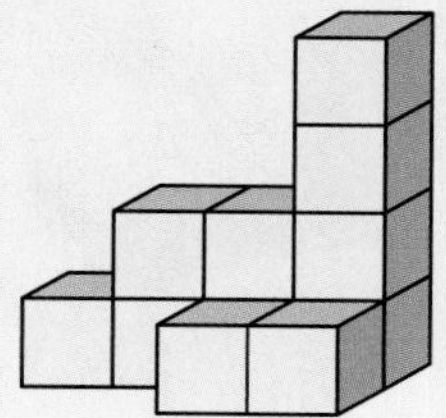

## Example 2

**Draw a foundation plan for this solid figure.**

Use squares to show a top view of the solid.

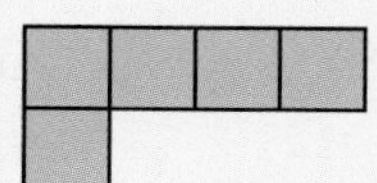

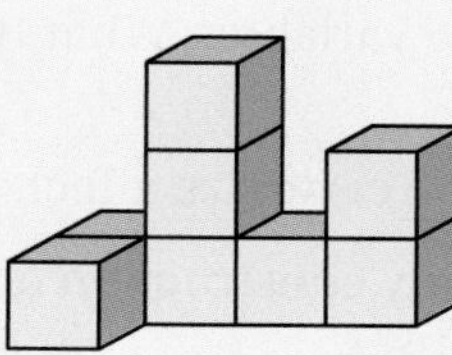

Put a number in each square to show the height at that point.

| 1 | 3 | 1 | 2 |
|---|---|---|---|
| 1 | | | |

## Try This

**Draw a foundation plan for each solid figure.**

**7.**

**8.**

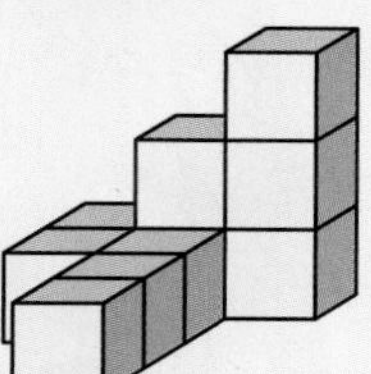

**9.**

**10.**

**11.**

**12.**

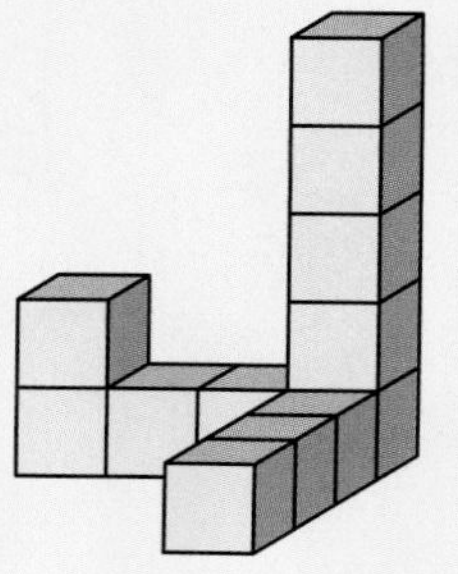

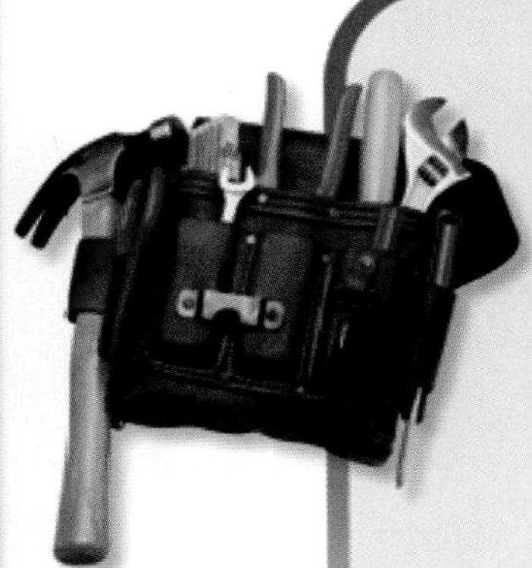

## Rational Functions and Expressions

### Construction Daze

Robert is part of a volunteer crew constructing houses for low-income families. The table shows how many construction days it takes to complete a house for work crews of various sizes.

| Crew Size | Construction Days | Workdays |
|---|---|---|
| 2 | 100 | 200 |
| 4 | 50 | 200 |
| 8 | 25 | 200 |
| 10 | 20 | 200 |
| 20 | 10 | 200 |

1. Working at the same rate, how many construction days should it take a crew of 40 people to build the house?
2. Express the number of construction days as a function of the crew size. Define the variables. What type of relationship is formed in the situation?
3. Explain how the crew size affects the number of construction days.
4. About how many construction days would it take a crew of 32 to complete a house?
5. If a crew can complete a house in 12.5 days, how many people are in the crew?
6. What are a reasonable domain and range of the function?
7. Suppose there are two managers that do not contribute to the work of building the house, yet are counted as part of the crew. Express the number of construction days as a function of the crew size. What are the asymptotes of this function? Graph the function.

# READY TO GO ON?



## Quiz for Lessons 12-1 Through 12-3

### 12-1 Inverse Variation

**Tell whether each relationship represents an inverse variation. Explain.**

1.

| $x$ | −5 | −4 | −3 |
|---|---|---|---|
| $y$ | 10 | −8 | 6 |

2.

| $x$ | 18 | 9 | 6 |
|---|---|---|---|
| $y$ | 2 | 4 | 6 |

3. $y = \frac{3}{x}$

4. $y + x = \frac{3}{4}$

5. $xy = -2$

6. $y = \frac{x}{5}$

7. Write and graph the inverse variation in which $y = 3$ when $x = 2$.

8. Write and graph the inverse variation in which $y = 4$ when $x = -1$.

9. The number of calculators Mrs. Hopkins can buy for the classroom varies inversely as the cost of each calculator. She can buy 24 calculators that cost \$60 each. How many calculators can she buy if they cost \$80 each?

### 12-2 Rational Functions

**Identify the excluded value and the vertical and horizontal asymptotes for each rational function. Then graph each function.**

10. $y = \frac{12}{x}$

11. $y = \frac{6}{x + 2}$

12. $y = \frac{4}{x - 1}$

13. $y = \frac{2}{x + 1} - 3$

14. Jeff builds model train layouts. He has \$75 to spend on packages of miniature landscape items. He receives 6 free packages with each order. The number of packages $y$ that Jeff can buy is given by $y = \frac{75}{x} + 6$, where $x$ represents the cost of each package in dollars. Describe the reasonable domain and range values and graph the function.

### 12-3 Simplifying Rational Expressions

**Find any excluded values of each rational expression.**

15. $\frac{15}{n}$

16. $\frac{p}{p - 8}$

17. $\frac{x + 2}{x^2 + 6x + 8}$

18. $\frac{t - 1}{t^2 + t}$

**Simplify each rational expression, if possible. Identify any excluded values.**

19. $\frac{3x^2}{6x^3}$

20. $\frac{2n}{n^2 - 3n}$

21. $\frac{s + 1}{s^2 - 4s - 5}$

22. $\frac{12 - 3x}{x^2 - 8x + 16}$

23. Suppose a cone and a cylinder have the same radius and that the slant height $l$ of the cone is the same as the height $h$ of the cylinder. Find the ratio of the cone's surface area to the cylinder's surface area.

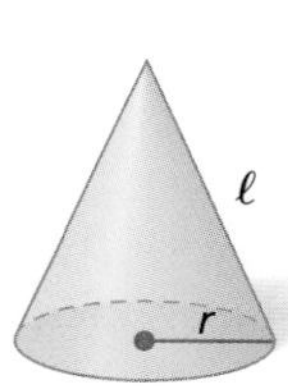


$S = \pi r\ell + \pi r^2$

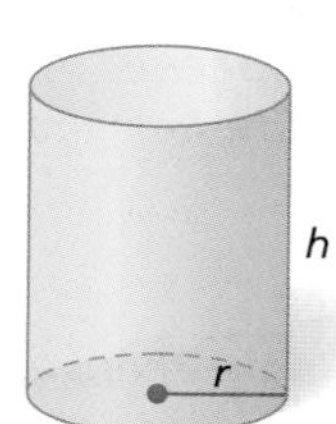


$S = 2\pi rh + 2\pi r^2$

# 12-4 Multiplying and Dividing Rational Expressions

**MA.A.1.1** Execute ... operations with algebraic expressions... *Also* **MA.A.1.3**

***Objective***
Multiply and divide rational expressions.

**Why learn this?**
You can multiply rational expressions to determine the probabilities of winning prizes at carnivals. (See Example 5.)

The rules for multiplying rational expressions are the same as the rules for multiplying fractions. You multiply the numerators, and you multiply the denominators.

**Multiplying Rational Expressions**

If $a$, $b$, $c$, and $d$ are nonzero polynomials, then $\frac{a}{b} \cdot \frac{c}{d} = \frac{ac}{bd}$.

## EXAMPLE 1 Multiplying Rational Expressions

**Multiply. Simplify your answer.**

**A** $\frac{a+3}{2} \cdot \frac{6}{3a+9}$

$\frac{6(a+3)}{2(3a+9)}$ *Multiply the numerators and denominators.*

$\frac{6(a+3)}{2 \cdot 3(a+3)}$ *Factor.*

$\frac{\cancel{6}^{1}\cancel{(a+3)}^{1}}{\cancel{6}^{1}\cancel{(a+3)}^{1}}$ *Divide out the common factors.*

$1$ *Simplify.*

**Remember!**
See the Quotient of Powers Property in Lesson 7-4.
$\frac{a^m}{a^n} = a^{m-n}$

**B** $\frac{12b^3c^2}{5ac} \cdot \frac{15a^2b}{3b^2c}$

$\frac{(12)(15)a^2(b^3 \cdot b)c^2}{(5)(3)ab^2(c \cdot c)}$ *Multiply the numerators and the denominators. Arrange the expression so like variables are together.*

$\frac{180a^2b^4c^2}{15ab^2c^2}$ *Simplify.*

$12a^1b^2c^0$ *Divide out common factors. Use properties of exponents.*

$12ab^2$ *Simplify. Remember that $c^0 = 1$.*

**C** $\frac{5x^2}{2y^3} \cdot \frac{3x}{2y^2}$

$\frac{15x^3}{4y^5}$ *Multiply. There are no common factors, so the product cannot be simplified.*

Multiply. Simplify your answer.

**1a.** $\frac{(c-4)}{5} \cdot \frac{45}{(-4c+16)}$  **1b.** $\frac{5y^5z}{3xy^2z} \cdot \frac{2x^4y^2}{4xy}$

## EXAMPLE 2 Multiplying a Rational Expression by a Polynomial

**Remember!**

Just as you can write an integer as a fraction, you can write any expression as a rational expression by writing it with a denominator of 1.

**Multiply $(x^2+8x+15)\frac{4}{2x+6}$. Simplify your answer.**

$\frac{x^2+8x+15}{1} \cdot \frac{4}{2x+6}$  *Write the polynomial over 1.*

$\frac{(x+3)(x+5)}{1} \cdot \frac{4}{2(x+3)}$  *Factor the numerator and denominator.*

$\frac{\cancel{(x+3)}^1 (x+5)\cancel{4}^2}{\cancel{2}^1\cancel{(x+3)}^1}$  *Divide out common factors.*

$2x+10$  *Multiply remaining factors.*

**2.** Multiply $\frac{m-5}{m^2-4m-12} \cdot 3m+6$. Simplify your answer.

There are two methods for simplifying rational expressions. You can **simplify first** by dividing out common factors and **then multiply** the remaining factors. You can also **multiply first** and **then simplify**. Using either method will result in the same answer.

## EXAMPLE 3 Multiplying Rational Expressions Containing Polynomials

**Multiply $\frac{4d^3+4d}{16f} \cdot \frac{2f}{7d^2f+7f}$. Simplify your answer.**

**Method 1** Simplify first.

$\frac{4d^3+4d}{16f} \cdot \frac{2f}{7d^2f+7f}$

$\frac{4d(d^2+1)}{16f} \cdot \frac{2f}{7f(d^2+1)}$  *Factor.*

$\frac{\cancel{4}^1 d\cancel{(d^2+1)}^1}{\cancel{16}^2 \cancel{f}^1} \cdot \frac{\cancel{2}^1\cancel{f}^1}{7f\cancel{(d^2+1)}^1}$  *Divide out common factors.*

Then multiply.

$\frac{d}{14f}$  *Simplify.*

**Method 2** Multiply first.

$\frac{4d^3+4d}{16f} \cdot \frac{2f}{7d^2f+7f}$

$\frac{(4d^3+4d)2f}{16f(7d^2f+7f)}$  *Multiply*

$\frac{8d^3f+8df}{112d^2f^2+112f^2}$  *Distribute.*

Then simplify.

$\frac{8df(d^2+1)}{112f^2(d^2+1)}$  *Factor.*

$\frac{\cancel{8}^1 d\cancel{f}^1\cancel{(d^2+1)}^1}{\cancel{112}^{14} \cancel{f^2}^1\cancel{(d^2+1)}^1}$  *Divide out common factors.*

$\frac{d}{14f}$  *Simplify.*

Multiply. Simplify your answer.

**3a.** $\frac{n-5}{n^2+4n} \cdot \frac{n^2+8n+16}{n^2-3n-10}$  **3b.** $\frac{p+4}{p^2+2p} \cdot \frac{p^2-3p-10}{p^2+16}$

The rules for dividing rational expressions are the same as the rules for dividing fractions. To divide by a rational expression, multiply by its reciprocal.

**Dividing Rational Expressions**

If $a$, $b$, $c$, and $d$ are nonzero polynomials, then $\frac{a}{b} \div \frac{c}{d} = \frac{a}{b} \cdot \frac{d}{c} = \frac{ad}{bc}$.

## EXAMPLE 4 Dividing by Rational Expressions and Polynomials

**Divide. Simplify your answer.**

**A** $\frac{1}{x} \div \frac{x-2}{2x}$

$\frac{1}{x} \cdot \frac{2x}{x-2}$ — *Write as multiplication by the reciprocal.*

$\frac{1(2x)}{x(x-2)}$ — *Multiply the numerators and the denominators.*

$\frac{2\cancel{x}^1}{\cancel{x}^1(x-2)}$ — *Divide out common factors.*

$\frac{2}{x-2}$ — *Simplify.*

**B** $\frac{x^2-2x}{x} \div \frac{2-x}{x^2+2x+1}$

$\frac{x^2-2x}{x} \cdot \frac{x^2+2x+1}{2-x}$ — *Write as multiplication by the reciprocal.*

$\frac{x(x-2)}{x} \cdot \frac{(x+1)(x+1)}{2-x}$ — *Factor.*

$\frac{x(x-2)}{x} \cdot \frac{(x+1)(x+1)}{-1(x-2)}$ — *Rewrite one opposite binomial.*

$\frac{\cancel{x}^1\cancel{(x-2)}^1}{\cancel{x}^1} \cdot \frac{(x+1)(x+1)}{-1\cancel{(x-2)}^1}$ — *Divide out common factors.*

$-(x+1)^2$ — *Multiply.*

**C** $\frac{3a^2b}{b} \div (3a^2+6a)$

$\frac{3a^2b}{b} \div \frac{3a^2+6a}{1}$ — *Write the binomial over 1.*

$\frac{3a^2b}{b} \cdot \frac{1}{3a^2+6a}$ — *Write as multiplication by the reciprocal.*

$\frac{3a^2b}{b(3a^2+6a)}$ — *Multiply the numerators and the denominators.*

$\frac{\cancel{3}^1 a^{\cancel{2}^1}\cancel{b}^1}{\cancel{b}^1[\cancel{3}^1\cancel{a}^1(a+2)]}$ — *Factor. Divide out common factors.*

$\frac{a}{(a+2)}$ — *Simplify.*

**Divide. Simplify your answer.**

**4a.** $\frac{3}{x^2} \div \frac{x^3}{(x-5)}$

**4b.** $\frac{18vw^2}{6v} \div \frac{3v^2x^4}{2w^4x}$

**4c.** $\frac{x^2-x}{x+2} \div (x^2+2x-3)$

## EXAMPLE 5 *Probability Application*

**Marty is playing a carnival game. He needs to pick two items out of a bag without looking. The bag has red and blue items. There are three more red items than blue items.**

**a. Write and simplify an expression that represents the probability that Marty will pick two blue items without replacing the first item.**

Let $x =$ the number of blue items.

| **Blue** + | **Red** = | **Total** |
|---|---|---|
| $x$ + | $x + 3$ = | $2x + 3$ |

*Write expressions for the number of each color item and for the total number of items.*

The probability of picking a blue item and then another blue item is the product of the probabilities of the individual events.

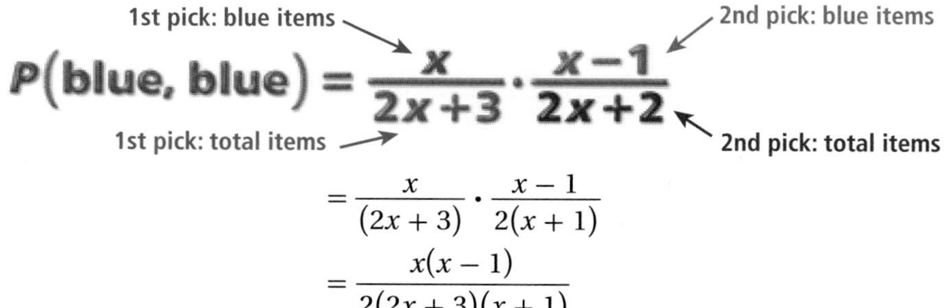


$$= \frac{x}{(2x+3)} \cdot \frac{x-1}{2(x+1)}$$

$$= \frac{x(x-1)}{2(2x+3)(x+1)}$$

**b. What is the probability that Marty picks two blue items if there are 10 blue items in the bag before his first pick?**

Use the probability of picking two blue items. Since $x$ represents the number of blue items, substitute 10 for $x$.

$$P(\text{blue, blue}) = \frac{10(10-1)}{2(2 \cdot 10 + 3)(10+1)}$$ *Substitute.*

$$= \frac{10(9)}{2(23)(11)} = \frac{90}{506} \approx 0.18$$ *Use the order of operations to simplify.*

The probability of picking two blue items if there are 10 blue items in the bag before the first pick is approximately 0.18.

**5. What if...?** There are 50 blue items in the bag before Marty's first pick. What is the probability that Marty picks two blue items?

**Remember!**

For a review of probability topics, see Chapter 10.

## THINK AND DISCUSS

**1.** Explain how to divide by a polynomial.

Know it! Note

**2. GET ORGANIZED** Copy and complete the graphic organizer. In each box, describe how to perform the operation with rational expressions.

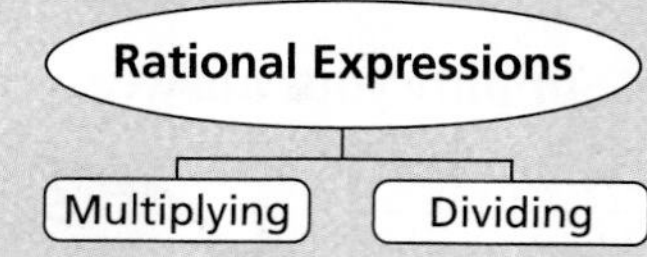

## 12-4 Exercises

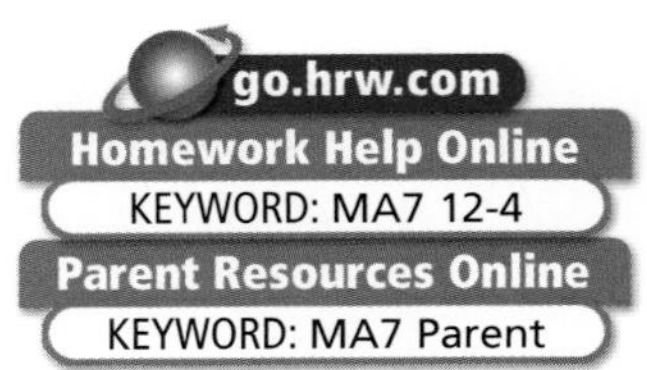


### GUIDED PRACTICE

SEE EXAMPLE 1 p. 878

**Multiply. Simplify your answer.**

1. $\frac{4hj^2}{10j^3} \cdot \frac{3h^3k}{h^3k^3}$
2. $\frac{4y}{x^5} \cdot \frac{2yz^2}{9x^2}$
3. $\frac{x-2}{x+3} \cdot \frac{4x+12}{6}$
4. $\frac{ab}{c} \cdot \frac{2a^2}{3c}$
5. $\frac{7c^4d}{10c} \cdot \frac{5a}{21c^3d}$
6. $\frac{12p^2q}{5p} \cdot \frac{15p^4q^3}{12q}$

SEE EXAMPLE 2 p. 879

7. $\frac{12}{4y+8}(y^2-4)$
8. $\frac{x+2}{6x^2}(5x+10)$
9. $\frac{3m}{6m+18}(m^2-7m-30)$
10. $\frac{4p}{8p+16}(p^2-5p-14)$
11. $\frac{a^2}{a}(a^2+10a+25)$
12. $\frac{-c}{4c+4}(c^2-c-2)$

SEE EXAMPLE 3 p. 879

13. $\frac{a^2+6ab}{b} \cdot \frac{5+3a}{3a^2b+5ab}$
14. $\frac{x^2+5x+4}{x-4} \cdot \frac{x^2-2x-8}{x^2+6x+8}$
15. $\frac{j-1}{j^2-4j+3} \cdot \frac{j^2-5j+6}{2j-4}$
16. $\frac{p^3+4pq}{p} \cdot \frac{6q^3-8}{2q}$
17. $\frac{r^2+15r+14}{r^2-16} \cdot \frac{2r+8}{r+1}$
18. $\frac{y-8}{y^2-1} \cdot \frac{y+2}{y^2-49}$

SEE EXAMPLE 4 p. 880

**Divide. Simplify your answer.**

19. $\frac{3a^4b}{2a^2c^3} \div \frac{12a^2c}{8c^4}$
20. $\frac{2m^3+2m}{m^2-2m} \div \frac{4m^2+4}{m-1}$
21. $\frac{x^2+4x-5}{3x-3} \div (x^2-25)$

SEE EXAMPLE 5 p. 881

22. **Probability** While playing a game, Rachel pulls two tiles out of a bag without looking and without replacing the first tile. The bag has two colors of tiles—black and white. There are 10 more white tiles than black tiles.
    a. Write and simplify an expression that represents the probability that Rachel will pick a black tile, then a white tile.
    b. What is the probability that Rachel pulls a black tile and then a white tile if there are 5 black tiles in the bag before her first pick?

### PRACTICE AND PROBLEM SOLVING

**Independent Practice**

| For Exercises | See Example |
|---|---|
| 23–25 | 1 |
| 26–28 | 2 |
| 29–31 | 3 |
| 32–34 | 4 |
| 35 | 5 |

**Extra Practice**
Skills Practice p. S27
Application Practice p. S39

**Multiply. Simplify your answer.**

23. $\frac{p^6q^2}{7r^3} \cdot \frac{-3p^2}{r}$
24. $\frac{3r^2t}{6st^3} \cdot \frac{2r^2s^3t^2}{8r^4s^2}$
25. $\frac{10}{y+5} \cdot \frac{y+2}{3}$
26. $\frac{3}{2a+6}(a^2+4a+3)$
27. $\frac{4m^2-8m}{m^2+6m-16}(m^2+7m-8)$
28. $\frac{x}{2x^2-12x+18}(2x^2-4x-6)$
29. $\frac{6n^2+18n}{n^2+9n+8} \cdot \frac{n^2-1}{2n+6}$
30. $\frac{3a^2b}{5a^3+10a^2b} \cdot \frac{2a+4b}{6a^3b+6a^2b^2}$
31. $\frac{t^2-100}{5t+50} \cdot \frac{5}{t-10}$

**Divide. Simplify your answer.**

32. $\frac{6j^2k^5}{5j} \div \frac{4j^3k^3}{3j}$
33. $\frac{a-4}{a^2} \div (8a-2a^2)$
34. $\frac{x^2-9}{x^2+6x+9} \div \frac{4x^2-12x}{16x}$

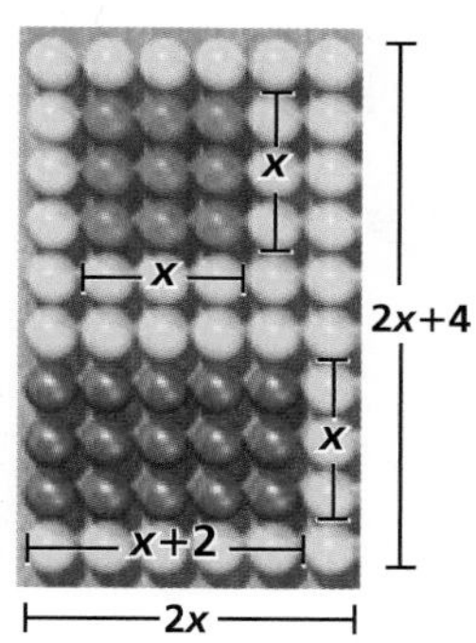


35. **Entertainment** A carnival game board is covered completely in small balloons. You throw darts at the board and try to pop the balloons.
    a. Write and simplify an expression describing the probability that the next two balloons popped are red and then blue. (*Hint:* Write the probabilities as ratios of the areas of rectangles.)
    b. What is the probability that the next two balloons popped are red and then blue if $x = 3$?

36. **ERROR ANALYSIS** Which is incorrect? Explain the error.

**A**

$$\frac{4a^2 - b^2}{a^2} \cdot \frac{a}{2a - b}$$

$$\frac{{}^{2}\cancel{4}\cancel{a^2} - b^2}{\cancel{a^2}} \cdot \frac{\cancel{a}}{2\cancel{a} - b} = \frac{2 - b^2}{b}$$

**B**

$$\frac{4a^2 - b^2}{a^2} \cdot \frac{a}{2a - b}$$

$$\frac{(\cancel{2a - b})(2a + b)}{{}_{a}\cancel{a^2}} \cdot \frac{\cancel{a}}{\cancel{2a - b}} = \frac{2a + b}{a}$$

37. **Critical Thinking** Which of the following expressions is NOT equivalent to the other three? Explain why.
    a. $\dfrac{4x^2}{x^2 - 3x} \cdot \dfrac{2x - 6}{8y^2}$
    b. $\dfrac{6xy^2}{x^2} \div \dfrac{3y^4}{2x^2}$
    c. $\dfrac{10x^4y}{5xy^2} \div 2x^2y$
    d. $\dfrac{4x}{xy^2 + 2y^2} \cdot \dfrac{x^2 - 4}{4x - 8}$

**Multiply or divide. Simplify your answer.**

38. $\dfrac{5p^3}{p^2q} \cdot \dfrac{2q^3}{p^2}$

39. $\dfrac{6m^2 - 18m}{12m^3 + 12m^2} \div \dfrac{m^2 - 9}{m^2 + 4m + 3}$

40. $\dfrac{2x^2}{4x - 8} \cdot \dfrac{x^2 - 5x + 6}{x^5}$

41. $\dfrac{x^2 - 9}{4x} \div \left(4x^2 - 36\right)$

42. $\dfrac{33m - 3m^2}{-2m - 4} \div \dfrac{6m - 66}{m^2 - 4m}$

43. $\dfrac{12w^4x^7}{3w^3} \cdot \dfrac{w^{-1}x^{-7}}{4}$

44. **Write About It** Explain how to divide $\frac{1}{m} \div \frac{3}{4m}$.

45. This problem will prepare you for the Multi-Step Test Prep on page 906.

The size of an image projected on a screen depends on how far the object is from the lens, the magnification of the lens, and the distance between the image and the lens. Magnification of a lens is $M = \frac{I}{O} = \frac{y}{x}$ where $I$ is the height of the image, $O$ is the height of the object, $x$ is the distance of the object from the lens, and $y$ is the distance of the image from the lens.

a. If an object 16 cm high is placed 15 cm from the lens, it forms an image 60 cm from the lens. What is the height of the image?
b. Marie moves the same object to a distance of 20 cm from the lens. If the image is the same size as part **a**, what is the distance between the image and the lens?
c. What is the magnification of the lens?

46. Which expression is equivalent to $\frac{t+4}{9} \cdot \frac{t+4}{3}$?

MA.A.1.1, MA.A.1.3

Ⓐ $\frac{(t+4)^2}{27}$ Ⓑ $\frac{t^2+16}{27}$ Ⓒ $\frac{1}{3}$ Ⓓ $\frac{1}{27}$

47. Identify the product $-\frac{20b^2}{a^2} \cdot \frac{3ab}{15b}$.

Ⓕ $-\frac{a}{4b^2}$ Ⓖ $-4b^2$ Ⓗ $-\frac{4b^2}{a}$ Ⓙ $-\frac{b^2}{4a}$

48. Which of the following is equivalent to $\frac{2x}{x+5}$?

Ⓐ $\frac{x-2}{8x} \cdot \frac{4}{x^2+3x-10}$ Ⓒ $\frac{x-2}{4} \div \frac{x^2+3x-10}{8x}$

Ⓑ $\frac{x^2-3x-10}{8x} \cdot \frac{4}{x-2}$ Ⓓ $\frac{x^2-3x-10}{4} \div \frac{x-2}{8x}$

49. **Short Response** Simplify $\frac{x^2-10x+24}{3x^2-12x} \div (x^2-3x-18)$. Show your work.

## CHALLENGE AND EXTEND

**Simplify.**

50. $\frac{x-3}{3x-6} \cdot \frac{3x+12}{x+1} \cdot \frac{2x-4}{x^2+x-12}$

51. $\frac{x^2-1}{x+2} \div \frac{3x+3}{x+2} \div (x-1)$

**A *complex fraction* is a fraction that contains one or more fractions in the numerator or the denominator. Simplify each complex fraction.**

(*Hint:* Use the rule $\frac{\frac{a}{b}}{\frac{c}{d}} = \frac{a}{b} \div \frac{c}{d}$.)

52. $\frac{\frac{c+5}{c^2-4}}{\frac{c^2+6c+5}{c+2}}$

53. $\frac{\frac{x^2y}{xz^3}}{\frac{x^2y}{x^2z}}$

54. $\frac{\frac{x^2}{2} \cdot \frac{x}{3}}{\frac{x}{6}}$

55. $\frac{\frac{a+1}{a^2+6a+5}}{\frac{2a+2}{a+5}}$

## SPIRAL REVIEW

56. Jillian's mother told her to preheat the oven to at least 325°F. When Jillian went into the kitchen, the oven was already set to 200°F. Write and solve an inequality to determine how many more degrees Jillian should increase the temperature. *(Lesson 3-2)*

57. Pierce has \$30 to spend on a night out. He already spent \$12 on dinner and \$9 on a movie ticket. He will spend some money *m* on movie-theatre snacks. Write and solve an inequality that will show all the values of *m* that Pierce can spend on snacks. *(Lesson 3-2)*

**Simplify each radical. Then add or subtract, if possible.** *(Lesson 11-7)*

58. $\sqrt{18} - \sqrt{8}$

59. $\sqrt{3t} + 5\sqrt{3t} + \sqrt{12t}$

60. $\sqrt{20} - \sqrt{80} + \sqrt{3}$

**Identify the excluded value and asymptotes for each rational function.** *(Lesson 12-2)*

61. $y = \frac{4}{x-3}$

62. $y = \frac{1}{2x+4}$

63. $y = -\frac{1}{x} + 3$

64. $y = -\frac{2}{x+5}$

65. $y = \frac{12}{4x}$

66. $y = -\frac{1}{3x-2}$

# 12-5 Adding and Subtracting Rational Expressions

**MA.A.1.1** Execute ... operations with algebraic expressions...
*Also* **MA.A.1.3, MA.N.1**

***Objectives***

Add and subtract rational expressions with like denominators.

Add and subtract rational expressions with unlike denominators.

**Who uses this?**

Kayakers can use rational expressions to figure out travel time for different river trips. (See Example 5.)

The rules for adding rational expressions are the same as the rules for adding fractions. If the denominators are the same, you add the numerators and keep the common denominator.

$$\frac{3}{8} + \frac{2}{8} = \frac{3+2}{8} = \frac{5}{8}$$

**Know it! Note**

**Adding Rational Expressions with Like Denominators**

If $a$, $b$, and $c$ represent polynomials and $c \neq 0$, then $\frac{a}{c} + \frac{b}{c} = \frac{a+b}{c}$.

## EXAMPLE 1 Adding Rational Expressions with Like Denominators

**Add. Simplify your answer.**

**A** $\frac{3b}{b^2} + \frac{5b}{b^2}$

$\frac{3b + 5b}{b^2} = \frac{8\cancel{b}^1}{b^{\cancel{2}1}}$ *Combine like terms in the numerator. Divide out common factors.*

$= \frac{8}{b}$ *Simplify.*

**B** $\frac{x^2 - 8x}{x - 4} + \frac{2x + 8}{x - 4}$

$\frac{x^2 - 8x + 2x + 8}{x - 4} = \frac{x^2 - 6x + 8}{x - 4}$ *Combine like terms in the numerator.*

$= \frac{(x-2)\cancel{(x-4)}^1}{\cancel{x-4}^1}$ *Factor. Divide out common factors.*

$= (x - 2)$ *Simplify.*

**C** $\frac{2m + 4}{m^2 - 9} + \frac{2}{m^2 - 9}$

$\frac{2m + 4 + 2}{m^2 - 9} = \frac{2m + 6}{m^2 - 9}$ *Combine like terms in the numerator.*

$= \frac{2\cancel{(m+3)}^1}{(m-3)\cancel{(m+3)}^1}$ *Factor. Divide out common factors.*

$= \frac{2}{m - 3}$ *Simplify.*

**Add. Simplify your answer.**

**1a.** $\frac{n}{2n} + \frac{3n}{2n}$ **1b.** $\frac{3y^2}{y+1} + \frac{3y}{y+1}$

To subtract rational expressions with like denominators, remember to add the opposite of *each* term in the second numerator.

## EXAMPLE 2 Subtracting Rational Expressions with Like Denominators

**Subtract. Simplify your answer.**

$$\frac{3m-6}{m^2+m-6} - \frac{-m+2}{m^2+m-6}$$

$$\frac{3m-6-(-m+2)}{m^2+m-6} = \frac{3m-6+m-2}{m^2+m-6}$$ *Subtract numerators.*

$$= \frac{4m-8}{m^2+m-6}$$ *Combine like terms.*

$$= \frac{4\cancel{(m-2)}^1}{(m+3)\cancel{(m-2)}^1}$$ *Factor. Divide out common factors.*

$$= \frac{4}{m+3}$$ *Simplify.*

**Caution!**

Make sure you add the opposite of all the terms in the numerator of the second expression when subtracting rational expressions.

**Subtract. Simplify your answer.**

**2a.** $\frac{5a+2}{a^2-4} - \frac{2a-4}{a^2-4}$ **2b.** $\frac{2b+14}{b^2+3b-4} - \frac{-2b+2}{b^2+3b-4}$

As with fractions, rational expressions must have a common denominator before they can be added or subtracted. If they do not have a common denominator, you can use the least common multiple, or LCM, of the denominators to find one.

To find the LCM, write the prime factorization of both expressions. Use each factor the greatest number of times it appears in either expression.

$$6x^2 = 2 \cdot 3 \cdot x \cdot x$$
$$8x = 2 \cdot 2 \cdot 2 \cdot x$$
$$\text{LCM} = 2 \cdot 2 \cdot 2 \cdot 3 \cdot x \cdot x = 24x^2$$

$$5x + 15 = 5(x+3)$$
$$x^2 - 9 = (x+3)(x-3)$$
$$\text{LCM} = 5(x+3)(x-3)$$

## EXAMPLE 3 Identifying the Least Common Multiple

**Find the LCM of the given expressions.**

**A** $24a^3, 4a$

$$24a^3 = 2 \cdot 2 \cdot 2 \cdot 3 \cdot a \cdot a \cdot a$$
$$4a = 2 \cdot 2 \cdot a$$
$$\text{LCM} = 2 \cdot 2 \cdot 2 \cdot 3 \cdot a \cdot a \cdot a = 24a^3$$

*Write the prime factorization of each expression. Use every factor of both expressions the greatest number of times it appears in either expression.*

**B** $2d^2 + 10d + 12, d^2 + 7d + 12$

$$2d^2 + 10d + 12 = 2(d^2 + 5d + 6)$$ *Factor each expression.*

$$= 2(d+3)(d+2)$$

$$d^2 + 7d + 12 = (d+3)(d+4)$$

$$\text{LCM} = 2(d+3)(d+2)(d+4)$$

*Use every factor of both expressions the greatest number of times it appears in either expression.*

**Find the LCM of the given expressions.**

**3a.** $5f^2h, 15fh^2$ **3b.** $x^2 - 4x - 12, (x-6)(x+5)$

The LCM of the denominators of fractions or rational expressions is also called the least common denominator, or LCD. You use the same method to add or subtract rational expressions.

| Adding or Subtracting Rational Expressions | |
|---|---|
| **Step 1** | Identify the LCD. |
| **Step 2** | Multiply each expression by an appropriate form of 1 so that each term has the LCD as its denominator. |
| **Step 3** | Write each expression using the LCD. |
| **Step 4** | Add or subtract the numerators, combining like terms as needed. |
| **Step 5** | Factor. |
| **Step 6** | Simplify as needed. |

## EXAMPLE 4 Adding and Subtracting with Unlike Denominators

**Add or subtract. Simplify your answer.**

**A** $\frac{3x}{6x^2} + \frac{2x}{4x}$

**Step 1** $6x^2 = 2 \cdot 3 \cdot x \cdot x$
$4x = 2 \cdot 2 \cdot x$
$\text{LCD} = 2 \cdot 2 \cdot 3 \cdot x \cdot x = 12x^2$ — *Identify the LCD.*

**Step 2** $\frac{3x}{6x^2}\left(\frac{2}{2}\right) + \frac{2x}{4x}\left(\frac{3x}{3x}\right)$ — *Multiply each expression by an appropriate form of 1.*

**Step 3** $\frac{6x}{12x^2} + \frac{6x^2}{12x^2}$ — *Write each expression using the LCD.*

**Step 4** $\frac{6x + 6x^2}{12x^2}$ — *Add the numerators.*

**Step 5** $\frac{\cancel{6}^1 \cancel{x}^1(1 + x)}{\cancel{6}^1 \cdot 2\cancel{x^2}^1}$ — *Factor and divide out common factors.*

**Step 6** $\frac{1 + x}{2x}$ — *Simplify.*

**B** $\frac{1}{m - 3} - \frac{5}{3 - m}$

**Step 1** The denominators are opposite binomials.
The LCD can be either $m - 3$ or $3 - m$. — *Identify the LCD.*

**Step 2** $\frac{1}{m - 3} - \frac{5}{3 - m}\left(\frac{-1}{-1}\right)$ — *Multiply the second expression by $\frac{-1}{-1}$ to get an LCD of $m - 3$.*

**Step 3** $\frac{1}{m - 3} - \frac{-5}{m - 3}$ — *Write each expression using the LCD.*

**Step 4** $\frac{1 - (-5)}{m - 3}$ — *Subtract the numerators.*

**Steps 5, 6** $\frac{6}{m - 3}$ — *No factoring is needed, so just simplify.*

**Remember!**

Expressions like $m - 3$ and $3 - m$ are opposite binominals.
$3 - m = -1(m - 3)$
and
$m - 3 = -1(3 - m)$

**Add or subtract. Simplify your answer.**

**4a.** $\frac{4}{3d} - \frac{2d}{2d^3}$ **4b.** $\frac{a^2 + 4a}{a^2 + 2a - 8} + \frac{8}{a - 2}$

## EXAMPLE 5 Recreation Application

**Katy wants to find out how long it will take to kayak 1 mile up a river and return to her starting point. Katy's average paddling rate is 4 times the speed of the river's current.**

**a. Write and simplify an expression for the time it will take Katy to kayak the round-trip in terms of the rate of the river's current.**

**Step 1** Write expressions for the distances and rates in the problem.

The distance in both directions is 1 mile.

Let $x$ represent the rate of the current, and let $4x$ represent Katy's paddling rate.

Katy's rate against the current is $4x - x$, or $3x$.

Katy's rate with the current is $4x + x$, or $5x$.

**Step 2** Use a table to write expressions for time.

| Direction | Distance (mi) | Rate (mi/h) | Time (h) $= \frac{\text{distance}}{\text{rate}}$ |
|---|---|---|---|
| Upstream (against current) | 1 | $3x$ | $\frac{1}{3x}$ |
| Downstream (with current) | 1 | $5x$ | $\frac{1}{5x}$ |

### Helpful Hint

To write expressions for time in terms of distance and rate, solve $d = rt$ for $t$.

$$t = \frac{d}{r}$$

**Step 3** Write and simplify an expression for the total time.

total time = time upstream + time downstream

$$\text{total time} = \frac{1}{3x} + \frac{1}{5x}$$ *Substitute known values.*

$$= \frac{1}{3x}\left(\frac{5}{5}\right) + \frac{1}{5x}\left(\frac{3}{3}\right)$$ *Multiply each fraction by an appropriate form of 1.*

$$= \frac{5}{15x} + \frac{3}{15x}$$ *Write each expression using the LCD, 15x.*

$$= \frac{8}{15x}$$ *Add the numerators.*

**b. If the rate of the river is 2 miles per hour, how long will it take Katy to kayak round trip?**

$$\frac{8}{15(2)} = \frac{4}{15}$$ *Substitute 2 for x. Simplify.*

It will take Katy $\frac{4}{15}$ of an hour, or 16 minutes, to kayak the round-trip.

5. **What if?...** Katy's average paddling rate increases to 5 times the speed of the current. Now how long will it take Katy to kayak the round trip?

## THINK AND DISCUSS

1. Explain how to find the least common denominator of rational expressions.

Know it! Note

2. **GET ORGANIZED** Copy and complete the graphic organizer. In each box, compare and contrast operations with fractions and rational expressions.

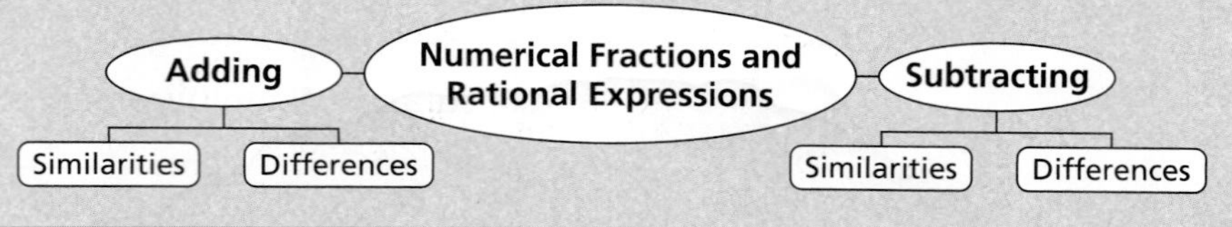

# 12-5 Exercises

MA.A.1.1, MA.A.1.3, MA.N.1

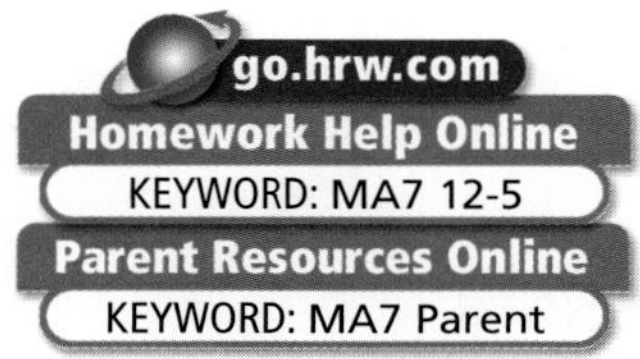


## GUIDED PRACTICE

SEE EXAMPLE 1 p. 885

**Add. Simplify your answer.**

1. $\dfrac{y}{3y^2} + \dfrac{5y}{3y^2}$
2. $\dfrac{4m+30}{m+5} + \dfrac{m^2+8m+5}{m+5}$
3. $\dfrac{x}{x^2-16} + \dfrac{4}{x^2-16}$

SEE EXAMPLE 2 p. 886

**Subtract. Simplify your answer.**

4. $\dfrac{7}{2x^3} - \dfrac{3}{2x^3}$
5. $\dfrac{7a-2}{a^2+3a+2} - \dfrac{5a-6}{a^2+3a+2}$
6. $\dfrac{3x^2+1}{2x+2} - \dfrac{2x^2-2x}{2x+2}$

SEE EXAMPLE 3 p. 886

**Find the LCM of the given expressions.**

7. $3xy^2, 6x^3yz$
8. $x^2+9x+20, (x+5)(x-4)$
9. $y^2-16, (y+9)(y-4)$

SEE EXAMPLE 4 p. 887

**Add or subtract. Simplify your answer.**

10. $\dfrac{3}{c} - \dfrac{4}{3c}$
11. $\dfrac{x^2+x}{x^2+3x+2} + \dfrac{3}{x+2}$
12. $\dfrac{2x}{x-5} + \dfrac{x}{5-x}$

SEE EXAMPLE 5 p. 888

13. **Travel** The Escobar family went on a car trip. They drove 100 miles on country roads and 240 miles on the highway. They drove 50% faster on the highway than on the country roads. Let $r$ represent their rate on country roads in miles per hour.
    a. Write and simplify an expression that represents the number of hours it took the Escobar family to complete their trip in terms of $r$. (*Hint:* 50% faster means 150% of the original rate.)
    b. Find their total travel time if they drove the posted speed limit.

## PRACTICE AND PROBLEM SOLVING

| Independent Practice | |
|---|---|
| For Exercises | See Example |
| 14–16 | 1 |
| 17–19 | 2 |
| 20–25 | 3 |
| 26–31 | 4 |
| 32 | 5 |

**Extra Practice**
Skills Practice p. S27
Application Practice p. S39

**Add. Simplify your answer.**

14. $\dfrac{4y}{y^3} + \dfrac{4y}{y^3}$
15. $\dfrac{a^2-3}{a+3} + \dfrac{2a}{a+3}$
16. $\dfrac{4x-13}{x^2-5x+6} + \dfrac{1}{x^2-5x+6}$

**Subtract. Simplify your answer.**

17. $\dfrac{m^2}{m-6} - \dfrac{6m}{m-6}$
18. $\dfrac{c+3}{4c^2-25} - \dfrac{-c+8}{4c^2-25}$
19. $\dfrac{-2a^2-9a}{a-2} - \dfrac{-5a^2-4a+2}{a-2}$

**Find the LCM of the given expressions.**

20. $4jk^4m, 25jm$
21. $12a^2+4a, 27a+9$
22. $p^2-3p, pqr^2$
23. $5xy^2z, 10y^3$
24. $5x^2, 7x-14$
25. $y^2+7y+10, y^2+9y+20$

**Add or subtract. Simplify your answer.**

26. $\dfrac{2x}{5x} + \dfrac{10x}{3x^2}$
27. $\dfrac{y^2-y}{y^2-4y+3} - \dfrac{2y-2}{3y-9}$
28. $\dfrac{-3t}{t-4} - \dfrac{2t+4}{4-t}$
29. $\dfrac{z}{3z^2} + \dfrac{4}{7z}$
30. $\dfrac{5x}{2x-6} + \dfrac{x+2}{3-x}$
31. $\dfrac{3m}{4m-8} - \dfrac{m^2}{m^2-4m+4}$

The first transcontinental railroad was completed in Utah on May 10, 1869. The occasion was commemorated with a golden spike that connected the eastern and western tracks.

32. **Fitness** Ira walks one mile from his house to the recreation center. After playing basketball, he walks home at only 85% of his normal walking speed. Let $w$ be Ira's normal rate of walking.
   a. Write an expression to represent Ira's round-trip walking time.
   b. If Ira's normal rate of walking is 3 miles per hour, how long did it take for him to complete his walking?

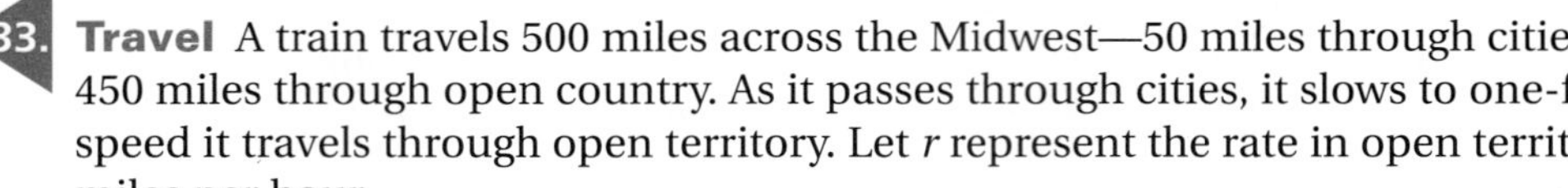

33. **Travel** A train travels 500 miles across the Midwest—50 miles through cities and 450 miles through open country. As it passes through cities, it slows to one-fifth the speed it travels through open territory. Let $r$ represent the rate in open territory in miles per hour.
   a. Write and simplify an expression that represents the number of hours it takes the train to travel 500 miles in terms of $r$.
   b. Find the total travel time if the train's rate through open territory is 50 miles per hour.
   c. **Critical Thinking** If you knew the time it took the train to make the round-trip, how could you find its average rate?

**Add or subtract. Simplify your answer.**

34. $\frac{10}{5+y}+\frac{2y}{5+y}$
35. $\frac{7}{49-c^2}-\frac{c}{49-c^2}$
36. $\frac{6a}{a-12}+\frac{4}{12-a}$
37. $\frac{b}{2b^3}+\frac{3}{3b^2}$
38. $\frac{r^2+2r}{r+3}-\frac{2r+9}{r+3}$
39. $\frac{x^2-2x}{3x-15}-\frac{8x-25}{3x-15}$
40. $\frac{2y}{8y^2}+\frac{9}{4y^3}$
41. $\frac{2}{x+2}+\frac{6}{x+4}$
42. $\frac{2y}{3y-9}-\frac{y+1}{y^2-9}$

43. **ERROR ANALYSIS** Two students were asked to find the excluded values of the expression $\frac{p}{p^2-p-12}-\frac{4}{p^2-p-12}$. Student A identified the excluded value as $p=-3$. Student B identified the excluded values as $p=-3$ and $p=4$. Who is incorrect? What is the error?

44. **Multi-Step** At the spring fair there is a square Velcro target as shown. A player tosses a ball, which will stick to the target in some random spot. If the ball sticks to a spot in either the small square or the circle, the player wins a prize. What is the probability that a player will win a prize, assuming the ball sticks somewhere on the target? Round your answer to the nearest hundredth.

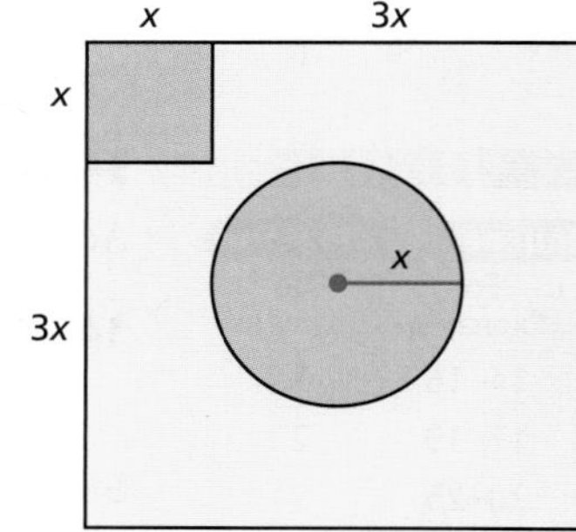


45. **Critical Thinking** Write two expressions whose sum is $\frac{x}{x+1}$.

46. This problem will prepare you for the Multi-Step Test Prep on page 906.

Jonathan is studying light in his science class. He finds that a magnifying glass can be used to project upside-down images on a piece of paper. The equation $\frac{1}{f}=\frac{1}{x}+\frac{1}{y}$ relates the focal length of the lens $f$, the distance of the object from the lens $x$, and the distance of the image from the lens $y$. The focal length of Jonathan's lens is 12 cm.
   a. Jonathan wants to write $y$, the distance of the image from the lens, as a function of $x$, the distance of the object from the lens. To begin, he rewrote the equation as $\frac{1}{y}=\frac{1}{12}-\frac{1}{x}$. Explain how he did this.
   b. Explain how Jonathan simplified the equation in part **a** to $\frac{1}{y}=\frac{x-12}{12x}$.

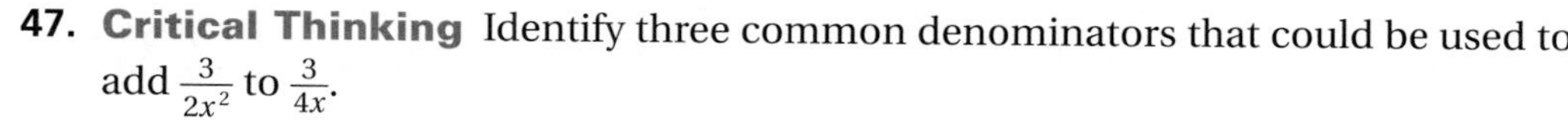

47. **Critical Thinking** Identify three common denominators that could be used to add $\frac{3}{2x^2}$ to $\frac{3}{4x}$.

48. **Write About It** Explain how to find the least common denominator of two rational expressions when the denominators are opposite binomials.

## TEST PREP

MA.A.1.1, MA.A.1.3, MA.N.1

49. What is the LCD of $\frac{6}{3p+3}$ and $\frac{4}{p+1}$?

Ⓐ $p+1$ Ⓑ $12$ Ⓒ $3p+1$ Ⓓ $3p+3$

50. Simplify $\frac{4}{2x} - \frac{1}{x}$.

Ⓕ $\frac{1}{x}$ Ⓖ $\frac{3}{x}$ Ⓗ $\frac{5}{x}$ Ⓙ $\frac{3}{2x}$

51. Which of the following is equivalent to $\frac{2x}{x-2}$?

Ⓐ $\frac{x}{x+2} + \frac{x}{x-2}$

Ⓑ $\frac{2x}{x^2-4} + \frac{4}{x-2}$

Ⓒ $\frac{x^2+4x}{x^2-4} + \frac{x}{x+2}$

Ⓓ $\frac{x}{x+2} + \frac{x^2+6x}{x^2-4}$

52. **Extended Response** Andrea biked 3 miles to the post office and 5 miles to the library. The rate at which she biked to the library was three times faster than her rate to the post office *r*.

a. Write an expression that represents Andrea's total biking time in hours. Explain what each part of your expression means in the situation.

b. Simplify the expression.

c. How long did it take Andrea to bike the 8 miles if her biking rate to the post office was 3 miles per hour?

## CHALLENGE AND EXTEND

**Add or subtract and simplify. Find the excluded values.**

53. $\frac{3}{x+y} - \frac{2x+y}{x^2-y^2}$

54. $\frac{3}{2m} + \frac{4}{m^2} + \frac{2}{5m}$

55. $\frac{a}{xy} + \frac{b}{xz} + \frac{c}{yz}$

56. Simplify the complex fraction $\dfrac{\frac{1}{x} - \frac{1}{y}}{\frac{x}{xy} - \frac{1}{x}}$. (*Hint:* Simplify the numerator and denominator of the complex fraction first.)

## SPIRAL REVIEW

**Sketch a graph for each situation.** *(Lesson 4-1)*

57. Snow falls lightly at first, then falls heavily at a steady rate.

58. Snow melts quickly during the afternoon, then stops melting at night.

59. Snow falls heavily, is shoveled away, and then a light snow falls.

**Solve each quadratic equation by factoring.** *(Lesson 9-6)*

60. $d^2 - 4d - 12 = 0$

61. $2g^2 - 9g = -4$

62. $9x^2 + 6x + 1 = 0$

**Simplify each rational expression, if possible. Identify any excluded values.** *(Lesson 12-3)*

63. $\frac{2t^2-8}{t^2-4}$

64. $\frac{n^2+5n}{n^2+3n-10}$

65. $\frac{4-x}{x^2-16}$

# Model Polynomial Division

Some polynomial divisions can be modeled by algebra tiles. If a polynomial can be modeled by a rectangle, then its factors are represented by the length and width of the rectangle. If one factor is a divisor, then the other factor is a quotient.

*Use with Lesson 12-6*

**MA.A.1.1** Execute … operations with algebraic expressions…

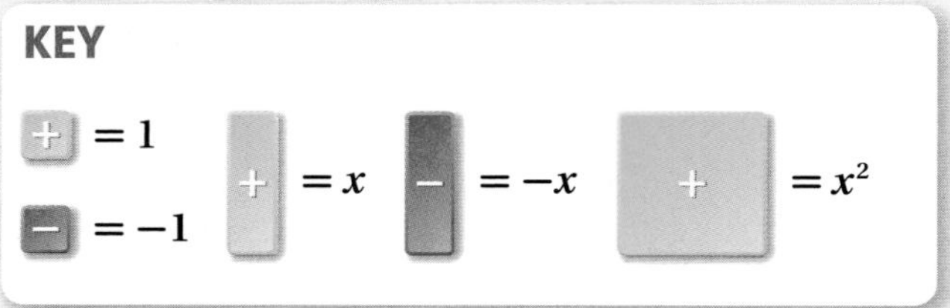


## Activity 1

**Use algebra tiles to find the quotient $(x^2 + 5x + 6) \div (x + 2)$.**

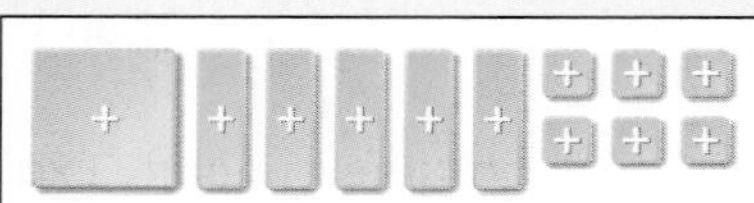

*Model $x^2 + 5x + 6$.*

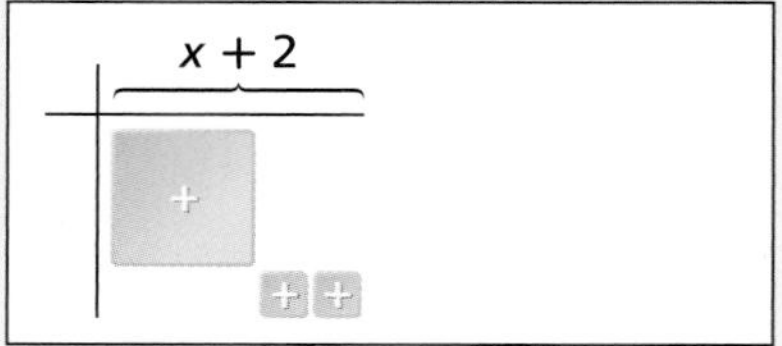


*Try to form a rectangle with a length of $x + 2$.*

*Place the $x^2$-tile in the upper-left corner. Then place two unit tiles in a row at the lower-right corner.*

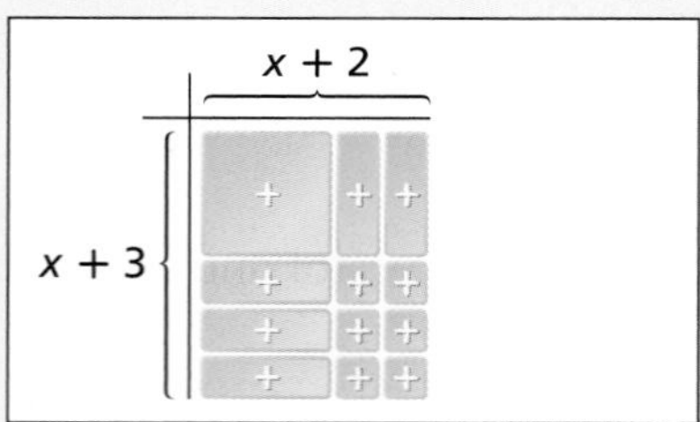


*Try to use all the remaining tiles to complete a rectangle.*

*If you can complete a rectangle, then the width of the rectangle is the quotient.*

The rectangle has length $x + 2$ and width $x + 3$. So, $(x^2 + 5x + 6) \div (x + 2) = x + 3$.

| You can check your answer by multiplying. | $(x + 3)(x + 2)$ | |
|---|---|---|
| | $x^2 + 2x + 3x + 6$ | *Use the FOIL method.* |
| | $x^2 + 5x + 6$ ✓ | |

## Try This

**Use algebra tiles to find each quotient.**

**1.** $(x^2 + 5x + 4) \div (x + 1)$ **2.** $(x^2 + 7x + 10) \div (x + 5)$ **3.** $(x^2 + 4x - 5) \div (x - 1)$

**4.** $(2x^2 + 5x + 2) \div (x + 2)$ **5.** $(x^2 - 6x + 8) \div (x - 2)$ **6.** $(2x^2 - x - 3) \div (x + 1)$

**7.** Describe what happens when you try to model $(x^2 - 4x + 3) \div (x + 1)$.

# 12-6 Dividing Polynomials

MA.A.1.1 Execute … operations with algebraic expressions…

***Objective***
Divide a polynomial by a monomial or binomial.

**Why learn this?**
Division of polynomials can be used to compare the energy produced by solar panels. (See Exercise 51.)

The electrical power (in watts) produced by a solar panel is directly proportional to the surface area of the solar panel. Division of polynomials can be used to compare energy production by solar panels of different sizes.

To divide a polynomial by a monomial, you can first write the division as a rational expression. Then divide each term in the polynomial by the monomial.

## EXAMPLE 1 Dividing a Polynomial by a Monomial

**Divide $(6x^3 + 8x^2 - 4x) \div 2x$.**

$\frac{6x^3 + 8x^2 - 4x}{2x}$ — *Write as a rational expression.*

$\frac{6x^3}{2x} + \frac{8x^2}{2x} - \frac{4x}{2x}$ — *Divide each term in the polynomial by the monomial 2x.*

$\frac{\cancel{6}^3 \cancel{x^3}^2}{\cancel{2}^1 \cancel{x}^1} + \frac{\cancel{8}^4 \cancel{x^2}^1}{\cancel{2}^1 \cancel{x}^1} - \frac{\cancel{4}^2 \cancel{x}^1}{\cancel{2}^1 \cancel{x}^1}$ — *Divide out common factors.*

$3x^2 + 4x - 2$ — *Simplify.*

**Divide.**

**1a.** $(8p^3 - 4p^2 + 12p) \div (-4p^2)$

**1b.** $(6x^3 + 2x - 15) \div 6x$

Division of a polynomial by a binomial is similar to division of whole numbers.

**Dividing Polynomials**

| | WORDS | NUMBERS | POLYNOMIALS |
|---|---|---|---|
| **Step 1** | Factor the numerator and/or denominator if possible. | $\frac{168}{3} = \frac{56 \cdot 3}{3}$ | $\frac{r^2 + 3r + 2}{r + 2} = \frac{(r + 2)(r + 1)}{(r + 2)}$ |
| **Step 2** | Divide out any common factors. | $\frac{56 \cdot \cancel{3}}{\cancel{3}}$ | $\frac{\cancel{(r + 2)}(r + 1)}{\cancel{(r + 2)}}$ |
| **Step 3** | Simplify. | 56 | $r + 1$ |

## EXAMPLE 2 Dividing a Polynomial by a Binomial

**Helpful Hint**

Put each term of the numerator over the denominator only when the denominator is a monomial. If the denominator is a polynomial, try to factor first.

**Divide.**

**A** $\dfrac{c^2 + 4c - 5}{c - 1}$

$\dfrac{(c+5)(c-1)}{c-1}$ *Factor the numerator.*

$\dfrac{(c+5)\cancel{(c-1)}^1}{\cancel{(c-1)}^1}$ *Divide out common factors.*

$c + 5$ *Simplify.*

**B** $\dfrac{3x^2 - 10x - 8}{4 - x}$

$\dfrac{(3x+2)(x-4)}{4-x}$ *Factor the numerator.*

$\dfrac{(3x+2)(x-4)}{-1(x-4)}$ *Factor one opposite binomial.*

$\dfrac{(3x+2)\cancel{(x-4)}^1}{-1\cancel{(x-4)}^1}$ *Divide out common factors.*

$-3x - 2$ *Simplify.*

**Divide.**

**2a.** $\dfrac{10 + 7k + k^2}{k + 2}$ **2b.** $\dfrac{b^2 - 49}{b + 7}$ **2c.** $\dfrac{s^2 + 12s + 36}{s + 6}$

Recall how you used long division to divide whole numbers as shown at right. You can also use long division to divide polynomials. An example is shown below.

$$\begin{array}{r} 15 \\ 23\overline{)345} \\ \underline{-23} \\ 115 \\ \underline{-115} \\ 0 \end{array}$$

$$(x^2+3x+2) \div (x+2)$$

$$\begin{array}{r} x+1 \\ x+2\overline{)x^2+3x+2} \\ \underline{-(x^2+2x)} \\ x+2 \\ \underline{-(x+2)} \\ 0 \end{array}$$

Divisor: $x+2$; Quotient: $x+1$; Dividend: $x^2+3x+2$

| Using Long Division to Divide a Polynomial by a Binomial | |
|---|---|
| **Step 1** | Write the binomial and polynomial in long division form. |
| **Step 2** | Divide the first term of the dividend by the first term of the divisor. This is the first term of the quotient. |
| **Step 3** | Multiply this first term of the quotient by the binomial divisor and place the product under the dividend, aligning like terms. |
| **Step 4** | Subtract the product from the dividend. |
| **Step 5** | Bring down the next term in the dividend. |
| **Step 6** | Repeat Steps 2–5 as necessary until you get 0 or until the degree of the remainder is less than the degree of the binomial. |

## EXAMPLE 3 Polynomial Long Division

**Divide using long division.**

**A** $(x^2 + 2 + 3x) \div (x + 2)$

**Step 1** $x + 2\overline{)x^2 + 3x + 2}$

*Write in long division form with expressions in standard form.*

**Step 2**
$$\begin{array}{r} x \\ x + 2\overline{)x^2 + 3x + 2} \end{array}$$

*Divide the first term of the dividend by the first term of the divisor to get the first term of the quotient.*

**Step 3**
$$\begin{array}{r} x \\ x + 2\overline{)x^2 + 3x + 2} \\ \underline{x^2 + 2x} \end{array}$$

*Multiply the first term of the quotient by the binomial divisor. Place the product under the dividend, aligning like terms.*

**Step 4**
$$\begin{array}{r} x \\ x + 2\overline{)x^2 + 3x + 2} \\ -(\underline{x^2 + 2x}) \\ 0 + x \end{array}$$

*Subtract the product from the dividend.*

**Step 5**
$$\begin{array}{r} x \\ x + 2\overline{)x^2 + 3x + 2} \\ -(\underline{x^2 + 2x}) \downarrow \\ x + 2 \end{array}$$

*Bring down the next term in the dividend.*

**Step 6**
$$\begin{array}{r} x + 1 \\ x + 2\overline{)x^2 + 3x + 2} \\ -(\underline{x^2 + 2x}) \\ x + 2 \\ \underline{-(x + 2)} \\ 0 \end{array}$$

*Repeat Steps 2–5 as necessary.*
*The remainder is 0.*

***Check*** Multiply the answer and the divisor.
$(x + 2)(x + 1)$
$x^2 + x + 2x + 2$
$x^2 + 3x + 2$ ✓

> **Helpful Hint**
> You can check your simplified answer by multiplying it by the divisor. When the remainder is 0, you should get the numerator.

**B** $\dfrac{x^2 + 4x + 3}{x + 1}$

$x + 1\overline{)x^2 + 4x + 3}$

*Write in long division form.*

$$\begin{array}{r} x + 3 \\ x + 1\overline{)x^2 + 4x + 3} \\ -(\underline{x^2 + x}) \downarrow \\ 3x + 3 \\ -(\underline{3x + 3}) \\ 0 \end{array}$$

*$x^2 \div x = x$*
*Multiply $x \cdot (x + 1)$. Subtract.*
*Bring down the 3. $3x \div x = 3$*
*Multiply $3(x + 1)$. Subtract.*
*The remainder is 0.*

***Check*** Multiply the answer and the divisor.
$(x + 1)(x + 3)$
$x^2 + 3x + 1x + 3$
$x^2 + 4x + 3$ ✓

**Divide using long division.**

**3a.** $(2y^2 - 5y - 3) \div (y - 3)$ **3b.** $(a^2 - 8a + 12) \div (a - 6)$

Sometimes the divisor is not a factor of the dividend, so the remainder is not 0. Then the remainder can be written as a rational expression.

## EXAMPLE 4 Long Division with a Remainder

**Divide $(2x^2 + 3x - 6) \div (x - 2)$.**

| | |
|---|---|
| $x - 2\overline{)2x^2 + 3x - 6}$ | *Write in long division form.* |
| $2x + 7$ over $x - 2\overline{)2x^2 + 3x - 6}$ | *$2x^2 \div x = 2x$* |
| $\underline{-(2x^2 - 4x)}\downarrow$ | *Multiply $2x(x - 2)$. Subtract.* |
| $7x - 6$ | *Bring down the $-6$. $7x \div x = 7$* |
| $\underline{-(7x - 14)}$ | *Multiply $7(x - 2)$. Subtract.* |
| $8$ | *The remainder is 8.* |
| $\dfrac{8}{x-2}$ | *Write the remainder as a rational expression using the divisor as the denominator.* |
| $2x + 7 + \dfrac{8}{x-2}$ | *Write the quotient with the remainder.* |

**Divide.**

**4a.** $(3m^2 + 4m - 2) \div (m + 3)$ **4b.** $(y^2 + 3y + 2) \div (y - 3)$

Sometimes you need to write a placeholder for a term using a zero coefficient. This is best seen if you write the polynomials in standard form.

## EXAMPLE 5 Dividing Polynomials That Have a Zero Coefficient

**Divide $(3x - 4x^3 - 15) \div (2x + 3)$.**

| | |
|---|---|
| $(-4x^3 + 3x - 15) \div (2x + 3)$ | *Write the polynomials in standard form.* |
| $2x + 3\overline{)-4x^3 + 0x^2 + 3x - 15}$ | *Write in long division form. Use $0x^2$ as a placeholder for the $x^2$ term.* |
| $-2x^2 + 3x - 3$ over $2x + 3\overline{)-4x^3 + 0x^2 + 3x - 15}$ | *$-4x^3 \div 2x = -2x^2$* |
| $\underline{-(-4x^3 - 6x^2)}\downarrow$ | *Multiply $-2x^2(2x + 3)$. Subtract.* |
| $6x^2 + 3x$ | *Bring down $3x$. $6x^2 \div 2x = 3x$* |
| $\underline{-(6x^2 + 9x)}\downarrow$ | *Multiply $3x(2x + 3)$. Subtract.* |
| $-6x - 15$ | *Bring down $-15$. $-6x \div 2x = -3$* |
| $\underline{-(-6x - 9)}$ | *Multiply $-3(2x + 3)$. Subtract.* |
| $-6$ | *The remainder is $-6$.* |

$$(3x - 4x^3 - 15) \div (2x + 3) = -2x^2 + 3x - 3 + \frac{-6}{2x+3}.$$

**Remember!**

Recall from Chapter 7 that a polynomial in one variable is written in standard form when the degrees of the terms go from greatest to least.

**Divide.**

**5a.** $(1 - 4x^2 + x^3) \div (x - 2)$

**5b.** $(4p - 1 + 2p^3) \div (p + 1)$

## THINK AND DISCUSS

1. When dividing a polynomial by a binomial, what does it mean when the remainder is 0?
2. Suppose that the final answer to a polynomial division problem is $x - 5 + \frac{3}{x+2}$. Find an excluded value. Justify your answer.

3. **GET ORGANIZED** Copy and complete the graphic organizer. In each box, show an example.

Long Division

Polynomials | Whole numbers

# 12-6 Exercises

MA.A.1.1

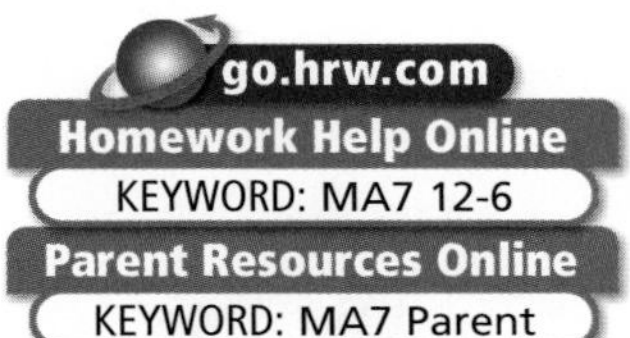


## GUIDED PRACTICE

SEE EXAMPLE 1 p. 893

**Divide.**

1. $(4x^2 - x) \div 2x$
2. $(16a^4 - 4a^3) \div 4a$
3. $(21b^2 - 14b + 24) \div 3b$
4. $(18r^2 - 12r + 6) \div -6r$
5. $(6x^3 + 12x^2 + 9x) \div 3x^2$
6. $(5m^4 + 15m^2 - 10) \div 5m^3$

SEE EXAMPLE 2 p. 894

7. $\frac{2x^2 - x - 3}{x + 1}$
8. $\frac{a^2 - a - 12}{a - 4}$
9. $\frac{6y^2 + 11y - 10}{3y - 2}$
10. $\frac{t^2 - 6t + 8}{t - 4}$
11. $\frac{x^2 + 16x + 15}{x + 15}$
12. $\frac{p^2 - p - 20}{p + 4}$

SEE EXAMPLE 3 p. 895

**Divide using long division.**

13. $(c^2 + 7c + 12) \div (c + 4)$
14. $(3s^2 - 12s - 15) \div (s - 5)$
15. $\frac{x^2 + 5x - 14}{x + 7}$
16. $\frac{x^2 + 4x - 12}{x - 2}$

SEE EXAMPLE 4 p. 896

17. $(a^2 + 4a + 3) \div (a + 2)$
18. $(2r^2 + 11r + 5) \div (r - 3)$
19. $(n^2 + 8n + 15) \div (n + 4)$
20. $(2t^2 - t + 4) \div (t - 1)$
21. $(8n^2 - 6n - 7) \div (2n + 1)$
22. $(b^2 - b + 1) \div (b + 2)$

SEE EXAMPLE 5 p. 896

23. $(3x - 2x^3 - 10) \div (3 + x)$
24. $(3p^3 - 2p^2 - 4) \div (p - 2)$
25. $(m^2 + 2) \div (m - 1)$
26. $(3x^2 + 4x^3 - 5) \div (5 + x)$
27. $(4k^3 - 2k - 8) \div (k + 1)$
28. $(j^3 + 6j + 2) \div (j + 4)$

## PRACTICE AND PROBLEM SOLVING

**Divide.**

29. $(9t^3 + 12t^2 - 6t) \div 3t^2$
30. $(5n^3 - 10n + 15) \div -5n$
31. $(-16p^4 + 4p^3 + 8) \div 4p^3$
32. $\frac{4r^2 - 9r + 2}{r - 2}$
33. $\frac{8t^2 + 2t - 3}{2t - 1}$
34. $\frac{3g^2 + 7g - 6}{g + 3}$

| Independent Practice | |
|---|---|
| For Exercises | See Example |
| 29–31 | 1 |
| 32–34 | 2 |
| 35–38 | 3 |
| 39–41 | 4 |
| 42–44 | 5 |

**Extra Practice**

Skills Practice p. S27
Application Practice p. S39

**Divide using long division.**

35. $(x^2 - 5x + 6) \div (x - 2)$
36. $(2m^2 + 8m + 8) \div (m + 2)$
37. $(6a^2 + 7a - 3) \div (2a + 3)$
38. $(3x^2 - 10x - 8) \div (x - 4)$
39. $(3x^2 - 2x + 6) \div (x - 2)$
40. $(2m^2 + 5m + 8) \div (m + 1)$
41. $(6x^2 - x - 3) \div (2x - 1)$
42. $(2m^3 - 4m - 30) \div (2m - 10)$
43. $(6t^3 + 21t + 9) \div (3t + 9)$
44. $(p^4 - 7p^2 + p + 1) \div (p - 3)$

45. **Multi-Step** Find the value of $n$, so that $x - 4$ is a factor of $x^2 + x + n$.

**Geometry The area of each of three rectangles is $2x^2 - 3x - 2$ cm$^2$. Below are the different widths of the rectangles. Find each corresponding length.**

46. $x - 2$
47. $x + 1$
48. $2x + 1$

49. **Graphing Calculator** Use the table of values for $f(x) = \frac{(x^2 + 3x + 4)}{x - 5}$ to answer the following.
   a. Describe what is happening to the values of $y$ as $x$ increases from 2 to 4.
   b. Describe what is happening to the values of $y$ as $x$ increases from 6 to 8.
   c. Explain why there is no value in the $y$ column when $x$ is 5.

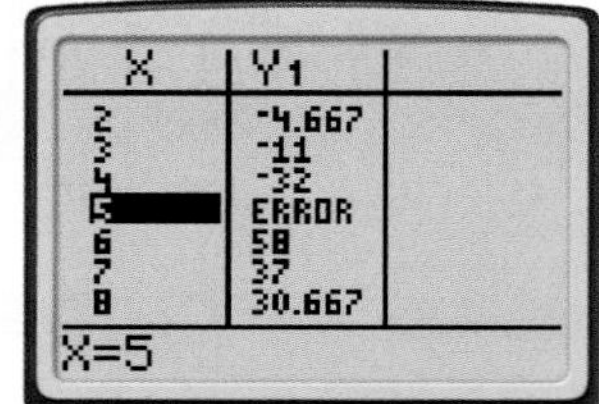


50. **Estimation** Estimate the value of $\frac{x^2 + 10x + 25}{x^2 - 25} \div \frac{x^4 - 4x^3 - 45x^2}{x^2 - 14x + 45}$ for $x = 2.88$.

**LINK**

**Solar Energy**

NASA is researching unmanned solar-powered aircraft. In the future, these aircraft may be able to stay in the air indefinitely.

51. **Solar Energy** The greater the area of a solar panel, the greater the number of watts of energy produced. The area of two solar panels $A$ and $B$, in square meters, can be represented by $A = m^2 + 3m + 2$ and $B = 2m + 2$. Divide the polynomials to find an expression that represents the ratio of the area of $A$ to the area of $B$.

52. **ERROR ANALYSIS** Two students attempted to divide $\frac{4x^2 - 6x + 12}{-2x}$. Which is incorrect? Explain the error.

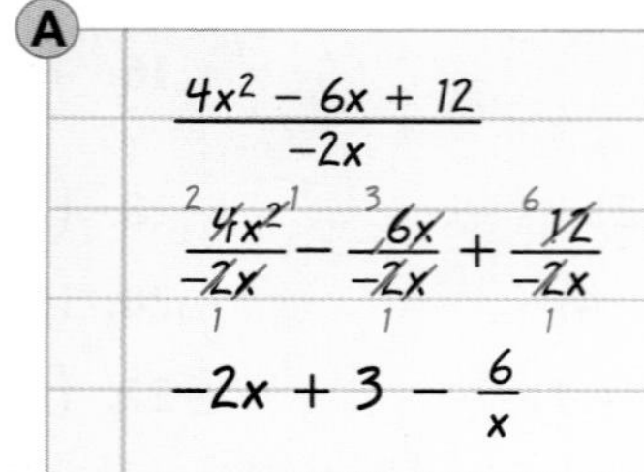


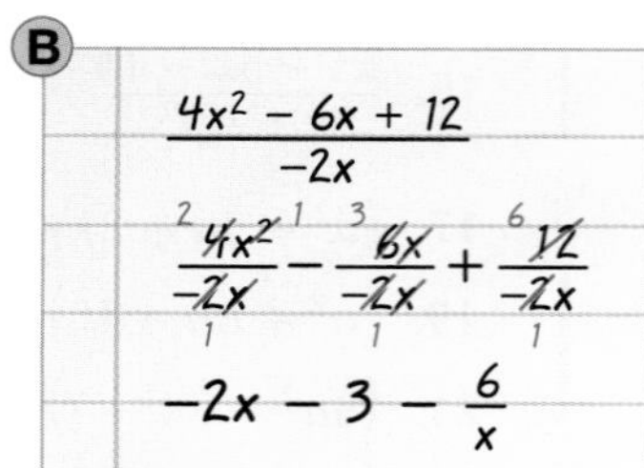


**MULTI-STEP TEST PREP**

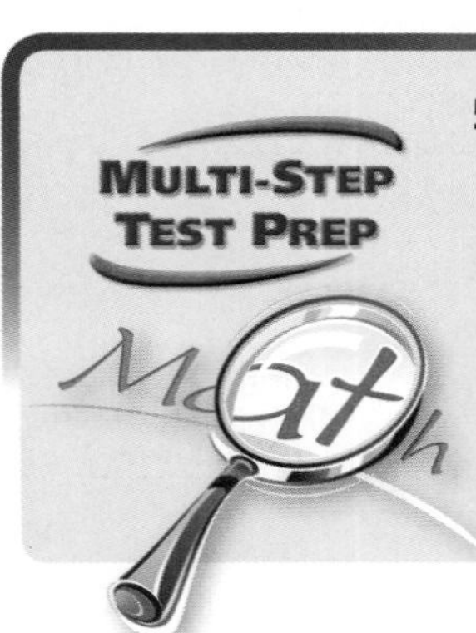

53. This problem will prepare you for the Multi-Step Test Prep on page 906.

Jonathan continues to study lenses and uses the equation $\frac{1}{y} = \frac{x - 12}{12x}$.
   a. Jonathan wants to write $y$, the distance of the image from the lens, as a function of $x$, the distance of the object from the lens. What is the equation solved for $y$?
   b. Use a graphing calculator to create a table of values for the function $y(x)$. For which value of $x$ is the function undefined?

54. **Write About It** When dividing a polynomial by a binomial, what does it mean when there is a remainder?

55. **Critical Thinking** Divide $2x + 3\overline{)2x^2 + 7x + 6}$. Find a value for each expression by substituting 10 for $x$ in the original problem. Repeat the division. Compare the results of each division.

56. **Write About It** Is $3x + 2$ a factor of $3x^2 + 14x + 8$? Explain.

## TEST PREP

MA.A.1.1

57. Which expression has an excluded value of $-\frac{1}{2}$?

(A) $\frac{4x^2 - 2x - 2}{4x - 2}$ (B) $\frac{4x^2 - 2x - 2}{2x - 4}$ (C) $\frac{4x^2 - 2x - 2}{4x + 2}$ (D) $\frac{4x^2 - 2x - 2}{2x + 4}$

58. Find $(x^2 - 1) \div (x + 2)$.

(F) $x - 2 + \frac{-5}{x + 2}$ (G) $x - 2 + \frac{3}{x + 2}$ (H) $x + 2 + \frac{-5}{x - 2}$ (J) $x + 2 + \frac{3}{x - 2}$

59. Which expression is a factor of $x^2 - 4x - 5$?

(A) $x - 1$ (B) $x + 1$ (C) $x - 4$ (D) $x + 5$

60. Which of the following expressions is equivalent to $(x^3 + 2x^2 + 3x + 1) \div (x - 1)$?

(F) $x^2 + 3x + 6 + \frac{7}{x - 1}$ (H) $x^2 + 3x + 6 + \frac{-5}{x - 1}$

(G) $x^2 + x + 2 + \frac{-1}{x - 1}$ (J) $x^2 + x + 2 + \frac{3}{x - 1}$

## CHALLENGE AND EXTEND

**Divide. Simplify your answer.**

61. $(6x^3y - x^2 + 4xy^2) \div (2x^2y)$

62. $(x^3 - 1) \div (x - 1)$

63. $(x^3 + 2x^2 - x - 2) \div (x^2 - 1)$

64. $(x^3 + 8) \div (x + 2)$

65. **Geometry** The base of a triangle is $2x + 4$ m and the area is $2x^2 + 5x + 2$ m². How much longer is the base than the height?

66. **Geometry** The formula for finding the volume of a cylinder is $V = BH$, where $B$ is the area of the base of the cylinder and $H$ is the height.

a. Find the height of the cylinder given that $V = \pi(x^3 + 4x^2 + 5x + 2)$ and $B = \pi(x^2 + 2x + 1)$.

b. Find an expression for the radius of the base.

## SPIRAL REVIEW

67. Find the probability that a point within the boundaries of the larger rectangle is in the shaded region. Express your answer as a simplified radical expression. *(Lesson 11-8)*

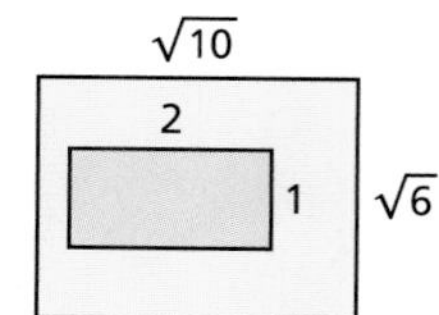


**Multiply. Write each product in simplest form.** *(Lesson 11-8)*

68. $3\sqrt{3} \cdot \sqrt{6}$

69. $\sqrt{5}(6 - \sqrt{10})$

70. $(\sqrt{3} + 2)(\sqrt{3} + 5)$

**Multiply. Simplify your answer.** *(Lesson 12-4)*

71. $(x^2 + 4x + 3) \cdot \frac{8}{2(x + 3)}$

72. $\frac{9xy^2}{2x^3} \cdot \frac{8y}{3x^4}$

73. $\frac{2k^2 + 4k^3}{k + 1} \cdot \frac{k^2 + 3k + 2}{2k^2}$

# 12-7 Solving Rational Equations

**Ext. MA.A.1.1** Execute all operations with algebraic expressions…
*Also* **MA.N.1**

***Objectives***
Solve rational equations.

Identify extraneous solutions.

***Vocabulary***
rational equation

**Why learn this?**

Rational equations can be used to find how much time it takes two or more people working together to complete a job. (See Example 3.)

A **rational equation** is an equation that contains one or more rational expressions. If a rational equation is a proportion, it can be solved using the Cross Product Property.

## EXAMPLE 1 Solving Rational Equations by Using Cross Products

**Solve $\frac{3}{t-3} = \frac{2}{t}$. Check your answer.**

$\frac{3}{t-3} = \frac{2}{t}$ *Use cross products.*

$3t = (t-3)(2)$

$3t = 2t - 6$ *Distribute 2 on the right side.*

$t = -6$ *Subtract 2t from both sides.*

***Check***

$$\frac{3}{t-3} = \frac{2}{t}$$

| | |
|---|---|
| $\frac{3}{-6-3}$ | $\frac{2}{-6}$ |
| $\frac{3}{-9}$ | $\frac{2}{-6}$ |
| $-\frac{1}{3}$ | $-\frac{1}{3}$ ✓ |

**Solve. Check your answer.**

**1a.** $\frac{1}{n} = \frac{3}{n+4}$ **1b.** $\frac{4}{h+1} = \frac{2}{h}$ **1c.** $\frac{21}{x-7} = \frac{3}{x}$

Some rational equations contain sums or differences of rational expressions. To solve these, you must find the LCD of all the rational expressions in the equation.

## EXAMPLE 2 Solving Rational Equations by Using the LCD

**Solve $\frac{1}{c} + \frac{3}{2c} = \frac{2}{c+1}$.**

**Step 1** Find the LCD.

$2c(c+1)$ *Include every factor of the denominators.*

**Step 2** Multiply both sides by the LCD.

$$2c(c+1)\left(\frac{1}{c} + \frac{3}{2c}\right) = 2c(c+1)\left(\frac{2}{c+1}\right)$$

$$2c(c+1)\left(\frac{1}{c}\right) + 2c(c+1)\left(\frac{3}{2c}\right) = 2c(c+1)\left(\frac{2}{c+1}\right)$$ *Distribute on the left side.*

**Step 3** Simplify and solve.

$$2\cancel{c}^1(c+1)\left(\frac{1}{\cancel{c}^1}\right) + \cancel{2c}^1(c+1)\left(\frac{3}{\cancel{2c}^1}\right) = 2c\cancel{(c+1)}^1\left(\frac{2}{\cancel{c+1}^1}\right) \quad \textit{Divide out common factors.}$$

$$2(c+1) + (c+1)3 = (2c)2 \quad \textit{Simplify.}$$

$$2c + 2 + 3c + 3 = 4c \quad \textit{Distribute and multiply.}$$

$$5c + 5 = 4c \quad \textit{Combine like terms.}$$

$$c + 5 = 0 \quad \textit{Subtract 4c from both sides.}$$

$$c = -5 \quad \textit{Subtract 5 from both sides.}$$

***Check*** Verify that your solution is not extraneous.

| $\frac{1}{c} + \frac{3}{2c}$ | $= \frac{2}{c+1}$ |
|---|---|
| $\frac{1}{-5} + \frac{3}{2(-5)}$ | $\frac{2}{-5+1}$ |
| $\frac{2}{-10} + \frac{3}{-10}$ | $\frac{2}{-4}$ |
| $-\frac{5}{10}$ | $-\frac{1}{2}$ |
| $-\frac{1}{2}$ | $-\frac{1}{2}$ ✓ |

**Solve each equation. Check your answer.**

**2a.** $\frac{2}{a+1} + \frac{1}{a+1} = \frac{4}{a}$

**2b.** $\frac{6}{j+2} - \frac{10}{j} = \frac{4}{2j}$

**2c.** $\frac{8}{t+3} = \frac{1}{t} + 1$

## EXAMPLE 3 *Problem-Solving Application*

**Greg can clean a house in 5 hours. It takes Armin 7 hours to clean the same house. How long will it take them to clean the house if they work together?**

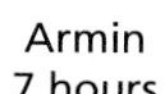

Armin
7 hours

Greg
5 hours

### 1 Understand the Problem

The **answer** will be the number of hours $h$ Greg and Armin need to clean the house.

**List the important information:**

- Greg cleans the house in 5 hours, so he cleans $\frac{1}{5}$ of the house per hour.
- Armin cleans the house in 7 hours, so he cleans $\frac{1}{7}$ of the house per hour.

### 2 Make a Plan

The part of the house Greg cleans plus the part of the house Armin cleans equals the complete job. Greg's rate times the number of hours worked plus Armin's rate times the number of hours worked will give the complete time to clean the house. Let $h$ represent the number of hours worked.

**(Greg's rate)** $h$ + **(Armin's rate)** $h$ = **complete job**

$$\frac{1}{5}h + \frac{1}{7}h = 1$$

**3 Solve**

$$35\left(\frac{1}{5}h + \frac{1}{7}h\right) = 35(1)$$ *Multiply both sides by the LCD, 35.*

$$7h + 5h = 35$$ *Distribute 35 on the left side.*

$$12h = 35$$ *Combine like terms.*

$$h = \frac{35}{12} = 2\frac{11}{12}$$ *Divide by 12 on both sides.*

Greg and Armin working together can clean the house in $2\frac{11}{12}$ hours, or 2 hours 55 minutes.

**4 Look Back**

Greg cleans $\frac{1}{5}$ of the house per hour and Armin cleans $\frac{1}{7}$ of the house per hour. So, in $2\frac{11}{12}$ hours, Greg cleans $\frac{35}{12} \cdot \frac{1}{5} = \frac{7}{12}$ of the house and Armin cleans $\frac{35}{12} \cdot \frac{1}{7} = \frac{5}{12}$ of the house. Together, they clean $\frac{7}{12} + \frac{5}{12} = 1$ house.

**3.** Cindy mows a lawn in 50 minutes. It takes Sara 40 minutes to mow the same lawn. How long will it take them to mow the lawn if they work together?

When you multiply each side of an equation by the LCD, you may get an extraneous solution. Recall from Chapter 11 that an extraneous solution is a solution to a resulting equation that is not a solution to the original equation.

**EXAMPLE 4** 

## Extraneous Solutions

**Solve $\frac{x-9}{x^2-9} = \frac{-3}{x-3}$. Identify any extraneous solutions.**

**Step 1** Solve.

$$(x-9)(x-3) = -3(x^2-9)$$ *Use cross products.*

$$x^2 - 12x + 27 = -3x^2 + 27$$ *Multiply the left side. Distribute −3 on the right side.*

$$4x^2 - 12x + 27 = 27$$ *Add $3x^2$ to both sides.*

$$4x^2 - 12x = 0$$ *Subtract 27 from both sides.*

$$4x(x-3) = 0$$ *Factor the quadratic expression.*

$$4x = 0 \text{ or } x - 3 = 0$$ *Use the Zero Product Property.*

$$x = 0 \text{ or } x = 3$$ *Solve for x.*

**Helpful Hint**

Extraneous solutions may be introduced by squaring both sides of an equation or by multiplying both sides of an equation by a variable expression.

**Step 2** Find extraneous solutions.

| $\frac{x-9}{x^2-9}$ | $= \frac{-3}{x-3}$ |
|---|---|
| $\frac{0-9}{0^2-9}$ | $\frac{-3}{0-3}$ |
| $\frac{-9}{-9}$ | $\frac{-3}{-3}$ |
| 1 | 1 ✓ |

| $\frac{x-9}{x^2-9}$ | $= \frac{-3}{x-3}$ |
|---|---|
| $\frac{3-9}{3^2-9}$ | $\frac{-3}{3-3}$ |
| $\frac{-6}{0}$ | $\frac{-3}{0}$ |

*Because both $\frac{-6}{0}$ and $\frac{-3}{0}$ are undefined, 3 is not a solution.*

The only solution is 0, so 3 is an extraneous solution.

**Solve. Identify any extraneous solutions.**

**4a.** $\frac{3}{x-7} = \frac{x-2}{x-7}$ **4b.** $\frac{x+1}{x-2} = \frac{4}{x-3}$ **4c.** $\frac{9}{x^2+2x} = \frac{6}{x^2}$

## THINK AND DISCUSS

1. Why is it important to check your answers to rational equations?
2. For what values of $x$ are the rational expressions in the equation $\frac{x}{x-3} = \frac{2}{x+3}$ undefined?
3. Explain why some rational equations, such as $\frac{x}{x-4} = \frac{4}{x-4}$, have no solutions.

4. **GET ORGANIZED** Copy and complete the graphic organizer. In each box, write the solution and check.

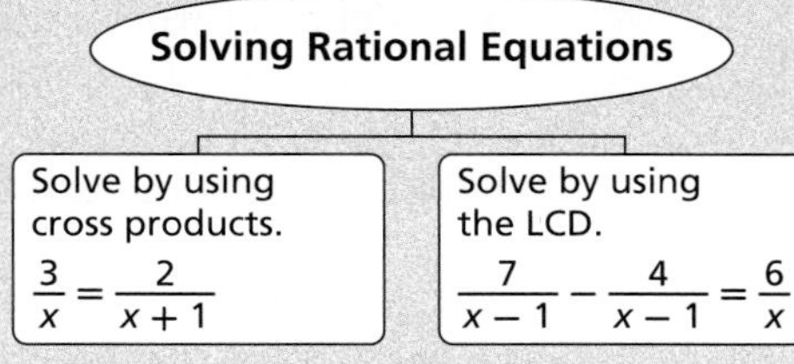


# 12-7 Exercises

Ext. MA.A.1.1, MA.N.1

## GUIDED PRACTICE

1. **Vocabulary** A(n) ___?___ contains one or more rational expressions. (*extraneous solution* or *rational equation*)

**Solve. Check your answer.**

SEE EXAMPLE 1 p. 900

2. $\frac{3}{x+4} = \frac{2}{x}$
3. $\frac{5}{s-6} = \frac{4}{s}$
4. $\frac{20}{p+100} = \frac{-10}{2p}$
5. $\frac{4}{j} = \frac{1}{j+2}$
6. $\frac{3}{x-4} = \frac{9}{x-2}$
7. $\frac{6}{2x-1} = 3$

SEE EXAMPLE 2 p. 900

8. $\frac{6}{x} - \frac{5}{x} = \frac{1}{3}$
9. $\frac{a}{9} + \frac{1}{3} = \frac{2}{5}$
10. $\frac{3}{x+1} = \frac{2}{x} + \frac{3}{x}$
11. $\frac{8}{d} = \frac{1}{d+2} - \frac{3}{d}$
12. $\frac{3}{s-6} = \frac{4}{s} + \frac{1}{2s}$
13. $\frac{7}{r} + \frac{2}{r-1} = \frac{-1}{2r}$
14. $\frac{3}{a-4} = \frac{a}{a-2}$
15. $\frac{r}{2} - \frac{2}{r} = \frac{5}{6}$
16. $\frac{6}{n} = \frac{7}{n^2} - 1$
17. $\frac{4}{x+1} = x - 2$
18. $\frac{5}{a^2} = \frac{-4}{a} + 1$
19. $\frac{1}{p} = \frac{-3}{p^2} + 2$

SEE EXAMPLE 3 p. 901

20. **Painting** Summer can paint a room in 3 hours. Louise can paint the room in 5 hours. How many hours will it take to paint the room if they work together?
21. **Technology** Lawrence's old robotic vacuum can clean his apartment in $1\frac{1}{2}$ hours. His new robotic vacuum can clean his apartment in 45 minutes. How long will it take both vacuums, working together, to clean his apartment?

SEE EXAMPLE 4 p. 902

**Solve. Identify any extraneous solutions.**

22. $\frac{3}{c-4} = \frac{c-1}{c-4}$
23. $\frac{w+3}{w^2-1} - \frac{2w}{w-1} = 1$
24. $\frac{3x-7}{x-5} + \frac{x}{2} = \frac{8}{x-5}$

## PRACTICE AND PROBLEM SOLVING

| Independent Practice | |
|---|---|
| For Exercises | See Example |
| 25–28 | 1 |
| 29–36 | 2 |
| 37 | 3 |
| 38–41 | 4 |

**Extra Practice**

Skills Practice p. S27

Application Practice p. S39

**Solve. Check your answer.**

**25.** $\frac{8}{x-2} = \frac{2}{x+1}$ **26.** $\frac{12}{3n-1} = \frac{3}{n}$ **27.** $\frac{x}{x+4} = \frac{x}{x-1}$ **28.** $\frac{9}{x+5} = \frac{4}{x}$

**29.** $\frac{6}{s} - \frac{2}{s} = 5$ **30.** $\frac{1}{2x} + \frac{1}{4x} = \frac{7}{8x}$ **31.** $\frac{7}{c} - \frac{2}{c} = \frac{4}{c-1}$ **32.** $\frac{9}{m} - \frac{3}{2m} = \frac{15}{m}$

**33.** $\frac{3}{x^2} = \frac{2}{x}$ **34.** $\frac{r}{3} - 3 = -\frac{6}{r}$ **35.** $\frac{6}{x^2} = \frac{1}{2} + \frac{1}{2x}$ **36.** $\frac{8}{3x^2} = \frac{2}{x} - \frac{1}{3}$

**37.** Mel can carpet a floor in 10 hours. Sandy can carpet the same floor in 15 hours. How many hours will it take them to carpet the floor if they work together?

**Solve. Identify any extraneous solutions.**

**38.** $\frac{5x}{x-3} = 8 + \frac{15}{x-3}$ **39.** $\frac{3t}{t-3} = \frac{t+4}{t-3}$

**40.** $\frac{2}{x} = \frac{x+1}{x^2-1}$ **41.** $\frac{1}{x} = \frac{x-4}{x^2-16}$

**42.** **Multi-Step** Clancy has been keeping his free throw statistics. Use his data to write the ratio of the number of free throws Clancy has made to the number of attempts.

| Clancy's Free Throws | |
|---|---|
| Attempts | Made |
| 45 | 39 |

a. What percentage has he made?

b. Write and solve an equation to find how many free throws *f* Clancy would have to make in a row to improve his free-throw percentage to 90%. (*Hint:* Clancy needs to make *f* more free throws in *f* more attempts.)

**43.** **Travel** A passenger train travels 20 mi/h faster than a freight train. It took the passenger train 2 hours less time than the freight train to travel 240 miles. The freight train took *t* hours. Copy and complete the chart. Then find the rate of the freight train.

| | Distance | Rate | Time |
|---|---|---|---|
| Passenger train | 240 | $\frac{240}{t-2}$ | ■ |
| Freight train | 240 | ■ | $t$ |

Suspecting that just such a word problem might be on the algebra midterm, Gary came prepared.



**44.** Pipe A fills a storage tank with a certain chemical in 12 hours. Pipe B fills the tank in 18 hours. How long would it take both pipes to fill the tank?

**MULTI-STEP TEST PREP**

**45.** This problem will prepare you for the Multi-Step Test Prep on page 906.

Blanca sets up a lens with a focal length *f* of 15 cm and places a candle 24 cm from the lens. She knows that $\frac{1}{f} = \frac{1}{x} + \frac{1}{y}$ where $x$ is the distance of the object from the lens and $y$ is the distance of the image from the lens.

a. Write the equation using the given values.

b. For the values of $f$ and $x$ given above, how far will the image appear from the lens?

c. How will distance between the image and the lens be affected if Blanca uses a lens with a focal length of 18 cm?

46. **Critical Thinking** Can you cross multiply to solve all rational equations? If so, explain. If not, how do you identify which ones can be solved using cross products?

47. **Write About It** Solve $\frac{1}{x} + \frac{3}{x} = \frac{3}{x-1}$. Explain each step and why you chose the method you used.

## TEST PREP

Ext. MA.A.1.1, MA.N.1

48. Which value is an extraneous solution to $\frac{x}{x+4} - \frac{4}{x-4} = \frac{x^2+16}{x^2-16}$?

Ⓐ $-16$ Ⓑ $-4$ Ⓒ $4$ Ⓓ $16$

49. Which is a solution to $\frac{x+2}{x-3} - \frac{1}{x} = \frac{3}{x^2-3x}$?

Ⓕ $-1$ Ⓖ $0$ Ⓗ $1$ Ⓙ $3$

50. What are the solutions of $\frac{5}{x^2} = \frac{1}{3} + \frac{2}{3x}$?

Ⓐ $-3$ and $5$ Ⓑ $-3$ and $2$ Ⓒ $2$ and $3$ Ⓓ $3$ and $-5$

## CHALLENGE AND EXTEND

51. Below is a solution to a rational equation. Use an algebraic property to justify each step.

Solve $\frac{3}{x} = \frac{6}{x+4}$.

| Statements | Reasons |
|---|---|
| a. $3(x+4) = 6x$ | |
| b. $3x + 12 = 6x$ | |
| c. $12 = 3x$ | |
| d. $4 = x$ | |

52. For what value of $a$ will the equation $\frac{x+4}{x-a} = \frac{7}{x-a}$ have no solution?

53. Luke, Eddie, and Ryan can do a job in 1 hour and 20 minutes if they work together. Working alone, it takes Ryan 1 hour more to do the job than it takes Luke, and Luke does the job twice as fast as Eddie. How much time would it take each to do the job working alone?

## SPIRAL REVIEW

**Identify which lines are parallel and which lines are perpendicular.** *(Lesson 5-8)*

54. $y = \frac{1}{3}x;\ y = 3x + 1;\ y = 3x - 1$

55. $y = -2x;\ y = 2x - 2;\ y = \frac{1}{2}x + 4$

56. $y = -x - 3;\ y = x - 2;\ y = x + 3$

57. $y = -\frac{2}{3}x + 2;\ y = \frac{3}{2}x + 3;\ y = -\frac{3}{2}x - 1$

**Solve each equation. Check your answer.** *(Lesson 11-9)*

58. $2\sqrt{x} = 24$

59. $\sqrt{x+15} = \sqrt{4x}$

60. $\sqrt{2-x} = x$

**Graph each rational function.** *(Lesson 12-2)*

61. $y = \frac{4}{x}$

62. $y = \frac{2}{x+1}$

63. $y = -\frac{1}{x} + 3$

CHAPTER 12

SECTION 12B

## Operations with Rational Expressions and Equations

**An Upside-Down World** Jamal is studying lenses and their images for a science project. He finds in a science book that a magnifying glass can be used to project upside-down images on a screen. The equation $\frac{1}{f} = \frac{1}{x} + \frac{1}{y}$ relates the focal length of the lens $f$, the distance of the object from the lens $x$, and the distance of the image from the lens $y$. The focal length of Jamal's lens is 10 cm.

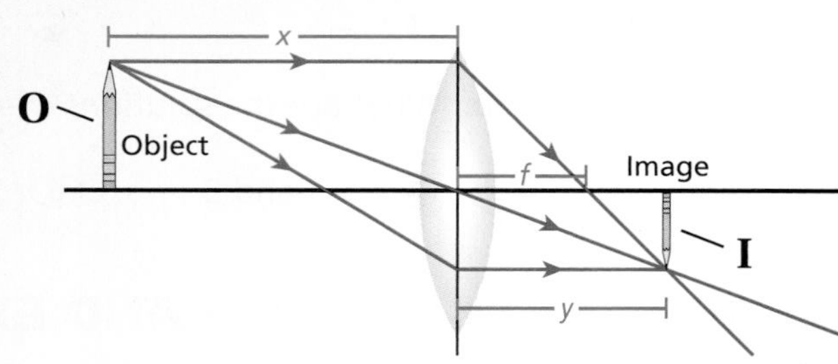


1. Solve the given equation for $y$ using the given value of $f$.
2. Jamal experiments with a candle, the lens, and a screen. Given that the focal length remains constant, use a table for the $x$-values 0, 2, 4, 6, 8, 10, 12, 14, and 16 cm. For which $x$-values are the $y$-values positive?
3. Graph the function $y(x)$. Label the axes.

Magnification for images is the ratio of the height of the image to the height of the object. This is also equal to the ratio of the distance between the image and the lens and the distance between the object and the lens: $M = \frac{I}{O} = \frac{y}{x}$. $I$ is the height of the image, $O$ is the height of the object, $y$ is the distance of the image from the lens, and $x$ is the distance of the object from the lens.

4. If the height of a candle is 15 cm and the projected image of that candle is 37.5 cm, what is the magnification of the lens?
5. As Jamal moves the candle further from the lens (increases $x$), and the distance between the lens and the screen decreases ($y$ decreases), does the magnification $M$ stay the same, increase, or decrease?

# READY TO GO ON?

CHAPTER 12

SECTION 12B

## Quiz for Lessons 12-4 Through 12-7

### 12-4 Multiplying and Dividing Rational Expressions

**Multiply. Simplify your answer.**

1. $\frac{n+3}{n-5} \cdot (n^2 - 5n)$

2. $\frac{8}{2x+6} \cdot (x^2 + 6x + 9)$

3. $\frac{5a^2b^3}{ab^5} \cdot \frac{2a^4bc^5}{20c}$

4. $\frac{6xy^2}{2x^2y^6} \cdot \frac{6x^4y^4}{9x^3}$

5. $\frac{3h^3 - 6h}{10g^2} \cdot \frac{4g}{gh^2 - 2g}$

6. $\frac{m^2 + m - 2}{m^2 - 2m - 8} \cdot \frac{m^2 - 8m + 16}{3m - 3}$

**Divide. Simplify your answer.**

7. $\frac{2}{n^3} \div \frac{n-6}{n^5}$

8. $\frac{2x^2 + 8x + 6}{x} \div \frac{2x^2 + 2x}{x^3 - x^2}$

9. $\frac{8b^3c}{b^2c} \div (4b^2 + 4b)$

### 12-5 Adding and Subtracting Rational Expressions

**Add or subtract. Simplify your answer.**

10. $\frac{15}{2p} - \frac{13}{2p}$

11. $\frac{3m^2}{4m^5} + \frac{5m^2}{4m^5}$

12. $\frac{x^2 + 8x}{x-2} - \frac{3x + 14}{x-2}$

13. $\frac{2t}{4t^2} + \frac{2}{t}$

14. $\frac{m^2 - m - 2}{m^2 + 6m + 5} - \frac{2}{m+5}$

15. $\frac{4x}{x-2} + \frac{3x}{2-x}$

16. Julianne competes in a biathlon that consists of a 25-mile running leg and a 45-mile biking leg. Julianne averages 3 times the rate of speed on her bike that she does on her feet. Let $r$ represent Julianne's running rate of speed. Write and simplify an expression, in terms of $r$, that represents the time it takes for Julianne to complete both legs of the race. Then determine how long it will take Julianne to complete the race if she runs an average of 10 mi/h.

### 12-6 Dividing Polynomials

**Divide.**

17. $(6d^2 + 4d) \div 2d$

18. $(15x^4 + 3x^3 - x) \div (-3x^2)$

19. $(2x^2 - 7x - 4) \div (2x + 1)$

**Divide using long division.**

20. $(a^2 + 3a - 10) \div (a - 2)$

21. $(4y^2 - 9) \div (2y - 3)$

22. $(2x^2 + 5x - 8) \div (x + 2)$

### 12-7 Solving Rational Equations

**Solve. Identify any extraneous solutions.**

23. $\frac{3}{x} = \frac{4}{x-1}$

24. $\frac{1}{x} = \frac{2}{x^2}$

25. $\frac{2}{t} + \frac{4}{3t} = \frac{4}{t+2}$

26. $\frac{4}{n^2} = \frac{7}{n} + 2$

27. $\frac{d+2}{d+8} = \frac{-6}{d+8}$

28. $\frac{x-6}{x^2-6} = \frac{-4}{x-4}$

29. It takes Dustin 2 hours to shovel the snow from his driveway and sidewalk. It takes his sister 3 hours to shovel the same area. How long will it take them to shovel the walk if they work together?

EXTENSION

# Trigonometric Ratios

**Objectives**

Find the three basic trigonometric ratios in a right triangle.

Use trigonometric ratios to find missing lengths.

**Vocabulary**

trigonometric ratios
sine
cosine
tangent

A **trigonometric ratio** is a ratio of the lengths of two sides in a right triangle. Three basic trigonometric ratios are *sine, cosine,* and *tangent,* abbreviated *sin, cos,* and *tan,* respectively.

**Trigonometric Ratios**

$$\sin A = \frac{\text{leg opposite } \angle A}{\text{hypotenuse}} = \frac{a}{c}$$

$$\cos A = \frac{\text{leg adjacent to } \angle A}{\text{hypotenuse}} = \frac{b}{c}$$

$$\tan A = \frac{\text{leg opposite } \angle A}{\text{side adjacent to } \angle A} = \frac{a}{b}$$

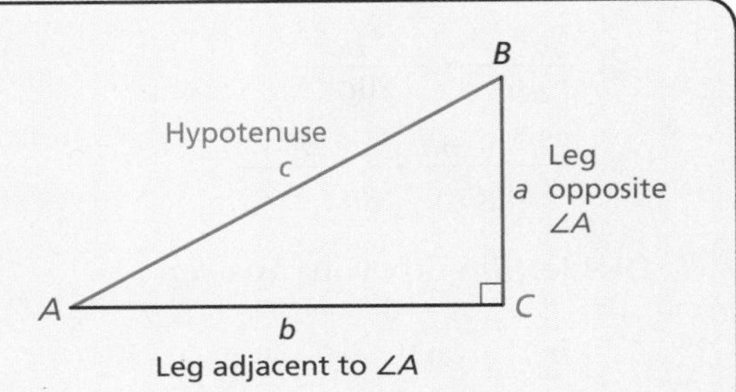


## EXAMPLE 1 Finding the Value of a Trigonometric Ratio

**Find each trigonometric ratio to the nearest thousandth.**

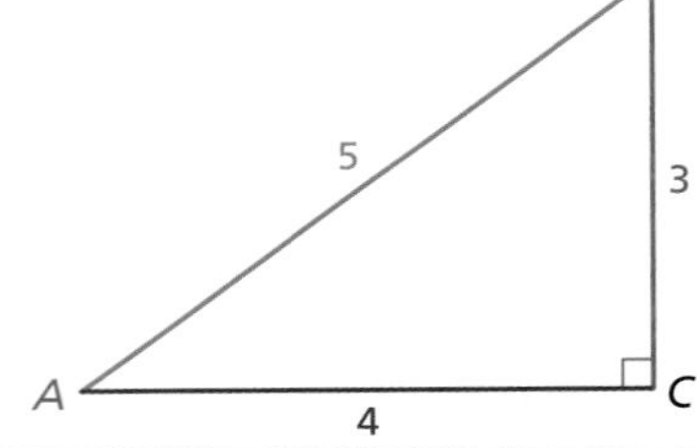


**A** sin $A$

$\sin A = \frac{\text{opposite}}{\text{hypotenuse}} = \frac{3}{5} = 0.600$

**B** cos $A$

$\cos A = \frac{\text{adjacent}}{\text{hypotenuse}} = \frac{4}{5} = 0.800$

**C** tan $A$

$\tan A = \frac{\text{opposite}}{\text{adjacent}} = \frac{3}{4} = 0.750$

CHECK IT OUT!

1. Use the figure above to find sin $B$, cos $B$ and tan $B$.

## EXAMPLE 2 *Aviation Application*

**A plane takes off with a 9° angle of ascent. What is the plane's altitude when it has covered a horizontal distance of 184,800 feet? Round your answer to the nearest foot.**

A — 9° — 184,800 ft — C — B — h

Draw a diagram to model the problem.

$\tan A = \frac{\text{opposite}}{\text{adjacent}}$

$\tan 9° = \frac{h}{184{,}800}$

$184{,}800(\tan 9°) = h$ *Multiply both sides by 184,800.*

$29{,}269.4 \approx h$ *Simplify the left side with a calculator.*

The plane's altitude is about 29,269 feet.

**Helpful Hint**

To find trigonometric ratios on a graphing calculator, press SIN, COS, or TAN and then the value of the degree. Be sure your calculator is in degrees.

2. **Construction** A 14-foot ladder is leaning against a building. The ladder makes a 70° angle with the ground. How far is the base of the ladder from the building? Round your answer to the nearest tenth of a foot.

## EXTENSION Exercises

**Use the diagram for Exercises 1 and 2.**

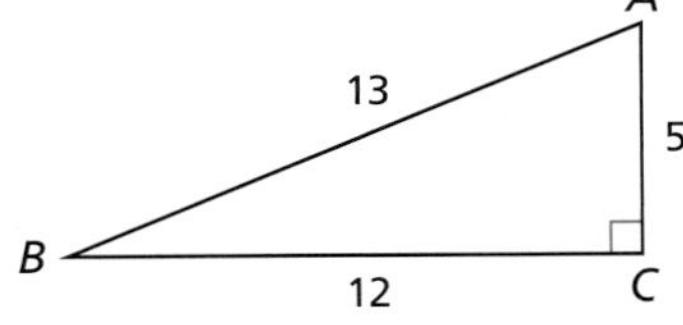


1. Find sin $A$, cos $A$, and tan $A$ to the nearest thousandth.
2. Find sin $B$, cos $B$, and tan $B$ to the nearest thousandth.

**Find the value of $x$. Round answers to the nearest tenth.**

3. 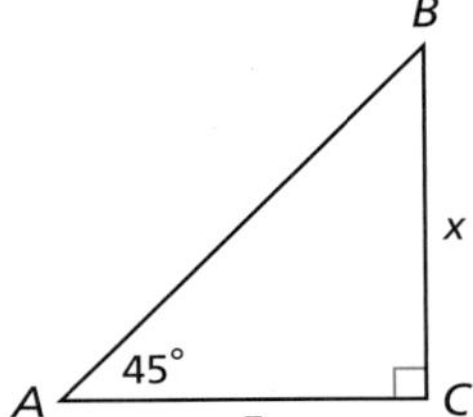


4. 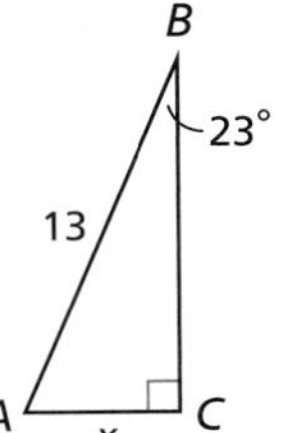


5. 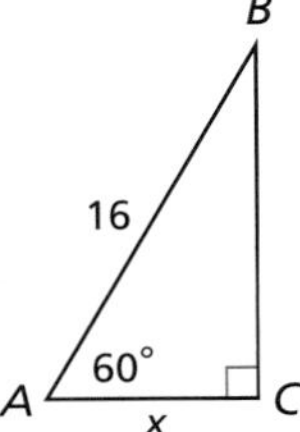


6. **Diving** If a submarine travels 3 miles while rising to the surface at a 9° angle, how deep was the submarine when it started? Round your answer to the nearest tenth of a mile.

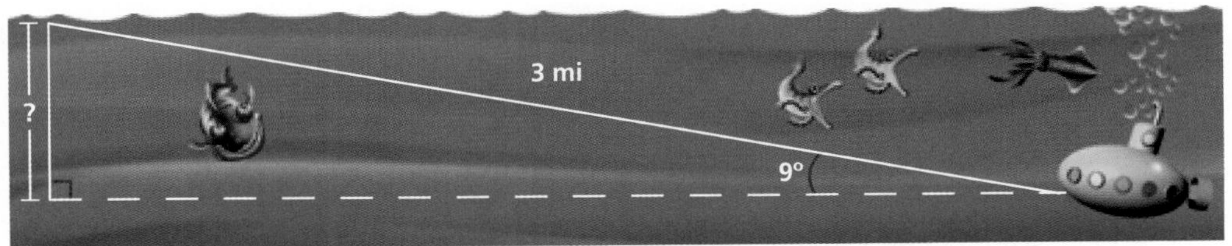


7. **Construction** A wheelchair ramp is to have an angle of 4.5° with the ground. The deck at the top of the ramp is 20 inches above ground level.
   a. Draw a diagram to illustrate the situation.
   b. How long should the ramp be? Round your answer to the nearest tenth of an inch.
   c. How far from the deck should the ramp begin? Round your answer to the nearest tenth of an inch.

8. **Navigation** The top of a lighthouse is 40 meters above sea level. The angle of elevation from a fishing boat to the top of the lighthouse is 20°. How far is the fishing boat from the base of the lighthouse? Round your answer to the nearest tenth of a meter.

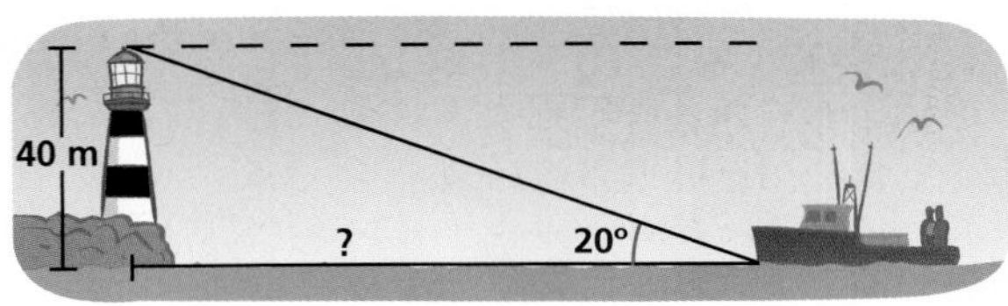

9. **Write About It** What would have to be true about the legs of a right triangle for an angle to have a tangent of 1? What would be the measure of that angle?

CHAPTER 12

# Study Guide: Review

## Vocabulary



**Complete the sentences below with vocabulary words from the list above.**

1. A(n) ___?___ is an algebraic expression whose numerator and denominator are polynomials.
2. A function whose rule is a quotient of polynomials in which the denominator has a degree of at least 1 is a(n) ___?___ .
3. A(n) ___?___ is an equation that contains one or more rational expressions.
4. A(n) ___?___ is a relationship that can be written in the form $y = \frac{k}{x}$, where $k$ is a nonzero constant.
5. A function is a ___?___ if its graph contains one or more jumps, breaks, or holes.

## 12-1 Inverse Variation *(pp. 851–857)*

MA.A.2, MA.A.2.1, MA.A.2.2

### EXAMPLE

- **Write and graph the inverse variation in which $y = 2$ when $x = 3$.**

$y = \frac{k}{x}$ *Use the form $y = \frac{k}{x}$.*

$2 = \frac{k}{3}$ *Substitute known values.*

$6 = k$ *Multiply by 3 to find the value of k.*

$y = \frac{6}{x}$ *Substitute 6 for k in $y = \frac{k}{x}$.*

| x | −6 | −3 | −2 | −1 | 0 | 1 | 2 | 3 | 6 |
|---|---|---|---|---|---|---|---|---|---|
| y | −1 | −2 | −3 | −6 | und. | 6 | 3 | 2 | 1 |

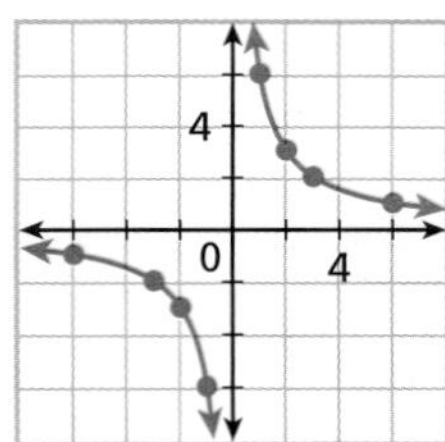


*Make a table of values and plot the points.*

### EXERCISES

**Tell whether each relationship represents an inverse variation. Explain.**

6.

| x | y |
|---|---|
| 4 | −3 |
| −12 | 1 |
| 6 | −2 |

7.

| x | y |
|---|---|
| 2 | 4 |
| 6 | 8 |
| 10 | 12 |

8. Write and graph the inverse variation in which $y = 4$ when $x = -1$.
9. Write and graph the inverse variation in which $y = \frac{1}{2}$ when $x = 2$.
10. Let $x_1 = 5$, $y_1 = -6$, and $x_2 = 2$. Let $y$ vary inversely as $x$. Find $y_2$.
11. The number of fleet vehicles a town can afford to buy varies inversely as the price of each car. If the town can afford 3 cars priced at $22,000 each, what must the price of a car be in order for the town to purchase 5 of them?

## 12-2 Rational Functions *(pp. 858–865)*

MA.A.4.2, MA.A.4.3

### EXAMPLE

■ **Graph the function $y = \frac{1}{x+1} + 3$.**

Since the numerator is 1, use the asymptotes and translate $y = \frac{1}{x}$.

Find the asymptotes.

$x = -1$    *$b = -1$*

$y = 3$    *$c = 3$*

Graph the asymptotes. Draw smooth curves to show the translation.

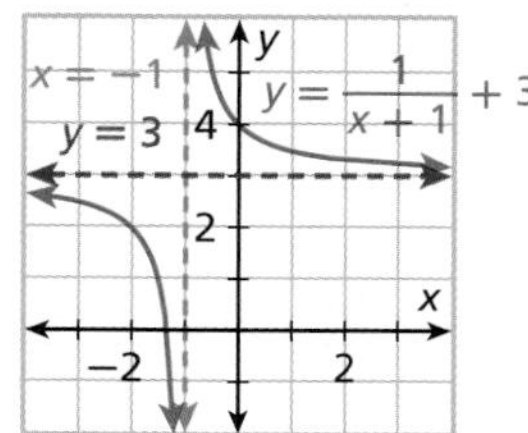


### EXERCISES

**Identify the excluded values and the vertical and horizontal asymptotes for each rational function.**

**12.** $y = \frac{1}{x+4}$

**13.** $y = \frac{1}{x+1} + 3$

**14.** $y = \frac{-5}{2x+6} - 4$

**15.** $y = \frac{2}{4x-7} + 5$

**Graph each function.**

**16.** $y = \frac{3}{x}$

**17.** $y = \frac{4}{x+5}$

**18.** $y = \frac{1}{x+4} - 2$

**19.** $y = \frac{1}{x-6} + 2$

**20.** A rectangle has an area of 24 $cm^2$. If $x$ represents the width, then $y = \frac{24}{x}$ represents the length $y$. Describe the reasonable domain and range values and graph the function.

## 12-3 Simplifying Rational Expressions *(pp. 866–872)*

MA.A.1.1, MA.A.1.3

### EXAMPLE

**Simplify the rational expression, if possible. Identify any excluded values.**

■ $\frac{x-1}{x^2+2x-3}$

$\frac{x-1}{(x+3)(x-1)}$    *Factor the denominator.*

$\frac{\cancel{x-1}^{1}}{(x+3)\cancel{(x-1)}^{1}}$    *Divide out common factors.*

$\frac{1}{(x+3)}$    *Simplify.*

Identify the excluded values.

$x^2 + 2x - 3 = 0$    *To find excluded values, set the denominator equal to 0.*

$(x+3)(x-1) = 0$    *Factor.*

$x + 3 = 0$ or $x - 1 = 0$    *Use the Zero Product Property.*

$x = -3$ or $x = 1$    *Solve each equation for x.*

The excluded values are −3 and 1.

### EXERCISES

**Find any excluded values of each rational expression.**

**21.** $\frac{3}{5p}$

**22.** $\frac{-2}{r-7}$

**23.** $\frac{t}{t^2-t}$

**24.** $\frac{-4}{x^2-4x-5}$

**25.** $\frac{x-1}{x^2-25}$

**26.** $\frac{x+4}{x^2-11x+28}$

**Simplify each rational expression, if possible. Identify any excluded values.**

**27.** $\frac{7r^2}{21r^3}$

**28.** $\frac{3k^2}{6k^3-9k^2}$

**29.** $\frac{x+6}{x^2+4x-12}$

**30.** $\frac{2x-6}{9-x^2}$

**31.** $\frac{3x+15}{x^2+4x-5}$

**32.** $\frac{x^2+9x+18}{x^2+x-30}$

**33.** What is the ratio of the area of the square to the area of the circle?

x

## 12-4 Multiplying and Dividing Rational Expressions *(pp. 878–884)*  MA.A.1.1, MA.A.1.3

### EXAMPLES

■ **Multiply. Simplify your answer.**

$\frac{5x^3-10x}{4x}\cdot\frac{6x^2}{7x^4-14x^2}$

$\frac{5x(x^2-2)}{4x}\cdot\frac{6x^2}{7x^2(x^2-2)}$ *Factor.*

$\frac{5\cancel{x}^1\cancel{(x^2-2)}^1}{\cancel{4}^2\cancel{x}^1}\cdot\frac{\cancel{6}^3\cancel{x^2}^1}{7\cancel{x^2}^1\cancel{(x^2-2)}^1}$ *Divide out common factors.*

$\frac{15}{14}$ *Simplify.*

■ **Divide. Simplify your answer.**

$\frac{32x^2y^2}{7z}\div\frac{2xy^2}{28xz^3}$

$\frac{32x^2y^2}{7z}\cdot\frac{28xz^3}{2xy^2}$ *Multiply by the reciprocal.*

$\frac{\cancel{32}^{16}x^2\cancel{y^2}^1}{\cancel{7}^1\cancel{z}^1}\cdot\frac{\cancel{28}^4\cancel{x}^1\cancel{z^3}^2}{\cancel{2}^1\cancel{x}^1\cancel{y^2}^1}$ *Divide out common factors.*

$64x^2z^2$ *Simplify.*

### EXERCISES

**Multiply. Simplify your answer.**

**34.** $\frac{2b}{3b-6}\cdot(b^2-b-2)$ **35.** $\frac{4x}{3x+9}\cdot(x^2-9)$

**36.** $\frac{5ab^2}{2ab}\cdot\frac{3a^2b^2}{a^2b}$ **37.** $\frac{3c}{2d}\cdot\frac{-4c^2d}{8d^2}$

**38.** $\frac{b+2}{2b^2+12b}\cdot\frac{b^2+2b-24}{b^2-16}$

**39.** $\frac{n^2-n-12}{n^2+2n-24}\cdot\frac{n^2+3n+2}{n^2-4n-21}$

**Divide. Simplify your answer.**

**40.** $\frac{3b+b^2}{b+3b^2}\div\frac{b^2-9}{3b+1}$ **41.** $\frac{7}{y}\div\frac{21}{y^3}$

**42.** $16n^3\div\frac{4m^2n}{3mn}$ **43.** $\frac{x^2+2x-3}{4x}\div\frac{x^2-4}{x}$

**44.** A bag contains red and blue marbles. It has 8 more red marbles than blue marbles. Veronica reaches into the bag and selects one marble at random. She sets the marble aside and then selects another. What is the probability that she selects two red marbles?

## 12-5 Adding and Subtracting Rational Expressions *(pp. 885–891)*  MA.A.1.1, MA.A.1.3, MA.N.1

### EXAMPLES

**Add or subtract. Simplify your answer.**

■ $\frac{7x}{3xy}-\frac{x^2-3x}{3xy}$

$\frac{7x-(x^2-3x)}{3xy}$ *Subtract numerators.*

$\frac{7x-x^2+3x}{3xy}$ *Distribute.*

$\frac{10x-x^2}{3xy}$ *Simplify.*

■ $\frac{3w}{w-5}+\frac{4}{w^2-2w-15}$

$\frac{3w}{w-5}+\frac{4}{(w-5)(w+3)}$ *Factor to find the LCD.*

$\frac{3w(w+3)}{(w-5)(w+3)}+\frac{4}{(w-5)(w+3)}$ *Write each expression using the LCD.*

$\frac{3w^2+9w}{(w-5)(w+3)}+\frac{4}{(w-5)(w+3)}$

$\frac{3w^2+9w+4}{(w-5)(w+3)}$ *Add and simplify.*

### EXERCISES

**Find the LCM of the given expressions.**

**45.** $5a^2b,\ 10ab^2$ **46.** $2x^2-6x,\ 5x-15$

**Add or subtract. Simplify your answer.**

**47.** $\frac{b^2}{2b}+\frac{8}{2b}$ **48.** $\frac{3x^2-4}{x^2-2}+\frac{2x}{x^2-2}$

**49.** $\frac{8p}{p^2-4p+2}-\frac{2}{p^2-4p+2}$

**50.** $\frac{3b+4}{7-b}-\frac{5-2b}{7-b}$ **51.** $\frac{n-5}{n^2-1}-\frac{n+5}{n^2-1}$

**52.** $\frac{3}{5m}+\frac{m+2}{10m^2}$ **53.** $\frac{h^2+2h}{h-5}-\frac{3h-1}{5-h}$

**54.** A scout troop hikes 10 miles to the top of a mountain. Because the return trip is downhill, the troop is able to hike 3 times faster on their way down. Let *r* represent the troop's rate to the mountaintop. Write and simplify an expression for the round-trip hiking time in terms of *r*.

## 12-6 Dividing Polynomials *(pp. 893–899)*

### EXAMPLES

**Divide.**

■ $(6x^4 - 9x^3 + 3x^2) \div 3x$

$\frac{6x^4 - 9x^3 + 3x^2}{3x}$ *Write as a rational expression.*

$\frac{6x^4}{3x} - \frac{9x^3}{3x} + \frac{3x^2}{3x}$ *Divide each term separately.*

$\frac{\cancel{6}^2 x^{\cancel{4}^3}}{\cancel{3}^1 x^1} - \frac{\cancel{9}^3 x^{\cancel{3}^2}}{\cancel{3}^1 x^1} + \frac{\cancel{3}^1 x^{\cancel{2}^1}}{\cancel{3}^1 x^1}$ *Divide out common factors.*

$2x^3 - 3x^2 + x$ *Simplify.*

■ $(4x^3 - 2x^2 + 5x - 1) \div (x - 2)$

$$
\begin{array}{r}
4x^2 + 6x + 17 \\
x - 2\,\overline{)\,4x^3 - 2x^2 + 5x - 1} \\
-(4x^3 - 8x^2) \qquad\qquad \\
\hline
6x^2 + 5x \qquad \\
-(6x^2 - 12x) \qquad \\
\hline
17x - 1 \\
-(17x - 34) \\
\hline
33
\end{array}
$$

$4x^2 + 6x + 17 + \frac{33}{x - 2}$

### EXERCISES

**Divide.**

55. $(4n^3 - 6n^2 - 10n) \div 2n$
56. $(-5x^3 + 10x - 25) \div (-5x^2)$
57. $\frac{x^2 - 8x - 20}{x - 10}$
58. $\frac{6n^2 - 13n - 5}{2n - 5}$
59. $\frac{h^2 - 144}{h - 12}$
60. $\frac{9x^2 + 12x + 4}{3x + 2}$
61. $\frac{m^2 - 2m - 24}{m + 4}$
62. $\frac{3m^2 + m - 4}{m - 1}$

**Divide using long division.**

63. $(x^2 + 5x + 6) \div (x + 3)$
64. $(x^2 + x - 30) \div (x - 5)$
65. $(p^2 + 2p - 8) \div (p + 4)$
66. $(2x^2 + 3x - 5) \div (x + 2)$
67. $(2n^2 - 3n + 1) \div (n - 5)$
68. $(3b^3 - 4b + 2) \div (b - 2)$
69. $(2x^2 - 4x^3 + 3x) \div (x + 2)$

## 12-7 Solving Rational Equations *(pp. 900–905)*

### EXAMPLE

**Solve. Identify any extraneous solutions.**

■ $\frac{3}{x + 3} - 4 = \frac{2}{x}$

$$x(x + 3)\left(\frac{3}{x + 3} - 4\right) = x(x + 3)\frac{2}{x}$$

$$x(x + 3)\left(\frac{3}{x + 3}\right) - x(x + 3)4 = x(x + 3)\frac{2}{x}$$

$$x\cancel{(x + 3)}^1\left(\frac{3}{\cancel{x + 3}^1}\right) - x(x + 3)4 = \cancel{x}^1(x + 3)\frac{2}{\cancel{x}^1}$$

$$3x - 4x(x + 3) = 2(x + 3)$$

$$3x - 4x^2 - 12x = 2x + 6$$

$$0 = 4x^2 + 11x + 6$$

$$0 = (4x + 3)(x + 2)$$

$4x + 3 = 0$ or $x + 2 = 0$

$x = -\frac{3}{4}$ or $x = -2$ *$x \neq -3$ or 0, so there are no extraneous solutions.*

### EXERCISES

**Solve. Identify any extraneous solutions.**

70. $-4 = \frac{3}{r}$
71. $\frac{6}{7} = \frac{x}{2}$
72. $\frac{6}{b} = \frac{-5}{3 + b}$
73. $\frac{7}{3y^2} = \frac{-2}{y}$
74. $\frac{2}{x - 1} = \frac{3x}{1 - x}$
75. $\frac{2x}{x^2} + \frac{1}{x^2} = 3$
76. $\frac{2}{3} + \frac{4}{x} = \frac{6}{3x}$
77. $-\frac{1}{3x} + \frac{x}{4} = -\frac{1}{12x}$
78. $\frac{2}{3b} + 4 = \frac{1}{3b}$
79. $\frac{4}{x - 4} = \frac{8}{x^2 - 16}$
80. $\frac{5x - 10}{x + 1} = \frac{x}{2}$
81. $\frac{2x}{x + 3} + \frac{x}{4} = \frac{3}{x + 3}$
82. $\frac{9m}{m - 5} = 7 - \frac{3}{m - 5}$
83. $\frac{x - 4}{x^2 - 4} = \frac{-2}{x - 2}$

CHAPTER 12

# CHAPTER TEST

1. Write and graph the inverse variation in which $y = -4$ when $x = 2$.
2. The number of posters the Spanish Club can buy varies inversely as the cost of each poster. The club can buy 15 posters that cost \$2.60 each. How many posters can the club buy if they cost \$3.25 each?

**Identify the excluded values and the vertical and horizontal asymptotes for each rational function.**

3. $y = \frac{3}{x+1}$
4. $y = \frac{1}{2x-1} + 5$
5. $y = \frac{1}{x+3} - 3$

**Simplify each rational expression, if possible. Identify any excluded values.**

6. $\frac{2b}{4b^2}$
7. $\frac{x^2 - 16}{x^2 + 3x - 4}$
8. $\frac{b^2 - 2b - 15}{5 - b}$
9. $\frac{x^2 + 4x - 5}{x^2 - 25}$

**Multiply. Simplify your answer.**

10. $\frac{-4}{x^2 - 9} \cdot (x - 3)$
11. $\frac{2a^2b^2}{5b^3} \cdot \frac{15a^2b}{8a^4}$
12. $\frac{x^2 - x - 12}{x^2 - 16} \cdot \frac{x^2 + x - 12}{x^2 + 3x + 2}$

**Divide. Simplify your answer.**

13. $\frac{4x^2y^4}{3xy^2} \div \frac{12xy}{15x^3y^2}$
14. $\frac{3b^2 - 6b}{2b^3 + 3b^2} \div \frac{2b - 4}{8b + 12}$
15. $\frac{x^2 + 2x - 15}{x^2 - 9} \div \frac{x^2 - 25}{x^2 + 3x + 2}$

**Add or subtract. Simplify your answer.**

16. $\frac{b^2 + 3}{5b} + \frac{4}{5b}$
17. $\frac{5x - 2}{x^2 + 2} - \frac{2x}{x^2 + 2}$
18. $\frac{2}{3x^2} - \frac{5 - 2x}{3x^2}$
19. $\frac{3m}{2m^2} + \frac{1}{2m}$
20. $\frac{3x}{2x + 4} - \frac{1}{x + 2}$
21. $\frac{y^2 + 4}{y - 3} + \frac{y^2}{3 - y}$

**Divide.**

22. $(8t^2 - 2t) \div 2t$
23. $\frac{3x^2 + 2x - 8}{x + 2}$
24. $\frac{k^2 - 2k - 35}{k + 5}$

**Divide using long division.**

25. $(2w^2 + 5w - 12) \div (w + 4)$
26. $(x^2 - 4x + 9) \div (x + 2)$
27. The area of a rectangle can be modeled by $A(x) = x^3 - 1$. The length is $x - 1$.
    a. Find a polynomial to represent the width of the rectangle.
    b. Find the width when $x$ is 6 cm.

**Solve. Identify any extraneous solutions.**

28. $\frac{2}{x - 1} = \frac{9}{2x - 3}$
29. $\frac{3}{n - 1} = \frac{n}{n + 4}$
30. $\frac{2}{n + 2} = \frac{n - 4}{n^2 - 4}$
31. Julio can wash and wax the family car in 2 hours. It takes Leo 3 hours to wash and wax the same car. How long will it take them to wash and wax the car if they work together?

CHAPTER 12

# College Entrance Exam Practice

## FOCUS ON SAT MATHEMATICS SUBJECT TESTS

The topics covered on each SAT Mathematics Subject Test vary only slightly each time the test is given. Find out the general distribution of test items across topics, and then identify the areas you need to concentrate on while studying.

**To prepare for the SAT Math Subject Tests, start reviewing material several months before your test date. Take sample tests to find the areas you need to focus on. You are not expected to have studied all topics on the test.**

**You may want to time yourself as you take this practice test. It should take you about 6 minutes to complete.**

**1.** Which set of ordered pairs satisfies an inverse variation?

**(A)** $(6, 3)$ and $(8, 4)$

**(B)** $(2, -3)$ and $(4, 5)$

**(C)** $(4, -2)$ and $(-5, 10)$

**(D)** $(2, 6)$ and $(-3, -4)$

**(E)** $\left(4, \frac{1}{4}\right)$ and $\left(-4, \frac{1}{4}\right)$

**2.** If $\dfrac{3}{x+3} = \dfrac{7x}{x^2-9}$, what is $x$?

**(A)** $-12$

**(B)** $-3$

**(C)** $-\dfrac{9}{4}$

**(D)** $\dfrac{9}{4}$

**(E)** 3

**3.** What is $h$ if $(x^3 + 2x^2 - 4x + h) \div (x + 1)$ has a remainder of 15?

**(A)** $-10$

**(B)** $-5$

**(C)** 5

**(D)** 10

**(E)** 20

**4.** The graph of which function is shown?

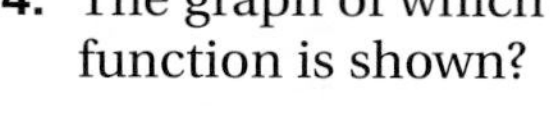

**(A)** $f(x) = \dfrac{2}{x+4} + 1$

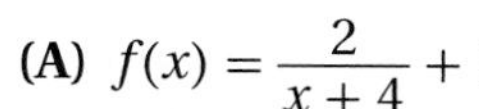

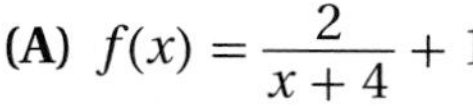

**(B)** $f(x) = \dfrac{4}{x+2} - 1$

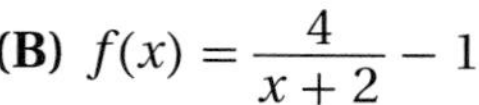

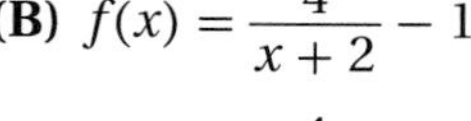

**(C)** $f(x) = \dfrac{4}{x-2} + 1$

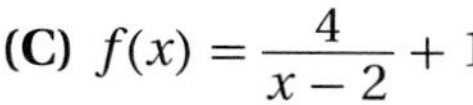

**(D)** $f(x) = \dfrac{4}{x-2} - 1$

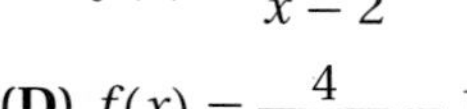

**(E)** $f(x) = \dfrac{2}{x-4} + 1$

**5.** Which function has the same graph as $f(x) = \dfrac{x^2 - 4x - 5}{x^2 - 3x - 10}$ except at $x = 5$?

**(A)** $g(x) = \dfrac{x-1}{x-2}$

**(B)** $g(x) = \dfrac{x+1}{x+2}$

**(C)** $g(x) = \dfrac{x+1}{(x-5)(x+2)}$

**(D)** $g(x) = \dfrac{(x+5)(x-1)}{x+2}$

**(E)** $g(x) = \dfrac{(x-5)(x+1)}{x-2}$

CHAPTER 12

# TEST TACKLER

### Standardized Test Strategies

## Multiple Choice: Choose Combinations of Answers

Some multiple-choice test items require selecting a combination of correct answers. The correct response is the most complete option available. To solve this type of test item, determine if each statement is true or false. Then choose the option that includes each correct statement.

### EXAMPLE 1

**Which of the following has an excluded value of −5?**

**I.** $\frac{5}{x-5}$

**II.** $\frac{8x^2+36x-20}{2(x+5)}$

**III.** $\frac{x^2-10}{5x+25} \cdot \frac{5}{x+10}$

**IV.** $\frac{2(x+2)}{2x^2+12x+10}$

Ⓐ I only

Ⓑ II and III

Ⓒ II, III, and IV

Ⓓ III and IV

*Look at each statement separately and determine whether it is true. You can keep track of which statements are true in a table.*

| Statement | True/False |
|---|---|
| I | False |
| II | True |
| III | True |
| IV | True |

**Statement I**
The denominator, $x - 5$, equals 0 when $x = 5$.

*Statement I does not answer the question, so it is false.*

**Statement II**
The denominator, $2(x + 5)$, equals 0 when $x = -5$.

*Statement II does answer the question, so it is true.*

**Statement III**
The denominator, $(5x + 25)(x + 10)$, equals 0 when $x = -5$ or $x = -10$.

*Statement III does answer the question, so it is true.*

**Statement IV**
The denominator, $2x^2 + 12x + 10$, can be factored as $2(x + 5)(x + 1)$. This expression equals 0 when $x = -5$ or $x = -1$.

*Statement IV does answer the question, so it is true.*

Statements II, III, and IV are all true. Option C is the correct response because it includes all the true statements.

Options B and D contain some of the true statements, but option C is the **most complete** answer.

**Evaluate all of the statements before deciding on an answer choice. Make a table to keep track of whether each statement is true or false.**

**Read each test item and answer the questions that follow.**

**Item A**

**Which dimensions represent a rectangle that has an area equivalent to the expression $2x^2 + 18x + 16$?**

I. $\ell = x + 8$

$w = 2(x + 1)$

II. $\ell = 2x + 2$

$w = \dfrac{x^2 + 3x - 40}{x - 5}$

III. $\ell = x + 2$

$w = \dfrac{(2x + 2)(x + 4)}{1} \cdot \dfrac{(3x - 1)}{(3x^2 - 11x - 4)}$

(A) I only

(B) III only

(C) I and II

(D) I, II, and III

1. How do you determine the area of a rectangle?
2. Daisy realized that the area of rectangle I was equivalent to the given area and selected option A as her response. Do you agree? Explain your reasoning.
3. Write a simplified expression for the width of rectangle II.
4. Explain each step for determining the area of rectangle III.
5. If rectangle II has an area equivalent to the given expression, then which options can you eliminate?

**Item B**

**Which expression is undefined for $x = 3$ or $x = -2$?**

I. $2x + 12 \cdot \dfrac{4}{2(x - 3)(x + 6)}$

II. $\dfrac{9x - 1}{x^2 + 3}$

III. $\dfrac{(x - 2)}{(x + 2)(x - 1)}$

IV. $\dfrac{14}{x^2 - x - 6}$

(F) I, III, and IV

(G) I and II

(H) III and IV

(J) I and IV

6. When is an expression undefined?
7. Henry determined that statement I is undefined when $x = 3$. He decides it is an incorrect answer because the expression is defined when $x = -2$. Should he select option H by process of elimination? Explain your reasoning.
8. Make a table to determine the correct response.

**Item C**

**Which rational function has a graph with a horizontal asymptote of $y = 4$?**

I. $y = \dfrac{-4}{x}$

II. $y = \dfrac{1}{x} + 4$

III. $y = \dfrac{1}{x - 4}$

IV. $y = -\dfrac{1}{x} + 4$

(A) I and III

(B) II only

(C) I and II

(D) II and IV

9. Where does the horizontal asymptote of the function in statement I occur?
10. Using your answer from Problem 9, which option(s) can you eliminate? Explain your reasoning.
11. Look at the options remaining. Which statement would be best to check next? Explain your reasoning.

go.hrw.com
State Test Practice Online
KEYWORD: MA7 TestPrep

## CUMULATIVE ASSESSMENT, CHAPTERS 1–12

### Multiple Choice

**1.** The number of packages that a freight elevator can hold varies inversely as the weight of each package. If the elevator can carry 14 packages that weigh 90 pounds each, how many packages can the elevator carry if each package weighs 52.5 pounds?

**A** 8 **C** 20

**B** 16 **D** 24

**2.** Terrence is considering investing \$2300 at a rate of 4.5% compounded annually. After 6 years, what will be his balance to the nearest cent?

**A** \$2995.20 **C** \$3072.44

**B** \$3033.82 **D** \$3111.06

**3.** Which function is shown in the graph?

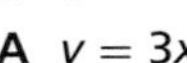
**A** $y = 3x$

**B** $y = \frac{x}{3}$

**C** $y = \sqrt{x} + 3$

**D** $y = \frac{1}{x} + 3$

**4.** The drama club needs to raise at least \$1400 for a field trip. The club was given \$150 by the school administration. Club members are selling key chains for \$5 each. Which inequality represents the number of key chains $k$ that the drama club needs to sell to go on its field trip?

**A** $150 + 5k \geq 1400$

**B** $5k - 150 \geq 1400$

**C** $5k + 150 \leq 1400$

**D** $150 \leq 5k + 1400$

**5.** Simplify: $(12 + \sqrt{14})(16 + \sqrt{18})$

**A** $192 + 36\sqrt{2}$

**B** $192 + 16\sqrt{14} + 6\sqrt{7} + 36\sqrt{2}$

**C** $192 + 6\sqrt{14} + 16\sqrt{7} + 36\sqrt{2}$

**D** $192 + 16\sqrt{14} + 36\sqrt{7} + 6\sqrt{2}$

**6.** Trina is buying flower pots. Two large flower pots cost the same as five small flower pots. The total cost of 11 large and 11 small flower pots is \$115.50. What is the cost of a large flower pot?

**A** \$3.00 **C** \$10.00

**B** \$7.50 **D** \$13.50

**7.** A bag contains red, white, and black tiles. There are two more red tiles than black tiles, and there are two more black tiles than white tiles. There are 24 tiles in total. What is the probability of randomly selecting a red tile, to the nearest hundredth?

**A** 0.58 **C** 0.33

**B** 0.42 **D** 0.25

**8.** What is the value of $f(x) = -11x^2 + 2x - 11$ when $x = -3$?

**A** $-116$ **C** 82

**B** $-82$ **D** 116

**9.** Which of the following has a slope of $-3$?

**A**
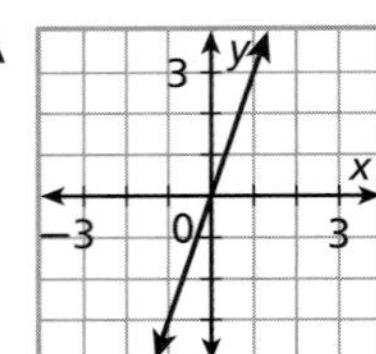


**C**
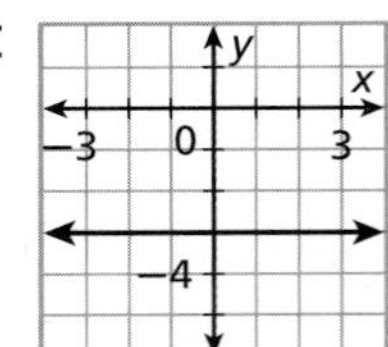


**B**
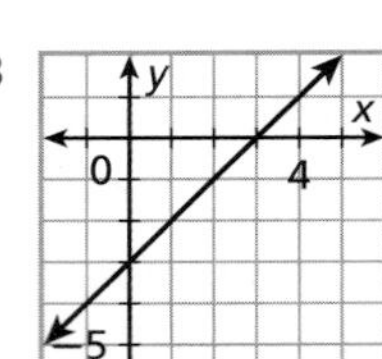


**D**
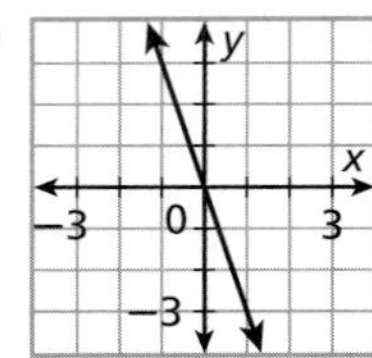


**10.** What is $(-12x^6 + x) \div (-4x^2)$?

**A** $3x^3 - \frac{1}{4x}$

**B** $3x^4 - \frac{1}{4x}$

**C** $3x^5$

**D** $3x^4 + x$

An extra minute spent checking your answers can result in a better test score.

**11.** Abe flips two coins. What is the probability of both coins landing heads up?

A $\frac{1}{2}$ C $\frac{1}{8}$

B $\frac{1}{4}$ D $\frac{1}{16}$

**12.** Which set of ordered pairs satisfies a linear function?

A

| x | −2 | 0 | 1 | 3 | 4 |
|---|---|---|---|---|---|
| y | −4 | 2 | 5 | 11 | 14 |

B

| x | −3 | −1 | 0 | 2 | 3 |
|---|---|---|---|---|---|
| y | 23 | 3 | 2 | 18 | 35 |

C

| x | −2 | −1 | 0 | 1 | 2 |
|---|---|---|---|---|---|
| y | 12 | 3 | 0 | 3 | 12 |

D

| x | −2 | 0 | 1 | 2 | 4 |
|---|---|---|---|---|---|
| y | −16 | 0 | 2 | 16 | 128 |

**13.** Which function describes the line with the least slope?

A $4x + 9y = 12$

B $12x - 4y = 9$

C $12x + 9y = 4$

D $4x - 12y = 9$

**14.** Which situation can be modeled by the function $y = \frac{140}{x}$?

A The cost of attending a ski trip is $140 for each person who attends.

B The area of a rectangle with a width of 140 meters varies directly as its length.

C The cost per person of a boat rental is $140 divided by the number of people.

D Attendance at this year's concert was 140 more people than at last year's concert.

**15.** Solve the quadratic equation $5x^2 - 30x - 35 = 0$.

A $x = -5$ or $x = 35$

B $x = -5$ or $x = 7$

C $x = -1$ or $x = 7$

D $x = 1$ or $x = -7$

**16.** What is the constant of variation if $y$ varies inversely as $x$ and $y = 3$ when $x = 6$?

A 2 C 15

B 3 D 18

## *STANDARDIZED TEST PREP*

## Short Response

**S1.** Mr. Lui wrote $\frac{15 - 5x}{x^2 - 9x + 18}$ on the board.

**a.** Explain what kind of expression this is.

**b.** Simplify the expression. Show your work.

**c.** Identify any excluded values.

**S2.** Describe the similarities and differences between the graph of $f(x) = x^2 + 4$ and the graph of $g(x) = \frac{1}{2}x^2 + 3$.

**S3.** What are 2 nonzero values of $b$ that will make $2x^2 - bx - 20$ factorable? Explain your answer.

**S4.** Brandee makes an hourly wage. In the last pay period, she earned $800 for regular hours and $240 for overtime hours. Her overtime rate of pay is 50% more per hour than her regular rate of pay $r$. Write and simplify an expression, in terms of $r$, that represents the number of hours $h$ Brandee worked in the pay period. Show your work.

## Extended Response

**E1.** Principal Farley has $200 to pay for some teachers to attend a technology conference. The company hosting the conference is allowing 2 teachers to attend for free. The number of teachers $y$ that can be sent to the conference is given by the function $y = \frac{200}{x} + 2$, where $x$ is the cost per teacher.

**a.** Describe the reasonable domain and range values for this function.

**b.** Identify the vertical and horizontal asymptotes.

**c.** Graph the function.

**d.** Give two whole-number solutions to the equation and describe what they mean in the context of this situation.

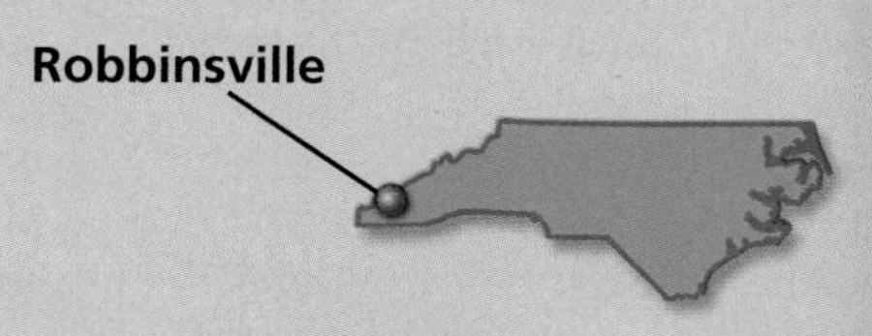


## North Carolina Agriculture

Agriculture plays a key role in both the daily life and the economy of North Carolina. More than 20% of the state's workers are employed by the agriculture industry, and the state is among the nation's top producers of sweet potatoes, cucumbers, and cotton. Farms account for nearly 9 million acres of the state's land.

**1.** As in many other states, the number of farms in North Carolina has decreased in recent years. The number of farms in the state (in thousands) can be modeled by the function $f(x) = 56.7(0.977)^x$, where $x$ is the number of years after 2000. According to the model, by what percent does the number of farms decrease each year?

**2.** Using the model, how many farms were there in 2004? How does your answer compare to the actual number of farms shown in the diagram?

**3.** Graph the function.

**4.** Use the model to predict the number of farms in North Carolina in 2010.

**5.** Based on the model, in what year will the number of farms in North Carolina be less than 40,000 for the first time?

**Farms in North Carolina**

| 2001 | 2002 | 2003 | 2004 | 2005 |
|---|---|---|---|---|
| 55,000 | 54,200 | 53,500 | 52,000 | 50,000 |

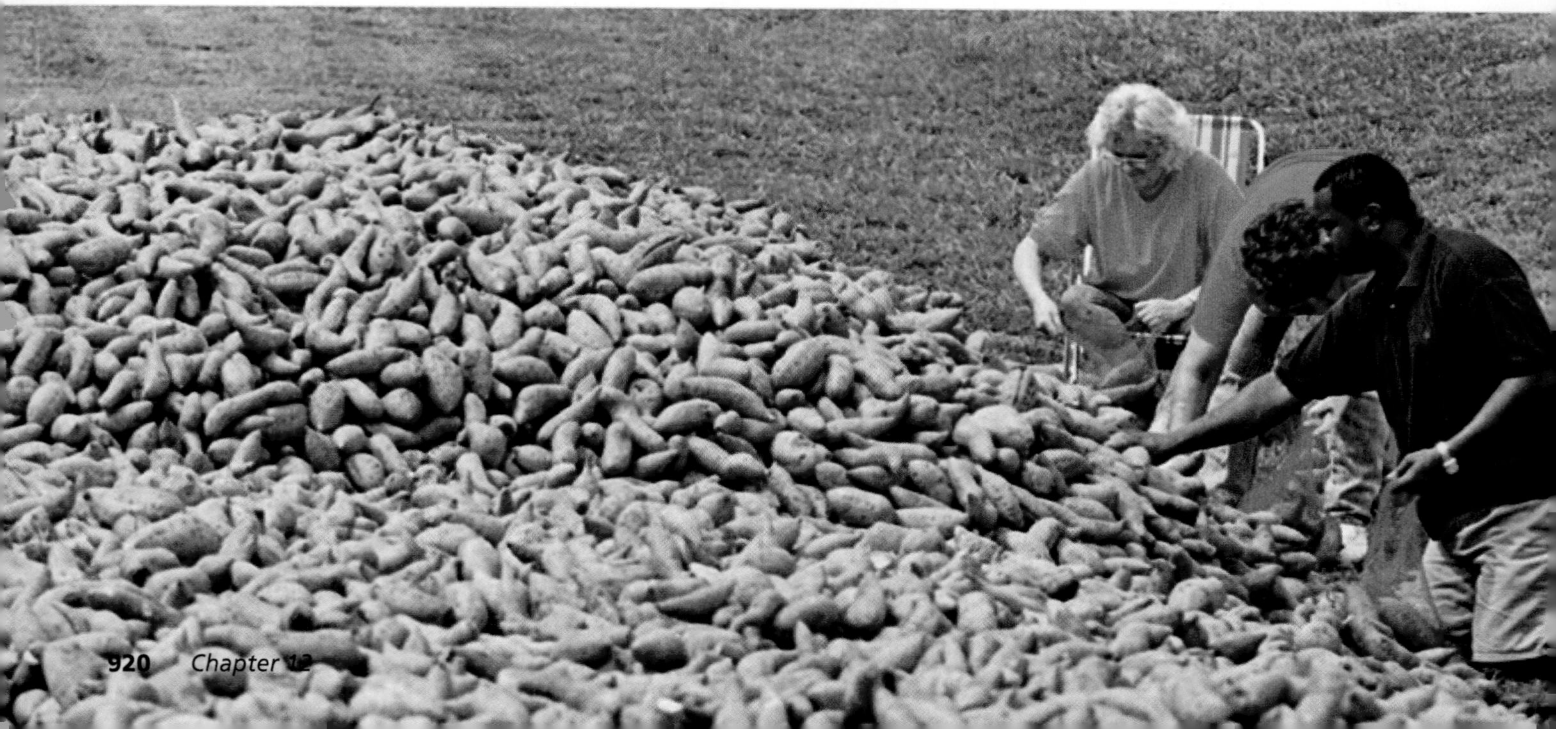

## Joyce Kilmer Memorial Forest

The Joyce Kilmer Memorial Forest, near Robbinsville, North Carolina, is home to one of the largest tracts of old-growth trees in the eastern United States. Many of the poplars, chestnuts, and oaks are more than 100 feet tall and more than 400 years old. A figure-eight trail leads visitors through this enchanted world.

1. The table shows the time it takes to complete the trail in the Joyce Kilmer Memorial Forest at various average rates of speed. Is the relationship an inverse variation? Why or why not?
2. What is the total length of the trail in miles? (*Hint:* 5280 ft = 1 mi)
3. Write a function $f(x)$ that gives the time it takes to complete the trail at an average rate of $x$ feet per minute.
4. What is the constant of variation for your function?
5. What is a reasonable domain and range for your function?
6. Graph the function.
7. Suppose that you walk at an average rate of 300 ft/min. Can you complete the trail in less than 35 minutes? Explain.

**Joyce Kilmer Memorial Forest Trail**

| Average Rate (ft/min) | Time to Complete Trail (min) |
|---|---|
| 440 | 24 |
| 352 | 30 |
| 264 | 40 |
| 176 | 60 |

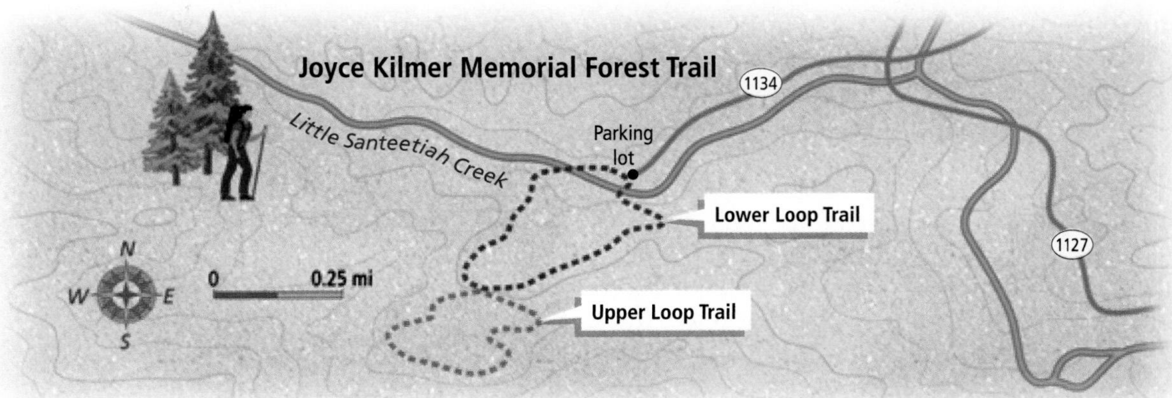

# Additional Topics in Geometry

# A-1 Understanding Points, Lines, and Planes

**Prep MA.G.1.2** Use geometric properties to identify geometric shapes. *Also* **Prep MA.G.2.1**

***Objectives***

Identify, name, and draw points, lines, segments, rays, angles, and planes.

Apply basic facts about points, lines, and planes.

***Vocabulary***

undefined term
point
line
plane
collinear
coplanar
segment
endpoint
ray
opposite rays
angle
postulate

The most basic figures in geometry are **undefined terms**, which cannot be defined by using other figures. The undefined terms *point, line,* and *plane* are the building blocks of geometry.

**Undefined Terms**

| TERM | NAME | DIAGRAM |
|---|---|---|
| A **point** names a location and has no size. It is represented by a dot. | A capital letter<br>point *P* | *P* • |
| A **line** is a straight path that has no thickness and extends forever. | A lowercase letter or two points on the line<br>line $\ell$, $\overleftrightarrow{XY}$ or $\overleftrightarrow{YX}$ | ←•X———•Y→ $\ell$ |
| A **plane** is a flat surface that has no thickness and extends forever. | A script capital letter or three points not on a line<br>plane $\mathcal{R}$ or plane *ABC* | parallelogram $\mathcal{R}$ with points A, B, C |

Points that lie on the same line are **collinear**. *K, L,* and *M* are collinear. *K, L,* and *N* are *noncollinear.* Points that lie in the same plane are **coplanar**. Otherwise they are *noncoplanar.*

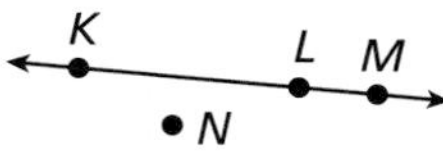


**EXAMPLE 1** **Naming Points, Lines, and Planes**

**Helpful Hint**

A plane may be named by any three noncollinear points on that plane. Plane *ABC* may also be named *BCA, CAB, CBA, ACB,* or *BAC.*

**A design of a stadium roof is shown at right.**

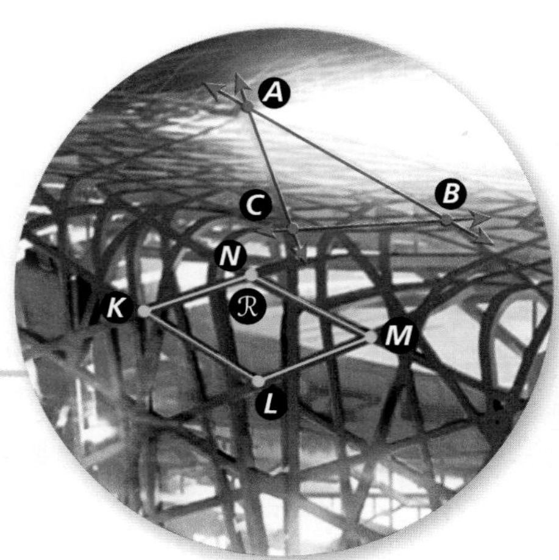


**A** **Name four coplanar points.**
*K, L, M,* and *N* all lie in plane $\mathcal{R}$.

**B** **Name three lines.**
$\overleftrightarrow{AB}$, $\overleftrightarrow{BC}$, and $\overleftrightarrow{CA}$

1. Use the diagram to name two planes.

## Segments, Rays, and Angles

| DEFINITION | NAME | DIAGRAM |
|---|---|---|
| A **segment**, or line segment, is the part of a line consisting of two points and all points between them. | The two endpoints $\overline{AB}$ or $\overline{BA}$ | A B |
| An **endpoint** is a point at one end of a segment or the starting point of a *ray.* | A capital letter *C* and *D* | C D |
| A **ray** is a part of a line that starts at an endpoint and extends forever in one direction. | Its endpoint and any other point on the ray $\overrightarrow{RS}$ | R S<br>S R |
| **Opposite rays** are two rays that have a common endpoint and form a line. | The common endpoint and any other point on each ray $\overrightarrow{EF}$ and $\overrightarrow{EG}$ | F E G |
| An **angle** is a figure formed by two rays, or sides, with a common endpoint called the **vertex**. | The vertex, or the vertex and one point on each side. In this case, the vertex must be the middle point. $\angle R$, $\angle SRT$, $\angle TRS$ | S R T |

EXAMPLE **2** **Drawing Segments, Rays, and Angles**

**Draw and label each of the following.**

**A** a segment with endpoints *U* and *V*

**B** opposite rays with a common endpoint *Q*

**C** an angle with vertex *V*

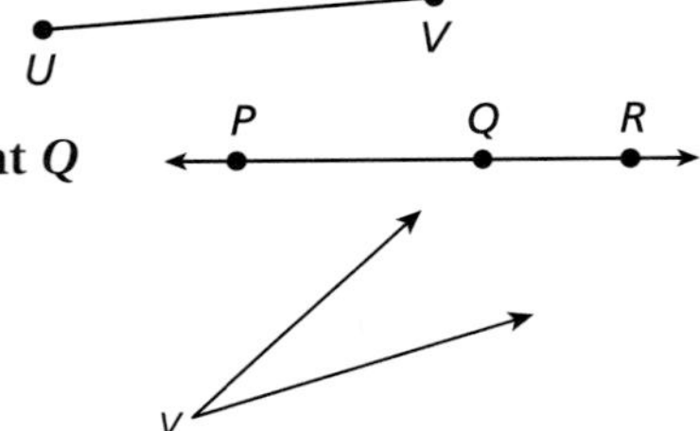

**2.** Draw and label a ray with endpoint *M* that contains *N*.

A **postulate**, or *axiom,* is a statement that is accepted as true without proof. Postulates about points, lines, and planes help describe geometric properties.

**Postulates** **Points, Lines, and Planes**

**1-1** Through any two points there is exactly one line.

**1-2** Through any three noncollinear points there is exactly one plane containing them.

**1-3** If two points lie in a plane, then the line containing those points lies in the plane.

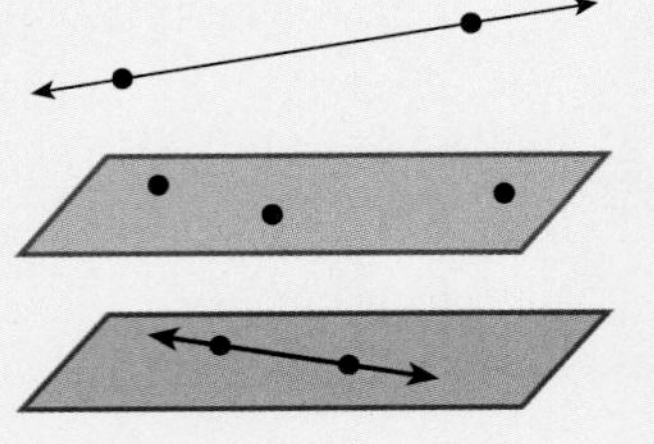

## EXAMPLE 3 Identifying Points and Lines in a Plane

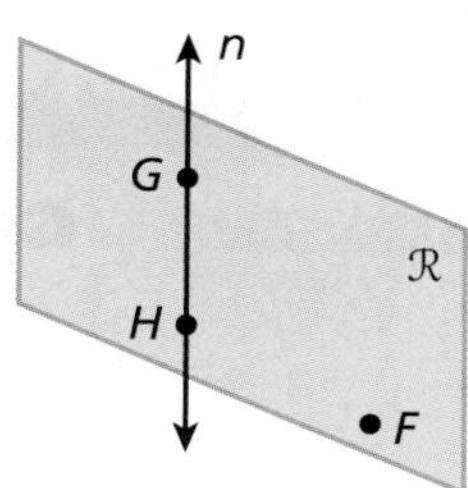


**Name a line that passes through two points.**

There is exactly one line $n$ passing through $G$ and $H$.

**3.** Name a plane that contains three noncollinear points.

Recall that a system of equations is a set of two or more equations containing two or more of the same variables. The coordinates of the solution of the system satisfy all equations in the system. These coordinates also locate the point where all the graphs of the equations in the system *intersect*.

An *intersection* is the set of all points that two or more figures have in common. The next two postulates describe intersections involving lines and planes.

**Postulates** — **Intersection of Lines and Planes**

| | |
|---|---|
| **1-4** | If two lines intersect, then they intersect in exactly one point. |
| **1-5** | If two planes intersect, then they intersect in exactly one line. |

Use a dashed line to show the hidden parts of any figure that you are drawing. A dashed line will indicate the part of the figure that is not seen.

## EXAMPLE  4 Representing Intersections

**Sketch a figure that shows each of the following.**

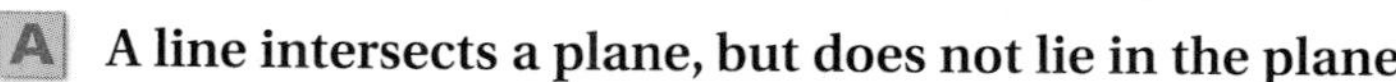

**A** **A line intersects a plane, but does not lie in the plane.**

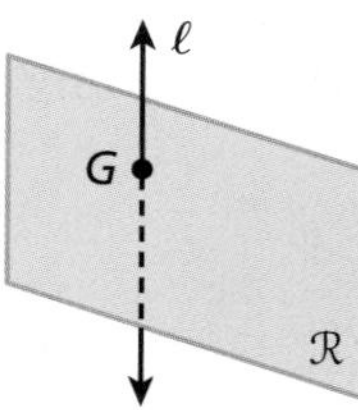


**B** **Two planes intersect in one line.**

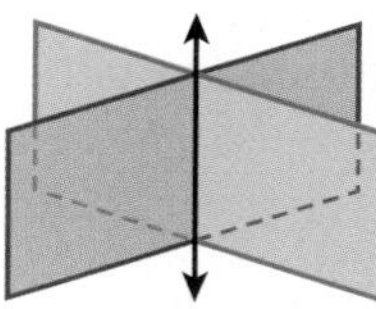

**4.** Sketch a figure that shows two lines intersect in one point in a plane, but only one of the lines lies in the plane.

# Exercises

Prep MA.G.1.2, Prep MA.G.2.1

## GUIDED PRACTICE

**Vocabulary Apply the vocabulary from this lesson to answer each question.**

1. Give an example from your classroom of three *collinear* points.
2. Make use of the fact that *endpoint* is a compound of *end* and *point* and name the *endpoint* of $\overrightarrow{ST}$.

SEE EXAMPLE 1 p. AT3

**Use the figure to name each of the following.**

3. five points
4. two lines
5. two planes
6. point on $\overleftrightarrow{BD}$

SEE EXAMPLE 2 p. AT4

**Draw and label each of the following.**

7. a segment with endpoints *M* and *N*
8. a ray with endpoint *F* that passes through *G*
9. angle *XYZ*

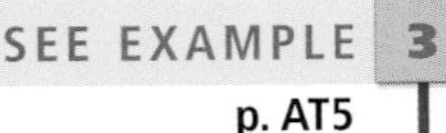

SEE EXAMPLE 3 p. AT5

**Use the figure to name each of the following.**

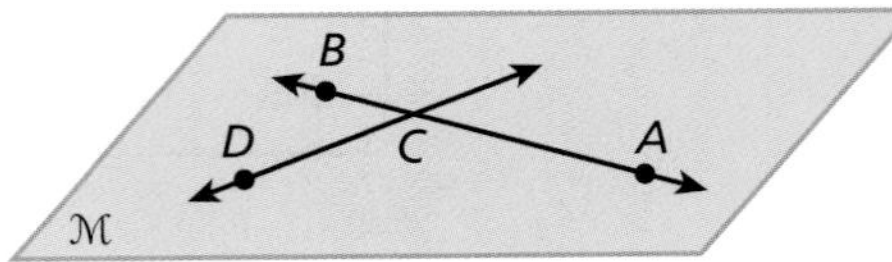


10. a line that contains *A* and *C*
11. a plane that contains *A, D,* and *C*
12. an angle

SEE EXAMPLE 4 p. AT5

**Sketch a figure that shows each of the following.**

13. three coplanar lines that intersect in a common point
14. two lines that do not intersect

## PRACTICE AND PROBLEM SOLVING

**Use the figure to name each of the following.**

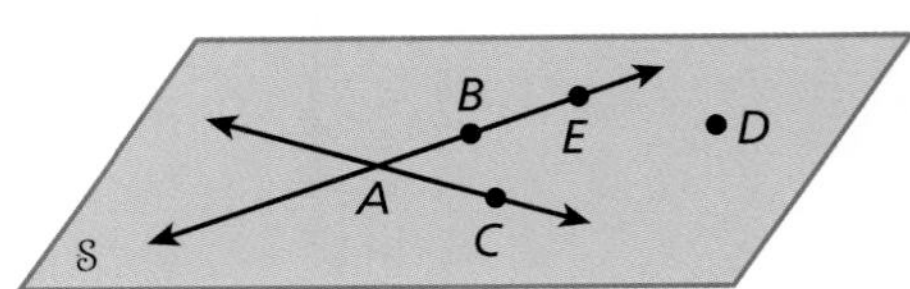


15. three collinear points
16. four coplanar points
17. a plane containing *E*

**Draw and label each of the following.**

18. a line containing *X* and *Y*
19. a pair of opposite rays that both contain *R*
20. angle *JKL*

**Use the figure to name each of the following.**

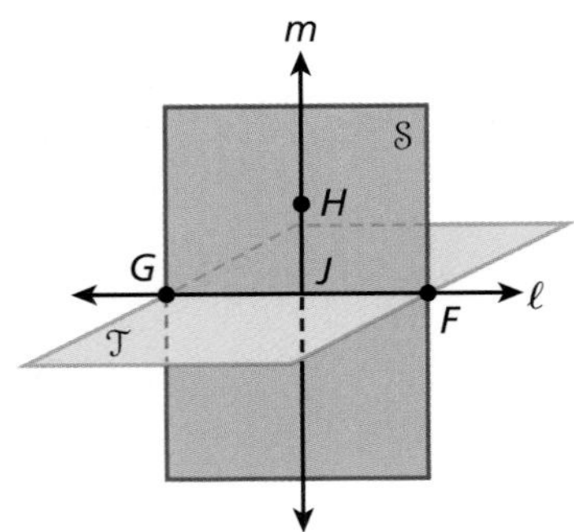


21. two points and a line that lie in plane $\mathcal{T}$
22. two planes that contain $\ell$

**Sketch a figure that shows each of the following.**

**23.** a line that intersects two nonintersecting planes

**24.** three coplanar lines that intersect in three different points

**Draw each of the following.**

**25.** plane $\mathcal{H}$ containing two lines that intersect at $M$

**26.** $\overleftrightarrow{ST}$ intersecting plane $\mathcal{M}$ at $R$

**Use the figure to name each of the following.**

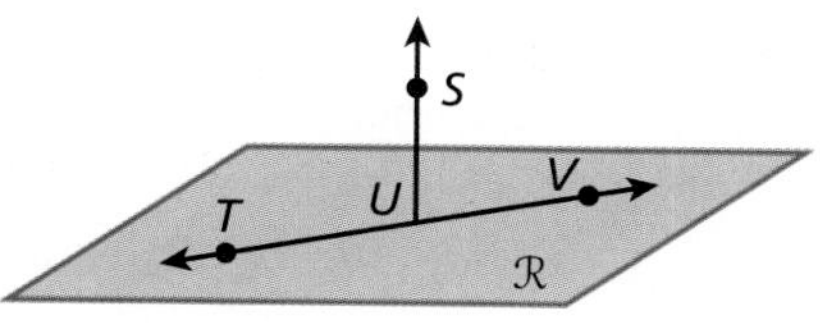


**27.** the intersection of $\overleftrightarrow{TV}$ and $\overrightarrow{US}$

**28.** the intersection of $\overrightarrow{US}$ and plane $\mathcal{R}$

**29.** the intersection of $\overline{TU}$ and $\overline{UV}$

**30. Music** Musicians use a metronome to keep time as they play. The metronome's needle swings back and forth in a fixed amount of time. Name all of the angles in the diagram.

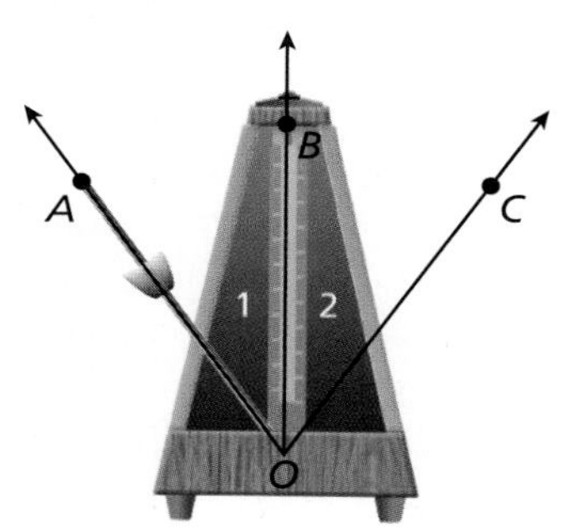


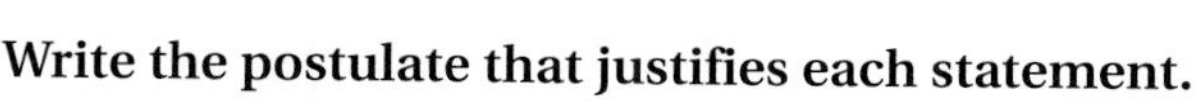

**Write the postulate that justifies each statement.**

**31.** The line connecting two dots on a sheet of paper lies on the same sheet of paper as the dots.

**32.** If two ants are walking in straight lines but in different directions, their paths cannot cross more than once.

**33. Critical Thinking** Is it possible to draw three points that are noncoplanar? Explain.

**Tell whether each statement is sometimes, always, or never true. Support your answer with a sketch.**

**34.** If two planes intersect, they intersect in a straight line.

**35.** If two lines intersect, they intersect at two different points.

**36.** $\overleftrightarrow{AB}$ is another name for $\overleftrightarrow{BA}$.

**37.** If two rays share a common endpoint, then they form a line.

**38. Physics** Pendulum clocks have been used since 1656 to keep time. The pendulum swings back and forth once or twice per second. Name all of the angles in the diagram.

**39. Write About It** Explain why three coplanar lines may have zero, one, two, or three points of intersection. Support your answer with a sketch.

**40. Challenge** Sketch and describe all possible intersections of three planes.

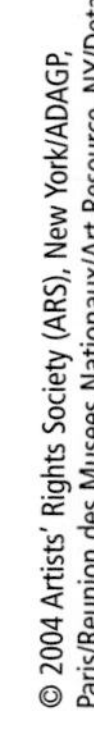

# A-2 Midpoint and Distance

**MA.G.1.1** Use strategies to calculate the … distance between points, coordinates of the midpoints and the distance from a point to a line.

***Objectives***
Develop and apply the formulas for midpoint and distance.

Describe the distance from a point to a line.

***Vocabulary***
midpoint
congruent segments
distance from a point to a line

In Lesson 5-4, you used the coordinates of points in the plane to determine the slopes of lines. You can also use coordinates to determine the *midpoint* of a line segment on the coordinate plane.

The **midpoint** of a line segment is the point that divides the segment into two *congruent segments*. **Congruent segments** are segments that have the same length.

You can find the midpoint of a segment by using the coordinates of its endpoints. Calculate the average of the *x*-coordinates and the average of the *y*-coordinates of the endpoints.

### Midpoint Formula

The midpoint $M$ of $\overline{AB}$ with endpoints $A(x_1, y_1)$ and $B(x_2, y_2)$ is found by

$$M\left(\frac{x_1 + x_2}{2}, \frac{y_1 + y_2}{2}\right).$$

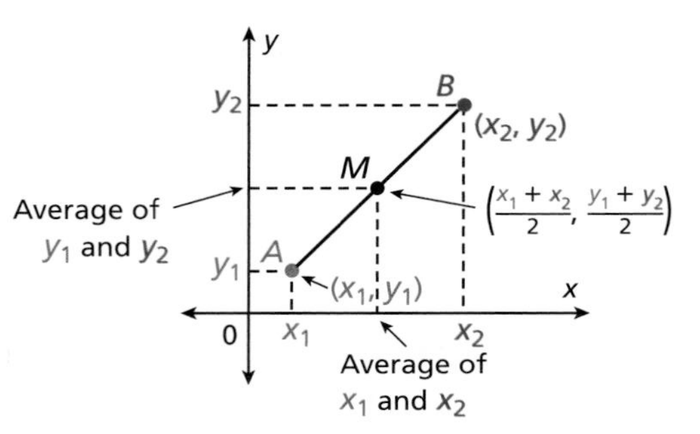


## EXAMPLE 1 Finding the Coordinates of a Midpoint

**Find the coordinates of the midpoint of $\overline{CD}$ with endpoints $C(-2, -1)$ and $D(4, 2)$.**

$$M\left(\frac{x_1 + x_2}{2}, \frac{y_1 + y_2}{2}\right)$$

$$\frac{-2 + 4}{2}, \frac{-1 + 2}{2} = \left(\frac{2}{2}, \frac{1}{2}\right)$$

$$= \left(1, \frac{1}{2}\right)$$

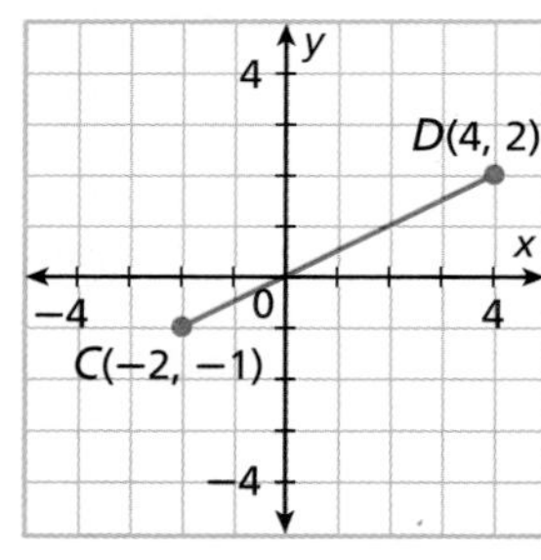


**Helpful Hint**

To make it easier to picture the problem, plot the segment's endpoints on a coordinate plane.

**1.** Find the coordinates of the midpoint of $\overline{EF}$ with endpoints $E(-2, 3)$ and $F(5, -3)$.

### Distance Formula

In a coordinate plane, the distance $d$ between two points $(x_1, y_1)$ and $(x_2, y_2)$ is

$$d = \sqrt{(x_2 - x_1)^2 + (y_2 - y_1)^2}.$$

## EXAMPLE 2 Using the Distance Formula

**Writing Math**

$\overline{AB}$ means "segment $AB$". $AB$ means "the length of segment $AB$".

**Find $AB$ and $CD$. Then determine if $\overline{AB}$ is congruent to $\overline{CD}$.**

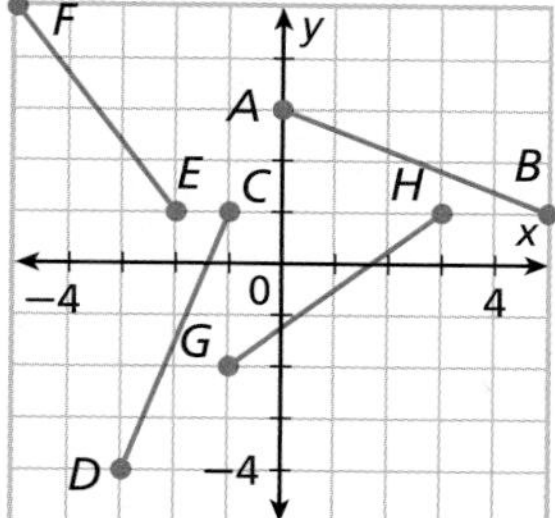


**Step 1** Find the coordinates of each point.

$A(0, 3)$, $B(5, 1)$, $C(-1, 1)$, and $D(-3, -4)$

**Step 2** Use the Distance Formula.

$$d = \sqrt{(x_2 - x_1)^2 + (y_2 - y_1)^2}$$

$$AB = \sqrt{(5-0)^2 + (1-3)^2} = \sqrt{5^2 + (-2)^2} = \sqrt{25+4} = \sqrt{29}$$

$$CD = \sqrt{[-3-(-1)]^2 + (-4-1)^2} = \sqrt{(-2)^2 + (-5)^2} = \sqrt{4+25} = \sqrt{29}$$

Since $AB = CD$, $\overline{AB}$ is congruent to $\overline{CD}$.

**2.** Find $EF$ and $GH$. Then determine if $\overline{EF}$ is congruent to $\overline{GH}$.

## EXAMPLE 3 *Sports Application*

**The four bases on a baseball field form a square with 90 ft sides. When a player throws the ball from home plate to second base, what is the distance of the throw, to the nearest tenth of a foot?**

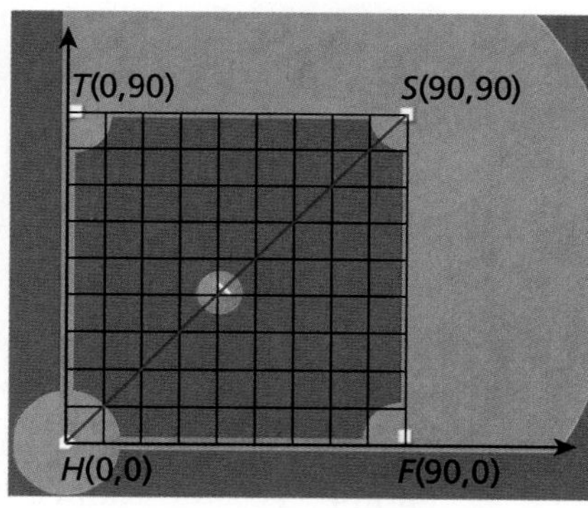

Set up the field on a coordinate plane so that home plate $H$ is at the origin, first base $F$ has coordinates $(90, 0)$, second base $S$ has coordinates $(90, 90)$, and third base $T$ has coordinates $(0, 90)$.

Use the Distance Formula.

$$HS = \sqrt{(x_2 - x_1)^2 + (y_2 - y_1)^2} = \sqrt{(90-0)^2 + (90-0)^2} = \sqrt{90^2 + 90^2} = \sqrt{8100 + 8100} = \sqrt{16{,}200} \approx 127.3 \text{ ft}$$

**3.** The center of the pitching mound has coordinates $(42.8, 42.8)$. When a pitcher throws the ball from the center of the mound to home plate, what is the distance of the throw, to the nearest tenth of a foot?

The shortest segment from a point to a line is perpendicular to the line. This fact is used to define the **distance from a point to a line** as the length of the perpendicular segment from the point to the line.

## EXAMPLE 4 Distance From a Point to a Line

**A** **Name the shortest segment from $P$ to $\overleftrightarrow{AC}$.**

The shortest distance from a point to a line is the length of the perpendicular segment, so $\overline{PB}$ is the shortest segment from $P$ to $\overleftrightarrow{AC}$.

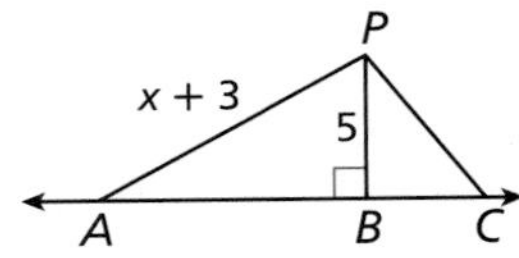


**B** **Write and solve an inequality for $x$.**

| | |
|---|---|
| $PA > PB$ | *$\overline{PB}$ is the shortest segment.* |
| $x + 3 > 5$ | *Substitute $x + 3$ for PA and 5 for PB.* |
| $-3 \quad -3$ | *Subtract 3 from both sides of the inequality.* |
| $x > 2$ | |

**4a.** Name the shortest segment from $A$ to $\overleftrightarrow{BC}$.

**4b.** Write and solve an inequality for $x$.

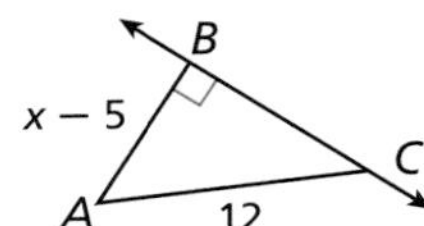


# Exercises

MA.G.1.1

## GUIDED PRACTICE

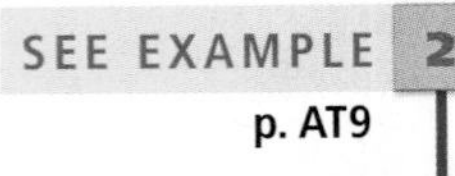

SEE EXAMPLE 1
p. AT8


**Find the coordinates of the midpoint of each segment.**

1. $\overline{AB}$ with endpoints $A(4, -6)$ and $B(-4, 2)$
2. $\overline{CD}$ with endpoints $C(0, -8)$ and $D(3, 0)$

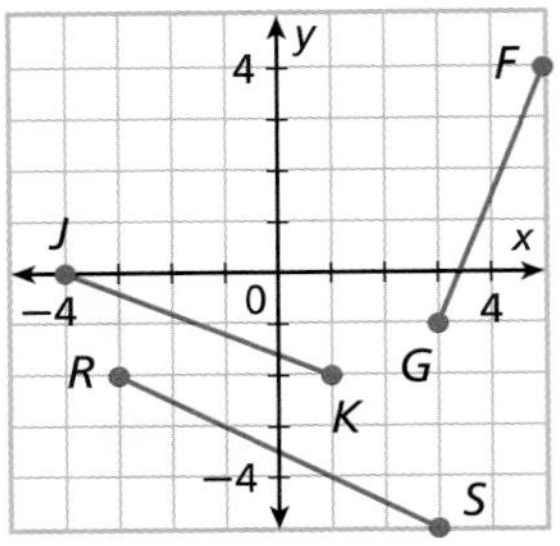

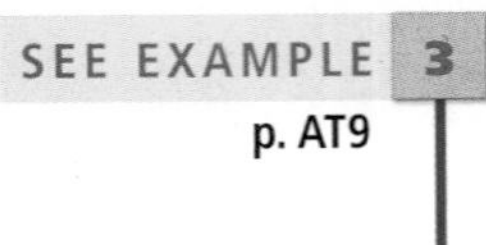

SEE EXAMPLE 2
p. AT9


**Multi-Step** **Find the length of the given segments and determine if they are congruent.**

3. $\overline{JK}$ and $\overline{FG}$
4. $\overline{JK}$ and $\overline{RS}$


SEE EXAMPLE 3
p. AT9


5. **Architecture** The plan for a rectangular living room shows electrical wiring will be run in a straight line from the entrance $E$ to a light $L$ at the opposite corner of the room. What is the length of the wire to the nearest tenth?

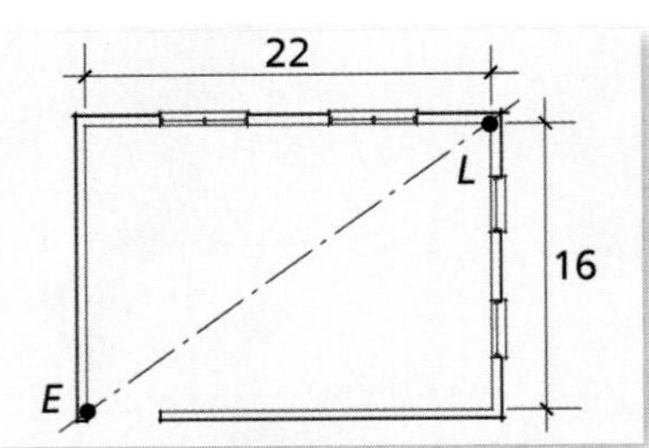


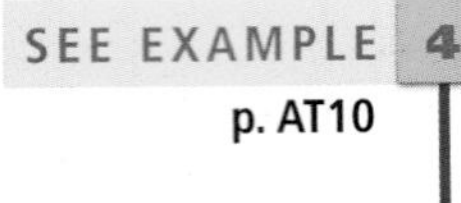

SEE EXAMPLE 4
p. AT10


6. Name the shortest segment from point $E$ to $\overleftrightarrow{AD}$.
7. Write and solve an inequality for $x$.

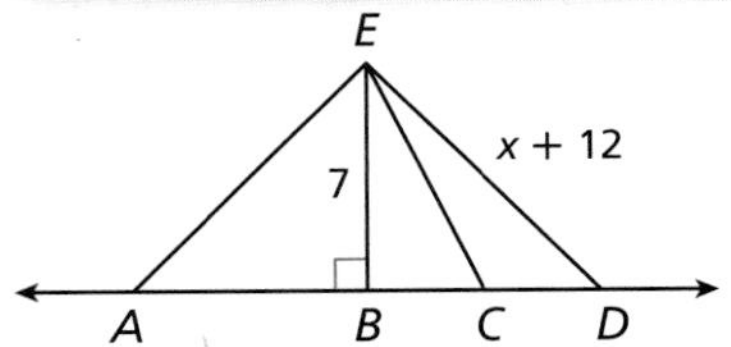

## PRACTICE AND PROBLEM SOLVING

**Find the coordinates of the midpoint of each segment.**

8. $\overline{XY}$ with endpoints $X(-3, -7)$ and $Y(-1, 1)$
9. $\overline{MN}$ with endpoints $M(12, -7)$ and $N(-5, -2)$

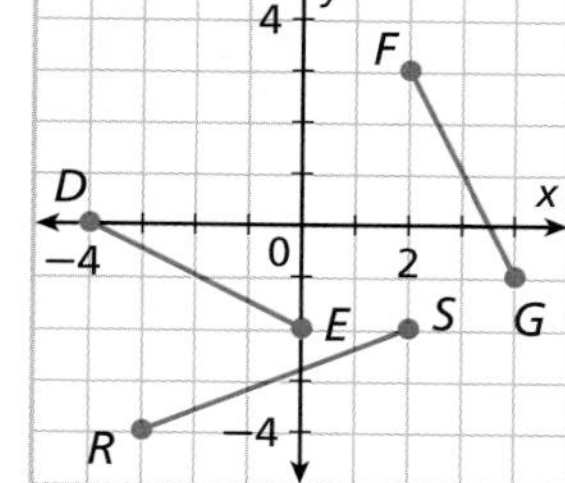


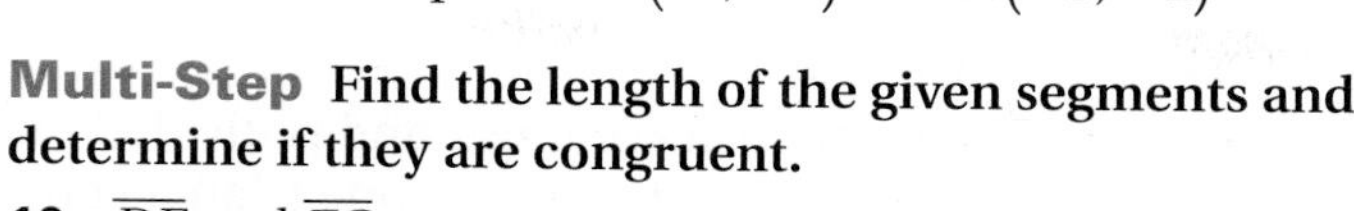

**Multi-Step** **Find the length of the given segments and determine if they are congruent.**

10. $\overline{DE}$ and $\overline{FG}$
11. $\overline{DE}$ and $\overline{RS}$
12. Name the shortest segment from point $W$ to $\overline{XZ}$. 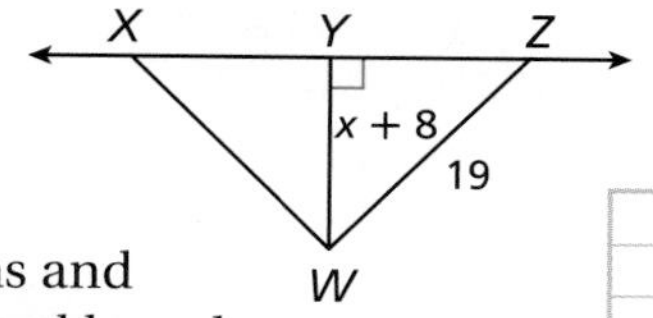
13. Write and solve an inequality for $x$.
14. **Consumer Application** Televisions and computer screens are usually advertised based on the length of their diagonals. If the height of a computer screen is 11 in. and the width is 14 in., what is the length of the diagonal? Round to the nearest inch.

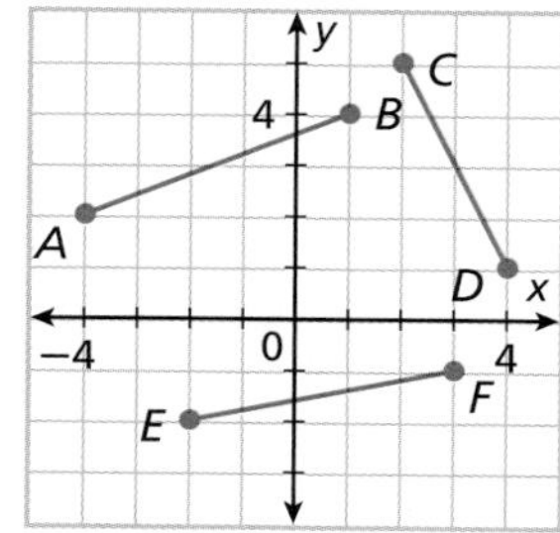


15. **Multi-Step** Use the Distance Formula to order $\overline{AB}$, $\overline{CD}$, and $\overline{EF}$ from shortest to longest.

**For each diagram, write and solve an inequality for $x$.**

16. 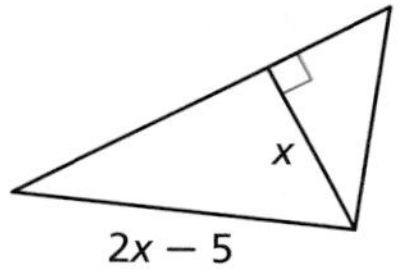


17. 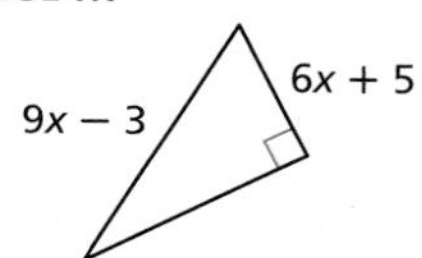


18. $X$ has coordinates $(a, 3a)$, and $Y$ has coordinates $(-5a, 0)$. Find the coordinates of the midpoint of $\overline{XY}$.
19. Describe a shortcut for finding the midpoint of a segment when one of its endpoints has coordinates $(a, b)$ and the other endpoint is the origin.

**On the map, each square of the grid represents 1 square mile. Find each distance to the nearest tenth of a mile.**

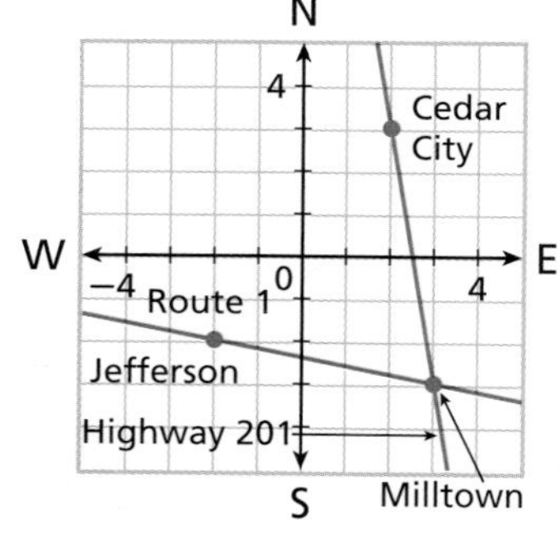


20. Find the distance along Highway 201 from Cedar City to Milltown.
21. A car breaks down on Route 1, at the midpoint between Jefferson and Milltown. A tow truck is sent out from Jefferson. How far does the truck travel to reach the car?
22. **History** The Forbidden City in Beijing, China, is the world's largest palace complex. Surrounded by a wall and a moat, the rectangular complex is 960 m long and 750 m wide. Find the distance, to the nearest meter, from one corner of the complex to the opposite corner.
23. **Critical Thinking** Give an example of a line segment with midpoint $(0, 0)$.

**The coordinates of the vertices of $\triangle ABC$ are $A(1, 4)$, $B(-2, -1)$, and $C(-3, -2)$.**

24. Find the perimeter of $\triangle ABC$ to the nearest tenth.
25. The height $h$ of $\triangle ABC$ is $\sqrt{2}$, and $b$ is the length of $\overline{BC}$. What is the area of $\triangle ABC$?
26. **Write About It** Explain why the Distance Formula is not needed to find the distance between two points that lie on a horizontal or a vertical line.

# A-3 Angle Relationships in Triangles

***Objectives***
Find the measures of interior and exterior angles of triangles.

Apply theorems about the interior and exterior angles of triangles.

***Vocabulary***
corollary
interior
exterior
interior angle
exterior angle
remote interior angle

Triangulation is a method used in surveying. Land is divided into adjacent triangles. By measuring the sides and angles of one triangle and applying properties of triangles, surveyors can gather information about adjacent triangles.

**Theorem 3-1** **Triangle Sum Theorem**

The sum of the angle measures of a triangle is 180°.

$m\angle A + m\angle B + m\angle C = 180°$

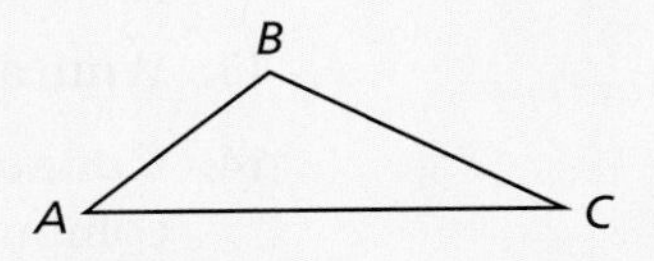


**EXAMPLE 1** ***Surveying Application***

**The map of France commonly used in the 1600s was significantly revised as a result of a triangulation land survey. The diagram shows part of the survey map. Use the diagram to find $m\angle NKM$.**

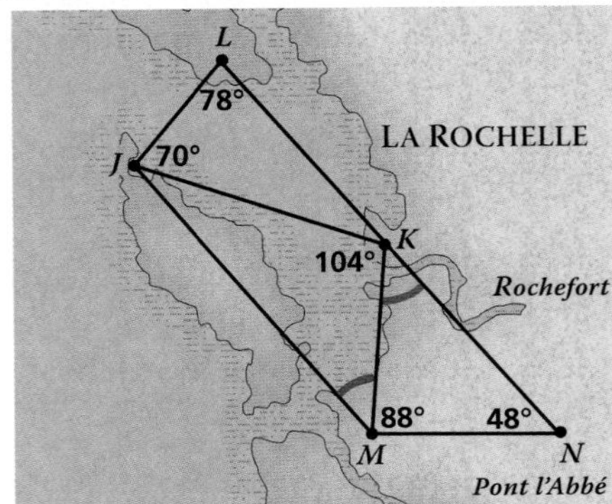


| | |
|---|---|
| $m\angle KMN + m\angle MNK + m\angle NKM = 180°$ | *Triangle Sum Theorem* |
| $88 + 48 + m\angle NKM = 180$ | *Substitute 88 for m∠KMN and 48 for m∠MNK.* |
| $136 + m\angle NKM = 180$ | *Simplify.* |
| $m\angle NKM = 44°$ | *Subtract 136 from both sides.* |

**1.** Use the diagram to find $m\angle JKL$.

A **corollary** is a theorem whose proof follows directly from another theorem. Here are two corollaries to the Triangle Sum Theorem.

**Corollaries**

| | COROLLARY | HYPOTHESIS | CONCLUSION |
|---|---|---|---|
| **3-2** | The acute angles of a right triangle are complementary. | (right triangle DFE with right angle at F) | $\angle D$ and $\angle E$ are complementary. $m\angle D + m\angle E = 90°$ |
| **3-3** | The measure of each angle of an equiangular triangle is 60°. | (equiangular triangle ABC) | $m\angle A = m\angle B = m\angle C = 60°$ |

## EXAMPLE 2 Finding Angle Measures in Right Triangles

**One of the acute angles in a right triangle measures 22.9°. What is the measure of the other acute angle?**

Let the acute angles be $\angle M$ and $\angle N$, with $m\angle M = 22.9°$.

| | |
|---|---|
| $m\angle M + m\angle N = 90$ | *Corollary 3-2* |
| $22.9 + m\angle N = 90$ | *Substitute 22.9 for m∠M.* |
| $m\angle N = 67.1°$ | *Subtract 22.9 from both sides.* |

**The measure of one of the acute angles in a right triangle is given. What is the measure of the other acute angle?**

**2a.** 63.7°  **2b.** $x°$  **2c.** $48\frac{2}{5}°$

The **interior** is the set of all points inside the figure. The **exterior** is the set of all points outside the figure. An **interior angle** is formed by two sides of a triangle. An **exterior angle** is formed by one side of the triangle and the extension of an adjacent side. Each exterior angle has two *remote interior angles*. A **remote interior angle** is an interior angle that is not adjacent to the exterior angle.

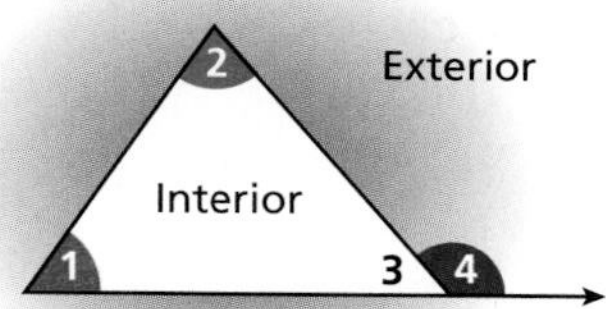


$\angle 4$ is an exterior angle. Its remote interior angles are $\angle 1$ and $\angle 2$.

**Theorem 3-4 Exterior Angle Theorem**

The measure of an exterior angle of a triangle is equal to the sum of the measures of its remote interior angles.

$m\angle 4 = m\angle 1 + m\angle 2$

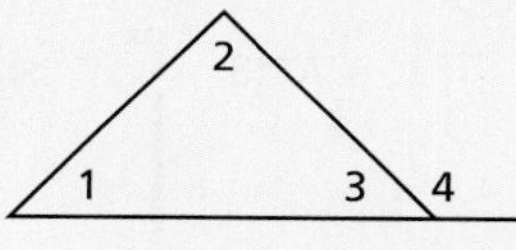


## EXAMPLE 3 Applying the Exterior Angle Theorem

**Find $m\angle J$.**

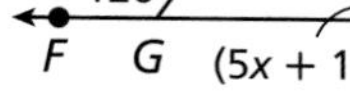


| | |
|---|---|
| $m\angle J + m\angle H = m\angle FGH$ | *Exterior Angle Theorem* |
| $5x + 17 + 6x - 1 = 126$ | *Substitute 5x + 17 for m∠J, 6x − 1 for m∠H, and 126 for m∠FGH.* |
| $11x + 16 = 126$ | *Simplify.* |
| $11x = 110$ | *Subtract 16 from both sides.* |
| $x = 10$ | *Divide both sides by 11.* |

$m\angle J = 5x + 17 = 5(10) + 17 = 67°$

**3.** Find $m\angle ACD$.

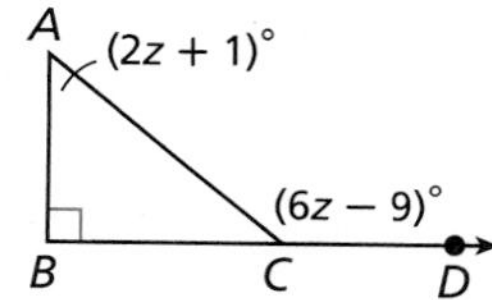

# Exercises

## GUIDED PRACTICE

**Vocabulary** **Apply the vocabulary from this lesson to answer each question.**

1. To remember the meaning of *remote interior angle*, think of a television remote control. What is another way to remember the term *remote*?
2. An *exterior angle* is drawn at vertex $E$ of $\triangle DEF$. What are its *remote interior angles*?

SEE EXAMPLE 1 p. AT12

**Astronomy** **Use the following information for Exercises 3 and 4.**

An *asterism* is a group of stars that is easier to recognize than a constellation. One popular asterism is the Summer Triangle, which is composed of the stars Deneb, Altair, and Vega.

3. What is the value of $y$?
4. What is the measure of each angle in the Summer Triangle?

SEE EXAMPLE 2 p. AT13

**The measure of one of the acute angles in a right triangle is given. What is the measure of the other acute angle?**

5. $20.8°$
6. $y°$
7. $24\frac{2}{3}°$

SEE EXAMPLE 3 p. AT13

**Find each angle measure.**

8. $m\angle M$

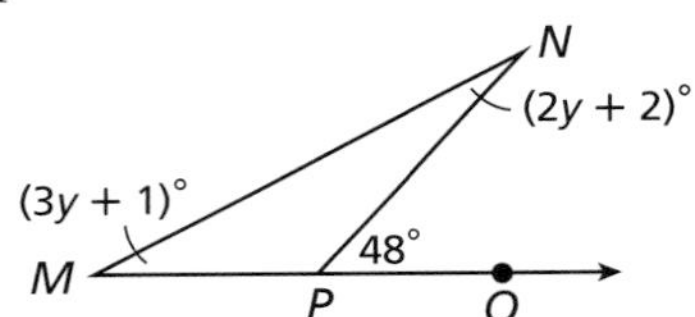


9. $m\angle L$

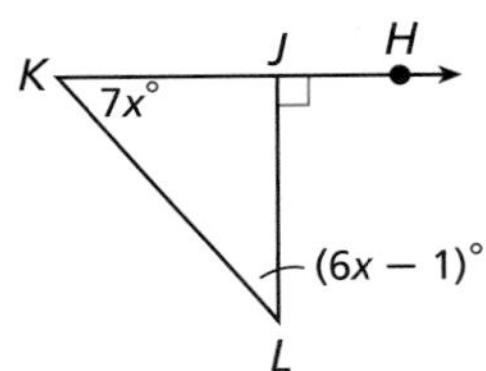


10. In $\triangle ABC$, $m\angle A = 65°$, and the measure of an exterior angle at $C$ is $117°$. Find $m\angle B$ and the $m\angle BCA$.

## PRACTICE AND PROBLEM SOLVING

11. **Navigation** A sailor on ship A measures the angle between ship B and the pier and finds that it is 39°. A sailor on ship B measures the angle between ship A and the pier and finds that it is 57°. What is the measure of the angle between ships A and B?

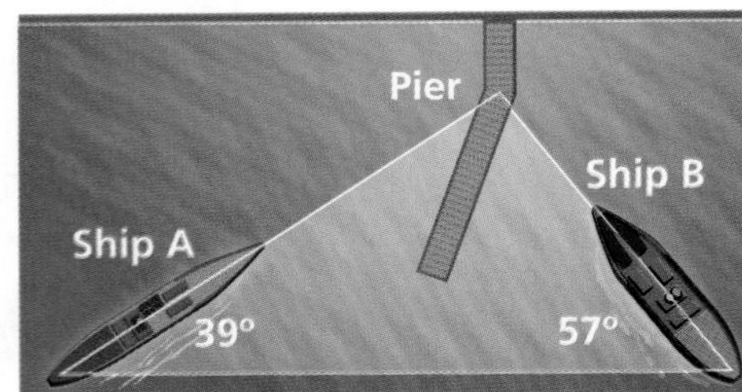

**The measure of one of the acute angles in a right triangle is given. What is the measure of the other acute angle?**

**12.** $76\frac{1}{4}^{\circ}$ **13.** $2x°$ **14.** 56.8°

**Find each angle measure.**

**15.** $m\angle XYZ$

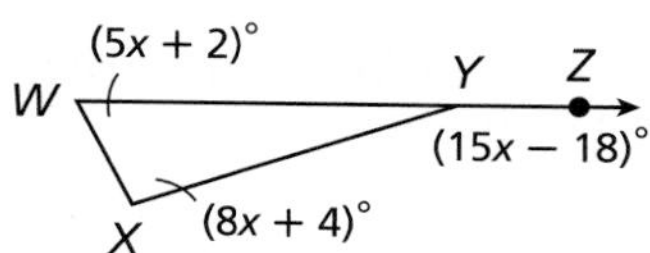


**16.** $m\angle C$

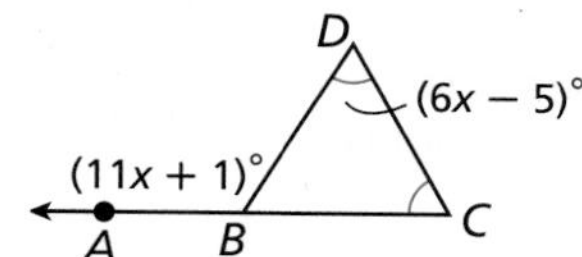


**17. Multi-Step** The measures of the angles of a triangle are in the ratio 1 : 4 : 7. What are the measures of the angles? (*Hint:* Let $x$, $4x$, and $7x$ represent the angle measures.)

**18. Multi-Step** The measure of one acute angle in a right triangle is $1\frac{1}{4}$ times the measure of the other acute angle. What is the measure of the larger acute angle?

**Find each angle measure.**

**19.** $\angle UXW$ **20.** $\angle UWY$

**21.** $\angle WZX$ **22.** $\angle XYZ$

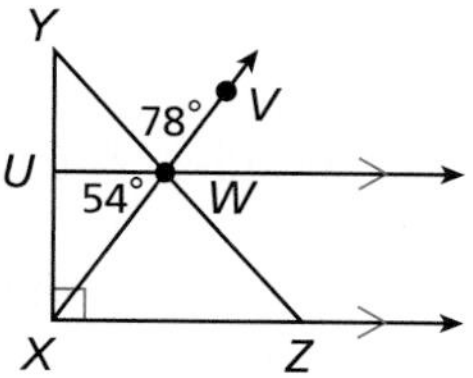


**23. Critical Thinking** What is the measure of any exterior angle of an equiangular triangle? What is the sum of the exterior angle measures?

**24.** Find $m\angle SRQ$, given that $\angle P \cong \angle U$, $\angle Q \cong \angle T$, and $m\angle RST = 37.5°$.

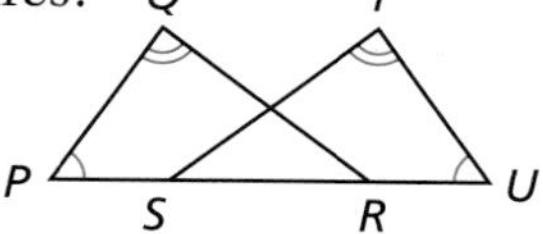


**25. Multi-Step** In a right triangle, one acute angle measure is 4 times the other acute angle measure. What is the measure of the smaller angle?

**26. Aviation** To study the forces of lift and drag, the Wright brothers built a glider, attached two ropes to it, and flew it like a kite. They modeled the two wind forces as the legs of a right triangle.

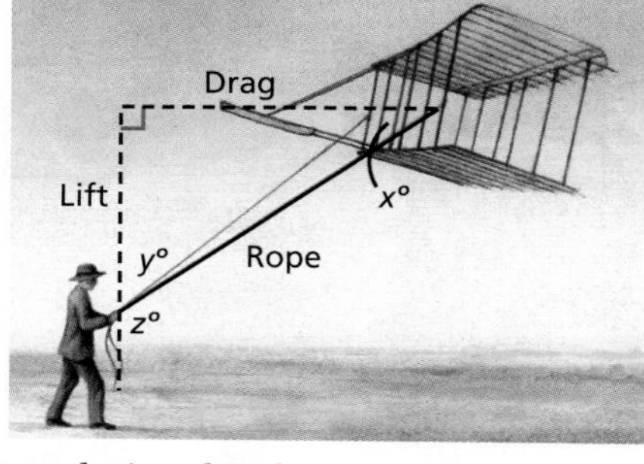


**a.** What part of a right triangle is formed by each rope?

**b.** Use the Triangle Sum Theorem to write an equation relating the angle measures in the right triangle.

**c.** Simplify the equation from part **b**. What is the relationship between $x$ and $y$?

**d.** Use the Exterior Angle Theorem to write an expression for $z$ in terms of $x$.

**e.** If $x = 37°$, use your results from parts **c** and **d** to find $y$ and $z$.

**27. Estimation** Draw a triangle and two exterior angles at each vertex. Estimate the measure of each angle. How are the exterior angles at each vertex related? Explain.

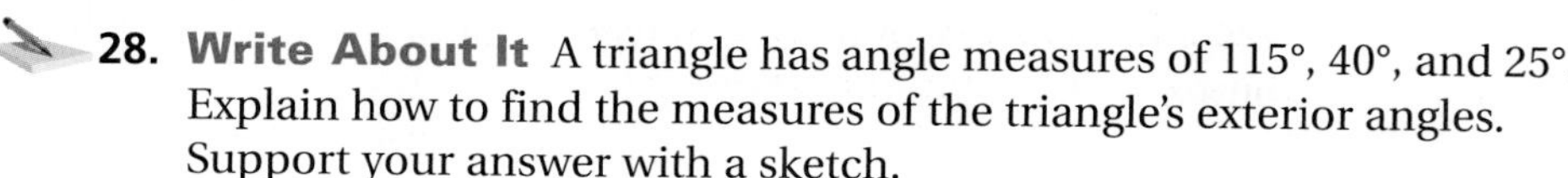

**28. Write About It** A triangle has angle measures of 115°, 40°, and 25°. Explain how to find the measures of the triangle's exterior angles. Support your answer with a sketch.

# A-4 Properties and Attributes of Polygons

**MA.G.1.2** Use geometric properties to identify geometric shapes.

***Objectives***
Classify polygons based on their sides and angles.

Find and use the measures of interior and exterior angles of polygons.

***Vocabulary***
polygon
side of a polygon
vertex of a polygon
diagonal
regular polygon
concave
convex

A **polygon** is a closed figure formed by three or more segments that intersect only at their endpoints. In this lesson, you will learn about the parts of a polygon and about ways to classify polygons.

Each segment that forms a polygon is a **side of the polygon**. The common endpoint of two sides is a **vertex of the polygon**. A segment that connects any two nonconsecutive vertices is a **diagonal**.

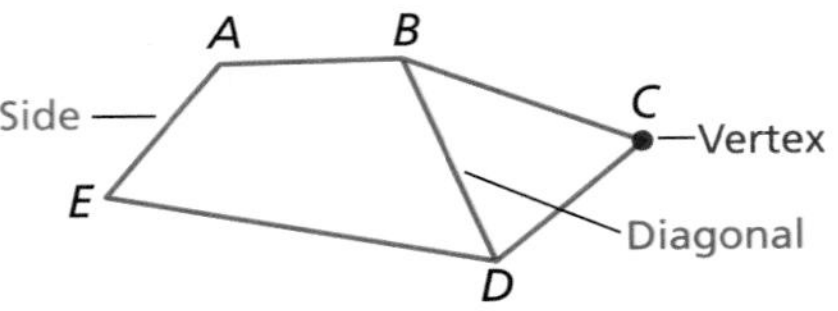


You can name a polygon by the number of its sides. The table shows the names of some common polygons. Polygon *ABCDE* is a pentagon.

| Number of Sides | Name of Polygon |
|---|---|
| 3 | Triangle |
| 4 | Quadrilateral |
| 5 | Pentagon |
| 6 | Hexagon |
| 7 | Heptagon |
| 8 | Octagon |
| 9 | Nonagon |
| 10 | Decagon |
| 12 | Dodecagon |
| *n* | *n*-gon |

## EXAMPLE 1 Identifying Polygons

**Tell whether each figure is a polygon. If it is a polygon, name it by the number of its sides.**

**A**

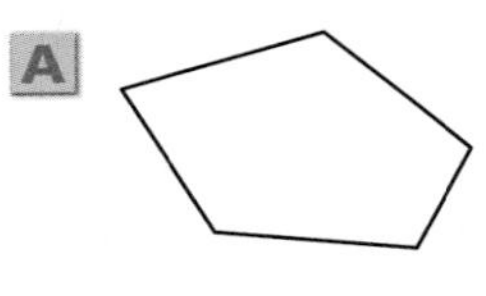

polygon, pentagon

**B**

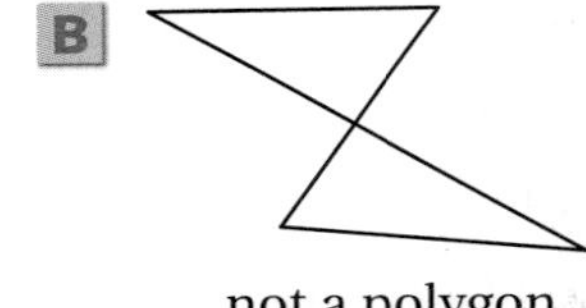

not a polygon

**C**

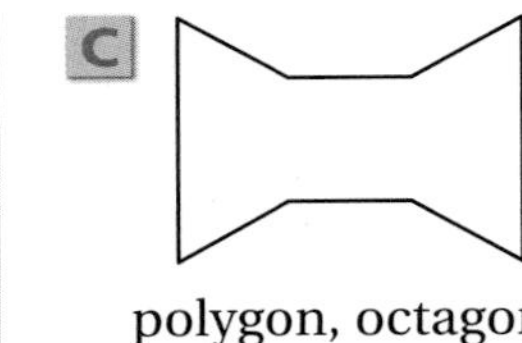

polygon, octagon

**Tell whether each figure is a polygon. If it is a polygon, name it by the number of its sides.**

**1a.** **1b.** **1c.**

All the sides are congruent in an equilateral polygon. All the angles are congruent in an equiangular polygon. A **regular polygon** is one that is both equilateral and equiangular. If a polygon is not regular, it is called irregular.

A polygon is **concave** if any part of a diagonal contains points in the exterior of the polygon. If no diagonal contains points in the exterior, then the polygon is **convex**. A regular polygon is always convex.

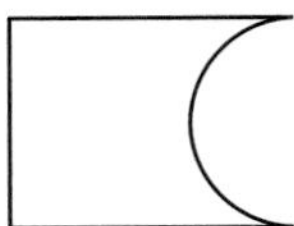

Concave quadrilateral

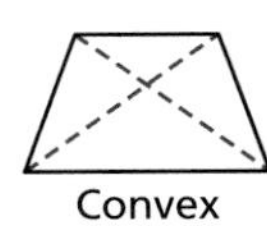

Convex quadrilateral

## EXAMPLE 2 Classifying Polygons

**Tell whether each polygon is regular or irregular. Tell whether it is concave or convex.**

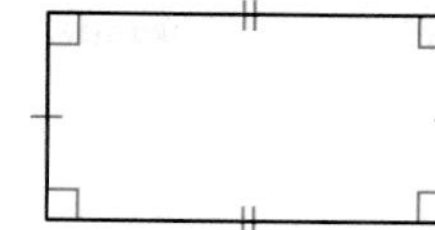

irregular, convex

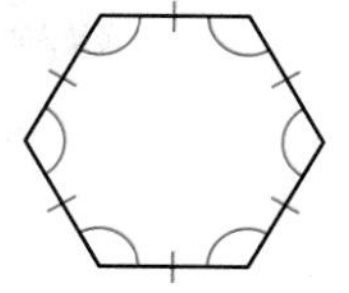

regular, convex

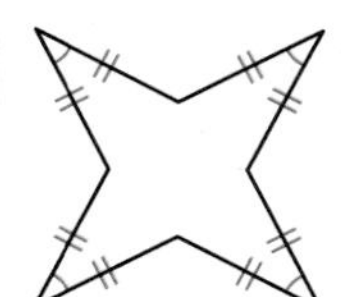

irregular, concave

**Tell whether each polygon is regular or irregular. Tell whether it is concave or convex.**

**2a.**

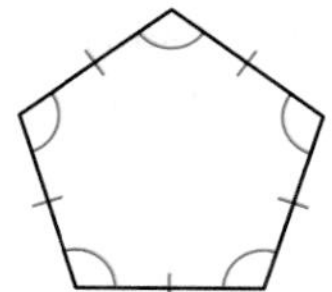

**2b.**

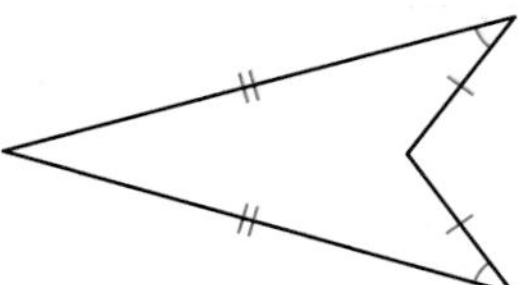

**Remember!**

By the Triangle Sum Theorem, the sum of the interior angle measures of a triangle is 180°.

To find the sum of the interior angle measures of a convex polygon, draw all possible diagonals from one vertex of the polygon. This creates a set of triangles. The sum of the angle measures of all the triangles equals the sum of the angle measures of the polygon.

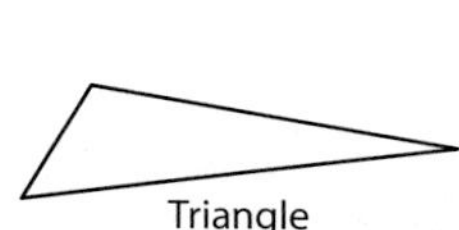

Triangle

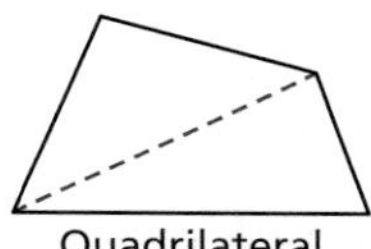

Quadrilateral

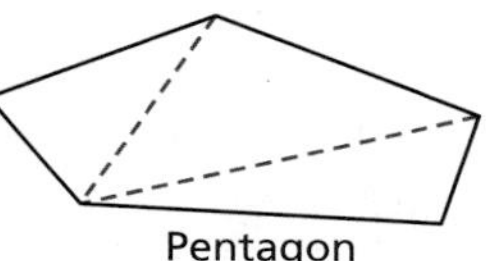

Pentagon

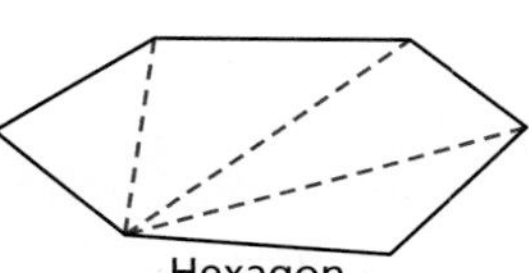

Hexagon

| Polygon | Number of Sides | Number of Triangles | Sum of Interior Angle Measures |
|---|---|---|---|
| Triangle | 3 | 1 | $(1)180° = 180°$ |
| Quadrilateral | 4 | 2 | $(2)180° = 360°$ |
| Pentagon | 5 | 3 | $(3)180° = 540°$ |
| Hexagon | 6 | 4 | $(4)180° = 720°$ |
| $n$-gon | $n$ | $n - 2$ | $(n - 2)180°$ |

In each convex polygon, the number of triangles formed is two less than the number of sides $n$. So the sum of the angle measures of all these triangles is $(n - 2)180°$.

**Theorem 4-1** **Polygon Angle Sum Theorem**

The sum of the interior angle measures of a convex polygon with $n$ sides is $(n - 2)180°$.

## EXAMPLE 3 Finding Interior Angle Measures and Sums in Polygons

**Find the sum of the interior angle measures of a convex octagon.**

$(n - 2)180°$ *Polygon Angle Sum Theorem*

$(8 - 2)180°$ *An octagon has 8 sides, so substitute 8 for n.*

$1080°$ *Simplify.*

**B** **Find the measure of each interior angle of a regular nonagon.**

**Step 1** Find the sum of the interior angle measures.

$(n - 2)180°$ *Polygon Angle Sum Theorem*

$(9 - 2)180° = \mathbf{1260°}$ *Substitute 9 for n and simplify.*

**Step 2** Find the measure of one interior angle.

$\frac{\mathbf{1260°}}{9} = 140°$ *The int. angles are congruent, so divide by 9.*

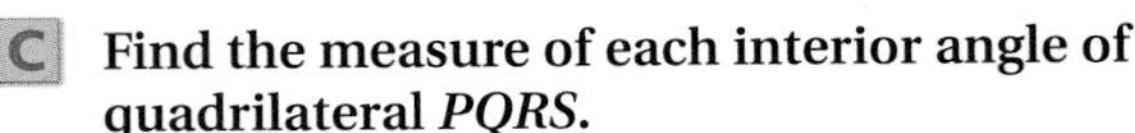

**C** **Find the measure of each interior angle of quadrilateral *PQRS*.**

$(4 - 2)180° = 360°$ *Polygon Angle Sum Theorem*

$m\angle P + m\angle Q + m\angle R + m\angle S = 360°$ *Polygon Angle Sum Theorem*

$c + 3c + c + 3c = 360$ *Substitute.*

$8c = 360$ *Combine like terms.*

$c = 45$ *Divide both sides by 8.*

$m\angle P = m\angle R = 45°$

$m\angle Q = m\angle S = 3(45°) = 135°$

**3a.** Find the sum of the interior angle measures of a convex 15-gon.

**3b.** Find the measure of each interior angle of a regular decagon.

**Remember!**

An exterior angle is formed by one side of a polygon and the extension of a consecutive side.

In the polygons below, an exterior angle has been measured at each vertex. Notice that in each case, the sum of the exterior angle measures is 360°.

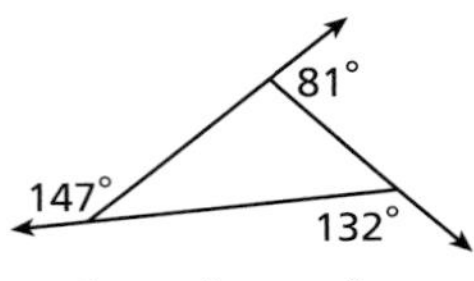


$147° + 81° + 132° = 360°$

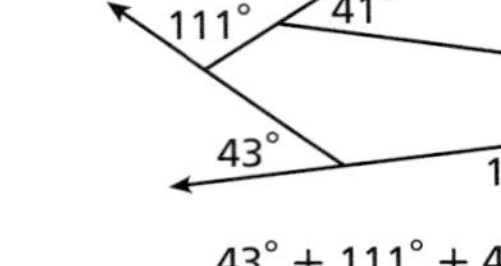


$43° + 111° + 41° + 55° + 110° = 360°$

**Theorem 4-2** **Polygon Exterior Angle Sum Theorem**

The sum of the exterior angle measures, one angle at each vertex, of a convex polygon is 360°.

## EXAMPLE  4 Finding Exterior Angle Measures in Polygons

**A** **Find the measure of each exterior angle of a regular hexagon.**

A hexagon has 6 sides and 6 vertices.

sum of ext. angles = **360°** *Polygon Ext. Angle Sum Theorem*

measure of one ext. $\angle = \frac{\mathbf{360°}}{6} = 60°$ *A regular hexagon has 6 congruent ext. angles, so divide the sum by 6.*

The measure of each exterior angle of a regular hexagon is 60°.

**B** **Find the value of $a$ in polygon $RSTUV$.**

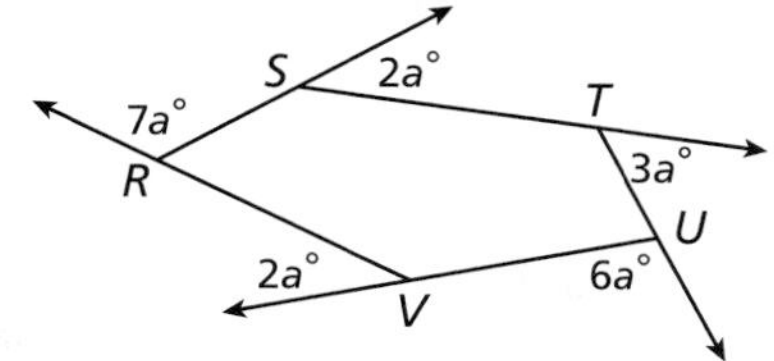


$$7a° + 2a° + 3a° + 6a° + 2a° = 360°$$ *Polygon Ext. Angle Sum Theorem*

$$20a = 360$$ *Combine like terms.*

$$a = 18$$ *Divide both sides by 20.*

**4a.** Find the measure of each exterior angle of a regular dodecagon.

**4b.** Find the value of $r$ in polygon $JKLM$.

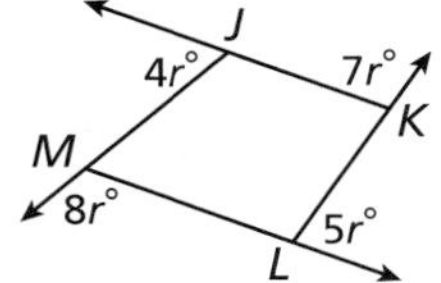


## EXAMPLE 5 *Photography Application*

**The aperture of the camera is formed by ten blades. The blades overlap to form a regular decagon. What is the measure of ∠$CBD$?**

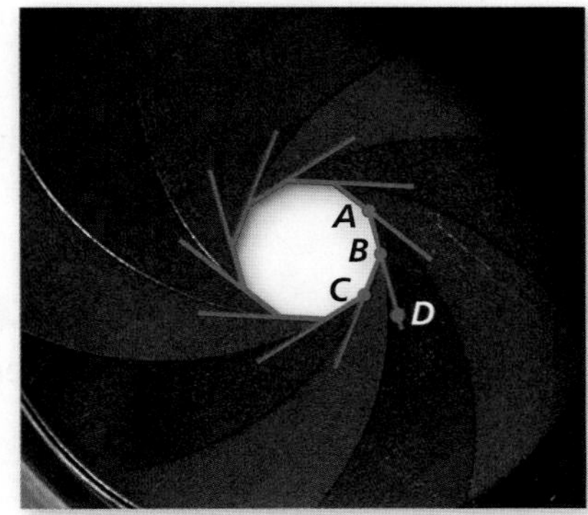


∠$CBD$ is an exterior angle of a regular decagon. By the Polygon Exterior Angle Sum Theorem, the sum of the exterior angle measures is 360°.

$$m\angle CBD = \frac{360°}{10} = 36°$$ *A regular decagon has 10 congruent ext. angles, so divide the sum by 10.*

**5. What if...?** Suppose the shutter were formed by 8 blades. What would the measure of each exterior angle be?

# Exercises

**MA.G.1.2**

## GUIDED PRACTICE

**1. Vocabulary** Explain why an equilateral polygon is not necessarily a *regular* polygon.

SEE EXAMPLE 1
p. AT16

**Tell whether each outlined shape is a polygon. If it is a polygon, name it by the number of its sides.**

**2.** 

**3.** 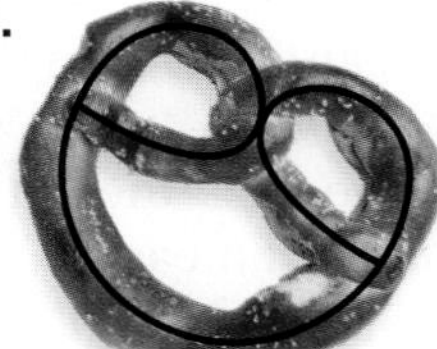

**4.** 

**5.** 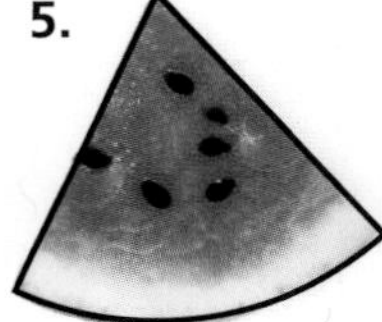

SEE EXAMPLE 2
p. AT17

**Tell whether each polygon is regular or irregular. Tell whether it is concave or convex.**

**6.** 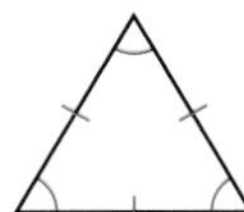

**7.** 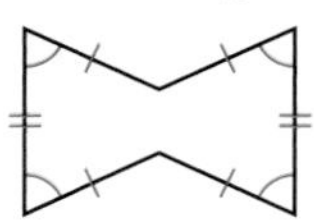

**8.** 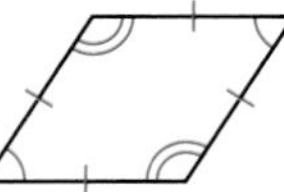

SEE EXAMPLE 3
p. AT17

**9.** Find the measure of each interior angle of pentagon *ABCDE*.

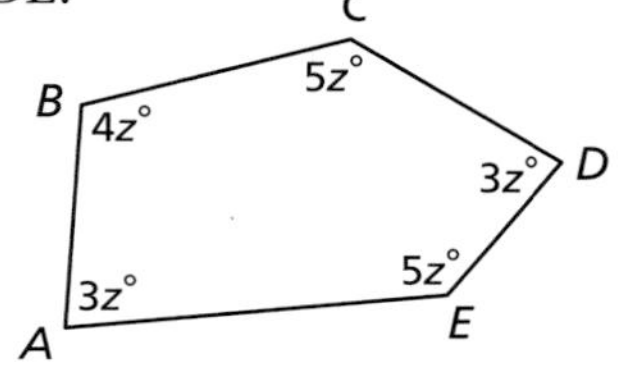


**10.** Find the measure of each interior angle of a regular dodecagon.

**11.** Find the sum of the interior angle measures of a convex 20-gon.

SEE EXAMPLE 4
p. AT18

**12.** Find the value of $y$ in polygon *JKLM*.

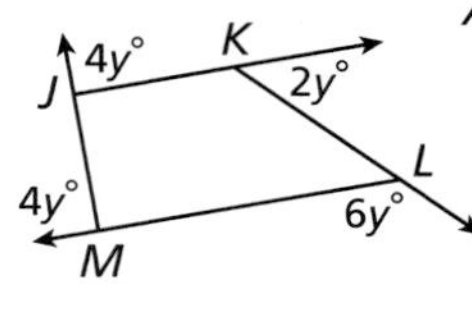


**13.** Find the measure of each exterior angle of a regular pentagon.

SEE EXAMPLE 5
p. AT19

**Safety** **Use the photograph of the traffic sign for Exercises 14 and 15.**

**14.** Name the polygon by the number of its sides.

**15.** In the polygon, $\angle P$, $\angle R$, and $\angle T$ are right angles, and $\angle Q \cong \angle S$. What are $m\angle Q$ and $m\angle S$?

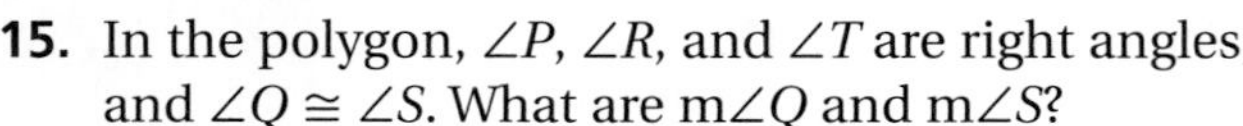

## PRACTICE AND PROBLEM SOLVING

**Tell whether each figure is a polygon. If it is a polygon, name it by the number of its sides.**

**16.** 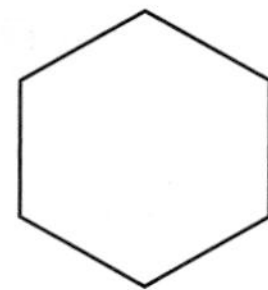

**17.** 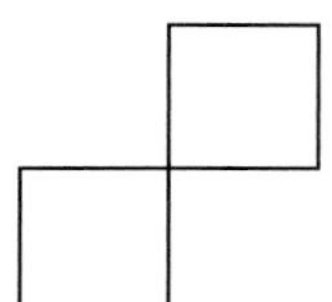

**18.** 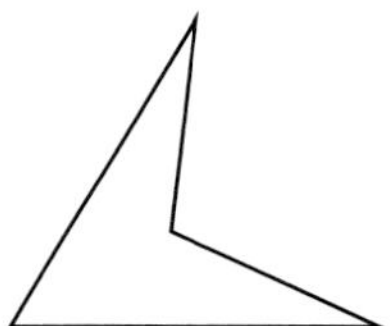

**Tell whether each polygon is regular or irregular. Tell whether it is concave or convex.**

**19.** 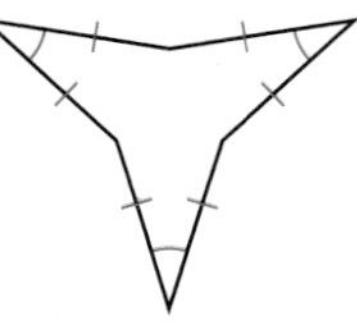

**20.** 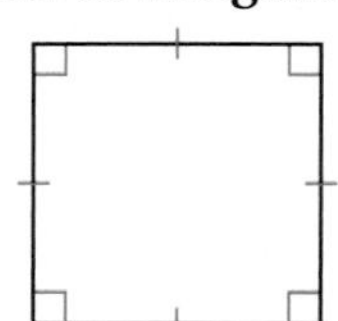

**21.** 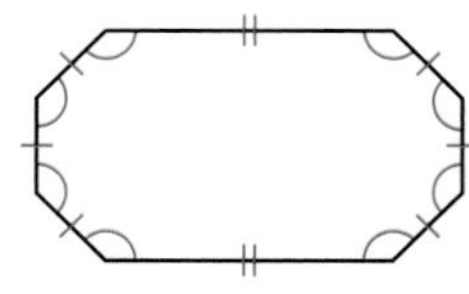

**22.** Find the measure of each interior angle of quadrilateral *RSTV*.

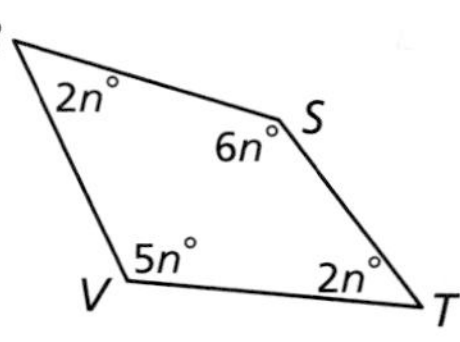


**23.** Find the measure of each interior angle of a regular 18-gon.

**24.** Find the sum of the interior angle measures of a convex heptagon.

**25.** Find the measure of each exterior angle of a regular nonagon.

**26.** A pentagon has exterior angle measures of $5a°$, $4a°$, $10a°$, $3a°$, and $8a°$. Find the value of $a$.

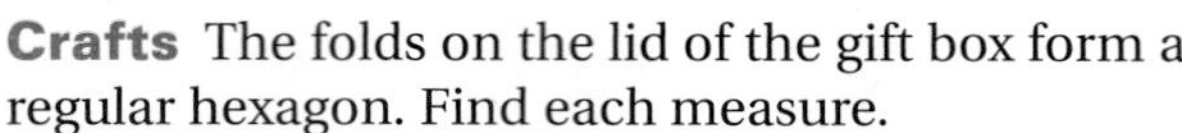

**Crafts** The folds on the lid of the gift box form a regular hexagon. Find each measure.

**27.** $m\angle JKM$

**28.** $m\angle MKL$

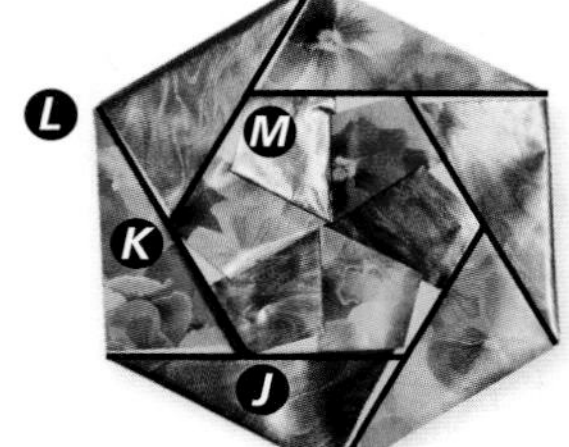

**Algebra** **Find the value of $x$ in each figure.**

29. 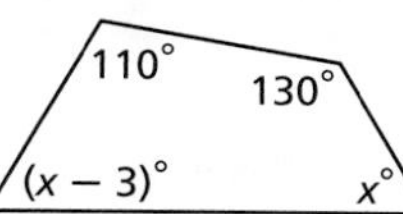


30. 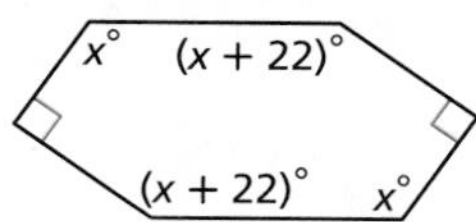


31. 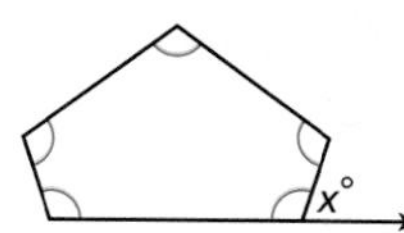


**Find the number of sides a regular polygon must have to meet each condition.**

32. Each interior angle measure equals each exterior angle measure.

33. Each interior angle measure is four times the measure of each exterior angle.

34. Each exterior angle measure is one eighth the measure of each interior angle.

**Name the convex polygon whose interior angle measures have each given sum.**

35. 540° 36. 900° 37. 1800° 38. 2520°

**Multi-Step** **An exterior angle measure of a regular polygon is given. Find the number of its sides and the measure of each interior angle.**

39. 120° 40. 72° 41. 36° 42. 24°

43. **ERROR ANALYSIS** Which conclusion is incorrect? Explain the error.

The figure is a polygon.

The figure is not a polygon.

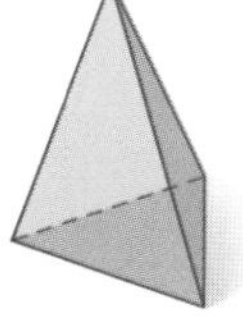

44. **Estimation** Graph the polygon formed by the points $A(-2, -6)$, $B(-4, -1)$, $C(-1, 2)$, $D(4, 0)$, and $E(3, -5)$. Estimate the measure of each interior angle. Make a conjecture about whether the polygon is equiangular. Now measure each interior angle with a protractor. Was your conjecture correct?

45. The perimeter of a regular polygon is 45 inches. The length of one side is 7.5 inches. Name the polygon by the number of its sides.

**Draw an example of each figure.**

46. a regular quadrilateral

47. an irregular concave heptagon

48. an irregular convex pentagon

49. an equilateral polygon that is not equiangular

50. **Write About It** Use the terms from the lesson to describe the figure as specifically as possible.

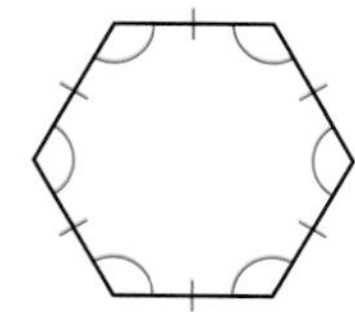

51. **Critical Thinking** What geometric figure does a regular polygon begin to resemble as the number of sides increases?

# A-5 Developing Formulas for Triangles and Quadrilaterals

**MA.G.2** Use formulas to solve problems involving area... *Also* **MA.G.2.2**

***Objectives***

Develop and apply the formulas for the areas of triangles and special quadrilaterals.

Solve problems involving perimeters and areas of triangles and special quadrilaterals.

A tangram is an ancient Chinese puzzle made from a square. The pieces can be rearranged to form many different shapes. The area of a figure made with all the pieces is the sum of the areas of the pieces.

**Postulate 5-1** **Area Addition Postulate**

The area of a region is equal to the sum of the areas of its nonoverlapping parts.

Recall that a rectangle with base $b$ and height $h$ has an area of $A = bh$. You can use the Area Addition Postulate to see that a parallelogram has the same area as a rectangle with the same base and height.

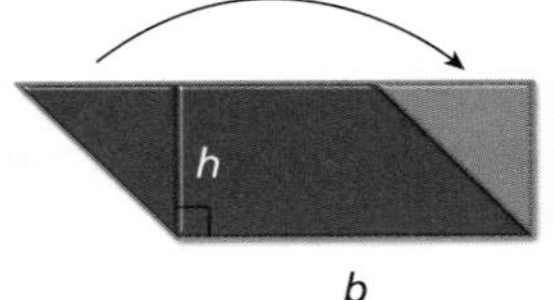


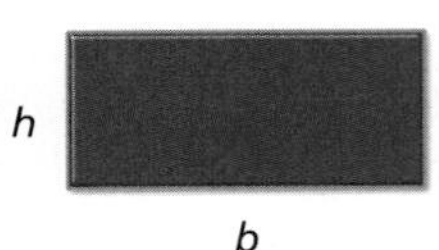


*A triangle is cut off one side and translated to the other side.*

**Area** **Parallelogram**

The area of a parallelogram with base $b$ and height $h$ is $A = bh$.

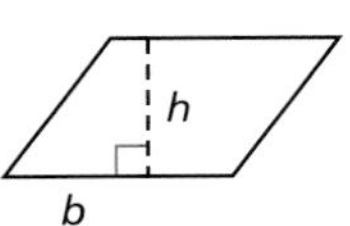


Rectangles and squares are also parallelograms. The area of a square with side $s$ is $A = s^2$, and the perimeter is $P = 4s$.

**EXAMPLE 1** **Finding Measurements of Parallelograms**

**Find each measurement.**

**A** **the area of the parallelogram**

**Step 1** Use the Pythagorean Theorem to find the height $h$.

$3^2 + h^2 = 5^2$

$h = 4$

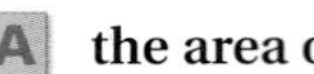

5 in. $h$ 6 in. 3 in.

**Step 2** Use $h$ to find the area of the parallelogram.

$A = bh$ — *Area of a parallelogram*

$A = 6(4)$ — *Substitute 6 for b and 4 for h.*

$A = 24 \text{ in}^2$ — *Simplify.*

**Remember!**

The height of a parallelogram is measured along a segment perpendicular to a line containing the base.

Find each measurement.

**B** **the height of a rectangle in which $b = 5$ cm and $A = (5x^2 - 5x)$ cm$^2$**

| | |
|---|---|
| $A = bh$ | *Area of a rectangle* |
| $5x^2 - 5x = 5h$ | *Substitute $5x^2 - 5x$ for A and 5 for b.* |
| $5(x^2 - x) = 5h$ | *Factor 5 out of the expression for A.* |
| $x^2 - x = h$ | *Divide both sides by 5.* |
| $h = (x^2 - x)$ cm | |

**C** **the perimeter of the rectangle, in which $A = 12x$ ft$^2$**

6 ft

**Step 1** Use the area and the height to find the base.

| | |
|---|---|
| $A = bh$ | *Area of a rectangle* |
| $12x = b(6)$ | *Substitute 12x for A and 6 for h.* |
| $2x = b$ | *Divide both sides by 6.* |

**Step 2** Use the base and the height to find the perimeter.

| | |
|---|---|
| $P = 2b + 2h$ | *Perimeter of a rectangle* |
| $P = 2(2x) + 2(6)$ | *Substitute 2x for b and 6 for h.* |
| $P = (4x + 12)$ ft. | *Simplify.* |

**Remember!**

The perimeter of a rectangle with base $b$ and height $h$ is $P = 2b + 2h$, or $P = 2(b + h)$.

**1.** Find the base of a parallelogram in which $h = 56$ yd and $A = 28$ yd$^2$.

To understand the formula for the area of a triangle or trapezoid, notice that two congruent triangles or two congruent trapezoids fit together to form a parallelogram. Thus the area of a triangle or trapezoid is half the area of the related parallelogram.

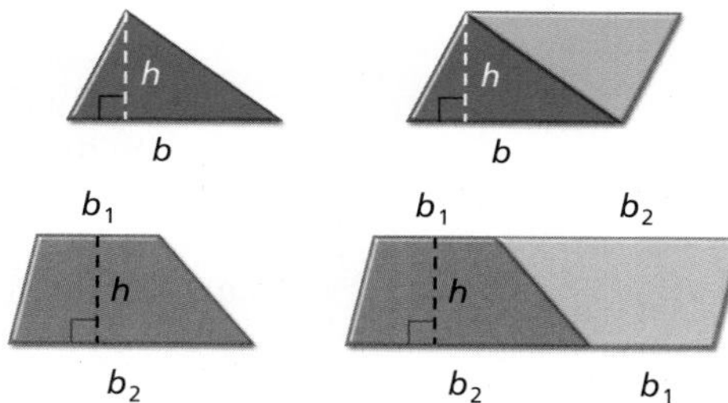


## Area — Triangles and Trapezoids

The area of a triangle with base $b$ and height $h$ is $A = \frac{1}{2}bh$.

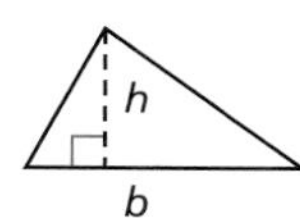


The area of a trapezoid with bases $b_1$ and $b_2$ and height $h$ is $A = \frac{1}{2}(b_1 + b_2)h$, or $A = \dfrac{(b_1 + b_2)h}{2}$.

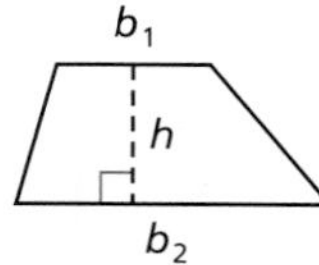


## EXAMPLE 2 Finding Measurements of Triangles and Trapezoids

Find each measurement.

**A** **the area of a trapezoid in which $b_1 = 9$ cm, $b_2 = 12$ cm, and $h = 3$ cm**

| | |
|---|---|
| $A = \frac{1}{2}(b_1 + b_2)h$ | *Area of a trapezoid* |
| $A = \frac{1}{2}(9 + 12)3$ | *Substitute 9 for $b_1$, 12 for $b_2$, and 3 for h.* |
| $A = 31.5$ cm$^2$ | *Simplify.* |

Find each measurement.

**B** **the base of the triangle, in which $A = x^2$ in$^2$**

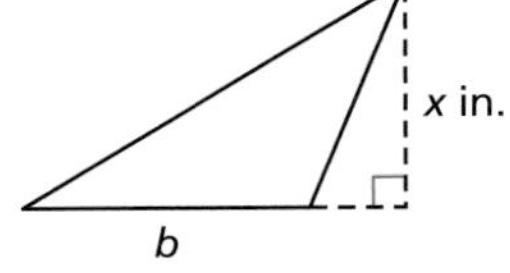


$A = \frac{1}{2}bh$ — *Area of a triangle*

$x^2 = \frac{1}{2}bx$ — *Substitute $x^2$ for A and x for h.*

$x = \frac{1}{2}b$ — *Divide both sides by x.*

$2x = b$ — *Multiply both sides by 2.*

$b = 2x$ in

**C** **$b_2$ of the trapezoid, in which $A = 8$ ft$^2$**

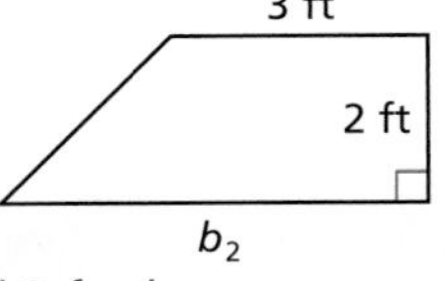


$A = \frac{1}{2}(b_1 + b_2)h$ — *Area of a trapezoid*

$8 = \frac{1}{2}(3 + b_2)(2)$ — *Substitute 8 for A, 3 for $b_1$, and 2 for h.*

$8 = 3 + b_2$ — *Multiply $\frac{1}{2}$ by 2.*

$5 = b_2$ — *Subtract 3 from both sides.*

$b_2 = 5$ ft

**2.** Find the area of the triangle.

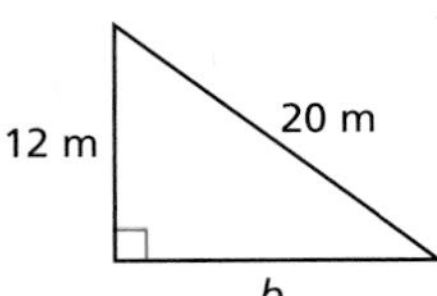


A kite or a rhombus with diagonals $d_1$ and $d_2$ can be divided into two congruent triangles with a base of $d_1$ and a height of $\frac{1}{2}d_2$.

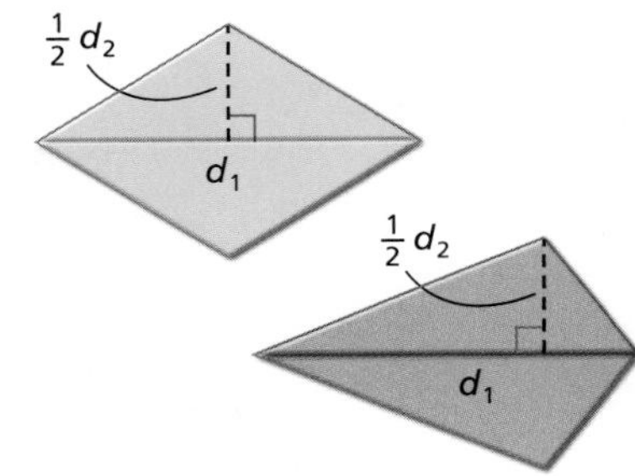


area of each triangle: $A = \frac{1}{2}d_1\left(\frac{1}{2}d_2\right) = \frac{1}{4}d_1d_2$

total area: $A = 2\left(\frac{1}{4}d_1d_2\right) = \frac{1}{2}d_1d_2$

**Area** | **Rhombuses and Kites**

The area of a rhombus or kite with diagonals $d_1$ and $d_2$ is $A = \frac{1}{2}d_1d_2$.

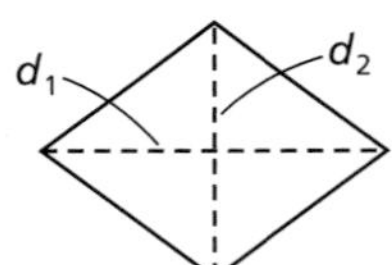


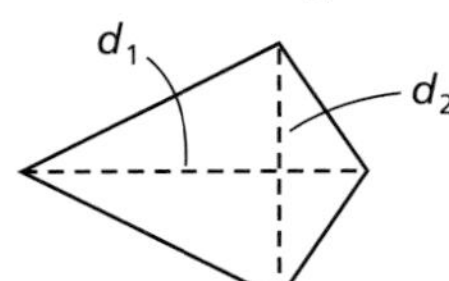


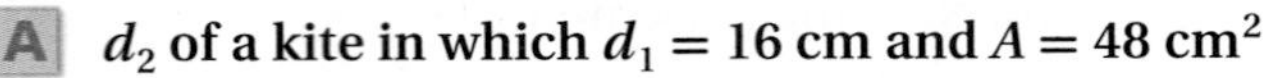

## EXAMPLE 3 Finding Measurements of Rhombuses and Kites

Find each measurement.

**A** **$d_2$ of a kite in which $d_1 = 16$ cm and $A = 48$ cm$^2$**

$A = \frac{1}{2}d_1d_2$ — *Area of a kite*

$48 = \frac{1}{2}(16)d_2$ — *Substitute 48 for A and 16 for $d_1$.*

$6 = d_2$ — *Solve for $d_2$.*

$d_2 = 6$ cm

**Find each measurement.**

**B** **the area of the rhombus**

$$A = \frac{1}{2}d_1d_2$$

$$A = \frac{1}{2}(6x + 4)(10x + 10) \quad \textit{Substitute } (6x + 4) \textit{ for } d_1 \textit{ and } (10x + 10) \textit{ for } d_2.$$

$$A = \frac{1}{2}(60x^2 + 100x + 40) \quad \textit{Multiply the binomials (FOIL).}$$

$$A = (30x^2 + 50x + 20) \text{ in}^2 \quad \textit{Distributive Property}$$

$d_1 = (6x + 4)$ in. $d_2 = (10x + 10)$ in.

**Helpful Hint**

The diagonals of a rhombus or kite are perpendicular, and the diagonals of a rhombus bisect each other.

**C** **the area of the kite**

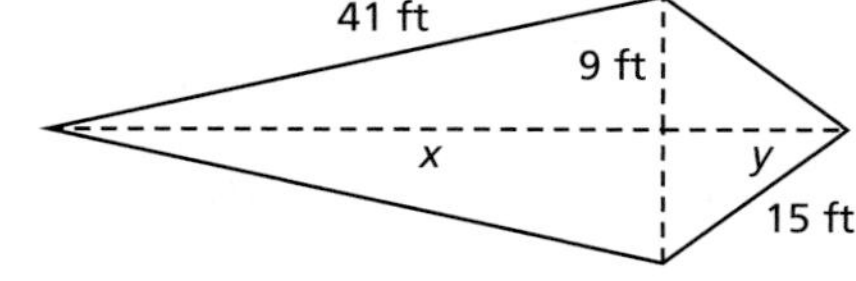


**Step 1** The diagonals $d_1$ and $d_2$ form four right triangles. Use the Pythagorean Theorem to find $x$ and $y$.

| | |
|---|---|
| $9^2 + x^2 = 41^2$ | $9^2 + y^2 = 15^2$ |
| $x^2 = 1600$ | $y^2 = 144$ |
| $x = 40$ | $y = 12$ |

**Step 2** Use $d_1$ and $d_2$ to find the area. $d_1$ is equal to $x + y$, which is 52. Half of $d_2$ is equal to 9, so $d_2$ is equal to 18.

$$A = \frac{1}{2}d_1d_2 \quad \textit{Area of a kite}$$

$$A = \frac{1}{2}(52)(18) \quad \textit{Substitute 52 for } d_1 \textit{ and 18 for } d_2.$$

$$A = 468 \text{ ft}^2 \quad \textit{Simplify.}$$

**3.** Find $d_2$ of a rhombus in which $d_1 = 3x$ m and $A = 12xy$ m$^2$.

**EXAMPLE 4** ***Games Application***

**The pieces of a tangram are arranged in a square in which $s = 4$ cm. Use the grid to find the perimeter and area of the red square.**

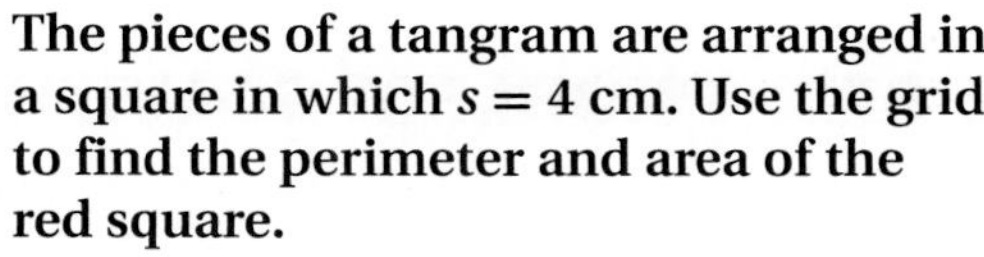

**Perimeter:**
Each side of the red square is the diagonal of a square of the grid. Each grid square has a side length of 1 cm, so the diagonal is $\sqrt{2}$ cm. The perimeter of the red square is $P = 4s = 4\sqrt{2}$ cm.

**Area:**

**Method 1** The red square is also a rhombus. The diagonals $d_1$ and $d_2$ each measure 2 cm. So its area is

$$A = \frac{1}{2}d_1d_2 = \frac{1}{2}(2)(2) = 2 \text{ cm}^2$$

**Method 2** The side length of the red square is $\sqrt{2}$ cm, so the area is

$$A = s^2 = \left(\sqrt{2}\right)^2 = 2 \text{ cm}$$

**4.** In the tangram above, find the perimeter and area of the large green triangle.

# Exercises

MA.G.2, MA.G.2.2

## GUIDED PRACTICE

**Find each measurement.**

SEE EXAMPLE 1
p. AT22

1. the area of the parallelogram

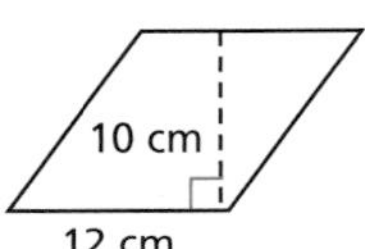


2. the height of the rectangle, in which $A = 10x^2$ ft$^2$

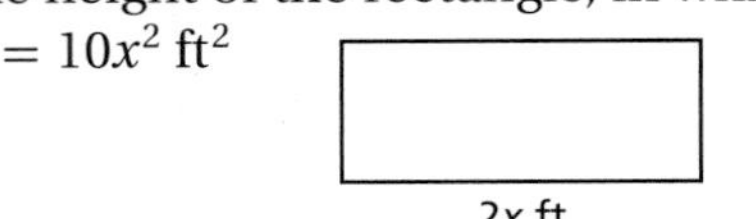


3. the perimeter of a square in which $A = 169$ cm$^2$

SEE EXAMPLE 2
p. AT23

4. the area of the trapezoid

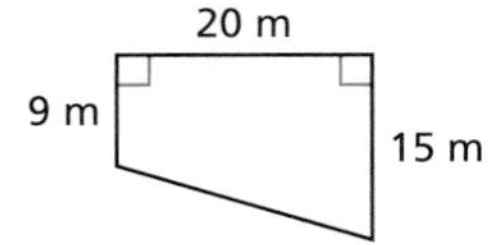


5. the base of the triangle, in which $A = 58.5$ in$^2$

9 in.

6. $b_1$ of a trapezoid in which $A = (48x + 68)$ in$^2$, $h = 8$ in., and $b_2 = (9x + 12)$ in.

SEE EXAMPLE 3
p. AT24

7. the area of the rhombus

8. $d_2$ of the kite, in which $A = 187.5$ m$^2$

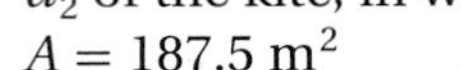

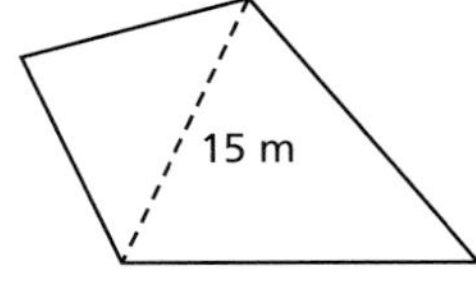


9. $d_2$ of a kite in which $A = 12x^2y^3$ cm$^2$, $d_1 = 3xy$ cm

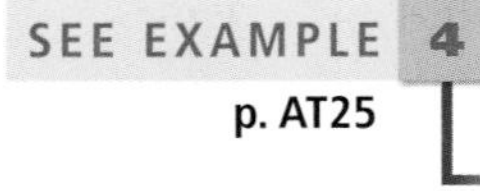

SEE EXAMPLE 4
p. AT25

10. **Art** The stained-glass window shown is a rectangle with a base of 4 ft and a height of 3 ft. Use the grid to find the area of each piece.

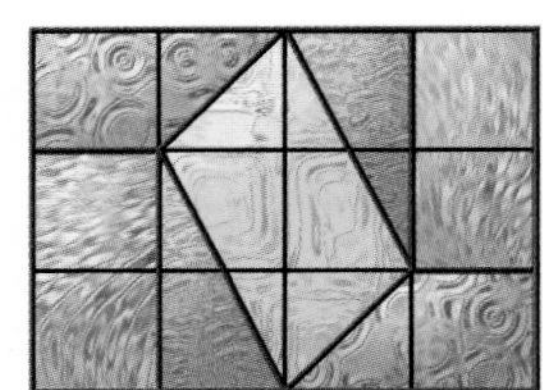

## PRACTICE AND PROBLEM SOLVING

**Find each measurement.**

11. the height of the parallelogram, in which $A = 7.5$ m$^2$

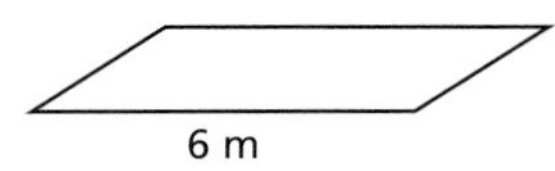


12. the perimeter of the rectangle

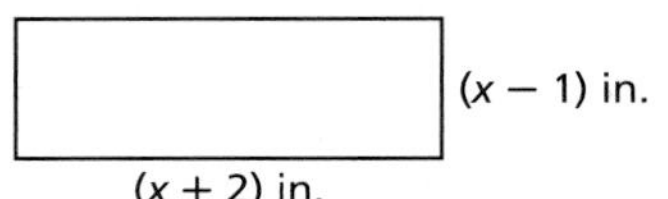


13. the area of a parallelogram in which $b = (3x + 5)$ ft and $h = (7x - 1)$ ft

14. the area of the triangle

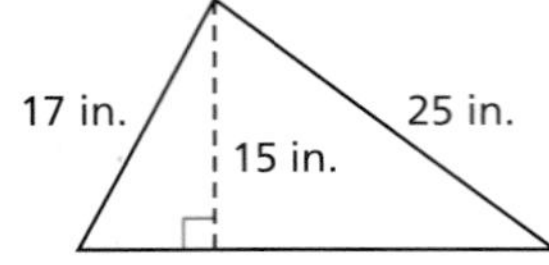


15. the height of the trapezoid, in which $A = 280$ cm$^2$

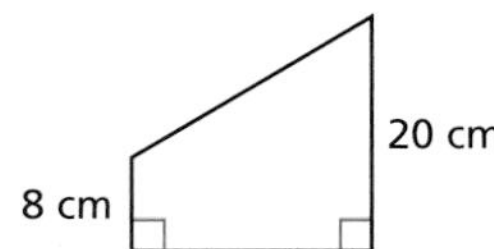


16. the area of a triangle in which $b = (x + 1)$ ft and $h = 8x$ ft

**Find each measurement.**

**17.** the area of the kite

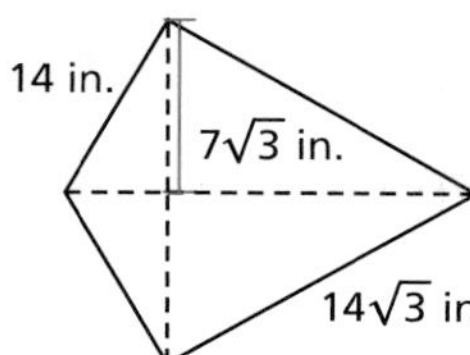


**18.** $d_2$ of the rhombus, in which $A = (3x^2 + 6x)\ \text{m}^2$

(x + 2) m

**19.** the area of a kite in which $d_1 = (6x + 5)$ ft and $d_2 = (4x + 8)$ ft

**Crafts** **In origami, a *square base* is the starting point for the creation of many figures, such as a crane. In the pattern for the square base, *ABCD* is a square, and *E, F, G,* and *H* are the midpoints of the sides. If *AB* = 6 in., find the area of each shape.**

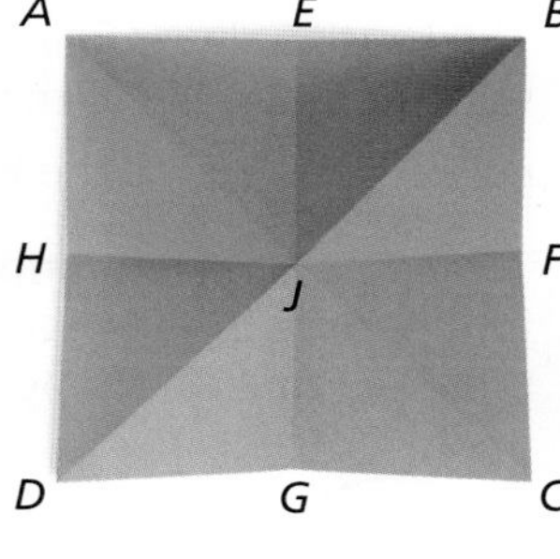

**20.** rectangle *ABFH*

**21.** $\triangle AEJ$

**22.** trapezoid *ABFJ*

**Multi-Step** **Find the area of each triangle.**

**23.**

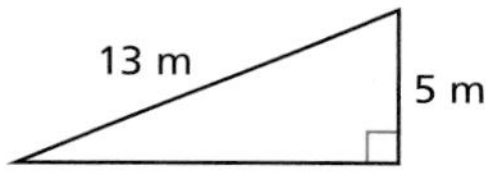


**24.**

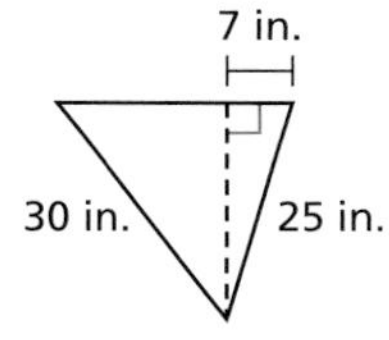


**Find the missing measurements for each rectangle.**

| | Base *b* | Height *h* | Area *A* | Perimeter *P* |
|---|---|---|---|---|
| **25.** | 12 | 16 | ■ | ■ |
| **26.** | 17 | ■ | 136 | ■ |
| **27.** | ■ | 11 | ■ | 50 |
| **28.** | ■ | ■ | 216 | 66 |

**29.** The perimeter of a rectangle is 72 in. The base is 3 times the height. Find the area of the rectangle.

**30.** The area of a triangle is 50 cm$^2$. The base of the triangle is 4 times the height. Find the height of the triangle.

**31.** The perimeter of an isosceles trapezoid is 40 ft. The bases of the trapezoid are 11 ft and 19 ft. Find the area of the trapezoid.

**Use the conversion table for Exercises 32–35.**

**32.** 1 yd$^2$ = __?__ ft$^2$

**33.** 1 m$^2$ = __?__ cm$^2$

**34.** 1 cm$^2$ = __?__ mm$^2$

**35.** 1 mi$^2$ = __?__ in$^2$

**36.** A triangle has a base of 3 yd and a height of 8 yd. Find the area in square feet.

| Conversion Factors | |
|---|---|
| **Metric** | **Customary** |
| 1 km = 1000 m | 1 mi = 1760 yd |
| 1 m = 100 cm | 1 mi = 5280 ft |
| 1 cm = 10 mm | 1 yd = 3 ft |
| | 1 ft = 12 in. |

# A-6 Developing Formulas for Circles and Regular Polygons

**MA.G.2** Use formulas to solve problems involving area… *Also* **MA.G.2.2**

***Objectives***

Develop and apply the formulas for the area and circumference of a circle.

Develop and apply the formula for the area of a regular polygon.

***Vocabulary***

circle
center of a circle
center of a regular polygon
apothem
central angle of a regular polygon

A **circle** is the set of all points in a plane that are a fixed distance from a point called the **center of the circle**. A circle is named by the symbol ⊙ and its center. ⊙$A$ has radius $r = AB$ and diameter $d = CD$.

The irrational number $\pi$ is defined as the ratio of the circumference $C$ to the diameter $d$, or $\pi = \frac{C}{d}$. Solving for $C$ gives the formula $C = \pi d$. Also $d = 2r$, so $C = 2\pi r$.

You can use the circumference of a circle to find its area. Divide the circle and rearrange the pieces to make a shape that resembles a parallelogram.

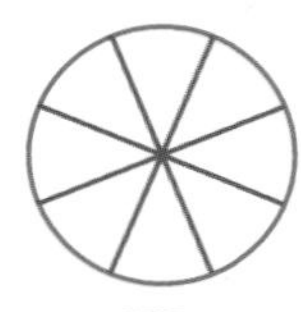

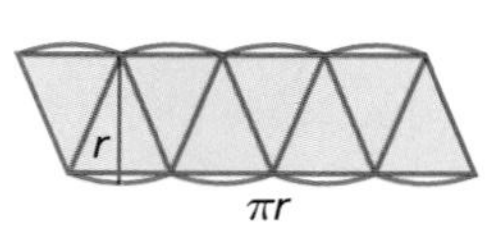


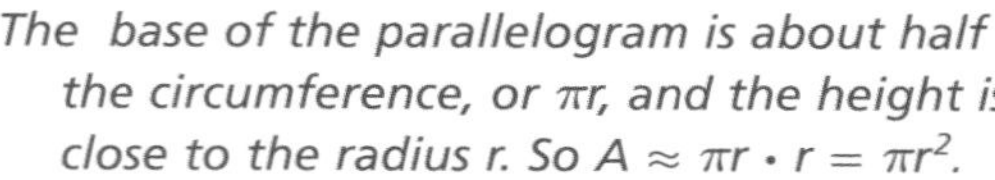

*The base of the parallelogram is about half the circumference, or $\pi r$, and the height is close to the radius r. So $A \approx \pi r \cdot r = \pi r^2$.*

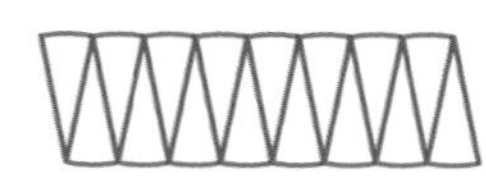

*The more pieces you divide the circle into, the more accurate the estimate will be.*

**Circumference and Area** | **Circle**

A circle with diameter $d$ and radius $r$ has circumference $C = \pi d$ or $C = 2\pi r$ and area $A = \pi r^2$.

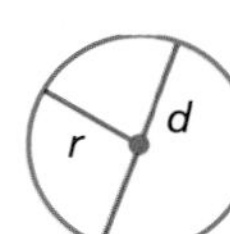


**EXAMPLE 1** **Finding Measurements of Circles**

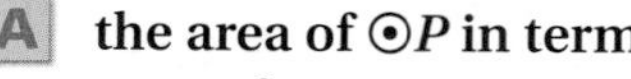

**Find each measurement.**

**A** **the area of ⊙$P$ in terms of $\pi$**

$A = \pi r^2$ — *Area of a circle*

$A = \pi(8)^2$ — *Divide the diameter by 2 to find the radius, 8.*

$A = 64\pi \text{ cm}^2$ — *Simplify.*

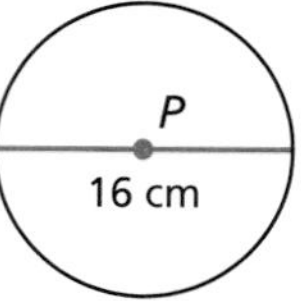


**B** **the circumference and area of ⊙$B$ in terms of $\pi$**

$C = 2\pi r = 2\pi(5xy)$

$= 10xy\pi \text{ m}$

$A = \pi r^2 = \pi(5xy)^2 = 25x^2y^2\pi \text{ m}^2$

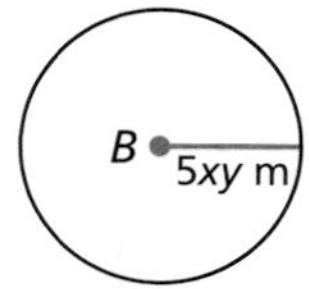

**Find each measurement.**

**C** **the radius of $\odot X$ in which $C = 24\pi$ in.**

| | |
|---|---|
| $C = 2\pi r$ | *Circumference of a circle* |
| $24\pi = 2\pi r$ | *Substitute $24\pi$ for C.* |
| $r = 12$ in. | *Divide both sides by $2\pi$.* |

**D** **the circumference of $\odot S$ in which $A = 9x^2\pi$ cm$^2$**

**Step 1** Use the given area to solve for $r$.

| | |
|---|---|
| $A = \pi r^2$ | *Area of a circle* |
| $9x^2\pi = \pi r^2$ | *Substitute $9x^2\pi$ for A.* |
| $9x^2 = r^2$ | *Divide both sides by $\pi$.* |
| $3x = r$ | *Take the square root of both sides.* |

**Step 2** Use the value of $r$ to find the circumference.

| | |
|---|---|
| $C = 2\pi r$ | |
| $C = 2\pi(3x)$ | *Substitute 3x for r.* |
| $C = 6x\pi$ cm | *Simplify.* |

**1.** Find the area of $\odot A$ in terms of $\pi$ in which $C = (4x - 6)\pi$ m.

**EXAMPLE 2** ***Music Application***

**Helpful Hint**

The $\pi$ key gives the best possible approximation for $\pi$ on your calculator. Always wait until the last step to round.

**A drum kit contains three drums with diameters of 10 in., 12 in., and 14 in. Find the area of the top of each drum. Round to the nearest tenth.**

| 10 in. diameter | 12 in. diameter | 14 in. diameter |
|---|---|---|
| $A = \pi(5^2)$ $\quad r = \frac{10}{2} = 5$ | $A = \pi(6^2)$ $\quad r = \frac{12}{2} = 6$ | $A = \pi(7)^2$ $\quad r = \frac{14}{2} = 7$ |
| $\approx 78.5$ in$^2$ | $\approx 113.1$ in$^2$ | $\approx 153.9$ in$^2$ |

**2.** Use the information above to find the circumference of each drum.

The **center of a regular polygon** is equidistant from the vertices. The **apothem** is the distance from the center to a side. A **central angle of a regular polygon** has its vertex at the center, and its sides pass through consecutive vertices. Each central angle measure of a regular $n$-gon is $\frac{360°}{n}$.

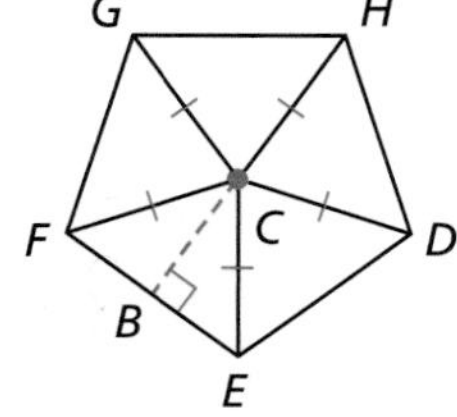


Regular pentagon *DEFGH* has center *C*, apothem *BC*, and central angle ∠*DCE*.

To find the area of a regular $n$-gon with side length $s$ and apothem $a$, divide it into $n$ congruent isosceles triangles.

area of each triangle: $\frac{1}{2}as$

total area of the polygon: $A = n\left(\frac{1}{2}as\right)$, or $A = \frac{1}{2}aP$ *The perimeter is $P = ns$.*

**Area** **Regular Polygon**

The area of a regular polygon with apothem $a$ and perimeter $P$ is $A = \frac{1}{2}aP$.

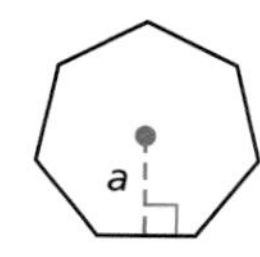

## EXAMPLE 3 Finding the Area of a Regular Polygon

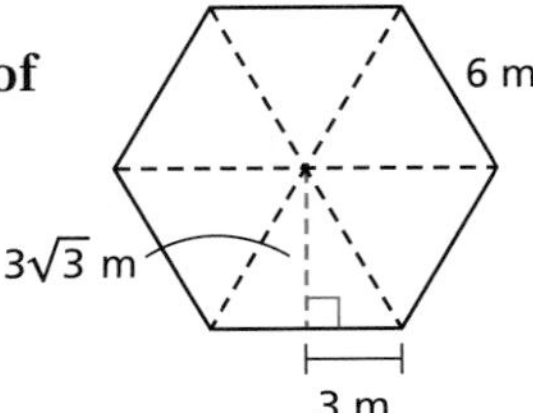


**Find the area of a regular hexagon with a side length of 6 m and an apothem of $3\sqrt{3}$ m. Round to the nearest tenth.**

The perimeter is $6(6) = 36$ m.

| | |
|---|---|
| $A = \frac{1}{2}aP$ | *Area of a regular polygon* |
| $A = \frac{1}{2}(3\sqrt{3})(36)$ | *Substitute $3\sqrt{3}$ for a and 36 for P.* |
| $A = 54\sqrt{3} \approx 93.5 \text{ m}^2$ | *Simplify.* |

**3.** Find the area of a regular octagon with a side length of 4 cm and an apothem of 4.83 cm.

# Exercises

**MA.G.2, MA.G.2.2**

## GUIDED PRACTICE

1. **Vocabulary** Describe how to find the *apothem* of a square with side length $s$.

SEE EXAMPLE 1 p. AT28

**Find each measurement.**

2. the circumference of $\odot C$

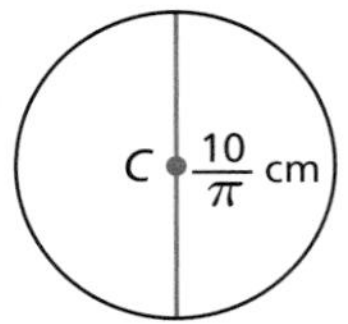


3. the area of $\odot A$ in terms of $\pi$

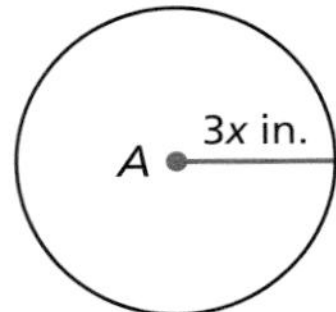


4. the circumference of $\odot P$ in which $A = 36\pi \text{ in}^2$

SEE EXAMPLE 2 p. AT29

5. **Food** A pizza parlor offers pizzas with diameters of 8 in., 10 in., and 12 in. Find the area of each size pizza. Round to the nearest tenth.

SEE EXAMPLE 3 p. AT30

**Find the area of each regular polygon. Round to the nearest tenth.**

6. an equilateral triangle with a side length of $4\sqrt{3}$ ft and an apothem of 2 ft
7. a regular dodecagon with a side length of 5 m and an apothem of 9.33 m

## PRACTICE AND PROBLEM SOLVING

**Find each measurement. Give your answers in terms of $\pi$.**

8. the area of $\odot M$

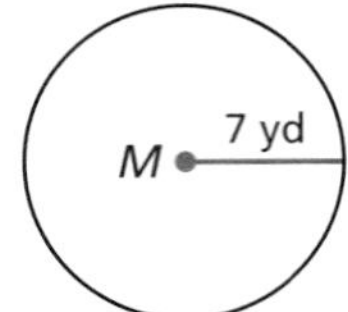


9. the circumference of $\odot Z$

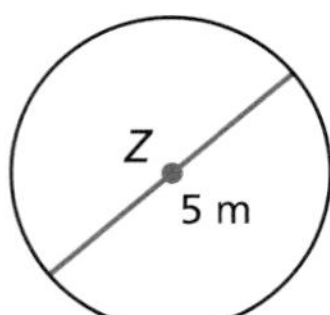


10. the diameter of $\odot G$ in which $C = 10$ ft.

11. **Sports** A horse trainer uses circular pens that are 35 ft, 50 ft, and 66 ft in diameter. Find the area of each pen. Round to the nearest tenth.

**Find the area of each regular polygon. Round to the nearest tenth, if necessary.**

12.
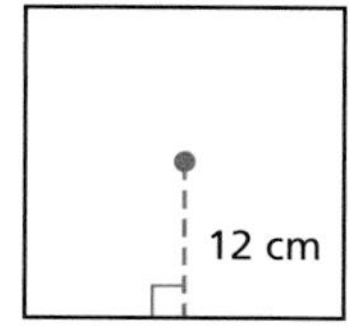


13.
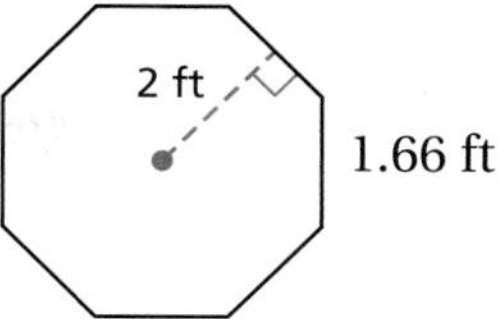


14. a regular nonagon with a perimeter of 144 in. and an apothem of 22 in.

15. a regular pentagon with a perimeter of 14.5 ft and an apothem of 2 ft

**Find the central angle measure of each regular polygon. (*Hint:* To review polygon names, see page AT16.)**

16. equilateral triangle
17. square
18. pentagon
19. hexagon
20. heptagon
21. octagon
22. nonagon
23. decagon

**Find the area of each regular polygon. Round to the nearest tenth, if necessary.**

24.
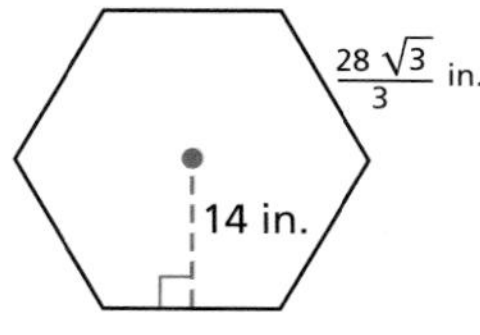


25.
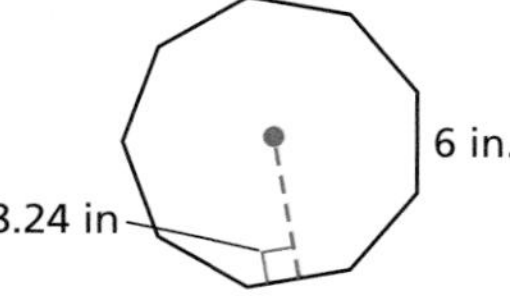


26.
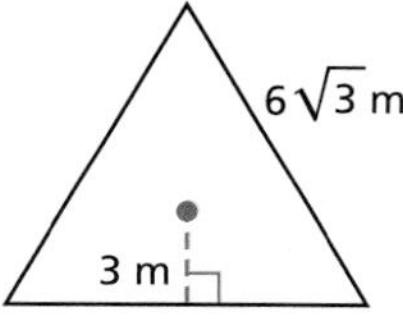


27.
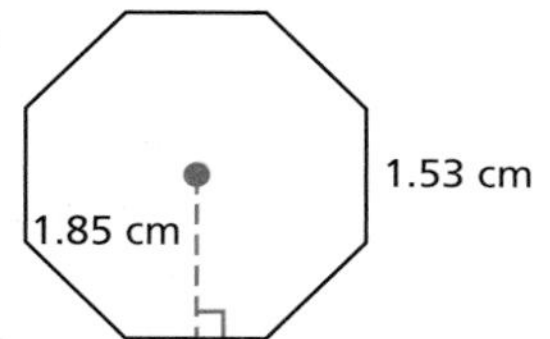


28. **Biology** You can estimate a tree's age in years by using the formula $a = \frac{r}{w}$, where $r$ is the tree's radius without bark and $w$ is the average thickness of the tree's rings. The circumference of a white oak tree is 100 in. The bark is 0.5 in. thick, and the average width of a ring is 0.2 in. Estimate the tree's age.

29. **/// ERROR ANALYSIS ///** A circle has a circumference of $2\pi$ in. Which calculation of the area is incorrect? Explain.

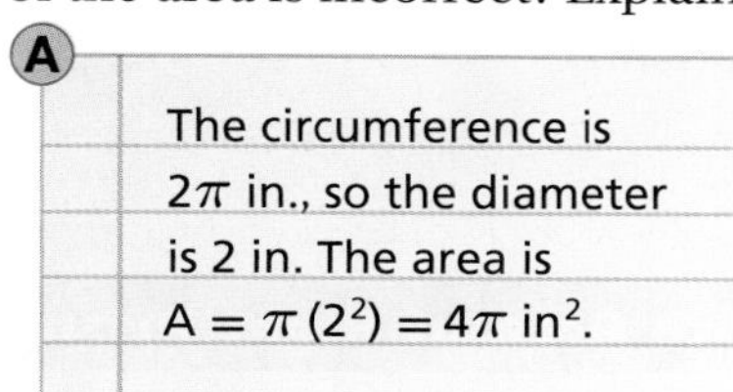
(A) The circumference is $2\pi$ in., so the diameter is 2 in. The area is $A = \pi(2^2) = 4\pi \text{ in}^2$.

(B) The circumference is $2\pi$ in., so the radius is 1 in. The area is $A = \pi(1^2) = 2\pi \text{ in}^2$.

**Find the missing measurements for each circle. Give your answers in terms of $\pi$.**

| | Diameter $d$ | Radius $r$ | Area $A$ | Circumference $C$ |
|---|---|---|---|---|
| 30. | 6 | | | |
| 31. | | | 100 | |
| 32. | | 17 | | |
| 33. | | | | $36\pi$ |

34. **Multi-Step** Janet is designing a garden around a gazebo that is a regular hexagon with side length 6 ft and apothem $3\sqrt{3}$ ft. The garden will be a circle that extends 10 feet from the vertices of the hexagon. What is the area of the garden? Round to the nearest square foot.

# A-7 Surface Area

**MA.G.2** Use formulas to solve problems involving area...
*Also* **MA.G.2.5**

***Objective***
Learn and apply the formula for the surface areas of a prism, cylinders, and pyramids.

***Vocabulary***
lateral face
lateral edge
right prism
altitude
surface area
lateral surface
axis of a cylinder
right cylinder
vertex of a pyramid
regular pyramid
slant height of a regular pyramid
altitude of a pyrmaid

Prisms and cylinders have 2 congruent parallel bases. A **lateral face** is not a base. The edges of the base are called *base edges*. A **lateral edge** is not an edge of a base. The lateral faces of a **right prism** are all rectangles.

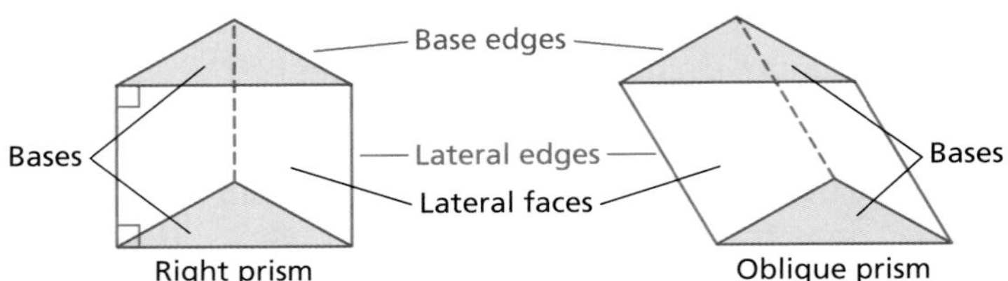


An **altitude** of a right prism is a perpendicular segment joining the bases. The *height* of a three-dimensional figure is the length of an altitude.

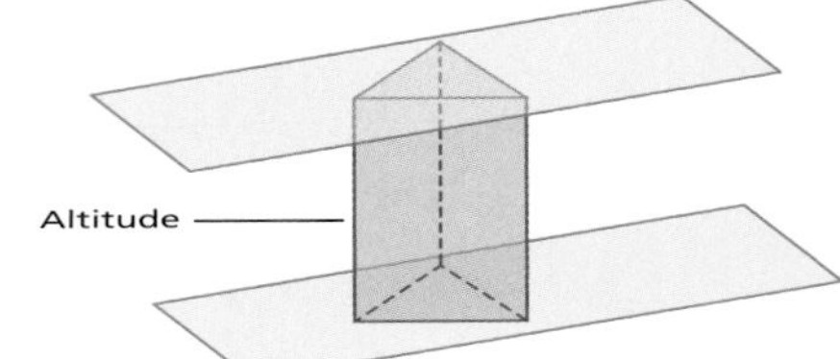


**Surface area** is the total area of all faces and curved surfaces of a three-dimensional figure. The *lateral area* of a prism is the sum of the areas of the lateral faces.

The net of a right prism can be drawn so that the lateral faces form a rectangle with the same height as the prism. The base of the rectangle is equal to the perimeter of the base of the prism.

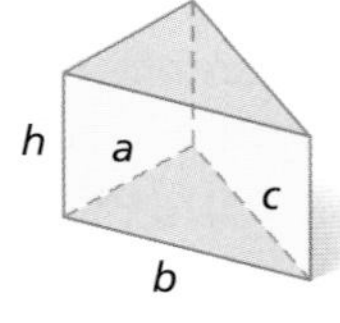


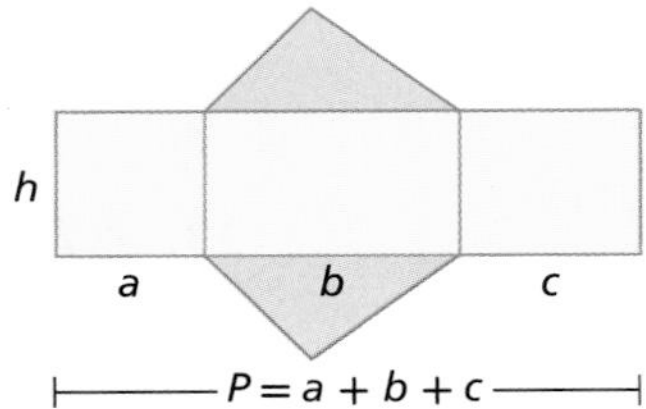


**Lateral Area and Surface Area of Right Prisms**

| |
|---|
| The lateral area of a right prism with base perimeter $P$ and height $h$ is $L = Ph$. |
| The surface area of a right prism with lateral area $L$ and base area $B$ is $S = L + 2B$, or $S = Ph + 2B$. |
| The surface area of a cube with edge length $s$ is $S = 6s^2$. |

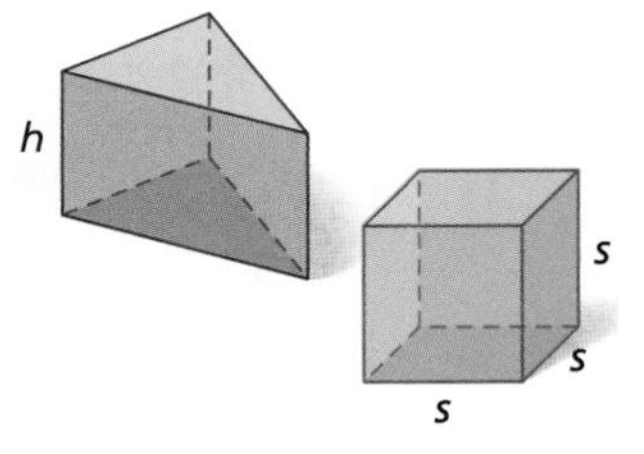


The surface area of a right rectangular prism with length $\ell$, width $w$, and height $h$ can be written as $S = 2\ell w + 2wh + 2\ell h$.

EXAMPLE 1

## Finding Lateral Areas and Surface Areas of Prisms

**Find the lateral area and surface area of each right prism. Round to the nearest tenth, if necessary.**

**A** **the rectangular prism**

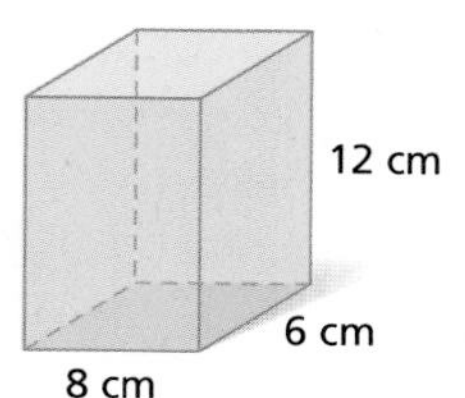


$L = Ph$

$= (28)12 = 336 \text{ cm}^2$   *$P = 2(8) + 2(6) = 28$ cm*

$S = Ph + 2B$

$= 336 + 2(6)(8)$

$= 432 \text{ cm}^2$

**B** **the regular hexagonal prism**

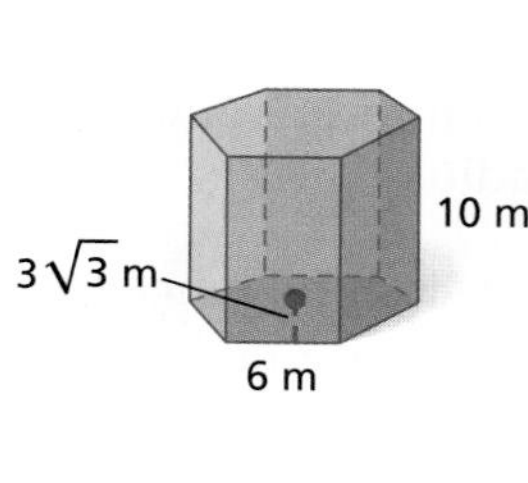


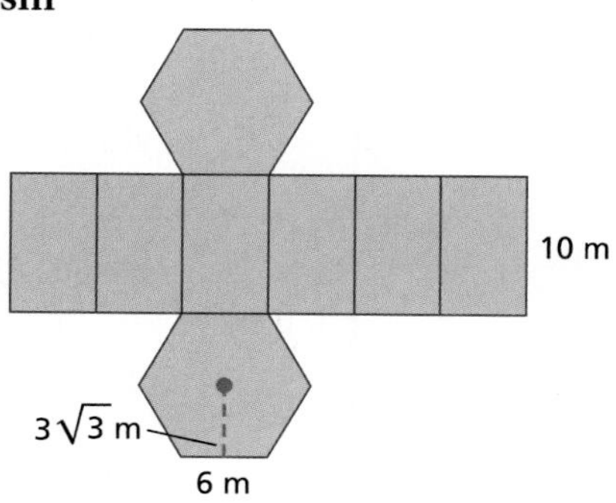


$L = Ph$

$= 36(10) = 360 \text{ m}^2$   *$P = 6(6) = 36$ m*

$S = Ph + 2B$

$= 360 + 2\left(54\sqrt{3}\right)$   *The base area is $B = \frac{1}{2}aP = 54\sqrt{3}$ m.*

$\approx 547.1 \text{ m}^2$

**1.** Find the lateral area and surface area of a cube with edge length 8 cm.

The **lateral surface** of a cylinder is the curved surface that connects the two bases. The **axis of a cylinder** is the segment with endpoints at the centers of the bases. The axis of a **right cylinder** is perpendicular to its bases and its length is the height of the cylinder.

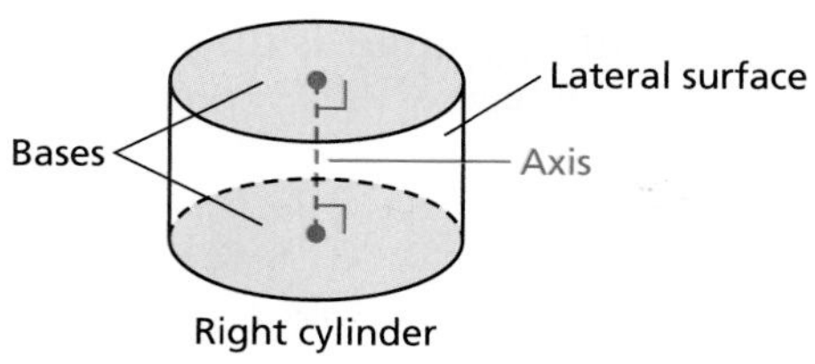


Right cylinder

### Lateral Area and Surface Area of Right Cylinders

| | |
|---|---|
| The lateral area of a right cylinder with radius $r$ and height $h$ is $L = 2\pi rh$. | |
| The surface area of a right cylinder with lateral area $L$ and base area $B$ is $S = L + 2B$, or $S = 2\pi rh + 2\pi r^2$. | |

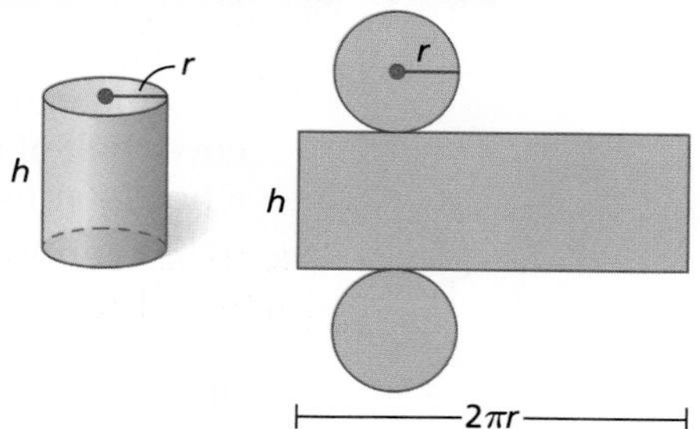

## EXAMPLE 2 Finding Lateral Areas and Surface Areas of Right Cylinders

**Find the lateral area and surface area of each right cylinder. Give your answers in terms of $\pi$.**

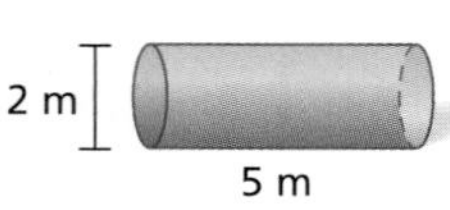


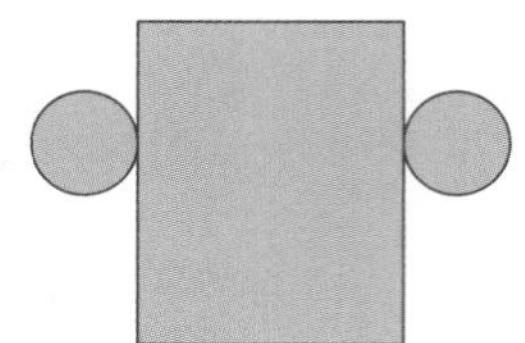

$L = 2\pi rh = 2\pi(1)(5) = 10\pi \text{ m}^2$ *The radius is half the diameter, or 1 m.*

$S = L + 2\pi r^2 = 10\pi + 2\pi(1)^2 = 12\pi \text{ m}^2$

**B a cylinder with a circumference of $10\pi$ cm and a height equal to 3 times the radius**

**Step 1** Use the circumference to find the radius.

$C = 2\pi r$ *Circumference of a circle*

$10\pi = 2\pi r$ *Substitute $10\pi$ for C.*

$r = 5$ *Divide both sides by $2\pi$.*

**Step 2** Use the radius to find the lateral area and surface area. The height is 3 times the radius, or 15 cm.

$L = 2\pi rh = 2\pi(5)(15) = 150\pi \text{ cm}^2$ *Lateral area*

$S = 2\pi rh + 2\pi r^2 = 150\pi + 2\pi(5)^2 = 200\pi \text{ cm}^2$ *Surface area*

**2.** Find the lateral area and surface area of a cylinder with a base area of $49\pi$ and a height that is 2 times the radius.

**Remember!**

Always round at the last step of the problem. Use the value of $\pi$ given by the $\pi$ key on your calculator.

The **vertex of a pyramid** is the point opposite the base of the pyramid. The base of a **regular pyramid** is a regular polygon, and the lateral faces are congruent isosceles triangles. The **slant height of a regular pyramid** is the distance from the vertex to the midpoint of an edge of the base. The **altitude of a pyramid** is the perpendicular segment from the vertex to the plane of the base.

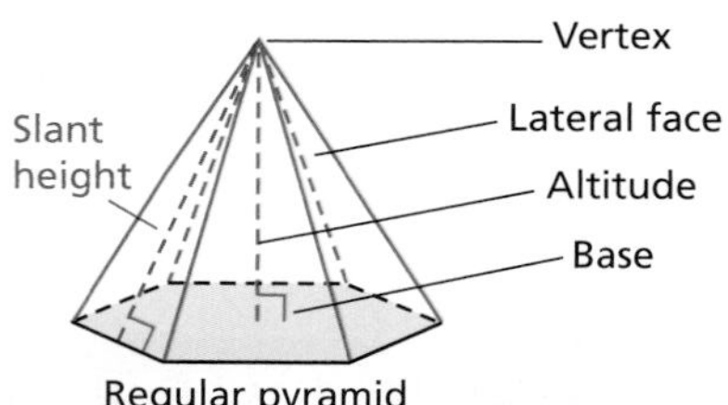

Regular pyramid

The lateral faces of a regular pyramid can be arranged to cover half of a rectangle with a height equal to the slant height of the pyramid. The width of the rectangle is equal to the base perimeter of the pyramid.

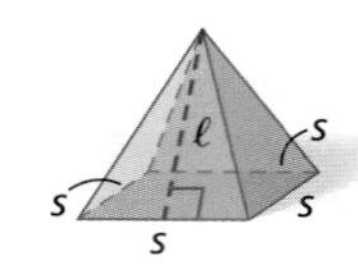


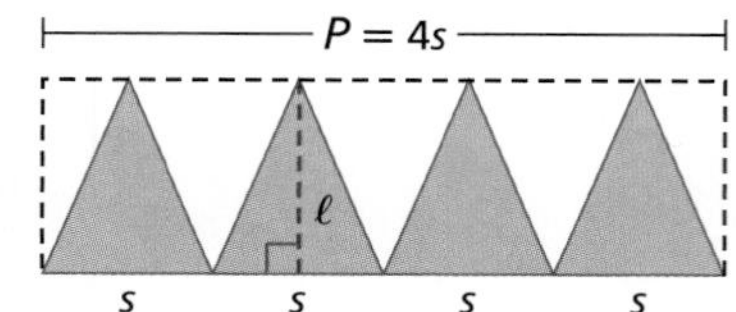

## Lateral and Surface Area of a Regular Pyramid

The lateral area of a regular pyramid with perimeter $P$ and slant height $\ell$ is $L = \frac{1}{2}P\ell$.

The surface area of a regular pyramid with lateral area $L$ and base area $B$ is $S = L + B$, or $S = \frac{1}{2}P\ell + B$.

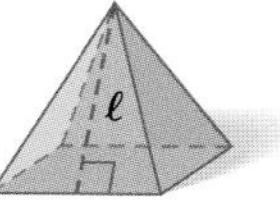


### EXAMPLE 3 Finding Lateral Area and Surface Area of Pyramids

**Find the lateral area and surface area of each pyramid. Round to the nearest tenth, if necessary.**

**A** **a regular square pyramid with base edge length 5 in. and slant height 9 in.**

$L = \frac{1}{2}P\ell$ — *Lateral area of a regular pyramid*

$= \frac{1}{2}(20)(9) = 90 \text{ in}^2$ — *$P = 4(5) = 20$ in.*

$S = \frac{1}{2}P\ell + B$ — *Surface area of a regular pyramid*

$= 90 + 25 = 115 \text{ in}^2$ — *$B = 5^2 = 25 \text{ in}^2$*

**B** **a regular hexagonal pyramid with base edge length 4 m, base apothem $2\sqrt{3}$ m, and slant height 7 m**

**Step 1** Find the base perimeter and apothem.
The base perimeter is $6(4) = 24$ m.
The apothem is $2\sqrt{3}$ m, so the base area is $\frac{1}{2}aP = \frac{1}{2}(2\sqrt{3})(24) = 24\sqrt{3} \text{ m}^2$.

**Step 2** Find the lateral area.

$L = \frac{1}{2}P\ell$ — *Lateral area of a regular pyramid*

$= \frac{1}{2}(24)(7) = 84 \text{ m}^2$ — *Substitute 24 for $P$ and 7 for $\ell$.*

**Step 3** Find the surface area.

$S = \frac{1}{2}P\ell + B$ — *Surface area of a regular pyramid*

$= 84 + 24\sqrt{3} \approx 125.6 \text{ m}^2$ — *Substitute $24\sqrt{3}$ for $B$.*

**3.** Find the lateral area and surface area of a regular triangular pyramid with base edge length 6 ft and slant height 10 ft. Round to the nearest tenth, if necessary.

# Exercises

## GUIDED PRACTICE

**1. Vocabulary** How many *lateral faces* does a pentagonal prism have?

SEE EXAMPLE 1
p. AT33

**Find the lateral area and surface area of each right prism.**

**2.**

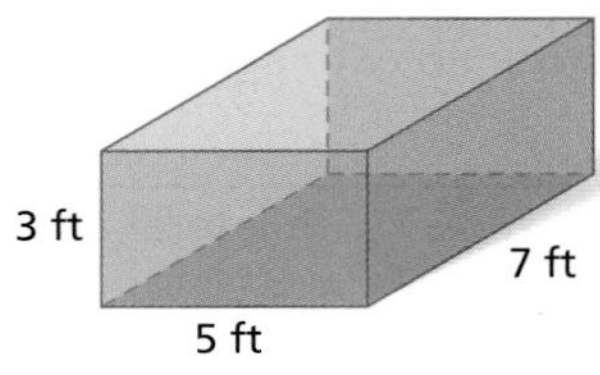


**3.** a cube with edge length 9 inches

SEE EXAMPLE 2
p. AT34

**Find the lateral area and surface area of each right cylinder. Give your answers in terms of $\pi$.**

**4.**

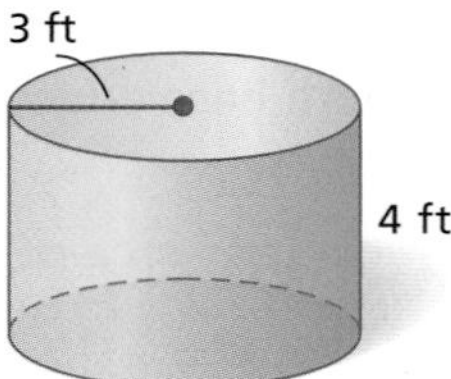


**5.**

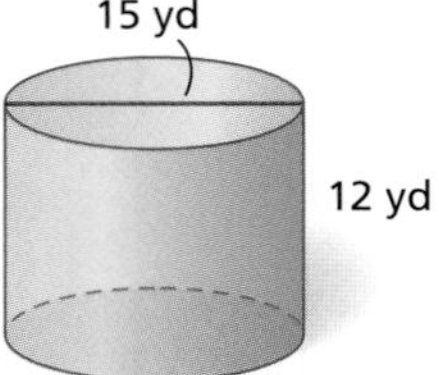


**6.** a cylinder with base area $64\pi$ m$^2$ and a height 3 meters less than the radius

SEE EXAMPLE 3
p. AT35

**Find the lateral area and surface area of each regular pyramid.**

**7.**

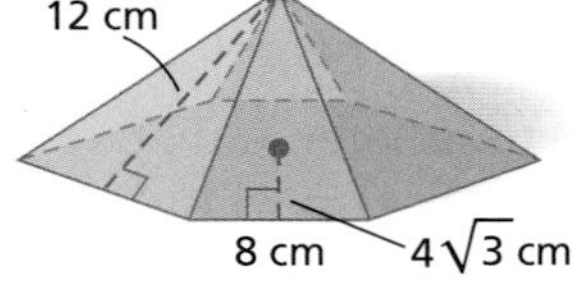


**8.**

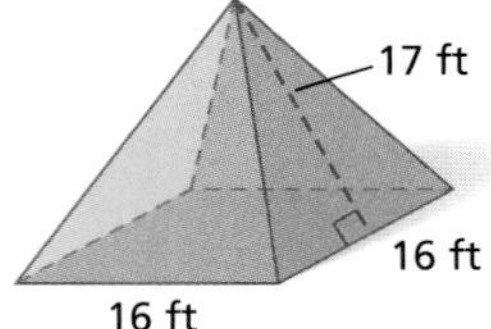


**9.** a regular triangular pyramid with base edge length 15 in. and slant height 20 in.

## PRACTICE AND PROBLEM SOLVING

**Find the lateral area and surface area of each right prism. Round to the nearest tenth, if necessary.**

**10.**

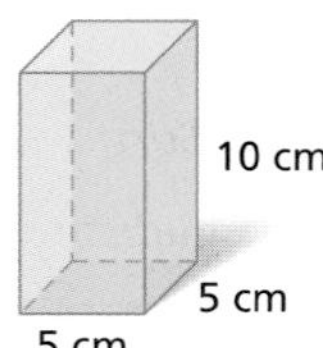


**11.**

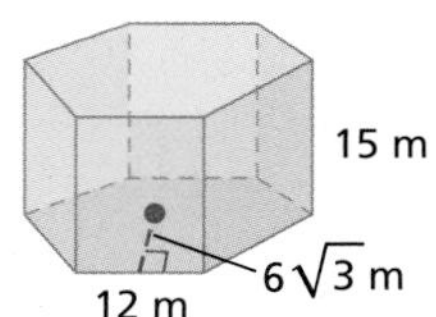


**12.** a right equilateral triangular prism with base edge length 8 ft and height 14 ft

**Find the lateral area and surface area of each right cylinder. Give your answers in terms of $\pi$.**

**13.**

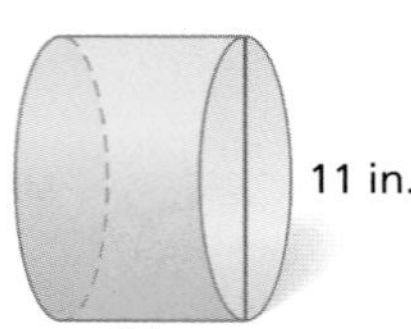


**14.**

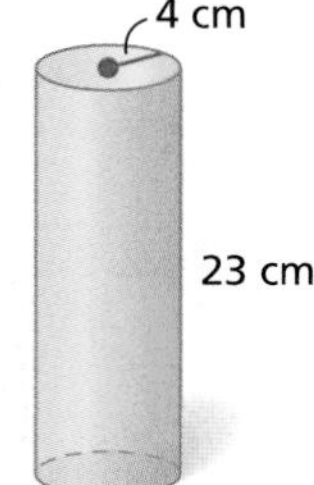


**15.** a cylinder with base circumference $16\pi$ yd and a height equal to 3 times the radius

**Find the lateral area and surface area of each regular pyramid.**

16.

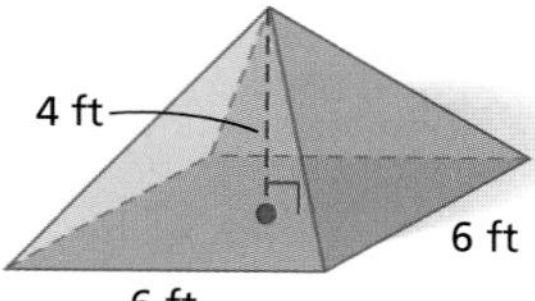


17. a regular hexagonal pyramid with base edge length 7 ft, base apothem $3.5\sqrt{3}$ ft, and slant height 15 ft

18. Find the height of a right cylinder with surface area $160\pi$ ft$^2$ and radius 5 ft.

19. Find the height of a right rectangular prism with surface area 286 m$^2$, length 10 m, and width 8 m.

20. Find the height of a right regular hexagonal prism with lateral area 1368 m$^2$ and base edge length 12 m.

21. Find the surface area of the right triangular prism with vertices at $(0, 0, 0)$, $(5, 0, 0)$, $(0, 2, 0)$, $(0, 0, 9)$, $(5, 0, 9)$, and $(0, 2, 9)$.

**The dimensions of various coins are given in the table. Find the surface area of each coin. Round to the nearest hundredth.**

| | Coin | Diameter (mm) | Thickness (mm) | Surface Area (mm$^2$) |
|---|---|---|---|---|
| 22. | Penny | 19.05 | 1.55 | ■ |
| 23. | Nickel | 21.21 | 1.95 | ■ |
| 24. | Dime | 17.91 | 1.35 | ■ |
| 25. | Quarter | 24.26 | 1.75 | ■ |

26. How can the edge lengths of a rectangular prism be changed so that the surface area is multiplied by 9?

27. How can the radius and height of a cylinder be changed so that the surface area is multiplied by $\frac{1}{4}$?

28. **Landscaping** Ingrid is building a shelter to protect her plants from freezing. She is planning to stretch plastic sheeting over the top and the ends of a frame. Which of the frames shown will require more plastic?

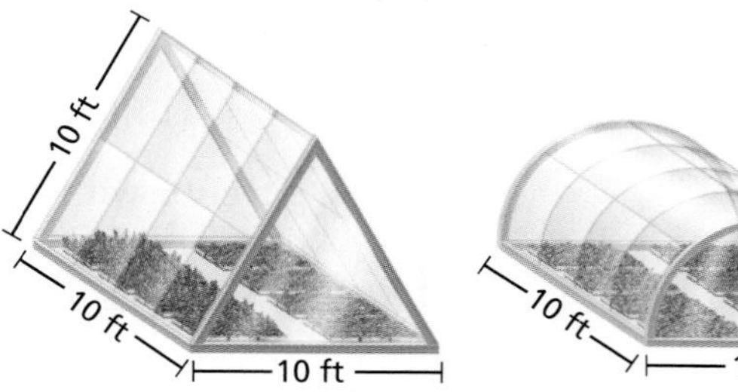


29. **Write About It** Explain how to use the net of a three-dimensional figure to find its surface area.

# A-8 Volume of Prisms and Cylinders

**MA.G.2** Use formulas to solve problems involving ... volume.
*Also* **MA.G.2.4**

***Objectives***

Learn and apply the formula for the volume of a prism.

Learn and apply the formula for the volume of a cylinder.

***Vocabulary***

volume

The **volume** of a three-dimensional figure is the number of nonoverlapping unit cubes of a given size that will exactly fill the interior.

*A cube built out of 27 unit cubes has a volume of 27 cubic units.*

**Volume of a Prism**

The volume of a prism with base area $B$ and height $h$ is $V = Bh$.

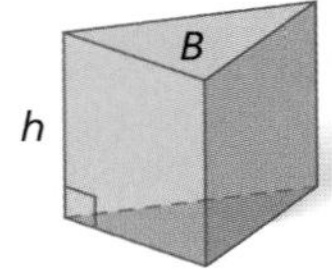


The volume of a right rectangular prism with length $\ell$, width $w$, and height $h$ is $V = \ell wh$.

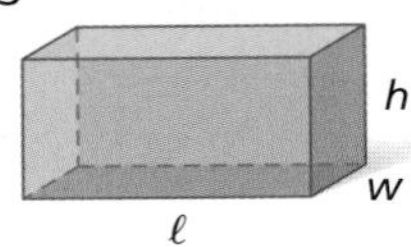


The volume of a cube with edge length $s$ is $V = s^3$.

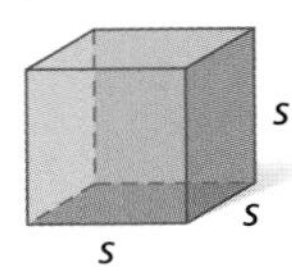


## EXAMPLE 1 Finding Volumes of Prisms

**Find the volume of each prism. Round to the nearest tenth, if necessary.**

**A**

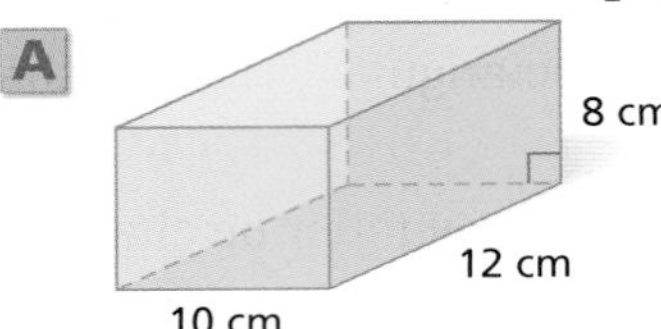


$V = \ell wh$ — *Volume of a right rectangular prism*

$= (10)(12)(8) = 960 \text{ cm}^3$ — *Substitute 10 for ℓ, 12 for w, and 8 for h.*

**B** **a cube with edge length 10 cm**

$V = s^3$ — *Volume of a cube*

$= 10^3 = 1000 \text{ cm}^3$ — *Substitute 10 for s.*

1. Find the volume of a triangular prism with a height of 9 yd whose base is a right triangle with legs 7 yd and 5 yd long.

## EXAMPLE 2 *Marine Biology Application*

**The aquarium at the right is a rectangular prism. Estimate the volume of the water in the aquarium in gallons. The density of water is about 8.33 pounds per gallon. Estimate the weight of the water in pounds. (*Hint:* 1 gallon ≈ 0.134 ft$^3$)**

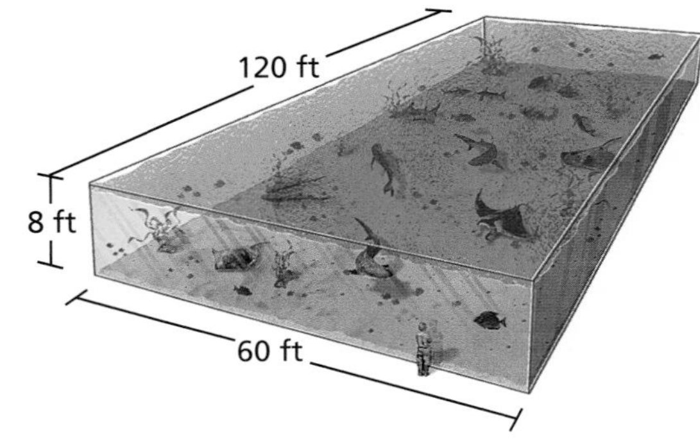

**Step 1** Find the volume of the aquarium in cubic feet.

$V = \ell wh = (120)(60)(8) = 57{,}600 \text{ ft}^3$

**Step 2** Use the conversion factor $\frac{1 \text{ gallon}}{0.134 \text{ ft}^3}$ to estimate the volume in gallons.

$57{,}600 \text{ ft}^3 \cdot \frac{1 \text{ gallon}}{0.134 \text{ ft}^3} \approx 429{,}851 \text{ gallons}$ *$\frac{1 \text{ gallon}}{0.134 \text{ ft}^3} = 1$*

**Step 3** Use the conversion factor $\frac{8.33 \text{ pounds}}{1 \text{ gallon}}$ to estimate the weight of the water.

$429{,}851 \text{ gallons} \cdot \frac{8.33 \text{ pounds}}{1 \text{ gallon}} \approx 3{,}580{,}659 \text{ pounds}$ *$\frac{8.33 \text{ pounds}}{1 \text{ gallon}} = 1$*

The aquarium holds about 429,851 gallons. The water in the aquarium weighs about 3,580,659 pounds.

**2. What if...?** Estimate the volume in gallons and the weight of the water in the aquarium above if the height were doubled.

## Volume of a Cylinder

The volume of a cylinder with base area $B$, radius $r$, and height $h$ is $V = Bh$, or $V = \pi r^2 h$.

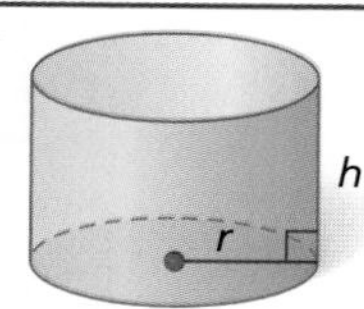


EXAMPLE  **3**

### Finding Volumes of Cylinders

**Find the volume of each cylinder. Give your answers both in terms of $\pi$ and rounded to the nearest tenth.**

**A**

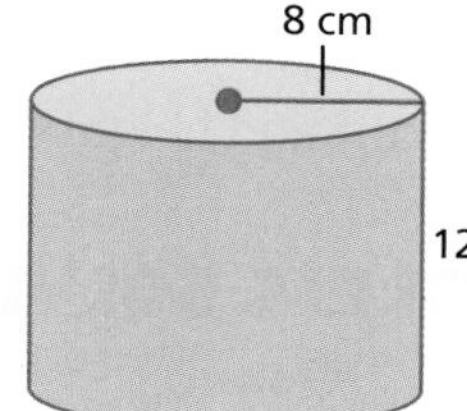


$V = \pi r^2 h$ *Volume of a cylinder*

$= \pi(8)^2(12)$ *Substitute 8 for r and 12 for h.*

$= 768\pi \text{ cm}^3 \approx 2412.7 \text{ cm}^3$

**B** **a cylinder with a base area of $36\pi$ in$^2$ and a height equal to twice the radius**

**Step 1** Use the base area to find the radius.

$\pi r^2 = 36\pi$ *Substitute $36\pi$ for the base area.*

$r = 6$ *Solve for r.*

**Step 2** Use the radius to find the height. The height is equal to twice the radius.

$h = 2r$

$= 2(6) = 12 \text{ cm}$

**Step 3** Use the radius and height to find the volume.

$V = \pi r^2 h$ *Volume of a cylinder*

$= \pi(6)^2(12) = 432\pi \text{ in}^3$ *Substitute 6 for r and 12 for h.*

$\approx 1357.2 \text{ in}^3$

**3.** Find the volume of a cylinder with a diameter of 16 in. and a height of 17 in. Give your answer both in terms of $\pi$ and rounded to the nearest tenth.

# Exercises

MA.G.2, MA.G.2.4

## GUIDED PRACTICE

SEE EXAMPLE 1 p. AT38

**Find the volume of each prism. Round to the nearest tenth, if necessary.**

1. 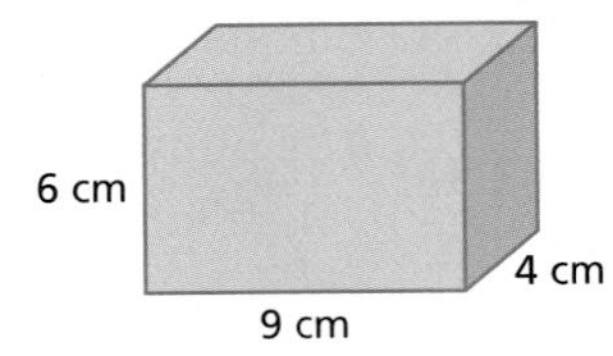


2. 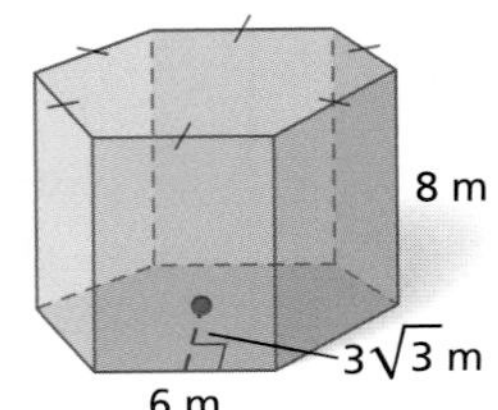


3. a cube with edge length 8 ft

SEE EXAMPLE 2 p. AT38

4. **Food** The world's largest ice cream cake, built in New York City on May 25, 2004, was approximately a 19 ft by 9 ft by 2 ft rectangular prism. Estimate the volume of the ice cream cake in gallons. If the density of the ice cream was 4.73 pounds per gallon, estimate the weight of the cake. (*Hint:* 1 gallon $\approx$ 0.134 cubic feet)

SEE EXAMPLE 3 p. AT39

**Find the volume of each cylinder. Give your answers both in terms of $\pi$ and rounded to the nearest tenth.**

5. 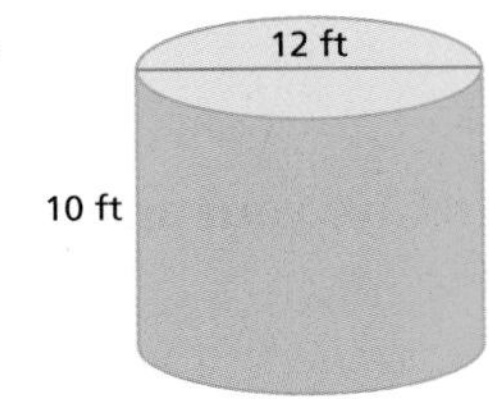


6. 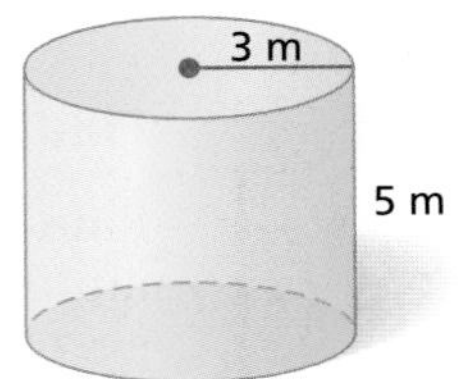


7. a cylinder with base area $25\pi$ cm$^2$ and height 3 cm more than the radius

## PRACTICE AND PROBLEM SOLVING

**Find the volume of each prism.**

8. 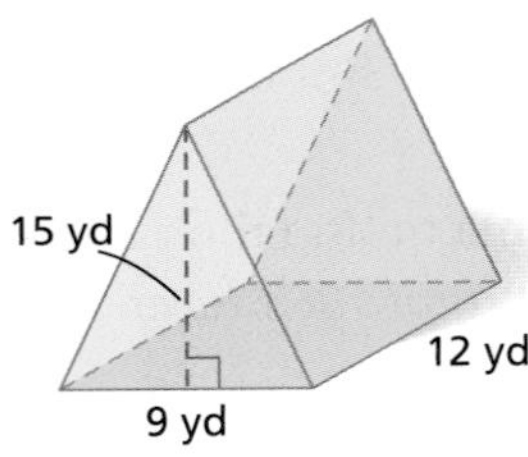


9. a square prism with a base area of 49 ft$^2$ and a height 2 ft less than the base edge length

10. **Landscaping** Colin is buying dirt to fill a garden bed that is a 9 ft by 16 ft rectangle. If he wants to fill it to a depth of 4 in., how many cubic yards of dirt does he need? If dirt costs \$25 per yd$^3$, how much will the project cost? (*Hint:* 1 yd$^3$ = 27 ft$^3$)

**Find the volume of each cylinder. Give your answers both in terms of $\pi$ and rounded to the nearest tenth.**

11. 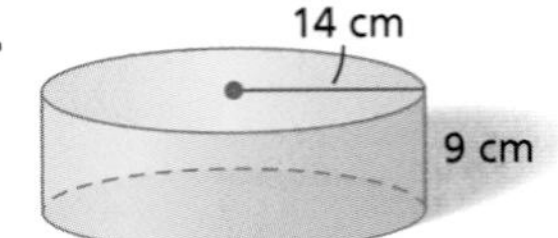


12. 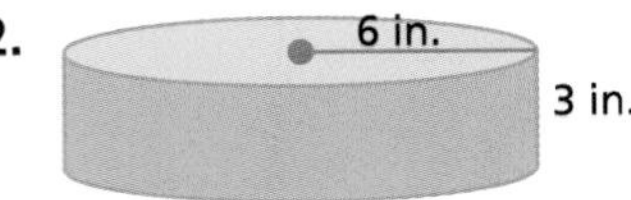


13. a cylinder with base area $24\pi$ cm$^2$ and height 16 cm

14. One cup is equal to 14.4375 $in^3$. If a 1 c cylindrical measuring cup has a radius of 2 in., what is its height? If the radius is 1.5 in., what is its height?

15. Find the volume of a cylinder with radius 8 yd and height 14 yd.

16. Find the height of a rectangular prism with length 5 ft, width 9 ft, and volume 495 $ft^3$.

17. Find the area of the base of a rectangular prism with volume 360 $in^3$ and height 9 in.

18. Find the volume of a cylinder with surface area $210\pi$ $m^2$ and height 8 m.

19. Find the volume of a rectangular prism with vertices $(0, 0, 0)$, $(0, 3, 0)$, $(7, 0, 0)$, $(7, 3, 0)$, $(0, 0, 6)$, $(0, 3, 6)$, $(7, 0, 6)$, and $(7, 3, 6)$.

20. You can use *displacement* to find the volume of an irregular object, such as a stone. Suppose the tank shown is filled with water to a depth of 8 in. A stone is placed in the tank so that it is completely covered, causing the water level to rise by 2 in. Find the volume of the stone.

21. **Food** A 1 in. cube of cheese is one serving. How many servings are in a 4 in. by 4 in. by $\frac{1}{4}$ in. slice?

22. **History** In 1919, a cylindrical tank containing molasses burst and flooded the city of Boston, Massachusetts. The tank had a 90 ft diameter and a height of 52 ft. How many gallons of molasses were in the tank? (*Hint:* 1 gal $\approx$ 0.134 $ft^3$)

23. **Meteorology** If 3 in. of rain fall on the property shown, what is the volume in cubic feet? In gallons? The density of water is 8.33 pounds per gallon. What is the weight of the rain in pounds? (*Hint:* 1 gal $\approx$ 0.134 $ft^3$)

24. A brick patio measures 10 feet by 12 feet by 4 inches. Find the volume of the bricks. If the density of brick is 130 pounds per cubic foot, what is the weight of the patio in pounds?

**Find the volume of each prism or cylinder. Round to the nearest tenth, if necessary.**

25.

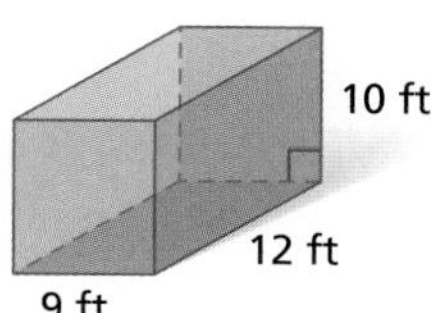


26.

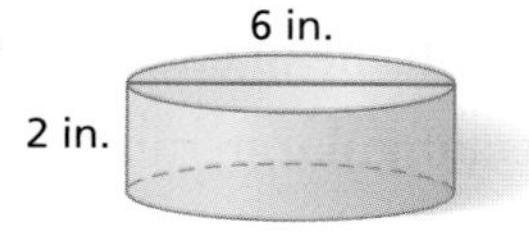


27.

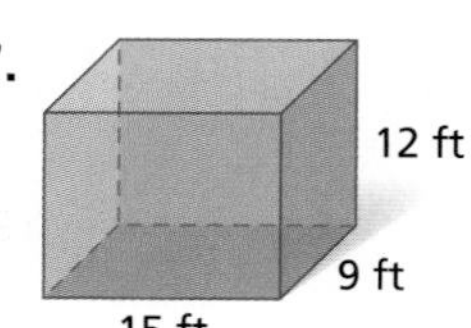

# A-9 Volume of Pyramids and Cones

**MA.G.2** Use formulas to solve problems involving ... volume. *Also* **MA.G.2.3, MA.G.2.4**

***Objectives***

Learn and apply the formula for the volume of a pyramid.

Learn and apply the formula for the volume of a cone.

The volume of a pyramid is related to the volume of a prism with the same base and height. The relationship can be verified by dividing a cube into three congruent square pyramids, as shown.

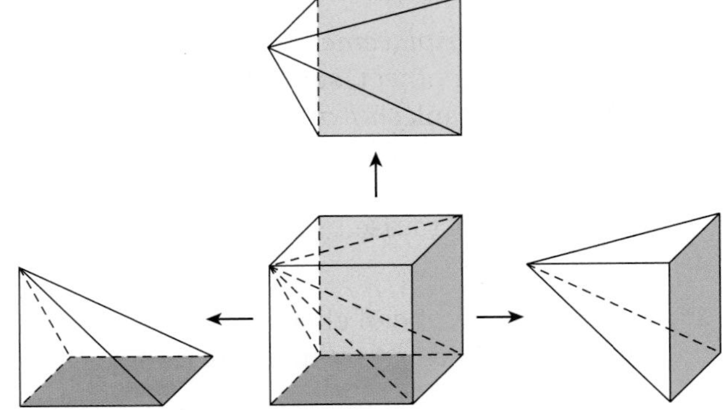

The square pyramids are congruent, so they have the same volume. The volume of each pyramid is one third the volume of the cube.

**Volume of a Pyramid**

The volume of a pyramid with base area $B$ and height $h$ is $V = \frac{1}{3}Bh$.

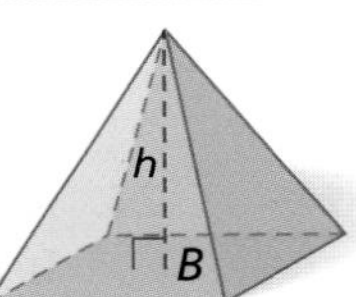


**EXAMPLE 1** **Finding Volumes of Pyramids**

**Find the volume of each pyramid.**

**A** **a rectangular pyramid with length 7 ft, width 9 ft, and height 12 ft**

$$V = \frac{1}{3}Bh = \frac{1}{3}(7 \cdot 9)(12) = 252 \text{ ft}^3$$

**B** **the square pyramid**

The base is a square with a side length of 4 in., and the height is 6 in.

$$V = \frac{1}{3}Bh = \frac{1}{3}(4^2)(6) = 32 \text{ in}^3$$

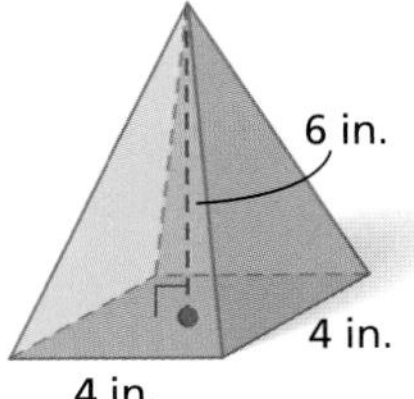

1. Find the volume of a regular hexagonal pyramid with a base edge length of 2 cm, a base apothem of $\sqrt{3}$ cm, and a height equal to the area of the base.

## EXAMPLE 2 Architecture Application

**The Rainforest Pyramid in Galveston, Texas, is a square pyramid with a base area of about 1 acre and a height of 10 stories. Estimate the volume in cubic yards and in cubic feet. (*Hint:* 1 acre = 4840 yd$^2$, 1 story ≈ 10 ft)**

The base is a square with an area of about 4840 yd$^2$. The base edge length is $\sqrt{4840} \approx 70$ yd. The height is about $10(10) = 100$ ft, or about 33 yd.

First find the volume in cubic yards.

$V = \frac{1}{3}Bh$ — *Volume of a regular pyramid*

$= \frac{1}{3}(70^2)(33) = 53{,}900 \text{ yd}^3$ — *Substitute $70^2$ for B and 33 for h.*

Then convert your answer to find the volume in cubic feet. The volume of one cubic yard is $(3 \text{ ft})(3 \text{ ft})(3 \text{ ft}) = 27 \text{ ft}^3$. Use the conversion factor $\frac{27 \text{ ft}^3}{1 \text{ yd}^3}$ to find the volume in cubic feet.

$$53{,}900 \text{ yd}^3 \cdot \frac{27 \text{ ft}^3}{1 \text{ yd}^3} \approx 1{,}455{,}300 \text{ ft}^3$$

**2.** **What if...?** What would be the volume of the Rainforest Pyramid if the height were doubled?

### Volume of Cones

The volume of a cone with base area $B$, radius $r$, and height $h$ is $V = \frac{1}{3}Bh$, or $V = \frac{1}{3}\pi r^2 h$.

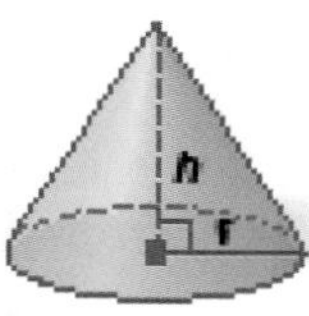


## EXAMPLE 3 Finding Volumes of Cones

**Find the volume of each cone. Give your answers both in terms of $\pi$ and rounded to the nearest tenth.**

**A** **a cone with radius 5 cm and height 12 cm**

$V = \frac{1}{3}\pi r^2 h$ — *Volume of a cone*

$= \frac{1}{3}\pi(5)^2(12)$ — *Substitute 5 for r and 12 for h.*

$= 100\pi \text{ cm}^3 \approx 314.2 \text{ cm}^3$ — *Simplify.*

**B** **a cone with a base circumference of $21\pi$ cm and a height 3 cm less than twice the radius**

**Step 1** Use the circumference to find the radius.

$2\pi r = 21\pi$ — *Substitute $21\pi$ for C.*

$r = 10.5$ cm — *Divide both sides by $2\pi$.*

**Step 2** Use the radius to find the height.

$2(10.5) - 3 = 18$ cm *The height is 3 cm less than twice the radius.*

**Step 3** Use the radius and height to find the volume.

$V = \frac{1}{3}\pi r^2 h$ *Volume of a cone*

$= \frac{1}{3}\pi(10.5)^2(18)$ *Substitute 10.5 for r and 18 for h.*

$= 661.5\pi \text{ cm}^3 \approx 2078.2 \text{ cm}^3$ *Simplify.*

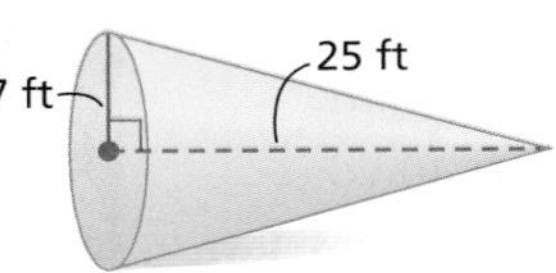


**Step 1** Use the Pythagorean Theorem to find the height.

$7^2 + h^2 = 25^2$ *Pythagorean Theorem*

$h^2 = 576$ *Subtract $7^2$ from both sides.*

$h = 24$ *Take the square root of both sides.*

**Step 2** Use the radius and height to find the volume.

$V = \frac{1}{3}\pi r^2 h$ *Volume of a cone*

$= \frac{1}{3}\pi(7)^2(24)$ *Substitute 7 for r and 24 for h.*

$= 392\pi \text{ ft}^3 \approx 1231.5 \text{ ft}^3$ *Simplify.*

3. Find the volume of the cone.

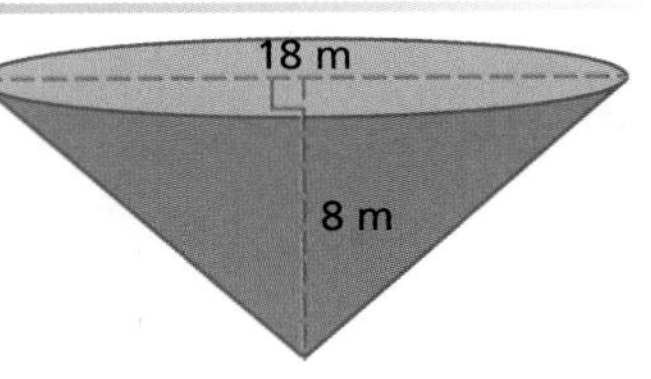


# Exercises

**MA.G.2., MA.G.2.3, MA.G.2.4**

## GUIDED PRACTICE

SEE EXAMPLE 1 p. AT42

**Find the volume of each pyramid. Round to the nearest tenth, if necessary.**

1.

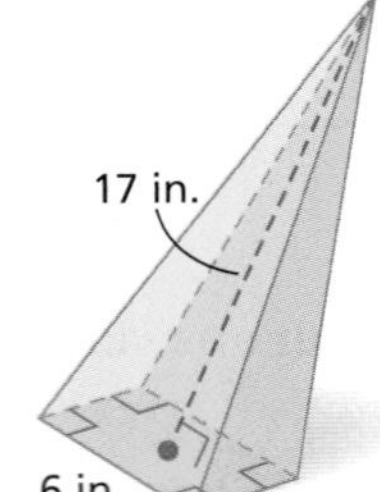


2. a hexagonal pyramid with a base area of 25 $\text{ft}^2$ and a height of 9 ft

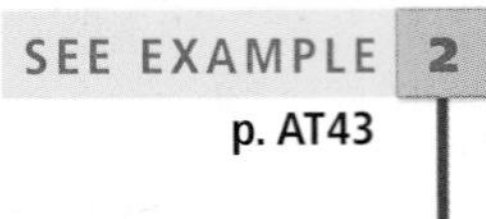


p. AT43

3. **Geology** A crystal is cut into the shape formed by two square pyramids joined at the base. Each pyramid has a base edge length of 5.7 mm and a height of 3 mm. What is the volume to the nearest cubic millimeter of the crystal?

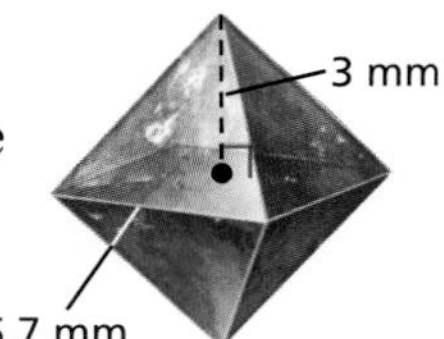

SEE EXAMPLE 3
p. AT43

**Find the volume of each cone. Give your answers both in terms of $\pi$ and rounded to the nearest tenth.**

**4.**

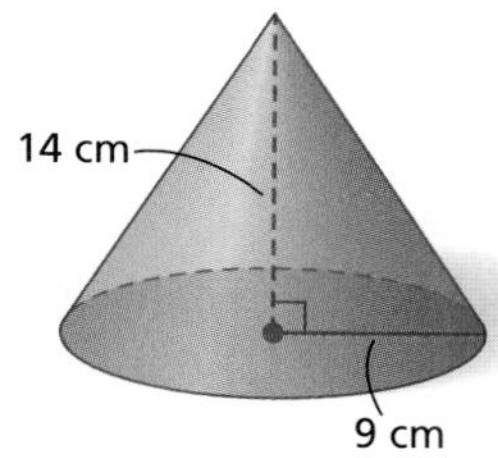


**5.**

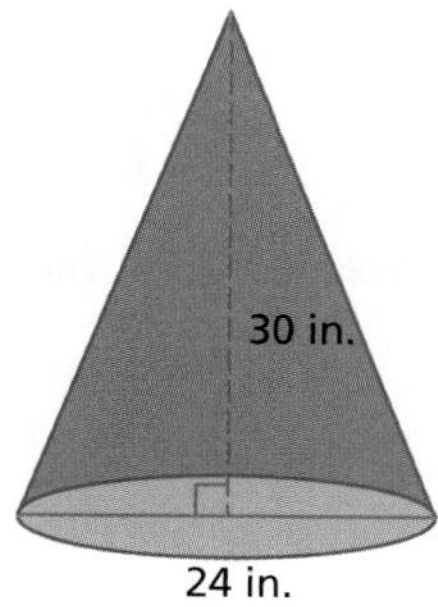


**6.** a cone with radius 12 m and height 20 m

## PRACTICE AND PROBLEM SOLVING

**Find the volume of each pyramid. Round to the nearest tenth, if necessary.**

**7.**

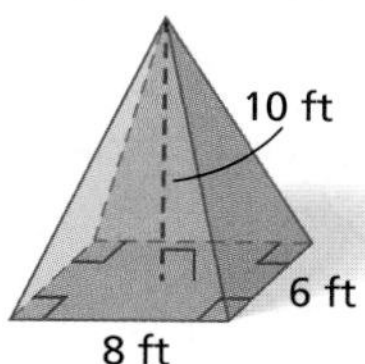


**8.** a regular square pyramid with base edge length 12 ft and slant height 10 ft

**9. Carpentry** A roof that encloses an attic is a square pyramid with a base edge length of 45 feet and a height of 5 yards. What is the volume of the attic in cubic feet? In cubic yards?

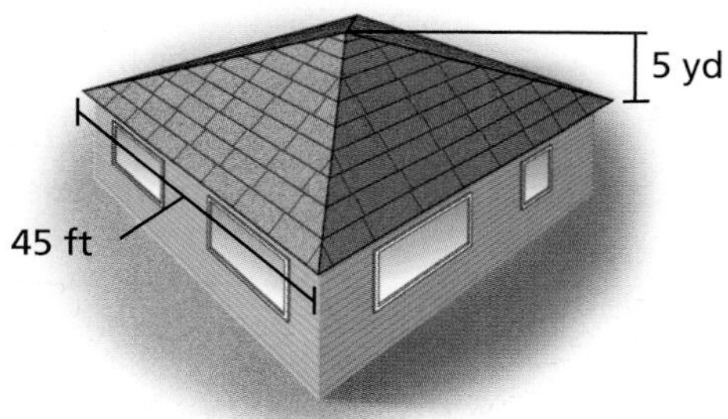


**Find the volume of each cone. Give your answers both in terms of $\pi$ and rounded to the nearest tenth.**

**10.**

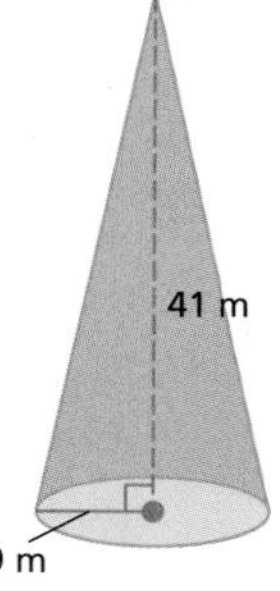


**11.**

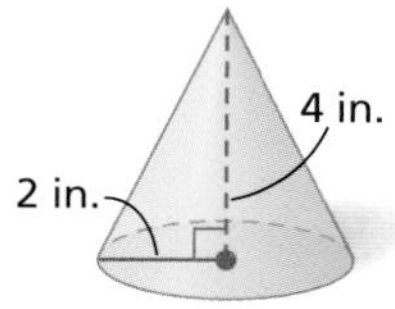


**12.** a cone with base area $36\pi$ ft$^2$ and a height equal to twice the radius

**Find the volume of each right cone with the given dimensions. Give your answers in terms of $\pi$.**

**13.** radius 3 in.
height 7 in.

**14.** diameter 5 m
height 2 m

**15.** radius 28 ft
slant height 53 ft

**16.** diameter 24 cm
slant height 13 cm

# A-10 Circles, Arcs, and Chords

**MA.G.2.1** Recognize examples of chord, tangent and secant in visual displays.

***Objectives***
Identify tangents, secants, and chords.

Use properties of tangents to solve problems.

***Vocabulary***
interior of a circle
exterior of a circle
chord
secant
tangent of a circle
point of tangency
central angle
arc
minor arc
major arc
semicircle
adjacent arcs

Recall that a circle is the set of all points in a plane that are equidistant from a given point, called the center of the circle. A circle with center $C$ is called circle $C$, or $\odot C$.

The **interior of a circle** is the set of all points inside the circle. The **exterior of a circle** is the set of all points outside the circle.

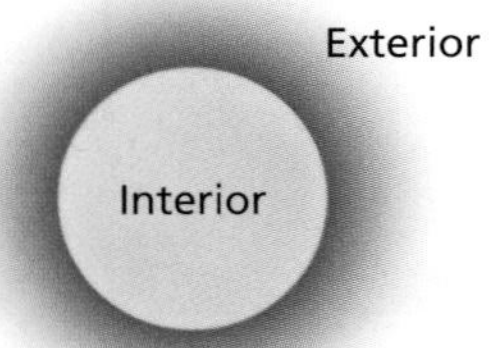


## Lines and Segments That Intersect Circles

| TERM | DIAGRAM |
| --- | --- |
| A **chord** is a segment whose endpoints lie on a circle. | |
| A **secant** is a line that intersects a circle at two points. | |
| A **tangent** is a line in the same plane as a circle that intersects it at exactly one point. | |
| The point where the tangent and a circle intersect is called the **point of tangency**. | |

## EXAMPLE 1 Identifying Lines and Segments That Intersect Circles

**Identify each line or segment that intersects ⊙A.**

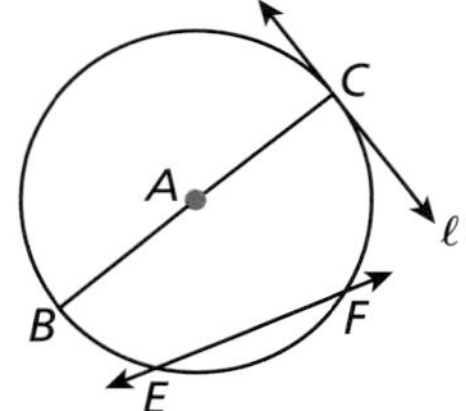


chords: $\overline{EF}$ and $\overline{BC}$

tangent: $\ell$

radii: $\overline{AC}$ and $\overline{AB}$

secant: $\overleftrightarrow{EF}$

diameter: $\overline{BC}$

**1.** Identify each line or segment that intersects $\odot P$.

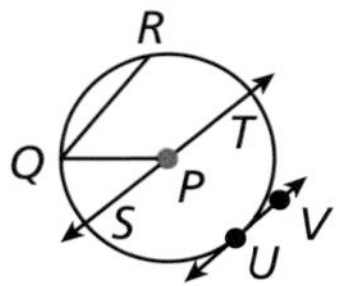

A **central angle** is an angle whose vertex is the center of a circle. An **arc** is an unbroken part of a circle consisting of two points called the endpoints and all the points on the circle between them.

## Arcs and Their Measure

| ARC | MEASURE | DIAGRAM |
|---|---|---|
| A **minor arc** is an arc whose points are on or in the interior of a central angle. | The measure of a minor arc is equal to the measure of its central angle. $m\overset{\frown}{AC} = m\angle ABC = x°$ | |
| A **major arc** is an arc whose points are on or in the exterior of a central angle. | The measure of a major arc is equal to 360° minus the measure of its central angle. $m\overset{\frown}{ADC} = 360° - m\angle ABC$ $= 360° - x°$ | |
| If the endpoints of an arc lie on a diameter, the arc is a **semicircle**. | The measure of a semicircle is equal to 180°. $m\overset{\frown}{EFG} = 180°$ | |

**EXAMPLE 2** ***Data Application***

**The circle graph shows the types of music sold during one week at a music store. Find $m\overset{\frown}{BC}$.**

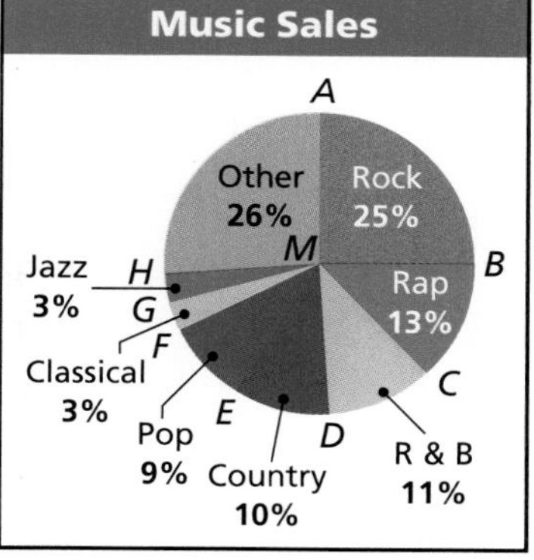


$m\overset{\frown}{BC} = m\angle BMC$ — *m of arc = m of central ∠.*

$m\angle BMC = 0.13(360°)$ — *Central ∠ is 13% of the ⊙.*

$= 46.8°$

**CHECK IT OUT!** **Use the graph to find each of the following.**

**2a.** $m\angle FMC$

**2b.** $m\overset{\frown}{AHB}$

**2c.** $m\angle EMD$

**Adjacent arcs** are arcs of the same circle that intersect at exactly one point. $\overset{\frown}{RS}$ and $\overset{\frown}{ST}$ are adjacent arcs.

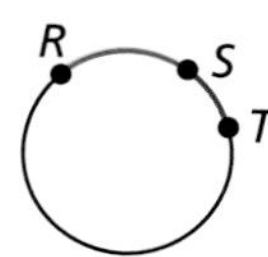

**Postulate 10-1** **Arc Addition Postulate**

The measure of an arc formed by two adjacent arcs is the sum of the measures of the two arcs.

$m\overset{\frown}{ABC} = m\overset{\frown}{AB} + m\overset{\frown}{BC}$

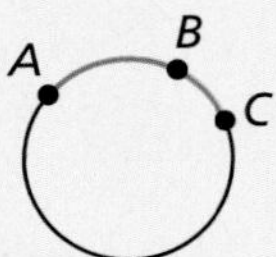


## EXAMPLE 3 Using the Arc Addition Postulate

Find $m\overset{\frown}{CDE}$

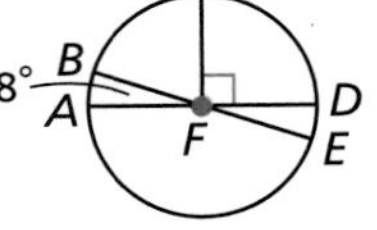


| | |
|---|---|
| $m\overset{\frown}{CD} = 90°$ | *m∠CFD = 90°* |
| $m\angle DFE = 18°$ | *Vert. ∠s Thm.* |
| $m\overset{\frown}{DE} = 18°$ | *m∠DFE = 18°* |
| $m\overset{\frown}{CE} = m\overset{\frown}{CD} + m\overset{\frown}{DE}$ | *Arc Add. Post.* |
| $= 90° + 18° = 108°$ | *Substitute and simplify.* |

**Find each measure.**

**3a.** $m\overset{\frown}{JKL}$ **3b.** $m\overset{\frown}{LJN}$

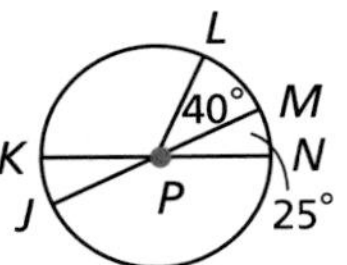


# Exercises

MA.G.2.1

## GUIDED PRACTICE

**Vocabulary** **Apply the vocabulary from this lesson to answer each question.**

1. A __?__ is a line in the plane of a circle that intersects the circle at two points. *(secant* or *tangent)*

2. An arc that joins the endpoints of a diameter is called a __?__. (*semicircle* or *major arc*)

3. How do you recognize a *central angle* of a circle?

4. In ⊙$P$ $m\overset{\frown}{ABC} = 205°$. Therefore $\overset{\frown}{ABC}$ is a __?__. (*major arc* or *minor arc*)

5. In a circle, an arc that is less than a semicircle is a __?__. (*major arc* or *minor arc*)

SEE EXAMPLE 1
p. AT46

**Identify each line or segment that intersects each circle.**

6.

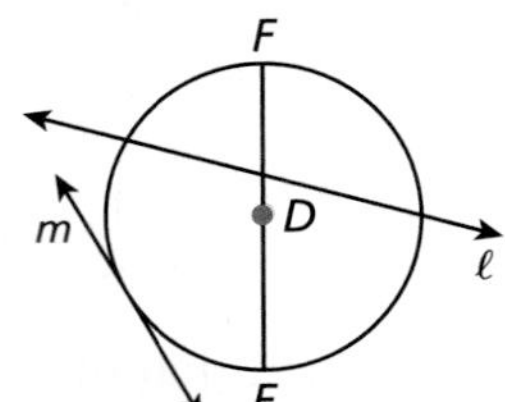


7.

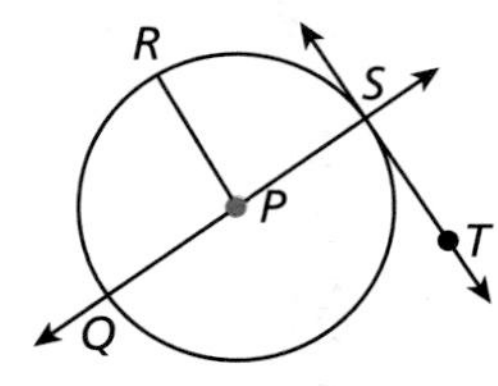

SEE EXAMPLE 2
p. AT47

**Consumer Application** **Use the following information for Exercises 8–13.**

The circle graph shows how a typical household spends money on energy. Find each of the following.

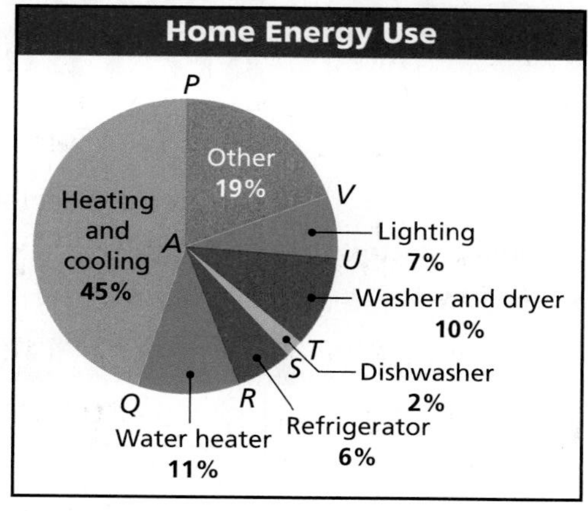


**8.** $m\angle PAQ$ **9.** $m\angle VAU$

**10.** $m\angle SAQ$ **11.** $m\widehat{UT}$

**12.** $m\widehat{RQ}$ **13.** $m\widehat{UPT}$

SEE EXAMPLE 3
p. AT48

**Find each measure.**

**14.** $m\widehat{DF}$

**16.** $m\widehat{DEB}$

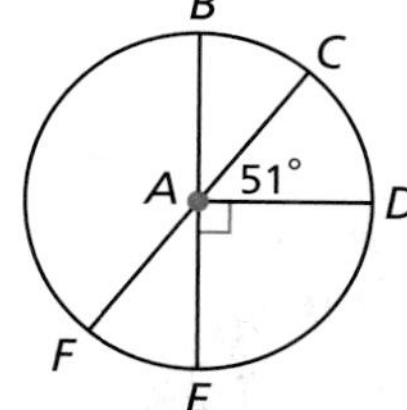


**15.** $m\widehat{JL}$

**17.** $m\widehat{HLK}$

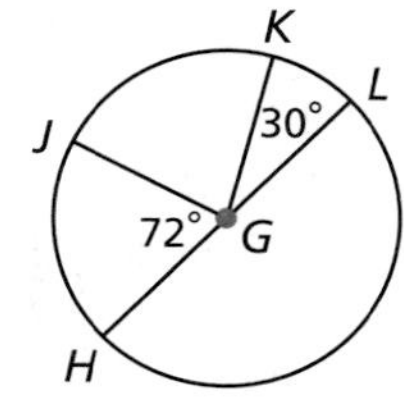


## PRACTICE AND PROBLEM SOLVING

**Identify each line or segment that intersects each circle.**

**18.**

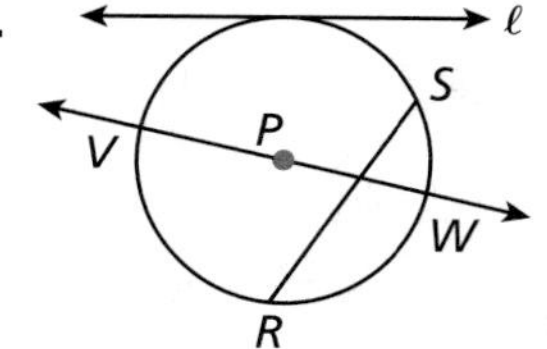


**19.**

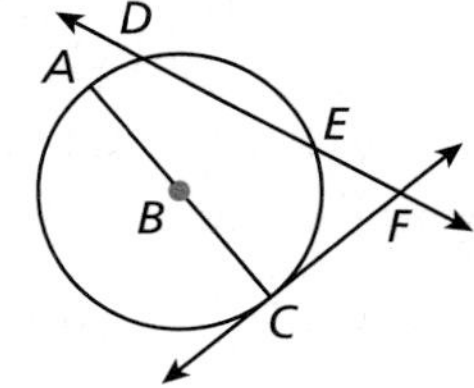


**Sports** **Use the following information for Exercises 20–25.**

The key shows the number of medals won by U.S. athletes at the 2004 Olympics in Athens. Find each of the following to the nearest tenth.

**20.** $m\angle ADB$ **21.** $m\angle ADC$

**22.** $m\widehat{AB}$ **23.** $m\widehat{BC}$

**24.** $m\widehat{ACB}$ **25.** $m\widehat{CAB}$

| Medals | |
|---|---|
| Gold | 35 |
| Silver | 39 |
| Bronze | 29 |

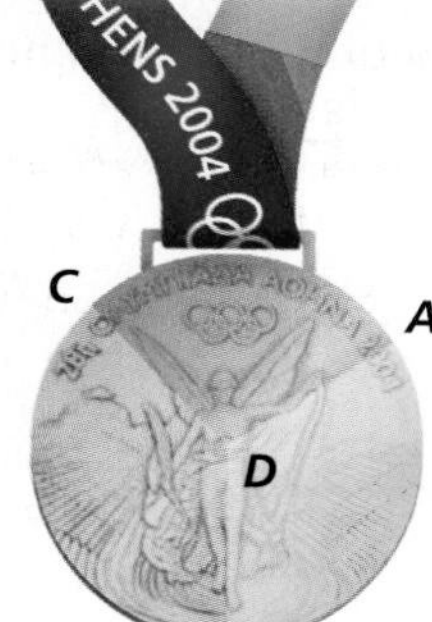


**Find each measure.**

**26.** $m\widehat{MP}$

**28.** $m\widehat{QNL}$

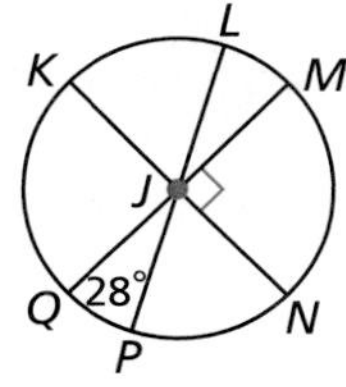


**27.** $m\widehat{WT}$

**29.** $m\widehat{WTV}$

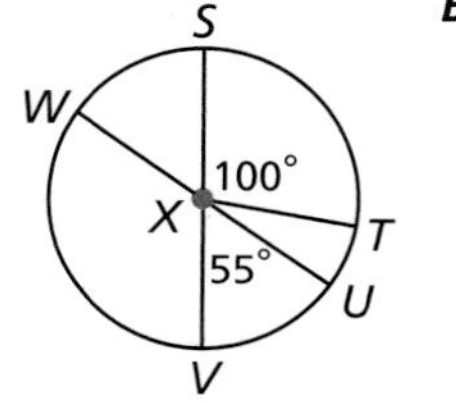

# A-11 Sector Area and Arc Length

**Objectives**
Find the area of sectors.

Find arc lengths.

**Vocabulary**
sector of a circle
arc length

The area of a sector is a fraction of the circle containing the sector. To find the area of a sector with arc measure $m°$, multiply the area of the circle by $\frac{m°}{360°}$.

## Sector of a Circle

| TERM | NAME | DIAGRAM | AREA |
|---|---|---|---|
| A **sector of a circle** is a region bounded by two radii of the circle and their intercepted arc. | sector *ACB* | A, r, C, m°, B | $A = \pi r^2\left(\frac{m°}{360°}\right)$ |

### EXAMPLE 1 Finding the Area of a Sector

**Find the area of each sector. Give your answer in terms of $\pi$ and rounded to the nearest hundredth.**

**A** sector *MPN*

$$A = \pi r^2\left(\frac{m°}{360°}\right)$$ *Use formula for area of a sector.*

$$= \pi(3)^2\left(\frac{80°}{360°}\right)$$ *Substitute 3 for r and 80 for m.*

$$= 2\pi \text{ in}^2 \approx 6.28 \text{ in}^2$$ *Simplify.*

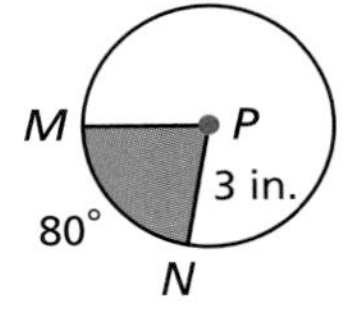


**Helpful Hint**

Write the degree symbol after *m* in the formula to help you remember to use degree measure not arc length.

**B** sector *EFG*

$$A = \pi r^2\left(\frac{m°}{360°}\right)$$ *Use formula for area of a sector.*

$$= \pi(6)^2\left(\frac{120°}{360°}\right)$$ *Substitute 6 for r and 120 for m.*

$$= 12\pi \approx 37.70 \text{ cm}^2$$ *Simplify.*

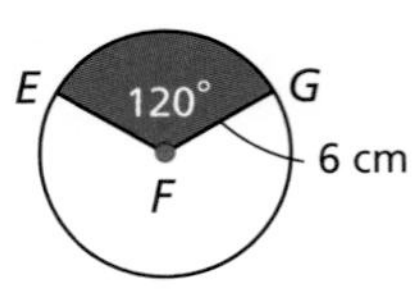

**Find the area of each sector. Give your answer in terms of $\pi$ and rounded to the nearest hundredth.**

**1a.** sector *ACB*

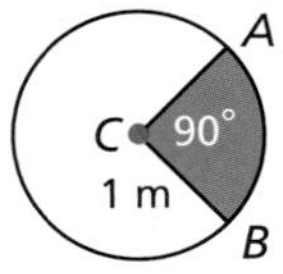


**1b.** sector *JKL*

J
36°
K
L
16 in.

## EXAMPLE 2 *Agriculture Application*

**A circular plot with a 720 ft diameter is watered by a spray irrigation system. To the nearest square foot, what is the area that is watered as the sprinkler rotates through an angle of 50°?**

$A = \pi r^2\left(\frac{m°}{360°}\right)$

$= \pi(360)^2\left(\frac{50°}{360°}\right)$ *$d = 720$ ft, $r = 360$ ft.*

$\approx 56{,}549 \text{ ft}^2$ *Simplify.*

2. To the nearest square foot, what is the area watered in Example 2 as the sprinkler rotates through a semicircle?

In the same way that the area of a sector is a fraction of the area of the circle, the length of an arc is a fraction of the circumference of the circle.

### Arc Length

| TERM | DIAGRAM | LENGTH |
|---|---|---|
| **Arc length** is the distance along an arc measured in linear units. | 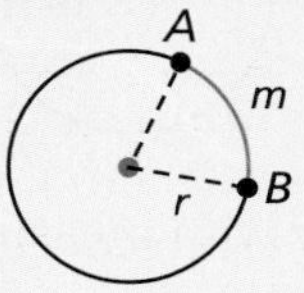 (circle with points A and B, arc m, radius r) | $L = 2\pi r\left(\frac{m°}{360°}\right)$ |

## EXAMPLE 3 Finding Arc Length

**Find each arc length. Give your answer in terms of $\pi$ and rounded to the nearest hundredth.**

 $\overparen{CD}$

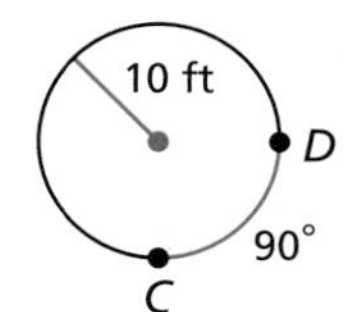


$L = 2\pi r\left(\frac{m°}{360°}\right)$ *Use formula for arc length.*

$= 2\pi(10)\left(\frac{90°}{360°}\right)$ *Substitute 10 for r and 90 for m.*

$= 5\pi \text{ ft} \approx 15.71 \text{ ft}$ *Simplify.*

**B an arc with measure 35° in a circle with radius 3 in.**

$L = 2\pi r\left(\frac{m°}{360°}\right)$ *Use formula for arc length.*

$= 2\pi(3)\left(\frac{35°}{360°}\right)$ *Substitute 3 for r and 35 for m.*

$= \frac{7}{12}\pi \text{ in.} \approx 1.83 \text{ in.}$ *Simplify.*

**Find each arc length. Give your answer in terms of $\pi$ and rounded to the nearest hundredth.**

**3a.** $\overparen{GH}$

**3b.** an arc with measure 135° in a circle with radius 4 cm

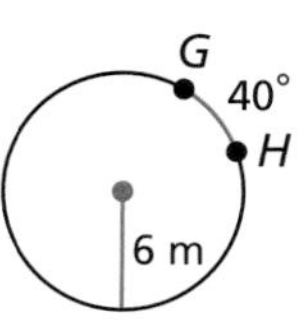

# Exercises

## GUIDED PRACTICE

SEE EXAMPLE 1 p. AT50

**Find the area of each sector. Give your answer in terms of $\pi$ and rounded to the nearest hundredth.**

1. sector $PQR$

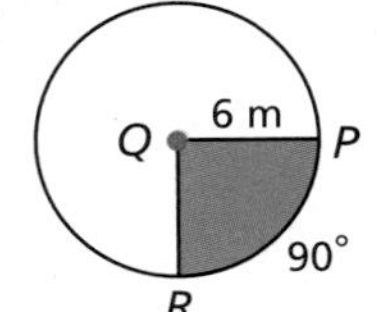


2. sector $JKL$

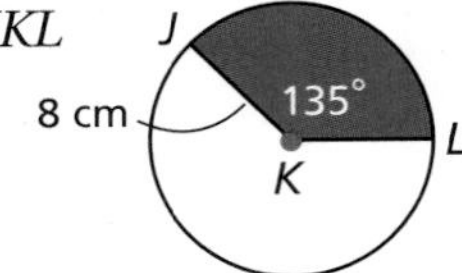


3. sector $ABC$

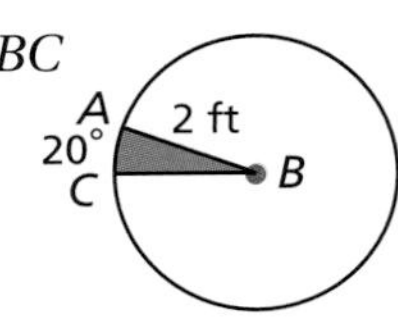


SEE EXAMPLE 2 p. AT50

4. **Navigation** The beam from a lighthouse is visible for a distance of 3 mi. To the nearest square mile, what is the area covered by the beam as it sweeps in an arc of 150°?

SEE EXAMPLE 3 p. AT51

**Find each arc length. Give your answer in terms of $\pi$ and rounded to the nearest hundredth.**

5. $\widehat{EF}$

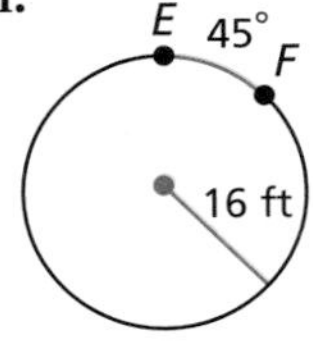


6. $\widehat{PQ}$

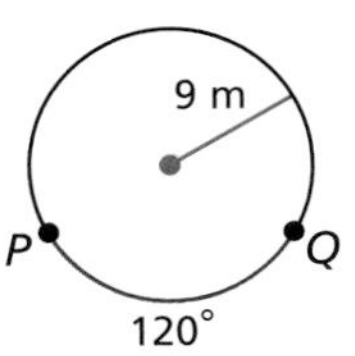


7. an arc with measure 20° in a circle with radius 6 in.

## PRACTICE AND PROBLEM SOLVING

**Find the area of each sector. Give your answer in terms of $\pi$ and rounded to the nearest hundredth.**

8. sector $DEF$

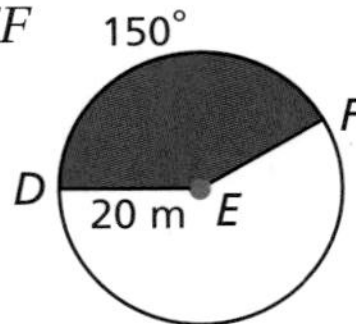


9. sector $GHJ$

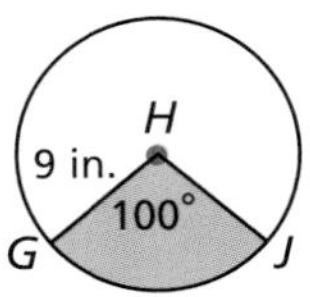


10. sector $RST$

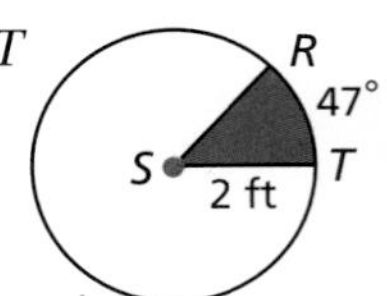


11. **Architecture** A *lunette* is a semicircular window that is sometimes placed above a doorway or above a rectangular window. To the nearest square inch, what is the area of the lunette?

**Find each arc length. Give your answer in terms of $\pi$ and rounded to the nearest hundredth.**

12. $\widehat{UV}$

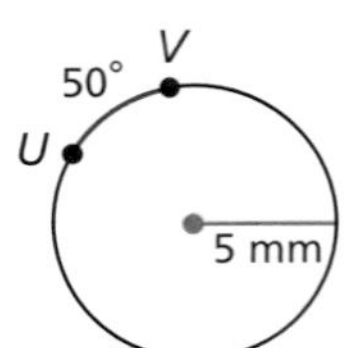


13. $\widehat{AB}$

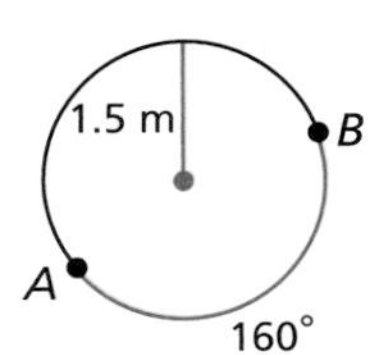


14. an arc with measure 9° in a circle with diameter 4 ft

# A-12 Graph Theory

**MA.D.1.1** Apply the properties of vertex-edge graphs. *Also* **MA.D.1.2**

***Objectives***

Explore and apply properties of vertex-edge graphs.

***Vocabulary***

graph
vertex
edge
path
connected graph
degree
Euler path
circuit
Euler circuit
coloring

In the branch of mathematics known as graph theory, a **graph** is a network of points and line segments or arcs that connect the points. A point of a graph is called a **vertex**. A line segment or arc that connects vertices is called an **edge**.

Graph theory has many real-world applications. For example, the graph at right shows the flights offered by a regional airline. The cities served by the airline are represented by vertices. Flights that connect cities are represented by edges.

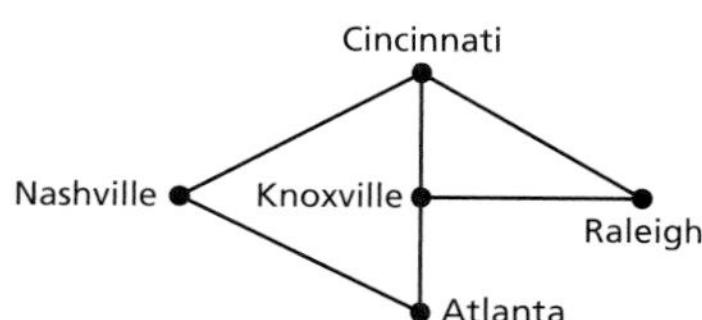


A **path** is a way to get from one vertex to another along one or more edges. A graph is a **connected graph** if there is a path between any two vertices. The **degree** of a vertex is the number of edges touching the vertex.

**EXAMPLE 1** **Analyzing a Graph**

**Use the graph at right for each problem.**

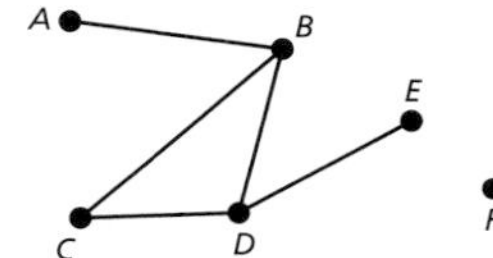


**A** **Find the degree of each vertex**

| Vertex | Degree |
|---|---|
| *A* | 1 |
| *B* | 3 |
| *C* | 2 |
| *D* | 3 |
| *E* | 1 |
| *F* | 0 |

**B** **Describe two different paths from vertex *A* to vertex *E*.**

Vertex *A* to vertex *B* to vertex *D* to vertex *E*

Vertex *A* to vertex *B* to vertex *C* to vertex *D* to vertex *E*

**C** **Determine whether the graph is connected. Explain.**

The graph is not connected. There is no path between vertex F and another vertex.

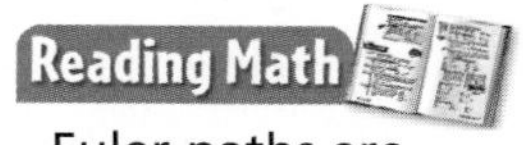

Euler paths are named after the mathematician Leonard Euler (1707–1783), (pronounced *oiler*).

**Use the airline graph above Example 1 for each problem.**

**1a.** Find the degree of each vertex.

**1b.** Describe two different paths from Atlanta to Raleigh.

**1c.** Determine whether the graph is connected. Explain.

An **Euler path** is a path that goes through every edge of a connected graph exactly once. A **circuit** is a path that ends at the same vertex at which it began and that does not go through any edge more than once. An **Euler circuit** is a circuit that goes through every edge of a connected graph exactly once.

In an Euler circuit, every vertex must have an even degree. To see why this is true, suppose a vertex of a graph has an odd degree. In an Euler circuit, two edges are required each time a path enters and exits the vertex. A vertex with an odd degree would have an edge that would be traveled twice or not at all.

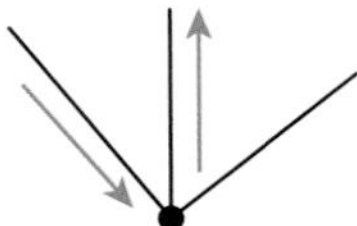

The Königsberg Bridge problem is one of the most famous problems in graph theory. The goal is to find a path that crosses every bridge only once and returns to the starting point. Solving the Königsberg Bridge problem is equivalent to finding an Euler circuit in a graph.

## EXAMPLE 2 *Social Studies Application*

**Determine whether the Königsberg Bridges, shown in the map below, can**

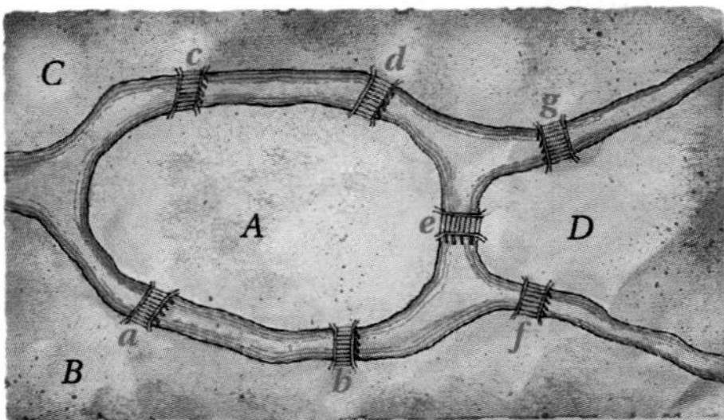


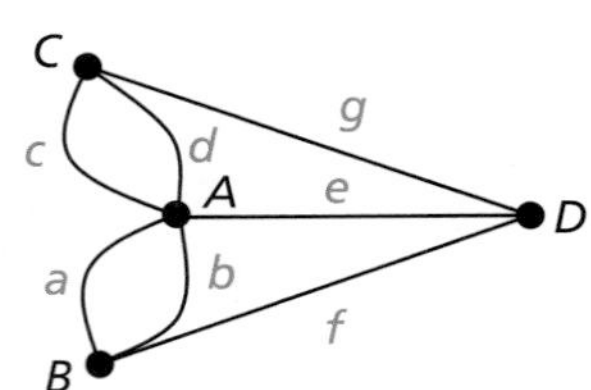


Create a graph to represent the land masses and bridges, as shown above. In the graph, the vertices represent land and edges represent bridges.

The bridges cannot be traversed through an Euler circuit because there is a vertex in the graph with an odd degree (in fact, all of the vertices have an odd degree).

**2.** Determine whether an Euler circuit exists for the graph shown here. If not, explain why not. If so, describe an Euler circuit of the graph.

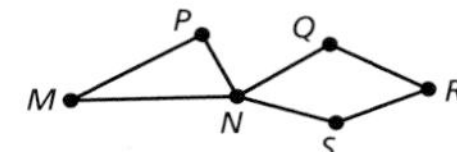


Some problems in graph theory can be solved using graph coloring. A **coloring** of a graph assigns a color to each vertex of the graph so that no two adjacent vertices have the same color.

The figures show colorings of several graphs. In each case, the minimum number of different colors is used to color the graph.

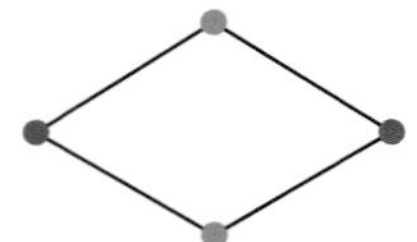

This graph can be colored with 2 colors.

Coloring this graph requires 3 colors.

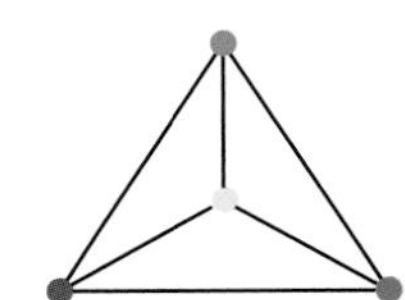

Coloring this graph requires 4 colors.

Graph coloring can be used to solve many problems about avoiding conflicts such as scheduling problems or problems about shared resources.

## EXAMPLE 3 Solving a Scheduling Problem

**A college offers five art courses: Art A, B, C, D, and E. An employee of the college must schedule final exams for the courses in either morning or afternoon time slots from Monday to Friday. However, some students are enrolled in more than one art course. In the table, an X means there is at least one student enrolled in both of the courses corresponding to that cell of the table. Show how the employee can schedule the exams using the least number of time slots.**

| | A | B | C | D | E |
|---|---|---|---|---|---|
| **A** | | X | X | | |
| **B** | X | | X | X | |
| **C** | X | X | | X | |
| **D** | | X | X | | X |
| **E** | | | | X | |

**Step 1** Represent the courses as the vertices of a graph.

**Step 2** Draw an edge between any two vertices that represent courses that have students in common.

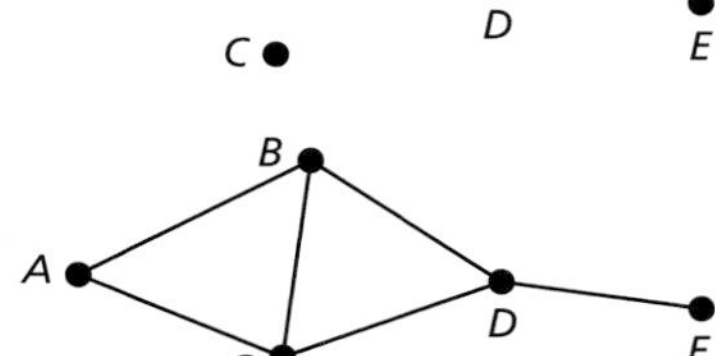


**Step 3** Color the graph using the minimum number of colors. Each color represents a different exam time.

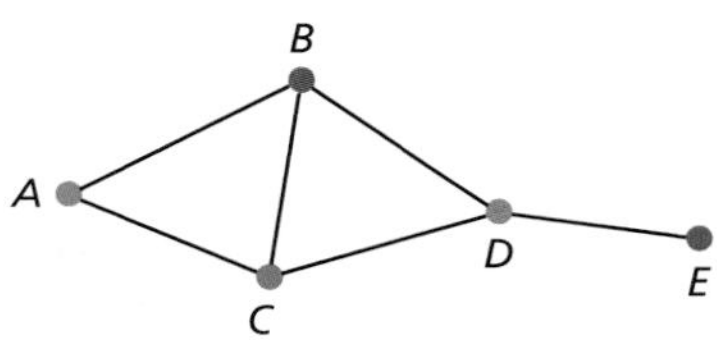


**Step 4** Interpret the coloring of the graph.

The employee can schedule the exams using a minimum of three time slots. For example, the exams could be scheduled as follows.

Monday morning (red vertices): Art A, Art D

Monday afternoon (blue vertices): Art B, Art E

Tuesday morning (green vertex): Art C

**3.** A parade organizer wants to schedule one-hour meetings for six different committees. The table shows the names of the committees and an X indicates committees that share one or more members. Show how the organizer can schedule the meetings using the least number of one-hour time slots.

| | Budget | Safety | Food | Music | Publicity | Clean Up |
|---|---|---|---|---|---|---|
| **Budget** | | X | X | | | |
| **Safety** | X | | | X | | |
| **Food** | X | | | X | | |
| **Music** | | X | X | | X | |
| **Publicity** | | | | X | | X |
| **Clean Up** | | | | | X | |

# Exercises

**Use the graph at right for Exercises 1–4.**

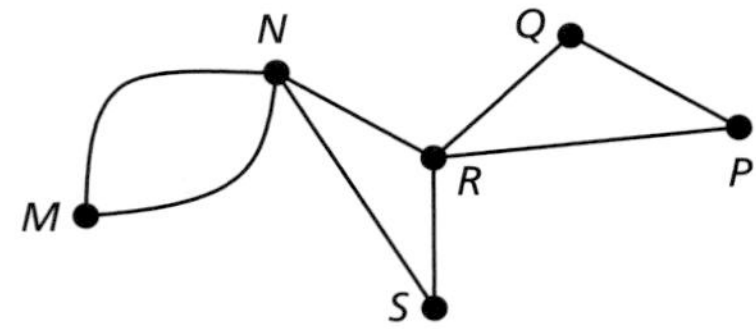


1. Find the degree of each vertex.
2. Describe two different paths from vertex M to vertex P.
3. Determine whether the graph is connected. Explain.
4. Determine whether an Euler circuit exists for the graph. If not, explain why not. If so, describe an Euler circuit of the graph.

**Use the graph at right for Exercises 5–8.**

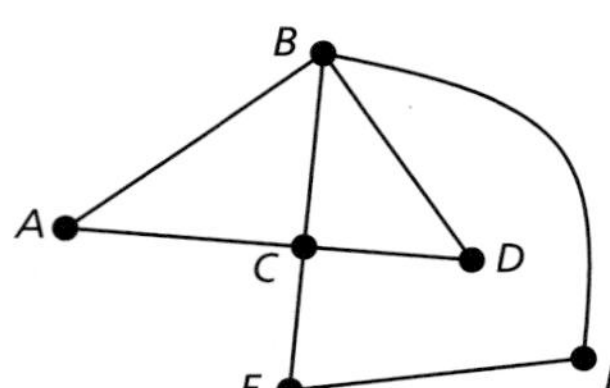


5. Find the degree of each vertex.
6. Describe a path from vertex A to vertex D that passes through every vertex of the graph.

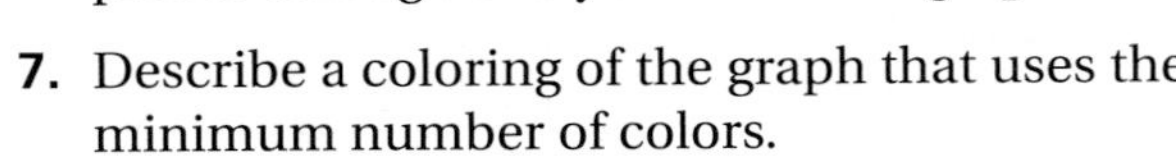

7. Describe a coloring of the graph that uses the minimum number of colors.
8. Determine whether an Euler circuit exists for the graph. If not, explain why not. If so, describe an Euler circuit of the graph.

**Describe a coloring of each graph that uses the minimum number of different colors.**

9. 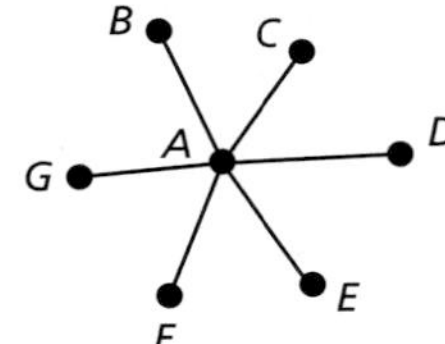


10. 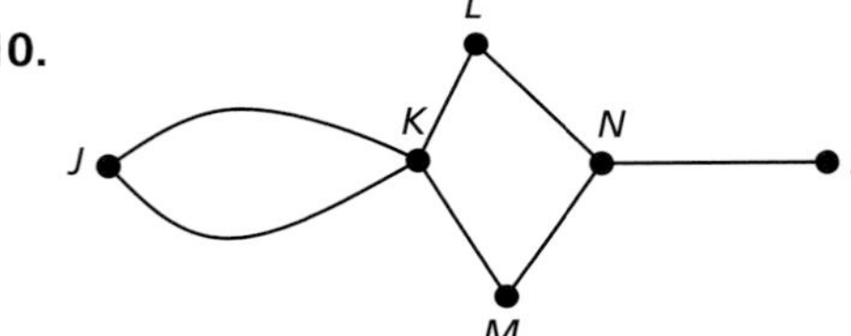


**Draw a graph with the given characteristics.**

11. a graph with 6 vertices and 7 edges
12. a graph with 4 vertices, all of degree 2
13. a connected graph for which there is no Euler circuit
14. a graph with 6 vertices that can be colored with 3 colors
15. The graph shows the homes on Chloe's paper route. The vertices represent the homes that receive a paper and the edges represent streets. Chloe would like to find a route that begins and ends at her house C. She would also like to go down each street exactly once. Is such a route possible? Explain.

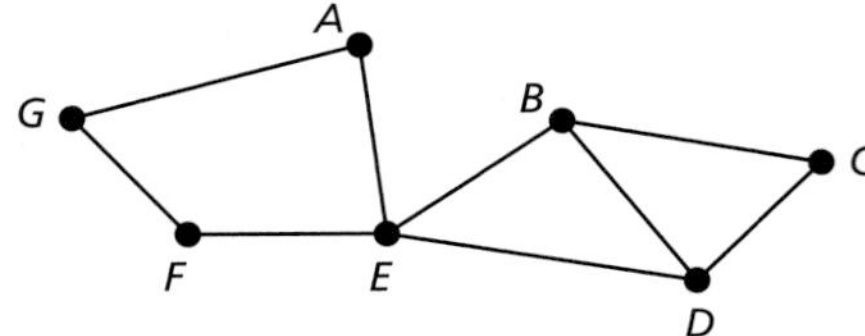

16. The map shows the coastline of a city $A$ and three islands $B$, $C$, and $D$. The landmasses are connected by bridges as shown.

**a.** If the information in the map is represented by a graph, what do the vertices represent? What do the edges represent?

**b.** Draw and label a graph to represent the information in the map.

**c.** Is the graph connected? Why or why not?

**d.** Is it possible to traverse the bridges in an Euler circuit? Explain.

17. A human-resources manager wants to schedule interviews for five job applicants named Alex ($A$), Brenda ($B$), Chan ($C$), Diego ($D$), and Erika ($E$). Multiple applicants can be interviewed at the same time, as long as they have not applied for the same job. In the table, an X means that the two candidates corresponding to that cell of the table have applied for the same job.

| | A | B | C | D | E |
|---|---|---|---|---|---|
| A | | X | X | X | X |
| B | X | | | X | |
| C | X | | | | |
| D | X | X | | | X |
| E | X | | | X | |

**a.** Draw a graph to represent the situation.

**b.** Explain how the director can schedule the interviews using the least number of time slots.

18. Viet is scheduling status meetings for six projects, known as Projects $J$, $K$, $L$, $M$, $N$, and $P$. Some team members work on more than one project at the same time. In the table, an X means that the two projects corresponding to that cell of the table share a team member. What is the least number of time slots Viet needs in order to schedule the meetings?

| | J | K | L | M | N | P |
|---|---|---|---|---|---|---|
| J | | X | | X | X | |
| K | X | | X | | | |
| L | | X | | X | | X |
| M | X | | X | | X | |
| N | X | | | X | | |
| P | | | X | | | |

**A graph is said to be $k$-colorable if there is a coloring of the graph that uses $k$ colors. The minimum value of $k$ for which a coloring of the graph exists is called the *chromatic number* of the graph. Find the chromatic number of each graph.**

19.

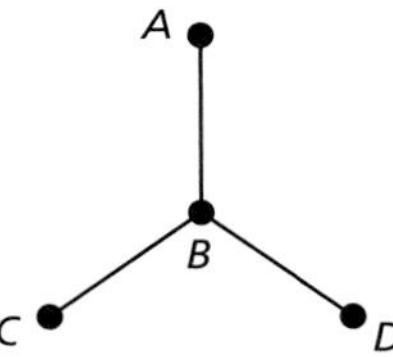


20.

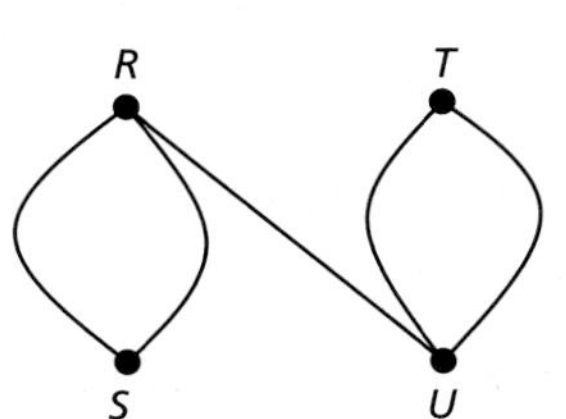


21.

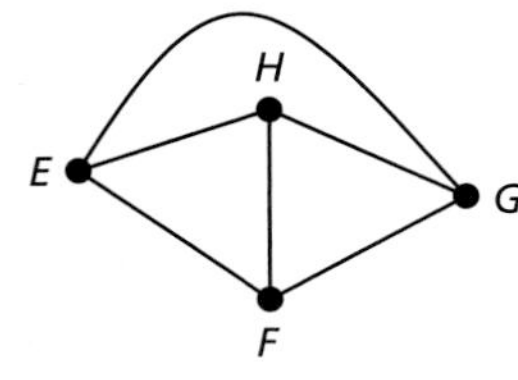


22. A *Hamiltonian circuit* is a path that ends at the beginning vertex and passes through each of the other vertices in the graph exactly once. A Hamiltonian circuit need not go through every edge. Describe a Hamiltonian circuit for the graph at right that begins and ends at vertex $A$.

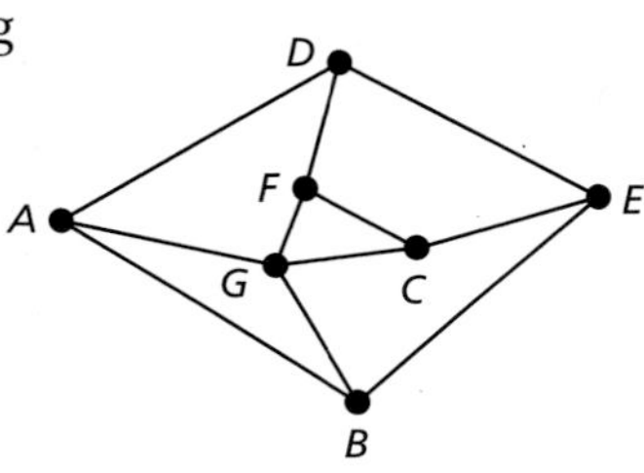


23. **Critical Thinking** Is it possible for an Euler path that is not a circuit to end at a vertex with an even degree? If so, draw an example. If not, explain why not.

# Student Handbook

# Extra Practice

## Chapter 1 ■ Skills Practice

**Lesson 1-1**

Give two ways to write each algebraic expression in words.

1. $x + 8$
2. $6(y)$
3. $g - 4$
4. $\frac{12}{h}$

Evaluate each expression for $a = 4$, $b = 2$, and $c = 5$.

5. $b + c$
6. $\frac{a}{b}$
7. $c - a$
8. $ab$

Write an algebraic expression for each verbal expression. Then evaluate the algebraic expression for the given values of $y$.

| | Verbal | Algebraic | $y = 9$ | $y = 6$ |
|---|---|---|---|---|
| 9. | $y$ reduced by 4 | ■ | ■ | ■ |
| 10. | the quotient of $y$ and 3 | ■ | ■ | ■ |
| 11. | 5 more than $y$ | ■ | ■ | ■ |
| 12. | the sum of $y$ and 2 | ■ | ■ | ■ |

**Lesson 1-2**

Add or subtract using a number line.

13. $-7 - 9$
14. $-2.2 + 4.3$
15. $-5\frac{1}{2} - 2\frac{1}{2}$
16. $3.4 - 6.5$

Subtract.

17. $12 - 47$
18. $1.3 - 9.2$
19. $y - 4\frac{2}{3}$ for $y = 1\frac{1}{3}$

Compare. Write <, >, or =.

20. $-5 - (-8)$ ■ $-4 - 9$
21. $|-6 - (-2)|$ ■ $7 - 4$
22. $-2 - 5$ ■ $7 - 14$

Evaluate the expression $g - (-7)$ for each value of $g$.

23. $g = 121$
24. $g = 1.25$
25. $g = -\frac{2}{5}$
26. $g = -8\frac{1}{3}$

**Lesson 1-3**

Find the value of each expression.

27. $-24 \div (-8)$
28. $5(-9)$
29. $-5.2 \div y$ for $y = -1.3$
30. $\frac{2}{7} \div \left(-\frac{6}{7}\right)$
31. $0 \div \left(-\frac{4}{5}\right)$
32. $\frac{9}{10} \div 0$

Evaluate each expression for $x = -8$, $y = 6$, and $z = -4$.

33. $xy$
34. $yz$
35. $\frac{y}{z}$
36. $\frac{z}{x}$

Let $a$ represent a positive number, $b$ represent a negative number, and $z$ represent zero. Tell whether each expression is positive, negative, zero, or undefined.

37. $ab$
38. $-bz$
39. $-\frac{a}{b}$
40. $\frac{ab}{z}$

**Lesson 1-4**

Write each expression as repeated multiplication. Then simplify the expression.

41. $3^3$
42. $-2^4$
43. $(-5)^3$
44. $(-1)^5$

Write each expression using a base and an exponent.

45. $5 \cdot 5 \cdot 5 \cdot 5 \cdot 5$
46. $4 \cdot 4 \cdot 4$
47. $2 \cdot 2 \cdot 2 \cdot 2$

Write the exponent that makes each equation true.

48. $2^{■} = 16$
49. $4^{■} = 256$
50. $(-3)^{■} = 81$
51. $-5^{■} = -125$

## Chapter 1 ■ Skills Practice

**Lesson 1-5**

**Find each square root.**

**52.** $-\sqrt{64}$ **53.** $\sqrt{144}$ **54.** $\sqrt{25}$

**Compare. Write <, >, or =.**

**55.** $\sqrt{118}$ ▒ 11 **56.** 6 ▒ $\sqrt{35}$ **57.** 14 ▒ $\sqrt{196}$ **58.** $\sqrt{50}$ ▒ 7

**Write all classifications that apply to each number.**

**59.** $-44$ **60.** $\sqrt{49}$ **61.** 15.982 **62.** $\frac{1}{9}$

**Lesson 1-6**

**Evaluate each expression for the given value of the variable.**

**63.** $22 - 3g + 5$ for $g = 4$ **64.** $12 - 30 \div h$ for $h = 6$ **65.** $\sqrt{(11j + j)} + 6$ for $j = 3$

**Simplify each expression.**

**66.** $4 + 12 \div |3 - 9|$ **67.** $-36 - \sqrt{4 + 15 \div 3}$ **68.** $\frac{5 - \sqrt{12(3)}}{-4 + \sqrt{2(8)}}$

**Translate each word phrase into an algebraic expression.**

**69.** the quotient of 8 and the difference of $a$ and 5

**70.** the sum of $-9$ and the square root of the product of 7 and $c$

**Lesson 1-7**

**Simplify each expression.**

**71.** $-5 + 38 + 5 + 62$ **72.** $2\frac{1}{3} - 42 + 7\frac{2}{3}$ **73.** $\frac{1}{5} \cdot 4 \cdot 25$

**Write each product using the Distributive Property. Then simplify.**

**74.** 12(108) **75.** 7(89) **76.** 11(33)

**Simplify each expression by combining like terms.**

**77.** $7a - 3a$ **78.** $-2b - 12b$ **79.** $4c + 5c^2 - c$

**Simplify each expression. Justify each step with an operation or property.**

**80.** $6(p - 2) + 3p$ **81.** $8q - 3 + 5q(2 + q)$ **82.** $-4 + 3r - 7(2s - r)$

**Lesson 1-8**

**Graph each point.**

**83.** $A(2, 3)$ **84.** $B(-4, 1)$ **85.** $C(0, -2)$ **86.** $D(-4, -1)$

**Name the quadrant in which each point lies.**

**87.** $J$ **88.** $K$ **89.** $L$

**90.** $M$ **91.** $N$ **92.** $P$

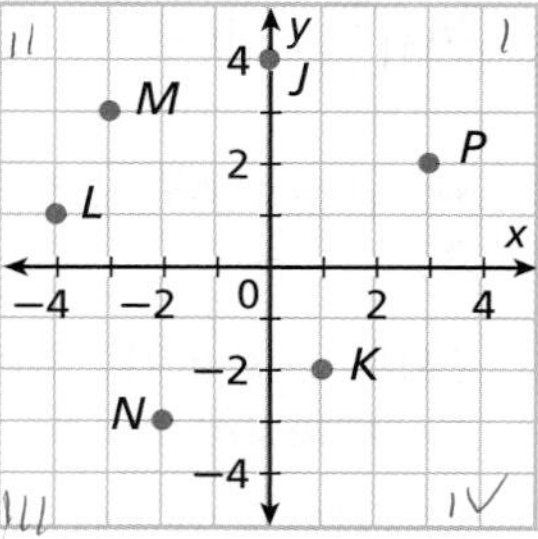


**Generate ordered pairs for each function for $x = -2, -1, 0, 1,$ and 2. Graph the ordered pairs and describe the pattern.**

**93.** $y = x - 3$ **94.** $y = -2x$ **95.** $y = -x^2$ **96.** $y = |3x|$

**Write an equation for each rule. Use the given values for $x$ to generate ordered pairs. Graph the ordered pairs and describe the pattern.**

**97.** $y$ is equal to the sum of one-third of $x$ and $-2$; $x = -6, -3, 0, 3,$ and 6.

**98.** $y$ is equal to 4 less than $x$ squared; $x = -2, -1, 0, 1,$ and 2.

Extra Practice

## Chapter 2 ■ Skills Practice



**Lesson 2-1**

**Solve each equation. Check your answer.**

1. $x - 9 = 5$
2. $4 = y - 12$
3. $a + \frac{3}{5} = 7$
4. $7.3 = b + 3.4$
5. $-6 + j = 5$
6. $-1.7 = -6.1 + k$

**Write an equation to represent each relationship. Then solve the equation.**

7. A number decreased by 7 is equal to 10.
8. The sum of 6 and a number is $-3$.

**Lesson 2-2**

**Solve each equation. Check your answer.**

9. $\frac{n}{5} = 15$
10. $-6 = \frac{k}{4}$
11. $\frac{r}{2.6} = 5$
12. $3b = 27$
13. $56 = -7d$
14. $-3.6 = -2f$
15. $\frac{1}{4}z = 3$
16. $12 = \frac{4}{5}g$
17. $\frac{1}{3}a = -5$

**Write an equation to represent each relationship. Then solve the equation.**

18. A number multiplied by 4 is $-20$.
19. The quotient of a number and 5 is 7.

**Use the equation $9y = -3x$ to find $y$ for each value of $x$.**

| | $x$ | $-3x$ | $9y = -3x$ | $y$ |
|---|---|---|---|---|
| 20. | $-6$ | $-3(-6) = 18$ | $9y = 18$ | |
| 21. | 0 | | | |
| 22. | 3 | | | |

**Lesson 2-3**

**Solve each equation. Check your answer.**

23. $2k + 7 = 15$
24. $11 - 5m = -4$
25. $23 = 9 - 2d$
26. $\frac{2}{5}b + 6 = 10$
27. $\frac{f}{3} - 4 = 2$
28. $6n + 4 = 22$
29. If $5(y - 2) = 30$, find the value of $\frac{1}{4}y$.
30. If $4 - 3b = 19$, find the value of $-2b$.

**Write an equation to represent each relationship. Solve each equation.**

31. The difference of 11 and 4 times a number equals 3.
32. Thirteen less than 5 times a number is equal to 7.

**Lesson 2-4**

**Solve each equation. Check your answer.**

33. $5b - 3 = 4b + 1$
34. $3g + 7 = 11g - 17$
35. $-8 + 4y = y - 6 + 3y - 2$
36. $7 + 3d - 5 = -1 + 2d - 12 + d$

**Write an equation to represent each relationship. Then solve the equation.**

37. Three more than one-half a number is the same as 17 minus three times the number.
38. Two times the difference of a number and 4 is the same as 5 less than the number.

# Chapter 2 ▪ Skills Practice

**Lesson 2-5**

**Solve each equation for the indicated variable.**

**39.** $q - 3r = 2$ for $r$

**40.** $\frac{5 - c}{6} = d - 7$ for $c$

**41.** $2x + 3\frac{y}{4} = 5$ for $y$

**42.** $2fgh - 3g = 10$ for $h$

**Lesson 2-6**

**Find each unit rate.**

**43.** A long-distance runner ran 9000 meters in 30 minutes.

**44.** A hummingbird flapped its wings 770 times in 14 seconds.

**Solve each proportion.**

**45.** $\frac{h}{4} = \frac{5}{6}$

**46.** $\frac{5}{m} = \frac{2}{5}$

**47.** $\frac{r}{3} = \frac{10}{7}$

**48.** $\frac{2}{3} = \frac{2x}{8}$

**49.** $\frac{5}{x - 3} = \frac{3}{10}$

**50.** $\frac{b - 2}{4} = \frac{7}{12}$

**Lesson 2-7**

**Find the value of $x$ in each diagram.**

**51.** $ABCD \sim EFGH$

**52.** $\triangle JKL \sim \triangle MNO$

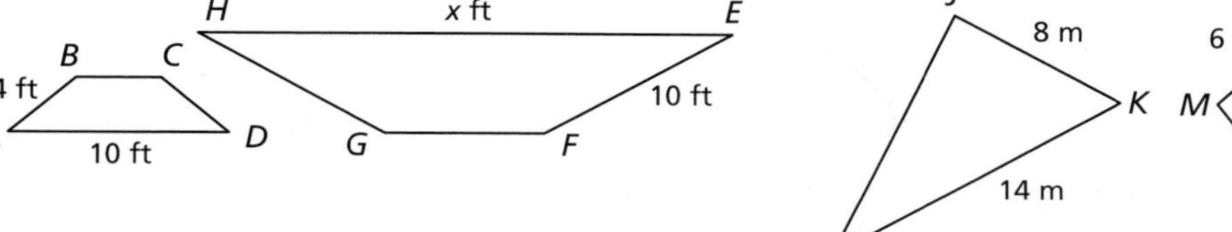


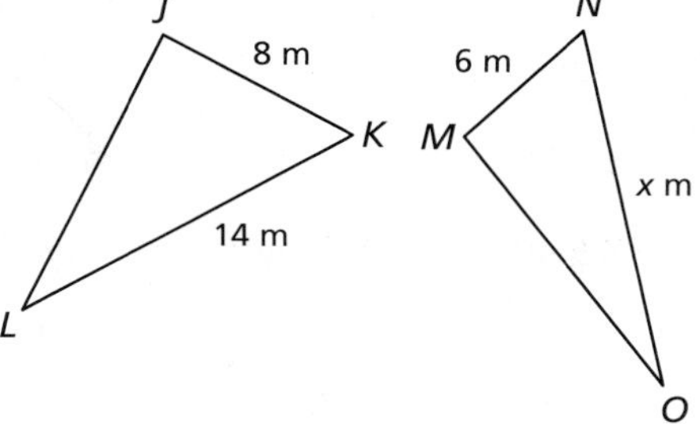


**Lesson 2-8**

**53.** Find 25% of 60.

**54.** Find 40% of 95.

**55.** What percent of 75 is 15?

**56.** What percent of 60 is 33?

**57.** 91 is what percent of 65?

**58.** 35% of what number is 24.5?

**Write each decimal or fraction as a percent.**

**59.** $\frac{4}{5}$

**60.** 0.55

**61.** $\frac{9}{6}$

**62.** 0.0375

**Write each percent as a decimal and as a fraction.**

**63.** 32%

**64.** 24%

**65.** 37.5%

**66.** 118.75%

**Write each list in order from least to greatest.**

**67.** $\frac{2}{17}$, 0.28, 1.9%, $\frac{6}{25}$, 0.19

**68.** $\frac{5}{3}$, 9.2, 117%, $\frac{9}{11}$, 8.8%

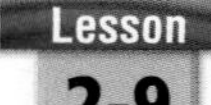


**69.** Estimate the tax on a $2438.00 clarinet when the sales tax is 7.9%.

**70.** Estimate the tip on a $21.32 check using a tip rate of 20%.

**Lesson 2-10**

**Find each percent change. Tell whether it is a percent increase or decrease.**

**71.** 10 to 25

**72.** 40 to 2

**73.** 800 to 160

**74.** 4 to 14

**75.** 8 to 30

**76.** 60 to 36

**77.** Find the result when 45 is increased by 40%.

**78.** Find the result when 120 is decreased by 70%.

Extra Practice

## Chapter 3 ■ Skills Practice

**Lesson 3-1**

**Describe the solutions of each inequality in words.**

**1.** $3 + v < -2$ **2.** $15 \leq k + 4$ **3.** $-3 + n > 6$ **4.** $1 - 4x \geq -2$

**Graph each inequality.**

**5.** $f \geq 2$ **6.** $m < -1$ **7.** $\sqrt{4^2 + 3^2} > c$ **8.** $(-1 - 1)^2 \leq p$

**Write the inequality shown by each graph.**

**9.** 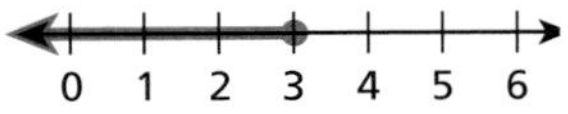 0 1 2 3 4 5 6

**10.** 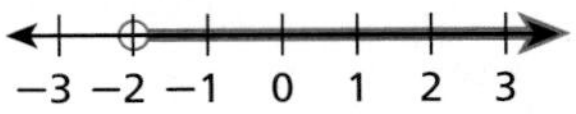 −3 −2 −1 0 1 2 3

**11.** 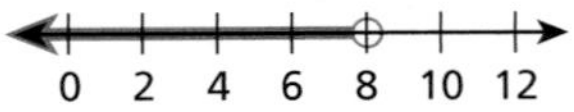 0 2 4 6 8 10 12

**12.** −6 −4 −2 0 2 4 6

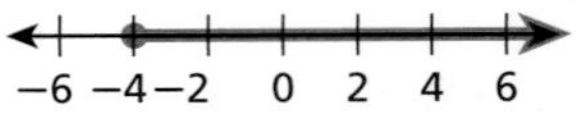

**13.** 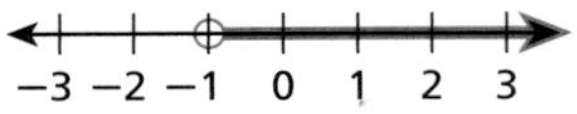 −3 −2 −1 0 1 2 3

**14.** 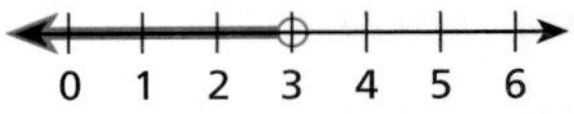 0 1 2 3 4 5 6

**Write each inequality with the variable on the left. Graph the solutions.**

**15.** $14 > b$ **16.** $9 \leq g$ **17.** $-2 < x$ **18.** $-4 \geq k$

**Lesson 3-2**

**Solve each inequality and graph the solutions.**

**19.** $8 \geq d - 4$ **20.** $-5 < 10 + w$ **21.** $a + 4 \leq 7$ **22.** $9 + j > 2$

**Write an inequality to represent each statement. Solve the inequality and graph the solutions.**

**23.** Five more than a number $v$ is less than or equal to 9.

**24.** A number $t$ decreased by 2 is at least 7.

**25.** Three less than a number $r$ is less than $-1$.

**26.** A number $k$ increased by 1 is at most $-2$.

**Use the inequality $4 + z \leq 11$ to fill in the missing numbers.**

**27.** $z \leq \blacksquare$ **28.** $z - \blacksquare \leq 4$ **29.** $z - 3 \leq \blacksquare$

**Lesson 3-3**

**Solve each inequality and graph the solutions.**

**30.** $24 > 4b$ **31.** $27g \leq 81$ **32.** $\frac{x}{5} < 3$ **33.** $10y \geq 2$

**34.** $4p < -2$ **35.** $\frac{3s}{8} > 3$ **36.** $0 \geq \frac{3}{7}d$ **37.** $\frac{a}{8} \geq \frac{3}{4}$

**38.** $-3k \leq -12$ **39.** $\frac{-2e}{5} \geq 4$ **40.** $8 < -12y$ **41.** $-3.5 > 14c$

**42.** $9 > \frac{h}{-2}$ **43.** $49 > -7m$ **44.** $60 \leq -12c$ **45.** $-\frac{1}{3}q < -6$

**Write an inequality for each statement. Solve the inequality and graph the solutions.**

**46.** The product of $\frac{1}{2}$ and a number is not more than 6.

**47.** The quotient of $r$ and $-5$ is greater than 3.

**48.** The product of $-11$ and a number is greater than $-33$.

**49.** The quotient of $w$ and $-4$ is less than or equal to $-6$.

# Chapter 3 ■ Skills Practice

**Lesson 3-4**

**Solve each inequality and graph the solutions.**

**50.** $3t - 2 < 5$ **51.** $4p + 4 \geq 12$ **52.** $10 > 4 - 3g$ **53.** $-6 < 5b - 4$

**54.** $\frac{m-2}{4} < -2$ **55.** $-1 > \frac{10x-4}{12}$ **56.** $9a + 6 \geq 3$ **57.** $4 < \frac{2f+3}{2}$

**58.** $10 \leq 3(4 - r)$ **59.** $\frac{2}{3} + \frac{3}{4}h < \frac{4}{3}$ **60.** $\frac{1}{5}(10k - 2) > 1$

**61.** $-n - 3 < -2^3$ **62.** $37 - 4d \leq \sqrt{3^2 + 4^2}$ **63.** $-\frac{3}{4}(8q - 2^2) < -3$

**Use the inequality $-6 - 2w \geq 10$ to fill in the missing numbers.**

**64.** $w \leq \square$ **65.** $w - 3 \leq \square$ **66.** $\square + w \leq 1$

**Write an inequality for each statement. Solve the inequality and graph the solutions.**

**67.** Twelve is less than or equal to the product of 6 and the difference of 5 and a number.

**68.** The difference of one-third a number and 8 is more than −4.

**69.** Seven more than a number is less than or equal to the square root of the sum of 9 and 7.

**70.** One-fourth of the sum of $2x$ and 4 is more than 5.

**Lesson 3-5**

**Solve each inequality and graph the solutions.**

**71.** $4v - 2 \leq 3v$ **72.** $9e > 7 - 2e$

**73.** $6j \geq 2j + 8$ **74.** $3z - 5 < 7z$

**75.** $2(7 - s) > 4(s + 2)$ **76.** $-3(3 + 2y) - 1 \leq 2(1 - 4y)$

**77.** $3n < 3(6 - 2n)$ **78.** $\frac{1}{3}u - \frac{5}{2} \geq \frac{1}{6}u$

**Solve each inequality.**

**79.** $3 + 3c < 6 + 3c$ **80.** $4(k + 2) \geq 4k + 5$ **81.** $2(5 - b) \leq 3 - 2b$

**Write an inequality to represent each relationship. Solve your inequality.**

**82.** The difference of three times a number and 5 is more than the number times 4.

**83.** Seven more than the product of four and a number is less than or equal to the number increased by 3.

**84.** one less than a number is greater than the product of 3 and the difference of 5 and the number.

**Lesson 3-6**

**Solve each compound inequality and graph the solutions.**

**85.** $6 < 3 + x < 8$ **86.** $-1 \leq b + 4 \leq 3$

**87.** $k + 5 \leq -3$ OR $k + 5 \geq 1$ **88.** $r - 3 > 2$ OR $r + 1 < 4$

**Write the compound inequality shown by each graph.**

**89.** 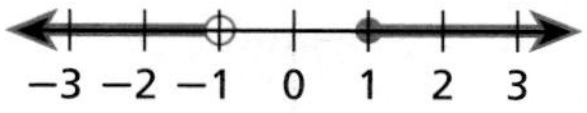


**90.** 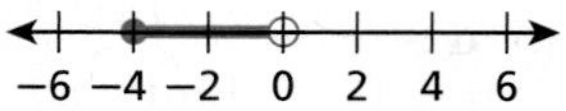


**Write and graph a compound inequality for the numbers described.**

**91.** all real numbers less than 2 and greater than or equal to −1

**92.** all real numbers between −3 and 1

**Solve each compound inequality and graph the solutions.**

**93.** $2r + 3 \geq 1$ AND $3r - 4 \leq 5$ **94.** $f - 2 > 6$ OR $f + 2 < 6$



Extra Practice

## Chapter 4 ■ Skills Practice

**Lesson 4-1**

**Choose the graph that best represents each situation.**

1. A person blows up a balloon with a steady airstream.
2. A person blows up a balloon steadily and then lets it deflate.
3. A person blows up a balloon slowly at first and then uses more and more air.

**Graph A**

Volume

Time

**Graph B**

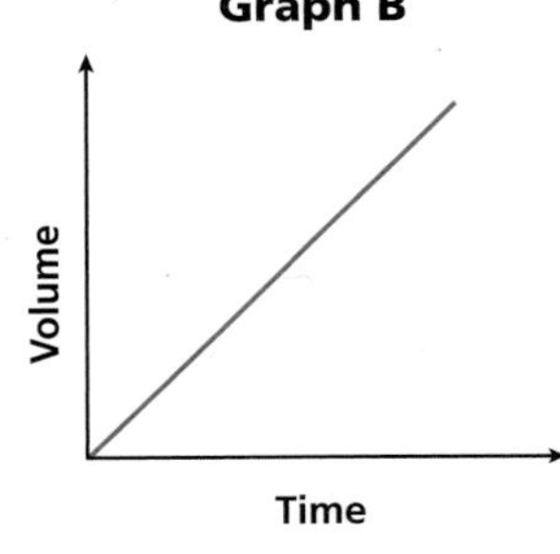


**Graph C**

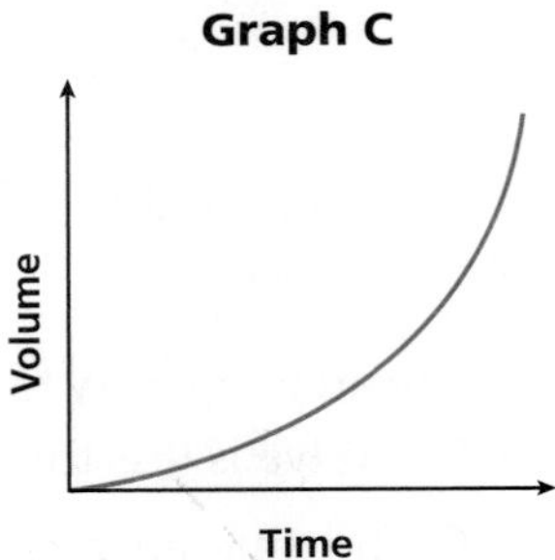


**Lesson 4-2**

**Express each relation as a table, as a graph, and as a mapping diagram.**

4. $\{(0, 2), (-1, 3), (-2, 5)\}$

5. $\{(2, 8), (4, 6), (6, 4), (8, 2)\}$

**Give the domain and range for each relation. Tell whether the relation is a function. Explain.**

6. $\{(3, 4), (-1, 2), (2, -3), (5, 0)\}$

7. $\{(5, 4), (0, 2), (5, -3), (0, 1)\}$

8.

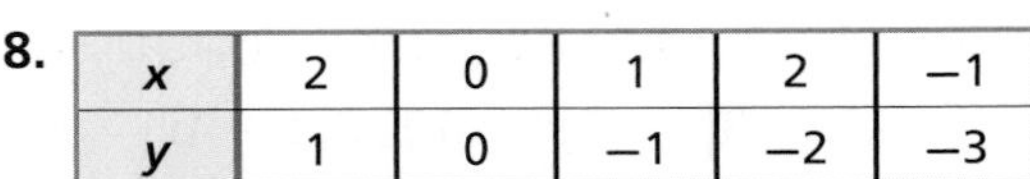

| *x* | 2 | 0 | 1 | 2 | −1 |
|---|---|---|---|---|---|
| *y* | 1 | 0 | −1 | −2 | −3 |

9.

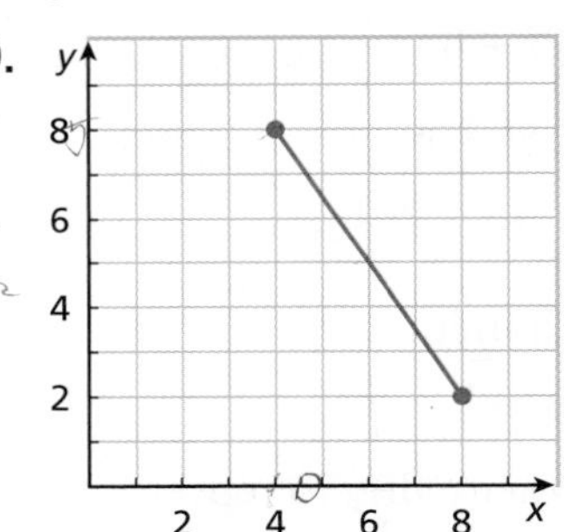


**Lesson 4-3**

**Determine a relationship between the *x*- and *y*-variables. Write an equation.**

10. $\{(1, 3), (2, 6), (3, 9), (4, 12)\}$

11.

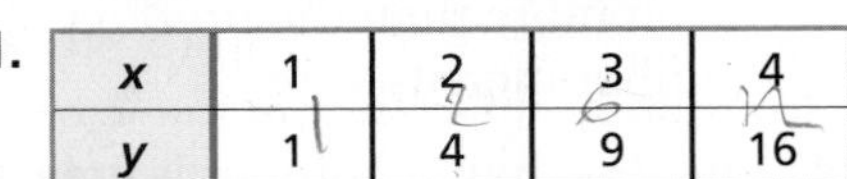

| *x* | 1 | 2 | 3 | 4 |
|---|---|---|---|---|
| *y* | 1 | 4 | 9 | 16 |

**Identify the independent and dependent variables. Write a rule in function notation for each situation.**

12. A science tutor charges students $15 per hour.
13. A circus charges a $10 entry fee and $1.50 for each pony ride.

**Evaluate each function for the given input values.**

14. For $f(a) = 6 - 4a$, find $f(a)$ when $a = 2$ and when $a = -3$.
15. For $g(d) = \frac{2}{5}d + 3$, find $g(d)$ when $d = 10$ and when $d = -5$.
16. For $h(w) = 2 - w^2$, find $h(w)$ when $w = -1$ and when $w = -2$.
17. Complete the table for $f(t) = 7 + 3t$.

| *t* | 0 | 1 | 2 | 3 |
|---|---|---|---|---|
| *f*(*t*) | ■ | ■ | ■ | ■ |

18. Complete the table for $h(s) = 2s + s^3 - 6$.

| *s* | −1 | 0 | 1 | 2 |
|---|---|---|---|---|
| *h*(*s*) | ■ | ■ | ■ | ■ |

# Chapter 4 ■ Skills Practice

Lesson **4-4**

**Graph each function for the given domain.**

**19.** $2x - y = 2$; D: $\{-2, -1, 0, 1\}$

**20.** $f(x) = x^2 - 1$; D: $\{-3, -1, 0, 2\}$

**Graph each function.**

**21.** $f(x) = 4 - 2x$

**22.** $y + 3 = 2x$

**23.** $y = -5 + x^2$

**24.** Use a graph of the function $f(x) = \frac{5}{2} - 2x$ to find the value of $f(x)$ when $x = \frac{1}{2}$. Check your answer.

**25.** Find the value of $x$ so that $(x, 4)$ satisfies $y = -x + 8$.

**26.** Find the value of $y$ so that $(-3, y)$ satisfies $y = 15 - 2x^2$.

**For each function, determine whether the given points are on the graph.**

**27.** $y = \frac{x}{3} + 4$; $(-3, 3)$ and $(3, 5)$

**28.** $y = x^2 - 1$; $(-2, 3)$ and $(2, 5)$

Lesson **4-5**

**Describe the correlation illustrated by each scatter plot.**

**29.**

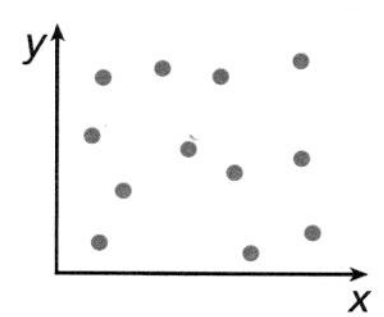


**30.**

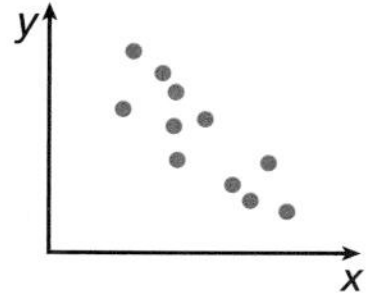


**31.**

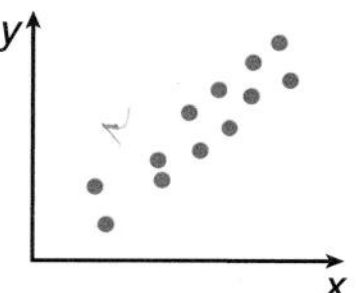


**Identify the correlation you would expect to see between each pair of data sets.**

**32.** the number of chess pieces captured and the number of pieces still on the board

**33.** a person's height and the color of the person's eyes

**Choose the scatter plot that best represents the described situation.**

**34.** the number of students in a class and the grades on a test

**35.** the number of students in a class and the number of empty desks

Graph A

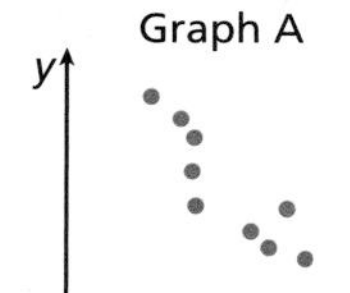


Graph B

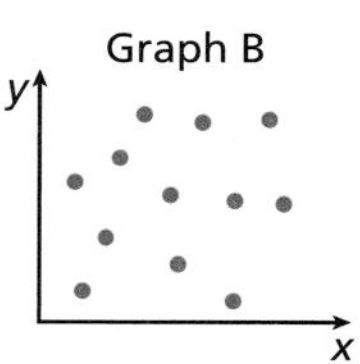


Lesson **4-6**

**Determine whether each sequence appears to be an arithmetic sequence. If so, find the common difference and the next three terms.**

**36.** $-10, -7, -4, -1, \ldots$

**37.** $8, 5, 1, -4, \ldots$

**38.** $1, -2, 3, -4, \ldots$

**39.** $-19, -9, 1, 11, \ldots$

**Find the indicated term of each arithmetic sequence.**

**40.** 15th term: $-5, -1, 3, 7, \ldots$

**41.** 20th term: $a_1 = 2$; $d = -5$

**42.** 12th term: $8, 16, 24, 32, \ldots$

**43.** 21st term: $5.2, 5.17, 5.14, 5.11, \ldots$

**Find the common difference for each arithmetic sequence.**

**44.** $0, 7, 14, 21, \ldots$

**45.** $132, 121, 110, 99, \ldots$

**46.** $\frac{1}{4}, 1, \frac{7}{4}, \frac{10}{4}, \ldots$

**47.** $1.4, 2.2, 3, 3.8, \ldots$

**48.** $-7, -2, 3, 8, \ldots$

**49.** $7.28, 7.21, 7.14, 7.07, \ldots$

**Find the next four terms in each arithmetic sequence.**

**50.** $-3, -6, -9, -12, \ldots$

**51.** $2, 9, 16, 23, \ldots$

**52.** $-\frac{1}{3}, \frac{1}{3}, 1, \frac{5}{3}, \ldots$

**53.** $-4.3, -3.2, -2.1, -1, \ldots$

## Chapter 5 ▪ Skills Practice

**Lesson 5-1**

**Identify whether each graph represents a function. Explain. If the graph does represent a function, is the function linear?**

**1.** 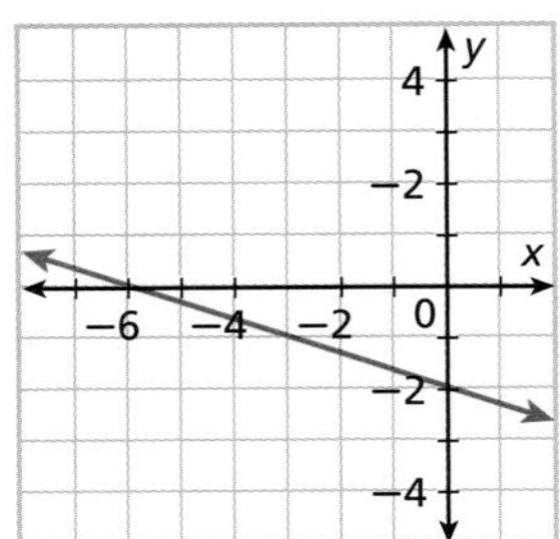

**2.** 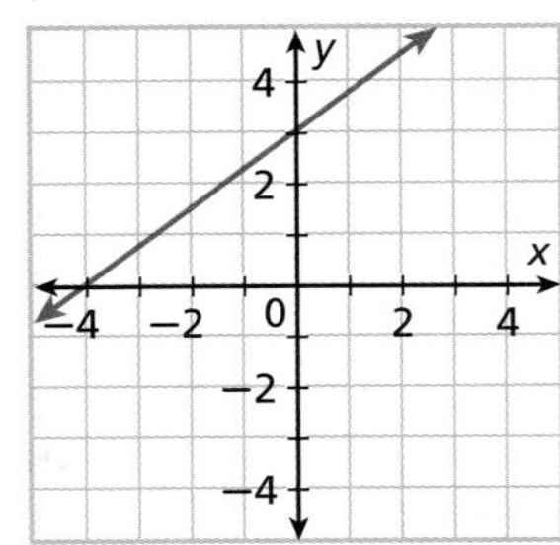

**3.** 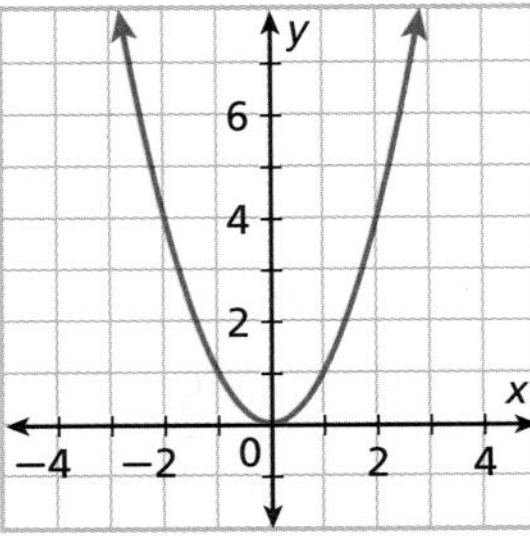

**Tell whether the given ordered pairs satisfy a linear function. Explain.**

**4.**

| x | −4 | −2 | 0 | 2 | 4 |
|---|---|---|---|---|---|
| y | 7 | 6 | 5 | 4 | 3 |

**5.**

| x | 2 | 5 | 8 | 11 | 14 |
|---|---|---|---|---|---|
| y | 12 | 8 | 7 | 3 | 3 |

**Tell whether each equation is linear. If so, write the equation in standard form and give the values of *A*, *B*, and *C*.**

**6.** $y = 8 - 3x$ **7.** $\frac{x}{3} = 4 - 2y$ **8.** $-3 + xy = 2$ **9.** $4x = -3 - 3y$

**Lesson 5-2**

**Find the *x*- and *y*-intercepts.**

**10.** 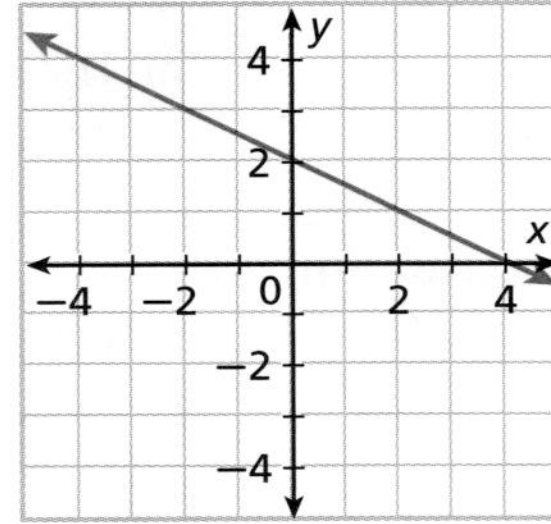

**11.** 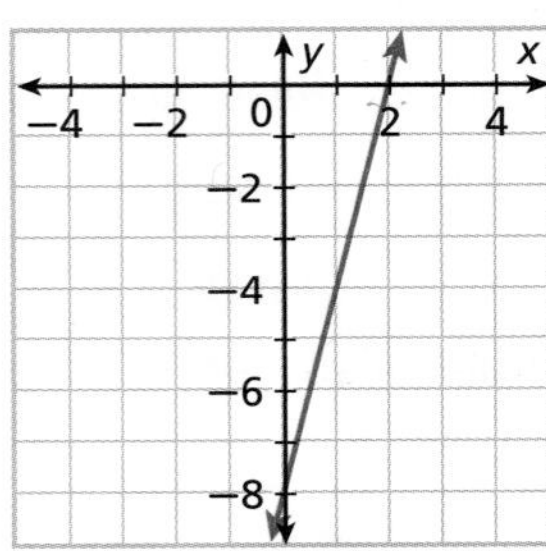

**12.** $-4x = 2y - 1$ **13.** $x - y = 3$ **14.** $2x - 3y = 12$ **15.** $2.5x + 2.5y = 5$

**Use intercepts to graph the line described by each equation.**

**16.** $15 = -3x - 5y$ **17.** $4y = 2x + 8$ **18.** $y = 6 - 3x$ **19.** $-2y = x + 2$

**Lesson 5-3**

**Find the slope of each line.**

**20.** 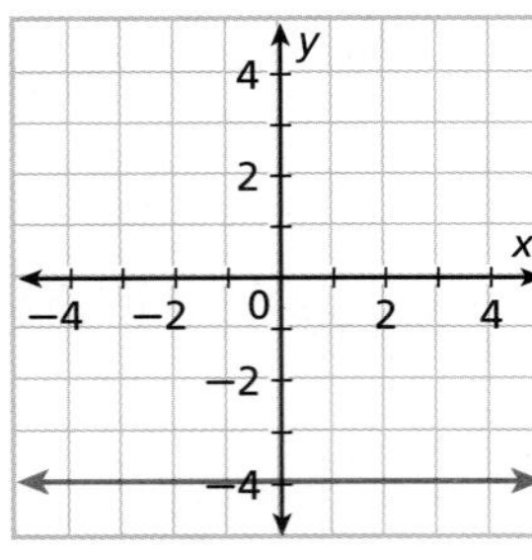

**21.** 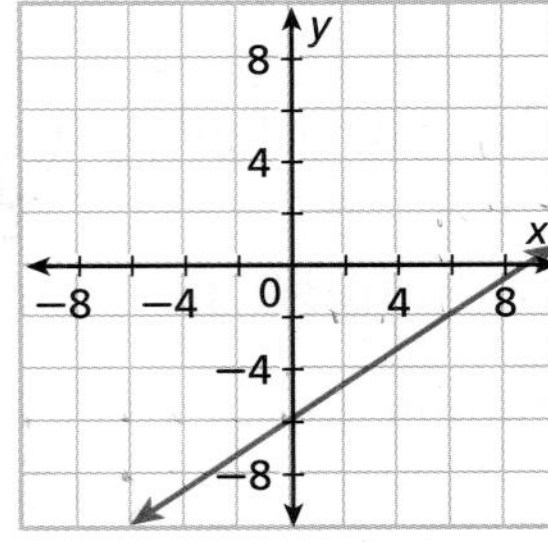

**Lesson 5-4**

**Find the slope of the line that contains each pair of points.**

**22.** $(-1, 2)$ and $(-4, 8)$ **23.** $(2, 6)$ and $(0, 1)$ **24.** $(-2, 3)$ and $(4, 0)$

**Find the slope of the line described by each equation.**

**25.** $2y = 42 - 6x$ **26.** $3x + 4y = 12$ **27.** $3x = 15 + 5y$

## Chapter 5 ■ Skills Practice

**Lesson 5-5**

**Tell whether each equation represents a direct variation. If so, identify the constant of variation.**

28. $x - 2y = 0$
29. $x - y = 3$
30. $3y = 2x$
31. The value of $y$ varies directly with $x$, and $y = 2$ when $x = -3$. Find $y$ when $x = 6$.
32. The value of $y$ varies directly with $x$, and $y = -3$ when $x = 9$. Find $y$ when $x = 12$.

**Each ordered pair is a solution of a direct variation. Write the equation of direct variation.**

33. $(1, 4)$
34. $(-2, 12)$
35. $\left(\frac{1}{2}, -3\right)$
36. $(5, 2)$
37. $(8, 12)$
38. $(7, -2)$
39. $(12, -3)$
40. $(5, 15)$

**Lesson 5-6**

**Write the equation that describes each line in slope-intercept form.**

41. slope $= 2$, $y$-intercept $= -2$
42. slope $= 0.25$, $y$-intercept $= 4$
43. slope $= -2$, $y$-intercept $= 3$
44. slope $= \frac{1}{3}$, $y$-intercept $= 2$

**Write each equation in slope-intercept form. Then graph the line described by the equation.**

45. $2y = x - 3$
46. $-3x - 2y = 1$
47. $2y - \frac{1}{2}x = 2$

**Lesson 5-7**

**Write an equation in point-slope form for the line with the given slope that contains the given point.**

48. slope $= 2$; $(0, 3)$
49. slope $= -1$; $(1, -1)$
50. slope $= \frac{1}{2}$; $(2, 4)$
51. slope $= \frac{1}{3}$; $(1, 2)$
52. slope $= -2$; $(3, 1)$
53. slope $= 3$; $(-2, -5)$

**Write an equation in slope-intercept form for the line through the two points.**

54. $(-1, 1)$ and $(1, -2)$
55. $(3, 1)$ and $(2, -3)$
56. $(4, -5)$ and $(2, -1)$

**Lesson 5-8**

57. Identify which lines are parallel: $y = 3x - 2$; $y = -2$; $y = 3x + 7$; $y = 0$
58. Identify which lines are perpendicular: $y = -2(2x - 1)$; $y = \frac{1}{2}(x + 3)$; $y = \frac{1}{4}(x + 8)$; $y - 4 = 2(3 - 2x)$

**Write an equation in slope-intercept form for the line that is parallel to the given line and that passes through the given point.**

59. $y = -2x + 3$; $(1, 4)$
60. $y = x - 5$; $(2, -4)$
61. $y = 3x$; $(-1, 5)$

**Write an equation in slope-intercept form for the line that is perpendicular to the given line and that passes through the given point.**

62. $y = x + 1$; $(3, -2)$
63. $y = -4x - 1$; $(-1, 0)$
64. $y = 4x + 5$; $(2, -1)$

**Lesson 5-9**

**Graph $f(x)$ and $g(x)$. Then describe the transformation(s) from the graph of $f(x)$ to the graph of $g(x)$.**

65. $f(x) = x$, $g(x) = x + 2$
66. $f(x) = x$, $g(x) = x - \frac{1}{2}$
67. $f(x) = 6x + 1$, $g(x) = 2x + 1$
68. $f(x) = 3x - 1$, $g(x) = 9x - 1$
69. $f(x) = x$, $g(x) = 2x - 1$
70. $f(x) = x + 1$, $g(x) = -\frac{1}{2}x$

**Graph $f(x)$. Then reflect the graph of $f(x)$ across the $y$-axis. Write a function $g(x)$ to describe the new graph.**

71. $f(x) = 2x + 3$
72. $f(x) = -3x - 1$
73. $f(x) = -4x$

Extra Practice

## Chapter 6 ■ Skills Practice

Extra Practice

**Lesson 6-1**

**Tell whether the ordered pair is a solution of the given system.**

**1.** $(1, 3); \begin{cases} 2x - 3y = -7 \\ -5x + 3y = 4 \end{cases}$

**2.** $(-2, 2); \begin{cases} 4x + 3y = -2 \\ -2x - 2y = 2 \end{cases}$

**3.** $(4, -3); \begin{cases} -2x - 3y = 1 \\ x + 2y = -2 \end{cases}$

**Use the given graph to find the solution of each system.**

**4.** $\begin{cases} y = \frac{1}{2}x - 1 \\ y = -\frac{1}{2}x + 3 \end{cases}$

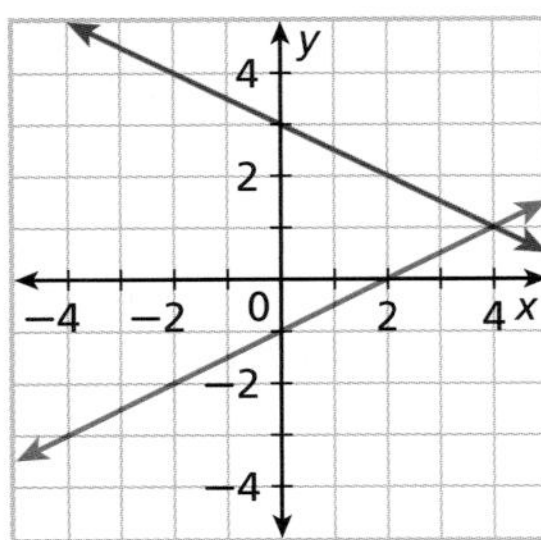


**5.** $\begin{cases} y = x + 1 \\ y = -x + 1 \end{cases}$

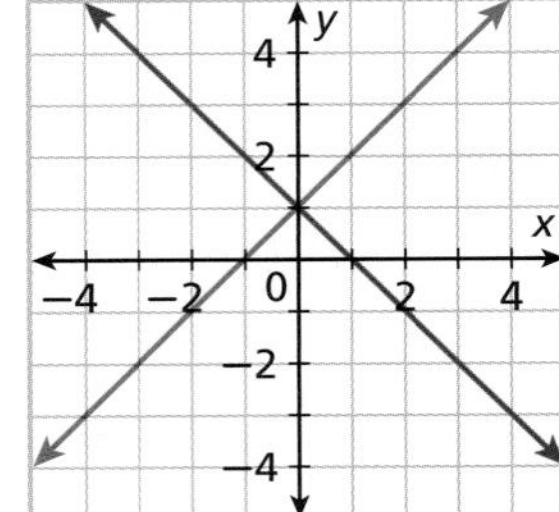


**Solve each system by graphing. Check your answer.**

**6.** $\begin{cases} y = x + 1 \\ y = -2x - 2 \end{cases}$

**7.** $\begin{cases} 3x + y = -8 \\ 3y = \frac{1}{2}x - 5 \end{cases}$

**8.** $\begin{cases} x = 2 - 2y \\ -1 = -2x - 3y \end{cases}$

**Lesson 6-2**

**Solve each system by substitution.**

**9.** $\begin{cases} y = 12 - 3x \\ y = 2x - 3 \end{cases}$

**10.** $\begin{cases} 2x + y = -6 \\ -5x + y = 1 \end{cases}$

**11.** $\begin{cases} y = 11 - 3x \\ -2x + y = 1 \end{cases}$

**12.** $\begin{cases} 2x + 3y = 2 \\ -\frac{1}{2}x + 2y = -6 \end{cases}$

**13.** $\begin{cases} 3x - 2y = -3 \\ y = 7 - 4x \end{cases}$

**14.** $\begin{cases} 4y - 2x = -2 \\ x + 3y = -4 \end{cases}$

**Two angles whose measures have a sum of 90° are called complementary angles. For Exercises 15–17, *x* and *y* represent complementary angles. Find the measure of each angle.**

**15.** $\begin{cases} x + y = 90 \\ y = 9x - 10 \end{cases}$

**16.** $\begin{cases} x + y = 90 \\ y - 4x = 15 \end{cases}$

**17.** $\begin{cases} x + y = 90 \\ y = 2x + 15 \end{cases}$

**Lesson 6-3**

**Solve each system by elimination.**

**18.** $\begin{cases} x - 3y = -1 \\ -x + 2y = -2 \end{cases}$

**19.** $\begin{cases} -3x - y = 1 \\ 5x + y = -5 \end{cases}$

**20.** $\begin{cases} -x - 3y = -1 \\ 3x + 3y = 9 \end{cases}$

**21.** $\begin{cases} 3x - 2y = 2 \\ 3x + y = 8 \end{cases}$

**22.** $\begin{cases} 5x - 2y = -15 \\ 2x - 2y = -12 \end{cases}$

**23.** $\begin{cases} -4x - 2y = -4 \\ -4x + 3y = -24 \end{cases}$

**24.** $\begin{cases} -3x - 3y = 3 \\ 2x + y = -4 \end{cases}$

**25.** $\begin{cases} 4x - 3y = -1 \\ 2x - 2y = -4 \end{cases}$

**26.** $\begin{cases} 3x + 6y = 0 \\ 7x + 4y = 20 \end{cases}$

Lesson 6-4

**Solve each system of linear equations.**

**27.** $\begin{cases} y = 2x + 4 \\ -2x + y = 6 \end{cases}$ **28.** $\begin{cases} -y = 3 - 5x \\ y - 5x = 6 \end{cases}$ **29.** $\begin{cases} y + 2 = 3x \\ 3x - y = -1 \end{cases}$

**30.** $\begin{cases} 2y = 6 - 6x \\ 3y + 9x = 9 \end{cases}$ **31.** $\begin{cases} y - 1 = -3x \\ 12x + 4y = 4 \end{cases}$ **32.** $\begin{cases} 4x - 2y = 4 \\ 3y = 6(x - 1) \end{cases}$

**Classify each system. Give the number of solutions.**

**33.** $\begin{cases} 2y = 2(4x - 3) \\ y - 1 = 4x \end{cases}$ **34.** $\begin{cases} 3y + 6x = 9 \\ 2(y - 3) = -4x \end{cases}$ **35.** $\begin{cases} 3x - 13 = 2y \\ -3y = 2x \end{cases}$

Lesson 6-5

**Tell whether the ordered pair is a solution of the given inequality.**

**36.** $(3, 6);\ y > 2x + 4$ **37.** $(-2, -8);\ y \leq 3x - 2$ **38.** $(-3, 3);\ y \geq -2x + 5$

**Graph the solutions of each linear inequality.**

**39.** $y > 2x$ **40.** $y \leq -3x + 2$ **41.** $y \geq 2x - 1$ **42.** $-y < -x + 4$

**43.** $y \geq -2x + 4$ **44.** $y > -x - 3$ **45.** $y < \frac{1}{2}x + 1\frac{1}{2}$ **46.** $y \leq 4x - (-1)$

**Write an inequality to represent each graph.**

**47.**

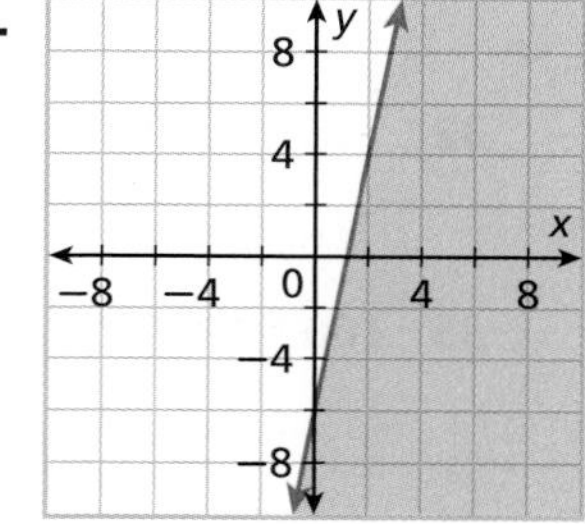


**48.**

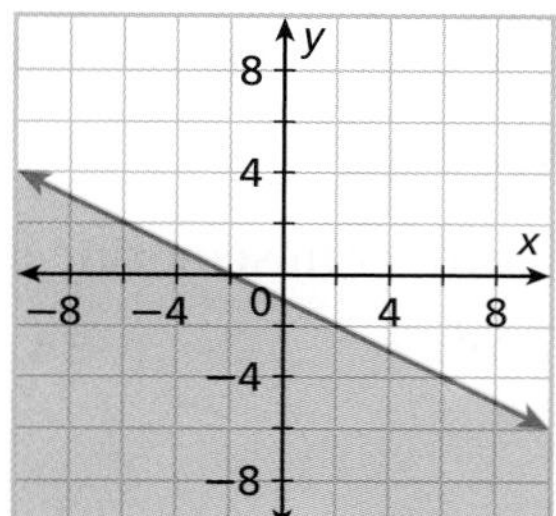


Lesson 6-6

**Tell whether the ordered pair is a solution of the given system.**

**49.** $(2, 5);\ \begin{cases} y > 3x - 3 \\ y \geq x + 1 \end{cases}$ **50.** $(3, 9);\ \begin{cases} y > -3x - 2 \\ y < 2x + 3 \end{cases}$ **51.** $(2, 3);\ \begin{cases} y > 2x \\ y \leq x - 3 \end{cases}$

**Graph each system of linear inequalities. Give two ordered pairs that are solutions and two that are not solutions.**

**52.** $\begin{cases} x + 4y < 2 \\ 2y > 3x + 8 \end{cases}$ **53.** $\begin{cases} y \leq 6 - 2x \\ x - 2y < -2 \end{cases}$ **54.** $\begin{cases} 2x - 2 > -3y \\ -x + 3y \geq -10 \end{cases}$

**Graph each system of linear inequalities.**

**55.** $\begin{cases} y > 2x + 1 \\ y < 2x - 2 \end{cases}$ **56.** $\begin{cases} y < 3x - 1 \\ y > 3x - 4 \end{cases}$ **57.** $\begin{cases} y \geq -x + 2 \\ y \geq -x + 5 \end{cases}$

**58.** $\begin{cases} y \geq 2x - 3 \\ y \geq 2x + 3 \end{cases}$ **59.** $\begin{cases} y > -4x - 2 \\ y \leq -4x - 5 \end{cases}$ **60.** $\begin{cases} y \geq -2x + 1 \\ y < -2x + 6 \end{cases}$

# Chapter 7 ■ Skills Practice

**Lesson 7-1**

**Simplify.**

1. $3^{-4}$
2. $5^{-3}$
3. $-4^{0}$
4. $-2^{-5}$
5. $6^{-3}$
6. $(-2)^{-4}$
7. $1^{-7}$
8. $(-4)^{-3}$
9. $(-5)^{0}$
10. $(-1)^{-5}$

**Evaluate each expression for the given value(s) of the variable(s).**

11. $x^{-4}$ for $x = 2$
12. $(c + 3)^{-3}$ for $c = -6$
13. $3j^{-7}k^{-1}$ for $j = -2$ and $k = 3$
14. $(2n - 2)^{-4}$ for $n = 3$

**Simplify.**

15. $b^4g^{-5}$
16. $\dfrac{k^{-3}}{r^5}$
17. $5s^{-3}c^0$
18. $\dfrac{z^{-4}}{5t^{-2}}$
19. $\dfrac{f^2}{3a^{-4}}$
20. $\dfrac{-3t^4}{q^{-5}}$
21. $\dfrac{a^0k^{-4}}{p^2}$
22. $3f^{-1}y^{-5}$

**Lesson 7-2**

**Find the value of each power of 10.**

23. $10^{-7}$
24. $10^{9}$
25. $10^{6}$
26. $10^{-8}$

**Write each number as a power of 10.**

27. 10,000,000
28. 0.00001
29. 10,000,000,000,000

**Find the value of each expression.**

30. $72.19 \times 10^{-2}$
31. $0.096 \times 10^{-7}$
32. $7384.5 \times 10^{6}$

**Write each number in scientific notation.**

33. 3,605,000
34. 0.0063
35. 100,500,000

**Lesson 7-3**

**Simplify.**

36. $3^4 \cdot 3^2$
37. $r^7 \cdot r^0$
38. $(k^4)^4$
39. $(b^4)^3$
40. $(c^3d^2)^3 \cdot (cd^2)^{-2}$
41. $(-3q^3)^{-2}$

**Find the missing exponent in each expression.**

42. $a^{■}a^6 = a^9$
43. $(a^3b^{■})^3 = \dfrac{a^9}{b^6}$
44. $(a^4b^{-2})^{■} \cdot a^3 = \dfrac{b^4}{a^5}$

**Lesson 7-4**

**Simplify.**

45. $\dfrac{3^{11}}{3^8}$
46. $\dfrac{4^4 \cdot 5^3}{3^2 \cdot 4^3 \cdot 5^3}$
47. $\dfrac{6h^4}{12h^3}$
48. $\dfrac{r^6s^5}{r^5s^6}$

**Simplify each quotient and write the answer in scientific notation.**

49. $(4 \times 10^7) \div (1.6 \times 10^5)$
50. $(10 \times 10^4) \div (2 \times 10^7)$
51. $(2.5 \times 10^8) \div (5 \times 10^3)$

**Simplify.**

52. $\left(\dfrac{2}{3}\right)^4$
53. $\left(\dfrac{x^2y^2}{y^3}\right)^2$
54. $\left(\dfrac{4}{5}\right)^{-3}$
55. $\left(\dfrac{2xy^2}{3(xy)^2}\right)^{-3}$

Extra Practice

# Chapter 7 ■ Skills Practice

**Lesson 7-5**

**Find the degree of each monomial.**

**56.** $4^7$ **57.** $x^3y$ **58.** $\frac{r^6st^2}{2}$ **59.** $9^0$

**Find the degree of each polynomial.**

**60.** $a^2b + b - 2^2$ **61.** $5x^4y^2 - y^5z^2$ **62.** $3g^4h + h^2 + 4j^6$ **63.** $4no^7 - o^6p^3 + p$

**Write each polynomial in standard form. Then give the leading coefficient.**

**64.** $4r - 5r^3 + 2r^2$ **65.** $-3b^2 + 7b^6 + 4 - b$ **66.** $\frac{1}{2}t^3 + t - \frac{1}{3}t^5 + 4$

**Classify each polynomial according to its degree and number of terms.**

**67.** $3x^2 + 4x - 5$ **68.** $-4x^2 + x^6 - 4 + x^3$ **69.** $x^3 - 7^2$

**Lesson 7-6**

**Add or subtract.**

**70.** $4y^3 - 2y + 3y^3$ **71.** $9k^2 + 5 - 10k^2 - 6$

**72.** $7 - 3n^2 + 4 + 2n^2$ **73.** $3a^2 + 4a^3 - 2a^2$

**74.** $(2 + x^2) + (5x^2 + 6)$ **75.** $(9x^6 - 5x^2 + 3) + (6x^2 - 5)$

**76.** $(2y^5 - 5y^2) + (3y^5 - y^3 + 2y^2)$ **77.** $(5y^3 - 6y + 2) + (2y^7 + y)$

**78.** $(r^3 + 2r + 1) - (2r^3 - 4)$ **79.** $(4r^4 - 3r^2 + 4) - (2r^4 - r^2)$

**80.** $(10s^2 + 5) - (5s^2 + 3s - 2)$ **81.** $(2s^7 - 6s^3 + 2) - (3s^7 + 2)$

**Lesson 7-7**

**Multiply.**

**82.** $(3a^7)(2a^4)$ **83.** $\left(\frac{3}{4}r^5\right)(12r^2)$ **84.** $(-3xy^3)(2x^2z)(yz^4)$

**85.** $(4kl^3m)(-2k^2m^2)$ **86.** $(-6c^2e)(-2de^2)$ **87.** $3jk^2(2j^2 + k)$

**88.** $4q^3r^2(2qr^2 + 3q)$ **89.** $-2c^3(c^3 + 3c - 2)$ **90.** $3xy^2(2x^2y - 3y)$

**91.** $(x - 3)(x + 1)$ **92.** $(x - 2)(x - 3)$ **93.** $(x - 4)(x - 4)$

**94.** $(2x^2 - 3y)(3x - y^2)$ **95.** $(x^2 + 2xy)(3x^2y - 2)$ **96.** $(x^2 - 3x)(2xy - 3y)$

**97.** $(x - 2)(x^2 + 3x - 4)$ **98.** $(2x - 1)(-2x^2 - 3x + 4)$ **99.** $(x + 3)(2x^4 - 3x^2 - 5)$

**100.** $(2a + 3)(a^2 + 2ab - b)$ **101.** $(3a + b)(2a^2 + ab - 2b^2)$ **102.** $(a^2 - b)(3a^2 - 2ab + 3b^2)$

**Lesson 7-8**

**Multiply.**

**103.** $(x + 3)^2$ **104.** $(3 + 2x)^2$ **105.** $(4x + 2y)^2$

**106.** $(3x - 2)^2$ **107.** $(5 - 2x)^2$ **108.** $(3x - 5y)^2$

**109.** $(3 + x)(3 - x)$ **110.** $(x - 5)(x + 5)$ **111.** $(2x + 1)(2x - 1)$

**112.** $(x^2 + 4)(x^2 - 4)$ **113.** $(2 + 3x^3)(2 - 3x^3)$ **114.** $(4x^3 - 3y)(4x^3 + 3y)$

# Chapter 8 ■ Skills Practice

**Lesson 8-1**

**Write the prime factorization of each number.**

**1.** 24 **2.** 78 **3.** 88 **4.** 63

**5.** 128 **6.** 102 **7.** 71 **8.** 125

**Find the GCF of each pair of numbers.**

**9.** 18 and 66 **10.** 24 and 104 **11.** 30 and 75

**12.** 24 and 120 **13.** 36 and 99 **14.** 42 and 72

**Find the GCF of each pair of monomials.**

**15.** $4a^3$ and $9a^4$ **16.** $6q^2$ and $15q^5$ **17.** $6x^2$ and $14y^3$

**18.** $4z^2$ and $10z^5$ **19.** $5g^3$ and $9g$ **20.** $12x^2$ and $21y^2$

**Lesson 8-2**

**Factor each polynomial. Check your answer.**

**21.** $6b^2 - 15b^3$ **22.** $11t^4 - 9t^3$ **23.** $10v^3 - 25v$

**24.** $12r + 16r^3$ **25.** $17a^4 - 35a^2$ **26.** $9f + 18f^5 + 12f^2$

**Factor each expression.**

**27.** $3(a + 3) + 4a(a + 3)$ **28.** $5(k - 4) - 2k(k - 4)$ **29.** $5(c - 3) + 4c^2(c - 3)$

**30.** $3(t - 4) + t(t - 4)$ **31.** $5(2r - 1) - s(2r - 1)$ **32.** $7(3d + 4) - 2e(3d + 4)$

**Factor each polynomial by grouping. Check your answer.**

**33.** $x^3 + 3x^2 - 2x - 6$ **34.** $2m^3 - 3m^2 + 8m - 12$ **35.** $3k^3 - k^2 + 15k - 5$

**36.** $15r^3 + 25r^2 - 6r - 10$ **37.** $12n^3 - 6n^2 - 10n + 5$ **38.** $4z^3 - 3z^2 + 4z - 3$

**39.** $2k^2 - 3k + 12 - 8k$ **40.** $3p^2 - 2p + 8 - 12p$ **41.** $10d^2 - 6d + 9 - 15d$

**42.** $6a^3 - 4a^2 + 10 - 15a$ **43.** $12s^3 - 2s^2 + 3 - 18s$ **44.** $4c^3 - 3c^2 + 15 - 20c$

**Lesson 8-3**

**Factor each trinomial. Check your answer.**

**45.** $x^2 + 15x + 36$ **46.** $x^2 + 13x + 40$ **47.** $x^2 + 10x + 16$

**48.** $x^2 - 9x + 18$ **49.** $x^2 - 11x + 28$ **50.** $x^2 - 13x + 42$

**51.** $x^2 + 4x - 21$ **52.** $x^2 - 5x - 36$ **53.** $x^2 - 7x - 30$

**54.** Factor $c^2 - 2c - 48$. Show that the original polynomial and the factored form describe the same sequence of values for $c = 0, 1, 2, 3,$ and 4.

**Complete the table.**

| | $x^2 + bx + c$ | Sign of $c$ | Binomial factors | Sign of Numbers in Binomials |
|---|---|---|---|---|
| | $x^2 + 9x + 20$ | Positive | $(x + 4)(x + 5)$ | Both positive |
| **55.** | $x^2 - x - 20$ | ? | $(x + ?)(x + ?)$ | ? |
| **56.** | $x^2 - 2x - 8$ | ? | $(x + ?)(x + ?)$ | ? |
| **57.** | $x^2 - 6x + 8$ | ? | $(x + ?)(x + ?)$ | ? |

## Chapter 8 ■ Skills Practice

**Lesson 8-4**

**Factor each trinomial. Check your answer.**

**58.** $2x^2 + 13x + 15$ **59.** $3x^2 + 14x + 16$ **60.** $8x^2 - 16x + 6$

**61.** $6x^2 + 11x + 4$ **62.** $3x^2 - 11x + 6$ **63.** $10x^2 - 31x + 15$

**64.** $6x^2 - 5x - 4$ **65.** $8x^2 - 14x - 15$ **66.** $4x^2 - 11x + 6$

**67.** $12x^2 - 13x + 3$ **68.** $6x^2 - 7x - 10$ **69.** $6x^2 + 7x - 3$

**70.** $2x^2 + 5x - 12$ **71.** $6x^2 - 5x - 6$ **72.** $8x^2 + 10x - 3$

**73.** $10x^2 - 11x - 6$ **74.** $4x^2 - x - 5$ **75.** $6x^2 - 7x - 20$

**76.** $-2x^2 + 11x - 5$ **77.** $-6x^2 - x + 12$ **78.** $-8x^2 - 10x - 3$

**79.** $-4x^2 + 16x - 15$ **80.** $-10x^2 + 21x + 10$ **81.** $-3x^2 + 13x - 14$

**Lesson 8-5**

**Determine whether each trinomial is a perfect square. If so, factor. If not, explain why.**

**82.** $x^2 - 8x + 16$ **83.** $4x^2 - 4x + 1$ **84.** $x^2 - 8x + 9$

**85.** $9x^2 - 14x + 4$ **86.** $4x^2 + 12x + 9$ **87.** $x^2 + 8x - 16$

**88.** $9x^2 - 42x + 49$ **89.** $4x^2 + 18x + 25$ **90.** $16x^2 - 24x + 9$

**Determine whether each trinomial is the difference of two squares. If so, factor. If not, explain why.**

**91.** $4 - 16x^4$ **92.** $-t^2 - 35$ **93.** $c^2 - 25$

**94.** $g^5 - 9$ **95.** $v^4 - 64$ **96.** $x^2 - 120$

**97.** $x^2 - 36$ **98.** $9m^2 - 15$ **99.** $25c^2 - 16$

**Find the missing term in each perfect-square trinomial.**

**100.** $4x^2 - 20x + \blacksquare$ **101.** $9x^2 + \blacksquare + 1$ **102.** $\blacksquare - 56x + 49$

**103.** $9b^2 - \blacksquare + 25$ **104.** $\blacksquare + 28a + 49$ **105.** $4a^2 + 4a + \blacksquare$

**Lesson 8-6**

**Tell whether each polynomial is completely factored. If not, factor.**

**106.** $5(16x^2 + 4)$ **107.** $3r(4x^2 - 9)$ **108.** $(9d - 6)(2d - 7)$

**109.** $(5 - h)(6 - 5h)$ **110.** $12y^2 - 2y - 24$ **111.** $3f(2f^2 + 5fg + 2g^2)$

**Factor each polynomial completely. Check your answer.**

**112.** $12b^3 - 48b$ **113.** $24w^4 - 20w^3 - 16w^2$ **114.** $18k^3 - 32k$

**115.** $4a^3 + 12a^2 - a^2b - 3ab$ **116.** $3x^3y - 6x^2y^2 + 3xy^3$ **117.** $36p^2q - 64q^3$

**118.** $32a^4 - 8a^2$ **119.** $m^3 + 5m^2n + 6mn^2$ **120.** $4x^2 - 3x^2 - 16x + 48x$

**121.** $18d^2 + 3d - 6$ **122.** $2r^2 - 9r - 18$ **123.** $8y^2 + 4y - 4$

**124.** $81 - 36u^2$ **125.** $8x^4 + 12x^2 - 20$ **126.** $10j^3 + 15j^2 - 70j$

**127.** $27z^3 - 18z^2 + 3z$ **128.** $4b^2 + 2b - 72$ **129.** $3f^2 - 3g^2$

# Chapter 9 ■ Skills Practice

Extra Practice

**Lesson 9-1**

**Tell whether each function is quadratic. Explain.**

**1.** $y + 4x^2 = 2x - 3$ **2.** $4x - y = 3$ **3.** $3x^2 - 4 = y + x$

**4.**

| x | −6 | −4 | −2 | −0 | 2 |
|---|---|---|---|---|---|
| y | −5 | −6 | −4 | 2 | 11 |

**5.**

| x | 0 | 1 | 2 | 3 | 4 |
|---|---|---|---|---|---|
| y | −5 | −5 | −3 | 1 | 7 |

**Tell whether the graph of each quadratic function opens upward or downward. Then use a table of values to graph each function.**

**6.** $y = -3x^2$ **7.** $y = \frac{2}{3}x^2$ **8.** $y = x^2 + 2$ **9.** $y = -4x^2 + 2x$

**Identify the vertex of each parabola. Then find the domain and range.**

**10.**

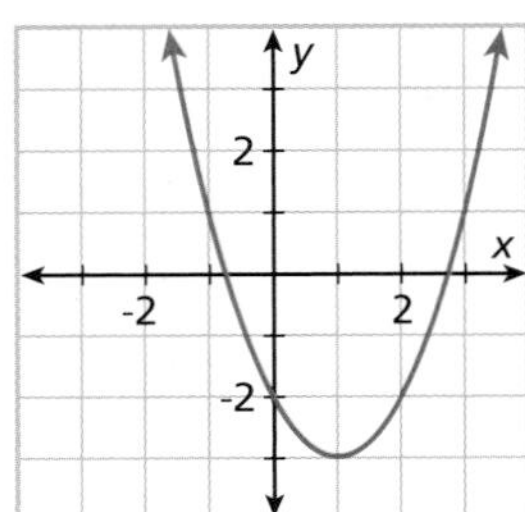

**11.**

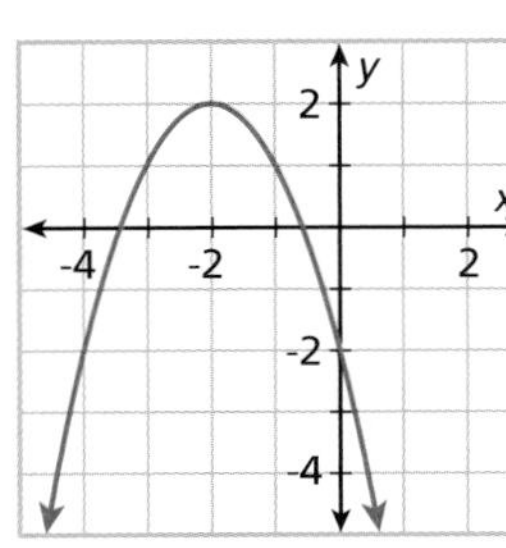

**12.**

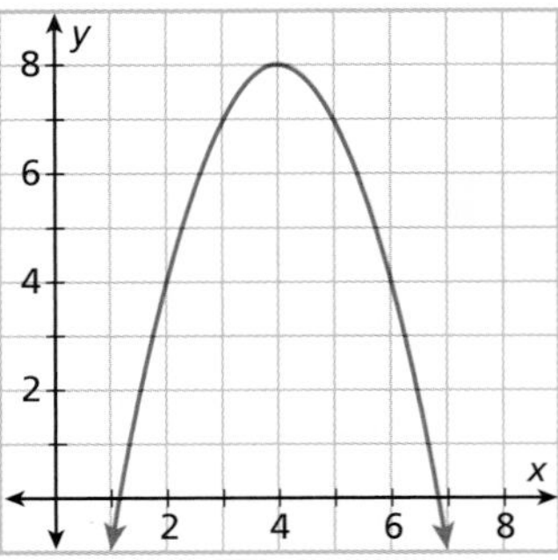

**Lesson 9-2**

**Find the zeros of each quadratic function and the axis of symmetry of each parabola from the graph.**

**13.**

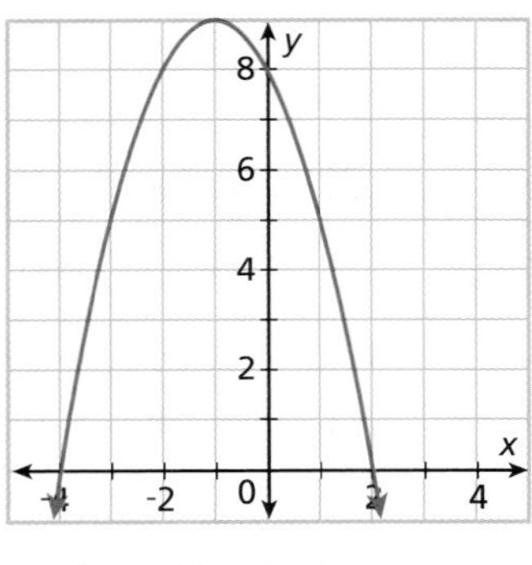

**14.**

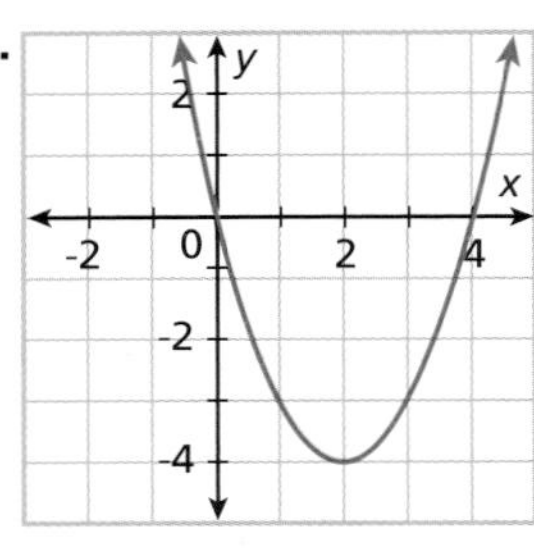

**15.**

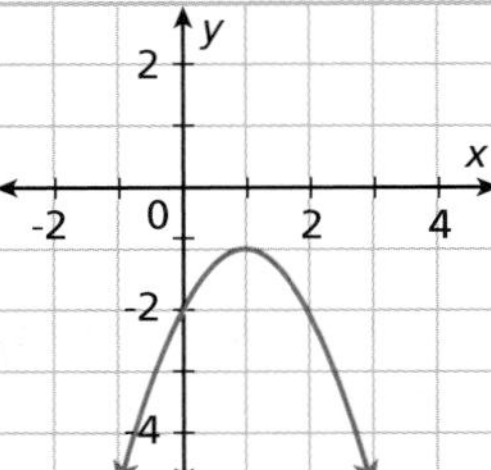

**For each quadratic function, find the vertex of its graph.**

**16.** $y = 3x^2 - 6x + 2$ **17.** $y = -2x^2 + 8x - 3$ **18.** $y = x^2 + 2x - 4$

**Lesson 9-3**

**Graph each quadratic function.**

**19.** $y = x^2 - 4x + 1$ **20.** $y = -x^2 - x + 4$ **21.** $y = 3x^2 - 3x + 1$

**22.** $y - 2 = 2x^2$ **23.** $y + 3x^2 = 3x - 1$ **24.** $y - 4 = x^2 + 2x$

**Lesson 9-4**

**Order the functions from narrowest to widest.**

**25.** $f(x) = 2x^2, g(x) = -4x^2, h(x) = -x^2$ **26.** $f(x) = 3x^2, g(x) = \frac{1}{2}x^2, h(x) = -2x^2$

**27.** $f(x) = 4x^2, g(x) = x^2, h(x) = -\frac{1}{4}x^2$ **28.** $f(x) = 2x^2, g(x) = 5x^2, h(x) = -3x^2$

**Compare the graph of each function with the graph of $f(x) = x^2$.**

**29.** $g(x) = 2x^2 - 2$ **30.** $g(x) = -\frac{1}{2}x^2$ **31.** $g(x) = -3x^2 + 1$

## Chapter 9 ■ Skills Practice

**Lesson 9-5**

**Solve each quadratic equation by graphing the related function.**

**32.** $x^2 - x - 2 = 0$ **33.** $x^2 - 2x + 8 = 0$ **34.** $2x^2 + 4x - 6 = 0$

**35.** $2x^2 + 9x = -4$ **36.** $2x^2 + 3 = 0$ **37.** $2x^2 - 2x - 12 = 0$

**38.** $3x^2 = -3x + 6$ **39.** $x^2 = 4$ **40.** $2x^2 + 6x - 20 = 0$

**41.** $-3x^2 - 2 = 0$ **42.** $x^2 = -2x + 8$ **43.** $x^2 - 2x = 15$

**Lesson 9-6**

**Use the Zero Product Property to solve each equation. Check your answer.**

**44.** $(x + 3)(x - 2) = 0$ **45.** $(x - 4)(x + 2) = 0$ **46.** $(x)(x - 4) = 0$

**47.** $(2x + 6)(x - 2) = 0$ **48.** $(3x - 1)(x + 3) = 0$ **49.** $(x)(2x - 4) = 0$

**Solve each quadratic equation by factoring. Check your answer.**

**50.** $x^2 + 5x + 6 = 0$ **51.** $x^2 - 3x - 4 = 0$ **52.** $x^2 + x - 12 = 0$

**53.** $x^2 + x - 6 = 0$ **54.** $x^2 - 6x + 5 = 0$ **55.** $x^2 + 4x - 12 = 0$

**56.** $x^2 = 6x - 9$ **57.** $2x^2 + 4x = 6$ **58.** $x^2 + 2x = -1$

**59.** $3x^2 = 3x + 6$ **60.** $x^2 = x + 12$ **61.** $4x^2 + 8x + 4 = 0$

**Lesson 9-7**

**Solve using square roots. Check your answer.**

**62.** $x^2 = 169$ **63.** $x^2 = 121$ **64.** $x^2 = 289$

**65.** $x^2 = -64$ **66.** $x^2 = 81$ **67.** $x^2 = -441$

**68.** $4x^2 - 196 = 0$ **69.** $0 = 3x^2 - 48$ **70.** $24x^2 + 96 = 0$

**71.** $10x^2 - 75 = 15$ **72.** $0 = 4x^2 + 144$ **73.** $5x^2 - 105 = 20$

**Solve. Round to the nearest hundredth.**

**74.** $4x^2 = 160$ **75.** $0 = 3x^2 - 66$ **76.** $250 - 5x^2 = 0$

**77.** $0 = 9x^2 - 72$ **78.** $48 - 2x^2 = 42$ **79.** $6x^2 = 78$

**Lesson 9-8**

**Complete the square to form a perfect square trinomial.**

**80.** $x^2 - 8x + \square$ **81.** $x^2 + x + \square$ **82.** $x^2 + 10x + \square$

**83.** $x^2 - 5x + \square$ **84.** $x^2 + 6x + \square$ **85.** $x^2 - 7x + \square$

**Solve by completing the square.**

**86.** $x^2 + 6x = 91$ **87.** $x^2 + 10x = -16$ **88.** $x^2 - 4x = 12$

**89.** $x^2 - 8x = -12$ **90.** $x^2 - 12x = -35$ **91.** $-x^2 - 6x = 5$

**92.** $-x^2 - 4x + 77 = 0$ **93.** $-x^2 = 10x + 9$ **94.** $-x^2 + 63 = -2x$

**Lesson 9-9**

**Solve using the quadratic formula.**

**95.** $x^2 + 3x - 4 = 0$ **96.** $x^2 - 2x - 8 = 0$ **97.** $x^2 + 2x - 3 = 0$

**98.** $x^2 - x - 10 = 0$ **99.** $2x^2 - x - 4 = 0$ **100.** $2x^2 + 3x - 3 = 0$

**Find the number of solutions of each equation using the discriminant.**

**101.** $x^2 + 4x + 1 = 0$ **102.** $2x^2 - 3x + 2 = 0$ **103.** $x^2 - 5x + 2 = 0$

**104.** $2x^2 - 4x + 2 = 0$ **105.** $x^2 + 2x - 5 = 0$ **106.** $2x^2 - 2x - 3 = 0$

# Chapter 10 ■ Skills Practice

**Lesson 10-1**

**Use the line graph for Exercises 1–4.**

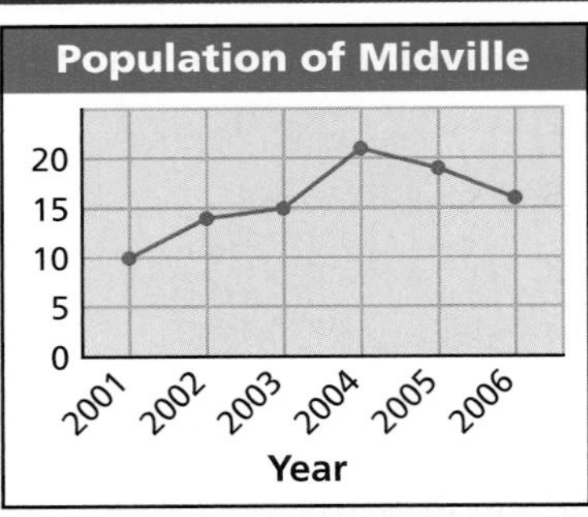


1. In what year was the population the greatest?
2. Estimate the population in 2005.
3. During which one-year period did the population increase by the greatest amount?
4. Estimate the amount by which the population decreased from 2005 to 2006.

**Use the circle graph for Exercises 5–7.**

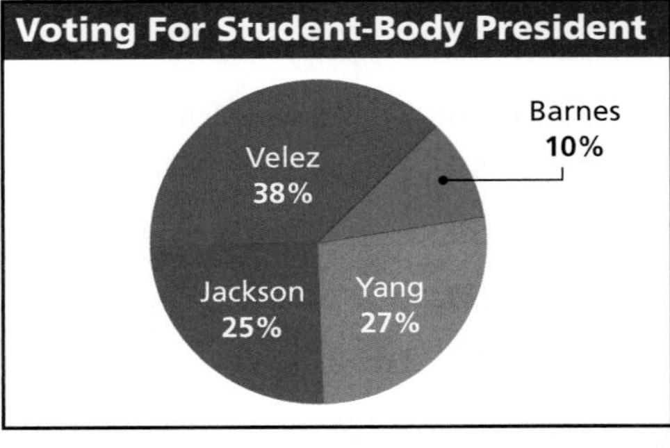


5. Which candidate received the fewest votes?
6. Which two candidates received approximately the same number of votes?
7. A total of 400 students voted in the election. How many votes did Velez receive?

**Lesson 10-2**

**The daily high temperatures in degrees Celsius during a two-week period in Madison, Wisconsin, are given at right.**

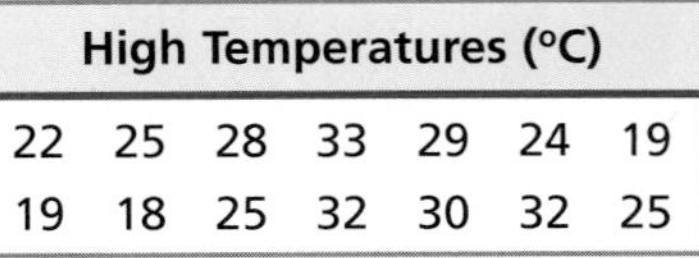

| High Temperatures (°C) | | | | | | |
|---|---|---|---|---|---|---|
| 22 | 25 | 28 | 33 | 29 | 24 | 19 |
| 19 | 18 | 25 | 32 | 30 | 32 | 25 |

8. Use the data to make a stem-and-leaf plot.
9. Use the data to make a frequency table with intervals.
10. Use the frequency table from Exercise 9 to make a histogram for the data.
11. Use the data to make a cumulative frequency table.

**Lesson 10-3**

**Find the mean, median, mode, and range of each data set.**

12. 42, 45, 48, 45
13. 66, 68, 68, 62, 61, 68, 65, 60
14. The numbers of customers who attended a reading at a bookstore on five different nights are 15, 23, 92, 15, 25. Use the mean, median, and mode of the data to answer each question.

    Mean = 34 Median = 23 Mode = 15

    a. Which value describes the average number of customers at the readings?
    b. Which value best describes the number of customers at the readings? Explain.

**Use the data set to make a box-and-whisker plot.**

15. 7, 8, 10, 2, 5, 1, 10, 8, 5, 5
16. 54, 64, 50, 48, 53, 55, 57

**Lesson 10-4**

17. The graph shows the ages of people who listen to a radio program.
    a. Explain why the graph is misleading.
    b. What might someone believe because of the graph?
    c. Who might want to use this graph?

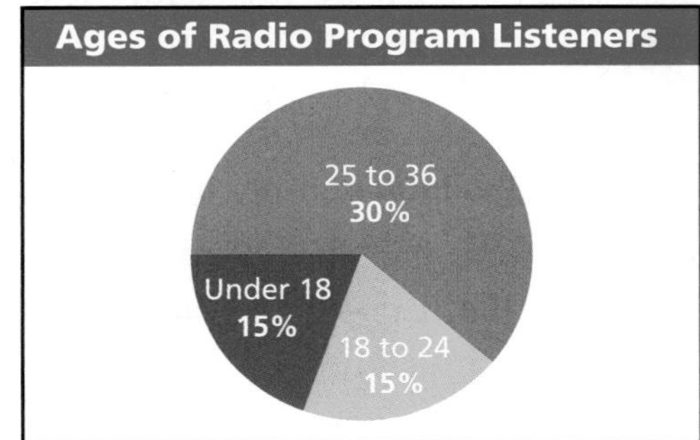


18. A researcher surveys people at the Elmwood library about the number of hours they spend reading each day. Explain why the following statement is misleading: "People in Elmwood read for an average of 1.5 hours per day."

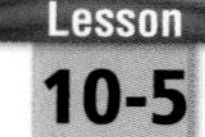

19. Identify the sample space and the outcome shown for the spinner at right.

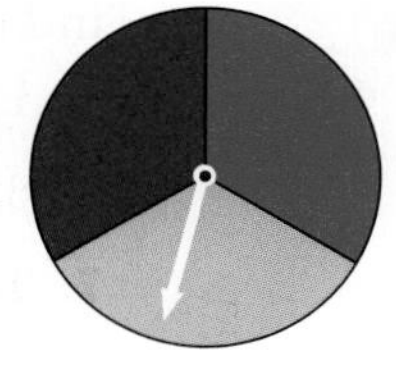

**Write *impossible, unlikely, as likely as not, likely,* or *certain* to describe each event.**

20. Two people sitting next to each other on a bus have the same birthday.
21. Dylan rolls a number greater than 1 on a standard number cube.

**An experiment consists of randomly choosing a fruit snack from a box. Use the results in the table to find the experimental probability of each event.**

| Outcome | Frequency |
|---|---|
| Cherry | 8 |
| Peach | 6 |
| Blueberry | 6 |

22. choosing a blueberry fruit snack.
23. choosing a cherry fruit snack
24. not choosing a cherry fruit snack

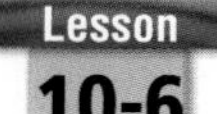

**Find the theoretical probability of each outcome.**

25. rolling an even number on a number cube
26. flipping two coins and both landing tails up
27. randomly choosing a prime number from a bag that contains ten slips of paper numbered 1 through 10
28. The probability of choosing a green marble from a bag is $\frac{3}{7}$. What is the probability of not choosing a green marble?
29. The odds against winning a game are 8:3. What is the probability of winning the game?

**Tell whether each set of events is independent or dependent. Explain your answer.**

30. You pick a bottle of orange juice from a basket containing chilled drinks, and then your friend chooses a bottle of apple juice.
31. You roll a 6 on a number cube and a coin lands heads up.
32. A number cube is rolled three times. What is the probability of rolling three numbers greater than 4?
33. An experiment consists of randomly selecting a marble from a bag, replacing it, and then selecting another marble. The bag contains 3 blue marbles, 2 orange marbles, and 5 yellow marbles. What is the probability of selecting a blue marble and then a yellow marble?
34. Madeleine has 3 nickels and 5 quarters in her pocket. She randomly chooses one coin and does not replace it. Then she randomly chooses another coin. What is the probability that she chooses two quarters?

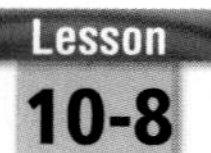

**Tell whether each situation involves combinations or permutations. Then give the number of possible outcomes.**

35. How many different ways can three photographs be arranged in a row on a wall?
36. How many different smoothies can be made by blending two of the following fruits: oranges, bananas, strawberries, and peaches?
37. There are 6 entrants in a livestock competition at a county fair. How many different ways can the first-place, second-place, and third-place ribbons be awarded?
38. An amusement park has 7 roller coasters. How many different ways can Jacinto choose 4 different roller coasters to ride?

# Chapter 11 ■ Skills Practice

**Lesson 11-1**

**Find the next three terms in each geometric sequence.**

1. 1, 5, 25, 125 ...
2. 736, 368, 184, 92, ...
3. −2, 6, −18, 54, ...
4. 8, 2, $\frac{1}{2}$, $\frac{1}{8}$, ...
5. 7, −14, 28, −56, ...
6. $\frac{1}{9}$, $\frac{1}{3}$, 1, 3, ...
7. The first term of a geometric sequence is 2, and the common ratio is 3. What is the 8th term of the sequence?
8. What is the 8th term of the sequence 600, 300, 150, 75, ...?

**Lesson 11-2**

**Tell whether each set of ordered pairs satisfies an exponential function. Explain your answer.**

9. $\left\{\left(-1, \frac{1}{2}\right), (0, 2), (1, 8), (2, 32)\right\}$
10. $\left\{\left(-1, -\frac{1}{2}\right), (0, 0), \left(1, \frac{1}{2}\right), (2, 4)\right\}$
11. $\left\{(-1, 4), (0, 1), \left(1, \frac{1}{4}\right), \left(2, \frac{1}{16}\right)\right\}$
12. $\{(0, 0), (1, 3), (2, 12), (3, 27)\}$

**Graph each exponential function.**

13. $y = 3(2)^x$
14. $y = \frac{1}{2}(4)^x$
15. $y = -3^x$
16. $y = -\frac{1}{2}(2)^x$
17. $y = 5\left(\frac{1}{2}\right)^x$
18. $y = -2(0.25)^x$

**Write an exponential growth function to model each situation. Then find the value of the function after the given amount of time.**

19. The rent for an apartment is \$6600 per year and increasing at a rate of 4% per year; 5 years.
20. A museum has 1200 members and the number of members is increasing at a rate of 2% per year; 8 years.

**Write a compound interest function to model each situation. Then find the balance after the given number of years.**

21. \$4000 invested at a rate of 4% compounded quarterly; 3 years
22. \$5200 invested at a rate of 2.5% compounded annually; 6 years

**Write an exponential decay function to model each situation. Then find the value of the function after the given amount of time.**

23. The cost of a stereo system is \$800 and is decreasing at a rate of 6% per year; 5 years.
24. The population of a town is 14,000 and is decreasing at a rate of 2% per year; 10 years.

**Lesson 11-4**

**Graph each data set. Which kind of model best describes the data?**

25. $\{(0, 3), (1, 0), (2, -1), (3, 0), (4, 3)\}$
26. $\{(-4, -4), (-3, -3.5), (-2, -3), (-1, -2.5), (0, -2), (1, -1.5)\}$
27. $\{(0, 4), (1, 2), (2, 1), (3, 0.5), (4, 0.25)\}$

**Look for a pattern in each data set to determine which kind of model best describes the data.**

28. $\{(-1, -5), (0, -5), (1, -3), (2, 1), (3, 7)\}$
29. $\{(0, 0.25), (1, 0.5), (2, 1), (3, 2), (4, 4)\}$
30. $\{(-2, 11), (-1, 8), (0, 5), (1, 2), (2, -1)\}$

# Chapter 11 ■ Skills Practice

**Lesson 11-5**

**Find the domain of each square-root function.**

**31.** $y = \sqrt{x + 1}$ **32.** $y = \sqrt{x - 2} + 4$ **33.** $y = \sqrt{4 + x}$

**34.** $y = \sqrt{3x - 6}$ **35.** $y = 1 + \sqrt{\frac{x}{3}}$ **36.** $y = \sqrt{4x - 1}$

**Graph each square-root function.**

**37.** $y = \sqrt{x + 2}$ **38.** $y = \sqrt{x} - 3$ **39.** $y = \sqrt{3x} + 1$

**40.** $y = -\sqrt{x}$ **41.** $y = 2\sqrt{x + 1}$ **42.** $y = 3\sqrt{x} - 2$

**Lesson 11-6**

**Simplify each expression.**

**43.** $\sqrt{\frac{128}{2}}$ **44.** $\sqrt{7^2 + 24^2}$ **45.** $\sqrt{(4 - x)^2}$

**46.** $\sqrt{\frac{3}{48}}$ **47.** $\sqrt{y^2 + 4y + 4}$ **48.** $\sqrt{5^2 - 4^2}$

**Simplify. All variables represent nonnegative numbers.**

**49.** $\sqrt{72}$ **50.** $\sqrt{75x^4y^3}$ **51.** $\sqrt{\frac{11}{81}}$

**52.** $\sqrt{\frac{64}{x^6}}$ **53.** $\sqrt{\frac{16a^4}{25b^2}}$ **54.** $\sqrt{\frac{18x^4}{49x^3}}$

**Lesson 11-7**

**Add or subtract.**

**55.** $5\sqrt{7} + 3\sqrt{7}$ **56.** $6\sqrt{2} + \sqrt{2}$ **57.** $5\sqrt{3} - 2\sqrt{3}$

**58.** $\sqrt{5} + 7\sqrt{5} - 9\sqrt{5}$ **59.** $2\sqrt{y} + 4\sqrt{y} - 3\sqrt{y}$ **60.** $5\sqrt{3} + 4\sqrt{2} - 3\sqrt{3}$

**Simplify each expression.**

**61.** $\sqrt{75} + \sqrt{27}$ **62.** $\sqrt{45} - \sqrt{20}$ **63.** $2\sqrt{12} + \sqrt{18}$

**64.** $3\sqrt{27x} + \sqrt{48x}$ **65.** $5\sqrt{20y} - 2\sqrt{80y}$ **66.** $\sqrt{28a} + 2\sqrt{63a} - \sqrt{175a}$

**67.** $\sqrt{50y} - 2\sqrt{18y} + 3\sqrt{8y}$ **68.** $\sqrt{12x} - \sqrt{27x} - \sqrt{5x}$ **69.** $5\sqrt{180s} - 6\sqrt{80s}$

**Lesson 11-8**

**Multiply. Write each product in simplest form.**

**70.** $\sqrt{5}\sqrt{10}$ **71.** $\sqrt{6}\sqrt{12}$ **72.** $\left(3\sqrt{3}\right)^2$

**73.** $\left(2\sqrt{7}\right)^2$ **74.** $\sqrt{6x}\sqrt{15x}$ **75.** $\sqrt{3}\left(2 + \sqrt{27}\right)$

**76.** $2\sqrt{5}\left(\sqrt{20} + 3\right)$ **77.** $\sqrt{2x}\left(3 + \sqrt{8x}\right)$ **78.** $\left(4 + \sqrt{3}\right)\left(1 - \sqrt{3}\right)$

**79.** $\left(3 + \sqrt{5}\right)\left(8 - \sqrt{5}\right)$ **80.** $\left(4 + \sqrt{2}\right)^2$ **81.** $\left(5 - \sqrt{3}\right)^2$

**Simplify each quotient.**

**82.** $\frac{\sqrt{5}}{\sqrt{3}}$ **83.** $\frac{2\sqrt{7}}{\sqrt{5}}$ **84.** $\frac{\sqrt{3}}{\sqrt{20}}$

**85.** $\frac{5\sqrt{7}}{\sqrt{50}}$ **86.** $\frac{\sqrt{12a}}{\sqrt{32}}$ **87.** $\frac{\sqrt{200x}}{\sqrt{28}}$

**Lesson 11-9**

**Solve each equation. Check your answer.**

**88.** $\sqrt{x} = 11$ **89.** $\sqrt{3x} = 9$ **90.** $\sqrt{-2x} = 10$

**91.** $5 = \sqrt{-4x}$ **92.** $\sqrt{x} + 5 = 12$ **93.** $\sqrt{x} - 4 = 1$

**94.** $\sqrt{3x + 1} = 4$ **95.** $\sqrt{2x + 5} = 3$ **96.** $\sqrt{x - 4} + 1 = 7$

**97.** $\sqrt{6 - 3x} - 2 = 4$ **98.** $\sqrt{6 - x} - 5 = -3$ **99.** $4\sqrt{x} = 20$

Extra Practice

# Chapter 12 ■ Skills Practice

**Lesson 12-1**

**Tell whether each relationship is an inverse variation. Explain.**

1.

| x | y |
|---|---|
| 4 | 8 |
| 8 | 16 |
| 16 | 32 |
| 32 | 64 |

2.

| x | y |
|---|---|
| 2 | 6 |
| 3 | 4 |
| 6 | 2 |
| 12 | 1 |

3.

| x | y |
|---|---|
| −1 | 24 |
| 2 | −12 |
| 4 | −6 |
| 8 | −3 |

4. $3xy = 10$
5. $y - x = 6$
6. $6xy = -1$
7. Write and graph the inverse variation in which $y = 4$ when $x = 3$.
8. Write and graph the inverse variation in which $y = \frac{1}{2}$ when $x = 6$.
9. Let $x_1 = 6$, $y_1 = 8$, and $x_2 = 12$. Let $y$ vary inversely as $x$. Find $y_2$.
10. Let $x_1 = -4$, $y_1 = -2$, and $y_2 = 16$. Let $y$ vary inversely as $x$. Find $x_2$.

**Lesson 12-2**

**Identify the excluded values for each rational function.**

11. $y = \frac{16}{x}$
12. $y = \frac{1}{x - 1}$
13. $y = -\frac{3}{x + 5}$
14. $y = \frac{20}{x + 20}$

**Identify the asymptotes.**

15. $y = \frac{2}{x - 4}$
16. $y = \frac{8}{x + 5}$
17. $y = \frac{7}{3x - 2} - 6$
18. $y = \frac{3}{2x - 2} + 4$

**Graph each function.**

19. $y = \frac{1}{x + 3}$
20. $y = \frac{1}{x - 2}$
21. $y = \frac{1}{x} + 4$
22. $y = \frac{3}{x - 2}$
23. $y = \frac{1}{x - 3} + 2$
24. $y = \frac{1}{x - 5} - 6$
25. $y = \frac{1}{x + 2} + 5$
26. $y = \frac{1}{x + 5} + 1$

**Lesson 12-3**

**Find the excluded value(s) of each rational expression.**

27. $\frac{3}{7x}$
28. $\frac{-2}{x^2 - x}$
29. $\frac{6}{x^2 + x - 12}$
30. $\frac{p + 1}{p^2 + 4p - 5}$

**Simplify each rational expression, if possible. Identify excluded values.**

31. $\frac{4m^2}{12m}$
32. $\frac{7x^5}{28x}$
33. $\frac{4x^2 - 8x}{x - 2}$
34. $\frac{2y}{y - 1}$
35. $\frac{5x^3 + 20x^2}{x + 4}$
36. $\frac{a + 1}{a - 2}$
37. $\frac{3y^3 + 3y}{y^2 + 1}$
38. $\frac{x^3 + 4x}{x^2 + 4}$

**Simply each rational expression, if possible.**

39. $\frac{b + 2}{b^2 + 5b + 6}$
40. $\frac{x - 3}{x^2 - 6x + 9}$
41. $\frac{y^2 - 4y - 5}{y^2 - 2y - 3}$
42. $\frac{(m + 2)^2}{m^2 - 6m - 16}$
43. $\frac{x^2 - 9}{x^2 + x - 12}$
44. $\frac{2 - m}{3m^2 - 6m}$
45. $\frac{x - 4}{12x^2 - 3x^3}$
46. $\frac{6 - 3x}{x^2 - 6x + 8}$

## Chapter 12 ■ Skills Practice

**Lesson 12-4**

**Multiply. Simplify your answer.**

**47.** $\frac{4a^3}{b^3} \cdot \frac{ab}{6a^2}$ **48.** $\frac{6x^3y}{4y^4} \cdot \frac{8x^2yz^2}{3xz^5}$ **49.** $\frac{x-3}{2} \cdot \frac{8}{4x-12}$

**50.** $\frac{x-2}{x-5} \cdot \frac{2x-10}{3}$ **51.** $\frac{a^2b^3}{6a^3c} \cdot \frac{9b^2}{12b^5c^2}$ **52.** $\frac{3x}{2x+4} \cdot \frac{3x+6}{9}$

**53.** $\frac{1}{2x+4}(x^2-2x-8)$ **54.** $\frac{3x}{4x-20}(x^2+x-30)$ **55.** $\frac{2y}{3y+15}(y^2+10y+25)$

**56.** $\frac{4r^3+8r}{r^3} \cdot \frac{r}{3r^2+6}$ **57.** $\frac{x^2+x}{x^2-x-6} \cdot \frac{x-3}{6x^2+6x}$ **58.** $\frac{a^2-3a-10}{a^2-a-6} \cdot \frac{a^2-2a-3}{a-5}$

**59.** $\frac{4b^2+4}{b-1} \cdot \frac{b^2-1}{8b^2+8}$ **60.** $\frac{pq+2q}{pq+1} \cdot \frac{3pq+3}{pq^2+2q^2}$ **61.** $\frac{r^2+3r+2}{4r+4} \cdot \frac{2r+6}{r^2-2r-8}$

**Divide. Simplify your answer.**

**62.** $\frac{3x^2y^3}{x^3z^2} \div \frac{6y^4}{x^2z^5}$ **63.** $\frac{x^2+4x+3}{3x^3+9x^2} \div (x^2-1)$ **64.** $\frac{p-1}{p^2+4p-5} \div \frac{p^2-2p}{p^2+3p-10}$

**Lesson 12-5**

**Add. Simplify your answer.**

**65.** $\frac{3x}{4x^3} + \frac{5x}{4x^3}$ **66.** $\frac{x^2+1}{x-1} + \frac{1-3x}{x-1}$ **67.** $\frac{2x^2}{x^2-2x-3} + \frac{2x}{x^2-2x-3}$

**Subtract. Simplify your answer.**

**68.** $\frac{5}{6y^4} - \frac{2}{6y^4}$ **69.** $\frac{5a^2+1}{a^2-a-6} - \frac{15a+1}{a^2-a-6}$ **70.** $\frac{m^2+2m}{m^2-9} - \frac{m+12}{m^2-9}$

**Find the LCM of the given expressions.**

**71.** $8x^5y^8, 6x^4y^9$ **72.** $x^2-4, x^2+7x+10$ **73.** $d^2-2d-3, d^2+d-12$

**Add or subtract. Simplify your answer.**

**74.** $\frac{5}{y^2} - \frac{3}{4y^2}$ **75.** $\frac{5}{x^2-x-6} + \frac{1}{x+2}$ **76.** $\frac{3x}{x-2} - \frac{x}{2-x}$

**Lesson 12-6**

**Divide.**

**77.** $(12y^5-16y^2+4y) \div 4y^2$ **78.** $(6m^4-18m+3) \div 6m^2$ **79.** $(16x^4+20x^3-4x) \div -4x^3$

**80.** $\frac{b^2-4b-5}{b+1}$ **81.** $\frac{2x^2+9x+4}{x+4}$ **82.** $\frac{6a^2-13a-5}{3a+1}$

**Divide using long division.**

**83.** $(a^2-5a-6) \div (a+1)$ **84.** $(2x^2+10x+8) \div (x+4)$ **85.** $(3y^2-11y+10) \div (y-2)$

**86.** $(3x^2-2x-7) \div (x-2)$ **87.** $(2x^2+2x-9) \div (x+3)$ **88.** $(5x^3+2x^2-4) \div (x-2)$

**Lesson 12-7**

**Solve. Check your answer.**

**89.** $\frac{5}{x+1} = \frac{4}{x-1}$ **90.** $\frac{4}{t} = \frac{10}{t+9}$ **91.** $\frac{8}{m} = \frac{6}{m+1}$

**92.** $\frac{4}{a-2} = \frac{8}{a+1}$ **93.** $\frac{3}{2y+4} = \frac{1}{y}$ **94.** $\frac{5}{4w-2} = \frac{6}{5w-2}$

**95.** $\frac{1}{2} + \frac{3}{2m} = -\frac{1}{m^2}$ **96.** $\frac{x}{2} + \frac{3}{2} = \frac{2}{x}$ **97.** $1 - \frac{3}{a} = \frac{10}{a^2}$

**Solve. Identify any extraneous solutions.**

**98.** $\frac{3}{x+4} = \frac{x-5}{x+4}$ **99.** $\frac{2}{x} = \frac{x+2}{x^2-4}$ **100.** $\frac{4x}{x-4} - 7 = \frac{16}{x-4}$

Extra Practice

# Extra Practice

## Chapter 1 ■ Applications Practice

**Biology** **Use the following information for Exercises 1 and 2.**

In general, every cell in the human body contains 46 chromosomes. *(Lesson 1-1)*

1. Write an expression for the number of chromosomes in $c$ cells.
2. Find the number of chromosomes in 8, 15, and 50 cells.
3. On a winter day in Fairbanks, Alaska, the temperature dropped from 12°F to $-16$°F. How many degrees did the temperature drop? *(Lesson 1-2)*
4. **Geography** The elevation of the Dead Sea in Jordan is $-411$ meters. The greatest elevation on Earth is Mt. Everest, at 8850 meters. What is the difference in elevation between these two locations? *(Lesson 1-2)*
5. Jeremy is raising money for his school by selling magazine subscriptions. Each subscription costs \$16.75. During the first week, he sells 12 subscriptions. How much money does he raise? *(Lesson 1-3)*
6. As a service charge, Nadine's checking account is adjusted by $-\$3$ each month. What is the total amount of the adjustment over the course of one year? *(Lesson 1-3)*
7. To go from one figure to the next in the sequence of figures, each square is split into four smaller squares. How many squares will be in Figure 5? *(Lesson 1-4)*

Figure 0

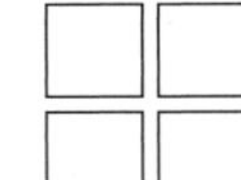
Figure 1

Figure 2

8. When you fold a sheet of paper in half and then open it, the crease creates 2 regions. Folding the paper in half 2 times creates 4 regions. How many regions do you create when you fold a sheet of paper in half 5 times? *(Lesson 1-4)*
9. Dan began his stamp collection with just 5 stamps in the first year. Every year thereafter, his collection grew 5 times as large as the year before. How many stamps were in Dan's collection after 4 years? *(Lesson 1-4)*
10. An art museum exhibits a square painting that has an area of 75 square feet. Find its side length to the nearest tenth. *(Lesson 1-5)*
11. **Travel** The base of the Washington Monument in Washington, D.C., is a square with an area of 336 yards. Find the length of one side of the monument's base to the nearest tenth. *(Lesson 1-5)*
12. The toll to cross a bridge is \$2 for cars, \$5 for trucks, and \$10 for buses. The total amount of money collected can be found using the expression $2C + 5T + 10B$. Use the table to find the total amount of money collected between 10 A.M. and 11 A.M. *(Lesson 1-6)*

**Bridge Tolls, 10 A.M. to 11 A.M.**

| Type of Vehicle | Number |
|---|---|
| Car $C$ | 104 |
| Truck $T$ | 20 |
| Bus $B$ | 3 |

13. The expression $\frac{5}{9}(F - 32)$ converts a temperature $F$ in degrees Fahrenheit to a temperature in degrees Celsius. Convert 77°F to degrees Celsius. *(Lesson 1-6)*

**Use the following information for Exercises 14 and 15.**

An airplane has 12 rows of seats in first class and 35 rows of seats in coach. Each row has the same number of seats. *(Lesson 1-7)*

14. The total number of seats in the plane is $12x + 35x$, where $x$ is the number of seats in a row. Simplify the expression.
15. Find the total number of seats in a plane that has 6 seats per row.

**Use the following information for Exercises 16 and 17.**

A sales representative earns \$680 per week plus a \$40 commission for each sale. *(Lesson 1-8)*

16. Write a rule for the sales representative's weekly earnings.
17. Write ordered pairs for the amount the sales representative earns for 5, 8, and 10 sales.

# Chapter 2 ■ Applications Practice

1. **Economics** In 2004, the average price of an ounce of gold was $47 more than the average price in 2003. The 2004 price was $410. Write and solve an equation to find the average price of an ounce of gold in 2003. *(Lesson 2-1)*

2. During a renovation, 36 seats were removed from a theater. The theater now seats 580 people. Write and solve an equation to find the number of seats in the theater before the renovation. *(Lesson 2-1)*

3. A case of juice drinks contains 12 bottles and costs $18. Write and solve an equation to find the cost of each drink. *(Lesson 2-2)*

4. **Astronomy** Objects weigh about 3 times as much on Earth as they do on Mars. A rock weighs 42 kg on Mars. Write and solve an equation to find the rock's weight on Earth. *(Lesson 2-2)*

5. The county fair's admission fee is $8 and each ride costs $2.50. Sonia spent a total of $25.50. How many rides did she go on? *(Lesson 2-3)*

6. At the beginning of a block party, the temperature was 84°. During the party, the temperature dropped 3° every hour. At the end of the party, the temperature was 66°. How long was the party? *(Lesson 2-3)*

7. **Consumer Economics** A health insurance policy costs $700 per year, plus a $15 payment for each visit to the doctor's office. A different plan costs $560 per year, but each office visit is $50. Find the number of office visits for which the two plans have the same total cost. *(Lesson 2-4)*

8. **Geometry** The formula $A = \frac{1}{2}bh$ gives the area $A$ of a triangle with base $b$ and height $h$. *(Lesson 2-5)*

   a. Solve $A = \frac{1}{2}bh$ for $h$.

   b. Find the height of a triangle with an area of 30 square feet and a base of 6 feet.

9. The ratio of students to adults on a school camping trip is 9:2. There are 6 adults on the trip. How many students are there? *(Lesson 2-6)*

10. A cheetah can reach speeds of up to 103 feet per second. What is the cheetah's speed in miles per hour? Round to the nearest tenth. *(Lesson 2-6)*

11. Write and solve a proportion to find the height of the flagpole. *(Lesson 2-7)*

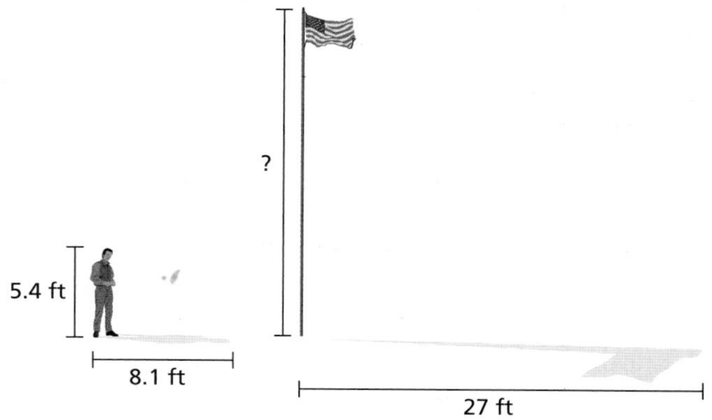


12. Paul has 8 jazz CDs. The jazz CDs are 5% of his collection. How many CDs does Paul have? *(Lesson 2-8)*

13. **Sports** During the 2004 season, the Texas Rangers baseball team had 32 players on their active roster, 3 of whom were catchers. To the nearest percent, what percent of the players were catchers? *(Lesson 2-8)*

14. Miguel earns an annual salary of $38,000 plus a 3.5% commission on sales. His sales for one year were $90,000. Find his total salary for the year. *(Lesson 2-9)*

15. How long would it take $3600 to earn simple interest of $450 at an annual interest rate of 5%? *(Lesson 2-9)*

16. At the end of summer, a store offers swimsuits at a 30% discount. What is the final price of a swimsuit that originally sold for $28? *(Lesson 2-10)*

17. Mei sells strawberry jam at a farmer's market for $4.20 per jar. Each jar costs Mei $3 to make. What is the markup as a percent? *(Lesson 2-10)*

## Chapter 3 ■ Applications Practice

1. At a food-processing factory, each box of cereal must weigh at least 15 ounces. Define a variable and write an inequality for the acceptable weights of the cereal boxes. Graph the solutions. *(Lesson 3-1)*

2. In order to qualify for a discounted entry fee at a museum, a visitor must be less than 13 years old. Define a variable and write an inequality for the ages that qualify for the discounted entry fee. Graph the solutions. *(Lesson 3-1)*

3. A restaurant can seat no more than 102 customers at one time. There are already 96 customers in the restaurant. Write and solve an inequality to find out how many additional customers could be seated in the restaurant. *(Lesson 3-2)*

4. **Meteorology** A hurricane is a tropical storm with a wind speed of at least 74 mi/h. A meteorologist is tracking a storm whose current wind speed is 63 mi/h. Write and solve an inequality to find out how much greater the wind speed must be in order for this storm to be considered a hurricane. *(Lesson 3-2)*

**Hobbies Use the following information for Exercises 5–7.**

When setting up an aquarium, it is recommended that you have no more than one inch of fish per gallon of water. For example, in a 30-gallon tank, the total length of the fish should be at most 30 inches. *(Lesson 3-3)*

| Freshwater Fish | |
|---|---|
| **Name** | **Length (in.)** |
| Red tail catfish | 3.5 |
| Blue gourami | 1.5 |

5. Write an inequality to show the possible numbers of blue gourami you can put in a 10-gallon aquarium.

6. Find the possible numbers of blue gourami you can put in a 10-gallon aquarium.

7. Find the possible numbers of red tail catfish you can put in a 20-gallon aquarium.

8. The admission fee at an amusement park is \$12, and each ride costs \$3.50. The park also offers an all-day pass with unlimited rides for \$33. For what numbers of rides is it cheaper to buy the all-day pass? *(Lesson 3-4)*

9. **Geometry** The perimeter of a rectangle with length $\ell$ and width $w$ is given by $2(\ell + w)$. The length of a rectangle is 18 inches. What must the width of the rectangle be in order for its perimeter to be at least 50 inches? *(Lesson 3-4)*

10. The table shows the cost of Internet access at two different cafes. For how many hours of access is the cost at Cyber Station less than the cost at Web World? *(Lesson 3-5)*

| Internet Access | |
|---|---|
| **Cafe** | **Cost** |
| Cyber Station | \$12 one-time membership fee<br>\$1.50 per hour |
| Web World | No membership fee<br>\$2.25 per hour |

11. Larissa is considering two summer jobs. A job at the mall pays \$400 per week plus \$15 for every hour of overtime. A job at the movie theater pays \$360 per week plus \$20 for every hour of overtime. How many hours of overtime would Larissa have to work in order for the job at the movie theater to pay a higher salary than the job at the mall? *(Lesson 3-5)*

12. **Health** For maximum safety, it is recommended that food be stored at a temperature between 34°F and 40°F inclusive. Write a compound inequality to show the temperatures that are within the recommended range. Graph the solutions. *(Lesson 3-6)*

13. **Physics** Color is determined by the wavelength of light. Wavelengths are measured in nanometers (nm). Our eyes see the color green when light has a wavelength between 492 nm and 577 nm inclusive. Write a compound inequality to show the wavelengths that produce green light. Graph the solutions. *(Lesson 3-6)*

Extra Practice

# Chapter 4 ■ Applications Practice

1. Donnell drove on the highway at a constant speed and then slowed down as she approached her exit. Sketch a graph to show the speed of Donnell's car. Tell whether the graph is continuous or discrete. *(Lesson 4-1)*

2. Lori is buying mineral water for a party. The bottles are available in six-packs. Sketch a graph showing the number of bottles Lori will have if she buys 1, 2, 3, 4, or 5 six-packs. Tell whether the graph is continuous or discrete. *(Lesson 4-1)*

3. **Health** To exercise effectively, it is important to know your maximum heart rate. You can calculate your maximum heart rate in beats per minute by subtracting your age from 220. *(Lesson 4-2)*
   a. Express the age $x$ and the maximum heart rate $y$ as a relation in table form by showing the maximum heart rate for people who are 20, 30, 35, and 40 years old.
   b. Is this relation a function? Why or why not?

4. **Sports** The table shows the number of games won by four baseball teams and the number of home runs each team hit. Is this relation a function? Explain. *(Lesson 4-2)*

| Season Statistics | |
|---|---|
| **Wins** | **Home Runs** |
| 95 | 185 |
| 93 | 133 |
| 80 | 140 |
| 93 | 167 |

5. Michael uses 5.5 cups of flour for each loaf of bread that he bakes. He plans to bake a maximum of 4 loaves. Write a function rule to describe the number of cups of flour used. Find a reasonable domain and range for the function. *(Lesson 4-3)*

6. A gym offers the following special rate. New members pay a $425 initiation fee and then pay $90 per year for 1, 2, or 3 years. Write a function rule to describe the situation. Find a reasonable domain and range for the function. *(Lesson 4-3)*

7. The function $y = 3.5x$ describes the number of miles $y$ that the average turtle can walk in $x$ hours. Graph the function. Use the graph to estimate how many miles a turtle can walk in 4.5 hours. *(Lesson 4-4)*

8. **Earth Science** The Kangerdlugssuaq glacier in Greenland is flowing into the sea at the rate of 1.6 meters per hour. The function $y = 1.6x$ describes the number of meters $y$ that flow into the sea in $x$ hours. Graph the function. Use the graph to estimate the number of meters that flow into the sea in 8 hours. *(Lesson 4-4)*

9. The scatter plot shows a relationship between the number of lemonades sold in a day and the day's high temperature. Based on this relationship, predict the number of lemonades that will be sold on a day when the high temperature is 96°F. *(Lesson 4-5)*

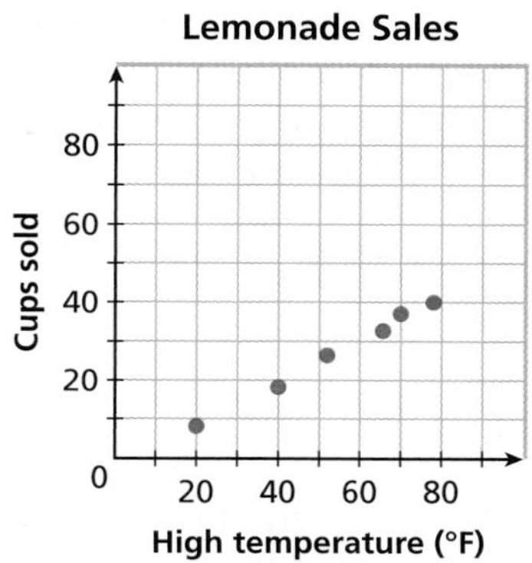


10. The Elmwood Public Library has 85 Spanish books in its collection. Each month, the librarian plans to order 8 new Spanish books. How many Spanish books will the library have after 15 months? *(Lesson 4-6)*

11. Nikki purchases a card that she can use to ride the bus in her town. The card costs $45, and each time she rides the bus $1.50 is deducted from the value of the card. How much money will be left on the card after Nikki has taken 12 bus rides? *(Lesson 4-6)*

# Chapter 5 ■ Applications Practice

1. Jennifer is having prints made of her photographs. Each print costs \$1.50. The function $f(x) = 1.50x$ gives the total cost of the $x$ prints. Graph this function and give its domain and range. *(Lesson 5-1)*

2. Rolando is serving on jury duty. He is paid \$40, plus \$15 for each day that he serves. The function $f(x) = 15x + 40$ gives Rolando's total pay for $x$ days. Graph this function and give its domain and range. *(Lesson 5-1)*

3. The Chang family lives 400 miles from Denver. They drive to Denver at a constant speed of 50 mi/h. The function $f(x) = 400 - 50x$ gives their distance in miles from Denver after $x$ hours. *(Lesson 5-2)*

   a. Graph this function and find the intercepts.

   b. What does each intercept represent?

4. **History** The table shows the number of nations in the United Nations in different years. Find the rate of change for each time interval. During which time interval did the U.N. grow at the greatest rate? *(Lesson 5-3)*

| Year | 1945 | 1950 | 1960 | 1975 |
|---|---|---|---|---|
| Number of Nations | 51 | 60 | 99 | 144 |

5. The graph shows the temperature of an oven at different times. Find the slope of the line. Then tell what the slope represents. *(Lesson 5-4)*

**Oven Temperature**

Temperature (°F): 450, 350, 250; points (10, 410), (40, 290); Time (min): 0, 20, 40

6. **Sports** Competitive race-walkers move at a speed of about 9 miles per hour. Write a direct variation equation for the distance $y$ that a race-walker will cover in $x$ hours. Then graph. *(Lesson 5-5)*

7. A bicycle rental costs \$10 plus \$1.50 per hour. The cost as a function of the number of hours is shown in the graph. *(Lesson 5-6)*

   a. Write an equation that represents the cost as a function of the number of hours.

   b. Identify the slope and $y$-intercept and describe their meaning.

   c. Find the cost of renting a bike for 6 hours.

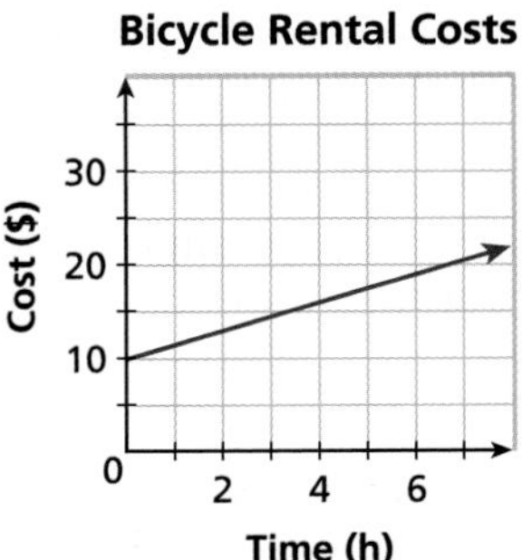


8. A hot-air balloon is moving at a constant rate. Its altitude is a linear function of time, as shown in the table. Write an equation in slope-intercept form that represents this function. Then find the balloon's altitude after 25 minutes. *(Lesson 5-7)*

| Balloon's Altitude | |
|---|---|
| **Time (min)** | **Altitude (m)** |
| 0 | 250 |
| 7 | 215 |
| 12 | 190 |

9. **Geometry** Show that the points $A(2, 3)$, $B(3, 1)$, $C(-1, -1)$, and $D(-2, 1)$ are the vertices of a rectangle. *(Lesson 5-8)*

10. A phone plan for international calls costs \$12.50 per month plus \$0.04 per minute. The monthly cost for $x$ minutes of calls is given by the function $f(x) = 0.04x + 12.50$. How will the graph change if the phone company raises the monthly fee to \$14.50? if the cost per minute is raised to \$0.05? *(Lesson 5-9)*

1. Net Sounds, an online music store, charges $12 per CD plus $3 for shipping and handling. Web Discs charges $10 per CD plus $9 for shipping and handling. For how many CDs will the cost be the same? What will that cost be? *(Lesson 6-1)*

2. At Rocco's Restaurant, a large pizza costs $12 plus $1.25 for each additional topping. At Pizza Palace, a large pizza costs $15 plus $0.75 for each additional topping. For how many toppings will the cost be the same? What will that cost be? *(Lesson 6-1)*

**Use the following information for Exercises 3 and 4.**

The coach of a baseball team is deciding between two companies that manufacture team jerseys. One company charges a $60 setup fee and $25 per jersey. The other company charges a $200 setup fee and $15 per jersey. *(Lesson 6-2)*

3. For how many jerseys will the cost at the two companies be the same? What will that cost be?

4. The coach is planning to purchase 20 jerseys. Which company is the better option? Why?

5. **Geometry** The length of a rectangle is 5 inches greater than the width. The sum of the length and width is 41 inches. Find the length and width of the rectangle. *(Lesson 6-2)*

6. At a movie theater, tickets cost $9.50 for adults and $6.50 for children. A group of 7 moviegoers pays a total of $54.50. How many adults and how many children are in the group? *(Lesson 6-3)*

7. **Business** A grocer is buying large quantities of fruit to resell at his store. He purchases apples at $0.50 per pound and pears at $0.75 per pound. The grocer spends a total of $17.25 for 27 pounds of fruit. How many pounds of each fruit does he buy? *(Lesson 6-3)*

8. Bricks are available in two sizes. Large bricks weigh 9 pounds, and small bricks weigh 4.5 pounds. A bricklayer has 14 bricks that weigh a total of 90 pounds. How many of each type of brick are there? *(Lesson 6-3)*

9. **Sports** The table shows the time it took two runners to complete the Boston Marathon in several different years. If the patterns continue, will Shanna ever complete the marathon in the same number of minutes as Maria? Explain. *(Lesson 6-4)*

| Marathon Times (min) | | | | |
|---|---|---|---|---|
| | 2003 | 2004 | 2005 | 2006 |
| Shanna | 190 | 182 | 174 | 166 |
| Maria | 175 | 167 | 159 | 151 |

10. Jordan leaves his house and rides his bike at 10 mi/h. After he goes 4 miles, his brother Tim leaves the house and rides in the same direction at 12 mi/h. If their rates stay the same, will Tim ever catch up to Jordan? Explain. *(Lesson 6-4)*

11. Charmaine is buying almonds and cashews for a reception. She wants to spend no more than $18. Almonds cost $4 per pound, and cashews cost $5 per pound. Write a linear inequality to describe the situation. Graph the solutions. Then give two combinations of nuts that Charmaine could buy. *(Lesson 6-5)*

12. Luis is buying T-shirts to give out at a school fund-raiser. He must spend less than $100 for the shirts. Child shirts cost $5 each, and adult shirts cost $8 each. Write a linear inequality to describe the situation. Graph the solutions. Then give two combinations of shirts that Luis could buy. *(Lesson 6-5)*

13. Nicholas is buying treats for his dog. Beef cubes cost $3 per pound, and liver cubes cost $2 per pound. He wants to buy at least 2 pounds of each type of treat, and he wants to spend no more than $14. Graph all possible combinations of the treats that Nicholas could buy. List two possible combinations. *(Lesson 6-6)*

14. **Geometry** The perimeter of a rectangle is at most 20 inches. The length and the width are each at least 3 inches. Graph all possible combinations of lengths and widths that result in such a rectangle. List two possible combinations. *(Lesson 6-6)*

## Chapter 7 ■ Applications Practice

1. **Biology** The eye of a bee is about $10^{-3}$ m in diameter. Simplify this expression. *(Lesson 7-1)*

2. A typical stroboscopic camera has a shutter speed of $10^{-6}$ seconds. Simplify this expression. *(Lesson 7-1)*

3. **Space Exploration** During a mission that took place in August, 2005, the Space Shuttle *Discovery* traveled a total distance of $9.3 \times 10^6$ km. The Space Shuttle's velocity was 28,000 km/h. *(Lesson 7-2)*
   a. Write the total distance that the Space Shuttle traveled in standard form.
   b. Write the Space Shuttle's velocity in scientific notation.

4. There are approximately 10,000,000 grains in a pound of salt. Write this number in scientific notation. *(Lesson 7-2)*

5. A high-speed centrifuge spins at a speed of $2 \times 10^4$ rotations per minute. How many rotations does the centrifuge make in one hour? Write your answer in scientific notation. *(Lesson 7-3)*

6. **Astronomy** Earth travels approximately $5.8 \times 10^8$ miles as it makes one orbit of the Sun. How far does Earth travel in 50 years? (*Note:* One year is one orbit of the Sun.) Write your answer in scientific notation. *(Lesson 7-3)*

7. **Geography** In 2005, the population of Indonesia was $2.4 \times 10^8$. This was 8 times the population of Afghanistan. What was the population of Afghanistan in 2005? Write your answer in standard form. *(Lesson 7-4)*

8. The Golden Gate Bridge weighs about $8 \times 10^8$ kg. The Eiffel Tower weighs about $1 \times 10^7$ kg. How many times heavier is the Golden Gate Bridge than the Eiffel Tower? Write your answer in standard form. *(Lesson 7-4)*

9. A rock is thrown off a 220-foot cliff with an initial velocity of 50 feet per second. The height of the rock above the ground is given by the polynomial $-16t^2 - 50t + 220$, where $t$ is the time in seconds. What is the height of the rock after 2 seconds? *(Lesson 7-5)*

10. The sum of the first $n$ natural numbers is given by the polynomial $\frac{1}{2}n^2 + \frac{1}{2}n$. Use this polynomial to find the sum of the first 9 natural numbers. *(Lesson 7-5)*

11. **Biology** The population of insects in a meadow depends on the temperature. A biologist predicts the population of insect A with the polynomial $0.02x^2 + 0.5x + 8$ and the population of insect B with the polynomial $0.04x^2 - 0.2x + 12$, where $x$ is the temperature in degrees Fahrenheit. *(Lesson 7-6)*
    a. Write a polynomial that represents the total population of both insects.
    b. Write a polynomial that represents the difference of the populations of insect B and insect A.

12. **Geometry** The length of the rectangle shown is 1 inch longer than 3 times the width.
    a. Write a polynomial that represents the area of the rectangle.
    b. Find the area of the rectangle when the width is 4 inches. *(Lesson 7-7)*

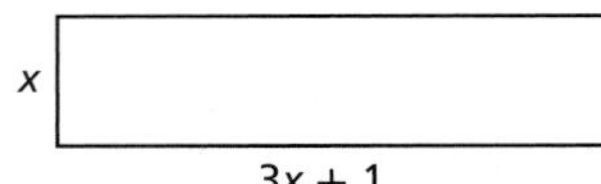


13. A cabinet maker starts with a square piece of wood and then cuts a square hole from its center as shown. Write a polynomial that represents the area of the remaining piece of wood. *(Lesson 7-8)*

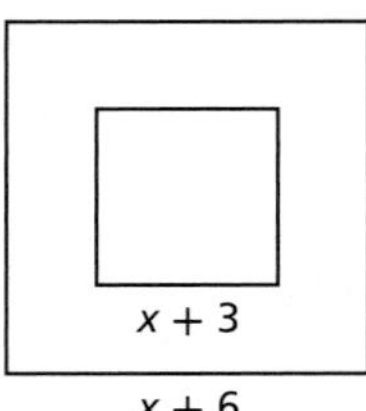

# Chapter 8 ■ Applications Practice

1. Ms. Andrews's class has 12 boys and 18 girls. For a class picture, the students will stand in rows on a set of steps. Each row must have the same number of students, and each row will contain only boys or girls. How many rows will there be if Ms. Andrews puts the maximum number of students in each row? *(Lesson 8-1)*

2. A museum director is planning an exhibit of Native American baskets. There are 40 baskets from North America and 32 baskets from South America. The baskets will be displayed on shelves so that each shelf has the same number of baskets. Baskets from North and South America will not be placed together on the same shelf. How many shelves will be needed if each shelf holds the maximum number of baskets? *(Lesson 8-1)*

3. The area of a rectangular painting is $(3x^2 + 5x)$ft$^2$. Factor this polynomial to find expressions for the dimensions of the painting. *(Lesson 8-2)*

4. **Geometry** The surface area of a cylinder with radius $r$ and height $h$ is given by the expression $2\pi r^2 + 2\pi rh$. Factor this expression. *(Lesson 8-2)*

5. The area of a rectangular classroom in square feet is given by $x^2 + 9x + 18$. The width of the classroom is $(x + 3)$ ft. What is the length of the classroom? *(Lesson 8-3)*

**Gardening Use the following information for Exercises 6 and 7.**

A rectangular flower bed has a width of $(x + 4)$ ft. The bed will be enlarged by increasing the length, as shown. *(Lesson 8-3)*

6. The original flower bed has an area of $(x^2 + 9x + 20)$ft$^2$. What is its length?

7. The enlarged flower bed will have an area of $(x^2 + 12x + 32)$ft$^2$. What will be the new length of the flower bed?

8. A rectangular poster has an area of $(6x^2 + 19x + 15)$ in$^2$. The width of the poster is $(2x + 3)$ in. What is the length of the poster? *(Lesson 8-4)*

9. **Physics** The height of an object thrown upward with a velocity of 38 feet per second from an initial height of 5 feet can be modeled by the polynomial $-16t^2 + 38t + 5$, where $t$ is the time in seconds. Factor this expression. Then use the factored expression to find the object's height after $\frac{1}{2}$ second. *(Lesson 8-4)*

10. A rectangular pool has an area of $(9x^2 + 30x + 25)$ ft$^2$. The dimensions of the pool are of the form $ax + b$, where $a$ and $b$ are whole numbers. Find an expression for the perimeter of the pool. Then find the perimeter when $x = 5$. *(Lesson 8-5)*

11. **Geometry** The area of a square is $9x^2 - 24x + 16$. Find the length of each side of the square. Is it possible for $x$ to equal 1 in this situation? Why or why not? *(Lesson 8-5)*

**Architecture Use the following information for Exercises 12–14.**

An architect is designing a rectangular hotel room. A balcony that is 5 feet wide runs along the length of the room, as shown in the figure. *(Lesson 8-6)*

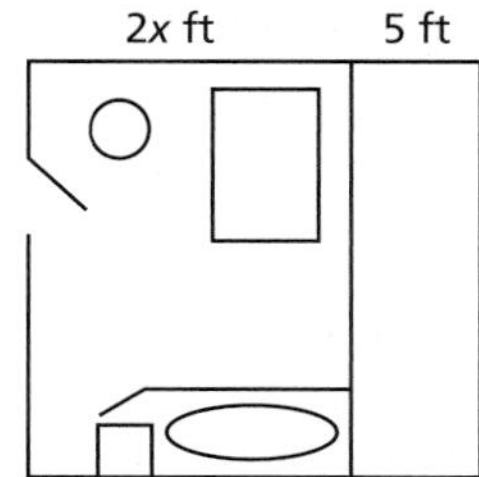


12. The area of the room, including the balcony, is $(4x^2 + 12x + 5)$ ft$^2$. Tell whether the polynomial is fully factored. Explain.

13. Find the length and width of the room (including the balcony).

14. How long is the balcony when $x = 9$?

Extra Practice

# Chapter 9 ■ Applications Practice

1. The table shows the height of a ball at various times after being thrown into the air. Tell whether the function is quadratic. Explain. *(Lesson 9-1)*

| Time (s) | 0 | 1 | 2 | 3 | 4 |
|---|---|---|---|---|---|
| Height (ft) | 200 | 204 | 176 | 116 | 24 |

2. The height of the curved roof of a camping tent can be modeled by $f(x) = -0.5x^2 + 3x$, where $x$ is the width in feet. Find the height of the tent at its tallest point. *(Lesson 9-2)*

3. **Engineering** A small bridge passes over a stream. The height in feet of the bridge's curved arch support can be modeled by $f(x) = -0.25x^2 + 2x + 1.5$, where the $x$-axis represents the level of the water. Find the height of the arch support. *(Lesson 9-2)*

4. **Sports** The height in meters of a football that is kicked from the ground is approximated by $f(x) = -5x^2 + 20x$, where $x$ is the time in seconds after the ball is kicked. Find the ball's maximum height and the time it takes the ball to reach this height. Then find how long the ball is in the air. *(Lesson 9-3)*

5. **Physics** Two golf balls are dropped, one from a height of 400 feet and the other from a height of 576 feet. *(Lesson 9-4)*
   a. Compare the graphs that show the time it takes each golf ball to reach the ground.
   b. Use the graphs to tell when each golf ball reaches the ground.

6. A model rocket is launched into the air with an initial velocity of 144 feet per second. The quadratic function $y = -16x^2 + 144x$ models the height of the rocket after $x$ seconds. How long is the rocket in the air? *(Lesson 9-5)*

7. A gymnast jumps on a trampoline. The quadratic function $y = -16x^2 + 24x$ models her height in feet above the trampoline after $x$ seconds. How long is the gymnast in the air? *(Lesson 9-5)*

8. A child standing on a rock tosses a ball into the air. The height of the ball above the ground is modeled by $h = -16t^2 + 28t + 8$, where $h$ is the height in feet and t is the time in seconds. Find the time it takes the ball to reach the ground. *(Lesson 9-6)*

9. A fireworks rocket is shot directly up from the edge of a rooftop. The height of the rocket above the ground is modeled by $h = -16t^2 + 40t + 24$, where $h$ is the height in feet and $t$ is the time in seconds. Find the time it takes the rocket to hit the ground. *(Lesson 9-6)*

10. **Geometry** The base of the triangle in the figure is five times the height. The area of the triangle is 400 in$^2$. Find the height of the triangle to the nearest tenth. *(Lesson 9-7)*

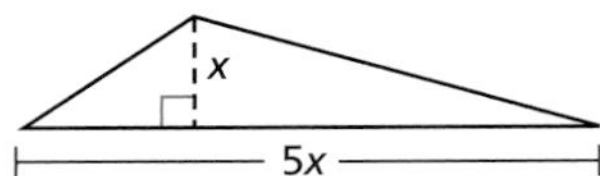


11. The length of a rectangular swimming pool is 8 feet greater than the width. The pool has an area of 240 ft$^2$. Find the length and width of the pool. *(Lesson 9-8)*

12. **Geometry** One base of a trapezoid is 4 ft longer than the other base. The height of the trapezoid is equal to the shorter base. The trapezoid's area is 80 ft$^2$. Find the height. $\left(Hint: A = \frac{1}{2}h(b_1 + b_2)\right)$ *(Lesson 9-8)*

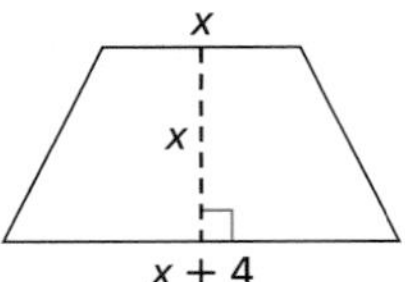


13. A referee tosses a coin into the air at the start of a football game to decide which team will get the ball. The height of the coin above the ground is modeled by $h = -16t^2 + 12t + 4$, where $h$ is the height in feet and $t$ is the time in seconds after the coin is tossed. Will the coin reach a height of 8 feet? Use the discriminant to explain your answer. *(Lesson 9-9)*

## Chapter 10 ■ Applications Practice

**Geography** **Use the following information for Exercises 1–3.**

The bar graph shows the areas of the Great Lakes. *(Lesson 10-1)*

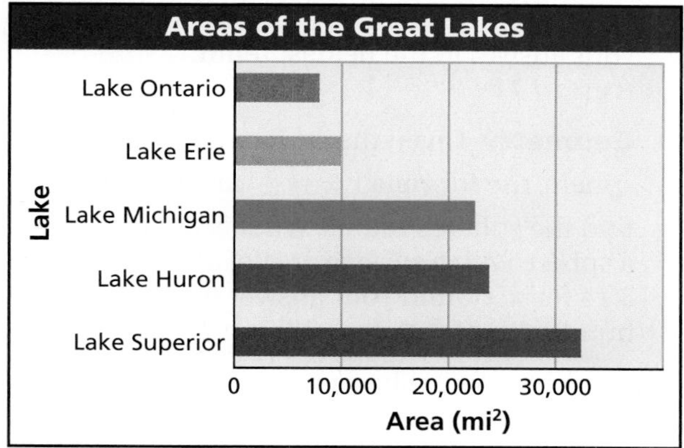


1. Estimate the difference in the areas between the lake with the greatest area and the lake with the least area.
2. Estimate the total area of the five lakes.
3. Approximately what percent of the total area is Lake Superior?
4. The scores of 18 students on a Spanish exam are given below. Use the data to make a stem-and-leaf plot. *(Lesson 10-2)*

| Exam Scores | | | | | | | | |
|---|---|---|---|---|---|---|---|---|
| 65 | 94 | 92 | 75 | 71 | 83 | 77 | 73 | 91 |
| 82 | 63 | 79 | 80 | 77 | 99 | 76 | 80 | 88 |

5. The numbers of customers who visited a hair salon each day are given below. Use the data to make a frequency table with intervals. *(Lesson 10-2)*

| Number of Customers Per Day | | | | | | |
|---|---|---|---|---|---|---|
| 32 | 35 | 29 | 44 | 41 | 25 | 35 |
| 40 | 41 | 32 | 33 | 28 | 33 | 34 |

**Sports** **Use the following information for Exercises 6 and 7.**

The numbers of points scored by a college football team in 11 games are given below. *(Lesson 10-3)*

**10 17 17 14 21 7 10 14 17 17 21**

6. Find the mean, median, mode, and range of the data set.
7. Use the data to make a box-and-whisker plot.
8. The weekly salaries of five employees at a restaurant are \$450, \$500, \$460, \$980, and \$520. Explain why the following statement is misleading: "The average salary is \$582." *(Lesson 10-4)*
9. The graph shows the sales figures for three sales representatives. Explain why the graph is misleading. What might someone believe because of the graph? *(Lesson 10-4)*

10. A manager inspects 120 stereos that were built at a factory. She finds that 6 are defective. What is the experimental probability that a stereo chosen at random will be defective? *(Lesson 10-5)*

**Travel** **Use the following information for Exercises 11–13.**

A row of an airplane has 2 window seats, 3 middle seats, and 4 aisle seats. You are randomly assigned a seat in the row. *(Lesson 10-6)*

11. Find the probability that you are assigned a window seat.
12. Find the odds in favor of being assigned a window seat.
13. Find the probability that you are not assigned a middle seat.
14. A class consists of 19 boys and 16 girls. The teacher selects one student at random to be the class president and then selects a different student to be vice president. What is the probability that both students are girls? *(Lesson 10-7)*

Extra Practice

# Chapter 11 ■ Applications Practice



1. Scientists who are developing a vaccine track the number of new infections of a disease each year. The values in the table form a geometric sequence. To the nearest whole number, how many new infections will there be in the 6th year? *(Lesson 11-1)*

| Year | Number of New Infections |
|---|---|
| 1 | 12,000 |
| 2 | 9000 |
| 3 | 6750 |

2. **Finance** For a savings account that earns 5% interest each year, the function $f(x) = 2000(1.05)^x$ gives the value of a \$2000 investment after $x$ years. *(Lesson 11-2)*

   a. Find the investment's value after 5 years.

   b. Approximately how many years will it take for the investment to be worth \$3100?

3. **Chemistry** Cesium-137 has a half-life of 30 years. Find the amount left from a 200-gram sample after 150 years. *(Lesson 11-3)*

4. The cost of tuition at a dance school is \$300 a year and is increasing at a rate of 3% a year. Write an exponential growth function to model the situation and find the cost of tuition after 4 years. *(Lesson 11-3)*

5. Use the data in the table to describe how the price of the company's stock is changing. Then write a function that models the data. Use your function to predict the price of the company's stock after 7 years. *(Lesson 11-4)*

| Stock Prices | | | | |
|---|---|---|---|---|
| Year | 0 | 1 | 2 | 3 |
| Price (\$) | 10.00 | 11.00 | 12.20 | 13.31 |

6. Use the data in the table to describe the rate at which Susan reads. Then write a function that models the data. Use your function to predict the number of pages Susan will read in 6 hours. *(Lesson 11-4)*

| Total Number of Pages Read | | | | |
|---|---|---|---|---|
| Time (h) | 1 | 2 | 3 | 4 |
| Pages | 48 | 96 | 144 | 192 |

7. The function $f(x) = \sqrt{1.44x}$ gives the approximate distance in miles to the horizon as observed by a person whose eye level is $x$ feet above the ground. Jamal stands on a tower so that his eyes are 180 ft above the ground. What is the distance to the horizon? Round your answer to the nearest tenth. *(Lesson 11-5)*

9. **Geometry** Given the surface area, $S$, of a sphere, the formula $r = \sqrt{\frac{S}{4\pi}}$ can be used to find the sphere's radius. What is the radius of a sphere with a surface area of 100 $m^2$? Use 3.14 for $\pi$. Round your answer to the nearest hundredth of a meter. *(Lesson 11-5)*

9. **Cooking** A chef has a square baking pan with sides 8 inches long. She wants to know if an 11-inch fish can fit in the pan. Find the length of the diagonal of the pan. Give the answer as a radical expression in simplest form. Then estimate the length to the nearest tenth of an inch. Tell whether the fish will fit in the pan. *(Lesson 11-6)*

10. Alicia wants to put a fence around the irregular garden plot shown. Find the perimeter of the plot. Give your answer as a radical in simplest form. *(Lesson 11-7)*

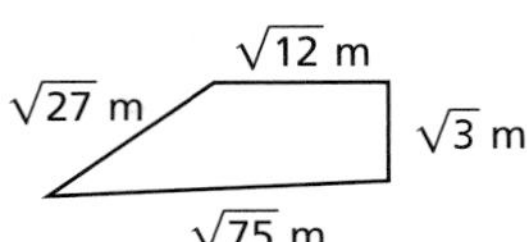


11. **Physics** The velocity of an object in meters per second is given by $\frac{\sqrt{2}\sqrt{E}}{\sqrt{m}}$, where $E$ is kinetic energy in Joules and $m$ is mass in kilograms. What is the velocity of an object that has 40 Joules of kinetic energy and a mass of 10 kilograms? Give the answer as a radical expression in simplest form. Then estimate the velocity to the nearest tenth. *(Lesson 11-8)*

12. A rectangular window has an area of 40 $ft^2$. The window is 8 feet long and its height is $\sqrt{x+2}$ ft. What is the value of $x$? What is the height of the window? *(Lesson 11-9)*

## Chapter 12 ■ Applications Practice

1. The inverse variation $xy = 200$ relates the number of words per minute $x$ at which a person types to the number of minutes $y$ that it takes to type a 200-word paragraph. Determine a reasonable domain and range and then graph this inverse variation. Use the graph to estimate how many minutes it would take to type the paragraph at a rate of 60 words per minute. *(Lesson 12-1)*

2. **Business** The owner of a deli finds that the number of sandwiches sold in one day varies inversely as the price of the sandwiches. When the price is \$4.50, the deli sells 60 sandwiches. How many sandwiches can the owner expect to sell when the price is \$3.60? *(Lesson 12-1)*

3. A gardener has \$30 in his budget to buy packets of seeds. He receives 3 free packets of seeds with his order. The number of packets $y$ he can buy is $y = \frac{30}{x} + 3$, where $x$ is the price per packet. Describe the reasonable domain and range values. Then graph the function. *(Lesson 12-2)*

4. Ashley wants to save \$1000 for a trip to Europe. She puts aside $x$ dollars per month, and her grandmother contributes \$10 per month. The number of months $y$ it will take to save \$1000 is $y = \frac{1000}{x + 10}$. Describe the reasonable domain and range values. Then graph the function. *(Lesson 12-2)*

5. **Geometry** Find the ratio of the area of a circle to the circumference of the circle. (*Hint:* For a circle, $A = \pi r^2$ and $C = 2\pi r$). For what radius is this ratio equal to 1? *(Lesson 12-3)*

6. **Geometry** For a cylinder with radius $r$ and height $h$, the volume is $V = \pi r^2 h$, and the surface area is $S = 2\pi r^2 + 2\pi rh$. What is the ratio of the volume to the surface area for a cylinder? What is this ratio when $r = h = 1$? *(Lesson 12-3)*

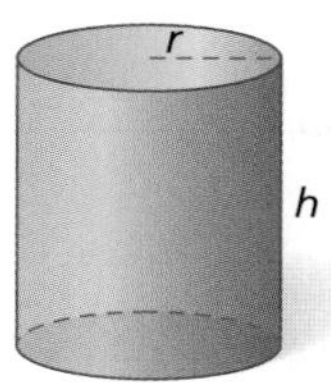


7. A committee consists of five more women than men. The chairperson randomly chooses one person to serve as secretary and a different person to serve as treasurer. Write and simplify an expression that represents the probability that both people who are chosen are men. What is the probability of choosing two men if there are 6 men on the committee? *(Lesson 12-4)*

8. **Transportation** A delivery truck makes a delivery to a town 150 miles away traveling $r$ miles per hour. On the return trip, the delivery truck travels 20% faster. Write and simplify an expression for the truck's round-trip delivery time in terms of $r$. Then find the round-trip delivery time if the truck travels 55 mi/h on its way to the delivery. *(Lesson 12-5)*

9. **Recreation** Jordan is hiking 2 miles to a vista point at the top of a hill and then back to his campsite at the base of the hill. His downhill rate is 3 times his uphill rate, $r$. Write and simplify an expression in terms of $r$ for the time that the round-trip hike will take. Then find how long the hike will take if Jordan's uphill rate is 2 mi/h. *(Lesson 12-5)*

10. **Geometry** The volume of a rectangular prism is the area of the base times the height. A rectangular prism has a volume given by $(2x^2 + 7x + 5)$ cm³ and a height given by $(x + 1)$ cm. What is the area of the base of the rectangular prism? *(Lesson 12-6)*

11. Tanya can deliver newspapers to all of the houses on her route in 1 hour. Her brother, Nick, can deliver newspapers along the same route in 2 hours. How long will it take to deliver the newspapers if they work together? *(Lesson 12-7)*

12. **Agriculture** Grains are harvested using a combine. A farm has two combines—one that can harvest the wheat field in 9 hours and another that can harvest the wheat field in 11 hours. How long will it take to harvest the wheat field using both combines? *(Lesson 12-7)*

# Problem Solving Handbook

## Draw a Diagram

**You can draw a diagram to help you visualize what the words of a problem are describing.**

**Problem Solving Strategies**

| | |
|---|---|
| Draw a Diagram | Make a Table |
| **Make a Model** | Solve a Simpler Problem |
| Guess and Test | Use Logical Reasoning |
| Work Backward | Use a Venn Diagram |
| Find a Pattern | Make an Organized List |

EXAMPLE

**A gardener wants to plant a 2.5-foot-wide border of flowers around a rectangular herb garden. The herb garden is 12 feet long and 7.5 feet wide. What is the area of the border?**

**1 Understand the Problem**

You need to find the area of the garden's border. You are given the garden's dimensions and the width of the border.

**2 Make a Plan**

Draw and label a diagram of the herb garden with the surrounding border. Find the dimensions of the outer rectangle. Then find the area of the inner rectangle and subtract to find the area of the border.

**3 Solve**

length of outer rectangle: 2.5 ft + 12 ft + 2.5 ft = **17 ft**
width of outer rectangle: 2.5 ft + 7.5 ft + 2.5 ft = **12.5 ft**

*Find the area of each rectangle:*

area of outer rectangle: **17 ft** × **12.5 ft** = 212.5 $ft^2$
area of inner rectangle: 12 ft × 7.5 ft = 90 $ft^2$

*Subtract:*

area of border: 212.5 $ft^2$ − 90 $ft^2$ = 122.5 $ft^2$

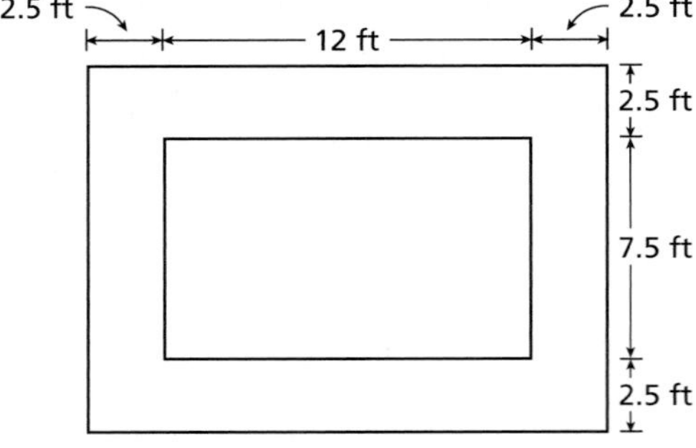

**4 Look Back**

To check your answer, solve the problem in a different way.

Divide the border into four parts and find the area of each part. Then add the areas.

**17 ft** × **2.5 ft** = **42.5 $ft^2$**  **7.5 ft** × **2.5 ft** = **18.75 $ft^2$**

**17 ft** × **2.5 ft** = **42.5 $ft^2$**  **7.5 ft** × **2.5 ft** = **18.75 $ft^2$**

**42.5 $ft^2$** + **42.5 $ft^2$** + **18.75 $ft^2$** + **18.75 $ft^2$** + = 122.5 $ft^2$

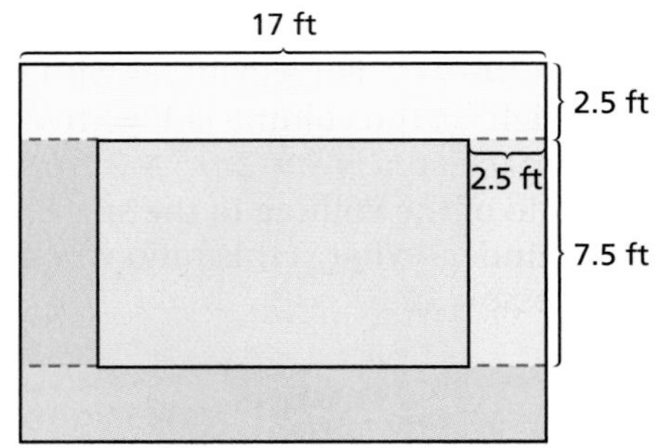


## PRACTICE

1. A circular fish pond is surrounded by a circular border of stones that is 18 inches wide. The fish pond is 4 feet in diameter. What is the area of the border? (Use 3.14 for $\pi$.)
2. Thirty-two teams are in the first round of a softball tournament. A team is eliminated as soon as it loses a game. How many games need to be played to determine the winner? (*Hint:* Use a tree diagram.)

# Make a Model

**You can make a model, or representation of the objects in a problem, to help you solve it.**

**Problem Solving Strategies**

| | |
|---|---|
| Draw a Diagram | Make a Table |
| **Make a Model** | Solve a Simpler Problem |
| Guess and Test | Use Logical Reasoning |
| Work Backward | Use a Venn Diagram |
| Find a Pattern | Make an Organized List |

## EXAMPLE

**Mr. Duncan is using blue and white square tiles to create a pattern on his kitchen wall. The entire design will have 8 rows with 15 tiles in each row. The bottom row alternates colors starting with blue, and the row above that alternates colors starting with white. He will continue this alternating pattern so that the same two colors are never next to each other. How many of each color tile does Mr. Duncan need to complete the entire design?**

### 1 Understand the Problem

You need to find how many of each color tile are needed. You know the number of rows and the number of tiles in each row. The colors alternate so that the same two colors are never next to each other.

### 2 Make a Plan

Use blocks (preferably blue and white, but any two colors would work) to make a model of the first two rows. Count how many of each color you use. Then multiply to find how many of each color would be used in the entire design.

### 3 Solve

Create the bottom row. Start with a blue block and alternate colors across the row until you have used 15 blocks.

Create the row above the bottom row. Start with a white block.

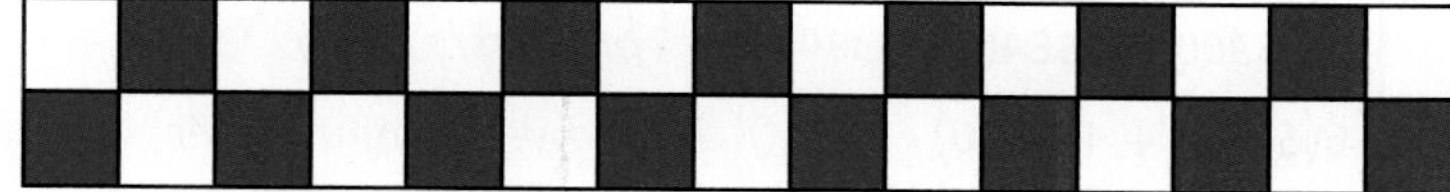

*You could build all 8 rows and just count the number of each color, but each group of two rows will be the same, so this way is quicker.*

There will be a total of 8 rows: 4 that start with blue and 4 that start with white. Count how many of each color are used above and multiply each number by 4.

blue: $15 \times 4 = 60$

white: $15 \times 4 = 60$

Mr. Duncan needs 60 blue tiles and 60 white tiles.

### 4 Look Back

The grid is 15 units by 8 units, so there are $15 \times 8 = 120$ squares in the grid. Add the number of blue and white tiles to see if the sum is 120: $60 + 60 = 120$.

## PRACTICE

1. Mr. Duncan decides to tile another area of his kitchen wall. This design will have 12 rows with 10 tiles in each row. The bottom row will repeat this pattern: blue, white, blue, blue, white. The row above the bottom row will repeat this pattern: white, green, white, white, green. He will use these two patterns for each of the remaining rows so that the first colors of each row always alternate. How many of each color tile will Mr. Duncan need?

# Guess and Test

**The guess and test strategy can be used when you cannot think of another way to solve the problem. Begin by making a reasonable guess, and then test it to see whether your guess is correct. If not, adjust the guess accordingly and test again. Keep guessing and testing until you correctly solve the problem.**

**Problem Solving Strategies**

| | |
|---|---|
| Draw a Diagram | Make a Table |
| Make a Model | Solve a Simpler Problem |
| **Guess and Test** | Use Logical Reasoning |
| Work Backward | Use a Venn Diagram |
| Find a Pattern | Make an Organized List |

## EXAMPLE

**The manager of a college computer lab purchased 24 printers at a total cost of \$3120. Some of the printers were laser, and some were ink jet. The laser printers cost \$250 each, and the ink jet printers cost \$70 each. How many of each type of printer did the manager purchase?**

### 1 Understand the Problem

You know the cost of each type of printer and the total number of printers. You need to find the number of each type of printer purchased.

### 2 Make a Plan

Make reasonable first guesses for each type of printer. The sum must be 24. Then multiply each guess by the cost of each printer. Find the total and compare it to \$3120. Adjust the guess as needed and continue until you find the solution.

### 3 Solve

Use a table to organize your guesses.

| | Laser Printers | Ink Jet Printers | Total Priners | Total Cost | |
|---|---|---|---|---|---|
| *1st guess* | 12 | 12 | 24 | 12(\$250) + 12(\$70)<br>\$3000 + \$840 = \$3840 | *Too high—try fewer laser printers.* |
| *2nd guess* | 6 | 18 | 24 | 6(\$250) + 18(\$70)<br>\$1500 + \$1260 = \$2760 | *Too low—try more laser printers.* |
| *3rd guess* | 8 | 16 | 24 | 8(\$250) + 16(\$70)<br>\$2000 + \$1120 = \$3120 | *Correct!* |

The manager purchased 8 laser printers and 16 ink jet printers.

### 4 Look Back

The total spent is \$3120, and the total number of printers is 24. The solution is correct.

## PRACTICE

1. All 350 seats were sold for a concert in the park. Adult tickets cost \$15, and child tickets cost \$5. Ticket sales totaled \$4350. How many of each type of ticket were sold?
2. Jane is 3 times as old as Theo. Luke is 5 years older than Theo. Zoe is 8 years younger than twice Theo's age, and Cassie is 6 years younger than Theo. The sum of their ages is 71. How old is each person?

# Work Backward

**You can work backward to solve a problem when you know the ending value and are asked to find the initial value.**

**Problem Solving Strategies**

| | |
|---|---|
| Draw a Diagram | Make a Table |
| Make a Model | Solve a Simpler Problem |
| Guess and Test | Use Logical Reasoning |
| **Work Backward** | Use a Venn Diagram |
| Find a Pattern | Make an Organized List |

## EXAMPLE

**Lee Ann is taking a vacation in Paris, France. Her flight arrived in Paris at 9:35 A.M. on Tuesday. The plane left New York City and flew for 7 hours and 55 minutes to Nice, France, where there was a layover of 1 hour 12 minutes. From Nice the plane flew 1 hour and 25 minutes to Paris. Paris time is 6 hours ahead of New York City time. What time did the plane leave New York City?**

### 1 Understand the Problem

You are asked to find the time that the plane left New York City. You know when the flight arrived in Paris, the length of the stops that were made along the way, and the time difference between New York City and Paris.

### 2 Make a Plan

Work backward from the time the plane arrived in Paris, using inverse operations. Then apply the time difference between the two cities.

### 3 Solve

Subtract the length of time it took to fly from Nice to Paris from the time Lee Ann arrived in Paris.

9:35 A.M. − 1 hour 25 minutes = 8:10 A.M.

Subtract the length of the layover in Nice.

8:10 A.M. − 1 hour 12 minutes = 6:58 A.M.

Subtract the length of the flight from New York to Nice.

6:58 A.M. – 7 hours 55 minutes = 11:03 P.M. Monday

Since Paris time is ahead of New York time, subtract the time difference.

11:03 P.M., Monday − 6 hours = 5:03 P.M. Monday

Lee Ann's flight left New York City on Monday at 5:03 P.M.

### 4 Look Back

Work forward to check your answer.

5:03 P.M. Monday + 6 h + 7 h 55 min + 1 h 12 min + 1 h 25 min
= 5:03 P.M. Monday + 16 h 32 min
= 9:35 A.M. Tuesday

This matches the information given in the problem.

## PRACTICE

1. A bus arrives in Dallas, Texas, at 10:59 A.M. on Friday. The bus left Atlanta, Georgia, and took 12 hours and 15 minutes to arrive in Shreveport, Louisiana, where there was a 45-minute layover. From Shreveport it took 4 hours and 29 minutes to get to Dallas. Dallas time is 1 hour behind Atlanta time. What time did the bus leave Atlanta?
2. Carolina bought a DVD player that was on sale for 90% of the original price. The total amount she paid was $135.72, which included a sales tax of $5.22. What was the original price of the DVD player?

# Find a Pattern

**If a problem involves a sequence of numbers or figures, it is often necessary to find a pattern to solve the problem.**

**Problem Solving Strategies**

| | |
|---|---|
| Draw a Diagram | Make a Table |
| Make a Model | Solve a Simpler Problem |
| Guess and Test | Use Logical Reasoning |
| Work Backward | Use a Venn Diagram |
| **Find a Pattern** | Make an Organized List |

## EXAMPLE

**Darian created the following sequence of stars:**

**How many stars will be in the 6th figure?**

### Understand the Problem

You need to find the number of stars in the 6th figure. You can find the number in the first four figures by counting.

### Make a Plan

Count the number of stars in each of the first four figures. Use the information to find a pattern and determine a general rule.

### Solve

Look for a pattern between the position of each figure in the sequence and the number of stars in that figure.

| Position | 1 | 2 | 3 | 4 |
|---|---|---|---|---|
| Stars | 2 | 6 | 12 | 20 |

The number of stars is the square of the position number plus the position number. This rule written algebraically is $n^2 + n$.

Evaluate the expression for $n = 6$: $n^2 + n$

$6^2 + 6 = 36 + 6 = 42$

There will be 42 stars in the 6th figure.

### Look Back

Look for another pattern. The number of stars in each position increases by 4, then by 6, then by 8. That is, the amount of increase always increases by 2. So the number of stars in the 5th position will be 20 + 10, or 30, and the number of stars in the 6th position will be 30 + 12, or 42.

## PRACTICE

1. The first three figures of a pattern are shown. How many circles will be in the 10th figure?

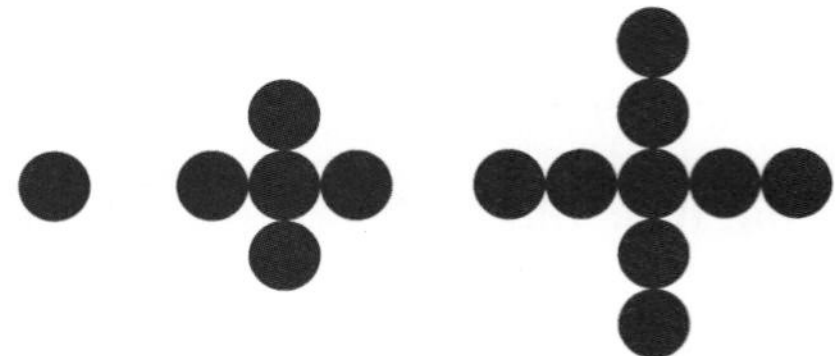

2. Lily drew the first four figures of a pattern. How many squares will be in the 7th figure?

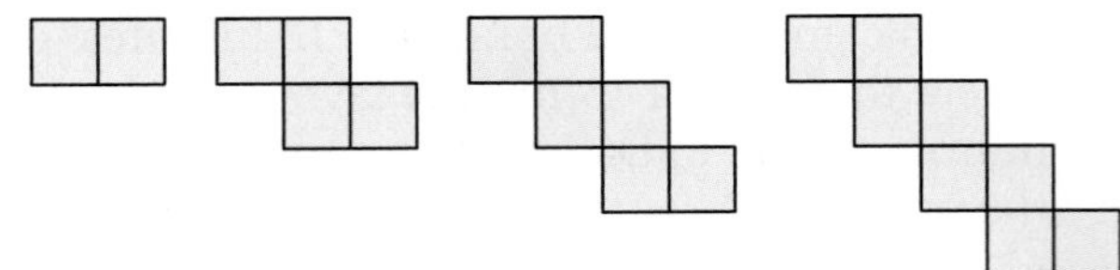

# Make a Table

**You can make a table to solve problems because the rows and columns can help you arrange information. Sometimes this also allows you to discover relationships that might otherwise be hard to notice.**

**Problem Solving Strategies**

| | |
|---|---|
| Draw a Diagram | **Make a Table** |
| Make a Model | Solve a Simpler Problem |
| Guess and Test | Use Logical Reasoning |
| Work Backward | Use a Venn Diagram |
| Find a Pattern | Make an Organized List |

## EXAMPLE

**A scientist begins a culture with 500 bacteria. The number of bacteria triples every 30 minutes. How many bacteria are in the culture after $2\frac{1}{2}$ hours?**

### 1 Understand the Problem

You are asked to find the number of bacteria in the culture after $2\frac{1}{2}$ hours. You know the initial number of bacteria, and you know that the population triples every half hour.

### 2 Make a Plan

Make a table with rows for time and number of bacteria. Start with the initial number in the culture. Increase the time in 30-minute increments and triple the number of bacteria with each increase. Keep extending the table until the time is $2\frac{1}{2}$ hours (150 minutes).

### 3 Solve

| Time (min) | 0 | 30 | 60 | 90 | 120 | 150 |
|---|---|---|---|---|---|---|
| Bacteria | 500 | 1500 | 4500 | 13,500 | 40,500 | 121,500 |

There are 121,500 bacteria in the culture after $2\frac{1}{2}$ hours.

### 4 Look Back

Check your answer by solving a simpler problem. The number of bacteria in the culture triples five times (150 min ÷ 30 min = 5). Start with 5 instead of 500 and triple the number five times.

$5 \times 3 = 15$

$15 \times 3 = 45$

$45 \times 3 = 135$

$135 \times 3 = 405$

$405 \times 3 = 1215$

Multiply by 100 to find the total if you had started with 500; $1215 \times 100 = 121{,}500$

## PRACTICE

1. A dietician's report states that a 125-pound woman needs to eat about 1750 Calories a day to maintain her weight. It also states that a 132-pound woman needs 1848 Calories and a 139-pound woman needs 1946 Calories a day. Based on these values, how many Calories does a 160-pound woman need to eat each day to maintain her weight?
2. Simon opened a savings account with an initial deposit of $200. At the end of each year, the account earns 4% interest. If he does not deposit or withdraw any additional money, what would his balance be at the end of 6 years?

# Solve a Simpler Problem

**Sometimes a problem contains numbers that make it seem difficult to solve. You can solve a simpler problem by rewriting the numbers so they are easier to compute.**

**Problem Solving Strategies**

| | |
|---|---|
| Draw a Diagram | Make a Table |
| Make a Model | **Solve a Simpler Problem** |
| Guess and Test | Use Logical Reasoning |
| Work Backward | Use a Venn Diagram |
| Find a Pattern | Make an Organized List |

## EXAMPLE

**During a skating competition, Jules skated around the track 35 times. One lap is 0.9 mile. If Jules finished in 1 hour 30 minutes, what was his average speed?**

### Understand the Problem

You are asked to find Jules's average speed for 35 laps. You know the distance of each lap and the amount of time it took him to finish the competition.

### Make a Plan

Solve a simpler problem by using easier numbers to do the computations.

### Solve

Find the total distance skated.

$$35(0.9)$$ *There were 35 laps that measured 0.9 mile.*

$$35(1 - 0.1)$$ *Write 0.9 as 1 − 0.1*

$$35(1) - 3.5(0.1)$$ *Use the Distributive Property.*

$$35 - 3.5$$

$$31.5$$

Use the distance formula to find the average speed.

$$d = rt$$

$$31.5 = r \times 1.5$$ *1 hour 30 minutes = 1.5 hours*

$$\frac{31.5}{1.5} = r$$ *Solve for r.*

$$\frac{315}{15} = r$$ *Multiply the numerator and denominator by 10 to eliminate the decimals.*

$$\frac{1}{15}(315) = r$$

$$\frac{1}{15}(300 + 15) = r$$ *Write 315 as 300 + 15.*

$$\frac{1}{15}(300) + \frac{1}{15}(15) = r$$ *Use the Distributive Property.*

$$20 + 1 = r$$

$$21 = r$$

Jules skated at an average speed of 21 miles per hour.

### Look Back

Each lap is a little less than 1 mile, so 35 laps is a little less than 35 miles. Round this distance to 30 miles and use $d = rt$ to find the rate when the time is 1.5 hours: $30 \text{ mi} = (1.5 \text{ h})r \longrightarrow r = 20 \text{ mi/h}$. This is close to 21 mi/h.

## PRACTICE

1. Diana swam 24 laps in the pool today. One lap is 200 feet. She swam at an average rate of 4 feet per second. How many minutes did Diana swim?

# Use Logical Reasoning

**Use logical reasoning to solve problems when you are given several facts and can use common sense to find a missing fact.**

**Problem Solving Strategies**

| | |
|---|---|
| Draw a Diagram | Make a Table |
| Make a Model | Solve a Simpler Problem |
| Guess and Test | **Use Logical Reasoning** |
| Work Backward | Use a Venn Diagram |
| Find a Pattern | Make an Organized List |

## EXAMPLE 1

**Five players on a baseball team wear the numbers 2, 12, 15, 34, and 42. Their positions are pitcher, catcher, first base, left field, and center field. The pitcher's number is less than the left fielder's number. The center fielder's number is greater than 25, and the left fielder wears an even number. The catcher wears number 34. What is the pitcher's number?**

### 1 Understand the Problem

You want to find the jersey number of the pitcher. You know there are five positions and five jersey numbers. Some information about who wears which number is given.

### 2 Make a Plan

Organize the information in a table. Start with the fact that the catcher wears number 34 and use logical reasoning to determine the numbers of the other positions.

### 3 Solve

The catcher wears number 34. No other player wears 34, and the catcher wears no other number. Enter *Y's* and *N's* in the chart as shown.

The center fielder's number is greater than 25, so he must wear number 42. The left fielder cannot wear number 15 (because it is odd), and he cannot have the least number (the pitcher's number is less than his). The left fielder must wear 12.

The pitcher's number is less than 12 (the left fielder's), so he must wear number 2.

| | 2 | 12 | 15 | 34 | 42 |
|---|---|---|---|---|---|
| Pitcher | Y | N | N | N | N |
| Catcher | N | N | N | Y | N |
| First Base | N | N | Y | N | N |
| Left Fielder | N | Y | N | N | N |
| Center Fielder | N | N | N | N | Y |

*Y = yes; N = no*

*Once you enter Y in a cell, enter N in the remaining cells for the row and the column that include it.*

The pitcher wears number 2.

### 4 Look Back

Complete the chart if needed. Read the problem while looking at the chart to make sure there are no contradictions.

## PRACTICE

1. Rose, Jill, Gaby, and Chloe bowled the scores 110, 125, 144, and 150. Jill did not bowl the 110. The person who bowled the 150 is Rose's sister and Jill's aunt. Chloe bowled the 125. What score did Jill bowl?

# Use a Venn Diagram

**You can use a Venn diagram to display relationships among sets of numbers. Circles are used to represent the individual sets.**

**Problem Solving Strategies**

| | |
|---|---|
| Draw a Diagram | Make a Table |
| Make a Model | Solve a Simpler Problem |
| Guess and Test | Use Logical Reasoning |
| Work Backward | **Use a Venn Diagram** |
| Find a Pattern | Make an Organized List |

## EXAMPLE

**At a local supermarket, 194 people were given samples of two brands of orange juice. Their opinions were as follows: 120 people liked brand A, 101 people liked brand B, and 15 people did not like either brand. How many people liked only brand A?**

### 1 Understand the Problem

The total number of people was 194, and 15 of them did not like either brand. The statement "120 people liked brand A" means some of the 120 people liked *only* brand A and some liked brand A *and* brand B. The statement "101 people liked brand B" means some of the 101 people liked *only* brand B and some liked brand A *and* brand B.

### 2 Make a Plan

Use a Venn diagram to show the relationship among the groups of people.

### 3 Solve

Brand A

Brand B

Both

Neither: 15

Draw and label two intersecting circles to show the sets of people who liked brand A and brand B. Write 15 in the area labeled "Neither."

Out of 194 people, 15 liked neither brand. Subtract 15 from 194 to find how many people liked at least one brand: $194 - 15 = 179$.

Add the number of people who liked brand A to the number of people who liked brand B: $120 + 101 = 221$. You know there are only 179 people who liked at least one brand, so subtract 179 from 221: $221 - 179 = 42$. This means 42 people were counted twice, and that 42 people liked both brands. Write 42 in the area labeled both.

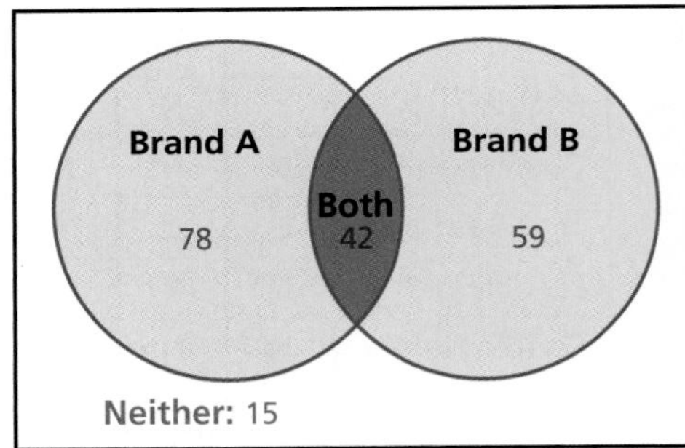


Out of 120 people who liked brand A, 42 also liked brand B. Subtract 42 from 120 to find the number of people who liked only brand A: $120 - 42 = 78$.

So 78 people liked only brand A.

### 4 Look Back

Find the number of people who liked brand B only: $101 - 42 = 59$. Add all the numbers in the Venn diagram. The sum of the number who liked only brand A, the number who liked only brand B, the number who liked both brands, and the number who liked neither brand should be the total number of people surveyed: $78 + 59 + 42 + 15 = 194$.

## PRACTICE

**In a group of 138 people, 55 own a cat, 27 own a cat and a dog, and 42 own neither pet.**

**1.** How many people own only a cat?

**2.** How many people own a dog?

# Make an Organized List

**If a problem asks you to find all the possible ways in which something can happen, you can make an organized list to keep track of the outcomes.**

**Problem Solving Strategies**

| | |
|---|---|
| Draw a Diagram | Make a Table |
| Make a Model | Solve a Simpler Problem |
| Guess and Test | Use Logical Reasoning |
| Work Backward | Use a Venn Diagram |
| Find a Pattern | **Make an Organized List** |

## EXAMPLE

**A fair coin is tossed 4 times. What is the probability that it lands heads up at least 3 times?**

### 1 Understand the Problem

You need to find the probability that a coin tossed 4 times lands heads up 3 or 4 times.

### 2 Make a Plan

The formula for probability is:

$$\text{probability} = \frac{\text{number of favorable outcomes}}{\text{total number of outcomes}}$$

The total number of outcomes is the number of items in the list. The number of favorable outcomes is the number of times the coin lands heads up 3 or 4 times.

Make an organized list of the coin tosses to find the total number of outcomes.

### 3 Solve

Start with heads for all 4 tosses, then heads for the first 3 tosses, then heads for the first 2 tosses, and then heads for the first toss. Repeat the pattern for tails.

| | | | |
|---|---|---|---|
| HHHH | HTHH | TTTT | THTT |
| HHHT | HTHT | TTTH | THTH |
| HHTH | HTTH | TTHT | THHT |
| HHTT | HTTT | TTHH | THHH |

*There are 16 total outcomes.*

*There are 5 favorable outcomes.*

The probability that the coin lands heads up 3 or 4 times is $\frac{5}{16}$.

### 4 Look Back

Double-check that each combination is listed and that no combination is written more than once. You can also use the Fundamental Counting Principle to check the total number of outcomes. For each of the 4 coin tosses, there are 2 possible outcomes, so the total number of outcomes is $2 \times 2 \times 2 \times 2 = 16$.

## PRACTICE

1. A beagle, a fox terrier, an Afghan hound, and a golden retriever are competing in the finals of a dog show. How many ways can the dogs finish in first, second, and third place?
2. Two number cubes are rolled. What is the probability that the sum of the numbers rolled is an odd number?

# Skills Bank

## Place Value

You can use a place-value chart to read and write numbers. The number 5,304,293,087,201.286 is shown below.

| Trillions | Billions | Millions | Thousands | Ones | . | Tenths | Hundredths | Thousandths |
|---|---|---|---|---|---|---|---|---|
| 5, | 304, | 293, | 087, | 201 | . | 2 | 8 | 6 |

**EXAMPLE 1** **Use the place-value chart to find the place value of the underlined digit.**

**A** **5,30$\underline{4}$,293,087,201.286** billions

**B** **5,304,2$\underline{9}$3,087,201.286** ten millions

**C** **5,304,293,087,201.28$\underline{6}$** thousandths

**Expanded form** shows the number as the sum of the values of each digit. The number 1463 written in expanded form is 1000 + 400 + 60 + 3.

**EXAMPLE 2** **Write 16,752,045.12 in expanded form.**

10,000,000 + 6,000,000 + 700,000 + 50,000 + 2,000 + 40 + 5 + 0.1 + 0.02

### PRACTICE

**Use the place-value chart to find the place value of the underlined digit.**

1. 22.3$\underline{8}$
2. 1,2$\underline{3}$8,400
3. $\underline{2}$,809,354.003

**Write each number in expanded form.**

4. 899,456
5. 1645.445
6. 3,009,844,002,359

## Compare and Order Rational Numbers

You can compare and order rational numbers by graphing them on a number line.

**EXAMPLE 1** **Order 0.25, $\frac{3}{4}$, 0.1, and $\frac{4}{5}$ from least to greatest.**

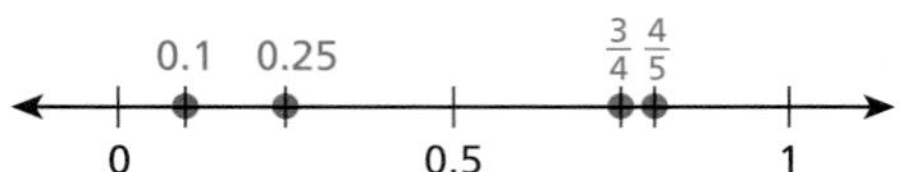


$\frac{3}{4} = 0.75$
$\frac{4}{5} = 0.8$

The values increase from left to right: 0.1, 0.25, $\frac{3}{4}$, $\frac{4}{5}$.

### PRACTICE

**Order each set of numbers from least to greatest.**

1. 2.6, $2\frac{2}{5}$, $2\frac{1}{2}$
2. 0.45, $\frac{3}{8}$, $\frac{4}{9}$
3. 0.55, $\frac{2}{3}$, 0.6
4. 5.25, $5\frac{1}{3}$, 5.05, 5.5
5. 0.4, $\frac{3}{5}$, $\frac{1}{4}$, 0.42
6. $\frac{5}{8}$, $\frac{4}{9}$, 0.6, $\frac{6}{7}$

## Times Tables

You can use a multiplication table to multiply and write *number families*. A **number family** is a group of related number sentences that use the same numbers.

**EXAMPLE 1**

**Find 8 × 9.**

Find where the 8's row and the 9's column intersect.

8 × 9 = 72

**EXAMPLE 2**

**Write a multiplication and division number family for 8, 9, and 72.**

8 × 9 = 72
9 × 8 = 72
72 ÷ 9 = 8
72 ÷ 8 = 9

| × | 1 | 2 | 3 | 4 | 5 | 6 | 7 | 8 | 9 | 10 | 11 | 12 |
|---|---|---|---|---|---|---|---|---|---|---|---|---|
| **1** | 1 | 2 | 3 | 4 | 5 | 6 | 7 | 8 | 9 | 10 | 11 | 12 |
| **2** | 2 | 4 | 6 | 8 | 10 | 12 | 14 | 16 | 18 | 20 | 22 | 24 |
| **3** | 3 | 6 | 9 | 12 | 15 | 18 | 21 | 24 | 27 | 30 | 33 | 36 |
| **4** | 4 | 8 | 12 | 16 | 20 | 24 | 28 | 32 | 36 | 40 | 44 | 48 |
| **5** | 5 | 10 | 15 | 20 | 25 | 30 | 35 | 40 | 45 | 50 | 55 | 60 |
| **6** | 6 | 12 | 18 | 24 | 30 | 36 | 42 | 48 | 54 | 60 | 66 | 72 |
| **7** | 7 | 14 | 21 | 28 | 35 | 42 | 49 | 56 | 63 | 70 | 77 | 84 |
| **8** | 8 | 16 | 24 | 32 | 40 | 48 | 56 | 64 | 72 | 80 | 88 | 96 |
| **9** | 9 | 18 | 27 | 36 | 45 | 54 | 63 | 72 | 81 | 90 | 99 | 108 |
| **10** | 10 | 20 | 30 | 40 | 50 | 60 | 70 | 80 | 90 | 100 | 110 | 120 |
| **11** | 11 | 22 | 33 | 44 | 55 | 66 | 77 | 88 | 99 | 110 | 121 | 132 |
| **12** | 12 | 24 | 36 | 48 | 60 | 72 | 84 | 96 | 108 | 120 | 132 | 144 |

### PRACTICE

**Find each product. Write a multiplication and division number family for each set of numbers.**

**1.** 4 × 8 **2.** 5 × 12 **3.** 3 × 11
**4.** 8 × 7 **5.** 9 × 6 **6.** 12 × 12

## Inverse Operations

**Inverse operations** "undo" each other. Addition and subtraction are inverse operations. Multiplication and division are inverse operations.

**EXAMPLE**  **Use inverse operations to check each answer.**

**A** **567 − 180 $\stackrel{?}{=}$ 487**

487 + 180
667
667 ≠ 557
incorrect

*Use addition to check subtraction.*

**B** **110 ÷ 11 $\stackrel{?}{=}$ 10**

10 × 11
110
110 = 110
correct

*Use multiplication to check division.*

### PRACTICE

**Use inverse operations to check each answer.**

**1.** 51 + 25 = 86 **2.** 14 × 4 = 48 **3.** 144 ÷ 4 = 36 **4.** 345 − 72 = 273
**5.** 134 + 653 = 787 **6.** 364 ÷ 7 = 52 **7.** 500 − 428 = 82 **8.** 6 × 25 = 150

## Translate from Words to Math

Some words indicate certain math operations. Common math words and phrases are shown below. Some are listed in more than one column, so always read the problem carefully.

| Addition | Subtraction | Multiplication | Division |
|---|---|---|---|
| add, plus, total, sum, more, more than, increased by, in all, combined | subtract, minus, difference, less, less than, more, more than, decreased by | multiply, times, of, product, per, for each, total | divide, divided by, quotient, divide equally, per, percent |

**EXAMPLE**

**A** **Caroline saved \$42 in September, \$25 in October, and \$33 in November. How much money did she save in all?**

*The words "in all" indicate addition.*

$42 + 25 + 33 = 100$

Caroline saved \$100 in all.

**B** **Jamal bought 13 gallons of gas for \$1.98 per gallon. What is the total amount he paid?**

*The word "per" could mean multiplication or division. But the word "total" indicates multiplication.*

$13 \times 1.98 = 25.74.$

Jamal paid a total of \$25.74.

### PRACTICE

**1.** Sarah worked 15 hours this week and earned a total of \$112.50. How much does she earn per hour? What words tell you which operation to use?

**2.** Lance biked 28.5 miles on Monday. On Thursday he biked 5.75 miles less than he did on Monday. How far did he bike on Thursday? What words tell you which operation to use?

## Mental Math

Mental math strategies include using the Distributive Property, using the Commutative Property, and using facts about powers of 10.

**EXAMPLE** **Use mental math to solve each problem.**

**A** $6 \times 17$

*Break 17 into 10 + 7. Then use the Distributive Property.*

$$\begin{aligned} 6 \times 17 &= 6(10 + 7) \\ &= 6(10) + 6(7) \\ &= 60 + 42 \\ &= 102 \end{aligned}$$

**B** $225 + 78 + 75$

*Use the Commutative Property to add or multiply numbers in a different order.*

$$\begin{aligned} 225 + 78 + 75 &= 225 + 75 + 78 \\ &= 300 + 78 \\ &= 378 \end{aligned}$$

**C** $132 \times 100{,}000$

*Count the number of zeros in 100,000. Move the decimal point that many places right.*

$$\begin{aligned} 132 \times 100{,}000 &= 13{,}200{,}000 \\ &= 13{,}200{,}000 \end{aligned}$$

### PRACTICE

**Use mental math to solve each problem.**

**1.** $3987 \times 10{,}000$

**2.** $5 \times 29$

**3.** $950 + 273 + 50$

**4.** $12 \times 41$

**5.** $25 \times 42 \times 4$

**6.** $4.5 \times 100 \times 2$

# Measurement

The measurements for time are the same worldwide.

1 min = 60 s
1 h = 60 min
1 day = 24 h

1 wk = 7 days
1 yr = 12 mo
1 yr = 365 days

1 leap yr = 366 days

The **customary system** of measurement is used in the United States.

**Length**
12 in. = 1 ft
3 ft = 1 yd
5280 ft = 1 mi

**Capacity**
8 oz = 1 c
2 c = 1 pt
2 pt = 1 qt

**Weight**
16 oz = 1 lb
2000 lb = 1 ton

The **metric system** is used elsewhere and in science worldwide.

**Length**
1 mm = 0.001 m
1 cm = 0.01 m
1 km = 1000 m

**Capacity**
1 mL = 0.001 L
1 kL = 1000 L

**Mass**
1 mg = 0.001 g
1 kg = 1000 g

Use the table below to convert from metric to customary measurements.

| Length | Capacity | Mass/Weight | Temperature |
|---|---|---|---|
| 1 cm ≈ 0.394 in. | 1 L ≈ 1.057 qt | 1 g ≈ 0.0353 oz | $F = \left(\frac{9}{5} \times C\right) + 32$ |
| 1 m ≈ 3.281 ft | 1 L ≈ 0.264 gal | 1 kg ≈ 2.205 lb | |
| 1 m ≈ 1.094 yd | 1 L ≈ 4.227 c | 1 kg ≈ 0.001 ton | |
| 1 km ≈ 0.621 mi | 1 mL ≈ 0.338 fl oz | 1 metric T ≈ 1.102 ton | |

Use the table below to convert from customary to metric measurements.

| Length | Capacity | Weight/Mass | Temperature |
|---|---|---|---|
| 1 in. ≈ 2.540 cm | 1 qt ≈ 0.946 L | 1 oz ≈ 28.350 g | $C = \frac{5}{9} \times (F - 32)$ |
| 1 ft ≈ 0.305 m | 1 gal ≈ 3.785 L | 1 lb ≈ 0.454 kg | |
| 1 yd ≈ 0.914 m | 1 c ≈ 0.237 L | 1 ton ≈ 907.185 kg | |
| 1 mi ≈ 1.609 km | 1 fl oz ≈ 29.574 mL | 1 ton ≈ 0.907 metric ton | |

**EXAMPLE**

**A** **Write <, =, or >.**

**35 in. ▒ 1 yd**
35 in. ▒ 3 ft *1 yd = 3 ft*
35 in. < 36 in. *3 ft = 36 in.*
35 in. < 1 yd

**B** **Convert 32 km/h to mi/h.**

1 km/h ≈ 0.621 mi/h
32 km/h ≈32 0.621 mi/h
32 km/h ≈ 19.872 mi/h

**C** **Convert 25°C to °F.**

$F = \left(\frac{9}{5} \times 25\right) + 32$
$F = 45 + 32$
$F = 77°F$

## PRACTICE

**Write <, >, or =.**

**1.** 3 lb ▒ 40 oz **2.** 200 cm ▒ 2 m **3.** 6 c ▒ 2 qt

**Convert.**

**4.** 15mi/h to km/h **5.** 2 weeks to hours **6.** 32 fl oz to mL **7.** 95°F to °C **8.** 14 tons to kg

Skills Bank

## Precision, Accuracy, and Significant Digits

**Significant digits** are those digits that are known to be correct in a measurement.

- All nonzero digits are significant.
- Zeros after the last nonzero number after the decimal point are significant.
- Zeros between significant digits are significant.
- Zeros at the end of a whole number are *not* significant

**EXAMPLE 1** **Determine the number of significant digits in each measurement.**

**A** **272 ft** Three significant digits: 272 *All digits are nonzero digits.*

**B** **0.0050 mm** Two significant digits: 0.0050 *The last zero is significant.*

**Accuracy** is determined by the exactness of a measurement—that is, how close it is to the actual or accepted value. **Precision** describes the level of detail an instrument measures. A measurement of 200 mm is more precise than a measurement of 20 cm because millimeters are a smaller unit of measurement. A measurement can be precise, but not accurate, and vice versa.

**EXAMPLE 2** **Three students measured the width of a dictionary. Their measurements were 21 cm, 8.5 in., and 212 mm. The publisher lists the width of the dictionary as 8.52 in.**

**A** **Which measurement is most accurate?**

8.5 in. *8.5 in. is closest to the accepted width of the dictionary.*

**B** **Which measurement is most precise?**

212 mm *Millimeters are the smallest unit of measurement used.*

- When *adding or subtracting measurements*, the answer must have the same number of decimal places as the measurement with the least number of decimal places.
- When *multiplying or dividing measurements*, the answer must have the same number of significant digits as the least precise measurement.

**EXAMPLE 3** **Perform the indicated operation. Write the answer with the correct number of significant digits.**

**A** **14 in. + 2.76 in.**

14 in. + 2.76 in. = 16.76 in.

*14 has zero decimal places.*
*2.76 has two decimal places.*

Round to zero decimal places: 17 in.

**B** **12.3 cm × 6.4 cm**

12.3 cm × 6.4 cm = 78.72 $cm^2$

*12.3 has three significant digits.*
*6.4 has two significant digits.*

Round to two significant digits: 79 $cm^2$

## PRACTICE

**Determine the number of significant digits in each measurement.**

1. 1,234.55 yd
2. 10,000 mi
3. 0.040 km
4. 102.045 ft
5. Three students measured the length of a classroom. Their measurements were 18.5 ft, 362 in., and 21 ft. A blueprint shows that the length of the classroom is 18.43 ft.
   a. Which measurement is most accurate?
   b. Which measurement is most precise?

**Perform the indicated operation. Write the answer with the correct number of significant digits.**

6. 244 in. + 4.58 in.
7. 155.02 ft ÷ 0.05 ft
8. 38.33 yd × 2.8 yd

## Absolute and Relative Error

It is never possible to measure quantities exactly—all measures are estimates. Accuracy refers to how close a measurement is to its actual or accepted value. **Absolute error** is the difference between the measured value and the actual or accepted value.

$$\text{absolute error} = |\text{measured value} - \text{actual value}|$$

EXAMPLE 1 **Carolyn used her car's odometer to measure the distance between her house and her grandmother's house. Carolyn's measurement was 1653 miles. The distance given on a map is 1642.2 miles. Find the absolute error in Carolyn's measurement.**

$$\begin{aligned}\text{absolute error} &= |\text{measured value} - \text{actual value}| \\ &= |1653 - 1642.2| \\ &= 10.8 \text{ miles}\end{aligned}$$

*Use the equation for absolute error.*

**Relative error** takes into account the size of the measurement by converting the error into a percent.

$$\text{relative error} = \frac{\text{absolute error}}{\text{actual value}}, \text{ written as a percent}$$

EXAMPLE 2 **What was the relative error in Carolyn's measurement?**

$$\begin{aligned}\text{relative error} &= \frac{\text{absolute error}}{\text{actual value}} \\ &= \frac{10.8}{1642.2} \\ &\approx 0.66\%\end{aligned}$$

*Use the equation for relative error.*

*Though the absolute error is 10.8 miles, it is a relatively small error (less than 1%) when compared to the total distance measured.*

**Tolerance** is the maximum amount that a measure may vary from an accepted standard. To find the maximum tolerated value for a measurement, add the tolerance to the measurement. To find the minimum tolerated value for a measurement, subtract the tolerance from the measurement. These two values give a tolerance interval.

EXAMPLE  **A pencil manufacturer specifies that the length of each pencil produced must be 18 cm, with a tolerance of 0.05 cm. What is the tolerance interval?**

$18 \pm 0.05$ *Add and subtract 0.05.*

The tolerance interval ranges from 17.95 cm to 18.05 cm.

## PRACTICE

1. Jerome measured the liquid in a filled eye dropper as 0.95 mL. The manufacturer's label says the capacity of the eye dropper is 1 mL. What are the absolute and relative errors in Jerome's measurement?

2. Julio used a metric ruler to take a measurement of 7.6 cm. The ruler has a precision of 0.1 cm. What is the tolerance interval for Julio's measurement?

# Points, Lines, Planes, and Angles

A **point** specifies an exact location in space. A **line** is a straight path that has no thickness and extends forever in two directions. A **ray** is a part of a line that extends forever in one direction. A **plane** is a flat surface that has no thickness and extends forever in all directions.

An **angle** is formed by two rays joined at their endpoints. Angles are classified by size and can be measured with a protractor.

**Parallel lines** are lines in the same plane that never intersect.
**Perpendicular lines** intersect to form right angles.

| Acute $< 90°$ | Obtuse $> 90°$ |
|---|---|
| **Right** $90°$ | **Straight** $180°$ |

**EXAMPLE 1** **Name a line, angle, ray, or plane. Then name the lines that are parallel or perpendicular.**

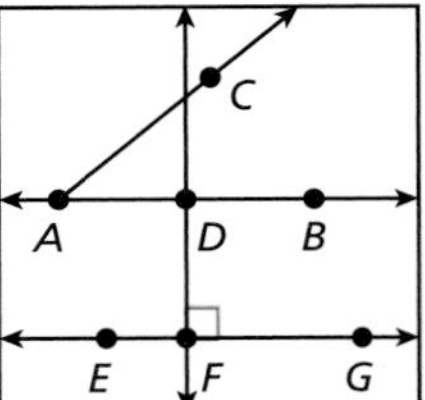


| | | |
|---|---|---|
| **Line** | *Choose two points on the line. Draw a bar with arrows over the letters.* | $\overleftrightarrow{AB}$ |
| **Angle** | *Use one point on one ray or line, then the vertex, then a point on the other ray or line.* | $\angle BAC$ |
| **Ray** | *Write the endpoint first. Then write another point the ray passes through.* | $\overline{AC}$ |
| **Plane** | *Use three points that are not all on the same line or ray.* | *plane ABE* |
| **Parallel** | *Choose two lines that will never intersect.* | $\overleftrightarrow{AB}$, $\overleftrightarrow{EG}$ |
| **Perpendicular** | *Choose two lines that form a right angle.* | $\overleftrightarrow{DF}$, $\overleftrightarrow{EG}$ |

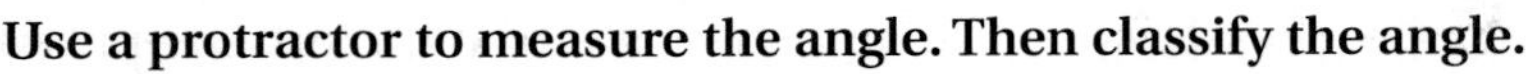

**EXAMPLE 2** **Use a protractor to measure the angle. Then classify the angle.**

*Align one ray along the base of the protractor, with the endpoint at the center. Read the protractor where the second ray crosses it, extending the ray if needed.*

120°; obtuse

## PRACTICE

**Name a line, angle, ray, or plane. Then name the lines that are parallel or perpendicular.**

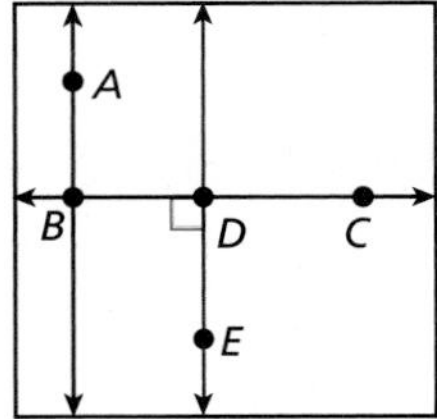


**1.** line **2.** angle **3.** ray

**4.** plane **5.** parallel **6.** perpendicular

**Use a protractor to measure each angle. Then classify the angle.**

**7.**

**8.**

**9.**

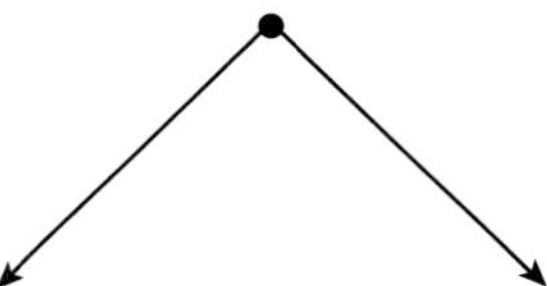

## Complementary and Supplementary Angles

**Complementary angles** are angles whose measures add to 90°. ∠1 and ∠2 are complementary.

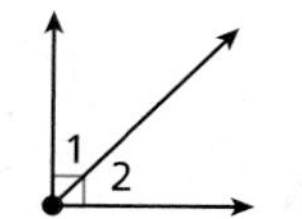


**Supplementary angles** are angles whose measures add to 180°. ∠3 and ∠4 are supplementary.

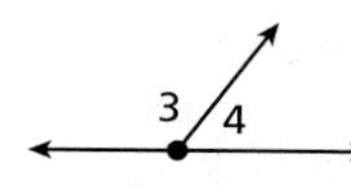


Complementary and supplementary angles may or may not be *adjacent* (have a ray in common).

EXAMPLE

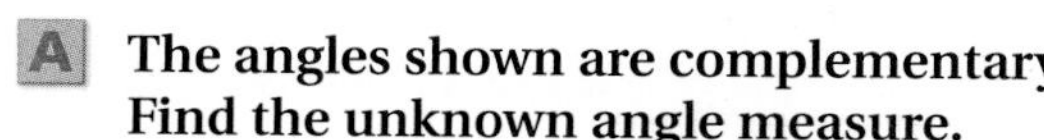

**A** **The angles shown are complementary. Find the unknown angle measure.**

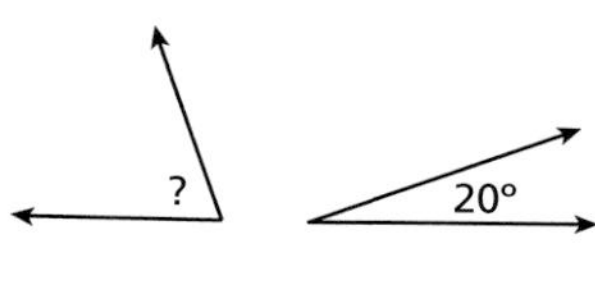


90 − 20 = 70°

**B** **The two angles that form a draw bridge are supplementary. One angle measures 30°. What is the measure of the other angle?**

180 − 30 = 150
The other angle measures 150°.

### PRACTICE

1. Find the complement and supplement of a 48° angle.

**Tell whether each pair of angles is complementary, supplementary, or neither.**

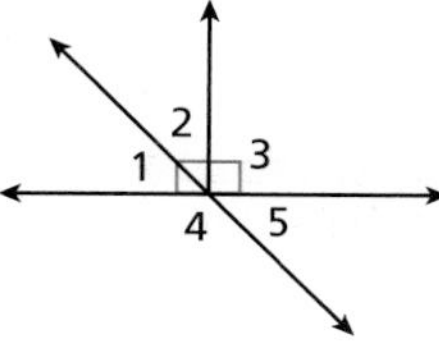


2. ∠1 and ∠4
3. ∠2 and ∠3
4. ∠1 and ∠2
5. ∠4 and ∠5

## Vertical Angles

When two lines intersect, the nonadjacent angles are called **vertical angles.** Vertical angles always have the same measure. In the section of fencing shown, there are two pairs of vertical angles: ∠1 and ∠3, ∠4 and ∠2.

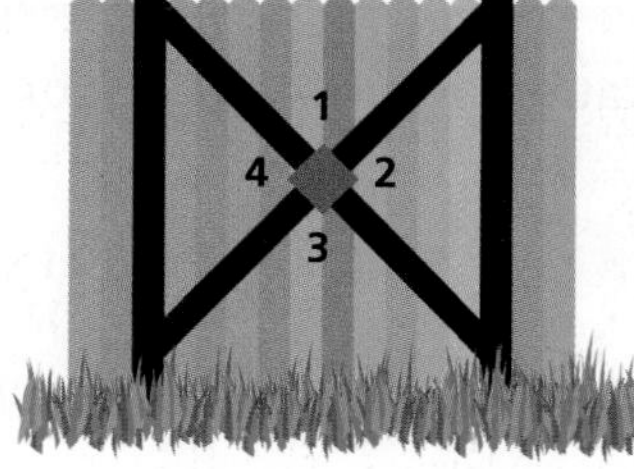

EXAMPLE

1

**Find the measures of ∠BEC, ∠AEB, and ∠DEC.**

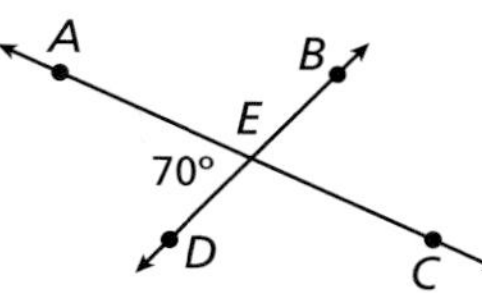


m∠*BEC* = 70° — *∠AED and ∠BEC are vertical.*
m∠*AEB* = 110° — *∠AED and ∠AEB are supplementary.*
m∠*DEC* = 110° — *∠AEB and ∠DEC are vertical.*

### PRACTICE

1. Name two pairs of vertical angles.

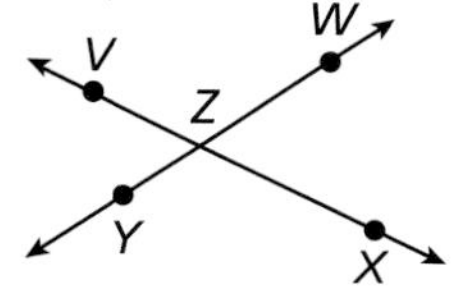


2. Find m∠*PTS*, m∠*PTQ*, and m∠*QTR*.

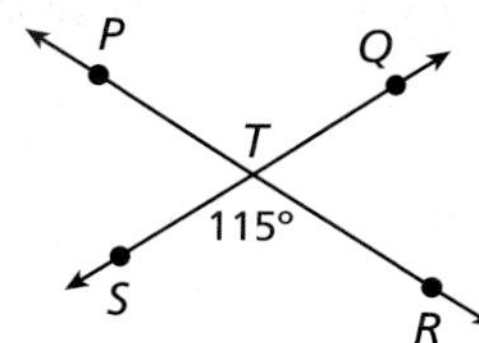


Skills Bank

## Polygons

A **polygon** is a closed figure with three or more sides. The name of a polygon is determined by its number of sides.

If all the sides are the same length, and all the angles have the same measure, the polygon is a **regular polygon.** Sides and angles with the same measures are marked with the same symbol.

| Number of Sides | Name | Number of Sides | Name |
|---|---|---|---|
| 3 | Triangle | 8 | Octagon |
| 4 | Quadrilateral | 9 | Nonagon |
| 5 | Pentagon | 10 | Decagon |
| 6 | Hexagon | 12 | Dodecagon |
| 7 | Heptagon | $n$ | $n$-gon |

**EXAMPLE** **Identify each polygon.**

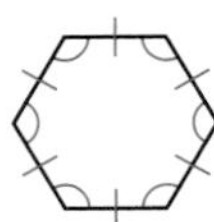

regular hexagon

*The mark on each side indicates that they are all the same length. The arch inside each angle indicates that they all have the same measure.*

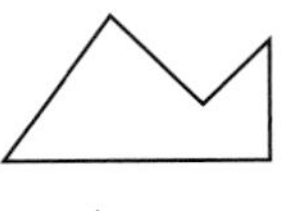

pentagon

### PRACTICE

**Identify each polygon.**

**1.**

**2.** 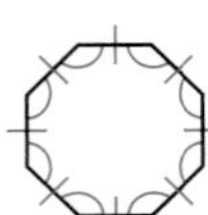

**3.** 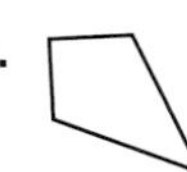

## Geometric Patterns

Patterns involving polygons may deal with size, color, position, or shape.

**EXAMPLE** **Predict the next term:** 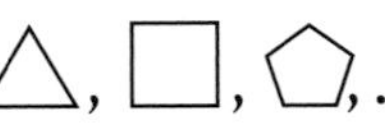

hexagon

*Each term has one more side than the previous term. The next term will have six sides.*

### PRACTICE

**1.** Predict the next term.

**2.** Describe the missing term.

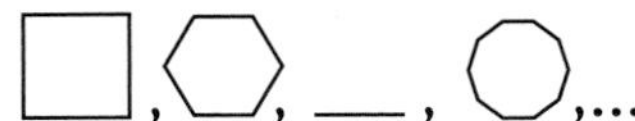

## Congruence

**Congruent segments** are segments that are the same length.

**Congruent angles** are angles that have the same measure.

Figures are **congruent** if all pairs of corresponding angles are congruent and all pairs of corresponding sides are congruent.

EXAMPLE **Identify the corresponding angles and sides.**

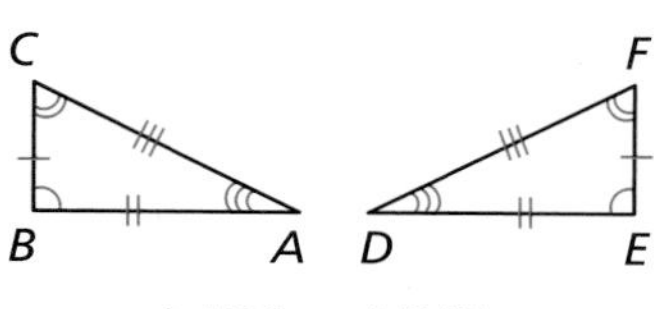

$\triangle ABC \cong \triangle DEF$

| | |
|---|---|
| $\angle A \cong \angle D$ | $\overline{AB} \cong \overline{DE}$ |
| $\angle B \cong \angle E$ | $\overline{BC} \cong \overline{EF}$ |
| $\angle C \cong \angle F$ | $\overline{AC} \cong \overline{DF}$ |

*The order of the letters in $\triangle ABC \cong \triangle DEF$ shows which angles and sides are congruent. Congruent sides and angles are also identified by the same mark.*

## PRACTICE

**Identify the corresponding angles and sides.**

1. 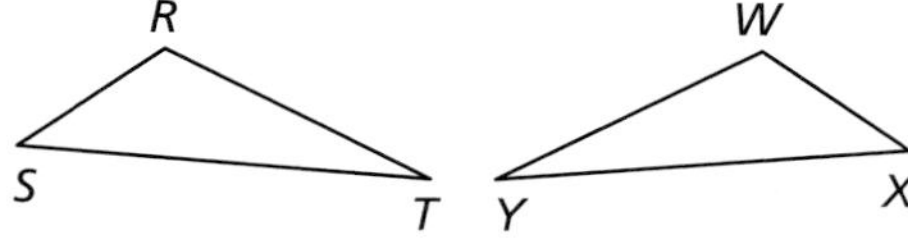


2. $\triangle JKL \cong \triangle OPQ$

## Symmetry

A **line of symmetry** is a line that can be drawn through a plane figure so that the figure on one side of the line is a reflection of the figure on the other side.

EXAMPLES

**A** **Determine the number of lines of symmetry.**

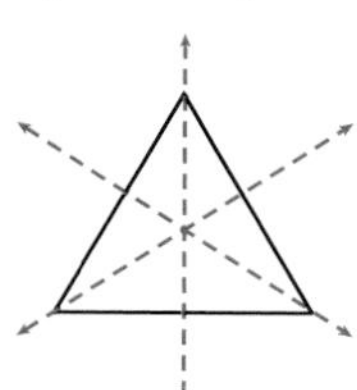

3 lines of symmetry

**B** **The line shown is a line of symmetry. Draw the reflection.**

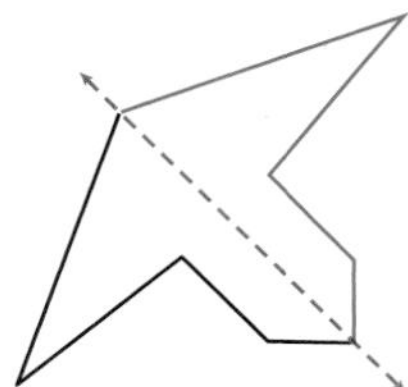

## PRACTICE

1. Determine the number of lines of symmetry.

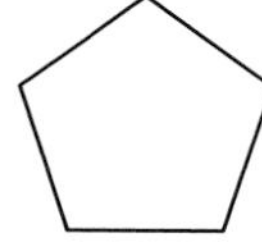

2. Determine the number of lines of symmetry.

3. The line shown is a line of symmetry. Draw the reflection.

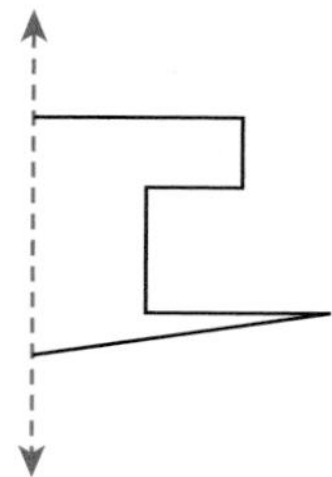

# Perimeter

The **perimeter** of a polygon is the sum of the lengths of its sides. The following formulas can be used to find the perimeters of rectangles and squares.

| Rectangle | $2\ell + 2w$ | Square | $4s$ |
|---|---|---|---|

**EXAMPLE 1** **Find the perimeter of each figure.**

**A**

6 ft

$P = 4s$
$= 4 \times 6$
$= 24$
$= 24$ ft

**B**

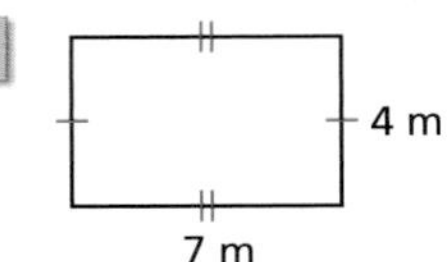


$P = 2\ell + 2w$
$= (2 \times 7) + (2 \times 4)$
$= 14 + 8$
$= 22$
$= 22$ m

**C**

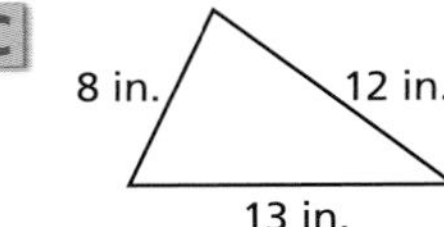


$P = 8 + 12 + 13$
$= 33$
$= 33$ in.

**EXAMPLE 2** **Estimate the perimeter of the figure.**

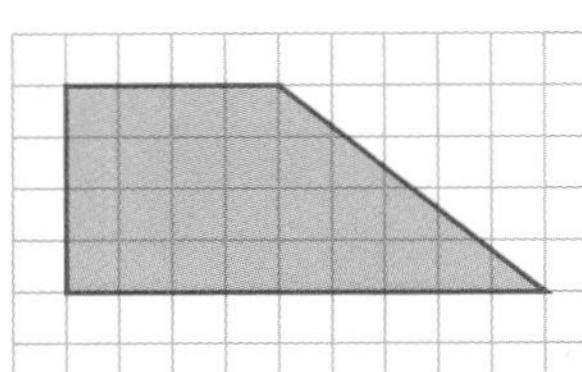

Find the length of the nondiagonal lines.
top: 4 units
left: 4 units
bottom: 9 units

Estimate the length of the diagonal line.
right: $\approx 6$ units

Add the lengths of all four sides:
$P \approx 4 + 4 + 9 + 6 \approx 23$ units

## PRACTICE

**Find the perimeter of each figure.**

1. 

2. 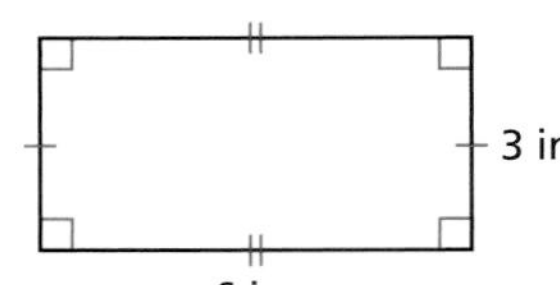


3. 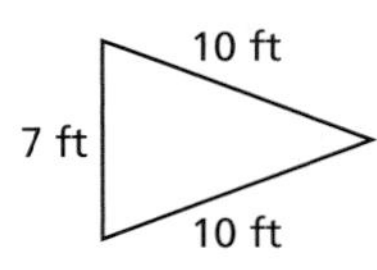


**Estimate the perimeter of each figure.**

4. 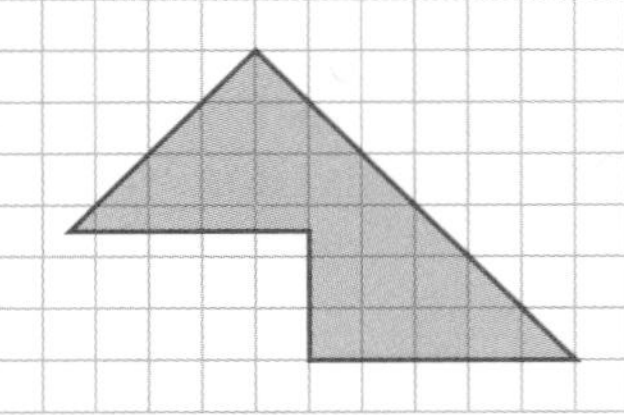

5. 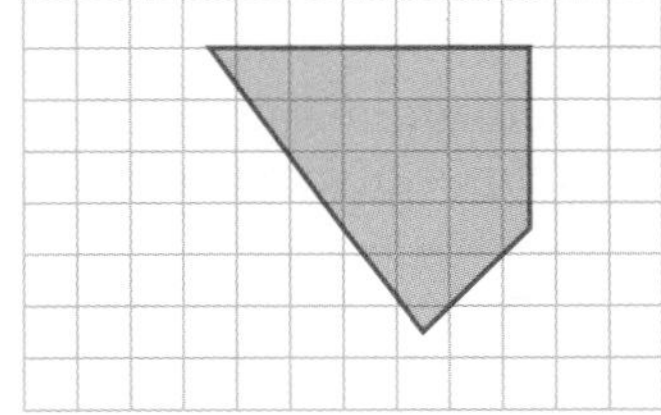

## Area

The **area** of a polygon is the number of nonoverlapping square units that will exactly cover its interior.

Formulas for the areas of some polygons are given at right.

| Square | $s^2$ | $s$: length of one side |
|---|---|---|
| Rectangle | $\ell w$ | $\ell$: length, $w$: width |
| Parallelogram | $bh$ | $b$: base, $h$: height |
| Triangle | $\frac{1}{2}bh$ | $b$: base, $h$: height |
| Trapezoid | $\frac{1}{2}h(b_1 + b_2)$ | $b_1$: top base, $b_2$: bottom base<br>$h$: height |

**EXAMPLE 1** Find the area of each polygon.

**A**

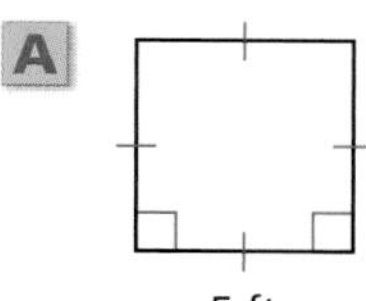


$$A = s^2 = 5^2 = 25 = 25 \text{ ft}^2$$

**B**

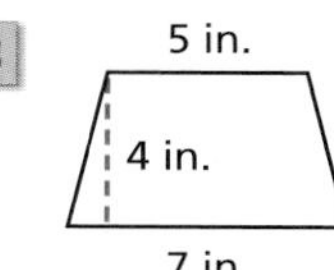


$$A = \frac{1}{2}h(b_1 + b_2) = \frac{1}{2}(4)(5 + 7) = 2 \times 12 = 24 = 24 \text{ in}^2$$

**EXAMPLE 2** Estimate the area of the figure.

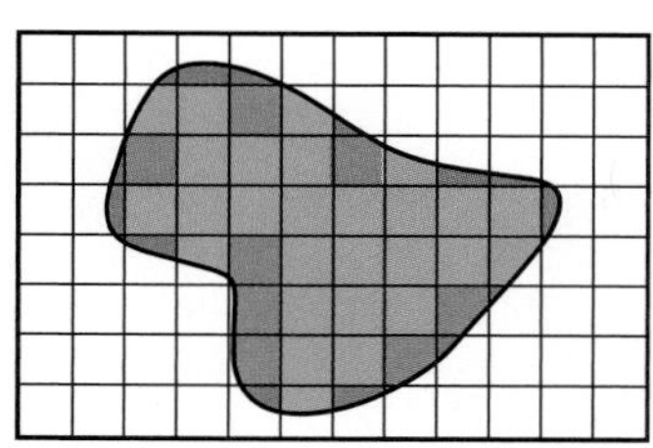

$A \approx 32$ square units

*Count full squares: 21 red squares*
*Count almost full squares: 8 blue squares*
*Count squares that are about half full: 6 green squares $\approx$ 3 full squares*
*Do not count almost empty purple squares.*
*Add: $21 + 8 + 3 \approx 32$*

## PRACTICE

**Find the area of each polygon.**

**1.**

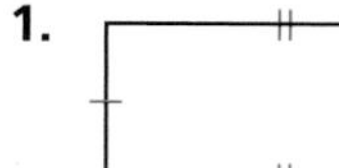
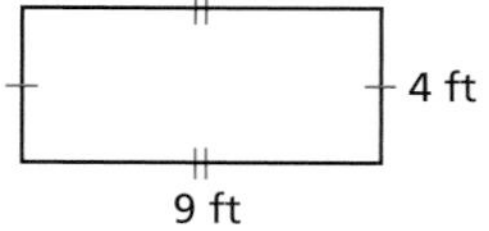


**2.**

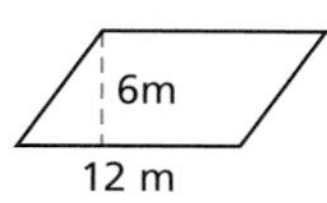


**3.**

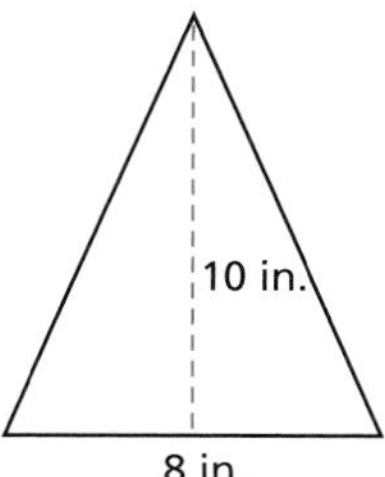


**Estimate the area of each figure.**

**4.**

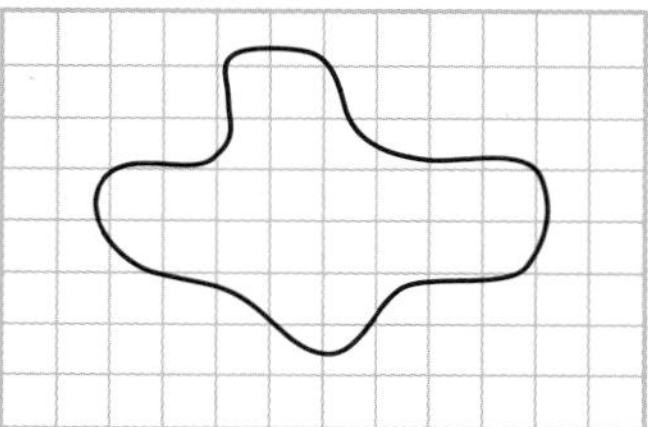

**5.**

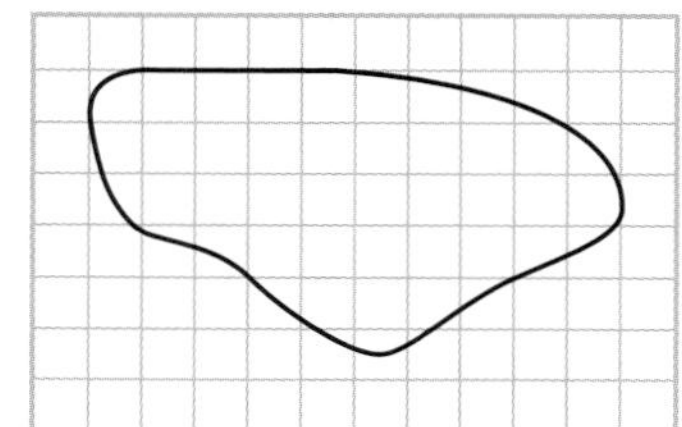

## Circles

A **circle** is the set of all points in a plane that are a given distance from a given point, known as the **center.** The center names the circle. The circle shown at right is referred to as circle *C*.

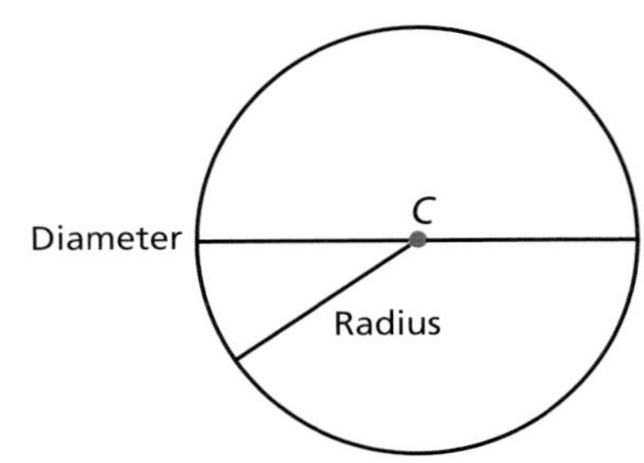


A **diameter** is a line segment that passes through the center and whose endpoints are points on the circle.

A **radius** is a segment whose endpoints are the center of the circle and a point on the circle. Any radius of a circle is half as long as any diameter of that circle.

**Circumference** is the distance around a circle. The ratio of circumference to diameter is the same for all circles and is denoted by the Greek letter $\pi$ (*pi*), which is approximately 3.14.

| Circle Formulas | |
|---|---|
| Area: $A = \pi r^2$ | Circumference: $C = \pi d$ or $C = 2\pi r$ |

**EXAMPLE 1** **Find the circumference of each circle. Use 3.14 for $\pi$.**

**A**

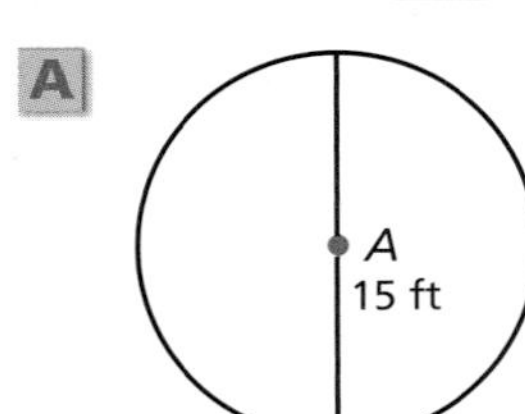


$C = \pi d$
$\approx 3.14(15)$
$\approx 47.1$ ft

**B**

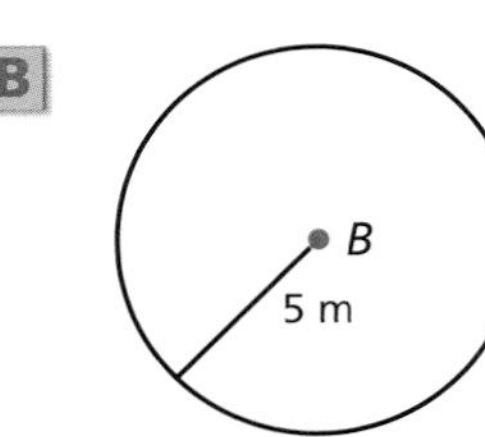


$C = 2\pi r$
$\approx 2(3.14)(5)$
$\approx 31.4$ m

**EXAMPLE 2** **Find the area of each circle. Use 3.14 for $\pi$.**

**A**

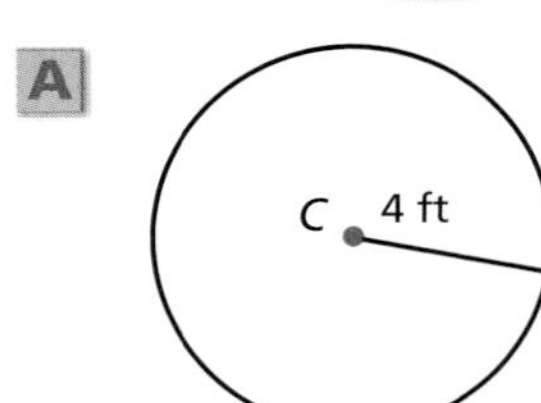


$A = \pi r^2$
$\approx 3.14(4)^2$
$\approx 3.14(16)$
$\approx 50.24 \text{ ft}^2$

**B**

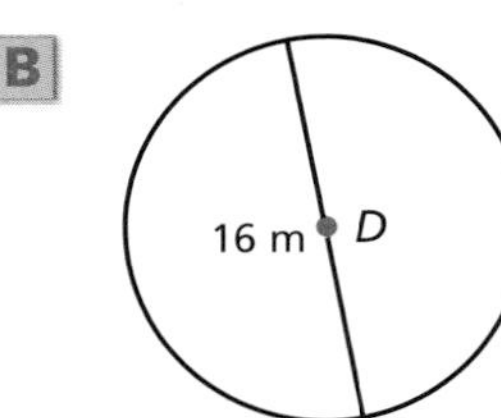


$A = \pi r^2$
$\approx 3.14(8)^2$
$\approx 3.14(64)$
$\approx 200.96 \text{ m}^2$

## PRACTICE

1. The radius of a circle is 13 inches. What is the diameter of the circle? Use 3.14 for $\pi$.
2. The diameter of a circle is 22 feet. What is the radius of the circle? Use 3.14 for $\pi$.

**Find the circumference and area of each circle.**

**3.**

E
3 m

**4.**

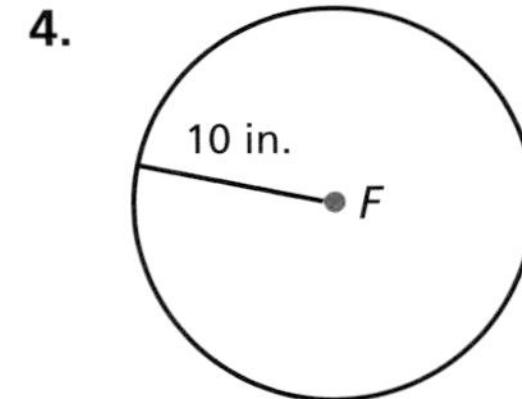


**5.**

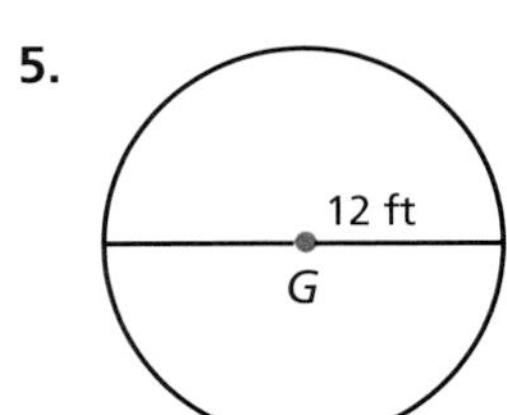

# Classify Triangles and Quadrilaterals

A triangle can be classified according to its angle measurements or according to the number of congruent sides it has.

| Classifying by Angles | | Classifying by Sides | |
|---|---|---|---|
| **Acute** | Three acute angles | **Scalene** | No sides congruent |
| **Right** | One right angle | **Isosceles** | At least 2 sides congruent |
| **Obtuse** | One obtuse angle | **Equilateral** | All sides congruent |

**EXAMPLE**  **Classify each triangle according to its angles and sides.**

acute isosceles

**B** 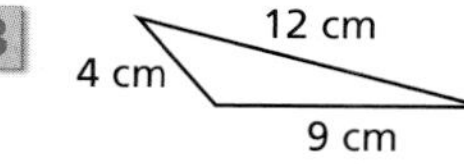


obtuse scalene

**C** 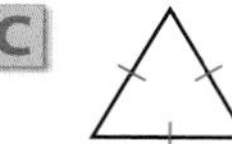

acute equilateral

Quadrilaterals can also be classified according to their sides and angles.

| Parallelograms | |
|---|---|
| **Parallelogram**<br>2 pairs of parallel, congruent sides | |
| **Rectangle**<br>4 right angles | |
| **Rhombus**<br>4 congruent sides | |
| **Square**<br>4 right angles and 4 congruent sides | |

| Other Quadrilaterals | |
|---|---|
| **Trapezoid**<br>exactly 1 pair of parallel sides | |
| **Isosceles Trapezoid**<br>congruent, nonparallel legs | |
| **Kite**<br>2 pairs of adjacent congruent sides | |

**EXAMPLE 2** **Tell whether the following statement is always, sometimes, or never true: A square is a rectangle.**

always *A rectangle must have four right angles, and a square always has four right angles.*

## PRACTICE

**Classify each triangle according to its angles and sides.**

**1.** 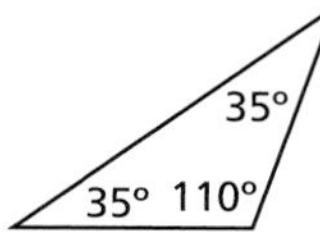


**2.** 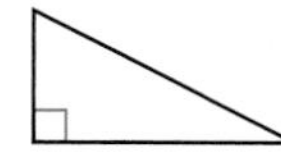

**3.** 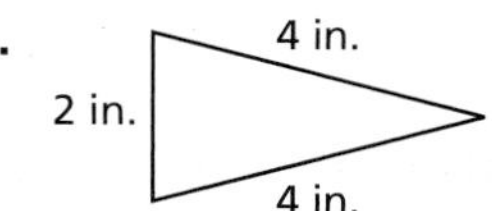


**Tell whether each statement is always, sometimes, or never true.**

**4.** A rectangle is a square.

**5.** A trapezoid is a parallelogram.

**Name the quadrilaterals that always meet the given conditions.**

**6.** All sides are congruent.

**7.** Two pairs of sides are congruent.

# Three-Dimensional Figures

**Polyhedrons** are three-dimensional figures made up of polygons which are called **faces.** The sides where faces intersect are **edges.** Any point where three or more edges intersect is a **vertex.**

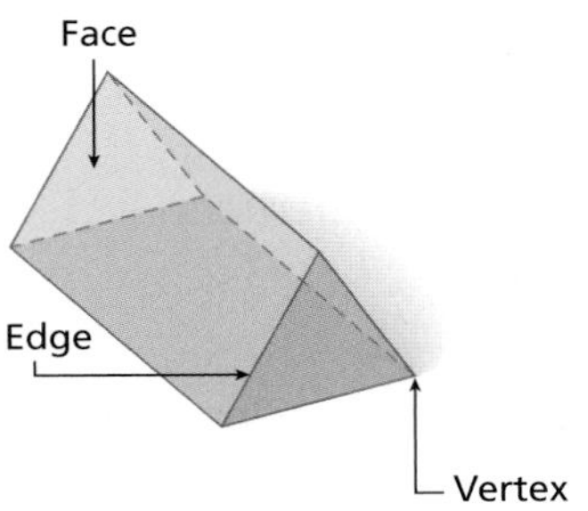


**EXAMPLE 1** **Tell how many faces, edges, and vertices the figure has.**

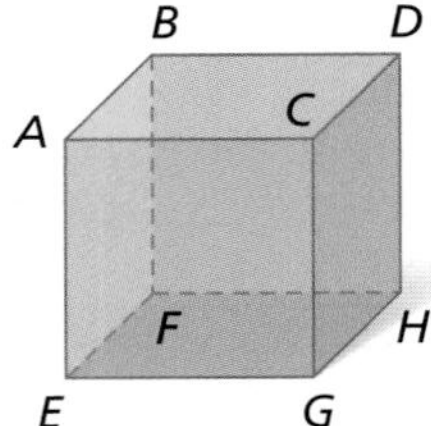


6 faces — *ABCD, ABFE, BFHD, DCGH, ACGE, FHGE*

12 edges — $\overline{AB}$, $\overline{BD}$, $\overline{DC}$, $\overline{AC}$, $\overline{AE}$, $\overline{BF}$, $\overline{DH}$, $\overline{CG}$, $\overline{EF}$, $\overline{FH}$, $\overline{HG}$, $\overline{EG}$

8 vertices — *A, B, C, D, E, F, G, H*

A **prism** has two faces called **bases.** The bases are congruent, parallel polygons. The faces that are not bases are parallelograms. **Pyramids** have only one base, and the faces other than the base are triangles. Both prisms and pyramids are named according to the polygon that forms the base or bases.

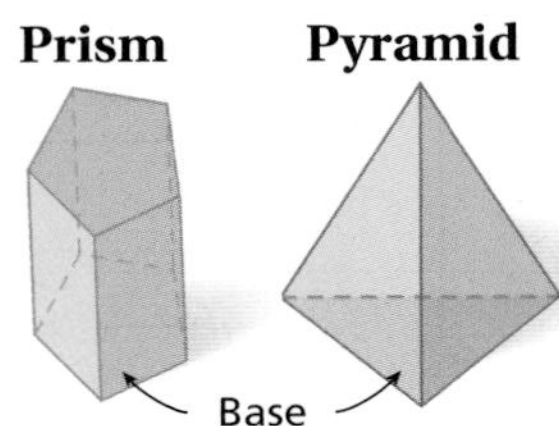


**EXAMPLE 2** **Name each figure.**

**A**

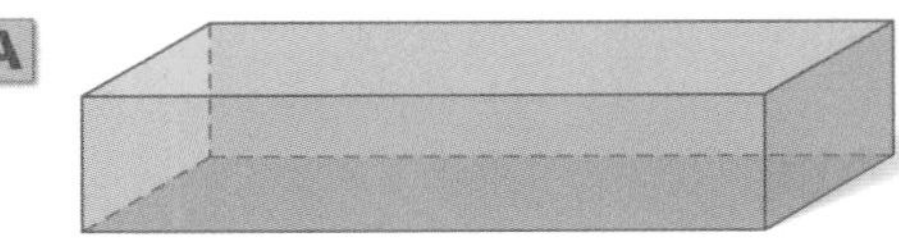

*Two congruent bases*
*Bases are rectangles.*
rectangular prism

**B**

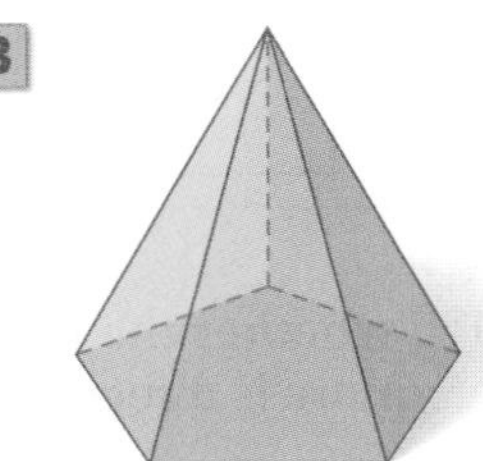

*One base*
*Base is a pentagon.*
pentagonal pyramid

Some three-dimensional figures are not polyhedrons because they are not made up of polygons. **Cones** and **cylinders** have circles as bases. A cone has one base, and a cylinder has two congruent bases.

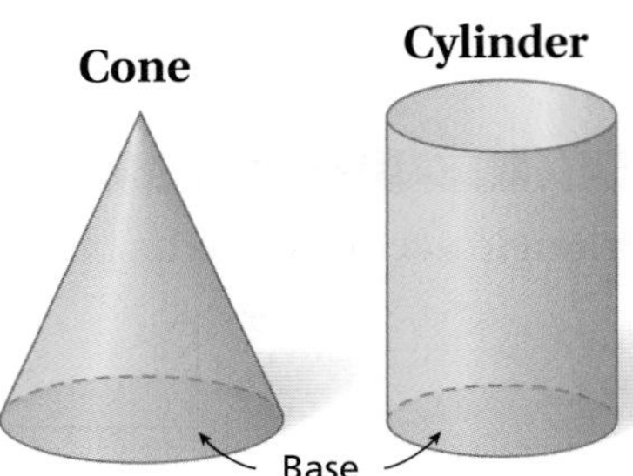


## PRACTICE

**Name each figure. If the figure is a polyhedron, tell how many faces, edges, and vertices the figure has.**

**1.**

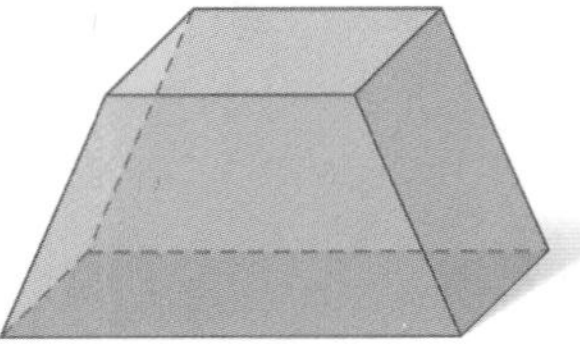

**2.**

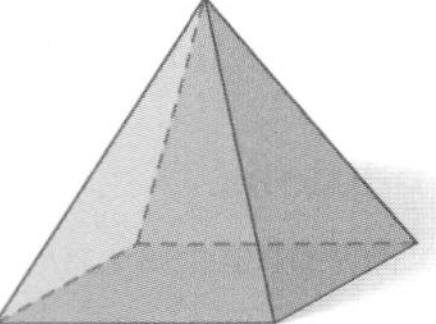

**3.**

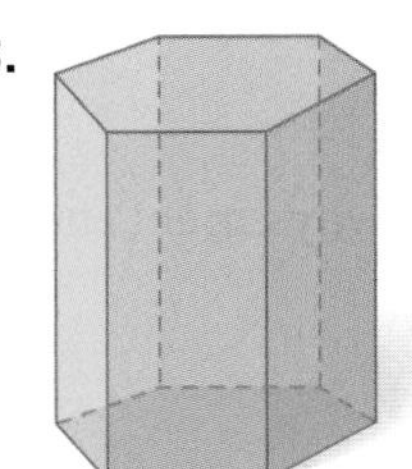

**4.**

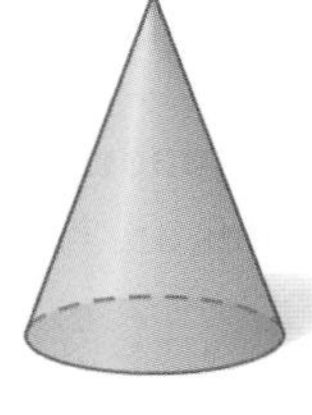

## Draw Three-Dimensional Figures

Three-dimensional figures appear different from different perspectives.

**EXAMPLE 1** **Side views are shown. Draw each figure as viewed from the bottom.**

A

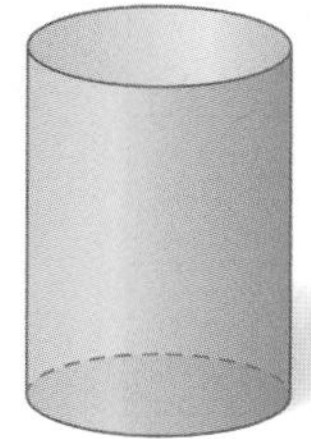

*Pretend you are directly below the figure. You would see only a circle.*

B

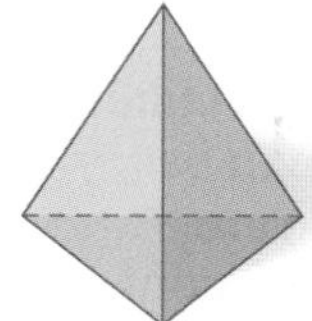

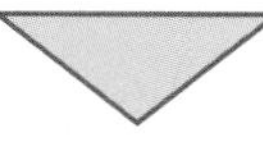

*The base would be seen from a bottom view.*

**EXAMPLE 2** **Draw the top, front, and side views of the figure.**

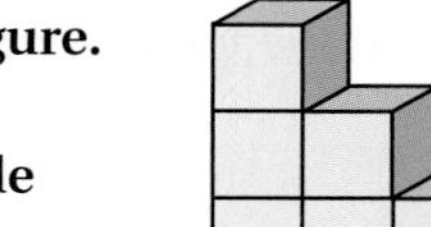

**Top**

*From the top, you can see the faces of 3 cubes.*

**Front**

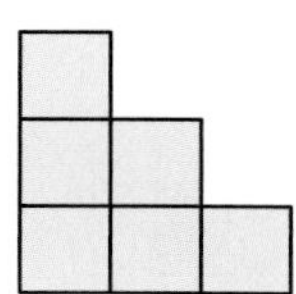

*From the front, you can see the faces of 6 cubes arranged in 3 stacks.*

**Side**

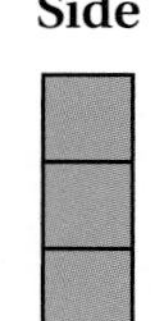

*From the side, you can see the faces of 3 cubes, one from each stack.*

## PRACTICE

**Side views are shown. Draw each figure as viewed from the top.**

**1.** 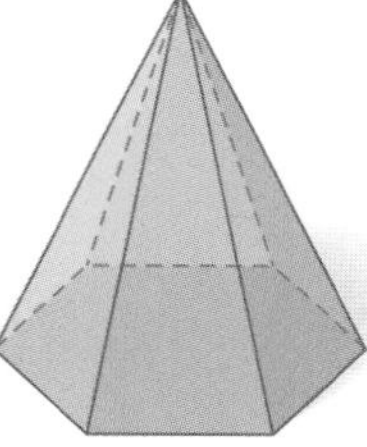

**2.** 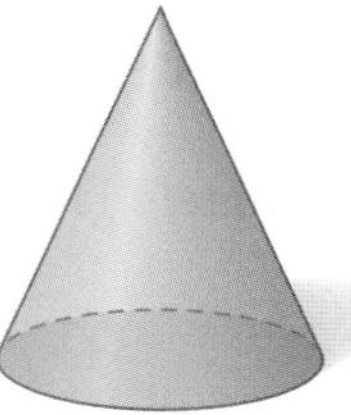

**3.** 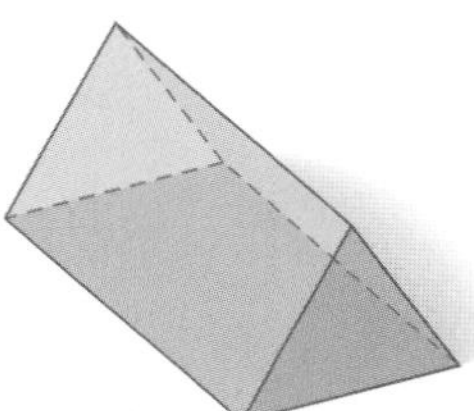

**Side views are shown. Draw each figure as viewed from the top and from the front.**

**4.** 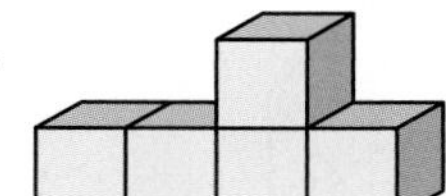

**5.** 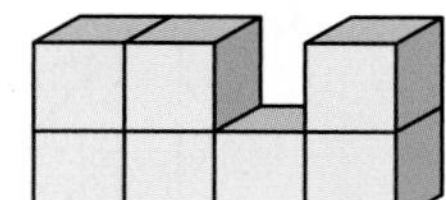

**6.** 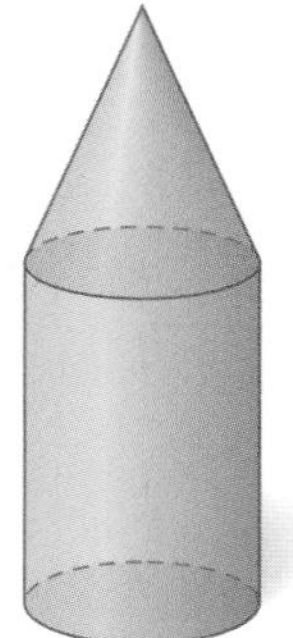

Skills Bank

# Volume

The **volume** of a three-dimensional figure is the number of nonoverlapping cubic units that will exactly fill its interior. The formulas for the volumes of some types of three-dimensional figures are given in the table.

Notice that a cube is listed in the table. A cube is a prism, so the formula for a prism can be used; however, since all sides in a cube are congruent, the formula $s^3$ is more convenient.

| | | |
|---|---|---|
| **Prism** | $Bh$ | $B$: area of base<br>$h$: height of prism |
| **Cube** | $s^3$ | $s$: length of one side |
| **Pyramid** | $\frac{1}{3}Bh$ | $B$: area of base<br>$h$: height of pyramid |
| **Cylinder** | $\pi r^2 h$ | $r$: radius<br>$h$: height |
| **Cone** | $\frac{1}{3}\pi r^2 h$ | $r$: radius<br>$h$: height |

**EXAMPLE 1** **Find the volume of each figure. Use 3.14 for $\pi$.**

**A**

4 in.

3 in.

3 in.

$$V = \frac{1}{3}Bh$$
$$= \frac{1}{3} \times 9 \times 4$$
$$= 3 \times 4$$
$$= 12 \text{ in}^3$$

**B**

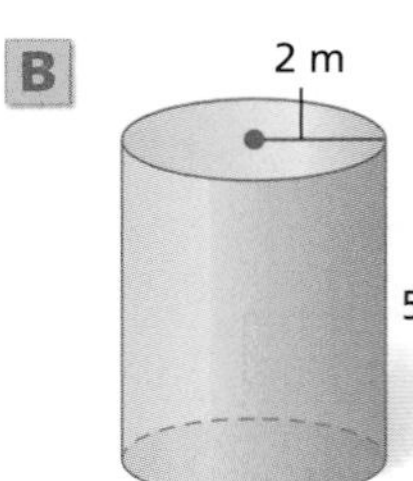


$$V = \pi r^2 h$$
$$\approx 3.14 \times (2^2) \times 5$$
$$\approx 3.14 \times 4 \times 5$$
$$\approx 62.8$$
$$62.8 \text{ m}^3$$

**EXAMPLE 2** **Estimate the volume of the figure.**

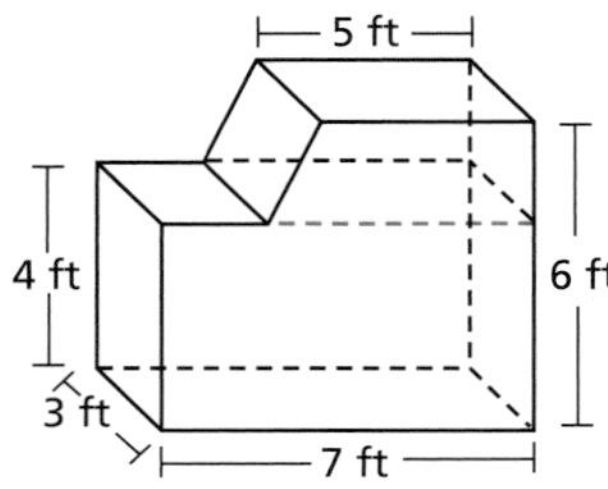


Find the volume of the rectangular prism (bottom part):

$Bh = 21 \times 4 = 84$

Pretend the top part is a rectangular prism with $w = 3$ ft, $\ell = 5$ ft, and $h = 6$ ft $-$ 4 ft $= 2$ ft.

$Bh = 15 \times 2 = 30.$

Add the volumes of the two prisms:

$84 + 30 = 114$

The volume is approximately 114 $\text{ft}^3$.

## PRACTICE

**Find or estimate the volume of each figure. Use 3.14 for $\pi$.**

**1.**

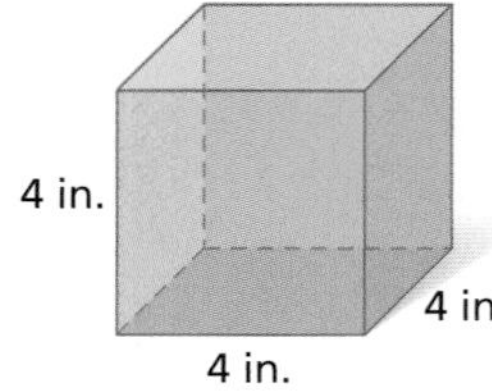


**2.**

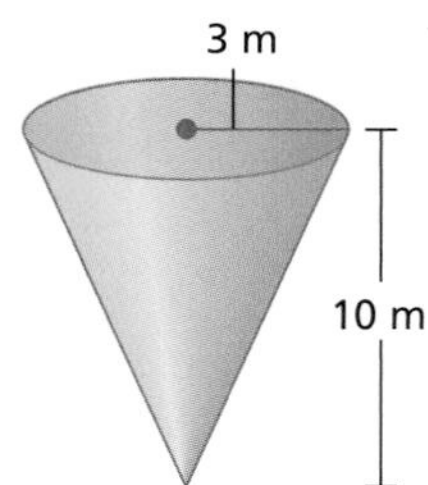


**3.**

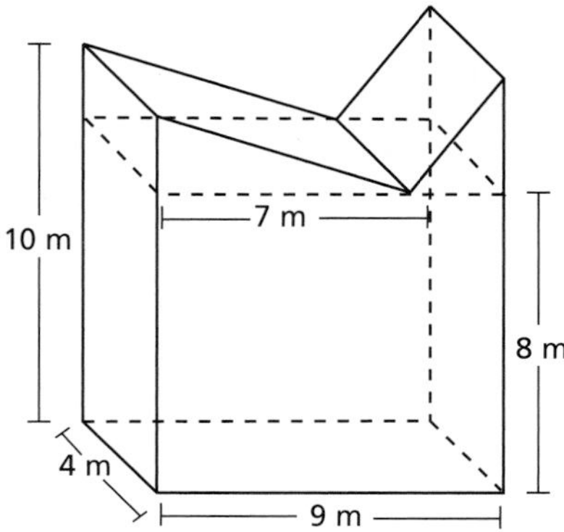

# Surface Area

The **surface area** of a three-dimensional figure is the sum of the areas of its surfaces.

Formulas for the surface areas of some three-dimensional figures are given in the table.

| | | |
|---|---|---|
| **Prism** | $2B + Ph$ | *B:* area of base<br>*h:* height |
| **Pyramid** | $B + \frac{1}{2}P\ell$ | *B:* area of base<br>*P:* perimeter of base<br>$\ell$: slant height |
| **Cube** | $6s^2$ | *s:* length of one side |
| **Cylinder** | $2\pi r^2 + 2\pi rh$ | *r:* radius; *h:* height |
| **Cone** | $\pi r^2 + \pi r\ell$ | *r:* radius; $\ell$: slant height |

**EXAMPLE 1** **Find the surface area of each figure. Use 3.14 for $\pi$.**

**A**

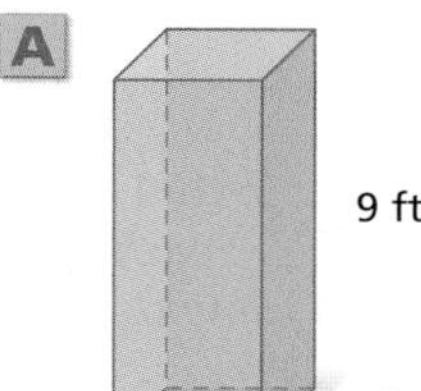


$S = 2B + Ph$
$= 2 \times 20 + 18 \times 9$
$= 40 + 162$
$= 202 \text{ ft}^2$

**B**

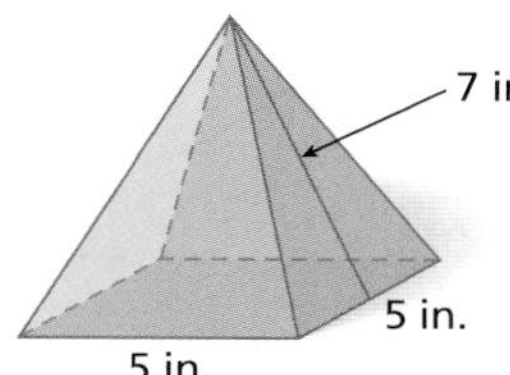

$S = B + \frac{1}{2}P\ell$
$= 25 + \frac{1}{2}(20 \times 7)$
$= 25 + 70$
$= 95 \text{ in}^2$

**C**

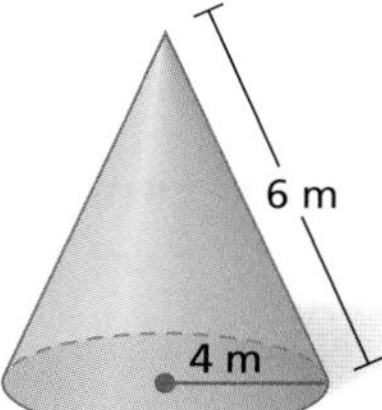


$S = \pi r^2 + \pi r\ell$
$\approx 3.14 \times 4^2 + (3.14 \times 4 \times 6)$
$\approx 50.24 + 75.36$
$\approx 125.6 \text{ m}^2$

**EXAMPLE 2** **The net of a prism is shown below. Estimate the surface area of the prism.**

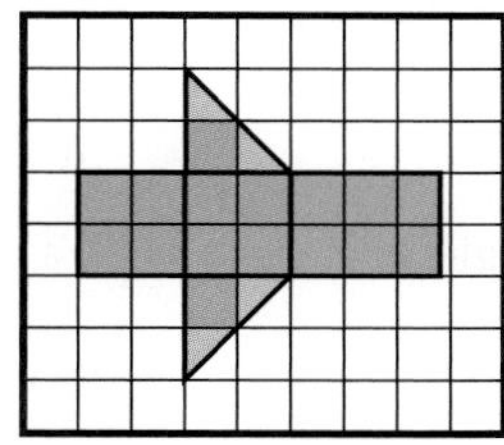

*Count full squares: 16 red squares*

*Count squares that are about half full: 4 blue squares ≈ 2 full squares*

*Add: 16 + 2 = 18*

S ≈ 18 square units

## PRACTICE

**Find or estimate the surface of each figure. Use 3.14 for $\pi$.**

**1.**

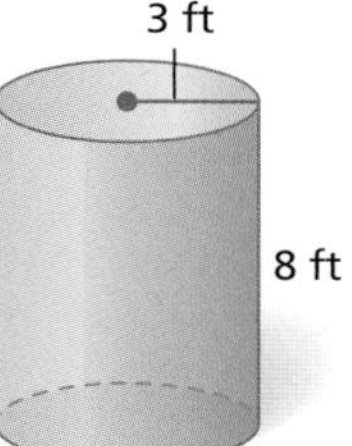


**2.**

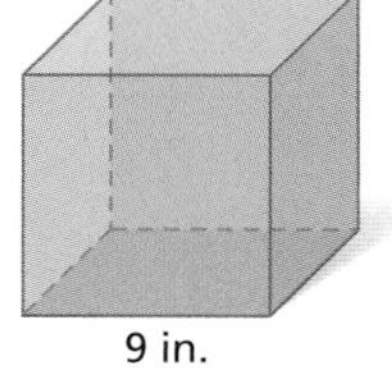


**3.**

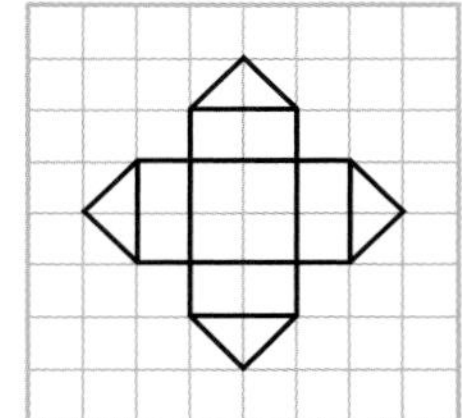

Skills Bank

## Pythagorean Theorem

In the right triangle shown, $a$ and $b$ are the lengths of the legs, and $c$ is the length of the hypotenuse. The **Pythagorean Theorem** states the following: If a triangle is a right triangle, then $a^2 + b^2 = c^2$. The converse of the theorem is also true: For any triangle, if $a^2 + b^2 = c^2$, then the triangle is a right triangle.

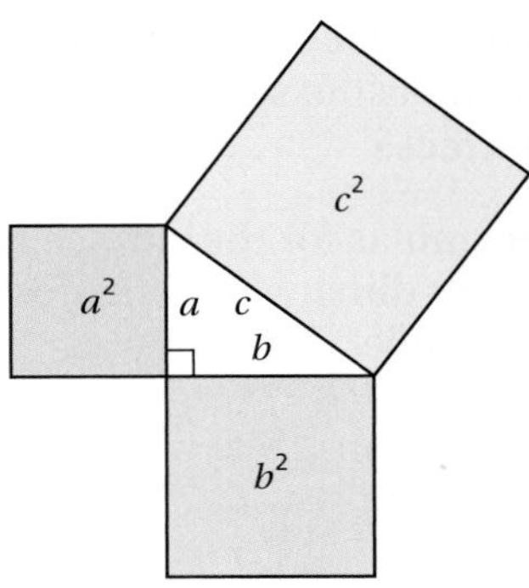


**EXAMPLE 1** **Find the missing measure. Round to the nearest tenth if necessary.**

**A**

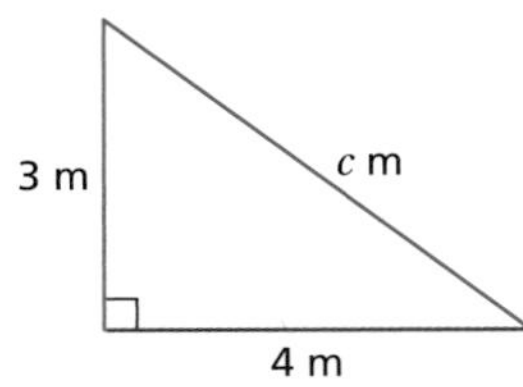


$$a^2 + b^2 = c^2$$
$$3^2 + 4^2 = c^2$$
$$9 + 16 = c^2$$
$$25 = c^2$$
$$\sqrt{25} = \sqrt{c^2}$$
$$5 \text{ m} = c$$

**B**

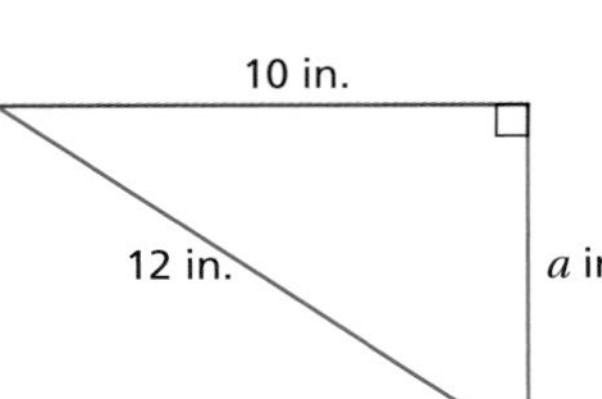


$$a^2 + b^2 = c^2$$
$$a^2 + 10^2 = 12^2$$
$$a^2 + 100 = 144$$
$$a^2 = 44 \quad \textit{Subtract 100 from each side.}$$
$$\sqrt{a^2} = \sqrt{44}$$
$$a \approx 6.6 \text{ in.} \quad \textit{Round.}$$

**EXAMPLE 2** **Determine whether a triangle with side lengths of 8 cm, 14 cm, and 20 cm is a right triangle.**

| $a^2 + b^2$ | $= c^2$ |
|---|---|
| $8^2 + 14^2$ | $20^2$ |
| $64 + 196$ | $400$ |
| $260$ | $400$ ✗ |

*The hypotenuse is always the longest side.*

The triangle is not a right triangle.

## PRACTICE

**Find the missing measure. Round to the nearest tenth if necessary.**

**1.**

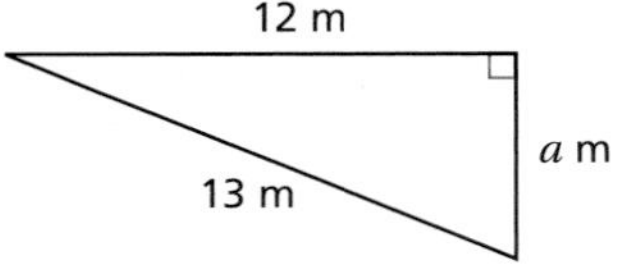


**2.**

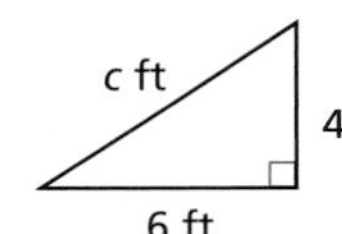


**3.** A leg is 6 ft long and the hypotenuse is 10 ft long.

**4.** Both legs are 20 mm long.

**5.** Determine whether a triangle with side lengths of 16 ft, 30 ft, and 34 ft is a right triangle.

## Midpoint Formula

If a segment in the coordinate plane has endpoints $(x_1, y_1)$ and $(x_2, y_2)$, the coordinates of the midpoint are $\left(\frac{x_1 + x_2}{2}, \frac{y_1 + y_2}{2}\right)$.

**EXAMPLE** **Find the coordinates of the midpoint of the segment with endpoints $A(2, 1)$ and $B(6, 5)$.**

Let $(x_1, y_1) = (2, 1)$.
Let $(x_2, y_2) = (6, 5)$.

$$\left(\frac{x_1 + x_2}{2}, \frac{y_1 + y_2}{2}\right) = \left(\frac{2 + 6}{2}, \frac{1 + 5}{2}\right) = \left(\frac{8}{2}, \frac{6}{2}\right) = (4, 3)$$

## PRACTICE

**Find the coordinates of the midpoint of segment $\overline{AB}$.**

**1.** $A(0, 5)$, $B(-4, 3)$

**2.** $A(6, -2)$, $B(3, -8)$

**3.** $A(4, 9)$, $B(-2, -3)$

# Transformations in the Coordinate Plane

A **transformation** is a change in the size or position of a figure. If the preimage, or original figure, is named *ABC*, then the transformed figure, or image, is named *A′B′C′*. Transformations include **translations** (slides), **reflections** (flips), and **rotations** (turns), for which preimages and images are congruent.

**EXAMPLE** 

**A Translate *ABC* 2 units right and 1 unit up.**

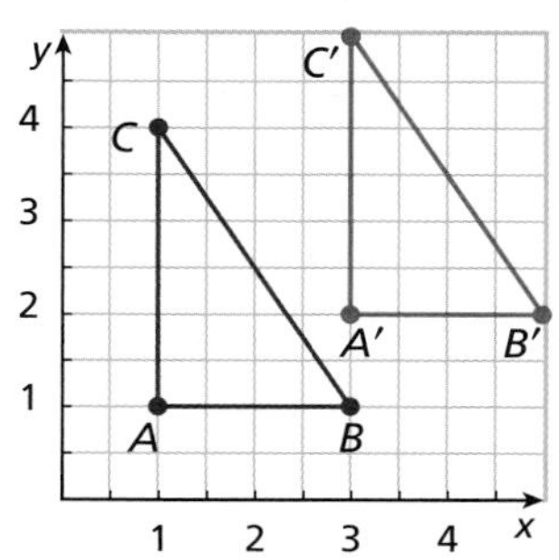


*Move each vertex 2 units right and 1 unit up.*

**B Reflect *ABC* across the *y*-axis.**

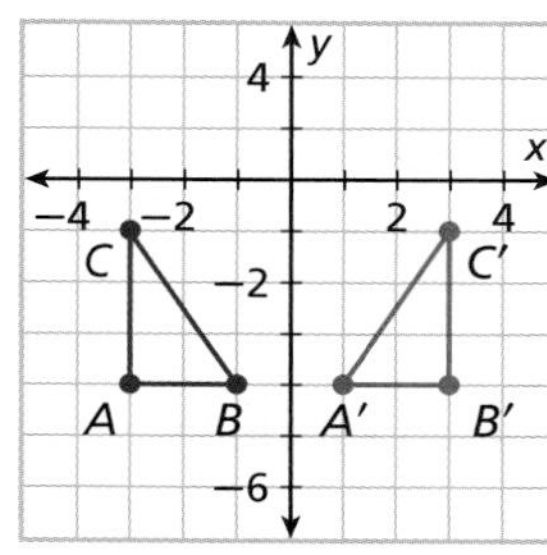


*The y-axis is a line of symmetry.*

**C Rotate *ABC* 90° clockwise about point *A*.**

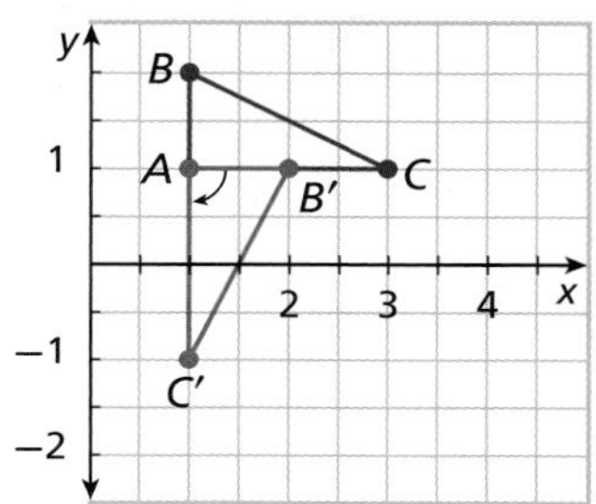


*A′ is the same as A. Maintain the same side lengths on the image.*

**EXAMPLE 2** **Could *ABCD* be transformed into *A′B′C′D′*? Explain.**

*The figures are congruent, so a translation, rotation, or reflection is possible. Study the figures. If A′ B′ C′ D′ is translated 1 unit right, both figures would be symmetric about the x-axis.*

*ABCD* can be transformed into *A′B′C′D′* by reflecting it across the *x*-axis and translating it 1 unit left.

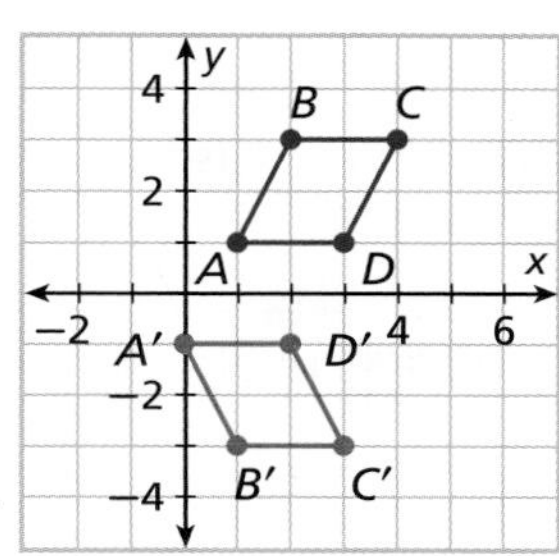


## PRACTICE

1. Translate *ABCD* 2 units left and 4 units down.

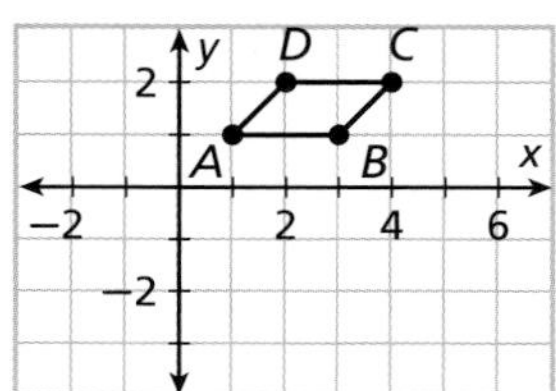


2. Graph triangle *ABC* with vertices $A(1, -2)$, $B(3, -2)$, and $C(2, -4)$. Rotate *ABC* 90° counterclockwise about *A* and reflect it across the *x*-axis.

**Use the graph for Exercises 3 and 4.**

3. Could *ABCD* be transformed into *A′B′C′D′*? Explain.
4. Could *FGHJKL* be transformed into *F′G′H′J′K′L′*? Explain.

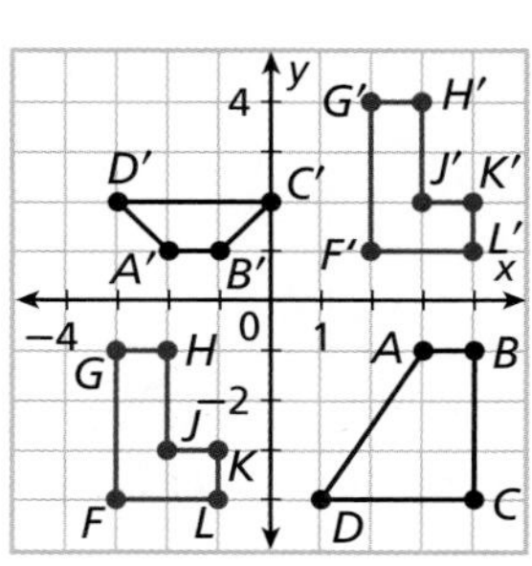

# Dilations in the Coordinate Plane

A **dilation** is a transformation that changes the size, but not the shape, of a figure.
A **scale factor,** $k$, describes how much a figure is enlarged or reduced.
Every dilation has a fixed point, $C$, that is the **center of dilation.**

If a dilation with center $C$ and scale factor $k$ is applied to the preimage, point $P(x, y)$, then the image will be point $(kx, ky)$.

k(CP)
P
P′
image
preimage
center of dilation

If $k$ is the scale factor and $C$ is the center of the dilation:

- when $|k| > 1$, the dilation is an enlargement.
- when $0 < |k| < 1$, the dilation is a reduction.
- when $k$ is positive, $k(x, y) = (kx, ky)$ and $(kx, ky)$ lies on $\overrightarrow{CP}$.
- when $k$ is negative, $|k|(x, y) = (kx, ky)$ and $(kx, ky)$ lies on the ray opposite $\overrightarrow{CP}$.

## EXAMPLES

**A** **Sketch the dilation image of $\overline{AB}$ with center $C$ and scale factor $\frac{1}{3}$.**

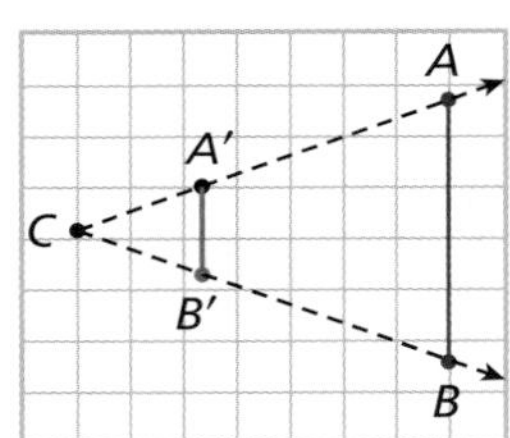


*$k$ is between 0 and 1, so it is a reduction.*

Draw $A'$ so that the length of $\overline{CA'}$ is $\frac{1}{3}$ the length of $\overline{CA}$, and draw $B'$ so that the length of $\overline{CB'}$ is $\frac{1}{3}$ the length of $\overline{CB}$.

**B** **The preimage is blue. The image is shown in red. What scale factor, with center $C$, was used?**

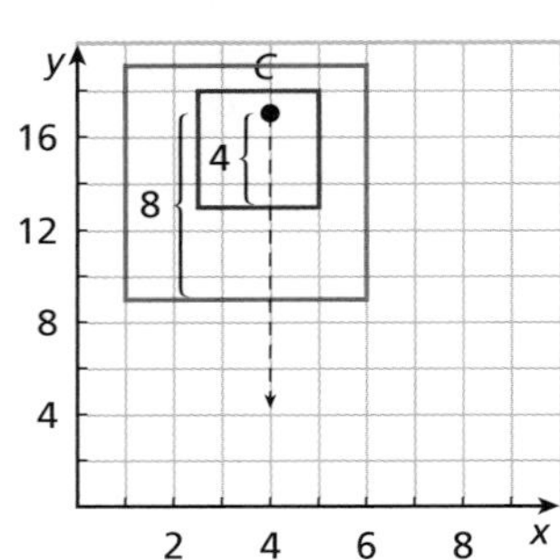


*Count the blocks from $C$ to a point on the image and then from $C$ to a point on the preimage that is on the same ray. Find the ratio.*

The scale factor was $\frac{8}{4} = 2$.

## PRACTICE

1. Sketch the dilation image of $MNO$ with center $C$ and scale factor 4.

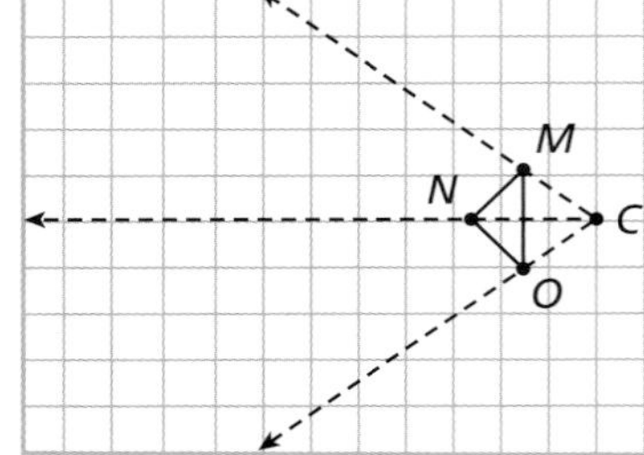


2. The preimage is blue. The image is red. What scale factor, with center $C$, was used?

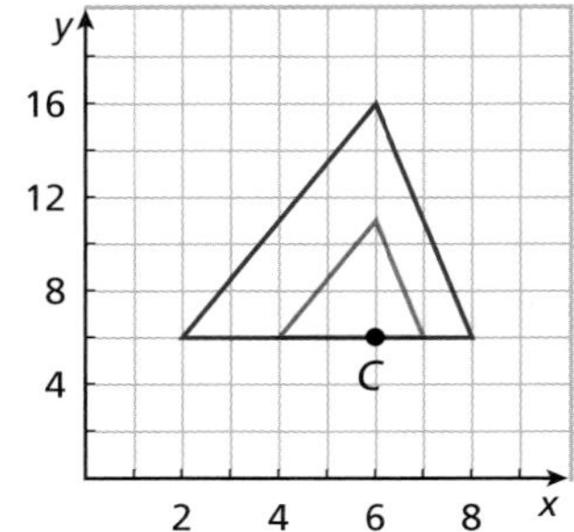

## Line Plots

How often a data value occurs in a data set is called its **frequency.** A **line plot** is a graph made up of a number line and columns of *X*'s (or other markers) to show frequency. Line plots make it easy to identify *gaps* and *clusters* in a data set. A **gap** is a large empty space in a graph. A **cluster** is an isolated group of data values bunched together.

EXAMPLE

**Twenty people went on a tour. Their ages are shown in the frequency table. Create a line plot. Identify any gaps and clusters.**

| Age | Frequency | Age | Frequency |
|---|---|---|---|
| 15 | 2 | 21 | 0 |
| 16 | 0 | 22 | 3 |
| 17 | 1 | 23 | 4 |
| 18 | 1 | 24 | 5 |
| 19 | 1 | 25 | 1 |
| 20 | 0 | 26 | 2 |

*Draw a number line that includes the minimum and maximum data values. Use an X to represent each person. Draw each X the same size. Title the axis and the graph.*

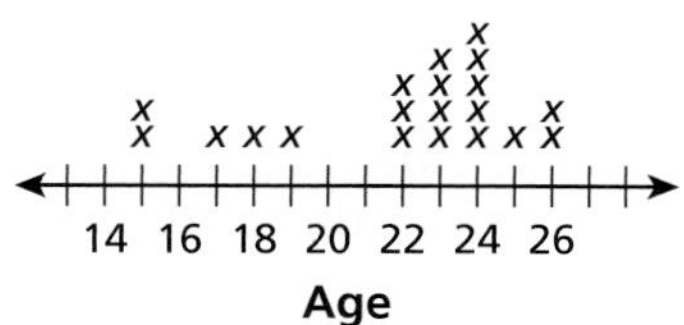


There is a gap between 19 and 22.
There is a cluster from 22 through 26.

## PRACTICE

**Create a line plot for each data set. Identify any gaps and clusters.**

**1.**

| High Temperatures for Two Weeks | | | |
|---|---|---|---|
| Temperature | Frequency | Temperature | Frequency |
| 55 | 2 | 60 | 0 |
| 56 | 0 | 61 | 2 |
| 57 | 0 | 62 | 4 |
| 58 | 0 | 63 | 3 |
| 59 | 2 | 64 | 1 |

**2.** scores on a math test: 75, 81, 82, 84, 92, 76, 77, 77, 81, 75, 95, 83, 84, 90, 84, 76, 76

**Use the line plot for Exercises 3–6.**

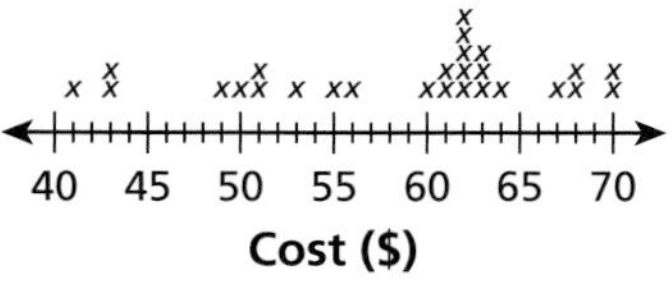


**3.** What are the minimum and maximum prices?

**4.** What is the most common price?

**5.** Where is the largest cluster?

**6.** Where is the largest gap?

# Measures of Central Tendency

**Measures of central tendency** are values that represent the center of a data set and can be considered typical of the set. These measures are the *mean, median,* and *mode.*

| | It is... | Find by... |
|---|---|---|
| **Mean** | The average. | Adding the data values and dividing by the number of values. |
| **Median** | The "middle value." | First ordering the data values from least to greatest.<br>If there are an *odd* number of values, the median is the middle number.<br>If there are an *even* number of values, the median is the mean of the two middle values. |
| **Mode** | The value or values that occur most often. If every value occurs the same number of times, the data set has no mode. | Choosing the value or values that occur more often than any other. |

EXAMPLES **Find the mean, median, and mode of each data set.**

**A** **18, 22, 13, 16, 15, 18, 10**

**mean:**

$$\frac{18 + 22 + 13 + 16 + 15 + 18 + 10}{7} = \frac{112}{7} = 16$$

The mean is 16.

**median:**

*Order the data values from least to greatest. There are an odd number of values. Choose the middle number.*

10, 13, 15, 16, 18, 18, 22

The median is 16.

**mode:**

*Every value occurs once except 18, which occurs twice.*

The mode is 18.

**B** **These are the number of people who attended a seminar each of four days: 102, 96, 88, 109.**

**mean:** $\frac{102 + 96 + 88 + 109}{4} = \frac{395}{4} = 98.75$

The mean is 98.75.

**median:**

*Order the data values from least to greatest. There are an even number of values. Find the mean of the two middle numbers.*

88, 96, 102, 109

$$\frac{96 + 102}{2} = \frac{198}{2} = 99$$

The median is 99.

**mode:**

*Every value occurs once.*

There is no mode.

## PRACTICE

**Find the mean, median, and mode of each data set.**

1.

| High Temperatures (°F) | | | | | | |
|---|---|---|---|---|---|---|
| **Sun** | **Mon** | **Tue** | **Wed** | **Thu** | **Fri** | **Sat** |
| 85 | 81 | 83 | 85 | 86 | 82 | 84 |

2. These are the ages of the students in an after-school club: 14, 15, 14, 16, 15, 17, 14, 15.

3. Jenny took a survey of her classmates to find out how much they each paid for their notebooks. Here are their responses: 85¢, 55¢, 80¢, 85¢, 75¢, 95¢, 85¢, 75¢, 67¢.

## Sampling

A **population** is a group that someone is gathering information about.

A **sample** is part of a population. For example, if 5 students are chosen to represent a class of 20 students, the 5 chosen students are a sample of the population of 20 students.

The sample is a **random sample** if every member of the population had an equal chance of being chosen.

**EXAMPLE** **Explain whether each sample is random.**

**A** **Carlos wrote the name of each student in his class on a slip of paper and put the papers into a hat. Then, without looking at the slips, he drew the names of the students who would complete his survey.**

Each name is in the hat once, so each has an equal chance of being selected. The sample is random.

**B** **Jamal telephoned people on a list of 100 names in the order in which they appeared. He surveyed the first 20 people who answered their phone.**

Names at the beginning of the list have a greater chance of being selected than those at the end of the list, so the sample is not random.

### PRACTICE

**Explain whether each sample is random.**

1. Rebecca surveyed every person in a theater who was sitting in a seat along the aisle.
2. Inez assigned 50 people a number from 1 to 50. Then she used a calculator to generate 10 random numbers from 1 to 50 and surveyed those with matching numbers.

## Bias

**Bias** is error that favors part of a population and/or does not accurately represent the population. Bias can occur from using sampling methods that are not random or from asking confusing or leading questions.

**EXAMPLE** **Explain why each survey is biased.**

**A** **Jenn went to a movie theater and asked people who exited if they agree that the theater should be torn down to build office space.**

People usually only go to movies if they enjoy them, so those exiting a movie theater would not want it torn down. People who do not use the theater did not have a chance to answer.

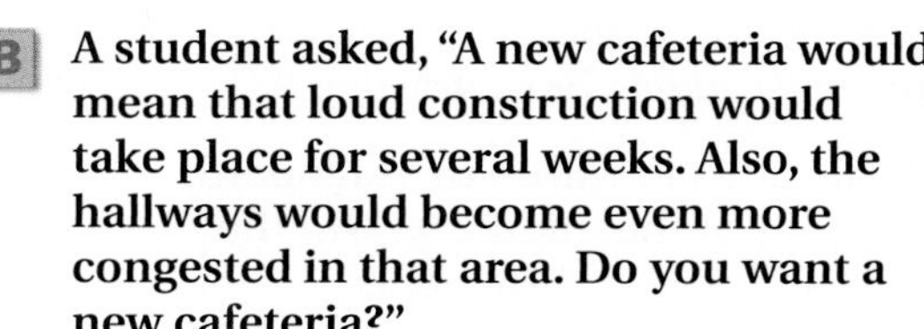

**B** **A student asked, "A new cafeteria would mean that loud construction would take place for several weeks. Also, the hallways would become even more congested in that area. Do you want a new cafeteria?"**

The question only mentions the bad things that could come from a new cafeteria, not the good ones, such as better food or more seats.

### PRACTICE

**Explain why each survey is biased.**

1. A surveyor asked, "Is it not true that you do not oppose the candidate's views?"
2. Brendan asked everyone on his track team how they thought the money from the athletic department fund-raiser should be spent.

## Standard Deviation and the Normal Curve

The **standard deviation** of a data set is a number that describes how spread out the data values are from the mean. Suppose two tests are given and both have the same mean score, but the standard deviations are 2.5 and 6.8. The scores on the test with the standard deviation of 6.8 are more spread out than the scores on the test with the standard deviation of 2.5.

**EXAMPLE 1** **Find the standard deviation of the following data set: 6, 5, 6, 7, 2, 4. Round to the nearest hundredth.**

**Step 1** Find the mean. $(6 + 5 + 6 + 7 + 2 + 4) \div 6 = 5$

**Step 2** Square the difference between each data value and the mean. Use a table to organize the information.

| Data Value | 6 | 5 | 6 | 7 | 2 | 4 |
|---|---|---|---|---|---|---|
| Data Value − Mean | $6 - 5 = 1$ | $5 - 5 = 0$ | $6 - 5 = 1$ | $7 - 5 = 2$ | $2 - 5 = -3$ | $4 - 5 = -1$ |
| (Data Value − Mean)$^2$ | $1^2 = 1$ | $0^2 = 0$ | $1^2 = 1$ | $2^2 = 4$ | $(-3)^2 = 9$ | $(-1)^2 = 1$ |

**Step 3** Find the mean of the squares of the differences. $\frac{1 + 0 + 1 + 4 + 9 + 1}{6} = \frac{16}{6} = 2.\overline{6}$

**Step 4** Take the square root of the quotient. $\sqrt{2.\overline{6}} \approx 1.63$
The standard deviation is approximately 1.63.

Some data sets are **normally distributed,** which means the graph of the distribution is a bell-shaped curve with the mean at the center. In a normal distribution:

- 68% of data fall within one standard deviation of the mean.
- 95% of data fall within two standard deviations of the mean.
- 99.7% of data fall within three standard deviations of the mean.

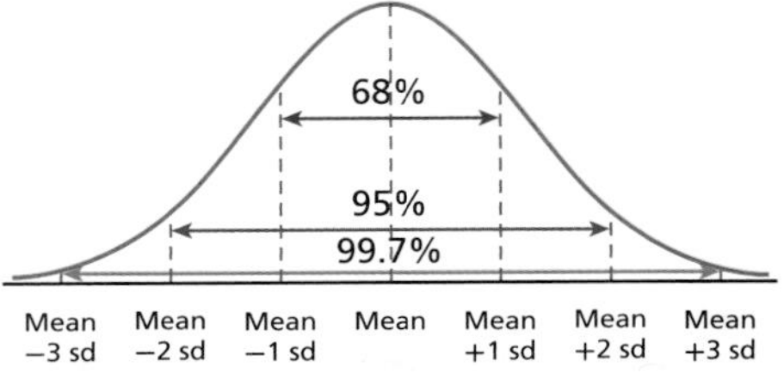


**EXAMPLE 2** **The heights of 1000 men are normally distributed, with a mean of 70 inches and a standard deviation of 3 inches. Between what heights do the middle 95% of the men fall?**

*Sketch a normal curve with 70 at the center. Label the standard deviations above and below the mean by repeatedly adding or subtracting 3.*

Because 95% of the data fall within two standard deviations, the heights of the middle 95% of the men fall between 64 inches and 76 inches.

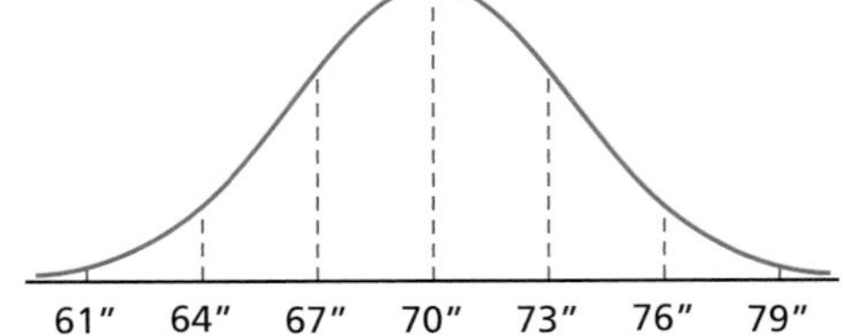


## PRACTICE

**Find the standard deviation of each data set.**

1. 12, 15, 20, 16, 32, 25
2. 10, 15, 9, 5, 8, 6, 10
3. A collection of test scores are normally distributed, with a mean of 80 and a standard deviation of 5. In what range do the middle 68% of the test scores lie?
4. The scores on a certain test are normally distributed, and 99.7% of the test takers scored between 92 and 128. The standard deviation is 6. What is the mean score?

## Cubic Functions

A **cubic function** contains a variable that is raised to the third power. The parent function is $y = x^3$. Its graph is shown at right. Cubic equations such as $x^3 - 2 = 0$ can be solved by graphing the related function $\left(y = x^3 - 2\right)$. Then the solution is the $x$-value where $y = 0$.

**EXAMPLE** **Graph the function $y = 2x^3$. Use the graph to solve the equation $2x^3 = 0$.**

Create a table of ordered pairs. Then plot each point and connect them with a smooth curve. To solve $2x^3 = 0$, find the value of $x$ when $y = 0$. The solution is $x = 0$.

| $x$ | $y = 2x^3$ | $(x, y)$ |
|---|---|---|
| −2 | $2(-2)^3 = 2(-8) = -16$ | (−2, −16) |
| −1 | $2(-1)^3 = 2(-1) = -2$ | (−1, −2) |
| 0 | $2(0)^3 = 2(0) = 0$ | (0, 0) |
| 1 | $2(1)^3 = 2(1) = 2$ | (1, 2) |
| 2 | $2(2)^3 = 2(8) = 16$ | (2, 16) |

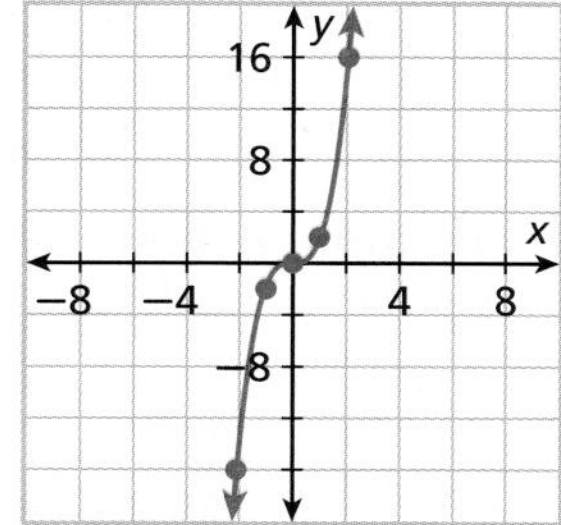


## PRACTICE

**Graph each cubic function.**

**1.** $y = x^3 - 2$ **2.** $y = \frac{1}{2}x^3$ **3.** $y = x^3 + 1$ **4.** $y = -x^3$

**5.** Use a graphing calculator to estimate the solution of $0 = x^3 + 4x - 8$ to the nearest tenth.

## Step Functions

A **step function** is a function whose graph looks like a series of steps. The graph of a step function is made up of unconnected line segments.

**EXAMPLE** **At a garage, parking costs \$5.50 for each hour or fraction of an hour. After 4 hours it costs \$25.00 to park for any amount of time up to 8 hours. Graph this step function.**

Create a table. Use $x$-values to represent time and $y$-values to represent the costs for those times. On the graph, an open circle indicates a value that is *not* included, and a closed circle indicates a value that is included.

| $x$ | $y$ |
|---|---|
| $0 < x \leq 1$ | \$5.50 |
| $1 < x \leq 2$ | \$11.00 |
| $2 < x \leq 3$ | \$16.50 |
| $3 < x \leq 4$ | \$22.00 |
| $4 < x \leq 8$ | \$25.00 |

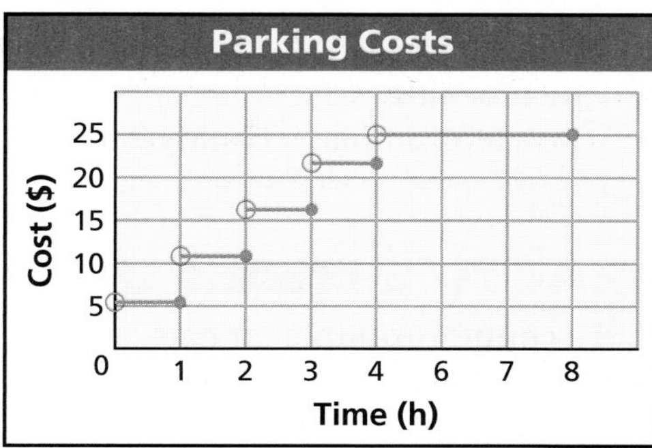


## PRACTICE

**1.** A bookseller gives discounts for book purchases made online and the amount of the discount is based on the cost of the book. A \$2 discount is applied to books costing at least \$20 but less than \$50. A \$5 discount is applied to books costing at least \$50 but less than \$100, and a \$10 discount is applied to books costing at least \$100. No book costs more than \$150. Graph this step function.

## Conditional Statements

If-then statements are called **conditional statements.** The phrase that follows *if* is called the **hypothesis,** and the phrase that follows *then* is called the **conclusion.**
If the hypothesis is true, the conclusion is also true.
If the conclusion is true, the hypothesis *may or may not* be true.

EXAMPLE

**A** **Identify the hypothesis and conclusion: If it is raining, then Jim will go to the movies.**
Hypothesis: It is raining today. Conclusion: Jim will go to the movies.

**B** **If it is raining, then Jim will go to the movies. It is raining. What can you conclude? Explain.**
Jim will go to the movies. The hypothesis is true, so the conclusion is also true.

**C** **If it is raining, then Jim will go to the movies. Jim goes to the movies. What can you conclude? Explain.**
Nothing can be concluded. Jim may have gone to the movies for reasons other than rain.

Skills Bank

### PRACTICE

1. Identify the hypothesis and conclusion: If it is Thursday, then Paulo has soccer practice.
2. If it is Thursday, then Paulo has soccer practice. Paulo has soccer practice today. What can you conclude? Explain.
3. Identify the hypothesis and conclusion: All dogs have four legs. (*Hint:* Write in if-then form first.)
4. All dogs have four legs. Barry is a dog. What can you conclude? Explain.

## Counterexamples

**Conjectures** are guesses and could be either true or false. If a conjecture is true, then it is *always* true. Therefore, just one example is enough to prove a conjecture false. An example that proves a conjecture false is called a **counterexample.**

EXAMPLE **Find a counterexample for each conjecture.**

**A** **If the clock reads 5:55, then it is early in the morning.**
Counterexample: It could be 5:55 P.M.

**B** **If $xy$ is a positive number, then $x$ and $y$ are both positive.**
Counterexample: $(-2)(-3) = 6$

### PRACTICE

**Find a counterexample for each conjecture.**

1. If an integer is divisible by 2, then it is also divisible by 4.
2. If the DVD recorder did not record the program, then the recorder is broken.

## Inductive and Deductive Reasoning

**Inductive reasoning** involves examining a set of data to determine a pattern and then making a conjecture about the data. Sometimes inductive reasoning can lead to different conclusions. In contrast, **deductive reasoning** uses logical reasoning based on given statements that are assumed to be true.

EXAMPLE **1** **Use inductive reasoning to predict the value of the 100th term in the sequence 1, 5, 9, 13, 17, ... .**

Examine the numbers and look for a pattern.

| Term | 1st | 2nd | 3rd | 4th | 5th |
|---|---|---|---|---|---|
| Value | 1 | 5 | 9 | 13 | 17 |
| Pattern | $1 + (0)(4)$ | $1 + (1)(4)$ | $1 + (2)(4)$ | $1 + (3)(4)$ | $1 + (4)(4)$ |

Each term is 4 more than the previous term. The rule $1 + (n - 1)(4)$ can be used to find any term $n$. So a reasonable prediction for the value of the 100th term is $1 + (99)(4) = 397$.

EXAMPLE **2** **Use deductive reasoning to make a conclusion based on the given statements.**

**Given: If it is raining, the grass is wet.**
**Given: It is raining.**

Conclusion: The grass is wet.

*Hypothesis: It is raining.Conclusion: The grass is wet.*

*If the hypothesis is true, the conclusion is always true.*

## PRACTICE

**Use inductive reasoning to predict the value of the given term in each sequence.**

1. 100th term: 2, 4, 6, 8, 10, ...
2. 50th term: 5, 10, 15, 20, 25, ...
3. 28th term: 0, 3, 6, 9, 12, ...
4. 77th term: 12, 8, 4, 0, −4, ...

**Use deductive reasoning to make a conclusion based on the given statements.**

5. **Given:** Darla bowls in a bowling league every Tuesday.
   **Given:** Today is Tuesday.
6. **Given:** A quadrilateral with two pairs of parallel sides is a parallelogram.
   **Given:** A rectangle is a quadrilateral with two pairs of parallel sides.

**Determine if the reasoning used was inductive or deductive. Explain.**

7. Sandra visited San Diego four times. Each time it was raining. Sandra concludes, “San Diego is a very rainy city.”
8. Charlie’s mother told him that if he wants to go out Friday night, then he has to clean his room. Charlie wants to go out Friday night. He concluded that he has to clean his room.
9. Looking at the series 3, 9, 27, 81, ..., Trina concludes that the next number is 243 because each term is three times the previous term.

Skills Bank

## Set Theory

A **set** is a collection of objects. Each object is called an **element** of the set. A set can have no elements, a finite number of elements, or an infinite number of elements. A set that contains no elements is called the **null** or **empty** set. The null set is symbolized by $\varnothing$ or $\{\}$.

Set $A$ is a **subset** of set $B$ $(A \subset B)$, if each element of $A$ is also in $B$.

The **intersection** of sets $A$ and $B$ $(A \cap B)$, is the set of all elements that are in both $A$ and $B$.

The **union** of $A$ and $B$ $(A \cup B)$, is the set of all elements that are in $A$ or $B$.

**EXAMPLE** **Tell whether $A \subset B$. Then find $A \cap B$ and $A \cup B$.**

$A = \{2, 7, 8, 10\}$; $B = \{2, 5, 7, 8, 9, 11, 13\}$

$A \not\subset B$ — *10 is an element of A but not an element of B.*

$A \cap B = \{2, 7, 8\}$ — *2, 7, and 8 are in both sets.*

$A \cup B = \{2, 5, 7, 8, 9, 10, 11, 13\}$ — *Elements belonging to both sets are listed only once.*

### PRACTICE

**Tell whether $A \subset B$, $B \subset A$, or neither. Then find $A \cap B$ and $A \cup B$.**

1. $A = \{\text{red, blue, yellow}\}$; $B = \{\text{green, red}\}$
2. $A = \{2, 14, 15, 20\}$; $B = \{2, 20\}$

## Field Properties

The table shows properties of addition and multiplication where $a$, $b$, and $c$ are real numbers. A property is said to hold for a set of numbers if it is true for each element of the set.

| | Addition | Multiplication |
|---|---|---|
| **Commutative** | $a + b = b + a$ | $ab = ba$ |
| **Associative** | $(a + b) + c = a + (b + c)$ | $(ab)c = a(bc)$ |
| **Inverse** | $a + (-a) = 0$ | $a \times \frac{1}{a} = 1, a \neq 0$ |
| **Identity** | $a + 0 = a$ | $a \times 1 = a$ |
| **Closure** | $a + b$ is a real number. | $ab$ is a real number. |
| **Distributive** | $a(b + c) = ab + ac$ | |

**EXAMPLE 1** **Name the property shown by $25 + (-25) = 0$.**

Inverse Property of Addition

**EXAMPLE 2** **Does the Closure Property hold for the set of negative integers under multiplication? Justify your answer.**

No; $(-2)(-3) = 6$, and since 6 is not an element of the set of negative integers, the property does not hold.

### PRACTICE

**Name the property shown.**

1. $7 + 4 = 4 + 7$
2. $23 \times 1 = 23$
3. $2(4 + 7) = 8 + 14$
4. $(9 \times 3)2 = 9(3 \times 2)$

**Tell whether the Closure Property holds for each set under the given operation. Justify your answer.**

5. whole numbers; multiplication
6. $\{1, 2, 3\}$; addition

# Selected Answers

## Chapter 1

### 1-1

**Check It Out!** **1a.** 4 decreased by $n$; $n$ less than 4 **1b.** the quotient of $t$ and 5; $t$ divided by 5 **1c.** the sum of 9 and $q$; $q$ added to 9 **1d.** the product of 3 and $h$; 3 times $h$ **2a.** $65t$ **2b.** $m + 5$ **2c.** $32d$ **3a.** 6 **3b.** 7 **3c.** 3 **4. a.** $63s$, **b.** 756 bottles; 1575 bottles; 3150 bottles

**Exercises** **1.** variable **3.** the quotient of $f$ and 3; $f$ divided by 3 **5.** 9 decreased by $y$; $y$ less than 9 **7.** the sum of $t$ and 12; $t$ increased by 12 **9.** $x$ decreased by 3; the difference of $x$ and 3 **11.** $w + 4$ **13.** 12 **15.** 6 **17.** the product of 5 and $p$; 5 groups of $p$ **19.** the sum of 3 and $x$; 3 increased by $x$ **21.** negative 3 times $s$; the product of negative 3 and $s$ **23.** 14 decreased by $t$; the difference of 14 and $t$ **25.** $t + 20$ **27.** 1 **29.** 2 **31a.** $h - 40$, **b.** 0; 4; 8; 12 **33.** $2x$ **35.** $y + 10$ **37.** $9w$; 9 in$^2$; 72 in$^2$; 81 in$^2$; 99 in$^2$ **39.** 13; 14; 15; 16 **41.** 6; 10; 13; 15 **43a.** $47.84 + m$; **b.** $58.53 - s$ **45.** $x + 7$; 19; 21 **47.** $x + 3$; 15; 17 **49.** F **51.** 36 **53.** 1 **55.** 45° **57.** 90° **59.** $\frac{1}{2}$ **61.** 1 **63.** Multiply the previous term by 3; 729, 2187, 6561.

### 1-2

**Check It Out!** **1a.** 4 **1b.** −10 **1c.** 1.5 **2a.** −12 **2b.** −35.8 **2c.** −16 **3a.** −8 **3b.** 4 **3c.** −2 **4.** 13,018 ft

**Exercises** **1.** opposite **3.** −8.5 **5.** $9\frac{1}{4}$ **7.** 1 **9.** −13 **11.** $-1\frac{3}{5}$ **13.** 4 **15.** $-11\frac{3}{4}$ **17.** −30 **19.** 14 **21.** $-\frac{1}{2}$ **23.** 23°F **25.** 0.75 **27.** $-12\frac{2}{5}$ **29.** −12 **31.** 37 **33.** 0 **35.** $\frac{1}{10}$ **37.** $>$ **39.** $>$ **41.** $<$ **43.** 11,331 ft **45.** always **47.** A **51.** F **53.** −9 **55.** 2 **57.** Subtract 4; −2, −6, −10. **59.** 12,660.5 ft **61.** 44 in$^2$ **63.** 13 cm **65.** 12 **67.** 4

### 1-3

**Check It Out!** **1a.** −7 **1b.** 44 **1c.** −42 **2a.** $\frac{1}{12}$ **2b.** $-\frac{1}{4}$ **2c.** $-\frac{1}{2}$ **3a.** 0 **3b.** undefined **3c.** 0 **4.** 7.875 mi

**Exercises** **3.** −121 **5.** 7 **7.** −2 **9.** undefined **11.** 0 **13.** about \$210,000,000 **15.** −32 **17.** $-\frac{3}{5}$ **19.** 3 **21.** 0 **23.** 0 **25.** −15°F **27.** −4 **29.** −62 **31.** 18.75 **33.** 1 **35.** −12 **37.** 6 **39.** negative **41.** negative **43.** positive **45.** undefined **47.** 1 **49.** $\frac{1}{2}$ **51.** $-\frac{1}{5}$ **53.** $\frac{9}{8}$ **55.** 15 h per semester **57.** $<$ **59.** $<$ **61.** $=$ **63a.** positive **b.** negative **c.** The product of two negative numbers is positive. The product of that positive number and a negative number is negative. **d.** no **65.** $75\left(\frac{1}{15}\right)$ **67.** $-121\left(\frac{1}{11}\right)$ **69.** sometimes **73.** B **75.** 16 quarter notes **77.** $\frac{25}{49}$ **79.** 5 **81.** 1 **83.** $-\frac{27}{64}$ **85.** Multiply by −2; −16, 32, −64. **87.** The numbers are alternating positive and negative multiples of 5; 30, −35, 40. **89.** \$85 **91.** hexagon **93.** triangle **95.** −6 **97.** 8

### 1-4

**Check It Out!** **1a.** $2^2$ **1b.** $x^3$ **2a.** −125 **2b.** −36 **2c.** $\frac{27}{64}$ **3a.** $8^2$ **3b.** $(-3)^3$ **4.** $2^8 = 256$

**Exercises** **1.** the number of times to use the base as a factor **3.** $2^3$ **5.** 49 **7.** −32 **9.** $9^2$ **11.** $(-4)^3$ **13.** $3^4$ **15.** $3^5 = 243$ **17.** $3^3$ **19.** 27 **21.** −16 **23.** $7^2$ **25.** $(-2)^3$ **27.** $4^3$ **29.** $2^4 = 16$ **31.** $<$ **33.** $=$ **35.** $=$ **37.** $>$ **39.** 8 **41.** −64 **43.** −1 **45.** $\frac{1}{27}$ **47a.** 36 in$^2$ **b.** 9 in$^2$ **c.** 27 in$^2$ **49.** $6^2$ **51.** $(-1)^4$ **53.** $\left(\frac{1}{9}\right)^3$ **55.** between 8000 cm$^3$ and 15,625 cm$^3$ **57.** 2 **59.** 4 **61.** 2 **63.** 4 **65a.** 100, 1000, 10,000 **b.** The exponent is the same as the number of zeros in the number. **67.** C **69.** B **71.** 64 **73.** 65,536 **75a.** $4 \cdot 4$; $4 \cdot 4 \cdot 4$ **b.** $4 \cdot 4 \cdot 4 \cdot 4 \cdot 4 = 4^5$ **c.** $2 + 3 = 5$; the sum of the exponents in $4^2$ and $4^3$ is the exponent in the product $4^5$. **77.** 5 **79.** 5 minus $x$; $x$ less than 5 **81.** $c$ divided by $d$; the quotient of $c$ and $d$ **83.** $\frac{5}{2}$ **85.** 280

### 1-5

**Check It Out!** **1a.** 2 **1b.** −5 **2.** about 6.2 **3a.** rational number, repeating decimal **3b.** rational number, terminating decimal, integer **3c.** irrational number

**Exercises** **1.** any negative integer **3.** 15 **5.** 13 **7.** rational number, terminating decimal, integer **9.** irrational number **11.** 11 **13.** −10 **15.** 14.9 yd **17.** rational number, terminating decimal, integer, whole number, natural number **19.** irr. **21.** $>$ **23.** $=$ **25.** 6 in. **27.** 45; rational number, terminating decimal, integer, whole number, natural number **29.** 34.625; rational number, terminating decimal **31.** always **33.** always **35.** whole numbers **37.** positive rational numbers **39.** positive rational numbers **41.** irrational numbers **43a.** $c^2 = 169$; $c = 13$ **b.** 130 ft **45.** A **47.** B **49.** 0.5 **51.** 1.5 **53.** no **55.** 168 in$^3$ **57.** $\frac{1}{2}$ **59.** −81 **61.** 196

### 1-6

**Check It Out!** **1a.** 48 **1b.** 2.6 **1c.** 2 **2a.** 15 **2b.** 3 **3a.** 1 **3b.** −3 **3c.** 21 **4.** $6.2(9.4 + 8)$ **5.** 400

**Exercises** **3.** 15 **5.** −9 **7.** 14 **9.** 1 **11.** 14 **13.** 92 **15.** 1.5 **17.** −3 **19.** −22 **21.** $12(-2 + 6)$ **23.** 188.4 ft$^2$ **25.** 19 **27.** −15 **29.** 3 **31.** −5 **33.** 24 **35.** 17 **37.** −9 **39.** 17 **41.** −7 **43.** 0 **45.** $\frac{1}{4}$ **47.** 1 **49.** 6 **51.** $3 - \frac{2}{5}$ **53.** $8 - |3 \cdot 5|$ **55a.** 55 **b.** 498 **c.** 250 **d.** 10 **e.** 30 **f.** 70 **57.** $2[9 + (-x)]$ **59.** $\frac{\sqrt{7}}{3 \cdot 10}$ **63.** $3 \cdot 5 - 6 \cdot 2 = 3$ **69.** H **71.** −3 **73.** 6 **77.** 20 **79.** acute **81.** 100 **83.** −11 **85.** 8 **87.** $\frac{6}{7}$

### 1-7

**Check It Out!** **1a.** 21 **1b.** 560 **1c.** 28 **2a.** $9(50) + 9(2) = 468$ **2b.** $12(100) - 12(2) = 1176$

Selected Answers

**2c.** $7(30) + 7(4) = 238$ **3a.** $100p$ **3b.** $-28.5t$ **3c.** $3m^2 + m^3$ **4a.** $6x - 15$ **4b.** $3a - 16x$

**Exercises** **1.** Associative Property of Addition **3.** 24 **5.** 56 **7.** 118,000 **9.** 304 **11.** 456 **13.** 763 **15.** $20x$ **17.** $-9r$ **19.** $7.9x$ **21.** $9a - 31$ **23.** $7x - 3x^2$ **25.** $2a + 2$ **39.** $-3x - 14$ **43.** $13y - 10$ **45a.** Amy: 98:21; Julie: 81:12; Mardi: 83:39; Sabine: 63:47 **b.** Sabine, Julie, Mardi, Amy **47.** Commutative Property of Addition **49.** Distributive Property **51.** Distributive Property **53.** $6p + 9$ **57a.** equal **b.** $96\pi$ **c.** $2(16\pi) + 96\pi = 128\pi$ **59.** J **61.** $12x + 116$ **63.** $-3b - 7$ **65a.** Commutative Property of Addition **b.** Associative Property of Addition **c.** Distributive Property **d.** Rule for subtraction **67.** 36 ft$^2$ **69.** 64

## 1-8

**Check It Out!**

**1a.**
**1b.**
**1c.**

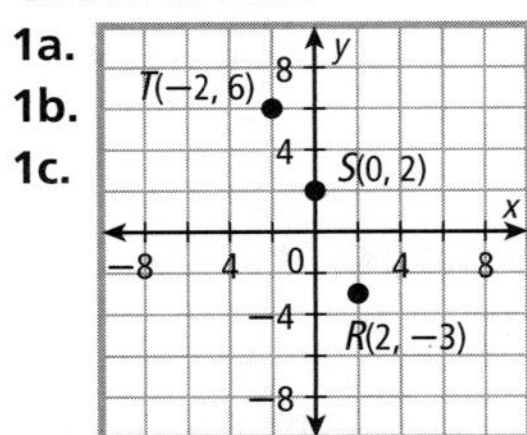


**2a.** none **2b.** I **2c.** III **2d.** II **3.** $y = 10 + 20x$; (1, 30), (2, 50), (3, 70), (4, 90) **4a.** (−4, −6), (−2, −5), (0, −4), (2, −3), (4, −2); line **4b.** (−3, 30), (−1, 6), (0, 3), (1, 6), (3, 30); U shape **4c.** (0, 2), (1, 1), (2, 0), (3, 1), (4, 2); V shape

**Exercises** **7.** none **9.** none **11.** I **13.** (−2, 0), (−1, 1), (0, 2), (1, 3), (2, 4); line **15.** (−2, −4), (−1, −2), (0, 0), (1, −2), (2, −4); V shape **21.** none **23.** none **25.** II **27.** $y = 500 + 0.10x$; (500, 550), (3000, 800), (5000, 1000), (7500, 1250) **29.** (−2, −4), (−1, −1), (0, 0), (1, −1), (2, −4); U shape **31.** (−2, 7), (−1, 4), (0, 3), (1, 4), (2, 7); U shape **33.** triangle **35.** rectangle **37a.** $f$ = yards; $c$ = total cost; $c = 2.90f$ **b.** $f$ is input; $c$ is output.

**c.**

| $f$ | $c$ |
|---|---|
| 1 | 2.90 |
| 2 | 5.80 |
| 3 | 8.70 |
| 4 | 11.60 |
| 5 | 14.50 |
| 6 | 17.40 |
| 7 | 20.30 |
| 8 | 23.20 |

**d.** 7 yards **39.** $y = \frac{1}{2}x + (-3)$; (−4,−5), (−2, −4), (0, −3), (2, −2), (4, −1); line **41a.** $y = 50 + 1.5x$ **b.** (100, 200); (150, 275); (200, 350); (250, 425); (300, 500) **43.** line **45.** line **51.** G **53.** H **57.** (−4, 4) **59.** The points make a horizontal line at $y = 6$. **61.** (−4, 5); 42 square units **63.** cylinder **65.** pentagon **67.** irrational **69.** rational, terminating decimal, integer **71.** $x^2 + 3x$

## Study Guide: Review

**1.** constant **2.** whole numbers **3.** coefficient **4.** origin **5.** $1.99g$ **6.** $t + 3$ **7.** 5 **8.** 5 **9.** 6 **10.** $150 \div m$; 30; 25; 15 **11.** −14 **12.** −4.6 **13.** $4\frac{1}{2}$ **14.** −1 **15.** −24 **16.** 14.3 **17.** 5 **18.** 2231 ft **19.** 90 **20.** 0 **21.** −15.2 **22.** −8 **23.** 0 **24.** undefined **25.** 9 **26.** $-\frac{2}{3}$ **27.** $\frac{15}{7}$ **28.** 3,650,000 steps **29.** 64 **30.** −27 **31.** 81 **32.** −25 **33.** $\frac{8}{27}$ **34.** $\frac{16}{25}$ **35.** $2^4$ **36.** $(-10)^3$ **37.** $(-8)^2$ **38.** $12^1$ **39.** 729 in$^3$ **40.** 6 **41.** 14 **42.** −7 **43.** −12 **44.** $\frac{5}{6}$ **45.** $\frac{1}{13}$ **46.** rational number, terminating decimal, integer, whole number, natural number **47.** rational number, terminating decimal, integer, whole number **48.** rational number, terminating decimal, integer **49.** rational number, terminating decimal **50.** irrational number **51.** rational number, repeating decimal **52.** 3.6 ft **53.** 23 **54.** 8 **55.** 6 **56.** $\frac{1}{2}$ **57.** −18 **58.** 0 **59.** 62 **60.** 10 **61.** 8 **62.** 10 **63.** $8 + 7(-2)$ **64.** $\frac{12}{8+3}$ **65.** $4\sqrt{20 - x}$ **66.** 168 ft **67.** 40 **68.** 270 **69.** $13(100) + 13(3) = 1339$ **70.** $18(100) - 18(1) = 1782$ **71.** $4x$ **72.** $7y^2$ **73.** $4x + 24$ **74.** $2x^2 + 2$ **75.** $-4y + 3y^2$ **76.** $8y - a$ **77.** $8.84

**78–81.**

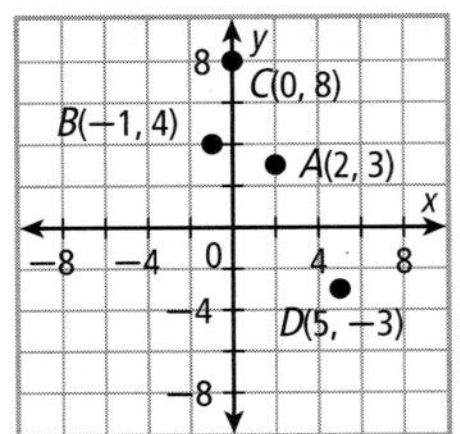


**82.** I **83.** IV **84.** I **85.** II **86.** III **87.** IV **88.** $y = p + \frac{1}{20}p$; $2.10; $15.75; $31.50; $42.00 **89.** (−4, 4), $\left(-1, \frac{1}{4}\right)$, (0, 0), $\left(1, \frac{1}{4}\right)$, (4, 4); U shape

# Chapter 2

## 2-1

**Check It Out!** **1a.** 8.8 **1b.** 0 **1c.** 25 **2a.** $\frac{1}{2}$ **2b.** −10 **2c.** 8 **3a.** 9.3 **3b.** 2 **3c.** 44 **4.** 35 years old

**Exercises** **3.** 21 **5.** 16.3 **7.** $\frac{1}{2}$ **9.** 0 **11.** 2.3 **13.** 1.2 **15.** 32 **17.** 3.7 **19.** $\frac{17}{6}$ **21.** 9 **23.** 17 **25.** $\frac{4}{7}$ **27.** 10.5 **29.** 9 **31.** 0 **33.** −17 **35.** −3100 **37.** −0.5 **39.** 0.05 **41.** 15 **43.** 1545 **45.** 30 **47.** $\frac{1}{3}$ **49.** $a + 500 = 4732$; $4232 **51.** $x - 10 = 12$; $x = 22$ **53.** $x + 8 = 16$; $x = 8$ **55.** $5 + x = 6$; $x = 1$ **57.** $x - 4 = 9$; $x = 13$ **59.** $m + 560 = 1680$; $1120 **61.** $63 + x = 90$; $x = 27$ **63.** $x + 15 = 90$; $x = 75$ **65.** $h - 47 = 28$; 75 **69.** J **71.** $-\frac{12}{5}$ **73.** $-\frac{13}{12}$ **75.** 10 **77.** 90 **79.** 9 **81.** 72 **83.** 6 ft **85.** −80 **87.** −3

## 2-2

**Check It Out!** **1a.** 50 **1b.** −39 **1c.** 56 **2a.** 4 **2b.** −20 **2c.** 5 **3a.** $-\frac{5}{4}$ **3b.** 1 **3c.** 612 **4.** 15,000 ft

**Exercises** **1.** 32 **3.** 14 **5.** 19 **7.** 7 **9.** 5 **11.** 2.5 **13.** 14 **15.** −9 **17.** $\frac{1}{8}$ **19.** $16c = 192$; $12 **21.** 24 **23.** −36 **25.** −150 **27.** 55 **29.** −3 **31.** 1 **33.** 13 **35.** 0.3 **37.** 2 **39.** −16 **41.** −3.5 **43.** −2 **45.** $\frac{7}{10}s = 392$; $560 **49.** $4s = 84$; 21 in. **51.** $4s = 16.4$; 4.1 cm **53.** $-3x = 12$; $x = -4$ **55.** $\frac{x}{3} = -8$; $x = -24$ **57.** $6.25h = 50$; 8 h **59.** $0.05m = 13.80$; 276 min **61.** −2 **63.** 0; $8y = 0$; 0 **65a.** number of data values **c.** 185,300 acres **67.** 7 **69.** 605 **71.** $\frac{3}{16}$ **73.** 5.7 **75.** $\frac{2}{3}g = 2$; 3 g **77.** D **79.** B **81a.** $6c = 4.80$ **b.** $c = \$0.80$ **83.** 2

**85.** 9 **87.** 2 **89.** −20 **91.** −132
**93.** Multiply both sides by *a*. **95.** 12
**97.** 25 **99.** 6 years old **101.** 6 **103.** 16

## 2-3

**Check It Out!** **1a.** 1 **1b.** 6 **1c.** 0
**2a.** $\frac{55}{4}$ **2b.** $\frac{1}{2}$ **2c.** 15 **3a.** $-\frac{5}{6}$ **3b.** 5
**3c.** 8 **4.** \$60 **5.** −42

**Exercises** **1.** 2 **3.** −18 **5.** 2 **7.** 66
**9.** $\frac{5}{4}$ **11.** −12 **13.** 16 **15.** −3.2 **17.** 4
**19.** 15 passes **21.** 4 **23.** −4 **25.** 4
**27.** 5 **29.** −9 **31.** $\frac{1}{4}$ **33.** 1 **35.** 3
**37.** $\frac{28}{5}$ **39.** 3 **41.** 8 **43.** 7 **45.** $-\frac{1}{2}$
**47.** $x = 40$ **49.** $x = 35$
**51.** $8 - 3n = 2$; $n = 2$
**53a.** $1963 - 5s = 1863$; $s = 20$ **53b.** 3
**55.** 8 **57.** 4.5 **59.** −10 **61.** 10
**63.** $5k - 70 = 60$; 26 in. **65.** Stan: 36; Mark: 37; Wayne: 38 **67a.** 45,000; 112,500; 225,000; 337,500; $225n$
**67b.** $c = 225n$ **71.** H **73.** 27 **75.** $6\frac{1}{5}$
**77.** 14.5 **79.** −6 **81.** irrational
**83.** repeating decimal, rational
**85.** $8(60) + 8(1) = 488$ **87.** $11(20) + 11(8) = 308$ **89.** 13 **91.** −18

## 2-4

**Check It Out!** **1a.** −2 **1b.** 2
**2a.** 4 **2b.** −2 **3a.** no solution
**3b.** all real numbers **4.** 10 years old

**Exercises** **1.** contradiction **3.** 1
**5.** 40 **7.** $-\frac{2}{3}$ **9.** 3 **11.** no solution
**13.** all real numbers **15.** 6 **17.** 6
**19.** 2.85 **21.** 10 **23.** 6 **25.** 14 **27.** $\frac{3}{4}$
**29.** −4 **31.** no solution **33a.** 15 weeks
**33b.** 180 lb **35.** $x - 30 = 14 - 3x$; $x = 11$ **37.** −4 **39.** 7 **41.** −3 **43.** 2
**45.** 1 **47.** $-\frac{7}{5}$ **49.** 4 **51.** no solution
**53.** 9 **59.** F **61.** H **63.** 2 **65.** no solution **67.** −20 **69.** 6, 7, 8 **71.** \$1.68
**73.** $3y$ cm **75.** −63 **77.** 4 **79.** 2
**81.** −125 **83.** 15 **85.** 3

## 2-5

**Check It Out!** **1.** about 1.46 h
**2.** $i = f + gt$ **3a.** $t = \frac{5-b}{2}$ **3b.** $V = \frac{m}{D}$

**Exercises** **3.** $w = \frac{V}{\ell h}$ **5.** $m = 4n + 8$
**7.** $a = \frac{10}{b+c}$ **9.** $I = A - P$
**11.** $x = \frac{k+5}{y}$ **13.** $\frac{x-2}{z} = y$
**15.** $x = 5(a + g)$ **17.** $x = \frac{y-b}{m}$
**19.** $T = \frac{PV}{nR}$ **21.** $T = M + R$
**23.** $b = \frac{c-2a}{2}$ **25.** $r = 7 - ax$
**27.** $x = \frac{5-4y}{3}$ **31.** $a = \frac{t-g}{-0.0035}$

**35.** C **37.** D **39.** $a = \frac{5}{2}\left(c + \frac{3}{4}b\right)$
**41.** $d = 500\left(t - \frac{1}{2}\right)$ **43.** $s = \frac{v^2 - u^2}{2a}$
**45.** 120 s **47.** 12 **49.** −6 **51.** 20 **53.** 12

## 2-6

**Check It Out!** **1.** 12 **2.** \$7.50/h
**3.** 20.5 ft/s **4a.** −20 **4b.** 5.75
**5.** 6 in.

**Exercises** **1.** The ratios are equivalent. **3.** 682 trillion **5.** 18,749 lb/cow **7.** 0.075 page/min
**9.** 18 mi/gal **11.** $\frac{3}{5}$ **13.** 39 **15.** 6.5
**17.** 23 **19.** $\frac{3}{5} = \frac{h}{4.9}$; 2.94 m **21.** 72
**23.** \$403.90/oz **25.** 2498.4 km/h
**27.** 10 **29.** −1 **31.** 13 **33.** 1.2 **35.** $\frac{1}{9}$
**37.** 45 **39.** \$84 **43.** 1.625 **45.** 3
**47.** $-\frac{2}{7}$ **49.** $\frac{11}{3}$ **51.** 3 **53.** 24
**55.** −120 **59.** A **61.** D **63.** 40°; 50°
**65.** 0.0006722 people/m$^2$ **67.** −27
**69.** $-\frac{1}{32}$ **71.** $10^2$ **73.** −5 **75.** 8
**77.** $V = \frac{nRT}{P}$

## 2-7

**Check It Out!** **1.** 2.8 in.
**2a.** $\frac{150}{x} = \frac{45}{195}$; 650 cm **2b.** $\frac{5.5}{x} = \frac{3.5}{28}$; 44 ft **3.** The ratio of the perimeters is equal to the ratio of the corresponding sides.

**Exercises** **3.** 10 ft **7.** 7 in. **11.** 480 ft$^2$
**13.** 4 **15.** 2.8 ft **17.** 4 cm
**21.** $\frac{1.5}{x} = \frac{4.5}{36}$; 12 m **23.** $k^2$ **25.** G
**27.** $w = 4$; $x = 7.5$; $y = 8$
**29.** 16.6 cm **31.** −12 **33.** −46
**35.** (−2, 4); (−1, 1); (0, 0); (1, 1); (2, 4) **37.** (−2, −7); (−1, −4); (0, −1); (1, 2); (2, 5) **39.** 32 **41.** 3.5

## 2-8

**Check It Out!** **1a.** 12 **1b.** 16.8
**1c.** 1.44 **2a.** 20% **2b.** 300% **3a.** 75
**3b.** 320 **4.** 10 karats

**Exercises** **3.** 21 **5.** 5.6 **7.** 80%
**9.** 12.5% **11.** 175 **13.** 36 **15.** 48
**17.** 2.5 **19.** 25% **21.** 50% **23.** 40
**25.** 511.1 **27.** 100 mg **29.** 2% **31.** 8%
**33.** 64% **35.** 85% **37.** 85% **39.** 0.52; $\frac{13}{25}$ **41.** 90.0; $\frac{90}{100}$ **43.** 1.12; $\frac{28}{25}$

**45.** 0.06; $\frac{3}{50}$ **47.** 0.006; $\frac{3}{500}$ **49.** 0.5 is greater than $\frac{1}{2}$% because $\frac{1}{2}$% = 0.005.
**51.** 0.001, 1%, $\frac{1}{10}$, 11%, 1.1 **53.** 0.49, $\frac{5}{9}$, $\frac{4}{5}$, 82%, 0.94 **55a.** 40%
**b.** action **c.** 3% **d.** 36.9%
**57.** box 1: 200; 100; 50
box 2: 12; 24; 148; 96
box 3: 25; 50; 100; 200
**59a.** $\frac{x}{90} = \frac{40}{100}$; \$36 **b.** \$54 **61.** F
**63.** G **65.** 17.2% **67.** 88.5 **71.** 120
**73.** 160 **75.** 6 in. **77.** 3

## 2-9

**Check It Out!** **1.** \$462.80 **2a.** \$270
**2b.** \$7650 **3a.** about \$3.30
**3b.** about \$5.60

**Exercises** **3.** \$41,775 **5.** $4\frac{1}{2}$ yr
**7.** about \$6.45 **9.** \$462.50
**11.** \$266.75 **13.** 5 yr **15.** about \$30
**17.** \$50,400 **19.** 2 yr **21.** \$2.89 **25.** A
**27.** D **29.** 900 **31.** \$47.17 **33.** \$93
**35.** $x - 2$ **37.** > **39.** > **41.** 24
**43.** 22.2%

## 2-10

**Check It Out!** **1a.** 45% decrease
**1b.** 20% increase **1c.** 43.75% increase
**2a.** 90 **2b.** 6 **3a.** \$88 **3b.** 20%
**4a.** \$15.30 **4b.** 130%

**Exercises** **3.** 20% decrease
**5.** 12.5% increase **7.** 20% decrease
**9.** 61.8 **11.** 8 **13.** 70% **15.** 90%
**17.** 25% decrease **19.** 400% increase
**21.** 30% increase **23.** 15% decrease
**25.** 20% increase **27.** $8\frac{1}{3}$% decrease
**29.** 252 **31.** 7.6 **33.** 15% **35.** 650%
**37.** 50% **41.** 18 **43.** 200% increase
**45.** 20 **47.** 60 **49.** 25% decrease
**51a.** 60% **b.** $\frac{60}{100} = \frac{18}{x}$; $x = \$30$
**53.** H **55.** G **57.** 200 **59.** 625
**61.** 64 fl oz **63.** \$9.43 **65.** 80°; 170°
**67.** 60°; 150° **69.** −20 **71.** 57 **73.** 36
**75.** −100 **77.** about \$4.20

## Extension Answers

**Check It Out!** **1a.** −7, 7 **1b.** −6, 10 **2a.** no solution **2b.** 4

**Exercises** **1.** −6, 6 **3.** 0 **5.** −2, 2
**7.** −11, 5 **9.** −9, 13 **11.** −57, 57
**13.** −3, 3 **15.** −16, 16 **17.** 0, 4
**19.** −5, 5 **21.** −5, 3 **23.** −3
**25.** 8, −2 **27.** 6.54 mm; 6.46 mm
**29.** $|x - 5| = 0.001$; 4.999 mm, 5.001 mm **31.** 18.8, 65.28

**33.** −9.5, 3.75 **35.** 0 **37.** no solution **39.** no solution **41.** −2.7, 10.3 **43.** $|x - 2| = 2.5$; −0.5°F; 4.5°F **45.** $|x - 168| = 3$; 165 lb, 171 lb

## Study Guide: Review

**1.** literal equation **2.** ratio **3.** 36 **4.** −2 **5.** −21 **6.** 18 **7.** $\frac{9}{8}$ **8.** $\frac{7}{3}$ **9.** $27 + s = 108$; 81 **10.** 7 **11.** $-\frac{10}{3}$ **12.** −90 **13.** 13 **14.** 0 **15.** −2 **16.** 17.5 **17.** −5 **18.** 40 **19.** −3 **20.** $-\frac{1}{2}$ **21.** 15 **22.** 18 **23.** 1 **24.** 41; 123°; 57° **25.** −2 **26.** −2 **27.** 1 **28.** $-\frac{2}{3}$ **29.** no solution **30.** all real numbers **31.** 9 **32.** $n = \frac{360}{c}$ **33.** $a = \frac{2S}{n} - \ell$ **34.** $x = \frac{225 - y}{0.25}$ **35.** 3.7 gal **36.** $\frac{1}{16}$ **37.** $3\frac{1}{3}$c **38.** \$1.83/golf ball **39.** \$0.18/oz. **40.** 1080 m/h **41.** 0.85 mi/min **42.** 1.6 **43.** 54 **44.** 5 **45.** −3 **46.** 3.85 in. **47.** 2.5 cm **48.** 16 ft **49.** The ratio of the areas is the square of the ratio of the radii. **50.** 5.29 **51.** 3105 **52.** 66.7% **53.** 400% **54.** 133.3 **55.** 240 **56.** 80% **57.** \$48,500 **58.** \$9000 **59.** about \$5.60 **60.** 37% increase **61.** 33% decrease **62.** 91 **63.** 127.5 **64.** \$3.75; \$6.25 **65.** 37.5%

# Chapter 3

## 3-1

**Check It Out! 1.** all real numbers greater than 4

**2a.**
2 $2\frac{1}{2}$ 3 $3\frac{1}{2}$ 4

**2b.**
−3 −2 −1 0 1 2 3

**2c.**
−6 −5 −4 −3 −2 −1 0

**3.** $x < 2.5$ **4.** $d$ = amount employee can earn per hour; $d \geq 8.25$

8.25
0 2 4 6 8 10 12

**Exercises 1.** A solution of an inequality makes the inequality true when substituted for the variable. **3.** all real numbers greater than −3 **5.** all real numbers greater than or equal to 3 **11.** $b > -8\frac{1}{2}$ **13.** $d < -7$ **15.** $f \leq 14$ **17.** $r < 140$ **19.** all real numbers less than 2 **21.** all real numbers less than or equal to 12 **27.** $v < -11$ **29.** $x > -3.3$ **31.** $z \geq 9$ **33.** $y$ = years of experience; $y \geq 5$ **35.** $h$ is less than −5. **37.** $r$ is greater than or equal to −2. **39.** $p \leq 17$ **41.** $f > 0$ **43.** $p$ = profits; $p < 10{,}000$ **45.** $e$ = elevation; $e \leq 5000$ **51.** D **53.** C **59.** D **61.** C **65.** < **71.** 10 **73.** 7 **75.** $3x + 3$ **77.** $g = 2b$; $g = 2(8) = 16$ **79.** $b = 9$ **81.** no solutions

## 3-2

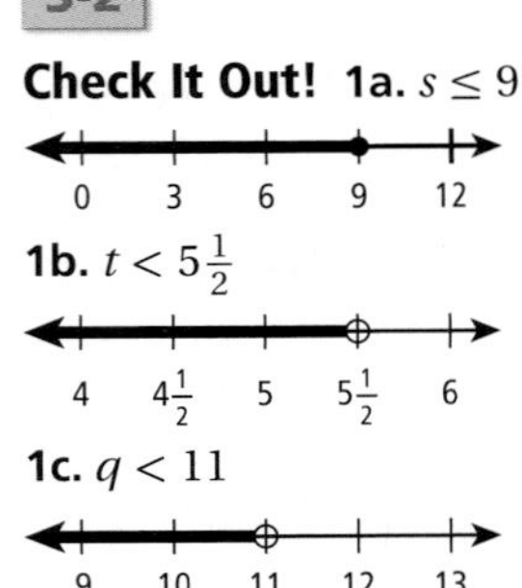


**2.** $11 + m \geq 15$; $m \geq 4$; Sarah must get at least 4 mg more iron to reach the RDA. **3.** $250 + p > 282$; $p > 32$; Josh needs to bench press more than 32 additional pounds to break the school record.

**Exercises 1.** $p > 6$ **3.** $x \leq -15$ **5.** $102 + t \leq 104$; $t \leq 2$ where $t$ is nonnegative **7.** $a \geq 5$ **9.** $x < 15$ **11.** $1400 + 243 + w \leq 2000$; $w \leq 357$ where $w$ is nonnegative **13.** $x - 10 > 32$; $x > 42$ **15.** $r - 13 \leq 15$; $r \leq 28$ **17.** $q > 51$ **19.** $p \leq 0.8$ **21.** $c > -202$ **23.** $x \geq 0$ **25.** $21 + d \leq 30$; $d \leq 9$ where $d$ is nonnegative **27.** $x < 3$; B **29.** $x \leq 3$; D **31.** $936 + 4254 + p \leq 45{,}611$; $5190 + p \leq 45{,}611$; $p \leq 40{,}421$ where $p$ is nonnegative **35. a.** $411 + 411 = 882$ miles **b.** $822 + m \leq 1000$ **c.** $m \leq 178$, but $m$ cannot be negative. **37.** F **39.** J **41.** $r \leq 5\frac{1}{10}$ **43.** sometimes **45.** always **47.** $y = 3 - \frac{2}{3}x$ **49.** $a = \frac{c}{2 + b}$ **51.** $k = 2s - 11$ **53.** $x = 10$ **55.** $x \geq -1$

## 3-3

**Check It Out! 1a.** $k > 6$

0 2 4 6 8 10 12

**1b.** $q \leq -10$

−18 −16 −14 −12 −10

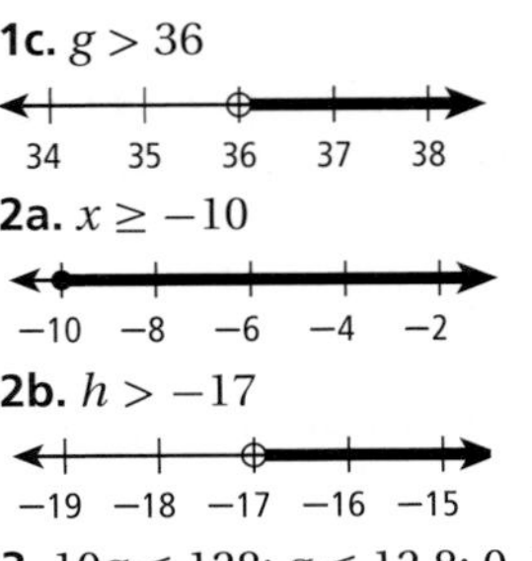


**3.** $10g \leq 128$; $g \leq 12.8$; 0, 1, 2, 3, 4, 5, 6, 7, 8, 9, 10, 11, or 12 servings

**Exercises 1.** $b > 9$ **3.** $d > 18$ **5.** $m \leq 1.1$ **7.** $s > -2$ **9.** $x > 5$ **11.** $n > -0.4$ **13.** $d > -3$ **15.** $t > -72$ **17.** $80n \leq 550$; $n \leq 6.875$; 0, 1, 2, 3, 4, 5, or 6 nights **19.** $j \leq 12$ **21.** $d < 7$ **23.** $h \leq \frac{8}{7}$ **25.** $c \leq -12$ **27.** $b \geq \frac{1}{10}$ **29.** $b \leq -16$ **31.** $r < -\frac{3}{2}$ **33.** $y < 2$ **35.** $t > 4$ **37.** $z < -11$ **39.** $k \leq -7$ **41.** $p \geq -12$ **43.** $x > -3$ **45.** $x < 20$ **47.** $p \leq -6$ **49.** $b < 2$ **51.** $7x \geq 21$; $x \geq 3$ **53.** $-\frac{4}{5}b \leq -16$; $b \geq 20$ **57.** C **59.** A **67.** B **71.** $g \leq \frac{-14}{5}$ **73.** $m > \frac{4}{15}$ **75.** $x = 5$ **79.** $2^3$ **81.** \$1.89/gal **83.** 25 words/min **85.** $t < 1$

## 3-4

**Check It Out! 1a.** $x \leq -6$

−8 −6 −4 −2 0

**1b.** $x < -11$

−13 −12 −11 −10 −9

**1c.** $n \leq -10$

−12 −11 −10 −9 −8

**2a.** $m > 10$

8 9 10 11 12

**2b.** $x > -4$

−6 −5 −4 −3 −2 −1 0

**2c.** $x > 2\frac{1}{3}$

$2\frac{1}{3}$
0 1 2 3 4

**3.** $\frac{95 + x}{2} \geq 90$; $95 + x \geq 180$; $x \geq 85$; Jim's score must be at least 85.

**Exercises 1.** $m > 6$ **3.** $x \leq -2$ **5.** $x > -16$ **7.** $x \geq -9$ **9.** $x > -\frac{1}{2}$ **11.** $x \leq 19$ **13.** $x > 1$ **15.** $300 + 0.1x > 1200$; sales of more than \$9000 **17.** $x \leq 1$ **19.** $w < -2$ **21.** $x < -6$ **23.** $f < -4.5$ **25.** $w > 0$ **27.** $v > \frac{2}{3}$ **29.** $x > -5$ **31.** $x < -2$ **33.** $a \geq 11$ **35.** $x > 3$

**37.** $29.99 < 19.99 + 0.35x$; $x > 28.57$; starting at 29 min **39.** $x \le 2$ **41.** $x < 4$ **43.** $x < -6$ **45.** $r < 8$ **47.** $x < 7$ **49.** $p \ge 18$ **51.** $\frac{1}{2}x + 9 < 33$; $x < 48$ **53.** $4(x + 12) \le 16$; $x \le -8$ **55.** B **57.** A **59.** $225 + 400 < 275 + 15m$; $23\frac{1}{3} < m$; 24 months or more

**61a.**

| Number | Process | Cost |
|---|---|---|
| 1 | 350 + 3 | 353 |
| 2 | 350 + 3(2) | 356 |
| 3 | 350 + 3(3) | 359 |
| 10 | 350 + 3(10) | 380 |
| $n$ | 350 + 3$n$ | 350 + 3$n$ |

**b.** $c = 350 + 3n$ **c.** $350 + 3n \le 500$; $n \le 50$; 50 CDs or fewer **65.** G **67.** 59 **69.** $x > 5$ **71.** $x > 0$ **73.** $x \ge 0$ **75.** $-3x > 0$ **77.** 7 **79.** $\frac{2}{3}$ **81.** $-1$ **83.** $25 + 2m = 10 + 2.5m$; $m = 30$ **85.** $a \ge 6$

## 3-5

**Check It Out! 1a.** $x \le -2$

−3 −2 −1 0 1 2 3

**1b.** $t < -1$

−3 −2 −1 0 1 2 3

**2.** more than 160 flyers

**3a.** $r \le 2$

−3 −2 −1 0 1 2 3

**3b.** $x < 3$

0 1 2 3 4 5 6

**4a.** no solutions **4b.** all real numbers

**Exercises 1.** $x < 3$ **3.** $x < 2$ **5.** $c < -2$ **7.** $100 + 4p < 7p$; $p > 33.33$; they'll have to sell at least 34 pizzas. **9.** $p < -17$ **11.** $x > 3$ **13.** $t < 6.8$ **15.** no solutions **17.** all real numbers **19.** no solutions **21.** $y > -2$ **23.** $b \ge -7$ **25.** $m > 5$ **27.** $x \ge 2$ **29.** $w \ge 6$ **31.** $r \ge -4$ **33.** no solutions **35.** all real numbers **37.** all real numbers **39.** $t < -7$ **41.** $x > 3$ **43.** $x < 2$ **45.** $x > -2$ **47.** $x \le -6$ **49.** $s > 26.67$; 27 s **51a.** $400 + 4.50n$ **b.** $12n$ **c.** $400 + 4.50n < 12n$; $n > 53\frac{1}{3}$; 54 CDs or more **53.** $5x - 10 < 6x - 8$; $x > -2$ **55.** $\frac{3}{4}x \ge x - 5$; $x \le 20$

**59.** $x$ can never be greater than itself plus 1. **61.** D **63.** A **67.** $x < -3$ **69.** $w \ge -1\frac{6}{7}$ **71.** The number in the square should be greater than the number in the circle. **73.** $\frac{2}{5} = \frac{w}{65}$; $w = 26$ in. **75.** $y$ = years; $y \ge 14$

## 3-6

**Check It Out! 1.** $1.0 < c < 3.0$

0 1 2 3 4 5 6

**2a.** $1 < x < 5$

0 1 2 3 4 5 6

**2b.** $-3 \le n < 2$

−3 −2 −1 0 1 2 3

**3a.** $r < 10$ OR $r > 14$

4 6 8 10 12 14 16

**3b.** $x \ge 3$ OR $x < -1$

−3 −2 −1 0 1 2 3

**4a.** $-9 < y < -2$

**4b.** $x \le -13$ or $x \ge 2$

**Exercises 1.** intersection **3.** $-5 < x < 5$ **5.** $0 < x < 3$ **7.** $x < -8$ OR $x > 4$ **9.** $n < 1$ OR $n > 4$ **11.** $-5 \le a \le -3$ **13.** $c < 1$ OR $c \ge 9$ **15.** $16 \le k \le 50$ **17.** $3 \le n \le 6$ **19.** $2 < x < 6$ **21.** $x < 0$ OR $x > 3$ **23.** $x < -3$ OR $x > 2$ **25.** $q < 0$ OR $q \ge 2$ **27.** $-2 < s < 1$ **29a.** $225 + 80n$; they will spend between \$200 and \$550. **b.** $-0.3125 \le n \le 4.0625$; $n$ cannot be a negative number **c.** 4.0625 h; they need an additional \$155 to use the studio for 6 h. **31.** $1 \le x \le 2$ **33.** $-10 \le x \le 10$ **35.** $t < 0$ OR $t > 100$ **37.** $-2 < x < 5$ **39.** $a < 0$ OR $a > 1$ **41.** $n < 2$ OR $n > 5$ **43.** $7 \le m \le 60$ **47.** D **49.** B **51.** $0.5 < c < 3$ **53.** $s \le 6$ OR $s \ge 9$ **55.** $-1 \le x \le 3$ **57.** $4x - 5$ **59.** $3a + 3$ **61.** $(-2, 3)$, $(-1, 0)$, $(0, -1)$, $(1, 0)$, $(2, 3)$; U-shaped **63.** $m < 2$ **65.** $x \le -2$

## Extension Answers

**Check It Out! 1a.** $-3 < x < 3$

−3 −2 −1 0 1 2 3

**1b.** $-1 < x < 1$

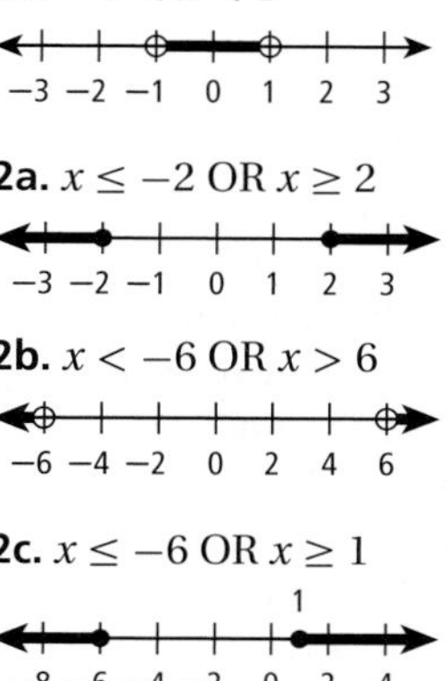


**2a.** $x \le -2$ OR $x \ge 2$

−3 −2 −1 0 1 2 3

**2b.** $x < -6$ OR $x > 6$

−6 −4 −2 0 2 4 6

**2c.** $x \le -6$ OR $x \ge 1$

1

−8 −6 −4 −2 0 2 4

**Exercises 1.** $-3 \le x \le 3$ **3.** $-15 < x < 13$ **5.** $-2 < x < 2$ **7.** $|x| \le 15$; $-15 \le x \le 15$ **9.** $|x - 2| < 3$; $-1 < x < 5$ **11a.** $-6 < x < 16$ **b.** $x \le 1$ OR $x \ge 9$ **c.** $-3 \le x \le 13$ **13.** no **15.** yes **17.** $|b| > 3$ **19.** $|d| < 7$

## Study Guide: Review

**1.** inequality **2.** union **3.** compound inequality **4.** intersection **5.** solution of an inequality

**6.**

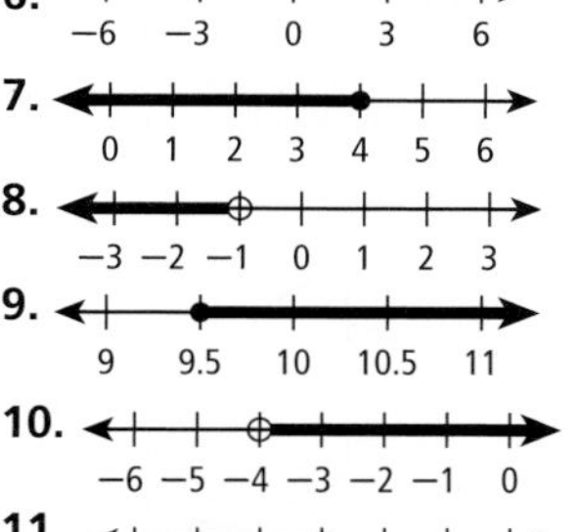


**7.** **8.** **9.** **10.** **11.**

**12.** $a < 2$ **13.** $k \ge -3.5$ **14.** $q < -10$ **15.** $t$ = temperature; $t \ge 72$ **16.** $s$ = students; $s \le 12$ where $s$ is a natural number **17.** $m$ = minutes; $m < 30$ where $m$ is nonnegative **18.** $t < 7$ **19.** $k \le 2$ **20.** $m > -5$ **21.** $x \ge 4.5$ **22.** $w < 9.5$ **23.** $a < 5$ **24.** $h < 1$ **25.** $v < -2$ **26.** $4.5 + m \ge 10$; $m \ge 5.5$; Tammy must run 5.5 mi or more. **27.** $32 + d \le 50$; $d \le 18$; Rob can spend \$18 or less. **28.** $a \le 5$ **29.** $t > -3$ **30.** $p > 8$ **31.** $x \le -25$ **32.** $n > 6$ **33.** $g < -12$ **34.** $k > -7$ **35.** $r < -9$ **36.** $h < -3$ **37.** $g < 2.5$ **38.** 0, 1, 2, 3, 4, 5, 6, 7 **39.** $0.75n \ge 250$; $n \ge 333\frac{1}{3}$; they must sell at least 334 lanyards. **40.** $x < 5$ **41.** $t \ge 6$ **42.** $m > -11$ **43.** $r < 6$ **44.** $p > -4$ **45.** $g > -7$ **46.** $x < -1$ **47.** $h > -3$

Selected Answers

**48.** $x > 1\frac{1}{2}$ **49.** $b \leq 10$ **50.** $y > 3\frac{1}{2}$ **51.** $n > -15$ **52.** 0, 1, 2, 3, 4, 5, 6, 7, 8, 9, 10, 11, 12, or 13 **53.** 26 mo total **54.** less than \$300,000 **55.** $m < -1$ **56.** $y \geq -2$ **57.** $c < -3$ **58.** $q \leq -4$ **59.** $x > 2$ **60.** $t < 3$ **61.** no solutions **62.** all real numbers **63.** $p > -\frac{1}{2}$ **64.** all real numbers **65.** $k > 2$ **66.** no solutions **67.** $210 + 16m > 175 + 20m$; $8.75 > m$ **68.** $-10 < t < 4$ **69.** $-6 < k \leq 7$ **70.** $r > 7$ OR $r < -2$ **71.** no solutions **72.** $-2 < p \leq 5$ **73.** all real numbers **74.** $68 \leq t \leq 84$ **75.** $102 \leq n \leq 183.6$

# Chapter 4

## 4-1

**Check It Out! 1.** graph C

**2a.** discrete;

Keyboarding

Words per minute

Weeks

**2b.** continuous;

Water Tank

Water level

Time

**3.** Possible answer: When the number of students reaches a certain point, the number of pizzas bought increases.

**Exercises 1.** continuous **3.** graph B **5.** graph C **11.** graph A **13.** continuous **19.** The point of intersection represents the time of day when you will be the same distance from the base of the mountain on both the hike up and the hike down. **23.** C **27.** Container C **29.** $-8$ **31.** $\frac{1}{9}$ **33.** $(-2, 5), (-1, 3), (0, 1), (1, -1), (2, -3)$; the points form a line. **35.** $(-2, 6), (-1, 3), (0, 2), (1, 3), (2, 6)$; the points form a U-shaped figure. **37.** $n - 5 = -2$; 3

## 4-2

**Check It Out! 1.**

| $x$ | $y$ |
|---|---|
| 1 | 3 |
| 2 | 4 |
| 3 | 5 |

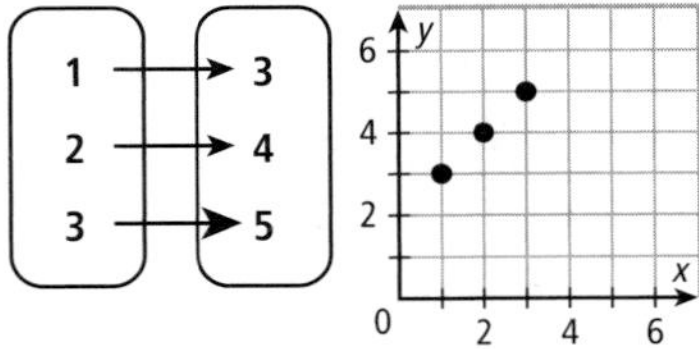

**2a.** D: {6, 5, 2, 1}; R: {−4, −1, 0} **2b.** D: {1, 4, 8}; R: {1, 4} **3a.** D: {−6, −4, 1, 8}; R: {1, 2, 9}; function; each domain value is paired with exactly one range value. **3b.** D: {2, 3, 4}; R: {−5, −4, −3}; not a function; the domain value 2 is paired with both −5 and −4.

### Exercises

**3.**

| $x$ | $y$ |
|---|---|
| 1 | 1 |
| 1 | 2 |

**5.**

| $x$ | $y$ |
|---|---|
| −7 | 7 |
| −3 | 3 |
| −1 | 1 |
| 5 | −5 |

**7.** D: {−5, 0, 2, 5}; R: {−20, −8, 0, 7} **9.** D: {2, 3, 5, 6, 8}; R: {4, 9, 25, 36, 81} **11.** D: {1}; R: {−2, 0, 3, 8}; not a function **13.** D: {−2, −1, 0, 1, 2}; R: {1}; function

**15.**

| $x$ | $y$ |
|---|---|
| −2 | −4 |
| −1 | −1 |
| 0 | 0 |
| 1 | −1 |
| 2 | −4 |

**17.** D: {3}; R: $1 \leq y \leq 5$ **19.** D: $-2 \leq x \leq 2$; R: $0 \leq y \leq 2$; not a function **21.** yes **23.** yes **25.** yes **27.** no **29a.** D: $0 \leq t \leq 5$; R: $0 \leq v \leq 750$ **b.** yes **c.** (2, 300); (3.5, 525) **33.** G **35a.** {(−3, 5), (−1, 7), (0, 9), (1, 11), (3, 13)} **b.** D: {−3, −1, 0, 1, 3}; R: {5, 7, 9, 11, 13} **c.** yes **37.** all real numbers **39.** $\frac{3}{4} = \frac{x}{36}$; 27 cm **41.** $x + 45 \geq 64$; $x \geq 19$

## 4-3

**Check It Out! 1.** $y = 3x$ **2a.** independent variable: time; dependent variable: cost **2b.** independent variable: pounds; dependent variable: cost **3a.** independent variable: pounds; dependent variable: cost; $f(x) = 1.69x$ **3b.** independent variable: people; dependent variable: cost; $f(x) = 6 + 29.99x$ **4a.** $h(1) = 1$; $h(-3) = -7$ **4b.** $g(-24) = -5$; $g(400) = 101$ **5.** $f(x) = 500x$; D: {0, 1, 2, 3}; R: {0, 500, 1000, 1500}

**Exercises 1.** dependent **3.** $y = x - 2$ **5.** independent variable: size of bottle; dependent variable: cost of water **7.** independent variable: hours; dependent variable: cost; $f(h) = 75h$ **9.** $f(0) = 2$; $f(1) = 9$ **11.** $h(27) = -1$; $h(-15) = -15$ **13.** $y = -2x$ **15.** independent variable: size of lawn; dependent variable: cost **17.** independent variable: days late; dependent variable: total cost; $f(x) = 3.99 + 0.99x$ **19.** independent variable: gallons of gas; dependent variable: miles; $f(x) = 28x$ **21.** $g(1) = 7$; $g(2) = 10$ **23.** $f(n) = 2n + 5$; D: {1, 2, 3, 4}; R: {\$7, \$9, \$11, \$13}

**25.**

| $z$ | 1 | 2 | 3 | 4 |
|---|---|---|---|---|
| $g(z)$ | −3 | −1 | 1 | 3 |

**27.** $f(-6.89) \approx -16$; $f(1.01) \approx 8$; $f(4.67) \approx 20$ **33.** D **35.** 3.5 **37.** 44.1 m **39.** $y = -3$ **41.** $x = 2$ **43.** D: $x \geq 0$; R: all real numbers; not a function

## 4-4

**Check It Out! 1a.**

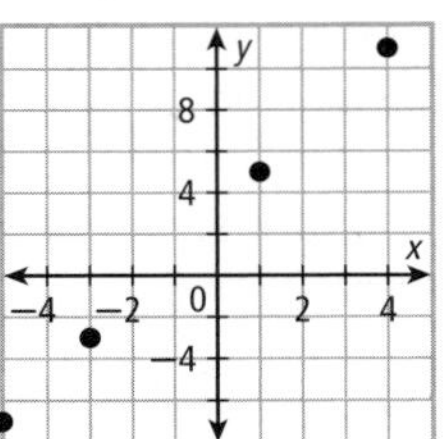

**1b.**

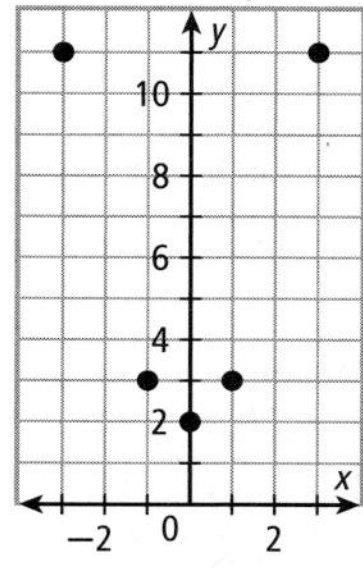

**2a.**

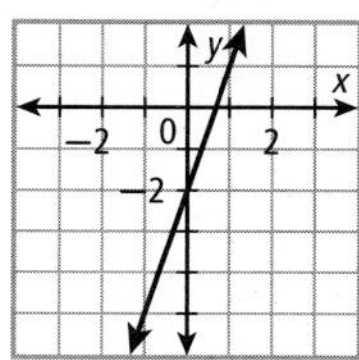

**2b.**

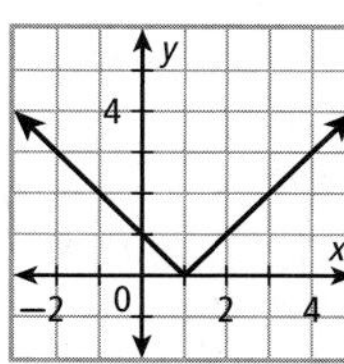

**3.** $x = 3$ **4.** Possible answer: about 32.5 mi

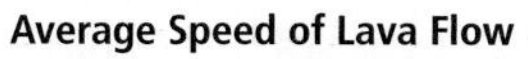


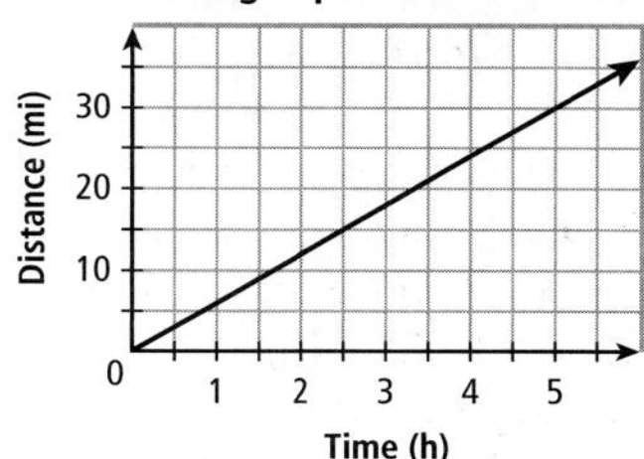


### Exercises

**1.**

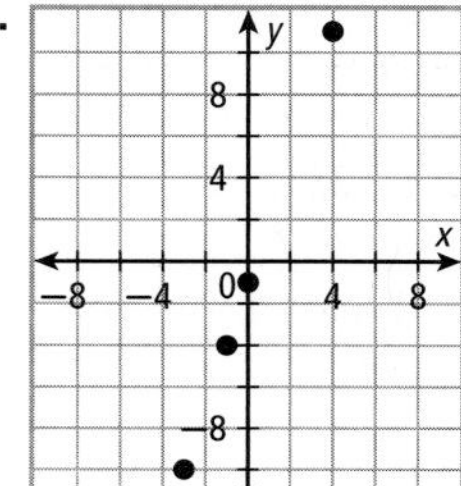

**3.**

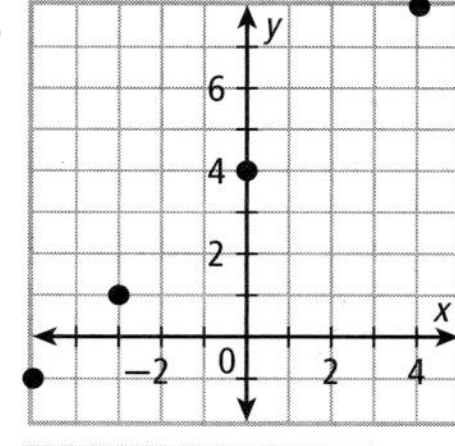

**5.**

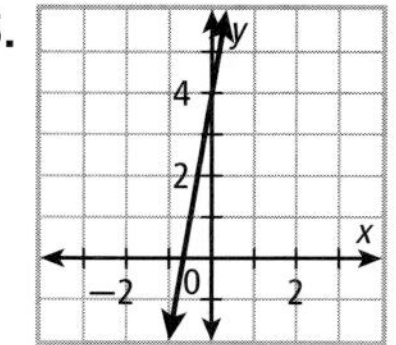

**7.**

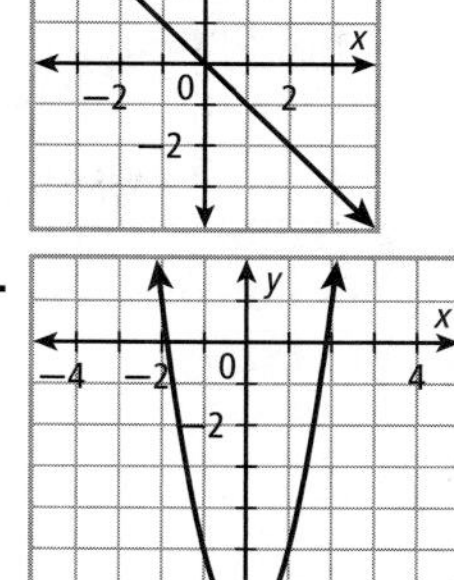

**9.**

**11.** $y = -1$

**13.**

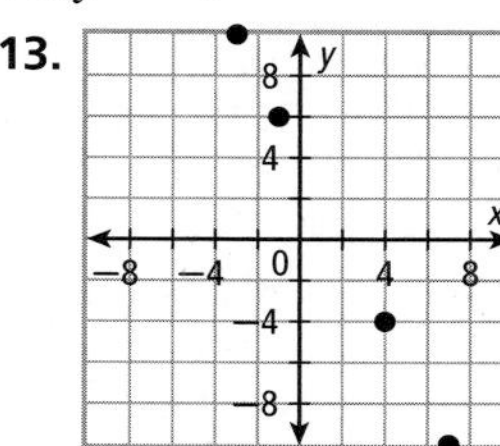

**15.**

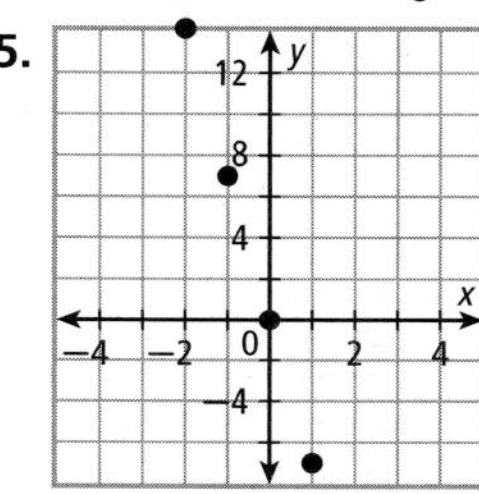

**17.**

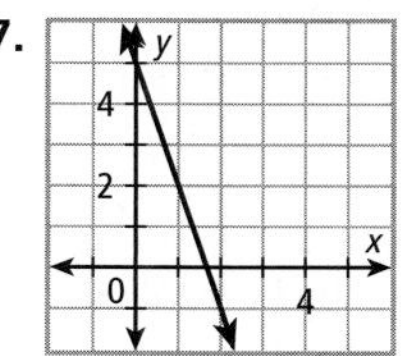

**19.**

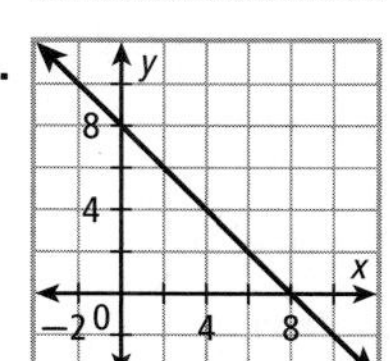

**21.**

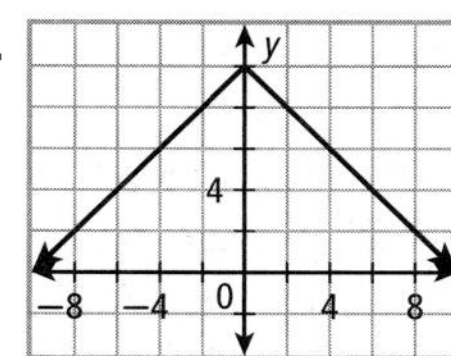

**23.**

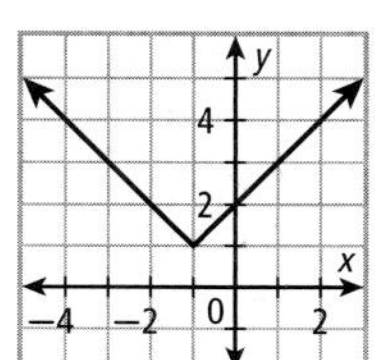

**25.** $y = 5$

**29.**

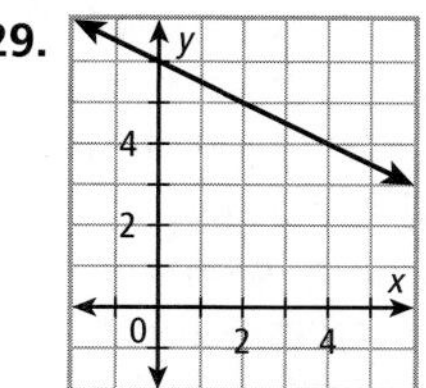

**31.**

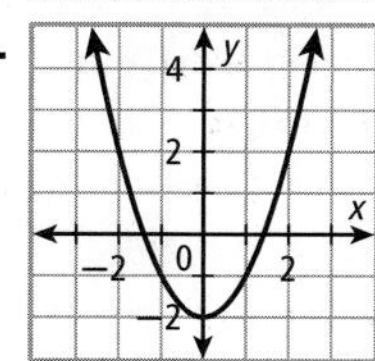

**33.**

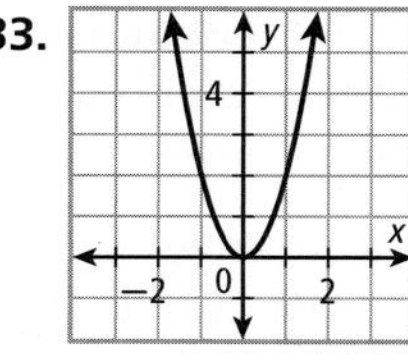

**35.**

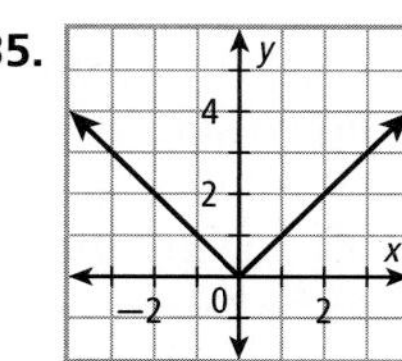

**37.** $x = 1$ **39.** $y = -8$ **41.** yes; yes **43.** no; yes **45.** no; yes; yes **47.** yes; no; yes **55a.** $v = 10{,}000 - 1500h$ **b.** 8500 gal

**c.**

| Time (h) | Volume (gal) |
|---|---|
| 0 | 10,000 |
| 1 | 8,500 |
| 2 | 7,000 |
| 3 | 5,500 |
| 4 | 4,000 |

**59.** J **61.** J **63.** $y = 4x + 64$ **65.** $2^3$ **67.** $p < -4$ **69.** $b \geq 20$ **71.** $h(-6) = -3$; $h(9) = 7$

## 4-5

### Check It Out!

**1.**

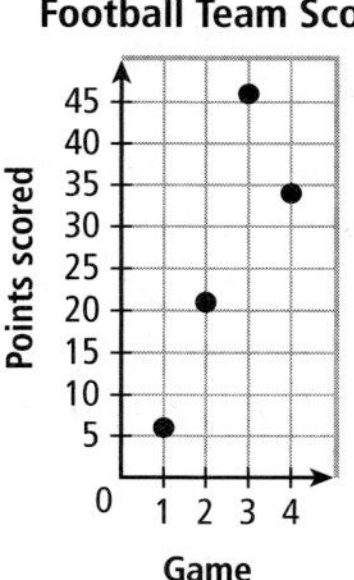


**2.** positive correlation **3a.** No correlation; the temperature in

Houston has nothing to do with the number of cars sold in Boston. **3b.** Positive correlation; as the number of family members increases, more food is needed, so the grocery bill increases too. **3c.** Negative correlation; as the number of times you sharpen your pencil increases, the length of the pencil decreases. **4.** Graph A; it cannot be graph B because graph B shows negative minutes; it cannot be graph C because graph C shows the temperature of the pie increasing, a positive correlation. **5.** about 75 rolls

**Exercises 3.** no **5.** positive correlation **7.** negative correlation **9.** positive correlation **11.** Graph A **15.** positive correlation **17.** positive correlation **19.** Graph A **23.** Positive correlation; as the number of left shoes sold increases, the number of right shoes sold also increases, because people need shoes for both feet. **25.** B

**27a.**

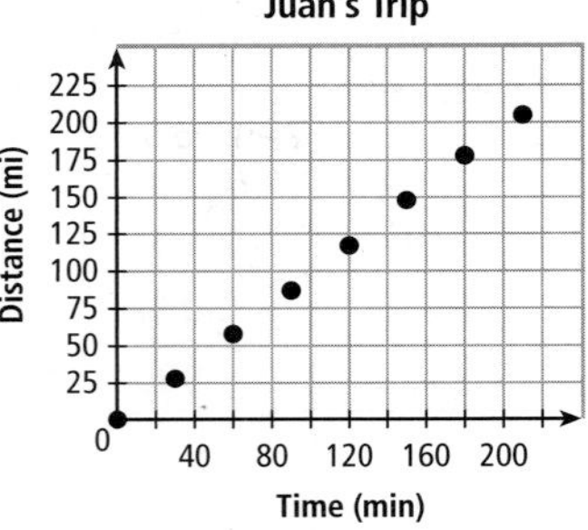


**b.** positive correlation **29.** C **35.** $5(n + 2) = 2n - 8, n = -6$ **37.** no solution

**39.**

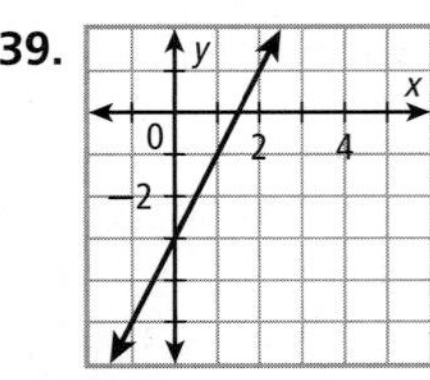

**41.**

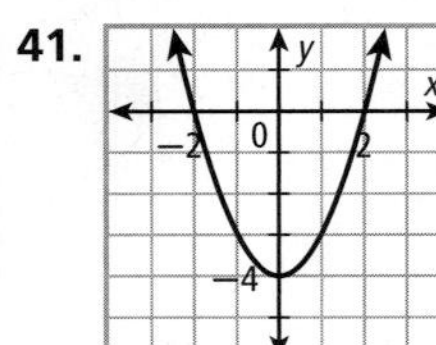

## 4-6

**Check It Out! 1a.** arithmetic; common difference: $\frac{1}{2}$ **1b.** not arithmetic **1c.** not arithmetic **1d.** arithmetic; common difference: $-3$ **2a.** $-343$ **2b.** 19.6 **3.** 750 lb

**Exercises 1.** common difference **3.** arithmetic; common difference: $-0.7$; $-0.7, -1.4, -2.1$ **5.** not arithmetic **7.** $-53$ **9.** not arithmetic **11.** arithmetic; common difference: $-9$; $-58, -67, -76$ **13.** 5.9 **15.** 9500 mi **17.** $\frac{1}{4}$ **19.** $-2.2$ **21.** 0.07 **23.** $-\frac{3}{8}, -\frac{1}{2}, -\frac{5}{8}, -\frac{3}{4}$ **25.** $-0.2, -0.7, -1.2, -1.7$ **27.** $-0.3, -0.1, 0.1, 0.3$ **29.** 22 **31.** 122 **33a.** It could be arithmetic because you pay $2 per lap, so the common difference could be 2. **b.** $9, $11, $13, $15; $a_n = 2n + 7$ **c.** $37 **d.** no **35.** $-104.5$ **37.** $\frac{20}{3}$ **39a.** $a_n = 6 + 3(n - 1)$ **b.** 48 **c.** $7800 **d.** $a_n = 7 + 3(n - 1)$; $8200 **41a.**

| Time Interval | Mile Marker |
|---|---|
| 1 | 520 |
| 2 | 509 |
| 3 | 498 |
| 4 | 487 |
| 5 | 476 |
| 6 | 465 |

**b.** $a_n = 520 + (n - 1)(-11)$ **c.** number of miles per interval **d.** 421 **43.** F **45.** 20th and 21st terms **47a.** session 16; yes **b.** Thursday **49.** $x = 16$ **51.** $t < -2$ OR $t > 2$ **53.** negative correlation

## Study Guide: Review

**1.** domain **2.** negative correlation **3.** term

**4.**

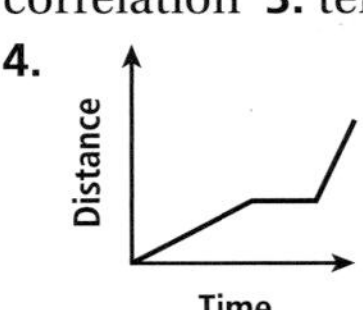


**5.**

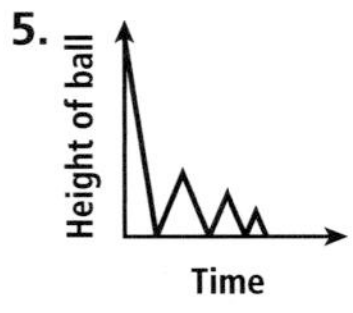


**6.**

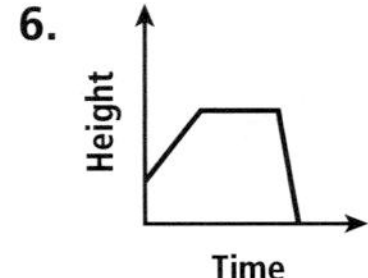


**7.** Possible answer: A family buys a fish tank and some fish. After two weeks, they buy some more fish. After two more weeks, they buy more fish. **8.** Possible answer: A monkey swings from a high branch to a lower branch. He climbs along the branch. Then he jumps to a higher branch and takes a nap.

**9.**

| x | −1 | 0 | 2 |
|---|---|---|---|
| y | 0 | 1 | 1 |

**10.**

| x | −2 | −1 | 2 | 3 |
|---|---|---|---|---|
| y | −1 | 1 | 3 | 4 |

**11.** D: $\{-4, -2, 0, 2\}$; R: $\{-1, 1, 3, 5\}$ **12.** D: $\{-2, -1, 0, 1, 2\}$; R: $\{-1, 0\}$ **13.** D: $\{0, 1, 4\}$; R: $\{-2, -1, 0, 1, 2\}$ **14.** D: $-4 \le x \le 3$; R: $-3 \le y \le 5$ **15.** D: $\{-5, -3, -1, 1\}$; R: $\{-3, -2, -1, 0\}$; function **16.** D: $\{-4, -2, 0, 2\}$; R: $\{-2, 1\}$; function **17.** D: $\{1, 2, 3, 4\}$; R: $\{-1, 0, 1, 2, 3\}$; not a function **18.** $\{(1, 5.00), (2, 6.50), (3, 8.00), (4, 9.50), (5, 11.00)\}$; yes **19.** yes **20.** The value of $y$ is 7 less than $x$; $y = x - 7$. **21.** The value of $y$ is 9 times $x$; $y = 9x$. **22.** independent variable: number of cakes; dependent variable: cost; $f(c) = 6c$ **23.** independent variable: number of CDs Raul will buy; dependent variable: number of CDs Tim will buy; $g(n) = 2n$ **24.** $f(5) = 14$ **25.** $g(-3) = -11$ **26.** $h(-4) = 6$; $h(5) = -1$

**27.**

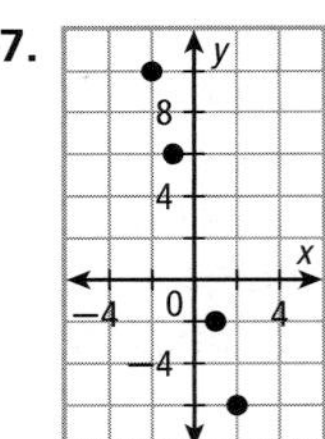

**28.**

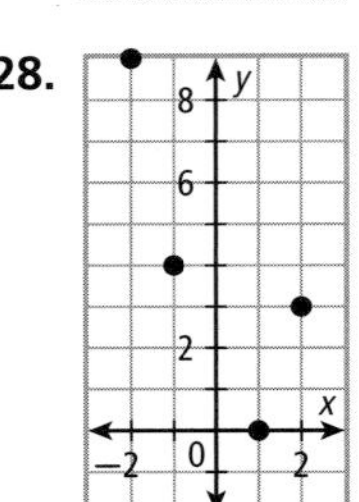

**29.**

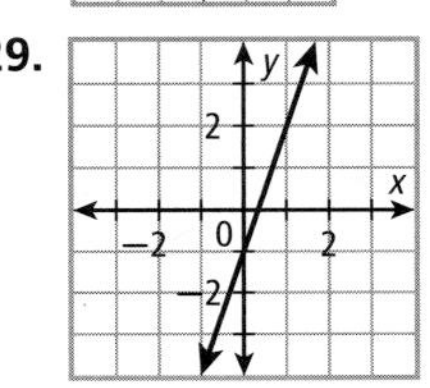

**30.**

**31.**

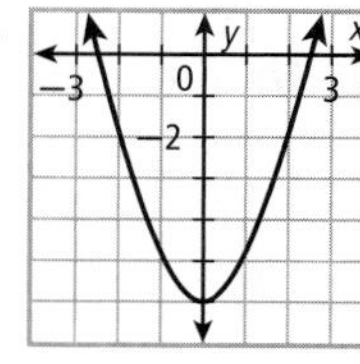

**32.**

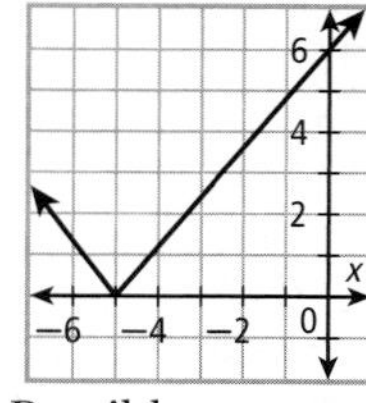

**33.** Possible answer: about \$43
**34.** negative correlation
**35.** Possible answer: 33 **36.** appears to be arithmetic; $-6$; $-4$, $-10$, $-16$
**37.** not arithmetic
**38.** not arithmetic **39.** appears to be arithmetic; 2.5; 2, 4.5, 7
**40.** 105 **41.** $-62$ **42.** 20 **43.** \$420
**44.** $-15.5$°C

# Chapter 5

## 5-1

**Check It Out!** **1a.** yes; each domain value is paired with exactly one range value; yes **1b.** yes; each domain value is paired with exactly one range value; yes **1c.** no; each domain value is not paired with exactly one range value
**2.** yes; a constant change of $+2$ in $x$ corresponds to a constant change of $-1$ in $y$.
**3a.** yes

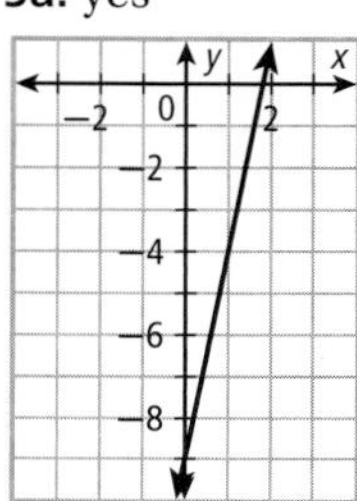

**3b.** yes

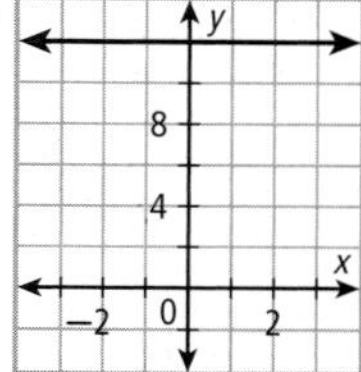

**3c.** no
**4.**

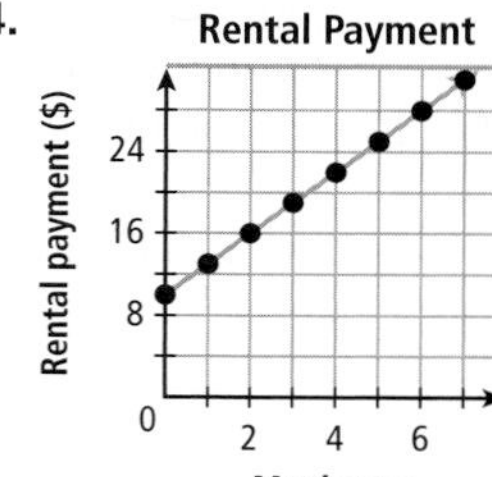


D: $\{0, 1, 2, 3, \ldots\}$
R: $\{\$10, \$13, \$16, \$19, \ldots\}$

**Exercises** **1.** No; it is not in the form $Ax + By = C$. **3.** Yes; each domain value is paired with exactly one range value; yes. **5.** yes **7.** yes **9.** yes **11.** no **15.** Yes; each domain value is paired with exactly one range value; no. **17.** Yes; each domain value is paired with exactly one range value; no. **19.** yes **23.** no **27.** yes; yes **29.** yes; yes **31.** yes; $-4x + y = 2$; $A = -4$; $B = 1$; $C = 2$ **33.** no **35.** yes; $x = 7$; $A = 1$; $B = 0$; $C = 7$ **37.** yes; $3x - y = 1$; $A = 3$; $B = -1$; $C = 1$ **39.** yes; $5x - 2y = -3$; $A = 5$, $B = -2$, $C = -3$ **41.** no **55.** no **57.** C **63.** not linear **65.** $-1$ **67.** $\frac{1}{9}$ **69.** 2 **71.** 9

## 5-2

**Check It Out!** **1a.** $x$-intercept: $-2$; $y$-intercept: 3 **1b.** $x$-intercept: $-10$; $y$-intercept: 6 **1c.** $x$-intercept: 4; $y$-intercept: 8
**2a.**

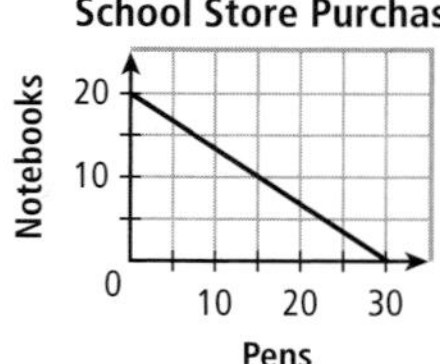


$x$-intercept: 30; $y$-intercept: 20
**2b.** $x$-intercept: number of pens that can be purchased if no notebooks are purchased; $y$-intercept: the number of notebooks that can be purchased if no pens are purchased.

**3a.**

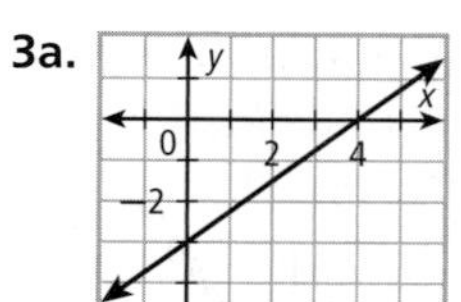

**3b.**

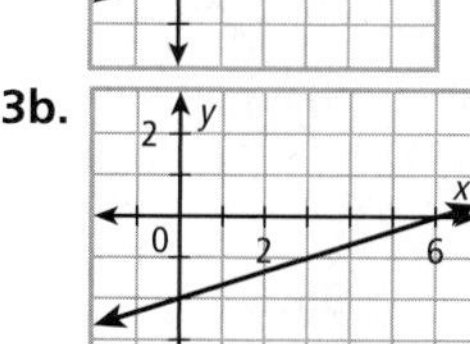

**Exercises** **1.** $y$-intercept
**3.** $x$-intercept: 2; $y$-intercept: $-4$
**5.** $x$-intercept: 2; $y$-intercept: $-1$
**7.** $x$-intercept: 2; $y$-intercept: 8
**13.** $x$-intercept: $-1$; $y$-intercept: 3
**15.** $x$-intercept: $-4$; $y$-intercept: 2
**17.** $x$-intercept: $-4$; $y$-intercept: 2 **19.** $x$-intercept: 2; $y$-intercept: 8 **21.** $x$-intercept: $\frac{1}{8}$; $y$-intercept: $-1$
**35.** A **37.** B **41.** F **47.** $x$-intercept: 950; $y$-intercept: $-55$

## 5-3

**Check It Out!** **1.** day 1 to day 6: $-53$; day 6 to day 16: $-7.5$; day 16 to day 22: 0; day 22 to day 30: $-4.375$; from day 1 to day 6
**2.**

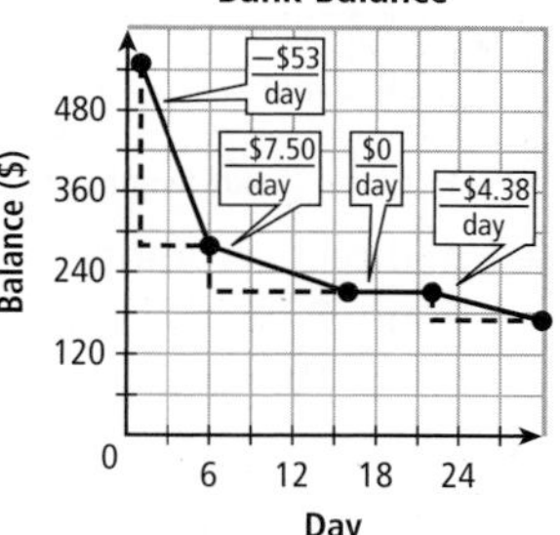


**3.** $-\frac{2}{5}$ **4a.** undefined **4b.** 0
**5a.** undefined **5b.** positive

**Exercises** **1.** constant **5.** $-\frac{3}{4}$
**7.** undefined **9.** undefined
**11.** positive **15.** 1 **17.** 0
**19.** positive **23.** $\frac{17}{18}$ **29.** C **31.** G
**35.** $-2$ **37.** D: $\{3\}$; R: $\{4, 2, 0, -2\}$; no **39.** $x$-intercept: 3; $y$-intercept: 6
**41.** $x$-intercept: $\frac{1}{4}$; $y$-intercept: $\frac{1}{2}$

## 5-4

**Check It Out!** **1a.** $m = 0$ **1b.** $m = 3$ **1c.** $m = 2$ **2a.** $m = \frac{1}{2}$ **2b.** $m = -3$ **2c.** $m = 2$ **2d.** $-\frac{3}{2}$ **3.** $m = \frac{1}{2}$; the height of the plant is increasing at a rate of 1 cm every 2 days.
**4.** $m = -\frac{2}{3}$

**Exercises** **1.** 1 **3.** $-\frac{1}{2}$ **5.** 10 **7.** $\frac{1}{540}$ **9.** $-\frac{5}{9}$ **11.** $-4$ **13.** undefined **15.** $-\frac{3}{4}$ **17.** $-\frac{9}{5000}$ **19.** $-\frac{13}{5}$ **21.** Student A is correct. **23a.** Car 1; 20 mi/h **b.** The speed and the slope are both equal to the distance divided by time. **c.** 20 mi/h **25a.** $y = 220 - x$ **27.** G **29.** $-\frac{b}{a}$ **31.** $\frac{3}{2} - y$ **33.** $x = \frac{1}{2}$ **35.** $x = -3$ **37.** $x = 0$ **39.** $p = 5$ **41.** $n = -11$ **43.** $a = 2$ **45.** yes

## 5-5

**Check It Out!** **1a.** no **1b.** yes; $-\frac{3}{4}$ **1c.** yes; $-3$ **2a.** No; possible answer: the value of $\frac{y}{x}$ is not the same for each ordered pair. **2b.** Yes; possible answer: the value of $\frac{y}{x}$ is the same for each ordered pair. **2c.** No; possible answer: the value of $\frac{y}{x}$ is not the same for each ordered pair. **3.** 90

**4.** $y = 4x$

Perimeter of a Square

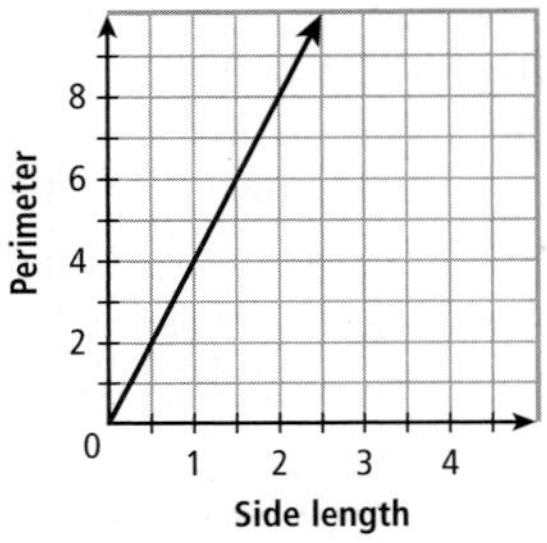

Perimeter

Side length

**Exercises** **1.** direct variation **3.** yes; $-4$ **5.** no **7.** 18 **11.** yes; $\frac{1}{4}$ **13.** yes **15.** $-16$ **19.** no **21.** $y = -3x$

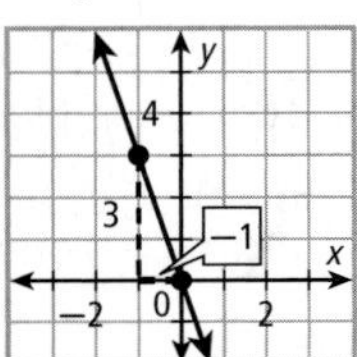

The value of $k$ is $-3$, and the graph shows that the slope of the line is $-3$.

**25.** $y = 2x$

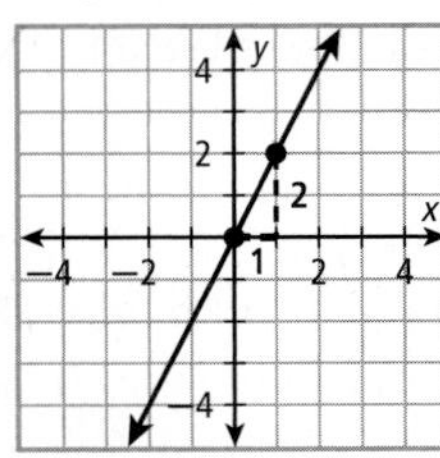

The value of $k$ is 2, and the graph shows that the slope of the line is 2.

**29.** $k = -\frac{2}{9}x$

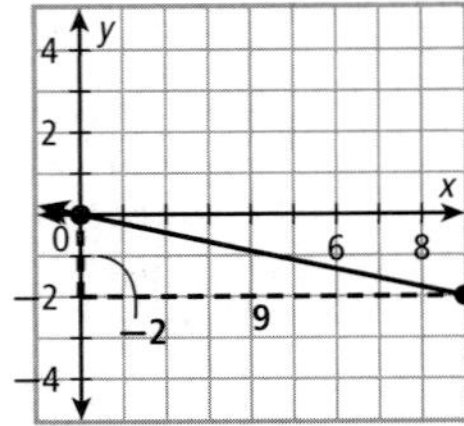

The value of $k$ is $-\frac{2}{9}$, and the graph shows that the slope of the line is $-\frac{2}{9}$.

**33.** $y = -6x$

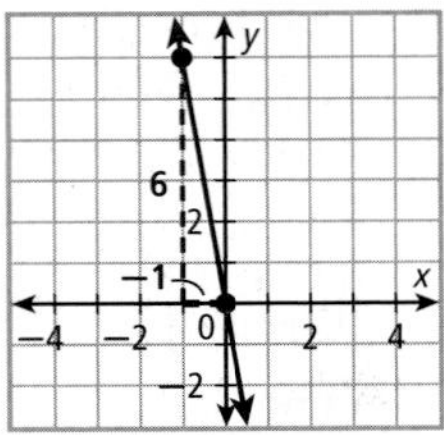

The value of $k$ is $-6$, and the graph shows that the slope of the line is $-6$. **41.** C **43.** B **47.** $p = 7 - 4q$ **49.** $x = \frac{4 - 2y}{y}$ **51.** $y = -2x$ **53.** $-4$ **55.** $\frac{1}{2}$

## 5-6

**Check It Out!**

**1a.**

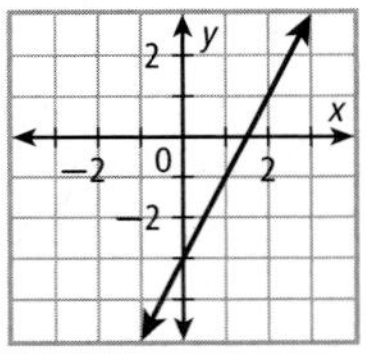

**1b.**

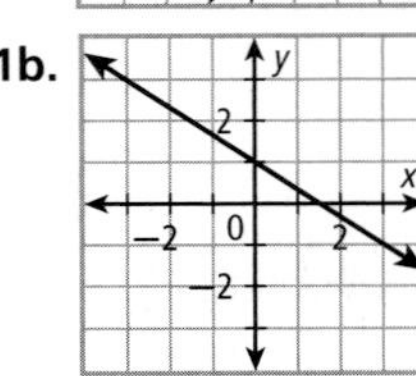

**2.** $y = 8x - 25$

**3a.** $y = \frac{2}{3}x$

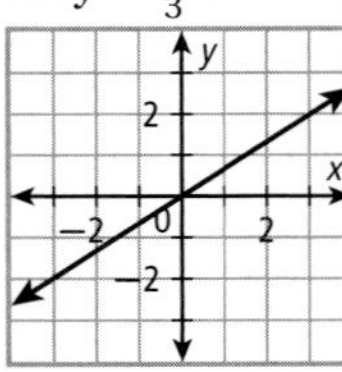

**3b.** $y = -3x + 5$

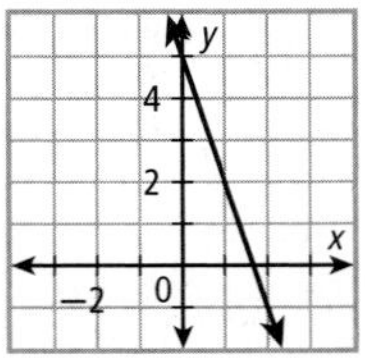

**3c.** $y = -4$

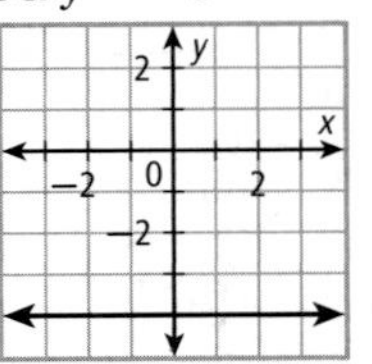

**4a.** $y = 18x + 200$ **4b.** slope: 18; cost per person; $y$-intercept: 200; fee **4c.** \$3800

**Exercises**

**1.**

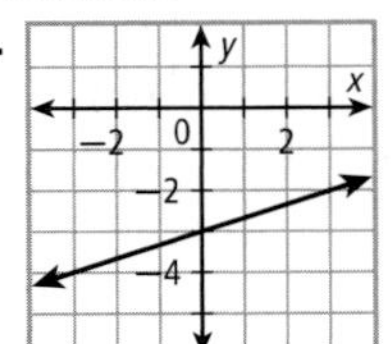

**5.** $y = 8x + 2$ **7.** $y = -3$

**9.** $y = \frac{2}{5}x - 6$

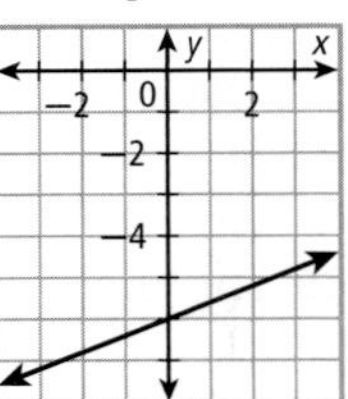

**13.**

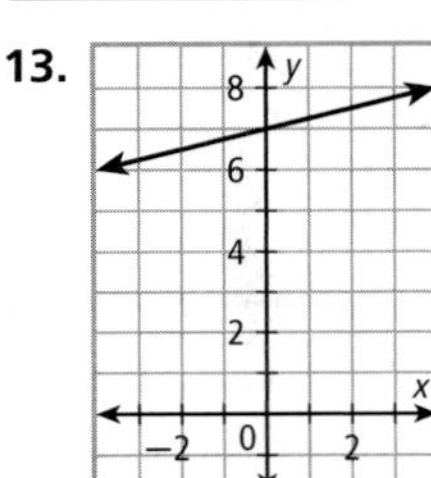

**17.** $y = 5x - 9$ **19.** $y = -\frac{1}{2}x + 7$

**21.** $y = -\frac{1}{2}x + 3$

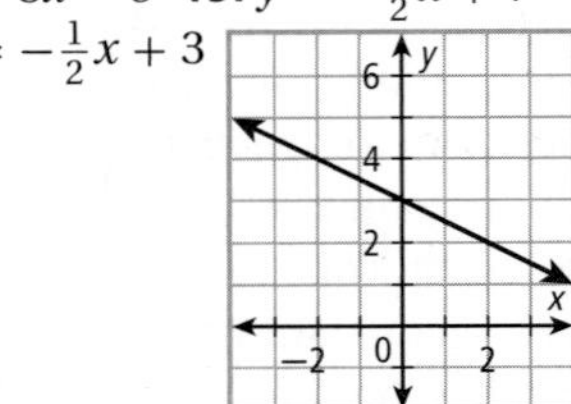

**25.** $y = \frac{7}{2}$

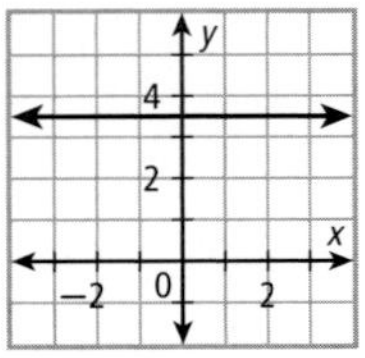

**29.** $y = -2x + 8$

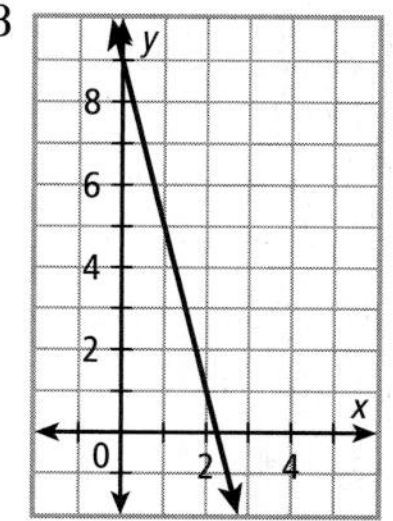

**31.** Student B is correct. **33.** possible **35.** impossible **37.** A **41.** B **43.** B **45.** $y = \frac{1}{3}x - 3$ **47.** $-6$ **51.** $n \leq 8$ **53.** $t < -3$ **55.** no

## 5-7

### Check It Out!

**1.**

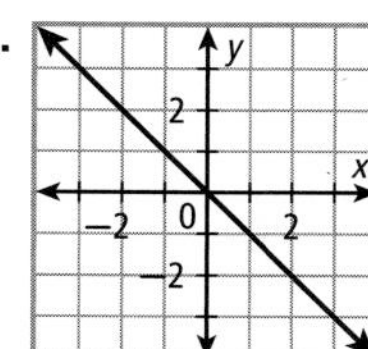

**2a.** $y - 1 = 2\left(x - \frac{1}{2}\right)$ **2b.** $y + 4 = 0(x - 3)$ **3.** $y = \frac{1}{3}x + 2$ **4a.** $y = 6x - 8$ **4b.** $y = \frac{2}{3}x - 1$ **5.** $y = 2.25x + 6$; $53.25

**Exercises** **5.** $y - 5 = -4(x - 1)$ **7.** $y = -\frac{1}{3}x + 7$ **9.** $y = \frac{1}{3}x$ **11.** $y = 3x - 13$ **13.** $y = -x$ **15.** $y = -\frac{1}{3}x + \frac{4}{3}$ **17.** $y = -x + 15$ **19.** $y = \frac{1}{5}x + 3$; 9 ft **23.** $y - 5 = \frac{2}{9}(x + 1)$ **25.** $y - 8 = 8(x - 1)$ **27.** $y - 7 = 3(x - 4)$ **29.** $y = -\frac{2}{7}x + 1$ **31.** $y = -\frac{1}{4}x$ **33.** $y = -5x + 13$ **35.** $y = \frac{1}{7}x + 7$ **37.** $y = -5x - 3$ **39.** $y = 2x + 11$ **41.** $y = -\frac{1}{500}x + 212$; 200°F **43.** $y = 6$; $x = 6$ **49.** D **51.** slope: $\frac{5}{2}$; $y$-intercept: 2 **53.** $y = \frac{2}{3}x$ **59.** $y = 3x - 5$

## 5-8

**Check It Out!** **1a.** $y = 2x + 2$ and $y = 2x + 1$ **1b.** $y = 3x$ and $y - 1 = 3(x + 2)$ **2.** slope of $\overline{AB} = 0$; slope of $\overline{BC} = \frac{5}{3}$; slope of $\overline{CD} = 0$; slope of $\overline{AD} = \frac{5}{3}$; $\overline{AB}$ is parallel to $\overline{CD}$ because they have the same slope. $\overline{AD}$ is parallel to $\overline{BC}$ because they have the same slope. Since opposite sides are parallel, $ABCD$ is a parallelogram. **3.** $y = -4$ and $x = 3$; $y - 6 = 5(x + 4)$ and $y = -\frac{1}{5}x + 2$ **4.** slope of $\overline{PQ} = 2$; slope of $\overline{QR} = -1$; slope of $\overline{PR} = -\frac{1}{2}$; $\overline{PQ}$ is perpendicular to $\overline{PR}$ because the product of their slopes is $-1$. Since $PQR$ contains a right angle, $PQR$ is a right triangle. **5a.** $y = \frac{4}{5}x + 3$ **5b.** $y = -\frac{1}{5}x + 2$

**Exercises** **1.** parallel **3.** $y = \frac{3}{4}x - 1$ and $y - 3 = \frac{3}{4}(x - 5)$ **5.** $y = \frac{2}{3}x - 4$ and $y = -\frac{3}{2}x + 2$; $y = -1$ and $x = 3$ **9.** $x = 7$ and $x = -9$; $y = -\frac{5}{6}x + 8$ and $y = -\frac{5}{6}x - 4$ **11.** $y = -3x + 2$ and $3x + y = 27$; $y = \frac{1}{2}x - 1$ and $-x + 2y = 17$ **13.** $y = 6x$ and $y = -\frac{1}{6}x$; $y = \frac{1}{6}x$ and $y = -6x$ **15.** $x - 6y = 15$ and $y = -6x - 8$; $y = 3x - 2$ and $3y = -x - 11$ **17.** $y = -\frac{6}{7}x$ **19.** neither **21.** parallel **23.** $y = \frac{1}{2}x - 5$ **25.** $y = 2x + 5$ **27.** $y = 3x + 13$ **29.** $y = -x + 5$ **31.** $y = 4x - 23$ **33.** $y = -\frac{3}{4}x$ **35.** $y = -x + 1$ **37.** $y = \frac{2}{5}x - \frac{31}{5}$ **39.** $y = -\frac{1}{5}x - \frac{11}{5}$ **41.** $y = -\frac{1}{2}x - \frac{1}{2}$ **43.** $y = \frac{1}{2}x + 6$ **45.** $y = x - 3$ **47.** $y = -4$ **51a.** $y = 50x$ **b.** $y = 50x + 30$ **53.** H **57.** $-\frac{1}{5}$ **59.** $94 + t > 112$; $t > 18$ **63.** $y = \frac{2}{3}x - 5$ **65.** $y = -\frac{1}{2}x - \frac{1}{2}$ **67.** $y = 3$

## 5-9

### Check It Out!

**1.**

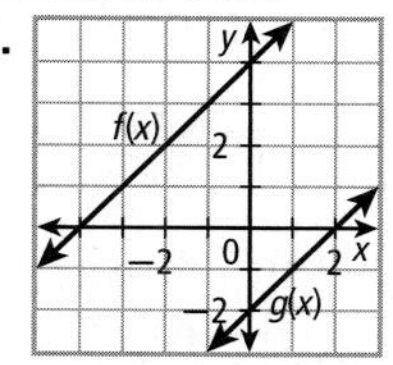

translation 6 units down

**2.**

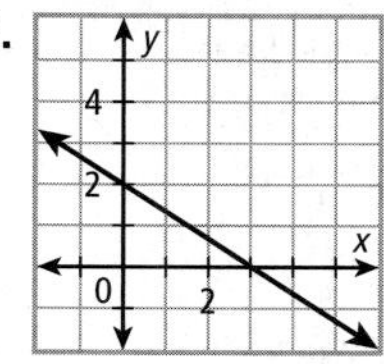

rotation about $(0, -1)$ (less steep)

**3.**

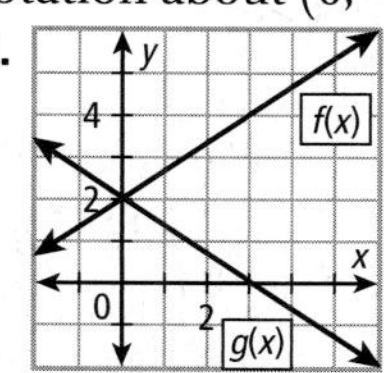

$g(x) = -\frac{2}{3}x + 2$

**4.**

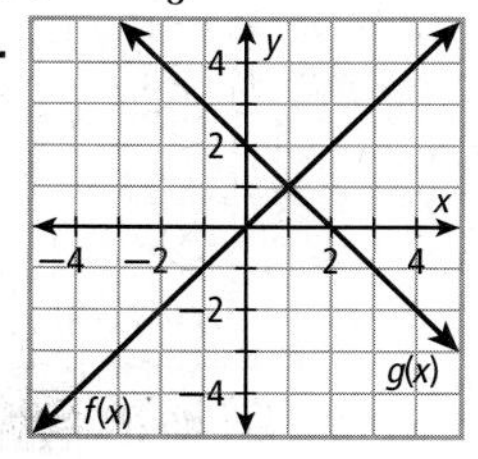

reflection across $y$-axis and translation 2 units up **5.** The graph will be rotated about $(0, 175)$ and become less steep; the graph will be translated 5 units up.

**Exercises** **1.** translation

**3.**

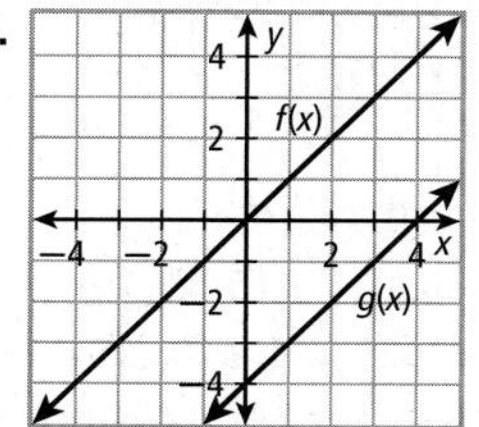

translation 4 units down

**7.**

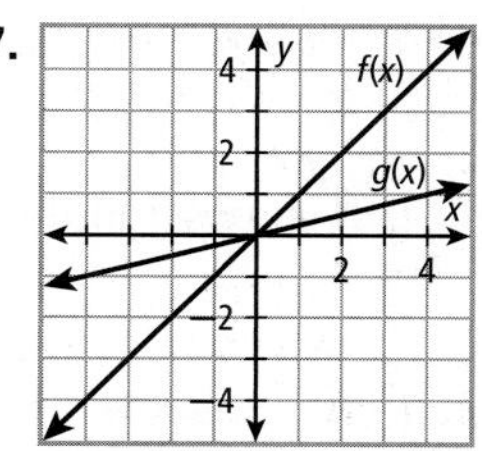

rotation about $(0, 0)$ (less steep)

**9.**

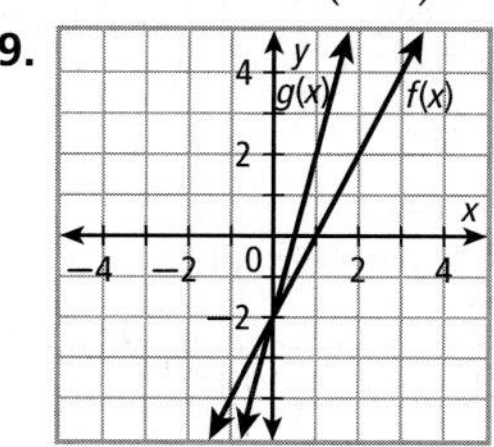

rotation about $(0, -2)$ (steeper)

**13.**

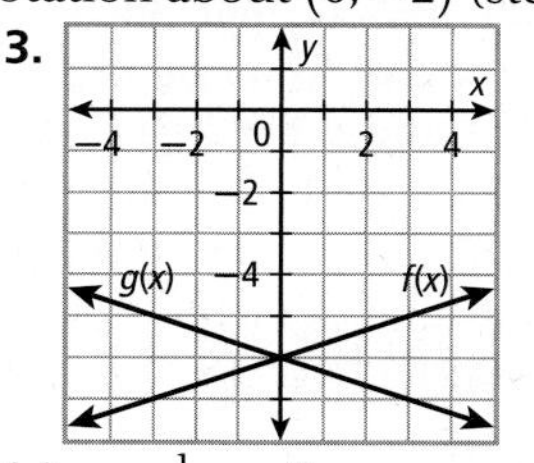

$g(x) = -\frac{1}{3}x - 6$

**17.**

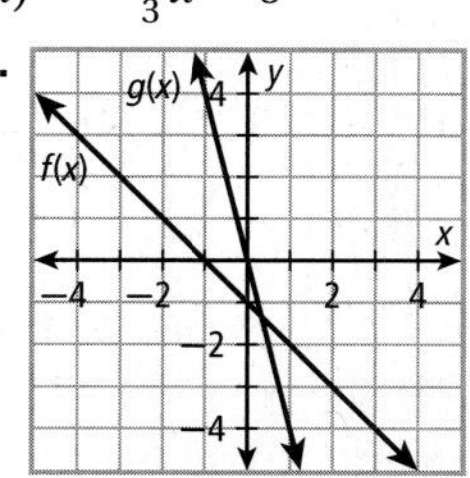

rotation about $(0, 0)$ (steeper) and translation 1 unit up

**23.**

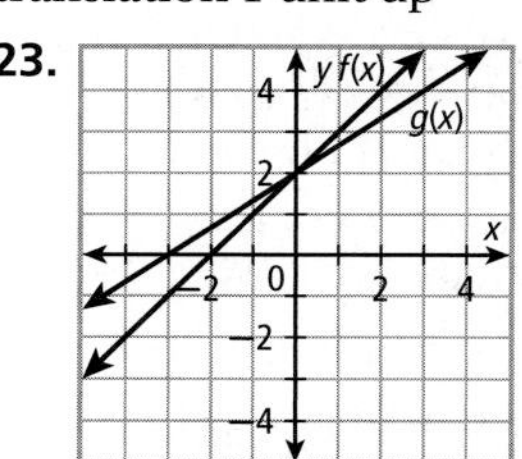

rotation about $(0, 2)$ (less steep)

Selected Answers

**27.**

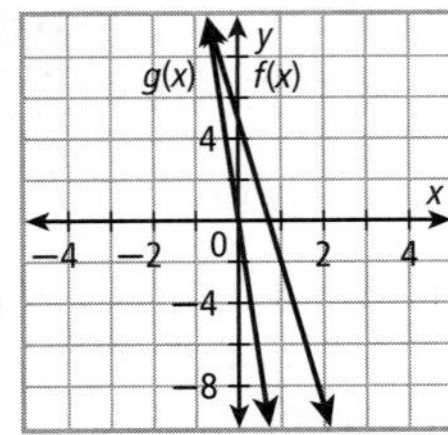


rotation about $(0, 0)$ (steeper) and translation 5 units down

**31.** rotation about $(0, 0)$ (steeper)

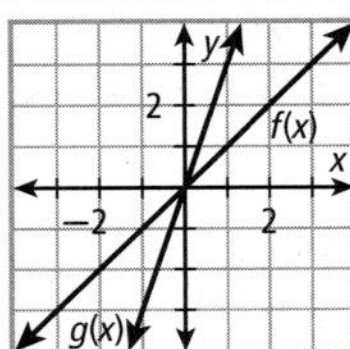


They have different slopes and the same $y$-intercept.

**37.**

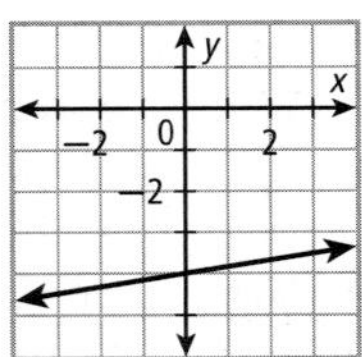


$g(x) = \frac{1}{6}x - 4$ **39.** translation 9 units down **41.** rotation about $(0, 0)$ (steeper) **43.** rotation about $(0, 0)$ (steeper) **45a.** \$300 **b.** 20% **c.** Commission changes to 25%. Base pay changes to \$400. **49.** D **53.** $15x$ **55.** positive **57.** negative **59.** $y = -\frac{3}{5}x$ and $y + 1 = -\frac{3}{5}(x - 2)$ **61.** $x = 4$ and $y = -3$; $2y + x = 6$ and $y = 2x + 3$

## Extension Answers

### Check It Out!

**1.**

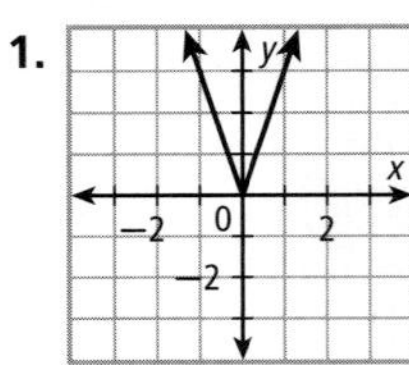


axis of symmetry: $x = 0$; vertex: $(0, 0)$; $x$-intercept: 0; $y$-intercept: 0; D: all real numbers; R: $y \geq 0$

**Exercises** **5.** D: all real numbers R: $y \geq 0$ **7.** D: all real numbers R: $y \geq 7$ **9.** never **11.** never

## Study Guide: Review

**1.** translation; rotation; reflection **2.** $y$-intercept **3.** slope; $y$-intercept **4.** No; a constant change of $+2$ in $x$ corresponds to different changes in $y$. **5.** Yes; a constant change of $+1$ in $x$ corresponds to a constant change of $+2$ in $y$. **6.** Yes; a constant change of $+1$ in $x$ corresponds to a constant change of $-2$ in $y$. **7.** No; a constant change of $-1$ in $y$ corresponds to different changes in $x$. **8.** $5x + y = 1$; $A = 5$; $B = 1$; $C = 1$ **9.** $x + 6y = -2$; $A = 1$; $B = 6$; $C = -2$ **10.** $7x - 4y = 0$; $A = 7$; $B = -4$; $C = 0$ **11.** $y = 9$; $A = 0$; $B = 1$; $C = 9$

**12.**

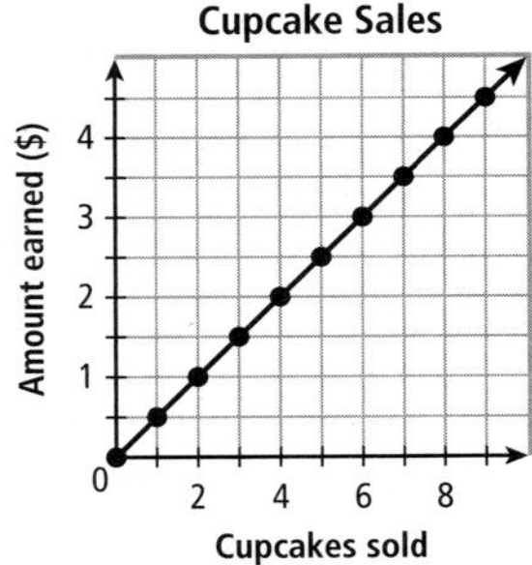


D: Whole numbers; R: positive multiples of 0.5

**13.** $x$-intercept: 2; $y$-intercept: $-4$ **14.** $x$-intercept: 5; $y$-intercept: 6 **15.** $x$-intercept: 3; $y$-intercept: $-9$ **16.** $x$-intercept: $-\frac{1}{2}$; $y$-intercept: 1 **17.** $x$-intercept: $-18$; $y$-intercept: 3 **18.** $x$-intercept: $\frac{1}{3}$; $y$-intercept: $-\frac{1}{4}$

**19.**

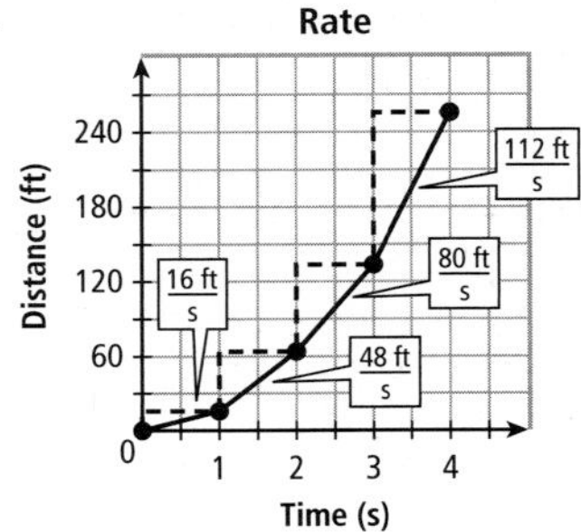


**20.** 5 **21.** $-\frac{4}{3}$ **22.** $-3$ **23.** $-\frac{1}{2}$ **24.** 3 **25.** 7 **26.** 4 **27.** $-5$ **28.** $-1$ **29.** 1 **30.** 2 **31.** undefined **32.** 0 **33.** yes; $-6$ **34.** yes; 1 **35.** no **36.** yes; $-\frac{1}{2}$ **37.** $-12$

**38.**

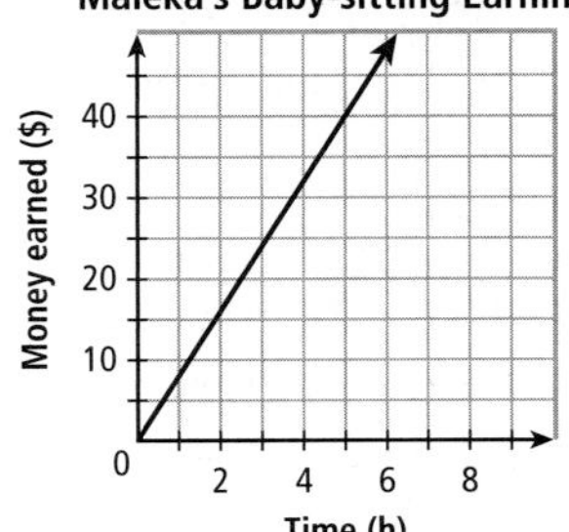


**39.**

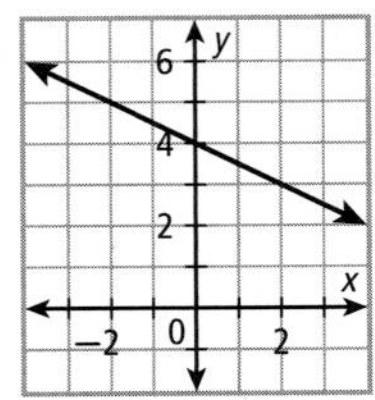


**40.**

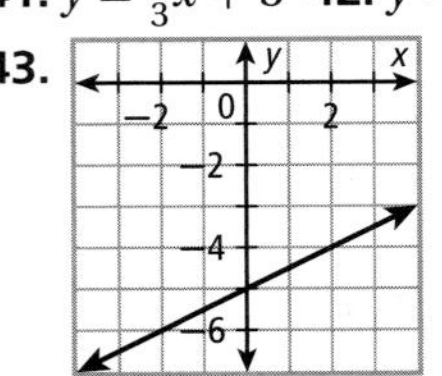


**41.** $y = \frac{1}{3}x + 5$ **42.** $y = 4x - 9$

**43.**

**44.**

**45.** $y - 3 = 2(x - 1)$ **46.** $y - 4 = -5(x + 6)$ **47.** $y = 2x + 2$ **48.** $y = -x + 3$ **49.** $y = 2x + 8$ **50.** $y = 2$ **51.** $y = -\frac{1}{3}x$ and $y = -\frac{1}{3}x - 6$ **52.** $y - 2 = -4(x - 1)$ and $y = -4x - 2$ **53.** $y - 1 = -5(x - 6)$ and $y = \frac{1}{5}x + 2$ **54.** $y - 2 = 3(x + 1)$ and $y = -\frac{1}{3}x$ **56.** $y = 2x - 3$

**57.**

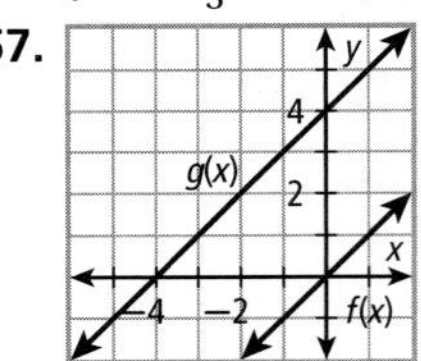


translation 4 units up

**58.**

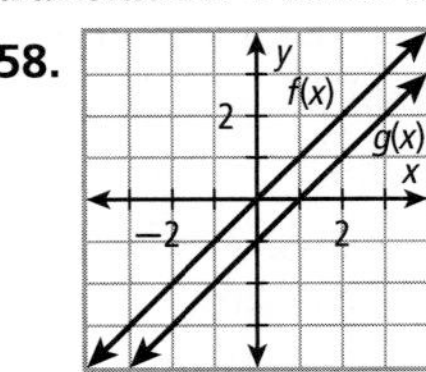


**59.**

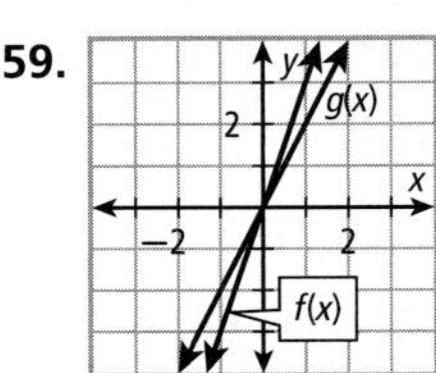


rotation about $(0, 0)$ (less steep)

60.

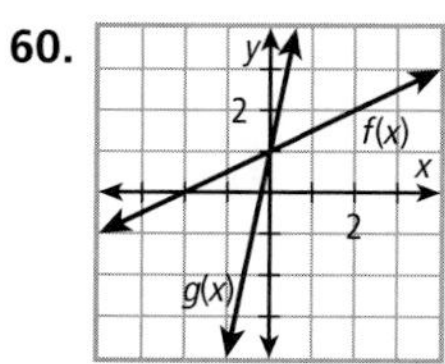


rotation about $(0, 0)$ (less steep)

61.

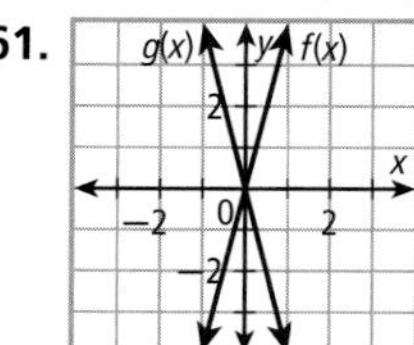


reflection across $y$-axis, rotation about $(0, 0)$

62.

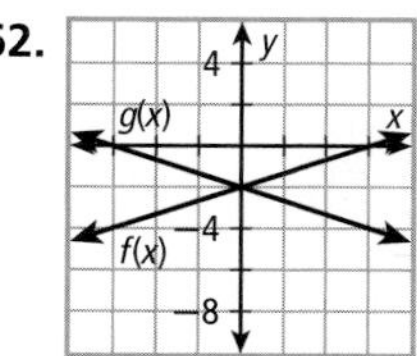


reflection across $y$-axis; rotation about $(0, -2)$

**63.** translation 2 units up; rotation about $(0, 3)$ (steeper)

# Chapter 6

## 6-1

**Check It Out! 1a.** yes **1b.** no **2a.** $(-2, 3)$ **2b.** $(3, -2)$ **3.** 5 movies; \$25

**Exercises 1.** an ordered pair that satisfies both equations **3.** yes **5.** $(2, 1)$ **7.** $(-4, 7)$ **9.** no **11.** yes **13.** $(3, 3)$ **15.** $(3, -1)$

**17a.** $\begin{cases} y = 2x \\ y = 16 + 0.50x \end{cases}$

**b.**

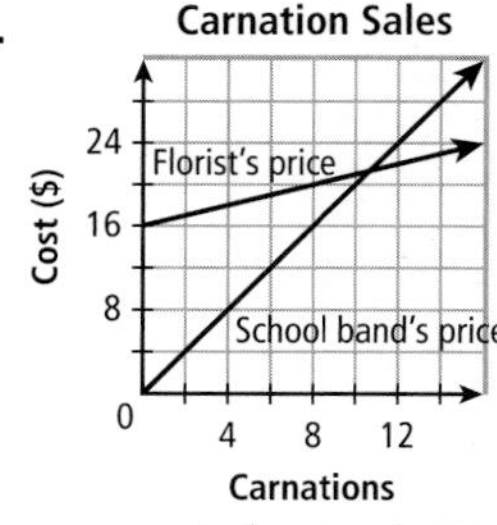


It represents how many carnations need to be sold to break even. **c.** No, because the solution is not a whole number of carnations; 11 carnations. **19.** $(-2.4, -9.3)$ **21.** $(0.3, -0.3)$ **23.** 45 white; 120 pink **25.** 8 yr **29.** C **31.** month 11; 400 **33.** 42 **35.** 2.2 **37.** numbers less than 5 **39.** numbers greater than 6 **41.** $c \leq -9$

## 6-2

**Check It Out! 1a.** $(-2, 1)$ **1b.** $(0, 2)$ **1c.** $(3, -10)$ **2.** $(-1, 6)$ **3.** 10 months; \$860; the first option; the first option is cheaper for the first 9 months; the second option is cheaper after 10 months.

**Exercises 1.** $(9, 35)$ **3.** $(3, 8)$ **5.** $(-3, -9)$ **7a.** 3 months; \$136 **b.** Green Lawn **9.** $(-4, 2)$ **11.** $(-1, 2)$ **13.** $(1, 5)$ **15.** $(3, -2)$ **17.** 6 months; \$360; the second option **19.** $(2, -2)$ **21.** $(8, 6)$ **23.** $(-9, -14.8)$ **25.** 12 nickels; 8 dimes **27.** $\begin{cases} x + y = 1000 \\ 0.05x + 0.06y = 58 \end{cases}$; \$200 at 5%; \$800 at 6%

**29.** $m\angle x = 60°$; $m\angle y = 30°$ **35.** Possible estimate: $(1.75, -2.5)$; $(1.8, -2.4)$ **37.** F **39.** $r = 5$; $s = -2$; $t = 4$ **41.** $a = 9$; $b = 5$; $c = 0$ **45.** $x$-intercept: 2; $y$-intercept: −6 **47.** $x$-intercept: 8; $y$-intercept: 10 **49.** yes

## 6-3

**Check It Out! 1.** $(-2, 4)$ **2.** $(4, 1)$ **3a.** $(2, 0)$ **3b.** $(3, 4)$ **4.** 9 lilies; 4 tulips

**Exercises 1.** $(-4, 1)$ **3.** $(-2, -4)$ **5.** $(-6, 30)$ **7.** $(3, 2)$ **9.** $(4, -3)$ **11.** $(-1, -2)$ **13.** $(1, 5)$ **15.** $\left(6, -\frac{1}{2}\right)$ **17.** $(-1, 2)$ **19.** $(-1, 2)$

**21.** $\begin{cases} \ell - w = 2 \\ 2\ell + 2w = 40 \end{cases}$; length: 11 units; width: 9 units

**25.** $(3, 3)$ **27.** $\left(\frac{46}{7}, \frac{8}{7}\right)$ **29.** $\left(\frac{15}{7}, \frac{9}{7}\right)$

**31a.** $\begin{cases} 3A + 2B = 16 \\ 2A + 3B = 14 \end{cases}$ **b.** $A = 4$; $B = 2$ **c.** Buying the first package will save \$8; buying the second package will save \$7. **33.** A **35a.** $s$ = number of student tickets; $n$ = number of nonstudent tickets; $\begin{cases} s + n = 358 \\ 1.50s + 3.25n = 752.25 \end{cases}$ **b.** $s = 235$; $n = 123$; 235 student tickets, 123 nonstudent tickets **37.** $x = 4$; $y = -1$; $z = 10$

**39.** $\begin{cases} x + y = 5 \\ 3(10x + y) = 42 \end{cases}$; $x = 1$; $y = 4$; the number is 14. **41.** $y = 3x$ **43.** yes; $\frac{1}{2}$ **45.** no **47.** $(4, 9)$

## 6-4

**Check It Out! 1.** no solution **2.** infinitely many solutions **3a.** consistent, dependent; infinitely many solutions **3b.** consistent, independent; one solution **3c.** inconsistent; no solution **4.** Yes; the graphs of the two equations have different slopes so they intersect.

**Exercises 1.** consistent **3.** no solutions **5.** infinitely many solutions **7.** infinitely many solutions **9.** inconsistent; no solutions **11.** Yes; the graphs of the two equations have different slopes so they intersect. **13.** no solutions **15.** no solutions **17.** infinitely many solutions **19.** infinitely many solutions **21.** consistent, independent; one solution **23.** Yes; the graphs of the two equations have different slopes, so they intersect. **27.** They will always have the same amount; both started with 2 and add 4 every year. **29.** The graph will be 2 parallel lines. **31.** A **33.** D **35.** $p = q$; $p \neq q$ **37.** 11 km **39.** not arithmetic **41.** $d = -1\frac{1}{2}$; −6, $-7\frac{1}{2}$, −9 **43.** $(-2, -4)$

## 6-5

**Check It Out! 1a.** no **1b.** yes

**2a.**

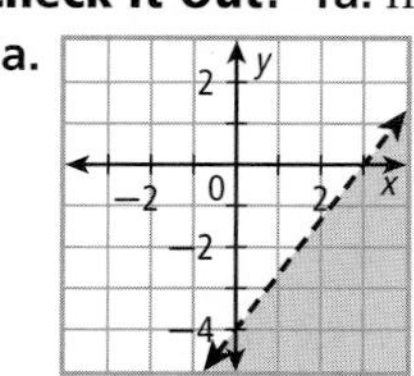


**2b.**

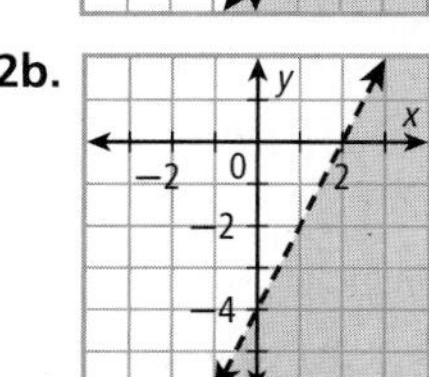


**2c.**

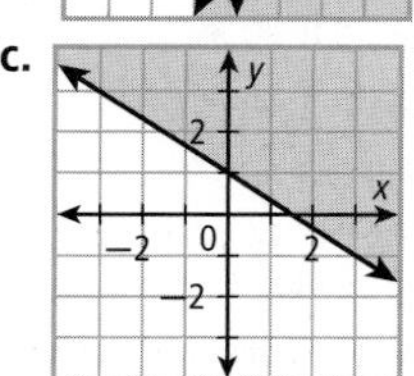


**3a.** $2.5b + 2g \leq 6$

Selected Answers

**3b.** Olive Combinations

Green olives

Black olives

**3c.** Possible answer: (1 lb black, 1 lb green), (0.5 lb black, 2 lb green)

**4a.** $y < -x$ **4b.** $y \geq -2x - 3$

**Exercises** **3.** yes

**5.**

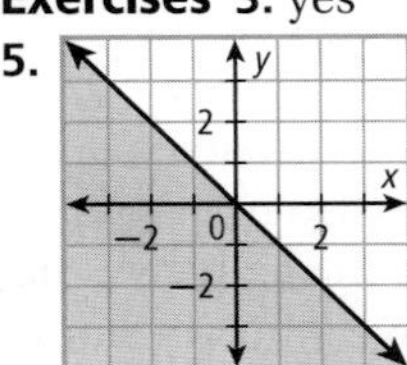

**7.**

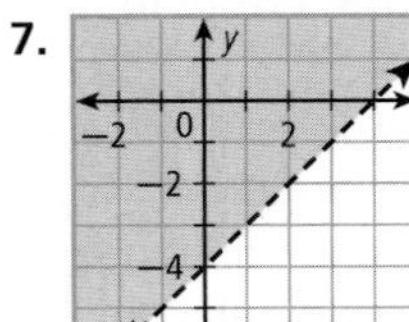

**9a.** $r + p \leq 16$

**b.**

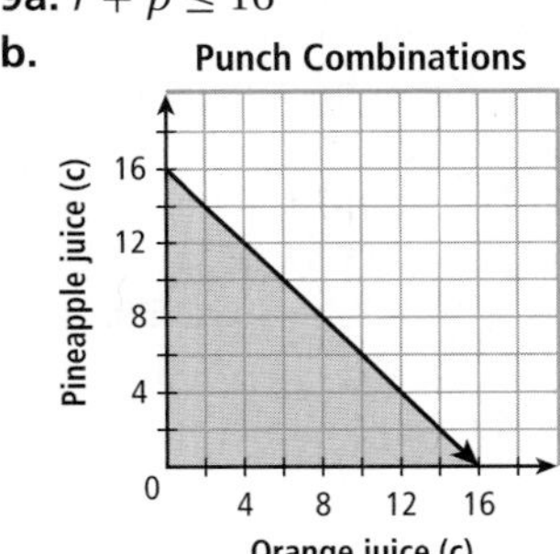


**c.** Possible answer: (2 c orange, 2 c pineapple), (4 c orange, 10 c pineapple) **11.** $y \geq x + 5$ **13.** yes

**15.**

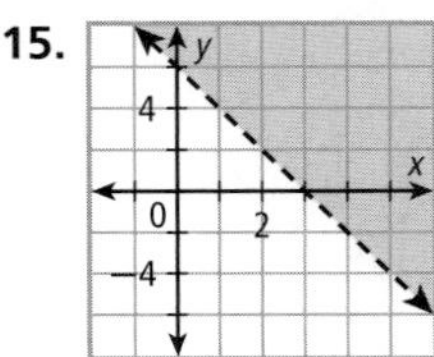

**19a.** $3b + 2d \leq 30$

**b.** Food Combinations

Hot dogs (lb)

Hamburger meat (lb)

**c.** Possible answer: (3 lb hamburger, 2 lb hot dogs), (5 lb hamburger, 6 lb hot dogs) **21.** $y \leq -\frac{1}{5}x + 3$

**23.**

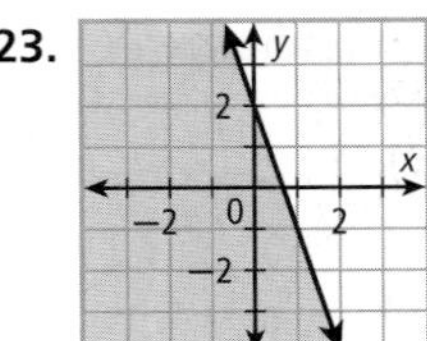

**25.**

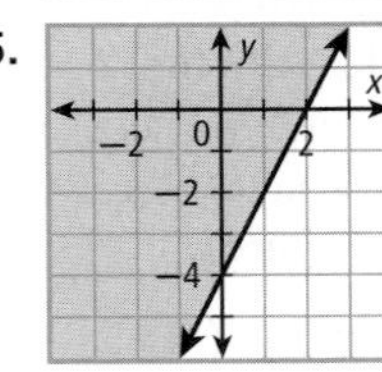

**29.**

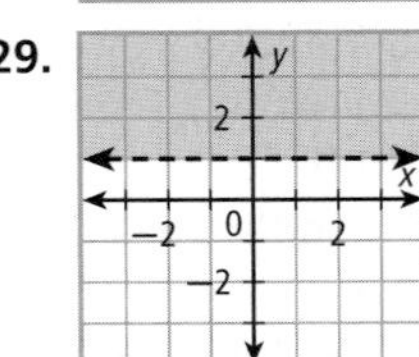

**31.**

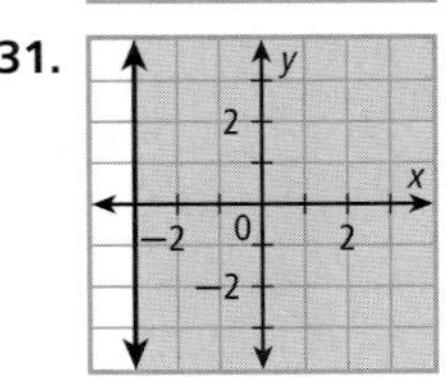

**33.**

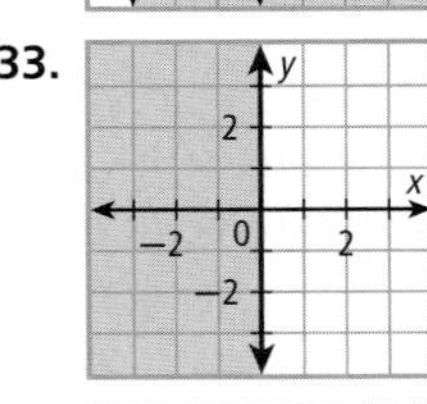

**35.**

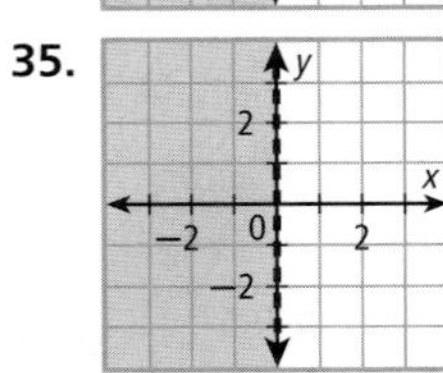

**37.** $7a + 4s \geq 280$ **41.** A **43.** B **45.** C

**47.**

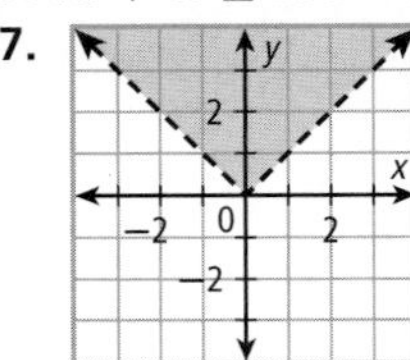

**49.** $y \geq \frac{1}{2}x + 3$ **51.** yes **53.** yes

**55.** $y = \frac{3}{4}x + \frac{7}{4}$ **57.** $y = 3x + 1$

**59.** $y = \frac{1}{2}x + \frac{1}{2}$ **61.** $(-2, 15)$ **63.** $(2, 5)$

**65.** $(12, 3)$

## 6-6

**Check It Out!** **1a.** yes **1b.** no

**2a.**

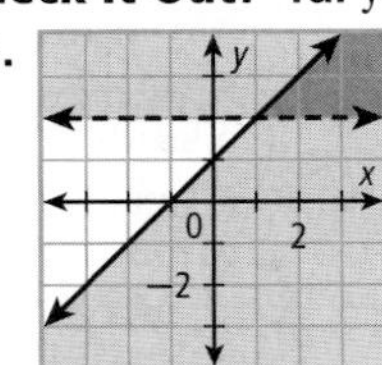

Possible answer: solutions: $(3, 3)$, $(4, 4)$; not solutions: $(-3, 1)$, $(-1, -4)$

**2b.**

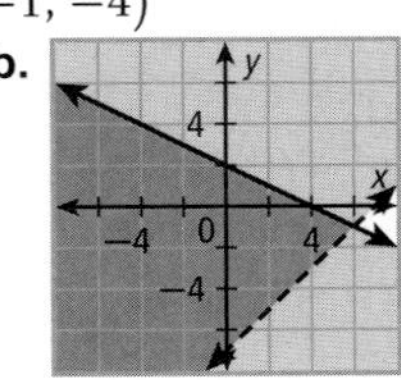

Possible answer: solutions: $(0, 0)$, $(3, -2)$; not solutions: $(4, 4)$, $(1, -6)$

**3a.**

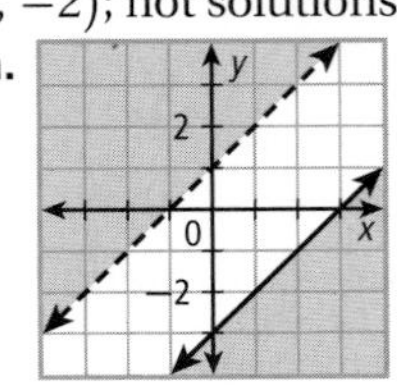

**3b.**

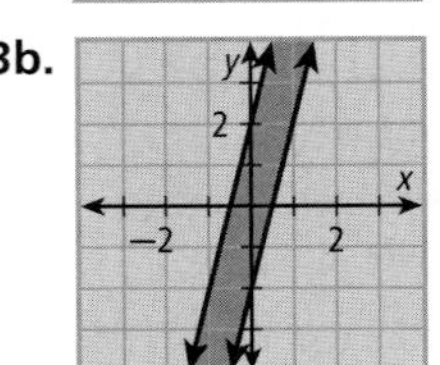

**3c.**

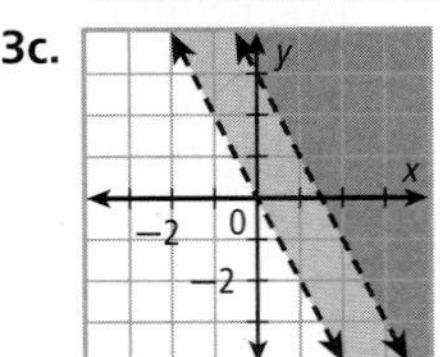

**4.**

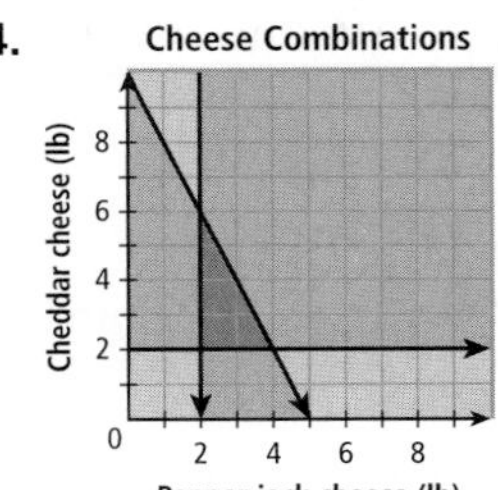


Possible answer: (3 lb pepper jack, 2 lb cheddar), (2.5 lb pepper jack, 4 lb cheddar)

**Exercises** **1.** all **3.** yes

**5.**

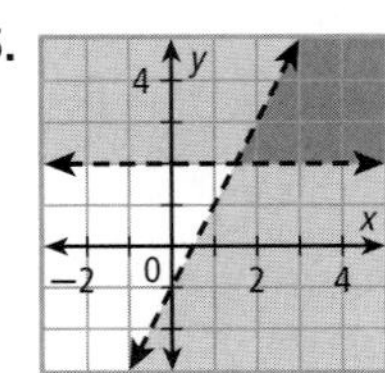

Possible answer: solutions: $(3, 3)$, $(4, 3)$; not solutions: $(0, 0)$, $(2, 1)$

**7.**

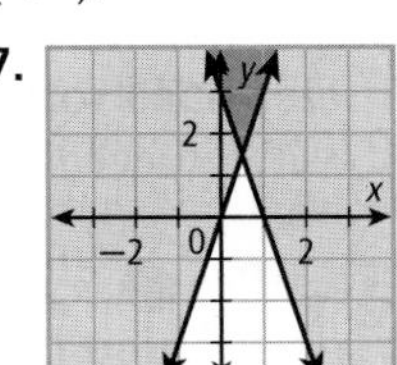

Possible answer: solutions: $(0, 4)$, $(1, 4)$; not solutions: $(2, -1)$, $(3, 1)$

**9.**
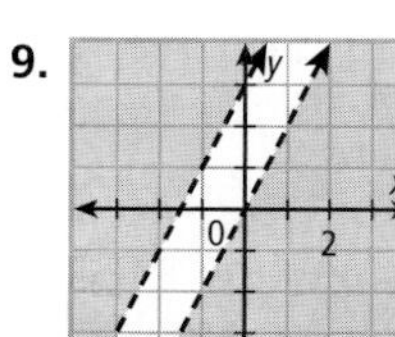

**11.**
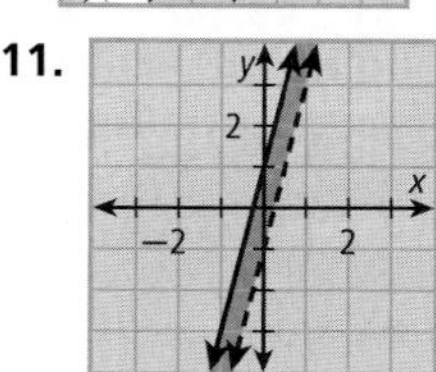

**13.**
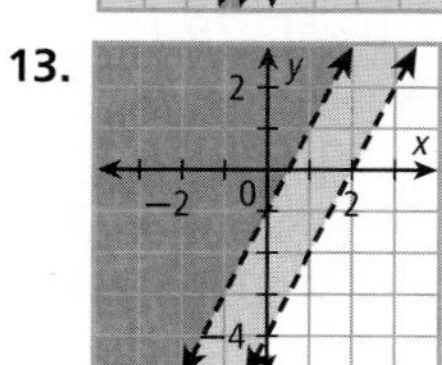

**15.**
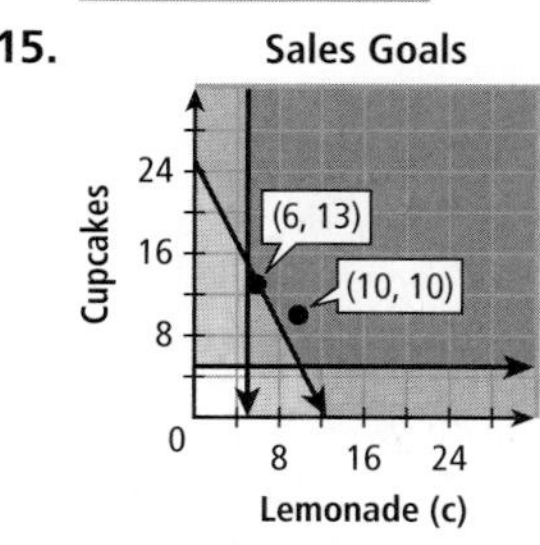


Possible answer: (6 lemonade, 13 cupcakes), (10 lemonade, 10 cupcakes) **17.** yes

**19.**
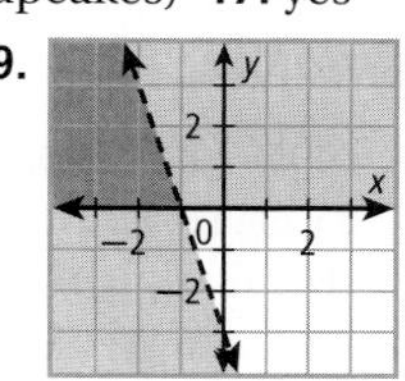

Possible answer: solutions: $(-2, 0)$, $(-3, 1)$; not solutions: $(0, 0)$, $(1, 4)$

**21.**
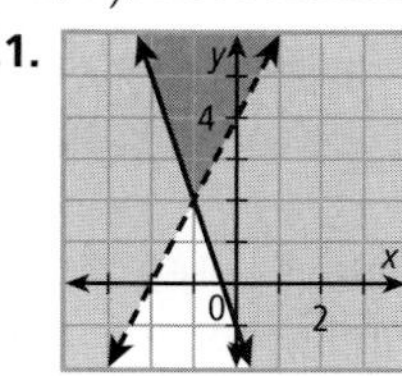

Possible answer: solutions: $(-1, 3)$, $(0, 5)$; not solutions: $(0, 0)$, $(1, 4)$

**23.**
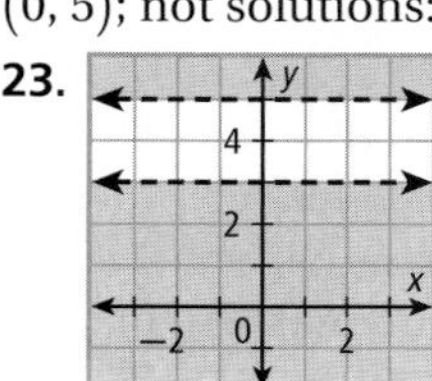

**25.**
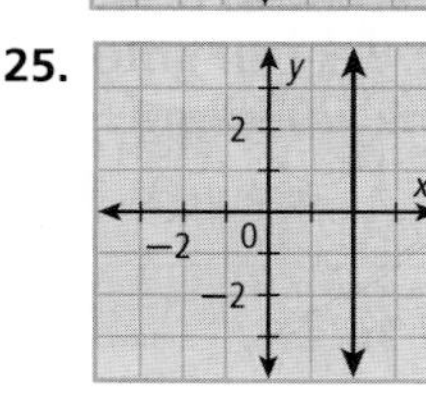

**27.**
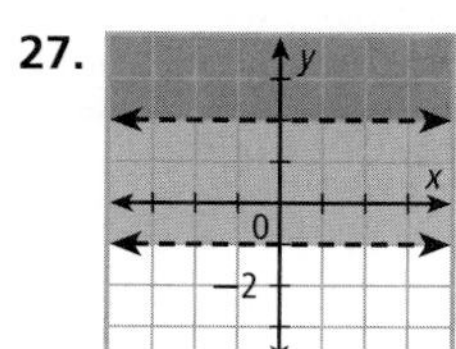

**29.**
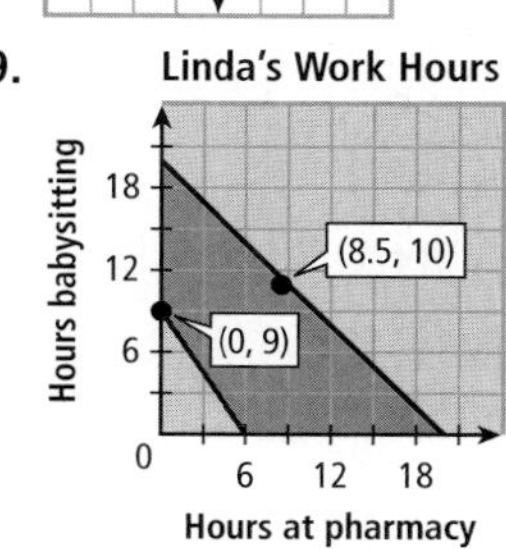


Possible answer: $(0, 9)$, $(8.5, 10)$

**31.**
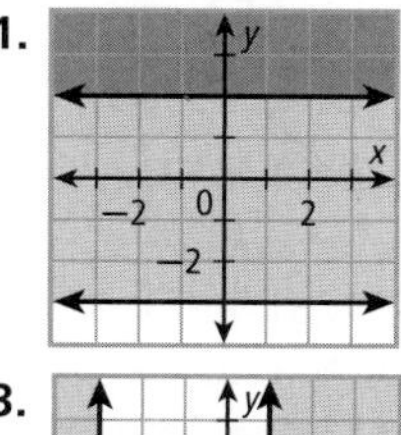

**33.**
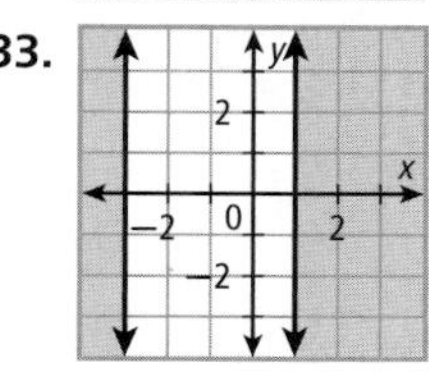

**35.** $\begin{cases} y > x + 1 \\ y < x + 3 \end{cases}$

**37.** $\begin{cases} y < 2 \\ x \geq -2 \end{cases}$

**39.** Student B **45.** G
**47.** about 12 square units

**49.**
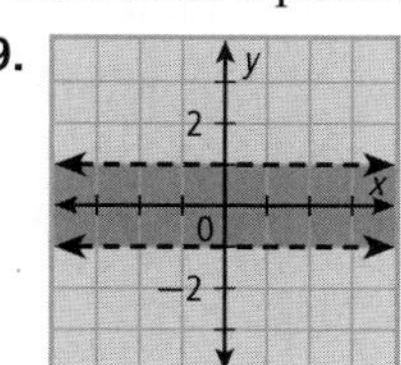

**51.** 25 cm$^2$ **53.** 12.5 cm$^2$ **55.** no
**57.** yes

## Study Guide: Review

**1.** independent system **2.** system of linear equations **3.** solution of a system of linear inequalities **4.** inconsistent system **5.** independent system **6.** no **7.** yes **8.** yes **9.** no **10.** $(-1, -1)$ **11.** $(3, 4)$ **12.** 8 h; \$10 **13.** $(-9, -6)$ **14.** $\left(\frac{1}{2}, -2\right)$ **15.** $(-1, 6)$ **16.** $(4, -5)$ **17.** $(-5, 2)$ **18.** $(6, 6)$ **19.** 10 h; \$1350; Motor Works **20.** $(-1, 3)$ **21.** $(5, -3)$ **22.** $(11, 1)$ **23.** $(0, 3)$ **24.** $(-2, 8)$ **25.** $(3, -5)$ **26.** $(4, -6)$ **27.** $(2, 2)$ **28.** no solution **29.** infinitely many solutions **30.** $(-2, -4)$ **31.** infinitely many solutions **32.** infinitely many solutions **33.** $(-1, -3)$ **34.** no **35.** consistent, independent; one solution **36.** inconsistent; no solution **37.** consistent, dependent; infinitely many solutions **38.** inconsistent; no solution **39.** consistent, independent; one solution **40.** consistent, dependent; infinitely many solutions **41.** inconsistent; no solution **42.** no **43.** yes **44.** yes **45.** no

**46.**
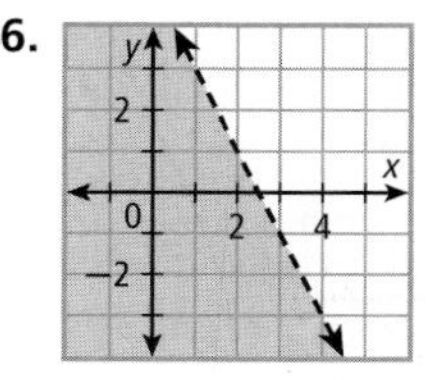

**47.**
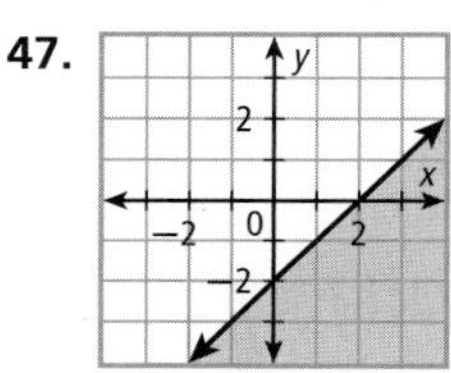

**48.**
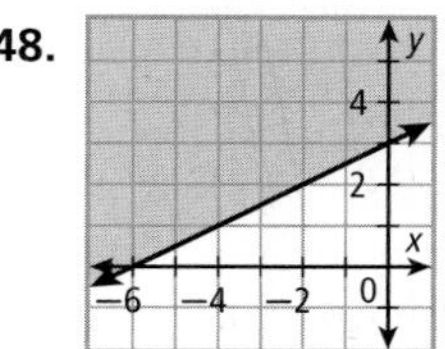

**49.**
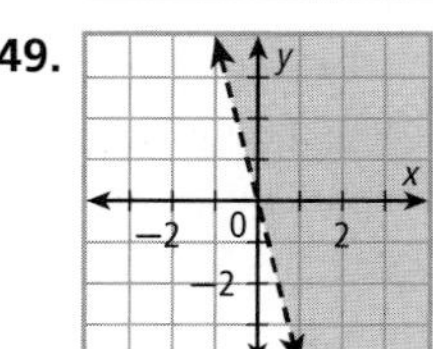

**50.**
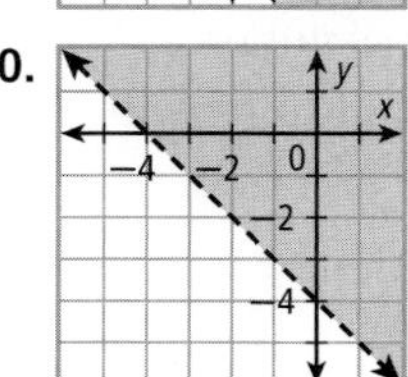

**51.**
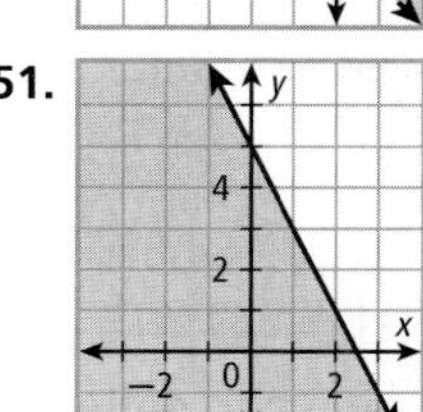

**52.** $x$ = slices of pizza; $y$ = bottles of soda; $2x + 1y \geq 450$

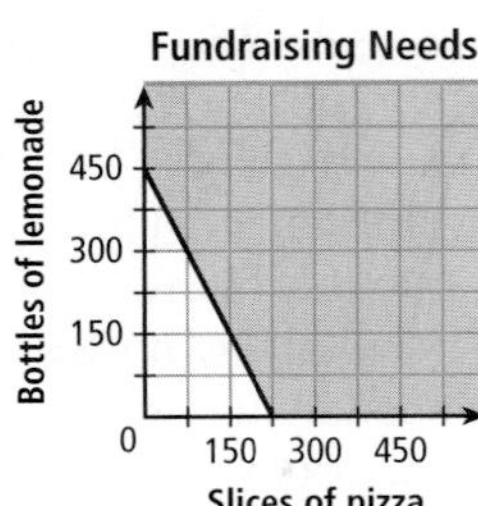


Possible answer: (200, 50), (150, 150) **53.** no **54.** yes

**55.**
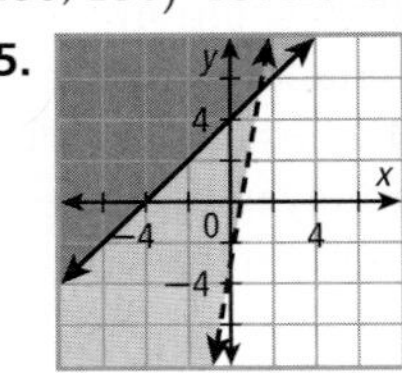

Possible answer: solutions: $(-6, 6)$, $(-10, 0)$; not solutions: $(0, 0)$, $(4, -4)$

**56.**
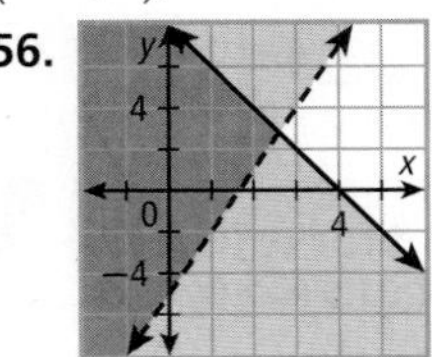

Possible answer: solutions: $(0, 0)$, $(-5, 0)$; not solutions: $(8, 0)$, $(3, -3)$

**57.**
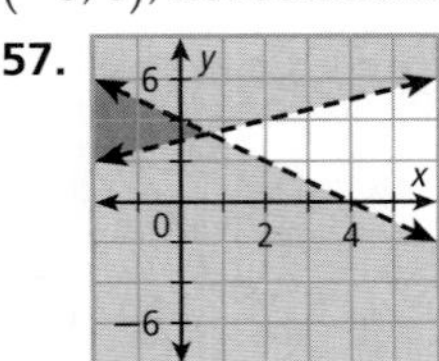

Possible answer: solutions: $(-6, 2)$, $(-8, 1)$; not solutions: $(0, 0)$, $(4, 1)$

**58.**
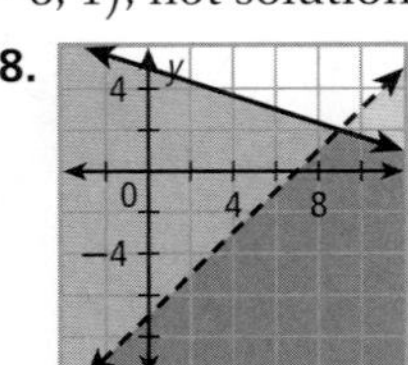

Possible answer: solutions: $(8, -8)$, $(9, 0)$; not solutions: $(0, 0)$, $(0, -4)$

**59.**
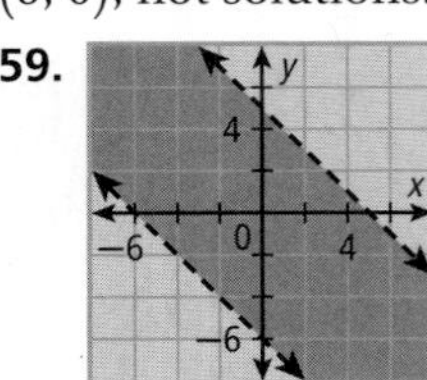

**60.**
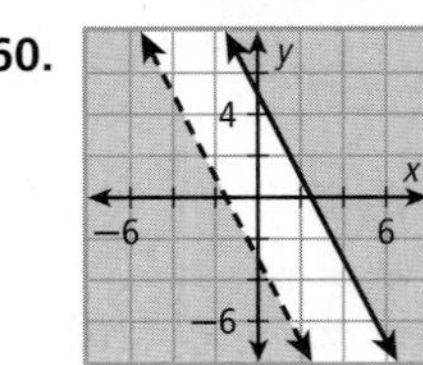

# Chapter 7

## 7-1

**Check It Out! 1.** $\frac{1}{125}$ m **2a.** $\frac{1}{10{,}000}$ **2b.** $\frac{1}{16}$ **2c.** $-\frac{1}{32}$ **2d.** $-\frac{1}{32}$ **3a.** $\frac{1}{64}$ **3b.** 2 **4a.** $\frac{2}{m^3}$ **4b.** $\frac{1}{7r^3}$ **4c.** $g^4h^6$

**Exercises 1.** $\frac{1}{10{,}000{,}000}$ m **3.** 1 **5.** $\frac{1}{27}$ **7.** $-\frac{1}{512}$ **9.** 1 **11.** $\frac{1}{16}$ **13.** $\frac{1}{256}$ **15.** $-\frac{1}{32}$ **17.** $\frac{3}{k^4}$ **19.** $x^{10}d^3$ **21.** $\frac{g^6}{f^4}$ **23.** $\frac{p^7}{q}$ **25.** 1 **27.** $\frac{1}{81}$ **29.** $-\frac{1}{36}$ **31.** 1 **33.** $-\frac{1}{3}$ **35.** 4 **37.** $\frac{1}{256}$ **39.** 1 **41.** $\frac{1}{144}$ **43.** $\frac{1}{k^4}$ **45.** $\frac{b^3}{2}$ **47.** $-\frac{5}{x^3}$ **49.** $\frac{2g^{10}}{7}$ **51.** $s^5t^{12}$ **53.** 1 **55.** $\frac{1}{q^2}$ **57.** $\frac{h^3}{6m^2k}$ **59.** $\frac{1}{16}$ **61.** $-\frac{1}{6}$ **63.** 3 **65.** 3 **67.** $\frac{a^3}{b^2}$ **69.** $\frac{w^2}{y}$ **71.** $-\frac{5}{y^6}$ **73.** $2a^3b$ **75.** $\frac{1}{3x^8y^{12}}$ **79.** never **81.** sometimes **83.** sometimes **87.** 81 **89.** 1 **91.** −3 **93.** −1 **95.** D **97.** A **103.** −2 **105.** 4 **107.** 28 **111.** $y = \frac{1}{3}x + 5$ **113.** $y = -4x + 9$

## 7-2

**Check It Out! 1a.** 0.01 **1b.** 100,000 **1c.** 10,000,000,000 **2a.** $10^8$ **2b.** $10^{-4}$ **2c.** $10^{-1}$ **3a.** 85,340,000 **3b.** 0.00163 **4a.** $1.43 \times 10^5$ km **4b.** 13,000 m/s **5.** $2 \times 10^{-12}$, $4 \times 10^{-3}$, $5.2 \times 10^{-3}$, $3 \times 10^{14}$, $4.5 \times 10^{14}$, $4.5 \times 10^{30}$

**Exercises 3.** 0.00001 **5.** 100,000,000 **7.** $10^{-6}$ **9.** 650,300,000 **11.** 0.092 **13.** $5.85 \times 10^{-3}$, $2.5 \times 10^{-1}$, $8.5 \times 10^{-1}$, $3.6 \times 10^{8}$, $8.5 \times 10^{8}$ **15.** 0.000000001 **17.** 100,000,000,000,000 **19.** $10^6$ **21.** 92,000 **23.** 0.00042 **25.** 10,000,000,000,000 **27.** $1.23 \times 10^{-3}$, $1.32 \times 10^{-3}$, $3.12 \times 10^{-3}$, $2.13 \times 10^{-1}$, $2.13 \times 10^{1}$, $3.12 \times 10^{2}$ **29.** $2.7 \times 10^7$ **31.** $2.35 \times 10^5$ **33.** $6 \times 10^{-7}$ **35.** $4.12 \times 10^{-2}$ **37.** yes **39.** no; $2.5 \times 10^2$ **41.** yes **43.** yes **47.** $10^{-3}$ **51.** F **55.** Let $m$ = number of minutes; $m \geq 45$. **59.** $(-2, 1)$ **61.** $\frac{1}{16}$ **63.** $\frac{3}{125}$

## 7-3

**Check It Out! 1a.** $7^{12}$ **1b.** $3 \times 5^{10}$ **1c.** $\frac{m^5}{n^4}$ **1d.** $\frac{1}{x^7}$ **2.** $6.696 \times 10^8$ mi **3a.** $3^{20}$ **3b.** 1 **3c.** $a^{18}$ **4a.** $64p^3$ **4b.** $25t^4$ **4c.** $\frac{1}{y^4}$

**Exercises 1.** $2^5$ **3.** $n^8$ **5.** $7.5 \times 10^8$ mi **7.** $y^{32}$ **9.** $\frac{1}{3^4}$, or $\frac{1}{81}$ **11.** $x^7y^{13}$ **13.** $36k^2$ **15.** $-8x^{15}$ **17.** $b^{10}$ **19.** $6^8$ **21.** $\frac{x}{y^3}$ **23.** $2^9$, or 512 **25.** $\frac{1}{x^2}$ **27.** $\frac{a^{12}}{b^5}$ **29.** $27x^3$ **31.** $p^{28}q^{14}$ **33.** $-256x^{12}$ **35.** 6 **37.** 3 **39.** 8 **41.** $2x^3$ **43.** $2m^{10}n^6$ **45.** $108x^{13}$ **47.** $125x^6$ **49.** $3a^6$ **51.** $10^3$, or 1000 **57.** $\frac{a^7}{b^5}$ **59.** $15m^{12}n^9$ **61.** $9s^2t^7$ **63.** $t^7$ **67.** yes **69.** $17k^2$ **71.** $6x^4$ **73.** $15a^2b^3$ **75a.** $6 \times 10^{-7}$ m **b.** $3 \times 10^8$ m/s **c.** Associative and Commutative Properties of Multiplication **77.** $(6ab)^2$ **79.** $\left(\frac{1}{2kmn}\right)^2$ **81.** H **83.** F **85.** $3^{2x}$ **87.** $x + 1$ **89.** $x^{3y+3z}$ **91.** $x^{x^2}$ **93.** $x = 4$ **95.** $x = 4$ **97.** $1.728 \times 10^{-6}$ **99.** 15 **101.** no **103.** 7,800,000 **105.** 98.3

## 7-4

**Check It Out! 1a.** $\frac{n^3}{m^5}$ **1b.** $\frac{1}{y^3}$ **1c.** $m^5n^3$ **1d.** $\frac{3}{16}$ **2.** $1.1 \times 10^{-2}$ **3.** \$12,800 **4a.** $\frac{2^6}{3^4}$, or $\frac{64}{81}$ **4b.** $\frac{a^5b^{20}}{c^{10}d^{15}}$ **4c.** $\frac{a^3}{b^3}$ **5a.** $\frac{9^3}{4^3}$, or $\frac{729}{64}$ **5b.** $\frac{b^8c^{12}}{16a^4}$ **5c.** $\frac{t}{s^4}$

**Exercises 1.** 25 **3.** 3 **5.** $7 \times 10^2$ **7.** 1 **9.** $\frac{4}{25}$ **11.** $\frac{1}{a^6b^4}$ **13.** $\frac{16}{9}$ **15.** $\frac{2b^2}{3a^2}$ **17.** 27 **19.** $x^5$ **21.** $5 \times 10^{-7}$ **23.** $7 \times 10^{-3}$ **25.** $2 \times 10^{27}$ kg **27.** $\frac{a^{12}}{b^6}$ **29.** $\frac{y^3}{x^6}$ **31.** $\frac{y^{25}}{x^{10}}$ **33.** $\frac{196}{9x^2}$ **35.** $2d^2$ **37.** $\frac{3x^5}{4}$ **39.** $\frac{c^4}{a^4}$ **41.** $\frac{25}{p^2}$ **43.** $\frac{1}{100}$ **45.** −1 **47.** 2000: $3 \times 10$; 1995: $2.84 \times 10$; 1990: $2.65 \times 10^1$ **51.** 3 **53.** 3; 4 **55.** B **57.** A **59.** 3 **61.** $m$; $(-n)$; $m$; $-n$; Definition of negative exponent; $a^n$ **63.** 1 **65.** 12 **67** $x = -\frac{1}{2}$ **69.** 1 **71.** $-125x^{12}$

## 7-5

**Check It Out! 1a.** 3 **1b.** 1 **1c.** 3 **2a.** 1 **2b.** 5 **3a.** $x^5 + 9x^3 - 4x^2 + 16$; 1 **3b.** $-3y^8 + 18y^5 + 14y$; −3 **4a.** cubic polynomial **4b.** constant monomial **4c.** 8th degree trinomial **5.** 1606 ft

**Exercises 1.** d **3.** a **5.** 3 **7.** 0 **9.** 8 **11.** 3 **13.** 4 **15.** $-8a^9 + 9a^8$; −8 **17.** $3x^2 + 2x - 1$; 3 **19.** $5c^4 + 5c^3 + 3c^2 - 4$; 5 **21.** linear binomial **23.** quartic polynomial **25.** quartic trinomial **27.** 4 **29.** 6 **31.** 7 **33.** 1 **35.** 4 **37.** 2 **39.** 3 **41.** $4.9t^3 - 4t^2 + t + 2.5$; 4.9 **43.** $x^{10} + x^7 - x^5 + x^3 - x$; 1 **45.** $5x^3 + 3x^2 + 5x - 4$; 5 **47.** $-d^3 + 3d^2 + 4d + 5$; −1 **49.** $-x^5 - x^3 + 4x^2 + 1$; −1

**51.** linear monomial **53.** quadratic trinomial **55.** quartic trinomial **57.** quadratic monomial **59.** always **61.** never **63a.** 58.5 in$^3$ **b.** 66 in$^3$ **c.** 0 **d.** yes **65.** –48; 0; 3270 **75.** A is incorrect **77.** J **79a.** 58 cm; 65 cm **b.** 50.310 cm **81.** $90 - m$ **83.** inconsistent; no solutions **85.** consistent and independent; one solution **87.** $\frac{x^2}{y^5}$ **89.** $\frac{p^8}{16}$

## 7-6

**Check It Out! 1a.** $5s^2 + s$ **1b.** $20z^4 - 6$ **1c.** $x^8 + 6y^8$ **1d.** $b^3c^2$ **2.** $12a^3 + 15a^2 - 16a$ **3.** $-2x^2 - x$ **4.** $-0.05x^2 + 46x - 3200$

**Exercises 1.** $-3a^2 + 9a$ **3.** $0.26r^4 + 0.32r^3$ **5.** $3b^3c$ **7.** $23n^3 + 3n + 15$ **9.** $9x^2 - x - 6$ **11.** $4c^4 + 8c + 6$ **13.** $-3r + 11$ **15.** $8a^2 + 5a + 9$ **17.** $12n^2 + 6n - 3m$ **19.** $d^5 + 1$ **21.** $5x$ **23.** $2x^3 - 5$ **25.** $10t^2 + t$ **27.** $x^5 + x^4$ **29.** $-2t^3 + 8t^2$ **31.** $-6m^3 + 2m^2 + 5m + 3$ **33.** $4w^2 + 6w + 4$ **35.** $t - 5$ **37.** $2n - 2$ **39.** $6x^2 - x - 1$ **41.** $-u^3 + 3u^2 + 3u + 6$ **43.** $x = \frac{3}{2}$, or 1.5 **45.** B is incorrect **47.** $3x + 6$ **49.** $6x + 14$ **51.** $2x^2 + x - 5$ **55.** G **57.** $3x^2 - 2$ **69.** $b^{11}$ **71.** $9z^{12}$

## 7-7

**Check It Out! 1a.** $18x^5$ **1b.** $10r^2t^4$ **1c.** $4x^5y^5z^7$ **2a.** $8x^2 + 2x + 6$ **2b.** $15a^3b + 3ab^2$ **2c.** $5r^3s^2 - 15r^2s^3$ **3a.** $a^2 - a - 12$ **3b.** $x^2 - 6x + 9$ **3c.** $2a^2 + 7ab^2 - 4b^4$ **4a.** $x^3 - x^2 - 6x + 18$ **4b.** $3x^3 - 4x^2 + 11x + 10$ **5a.** $x^2 - 4x$ **5b.** 12 m$^2$

**Exercises 1.** $14x^6$ **3.** $3r^5s^5t^5$ **5.** $21x^7y^3$ **7.** $4x^2 + 8x + 4$ **9.** $6a^5b^2 + 2a^4b^3$ **11.** $10x^3y^4 - 5x^2y^2$ **13.** $x^2 - x - 2$ **15.** $x^2 - 4x + 4$ **17.** $4a^4 - 2ab - 12a^3b^2 + 6b^3$ **19.** $x^3 + 3x^2 - 7x + 15$ **21.** $-6x^4 + 12x^3 + 4x^2 - 18x + 20$ **23.** $x^3 - 4x^2 - 4x - 5$ **25a.** $2x^2 - 3x$ **b.** 20 in$^2$ **27.** $-12r^5s^5$ **29.** $10a^4$ **31.** $-6a^5b^6$ **33.** $-12a^7b^7c^8$ **35.** $9s^2 + 54s$ **37.** $27x^3 - 12x^2$ **39.** $10s^3t^3 - 15s^2t^5$ **41.** $-10x^3 + 15x^2 + 5x$ **43.** $-14x^6y^3 + 7x^5y^4$ **45.** $x^2 + 8x + 16$ **47.** $5x^2 + 13x - 6$ **49.** $10x^2 - x - 2$ **51.** $7x^2 - 52x - 32$ **53.** $x^3 - x^2 - x + 10$ **55.** $-10x^4 + 2x^3 + 20x^2 - 19x + 3$ **57.** $8x^5 - 12x^3 - 2x^4 + 17x^2 - 21$ **59.** $x^3 - 3x - 2$ **61.** $-x^3 + 3x^2 - 3x + 1$ **63.** $16x^2 - 48x + 36$ **65a.** 3; 2; $10x^5 + 5x^3$; 5 **b.** 2; 2; $x^4 - x^3 + 2x^2 - 2x$; 4 **c.** 1; 3; $x^4 - 5x^3 + 6x^2 + x - 3$; 4 **d.** $m + n$ **67.** $12x^2 + 12x + 3$ **69a.** $2x^2$ **b.** 800 m$^2$ **71.** $2x^2 - 7x - 30$ **73.** $8x^2 - 16xy + 6y^2$ **75.** $6x^2 - 9x - 6$ **77.** $x^3 + 3x^2$ **79.** $2x^3 - 7x^2 - 10x + 24$ **81.** $8p^3 - 36p^2q + 54pq^2 - 27q^3$ **87.** C **89.** D **91.** $-x^2 - 6$ **93. a.** $x^2 - 1$ **b.** $8x + 16$ **95.** $x^3 + 3x^2 + 2x$ **97.** $a = 2$ **103.** quadratic monomial

## 7-8

**Check It Out! 1a.** $x^2 + 12x + 36$ **1b.** $25a^2 + 10ab + b^2$ **1c.** $1 + 2c^3 + c^6$ **2a.** $x^2 - 14x + 49$ **2b.** $9b^2 - 12bc + 4c^2$ **2c.** $a^4 - 8a^2 + 16$ **3a.** $x^2 - 64$ **3b.** $9 - 4y^4$ **3c.** $81 - r^2$ **4.** 25

**Exercises 3.** $4 + 4x + x^2$ **5.** $4x^2 + 24x + 36$ **7.** $4a^2 + 28ab + 49b^2$ **9.** $x^2 - 4x + 4$ **11.** $64 - 16x + x^2$ **13.** $49a^2 - 28ab + 4b^2$ **15.** $x^2 - 36$ **17.** $4x^4 - 9$ **19.** $4x^2 - 25y^2$ **21.** $x^2 + 6x + 9$ **23.** $x^4 + 2x^2y^2 + y^4$ **25.** $4 + 12x + 9x^2$ **27.** $s^4 - 14s^2 + 49$ **29.** $a^2 - 16a + 64$ **31.** $9x^2 - 24x + 16$ **33.** $a^2 - 100$ **35.** $49x^2 - 9$ **37.** $25a^4 - 81$ **39.** $\pi x^2 + 8\pi x + 16\pi$ **41.** $x^2 + 2xy + y^2$ **43.** $x^4 - 16$ **45.** $x^4 - 8x^2 + 16$ **47.** $1 + 2x + x^2$ **49.** $x^6 - 2a^3x^3 + a^6$ **51.** $36a^2 - 25b^2$ **53.** 4; 4 **55.** 25; 25 **57.** 9; 9 **59.** –5; –5 **61.** 840 **65.** 1, 4, 9, 16, 25, 36, 49, 64, 81, 100 **67.** B **69.** D **71.** $x^3 + 4x^2 - 16x - 64$ **73.** $b = \pm 2\sqrt{c}$ **75.** 13 cm

## Study Guide: Review

**1.** cubic **2.** standard form of a polynomial **3.** monomial **4.** trinomial **5.** scientific notation **6.** $\frac{1}{32}$ in. **7.** 1 **8.** 1 **9.** $\frac{1}{125}$ **10.** $\frac{1}{10{,}000}$, or 0.0001 **11.** $\frac{1}{16}$ **12.** $\frac{1}{256}$ **13.** $\frac{27}{4}$ **14.** $\frac{1}{m^2}$ **15.** $b$ **16.** $-\frac{1}{2x^2y^4}$ **17.** $2b^6c^4$ **18.** $\frac{3a^2}{4c^2}$ **19.** $\frac{s^3}{qr^2}$ **20.** 10,000,000 **21.** 0.00001 **22.** $10^2$ **23.** $10^{-11}$ **24.** 325,000 **25.** 1800 **26.** 0.17 **27.** 0.000299 **28.** $5.8 \times 10^{-7}$, $6.3 \times 10^{-3}$, $2.2 \times 10^2$, $1.2 \times 10^4$ **29.** $38,500,000,000 **30.** $5^9$ **31.** $2^3 \cdot 3^4$ **32.** $b^{10}$ **33.** $r^5$ **34.** $x^{12}$ **35.** 1 **36.** $\frac{1}{2^3}$, or $\frac{1}{8}$ **37.** $\frac{1}{5^4}$, or $\frac{1}{625}$ **38.** $\frac{1}{16b^6}$ **39.** $g^{12}h^8$ **40.** $x^4y^2$ **41.** $-x^4y^2$ **42.** $x^6y^{15}$ **43.** $j^6k^9$ **44.** $\frac{1}{5}$ **45.** $m^8n^{30}$ **46.** $8 \times 10^{11}$ **47.** $9 \times 10^7$ **48.** $1 \times 10^{10}$ **49.** $2.8 \times 10^{15}$ **50.** $6 \times 10^1$ **51.** $1.8 \times 10^{-8}$ **52.** $3.55 \times 10^7$ **53.** 64 **54.** 4 **55.** $m^5$ **56.** 1 **57.** $\frac{7}{32}$ **58.** $6b$ **59.** $t^3v^4$ **60.** 16 **61.** $5 \times 10^1$ **62.** $2.5 \times 10^7$ **63.** $2 \times 10^4$ **64.** $2.25 \times 10^7$ **65.** 0 **66** 4 **67.** 6 **68.** 7 **69.** 2 **70.** 1 **71.** $3n^2 + 2n - 4$; 3 **72.** $-a^6 - a^4 + 3a^3 + 2a$; –1 **73.** $-5t^2 - t + 1$; –5 **74.** $6v^4 + 12v + 3$; 6 **75.** $-2x^2 + x + 5$; –2 **76.** $-2w^6 - w^3 + w^2 - w$; –2 **77.** linear binomial **78.** quintic monomial **79.** quadratic trinomial **80.** cubic polynomial **81.** quartic trinomial **82.** constant monomial **83.** quintic trinomial **84.** 7th-degree polynomial **85.** $-4t + 3$ **86.** $-6x^6 - x^5$ **87.** $3h^3 - 3h^2 + 5$ **88.** $2m^2 - 5m - 1$ **89.** $p^2 + 5p + 8$ **90.** $-7z^2 - z + 10$ **91.** $3g^2 + 2g + 4$ **92.** $-x^2 + 4x + 8$ **93.** $8r^2$ **94.** $6a^6b$ **95.** $18x^3y^2$ **96.** $3s^6t^{14}$ **97.** $2x^2 - 8x + 12$ **98.** $-3a^2b^2 + 6a^3b^2 - 15a^2b$ **99.** $a^2 - 3a - 18$ **100.** $b^2 - 6b - 27$ **101.** $x^2 - 12x + 20$ **102.** $t^2 - 1$ **103.** $8q^2 + 34q + 30$ **104.** $20g^2 - 37g + 8$ **105.** $p^2 - 8p + 16$ **106.** $x^2 + 24x + 144$ **107.** $m^2 + 12m + 36$ **108.** $9c^2 + 42c + 49$ **109.** $4r^2 - 4r + 1$ **110.** $9a^2 - 6ab + b^2$ **111.** $4n^2 - 20n + 25$ **112.** $h^2 - 26h + 169$ **113.** $x^2 - 1$ **114.** $z^2 - 225$ **115.** $c^4 - d^2$ **116.** $9k^4 - 49$

# Chapter 8

## 8-1

**Check It Out! 1a.** $2^3 \cdot 5$ **1b.** $3 \cdot 11$ **1c.** $7^2$ **1d.** 19 **2a.** 4 **2b.** 5 **3a.** $9g^2$ **3b.** 1 **3c.** 1 **4.** 7

**Exercises 3.** $3^2 \cdot 2^2$ **5.** $3^3 \cdot 2$ **7.** 7 (prime) **9.** $3 \cdot 5^2$ **11.** 7 **13.** $x^2$ **15.** 1 **17.** $2 \cdot 3^2$ **19.** $2^2 \cdot 3$ **21.** 17 **23.** $7^2$ **25.** 9 **27.** 10 **29.** $9s$ **31.** 5 **33.** $4x^2$ **35.** $2n$ **39.** 15 rows **41.** 8 and 20; 4 **43.** 63 and 105; 21 **45.** 54 and 72; 18 **47.** 36; 2; 9; 3 **49.** 105; 5; 7 **51.** 2; 2; 27; 3

**53.** 24; 2; 6; 3 **55.** 2; 2; 10, 5 **57.** D
**61.** $9y$ **63.** $2p^2r$ **65.** $4a^2b^3$ **69.** 24
**71.** 25% **73.** no **75.** $3x^2 + 14x - 3$

## 8-2

**Check It Out! 1a.** $b(5 + 9b^2)$
**1b.** cannot be factored
**1c.** $-y^2(18y + 7)$
**1d.** $2x^2(4x^2 + 2x - 1)$
**2.** $2x$ cm; $(x + 2)$ cm
**3a.** $(4s - 5)(s + 6)$ **3b.** $(7x + 1)(2x + 3)$
**3c.** cannot be factored **3d.** $(5x - 2)^2$
**4a.** $(2b^2 + 3)(3b + 4)$
**4b.** $(4r + 1)(r^2 + 6)$
**5a.** $(5x^2 - 4)(3 - 2x)$
**5b.** $(8 - x)(y - 1)$

**Exercises 1.** $5a(3 - a)$ **3.** $7(-5x + 6)$
**5.** $2h(6h^3 + 4h - 3)$ **7.** $m(9m + 1)$
**9.** $3(12f + 6f^2 + 1)$ **11.** $16t(-t + 20)$
**13.** $(2b + 5)(b + 3)$
**15.** $(x^2 + 2)(x + 4)$
**17.** $(2b^2 + 5)(2b - 3)$
**19.** $(7r^2 + 6)(r - 5)$
**21.** $2(r - 2)(r - 3)$
**23.** $(7q - 2)(2q - 3)$
**25.** $(2m^2 - 3)(m - 3)$ **27.** $9y(y + 5)$
**29.** $x^2(-14x^2 + 5)$
**31.** $-d^2(4d^2 - d + 3)$
**33.** $7c(3c + 2)$ **35.** $-5g^2(g + 3)$
**37.** cannot be factored
**39.** $(6y + 1)(y - 7)$
**41.** $(-3 + 4b)(b + 2)$
**43.** $(2a^2 + 3)(a - 4)$
**45.** $(6x^2 + 1)(x + 3)$
**47.** $(n^2 + 5)(n - 2)$
**49.** $(2m^2 - 3)(m - 1)$
**51.** $(2f^2 - 5)(3f - 4)$
**53.** $(b^2 - 2)(b + 4)$ **55.** $3v$
**57.** $2k$ **59.** 2; binomial; $x(x + 5)$
**61.** 3; trinomial; $a^2(a^2 + a + 1)$
**63a.** $100x^3$; $200x^2$; $400x$
**b.** $100x^3 + 200x^2 + 400x + 800$
**c.** $100(x^2 + 4)(x + 2)$; \$1603.12
**67.** The sum of opposite binomials is 0. **69a.** Commutative Property of Addition **b.** Associative Property of Addition **c.** Distributive Property **d.** Distributive Property
**71.** D **73.** C **75.** $-9ab(8ab + 5)$
**77.** $(a + c)(b + d)$
**79.** $(x^2 + 3)(x - 4)$ **83.** $2^2 \cdot 13$
**85.** $2^3 \cdot 3$

## 8-3

**Check It Out! 1a.** $(x + 4)(x + 6)$
**1b.** $(x + 4)(x + 3)$ **2a.** $(x + 6)(x + 2)$
**2b.** $(x - 6)(x + 1)$ **2c.** $(x + 6)(x + 7)$
**2d.** $(x - 8)(x - 5)$ **3a.** $(x + 5)(x - 3)$
**3b.** $(x - 4)(x - 2)$ **3c.** $(x - 10)(x + 2)$

**4.**

| $n$ | $n^2 - 7n + 10$ |
|---|---|
| 0 | $0^2 - 7(0) + 10 = 10$ |
| 1 | $1^2 - 7(1) + 10 = 4$ |
| 2 | $2^2 - 7(2) + 10 = 0$ |
| 3 | $3^2 - 7(3) + 10 = -2$ |
| 4 | $4^2 - 7(4) + 10 = -2$ |

| $n$ | $(n - 5)(n - 2)$ |
|---|---|
| 0 | $(0 - 5)(0 - 2) = 10$ |
| 1 | $(1 - 5)(1 - 2) = 4$ |
| 2 | $(2 - 5)(2 - 2) = 0$ |
| 3 | $(3 - 5)(3 - 2) = -2$ |
| 4 | $(4 - 5)(4 - 2) = -2$ |

**Exercises 1.** $(x + 4)(x + 9)$
**3.** $(x + 4)(x + 10)$ **5.** $(x + 2)(x + 8)$
**7.** $(x - 1)(x - 6)$ **9.** $(x - 3)(x - 8)$
**11.** $(x + 9)(x - 3)$ **13.** $(x - 2)(x + 1)$
**15.** $(x - 9)(x + 5)$ **17.** $(x + 3)(x + 10)$
**19.** $(x + 4)(x + 12)$
**21.** $(x + 2)(x + 14)$ **23.** $(x - 1)(x - 5)$
**25.** $(x - 4)(x - 8)$ **27.** $(x + 7)(x - 3)$
**29.** $(x - 13)(x + 1)$ **31.** $(x - 7)(x + 5)$
**33.** C **35.** D **37.** They are inverse operations. **39.** $(x - 2)(x - 9)$
**41.** $(x + 1)(x + 9)$ **43.** $(x + 6)(x + 7)$
**45.** $(x + 2)(x + 9)$ **47.** $(x - 3)(x + 8)$
**49.** $(x - 5)(x + 9)$ **51.** approximately 1.5 **55.** $x^2 + 6x + 8$; $(x + 4)(x + 2)$
**57.** Positive; $-$, $-$; Both negative
**59.** Negative; $+$, $-$; Positive; negative **61a.** $d = t^2$ **b.** $d = 4t$
**c.** $t(t - 4)$ **63.** true **65.** false **67.** 4
**69.** 4 **71a.** $(x + 10)$ ft **b.** $\ell = (x + 14)$ ft; $w = (x + 6)$ ft **c.** $A = (x^2 + 20x + 84)\text{ ft}^2$
**73.** D **75.** C **77.** $(x^2 + 9)(x^2 + 9)$
**79.** $(d^2 + 21)(d^2 + 1)$
**81.** $(de - 5)(de + 4)$ **83.** 16; 11; 29
**85a.** $(x + 7)$ ft **b.** $(4x + 26)$ ft **c.** \$92.00
**d.** \$36.96 **e.** \$128.96 **87.** $x^5$ **89.** $t^{12}$
**91.** $(x + 2)(x^2 + 5)$
**93.** $(p - 2)(2p^3 + 7)$

## 8-4

**Check It Out! 1a.** $(3x + 1)(2x + 3)$
**1b.** $(3x + 4)(x - 2)$
**2a.** $(2x + 5)(3x + 1)$
**2b.** $(3x - 4)(3x - 1)$
**2c.** $(3x + 4)(x + 3)$
**3a.** $(3x - 1)(2x + 3)$
**3b.** $(4n + 3)(n - 1)$
**4a.** $-1(2x + 3)(3x + 4)$
**4b.** $-1(3x + 2)(x + 5)$

**Exercises 1.** $(2x + 5)(x + 2)$
**3.** $(5x - 3)(x + 2)$ **5.** $(3x + 4)(x - 6)$
**7.** $(x + 2)(5x + 1)$
**9.** $(4x - 5)(x - 1)$
**11.** $(5x + 4)(x + 1)$
**13.** $(2a - 1)(2a + 5)$
**15.** $(2x - 3)(x + 2)$
**17.** $(10x + 1)(x - 1)$
**19.** $(2x + 3)(4 - x)$
**21.** $-1(5x + 3)(x - 2)$
**23.** $-1(2x - 1)(2x + 5)$
**25.** $(3x + 2)(3x + 1)$
**27.** $(n + 2)(3n + 2)$
**29.** $(4c - 5)(c - 3)$
**31.** $(2x + 5)(4x + 1)$
**33.** $(5x - 6)(x + 3)$
**35.** $(10n - 7)(n - 1)$
**37.** $(7x + 1)(x + 2)$
**39.** $(3x - 4)(x - 5)$
**41.** $(x - 7)(4x - 3)$
**43.** $(4y - 1)(3y + 5)$
**45.** $(2x - 1)(2x + 3)$
**47.** $(3x + 5)(x - 3)$
**49.** $-1(2x - 3)(2x + 5)$
**51.** $-1(3x - 2)(x + 1)$
**53.** $2x^2 - 5x + 2$; $(x - 2)(2x - 1)$
**55.** $(9n + 8)(n + 1)$
**57.** $(2x - 1)(2x - 5)$
**59.** $(3x + 8)(x + 2)$
**61.** $(3x + 4)(2x - 3)$
**63.** $(2x - 3)(2x - 3)$
**65.** $(2x + 3)(3x + 2)$
**69a.** $-16t^2 + 20t + 6$
**b.** $-2(4t + 1)(2t - 3)$ **c.** 10 ft **71.** D
**73.** B **77.** B **79.** A **81.** $(2x + 1)(2x + 1)$ **83.** $(9x + 1)(9x + 1)$
**85.** $(5x + 2)(5x + 2)$ **87.** $-7$; $-5$; 5; 7
**89.** $-6$; 6 **95.** $(x + 1)(x - 9)$

## 8-5

**Check It Out! 1a.** $(x + 2)^2$
**1b.** $(x - 7)^2$ **1c.** no; $-6x \neq 2(3x)(2)$
**2.** $4(3x + 1)$ m; 40 m
**3a.** $(1 - 2x)(1 + 2x)$
**3b.** $(p^4 + 7q^3)(p^4 - 7q^3)$ **3c.** no; $4y^5$ is not a perfect square.

**Exercises 1.** yes; $(x - 2)^2$ **3.** yes; $(3x - 2)^2$ **5.** yes; $(x - 3)^2$
**7.** $4(x + 12)$; 88 yd **9.** yes; $(s + 4)(s - 4)$ **11.** yes; $(2x^2 + 3y)(2x^2 - 3y)$
**13.** yes; $(x^3 + 3)(x^3 - 3)$ **15.** No; the last term must be positive. **17.** no; $10x \neq 2(5x)(2)$ **19.** yes; $(4x - 5)^2$
**21.** yes; $(1 + 2x)(1 - 2x)$ **23.** No;

4$x$ and 9$y$ are not perfect squares. **25.** yes; $(9 - 10x^2)(9 + 10x^2)$ **27.** 49 **29.** $4y^2$ **31.** $(10x + 9y)(10x - 9y)$; difference of 2 squares **33.** $(2r^3 + 5s^3)(2r^3 - 5s^3)$; difference of 2 squares **35.** $(x^7 + 12)(x^7 - 12)$; difference of 2 squares **39.** $c = 32$ **41a.** $5z - 4$ **b.** $20z - 16$ **c.** 11; 44; 121 **43a.** 0; 0; 100; 100; 0 **b.** 16; 16; 36; 36; −24 **c.** 25; 25; 25; 25; −25 **d.** 36; 36; 16; 16; −24 **e.** 100; 100; 0; 0; 0 **45.** $a - b$; $a + b$ **47.** C **49.** 1 **51a.** $a = 2$; $b = (v + 2)$ **b.** $[2 + (v + 2)][2 - (v + 2)] = (v + 4)(-v) = -v^2 - 4v$ **53.** $a = 3y$; $b = y$; $(3y - 4)(9y^2 + 12y + 16)$ **55.** D: {5, 4, 3, 2}; R: {2, 1, 0, −1}; yes **57.** D: {2}; R: {−8, −2, 4, 10}; no **59.** $6a^3 + 14a^2 - 10a$ **61.** $t^2 - 8t + 16$ **63.** 8

## 8-6

**Check It Out!** **1a.** yes **1b.** no; $4(x + 1)^2$ **2a.** $4x(x + 2)^2$ **2b.** $2y(x - y)(x + y)$ **3a.** $(3x + 4)(x + 1)$ **3b.** $2p^3(p + 6)(p - 1)$ **3c.** $3q^4(3q + 4)(q + 2)$ **3d.** $2(x^4 + 9)$

**Exercises** **1.** yes **3.** yes **5.** no; $4(2p^2 + 1)(2p^2 - 1)$ **7.** $3x^3(x + 2)(x - 2)$ **9.** $2p(2q + 1)^2$ **11.** $mn(n^2 + m)(n^2 - m)$ **13.** $3x^2(2x - 3)(x + 1)$ **15.** $(p^3 + 1)(p^2 + 3)$ **17.** unfactorable **19.** no; $2xy(y^2 - 4y + 5)$ **21.** no; $3n^2(n + 5)(n - 5)$ **23.** yes **25.** $-4x(x - 3)^2$ **27.** $5(d - 3)(d - 9)$ **29.** $2x(7x + 5y)(7x - 5y)$ **31.** unfactorable **33.** $(p^2 + 4)(p + 2)(p - 2)$ **35.** $(k^2 + 3)(2k + 3)$ **37.** $x^2 + 12x + 36 = (x + 6)^2$ **39.** $s^2 - 16s + 28 = (s - 2)(s - 14)$ **41.** $b^2 - 49 = (b + 7)(b - 7)$ **45.** $(3x - 1)(x + 7)$ **47.** $(3x + y - 3)(3x - y - 7)$ **53.** 8 **55.** C **57.** C **59a.** $V = 8p[\pi(3p + 1)^2]$ **b.** $r = (3p + 1)$ cm **c.** $h = 8$ cm; $V = 128\pi$ cm$^3$ **61.** $h^2(h^4 + 1)(h^2 + 1)$ **63.** $x^{n+3}(x^2 + x + 1)$ **65.** $-2n$ **67.** $12.3r$ **69.** $\frac{23}{2} = \frac{x}{3}$; 34.5 cm **71.** $(2x - 1)(2x + 3)$

## Study Guide: Review

**1.** prime factorization **2.** greatest common factor **3.** $2^2 \cdot 3$ **4.** $2^2 \cdot 5$ **5.** $2^5$ **6.** prime **7.** $2^3 \cdot 5$ **8.** $2^6$ **9.** $2 \cdot 3 \cdot 11$ **10.** $2 \cdot 3 \cdot 19$ **11.** 5 **12.** 12 **13.** 1 **14.** 27 **15.** 4 **16.** 3 **17.** $2x$ **18.** $9b^2$ **19.** $25r$ **20.** 6 boxes; 13 rows **21.** $5x(1 - 3x^2)$ **22.** $16(-b + 2)$ **23.** $-7(2v + 3)$ **24.** $4(a^2 - 3a - 2)$ **25.** $5g(g^2 - 3)(g^2 + 1)$ **26.** $10(4p^2 - p + 3)$ **27.** $(6x + 5)$ ft by $x$ ft **28.** $(2x + 9)(x - 4)$ **29.** $(t - 6)(3t + 5)$ **30.** $(5 - 3n)(6 - n)$ **31.** $(b + 2)(b + 4)$ **32.** $(x^2 + 7)(x - 3)$ **33.** $(n^2 + 1)(n - 4)$ **34.** $(2b + 5)(3b - 4)$ **35.** $(2h^2 - 7)(h + 7)$ **36.** $(3t + 1)(t + 6)$ **37.** $(5m^2 - 1)(2m + 3)$ **38.** $(4p - 3)(2p^2 + 1)$ **39.** $-1(r - 5)(r - 2)$ **40.** $(b^2 - 5)(b - 3)$ **41.** $(t + 4)(-t^2 + 6)$ **42.** $-1(3h - 1)(h - 4)$ **43.** $-1(d - 1)^2$ **44.** $(2 - b)(5b - 6)$ **45.** $(t + 1)(5 - t)$ **46.** $(2b^2 + 5)(4 - b)$ **47.** $-1(3r - 1)(r - 1)$ **48.** left rectangle: $2x^2 + 3x$; right rectangle: $8x + 12$; combined: $2x^2 + 8x + 3x + 12$; $(2x + 3)(x + 4)$ **49.** $(x + 1)(x + 5)$ **50.** $(x + 2)(x + 4)$ **51.** $(x + 3)(x + 5)$ **52.** $(x - 6)(x - 2)$ **53.** $(x + 5)^2$ **54.** $(x - 2)(x - 11)$ **55.** $(x + 4)(x + 20)$ **56.** $(x - 6)(x - 20)$ **57.** $(x + 12)(x - 7)$ **58.** $(x + 3)(x - 8)$ **59.** $(x + 4)(x - 7)$ **60.** $(x - 1)(x + 5)$ **61.** $(x + 3)(x - 2)$ **62.** $(x + 5)(x - 4)$ **63.** $(x - 8)(x + 6)$ **64.** $(x - 9)(x + 4)$ **65.** $(x - 12)(x + 6)$ **66.** $(x - 10)(x + 7)$ **67.** $(x + 20)(x - 6)$ **68.** $(x + 7)(x - 1)$ **69.** $(y + 3)$ m **70.** $(2x + 1)(x + 5)$ **71.** $(3x + 7)(x + 1)$ **72.** $(2x - 1)(x - 1)$ **73.** $(3x + 2)(x + 2)$ **74.** $(5x + 3)(x + 5)$ **75.** $(2x - 3)(3x - 5)$ **76.** $(4x + 5)(x + 2)$ **77.** $(3x + 4)(x + 2)$ **78.** $(7x - 2)(x - 5)$ **79.** $(3x + 2)(3x + 4)$ **80.** $(2x + 1)(x - 1)$ **81.** $(3x + 1)(x - 4)$ **82.** $(2x - 1)(x - 5)$ **83.** $(7x + 2)(x - 3)$ **84.** $(5x + 1)(x - 2)$ **85.** $-1(2x - 1)(3x + 2)$ **86.** $(6x + 5)(x - 1)$ **87.** $(3x - 2)(2x + 7)$ **88.** $-1(2x + 1)(2x - 5)$ **89.** $-1(2x - 3)(5x + 2)$ **90.** $12x^2 - 11x - 5$; $(4x - 5)(3x + 1)$ **91.** yes; $(x + 6)^2$ **92.** no; $5x \neq 2(x)(5)$ **93.** no; $-2x \neq 2(2x)(1)$ **94.** yes; $(3x + 2)^2$ **95.** no; $8x \neq 2(4x)(2)$ **96.** yes; $(x + 7)^2$ **97.** yes; $(10x - 9)(10x + 9)$ **98.** No; 2 is not a perfect square. **99.** No; 5 and 10 are not perfect squares. **100.** yes; $(-12 + x^3)(-12 - x^3)$ **101.** no; terms must be subtracted **102.** yes; $(10p - 5q)(10p + 5q)$ **103.** $(x - 5)(x + 5)$; difference of 2 squares **104.** $(x + 10)^2$; perfect-square trinomial **105.** $(j - k^2)(j + k^2)$; difference of 2 squares **106.** $(3x - 7)^2$; perfect-square trinomial **107.** $(9x + 8)^2$; perfect-square trinomial **108.** $(4b^2 - 11c^3)(4b^2 + 11c^3)$; difference of 2 squares **109.** no; $2(2x + 3)(x + 1)$ **110.** yes **111.** no; $(b^2 + 9)(b - 3)(b + 3)$ **112.** yes **113.** $4(x - 4)(x + 4)$ **114.** $3b^3(b - 4)(b + 2)$ **115.** $a^2b^3(a - b)(a + b)$ **116.** $t^4(t^8 + 1)(t^4 + 1)(t^2 + 1)(t + 1)(t - 1)$ **117.** $5(x + 3)(x + 1)$ **118.** $2x^2(x - 5)(x + 5)$ **119.** $2(s + 4)(t + 4)$ **120.** $5m(5m + 2)(m - 4)$ **121.** $4x(4x^2 + 1)(2x - 3)$ **122.** $6s^2t(s + t^2)$ **123.** $2(m + 3)(m - 3)(5m + 2)$

# Chapter 9

## 9-1

**Check It Out!** **1a.** Yes; the second differences are constant. **1b.** Yes; the function can be written in the form $y = ax^2 + bx + c$.

**2a.** 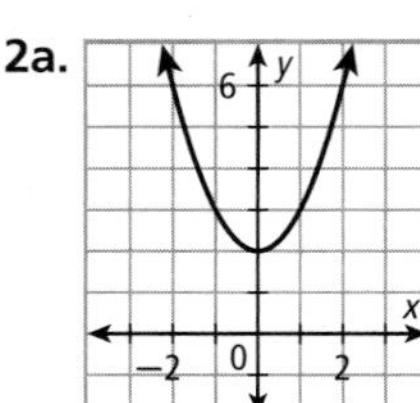


**2b.** 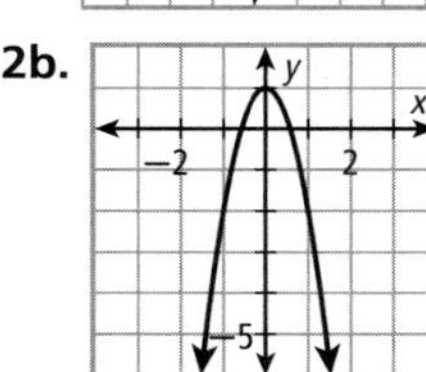


**3a.** Because $a < 0$, the parabola opens downward. **3b.** Because $a > 0$, the parabola opens upward. **4a.** Vertex: $(-2, 5)$; maximum: 5 **4b.** Vertex: $(3, -1)$; minimum: $-1$ **5a.** D: all real numbers; R: $y \geq 4$ **5b.** D: all real numbers; R: $y \leq 3$

**Exercises** **1.** minimum **3.** yes **5.** no

**7.** 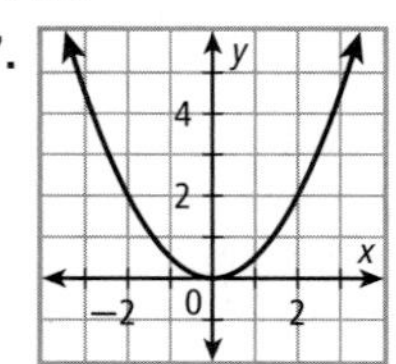


**9.** 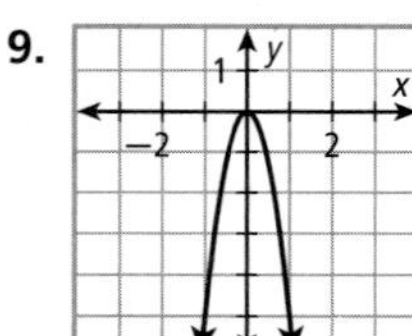


**11.** upward; $a > 0$ **13.** upward; $a > 0$ **15.** downward; $a < 0$ **17.** $(-3, -4)$; minimum: $-4$ **19.** D: all real numbers; R: $y \leq 4$ **21.** D: all real numbers; R: $y \geq -4$ **23.** yes **25.** yes **31.** upward; $a > 0$ **33.** vertex: $(0, -5)$; minimum: $-5$ **35.** D: all real; numbers; R: $y \leq 0$ **37.** D: all real numbers; R: $y \geq -2$ **39.** never **41.** always **43.** sometimes **45.** no **47.** yes **49.** yes **53.** quadratic **55.** quadratic **57.** neither **59.** linear **61b.** $t \geq 0$ **c.** 16 ft **d.** 2 s **65.** C **67.** yes **71.** $(-2)^4$ **73.** $42\frac{3}{4}$ mi

## 9-2

**Check It Out!** **1a.** no zeros **1b.** 3 **2a.** $x = -3$ **2b.** $x = 1$ **3.** $x = -\frac{1}{4}$ **4.** $(2, -14)$ **5.** 7 ft

**Exercises** **3.** $-1$ **5.** no zeros **7.** $x = 2$ **9.** $x = -2$ **11.** $x = -\frac{3}{4}$ **13.** $(1, 8)$ **15.** $(-2, -2)$ **17.** $(-2, -9)$ **19.** no zeros **21.** $-8, -2$ **23.** $x = 6$ **25.** $x = -\frac{1}{2}$ **27.** $x = 5$ **29.** $(-3.5, -12.25)$ **31.** $(-2, 5)$ **33.** $(1, 4.5)$ **35.** $x = 0.$ **37.** 0 **39.** 2 **41.** B **43.** 2 **45.** 25 ft; 100 ft **47.** $y = -2x + 3$ **49.** $y = -4x + 2$ **51.** yes

## 9-3

**Check It Out!**

**1a.** 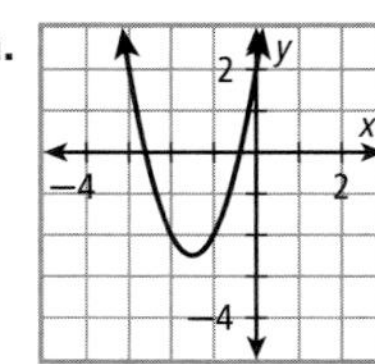


**1b.** 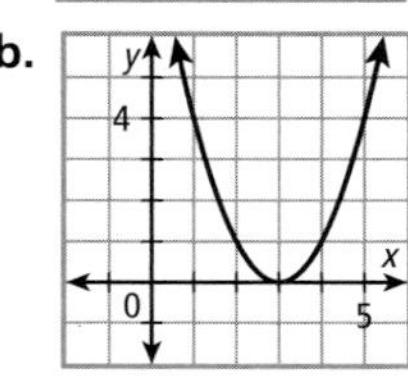


**2.** maximum height: 9 ft at 0.75 s; time it takes to reach the pool: 1.5 s

**Exercises** **1.** 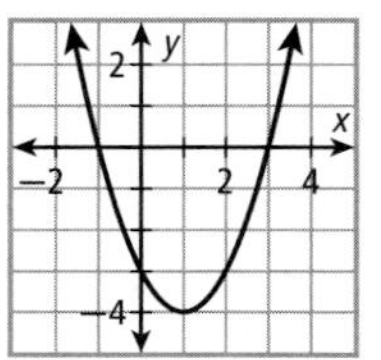


**3.** 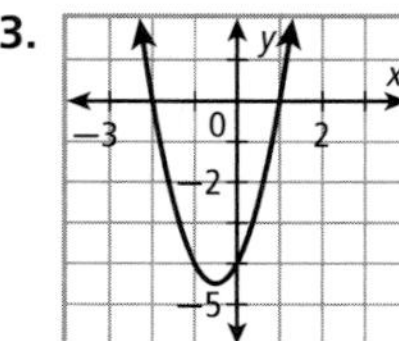


**5.** 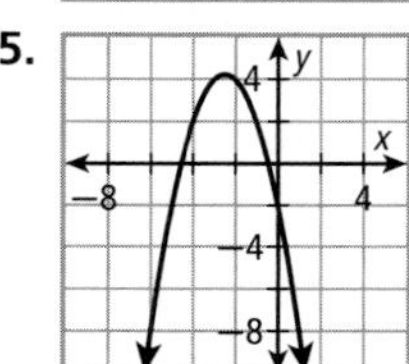


**7.** Maximum height: 144 ft at 3 s; time in the air: 6 s

**9.** 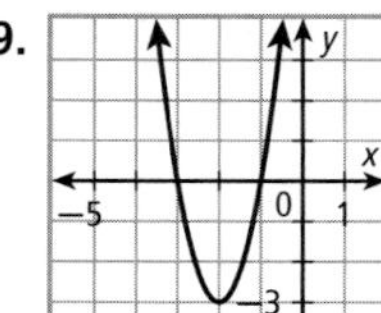


**11.** 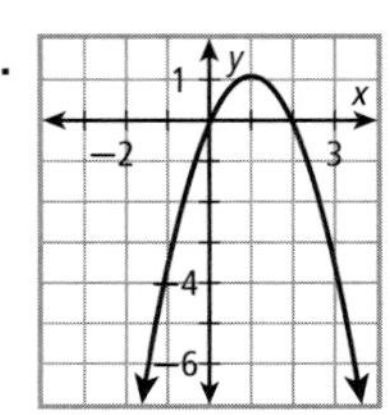


**13.** 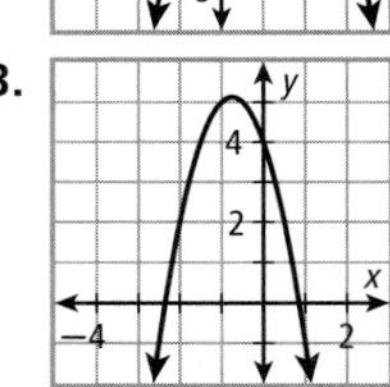


**15.** $x = 4$; $(4, -16)$ **17.** $x = 0$; $(0,4)$ **19.** $x = -\frac{1}{2}$; $\left(-\frac{1}{2}, -\frac{15}{4}\right)$ **21.** vertex: $(0, 0)$; axis of symmetry $x = 0$ **23.** vertex: $(3, -5)$; axis of symmetry $x = 3$ **25.** vertex: $(0, -4)$; axis of symmetry $x = 0$ **27b.** D: $\{x \mid 0 \leq x \leq 3.16\}$; R: $\{y \mid 0 \leq x \leq 50\}$ **c.** 3.16 s **35a.** $h(t) = -16t^2 + 45t + 50$ **b.** $(1.4, 81.6)$ **37.** A **39.** D **41.** $-1$ **43.** 3; 6 **45.** none; 3 **47.** $(3, -1)$ **49.** $(-1, -16)$ **51.** $(-1, 4)$

## 9-4

**Check It Out!** **1a.** $f(x)$, $g(x)$ **1b.** $g(x)$, $f(x)$, $h(x)$ **2a.** same width, same axis of symmetry, opens upward, vertex is translated 4 units down **2b.** narrower, same axis of symmetry, opens upward, vertex is translated 9 units up **2c.** wider, same axis of symmetry, opens upward, vertex is translated 2 units up **3a.** The graph of the ball that is dropped from a height of 100 ft is a vertical translation of the graph of the ball that is dropped from a height of 16 ft. The $y$-intercept of the graph of the ball that is dropped from 100 ft is 84 units higher. **3b.** The ball that is dropped from 16 ft reaches the ground in 1 s. The ball that is dropped from 100 ft reaches the ground in 2.5 s.

**Exercises** **1.** $f(x)$, $g(x)$ **3.** $h(x)$, $g(x)$, $f(x)$ **5.** same width, same axis of symmetry, opens upward, vertex is translated 6 units up **7.** wider, same axis of symmetry, opens upward, same vertex **9a.** $h_1(t) = -16t^2 + 16$, $h_2(t) = -16t^2 + 256$; The graph of $h_2$ is a vertical translation of the graph of $h_1$. The $y$-intercept of $h_2$ is 240 units higher. **b.** The baseball that is dropped from 256 ft reaches the ground in 4 s. The baseball that is dropped from 16 ft reaches the ground in 1 s. **11.** $f(x)$, $g(x)$ **13.** $f(x)$, $h(x)$, $g(x)$ **19.** always **21.** never **25.** $f(x) = 3x^2 - 6$ **39.** D **41.** 0 **43a.** $f(x) = x^2 - 7$ **b.** $f(x) = -x^2 + 2$ **c.** $f(x) = \frac{1}{2}x^2 + 1$ **45.** no correlation

## 9-5

**Check It Out!** **1a.** $x = -4$ **1b.** no zeros **1c.** $x = -2$ or $x = 2$ **2.** 2 s

**Exercises** **1.** zeros, $x$-intercepts **3.** $-4, 4$ **5.** 6 **7.** $-2, 4$ **9.** $-1$ **11.** no real solutions **13.** no real solutions **15.** $x = -4$ or $x = 4$ **17.** $x = \frac{1}{2}$ or $x = 5$ **19.** $x = -3$ **21.** no real solutions **23.** no real solutions **25.** always **27.** always **29.** never **31a.** 4 s **b.** 10 ft **33.** 1.4 s **35.** $-1, 1$ **41.** C **45.** no real solutions **47.** $x \approx -1.6$ or $x \approx 0.86$ **49.** $y = -3x - 2$ **51.** 27 **53.** $x^{11}$ **55.** $a^3b^3$ **57.** $\frac{27b^2}{8a^6}$

## 9-6

**Check It Out!** **1a.** $0, -4$ **1b.** $-4, 3$ **2a.** 3 **2b.** $1, -5$ **2c.** $-\frac{5}{3}$ **2d.** $\frac{1}{3}, 1$ **3.** 1.5 s

**Exercises** **1.** $-2, 8$ **3.** $-7, -9$ **5.** $-11, 0$ **7.** $-6, 2$ **9.** 2, 3 **11.** $-8, -2$ **13.** 4 **15.** 6 **17.** 8 **19.** 1 s **21.** $-4, -7$ **23.** 0, 9 **25.** $-\frac{1}{2}, \frac{1}{3}$ **27.** $-2, 4$ **29.** $-5$ **31.** $-2$ **33.** 1 **35.** 1 **37.** 1 **39.** A is correct **41.** 6 m **43.** 6 s **45.** no **47a.** 3 s **b.** 64 ft **c.** yes **49.** F **51.** $-5, -1$ **53.** $\frac{1}{2}, -3$ **55.** $-2, 5$ **57.** $3x$ **59.** $f - 4$ **61.** 11 **63.** $-10$ **65.** $-7, 7$ **67.** 3, 5

## 9-7

**Check It Out!** **1a.** $\pm 11$ **1b.** 0 **1c.** no real solutions **2a.** no real solutions **2b.** $\pm\frac{1}{6}$ **3a.** $\pm 9.49$ **3b.** $\pm 5.66$ **3c.** no real solutions **4.** 45 ft

**Exercises** **1.** $\pm 15$ **3.** no real solutions **5.** no real solutions **7.** $\pm 5$ **9.** no real solutions **11.** $\pm 2$ **13.** $\pm 5.20$ **15.** $\pm 4.47$ **17.** $\pm 13$ **19.** no real solutions **21.** no real solutions **23.** $\pm\frac{2}{9}$ **25.** $\pm\frac{5}{8}$ **27.** $\pm\frac{13}{7}$ **29.** $\pm 4.69$ **31.** $\pm 10.20$ **33.** $\pm 7.07$ **35.** 6.1 s **37.** $a = -6$ and $b = -3$ or $a = 6$ and $b = 3$ **39.** about 4.2 ft by 8.4 ft **41.** A **43.** sometimes **45a.** $a$ must be greater than 0. **b.** $a$ must be equal to 0. **c.** $a$ must be less than 0. **47.** no; $x = \pm\frac{\sqrt{2}}{2}$, irrational **49.** yes; $x = \pm\frac{1}{2}$, rational **53.** H **55.** $\pm\frac{1}{4}$ **57.** $\pm\frac{8}{11}$ **59.** 13 **61.** 2, 4 **63.** $-2, 7$

## 9-8

**Check It Out!** **1a.** 36 **1b.** $\frac{25}{4}$ **1c.** 16 **2a.** $-9, -1$ **2b.** $4 \pm \sqrt{21}$ **3a.** $-\frac{1}{3}, 2$ **3b.** no real solutions **4.** 16.4 ft by 24.4 ft

**Exercises** **3.** 4 **5.** $-5, -1$ **7.** $-6, 5$ **9.** 1, 9 **11.** $\frac{-5 \pm 3\sqrt{5}}{2}$ **13.** no real solutions **15.** $4 \pm \sqrt{10}$ **17.** 7.2 m; 11.2 m **19.** 1 **21.** $-2, 12$ **23.** $-13, -2$ **25.** $-6, 8$ **27.** $-2, 3$ **29.** $\frac{-1 \pm \sqrt{5}}{2}$ **31.** $\frac{-15 \pm \sqrt{105}}{2}$ **33.** 4 in. **35.** $1 \pm \sqrt{7}$ **37.** $-3, \frac{1}{2}$ **39.** $-10, 2$ **41.** 81 **43.** $\frac{49}{4}$ **45.** 9 **47a.** $(10 + 2x)(24 + 2x) = 640$ **b.** 3 ft **51.** $-6 \pm 3\sqrt{3}$ **53.** $-6$ **55.** no real solutions **57.** no real solutions **61a.** $-16t^2 + 64t + 32 = 0$ **b.** 4 **c.** $\approx 4.4$ s **63.** B **65.** B **67.** $-\frac{3}{2}, \frac{2}{3}$ **69.** $-\frac{2}{3} - \frac{\sqrt{7}}{3}, -\frac{2}{3} + \frac{\sqrt{7}}{3}$ **71.** $0, -\frac{b}{a}$ **77.** $x^2 - 8x + 16$ **79.** $t^2 - 8t + 16$ **81.** $64b^4 - 4$ **83.** $\pm 1$ **85.** $\pm 4$ **87.** $\pm 15$ **89.** $\pm 1.55$ **91.** $\pm 5.10$ **93.** $\pm 1.48$

## 9-9

**Check It Out!** **1a.** $2, -\frac{1}{3}$ **1b.** $2, -\frac{1}{5}$ **2.** $\approx 0.13$, $\approx 3.87$ **3a.** 0 **3b.** 1 **3c.** 2 **4.** No; for the equation $45 = -16t^2 + 20t + 0$, the discriminant is negative, so the weight will not ring the bell. **5a.** $-2, -5$ **5b.** $-2, 7$ **5c.** $\approx -4.39$, $\approx 2.39$

**Exercises** **1.** no **3.** $\frac{1}{2}, 3$ **5.** $-4, -10$ **7.** $-\frac{1}{2}, \frac{3}{2}$ **9.** $\approx -5.45$, $\approx -0.55$ **11.** $\approx 1.14$, $\approx -1.47$ **13.** $\approx -1.85$, $\approx 1.35$ **15.** 1 **17.** 0 **19.** 2 **21.** 0 **23.** yes **25.** $-3$ **27.** $-\frac{1}{2}$ **29.** $-3, \frac{3}{2}$ **31.** 1, 9 **33.** $\approx 0.27$, $\approx 3.73$ **35.** $\approx 2.78$, $\approx -0.72$ **37.** 2 **39.** no **41.** $-5, 3$ **43.** no real solutions **45.** 2 solutions; $-2, \frac{1}{4}$ **47.** 1 solution; $\frac{2}{3}$ **49.** 2 $x$-intercepts; $\frac{7}{2}, -3$ **51.** 1 $x$-intercept; 5 **57.** A **59a.** 1 **b.** $-1$ **c.** $-1$ **d.** $-1$ **63.** $-10, 4$ **65.** $(r^3 + t)(s^2 + 5)$ **67.** $(n^4 - 2)(n - 6)$ **69.** $f(x)$, $g(x)$

## Study Guide: Review

**1.** vertex **2.** minimum; maximum **3.** zero of a function **4.** discriminant of a quadratic equation **5.** completing the square **6.** Yes; it is in standard form. **7.** No; there is no $ax^2$ term. **8.** Yes; it is in standard form. **9.** No; a quadratic function does not have a term to the third power.

**10.**

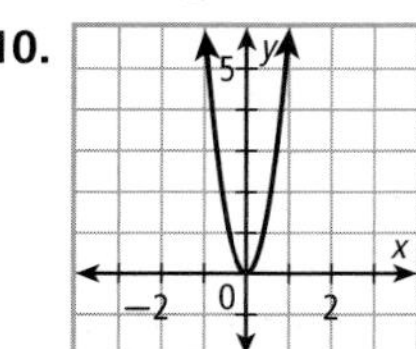

**11.**

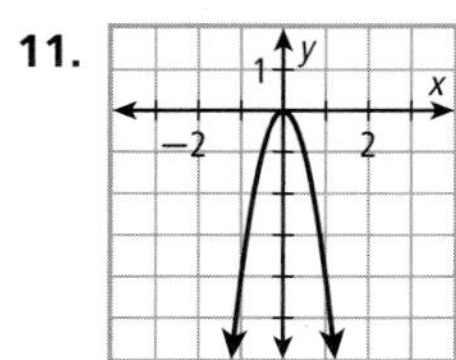

**12.**

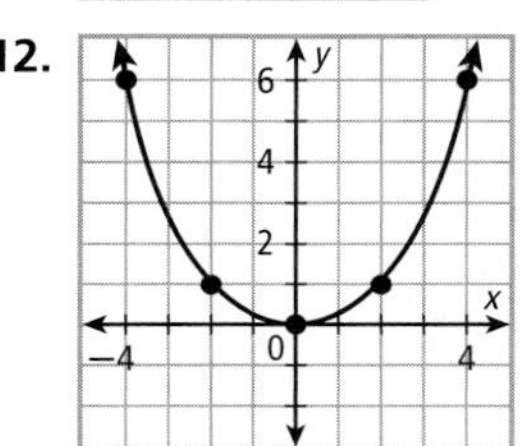

**13.**

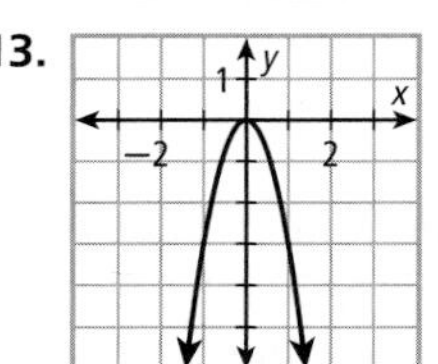

**14.** upward **15.** downward **16.** $(-2, -4)$; minimum: $-4$ **17.** $-5$ and 2 **18.** $-1$ and 2 **19.** $x = 6$; $(6, 4)$ **20.** $x = -1$; $(-1, -18)$

**21.**

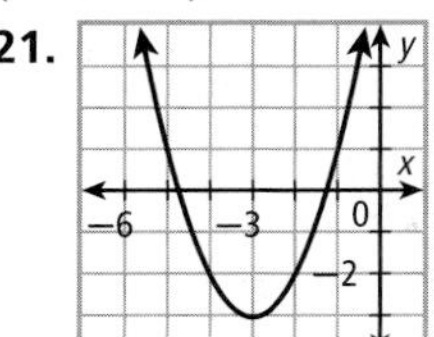

**22.**

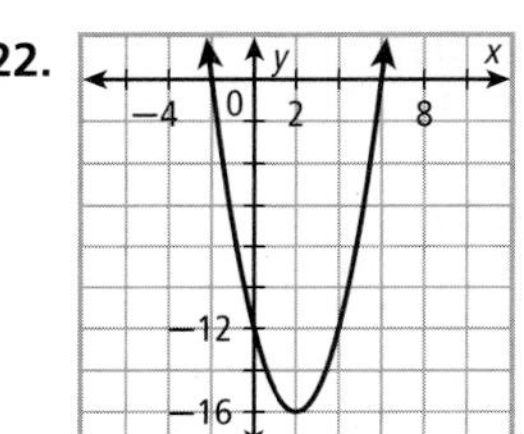

Selected Answers

**23.** 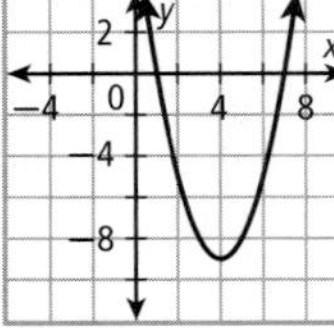

**24.** 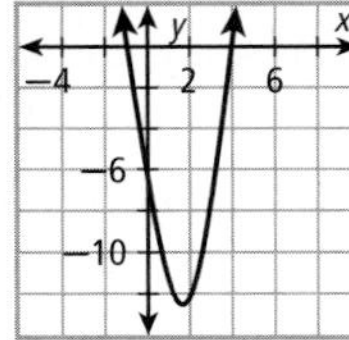

**25.** 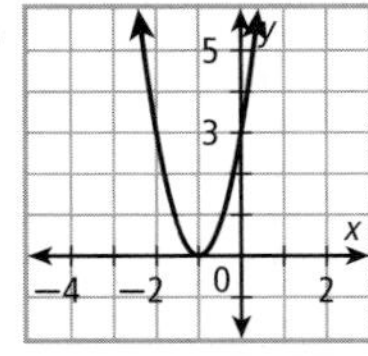

**26.** 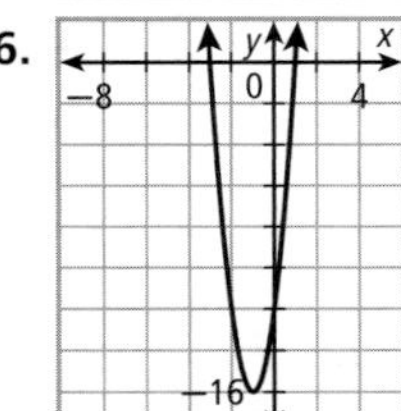

**27.** 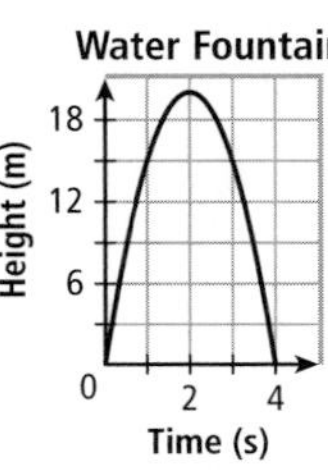


In 2 seconds, the water reaches its maximum height of 20 meters. It takes a total of 4 seconds for the water to reach the ground. **28.** $g(x)$, $f(x)$ **29.** The graphs have the same width. **30.** $h(x)$, $f(x)$, $g(x)$ **31.** same width, same axis of symmetry, opens upward, vertex translated 5 units up **32.** narrower, same axis of symmetry, opens upward, vertex translated 1 unit down **33.** narrower, same axis of symmetry, opens upward, vertex translated 3 units up

**34.** 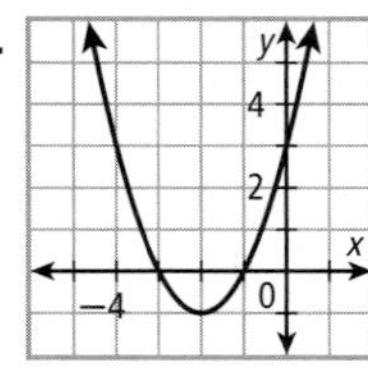

$x = -3$ or $x = -1$

**35.** 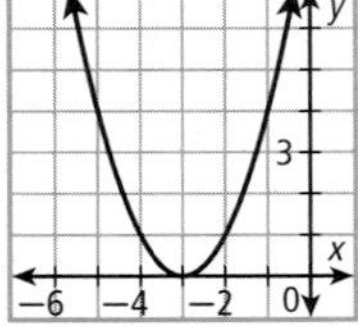

$x = -3$

**36.** 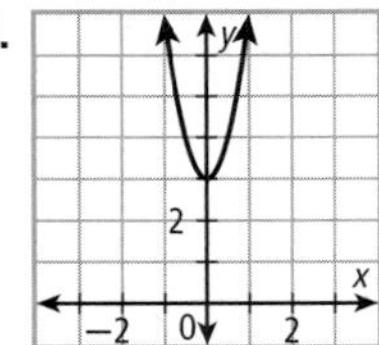

no real solutions

**37.** 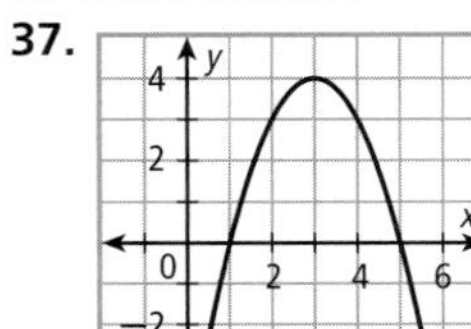

$x = 1$ or $x = 5$

**38.** 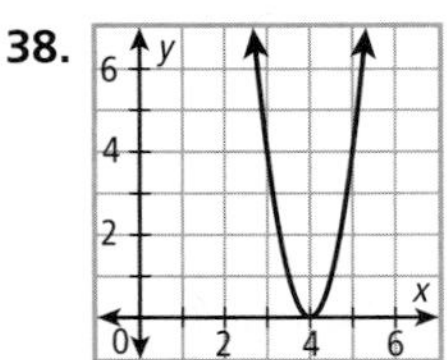

$x = 4$

**39.** 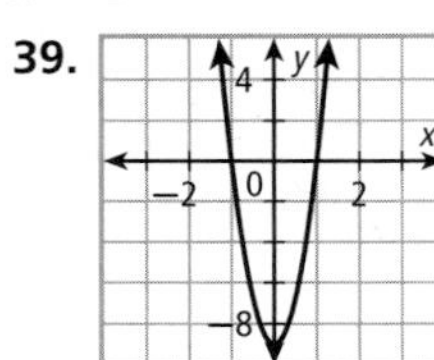

$x = 1$ or $x = -1$

**40.** 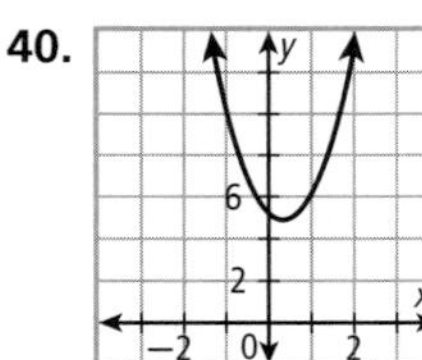

no real solutions **41.** $x = -5$ or $x = -1$ **42.** $x = -7$ or $x = -2$ **43.** $x = -3$ or $x = 5$ **44.** $x = -1$ or $x = 2$ **45.** $x = -5$ **46.** $x = 4.5$ **47.** $x^2 + 2x = 48$; 6 ft **48.** $x = -8$ or $x = 8$ **49.** $x = -12$ or $x = 12$ **50.** no real solutions **51.** $x = 0$ **52.** $x = -5$ or $x = 5$ **53.** $x = -\frac{5}{2}$ or $x = \frac{5}{2}$ **54.** 4 ft **55.** $x = -8$ or $x = 6$ **56.** $x = -7$ or $x = 3$ **57.** $x = 1$ or $x = 5$ **58.** $x = 5 \pm \sqrt{5}$ **59.** 16 ft by 12 ft **60.** $x = -1$ or $x = 6$ **61.** $x = -\frac{1}{2}$ or $x = 5$ **62.** $x = 1$ **63.** $x = \frac{6 \pm \sqrt{8}}{2}$ **64.** 1 **65.** 0 **66.** 2 **67.** 2

# Chapter 10

## 10-1

**Check It Out! 1a.** bread **1b.** cheese and mayonnaise **2.** 2001, 2002, and 2005; about 13,000 **3.** about 18°F **4.** Prices increased from January through July or August, and then prices decreased through November. **5.** 31.25%

**6.** 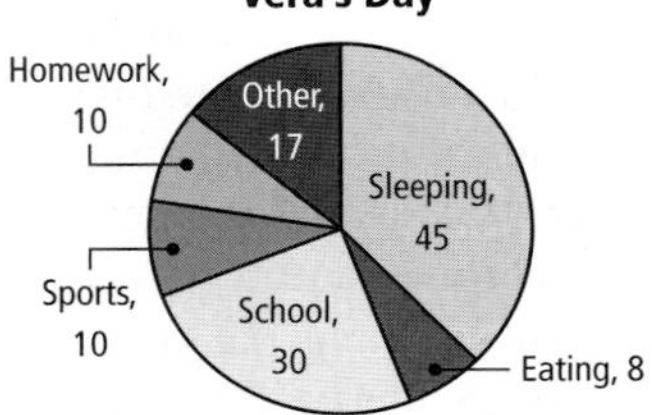


A circle graph shows parts of a whole.

**Exercises 1.** one part of a whole **3.** 82 animals **5.** \$15 **7.** Prices at stadium A are greater than prices at stadium B. **9.** between weeks 4 and 5 **11.** 18% **13.** purple **15.** blue and green **17.** 225,000 **19.** Friday **21.** 3.5 times **23.** games 3, 4, and 5 **25.** Stock Y changed the most between April and July of 2004. **27.** $8\frac{1}{3}$% **31.** double line **33.** circle **35a.** Greece; about 40% **b.** United States; about 15% **37.** D **41.** 19 girls **43.** D: $\{-3, -1, 0, 1, 3\}$; R: $\{0, 1, 3\}$; yes **47.** quadratic binomial

## 10-2

**Check It Out!**

**1.** **Temperature (°C)**

| Stem | Leaves |
|---|---|
| 0 | 7 |
| 1 | 9 |
| 2 | 2 3 6 7 9 |
| 3 | 0 1 1 2 4 5 6 6 |

*Key: 1|9 means 19*

**2.**

| Interval | Frequency |
|---|---|
| 4–6 | 5 |
| 7–9 | 4 |
| 10–12 | 4 |
| 13–15 | 2 |

3.

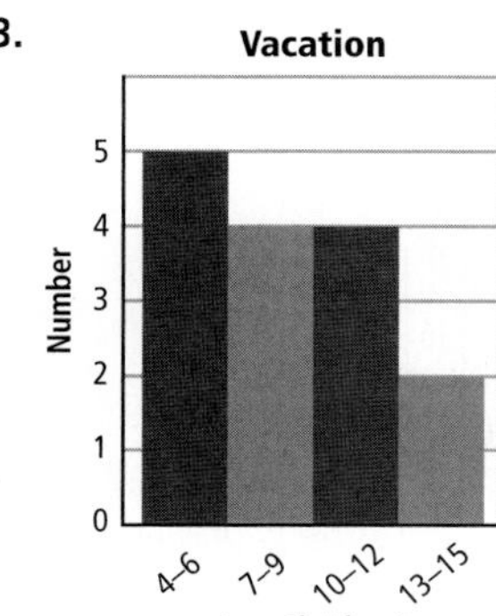


4a.

| Interval | Frequency | Cumulative Frequency |
|---|---|---|
| 28–31 | 2 | 2 |
| 32–35 | 7 | 9 |
| 36–39 | 5 | 14 |
| 40–43 | 3 | 17 |

**4b.** 9

**Exercises 1.** stem-and-leaf plot

3.

| Austin | Stem | New York |
|---|---|---|
| 9 9 9 | 1 | |
| 4 3 2 1 | 2 | |
| 6 5 3 2 0 | 3 | 1 3 3 3 6 6 7 9 |
| | 4 | 1 1 2 2 |

5.

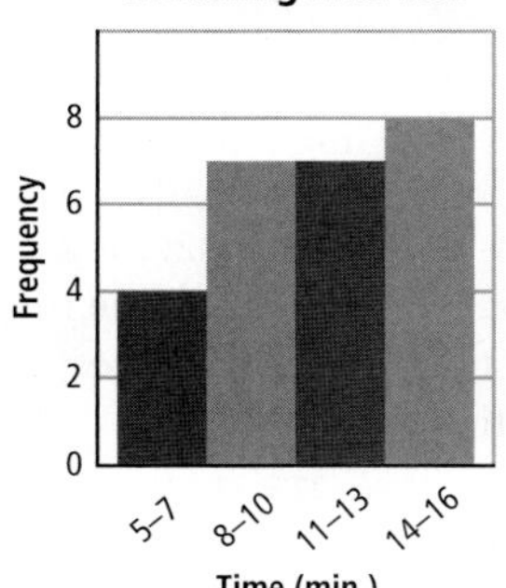


7.

| Summer | Stem | Winter |
|---|---|---|
| | 0 | 4 9 9 |
| | 1 | 1 2 3 4 9 9 |
| 9 7 7 6 5 5 3 3 2 2 | 2 | 1 7 |
| | 3 | 0 3 5 |
| | 4 | |
| 9 7 4 3 | 5 | |

*Key: |2|1 means 21*
*7|2| means 27*

9.

| Interval | Frequency |
|---|---|
| 2.0–2.4 | 2 |
| 2.5–2.9 | 7 |
| 3.0–3.4 | 5 |
| 3.5–3.9 | 3 |

**11a.**

| Interval | Frequency | Cumulative Frequency |
|---|---|---|
| 36–38 | 4 | 4 |
| 39–41 | 6 | 10 |
| 42–44 | 5 | 15 |
| 45–47 | 1 | 16 |

**b.** 10

**15a.**

| Interval | Frequency |
|---|---|
| 160–169.9 | 2 |
| 170–179.9 | 4 |
| 180–189.9 | 3 |
| 190–199.9 | 1 |
| 200–209.9 | 2 |
| 210–219.9 | 1 |

**19.** G **21.** 8; 8; 41; 66 **23.** −2.3 **25.** 0.5 in. **27.** books

## 10-3

**Check It Out! 1a.** mean: 9; median: 8; mode: 8; range: 8 **1b.** mean: 3.6; median: 3; mode: none **1c.** mean: $15\frac{1}{6}$; median: $15\frac{1}{2}$; mode: 12 and 18; range: 6 **2a.** mode: 75 **2b.** Median; the mean is lowered by the 2 scores of 75, and the mode is the lowest score.

3.

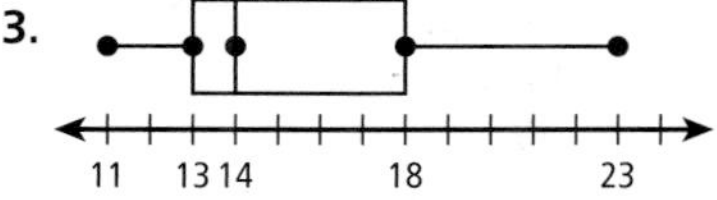


**Exercises 3.** mean: 31.5; median: 33.5; mode: 44; range: 32 **5.** mean: 78.25; median: 78; mode: 78; range: 15

7.

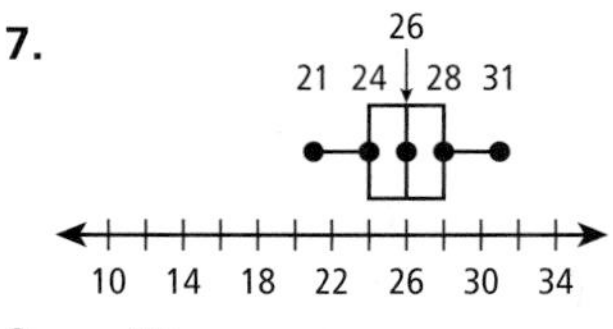


9.

1.5
1 2 3.5 6
1 2 3 4 5 6

**11.** mean: 79.5; median: 82; mode: none; range: 28 **13.** mean: 26.875; median: 28; modes: 19, 31, and 34; range: 15 **15a.** mean: 151 **b.** mean

17.

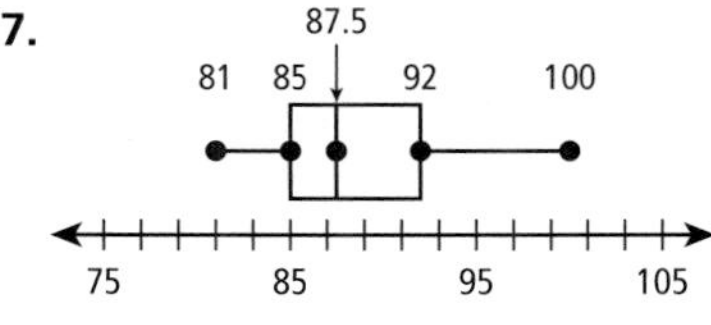


**21.** mean: 5.4; median: 5; mode: 5; range: 1 **23.** mean: $\frac{1}{2}$; median: $\frac{1}{2}$; mode: none; range: 1 **25.** mean: $-2\frac{1}{3}$; median: $-2\frac{1}{2}$; mode: −3; range: 2 **27.** mean: 51.8; median: 51; mode: 51; range: 2 **31a.** mean: 5.6875; median: 5.65; mode: 5.55; range: 0.4 **b.** 5.95 m **c.** mean **37.** increase the mean; decrease the mean **39.** sometimes **41.** always **43.** never **45.** B **47.** C **51.** 32; Typing speed is 32 words per minute. **53.** length: 5 yd; width: 3 yd

## 10-4

**Check It Out! 1.** Company D; the fertilizer from company D appears to be more effective than the other fertilizers. **2.** Possible answer: taxi drivers; the drivers could justify charging higher rates by using this graph, which seems to show that gas prices have increased dramatically. **3.** Smith; Smith might want to show that he or she got many more votes than Atkins or Napier. **4.** The sample size is much too small.

**Exercises 3a.** The vertical scale does not start at 0, and the categories on the horizontal scale are not at equal time intervals. **b.** Tourism is decreasing rapidly. **c.** someone who wants to run a campaign to increase tourism **5.** The sample size is too small. **7a.** The vertical scale does not start at 0. **b.** Single men pay significantly more than single women. **9a.** The sectors of the graph do not add to 100%. **b.** Someone might believe that half of the state's spending was for welfare. **c.** someone who wants to justify cutting spending on welfare **15.** B **19.** $w \leq 1500$ **21.** $b \leq 20$ **23.** $t \geq -4$

## 10-5

**Check It Out! 1.** sample space: {1, 2, 3, 4, 5, 6}; outcome shown: 3 **2.** certain **3a.** $\frac{7}{20}$ **3b.** $\frac{13}{20}$ **4a.** 99.8% **4b.** 34,930

**Exercises 3.** sample space: {blue, red, yellow, green}; outcome shown: red **5.** impossible **7.** unlikely

**9.** $\frac{3}{5}$ **11a.** 30% **b.** 54 **13.** sample space: {blue, red, yellow}; outcome shown: blue **15.** as likely as not **17.** likely **19.** $\frac{6}{25}$ **21a.** 5% **b.** 21 **25.** as likely as not **27.** 1%; 57 **29.** B **31.** B **33.** as likely as not **35.** unlikely **37a.** 7 **b.** 8 **39.** $14 **41.** reflected across the $x$-axis **43.** mean: 6; median: 5; mode: 5

## 10-6

**Check It Out! 1a.** 50% **1b.** $33\frac{1}{3}$% **2.** 0.4 **3.** $\frac{1}{25}$

**Exercises 1.** complement **3.** 25% **5.** $\frac{1}{2}$ **7.** $\frac{2}{3}$ **9.** $\frac{9}{10}$ **11.** 1:12 **13.** $\frac{1}{4}$ **15.** 50% **17.** $\frac{5}{9}$ **19.** 70% **21.** $\frac{9}{10}$ **23.** $\frac{1}{5}$ **25.** $\frac{4}{5}$ **27.** 4:1 **31.** $\frac{1}{2}$ **35.** D **37.** B **41.** $(4x - 3)(x - 1)$ **43.** $\frac{1}{10}$ **45.** $\frac{13}{20}$

## 10-7

**Check It Out! 1a.** Independent; the result of rolling the number cube the first time does not affect the result of the second roll. **1b.** Dependent; choosing the first student leaves fewer students to choose from the second time. **2.** $\frac{1}{4}$ **3.** $\frac{8}{87}$

**Exercises 1.** dependent **3.** independent **5.** independent **7.** $\frac{1}{8}$ **9.** $\frac{1}{6}$ **11.** $\frac{1}{16}$ **13.** $\frac{2}{7}$ **15.** dependent **17.** $\frac{1}{8}$ **19.** $\frac{1}{12}$ **21.** $\frac{2}{9}$ **23a.** $\frac{27}{64}$ **b.** $\frac{1}{64}$ **25.** dependent **27.** independent **29a.** $\frac{3}{20}$ **b.** $\frac{1}{6}$ **c.** $\frac{9}{100}$ **d.** $\frac{1}{15}$ **31.** $\frac{2}{15}$ **35.** D **37.** A **39.** 72.9% **41.** 80% **43.** 48% **45.** 24 **47.** wider **49.** $\frac{3}{5}$ **51.** $\frac{5}{26}$

## 10-8

**Check It Out! 1.** 15,600 **2a.** permutation; 6 **2b.** combination; 6 **3.** 362,880 **4.** 792

**Exercises 1.** combination **3.** 8 **5.** combination; 6 **7.** 20,160 **9.** 35 **11.** 15,504 **13.** 441,000 **15.** combination; 10 **17.** 120 **19.** 133,784,560 **21.** ${}_nP_r$ **25a.** $\frac{1}{308,915,776}$ **b.** 85,810 h **27.** J **29.** 227,920 **31.** 168 **39.** independent: minutes, $t$; dependent: volume of water in tub, $v$ : $v(t) = 15t$

**41.** independent: hours; dependent: total fee; $f(x) = 300 + 8x$

## Extension Answers

**Check It Out! 1.**
$$\begin{array}{c} \\ P \\ B \\ W \end{array}\begin{array}{c} \text{North} \quad \text{West} \\ \begin{bmatrix} 14 & 19 \\ 23 & 36 \\ 16 & 41 \end{bmatrix} \end{array}$$

**2a.** 217 **2b.** 21

**3.**
$$\begin{array}{r} \\ \\ \text{Small} \\ \text{Medium} \\ \text{Large} \end{array}\begin{array}{c} \text{Short} \quad \text{Long} \\ \text{sleeve} \quad \text{sleeve} \\ \begin{bmatrix} 126 & 156 \\ 228 & 129 \\ 57 & 78 \end{bmatrix} \end{array}$$

**Exercises**

**1.**
$$\begin{array}{r} \\ \text{Tetrahedron} \\ \text{Cube} \\ \text{Octahedron} \\ \text{Icosahedron} \end{array}\begin{array}{c} \text{F} \quad \text{V} \quad \text{E} \\ \begin{bmatrix} 4 & 4 & 6 \\ 6 & 8 & 12 \\ 8 & 6 & 12 \\ 20 & 12 & 30 \end{bmatrix} \end{array}$$

**3.**
$$\begin{array}{r} \\ \text{Johnson} \\ \text{Crabtree} \\ \text{Aguirre} \end{array}\begin{array}{c} \text{At bats} \quad \text{Hits} \\ \begin{bmatrix} 69 & 22 \\ 108 & 31 \\ 47 & 13 \end{bmatrix} \end{array}$$

**5.** $1 \times 1$ **7.** $2 \times 4$ **9.** $3 \times 3$

**11.** $\begin{bmatrix} 3 & 10 \\ -1 & 2 \end{bmatrix}$ **13.** $\begin{bmatrix} -1.4 \\ 0.7 \end{bmatrix}$

**15a.**
$$\begin{array}{r} \\ \text{Day 1} \\ \text{Day 2} \\ \text{Day 3} \end{array}\begin{array}{c} \text{Km} \\ \begin{bmatrix} 16.32 \\ 29.76 \\ 6.88 \end{bmatrix} \end{array}$$

**b.** 52.96 km

**17.** $\begin{bmatrix} -4 & 0 & 16 \\ -12 & 12 & -20 \\ 0 & -24 & 4 \end{bmatrix}$

**19.** $\begin{bmatrix} -4.92 & -6 & 1.68 \end{bmatrix}$

**21.** $\begin{bmatrix} 12\frac{1}{2} & -7\frac{1}{2} & -2 \\ -\frac{1}{2} & 10 & -5 \end{bmatrix}$

## Study Guide: Review

**1.** outcome **2.** interquartile range **3.** independent events **4.** 2003 **5.** 14 more boys

**6.**

| Stem | Leaves |
|---|---|
| 0 | 1 7 9 |
| 1 | 2 4 8 9 |
| 2 | 2 2 4 8 |

*Key: 1|2 means 12*

**7.**

| Comedy Camp | | Days and Days |
|---|---|---|
| 2 | 6 | |
| | 7 | |
| 3 1 | 8 | 0 2 |
| | 9 | |
| 4 4 2 | 10 | 3 5 9 |
| | 11 | |
| 6 2 0 | 12 | 8 |
| | 13 | 2 5 9 |

*Key: |12|8 means 128*
*4|10| means 104*

**8.**

| Gas Tank Capacities | | |
|---|---|---|
| Capacity | Tally | Frequency |
| 10–14 | 卌 I | 6 |
| 15–19 | 卌 卌 | 10 |
| 20–24 | III | 3 |
| 25–29 | III | 3 |

**9.**

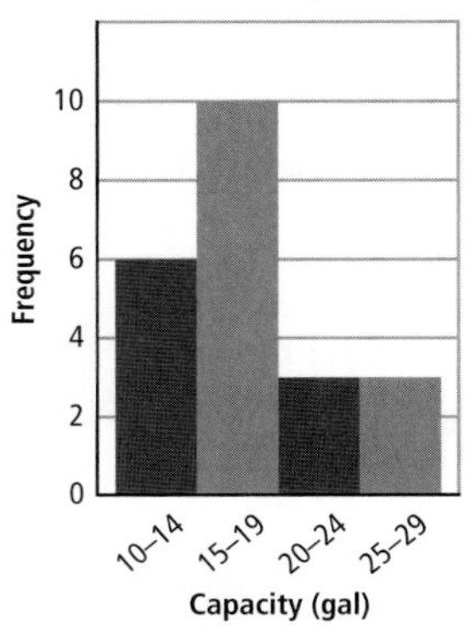


**10.** mean: 14; median: 12; mode: 12; range: 28 **11.** Median; the mean is higher than 4 of the 5 prices; the mode is the lowest price.

**12.**

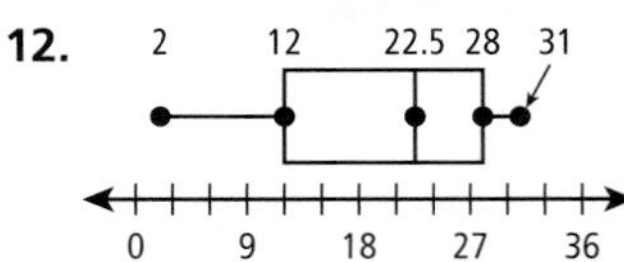


**13.** The scale on the vertical axis is too large. This makes the slopes of the segments less steep.
**14.** Someone might believe that the price has been relatively stable, when in fact it has doubled.
**15.** 99.5% **16.** 24,875 **17.** 250 **18.** $\frac{1}{2}$ **19.** $\frac{1}{4}$ **20.** $\frac{5}{8}$ **21.** independent **22.** independent **23.** dependent **24.** $\frac{2048}{9555}$ **25.** 0 **26.** $\frac{256}{2401}$ **27.** 60 **28.** permutation; 604,800 **29.** combination; 220 **30.** combination; 1365

# Chapter 11

## 11-1

**Check It Out!** **1a.** 80, −160, 320 **1b.** 216, 162, 121.5 **2.** 7.8125 **3.** \$1342.18

**Exercises** **3.** 25, 12.5, 6.25 **5.** 1,000,000,000 **7.** 4 **9.** 162, 243, 364.5 **11.** 2058; 14,406; 100,842 **13.** $\frac{5}{32}, \frac{5}{128}, \frac{5}{512}$ **15.** 0.0000000001, or $1 \times 10^{-10}$ **17.** 80; 160 **19.** $\frac{1}{3}$ **21.** $\frac{1}{7}; \frac{1}{49}$ **23.** 6; −48 **25.** 4913 **27.** yes; $\frac{1}{3}$ **29.** no **31.** no **33a.** 1.28 cm **b.** 40.96 cm **35.** −2, −8, −32, −128 **37.** 2, 4, 8, 16 **39.** 12, 3, $\frac{3}{4}, \frac{3}{16}$ **43a.** \$3993; \$4392.30 **b.** 1.1 **c.** \$2727.27 **45.** J **47.** $x^4, x^5, x^6$ **49.** $1, y, y^2$ **51.** −400 **53.** the 7th term **55.** $b > 10$ **57.** $c < -\frac{1}{3}$ **61.** $f(x) = x^2 + 4$

## 11-2

**Check It Out!** **1.** 3.375 in. **2a.** no **2b.** yes

**3a.**

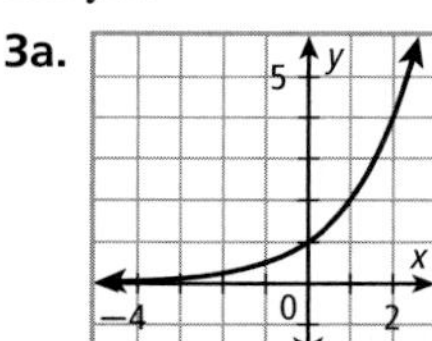

**3b.**

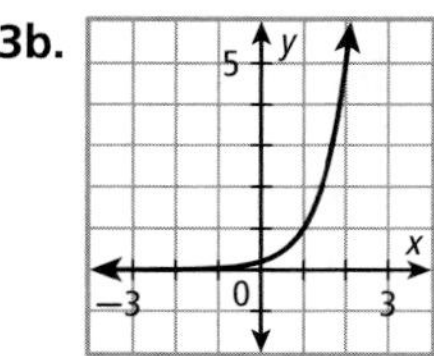

**4a.**

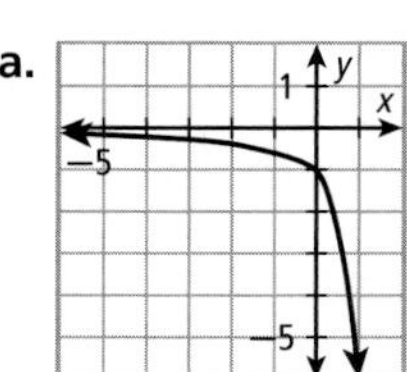

**4b.**

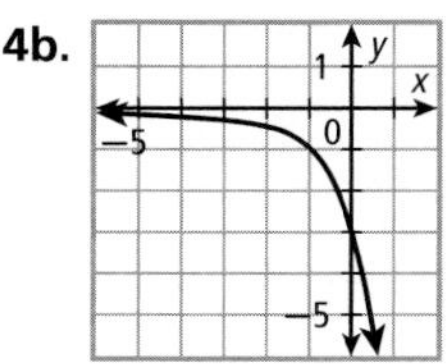

**5a.**

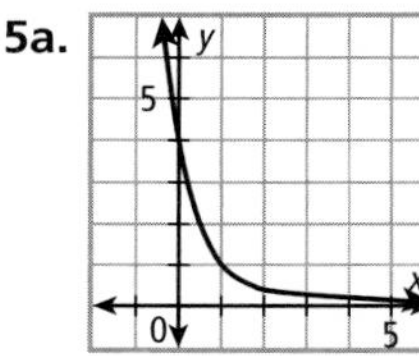

**5b.**

**6.** after about 13 yr

**Exercises** **1.** no **3.** no **17.** about 2023 **19.** 289 ft **21.** yes **23.** no **35.** $y = 4.8\,(2)^x$ **41.** −0.125 **45.** C **47.** D **49.** 3 **51.** The value of $a$ is the $y$-intercept. **53.** 25 **55.** $9x^2$

## 11-3

**Check It Out!** **1.** $y = 1200(1.08)^t$; \$1904.25 **2a.** $A = 1200(1.00875)^{4t}$; \$1379.49 **2b.** $A = 4000(1.0025)^{12t}$; \$5083.47 **3.** $y = 48{,}000(0.97)^t$; 38,783 **4a.** 1.5625 mg **4b.** 0.78125 g

**Exercises** **1.** exponential growth **3.** $y = 300(1.08)^t$; 441 **5.** $A = 4200(1.007)^{4t}$; \$4965.43 **7.** $y = 10(0.84)^t$; 4.98 mg **9.** 5.5 g **11.** $y = 1600(1.03)^t$; 2150 **13.** $A = 30(1.078)^t$; 47 members **15.** $A = 7000(1.0075)^{4t}$; \$9438.44 **17.** $A = 12{,}000(1.026)^t$; \$17,635.66 **19.** $y = 58(0.9)^t$; \$24.97 **21.** growth; 61% **23.** decay; $33\frac{1}{3}$% **25.** growth; 10% **27.** growth; 25% **29.** $y = 58{,}000{,}000(1.001)^t$; 58,174,174 **31.** $y = 8200(0.98)^t$; \$7118.63 **33.** $y = 970(1.012)^t$; 1030 **35.** B **37.** 18 yr **39.** A; B **45.** D **47.** D **49.** about 20 yr **51.** 100 min, or 1 h 40 min **53.** \$225,344 **55.** 16 ft

## 11-4

**Check It Out!**

**1a.**

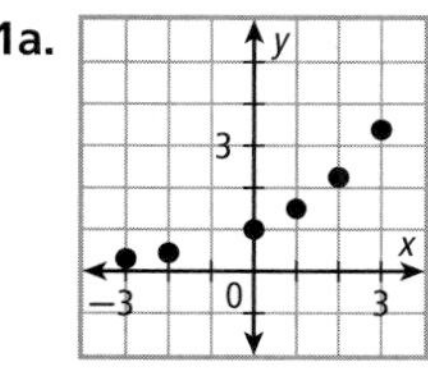

exponential

**1b.**

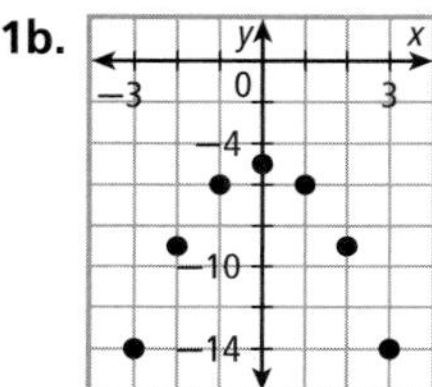

quadratic **2.** quadratic **3.** The oven temperature decreases by 50°F every 10 min; $y = -5x + 375$; 75°F

**Exercises** **5.** exponential **7.** Grapes cost \$1.79/lb; $y = 1.79x$; \$10.74 **11.** linear **13.** exponential **15.** $\ell = 6k$; linear **17.** linear **19.** $y = 0.2(4)^x$ **21.** linear **33.** $\frac{145}{g}$ **35.** 5, −5 **37.** $\frac{9}{4}, -\frac{9}{4}$

## 11-5

**Check It Out!** **1a.** 40 ft/s **1b.** 30.98 ft/s **2a.** $x \geq \frac{1}{2}$ **2b.** $x \geq \frac{5}{3}$

**3a.**

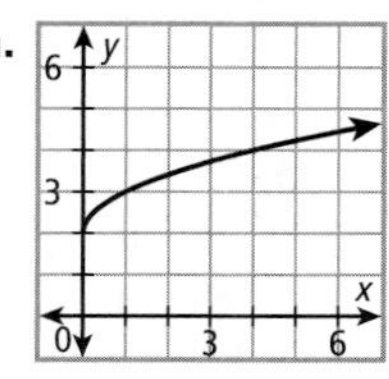

**3b.**

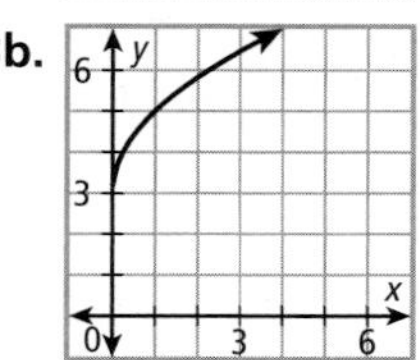

**Exercises** **1.** There is no variable under the square-root sign. **3.** $x \geq -6$ **5.** $x \geq 0$ **7.** $x \geq -3$ **15.** 49.96 mi/h **17.** $x \geq 0$ **19.** $x \leq \frac{3}{2}$ **21.** $x \geq -\frac{5}{3}$ **23.** $x \geq 40$ **25.** $x \geq 9$ **45.** A **47.** C **49.** $x \leq -5$ OR $x \geq 5$ **51.** $x \leq -4$ OR $x \geq \frac{3}{2}$ **53.** D: $x \leq 3$; R: $y \leq 4$ **57a.** 2 and 4 **b.** 3, 1 **61.** $9x^2 - 6x + 1$ **63.** $a^2 - 2ab^2c + b^4c^2$ **65.** $9r^2 - 4s^2$ **67.** $A = 42{,}000(1.0125)^{4t}$; \$48,751.69

## 11-6

**Check It Out!** **1a.** 8 **1b.** 7 **1c.** 13 **1d.** $|3 - x|$ **2a.** $8\sqrt{2}$ **2b.** $xy\sqrt{x}$ **2c.** $4a\sqrt{3b}$ **3a.** $\frac{2}{3}$ **3b.** $\frac{6}{x^2}$ **3c.** $\frac{y^3}{2}$ **4a.** $\frac{2\sqrt{5}}{7}$ **4b.** $\frac{z^2\sqrt{z}}{5y}$ **4c.** $\frac{p^3}{q^5}$ **5.** $60\sqrt{2}$ ft; 84.9 ft

**Exercises** **1.** $3x - 6$ **3.** 7 **5.** $6\sqrt{5}$ **7.** $18\sqrt{2}$ **9.** $4x^2y\sqrt{2y}$ **11.** $\frac{\sqrt{17}}{5}$ **13.** $\frac{\sqrt{6}}{7}$ **15.** $\frac{\sqrt{x}}{3}$ **17.** $\frac{6\sqrt{3}}{7}$ **19.** $\frac{16\sqrt{2}}{9}$ **21.** $\frac{5x\sqrt{2}}{13}$ **23.** $5\sqrt{41}$ mi; 32 mi **25.** 20 **27.** 9 **29.** $|x + 1|$ **31.** $|x - 3|$ **33.** $20\sqrt{10}$ **35.** $8rs\sqrt{5}$ **37.** $\frac{3\sqrt{5}}{2}$ **39.** $\frac{\sqrt{14}}{3}$ **41.** $\frac{x\sqrt{x}}{y^3}$ **43.** $\frac{8s\sqrt{3}}{7}$ **45.** $-20\sqrt{3}$ **47.** $15x\sqrt{7}$ **49.** $x$ **51.** $\frac{x^3\sqrt{x}}{3}$ **53.** $\sqrt{36}$; 6 **55.** $\sqrt{50}$; $5\sqrt{2}$ **57.** $\sqrt{3}$ **59.** $\sqrt{20}$; $2\sqrt{5}$ **67.** C **69.** C **71.** $x\sqrt{x + 1}$ **73a.** $|x|$ **b.** $x^2$ **c.** $|x^3|$ **d.** $x^4$ **e.** $|x^5|$ **f.** $x^n$; $|x^n|$ **77.** exponential

## 11-7

**Check It Out!** **1a.** $-\sqrt{7}$ **1b.** $3\sqrt{3}$ **1c.** $8\sqrt{n}$ **1d.** $\sqrt{2s}+8\sqrt{5s}$ **2a.** $5\sqrt{6}$ **2b.** $12\sqrt{3}-3\sqrt{2}$ **2c.** $5\sqrt{3y}$ **3.** $10\sqrt{b}$ in.

**Exercises** **3.** $10\sqrt{5}$ **5.** $3\sqrt{7}+5\sqrt{2}$ **7.** $5\sqrt{6a}+6\sqrt{5a}$ **9.** $13\sqrt{3}$ **11.** $-\sqrt{5x}$ **13.** $8\sqrt{2t}-4\sqrt{3t}$ **15.** $6\sqrt{3}$ **17.** $-3\sqrt{11}$ **19.** $-4\sqrt{n}$ **21.** $7\sqrt{7}$ **23.** $12\sqrt{2}$ **25.** $3\sqrt{7x}-12\sqrt{3x}$ **27.** $3\sqrt{5j}$ **29.** $2\sqrt{3m}$ **31.** $12\sqrt{7}$ **33.** 0 **35.** $7\sqrt{3}$ **37.** $7\sqrt{2}$ **41.** $2\sqrt{3}+5\sqrt{5}+5$ **43.** $8\sqrt{7x}-\sqrt{70x}$ **45.** $35\sqrt{5k}$ **47.** $5\sqrt{3}+5\sqrt{5}$ **51.** 9 **53.** 18 **55.** $36x^2$ **57.** $16\sqrt{3}$ in.; $8\sqrt{3}$ in.; $24\sqrt{3}$ in. **59.** B **61.** A **63.** $\sqrt{x}(x+2)$ **65.** 0 **67.** $(x+2)\sqrt{x-1}$ **69.** $3\sqrt{x+1}-x\sqrt{x+2}$ **73.** $\frac{1}{12}$ **75.** $x \geq -3$

## 11-8

**Check It Out!** **1a.** $5\sqrt{2}$ **1b.** 63 **1c.** $2m\sqrt{7}$ **2a.** $4\sqrt{3}-3\sqrt{6}$ **2b.** $5\sqrt{2}+4\sqrt{15}$ **2c.** $7\sqrt{k}-5\sqrt{7k}$ **2d.** $150-20\sqrt{5}$ **3a.** $21-5\sqrt{3}$ **3b.** $83+18\sqrt{2}$ **3c.** $11-6\sqrt{2}$ **3d.** $17-\sqrt{3}$ **4a.** $\frac{\sqrt{65}}{5}$ **4b.** $\frac{\sqrt{21a}}{6}$ **4c.** $\frac{8\sqrt{35}}{7}$

**Exercises** **1.** $\sqrt{6}$ **3.** 125 **5.** $3\sqrt{30a}$ **7.** $2\sqrt{6}+\sqrt{42}$ **9.** $\sqrt{35}-\sqrt{21}$ **11.** $5\sqrt{3y}+4\sqrt{5y}$ **13.** $12+7\sqrt{2}$ **15.** $-5-2\sqrt{3}$ **17.** $81-30\sqrt{2}$ **19.** $\frac{\sqrt{26}}{2}$ **21.** $\frac{\sqrt{33}}{18}$ **27.** $3\sqrt{10}$ **29.** 8 **31.** $6d\sqrt{7}$ **33.** $4\sqrt{5}-5\sqrt{2}$ **35.** $2\sqrt{3}-2\sqrt{5}$ **37.** $3\sqrt{f}+12\sqrt{3f}$ **39.** $75+19\sqrt{15}$ **41.** $10-\sqrt{2}$ **43.** $67+16\sqrt{3}$ **45.** $\frac{5\sqrt{6}}{2}$ **47.** $\frac{\sqrt{3x}}{x}$ **49.** $\frac{7\sqrt{2x}}{2}$ **51.** $2\sqrt{y}$ **53.** 180 $\text{in}^2$ **55.** $6\sqrt{10}-2\sqrt{5}$ $\text{cm}^2$ **57.** $\sqrt{30}$ **59.** $-5-2\sqrt{3}$ **61.** $3\sqrt{2}$ **63.** $134\sqrt{3}+96$ **65.** $x-2\sqrt{xy}+y$ **67.** $3+2\sqrt{3x}+x$ **69.** $\frac{\pi\sqrt{6}}{4}$ s $\approx$ 1.9 s **71.** 269.5 $\text{ft}^2$ **73.** $\frac{1}{\sqrt{3}}$ **75.** B **77.** D **79.** $-4\sqrt{3}+4\sqrt{5}$ **81.** $-5-2\sqrt{6}$ **83.** $2-\sqrt{3}$ **85.** $2\sqrt{6}+2\sqrt{5}$ **87.** translation 4 units down

## 11-9

**Check It Out!** **1a.** 36 **1b.** 3 **1c.** $\frac{1}{3}$ **2a.** 9 **2b.** 18 **2c.** 3 **3a.** 121 **3b.** 64 **3c.** 100 **4a.** 2 **4b.** $\frac{11}{2}$ **5a.** no solution **5b.** no solution **5c.** 4 **6.** 8; 3 cm

**Exercises** **1.** No; it does not contain a variable under the radical sign. **3.** −8 **5.** −144 **7.** 27 **9.** 50 **11.** −2 **13.** 9 **15.** 64 **17.** 16 **19.** 16 **21.** $\frac{4}{9}$ **23.** 100 **25.** 5 **27.** 13 **29.** 6 **31.** 2 **33.** no solution **35.** 4 **37.** 2 **39.** no solution **41.** 48 **43.** −25 **45.** 71 **47.** −8 **49.** 36 **51.** −16 **53.** 8 **55.** 9 **57.** 2 **59.** −5 **61.** 5 **63.** 1 **65.** 1 **67.** $x = 144$; 12 in. **69.** $\sqrt{x}-3=4$; 49 **71.** $x=\sqrt{x+6}$; 3 **73.** 3 in. by 1 in. **75a.** 54.88 joules **b.** 0 joules **77.** 1690 ft **79.** $x = 25$; $y = 16$ **87.** A **89.** C **95.** 2

## Extension Answers

**Check It Out!** **1a.** 3 **1b.** 0 **1c.** 2 **1d.** 12 **2a.** 11 **2b.** 3 **2c.** 4 **3a.** 8 **3b.** 1 **3c.** 81

**Exercises** **1.** 13 **3.** 5 **5.** 2 **7.** 20 **9.** 7 **11.** 2 **13.** 6 **15.** 8 **17.** 2 **19.** 4 **25.** \$9698 **27.** 4 **29.** 9 **31.** 1 **33.** 27 **35.** 14 **37.** 17 **39.** 20 **41.** 25 **43.** 216 **45.** 64 **47.** 125 **49.** 32 **51.** 113.04 $\text{cm}^2$ **53.** $\frac{2}{3}$ **55.** $\frac{1}{4}$ **57.** $\frac{4}{9}$ **59.** $\frac{8}{343}$ **61.** $\frac{1}{27}$ **63.** $\frac{16}{625}$ **65.** 1 **67.** 0 **69.** 625 **71.** −1 **73.** 11% **75.** $x^4$

## Study Guide: Review

**1.** square-root function **2.** exponential decay **3.** common ratio **4.** exponential function **5.** 81, 243, 729 **6.** 48, −96, 192 **7.** 5, 2.5, 1.25 **8.** −256, −1024, −4096 **9.** 7,812,500 **10.** 19,131,876 **11.** yes **12.** no

**13.**

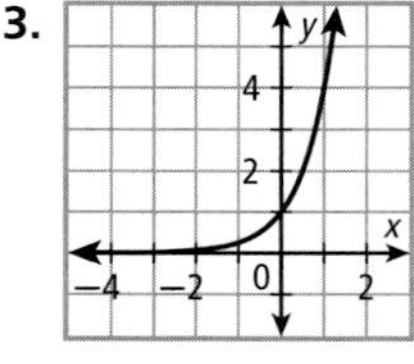


**14.**

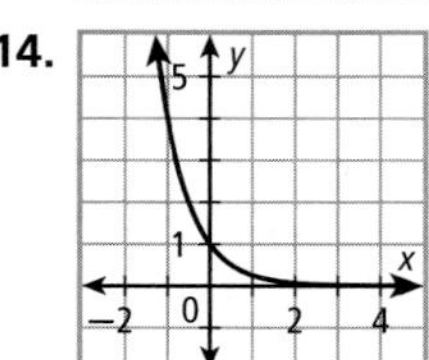


**15.** $y = 9(1.15)^t$; 24
**16.** $y = 24{,}500(0.96)^t$; 3182

**17.** quadratic **18.** linear **19.** exponential **20.** exponential **21.** quadratic **22.** linear **23.** $y = 1.5x$; 15 h **24.** 4.74 cm **25.** $x \geq 0$ **26.** $x \geq -4$ **27.** $x \geq 0$ **28.** $x \geq -2$ **29.** $x \geq \frac{4}{3}$ **30.** $x \geq -3$ **31.** $x \geq \frac{7}{2}$ **32.** $x \geq -\frac{18}{5}$ **33.** $x \geq \frac{3}{4}$ **34.** $x \geq 1$

**35.**

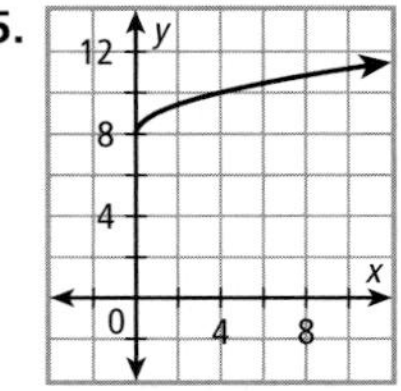


**36.**

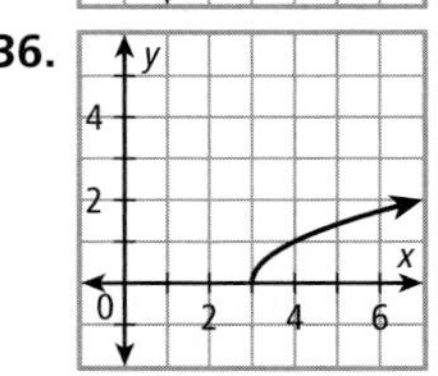


**37.**

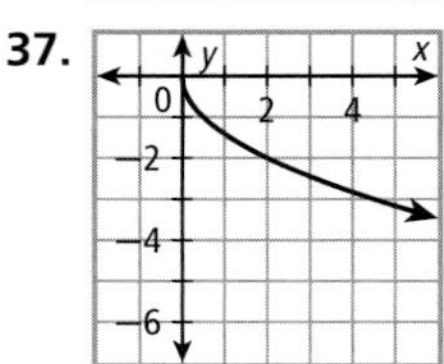


**38.**

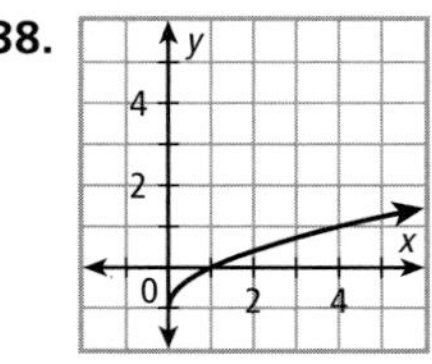


**39.**

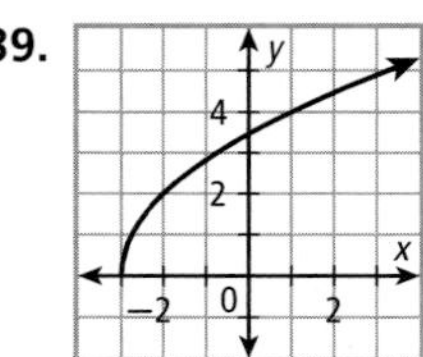


**40.**

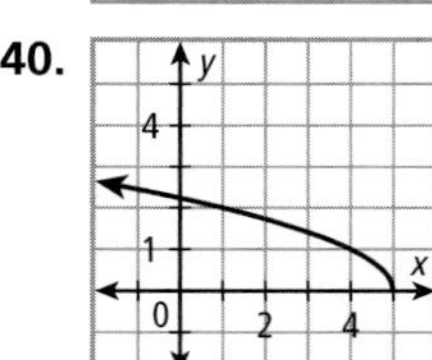


**41.**

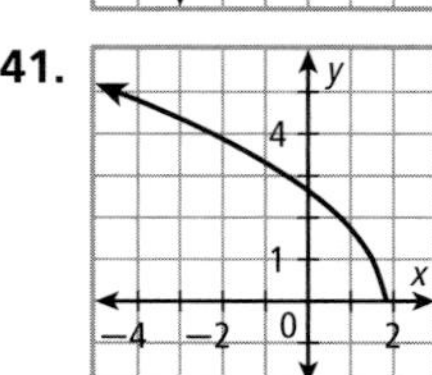


**42.**

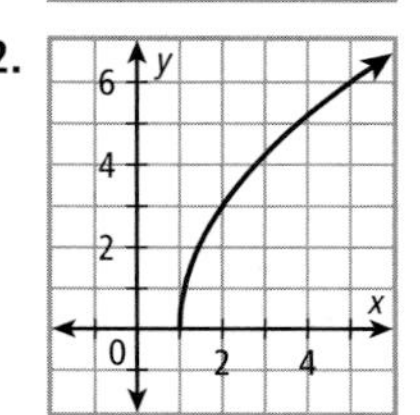

**43.** 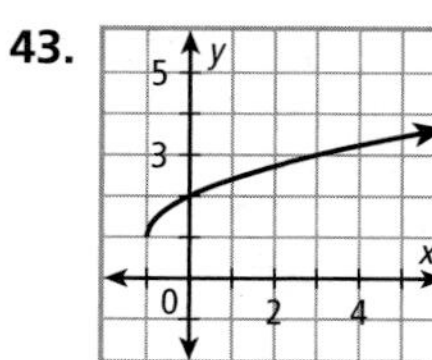

**44.** 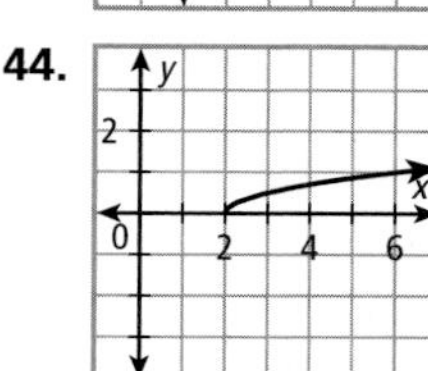

**45.** 11 **46.** $n^2$ **47.** $x + 3$ **48.** 5 **49.** $6d$ **50.** $y^3\sqrt{x}$ **51.** $2\sqrt{3}$ **52.** $4b^2\sqrt{2ab}$ **53.** $\frac{\sqrt{5}}{2}$ **54.** $\frac{t}{10}$ **55.** $\frac{2}{3}$ **56.** $\frac{4p^2\sqrt{2}}{7}$ **57.** $\frac{t^4\sqrt{t}}{s}$ **58.** $\frac{2b^3\sqrt{2}}{5}$ **59.** $9\sqrt{7}$ **60.** $3\sqrt{3}$ **61.** $3\sqrt{2} + 2\sqrt{3}$ **62.** $\sqrt{5t}$ **63.** $2\sqrt{2}$ **64.** $2\sqrt{3} + 2\sqrt{5}$ **65.** $-2\sqrt{5x}$ **66.** $10\sqrt{6}$ **67.** $\sqrt{14}$ **68.** $3\sqrt{2}$ **69.** $6\sqrt{7x}$ **70.** 150 **71.** $4\sqrt{2} - 4$ **72.** $71 + 16\sqrt{7}$ **73.** $\frac{4\sqrt{5}}{5}$ **74.** $\frac{3a\sqrt{2}}{2}$ **75.** $\frac{\sqrt{3}}{3}$ **76.** $\frac{\sqrt{10n}}{2n}$ **77.** $\frac{\sqrt{6}}{2}$ **78.** $-\sqrt{3}$ **79.** 64 **80.** 8 **81.** 3 **82.** 25 **83.** $-81$ **84.** 100 **85.** 3 **86.** no solution **87.** $x = 4$ **88.** $x = 6$ **89.** $x = 7$ **90.** $x = \frac{19}{2}$ **91.** $x = 12$ **92.** $x = 3$ **93.** $x = 4$ **94.** $x = 5$

# Chapter 12

## 12-1

**Check It Out! 1a.** No; the product $xy$ is not constant. **1b.** Yes; the product $xy$ is constant. **1c.** No; the equation cannot be written in the form $y = \frac{k}{x}$. **2.** $y = \frac{5}{x}$

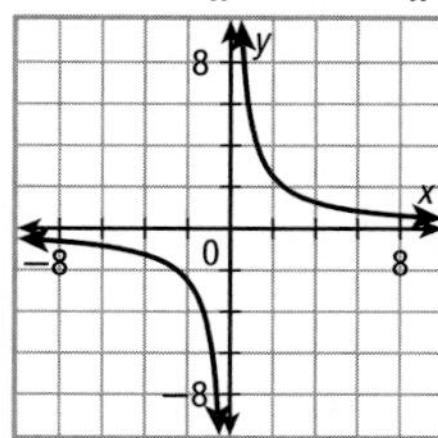

**3.** D: $x > 0$; R: $y > 0$; 2.5 mm$^3$

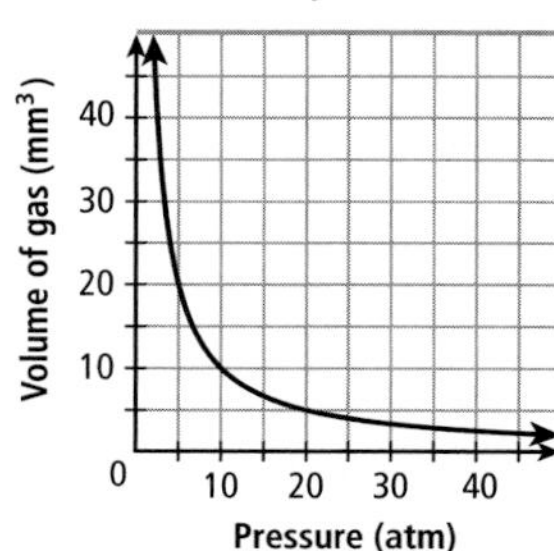


**4.** 3 **5.** 80.625 lb

**Exercises 3.** no **5.** yes **9.** 4 **11.** 16 teeth **13.** yes **15.** no **19.** 2 **21.** 12 yd **23.** direct; 8 **25.** neither **27.** inverse; 12 **29.** inverse; 15 **31.** $d = \frac{10}{n}$; inverse **33.** neither **41.** C **43.** C **49.** D: $\{-4, -2, 0, 2, 4\}$; R: $\{1, 3, 5\}$; yes **51.** $-1, 7$ **53.** $2\sqrt{10}$ cm

## 12-2

**Check It Out! 1a.** 0 **1b.** 1 **1c.** $-4$ **2a.** $x = 5$; $y = 0$ **2b.** $x = -4$; $y = 5$ **2c.** $x = -77$; $y = -15$

**3a.** 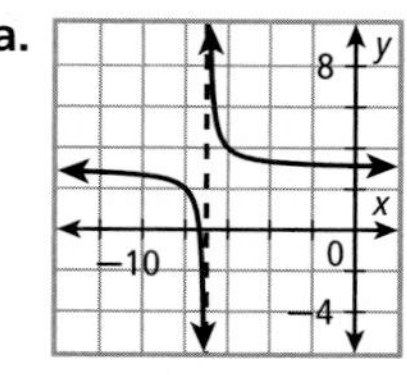

**3b.** 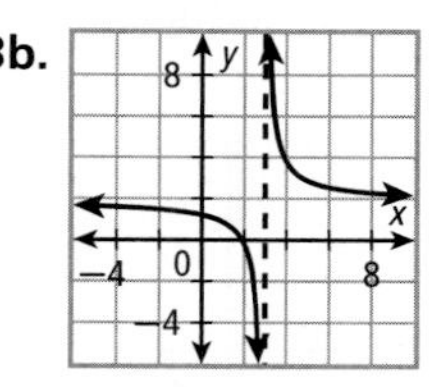

**4a.** D: $x > 0$; R: natural numbers $> 10$

**4b.** 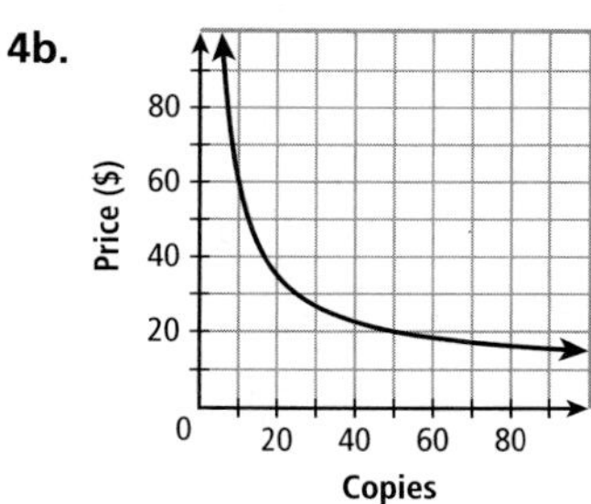


**Exercises 1.** excluded value **3.** $-3$ **5.** 4 **7.** $x = -5$; $y = 0$ **9.** $x = -9$; $y = -10$ **15.** 0 **17.** 0 **19.** $x = 4$; $y = 0$ **21.** $x = 3$; $y = 4$ **29.** 7 **39.** $x = 2$; $y = 5$ **41.** B **43.** C **51.** D: $x > 2$ **53.** D: $x > -\frac{1}{5}$ **55.** I and III; II and IV **59.** J **61a.** yes **b.** D: all real numbers **c.** R: $0 < y \leq 1$ **d.** no **63.** $y = \frac{3}{x+2} + 3$ **65.** $-2, 3$ **67.** 0.46875 cm **69.** No; the product $xy$ is not constant.

## 12-3

**Check It Out! 1a.** $-5$ **1b.** $0, -5$ **1c.** $-3, -4$ **2a.** $\frac{m}{3}$; $m \neq 0$ **2b.** $6p$ **2c.** $\frac{3n}{n-2}$; $n \neq 2$ **3a.** $\frac{1}{r+5}$ **3b.** $\frac{b-5}{b+5}$ **4a.** $-\frac{3}{4+x}$ **4b.** $-\frac{1}{x+1}$ **4c.** $\frac{3}{x+11}$ **5.** The barrel cactus with a radius of 3 inches has less of a chance to survive. Its surface-area-to-volume ratio is greater than for a cactus with a radius of 6 inches.

**Exercises 3.** 0, 8 **5.** $\frac{a}{2}$; $a \neq 0$ **7.** $\frac{2}{y+3}$; $y \neq -3$ **9.** $\frac{h}{h+2}$; $h \neq -2$ **11.** $\frac{1}{b+1}$ **13.** $\frac{c+2}{c-4}$ **15.** $\frac{j-5}{j-3}$ **17.** $-\frac{2}{8+n}$ **19.** not possible **21.** $-\frac{5}{10+q}$ **23a.** $\frac{b_2}{b_1+b_2}$ **b.** They will be the same: $\frac{b_2}{b_1+b_2}$. **25.** 0 **27.** $-\frac{1}{2}, 4$ **29.** already simplified; $m \neq 4$ **31.** $\frac{t}{8}$; $t \neq 0$ **33.** $\frac{z-1}{z+1}$ **35.** $\frac{p-7}{p-5}$ **37.** $\frac{2}{x-4}$ **39.** $-\frac{1}{b+7}$ **43.** $\frac{p+6}{12}$ **45.** $\frac{1}{3}$ **47.** $\frac{3w+7}{3}$ **49.** 1 **51.** $-\frac{5+x}{x+2}$ **53a.** $\frac{6}{s}$ **b.** 3 **c.** 1 **57.** F **63.** $\frac{a-3}{a+5}$ **65.** $\pm 14$ **67.** $-2, 0$ **73.** $-6$

## 12-4

**Check It Out! 1a.** $-\frac{9}{4}$ **1b.** $\frac{5x^2y^4}{6}$ **2.** $\frac{3m-15}{m-6}$ **3a.** $\frac{n+4}{n^2+2n}$ **3b.** $\frac{p^2-p-20}{p^3+16p}$ **4a.** $\frac{3x-15}{x^5}$ **4b.** $\frac{2w^6}{v^2x^3}$ **4c.** $\frac{x}{x^2+5x+6}$ **5.** approximately 0.23

**Exercises 1.** $\frac{6h}{5jk^2}$ **3.** $\frac{2x-4}{3}$ **5.** $\frac{a}{6}$ **7.** $3y - 6$ **9.** $\frac{m^2-10m}{2}$ **11.** $a^3 + 10a^2 + 25a$ **13.** $\frac{a+6b}{b^2}$ **15.** $\frac{1}{2}$ **17.** $\frac{2r+28}{r-4}$ **19.** $b$ **21.** $\frac{1}{3x-15}$ **23.** $-\frac{3p^8q^2}{7r^4}$ **25.** $\frac{10y+20}{3y+15}$ **27.** $4m^2 - 4m$ **29.** $\frac{3n^2-3n}{n+8}$ **31.** 1 **33.** $-\frac{1}{2a^3}$ **35a.** $\frac{x^2}{4(4x^2+8x-1)}$ **b.** $\frac{9}{236}$ **37.** B **39.** $\frac{1}{2m}$ **41.** $\frac{1}{16x}$ **43.** 1 **45a.** 64 cm **b.** 80 cm **c.** 4 **47.** H **49.** $\frac{1}{3x^2+9x}$ **51.** $\frac{1}{3}$ **53.** $\frac{x}{z^2}$ **55.** $\frac{1}{2a+2}$ **57.** $12 + 9 + m \leq 30$; $m \leq 9$ **59.** $8\sqrt{3t}$ **61.** $x \neq 3$; $x = 3$ and $y = 0$ **63.** $x \neq 0$; $x = 0$ and $y = 3$ **65.** $x \neq 0$; $x = 0$ and $y = 0$

## 12-5

**Check It Out! 1a.** 2 **1b.** $3y$ **2a.** $\frac{3}{a-2}$ **2b.** $\frac{4b+12}{b^2+3b-4}$ **3a.** $15f^2h^2$ **3b.** $(x-6)(x+2)(x+5)$ **4a.** $\frac{4d-3}{3d^2}$ **4b.** $\frac{a+8}{a-2}$ **5.** $\frac{5}{24}$ h or 12.5 min

**Exercises 1.** $\frac{2}{y}$ **3.** $\frac{1}{x-4}$ **5.** $\frac{2}{a+1}$ **7.** $6x^3y^2z$ **9.** $(y+4)(y-4)(y+9)$ **11.** $\frac{x+3}{x+2}$ **13a.** $\frac{260}{r}$ **b.** $6\frac{1}{2}$ h **15.** $a - 1$ **17.** $m$ **19.** $3a + 1$ **21.** $36a(3a + 1)$ **23.** $10xy^3z$ **27.** $\frac{y+2}{3(y-3)}$

**29.** $\frac{19}{21z}$ **31.** $\frac{-m^2-6m}{4(m-2)^2}$ **33a.** $\frac{700}{r}$ **b.** 14 h **35.** $\frac{1}{7+c}$ **37.** $\frac{3}{2b^2}$ **39.** $\frac{x-5}{3}$ **41.** $\frac{8x+20}{(x+4)(x+2)}$ **43.** A **47.** $4x^2$; $8x^2$; $8x^3$ **49.** A **51.** D **53.** $\frac{x-4y}{(x+y)(x-y)}$; $x \neq y$ and $x \neq -y$ **55.** $\frac{az+by+cx}{xyz}$; $x \neq 0$, $y \neq 0$, and $z \neq 0$ **61.** $\frac{1}{2}$, 4 **63.** 2; $t \neq \pm 2$ **65.** $-\frac{1}{x+4}$; $x \neq \pm 4$

## 12-6

**Check It Out! 1a.** $-2p+1-\frac{3}{p}$ **1b.** $x^2+\frac{1}{3}-\frac{5}{2x}$ **2a.** $k+5$ **2b.** $b-7$ **2c.** $s+6$ **3a.** $2y+1$ **3b.** $a-2$ **4a.** $3m-5+\frac{13}{m+3}$ **4b.** $y+6+\frac{20}{y-3}$ **5a.** $x^2-2x-4+\frac{-7}{x-2}$ **5b.** $2p^2-2p+6+\frac{-7}{p+1}$

**Exercises 1.** $2x-\frac{1}{2}$ **3.** $7b-\frac{14}{3}+\frac{8}{b}$ **5.** $2x+4+\frac{3}{x}$ **7.** $2x-3$ **9.** $2y+5$ **11.** $x+1$ **13.** $c+3$ **15.** $x-2$ **17.** $a+2+\frac{-1}{a+2}$ **19.** $n+4+\frac{-1}{n+4}$ **21.** $4n-5+\frac{-2}{2n+1}$ **23.** $-2x^2+6x-15+\frac{35}{x+3}$ **25.** $m+1+\frac{3}{m-1}$ **27.** $4k^2-4k+2+\frac{-10}{k+1}$ **29.** $3t+4-\frac{2}{t}$ **31.** $-4p+1+\frac{2}{p^3}$ **33.** $4t+3$ **35.** $x-3$ **37.** $3a-1$ **39.** $3x+4+\frac{14}{x-2}$ **41.** $3x+1+\frac{-2}{2x-1}$ **43.** $2t^2-6t+25+\frac{-216}{3t+9}$ **45.** $-20$ **47.** $2x-5+\frac{3}{x+1}$ **51.** $0.5m+1$ **57.** C **59.** B **61.** $3x-\frac{1}{2y}+\frac{2y}{x}$ **63.** $x+2$ **65.** 3 m **67.** $\frac{\sqrt{15}}{15}$ **69.** $6\sqrt{5}-5\sqrt{2}$ **71.** $4(x+1)$ **73.** $2k^2+5k+2$

## 12-7

**Check It Out! 1a.** 2 **1b.** 1 **1c.** $-\frac{7}{6}$ **2a.** $-4$ **2b.** $-4$ **2c.** 1, 3 **3.** $22\frac{2}{9}$ min **4a.** 5; 7 is an extraneous solution. **4b.** 1 and 5; no extraneous solutions. **4c.** 4; 0 is an extraneous solution.

**Exercises 1.** rational equation **3.** $-24$ **5.** $-\frac{8}{3}$ **7.** $\frac{3}{2}$ **9.** $\frac{3}{5}$ **11.** $-\frac{11}{5}$ **13.** $\frac{15}{19}$ **15.** 3, $-\frac{4}{3}$ **17.** $-2$, 3 **19.** $-1$, $\frac{3}{2}$ **21.** $\frac{1}{2}$ h, or 30 min **23.** $-\frac{4}{3}$; 1 is extraneous. **25.** $-2$ **27.** 0 **29.** $\frac{4}{5}$ **31.** 5 **33.** $\frac{3}{2}$ **35.** $-4$, 3 **37.** 6 h **39.** 2; 3 is extraneous. **41.** no solution; 4 is extraneous. **43.** $\frac{240}{t}$; $t-2$; 40 mi/h **45a.** $\frac{1}{15}=\frac{1}{24}+\frac{1}{y}$ **b.** 40 cm **c.** It will increase to 72 cm. **49.** F **53.** Eddie: 6 h; Luke 3 h; Ryan: 4 h **55.** $y=-2x$ and $y=\frac{1}{2}x+4$ are perpendicular. **59.** 5

## Extension Answers

**Check It Out! 1.** $\frac{4}{5}=0.800$; $\frac{3}{5}=0.600$; $\frac{4}{3}\approx 1.333$ **2.** 4.8 ft

**Exercises 1.** 0.923; 0.385; 2.400 **3.** 5.0 **5.** 8.0

## Study Guide: Review

**1.** rational expression **2.** rational function **3.** rational equation **4.** inverse variation **5.** discontinuous function **6.** Yes; the product $xy$ is constant. **7.** No; the product $xy$ is not constant.

**8.** $y=-\frac{4}{x}$

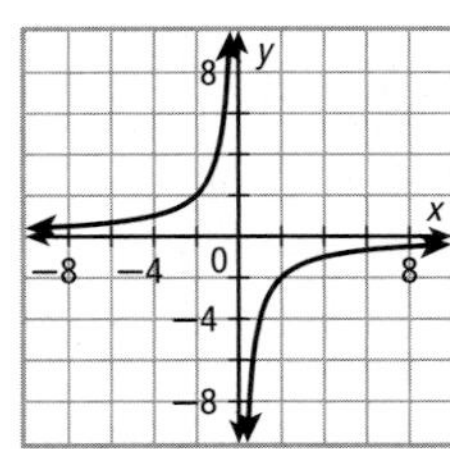

**9.** $y=\frac{1}{x}$

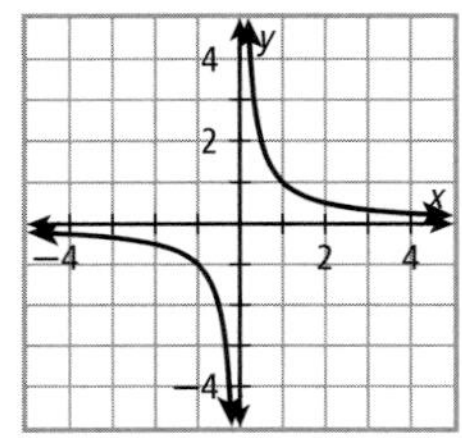

**10.** $-15$ **11.** $13,200 **12.** $-4$; $x=-4$ and $y=0$ **13.** $-1$; $x=-1$ and $y=3$ **14.** $-3$; $x=-3$ and $y=-4$ **15.** $\frac{7}{4}$; $x=\frac{7}{4}$ and $y=5$

**16.**

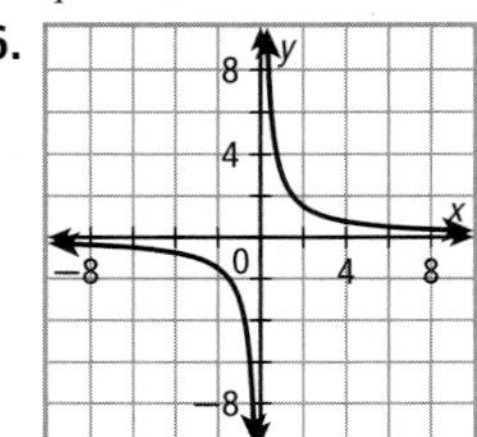

**17.**

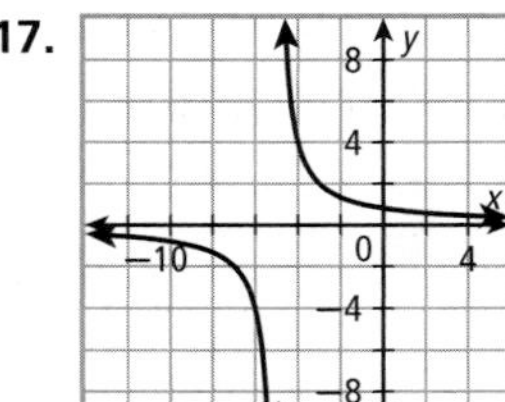

**18.**

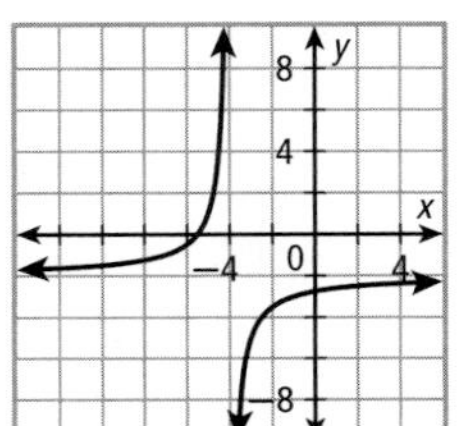

**19.**

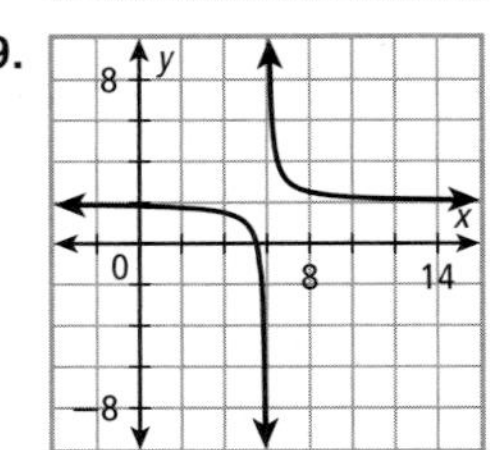

**20.** D: $x>0$; R: $y>0$

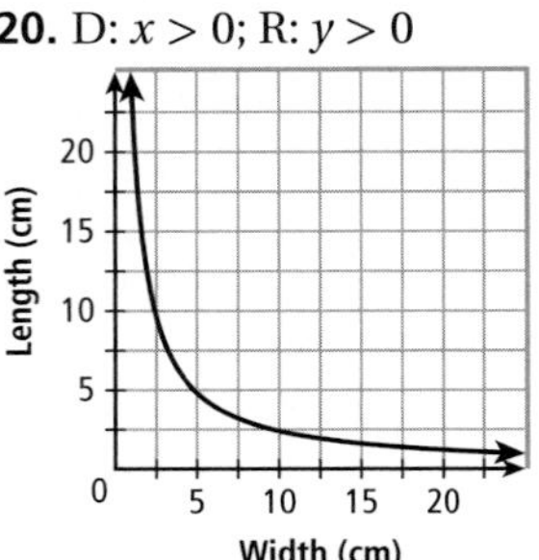


**21.** 0 **22.** 7 **23.** 0, 1 **24.** $-1$, 5 **25.** 5, $-5$ **26.** 4, 7 **27.** $\frac{1}{3r}$; $r \neq 0$ **28.** $\frac{1}{2k-3}$; $k \neq 0$ and $k \neq \frac{3}{2}$ **29.** $\frac{1}{x-2}$; $x \neq -6$ and $x \neq 2$ **30.** $\frac{-2}{x+3}$; $x \neq \pm 3$ **31.** $\frac{3}{x-1}$; $x \neq -5$ and $x \neq 1$ **32.** $\frac{x+3}{x-5}$; $x \neq -6$ and $x \neq 5$ **33.** $\frac{4}{\pi}$ **34.** $\frac{2b^2+2b}{3}$ **35.** $\frac{4x^2-12x}{3}$ **36.** $\frac{15b^2}{2}$ **37.** $\frac{-3c^3}{4d^2}$ **38.** $\frac{b+2}{2b^2+8b}$ **39.** $\frac{n^2+3n+2}{n^2-n-42}$ **40.** $\frac{1}{b-3}$ **41.** $\frac{y^2}{3}$ **42.** $\frac{12n^3}{m}$ **43.** $\frac{x^2+2x-3}{4x^2-16}$ **44.** $\frac{(b+8)(b+7)}{2(b+4)(2b+7)}$ **45.** $10a^2b^2$ **46.** $10x(x-3)$ **47.** $\frac{b^2+8}{2b}$ **48.** $\frac{3x^2+2x-4}{x^2-2}$ **49.** $\frac{8p-2}{p^2-4p+2}$ **50.** $\frac{5b-1}{7-b}$ **51.** $\frac{-10}{n^2-1}$ **52.** $\frac{7m+2}{10m^2}$ **53.** $\frac{h^2+5h-1}{h-5}$ **54.** $\frac{40}{3r}$ **55.** $2n^2-3n-5$ **56.** $x-\frac{2}{x}+\frac{5}{x^2}$ **57.** $x+2$ **58.** $3n+1$ **59.** $h+12$ **60.** $3x+2$ **61.** $m-6$ **62.** $3m+4$ **63.** $x+2$ **64.** $x+6$ **65.** $p-2$ **66.** $2x-1+\frac{-3}{x+2}$ **67.** $2n+7+\frac{36}{n-5}$ **68.** $3b^2+6b+8+\frac{18}{b-2}$ **69.** $-4x^2+10x-17+\frac{34}{x+2}$ **70.** $-\frac{3}{4}$ **71.** $\frac{12}{7}$ **72.** $-\frac{18}{11}$ **73.** $-\frac{7}{6}$; 0 is extraneous. **74.** $-\frac{2}{3}$; 1 is extraneous. **75.** $-\frac{1}{3}$, 1 **76.** $-3$ **77.** $\pm 1$ **78.** $-\frac{1}{12}$ **79.** $-2$; 4 is extraneous. **80.** 4, 5 **81.** $-12$, 1 **82.** $-19$ **83.** 0; 2 is extraneous.

# Glossary/Glosario

go.hrw.com
Multilingual Glossary Online
KEYWORD: MA7 Glossary

## A

| ENGLISH | SPANISH | EXAMPLES |
|---|---|---|
| **absolute value** (p. 14) The absolute value of $x$ is the distance from zero to $x$ on a number line, denoted $\|x\|$. $\|x\| = \begin{cases} x & \text{if } x \geq 0 \\ -x & \text{if } x < 0 \end{cases}$ | **valor absoluto** El valor absoluto de $x$ es la distancia de cero a $x$ en una recta numérica, y se expresa $\|x\|$. $\|x\| = \begin{cases} x & \text{si } x \geq 0 \\ -x & \text{si } x < 0 \end{cases}$ | $\|3\| = 3$ <br> $\|-3\| = 3$ |
| **absolute-value equation** (p. 148) An equation that contains absolute-value expressions. | **ecuación de valor absoluto** Ecuación que contiene expresiones de valor absoluto. | $\|x + 4\| = 7$ |
| **absolute-value function** (p. 366) A function whose rule contains absolute-value expressions. | **función de valor absoluto** Función cuya regla contiene expresiones de valor absoluto. | $y = \|x + 4\|$ |
| **absolute-value inequality** (p. 212) An inequality that contains absolute-value expressions. | **desigualdad de valor absoluto** Desigualdad que contiene expresiones de valor absoluto. | $\|x + 4\| > 7$ |
| **acute angle** (p. S56) An angle that measures greater than 0° and less than 90°. | **ángulo agudo** Ángulo que mide más de 0° y menos de 90°. | |
| **acute triangle** (p. S63) A triangle with three acute angles. | **triángulo acutángulo** Triángulo con tres ángulos agudos. | |
| **Addition Property of Equality** (p. 79) For real numbers $a$, $b$, and $c$, if $a = b$, then $a + c = b + c$. | **Propiedad de igualdad de la suma** Dados los números reales $a$, $b$ y $c$, si $a = b$, entonces $a + c = b + c$. | $x - 6 = 8$ <br> $+6 \quad +6$ <br> $x = 14$ |
| **Addition Property of Inequality** (p. 174) For real numbers $a$, $b$, and $c$, if $a < b$, then $a + c < b + c$. Also holds true for $>$, $\leq$, $\geq$, and $\neq$. | **Propiedad de desigualdad de la suma** Dados los números reales $a$, $b$ y $c$, si $a < b$, entonces $a + c < b + c$. Es válido también para $>$, $\leq$, $\geq$ y $\neq$. | $x - 6 < 8$ <br> $+6 \quad +6$ <br> $x < 14$ |
| **additive inverse** (p. 15) The opposite of a number. Two numbers are additive inverses if their sum is zero. | **inverso aditivo** El opuesto de un número. Dos números son inversos aditivos si su suma es cero. | The additive inverse of 5 is −5. <br> The additive inverse of −5 is 5. |
| **algebraic expression** (p. 6) An expression that contains at least one variable. | **expresión algebraica** Expresión que contiene por lo menos una variable. | $2x + 3y$ <br> $4x$ |
| **algebraic order of operations** *See* order of operations. | **orden algebraico de las operaciones** *Ver* orden de las operaciones. | |

| ENGLISH | SPANISH | EXAMPLES |
|---|---|---|

**AND** (p. 202) A logical operator representing the intersection of two sets.

**Y** Operador lógico que representa la intersección de dos conjuntos.

$A = \{2, 3, 4, 5\}$ $B = \{1, 3, 5, 7\}$ The set of values that are in $A$ AND $B$ is $A \cap B = \{3, 5\}$.

---

**angle** (p. S56) A figure formed by two rays with a common endpoint.

**ángulo** Figura formada por dos rayos con un extremo común.

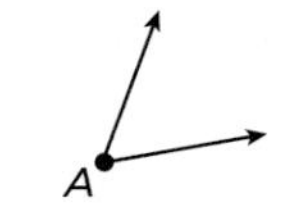


---

**area** (p. S61) The number of nonoverlapping unit squares of a given size that will exactly cover the interior of a plane figure.

**área** Cantidad de cuadrados unitarios de un determinado tamaño no superpuestos que cubren exactamente el interior de una figura plana.

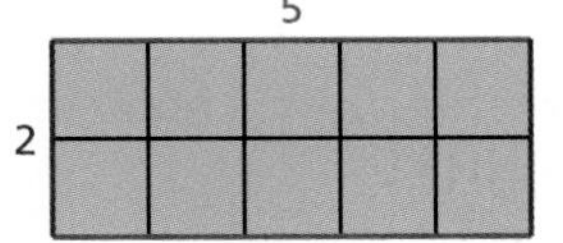


The area is 10 square units.

---

**arithmetic sequence** (p. 272) A sequence whose successive terms differ by the same nonzero number $d$, called the *common difference*.

**sucesión aritmética** Sucesión cuyos términos sucesivos difieren en el mismo número distinto de cero $d$, denominado *diferencia común*.

4, 7, 10, 13, 16, ...

+3 +3 +3 +3

$d = 3$

---

**Associative Property of Addition** (p. 46) For all numbers $a$, $b$, and $c$, $a + b + c = (a + b) + c = a + (b + c)$.

**Propiedad asociativa de la suma** Dados tres números cualesquiera $a$, $b$ y $c$, $a + b + c = (a + b) + c = a + (b + c)$.

$5 + 3 + 7 = (5 + 3) + 7 = 5 + (3 + 7)$

---

**Associative Property of Multiplication** (p. 46) For all numbers $a$, $b$, and $c$, $a \cdot b \cdot c = (a \cdot b) \cdot c = a \cdot (b \cdot c)$.

**Propiedad asociativa de la multiplicación** Dados tres números cualesquiera $a$, $b$ y $c$, $a \cdot b \cdot c = (a \cdot b) \cdot c = a \cdot (b \cdot c)$.

$5 \cdot 3 \cdot 7 = (5 \cdot 3) \cdot 7 = 5 \cdot (3 \cdot 7)$

---

**asymptote** (p. 858) A line that a graph gets closer to as the value of a variable becomes extremely large or small.

**asíntota** Línea recta a la cual se aproxima una gráfica a medida que el valor de una variable se hace sumamente grande o pequeño.

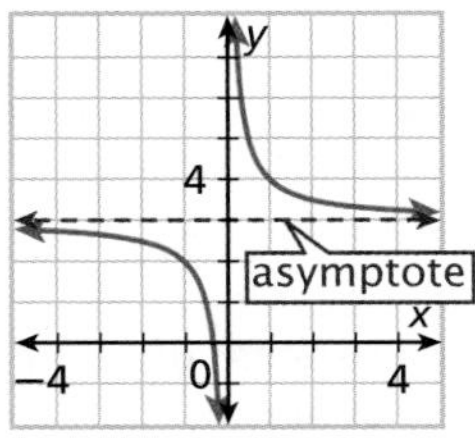


---

**average** *See* mean.

**promedio** *Ver* media.

---

**axis of a coordinate plane** (p. 54) One of two perpendicular number lines, called the $x$-axis and the $y$-axis, used to define the location of a point in a coordinate plane.

**eje de un plano cartesiano** Una de las dos rectas numéricas perpendiculares, denominadas eje $x$ y eje $y$, utilizadas para definir la ubicación de un punto en un plano cartesiano.

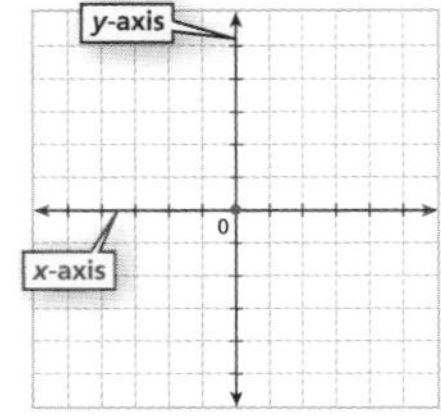


---

**axis of symmetry** (p. 366, p. 600) A line that divides a plane figure or a graph into two congruent reflected halves.

**eje de simetría** Línea que divide una figura plana o una gráfica en dos mitades reflejadas congruentes.

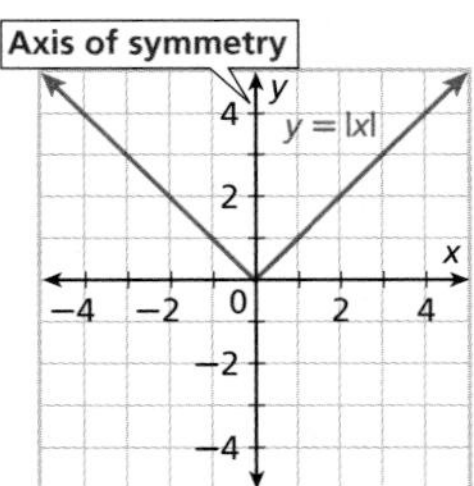

# B

| ENGLISH | SPANISH | EXAMPLES |
|---|---|---|
| **back-to-back stem-and-leaf plot** (p. 687) A graph used to organize and compare two sets of data so that the frequencies can be compared. *See also* stem-and-leaf plot. | **diagrama doble de tallo y hojas** Gráfica utilizada para organizar y comparar dos conjuntos de datos para poder comparar las frecuencias. *Ver también* diagrama de tallo y hojas. | Data set A: 9, 12, 14, 16, 23, 27<br>Data set B: 6, 8, 10, 13, 15, 16, 21<br>Set A \| \| Set B<br>9 \| 0 \| 6 8<br>6 4 2 \| 1 \| 0 3 5 6<br>3 7 \| 2 \| 1<br>*Key:* \|2\|1 means 21<br>7\|2\| means 27 |
| **bar graph** (p. 678) A graph that uses vertical or horizontal bars to display data. | **gráfica de barras** Gráfica con barras horizontales o verticales para mostrar datos. | 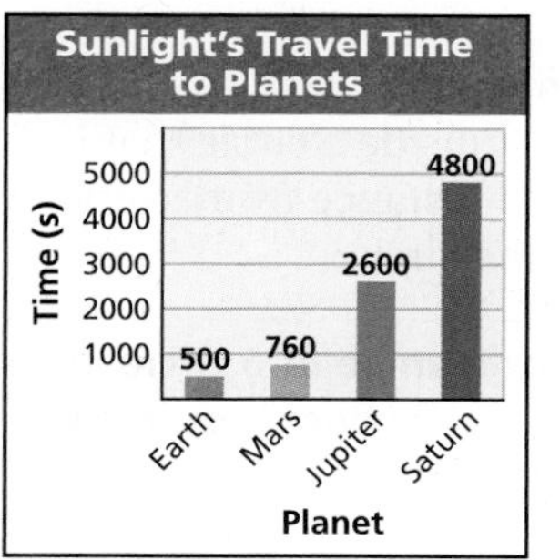 |
| **base of a power** (p. 26) The number in a power that is used as a factor. | **base de una potencia** Número de una potencia que se utiliza como factor. | $3^4 = 3 \cdot 3 \cdot 3 \cdot 3 = 81$<br>3 is the base. |
| **base of an exponential function** (p. 772) The value of $b$ in a function of the form $f(x) = ab^x$, where $a$ and $b$ are real numbers with $a \neq 0$, $b > 0$, and $b \neq 1$. | **base de una función exponencial** Valor de $b$ en una función del tipo $f(x) = ab^x$, donde $a$ y $b$ son números reales con $a \neq 0$, $b > 0$ y $b \neq 1$. | In the function $f(x) = 5(2)^x$, the base is 2. |
| **biased sample** (p. 709) A sample that does not fairly represent the population. | **muestra no representativa** Muestra que no representa adecuadamente una población. | To find out about the exercise habits of average Americans, a fitness magazine surveyed its readers about how often they exercise. The population is all Americans and the sample is readers of the fitness magazine. This sample will likely be biased because readers of fitness magazines may exercise more often than other people do. |
| **binomial** (p. 477) A polynomial with two terms. | **binomio** Polinomio con dos términos. | $x + y$<br>$2a^2 + 3$<br>$4m^3n^2 + 6mn^4$ |
| **boundary line** (p. 414) A line that divides a coordinate plane into two half-planes. | **línea de límite** Línea que divide un plano cartesiano en dos semiplanos. | 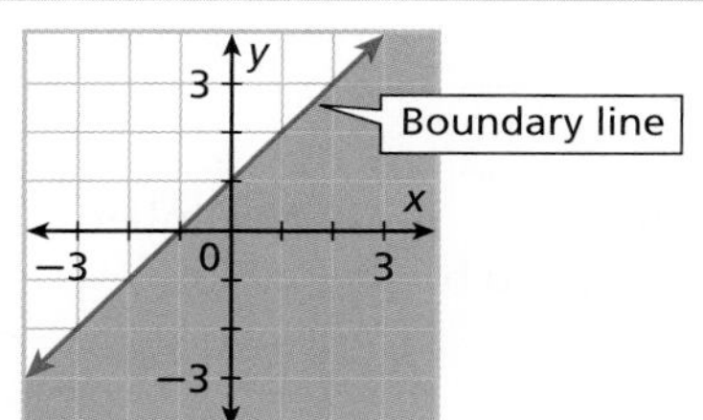 |

| ENGLISH | SPANISH | EXAMPLES |
| --- | --- | --- |
| **box-and-whisker plot** (p. 695) A method of showing how data is distributed by using the median, quartiles, and minimum and maximum values; also called a *box plot.* | **gráfica de mediana y rango** Método para mostrar la distribución de datos utilizando la mediana, los cuartiles y los valores mínimo y máximo; también llamado *gráfica de caja.* | 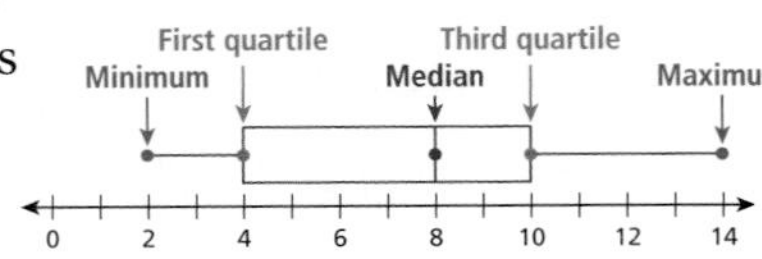 |

| | | |
| --- | --- | --- |
| **Cartesian coordinate system** *See* coordinate plane. | **sistema de coordenadas cartesianas** *Ver* plano cartesiano. | |
| **center of a circle** (p. S62) The point inside a circle that is the same distance from every point on the circle. | **centro de un círculo** Punto dentro de un círculo que se encuentra a la misma distancia de todos los puntos del círculo. | 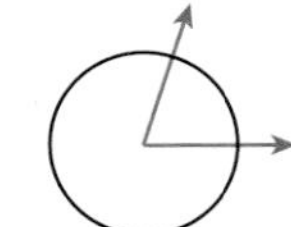 |
| **central angle of a circle** (p. 681) An angle whose vertex is the center of a circle. | **ángulo central de un círculo** Ángulo cuyo vértice es el centro de un círculo. | 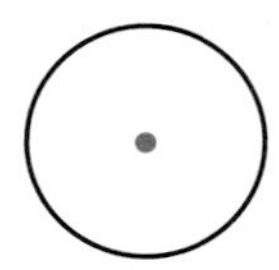 |
| **circle** (p. S62) The set of points in a plane that are a fixed distance from a given point called the center of the circle. | **círculo** Conjunto de puntos en un plano que se encuentran a una distancia fija de un punto determinado denominado centro del círculo. | |
| **circle graph** (p. 680) A way to display data by using a circle divided into non-overlapping sectors. | **gráfica circular** Forma de mostrar datos mediante un círculo dividido en sectores no superpuestos. | 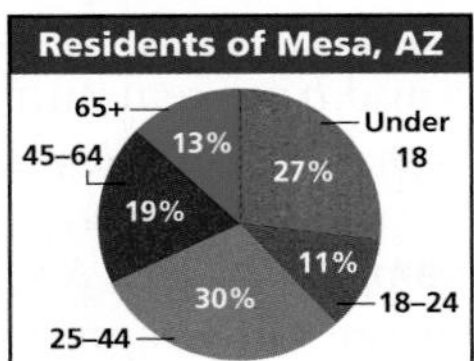 |
| **circumference** (p. S62) The distance around a circle. | **circunferencia** Distancia alrededor de un círculo. |  |
| **closure** (p. 37) A set of numbers is said to be closed, or to have closure, under a given operation if the result of the operation on any two numbers in the set is also in the set. | **cerradura** Se dice que un conjunto de números es cerrado, o tiene cerradura, respecto de una operación determinada, si el resultado de la operación entre dos números cualesquiera del conjunto también está en el conjunto. | The set of integers is closed under addition because the sum of any two integers is also an integer.<br>The set of whole numbers is not closed under subtraction because the difference of any two whole numbers may not be another whole number; for example, $2 - 4 = -2$. |
| **coefficient** (p. 48) A number multiplied by a variable. | **coeficiente** Número multiplicado por una variable. | In the expression $2x + 3y$, 2 is the coefficient of $x$ and 3 is the coefficient of $y$. |

| ENGLISH | SPANISH | EXAMPLES |
| --- | --- | --- |
| **combination** (p. 737) A selection of a group of objects in which order is *not* important. The number of combinations of $r$ objects chosen from a group of $n$ objects is denoted $_nC_r$. | **combinación** Selección de un grupo de objetos en la cual el orden *no* es importante. El número de combinaciones de $r$ objetos elegidos de un grupo de $n$ objetos se expresa así: $_nC_r$. | For objects $A$, $B$, $C$, and $D$, there are 6 different combinations of 2 objects. $AB$, $AC$, $AD$, $BC$, $BD$, $CD$ |
| **commission** (p. 133) Money paid to a person or company for making a sale, usually a percent of the sale amount. | **comisión** Dinero que se paga a una persona o empresa por realizar una venta; generalmente se trata de un porcentaje del total de la venta. | |
| **common difference** (p. 272) In an arithmetic sequence, the nonzero constant difference of any term and the previous term. | **diferencia común** En una sucesión aritmética, diferencia constante distinta de cero entre cualquier término y el término anterior. | In the arithmetic sequence 3, 5, 7, 9, 11, ..., the common difference is 2. |
| **common factor** (p. 525) A factor that is common to all terms of an expression or to two or more expressions. | **factor común** Factor que es común a todos los términos de una expresión o a dos o más expresiones. | Expression: $4x^2 + 16x^3 - 8x$<br>Common factor: $4x$<br>Expressions: 12 and 18<br>Common factors: 2, 3, and 6 |
| **common ratio** (p. 766) In a geometric sequence, the constant ratio of any term and the previous term. | **razón común** En una sucesión geométrica, la razón constante entre cualquier término y el término anterior. | In the geometric sequence 32, 16, 8, 4, 2, . . ., the common ratio is $\frac{1}{2}$. |
| **Commutative Property of Addition** (p. 46) For any two numbers $a$ and $b$, $a + b = b + a$. | **Propiedad conmutativa de la suma** Dados dos números cualesquiera $a$ y $b$, $a + b = b + a$. | $3 + 4 = 4 + 3 = 7$ |
| **Commutative Property of Multiplication** (p. 46) For any two numbers $a$ and $b$, $a \cdot b = b \cdot a$. | **Propiedad conmutativa de la multiplicación** Dados dos números cualesquiera $a$ y $b$, $a \cdot b = b \cdot a$. | $3 \cdot 4 = 4 \cdot 3 = 12$ |
| **complement of an event** (p. 721) All outcomes in the sample space that are not in an event $E$, denoted $\overline{E}$. | **complemento de un suceso** Todos los resultados en el espacio muestral que no están en el suceso $E$, y se expresan $\overline{E}$. | In the experiment of rolling a number cube, the complement of rolling a 3 is rolling a 1, 2, 4, 5, or 6. |
| **complementary angles** (p. S57) Two angles whose measures have a sum of 90°. | **ángulos complementarios** Dos ángulos cuyas medidas suman 90°. | 37° B 53° A |
| **completing the square** (p. 645) A process used to form a perfect-square trinomial. To complete the square of $x^2 + bx$, add $\left(\frac{b}{2}\right)^2$. 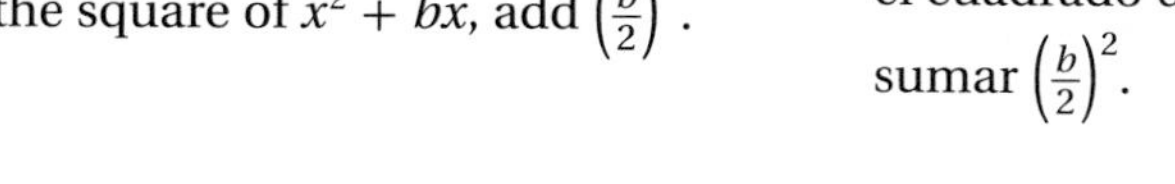 | **completar el cuadrado** Proceso utilizado para formar un trinomio cuadrado perfecto. Para completar el cuadrado de $x^2 + bx$, hay que sumar $\left(\frac{b}{2}\right)^2$. | $x^2 + 6x + \square$<br>Add $\left(\frac{6}{2}\right)^2 = 9$.<br>$x^2 + 6x + 9$ |

| ENGLISH | SPANISH | EXAMPLES |
|---|---|---|
| **composite figure** (p. 83) A plane figure made up of triangles, rectangles, trapezoids, circles, and other simple shapes, or a three-dimensional figure made up of prisms, cones, pyramids, cylinders, and other simple three-dimensional figures. | **figura compuesta** Figura plana compuesta por triángulos, rectángulos, trapecios, círculos y otras figuras simples, o figura tridimensional compuesta por prismas, conos, pirámides, cilindros y otras figuras tridimensionales simples. | 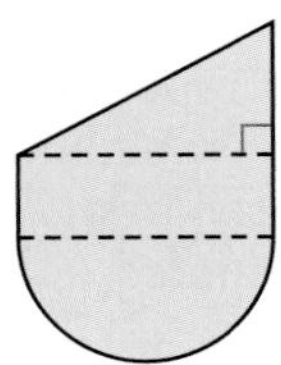 |
| **compound event** (p. 737) An event made up of two or more simple events. | **suceso compuesto** Suceso formado por dos o más sucesos simples. | In the experiment of tossing a coin and rolling a number cube, the event of the coin landing heads and the number cube landing on 3. |
| **compound inequality** (p. 202) Two inequalities that are combined into one statement by the word *and* or *or*. | **desigualdad compuesta** Dos desigualdades unidas en un enunciado por la palabra *y* u *o*. | $x \geq 2$ AND $x < 6$ (also written $2 \leq x < 6$)<br>0 2 4 6 8<br>$x < 2$ OR $x > 6$<br>0 2 4 6 8 |
| **compound interest** (p. 782) Interest earned or paid on both the principal and previously earned interest. The formula for compound interest is $A = P\left(1 + \frac{r}{n}\right)^{nt}$, where $A$ is the final amount, $P$ is the principal, $r$ is the interest rate expressed as a decimal, $n$ is the number of times interest is compounded, and $t$ is the time. | **interés compuesto** Intereses ganados o pagados sobre el capital y los intereses ya devengados. La fórmula de interés compuesto es $A = P\left(1 + \frac{r}{n}\right)^{nt}$, donde $A$ es la cantidad final, $P$ es el capital, $r$ es la tasa de interés expresada como un decimal, $n$ es la cantidad de veces que se capitaliza el interés y $t$ es el tiempo. | If \$100 is put into an account with an interest rate of 5% compounded monthly, then after 2 years, the account will have $100\left(1 + \frac{0.05}{12}\right)^{12 \cdot 2} = \$110.49$. |
| **compound statement** (p. 201) Two statements that are connected by the word *and* or *or*. | **enunciado compuesto** Dos enunciados unidos por la palabra *y* u *o*. | The sky is blue and the grass is green.<br>I will drive to school or I will take the bus. |
| **cone** (p. 874, p. S64) A three-dimensional figure with a circular base and a curved surface that connects the base to a point called the vertex. | **cono** Figura tridimensional con una base circular y una superficie lateral curva que conecta la base con un punto denominado vértice. | 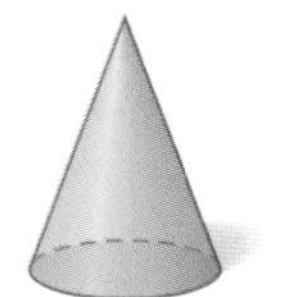 |
| **congruent** (p. S59) Having the same size and shape, denoted by $\cong$. | **congruente** Que tiene el mismo tamaño y la misma forma, expresado por $\cong$. | 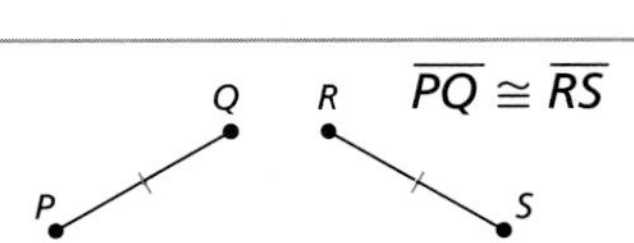 |
| **conjugate of an irrational number** (p. 821) The conjugate of a number in the form $a + \sqrt{b}$ is $a - \sqrt{b}$. | **conjugado de un número irracional** El conjugado de un número en la forma $a + \sqrt{b}$ es $a - \sqrt{b}$. | The conjugate of $1 + \sqrt{2}$ is $1 - \sqrt{2}$. |

| ENGLISH | SPANISH | EXAMPLES |
|---|---|---|
| **consistent system** (p. 406) A system of equations or inequalities that has at least one solution. | **sistema consistente** Sistema de ecuaciones o desigualdades que tiene por lo menos una solución. | $\begin{cases} x + y = 6 \\ x - y = 4 \end{cases}$ solution: $(5, 1)$ |
| **constant** (p. 6) A value that does not change. | **constante** Valor que no cambia. | $3, 0, \pi$ |
| **constant of variation** (p. 326) The constant *k* in direct and inverse variation equations. | **constante de variación** La constante *k* en ecuaciones de variación directa e inversa. | $y = 5x$ (5 ↑ constant of variation) |
| **continuous graph** (p. 231) A graph made up of connected lines or curves. | **gráfica continua** Gráfica compuesta por líneas rectas o curvas conectadas. | 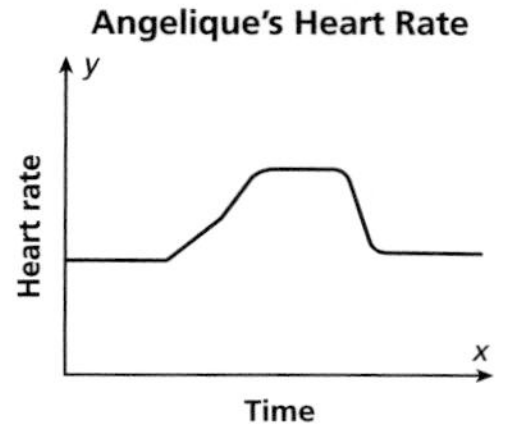  |
| **contradiction** (p. 101) An equation that has no solutions. | **contradicción** Ecuación que no tiene soluciones. | $x + 1 = x$<br>$1 = 0$ ✗ |
| **conversion factor** (p. 115) The ratio of two equal quantities, each measured in different units. | **factor de conversión** Razón entre dos cantidades iguales, cada una medida en unidades diferentes. | $\frac{12\text{ inches}}{1\text{ foot}}$ |
| **coordinate** (p. 54) A number used to identify the location of a point. On a number line, one coordinate is used. On a coordinate plane, two coordinates are used, called the *x*-coordinate and the *y*-coordinate. | **coordenada** Número utilizado para identificar la ubicación de un punto. En una recta numérica se utiliza una coordenada. En un plano cartesiano se utilizan dos coordenadas, denominadas coordenada *x* y coordenada *y*. | 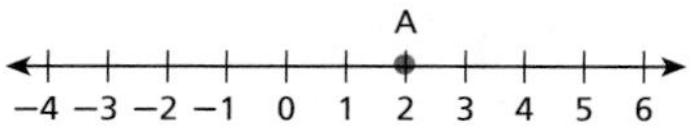  The coordinate of *A* is 2. 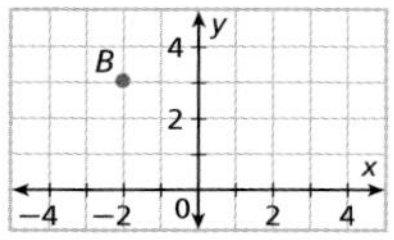  The coordinates of *B* are $(-2, 3)$. |
| **coordinate plane** (p. 54) A plane that is divided into four regions by a horizontal line called the *x*-axis and a vertical line called the *y*-axis. | **plano cartesiano** Plano dividido en cuatro regiones por una línea horizontal denominada eje *x* y una línea vertical denominada eje *y*. | 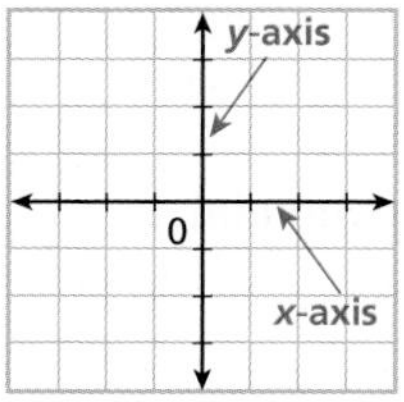  |
| **correlation** (p. 262) A measure of the strength and direction of the relationship between two variables or data sets. | **correlación** Medida de la fuerza y dirección de la relación entre dos variables o conjuntos de datos. | 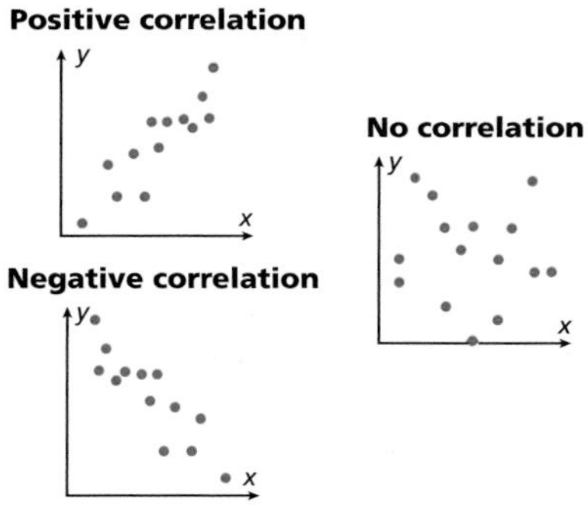  |

| ENGLISH | SPANISH | EXAMPLES |
|---|---|---|
| **corresponding angles of polygons** (p. 121) Angles in the same position in two different polygons that have the same number of angles. | **ángulos correspondientes de los polígonos** Ángulos que tienen la misma posición relativa en dos polígonos diferentes que tienen el mismo número de ángulos. | 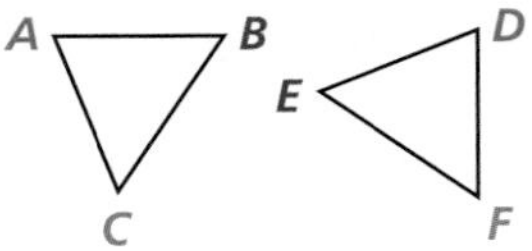  $\angle A$ and $\angle D$ are corresponding angles. |
| **corresponding sides of polygons** (p. 121) Sides in the same position in two different polygons that have the same number of sides. | **lados correspondientes de los polígonos** Lados que tienen la misma posición en dos polígonos diferentes que tienen el mismo número de lados. | 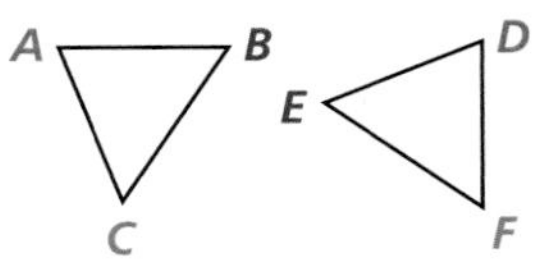  $\overline{AB}$ and $\overline{DE}$ are corresponding sides. |
| **cosine** (p. 908) In a right triangle, the cosine of angle *A* is the ratio of the length of the leg adjacent to angle *A* to the length of the hypotenuse. | **coseno** En un triángulo rectángulo, el coseno del ángulo *A* es la razón entre la longitud del cateto adyacente al ángulo *A* y la longitud de la hipotenusa. | 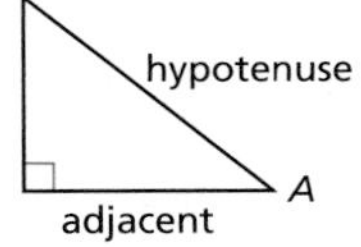  $\cos A = \frac{\text{adjacent}}{\text{hypotenuse}}$ |
| **counterexample** (p. S76) An example that proves that a conjecture or statement is false. | **contraejemplo** Ejemplo que demuestra que una conjetura o enunciado es falso. | |
| **cross products** (p. 115) In the statement $\frac{a}{b} = \frac{c}{d}$, *bc* and *ad* are the cross products. | **productos cruzados** En el enunciado $\frac{a}{b} = \frac{c}{d}$, *bc* y *ad* son productos cruzados. | $\frac{1}{2} = \frac{3}{6}$ Cross products: $2 \cdot 3 = 6$ and: $1 \cdot 6 = 6$ |
| **Cross Product Property** (p. 115) For any real numbers *a, b, c,* and *d*, where $b \neq 0$ and $d \neq 0$, if $\frac{a}{b} = \frac{c}{d}$, then $ad = bc$. | **Propiedad de productos cruzados** Dados los números reales *a, b, c* y *d*, donde $b \neq 0$ y $d \neq 0$, si $\frac{a}{b} = \frac{c}{d}$, entonces $ad = bc$. | If $\frac{4}{6} = \frac{10}{x}$, then $4x = 60$, so $x = 15$. |
| **cube** (p. S66) A prism with six square faces. | **cubo** Prisma con seis caras cuadradas. | 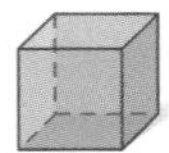 |
| **cube in numeration** (p. 26) The third power of a number. | **cubo en numeración** Tercera potencia de un número. | 8 is the cube of 2. |
| **cube root** (p. 832) A number, written as $\sqrt[3]{x}$, whose cube is *x*. | **raíz cúbica** Número, expresado como $\sqrt[3]{x}$, cuyo cubo es *x*. | $\sqrt[3]{64} = 4$, because $4^3 = 64$; 4 is the cube root of 64. |
| **cubic polynomial** (p. 477) A polynomial of degree 3. | **polinomio cúbico** Polinomio de grado 3. | $x^3 + 4x^2 - 6x + 2$ |
| **cumulative frequency** (p. 689) The frequency of all data values that are less than or equal to a given value. | **frecuencia acumulativa** Frecuencia de todos los valores de los datos que son menores que o iguales a un valor dado. | For the data set 2, 2, 3, 5, 5, 6, 7, 7, 8, 8, 8, 9, the cumulative frequency table is shown below. |

| Data | Frequency | Cumulative Frequency |
|---|---|---|
| 2 | 2 | 2 |
| 3 | 1 | 3 |
| 5 | 2 | 5 |
| 6 | 1 | 6 |
| 7 | 2 | 8 |
| 8 | 3 | 11 |
| 9 | 1 | 12 |

| ENGLISH | SPANISH | EXAMPLES |
|---|---|---|
| **cylinder** (p. S64) A three-dimensional figure with two parallel congruent circular bases and a curved surface that connects the bases. | **cilindro** Figura tridimensional con dos bases circulares congruentes paralelas y una superficie lateral curva que conecta las bases. | 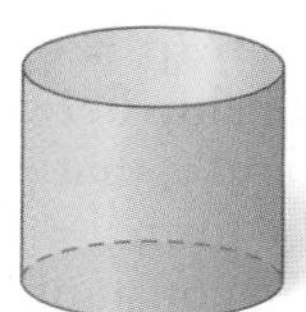 |

## D

| ENGLISH | SPANISH | EXAMPLES |
|---|---|---|
| **data** (p. 678) Information gathered from a survey or experiment. | **datos** Información reunida en una encuesta o experimento. | |
| **degree measure of an angle** (p. S56) A unit of angle measure; one degree is $\frac{1}{360}$ of a circle. | **medida en grados de un ángulo** Unidad de medida de los ángulos; un grado es $\frac{1}{360}$ de un círculo. | |
| **degree of a monomial** (p. 476) The sum of the exponents of the variables in the monomial. | **grado de un monomio** Suma de los exponentes de las variables del monomio. | $4x^2y^5z^3$ Degree: $2 + 5 + 3 = 10$<br>$5 = 5x^0$ Degree: 0 |
| **degree of a polynomial** (p. 476) The degree of the term of the polynomial with the greatest degree. | **grado de un polinomio** Grado del término del polinomio con el grado máximo. | $3x^2y^2 + 4xy^5 - 12x^3y^2$<br>Degree 4 Degree 6 Degree 5<br>Degree 6 |
| **dependent events** (p. 726) Events for which the occurrence or nonoccurrence of one event affects the probability of the other event. | **sucesos dependientes** Dos sucesos son dependientes si el hecho de que uno de ellos ocurra o no afecta la probabilidad del otro suceso. | From a bag containing 3 red marbles and 2 blue marbles, drawing a red marble, and then drawing a blue marble without replacing the first marble. |
| **dependent system** (p. 407) A system of equations that has infinitely many solutions. | **sistema dependiente** Sistema de ecuaciones que tiene infinitamente muchas soluciones. | $\begin{cases} x + y = 2 \\ 2x + 2y = 4 \end{cases}$ |
| **dependent variable** (p. 246) The output of a function; a variable whose value depends on the value of the input, or independent variable. | **variable dependiente** Salida de una función; variable cuyo valor depende del valor de la entrada, o variable independiente. | For $y = 2x + 1$, $y$ is the dependent variable.<br>input: $x$ output: $y$ |
| **diameter** (p. S62) A segment that has endpoints on the circle and that passes through the center of the circle; also the length of that segment. | **diámetro** Segmento que atraviesa el centro de un círculo y cuyos extremos están sobre la circunferencia; longitud de dicho segmento. | 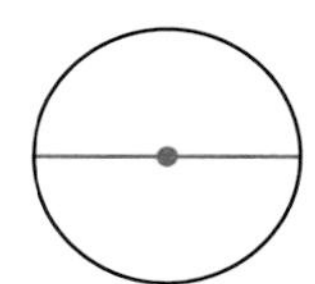 |
| **difference of two cubes** (p. 564) A polynomial of the form $a^3 - b^3$, which may be written as the product $(a - b)(a^2 + ab + b^2)$. | **diferencia de dos cubos** Polinomio del tipo $a^3 - b^3$, que se puede expresar como el producto $(a - b)(a^2 + ab + b^2)$. | $x^3 - 8 = (x - 2)(x^2 + 2x + 4)$ |
| **difference of two squares** (p. 503) A polynomial of the form $a^2 - b^2$, which may be written as the product $(a + b)(a - b)$. | **diferencia de dos cuadrados** Polinomio del tipo $a^2 - b^2$, que se puede expresar como el producto $(a + b)(a - b)$. | $x^2 - 4 = (x + 2)(x - 2)$ |

| ENGLISH | SPANISH | EXAMPLES |
|---|---|---|
| **direct variation** (p. 326) A linear relationship between two variables, $x$ and $y$, that can be written in the form $y = kx$, where $k$ is a nonzero constant. | **variación directa** Relación lineal entre dos variables, $x$ e $y$, que puede expresarse en la forma $y = kx$, donde $k$ es una constante distinta de cero. | 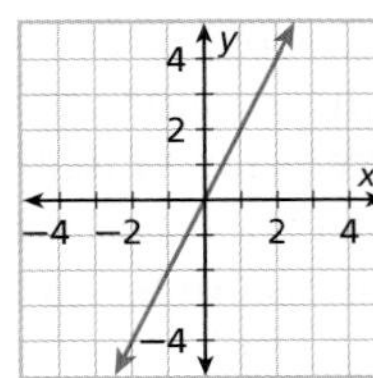 $y = 2x$ |
| **discontinuous function** (p. 858) A function whose graph has one or more jumps, breaks, or holes. | **función discontinua** Función cuya gráfica tiene uno o más saltos, interrupciones u hoyos. | 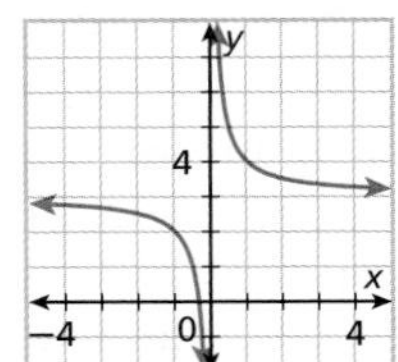 |
| **discount** (p. 139) An amount by which an original price is reduced. | **descuento** Cantidad por la que se reduce un precio original. | |
| **discrete graph** (p. 231) A graph made up of unconnected points. | **gráfica discreta** Gráfica compuesta de puntos no conectados. | 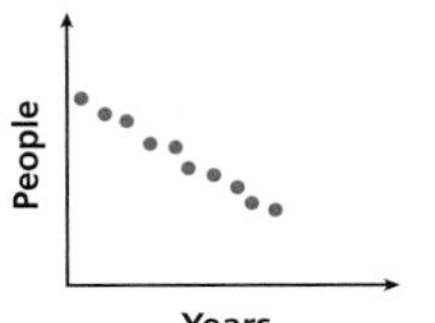  |
| **discriminant** (p. 654) The discriminant of the quadratic equation $ax^2 + bx + c = 0$ is $b^2 - 4ac$. | **discriminante** El discriminante de la ecuación cuadrática $ax^2 + bx + c = 0$ es $b^2 - 4ac$. | The discriminant of $2x^2 - 5x - 3$ is $(-5)^2 - 4(2)(-3)$ or 49. |
| **Distance Formula** (p. 642) In a coordinate plane, the distance from $(x_1, y_1)$ to $(x_2, y_2)$ is $d = \sqrt{(x_2 - x_1)^2 + (y_2 - y_1)^2}$. | **Fórmula de distancia** En un plano cartesiano, la distancia desde $(x_1, y_1)$ hasta $(x_2, y_2)$ es $d = \sqrt{(x_2 - x_1)^2 + (y_2 - y_1)^2}$. | 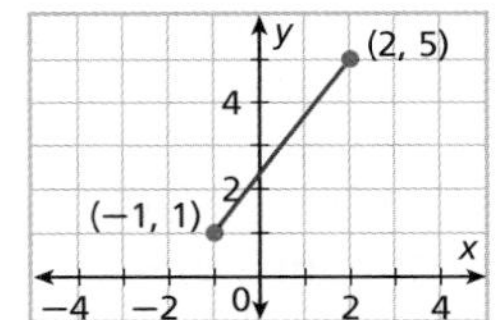  The distance from $(2, 5)$ to $(-1, 1)$ is $d = \sqrt{(-1 - 2)^2 + (1 - 5)^2} = \sqrt{(-3)^2 + (-4)^2} = \sqrt{9 + 16} = \sqrt{25} = 5$. |
| **Distributive Property** (p. 47) For all real numbers $a$, $b$, and $c$, $a(b + c) = ab + ac$, and $(b + c)a = ba + ca$. | **Propiedad distributiva** Dados los números reales $a$, $b$ y $c$, $a(b + c) = ab + ac$, y : $(b + c)a = ba + ca$. | $3(4 + 5) = 3 \cdot 4 + 3 \cdot 5$<br>$(4 + 5)3 = 4 \cdot 3 + 5 \cdot 3$ |
| **Division Property of Equality** (p. 86) For real numbers $a$, $b$, and $c$, where $c \neq 0$, if $a = b$, then $\frac{a}{c} = \frac{b}{c}$. | **Propiedad de igualdad de la división** Dados los números reales $a$, $b$ y $c$, donde $c \neq 0$, si $a = b$, entonces $\frac{a}{c} = \frac{b}{c}$. | $4x = 12$<br>$\frac{4x}{4} = \frac{12}{4}$<br>$x = 3$ |

| ENGLISH | SPANISH | EXAMPLES |
|---|---|---|
| **Division Property of Inequality** (p. 180) If both sides of an inequality are divided by the same positive quantity, the new inequality will have the same solution set. If both sides of an inequality are divided by the same negative quantity, the new inequality will have the same solution set if the inequality symbol is reversed. | **Propiedad de desigualdad de la división** Cuando ambos lados de una desigualdad se dividen entre el mismo número positivo, la nueva desigualdad tiene el mismo conjunto solución. Cuando ambos lados de una desigualdad se dividen entra el mismo número negativo, la nueva desigualdad tiene el mismo conjunto solución si se invierte el símbolo de desigualdad. | $4x \geq 12$<br>$\frac{4x}{4} \geq \frac{12}{4}$<br>$x \geq 3$<br>$-4x \geq 12$<br>$\frac{4x}{-4} \geq \frac{12}{-4}$<br>$x \leq -3$ |
| **domain** (p. 236) The set of all possible input values of a relation or function. | **dominio** Conjunto de valores de entrada de una función o relación. | The domain of the function $f(x) = \sqrt{x}$ is $x \geq 0$. |

## E

| ENGLISH | SPANISH | EXAMPLES |
|---|---|---|
| **element** Each member in a set or matrix. *See also* entry. | **elemento** Cada miembro en un conjunto o matriz. *Ver también* entrada. | |
| **elimination method** (p. 397) A method used to solve systems of equations in which one variable is eliminated by adding or subtracting two equations of the system. | **eliminación** Método utilizado para resolver sistemas de ecuaciones por el cual se elimina una variable sumando o restando dos ecuaciones del sistema. | |
| **empty set** (p. 102) A set with no elements. | **conjunto vacío** Conjunto sin elementos. | The solution set of $\|x\| < 0$ is the empty set, { }, or ∅. |
| **entry** (p. 746) Each value in a matrix; also called an element. | **entrada** Cada valor de una matriz, también denominado elemento. | 3 is the entry in the first row and second column of $A = \begin{bmatrix} 2 & 3 \\ 0 & 1 \end{bmatrix}$, denoted $a_{12}$. |
| **equally likely outcomes** (p. 720) Outcomes are equally likely if they have the same probability of occurring. If an experiment has $n$ equally likely outcomes, then the probability of each outcome is $\frac{1}{n}$. | **resultados igualmente probables** Los resultados son igualmente probables si tienen la misma probabilidad de ocurrir. Si un experimento tiene $n$ resultados igualmente probables, entonces la probabilidad de cada resultado es $\frac{1}{n}$. | If a fair coin is tossed, then $P(\text{heads}) = P(\text{tails}) = \frac{1}{2}$.<br>So the outcome "heads" and the oucome "tails" are equally likely. |
| **equation** (p. 77) A mathematical statement that two expressions are equivalent. | **ecuación** Enunciado matemático que indica que dos expresiones son equivalentes. | $x + 4 = 7$<br>$2 + 3 = 6 - 1$<br>$(x - 1)^2 + (y + 2)^2 = 4$ |
| **equilateral triangle** (p. S63) A triangle with three congruent sides. | **triángulo equilátero** Triángulo con tres lados congruentes. | |
| **equivalent ratios** (p. 114) Ratios that name the same comparison. | **razones equivalentes** Razones que expresan la misma comparación. | $\frac{1}{2}$ and $\frac{2}{4}$ are equivalent ratic |

| ENGLISH | SPANISH | EXAMPLES |
| --- | --- | --- |
| **evaluate** (p. 7) To find the value of an algebraic expression by substituting a number for each variable and simplifying by using the order of operations. | **evaluar** Calcular el valor de una expresión algebraica sustituyendo cada variable por un número y simplificando mediante el orden de las operaciones. | Evaluate $2x + 7$ for $x = 3$.<br>$2x + 7$<br>$2(3) + 7$<br>$6 + 7$<br>$13$ |
| **event** (p. 713) An outcome or set of outcomes in a probability experiment. | **suceso** Resultado o conjunto de resultados en un experimento de probabilidad. | In the experiment of rolling a number cube, the event "an odd number" consists of the outcomes 1, 3, and 5. |
| **excluded values** (p. 858) Values of $x$ for which a function or expression is not defined. | **valores excluidos** Valores de $x$ para los cuales no está definida una función o expresión. | The excluded values of $f(x) = \frac{(x+2)}{(x-1)(x+4)}$ are $x = 1$ and $x = -4$, which would make the denominator equal to 0. |
| **experiment** (p. 713) An operation, process, or activity in which outcomes can be used to estimate probability. | **experimento** Una operación, proceso o actividad en la que se usan los resultados para estimar una probabilidad. | Tossing a coin 10 times and noting the number of heads. |
| **experimental probability** (p. 714) The ratio of the number of times an event occurs to the number of trials, or times, that an activity is performed. | **probabilidad experimental** Razón entre la cantidad de veces que ocurre un suceso y la cantidad de pruebas, o veces, que se realiza una actividad. | Kendra attempted 27 free throws and made 16 of them. The probability that she will make her next free throw can be estimated by $P(\text{free throw}) \approx \frac{\text{number made}}{\text{number attempted}} = \frac{16}{27} \approx 0.59$. |
| **exponent** (p. 26) The number that indicates how many times the base in a power is used as a factor. | **exponente** Número que indica la cantidad de veces que la base de una potencia se utiliza como factor. | $3^4 = 3 \cdot 3 \cdot 3 \cdot 3 = 81$<br>4 is the exponent. |
| **exponential decay** (p. 783) An exponential function of the form $f(x) = ab^x$ in which $0 < b < 1$. If $r$ is the rate of decay, then the function can be written $y = a(1 - r)^t$, where $a$ is the initial amount and $t$ is the time. | **decremento exponencial** Función exponencial del tipo $f(x) = ab^x$ en la cual $0 < b < 1$. Si $r$ es la tasa decremental, entonces la función se puede expresar como $y = a(1 - r)^t$,donde $a$ es la cantidad inicial y $t$ es el tiempo. | $f(x) = 3\left(\frac{1}{2}\right)^x$<br>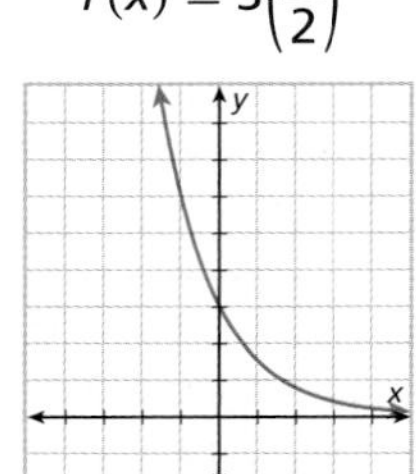 |
| **exponential expression** An algebraic expression in which the variable is in an exponent with a fixed number as the base. | **expresión exponencial** Expresión algebraica en la que la variable está en un exponente y que tiene un número fijo como base. | $2^{x+1}$ |
| **exponential function** (p. 772) A function of the form $f(x) = ab^x$, where $a$ and $b$ are real numbers with $a \neq 0$, $b > 0$, and $b \neq 1$. | **función exponencial** Función del tipo $f(x) = ab^x$, donde $a$ y $b$ son números reales con a $\neq 0$, $b > 0$ y $b \neq 1$. | $f(x) = 3 \cdot 4^x$<br>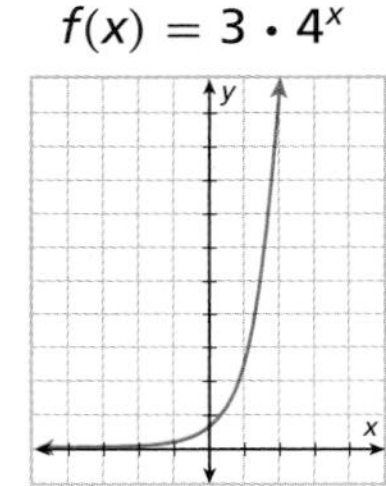 |

| ENGLISH | SPANISH | EXAMPLES |
|---|---|---|

**exponential growth** (p. 781) An exponential function of the form $f(x) = ab^x$ in which $b > 1$. If $r$ is the rate of growth, then the function can be written $y = a(1 + r)^t$, where $a$ is the initial amount and $t$ is the time.

**crecimiento exponencial** Función exponencial del tipo $f(x) = ab^x$ en la que $b > 1$. Si $r$ es la tasa de crecimiento, entonces la función se puede expresar como $y = a(1 + r)^t$, donde $a$ es la cantidad inicial y $t$ es el tiempo.

$f(x) = 2^x$

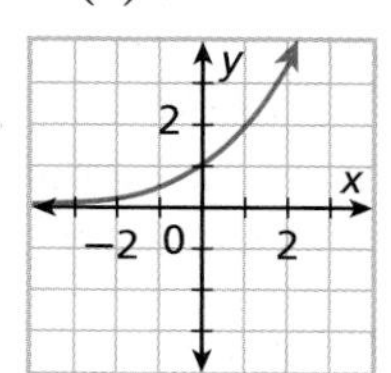


---

**expression** (p. 6) A mathematical phrase that contains operations, numbers, and/or variables.

**expresión** Frase matemática que contiene operaciones, números y/o variables.

$6x + 1$

---

**extraneous solution** (p. 824) A solution of a derived equation that is not a solution of the original equation.

**solución extraña** Solución de una ecuación derivada que no es una solución de la ecuación original.

To solve $\sqrt{x} = -2$, square both sides; $x = 4$.
***Check*** $\sqrt{4} = -2$ is false; so 4 is an extraneous solution.

## F

**factor** A number or expression that is multiplied by another number or expression to get a product. *See also* factoring.

**factor** Número o expresión que se multiplica por otro número o expresión para obtener un producto. *Ver también* factoreo.

$12 = 3 \cdot 4$
3 and 4 are factors of 12.

$x^2 - 1 = (x - 1)(x + 1)$
$(x - 1)$ and $(x + 1)$ are factors of $x^2 - 1$.

---

**factorial** (p. 738) If $n$ is a positive integer, then $n$ factorial, written $n!$, is $n \cdot (n - 1) \cdot (n - 2) \cdot \ldots \cdot 2 \cdot 1$. The factorial of 0 is defined to be 1.

**factorial** Si $n$ es un entero positivo, entonces el factorial de $n$, expresado como $n!$, es $n \cdot (n - 1) \cdot (n - 2) \cdot \ldots \cdot 2 \cdot 1$. Por definición, el factorial de 0 será 1.

$7! = 7 \cdot 6 \cdot 5 \cdot 4 \cdot 3 \cdot 2 \cdot 1$
$= 5040$

---

**factoring** (p. 524) The process of writing a number or algebraic expression as a product.

**factorización** Proceso por el que se expresa un número o expresión algebraica como un producto.

$x^2 - 4x - 21 = (x - 7)(x + 3)$

---

**fair** (p. 720) When all outcomes of an experiment are equally likely.

**justo** Cuando todos los resultados de un experimento son igualmente probables.

When tossing a fair coin, heads and tails are equally likely. Each has a probability of $\frac{1}{2}$.

---

**family of functions** (p. 357) A set of functions whose graphs have basic characteristics in common. Functions in the same family are transformations of their parent function.

**familia de funciones** Conjunto de funciones cuyas gráficas tienen características básicas en común. Las funciones de la misma familia son transformaciones de su función madre.

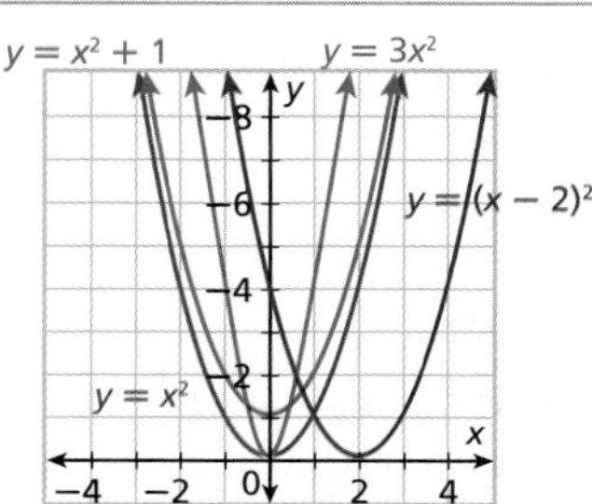

| ENGLISH | SPANISH | EXAMPLES |
|---|---|---|

**first differences** (p. 590) The differences between $y$-values of a function for evenly spaced $x$-values.

**primeras diferencias** Diferencias entre los valores de $y$ de una función para valores de $x$ espaciados uniformemente.

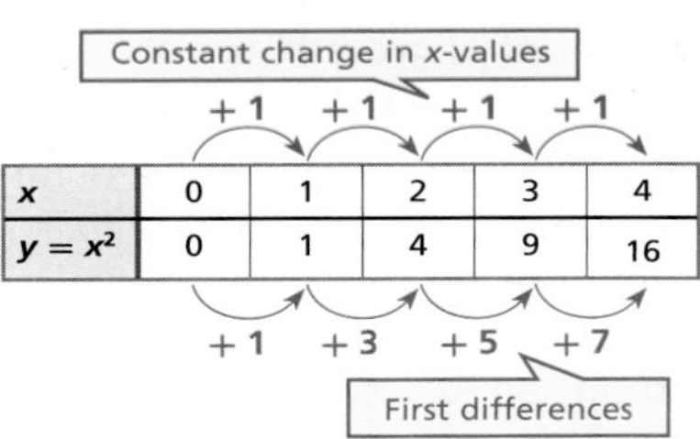


---

**first quartile** (p. 695) The median of the lower half of a data set, denoted $Q_1$. Also called *lower quartile*.

**primer cuartil** Mediana de la mitad inferior de un conjunto de datos, expresada como $Q_1$. También se llama *cuartil inferior*.

Lower half Upper half
18, (23), 28, 49, 36, 42
First quartile

---

**FOIL** (p. 493) A mnemonic (memory) device for a method of multiplying two binomials:
Multiply the **First** terms.
Multiply the **Outer** terms.
Multiply the **Inner** terms.
Multiply the **Last** terms.

**FOIL** Regla mnemotécnica para recordar el método de multiplicación de dos binomios:
Multiplicar los términos **Primeros** (***First***).
Multiplicar los términos **Externos** (***Outer***).
Multiplicar los términos **Internos** (***Inner***).
Multiplicar los términos **Últimos** (***Last***).

F L I O

$(x + 2)(x - 3) = x^2 - 3x + 2x - 6$
$= x^2 - x - 6$

---

**formula** (p. 107) A literal equation that states a rule for a relationship among quantities.

**fórmula** Ecuación literal que establece una regla para una relación entre cantidades.

$A = \pi r^2$

---

**fractional exponent** *See* rational exponent.

**exponente fraccionario** *Ver* exponente racional.

---

**frequency** (p. 688, p. S71) The number of times the value appears in the data set.

**frecuencia** Cantidad de veces que aparece el valor en un conjunto de datos.

In the data set 5, 6, 6, 7, 8, 9, the data value 6 has a frequency of 2.

---

**frequency table** (p. 688) A table that lists the number of times, or frequency, that each data value occurs.

**tabla de frecuencia** Tabla que enumera la cantidad de veces que ocurre cada valor de datos, o la frecuencia.

Data set: 1, 1, 2, 2, 3, 4, 5, 5, 5, 6, 6, 6, 6
Frequency table:

| Data | Frequency |
|---|---|
| 1 | 2 |
| 2 | 2 |
| 3 | 1 |
| 4 | 1 |
| 5 | 3 |
| 6 | 4 |

---

**function** (p. 237) A relation in which every input is paired with exactly one output.

**función** Una relación en la que cada entrada corresponde exactamente a una salida.

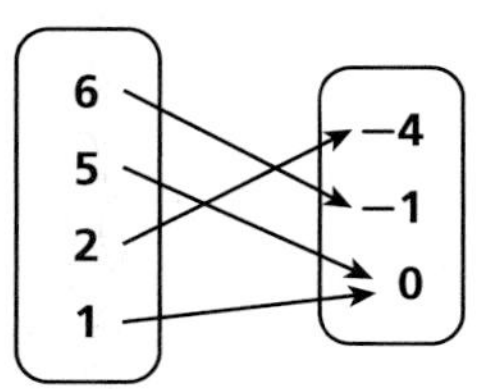

| ENGLISH | SPANISH | EXAMPLES |
|---|---|---|
| **function notation** (p. 246) If $x$ is the independent variable and $y$ is the dependent variable, then the function notation for $y$ is $f(x)$, read "$f$ of $x$," where $f$ names the function. | **notación de función** Si $x$ es la variable independiente e $y$ es la variable dependiente, entonces la notación de función para $y$ es $f(x)$, que se lee "$f$ de $x$," donde $f$ nombra la función. | equation: $y = 2x$<br>function notation: $f(x) = 2x$ |
| **function rule** (p. 246) An algebraic expression that defines a function. | **regla de función** Expresión algebraica que define una función. | $f(x) = \underline{2x^2 + 3x - 7}$<br>function rule |
| **Fundamental Counting Principle** (p. 736) For $n$ items, if there are $m_1$ ways to choose a first item, $m_2$ ways to choose a second item after the first item has been chosen, and so on, then there are $m_1 \cdot m_2 \cdot \ldots \cdot m_n$ ways to choose $n$ items. | **Principio fundamental de conteo** Dados $n$ elementos, si existen $m_1$ formas de elegir un primer elemento, $m_2$ formas de elegir un segundo elemento después de haber elegido el primero, y así sucesivamente, entonces existen $m_1 \cdot m_2 \cdot \ldots \cdot m_n$ formas de elegir $n$ elementos. | If there are 4 colors of shirts, 3 colors of pants, and 2 colors of shoes, then there are $4 \cdot 3 \cdot 2 = 24$ possible outfits. |

| | | |
|---|---|---|
| **geometric sequence** (p. 766) A sequence in which the ratio of successive terms is a constant $r$, called the common ratio, where $r \neq 0$ and $r \neq 1$. | **sucesión geométrica** Sucesión en la que la razón de los términos sucesivos es una constante $r$, denominada razón común, donde $r \neq 0$ y $r \neq 1$. | 1, 2, 4, 8, 16, ...<br>$\cdot 2$ $\cdot 2$ $\cdot 2$ $\cdot 2$ $r = 2$ |
| **graph of a function** (p. 252) The set of points in a coordinate plane with coordinates $(x, y)$, where $x$ is in the domain of the function $f$ and $y = f(x)$. | **gráfica de una función** Conjunto de los puntos de un plano cartesiano con coordenadas $(x, y)$, donde $x$ está en el dominio de la función $f$ e $y = f(x)$. | 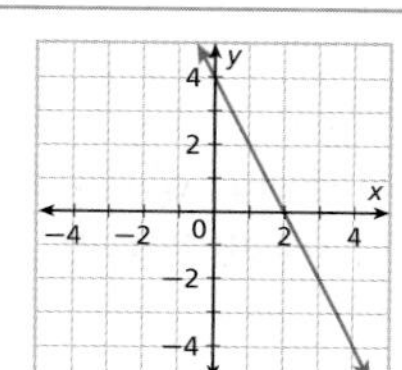 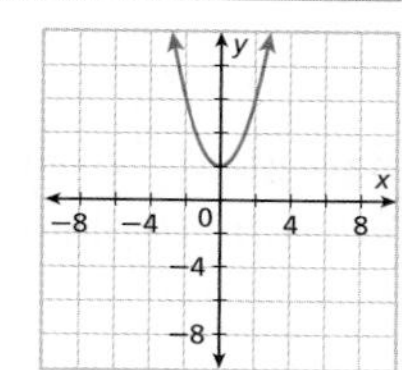 |
| **graph of a system of linear inequalities** (p. 421) The region in a coordinate plane consisting of points whose coordinates are solutions to all of the inequalities in the system. | **gráfica de un sistema de desigualdades lineales** Región de un plano cartesiano que consta de puntos cuyas coordenadas son soluciones de todas las desigualdades del sistema. | (2, 1) is in the overlapping shaded regions, so it is a solution. |
| **graph of an inequality in one variable** (p. 169) The set of points on a number line that are solutions of the inequality. | **gráfica de una desigualdad en una variable** Conjunto de los puntos de una recta numérica que representan soluciones de la desigualdad. | $x \geq 2$<br>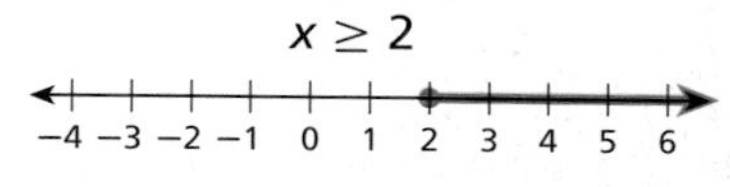 |
| **graph of an inequality in two variables** (p. 414) The set of points in a coordinate plane whose coordinates $(x, y)$ are solutions of the inequality. | **gráfica de una desigualdad en dos variables** Conjunto de los puntos de un plano cartesiano cuyas coordenadas $(x, y)$ son soluciones de la desigualdad. | $y \leq x + 1$<br>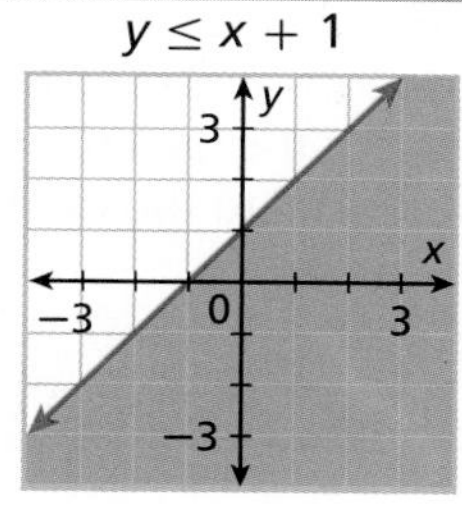 |

| ENGLISH | SPANISH | EXAMPLES |
|---|---|---|
| **graph of an ordered pair** (p. 54) For the ordered pair $(x, y)$, the point in a coordinate plane that is a horizontal distance of $x$ units from the origin and a vertical distance of $y$ units from the origin. | **gráfica de un par ordenado** Dado el par ordenado $(x, y)$, punto en un plano cartesiano que está a una distancia horizontal de $x$ unidades desde el origen y a una distancia vertical de $y$ unidades desde el origen. | 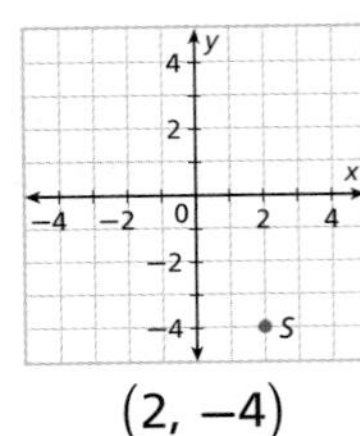 (2, −4) |
| **greatest common factor (GCF)** (p. 525) The product of the greatest integer and the greatest power of each variable that divide evenly into each term. | **máximo común divisor (MCD)** Producto del entero mayor y la potencia mayor de cada variable que divide exactamente cada término de la expresión. | The GCF of $4x^3y$ and $6x^2y$ is $2x^2y$. The GCF of 27 and 45 is 9. |
| **grouping symbols** (p. 40) Symbols such as parentheses ( ), brackets [ ], and braces { } that separate part of an expression. A fraction bar, absolute-value symbols, and radical symbols may also be used as grouping symbols. | **símbolos de agrupación** Símbolos tales como paréntesis ( ), corchetes [ ] y llaves { } que separan parte de una expresión. La barra de fracciones, los símbolos de valor absoluto y los símbolos de radical también se pueden utilizar como símbolos de agrupación. | $6 + \{3 - [(4 - 3) + 2] + 1\} - 5$<br>$6 + \{3 - [1 + 2] + 1\} - 5$<br>$6 + \{3 - 3 + 1\} - 5$<br>$6 + 1 - 5$<br>$2$ |

## H

| ENGLISH | SPANISH | EXAMPLES |
|---|---|---|
| **half-life** (p. 783) The half-life of a substance is the time it takes for one-half of the substance to decay into another substance. | **vida media** La vida media de una sustancia es el tiempo que tarda la mitad de la sustancia en desintegrarse y transformarse en otra sustancia. | Carbon-14 has a half-life of 5730 years, so 5 g of an initial amount of 10 g will remain after 5730 years. |
| **half-plane** (p. 414) The part of the coordinate plane on one side of a line, which may include the line. | **semiplano** La parte del plano cartesiano de un lado de una línea, que puede incluir la línea. | 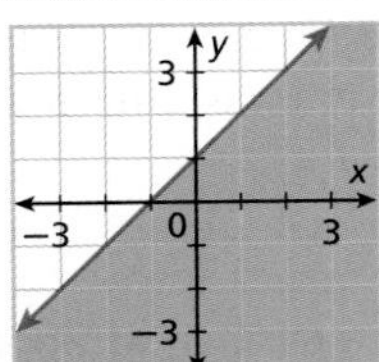 |
| **Heron's Formula** (p. 810) A triangle with side lengths $a$, $b$, and $c$ has area $A = \sqrt{s(s - a)(s - b)(s - c)}$, where $s$ is one-half the perimeter, or $s = \frac{1}{2}(a + b + c)$. | **fórmula de Herón** Un triángulo con longitudes de lado $a$, $b$ y $c$ tiene un área $A = \sqrt{s(s - a)(s - b)(s - c)}$, donde $s$ es la mitad del perímetro ó $s = \frac{1}{2}(a + b + c)$. | |
| **histogram** (p. 688) A bar graph used to display data grouped in class intervals. The width of each bar is proportional to the class interval, and the area of each bar is proportional to the frequency. | **histograma** Gráfica de barras utilizada para mostrar datos agrupados en intervalos de clases. El ancho de cada barra es proporcional al intervalo de clase y el área de cada barra es proporcional a la frecuencia. | 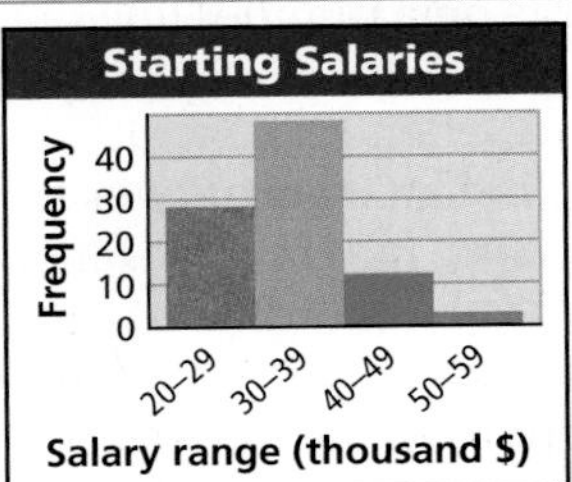  |

| ENGLISH | SPANISH | EXAMPLES |
|---|---|---|

**horizontal line** (p. 312) A line described by the equation $y = b$, where $b$ is the $y$-intercept.

**línea horizontal** Línea descrita por la ecuación $y = b$, donde $b$ es la intersección con el eje $y$.

$y = 4$

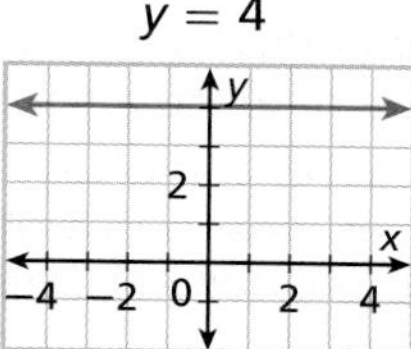


**hypotenuse** (p. S68) The side opposite the right angle in a right triangle.

**hipotenusa** Lado opuesto al ángulo recto de un triángulo rectángulo.

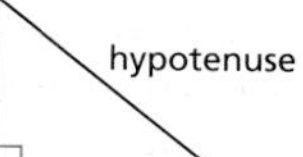

## I

**identity** (p. 101) An equation that is true for all values of the variables.

**identidad** Ecuación verdadera para todos los valores de las variables.

$3 = 3$
$2(x - 1) = 2x - 2$

**inclusive events** (p. 734) Events that have one or more outcomes in common.

**sucesos inclusivos** Sucesos que tienen uno o más resultados en común.

In the experiment of rolling a number cube, rolling an even number and rolling a number less than 3 are inclusive events because both contain the outcome 2.

**inconsistent system** (p. 406) A system of equations or inequalities that has no solution.

**sistema inconsistente** Sistema de ecuaciones o desigualdades que no tiene solución.

$$\begin{cases} x + y = 0 \\ x + y = 1 \end{cases}$$

**independent events** (p. 726) Events for which the occurrence or nonoccurrence of one event does not affect the probability of the other event.

**sucesos independientes** Dos sucesos son independientes si el hecho de que se produzca o no uno de ellos no afecta la probabilidad del otro suceso.

From a bag containing 3 red marbles and 2 blue marbles, drawing a red marble, replacing it, and then drawing a blue marble.

**independent system** (p. 407) A system of equations that has exactly one solution.

**sistema independiente** Sistema de ecuaciones que tiene sólo una solución.

$$\begin{cases} x + y = 7 \\ x - y = 1 \end{cases}$$
Solution: $(4, 3)$

**independent variable** (p. 246) The input of a function; a variable whose value determines the value of the output, or dependent variable.

**variable independiente** Entrada de una función; variable cuyo valor determina el valor de la salida, o variable dependiente.

For $y = 2x + 1$, $x$ is the independent variable.

**index** (p. 832) In the radical $\sqrt[n]{x}$, which represents the $n$th root of $x$, $n$ is the index. In the radical $\sqrt{x}$, the index is understood to be 2.

**índice** En el radical $\sqrt[n]{x}$, que representa la enésima raíz de $x$, $n$ es el índice. En el radical $\sqrt{x}$, se da por sentado que el índice es 2.

The radical $\sqrt[3]{8}$ has an index of 3.

**indirect measurement** (p. 122) A method of measurement that uses formulas, similar figures, and/or proportions.

**medición indirecta** Método de medición en el que se usan fórmulas, figuras semejantes y/o proporciones.

| ENGLISH | SPANISH | EXAMPLES |
|---|---|---|

**inequality** (p. 168) A statement that compares two expressions by using one of the following signs: $<, >, \leq, \geq$, or $\neq$.

**desigualdad** Enunciado que compara dos expresiones utilizando uno de los siguientes signos: $<, >, \leq, \geq$, o $\neq$.

$x \geq 2$

−4 −3 −2 −1 0 1 2 3 4 5 6

---

**input** (p. 55) A value that is substituted for the independent variable in a relation or function.

**entrada** Valor que sustituye a la variable independiente en una relación o función.

For the function $f(x) = x + 5$, the input 3 produces an output of 8.

---

**input-output table** A table that displays input values of a function or expression together with the corresponding outputs.

**tabla de entrada y salida** Tabla que muestra los valores de entrada de una función o expresión junto con las correspondientes salidas.

| | | | | | |
|---|---|---|---|---|---|
| Input | x | 1 | 2 | 3 | 4 |
| Output | y | 4 | 7 | 10 | 13 |

---

**integer** (p. 34) A member of the set of whole numbers and their opposites.

**entero** Miembro del conjunto de números cabales y sus opuestos.

$\ldots -3, -2, -1, 0, 1, 2, 3, \ldots$

---

**intercept** *See* $x$-intercept and $y$-intercept.

**intersección** *Ver* intersección con el eje $x$ e intersección con el eje $y$.

---

**interest** (p. 133) The amount of money charged for borrowing money or the amount of money earned when saving or investing money. *See also* compound interest, simple interest.

**interés** Cantidad de dinero que se cobra por prestar dinero o cantidad de dinero que se gana cuando se ahorra o invierte dinero. *Ver también* interés compuesto, interés simple.

---

**interquartile range (IQR)** (p. 695) The difference of the third (upper) and first (lower) quartiles in a data set, representing the middle half of the data.

**rango entre cuartiles** Diferencia entre el tercer cuartil (superior) y el primer cuartil (inferior) de un conjunto de datos, que representa la mitad central de los datos.

| Lower half | Upper half |
|---|---|
| 18, (23), 28, | 29, (36), 42 |
| First quartile | Third quartile |

Interquartile range:
$36 - 23 = 13$

---

**intersection** (p. 203) The intersection of two sets is the set of all elements that are common to both sets, denoted by $\cap$.

**intersección de conjuntos** La intersección de dos conjuntos es el conjunto de todos los elementos que son comunes a ambos conjuntos, expresado por $\cap$.

$A = \{1, 2, 3, 4\}$
$B = \{1, 3, 5, 7, 9\}$
$A \cap B = \{1, 3\}$

---

**inverse operations** Operations that undo each other.

**operaciones inversas** Operaciones que se anulan entre sí.

Addition and subtraction are inverse operations:
$5 + 3 = 8, 8 - 3 = 5$
Multiplication and division are inverse operations:
$2 \cdot 3 = 6, 6 \div 3 = 2$

---

**inverse variation** (p. 851) A relationship between two variables, $x$ and $y$, that can be written in the form $y = \frac{k}{x}$, where $k$ is a nonzero constant and $x \neq 0$.

**variación inversa** Relación entre dos variables, $x$ e $y$, que puede expresarse en la forma $y = \frac{k}{x}$, donde $k$ es una constante distinta de cero y $x \neq 0$.

$y = \frac{8}{x}$

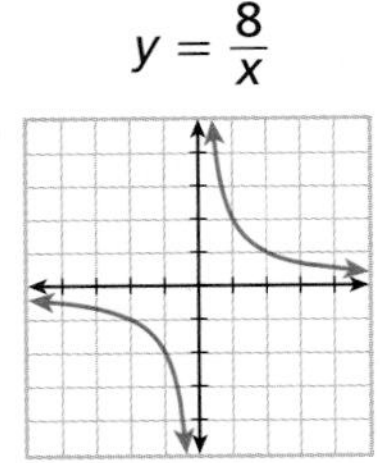

---

**irrational number** (p. 34) A real number that cannot be expressed as the ratio of two integers.

**número irracional** Número real que no se puede expresar como una razón de enteros.

$\sqrt{2}, \pi, e$

| ENGLISH | SPANISH | EXAMPLES |
|---|---|---|
| **isolate the variable** (p. 77) To isolate a variable in an equation, use inverse operations on both sides until the variable appears by itself on one side of the equation and does not appear on the other side. | **despejar la variable** Para despejar la variable de una ecuación, utiliza operaciones inversas en ambos lados hasta que la variable aparezca sola en uno de los lados de la ecuación y no aparezca en el otro lado. | $10 = 6 - 2x$<br>$\underline{-6 \quad -6}$<br>$4 = -2x$<br>$\frac{4}{-2} = \frac{-2x}{-2}$<br>$-2 = x$ |
| **isosceles triangle** (p. S63) A triangle with at least two congruent sides. | **triángulo isósceles** Triángulo que tiene al menos dos lados congruentes. |  |

| | | |
|---|---|---|
| **leading coefficient** (p. 477) The coefficient of the first term of a polynomial in standard form. | **coeficiente principal** Coeficiente del primer término de un polinomio en forma estándar. | $3x^2 + 7x - 2$<br>Leading coefficient: 3 |
| **least common denominator (LCD)** (p. 887) The least common multiple of the denominators of two or more given fractions. | **mínimo común denominador (MCD)** Mínimo común múltiplo de los denominadores de dos o más fracciones dadas. | The LCD of $\frac{3}{4}$ and $\frac{5}{6}$ is 12. |
| **least common multiple (LCM)** (p. 886) The product of the smallest positive number and the lowest power of each variable that divide evenly into each term. | **mínimo común múltiplo (MCM)** El producto del número positivo más pequeño y la menor potencia de cada variable que divide exactamente cada término. | The LCM of 10 and 18 is 90. |
| **leg of a right triangle** (p. S68) One of the two sides of a right triangle that form the right angle. | **cateto de un triángulo rectángulo** Uno de los dos lados de un triángulo rectángulo que forman el ángulo recto. | 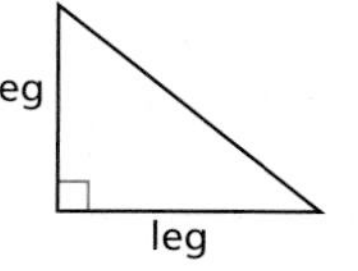 |
| **like radicals** (p. 811) Radical terms having the same radicand and index. | **radicales semejantes** Términos radicales que tienen el mismo radicando e índice. | $3\sqrt{2x}$ and $\sqrt{2x}$ |
| **like terms** (p. 47) Terms with the same variables raised to the same exponents. | **términos semejantes** Términos con las mismas variables elevadas a los mismos exponentes. | $3a^3b^2$ and $7a^3b^2$ |
| **line** (p. S56) An undefined term in geometry, a line is a straight path that has no thickness and extends forever in two directions. | **recta** Término indefinido en geometría, una recta es un trazo recto que no tiene grosor y se extiende infinitamente. | $\ell$ |
| **line graph** (p. 679) A graph that uses line segments to show how data changes. | **gráfica lineal** Gráfica que se vale de segmentos de recta para mostrar cambios en los datos. | 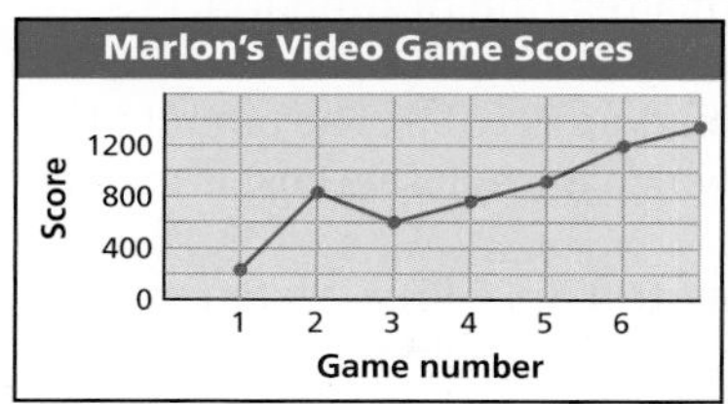 |

| ENGLISH | SPANISH | EXAMPLES |
| --- | --- | --- |
| **linear equation in one variable** (p. 298) An equation that can be written in the form $ax = b$ where $a$ and $b$ are constants and $a \neq 0$. | **ecuación lineal en una variable** Ecuación que puede expresarse en la forma $ax = b$ donde $a$ y $b$ son constantes y $a \neq 0$. | $x + 1 = 7$ |
| **linear equation in two variables** (p. 298) An equation that can be written in the form $Ax + By = C$ where $A$, $B$, and $C$ are constants and $A$ and $B$ are not both 0. | **ecuación lineal en dos variables** Ecuación que puede expresarse en la forma $Ax + By = C$ donde $A$, $B$ y $C$ son constantes y $A$ y $B$ no son ambas 0. | $2x + 3y = 6$ |
| **linear function** (p. 296) A function that can be written in the form $y = mx + b$, where $x$ is the independent variable and $m$ and $b$ are real numbers. Its graph is a line. | **función lineal** Función que puede expresarse en la forma $y = mx + b$, donde $x$ es la variable independiente y $m$ y $b$ son números reales. Su gráfica es una línea. | $y = x - 1$ |
| **linear inequality in one variable** (p. 414) An inequality that can be written in one of the following forms: $ax < b$, $ax > b$, $ax \leq b$, $ax \geq b$, or $ax \neq b$, where $a$ and $b$ are constants and $a \neq 0$. | **desigualdad lineal en una variable** Desigualdad que puede expresarse de una de las siguientes formas: $ax < b$, $ax > b$, $ax \leq b$, $ax \geq b$ o $ax \neq b$, donde $a$ y $b$ son constantes y $a \neq 0$. | $3x - 5 \leq 2(x + 4)$ |
| **linear inequality in two variables** (p. 414) An inequality that can be written in one of the following forms: $Ax + By < C$, $Ax + By > C$, $Ax + By \leq C$, $Ax + By \geq C$, or $Ax + By \neq C$, where $A$, $B$, and $C$ are constants and $A$ and $B$ are not both 0. | **desigualdad lineal en dos variables** Desigualdad que puede expresarse de una de las siguientes formas: $Ax + By < C$, $Ax + By > C$, $Ax + By \leq C$, $Ax + By \geq C$ o $Ax + By \neq C$, donde $A$, $B$ y $C$ son constantes y $A$ y $B$ no son ambas 0. | $2x + 3y > 6$ |
| **literal equation** (p. 108) An equation that contains two or more variables. | **ecuación literal** Ecuación que contiene dos o más variables. | $d = rt$<br>$A = \frac{1}{2}h(b_1 + b_2)$ |
| **lower quartile** *See* first quartile. | **cuartil inferior** *Ver* primer cuartil. | |

## M

| ENGLISH | SPANISH | EXAMPLES |
| --- | --- | --- |
| **mapping diagram** (p. 236) A diagram that shows the relationship of elements in the domain to elements in the range of a relation or function. | **diagrama de correspondencia** Diagrama que muestra la relación entre los elementos del dominio y los elementos del rango de una función. | **Mapping Diagram**<br>Domain: 2<br>Range: A, B, C |
| **markup** (p. 139) The amount by which a wholesale cost is increased. | **margen de ganancia** Cantidad que se agrega a un costo mayorista. | |
| **matrix** (p. 746) A rectangular array of numbers. | **matriz** Arreglo rectangular de números. | $\begin{bmatrix} 1 & 0 & 3 \\ -2 & 2 & -5 \\ 7 & -6 & 3 \end{bmatrix}$ |

| ENGLISH | SPANISH | EXAMPLES |
|---|---|---|
| **maximum of a function** (p. 592) The $y$-value of the highest point on the graph of the function. | **máximo de una función** Valor de $y$ del punto más alto en la gráfica de la función. | 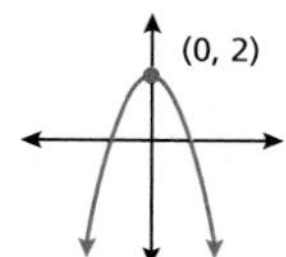  The maximum of the function is 2. |
| **mean** (p. 694) The sum of all the values in a data set divided by the number of data values. Also called the *average*. | **media** Suma de todos los valores de un conjunto de datos dividida entre el número de valores de datos. También llamada *promedio*. | Data set: 4, 6, 7, 8, 10<br>Mean: $\frac{4+6+7+8+10}{5}$<br>$= \frac{35}{5} = 7$ |
| **measure of an angle** (p. S56) Angles are measured in degrees. A degree is $\frac{1}{360}$ of a complete circle. | **medida de un ángulo** Los ángulos se miden en grados. Un grado es $\frac{1}{360}$ de un círculo completo. | 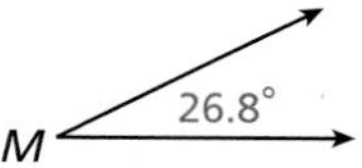  |
| **measure of central tendency** (p. 694) A measure that describes the center of a data set. | **medida de tendencia dominante** Medida que describe el centro de un conjunto de datos. | mean, median, or mode |
| **median** (p. 694) For an ordered data set with an odd number of values, the median is the middle value. For an ordered data set with an even number of values, the median is the average of the two middle values. | **mediana** Dado un conjunto de datos ordenado con un número impar de valores, la mediana es el valor medio. Dado un conjunto de datos con un número par de valores, la mediana es el promedio de los dos valores medios. | 8, 9, (9,) 12, 15 Median: 9<br>4, 6, (7, 10) 10, 12<br>Median: $\frac{7+10}{2} = 8.5$ |
| **minimum of a function** (p. 592) The $y$-value of the lowest point on the graph of the function. | **mínimo de una función** Valor de $y$ del punto más bajo en la gráfica de la función. | 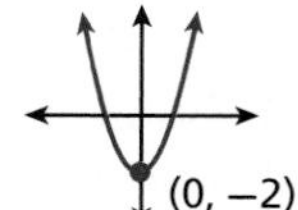  The minimum of the function is −2. |
| **mode** (p. 694) The value or values that occur most frequently in a data set; if all values occur with the same frequency, the data set is said to have no mode. | **moda** El valor o los valores que se presentan con mayor frecuencia en un conjunto de datos. Si todos los valores se presentan con la misma frecuencia, se dice que el conjunto de datos no tiene moda. | Data set: 3, 6, 8, 8, 10 Mode: 8<br>Data set: 2, 5, 5, 7, 7 Modes: 5 and 7<br>Data set: 2, 3, 6, 9, 11 No mode |
| **monomial** (p. 476) A number or a product of numbers and variables with whole-number exponents, or a polynomial with one term. | **monomio** Número o producto de números y variables con exponentes de números cabales, o polinomio con un término. | $3x^2y^4$ |
| **Multiplication Property of Equality** (p. 86) If $a$, $b$, and $c$ are real numbers and $a = b$, then $ac = bc$. | **Propiedad de igualdad de la multiplicación** Si $a$, $b$ y $c$ son números reales y $a = b$, entonces $ac = bc$. | $\frac{1}{3}x = 7$<br>$(3)\left(\frac{1}{3}x\right) = (3)(7)$<br>$x = 21$ |

| ENGLISH | SPANISH | EXAMPLES |
|---|---|---|
| **Multiplication Property of Inequality** (p. 180) If both sides of an inequality are multiplied by the same positive quantity, the new inequality will have the same solution set.<br>If both sides of an inequality are multiplied by the same negative quantity, the new inequality will have the solution set if the inequality symbol is reversed. | **Propiedad de desigualdad de la multiplicación** Si ambos lados de una desigualdad se multiplican por el mismo número positivo, la nueva desigualdad tendrá el mismo conjunto solución.<br>Si ambos lados de una desigualdad se multiplican por el mismo número negativo, la nueva desigualdad tendrá el mismo conjunto solución si se invierte el símbolo de desigualdad. | $\frac{1}{3}x > 7$<br>$(3)\left(\frac{1}{3}x\right) > (3)(7)$<br>$x > 21$<br>$-x \leq 2$<br>$(-1)(-x) \geq (-1)(2)$<br>$x \geq -2$ |
| **multiplicative inverse** (p. 21) The reciprocal of the number. | **inverso multiplicativo** Recíproco de un número. | The multiplicative inverse of 5 is $\frac{1}{5}$. |
| **mutually exclusive events** (p. 734) Two events are mutually exclusive if they cannot both occur in the same trial of an experiment. | **sucesos mutuamente excluyentes** Dos sucesos son mutuamente excluyentes si ambos no pueden ocurrir en la misma prueba de un experimento. | In the experiment of rolling a number cube, rolling a 3 and rolling an even number are mutually exclusive events. |

| ENGLISH | SPANISH | EXAMPLES |
|---|---|---|
| **natural number** (p. 34) A counting number. | **número natural** Número que se utiliza para contar. | 1, 2, 3, 4, 5, 6, ... |
| **negative correlation** (p. 263) Two data sets have a negative correlation if one set of data values increases as the other set decreases. | **correlación negativa** Dos conjuntos de datos tienen una correlación negativa si un conjunto de valores de datos aumenta a medida que el otro conjunto disminuye. | y, x |
| **negative exponent** (p. 446) For any nonzero real number $x$ and any integer $n$, $x^{-n} = \frac{1}{x^n}$. | **exponente negativo** Para cualquier número real distinto de cero $x$ y cualquier entero $n$, $x^{-n} = \frac{1}{x^n}$. | $x^{-2} = \frac{1}{x^2}$; $3^{-2} = \frac{1}{3^2}$ |
| **negative number** A number that is less than zero. Negative numbers lie to the left of zero on a number line. | **número negativo** Número menor que cero. Los números negativos se ubican a la izquierda del cero en una recta numérica. | −2 is a negative number.<br>−4 −3 −2 −1 0 1 2 3 4 |
| **negative square root** (p. 32) The opposite of the principal square root of a number $a$, written as $-\sqrt{a}$. | **raíz cuadrada negativa** Opuesto de la raíz cuadrada principal de un número $a$, que se expresa como $-\sqrt{a}$. | The negative square root of 9 is $-\sqrt{9} = -3$. |
| **net** (p. S67) A diagram of the faces of a three-dimensional figure arranged in such a way that the diagram can be folded to form the three-dimensional figure. | **plantilla** Diagrama de las caras de una figura tridimensional que se puede plegar para formar la figura tridimensional. | 10 m, 6 m, 10 m, 6 m |
| **no correlation** (p. 263) Two data sets have no correlation if there is no relationship between the sets of values. | **sin correlación** Dos conjuntos de datos no tienen correlación si no existe una relación entre los conjuntos de valores. | 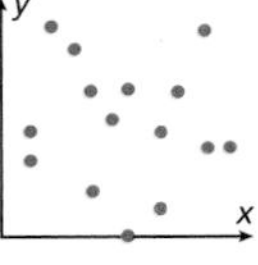 |

| ENGLISH | SPANISH | EXAMPLES |
|---|---|---|
| ***n*th root** (p. 832) The $n$th root of a number $a$, written as $\sqrt[n]{a}$ or $a^{\frac{1}{n}}$, is a number that is equal to $a$ when it is raised to the $n$th power. | **enésima raíz** La enésima raíz de un número $a$, que se escribe $\sqrt[n]{a}$ o $a^{\frac{1}{n}}$, es un número igual a $a$ cuando se eleva a la enésima potencia. | $\sqrt[5]{32} = 2$, because $2^5 = 32$. |
| **number line** (p. 14) A line used to represent the real numbers. | **recta numérica** Línea utilizada para representar los números reales. | −4 −3 −2 −1 0 1 2 3 4 5 6 |
| **numerical expression** (p. 6) An expression that contains only numbers and operations. | **expresión numérica** Expresión que contiene únicamente números y operaciones. | $2 \cdot 3 + (4 - 6)$ |

| ENGLISH | SPANISH | EXAMPLES |
|---|---|---|
| **obtuse angle** (p. S56) An angle that measures greater than 90° and less than 180°. | **ángulo obtuso** Ángulo que mide más de 90° y menos de 180°. | 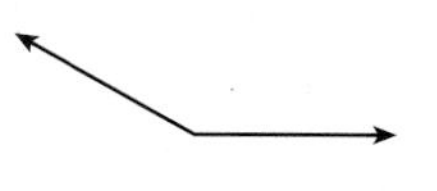 |
| **obtuse triangle** (p. S63) A triangle with one obtuse angle. | **triángulo obtusángulo** Triángulo con un ángulo obtuso. | 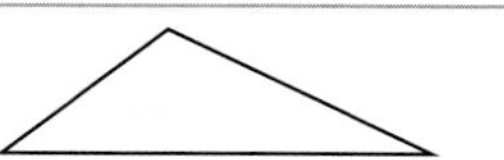 |
| **odds** (p. 722) A comparison of favorable and unfavorable outcomes. The odds in favor of an event are the ratio of the number of favorable outcomes to the number of unfavorable outcomes. The odds against an event are the ratio of the number of unfavorable outcomes to the number of favorable outcomes. | **probabilidades a favor y en contra** Comparación de los resultados favorables y desfavorables. Las probabilidades a favor de un suceso son la razón entre la cantidad de resultados favorables y la cantidad de resultados desfavorables. Las probabilidades en contra de un suceso son la razón entre la cantidad de resultados desfavorables y la cantidad de resultados favorables. | The odds in favor of rolling a 3 on a number cube are 1:5. The odds against rolling a 3 on a number cube are 5:1. |
| **opposite** (p. 15) The opposite of a number $a$, denoted $-a$, is the number that is the same distance from zero as $a$, on the opposite side of the number line. The sum of opposites is 0. | **opuesto** El opuesto de un número $a$, expresado $-a$, es el número que se encuentra a la misma distancia de cero que $a$, del lado opuesto de la recta numérica. La suma de los opuestos es 0. | 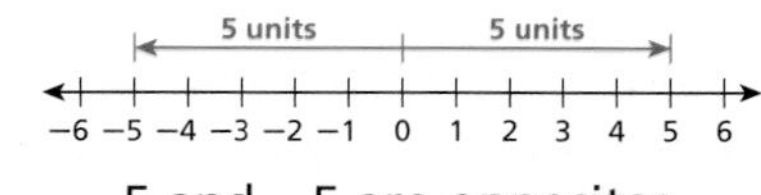  5 and −5 are opposites. |
| **opposite reciprocal** (p. 352) The opposite of the reciprocal of a number. The opposite reciprocal of any nonzero number $a$ is $-\frac{1}{a}$. | **recíproco opuesto** Opuesto del recíproco de un número. El recíproco opuesto de $a$ es $-\frac{1}{a}$. | The opposite reciprocal of $\frac{2}{3}$ is $-\frac{3}{2}$. |
| **OR** (p. 202) A logical operator representing the union of two sets. | **O** Operador lógico que representa la unión de dos conjuntos. | $A = \{2, 3, 4, 5\}$ $B = \{1, 3, 5, 7\}$ The set of values that are in $A$ OR $B$ is $A \cup B = \{1, 2, 3, 4, 5, 7\}$. |

| ENGLISH | SPANISH | EXAMPLES |
|---|---|---|
| **order of operations** (p. 40) A process for evaluating expressions:<br>First, perform operations in parentheses or other grouping symbols.<br>Second, evaluate powers and roots.<br>Third, perform all multiplication and division from left to right.<br>Fourth, perform all addition and subtraction from left to right. | **orden de las operaciones** Regla para evaluar las expresiones:<br>Primero, realizar las operaciones entre paréntesis u otros símbolos de agrupación.<br>Segundo, evaluar las potencias y las raíces.<br>Tercero, realizar todas las multiplicaciones y divisiones de izquierda a derecha.<br>Cuarto, realizar todas las sumas y restas de izquierda a derecha. | $2 + 3^2 - (7 + 5) \div 4 \cdot 3$<br>$2 + 3^2 - 12 \div 4 \cdot 3$ Add inside parentheses.<br>$2 + 9 - 12 \div 4 \cdot 3$ Evaluate the power.<br>$2 + 9 - 3 \cdot 3$ Divide.<br>$2 + 9 - 9$ Multiply.<br>$11 - 9$ Add.<br>$2$ Subtract. |
| **ordered pair** (p. 54) A pair of numbers $(x, y)$ that can be used to locate a point on a coordinate plane. The first number $x$ indicates the distance to the left or right of the origin, and the second number $y$ indicates the distance above or below the origin. | **par ordenado** Par de números $(x, y)$ que se pueden utilizar para ubicar un punto en un plano cartesiano. El primer número, $x$, indica la distancia a la izquierda o derecha del origen y el segundo número, $y$, indica la distancia hacia arriba o hacia abajo del origen. | 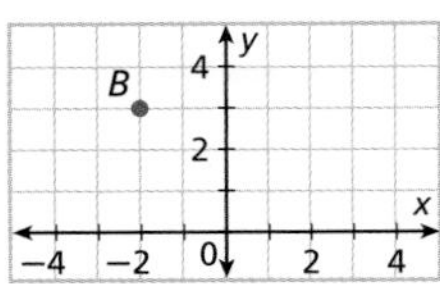<br>The coordinates of $B$ are $(-2, 3)$. |
| **origin** (p. 54) The intersection of the $x$- and $y$-axes in a coordinate plane. The coordinates of the origin are $(0, 0)$. | **origen** Intersección de los ejes $x$ e $y$ en un plano cartesiano. Las coordenadas de origen son $(0, 0)$. | 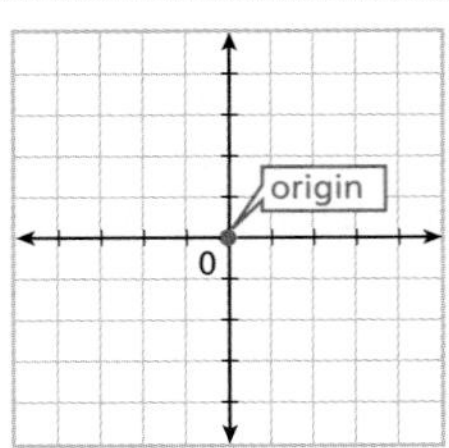 |
| **outcome** (p. 713) A possible result of a probability experiment. | **resultado** Resultado posible de un experimento de probabilidad. | In the experiment of rolling a number cube, the possible outcomes are 1, 2, 3, 4, 5, and 6. |
| **outlier** (p. 695) A data value that is far removed from the rest of the data. | **valor extremo** Valor de datos que está muy alejado del resto de los datos. |  |
| **output** (p. 55) The result of substituting a value for a variable in a function. | **salida** Resultado de la sustitución de una variable por un valor en una función. | For the function $f(x) = x^2 + 1$, the input 3 produces an output of 10. |

## P

| ENGLISH | SPANISH | EXAMPLES |
|---|---|---|
| **parabola** (p. 591) The shape of the graph of a quadratic function. | **parábola** Forma de la gráfica de una función cuadrática. | 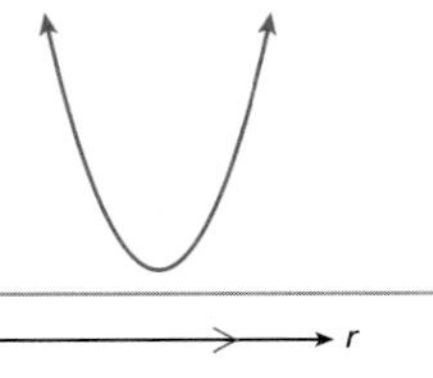 |
| **parallel lines** (p. 349, p. S56) Lines in the same plane that do not intersect. | **rectas paralelas** Rectas en el mismo plano que no se cruzan. | 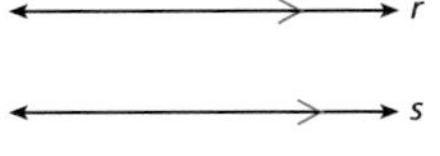 |
| **parallelogram** (p. S63) A quadrilateral with two pairs of parallel sides. | **paralelogramo** Cuadrilátero con dos pares de lados paralelos. |  |

| ENGLISH | SPANISH | EXAMPLES |
|---|---|---|
| **parent function** (p. 357) The simplest function with the defining characteristics of the family. Functions in the same family are transformations of their parent function. | **función madre** La función más básica que tiene las características distintivas de una familia. Las funciones de la misma familia son transformaciones de su función madre. | $f(x) = x^2$ is the parent function for $g(x) = x^2 + 4$ and $h(x) = (5x + 2)^2 - 3$. |
| **Pascal's triangle** (p. 570) A triangular arrangement of numbers in which every row starts and ends with 1 and each other number is the sum of the two numbers above it. | **triángulo de Pascal** Arreglo triangular de números en el cual cada fila comienza y termina con 1 y los demás números son la suma de los dos valores que están arriba de cada uno. | 1<br>1 1<br>1 2 1<br>1 3 3 1<br>1 4 6 4 1 |
| **percent** (p. 127) A ratio that compares a number to 100. | **porcentaje** Razón que compara un número con 100. | $\frac{17}{100} = 17\%$ |
| **percent change** (p. 138) An increase or decrease given as a percent of the original amount. *See also* percent decrease, percent increase. | **porcentaje de cambio** Incremento o disminución dada como un porcentaje de la cantidad original. *Ver también* porcentaje de disminución, porcentaje de incremento. | |
| **percent decrease** (p. 138) A decrease given as a percent of the original amount. | **porcentaje de disminución** Disminución dada como un porcentaje de la cantidad original. | If an item that costs \$8.00 is marked down to \$6.00, the amount of the decrease is \$2.00, so the percent decrease is $\frac{2.00}{8.00} = 0.25 = 25\%$. |
| **percent increase** (p. 138) An increase given as a percent of the original amount. | **porcentaje de incremento** Incremento dado como un porcentaje de la cantidad original. | If an item's wholesale cost of \$8.00 is marked up to \$12.00, the amount of the increase is \$4.00, so the percent increase is $\frac{4.00}{8.00} = 0.5 = 50\%$. |
| **perfect square** (p. 32) A number whose positive square root is a whole number. | **cuadrado perfecto** Número cuya raíz cuadrada positiva es un número cabal. | 36 is a perfect square because $\sqrt{36} = 6$. |
| **perfect-square trinomial** (p. 501) A trinomial whose factored form is the square of a binomial. A perfect-square trinomial has the form $a^2 - 2ab + b^2 = (a - b)^2$ or $a^2 + 2ab + b^2 = (a + b)^2$. | **trinomio cuadrado perfecto** Trinomio cuya forma factorizada es el cuadrado de un binomio. Un trinomio cuadrado perfecto tiene la forma $a^2 - 2ab + b^2 = (a - b)^2$ o $a^2 + 2ab + b^2 = (a + b)^2$. | $x^2 + 6x + 9$ is a perfect-square trinomial, because $x^2 + 6x + 9 = (x + 3)^2$. |
| **perimeter** (p. S60) The sum of the side lengths of a closed plane figure. | **perímetro** Suma de las longitudes de los lados de una figura plana cerrada. | 18 ft<br>6ft<br>Perimeter = 18 + 6 + 18 + 6 = 48 ft |
| **permutation** (p. 737) An arrangement of a group of objects in which order is important. | **permutación** Arreglo de un grupo de objetos en el cual el orden es importante. | For objects *A*, *B*, *C*, and *D*, there are 12 different permutations of 2 objects.<br>*AB*, *AC*, *AD*, *BC*, *BD*, *CD*<br>*BA*, *CA*, *DA*, *CB*, *DB*, *DC* |

| ENGLISH | SPANISH | EXAMPLES |
|---|---|---|
| **perpendicular** Intersecting to form 90° angles. | **perpendicular** Que se cruza para formar ángulos de 90°. | 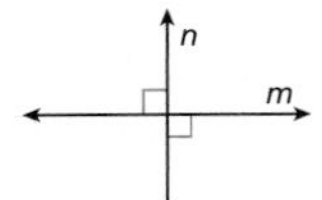 |
| **perpendicular lines** (p. 351, p. S56) Lines that intersect at 90° angles. | **rectas perpendiculares** Rectas que se cruzan en ángulos de 90°. | 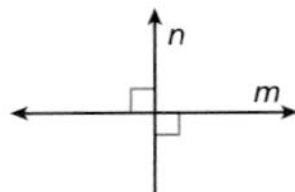 |
| **plane** (p. S56) An undefined term in geometry, it is a flat surface that has no thickness and extends forever in all directions. | **plano** Término indefinido en geometría; un plano es una superficie plana que no tiene grosor y se extiende infinitamente en todas direcciones. | 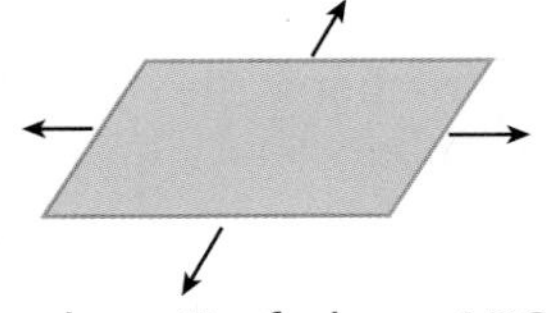<br>plane $\mathcal{R}$ of plane *ABC* |
| **point** (p. S56) An undefined term in geometry, it names a location and has no size. | **punto** Término indefinido en geometría que denomina una ubicación y no tiene tamaño. | *P* •<br>point *P* |
| **point-slope form** (p. 342) The point-slope form of a linear equation is $y - y_1 = m(x - x_1)$, where $m$ is the slope and $(x_1, y_1)$ is a point on the line. | **forma de punto y pendiente** La forma de punto y pendiente de una ecuación lineal es $y - y_1 = m(x - x_1)$, donde $m$ es la pendiente y $(x_1, y_1)$ es un punto en la línea. | $y - 3 = 2(x - 3)$ |
| **polygon** (p. S58) A closed plane figure formed by three or more segments such that each segment intersects exactly two other segments only at their endpoints and no two segments with a common endpoint are collinear. | **polígono** Figura plana cerrada formada por tres o más segmentos tal que cada segmento se cruza únicamente con otros dos segmentos sólo en sus extremos y ningún segmento con un extremo común a otro es colineal con éste. | 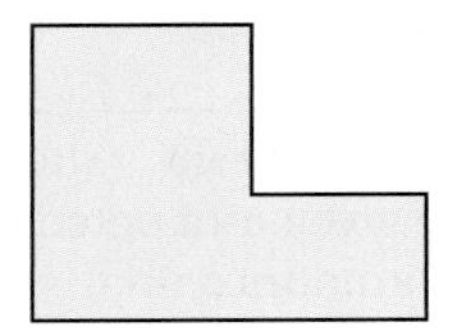 |
| **polynomial** (p. 476) A monomial or a sum or difference of monomials. | **polinomio** Monomio o suma o diferencia de monomios. | $2x^2 + 3xy - 7y^2$ |
| **polynomial long division** (p. 893) A method of dividing one polynomial by another. | **división larga polinomial** Método por el que se divide un polinomio entre otro. | $x + 1$<br>$x + 2\overline{)\; x^2 + 3x + 5}$<br>$\underline{-(x^2 + 2x)}$<br>$x + 5$<br>$\underline{-(x + 2)}$<br>$3$<br>$\frac{x^2 + 3x + 5}{x + 2} = x + 1 + \frac{3}{x + 2}$ |
| **positive correlation** (p. 263) Two data sets have a positive correlation if both sets of data values increase. | **correlación positiva** (p. 264) Dos conjuntos de datos tienen correlación positiva si los valores de ambos conjuntos de datos aumentan. | 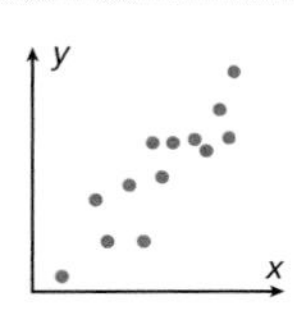 |
| **positive number** A number greater than zero. | **número positivo** Número mayor que cero. | 2 is a positive number.<br>−4 −3 −2 −1 0 1 2 3 4 |

| ENGLISH | SPANISH | EXAMPLES |
|---|---|---|
| **positive square root** (p. 32) The positive square root of a number, indicated by the radical sign. | **raíz cuadrada positiva** Raíz cuadrada positiva de un número, expresada por el signo de radical. | The positive square root of 36 is $\sqrt{36} = 6$. |
| **power** (p. 26) An expression written with a base and an exponent or the value of such an expression. | **potencia** Expresión escrita con una base y un exponente o el valor de dicha expresión. | $2^3 = 8$, so 8 is the third power of 2. |
| **Power of a Power Property** (p. 462) If $a$ is any nonzero real number and $m$ and $n$ are integers, then $(a^m)^n = a^{mn}$. | **Propiedad de la potencia de una potencia** Dado un número real $a$ distinto de cero y los números enteros $m$ y $n$, entonces $(a^m)^n = a^{mn}$. | $(6^7)^4 = 6^{7 \cdot 4} = 6^{28}$ |
| **Power of a Product Property** (p. 463) If $a$ and $b$ are any nonzero real numbers and $n$ is any integer, then $(ab)^n = a^n b^n$. | **Propiedad de la potencia de un producto** Dados los números reales $a$ y $b$ distintos de cero y un número entero $n$, entonces $(ab)^n = a^n b^n$. | $(2 \cdot 4)^3 = 2^3 \cdot 4^3 = 8 \cdot 64 = 512$ |
| **Power of a Quotient Property** (p. 469, p. 470) If $a$ and $b$ are any nonzero real numbers and $n$ is an integer, then $\left(\frac{a}{b}\right)^n = \frac{a^n}{b^n}$. | **Propiedad de la potencia de un cociente** Dados los números reales $a$ y $b$ distintos de cero y un número entero $n$, entonces $\left(\frac{a}{b}\right)^n = \frac{a^n}{b^n}$. | $\left(\frac{3}{5}\right)^4 = \frac{3}{5} \cdot \frac{3}{5} \cdot \frac{3}{5} \cdot \frac{3}{5} = \frac{3 \cdot 3 \cdot 3 \cdot 3}{5 \cdot 5 \cdot 5 \cdot 5} = \frac{3^4}{5^4}$ |
| **prediction** (p. 715) An estimate or guess about something that has not yet happened. | **predicción** Estimación o suposición sobre algo que todavía no ha sucedido. | |
| **prime factorization** (p. 524) A representation of a number or a polynomial as a product of primes. | **factorización prima** Representación de un número o de un polinomio como producto de números primos. | The prime factorization of 60 is $2 \cdot 2 \cdot 3 \cdot 5$ |
| **prime number** (p. 524) A whole number greater than 1 that has exactly two factors, itself and 1. | **número primo** Número cabal mayor que 1 que es divisible únicamente entre sí mismo y entre 1. | 5 is prime because its only factors are 5 and 1. |
| **principal** (p. 133) An amount of money borrowed or invested. | **capital** Cantidad de dinero que se pide prestado o se invierte. | |
| **prism** (p. 874, p. S64) A polyhedron formed by two parallel congruent polygonal bases connected by faces that are parallelograms. | **prisma** Poliedro formado por dos bases poligonales congruentes y paralelas conectadas por caras laterales que son paralelogramos. | |
| **probability** (p. 713) A number from 0 to 1 (or 0% to 100%) that is the measure of how likely an event is to occur. | **probabilidad** Número entre 0 y 1 (o entre 0% y 100%) que describe cuán probable es que ocurra un suceso. | A bag contains 3 red marbles and 4 blue marbles. The probability of randomly choosing a red marble is $\frac{3}{7}$. |
| **Product of Powers Property** (p. 460) If $a$ is any nonzero real number and $m$ and $n$ are integers, then $a^m \cdot a^n = a^{m+n}$. | **Propiedad del producto de potencias** Dado un número real $a$ distinto de cero y los números enteros $m$ y $n$, entonces $a^m \cdot a^n = a^{m+n}$. | $6^7 \cdot 6^4 = 6^{7+4} = 6^{11}$ |

| ENGLISH | SPANISH | EXAMPLES |
|---|---|---|
| **Product Property of Square Roots** (p. 806) For $a \geq 0$ and $b \geq 0$, $\sqrt{ab} = \sqrt{a} \cdot \sqrt{b}$. | **Propiedad del producto de raíces cuadradas** Dados $a \geq 0$ y $b \geq 0$, $\sqrt{ab} = \sqrt{a} \cdot \sqrt{b}$. | $\sqrt{9 \cdot 25} = \sqrt{9} \cdot \sqrt{25}$ <br> $= 3 \cdot 5 = 15$ |
| **proportion** (p. 114) A statement that two ratios are equal; $\frac{a}{b} = \frac{c}{d}$. | **proporción** Ecuación que establece que dos razones son iguales; $\frac{a}{b} = \frac{c}{d}$. | $\frac{2}{3} = \frac{4}{6}$ |
| **pyramid** (p. 874, p. S64) A polyhedron formed by a polygonal base and triangular lateral faces that meet at a common vertex. | **pirámide** Poliedro formado por una base poligonal y caras laterales triangulares que se encuentran en un vértice común. | 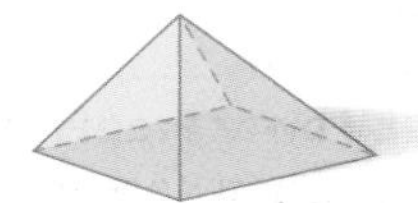 |
| **Pythagorean Theorem** (p. S68) If a right triangle has legs of lengths $a$ and $b$ and a hypotenuse of length $c$, then $a^2 + b^2 = c^2$. | **Teorema de Pitágoras** Dado un triángulo rectángulo con catetos de longitudes $a$ y $b$ y una hipotenusa de longitud $c$, entonces $a^2 + b^2 = c^2$. | 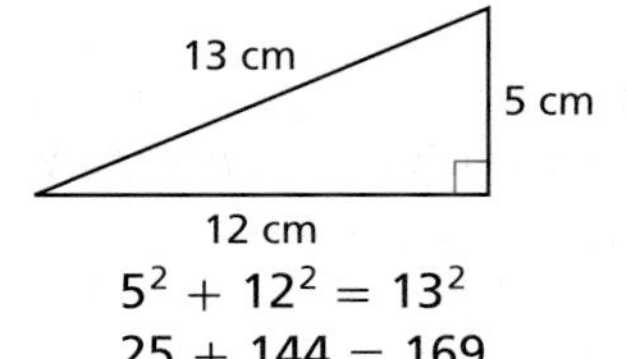  <br> $5^2 + 12^2 = 13^2$ <br> $25 + 144 = 169$ |
| **Pythagorean triple** (p. 519) A set of three nonzero whole numbers $a$, $b$, and $c$ such that $a^2 + b^2 = c^2$. | **Tripleta de Pitágoras** Conjunto de tres números cabales distintos de cero $a$, $b$ y $c$ tal que $a^2 + b^2 = c^2$. | The numbers 3, 4, and 5 form a Pythagorean triple because $3^2 + 4^2 = 5^2$. |

## Q

| ENGLISH | SPANISH | EXAMPLES |
|---|---|---|
| **quadrant** (p. 54) One of the four regions into which the $x$- and $y$-axes divide the coordinate plane. | **cuadrante** Una de las cuatro regiones en las que los ejes $x$ e $y$ dividen el plano cartesiano. | 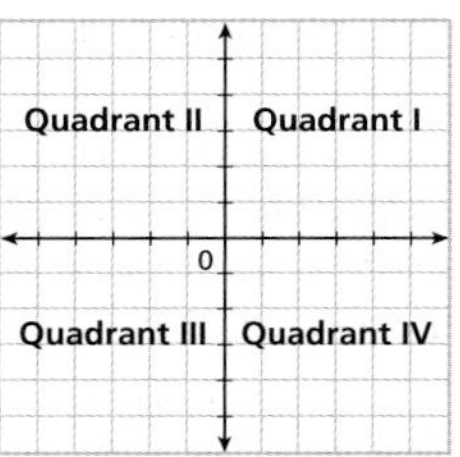  |
| **quadratic equation** (p. 622) An equation that can be written in the form $ax^2 + bx + c = 0$, where $a$, $b$, and $c$ are real numbers and $a \neq 0$. | **ecuación cuadrática** Ecuación que se puede expresar como $ax^2 + bx + c = 0$, donde $a$, $b$ y $c$ son números reales y $a \neq 0$. | $x^2 + 3x - 4 = 0$ <br> $x^2 - 9 = 0$ |
| **Quadratic Formula** (p. 652) The formula $x = \frac{-b \pm \sqrt{b^2 - 4ac}}{2a}$, which gives solutions, or roots, of equations in the form $ax^2 + bx + c = 0$, where $a \neq 0$. | **fórmula cuadrática** La fórmula $x = \frac{-b \pm \sqrt{b^2 - 4ac}}{2a}$, que da soluciones, o raíces, para las ecuaciones del tipo $ax^2 + bx + c = 0$, donde $a \neq 0$. | The solutions of $2x^2 - 5x - 3 = 0$ are given by <br> $x = \frac{-(-5) \pm \sqrt{(-5)^2 - 4(2)(-3)}}{2(2)}$ <br> $= \frac{5 \pm \sqrt{25 + 24}}{4} = \frac{5 \pm 7}{4}$ <br> $x = 3$ or $x = -\frac{1}{2}$. |
| **quadratic function** (p. 590) A function that can be written in the form $f(x) = ax^2 + bx + c$, where $a$, $b$, and $c$ are real numbers and $a \neq 0$. | **función cuadrática** Función que se puede expresar como $f(x) = ax^2 + bx + c$, donde $a$, $b$ y $c$ son números reales y $a \neq 0$. | $f(x) = x^2 - 6x + 8$ |

| ENGLISH | SPANISH | EXAMPLES |
| --- | --- | --- |
| **quadratic polynomial** (p. 477) A polynomial of degree 2. | **polinomio cuadrático** Polinomio de grado 2. | $x^2 - 6x + 8$ |
| **quartile** (p. 695) The median of the upper or lower half of a data set. *See also* first quartile, third quartile. | **cuartil** La mediana de la mitad superior o inferior de un conjunto de datos. *Ver también* primer cuartil, tercer cuartil. | 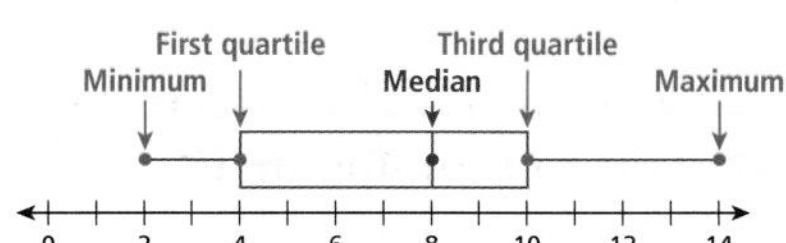  |
| **Quotient of Powers Property** (p. 467) If $a$ is a nonzero real number and $m$ and $n$ are integers, then $\frac{a^m}{a^n} = a^{m-n}$. | **Propiedad del cociente de potencias** Dado un número real $a$ distinto de cero y los números enteros $m$ y $n$, entonces $\frac{a^m}{a^n} = a^{m-n}$. | $\frac{6^7}{6^4} = 6^{7-4} = 6^3$ |
| **Quotient Property of Square Roots** (p. 806) For $a \geq 0$ and $b > 0$, $\sqrt{\frac{a}{b}} = \frac{\sqrt{a}}{\sqrt{b}}$. | **Propiedad del cociente de raíces cuadradas** Dados $a \geq 0$ y $b > 0$, $\sqrt{\frac{a}{b}} = \frac{\sqrt{a}}{\sqrt{b}}$. | $\sqrt{\frac{9}{25}} = \frac{\sqrt{9}}{\sqrt{25}} = \frac{3}{5}$ |

## R

| ENGLISH | SPANISH | EXAMPLES |
| --- | --- | --- |
| **radical equation** (p. 822) An equation that contains a variable within a radical. | **ecuación radical** Ecuación que contiene una variable dentro de un radical. | $\sqrt{x+3} + 4 = 7$ |
| **radical expression** (p. 805) An expression that contains a radical sign. | **expresión radical** Expresión que contiene un signo de radical. | $\sqrt{x+3} + 4$ |
| **radical symbol** (p. 32) The symbol $\sqrt{\phantom{x}}$ used to denote a root. The symbol is used alone to indicate a square root or with an index, $\sqrt[n]{\phantom{x}}$, to indicate the $n$th root. | **símbolo de radical** Símbolo $\sqrt{\phantom{x}}$ que se utiliza para expresar una raíz. Puede utilizarse solo para indicar una raíz cuadrada, o con un índice, $\sqrt[n]{\phantom{x}}$, para indicar la enésima raíz. | $\sqrt{36} = 6$<br>$\sqrt[3]{27} = 3$ |
| **radicand** (p. 805) The expression under a radical sign. | **radicando** Número o expresión debajo del signo de radical. | Expression: $\sqrt{x} + 3$<br>Radicand: $x + 3$ |
| **radius** (p. S62) A segment whose endpoints are the center of a circle and a point on the circle; the distance from the center of a circle to any point on the circle. | **radio** Segmento cuyos extremos son el centro de un círculo y un punto de la circunferencia; distancia desde el centro de un círculo hasta cualquier punto de la circunferencia. |   |
| **random sample** (p. 703) A sample selected from a population so that each member of the population has an equal chance of being selected. | **muestra aleatoria** Muestra seleccionada de una población tal que cada miembro de ésta tenga igual probabilidad de ser seleccionada. | Mr. Hansen chose a random sample of the class by writing each student's name on a slip of paper, mixing up the slips, and drawing five slips without looking. |
| **range of a data set** (p. 694) The difference of the greatest and least values in the data set. | **rango de un conjunto de datos** La diferencia del mayor y menor valor en un conjunto de datos. | The data set {3, 3, 5, 7, 8, 10, 11, 11, 12} has a range of $12 - 3 = 9$. |

| ENGLISH | SPANISH | EXAMPLES |
|---|---|---|
| **range of a function or relation** (p. 236) The set of output values of a function or relation. | **rango de una función o relación** Conjunto de todos los valores de salida posibles de una función o relación. | The range of $y = x^2$ is $y \geq 0$. |
| **rate** (p. 114) A ratio that compares two quantities measured in different units. | **tasa** Razón que compara dos cantidades medidas en diferentes unidades. | $\frac{55 \text{ miles}}{1 \text{ hour}} = 55\text{mi/h}$ |
| **rate of change** (p. 310) A ratio that compares the amount of change in a dependent variable to the amount of change in an independent variable. | **tasa de cambio** Razón que compara la cantidad de cambio de la variable dependiente con la cantidad de cambio de la variable independiente. | The cost of mailing a letter increased from 22 cents in 1985 to 25 cents in 1988. During this period, the rate of change was $\frac{\text{change in cost}}{\text{change in year}} = \frac{25 - 21}{1988 - 1985} = \frac{3}{3}$ $= 1$ cent per year. |
| **ratio** (p. 114) A comparison of two quantities by division. | **razón** Comparación de dos cantidades mediante una división. | $\frac{1}{2}$ or 1:2 |
| **rational equation** (p. 900) An equation that contains one or more rational expressions. | **ecuación racional** Ecuación que contiene una o más expresiones racionales. | $\frac{x + 2}{x^2 + 3x - 1} = 6$ |
| **rational exponent** (p. 832) An exponent that can be expressed as $\frac{m}{n}$ such that if $m$ and $n$ are integers, then $b^{\frac{m}{n}} = \sqrt[n]{b^m} = \left(\sqrt[n]{b}\right)^m$. | **exponente racional** Exponente que se puede expresar como $\frac{m}{n}$ tal que si $m$ y $n$ son números enteros, entonces $b^{\frac{m}{n}} = \sqrt[n]{b^m} = \left(\sqrt[n]{b}\right)^m$. | $64^{\frac{1}{6}} = \sqrt[6]{64}$ |
| **rational expression** (p. 866) An algebraic expression whose numerator and denominator are polynomials and whose denominator has a degree $\geq 1$. | **expresión racional** Expresión algebraica cuyo numerador y denominador son polinomios y cuyo denominador tiene un grado $\geq 1$. | $\frac{x + 2}{x^2 + 3x - 1}$ |
| **rational function** (p. 858) A function whose rule can be written as a rational expression. | **función racional** Función cuya regla se puede expresar como una expresión racional. | $f(x) = \frac{x + 2}{x^2 + 3x - 1}$ |
| **rational number** (p. 34) A number that can be written in the form $\frac{a}{b}$, where $a$ and $b$ are integers and $b \neq 0$. | **número racional** Número que se puede expresar como $\frac{a}{b}$, donde $a$ y $b$ son números enteros y $b \neq 0$. | $3, 1.75, 0.\overline{3}, -\frac{2}{3}, 0$ |
| **rationalizing the denominator** (p. 818) A method of rewriting a fraction by multiplying by another fraction that is equivalent to 1 in order to remove radical terms from the denominator. | **racionalizar el denominador** Método que consiste en escribir nuevamente una fracción multiplicándola por otra fracción equivalente a 1 a fin de eliminar los términos radicales del denominador. | $\frac{1}{\sqrt{2}} \cdot \frac{\sqrt{2}}{\sqrt{2}} = \frac{\sqrt{2}}{2}$ |
| **ray** (p. S56) A part of a line that starts at an endpoint and extends forever in one direction. | **rayo** Parte de una recta que comienza en un extremo y se extiende infinitamente en una dirección. | D |

| ENGLISH | SPANISH | EXAMPLES |
|---|---|---|
| **real number** (p. 34) A rational or irrational number. Every point on the number line represents a real number. | **número real** Número racional o irracional. Cada punto de la recta numérica representa un número real. | 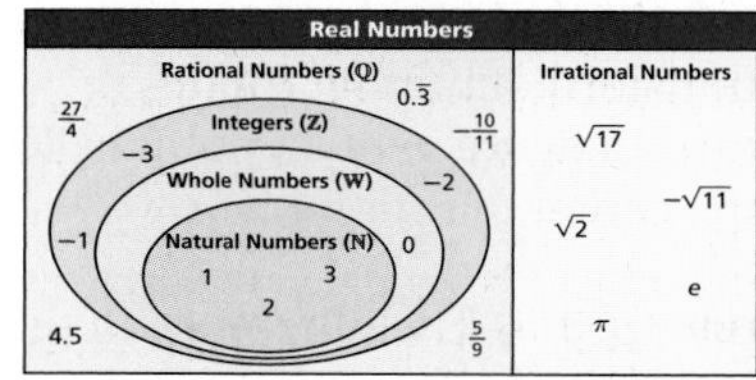  |
| **reciprocal** (p. 21) For a real number $a \neq 0$, the reciprocal of $a$ is $\frac{1}{a}$. The product of reciprocals is 1. | **recíproco** Dado el número real $a \neq 0$, el recíproco de $a$ es $\frac{1}{a}$. El producto de los recíprocos es 1. | Number: 2, 1, −1, 0 / Reciprocal: $\frac{1}{2}$, 1, −1, No reciprocal |
| **rectangle** (p. S63) A quadrilateral with four right angles. | **rectángulo** Cuadrilátero con cuatro ángulos rectos. | 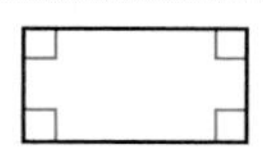 |
| **rectangular prism** (p. 874) A prism whose bases are rectangles. | **prisma rectangular** Prisma cuyas bases son rectángulos. | 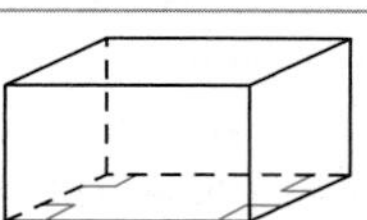 |
| **rectangular pyramid** (p. 874) A pyramid whose base is a rectangle. | **pirámide rectangular** Pirámide cuya base es un rectángulo. | 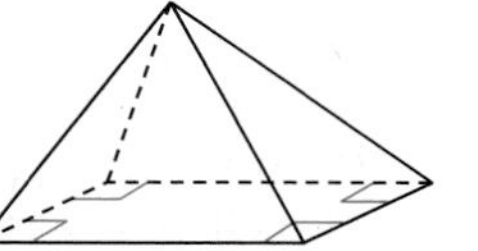 |
| **reflection** (p. 359, p. S69) A transformation that reflects, or "flips," a graph or figure across a line, called the line of reflection. | **reflexión** Transformación en la que una gráfica o figura se refleja o se invierte sobre una línea, denominada la línea de reflexión. | 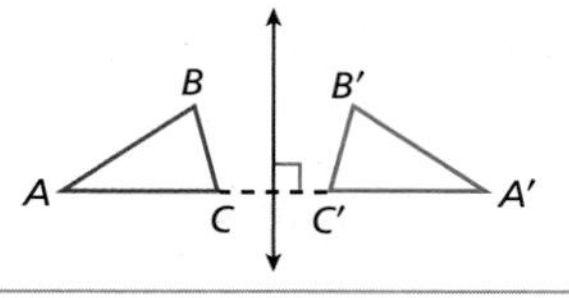  |
| **regular polygon** (p. S58) A polygon that is both equilateral and equiangular. | **polígono regular** Polígono equilátero de ángulos iguales. | 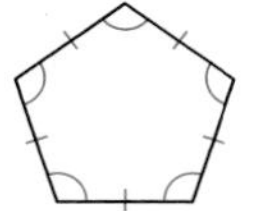 |
| **relation** (p. 236) A set of ordered pairs. | **relación** Conjunto de pares ordenados. | $\{(0, 5), (0, 4), (2, 3), (4, 0)\}$ |
| **repeating decimal** (p. 34) A rational number in decimal form that has a block of one or more digits that repeat continuously. | **decimal periódico** Número racional en forma decimal que tiene un bloque de uno o más dígitos que se repite continuamente. | $1.\overline{3}, 0.\overline{6}, 2.\overline{14}, 6.77\overline{3}$ |
| **replacement set** (p. 8) A set of numbers that can be substituted for a variable. | **conjunto de reemplazo** Conjunto de números que pueden sustituir una variable. | |
| **rhombus** (p. S63) A quadrilateral with four congruent sides. | **rombo** Cuadrilátero con cuatro lados congruentes. | 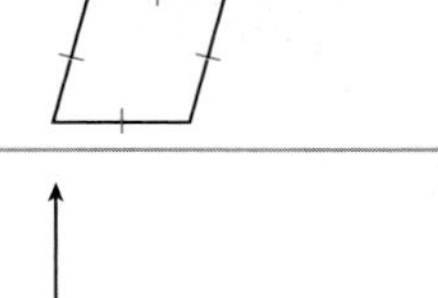 |
| **right angle** (p. S56) An angle that measures 90°. | **ángulo recto** Ángulo que mide 90°. | 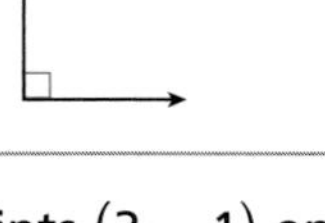 |
| **rise** (p. 311) The difference in the $y$-values of two points on a line. | **distancia vertical** Diferencia entre los valores de $y$ de dos puntos de una línea. | For the points $(3, -1)$ and $(6, 5)$, the rise is $5 - (-1) = 6$. |

Glossary/Glosario

| ENGLISH | SPANISH | EXAMPLES |
|---|---|---|
| **rotation** (p. 358, p. S69) A transformation that rotates or turns a figure about a point called the center of rotation. | **rotación** Transformación que rota o gira una figura sobre un punto llamado centro de rotación. | 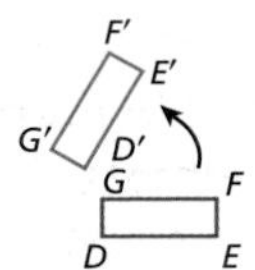 |
| **run** (p. 311) The difference in the $x$-values of two points on a line. | **distancia horizontal** Diferencia entre los valores de $x$ de dos puntos de una línea. | For the points $(3, -1)$ and $(6, 5)$, the run is $6 - 3 = 3$. |

## S

| ENGLISH | SPANISH | EXAMPLES |
|---|---|---|
| **sales tax** (p. 134) A percent of the cost of an item that is charged by governments to raise money. | **impuesto sobre la venta** Porcentaje del costo de un artículo que cobran los gobiernos para recaudar dinero. | |
| **sample space** (p. 713) The set of all possible outcomes of a probability experiment. | **espacio muestral** Conjunto de todos los resultados posibles de un experimento de probabilidad. | In the experiment of rolling a number cube, the sample space is $\{1, 2, 3, 4, 5, 6\}$. |
| **scale** (p. 116) The ratio between two corresponding measurements. | **escala** Razón entre dos medidas correspondientes. | 1 cm : 5 mi |
| **scale drawing** (p. 116) A drawing that uses a scale to represent an object as smaller or larger than the actual object. | **dibujo a escala** Dibujo que utiliza una escala para representar un objeto como más pequeño o más grande que el objeto original. | 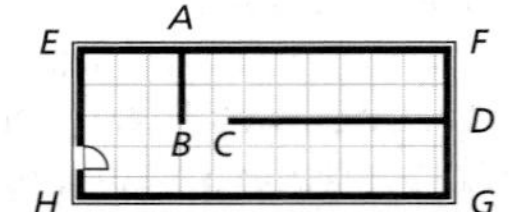 A blueprint is an example of a scale drawing. |
| **scale factor** (p. 123) The multiplier used on each dimension to change one figure into a similar figure. | **factor de escala** El multiplicador utilizado en cada dimensión para transformar una figura en una figura semejante. | 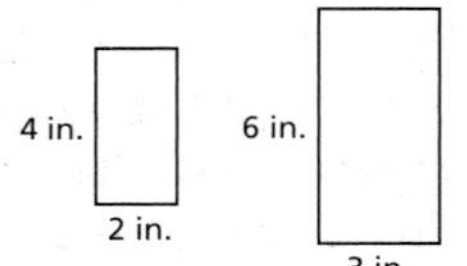 Scale factor: $\frac{3}{2} = 1.5$ |
| **scale model** (p. 116) A three-dimensional model that uses a scale to represent an object as smaller or larger than the actual object. | **modelo a escala** Modelo tridimensional que utiliza una escala para representar un objeto como más pequeño o más grande que el objeto real. | |
| **scalene triangle** (p. S63) A triangle with no congruent sides. | **triángulo escaleno** Triángulo sin lados congruentes. | 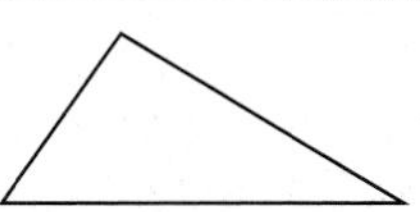 |
| **scatter plot** (p. 262) A graph with points plotted to show a possible relationship between two sets of data. | **diagrama de dispersión** Gráfica con puntos que se usa para demostrar una relación posible entre dos conjuntos de datos. | 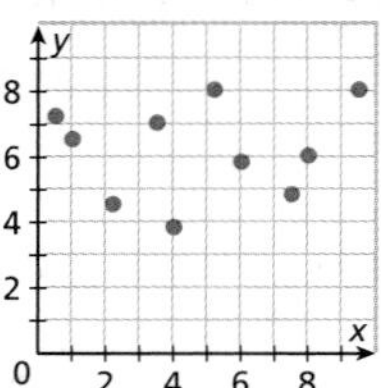 |

| ENGLISH | SPANISH | EXAMPLES |
|---|---|---|

**scientific notation** (p. 453) A method of writing very large or very small numbers, by using powers of 10, in the form $m \times 10^n$, where $1 \leq m < 10$ and $n$ is an integer.

**notación científica** Método que consiste en escribir números muy grandes o muy pequeños utilizando potencias de 10 del tipo $m \times 10^n$, donde $1 \leq m < 10$ y $n$ es un número entero.

$12{,}560{,}000{,}000{,}000 = 1.256 \times 10^{13}$

$0.0000075 = 7.5 \times 10^{-6}$

---

**second differences** (p. 590) Differences between first differences of a function.

**segundas diferencias** Diferencias entre las primeras diferencias de una función.

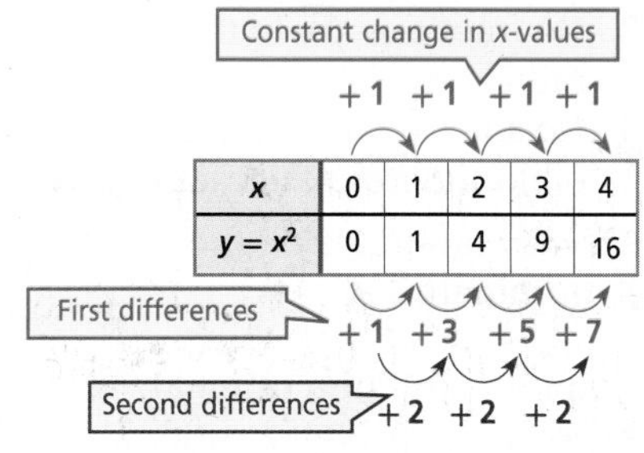


---

**sequence** (p. 272) A list of numbers that often form a pattern.

**sucesión** Lista de números que generalmente forman un patrón.

1, 2, 4, 8, 16, ...

---

**set-builder notation** (p. 168) A notation for a set that uses a rule to describe the properties of the elements of the set.

**notación de conjuntos** Notación para un conjunto que se vale de una regla para describir las propiedades de los elementos del conjunto.

$\{x | x > 3\}$ is read "The set of all $x$ such that $x$ is greater than 3."

---

**similar** (p. 121) Two figures are similar if they have the same shape but not necessarily the same size.

**semejantes** Dos figuras con la misma forma pero no necesariamente del mismo tamaño.

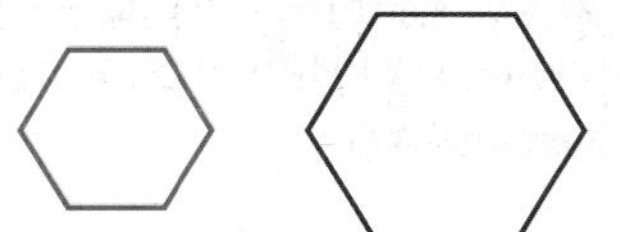

---

**similarity statement** (p. 121) A statement that indicates that two polygons are similar by listing the vertices in the order of correspondence.

**enunciado de semejanza** Enunciado que indica que dos polígonos son semejantes enumerando los vértices en orden de correspondencia.

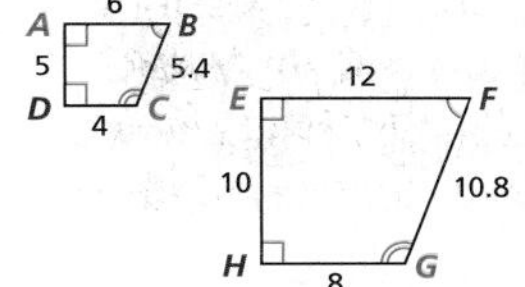


quadrilateral $ABCD \sim$ quadrilateral $EFGH$

---

**simple event** (p. 737) An event consisting of only one outcome.

**suceso simple** Suceso que tiene sólo un resultado.

In the experiment of rolling a number cube, the event consisting of the outcome 3 is a simple event.

---

**simple interest** (p. 133) A fixed percent of the principal. For principal $P$, interest rate $r$, and time $t$ in years, the simple interest is $I = Prt$.

**interés simple** Porcentaje fijo del capital. Dado el capital $P$, la tasa de interés $r$ y el tiempo $t$ expresado en años, el interés simple es $I = Prt$.

If \$100 is put into an account with a simple interest rate of 5%, then after 2 years, the account will have earned $I = 100 \cdot 0.05 \cdot 2 = \$10$ in interest.

| ENGLISH | SPANISH | EXAMPLES |
| --- | --- | --- |

**simplest form of a square root expression** (p. 805) A square root expression is in simplest form if it meets the following criteria:

1. No perfect squares are in the radicand.
2. No fractions are in the radicand.
3. No square roots appear in the denominator of a fraction.

*See also* rationalizing the denominator.

**forma simplificada de una expresión de raíz cuadrada** Una expresión de raíz cuadrada está en forma simplificada si reúne los siguientes requisitos:

1. No hay cuadrados perfectos en el radicando.
2. No hay fracciones en el radicando.
3. No aparecen raíces cuadradas en el denominador de una fracción.

*Ver también* racionalizar el denominador.

| Not Simplest Form | Simplest Form |
| --- | --- |
| $\sqrt{180}$ | $6\sqrt{5}$ |
| $\sqrt{216a^2b^2}$ | $6ab\sqrt{6}$ |
| $\frac{\sqrt{7}}{\sqrt{2}}$ | $\frac{\sqrt{14}}{2}$ |

---

**simplest form of a rational expression** (p. 867) A rational expression is in simplest form if the numerator and denominator have no common factors.

**forma simplificada de una expresión racional** Una expresión racional está en forma simplificada cuando el numerador y el denominador no tienen factores comunes.

$$\frac{x^2 - 1}{x^2 + x - 2} = \frac{(x-1)(x+1)}{(x+1)(x+2)} = \frac{x-1}{x+2}$$

Simplest form

---

**simplest form of an exponential expression** (p. 460) An exponential expression is in simplest form if it meets the following criteria:

1. There are no negative exponents.
2. The same base does not appear more than once in a product or quotient.
3. No powers, products, or quotients are raised to powers.
4. Numerical coefficients in a quotient do not have any common factor other than 1.

**forma simplificada de una expresión exponencial** Una expresión exponencial está en forma simplificada si reúne los siguientes requisitos:

1. No hay exponentes negativos.
2. La misma base no aparece más de una vez en un producto o cociente.
3. No se elevan a potencias productos, cocientes ni potencias.
4. Los coeficientes numéricos en un cociente no tienen ningún factor común que no sea 1.

| Not Simplest Form | Simplest Form |
| --- | --- |
| $7^8 \cdot 7^4$ | $7^{12}$ |
| $(x^2)^{-4} \cdot x^5$ | $\frac{1}{x^3}$ |
| $\frac{a^5b^9}{(ab)^4}$ | $ab^5$ |

---

**simplify** (p. 40) To perform all indicated operations.

**simplificar** Realizar todas las operaciones indicadas.

$13 - 20 + 8$
$-7 + 8$
$1$

---

**simulation** (p. 712) A model of an experiment, often one that would be too difficult or time-consuming to actually perform.

**simulación** Modelo de un experimento; generalmente se recurre a la simulación cuando realizar dicho experimento sería demasiado difícil o llevaría mucho tiempo.

---

**sine** (p. 908) In a right triangle, the ratio of the length of the leg opposite $\angle A$ to the length of the hypotenuse.

**seno** En un triángulo rectángulo, razón entre la longitud del cateto opuesto a $\angle A$ y la longitud de la hipotenusa.

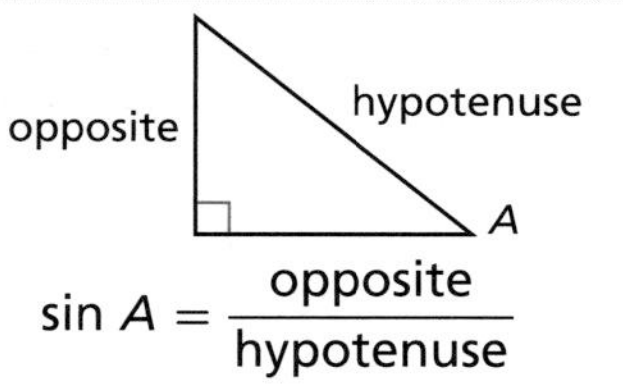


$$\sin A = \frac{\text{opposite}}{\text{hypotenuse}}$$

| ENGLISH | SPANISH | EXAMPLES |
|---|---|---|
| **slope** (p. 311) A measure of the steepness of a line. If $(x_1, y_1)$ and $(x_2, y_2)$ are any two points on the line, the slope of the line, known as $m$, is represented by the equation $m = \frac{y_2 - y_1}{x_2 - x_1}$. | **pendiente** Medida de la inclinación de una línea. Dados dos puntos $(x_1, y_1)$ y $(x_2, y_2)$ en una línea, la pendiente de la línea, denominada $m$, se representa con la ecuación $m = \frac{y_2 - y_1}{x_2 - x_1}$. | 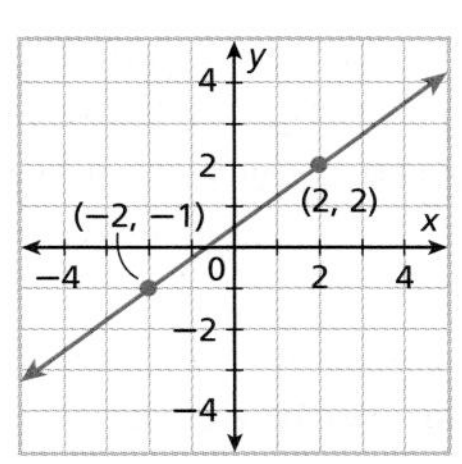  $m = \frac{y_2 - y_1}{x_2 - x_1} = \frac{-1 - 2}{-2 - 2} = \frac{3}{4}$ |
| **slope-intercept form** (p. 335) The slope-intercept form of a linear equation is $y = mx + b$, where $m$ is the slope and $b$ is the $y$-intercept. | **forma de pendiente-intersección** La forma de pendiente-intersección de una ecuación lineal es $y = mx + b$, donde $m$ es la pendiente y $b$ es la intersección con el eje $y$. | $y = -2x + 4$<br>The slope is $-2$.<br>The $y$-intercept is 4. |
| **solution of a linear equation in two variables** (p. 245) An ordered pair or ordered pairs that make the equation true. | **solución de una ecuación lineal en dos variables** Un par ordenado o pares ordenados que hacen que la ecuación sea verdadera. | Equation: $x + y = 6$<br>Solution: $(4, 2)$ (one possible solution) |
| **solution of a linear inequality in two variables** (p. 414) An ordered pair or ordered pairs that make the inequality true. | **solución de una desigualdad lineal en dos variables** Un par ordenado o pares ordenados que hacen que la desigualdad sea verdadera. | Inequality: $x + y < 6$<br>Solution: $(3, 1)$ (one possible solution) |
| **solution of a system of linear equations** (p. 383) Any ordered pair that satisfies all the equations in a system. | **solución de un sistema de ecuaciones lineales** Cualquier par ordenado que resuelva todas las ecuaciones de un sistema. | $\begin{cases} x + y = -1 \\ -x + y = -3 \end{cases}$<br>Solution: $(1, -2)$ |
| **solution of a system of linear inequalities** (p. 421) Any ordered pair that satisfies all the inequalities in a system. | **solución de un sistema de desigualdades lineales** Cualquier par ordenado que resuelva todas las desigualdades de un sistema. | 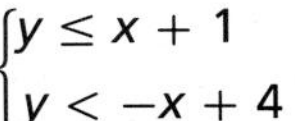 $\begin{cases} y \leq x + 1 \\ y < -x + 4 \end{cases}$<br>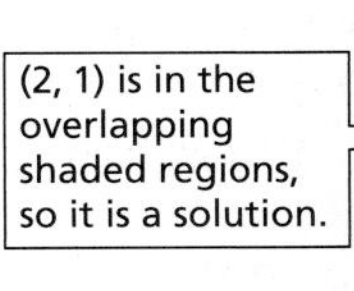  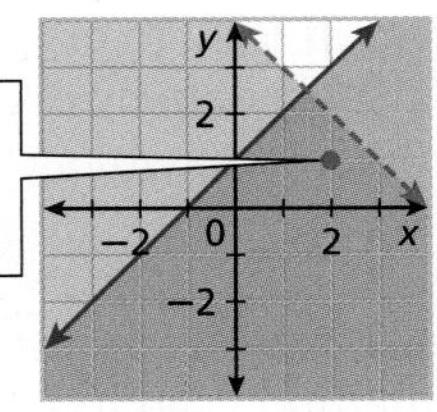 |
| **solution of an equation in one variable** (p. 77) A value or values that make the equation true. | **solución de una ecuación en una variable** Valor o valores que hacen que la ecuación sea verdadera. | Equation: $x + 2 = 6$<br>Solution: $x = 4$ |
| **solution of an inequality in one variable** (p. 168) A value or values that make the inequality true. | **solución de una desigualdad en una variable** Valor o valores que hacen que la desigualdad sea verdadera. | Inequality: $x + 2 < 6$<br>Solution: $x < 4$ |
| **solution set** (p. 77) The set of values that make a statement true. | **conjunto solución** Conjunto de valores que hacen verdadero un enunciado. | Inequality: $x + 3 \geq 5$<br>Solution set: $\{x \mid x \geq 2\}$<br>−4 −3 −2 −1 0 1 2 3 4 5 6 |

| ENGLISH | SPANISH | EXAMPLES |
|---|---|---|
| **square** (p. S63) A quadrilateral with four congruent sides and four right angles. | **cuadrado** Cuadrilátero con cuatro lados congruentes y cuatro ángulos rectos. | 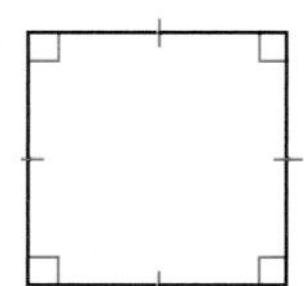 |
| **square in numeration** (p. 26) The second power of a number. | **cuadrado en numeración** La segunda potencia de un número. | 16 is the square of 4. |
| **square root** (p. 32) A number that is multiplied to itself to form a product is called a square root of that product. | **raíz cuadrada** El número que se multiplica por sí mismo para formar un producto se denomina la raíz cuadrada de ese producto. | $\sqrt{16} = 4$, because $4^2 = 4 \cdot 4 = 16$. |
| **square-root function** (p. 798) A function whose rule contains a variable under a square-root sign. | **función de raíz cuadrada** Función cuya regla contiene una variable bajo un signo de raíz cuadrada. | $y = \sqrt{3x} - 5$ |
| **standard form of a linear equation** (p. 298) $Ax + By = C$, where $A$, $B$, and $C$ are real numbers. | **forma estándar de una ecuación lineal** $Ax + By = C$, donde $A$, $B$ y $C$ son números reales. | $2x + 3y = 6$ |
| **standard form of a polynomial** (p. 477) A polynomial in one variable is written in standard form when the terms are in order from greatest degree to least degree. | **forma estándar de un polinomio** Un polinomio de una variable se expresa en forma estándar cuando los términos se ordenan de mayor a menor grado. | $4x^5 - 2x^4 + x^2 - x + 1$ |
| **standard form of a quadratic equation** (p. 622) $ax^2 + bx + c = 0$, where $a$, $b$, and $c$ are real numbers and $a \neq 0$. | **forma estándar de una ecuación cuadrática** $ax^2 + bx + c = 0$, donde $a$, $b$ y $c$ son números reales y $a \neq 0$. | $2x^2 + 3x - 1 = 0$ |
| **stem-and-leaf plot** (p. 687) A graph used to organize and display data by dividing each data value into two parts, a stem and a leaf. | **diagrama de tallo y hojas** Gráfica utilizada para organizar y mostrar datos dividiendo cada valor de datos en dos partes, un tallo y una hoja. | **Stem \| Leaves**<br>3 \| 2 3 4 4 7 9<br>4 \| 0 1 5 7 7 7 8<br>5 \| 1 2 2 3<br>*Key: 3\|2 means 3.2* |
| **substitution method** (p. 390) A method used to solve systems of equations by solving an equation for one variable and substituting the resulting expression into the other equation(s). | **sustitución** Método utilizado para resolver sistemas de ecuaciones resolviendo una ecuación para una variable y sustituyendo la expresión resultante en las demás ecuaciones. | |
| **Subtraction Property of Equality** (p. 79) If $a$, $b$, and $c$ are real numbers and $a = b$, then $a - c = b - c$. | **Propiedad de igualdad de la resta** Si $a$, $b$ y $c$ son números reales y $a = b$, entonces $a - c = b - c$. | $x + 6 = 8$<br>$\underline{-6} \quad \underline{-6}$<br>$x = 2$ |
| **Subtraction Property of Inequality** (p. 174) For real numbers $a$, $b$, and $c$, if $a < b$, then $a - c < b - c$. Also holds true for $>$, $\leq$, $\geq$, and $\neq$. | **Propiedad de desigualdad de la resta** Dados los números reales $a$, $b$ y $c$, si $a < b$, entonces $a - c < b - c$. Es válido también para $>$, $\leq$, $\geq$ y $\neq$. | $x + 6 < 8$<br>$\underline{-6} \quad \underline{-6}$<br>$x < 2$ |

| ENGLISH | SPANISH |  EXAMPLES |
|---|---|---|
| **supplementary angles** (p. S57) Two angles whose measures have a sum of 180°. | **ángulos suplementarios** Dos ángulos cuyas medidas suman 180°. | 30° 150° |
| **surface area** (p. S67) The total area of all faces and curved surfaces of a three-dimensional figure. | **área total** Área total de todas las caras y superficies curvas de una figura tridimensional. | 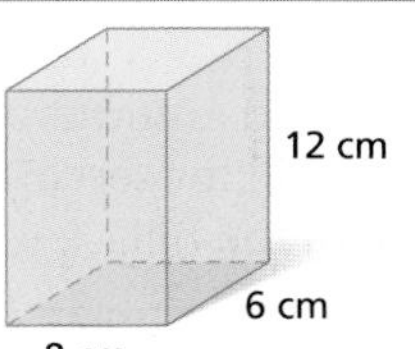 12 cm, 6 cm, 8 cm<br>Surface area $= 2(8)(12) + 2(8)(6) + 2(12)(6)$ $= 432\text{ cm}^2$ |
| **system of linear equations** (p. 383) A system of equations in which all of the equations are linear. | **sistema de ecuaciones lineales** Sistema de ecuaciones en el que todas las ecuaciones son lineales. | $\begin{cases} 2x + 3y = -1 \\ x - 3y = 4 \end{cases}$ |
| **system of linear inequalities** (p. 421) A system of inequalities in two or more variables in which all of the inequalities are linear. | **sistema de desigualdades lineales** Sistema de desigualdades en dos o más variables en el que todas las desigualdades son lineales. | $\begin{cases} 2x + 3y > -1 \\ x - 3y \le 4 \end{cases}$ |

## T

| | | |
|---|---|---|
| **tangent** (p. 908) In a right triangle, the ratio of the length of the leg opposite $\angle A$ to the length of the leg adjacent to $\angle A$. | **tangente** En un triángulo rectángulo, razón entre la longitud del cateto opuesto a $\angle A$ y la longitud del cateto adyacente a $\angle A$. | 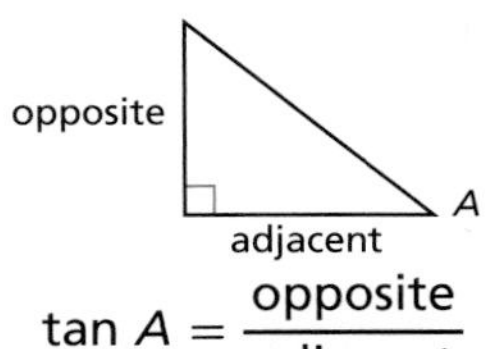 opposite, adjacent, A<br>$\tan A = \frac{\text{opposite}}{\text{adjacent}}$ |
| **term of an expression** (p. 47) The parts of the expression that are added or subtracted. | **término de una expresión** Parte de una expresión que debe sumarse o restarse. | 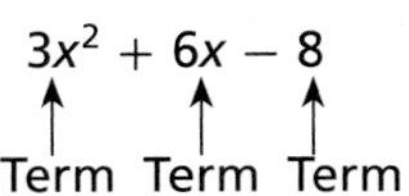 $3x^2 + 6x - 8$<br>Term Term Term |
| **term of a sequence** (p. 272) An element or number in the sequence. | **término de una sucesión** Elemento o número de una sucesión. | 5 is the third term in the sequence 1, 3, 5, 7, ... |
| **terminating decimal** (p. 34) A rational number in decimal form that has a finite number of digits after the decimal point. | **decimal finito** Número racional en forma decimal que tien un número finito de dígitos después del punto decimal. | 1.5, 2.75, 4.0 |
| **theoretical probability** (p. 720) The ratio of the number of equally likely outcomes in an event to the total number of possible outcomes. | **probabilidad teórica** Razón entre el número de resultados igualmente probables de un suceso y el número total de resultados posibles. | In the experiment of rolling a number cube, the theoretical probability of rolling an odd number is $\frac{3}{6} = \frac{1}{2}$. |

Glossary/Glosario

| ENGLISH | SPANISH | EXAMPLES |
|---|---|---|
| **third quartile** (p. 695) The median of the upper half of a data set. Also called *upper quartile.* | **tercer cuartil** La mediana de la mitad superior de un conjunto de datos. También se llama *cuartil superior.* | Lower half Upper half<br>18, 23, 28, 49, 36, 42<br>Third quartile |
| **tip** (p. 134) An amount of money added to a bill for service; usually a percent of the bill. | **propina** Cantidad que se agrega a una factura por servicios; generalmente, un porcentaje de la factura. | |
| **transformation** (p. 357, p. S69) A change in the position, size, or shape of a figure or graph. | **transformación** Cambio en la posición, tamaño o forma de una figura o gráfica. | Preimage, Image<br>$\triangle ABC \rightarrow \triangle A'B'C'$ |
| **translation** (p. 357, p. S69) A transformation that shifts or slides every point of a figure or graph the same distance in the same direction. | **traslación** Transformación en la que todos los puntos de una figura o gráfica se mueven la misma distancia en la misma dirección. | |
| **trapezoid** (p. S63) A quadrilateral with exactly one pair of parallel sides. | **trapecio** Cuadrilátero con sólo un par de lados paralelos. | |
| **tree diagram** (p. 736) A branching diagram that shows all possible combinations or outcomes of an experiment. | **diagrama de árbol** Diagrama con ramificaciones que muestra todas las combinaciones o resultados posibles de un experimento. | H: 1 2 3 4 5 6 T: 1 2 3 4 5 6<br>The tree diagram shows the possible outcomes when tossing a coin and rolling a number cube. |
| **trend line** (p. 265) A line on a scatter plot that helps show the correlation between data sets more clearly. | **línea de tendencia** Línea en un diagrama de dispersión que sirve para mostrar la correlación entre conjuntos de datos más claramente. | Fund-raiser<br>Money raised ($) vs. Rolls sold |
| **trial** (p. 713) In probability, a single repetition or observation of an experiment. | **prueba** En probabilidad, una sola repetición u observación de un experimento. | In the experiment of rolling a number cube, each roll is one trial. |
| **triangle** (p. 209) A three-sided polygon. | **triángulo** Polígono de tres lados. | |

| ENGLISH | SPANISH | EXAMPLES |
|---|---|---|
| **triangular prism** (p. 874) A prism whose bases are triangles. | **prisma triangular** Prisma cuyas bases son triángulos. |  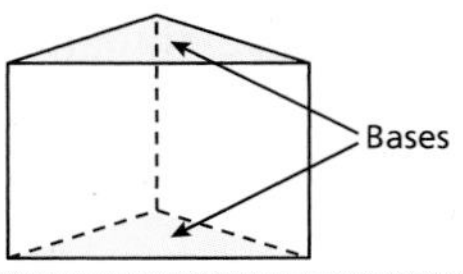  |
| **triangular pyramid** (p. 874) A pyramid whose base is a triangle. | **pirámide triangular** Pirámide cuya base es un triángulo. | 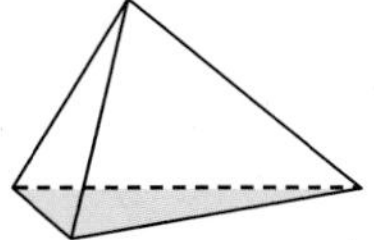 |
| **trigonometric ratio** (p. 908) Ratio of the lengths of two sides of a right triangle. | **razón trigonométrica** Razón entre dos lados de un triángulo rectángulo. | 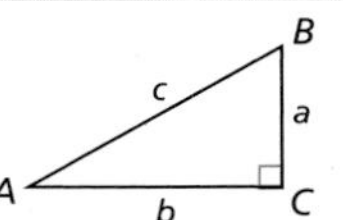  $\sin A = \frac{a}{c}$, $\cos A = \frac{b}{c}$, $\tan A = \frac{a}{b}$ |
| **trinomial** (p. 477) A polynomial with three terms. | **trinomio** Polinomio con tres términos. | $4x^2 + 3xy - 5y^2$ |

## U

| ENGLISH | SPANISH | EXAMPLES |
|---|---|---|
| **union** (p. 204) The union of two sets is the set of all elements that are in either set, denoted by ∪. | **unión** La unión de dos conjuntos es el conjunto de todos los elementos que se encuentran en ambos conjuntos, expresado por ∪. | $A = \{1, 2, 3, 4\}$<br>$B = \{1, 3, 5, 7, 9\}$<br>$A \cup B = \{1, 2, 3, 4, 5, 7, 9\}$ |
| **unit rate** (p. 114) A rate in which the second quantity in the comparison is one unit. | **tasa unitaria** Tasa en la que la segunda cantidad de la comparación es una unidad. | $\frac{30\text{ mi}}{1\text{h}} = 30\text{ mi/h}$ |
| **unlike radicals** (p. 811) Radicals with a different quantity under the radical. | **radicales distintos** Radicales con cantidades diferentes debajo del signo de radical. | $2\sqrt{2}$ and $2\sqrt{3}$ |
| **unlike terms** Terms with different variables or the same variables raised to different powers. | **términos distintos** Términos con variables diferentes o las mismas variables elevadas a potencias diferentes. | $4xy^2$ and $6x^2y$ |
| **upper quartile** *See* third quartile. | **cuartil superior** *Ver* tercer cuartil. | |

## V

| ENGLISH | SPANISH | EXAMPLES |
|---|---|---|
| **value of a function** (p. 247) The result of replacing the independent variable with a number and simplifying. | **valor de una función** Resultado de reemplazar la variable independiente por un número y luego simplificar. | The value of the function $f(x) = x + 1$ for $x = 3$ is 4. |
| **value of a variable** (p. 7) A number used to replace a variable to make an equation true. | **valor de una variable** Número utilizado para reemplazar una variable y hacer que una ecuación sea verdadera. | In the equation $x + 1 = 4$, the value of $x$ is 3. |

| ENGLISH | SPANISH | EXAMPLES |
|---|---|---|
| **value of an expression** (p. 7) The result of replacing the variables in an expression with numbers and simplifying. | **valor de una expresión** Resultado de reemplazar las variables de una expresión por un número y luego simplificar. | The value of the expression $x + 1$ for $x = 3$ is 4. |
| **variable** (p. 6) A symbol used to represent a quantity that can change. | **variable** Símbolo utilizado para representar una cantidad que puede cambiar. | In the expression $2x + 3$, $x$ is the variable. |
| **Venn diagram** (p. S48) A diagram used to show relationships between sets. | **diagrama de Venn** Diagrama utilizado para mostrar la relación entre conjuntos. | 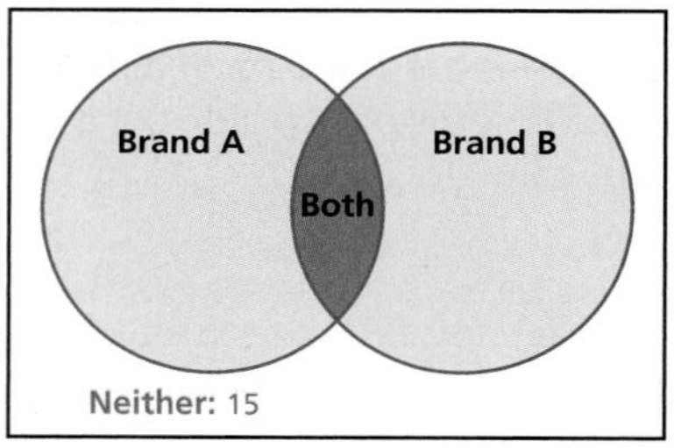 Brand A / Both / Brand B; Neither: 15 |
| **vertex of a cone** (p. S64) The point opposite the base of the cone. | **vértice de un cono** Punto opuesto a la base del cono. | 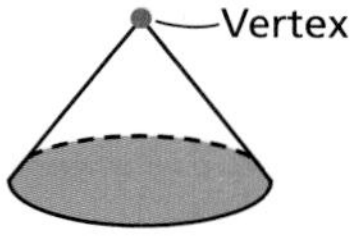 Vertex |
| **vertex of a parabola** (p. 592) The highest or lowest point on the parabola. | **vértice de una parábola** Punto más alto o más bajo de una parábola. | (0, −2)<br>The vertex is $(0, -2)$. |
| **vertex of an absolute-value graph** (p. 366) The point on the axis of symmetry of the graph. | **vértice de una gráfica de valor absoluto** Punto en el eje de simetría de la gráfica. | 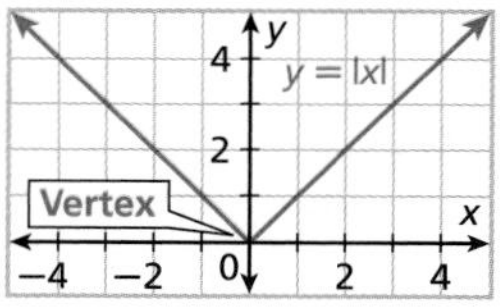 $y = \|x\|$; Vertex |
| **vertical angles** (p. S57) The nonadjacent angles formed by two intersecting lines. | **ángulos opuestos por el vértice** Ángulos no adyacentes formados por dos líneas que se cruzan. | $\angle 1$ and $\angle 3$ are vertical angles.<br>$\angle 2$ and $\angle 4$ are vertical angles. |
| **vertical line** (p. 312) A line whose equation is $x = a$, where $a$ is the $x$-intercept. | **línea vertical** Línea cuya ecuación es $x = a$, donde $a$ es la intersección con el eje $x$. | $x = 2$ |

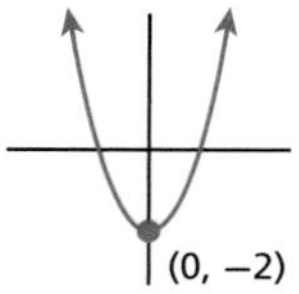

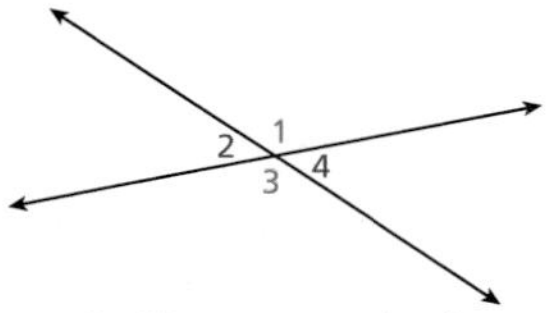

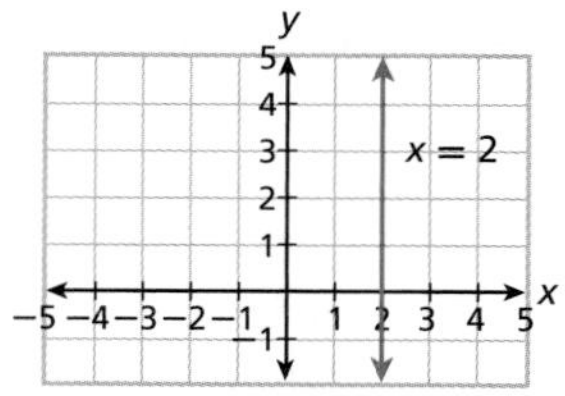

| ENGLISH | SPANISH | EXAMPLES |
|---|---|---|
| **vertical-line test** (p. 243) A test used to determine whether a relation is a function. If any vertical line crosses the graph of a relation more than once, the relation is not a function. | **prueba de la línea vertical** Prueba utilizada para determinar si una relación es una función. Si una línea vertical corta la gráfica de una relación más de una vez, la relación no es una función. | 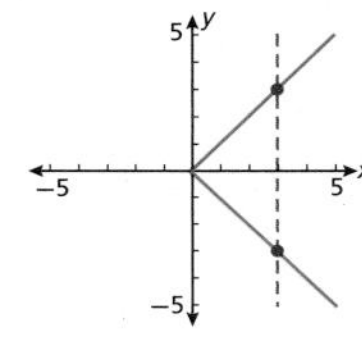  Function Not a function |
| **volume** (p. S66) The number of nonoverlapping unit cubes of a given size that will exactly fill the interior of a three-dimensional figure. | **volumen** Cantidad de cubos unitarios no superpuestos de un determinado tamaño que llenan exactamente el interior de una figura tridimensional. | 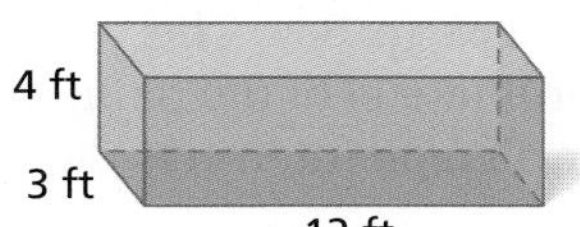  Volume = $(3)(4)(12) = 144\text{ ft}^3$ |

## W

| | | |
|---|---|---|
| **whole number** (p. 34) The set of natural numbers and zero. | **número cabal** Conjunto de los números naturales y cero. | 0, 1, 2, 3, 4, 5, ... |

## X

| | | |
|---|---|---|
| ***x*-axis** (p. 54) The horizontal axis in a coordinate plane. | **eje *x*** Eje horizontal en un plano cartesiano. | 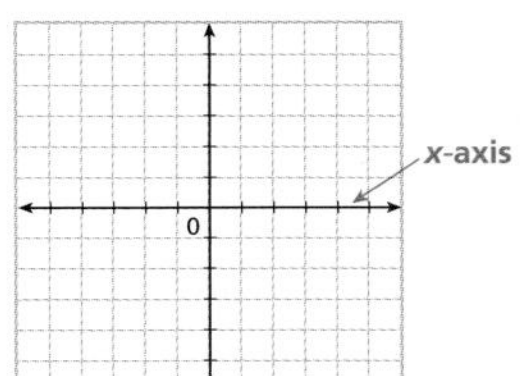  |
| ***x*-coordinate** (p. 54) The first number in an ordered pair, which indicates the horizontal distance of a point from the origin on the coordinate plane. | **coordenada *x*** Primer número de un par ordenado, que indica la distancia horizontal de un punto desde el origen en un plano cartesiano. | 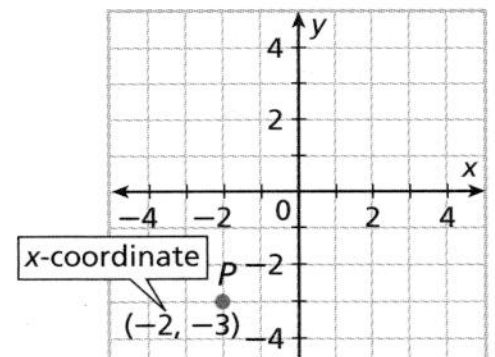  |
| ***x*-intercept** (p. 303) The *x*-coordinate(s) of the point(s) where a graph intersects the *x*-axis. | **intersección con el eje *x*** Coordenada(s) *x* de uno o más puntos donde una gráfica corta el eje *x*. | 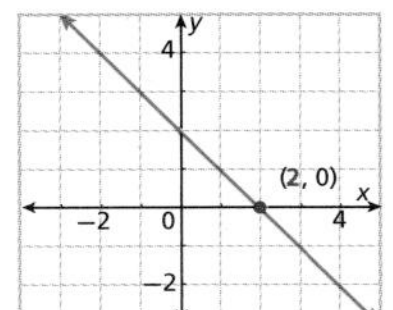  The *x*-intercept is 2. |

## Y

| | | |
|---|---|---|
| ***y*-axis** (p. 54) The vertical axis in a coordinate plane. | **eje *y*** Eje vertical en un plano cartesiano. | 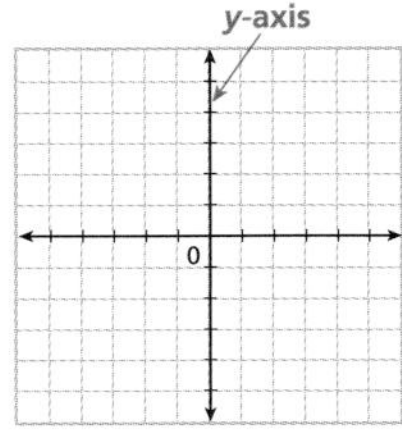  |

Glossary/Glosario

| ENGLISH | SPANISH | EXAMPLES |
|---|---|---|
| ***y*-coordinate** (p. 54) The second number in an ordered pair, which indicates the vertical distance of a point from the origin on the coordinate plane. | **coordenada *y*** Segundo número de un par ordenado, que indica la distancia vertical de un punto desde el origen en un plano cartesiano. | 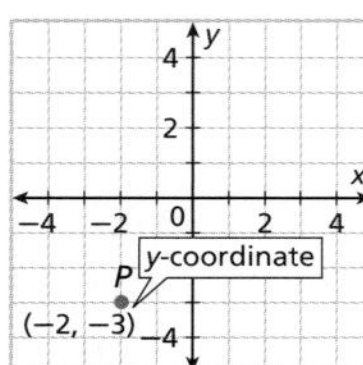  |
| ***y*-intercept** (p. 303) The *y*-coordinate(s) of the point(s) where a graph intersects the *y*-axis. | **intersección con el eje *y*** Coordenada(s) *y* de uno o más puntos donde una gráfica corta el eje *y*. | 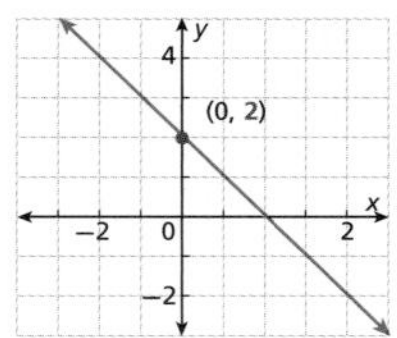  The *y*-intercept is 2. |

## Z

| ENGLISH | SPANISH | EXAMPLES |
|---|---|---|
| **zero exponent** (p. 446) For any nonzero real number $x$, $x^0 = 1$. | **exponente cero** Dado un número real distinto de cero $x$, $x^0 = 1$. | $5^0 = 1$ |
| **zero of a function** (p. 599) For the function $f$, any number $x$ such that $f(x) = 0$. | **cero de una función** Dada la función $f$, todo número $x$ tal que $f(x) = 0$. | 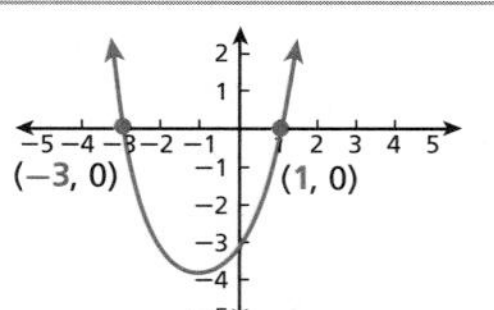  The zeros are −3 and 1. |
| **Zero Product Property** (p. 630) For real numbers $p$ and $q$, if $pq = 0$, then $p = 0$ or $q = 0$. | **Propiedad del producto cero** Dados los números reales $p$ y $q$, si $pq = 0$, entonces $p = 0$ o $q = 0$. | If $(x - 1)(x + 2) = 0$, then $x - 1 = 0$ or $x + 2 = 0$. so $x = 1$ or $x = -2$. |

# Index 

## A

## B

Index

Index

## G

Index

## M



Index

Index

## S

Index

Index

# Credits

***Abbreviations used: (t) top, (c) center, (b) bottom, (l) left, (r) right, (bkgd) background***

## Photo

**All images HRW Photo unless otherwise noted.**

**Master Icons—**(flower border), Kim Steele/PhotoDisc/Getty Images; (lighthouse), Ellen Isaacs/Alamy; (road), Creatas/Jupiterimages; (skyline), Digital Vision/Alamy; (beach), Photodisc/Alamy

**Table of content:** (chapter one), ©David Forbert/SuperStock; (chapter two), ©Tom Brakefield/SuperStock; (chapter three), Jeff Greenberg/The image Works; (chapter four), Kim Taylor/npl/Minden Pictures; (chapter five), Harrison Shull/Aurora Photos; (chapter six), Sports Illustrsted; (chapter seven), Frank Boellmann Photography, photographersdirect.com; (chapter eight), ©James Schwabel/Alamy; (chapter nine), Bates Littlehales/National Geographic Image Collection; (chapter 10), Jane Faircloth/Transparencies, Inc.; (chapter eleven), ©Reuters/CORBIS; (chapter twelve), ©Pat and Chuck Blackley

**Chapter Zero:** Page Z26 (t), Victoria Smith/HRW.

**Chapter One:** Page 2–3 (bkgd), ©David Forbert/SuperStock; 6 (tr), ©Ray Roberts/Alamy Photos; 6 (sky), PhotoDisc/Getty Images; 8 (tc), Sam Dudgeon/HRW; 8 (tr), ©Thinkstock; 10 (bl), AP Photo/NASA Haughton-Mars Project 2001, Pascal Lee; 10 (tl), ©Royalty Free/CORBIS; 14 (tr), ©Paul A. Souders/CORBIS; 18 (c), John Sullivan/Ribbit Photography; 18 (bl), ©Royalty Free/CORBIS; 20 (tr), ©Craig Aurness/CORBIS; 20 (tc), Derek & Garry Walker/Adams/PictureQuest; 22 (cr), ©Dave G. Houser/CORBIS; 24 (cl), ©M. Timothy O'Keefe/Alamy; 24 (bl), ©Royalty Free/CORBIS; 26 (tr), ©Ted Horowitz/CORBIS; 29 (br), Michael Abbey/Photo Researchers, Inc.; 30 (cl), ©The Newark Museum/Art Resource, NY; 30 (bl), ©Royalty Free/CORBIS; 30 (cr), PhotoDisc/Getty Images; 32 (tr), ON-PAGE CREDIT; 33 (tr), ©Craig Tuttle/CORBIS; 36 (bl), ©Royalty Free/CORBIS; 37 (tr), Stephanie Friedman/HRW; 38 (tl), ©Royalty Free/CORBIS; 38 (cr), ©Federico Cabello/SuperStock; 40 (tr), AP Photo/Mark Lennihan; 42 (cr), AP/Wide World Photos; 44 (cl), ©Lucy Nicholson/Reuters/Corbis; 44 (bl), PhotoDisc/gettyimages; 46 (tr), ©Sergio Moraes/Reuters/Corbis; 47 (tl), ©BananaStock Ltd.; 50 (bl), PhotoDisc/gettyimages; 58 (tl), PhotoDisc/gettyimages; 58 (cl), ©Stapleton Collection/CORBIS; 60 (tl), PhotoDisc/gettyimages; 60 (tr), Sam Dudgeon/HRW.

**Appendix:** 71B (cl), Brian Fleming/Courtesy of Durham Bulls; 71K (b), Sam Dudgeon/Harcourt

**Chapter Two:** Page 72–73 (all), ©Tom Brakefield/SuperStock 75 (cr), Sam Dudgeon/HRW; 77 (tr), ©Duomo/CORBIS; 78 (bl), RubberBall/Alamy; 79 (tl), Sam Dudgeon/HRW; 81 (tl), ©Dante Fenolio/Photo Researchers, Inc.; 81 (bl), ©Image Ideas, Inc.; 84 (tr), ©Lester Lefkowitz/CORBIS; 88 (cl), ©Bettmann/CORBIS; 89 (tl), ©Image Ideas, Inc.; 89 (cr), PhotoDisc/gettyimages; 92 (tr), ©Tom Stewart/CORBIS; 94 (cr), ©Tom Stewart/CORBIS; 97 (tl), ©Robert W. Kelley/Time Life Pictures/Getty Images; 97 (cr), ©Corel; 97 (bl), ©Image Ideas, Inc.; 100 (tc), ©Ingram Publishing; 104 (bl), ©Image Ideas, Inc.; 105 (tl), ©Royalty-Free/CORBIS; 106 (bl), Rob Melnychuk/gettyimages; 107 (tr), ©Ezra Shaw/Getty Images; 110 (bl), ©Image Ideas, Inc.; 110 (cr), Aflo Foto Agency/Alamy; 111 (cr), Pixar Animation Studios/ZUMA Press; 112 (tl), ©Image Ideas, Inc.; 112 (cr), FRANCIS SPECKER/NewsCom; 115 (cl), Shedd Aquarium/Lines Jr./SeaPics.com; 118 (tr), Linda Owen; 119 (cl), ©Duomo/CORBIS; 119 (bl), PhotoDisc/gettyimages; 121 (tr), Robert Harding Picture Library Ltd/Alamy; 125 (bl), PhotoDisc/gettyimages; 127 (tr), Spencer Platt/Getty Images/NewsCom; 129 (cr), Sam Dudgeon/HRW; 131 (bl), PhotoDisc/gettyimages; 136 (cl), Jessica Hill/AP/Wide World Photos; 136 (bl), PhotoDisc/gettyimages; 138 (tr), Terry Warner/www.cartoonstock.com; 142 (tr), ©Rubberball Productions; 142 (bl), PhotoDisc/gettyimages; 146 (tl), PhotoDisc/gettyimages; 146 (cr), Sam Dudgeon/HRW; 146 (bl, br), ©COMSTOCK, Inc.; 151 (cr), David Guttenfelder/AP/Wide World Photos; 162 (c), ©E.R. Degginger/Animals Animals/Earth Scenes; 163 (c), Library of congress; 163 (cr), ©Raymond Gehman/CORBIS

**Chapter Three:** Page 164–165 (all), ©Jeff Greenberg/The Image Works; 168 (tr), ©Charles Crust; 169 (bl), Digital Vision/gettyimages; 172 (bl), ©Creatas; 174 (tr), ©Mingasson/Getty/HRW; 174 (cellphone), ©Mingasson/Getty/HRW; 175 (bc, br), ©Mingasson/Getty/HRW; 178 (tl), Buzz Orr/The Gazette/AP/Wide World Photos; 178 (cr), PhotoDisc/gettyimages; 178 (bl), ©Creatas; 180 (tr), on-page credit; 182 (cl), Sam Dudgeon/HRW; 184 (cl), ©Reuters/CORBIS; 184 (bl), ©Creatas; 186 (br), Scott Vallance/VIP Photographic/HRW; 187 (tl), ©Creatas; 188 (tr), ©Peter Beck/CORBIS; 190 (tr), Paul Sakuma/AP/Wide World Photos; 192 (bl), ©Brand X Pictures; 194 (tr), ©Ariel Skelley/CORBIS; 198 (cl), Brad Mitchell/Alamy; 198 (bl), ©Brand X Pictures; 200 (bl), ©Jose Luis Pelaez, Inc./CORBIS; 202 (tr), ©Michele Westmorland/CORBIS; 202 (br), Sam Dudgeon/HRW; 207 (tl), ©Brand X Pictures; 207 (cl), Richard Megna/Fundamental Photographs; 210 (tl), ©Brand X Pictures; 210 (br), Peter Beavis/Taxi/Getty Images; 210 (cr, bl), PhotoDisc/Getty Images.

**Chapter Four:** Page 226–227 (all), ©Kim Taylor/npl/Minden Pictures; 230 (tr), ©Royalty-Free/CORBIS; 234 (cl), ©Bettmann/CORBIS; 234 (bl), Sam Dudgeon/HRW; 235 (bc, bl), Sam Dudgeon/HRW; 236 (tr), Aflo Foto Agency; 238 (cl), ©Comstock Images/Alamy Photos; 241 (tl), Sam Dudgeon/HRW; 245 (tr), RubberBall/Alamy; 250 (tl), ©Bettmann/CORBIS; 250 (bl), Sam Dudgeon/HRW; 257 (bl), Sam Dudgeon/HRW; 260 (br), Big Cheese Photo/Alamy Photos; 260 (tl), Sam Dudgeon/HRW; 262 (tr), David Welling/Animals Animals; 267 (bl), Roy Toft; 268 (bl), comstock.com; 272 (tr), ©COMSTOCK, Inc.; 276 (tl), Digital Vision/gettyimages; 276 (bl), comstock.com; 278 (tl), comstock.com; 278 (bl), AP Photo/Daniel Hulshizer; 290 (br), ©Ellen McCall/TRANSPARENCIES, Inc.; 290 (cr), Jane Faircloth/Transparencies, Inc.; 291 (c), ©Paul Buck/epa/CORBIS; 291 (b), ©POOL/Reuters/CORBIS

**Chapter Five:** Page 292–293 (all), ©Harrison Shull/Aurora Photos; 296 (tr), ©Aldo Torelli/Getty Images; 301 (bl), Victoria Smith/HRW; 304 (tl), ©LWA-Dann Tardif/CORBIS; 304 (cr), ©Buddy Mays/CORBIS; 307 (tl), ©John and Lisa Merrill/CORBIS; 308 (tl), Victoria Smith/HRW; 310 (c), ©elaineitalia/Alamy; 310 (b), ©imageZebra/Alamy; 315 (bl), ©Dave G. Houser/CORBIS; 316 (tl), Victoria Smith/HRW; 320 (tr), ©Patrick Eden/Alamy Photos; 325 (tl), ©Patrick Eden/Alamy Photos; 326 (tr), ©Royalty-Free/Corbis; 328 (bl), Genevieve Vallee/Alamy; 330 (cl), Courtesy NASA/JPL-Caltech; 330 (bl), Victoria Smith/HRW; 332 (tl), Victoria Smith/HRW; 332 (br), ©Rick Gomez/CORBIS; 332 (tr), ©age fotostock/SuperStock; 339 (bl), ©Brand X Pictures; 341 (tr), ©Pixtal/SuperStock; 346 (tl), Jake Norton; 346 (bl), ©Brand X Pictures; 347 (bl), image100/Alamy; 349 (tr), ©Owen Franken/CORBIS; 354 (bl), ©Brand X Pictures; 357 (tr), ©Jim Cummins/CORBIS; 360 (c), Victoria Smith/HRW; 362 (bl), ©Brand X Pictures; 362 (cl), AP Photo/Ted S. Warren; 364 (tl), ©Brand X Pictures; 364 (b), ©Tim Pannell/CORBIS; 364 (tr), Andy Christiansen/HRW.

**Chapter Six:** Page 378–379 (all), Sports Illustrated; 383 (tr), ©Kwame Zikomo/SuperStock; 386 (bl), Victoria Smith/HRW; 387 (tl), ©Lee Snider/Photo Images/CORBIS; 388 (bl), ©R. Holz/CORBIS; 390 (tr), Cartoon copyrighted by Mark Parisi, printed with permission.; 392 (bl), ©Michael Pole/SuperStock; 395 (bl), Victoria Smith/HRW; 397 (tr), Photofusion Picture Library/Alamy; 400 (tl), Victoria Smith/HRW; 402 (cl), ©UNICOVER CORPORATION 1986; 402 (bl), Victoria Smith/HRW; 410 (cl), David R. Frazier Photolibrary, Inc./Alamy; 410 (bl), Victoria Smith/HRW; 412 (tl), Victoria Smith/HRW; 412 (cr), David Madison ©2005; 412 (b), ©Les Stone/CORBIS; 414 (tr), ©Susan Werner/Getty Images; 419 (tl), Max Gibbs/photolibrary.com; 419 (bl), Nathan Kaey/HRW; 419 (cl), PhotoDisc Blue/Getty Images; 421 (tr), ©Justin Pumfrey/Taxi/Getty Images; 425 (cl), ©Reuters/CORBIS; 425 (bl), Nathan Kaey/HRW; 428 (all), Nathan Kaey/HRW; 440 (b), ©Daniel Dempster Photography/Alamy; 441 (c), Gary Burke

**Chapter Seven:** Page 442–423 (all), ©Frank Boellmann Photography, photographersdirect.com; 446 (tr), Advertising Archive; 449 (cr), B. G. Thomson/Photo Researchers, Inc.; 450 (cl), ©PHOTOTAKE Inc./Alamy; 452 (tr), Arscimed/Photo Researchers, Inc.; 454 (tr), Courtesy NASA/JPL-Caltech; 455 (br), ©Mediscan/Corbis; 456 (tl), Cern/Photo Researchers, Inc.; 460 (tr), D. Parker/Photo Researchers, Inc.; 461 (bl), ©Brand X Pictures; 462 (bl), ©BananaStock Ltd.; 474 (br), Robert Flusic/PhotoDisc/Getty Images; 476 (tr), ©Jeff Hunter/Getty Images; 480 (tl), ©Don Johnston/Stone/Getty Images; 480 (bl), ©Comstock, Inc.; 484 (tr), www.cartoonstock.com; 487 (frame), ©1998 Image Farm Inc.; 487 (girls), Artville/Getty Images; 488 (bl), ©Comstock, Inc.; 492 (tr), ©Pat and Chuck Blackley; 496 (cr), Royalty-Free/Corbis; 498 (cl), PHILIPPE DESMAZES/AFP/Getty Images; 498 (tl), ©Comstock, Inc.; 501 (tr), Juniors Bildarchiv/Alamy; 506 (tr), Molly Eckler–puzzle, photo by Victoria Smith/HRW; 506 (bl), ©Ruggero Vanni/CORBIS; 507 (tl), ©Comstock, Inc.; 508 (tl), ©Comstock, Inc.; 508 (tr), SuperStock; 508 (b), Ryan McVay/PhotoDisc/Getty Images.

**Chapter Eight:** Page 520–521 (all), ©Hugh Sitton/Getty Images; 523 Sam Dudgeon/HRW; 527 (tr), Sam Dudgeon/HRW; 527 (b), Brian Hagiwara/FoodPix; 528 (tr), Photo by Jolesch Photography. ©2004 Drum Corps International. All rights reserved.; 528 (tl), Photo by Jolesch Photography. ©2004 Drum Corps International. All rights reserved.; 529 (t), ©Royalty-Free/Corbis; 531 (tr), PhotoDisc/Getty Images; 532 (br, bc), Victoria Smith/HRW; 535 (tr), Tony Freeman/Photoedit; 536 (bl), ©Royalty-Free/Corbis; 537 (cr), Sam Dudgeon/HRW; 540 (tr), Travel-Shots/Alamy; 545 (cl), Composition 17, 1919 (oil on canvas) by Doesburg, Theo van (1883–1931) ©Haags Gemeentemuseum, The Hague, Netherlands/The Bridgeman Art Library Nationality/copyright status: Dutch/out of copyright; 547 (bl), Janine Wiedel

Photolibrary/Alamy; 548 (tr), AP Photo/Peter Cosgrove; 551 (tl), ©Stockbyte; 553 (bl), ©Royalty-Free/Corbis; 556 (tl), ©Royalty-Free/Corbis; 556 (br), ©Peter ©Comstock, Inc.; 508 (tl), ©Comstock, Inc.; 508 (tr), SuperStock; 508 (b), Ryan McVay/PhotoDisc/ Getty Images

**Chapter Eight:** Page 520–521 (all), James Schwabel/Alamy; 523 Sam Dudgeon/ HRW; 527 (tr), Sam Dudgeon/HRW; 527 (b), Brian Hagiwara/FoodPix; 528 (tr), Photo by Jolesch Photography. ©2004 Drum Corps International. All rights reserved.; 528 (tl), Photo by Jolesch Photography. ©2004 Drum Corps International. All rights reserved.; 529 (t), ©Royalty-Free/Corbis; 531 (tr), PhotoDisc/Getty Images; 532 (br, bc), Victoria Smith/HRW; 535 (tr), Tony Freeman/Photoedit; 536 (bl), ©Royalty-Free/Corbis; 537 (cr), Sam Dudgeon/HRW; 540 (tr), Travel-Shots/Alamy; 545 (cl), Alinari/Art Resource, NY; 547 (bl), Janine Wiedel Photolibrary/Alamy; 548 (tr), AP Photo/Peter Cosgrove; 551 (tl), ©Stockbyte; 553 (bl), ©Royalty-Free/Corbis; 556 (tl), ©Royalty-Free/Corbis; 556 (br), ©Peter Adams/Getty Images; 558 (tr), ©Lee Snider/Photo Images/CORBIS; 559 (cr), ©Yann Arthus-Bertrand/CORBIS; 563 (tl), ©Stockbyte; 566 (tr), ©Robbie Jack/CORBIS; 570 (tl), ©Stockbyte; 570 (cl), Sheila Terry/Science Photo Library/Photo Researchers, Inc.; 572 (tl), ©Stockbyte; 572 (br), David Young Wolff/Photoedit; 584 (b), ©Raymond Gehman/CORBIS; 585 (b), ©Jane Faircloth/TRANSPARENCIES, Inc.

**Chapter Nine:** Page 586–587 (all), Bates Littlehales/National Geographic Image Collection; 590 (tr), Aflo Foto Agency; 596 (bl), Sam Dudgeon/HRW; 599 (tr), Gary Crabbe/Alamy; 604 (bl), ©Gensaku Izumiya/Sebun Photo/Getty Images; 605 (tl), Sam Dudgeon/HRW; 606 (tr), ©Michael S. Yamashita/CORBIS; 610 (tl), AP Photo/Fabio Muzzi; 610 (bl), Sam Dudgeon/HRW; 613 (tr), ©Craig Tuttle/CORBIS; 618 (bl), Sam Dudgeon/HRW; 620 (all), Sam Dudgeon/HRW; 622 (tr), ©MedioImages/SuperStock; 624 (tr), ©Digital Vision; 626 (cl), ©Theo Allofs/CORBIS; 626 (bl), PhotoDisc/Getty Images; 626 (bc), ©COMSTOCK, Inc.; 630 (tr), Dynamic Graphics Group/IT Stock Free/Alamy; 634 (cr), imagebroker/Alamy; 634 (bl), PhotoDisc/Getty Images; 634 (bc), ©COMSTOCK, Inc.; 636 (t), ©Gerald French/CORBIS; 640 (cl), ©Phil Degginger/ Alamy; 640 (bl), PhotoDisc/Getty Images; 640 (bc), ©COMSTOCK, Inc.; 645 (tr), The Garden Picture Library/Alamy; 650 (bl), PhotoDisc/Getty Images; 650 (bl), ©COMSTOCK, Inc.; 652 (tr), ©Powerstock/SuperStock; 656 (bl), Comstock Images/ Alamy; 659 (tl), PhotoDisc/Getty Images; 659 (tc), ©COMSTOCK, Inc.; 660 (tl), PhotoDisc/Getty Images; 660 (tc), ©COMSTOCK, Inc.; 660 (tr), Stuart Franklin/Getty Images; 660 (b), Robert Laberge/Getty Images.

**Chapter Ten:** Page 672–673 (all), Jane Faircloth/Transparencies, Inc.; 678 (tr), Victoria Smith/HRW; 680 (all), Sam Dudgeon/HRW; 687 (tr), ©Tom Stewart/CORBIS; 691 (cl), ©Reuters/CORBIS; 694 (tr), AP Photo/Dave Martin; 696 (tr), Victoria Smith/ HRW; 698 (cr), ©Michael Prince/CORBIS; 707 (tl), ©Bettmann/CORBIS; 710 (cr), Stuart Franklin/Getty Images; 710 (bl), Stuart Franklin/Getty Images; 712 (tr), Sam Dudgeon/HRW; 713 (tl), Sam Dudgeon/HRW; 713 (tc), United States Mint image; 713 (tc), United States Mint image; 713 (tr), Sam Dudgeon/HRW; 713 (c), United States Mint image; 713 (c), United States Mint image; 713 (bc, br), Sam Dudgeon/ HRW; 716 (tl, tc), Sam Dudgeon/HRW; 716 (penny), PhotoDisc/Getty Images; 716 (dime), PhotoDisc/Getty Images; 716 (nickel), PhotoDisc/Getty Images; 716 (bl), PhotoDisc/Getty Images; 716 (bc), Sam Dudgeon/HRW; 716 (br), Victoria Smith/HRW; 717 (bl), Sam Dudgeon/HRW; 718 (cr), ©European Communities; 720 (tr), ©Warren Faidley/Weatherstock; 721 (bl), Aflo Foto Agency/Alamy; 722 (cr), Victoria Smith/HRW; 724 (bl), Sam Dudgeon/HRW; 727 (tl), David Young-Wolff/Alamy; 728 (tl), Peter Van Steen/HRW; 728 (bl, bc), Victoria Smith/HRW; 729 (tr), Victoria Smith/HRW; 730 (cr), Sam Dudgeon/HRW; 731 (bl), ©Jose Luis Pelaez, Inc./CORBIS; 732 (tl), Sam Dudgeon/HRW; 735 (all), Sam Dudgeon/HRW; 736 (all), Sam Dudgeon/HRW; 741 (cr), Sam Dudgeon/HRW; 741 (cl), ©Underwood & Underwood/CORBIS; 742 (tl), Sam Dudgeon/HRW; 743 (tr), Foodcollection.com/Alamy; 743 (bl), ©Comstock Images; 744 (tl), Sam Dudgeon/HRW; 744 (b), ©Handout/Hasbro/Ray Stubblebine/Reuters/ CORBIS; 749 (cl), Courtesy of Blue Sky Studios/ZUMA Press; 760 (bl), Billy E. Barnes/ TRANSPARENCIES, Inc.; 760 (br), Courtesy of North Carolina General Assembly; 761 (c), Courtesy of North Carolina Symphony

**Chapter Eleven:** Page 762–763 (all), Reuters/CORBIS; 766 (tr), Randy Lincks/ Masterfile; 777 (tl), Lucidio Studio, Inc./Alamy; 781 (tr), ©Wendy Stone/CORBIS; 786 (cr), Elaine Wakefield, Wessex Archaeology; 789 (tr), ©Stan Liu/Icon SMI/ZUMA Press; 791 (tr), Stephen Dalton/Photo Researchers, Inc.; 792 (cl), age fotostock; 796 (c), Laimute Druskis/Stock Boston/IPN; 796 (bc), ©D. Hurst/Alamy; 796 (br), ©Brian Hagiwara/Brand X Pictures/Alamy; 798 (tr), NASA; 802 (tl), AP Photo/Andy Eames; 802 (bl), ©Brand X Pictures; 805 (tr), Steve Gottlieb/PictureQuest; 809 (bl), ©Brand X Pictures; 814 (bl), ©Brand X Pictures; 816 (tr), ON-PAGE CREDIT; 820 (tl), ©Richard Cummins /SuperStock; 820 (bl), ©Brand X Pictures; 827 (bl), AP Photo/Gregory Smith; 828 (bl), ©Brand X Pictures; 830 (cr), Walker/PictureQuest; 830 (tl), ©Brand X Pictures; 830 (bc), AP Photo/Anna Branthwaite

**Chapter Twelve:** Page 846–847 (all), Pat and Chuck Blackley; 849 Sam Dudgeon/ HRW; 851 (tr), ©RubberBall/Alamy; 853 (tl), MedioImages/Alamy; 856 (tl), AP Photo/ Robert F. Bukaty; 856 (bl), PhotoDisc/Getty Images; 858 (tr), ©Steve Hamblin/Alamy; 864 (bl), PhotoDisc/Getty Images; 866 (tr), Gerald C. Kelley/Photo Researchers, Inc.; 868 (bl), ©Paul Barton/CORBIS; 869 (tl), ©SuperStock; 871 (cl), AP Photo/Lou Krasky; 871 (bl), PhotoDisc/Getty Images; 876 (tl), PhotoDisc/Getty Images; 876 (br), AP Photo/Tyler Morning Telegraph, Tom Worner; 876 (sky), PhotoDisc/Getty Images; 878 (tr), ©Stock Connection Distribution/Alamy; 885 (tr), Philippe Blondel/Photo Researchers, Inc.; 890 (tl), Photo Researchers, Inc.; 893 (tc), AP Photo/Dolores Ochoa; 893 (tr), ©Nigel Francis/Robert Harding/Alamy Photos; 898 (cl), AP Photo /NASA, Nick Galante, PMRF; 900 (tr), ©Tom Stewart/CORBIS; 904 (br), ON-PAGE CREDIT; 906 (b), ©Dynamic Graphics Group/i2i/Alamy; 906 (movie screen), ©Ralph Nelson/ Imagine Entertainment/ZUMA/CORBIS; 920 (b), AP Photo/Grant Halverson; 921 (c), ©Todd Patrick Photography

**Student Handbook:** S2 (tl), PhotoDisc/Getty Images; S3 (br), Sam Dudgeon/HRW.

# Symbols

## Relation Symbols

|  |  |
|---|---|
| $<$ | is less than |
| $>$ | is greater than |
| $\leq$ | is less than or equal to |
| $\geq$ | is greater than or equal to |
| $\neq$ | is not equal to |
| $\approx$ | is approximately equal to |
| $\cong$ | is congruent to |
| $\sim$ | is similar to |

## Real Numbers

|  |  |
|---|---|
| $\mathbb{R}$ | the set of real numbers |
| $\mathbb{Q}$ | the set of rational numbers |
| $\mathbb{Z}$ | the set of integers |
| $\mathbb{W}$ | the set of whole numbers |
| $\mathbb{N}$ | the set of natural numbers |

## Geometry

|  |  |
|---|---|
| $\angle ABC$ | angle $ABC$ |
| $m\angle ABC$ | the measure of angle $ABC$ |
| $\triangle ABC$ | triangle $ABC$ |
| $\overline{AB}$ | segment $AB$ |

## Other

|  |  |
|---|---|
| $\pm$ | plus or minus |
| $\|-4\|$ | the absolute value of $-4$ |
| $\{$ | system |
| $\pi$ | pi; $\pi \approx 3.14$ or $\pi \approx \frac{22}{7}$ |
| $\varnothing$ | empty set |
| $f(x)$ | function notation; $f$ of $x$ |
| $a_n$ | the $n$th term of a sequence |
| $n!$ | $n$ factorial |
| $P(\text{event})$ | the probability of an event |

# Table of Measures

## METRIC

### Length

1 kilometer (km) = 1000 meters (m)
1 meter = 100 centimeters (cm)
1 centimeter = 10 millimeters (mm)

### Capacity and Volume

1 liter (L) = 1000 milliliters (mL)

### Mass and Weight

1 kilogram (kg) = 1000 grams (g)
1 gram = 1000 milligrams (mg)

## CUSTOMARY

### Length

1 mile (mi) = 1760 yards (yd)
1 yard = 3 feet (ft)
1 foot = 12 inches (in.)

### Capacity and Volume

1 gallon (gal) = 4 quarts (qt)
1 quart = 2 pints (pt)
1 pint = 2 cups (c)
1 cup = 8 fluid ounces (fl oz)

### Mass and Weight

1 ton = 2000 pounds (lb)
1 pound = 16 ounces (oz)

## TIME

1 year (yr) = 365 days (d)
1 year = 12 months (mo)
1 year = 52 weeks (wk)
1 week = 7 days
1 day = 24 hours (h)
1 hour = 60 minutes (min)
1 minute = 60 seconds (s)